Baseball Prospectus 2008

CLAY DAVENPORT · STEVEN GOLDMAN · KEVIN GOLDSTEIN

CHRISTINA KAHRL · JOE SHEEHAN · NATE SILVER

WILLIAM BURKE · DAN FOX · DEREK JACQUES

JAY JAFFE · RANY JAZAYERLI

MARC NORMANDIN · JOHN PERROTTO

A PLUME BOOK

PLUME
Published by Penguin Group
Penguin Group (USA) Inc., 375 Hudson Street, New York, New York 10014, U.S.A.
Penguin Group (Canada), 90 Eglinton Avenue East, Suite 700, Toronto, Ontario, Canada M4P 2Y3
(a division of Pearson Penguin Canada Inc.)
Penguin Books Ltd., 80 Strand, London WC2R 0RL, England
Penguin Ireland, 25 St. Stephen's Green, Dublin 2, Ireland (a division of Penguin Books Ltd.)
Penguin Group (Australia), 250 Camberwell Road, Camberwell, Victoria 3124, Australia
(a division of Pearson Australia Group Pty. Ltd.)
Penguin Books India Pvt. Ltd., 11 Community Centre, Panchsheel Park, New Delhi – 110 017, India
Penguin Group (NZ), 67 Apollo Drive, Rosedale, North Shore 0632, New Zealand
(a division of Pearson New Zealand Ltd.)
Penguin Books (South Africa) (Pty.) Ltd., 24 Sturdee Avenue, Rosebank, Johannesburg 2196, South Africa

Penguin Books Ltd., Registered Offices:
80 Strand, London WC2R 0RL, England

First published by Plume, a member of Penguin Group (USA) Inc.

First Printing (2008 edition), February 2008
10 9 8 7 6 5 4 3 2 1

 REGISTERED TRADEMARK—MARCA REGISTRADA

ISBN 978-0-452-28903-1

Printed in the United States of America
Set in Utopia
Design by Jane Raese

Contents

Fungoes

Foreword

Thank you for purchasing *Baseball Prospectus 2008*. *Baseball Prospectus* is a much different book than it was 13 years ago, when we produced the first version of this annual. Although rumors that *Baseball Prospectus 1996* was published on a mimeograph machine are untrue, it did leave out the St. Louis Cardinals chapter and sold fewer copies than *Cooking with Armin Meiwes*. Today, *Baseball Prospectus* has become the best selling baseball annual on the market, and for that we want to thank you, our loyal readers.

Our goal, both here in this annual and on our website, BaseballProspectus.com, is to provide a refreshingly informed, independent, and honest perspective on professional baseball. Increasingly, that is a perspective that takes advantage of multiple points of view. A single player comment in this book might be informed by a statistical analysis or PECOTA projection, a discussion with an executive or a scout, a firsthand observation, or a conversation with one of our experts, be it Kevin Goldstein on prospects, Will Carroll on injuries, or Christina Kahrl on the significance of a team's sequence of player transactions. Increasingly, we have been less concerned about where we fall on an imagined ideological spectrum between objective and subjective evaluation techniques, preferring instead to focus on delivering good, smart baseball writing and analysis, period.

Just good, smart baseball, period. That's become the modus operandi not just here at Baseball Prospectus, but also among those teams that have tended to have the most success. The four organizations that reached their respective League Championship Series last fall each embodied that philosophy in one way or another. Whether it was the Rockies' discovery of how important a great defense could be in Coors Field, the Indians' knack for spending their limited resources wisely, the Diamondbacks' ability to build a bullpen that was more than the sum of its parts, or the Red Sox' willingness to trust an undersized, underscouted player such as Dustin Pedroia to be a critical cog in their everyday lineup, all four clubs have demonstrated that a cohesive organizational philosophy and a willingness to listen to arguments from both sides of the aisle have far more to do with success in baseball than do a big budget or a famous manager. As a result, last year we saw one of the most competitive baseball seasons in recent memory, and also one of the most gratifying.

In other quarters, the 2007 season will be remembered primarily for Barry Bonds, the Mitchell Report, and the concomitant controversy over performance-enhancing drugs. Although we have not shied away from this subject, we have come to believe that it is not the thing that you are most interested in reading about. When we track steroids-related stories on our website, we have found that they cause people to hit the collective snooze button; they do not generate the level of interest that accompanies the release of PECOTA, the Top 10 prospects lists, Jay Jaffe's take on the Hall of Fame candidates, or Joe Sheehan's reports from the World Series or winter meetings.

That is not to say that the Mitchell Report is unimportant, but at this stage, it is primarily a legal, political, and historical story, rather than a baseball story. None of the bright young stars that made 2007 such an exciting season—Jimmy Rollins or Matt Holliday, Curtis Granderson or Danny Haren, C. C. Sabathia or Jose Reyes—are implicated in the report, nor have they ever been suspected of steroid use. In fact, not a single player accused by the Mitchell Report—not one—received a single vote in the MVP, Cy Young, or Rookie of the Year balloting last season. We love baseball and we hate what steroids have done to the game, and through the tireless work of folks like Will Carroll we will continue to stay involved in the story, but we trust that, once the first pitch is tossed out at the Tokyo Dome to begin the season-opening meeting between the A's and the Red Sox on March 25, the focus will be back on the field, where it belongs.

Baseball Prospectus 2008 would not be possible without the tireless devotion of dozens of people, many of whom give up their holidays to make sure that the book gets into your hands in time for spring training. The most important people of all might not be those whose names you see on the back cover, but those who work behind the scenes to build our databases and infrastructure. Thus, special commendation must go out to William Burke, our director of research and development, as well as Dave Pease, Clay Davenport, Dan Fox, Ben Murphy, Tom Fontaine, and our crack team of interns. I also must provide an emeritus acknowledgement of the highest order to Keith Woolner, who has gone on to bigger and better things with the Cleveland Indians, but who was essential in making *Baseball Prospectus* what it is today, and—through our frequent conversations with him over instant messenger and e-mail—was still a major help in putting this edition together.

The other people that the book could not survive without are our editors. So a special thank you to our three-headed editorial hydra of Cliff Corcoran, Steven Goldman, and Christina Kahrl. For these three people, the book is quite literally a year-round project, and there are a number of changes that they have shepherded this year—most subtle, some more obvious—that we hope will make *Baseball Prospectus 2008* the best edition of the annual yet. Managing a team of a dozen-plus writers is like herding cats, and yet somehow, in spite of crossed wires and missed deadlines and one very cranky analyst who can never quite seem to get the PECOTAs out on time, Cliff, Steven, and Christina manage to get it done.

Thanks also to Christine Marra, our project manager, Sydelle Kramer, our agent, Cherise Davis, our editor and champion at Plume, and Marie Coolman and Mary Pomponio, our publicists.

I am writing this on the evening of the Iowa Caucus, a process that, even if it's largely a matter of tossing the old rascals out to just to elect new ones, has come to symbolize a certain kind of renewal in American life. In many ways, that is how I feel about the baseball season. The 2008 season will bring new heroes and new controversies; it will be just the same as every other baseball season and yet just as different. We are happy that you have chosen to join us for it. We hope that you will continue to do so throughout the season at Baseball Prospectus.com, and that your copy of this book will become just as beat-up and dog-eared as our own.

Nate Silver
Chicago, Illinois
January 3, 2008

Statistical Introduction

In our 2005 book, *Mind Game,* we began with a page titled "A Comforting Note about Statistics." The comforting message was, "You can enjoy this book without an advanced degree in mathematics." We've subsequently repeated that message in every book we've done except previous editions of the one that you're holding your hands, the *Baseball Prospectus* annual. That's because the ratio of numbers to letters is higher in this series than it is in our one-off projects such as *Baseball Between the Numbers* or *It Ain't Over 'Til It's Over.* Open to almost any page and you'll see it: big chunks of text alternating with big chunks of numbers. Despite this, the comforting note still applies: if you're not familiar with any statistics that aren't on the back of a baseball card, and even if you're not familiar with *those,* you can find just as much information between these covers about the state of baseball today as if you had just walked out of the astrophysics lab at NASA.

For those readers who do want to know more about the statistics we utilize within these pages, this section of the book is designed to introduce you to the tools we use for player analysis and to explain how they fit together. We'll start by introducing a few key concepts, including our PECOTA projection system and the new features we're unveiling this year; then we'll go over the statistics used in the thirty team chapters that follow.

Types of Statistics

In this book we refer to two distinct types of baseball metrics: cumulative statistics and rate statistics. **Cumulative statistics** tally individual events such as hits, walks, strikeouts, home runs, errors, or wins over the course of the season. Cumulative statistics are the backbone of all the other baseball metrics, because they represent a record of the events that happened on the field. Knowing that a player hit 14 home runs, however, does us little good on its own. Thus we need to place our cumulative statistics in context. If the player in question hit his 14 home runs over the course of a six-year career, that total would be an indication of a severe lack of power. If he hit those 14 dingers over the course of a single month, however, they would be the calling card of a big-time slugger.

That brings us to **rate statistics**, which measure the frequency of events, and are thus often expressed as percentages, averages, or ratios. Slugging percentage, for example, is a measure of a hitter's power determined by total bases divided by at-bats. Returning to our example of 14 home runs, career backup catcher and cutup Bob Ueker hit 14 home runs in his entire six-year career and posted a .287 slugging percentage. Meanwhile, AL MVP Alex Rodriguez hit 14 home runs in April of last season and posted a .882 slugging percentage. While the cumulative statistic needs context to show us the difference between the two players, the rate statistic does it all on its own.

Of course, rate statistics sometimes need a context of their own. Rodriguez's .882 slugging percentage last April is a good example. The single-season record for slugging percentage is .863, set by Barry Bonds in 2001. Rodriguez's .882 would thus suggest that he's the greatest power hitter who ever lived, but over the course of the entire 2007 season his SLG was .645, merely the 109th best mark. What changed wasn't Rodriguez's power, but the **sample size**. If you flip a coin four times you might get heads every time, but if you flip it 400 times, you're most likely to get 200 heads and 200 tails. The same probability effect occurs in baseball; the larger the sample, the closer the result will reflect the true probability of a given outcome. For that reason you'll often see us describe something as a "small-sample fluke," which simply means a result akin to having a coin flip come up heads four times in a row.

Translating Baseball Performance

While statistics become increasingly more informative when placed in the context of frequency and sample size, there is yet another context to be considered, and that is quite literally the context in which they were achieved. As a player rises through the minor leagues, plays in foreign leagues, or even simply moves around the majors, the quality of his competition changes, as do the physical environments in which he performs, whether it be a small ball park at a high elevation in a dry climate in which batted balls seem to rocket over the fence, or a large park on the water in which potential home runs get hung up by the thick sea air or lake-effect winds. What's more, the effects of a ballpark's environment or the competition level of a given league can fluctuate from year to year, and can vary quite significantly over a period of several years. As a result, players' statistical records are awash with distortions and statistical noise. The need to correct these distortions has given rise to an entire family of advanced statistics that attempts to translate statistics complied in different contexts to a common standard. Our translated statistics (sometimes called "normalized" or "adjusted" statistics) were devised by Clay Davenport and are typically signified by the prefix "Equivalent," such as Equivalent Slugging Percentage (EqSLG). These statistics adjust every player's performance—whether it took place in the major leagues, minor leagues, Japanese or Mexican leagues—to show us what it would have looked like had it happened in a neutral ballpark (one that doesn't favor either pitchers or hitters) in the major leagues, in a season in which the average hitter hit for a .260 batting average, .330 on-base percentage, and .420 slugging percentage. Translated statistics are found in the gray shaded areas on the right side of the statistical tables in the player comments in the team chapters.

Predicting Future Performance— PECOTA and Its New Features

Having translated all player performances to a neutral context, we have a uniform body of data that allows us to see trends and to forecast performance. Our main tool for this purpose is **PECOTA** (which stands for **P**layer **E**mpirical **C**omparison and **O**ptimization **T**est **A**lgorithm), a system created by Nate Silver that projects future player performance based on existing trends in the historical record. PECOTA works by analyzing a number of quantifiable factors, including production metrics (batting average, isolated power), usage metrics (plate appearances, major league career length, minor league level), phenotypic attributes (handedness, height, and weight), and a player's defensive position. With this data, PECOTA identifies as many as a hundred of the hitters or pitchers who are most comparable to the player being projected. The career trends of those players are then used in producing that player's forecast.

The PECOTA projections also incorporate an adjustment for the discrepancy of difficulty between the National and American leagues, as the American League is currently quite a bit tougher than the National League (roughly 10 points worth of EqA, or 25 points of EqERA above and beyond the adjustment required by the inclusion of the designated hitter in place of the pitcher in opposing lineups). A player migrating from the AL to the NL can expect a boost in his projection, while a player moving from the senior to the junior circuit can expect a corresponding drop in production; in both

cases, that change will be reflected in his PECOTA projection.

That league adjustment was a new feature that we added to PECOTA last year. We always treat PECOTA as a work in progress and try to improve it whenever possible. The three most significant new features that have been added for this year are:

Platoon Splits. PECOTA now incorporates an adjustment for a player's platoon splits. From season to season, there may be differences in the ratio of left-handed and right-handed pitchers that a batter faces, or left-handed and right-handed batters that a pitcher faces. These differences may result from a change in a player's role (for example, a left-handed hitter who goes from a platoon role in which he faced a reduced number of left-handed pitchers, to a full-time job in which he faces a more typical number of lefties, can expect a corresponding decline in his overall numbers), or a change in team context (for example, left-handed batters on the Astros took just 12 percent of their plate appearances against left-handed pitchers last year, while left-handed batters on the White Sox took 23 percent). In many ways, the platoon adjustment behaves similarly to a park adjustment, in that it is trying to place players into a context-neutral environment.

After determining the potential change in the ratio of lefties to righties a given player is likely to face, the specific degree to which the player's statistics are adjusted is determined by a combination of his "personal" platoon split, which is based on his career numbers, and a "generic" platoon split based on the average performance of all batters that hit from his side of the plate. The extent to which the "personal" platoon split is weighted compared to the "generic" platoon split depends on several factors, including the statistic involved (homers, strikeouts, walks, etc.), the length of a player's career (sample size), his handedness (for example, left-handed batters tend to be at a larger disadvantage against like-handed pitching than righties because they have less opportunity to face lefty pitching), and whether he is a pitcher or a hitter (by that same measure, left-handed pitchers have an increased platoon advantage compared to righty hurlers).

First–Second Half Splits. Statistics from the second half of the season—which we define as beginning on July 1 for major league players, and on June 16 for minor league players—are correlated somewhat more strongly with future performance than statistics from the first half of the season. We now incorporate a simple adjustment that weights second-half statistics from the preceding season somewhat more heavily. The specific amount of the adjustment depends on the statistic, and the second-half weighting is generally greater for pitchers than for hitters. For example, for a pitcher's strikeout rate, the second half receives a 59:41 weighting, whereas for a hitter's home run rate, it receives a more modest 52:48 weighting.

Draft Slot Information for Minor League Comparables. The overall pick number with which a minor league player was selected in the amateur draft can serve as a proxy for scouting variables that are otherwise difficult to pick up from his statistics. All else being equal, a first-round pick has a brighter future than a 20th-round pick. We have therefore introduced a new variable for minor league comparables, which is based on the amount of the player's signing bonus when he was drafted. Using a player's bonus should be a more reliable evaluation technique than using his actual draft position, because players can move upward or downward in the draft based on "signability" concerns.

All signing bonuses are inflation-adjusted to account for typical 2007 bonus schedules. For example, Chipper Jones's $275,000 bonus in 1990 is adjusted upward to $2,275,000 in 2007 terms. Where we do not have specific information about a player's signing bonus, we estimate it based on his draft slot. Latin American free agents who were not selected in the amateur draft are not evaluated by the draft bonus variable, although PECOTA slightly prefers to compare them to other Latin American free agents.

The Team Prospectus

The bulk of this book is composed of thirty team chapters, one for each major league franchise. On the first page of each chapter, you'll find the Team Prospectus box, which looks like Figure 1.

2007 Record is quite simply the team's win-loss record for last season, their final place in their division, and postseason results, if any. **Pythagenport record** is an adjusted win-loss record based on the team's runs scored and allowed that better represents the actual performance of the team in question by correcting for some of the luck involved in its actual record. The relationship between run differential and winning percentage was first demonstrated by Bill James in his 1980 *Baseball Abstract*. James dubbed his translation of runs scored and allowed into wins and losses "Pythagorean record" because of the resemblance of the use of squares in his equation to the Pythagorean theorem $(a^2 + b^2 = c^2)$. Further research has refined the coefficients in the equation and our version, created and calculated by Clay Davenport (thus "Pythag*enport*"), uses the context-neutral Equivalent Runs in place of actual runs scored and allowed for an even more accurate

---

ROCKIES PROSPECTUS

2007 record: 90-73; Second place, NL West; Lost to Red Sox in World Series

Pythagenport record: 91-72

Runs scored per game: 5.28 (2nd in NL)

Runs allowed per game: 4.65 (8th in NL)

Team EqA: .264 (6th in NL)

2007 Batters Age: 28.4 (7th youngest in NL)

2007 Pitchers Age: 28.4 (5th youngest in NL)

Ballpark: Coors Field; Strong hitter's park; Park Factor of 1.067

2007: Having exhausted the gimmicks, the Rockies finally win with balance.

2008: Emerging young arms in the rotation keep the Rox in the mix.

Figure 1. Example of a Team Prospectus box

---

measure of a team's expected wins and losses. Indeed, the Pythagenport record correlates better to a team's performance in the coming season than does its actual record.

Runs scored/allowed per game are the team actual runs scored/allowed divided by total games played, followed by their league ranking in parentheses (with the top figure in the league being the highest runs-scored total but the lowest runs-allowed total). While runs scored per game gives us a basic sense of the team's offensive prowess, the next line, **Team EqA**, gives us a more advanced measure. Equivalent Average (EqA) is a rate statistic that combines all the components of offense, including baserunning, into a number on the same scale as batting average. For teams, a .260 EqA is league average, a .280 EqA is very good, and a .240 EqA is very poor. Like other Equivalent statistics, EqA is normalized for ballpark and league offensive levels. As you can see above, although the Rockies were second in the National League in runs scored, they were only sixth in EqA, which is indicative of the significant advantage their home ballpark gave them in terms of run scoring.

2007 Pitchers/Batters Age give the weighted average ages for each team, using the players' "baseball ages"—that is, the age each player was as of July 1 of the given season—weighted by playing time (plate appearances for batters, batters faced for pitchers) so that outliers don't skew the average disproportionately to the role they played on the team. In other words, weighted averaging ensures that 45 plate appearances by the baseball Methuselah, Julio Franco, didn't make the Braves the oldest team in the National League.

The **Ballpark** line in the team box tells us the name of the team's home park for the previous season as well as both a description and a **Park Factor** indicating that park's effect on run scoring. Park Factor is calculated by comparing the differences in run scoring by the team in question and their opponents both at and away from the ballpark in question. A neutral ballpark that doesn't favor hitters or pitchers gets a rating of 1.000, while a park that favors hitters has a higher rating, and a park that favors pitchers has a lower rating. When we term Coors Field a "strong hitter's park," what we're saying is that its 1.067 park factor was among the highest in the major leagues (in this particular case, it was *the* highest).

The Hitters' Statistics

After an opening essay, each chapter moves on to the player comments. Position players are listed first, in alphabetical order, and each player is listed with the major league team with which he finished the 2007 season (so Chris Snelling, who started the 2007 season with the Nationals, was traded to Oakland at midseason, was picked up by the Devil Rays on waivers in October, and was then dealt to the Phillies in November, is listed as an Athletic, as are both Nick Swisher and Dan Haren). If you can't quite remember where a player ended up as of last September, there's an index in the back. Each player is represented by his statistics from every significant stint in the majors, minors, or prominent international leagues (Japanese and Mexican) between 2005 and 2007. Let's use the 2007 NL Rookie of the Year as an example of a hitter statistics table, as shown in Figure 2.

The first line of the entry contains the player's name and some basic biographical information. The next line shows the headers for the columns of data that follow, with each horizontal line representing one season or

fraction of a season with a given team. If a player had significant playing time with two teams in one season, as Braun did last year, dividing his time between the Brewers and their Triple-A team in Nashville, both statistical lines will be listed. Note that extremely short stints, such as rehab assignments or year-end cups of coffee in a higher league, have been trimmed out in the interest of space and because of the lack of meaningful data provided by those small samples.

The first few columns of data show time and assignment data—the year (**YEAR**), team (**TEAM**), and level (**LVL**) at which the hitter played. Levels are designated as the major leagues (MLB), the Japanese leagues (JPL, JCL), Mexican League (MEX), Triple-A (AAA), Double-A (AA), High A-ball (A+), A-ball (A), Short-Season A-ball, aka Low-A (A-), and Rookie ball (Rk). For each season, we also show how old the player was at the time, using his baseball **Age** that season as per the team age information in the Team Prospectus boxes.

The next few columns—**PA** (Plate Appearances), **R** (Runs), **2B** (doubles), **3B** (triples), **HR** (home runs), **RBI** (runs batted in), **BB** (walks), **SO** (strikeouts), **SB** (stolen bases), and **CS** (caught stealing)—show the actual and familiar statistical totals the player compiled in those cumulative categories during the given playing stint. Like the other items in the "unshaded" side of the statistical table, these are raw, untranslated statistics.

Next is Equivalent Baserunning Runs (**EqBRR**), a new feature in this edition of *Baseball Prospectus*. EqBRR is explained by its creator, Dan Fox, in the essay *The Tortoise, the Hare, and Juan Pierre: Translating Baserunning into Runs* in the back of this book. In essence, EqBRR measures how often a player takes an extra base relative to the average player—be it on a hit, a groundball, a fly ball, a passed ball or wild pitch, a stolen base, or even a balk—as well as how often a player is thrown out attempting to take that extra base and translates those extra bases gained and lost into Equivalent Runs (thus Equivalent Baserunning Runs).

														Bats: R	Throws: R	Height: 6' 2"		Weight: 200		Born: November 17, 1983		Age: 24
Ryan Braun						**3B**																

YEAR	TEAM	LVL	AGE	PA	R	2B	3B	HR	RBI	BB	SO	SB	CS	EqBRR	AVG	OBP	SLG	MLVr	EqAVG	EqOBP	EqSLG	EqA	VORP	DEFENSE
2005	WVA	A	21	166	21	16	2	8	35	9	34	2	4	-1.6	.355	.396	.645	.540	.244	.279	.449	.240	2.9	34-3B -5
2006	BRV	A+	22	260	34	12	2	7	37	23	54	14	4	0.1	.274	.346	.438	.156	.241	.302	.392	.246	1.6	58-3B -4
2006	HUN	AA	22	257	42	19	1	15	40	21	46	12	0	1.4	.303	.367	.589	.386	.289	.346	.583	.308	30.0	57-3B -15
2007	NAS	AAA	23	134	28	12	0	10	22	15	11	4	3	0.0	.342	.418	.701	.620	.314	.388	.636	.324	21.4	29-3B 1
2007	MIL	MLB	23	492	91	26	6	34	97	29	112	15	5	0.8	.324	.370	.634	.404	.325	.374	.653	.326	57.2	106-3B -24
2008	*MIL*	*MLB*	*24*	*678*	*111*	*40*	*4*	*39*	*117*	*60*	*137*	*16*	*6*	*0.8*	*.300*	*.367*	*.575*	*.251*	*.300*	*.365*	*.579*	*.307*	*60.6*	*158-3B -14*

Breakout: 30%   *Improve: 60%*   *Collapse: 9%*   *Attrition: 5%*   *Comparables: Tony Conigliaro, Alex Rodriguez, Del Ennis, Eric Chavez*

Figure 2. Example of Hitter Statistics Table

The next three columns show the three most commonly used rate statistics in their raw, unadjusted form: batting average (**BA**), on base percentage (**OBP**), and slugging percentage (**SLG**). Throughout the book you may see these three statistics presented as what we call the "slash stats." For example, "Last year, Braun hit .324/.370/.634," by which we mean he had a .324 batting average, a .370 on-base percentage, and a .634 slugging percentage. These three statistics are the best short-hand summary of a hitter's season as they tell us how often he got a hit, how often he reached base (or, inversely, avoided making an out), and how successful he was at hitting for extra bases by measuring the total bases he gained on a per-at-bat basis.

The remaining columns contain Baseball Prospectus's most useful original statistics. The next column is Marginal Lineup Value rate, or **MLVr**. Marginal Lineup Value estimates the value of a player by computing the change in expected run scoring between an average team, and a team with eight average players, plus our "hero." If we were to swap one of the nine average players for the 2007 version of Magglio Ordoñez we would, naturally, expect the team to score more runs. Similarly, if you replaced one of the nine average players with Nick Punto, we would expect it's scoring to decrease. This is demonstrated in Table 1.

Table 1. Marginal Lineup Value rate (MLVr)

Batting Order	Team A	Team B	Team C
1	Joe Average	Joe Average	Joe Average
2	Joe Average	Joe Average	Joe Average
3	Joe Average	Joe Average	Joe Average
4	Joe Average	Joe Average	Joe Average
5	Joe Average	MAGGLIO ORDOÑEZ	NICK PUNTO
6	Joe Average	Joe Average	Joe Average
7	Joe Average	Joe Average	Joe Average
8	Joe Average	Joe Average	Joe Average
9	Joe Average	Joe Average	Joe Average
Expected runs/game	4.797	5.297	4.466
Difference in runs/game versus Team A	0	+0.500	-0.331

Since the difference in expected run scoring between Team A and Team B is entirely due to having Ordoñez in the lineup, we call this difference his Marginal Lineup Value Rate (MLVr). MLVr is the number of runs a player adds or subtracts over an entire season divided by the number of games that the he participated in.

As you can see in the case of Punto, contributing an MLVr below zero is certainly possible, and actually quite common, as any below-average hitter will have a negative MLVr. Unlike statistics in the shaded righthand side of the table, MLVr for hitters in minor or foreign leagues is not based on translated statistics—those players are being evaluated against their own league averages, not for the equivalent performance in the majors.

The next three columns are **EqBA**, **EqOBP**, **EqSLG**. These are our "translated" versions of the three slash stats discussed before. **EqA** is the same stat that appears in the Team Prospectus boxes, but whereas team totals generally fall between .280 and .240, individual hitters' EqAs show a much wider spread, again reflecting typical batting averages. Something in the area of .350 is a typical league-leading total, as it was last year when Barry Bonds led the National League with a .353 EqA and Alex Rodriguez led the AL with a .354. A .400 EqA is exceptionally rare, but the greatest hitters in history—Babe Ruth, Mickey Mantle, Ted Williams, Bonds—have pulled it off in their best seasons. On the other hand, if your EqA is .220, you'd better be a great defensive player, or you'll be heading back to the minors.

The second-to-last column in the statistical record is **VORP**, which stands for Value Over Replacement Level. VORP is an estimate of total player value, which builds on MLVr and incorporates the position the player plays, how many games he played, and what "replacement level" is for his position.

Replacement level is a concept discussed in great detail in the article "Understanding and Measuring Replacement Level" by Keith Woolner, which was published in *Baseball Prospectus 2002*, so we'll only summarize the main points here. We define replacement level as "the expected level of performance a major league team can receive from one or more of the best available players who substitute for a suddenly unavailable starting player at the same position and who can be (or were) obtained with minimal expenditure of team resources." Metrics such as MLVr, which compare a player to league-average offense, are incomplete because they do not account for the value of having a player healthy and in the lineup. Losing a starting player typically results in more starts being given to a bench player who is significantly below average (like Nick Punto). By comparing a player's production to the level of a typical bench player or "Quadruple-A" journeyman (which we dub replacement level), we recognize the value of a player's durability. The concept of VORP is equally applicable to position players and pitchers.

VORP is available on BaseballProspectus.com for all players and seasons going back over 40 years, and is updated daily during the season. A couple of additional details about how VORP is presented for *minor* league players:

- VORP for minor leaguers is computed using their translated rates of production, and so should be considered to be their major-league equivalent VORP, not their VORP relative to the minor league they actually played in.
- Minor league players are rated at their most frequently played position, rather than a weighted average across all positions they appeared at (as is done with major league players). That is, if a minor league player plays 100 games at second base, and 20 at shortstop, he would be considered to be purely a second baseman in calculating his VORP. (This is *not* true for major league players: If a major league player played 100 games at second, and 20 at shortstop, we would his compute his VORP on a weighted average basis, with second base having five times the weight of shortstop).
- Minor leagues have shorter seasons than the majors do, and as a result, even excellent translated rates of production may not produce as high a VORP as for a player with the benefit of a 162-game schedule.

Although VORP looks at what position a player plays, it does not directly consider how well he fields that position. Thus we turn to the final column in hitter table, **Defense**, to show the position, number of games, and fielding rating for the player at his primary position(s). The fielding rating is denominated in runs, thus Braun's 2007 line in Milwaukee which reads "106-3B -24" means he played the equivalent of 106 full games at the hot corner, with a defensive performance that was twenty-four runs below average for third basemen (more on that in the Brewers chapter).

The 2008 line is the PECOTA projection for the player in the upcoming season. Note that the player is projected into the league and park context as indicated by his team abbreviation; for example, Delmon Young is projected as a Twin, even though he appears in the Rays' chapter. All PECOTAs represent a player's projected major league performance.

The numbers beneath the 2008 forecast line—Breakout, Improve, Collapse, and Attrition—are also a part of PECOTA, and estimate the likelihood of changes in performance relative to a player's previously established level of production. PECOTA differs from other projection systems in that it uses historical comparables data to generate a probability distribution, rather than just a single forecast line. History might tell us, for example, that an old, slow hitter will manage just fine eighty percent of the time, but will have a disastrous, career-ending season (a "collapse") twenty percent of the time. Conversely, a young pitcher with a high walk rate might show a sudden and marked improvement (a "breakout") fifteen percent of the time, while failing to improve much at all in his other seasons. The Breakout, Collapse, Improve, and Attrition numbers are an attempt to quantify these sorts of performance changes. To be more precise about it:

- **Breakout Rate** is the percent chance that a hitter's equivalent runs produced per PA, or a pitcher's EqERA (see more on our pitcher stats below), will improve by at least 20 percent relative to the weighted average of his performance over his most recent seasons of 2005-2007 (with 2007 performance weighted more heavily). High breakout rates are indicative of upside potential.
- **Improve Rate** is the percent chance that a hitter's equivalent runs produced per PA, or a pitcher's EqERA, will improve *at all* relative to his baseline performance. A player who is expected to perform just the same as he has in the recent past will have an Improve Rate of 50 percent. Note that Breakout Rate is a subset of Improve Rate; Improve Rate is the chance that a player improves *at all*; Breakout Rate is the chance that he improves *a lot*.
- **Collapse Rate** is the percent chance that a position player's equivalent runs produced per PA, or a pitcher's EqERA, will decline by at least 25 percent relative to his baseline performance over his past three seasons. High collapse rates are indicative of downside risk.
- **Attrition Rate** operates on playing time rather than performance. Specifically, it measures the likelihood that a hitter's plate appearances, or a pitcher's innings pitched, will decrease by at least 50 percent relative to his established level. Attrition Rate captures any reason for substantial playing time decline, including catastrophic injuries, but also a player being benched, retiring in midseason, or anything similar.

Breakout Rate and Collapse Rate can sometimes be counterintuitive for players who have already experienced a radical change in their performance levels. For example, PECOTA assigns Braun a Breakout Rate of 30%, even though it expects his rate statistics to *decline* from their 2007 levels. This is because PECOTA is comparing Braun's 2008 performance to a weighted average of the past *three* years, including a season and a half in the low minors playing against competition so weak that his major league translations bordered on replacement level. It's also worth noting that the projected decline in his rate performances is not indicative of an expected decline in underlying ability or skill, but rather something of an anticipated correction following his spectacular rookie season. Braun's batting average on balls in play last year was very high (.367), which is often an indicator that the player has been somewhat hit-lucky. PECOTAs projections will almost always correct for such extreme performances, much like Pythagenport record does at the team level.

The final piece of information, listed just to the right of the hitter's Attrition Rate, are his four highest scoring comparable players, as determined by PECOTA. Note that these are simply the four most similar comparables, and not the entire sample from which PECOTA generates its projection. Occasionally, a player's top comparables will not be representative of the larger sample that PECOTA uses. It's also important to note that established major leaguers are compared to other major leaguers only, while minor league players may be compared to major league or minor league players, with PECOTA strongly preferring the latter (in fact, PECOTA prefers to compare a player at the same level of competition: a Double-A player to other Double-A players, for example). All comparables represent a snapshot of how the listed player was performing at the same age as the current player, so if a 23-year-old hitter is compared to Sammy Sosa, he's actually being compared to a 23-year-old Sammy Sosa, which is much different than being compared to Sosa at the age of 31, when he was one of the best hitters on the planet, or 38, when he was an adequate DH who could stand to be platooned, though one could infer from the comparison that the current player has at least some chance of following Sosa's career path.

The Pitchers' Statistics

Now let's take a look at a sample pitcher's statistics table, this time from last season's most anticipated foreign import.

The first line and the **YEAR**, **TM**, **LVL**, and **AGE** columns of Figure 4 are the same as in the hitter's example in Figure 2, and should be self-explanatory. The next set of columns—**W** (Wins), **L** (Losses), **SV** (Saves), **G** (Games pitched), **GS** (Games Started), **IP** (Innings Pitched), **H** (Hits), **BB**, **SO**, **HR**—are the actual, unadjusted cumulative stats compiled by the pitcher during his stint.

Next is **GB%**, which is the percentage of all batted balls that were hit on the ground, including both outs and base hits. Because groundballs are more likely to be turned into outs than fly balls, the average GB% measured only from outs will be higher than for all batted balls. Furthermore, measuring GB% using just outs can be skewed by having an unusually good (or bad) infield or outfield defense. Therefore, we prefer to measure GB% using all batted balls, including both outs and hits. The average GB% for a major league pitcher in 2007 was about 45%; a pitcher with a GB% anywhere north of 50% can be considered a good ground-ball pitcher.

BABIP is batting average on balls in play, a statistic recently popularized by research indicating that pitchers exert a relatively small influence over the outcomes of balls in play (everything except home runs, strikeouts, walks, and times hit by pitch). A high BABIP is most likely due to a poor defense, or bad luck, rather than a pitcher's own abilities, and may be a good indicator of a potential rebound. A typical league-average BABIP is about .290, although in 2007, that number was .306. BABIP is not necessarily a strong indicator of a pitcher's overall performance—the pitcher with the lowest BABIP among AL ERA title qualifiers (A. J. Burnett, .262) allowed roughly the same number of runs per game as the qualifier with the second-highest BABIP (Scott Kazmir, .339)—but it can help explain performances that exceed or fall short of expectations.

The next column is **STUFF**. Our definition of STUFF is a mathematical formula and not quite the same as

YEAR	TEAM	LVL	AGE	W	L	SV	G	GS	IP	H	BB	SO	HR	GB%	BABIP	STUFF	WHIP	ERA	PERA	EqERA	EqH9	EqBB9	EqSO9	EqHR9	VORP	SN/WX
2005	SEI	JP	24	14	13	0	28	28	215	172	49	226	13	0.0%	.275	32	1.03	2.30	3.41	3.33	7.5	2.7	7.6	0.7	51.1	—
2006	SEI	JP	25	17	5	0	25	25	186¹	138	34	200	13	0.0%	.265	27	0.92	2.13	3.61	3.59	7.6	2.3	7.8	0.9	39.2	—
2007	BOS	MLB	26	15	12	0	32	32	204²	191	80	201	25	39.3%	.302	21	1.32	4.40	4.54	4.19	8.7	3.2	8.3	1.1	37.0	5.14
2008	*BOS*	*MLB*	*27*	*13*	*8*	*0*	*30*	*30*	*191*	*179*	*67*	*170*	*21*	*41.9%*	*.290*	*24*	*1.29*	*3.90*	*3.71*	*3.91*	*7.9*	*2.9*	*7.4*	*1.0*	*36.8*	*5.40*

Daisuke Matsuzaka — Bats: R Throws: R Height: 6' 0" Weight: 190 Born: September 13, 1980 Age: 27

Breakout: 12% Improve: 43% Collapse: 24% Attrition: 11%   Comparables: David Cone, Pete Harnisch, Bob Welch, Jim Bunning

Figure 3. Example of a Pitcher Statistics Table

the scouting term "stuff"; we aren't using radar guns or trying to evaluate the break on a curveball. STUFF is a shorthand rating of a pitcher's demonstrated skills, relative to his age and level; its primary use is to evaluate prospects, not established major league pitchers. An average major league starter, or a minor league pitcher who has shown the talent to develop into an average major league starter, will score a 10. Pitchers who score above 20 are excellent prospects; those above 30 belong in the ranks of the truly elite. Matsuzaka's STUFF ratings in Japan justified the anticipation with which he was received last year, and even in what some considered a disappointing year, his rating remained in the 20s. The largest single component of STUFF is strikeout rate, but walk rate, home run rate, hit rate, ERA, innings pitched per game, age, and age relative to league all figure into the final STUFF rating.

The **WHIP** and **ERA** columns are familiar to most fans, particularly those who play fantasy baseball. WHIP is the number of baserunners allowed per inning ([**Walks** + **Hits**] / **IP**), which makes it analogous to OBP. ERA is the pitcher's earned run average. Both of these statistics are unadjusted and untranslated.

The next column is Peripheral ERA, abbreviated as **PERA**. PERA is the Equivalent ERA (EqERA) a pitcher would be expected to have given his Equivalent rate stats: EqH9, EqBB9, EqSO9, and EqHR9 (see below). A PERA lower than a pitcher's actual EqERA may indicate that he was somewhat unlucky and could be expected to improve his EqERA next season even without substantial change in peripheral rates of production.

The next five columns, all starting with "Eq," are the pitcher's rates of production (hits allowed per nine innings, strikeouts per nine innings, etc.) based on his "translated" statistics. As with the hitter example above, a pitcher's raw statistics are adjusted and converted to a neutral-park major league equivalent performance. We present the translated (or equivalent) ERA (**EqERA**), as well as the per 9 inning rates of hits allowed (**EqH9**), walks issued (**EqBB9**), strikeouts recorded (**EqSO9**), and home runs surrendered (**EqHR9**).

VORP, again, is Value Over Replacement Player. A pitcher's VORP is the number of extra runs that a replacement level pitcher would have allowed to score if he pitched the same number of innings as this pitcher, based on his translated statistics. Slightly different standards are applied for starting and relief pitchers because of the different replacement levels for the two roles.

The final column, **SN/WX**, actually represents two statistics, each of which tell us how many wins the pitcher contributed to his team by applying a concept called "Win Expectation," which was discussed in the 2005 and 2006 editions of this book. The **WX** is short for **WXRL**, which refers to "**W**ins e**X**pected above **R**eplacement and adjusted for **L**ineup faced" for relief pitchers. For each bullpen appearance, Win Expectation looks at the situation the reliever faced when he entered the game—the score; the number and placement of men on base, if any; the inning and number of outs—and compares that to the situation when the reliever leaves the game, whether because he was replaced by another pitcher or because the game ended. By measuring the chances of his team winning at the beginning and the end of the appearance and taking the difference, Win Expectation determines the percentage of a win that the reliever contributed during his appearance. Since a 100 percent chance equals a win and a zero percent chance equals a loss, all chances in between follow suit. Thus if a reliever enters a game when his team has an 85 percent chance of winning and leaves with them holding a 95 percent chance, as determined by Win Expectation, he contributed 0.1 wins. If he left with his team holding a 75 percent chance he would have contributed -0.1 wins. All of these fractional wins are then adjusted for the strength of the actual hitters faced, compared to replacement level, then added up to produce the pitcher's cumulative season total of expected wins above replacement adjusted for lineup, or WXRL.

WXRL has benefits over other statistics used to evaluate bullpen performance. Because it relies on the Win Expectation framework, it is sensitive to leverage, and will assign more value to a reliever who pitches well in a close game than to a reliever who is just as effective in a blowout. Unlike ERA, WXRL rewards a reliever for keeping any runners he inherits from scoring—it also punishes a reliever for leaving runners on base for the next pitcher to take care of, regardless of whether or not those runners come around to score. In this way, the reliever's contribution is isolated from that of both the pitcher that preceded him and the one that that followed him.

The **SN** in this final column is short for **SNLVAR**, which stands for "Support Neutral Lineup-adjusted Value Added above Replacement" and measures the performance of starting pitchers. Like WXRL, SNLVAR is based on Win Expectation is adjusted according to the actual hitters faced, and is compared to replacement level. For example, facing the slugging lineups of the AL East in the majority of his starts, Roy Halladay pitched against batters who averaged a .273/.346/.429 line last year; Dave Bush, pitching in the weaker National League and the particularly weak NL Central, faced opposing hitters who batted .256/.326/.402. Both SNLVAR and WXRL adjust for such differences, and both statistics are only listed for a player's major league appearances.

As with hitters, the pitcher's 2008 line and the one below it represent his PECOTA projection for the upcoming season and list his four most comparable pitchers.

The Managers' Statistics

Each team chapter ends with a manager's comment. Fact-based analysis of managers has been a sketchy proposition throughout baseball history. There are many aspects of a manager's job that defy enumeration, and as a result, few bother to try. For the most part, only two statistics are ever brought to bear in evaluating managers' performances: wins and losses.

However, we're a stubborn lot, so we've devised a series of statistics to look at various aspects of managerial performance. Most of these statistics fall into two broad categories: managerial decisions—that is, how long did the manager stick with his starters, how often did he use pinch-hitters and relievers, how frequently did his teams sacrifice and steal—and some of the results of those decisions. While the manager is not directly in control of the results—a good manager can be done in by poor execution on his team's part—those statistics can provide insight as to the manager's ability to identify and adapt to his team's strengths and weaknesses. Let's take a look at Figure 4, of the NL Manager of the Year, Bob Melvin:

Taking the columns from left to right, we start off with the **YEAR**, **TEAM**, and the team's actual record (**W-L**). **Pythag +/-** tells us by how many games the team under or over performed its Pythagenport record. As you can see above, Melvin's Diamondbacks greatly exceeded their Pythagenport record, a phenomenon further discussed in the D'Backs chapter which immediately follows this introduction. Keep in mind that Pythag +/- is a mathematical expression of team performance, not an interpretation of the manager's work. That being said, it can be interesting to try to figure out how or why a team greatly under or over performed it's Pythagenport record.

Next comes a group of statistics that measure a manager's use of and success with his pitching staff. **Avg PC** is the average pitch count of his starting pitchers in that particular year, and **100+P** and **120+P** are the numbers of games in which a manager had his starter exceed 100 or 120 pitches. **QS** is the total number of quality starts a manager received from his starting pitchers. We define a quality start as any game in which the starter lasted a minimum of six innings pitched and allowed no more than three runs. We prefer to use runs instead of the more commonly accepted unearned runs because the former are irrefutable fact—the runs scored—as opposed to a statistic dependent on judgment calls made by individual official scorers. **BQS** is Blown Quality Starts, a Baseball Prospectus invention that measures games in which the starter delivered a quality start through six innings, then lost it in the seventh inning or later by allowing a fourth run. The fault for a Blown Quality Start lies primarily at the feet of the manager who left his starter in the game after the minimum requirements of the Quality Start had met. That said, a Blown Quality Start is not necessarily an indictment of the manager's abilities or tactics—a number of factors ranging from excellent offensive support to extremely poor bullpen support, can lead a manager to leave his starter in a game after they've thrown six quality innings. Conversely, the decision by a manager to "bank" quality starts by restricting his starters to only six innings can have downsides as well as it increases his bullpen's workload and increases the opportunity for the pen to blow a game in which a starter was cruising. Ozzie Guillen led the majors in BQS last year with 15.

Speaking of bullpen support, the next stats in the manager table tally how many pitching changes a manager made over the course of the season (**REL**) and how many times the reliever called upon didn't allow any runners, be they his own or inherited, to score (**REL w Zero R**). Bequeathed runners also count against REL w Zero R, which means even if a reliever did not allow a run to score on his watch, but left the game with a man on base, and the pitcher who replaced him allowed that runner to score, he does not earn his manager a tick in

MANAGER: BOB MELVIN

YEAR	TEAM	W-L	Pythag +/-	Avg PC	100+ P	120+ P	QS	BQS	REL	REL w Zero R	IBB	Subs	PH	PH Avg	PH HR	SB2	CS2	SB3	CS3	SAC Att	SAC %	POS SAC	Squeeze	Swing	In Play
2005	ARI	77-85	13	96.8	66	3	81	18	458	274	43	57	310	.231	9	64	21	3	4	104	68.3%	30	5	122	86
2006	ARI	76-86	-3	95.2	70	3	76	13	461	299	44	56	275	.193	7	64	26	11	4	84	72.6%	21	1	105	80
2007	ARI	90-72	11	94.9	68	4	80	9	469	314	38	77	240	.243	12	90	16	18	8	79	69.6%	26	0	118	89

Figure 4. Example of a Manager Statistics Table

this column. Concluding the pitching section **IBB** is quite simply the number of intentional walks the manager ordered during the given season. Like some other strategic elements, you'll see large differences between leagues and between specific managers: Terry Francona called for four wide only 20 times in 2007, while Bobby Cox's Braves gave out free passes more than four times as often (89 IBB).

The next group of statistics deals with the manager's use of his bench. The first stat is **Subs**, which is the number of defensive substitutes the manager employed during the season. The next three stats tell us how often the manager used pinch hitters (**PH**), the combined batting average of those pinch-hitters (**PH Avg**), and how many home runs they hit (**PH HR**). Again, these aren't reflective of any particular genius or lack of it; some managers simply like to pinch hit more than others. It's also important to keep in mind the differences between leagues; on average, NL managers pinch hit almost three times as often as their AL counterparts.

We then turn to the so-called "small ball" tactics, starting with the running game. The manager's aggressiveness on the bases is broken down by successful steals of second base (**SB2**) and times caught (**CS2**) and the times hit team was successful and not successful stealing third (**SB3** and **CS3**). Bunts, perhaps the most controversial tactic in the book, come next. We provide the number of sacrifices a team attempted (**SAC Att**) and their success rate (**SAC %**). Again, be sure to keep in mind the differences between leagues, as National League sacrifice attempts are greatly inflated by the fact that the pitchers hit in the senior circuit. To correct for this, we list the number of times a manager got a suc-cessful sacrifice from a position player (**POS SAC**), which allows for comparisons between the two leagues. For example, the Texas Rangers finished behind thirteen National League teams in sacrifice hits last year, but when we look at only sacrifices by position players, Ron Washington's team led the majors by a wide margin with 54. We finish up with **Squeeze**, which counts the number of successful squeeze plays the team executed over the season. In 2006, Dusty Baker led the majors in squeeze plays, with seven, and found himself unemployed after the season's end. Last year Dodgers manager Grady Little blew away the field with ten squeezes, and was replaced by Joe Torre before Veterans' Day. As the saying goes, correlation does not equal causation. But fluke or not, that's pretty darn spooky. Finally, we have a couple of statistics that attempt to measure the manager's investment in hit-and-run tactics and how well his team executed them. **Swing** is the number of times a hitter swung at a pitch while the runners were in motion, while **In Play** reflects how many times his hitters swung and made contact while those runners were off to the races.

The better you understand the statistical tools detailed above, the more you'll get out of this book. If you want more details about the statistics we use, you can consult the glossary at BaseballProspectus.com (www.baseballprospectus.com/glossary), or read our book *Baseball Between the Numbers*. BaseballProspectus.com also features daily articles and statistics updated throughout the regular season.

Derek Jacques with
Nate Silver, Clay Davenport, and Christina Kahrl

Arizona Diamondbacks

The Diamondbacks won the West last year, shooting past a poorly directed Dodgers team and the defending back-to-back division champion Padres, while keeping just barely ahead of the equally surprising Rockies. While that performance surpassed the expectations most pundits had for the club, we were not among them. In this space last year, we stated flatly that the Diamondbacks would be "the best team in the division." However, if you'd told us then that the Snakes were going to allow more runs than they scored, we'd have said they wouldn't be a contender.

As Derek Jacques explains in the Statistical Introduction at the front of this book, teams' won-loss records generally reflect their run differentials. A team that allows more runs than it scores is almost always going to have a losing record. If you glance over at the Diamondbacks Prospectus box, you'll notice that the Diamondbacks allowed 732 runs last year and scored just 712, yet still won the division with a 90-72 record. When we adjust for the strength of their schedule, we find that the Diamondbacks' record was nearly 11 games better than their run differential would have suggested. That sounds like a lot, and it is, but it's not unprecedented either in the history of the game or in the history of the franchise (see Table 1).

Still, what the Diamondbacks did last year goes against our accepted beliefs about how baseball teams win. The relationship between run differential and overall record is so consistent that it has created a measure of certainty among performance analysts. When that relationship is fractured to the degree that it was by the Snakes last year, it's almost enough to make us wonder if we've taken a bite out of the right apple. Rather

than try to fob off the 2007 Diamondbacks a fluke, let's pop the hood and try and sort out exactly how they managed to undermine sabermetric orthodoxy to such an alarming degree.

For starters, the Diamondbacks' runs-allowed total was actually fifth best in the National League last year, as was their park-adjusted total. Contributing to that was one of the game's best bullpens. The Arizona relievers ranked second in baseball last year with cumulative 14.52 WXRL, a total surpassed only by that of the Padres' pen. Better still, from 1959 to last year, only 21 teams had the benefit of a bullpen with a higher cumulative WXRL total than last year's Diamondbacks (for the curious, the list is topped Eric Gagné's 2003 Dodgers, while the 2007 D'backs rank just a hair behind the 1984 Tigers' pen led by Willie Hernandez).

That's an asset, to be sure, especially when you want to argue that one of the things that helps a team like this win games is a unit that protects the few leads it gets, but focusing on the strength of the pen sells the performance of the Diamondbacks' rotation short, while also neglecting how the offense maximized it's ability to generate those leads even though it scored the third fewest runs in the league.

Despite the continuing decline of Livan Hernandez and the season-long drama over whether or not they could rely on Randy Johnson, the D'backs' starting rotation kept the team in games all year. Certainly having a dominant ace like Brandon Webb is a huge part of that, but some of the credit is also due to manager Bob Melvin for refusing to push matters with some of his fill-in starters, a luxury afforded him by his outstanding

---

DIAMONDBACKS PROSPECTUS

2007 record: 90-72; First place, NL West; Lost to Rockies in Championship Series

Pythagenport record: 79-83

Runs scored per game: 4.40 (14th in NL)

Runs allowed per game: 4.52 (4th in NL)

Team EqA: .248 (15th in NL)

2007 Batters Age: 27.0 (2nd youngest in NL)

2007 Pitchers Age: 28.8 (7th youngest in NL)

Ballpark: Chase Field; Strong hitter's park; Park Factor of 1.049

2007: They were outscored, their rookies didn't hit, Randy Johnson barely pitched, and still they made the NLCS.

2008: If the kids build on their experience, they'll win again—this time with Pythagoras's blessing.

Table 1. Beating Pythagoras:
Baseball's biggest over- and underperforming teams

	Best			Worst	
Team	Actual W-L	Plus	Team	Actual W-L	Minus
2005 D'backs	77-85	+14.5	1993 Mets	59-103	-15.1
2004 Yankees	101-61	+12.7	1935 Braves	38-115	-14.6
1970 Reds	102-60	+12.6	1986 Pirates	64-98	-13.6
1954 Dodgers	92-62	+12.1	1946 A's	49-105	-12.8
1905 Tigers	79-74	+11.9	1905 Browns	54-99	-12.7
1924 Dodgers	92-62	+11.7	2006 Indians	78-84	-12.4
2002 Twins	94-67	+11.7	1937 Reds	56-98	-12.4
1954 Indians	111-43	+11.4	1939 Browns	43-111	-12.2
1907 Cubs	108-44	+11.2	1962 Mets	40-120	-12.1
1961 Reds	93-61	+11.2	1917 Pirates	51-103	-11.9
1972 Mets	83-73	+11.0	1984 Pirates	75-87	-11.8
1931 A's	107-45	+11.0	1975 Astros	64-97	-11.8
2007 D'backs	90-72	+10.9	2001 Rockies	73-89	-11.5

bullpen. For example, in his first five starts after being called up, Yusmeiro Petit only pitched past the sixth inning once, despite never allowing more than three runs or throwing more than 90 pitches in a game. Edgar Gonzalez was handled similarly in spot starts in May and June and upon his return to the rotation in September.

Melvin's careful handling of his staff contributed to the D'backs' ability to hold their opponents to four runs or fewer, doing so 96 times, the third-best mark in the majors last year and ten more than the major league average. On average, teams win such games almost 75 percent of the time, but Arizona not only had more of those games than the average team, they also won slightly more of them than average, posting a .771 winning percentage when holding their opponents to four runs or less. Then again, the D'backs also won more often than would be expected when allowing five or more runs, winning such games at a .242 clip against a .221 major league mark, but as those winning percentages indicate, the real secret to their success was avoiding such games in the first place.

Holding opponents to four runs or fewer as often as the Diamondbacks did is quite an accomplishment, but it wouldn't have gotten them anywhere had their offense not repeatedly found a way to win those games despite its poor overall performance. Offensively, the D'backs were a weak lot, but nudge around, and you see statistical clues to the little things they did to win. Even though they weren't especially good with runners in scoring position, the Diamondbacks were a little better than average late in close games. This was also true of their offense in 2005, when the club set a major league record by outperforming their Pythagorean

record by 14.5 games. In both years, Arizona's pinch-hitters were among the best in the National League. Last year's Snakes were also one of the better running teams around, thanks to players such as left fielder Eric Byrnes (5.8 EqBRR), second baseman Orlando Hudson (2.5), and shortstop Stephen Drew (2.4), who helped them rank fourth in the NL in Equivalent Baserunning Runs. Such small positives wouldn't have been enough to make a bad team good, but for a team living on slender margins afforded by its pitching, they added up to just enough.

The reason the Diamondbacks offense scuffled so badly that it had to get by on these bells and whistles was that the collection of highly touted youngsters that was supposed to rejuvenate it instead disappointed. Sophomores Drew and right fielder Carlos Quentin, and rookies Chris Young in center field, Justin Upton in right, infielder Alberto Callaspo, and catcher Miguel Montero all struggled terribly, while veterans such as third baseman Chad Tracy and first baseman Tony Clark also delivered less than expected. Counterintuitive though it may be, that is actually a positive for their hopes of repeating in 2008, as there's plenty of reason to expect improvement with a minimum of player turnover. Though the team's hitting prospects may be slightly overrated as a result of having too many minor league affiliates playing in hitter's ballparks, the kids are clearly talented and still have the potential to fulfill expectations. Young and Drew could give the team a pair of stars at key up-the-middle positions, and if 20-year-old right fielder Justin Upton delivers on his potential, Arizona may even have a genuine superstar in the heart of their lineup. What's noteworthy isn't that the kids struggled, it's that the organization had the vision to trust them with big-league jobs both in last year's pennant race and during the club's long-odds stretch run in 2006. The Diamondbacks know who their stars will be and know where their future lies—with their home-grown cadre, not with stretch-drive pickups like Shannon Stewart.

If there's a source of concern, it's that the organization's frequently touted talent pipeline, while good, is a bit short of its hype. The player development program is still generating talent, but not as much as it did on scouting director Mike Rizzo's watch before he left to become the Nationals' assistant GM. With the exception of Webb, the prospects who have already joined the big-league club still have a lot left to prove, and, behind them, the organization's lower levels seem to be stocked with corner outfielders with questionable power and a number of pitchers whose eventual destination seems to be the bullpen.

General manager Josh Byrnes knows all of this, which is why he was willing to let it ride on the offensive side of the ledger in the continuing hope that the kids fulfill their promise while focusing his efforts on adding a starting pitcher to slot between perennial Cy Young contender Webb and mid-rotation starters Doug Davis and Micah Owings. He achieved this dramatically in December by acquiring Dan Haren from Oakland in an eight-player exchange. While the risk involved with putting a fly-ball pitcher like Haren in Arizona's homer-happy ballpark seems obvious, Haren's combination of talent, durability, and affordability (including his 2010 option, he could cost as little as $16.25 million over the next three seasons, a bargain in today's market) was irresistible. With Haren in the fold, the Diamondbacks will continue to contend with a young lineup, a deep pen, and a sound rotation, putting their days as a minor sabermetric curiosity behind them.

Some Snakes Go Both Ways

As if the Diamondbacks weren't already entertaining enough, they also have Micah Owings. If you were inclined to get worked up over the Brewers' recent experiment with using Brooks Kieschnick as a two-way player, Owings is the player you've really been waiting for.

The idea of a true two-way player, one who can contribute regularly both on the mound and at the plate, has always excited baseball fans. Before Owings, Kieschnick was the great two-way hope. A two-way star at the University of Texas, Kieschnick was drafted tenth-overall by the Cubs in 1993 and converted into an outfielder, but was never given a proper major league opportunity with the team and drifted through five organizations before the White Sox let him pitch in the minors in 2002. He parlayed that into a two-year stint in Milwaukee as the ultimate 25th man, a mop-up reliever who was also a dangerous pinch-hitter.

Ultimately, Kieschnick was only marginally useful on the mound and proved to be little more than a carny-level sideshow. If you like seeing pitchers—real pitchers—who hit well enough that it makes you wonder about their ability to transcend their primary roles as moundsmen, you're probably the sort who remembers fondly the last day of the 1984 season, when reliever Don Robinson started in left field for the Pirates in the second game of a doubleheader, or when Billy Martin used Robinson's former teammate Rick Rhoden as the Yankees' designated hitter in a June 1988 game. Those are footnotes in a narrative otherwise appropriately defined by the specialization of our age. True pitchers who

hit well enough to make you wonder what else you could do with them are few and far between.

Now we have Owings, and after his rookie season he appears to be a legit two-way star, someone who hits well enough to bat higher than eighth in a lot of line-ups, and who pitches well enough that he belongs in almost anybody's rotation. For Arizona, making him a pitcher wasn't an automatic choice—if he hadn't been drafted out of Tulane as a pitcher by the Diamondbacks in the third round of the 2005 draft, he probably would have been picked as a first baseman by another team in the fourth. That's because he batted cleanup in college, even on the days he pitched. After Owings hit .333/.349/.683 in the majors in his rookie season, D'backs fans might understandably wonder if the Green Wave wasn't onto something.

At the plate, Owings' 2007 season wasn't just good—it was historic. Table 2 is a list of the best hitting seasons by pitchers in the era of divisional play ranked by VORP. Not only does Owings' 2007 rank second on the list in VORP, but it was easily the best single-season Equivalent Average for any pitcher with more than 50 plate appearances since the advent of divisional play. Second place is held by Kieschnick (.314 EqA in 2003); the next real pitcher on the list is Mark Portugal, who had a .294 EqA in 1994.

Looking beyond Owings, we see via the career EqA column that Rick Rhoden was arguably the best-hitting pitcher to have played in the divisional era before Mike Hampton hit his stride after the 1994 strike. If we were to expand Table 2 to the top 21, we would add Rhoden's 1986 season, Hampton's 2002, and two more seasons by Rhoden's contemporary, Bob Forsch (1980 and 1987). Don Robinson's best single season clocks in at 28th, with a VORP of 11.5.

Table 2. No Sacrifice:
The 15 best hitting pitchers (single season),
1969-2007, ranked by VORP

Pitcher	Year	Team	PA	EqA	VORP	Career EqA
Catfish Hunter	1971	OAK	109	.287	17.3	.203
Micah Owings	2007	ARI	64	.323	16.5	.323
Mike Hampton	1999	HOU	88	.276	16.4	.224
Fergie Jenkins	1971	.CHN	132	.261	16.3	.170
Bob Gibson	1970	SLN	124	.262	16.1	.208
Mike Hampton	2001	COL	86	.258	15.4	.224
Dontrelle Willis	2007	FLO	80	.287	14.7	.230
Jason Marquis	2005	SLN	81	.268	14.6	.180
Orel Hershiser	1993	LAN	83	.280	14.3	.192
Bob Forsch	1975	SLN	88	.283	14.1	.215
Rick Rhoden	1984	PIT	92	.277	14.0	.216
Sonny Siebert	1971	BOS	90	.276	13.7	.176
Blue Moon Odom	1969	OAK	90	.280	13.6	.214
Jim Rooker	1974	PIT	106	.275	13.5	.191

The most compelling thing about Table 2, however, is that the best-hitting pitchers of the divisional era are still active. Outside of the rookie Owings, Dontrelle Willis has the best career EqA of anybody on the list, while Hampton's is only a few ticks behind. Tragically, Willis was relocated to the DH league at the Winter Meetings, and Hampton may never return from his endless parade of injuries, but we now have somebody even better.

Though he's done it only for one season, Owings' level of offensive production is unprecedented for a pitcher. Even if the league catches up to him in 2008, he still provides his team an exciting tactical possibility. Regardless of whether or not some of the young Ari-zona hitters fail to develop, Owings' hitting is strong enough to merit consideration for a spot in the order much higher than ninth and certainly higher than eighth—that's mere La Russian gamesmanship, that. As a club whose offense ranked next to last in the National League in EqA last year, the Diamondbacks can't afford to be close-minded about where they get their offensive help. To their credit, it appears they won't be, as the team suggested over the winter that they would let Owings log some time at first base. That's not simply a way to score more runs—though, for the propeller-heads amongst us, it will give Owings a great shot at the single-season offensive VORP record for a pitcher—it's yet another entertaining thing about this team.

HITTERS

Emilio Bonifacio　　2B　　　Bats: S　　Throws: R　　Height: 5' 11"　　Weight: 180　　Born: April 23, 1985　　Age: 23

YEAR	TEAM	LVL	AGE	PA	R	2B	3B	HR	RBI	BB	SO	SB	CS	EqBRR	AVG	OBP	SLG	MLVr	EqAVG	EqOBP	EqSLG	EqA	VORP	DEFENSE	
2005	SBN	A	20	591	81	14	7	1	44	56	90	55	17	0.8	.270	.341	.330	-.039	.225	.282	.273	.204	-31.8	119-2B -14	
2006	LNC	A+	21	608	117	35	7	7	50	44	104	61	14	4.4	.321	.375	.449	.068	.250	.296	.351	.235	-7.7	127-2B 7	
2007	MOB	AA	22	596	84	21	5	2	40	38	105	41	13	6.2	.285	.333	.352	-.033	.252	.293	.321	.222	-16.1	75-2B 4	55-SS 4
2007	ARI	MLB	22	27	2	1	0	0	2	4	3	0	1	0.1	.217	.333	.261	-.257	.217	.333	.261	.207	-1.5		
2008	ARI	MLB	23	619	82	26	7	5	43	50	108	32	9	2.3	.264	.327	.361	-.136	.253	.317	.344	.236	3.4	145-2B 3	

Breakout: 42% Improve: 72% Collapse: 13% Attrition: 7%　　　*Comparables: Alejandro Machado, Anderson Hernandez, Alexi Casilla, Alfredo Amezaga*

Even though he didn't hit in the California League or at Double-A, it's too early to write off Bonifacio. Gifted with blazing speed and a certain brio, he's what some might call a gamer, but despite the slappy-speed-guy profile, the bat doesn't get knocked out of his hands in tight spots. His upside is something in the Tony Womack/Miguel Cairo range. His glovework at second is better than those two, but he's not able to handle shortstop as a regular.

Javier Brito　　1B　　　Bats: R　　Throws: R　　Height: 6' 3"　　Weight: 210　　Born: March 25, 1983　　Age: 25

YEAR	TEAM	LVL	AGE	PA	R	2B	3B	HR	RBI	BB	SO	SB	CS	EqBRR	AVG	OBP	SLG	MLVr	EqAVG	EqOBP	EqSLG	EqA	VORP	DEFENSE	
2005	SBN	A	22	338	43	18	1	5	52	41	37	1	2	-1.2	.296	.389	.419	.177	.253	.326	.364	.244	-5.5	40-1B -7	28-LF -1
2005	LNC	A+	22	101	17	6	0	2	11	10	17	0	0	-1.9	.292	.376	.427	-.053	.228	.297	.326	.218	-4.9	18-1B -2	
2006	LNC	A+	23	319	63	20	1	16	60	44	48	1	2	-1.9	.356	.448	.621	.445	.280	.362	.484	.287	16.1	25-1B -1	12-RF 0
2007	MOB	AA	24	528	72	29	2	11	72	78	90	1	0	-4.5	.327	.433	.477	.320	.294	.388	.442	.292	28.7	102-1B 0	
2008	ARI	MLB	25	536	69	28	2	15	67	59	91	3	2	-1.1	.280	.364	.444	.051	.269	.353	.423	.268	11.5	126-1B 1	

Breakout: 6% Improve: 32% Collapse: 35% Attrition: 11%　　　*Comparables: Justin Huber, Olmedo Saenz, Luis Jimenez, Bo Dodson*

Brito is a good example of the kind of organizational player cranked out by this system. Another Venezuelan import, he's not gifted with the kind of power it takes to really make it as a first baseman, but he has fine plate coverage and patience. In days gone by, that would have made for a productive career as a pinch-hitter and spare part in the majors. Today, the ability to play the outfield could make all the difference between Brito's playing for titles in the PCL and making it to The Show. He has kicked around the pastures briefly, but as long as he's in an organization, such as this one, that lacks a first baseman with star potential, that may not be a necessity.

Eric Byrnes   LF

Bats: R   Throws: R   Height: 6' 2"   Weight: 210   Born: February 16, 1976   Age: 32

YEAR	TEAM	LVL	AGE	PA	R	2B	3B	HR	RBI	BB	SO	SB	CS	EqBRR	AVG	OBP	SLG	MLVr	EqAVG	EqOBP	EqSLG	EqA	VORP	DEFENSE			
2005	OAK	MLB	29	215	30	15	2	7	24	14	27	2	2	-0.4	.266	.336	.474	.077	.274	.350	.500	.285	7.0	43-LF	10		
2005	COL	MLB	29	60	2	2	0	0	5	7	11	2	0	0.0	.189	.283	.226	-.382	.170	.267	.208	.178	-3.9				
2005	BAL	MLB	29	181	17	7	1	3	11	11	33	3	0	0.4	.192	.246	.299	-.365	.195	.263	.323	.208	-11.8	43-LF	-1		
2006	ARI	MLB	30	606	82	37	3	26	79	34	88	25	3	2.7	.267	.313	.482	.024	.258	.306	.469	.267	25.1	116-CF	0		
2007	ARI	MLB	31	698	103	30	8	21	83	57	98	50	7	5.8	.286	.353	.460	.084	.279	.350	.461	.285	35.2	109-LF	17	28-RF	2
2008	ARI	MLB	32	514	75	27	4	17	66	40	75	22	6	1.3	.279	.342	.468	.045	.268	.331	.446	.267	13.9	121-LF	4		

Breakout: 13% Improve: 42% Collapse: 30% Attrition: 18%   Comparables: Raul Mondesi, Glenallen Hill, Al Smith, Gerald Williams

The margin between being good-enough and a millstone is pretty slim. Unfortunately, Byrnes is on that knife-edge, in no small part because of his new three-year, $30-million contract. That he didn't deliver his usual monster mash off of lefties last year provides hope that he can improve on his overall performance in 2008. Still, even his usual platoon advantage would have gotten his 2007 slugging percentage up only around .490, not great for a left fielder playing in a hitter's park. He has his virtues, things that don't always show up in his stat line—speed and a good sense of how to use it on the bases, outstanding glovework in left, and a nice blend of contact and power on contact—but all they add up to is a player who doesn't hurt you only when he's at his best. That's a tough proposition at a position at which you'd expect to employ a real difference-maker, particularly at these prices.

Alberto Callaspo   UT

Bats: S   Throws: R   Height: 5' 10"   Weight: 175   Born: April 19, 1983   Age: 25

YEAR	TEAM	LVL	AGE	PA	R	2B	3B	HR	RBI	BB	SO	SB	CS	EqBRR	AVG	OBP	SLG	MLVr	EqAVG	EqOBP	EqSLG	EqA	VORP	DEFENSE			
2005	ARK	AA	22	385	53	9	0	10	49	28	17	9	8	-4.4	.297	.346	.409	.024	.278	.327	.374	.245	6.9	87-2B	-3		
2005	SLC	AAA	22	228	28	21	2	1	31	10	13	2	5	-2.2	.316	.345	.448	-.023	.265	.291	.377	.225	-0.6	46-2B	-1		
2006	TUC	AAA	23	554	93	24	12	7	68	56	27	8	5	0.3	.337	.404	.478	.225	.296	.360	.429	.274	31.0	68-2B	0	22-SS	0
2006	ARI	MLB	23	47	2	1	1	0	6	4	6	0	1	-0.7	.238	.298	.310	-.256	.238	.298	.310	.211	-1.8				
2007	TUC	AAA	24	261	48	15	2	5	30	28	17	1	2	-0.7	.341	.406	.491	.226	.294	.363	.430	.276	17.1	33-SS	0	17-2B	0
2007	ARI	MLB	24	156	10	8	0	0	7	9	14	1	1	-0.6	.215	.265	.271	-.380	.215	.269	.264	.185	-10.8	13-3B	1		
2008	KCA	MLB	25	392	43	20	2	4	37	29	30	4	2	0.3	.272	.327	.372	-.087	.267	.324	.382	.252	3.1	94-2B	2		

Breakout: 24% Improve: 48% Collapse: 17% Attrition: 19%   Comparables: Alex Cintron, Chico Carrasquel, Joey Cora, Walt Weiss

The 2007 season was one that Callaspo may well wish to forget. After drawing a suspension for an alleged assault on his wife and a subsequent mid-June demotion, a late-season hamstring injury kept him from being able to step into Orlando Hudson's job when the starting second baseman went down in September. Callaspo's the infield version of an outfield tweener; he doesn't have the power for everyday play at third, and, while his ability to get on base makes him an asset at either second or short, there's no one extra feature to his game that would encourage many managers to be patient with him. He's in danger of heading down the D'Angelo Jimenez path, though his chances improved after he got dealt to the Royals in a December deal for pitcher Billy Buckner.

Jeff Cirillo   1B/3B

Bats: R   Throws: R   Height: 6' 1"   Weight: 205   Born: September 23, 1969   Age: 38

YEAR	TEAM	LVL	AGE	PA	R	2B	3B	HR	RBI	BB	SO	SB	CS	EqBRR	AVG	OBP	SLG	MLVr	EqAVG	EqOBP	EqSLG	EqA	VORP	DEFENSE			
2005	MIL	MLB	35	219	29	15	0	4	23	23	22	4	2	1.5	.281	.373	.427	.104	.277	.367	.426	.275	9.6	41-3B	-1		
2006	MIL	MLB	36	290	33	16	0	3	23	21	33	1	1	-0.5	.319	.369	.414	.083	.319	.372	.414	.276	11.1	31-3B	5	11-1B	1
2007	MIN	MLB	37	174	18	9	2	2	21	15	13	2	0	0.8	.261	.327	.386	-.071	.270	.339	.414	.266	1.0	12-3B	3		
2007	ARI	MLB	37	44	6	4	0	0	6	4	6	0	0	0.3	.200	.273	.300	-.335	.200	.273	.300	.199	-2.4				
2008	ARI	MLB	38	139	16	7	1	2	15	12	14	2	0	0.0	.266	.335	.382	-.091	.256	.325	.364	.241	1.1				

Breakout: 16% Improve: 28% Collapse: 49% Attrition: 53%   Comparables: B. J. Surhoff, Bill Baker, Hank Bauer, Andy Pafko

Some things have a timeless sameness to them. Whether you're talking Spam from the can, Bazooka Joe comics, or role players, this can be immensely reassuring. Cirillo can still play a decent third base, he'll still put a charge into the occasional offering from a lefty, and his line-drive stroke has translated into a useful four-year run as a pinch-hitter. Knock any one of those props out of his game, and he's done.

Tony Clark — 1B

Bats: S   Throws: R   Height: 6' 7"   Weight: 245   Born: June 15, 1972   Age: 36

YEAR	TEAM	LVL	AGE	PA	R	2B	3B	HR	RBI	BB	SO	SB	CS	EqBRR	AVG	OBP	SLG	MLVr	EqAVG	EqOBP	EqSLG	EqA	VORP	DEFENSE		
2005	ARI	MLB	33	393	47	22	2	30	87	37	88	0	0	-0.8	.304	.366	.636	.382	.291	.356	.625	.317	39.3	72-1B	-7	
2006	ARI	MLB	34	147	13	4	0	6	16	13	40	0	0	-0.7	.197	.279	.364	-.246	.189	.277	.348	.217	-6.5	29-1B	-1	
2007	ARI	MLB	35	245	31	5	1	17	51	21	59	0	0	-0.5	.249	.310	.511	.051	.242	.307	.507	.272	7.3	51-1B	-2	
2008	ARI	MLB	36	173	21	6	1	10	29	16	40	0	0	-0.5	.256	.325	.493	.031	.246	.315	.470	.261	4.8	45-1B	-2	

Breakout: 10% Improve: 24% Collapse: 52% Attrition: 41%   Comparables: Walt Dropo, Eduardo Perez, Gus Zernial, Mark Parent

It's the park that gives him value. Clark launched 14 of his 17 homers last season (and 36 of his 53 as a Snake) in Phoenix. That's not a bad thing in itself; carrying Clark for some home-based power is better than carrying someone who can't exploit the park. The problem is the expectation that he's something more than that. Clark needed to re-sign with the Diamondbacks more than the Diamondbacks needed to re-sign him as a free agent. They've let him know they're no longer interested; he won't be nearly as valuable for anybody else.

Aaron Cunningham — OF

Bats: R   Throws: R   Height: 5' 11"   Weight: 195   Born: April 24, 1986   Age: 22

YEAR	TEAM	LVL	AGE	PA	R	2B	3B	HR	RBI	BB	SO	SB	CS	EqBRR	AVG	OBP	SLG	MLVr	EqAVG	EqOBP	EqSLG	EqA	VORP	DEFENSE				
2005	BRI	Rk	19	255	41	10	2	5	25	16	45	6	5	-1.4	.315	.392	.446	.224	.224	.271	.291	.193	-43.5	36-RF	-6	14-LF	-2
2006	KAN	A	20	402	58	26	3	11	41	34	72	19	10	2.9	.305	.386	.496	.278	.250	.309	.400	.246	-8.4	79-LF	-8		
2007	WNS	A+	21	306	51	12	5	8	37	34	39	22	8	3.1	.294	.376	.476	.166	.245	.313	.389	.250	-6.3	36-RF	-5	26-LF	-6
2007	VIS	A+	21	135	25	11	2	3	20	5	23	5	3	-0.8	.358	.386	.553	.358	.278	.303	.413	.244	1.7	16-CF	1		
2007	MOB	AA	21	132	25	8	3	5	20	12	27	1	3	-0.2	.288	.364	.534	.262	.258	.321	.475	.264	2.6	19-RF	0		
2008	OAK	MLB	22	630	65	31	4	10	60	41	132	19	8	2.2	.245	.300	.365	-.163	.248	.305	.390	.248	-9.7	147-RF	1		

Breakout: 40% Improve: 63% Collapse: 18% Attrition: 9%   Comparables: Damon Buford, Darren Burton, Garey Ingram, Cody Ross

Cunningham is a tough call as outfield prospects go, which might help explain why first the White Sox and then the Snakes dealt him. He stands on the inside corner of the batter's box and covers the plate well (taking a number of HBPs as a result), but, at age 21, the resultant power is already showing a mature spread of extra-base hits. He doesn't have big doubles totals that project as future home runs, which takes some of the bite out of his otherwise outstanding power numbers. Cunningham impressed by making it up to Double-A by season's end, but he didn't hit with any power in the Arizona Fall League. One of the six dealt to Oakland in the Haren deal, he's in an organization that appreciates his gifts. If he hits at Double-A this year, he'll silence some of the skeptics, but as a corner outfielder without the arm for right, he'll have to keep slugging in the .500s to be an asset in left.

Stephen Drew — SS

Bats: L   Throws: R   Height: 6' 1"   Weight: 185   Born: March 16, 1983   Age: 25

YEAR	TEAM	LVL	AGE	PA	R	2B	3B	HR	RBI	BB	SO	SB	CS	EqBRR	AVG	OBP	SLG	MLVr	EqAVG	EqOBP	EqSLG	EqA	VORP	DEFENSE	
2005	LNC	A+	22	177	33	16	3	10	39	26	25	1	1	-0.7	.389	.486	.738	.666	.290	.379	.535	.302	19.4	37-SS	-5
2005	TEN	AA	22	113	11	5	0	4	13	12	24	2	3	-1.6	.218	.301	.386	-.117	.184	.257	.330	.198	-5.4	26-SS	-1
2006	TUC	AAA	23	383	55	16	3	13	51	33	50	3	3	1.5	.284	.340	.462	.055	.251	.306	.419	.249	9.3	80-SS	-21
2006	ARI	MLB	23	226	27	13	7	5	23	14	50	2	0	1.5	.316	.357	.517	.191	.306	.351	.498	.288	18.1	54-SS	-1
2007	ARI	MLB	24	619	60	28	4	12	60	60	100	9	0	2.4	.238	.313	.370	-.142	.231	.311	.372	.245	2.8	144-SS	-3
2008	ARI	MLB	25	542	72	28	4	19	68	50	84	6	3	0.6	.270	.340	.463	.029	.259	.330	.441	.262	22.3	127-SS	-1

Breakout: 28% Improve: 58% Collapse: 14% Attrition: 16%   Comparables: Bernie Allen, Jay Bell, Dick McAuliffe, Chase Utley

It wasn't lefties or righties, or power pitches or off-speed stuff, or the park or not hitting in the park that troubled Drew last year—he just didn't hit anything off anybody anywhere. That's on top of concerns that he might not be able to cut it at shortstop. He's got the arm strength and accuracy, but most metrics suggest that his range is bad despite good first-step quickness, and there's concern that he doesn't always give his all. Making matters worse is the fact that his 2007 big-league line is uncomfortably close to his 2006 performance in Tucson, creating a dangerous disparity between his high-pressure performances in his 2006 call-up and the 2007 postseason, and what appears to be his "relaxed" level of production. If it's a matter of getting him to be "up" for a whole season, that's a problem only the D'backs themselves can address, but at age 25, his future is now. If he doesn't take a major step forward in 2008, Drew's more likely to conjure up comparisons to Russ Adams than to older brother J.D.

Carlos Gonzalez   OF

Bats: L   Throws: L   Height: 6' 1"   Weight: 200   Born: October 17, 1985   Age: 22

YEAR	TEAM	LVL	AGE	PA	R	2B	3B	HR	RBI	BB	SO	SB	CS	EqBRR	AVG	OBP	SLG	MLVr	EqAVG	EqOBP	EqSLG	EqA	VORP	DEFENSE	
2005	SBN	A	19	569	91	28	6	18	92	48	86	7	3	1.0	.307	.371	.489	.257	.255	.306	.410	.244	-8.0	126-RF	6
2006	LNC	A+	20	452	82	35	4	21	94	30	104	15	8	0.5	.300	.356	.563	.179	.236	.279	.428	.242	-10.7	95-RF	-6
2006	TEN	AA	20	69	11	6	0	2	5	7	12	1	0	1.6	.213	.294	.410	-.025	.226	.294	.435	.251	-1.2	15-RF	1
2007	MOB	AA	21	499	63	33	3	16	75	32	103	9	5	-0.9	.286	.330	.476	.134	.258	.297	.439	.251	-3.4	92-RF -6 22-CF	1
2007	TUC	AAA	21	48	9	5	0	1	11	6	6	1	0	-1.4	.310	.396	.500	.190	.262	.354	.429	.276	2.0	11-CF	-1
2008	*OAK*	*MLB*	*22*	*606*	*63*	*35*	*3*	*16*	*74*	*38*	*131*	*9*	*4*	*0.8*	*.249*	*.299*	*.407*	*-.105*	*.253*	*.304*	*.434*	*.256*	*-2.2*	*142-RF*	*0*

Breakout: 33% Improve: 60% Collapse: 16% Attrition: 5%   *Comparables: Juan Encarnacion, Edgard Clemente, FelixPie, Brandon Moss*

While many of the D'backs' prospects have disappointed upon reaching the Show, there's some sense that Gonzalez is in danger of doing so before even getting there. This isn't entirely fair. While his limited ability to get deep into counts might hurt his projections among stat-heads, he's still pretty young, and he punishes right-handed pitching (.326/.373/.554 against Double-A right-handers). Gonzalez might need the occasional platoon partner, but if you consider that most pitchers are right-handed, then mix in his age and tremendous throwing arm—tailor-made for right—you've still got somebody with future All-Star potential. The headline player sent to Oakland in the Haren deal, he'll get a long look as a center fielder, where he'll be adequate afield and a star at the plate.

Orlando Hudson   2B

Bats: S   Throws: R   Height: 6' 0"   Weight: 185   Born: December 12, 1977   Age: 30

YEAR	TEAM	LVL	AGE	PA	R	2B	3B	HR	RBI	BB	SO	SB	CS	EqBRR	AVG	OBP	SLG	MLVr	EqAVG	EqOBP	EqSLG	EqA	VORP	DEFENSE
2005	TOR	MLB	27	501	62	25	5	10	63	30	65	7	1	-0.6	.271	.315	.412	-.047	.272	.325	.426	.263	10.8	120-2B 19
2006	ARI	MLB	28	650	87	34	9	15	67	61	78	9	6	3.7	.287	.354	.454	.072	.279	.350	.441	.272	30.8	150-2B 14
2007	ARI	MLB	29	601	69	28	9	10	63	70	87	10	2	2.5	.294	.376	.441	.104	.287	.374	.439	.286	32.8	133-2B 13
2008	*ARI*	*MLB*	*30*	*570*	*77*	*28*	*5*	*11*	*57*	*56*	*75*	*9*	*3*	*0.5*	*.283*	*.355*	*.425*	*.014*	*.272*	*.344*	*.405*	*.260*	*18.9*	*134-2B 7*

Breakout: 11% Improve: 19% Collapse: 49% Attrition: 15%   *Comparables: Mark McLemore, Bill Mueller, Ron Oester, Tony Fernandez*

Like Byrnes, Hudson became a signature player on a contending team that lacked any real offensive stars, an unexpected development as (also like Byrnes) Hudson is a player whose assets don't leap out at you from his Baseball-Reference page. Hudson's still a contact hitter with solid power from both sides of the plate, but last year he had better results on his balls in play. That, plus his improved walk rate, fueled the best season of his career. His average might jump around going forward, but if he's walking in ten percent of his plate appearances, he'll still be in the front rank offensively at second base among the non-Utleys. Given his contributions in the field, that makes him one of the elite second basemen in the game.

Conor Jackson   1B

Bats: R   Throws: R   Height: 6' 2"   Weight: 225   Born: May 7, 1982   Age: 26

YEAR	TEAM	LVL	AGE	PA	R	2B	3B	HR	RBI	BB	SO	SB	CS	EqBRR	AVG	OBP	SLG	MLVr	EqAVG	EqOBP	EqSLG	EqA	VORP	DEFENSE	
2005	TUC	AAA	23	409	66	38	2	8	73	69	32	3	2	-2.3	.354	.457	.553	.364	.299	.401	.463	.300	26.6	71-1B -4 17-LF	-1
2005	ARI	MLB	23	99	8	3	0	2	8	12	11	0	0	0.4	.200	.303	.306	-.234	.188	.293	.282	.208	-4.1	18-1B	-3
2006	ARI	MLB	24	556	75	26	1	15	79	54	73	1	0	-1.2	.291	.368	.441	.081	.283	.360	.430	.278	14.1	120-1B	-12
2007	ARI	MLB	25	477	56	29	1	15	60	53	50	2	2	-0.6	.284	.368	.467	.119	.278	.366	.465	.285	20.5	98-1B	-9
2008	*ARI*	*MLB*	*26*	*525*	*76*	*32*	*2*	*18*	*70*	*62*	*59*	*4*	*2*	*-0.7*	*.298*	*.385*	*.493*	*.166*	*.286*	*.373*	*.469*	*.288*	*24.0*	*124-1B*	*-6*

Breakout: 24% Improve: 62% Collapse: 13% Attrition: 11%   *Comparables: Ryan Garko, John Ellis, Carmelo Martinez, Paul Konerko*

"Mostly harmless" isn't a term you want to see applied to a first baseman who's supposed to be entering his prime, but Conor Jackson is the Dermot Mulroney of first basemen: he's there, and . . . yeah, he's there. Jackson walks, but it's not a major feature of his game. He has power, but not enough to be a leading man in an offense, which would be that much more obvious if he didn't get to call Phoenix home. He handles the bat well enough in situational hitting—making contact but avoiding double plays—but not so well that you can overlook his other limitations. He's not an asset in the field; he's just good enough to avoid attention.

Miguel Montero — C

Bats: L Throws: R Height: 5' 11" Weight: 195 Born: July 9, 1983 Age: 24

YEAR	TEAM	LVL	AGE	PA	R	2B	3B	HR	RBI	BB	SO	SB	CS	EqBRR	AVG	OBP	SLG	MLVr	EqAVG	EqOBP	EqSLG	EqA	VORP	DEFENSE	
2005	LNC	A+	21	399	73	24	1	24	82	26	52	1	2	-1.0	.349	.403	.625	.333	.265	.310	.443	.256	12.0	59-C	-1
2005	TEN	AA	21	120	13	1	2	2	13	7	26	1	0	0.9	.250	.311	.352	-.126	.216	.267	.315	.204	-5.9	28-C	-1
2006	TEN	AA	22	337	24	18	0	10	46	39	44	0	3	0.0	.270	.362	.436	.139	.255	.338	.432	.265	13.9	73-C	1
2006	TUC	AAA	22	154	21	5	0	7	29	14	21	1	1	-3.2	.321	.396	.515	.249	.285	.355	.467	.282	9.7	28-C	-1
2007	ARI	MLB	23	244	30	7	0	10	37	20	35	0	0	-1.2	.224	.292	.397	-.152	.216	.287	.394	.239	0.5	57-C	-5
2008	ARI	MLB	24	303	38	13	1	15	46	25	44	2	1	-0.4	.270	.337	.491	.061	.260	.327	.468	.267	13.8	74-C	-2

Breakout: 35% Improve: 65% Collapse: 17% Attrition: 27%   Comparables: Joe Garagiola, Frank House, Dave Nilsson, Rube Walker

Montero was another in the club's cadre of rookie disappointments. His power was pure park fiction, and his value as a platoon player isn't much when he's reaching base against right-handers only at a .291 clip. Montero also struggled to contain the running game, and, since he's not the most polished receiver around, every weakness behind the plate gets magnified. If he's just the new Greg Myers, that's valuable, but his projection should help his believers keep their faith.

Augie Ojeda — INF

Bats: S Throws: R Height: 5' 8" Weight: 170 Born: December 20, 1974 Age: 33

YEAR	TEAM	LVL	AGE	PA	R	2B	3B	HR	RBI	BB	SO	SB	CS	EqBRR	AVG	OBP	SLG	MLVr	EqAVG	EqOBP	EqSLG	EqA	VORP	DEFENSE			
2005	ROC	AAA	30	370	42	16	0	3	33	33	33	3	2	1.5	.224	.322	.304	-.221	.243	.328	.312	.232	-1.5	64-SS	4	25-2B	1
2006	IOW	AAA	31	378	40	11	1	3	25	46	38	4	1	1.0	.248	.356	.320	-.099	.230	.329	.300	.234	-3.6	90-SS	-9		
2007	TUC	AAA	32	118	20	8	0	0	17	10	11	1	0	0.6	.323	.395	.404	.066	.284	.353	.343	.256	3.0	28-SS	6		
2007	ARI	MLB	32	132	16	2	2	1	12	15	13	1	0	0.7	.274	.354	.354	-.067	.265	.351	.345	.255	2.1	19-2B	7		
2008	ARI	MLB	33	193	21	7	1	1	15	18	21	2	1	0.1	.255	.333	.332	-.168	.245	.323	.316	.226	0.3	49-SS	2		

Breakout: 11% Improve: 33% Collapse: 45% Attrition: 38%   Comparables: Denny Hocking, Spike Owen, Wayne Tolleson, Jose Uribe

Pressed into action when Hudson broke down, this well-traveled utility man got be Walter Mitty in snake skin down the stretch, only to see the fantasy of getting to the World Series come up short. Nearing the end, he's not too different from what he was when he first came up with the Cubs: a good pair of hands to catch the ball in the field and to attempt sac bunts at the plate. That was apparently enough for the D'backs, who re-signed him to a one-year deal.

Gerardo Parra — OF

Bats: L Throws: L Height: 6' 1" Weight: 186 Born: May 6, 1987 Age: 21

YEAR	TEAM	LVL	AGE	PA	R	2B	3B	HR	RBI	BB	SO	SB	CS	EqBRR	AVG	OBP	SLG	MLVr	EqAVG	EqOBP	EqSLG	EqA	VORP	DEFENSE			
2006	MSO	Rk	19	303	46	18	4	4	43	25	30	23	7	2.7	.328	.386	.469	.229	.251	.290	.357	.227	-24.5	65-RF	6		
2007	SBN	A	20	488	64	25	4	6	57	30	51	24	8	-3.0	.320	.370	.435	.196	.262	.304	.355	.233	-17.4	91-RF	4	15-CF	1
2007	VIS	A+	20	109	11	2	1	2	14	4	17	2	3	-1.4	.284	.303	.382	-.111	.240	.257	.337	.201	-5.2	20-CF	2		
2008	ARI	MLB	21	628	73	31	5	7	55	33	88	22	9	1.0	.267	.308	.378	-.143	.257	.299	.360	.228	-10.6	147-RF	-1		

Breakout: 25% Improve: 58% Collapse: 15% Attrition: 8%   Comparables: Trent Oeltjen, Melky Cabrera, Willie Cañate, Alex Fernandez

Already considered the new Carlos Gonzalez, Parra's another Venezuelan import with a cannon arm. He didn't disappoint while making his full-season debut at age 20 last year, and he surprised people with how well he handled center when pressed into action there. He's still very raw, but toolsy enough that people are excited about what he might grow up to be. Gonzalez's power potential doesn't seem to be there yet, but if Parra can play center, that radically changes his possibilities within an organization that already has Justin Upton in-house.

Carlos Quentin — RF

Bats: R Throws: R Height: 6' 2" Weight: 220 Born: August 28, 1982 Age: 25

YEAR	TEAM	LVL	AGE	PA	R	2B	3B	HR	RBI	BB	SO	SB	CS	EqBRR	AVG	OBP	SLG	MLVr	EqAVG	EqOBP	EqSLG	EqA	VORP	DEFENSE			
2005	TUC	AAA	22	561	98	28	4	21	89	72	71	9	1	-2.1	.301	.422	.520	.210	.256	.365	.429	.280	11.8	73-RF	7	48-CF	-4
2006	TUC	AAA	23	396	66	30	3	9	52	45	46	5	0	-1.9	.289	.424	.487	.227	.257	.374	.438	.286	10.8	73-RF	-6		
2006	ARI	MLB	23	191	23	13	3	9	32	15	34	1	0	0.1	.253	.342	.530	.123	.246	.332	.521	.285	8.4	42-RF	4		
2007	TUC	AAA	24	135	30	12	1	4	27	9	14	0	1	-0.6	.348	.430	.574	.389	.308	.385	.513	.303	9.4	26-RF	-1		
2007	ARI	MLB	24	263	29	16	0	5	31	18	54	2	2	-1.1	.214	.298	.349	-.212	.214	.300	.354	.230	-10.8	65-RF	1		
2008	CHA	MLB	25	365	48	20	1	11	45	31	58	4	1	-0.2	.263	.349	.439	.030	.260	.348	.443	.279	6.4	88-RF	1		

Breakout: 22% Improve: 51% Collapse: 25% Attrition: 27%   Comparables: Charlie Spikes, Bill Robinson, Dave Henderson, Gabe Kapler

Quentin simply never got on track in 2007, as he opened the year recovering from a torn labrum, lost August to a strained hamstring, and struggled to control his at-bats or hit his pitch with any authority during his stints in the bigs. With Justin Upton already up, Quentin was dealt to the White Sox for first-base prospect Chris Carter (the younger one with more upside, not the one they traded away last year). In his new organization, Quentin's at the top of the Sox stack of guys competing for playing time in left, but corner outfielders with middling power are good, not great, prospects. For the curious, Quentin managed to take one for the team 20 times in less than 400 plate appearances in 2007; his career rate as a pro is now at one hit-by-pitch every 15.9 PA, insanely more often than modern career leaders Craig Biggio (every 43.8), Don Baylor (every 35.2), and Ron Hunt (every 25.3).

Mark Reynolds — 3B

Bats: R Throws: R Height: 6'1" Weight: 200 Born: August 3, 1983 Age: 24

YEAR	TEAM	LVL	AGE	PA	R	2B	3B	HR	RBI	BB	SO	SB	CS	EqBRR	AVG	OBP	SLG	MLVr	EqAVG	EqOBP	EqSLG	EqA	VORP	DEFENSE			
2005	SBN	A	21	484	65	26	2	19	76	37	107	4	1	-0.3	.253	.319	.454	.084	.210	.260	.371	.216	-11.4	55-SS	-11	32-3B	-8
2006	LNC	A+	22	322	64	18	2	23	77	41	72	1	1	-1.0	.337	.422	.670	.456	.261	.339	.512	.284	24.9	29-SS	0	15-3B	-2
2006	TEN	AA	22	127	23	7	0	8	21	11	37	0	1	1.0	.272	.346	.544	.254	.267	.331	.552	.285	7.0	12-LF	2		
2007	MOB	AA	23	155	28	9	2	6	22	20	32	2	1	0.3	.306	.394	.537	.325	.277	.355	.482	.285	12.0	31-3B	-4		
2007	ARI	MLB	23	414	62	20	4	17	62	37	129	0	1	-1.1	.279	.349	.495	.119	.269	.344	.492	.283	19.2	95-3B	-1		
2008	ARI	MLB	24	579	77	29	3	28	87	52	148	6	3	0.2	.265	.337	.495	.061	.255	.327	.471	.268	20.4	136-3B	-5		

Breakout: 14% Improve: 42% Collapse: 27% Attrition: 13%   Comparables: Russ Davis, Jared Sandberg, Jim Chamblee, Dean Palmer

The mystery of what position Reynolds would play in the majors answered itself in mid-May when his hot hitting and Chad Tracy's bad knee made the rookie the regular third baseman. He's not especially good at the hot corner, but he's not really an ideal second baseman either, so the issue of where he'll ultimately reside remains open-ended. After his hot start, the league appeared to figure Reynolds out in June and July, but he returned the favor in August and September, hitting .319/.399/.530. For now, what matters is that his line-drive power stroke works everywhere against everybody, so until the D'backs find somewhere else to put him, third base should be his.

Jeff Salazar — OF

Bats: L Throws: L Height: 6'0" Weight: 190 Born: November 24, 1980 Age: 27

YEAR	TEAM	LVL	AGE	PA	R	2B	3B	HR	RBI	BB	SO	SB	CS	EqBRR	AVG	OBP	SLG	MLVr	EqAVG	EqOBP	EqSLG	EqA	VORP	DEFENSE			
2005	TUL	AA	24	319	47	13	2	6	35	44	49	12	8	-3.4	.278	.381	.410	.087	.239	.335	.349	.246	-0.8	50-CF	5	17-LF	2
2005	CSP	AAA	24	272	42	17	3	6	26	32	58	5	2	0.8	.263	.349	.436	-.058	.220	.300	.361	.232	-5.4	51-CF	3		
2006	CSP	AAA	25	381	62	14	7	9	39	46	64	12	5	0.0	.265	.357	.433	.002	.234	.319	.383	.248	0.2	82-CF	-8		
2006	COL	MLB	25	67	13	4	0	1	8	11	16	2	0	1.8	.283	.409	.415	.083	.264	.394	.377	.288	3.8	12-CF	-2		
2007	TUC	AAA	26	472	76	31	9	10	68	56	56	18	5	1.4	.299	.385	.495	.154	.260	.346	.437	.275	18.0	91-CF	3	12-LF	2
2007	ARI	MLB	26	103	13	6	1	1	10	9	19	2	0	1.1	.277	.340	.394	-.038	.269	.340	.387	.259	1.2	20-RF	3		
2008	ARI	MLB	27	516	73	28	6	14	59	58	86	12	4	1.4	.263	.349	.449	.020	.253	.339	.428	.265	12.9	122-CF	0		

Breakout: 25% Improve: 61% Collapse: 15% Attrition: 19%   Comparables: Terry Bradshaw, Terrmel Sledge, Gabe Whatley, Derek Lee

Snagging guys on waivers is as useful to a team at the top as one at the bottom. The left-handed Salazar is a good fit as a fourth outfielder for this team with three right-handed outfield regulars. He has the range to handle center, good speed, solid plate coverage, the sort of approach that can work while pinch-hitting, and a useful blend of patience and some sock against righties.

Chris Snyder — C

Bats: R Throws: R Height: 6'3" Weight: 230 Born: February 12, 1981 Age: 27

YEAR	TEAM	LVL	AGE	PA	R	2B	3B	HR	RBI	BB	SO	SB	CS	EqBRR	AVG	OBP	SLG	MLVr	EqAVG	EqOBP	EqSLG	EqA	VORP	DEFENSE	
2005	ARI	MLB	24	373	24	14	0	6	28	40	87	0	1	-1.7	.202	.297	.301	-.252	.196	.293	.297	.209	-9.5	102-C	-3
2006	ARI	MLB	25	213	19	9	0	6	32	22	39	0	0	-0.5	.277	.349	.424	.013	.268	.343	.415	.268	6.1	54-C	6
2007	ARI	MLB	26	380	37	20	0	13	47	40	67	0	1	-3.4	.252	.342	.433	.002	.245	.339	.433	.267	14.1	100-C	10
2008	ARI	MLB	27	282	30	13	1	9	35	29	52	1	1	-0.9	.254	.337	.423	-.043	.244	.327	.403	.250	7.6	69-C	3

Breakout: 27% Improve: 41% Collapse: 38% Attrition: 40%   Comparables: Randy Knorr, Ramon Castro, Ramon Hernandez, Charles Johnson

Snyder chose the right time to get hot, picking things up in July just as Bob Melvin was becoming frustrated with Miguel Montero, the other half of the Diamondbacks' catching duo. That fortuitous timing helped Snyder gain Melvin's confidence and a larger share of the catching timeshare. Snyder has matured into a smooth and strong-armed receiver behind the plate, but he could still use the platoon support when stepping up to it. Then again, you can't wait around to find a star at every position, and the offensive standard is so low among NL backstops (they averaged .256/.318/.394 in 2007) that it's worth giving Snyder a chance to close the gap in his splits.

Chad Tracy — 3B/1B

Bats: L Throws: R Height: 6' 2" Weight: 200 Born: May 22, 1980 Age: 28

YEAR	TEAM	LVL	AGE	PA	R	2B	3B	HR	RBI	BB	SO	SB	CS	EqBRR	AVG	OBP	SLG	MLVr	EqAVG	EqOBP	EqSLG	EqA	VORP	DEFENSE			
2005	ARI	MLB	25	553	73	34	4	27	72	35	78	3	1	-0.1	.308	.359	.553	.266	.299	.350	.548	.298	40.0	73-1B	-2	42-RF	2
2006	ARI	MLB	26	662	91	41	0	20	80	54	129	5	1	-0.6	.281	.343	.451	.043	.272	.337	.437	.268	16.3	142-3B	-18		
2007	ARI	MLB	27	260	30	18	2	7	35	29	43	0	0	-1.3	.264	.346	.454	.046	.253	.342	.449	.274	7.8	42-3B	-1	13-1B	-1
2008	ARI	MLB	28	397	54	23	2	17	61	35	66	3	1	-0.4	.284	.352	.505	.117	.273	.341	.481	.277	17.4	95-3B	-2		

Breakout: 17% Improve: 39% Collapse: 33% Attrition: 23%   Comparables: Pete Ward, Scott Cooper, J. T. Snow, Rico Brogna

Tracy's gunning for an Opening Day return after surgery to repair microfractures in his knee, but whether he's ready by April or June, he'll deserve the chance to reclaim playing time at both infield corners. The club has a first baseman who doesn't hit all that well and a third baseman who isn't great in the field, and both bat right-handed, as do the catcher and all three outfielders. Tracy's lefty pop and career .307/.366/.502 line against right-handed pitching is precisely what this offense needs.

Justin Upton — RF

Bats: R Throws: R Height: 6' 3" Weight: 205 Born: August 25, 1987 Age: 20

YEAR	TEAM	LVL	AGE	PA	R	2B	3B	HR	RBI	BB	SO	SB	CS	EqBRR	AVG	OBP	SLG	MLVr	EqAVG	EqOBP	EqSLG	EqA	VORP	DEFENSE	
2006	SBN	A	18	501	71	28	1	12	66	52	96	15	7	-5.0	.263	.343	.413	.110	.212	.278	.334	.216	-22.3	103-CF	4
2007	VIS	A+	19	150	27	6	2	5	17	19	28	9	4	-1.1	.341	.433	.540	.387	.267	.353	.412	.267	5.2	28-CF	1
2007	MOB	AA	19	306	48	17	4	13	53	37	51	10	7	1.3	.309	.399	.556	.359	.278	.356	.504	.288	23.1	58-CF	-2
2007	ARI	MLB	19	152	17	8	3	2	11	11	37	2	0	-0.4	.221	.283	.364	-.211	.216	.283	.360	.226	-5.3	35-RF	-4
2008	ARI	MLB	20	642	92	37	7	20	78	64	118	18	8	1.1	.271	.349	.471	.054	.261	.338	.448	.267	19.2	150-CF	-5

Breakout: 56% Improve: 76% Collapse: 2% Attrition: 9%   Comparables: Delmon Young, B. J. Upton, Michael Cuddyer, Adrian Gonzalez

After making his professional debut at age 18 in a full-season league in 2006, Upton snapped back in 2007 to pound his way through the Californa League up to Double-A, then got sucked upwards into the Diamondback's vacuum in right field at the beginning of August. He went 7-for-16 with five extra-base hits in his first four starts, but then showed that he's still got a few things to learn, especially about biting on sinkers and pounding them into the dirt. He has tremendous gifts and aptitude to match, so comparisons to Griffey or A-Rod aren't misplaced. The challenge will be for him to decisively earn the job in right this spring, instead of having it handed to him.

Chris Young — CF

Bats: R Throws: R Height: 6' 2" Weight: 180 Born: September 5, 1983 Age: 24

YEAR	TEAM	LVL	AGE	PA	R	2B	3B	HR	RBI	BB	SO	SB	CS	EqBRR	AVG	OBP	SLG	MLVr	EqAVG	EqOBP	EqSLG	EqA	VORP	DEFENSE	
2005	BIR	AA	21	553	100	41	3	26	77	70	129	32	6	1.5	.277	.377	.545	.297	.241	.329	.483	.277	24.6	121-CF	-2
2006	TUC	AAA	22	466	78	32	4	21	77	52	71	17	5	0.9	.276	.363	.532	.179	.244	.326	.477	.273	17.9	100-CF	2
2006	ARI	MLB	22	78	10	4	0	2	10	6	12	2	1	0.4	.243	.308	.386	-.120	.243	.308	.371	.241	0.0	17-CF	3
2007	ARI	MLB	23	624	85	29	3	32	68	43	141	27	6	0.4	.237	.295	.467	-.042	.233	.295	.468	.261	15.5	142-CF	-7
2008	ARI	MLB	24	539	84	32	3	27	81	53	105	22	6	1.2	.274	.352	.523	.132	.263	.342	.498	.283	29.2	127-CF	-1

Breakout: 36% Improve: 63% Collapse: 8% Attrition: 17%   Comparables: Roger Maris, Jim Landis, Richard Hidalgo, Andruw Jones

How many guys get touted for the Rookie of the Year award before the season, hit 32 homers during the season, and are seen as disappointments after? Like Byrnes and Hudson, there's more here than meets the eye—Young's a very effective baserunner and a good center fielder with the tools to be a very good one, and his power isn't merely park-generated. The problem is that he squandered too many at-bats by popping up instead of making solid contact, proving half again as likely to pop up on contact as your average right-handed hitter (doing so 12.5 percent of the time against an average mark of 8.6 percent for all right-handed batters from 2003-2007). He can do much better, and he's gotten good marks for his coachability in the past.

PITCHERS

Hector Ambriz

Bats: L   Throws: R   Height: 6' 1"   Weight: 210   Born: May 24, 1984   Age: 24

YEAR	TEAM	LVL	AGE	W	L	SV	G	GS	IP	H	BB	SO	HR	GB%	BABIP	STUFF	WHIP	ERA	PERA	EqERA	EqH9	EqBB9	EqSO9	EqHR9	VORP	SN/WX
2006	MSO	Rk	22	1	3	3	15	4	42	29	11	52	1	50.0%	.270	0	0.95	1.93	5.20	4.46	8.9	4.7	5.9	0.7	4.6	—
2007	VIS	A+	23	10	8	0	28	26	150	137	50	133	12	43.9%	.295	-11	1.25	4.08	5.49	5.99	9.6	4.4	4.6	1.2	-6.1	—
2008	ARI	MLB	24	6	10	0	32	22	130	155	65	81	25	42.6%	.306	-7	1.69	6.32	6.15	6.12	10.1	4.0	5.2	1.6	-5.1	0.30

Breakout: 12% Improve: 42% Collapse: 28% Attrition: 14%   Comparables: Brian Sikorski, Paul Byrd, Brian Boehringer, Greg Keagle

Your basic command-and-control right-hander spat out by innumerable college programs, Ambriz is a UCLA product the Snakes snagged in the fifth round of the 2006 draft who mixes his off-speed stuff well and spots his fastball. Challenged to work deeper in games in the second half of his full-season debut, he not only averaged an inning more per start, but his strikeout rate improved from 7.5 per 9 to 8.2, and he generated more grounders. High-pick, big-program pitchers are supposed to be able to handle High-A competition, but if he can pick up more steam while getting up to Double-A, he'll sneak onto people's prospect radars.

Brett Anderson

Bats: L   Throws: L   Height: 6' 4"   Weight: 215   Born: February 1, 1988   Age: 20

YEAR	TEAM	LVL	AGE	W	L	SV	G	GS	IP	H	BB	SO	HR	GB%	BABIP	STUFF	WHIP	ERA	PERA	EqERA	EqH9	EqBB9	EqSO9	EqHR9	VORP	SN/WX
2007	SBN	A	19	8	4	0	14	14	81¹	76	10	85	3	60.7%	.335	16	1.06	2.21	5.72	5.43	11.0	3.0	4.9	1.0	1.3	—
2007	VIS	A+	19	3	3	0	9	9	39	50	11	40	6	53.3%	.383	-4	1.56	4.85	11.36	8.21	14.8	4.2	5.8	2.4	-9.9	—
2008	OAK	MLB	20	6	11	0	26	26	140¹	183	61	76	19	50.5%	.336	-1	1.74	6.06	6.25	6.13	11.4	3.5	4.6	1.2	-12.0	-0.20

Breakout: 20% Improve: 64% Collapse: 14% Attrition: 10%   Comparables: Chris George, Aaron Thompson, Michael Bowden, Anthony Swarzak

A second-round pick in 2006, Anderson is the son of the head baseball coach at Oklahoma State, so it's no surprise that he's arguably the most polished high school pitcher to be drafted in years. How often do you find a teenager with plus-plus command? How often do you find one with an outstanding changeup? Anderson has both, as well as a plus curve and average-velocity fastball. He's not a pure power pitcher, and he's also a little pudgy, but if you had to gamble on any teenage pitcher to reach the majors (not star, mind you, just get there), Anderson might be your best bet. That ability to move up fast may serve him particulary well now that he's been transplanted as part of the Haren deal to an Oakland team that needs pitching.

Brooks Brown

Bats: L   Throws: R   Height: 6' 3"   Weight: 205   Born: June 20, 1985   Age: 23

YEAR	TEAM	LVL	AGE	W	L	SV	G	GS	IP	H	BB	SO	HR	GB%	BABIP	STUFF	WHIP	ERA	PERA	EqERA	EqH9	EqBB9	EqSO9	EqHR9	VORP	SN/WX
2006	YAK	A-	21	0	2	0	13	1	23	23	12	30	2	55.6%	.350	-10	1.52	3.52	10.79	8.69	12.8	8.7	6.4	2.3	-6.8	—
2007	VIS	A+	22	6	3	0	14	14	80	66	23	74	2	58.4%	.292	10	1.11	2.81	4.44	4.54	8.8	3.9	4.9	0.5	8.6	—
2007	MOB	AA	22	4	4	0	12	12	66¹	64	36	54	2	52.5%	.328	7	1.51	3.67	5.19	5.00	9.4	5.4	4.7	0.6	4.2	—
2008	ARI	MLB	23	6	11	0	25	25	134²	157	79	85	17	52.0%	.318	0	1.75	5.91	5.75	5.86	9.9	4.7	5.3	1.0	-1.4	0.90

Breakout: 10% Improve: 31% Collapse: 40% Attrition: 9%   Comparables: Brian Williams, Marc Valdes, Sean Bergman, Brad Rigby

Brown was a closer at the University of Georgia, but Arizona had designs on making him a starter when they drafted him in the supplemental round in 2006. It looks like a smart decision thus far as he reached Double-A in his full-season debut last year. He's a classic sinker/slider pitcher who is still working on a changeup, but, even without one, he was still effective enough against left-handers to avoid getting into too much trouble. He projects as somewhere between a third and fifth starter.

Juan Cruz

Bats: R   Throws: R   Height: 6' 2"   Weight: 155   Born: October 15, 1978   Age: 29

YEAR	TEAM	LVL	AGE	W	L	SV	G	GS	IP	H	BB	SO	HR	GB%	BABIP	STUFF	WHIP	ERA	PERA	EqERA	EqH9	EqBB9	EqSO9	EqHR9	VORP	SN/WX
2005	SAC	AAA	26	5	1	0	13	13	75	51	28	90	4	49.5%	.273	29	1.05	2.40	3.40	3.15	6.4	3.7	7.9	0.6	19.4	—
2005	OAK	MLB	26	0	3	0	28	0	32²	38	22	34	5	43.4%	.359	-1	1.84	7.43	8.22	9.66	11.1	6.3	9.4	1.4	-12.1	-0.54
2006	ARI	MLB	27	5	6	0	31	15	94²	80	47	88	7	43.1%	.289	20	1.34	4.18	3.51	3.67	7.2	3.9	7.5	0.6	19.8	2.94
2007	ARI	MLB	28	6	1	0	53	0	61	45	32	87	7	35.0%	.302	24	1.26	3.10	3.67	3.69	6.9	4.0	10.8	0.9	12.3	0.81
2008	ARI	MLB	29	3	4	3	53	1	68²	62	39	78	10	41.8%	.300	14	1.47	4.55	4.44	4.44	7.7	4.5	9.4	1.2	9.2	0.90

Breakout: 28% Improve: 59% Collapse: 17% Attrition: 4%   Comparables: Jack Meyer, Felix Rodriguez, Armando Benitez, Jeff Brantley

Left alone in a relief role for a full season, Cruz was throwing mid-90s bullets consistently after missing three weeks with an early shoulder injury, showing what the stringbean can do when all he has to worry about is putting every ounce of mustard on his stuff. The problem is that he seems to be degenerating into a right-handed specialist—last year he held righties to .143/.211/.277 while striking them out 42 percent of the time, but lefties hit .269/.412/.454 against him. That's still pretty useful, but his manager kept him away from late or really tight situations.

Doug Davis

Bats: R   Throws: L   Height: 6' 4"   Weight: 210   Born: September 21, 1975   Age: 32

YEAR	TEAM	LVL	AGE	W	L	SV	G	GS	IP	H	BB	SO	HR	GB%	BABIP	STUFF	WHIP	ERA	PERA	EqERA	EqH9	EqBB9	EqSO9	EqHR9	VORP	SN/WX
2005	MIL	MLB	29	11	11	0	35	35	222²	196	93	208	26	46.8%	.283	19	1.30	3.84	4.04	4.12	8.1	3.4	7.7	1.0	35.6	4.98
2006	MIL	MLB	30	11	11	0	34	34	203¹	206	102	159	19	46.7%	.314	15	1.51	4.91	4.28	4.44	8.8	3.9	6.4	0.7	18.8	3.01
2007	ARI	MLB	31	13	12	0	33	33	192²	211	95	144	21	48.7%	.325	10	1.59	4.25	5.08	4.30	9.7	3.8	6.4	0.9	28.6	4.00
2008	ARI	MLB	32	9	11	0	29	29	173²	188	78	126	23	47.1%	.305	8	1.53	5.00	4.94	4.91	9.1	3.6	6.1	1.1	15.0	3.00

Breakout: 5% Improve: 22% Collapse: 37% Attrition: 11%   Comparables: Rudy May, Chuck Finley, Brian Bohanon, Mike Moore

Credit Josh Byrnes for taking a chance on Davis, who moved into a more difficult home park last year and nevertheless delivered a Doug Davis sort of season. As expected, Phoenix wasn't kind to him; though he split his starts evenly between home and the road, two-thirds of the homers he allowed came at Chase Field. What has separated Davis from 90 percent of the guys we say might be fourth starters is that he's made the Jamie Moyer Leap of Understanding: he gets what his limitations are and works within them, giving his team quality starts more than half the time while relying on his low-velocity curveball-driven mix. He also has one of the best pickoff moves around. He's not quite what you want at the front of your rotation, but he provides the sort of stability that lets the Diamondbacks take their chances with Randy Johnson.

Dana Eveland

Bats: L   Throws: L   Height: 6' 1"   Weight: 240   Born: October 29, 1983   Age: 24

YEAR	TEAM	LVL	AGE	W	L	SV	G	GS	IP	H	BB	SO	HR	GB%	BABIP	STUFF	WHIP	ERA	PERA	EqERA	EqH9	EqBB9	EqSO9	EqHR9	VORP	SN/WX
2005	HUN	AA	21	10	4	0	18	18	109	96	38	98	4	61.7%	.304	18	1.23	2.72	4.13	4.15	8.2	3.8	5.2	0.7	16.4	—
2005	MIL	MLB	21	1	1	1	27	0	31²	40	18	23	2	52.9%	.376	-4	1.83	5.96	7.24	6.75	12.6	4.9	6.4	0.6	-1.6	0.68
2006	NAS	AAA	22	6	5	0	20	19	105²	71	41	110	4	55.1%	.275	28	1.06	2.74	3.58	4.23	7.0	3.9	7.1	0.5	15.2	—
2006	MIL	MLB	22	0	3	0	9	5	27²	39	16	32	4	47.7%	.427	6	1.99	8.12	8.93	8.04	12.5	4.5	9.3	1.0	-6.0	-0.95
2007	TUC	AAA	23	1	0	0	7	5	27²	29	10	15	0	57.4%	.315	-2	1.41	1.95	3.61	2.28	8.5	3.6	3.6	0.3	10.2	—
2008	OAK	MLB	24	5	7	1	47	13	101	107	51	66	9	53.7%	.305	-4	1.57	5.04	4.88	5.21	9.3	4.1	5.5	0.8	1.9	0.70

Breakout: 42% Improve: 65% Collapse: 16% Attrition: 15%   Comparables: Chris Capuano, Omar Daal, Rafael Perez, Juan Dominguez

Last year was a lost season for Eveland, as a torn tendon in the middle finger of his pitching hand cost him three months. He's also handicapped by his propensity to observe the first law of thermodynamics by converting potential energy into flab instead of pure performance. Still, he's a lefty who throws over 90 mph, and that buys a guy a lot of forgiveness, even among picky physicists. He'll get his opportunities, but if they're going to come in the rotation he has to improve his durability. That's why he was logging innings as a starter in the Mexican winter league, and now that he's been sent to the A's in the Haren deal, he might get his next shot as a starter as soon as April.

Emiliano Fruto

Bats: R **Throws:** R **Height:** 6' 3" **Weight:** 230 **Born:** June 6, 1984 **Age:** 24

YEAR	TEAM	LVL	AGE	W	L	SV	G	GS	IP	H	BB	SO	HR	GB%	BABIP	STUFF	WHIP	ERA	PERA	EqERA	EqH9	EqBB9	EqSO9	EqHR9	VORP	SN/WX
2005	SAN	AA	21	2	3	12	40	0	66²	56	22	63	6	41.5%	.289	-4	1.17	2.56	4.85	4.15	8.5	4.3	6.1	1.3	9.8	—
2006	TAC	AAA	22	1	3	10	28	0	45¹	33	21	55	1	51.4%	.302	15	1.20	3.19	3.71	5.52	7.2	4.5	8.2	0.4	0.4	—
2006	SEA	MLB	22	2	2	1	23	0	36	34	24	34	4	37.1%	.300	11	1.61	5.50	4.70	5.50	8.2	5.5	8.0	1.0	-0.1	0.54
2007	COH	AAA	23	3	9	0	18	16	87¹	78	59	68	6	46.3%	.301	1	1.57	5.26	5.70	6.39	9.0	6.7	5.2	1.0	-7.2	—
2007	TUC	AAA	23	0	1	0	6	0	11	8	10	14	0	40.0%	.348	10	1.64	2.45	4.24	2.61	7.0	8.7	9.6	0.0	3.4	—
2008	ARI	MLB	24	4	7	0	27	14	83²	87	57	63	12	44.2%	.295	-4	1.71	5.95	5.59	5.85	8.8	5.4	6.3	1.2	-0.9	0.40

Breakout: 22% **Improve:** 54% **Collapse:** 20% **Attrition:** 13% **Comparables:** Rafael Medina, Mac Suzuki, Juan Morillo, Ray Ricken

As frustrating a project pitcher as Eveland, Fruto was dealt twice in a nine-month span, first from Seattle to D.C. in the Jose Vidro deal, then to Arizona for minor league first baseman Chris Carter the Elder. In between, the Nats tried to turn him into a starter to exploit his mix of occasionally tasty breaking stuff, a plus changeup, and consistent low-90s heat. That failed, and Fruto's ongoing control problems showed no sign of letting up even after his return to the pen. He's young and talented, but handicapped by something of a short fuse, and he has no track record for success. Still, anything is possible with some good coaching, hard work, and the occasional timeout.

Edgar Gonzalez

Bats: R **Throws:** R **Height:** 6' 0" **Weight:** 225 **Born:** February 23, 1983 **Age:** 25

YEAR	TEAM	LVL	AGE	W	L	SV	G	GS	IP	H	BB	SO	HR	GB%	BABIP	STUFF	WHIP	ERA	PERA	EqERA	EqH9	EqBB9	EqSO9	EqHR9	VORP	SN/WX
2005	TUC	AAA	22	11	6	0	28	24	167	185	38	116	20	45.6%	.319	-4	1.34	4.37	5.27	5.32	10.2	2.4	4.3	1.2	4.9	—
2006	TUC	AAA	23	3	8	0	24	24	138¹	142	27	107	11	46.0%	.319	6	1.22	3.91	4.77	5.00	9.7	2.1	5.1	1.0	8.8	—
2006	ARI	MLB	23	3	4	0	11	5	42²	45	9	28	7	40.1%	.292	5	1.27	4.22	4.21	3.53	8.7	1.7	5.4	1.2	8.6	0.82
2007	ARI	MLB	24	8	4	0	32	12	102	110	28	62	18	45.3%	.288	-13	1.35	5.03	4.91	4.87	9.3	2.1	5.1	1.4	7.3	1.89
2008	ARI	MLB	25	5	8	0	42	12	108¹	130	33	67	23	43.5%	.303	-7	1.50	5.93	5.57	5.76	10.2	2.4	5.2	1.7	-0.1	0.40

Breakout: 17% **Improve:** 46% **Collapse:** 28% **Attrition:** 6% **Comparables:** Jose Bautista, Amaury Telemaco, Brian Rose, Tim Stauffer

Gonzalez has been valuable as a utility pitcher of sorts, flipping between long relief and the rotation on an as-needed basis (which was often last year, given Randy Johnson's back problems). Gonzalez is a short right-hander without an out pitch; he throws strikes, but doesn't have a lot of movement or angle on his fastball, and his merely nice breaking stuff doesn't freeze lefties. An escape from Chase Field to a roomier ballpark would help, as was illustrated by the extra 46 points of isolated power he allowed at home in 2007.

Matthew Green

Bats: R **Throws:** R **Height:** 6' 5" **Weight:** 195 **Born:** January 5, 1982 **Age:** 26

YEAR	TEAM	LVL	AGE	W	L	SV	G	GS	IP	H	BB	SO	HR	GB%	BABIP	STUFF	WHIP	ERA	PERA	EqERA	EqH9	EqBB9	EqSO9	EqHR9	VORP	SN/WX
2005	MSO	Rk	23	4	3	0	15	12	60	77	26	59	6	48.7%	.397	-40	1.72	5.55	11.79	10.33	14.5	8.5	3.4	2.4	-26.1	—
2006	LNC	A+	24	5	12	0	27	27	136¹	182	51	96	18	40.9%	.358	-49	1.71	5.16	8.55	7.94	12.2	4.8	3.1	2.0	-33.9	—
2007	MOB	AA	25	12	6	0	28	28	148	151	55	128	15	45.1%	.319	-18	1.39	3.95	6.20	5.74	10.3	3.8	5.0	1.5	-2.2	—
2008	ARI	MLB	26	3	7	0	24	14	83	107	47	48	18	44.5%	.319	-16	1.86	7.16	7.04	6.89	10.9	4.6	4.9	1.8	-10.8	-0.50

Breakout: 21% **Improve:** 55% **Collapse:** 27% **Attrition:** 22% **Comparables:** Patrick Coogan, Ryan Mottl, Brian Rogers, Jeff Farnsworth

Green is a tall right-hander with a plus fastball. That was enough for him to put together a solid (at best) showing at Double-A last year, but therein lies the problem; he's becoming a one-pitch pitcher, since his below-average slider and changeup fool fewer and fewer hitters as he's moved up the ladder. Expect a move to the bullpen sooner than later.

Livan Hernandez

Bats: R **Throws:** R **Height:** 6' 2" **Weight:** 245 **Born:** February 20, 1975 **Age:** 33

YEAR	TEAM	LVL	AGE	W	L	SV	G	GS	IP	H	BB	SO	HR	GB%	BABIP	STUFF	WHIP	ERA	PERA	EqERA	EqH9	EqBB9	EqSO9	EqHR9	VORP	SN/WX
2005	WAS	MLB	30	15	10	0	35	35	246¹	268	84	147	25	42.3%	.315	4	1.43	3.98	5.05	4.61	10.0	2.9	5.0	0.9	33.6	5.21
2006	WAS	MLB	31	9	8	0	24	24	146²	176	52	89	22	40.0%	.322	-5	1.55	5.34	5.55	5.47	10.3	2.7	5.0	1.2	2.5	1.50
2006	ARI	MLB	31	4	5	0	10	10	69¹	70	26	39	7	36.8%	.290	8	1.38	3.77	3.92	3.37	8.6	2.9	4.7	0.8	16.1	1.66
2007	ARI	MLB	32	11	11	0	33	33	204¹	247	79	90	34	41.5%	.314	-16	1.60	4.93	6.13	4.86	10.5	3.0	3.8	1.4	20.4	3.11
2008	ARI	MLB	33	7	11	0	26	26	149	178	54	73	25	43.0%	.300	-5	1.55	5.54	5.46	5.39	10.1	2.9	4.1	1.4	5.8	1.80

Breakout: 8% **Improve:** 29% **Collapse:** 43% **Attrition:** 23% **Comparables:** Jaime Navarro, Brett Tomko, Aaron Sele, Tim Belcher

As expected, Livan delivered innings and starts, but a strikeout rate that low is flirting with the sort of "only fooling himself" point of no return that swallowed up the tail ends of the careers of Jaime Navarro, Craig Biggio, and Robin Williams. Last year brought Hernandez's lowest innings total since 1999; if durability is the basis of his value now that he's not overpowering anybody, that's not a good sign. He still throws four pitches for strikes, and he did produce 20 quality starts in 33 outings if you include quality starts lost after the sixth inning, but he's now no more than a back-end stalwart, sort of like Sir Mix-A-Lot in spikes.

Randy Johnson

Bats: R   Throws: L   Height: 6' 10"   Weight: 231   Born: September 10, 1963   Age: 44

YEAR	TEAM	LVL	AGE	W	L	SV	G	GS	IP	H	BB	SO	HR	GB%	BABIP	STUFF	WHIP	ERA	PERA	EqERA	EqH9	EqBB9	EqSO9	EqHR9	VORP	SN/WX
2005	NYA	MLB	41	17	8	0	34	34	225²	207	47	211	32	45.2%	.288	24	1.13	3.79	3.74	3.71	7.9	1.9	8.2	1.2	43.8	5.63
2006	NYA	MLB	42	17	11	0	33	33	205	194	60	172	28	42.7%	.288	15	1.24	5.00	4.08	5.11	8.3	2.5	7.1	1.1	12.3	2.42
2007	ARI	MLB	43	4	3	0	10	10	56²	52	13	72	7	43.1%	.338	39	1.15	3.81	3.96	3.74	8.6	1.8	10.1	1.0	12.3	1.48
2008	ARI	MLB	44	5	4	0	14	14	75²	72	22	78	10	43.9%	.301	26	1.23	3.94	3.71	3.88	8.0	2.3	8.6	1.1	17.8	2.20

Breakout: 37%   Improve: 60%   Collapse: 28%   Attrition: 40%   Comparables: Satchel Paige, Don McMahon, Gaylord Perry, Hoyt Wilhelm

Johnson is the fulcrum around which the Diamondbacks' fortunes revolve, but he could turn their fearsome one-two punch in the rotation into a great front three if he can stay healthy. Johnson's back surgery in August went well, and he was rehabbing in September, but it was his second such surgery in less than a year. The challenge for the D'backs is avoiding a third, which would likely be career-ending. A reduced workload seems like the best answer; if Roger Clemens could be a six-inning ace for four months in Houston, Johnson could be the best five-inning starter in the game's history. That might seem like an odd modern artifact, but if it reduces the strain on Johnson's back, it could allow him to work deeper into games in September and October, and could get him to 300 wins in the process (he needs 16 more). There's still the chance that he'll simply break down for good no matter what Arizona does; the standard assertions about what sort of workload should be assigned to a pitcher Johnson's age are sort of hard to apply to such a physical anomaly as the Big Unit, especially when he's still overpowering this many people at the plate.

Brandon Lyon

Bats: R   Throws: R   Height: 6' 1"   Weight: 195   Born: August 10, 1979   Age: 28

YEAR	TEAM	LVL	AGE	W	L	SV	G	GS	IP	H	BB	SO	HR	GB%	BABIP	STUFF	WHIP	ERA	PERA	EqERA	EqH9	EqBB9	EqSO9	EqHR9	VORP	SN/WX
2005	ARI	MLB	25	0	2	14	32	0	29¹	44	10	17	6	43.5%	.358	-32	1.84	6.45	8.37	7.63	12.3	2.6	4.4	1.8	-6.6	1.45
2006	ARI	MLB	26	2	4	0	68	0	69¹	68	22	46	7	44.0%	.289	0	1.30	3.90	3.57	3.47	8.2	2.4	5.4	0.8	15.4	1.64
2007	ARI	MLB	27	6	4	2	73	0	74	70	22	40	2	43.4%	.287	7	1.24	2.68	3.10	2.81	8.2	2.3	4.6	0.2	24.0	4.36
2008	ARI	MLB	28	3	3	2	58	0	66¹	76	23	39	9	45.0%	.303	-10	1.50	5.04	4.90	4.96	9.7	2.8	4.9	1.2	5.6	0.50

Breakout: 8%   Improve: 20%   Collapse: 56%   Attrition: 7%   Comparables: Tom Hume, Chuck Crim, Randy Moffitt, Carlos Reyes

He's not the classic set-up man who either throws almost as hard as the closer or is polishing his craft as the closer-in-waiting. Instead, Lyon merely pitches exceptionally well from the stretch and doesn't bat an eye with runners on base. It makes for an unusual eighth-inning hero, and despite our low expectations, he put up his best year yet in 2007. Two years ago, nobody would have rated Lyon over Scott Linebrink, but it was the former, not the latter who finished in major league's top ten in WXRL in 2007. Such is the nature of the frequent turnover within the ranks of the game's top relievers.

Brandon Medders

Bats: R   Throws: R   Height: 6' 1"   Weight: 190   Born: January 26, 1980   Age: 28

YEAR	TEAM	LVL	AGE	W	L	SV	G	GS	IP	H	BB	SO	HR	GB%	BABIP	STUFF	WHIP	ERA	PERA	EqERA	EqH9	EqBB9	EqSO9	EqHR9	VORP	SN/WX
2005	TUC	AAA	25	3	2	8	36	0	36¹	31	18	44	3	55.3%	.318	10	1.35	2.48	4.61	2.91	8.5	4.8	8.2	0.8	10.2	—
2005	ARI	MLB	25	4	1	0	27	0	30¹	21	11	31	2	46.8%	.253	20	1.05	1.78	2.65	1.76	5.9	2.9	8.2	0.6	12.6	0.73
2006	ARI	MLB	26	5	3	0	60	0	71²	76	28	47	5	43.9%	.310	0	1.45	3.64	3.93	4.09	8.9	3.0	5.3	0.5	12.0	0.92
2007	TUC	AAA	27	5	3	5	35	0	48	55	24	38	3	43.9%	.344	-9	1.65	4.69	4.98	5.10	9.6	4.7	5.3	0.8	2.7	—
2007	ARI	MLB	27	1	2	0	30	0	29¹	30	16	23	9	29.5%	.269	-19	1.57	4.30	7.84	5.08	9.2	4.4	7.0	2.5	3.6	-0.41
2008	ARI	MLB	28	3	3	2	57	1	61²	66	31	44	8	41.0%	.300	-6	1.56	4.91	4.89	4.81	9.0	4.0	6.0	1.0	6.7	0.60

Breakout: 14%   Improve: 34%   Collapse: 38%   Attrition: 7%   Comparables: Jim Dickson, Gabe Molina, Jason Anderson, Todd Erdos

Medders isn't gifted with an overpowering pitch, so early last year when he struggled with his command against right-handers and still couldn't fool lefties, it was enough to punch his ticket back to Tucson. Because he doesn't have a strong breaking pitch, the mistakes he was making up in the zone with a fastball/cutter mix were getting tattooed (eight homers in 22⅓ innings prior to his June demotion). If he can keep the ball down, he can get back to being a useful arm in the back of the bullpen.

Bill Murphy

Bats: L   Throws: L   Height: 5' 11"   Weight: 215   Born: May 9, 1981   Age: 27

YEAR	TEAM	LVL	AGE	W	L	SV	G	GS	IP	H	BB	SO	HR	GB%	BABIP	STUFF	WHIP	ERA	PERA	EqERA	EqH9	EqBB9	EqSO9	EqHR9	VORP	SN/WX
2005	TUC	AAA	24	6	8	0	23	21	121	135	78	87	14	49.2%	.324	-11	1.76	5.65	6.63	6.36	10.4	6.1	4.4	1.2	-9.7	—
2006	TEN	AA	25	0	1	0	5	4	21	22	9	26	2	47.4%	.377	0	1.48	5.57	7.61	7.91	11.6	4.7	7.9	1.4	-5.0	—
2006	TUC	AAA	25	5	4	0	37	9	80^1	86	38	72	5	41.8%	.339	-7	1.55	5.62	5.45	6.57	10.2	4.7	5.9	0.8	-8.3	—
2007	TUC	AAA	26	3	3	1	54	9	100^1	93	43	102	10	50.5%	.312	-1	1.36	3.68	4.43	4.58	8.0	4.1	7.0	1.0	11.1	—
2007	ARI	MLB	26	0	0	0	10	0	6^1	9	7	2	0	50.0%	.375	-20	2.53	5.71	9.90	6.00	13.5	9.0	3.0	0.0	0.3	-0.03
2008	ARI	MLB	27	3	5	4	51	6	63^1	66	39	50	8	47.3%	.304	-5	1.65	5.13	5.12	5.07	8.8	5.0	6.6	1.0	4.9	0.70

Breakout: 40% Improve: 68% Collapse: 17% Attrition: 13%   Comparables: Tim Byrdak, Len Whitehouse, Kenny Rogers, Travis Miller

Maybe it's a reflection of Murphy's ambiguous role on a pitching staff and in the organization, but some people think he might make a good pitching coach. Teams seem to want him—he's been packaged in three major trades during his career, coming to Arizona in the deal that sent Steve Finley to L.A.—but where he fits is an open question. If a staff needed a lefty utility pitcher, Murphy would do, as he's got a decent fastball for a southpaw, works in a good curveball and change to keep hitters off balance, and gets good marks for his aptitude. But how many lefty utility pitchers do you see these days?

Dustin Nippert

Bats: R   Throws: R   Height: 6' 8"   Weight: 225   Born: May 6, 1981   Age: 27

YEAR	TEAM	LVL	AGE	W	L	SV	G	GS	IP	H	BB	SO	HR	GB%	BABIP	STUFF	WHIP	ERA	PERA	EqERA	EqH9	EqBB9	EqSO9	EqHR9	VORP	SN/WX
2005	TEN	AA	24	8	3	0	18	18	117^1	95	42	97	4	55.3%	.285	11	1.17	2.38	3.86	3.28	7.5	3.9	4.7	0.7	28.3	—
2005	ARI	MLB	24	1	0	0	3	3	14^2	10	13	11	1	46.5%	.214	10	1.57	5.51	3.33	4.70	5.3	7.0	5.9	0.6	0.1	0.31
2006	TUC	AAA	25	13	8	0	25	24	140	161	52	130	11	47.0%	.353	1	1.52	4.89	6.02	6.24	11.1	3.8	6.2	0.9	-9.4	—
2006	ARI	MLB	25	0	2	0	2	2	10	15	7	9	5	57.1%	.345	-35	2.20	11.70	17.74	13.94	12.2	5.2	7.0	3.5	-5.7	-0.41
2007	TUC	AAA	26	0	3	0	10	8	36	23	23	46	3	39.7%	.274	26	1.28	4.75	3.68	4.76	5.8	6.1	9.3	0.8	3.2	—
2007	ARI	MLB	26	1	1	0	36	0	45^1	48	16	38	5	39.4%	.314	2	1.41	5.56	4.34	5.36	9.1	2.8	6.9	0.8	0.4	0.65
2008	ARI	MLB	27	3	4	1	47	3	71	77	32	56	10	45.6%	.310	-1	1.54	5.34	5.02	5.26	9.3	3.7	6.6	1.2	3.8	0.40

Breakout: 38% Improve: 54% Collapse: 15% Attrition: 5%   Comparables: Jim Britton, Tom Davey, Jeff Nelson, Rick Bauer

Nipper's power curve flattens out at times, and there's concern that he isn't aggressive enough with his fastball, strange as that may seem for a guy this big. That might mean he's better off staying in the pen, where mid-90s heat and a sometime plus bender can be enough; he might even grow into a great big-league reliever. Still, it's worth wondering whether putting him in a park with a more spacious outfield would give you a poor man's version of San Diego's Chris Young.

Micah Owings

Bats: R   Throws: R   Height: 6' 5"   Weight: 220   Born: September 28, 1982   Age: 25

YEAR	TEAM	LVL	AGE	W	L	SV	G	GS	IP	H	BB	SO	HR	GB%	BABIP	STUFF	WHIP	ERA	PERA	EqERA	EqH9	EqBB9	EqSO9	EqHR9	VORP	SN/WX
2005	LNC	A+	22	1	1	0	16	0	22	17	4	30	0	42.9%	.362	15	0.95	2.45	3.82	3.60	8.1	2.7	7.7	0.4	4.4	—
2006	TEN	AA	23	6	2	0	12	12	74	66	17	69	4	46.8%	.318	12	1.12	2.92	4.69	4.14	9.5	2.5	5.7	0.9	10.9	—
2006	TUC	AAA	23	10	0	0	15	15	87^2	96	34	61	4	39.6%	.338	3	1.49	3.72	5.35	4.74	10.5	4.0	4.5	0.6	7.8	—
2007	ARI	MLB	24	8	8	0	29	27	152^2	146	50	106	20	38.7%	.279	8	1.28	4.30	4.08	4.19	8.3	2.5	5.8	1.1	21.1	2.92
2008	ARI	MLB	25	8	10	0	26	26	147	163	53	103	24	42.5%	.300	9	1.46	5.19	5.03	5.06	9.4	2.9	5.8	1.4	11.5	2.30

Breakout: 6% Improve: 23% Collapse: 38% Attrition: 3%   Comparables: Bob Heffner, Ryan Rupe, Doc Medich, Bob Milacki

Owings is the new Don Robinson, with a bat good enough to sneak into the lineup now and again, and a good power pitcher's assortment of low-90s heat and a snappy slider. If there's a major difference, it's Owings' mean streak when it comes to the inside corner; he was tied for second in the NL in hit batsmen last year with 14, behind only a cranky Byung-Hyun Kim. After posting eight quality starts in his last ten (one blown), he's prepped for a better sophomore season.

Jarrod Parker

Bats: R   Throws: R   Height: 6' 1"   Weight: 180   Born: November 24, 1988   Age: 19

YEAR	TEAM	LVL	AGE	W	L	SV	G	GS	IP	H	BB	SO	HR	GB%	BABIP	STUFF	WHIP	ERA	PERA	EqERA	EqH9	EqBB9	EqSO9	EqHR9	VORP	SN/WX
2008	ARI	MLB	19	4	11	0	25	25	124¹	153	96	74	26	46.0%	.312	-13	2.00	7.44	7.27	7.21	10.5	6.2	5.0	1.7	-19.3	-1.10

Breakout: NA   Improve: NA   Collapse: NA   Attrition: NA   Comparables: Clint Everts, Brian Barber, Luis Cota, Gil Meche

The Diamondbacks' first-round pick in June, Parker was the late bloomer of the 2007 draft. As word spread of the little right-hander in the small Indiana town who was pumping out upper-90s gas, his last few starts began to have more scouts than actual fans in attendance. The Cubs loved him and almost took him third overall, making it somewhat surprising that he fell into the Snakes' lap at number nine. He's a little raw when it comes to command and secondary stuff, but his arm speed is a rare commodity. He'll likely be treated with kid gloves in 2008, so be patient.

Jailen Peguero

Bats: R   Throws: R   Height: 6' 0"   Weight: 195   Born: January 4, 1981   Age: 27

YEAR	TEAM	LVL	AGE	W	L	SV	G	GS	IP	H	BB	SO	HR	GB%	BABIP	STUFF	WHIP	ERA	PERA	EqERA	EqH9	EqBB9	EqSO9	EqHR9	VORP	SN/WX
2005	CCH	AA	24	2	2	12	50	0	64¹	62	25	63	3	46.3%	.331	-5	1.35	2.94	6.04	5.08	10.8	5.1	6.4	0.8	3.3	—
2006	CCH	AA	25	2	0	14	27	0	38²	18	16	48	0	39.2%	.234	19	0.89	0.71	3.25	2.04	5.3	4.6	8.2	0.3	14.0	—
2006	ROU	AAA	25	1	2	1	21	0	36	34	8	30	3	48.0%	.299	-12	1.44	3.50	5.29	5.60	9.4	4.8	5.3	1.0	0.0	—
2007	TUC	AAA	26	6	2	4	53	0	66²	47	26	68	5	50.0%	.261	8	1.09	1.89	3.17	2.60	5.9	3.7	7.0	0.8	21.9	—
2007	ARI	MLB	26	1	0	0	18	0	14²	17	13	9	2	29.2%	.341	-22	2.05	9.18	7.98	9.00	10.9	7.1	5.1	1.3	-4.9	0.13
2008	ARI	MLB	27	3	4	3	57	3	60¹	58	34	49	8	43.4%	.286	-3	1.53	4.78	4.67	4.71	8.2	4.5	6.8	1.1	6.9	0.70

Breakout: 26%   Improve: 51%   Collapse: 29%   Attrition: 10%   Comparables: Jesus Colome, Hector Carrasco, Felix Rodriguez, Jorge Vasquez

No plus pitch, generic arm, generic stuff . . . for Peguero to get any more nondescript he'd have to trade names with Tony Peña. And why not? Peguero is another Age-gate Dominican. Your basic command guy, Peguero threw strikes on 66 percent of his pitches for Triple-A Tucson. He might surface as somebody's middle-relief innings-eater, but he's not a great bet to push his way into a pen as well-stocked as Arizona's.

Tony Peña

Bats: R   Throws: R   Height: 6' 1"   Weight: 220   Born: January 9, 1982   Age: 26

YEAR	TEAM	LVL	AGE	W	L	SV	G	GS	IP	H	BB	SO	HR	GB%	BABIP	STUFF	WHIP	ERA	PERA	EqERA	EqH9	EqBB9	EqSO9	EqHR9	VORP	SN/WX
2005	TEN	AA	23	7	13	0	25	25	148¹	165	40	95	17	42.3%	.314	-30	1.38	4.43	6.58	6.42	10.6	3.1	3.5	1.8	-12.5	—
2006	TEN	AA	24	2	0	6	17	0	20²	18	5	17	0	60.3%	.295	-1	1.14	0.89	3.43	1.77	8.0	2.7	4.9	0.0	8.6	—
2006	TUC	AAA	24	3	1	7	24	0	26²	17	2	21	1	48.5%	.212	5	0.73	1.72	2.65	2.81	5.6	1.1	5.3	0.4	8.0	—
2006	ARI	MLB	24	3	4	1	25	0	30²	36	8	21	6	41.5%	.309	-12	1.43	5.57	5.10	5.46	9.8	2.0	5.5	1.4	0.3	0.89
2007	ARI	MLB	25	5	4	2	75	0	85¹	63	31	63	8	48.6%	.236	7	1.10	3.27	2.92	3.40	6.4	2.8	6.3	0.7	20.7	4.10
2008	ARI	MLB	26	3	4	3	64	0	73	73	28	51	11	44.3%	.280	-4	1.38	4.68	4.35	4.63	8.5	3.1	5.8	1.2	8.8	0.70

Breakout: 19%   Improve: 41%   Collapse: 27%   Attrition: 4%   Comparables: Steve Foucault, Turk Farrell, Steve Ontiveros, Bobby Thigpen

Along with Doug Slaten, Peña was the NL West champions' cleaner, the guy who inherited ugly situations and fixed them. That was all the more impressive given how close he was to not even having a career under his pre-Age-gate *nomme de mound*, Adriano Rosario. Is it ironic, given the other Tony Peñas running around out there, that this one's found a home in the equally nondescript realm of middle relief only after reverting to that name? If so, the irony might not last; Peña's hard heat and solid slider make him the best closer candidate of all of the guys who were knocking around in front of Jose Valverde before the closer was dealt to Houston.

Yusmeiro Petit

Bats: R   Throws: R   Height: 6' 0"   Weight: 230   Born: November 22, 1984   Age: 23

YEAR	TEAM	LVL	AGE	W	L	SV	G	GS	IP	H	BB	SO	HR	GB%	BABIP	STUFF	WHIP	ERA	PERA	EqERA	EqH9	EqBB9	EqSO9	EqHR9	VORP	SN/WX
2005	BIN	AA	20	9	3	0	21	21	117²	90	18	130	15	35.0%	.262	13	0.92	2.91	4.37	4.08	7.8	2.2	6.4	1.8	18.2	—
2005	NOR	AAA	20	0	3	0	3	3	14²	24	6	14	5	33.3%	.422	-29	2.04	9.18	22.26	17.31	17.3	4.8	6.2	4.2	-16.9	—
2006	ABQ	AAA	21	4	6	0	17	17	96²	101	20	68	14	42.5%	.295	-6	1.26	4.30	4.86	5.04	9.1	2.2	4.5	1.6	5.9	—
2006	FLO	MLB	21	1	1	0	15	1	26¹	46	9	20	7	32.0%	.429	-28	2.09	9.58	15.07	12.27	15.4	2.8	6.3	2.1	-11.1	-0.37
2007	TUC	AAA	22	8	4	0	17	17	93²	83	38	60	11	27.5%	.258	-4	1.29	4.03	3.81	4.10	7.0	3.8	4.1	1.1	15.7	—
2007	ARI	MLB	22	3	4	0	14	10	57	58	18	40	12	34.1%	.269	0	1.33	4.58	4.76	4.21	8.6	2.3	5.8	1.7	8.0	1.07
2008	ARI	MLB	23	7	10	1	40	24	144¹	154	54	95	29	37.1%	.278	0	1.44	5.26	5.16	5.06	9.1	3.0	5.5	1.7	11.1	2.10

Breakout: 20%   Improve: 51%   Collapse: 19%   Attrition: 6%   Comparables: Luke Prokopec, Rafael Soriano, Amaury Telemaco, Sidney Ponson

Petit fires up the stats-versus-scouts debate, as stat-heads look with enthusiasm upon Petit's youth and collection of excellent ERAs and strikeout rates in the low minors, while scouts warn that he's a changeup pitcher with a funky delivery, mediocre breaking stuff, and no fastball. Lefties crushed him in Triple-A and the majors last year, and while his weak assortment might have gotten him strikes against right-handed bats in the majors, it still landed in the cheap seats with alarming regularity. Add in the usual doubts about short right-handers, and you've got a guy who might grow up to be only staff filler.

Max Scherzer

Bats: R   Throws: R   Height: 6' 3"   Weight: 190   Born: July 27, 1984   Age: 23

YEAR	TEAM	LVL	AGE	W	L	SV	G	GS	IP	H	BB	SO	HR	GB%	BABIP	STUFF	WHIP	ERA	PERA	EqERA	EqH9	EqBB9	EqSO9	EqHR9	VORP	SN/WX
2007	VIS	A+	22	2	0	0	3	3	17	5	2	30	0	53.8%	.192	16	0.41	0.53	2.99	0.00	3.9	1.7	9.0	0.0	10.0	—
2007	MOB	AA	22	4	4	0	14	14	73²	64	40	76	3	50.5%	.316	13	1.41	3.91	4.91	5.61	9.0	5.5	6.3	0.7	-0.1	—
2008	ARI	MLB	23	7	9	0	24	24	134	132	71	106	16	49.3%	.294	13	1.52	4.88	4.70	4.84	8.4	4.3	6.6	1.0	13.4	2.40

Breakout: 12% Improve: 38% Collapse: 25% Attrition: 15%   Comparables: Mike Pelfrey, Steve Soderstrom, Dan Reichert, Jason Young

With the new signing deadline in place, Scherzer holds the distinction of being the last of the yearlong draft hold-outs. Signed just before this year's draft after being picked eleventh overall in 2006, Scherzer was nothing short of spectacular in his first three professional starts at High-A, but when he got bumped up to Double-A Mobile, he found it harder going. Scherzer has an outstanding fastball that gets into the mid-90s and features heavy sink, but the good things to say about him end there, as his command and secondary stuff need a lot of work. Most scouts see him as a reliever in the end, but the good news is that he might prove to be good enough to close if he can develop just one solid second offering.

Doug Slaten

Bats: L   Throws: L   Height: 6' 5"   Weight: 200   Born: February 4, 1980   Age: 28

YEAR	TEAM	LVL	AGE	W	L	SV	G	GS	IP	H	BB	SO	HR	GB%	BABIP	STUFF	WHIP	ERA	PERA	EqERA	EqH9	EqBB9	EqSO9	EqHR9	VORP	SN/WX
2005	TEN	AA	25	2	2	1	58	0	61¹	61	26	72	2	53.8%	.371	-4	1.42	4.26	5.28	7.83	10.2	4.6	7.0	0.6	-13.9	—
2006	TEN	AA	26	2	3	8	40	0	43	31	15	59	1	46.2%	.341	16	1.07	1.88	3.98	3.76	8.5	3.8	8.9	0.5	7.8	—
2006	TUC	AAA	26	2	1	2	18	0	20²	10	7	21	0	51.0%	.222	10	0.84	0.45	2.59	1.80	4.5	3.2	6.8	0.0	8.4	—
2007	ARI	MLB	27	3	2	0	61	0	36¹	41	14	28	4	43.8%	.316	-1	1.51	2.73	4.56	3.38	9.6	2.9	6.3	1.0	9.1	0.10
2008	ARI	MLB	28	2	3	2	62	0	53	57	27	42	6	45.0%	.315	-3	1.58	4.84	4.88	4.76	9.1	4.0	6.6	0.9	5.6	0.50

Breakout: 15% Improve: 33% Collapse: 34% Attrition: 7%   Comparables: Hank Aguirre, Scott Ruskin, Mike Myers, Fred Green

Along with Tony Peña, Slaten drew the rough trade as the reliever brought into the seventh or eight inning with men on base (Peña came in with a team-leading 38 runners aboard, Slaten 36). Using a rookie in the situational lefty role isn't something a lot of teams are willing to try, and even the Diamondbacks didn't use Slaten that aggressively last year. Bob Melvin frequently went to the rookie southpaw to gain the platoon advantage when behind in tight games, but when the Snakes had a lead, he generally went straight to Peña or Brandon Lyon.

Greg Smith

Bats: L   Throws: L   Height: 6' 2"   Weight: 190   Born: December 22, 1983   Age: 24

YEAR	TEAM	LVL	AGE	W	L	SV	G	GS	IP	H	BB	SO	HR	GB%	BABIP	STUFF	WHIP	ERA	PERA	EqERA	EqH9	EqBB9	EqSO9	EqHR9	VORP	SN/WX
2005	MSO	Rk	21	8	5	0	16	14	82¹	69	18	100	8	54.2%	.319	-21	1.06	4.16	6.76	7.07	9.6	4.9	5.0	2.2	-11.4	—
2006	LNC	A+	22	9	0	0	13	13	88	57	31	71	3	54.5%	.239	9	1.00	1.64	3.60	2.96	5.5	4.5	4.1	0.7	24.1	—
2006	TEN	AA	22	5	4	0	11	11	60	65	23	38	4	35.2%	.326	-15	1.47	3.90	6.31	6.34	10.9	4.1	3.6	1.1	-4.5	—
2007	MOB	AA	23	5	3	0	12	12	69²	64	14	62	7	43.5%	.306	0	1.12	3.36	5.10	4.92	9.6	2.2	5.5	1.5	4.8	—
2007	TUC	AAA	23	4	2	0	10	10	52¹	61	18	34	4	40.7%	.339	-2	1.51	3.79	5.05	4.53	10.1	3.4	4.5	0.9	5.9	—
2008	OAK	MLB	24	6	8	0	31	19	119	140	51	66	19	44.3%	.304	-7	1.61	5.68	5.84	5.69	10.3	3.5	4.7	1.5	-4.3	0.30

Breakout: 10% Improve: 30% Collapse: 36% Attrition: 8%   Comparables: Dennis Moeller, Eddie Pierce, Brad Halsey, Rick Krivda

Smith missed the first month of 2007 with some shoulder weakness, but that didn't stop him from earning a promotion to Triple-A, where he finished strong, allowing only four runs in his last four starts (23 IP). Armed with only standard lefty velocity, Smith might aspire to being the next Doug Davis, as he relies on a nifty curve and change and has a top-notch pickoff move. He was outstanding as a starter in the Arizona Fall League, but he's got the stuff to be a quality situational lefty right now. Figuring out how to employ him is Oakland's problem, as Smith was the third southpaw swapped to the A's in the Haren deal.

Jose Valverde

Bats: R   Throws: R   Height: 6' 4"   Weight: 255   Born: July 24, 1979   Age: 28

YEAR	TEAM	LVL	AGE	W	L	SV	G	GS	IP	H	BB	SO	HR	GB%	BABIP	STUFF	WHIP	ERA	PERA	EqERA	EqH9	EqBB9	EqSO9	EqHR9	VORP	SN/WX
2005	ARI	MLB	25	3	4	15	61	0	66¹	51	20	75	5	36.8%	.284	27	1.07	2.44	2.87	2.43	6.6	2.4	9.0	0.7	21.9	2.89
2006	TUC	AAA	26	1	0	3	15	0	17	13	10	18	1	46.8%	.261	-2	1.35	3.18	3.79	5.19	6.7	5.2	6.7	0.5	0.8	—
2006	ARI	MLB	26	2	3	18	44	0	49¹	50	22	69	6	35.4%	.367	20	1.46	5.84	4.53	5.15	9.1	3.4	10.5	0.9	2.1	0.91
2007	ARI	MLB	27	1	4	47	65	0	64¹	46	26	78	7	36.7%	.260	24	1.12	2.66	3.02	2.49	6.4	3.0	9.6	0.8	21.6	4.27
2008	HOU	MLB	28	4	6	39	63	0	69¹	60	31	74	8	39.5%	.287	13	1.30	3.43	4.02	3.60	7.7	3.5	8.5	1.0	14.7	2.50

Breakout: 21%   Improve: 35%   Collapse: 29%   Attrition: 3%   Comparables: Dick Radatz, Lee Smith, Roberto Hernandez, Brian Fuentes

Valverde finally put everything together in 2007, as he was both healthy and the closer all season long. His eleventh-inning meltdown in Game Two of the NLCS caused some to complain about over-specialization because it came in what was only his fourth appearance during the year to last longer than an inning, but he'd done fine the first three times. One could easily flip that argument around and say that the brevity of his outings throughout the year is what kept him healthy and effective enough to set a career high in appearances and help the team get to the NLCS in the first place. With his mid-90s heat and that sort of handling, we should see more great work from Papa Grande as the Astros closer, since he was dealt to Houston over the winter for utilityman Chris Burke and right-handers Chad Qualls and Juan Gutierrez. Valverde should be helped by the move; both parks are homer havens, but Houston's tougher on lefty power hitters.

Brandon Webb

Bats: R   Throws: R   Height: 6' 2"   Weight: 230   Born: May 9, 1979   Age: 29

YEAR	TEAM	LVL	AGE	W	L	SV	G	GS	IP	H	BB	SO	HR	GB%	BABIP	STUFF	WHIP	ERA	PERA	EqERA	EqH9	EqBB9	EqSO9	EqHR9	VORP	SN/WX
2005	ARI	MLB	26	14	12	0	33	33	229	229	59	172	21	65.8%	.310	21	1.26	3.54	3.78	3.53	8.6	2.1	6.2	0.8	46.2	5.32
2006	ARI	MLB	27	16	8	0	33	33	235	216	50	178	15	67.3%	.293	32	1.13	3.10	3.07	3.13	7.9	1.7	6.3	0.5	68.9	7.22
2007	ARI	MLB	28	18	10	0	34	34	236¹	209	72	194	12	63.6%	.291	35	1.19	3.01	3.05	3.24	7.7	2.3	6.9	0.4	66.1	7.12
2008	ARI	MLB	29	14	9	0	32	32	214²	209	57	167	16	60.5%	.299	23	1.24	3.39	3.36	3.44	8.3	2.1	6.5	0.6	52.8	7.30

Breakout: 9%   Improve: 44%   Collapse: 21%   Attrition: 8%   Comparables: Rick Reuschel, Roy Halladay, Dave Goltz, Mark Gubicza

Although he started going to his off-speed stuff slightly more often in 2007, Webb produced a season almost identical to his 2006 campaign. When lefties pulled the ball against Webb last year, they put it on the ground more often than ever before, playing right into the trap set by the team when they acquired Orlando Hudson two winters ago. Webb further helps his cause by being one of the better-fielding pitchers in the league; when you're generating this many groundballs, who wouldn't want a fifth infielder? If there's one thing he could work on, it might be holding runners. One can understand the opposition's desperation; Webb doesn't put many guys on base and his ground-ball rate is perfect for twin killings, so opposing teams need to live a little more dangerously.

LINEOUTS

Hitters

	PLAYER	TEAM	LVL	AGE	PA	R	2B	3B	HR	RBI	BB	SO	SB-CS	EqBRR	AVG/OBP/SLG	MLVr	EqAVG/EqOBP/EqSLG	EqA	VORP
UT	W. Castillo#	MOB	AA	23	449	50	31	3	6	46	17	62	18-14	-4.4	.302/.333/.437	.097	.270/.294/.400	.238	3.9
INF	J. D'Antona	TUC	AAA	25	533	79	43	5	13	86	40	57	3-2	-2.8	.308/.362/.499	.131	.270/.324/.444	.264	22.2
C	E. Easley	YAK	A-	21	141	21	1	1	6	20	9	30	1-0	0.8	.250/.319/.419	.062	.189/.227/.311	.181	-19.0
UT	R. Hammock	TUC	AAA	30	293	34	17	1	4	35	43	34	3-2	-2.8	.325/.427/.451	.190	.281/.384/.394	.278	15.5
		ARI	MLB	30	49	5	2	0	0	0	3	7	0-0	0.5	.244/.306/.289	-.260	.244/.306/.289	.210	-1.7
OF	C. Hankerd	VIS	A+	22	446	55	27	1	8	54	35	60	2-3	-3.0	.285/.368/.422	.063	.236/.300/.342	.226	-21.3
C	O. Mercado	VIS	A+	22	275	27	12	0	6	37	51	42	2-2	-6.7	.256/.418/.398	.098	.210/.348/.308	.241	-2.0
OF	D. Perales*	SBN	A	22	609	80	32	10	16	92	42	100	7-7	2.3	.282/.338/.462	.157	.224/.271/.360	.217	-37.7
OF	C. Rahl	MOB	AA	23	458	64	26	5	8	51	15	87	15-5	2.5	.259/.286/.398	-.063	.233/.254/.365	.215	-31.0
OF	A. Romero*	TUC	AAA	23	584	82	32	6	5	66	37	53	12-10	-4.3	.310/.354/.421	.005	.269/.314/.369	.237	-13.0

The Snakes are grooming **Wilkin Castillo** to be something like the newer, better version of Eli Marrero or Robby Hammock; he catches most of the time, but can also play second, third, and short. ⏀ Like Castillo, **Jamie**

D'Antona can catch, but a strong arm has him trying (and failing) at third base; he's more strong than athletic, so he won't be the next B. J. Surhoff. ⊘ Yet another backstop of sorts, **Ed Easley** was a supplemental first-rounder out of Mississippi State last June because of his decent approach and power at the plate, and despite concerns about his defense behind it. ⊘ Speaking of **Robby Hammock**, he's baseball's one true five-corners player, capable of playing anywhere but middle infield or center field, and he would be a valuable spacesaver on a lot of rosters. ⊘ **Cyle Hankerd** was picked out of USC in the third round in 2006, but didn't graduate from the California League in his first full season. He's best suited for left field, but he hasn't hit well enough to inspire confidence in his future. ⊘ Not unlike his old man of the same name, **Orlando Mercado** is a good-fielding backstop, with the added virtue of tremendous patience at the plate; he has potential as a big-league backup backstop. ⊘ **Daniel Perales** is your basic power-only guy who outmuscled the Midwest League last year without showing a lot of upside. ⊘ After leading the Cal League in hits, total bases, and average in 2006, only to fall flat on his face in Double-A last year, **Chris Rahl** is Cyle Hankerd one year into the future. Don't get too excited about guys coming out of college who rock in the Cal League. ⊘ Briefly seen as a prospect in the Twins organization, **Alex Romero** is now just hoping to get a shot to be somebody's fourth outfielder someday.

Pitchers

PLAYER	TEAM	LVL	AGE	W	L	SV	IP	H	BB	SO	HR	GB%	BABIP	STUFF	WHIP	ERA	PERA	EqERA	EqH9	EqBB9	EqSO9	EqHR9	VORP
D. Buck	VIS	A+	22	4	4	0	97²	84	31	88	10	62.1%	.278	-12	1.18	3.41	5.61	5.79	9.3	4.3	4.8	1.5	-1.9
R. Choate*	TUC	AAA	31	3	1	3	63¹	68	16	61	3	60.0%	.346	8	1.33	2.99	4.04	3.68	9.0	2.5	6.5	0.6	13.6
C. Goocher*	MOB	AA	25	5	4	6	76¹	70	23	66	7	48.3%	.289	-19	1.22	3.42	4.85	5.25	8.9	3.1	5.0	1.3	2.9
W. Roemer	YAK	A-	20	1	0	0	12	11	2	18	1	36.7%	.357	-1	1.08	4.50	7.57	7.59	11.8	3.4	6.8	2.5	-2.4
L. Rosales	POR	AAA	26	1	1	14	24²	23	10	27	3	43.3%	.313	2	1.34	3.28	4.52	3.38	8.2	3.8	7.5	1.1	5.9
M. Rosen*	MOB	AA	23	4	4	7	66¹	80	22	78	6	54.7%	.411	-15	1.54	3.12	8.53	7.13	13.3	3.6	7.4	1.4	-10.1
M. Torra	VIS	A+	23	12	10	0	158²	186	43	137	15	45.8%	.353	-25	1.44	6.01	7.65	8.48	12.7	3.9	4.5	1.4	-45.9
E. Vasquez	MOB	AA	23	10	6	0	165¹	125	60	151	11	46.6%	.275	5	1.12	2.99	4.27	4.19	7.8	3.8	5.6	1.1	23.9

Briefly seen as a top prospect, Oregon State product **Dallas Buck** struggled to avoid elbow surgery and failed, breaking down in July. He'll miss the first half of 2008. ⊘ Your classic "have left arm, will travel" specialist, side-armer **Randy Choate** has already drifted to the Brewers' 40-man roster, reflecting his better chance to stick there. ⊘ **Clint Goocher** is an organizational lefty in a system in which being a LOOGY isn't an insult or a dead-end career option. ⊘ After starring as the ace at Cal State–Fullerton, **Wes Roemer** was picked 50th overall last June as a supplemental first-rounder. Although his fastball reaches only the upper 80s, he spins a nice slider, and he had the best command of anybody in the draft. ⊘ The bounty received from San Diego for Scott Hairston, **Leo Rosales** is a backward reliever, relying on a changeup as his out pitch. You can add him to the pile of pitchers wishing they could be the next Doug Jones. ⊘ **Mark Rosen** is the sort of power groundballer stat-heads can get worked up about. Perhaps with a quality infield defense, he'll exceed scouts' expectations; his terrible AFL stint certainly didn't surprise them. ⊘ His line looks awful, but former first-round pick **Matt Torra** had a decent second half coming back from a full torn labrum, throwing strikes with his low-90s heat and going 10-3 with a 4.01 ERA in his last 14 starts and posting a 5.7 (91/16) K/UIBB ratio in 93 1/3 IP. ⊘ **Esmerling Vasquez** dove for a popped-up bunt in the Arizona Fall League and tore his labrum. The Diamondbacks hope that he'll be able to rehab it nonsurgically and be ready to go in spring training, but with an only average fastball, he's probably not anything more than a reliever even if he gets back to full strength.

MANAGER: BOB MELVIN

YEAR	TEAM	W-L	Pythag +/–	Avg PC	100+ P	120+ P	QS	BQS	REL	REL w Zero R	IBB	Subs	PH	PH Avg	PH HR	SB2	CS2	SB3	CS3	SAC Att	SAC %	POS SAC	Squeeze	Swing	In Play
2005	ARI	77-85	13	96.8	66	3	81	18	458	274	43	57	310	.231	9	64	21	3	4	104	68.3%	30	5	122	86
2006	ARI	76-86	-3	95.2	70	3	76	13	461	299	44	56	275	.193	7	64	26	11	4	84	72.6%	21	1	105	80
2007	ARI	90-72	11	94.9	68	4	80	9	469	314	38	77	240	.243	12	90	16	18	8	79	69.6%	26	0	118	89

As our colleague Steven Goldman reminded us in his wonderful biography of Casey Stengel's pre-Yankees career, *Forging Genius*, managers can be made. That may be the case with Melvin, who was never seen as one of the game's top skippers before winning the NL Manager of the Year award for leading a very young team to the NLCS last year. Whether by design or adaptation, Melvin's nicely executed combinations of double-switches and pitching changes kept his bench active while employing his pen to good effect. His lineups were unsettled, but between a couple of platoons, no true leadoff or cleanup hitter, injuries, and some profound slumps, that was less a matter of design than a reflection of a weak offense. Despite all that, he wasn't a tactical spaz, avoiding issuing many intentional walks or having his position players bunt in excess.

Atlanta Braves

No, no, he's not dead. He's resting.

—MICHAEL PALIN, Monty Python's Parrot Sketch

For years, practically since the shocking beginning back in 1991, oceans of ink have been spilled predicting the end of the Braves' dynastic run. Fifteen years later, the prediction finally came true. The team's run of first-place finishes in the National League East came to a thudding end in 2006 with a third-place finish and a 79-83 record.

It seemed reasonable at the time to conclude that the Braves would not find greatness again anytime soon, and that when they did, it would be for a more typical run up and down the standings in the style of most latter-day champions —win, age, divest, rebuild, all in the space of a year or two. Besides, fallen dynasties don't just leap to their feet again. When the Roman Empire went down for the count, it stayed down, and so did the Yankees after 1964. Whether we recognize entropy by its name or not, we intuitively know that it's the dominant force in the universe. Things tend toward disorder. As such, we know that sustained success is unnatural, that the circumstances that permit defiance of entropy don't roll up too often. When they vanish, we don't expect them to reappear quickly and certainly not in the same place.

However, what if the Braves' run wasn't over, but had just hit a momentary speed bump? What if, to paraphrase Samuel Clemens, reports of their death had been greatly exaggerated? We instinctively reject the conclusion that the Braves are simply on hiatus because dynasties are a merely temporary truce with nature, and the circumstances that made the dynasty possible have changed: Tom Glavine, Greg Maddux, and

> ## BRAVES PROSPECTUS
>
> **2007 record:** 84-78; Third place, NL East
>
> **Pythagenport record:** 89-73
>
> **Runs scored per game:** 5.00 (3rd in NL)
>
> **Runs allowed per game:** 4.52 (3rd in NL)
>
> **Team EqA:** .267 (4th in NL)
>
> **2007 Batters Age:** 28.1 (5th youngest in NL)
>
> **2007 Pitchers Age:** 30.2 (6th oldest in NL)
>
> **Ballpark:** Turner Field; Slight pitcher's park; Park Factor of .972
>
> **2007:** Dynasty in the wilderness lacks native arms to guide it home.
>
> **2008:** Recapturing Glavine won't recapture the magic of Glavine-Maddux-Smoltz.

John Smoltz, the trio of starting pitchers who were the key element in perpetuating the run, have aged and dispersed (the Glavine who returned to the Braves this winter in no way resembles his 25-year-old self); Ted Turner's munificence was replaced by the careful bottom-line watching of Time-Warner and then Liberty Media. At the same time, some things haven't changed: the ingenuity of the front office and the absence of another dominant team in the NL East. With the proper moves, the Braves' 84-78 third-place finish could prove to have been a harbinger of things to come.

The decline of the Braves along with that of Maddux-Glavine-Smoltz was likely but not inevitable. What forced the issue was the dearth of quality, low-cost replacement pitchers coming out of their farm system. In truth, the Braves have been out of the pitcher development business for years, having boarded up after successfully establishing Kevin Millwood, who posted a 3.73 ERA in just over a thousand innings from 1997 through 2002. Since Millwood's arrival in 1997, a number of other homegrown starters have been tried, found wanting, and scattered to the other 29 teams. The Braves' product who started the most games for the big club subsequent to 1997 was Horacio Ramirez. Other farm-raised hurlers in that time have included Odalis Perez, Jason Marquis, Damian Moss, and Kyle Davies. As a result of the team's inability to develop young pitching, what was once an elite staff has been increasingly populated by mediocre veteran imports in the years since Glavine's departure broke up the holy trinity (see Table 1).

Table 1. After the Big Three, the Minus 5: Braves' starters in the post-trinity years

Pitcher	GS	SNLVAR
John Smoltz	100	21.25
Tim Hudson	98	16.72
Mike Hampton	72	11.35
Horacio Ramirez	**84**	**11.23**
Russ Ortiz	68	10.35
Chuck James	**48**	**7.32**
John Thomson	65	7.29
Jaret Wright	32	5.51
Greg Maddux	36	4.74
Jorge Sosa	33	4.48
Paul Byrd	19	2.58
Kyle Davies	**45**	**2.17**
Shane Reynolds	29	1.83
Buddy Carlyle	20	1.15
Lance Cormier	18	0.84
Roman Colon	**4**	**0.66**
Oscar Villarreal	4	0.63
Travis Smith	5	0.5
Jeff Bennett	2	0.43
Jason Marquis	**2**	**0.32**
Trey Hodges	**1**	**0.2**
Jo-Jo Reyes	10	0.18
Seth Greisinger	1	0.13
Anthony Lerew	**3**	**-0.08**
Jose Capellan	**2**	**-0.22**
Kevin Barry	**1**	**-0.24**
Jason Shiell	3	-0.26
Mark Redman	5	-0.39

In addition to poor drafting and an inability to establish young pitchers in the bigs, two long-ago trades have had continuing consequences for the present-day Braves. Kevin Millwood's post-Braves career has been spotty, but in the winter of 2002 he was a 27-year-old with 75 career wins coming off of an 18-8, 3.24 ERA season. That offseason, the Braves offered arbitration to free agent Maddux in the hope of landing a couple of draft picks with which to restock the system, then were shocked when he accepted. In an apparent panic about the payroll, general manager John Schuerholz dealt Millwood to the Philadelphia Phillies for catcher Johnny Estrada, at the time a singles hitter as yet unestablished in the majors, entering his age-27 season. That same winter, Mark Redman—also 27 and coming off of an 8-15, 4.21 season—netted the Tigers three prospects from the Marlins, including Nate Robertson, who has started 30 games or more for Detroit in each of the past four seasons. The failure to acquire any prospects in return for Millwood affects the Braves to this day, as any players in their early 20s the Braves

might have acquired at that time would now be in the prime of their careers.

A year later, Schuerholz undertook another gamble. With affable right fielder Gary Sheffield set to depart as a free agent, the Braves swapped three pitchers—starter Jason Marquis, LOOGY Ray King, and prospect Adam Wainwright—to the Cardinals for outfielder J.D. Drew, who was entering his walk year, and utilityman Eli Marrero. The Braves got a good season out of Drew, but at the end of the year he took Dodger Dollars over Brave Bucks, leaving Atlanta with nothing to show for the deal (Marrero was flipped to the Royals for right-hander Jorge Vasquez, who would toss just nine innings for Atlanta). The Cardinals, meanwhile, got three pitchers, including two former first-round picks in Marquis and Wainwright, who would help drive their team to three consecutive playoff appearances and the 2006 championship. In 2007, Wainwright established himself as a capable starter, something of which the Braves are in desperate need. As a result of transactions such as these, the list in Table 1 is more notable for names not on it, such as Millwood's and Wainwright's, as well as names that we literally cannot mention because we don't know them, names of players the team failed to acquire in trades, failed to draft, or failed to develop.

The Braves' record with young position players stands in direct contrast to these struggles with pitching. In recent seasons, the Braves have promoted catcher Brian McCann, right fielder Jeff Francoeur, outfielder-turned-second baseman Kelly Johnson, and shortstop Yunel Escobar to regular spots in the lineup, and also produced a second top catching prospect in baseball in Jarrod Saltalamacchia, a player attractive enough to be the main draw in the Mark Teixeira trade. In the coming seasons, they will attempt to turn the same trick in the outfield, with Brandon Jones challenging Matt Diaz in left field this year and center field prospect Jordan Schafer working his way up the ladder to fill Andruw Jones's vacated position.

The 2007 lineup was a relative strength, finishing third in the league in runs per game, though that was troublingly driven more by the team's .275 batting average than it was by repeatable offensive prowess—the Braves ranked sixth in the league in home runs, seventh in walks, and seventh in isolated power. They also had a largely successful bullpen in 2007. Led by Rafael Soriano, who was filched from the Mariners in a daring broad-daylight robbery, the Braves ranked tenth in the majors and sixth in the National League in WXRL. It wasn't always pretty, with manager Bobby Cox needing to do a lot of mixing and matching, a condition exacerbated by the midseason downfall of Bob Wickman, who objected to being demoted from the closing role. Bullpen success is ephemeral, but the Braves at least seem to be on the right path. The only thing, then, that stands between the Braves and a revival of their post-season tradition in a mediocre division is their starting pitching, which can be fairly described as "Tim Hudson, two old guys, and 'staff.'"

After the season, longtime general manager Schuerholz became team president and relinquished his former position to assistant GM Frank Wren. Wren initially resisted making a splash to mark his elevation, staying out of such contentious scenes as the Johan Santana auction, despite the fact that his team would have benefited from the addition of Santana disproportionately to many of others in pursuit of the Twins lefty. As is, the Braves really have only one candidate for ace, the redoubtable Smoltz, who turns 41 on May 15. Hudson had his best season since leaving Oakland last year and may or may not repeat it. The rest of the rotation makes Atlanta's desperate need for rain all the more poignant.

Wren did make two moves to deepen the pitching staff. The more prominent of the two brought prodigal son Tom Glavine back home on a one-year, $8-million deal. Given Glavine's age, plunging strikeout rate, and woeful pounding in his last three starts of 2007 (he put up a 14.81 ERA against the Litterbugs' Row lineups of the Marlins and Nationals), the deal is more like a multimillion-dollar version of Phil Niekro's 1987 one-start encore/mercy killing than anything that's going to advance the team back to the division title.

More promising was the October 29 deal that sent shortstop Edgar Renteria, rendered redundant by Escobar's emergence, to the Tigers in return for right-handed starter Jair Jurrjens and another center field prospect in Gorkys Hernandez. Jurrjens probably isn't the ace-in-the-making that the Braves need, but he's a solid prospect with a low-90s fastball. If nothing else, he should allow them to stay one step further removed from the Lance Cormiers of the world. Going into camp Jurrjens will compete with southpaw Chuck James, an occasionally effective home-run machine, and the control-impaired Jo-Jo Reyes for one of the last two spots in this year's rotation (barring the unlikely occurance that one of those slots is claimed by the resurrection of 35-year-old infirmary case Mike "Brigadoon" Hampton, who is still rehabbing his way through the eight-year contract he signed with the Rockies back in 2001).

With the Phillies' and Mets' pitching every bit as dubious, the Braves' inability to assemble a solid staff has robbed them of the opportunity to pick up where they left off in 2005. Having included three of their better pitching prospects in the Teixeira deal, immediate salvation won't be coming from the minor leagues. If everything clicks in just the right way (or nothing does for their rivals), the Braves will be back on top. If not, they may come to see the 2008 season as a missed opportunity to prove that the dynasty was not dead, but merely shagged out following a prolonged squawk.

HITTERS

Gregor Blanco   **CF**   Bats: L   Throws: L   Height: 5' 11"   Weight: 170   Born: December 24, 1983   Age: 24

YEAR	TEAM	LVL	AGE	PA	R	2B	3B	HR	RBI	BB	SO	SB	CS	EqBRR	AVG	OBP	SLG	MLVr	EqAVG	EqOBP	EqSLG	EqA	VORP	DEFENSE
2005	MIS	AA	21	486	64	11	12	6	37	73	124	28	12	-3.9	.252	.367	.384	.056	.221	.323	.346	.242	-6.9	108-CF -4
2006	MIS	AA	22	302	45	16	3	0	9	43	57	17	6	1.7	.287	.397	.375	.172	.270	.370	.378	.270	10.1	66-CF 3
2006	RIC	AAA	22	327	43	12	1	0	19	52	53	14	9	-1.4	.294	.408	.346	.106	.271	.384	.326	.260	6.8	64-CF -6
2007	RIC	AAA	23	545	81	18	5	3	35	63	85	23	18	-3.2	.282	.369	.362	.042	.262	.346	.345	.246	3.2	118-CF -6
2008	ATL	MLB	24	506	73	18	5	4	33	60	95	23	8	2.4	.264	.355	.352	-.096	.261	.353	.360	.256	9.3	119-CF -1

Breakout: 27%   Improve: 51%   Collapse: 26%   Attrition: 17%   Comparables: Michael Bourn, Luis Mercedes, Mike Curry, Jim Buccheri

Players such as Blanco, who have high walk and strikeout totals but no power, usually lose the walks and keep the strikeouts as they advance because pitchers at the higher levels are willing to challenge them. Blanco, however, has improved his contact rate over the past two years, which given his speed and on-base ability, makes him projectable as a fourth outfielder. With the Braves lacking an obvious center-field solution following Andruw Jones' departure, he could even slide in as the starter in 2008. He's better than Willie Harris.

Matt Diaz — LF

Bats: R   Throws: R   Height: 6' 1"   Weight: 205   Born: March 3, 1978   Age: 30

YEAR	TEAM	LVL	AGE	PA	R	2B	3B	HR	RBI	BB	SO	SB	CS	EqBRR	AVG	OBP	SLG	MLVr	EqAVG	EqOBP	EqSLG	EqA	VORP	DEFENSE	
2005	OMA	AAA	27	277	48	22	4	14	56	12	49	10	3	-2.8	.371	.408	.649	.554	.308	.339	.540	.291	17.3	58-LF	1
2005	KCA	MLB	27	97	7	4	2	1	9	4	15	0	1	-1.0	.281	.323	.404	-.028	.284	.333	.409	.256	0.7	16-LF	-2
2006	ATL	MLB	28	322	37	15	4	7	32	11	49	5	5	-1.4	.327	.364	.475	.181	.332	.368	.483	.286	16.1	66-LF	12
2007	ATL	MLB	29	384	44	21	0	12	45	16	63	4	0	-1.5	.338	.368	.497	.233	.342	.373	.513	.302	27.6	76-LF	8
2008	ATL	MLB	30	373	48	21	2	11	53	18	61	5	2	-0.5	.297	.338	.466	.053	.294	.336	.476	.272	15.4	89-LF	2

Breakout: 4%   Improve: 23%   Collapse: 41%   Attrition: 18%   Comparables: Tommy Davis, Rondell White, Lou Piniella, Alex Johnson

Matt Diaz has batted .401 on contact over the past two seasons, sixth-best in MLB. That is an extremely high figure that, coupled with his a 6:1 K/UIBB ratio, indicates that his batting average will be coming down. Because Diaz's high batting average represents so much of his value—he has middling power, no speed, and very little defensive skill—you can expect his playing time to be reduced accordingly. Still, Diaz should have a long career as a pinch-hitter and platoon corner guy.

Yunel Escobar — SS

Bats: R   Throws: R   Height: 6' 2"   Weight: 200   Born: November 2, 1982   Age: 25

YEAR	TEAM	LVL	AGE	PA	R	2B	3B	HR	RBI	BB	SO	SB	CS	EqBRR	AVG	OBP	SLG	MLVr	EqAVG	EqOBP	EqSLG	EqA	VORP	DEFENSE			
2005	ROM	A	22	214	30	13	3	4	19	14	30	0	2	-0.5	.313	.358	.470	.239	.252	.288	.376	.224	0.1	47-SS	8		
2006	MIS	AA	23	501	55	21	4	2	45	59	77	7	9	-0.5	.264	.361	.346	.067	.247	.334	.341	.240	5.4	60-SS	-1	33-3B	2
2007	RIC	AAA	24	195	20	10	3	2	29	14	27	7	3	0.8	.333	.379	.456	.226	.309	.354	.453	.277	15.6	45-SS	0		
2007	ATL	MLB	24	355	54	25	0	5	28	27	44	5	3	0.6	.326	.385	.451	.183	.336	.397	.478	.298	24.4	40-SS	-2	18-3B	-2
2008	ATL	MLB	25	493	63	24	3	7	49	39	73	9	4	0.8	.287	.348	.402	-.026	.284	.346	.411	.261	18.8	116-SS	0		

Breakout: 14%   Improve: 37%   Collapse: 29%   Attrition: 21%   Comparables: Phil Linz, Royce Clayton, Julio Gotay, Jose Castillo

Now that Edgar Renteria is gone, the shortstop job belongs to Escobar, but it's not clear that he's good enough to hold it. Setting aside the batting average, which will be closer to .280, he'd never before shown the kind of power he did in his four months in Atlanta. Unless those doubles are real (not likely), you're looking at a mostly empty average. Escobar is not a superior defensive player, either. Brent Lillibridge could pass him by August.

Jeff Francoeur — RF

Bats: R   Throws: R   Height: 6' 4"   Weight: 220   Born: January 8, 1984   Age: 24

YEAR	TEAM	LVL	AGE	PA	R	2B	3B	HR	RBI	BB	SO	SB	CS	EqBRR	AVG	OBP	SLG	MLVr	EqAVG	EqOBP	EqSLG	EqA	VORP	DEFENSE			
2005	MIS	AA	21	367	40	28	2	13	62	21	76	13	4	-1.2	.275	.322	.487	.145	.238	.275	.425	.240	-10.9	71-RF	-6	11-CF	0
2005	ATL	MLB	21	274	41	20	1	14	45	11	58	3	2	-0.9	.300	.336	.549	.227	.297	.333	.559	.291	17.5	66-RF	1		
2006	ATL	MLB	22	686	83	24	6	29	103	23	132	1	6	-0.4	.260	.293	.449	-.041	.262	.296	.454	.250	-1.0	160-RF	-13		
2007	ATL	MLB	23	696	84	40	0	19	105	42	129	5	2	0.2	.293	.338	.444	.063	.298	.345	.461	.276	17.9	160-RF	1		
2008	ATL	MLB	24	590	75	33	2	22	84	35	108	8	3	0.0	.284	.331	.474	.040	.281	.329	.483	.271	18.2	138-RF	-1		

Breakout: 30%   Improve: 49%   Collapse: 22%   Attrition: 23%   Comparables: Charlie Spikes, George Hendrick, Vernon Wells, Carlos Lee

Don't look now, but Francoeur is developing as a hitter. He's becoming more disciplined, evidenced by his seeing a few more pitches (up 3.6 percent) and drawing more walks. Just counting unintentional passes, he walked more than twice as often in 2007 as the year before, while holding his strikeout rate steady and upping his batting average. While his slugging was down, he actually had the same number of extra-base hits, and essentially the same XBH rate as in 2006; the homers and triples just became doubles, which happens. Just 24 years old, he may well become a star in 2008.

Willie Harris — OF

Bats: L   Throws: R   Height: 5' 9"   Weight: 170   Born: June 22, 1978   Age: 30

YEAR	TEAM	LVL	AGE	PA	R	2B	3B	HR	RBI	BB	SO	SB	CS	EqBRR	AVG	OBP	SLG	MLVr	EqAVG	EqOBP	EqSLG	EqA	VORP	DEFENSE			
2005	CHR	AAA	27	129	21	11	1	1	10	16	27	10	2	0.1	.266	.360	.413	.024	.234	.331	.378	.256	1.6	27-2B	1		
2005	CHA	MLB	27	139	17	2	1	1	8	13	25	10	3	0.5	.256	.333	.314	-.153	.261	.348	.319	.249	0.4	27-2B	0		
2006	PAW	AAA	28	253	32	6	1	8	17	29	56	11	3	2.8	.220	.319	.367	-.069	.209	.303	.364	.239	-2.9	21-2B	-3	19-LF	-1
2006	BOS	MLB	28	52	17	2	0	0	1	4	11	6	3	0.8	.156	.250	.200	-.568	.156	.264	.200	.186	-5.1	10-CF	0		
2007	RIC	AAA	29	70	17	7	2	1	7	8	6	7	3	1.1	.362	.457	.603	.562	.322	.414	.576	.321	9.3				
2007	ATL	MLB	29	391	56	20	8	2	32	40	71	17	11	0.1	.270	.349	.392	-.007	.287	.367	.424	.269	4.0	69-LF	5	12-CF	1
2008	WAS	MLB	30	315	45	15	3	6	28	33	56	12	5	1.7	.267	.351	.412	-.022	.267	.352	.420	.268	9.7	76-LF	0		

Breakout: 24% Improve: 55% Collapse: 20% Attrition: 31%   Comparables: John Lowenstein, Eddie Milner, Rick Miller, Don Landrum

The Braves allowed themselves to be fooled by a fluke, a random spike in Harris's career in which he hit .412 from his call-up on April 30 through June 12. Installed as the platoon left fielder and leadoff man on June 23, he began killing the team, hitting .228/.319/.360 through September 9 and canceling out much of the benefit of the Teixeira trade. He's a decent utilityman, but nothing more. Designated for assignment in December to make room for Omar Infante, he signed a one-year contract to play for the Nationals.

Diory Hernandez — SS

Bats: R   Throws: R   Height: 5' 11"   Weight: 170   Born: April 8, 1984   Age: 24

YEAR	TEAM	LVL	AGE	PA	R	2B	3B	HR	RBI	BB	SO	SB	CS	EqBRR	AVG	OBP	SLG	MLVr	EqAVG	EqOBP	EqSLG	EqA	VORP	DEFENSE			
2005	MYR	A+	21	300	30	15	1	5	30	18	53	5	5	0.8	.253	.314	.374	-.052	.210	.252	.308	.193	-15.4	68-SS	2		
2006	MYR	A+	22	312	37	10	0	6	47	19	51	11	1	2.4	.238	.295	.336	-.113	.211	.250	.303	.196	-17.7	68-SS	-5		
2007	MYR	A+	23	67	9	8	2	0	9	2	11	2	2	-0.9	.313	.343	.500	.234	.262	.273	.385	.221	-0.7	14-2B	2		
2007	MIS	AA	23	481	50	25	1	7	59	29	68	22	20	-4.6	.307	.370	.418	.163	.279	.328	.389	.246	15.0	78-SS	-11	33-2B	7
2008	ATL	MLB	24	563	59	26	2	8	52	29	101	17	8	1.2	.252	.299	.359	-.196	.250	.297	.366	.228	2.8	132-SS	-4		

Breakout: 28% Improve: 57% Collapse: 21% Attrition: 10%   Comparables: Orlando Miller, Luis Maza, Alberto Gonzalez, Fausto Cruz

An injury to second baseman J. C. Holt opened up a spot for Hernandez at Double-A, and he played well enough to stay there after Holt returned, sliding to shortstop after Brent Lillibridge's promotion. Hernandez is more extra infielder than starter, with good hands and a low-power approach at the plate.

Jason Heyward — RF

Bats: L   Throws: L   Height: 6' 4"   Weight: 220   Born: August 9, 1989   Age: 18

YEAR	TEAM	LVL	AGE	PA	R	2B	3B	HR	RBI	BB	SO	SB	CS	EqBRR	AVG	OBP	SLG	MLVr	EqAVG	EqOBP	EqSLG	EqA	VORP	DEFENSE	
2007	BRA	Rk	17	31	1	4	0	1	5	2	4	1	1	-0.7	.296	.355	.556	.352	.241	.258	.448	.237	-0.7		
2007	DNV	Rk	17	17	3	1	0	0	1	1	5	0	0	-0.2	.313	.353	.375	.132	.125	.176	.125	.000	-6.9		
2008	ATL	MLB	18	535	36	23	2	7	44	34	149	9	4	0.1	.206	.259	.302	-.373	.204	.258	.308	.189	-30.1	126-RF	0

Breakout: NA Improve: NA Collapse: NA Attrition: NA   Comparables: Carl Crawford, Chris Parmelee, James Loney, Kyler Burke

The Braves' top pick last year (number 14 overall) didn't turn 18 until two months after the draft, which is just one reason why he's already a fixture on prospect lists. The best tools in his draft class don't hurt, either. Beyond profiling as a prototypical right fielder with size, hitting ability, and great power, Heyward drew a ton of walks in high school, but it will take a year of pro ball for us to figure out if that was plate discipline or guys with no baseball future pitching scared.

Cody Johnson — LF

Bats: L   Throws: R   Height: 6' 4"   Weight: 195   Born: August 18, 1988   Age: 19

YEAR	TEAM	LVL	AGE	PA	R	2B	3B	HR	RBI	BB	SO	SB	CS	EqBRR	AVG	OBP	SLG	MLVr	EqAVG	EqOBP	EqSLG	EqA	VORP	DEFENSE	
2006	BRA	Rk	17	127	13	6	1	1	16	12	49	2	0	0.7	.184	.260	.281	-.176	.127	.188	.220	.114	-62.1	23-LF	-3
2007	DNV	Rk	18	270	51	18	5	17	57	26	72	7	0	-1.0	.305	.374	.630	.509	.206	.259	.393	.223	-32.4	50-LF	0
2008	ATL	MLB	19	554	54	30	4	13	51	38	160	9	4	0.6	.218	.274	.369	-.250	.216	.272	.377	.219	-16.6	130-LF	-1

Breakout: 58% Improve: 74% Collapse: 10% Attrition: 5%   Comparables: Colby Rasmus, Jeff Key, LaRue Baber, Tate Seefried

Many teams rolled their eyes when the Braves took Johnson with their first-round pick in 2006. Indeed, the big athlete with tons of power and huge holes in his swing was awful in the Gulf Coast League. Last year, the Braves held him back in extended spring training to work on controlling his approach and letting his natural strength work for him. Once he joined Rookie League Danville, the results were immediate and obvious. Johnson is hardly a contact hitter, but the organization has found a way to tap into his power. He just might have a little Adam Dunn in him.

Kelly Johnson 2B Bats: L Throws: R Height: 6′ 1″ Weight: 205 Born: February 22, 1982 Age: 26

YEAR	TEAM	LVL	AGE	PA	R	2B	3B	HR	RBI	BB	SO	SB	CS	EqBRR	AVG	OBP	SLG	MLVr	EqAVG	EqOBP	EqSLG	EqA	VORP	DEFENSE
2005	RIC	AAA	23	192	35	12	3	8	22	34	22	7	1	0.0	.310	.438	.581	.414	.278	.401	.525	.314	14.9	15-LF 0 12-RF 1
2005	ATL	MLB	23	334	46	12	3	9	40	40	75	2	1	-0.4	.241	.334	.397	-.033	.238	.333	.400	.257	1.5	73-LF 15
2006	RIC	AAA	24	47	3	4	0	1	7	6	6	1	0	-0.1	.333	.426	.513	.375	.308	.404	.462	.308	3.8	
2007	ATL	MLB	25	608	91	26	10	16	68	79	117	9	5	-0.1	.276	.375	.457	.127	.284	.384	.477	.294	33.1	128-2B 5
2008	ATL	MLB	26	575	89	29	6	17	69	74	106	11	4	0.9	.279	.375	.466	.098	.276	.373	.475	.288	36.0	135-2B 5

Breakout: 18% Improve: 44% Collapse: 15% Attrition: 6%   Comparables: Eric Hinske, Wayne Garrett, Trot Nixon, Joe Foy

The decision to move Johnson to second base worked out beautifully, as he played plus defense while providing OBP in the top two lineup spots for most of the year. That he faded in September may be attributable the fact that he came off of a season lost to injury and played a full year at a new position. There's upside here; he could develop like Bill Doran and be a leadoff guy, or keep the power and be Jeff Kent from the left side.

Andruw Jones CF Bats: R Throws: R Height: 6′ 1″ Weight: 210 Born: April 23, 1977 Age: 31

YEAR	TEAM	LVL	AGE	PA	R	2B	3B	HR	RBI	BB	SO	SB	CS	EqBRR	AVG	OBP	SLG	MLVr	EqAVG	EqOBP	EqSLG	EqA	VORP	DEFENSE
2005	ATL	MLB	28	672	95	24	3	51	128	64	112	5	3	0.8	.263	.347	.575	.240	.260	.344	.583	.301	52.8	153-CF 7
2006	ATL	MLB	29	669	107	29	0	41	129	82	127	5	1	1.2	.262	.363	.531	.191	.262	.363	.535	.302	49.3	148-CF 0
2007	ATL	MLB	30	659	83	27	2	26	94	70	138	5	2	-2.3	.222	.311	.413	-.082	.227	.319	.430	.259	5.4	150-CF 9
2008	LAN	MLB	31	568	77	24	1	29	92	61	109	7	2	-0.3	.256	.344	.486	.053	.254	.341	.491	.278	27.9	133-CF -1

Breakout: 12% Improve: 47% Collapse: 30% Attrition: 9%   Comparables: Tom Brunansky, Richie Zisk, Jermaine Dye, Jim Dyck

What's strange about Jones's 2007 season is that all he lost were the homers. Look at those lines: 2007 is a typical Andruw Jones season, less 15 homers, five singles, and some intentional walks. His fly-ball rate was unchanged, so it wasn't that. Now, the $90 million question: was it a change in his skills, or just one of those fluke seasons? Given his age and the stability of everything else, lean toward the latter. Despite the down season, Jones was still the best of the winter's free-agent center fielders, and because of it, a bargain for the Dodgers, who signed him to a two-year, $36.2-million contract.

Brandon Jones LF Bats: L Throws: R Height: 6′ 2″ Weight: 195 Born: December 10, 1983 Age: 24

YEAR	TEAM	LVL	AGE	PA	R	2B	3B	HR	RBI	BB	SO	SB	CS	EqBRR	AVG	OBP	SLG	MLVr	EqAVG	EqOBP	EqSLG	EqA	VORP	DEFENSE
2005	ROM	A	21	189	37	12	3	8	27	29	29	4	1	0.8	.308	.423	.577	.468	.248	.339	.448	.270	3.0	35-RF -4
2005	MYR	A+	21	71	7	4	0	0	5	9	9	0	1	-0.1	.350	.437	.417	.288	.302	.366	.349	.254	1.4	
2006	MYR	A+	22	255	27	10	3	7	35	25	49	11	6	-1.2	.257	.329	.420	.069	.223	.282	.369	.226	-13.6	49-LF -6
2006	MIS	AA	22	194	18	9	3	7	25	15	38	4	2	-2.1	.273	.326	.477	.196	.264	.311	.489	.267	4.3	30-RF 3 17-LF 1
2007	MIS	AA	23	418	58	21	6	15	74	44	84	12	7	0.6	.293	.368	.507	.271	.268	.335	.472	.274	10.2	89-LF 5
2007	RIC	AAA	23	191	26	12	1	4	26	17	36	5	0	2.0	.300	.363	.453	.168	.279	.340	.453	.275	4.3	43-LF -3
2007	ATL	MLB	23	21	0	1	0	0	4	0	8	0	0	-0.1	.158	.190	.211	-.614	.158	.190	.211	.127	-2.7	
2008	ATL	MLB	24	598	79	32	5	17	76	51	124	13	5	1.0	.271	.335	.446	-.003	.268	.333	.455	.266	13.5	140-LF -2

Breakout: 29% Improve: 60% Collapse: 11% Attrition: 7%   Comparables: Curtis Granderson, Bobby Higginson, Chin-Feng Chen, Ryan Church

The third Jones timed his arrival well, reaching Atlanta just as the second Jones headed out the door and left the outfield to Jeff Francoeur and "staff." Brandon was healthy last season for the first time, putting up good lines while impressing scouts with his tools. The big drop-off in his power at Triple-A is a mild concern; watch his power and his contact rate this year.

Chipper Jones　　　3B

Bats: S　Throws: R　Height: 6' 4"　Weight: 210　Born: April 24, 1972　Age: 36

YEAR	TEAM	LVL	AGE	PA	R	2B	3B	HR	RBI	BB	SO	SB	CS	EqBRR	AVG	OBP	SLG	MLVr	EqAVG	EqOBP	EqSLG	EqA	VORP	DEFENSE	
2005	ATL	MLB	33	432	66	30	0	21	72	72	56	5	1	-0.1	.296	.412	.556	.343	.292	.411	.562	.326	43.6	93-3B	-8
2006	ATL	MLB	34	477	87	28	3	26	86	61	73	6	1	-1.2	.324	.409	.596	.417	.325	.413	.597	.334	53.8	100-3B	-10
2007	ATL	MLB	35	600	108	42	4	29	102	82	75	5	1	1.7	.337	.425	.604	.467	.340	.432	.625	.348	76.0	120-3B	2
2008	ATL	MLB	36	567	99	34	3	24	89	78	76	7	2	-0.4	.315	.410	.547	.294	.313	.408	.558	.321	57.1	133-3B	-6

Breakout: 3%　Improve: 14%　Collapse: 30%　Attrition: 10%　　　Comparables: George Brett, Frank Robinson, Reggie Smith, Chili Davis

Despite losing his durability, Chipper is not showing any erosion in his skills. Due to thumb and groin problems, Jones missed 28 games last year, most of them in June, but still finished fourth in the NL in VORP and sixth in the MVP voting. Look for more of the same this year. It's not whether he's a Hall of Famer; it's whether he goes in on the first ballot.

Kala Kaaihue　　　1B

Bats: R　Throws: R　Height: 6' 2"　Weight: 230　Born: March 29, 1985　Age: 23

YEAR	TEAM	LVL	AGE	PA	R	2B	3B	HR	RBI	BB	SO	SB	CS	EqBRR	AVG	OBP	SLG	MLVr	EqAVG	EqOBP	EqSLG	EqA	VORP	DEFENSE	
2006	ROM	A	21	284	44	16	2	15	49	52	66	3	0	-1.0	.329	.458	.614	.580	.237	.349	.444	.276	6.3	64-1B	3
2006	MYR	A+	21	222	37	8	0	13	31	30	49	0	1	-2.8	.223	.342	.473	.132	.189	.284	.388	.229	-9.5	49-1B	-1
2007	MYR	A+	22	376	57	20	1	22	61	53	92	2	0	-3.2	.298	.410	.583	.421	.240	.332	.465	.273	8.1	81-1B	-3
2007	MIS	AA	22	133	14	5	1	0	8	11	51	0	0	-0.2	.127	.211	.186	-.521	.124	.188	.190	.088	-23.2	32-1B	-1
2008	ATL	MLB	23	573	62	25	2	23	75	63	166	3	1	-1.3	.226	.317	.418	-.105	.224	.315	.426	.251	-0.1	134-1B	1

Breakout: 49%　Improve: 81%　Collapse: 7%　Attrition: 10%　　　Comparables: Bobby Estalella, Mike Glendenning, Chad Rupp, Mike Napoli

It comes down to what's bigger: his power, or the holes in his swing. You don't put up 35 homers in a year at Myrtle Beach without having real power. You also don't strike out as often as Kaaihue does (a rate that is increasing) and play in the majors. What the Southern League did to him is usually only available for $14.95 on channels you don't let your spouse catch you watching. Still, his glove isn't bad and could give him a shot at a platoon/defense job if Teixeira leaves next winter.

Brent Lillibridge　　　SS

Bats: R　Throws: R　Height: 5' 11"　Weight: 190　Born: September 18, 1983　Age: 24

YEAR	TEAM	LVL	AGE	PA	R	2B	3B	HR	RBI	BB	SO	SB	CS	EqBRR	AVG	OBP	SLG	MLVr	EqAVG	EqOBP	EqSLG	EqA	VORP	DEFENSE	
2005	WPT	A-	21	191	19	12	4	4	18	14	35	10	3	1.3	.243	.305	.432	.066	.182	.228	.324	.193	-21.9	41-SS	5
2006	HIC	A	22	333	59	18	5	11	43	51	61	29	8	4.1	.299	.414	.522	.354	.243	.337	.417	.265	13.5	72-SS	14
2006	LYN	A+	22	252	47	10	3	2	28	36	43	24	5	7.2	.313	.426	.423	.235	.262	.355	.350	.261	6.9	54-SS	-5
2007	MIS	AA	23	237	31	8	3	3	17	20	60	14	7	0.7	.275	.355	.387	.071	.236	.303	.349	.233	-1.2	52-SS	-6
2007	RIC	AAA	23	355	47	14	2	10	41	20	59	28	5	7.4	.287	.331	.436	.085	.270	.313	.426	.262	13.0	84-SS	2
2008	ATL	MLB	24	578	77	28	5	13	56	48	123	34	9	2.7	.256	.324	.403	-.089	.254	.322	.411	.258	18.4	135-SS	1

Breakout: 34%　Improve: 59%　Collapse: 14%　Attrition: 16%　　　Comparables: Mike Lansing, Craig Stansberry, Ryan Klosterman, Tony Manahan

If Yunel Escobar hadn't hit .326 in the majors last season, Lillibridge would be going into spring training fighting for the starting shortstop job. Lillibridge is the better defensive player and has stronger secondary skills. Still, it might be for the best that he'll start the year at Triple-A; his plate discipline has been in reverse for three levels, and he's never spent more than three months in one place.

Brian McCann　　　C

Bats: L　Throws: R　Height: 6' 3"　Weight: 210　Born: February 20, 1984　Age: 24

YEAR	TEAM	LVL	AGE	PA	R	2B	3B	HR	RBI	BB	SO	SB	CS	EqBRR	AVG	OBP	SLG	MLVr	EqAVG	EqOBP	EqSLG	EqA	VORP	DEFENSE	
2005	MIS	AA	21	198	27	13	2	6	26	25	26	2	3	-1.4	.265	.359	.476	.176	.234	.313	.415	.253	3.5	43-C	1
2005	ATL	MLB	21	204	20	7	0	5	23	18	26	1	1	-2.1	.278	.345	.400	.016	.271	.342	.398	.259	7.6	50-C	-2
2006	ATL	MLB	22	492	61	34	0	24	93	41	54	2	0	-4.4	.333	.388	.572	.362	.332	.388	.575	.321	54.8	114-C	-1
2007	ATL	MLB	23	552	51	38	0	18	92	35	74	0	1	-4.2	.270	.320	.452	.024	.273	.325	.468	.270	22.8	127-C	-1
2008	ATL	MLB	24	540	65	32	1	19	79	45	70	3	2	-1.6	.281	.344	.471	.056	.279	.342	.481	.275	29.7	127-C	2

Breakout: 13%　Improve: 36%　Collapse: 31%　Attrition: 11%　　　Comparables: Ed Herrmann, Matt Nokes, Del Crandall, Ray Fosse

You could say he took a step backward last year, but it would be more accurate to say that McCann's 2006 season was the one out of line, and that his 2007 was a better fit with his career progression. Forget '06 and look at him as a 23-year-old, left-handed-hitting catcher who provides league-average offense and defense but needs to get back to being a bit more selective at the plate. He's still a star in the making.

Martin Prado — 2B — Bats: R — Throws: R — Height: 6' 1" — Weight: 190 — Born: October 27, 1983 — Age: 24

YEAR	TEAM	LVL	AGE	PA	R	2B	3B	HR	RBI	BB	SO	SB	CS	EqBRR	AVG	OBP	SLG	MLVr	EqAVG	EqOBP	EqSLG	EqA	VORP	DEFENSE			
2005	MYR	A+	21	326	44	13	3	4	34	24	48	9	6	-4.9	.306	.353	.411	.107	.257	.294	.336	.221	-6.3	72-2B	3		
2005	MIS	AA	21	162	17	7	1	1	11	17	17	3	3	-0.8	.280	.354	.364	.026	.240	.304	.322	.218	-3.8	37-2B	4		
2006	MIS	AA	22	191	17	6	2	1	15	14	35	2	2	-1.3	.278	.330	.352	.039	.258	.307	.337	.226	-2.3	27-2B	-3	16-3B	-2
2006	RIC	AAA	22	257	30	12	1	2	23	12	28	2	2	1.0	.282	.314	.365	-.027	.261	.297	.357	.227	-2.1	45-2B	4	13-3B	0
2006	ATL	MLB	22	49	3	1	1	1	9	5	7	0	0	-1.7	.262	.340	.405	-.025	.256	.333	.395	.255	1.1				
2007	RIC	AAA	23	443	61	23	3	4	41	34	41	5	4	5.2	.316	.374	.420	.153	.290	.346	.398	.260	17.5	85-2B	9		
2007	ATL	MLB	23	62	5	3	0	0	2	3	6	0	0	0.4	.288	.323	.339	-.123	.288	.323	.339	.232	-0.2				
2008	ATL	MLB	24	502	56	24	2	5	46	35	62	7	3	0.7	.273	.326	.372	-.117	.271	.324	.379	.243	8.4	118-2B	3		

Breakout: 21%   Improve: 49%   Collapse: 23%   Attrition: 13%   Comparables: Jose Lind, Chico Carrasquel, William Bergolla, Luis Gonzalez

The exceptionally sure-handed Prado has posted a career fielding percentage of .980 in the minor leagues. If he could play shortstop, that might be enough to project a fifth infielder's career for him. As a second baseman, however, he won't hit enough to start.

Edgar Renteria — SS — Bats: R — Throws: R — Height: 6' 1" — Weight: 200 — Born: August 7, 1975 — Age: 32

YEAR	TEAM	LVL	AGE	PA	R	2B	3B	HR	RBI	BB	SO	SB	CS	EqBRR	AVG	OBP	SLG	MLVr	EqAVG	EqOBP	EqSLG	EqA	VORP	DEFENSE	
2005	BOS	MLB	29	692	100	36	4	8	70	55	100	9	4	3.3	.276	.335	.385	-.046	.279	.348	.395	.262	19.6	147-SS	-23
2006	ATL	MLB	30	673	100	40	2	14	70	62	89	17	6	-1.1	.293	.361	.436	.087	.295	.365	.442	.280	37.6	142-SS	-9
2007	ATL	MLB	31	543	87	30	1	12	57	46	77	11	2	4.9	.332	.390	.470	.223	.339	.400	.486	.306	47.5	113-SS	-1
2008	DET	MLB	32	495	63	23	3	7	48	42	72	8	3	0.6	.279	.343	.393	-.028	.279	.346	.410	.269	18.1	117-SS	-4

Breakout: 2%   Improve: 28%   Collapse: 50%   Attrition: 11%   Comparables: Jeff Cirillo, Dave Concepcion, Kevin Seitzer, Tadahito Iguchi

If you thought Hall of Fame voters dodged a bullet when Harold Baines retired with 2,866 hits, wait a few years. Edgar Renteria made his major league debut three months before his 21st birthday, has been a regular ever since, and will pick up his 2000th hit sometime in June, or just after he turns 32. That doesn't mean he'll get to 3000, but his chances are real; the *2008 Bill James Handbook* gives him a 37 percent shot at the milestone. It's not like Renteria is a scrub—his career WARP3 will edge over 70 this year—he's just not anyone's idea of even a fringe Hall of Famer. The Tigers are better for having him, but not by that much; he's only a marginally better defender than Carlos Guillen, though he is likely to out hit Sean Casey.

Clint Sammons — C — Bats: R — Throws: R — Height: 6' 0" — Weight: 200 — Born: May 15, 1983 — Age: 25

YEAR	TEAM	LVL	AGE	PA	R	2B	3B	HR	RBI	BB	SO	SB	CS	EqBRR	AVG	OBP	SLG	MLVr	EqAVG	EqOBP	EqSLG	EqA	VORP	DEFENSE	
2005	ROM	A	22	494	60	29	0	4	62	55	66	4	1	1.0	.286	.368	.382	.106	.234	.300	.300	.215	-17.0	79-C	3
2006	MYR	A+	23	407	36	21	0	8	56	32	65	4	4	0.0	.258	.323	.383	.010	.231	.279	.346	.218	-11.5	94-C	1
2007	MYR	A+	24	91	13	6	0	4	13	10	14	1	1	-0.5	.269	.363	.500	.218	.235	.308	.420	.250	1.5	18-C	5
2007	MIS	AA	24	328	27	10	0	5	36	26	72	1	1	-2.9	.243	.304	.328	-.116	.222	.274	.301	.201	-16.3	80-C	7
2008	ATL	MLB	25	365	31	14	1	7	37	27	76	3	1	-0.4	.231	.293	.345	-.239	.229	.291	.352	.221	-2.6	88-C	3

Breakout: 34%   Improve: 56%   Collapse: 21%   Attrition: 17%   Comparables: Joe Perona, Jason Hill, Dan Conway, Sean Mulligan

Despite a nice second look in the Carolina League, Sammons isn't a threat to McCann, but with gap power, a good catchers' body, and enough arm to throw out half of the runners who tried to steal against him last season, he's a credible contender for Brayan Peña's backup job.

Jordan Schafer — CF

Bats: L   Throws: L   Height: 6' 1"   Weight: 190   Born: September 4, 1986   Age: 21

YEAR	TEAM	LVL	AGE	PA	R	2B	3B	HR	RBI	BB	SO	SB	CS	EqBRR	AVG	OBP	SLG	MLVr	EqAVG	EqOBP	EqSLG	EqA	VORP	DEFENSE	
2006	ROM	A	19	422	49	15	7	8	60	28	95	15	9	-2.7	.240	.293	.376	-.031	.199	.239	.310	.187	-33.3	106-CF	-3
2007	ROM	A	20	145	16	15	2	5	20	16	31	4	4	-3.0	.372	.441	.636	.620	.242	.310	.432	.249	2.4	32-CF	-8
2007	MYR	A+	20	481	70	34	8	10	43	40	95	19	11	0.7	.294	.354	.477	.197	.237	.286	.387	.231	-7.3	101-CF	-2
2008	ATL	MLB	21	633	67	37	5	11	60	45	159	16	7	1.6	.240	.295	.375	-.191	.237	.293	.383	.229	-3.1	148-CF	-2

Breakout: 42% Improve: 70% Collapse: 14% Attrition: 6%   Comparables: K.C. Gillum, Laynce Nix, Jason Robertson, Brandon Moss

Schafer profiles like a lot of the Braves' high draft choices from the Atlanta region, except he hails from Indiana. Already noted for a great glove in center field, Schafer hit for the first time in 2007, showing newfound power (in a home park that usually kills it) and better plate discipline. Schafer gets overlooked in a deep pool of center-field prospects, but he's someone to watch at Double-A this year.

Mark Teixeira — 1B

Bats: S   Throws: R   Height: 6' 3"   Weight: 220   Born: April 11, 1980   Age: 28

YEAR	TEAM	LVL	AGE	PA	R	2B	3B	HR	RBI	BB	SO	SB	CS	EqBRR	AVG	OBP	SLG	MLVr	EqAVG	EqOBP	EqSLG	EqA	VORP	DEFENSE	
2005	TEX	MLB	25	730	112	41	3	43	144	72	124	4	0	2.0	.301	.379	.575	.298	.300	.388	.590	.322	62.0	153-1B	0
2006	TEX	MLB	26	727	99	45	1	33	110	89	128	2	0	-0.3	.282	.371	.514	.160	.274	.373	.511	.300	37.4	158-1B	6
2007	TEX	MLB	27	335	48	24	1	13	49	45	66	0	0	0.9	.297	.397	.524	.254	.297	.403	.544	.319	26.0	71-1B	-5
2007	ATL	MLB	27	240	38	9	1	17	56	27	46	0	0	-0.8	.317	.404	.615	.429	.324	.412	.647	.343	27.1	53-1B	-1
2008	ATL	MLB	28	632	102	34	2	32	103	85	110	3	1	-0.6	.295	.394	.547	.247	.292	.391	.558	.312	48.8	148-1B	-2

Breakout: 15% Improve: 45% Collapse: 22% Attrition: 7%   Comparables: Eddie Murray, Lance Berkman, Willie Aikens, Willie McCovey

When you look at the prices paid for free agents this winter, it becomes clear that Teixeira is going to be the next player to top $20 million in annual compensation. He'll hit the market at 28, presumably off of yet another .300/.400/.500 season, with a Gold Glove reputation—his range is declining, but his hands are still good—as the best free-agent hitter available. There's very little chance he won't test the market, which makes it imperative that the Braves choose wisely at the trading deadline if they're on the contention bubble.

Scott Thorman — 1B

Bats: L   Throws: R   Height: 6' 3"   Weight: 235   Born: January 6, 1982   Age: 26

YEAR	TEAM	LVL	AGE	PA	R	2B	3B	HR	RBI	BB	SO	SB	CS	EqBRR	AVG	OBP	SLG	MLVr	EqAVG	EqOBP	EqSLG	EqA	VORP	DEFENSE			
2005	MIS	AA	23	383	49	21	2	15	65	28	76	2	2	-2.3	.305	.360	.506	.259	.263	.311	.449	.257	4.3	90-1B	-3		
2005	RIC	AAA	23	224	23	10	3	6	27	9	42	0	0	-2.1	.276	.313	.438	-.009	.251	.289	.398	.235	-5.2	52-1B	-3		
2006	RIC	AAA	24	344	38	16	2	15	48	31	48	4	2	0.4	.298	.360	.508	.246	.281	.345	.503	.285	18.1	49-1B	-6	24-LF	-2
2006	ATL	MLB	24	133	13	11	0	5	14	5	21	1	0	-1.3	.234	.263	.438	-.133	.234	.269	.438	.238	-2.3	15-LF	-1	13-1B	0
2007	ATL	MLB	25	307	37	18	0	11	36	14	70	1	1	-1.3	.216	.258	.394	-.206	.220	.267	.402	.227	-9.6	68-1B	-5		
2008	ATL	MLB	26	262	32	14	1	10	38	19	52	2	1	-0.3	.268	.324	.458	-.008	.265	.322	.467	.263	7.7	65-1B	-2		

Breakout: 40% Improve: 66% Collapse: 19% Attrition: 29%   Comparables: Daryle Ward, Pat Putnam, Bob Chance, Gail Harris

If Thorman had come anywhere close to an acceptable performance in early 2007, Teixeira would not be a Brave. Instead, after a strong April, Thorman was a disaster, batting just .203/.242/.366 from the start of May through Teixeira's arrival at the deadline. Thorman is Russell Branyan without the walks or homers, which means the Braves will be back to square one if Teixeira leaves next winter.

PITCHERS

Manny Acosta

Bats: R   Throws: R   Height: 6' 4"   Weight: 170   Born: May 1, 1981   Age: 27

YEAR	TEAM	LVL	AGE	W	L	SV	G	GS	IP	H	BB	SO	HR	GB%	BABIP	STUFF	WHIP	ERA	PERA	EqERA	EqH9	EqBB9	EqSO9	EqHR9	VORP	SN/WX
2005	MYR	A+	24	2	2	7	18	0	22¹	22	9	18	1	60.6%	.309	-24	1.39	4.44	6.32	7.32	11.0	5.5	3.7	0.9	-3.8	—
2006	MIS	AA	25	0	0	4	13	0	15¹	7	15	13	1	63.2%	.162	-3	1.46	2.38	4.38	3.14	5.0	9.4	5.0	1.3	3.9	—
2006	RIC	AAA	25	1	6	17	38	0	44¹	38	32	44	4	59.7%	.304	-4	1.59	3.67	6.07	4.93	8.6	7.5	6.4	1.3	3.1	—
2007	RIC	AAA	26	9	3	12	40	0	59²	46	35	56	0	56.4%	.297	12	1.36	2.26	4.03	3.64	8.0	6.0	6.5	0.2	11.8	—
2007	ATL	MLB	26	1	1	0	21	0	23²	13	14	22	2	59.6%	.200	16	1.14	2.28	2.76	1.99	5.2	4.8	7.9	0.8	9.5	0.59
2008	ATL	MLB	27	3	3	2	58	2	57²	57	44	48	4	53.1%	.310	-7	1.76	4.53	5.51	4.87	8.7	6.2	6.7	0.7	5.2	0.50

Breakout: 8%   Improve: 17%   Collapse: 65%   Attrition: 8%   Comparables: Greg Aquino, Gary Wagner, Jose Paniagua, Tim Layana

This rail-thin Panamanian was one of many Richmond Braves to come up and support a tiring bullpen late in the season. Credit the Braves for picking up a castoff from the Yankees' system—Acosta was signed by the Yanks at 16—and slowly turning him into a useful bullpen arm. Persistent command problems plague him, but as a $400,000 solution in the seventh inning, he'll do nicely.

Buddy Carlyle

Bats: L   Throws: R   Height: 6' 3"   Weight: 185   Born: December 21, 1977   Age: 30

YEAR	TEAM	LVL	AGE	W	L	SV	G	GS	IP	H	BB	SO	HR	GB%	BABIP	STUFF	WHIP	ERA	PERA	EqERA	EqH9	EqBB9	EqSO9	EqHR9	VORP	SN/WX
2005	LVG	AAA	27	1	2	2	20	6	48	51	21	53	7	32.1%	.361	-7	1.50	4.88	5.70	5.05	9.3	4.3	7.0	1.4	2.8	—
2005	LAN	MLB	27	0	0	0	10	0	14	16	4	13	4	31.8%	.316	-14	1.43	8.36	8.10	9.22	10.5	2.6	7.9	2.6	-4.4	-0.44
2006	ABQ	AAA	28	3	1	0	13	2	28¹	17	7	22	3	35.5%	.197	-1	0.85	1.92	2.99	2.30	4.9	2.6	4.9	1.3	10.0	—
2007	RIC	AAA	29	5	2	0	9	9	48²	40	9	56	5	46.7%	.299	20	1.01	2.59	4.51	3.83	8.7	2.0	8.1	1.4	8.8	—
2007	ATL	MLB	29	8	7	0	22	20	107	117	32	74	19	35.0%	.307	-8	1.39	5.21	5.32	5.42	9.6	2.3	5.8	1.5	2.4	1.26
2008	ATL	MLB	30	8	9	0	42	21	137²	149	40	99	26	37.3%	.290	-1	1.38	5.01	5.20	5.25	9.5	2.4	5.8	1.6	6.4	1.60

Breakout: 24%   Improve: 45%   Collapse: 24%   Attrition: 13%   Comparables: Dennis Cook, Dick Hall, Rick Reed, Shawn Boskie

When the Braves placed Carlyle in the rotation in June, it went well for a while: six quality starts in nine, with a 3.00 K/BB in 55 innings. After that, it was ugly: 39 runs in 45 innings over ten starts, with a .603 opposition SLG. He's a strike-throwing swingman who needs a big outfield patrolled by young legs just to survive.

Lance Cormier

Bats: R   Throws: R   Height: 6' 1"   Weight: 200   Born: August 19, 1980   Age: 27

YEAR	TEAM	LVL	AGE	W	L	SV	G	GS	IP	H	BB	SO	HR	GB%	BABIP	STUFF	WHIP	ERA	PERA	EqERA	EqH9	EqBB9	EqSO9	EqHR9	VORP	SN/WX
2005	ARI	MLB	24	7	3	0	67	0	79¹	86	43	63	7	50.4%	.341	-2	1.63	5.11	5.24	5.38	9.7	4.6	6.7	0.8	-0.7	2.15
2006	RIC	AAA	25	4	3	0	9	9	54¹	65	14	27	4	58.5%	.330	-15	1.46	3.99	6.04	5.47	11.3	3.0	3.0	1.1	0.7	—
2006	ATL	MLB	25	4	5	0	29	9	73²	90	39	43	8	50.6%	.347	-13	1.75	4.88	6.28	5.35	11.0	4.3	5.0	0.9	4.9	1.32
2007	RIC	AAA	26	4	2	0	10	10	52	56	15	31	4	67.3%	.325	-12	1.37	3.46	6.02	5.28	11.2	3.1	4.1	1.2	1.6	—
2007	ATL	MLB	26	2	6	0	10	9	45²	56	22	27	16	51.6%	.282	-43	1.71	7.09	10.33	8.47	10.8	3.7	4.9	3.0	-8.2	-0.03
2008	ATL	MLB	27	6	9	0	58	16	123²	160	52	69	18	48.7%	.330	-16	1.71	6.25	6.47	6.68	11.3	3.4	4.5	1.3	-11.1	-0.70

Breakout: 29%   Improve: 55%   Collapse: 29%   Attrition: 22%   Comparables: Chris Baker, Jared Gothreaux, Frank Seminara, Mike Brown

If you're wondering why the Braves signed Tom Glavine, it wasn't for his vivid memories of the Civil War. It was because Carlyle and Cormier combined to make 29 starts last year, posting a combined 5.81 ERA and averaging barely more than five innings per start—and that was above average for the back end of the rotation, because Redman, Davies, and Reyes were all worse. Cormier is a ground-ball pitcher who somehow allows a homer every five innings. It's no surprise that he was designated for assignment in December.

Joey Devine

Bats: R   **Throws:** R   **Height:** 6' 1"   **Weight:** 225   **Born:** September 19, 1983   **Age:** 24

YEAR	TEAM	LVL	AGE	W	L	SV	G	GS	IP	H	BB	SO	HR	GB%	BABIP	STUFF	WHIP	ERA	PERA	EqERA	EqH9	EqBB9	EqSO9	EqHR9	VORP	SN/WX
2005	MIS	AA	21	1	1	5	18	0	20	19	12	28	2	46.0%	.370	1	1.55	2.70	8.85	8.50	11.0	6.5	8.5	1.5	-5.8	—
2005	ATL	MLB	21	0	1	0	5	0	5	6	5	3	2	38.9%	.250	-24	2.20	12.60	12.81	13.50	10.1	6.8	5.1	3.4	-4.0	-0.32
2006	MYR	A+	22	1	3	0	13	2	18¹	13	11	28	1	30.8%	.343	16	1.33	5.97	5.90	8.27	8.8	7.2	9.9	1.1	-4.8	—
2006	MIS	AA	22	2	0	0	6	0	11¹	2	4	20	1	30.8%	.100	10	0.54	0.81	2.77	1.80	2.7	3.6	9.9	1.8	4.2	—
2006	ATL	MLB	22	0	0	0	10	0	6¹	8	9	10	1	12.5%	.467	6	2.68	10.00	12.71	11.37	12.8	11.4	12.8	1.4	-2.7	-0.35
2007	MIS	AA	23	2	4	16	33	0	35	26	13	51	1	50.7%	.352	18	1.11	2.06	4.32	3.38	8.4	3.9	9.3	0.6	7.9	—
2007	RIC	AAA	23	3	0	4	17	0	22	15	6	27	1	54.5%	.269	16	0.95	1.64	3.10	2.86	6.5	2.9	7.8	0.8	6.7	—
2007	ATL	MLB	23	1	0	0	10	0	8¹	7	8	7	0	58.3%	.318	8	1.80	1.08	4.12	1.08	7.6	7.6	7.6	0.0	4.4	0.23
2008	OAK	MLB	24	3	3	5	49	3	54¹	48	31	52	5	46.3%	.293	9	1.46	3.90	4.14	3.97	7.8	4.6	8.0	0.8	10.0	1.00

Breakout: 31% **Improve:** 54% **Collapse:** 22% **Attrition:** 10%   **Comparables:** Chris Ray, Taylor Tankersley, Lance McCullers, Logan Kensing

Healthy again, Devine pitched like the first-round pick he was in 2005, before some back problems and a bit of mis-handling by the Braves made his professional career an adventure. A groundballer who kills righties, he should handle lefties well enough and, having been dealt for Mark Kotsay, will get a chance to prove it in Oakland.

Octavio Dotel

Bats: R   **Throws:** R   **Height:** 6' 0"   **Weight:** 210   **Born:** November 25, 1973   **Age:** 34

YEAR	TEAM	LVL	AGE	W	L	SV	G	GS	IP	H	BB	SO	HR	GB%	BABIP	STUFF	WHIP	ERA	PERA	EqERA	EqH9	EqBB9	EqSO9	EqHR9	VORP	SN/WX
2005	OAK	MLB	31	1	2	7	15	0	15¹	10	11	16	2	26.3%	.222	15	1.37	3.53	4.05	3.68	6.1	6.8	9.2	1.2	3.8	0.09
2006	NYA	MLB	32	0	0	0	14	0	10	18	11	7	2	36.6%	.421	-36	2.90	10.80	16.58	13.94	15.7	8.7	6.1	1.7	-6.4	-0.43
2007	KCA	MLB	33	2	1	11	24	0	23	24	11	29	3	46.0%	.356	16	1.52	3.91	5.11	3.80	9.1	3.8	9.9	1.1	4.4	0.51
2007	ATL	MLB	33	0	0	0	9	0	7²	5	1	12	1	17.6%	.250	8	0.78	4.68	2.60	5.62	5.6	1.1	10.1	1.1	-0.0	0.18
2008	ATL	MLB	34	3	4	11	51	0	57	53	26	62	8	37.2%	.301	10	1.38	4.18	4.39	4.43	8.2	3.7	8.7	1.1	8.0	0.90

Breakout: 54% **Improve:** 87% **Collapse:** 6% **Attrition:** 4%   **Comparables:** Mike Trombley, Doug Bair, Todd Worrell, Alejandro Peña

Whoops! Dotel was healthy just long enough—less than three months between an oblique injury in the spring and one to his beleaguered shoulder in early August—to entice the Braves into trading Kyle Davies for him at the deadline in an attempt to shore up their bullpen. He lasted 4⅓ innings over his first week as a Brave before heading to the DL. A free agent, he's still effective on the increasingly rare days that he's available to pitch.

Mike Gonzalez

Bats: R   **Throws:** L   **Height:** 6' 2"   **Weight:** 215   **Born:** May 23, 1978   **Age:** 30

YEAR	TEAM	LVL	AGE	W	L	SV	G	GS	IP	H	BB	SO	HR	GB%	BABIP	STUFF	WHIP	ERA	PERA	EqERA	EqH9	EqBB9	EqSO9	EqHR9	VORP	SN/WX
2005	PIT	MLB	27	1	3	3	51	0	50	35	31	58	2	50.0%	.280	28	1.32	2.70	3.20	2.74	6.6	5.1	9.5	0.4	15.5	2.39
2006	PIT	MLB	28	3	4	24	54	0	54	42	31	64	1	40.1%	.311	32	1.35	2.17	2.87	1.79	6.5	4.4	9.4	0.2	23.3	3.49
2007	ATL	MLB	29	2	0	2	18	0	17	15	8	13	0	40.8%	.313	7	1.35	1.59	3.50	1.69	8.4	3.9	6.8	0.0	8.1	1.08
2008	ATL	MLB	30	3	2	6	51	0	50	44	30	54	3	43.8%	.305	10	1.48	3.73	4.23	4.01	7.7	4.9	8.7	0.6	9.0	0.90

Breakout: 3% **Improve:** 6% **Collapse:** 89% **Attrition:** 3%   **Comparables:** Don McMahon, Randy Myers, Jim Kern, Will Ohman

Whoops! Gonzalez was healthy just long enough—he missed time in 2005 to a sprained knee and at the end of 2006 to a sore elbow—to entice the Braves into trading Adam LaRoche for him (and, to their credit, Lillibridge) in an attempt to shore up their bullpen. Gonzalez lasted 17 innings over seven weeks before heading to the DL for Tommy John surgery. He'll be out until at least June.

Thomas Hanson

Bats: R   **Throws:** R   **Height:** 6' 6"   **Weight:** 210   **Born:** August 28, 1986   **Age:** 21

YEAR	TEAM	LVL	AGE	W	L	SV	G	GS	IP	H	BB	SO	HR	GB%	BABIP	STUFF	WHIP	ERA	PERA	EqERA	EqH9	EqBB9	EqSO9	EqHR9	VORP	SN/WX
2006	DNV	Rk	19	4	1	0	13	8	51¹	42	9	56	2	41.1%	.302	0	1.00	2.11	6.02	5.76	9.9	4.4	4.6	1.4	-0.8	—
2007	ROM	A	20	2	6	0	15	14	73	51	26	90	6	44.3%	.269	9	1.05	2.59	5.48	5.26	8.2	5.3	6.6	1.5	2.5	—
2007	MYR	A+	20	3	3	0	11	11	60	53	32	64	10	39.0%	.299	-16	1.42	4.20	10.58	8.65	11.1	7.4	6.5	3.4	-17.3	—
2008	ATL	MLB	21	6	9	0	23	23	122¹	129	82	100	23	40.0%	.294	1	1.72	5.91	6.49	6.17	9.2	5.4	6.6	1.6	-5.5	0.30

Breakout: 30% **Improve:** 54% **Collapse:** 25% **Attrition:** 11%   **Comparables:** Travis Buckley, Domingo Valdez, Fernando Cabrera, Kris Detmers

Whoops! (Just kidding.) Hanson was part of the penultimate last class of draft-and-follows in 2005. Last year, the big righty led the organization in strikeouts, although his home run rate was notably high for his levels, particularly the half season he pitched at Myrtle Beach. His size and mid-90s fastball mean he'll get lots of chances.

Tim Hudson — Bats: R   Throws: R   Height: 6' 1"   Weight: 170   Born: July 14, 1975   Age: 32

YEAR	TEAM	LVL	AGE	W	L	SV	G	GS	IP	H	BB	SO	HR	GB%	BABIP	STUFF	WHIP	ERA	PERA	EqERA	EqH9	EqBB9	EqSO9	EqHR9	VORP	SN/WX
2005	ATL	MLB	29	14	9	0	29	29	192	194	65	115	20	59.2%	.291	7	1.35	3.52	4.37	3.83	9.0	2.8	5.0	0.9	41.2	5.33
2006	ATL	MLB	30	13	12	0	35	35	218¹	235	79	141	25	58.6%	.303	7	1.44	4.86	4.36	4.81	9.1	2.8	5.3	0.9	17.0	3.48
2007	ATL	MLB	31	16	10	0	34	34	224¹	221	53	132	10	62.7%	.299	25	1.22	3.33	3.45	3.48	8.8	1.8	5.1	0.4	59.7	7.91
2008	ATL	MLB	32	12	10	0	30	30	192²	206	57	110	17	55.5%	.299	7	1.36	4.01	4.28	4.38	9.4	2.4	4.6	0.7	27.4	4.50

Breakout: 11% Improve: 32% Collapse: 33% Attrition: 11%   Comparables: Joe Horlen, Larry Jackson, Andy Ashby, Mel Stottlemyre

He was as good last year as he's been since his rookie season, for the first time resembling the pitcher the Braves traded for three years ago, the one who didn't walk people or give up homers. Lacking the stuff he entered the league with, Hudson has to limit those two elements to succeed. Healthy in 2007, he did just that, and you can expect more of the same this year.

Chuck James — Bats: L   Throws: L   Height: 6' 0"   Weight: 170   Born: November 9, 1981   Age: 26

YEAR	TEAM	LVL	AGE	W	L	SV	G	GS	IP	H	BB	SO	HR	GB%	BABIP	STUFF	WHIP	ERA	PERA	EqERA	EqH9	EqBB9	EqSO9	EqHR9	VORP	SN/WX
2005	MYR	A+	23	3	3	0	7	7	41²	20	8	59	1	35.3%	.226	30	0.67	1.08	3.48	3.13	5.8	2.9	8.0	0.5	10.2	—
2005	MIS	AA	23	9	1	0	16	16	86	62	18	104	4	28.6%	.286	24	0.93	2.09	3.83	3.91	7.8	2.5	7.5	0.8	14.7	—
2005	RIC	AAA	23	1	3	0	6	6	33²	21	10	30	4	20.0%	.200	9	0.92	3.47	3.61	4.06	6.4	3.5	6.1	1.5	5.3	—
2006	RIC	AAA	24	1	0	0	7	6	33	30	6	25	3	37.5%	.273	1	1.09	2.73	4.13	3.34	8.4	2.2	4.7	1.4	8.1	—
2006	ATL	MLB	24	11	4	0	25	18	119	101	47	91	20	29.5%	.250	3	1.24	3.78	3.65	3.48	7.0	3.0	6.1	1.3	25.2	3.09
2007	ATL	MLB	25	11	10	0	30	30	161¹	164	58	116	32	32.8%	.280	-7	1.38	4.24	5.18	4.10	9.0	2.8	6.1	1.7	28.7	4.26
2008	ATL	MLB	26	8	9	0	39	22	150²	157	53	111	23	35.3%	.289	4	1.39	4.79	5.03	5.03	9.1	2.9	5.9	1.3	11.0	2.10

Breakout: 6%   Improve: 26% Collapse: 51% Attrition: 11%   Comparables: Dan Schatzeder, Jarrod Washburn, Rick Krivda, Tom Browning

Fully formed at 26, James is a fly ball–tossing southpaw whose ERA will fluctuate with his home-run-to-fly-ball rate. That figure ticked upward from 10.4 percent to 13.2 percent last year, accounting for the bump in his ERA. The Braves could use more innings from him; he averaged just 5⅓ frames per start last season, and had a dramatic falloff in his performance after 60 pitches.

Ron Mahay — Bats: L   Throws: L   Height: 6' 2"   Weight: 190   Born: June 28, 1971   Age: 37

YEAR	TEAM	LVL	AGE	W	L	SV	G	GS	IP	H	BB	SO	HR	GB%	BABIP	STUFF	WHIP	ERA	PERA	EqERA	EqH9	EqBB9	EqSO9	EqHR9	VORP	SN/WX
2005	FRI	AA	34	1	3	0	5	5	19²	24	9	20	3	45.9%	.368	-17	1.68	7.77	9.80	11.21	12.7	6.1	6.6	2.0	-11.0	—
2005	TEX	MLB	34	0	2	1	30	0	35²	47	16	30	8	49.6%	.348	-18	1.74	6.81	7.59	6.75	11.0	4.0	7.2	1.8	-4.3	-0.31
2006	TEX	MLB	35	1	3	0	62	0	57	54	28	56	7	42.6%	.307	6	1.44	3.95	4.09	4.13	7.9	4.1	8.3	1.0	9.2	0.25
2007	TEX	MLB	36	2	0	1	28	0	39	33	21	32	3	52.7%	.286	7	1.38	2.77	3.73	2.39	7.4	4.5	6.9	0.7	14.3	0.62
2007	ATL	MLB	36	1	0	0	30	0	28	19	16	23	1	47.4%	.243	10	1.25	2.25	2.72	2.54	6.0	4.4	6.7	0.3	10.2	0.48
2008	KCA	MLB	37	3	4	3	70	0	69²	73	38	56	8	48.2%	.310	-6	1.59	4.90	4.81	4.67	8.9	4.4	6.7	1.0	5.0	0.50

Breakout: 20% Improve: 43% Collapse: 38% Attrition: 14%   Comparables: Tommy Byrne, Mike Myers, Norm Charlton, Turk Lown

Isn't there a book in Ron Mahay's story? He was a replacement player in the spring of 1995 and got a call-up later that season as an extra outfielder for the Red Sox, who treated him better than the Dodgers treated Mike Busch, but not by much. He then returned to the minors and converted to relief pitching, making his way back to the bigs by 1997. Since then, he's made 359 career appearances with an ERA of 3.87. A shutdown guy against lefty batters, he was good enough to be desired at the trade deadline last season, and should stay in the league for a while longer.

Kristopher Medlen

Bats: S   Throws: R   Height: 5' 10"   Weight: 175   Born: October 7, 1985   Age: 22

YEAR	TEAM	LVL	AGE	W	L	SV	G	GS	IP	H	BB	SO	HR	GB%	BABIP	STUFF	WHIP	ERA	PERA	EqERA	EqH9	EqBB9	EqSO9	EqHR9	VORP	SN/WX
2006	DNV	Rk	20	1	0	0	10	20	0	22²	14	2	36	0	61.7%	.298	19	0.72	0.41	4.88	3.32	9.0	3.3	8.1	0.5	4.8	—
2007	ROM	A	21	0	1	0	8	17	0	20²	13	3	33	1	54.5%	.279	20	0.77	0.87	3.92	3.20	7.3	2.7	8.2	0.9	5.3	—
2007	MYR	A+	21	2	0	0	2	18	0	24	22	7	28	1	53.0%	.333	2	1.21	1.13	5.43	4.50	10.2	4.1	6.5	0.8	2.7	—
2008	ATL	MLB	22	4	4	3	27	5	59²	63	28	46	6	51.6%	.313	3	1.52	4.25	4.85	4.58	9.3	3.8	6.3	0.8	8.0	1.00

Breakout: 22%   Improve: 45%   Collapse: 33%   Attrition: 7%   Comparables: Fernando Hernandez, Cory Bailey, Ryan Larson, Sean Spencer

Primarily a shortstop in college, Medlen was drafted by the Braves to pitch, and it looks like it was the right decision. It's hard for scouts to get worked up about a 5-foot-10 right-hander, but easy when that pitcher dominates out of the pen with a fastball that touches 94 mph and an outstanding curveball, as Medlen does. He doesn't have the body or the arsenal to start, nor the pure stuff to close, but he's going to be a big-league reliever in short order.

Peter Moylan

Bats: R   Throws: R   Height: 6' 3"   Weight: 220   Born: February 12, 1978   Age: 30

YEAR	TEAM	LVL	AGE	W	L	SV	G	GS	IP	H	BB	SO	HR	GB%	BABIP	STUFF	WHIP	ERA	PERA	EqERA	EqH9	EqBB9	EqSO9	EqHR9	VORP	SN/WX
2006	RIC	AAA	28	1	7	1	35	0	56²	61	38	54	4	63.4%	.343	-10	1.76	6.41	6.98	8.23	10.4	6.9	6.1	1.0	-16.0	—
2006	ATL	MLB	28	0	0	0	15	0	15	18	5	14	1	59.2%	.362	5	1.53	4.80	4.44	4.70	10.0	2.3	7.6	0.6	2.0	0.24
2007	ATL	MLB	29	5	3	1	80	0	90	65	31	63	6	64.0%	.242	12	1.07	1.80	2.86	2.56	6.4	2.7	6.0	0.6	31.7	3.04
2008	ATL	MLB	30	4	3	3	67	0	73	77	32	53	6	55.8%	.311	-3	1.49	4.05	4.43	4.44	9.2	3.5	5.9	0.7	9.8	0.90

Breakout: 19%   Improve: 44%   Collapse: 29%   Attrition: 8%   Comparables: Luis Sanchez, Lou Pote, Tom Tellmann, Jim Corsi

Moylan owes his well-paying job to the World Baseball Classic. After washing out of the Twins' system a decade ago, Moylan found himself out of baseball and back in his native Australia. He picked up the game again a few years ago, made the Australian national team, and pitched well against Venezuela in the WBC. His ERA last year was artificially low, as a third of his runs allowed were unearned. Still, he's a ground-ball machine who owns righties and can pitch two days out of three (he had a 1.32 ERA on zero day's rest). He'll make more than $400,000 pretty soon.

Chad Paronto

Bats: R   Throws: R   Height: 6' 5"   Weight: 250   Born: July 28, 1975   Age: 32

YEAR	TEAM	LVL	AGE	W	L	SV	G	GS	IP	H	BB	SO	HR	GB%	BABIP	STUFF	WHIP	ERA	PERA	EqERA	EqH9	EqBB9	EqSO9	EqHR9	VORP	SN/WX
2005	NAS	AAA	29	3	1	4	27	0	39¹	40	19	38	1	55.1%	.345	-1	1.50	2.75	4.87	4.38	9.7	4.6	6.3	0.2	5.0	—
2005	RIC	AAA	29	3	1	0	26	0	41	43	17	28	4	51.6%	.322	-22	1.46	3.95	6.13	5.02	10.5	4.5	4.3	1.2	2.4	—
2006	RIC	AAA	30	1	1	4	12	0	17	17	3	15	1	56.6%	.308	1	1.18	1.06	4.34	2.16	9.2	2.2	5.4	1.1	6.4	—
2006	ATL	MLB	30	2	3	0	65	0	56²	53	19	41	5	44.3%	.293	3	1.27	3.17	3.59	3.38	8.0	2.6	5.9	0.6	14.8	-0.42
2007	RIC	AAA	31	0	0	2	11	0	16²	18	4	11	1	51.8%	.321	-16	1.32	3.77	5.00	5.51	9.9	2.2	3.9	0.6	0.2	—
2007	ATL	MLB	31	3	1	1	41	0	40¹	47	19	14	1	51.4%	.333	-19	1.64	3.57	5.11	4.46	10.8	3.8	3.1	0.2	6.3	0.22
2008	HOU	MLB	32	2	3	1	48	0	52	61	25	27	5	48.0%	.310	-21	1.64	5.55	5.69	5.99	10.5	3.8	4.1	0.9	-2.2	-0.20

Breakout: 8%   Improve: 21%   Collapse: 60%   Attrition: 11%   Comparables: Kevin Gryboski, Ben Weber, Mike Barlow, Matt Karchner

Paronto lost his middle-innings job to Moylan in July and was designated for assignment after the season. A big guy, Paronto's back-to-back good ERAs should land him a low-leverage role in an MLB bullpen this spring, but don't look for him to make it three in a row; he may be a big guy, but he doesn't have big-guy stuff.

Jo-Jo Reyes

Bats: L   Throws: L   Height: 6' 2"   Weight: 230   Born: November 20, 1984   Age: 23

YEAR	TEAM	LVL	AGE	W	L	SV	G	GS	IP	H	BB	SO	HR	GB%	BABIP	STUFF	WHIP	ERA	PERA	EqERA	EqH9	EqBB9	EqSO9	EqHR9	VORP	SN/WX
2005	DNV	Rk	20	3	0	0	9	8	43¹	37	6	27	3	32.1%	.258	-36	0.99	3.53	7.72	8.74	12.2	4.8	1.6	2.1	-11.9	—
2006	ROM	A	21	8	1	0	13	13	75²	62	25	84	5	50.8%	.305	-2	1.16	2.99	6.52	5.65	9.9	5.4	5.8	1.7	-0.4	—
2006	MYR	A+	21	4	4	0	14	14	65²	52	36	58	0	41.3%	.292	11	1.35	4.14	4.76	6.75	8.4	6.4	5.1	0.3	-7.7	—
2007	MIS	AA	22	8	1	0	13	13	73¹	63	35	71	5	46.2%	.310	5	1.34	3.56	5.18	4.95	9.0	4.9	5.9	1.1	4.9	—
2007	RIC	AAA	22	4	0	0	6	6	36	25	12	39	2	53.3%	.258	27	1.03	1.00	3.40	2.60	6.7	3.4	7.3	0.8	11.6	—
2007	ATL	MLB	22	2	2	0	11	10	50²	55	30	27	9	45.3%	.295	-15	1.68	6.21	6.33	6.84	9.7	4.7	4.7	1.4	-5.8	0.26
2008	ATL	MLB	23	8	10	0	39	26	147¹	153	84	113	19	44.2%	.300	1	1.60	5.19	5.53	5.53	9.1	4.6	6.2	1.1	3.4	1.30

Breakout: 36%   Improve: 59%   Collapse: 16%   Attrition: 6%   Comparables: Tom Gorzelanny, Noah Lowry, Gary Rath, Eric DuBose

Just the second-most desperate act the Braves pulled in trying to save their rotation (the first being employing Mark Redman), bringing Reyes up in July after six International League starts didn't work. Reyes' command wasn't as good as his minor league ERAs, and it declined to awful in the majors. Given another 20 to 30 starts in the minors to work on this, he can eventually become a midrotation starter.

Jamie Richmond

Bats: R Throws: R Height: 6' 3" Weight: 185 Born: March 23, 1986 Age: 22

YEAR	TEAM	LVL	AGE	W	L	SV	G	GS	IP	H	BB	SO	HR	GB%	BABIP	STUFF	WHIP	ERA	PERA	EqERA	EqH9	EqBB9	EqSO9	EqHR9	VORP	SN/WX
2006	DNV	Rk	20	7	1	0	14	12	67	51	4	52	0	61.1%	.272	3	0.82	1.21	4.59	3.99	8.6	2.6	2.9	0.6	10.5	—
2007	ROM	A	21	7	6	0	25	24	138²	141	25	98	9	51.4%	.296	-15	1.20	3.05	5.43	6.27	10.0	3.1	3.0	1.2	-9.8	—
2008	OAK	MLB	22	6	10	0	34	22	132²	170	56	45	19	50.2%	.311	-17	1.71	6.24	6.20	6.34	11.3	3.4	2.9	1.3	-14.2	-0.70

Breakout: 9% Improve: 37% Collapse: 36% Attrition: 17%   Comparables: Keith Evans, Ronald Bay, John Carter, Keith Dunn

A long, lanky Canadian who is still a bit rough around the edges, Richmond has two things going for him: he throws strikes, and he keeps the ball on the ground. That was enough to stymie hitters in the Sally League, but he'll need to work on his secondary pitches to project as more than a back-of-the-rotation type.

Royce Ring

Bats: L Throws: L Height: 6' 0" Weight: 220 Born: December 21, 1980 Age: 27

YEAR	TEAM	LVL	AGE	W	L	SV	G	GS	IP	H	BB	SO	HR	GB%	BABIP	STUFF	WHIP	ERA	PERA	EqERA	EqH9	EqBB9	EqSO9	EqHR9	VORP	SN/WX
2005	NOR	AAA	24	3	0	2	33	0	38²	34	13	26	2	56.7%	.281	-15	1.21	3.26	4.35	4.79	8.8	3.8	4.3	0.8	3.2	—
2005	NYN	MLB	24	0	2	0	15	0	10²	10	10	8	0	54.5%	.313	-1	1.88	5.05	4.79	5.06	8.4	7.6	5.9	0.0	0.4	0.12
2006	NOR	AAA	25	2	2	11	36	0	39	30	15	40	2	66.3%	.286	-1	1.15	3.00	3.78	4.23	7.0	4.0	6.6	0.7	5.8	—
2006	NYN	MLB	25	0	0	0	11	0	12²	7	3	8	2	62.2%	.143	1	0.79	2.13	2.37	2.08	4.8	2.1	4.8	1.4	5.4	0.18
2007	POR	AAA	26	4	0	1	27	0	31²	22	11	44	0	60.8%	.301	26	1.04	1.99	2.77	2.53	5.9	3.4	9.3	0.3	10.9	—
2007	SDN	MLB	26	1	0	0	15	0	15	11	14	17	1	63.2%	.270	15	1.67	3.60	3.81	4.11	6.5	7.0	9.4	0.6	1.3	0.24
2007	RIC	AAA	26	1	2	1	15	0	12²	17	7	14	2	64.1%	.429	-26	1.89	5.67	13.17	10.03	13.9	5.4	7.7	2.3	-5.8	—
2007	ATL	MLB	26	0	0	0	11	0	5	2	3	4	0	50.0%	.182	5	1.00	0.00	0.08	0.00	3.9	5.8	7.7	0.0	3.3	0.04
2008	ATL	MLB	27	3	3	3	70	1	55¹	55	32	47	5	54.0%	.309	-2	1.58	4.51	4.83	4.91	8.8	4.7	6.8	0.7	5.1	0.50

Breakout: 4% Improve: 32% Collapse: 45% Attrition: 3%   Comparables: Gary Lavelle, John Parrish, J. C. Romero, Gene Walter

Even though he's a closer-turned-LOOGY, this stat is pretty weird: Ring has never thrown 40 innings for any team in any season as a professional. That's a combination of how he's been handled, a couple of midseason trades, and the occasional injury. Now years removed from the first-round-pick hype, he's become a power lefty who's ready for Arthur Rhodes' old job. Ring has that kind of stuff, and will be a key part of the Braves' bullpen this year.

Cole Rohrbough

Bats: L Throws: L Height: 6' 3" Weight: 205 Born: May 23, 1987 Age: 21

YEAR	TEAM	LVL	AGE	W	L	SV	G	GS	IP	H	BB	SO	HR	GB%	BABIP	STUFF	WHIP	ERA	PERA	EqERA	EqH9	EqBB9	EqSO9	EqHR9	VORP	SN/WX
2007	ROM	A	20	2	0	0	6	6	28	13	12	38	1	33.9%	.218	25	0.89	1.29	4.16	3.96	5.4	6.1	7.6	0.7	4.6	—
2007	DNV	Rk	20	3	2	0	8	7	33¹	20	8	58	1	55.6%	.311	21	0.84	1.08	6.08	5.53	9.4	5.5	8.1	1.3	0.2	—
2008	ATL	MLB	21	7	7	0	30	20	125²	109	85	131	15	42.2%	.287	16	1.54	4.42	5.01	4.67	7.6	5.5	8.4	1.0	13.4	2.40

Breakout: 27% Improve: 53% Collapse: 25% Attrition: 10%   Comparables: Gio Gonzalez, Terrell Wade, Bill Pulsipher, Yovani Gallardo

Rohrbough joined Hanson as one of the Braves' last draft-and-follow finds, and could be a gem. Given nearly $700,000 to not go back into the draft last June, Rohrbough overmatched hitters after signing. A big, physical lefty who already has a plus fastball, outstanding curve, and tons of command, he has a very high ceiling.

John Smoltz

Bats: R Throws: R Height: 6' 3" Weight: 220 Born: May 15, 1967 Age: 41

YEAR	TEAM	LVL	AGE	W	L	SV	G	GS	IP	H	BB	SO	HR	GB%	BABIP	STUFF	WHIP	ERA	PERA	EqERA	EqH9	EqBB9	EqSO9	EqHR9	VORP	SN/WX
2005	ATL	MLB	38	14	7	0	33	33	229²	210	53	169	18	49.4%	.284	24	1.15	3.06	3.33	3.41	8.1	1.9	6.1	0.7	60.1	6.74
2006	ATL	MLB	39	16	9	0	35	35	232	221	55	211	23	47.6%	.306	31	1.19	3.49	3.49	3.30	8.2	1.8	7.4	0.8	61.9	7.51
2007	ATL	MLB	40	14	8	0	32	32	205²	196	47	197	18	47.0%	.312	35	1.18	3.11	3.51	3.28	8.4	1.7	8.0	0.7	56.7	7.00
2008	ATL	MLB	41	15	8	0	32	32	214¹	203	50	180	22	46.7%	.289	20	1.18	3.29	3.58	3.53	8.3	1.9	6.7	0.9	44.7	7.00

Breakout: 5% Improve: 29% Collapse: 21% Attrition: 22%   Comparables: Gaylord Perry, Roger Clemens, Tom Seaver, Phil Niekro

Is there actually a debate about his Hall of Fame credentials? While he doesn't have the split career that Dennis Eckersley did, he was arguably the best closer in the National League during his four years in the role. Smoltz's case, like those of Bernie Williams and Jorge Posada, also leans heavily on his extensive body of post-season work: 207 innings with a 2.64 ERA. He's still adding to his case, as well, coming off a season in which he was one of the top six starters in the NL. Given his rates and durability, Smoltz looks to have at least another two seasons of above-average work in him.

Rafael Soriano

Bats: R   Throws: R   Height: 6' 1"   Weight: 220   Born: December 19, 1979   Age: 28

YEAR	TEAM	LVL	AGE	W	L	SV	G	GS	IP	H	BB	SO	HR	GB%	BABIP	STUFF	WHIP	ERA	PERA	EqERA	EqH9	EqBB9	EqSO9	EqHR9	VORP	SN/WX
2005	SEA	MLB	25	0	0	0	7	0	7^1	6	1	9	0	31.6%	.333	7	0.95	2.47	2.82	2.45	7.4	1.2	9.8	0.0	2.7	0.12
2006	SEA	MLB	26	1	2	2	53	0	60	44	21	65	6	28.8%	.262	24	1.08	2.25	3.00	2.12	6.4	2.9	9.1	0.8	25.3	3.19
2007	ATL	MLB	27	3	3	9	71	0	72	47	15	70	12	33.3%	.198	11	0.86	3.00	2.76	3.00	5.6	1.6	8.1	1.4	20.9	3.71
2008	ATL	MLB	28	4	3	8	65	0	72	61	21	67	8	35.3%	.266	12	1.14	3.14	3.36	3.33	7.4	2.4	7.5	1.0	18.6	1.90

Breakout: 14% Improve: 27% Collapse: 39% Attrition: 2%   Comparables: Trevor Hoffman, Jeff Zimmerman, Keith Foulke, Roberto Hernandez

Stolen from the Mariners for Horacio Ramirez, Soriano saw his ERA bounce up as his HR/FB rate returned to non-Safeco levels. Everything else about his game improved, including his role. Even though he had just four saves after Bob Wickman's release on August 23, he was clearly the closer, and pitched well in the role: 14⅓ innings, one run allowed, 19/3 K/BB. He's the ninth-inning guy in an extremely deep bullpen, and could be the best closer in the NL this year.

Oscar Villarreal

Bats: L   Throws: R   Height: 6' 0"   Weight: 215   Born: November 22, 1981   Age: 26

YEAR	TEAM	LVL	AGE	W	L	SV	G	GS	IP	H	BB	SO	HR	GB%	BABIP	STUFF	WHIP	ERA	PERA	EqERA	EqH9	EqBB9	EqSO9	EqHR9	VORP	SN/WX
2005	TUC	AAA	23	0	3	0	12	8	17^1	19	4	8	1	68.3%	.321	-25	1.33	5.20	4.38	6.61	9.9	2.2	2.8	0.6	-1.8	—
2005	ARI	MLB	23	2	0	0	11	0	13^2	11	6	5	2	35.6%	.225	-22	1.24	5.26	3.62	4.61	6.6	3.3	3.3	1.3	0.7	0.14
2006	ATL	MLB	24	9	1	0	58	4	92^1	93	27	55	13	48.1%	.278	-8	1.30	3.61	3.96	3.43	8.3	2.2	4.8	1.1	20.7	1.52
2007	ATL	MLB	25	2	2	1	51	0	76^1	75	32	58	6	46.7%	.308	5	1.40	4.25	3.97	4.42	8.6	3.1	6.3	0.7	9.6	0.44
2008	ATL	MLB	26	4	4	2	51	2	76^1	80	28	50	9	46.1%	.294	-4	1.41	4.32	4.57	4.66	9.2	2.9	5.3	1.0	8.6	0.80

Breakout: 16% Improve: 33% Collapse: 39% Attrition: 7%   Comparables: Willie Fraser, Steve Foucault, Mark Grant, Duaner Sanchez

Villarreal has pitched reasonably well in low-leverage relief the past two seasons, making 47 of his 109 entrances with the Braves trailing by at least two runs. Traded to the Astros for outfielder Josh Anderson, he'll be used in higher-leverage spots in Chad Qualls's old seventh-inning role. The new role is slightly above Villarreal's skill set.

Tyler Yates

Bats: R   Throws: R   Height: 6' 4"   Weight: 240   Born: August 7, 1977   Age: 30

YEAR	TEAM	LVL	AGE	W	L	SV	G	GS	IP	H	BB	SO	HR	GB%	BABIP	STUFF	WHIP	ERA	PERA	EqERA	EqH9	EqBB9	EqSO9	EqHR9	VORP	SN/WX
2006	ATL	MLB	28	2	5	1	56	0	50	42	31	46	6	42.1%	.273	5	1.46	3.96	3.87	3.60	7.2	4.9	7.6	0.9	10.4	-0.63
2007	ATL	MLB	29	2	3	2	75	0	66	64	31	69	6	47.1%	.322	10	1.44	5.18	4.17	5.64	8.6	3.5	8.6	0.8	-1.1	1.11
2008	ATL	MLB	30	3	3	3	62	0	67^2	64	32	60	7	45.2%	.295	2	1.41	4.57	4.27	4.97	8.3	3.8	7.2	0.8	5.2	0.50

Breakout: 35% Improve: 62% Collapse: 22% Attrition: 6%   Comparables: Tim Stoddard, Ted Power, Matt Karchner, Roger Mason

It's tempting to be dismissive here, having commented on seemingly half the relievers in the NL in this chapter. Yates, however, deserves better, having struck out a man every inning over two seasons of middle relief, with a 2.50 K/BB after 16 intentional passes are removed. Moylan is ahead of him for the set-up job, and Yates doesn't look like a high-leverage guy, but then neither did Bob Wickman.

LINEOUTS

Hitters

PLAYER	TEAM	LVL	AGE	PA	R	2B	3B	HR	RBI	BB	SO	SB-CS	EqBRR	AVG/OBP/SLG	MLVr	EqAVG/EqOBP/EqSLG	EqA	VORP
2B W. Aybar '08	ATL	MLB	25	322	36	16	1	7	36	31	42	3-1	-0.5	.267/.342/.400	-.055	.264/.339/.408	.258	8.7
SS C. Fontaine*	ROM	A	21	375	60	14	6	3	26	58	75	10-9	-2.4	.288/.402/.399	.156	.224/.322/.307	.224	-7.5
	MYR	A+	21	88	6	4	0	0	7	8	26	1-0	-0.5	.205/.284/.256	-.280	.173/.227/.222	.144	-11.3
1B J. Franco	NYN	MLB	48	61	7	0	0	1	8	10	13	2-1	-0.1	.200/.328/.260	-.251	.200/.328/.260	.226	-2.0
	ATL	MLB	48	45	1	3	0	0	8	4	10	0-0	-0.2	.250/.311/.325	-.190	.250/.311/.325	.229	-1.2
SS B. Hicks	DNV	Rk	21	74	14	3	1	3	13	12	18	1-2	-0.6	.224/.370/.466	.206	.159/.270/.222	.178	-11.7
	ROM	A	21	157	26	11	0	4	15	27	26	5-3	0.2	.313/.433/.492	.345	.261/.363/.396	.268	7.7
C C. Miller	RIC	AAA	31	222	12	8	0	4	25	25	26	4-0	-0.7	.210/.342/.320	-.099	.237/.347/.355	.257	2.8
	ATL	MLB	31	29	3	2	0	1	4	1	5	0-0	0.2	.259/.310/.444	-.005	.259/.310/.444	.256	1.0
UT P. Orr*	RIC	AAA	28	169	26	6	4	1	8	14	39	7-3	0.7	.240/.308/.351	-.102	.219/.284/.335	.219	-6.8
	ATL	MLB	28	69	11	1	0	0	2	3	14	1-0	1.1	.200/.235/.215	-.506	.200/.235/.215	.148	-5.8
C B. Peña#	RIC	AAA	25	370	42	20	2	6	48	19	38	5-7	-4.6	.301/.341/.423	.094	.277/.315/.409	.246	9.3
	ATL	MLB	25	33	2	0	0	1	3	0	3	0-1	-0.2	.212/.212/.303	-.424	.212/.212/.303	.152	-2.6
2B J. Schuerholz	RIC	AAA	27	153	19	7	0	3	19	14	23	7-1	-1.0	.215/.295/.338	-.154	.226/.298/.353	.239	-2.3
UT C. Woodward	ATL	MLB	31	151	16	6	1	1	8	10	29	1-0	1.6	.199/.252/.279	-.382	.204/.262/.285	.193	-8.9

After a lost season, **Willy Aybar**'s clean, sober, and back in action in the Dominican Winter League. He's out of options, so he'll have to stick or clear waivers, but at least he's headed in the right direction. ⊘ **Chase Fontaine**'s lack of power and high strikeout rate won't continue to support his walk rate. ⊘ The 90 at-bats **Julio Franco** had in 2007 aren't enough to prove he's done, no matter how old he is. ⊘ The 2007 draft was not an especially good one for infielders, but the Braves got one of the better ones in the third round with **Brandon Hicks**, who performed very well in his pro debut. The sum is greater than the parts, as he can hit a little, can draw walks, and is decent but hardly flashy in the field. ⊘ Minor league free agent **Corky Miller** hits a little better than the average backup catcher. ⊘ **Pete Orr** milked two years out of hitting .300 in 2005, but was released over the winter. ⊘ **Brayan Peña**'s empty .300 averages in Triple-A haven't translated yet, and Clint Sammons is about to pass him, but Peña will have other chances. ⊘ **Jon Schuerholz**'s career has become a shameful display of nepotism as the former GM's son has surpassed a 700 OPS only once on his way to Triple-A, and never done so over a full season. ⊘ **Chris Woodward** slugged .468 in 2002, but only .353 over the rest of his career. He keeps getting jobs, though.

Pitchers

PLAYER	TEAM	LVL	AGE	W	L	SV	IP	H	BB	SO	HR	GB%	BABIP	STUFF	WHIP	ERA	PERA	EqERA	EqH9	EqBB9	EqSO9	EqHR9	VORP
J. Ascanio	MIS	AA	22	2	2	10	78	66	18	71	1	46.8%	.310	12	1.08	2.54	3.61	3.89	8.3	2.6	5.4	0.2	14.1
	ATL	MLB	22	1	1	0	16	17	6	13	3	30.9%	.275	-2	1.44	5.06	4.56	5.71	8.8	2.6	6.2	1.6	-0.6
J. Bennett	RIC	AAA	27	3	5	1	86	84	34	45	5	56.5%	.297	-19	1.37	3.35	5.17	4.44	9.6	4.1	3.3	0.8	10.2
	ATL	MLB	27	2	1	0	13	14	3	14	3	57.5%	.314	14	1.31	3.46	5.05	3.29	9.2	2.0	8.6	2.0	3.6
B. Boyer	RIC	AAA	25	4	3	2	73¹	76	50	62	1	49.1%	.373	10	1.72	4.30	6.24	6.30	10.8	7.0	5.9	0.3	-5.1
	ATL	MLB	25	0	0	0	5¹	10	1	3	0	59.1%	.476	-23	2.06	3.40	10.16	7.20	18.0	1.8	5.4	0.0	0.5
J. Cuevas	MYR	A+	23	6	12	0	132	113	71	116	9	41.1%	.275	-12	1.39	3.55	6.08	7.21	9.1	6.8	4.6	1.4	-21.9
S. Evarts*	DNV	Rk	19	4	0	0	37	29	4	34	0	68.9%	.284	2	0.89	1.95	5.17	5.68	9.7	3.4	3.4	0.6	-0.3
B. Hernandez	RIC	AAA	28	9	3	3	74²	76	18	71	7	35.1%	.329	-8	1.26	3.13	5.31	4.84	10.1	2.5	6.4	1.3	6.0
M. Hampton '08	ATL	MLB	35	3	3	0	48²	60	16	22	6	49%	.316	-16	1.56	5.00	5.48	5.36	10.8	2.7	3.7	1.0	2.0
A. Lerew	RIC	AAA	24	1	0	0	26¹	20	8	15	0	51.9%	.250	4	1.06	1.37	3.22	2.49	7.1	3.2	3.6	0.4	8.7
	ATL	MLB	24	0	2	0	11²	14	7	9	4	39.0%	.294	-22	1.80	7.69	8.97	8.03	10.2	4.4	5.8	2.9	-2.3
J. Locke*	DNV	Rk	19	7	1	1	61	48	8	74	2	55.3%	.309	6	0.92	2.66	6.34	7.11	10.8	4.1	5.2	1.2	-8.5
C. Morton	MIS	AA	23	4	6	0	79²	80	37	67	3	48.3%	.341	-8	1.47	4.29	5.39	5.81	10.0	4.7	5.0	0.6	-1.7
Z. Schreiber	MIS	AA	25	3	5	5	44²	26	22	38	3	36.7%	.211	-9	1.07	2.21	3.41	3.30	5.4	4.7	4.7	1.0	11.2
	RIC	AAA	25	1	1	1	33¹	25	11	38	1	43.7%	.289	10	1.08	2.43	3.39	4.13	7.2	3.3	7.4	0.6	5.3
P. Stockman	MIS	AA	27	1	0	3	15¹	8	7	17	0	29.7%	.216	3	0.98	0.59	2.88	2.40	4.8	4.2	6.6	0.0	5.3
	RIC	AAA	27	1	0	0	15²	7	6	15	1	28.9%	.162	4	0.83	1.72	2.73	2.35	4.1	3.5	6.5	0.6	5.5
S. Valenzuela	ROM	A	22	1	3	0	36²	55	19	19	5	42.3%	.376	-59	2.02	7.11	15.35	13.08	15.9	7.5	1.7	2.5	-26.8
	MYR	A+	22	0	0	0	35¹	47	18	19	3	49.6%	.349	-50	1.84	6.88	11.14	12.38	14.1	6.8	2.2	1.7	-24.1

Jose Ascanio is a project with a big-league fastball and a solid slider who was rushed last summer and dealt to the Cubs over the winter. ⊘ **Jeff Bennett** keeps the ball down and could be a back-end-of-the-rotation solution. ⊘ Though he still throws hard, **Blaine Boyer**'s return from shoulder problems was marred by disastrous control. ⊘ A converted third baseman, **Jairo Cuevas** has shown the ability to miss some bats in the minors thanks to good velocity and a plus changeup, but he's still a raw product who needs command and a breaking ball. ⊘ The Braves' supplementary first-round pick in 2006, **Steven Evarts** pitched well in the Appalachian League while being babied. ⊘ The highest-paid Brave (Atlanta's responsible for his entire $15-million salary this year), **Mike Hampton** hasn't thrown a pitch in competition since 2005, and the hamstring he tore in the first inning of his first start in the Mexican League this winter should be an indication of how likely he is to contribute in 2008. ⊘ **Buddy Hernandez** bounced back after two lost years to pitch well at Richmond. He could be the next Heath Bell if he gets a chance. ⊘ Tommy John surgery shut down **Anthony Lerew** in May and will cost him the 2008 season as well. ⊘ The Braves' second-round pick in 2006, **Jeffrey Locke** has a career 8.62 (112:13) K/BB ratio in two low-level seasons. ⊘ Always seen as big and projectable, **Charlie Morton** struggled in a regular-season conversion to the bullpen, but generated a ton of buzz in the Arizona Fall League by flashing a mid-90s fastball and a plus changeup. The Braves think he might be turning the corner. ⊘ A product of Duke, **Zach Schreiber** has put up some solid minor league numbers thanks to a plus slider that he sets up with an average fastball. He should get to the majors, but doesn't project as more than a middle-relief type. ⊘ A big Aussie, **Phil Stockman** has plus heat and a nice curve, but hampered by hamstring and back problems, he's had trouble getting onto the mound. ⊘ **Sergio Valenzuela** was a Rule 5 pick by the Reds despite posting a 7.00 ERA across two A-ball levels during the regular season. Some things you just can't explain.

MANAGER: BOBBY COX

YEAR	TEAM	W-L	Pythag +/–	Avg PC	100+ P	120+ P	QS	BQS	REL	REL w Zero R	IBB	Subs	PH	PH Avg	PH HR	SB2	CS2	SB3	CS3	SAC Att	SAC %	POS SAC	Squeeze	Swing	In Play
2005	ATL	90-72	-2	93.9	69	1	75	14	483	319	52	54	245	.226	3	81	31	11	1	107	70.1%	29	3	109	84
2006	ATL	79-83	-6	92.6	61	8	70	6	522	342	69	51	299	.277	8	49	34	4	1	105	74.3%	25	6	106	78
2007	ATL	84-78	-5	89.2	43	2	78	6	527	346	89	36	288	.213	3	60	25	4	3	77	71.4%	16	2	110	82

You don't keep your job for 17 years without learning how to adjust. Bobby Cox has had to adjust more than most, especially in his handling of the pitching staff. In 1991, his first full season, his starters accounted for 69 percent of the Braves' innings, averaging about 6⅓ innings per start. By 1997, their number was up to 1096⅔ innings, just shy of 75 percent of the total. Last season, Cox wore out a path to the mound; his starters averaged just 5⅔ innings and accounted for only 63 percent of the Braves' innings. He's had to build and use his bullpen much differently over the last few seasons, not always with prime talent, but has still kept the Braves in contention. He continues to break in young players successfully—Kelly Johnson being the latest—which, looking back, may be Cox's signature talent. Put it all together, and you have a man who has successfully changed with the game, and with his personnel, for nearly two decades. Having Cox is a competitive advantage for the Braves, and it makes them a threat even in a year, including 2008, when their talent will be just third-best in the division.

Baltimore Orioles

30-3. The 2007 Orioles are likely to be remembered by those numbers for a very long time. The last time a team had allowed 30 or more runs in a game was June 29, 1897, when the Louisville Colonels lost to the Chicago Colts by a score of 36-7 (obviously in need of talent, the Colonels bought a kid named Honus Wagner from the minor leagues a couple of weeks later). In the 20th century, the closest any team came was the 1950 St. Louis Browns, who lost to the Red Sox 29-4 on June 8. Four years later, the Browns moved to Baltimore and became the Orioles, and 53 years after that the Orioles earned the dubious distinction of becoming the first team in 110 years to allow 30 runs in a game.

It took only four pitchers to run up that momentous score. The game was the first of an August 22 doubleheader at Camden Yards, and Orioles manager Dave Trembley didn't want to burn his bullpen before the nightcap. In the early going, the game seemed just like any other. The visiting Texas Rangers led 5-3 after five innings. Baltimore starter Daniel Cabrera was continuing to disappoint fans of baseball in general and the Baltimore fans in particular by accomplishing so little with such great talent. Cabrera was relieved by Brian Burres and Rob Bell, two forgettable pitchers who had been pitching well above expectations up until then, but would do so no more. Burres broke the game open in the sixth by inflating the 6-3 deficit he inherited to 14-3, the final run scoring on Bell's watch. Bell set the side down in order in the seventh, but let all seven batters he faced in the eighth reach base and left with his team down 20-3. The final pitcher of the night was Paul Shuey, a former retiree who had no business being on that mound, but was left out there as if part of some misdirected Rope-A-Dope strat-

egy designed to make the Rangers wear themselves out running the bases. It was a microcosm of the entire season, as the Orioles, a team that has specialized in unhappy endings over the past decade, stumbled to one of the worst finishes in history.

The Orioles opened the season with Sam Perlozzo as their manager. On June 18, the team was 29-40 and in last place, and Perlozzo's decision-making skills (particularly the way he managed his bullpen) were being questioned by everyone from the Boog's Barbecue stand to the dugout. That day, Perlozzo became the first major league manager fired in the 2007 season. Dave Trembley, a longtime minor league manager in his first year coaching at the major league level, was named interim manager.

On that very same day, word got out that the Orioles had hired Andy MacPhail, formerly of the Cubs and before that the Twins, as their new president of baseball operations. The move shifted the center of power in the front office away from co–general managers Jim Duquette and Mike Flanagan (Duquette would resign after the season). Speculation was rampant that highly coveted managerial candidate Joe Girardi, who played for the Cubs while MacPhail was the team president, would soon be hired, but within the week, Girardi turned the job down cold.

Meanwhile, the Orioles showed a glimmer of life under new manager Trembley, getting their skipper's major league managerial career off to a 29-25 start. Then that ominous August 22 date rolled around. That morning, MacPhail and company removed the interim tag by naming Trembley manager for the 2008 season. That evening, Trembley's team lost 30-3.

Then they lost the second game of the doubleheader. And the game after that. And six more after that. Even

---

ORIOLES PROSPECTUS

2007 record: 69-93; Fourth place, AL East

Pythagenport record: 70-92

Runs scored per game: 4.67 (9th in AL)

Runs allowed per game: 5.36 (13th in AL)

Team EqA: .256 (10th in AL)

2007 Batters Age: 30.8 (4th oldest in AL)

2007 Pitchers Age: 29.2 (3rd oldest in AL)

Ballpark: Oriole Park at Camden Yards; Slight hitter's park; Park Factor of 1.010

2007: It's a bad year when a 30-3 loss is representative of your season.

2008: Baltimore's rebuilding finally begins under Andy MacPhail, but the foundation's weak.

putting aside that historic game in Baltimore, these weren't your average, run-of-the-mill 4-2 losses. The Orioles lost by scores such as 11-3, 15-8, and 17-2. On September 1, they lost 10-0 to the Red Sox and were no-hit by a kid making his second major league start. When the beatings finally stopped at season's end, the Orioles had gone 10-29 dating back to August 22. The timing of the collapse generated the popular assumption that the players had quit on Trembley once he was named the 2008 manager, but there were other forces at work.

The biggest problem, which had nothing to do with Trembley, was the disintegration of the pitching staff. Pitching injuries hit the Orioles early and often in 2007. Kris Benson's season ended with a torn rotator cuff in February. Off-season pickup Jaret Wright made just two starts before landing on the disabled list with more of the shoulder problems that have plagued his career. He made just one more aborted start in late April before returning to the DL for good. Twenty-three-year-old lefty Adam Loewen broke his arm in his sixth start and was done for the year.

Despite losing three-fifths of their intended rotation by May 1, the Orioles managed to piece things together, signing free agent Steve Trachsel in the wake of Benson's injury and replacing Wright in the rotation with off-season waiver claim Jeremy Guthrie, who emerged as a dominant number-two starter behind staff ace Erik Bedard. It was a trick they could do only once. When another rash of injuries hit later in the season, the Orioles simply ran out of options. In his first start after August 22, Bedard strained an oblique and was done for the season. A month before the disastrous double-header, closer Chris Ray hit the disabled list. He ultimately underwent Tommy John surgery, which not only ended his 2007 season, but wiped out 2008 as well. In mid-September, set-up man Danys Baez did the same. Even Guthrie missed three starts in September with an oblique injury of his own. The Orioles used just eight starters in their first 123 games, but needed 11 to get through their last 39. As a whole, the pitching staff, which had allowed 4.55 runs per game through August 21, yielded 7.90 runs per game thereafter.

The changeover on the staff is illustrated in Table 1, which compares the performances of the pitchers who threw 90 percent of their innings for the Orioles before August 22 with those who pitched primarily afterwards (using a 60 percent minimum). The two groups represent a similar proportion of the team's total innings relative to the time span in question, with the ante-diluvian pitchers prorating to 669 innings per 162 games, and the followers prorating to 701. As the entire Orioles staff threw 1438⅔ innings on the year, what the

Table 1. Après Erik Bedard, Le Déluge

Pitched mostly before August 22				Pitched mostly after August 22			
	IP	R	RA		IP	R	RA
Erik Bedard	182	66	3.26	Kurt Birkins	34.1	31	8.13
Steve Trachsel	140.2	73	4.67	Jon Leicester	32	27	7.59
Chris Ray	42.2	22	4.64	Jim Hoey	24.2	21	7.66
John Parrish	41.2	26	5.62	Radhames Liz	24.2	21	7.66
Adam Loewen	30.1	14	4.16	Rocky Cherry	16.1	14	7.73
Paul Shuey	25.2	28	9.82	Victor Santos	14.1	13	8.18
Todd Williams	14.1	12	7.55	Victor Zambrano	12.1	13	9.51
Scott Williamson	14.1	8	5.02	Fernando Cabrera	10	14	12.60
Jaret Wright	10.1	11	9.58				
Cory Doyne	3.2	6	14.71				
Jim Johnson	2	2	9.00				
TOTAL	**507.2**	**268**	**4.75**	Total	168.2	154	8.22

table is really showing us is that, after August 22, nearly half of the team's innings were thrown by pitchers three and a half runs worse than their predecessors. Not even a combination of Dale Carnegie, Tony Robbins, Zig Ziglar, and Randolph Dupree could motivate a team out of that kind of hole.

No offense could have outhit that sort of collapse by the pitching staff; thus the Orioles' hitters, who actually scored runs at a slightly better pace during the collapse (4.74 R/G) than they had up until then (4.64), are absolved. Still, theirs was a distinctly mediocre performance. Despite the aggressive baserunning of Brian Roberts and Corey Patterson, which helped the team lead the AL in stolen bases, and the continued emergence of Nick Markakis, the Orioles simply had too many nondescript players at key offensive positions.

So what does one do with such a lousy team? The Orioles have always been reluctant to start over again, but it seems they now have little choice. Owner Peter Angelos was always the primary obstacle to rebuilding, but it seems possible that MacPhail—a strong, established baseball executive whom Angelos came to trust while the two were working together on baseball's labor committee—has become the first Oriole executive in a decade to get true operating autonomy. What that means is that he is cleared to make moves on his own authority; he doesn't have to go back to Angelos for final approval. When MacPhail says yes, the deal is done.

MacPhail has the added advantage of being a new arrival to the team. He doesn't have to worry about past perceptions created by the team's misguided contracts (Jay Gibbons, Aubrey Huff), or by the players that they let get away (Jack Cust, Eric Byrnes). He can easily identify, admit, and go about rectifying past mistakes because they weren't his. Similarly, he can operate without the ego-driven attachment to players he signed himself, a phenomenon that frequently develops in front offices in the major leagues.

To accomplish his mission of rebuilding the Orioles, a team that has now endured ten consecutive losing seasons, MacPhail's going to have to take a step backward first. Using the Tigers' dramatic turnaround as a model, a serious rebuilding is going to take a minimum of three years, which puts off any real hope of winning until 2010 at the earliest. Taking stock of the Orioles' offense, they have one player, Markakis, who is both young enough and good enough to be a keeper. Everyone else should be considered expendable in favor of players who will be valuable in three years.

That brings us to a peculiar aspect of the Orioles' salary structure: it seems that just about every contract they've handed out in the past few years is due to expire after the 2009 season. Among signed, veteran players, the Orioles have $56 million of obligations in 2008 and $53 million of that (all but Kevin Millar and Jay Payton) carries over to 2009. In 2010, however, those commitments come down to practically nothing, just some buyouts on options that would add up to less than $2 million. Therein lies some serious opportunity. Just as they did with Miguel Tejada, who is signed through 2009 and was shipped to the Astros in a six-player deal in December, the Orioles need to trade their veterans while their value is still enhanced by their being under contract for another season.

The trouble is that most of the players who would otherwise be desired by other teams are overpriced, which means MacPhail is going to have to ship a lot of cash around the league to cover the difference between those players' salaries and their actual value. Still, replacing those vets with younger, cheaper, hungrier players is going to save the team a nice chunk of change over the next couple of years, and the O's should be able to dive deep into the free-agent pool when all those responsibilities come off the books after 2009.

The pitching is a different story. The veteran starters—Benson, Wright, Trachsel—have already been dispersed, leaving Bedard as the old man at 28. Bedard is also due to be a part of that free-agent class of 2009, and negotiations to sign him beyond that have been unsuccessful so far. He's certainly good enough to want to keep, but as he'll be an over-30 pitcher with a checkered injury history by the time he becomes a free agent, it may not be a good idea to treat him as an untouchable cornerstone of the next winning Orioles team. Bedard is highly coveted by teams across the majors, and, if someone offers enough in a trade, MacPhail should probably shake hands. Beyond Bedard, the Orioles have a slew of younger pitchers who have either established a major league presence, such as Guthrie and Loewen, or are getting their first taste of The Show, such as Radhames Liz and Garrett Olson. As for the bullpen, it almost has to be better in 2008, even if they take the approach of their regional rivals the Nationals by inviting everyone under the sun and then keeping the hottest hands.

Of course, whether MacPhail and company can pull all of that off depends on the whims of the trade market. Teams will try to lowball him because they know he wants to unload, and we don't yet know how disciplined he will be when it comes to holding out for full value. There are risks on either side. Taking a bad offer leaves you with players who won't contribute to the club's future, and holding out leaves you stuck with your current hand. Either way, the Orioles are as likely as 5¼-inch floppy disks to make a comeback in 2008. Success in Baltimore won't be measured by how many games the team wins this season, but by what kind of foundation it can build for the future.

HITTERS

Paul Bako   C   Bats: L   Throws: R   Height: 6' 2"   Weight: 205   Born: June 20, 1972   Age: 36

YEAR	TEAM	LVL	AGE	PA	R	2B	3B	HR	RBI	BB	SO	SB	CS	EqBRR	AVG	OBP	SLG	MLVr	EqAVG	EqOBP	EqSLG	EqA	VORP	DEFENSE
2005	LAN	MLB	33	47	1	2	0	0	4	7	12	0	0	-0.6	.250	.362	.300	-.095	.250	.362	.300	.245	0.6	12-C 0
2006	KCA	MLB	34	167	7	3	0	0	10	11	46	0	0	-1.6	.209	.261	.229	-.488	.205	.267	.225	.170	-13.3	45-C 0
2007	BAL	MLB	35	174	13	3	1	1	8	15	50	0	1	-0.8	.205	.277	.256	-.375	.213	.293	.265	.198	-8.7	47-C -2
2008	BAL	MLB	36	120	8	3	0	1	9	10	32	0	0	-0.5	.217	.287	.279	-.312	.215	.288	.288	.205	-3.9	33-C -1

Breakout: 45% Improve: 53% Collapse: 41% Attrition: 61%   Comparables: Larry Haney, Brent Mayne, Joe Ginsberg, Chad Kreuter

Bako was the primary backup to Ramon Hernandez last year. He and the Orioles' other reserve backstops—Alberto Castillo, Gus Molina, and J.R. House—combined to hit .201/.267/.308 in 2007, turning the catcher spot into the

Springfield Mystery Spot whenever Hernandez was unavailable, which turned out to be more than a third of the season altogether. The Orioles have bought into the idea that their backup catcher must be a strong defender and guide the young pitchers. The results have been *so spectacular*, haven't they?

Freddie Bynum   **UT**   Bats: L   Throws: R   Height: 6' 1"   Weight: 190   Born: March 15, 1980   Age: 28

YEAR	TEAM	LVL	AGE	PA	R	2B	3B	HR	RBI	BB	SO	SB	CS	EqBRR	AVG	OBP	SLG	MLVr	EqAVG	EqOBP	EqSLG	EqA	VORP	DEFENSE			
2005	SAC	AAA	25	428	56	16	9	2	40	38	83	23	7	3.7	.278	.347	.384	-.041	.243	.304	.328	.229	-10.5	51-CF	1	21-SS	-6
2006	CHN	MLB	26	148	20	5	5	4	12	9	44	8	4	-0.6	.257	.308	.456	-.017	.255	.311	.460	.259	3.3	13-2B	-2		
2007	BAL	MLB	27	101	21	8	2	2	11	2	30	8	1	0.4	.260	.290	.448	-.055	.271	.307	.490	.275	3.2	11-LF	3		
2008	BAL	MLB	28	131	14	6	1	2	12	8	32	5	1	0.7	.241	.293	.364	-.177	.239	.294	.375	.241	-0.5				

Breakout: 24% Improve: 39% Collapse: 40% Attrition: 47%   Comparables: Reggie Taylor, Gil Coan, Herm Winningham, Jeff Stone

A useful player to have, Bynum is fast, with surprising power (more than we'd thought he'd have, based on his minor league career), and the positional flexibility you can find only on unmentionable websites. If he would take a walk more than twice a month, he'd be pushing into Chone Figgins territory, but he's much more likely to stay in the pinch-runner/defensive replacement slot he occupied last year.

Jay Gibbons   **LF**   Bats: L   Throws: L   Height: 6' 0"   Weight: 195   Born: March 2, 1977   Age: 31

YEAR	TEAM	LVL	AGE	PA	R	2B	3B	HR	RBI	BB	SO	SB	CS	EqBRR	AVG	OBP	SLG	MLVr	EqAVG	EqOBP	EqSLG	EqA	VORP	DEFENSE			
2005	BAL	MLB	28	518	72	33	3	26	79	28	56	0	0	-1.2	.277	.317	.516	.119	.283	.334	.542	.289	24.4	63-RF	6	19-1B	-3
2006	BAL	MLB	29	378	34	23	0	13	46	32	48	0	0	-0.1	.277	.341	.458	.042	.277	.349	.472	.280	11.8	40-RF	4		
2007	BAL	MLB	30	290	28	14	0	6	28	15	52	0	0	-2.1	.230	.272	.348	-.246	.231	.279	.369	.225	-11.8	37-LF	2		
2008	BAL	MLB	31	289	31	15	1	9	40	21	44	1	1	-0.6	.263	.320	.426	-.034	.261	.321	.439	.264	3.6	70-DH			

Breakout: 27% Improve: 49% Collapse: 24% Attrition: 33%   Comparables: Wes Covington, Robert Fick, Jim Spencer, Fred Whitfield

If we followed the old adage "If you can't say anything nice, don't say anything at all," this entry would be blank. Gibbons is an average hitter at best. He's limited defensively. He can't stay healthy (adding a torn labrum to his chronic back injuries last year). He has an albatross contract that will pay him around $6 million both this year and in 2009, and a September news report identified him as the recipient of a variety of performance-enhancing drugs from an Orlando-based pharmacy that's under federal investigation.

Luis Hernandez   **SS**   Bats: S   Throws: R   Height: 5' 10"   Weight: 180   Born: June 26, 1984   Age: 24

YEAR	TEAM	LVL	AGE	PA	R	2B	3B	HR	RBI	BB	SO	SB	CS	EqBRR	AVG	OBP	SLG	MLVr	EqAVG	EqOBP	EqSLG	EqA	VORP	DEFENSE			
2005	MIS	AA	21	469	47	12	5	2	32	41	56	5	5	-0.4	.243	.315	.311	-.137	.216	.277	.286	.197	-23.3	113-SS	-5		
2006	MIS	AA	22	413	39	12	4	1	29	20	46	4	4	-1.0	.268	.308	.329	-.032	.251	.285	.320	.211	-10.0	65-SS	2	33-2B	-2
2006	RIC	AAA	22	74	3	4	0	1	5	0	8	0	1	-0.8	.192	.192	.288	-.384	.233	.243	.329	.187	-3.4	19-SS	4		
2007	BOW	AA	23	393	42	15	6	0	37	18	50	6	5	0.2	.242	.276	.316	-.202	.217	.249	.293	.185	-23.5	89-SS	12		
2007	BAL	MLB	23	71	5	2	0	1	7	1	10	2	2	-0.6	.290	.300	.362	-.133	.304	.314	.377	.231	-0.3	16-SS	1		
2008	BAL	MLB	24	521	45	20	3	2	38	23	73	8	5	1.0	.238	.275	.306	-.288	.236	.276	.316	.209	-14.2	123-SS	1		

Breakout: 45% Improve: 68% Collapse: 15% Attrition: 10%   Comparables: Alex Cintron, Juan Lorenzo, Javier Guzman, Luis Lopez

The Orioles claimed Hernandez off of waivers when the Braves dropped him from their 40-man roster following the 2006 season. He's as light-hitting an infielder as you'll find, with three years of Double-A ball under his belt and no apparent improvement. Tejada's injury gave him a chance to play in the majors last year, and he hit .290, but it was almost all singles and was accompanied by a single solitary walk. Typically, the O's are more impressed by the number than concerned about its emptiness. Hernandez *is* a much better fielder than Tejada, but he's no major league starter.

Ramon Hernandez   C   Bats: R   Throws: R   Height: 6' 0"   Weight: 235   Born: May 20, 1976   Age: 32

YEAR	TEAM	LVL	AGE	PA	R	2B	3B	HR	RBI	BB	SO	SB	CS	EqBRR	AVG	OBP	SLG	MLVr	EqAVG	EqOBP	EqSLG	EqA	VORP	DEFENSE	
2005	SDN	MLB	29	392	36	19	2	12	58	18	40	1	0	-3.0	.290	.322	.450	.076	.300	.334	.474	.276	20.7	90-C	-2
2006	BAL	MLB	30	560	66	29	2	23	91	43	79	1	0	-0.9	.275	.343	.479	.074	.276	.350	.490	.286	28.8	125-C	3
2007	BAL	MLB	31	409	40	18	0	9	62	36	59	1	3	-2.9	.258	.333	.382	-.070	.266	.345	.410	.261	8.4	96-C	-6
2008	BAL	MLB	32	378	40	18	1	9	44	30	55	3	2	-0.9	.262	.327	.399	-.060	.260	.327	.411	.261	8.0	91-C	-3

Breakout: 12% Improve: 30% Collapse: 33% Attrition: 27%   Comparables: Javy Lopez, Don Leppert, Lance Parrish, Terry Steinbach

Last year we mentioned that reaching a career high in at-bats, as Hernandez did in 2006, was a bad thing for a 30-year-old catcher. Hernandez backed us up in 2007 by making two trips to the DL and suffering a drop-off in virtually every facet of his game. All that may have been the fault of the strained oblique he suffered in the spring, but his 2006 workload surely didn't help matters. Hernandez was the subject of trade talks during the season, and, despite not having any major league–ready in-house alternatives, the O's would be smart to parlay any Hernandez hot streak into a deal.

J.R. House   C   Bats: R   Throws: R   Height: 5' 10"   Weight: 210   Born: November 11, 1979   Age: 28

YEAR	TEAM	LVL	AGE	PA	R	2B	3B	HR	RBI	BB	SO	SB	CS	EqBRR	AVG	OBP	SLG	MLVr	EqAVG	EqOBP	EqSLG	EqA	VORP	DEFENSE			
2006	CCH	AA	26	423	58	23	2	10	69	32	44	2	2	-2.2	.325	.376	.475	.214	.284	.329	.416	.259	15.2	65-C	-9	29-1B	-1
2006	ROU	AAA	26	128	25	15	0	5	36	9	15	0	0	-1.5	.412	.445	.675	.775	.365	.398	.609	.333	17.7	24-1B	-1		
2007	NOR	AAA	27	471	52	32	2	11	66	43	59	1	5	-6.2	.298	.365	.463	.254	.284	.348	.469	.276	31.2	50-C	-6	25-1B	0
2007	BAL	MLB	27	41	5	2	0	3	3	1	11	0	0	-0.1	.211	.268	.500	-.066	.211	.268	.500	.253	0.7				
2008	BAL	MLB	28	489	55	29	2	14	68	35	73	3	2	-0.9	.273	.330	.442	.010	.271	.331	.455	.272	14.0	115-C	-5		

Breakout: 17% Improve: 50% Collapse: 17% Attrition: 14%   Comparables: Carlos Ruiz, Ron Jackson, Earl Battey, Terry Steinbach

House was the only backup catcher the Orioles had last year who had any chance of contributing at the plate, but they were so afraid of his glove work behind it that they let him spend most of the year being Norfolk's best hitter. Yes, he catches like a first baseman, but in a good year, he'll also hit like one. Some teams need to learn that both sides matter; House's bat can make up for his fielding, at least when the competition is Paul Bako.

Aubrey Huff   DH   Bats: L   Throws: R   Height: 6' 4"   Weight: 235   Born: December 20, 1976   Age: 31

YEAR	TEAM	LVL	AGE	PA	R	2B	3B	HR	RBI	BB	SO	SB	CS	EqBRR	AVG	OBP	SLG	MLVr	EqAVG	EqOBP	EqSLG	EqA	VORP	DEFENSE			
2005	TBA	MLB	28	636	70	26	2	22	92	49	88	8	7	-2.1	.261	.321	.428	-.008	.269	.336	.452	.269	8.5	90-RF	-5	18-1B	-2
2006	TBA	MLB	29	256	26	15	1	8	28	24	25	0	0	1.2	.283	.348	.461	.062	.282	.355	.471	.283	9.4	55-3B	1		
2006	HOU	MLB	29	261	31	10	1	13	38	26	39	0	0	-0.1	.250	.341	.478	.066	.250	.338	.487	.281	7.5	29-RF	-5	24-3B	-2
2007	BAL	MLB	30	603	68	34	5	15	72	48	87	1	1	1.4	.280	.337	.442	.039	.283	.345	.464	.277	15.8	47-1B	-3	14-3B	-2
2008	BAL	MLB	31	523	61	26	2	14	68	43	76	4	2	-0.3	.269	.332	.422	-.015	.267	.333	.435	.269	8.6	123-DH			

Breakout: 4% Improve: 37% Collapse: 28% Attrition: 16%   Comparables: Travis Lee, Chris Chambliss, Paul O'Neill, Gordy Coleman

In the end, Huff's 2007 stats were right where they were expected to be, but only because he got hot down the stretch—something he's made a habit of doing, averaging a .247 EqA in the first halves of the past four seasons and .295 in the second halves. Huff reportedly promised the front office that he'd work harder in the offseason to prevent another slow start, but in an off-color radio appearance in November, in which he slammed the city of Baltimore, he seemed more concerned about his off-field scoring than his on-field performance. The ten-cent-head label applies, but the most problematic statistic may prove to be the $16 million he'll earn over the next two seasons.

Jon Knott   LF   Bats: R   Throws: R   Height: 6' 3"   Weight: 240   Born: August 4, 1978   Age: 29

YEAR	TEAM	LVL	AGE	PA	R	2B	3B	HR	RBI	BB	SO	SB	CS	EqBRR	AVG	OBP	SLG	MLVr	EqAVG	EqOBP	EqSLG	EqA	VORP	DEFENSE			
2005	POR	AAA	26	577	81	34	4	25	78	55	112	1	0	-1.0	.250	.333	.483	.041	.218	.291	.411	.242	-17.9	66-LF	1	38-1B	0
2006	POR	AAA	27	544	80	32	6	32	113	52	103	3	3	-2.6	.280	.353	.572	.279	.253	.322	.521	.279	20.9	69-1B	3	31-RF	-3
2007	NOR	AAA	28	340	42	15	2	13	34	48	80	4	2	-0.5	.250	.356	.451	.179	.244	.346	.460	.277	6.7	62-LF	1	12-1B	0
2007	BAL	MLB	28	19	3	0	0	1	4	4	3	0	0	-0.1	.214	.368	.429	.029	.214	.368	.429	.288	0.5				
2008	BAL	MLB	29	343	37	15	1	13	48	31	83	3	1	-0.5	.237	.311	.422	-.074	.235	.312	.434	.260	-0.6	83-LF	-1		

Breakout: 11% Improve: 34% Collapse: 33% Attrition: 24%   Comparables: Bucky Jacobsen, Ernie Young, Tim Laker, Rich Rowland

Look at what Jon Knott, Jay Gibbons, and Aubrey Huff have done over the past three years and try to discern any significant differences among them. In terms of total production, the difference is slight: the others don't strike out as much and have prettier batting averages, but Knott draws more walks and hits more homers. Gibbons and Huff have guaranteed multimillion-dollar contracts; Knott earns a Triple-A salary. We're not saying he's as good as they are; we're saying the difference isn't worth the money.

Nick Markakis RF

Bats: L   Throws: L   Height: 6' 2"   Weight: 215   Born: November 17, 1983   Age: 24

YEAR	TEAM	LVL	AGE	PA	R	2B	3B	HR	RBI	BB	SO	SB	CS	EqBRR	AVG	OBP	SLG	MLVr	EqAVG	EqOBP	EqSLG	EqA	VORP	DEFENSE			
2005	FRD	A+	21	401	59	25	1	12	62	43	65	2	1	-0.7	.300	.379	.480	.190	.246	.309	.376	.240	-11.1	86-RF	-1		
2005	BOW	AA	21	143	19	16	2	3	30	18	30	0	1	-1.0	.339	.420	.573	.478	.262	.347	.476	.278	8.1	19-CF	2	15-RF	-1
2006	BAL	MLB	22	542	72	25	2	16	62	43	72	2	0	2.1	.291	.351	.448	.059	.291	.358	.458	.281	19.4	105-RF	12	23-LF	3
2007	BAL	MLB	23	710	97	43	3	23	112	61	112	18	6	0.4	.300	.362	.485	.162	.304	.371	.515	.299	38.4	158-RF	10		
2008	BAL	MLB	24	641	86	37	2	18	86	58	105	10	4	0.3	.287	.354	.455	.079	.285	.355	.469	.287	18.2	150-RF	9		

Breakout: 24% Improve: 49% Collapse: 16% Attrition: 12%   Comparables: Bruce Bochte, Carlos May, Willie Montañez, Mel Hall

As a rookie, Markakis had a .213 EqA in the first half of 2006, but has posted a .303 mark ever since despite a relatively slow start in 2007 as well (.272 EqA). Just 24, he's already hitting for average and increasing power and he doesn't seem overly troubled by lefty pitching. Last year he also showed off some stolen-base skills we'd never seen before and established himself as one of the best defensive right fielders in the league. Markakis has consistently matched and even exceeded our more optimistic forecasts for him. He's the stud to build the next good Oriole team around.

Kevin Millar 1B

Bats: R   Throws: R   Height: 6' 0"   Weight: 215   Born: September 24, 1971   Age: 36

YEAR	TEAM	LVL	AGE	PA	R	2B	3B	HR	RBI	BB	SO	SB	CS	EqBRR	AVG	OBP	SLG	MLVr	EqAVG	EqOBP	EqSLG	EqA	VORP	DEFENSE			
2005	BOS	MLB	33	519	57	28	1	9	50	54	74	0	1	-3.7	.272	.355	.399	.002	.274	.365	.410	.275	7.0	90-1B	11	14-LF	-3
2006	BAL	MLB	34	503	64	26	0	15	64	59	74	1	1	-2.8	.272	.374	.437	.068	.273	.382	.447	.289	15.5	91-1B	4		
2007	BAL	MLB	35	562	63	26	1	17	63	76	94	1	1	-2.8	.254	.365	.420	.037	.259	.375	.442	.285	14.4	98-1B	-2		
2008	BAL	MLB	36	403	46	18	1	13	53	51	68	2	1	-1.4	.249	.351	.417	-.004	.247	.352	.430	.278	6.6	96-1B	-2		

Breakout: 15% Improve: 35% Collapse: 37% Attrition: 32%   Comparables: Andre Thornton, Mike Stanley, Jeff Bagwell, J. T. Snow

In each of the past two years, the Orioles entered the season with a crowded first-base/DH/outfield-corner situation, and each time it was Millar who stayed healthy and out-hit his competition to claim the first-base job by the All-Star break. It's the walks that make him valuable, allowing him to set an Orioles record by reaching base in 52 straight games. Walk increases by older players are frequently a sign of declining skills, and we do see some declines in fielding and in BABIP. Still, he should be back fighting Huff and Gibbons for playing time again this year.

Scott Moore 3B

Bats: L   Throws: R   Height: 6' 2"   Weight: 195   Born: November 17, 1983   Age: 24

YEAR	TEAM	LVL	AGE	PA	R	2B	3B	HR	RBI	BB	SO	SB	CS	EqBRR	AVG	OBP	SLG	MLVr	EqAVG	EqOBP	EqSLG	EqA	VORP	DEFENSE			
2005	DAY	A+	21	536	77	31	2	20	82	55	134	22	7	2.6	.281	.358	.485	.174	.230	.300	.395	.243	2.1	116-3B	-20		
2006	WTN	AA	22	532	52	28	0	22	75	55	126	12	7	-0.4	.276	.360	.479	.218	.265	.340	.480	.278	34.5	121-3B	-7		
2006	CHN	MLB	22	42	6	2	0	2	5	2	10	0	0	-0.1	.263	.317	.474	.015	.256	.310	.462	.260	0.7				
2007	IOW	AAA	23	382	61	19	4	19	69	48	100	4	3	3.1	.265	.373	.526	.166	.239	.343	.472	.277	20.1	73-3B	-5	16-LF	-1
2007	BAL	MLB	23	50	2	2	0	1	11	1	15	0	1	-1.0	.255	.260	.362	-.239	.255	.260	.362	.212	-2.3				
2008	BAL	MLB	24	423	52	20	2	16	57	40	109	6	3	0.6	.248	.326	.441	-.017	.246	.327	.454	.272	8.7	101-3B	-4		

Breakout: 31% Improve: 55% Collapse: 20% Attrition: 21%   Comparables: Willie Greene, Carlos Peña, Michael Cuddyer, Larry Walker

Moore came from the Cubs in the Steve Trachsel trade and got some face time at Camden Yards filling in for a dinged-up Melvin Mora at third base in September. He is what he is: a strikeout-prone, power-hitting lefty who should provide a respectable bat from either infield corner. He's not going to beat out any of the players ahead of him, but some combination of injuries and trades could open up a spot.

Melvin Mora   3B

Bats: R   Throws: R   Height: 5' 11"   Weight: 200   Born: February 2, 1972   Age: 36

YEAR	TEAM	LVL	AGE	PA	R	2B	3B	HR	RBI	BB	SO	SB	CS	EqBRR	AVG	OBP	SLG	MLVr	EqAVG	EqOBP	EqSLG	EqA	VORP	DEFENSE	
2005	BAL	MLB	33	664	86	30	1	27	88	50	112	7	4	-4.9	.283	.348	.474	.119	.293	.366	.498	.292	33.5	146-3B	-4
2006	BAL	MLB	34	705	96	25	0	16	83	54	99	11	1	1.6	.274	.342	.391	-.053	.276	.350	.404	.268	8.9	151-3B	-20
2007	BAL	MLB	35	527	67	23	1	14	58	47	83	9	3	-1.0	.274	.341	.418	.009	.279	.351	.443	.275	13.4	118-3B	3
2008	BAL	MLB	36	398	46	17	1	10	48	34	63	6	2	-0.4	.259	.328	.401	-.058	.257	.328	.413	.263	5.9	95-3B	-4

Breakout: 8%   Improve: 27%   Collapse: 39%   Attrition: 35%   Comparables: Joe Randa, Ken Boyer, Brooks Robinson, Bill Madlock

Mora missed about a month of the season following a feet-first slide into Angels catcher Mike Napoli in early July. The original diagnosis was that Mora had a mild sprain and wouldn't need to go on the DL; he sat out a week, played *one inning*, and left the game with a torn tendon in the same foot that had been bothering him all week. Like the rest of the team, he's signed through 2009, and his production and durability have declined since he signed his extension in May 2006. While Mora prefers to stay at third, he has a history of playing elsewhere if the Orioles want to take advantage of his flexibility to work other bats into the lineup.

Corey Patterson   CF

Bats: L   Throws: R   Height: 5' 9"   Weight: 175   Born: August 13, 1979   Age: 28

YEAR	TEAM	LVL	AGE	PA	R	2B	3B	HR	RBI	BB	SO	SB	CS	EqBRR	AVG	OBP	SLG	MLVr	EqAVG	EqOBP	EqSLG	EqA	VORP	DEFENSE	
2005	CHN	MLB	25	481	47	15	3	13	34	23	118	15	5	0.4	.215	.254	.348	-.256	.211	.253	.348	.210	-16.8	111-CF	-1
2006	BAL	MLB	26	498	75	19	5	16	53	21	94	45	9	5.5	.276	.314	.443	-.027	.277	.322	.456	.273	23.3	123-CF	6
2007	BAL	MLB	27	503	65	26	2	8	45	21	65	37	9	1.5	.269	.304	.386	-.105	.277	.316	.413	.259	8.4	119-CF	-6
2008	BAL	MLB	28	458	57	21	3	10	46	22	75	29	8	1.4	.268	.307	.402	-.084	.265	.308	.414	.260	5.4	109-CF	0

Breakout: 27%   Improve: 54%   Collapse: 20%   Attrition: 21%   Comparables: Gil Coan, Bobby Tolan, Ray Coleman, Catfish Metkovich

Patterson started out cold and got worse, bottoming out at .205/.258/.285 on June 17. He salvaged his season with a hot July, but cooled off from there before an ankle strain ended his season in early September. Surprisingly, his struggles had nothing to do with his usual nemesis, the Southpawed Hurler, as he cut his strikeout rate against them by two-thirds and hit a respectable .310/.344/.451 against them on the season. He just stopped hitting with any authority, posting a full-season worst of .117 isolated power. Though Patterson was a free agent at press time, there are plenty of teams willing to sign him for his speed, which is about all he offers anyway.

Jay Payton   OF

Bats: R   Throws: R   Height: 5' 10"   Weight: 205   Born: November 22, 1972   Age: 35

YEAR	TEAM	LVL	AGE	PA	R	2B	3B	HR	RBI	BB	SO	SB	CS	EqBRR	AVG	OBP	SLG	MLVr	EqAVG	EqOBP	EqSLG	EqA	VORP	DEFENSE				
2005	BOS	MLB	32	144	24	7	0	5	21	10	14	0	0	0.5	.263	.313	.429	-.036	.260	.319	.435	.259	1.6	21-RF	4			
2005	OAK	MLB	32	291	38	9	1	13	42	14	33	0	1	-0.8	.269	.302	.451	-.010	.273	.316	.465	.264	4.4	46-LF	5	24-CF	-1
2006	OAK	MLB	33	588	78	32	3	10	59	22	52	8	4	0.5	.296	.325	.418	-.027	.301	.337	.434	.265	10.7	51-LF	7	43-CF	-6
2007	BAL	MLB	34	470	48	21	5	7	58	22	42	5	2	-1.1	.256	.292	.376	-.152	.262	.303	.397	.244	-8.1	102-LF	12	12-CF	2
2008	BAL	MLB	35	353	38	17	2	6	41	18	35	4	2	0.0	.270	.309	.388	-.099	.267	.309	.400	.249	-1.8	85-LF	1		

Breakout: 9%   Improve: 40%   Collapse: 34%   Attrition: 35%   Comparables: Andy Pafko, Dan Gladden, Brian Jordan, Darrin Jackson

Payton didn't hit as well as the Orioles thought he would when they signed him for two years of starter money. Kevin Millar notwithstanding, most players experience significant declines in their mid-30s, and Payton wasn't an All-Star to begin with. He's a good fourth outfielder, as he can handle center and is a plus defender in left, but what you see is what you get from him at the plate. The only thing that changed in Payton's production in 2007 was that his BABIP snapped back to his normal level (.268), from a fluke high of .312 in 2006.

Tike Redman — CF

Bats: L Throws: L Height: 5' 11" Weight: 175 Born: March 10, 1977 Age: 31

YEAR	TEAM	LVL	AGE	PA	R	2B	3B	HR	RBI	BB	SO	SB	CS	EqBRR	AVG	OBP	SLG	MLVr	EqAVG	EqOBP	EqSLG	EqA	VORP	DEFENSE	
2005	PIT	MLB	28	344	33	12	4	2	26	19	27	4	1	1.9	.251	.292	.332	-.184	.252	.297	.333	.224	-6.4	59-CF	3
2006	CCH	AA	29	121	17	3	0	1	6	16	6	4	2	2.0	.311	.408	.369	.105	.274	.364	.321	.251	-1.7	15-RF	3
2006	TOL	AAA	29	315	30	15	2	1	13	13	35	12	4	-0.1	.253	.287	.327	-.108	.237	.273	.313	.207	-15.8	49-CF	-2
2007	NOR	AAA	30	336	53	15	6	2	27	32	24	25	8	1.2	.304	.372	.416	.203	.284	.350	.415	.271	13.1	70-CF	-11
2007	BAL	MLB	30	139	23	9	2	2	16	5	18	7	1	2.3	.318	.341	.462	.107	.328	.355	.496	.293	8.8	26-CF	2
2008	BAL	MLB	31	436	53	21	4	4	35	27	44	16	6	1.5	.268	.316	.367	-.117	.266	.317	.378	.250	0.1	103-CF	0

Breakout: 19% Improve: 48% Collapse: 26% Attrition: 29%   Comparables: Bobby Darula, Scott Podsednik, Lance Johnson, Darryl Hamilton

Tike Redman was hungry in 2007. After being forced to start the year in independent ball, he was picked up by the Orioles after hitting .464 in just seven games. Assigned to Triple-A Norfolk, he had his best minor league season, earning him a call-up when Gibbons went down for the year in August. After hitting .324/.359/.432 off the bench, he was then installed as the regular center fielder after Patterson sprained his ankle and hit .308/.330/.462 in September. He did all of that with an unsustainable hit rate on balls in play, and he's still all singles and steals with a large platoon split, but it made for a nice story on a team desperately in need of a little hunger.

Nolan Reimold — OF

Bats: R Throws: R Height: 6' 4" Weight: 207 Born: October 12, 1983 Age: 24

YEAR	TEAM	LVL	AGE	PA	R	2B	3B	HR	RBI	BB	SO	SB	CS	EqBRR	AVG	OBP	SLG	MLVr	EqAVG	EqOBP	EqSLG	EqA	VORP	DEFENSE			
2005	ABE	A-	21	212	33	15	2	9	30	29	44	2	0	-3.2	.294	.392	.550	.384	.221	.292	.395	.237	-13.5	29-RF	0	15-CF	-2
2005	FRD	A+	21	97	17	6	0	6	11	12	27	3	0	0.5	.265	.371	.554	.243	.218	.299	.414	.248	-0.1	13-CF	-2		
2006	FRD	A+	22	504	73	26	0	19	75	76	107	14	8	-0.9	.255	.379	.455	.150	.219	.320	.387	.248	-11.5	94-RF	-13	19-CF	0
2007	BOW	AA	23	203	30	15	0	11	34	17	47	2	3	-1.8	.306	.365	.565	.339	.266	.320	.495	.269	6.0	45-RF	0		
2008	BAL	MLB	24	271	30	13	1	10	35	24	74	3	2	0.0	.234	.308	.414	-.092	.233	.309	.426	.256	-1.9	66-RF	0		

Breakout: 22% Improve: 54% Collapse: 22% Attrition: 14%   Comparables: Danny Peoples, Ryan Ludwick, Tydus Meadows, Paul Carey

Reimold missed more than half the year with oblique injuries, but otherwise had his best season yet. He has excellent power, especially against lefties, but needs to learn to handle breaking pitches better. If he can, he'll improve both his strikeout rate and his platoon splits. Odds are the strikeouts will stay high, which will limit him to being a fairly average major league outfielder, but that wouldn't prevent him from supplanting Jay Payton sometime this year.

Brian Roberts — 2B

Bats: S Throws: R Height: 5' 9" Weight: 180 Born: October 9, 1977 Age: 30

YEAR	TEAM	LVL	AGE	PA	R	2B	3B	HR	RBI	BB	SO	SB	CS	EqBRR	AVG	OBP	SLG	MLVr	EqAVG	EqOBP	EqSLG	EqA	VORP	DEFENSE	
2005	BAL	MLB	27	640	92	45	7	18	73	67	83	27	10	-1.1	.314	.387	.515	.268	.323	.405	.544	.317	62.0	137-2B	13
2006	BAL	MLB	28	629	85	34	3	10	55	55	66	36	7	4.1	.286	.347	.410	-.008	.288	.356	.423	.278	31.3	133-2B	-4
2007	BAL	MLB	29	716	103	42	5	12	57	89	99	50	7	8.4	.290	.377	.432	.102	.295	.388	.456	.300	48.6	150-2B	2
2008	BAL	MLB	30	651	101	37	5	14	69	72	82	35	8	1.9	.284	.366	.439	.074	.282	.367	.453	.293	33.5	152-2B	-2

Breakout: 12% Improve: 40% Collapse: 20% Attrition: 8%   Comparables: Ray Durham, Don Buford, Bill Doran, Chuck Knoblauch

If Roberts can finish out his contract with two more years remotely like his last two, he could pass Bobby Grich as the best second baseman in Orioles history, despite his playing during a much more bleak period in the franchise's existence. That assumes that he'll stay an Oriole; with a salary roughly half of Miguel Tejada's, he might actually be the team's most valuable trade commodity. An underrated player and an absolute workout fanatic, he could be a steal for whatever team acquires him.

Billy Rowell — 3B

Bats: L Throws: R Height: 6' 5" Weight: 205 Born: September 10, 1988 Age: 19

YEAR	TEAM	LVL	AGE	PA	R	2B	3B	HR	RBI	BB	SO	SB	CS	EqBRR	AVG	OBP	SLG	MLVr	EqAVG	EqOBP	EqSLG	EqA	VORP	DEFENSE	
2006	BLU	Rk	17	180	38	15	3	2	26	25	47	3	0	1.4	.329	.422	.507	.362	.180	.256	.280	.191	-27.2	36-3B	4
2006	ABE	A-	17	49	8	4	0	1	6	4	12	0	0	1.2	.326	.388	.488	.371	.200	.245	.333	.193	-5.0	11-3B	-2
2007	DEL	A	18	388	47	21	3	9	57	31	104	3	2	-3.6	.273	.335	.426	.095	.211	.263	.328	.203	-17.9	80-3B	-12
2008	BAL	MLB	19	454	38	23	2	7	39	30	126	5	3	0.1	.217	.270	.331	-.275	.215	.271	.341	.215	-17.4	108-3B	-6

Breakout: 57% Improve: 74% Collapse: 15% Attrition: 6%   Comparables: Matt Tuiasosopo, Austin Kearns, Corey Smith, Chris Lubanski

The Orioles' first-round pick in 2006, Rowell missed a big chunk of the season to an oblique injury and didn't impress anyone when he got back. He's a big, big guy who will probably have to move to first base somewhere down the line. As such, he has enormous power potential that hasn't yet translated into results. His strikeouts are way too high, and he literally can't touch lefties: 56 of his 165 career plate appearances against them ended in a whiff. Still, time is very much on his side.

Brandon Snyder 1B Bats: R Throws: R Height: 6' 2" Weight: 205 Born: November 23, 1986 Age: 21

YEAR	TEAM	LVL	AGE	PA	R	2B	3B	HR	RBI	BB	SO	SB	CS	EqBRR	AVG	OBP	SLG	MLVr	EqAVG	EqOBP	EqSLG	EqA	VORP	DEFENSE	
2005	BLU	Rk	18	180	26	8	0	8	35	28	36	7	2	-1.7	.271	.380	.493	.196	.181	.264	.265	.196	-27.6	19-C	1
2006	ABE	A-	19	131	14	8	1	1	11	5	43	2	1	0.2	.234	.267	.339	-.034	.168	.198	.256	.139	-29.2	26-C	-4
2006	DEL	A	19	159	12	12	0	3	20	9	55	0	0	-1.5	.194	.237	.340	-.198	.169	.203	.284	.159	-16.9	23-C	-2
2007	DEL	A	20	501	63	23	3	11	58	44	107	0	2	-3.0	.283	.354	.422	.129	.230	.287	.343	.218	-25.5	63-1B	-5
2008	BAL	MLB	21	585	45	27	2	10	58	39	157	4	2	-0.7	.217	.272	.332	-.271	.215	.273	.343	.216	-23.6	137-1B	-3

Breakout: 59% Improve: 75% Collapse: 15% Attrition: 9%   Comparables: Adam Hyzdu, Mark Trumbo, Corey Smith, Corey Myers

Snyder was a first-round pick in 2005, but a bad shoulder injury stunted his development and forced him away from catching. He played first base for Delmarva in the Sally League last year and tried third base in Hawaii Winter League. His bat was as pedestrian as ever in the first half, but he apparently found a higher gear in June that lasted through Hawaii, where he outhit the O's 2007 top pick, Matt Wieters.

Miguel Tejada SS Bats: R Throws: R Height: 5' 9" Weight: 215 Born: May 25, 1976 Age: 32

YEAR	TEAM	LVL	AGE	PA	R	2B	3B	HR	RBI	BB	SO	SB	CS	EqBRR	AVG	OBP	SLG	MLVr	EqAVG	EqOBP	EqSLG	EqA	VORP	DEFENSE	
2005	BAL	MLB	29	704	89	50	5	26	98	40	83	5	1	0.8	.304	.349	.515	.199	.311	.364	.540	.302	62.3	158-SS	4
2006	BAL	MLB	30	709	99	37	0	24	100	46	79	6	2	-0.5	.330	.379	.498	.219	.331	.386	.509	.304	65.9	148-SS	0
2007	BAL	MLB	31	568	72	19	1	18	81	41	55	2	1	-0.4	.296	.357	.442	.090	.299	.366	.464	.286	31.8	120-SS	-14
2008	BAL	MLB	32	565	67	27	1	14	74	35	62	4	2	-0.7	.290	.340	.428	.022	.288	.341	.441	.273	24.0	133-SS	-5

Breakout: 3% Improve: 17% Collapse: 44% Attrition: 7%   Comparables: Hubie Brooks, Ron Coomer, Hank Majeski, Kirby Puckett

Almost everything was down for Tejada this past year: his average, his speed, his fielding, his playing time, his trade value. You may be inclined to blame it all on the pitch that broke his wrist in June, ending a seven-year consecutive game streak, but the fact is that he didn't hit any differently before or after that. Instead, 2007 continued a multi-year slide, especially in foot speed. One thing that wasn't actually down was Tejada's power—it looks worse than it was thanks to the time he missed and the league-wide power drop-off. Dealt to Houston for five Astros, he'll receive only marginal benefit from Minute Maid's Crawford Boxes (Camden's friendly to righty power too), but moving to the weakest division of the weaker league won't hurt any. He'll remain at shortstop for his new club, ending speculation that he's headed for the hot corner.

Brandon Tripp RF Bats: L Throws: R Height: 6' 2" Weight: 200 Born: April 2, 1985 Age: 23

YEAR	TEAM	LVL	AGE	PA	R	2B	3B	HR	RBI	BB	SO	SB	CS	EqBRR	AVG	OBP	SLG	MLVr	EqAVG	EqOBP	EqSLG	EqA	VORP	DEFENSE			
2006	ABE	A-	21	174	20	8	0	2	15	16	49	1	2	-0.5	.221	.345	.317	.039	.199	.276	.288	.199	-19.9	26-CF	-3	14-RF	0
2007	DEL	A	22	433	72	25	4	19	79	43	112	7	1	0.7	.288	.377	.531	.319	.225	.296	.406	.243	-11.6	89-RF	-12		
2008	BAL	MLB	23	466	43	24	2	11	48	34	143	5	3	0.3	.216	.282	.363	-.215	.215	.282	.374	.229	-16.5	110-RF	0		

Breakout: 31% Improve: 58% Collapse: 21% Attrition: 11%   Comparables: Justin Nelson, Steve Murphy, John Rodriguez, Brad Hawpe

Tripp, a twelfth-round pick in 2006, shrugged off a lousy debut season to become the Orioles' Minor League Player of the Year in 2007. Optimistically speaking, he fixed a flaw in his swing and took off; pessimistically speaking, he was a college vet beating up on younger competition. His tools are good, but it would be nice to see how they work against someone his own age.

Matt Wieters   C   Bats: S   Throws: R   Height: 6′ 5″   Weight: 230   Born: May 21, 1986   Age: 21

YEAR	TEAM	LVL	AGE	PA	R	2B	3B	HR	RBI	BB	SO	SB	CS	EqBRR	AVG	OBP	SLG	MLVr	EqAVG	EqOBP	EqSLG	EqA	VORP	DEFENSE
2007	HON	HWB	22	121	13	9	1	1	17	12	15	0	1	0.0	.283	.364	.415	—	.236	.298	.345	.223		
2008	BAL	MLB	22	603	65	29	2	13	69	49	144	10	4	0.3	.240	.306	.373	-.145	.238	.307	.384	.246	1.2	141-C	-6

Breakout: NA   Improve: NA   Collapse: NA   Attrition: NA   Comparables: Jose Cruz Jr., Ryan Zimmerman, Mike Kelly, Carlos Peña

Wieters was regarded as the best position player in last year's draft and possibly the best college catcher in recent memory, combining good defense, a high average, and good power. The Orioles got him with the fifth overall pick because the top four teams were scared away by his bonus demands and his agent, Scott Boras. Indeed, the O's wound up giving Wieters a record signing bonus, inking him too late to play last season, but he did have a solid debut in Hawaii over the winter.

PITCHERS

Jake Arrieta   Bats: R   Throws: R   Height: 6′ 4″   Weight: 225   Born: March 6, 1986   Age: 22

YEAR	TEAM	LVL	AGE	W	L	SV	G	GS	IP	H	BB	SO	HR	GB%	BABIP	STUFF	WHIP	ERA	PERA	EqERA	EqH9	EqBB9	EqSO9	EqHR9	VORP	SN/WX
2008	BAL	MLB	22	4	13	0	27	27	134	184	85	64	29	47.0%	.327	-19	2.00	8.00	7.49	7.66	11.8	5.2	4.0	1.9	-32.7	-2.70

Breakout: NA   Improve: NA   Collapse: NA   Attrition: NA   Comparables: Colby Lewis, Benjamin Fritz, Chris Clemons, Aaron Sele

Arrieta had a poorer-than-expected season at Texas Christian last year. That plus Scott Boras' representation dropped him into the fifth round in the draft. The Orioles went way over slot, giving him first-round money to sign, and Arrieta buried the memory of his college season with a spectacular debut in the Arizona Fall League (16 innings, no runs). That should mean he'll start 2008 at an advanced level, High-A Frederick at least. He mostly works off of a sinking fastball.

Danys Baez   Bats: R   Throws: R   Height: 6′ 1″   Weight: 235   Born: September 10, 1977   Age: 30

YEAR	TEAM	LVL	AGE	W	L	SV	G	GS	IP	H	BB	SO	HR	GB%	BABIP	STUFF	WHIP	ERA	PERA	EqERA	EqH9	EqBB9	EqSO9	EqHR9	VORP	SN/WX
2005	TBA	MLB	27	5	4	41	67	0	72¹	66	30	51	7	48.4%	.278	1	1.33	2.86	3.68	2.88	7.6	3.6	6.1	0.8	19.1	4.48
2006	LAN	MLB	28	5	5	9	46	0	49²	53	11	29	3	40.7%	.323	-1	1.29	4.35	3.76	4.71	9.1	1.6	4.9	0.5	4.1	-0.03
2006	ATL	MLB	28	0	1	0	11	0	10	7	6	10	0	37.0%	.259	5	1.30	5.40	2.79	5.23	6.1	4.4	7.8	0.0	0.6	0.07
2007	BAL	MLB	29	0	6	3	53	0	50¹	50	29	29	8	52.4%	.269	-23	1.57	6.44	5.17	5.61	8.2	4.6	4.7	1.4	-1.9	0.11
2008	BAL	MLB	30	2	2	2	41	0	47	52	20	30	5	47.9%	.304	-8	1.52	4.88	4.62	4.76	9.4	3.5	5.4	1.0	3.5	0.30

Breakout: 24%   Improve: 46%   Collapse: 34%   Attrition: 29%   Comparables: Bob Lee, Larry Sherry, Anthony Young, Dave Heaverlo

One of a trio of relievers the Orioles signed prior to the 2007 season to save their bullpen, Baez was guaranteed $41 million over three years to work the seventh and eighth innings. It was a ludicrous contract made far worse by Baez's performance. The O's got a good month out of him before he turned into an arsonist. He then tore an elbow ligament and will miss the entire 2008 season following Tommy John surgery, so you can ignore that projection.

Pedro Beato   Bats: R   Throws: R   Height: 6′ 5″   Weight: 210   Born: October 27, 1986   Age: 21

YEAR	TEAM	LVL	AGE	W	L	SV	G	GS	IP	H	BB	SO	HR	GB%	BABIP	STUFF	WHIP	ERA	PERA	EqERA	EqH9	EqBB9	EqSO9	EqHR9	VORP	SN/WX
2006	ABE	A-	19	3	2	0	14	10	57	47	23	52	6	53.3%	.266	-50	1.23	3.63	15.14	12.69	13.1	8.3	4.4	4.6	-35.2	—
2007	DEL	A	20	7	8	0	27	27	142¹	139	59	106	10	53.1%	.301	-22	1.39	4.05	7.19	7.38	11.1	6.2	3.4	1.4	-24.9	—
2008	BAL	MLB	21	4	12	0	25	25	126²	157	92	56	22	49.9%	.307	-19	1.97	7.36	6.83	7.15	10.6	6.0	3.7	1.5	-23.9	-1.70

Breakout: 37%   Improve: 68%   Collapse: 13%   Attrition: 9%   Comparables: David Coggin, Zach Miner, Brian West, Jamie Arnold

More was expected from Beato in his first full season. A supplemental first-round pick from 2006, he was consistently okay last year, but never impressive. That's troubling because organizations want their young pitchers to show some dominant skills, which coaches can then help them figure out how to access repeatedly. Part of Beato's problem was conditioning; he picked up some weight and that threw off his mechanics, costing him velocity on his fastball and differential on his change.

Erik Bedard

Bats: L   Throws: L   Height: 6' 1"   Weight: 195   Born: March 6, 1979   Age: 29

YEAR	TEAM	LVL	AGE	W	L	SV	G	GS	IP	H	BB	SO	HR	GB%	BABIP	STUFF	WHIP	ERA	PERA	EqERA	EqH9	EqBB9	EqSO9	EqHR9	VORP	SN/WX
2005	BAL	MLB	26	6	8	0	24	24	141²	139	57	125	10	41.3%	.323	28	1.38	4.00	4.15	4.06	8.8	3.7	7.9	0.6	24.7	3.71
2006	BAL	MLB	27	15	11	0	33	33	196¹	196	69	171	16	49.9%	.314	28	1.35	3.76	3.65	3.72	8.2	2.9	7.3	0.6	40.2	5.42
2007	BAL	MLB	28	13	5	0	28	28	182	141	57	221	19	49.8%	.287	40	1.09	3.16	3.18	2.95	6.9	2.5	9.6	0.9	54.9	6.02
2008	BAL	MLB	29	13	9	0	30	30	193²	175	72	196	17	48.3%	.302	31	1.27	3.58	3.43	3.50	7.8	3.0	8.5	0.8	42.2	6.00

Breakout: 18% Improve: 50% Collapse: 24% Attrition: 10%   Comparables: Mark Langston, Floyd Bannister, Harvey Haddix, Sonny Siebert

Bedard missed all of September with a strained oblique muscle. In the game of "what if," we're talking about five starts, maybe six, which could have bumped Bedard's season totals up to, say, a 15-6 record and a majors-leading 260 strikeouts, still not quite enough to pry the Cy Young award away from C. C. Sabathia. The only reason not to think of Bedard as a favorite for the 2008 Cy Young is the lack of support he's likely to get from the Orioles. Amazingly, he's been mentioned in trade talks; it should take a truly extraordinary package of players to get him.

Kurt Birkins

Bats: L   Throws: L   Height: 6' 2"   Weight: 190   Born: August 11, 1980   Age: 27

YEAR	TEAM	LVL	AGE	W	L	SV	G	GS	IP	H	BB	SO	HR	GB%	BABIP	STUFF	WHIP	ERA	PERA	EqERA	EqH9	EqBB9	EqSO9	EqHR9	VORP	SN/WX
2005	BOW	AA	24	7	11	0	26	24	129	134	42	114	8	55.9%	.336	-10	1.36	3.91	6.52	6.99	11.5	4.3	5.0	0.9	-17.7	—
2006	OTT	AAA	25	1	3	0	5	5	25²	20	11	19	2	64.3%	.265	-3	1.23	3.21	4.95	4.84	8.5	4.8	5.2	1.2	1.9	—
2006	BAL	MLB	25	5	2	0	35	0	31	25	16	27	4	42.2%	.256	-1	1.32	4.94	3.50	4.78	6.5	4.2	7.0	1.1	1.9	0.22
2007	NOR	AAA	26	8	4	0	20	19	105²	102	38	98	6	54.9%	.324	9	1.32	3.07	5.04	4.45	9.7	3.7	6.3	0.8	12.7	—
2007	BAL	MLB	26	1	2	0	19	2	34¹	52	14	30	3	50.4%	.408	-8	1.92	8.13	7.57	7.97	12.9	3.1	6.9	0.8	-8.1	-0.83
2008	TBA	MLB	27	3	5	1	38	9	75²	89	35	56	8	50.2%	.333	-4	1.64	5.52	5.42	5.24	10.4	3.8	6.0	1.0	-1.6	0.10

Breakout: 36% Improve: 60% Collapse: 20% Attrition: 33%   Comparables: Steve Searcy, Alex Graman, Mark Mimbs, Woodie Fryman

Birkins looked good at Triple-A Norfolk, one of the most forgiving places to pitch in the minor leagues, but major league hitters picked up right where they left off against him in 2006. The Rays claimed him on waivers after the season. He might survive if they can get him into a strict LOOGY role, but if a team is going to devote a roster spot to such a restricted role, they need to give it to a pitcher who dominates lefties. That's not Birkins.

Chad Bradford

Bats: R   Throws: R   Height: 6' 5"   Weight: 205   Born: September 14, 1974   Age: 33

YEAR	TEAM	LVL	AGE	W	L	SV	G	GS	IP	H	BB	SO	HR	GB%	BABIP	STUFF	WHIP	ERA	PERA	EqERA	EqH9	EqBB9	EqSO9	EqHR9	VORP	SN/WX
2005	BOS	MLB	30	2	1	0	31	0	23¹	29	4	10	1	69.0%	.341	-9	1.41	3.86	4.30	3.42	10.3	1.5	3.8	0.4	5.1	0.34
2006	NYN	MLB	31	4	2	2	70	0	62	59	13	45	1	65.5%	.312	15	1.16	2.90	3.14	3.26	8.8	1.6	6.1	0.1	19.2	1.83
2007	BAL	MLB	32	4	7	2	78	0	64²	77	16	29	1	63.9%	.328	0	1.44	3.34	3.90	3.41	9.8	1.9	3.7	0.1	15.0	1.03
2008	BAL	MLB	33	2	3	3	49	0	53	65	14	25	3	59.3%	.324	-12	1.48	4.46	4.23	4.46	10.5	2.2	3.9	0.6	6.0	0.50

Breakout: 4% Improve: 15% Collapse: 60% Attrition: 19%   Comparables: Nate Snell, Dale Murray, Ben Weber, Clay Carroll

By the end of the season, Bradford and Jamie Walker were the only effective pitchers left in the Orioles pen, and they were worked hard as a result; the left-handed Walker finished in a tie for the AL lead with 81 appearances, and Bradford was right behind him with 78. It was a pretty typical year for the submarining righty, stifling right-handed hitters while keeping his pitches down, down, and farther down. Assuming the workload doesn't get to him, expect more of the same.

Brian Burres | Bats: L | Throws: L | Height: 6' 1" | Weight: 180 | Born: April 8, 1981 | Age: 27

YEAR	TEAM	LVL	AGE	W	L	SV	G	GS	IP	H	BB	SO	HR	GB%	BABIP	STUFF	WHIP	ERA	PERA	EqERA	EqH9	EqBB9	EqSO9	EqHR9	VORP	SN/WX
2005	NRW	AA	24	9	6	0	26	24	128²	130	57	105	13	39.3%	.312	-21	1.45	4.20	6.93	6.46	10.6	5.6	4.5	1.5	-11.1	—
2006	OTT	AAA	25	10	6	0	26	26	139²	133	57	110	14	42.9%	.300	-15	1.36	3.75	5.94	5.44	9.6	4.5	5.2	1.5	2.3	—
2006	BAL	MLB	25	0	0	0	11	0	8	6	1	6	1	54.2%	.217	8	0.88	2.25	2.44	2.16	5.4	1.1	6.5	1.1	3.4	0.50
2007	BAL	MLB	26	6	8	0	37	17	121	140	66	96	14	39.0%	.335	-3	1.70	5.95	5.72	5.59	10.1	4.3	6.6	1.0	-0.9	1.64
2008	BAL	MLB	27	2	4	1	23	6	49¹	57	25	35	7	42.6%	.319	-6	1.66	5.77	5.42	5.56	9.9	4.2	6.0	1.2	-1.2	0.10

Breakout: 17% Improve: 39% Collapse: 40% Attrition: 54%   Comparables: Angel Miranda, Paul Mirabella, Frank Kreutzer, Mike Kekich

Burres was great in April, making him the natural choice to move up when injuries hit the rotation. He pitched decently until July, then the league caught up in a big way. He's an unusual pitcher, with a fairly large fly-ball bias and a severe reverse platoon split. The overall picture looks like a pitcher who will always be in danger of a demotion back to the minor leagues.

Daniel Cabrera | Bats: R | Throws: R | Height: 6' 9" | Weight: 270 | Born: May 28, 1981 | Age: 27

YEAR	TEAM	LVL	AGE	W	L	SV	G	GS	IP	H	BB	SO	HR	GB%	BABIP	STUFF	WHIP	ERA	PERA	EqERA	EqH9	EqBB9	EqSO9	EqHR9	VORP	SN/WX
2005	BAL	MLB	24	10	13	0	29	29	161¹	144	87	157	14	52.3%	.294	28	1.43	4.52	4.07	4.75	7.8	4.8	8.4	0.7	11.4	2.87
2006	OTT	AAA	25	3	1	0	4	4	24¹	20	9	27	1	40.9%	.302	14	1.20	4.11	3.99	6.08	8.0	3.8	7.2	0.8	-1.3	—
2006	BAL	MLB	25	9	10	0	26	26	148	130	104	157	11	42.4%	.320	38	1.58	4.74	4.07	4.43	7.5	6.0	9.0	0.6	18.0	3.33
2007	BAL	MLB	26	9	18	0	34	34	204¹	207	108	166	25	50.7%	.308	7	1.54	5.55	4.83	5.22	8.7	4.2	6.7	1.1	2.2	2.47
2008	BAL	MLB	27	10	11	0	29	29	177¹	172	88	152	18	48.3%	.299	18	1.46	4.54	4.25	4.44	8.3	4.1	7.2	0.9	18.3	3.50

Breakout: 29% Improve: 66% Collapse: 12% Attrition: 19%   Comparables: J.R. Richard, Jeff Juden, Jeff Robinson, Rich Gale

Cabrera pitched more than 200 innings for the first time last year, so he can claim a workhorse label. He can also point fingers at his teammates for giving him the worst bullpen support of any starter in the majors last year and putting him in the top 20 in difference between Support-Neutral record and actual record. Who are we kidding? He stunk last year. Cabrera led the majors in earned runs and walks, was second-worst in runs and hit batsmen, and earned serious punk points by throwing at Dustin Pedroia and inciting a brawl. There's still talent there, but mostly there's slack.

Fernando Cabrera | Bats: R | Throws: R | Height: 6' 4" | Weight: 220 | Born: November 16, 1981 | Age: 26

YEAR	TEAM	LVL	AGE	W	L	SV	G	GS	IP	H	BB	SO	HR	GB%	BABIP	STUFF	WHIP	ERA	PERA	EqERA	EqH9	EqBB9	EqSO9	EqHR9	VORP	SN/WX
2005	BUF	AAA	23	6	1	3	30	0	51¹	36	11	68	3	35.0%	.292	28	0.92	1.23	3.24	2.06	6.9	2.4	9.0	0.8	18.9	—
2005	CLE	MLB	23	2	1	0	15	0	30²	24	11	29	1	38.1%	.277	24	1.14	1.47	3.09	2.43	7.3	3.3	8.5	0.3	12.4	0.56
2006	CLE	MLB	24	3	3	0	51	0	60²	53	32	71	12	34.9%	.304	8	1.40	5.19	4.78	4.76	7.7	4.6	10.0	1.7	4.7	0.02
2007	CLE	MLB	25	1	2	0	24	0	33²	38	22	39	7	35.4%	.356	2	1.78	5.61	7.44	5.94	10.0	5.1	9.7	1.9	-0.1	0.11
2007	BAL	MLB	25	0	0	1	9	0	10	12	9	9	2	21.9%	.333	-12	2.10	12.60	8.50	12.60	10.8	7.2	7.2	1.8	-7.4	0.12
2008	BAL	MLB	26	3	3	2	45	0	55	51	25	51	8	38.4%	.283	7	1.38	4.31	4.10	4.14	8.0	3.7	7.8	1.2	8.4	0.70

Breakout: 55% Improve: 73% Collapse: 12% Attrition: 21%   Comparables: Jeff Parrett, Robb Nen, Stan Belinda, Kurt Knudsen

His arm is still electric, but Cabrera has lost more and more control over the past two years. The Indians finally gave up on him in August—they'd kept him on their 25-man roster despite barely using him for more than two months—triggering a waiver war between the Orioles and the Rays that ended in the Orioles' favor. You'd like to think that the Orioles are desperately trying to get their hands on every tape of Cabrera pitching in 2005 they can find in order to figure out what's changed.

Cory Doyne

Bats: R   Throws: R   Height: 6' 2"   Weight: 240   Born: August 13, 1981   Age: 26

YEAR	TEAM	LVL	AGE	W	L	SV	G	GS	IP	H	BB	SO	HR	GB%	BABIP	STUFF	WHIP	ERA	PERA	EqERA	EqH9	EqBB9	EqSO9	EqHR9	VORP	SN/WX
2005	SFD	AA	23	2	1	19	48	0	55¹	37	36	53	5	43.5%	.230	0	1.32	1.95	5.25	3.26	6.9	8.0	6.2	1.3	12.9	—
2006	SFD	AA	24	1	7	6	54	0	66¹	48	42	78	1	45.0%	.301	18	1.36	3.40	4.39	5.04	7.9	6.8	7.7	0.3	3.8	—
2007	NOR	AAA	25	0	1	29	42	0	44¹	23	16	49	0	47.1%	.225	15	0.88	2.23	2.76	3.16	5.1	3.6	7.4	0.2	11.6	—
2007	BAL	MLB	25	0	0	0	5	0	3²	7	3	2	1	31.3%	.429	-78	2.73	14.59	19.92	18.00	15.8	6.8	4.5	2.2	-3.6	-0.08
2008	BAL	MLB	26	2	3	2	26	2	44²	44	27	35	5	43.0%	.290	-3	1.58	5.03	4.80	4.87	8.4	5.0	6.6	1.1	3.2	0.30

Breakout: 36% Improve: 58% Collapse: 22% Attrition: 27%   Comparables: Ken Wright, Rich Garces, Jim Britton, Bob Gibson

After turning in one of the best minor league relief-pitching seasons of 2007 (and leading the International League in tattoos), Doyne was called up to Baltimore and almost immediately came down with a sore shoulder. He tried pitching through it with disastrous results, and it wasn't until he was sent back to the minors that he was diagnosed with a SLAP lesion. Full recovery from the surgery should take until March, at which point we'll see if his 98 mph fastball still exists.

Brandon Erbe

Bats: R   Throws: R   Height: 6' 4"   Weight: 180   Born: December 25, 1987   Age: 20

YEAR	TEAM	LVL	AGE	W	L	SV	G	GS	IP	H	BB	SO	HR	GB%	BABIP	STUFF	WHIP	ERA	PERA	EqERA	EqH9	EqBB9	EqSO9	EqHR9	VORP	SN/WX
2005	BLU	Rk	17	1	1	1	11	3	23¹	8	10	48	1	33.3%	.241	19	0.77	3.09	6.19	7.71	5.8	9.6	9.6	1.4	-4.4	—
2006	DEL	A	18	5	9	0	28	27	114¹	88	47	133	2	36.0%	.319	32	1.18	3.23	5.70	6.19	9.7	6.5	6.3	0.7	-6.3	—
2007	FRD	A+	19	6	8	0	25	25	119¹	127	62	111	14	47.8%	.331	-29	1.58	6.26	9.47	10.22	11.9	7.0	5.2	2.3	-54.3	—
2008	BAL	MLB	20	4	11	0	24	24	114¹	139	96	79	21	43.7%	.324	-11	2.06	7.59	7.25	7.26	10.5	6.9	5.8	1.6	-22.9	-1.70

Breakout: 56% Improve: 81% Collapse: 4%   Attrition: 9%   Comparables: Chris Seelbach, Corey Avrard, Kyle Davies, Dave Doorneweerd

Youth is still on Erbe's side, but 2007 was a terrible year for Baltimore's 2005 third-round pick. His control deserted him, which is not the most surprising thing given that he's a tall, skinny kid who's still growing. His fastball was still reaching the upper 90s, so he hasn't lost any velocity, his slider bites (we mean that in a good way), and his changeup is decent, but he was always behind in the count and hitters sat and waited.

Jeremy Guthrie

Bats: R   Throws: R   Height: 6' 1"   Weight: 195   Born: April 8, 1979   Age: 29

YEAR	TEAM	LVL	AGE	W	L	SV	G	GS	IP	H	BB	SO	HR	GB%	BABIP	STUFF	WHIP	ERA	PERA	EqERA	EqH9	EqBB9	EqSO9	EqHR9	VORP	SN/WX
2005	BUF	AAA	26	12	10	0	25	25	136¹	152	49	100	15	44.0%	.329	-14	1.47	5.08	5.97	6.45	10.4	4.0	4.6	1.2	-12.1	—
2005	CLE	MLB	26	0	0	0	1	0	6	9	2	3	2	45.8%	.350	-31	1.83	6.00	13.25	9.00	13.5	3.0	4.5	3.0	-0.3	-0.04
2006	BUF	AAA	27	9	5	0	21	20	123	104	48	88	6	53.0%	.271	3	1.24	3.15	4.51	4.70	8.6	4.3	4.6	0.7	11.5	—
2006	CLE	MLB	27	0	0	0	9	1	19¹	24	15	14	2	48.4%	.367	-4	2.02	6.99	7.76	6.87	11.3	6.9	6.4	1.0	-2.2	-0.16
2007	BAL	MLB	28	7	5	0	32	26	175¹	165	47	123	23	43.7%	.275	9	1.21	3.70	3.75	3.45	7.9	2.1	5.8	1.1	38.2	4.24
2008	BAL	MLB	29	6	8	0	30	18	124²	140	46	78	17	45.6%	.303	0	1.49	5.07	4.86	4.90	9.6	3.0	5.3	1.2	7.5	1.50

Breakout: 8% Improve: 31% Collapse: 38% Attrition: 19%   Comparables: Scott Kamieniecki, Armando Reynoso, Ramon Ortiz, Bob Porterfield

After a poor April in the pen, Guthrie moved to the rotation in place of the injured Jaret Wright and became one of the Orioles' few pleasant surprises, giving us a taste of why he'd been a first-round draft pick way back in 2002; only his pedestrian 7-5 record kept him from ranking higher on Rookie of the Year lists. Guthrie had shown substantial improvement in 2006, and 2007 was better still, but there was a lot of luck in his line—he gave up 17 fewer hits than expected, fifth-most in the AL, and was still six runs below expectation even after allowing for those missing hits. He's liable to give those gains up in 2008, but that won't be enough to knock him out of the O's rotation.

David Hernandez

Bats: R   Throws: R   Height: 6' 3"   Weight: 214   Born: May 13, 1985   Age: 23

YEAR	TEAM	LVL	AGE	W	L	SV	G	GS	IP	H	BB	SO	HR	GB%	BABIP	STUFF	WHIP	ERA	PERA	EqERA	EqH9	EqBB9	EqSO9	EqHR9	VORP	SN/WX
2005	ABE	A-	20	1	2	0	12	8	41²	41	17	47	2	47.0%	.348	-13	1.39	3.88	9.23	8.74	12.7	7.9	5.0	1.6	-11.9	—
2006	DEL	A	21	7	8	0	28	28	145	134	71	154	13	39.0%	.316	-25	1.41	4.16	8.84	8.71	11.5	7.5	5.4	2.2	-42.8	—
2007	FRD	A+	22	7	11	0	28	27	145¹	139	47	168	16	37.4%	.328	-21	1.28	4.96	7.51	7.62	11.0	4.6	6.8	2.1	-29.2	—
2008	BAL	MLB	23	5	11	0	25	25	131¹	155	84	93	27	39.2%	.311	-4	1.82	6.77	6.55	6.41	10.2	5.3	5.9	1.8	-14.4	-0.60

Breakout: 49% Improve: 80% Collapse: 9%   Attrition: 13%   Comparables: Garrett Stephenson, Eric Gagné, Brandon Knight, Claudio Vargas

Hernandez is a power pitcher with a good fastball/slider combo; he's durable, and he's inconsistent. That creates a split between the stat and scout perspectives, with the scouts drooling over the good outings and the analysts backing off because of the bad ones. He could be just a few adjustments from taking off, but he could also never make those adjustments and go nowhere.

James Hoey   Bats: R   Throws: R   Height: 6' 6"   Weight: 210   Born: December 30, 1982   Age: 25

YEAR	TEAM	LVL	AGE	W	L	SV	G	GS	IP	H	BB	SO	HR	GB%	BABIP	STUFF	WHIP	ERA	PERA	EqERA	EqH9	EqBB9	EqSO9	EqHR9	VORP	SN/WX
2005	ABE	A-	22	1	1	0	9	0	15	11	10	15	1	46.2%	.286	-14	1.40	4.80	8.77	10.22	9.5	11.7	4.4	2.2	-6.3	—
2006	DEL	A	23	2	1	18	27	0	28²	17	10	46	2	54.4%	.306	7	0.96	2.55	5.41	5.04	8.3	5.4	9.0	1.8	1.6	—
2006	FRD	A+	23	0	0	11	14	0	14	13	5	16	0	43.9%	.317	-4	1.29	0.64	4.85	3.29	9.9	4.6	6.6	0.0	3.5	—
2006	BAL	MLB	23	0	1	0	12	0	9²	14	5	6	1	52.8%	.406	-28	1.97	10.21	7.63	10.24	12.1	4.7	5.6	0.9	-4.6	-0.57
2007	BOW	AA	24	1	0	14	20	0	18²	13	4	28	0	56.4%	.351	17	0.91	0.00	0.23	0.00	7.9	2.6	10.1	0.7	10.6	—
2007	NOR	AAA	24	2	0	2	20	0	27	15	10	41	1	42.6%	.275	25	0.93	1.33	3.17	2.45	6.3	3.9	9.8	0.7	9.0	—
2007	BAL	MLB	24	3	4	0	23	0	24²	25	18	18	2	39.7%	.319	-9	1.74	7.29	4.89	6.93	8.8	5.8	6.2	0.7	-4.7	-0.81
2008	BAL	MLB	25	2	3	3	51	1	53¹	49	28	48	5	43.2%	.289	5	1.44	4.41	4.03	4.31	7.9	4.3	7.5	0.9	7.6	0.70

Breakout: 49% Improve: 76% Collapse: 13% Attrition: 25%   Comparables: *Jeff Jones, Russ Kemmerer, Sammy Stewart, Bill Simas*

Hoey came back from TJ surgery a couple of years ago and has since teased the Orioles with minor league dominance and major league submissiveness. He's a one-pitch guy, that pitch being a fastball that can reach 100 on a kind gun but that lacks movement. It doesn't help that he's been a lot worse from the stretch, but it does account somewhat for the gap between his major and minor league performances; once runners start reaching base against him, the boulder starts rolling downhill.

Luis Lebron   Bats: R   Throws: R   Height: 6' 1"   Weight: 172   Born: March 15, 1985   Age: 23

YEAR	TEAM	LVL	AGE	W	L	SV	G	GS	IP	H	BB	SO	HR	GB%	BABIP	STUFF	WHIP	ERA	PERA	EqERA	EqH9	EqBB9	EqSO9	EqHR9	VORP	SN/WX
2005	BLU	Rk	20	2	4	0	14	7	25	34	22	45	2	41.5%	.533	-21	2.24	11.16	27.73	28.10	22.0	22.6	9.4	2.8	-40.8	—
2006	ABE	A-	21	0	2	20	32	0	30	17	15	46	2	38.7%	.268	5	1.07	1.20	8.94	6.00	9.4	9.8	8.6	3.0	-1.1	—
2007	DEL	A	22	1	2	5	46	0	55¹	48	55	86	1	41.5%	.395	24	1.86	5.05	9.60	9.34	12.0	14.6	9.3	0.6	-18.4	—
2008	BAL	MLB	23	2	4	0	23	7	48¹	52	67	52	7	41.2%	.342	-15	2.46	8.01	8.06	7.66	9.2	11.4	9.1	1.4	-13.3	-1.00

Breakout: 60% Improve: 76% Collapse: 18% Attrition: 13%   Comparables: *Bryan Wolff, Lesli Brea, Julio Soriano, Brad Pennington*

Lebron is an exciting pitcher to watch, but it can't be terribly stimulating to play the field behind him. He's all strikeouts and walks, flinging the ball at mid- to upper-90s speeds without much regard for where it ends up. He doesn't look as big as his listed height, and there's a cognitive dissonance effect for hitters when a guy his size brings it that hard.

Jon Leicester   Bats: R   Throws: R   Height: 6' 3"   Weight: 220   Born: February 7, 1979   Age: 29

YEAR	TEAM	LVL	AGE	W	L	SV	G	GS	IP	H	BB	SO	HR	GB%	BABIP	STUFF	WHIP	ERA	PERA	EqERA	EqH9	EqBB9	EqSO9	EqHR9	VORP	SN/WX
2005	IOW	AAA	26	3	8	1	24	16	98	115	42	73	17	50.0%	.326	-33	1.60	5.51	7.04	6.53	10.8	4.2	4.7	1.8	-9.5	—
2005	CHN	MLB	26	0	2	0	6	1	9	11	9	7	2	53.6%	.360	-20	2.22	9.00	13.92	11.88	11.9	8.6	6.5	2.2	-4.3	-0.31
2007	NOR	AAA	28	3	3	0	13	11	65	48	22	54	5	45.8%	.257	3	1.08	2.22	4.12	3.90	7.5	3.6	5.7	1.2	11.3	—
2007	BAL	MLB	28	2	3	0	10	5	32²	36	13	16	3	38.9%	.306	-14	1.53	7.59	4.75	6.96	9.5	3.1	4.2	0.8	-5.6	0.39
2008	BAL	MLB	29	3	6	1	28	13	73²	86	36	47	11	45.1%	.313	-9	1.65	5.89	5.51	5.69	10.0	4.0	5.4	1.3	-3.1	0.20

Breakout: 37% Improve: 63% Collapse: 16% Attrition: 30%   Comparables: *Jason Middlebrook, Eric Junge, Shane Bowers, Jason Roach*

Last year, Leicester overcame a knee injury that effectively cost him all of 2006 and made it back to the major leagues, pitching substantially better than his ERA suggests. While the opportunity came only after a slew of injuries to the Oriole staff, his Norfolk performance certainly warranted the trial. He doesn't figure to crack the 2008 rotation, but could have value in a swing role.

Radhames Liz

Bats: R   Throws: R   Height: 6' 2"   Weight: 185   Born: June 10, 1983   Age: 25

YEAR	TEAM	LVL	AGE	W	L	SV	G	GS	IP	H	BB	SO	HR	GB%	BABIP	STUFF	WHIP	ERA	PERA	EqERA	EqH9	EqBB9	EqSO9	EqHR9	VORP	SN/WX
2005	DEL	A	22	2	3	0	10	10	38¹	33	23	55	2	36.3%	.360	13	1.46	4.46	7.29	8.35	10.3	9.2	7.8	1.4	-9.9	—
2005	ABE	A-	22	5	4	0	11	11	56	36	19	82	1	45.0%	.324	18	0.98	1.77	5.60	5.05	8.7	6.6	7.2	0.8	2.8	—
2006	FRD	A+	23	6	5	0	16	16	83²	57	44	95	8	41.6%	.261	0	1.21	2.81	6.33	5.25	8.6	6.6	7.2	1.9	2.8	—
2006	BOW	AA	23	3	1	0	10	10	50²	55	31	54	9	42.0%	.346	-23	1.71	5.38	13.14	9.97	12.9	7.5	6.9	2.9	-21.0	—
2007	BOW	AA	24	11	4	0	25	25	137	101	70	161	13	37.5%	.273	7	1.25	3.22	5.10	4.98	7.9	5.4	7.6	1.4	8.8	—
2007	BAL	MLB	24	0	2	0	9	4	24²	25	23	24	3	23.0%	.319	10	1.95	6.92	5.73	6.75	8.5	7.1	7.8	1.1	-4.5	-0.53
2008	BAL	MLB	25	5	9	0	35	21	115²	113	82	102	17	37.1%	.291	2	1.68	5.69	5.38	5.45	8.4	5.9	7.4	1.3	-0.6	0.60

Breakout: 38% Improve: 59% Collapse: 23% Attrition: 27%   Comparables: Joaquin Benoit, Kevin Foster, Steve Shoemaker, Miguel Jimenez

Liz has the best fastball in the Orioles system. At 95 mph, it's not necessarily the fastest, but it has good movement. He got a chance in Baltimore last summer, making four awful starts before doing some good work in relief. Mechanical issues and limited breaking pitches may eventually push him to the pen to stay, but the Orioles will try to keep him a starter for now.

Adam Loewen

Bats: L   Throws: L   Height: 6' 5"   Weight: 225   Born: April 9, 1984   Age: 24

YEAR	TEAM	LVL	AGE	W	L	SV	G	GS	IP	H	BB	SO	HR	GB%	BABIP	STUFF	WHIP	ERA	PERA	EqERA	EqH9	EqBB9	EqSO9	EqHR9	VORP	SN/WX
2005	FRD	A+	21	10	8	0	28	27	142	130	86	146	8	62.0%	.324	2	1.52	4.12	6.87	7.07	10.3	7.8	5.2	1.1	-20.4	—
2006	BOW	AA	22	4	2	0	9	8	49²	46	26	55	3	55.3%	.341	14	1.46	2.74	6.51	4.91	10.6	6.3	7.0	1.0	3.4	—
2006	OTT	AAA	22	2	0	0	3	3	21¹	10	3	21	0	69.4%	.204	20	0.62	1.28	2.51	2.75	4.6	1.8	6.9	0.0	6.2	—
2006	BAL	MLB	22	6	6	0	22	19	112¹	111	62	98	8	50.0%	.319	25	1.54	5.37	4.20	5.14	8.3	4.7	7.4	0.6	3.5	1.66
2007	BAL	MLB	23	2	0	0	6	6	30¹	27	26	22	1	53.3%	.289	19	1.75	3.56	4.19	3.52	7.6	6.8	5.9	0.3	6.1	1.08
2008	BAL	MLB	24	3	5	0	22	10	68	65	42	58	6	51.7%	.303	7	1.58	4.77	4.47	4.71	8.2	5.1	7.1	0.7	6.4	1.00

Breakout: 26% Improve: 47% Collapse: 29% Attrition: 38%   Comparables: Mike Thompson, Mike Torrez, Mike Wegener, Jim Hannan

Loewen got off to a good start last year, proving effective despite severe wildness. Then elbow pain ended his season at the beginning of May. The pain turned out to be caused by a stress fracture, and, when it was discovered that it wasn't healing properly, he had to get a screw put in the elbow. Although rare, the injury isn't career-threatening; other pitchers have made strong recoveries from similar injuries. Loewen should be fully healed by the time you read this, reducing concerns to that early season wildness, which the Orioles hope was nothing but a symptom.

Robert McCrory

Bats: R   Throws: R   Height: 6' 1"   Weight: 205   Born: May 3, 1982   Age: 26

YEAR	TEAM	LVL	AGE	W	L	SV	G	GS	IP	H	BB	SO	HR	GB%	BABIP	STUFF	WHIP	ERA	PERA	EqERA	EqH9	EqBB9	EqSO9	EqHR9	VORP	SN/WX
2005	ABE	A-	23	2	1	0	5	5	24²	21	8	21	2	43.5%	.284	-19	1.17	3.28	8.07	6.53	10.5	6.5	3.5	2.6	-2.1	—
2006	ABE	A-	24	2	2	2	20	1	38²	32	16	57	2	50.0%	.375	-10	1.26	2.36	11.90	8.38	13.7	8.7	8.7	2.5	-9.0	—
2007	FRD	A+	25	0	0	14	22	0	22	16	12	22	1	57.9%	.273	-5	1.27	1.23	5.32	3.20	7.8	6.9	5.9	0.9	5.3	—
2007	BOW	AA	25	1	2	13	22	0	23	23	16	22	0	60.0%	.333	-6	1.70	3.91	5.41	7.83	9.8	6.7	5.5	0.4	-5.7	—
2008	BAL	MLB	26	2	5	2	25	6	55	62	42	42	7	50.0%	.324	-10	1.90	6.25	6.06	6.08	9.7	6.3	6.4	1.1	-4.2	-0.20

Breakout: 38% Improve: 63% Collapse: 23% Attrition: 21%   Comparables: Marcus Gwyn, Jason Bulger, Ruddy Lugo, Pete Sikaras

McCrory is old for a prospect, thanks to his entering pro ball after a full college tour and losing two years to elbow injuries after that. He started last year closing for High-A Frederick while relying on a solid fastball, then moved up and did the same for Double-A Bowie. The Orioles added him to their 40-man roster after the season, but he still needs more work in the minors.

Garrett Olson

Bats: R　Throws: L　Height: 6' 1"　Weight: 195　Born: October 18, 1983　Age: 24

YEAR	TEAM	LVL	AGE	W	L	SV	G	GS	IP	H	BB	SO	HR	GB%	BABIP	STUFF	WHIP	ERA	PERA	EqERA	EqH9	EqBB9	EqSO9	EqHR9	VORP	SN/WX
2005	ABE	A-	21	2	1	1	11	6	40	22	13	40	1	61.2%	.226	-1	0.88	1.58	4.93	3.93	6.3	6.0	4.2	1.0	6.4	—
2005	FRD	A+	21	0	0	0	3	3	14¹	10	7	19	0	63.6%	.303	13	1.19	3.15	5.01	4.97	8.5	6.4	7.1	0.7	0.9	—
2006	FRD	A+	22	4	4	0	14	14	81	81	19	77	7	46.4%	.336	-8	1.23	2.78	7.32	5.65	11.8	3.4	5.7	1.8	-0.4	—
2006	BOW	AA	22	6	5	0	14	14	84	78	31	85	5	46.8%	.327	7	1.30	3.43	5.71	5.19	10.1	4.5	6.1	0.9	3.5	—
2007	NOR	AAA	23	9	7	0	22	22	128	95	39	120	13	45.1%	.253	3	1.05	3.16	4.18	4.39	7.5	3.1	6.3	1.4	16.3	—
2007	BAL	MLB	23	1	3	0	7	7	32¹	42	28	28	4	34.6%	.392	3	2.16	7.80	8.96	8.04	11.8	7.2	7.5	1.1	-6.3	-0.34
2008	*BAL*	*MLB*	*24*	*6*	*9*	*0*	*34*	*22*	*123¹*	*130*	*63*	*95*	*16*	*42.4%*	*.303*	*4*	*1.56*	*5.04*	*4.89*	*4.85*	*9.0*	*4.2*	*6.4*	*1.2*	*7.8*	*1.60*

Breakout: 39% Improve: 71% Collapse: 13% Attrition: 30%　　　Comparables: Arthur Rhodes, Matt Perisho, Pete Falcone, Ed Yarnall

The real Garret Olson lies somewhere between the one who throttled Triple-A and the one who stunk in the majors. A polished college lefty, Olson has three good pitches but no devastating out pitch, which limits his upside. In Baltimore, he fell into the common trap of trying to be very fine, afraid to trust the approach and pitches that got him there in the first place. At worst, he should enter 2008 as the first starter-in-waiting at Norfolk, but he has nothing left to prove in the minors.

Hayden Penn

Bats: R　Throws: R　Height: 6' 3"　Weight: 200　Born: October 13, 1984　Age: 23

YEAR	TEAM	LVL	AGE	W	L	SV	G	GS	IP	H	BB	SO	HR	GB%	BABIP	STUFF	WHIP	ERA	PERA	EqERA	EqH9	EqBB9	EqSO9	EqHR9	VORP	SN/WX
2005	BOW	AA	20	7	6	0	20	19	110¹	101	37	120	11	47.8%	.326	6	1.25	3.84	6.32	6.20	10.4	4.4	6.5	1.5	-6.5	—
2005	BAL	MLB	20	3	2	0	8	8	38¹	46	21	18	6	44.6%	.303	-9	1.75	6.34	6.59	6.87	10.4	5.0	4.0	1.4	-5.4	0.12
2006	OTT	AAA	21	7	4	0	14	14	87	71	27	85	5	47.3%	.286	24	1.13	2.28	4.03	3.62	8.1	3.4	6.5	0.9	18.0	—
2006	BAL	MLB	21	0	4	0	6	6	19²	38	13	8	8	37.1%	.370	-69	2.59	15.08	20.73	18.86	15.0	5.1	3.4	3.0	-20.0	-0.89
2007	NOR	AAA	22	2	1	0	4	4	21	26	5	20	2	44.6%	.387	2	1.48	5.14	8.14	7.58	13.3	2.8	6.6	1.4	-4.2	—
2007	ORI	Rk	22	0	0	0	5	5	15	17	4	17	0	56.8%	.386	-15	1.40	2.40	8.42	7.11	14.9	5.7	5.0	0.7	-2.1	—
2008	*BAL*	*MLB*	*23*	*4*	*9*	*0*	*28*	*18*	*107²*	*136*	*53*	*63*	*18*	*48.0%*	*.324*	*-8*	*1.75*	*6.47*	*6.08*	*6.24*	*10.8*	*4.0*	*4.9*	*1.5*	*-10.2*	*-0.40*

Breakout: 64% Improve: 87% Collapse: 8% Attrition: 16%　　　Comparables: Rob Bell, Chris Ray, Scott Klingenbeck, Merkin Valdez

Penn used to be a highly regarded prospect, but after missing large chunks of 2006 (appendicitis) and 2007 (elbow surgery) he's back to be being an untested minor leaguer. He returned from the latter surgery to pitch at the very end of last season, then went on to the Arizona Fall League, where he looked predictably rusty. He's a true wild card for 2008.

Wilfrido Perez

Bats: L　Throws: L　Height: 6' 0"　Weight: 145　Born: August 12, 1984　Age: 23

YEAR	TEAM	LVL	AGE	W	L	SV	G	GS	IP	H	BB	SO	HR	GB%	BABIP	STUFF	WHIP	ERA	PERA	EqERA	EqH9	EqBB9	EqSO9	EqHR9	VORP	SN/WX
2005	BLU	Rk	20	3	4	0	12	12	58	54	27	75	4	46.0%	.347	-7	1.40	3.26	9.75	9.07	12.1	11.1	5.2	2.0	-17.2	—
2006	ABE	A-	21	1	1	0	7	5	24	23	12	31	1	55.0%	.379	-2	1.46	3.38	13.38	9.68	15.3	10.7	7.1	2.0	-8.0	—
2007	DEL	A	22	5	3	5	27	8	81	53	28	108	3	58.6%	.281	13	1.00	1.67	4.83	3.86	8.2	5.2	7.2	0.9	14.0	—
2008	*BAL*	*MLB*	*23*	*3*	*5*	*2*	*25*	*9*	*65*	*67*	*48*	*54*	*7*	*51.6%*	*.313*	*-1*	*1.77*	*5.30*	*5.34*	*5.16*	*8.9*	*6.1*	*6.9*	*0.9*	*1.9*	*0.50*

Breakout: 38% Improve: 51% Collapse: 27% Attrition: 15%　　　Comparables: Saul Rivera, Jonathan Sanchez, Adam Gardner, J. C. Romero

Perez has fought injuries throughout his career and may not have the durability to make it as a starter; he was used either from the pen or on tight pitch counts all year. He's a junker, with an excellent curve and changeup offsetting a below-average fastball. It's not clear that he'll be able to fool more advanced hitters as thoroughly as he manhandled the Sally League. Unlike the *Baseball Prospectus* Team of Experts, he definitely needs to put on some weight.

Chris Ray

| | | | | | | | | | | | | | | | Bats: R | | Throws: R | | Height: 6' 3" | | Weight: 215 | | Born: January 12, 1982 | | Age: 26 |

YEAR	TEAM	LVL	AGE	W	L	SV	G	GS	IP	H	BB	SO	HR	GB%	BABIP	STUFF	WHIP	ERA	PERA	EqERA	EqH9	EqBB9	EqSO9	EqHR9	VORP	SN/WX
2005	BOW	AA	23	1	2	18	31	0	37¹	17	7	40	3	51.2%	.179	4	0.64	0.97	3.23	2.36	5.0	2.6	6.3	1.0	12.3	—
2005	BAL	MLB	23	1	3	0	41	0	40²	34	18	43	5	34.8%	.276	16	1.28	2.65	3.69	3.07	7.2	4.0	9.0	1.1	10.9	-0.32
2006	BAL	MLB	24	4	4	33	61	0	66	45	27	51	10	37.2%	.203	0	1.09	2.73	2.85	2.41	5.2	3.3	6.4	1.2	22.7	4.25
2007	BAL	MLB	25	5	6	16	43	0	42²	35	18	44	5	45.2%	.275	11	1.24	4.43	3.54	4.01	7.0	3.4	8.4	1.1	6.2	-0.16
2008	BAL	MLB	26	3	4	17	51	0	56¹	49	22	53	6	42.6%	.276	13	1.25	3.52	3.34	3.42	7.4	3.3	7.9	0.9	14.9	1.70

Breakout: 18% Improve: 40% Collapse: 37% Attrition: 6%   Comparables: Bobby Howry, Danys Baez, Steve Bedrosian, Victor Zambrano

With nobody on, Ray's opponents collectively hit like career backup catcher Josh Paul; once a man reached base, though, they hit a lot like future Hall of Famer Jim Thome, with four times the walks and one-third the strikeouts. This was never a problem before. Things got really bad in July, when what was initially diagnosed and treated as a bone spur turned out to be a torn ulnar collateral ligament. He's slated to miss all of 2008 following Tommy John surgery, so consider his projection what the Orioles' pen will be missing this year.

Chorye Spoone

| | | | | | | | | | | | | | | | Bats: R | | Throws: R | | Height: 6' 1" | | Weight: 215 | | Born: September 16, 1985 | | Age: 22 |

YEAR	TEAM	LVL	AGE	W	L	SV	G	GS	IP	H	BB	SO	HR	GB%	BABIP	STUFF	WHIP	ERA	PERA	EqERA	EqH9	EqBB9	EqSO9	EqHR9	VORP	SN/WX
2005	BLU	Rk	19	2	5	0	15	3	24²	27	13	27	3	59.5%	.348	-34	1.62	8.02	13.50	15.63	13.7	12.3	3.8	3.3	-21.2	—
2006	DEL	A	20	7	9	0	26	25	129¹	118	80	90	5	59.4%	.285	-14	1.53	3.56	7.10	7.76	10.1	8.9	2.9	1.1	-27.3	—
2007	FRD	A+	21	10	9	0	26	25	152	108	67	133	8	66.9%	.250	3	1.15	3.26	4.80	5.26	7.4	5.7	4.7	1.1	5.3	—
2008	BAL	MLB	22	5	12	0	26	26	137¹	159	103	73	16	56.8%	.311	-11	1.91	6.42	6.10	6.32	9.9	6.2	4.4	1.0	-14.9	-0.50

Breakout: 14% Improve: 46% Collapse: 24% Attrition: 10%   Comparables: Adam Harben, Ben Hendrickson, Preston Larrison, Brandon Webb

His name is pronounced "Cory," it's just spelled creatively. A local product, Spoone is a projectable righty who started fulfilling that projection last year and was arguably the organization's most improved player. The improvement comes from refined control, mechanics, temperament, maturity . . . you name an aspect of his game the Orioles were concerned about prior to 2007, and Spoone got better at it last year. He throws four pitches and keeps them all down, generating plenty of grounders.

Jamie Walker

| | | | | | | | | | | | | | | | Bats: L | | Throws: L | | Height: 6' 2" | | Weight: 195 | | Born: July 1, 1971 | | Age: 37 |

YEAR	TEAM	LVL	AGE	W	L	SV	G	GS	IP	H	BB	SO	HR	GB%	BABIP	STUFF	WHIP	ERA	PERA	EqERA	EqH9	EqBB9	EqSO9	EqHR9	VORP	SN/WX
2005	DET	MLB	34	4	3	0	66	0	48²	49	13	30	5	43.6%	.282	-5	1.27	3.70	3.96	3.86	8.6	2.4	5.3	0.9	8.9	1.10
2006	DET	MLB	35	0	1	0	56	0	48	47	8	37	8	33.8%	.275	3	1.15	2.81	4.06	2.64	8.7	1.3	6.6	1.3	17.5	0.75
2007	BAL	MLB	36	3	2	7	81	0	61¹	57	17	41	6	34.8%	.273	0	1.21	3.23	3.35	3.16	7.6	2.2	5.5	0.9	14.7	1.71
2008	BAL	MLB	36	2	2	6	49	0	45¹	48	13	31	6	39.9%	.295	-4	1.34	3.97	4.01	3.81	9.1	2.3	5.7	1.1	8.4	0.80

Breakout: 14% Improve: 26% Collapse: 47% Attrition: 29%   Comparables: Joe Hoerner, Bob Patterson, Grant Jackson, Alan Embree

One of three men brought in to save the Oriole bullpen, Walker was the team's best reliever last year according to WXRL, but his 1.71 total was a mere 68th in the majors, giving the Orioles far and away the worst best reliever in baseball. Despite his three-year, $12-million contract, he was frequently used as a LOOGY, but his role expanded as his penmates fell like plague victims around him, and he wound up leading the AL with 81 appearances.

Jaret Wright

| | | | | | | | | | | | | | | | Bats: R | | Throws: R | | Height: 6' 2" | | Weight: 245 | | Born: December 29, 1975 | | Age: 32 |

YEAR	TEAM	LVL	AGE	W	L	SV	G	GS	IP	H	BB	SO	HR	GB%	BABIP	STUFF	WHIP	ERA	PERA	EqERA	EqH9	EqBB9	EqSO9	EqHR9	VORP	SN/WX
2005	NYA	MLB	29	5	5	0	13	13	63²	81	32	34	8	46.1%	.336	-15	1.77	6.08	6.77	7.14	11.0	4.4	4.7	1.0	-10.0	0.08
2006	NYA	MLB	30	11	7	0	30	27	140¹	157	57	84	10	39.6%	.319	7	1.52	4.49	4.83	4.77	10.0	3.5	5.2	0.6	18.1	3.48
2007	BAL	MLB	31	0	3	0	3	3	10¹	12	9	7	1	37.5%	.355	-5	2.03	6.99	7.79	9.64	11.6	7.7	5.8	1.0	-4.3	0.04
2008	BAL	MLB	32	3	4	0	21	7	57	65	28	39	7	43.9%	.315	-6	1.63	5.58	5.25	5.40	9.8	4.0	5.7	1.1	0.0	0.30

Breakout: 23% Improve: 45% Collapse: 28% Attrition: 36%   Comparables: Don Larsen, Pete Vuckovich, Don McMahon, Pat Rapp

Jaret Wright pitched three games—all losses—for the Orioles last year before succumbing to shoulder trouble. He did come back to pitch minor league rehab games in August, but as desperate as the Orioles were for pitchers in

September, they weren't that desperate. Still, at the low, low price of $3 million and reliever Chris Britton, Wright wasn't the worst Oriole acquisition of the last few years (see Kris Benson).

LINEOUTS

Hitters

PLAYER	TEAM	LVL	AGE	PA	R	2B	3B	HR	RBI	BB	SO	SB-CS	EqBRR	AVG/OBP/SLG	MLVr	EqAVG/EqOBP/EqSLG	EqA	VORP
C A. Castillo	NOR	AAA	37	240	24	6	0	3	24	32	34	0-0	-1.6	.271/.367/.345	.070	.257/.351/.335	.250	2.6
	BAL	MLB	37	36	5	2	0	1	3	3	10	0-0	-0.1	.161/.229/.323	-.398	.161/.229/.323	.196	-1.9
SS B. Fahey*	NOR	AAA	26	383	37	8	8	2	28	30	46	12-5	-0.9	.236/.301/.324	-.099	.225/.286/.326	.218	-9.5
	BAL	MLB	26	56	10	1	1	0	1	2	9	2-1	0.3	.167/.196/.222	-.605	.167/.196/.222	.127	-6.1
OF J. Fiorentino*	BOW	AA	24	496	68	18	4	15	65	44	89	8-4	1.3	.282/.346/.445	.121	.256/.315/.416	.253	7.8
C G. Molina	CHR	AAA	25	156	13	4	0	2	9	9	27	0-2	-1.6	.209/.265/.281	-.302	.204/.255/.289	.185	-10.0
	BOW	AA	25	80	5	4	0	0	6	3	10	0-0	-0.2	.364/.388/.416	.219	.312/.338/.364	.242	2.2
1B C. Vinyard	DEL	A	21	547	61	34	0	16	82	48	115	1-0	-2.3	.269/.340/.440	.119	.222/.278/.351	.221	-29.1

At 38, **Alberto Castillo** catches and hits as well as ever. The former's a good thing, not so much for the latter. ⊘ **Brandon Fahey** is overmatched in the majors, but at least the Orioles used him at shortstop last year instead of left field. ⊘ **Jeff Fiorentino** was once one of the Orioles' top prospects, but the organization has drafted better in the past few years, while Fiorentino hasn't shown any improvement, particularly against left-handed pitchers. He'd be decent in a platoon. ⊘ **Gus Molina** could be an acceptable catcher (barely) if he never had to face right-handed pitchers, but that's an awfully narrow niche, and narrow niches are always vulnerable to extinction. ⊘ **Chris Vinyard** has been a power threat in the low minors and, with the way he fields, he's going to have to slug his way to the majors.

Pitchers

PLAYER	TEAM	LVL	AGE	W	L	SV	IP	H	BB	SO	HR	GB%	BABIP	STUFF	WHIP	ERA	PERA	EqERA	EqH9	EqBB9	EqSO9	EqHR9	VORP
R. Bell	NOR	AAA	30	4	3	0	66²	61	17	59	5	47.2%	.296	8	1.17	2.97	4.43	4.34	9.0	2.7	5.7	1.1	9.0
	BAL	MLB	30	4	3	0	53	73	24	28	7	50.3%	.351	-25	1.83	5.94	6.87	6.04	11.6	3.5	4.4	1.2	-1.7
K. Benson '08	BAL	MLB	33	2	4	0	53	61	17	27	8	45.2%	.297	-11	1.48	5.24	4.90	5.07	9.9	2.7	4.2	1.3	2.5
R. Cherry	IOW	AAA	27	2	0	7	51	50	18	56	5	45.1%	.324	2	1.33	4.59	4.35	4.80	8.5	3.4	7.5	1.1	4.5
	CHN	MLB	27	1	1	0	15	13	6	13	1	30.4%	.273	8	1.27	3.00	3.31	3.45	7.5	2.9	6.9	0.6	3.9
	BAL	MLB	27	0	0	0	16¹	17	13	10	3	44.4%	.292	-17	1.84	7.73	6.50	7.02	8.6	6.5	4.9	1.6	-3.1
F. Deza	BOW	AA	24	7	8	0	124	131	43	101	22	47.5%	.292	-54	1.40	4.43	8.46	7.04	11.0	3.9	5.1	2.5	-18.4
J. Johnson	NOR	AAA	24	6	12	0	148	164	48	109	15	47.7%	.320	-17	1.43	4.07	6.45	6.16	10.9	3.3	4.7	1.4	-8.8
	BAL	MLB	24	0	0	0	2	3	2	1	0	62.5%	.429	-44	2.50	9.00	7.52	9.00	13.5	9.0	4.5	0.0	-0.7
V. Santos	CIN	MLB	30	1	4	0	49	51	23	44	10	46.3%	.313	-5	1.51	5.14	5.24	4.20	8.6	3.6	7.5	1.6	4.5
	BAL	MLB	30	0	2	0	14¹	20	10	4	5	35.8%	.326	-68	2.09	8.18	18.36	11.77	13.2	6.2	2.8	3.5	-3.2
P. Shuey	NOR	AAA	36	0	0	1	23	30	9	24	2	54.1%	.400	-18	1.70	4.70	8.34	7.48	13.3	4.2	7.1	1.2	-4.5
	BAL	MLB	36	0	1	1	25²	33	21	22	3	54.2%	.380	-10	2.10	9.81	8.11	9.72	11.5	6.8	7.2	1.1	-10.9
V. Zambrano	SYR	AAA	31	3	2	0	41¹	50	22	38	4	51.6%	.371	-9	1.74	7.41	8.49	8.92	12.0	5.4	6.1	1.4	-14.1
	TOR	MLB	31	0	2	0	10²	20	11	5	5	46.7%	.395	-73	2.91	10.93	26.91	17.42	17.4	8.7	4.4	4.4	-5.9
	IND	AAA	31	2	0	0	26²	17	9	25	1	47.1%	.242	14	0.97	2.70	3.09	3.91	6.0	3.6	6.4	0.7	4.8
	BAL	MLB	31	0	1	0	12¹	12	11	11	1	62.2%	.324	3	1.86	9.51	5.69	8.53	8.5	7.1	7.1	0.7	-4.6

Rob Bell pitched well in Triple-A Norfolk, but had the same old ring in the majors; he refused a minor league assignment after the season, preferring to find another Triple-A shuttle to ride. ⊘ The Orioles chose not to exercise their 2008 option on **Kris Benson** after he missed all of 2007 due to rotator cuff surgery, thus closing the book on the John Maine trade. There's no telling how effective Benson will be in his comeback until he actually pitches. ⊘ Picked up in the Steve Trachsel trade, **Rocky Cherry** provides a serviceable bullpen arm and a funky name. ⊘ **Fredy Deza** was a late add to the 40-man roster, as the O's feared that another team would try to nab him in the Rule 5 draft and turn him into a reliever, which is what most scouts project him to be given his fastball/slider combination. ⊘ **Jim Johnson** is the same pitcher he was three years ago; that made him one of the better pitchers in A-ball in 2005, but he was supposed to build on that, not stall. ⊘ **Victor Santos** was a piece of chewing gum (or was he bailing wire?) that the Orioles sent to the mound last September following his marginally respectable summer with the Reds. ⊘ **Paul Shuey** came out of retirement to join the Orioles last year. That was a bad idea, like storing nitroglycerin in a piñata. ⊘ **Victor Zambrano** was purchased from the Pirates organization in September as an alternative to calling someone down from the stands to pitch; the Shaky Lemonade Guy would have been cheaper and only marginally less effective.

MANAGER: DAVE TREMBLEY

YEAR	TEAM	W-L	Pythag +/–	Avg PC	100+ P	120+ P	QS	BQS	REL	REL w Zero R	IBB	Subs	PH	PH Avg	PH HR	SB2	CS2	SB3	CS3	SAC Att	SAC %	POS SAC	Squeeze	Swing	In Play
2007	BAL	40-53	2	94.0	43	1	38	3	279	149	29	24	62	.190	0	76	29	16	3	38	52.6%	19	2	83	63

Trembley took a most unusual route to being a major league manager, one which never included playing professional baseball. He started as a high school baseball coach, then managed a community college team, was recruited by the Cubs as a scout, then spent twenty years as a coach and minor league manager in the Cubs, Padres, Pirates, and Orioles organizations. The Orioles initially tabbed him to be their major league field coordinator for 2007, but he moved up to bullpen coach when Rick Dempsey returned to the broadcast booth, and then filled in as bench coach during Tom Trebelhorn's frequent absences to attend to his ailing wife. Both Dempsey and Trebelhorn were considered ahead of Trembley in the line to be Sam Perlozzo's successor, but ironically, while the bullpen may have helped cost Perlozzo his job, it was bullpen coach Trembley who wound up taking over the team. Trembley's a very old-school guy with a fetish for attention to detail and professionalism and a fondness for small ball. Given that the Orioles might wind up fielding little more than a glorified minor league team once their rebuilding process kicks in, those qualities along with his long minor league managerial track record just might make Trembley the ideal man for the job.

Boston Red Sox

Could you have seen this coming four years ago? Four years ago, the Red Sox were floundering. They'd just finished in second place for the fifth consecutive season. They'd just been through the Dan Duquette era, which began promisingly and amid great praise from analytical circles, only to end up marked mostly by questionable player-personnel decisions, rampant criticism of Duquette's management style, and perpetual on-field disappointment.

Duquette was let go after the 2001 season and replaced on an interim basis by vice president of baseball operations Mike Port, a veteran executive who ran the team through the 2002 campaign, the third consecutive one that ended without a postseason appearance by the Red Sox and the second straight in which they'd had one of the top two payrolls in the game. Despite having three of the most valuable players in the sport in left fielder Manny Ramirez, ace Pedro Martinez, and shortstop Nomar Garciaparra, the Red Sox seemed destined to remain a bridesmaid to the Yankees and a second-tier franchise in an increasingly bifurcated league.

On November 25, 2002, the Red Sox promoted 28-year-old assistant GM Theo Epstein to the general manager's job. Noted at the time mostly for his youth, Epstein was already a veteran of nearly a decade in major league front offices and had previous experience working with Red Sox President and CEO Larry Lucchino while both were with the San Diego Padres. Epstein quickly became a symbol of the vanguard of young executives raised in classrooms rather than on ballfields, who were as comfortable with performance analysis and financial projections as scouting reports. The Sox surrounded him with a bevy of veteran execs, including

---

RED SOX PROSPECTUS

2007 record: 96-66; First place AL East; Beat Rockies in World Series 4-0

Pythagenport record: 102-60

Runs scored per game: 5.35 (3rd in AL)

Runs allowed per game: 4.06 (1st in AL)

Team EqA: .270 (3rd in AL)

2007 Batters Age: 30.7 (5th oldest in AL)

2007 Pitchers Age: 31.9 (Oldest in AL)

Ballpark: Fenway Park; Hitter's park; Park Factor of 1.039

2007: Sox reverse the Curse of the Bellhorn, snap two-year title drought.

2008: First the Patriots, now the Red Sox, so when does the Bruins' dynasty begin?

Port, Lucchino, and Special Advisor Bill Lajoie, but it was Epstein, displaying a gravitas belying his age, who ran the show.

Upon taking the reins, Epstein said that he wanted to turn the Red Sox into "a scouting and player development machine." To say that he has succeeded in doing so would be an understatement. Boston's 2004 title, the one for which Epstein garnered so much praise, was won by a roster that was largely built upon players acquired by Duquette from outside the organization. Those champions were led by one of the highest-priced free agents ever in Ramirez and included another big-dollar Duquette player in center fielder Johnny Damon. Trade and waiver-pickup successes from that era including Martinez, catcher/captain Jason Varitek, and starters Derek Lowe and Tim Wakefield were among the very best players on the 2004 team. Right fielder Trot Nixon was the only Sox farm product to make a contribution during the World Series.

Epstein made his mark on that roster, of course, adding second baseman Mark Bellhorn and, most famously, a second ace in Curt Schilling in his first off-season of running the show himself. A year before, he'd been part of the front office that acquired first baseman Kevin Millar, third-sacker Bill Mueller, and DH David Ortiz as inexpensive free agents. The 2004 champions, however, were not his team so much as a co-production of his and Duquette's.

The current title-holders, though, are much more Epstein's team and, more importantly, feature drafted-and-developed Red Sox in a way the 2004 team didn't, a fact which makes David Chadd, the Sox' scouting director from 2002 to 2004, a key contributor to the creation of the 2007 world champions. Sure, certain stars from 2004 reprised their roles, with Ortiz, Ramirez, Varitek, Schilling, Wakefield, and reliever Mike Timlin each earning their second Red Sox rings. Around them, however, were the first products of the machine, the first signs that, after a fitful start—the Sox' 2003 draft left something to be desired as the team was a bit too college-centric and risk-averse—Epstein's vision was becoming a reality. Draftees Dustin Pedroia (2004, second base) and outfielder Jacoby Ellsbury (2005) were two of the team's best players in October. Supplemental first-round pick Clay Buchholz (2005) threw a no-hitter down the stretch. Duquette-era draftee Kevin Youkilis won the AL Gold Glove award at first base, made the All-Star team, and provided good offense. Closer Jonathan Papelbon, a 2003 selection, was devastating out of the bullpen, and fellow reliever Manny Delcarmen, a second-round pick under Duquette in 2000, had his best season.

That transition will continue in 2008. The Red Sox now sport one of the best farm systems in the industry and are beginning to transition away from the Manny Ramirez/Dan Duquette era to one in which more and more playing time will go to players they have always controlled. Ellsbury and Buchholz are assured of major roles this season. Jon Lester, a Duquette-era draftee in 2002 and winner of Game Four of the World Series, should be in the rotation. Shortstop prospect Jed Lowrie waits in the wings should incumbent Julio Lugo falter. Recent draftees Justin Masterson, a right-handed starter, center fielder Ryan Kalish, and first baseman Lars Anderson are among the game's better prospects.

Many of these names might be familiar because they were in the news throughout the offseason, bandied about as part of potential trade packages for the best pitcher in baseball, the Twins' Johan Santana. With Santana a free agent at the end of the 2008 season, the Twins have been open to the idea of dealing him, and the Red Sox were prominently featured in rumors throughout the fall. It's significant that the Red Sox didn't close on a Santana deal. They wouldn't have been trading for Santana in some abstract sense, for his stat lines or his Cy Young awards, but for one year of his services and the right to negotiate a contract extension for $150 million or more. Because of the success the Red Sox have had in drafting and developing their own talent, they had the chips to buy in to the Santana sweepstakes, but also the ability to bow out if the price was too high. Theo Epstein has built a system that reduces his need to overpay, in coin or in talent, for anything. It's one which allows the Red Sox to turn inward or outward for solutions and always have the leverage to make a good deal for themselves. It is the sweet spot for a baseball front office.

Player personnel is not the only area in which the Red Sox have set the pace for the league. Since John Henry bought the Red Sox in 2002, he has remade the way the team does business. Rather than press for a replacement for small, ancient Fenway Park, as previous owners had done, he set about squeezing as much revenue from the old park as possible. The Monster Seats, situated atop the park's famed left-field wall, were put in place for the 2003 season and became highly sought after. More seating was added in 2004, and with the sale of standing-room-only tickets, capacity in Fenway is now 13 percent greater than it was when Henry purchased the team. The Red Sox have the highest ticket prices in the sport, sell out every game (something nearly unheard of in baseball), and given the secondary market for Sox tickets, it's obvious that Henry isn't actually extracting the maximum revenue he could from the park. There's a plan to add another 1,400 seats in the near future, with a significant number of them premium seats, the golden goose of sports venues in the 21st century.

Henry has also tried to make the park a better experience beyond the stands, creating concourses with picnic tables and increasing the number and variety of concession stands. While there's only so much that can be done with the small wooden seats in much of the park, the experience once out of your seat is much like it is in one of the newer ballparks, the important difference being that you're at Fenway, a beautiful and historic ballpark that has been hosting major league games for nearly a century. Just as his general manager leverages his talent edge to make or not make deals, Henry leverages the best things about his ballpark to fill it game after game.

Like the Yankees, the Red Sox have a synergistic relationship with their primary broadcast outlet, the New England Sports Network, 80 percent of which is owned by the team. NESN has seen its ratings rise with the popularity of the Sox, and while the assignation of NESN revenues within the larger corporate entity isn't entirely transparent, it's clear that the Sox get some benefit from being a majority owner of their regional sports network. The Red Sox have also expanded their corporate reach, with the Fenway Sports Group adding a NASCAR team and a minor league franchise. That kind of diversification, common in large business but new in baseball, signifies the evolution of the Red Sox from family-owned quasi-public trust to modern conglomerate.

In their primary business of winning major league baseball games, the Sox are innovating throughout their organization. Their sweep of the Rockies in last year's World Series was credited in part to their advance scouting, which enabled them to be completely prepared for a foe they saw just once all year. As Tom Verducci wrote in the November 5 edition of *Sports Illustrated*:

"The Red Sox changed their approach this season to include two advance scouts, Todd Claus and Dana Levangie, who were assigned alternating opponents. Instead of faxing or e-mailing reports as some teams do, the Red Sox had Claus or Levangie deliver the report in person while the other scout watched the next opponent. The Red Sox also assign scouts to watch their own club to look for tendencies other teams might use against them."

The cost of dedicating scouts to such tasks over the course of a season is a rounding error in the context of running a major league team, perhaps $300,000 total in salaries, benefits, and travel expenses. In Baseball Prospectus's *Baseball Between the Numbers*, Nate Silver estimates the value of a win at about $750,000, but for a team such as the Red Sox, for whom each additional win could mean the difference between a playoff berth and an October at home on the couch, those marginal wins are worth closer to $4-5 million. Even if the value of the advance and self-scouting is just one win, they're getting a better than 13-to-1 return on their money. If the benefit is even a fraction of a win, it's worth doing.

Down in the trainer's room, the Sox are also investing on the front end in an effort to get results on the back end. They have had great success managing and maintaining their pitchers. With Mike Reinold, a physical therapist that the Red Sox hired away from famed sports surgeon Dr. James Andrews' Birmingham complex, the team has implemented a system which on the surface seems like common sense, but is nevertheless nearly singular in baseball. Using simple and inexpensive hands-on testing methods, the medical staff is able to set individual baselines for the strength, flexibility, and stamina of each of its pitchers. By monitoring the change in those areas relative to those baselines, the trainers are able to work closely with pitching coach John Farrell and manager Terry Francona to manage the pitchers' workloads. The result has not only been a decrease in pitching injuries, but an increase in effectiveness.

Everywhere you look, the Red Sox are finding small edges, putting new practices in place, and investing in their organization. Analysts were excited when Theo Epstein was hired as GM because they saw him as someone who understood the value of statistics in evaluating players and running a team, but Epstein brings more than just that to the table. Along with John Henry, himself open to new ideas, Epstein has applied thought to all areas of running a baseball team with an eye toward improving what can be improved and spending money where it will help, all with one goal in mind: winning championships. A bit more than four years since taking the job, he's won two. More than that, though, he's built the model organization in baseball and arguably in sports. No franchise combines on-field success, off-field processes, and profitability the way the Boston Red Sox do. This is what the start of a dynasty looks like. Could you have seen this coming four years ago?

HITTERS

Lars Anderson — 1B

Bats: L Throws: L Height: 6' 4" Weight: 215 Born: September 25, 1987 Age: 20

YEAR	TEAM	LVL	AGE	PA	R	2B	3B	HR	RBI	BB	SO	SB	CS	EqBRR	AVG	OBP	SLG	MLVr	EqAVG	EqOBP	EqSLG	EqA	VORP	DEFENSE	
2007	GRN	A	19	533	69	35	3	10	69	71	112	2	4	-2.7	.288	.385	.443	.149	.228	.310	.348	.231	-19.1	110-1B	8
2007	LNC	A+	19	47	13	2	0	1	9	11	9	0	0	0.2	.343	.489	.486	.304	.243	.383	.378	.273	1.2		
2008	BOS	MLB	20	630	63	38	3	8	62	61	164	4	4	0.0	.242	.317	.361	-.141	.235	.313	.369	.242	-14.5	147-1B	7

Breakout: 43% Improve: 69% Collapse: 11% Attrition: 7%   Comparables: Chris Weinke, Mike Darr, Mike Whitlock, Bronson Sardinha

Anderson showed extraordinary plate discipline in his first pro season; he's expected to hit for more power as he ages as well. So, while he's maxed out defensively at first base, he may well hit enough to be a monster there.

Chris Carter   1B

Bats: L   **Throws:** L   **Height:** 6' 0"   **Weight:** 210   **Born:** September 16, 1982   **Age:** 25

YEAR	TEAM	LVL	AGE	PA	R	2B	3B	HR	RBI	BB	SO	SB	CS	EqBRR	AVG	OBP	SLG	MLVr	EqAVG	EqOBP	EqSLG	EqA	VORP	DEFENSE			
2005	LNC	A+	22	470	71	26	2	21	85	46	66	0	0	0.4	.296	.370	.522	.071	.222	.287	.370	.228	-18.0	67-1B	-9	23-LF	-4
2005	TEN	AA	22	151	21	4	0	10	30	19	11	0	3	-0.9	.297	.397	.563	.323	.288	.371	.523	.295	11.4	22-1B	-1		
2006	TUC	AAA	23	588	87	30	3	19	97	78	69	10	4	-6.3	.301	.395	.483	.185	.264	.354	.428	.272	13.3	118-1B	-19		
2007	TUC	AAA	24	561	74	39	3	18	84	50	68	2	0	-7.1	.324	.383	.521	.214	.283	.343	.455	.276	18.0	82-1B	-18	20-LF	-1
2007	PAW	AAA	24	52	6	1	0	1	4	4	7	0	0	-0.2	.234	.308	.319	-.169	.213	.288	.298	.206	-3.5	12-1B	2		
2008	BOS	MLB	25	557	59	31	1	11	71	48	87	3	2	-1.0	.259	.325	.394	-.072	.252	.322	.402	.256	-2.8	131-1B	-9		

Breakout: 13% **Improve:** 37% **Collapse:** 33% **Attrition:** 22%   **Comparables:** Dan Johnson, J. T. Snow, Steve Cox, Jamie Dismuke

Not to be confused with the first-base prospect of the same name who was traded from the White Sox to the Diamondbacks and then to the A's in the Dan Haren deal in December, this Chris Carter was traded from the Diamondbacks to the Nationals and then to the Red Sox in the Wily Mo Peña deal in August. Got that? To make it simpler, this is the older, less talented, left-handed Chris Carter. Scouts don't like anything about him, he doesn't have the home-run power he'll need to impress, and after escaping the Diamondbacks' hitter factory, he's found himself in an even worse situation with the Red Sox. So, he's waiting it out until minor league free agency comes after the 2009 season. He'd be the Twins' fourth-best hitter, and he could bat third for the Giants.

Alex Cora   2B/SS

Bats: L   **Throws:** R   **Height:** 6' 0"   **Weight:** 200   **Born:** October 18, 1975   **Age:** 32

YEAR	TEAM	LVL	AGE	PA	R	2B	3B	HR	RBI	BB	SO	SB	CS	EqBRR	AVG	OBP	SLG	MLVr	EqAVG	EqOBP	EqSLG	EqA	VORP	DEFENSE			
2005	CLE	MLB	29	157	11	5	2	1	8	5	18	6	0	2.0	.205	.250	.288	-.359	.215	.265	.299	.209	-5.8	22-SS	5	13-2B	4
2005	BOS	MLB	29	116	14	3	2	2	16	6	12	1	2	-0.3	.269	.310	.394	-.083	.275	.327	.402	.252	0.3	24-2B	-3		
2006	BOS	MLB	30	264	31	7	2	1	18	19	29	6	2	0.6	.238	.312	.298	-.272	.236	.315	.296	.224	-5.4	49-SS	8	11-2B	-4
2007	BOS	MLB	31	232	30	10	5	3	18	7	23	1	1	0.2	.246	.298	.386	-.143	.246	.298	.401	.242	-0.6	34-2B	2	23-SS	1
2008	BOS	MLB	32	181	17	7	2	1	16	9	20	2	1	0.3	.245	.291	.331	-.223	.238	.288	.338	.223	-2.8	46-2B	1		

Breakout: 20% **Improve:** 40% **Collapse:** 40% **Attrition:** 42%   **Comparables:** Rob Wilfong, John McDonald, Jeff Huson, Jose Vizcaino

His older brother, Joey, was the better player, a regular second baseman with a career .348 OBP. Alex is likely to play a lot longer, though, because he's a true middle infielder who can play both second and short. Joey was done once he wasn't a regular any longer (which happened abruptly at 34) because you can't carry a utility infielder who can't handle any position but second. Alex has that in his favor, plus better speed than his stolen base numbers indicate, and a decent lefty bat for a fifth infielder. He'll be around for a while.

Coco Crisp   CF

Bats: S   **Throws:** R   **Height:** 6' 0"   **Weight:** 180   **Born:** November 1, 1979   **Age:** 28

YEAR	TEAM	LVL	AGE	PA	R	2B	3B	HR	RBI	BB	SO	SB	CS	EqBRR	AVG	OBP	SLG	MLVr	EqAVG	EqOBP	EqSLG	EqA	VORP	DEFENSE	
2005	CLE	MLB	25	656	86	42	4	16	69	44	81	15	6	2.4	.300	.345	.465	.128	.310	.364	.493	.291	31.6	134-LF	15
2006	BOS	MLB	26	452	58	22	2	8	36	31	67	22	4	3.3	.264	.317	.385	-.125	.260	.321	.385	.253	7.5	101-CF	-1
2007	BOS	MLB	27	591	85	28	7	6	60	50	84	28	6	7.9	.268	.330	.382	-.075	.267	.335	.393	.261	11.9	137-CF	29
2008	BOS	MLB	28	549	73	29	4	8	53	44	78	19	5	1.9	.278	.338	.407	-.019	.271	.335	.416	.269	10.0	129-CF	10

Breakout: 17% **Improve:** 50% **Collapse:** 16% **Attrition:** 10%   **Comparables:** Brian McRae, Dave Philley, Randy Winn, Tony Scott

Crisp's glovework in center field last year was astounding, a defensive performance that wouldn't have looked out of line in Andruw Jones' peak. That league-leading ERA the Sox pitchers posted had everything to do with the team's league-best defense, which was anchored by Crisp. It's assumed that he'll be elsewhere by the time you read this, but the Sox could keep him around as a fourth outfielder to cover for the 50 games Drew and Ramirez will miss and as a defensive replacement for Manny.

J. D. Drew — RF

Bats: L Throws: R Height: 6' 1" Weight: 200 Born: November 20, 1975 Age: 32

YEAR	TEAM	LVL	AGE	PA	R	2B	3B	HR	RBI	BB	SO	SB	CS	EqBRR	AVG	OBP	SLG	MLVr	EqAVG	EqOBP	EqSLG	EqA	VORP	DEFENSE			
2005	LAN	MLB	29	311	48	12	1	15	36	51	50	1	1	-1.6	.286	.412	.520	.302	.286	.410	.528	.319	26.9	43-RF	1	27-CF	0
2006	LAN	MLB	30	594	84	34	6	20	100	89	106	2	3	1.1	.283	.393	.498	.210	.280	.392	.492	.302	34.9	125-RF	16		
2007	BOS	MLB	31	552	84	30	4	11	64	79	100	4	2	0.1	.270	.373	.423	.058	.263	.375	.433	.284	15.1	120-RF	-8		
2008	BOS	MLB	32	485	65	26	2	11	60	65	87	4	2	0.1	.267	.367	.421	.041	.260	.364	.430	.282	8.7	115-RF	0		

Breakout: 5% Improve: 25% Collapse: 32% Attrition: 15%   Comparables: Charlie Maxwell, Gene Woodling, Von Hayes, Dwayne Murphy

The value of drawing walks is that, even when you don't do much else at the plate, just not making outs means that you won't be that big a drag on the offense. Drew's .373 on-base percentage kept the line moving last year. Cut him some slack; he spent much of the summer worried about his year-old son, who required surgery on both his collarbone and hip in July. Drew is a strong bounceback candidate.

Jacoby Ellsbury — CF

Bats: L Throws: L Height: 6' 1" Weight: 185 Born: September 11, 1983 Age: 24

YEAR	TEAM	LVL	AGE	PA	R	2B	3B	HR	RBI	BB	SO	SB	CS	EqBRR	AVG	OBP	SLG	MLVr	EqAVG	EqOBP	EqSLG	EqA	VORP	DEFENSE			
2005	LOW	A-	21	165	28	3	5	1	19	24	20	23	3	2.2	.317	.418	.432	.256	.245	.321	.340	.249	-3.8	26-CF	-2		
2006	WIL	A+	22	281	35	7	5	4	32	25	28	25	9	1.9	.299	.379	.418	.159	.263	.323	.369	.245	0.8	58-CF	4		
2006	PME	AA	22	225	29	10	3	3	19	24	25	16	8	-1.7	.308	.387	.434	.199	.284	.356	.408	.267	9.2	47-CF	6		
2007	PME	AA	23	83	16	10	2	0	13	6	7	8	1	1.8	.452	.518	.644	.782	.360	.422	.533	.330	11.1	18-CF	3		
2007	PAW	AAA	23	401	66	14	5	2	28	32	47	33	6	4.3	.298	.360	.380	.036	.270	.332	.358	.253	1.9	66-CF	-10	12-LF	-1
2007	BOS	MLB	23	127	20	7	1	3	18	8	15	9	0	1.5	.353	.394	.509	.285	.348	.394	.530	.322	13.6	16-LF	0	12-CF	3
2008	BOS	MLB	24	590	86	29	7	5	52	45	78	32	9	2.5	.287	.346	.395	-.014	.279	.343	.404	.271	11.1	138-CF	2		

Breakout: 32% Improve: 53% Collapse: 15% Attrition: 15%   Comparables: Gene Richards, Johnny Damon, Richie Ashburn, Vince Coleman

Ellsbury is one of the fastest players in baseball, and that speed enables him to outrun the misreads he makes in center field. He will also be good for 20 to 30 infield hits a year. Along with a lefty stroke designed for his new home park, that makes him a threat to win a batting title right out of the gate. He doesn't have much power, and his rawness in center will lead to some embarrassing moments, but he's still the Rookie of the Year favorite.

Eric Hinske — 4C

Bats: L Throws: R Height: 6' 2" Weight: 235 Born: August 5, 1977 Age: 30

YEAR	TEAM	LVL	AGE	PA	R	2B	3B	HR	RBI	BB	SO	SB	CS	EqBRR	AVG	OBP	SLG	MLVr	EqAVG	EqOBP	EqSLG	EqA	VORP	DEFENSE			
2005	TOR	MLB	27	537	79	31	2	15	68	46	121	8	4	1.3	.262	.333	.430	.000	.262	.342	.440	.271	8.9	96-1B	-1		
2006	TOR	MLB	28	224	35	9	2	12	29	27	49	1	1	-1.1	.264	.353	.513	.109	.258	.357	.521	.293	10.4	24-RF	0		
2006	BOS	MLB	28	88	8	8	0	1	5	8	30	1	1	1.3	.288	.352	.425	.018	.278	.352	.443	.272	1.6				
2007	BOS	MLB	29	218	25	12	3	6	21	28	54	3	0	-0.2	.204	.317	.398	-.125	.201	.321	.408	.257	-1.5	31-1B	3	11-LF	0
2008	BOS	MLB	30	183	22	10	1	5	23	20	44	3	1	0.1	.246	.334	.415	-.039	.239	.330	.424	.267	2.2	47-1B	0		

Breakout: 18% Improve: 40% Collapse: 43% Attrition: 42%   Comparables: Mark Johnson, Greg Walker, Kevin Maas, Bob Hamelin

Hinske hit .279/.365/.481 in his 2002 Rookie of the Year campaign. In the five years that followed, all covered by a $14.75 million contract, he surpassed exactly one of those marks, slugging .487 in part-time play in 2006. Hinske would fit better in a world in which teams carried 15 position players rather than 13, because he has bench value as a lefty bat who can play the four corners.

Bobby Kielty — OF

Bats: S Throws: R Height: 6' 1" Weight: 225 Born: August 5, 1976 Age: 31

YEAR	TEAM	LVL	AGE	PA	R	2B	3B	HR	RBI	BB	SO	SB	CS	EqBRR	AVG	OBP	SLG	MLVr	EqAVG	EqOBP	EqSLG	EqA	VORP	DEFENSE			
2005	OAK	MLB	28	433	55	20	0	10	57	50	67	3	2	1.0	.263	.350	.395	-.004	.267	.364	.415	.273	6.9	51-LF	4	36-RF	-1
2006	OAK	MLB	29	297	35	20	1	8	36	22	49	2	0	0.2	.270	.329	.441	-.011	.273	.339	.449	.272	5.4	38-LF	2	29-RF	-1
2007	OAK	MLB	30	40	4	1	0	0	3	3	9	0	0	-0.1	.200	.275	.229	-.416	.200	.275	.229	.183	-3.2				
2007	BOS	MLB	30	61	6	2	0	1	9	5	17	0	0	-0.1	.231	.295	.327	-.246	.231	.306	.327	.235	-2.5				
2008	BOS	MLB	31	159	18	9	0	4	19	15	33	1	0	-0.2	.260	.335	.410	-.034	.253	.331	.419	.265	2.5	41-LF	0		

Breakout: 28% Improve: 51% Collapse: 33% Attrition: 49%   Comparables: Mark Whiten, Marty Cordova, Jack Daugherty, Steve Kemp

Kielty has become a switch-hitter in name only, with career splits of .228/.329/.348 from the left side and .296/.379/.503 from the right, and even those lefty marks are inflated by one good season back in 2002. As a very good extra outfielder who plays the corners well, is okay in center, and socks southpaws, he's a bargain for whoever signs him.

Che-Hsuan Lin   **OF**   Bats: R   Throws: R   Height: 6' 0"   Weight: 180   Born: September 21, 1988   Age: 19

YEAR	TEAM	LVL	AGE	PA	R	2B	3B	HR	RBI	BB	SO	SB	CS	EqBRR	AVG	OBP	SLG	MLVr	EqAVG	EqOBP	EqSLG	EqA	VORP	DEFENSE	
2007	LOW	A-	18	50	7	2	0	0	3	5	10	3	2	-0.9	.163	.265	.209	-.319	.156	.224	.200	.153	-11.8	11-CF	3
2007	RSX	Rk	18	200	33	10	6	4	22	17	42	14	3	0.6	.263	.330	.457	.135	.202	.250	.339	.213	-29.6	28-CF -5	14-RF -2
2008	BOS	MLB	19	472	42	28	4	5	36	28	118	17	9	0.9	.213	.263	.333	-.288	.207	.260	.341	.214	-21.3	112-CF	-1

Breakout: 56% Improve: 80% Collapse: 12% Attrition: 8%   *Comparables: Richard Peña, Javier Herrera, LaRue Baber, Joe Benson*

Loosely comparable to Ellsbury, the toolsy Lin signed with the Red Sox last spring for $400,000. A very raw talent, he's a long way from contributing, but signing the best player in Taiwan is another way in which the Red Sox have leveraged their revenue to improve the team.

Mike Lowell   **3B**   Bats: R   Throws: R   Height: 6' 3"   Weight: 210   Born: February 24, 1974   Age: 34

YEAR	TEAM	LVL	AGE	PA	R	2B	3B	HR	RBI	BB	SO	SB	CS	EqBRR	AVG	OBP	SLG	MLVr	EqAVG	EqOBP	EqSLG	EqA	VORP	DEFENSE
2005	FLO	MLB	31	558	56	36	1	8	58	46	58	4	0	-3.0	.236	.298	.360	-.126	.239	.303	.372	.241	-5.1	127-3B 16
2006	BOS	MLB	32	631	79	47	1	20	80	47	61	2	2	-1.3	.284	.339	.475	.058	.279	.342	.479	.279	20.7	146-3B 21
2007	BOS	MLB	33	653	79	37	2	21	120	53	71	3	2	-6.2	.324	.378	.501	.223	.320	.380	.515	.303	46.5	149-3B 15
2008	BOS	MLB	34	570	66	35	1	14	79	46	64	4	2	-1.4	.285	.345	.437	.039	.278	.341	.447	.276	16.9	134-3B 8

Breakout: 6% Improve: 35% Collapse: 26% Attrition: 11%   *Comparables: Brooks Robinson, Keith Moreland, Ray Boone, Cal Ripken*

In the same way that Adrian Beltre's 2004 season stands out to the good, Lowell's 2005 season stands out to the bad. The Red Sox were forced to take on his contract following that dud as part of the Beckett deal, but they've now volunteered to pay him $37.5 million over the next three seasons. The price is right in this market, and they're protected against a decline by the brevity of the deal (Lowell had wanted a fourth year, but ultimately agreed to return for three). This year, look for his average to return to .280 and everything else to stay about the same.

Jed Lowrie   **SS**   Bats: S   Throws: R   Height: 6' 0"   Weight: 180   Born: April 17, 1984   Age: 24

YEAR	TEAM	LVL	AGE	PA	R	2B	3B	HR	RBI	BB	SO	SB	CS	EqBRR	AVG	OBP	SLG	MLVr	EqAVG	EqOBP	EqSLG	EqA	VORP	DEFENSE	
2005	LOW	A-	21	240	36	12	0	4	32	34	30	7	5	1.5	.328	.429	.448	.301	.254	.331	.343	.237	4.7	40-SS -3	11-2B 0
2006	WIL	A+	22	438	43	21	6	3	50	54	65	2	2	-1.6	.262	.352	.374	.032	.227	.302	.328	.224	-6.7	88-SS -10	
2007	PME	AA	23	408	61	31	7	8	49	65	58	5	3	2.1	.297	.410	.501	.272	.266	.371	.460	.286	31.3	84-SS -7	
2007	PAW	AAA	23	177	21	16	1	5	21	12	33	0	1	-2.1	.300	.356	.506	.200	.280	.333	.497	.277	13.3	31-SS 8	
2008	BOS	MLB	24	604	70	38	3	11	68	60	114	6	3	0.5	.259	.335	.407	-.038	.252	.332	.416	.265	15.4	141-SS -4	

Breakout: 24% Improve: 61% Collapse: 10% Attrition: 9%   *Comparables: Felipe Crespo, Mike Rouse, Kurt Stillwell, Russ Johnson*

Lowrie is a rarity, a college second baseman who has become a professional shortstop. Just what kind of shortstop is a matter of debate, however, as there is a range of opinions about his defense. The Sox have no room for him at the moment. Given the big drop in his strikeout-to-walk ratio with Pawtucket, that may be for the best.

Julio Lugo   **SS**   Bats: R   Throws: R   Height: 6' 1"   Weight: 175   Born: November 16, 1975   Age: 32

YEAR	TEAM	LVL	AGE	PA	R	2B	3B	HR	RBI	BB	SO	SB	CS	EqBRR	AVG	OBP	SLG	MLVr	EqAVG	EqOBP	EqSLG	EqA	VORP	DEFENSE	
2005	TBA	MLB	29	690	89	36	6	6	57	61	72	39	11	5.1	.295	.362	.403	.059	.310	.385	.432	.290	42.5	153-SS 10	
2006	TBA	MLB	30	322	53	17	1	12	27	27	47	18	4	2.0	.308	.373	.498	.184	.311	.382	.521	.306	31.3	71-SS 0	
2006	LAN	MLB	30	164	16	5	1	0	10	12	29	6	5	-1.5	.219	.278	.267	-.348	.226	.288	.274	.203	-10.3	18-2B 2	13-3B 1
2007	BOS	MLB	31	630	71	36	2	8	73	48	82	33	6	1.6	.237	.294	.349	-.208	.235	.299	.361	.240	-1.3	138-SS -12	
2008	BOS	MLB	32	501	65	27	3	6	46	41	66	21	7	1.2	.275	.337	.384	-.053	.267	.333	.393	.263	12.5	118-SS -2	

Breakout: 24% Improve: 45% Collapse: 25% Attrition: 17%   *Comparables: Rich Amaral, Tony Graffanino, Mark Belanger, Dave Concepcion*

Lugo had a massive home/road split in 2007 that was almost entirely contained in his batting average (.286 home, .190 away). That could reflect an attempt by Lugo to tailor his swing to Fenway that failed to help that much at home (he only slugged .395 in Boston) and completely screwed him up everywhere else. His overall falloff last year was also all in batting average, so he should bounce back—which he pretty much did in the second half (.280/.322/.406) anyway.

Doug Mirabelli   C   Bats: R   Throws: R   Height: 6' 1"   Weight: 220   Born: October 18, 1970   Age: 37

YEAR	TEAM	LVL	AGE	PA	R	2B	3B	HR	RBI	BB	SO	SB	CS	EqBRR	AVG	OBP	SLG	MLVr	EqAVG	EqOBP	EqSLG	EqA	VORP	DEFENSE
2005	BOS	MLB	34	152	16	7	0	6	18	14	48	2	0	0.4	.228	.309	.412	-.092	.231	.322	.425	.260	3.0	35-C 1
2006	SDN	MLB	35	26	1	1	0	0	0	4	5	0	0	0.0	.182	.308	.227	-.327	.182	.308	.227	.197	-1.2	
2006	BOS	MLB	35	176	12	6	0	6	25	11	54	0	0	-1.8	.193	.261	.342	-.339	.188	.266	.344	.210	-7.6	45-C -5
2007	BOS	MLB	36	127	9	3	0	5	16	11	41	0	0	-2.0	.202	.278	.360	-.247	.204	.286	.381	.230	-2.2	33-C -2
2008	BOS	MLB	37	87	7	4	0	2	10	8	26	0	0	-0.4	.214	.294	.354	-.206	.208	.291	.362	.231	-1.3	25-C -2

Breakout: 32% Improve: 51% Collapse: 28% Attrition: 38%   Comparables: Lance Parrish, Jim Hegan, Kelly Stinnett, Buck Martinez

Varitek can't catch the knuckleball, but as long as the Sox employ Tim Wakefield, they need someone who can. Still, it doesn't have to be Mirabelli, who strikes out in a third of his at-bats these days. Popular is nice; runs are better.

Brandon Moss   OF   Bats: L   Throws: R   Height: 6' 0"   Weight: 205   Born: September 16, 1983   Age: 24

YEAR	TEAM	LVL	AGE	PA	R	2B	3B	HR	RBI	BB	SO	SB	CS	EqBRR	AVG	OBP	SLG	MLVr	EqAVG	EqOBP	EqSLG	EqA	VORP	DEFENSE	
2005	PME	AA	21	568	87	31	4	16	61	53	129	6	3	2.0	.268	.337	.441	.074	.236	.303	.388	.240	-15.8	126-RF -4	
2006	PME	AA	22	573	76	36	3	12	83	56	108	8	5	-2.0	.285	.357	.439	.145	.262	.330	.416	.259	1.1	128-RF -13	
2007	PAW	AAA	23	559	66	41	2	16	78	61	148	3	5	-1.5	.282	.363	.471	.147	.245	.326	.437	.260	2.3	99-RF 1	12-CF 1
2007	BOS	MLB	23	29	6	2	1	0	1	4	6	0	0	0.5	.280	.379	.440	.101	.280	.379	.440	.286	1.1		
2008	BOS	MLB	24	577	61	35	3	14	72	53	148	5	3	0.4	.246	.317	.402	-.083	.239	.314	.411	.255	-6.2	135-RF -2	

Breakout: 16% Improve: 48% Collapse: 20% Attrition: 8%   Comparables: Bobby Higginson, Doug Deeds, Eric Gillespie, Mike O'Keefe

Moss is in the wrong organization; there are other teams that could get some value from his skills as a fourth outfielder. Moss' power never developed, he doesn't make enough contact to hit .300 in the majors, and he's not so good with the glove you'd carry him for it.

David Ortiz   DH   Bats: L   Throws: L   Height: 6' 4"   Weight: 230   Born: November 18, 1975   Age: 32

YEAR	TEAM	LVL	AGE	PA	R	2B	3B	HR	RBI	BB	SO	SB	CS	EqBRR	AVG	OBP	SLG	MLVr	EqAVG	EqOBP	EqSLG	EqA	VORP	DEFENSE
2005	BOS	MLB	29	713	119	40	1	47	148	102	124	1	0	-6.3	.300	.397	.604	.365	.298	.405	.614	.334	75.8	
2006	BOS	MLB	30	686	115	29	2	54	137	119	117	1	0	-1.8	.287	.413	.636	.400	.275	.411	.627	.337	76.8	
2007	BOS	MLB	31	667	116	52	1	35	117	111	103	3	1	-2.5	.332	.445	.621	.495	.323	.445	.627	.353	86.2	
2008	BOS	MLB	32	681	109	38	1	35	119	111	120	6	1	-1.8	.282	.402	.541	.259	.275	.398	.553	.323	51.3	159-DH

Breakout: 2% Improve: 18% Collapse: 32% Attrition: 4%   Comparables: Willie McCovey, Jason Giambi, Ted Williams, Jim Thome

It was the best year of his career, and no one noticed. Ortiz didn't have 52 homers, or 148 RBI, or 22 memorable late-inning hits. He just went out and raked, setting career highs in batting average, OBP, WARP, hits, and doubles. The knee problems he played through are a major concern for a player who carries a lot of weight, but with maybe two more good years, he becomes a very interesting Hall of Fame case based on peak, postseason, and soft factors (such as his reputation for clutch hits and his contribution to the Red Sox' dramatic 2004 World Championship).

Dustin Pedroia   2B   Bats: R   Throws: R   Height: 5' 9"   Weight: 180   Born: August 17, 1983   Age: 24

YEAR	TEAM	LVL	AGE	PA	R	2B	3B	HR	RBI	BB	SO	SB	CS	EqBRR	AVG	OBP	SLG	MLVr	EqAVG	EqOBP	EqSLG	EqA	VORP	DEFENSE	
2005	PME	AA	21	298	39	19	2	8	40	34	26	7	3	-2.0	.324	.409	.508	.312	.287	.367	.448	.283	20.2	56-2B 1	
2005	PAW	AAA	21	240	39	9	1	5	24	24	17	1	0	0.1	.255	.356	.382	-.033	.260	.350	.385	.261	6.6	38-2B 4	
2006	PAW	AAA	22	493	55	30	3	5	50	48	27	1	4	-6.7	.305	.384	.426	.162	.282	.358	.417	.269	27.7	74-SS 6	32-2B 4
2006	BOS	MLB	22	98	5	4	0	2	7	7	7	0	1	-2.7	.191	.258	.303	-.396	.182	.258	.284	.184	-5.5	19-2B 2	
2007	BOS	MLB	23	581	86	39	1	8	50	47	42	7	1	0.3	.317	.380	.442	.137	.316	.384	.457	.293	35.9	129-2B 3	
2008	BOS	MLB	24	616	81	39	2	10	70	53	50	7	3	-0.3	.295	.361	.430	.063	.287	.357	.439	.282	26.2	144-2B 2	

Breakout: 21% Improve: 58% Collapse: 11% Attrition: 7%   Comparables: Ron Belliard, Cass Michaels, Rich Rollins, Aaron Hill

Pedroia's Rookie of the Year season almost never was. After a .182/.308/.236 April, he was losing playing time to Alex Cora as May began. On a road trip to Minnesota and Toronto, he went 9-for-14, saving his job, and by June he was established as a regular hitting in one of the top two lineup spots. He should have more walks and thus a higher OBP in him, but could lose some power, most of which is a Fenway effect (.151 ISO at home, .098 on the road).

Manny Ramirez   **LF**   Bats: R   Throws: R   Height: 6' 0"   Weight: 200   Born: May 30, 1972   Age: 36

YEAR	TEAM	LVL	AGE	PA	R	2B	3B	HR	RBI	BB	SO	SB	CS	EqBRR	AVG	OBP	SLG	MLVr	EqAVG	EqOBP	EqSLG	EqA	VORP	DEFENSE
2005	BOS	MLB	33	650	112	30	1	45	144	80	119	1	0	-0.8	.292	.388	.594	.331	.292	.396	.609	.329	59.7	139-LF -19
2006	BOS	MLB	34	558	79	27	1	35	102	100	102	0	1	-2.6	.321	.439	.619	.456	.308	.436	.611	.346	66.1	116-LF -20
2007	BOS	MLB	35	569	84	33	1	20	88	71	92	0	0	-2.2	.296	.388	.493	.200	.289	.388	.496	.304	34.6	112-LF -13
2008	BOS	MLB	36	537	72	29	1	21	84	72	96	1	1	-1.8	.281	.381	.486	.156	.273	.377	.497	.302	23.3	126-LF -14

Breakout: 4% Improve: 15% Collapse: 38% Attrition: 14%   Comparables: Sid Gordon, Frank Robinson, Sammy Sosa, Roy Sievers

So much attention is paid to the silly things Ramirez does that it's hard both to keep them in context and to properly identify the ones that actually hurt the team. In the postseason, he made some very smart plays on the bases, then got thrown out at home because he was too busy playing with his helmet while running. What's fundamental is that he is in decline and, given his negative defensive value, could have a limited amount of time left in his Hall of Fame career.

Oscar Tejeda   **SS**   Bats: R   Throws: R   Height: 6' 1"   Weight: 177   Born: December 12, 1989   Age: 18

YEAR	TEAM	LVL	AGE	PA	R	2B	3B	HR	RBI	BB	SO	SB	CS	EqBRR	AVG	OBP	SLG	MLVr	EqAVG	EqOBP	EqSLG	EqA	VORP	DEFENSE
2007	LOW	A-	17	101	14	5	2	0	12	6	26	4	1	0.2	.298	.347	.394	.116	.208	.240	.281	.176	-13.2	19-SS -5
2007	RSX	Rk	17	193	23	13	1	1	21	15	27	6	2	0.8	.295	.344	.399	.102	.229	.266	.318	.205	-18.9	43-SS -4
2008	BOS	MLB	18	491	37	28	2	3	39	22	101	9	5	0.3	.229	.264	.317	-.298	.223	.261	.324	.206	-16.4	116-SS -11

Breakout: 61% Improve: 68% Collapse: 16% Attrition: 11%   Comparables: Eddy Martinez, Mitch Root, Jorge Cantu, Billy Schmitt

The Red Sox compete with the Yankees to acquire the best talent not only through trades and free agency, but in the international talent market as well. This Dominican shortstop was one of Boston's big finds in 2006. In his pro debut last year, he looked to be worth the half-million or so he got to sign. Scouts adore his tools, both offensively and defensively, and his numbers are pretty good as well considering that when he got to the New York-Penn League he was the youngest player in team history. Tons of upside, but tons of development still to go.

Jason Varitek   **C**   Bats: S   Throws: R   Height: 6' 2"   Weight: 230   Born: April 11, 1972   Age: 36

YEAR	TEAM	LVL	AGE	PA	R	2B	3B	HR	RBI	BB	SO	SB	CS	EqBRR	AVG	OBP	SLG	MLVr	EqAVG	EqOBP	EqSLG	EqA	VORP	DEFENSE
2005	BOS	MLB	33	539	70	30	1	22	70	62	117	2	0	-2.4	.281	.366	.489	.149	.281	.377	.502	.300	39.6	124-C 1
2006	BOS	MLB	34	416	46	19	2	12	55	46	87	1	2	-2.0	.238	.325	.400	-.109	.231	.328	.397	.252	2.8	92-C 0
2007	BOS	MLB	35	518	57	15	3	17	68	71	122	1	2	-3.4	.255	.367	.421	.033	.248	.367	.432	.278	23.4	120-C 8
2008	BOS	MLB	36	384	45	17	1	11	49	47	86	2	1	-1.0	.255	.352	.420	.004	.248	.348	.429	.274	13.1	92-C -2

Breakout: 19% Improve: 43% Collapse: 36% Attrition: 37%   Comparables: Todd Pratt, Jorge Posada, Lance Parrish, Jamie Quirk

The four-year extension he received after 2004 has worked out reasonably well, with Varitek having had two good years and one poor one thus far. Having a better backup to take 15 to 20 more starts from him would help, as he's worn down in his last two full seasons. The mileage is definitely taking a toll on his power, which may not bounce back without more time off.

Mark Wagner   **C**   Bats: R   Throws: R   Height: 6' 1"   Weight: 205   Born: June 11, 1984   Age: 24

YEAR	TEAM	LVL	AGE	PA	R	2B	3B	HR	RBI	BB	SO	SB	CS	EqBRR	AVG	OBP	SLG	MLVr	EqAVG	EqOBP	EqSLG	EqA	VORP	DEFENSE
2005	LOW	A-	21	81	10	2	1	0	6	9	7	1	1	-1.0	.203	.309	.261	-.190	.205	.272	.288	.192	-8.4	21-C -3
2006	GRN	A	22	407	49	32	1	7	45	42	52	1	3	-0.4	.301	.386	.456	.216	.249	.314	.382	.241	3.0	64-C -4
2006	WIL	A+	22	74	8	4	0	1	5	7	9	0	0	-2.0	.169	.243	.277	-.323	.209	.267	.313	.206	-3.8	13-C -3
2007	LNC	A+	23	431	71	35	1	14	82	55	46	0	1	-1.3	.318	.406	.533	.214	.255	.333	.409	.258	11.4	81-C 0
2008	BOS	MLB	24	459	42	28	1	7	51	39	72	2	2	-0.5	.247	.314	.369	-.131	.240	.310	.377	.245	0.2	109-C -3

Breakout: 27% Improve: 39% Collapse: 21% Attrition: 14%   Comparables: Jim Foster, Adan Millan, Kiki Hernandez, Joe Durso

When a catcher posts a 939 OPS, you take notice, but Wagner's 2007 performance comes with so many caveats that it's hard to take it seriously. He was old for his league, he didn't actually hit for impressive power given his environment, and he didn't warrant a promotion. In other words, Wagner looks like an organizational player.

Kevin Youkilis 1B

Bats: R Throws: R Height: 6' 1" Weight: 220 Born: March 15, 1979 Age: 29

YEAR	TEAM	LVL	AGE	PA	R	2B	3B	HR	RBI	BB	SO	SB	CS	EqBRR	AVG	OBP	SLG	MLVr	EqAVG	EqOBP	EqSLG	EqA	VORP	DEFENSE				
2005	PAW	AAA	26	194	30	15	1	8	27	35	29	1	2	-0.2	.322	.459	.592	.461	.295	.426	.545	.325	24.3	22-3B	-3	16-1B	2	
2005	BOS	MLB	26	95	11	7	0	1	9	14	19	0	1	0.5	.278	.400	.405	.093	.282	.417	.397	.290	3.4	16-3B	1			
2006	BOS	MLB	27	680	100	42	2	13	72	91	120	5	2	0.8	.279	.381	.429	.064	.275	.384	.428	.288	19.6	116-1B	5	15-LF	2	
2007	BOS	MLB	28	625	85	35	2	16	83	77	105	4	2	4.6	.288	.390	.453	.142	.285	.393	.467	.298	31.1	123-1B	19	12-3B	3	
2008	BOS	MLB	29	616	84	36	2	17	81	79	107	6	3	0.2	.272	.373	.448	.088	.265	.369	.458	.292	17.5	144-1B	8			

Breakout: 13% Improve: 36% Collapse: 24% Attrition: 8%   Comparables: Sal Bando, Tim Salmon, Derrek Lee, Bob Allison

Youkilis was an All-Star because he had the month of his life in May (.402/.447/.679), not because he really deserved the label; thereafter he hit .248/.370/.388. He doesn't hit enough to play first base and is an asset there only because he plays the position like a converted third baseman should, but he's locked in at the position following the Lowell re-signing. That leaves the Red Sox with a package comparable to Mark Grace or Wally Joyner at their peaks.

PITCHERS

Daniel Bard

Bats: R Throws: R Height: 6' 4" Weight: 195 Born: June 25, 1985 Age: 23

YEAR	TEAM	LVL	AGE	W	L	SV	G	GS	IP	H	BB	SO	HR	GB%	BABIP	STUFF	WHIP	ERA	PERA	EqERA	EqH9	EqBB9	EqSO9	EqHR9	VORP	SN/WX
2007	GRN	A	22	3	5	0	17	17	61²	55	56	38	3	44.7%	.291	-13	1.80	6.42	7.75	9.40	9.1	12.6	2.6	1.0	-22.3	—
2007	LNC	A+	22	0	2	0	5	5	13¹	21	22	9	2	51.9%	.388	-31	3.23	10.15	17.82	20.08	14.5	18.0	2.8	2.1	-20.9	—
2008	BOS	MLB	23	2	5	0	18	11	55¹	70	68	18	12	46.4%	.296	-52	2.49	9.18	9.02	8.95	10.7	10.0	2.6	1.9	-27.7	-1.80

Breakout: 63% Improve: 73% Collapse: 24% Attrition: 40%   Comparables: Melido Dotel, Ryan Mills, Anthony Pearson, Mark Woodyard

The team's second first-round pick in 2006, Bard never found the strike zone in 2007. He washed out of the California League in a month and wasn't any better in the Sally after his demotion. He's suspect until further notice.

Josh Beckett

Bats: R Throws: R Height: 6' 5" Weight: 220 Born: May 15, 1980 Age: 28

YEAR	TEAM	LVL	AGE	W	L	SV	G	GS	IP	H	BB	SO	HR	GB%	BABIP	STUFF	WHIP	ERA	PERA	EqERA	EqH9	EqBB9	EqSO9	EqHR9	VORP	SN/WX
2005	FLO	MLB	25	15	8	0	29	29	178²	153	58	166	14	43.9%	.294	31	1.18	3.37	3.29	3.59	7.4	2.7	7.7	0.7	34.0	5.23
2006	BOS	MLB	26	16	11	0	33	33	204²	191	73	158	36	46.4%	.265	6	1.29	5.01	3.92	4.30	7.4	3.0	6.4	1.3	19.9	3.87
2007	BOS	MLB	27	20	7	0	30	30	200²	189	40	194	17	47.9%	.307	36	1.14	3.27	3.62	3.37	8.7	1.6	8.1	0.7	58.6	6.25
2008	BOS	MLB	28	14	8	0	31	31	205	191	60	176	20	45.8%	.289	24	1.22	3.64	3.41	3.69	7.9	2.4	7.1	0.8	44.6	6.40

Breakout: 16% Improve: 46% Collapse: 20% Attrition: 11%   Comparables: Andy Benes, John Smoltz, Pete Vuckovich, Bill Singer

Beckett's inflated home run rate in 2006 proved to be an anomaly, but it was the improvement in his control (1.8 BB/9 in 2007 vs. 3.1 BB/9 from 2004 to 2006) that made him the second-best starter in the AL last year. That dramatic step forward is comparable to those taken by Curt Schilling and Greg Maddux at similar ages, and it foretells a coming period of dominance.

Michael Bowden

Bats: R Throws: R Height: 6' 3" Weight: 215 Born: September 9, 1986 Age: 21

YEAR	TEAM	LVL	AGE	W	L	SV	G	GS	IP	H	BB	SO	HR	GB%	BABIP	STUFF	WHIP	ERA	PERA	EqERA	EqH9	EqBB9	EqSO9	EqHR9	VORP	SN/WX
2006	GRN	A	19	9	6	0	24	24	107²	91	31	118	9	52.7%	.293	-8	1.14	3.53	7.27	7.19	11.1	4.9	5.6	1.9	-16.4	—
2007	LNC	A+	20	2	0	0	8	8	46	35	8	46	1	45.9%	.288	28	0.93	1.37	3.77	2.98	7.9	2.6	5.5	0.4	12.3	—
2007	PME	AA	20	8	6	0	19	19	96²	105	33	82	9	37.5%	.337	0	1.43	4.28	6.53	6.07	11.0	3.8	5.4	1.4	-4.6	—
2008	BOS	MLB	21	8	9	0	24	24	137	155	60	91	20	41.2%	.307	6	1.57	5.39	5.22	5.32	9.6	3.6	5.5	1.3	5.0	1.60

Breakout: 20% Improve: 57% Collapse: 12% Attrition: 12%   Comparables: Jeff Suppan, Eric Hurley, Jose Lima, Javier Vazquez

For the first six weeks of last season, Michael Bowden was the one pitcher known to man who could actually succeed in the pinball-machine atmosphere of Lancaster. From there, he went to Double-A, where he wasn't nearly as good. The mitigating factor is that Bowden was among the youngest starters in the Eastern League. There is still some work to be done, particularly on his changeup and his anything-but-ideal mechanics, but he's a future rotation piece.

Clay Buchholz

Bats: L   Throws: R   Height: 6' 3"   Weight: 190   Born: August 14, 1984   Age: 23

YEAR	TEAM	LVL	AGE	W	L	SV	G	GS	IP	H	BB	SO	HR	GB%	BABIP	STUFF	WHIP	ERA	PERA	EqERA	EqH9	EqBB9	EqSO9	EqHR9	VORP	SN/WX
2005	LOW	A-	20	0	1	0	15	15	41¹	34	9	45	2	51.4%	.296	-10	1.04	2.62	6.49	6.29	10.5	4.7	5.0	1.6	-2.6	—
2006	GRN	A	21	9	4	0	21	21	103	78	29	117	10	46.5%	.281	-18	1.04	2.62	7.23	5.79	10.4	4.8	6.1	2.3	-1.8	—
2006	WIL	A+	21	2	0	0	3	3	16¹	10	4	23	0	53.3%	.302	15	0.87	1.12	3.64	3.68	7.4	3.1	9.2	0.0	3.1	—
2007	PME	AA	22	7	2	0	16	15	86²	55	22	116	4	46.9%	.276	40	0.89	1.76	3.36	2.88	6.6	2.9	8.9	0.7	24.6	—
2007	PAW	AAA	22	1	3	0	8	8	38²	32	13	55	5	47.4%	.318	23	1.16	3.95	5.02	5.73	8.6	3.3	9.6	1.7	-0.5	—
2007	BOS	MLB	22	3	1	0	4	3	22²	14	10	22	0	40.0%	.259	21	1.06	1.59	2.66	2.53	5.9	3.8	8.4	0.0	9.3	1.02
2008	BOS	MLB	23	8	7	0	38	22	130²	121	56	119	13	44.5%	.292	17	1.35	4.08	3.86	4.09	7.8	3.5	7.5	0.9	22.8	3.10

Breakout: 11% Improve: 40% Collapse: 24% Attrition: 21%   Comparables: Clay Kirby, Jose Rijo, Erv Palica, Dave Boswell

First things first: Buchholz is healthy. The Red Sox shut him down at the end of the year not because he was injured, but because they believed it was the best way to manage his career. Somehow they managed to scuffle their way to 11 wins in October without him. There's nothing not to like here; Buchholz has the performance record and skill set—fastball that touches 97, amazing curve, above-average changeup, slider, good mechanics—to be the Sox' number-two starter this year.

Bryce Cox

Bats: R   Throws: R   Height: 6' 4"   Weight: 205   Born: August 10, 1984   Age: 23

YEAR	TEAM	LVL	AGE	W	L	SV	G	GS	IP	H	BB	SO	HR	GB%	BABIP	STUFF	WHIP	ERA	PERA	EqERA	EqH9	EqBB9	EqSO9	EqHR9	VORP	SN/WX
2006	WIL	A+	21	2	0	0	13	0	24	14	9	25	0	75.8%	.215	7	0.96	0.75	3.63	2.78	6.4	4.4	6.0	0.4	7.1	—
2007	GRN	A	22	1	1	0	21	0	33¹	31	10	24	4	61.1%	.265	-36	1.23	5.41	6.14	7.59	9.0	4.5	3.1	2.0	-7.1	—
2007	PME	AA	22	1	1	0	9	0	14²	15	11	3	1	63.6%	.275	-42	1.77	4.90	6.23	9.42	9.4	7.5	0.6	1.3	-6.1	—
2008	BOS	MLB	23	3	4	0	28	7	62	75	37	22	8	57.5%	.302	-25	1.80	6.33	5.84	6.43	10.2	4.9	2.9	1.1	-5.7	-0.30

Breakout: 39% Improve: 62% Collapse: 17% Attrition: 10%   Comparables: Chad Bradford, Carlos Hines, Patrick Ryan, Michael Gardner

There might be a lesson here about judging amateurs. Cox wasn't a highly touted prospect at Rice until his junior season in 2006, when he closed for a team that reached the College World Series. He was subsequently drafted by the Sox in the third round. Last year was a disaster, as he failed at Double-A and then at Low-A. Perhaps too much was made of a handful of innings that were in close proximity to the draft, the same way that we often overrate professionals based on insufficient samples.

Manny Delcarmen

Bats: R   Throws: R   Height: 6' 2"   Weight: 190   Born: February 16, 1982   Age: 26

YEAR	TEAM	LVL	AGE	W	L	SV	G	GS	IP	H	BB	SO	HR	GB%	BABIP	STUFF	WHIP	ERA	PERA	EqERA	EqH9	EqBB9	EqSO9	EqHR9	VORP	SN/WX
2005	PME	AA	23	4	4	3	31	0	39	31	20	49	3	58.0%	.298	2	1.31	3.23	5.71	7.08	9.2	6.6	7.6	1.0	-5.6	—
2005	PAW	AAA	23	3	1	2	15	0	21	17	13	23	0	34.5%	.309	16	1.43	1.29	4.41	1.86	7.9	6.5	7.4	0.0	8.0	—
2005	BOS	MLB	23	0	0	0	10	0	9	8	7	9	0	62.5%	.333	9	1.67	3.00	4.40	3.12	8.3	7.3	9.3	0.0	2.8	-0.07
2006	PAW	AAA	24	0	1	0	10	0	17²	9	6	19	0	41.0%	.231	12	0.87	2.09	2.92	3.38	5.6	3.9	7.3	0.0	3.9	—
2006	BOS	MLB	24	2	0	0	50	0	53¹	68	17	45	2	46.9%	.382	10	1.59	5.07	4.49	4.80	10.4	2.7	7.0	0.3	4.3	0.60
2007	PAW	AAA	25	3	2	0	20	0	29¹	28	14	37	1	46.8%	.351	10	1.43	3.38	4.85	4.76	9.8	4.8	8.3	0.6	2.6	—
2007	BOS	MLB	25	0	0	1	44	0	44	28	17	41	4	47.4%	.222	14	1.02	2.05	2.80	2.06	5.8	3.1	7.6	0.8	18.4	1.65
2008	BOS	MLB	26	3	2	3	57	0	58²	54	25	53	5	46.5%	.295	10	1.34	3.81	3.57	3.89	7.7	3.5	7.5	0.7	13.0	1.10

Breakout: 10% Improve: 34% Collapse: 38% Attrition: 15%   Comparables: Jack Baldschun, Jack Lamabe, Jose Paniagua, Paul Shuey

Delcarmen pitched better in 2007, just not by as much as the three runs that dropped off his ERA would have you believe. No, the secret was going from a .379 BABIP to a .218, an improvement that was part team defense and part good fortune; as is often the case, the truth lies in between. Delcarmen is well-suited to high-leverage relief and should move into a setup tandem with Hideki Okajima this year.

Eric Gagné   Bats: R   Throws: R   Height: 6' 0"   Weight: 240   Born: January 7, 1976   Age: 32

YEAR	TEAM	LVL	AGE	W	L	SV	G	GS	IP	H	BB	SO	HR	GB%	BABIP	STUFF	WHIP	ERA	PERA	EqERA	EqH9	EqBB9	EqSO9	EqHR9	VORP	SN/WX
2005	LAN	MLB	29	1	0	8	14	0	13¹	10	3	22	2	53.6%	.308	13	0.98	2.71	3.88	2.77	8.3	2.1	11.1	1.4	4.0	1.09
2007	TEX	MLB	31	2	0	16	34	0	33¹	23	12	29	2	41.8%	.236	14	1.02	2.16	2.58	1.89	5.7	3.0	7.3	0.5	14.4	2.77
2007	BOS	MLB	31	2	2	0	20	0	18²	26	9	22	1	36.2%	.439	5	1.88	6.74	7.46	7.50	13.5	4.0	10.0	0.5	-1.4	-1.41
2008	*MIL*	*MLB*	*32*	*3*	*5*	*34*	*46*	*0*	*52¹*	*47*	*20*	*56*	*5*	*42.6%*	*.297*	*14*	*1.28*	*3.38*	*3.75*	*3.42*	*7.9*	*3.0*	*8.4*	*0.9*	*12.8*	*2.20*

Breakout: 35%   Improve: 58%   Collapse: 20%   Attrition: 9%   Comparables: Roberto Hernandez, Alejandro Peña, Jeff Russell, Francisco Cordero

Gagné's 2007 season is an interesting case study in how we perceive things. His overall numbers were right in line with what you would expect from a good reliever coming off two seasons lost to surgeries and rehab. Pitching for Texas in the first four months, Gagné was effective, if not dominant, and his low ERA (2.16) was as much a function of low BABIP (.236) as anything else. With the Red Sox, the latter number jumped to .439, including a whopping .515 in August. Would that have happened in Texas? We'll never know, but connecting the change to the trade is implausible. Gagné was due for a correction, and having it come while he was pitching high-leverage innings for a high-profile team after a high-visibility trade made it seem like the two were related, or that there had to be a cause. Neither is necessarily true. Signed to a one-year, $10 million deal with Milwaukee, Gagné should have an unexceptional but successful season as the Brewers' closer.

Nick Hagadone   Bats: L   Throws: L   Height: 6' 5"   Weight: 230   Born: January 1, 1986   Age: 22

YEAR	TEAM	LVL	AGE	W	L	SV	G	GS	IP	H	BB	SO	HR	GB%	BABIP	STUFF	WHIP	ERA	PERA	EqERA	EqH9	EqBB9	EqSO9	EqHR9	VORP	SN/WX
2007	LOW	A-	21	0	1	0	10	10	24¹	14	8	33	1	60.4%	.250	11	0.91	1.85	4.85	3.80	7.6	5.1	7.2	1.3	4.3	—
2008	*BOS*	*MLB*	*22*	*7*	*7*	*0*	*30*	*18*	*111²*	*112*	*68*	*87*	*10*	*54.2%*	*.305*	*6*	*1.61*	*4.62*	*4.70*	*4.66*	*8.5*	*5.0*	*6.5*	*0.8*	*11.9*	*2.00*

Breakout: 12%   Improve: 27%   Collapse: 50%   Attrition: 19%   Comparables: Scott Downs, A. J. Burnett, Jay Witasick, Jim Parque

The Red Sox had no first-round pick in last year's draft (the Dodgers got it as compensation for losing Julio Lugo). They used their first supplemental-round selection on Hagadone. In his professional debut, he gave up five runs in one inning, but was unscored upon after that, finishing the year with 23 consecutive scoreless innings stretched over nine games in which he gave up just eight hits and struck out 32. He's a huge left-hander who can get into the mid-90s at times and has a plus slider, so he could move quickly through the system as a reliever, but Boston wants to see how he develops as a starter first.

Devern Hansack   Bats: R   Throws: R   Height: 6' 2"   Weight: 185   Born: February 5, 1978   Age: 30

YEAR	TEAM	LVL	AGE	W	L	SV	G	GS	IP	H	BB	SO	HR	GB%	BABIP	STUFF	WHIP	ERA	PERA	EqERA	EqH9	EqBB9	EqSO9	EqHR9	VORP	SN/WX
2006	PME	AA	28	8	7	1	31	18	132	122	36	124	14	40.4%	.287	-19	1.20	3.27	6.20	5.56	10.4	3.4	5.6	1.6	0.5	—
2006	BOS	MLB	28	1	1	0	2	2	10	6	1	8	2	48.1%	.160	10	0.70	2.70	2.30	1.80	4.5	0.9	6.3	1.8	3.9	0.44
2007	PAW	AAA	29	10	7	0	25	23	139²	126	40	131	16	43.4%	.292	-3	1.19	3.61	5.06	4.76	9.1	3.0	6.3	1.5	12.3	—
2007	BOS	MLB	29	0	1	0	3	1	7²	9	5	5	2	46.4%	.269	-22	1.83	4.68	7.26	5.40	9.7	4.3	5.4	2.2	0.2	-0.05
2008	*BOS*	*MLB*	*30*	*5*	*5*	*0*	*29*	*12*	*89*	*98*	*35*	*60*	*13*	*43.1%*	*.301*	*-3*	*1.49*	*5.09*	*4.87*	*5.04*	*9.3*	*3.2*	*5.6*	*1.3*	*6.1*	*1.10*

Breakout: 17%   Improve: 41%   Collapse: 28%   Attrition: 19%   Comparables: Javier De La Hoya, Rodrigo Lopez, Victor Santos, Julio Manon

Hansack pitched just as well last year as he did in 2006, this time a level higher. The relative stability of the Sox' rotation and the emergence of Buchholz kept him from having much impact in Boston. The organization's pitching depth may mean that he has to go elsewhere to get a shot, especially with swing-man Julian Tavarez returning in 2008.

Craig Hansen

									Bats: R		Throws: R		Height: 6' 5"		Weight: 185		Born: November 15, 1983				Age: 24	

YEAR	TEAM	LVL	AGE	W	L	SV	G	GS	IP	H	BB	SO	HR	GB%	BABIP	STUFF	WHIP	ERA	PERA	EqERA	EqH9	EqBB9	EqSO9	EqHR9	VORP	SN/WX
2005	PME	AA	21	0	0	1	8	0	9²	9	1	10	0	55.6%	.333	9	1.03	0.00	0.32	0.00	10.4	2.1	6.2	0.0	5.4	—
2005	BOS	MLB	21	0	0	0	4	0	3	6	1	3	1	50.0%	.500	-12	2.33	6.00	18.97	9.00	18.0	3.0	9.0	3.0	-0.1	-0.29
2006	PME	AA	22	1	0	0	5	0	11	4	4	12	0	53.8%	.154	9	0.73	0.82	2.96	1.64	4.1	4.1	5.7	0.0	4.8	—
2006	PAW	AAA	22	1	2	0	14	4	36²	31	19	26	0	52.3%	.298	1	1.38	2.73	4.27	4.36	8.5	5.7	4.9	0.3	4.5	—
2006	BOS	MLB	22	2	2	0	38	0	38	46	15	30	5	46.5%	.353	-5	1.61	6.63	5.30	6.75	9.8	3.3	6.5	0.9	-6.0	-0.68
2007	PAW	AAA	23	3	1	3	40	0	51¹	58	32	48	2	65.9%	.348	-4	1.75	3.86	6.28	5.94	11.0	5.9	5.9	0.5	-1.9	—
2008	BOS	MLB	24	3	4	2	31	6	59¹	61	32	44	4	55.1%	.311	0	1.56	4.65	4.36	4.79	8.7	4.4	6.2	0.6	6.1	0.80

Breakout: 40% Improve: 69% Collapse: 15% Attrition: 19%   Comparables: Ryan Wagner, Ron Willis, Dave Wainhouse, Ed Farmer

A bit more than two years after being a first-round pick, Hansen is just another minor league pitcher, ineffective at Pawtucket most of the year and roped in the Arizona Fall League. One problem with taking relievers high in the draft is that there's no fallback position; a comparable starting pitcher can move to the bullpen and have a career. If you flop as a reliever, the next step is scout.

Jon Lester

									Bats: L		Throws: L		Height: 6' 2"		Weight: 190		Born: January 7, 1984				Age: 24	

YEAR	TEAM	LVL	AGE	W	L	SV	G	GS	IP	H	BB	SO	HR	GB%	BABIP	STUFF	WHIP	ERA	PERA	EqERA	EqH9	EqBB9	EqSO9	EqHR9	VORP	SN/WX
2005	PME	AA	21	11	6	0	26	26	148¹	114	57	163	10	47.9%	.291	15	1.15	2.61	4.84	4.48	8.5	4.9	6.4	1.0	16.5	—
2006	PAW	AAA	22	3	4	0	11	11	46	43	25	43	5	43.9%	.290	-1	1.48	2.74	5.82	4.43	9.1	5.6	6.0	1.4	5.8	—
2006	BOS	MLB	22	7	2	0	15	15	81¹	91	43	60	7	40.5%	.347	15	1.65	4.76	4.98	4.18	9.5	4.5	6.3	0.7	12.3	1.73
2007	PAW	AAA	23	4	5	0	14	14	71²	67	31	51	4	46.2%	.296	-1	1.37	3.89	4.85	4.68	9.2	4.4	4.7	0.8	6.9	—
2007	BOS	MLB	23	4	0	0	12	11	63	61	31	50	10	35.8%	.288	3	1.46	4.57	5.23	4.52	8.9	3.9	6.7	1.5	9.0	1.19
2008	BOS	MLB	24	8	8	1	34	23	128²	135	65	92	15	42.1%	.302	3	1.56	4.93	4.78	4.90	8.9	4.2	5.9	1.0	10.9	2.00

Breakout: 9% Improve: 30% Collapse: 40% Attrition: 28%   Comparables: Arthur Rhodes, Dave LaPoint, Casey Fossum, Allen Watson

Simply pitching so soon after undergoing chemotherapy to treat lymphoma was a feat, so reading too much into Lester's 2007 performance would be a mistake. He was up and down after his July promotion, turning in consecutive effective outings just once. His World Series start—5⅔ shutout innings in Colorado touching 93 mph at times—was a revelation. He's not Buchholz, but he can play Sid Fernandez to Buchholz's Dwight Gooden.

Javier Lopez

									Bats: L		Throws: L		Height: 6' 4"		Weight: 220		Born: July 11, 1977				Age: 30	

YEAR	TEAM	LVL	AGE	W	L	SV	G	GS	IP	H	BB	SO	HR	GB%	BABIP	STUFF	WHIP	ERA	PERA	EqERA	EqH9	EqBB9	EqSO9	EqHR9	VORP	SN/WX
2005	TUC	AAA	27	0	1	2	27	0	24¹	17	12	16	0	70.6%	.266	-10	1.19	2.22	3.24	3.13	6.3	4.7	3.9	0.4	6.3	—
2005	ARI	MLB	27	1	1	2	29	0	14¹	19	11	11	2	52.9%	.354	-16	2.09	9.44	7.48	9.00	10.8	6.0	6.0	1.2	-5.8	0.25
2006	CHR	AAA	28	2	1	12	26	0	33	28	6	26	1	73.1%	.293	3	1.03	0.55	4.19	1.55	9.6	2.2	5.6	0.6	13.1	—
2006	PAW	AAA	28	0	0	4	13	0	16	20	8	12	1	61.4%	.352	-23	1.75	5.06	6.79	6.75	11.2	5.1	4.5	1.1	-2.0	—
2006	BOS	MLB	28	1	0	1	27	0	16²	13	10	11	1	67.4%	.273	-5	1.38	2.69	3.71	4.70	7.0	5.3	5.9	0.6	1.4	0.82
2007	PAW	AAA	29	2	1	0	17	0	16²	19	8	15	0	70.6%	.396	-6	1.62	3.77	6.25	4.70	11.7	4.7	5.9	0.0	1.5	—
2007	BOS	MLB	29	2	1	0	61	0	40²	36	18	26	2	53.2%	.279	-3	1.33	3.10	3.80	3.40	8.2	3.6	5.4	0.5	11.3	0.50
2008	BOS	MLB	30	2	2	2	52	0	41²	44	20	28	3	54.9%	.308	-6	1.52	4.30	4.20	4.43	8.8	3.9	5.6	0.6	6.0	0.50

Breakout: 31% Improve: 56% Collapse: 24% Attrition: 30%   Comparables: Russ Swan, Paul Mirabella, John O'Donoghue, Kevin Gryboski

Evaluating a LOOGY by his ERA is a bit like evaluating a baseball book by its use of gerunds. Lopez has the mechanics and repertoire to fill the role, and struck out 19 percent of the left-handed batters he faced. His weird opponent's average split (.293 vs. LHB, .176 vs. RHB) was a fluke. He's an effective specialist and number-two lefty.

Justin Masterson

Bats: R   Throws: R   Height: 6' 6"   Weight: 250   Born: March 22, 1985   Age: 23

YEAR	TEAM	LVL	AGE	W	L	SV	G	GS	IP	H	BB	SO	HR	GB%	BABIP	STUFF	WHIP	ERA	PERA	EqERA	EqH9	EqBB9	EqSO9	EqHR9	VORP	SN/WX
2006	LOW	A-	21	3	1	0	14	0	31	20	2	33	0	74.4%	.244	4	0.71	0.87	4.08	3.41	7.4	2.2	4.7	0.3	7.1	—
2007	LNC	A+	22	8	5	0	17	17	95²	103	22	56	4	54.9%	.314	-9	1.31	4.33	5.08	6.18	10.3	3.3	2.6	0.7	-5.8	—
2007	PME	AA	22	4	3	0	10	10	58	49	18	59	4	68.5%	.296	12	1.16	4.34	4.42	5.56	8.5	3.4	6.4	1.0	0.2	—
2008	BOS	MLB	23	9	10	0	27	27	155¹	181	63	82	15	55.9%	.313	2	1.57	5.33	4.88	5.44	9.8	3.4	4.3	0.9	3.8	1.60

Breakout: 27% Improve: 58% Collapse: 18% Attrition: 7%   Comparables: Nate Minchey, Richie Gardner, Chris Reitsma, Sean Bergman

Can we get him nicknamed "Monsterson"? At 6-foot-6, 250 pounds, he's more than qualified for the moniker. Masterson's sinker is as scary as any movie creation and arguably the best in the minors. Finding a second pitch and refining his mechanics are on the to-do list for 2008.

Daisuke Matsuzaka

Bats: R   Throws: R   Height: 6' 0"   Weight: 190   Born: September 13, 1980   Age: 27

YEAR	TEAM	LVL	AGE	W	L	SV	G	GS	IP	H	BB	SO	HR	GB%	BABIP	STUFF	WHIP	ERA	PERA	EqERA	EqH9	EqBB9	EqSO9	EqHR9	VORP	SN/WX
2005	SEI	JP	24	14	13	0	28	28	215	172	49	226	13	0.0%	.275	32	1.03	2.30	3.41	3.33	7.5	2.7	7.6	0.7	51.1	—
2006	SEI	JP	25	17	5	0	25	25	186¹	138	34	200	13	0.0%	.265	27	0.92	2.13	3.61	3.59	7.6	2.3	7.8	0.9	39.2	—
2007	BOS	MLB	26	15	12	0	32	32	204²	191	80	201	25	39.3%	.302	21	1.32	4.40	4.54	4.19	8.7	3.2	8.3	1.1	37.0	5.14
2008	BOS	MLB	27	13	8	0	30	30	191	179	67	170	21	41.9%	.290	24	1.29	3.90	3.71	3.91	7.9	2.9	7.4	1.0	36.8	5.40

Breakout: 12% Improve: 43% Collapse: 24% Attrition: 11%   Comparables: David Cone, Pete Harnisch, Bob Welch, Jim Bunning

It seems silly to invest $100 million in a player and then try to change him, but the Sox did that with Matsuzaka. They limited his repertoire and attempted to adjust his training regimen to major league standards. In return, they got a pitcher with less effectiveness, less command, and who wilted in the second half. The Sox have let Manny be Manny; they need to let Dice-K be Dice-K. He'll shave at least a half-run off of his ERA this year if they do.

Hideki Okajima

Bats: L   Throws: L   Height: 6' 1"   Weight: 194   Born: December 25, 1975   Age: 32

YEAR	TEAM	LVL	AGE	W	L	SV	G	GS	IP	H	BB	SO	HR	GB%	BABIP	STUFF	WHIP	ERA	PERA	EqERA	EqH9	EqBB9	EqSO9	EqHR9	VORP	SN/WX
2005	YOM	JP	29	1	0	0	42	0	53	55	19	56	10	0.0%	.304	-14	1.40	4.75	5.65	5.86	9.2	3.7	7.1	1.8	-1.5	—
2006	NIP	JP	30	2	2	4	55	0	54²	46	14	63	5	0.0%	.299	7	1.10	2.14	4.83	3.75	9.1	3.2	8.6	1.3	10.3	—
2007	BOS	MLB	31	3	2	5	66	0	69	50	17	63	6	47.1%	.246	18	0.97	2.22	2.79	2.23	6.6	2.0	7.6	0.8	29.3	4.43
2008	BOS	MLB	32	3	3	6	56	0	56¹	54	19	50	6	44.8%	.297	7	1.29	3.71	3.62	3.76	8.1	2.7	7.3	0.9	12.1	1.20

Breakout: 15% Improve: 47% Collapse: 26% Attrition: 20%   Comparables: Mike Stanton, Paul Assenmacher, Tug McGraw, Jamie Walker

The Sox shut down a winded Okajima in September and were rewarded with lights-out pitching in October, including a dominating seven-out appearance to hold a 2-1 lead in Game Two of the World Series. An overhand thrower without a side-to-side breaking ball, he's correctly used in full-inning and multi-inning roles rather than as a specialist. Indeed, nearly two-thirds of the batters he faced last year were right-handed.

Jonathan Papelbon

Bats: R   Throws: R   Height: 6' 4"   Weight: 230   Born: November 23, 1980   Age: 27

YEAR	TEAM	LVL	AGE	W	L	SV	G	GS	IP	H	BB	SO	HR	GB%	BABIP	STUFF	WHIP	ERA	PERA	EqERA	EqH9	EqBB9	EqSO9	EqHR9	VORP	SN/WX
2005	PME	AA	24	5	2	0	14	14	87	59	23	83	9	44.8%	.234	-2	0.94	2.48	4.29	3.99	7.3	3.5	5.5	1.5	14.1	—
2005	PAW	AAA	24	1	2	1	7	4	27²	21	3	27	2	44.7%	.264	16	0.87	2.92	3.28	3.46	7.3	1.4	6.6	0.7	6.2	—
2005	BOS	MLB	24	3	1	0	17	3	34	33	17	34	4	36.2%	.326	16	1.47	2.65	4.81	2.76	8.5	4.7	9.1	1.1	11.0	1.10
2006	BOS	MLB	25	4	2	35	59	0	68¹	40	13	75	3	38.7%	.228	37	0.78	0.92	2.03	1.16	4.7	1.6	8.7	0.4	38.6	6.61
2007	BOS	MLB	26	1	3	37	59	0	58¹	30	15	84	5	28.9%	.216	34	0.77	1.85	2.42	2.02	5.1	2.0	10.1	0.8	27.1	5.14
2008	BOS	MLB	27	5	5	39	62	0	67¹	51	21	81	6	37.6%	.273	29	1.06	2.55	2.51	2.58	6.4	2.5	9.9	0.8	25.4	4.00

Breakout: 8% Improve: 28% Collapse: 39% Attrition: 8%   Comparables: Dick Radatz, John Wetteland, Troy Percival, Rob Dibble

Papelbon is not literally "unhittable." Nearly two-thirds of batters who faced him last year didn't strike out, and about 14 percent actually got hits. To watch him, however, is to wonder how those events happened. By the end of the year he was mixing his splitter in with his fastball with such effectiveness that hitters had no chance, thus his 10⅔ shutout innings in the postseason. The only negative is his low innings totals, which keep him behind Joe Nathan on the "best closers" list.

Curt Schilling

Bats: R   Throws: R   Height: 6' 5"   Weight: 235   Born: November 14, 1966   Age: 41

YEAR	TEAM	LVL	AGE	W	L	SV	G	GS	IP	H	BB	SO	HR	GB%	BABIP	STUFF	WHIP	ERA	PERA	EqERA	EqH9	EqBB9	EqSO9	EqHR9	VORP	SN/WX
2005	BOS	MLB	38	8	8	9	32	11	93¹	121	22	87	12	36.3%	.381	10	1.53	5.69	5.59	5.30	11.0	2.0	8.1	1.1	2.1	0.03
2006	BOS	MLB	39	15	7	0	31	31	204	220	28	183	28	41.3%	.328	26	1.22	3.97	3.94	3.39	8.9	1.2	7.6	1.1	48.6	5.08
2007	BOS	MLB	40	9	8	0	24	24	151	165	23	101	21	39.3%	.301	8	1.25	3.87	4.66	4.04	9.9	1.2	5.6	1.2	33.5	4.29
2008	BOS	MLB	41	8	6	0	30	19	123¹	133	26	87	16	42.9%	.301	6	1.29	4.18	4.04	4.18	9.1	1.7	5.8	1.1	20.2	3.00

Breakout: 2%   Improve: 34%   Collapse: 29%   Attrition: 34%   Comparables: Rick Reuschel, Gaylord Perry, Bert Blyleven, Danny Darwin

After he came off of the DL last August, Schilling appeared to make a conscious decision to throw strikes, and only strikes, and force the hitters to beat him. Counting the postseason, Schilling walked just seven men in his last 80⅔ innings. It's an approach that will make him a league-average innings guy at age 40, and well worth the $11-13 million his incentive-laden contract will end up paying him.

Kyle Snyder

Bats: S   Throws: R   Height: 6' 8"   Weight: 215   Born: September 9, 1977   Age: 30

YEAR	TEAM	LVL	AGE	W	L	SV	G	GS	IP	H	BB	SO	HR	GB%	BABIP	STUFF	WHIP	ERA	PERA	EqERA	EqH9	EqBB9	EqSO9	EqHR9	VORP	SN/WX
2005	OMA	AAA	27	2	3	0	15	12	66	61	22	48	3	56.9%	.291	2	1.26	3.55	3.94	4.74	8.3	3.3	4.6	0.6	6.0	—
2005	KCA	MLB	27	1	3	0	13	3	36	55	10	19	3	46.0%	.388	-12	1.81	6.75	6.28	6.44	12.4	2.5	4.5	0.7	-6.1	-0.47
2006	OMA	AAA	28	0	4	1	10	9	60¹	63	9	43	4	56.0%	.307	5	1.20	3.89	4.08	5.70	9.3	1.6	4.3	0.8	-0.7	—
2006	PAW	AAA	28	1	1	0	3	3	20¹	24	2	7	1	59.7%	.324	-12	1.29	3.58	5.66	5.00	12.0	1.5	2.0	1.0	1.2	—
2006	BOS	MLB	28	4	5	0	16	10	58¹	77	19	55	11	42.2%	.369	2	1.65	5.87	6.40	5.80	10.8	2.7	7.8	1.5	-1.6	0.28
2007	BOS	MLB	29	2	3	0	46	0	54¹	45	32	41	7	38.7%	.247	-6	1.42	3.81	4.39	4.31	7.5	4.6	6.3	1.2	7.5	0.39
2008	BOS	MLB	30	2	2	1	28	2	42¹	46	18	31	4	44.1%	.310	-3	1.49	4.82	4.53	4.84	9.1	3.5	6.1	0.9	4.6	0.40

Breakout: 38%   Improve: 61%   Collapse: 20%   Attrition: 35%   Comparables: Doug Brocail, Roger Mason, Jerry Spradlin, Tim Worrell

The definition of a low-leverage reliever, Snyder made 36 of his 46 appearances when the Red Sox were up at least four runs or down at least two. He'll be back for more of the same in 2008. There's nothing to indicate he can move up to a more important role.

Julian Tavarez

Bats: L   Throws: R   Height: 6' 2"   Weight: 195   Born: May 22, 1973   Age: 35

YEAR	TEAM	LVL	AGE	W	L	SV	G	GS	IP	H	BB	SO	HR	GB%	BABIP	STUFF	WHIP	ERA	PERA	EqERA	EqH9	EqBB9	EqSO9	EqHR9	VORP	SN/WX
2005	SLN	MLB	32	2	3	4	74	0	65²	68	19	47	6	52.0%	.323	-2	1.32	3.42	5.06	4.38	10.1	2.5	6.1	0.9	12.0	2.26
2006	BOS	MLB	33	5	4	1	58	6	98²	110	44	56	10	58.5%	.324	-9	1.56	4.56	4.95	4.45	9.5	3.9	4.9	0.9	12.4	0.35
2007	BOS	MLB	34	7	11	0	34	23	134²	151	51	77	14	54.8%	.306	-6	1.50	5.14	5.15	5.90	10.1	3.0	4.8	0.9	1.7	1.01
2008	BOS	MLB	35	4	5	0	34	10	80¹	94	31	45	8	52.0%	.315	-10	1.55	5.14	4.83	5.20	9.9	3.2	4.6	0.9	4.5	0.80

Breakout: 14%   Improve: 43%   Collapse: 29%   Attrition: 37%   Comparables: Charles Nagy, Pat Hentgen, Bobby Witt, Dick Ruthven

True swingmen aren't common in this era of all-specialist bullpens. Tavarez played that role last year with modest effectiveness, dropping in and out of the rotation as the Red Sox rehabbed Lester, then Schilling, then Tim Wakefield throughout the season. The team picked up his $3.85 million option for 2008 as a cheap insurance policy, even though the team has six starters ready to go.

Mike Timlin

Bats: R   Throws: R   Height: 6' 4"   Weight: 210   Born: March 10, 1966   Age: 42

YEAR	TEAM	LVL	AGE	W	L	SV	G	GS	IP	H	BB	SO	HR	GB%	BABIP	STUFF	WHIP	ERA	PERA	EqERA	EqH9	EqBB9	EqSO9	EqHR9	VORP	SN/WX
2005	BOS	MLB	39	7	3	13	81	0	80¹	86	20	59	2	46.0%	.336	19	1.32	2.24	3.47	2.35	9.0	2.2	6.4	0.2	28.9	2.24
2006	BOS	MLB	40	6	6	9	68	0	64	78	17	30	7	39.8%	.324	-13	1.48	4.36	4.63	3.94	9.8	2.2	3.9	0.8	10.6	1.56
2007	BOS	MLB	41	2	1	1	50	0	55¹	46	14	31	7	40.8%	.244	-8	1.08	3.42	3.56	3.50	7.5	2.0	4.7	1.2	14.0	1.57
2008	BOS	MLB	42	2	2	2	39	0	45	49	13	23	5	42.8%	.291	-14	1.36	4.40	4.09	4.46	9.2	2.3	4.3	1.0	6.8	0.50

Breakout: 0%   Improve: 6%   Collapse: 55%   Attrition: 25%   Comparables: Kent Tekulve, Roberto Hernandez, Ellis Kinder, Dutch Leonard

It was Timlin's strained oblique in spring training that forced Papelbon, then slated to start, back into the bullpen, a move which arguably led to the Red Sox's championship. Timlin also had shoulder problems in the early going, but after a trip to the DL in May, he posted a 2.89 ERA and 2.25 K/BB in 46⅔ innings. Back with the Sox for another go-round, he remains a useful third right-hander even at his advanced age.

Tim Wakefield

			Bats: R	Throws: R	Height: 6′ 2″	Weight: 210	Born: August 2, 1966	Age: 41

YEAR	TEAM	LVL	AGE	W	L	SV	G	GS	IP	H	BB	SO	HR	GB%	BABIP	STUFF	WHIP	ERA	PERA	EqERA	EqH9	EqBB9	EqSO9	EqHR9	VORP	SN/WX
2005	BOS	MLB	38	16	12	0	33	33	225¹	210	68	151	35	43.6%	.261	6	1.23	4.15	3.88	3.83	7.6	2.6	5.8	1.3	34.5	4.49
2006	BOS	MLB	39	7	11	0	23	23	140	135	51	90	19	40.1%	.266	7	1.33	4.63	3.70	4.17	7.5	2.9	5.2	1.0	15.2	2.06
2007	BOS	MLB	40	17	12	0	31	31	189	191	64	110	22	40.8%	.285	2	1.35	4.76	4.62	4.86	9.3	2.7	5.0	1.0	23.2	3.92
2008	BOS	MLB	41	8	7	0	23	23	131	140	49	76	18	42.9%	.288	-1	1.44	4.86	4.56	4.86	9.0	3.1	4.8	1.2	11.2	2.30

Breakout: 4%   Improve: 31%   Collapse: 38%   Attrition: 31%   Comparables: Joe Niekro, Don Sutton, Tom Seaver, Luis Tiant

Wakefield opened the year with 26 decisions in 26 outings before a bad start against the Orioles combined with the Orioles' forgiving pitching staff to yield a no-decision. That outing kicked off a brutal end to his season—an 8.76 ERA in 24⅔ innings over five starts—that was blamed on a sore shoulder, as he had posted a 4.16 ERA in 164 1/3 IP before that game. He's expected back this year, although he's the team's sixth starter, at best.

LINEOUTS

Hitters

PLAYER		TEAM	LVL	AGE	PA	R	2B	3B	HR	RBI	BB	SO	SB-CS	EqBRR	AVG/OBP/SLG	MLVr	EqAVG/EqOBP/EqSLG	EqA	VORP
1B	A. Bates	LNC	A+	23	465	89	21	2	24	88	69	83	0-1	-1.7	.332/.456/.592	.378	.263/.369/.443	.283	15.1
		PME	AA	23	112	16	9	0	4	13	17	29	0-0	0.2	.198/.348/.429	.012	.191/.321/.415	.256	-1.3
C	D. Brown	PME	AA	25	285	43	16	2	9	43	28	64	0-0	-0.1	.268/.344/.453	.086	.236/.305/.411	.246	3.2
C	K. Cash	PAW	AAA	29	208	22	7	0	7	25	23	56	0-0	-0.1	.176/.276/.335	-.232	.178/.268/.339	.214	-9.1
		BOS	MLB	29	33	2	1	0	0	4	4	13	0-0	-0.1	.111/.242/.148	-.628	.111/.242/.148	.140	-3.4
SS	R. Clayton	TOR	MLB	37	210	23	14	0	1	12	14	50	2-1	-0.4	.254/.304/.344	-.188	.262/.319/.358	.242	-1.6
LF	Z. Daeges*	LNC	A+	23	614	124	55	5	21	113	82	97	4-1	1.1	.330/.423/.579	.312	.261/.345/.440	.272	8.6
SS	A. Diaz	GRN	A	20	447	62	25	5	2	40	36	92	5-9	-5.3	.279/.342/.380	-.007	.222/.273/.301	.195	-18.6
CF	R. Kalish*	LOW	A-	19	104	27	4	1	3	13	16	12	18-3	2.5	.368/.471/.540	.532	.308/.388/.440	.295	14.2
C	G. Kottaras*	PAW	AAA	24	334	32	22	0	9	39	32	71	1-1	-1.6	.241/.316/.408	-.036	.229/.300/.391	.242	-0.0
INF	J. Natale	PME	AA	24	524	66	28	1	5	64	88	36	5-3	0.9	.270/.417/.381	.112	.252/.380/.361	.272	5.2
SS	Y. Navarro	LOW	A-	19	253	36	10	1	5	37	22	52	12-6	0.1	.289/.357/.409	.144	.236/.289/.348	.223	-6.0
RF	J. Reddick*	GRN	A	20	403	60	17	6	18	72	26	51	8-5	0.4	.306/.352/.531	.236	.249/.288/.416	.240	-8.8

Aaron Bates raked in the California League and was raked in the Eastern League, although he sustained good secondary skills after the promotion. ⊘ **Dusty Brown** is an organizational backup catcher who can draw a few walks. ⊘ In five partial seasons in the majors (as well as his last two years in the minors), **Kevin Cash** has never gotten his batting average off the interstate (MLB career .167 AVG). ⊘ As **Royce Clayton**'s career comes to a close, it's worth mentioning that he had more than 7,000 at-bats, nearly 2,000 hits, and more than 200 steals. Moreover, he played very good defense at shortstop, good enough to justify his lineup spot for a decade from 1993 to 2003. ⊘ **Zachary Daeges** led pro baseball with 55 doubles as a 23-year-old in the Cal League. ⊘ Venezuelan **Argenis Diaz** was unimpressive in his first full season in the U.S., hitting poorly as a 20-year-old at Greenville. ⊘ The definition of athletic and toolsy, **Ryan Kalish** was considered by some to be the best position player in the New York-Penn League last year before a hand injury shortened his season. Teams are already asking about him in trades, and his ceiling is of the cathedral variety. ⊘ **George Kottaras** takes his walks, but that's now his only skill. He is no longer a prospect. ⊘ The 0.41 K/BB ratio at Double-A is terrific, but it's all **Jeff Natale** brings to the table. ⊘ **Yomaico Navarro** is another of the plethora of impressive young Latin American talents in the Red Sox' system. He has plenty of tools and can play anywhere in the infield. If there's one knock against him, it's that, at 5-foot-11, 170 pounds, he's a little small. ⊘ **Josh Reddick** is a raw athlete who played well in the Sally League at age 20. He'll put up some nice numbers at Lancaster this year.

Pitchers

PLAYER	TEAM	LVL	AGE	W	L	SV	IP	H	BB	SO	HR	GB%	BABIP	STUFF	WHIP	ERA	PERA	EqERA	EqH9	EqBB9	EqSO9	EqHR9	VORP
A. Alvarez*	PAW	AAA	24	5	8	0	100	102	45	69	9	40.6%	.307	-18	1.47	4.77	5.83	5.97	10.0	4.5	4.5	1.2	-3.9
C. Breslow*	PAW	AAA	26	2	3	1	68²	70	25	73	6	43.3%	.340	-8	1.38	4.06	5.67	5.89	10.3	3.7	7.1	1.1	-2.1
J. Capellan*	LOW	A-	20	4	3	0	75²	68	11	71	1	56.9%	.313	10	1.04	3.69	5.11	6.55	10.6	2.8	4.4	0.5	-7.1
M. Clement '08	SLN	MLB	33	4	4	0	71¹	73	29	50	8	47.4%	.294	0	1.42	4.54	4.77	5.01	9.0	3.3	5.9	0.9	5.7
B. Corey	PAW	AAA	33	6	8	3	68¹	57	20	67	6	52.9%	.288	-5	1.13	3.69	4.36	4.68	8.4	3.0	6.5	1.1	6.7
	BOS	MLB	33	1	0	0	9¹	6	4	6	0	63.6%	.300	2	1.07	1.94	3.17	2.45	7.4	4.9	6.1	0.0	4.3
L. Holdzkom	PME	AA	25	4	1	1	46²	35	30	41	5	59.4%	.250	-11	1.39	3.47	5.26	5.40	7.5	6.9	5.6	1.5	1.0
	PAW	AAA	25	1	0	0	17	19	14	13	0	73.7%	.345	-8	1.94	1.59	6.37	3.24	10.8	7.6	4.9	0.0	4.4
K. Jackson	PME	AA	24	4	9	1	70²	69	48	83	9	28.8%	.331	-16	1.65	5.98	7.87	8.45	10.4	7.1	7.6	1.8	-20.9
E. Martinez	PAW	AAA	25	2	6	1	68	69	28	58	11	46.2%	.302	-37	1.43	5.16	7.45	7.31	10.4	4.2	5.6	2.1	-12.2
J. Papelbon	GRN	A	24	5	8	18	76	86	21	57	4	58.5%	.346	-33	1.41	3.91	6.36	6.46	11.2	4.3	3.2	1.0	-6.8
D. Pauley	PAW	AAA	24	6	6	0	153²	164	49	110	18	55.2%	.304	-19	1.39	4.33	6.14	6.17	10.4	3.2	4.6	1.5	-9.3
C. Zink	PME	AA	27	9	3	0	92²	92	44	55	6	52.3%	.301	-11	1.47	3.98	5.72	5.86	9.7	5.1	3.5	0.9	-2.5
	PAW	AAA	27	2	3	0	47¹	51	27	23	8	42.6%	.269	-34	1.65	5.90	8.04	8.35	10.3	5.4	2.9	2.1	-14.1

Abe Alvarez is just an organizational arm now that he's been lapped by the real pitching prospects in the system. ⊘ Yale product **Craig Breslow** had another serviceable year relieving in Triple-A. He could help 20 other teams in the pen. ⊘ Lefty **Jose Capellan** has very good command of average stuff. He was pretty impressive in the New York-Penn League, but it seems like a bit of a stretch for the Giants to have used the third overall pick of the Rule 5 draft on someone who has never even played in a full-season league. ⊘ **Matt Clement** missed the 2007 season, but should be ready to go in the Cardinals' camp after signing a one-year-plus-option deal. ⊘ Veteran **Bryan Corey** was even better than Breslow and almost made the Sox' playoff roster. ⊘ **Lincoln Holdzkom** has a lot of uniforms in his closet. In December 2006, the Astros took him in the Rule 5 draft from the Cubs, but returned him in spring training. The Cubs tried to slip him through waivers, but the Red Sox snatched him up. This past December, the Phillies took him in the Rule 5 draft. He has the velocity to keep getting chances, but lacks the pitching ability to do anything with them. ⊘ Right-hander **Kyle Jackson** couldn't sustain the success of his strong 2006 showing as his ever-increasing walk rate boiled over to ridiculous (6.1 BB/9). ⊘ A converted catcher who didn't start pitching until 2004, **Edgar Martinez** has a very good fastball, but is limited by his lack of a dependable secondary offering. ⊘ At this point, **Josh Papelbon**'s name is more interesting than his pitching, as he struggled in the Sally League at the age of 24. ⊘ Command lefty **David Pauley** needs a trade to see if his number-four starter act will play in the majors. ⊘ At 27, **Charlie Zink** is still young for a knuckleballer, which is good because he's still trying to control the pitch.

MANAGER: TERRY FRANCONA

YEAR	TEAM	W-L	Pythag +/-	Avg PC	100+ P	120+ P	QS	BQS	REL	REL w Zero R	IBB	Subs	PH	PH Avg	PH HR	SB2	CS2	SB3	CS3	SAC Att	SAC %	POS SAC	Squeeze	Swing	In Play
2005	BOS	95-67	4	99.9	93	3	74	7	442	255	28	59	108	.202	1	42	12	3	0	24	58.3%	13	0	139	98
2006	BOS	86-76	5	95.6	64	2	67	11	453	263	25	71	93	.221	0	46	22	5	1	39	56.4%	22	0	126	106
2007	BOS	96-66	-7	97.9	68	4	81	10	451	323	20	43	83	.203	0	83	20	13	4	54	55.6%	30	3	149	100

You can't say enough about the job Terry Francona did in September of last season after his team had locked up a postseason berth. With the support of the front office, Francona spent the last four weeks of the season getting his roster ready for October. He rested Manny Ramirez and Hideki Okajima almost all month, went to a six-man rotation at times to lighten the load on Josh Beckett and Daisuke Matsuzaka, and stuck to doing so as the Sox' lead over the Yankees dwindled and created an atmosphere of panic around—but not on—the team. All four of those players were stars for the Sox as they went 11-3 in the postseason on their way to another championship. Francona has the confidence of both the people above and below him, giving him latitude to make the right decisions without fear of being undermined.

Chicago Cubs

Four years after the Cubs' loss in the 2003 NLCS, the shadow of the Bartman Ball and the team's unlikely collapse five outs away from the World Series still looms large over the organization. Few teams in recent memory had their expectations raised so quickly, only to see them undermined so dramatically.

The Cubs had experienced fleeting moments of success before. In 1984 the Cubs were eight outs from the World Series when Padre Tim Flannery's grounder found its way through first baseman Leon Durham's legs. Those Cubs were a veteran club cobbled together through trades engineered by general manager Dallas Green, a team that looked the whole while like it might have just that one moment in the sun, squeezed by the contending Cardinals and Mets dynasties in the NL East. The 1989 team that lost the NLCS in less memorable fashion was younger and more promising, but with major contributions from similarly forgettable players such as closer Mitch Williams and outfielders Jerome Walton and Dwight Smith, it still had something of a Bad News Bears feel to it. The 1998 Cubs were a motley crew that snuck into the playoffs by means of the wild card and Sammy Sosa's 66 home runs; even Cubs diehards regarded that edition as an average team that had overachieved.

It was different in 2003. Although that team was not particularly young—the average age of its position players was 31.3—it seemed all but certain that Kerry Wood, Mark Prior, and Carlos Zambrano, the trio of young flamethrowers who formed the core of the starting rotation, would keep the club competitive for at least the next half-dozen seasons. It was in 2003 that the Cubs, always reasonably popular, became a phe-

nomenon, selling out chilly Tuesday afternoon games against the Pirates and graduating into a megabrand to rival the AL East's superpowers.

The Cubs spent the next three seasons trying to chase down the promise of 2003, trading off the same assumption that their fans had made: that Prior, Wood, and Zambrano, paired with a league-average offense, would be enough to lead them back into the playoffs. They came tantalizingly close in 2004 with a team that, because of the additions of first baseman Derrek Lee and prodigal son Greg Maddux, was probably stronger on paper than the 2003 version, but things never went according to plan. The headlines in the first half of that season were Prior's Achilles' tendon injury and Sosa's corked bat, and the Cubs traded winning and losing streaks all year before ultimately seeing the wheel land on the bankrupt space. In 2005, it was Wood's turn to be injured, and with Sosa having departed to Baltimore, the offense was dragged under by the weight of manager Dusty Baker's pets (such as shortstop Neifi Perez and left fielder Todd Hollandsworth), leading to a sub-.500 finish. By 2006, nothing at all was going right: Prior and Wood combined to make just 13 appearances that year, while the offense, handicapped by Lee's broken wrist and uninspired acquisitions such as outfielders Jacque Jones and Juan Pierre, scored just 716 runs, second-to-last in the National League.

This left the Cubs with not only a baseball crisis, but also an identity crisis. Faced with ticket prices that had increased by more than 40 percent since 2003, an attractive competitor in the 2005 world champion White Sox, and an organization that had increasingly begun to

---

CUBS PROSPECTUS

2007 record: 85-77; First place, NL Central; Lost to Diamondbacks in Division Series

Pythagenport record: 87-75

Runs scored per game: 4.64 (8th in NL)

Runs allowed per game: 4.26 (2nd in NL)

Team EqA: .253 (14th in NL)

2007 Batters Age: 29.8 (8th oldest in NL)

2007 Pitchers Age: 28.6 (6th youngest in NL)

Ballpark: Wrigley Field; Hitter's park; Park Factor of 1.032

2007: Cubs back into the playoffs and then promptly back out.

2008: If Lou learns to trust the kids, the Cubs might actually win a playoff game.

behave more like a big corporation and less like a quasi-community trust, fans were calling for the ouster of both Baker and GM Jim Hendry. By the end of the year, whole rows of empty seats could be observed at Wrigley Field for the first time in several seasons. Compounding matters further, the Tribune Company was preparing to sell the Cubs, ending a 30-year relationship with the club. The promise of 2003 had changed everything. Being baseball's lovable losers was no longer going to be enough.

It's in this context that we must view the Cubs' decision following the 2006 season to commit $285 million to long-term contracts for sluggers Alfonso Soriano and Aramis Ramirez, utilityman Mark DeRosa, and starters Ted Lilly and Jason Marquis. The Cubs had never gone on a spending spree before. Rather, their strategy, at least since Green resigned after the 1987 season, had been to put together a modestly competitive team on a modestly significant budget, a haphazard mix of youth and veteran talent gathered around one or two superstars and thus prone to rise and fall depending on the fluctuating performances of those stars or the odd career year from one of their supporting players.

If the phrase "modestly significant budget" sounds strange, it's because the Tribune Company was never exactly unwilling to spend; the Cubs have ranked in the top 15 in the majors in payroll in every year since 1991 (see Table 1). At the same time, the organization was only willing to spend so much, as the Cubs have never ranked in the top five in payroll, a streak that has yet to be broken but probably will be once the back-loaded contracts of players such as Soriano come into full effect. The result has been a whole lot of Jeff Blausers,

Henry Rodriguezes, and Jacque Joneses, players who were not without their uses, but were not enough to carry a team into contention. The worst transgression came before the 2006 season, when the Cubs came very close to matching the Dodgers' offer to shortstop Rafael Furcal. Instead, they came up a little short and opted to spend their money instead on Jones and a couple of middle relievers. That year, Cubs shortstops combined for a ghastly -22.4 VORP.

The break between the construction of the 2007 Cubs and the organization's usual way of doing business is easier to see if we split last year's roster into the following four categories:

- Players selected in the amateur draft or signed as amateur free agents who have remained with the club ever since.
- Players who were acquired and developed (A&D). This means players who were picked up in trade before they had established themselves in the major leagues, which we define as having fewer than 400 career innings pitched, 100 pitching appearances, or 1200 plate appearances at the time of their acquisition. Players picked up off the waiver wire, signed as minor league free agents, purchased from another club, or acquired in the Rule 5 draft are also assigned to this category.
- Established major leaguers who are acquired in trade.
- Major league free agents.

Note that these four categories form a continuum of sorts. The draft end of the spectrum represents minimal financial investment beyond the team's long-term commitments to scouting and development. The free agents at the other end of the spectrum can only be obtained through large and immediate expenditures. In between, it is important to separate the A&D players from the established major leaguers acquired in trade because the former are much closer to players selected in the draft in terms of cost and team control, while the latter are not unlike free-agent signings in that they're already earning major league salaries and have already put time on their clocks toward the next time they will be eligible for free agency.

The breakdown for the 2007 Cubs can be found in Table 2. Players are listed by their 2007 Wins Above Replacement (WARP) scores, with the handful of players who posted negative WARPs excluded from the analysis. The numbers in parentheses before each category's WARP total indicate the percentage of the team's total WARP value that was obtained through that method. As

Table 1. Cubs Payroll, 1988–2007

Year	Payroll ($M)	MLB Rank
1991	$26.9	10
1992	$29.0	15
1993	$38.3	6
1994	$35.7	12
1995	$32.5	12
1996	$31.0	14
1997	$39.8	14
1998	$49.4	10
1999	$55.4	10
2000	$62.1	12
2001	$64.5	15
2002	$75.7	12
2003	$79.9	11
2004	$90.6	7
2005	$87.0	9
2006	$94.4	7
2007	$99.7	8

Table 2. Means of Acquisition for 2007 Cubs

Draft	WARP	A&D	WARP	Trade	WARP	Free Agent	WARP
Carlos Zambrano	7.5	Matt Murton	1.7	Aramis Ramirez	7.3	Alfonso Soriano	7.1
Rich Hill	4.8	Mike Fontenot	1.1	Derrek Lee	7.2	Ted Lilly	5.9
Carlos Marmol	4.2	Angel Guzman	0.8	Jason Kendall	0.4	Bob Howry	4.9
Sean Marshall	2.8	Angel Pagan	0.6	Neal Cotts	0.3	Mark DeRosa	4.5
Michael Wuertz	2.4	Kevin Hart	0.4			Ryan Dempster	3.2
Ryan Theriot	2.1	Koyie Hill	0.2			Jacque Jones	3.0
Geovany Soto	1.5					Jason Marquis	2.9
Will Ohman	1.3					Daryle Ward	1.8
Kerry Wood	0.8					Cliff Floyd	1.4
Rocky Cherry	0.5					Scott Eyre	1.2
Felix Pie	0.5					Michael Barrett	0.9
Clay Rapada	0.5						
Sam Fuld	0.2						
Ronny Cedeño	0.1						
Total (39.2%)	**29.2**	**Total (5.6%)**	**4.8**	**Total (17.7%)**	**15.2**	**Total (42.8%)**	**36.8**

we can see, the largest fraction of the 2007 Cubs' value—about 43 percent—came from the free-agent market. By comparison, the draft category registers at 39 percent, about half of which is international amateur free-agent signings from Latin America. With the notable exceptions of Derrek Lee and Aramis Ramirez, both of whom were acquired in trades that proved to be steals, there is little of note in the middle two categories; Hendry has gone a couple of years without making a truly high-impact trade, and the Cubs have gotten very little from the A&D channel.

To place these numbers in context, compare them to those of the Cubs' other playoff teams from the divisional era in Table 3. The Cubs derived a much larger percentage of their value from free agents in 2007 than in any of their other playoff seasons. Even the 1998 team, which was buoyed by a $10-million increase in payroll, realized only a quarter of its value from free agents. At the same time, the contributions of talent acquired from the draft last year were not especially low by Cubs standards. The Cubs have rarely been a scouting-and-development machine, but they have had some rather notable successes with acquiring and developing players, specifically Sosa and Hall of Fame second baseman Ryne Sandberg. As in the cases of Lee and Ramirez, they also have a legacy of winning trades. The ultimate manifestation of these strengths was the 1984 team, which was put together almost entirely via trades and A&D. For better or for worse, the Cubs have broken from that legacy.

A second comparison, this to the other seven playoff clubs from 2007, provides a greater understanding of the extent to which last year's Cubs were dependent upon their free agents, as the team's 43 percent figure

for free-agent contributors is the highest of the eight playoff clubs in Table 4. Their closest competitors in that category, the Red Sox, have had their figure significantly boosted by David Ortiz, who signed to a deeply discounted contract in 2003 after the Twins nontendered him. Ortiz made 1,693 plate appearances for the Twins, barely a full season more than our cutoff for A&D players. Although the Yankees have had to spend a lot to re-sign their own free agents, both of the other big-budget teams on the list have gotten more out of their homegrown talent than the Cubs, while moderate to low spenders such as the Indians, Rockies, Phillies, and Diamondbacks all reached the playoffs while hardly having to use the free agent market at all.

Predictably, the Cubs' foray into the free-agent market was met with a certain ambivalence. Without Dusty Baker to kick around anymore, some of the same columnists who had spent years lamenting that the Cubs were too cheap were instead taking jabs at the club for being spendthrifts. In some respects, the Cubs' results in 2007 played perfectly into this witches' brew of cynicism and heightened expectations. On the one hand, the Cubs improved by 19 wins, made the playoffs, and registered a modest gain in attendance. On the other hand, they won only 85 games, won the weakest division in baseball by a mere two games with a worse record than the league's wild-card team, and were summarily swept in three lackluster NLDS games by the overachieving Diamondbacks. The 2007 Cubs did everything possible to test the proposition that reaching the playoffs is the ultimate measure of success or failure in the wild-card era.

How could the Cubs spend $300 million on free agents to add to a reasonable if not spectacular core of

Table 3. Means of Acquisition for Cubs Playoff Teams

Method	1984	1989	1998	2003	2007
Draft	9.8%	44.7%	31.5%	38.7%	34.0%
A&D	37.3%	17.3%	31.1%	12.8%	5.6%
Trade	50.4%	19.0%	12.8%	26.5%	17.7%
Free Agent	2.5%	19.0%	24.7%	22.0%	42.8%

Table 4. Means of Acqusition for 2007 MLB Playoff Teams

Method	Cubs	Red Sox	Angels	Yankees	Indians	Rockies	Phillies	D'backs
Draft	34.0%	23.9%	57.0%	47.8%	47.9%	63.4%	58.0%	52.5%
A&D	5.6%	8.4%	9.7%	5.7%	38.4%	14.7%	13.2%	12.7%
Trade	17.7%	26.0%	0.0%	19.9%	0.8%	9.0%	16.5%	24.1%
Free Agent	42.8%	41.8%	33.3%	26.6%	12.9%	12.9%	12.3%	10.7%

talent and still have nothing better than a winless first-round playoff exit to show for it? What may be showing through is the Cubs' tendency to think a bit too linearly. Free-agent signings are nice, and so are players from your farm system, but those are not the only ways to acquire talent in baseball. Judging by their poor performance in the A&D category, the Cubs seem to have very little appreciation for the value available in the free-talent pool. Similarly, Hendry has a pretty good record in trades when he's made them, but he's become strangely gun-shy since stealing Lee from the Marlins for Hee Seop Choi and a minor league throw-in.

Moreover, there is still an unhealthy skepticism at the major league level toward the organization's minor league talent. Although current manager Lou Piniella is more tolerant of the young than Baker was, center fielder Felix Pie still found himself flying to and from Des Moines far too often last year for someone not competing in the Iowa Caucus. Similarly, the potential contributions of players such as outfielder Matt Murton and shortstop Ronny Cedeño were largely ignored. The Cubs also made one outright terrible trade when third baseman Scott Moore and reliever Rocky Cherry, both of whom should become quality major leaguers, were sent to Baltimore for a handful of starts from Steve Trachsel, who was only doing the rest of the NL Central a favor when he took the mound for the Cubs.

On this front, the Cubs' late-season warming to catcher Geovany Soto should be taken as a sign of progress. So too should their signing of outfielder Kosuke Fukudome, who will become the first Japanese player ever to suit up for the Cubs. Although Fukudome still qualifies as a free agent acquisition, and received a salary that reflects that, it suggests that the Cubs are willing to put their faith in something other than a major league track record when it comes to acquiring players.

While their execution needs improvement, the Cubs had little choice but to increase their payroll. Their near-miss in 2003 raised the stakes, but the Prior/Wood/Sosa era is over and gone. While in certain respects the Cubs' brand is stronger than it has ever been, its dimensions have changed. No longer are fans liable to find the team cuddly and cute in its leaner years; the Cubs have increased ticket prices as though they are Red Sox West, and the fans are going to expect a level of performance to match. Yes, near-sellout attendance at Wrigley Field seems like a given these days, but the same might have been said of the Orioles during their string of sellouts in the early years of Camden Yards, or the Blue Jays in the early days of SkyDome. That Wrigley Field will soon be one of just two major league parks built before the 1960s gives the venue a considerable cachet, but as in Baltimore and Toronto, or in a different way, Pittsburgh and Cincinnati, a prestigious ballpark populated by a poor team will not draw fans on its own. At its most basic level, a brand is a set of expectations associated with a product, and if those expectations are not met, the results can be quite damaging.

While high expectations can be a curse, they can also be a blessing. If the signing of Fukudome and the trust afforded to Soto are indeed indicative of a new way of thinking, one open to a broader, more aggressive spread of talent acquisition, Cubs fans may soon have reason to forget all about Steve Bartman.

HITTERS

Henry Blanco   C

Bats: R   Throws: R   Height: 5' 11"   Weight: 220   Born: August 29, 1971   Age: 36

YEAR	TEAM	LVL	AGE	PA	R	2B	3B	HR	RBI	BB	SO	SB	CS	EqBRR	AVG	OBP	SLG	MLVr	EqAVG	EqOBP	EqSLG	EqA	VORP	DEFENSE	
2005	CHN	MLB	33	178	16	6	0	6	25	11	24	0	0	-0.1	.242	.287	.391	-.123	.235	.284	.389	.233	1.0	48-C	9
2006	CHN	MLB	34	261	23	15	2	6	37	14	38	0	0	-1.6	.266	.304	.419	-.076	.260	.301	.409	.245	1.7	59-C	7
2007	CHN	MLB	35	58	3	3	0	0	4	2	12	0	0	0.0	.167	.193	.222	-.598	.167	.193	.222	.123	-6.1	12-C	1
2008	CHN	MLB	36	59	5	3	0	1	6	3	10	0	0	-0.1	.224	.267	.350	-.285	.219	.263	.343	.204	-1.4	19-C	2

Breakout: 24% Improve: 38% Collapse: 43% Attrition: 53%   Comparables: John Flaherty, Bill Haselman, Ray Murray, Tim Laker

One of the prouder representatives of *backuptis catcherus*, Blanco missed most of last season due to a herniated disc. In an odd way, not having the security blanket of Blanco's arm off the bench might have forced the Cubs to look at Michael Barrett's defense in a harsher light, thus leading to Barrett's being run out of town. Blanco is under contract for $2.8 million this season, but now that the equally strong-armed Soto is the regular the Cubs might be better off finding a backup catcher with a little more life in his bat.

Kyler Burke   RF

Bats: L   Throws: L   Height: 6' 3"   Weight: 205   Born: April 20, 1988   Age: 20

YEAR	TEAM	LVL	AGE	PA	R	2B	3B	HR	RBI	BB	SO	SB	CS	EqBRR	AVG	OBP	SLG	MLVr	EqAVG	EqOBP	EqSLG	EqA	VORP	DEFENSE	
2006	PDR	Rk	18	192	24	3	4	1	15	26	56	1	3	-4.2	.209	.313	.294	-.189	.155	.224	.207	.132	-66.9	40-RF	-8
2007	FTW	A	19	243	24	7	1	1	21	26	73	3	1	-0.3	.211	.305	.268	-.169	.182	.255	.232	.168	-30.3	59-RF	-13
2007	BOI	A-	19	259	35	11	1	10	41	24	63	1	3	-2.2	.254	.340	.446	.054	.189	.245	.294	.182	-47.3	55-RF	-5
2008	CHN	MLB	20	538	42	25	2	9	43	41	154	6	3	-0.3	.201	.265	.315	-.348	.196	.260	.309	.191	-29.9	127-RF	0

Breakout: 68% Improve: 77% Collapse: 13% Attrition: 10%   Comparables: Terrence Long, Carlos Beltran, Bronson Sardinha, Sean Swedlow

An extremely raw import from the Padres organization, Burke struggled in the first half of last year following an aggressive promotion to the Midwest League. After the Cubs acquired him in the Barrett deal, they sent him down to the Northwest League, and he rewarded them with flashes of power and plate discipline. His tools are very good, and he bears watching.

Ronny Cedeño   SS

Bats: R   Throws: R   Height: 6' 0"   Weight: 180   Born: February 2, 1983   Age: 25

YEAR	TEAM	LVL	AGE	PA	R	2B	3B	HR	RBI	BB	SO	SB	CS	EqBRR	AVG	OBP	SLG	MLVr	EqAVG	EqOBP	EqSLG	EqA	VORP	DEFENSE			
2005	IOW	AAA	22	275	42	14	1	8	36	20	31	11	3	1.6	.355	.403	.518	.302	.307	.351	.446	.276	19.8	64-SS	5		
2005	CHN	MLB	22	89	13	3	0	1	6	5	11	1	0	0.2	.300	.356	.375	.019	.296	.352	.370	.258	3.8	18-SS	-2		
2006	CHN	MLB	23	572	51	18	7	6	41	17	109	8	8	-0.7	.245	.271	.339	-.258	.243	.270	.337	.207	-17.8	127-SS	1	14-2B	0
2007	IOW	AAA	24	327	52	15	3	10	37	30	46	6	4	-0.4	.359	.422	.537	.363	.316	.381	.478	.292	31.5	72-SS	-4		
2007	CHN	MLB	24	80	6	2	0	4	13	3	18	2	1	-0.2	.203	.231	.392	-.281	.203	.231	.392	.214	-2.8	12-SS	-2		
2008	CHN	MLB	25	435	53	20	3	11	50	27	72	8	3	0.5	.278	.326	.422	-.044	.272	.321	.414	.251	13.3	103-SS	0		

Breakout: 18% Improve: 45% Collapse: 25% Attrition: 19%   Comparables: Rafael Ramirez, Chico Carrasquel, Jose Castillo, Orlando Cabrera

As much as it might have chapped Cedeño to see Ryan Theriot emerge with the shortstop job after Cesar Izturis was declared unfit for duty, the truth is that he only has so much room for complaint; over nearly 750 plate appearances in the big leagues, Cedeño's career VORP stands at -16.8. Still, as his good doings in Triple-A Iowa last year attest, he's fundamentally a better player than Theriot, the major differences being the doubles power that Cedeño has and Theriot lacks, and also Cedeño's better footwork at shortstop. Cedeño's is a tried and true skill set—the same one that's earning Orlando Cabrera millions of dollars every season—and the Cubs will give it another long look come spring training.

Tyler Colvin — OF

Bats: L   Throws: L   Height: 6' 3"   Weight: 190   Born: September 5, 1985   Age: 22

YEAR	TEAM	LVL	AGE	PA	R	2B	3B	HR	RBI	BB	SO	SB	CS	EqBRR	AVG	OBP	SLG	MLVr	EqAVG	EqOBP	EqSLG	EqA	VORP	DEFENSE			
2006	BOI	A-	20	288	50	12	6	11	53	17	55	12	5	-1.4	.268	.313	.483	.130	.210	.247	.358	.207	-41.0	46-LF	-5	18-CF	0
2007	DAY	A+	21	262	38	24	3	7	50	10	47	10	4	0.4	.306	.336	.514	.198	.259	.290	.449	.250	4.6	61-CF	7		
2007	TEN	AA	21	257	34	11	2	9	31	5	54	7	1	2.6	.291	.313	.462	.059	.256	.272	.412	.234	-2.1	44-CF	8	12-RF	-1
2008	CHN	MLB	22	592	68	34	4	18	71	27	133	15	6	1.3	.257	.295	.429	-.106	.251	.290	.420	.239	3.4	139-CF	0		

Breakout: 44% Improve: 67% Collapse: 10% Attrition: 9%   Comparables: Nic Jackson, Terrence Long, Jacque Jones, Aaron Rowand

At this stage of his development, Colvin has a couple of significant holes in his swing; anytime your strikeout-to-walk ratio looks like Tom Brady's touchdown-to-interception ratio, that's bad news. While the power and speed tools are there, they're not off the charts. Colvin's upside is being a .280/.320/.500-type of hitter; that's valuable in center field, but less so in an outfield corner, so his defensive progress is the key. Although our translations suggest Colvin took quite well to center last year, the scouting reports were mixed.

Mark DeRosa — 2B

Bats: R   Throws: R   Height: 6' 1"   Weight: 205   Born: February 26, 1975   Age: 33

YEAR	TEAM	LVL	AGE	PA	R	2B	3B	HR	RBI	BB	SO	SB	CS	EqBRR	AVG	OBP	SLG	MLVr	EqAVG	EqOBP	EqSLG	EqA	VORP	DEFENSE			
2005	TEX	MLB	30	166	26	5	0	8	20	16	35	1	0	-0.1	.243	.325	.439	-.018	.240	.335	.452	.271	3.6	21-RF	0		
2006	TEX	MLB	31	572	78	40	2	13	74	44	102	4	4	-2.8	.296	.357	.456	.065	.294	.361	.459	.280	21.9	58-RF	5	39-3B	-3
2007	CHN	MLB	32	574	64	28	3	10	72	58	93	1	2	0.1	.293	.371	.420	.071	.288	.371	.418	.276	21.3	79-2B	1	32-3B	3
2008	CHN	MLB	33	488	62	26	2	12	59	47	79	3	2	-0.7	.286	.360	.439	.043	.280	.354	.430	.270	18.9	115-2B	-2		

Breakout: 10% Improve: 38% Collapse: 32% Attrition: 17%   Comparables: Randy Velarde, Travis Fryman, Kevin Seitzer, Jerry Priddy

DeRosa did exactly what should have been expected of him last year: he got into the lineup four or five times a week, had smart at-bats, found ways to get on base, banged out the occasional extra-base hit, and fielded competently wherever he played. Whether or not he's an "everyday second baseman" is a silly argument; he hits and fields as well as half the regulars at that position. If the Cubs bring in a Brian Roberts-type and bump DeRosa into a utility role, the gains will be less than they might appear at first glance.

Josh Donaldson — C

Bats: R   Throws: R   Height: 6' 0"   Weight: 195   Born: December 8, 1985   Age: 22

YEAR	TEAM	LVL	AGE	PA	R	2B	3B	HR	RBI	BB	SO	SB	CS	EqBRR	AVG	OBP	SLG	MLVr	EqAVG	EqOBP	EqSLG	EqA	VORP	DEFENSE	
2007	BOI	A-	21	202	37	11	2	9	35	37	34	6	2	2.1	.346	.470	.605	.512	.251	.350	.417	.269	14.7	41-C	4
2008	CHN	MLB	22	536	60	28	3	12	54	52	128	9	4	0.6	.236	.314	.378	-.155	.231	.309	.371	.235	2.8	126-C	3

Breakout: 4% Improve: 20% Collapse: 48% Attrition: 3%   Comparables: Curtis Thigpen, Brad Ripplemeyer, Mike Daniel, Dan Gray

Donaldson's numbers were awesome at Low-A Boise last year. Although he just missed qualifying for the Pioneer League batting title, he would have ranked second in that department and first in the league in both on-base percentage and slugging had he qualified. PECOTA hedges on those numbers a bit, with its inherent skepticism toward accomplished college players playing short-season ball, but Donaldson is a considerably better athlete than comparables such as Thigpen. If he can catch—and the jury is still out on that—he could emerge as one of the major sleepers of the 2007 draft.

Cliff Floyd — OF

Bats: L   Throws: R   Height: 6' 4"   Weight: 230   Born: December 5, 1972   Age: 35

YEAR	TEAM	LVL	AGE	PA	R	2B	3B	HR	RBI	BB	SO	SB	CS	EqBRR	AVG	OBP	SLG	MLVr	EqAVG	EqOBP	EqSLG	EqA	VORP	DEFENSE			
2005	NYN	MLB	32	626	85	22	2	34	98	63	98	12	2	0.5	.273	.358	.505	.185	.271	.358	.517	.295	37.3	143-LF	13		
2006	NYN	MLB	33	376	45	19	1	11	44	29	58	6	0	0.7	.244	.324	.407	-.045	.249	.327	.414	.261	1.3	85-LF	-1		
2007	CHN	MLB	34	322	40	10	1	9	45	35	47	0	0	-2.3	.284	.373	.422	.071	.274	.366	.420	.276	9.6	46-RF	-7	15-LF	2
2008	TBA	MLB	35	214	26	9	1	6	27	20	35	2	1	-0.2	.257	.332	.406	-.046	.260	.338	.426	.268	3.0	54-LF	-3		

Breakout: 14% Improve: 34% Collapse: 37% Attrition: 47%   Comparables: Walt Moryn, Al Martin, Gates Brown, Leon Wagner

This is sort of what it's like when you finally get with your dream girl from sophomore year, only it happens twenty years, three children, and forty pounds later after one too many rum-and-Cokes at your high school reunion.

Hendry had long courted Chicago native Floyd, and jumped at the opportunity to add him to the roster in late January, a superfluous move that left all the Chicago outfielders feeling like the glass was half-empty. Floyd is a consummate professional who can still hold his own against right-handed pitching, but his knees are completely gone, making him a major liability on the basepaths and in the field. Signed to a one-year deal with the Rays, he could form a decent DH platoon with Jonny Gomes.

Mike Fontenot — 2B

Bats: L Throws: R Height: 5' 8" Weight: 170 Born: June 9, 1980 Age: 28

YEAR	TEAM	LVL	AGE	PA	R	2B	3B	HR	RBI	BB	SO	SB	CS	EqBRR	AVG	OBP	SLG	MLVr	EqAVG	EqOBP	EqSLG	EqA	VORP	DEFENSE			
2005	IOW	AAA	25	449	60	22	10	6	39	59	77	3	2	-1.1	.272	.377	.430	.043	.237	.333	.373	.249	5.6	58-2B	2	35-3B	-4
2006	IOW	AAA	26	418	54	28	2	8	36	47	64	5	4	-3.5	.296	.375	.450	.145	.264	.338	.410	.261	14.0	87-2B	-1		
2007	IOW	AAA	27	231	46	17	4	6	34	16	32	3	1	1.9	.336	.384	.540	.283	.296	.343	.479	.280	17.4	20-SS	-1	18-2B	-2
2007	CHN	MLB	27	260	32	12	4	3	29	22	43	5	4	0.4	.278	.336	.402	-.031	.275	.338	.412	.257	4.3	52-2B	1		
2008	CHN	MLB	28	349	48	20	3	7	37	35	57	5	2	0.6	.282	.357	.431	.024	.276	.352	.422	.267	15.4	84-2B	0		

Breakout: 23% Improve: 53% Collapse: 20% Attrition: 17%   Comparables: Chuck Hiller, Mike Cubbage, Todd Walker, Rob Wilfong

Is Jim Hendry a closet Francophile? Two years ago, he acquired outfielders named Jacque and Pierre, and at times last season, his double-play combination was a diminutive duo named Theriot and Fontenot. Fontenot is a mildly underrated player, with a skill set not unlike DeRosa's (minus some positional flexibility), or ex-Cub Todd Walker (minus about ten points of batting average). If Fontenot does not win an everyday job out of spring training, teams looking for a second baseman on the cheap could do worse than to try to pry him away from Hendry.

Jake Fox — 1B/OF

Bats: R Throws: R Height: 6' 0" Weight: 210 Born: July 20, 1982 Age: 25

YEAR	TEAM	LVL	AGE	PA	R	2B	3B	HR	RBI	BB	SO	SB	CS	EqBRR	AVG	OBP	SLG	MLVr	EqAVG	EqOBP	EqSLG	EqA	VORP	DEFENSE			
2005	DAY	A+	22	309	37	20	0	9	40	26	48	5	2	-2.9	.281	.357	.456	.135	.237	.301	.381	.239	-0.6	60-C	-3		
2006	DAY	A+	23	291	45	15	1	16	61	27	49	4	1	-2.6	.313	.383	.574	.359	.273	.334	.504	.284	20.6	48-C	-2		
2006	WTN	AA	23	204	20	17	0	5	25	9	44	0	0	-0.6	.269	.304	.435	.081	.258	.289	.433	.245	3.5	41-C	0		
2007	TEN	AA	24	388	60	23	1	18	60	17	72	6	2	-3.4	.284	.327	.504	.131	.252	.286	.452	.250	-1.4	35-1B	4	17-LF	3
2007	IOW	AAA	24	108	18	7	0	6	19	5	23	2	0	0.2	.283	.343	.535	.146	.260	.315	.490	.273	2.3	13-RF	0		
2007	CHN	MLB	24	15	3	2	0	0	1	1	2	0	0	0.0	.143	.200	.286	-.511	.143	.200	.214	.112	-1.5				
2008	CHN	MLB	25	540	63	28	2	21	80	32	110	8	3	-0.9	.262	.313	.453	-.038	.256	.308	.444	.254	8.7	127-C	1		

Breakout: 15% Improve: 49% Collapse: 23% Attrition: 17%   Comparables: Riccardo Ingram, David Gibralter, Ryan Garko, Stan Royer

Jake Fox's power is very real, but it is his only tool; he has no concept of the strike zone and a cumbersome body that tried and failed to take to catching. PECOTA is thinking in the right direction in terms of Garko, but that's really the best-case scenario. More likely, Fox will be useful to a team looking to conserve roster space that is willing to employ him as a lefty-mashing pinch-hitter and emergency catcher.

Kosuke Fukudome — RF

Bats: L Throws: R Height: 6' 0" Weight: 190 Born: April 26, 1977 Age: 31

YEAR	TEAM	LVL	AGE	PA	R	2B	3B	HR	RBI	BB	SO	SB	CS	EqBRR	AVG	OBP	SLG	MLVr	EqAVG	EqOBP	EqSLG	EqA	VORP	DEFENSE	
2005	CHU	JP	28	608	102	39	6	28	103	93	128	13	5	0.0	.328	.431	.590	.504	.271	.364	.458	.285	31.7		
2006	CHU	JP	29	578	117	47	5	31	104	76	94	11	2	0.0	.351	.438	.653	.638	.314	.399	.543	.318	63.7		
2007	CHU	JP	30	348	64	22	0	13	48	69	66	5	2	0.0	.294	.443	.520	.392	.280	.431	.455	.314	29.4		
2008	CHN	MLB	31	465	80	30	4	15	58	70	94	9	3	0.9	.289	.401	.504	.198	.282	.395	.494	.303	29.2	110-RF	0

Breakout: 7% Improve: 29% Collapse: 29% Attrition: 9%   Comparables: J.D. Drew, Gene Hermanski, Jim Edmonds, Fred Lynn

An inspired acquisition by Hendry, Fukudome is a J.D. Drew/Bobby Abreu-type of player, not a huge power threat, but someone who can get on base at a .390 or .400 clip while contributing in all facets of the game. The Cubs have had limited experience with Asian players—Fukudome is the first Japanese player on their roster, and the engagements with Koreans Hee Seop Choi and Jae Kuk Ryu ended bitterly—but it's worth remembering that Lou Piniella was Ichiro Suzuki's first manager in the States. The question is whether Fukudome can handle center or will be limited to right field, the position he played most often in Japan. Japanese-based observers such as new Royals manager Trey Hillman think Fukudome has the speed and instincts to handle center competently, if perhaps not on an everyday basis.

Sam Fuld   OF

Bats: L   Throws: L   Height: 5' 10"   Weight: 180   Born: November 20, 1981   Age: 26

YEAR	TEAM	LVL	AGE	PA	R	2B	3B	HR	RBI	BB	SO	SB	CS	EqBRR	AVG	OBP	SLG	MLVr	EqAVG	EqOBP	EqSLG	EqA	VORP	DEFENSE		
2005	PEO	A	23	508	82	32	6	5	37	50	44	18	11	-1.3	.300	.377	.433	.165	.255	.315	.373	.239	-0.6	118-CF	15	
2006	DAY	A+	24	405	63	19	6	4	40	40	54	22	3	7.9	.300	.378	.422	.149	.259	.328	.377	.253	3.3	84-CF	14	
2007	TEN	AA	25	392	56	23	2	2	27	41	38	10	3	0.8	.290	.372	.388	.049	.251	.325	.341	.241	-3.5	57-CF	13	20-RF 3
2007	IOW	AAA	25	63	13	4	1	1	2	9	5	2	0	2.0	.269	.397	.442	.099	.245	.375	.434	.285	2.6			
2008	CHN	MLB	26	498	63	28	3	4	39	43	63	13	4	1.5	.265	.334	.369	-.112	.259	.329	.362	.243	2.8	117-CF	1	

Breakout: 17% Improve: 40% Collapse: 26% Attrition: 15%   Comparables: Brian Kowitz, Kevin Reese, Chris Prieto, Dustin Delucchi

Fuld is a hard-working, smart, fundamentally sound player who takes enough walks to be useful as a fourth outfielder, but whose manager could very easily fall in love with him to the ultimate detriment of the club—think Scott Podsednik. Apart from Felix Pie, Fuld and Angel Pagan are the only guys on the Cubs' 40-man roster who can legitimately play center field, and Fuld may be used as Pie's foil in spring training.

Jacque Jones   OF

Bats: L   Throws: L   Height: 5' 10"   Weight: 200   Born: April 25, 1975   Age: 33

YEAR	TEAM	LVL	AGE	PA	R	2B	3B	HR	RBI	BB	SO	SB	CS	EqBRR	AVG	OBP	SLG	MLVr	EqAVG	EqOBP	EqSLG	EqA	VORP	DEFENSE		
2005	MIN	MLB	30	585	74	22	4	23	73	51	120	13	4	1.7	.249	.319	.438	-.014	.249	.329	.449	.268	9.7	120-RF	15	
2006	CHN	MLB	31	577	73	31	1	27	81	35	116	9	1	1.2	.285	.334	.499	.108	.278	.328	.490	.277	24.6	136-RF	5	
2007	CHN	MLB	32	495	52	33	2	5	66	34	70	6	3	-3.2	.285	.335	.400	-.027	.279	.334	.396	.255	7.6	72-CF	8	39-RF -2
2008	DET	MLB	33	379	42	17	2	6	39	25	64	5	2	-0.3	.267	.318	.380	-.096	.267	.320	.397	.253	0.9	91-RF	0	

Breakout: 6% Improve: 26% Collapse: 39% Attrition: 28%   Comparables: Ralph Garr, Cleon Jones, Jim Eisenreich, Milt Thompson

Last year we learned that Jones can still play a pretty good center field. He's always gotten good jumps on the ball, and by the second half of the year, he looked confident and natural at his new position. Indeed, Jones might well be among the 30 best center fielders in baseball, but as a corner guy, he needs to be platooned carefully and monitored for any further signs of decline. Fortunately he has a suitable partner in the Tigers' expected left-field platoon in Marcus Thames. Jones' PECOTA projection looks harsh, but the 37 points of OPS it expects him to lose off last year's numbers are about the going rate for a left-handed hitter coming back to the more difficult league.

Jason Kendall   C

Bats: R   Throws: R   Height: 6' 0"   Weight: 205   Born: June 26, 1974   Age: 34

YEAR	TEAM	LVL	AGE	PA	R	2B	3B	HR	RBI	BB	SO	SB	CS	EqBRR	AVG	OBP	SLG	MLVr	EqAVG	EqOBP	EqSLG	EqA	VORP	DEFENSE	
2005	OAK	MLB	31	676	70	28	1	0	53	50	39	8	3	3.2	.271	.345	.321	-.108	.282	.361	.339	.255	9.9	144-C	-5
2006	OAK	MLB	32	626	76	23	0	1	50	53	54	11	5	1.0	.295	.367	.342	-.058	.302	.379	.353	.266	13.2	140-C	5
2007	OAK	MLB	33	312	24	10	0	2	22	12	27	3	1	-0.7	.226	.261	.281	-.363	.238	.277	.303	.205	-13.2	80-C	-7
2007	CHN	MLB	33	202	21	10	1	1	19	19	15	0	3	-0.5	.270	.362	.356	-.053	.263	.355	.349	.248	3.3	48-C	-7
2008	MIL	MLB	34	293	30	12	1	1	22	22	25	4	1	-0.2	.255	.324	.321	-.198	.255	.322	.324	.228	0.6	72-C	-3

Breakout: 7% Improve: 30% Collapse: 51% Attrition: 42%   Comparables: Joe Girardi, Brad Ausmus, Jerry Grote, Paul Lo Duca

Although Kendall performed reasonably well for the Cubs after they acquired him in mid-July, he'll best help Chicago by hurting Milwaukee as the Brewers' regular catcher this year. Kendall's only real skill is his ability to get on base by taking ball four and being hit by pitches, yet he posted a .301 OBP last season. Moreover, Kendall's throwing arm is now a major liability, as he allowed 111 of 131 baserunners to steal successfully against him last year, including 52 of 57 after returning to the NL. At age 33 and with a pair of gimpy knees, Kendall has little chance of escaping the pull of the undertow that's about to sink his career.

Derrek Lee   1B

Bats: R   Throws: R   Height: 6' 5"   Weight: 245   Born: September 6, 1975   Age: 32

YEAR	TEAM	LVL	AGE	PA	R	2B	3B	HR	RBI	BB	SO	SB	CS	EqBRR	AVG	OBP	SLG	MLVr	EqAVG	EqOBP	EqSLG	EqA	VORP	DEFENSE	
2005	CHN	MLB	29	691	120	50	3	46	107	85	109	15	3	0.5	.335	.418	.662	.533	.323	.408	.649	.341	96.4	156-1B	16
2006	CHN	MLB	30	204	30	9	0	8	30	25	41	8	4	0.0	.286	.368	.474	.127	.282	.368	.471	.287	7.5	44-1B	4
2007	CHN	MLB	31	650	91	43	1	22	82	71	114	6	5	-5.2	.317	.400	.513	.265	.310	.397	.511	.306	48.6	143-1B	11
2008	CHN	MLB	32	582	94	34	2	25	91	66	100	13	3	-0.5	.303	.387	.527	.219	.296	.381	.517	.302	37.7	136-1B	5

Breakout: 3% Improve: 32% Collapse: 24% Attrition: 7%   Comparables: Orlando Cepeda, Eric Karros, Donn Clendenon, George Scott

Lee's 2006 wrist injury seemed to have sapped him of his power early last year, but he banged out 16 home runs after the All-Star break, quieting most of those concerns. Still, while Lee is a good athlete who should age better than your typical burly first baseman, he doesn't run as well as he used to, and 32 is an age at which most hitters can't avoid some symptoms of decline. Expect a little more in the home run department, but perhaps a little less of everything else.

Craig Monroe — OF — Bats: R — Throws: R — Height: 6' 1" — Weight: 205 — Born: February 27, 1977 — Age: 31

YEAR	TEAM	LVL	AGE	PA	R	2B	3B	HR	RBI	BB	SO	SB	CS	EqBRR	AVG	OBP	SLG	MLVr	EqAVG	EqOBP	EqSLG	EqA	VORP	DEFENSE			
2005	DET	MLB	28	623	69	30	3	20	89	40	95	8	3	1.8	.277	.322	.446	.034	.285	.339	.472	.278	17.0	71-RF	-4	57-LF	-1
2006	DET	MLB	29	585	89	35	2	28	92	37	126	2	2	0.2	.255	.301	.482	-.012	.252	.306	.492	.266	8.6	104-LF	-7		
2007	DET	MLB	30	372	47	19	0	11	55	20	94	0	3	-1.6	.222	.264	.373	-.231	.226	.275	.397	.229	-15.7	89-LF	-7		
2007	CHN	MLB	30	55	6	4	0	1	4	6	13	0	1	0.6	.204	.291	.347	-.229	.204	.291	.327	.211	-2.4				
2008	MIN	MLB	31	355	35	18	1	11	48	25	79	2	1	-0.2	.245	.300	.412	-.100	.246	.304	.435	.256	-0.3	85-LF	-3		

Breakout: 30% Improve: 53% Collapse: 32% Attrition: 34%   Comparables: Wally Post, Rip Repulski, Jeffrey Hammonds, Jermaine Dye

In Detroit, Monroe went from post-season hero to persona non grata in a hurry last year, but such a thing was the inevitable consequence of the late start that Monroe got on his career, which meant that the start of his decline cycle coincided with his escalating costs via arbitration. After picking him up from the Cubs for a player to be named later, the Twins signed him for $3.8 million, a million less than he earned last year. PECOTA doesn't like how his bat will play in the Metrodome, a park that can be tough on right-handed power, and regards him as no better than a replacement-level option at this stage.

Matt Murton — OF — Bats: R — Throws: R — Height: 6' 1" — Weight: 220 — Born: October 3, 1981 — Age: 26

YEAR	TEAM	LVL	AGE	PA	R	2B	3B	HR	RBI	BB	SO	SB	CS	EqBRR	AVG	OBP	SLG	MLVr	EqAVG	EqOBP	EqSLG	EqA	VORP	DEFENSE			
2005	WTN	AA	23	350	46	17	4	8	46	29	42	18	5	-0.7	.342	.403	.498	.319	.293	.347	.452	.275	10.1	61-LF	4	14-RF	-1
2005	CHN	MLB	23	160	19	3	2	7	14	16	22	2	1	-0.4	.321	.386	.521	.283	.307	.377	.507	.300	12.8	37-LF	-1		
2006	CHN	MLB	24	508	70	22	3	13	62	45	62	5	2	-0.5	.297	.365	.444	.092	.291	.361	.436	.277	16.2	118-LF	10		
2007	IOW	AAA	25	172	30	16	1	6	27	18	18	1	0	0.5	.331	.407	.570	.354	.289	.366	.513	.296	10.4	37-RF	-1		
2007	CHN	MLB	25	261	35	13	0	8	22	26	39	1	0	-0.1	.281	.352	.438	.052	.275	.352	.429	.272	7.3	32-RF	-2	21-LF	4
2008	CHN	MLB	26	287	41	16	1	8	37	25	41	5	1	0.0	.295	.359	.462	.080	.288	.354	.453	.276	12.8	70-LF	1		

Breakout: 14% Improve: 46% Collapse: 31% Attrition: 15%   Comparables: Herb Perry, Aaron Rowand, Mark Brouhard, Leon Roberts

Let's be honest, Matt Murton is a good, well-rounded hitter, but it looks as though he's going to peak as about a .275-EqA bat, and you can subtract a few points from that for his propensity to make boneheaded plays in the outfield. That number is right in the area in which a corner outfielder can be a regular for some, and a platoon guy for others. The Cubs, who aspire to first-division status, are making no great mistake if they choose the latter course with Murton. Indeed, he may struggle for even platoon work if the Cubs are uncomfortable playing Kosuke Fukudome in center field on occasion, in which case Murton becomes a good bet to be traded.

Angel Pagan — OF — Bats: S — Throws: R — Height: 6' 1" — Weight: 180 — Born: July 2, 1981 — Age: 26

YEAR	TEAM	LVL	AGE	PA	R	2B	3B	HR	RBI	BB	SO	SB	CS	EqBRR	AVG	OBP	SLG	MLVr	EqAVG	EqOBP	EqSLG	EqA	VORP	DEFENSE			
2005	NOR	AAA	24	579	69	20	10	8	40	49	111	27	15	-1.0	.271	.333	.395	.025	.248	.312	.363	.237	-4.5	102-CF	20		
2006	CHN	MLB	25	187	28	6	2	5	18	15	28	4	2	-0.3	.247	.306	.394	-.119	.241	.305	.382	.240	-2.7	24-LF	1	15-RF	3
2007	IOW	AAA	26	127	18	4	3	3	9	10	20	6	1	0.1	.250	.310	.414	-.117	.222	.283	.359	.230	-3.6	19-CF	2		
2007	CHN	MLB	26	161	21	10	2	4	21	10	32	4	1	0.3	.264	.306	.439	-.033	.259	.306	.449	.260	3.2	26-CF	-1	10-RF	-1
2008	NYN	MLB	26	174	21	8	1	4	18	14	32	6	2	0.7	.249	.313	.389	-.134	.252	.316	.405	.249	2.7	45-CF	-2		

Breakout: 41% Improve: 59% Collapse: 26% Attrition: 39%   Comparables: Milt Cuyler, John Shelby, Stan Jefferson, John Moses

If you're going to have a generic fourth outfielder, better that he have a slightly blasphemous name. Indeed, until baseball becomes really big in Slovakia, this is the closest we're going to come to having our own Miroslav Satan. Pagan runs quite well and switch-hits, both of which are nifty tricks, but there's little here that you can't get elsewhere just as cheaply. Dealt to the Mets for a pair of nondescript minor leaguers.

Eric Patterson　　2B

Bats: L　Throws: R　Height: 5' 11"　Weight: 170　Born: April 8, 1983　Age: 25

YEAR	TEAM	LVL	AGE	PA	R	2B	3B	HR	RBI	BB	SO	SB	CS	EqBRR	AVG	OBP	SLG	MLVr	EqAVG	EqOBP	EqSLG	EqA	VORP	DEFENSE	
2005	PEO	A	22	500	90	26	11	13	71	53	94	40	11	7.1	.333	.405	.535	.374	.250	.312	.413	.254	9.5	103-2B	6
2006	WTN	AA	23	501	66	22	9	8	48	46	89	38	12	4.2	.263	.330	.408	.077	.249	.311	.409	.255	8.6	111-2B	13
2006	IOW	AAA	23	76	14	1	1	2	12	6	9	8	0	3.0	.358	.395	.493	.301	.324	.364	.456	.301	5.8	17-2B	1
2007	IOW	AAA	24	582	94	28	6	14	65	54	85	24	9	1.3	.297	.362	.455	.078	.261	.327	.405	.257	14.5	79-2B -9	23-CF 2
2008	CHN	MLB	25	532	74	29	5	13	54	48	94	21	6	2.5	.268	.337	.429	-.023	.262	.332	.421	.261	17.9	125-2B	2

Breakout: 18%　Improve: 52%　Collapse: 21%　Attrition: 15%　　　　Comparables: James Mouton, Jermaine Clark, Eric Owens, Ray Durham

Patterson forms an interesting little case study with older brother Corey. The less athletic of the brothers, Eric is by far the sounder fundamental player, with a very good plate approach and a high baseball IQ. Of course, Eric also played college ball and Corey didn't. One wonders if Corey might have picked up the same skills that Eric did had he too gone to college and, if so, would his career have turned out differently? As for Eric, the Cubs need to get over their fear of the Ghost of Pattersons Past and either hand him the second-base job or deal him to a team that will. Eric's is almost certainly a major league-quality skill set, but also one that isn't likely to get much better.

Felix Pie　　CF

Bats: L　Throws: L　Height: 6' 2"　Weight: 170　Born: February 8, 1985　Age: 23

YEAR	TEAM	LVL	AGE	PA	R	2B	3B	HR	RBI	BB	SO	SB	CS	EqBRR	AVG	OBP	SLG	MLVr	EqAVG	EqOBP	EqSLG	EqA	VORP	DEFENSE	
2005	WTN	AA	20	262	41	17	5	11	25	16	53	13	9	-1.3	.304	.349	.554	.282	.262	.299	.484	.259	9.4	55-CF	-8
2006	IOW	AAA	21	623	78	33	8	15	57	46	126	17	11	-1.8	.283	.341	.451	.078	.255	.308	.417	.249	7.3	122-CF 10	13-RF 5
2007	IOW	AAA	22	250	51	9	5	9	43	19	40	9	6	2.7	.362	.410	.563	.389	.317	.365	.504	.290	21.7	49-CF	3
2007	CHN	MLB	22	194	26	9	3	2	20	14	43	8	1	2.7	.215	.271	.333	-.282	.209	.269	.328	.217	-5.7	48-CF	2
2008	CHN	MLB	23	429	62	25	4	14	53	31	84	13	5	2.3	.291	.344	.479	.076	.284	.339	.470	.273	21.4	102-CF	0

Breakout: 46%　Improve: 72%　Collapse: 5%　Attrition: 10%　　　　Comparables: David Green, Junior Felix, Gary Geiger, Bobby Tolan

Piniella tends to ride the hot hand, or bury the cold one on the bench for days at a time, and that put Pie under a great deal of pressure to perform last year lest he be shipped back on the next flight to Des Moines. This may have been optimal from the standpoint of steering the Cubs into the playoffs, but it probably wasn't optimal for Pie's development, and it helps to explain the big split in his major and minor league numbers. There's still a ton of upside here in the form of an exciting throwback player—nearly all of Pie's PECOTA comps date from the 1960s through 1980s—who can win a baseball game in a number of different ways. As of this writing, Pie is the favorite to win the Cubs' center-field job. It wouldn't kill the Cubs to sit him from time to time against tough lefties, but they need to make a commitment to him as a big-league regular.

Aramis Ramirez　　3B

Bats: R　Throws: R　Height: 6' 1"　Weight: 215　Born: June 25, 1978　Age: 30

YEAR	TEAM	LVL	AGE	PA	R	2B	3B	HR	RBI	BB	SO	SB	CS	EqBRR	AVG	OBP	SLG	MLVr	EqAVG	EqOBP	EqSLG	EqA	VORP	DEFENSE	
2005	CHN	MLB	27	506	72	30	0	31	92	35	60	0	1	-3.3	.302	.358	.568	.285	.294	.352	.567	.301	42.6	115-3B	-12
2006	CHN	MLB	28	660	93	38	4	38	119	50	63	2	1	-1.7	.291	.352	.561	.227	.285	.346	.550	.297	44.5	152-3B	-4
2007	CHN	MLB	29	558	72	35	4	26	101	43	66	0	0	-1.5	.310	.366	.549	.258	.300	.359	.541	.300	43.9	122-3B	18
2008	CHN	MLB	30	593	85	35	2	28	103	49	70	3	1	-1.1	.301	.363	.536	.193	.294	.358	.526	.293	40.7	139-3B	3

Breakout: 13%　Improve: 39%　Collapse: 19%　Attrition: 6%　　　　Comparables: Mike Lowell, Frank Thomas, Gary Gaetti, Brooks Robinson

Given that he once had a reputation as an erratic performer, it's ironic that Ramirez has developed into one of the most consistent hitters in baseball. Even more shocking is the fact that he was 18 fielding runs above average at the hot corner last year, a positive result not unique to our system; David Pinto's Probabilistic Model of Range (PMR) listed Ramirez as the fourth-best defensive third baseman in baseball in 2007. Ramirez's defensive issues had always been more a lack of concentration than a lack of ability, and some observers insist he was simply more engaged in the field last year. On the other hand, players can have fluke seasons with the glove just as with the stick, and this could have been the fielding equivalent of Brady Anderson's 1996. In either event, he's one of the more underappreciated stars of the NL.

Alfonso Soriano — LF

Bats: R Throws: R Height: 6' 1" Weight: 180 Born: January 7, 1976 Age: 32

YEAR	TEAM	LVL	AGE	PA	R	2B	3B	HR	RBI	BB	SO	SB	CS	EqBRR	AVG	OBP	SLG	MLVr	EqAVG	EqOBP	EqSLG	EqA	VORP	DEFENSE		
2005	TEX	MLB	29	682	102	43	2	36	104	33	125	30	2	5.9	.268	.309	.512	.072	.266	.317	.523	.285	38.9	152-2B	-20	
2006	WAS	MLB	30	728	119	41	2	46	95	67	160	41	17	-4.0	.277	.351	.560	.236	.286	.360	.578	.303	48.2	156-LF	-10	
2007	CHN	MLB	31	617	97	42	5	33	70	31	130	19	6	-0.4	.299	.337	.560	.217	.293	.334	.559	.293	42.1	119-LF	18	11-CF 1
2008	CHN	MLB	32	605	89	35	3	35	104	44	126	17	4	1.1	.278	.336	.544	.138	.272	.331	.534	.286	31.0	141-LF	-1	

Breakout: 6% Improve: 34% Collapse: 31% Attrition: 8% Comparables: Joe Carter, Andre Dawson, Dusty Baker, Jeff Kent

Virtually all of Soriano's PECOTA comparables have some or another kind of Cubs connection: Joe Carter (1), Andre Dawson (2), Dusty Baker (3), Don Baylor (5), Glenallen Hill (8), and Ernie Banks (9). Perhaps Soriano was predestined to be a Cub his entire life; there's nothing more Cubby than being a very good player who sometimes gets mistaken for a great one. The only thing that can honestly be considered disappointing about Soriano's 2007 season is that he didn't retain the walk-rate spike that he experienced with the Nationals in 2006, which makes it all the more important that he be removed from the leadoff spot. No, he didn't stick in center field, but he was by no means terrible for someone who hadn't played the position before; as with Pie, the whole incident reflected the Cubs' lack of patience more than any fault of the player's.

Geovany Soto — C

Bats: R Throws: R Height: 6' 1" Weight: 230 Born: January 20, 1983 Age: 25

YEAR	TEAM	LVL	AGE	PA	R	2B	3B	HR	RBI	BB	SO	SB	CS	EqBRR	AVG	OBP	SLG	MLVr	EqAVG	EqOBP	EqSLG	EqA	VORP	DEFENSE		
2005	IOW	AAA	22	345	30	14	0	4	39	48	77	0	1	1.3	.253	.357	.342	-.130	.221	.317	.298	.220	-9.4	86-C	0	
2006	IOW	AAA	23	391	34	21	0	6	38	41	74	0	1	-0.5	.272	.353	.386	-.001	.247	.323	.353	.240	0.4	96-C	-2	
2006	CHN	MLB	23	26	1	1	0	0	2	0	5	0	0	-0.1	.200	.231	.240	-.499	.200	.231	.240	.145	-2.3			
2007	IOW	AAA	24	449	75	31	3	26	109	53	94	0	0	-3.1	.353	.424	.652	.528	.296	.371	.563	.311	49.7	70-C	0	20-1B 0
2007	CHN	MLB	24	60	12	6	0	3	8	5	14	0	0	-0.1	.389	.433	.667	.621	.370	.417	.667	.351	10.9	14-C	2	
2008	CHN	MLB	25	483	60	25	1	19	69	51	105	2	1	-0.9	.273	.352	.470	.060	.267	.347	.461	.274	23.5	114-C	3	

Breakout: 10% Improve: 39% Collapse: 20% Attrition: 21% Comparables: Ronny Paulino, Charles Johnson, Justin Huber, Steve Bilko

Without qualification, Soto is one of the more valuable prospects in baseball. Catchers who can slug in the .450 to .500 range are unusual enough, but slugging catchers who also boast a well-above-average throwing arm and a pretty good batting eye are among the elite. PECOTA sees some potential for a slightly late, Jorge Posada-style peak, but even at Soto's present level of ability, he's already the best catcher in the division.

Ryan Theriot — SS/2B

Bats: R Throws: R Height: 5' 11" Weight: 175 Born: December 7, 1979 Age: 28

YEAR	TEAM	LVL	AGE	PA	R	2B	3B	HR	RBI	BB	SO	SB	CS	EqBRR	AVG	OBP	SLG	MLVr	EqAVG	EqOBP	EqSLG	EqA	VORP	DEFENSE		
2005	WTN	AA	25	503	52	28	4	1	53	45	38	24	10	-2.6	.304	.365	.391	.074	.258	.313	.341	.234	-3.3	82-2B	1	31-SS -1
2006	IOW	AAA	26	312	41	11	5	0	22	27	34	14	3	2.0	.304	.367	.379	.036	.268	.327	.335	.242	2.5	40-SS	-4	19-2B -2
2006	CHN	MLB	26	159	34	11	3	3	16	17	18	13	2	1.3	.328	.412	.522	.298	.321	.408	.511	.317	19.2	32-2B	-6	
2007	CHN	MLB	27	597	80	30	2	3	45	49	50	28	4	1.0	.266	.326	.346	-.128	.263	.327	.348	.247	6.6	96-SS	-6	26-2B 2
2008	CHN	MLB	28	557	70	25	3	2	40	44	54	20	5	0.9	.270	.330	.347	-.144	.264	.325	.340	.237	6.4	131-SS	-2	

Breakout: 10% Improve: 25% Collapse: 42% Attrition: 13% Comparables: Scott Fletcher, Doug Griffin, Ron Theobald, Joey Amalfitano

Ryan the Riot is overrated for a variety of reasons ranging from his lack of any discernible home run power, to his tendency to party a little too hard on the bases, to his second baseman's glove stuck at shortstop. Piniella can't be blamed for sticking with him last year—Theriot's average got up as high as .290 on August 21 and was largely undone by a dreadful slump over the season's final three weeks (.171/.231/.186)—but the Cubs need to upgrade at shortstop.

Josh Vitters — 3B

Bats: R Throws: R Height: 6' 3" Weight: 200 Born: August 27, 1989 Age: 18

YEAR	TEAM	LVL	AGE	PA	R	2B	3B	HR	RBI	BB	SO	SB	CS	EqBRR	AVG	OBP	SLG	MLVr	EqAVG	EqOBP	EqSLG	EqA	VORP	DEFENSE	
2007	CUB	Rk	17	32	0	0	0	0	2	1	9	0	0	0.0	.067	.094	.067	-.915	.129	.125	.129	.000	-17.3		
2007	BOI	A-	17	23	2	0	0	0	1	2	5	1	1	-0.5	.190	.261	.190	-.438	.136	.174	.136	.000	-8.2		
2008	CHN	MLB	18	537	40	22	2	7	45	32	151	10	5	0.2	.201	.251	.296	-.399	.197	.247	.290	.177	-28.7	126-3B	-3

Breakout: NA Improve: NA Collapse: NA Attrition: NA Comparables: Corey Smith, John Oliver, Billy Rowell, Dmitri Young

Vitters was the third overall pick in last June's amateur draft. Scouts love his bat speed and quick hands and expect him to develop into a Howie Kendrick-type of bat. They also think he's more likely than not to become a decent third baseman. Our highly experimental PECOTA dings him a bit for his brief, unproductive pro debut in the rookie leagues and the somewhat mixed track record of past high school third basemen, but apart from the obvious conclusion that Vitters is liable to take several years to develop, there's no reason to be worried at this stage.

Daryle Ward   **DH**   Bats: L   Throws: L   Height: 6' 2"   Weight: 240   Born: June 27, 1975   Age: 33

YEAR	TEAM	LVL	AGE	PA	R	2B	3B	HR	RBI	BB	SO	SB	CS	EqBRR	AVG	OBP	SLG	MLVr	EqAVG	EqOBP	EqSLG	EqA	VORP	DEFENSE
2005	PIT	MLB	30	453	46	21	1	12	63	37	60	0	2	-4.0	.260	.318	.405	-.031	.255	.316	.408	.252	0.1	101-1B -4
2006	WAS	MLB	31	123	15	9	0	6	19	14	21	0	1	-0.3	.308	.390	.567	.340	.317	.403	.587	.325	11.9	
2006	ATL	MLB	31	27	2	1	0	1	7	1	6	0	0	0.1	.308	.333	.462	.081	.308	.333	.462	.270	1.1	
2007	CHN	MLB	32	133	16	13	0	3	19	22	23	0	0	-0.1	.327	.436	.527	.352	.303	.421	.495	.318	13.7	10-1B 1
2008	CHN	MLB	33	109	13	7	0	3	16	12	18	0	0	-0.4	.277	.358	.459	.059	.271	.352	.450	.271	4.8	

Breakout: 8%   Improve: 26%   Collapse: 40%   Attrition: 40%   Comparables: Gordy Coleman, Sid Bream, Greg Colbrunn, Terry Whitfield

Ward's performance over the past two seasons shouldn't be taken completely for granted. Yeah, there are at least several dozen defensively challenged sluggers throughout baseball with the same fundamental skill set, but not all of them would take so well to being used off the bench just a couple of times a week. Piniella used Ward in right field a couple of times last year, a sight that was not to be witnessed by children under the age of 13.

PITCHERS

Jose Ceda   Bats: R   Throws: R   Height: 6' 4"   Weight: 205   Born: January 28, 1987   Age: 21

YEAR	TEAM	LVL	AGE	W	L	SV	G	GS	IP	H	BB	SO	HR	GB%	BABIP	STUFF	WHIP	ERA	PERA	EqERA	EqH9	EqBB9	EqSO9	EqHR9	VORP	SN/WX
2006	BOI	A-	19	1	0	0	3	3	11²	5	2	11	1	28.6%	.250	10	0.63	3.21	5.17	5.59	6.5	3.7	4.7	1.9	0.0	—
2006	CUB	Rk	19	0	0	0	5	3	12²	6	7	21	0	36.8%	.333	9	1.07	0.74	6.10	3.86	7.7	10.6	9.6	1.0	1.8	—
2006	PDR	Rk	19	2	0	0	8	4	23¹	20	13	31	1	30.9%	.358	-2	1.43	5.06	11.01	10.70	12.7	10.7	6.6	2.5	-10.0	—
2007	PEO	A	20	2	2	0	21	6	46¹	14	31	66	1	49.4%	.155	22	0.97	3.11	4.91	6.58	4.3	10.7	7.5	0.7	-4.3	—
2008	CHN	MLB	21	3	4	0	22	9	61	44	74	68	7	42.0%	.258	-1	1.93	5.55	5.88	5.80	6.2	9.7	8.8	0.9	0.3	0.40

Breakout: 45%   Improve: 70%   Collapse: 12%   Attrition: 11%   Comparables: Shane Lindsay, Nick Neugebauer, Manny Acosta, Anibal Sanchez

Ceda is very raw and doesn't throw a lot of strikes, but his combination of youth, size, and velocity is rare, and he was touching 98 mph on the radar gun by the end of the year at Peoria. The Cubs see him as a relief pitcher, a role that can sometimes give pitchers with command problems a bit of a break, and his ceiling is that of a big-league closer.

Neal Cotts   Bats: L   Throws: L   Height: 6' 1"   Weight: 200   Born: March 25, 1980   Age: 28

YEAR	TEAM	LVL	AGE	W	L	SV	G	GS	IP	H	BB	SO	HR	GB%	BABIP	STUFF	WHIP	ERA	PERA	EqERA	EqH9	EqBB9	EqSO9	EqHR9	VORP	SN/WX
2005	CHA	MLB	25	4	0	0	69	0	60¹	38	29	58	1	46.5%	.242	25	1.11	1.94	2.75	2.43	5.9	4.2	8.5	0.2	23.8	2.03
2006	CHA	MLB	26	1	2	1	70	0	54	64	24	43	12	43.6%	.315	-19	1.63	5.17	6.52	5.07	10.0	3.6	6.5	1.6	4.1	0.06
2007	CHN	MLB	27	0	1	0	16	0	16²	15	9	14	1	46.0%	.304	1	1.44	4.85	4.07	4.24	7.9	4.2	6.9	0.5	2.0	0.22
2007	IOW	AAA	27	2	2	0	24	6	50¹	43	30	48	4	47.8%	.300	4	1.45	4.83	4.32	5.03	7.4	5.8	6.7	0.9	3.1	—
2008	CHN	MLB	28	2	2	3	42	1	41	39	22	35	5	44.1%	.286	-2	1.47	4.31	4.48	4.57	8.1	4.2	6.7	1.0	6.4	0.60

Breakout: 16%   Improve: 32%   Collapse: 37%   Attrition: 26%   Comparables: Mike Stanton, Larry Thomas, Brad Havens, Randy Choate

Even in his best seasons on the South Side, Cotts always walked a tightrope because of his spotty command. His innings-pitched totals were never high with the White Sox, but Ozzie Guillen had a habit of using him in back-to-back appearances, and that, coupled with Cotts's high-effort mechanics, seem to have reduced his arm strength to the point at which Cotts was doing as much harm as good when he took the mound for the Cubs last year. The Cubs farmed him out to Iowa and tried to make him a starter, but after a 7.33 ERA in six starts, he was returned to the bullpen, where he registered a solid second half.

Ryan Dempster

Bats: R   Throws: R   Height: 6' 2"   Weight: 215   Born: May 3, 1977   Age: 31

YEAR	TEAM	LVL	AGE	W	L	SV	G	GS	IP	H	BB	SO	HR	GB%	BABIP	STUFF	WHIP	ERA	PERA	EqERA	EqH9	EqBB9	EqSO9	EqHR9	VORP	SN/WX
2005	CHN	MLB	28	5	3	33	63	6	92	83	49	89	4	59.8%	.316	21	1.43	3.13	4.04	3.51	8.5	4.4	8.0	0.4	21.8	5.53
2006	CHN	MLB	29	1	9	24	74	0	75	77	36	67	5	55.1%	.324	7	1.51	4.80	4.19	5.14	9.1	3.6	7.1	0.5	3.9	-1.26
2007	CHN	MLB	30	2	7	28	66	0	66²	59	30	55	8	49.5%	.279	0	1.34	4.72	4.08	4.55	8.1	3.6	7.0	1.0	8.2	2.66
2008	CHN	MLB	31	3	4	15	51	0	58	57	29	47	5	51.5%	.302	-2	1.48	4.24	4.39	4.57	8.6	4.0	6.4	0.8	8.2	1.00

Breakout: 16% Improve: 42% Collapse: 28% Attrition: 18%   Comparables: Jay Powell, Clay Carroll, Bob Wickman, Todd Jones

A closer by assignment only, Dempster may not even be that for much longer. He has experienced a steady decline in his groundball rates over the past three seasons which, coupled with command that was never very good to begin with, has rendered him an unreliable ninth-inning option. The Cubs are considering trying him in the rotation, which might not be the worst idea; his PECOTA as a starter includes a 4.78 ERA and sees his VORP improve slightly from the 8.2 above to 10.9.

Scott Eyre

Bats: L   Throws: L   Height: 6' 1"   Weight: 215   Born: May 30, 1972   Age: 36

YEAR	TEAM	LVL	AGE	W	L	SV	G	GS	IP	H	BB	SO	HR	GB%	BABIP	STUFF	WHIP	ERA	PERA	EqERA	EqH9	EqBB9	EqSO9	EqHR9	VORP	SN/WX
2005	SFN	MLB	33	2	2	0	86	0	68¹	48	26	65	3	39.6%	.262	20	1.10	2.64	2.83	2.94	6.4	3.1	7.9	0.4	20.9	3.71
2006	CHN	MLB	34	1	3	0	74	0	61¹	61	30	73	11	44.8%	.342	9	1.48	3.38	5.52	3.49	9.4	3.9	10.0	1.4	16.5	1.26
2007	CHN	MLB	35	2	1	0	55	0	52¹	59	35	45	3	40.9%	.366	7	1.80	4.13	6.08	4.53	10.9	5.4	7.6	0.5	8.7	-0.60
2008	CHN	MLB	36	2	2	3	42	0	41²	38	25	40	4	43.0%	.290	0	1.49	4.08	4.38	4.33	7.8	4.7	7.5	0.9	6.9	0.60

Breakout: 14% Improve: 29% Collapse: 53% Attrition: 29%   Comparables: Ricardo Rincon, Norm Charlton, Ron Mahay, Ron Villone

Eyre has always had some trouble with control, but not to the extent that he did last season when he walked 5.2 men unintentionally per nine innings, his highest figure in years. Given Eyre's BABIP marks over the past two seasons, that increased walk rate may be indicative of a pitcher who is afraid to work in the strike zone for fear that he'll get creamed. Eyre did improve some in the second half of last season, but by that point he'd been demoted to mop-up work, and his very appearance in the ballgame was a signal for the Wrigley faithful to drink up, head for the exits, and beat the crowd to the Cubby Bear.

Sean Gallagher

Bats: R   Throws: R   Height: 6' 2"   Weight: 225   Born: December 30, 1985   Age: 22

YEAR	TEAM	LVL	AGE	W	L	SV	G	GS	IP	H	BB	SO	HR	GB%	BABIP	STUFF	WHIP	ERA	PERA	EqERA	EqH9	EqBB9	EqSO9	EqHR9	VORP	SN/WX
2005	PEO	A	19	14	5	0	26	26	146	107	55	139	10	48.6%	.262	8	1.11	2.71	5.25	4.82	8.1	5.2	5.2	1.4	11.3	—
2006	DAY	A+	20	4	0	0	13	13	78¹	75	21	80	5	58.8%	.345	11	1.23	2.30	6.52	4.76	11.2	4.0	5.8	1.3	6.3	—
2006	WTN	AA	20	7	5	0	15	15	86²	74	55	91	4	51.5%	.326	22	1.50	2.71	5.86	4.77	9.8	6.6	6.8	0.8	7.1	—
2007	TEN	AA	21	7	2	0	11	11	61	54	24	54	3	48.6%	.291	9	1.28	3.39	4.82	4.87	9.4	4.1	5.2	0.8	4.6	—
2007	IOW	AAA	21	3	1	0	8	8	40²	33	13	37	1	45.5%	.308	27	1.13	2.65	3.31	3.03	7.2	3.3	6.5	0.2	11.1	—
2007	CHN	MLB	21	0	0	1	8	0	14²	19	12	5	3	41.1%	.308	-37	2.11	8.57	9.72	9.82	11.7	6.1	3.1	1.8	-5.1	-0.16
2008	CHN	MLB	22	6	8	1	34	17	121¹	126	62	89	16	45.2%	.297	1	1.55	4.91	5.17	5.17	9.0	4.1	5.8	1.1	8.7	1.60

Breakout: 25% Improve: 56% Collapse: 21% Attrition: 20%   Comparables: Jason Bere, Hayden Penn, Albie Lopez, Grant Roberts

Gallagher will be just 22 next season and already possesses an average fastball and breaking pitch, but both PECOTA and scouts are dubious about how much better he's likely to get. Gallagher's command isn't good, and physically he's stocky and perhaps somewhat overbuilt. Deeper down on his PECOTA comparables list are a couple of encouraging names such as Jason Schmidt's, but for the most part it's just more guys like Bere, Lopez, and Roberts, who often proved frustrating to their employers.

Angel Guzman

Bats: R   Throws: R   Height: 6' 3"   Weight: 195   Born: December 14, 1981   Age: 26

YEAR	TEAM	LVL	AGE	W	L	SV	G	GS	IP	H	BB	SO	HR	GB%	BABIP	STUFF	WHIP	ERA	PERA	EqERA	EqH9	EqBB9	EqSO9	EqHR9	VORP	SN/WX
2006	IOW	AAA	24	4	4	0	15	15	75²	72	24	77	5	40.6%	.328	12	1.28	4.07	4.42	5.05	9.0	3.2	6.8	0.9	4.5	—
2006	CHN	MLB	24	0	6	0	15	10	56	68	37	60	9	34.9%	.388	3	1.88	7.39	7.92	7.64	11.4	5.2	8.9	1.3	-9.7	0.26
2007	IOW	AAA	25	0	2	0	3	3	10¹	14	6	7	1	51.4%	.361	-26	1.94	12.23	7.25	13.06	11.3	5.2	4.4	0.9	-8.5	—
2007	CHN	MLB	25	0	1	0	12	3	30¹	32	9	26	2	47.3%	.345	14	1.35	3.56	4.63	3.77	10.0	2.5	7.5	0.6	8.0	0.38
2008	CHN	MLB	26	3	4	1	25	6	61¹	63	25	51	8	44.1%	.301	5	1.43	4.57	4.59	4.84	8.8	3.3	6.6	1.1	7.8	0.90

Breakout: 46% Improve: 73% Collapse: 12% Attrition: 35%   Comparables: Dan Smith, Rafael Carmona, Vinnie Chulk, Wayne Simpson

Never a stranger to the trainer's table, Guzman quietly underwent reconstructive elbow surgery as the Cubs were busy wrapping up the Central and is unlikely to pitch professionally in 2008. What's especially discouraging is that his previous injuries had been to his shoulder and forearm, so this latest is a new area of concern. Guzman's mechanics have never been pristine, particularly on his follow-though, and once he returns, it's probably in the Cubs' best interest to hedge against the injury risk by using him strictly as a reliever.

Rich Hill

Bats: L   Throws: L   Height: 6' 5"   Weight: 205   Born: March 11, 1980   Age: 28

YEAR	TEAM	LVL	AGE	W	L	SV	G	GS	IP	H	BB	SO	HR	GB%	BABIP	STUFF	WHIP	ERA	PERA	EqERA	EqH9	EqBB9	EqSO9	EqHR9	VORP	SN/WX
2005	WTN	AA	25	4	3	0	10	10	57²	42	21	90	9	43.0%	.297	6	1.09	3.28	6.75	5.26	9.1	4.0	10.0	2.6	1.9	—
2005	IOW	AAA	25	6	1	0	11	10	65	53	14	92	11	44.1%	.300	22	1.03	3.60	4.63	4.28	8.3	2.4	9.6	1.8	8.9	—
2005	CHN	MLB	25	0	2	0	10	4	23²	25	17	21	3	39.5%	.306	-6	1.77	9.11	5.69	8.88	9.2	5.5	7.0	1.1	-9.1	-0.42
2006	IOW	AAA	26	7	1	0	15	15	100²	62	21	135	3	48.4%	.282	49	0.83	1.80	2.87	2.82	6.2	2.3	9.1	0.4	29.6	—
2006	CHN	MLB	26	6	7	0	17	16	99¹	83	39	90	16	33.2%	.259	14	1.23	4.17	3.75	3.96	7.4	3.1	7.4	1.3	16.8	2.50
2007	CHN	MLB	27	11	8	0	32	32	195	170	63	183	27	39.4%	.278	22	1.19	3.92	3.93	3.74	8.0	2.5	7.9	1.1	40.3	4.84
2008	CHN	MLB	28	11	9	0	28	28	175¹	161	59	160	25	40.0%	.279	21	1.25	4.02	4.02	4.22	7.9	2.7	7.2	1.2	29.5	4.60

Breakout: 9%   Improve: 41% Collapse: 23% Attrition: 17%   Comparables: Rudy May, Dick Stigman, Vinegar Bend Mizell, Bob Kuzava

Hill's curve is simply an excellent pitch. It's not the gimmicky Barry Zito lollipop variety, but its sudden break leaves lots of batters looking confused. To his credit, Hill doesn't overuse the pitch, but since his fastball tops out at about 90 mph, he's probably going to need to work on another offering if he wants to be an ace instead of a very solid number two. PECOTA cannily throws out a number of other comparables who also worked primarily off of a breaking pitch, but his chances of taking another step forward are probably better than the system gives him credit for.

Bob Howry

Bats: L   Throws: R   Height: 6' 5"   Weight: 220   Born: August 4, 1973   Age: 34

YEAR	TEAM	LVL	AGE	W	L	SV	G	GS	IP	H	BB	SO	HR	GB%	BABIP	STUFF	WHIP	ERA	PERA	EqERA	EqH9	EqBB9	EqSO9	EqHR9	VORP	SN/WX
2005	CLE	MLB	31	7	4	3	79	0	73	49	16	48	4	40.8%	.221	11	0.89	2.47	2.56	3.18	6.2	2.0	5.9	0.5	23.3	3.11
2006	CHN	MLB	32	4	5	5	84	0	76²	70	17	71	8	39.9%	.300	16	1.13	3.17	3.52	2.96	8.3	1.7	7.7	0.8	23.8	2.17
2007	CHN	MLB	33	6	7	8	78	0	81¹	76	19	72	8	32.9%	.296	15	1.17	3.32	3.61	3.24	8.5	1.8	7.5	0.8	22.7	3.13
2008	CHN	MLB	34	4	3	8	59	0	66	62	18	54	8	39.0%	.280	3	1.21	3.60	3.68	3.83	8.2	2.1	6.4	1.1	14.8	1.40

Breakout: 8%   Improve: 22% Collapse: 50% Attrition: 17%   Comparables: Stan Williams, Ron Reed, Jeff Russell, Jay Howell

Proof that an old pitcher can learn new tricks, Howry made the commonsensical adjustment of throwing more first-pitch strikes after recognizing that, while his fastball might not quite be good enough to blow by people, it is good enough to generate a lot of foul balls and other weak contact, setting him up to work the corners later in the at-bat. Although this approach is a bit risky because it results in a lot of fly balls, Howry is probably the Cubs' best relief pitcher entering the season, at least when the wind is blowing in.

Ted Lilly

Bats: L   Throws: L   Height: 6' 1"   Weight: 190   Born: January 4, 1976   Age: 32

YEAR	TEAM	LVL	AGE	W	L	SV	G	GS	IP	H	BB	SO	HR	GB%	BABIP	STUFF	WHIP	ERA	PERA	EqERA	EqH9	EqBB9	EqSO9	EqHR9	VORP	SN/WX
2005	TOR	MLB	29	10	11	0	25	25	126¹	135	58	96	23	38.9%	.296	-9	1.53	5.56	5.77	5.60	9.4	4.1	6.6	1.5	4.0	1.69
2006	TOR	MLB	30	15	13	0	32	32	181²	179	81	160	28	38.9%	.292	10	1.43	4.31	4.63	4.40	8.6	3.7	7.4	1.2	26.4	3.85
2007	CHN	MLB	31	15	8	0	34	34	207	181	55	174	28	36.2%	.270	20	1.14	3.83	3.61	3.63	7.9	2.0	7.1	1.1	46.7	5.44
2008	CHN	MLB	32	10	10	0	27	27	168²	165	57	139	25	39.5%	.284	14	1.32	4.25	4.38	4.44	8.4	2.7	6.5	1.3	25.7	4.10

Breakout: 10% Improve: 44% Collapse: 24% Attrition: 10%   Comparables: Floyd Bannister, Gary Peters, Frank Castillo, Denny Neagle

Lilly went from unintentionally walking 9.4 percent of the batters he faced in 2006 to 5.6 percent in 2007. That not only helped his ERA, it allowed his workload to exceed the 200-innings barrier for the first time, since that improved command translated to lower pitch counts. Then again, he did tire a bit down the stretch following a 127-pitch outing in Colorado on August 9 (his ERA for the last quarter of the season was 4.69), and you can expect his walk rate to bounce back a bit. Still, his should prove to be one of the best contracts signed between the 2006 and 2007 seasons.

Carlos Marmol

| | | | | | | Bats: R | | Throws: R | | Height: 6' 2" | | Weight: 180 | | Born: October 14, 1982 | | | Age: 25 |

YEAR	TEAM	LVL	AGE	W	L	SV	G	GS	IP	H	BB	SO	HR	GB%	BABIP	STUFF	WHIP	ERA	PERA	EqERA	EqH9	EqBB9	EqSO9	EqHR9	VORP	SN/WX
2005	DAY	A+	22	6	2	0	13	13	72¹	60	37	71	7	42.1%	.285	-5	1.34	2.99	6.54	5.54	8.8	7.4	5.1	1.8	0.4	—
2005	WTN	AA	22	3	4	0	14	14	81¹	70	40	70	10	47.2%	.282	-15	1.35	3.65	6.72	5.25	9.3	5.3	5.0	2.1	2.9	—
2006	WTN	AA	23	3	2	0	11	11	58	42	25	67	1	46.8%	.304	23	1.16	2.33	3.97	4.08	8.2	4.4	7.3	0.3	9.0	—
2006	CHN	MLB	23	5	7	0	19	13	77	71	59	59	14	33.0%	.270	-2	1.69	6.08	5.61	5.63	8.3	6.0	6.3	1.4	-1.3	0.46
2007	IOW	AAA	24	4	1	0	8	7	41	30	12	48	4	29.5%	.274	23	1.02	3.95	3.44	3.89	6.0	2.8	8.0	1.1	7.9	—
2007	CHN	MLB	24	5	1	1	59	0	69¹	41	35	96	3	32.7%	.264	38	1.10	1.43	2.74	1.43	5.9	3.9	10.4	0.4	34.5	3.69
2008	CHN	MLB	25	4	4	3	40	5	68¹	59	36	72	9	37.9%	.284	12	1.39	4.06	4.29	4.24	7.5	4.2	8.4	1.1	13.0	1.30

Breakout: 8%   Improve: 25%   Collapse: 51%   Attrition: 30%   Comparables: Jack Meyer, Tracy Stallard, Larry Sherry, Steve Mura

A lot of Cubs fans were up in arms that Marmol was not the team's closer by the end of the season, comparing the situation to that of the 2006 Tigers, who had Joel Zumaya in the Marmol role and Todd Jones playing Dempster. The analogy is a pretty good one, but one needs to remember what happened to Zumaya in 2007: his ERA spiked, and he suffered a career-threatening shoulder injury. Although Marmol is not likely to duplicate Zumaya's history of fluke injuries, he can expect to see his ERA rise, mostly because the high heat he throws is good, but not good enough to let him repeat the mere three home runs he allowed in 2007. To build on his breakout season, Marmol will have to rely less on his fastball and instead work on throwing his good curveball down in the zone.

Jason Marquis

| | | | | | | Bats: L | | Throws: R | | Height: 6' 1" | | Weight: 210 | | Born: August 21, 1978 | | | Age: 29 |

YEAR	TEAM	LVL	AGE	W	L	SV	G	GS	IP	H	BB	SO	HR	GB%	BABIP	STUFF	WHIP	ERA	PERA	EqERA	EqH9	EqBB9	EqSO9	EqHR9	VORP	SN/WX
2005	SLN	MLB	26	13	14	0	33	32	207	206	69	100	29	53.2%	.269	-10	1.33	4.13	4.93	5.21	9.3	2.8	4.1	1.3	18.2	4.20
2006	SLN	MLB	27	14	16	0	33	33	194¹	221	75	96	35	44.5%	.294	-18	1.52	6.02	6.00	6.21	10.1	3.0	4.1	1.4	-5.7	2.12
2007	CHN	MLB	28	12	9	0	34	33	191²	190	76	109	22	52.5%	.275	3	1.39	4.60	4.33	4.82	8.8	3.0	4.8	0.9	16.5	3.06
2008	CHN	MLB	29	7	9	0	31	21	132¹	147	49	76	19	48.4%	.296	-4	1.48	5.04	5.07	5.35	9.6	2.9	4.5	1.2	8.1	1.70

Breakout: 18%   Improve: 46%   Collapse: 30%   Attrition: 22%   Comparables: Stan Bahnsen, Dustin Hermanson, Richard Dotson, Herm Wehmeier

As successful as Marquis was in the first half of last season, keeping his ERA below 4.00 as late as July 20, it was only a matter of time before his ERA caught up with his middling peripherals. Although he's nominally better than replacement level, he's also a borderline liability for a team that aspires to reach the playoffs, something the 2006 world champion Cardinals recognized by not letting Marquis throw a single pitch in that postseason. The Cubs need to be willing to ignore the $16.25 million they'll be paying him between this season and next and bump him from the rotation should a better alternative present itself.

Sean Marshall

| | | | | | | Bats: L | | Throws: L | | Height: 6' 7" | | Weight: 205 | | Born: August 30, 1982 | | | Age: 25 |

YEAR	TEAM	LVL	AGE	W	L	SV	G	GS	IP	H	BB	SO	HR	GB%	BABIP	STUFF	WHIP	ERA	PERA	EqERA	EqH9	EqBB9	EqSO9	EqHR9	VORP	SN/WX
2005	DAY	A+	22	4	4	0	12	12	69	63	26	61	7	59.7%	.298	-12	1.29	2.74	6.46	4.87	9.6	5.6	4.4	1.9	4.9	—
2005	WTN	AA	22	0	1	0	4	4	25	16	5	24	1	47.0%	.234	18	0.84	2.52	3.31	3.91	6.7	2.3	5.9	0.8	4.3	—
2006	IOW	AAA	23	0	2	0	4	4	21²	17	14	21	1	57.9%	.291	18	1.46	3.40	4.35	4.87	7.5	6.2	6.6	0.4	1.6	—
2006	CHN	MLB	23	6	9	0	24	24	125²	132	59	77	20	48.6%	.286	-8	1.52	5.58	5.25	5.44	9.3	3.7	5.1	1.2	-0.2	1.58
2007	IOW	AAA	24	2	0	0	4	4	24²	17	8	15	2	47.3%	.208	5	1.01	1.82	2.86	2.19	5.5	2.9	4.0	0.7	9.4	—
2007	CHN	MLB	24	7	8	0	21	19	103¹	107	35	67	13	49.9%	.293	4	1.37	3.92	4.51	4.28	9.3	2.6	5.5	1.0	16.7	2.63
2008	CHN	MLB	25	6	7	0	30	18	112	119	44	73	14	48.8%	.294	0	1.45	4.74	4.75	5.05	9.1	3.1	5.1	1.1	10.6	1.80

Breakout: 5%   Improve: 35%   Collapse: 37%   Attrition: 19%   Comparables: Jim Umbarger, Bill Travers, Dean Stone, Andy Hassler

Facially, Sean Marshall looks just a tiny bit like a young Kerry Wood, and that coupled with his sturdy 6-foot-7 frame makes him seem like he should be an overpowering starter. He's not. Instead, he depends on a variety pack of breaking stuff, which he's become increasingly adept at throwing for strikes. The pitcher he most resembles is not Wood, but a taller, left-handed version of Jason Marquis. That's not entirely a bad thing, especially when he comes at a fraction of Marquis' price.

Will Ohman

| | | | | | | | Bats: L | | Throws: L | | Height: 6' 2" | | Weight: 205 | | Born: August 13, 1977 | | | Age: 30 |

YEAR	TEAM	LVL	AGE	W	L	SV	G	GS	IP	H	BB	SO	HR	GB%	BABIP	STUFF	WHIP	ERA	PERA	EqERA	EqH9	EqBB9	EqSO9	EqHR9	VORP	SN/WX
2005	CHN	MLB	27	2	2	0	69	0	43¹	32	24	45	6	52.2%	.241	8	1.29	2.91	3.87	2.70	6.9	4.6	8.5	1.2	12.6	0.09
2006	CHN	MLB	28	1	1	0	78	0	65¹	51	34	74	6	34.1%	.273	18	1.30	4.13	3.43	3.63	7.0	3.9	9.0	0.7	14.2	1.70
2007	CHN	MLB	29	2	4	1	56	0	36¹	42	16	33	3	41.5%	.345	2	1.60	4.96	5.07	4.86	10.5	3.4	7.5	0.7	4.1	-0.73
2008	ATL	MLB	30	3	2	3	51	1	48²	46	22	43	5	41.4%	.293	3	1.40	4.05	4.33	4.34	8.3	3.7	7.2	0.9	7.3	0.70

Breakout: 14%　Improve: 36%　Collapse: 38%　Attrition: 24%　　Comparables: Dave Hamilton, Trever Miller, Ricardo Rincon, Alan Embree

The Cubs waited on Ohman for quite a long time, nursing him back to health after an elbow injury cost him essentially all of his 2002 and 2003 seasons. For their trouble they got a pitcher who has limited lefties to a .196/.294/.319 line over the course of his major league career. He's a more reliable LOOGY than Scott Eyre, but it's Eyre who's making the big bucks, and so Ohman was shipped to the Braves in December for live arm Jose Ascanio. The Cubs could miss him more than you'd think.

Mark Pawelek

| | | | | | | | Bats: L | | Throws: L | | Height: 6' 3" | | Weight: 190 | | Born: August 18, 1986 | | | Age: 21 |

YEAR	TEAM	LVL	AGE	W	L	SV	G	GS	IP	H	BB	SO	HR	GB%	BABIP	STUFF	WHIP	ERA	PERA	EqERA	EqH9	EqBB9	EqSO9	EqHR9	VORP	SN/WX
2006	BOI	A-	19	3	5	0	15	12	61¹	54	23	52	1	50.5%	.283	-3	1.26	2.50	6.34	6.13	10.6	6.3	3.6	0.7	-3.2	—
2007	BOI	A-	20	1	2	0	8	1	12²	13	10	10	1	63.2%	.333	-37	1.81	9.21	13.36	15.30	13.5	13.5	2.7	2.7	-10.8	—
2008	CHN	MLB	21	2	4	0	26	7	55¹	64	53	25	7	52.5%	.303	-34	2.11	8.14	7.21	8.80	10.0	7.6	3.6	1.0	-14.6	-1.50

Breakout: 28%　Improve: 56%　Collapse: 27%　Attrition: 35%　　Comparables: Josh Girdley, Scott Rice, Kirk Presley, Chris Ochsenfeld

There's being stuck in neutral, and then there's Pawelek, the former Scott Boras client and first-round draft pick who, according to our friends at Rotowire.com, "sustained a fractured radial head in his non-throwing right elbow after tripping over his PlayStation." Suffered in early October, the injury seems worthy of the Glenallen Hill/Clint Barmes/Joel Zumaya Hall of Shame, but it was all too typical of Pawelek, who has failed to keep himself in shape and has regressed from a relatively polished prospect to a complete project. His odds of putting together a meaningful career at this point are probably 50:1 against.

Carmen Pignatiello

| | | | | | | | Bats: R | | Throws: L | | Height: 6' 0" | | Weight: 205 | | Born: September 12, 1982 | | | Age: 25 |

YEAR	TEAM	LVL	AGE	W	L	SV	G	GS	IP	H	BB	SO	HR	GB%	BABIP	STUFF	WHIP	ERA	PERA	EqERA	EqH9	EqBB9	EqSO9	EqHR9	VORP	SN/WX
2005	WTN	AA	22	5	4	0	16	10	80²	67	28	77	3	58.3%	.299	11	1.18	2.68	4.38	4.17	8.7	3.9	5.8	0.7	11.6	—
2005	IOW	AAA	22	1	5	0	22	5	47¹	52	20	43	6	48.6%	.326	-14	1.52	5.52	6.09	6.85	10.3	4.2	5.8	1.4	-6.2	—
2006	WTN	AA	23	3	1	0	38	1	60¹	52	19	74	3	58.7%	.329	7	1.18	2.70	5.00	4.34	9.6	3.4	7.7	0.8	7.8	—
2007	IOW	AAA	24	1	0	2	45	0	49	40	16	44	5	52.8%	.257	-3	1.14	2.76	3.36	3.58	6.4	3.0	5.9	1.1	11.3	—
2008	CHN	MLB	25	3	3	3	28	4	54	51	22	43	5	51.5%	.289	5	1.36	3.72	3.92	4.02	8.2	3.3	6.3	0.8	11.6	1.20

Breakout: 38%　Improve: 70%　Collapse: 15%　Attrition: 18%　　Comparables: John Franco, Joe Thatcher, Ron Perranoski, John Riedling

A local kid and 20th-round draft pick who has never been a favorite of scouts, Pignatiello has nevertheless managed to impress PECOTA with his ability to generate groundballs off his plus curve. He was also particularly effective against lefties last season, limiting them to a .173 batting average against. Although he hadn't displayed that kind of split in the past, some pretty decent left-handed setup men have gotten away with less.

Mark Prior

| | | | | | | | Bats: R | | Throws: R | | Height: 6' 5" | | Weight: 230 | | Born: September 7, 1980 | | | Age: 27 |

YEAR	TEAM	LVL	AGE	W	L	SV	G	GS	IP	H	BB	SO	HR	GB%	BABIP	STUFF	WHIP	ERA	PERA	EqERA	EqH9	EqBB9	EqSO9	EqHR9	VORP	SN/WX
2005	CHN	MLB	24	11	7	0	27	27	166²	143	59	188	25	38.9%	.283	24	1.21	3.67	4.03	3.78	7.8	2.9	9.2	1.3	31.8	4.14
2006	CHN	MLB	25	1	6	0	9	9	43²	46	28	38	9	38.0%	.298	-3	1.69	7.21	6.49	7.20	9.2	4.8	7.0	1.6	-9.5	-0.48
2008	SDN	MLB	27	5	4	0	24	10	77	69	31	73	9	39.5%	.284	13	1.29	3.90	4.36	4.47	8.1	3.3	7.4	1.0	11.1	1.50

Breakout: 35%　Improve: 57%　Collapse: 20%　Attrition: 30%　　Comparables: Bobby Bolin, Joaquin Benoit, Wayne Twitchell, Ron Schueler

The Mark Prior Era officially ended when the clock struck midnight on Wednesday, December 12, 2007, when the Cubs declined to tender him a contract. It's probably a healthy breakup for both parties. Prior was unfairly maligned by the local press for being soft, which was more a reflection of his low-key California personality than any lack of work ethic; he busted his butt to get back into shape. Nevertheless, there is something to the notion that a pitcher to whom things came so easily was more likely to struggle once he found adversity; Prior's mechanics were so consistent that he had never had to learn how to pitch when his stuff was less than 100 percent. He has signed a one-year, incentive-laden deal to pitch in San Diego, one of the better possible fits for him, but the Padres need to remember to ease him back in slowly.

Jeff Samardzija

Bats: R Throws: R Height: 6' 5" Weight: 220 Born: January 23, 1985 Age: 23

YEAR	TEAM	LVL	AGE	W	L	SV	G	GS	IP	H	BB	SO	HR	GB%	BABIP	STUFF	WHIP	ERA	PERA	EqERA	EqH9	EqBB9	EqSO9	EqHR9	VORP	SN/WX
2006	PEO	A	21	0	1	0	2	2	11¹	6	6	4	1	54.5%	.161	-19	1.08	3.24	6.65	8.00	7.0	9.0	1.0	3.0	-2.4	—
2006	BOI	A-	21	1	1	0	5	5	19	18	6	13	1	58.3%	.288	-21	1.26	2.37	7.75	4.86	11.3	5.4	2.7	1.6	1.4	—
2007	DAY	A+	22	3	8	0	24	20	107¹	142	35	45	8	52.8%	.347	-46	1.65	4.95	8.92	8.40	13.6	4.5	1.9	1.5	-29.6	—
2007	TEN	AA	22	3	3	0	6	6	34¹	33	9	20	8	40.0%	.240	-25	1.22	3.41	8.29	5.79	10.2	2.8	3.3	3.3	-0.7	—
2008	CHN	MLB	23	4	9	0	30	16	100	136	49	34	22	46.9%	.312	-28	1.86	7.43	7.42	7.71	11.7	3.9	2.7	1.9	-20.0	-1.40

Breakout: 20% Improve: 49% Collapse: 25% Attrition: 6%   Comparables: Andrew Baldwin, Mike Thompson, Chris Mears, Peter Fisher

A mystery wrapped in an enigma, 2006 fifth-round pick Samardzija received one of the largest total dollar packages in draft history, then proceeded to get lambasted in the Florida State League last year before pitching a little better at Double-A. On pure talent, most teams saw Samardzija as a late-first-round talent. The Cubs had to buy him out of an NFL career, but that doesn't necessarily mean they should have (though it continued the Cubs' trend of overpaying for Notre Dame talent and/or clients of agent Mark Rodgers). A few hundred thousand here or there to get Samardzija into the system would have made sense, but the Cubs paid $7.25 million for a $1-million arm, and that's indefensible. Samardzija's scouting reports remain excellent, as he's big, extremely athletic, and touches 98 mph with his fastball. That said, scouts have little explanation as to why he simply doesn't miss any bats. Sure, his secondary pitches could use improvement, but they're not awful, and yes he could add a little movement to his fastball, but it's got plenty of zip. For every insider who thinks Samardzija could become a dominant big leaguer, there's one who thinks he'll never get out of the minors.

Steve Trachsel

Bats: R Throws: R Height: 6' 4" Weight: 205 Born: October 31, 1970 Age: 37

YEAR	TEAM	LVL	AGE	W	L	SV	G	GS	IP	H	BB	SO	HR	GB%	BABIP	STUFF	WHIP	ERA	PERA	EqERA	EqH9	EqBB9	EqSO9	EqHR9	VORP	SN/WX
2005	NYN	MLB	34	1	4	0	6	6	37	37	12	24	6	41.7%	.282	0	1.32	4.14	5.07	5.00	9.2	2.8	5.5	1.5	3.0	0.66
2006	NYN	MLB	35	15	8	0	30	30	164²	185	78	79	23	43.3%	.299	-14	1.60	4.97	5.86	5.15	10.3	3.8	4.1	1.2	14.9	2.89
2007	BAL	MLB	36	6	8	0	25	25	140²	151	69	45	16	44.0%	.281	-15	1.56	4.48	4.74	4.11	9.0	3.9	2.7	1.0	20.3	3.03
2007	CHN	MLB	36	1	3	0	4	4	17¹	25	7	11	3	42.6%	.407	-23	1.85	8.32	10.51	9.56	14.1	3.4	5.6	1.7	-4.7	-0.06
2008	CHN	MLB	37	3	5	0	22	12	73	89	32	34	11	44.1%	.307	-19	1.66	5.74	5.99	6.00	10.5	3.5	3.7	1.3	-0.8	0.40

Breakout: 3% Improve: 12% Collapse: 57% Attrition: 41%   Comparables: Mike Torrez, Bob Welch, Rick Sutcliffe, Bob Buhl

Trachsel made some kind of deal with the devil to sustain an ERA in the mid-fours in Baltimore while posting an unholy 0.65 strikeout-to-walk ratio. The Cubs fell under that spell and were foolish enough to trade two pretty decent prospects for him in third baseman Scott Moore and reliever Rocky Cherry. Trachsel rewarded them by turning in a sub-replacement level performance over four starts. To put it kindly, this was a serious mistake of valuation. One hopes the Cubs have learned from it and will pay more attention to peripheral statistics and less to things such as ERA and win-loss record going forward.

Donald Veal

Bats: L   Throws: L   Height: 6′ 4″   Weight: 215   Born: September 18, 1984   Age: 23

YEAR	TEAM	LVL	AGE	W	L	SV	G	GS	IP	H	BB	SO	HR	GB%	BABIP	STUFF	WHIP	ERA	PERA	EqERA	EqH9	EqBB9	EqSO9	EqHR9	VORP	SN/WX
2005	BOI	A-	20	1	2	0	7	6	29	18	15	34	2	44.1%	.250	4	1.14	2.48	6.62	6.46	7.6	9.5	5.3	1.9	-2.3	—
2006	PEO	A	21	5	3	0	14	14	73²	45	40	86	4	36.3%	.255	8	1.16	2.70	6.70	6.34	8.6	8.9	6.5	1.7	-4.9	—
2006	DAY	A+	21	6	2	0	14	14	80²	46	42	88	3	41.1%	.240	23	1.10	1.68	4.45	3.47	6.6	6.9	6.4	0.9	16.6	—
2007	TEN	AA	22	8	10	0	28	27	130¹	126	73	131	11	42.9%	.329	-5	1.53	4.97	6.76	7.09	10.7	5.7	6.0	1.3	-20.0	—
2008	CHN	MLB	23	5	8	0	28	19	110	113	72	91	17	41.8%	.298	0	1.68	5.63	5.79	5.86	8.8	5.2	6.6	1.3	0.4	0.80

Breakout: 36% Improve: 62% Collapse: 16% Attrition: 11%   Comparables: Chris Capuano, Matthew Maloney, Tom Gorzelanny, Ed Yarnall

That Veal is the best pitching prospect the Cubs have is irrefutable evidence that their farm system is no longer the pitching factory that it once was. He failed to take a step forward last year, particularly in terms of his command. The silver lining is that there's a school of thought that says big lefties develop slowly, with top PECOTA comparable Chris Capuano being one of the better examples.

Randy Wells

Bats: R   Throws: R   Height: 6′ 5″   Weight: 230   Born: August 28, 1982   Age: 25

YEAR	TEAM	LVL	AGE	W	L	SV	G	GS	IP	H	BB	SO	HR	GB%	BABIP	STUFF	WHIP	ERA	PERA	EqERA	EqH9	EqBB9	EqSO9	EqHR9	VORP	SN/WX
2005	DAY	A+	22	10	2	2	41	10	98²	93	22	106	5	46.7%	.328	-5	1.17	2.74	5.37	4.60	10.0	3.7	5.6	1.0	9.8	—
2006	WTN	AA	23	4	2	0	12	12	62¹	45	13	54	2	48.6%	.253	15	0.93	1.59	3.31	2.98	7.3	2.2	5.1	0.6	17.6	—
2006	IOW	AAA	23	5	5	0	13	12	69²	87	23	59	7	46.3%	.370	-7	1.59	4.94	6.71	6.45	11.8	3.4	5.5	1.2	-6.3	—
2007	IOW	AAA	24	5	6	2	40	9	95²	100	41	101	11	46.4%	.341	-4	1.47	4.51	5.22	5.17	9.2	4.1	7.3	1.1	4.5	—
2008	TOR	MLB	25	4	5	4	23	10	72	72	34	61	8	47.9%	.303	7	1.47	4.42	4.29	4.49	8.6	3.9	6.6	1.0	10.8	1.40

Breakout: 37% Improve: 61% Collapse: 13% Attrition: 13%   Comparables: Brent Stentz, Roy Smith, Chad Ricketts, Steve Rain

The Cubs gave up too quickly on Wells, who was taken by the Blue Jays in December's Rule 5 draft. While he does not have that one plus-plus offering that makes scouts do a Tex Avery double take, he mixes and matches well enough to be a league-average reliever and has struck out more than a batter an inning in his minor league career. Once again, the Cubs' focus appeared to be on his ERA, which has been inflated by some high BABIP marks, rather than on his more informative and encouraging peripheral stats.

Kerry Wood

Bats: R   Throws: R   Height: 6′ 5″   Weight: 225   Born: June 16, 1977   Age: 31

YEAR	TEAM	LVL	AGE	W	L	SV	G	GS	IP	H	BB	SO	HR	GB%	BABIP	STUFF	WHIP	ERA	PERA	EqERA	EqH9	EqBB9	EqSO9	EqHR9	VORP	SN/WX
2005	CHN	MLB	28	3	4	0	21	10	66	52	26	77	14	36.9%	.252	10	1.18	4.23	4.42	4.15	7.3	3.2	9.6	1.8	9.2	1.01
2006	CHN	MLB	29	1	2	0	4	4	19²	19	8	13	5	42.2%	.246	-5	1.37	4.11	5.26	4.95	8.1	3.2	5.4	1.8	0.2	0.17
2007	CHN	MLB	30	1	1	0	22	0	24¹	18	13	24	0	35.9%	.286	16	1.27	3.33	2.97	3.42	7.2	4.2	8.4	0.0	7.1	0.01
2008	CHN	MLB	31	2	2	2	39	0	44¹	41	21	43	6	40.1%	.285	4	1.38	4.25	4.36	4.47	7.9	3.8	7.7	1.1	7.2	0.60

Breakout: 11% Improve: 36% Collapse: 42% Attrition: 15%   Comparables: Todd Van Poppel, Eric Plunk, Dwayne Henry, Steve Bedrosian

Don't expect miracles. Although Wood should be a decent major league reliever, he will always be fighting uphill because of his fly-ball tendencies and middling command. He now tops out at around 93 to 95 mph, and his breaking stuff is no longer as sharp; even that small drop in velocity probably limits his upside to an ERA in the high threes. That might still be enough to make him better than Dempster, but that's damning him with faint praise.

Michael Wuertz

Bats: R   Throws: R   Height: 6′ 3″   Weight: 205   Born: December 15, 1978   Age: 29

YEAR	TEAM	LVL	AGE	W	L	SV	G	GS	IP	H	BB	SO	HR	GB%	BABIP	STUFF	WHIP	ERA	PERA	EqERA	EqH9	EqBB9	EqSO9	EqHR9	VORP	SN/WX
2005	CHN	MLB	26	6	2	0	75	0	75²	60	40	89	6	43.7%	.302	22	1.32	3.80	3.72	4.28	7.6	4.4	9.8	0.7	10.4	1.20
2006	IOW	AAA	27	6	0	10	30	0	41	30	9	67	2	44.0%	.318	30	0.95	1.76	3.33	2.85	7.5	2.2	9.9	0.7	12.5	—
2006	CHN	MLB	27	3	1	0	41	0	40²	35	16	42	5	55.2%	.278	14	1.25	2.65	3.53	2.57	7.5	3.0	8.1	0.9	13.5	0.26
2007	CHN	MLB	28	2	3	0	73	0	72¹	64	35	79	8	46.5%	.301	16	1.37	3.49	3.99	3.36	8.1	3.7	9.1	0.9	17.8	0.89
2008	CHN	MLB	29	3	3	4	50	0	55²	49	25	57	5	45.1%	.288	11	1.32	3.47	3.68	3.72	7.5	3.6	8.0	0.8	14.2	1.20

Breakout: 14% Improve: 37% Collapse: 36% Attrition: 17%   Comparables: Derrick Turnbow, Darren Holmes, Rich Croushore, Curt Leskanic

Wuertz generates a great deal of movement on his pitches, which causes both left- and right-handed hitters a fair amount of trouble; indeed, he has a slight reverse platoon split over the course of his career. He's finally developed decent command over that slippy-slidey arsenal, and if the Cubs are so inclined, that platoon neutrality could make him better suited than most middle relievers to the closer's role, as closers tend to get the platoon advantage less often.

Carlos Zambrano

Bats: S   Throws: R   Height: 6' 5"   Weight: 255   Born: June 1, 1981   Age: 27

YEAR	TEAM	LVL	AGE	W	L	SV	G	GS	IP	H	BB	SO	HR	GB%	BABIP	STUFF	WHIP	ERA	PERA	EqERA	EqH9	EqBB9	EqSO9	EqHR9	VORP	SN/WX
2005	CHN	MLB	24	14	6	0	33	33	223^1	170	86	202	21	52.7%	.258	26	1.15	3.26	3.37	3.51	7.1	3.2	7.5	0.8	51.2	6.76
2006	CHN	MLB	25	16	7	0	33	33	214	162	115	210	20	49.2%	.259	29	1.29	3.41	3.36	3.33	6.8	4.1	8.0	0.7	53.8	6.31
2007	CHN	MLB	26	18	13	0	34	34	216^1	187	101	177	23	48.2%	.273	19	1.33	3.95	4.00	3.80	8.0	3.6	7.0	0.9	43.5	5.62
2008	CHN	MLB	27	12	10	0	30	30	195^2	176	84	173	19	48.3%	.284	20	1.33	3.81	3.90	4.08	7.8	3.4	7.0	0.8	35.8	5.50

Breakout: 5%   Improve: 18%   Collapse: 33%   Attrition: 13%   Comparables: Mark Gubicza, Joey Jay, Jim Clancy, Stan Williams

Zambrano had been outpitching his peripheral statistics for several seasons, so the main cause of the uptick in his ERA last year was simple regression to the mean. That said, both his velocity and strikeout rate were off a bit as well. There were clearly times when Zambrano seemed flustered last season, most notably his much-publicized dugout fight with Michael Barrett, so there was some hope that his performance would improve after being granted peace of mind by the contract extension he signed in August, but his strikeout rate was incrementally worse down the stretch. Maybe Zambrano's a guy who's better when he's pitching a little angry. Either way, he's a pitcher of legendary durability, but is probably closer to a number two than a true ace in most other respects.

LINEOUTS

Hitters

	PLAYER	TEAM	LVL	AGE	PA	R	2B	3B	HR	RBI	BB	SO	SB-CS	EqBRR	AVG/OBP/SLG	MLVr	EqAVG/EqOBP/EqSLG	EqA	VORP
C	W. Castillo	PEO	A	20	353	41	11	2	11	44	23	77	1-3	-3.9	.271/.334/.423	.118	.221/.271/.337	.210	-13.7
INF	R. Chirinos	DAY	A+	23	293	35	14	2	3	20	37	48	8-5	-0.7	.259/.385/.372	.052	.225/.332/.337	.241	1.3
		TEN	AA	23	146	11	4	2	2	16	13	31	1-1	-0.9	.220/.298/.331	-.185	.197/.264/.288	.192	-8.1
3B	M. Craig#	TEN	AA	26	323	41	20	1	10	44	40	58	1-0	-4.3	.326/.416/.514	.306	.290/.372/.473	.291	27.1
		IOW	AAA	26	121	16	7	1	4	25	10	29	0-0	1.2	.273/.331/.464	.012	.243/.303/.423	.250	2.2
RF	R. Harvey	DAY	A+	22	234	30	10	1	11	35	7	53	0-1	-0.5	.246/.269/.446	-.039	.209/.234/.391	.209	-17.2
C	K. Hill#	IOW	AAA	28	162	22	16	0	2	24	11	23	1-1	1.9	.322/.364/.470	.129	.287/.331/.413	.258	5.7
		CHN	MLB	28	105	7	4	0	2	12	8	18	0-0	-0.6	.161/.231/.269	-.465	.161/.238/.258	.174	-7.4
RF	J. Kroeger*	TEN	AA	24	256	40	14	2	11	50	27	35	8-3	0.8	.382/.449/.609	.533	.339/.398/.543	.316	27.3
		IOW	AAA	24	198	27	7	0	10	31	21	38	0-1	-2.6	.263/.338/.474	.032	.233/.308/.415	.248	-3.6

Welington Castillo was perhaps the best defensive catcher in the Midwest League last year. He's not going to be a stud, but he may have just enough line-drive power to become something interesting. ⊘ **Robinson Chirinos** can take a walk, but he'll likely fall victim to the "Rexrode Threshold," as his insufficient power will allow pitchers at higher levels to throw him more strikes, thus decreasing his walk rate. Still, his glove isn't bad, so he could make it as a utility player. ⊘ A reasonably promising prospect before he tested positive for steroids at the start of the 2005 season, **Matt Craig** offers a decent bat at the corner infield positions but little else; think Kevin Orie. ⊘ The sixth overall pick in the 2003 draft, hulking **Ryan Harvey** became an official bust last year after repeating the Florida State League in his fifth professional season without showing any improvement at the level. A hamstring injury didn't help, but he has yet to demonstrate any idea of how to hit a breaking ball. ⊘ **Koyie Hill** took advantage of the Cubs' revolving door at catcher last year to record his longest stint as a big-leaguer, but didn't do himself any favors by posting a .174 EqA. As a backup catcher, he's neither any better nor any worse than most of the scrubs in the league. ⊘ Playing for his third organization in as many seasons, **Josh Kroeger** showed unexpected life in his bat at Double-A West Tennessee last year, but was less impressive in the second half after a promotion to Triple-A Iowa and an injury to his left oblique.

Pitchers

PLAYER	TEAM	LVL	AGE	W	L	SV	IP	H	BB	SO	HR	GB%	BABIP	STUFF	WHIP	ERA	PERA	EqERA	EqH9	EqBB9	EqSO9	EqHR9	VORP
A. Harben	CUB	Rk	23	0	1	0	5	2	4	6	0	77.8%	.222	4	1.20	1.80	2.73	2.45	4.9	14.7	4.9	0.0	1.3
K. Hart	TEN	AA	24	8	5	0	102	100	27	92	13	52.6%	.303	-21	1.25	4.24	6.54	6.82	10.6	2.8	5.4	1.8	-12.9
	IOW	AAA	24	4	1	0	56	56	23	39	6	50.3%	.309	-2	1.41	3.54	4.56	3.62	8.4	4.0	4.6	1.2	12.0
	CHN	MLB	24	0	0	0	11	7	4	13	0	40.0%	.292	10	1.00	0.82	2.57	0.87	7.0	2.6	9.6	0.0	6.2
G. Johnson	DAY	A+	24	1	1	0	22²	19	11	25	2	40.0%	.288	-11	1.32	3.57	5.76	6.14	8.6	5.7	6.1	1.6	-1.3
	TEN	AA	24	1	1	3	47¹	36	20	43	5	45.9%	.246	-21	1.18	4.38	4.94	6.00	8.2	4.2	5.4	1.6	-2.0
J. Mateo	PEO	A	24	2	1	0	22¹	27	8	14	1	57.1%	.351	-39	1.57	5.25	10.42	10.80	15.2	6.9	2.5	1.5	-10.6
	IOW	AAA	24	2	3	0	40	50	11	29	8	41.7%	.323	-17	1.53	4.05	6.53	6.07	10.6	2.7	4.7	2.0	-2.1
W. Miller	CHN	MLB	30	0	1	0	13²	24	6	6	5	29.3%	.365	-66	2.20	10.51	18.96	14.49	15.8	3.3	4.0	3.3	-6.7
B. Petrick	DAY	A+	23	0	1	0	11²	12	2	10	0	55.6%	.343	-6	1.20	3.08	4.83	4.22	11.0	2.5	5.1	0.0	1.6
	TEN	AA	23	1	1	2	30¹	22	8	33	3	53.8%	.260	0	0.99	2.38	4.44	4.13	7.9	2.9	6.7	1.6	4.6
	IOW	AAA	23	1	1	0	12¹	17	2	7	3	41.9%	.368	-28	1.54	5.12	10.96	7.15	12.7	1.6	4.0	2.4	-1.9
	CHN	MLB	23	0	0	0	9²	8	7	6	3	55.2%	.192	-15	1.55	7.42	6.73	6.75	7.7	5.8	5.8	2.9	-1.6

The player to be named later for Phil Nevin in late 2006, **Adam Harben** underwent Tommy John surgery after just three Arizona Fall League starts that fall. Added to the 40-man roster in November, he'll be working his way back this year. ⊘ More a grinder than any sort of prospect, **Kevin Hart** is a smart pitcher who makes the most out of middling stuff, but will likely be exposed in the big leagues because of his propensity to give up home runs. ⊘ **Grant Johnson** has never quite found the velocity he flashed in his sophomore year at Notre Dame, and this year is perhaps his last chance to do so. ⊘ After spending considerable time with the Cubs in 2006, **Juan Mateo** got lost in baggage claim last year, starting the season in A-ball because of a shoulder impingement before eventually posting lukewarm numbers in Iowa. The organization still likes him long-term, probably in the bullpen, where his lack of secondary stuff would be less exposed. ⊘ **Wade Miller** is now five years removed from his last healthy season, and even teams that are desperate for pitching can probably find more interesting alternatives. ⊘ **Billy Petrick** has a good pitcher's body and respectable stuff. He's started to use his curveball to better effect, increasing his strikeout rates accordingly. His ceiling is probably that of a league-average middle reliever; having been added to the 40-man roster, he may get that opportunity sooner rather than later.

MANAGER: LOU PINIELLA

YEAR	TEAM	W-L	Pythag +/-	Avg PC	100+ P	120+ P	QS	BQS	REL	REL w Zero R	IBB	Subs	PH	PH Avg	PH HR	SB2	CS2	SB3	CS3	SAC Att	SAC %	POS SAC	Squeeze	Swing	In Play
2005	TBA	67-95	4	93.9	66	9	53	10	400	219	41	74	118	.309	4	129	43	22	5	59	57.6%	32	0	136	106
2007	CHN	85-77	-3	95.0	69	6	81	4	478	323	46	85	257	.208	6	78	24	8	9	64	75.0%	28	4	126	98

With the exception of a couple of incidents around Memorial Day, when the Cubs were not playing well, Chicago got a calmer, more sedate version of Piniella. Though he avoided any Lee Elia moments, Piniella represented a welcome change of pace from the passive-aggressive "What, me worry?" ways of Dusty Baker. Piniella's greatest strength as a manager is his ability to juggle component parts in a relatively apolitical way, something that should come in handy as the team may want to take advantage of some platoons this year. He's not anti-youth, as evidenced by his decision to make Geovany Soto the starting catcher down the stretch run, but he's also not inclined to stick a player like Felix Pie in the lineup unless he thinks the kid's ready. Thus, if a decision is going to be made about giving players such as Pie or Carlos Marmol a larger role with the club this year, it will probably need to come from the top down.

Chicago White Sox

"Value" has no meaning other than in relation to living beings. The value of a thing is always relative to a particular person . . . "market value" is a fiction, merely a rough guess at the average of personal values, all of which must be quantitatively different or trade would be impossible.
—ROBERT HEINLEIN, *Starship Troopers*

And so, with a thump, the White Sox fell. It wasn't particularly remarkable; in his spring PECOTA-driven predictions on BaseballProspectus.com, Nate Silver pegged the Sox to win 72 games, and win 72 games they did. It wasn't a particularly remarkable prediction—unless of course you were the White Sox. From the moment that prediction was published, the White Sox noisily, publicly, and appropriately rejected the suggestion that they were anything less than contenders. General manager Kenny Williams immediately shot back: "That's a good sign for us because usually they're wrong about everything regarding our dealings." Team owner Jerry Reinsdorf chimed in, "We ought to win the division."

To be fair, what was their alternative—read that projection and run up a(nother) white flag? In March? Nobody should have been surprised at the public posturing with which the White Sox responded—to do so was a necessity; even the derision was entirely understandable. They flat-out didn't agree with the forecast, and to be frank, even we were a little surprised PECOTA was as negative about the team as it was. Where the problem lies isn't with a prediction that hit the bull's-eye, but with the more important issue of whether or not the Sox really believed they were contenders, because on the face of it, their confidence might not do them any credit, especially given the results.

Understanding the White Sox' confidence that they were and are a contending ballclub depends upon un-

derstanding their sense of player value, one that isn't like that of many other teams. In every aspect of designing a roster, the Sox take chances that few other teams would. While that has been seen as a reason for their success in the past, right now it's a contributing cause to their failures. Whether we're talking about employing singles-hitting Scott Podsednik as a left fielder, carrying multiple infield reserves with modest power, or trying to breathe new life into Darin Erstad's career, the Sox have made their share of choices that leave performance analysts howling. Some of these moves didn't work, but some did—some in baseball had given up on shortstop Juan Uribe after three years in Colorado yielded just 24 home runs and a .298 on-base percentage, but the Sox recognized him for his merits as a defender and as a hitter whose stroke was best-suited for delivering power in their park. Less an issue of orthodoxy than of solid scouting, Williams landed Tadahito Iguchi to fill his need for a second baseman at less than half the price the Mets paid for Kaz Matsui, while receiving significantly more value.

As for the pitching staff, some thought that Williams got snookered when he gave up top center-field prospect Jeremy Reed in a five-player trade for disappointing starter Freddy Garcia, but Garcia improved on the Sox' watch while Reed, now entering his age-27 season, has been a complete bust in the major leagues. Many had given up on Jose Contreras after his failures with the Yankees, but the big Cuban stepped up his game after

---

WHITE SOX PROSPECTUS

2007 record: 72-90; Fourth place, AL Central

Pythagenport record: 67-95

Runs scored per game: 4.28 (14th in AL)

Runs allowed per game: 5.18 (12th in AL)

Team EqA: .243 (13th in AL)

2007 Batters Age: 30.3 (7th oldest in AL)

2007 Pitchers Age: 28.5 (7th oldest in AL)

Ballpark: U.S. Cellular Park; Hitter's park; Park Factor of 1.046

2007: The Sox doth protest too much and win too little.

2008: The Pale Hose refuse to settle in as also-rans, but might not escape that fate.

being picked up in a trade by Chicago. The bullpen was an area of special success, as the Sox had conjured up an outstanding relief corps for their championship team almost out of thin air—closer Bobby Jenks was a waiver claim, righties Dustin Hermanson and Cliff Politte relatively cheap free agency finds, lefty Damaso Marte a straight-up steal in a trade with the Pirates for minor league right-hander Matt Guerrier, and Luis Vizcaino and lefty Neal Cotts throw-ins on deals that otherwise didn't work out all that well (the Podsednik swap with the Brewers and the Keith Foulke/Billy Koch exchange with the A's, respectively). In sum, the assembly of that pen was a vindication of the White Sox' balance of risk and good scouting, a compliment it would be fair to extend to Williams' roster management in general. The Sox had reasons to believe in their ability to identify players who could help them, and get value.

By 2007, those risks had stopped paying off. The hazards of playing Uribe regularly had gone back to outweighing the benefits. Podsednik and Erstad punished the faith placed in them, and speed guy Jerry Owens, acquired in a low-profile trade with the Nationals, did no better when plugged into the team's hole in center field. The lineup was already heavily dependent on the core trio of first baseman Paul Konerko, right fielder Jermaine Dye, and designated hitter Jim Thome, but adding the complete lack of production from shortstop, left, and center to the stone-cold starts of both Dye and third baseman Joe Crede (before he broke down entirely) left the Sox with very little offense; they finished next-to-last in the majors with a team .243 Equivalent Average, ahead of only the Royals.

The pitching staff responded in kind. Contreras, in particular, started to look like a pitcher of indeterminate age who had been used up, but the worst setbacks weren't with the staff's veterans, but with the crowd of hard-throwing youngsters who had been added in a quick bit of retooling before the 2007 season. Raw arms such as lefties Andy Sisco and John Danks, and righties David Aardsma, Nick Masset, and Gavin Floyd—acquired in four different trades—all throw hard and all hold promise, but all have command problems that could get the better of each of them. Taking a chance on a pitcher like that can be a good thing for an organization, especially one with past experience ironing out a wild reliever or two, as the Sox have had with pitching coach Don Cooper and Jenks and Cotts. When you take that risk on one pitcher, and he fails, that's endurable. When you risk a full slate of longshots and they all blow up in your face, you wind up with one of the worst bullpens in baseball, as the Sox did last year despite compressing those failures into the fewest relief innings thrown by any team in baseball (424 2/3, more than 80 fewer than the average team's 510) *and* getting an exceptional season from Jenks. Last year's White Sox bullpen allowed the second most inherited runners to score in the majors (116, second only to the Orioles), posted the second-worst Fair Run Average (6.20, second only to the Devil Rays), and ranked 27th in WXRL with a 3.214 mark that surpassed only those of the O's, D-Rays and Reds.

Winning only 72 games was a massive disappointment to the Sox, but to get even that far, they had to run up an 18-7 record against the Royals and Devil Rays, two of the three teams in the league with a worse final record. Against the rest of the world, the Sox were under .400. If anything, last year's 90 losses might have only been the start of a period of prolonged losing on the South Side of Chicago that will necessitate an especially ugly, extended rebuilding in the near future. Add in that the Cubs are riding high off a division title, and you can forgive the Sox—and their fans—if they're a little cranky about the prospect of going back to being the Second City's second team as if the 2005 title had never happened.

After the season, Williams was quick to change things up. Having failed to leverage any of his starting pitchers for future-minded help at last year's trading deadline, he quickly worked a deal for Jon Garland, the one disposable starter with the best balance of value, salary, and acceptable risk. The problem was, with only one year left on his contract, Garland wasn't going to yield much, and he didn't, going to the Angels in exchange for an equally expensive, semi-valuable, acceptably risky, low-upside player in shortstop Orlando Cabrera, also on the final year of his contract. To want Cabrera, you don't have to be the kind of organization that values the Alex Cintrons and Pablo Ozunas, or the odd Podzilla, but it helps. With Garland deleted from the rotation, there is the considerable question of who will be among their starting five after Vazquez and Buehrle. Contreras left shoppers cold, so the Sox are stuck with him. It isn't a bad thing to have to choose two or three from among youngsters John Danks, Gavin Floyd, Lance Broadway, and Charlie Haeger initially, and perhaps Jack Egbert eventually. The problem is that it's not the choice a self-anointed contender should be making, and as interesting as all of them are, none of them are surefire talents of the caliber of the Yankees' Phil Hughes, Boston's Clay Buchholz, or Seattle's Felix Hernandez. There is a very real possibility that last year's frustrations with talented young arms will be repeated, only this time around with a greater emphasis in the rotation.

That said, the White Sox are in position to do a number of things that might be semi-surprising. At a time when platooning isn't popular—it's difficult to afford the roster space when pitchers number an even dozen on most teams—the Sox have the potential to carry a pair, one at catcher, with veterans A. J. Pierzynski and Toby Hall, and another at second base. With Cabrera taking over at shortstop, there is a possibility (some might say danger) that Uribe will claim the second base job, but a platoon of Uribe and the lefty-swinging Danny Richar, who took over at the keystone after Iguchi was dealt to the Phillies, would have the value of actively employing the team's backup shortstop while giving Richar a cushion as he attempts to build on his rough 2007 debut and become the line-drive power source that Kenny Williams believed he had acquired in a deal with the Diamondbacks in June. There's also the winter addition of Cuban defector Alexei Ramirez, a potential power source versatile enough to play second, short, or center.

Richar and another former Snakeling, outfielder Carlos Quentin (acquired this past winter for slugging Low-A first-baseman Chris Carter), give the Sox a pair of ready-now youngsters to plug into a lineup which should also feature Josh Fields, the homegrown prospect who, having delivered on the power potential he flashed in the minors, is ready to settle in at third base after a solid rookie season. Quentin, Richar, and Fields are all entering their age-25 seasons, so they're coming into what should be their most productive seasons while still earning close to the league minimum. That's worth taking some credit for, but the problem is that none of them are really high-upside players with anything like the MVP potential that Thome, Konerko, or Dye had in their best years. In fact, the Sox' farm system is dreadfully lacking in position players with promise. Thus, while in the broad view Williams has made an effort to weave in younger players to complement his older stars, the members of the lineup's core aren't great bets to match or top their past achievements, potentially trapping the Sox in a loop in which they're hoping that their individually good-enough youngster add-ons can sufficiently compensate for the creeping decline of their best hitters. Consider the contrasts in productivity between the White Sox' typical 2007 and projected 2008 lineups (see Table 1).

Where the Sox, perhaps, should have made a meaningful upgrade was center field. In what was seen as a fine market for free-agent help at the position, Williams was voluble in his interest in first Torii Hunter, and maybe Andruw Jones, and then former Sock Aaron Rowand, but he didn't sign any of them and was left using poverty as his excuse. You can consider the failure to

Table 1. Racing Against Father Time: White Sox lineup productivity, then and now

Position	Avg EqA	2007 Regular	2007 EqA	2008 Regular	2008 EqA
DH	.279	Thome	.327	Thome	.309
C	.244	Pierzynski	.252	Pierzynski	.245
1B	.279	Konerko	.290	Konerko	.289
2B	.259	Iguchi	.267	Richar	.257
3B	.269	Fields	.271	Fields	.279
SS	.255	Uribe	.237	Cabrera	.252
LF	.269	Podsednik	.246	Quentin	.278
CF	.263	Owens	.246	Swisher	.301
RF	.272	Dye	.277	Dye	.282

Avg EqA is the major league average EqA for the given position in 2007; 2008 EqAs are taken from the respective players' PECOTA projections

land a premium center fielder a massive misread of the market, but that failure proved inspirational, as Williams subsequently swung a deal with Billy Beane that sent Oakland his two top pitching prospects, Gio Gonzalez and Fautino De Los Santos, and outfielder Ryan Sweeney for outfielder/first baseman Nick Swisher, a move that should give the Sox a slugger already under contract for five productive years at a cheaper price than any of the free agent alternatives.

To some extent, Williams' spending was handicapped by his having spent the second half of the season handing out multi-year extensions first to Mark Buehrle (July, fours years for $56 million, running through 2011), then Dye (August, two years, $22 million, through 2009), and finally A. J. Pierzynski ($12.5 million for the 2009 and 2010 seasons). Still, each of those extensions can be seen as the product of reasonable decision-making. That's less true of the decisions to retain both Uribe and Crede, neither likely to start or be especially good should they start, for a combined total of more than $9 million in 2008. If Williams' financial freedom was limited, as he now claims, it was his decision to circumscribe his options, first by jumping the gun and signing Uribe before he had to tender him a contract or had acquired Miguel Cabrera, then by retaining Crede when he already had Fields. At best, Crede gives Williams the option to supplement his roster through a mid-level deal—Williams could shop him from March through July and get value, knowing that Fields is the future—which is small consolation. Even in the pursuit of a Crede trade, the Sox are in danger of having a march stolen on them by a division rival—the Tigers can shop displaced third baseman Brandon Inge, and the Indians might do likewise with failed third-base prospect Andy Marte.

The confidence the White Sox displayed entering the 2007 season brings to mind the rallying speech of a newly minted football coach upon taking over a desperately bad team in 1984: "This is a new era; we're starting over. We're getting it going, and we're going to win. We're going to win for the people; we're going to win for our fans!" That sort of commitment is admirable, to be sure. Unfortunately, Hank Bullough never coached a single Pittsburgh Maulers game—the United States Football League franchise ceased to exist before the next season came around.

It's fine to have confidence, but it's also important to recognize when those confident words represent little more than empty promises. The future provides no guarantees. The Sox—and Kenny Williams—can posture all they like, but 2005 is gone, and their farm system is desperately shallow. The near-term goal is to contend and squeeze some last bit of glory out of a core built around Swisher, Thome, Konerko, Dye, Buehrle, Vazquez, and Jenks, but the White Sox' winter activity might have been only the last desperate throw before an extended collapse.

HITTERS

Brian Anderson OF   Bats: R   Throws: R   Height: 6' 2"   Weight: 220   Born: March 11, 1982   Age: 26

YEAR	TEAM	LVL	AGE	PA	R	2B	3B	HR	RBI	BB	SO	SB	CS	EqBRR	AVG	OBP	SLG	MLVr	EqAVG	EqOBP	EqSLG	EqA	VORP	DEFENSE	
2005	CHR	AAA	23	501	71	24	3	16	57	44	115	4	2	3.8	.295	.360	.469	.122	.257	.322	.415	.254	9.3	111-CF	-6
2006	CHA	MLB	24	406	46	23	1	8	33	30	91	4	7	-0.6	.224	.290	.358	-.247	.221	.295	.356	.223	-11.3	108-CF	10
2007	CHA	MLB	25	19	3	1	0	0	0	2	7	0	0	0.1	.118	.211	.176	-.654	.118	.211	.176	.100	-2.4		
2007	CHR	AAA	25	223	29	8	2	8	31	19	47	3	2	-1.3	.255	.318	.435	.015	.239	.300	.418	.247	1.1	35-CF	0
2008	CHA	MLB	26	266	29	12	1	8	30	21	64	3	2	0.2	.240	.305	.395	-.117	.238	.304	.398	.247	-0.5	65-CF	1

Breakout: 31% Improve: 60% Collapse: 21% Attrition: 26%   Comparables: Mark Smith, Dee Brown, Jeff Liefer, Steve Hosey

If Mother Nature is red in tooth and claw, it's in part because her nastier predators make easy meals out of aspiring fourth outfielders who are just shy of playable. Anderson has fallen out of favor after a pair of crushingly disappointing seasons, and being slow, underpowered, and a right-handed hitter doesn't put him ahead of the other equally flawed wildebeests.

Chris Carter 1B   Bats: R   Throws: R   Height: 6' 4"   Weight: 210   Born: December 18, 1986   Age: 21

YEAR	TEAM	LVL	AGE	PA	R	2B	3B	HR	RBI	BB	SO	SB	CS	EqBRR	AVG	OBP	SLG	MLVr	EqAVG	EqOBP	EqSLG	EqA	VORP	DEFENSE			
2005	BRI	Rk	18	262	33	17	0	10	37	17	64	2	1	0.4	.283	.350	.485	.184	.197	.242	.283	.177	-41.0	36-3B	-9	20-1B	-1
2006	GRF	Rk	19	294	37	21	1	15	59	34	70	4	4	-3.1	.299	.398	.570	.370	.221	.289	.397	.233	-16.0	59-1B	-12		
2006	KAN	A	19	52	4	3	0	1	5	5	17	0	0	-0.8	.130	.231	.261	-.357	.125	.192	.250	.132	-7.8				
2007	KAN	A	20	545	84	27	3	25	93	67	112	3	2	-0.7	.291	.383	.522	.260	.229	.306	.394	.243	-11.3	73-1B	-10		
2008	OAK	MLB	21	595	49	28	2	13	61	49	162	4	3	-0.3	.212	.281	.345	-.241	.215	.286	.368	.229	-18.5	139-1B	-4		

Breakout: 32% Improve: 56% Collapse: 19% Attrition: 12%   Comparables: Wes Bankston, Mike Little, Jake Blalock, Ron Wright

A hulking high school draftee tabbed in the 15th round in 2005, Carter had an excellent first full professional season last year, showing the power that got him picked but also improved command of the strike zone. If he has a handicap, it's his fielding, which is a bit stiff and clumsy, but at his age, he's got years to work on that. Traded twice in the offseason—first to Arizona for Carlos Quentin, then to Oakland in the Dan Haren deal—Carter now finds himself in an organization that's committed to coaching hitters to work for their pitch, so his potential to break out just got a little bit better.

Alex Cintron INF   Bats: S   Throws: R   Height: 6' 1"   Weight: 205   Born: December 17, 1978   Age: 29

YEAR	TEAM	LVL	AGE	PA	R	2B	3B	HR	RBI	BB	SO	SB	CS	EqBRR	AVG	OBP	SLG	MLVr	EqAVG	EqOBP	EqSLG	EqA	VORP	DEFENSE			
2005	ARI	MLB	26	348	36	19	2	8	48	12	33	1	2	0.8	.273	.298	.415	-.055	.264	.293	.413	.241	4.1	30-SS	-2	21-3B	0
2006	CHA	MLB	27	304	35	10	3	5	41	10	35	10	3	-1.1	.285	.310	.392	-.118	.281	.314	.396	.249	4.6	36-SS	-2	23-2B	-4
2007	CHA	MLB	28	196	23	7	1	2	19	9	35	2	1	-0.5	.243	.281	.324	-.267	.245	.286	.342	.219	-6.8	15-SS	3	13-3B	-1
2008	CHA	MLB	29	211	20	9	1	3	20	10	31	3	1	0.0	.252	.290	.358	-.185	.249	.288	.361	.229	-2.9	53-SS	-3		

Breakout: 21% Improve: 37% Collapse: 36% Attrition: 34%   Comparables: Cristian Guzman, Garry Templeton, Greg Pryor, Roy Staiger

A classic Ozzie Guillen filler player released by the White Sox in November, Cintron has a decent set of virtues—some speed, modest sock for a non-star shortstop, and an ability to play the middle infield and third well enough. If he got an opportunity to play regularly, hitting closer to his career rates of .277/.315/.401 wouldn't be out of reach, but getting that chance is a bit of a longshot.

Joe Crede — 3B

Bats: R   Throws: R   Height: 6' 2"   Weight: 230   Born: April 26, 1978   Age: 30

YEAR	TEAM	LVL	AGE	PA	R	2B	3B	HR	RBI	BB	SO	SB	CS	EqBRR	AVG	OBP	SLG	MLVr	EqAVG	EqOBP	EqSLG	EqA	VORP	DEFENSE	
2005	CHA	MLB	27	471	54	21	0	22	62	25	66	1	1	3.0	.252	.303	.454	-.023	.251	.311	.462	.262	7.8	123-3B	14
2006	CHA	MLB	28	586	76	31	0	30	94	28	58	0	2	-3.5	.283	.323	.506	.067	.277	.323	.506	.277	20.2	141-3B	24
2007	CHA	MLB	29	178	13	5	0	4	22	10	24	0	1	-0.1	.216	.258	.317	-.332	.217	.264	.325	.201	-10.8	44-3B	9
2008	CHA	MLB	30	339	34	16	0	12	47	22	47	1	1	-0.5	.252	.307	.419	-.075	.249	.306	.422	.254	2.1	82-3B	6

Breakout: 16% Improve: 48% Collapse: 25% Attrition: 26%   Comparables: Dave Roberts, Kevin Orie, Tim Wallach, Tim Hulett

The Tim Wallach comp isn't too shabby—like the former Expo great, Crede's a gifted defender, the sort of third baseman who covers the line well, can take away the bunt, and does an outstanding job starting double plays. He's also not on base as often as you'd like, and if his power fades, he becomes a luxury a lot of lineups can't afford. Assuming that he's fully healed from last year's back surgery, the White Sox should move him quickly, because even before the operation, Crede's career arc didn't seem likely to involve a glorious run deep into his 30s.

Jermaine Dye — RF

Bats: R   Throws: R   Height: 6' 5"   Weight: 240   Born: January 28, 1974   Age: 34

YEAR	TEAM	LVL	AGE	PA	R	2B	3B	HR	RBI	BB	SO	SB	CS	EqBRR	AVG	OBP	SLG	MLVr	EqAVG	EqOBP	EqSLG	EqA	VORP	DEFENSE	
2005	CHA	MLB	31	579	74	29	2	31	86	39	99	11	4	-2.3	.274	.333	.512	.126	.273	.342	.526	.289	27.7	136-RF	-7
2006	CHA	MLB	32	611	103	27	3	44	120	59	118	7	3	-3.0	.315	.385	.622	.367	.308	.385	.624	.326	64.6	139-RF	3
2007	CHA	MLB	33	561	68	34	0	28	78	45	107	2	1	-1.7	.254	.317	.486	.032	.252	.322	.508	.277	12.2	130-RF	10
2008	CHA	MLB	34	490	63	23	1	24	78	43	94	6	2	-0.9	.265	.334	.484	.066	.262	.333	.489	.282	11.5	116-RF	0

Breakout: 5% Improve: 18% Collapse: 35% Attrition: 19%   Comparables: Dave Henderson, Joe Adcock, Jose Canseco, Juan Gonzalez

Although his performance at the plate last year was uneven, Dye's big second half (.298/.368/.579) provided hope that a return to his 2006 levels isn't out of reach. Having given him a new two-year, $22 million extension with a $12 million mutual option for 2010, the Sox are banking on that second half. Dye's aging better than some might have expected during his brief string of misfortunes with the A's, but there's a very real danger that he's going to be a barely adequate regular from here on out, especially if he's once again struggling to post an OBP over .300 against right-handers.

Darin Erstad — OF/1B

Bats: L   Throws: L   Height: 6' 2"   Weight: 220   Born: June 4, 1974   Age: 34

YEAR	TEAM	LVL	AGE	PA	R	2B	3B	HR	RBI	BB	SO	SB	CS	EqBRR	AVG	OBP	SLG	MLVr	EqAVG	EqOBP	EqSLG	EqA	VORP	DEFENSE			
2005	ANA	MLB	31	663	86	33	3	7	66	47	109	10	3	2.2	.273	.325	.371	-.067	.280	.343	.386	.258	0.3	142-1B	17		
2006	ANA	MLB	32	105	8	8	1	0	5	6	18	1	1	0.0	.221	.279	.326	-.291	.223	.288	.319	.215	-3.7	25-CF	2		
2007	CHA	MLB	33	345	33	13	1	4	32	28	44	7	2	0.9	.248	.310	.335	-.187	.251	.319	.349	.239	-6.2	42-CF	-5	20-1B	1
2008	HOU	MLB	34	213	22	8	1	2	19	19	32	3	1	0.2	.246	.314	.333	-.207	.248	.317	.339	.230	-2.1	54-CF	-4		

Breakout: 31% Improve: 49% Collapse: 34% Attrition: 48%   Comparables: Gino Cimoli, Darren Lewis, Larry Biittner, Joe Orsulak

The White Sox signing Erstad was a decisively bad idea and a solid sabermetric parlor trick for anyone who wants to argue that chemistry doesn't matter. Maybe it does, maybe it doesn't, but the problem with Erstad isn't whether or not he adds something to a team, it's that whatever it is he does add isn't something you can measure, and it's really doubtful that it overcomes the obvious, measurable handicap that playing him places on a lineup. His charm is such that he'll be on the Astro's bench in 2008, but lord have mercy on them if he gets another 300 plate appearances.

Josh Fields 3B

Bats: R   Throws: R   Height: 6' 1"   Weight: 215   Born: December 14, 1982   Age: 25

YEAR	TEAM	LVL	AGE	PA	R	2B	3B	HR	RBI	BB	SO	SB	CS	EqBRR	AVG	OBP	SLG	MLVr	EqAVG	EqOBP	EqSLG	EqA	VORP	DEFENSE	
2005	BIR	AA	22	560	76	27	0	16	79	55	142	7	6	-1.2	.252	.341	.409	.036	.224	.300	.376	.235	-2.6	127-3B -12	
2006	CHR	AAA	23	526	85	32	4	19	70	54	136	28	5	-0.7	.305	.379	.515	.274	.252	.329	.462	.274	25.7	113-3B -14	
2006	CHA	MLB	23	25	4	2	0	1	2	5	8	0	0	0.0	.150	.320	.400	-.168	.150	.320	.350	.241	-0.4		
2007	CHR	AAA	24	249	28	14	0	10	37	39	60	8	5	-1.4	.283	.394	.498	.231	.266	.373	.473	.290	18.8	53-3B -1	
2007	CHA	MLB	24	418	54	17	1	23	67	35	125	1	1	-2.6	.244	.308	.480	-.002	.243	.313	.497	.271	8.2	78-3B 0	20-LF -4
2008	CHA	MLB	25	523	68	25	2	22	71	51	134	11	3	-0.1	.256	.334	.463	.031	.253	.332	.467	.279	13.8	123-3B -2	

Breakout: 29% Improve: 62% Collapse: 11% Attrition: 21%   Comparables: Gary Gaetti, Nick Esasky, Dick Gernert, Craig Worthington

If you were God and fashioning molds, and you had your Joe Crede mold right there, you might be forgiven for succumbing to the temptation to just pour some more clay into it and send the Fields a very similar bouncing baby boy. Fields isn't quite as nimble or instinctual at third, but he's faster on the bases and, given his athleticism as a former quarterback, there's hope that he'll improve his glove work. He generates a tick more power than Crede from a pull-oriented fly-ball stroke, but he can rush himself out of at-bats by getting out in front on breaking stuff. What's clear is that the left-field experiment is over, although that might mean he's headed back to Charlotte for a third season if Kenny Williams can't move Crede.

Chris Getz 2B

Bats: L   Throws: R   Height: 6' 0"   Weight: 175   Born: August 30, 1983   Age: 24

YEAR	TEAM	LVL	AGE	PA	R	2B	3B	HR	RBI	BB	SO	SB	CS	EqBRR	AVG	OBP	SLG	MLVr	EqAVG	EqOBP	EqSLG	EqA	VORP	DEFENSE	
2005	KAN	A	21	253	38	13	2	1	28	35	10	11	4	1.8	.304	.407	.397	.161	.254	.336	.330	.241	0.3	35-2B 4	19-SS -1
2006	BIR	AA	22	573	67	15	6	2	36	52	47	19	6	4.4	.256	.326	.321	-.021	.245	.308	.318	.227	-12.0	127-2B -10	
2007	BIR	AA	23	319	40	10	2	3	29	36	30	13	7	0.6	.299	.382	.381	.123	.267	.340	.354	.247	4.7	67-2B 0	
2008	CHA	MLB	24	349	39	13	1	2	23	28	37	8	3	1.1	.251	.314	.318	-.195	.248	.313	.321	.231	-4.4	84-2B 1	

Breakout: 14% Improve: 43% Collapse: 28% Attrition: 12%   Comparables: Carlton Fleming, Craig Counsell, Dominic Rich, Tim Hyers

Getz was off to a torrid start in his repeat assignment at Double-A last year, hitting .316/.408/.426 over the first six weeks, when he went down with an injured ankle. After returning for the season's final month, he wasn't quite so red-hot, but he did well getting on base in his AFL stint after the season. He's not a prospect, but he's a scrapper who understands that his job is to reach first base and gives his approach at the plate a lot of thought. The Sox don't have an established starter at second base, so you never know—every once in a while a dark horse getz his shot.

Toby Hall C

Bats: R   Throws: R   Height: 6' 3"   Weight: 240   Born: October 21, 1975   Age: 32

YEAR	TEAM	LVL	AGE	PA	R	2B	3B	HR	RBI	BB	SO	SB	CS	EqBRR	AVG	OBP	SLG	MLVr	EqAVG	EqOBP	EqSLG	EqA	VORP	DEFENSE
2005	TBA	MLB	29	463	28	20	0	5	48	16	39	0	0	-3.6	.287	.315	.368	-.082	.299	.335	.384	.254	9.5	121-C 3
2006	TBA	MLB	30	234	15	13	0	8	23	8	17	0	2	-2.0	.231	.261	.398	-.233	.228	.265	.406	.226	-6.1	57-C -8
2006	LAN	MLB	30	60	2	4	0	0	8	2	5	0	0	-1.6	.368	.383	.439	.204	.351	.367	.404	.272	4.4	14-C 0
2007	CHA	MLB	31	120	8	4	0	0	3	3	12	0	0	-1.0	.207	.225	.241	-.510	.209	.233	.243	.152	-9.6	33-C -6
2008	CHA	MLB	32	164	12	7	0	3	18	8	17	0	0	-0.6	.243	.280	.345	-.225	.240	.279	.348	.218	-2.3	43-C -3

Breakout: 19% Improve: 43% Collapse: 42% Attrition: 46%   Comparables: Ray Fosse, Carlos Hernandez, Danny Sheaffer, Sandy Alomar

Last year was ghastly looking for Hall in terms of the final tally, but his taking the field was an achievement in itself after he shredded the labrum of his throwing shoulder in spring training. He chose rehabilitation over season-ending surgery, and surprised everyone by making it back before the end of May. His bat was already going slack years earlier, but the Sox are on the hook for at least another $1.9 million before they can part ways with him (2008's guaranteed salary plus a buyout of 2009), so he's an expensive profile in courage.

Francisco Hernandez   C

Bats: S   Throws: R   Height: 5' 9"   Weight: 160   Born: February 4, 1986   Age: 22

YEAR	TEAM	LVL	AGE	PA	R	2B	3B	HR	RBI	BB	SO	SB	CS	EqBRR	AVG	OBP	SLG	MLVr	EqAVG	EqOBP	EqSLG	EqA	VORP	DEFENSE	
2005	KAN	A	19	171	15	5	0	3	18	13	29	0	0	-0.1	.222	.292	.314	-.188	.171	.222	.234	.145	-19.9	39-C	3
2005	GRF	Rk	19	237	37	19	0	6	34	19	25	0	1	-0.8	.349	.405	.524	.351	.249	.288	.344	.218	-8.9	37-C	5
2006	KAN	A	20	351	29	16	1	6	34	22	31	3	1	-0.9	.247	.305	.361	-.056	.233	.275	.331	.212	-13.2	86-C	3
2007	KAN	A	21	310	42	23	1	4	36	35	29	0	1	-1.7	.277	.362	.413	.073	.225	.297	.332	.219	-7.8	66-C	-3
2008	CHA	MLB	22	307	24	14	0	4	27	20	47	1	1	-0.3	.233	.286	.325	-.246	.230	.285	.328	.216	-7.3	74-C	3

Breakout: 35% **Improve:** 56% **Collapse:** 24% **Attrition:** 16%   *Comparables: Omar Fuentes, Victor Martinez, Jaime Torres, Mitch Meluskey*

Catching prospects are few and far between, but Hernandez doesn't merely deserve consideration because supply lags so far behind demand. He's a solid line-drive hitter with adequate receiving skills and a strong arm behind the plate (killing off 29 percent of attempting base stealers), although he's almost tiny by backstop standards, which handicaps any projection of future power. He's young, but not so young that he can afford to stumble on his way up.

Paul Konerko   1B

Bats: R   Throws: R   Height: 6' 2"   Weight: 215   Born: March 5, 1976   Age: 32

YEAR	TEAM	LVL	AGE	PA	R	2B	3B	HR	RBI	BB	SO	SB	CS	EqBRR	AVG	OBP	SLG	MLVr	EqAVG	EqOBP	EqSLG	EqA	VORP	DEFENSE	
2005	CHA	MLB	29	664	98	24	0	40	100	81	109	0	0	-3.8	.283	.375	.534	.230	.279	.381	.539	.308	46.1	140-1B	16
2006	CHA	MLB	30	643	97	30	0	35	113	60	104	1	0	-5.4	.313	.381	.551	.259	.306	.381	.553	.313	47.7	132-1B	7
2007	CHA	MLB	31	636	71	34	0	31	90	78	102	0	1	-3.4	.259	.351	.490	.096	.256	.355	.503	.290	25.4	138-1B	-2
2008	CHA	MLB	32	597	75	28	0	27	90	69	103	2	1	-2.2	.267	.355	.479	.094	.264	.354	.483	.289	17.8	140-1B	0

Breakout: 7% **Improve:** 27% **Collapse:** 30% **Attrition:** 9%   *Comparables: Kevin Millar, Gil Hodges, Jeff Conine, Eric Karros*

Konerko's comparables may seem to be damning him with faint praise, but when a slow slugger chugs into his 30s, his game starts spitting pistons and losing power. Konerko is a GIDP waiting to happen at the plate and last year was the third most likely batter in the AL to turn a DP opportunity into a twin killing. However, while he's not especially mobile at first base, he still throws out lead runners and starts double plays on defense much more often than, say, the more highly regarded Derrek Lee does for the crosstown Cubs, so it isn't like Konerko's a total slug. Even if his best days are behind him, this guy's still a ballplayer.

Jose Martinez   OF

Bats: R   Throws: R   Height: 6' 5"   Weight: 170   Born: July 25, 1988   Age: 19

YEAR	TEAM	LVL	AGE	PA	R	2B	3B	HR	RBI	BB	SO	SB	CS	EqBRR	AVG	OBP	SLG	MLVr	EqAVG	EqOBP	EqSLG	EqA	VORP	DEFENSE	
2007	BRI	Rk	18	275	34	11	3	7	37	22	53	12	2	1.6	.282	.348	.437	.146	.203	.248	.293	.189	-59.7	45-RF	1
2008	CHA	MLB	19	521	39	19	2	5	34	27	134	11	5	0.4	.202	.246	.280	-.394	.199	.245	.283	.183	-39.5	123-RF	-2

Breakout: 38% **Improve:** 54% **Collapse:** 29% **Attrition:** 9%   *Comparables: Cristian Guerrero, Ardley Jansen, Florentino Nuñez, Ricardo Rojas*

You can indict the White Sox system for many failings, but not for the fact that this Venezuelan import, who made his state-side debut just last year, already ranks among their best. Toolsy but talented, Martinez is fluid in the field with a strong enough arm for right. His long, fluid swing delivers plenty of power once he gets his arms extended, but he's still learning how to handle off-speed stuff (creating a problem with lefties for the time being). Fortunately, he gets good marks for working on his approach. He's years from the majors, but Martinez is the team's hitting prospect with the most potential for stardom.

Jerry Owens   CF

Bats: L   Throws: L   Height: 6' 3"   Weight: 190   Born: February 16, 1981   Age: 27

YEAR	TEAM	LVL	AGE	PA	R	2B	3B	HR	RBI	BB	SO	SB	CS	EqBRR	AVG	OBP	SLG	MLVr	EqAVG	EqOBP	EqSLG	EqA	VORP	DEFENSE		DEFENSE	
2005	BIR	AA	24	587	99	21	6	2	52	52	72	38	20	2.2	.331	.393	.406	.179	.284	.338	.360	.246	-8.3	116-LF	9		
2006	CHR	AAA	25	493	75	15	5	4	48	45	61	40	12	6.5	.262	.330	.346	-.050	.242	.310	.328	.235	-11.7	83-CF	0	26-LF	3
2007	CHR	AAA	26	267	39	10	0	3	21	29	37	23	8	2.1	.284	.361	.366	.014	265	.341	.355	.255	-4.7	57-LF	3		
2007	CHA	MLB	26	389	44	9	2	1	17	27	63	32	8	3.1	.267	.324	.312	-.189	.275	.337	.323	.246	-1.1	80-CF	-9		
2008	CHA	MLB	27	424	55	14	2	3	30	31	64	26	8	2.2	.264	.321	.338	-.149	.261	.319	.341	.245	-4.5	101-CF	-4		

Breakout: 22% **Improve:** 44% **Collapse:** 28% **Attrition:** 25%   *Comparables: David Hulse, Alex Sanchez, Marvin Benard, Randy Winn*

You've seen this sort of guy before, and while 2007 seemed to feature a lot of speed guys getting shots—Rajai Davis, Tike Redman, Nook Logan, even Timo Perez one more time—most of them just aren't all that useful. As does Endy

Chavez, Owens makes a nifty fourth outfielder on a team on which all of the regulars bat right-handed and don't run especially well. The addition of Nick Swisher might reduce Owens to a defensive replacement, a role he's eminently suited for.

Pablo Ozuna   UT   Bats: R   Throws: R   Height: 5' 11"   Weight: 190   Born: August 25, 1974   Age: 33

YEAR	TEAM	LVL	AGE	PA	R	2B	3B	HR	RBI	BB	SO	SB	CS	EqBRR	AVG	OBP	SLG	MLVr	EqAVG	EqOBP	EqSLG	EqA	VORP	DEFENSE			
2005	CHA	MLB	30	217	27	7	2	0	11	7	26	14	7	1.0	.276	.313	.330	-.158	.280	.324	.335	.236	-2.5	29-3B	3	11-SS	2
2006	CHA	MLB	31	203	25	12	2	2	17	7	16	6	6	0.2	.328	.365	.444	.097	.332	.375	.449	.276	6.9	30-LF	-5		
2007	CHA	MLB	32	85	9	3	0	0	3	3	9	3	0	0.3	.244	.280	.282	-.323	.244	.289	.282	.213	-3.9				
2008	CHA	MLB	33	105	12	4	1	1	9	4	11	3	1	0.4	.269	.305	.341	-.170	.266	.304	.344	.235	-1.3	29-LF	-1		

Breakout: 21% Improve: 35% Collapse: 44% Attrition: 43%   Comparables: Craig Shipley, Tommy Davis, Alex Johnson, Mario Diaz

As nice as it was for the Sox to scrape the gunk off Ozuna and give him a shot, there comes a point at which you shouldn't go out of your way to keep doing a guy favors. He's a utility scrub making seven figures, and while he can make contact and run a little, the team has to ask itself why it's paying so much for a manager's pet capable of only modest contributions.

A. J. Pierzynski   C   Bats: L   Throws: R   Height: 6' 3"   Weight: 240   Born: December 30, 1976   Age: 31

YEAR	TEAM	LVL	AGE	PA	R	2B	3B	HR	RBI	BB	SO	SB	CS	EqBRR	AVG	OBP	SLG	MLVr	EqAVG	EqOBP	EqSLG	EqA	VORP	DEFENSE	
2005	CHA	MLB	28	497	61	21	0	18	56	23	68	0	2	-1.0	.257	.308	.420	-.057	.256	.315	.432	.254	11.9	123-C	3
2006	CHA	MLB	29	543	65	24	0	16	64	22	72	1	0	-2.7	.295	.333	.436	-.005	.288	.332	.437	.264	18.3	126-C	-8
2007	CHA	MLB	30	509	54	24	0	14	50	25	66	1	1	-2.1	.263	.309	.403	-.092	.262	.313	.418	.252	9.6	119-C	4
2008	CHA	MLB	31	384	37	18	0	10	46	19	54	2	1	-0.8	.260	.304	.396	-.103	.257	.303	.399	.245	3.4	92-C	-1

Breakout: 10% Improve: 32% Collapse: 42% Attrition: 29%   Comparables: Terry Kennedy, Javy Lopez, Greg Myers, John Bateman

Pierzynski's the catcher people love to hate, but also exactly the sort of guy Sox fans can relate to. Sure, he's obnoxious, combative, and vowel-challenged, but those things go over just fine in Bridgeport. Although he's been a useful enough hitter in his Chicago career, his two-year, $12.5 million extension which kicks in after this season was a contract too far for the Sox. A platoon wouldn't help Pierzynski appreciably at the plate beyond keeping him fresh; he's a spray hitter with line-drive power who kills you with double-play grounders. His receiving skills are also losing something to Father Time, which is another argument for the effective veteran caddy the Sox don't have.

Scott Podsednik   LF   Bats: L   Throws: L   Height: 6' 1"   Weight: 190   Born: March 18, 1976   Age: 32

YEAR	TEAM	LVL	AGE	PA	R	2B	3B	HR	RBI	BB	SO	SB	CS	EqBRR	AVG	OBP	SLG	MLVr	EqAVG	EqOBP	EqSLG	EqA	VORP	DEFENSE	
2005	CHA	MLB	29	568	80	28	1	0	25	47	75	59	23	4.8	.290	.351	.349	-.055	.295	.365	.359	.264	6.3	117-LF	10
2006	CHA	MLB	30	591	86	27	6	3	45	54	95	40	19	0.2	.262	.331	.354	-.150	.260	.337	.357	.249	-9.9	122-LF	-10
2007	CHA	MLB	31	235	30	13	4	2	11	13	36	12	5	0.2	.243	.299	.369	-.168	.249	.310	.394	.246	-4.9	52-LF	-5
2008	CHA	MLB	32	319	41	14	2	3	24	25	48	16	5	1.1	.263	.325	.351	-.127	.260	.323	.354	.249	-5.2	77-LF	-3

Breakout: 17% Improve: 35% Collapse: 31% Attrition: 27%   Comparables: Russ Snyder, Milt Thompson, Harry Walker, Tom Goodwin

Even at the best of times, Podzilla was a guy who made his dollar legging out grounders; if he ever got under anything all he'd do is tap it to the opposite field. Now that he's increasingly fragile and not as speedy, not even the White Sox believe the dubious proposition that his bat is affordable in an outfield corner. Cut loose in November, he could hang around by reinventing himself as a sort of Orlando Palmeiro-type pinch-singles-hitter on wheels, but if he can't adapt to a bench role, he'll disappear quickly.

Danny Richar — 2B — Bats: L — Throws: R — Height: 6' 0" — Weight: 170 — Born: June 9, 1983 — Age: 25

YEAR	TEAM	LVL	AGE	PA	R	2B	3B	HR	RBI	BB	SO	SB	CS	EqBRR	AVG	OBP	SLG	MLVr	EqAVG	EqOBP	EqSLG	EqA	VORP	DEFENSE			
2005	LNC	A+	22	503	78	32	8	20	79	32	64	9	3	-2.8	.300	.347	.537	.056	.224	.265	.381	.222	-7.1	61-SS	-12	47-2B	5
2006	TEN	AA	23	548	79	25	5	8	42	52	77	15	5	0.9	.292	.360	.415	.125	.272	.334	.409	.262	18.9	120-2B	-14		
2007	TUC	AAA	24	299	40	20	4	8	46	27	47	4	5	-4.9	.285	.348	.479	.055	.249	.313	.424	.250	6.8	50-2B	-10	13-SS	-3
2007	CHR	AAA	24	145	21	5	4	5	15	10	24	4	0	1.0	.346	.400	.556	.380	.321	.372	.537	.307	16.4	26-2B	-1		
2007	CHA	MLB	24	206	30	9	3	6	15	16	33	1	3	0.8	.230	.289	.406	-.145	.232	.299	.438	.245	-2.5	55-2B	-7		
2008	CHA	MLB	25	589	70	30	4	15	65	42	100	8	4	0.7	.260	.315	.415	-.060	.257	.314	.418	.257	9.8	138-2B	-9		

Breakout: 18% Improve: 51% Collapse: 15% Attrition: 19%   Comparables: Jorge Orta, Antonio Perez, Roberto Mejia, Zoilo Versalles

In one of several interesting prospect exchanges with the D'backs, the Sox sent Arizona intriguing outfield prospect Aaron Cunningham to land a ready-now replacement for Tadahito Iguchi in Richar. Richar came with the line-drive-power gift package and sprays balls around the diamond with his solid stroke. The Snakes worked hard to get him to improve his approach and especially to learn to lay off bad pitches; that hasn't translated into lots of walks, but it has taught him how to wait for his pitch and drive it. Don't let that monster year in the California League distract you—Richar will be a perfectly acceptable starter, but he's not the next Robinson Cano.

John Shelby Jr. — CF — Bats: R — Throws: R — Height: 5' 10" — Weight: 185 — Born: August 6, 1985 — Age: 22

YEAR	TEAM	LVL	AGE	PA	R	2B	3B	HR	RBI	BB	SO	SB	CS	EqBRR	AVG	OBP	SLG	MLVr	EqAVG	EqOBP	EqSLG	EqA	VORP	DEFENSE			
2006	GRF	Rk	20	279	37	12	3	8	36	18	55	8	4	-2.3	.272	.332	.440	.071	.202	.238	.308	.186	-34.9	42-2B	5	23-SS	0
2007	KAN	A	21	538	83	35	9	16	79	35	77	19	8	1.0	.301	.352	.508	.205	.244	.285	.396	.235	-5.5	61-CF	-1	54-2B	-9
2008	CHA	MLB	22	604	57	31	4	11	59	31	131	11	6	0.7	.235	.279	.364	-.205	.232	.278	.368	.226	-11.6	141-2B	-5		

Breakout: 44% Improve: 61% Collapse: 14% Attrition: 10%   Comparables: Andy Burress, German Duran, Chris Aguila, Felix Escalona

The son of the former major league outfielder, John Shelby Jr. started out a second baseman, but after moving to the outfield in June seemed to adopt an outfielder's approach, hitting for more power while getting less patient and finishing with a flourish by socking ten homers in his last month. He's not the gifted glove in center that his father was, but he might improve his route-running through the hard work he's already respected for. If he takes that season-ending hot streak into his High-A debut, he could play his way to Double-A this summer, which would put him on the fringes of the big-league picture for 2009 and beyond. That's a lot on his plate, but he's the organization's best current candidate for a homegrown Center Fielder of the Future.

Ryan Sweeney — OF — Bats: L — Throws: L — Height: 6' 4" — Weight: 215 — Born: February 20, 1985 — Age: 23

YEAR	TEAM	LVL	AGE	PA	R	2B	3B	HR	RBI	BB	SO	SB	CS	EqBRR	AVG	OBP	SLG	MLVr	EqAVG	EqOBP	EqSLG	EqA	VORP	DEFENSE			
2005	BIR	AA	20	483	64	22	3	1	47	35	53	6	6	0.6	.298	.357	.371	.045	.254	.304	.322	.220	-23.7	107-RF	0		
2006	CHR	AAA	21	492	64	25	3	13	70	35	73	7	7	-1.8	.296	.350	.452	.143	.275	.329	.439	.261	17.8	57-CF	0	42-RF	4
2006	CHA	MLB	21	35	1	0	0	0	5	0	7	0	0	0.5	.229	.229	.229	-.549	.200	.200	.200	.078	-3.4				
2007	CHR	AAA	22	450	50	17	2	10	47	48	71	8	5	-1.6	.270	.348	.398	.024	.250	.327	.390	.250	4.7	46-CF	5	34-RF	6
2007	CHA	MLB	22	49	5	3	0	1	5	4	5	0	1	0.3	.200	.265	.333	-.304	.200	.265	.333	.199	-3.2	10-LF	-1		
2008	OAK	MLB	23	541	61	28	2	10	60	44	85	7	4	0.7	.263	.326	.393	-.068	.267	.331	.419	.264	4.5	127-CF	-7		

Breakout: 57% Improve: 81% Collapse: 6% Attrition: 4%   Comparables: Jacob Cruz, James Loney, Travis Buck, Trey Beamon

Though only 23, Sweeney is already seen as a disappointment for his failure to develop any kind of meaningful power. What thumping he did do last year was all done in hitter-friendly Charlotte, and following up that season with a punchless Arizona Fall League campaign only reinforced concern that he has little or no projection other than as a fourth outfielder. Sweeney has a fine throwing arm, good plate coverage, and can play center in a pinch, so there's certainly enough there to recommend him for the bench. It's just that so much more was expected. Dealt to the A's in the Swisher deal, he'll get a shot because they're still looking at his birth certificate.

Jim Thome — DH

Bats: L Throws: R Height: 6' 3" Weight: 250 Born: August 27, 1970 Age: 37

YEAR	TEAM	LVL	AGE	PA	R	2B	3B	HR	RBI	BB	SO	SB	CS	EqBRR	AVG	OBP	SLG	MLVr	EqAVG	EqOBP	EqSLG	EqA	VORP	DEFENSE	
2005	PHI	MLB	34	242	26	7	0	7	30	45	59	0	0	-1.7	.207	.360	.352	-.067	.198	.355	.349	.258	-1.3	49-1B	3
2006	CHA	MLB	35	610	108	26	0	42	109	107	147	0	0	-1.5	.288	.416	.598	.351	.275	.415	.588	.332	62.6		
2007	CHA	MLB	36	536	79	19	0	35	96	95	134	0	1	-2.9	.275	.410	.563	.302	.269	.412	.574	.327	47.4		
2008	CHA	MLB	37	474	72	18	0	29	79	69	115	1	1	-1.3	.267	.379	.531	.197	.264	.378	.535	.309	29.5	112-DH	

Breakout: 8% Improve: 34% Collapse: 37% Attrition: 24% Comparables: Cliff Johnson, Willie McCovey, Darrell Evans, Frank Thomas

To this day, Thome remains the kind of hitter who beats you. Put a righty on the mound, and Thome can still power fastballs out of the yard in any direction, killing mistakes and challenges alike as though he was gifted with some sort of wizardly talisman—the eyes of Johnny Mize, perhaps? His weaknesses are that he's going to miss a few weeks in even the healthiest of seasons, and he effectively goes away against southpaws; Thome hasn't slugged better than .361 in a season against the *gaucheoisie* since 2004. As dangerous difference-makers go, he's thus a bit too easily de-fanged in our age of situational obsessions. Still, he's gotten past 500 career homers without any speculation about something extra in his corn flakes, which means we should start considering where he ranks among the all-time greats at first base (where, unlike Frank Thomas, he played the overwhelming bulk of his career) and his case for Cooperstown. One holdup will be that the Indians teams he starred on never won it all, but that's between the man and Jose Mesa.

Juan Uribe — SS

Bats: R Throws: R Height: 6' 0" Weight: 220 Born: March 22, 1979 Age: 29

YEAR	TEAM	LVL	AGE	PA	R	2B	3B	HR	RBI	BB	SO	SB	CS	EqBRR	AVG	OBP	SLG	MLVr	EqAVG	EqOBP	EqSLG	EqA	VORP	DEFENSE	
2005	CHA	MLB	26	540	58	23	3	16	71	34	77	4	6	0.4	.252	.301	.412	-.086	.252	.311	.426	.253	8.2	142-SS	15
2006	CHA	MLB	27	495	53	28	2	21	71	13	82	1	1	0.0	.235	.257	.441	-.184	.231	.261	.445	.239	-0.6	126-SS	8
2007	CHA	MLB	28	563	55	18	2	20	68	34	112	1	9	-2.1	.234	.284	.394	-.170	.236	.291	.417	.237	-7.1	147-SS	18
2008	CHA	MLB	29	463	47	21	1	16	60	29	80	2	2	-0.1	.249	.299	.419	-.088	.246	.298	.423	.250	7.2	110-SS	4

Breakout: 34% Improve: 64% Collapse: 16% Attrition: 27% Comparables: Ed Sprague, Charlie Hayes, Dale Berra, Jim Presley

It was a bit of a surprise that the Sox quickly re-signed Uribe, especially after complaints about his work ethic and weight followed a couple of years of really uninspired batsmanship. He's now out of a job in the wake of the acquisition of shortstop Orlando Cabrera, but he might be seen as something resembling veteran insurance against Richar's potential failure to hold the job at the keystone. Uribe's a decidedly strange sort of shortstop, an impatient pull hitter whose offensive game depends on getting around on a pitch and punching it into the left-field corner. It's a fun gambit in the Cell, but you can count on one hand the stadia in which his style works: the Cell, Minute Maid . . . hmm, half a hand, maybe?

PITCHERS

David Aardsma

Bats: R Throws: R Height: 6' 4" Weight: 205 Born: December 27, 1981 Age: 26

YEAR	TEAM	LVL	AGE	W	L	SV	G	GS	IP	H	BB	SO	HR	GB%	BABIP	STUFF	WHIP	ERA	PERA	EqERA	EqH9	EqBB9	EqSO9	EqHR9	VORP	SN/WX
2005	NRW	AA	23	6	2	0	9	8	46	44	13	30	2	51.4%	.300	-9	1.24	2.93	4.71	4.75	9.5	3.7	3.5	0.6	3.9	—
2005	WTN	AA	23	4	1	2	33	3	50²	48	32	43	3	55.5%	.324	-12	1.58	3.91	6.37	5.48	10.0	6.7	4.9	1.0	0.6	—
2006	IOW	AAA	24	2	3	8	29	0	36	31	15	36	1	55.6%	.326	1	1.28	3.25	3.87	4.46	8.1	4.2	6.8	0.5	4.3	—
2006	CHN	MLB	24	3	0	0	45	0	53	41	28	49	9	38.1%	.239	0	1.30	4.08	3.82	3.54	6.8	4.1	7.6	1.4	11.0	1.32
2007	CHA	MLB	25	2	1	0	25	0	32¹	39	17	36	4	39.2%	.389	3	1.73	6.41	6.18	6.12	10.6	4.2	9.2	1.1	-2.1	-0.02
2007	CHR	AAA	25	3	2	15	28	0	35¹	26	11	45	7	32.2%	.241	-6	1.05	4.33	5.38	5.56	7.7	3.2	8.5	2.6	0.2	—
2008	CHA	MLB	26	2	2	3	48	0	47²	46	22	43	7	42.3%	.287	4	1.40	4.52	4.12	4.22	8.2	3.7	7.3	1.3	6.8	0.60

Breakout: 47% Improve: 60% Collapse: 19% Attrition: 26% Comparables: Jeff Parrett, Roberto Novoa, Robb Nen, Jim Ray

Aardsma is one of a group of hard-throwing arms the Sox fancy they can make something out of. The same things are true about him that were true four years ago: he pumps gas and has a snappy curve, but command is a problem.

To make matters worse, he rattles easily, turning a bad situation worse once men are aboard. After being demoted in early July, he didn't earn even a September cup of coffee with the big club, which doesn't bode well for his future.

Lance Broadway

Bats: R   Throws: R   Height: 6' 2"   Weight: 210   Born: August 20, 1983   Age: 24

YEAR	TEAM	LVL	AGE	W	L	SV	G	GS	IP	H	BB	SO	HR	GB%	BABIP	STUFF	WHIP	ERA	PERA	EqERA	EqH9	EqBB9	EqSO9	EqHR9	VORP	SN/WX
2005	WNS	A+	21	1	3	0	11	11	55	68	20	58	4	53.0%	.400	-11	1.60	4.58	8.72	7.77	13.5	5.2	5.4	1.3	-11.7	—
2006	BIR	AA	22	8	8	0	25	25	154²	160	40	111	10	48.6%	.316	-3	1.30	2.74	5.36	4.80	10.2	2.8	4.1	1.1	13.0	—
2007	CHR	AAA	23	8	9	0	26	26	155	155	78	108	17	49.4%	.299	-16	1.50	4.65	6.54	6.28	10.1	5.1	4.5	1.5	-10.9	—
2007	CHA	MLB	23	1	1	0	4	1	10¹	5	5	14	0	36.4%	.238	11	0.97	0.87	2.08	1.69	4.2	3.4	9.3	0.0	5.0	0.54
2008	CHA	MLB	24	4	8	0	32	16	102	121	57	63	15	48.1%	.315	-9	1.74	6.15	5.71	5.76	10.1	4.5	5.0	1.3	-4.6	0.10

Breakout: 14%   Improve: 39%   Collapse: 24%   Attrition: 18%   Comparables: Jamie McAndrew, Greg Gohr, Marc Valdes, Brian Williams

You might not be able to find a more generic right-hander. Picking Broadway in the first round of the 2005 draft might be the best example of the organization's former bad habit of picking low-upside pitchability types. Although he's come back from Tommy John surgery unimpaired, his heat only gets into the high 80s, so he relies instead on a curve and change. Broadway's not a prospect, but with at least two slots in the rotation up for grabs, he is on the margins of the picture—you know, the part you crop out in Photoshop.

Mark Buehrle

Bats: L   Throws: L   Height: 6' 2"   Weight: 220   Born: March 23, 1979   Age: 29

YEAR	TEAM	LVL	AGE	W	L	SV	G	GS	IP	H	BB	SO	HR	GB%	BABIP	STUFF	WHIP	ERA	PERA	EqERA	EqH9	EqBB9	EqSO9	EqHR9	VORP	SN/WX
2005	CHA	MLB	26	16	8	0	33	33	236²	240	40	149	20	48.1%	.295	19	1.18	3.12	4.01	4.05	9.5	1.5	5.6	0.7	54.8	5.72
2006	CHA	MLB	27	12	13	0	32	32	204	247	48	98	36	46.0%	.313	-12	1.45	4.99	5.86	5.19	10.7	2.0	4.2	1.4	16.1	2.41
2007	CHA	MLB	28	10	9	0	30	30	201	208	45	115	22	45.2%	.292	10	1.26	3.63	3.87	3.25	8.7	1.8	4.8	0.9	49.3	5.65
2008	CHA	MLB	29	9	11	0	28	28	172²	202	43	98	24	45.9%	.308	6	1.41	4.77	4.49	4.46	10.0	2.0	4.6	1.2	18.3	3.30

Breakout: 4%   Improve: 30%   Collapse: 27%   Attrition: 16%   Comparables: Ken Holtzman, Greg Swindell, Jim Abbott, Curt Simmons

Delivering 18 quality starts (two blown after the sixth inning) in his first 22 games helped Buehrle earn a multi-year extension last July. The big money might have encouraged the Sox to give him a literal pass with the team out of contention in September, as he made only three starts on long rest that month. Buehrle is effectively in Jamie Moyer territory, where his margin for error can't get any more slim without costing him his status as a top starter. The park doesn't do him any favors, and he's more about changing speeds and location than movement—his breaking stuff isn't his strong suit—so he gets hurt by lefties now and again, but like a lot of wise lefties, he's got the full spread of Jedi skills when it comes to choking off the running game and fielding his position.

Jose Contreras

Bats: R   Throws: R   Height: 6' 4"   Weight: 245   Born: December 12, 1971   Age: 36

YEAR	TEAM	LVL	AGE	W	L	SV	G	GS	IP	H	BB	SO	HR	GB%	BABIP	STUFF	WHIP	ERA	PERA	EqERA	EqH9	EqBB9	EqSO9	EqHR9	VORP	SN/WX
2005	CHA	MLB	33	15	7	0	32	32	204²	177	75	154	23	46.0%	.263	16	1.23	3.61	3.99	4.02	8.1	3.3	6.7	0.9	42.1	5.03
2006	CHA	MLB	34	13	9	0	30	30	196	194	55	134	20	45.7%	.288	16	1.27	4.27	3.80	4.17	8.4	2.3	5.7	0.8	33.1	4.19
2007	CHA	MLB	35	10	17	0	32	30	189	232	62	113	21	47.0%	.335	1	1.56	5.57	5.27	5.61	10.3	2.6	4.9	0.9	-6.1	0.97
2008	CHA	MLB	36	6	9	0	30	19	127¹	143	45	81	17	46.2%	.304	-1	1.48	5.00	4.62	4.69	9.6	2.9	5.2	1.2	11.0	1.90

Breakout: 16%   Improve: 40%   Collapse: 21%   Attrition: 21%   Comparables: Sonny Siebert, Tim Belcher, Steve Renko, Dave Burba

Contreras is almost Buehrle's exact opposite—a painfully slow worker who doesn't give baserunners much thought, and after committing six errors last year, seems to have picked up Matt Young's cursed -6 Glove of Disaster as an heirloom. To be fair, Contreras pitched pretty well last year for somebody as likely to be 46 as 36, but while the Sox get props for seeing something in the big Cuban and fixing him after acquiring him from New York, that was four years ago, and he hasn't been terribly effective since May of 2006. In an effort to keep right-handers from digging in and crowding the plate, Contreras has been hitting more batters, which is an indication of declining velocity. He's an even more important part of the rotation now that Garland's been dealt, but it's doubtful that he can deliver.

John Danks

| | | | | | | | | | | | | | Bats: L | Throws: L | Height: 6' 1" | | Weight: 200 | | Born: April 15, 1985 | | Age: 23 |

YEAR	TEAM	LVL	AGE	W	L	SV	G	GS	IP	H	BB	SO	HR	GB%	BABIP	STUFF	WHIP	ERA	PERA	EqERA	EqH9	EqBB9	EqSO9	EqHR9	VORP	SN/WX
2005	BAK	A+	20	3	3	0	10	10	57²	50	16	53	5	48.8%	.280	8	1.14	2.50	5.04	4.13	8.8	4.0	4.8	1.2	8.5	—
2005	FRI	AA	20	4	10	0	18	17	98¹	117	34	85	12	43.5%	.354	-10	1.54	5.49	7.76	7.76	11.8	4.5	5.3	1.7	-21.4	—
2006	FRI	AA	21	5	4	0	13	13	69	74	22	82	11	39.2%	.354	3	1.39	4.17	7.27	6.30	11.1	3.6	7.6	2.0	-5.0	—
2006	OKL	AAA	21	4	5	0	14	13	70²	67	34	72	11	39.2%	.299	-3	1.44	4.36	6.13	6.32	9.2	4.7	6.7	1.8	-5.5	—
2007	CHA	MLB	22	6	13	0	26	26	139	160	54	109	28	37.6%	.317	-6	1.54	5.50	6.03	5.27	9.7	3.1	6.4	1.7	1.8	0.70
2008	CHA	MLB	23	5	8	0	28	19	113¹	128	47	88	21	40.6%	.307	5	1.54	5.54	5.18	5.11	9.6	3.3	6.2	1.6	3.8	1.20

Breakout: 27%   Improve: 58%   Collapse: 19%   Attrition: 25%   Comparables: Bob Owchinko, Bob Kipper, Javier Vazquez, Jerry Garvin

Some see Danks as a rookie who started off hot but later melted down. The reality is that he just went from nearly mediocre to bad. Danks gives in far too easily on hitter's counts and major league hitters learned to wait him out to get their pitch. He does have a good four-pitch assortment and better velocity than most lefties, but none of his offerings are dominant out-pitches, and he falls apart with men on base. Still very young, he's a work in progress the Sox need to polish up to see if they've got a diamond in the rough, or another lump of coal for Charlie Brown's collection.

Dewon Day

| | | | | | | | | | | | | | Bats: R | Throws: R | Height: 6' 4" | | Weight: 210 | | Born: September 29, 1980 | | Age: 27 |

YEAR	TEAM	LVL	AGE	W	L	SV	G	GS	IP	H	BB	SO	HR	GB%	BABIP	STUFF	WHIP	ERA	PERA	EqERA	EqH9	EqBB9	EqSO9	EqHR9	VORP	SN/WX
2005	LNS	A	24	0	0	0	9	0	13¹	15	9	14	2	51.4%	.382	-27	1.80	4.06	14.01	7.94	13.5	8.7	5.6	3.2	-2.9	—
2006	WNS	A+	25	1	4	8	40	0	47	40	21	63	3	54.5%	.325	-3	1.30	3.45	6.11	6.14	10.0	5.3	8.0	1.2	-2.6	—
2007	BIR	AA	26	2	3	3	20	0	25	26	12	48	1	63.0%	.481	20	1.52	3.60	7.31	6.65	12.9	5.1	11.7	0.8	-2.7	—
2007	CHR	AAA	26	0	2	0	14	0	14¹	10	20	15	0	54.1%	.270	12	2.10	6.29	5.86	7.07	7.1	12.9	6.4	0.0	-2.3	—
2007	CHA	MLB	26	0	1	0	13	0	12	19	9	7	1	51.1%	.391	-34	2.33	11.25	9.48	10.95	13.1	5.8	4.4	0.7	-6.8	0.06
2008	CHA	MLB	27	0	1	1	13	0	12¹	14	10	11	1	50.6%	.353	-7	1.94	6.62	5.99	6.29	10.0	6.4	7.6	1.0	-2.7	-0.10

Breakout: 32%   Improve: 47%   Collapse: 36%   Attrition: 68%   Comparables: Ted Abernathy, John Davis, Mike Madden, Jaret Wright

After missing most of the 2005 season, Day was fished out of the Blue Jays' system in the minor league portion of the Rule 5 draft, spent 2006 getting reacquainted with his craft, and 2007 pitching rock'em sock'em baseball, alternately punching batters out and getting lit up. The Sox knew he was guy capable of throwing a heavy fastball consistently in the mid 90s, but his command is a problem, and his slider isn't a reliable enough second offering. He might be the team's best hope for a relief-pitching scouting coup, but that doesn't mean the odds are in his favor.

Fautino De Los Santos

| | | | | | | | | | | | | | Bats: R | Throws: R | Height: 6' 1" | | Weight: 210 | | Born: February 15, 1986 | | Age: 22 |

YEAR	TEAM	LVL	AGE	W	L	SV	G	GS	IP	H	BB	SO	HR	GB%	BABIP	STUFF	WHIP	ERA	PERA	EqERA	EqH9	EqBB9	EqSO9	EqHR9	VORP	SN/WX
2007	KAN	A	21	9	4	0	21	15	97²	49	36	121	5	45.7%	.214	13	0.87	2.40	4.05	4.52	5.0	5.2	6.4	1.0	11.0	—
2007	WNS	A+	21	1	1	0	5	5	24²	20	7	32	3	45.8%	.304	12	1.09	3.64	6.98	6.75	10.1	4.2	8.0	2.5	-2.7	—
2008	OAK	MLB	22	7	8	0	30	20	127	117	75	97	16	44.7%	.271	5	1.50	4.84	4.82	4.91	8.1	4.7	6.4	1.2	6.7	1.60

Breakout: 29%   Improve: 51%   Collapse: 28%   Attrition: 15%   Comparables: Anibal Sanchez, Mike Meyers, Seung Song, Rafael Soriano

De Los Santos went from being a little-known Dominican arm to the best prospect in the White Sox' system last year—153 strikeouts in 122⅓ innings can do that to a guy. With a powerful build and lightning-quick arm, De Los Santos pounds the strike zone with a mid 90s fastball that can touch 98, and his curve ball is a big power breaker that makes hitters look silly. He's still an unrefined product that will take another two years or so to be ready, but the A's can afford to wait as he was the key to the Swisher deal.

Jack Egbert

| | | | | | | | | | | | | | Bats: L | Throws: R | Height: 6' 3" | | Weight: 205 | | Born: May 12, 1983 | | Age: 25 |

YEAR	TEAM	LVL	AGE	W	L	SV	G	GS	IP	H	BB	SO	HR	GB%	BABIP	STUFF	WHIP	ERA	PERA	EqERA	EqH9	EqBB9	EqSO9	EqHR9	VORP	SN/WX
2005	KAN	A	22	10	5	0	30	24	147	127	48	107	5	56.8%	.286	-13	1.19	3.12	6.00	6.63	10.2	5.5	3.1	0.9	-14.5	—
2006	WNS	A+	23	9	8	0	25	25	140	131	46	120	2	58.3%	.315	10	1.26	2.96	5.14	5.19	10.3	4.3	4.9	0.4	5.8	—
2006	BIR	AA	23	0	2	0	4	4	21¹	17	8	24	0	50.0%	.309	19	1.18	0.85	3.67	2.66	8.0	4.0	6.6	0.0	6.6	—
2007	BIR	AA	24	12	8	0	28	28	161²	138	44	165	3	54.7%	.315	26	1.13	3.06	3.79	4.20	8.4	2.9	6.2	0.4	23.6	—
2008	CHA	MLB	25	6	9	0	31	20	128¹	141	59	91	14	52.6%	.314	5	1.55	4.99	4.64	4.74	9.4	3.7	5.8	1.0	9.0	1.90

Breakout: 15%   Improve: 48%   Collapse: 23%   Attrition: 27%   Comparables: Sean Bergman, Brian Lawrence, Brian Bannister, Matt Maysey

Egbert is the sort of pitcher whose stats tend to get people worked up a bit more than they should be. The strikeout totals and the ERA are nice, but they're not indicative of a power pitcher as much as a finished product. Egbert's got a dandy sinker and a plus changeup, and he can occasionally reach for a low-90s fastball, but he's not going to blow people away as much as grind them down, and that doesn't get easier as you get closer to the Show. It's not hard to envision his getting into the big-league rotation at some point this summer, but he won't dominate, now, or ever.

Gavin Floyd

Bats: R   Throws: R   Height: 6' 4"   Weight: 225   Born: January 27, 1983   Age: 25

YEAR	TEAM	LVL	AGE	W	L	SV	G	GS	IP	H	BB	SO	HR	GB%	BABIP	STUFF	WHIP	ERA	PERA	EqERA	EqH9	EqBB9	EqSO9	EqHR9	VORP	SN/WX
2005	SWB	AAA	22	6	9	0	24	23	137¹	155	66	97	11	49.3%	.338	-7	1.61	6.16	6.43	7.90	10.8	5.2	4.5	0.9	-32.9	—
2005	PHI	MLB	22	1	2	0	7	4	26	30	16	17	5	40.7%	.298	-18	1.77	10.04	7.31	10.80	10.1	4.7	5.1	1.7	-14.9	0.01
2006	SWB	AAA	23	7	4	0	17	17	115	117	38	85	9	42.1%	.320	-10	1.35	4.23	6.72	6.58	11.4	3.8	4.9	1.2	-11.3	—
2006	PHI	MLB	23	4	3	0	11	11	54¹	70	32	34	14	36.4%	.322	-24	1.88	7.29	7.91	7.55	10.6	4.5	5.0	1.9	-10.9	-0.20
2007	CHR	AAA	24	7	3	0	17	17	106²	93	35	96	9	43.3%	.288	5	1.20	3.12	4.75	4.22	8.9	3.4	6.0	1.2	15.4	—
2007	CHA	MLB	24	1	5	0	16	10	70	85	19	49	17	43.3%	.312	-17	1.49	5.27	6.83	5.22	10.2	2.2	5.7	2.0	2.4	0.82
2008	*CHA*	*MLB*	*25*	*5*	*7*	*0*	*30*	*16*	*102*	*115*	*40*	*70*	*15*	*44.2%*	*.306*	*0*	*1.52*	*5.23*	*4.91*	*4.87*	*9.6*	*3.2*	*5.6*	*1.3*	*6.5*	*1.20*

Breakout: 38% Improve: 68% Collapse: 15% Attrition: 29%   *Comparables: Don Larsen, Alan Benes, Dan Wright, Rob Bell*

The payoff in the Freddy Garcia deal, Floyd is another one of Chicago's very talented yet immensely frustrating pitchers. Floyd can be agonizing to watch because he's so inconsistent from pitch to pitch, alternating between a sometimes-plus fastball and an occasional 70-grade curve, and then blowing it against the very same batter by leaving something up in the zone, or flattening out his curve. Forget gray hair—pitching coach Don Cooper could wind up pulling it all out before it changes color. Thanks in part to Floyd's turning in five quality starts in the six he made after being put in the rotation at the end of August, he's first in line for the fifth slot in the rotation in the wake of the Garland deal. That's not as meaningful as it sounds; he's just as likely to still be starting games next September as anybody on the roster after Buehrle and Vazquez.

Jon Garland

Bats: R   Throws: R   Height: 6' 6"   Weight: 215   Born: September 27, 1979   Age: 28

YEAR	TEAM	LVL	AGE	W	L	SV	G	GS	IP	H	BB	SO	HR	GB%	BABIP	STUFF	WHIP	ERA	PERA	EqERA	EqH9	EqBB9	EqSO9	EqHR9	VORP	SN/WX
2005	CHA	MLB	25	18	10	0	32	32	221	212	47	115	26	47.7%	.270	6	1.17	3.50	4.17	3.98	9.0	1.9	4.7	1.0	50.7	5.99
2006	CHA	MLB	26	18	7	0	33	32	211¹	247	41	112	26	43.5%	.315	5	1.36	4.51	4.75	4.42	10.1	1.6	4.6	1.0	32.4	3.90
2007	CHA	MLB	27	10	13	0	32	32	208¹	219	57	98	19	41.4%	.288	6	1.32	4.23	3.80	4.13	8.7	2.1	3.9	0.8	26.6	4.30
2008	*LAA*	*MLB*	*28*	*11*	*11*	*0*	*29*	*29*	*183²*	*214*	*48*	*99*	*21*	*44.2%*	*.308*	*6*	*1.42*	*4.72*	*4.59*	*4.65*	*10.0*	*2.1*	*4.4*	*1.0*	*15.4*	*3.10*

Breakout: 6% Improve: 31% Collapse: 31% Attrition: 12%   *Comparables: Jeff Weaver, Bill Gullickson, Mike Moore, Mike Witt*

You can argue that the Sox might have gotten more back by trading Garland a year earlier, but he took the ball every fifth game last year for the sixth straight season, and that didn't hurt his value. Seemingly unlovable for being a gentle giant who doesn't overpower people, Garland allowed line-drives on more than 25 percent of his balls in play last season; that sort of thing gets deadly, as it means you're just not fooling people. While Anaheim's a much better place to pitch, things are about to get really ugly for the big righty.

Gio Gonzalez

Bats: R   Throws: L   Height: 5' 11"   Weight: 185   Born: September 19, 1985   Age: 22

YEAR	TEAM	LVL	AGE	W	L	SV	G	GS	IP	H	BB	SO	HR	GB%	BABIP	STUFF	WHIP	ERA	PERA	EqERA	EqH9	EqBB9	EqSO9	EqHR9	VORP	SN/WX
2005	KAN	A	19	5	3	0	11	10	57²	36	22	84	3	48.8%	.277	33	1.01	1.87	5.67	5.03	8.8	6.3	8.2	1.3	3.1	—
2005	WNS	A+	19	8	3	0	13	13	73¹	61	25	79	5	40.1%	.304	17	1.17	3.56	5.19	5.79	8.8	4.7	5.6	1.1	-1.4	—
2006	REA	AA	20	7	12	0	27	27	154	140	81	166	24	42.9%	.293	-19	1.44	4.68	8.57	7.73	10.6	6.1	6.5	2.4	-33.1	—
2007	BIR	AA	21	9	7	0	27	27	150	116	57	185	10	54.2%	.309	24	1.15	3.18	4.25	4.20	8.0	3.9	7.6	1.0	22.0	—
2008	*OAK*	*MLB*	*22*	*7*	*8*	*0*	*31*	*21*	*130²*	*127*	*66*	*110*	*14*	*47.4%*	*.296*	*13*	*1.47*	*4.53*	*4.63*	*4.60*	*8.5*	*4.0*	*7.1*	*1.0*	*11.6*	*2.10*

Breakout: 31% Improve: 68% Collapse: 18% Attrition: 17%   *Comparables: Pete Falcone, Arthur Rhodes, Jon Lester, Lance Dickson*

In a perfect case of not having to regret the one who got away, the White Sox reacquired Gonzalez, the prize surrendered to the Phillies in the Jim Thome trade, in the package for Chief Garcia. The timing was good; Gonzalez dominated Double-A in his second go-round, leading the Southern League in strikeouts. His out pitch is a big bender, but he's got a little more velocity than most lefties and a changeup he's still mastering. Best of all, he doesn't have a problem going in on righties and winning that confrontation. Traded to Oakland in the Swisher deal, although he's not likely to win a job in camp, Gonzalez will be in the first rank of reinforcements when the Opening Day rotation starts getting smashed to flinders. There's concern that his ceiling isn't that high, but it's high enough and getting higher.

Charlie Haeger

Bats: R Throws: R Height: 6' 1" Weight: 220 Born: September 19, 1983 Age: 24

YEAR	TEAM	LVL	AGE	W	L	SV	G	GS	IP	H	BB	SO	HR	GB%	BABIP	STUFF	WHIP	ERA	PERA	EqERA	EqH9	EqBB9	EqSO9	EqHR9	VORP	SN/WX
2005	WNS	A+	21	8	2	0	14	13	81²	82	40	64	3	53.2%	.329	0	1.49	3.19	5.97	5.28	10.1	6.4	3.6	0.7	2.6	—
2005	BIR	AA	21	6	3	0	13	13	85²	84	45	48	1	51.1%	.307	4	1.51	3.78	4.66	5.62	9.0	5.5	2.9	0.3	-0.2	—
2006	CHR	AAA	22	14	6	0	26	25	170²	143	78	130	9	47.0%	.279	7	1.30	3.07	5.13	5.26	9.2	5.1	5.1	0.8	5.8	—
2006	CHA	MLB	22	1	1	1	7	1	18¹	12	13	19	0	46.8%	.255	18	1.36	3.44	2.89	4.42	5.9	5.9	8.8	0.0	2.7	0.00
2007	CHR	AAA	23	5	16	0	24	23	147²	138	67	126	16	41.8%	.298	-8	1.39	4.08	5.86	6.18	9.6	4.6	5.7	1.4	-8.9	—
2007	CHA	MLB	23	0	1	0	8	0	11¹	17	8	1	3	40.8%	.318	-56	2.21	7.17	11.51	9.26	12.3	5.4	0.8	2.3	-3.5	-0.14
2008	CHA	MLB	24	4	8	0	35	16	106¹	123	64	69	17	45.3%	.311	-10	1.76	6.29	5.76	5.89	9.9	4.8	5.3	1.4	-5.9	0.00

Breakout: 24% Improve: 55% Collapse: 14% Attrition: 19%   Comparables: Reid Cornelius, Justin Miller, Nick Pereira, Rett Johnson

Everybody loves a knuckleballer, but no amount of heavy breathing is going to get him to the Show. According to past master of the flutterball Charlie Hough, Haeger's got the best knuckler since Tim Wakefield first arrived, but it's still a work in progress. Haeger had his moments in a brief July stint, and had his best run in Charlotte's rotation after being sent back down for August, making five quality starts in six and putting up a 34/10 K/BB ratio in 46 2/3 IP, but as you can see above, it was a rough year overall. Sox catchers gave up a quarter of their season total of 20 passed balls in his 11 1/3 IP with the big club, which complicates his chances of making a rotation he could help.

Fernando Hernandez

Bats: R Throws: R Height: 5' 11" Weight: 190 Born: July 31, 1984 Age: 23

YEAR	TEAM	LVL	AGE	W	L	SV	G	GS	IP	H	BB	SO	HR	GB%	BABIP	STUFF	WHIP	ERA	PERA	EqERA	EqH9	EqBB9	EqSO9	EqHR9	VORP	SN/WX
2005	WNS	A+	20	4	1	1	45	0	70	83	30	59	6	46.0%	.368	-30	1.61	5.14	8.08	8.09	12.4	5.8	4.0	1.4	-17.2	—
2006	WNS	A+	21	7	5	13	57	0	65²	50	32	81	4	56.1%	.293	5	1.26	1.93	5.62	4.95	9.0	5.8	7.5	1.2	4.3	—
2007	BIR	AA	22	1	3	9	60	0	85¹	73	23	84	4	50.4%	.301	5	1.13	3.06	3.86	3.83	8.1	2.8	5.8	0.8	16.2	—
2008	OAK	MLB	23	4	4	2	27	6	61²	62	27	41	3	69.7%	.303	3	1.45	3.86	4.05	4.06	8.9	3.6	5.6	0.4	10.0	1.20

Breakout: 33% Improve: 53% Collapse: 21% Attrition: 16%   Comparables: Brandon League, Tim Layden, Franquelis Osoria, Brian Reed

Hernandez had a pretty solid season as a reliever in Double-A last year, but he really opened some eyes in the Arizona Fall League. Some of those eyes belonged to Oakland scouts, and the Athletics subsequently took a flyer on him in the Rule 5 draft. He's a classic sinker/slider guy, and the slider is awfully good, but some wonder if his heater has enough velocity to be used as a set-up pitch. Given the state of the A's bullpen, he could definitely stick.

Bobby Jenks

Bats: R Throws: R Height: 6' 3" Weight: 275 Born: March 14, 1981 Age: 27

YEAR	TEAM	LVL	AGE	W	L	SV	G	GS	IP	H	BB	SO	HR	GB%	BABIP	STUFF	WHIP	ERA	PERA	EqERA	EqH9	EqBB9	EqSO9	EqHR9	VORP	SN/WX
2005	BIR	AA	24	1	2	19	35	0	41	34	20	48	1	61.3%	.320	3	1.32	2.85	4.64	5.02	8.6	5.3	7.2	0.5	2.4	—
2005	CHA	MLB	24	1	1	6	32	0	39¹	34	15	50	3	47.1%	.316	26	1.25	2.75	3.79	3.46	8.3	3.5	10.4	0.7	10.4	1.41
2006	CHA	MLB	25	3	4	41	67	0	69²	66	31	80	5	60.4%	.347	24	1.39	4.00	4.00	3.82	8.6	3.8	9.9	0.5	15.9	3.94
2007	CHA	MLB	26	3	5	40	66	0	65	45	13	56	2	56.4%	.254	24	0.89	2.77	2.22	2.62	5.6	1.5	7.0	0.3	23.7	2.47
2008	CHA	MLB	27	4	5	37	56	0	60¹	56	21	59	4	53.5%	.308	16	1.27	3.38	3.11	3.24	8.0	2.8	7.9	0.6	16.1	2.60

Breakout: 24% Improve: 46% Collapse: 30% Attrition: 13%   Comparables: Greg McMichael, Mark Eichhorn, Gregg Olson, Lee Smith

The Human Barrel was the one effective member of the Sox' pen last year, as Jenks silenced doubters with his best year yet, in no small part because of his record-tying 41 straight batters retired (joining 1970s Giants starter Jim Barr at the head of the class). Remove those 41 consecutive outs from his record, and his season line was a still-dominant .242/.291/.301. The secret to his success was that he started putting his fastball in the zone with much more regularity. That meant both fewer walks and fewer strikeouts, but it was a worthwhile tradeoff as it's almost impossible to catch up with and pull his heater. It might not be beyond the realm of possibility for him to improve yet again this year; he was raw when he first got to the Sox in 2005, after all, and he's really only just putting everything together.

Boone Logan

Bats: R   Throws: L   Height: 6′ 5″   Weight: 200   Born: August 13, 1984   Age: 23

YEAR	TEAM	LVL	AGE	W	L	SV	G	GS	IP	H	BB	SO	HR	GB%	BABIP	STUFF	WHIP	ERA	PERA	EqERA	EqH9	EqBB9	EqSO9	EqHR9	VORP	SN/WX
2005	GRF	Rk	20	1	1	2	21	0	35¹	34	4	29	1	54.3%	.324	-21	1.08	3.31	5.64	6.16	10.6	3.5	2.6	0.9	-1.9	—
2006	CHR	AAA	21	3	1	11	38	0	42¹	35	12	57	1	44.7%	.340	27	1.12	3.42	4.59	5.22	9.3	3.2	9.3	0.5	1.7	—
2006	CHA	MLB	21	0	0	1	21	0	17¹	21	15	15	2	46.7%	.339	-2	2.08	8.32	6.59	8.68	9.6	6.8	6.8	1.0	-6.3	-0.55
2007	CHA	MLB	22	2	1	0	68	0	50²	59	20	35	7	52.0%	.333	-9	1.56	4.97	5.22	4.59	9.9	3.2	5.6	1.2	4.2	0.23
2008	CHA	MLB	23	2	2	2	45	1	47	46	18	35	5	48.1%	.291	3	1.35	3.89	3.68	3.67	8.4	3.0	6.0	0.9	10.7	0.90

Breakout: 48% Improve: 67% Collapse: 15% Attrition: 33%   Comparables: Bill Bray, Dennis Powell, Jung Bong, Jimmy Key

Like so many of the Sox' projects, Logan can throw in the 90s. That means he's not your standard-issue organizational lefty looking for tenure as a situational specialist. He has some problems with focus, however; he's been asked to make adjustments, but just doesn't seem to apply the lessons in-game. He's also a haphazard fielder and has trouble holding baserunners. Still, he's a big lefty with velocity, and in the absence of any veteran to challenge him for his perch, he's the second southpaw in the pen until the Sox fix Sisquatch.

Mike MacDougal

Bats: S   Throws: R   Height: 6′ 3″   Weight: 180   Born: March 5, 1977   Age: 31

YEAR	TEAM	LVL	AGE	W	L	SV	G	GS	IP	H	BB	SO	HR	GB%	BABIP	STUFF	WHIP	ERA	PERA	EqERA	EqH9	EqBB9	EqSO9	EqHR9	VORP	SN/WX
2005	KCA	MLB	28	5	6	21	68	0	70¹	69	24	72	6	55.8%	.330	20	1.34	3.33	3.63	3.47	8.0	3.0	8.9	0.6	13.0	1.23
2006	KCA	MLB	29	0	0	1	4	0	4	2	0	2	0	72.7%	.182	4	0.50	0.00	0.08	0.00	4.9	0.0	4.9	0.0	2.7	0.24
2006	CHA	MLB	29	1	1	0	25	0	25	19	6	19	1	63.4%	.261	13	1.00	1.80	2.64	1.85	6.7	2.2	6.7	0.4	12.1	0.88
2007	CHA	MLB	30	2	5	0	54	0	42¹	50	33	39	3	58.2%	.362	1	1.96	6.81	5.93	7.12	10.3	6.1	7.5	0.6	-8.3	-0.14
2008	CHA	MLB	31	2	2	3	46	0	49	47	25	43	4	54.9%	.304	3	1.47	4.07	3.86	3.89	8.2	4.1	7.1	0.7	9.3	0.80

Breakout: 41% Improve: 70% Collapse: 16% Attrition: 11%   Comparables: Todd Jones, Mike Stanton, Mike Fetters, Frank Williams

While MacDougal's past success as the Royals' closer suggests that he should be better than the rest of the Sox' exasperating collection of hard-throwing gas cans, he instead contributed to last year's conflagration as the entire pen went up with a noisy *Whoomph!* MacDougal endured the full spread of his past failings last year, struggling to stay healthy, struggling to throw strikes, and making too many mistakes in the zone on the few occasions that he did find it. With the addition of Scott Linebrink and Ehren Wasserman to the roster, what's preserving MacDougal for now is a contract that runs through 2009, and the memory of the couple of seasons in which he was healthy enough for Kansas City fans to dub him "Mac the Ninth."

Kyle McCulloch

Bats: R   Throws: R   Height: 6′ 3″   Weight: 180   Born: March 20, 1985   Age: 23

YEAR	TEAM	LVL	AGE	W	L	SV	G	GS	IP	H	BB	SO	HR	GB%	BABIP	STUFF	WHIP	ERA	PERA	EqERA	EqH9	EqBB9	EqSO9	EqHR9	VORP	SN/WX
2006	WNS	A+	21	2	5	0	7	7	35¹	37	17	21	4	53.3%	.289	-26	1.54	4.10	8.54	7.52	11.4	5.8	3.1	2.2	-6.9	—
2006	GRF	Rk	21	1	1	0	6	5	22²	19	7	27	1	61.3%	.295	-11	1.17	1.62	5.55	8.44	8.9	5.1	5.1	1.3	-6.7	—
2007	WNS	A+	22	7	7	0	22	22	121	116	42	88	7	61.8%	.297	-15	1.31	3.64	6.01	6.40	10.3	4.8	3.8	1.1	-9.8	—
2007	BIR	AA	22	1	2	0	6	6	26²	38	11	16	4	58.3%	.362	-38	1.84	6.40	9.71	10.12	12.8	4.1	3.0	2.0	-13.4	—
2008	CHA	MLB	23	5	12	0	25	25	127¹	166	74	58	22	53.9%	.321	-15	1.88	7.05	6.46	6.65	11.2	4.7	3.7	1.5	-18.6	-1.00

Breakout: 30% Improve: 60% Collapse: 14% Attrition: 10%   Comparables: Logan Kensing, Aaron Cook, Jake Dittler, Chris Mason

McCulloch is the reason that the White Sox overhauled their scouting department before the 2007 draft. They were tired of first-round picks like this—safe, unprojectable, and downright boring. McCulloch is a right-hander with an upper-80s fastball, a solid curve, very good command, and an excellent feel for pitching. In other words, he's a classic back-of-the-rotation starter. That's not a horrible thing, mind you, it's just not what you spend your first round picks on.

Brian Omogrosso

Bats: R   Throws: R   Height: 6' 3"   Weight: 230   Born: April 26, 1984   Age: 24

YEAR	TEAM	LVL	AGE	W	L	SV	G	GS	IP	H	BB	SO	HR	GB%	BABIP	STUFF	WHIP	ERA	PERA	EqERA	EqH9	EqBB9	EqSO9	EqHR9	VORP	SN/WX
2006	KAN	A	22	1	2	2	22	0	36	27	13	23	2	53.6%	.240	-27	1.11	3.25	5.06	4.86	7.6	5.4	2.4	1.4	2.7	—
2007	WNS	A+	23	8	8	5	40	14	120¹	94	57	108	7	50.1%	.263	-12	1.26	3.74	5.42	6.11	8.4	6.1	4.7	1.1	-6.3	—
2008	CHA	MLB	24	3	6	0	26	12	76²	88	56	44	13	47.9%	.301	-19	1.88	6.69	6.23	6.27	9.8	5.9	4.6	1.5	-7.7	-0.40

Breakout: 22% Improve: 44% Collapse: 34% Attrition: 23%   Comparables: Keith Surkont, Richard Dishman, Steven White, Gary Goldsmith

Omogrosso found success in both relief and starting roles in 2007, but the bullpen is where his future lies. He's a side-armer, but the thing that separates him from most of his ilk is that he also throws hard, often in the low 90s. The thing that doesn't separate him from most side-armers is that opposite-handed hitters hit him hard because they just see the ball for too long. Not that there's no use for a ROOGY; just ask the Twins or Chad Bradford's accountant.

Oneli Perez

Bats: R   Throws: R   Height: 6' 2"   Weight: 190   Born: May 26, 1983   Age: 25

YEAR	TEAM	LVL	AGE	W	L	SV	G	GS	IP	H	BB	SO	HR	GB%	BABIP	STUFF	WHIP	ERA	PERA	EqERA	EqH9	EqBB9	EqSO9	EqHR9	VORP	SN/WX
2005	KAN	A	22	4	2	2	36	2	80	84	32	62	7	38.6%	.310	-39	1.45	3.71	9.33	8.19	12.9	6.7	3.5	1.9	-19.3	—
2006	KAN	A	23	3	1	8	30	0	36	23	8	42	1	35.9%	.242	-4	0.86	1.00	4.05	2.86	6.7	3.6	5.5	0.8	10.6	—
2006	WNS	A+	23	1	0	0	17	0	25¹	17	5	29	1	48.5%	.250	6	0.88	0.72	3.94	2.92	7.3	2.6	6.6	0.7	7.4	—
2006	BIR	AA	23	0	1	1	7	0	16²	6	6	20	1	57.6%	.161	15	0.74	0.56	3.04	1.17	4.1	3.5	7.6	1.2	7.5	—
2007	BIR	AA	24	6	2	16	59	0	77	62	20	89	5	39.6%	.302	5	1.06	2.10	3.96	2.89	7.8	2.7	6.9	1.0	22.5	—
2008	CHA	MLB	25	4	5	4	27	7	65²	68	28	53	11	40.7%	.292	2	1.46	4.62	4.73	4.24	8.9	3.4	6.5	1.5	9.6	1.20

Breakout: 18% Improve: 40% Collapse: 33% Attrition: 7%   Comparables: Julian Heredia, Carlos Almanzar, Jeff Pierce, Francisco Cordero

A Dominican retread found after he was discarded by the Pads, Keith Jackson's favorite pitcher has made himself a relief prospect (as much as there is such a thing) with his command of low-90s heat and a solid slider. He had a great finishing kick last year, striking out 50 and walking only four unintentionally in 33 1/3 IP over the final two months. If the Sox decide to completely make over their pen, Perez has an excellent shot to push past the crowd of guys who lack his command and stick in a middle relief role.

Aaron Poreda

Bats: L   Throws: L   Height: 6' 6"   Weight: 240   Born: October 1, 1986   Age: 21

YEAR	TEAM	LVL	AGE	W	L	SV	G	GS	IP	H	BB	SO	HR	GB%	BABIP	STUFF	WHIP	ERA	PERA	EqERA	EqH9	EqBB9	EqSO9	EqHR9	VORP	SN/WX
2007	GRF	Rk	20	4	0	0	12	8	46¹	29	10	48	1	67.3%	.252	7	0.84	1.17	4.45	3.35	6.7	4.5	4.7	0.7	10.1	—
2008	CHA	MLB	21	5	12	0	25	25	133	159	86	74	22	51.8%	.309	-9	1.84	6.49	6.11	6.09	10.2	5.2	4.5	1.5	-10.8	-0.10

Breakout: NA   Improve: NA   Collapse: NA   Attrition: NA   Comparables: Kelly Wunsch, Ray Liotta, Matt Beaumont, Nick Webber

Kenny Williams insisted that the scouting department select a power arm with the Sox' first-round pick last June, and they delivered with Poreda. The list of left-handers who can get into the upper 90s is a short one, but Poreda is on it. He needs to find some secondary offerings to accompany his plus-plus fastball, but even if that doesn't happen, he could develop into a closer.

Andy Sisco

Bats: L   Throws: L   Height: 6' 10"   Weight: 270   Born: January 13, 1983   Age: 25

YEAR	TEAM	LVL	AGE	W	L	SV	G	GS	IP	H	BB	SO	HR	GB%	BABIP	STUFF	WHIP	ERA	PERA	EqERA	EqH9	EqBB9	EqSO9	EqHR9	VORP	SN/WX
2005	KCA	MLB	22	2	5	0	67	0	75¹	68	42	76	6	42.1%	.313	24	1.46	3.11	3.70	2.63	7.2	4.9	8.7	0.6	21.3	0.22
2006	KCA	MLB	23	1	3	1	65	0	58¹	66	40	52	8	40.0%	.345	-2	1.82	7.10	5.53	6.49	9.2	5.6	7.4	1.1	-7.1	-1.23
2007	CHA	MLB	24	0	1	0	19	0	14	19	11	13	2	36.7%	.362	-6	2.14	8.36	7.61	7.80	10.8	6.0	7.2	1.2	-3.5	0.02
2007	CHR	AAA	24	3	6	0	23	15	78²	76	44	76	10	39.6%	.319	-14	1.52	4.35	7.33	6.53	10.3	5.8	6.7	1.8	-7.4	—
2008	CHA	MLB	25	2	3	1	50	3	58	60	36	48	9	41.5%	.301	-6	1.66	5.70	5.25	5.31	8.9	5.0	6.8	1.4	0.6	0.10

Breakout: 27% Improve: 58% Collapse: 15% Attrition: 22%   Comparables: David West, Tim Birtsas, Mark Redman, Gary Kroll

On the Sox' too-long list of interesting science experiments gone bad, there's still reason to invest some hope in Sisquatch. After all, he's still 6-foot-10 and still throws hard. The Rule 5 draft interrupted his development—providing another reminder of how it can derail a guy—but Sisco has still managed to have his moments. The team has attempted to help him harness his power assortment by giving him more innings to pitch, but it isn't working; he hasn't shown progress with his heat or his slider in Triple-A or a repeat engagement in the Mexican Winter League. He'll never make it through waivers, but riding around on the wire could be his fate.

Matt Thornton

Bats: L   Throws: L   Height: 6' 6"   Weight: 230   Born: September 15, 1976   Age: 31

YEAR	TEAM	LVL	AGE	W	L	SV	G	GS	IP	H	BB	SO	HR	GB%	BABIP	STUFF	WHIP	ERA	PERA	EqERA	EqH9	EqBB9	EqSO9	EqHR9	VORP	SN/WX
2005	SEA	MLB	28	0	4	0	55	0	57	54	42	57	13	45.4%	.277	-3	1.68	5.21	6.61	5.30	8.5	6.6	8.8	1.9	2.8	-0.35
2006	CHA	MLB	29	5	3	2	63	0	54	46	21	49	5	50.0%	.279	11	1.24	3.33	3.35	2.98	7.3	3.1	7.6	0.7	17.0	1.74
2007	CHA	MLB	30	4	4	2	68	0	56¹	59	26	55	4	45.8%	.344	10	1.51	4.80	4.37	4.34	9.2	3.7	8.0	0.6	7.1	0.03
2008	CHA	MLB	31	2	3	4	55	0	52²	53	23	48	6	45.6%	.306	4	1.44	4.37	4.11	4.11	8.5	3.6	7.4	1.1	8.2	0.70

Breakout: 26%   Improve: 55%   Collapse: 27%   Attrition: 20%   Comparables: Dan Plesac, Mike Myers, Mike Muñoz, Andy Hassler

Once Don Cooper's prize reclamation project, Thornton endured a blend of cascading ill fortune and some perhaps interrelated bad luck last year. He was a bit hit-unlucky, but part of the problem was that he wasn't any good with men on base yet was the year's leading recipient of Ozzie Guillen's special brand of love, walking six men under orders. Subtract those six passes, and Thornton struck out a man per inning and three times as many as he walked. Pitchers who do that have value, and Thornton should bounce back.

Javier Vazquez

Bats: R   Throws: R   Height: 6' 1"   Weight: 210   Born: July 25, 1976   Age: 31

YEAR	TEAM	LVL	AGE	W	L	SV	G	GS	IP	H	BB	SO	HR	GB%	BABIP	STUFF	WHIP	ERA	PERA	EqERA	EqH9	EqBB9	EqSO9	EqHR9	VORP	SN/WX
2005	ARI	MLB	28	11	15	0	33	33	215²	223	46	192	35	44.6%	.308	13	1.25	4.42	4.34	4.21	8.8	1.7	7.2	1.4	22.7	4.05
2006	CHA	MLB	29	11	12	0	33	32	202²	206	56	184	23	41.7%	.311	24	1.29	4.84	4.10	4.66	8.8	2.3	7.6	0.9	22.8	3.29
2007	CHA	MLB	30	15	8	0	32	32	216²	197	50	213	29	41.2%	.294	26	1.14	3.74	3.61	3.34	7.8	1.8	8.2	1.2	51.1	5.25
2008	CHA	MLB	31	13	10	0	31	31	205	199	55	177	26	43.4%	.292	22	1.24	3.94	3.60	3.69	8.3	2.2	7.0	1.1	38.7	5.90

Breakout: 22%   Improve: 62%   Collapse: 12%   Attrition: 12%   Comparables: Jack Morris, Bob Feller, Mike Mussina, Bob Welch

Although Vazquez has the benefits of a clean delivery, heat that touches the mid 90s, and a plus change, it's only when his breaking stuff is on that he resembles a staff ace. While a fly-ball pitcher in the Cell can be a dangerous thing, he doesn't get pulled that often and keeps hitters from exploiting the Cell's tight corners. He still has trouble getting over that sixth-inning hump (his eight sixth-inning souvenirs were the most he allowed in any single frame), but he was much better at getting deeper into ballgames in his second season with the Pale Hose, leading to relative quiescence from his generally noisy skipper, and Vazquez's best year since his youthful Expos heyday.

Ehren Wasserman

Bats: S   Throws: R   Height: 6' 0"   Weight: 185   Born: December 6, 1980   Age: 27

YEAR	TEAM	LVL	AGE	W	L	SV	G	GS	IP	H	BB	SO	HR	GB%	BABIP	STUFF	WHIP	ERA	PERA	EqERA	EqH9	EqBB9	EqSO9	EqHR9	VORP	SN/WX
2005	WNS	A+	24	4	2	20	42	0	46	41	9	37	0	56.3%	.318	-11	1.09	1.37	4.27	3.24	8.9	3.0	3.9	0.4	10.9	—
2005	BIR	AA	24	2	0	0	14	0	21	23	7	18	0	65.1%	.377	-10	1.43	2.14	5.18	3.72	10.7	3.7	5.1	0.5	4.0	—
2006	BIR	AA	25	4	8	22	61	0	63¹	60	25	47	3	55.1%	.305	-19	1.35	2.57	4.99	4.95	9.3	4.1	4.3	0.9	4.3	—
2007	CHR	AAA	26	2	4	5	38	0	42²	34	18	33	0	62.3%	.296	-4	1.22	2.11	3.89	3.63	8.2	4.3	5.2	0.2	8.7	—
2007	CHA	MLB	26	1	1	0	33	0	23	20	7	14	0	70.4%	.286	0	1.17	2.74	2.96	3.22	7.7	2.4	5.2	0.0	6.4	1.08
2008	CHA	MLB	27	2	2	2	49	1	48²	51	19	29	4	57.4%	.296	-6	1.43	4.12	3.83	3.96	8.9	3.1	4.8	0.7	9.1	0.80

Breakout: 12%   Improve: 33%   Collapse: 40%   Attrition: 25%   Comparables: Phil Niekro, Frank Linzy, Mike Trujillo, Dave Sells

He's not Chad Bradford, but Wasserman could fill the same role by providing the unstable Sox pen with some side-arming special goodness, scything down right-handed batters with a fastball that sometimes touches 90 mph. Wasserman limited Triple-A right-handers to .186/.260/.267 and managed to avoid giving up power to lefties, although he did walk them (.290/.421/.355). If the Sox decide to break with their bullpen monoculture of big, explosive/exploding power pitchers and settle for a situational star in the making, Wasserman's their man.

LINEOUTS

Hitters

PLAYER	TEAM	LVL	AGE	PA	R	2B	3B	HR	RBI	BB	SO	SB-CS	EqBRR	AVG/OBP/SLG	MLVr	EqAVG/EqOBP/EqSLG	EqA	VORP
C C. Armstrong*	WNS	A+	23	316	35	17	0	12	39	23	69	1-1	-3.5	.288/.342/.474	.108	.235/.280/.372	.225	-5.5
	BIR	AA	23	79	2	6	0	1	12	3	20	0-0	-2.2	.239/.273/.366	-.118	.219/.253/.329	.204	-3.9
OF T. Collaro	BIR	AA	24	471	55	26	2	19	67	27	129	7-3	-0.4	.257/.306/.456	.074	.239/.278/.429	.240	-11.6
	CHR	AAA	24	110	9	7	0	4	13	7	29	0-1	-0.1	.291/.336/.476	.127	.252/.300/.447	.249	-0.4
OF D. Cook	WNS	A+	25	400	73	22	3	16	50	51	77	10-8	-1.8	.279/.373/.503	.184	.224/.303/.397	.241	-12.5
	BIR	AA	25	126	19	5	2	8	25	24	22	2-2	0.1	.293/.437/.626	.514	.272/.397/.563	.315	11.5
OF J. Gallagher*	GRF	Rk	21	295	52	21	1	9	44	35	38	7-4	-1.5	.332/.418/.534	.340	.242/.313/.362	.239	-17.5
OF S. Gartrell	KAN	A	23	383	67	20	3	12	57	37	77	12-2	1.8	.301/.374/.484	.204	.238/.298/.375	.236	-13.6
	WNS	A+	23	81	13	1	1	2	6	6	17	2-0	0.3	.288/.358/.411	.049	.240/.296/.360	.231	-3.5
UT A. Gonzalez	CHR	AAA	25	148	15	7	1	3	17	22	39	6-1	0.0	.242/.358/.387	.008	.232/.345/.392	.265	3.6
	CHA	MLB	25	215	17	6	0	2	11	25	61	1-5	0.4	.185/.280/.249	-.399	.193/.294/.267	.193	-18.6
C D. Lucy	BIR	AA	24	326	42	17	0	6	27	30	59	13-1	1.4	.269/.343/.390	.049	.247/.311/.365	.244	-0.3
	CHR	AAA	24	78	5	3	0	0	3	3	25	0-0	0.4	.200/.231/.240	-.419	.187/.218/.227	.130	-8.9
1B C. Marrero*	GRF	Rk	20	313	53	21	6	12	63	36	43	3-2	1.7	.305/.383/.561	.296	.221/.288/.375	.230	-21.3
SS S. Miranda#	KAN	A	20	283	45	9	2	1	30	37	27	5-3	-1.2	.282/.384/.349	.026	.230/.314/.286	.216	-6.7
A.Ramirez '08	CHA	MLB	26	505	67	28	2	14	65	32	64	9-3	0.3	.295/.342/.452	.062	.291/.340/.457	.278	18.9
CF L. Terrero	CHR	AAA	27	67	7	4	0	4	9	1	15	3-1	0.2	.231/.254/.477	-.047	.215/.239/.446	.232	-1.3
	CHA	MLB	27	139	18	2	0	5	12	12	35	4-3	-1.3	.231/.348/.376	-.096	.239/.355/.410	.263	0.1

A Canadian catcher, **Cole Armstrong** was a little old for his level in 2007 but can be seen as a possible late bloomer. He's a good defensive catcher with a decent amount of power with backup possibilities down the road. ⊘ A one-dimensional organizational slugger, **Tom Collaro**'s best and only hope is that he somehow falls into a left-field platoon on a team gunning for that always-tasty International League title. ⊘ **David Cook** has done nothing but hit in three years in A-ball, but last year was his first sniff of Double-A. Now five years removed from being drafted out of Miami of Ohio, he's not somebody with a high upside. ⊘ Drafted out of Duke in the seventh round of last summer's draft, **Jimmy Gallagher** is already being forced to contend with the "tweener" label. He's not athletic enough for center, and there are questions as to whether he'll show enough power to play in a corner. ⊘ The outfielder formerly known as Stefan, **Maurice Gartrell** did nicely last year in his first full professional season, with a nice spread of production and athleticism. ⊘ **Andy Gonzalez** is a strong-armed middle-infield organizational soldier, and his greatest endorsement is that he lasted long enough to make it to the majors, if only briefly. He was non-tendered in December. ⊘ Although he threw out 34 percent of opposing base thieves in the minors, **Donny Lucy**'s a bad use of a 40-man roster spot. ⊘ The older brother of Nationals prospect Christopher, **Christian Marrero** is a 2006 draft-and-follow with plus power. His future anywhere but first base is hopeless, so he'll have to slug his way up the ladder. ⊘ A diminutive shortstop taken in the 13th round of the 2007 draft, **Sergio Miranda** is the sort of fundamentally sound scrapper who might surprise you. ⊘ When the White Sox lost out on Torii Hunter, they signed Cuban **Alexei Ramirez** in an attempt to fill their center field hole. He led the Cuban pro league in home runs last year, but scouts see him as more of a gap power type in the majors. Unlike most Cubans who come over, Ramirez is in his prime (somewhere in his late 20s—as usual his birthdate is in some dispute) and an outstanding athlete to boot, capable of playing shortstop, second, or the outfield. ⊘ It speaks volumes about how **Luis Terrero**'s career is going that last year he was a center fielder on a team that didn't have one and still couldn't earn a shot.

Pitchers

PLAYER	TEAM	LVL	AGE	W	L	SV	IP	H	BB	SO	HR	GB%	BABIP	STUFF	WHIP	ERA	PERA	EqERA	EqH9	EqBB9	EqSO9	EqHR9	VORP
R. Bukvich	CHR	AAA	29	1	3	9	28	24	9	32	2	48.1%	.306	5	1.18	2.89	4.25	3.62	8.6	3.3	7.6	1.0	6.0
	CHA	MLB	29	1	0	0	35²	36	24	18	5	46.4%	.265	-21	1.68	5.04	4.78	4.78	7.9	5.0	4.1	1.2	0.1
M. Dubee	LWD	A	21	4	4	1	55²	52	22	54	2	54.4%	.325	-11	1.33	3.88	6.40	6.52	11.0	6.0	5.0	0.9	-4.9
	KAN	A	21	3	0	0	33	34	13	35	3	44.6%	.356	-6	1.42	4.09	7.81	6.67	11.4	6.0	5.7	1.9	-3.4
J. Ely	GRF	Rk	21	6	1	0	56	55	14	56	6	49.0%	.327	-23	1.23	3.86	8.27	7.33	11.8	5.4	4.4	2.3	-9.0
N. Masset	CHA	MLB	25	2	3	0	39¹	52	26	21	2	43.1%	.362	-15	1.98	7.10	6.15	6.81	11.1	5.2	4.3	0.5	-5.2
	CHR	AAA	25	0	4	0	45¹	51	9	33	6	48.0%	.321	-18	1.32	4.57	6.88	6.86	11.6	2.1	4.9	1.7	-5.9
M. Myers*	NYA	MLB	38	3	0	0	40²	38	16	21	3	59.6%	.269	-9	1.33	2.65	3.52	2.83	7.8	3.0	4.1	0.7	13.0
	CHA	MLB	38	1	0	0	13²	21	7	6	3	53.6%	.360	-51	2.05	11.17	9.64	11.93	12.6	3.8	3.8	1.9	-9.5
H. Phillips*	CHR	AAA	25	13	7	0	173²	198	56	108	23	46.3%	.313	-30	1.46	4.30	7.32	6.26	11.4	3.4	4.0	1.8	-11.9
	CHA	MLB	25	1	1	0	7¹	10	4	2	1	50.0%	.333	-38	1.91	3.70	7.88	3.86	11.6	5.1	2.6	1.3	2.0
A. Russell	BIR	AA	24	9	11	1	138²	159	58	95	8	53.3%	.339	-18	1.56	4.80	5.89	6.05	10.7	4.2	3.8	0.9	-6.6
C. Vasquez*	BIR	AA	24	0	0	2	14²	8	3	14	0	67.6%	.222	6	0.75	1.22	2.67	1.88	5.0	1.9	5.7	0.0	5.9
	CHR	AAA	24	4	3	2	62	50	33	43	2	62.5%	.274	-6	1.34	3.05	4.31	4.78	8.0	5.2	4.5	0.5	5.3

In their hour of most desperate need, the Sox turned to **Ryan Bukvich**, not because he would solve their bullpen problems, but because he was a familiar name and throws hard. ⊘ The prize fetched from the Phillies in exchange for two months of Tadahito Iguchi, **Michael Dubee** throws in the low 90s with a decent curve. ⊘ Selected in the third round of the 2007 draft out of Miami of Ohio, **John Ely** can touch 94 mph while sitting in the low 90s and supplements that with a nice change and curve. He figures to be a reliever. ⊘ After a dominating showing in 2006, **Lucas Harrell** missed all of 2007 recovering from elbow surgery, so his last performance was great, but also 18 months ago. ⊘ The Sox' fascination with having unpleasantly wild flameouts in the pen led to some rather nondescript additions last year, but **Nick Masset** deserves some notice for mixing mid-90s velocity with a sharp curve. ⊘ Things get messy for every situational hero toward the end, but at times it seems like side-arming southpaw **Mike Myers** will give that pink bunny a run for his money. ⊘ Your stock organizational lefty changeup artist has his uses, but **Heath Phillips'** assortment is so mediocre that he has little value as a situational reliever, not even with his brilliant pickoff move. ⊘ A 6-foot-8 right-hander who can get up to 95 mph with his fastball, **Adam Russell** has been hampered as a starter because of his lack of a secondary pitch, but the White Sox have moved him to the pen; the more optimistic people in the front office think he could be ready in that role this year. ⊘ **Carlos Vasquez** has a similar problem to Phillips'—he's useful enough at an upper-level affiliate, but there's not a lot of projection in the arm of this Venezuelan southpaw.

MANAGER: OZZIE GUILLEN

YEAR	TEAM	W-L	Pythag +/−	Avg PC	100+ P	120+ P	QS	BQS	REL	REL w Zero R	IBB	Subs	PH	PH Avg	PH HR	SB2	CS2	SB3	CS3	SAC Att	SAC %	POS SAC	Squeeze	Swing	In Play
2005	CHA	99-63	7	101.9	105	3	89	13	410	272	42	36	100	.205	2	115	61	21	5	78	67.9%	51	4	159	121
2006	CHA	90-72	2	100.9	93	4	76	12	398	222	59	51	135	.225	6	83	43	10	4	72	61.1%	39	2	127	100
2007	CHA	72-90	6	100.7	98	2	82	15	463	258	50	31	100	.227	3	75	38	3	6	61	67.2%	36	0	128	108

Assertions that Guillen is pure little ball as a manager can't be readily reconciled with his lineup cards; Thome-Konerko-Pierzynski in the three, four, and five slots might provide sufficient lefty/righty alternation and runners on base in front of Konerko, but it is also murderously reliable when it comes to the rally-killing double play. Ozzie might be very much an entertainer, but Ozzieball still isn't likely to be mistaken for Whiteyball or Billyball, as the Sox are still very much a team that gets by on power, not speed, just as they did in their championship season of 2005. It's hard to pin last year's pen's massive failures on Guillen—he didn't bring in a bunch of wild kids on his own, after all—and his willingness to push his starters to go deeper into games isn't anywhere close to abusive. Not being a small ball guy and not abusing your pitchers are two virtues; one among many things a manager should strive for is to "do no harm." Beyond Guillen's value as an amusement and his resulting local popularity, he's an asset in the dugout as well.

Cincinnati Reds

Whoever wants to know the heart and mind of America
had better learn baseball, the rules and realities of the game.
—**JACQUES BARZUN**, *God's Country and Mine:*
A Declaration of Love Spiced with a Few Harsh Words (1954)

Jacques Barzun made his observation about baseball as the meme leading to America's heart and mind more than fifty years ago, but his statement still rings true, though perhaps not quite in the same way. Today, in the game as in society, we have the phenomenon of the super-rich getting richer—Red Sox and Yankees, Paul Allen and Larry Ellison—seemingly holding themselves aloft by the sheer mass of their financial muscle. Where this comparison fails is in the National League, because while the arguments over the shrinking middle class might reflect life in the wider American world, in the senior circuit the number of teams with realizable aspirations has only grown in recent years.

While there still exists a small cadre of teams that are truly without any immediate hope—the Giants and the Marlins, the Astros and the Pirates—that group is dwarfed by the more amorphous gaggle of potential contenders. In the current National League environment, all four playoff spots can turn over from one season to the next, as they did from 2006 to 2007, and there are additional teams beyond those eight with playoff possibilities of their own. This phenomenon may be attributable to realignment, revenue sharing, increased revenues due to improved and new media exposure, new stadia, and the recapturing of the last of the ground lost to the labor wars of the 1990s, or simply better management practices, but despite expanding by four teams in the last 15 years, the NL now contains more teams that can consider themselves contenders, not less.

Despite this increased upward mobility, the Reds have more often than not found themselves among that small cadre of teams that are on the outside looking in. For a team of modest means, this is a most dangerous place to be. A team such as the Reds, with more hope than none, but less hope than most, is constantly faced with the desperate decision of whether to play for big stakes by risking all of its resources on one throw of the dice, or to embark on a rebuilding program that may never end. Complicating this decision is the lack of job security of the man charged with making it. Few general managers can wait out that long night of 90-loss seasons without ownership's uncritical buy-in, even if rebuilding really is the right choice to make.

Entering his third season as the Reds GM, Wayne Krivsky is now faced with that desperate decision, but despite dropping from 80 wins in Krivsky's first year to 72 last year, the Reds are much closer to October action than they are to permanent membership in that hopeless cadre. Indeed, the Reds expected to contend in 2007, only to have their plans foiled by a number of disappointing pitching performances. In the rotation, free agent disaster Eric Milton broke down only six starts into his season, closing the book on the biggest mistake made by the team during the tenure of Krivsky's predecessor, Dan O'Brien. Bronson Arroyo declined from

---

REDS PROSPECTUS

2007 record: 72-90; Fifth place, NL Central

Pythagenport record: 74-88

Runs scored per game: 4.83 (7th in NL)

Runs allowed per game: 5.27 (15th in NL)

Team EqA: .259 (9th in NL)

2007 Batters Age: 30.6 (5th oldest in NL)

2007 Pitchers Age: 29.2 (8th oldest in NL)

Ballpark: Great American Ball Park; Strong hitter's park; Park Factor of 1.049

2007: In a division there for the taking, the Reds take it on the chin.

2008: Reinforcements arrive, but will Dusty use them, abuse them, or ignore them?

staff ace to above-average innings-eater, falling from 3rd to 24th in the league in Support-Neutral Lineup-adjusted Value Above Replacement (SNLVAR). Rookie Homer Bailey came into the season as one of the game's top young arms; he finished it as a cipher. These and lesser setbacks combined to push the Reds' rotation from solidly middle-of-the-pack at 14th in the majors in SNLVAR in 2006 down to 21st.

The bigger pitching problem, however, was the bullpen. Despite, and perhaps in part because of Krivsky's desperate attempts to fix the pen at the tail end of 2006, most notably via the still-lamentable deal with the Nationals that fetched relievers Gary Majewski and Bill Bray in exchange for two members of the starting lineup, the Reds' relief staff got worse even though it also became notionally more stable. The Reds used a remarkable 25 different relievers in 2006, but didn't get any better using "only" 17 in 2007, as the pen dropped from 12th in the NL in WXRL to last. A stable and effective pen acquired on the cheap is usually a testament to good scouting, managerial acumen, and front office judgment. All three of Cincinnati's decision-making elements can duck the blame for the pen's failures by saying, as Casey Stengel would, that "they could'na dunnit without the players," but the team's desperate lurching from one bad idea to the next speaks for itself. When washed-up veterans such as Mike Stanton or Victor Santos are seen as trustworthy, poor judgment is reaping what it has sown.

It's puzzling that Krivsky would have so much trouble with his bullpen given his continued success in digging up low-cost, free talent pickups to employ elsewhere. Two years ago, he nabbed Arroyo from the Red Sox for baseball's equivalent of a shiny, distracting object (Wily Mo Peña) and swiped Brandon Phillips from the Indians for a fringy minor league right-hander. Last winter, his feats were less productive, but no less inspired. Krivsky took an especially bold risk in taking troubled prodigy Josh Hamilton in the Rule 5 draft, thus forcing Hamilton to make it at the major league level after three years out of the game and a mere 15 games in the New York–Penn League in late 2006. Hamilton didn't just earn his keep, he reminded people why he was the top overall pick of the 1999 amateur draft, proving that his natural gifts as a baseball player are so tremendous as to defy easy interpretation or forecasting.

Still, Krivsky chose discretion over unyielding faith, flipping Hamilton to Texas over the winter for pitcher Edinson Volquez. In his other lower-stakes, lower-upside pickups, Krivsky also added utility infielder Jeff Keppinger in a minor swap, and a pair of real-life reliev-

ers in Jared Burton (another Rule 5 pick) and Marcus McBeth (for injured surplus outfield prospect Chris Denorfia), all of whom figure to play roles in 2008.

Krivsky's moves following the 2007 season leave no doubt that the Reds once again see themselves as a team primed for a quick reversal of fortune. Having fired incumbent manger Jerry Narron in early July, Krivsky's first move this winter was to tab Dusty Baker to be the club's new manager. While Baker's hiring during the League Championship Series might seem to have only symbolic import, Baker is one of the few managers in the game who comes to a new job expecting to get his way in personnel decisions and expecting to win. He is a classic solution for a general manager with a background in player development—a high-profile manager with some sort of media savvy who can be a true partner in major league operations and thus allow Krivsky to burrow back into the lower-profile spadework of rebuilding a farm system. Cubs GM Jim Hendry had similar intentions when he hired first Baker and then Lou Piniella to manage in Chicago.

Cynics might be quick to note that Baker's past success has coincided with major outlays in cash and/or having Barry Bonds in his lineup and has often resulted in burning out a pitcher or two in the name of the cause. They might also note how quickly things went sour for Baker in Wrigleyville, as his ever-expanding doghouse, frequently capricious judgment calls on younger players, and increasingly surly relationship with a generally cuddly local press corps seemed to get the better of him. Baker nevertheless commands some sort of respect within the game, and bringing him in before the wooing of free agents and season ticket holders began had the potential to reap benefits in a way few managerial alternatives could. Making a good impression on ticket holders is especially important to the Reds, who never received an appreciable "new stadium" boost from the Great American Ball Park. Their annual attendance not only bobs down around 12th or 13th in the league, but falls short of the crowds the team drew at old Riverfront Stadium in the early '90s or mid '70s, which is proof of what winning, or even the suggestion of winning, can do for attendance.

The Reds' second-biggest move this winter was to address their perpetual bullpen problem by signing the best closer on the free agent market, Francisco Cordero, to a four-year, $46 million deal. Cordero comes over from the Brewers with a record of durability and a dominant fastball/slider combination. The danger is that he allows fly balls and liners to lefties, and the GABP rewards lefty hitters who get balls past the infield. Still, it isn't hard to envision a positive cascade effect in which the addition of Cordero pushes last year's closer David Weathers into his more familiar set-up role, and so on down the line as some of the hard-throwing youngsters the club has on hand establish themselves by tackling lower-leverage sixth- and seventh-inning assignments—if Dusty lets them; his track record with the Cubs on this score was spotty, to say the least.

Another reason to be optimistic about the Reds' near-term outlook is that help is on the way from within. While the Cincinnati organization doesn't get high marks for its breadth and depth of talent, it does have nearly ready homegrown blue-chippers in first baseman Joey Votto, outfielder Jay Bruce, and right-hander Johnny Cueto. The challenge here isn't simply bringing them up once they're ready, but convincing the new skipper to play them once they're on the roster. Baker is no great fan of young talent. Whether the Reds contend or not, it remains to be seen if he'll be willing to slot in Votto over veteran Scott Hatteberg at first, or invest Cueto or Bailey with much trust (or, perversely, avoid trusting them so much that their careers follow the same tragic trajectory of the young pair of prospective aces Baker was entrusted with as the Cubs' skipper). Certainly, having Bruce ready creates an additional incentive for Krivksy to explore his slender window of opportunity to deal left fielder Adam Dunn this summer should the Reds fall out of the race, but even convincing Baker to ride out retooling is no easy proposition.

If there's a danger, it's that the Reds may not recognize how much room for improvement they have yet to make on offense. Despite Hamilton's breakthrough, an almost full season from Ken Griffey Jr., and a nifty bounce-back season from Dunn, the Reds were not an especially good offensive ballclub last year, ranking only ninth in the league in Equivalent Average at .259, a point below mediocrity. Yes, they were third in the league in homers and sixth in isolated power, but those rankings were products of their home park, which overstated the contributions of several regulars (see Table 1).

Some of this isn't really bad news—the big splits of Griffey and Hamilton can be forgiven due to their still-

Table 1. Coors Brewed on the Banks of the Ohio? Reds home and road slugging

Hitter	Home ISO	Road ISO	Diff.
C Ross	.242	.176	+.066
1B Hatteberg	.201	.122	+.079
2B Phillips	.218	.176	+.042
3B Encarnacion	.168	.130	+.030
SS Gonzalez	.198	.194	-.004
RF Griffey	.263	.181	+.082
CF Hamilton	.305	.223	+.082
LF Dunn	.293	.286	+.007
Team	.191	.149	+.042

solid production on the road, while exceptional three-true-outcomes hitter Dunn delivers everywhere. However, Hatteberg goes from dangerous in Cincinnati's bandbox (.370/.436/.571) to near uselessness on the road (.244/.351/.366), making it all the more imperative that the Reds replace him in the lineup with Votto's more broad-based and park-independent collection of offensive skills and far greater upside. Hatteberg remains a low-cost contingency should Votto falter, and a dangerous bat off the bench during home games, but if the Reds are going to improve their production at the plate, it will have to start with Votto. Otherwise, the lineup is well established, and wishful thinking that everyone will just get better has a way of being disappointed.

Krivsky's had his stumbles in his first two years as the Reds GM, most notably his hyperactive accumulation of relief help in late 2006, but despite whispers that his job was being threatened by newly available former Cardinals GM Walt Jocketty, he's put his team in position to make rapid improvements thanks to his knack for adept free-talent pickups and cultivation of the farm system. If Cueto and Bailey develop into starters good enough to round out the Reds rotation and shore up that unit as much as Cordero will the pen and Votto should the lineup, it isn't hard to see the Reds posting a winning record this year. In a division that's been won by 83- and 85-win teams in the last two years, that doesn't simply put them back in baseball's middle class, it puts them solidly in contention.

HITTERS

Jay Bruce — OF

Bats: L Throws: L Height: 6' 2" Weight: 218 Born: April 3, 1987 Age: 21

YEAR	TEAM	LVL	AGE	PA	R	2B	3B	HR	RBI	BB	SO	SB	CS	EqBRR	AVG	OBP	SLG	MLVr	EqAVG	EqOBP	EqSLG	EqA	VORP	DEFENSE			
2005	BIL	Rk	18	81	16	2	0	4	13	11	22	2	2	-2.7	.257	.358	.457	.082	.176	.247	.284	.175	-15.9	10-RF	2		
2006	DYT	A	19	498	69	42	5	16	81	44	106	19	9	-0.9	.291	.355	.516	.266	.237	.291	.412	.243	-12.6	52-RF	-3	41-CF	5
2007	SAR	A+	20	298	49	27	5	11	49	24	67	4	4	0.0	.325	.379	.586	.381	.250	.305	.478	.262	10.0	49-CF	-2	18-RF	-1
2007	CHT	AA	20	74	10	7	1	4	15	8	20	2	1	-0.1	.333	.405	.652	.494	.254	.324	.552	.286	5.3	11-CF	-1		
2007	LOU	AAA	20	204	28	12	2	11	25	15	48	2	2	-1.5	.305	.358	.567	.321	.282	.333	.548	.287	16.4	40-CF	0		
2008	CIN	MLB	21	652	91	45	4	29	99	57	154	11	5	1.2	.269	.336	.512	.085	.265	.332	.503	.277	29.9	152-CF	-4		

Breakout: 47% Improve: 77% Collapse: 2% Attrition: 5%   Comparables: Cliff Floyd, Eric Chavez, Ian Stewart, Manny Ramirez

Perhaps the top prospect in all of baseball, Bruce is certainly the top dog in the Reds' organization. He's been playing center in the minors and holding his own, but his bat will play anywhere; he tallied 80 extra-base hits across three levels in 2007. Bruce won't be old enough to buy a drink in most major league cities until after the season starts, but if he's not patrolling some portion of the Cincinnati outfield by then, it won't be because of his performance. The kid is ready, and the Hamilton deal creates an opening.

Jorge Cantu — INF

Bats: R Throws: R Height: 6' 3" Weight: 200 Born: January 30, 1982 Age: 26

YEAR	TEAM	LVL	AGE	PA	R	2B	3B	HR	RBI	BB	SO	SB	CS	EqBRR	AVG	OBP	SLG	MLVr	EqAVG	EqOBP	EqSLG	EqA	VORP	DEFENSE			
2005	TBA	MLB	23	630	73	40	1	28	117	19	83	1	0	-0.2	.286	.311	.497	.094	.295	.329	.523	.285	31.2	76-2B	-9	57-3B	-11
2006	TBA	MLB	24	448	40	18	2	14	62	26	91	1	1	-0.6	.249	.295	.404	-.144	.250	.304	.419	.249	3.0	102-2B	-12		
2007	DUR	AAA	25	100	12	5	1	1	10	8	21	0	0	-0.2	.242	.300	.352	-.145	.220	.280	.330	.214	-4.9				
2007	TBA	MLB	25	65	4	1	0	0	4	5	16	0	0	0.2	.207	.277	.224	-.424	.207	.288	.224	.185	-5.1				
2007	LOU	AAA	25	102	12	9	0	2	13	5	15	0	0	-1.0	.309	.363	.468	.195	.295	.343	.463	.275	6.3	12-2B	2		
2007	CIN	MLB	25	68	8	8	0	1	9	7	10	0	0	-1.1	.298	.382	.491	.183	.298	.382	.526	.309	4.1	12-1B	-1		
2008	FLO	MLB	26	322	35	18	1	10	43	22	56	2	1	-0.7	.271	.327	.437	-.028	.271	.326	.448	.261	11.2	78-2B	-8		

Breakout: 22% Improve: 51% Collapse: 25% Attrition: 22%   Comparables: Francisco Cabrera, Mike Lowell, Guillermo Velasquez, Rob Cosby

Cantu is a butcher in the field, so after a poor season at the plate in 2006, the Devil Rays made him fight for his job in spring training. That didn't work out, and after struggling in the minors, he was dealt to the Reds at the deadline. Cantu's power on contact was a good match for Cincinnati's home park, but he didn't get much opportunity there despite much better results at the plate. Released in December, Cantu caught on with Florida on a minor league deal with a hope of taking advantage of their wide open third-base situation.

Chris Dickerson — OF

Bats: L Throws: L Height: 6' 4" Weight: 212 Born: April 10, 1982 Age: 26

YEAR	TEAM	LVL	AGE	PA	R	2B	3B	HR	RBI	BB	SO	SB	CS	EqBRR	AVG	OBP	SLG	MLVr	EqAVG	EqOBP	EqSLG	EqA	VORP	DEFENSE			
2005	SAR	A+	23	505	68	17	7	11	43	53	124	19	3	5.1	.236	.325	.383	-.018	.199	.276	.324	.215	-27.6	91-CF	-4	16-LF	-2
2006	CHT	AA	24	465	65	21	7	12	48	65	129	21	6	1.2	.242	.355	.424	.104	.236	.338	.432	.269	13.7	107-CF	4		
2007	CHT	AA	25	123	11	4	1	1	11	7	31	7	2	-0.5	.272	.325	.351	-.077	.233	.276	.310	.209	-6.1	29-CF	-3		
2007	LOU	AAA	25	416	58	11	6	13	44	52	131	23	5	2.2	.260	.361	.435	.107	.223	.323	.401	.259	2.9	57-CF	-3	27-LF	-1
2008	CIN	MLB	26	526	68	23	5	15	54	51	147	21	6	1.7	.240	.319	.408	-.104	.237	.315	.402	.249	4.3	124-CF	0		

Breakout: 17% Improve: 52% Collapse: 22% Attrition: 13%   Comparables: George Lombard, Colin Porter, Kinnis Pledger, Abraham Nuñez

In a system full of athletes, the Reds think Dickerson might be their best. If so, it makes you wonder about their ability to perceive the difference between athletic ability and useful baseball skills. Dickerson is a fourth outfielder at most, in large part because of his struggles against his fellow lefties. Dickerson has the potential to play once a week in the bigs, but he could also spend his prime years becoming a local hero in Louisville.

Adam Dunn — LF

Bats: L   Throws: R   Height: 6' 6"   Weight: 275   Born: November 9, 1979   Age: 28

YEAR	TEAM	LVL	AGE	PA	R	2B	3B	HR	RBI	BB	SO	SB	CS	EqBRR	AVG	OBP	SLG	MLVr	EqAVG	EqOBP	EqSLG	EqA	VORP	DEFENSE	
2005	CIN	MLB	25	671	107	35	2	40	101	114	168	4	2	-2.6	.247	.387	.540	.241	.241	.383	.541	.308	45.0	124-LF -11	29-1B -2
2006	CIN	MLB	26	683	99	24	0	40	92	112	194	7	0	-0.8	.234	.365	.490	.098	.223	.359	.470	.286	23.5	148-LF -13	
2007	CIN	MLB	27	632	101	27	2	40	106	101	165	9	2	1.6	.264	.386	.554	.245	.257	.384	.552	.312	45.5	133-LF -17	
2008	CIN	MLB	28	579	96	26	2	36	97	95	143	7	2	-0.2	.261	.388	.549	.208	.257	.384	.540	.306	35.8	136-LF -10	

Breakout: 18% Improve: 51% Collapse: 16% Attrition: 16%   Comparables: Calvin Pickering, Troy Glaus, Mike Epstein, Bob Hamelin

It says all you need to know about the relationship between Dunn and the Reds that picking up the big slugger's $13 million contract option for 2008 wasn't a foregone conclusion. His low batting averages and high strikeout totals still cloud people's judgment about his value; meanwhile, he just keeps on notching 40-homer/100-walk seasons. It doesn't help his cause that he's now built like an NFL linebacker, rather than the more streamlined high school quarterback he used to be. Given the outfield talent the Reds have at the major league level and coming through the pipeline, it would be a surprise to see Dunn in a Reds uniform come August 1.

Edwin Encarnacion — 3B

Bats: R   Throws: R   Height: 6' 1"   Weight: 215   Born: January 7, 1983   Age: 25

YEAR	TEAM	LVL	AGE	PA	R	2B	3B	HR	RBI	BB	SO	SB	CS	EqBRR	AVG	OBP	SLG	MLVr	EqAVG	EqOBP	EqSLG	EqA	VORP	DEFENSE
2005	LOU	AAA	22	330	44	23	0	15	54	33	53	7	2	0.2	.314	.388	.548	.301	.287	.358	.491	.289	26.6	75-3B -2
2005	CIN	MLB	22	234	25	16	0	9	31	20	60	3	0	-1.1	.232	.308	.436	-.026	.227	.303	.436	.255	3.7	54-3B 4
2006	CIN	MLB	23	463	60	33	1	15	72	41	78	6	3	-0.2	.276	.359	.473	.099	.270	.352	.467	.280	17.0	104-3B -11
2007	LOU	AAA	24	47	12	3	0	3	7	1	4	1	0	0.7	.413	.426	.674	.705	.391	.404	.696	.354	10.3	11-3B -3
2007	CIN	MLB	24	556	66	25	1	16	76	39	86	8	1	0.7	.289	.356	.438	.062	.283	.353	.435	.275	20.3	131-3B -10
2008	CIN	MLB	25	561	80	31	2	23	81	48	89	8	2	0.1	.285	.356	.493	.109	.282	.352	.486	.282	30.2	132-3B -3

Breakout: 19% Improve: 53% Collapse: 16% Attrition: 7%   Comparables: Khalil Greene, Doug Rader, Don Money, Larry Parrish

After wearing out Jerry Narron's good will in 2007, Edwin Encarnacion will get a fresh start with a new manager. A mid-May demotion to Triple-A lit a fire under the young third baseman, who took out his frustrations on the International League for a couple of weeks, then went on to bat .307/.370/.476 after his return to the majors. He'd be well advised to keep the initiative—the new boss, Dusty Baker, has a doghouse twice as roomy as his predecessors' and is particularly ill-disposed toward talented youths who don't give their all on defense.

Juan Francisco — 3B

Bats: S   Throws: R   Height: 6' 2"   Weight: 180   Born: June 24, 1987   Age: 21

YEAR	TEAM	LVL	AGE	PA	R	2B	3B	HR	RBI	BB	SO	SB	CS	EqBRR	AVG	OBP	SLG	MLVr	EqAVG	EqOBP	EqSLG	EqA	VORP	DEFENSE
2006	RDS	Rk	19	190	24	14	0	3	30	6	35	2	0	1.8	.280	.305	.407	.101	.227	.242	.335	.195	-26.9	37-3B 0
2007	DYT	A	20	562	69	21	4	25	90	23	161	12	6	-3.5	.268	.301	.463	.104	.212	.240	.353	.200	-27.4	116-3B -5
2008	CIN	MLB	21	588	48	27	2	14	57	23	167	9	4	-0.1	.221	.254	.355	-.303	.218	.252	.349	.198	-20.2	138-3B -1

Breakout: 33% Improve: 59% Collapse: 22% Attrition: 12%   Comparables: Wilkin Ramirez, Juan Melo, Jose Lopez, Tony Blanco

Juan Francisco is very young, has power from both sides of the plate, and is about as raw as carpaccio. Still, a twenty-year-old who leads the Midwest League in homers is definitely doing something right, even if he's sporting a nearly eight-to-one whiff-to-walk ratio. It's too soon to say if this cannon-armed infielder's destiny is to be the next Cory Snyder, but a move to the outfield is likely in his future.

Todd Frazier — SS

Bats: R   Throws: R   Height: 6' 3"   Weight: 215   Born: February 12, 1986   Age: 22

YEAR	TEAM	LVL	AGE	PA	R	2B	3B	HR	RBI	BB	SO	SB	CS	EqBRR	AVG	OBP	SLG	MLVr	EqAVG	EqOBP	EqSLG	EqA	VORP	DEFENSE
2007	BIL	Rk	21	186	29	6	5	5	25	18	22	3	3	0.2	.319	.409	.513	.304	.237	.301	.349	.227	-2.0	34-SS -6
2008	CIN	MLB	22	590	65	32	3	12	60	49	117	9	4	0.8	.242	.310	.383	-.152	.239	.306	.376	.235	6.3	138-SS -5

Breakout: 27% Improve: 59% Collapse: 22% Attrition: 2%   Comparables: Hunter Pence, Mike Gulan, Scott Hairston, Tim Hummel

Scouts spend too much time finding stuff not to like about Frazier. Sure, the Reds' supplemental first-round pick out of Rutgers last June isn't really a shortstop. Sure everything he does, from fielding to throwing to swinging a bat, just looks a little . . . abnormal. What they ignore is that he's been getting the job done as an amateur for what seems like forever; he played his first nationally televised game almost a decade ago when he led his team to the Little League World Series. Frazier could end up an offensive force and should have no problem carrying third or second base (though the former is more likely).

Ryan Freel — UT

Bats: R **Throws:** R **Height:** 5′ 10″ **Weight:** 185 **Born:** March 8, 1976 **Age:** 32

YEAR	TEAM	LVL	AGE	PA	R	2B	3B	HR	RBI	BB	SO	SB	CS	EqBRR	AVG	OBP	SLG	MLVr	EqAVG	EqOBP	EqSLG	EqA	VORP	DEFENSE			
2005	CIN	MLB	29	431	69	19	3	4	21	51	59	36	10	5.6	.271	.371	.371	.020	.273	.373	.381	.275	15.4	44-2B	3	19-LF	3
2006	CIN	MLB	30	523	67	30	2	8	27	57	98	37	11	-1.3	.271	.363	.399	.007	.268	.362	.398	.272	16.4	45-CF	1	40-RF	6
2007	CIN	MLB	31	304	44	13	3	3	16	18	47	15	8	-0.2	.245	.308	.347	-.171	.253	.317	.365	.236	-4.7	50-CF	-4	14-3B	1
2008	CIN	MLB	32	334	45	15	2	5	28	30	51	15	4	1.1	.261	.334	.371	-.111	.257	.330	.365	.247	3.6	81-CF	1		

Breakout: 9% **Improve:** 26% **Collapse:** 40% **Attrition:** 30% **Comparables:** Darren Lewis, Alan Bannister, Lonnie Smith, Jacob Brumfield

At the end of May, Freel got his bell rung in a full-tilt outfield collision with Norris Hopper and suffered what Freel cheerfully claims was the "eighth or ninth" concussion of his career. It's injuries like this, caused by Freel's hard-charging style of play, that everyone believes will be the end of him. However, it was the innocuous-sounding "loose cartilage" in Freel's right knee that required surgery and actually ended his 2007 season. Freel's game depends on his wheels, and he's already at a dangerous age for a speed player. Much of his value is gone if he's left his explosive first step on the operating table.

Alex Gonzalez — SS

Bats: R **Throws:** R **Height:** 6′ 0″ **Weight:** 200 **Born:** February 15, 1977 **Age:** 31

YEAR	TEAM	LVL	AGE	PA	R	2B	3B	HR	RBI	BB	SO	SB	CS	EqBRR	AVG	OBP	SLG	MLVr	EqAVG	EqOBP	EqSLG	EqA	VORP	DEFENSE	
2005	FLO	MLB	28	478	45	30	0	5	45	31	81	5	3	-2.8	.264	.319	.368	-.061	.267	.321	.377	.245	9.5	122-SS	0
2006	BOS	MLB	29	429	48	24	2	9	50	22	67	1	0	0.4	.255	.299	.397	-.151	.251	.302	.397	.245	3.2	109-SS	-4
2007	CIN	MLB	30	430	55	27	1	16	55	24	75	0	1	1.0	.272	.325	.468	.039	.268	.322	.467	.267	17.4	98-SS	-7
2008	CIN	MLB	31	377	41	22	1	11	47	25	62	2	1	-0.3	.261	.315	.424	-.075	.257	.312	.417	.247	11.3	90-SS	-4

Breakout: 12% **Improve:** 38% **Collapse:** 34% **Attrition:** 28% **Comparables:** Greg Gagne, Travis Fryman, Max Alvis, Pat Meares

It's tempting to chalk up Gonzalez's power surge to his new ballpark, but that would be a mistake: he was awful at the GABP in his first year as a Red (.242/.309/.440) and hit as many homers on the road as he did at home. Gonzalez missed parts of the season caring for his infant son, who was ill, and in September he was limited by a bone bruise. Jeff Keppinger might have Pipped him in that time, but with a new manager in place, that slate is wiped clean; Gonzalez's defensive reputation should give him the leg up.

Ken Griffey Jr. — RF

Bats: L **Throws:** L **Height:** 6′ 3″ **Weight:** 230 **Born:** November 21, 1969 **Age:** 38

YEAR	TEAM	LVL	AGE	PA	R	2B	3B	HR	RBI	BB	SO	SB	CS	EqBRR	AVG	OBP	SLG	MLVr	EqAVG	EqOBP	EqSLG	EqA	VORP	DEFENSE	
2005	CIN	MLB	35	555	85	30	0	35	92	54	93	0	1	-4.4	.301	.369	.576	.316	.297	.366	.582	.311	52.4	121-CF	-18
2006	CIN	MLB	36	472	62	19	0	27	72	39	78	0	0	-0.2	.252	.316	.486	.026	.244	.311	.472	.265	16.0	98-CF	-14
2007	CIN	MLB	37	623	78	24	1	30	93	85	99	6	1	-4.8	.277	.372	.496	.159	.267	.369	.489	.295	31.1	130-RF	2
2008	CIN	MLB	38	435	59	20	1	20	64	47	70	5	2	-1.0	.268	.350	.480	.065	.264	.346	.472	.276	16.5	103-RF	-7

Breakout: 5% **Improve:** 28% **Collapse:** 40% **Attrition:** 28% **Comparables:** Paul O'Neill, Fred McGriff, Cliff Johnson, Luis Gonzalez

Griffey's season ended, like so many before it, with the slugging outfielder prostrated on the turf in pain and needing to be helped off the field. The injury, a "high groin pull," wasn't that gruesome by Griffey standards, but it ended his chances of finishing a season without a major injury for the first time since 2000. Still, the 144 games he was able to complete and his highest WARP score since 2000 justify the decision to move him to right field, where he should remain when healthy. As he's only seven homers away from 600, it's unlikely that Griffey's going to be dealt anywhere in the immediate future, but once that milestone is reached, all bets are off.

Josh Hamilton — CF

Bats: L Throws: L Height: 6' 4" Weight: 235 Born: May 21, 1981 Age: 27

YEAR	TEAM	LVL	AGE	PA	R	2B	3B	HR	RBI	BB	SO	SB	CS	EqBRR	AVG	OBP	SLG	MLVr	EqAVG	EqOBP	EqSLG	EqA	VORP	DEFENSE	
2006	HUD	A-	25	55	7	3	1	0	5	5	11	0	1	0.3	.260	.327	.360	.091	.216	.273	.333	.203	-5.7		
2007	LOU	AAA	26	45	9	1	0	4	8	5	9	3	0	0.6	.350	.422	.675	.604	.325	.400	.650	.342	7.1		
2007	CIN	MLB	26	337	52	17	2	19	47	33	65	3	3	-0.9	.292	.368	.554	.245	.287	.366	.554	.301	26.4	62-CF	-4
2008	TEX	MLB	27	516	72	29	3	19	73	44	108	6	4	0.5	.283	.349	.482	.104	.280	.349	.495	.289	23.2	122-CF	-3

Breakout: 18% Improve: 53% Collapse: 14% Attrition: 8%   Comparables: Cliff Floyd, Paul O'Neill, Harry Anderson, Ryan Klesko

Anyone who's been trapped under a rock since *Seinfeld* went off the air might've missed the story of Josh Hamilton, the 1999 number-one draft pick who became addicted to crack while sidelined with a back injury, then spent close to three years out of organized baseball before finding sobriety and returning to the Devil Rays system in mid-2006. It took a major leap of faith for the Reds to use a major league Rule 5 pick on a player whose only action above A-ball was 23 games at Double-A five years earlier, but their faith was quickly rewarded. Hamilton lit up spring training to stick with the team, and the promise he showed in center field helped justify moving Griffey to a corner. Hamilton's hitting got better as the year went along. If he can learn to hit left-handers, he'll go from very good to outright dangerous given his .637 slugging percentage against right-handers in his rookie season. One Reds source compared Hamilton to Wily Mo Peña in that, "he's doing it all on talent. The difference with Josh is that he'll learn and adjust." A more cynical point of view would be that the Reds should cash in their chips now and deal Hamilton while he's still clean, and his potential still seems unlimited—which is what they did, dealing him to Texas for Edinson Volquez.

Ryan Hanigan — C

Bats: R Throws: R Height: 6' 0" Weight: 195 Born: August 16, 1980 Age: 27

YEAR	TEAM	LVL	AGE	PA	R	2B	3B	HR	RBI	BB	SO	SB	CS	EqBRR	AVG	OBP	SLG	MLVr	EqAVG	EqOBP	EqSLG	EqA	VORP	DEFENSE			
2005	CHT	AA	24	390	45	14	1	4	29	50	41	4	1	-2.2	.321	.418	.405	.166	.271	.357	.359	.256	0.4	44-1B	-2	44-C	-4
2006	CHT	AA	25	150	17	2	0	0	14	19	23	0	0	0.6	.246	.347	.262	-.101	.227	.315	.242	.208	-7.2	23-C	3		
2007	CHT	AA	26	247	30	14	1	3	27	41	30	0	2	-0.6	.299	.420	.426	.188	.265	.374	.377	.270	9.6	55-C	2		
2007	LOU	AAA	26	150	16	5	0	1	9	14	15	0	0	-0.5	.252	.333	.315	-.099	.237	.313	.321	.226	-2.5	31-C	10		
2007	CIN	MLB	26	11	3	1	0	0	2	1	2	0	0	0.7	.300	.364	.400	.031	.300	.364	.400	.269	0.5				
2008	CIN	MLB	27	362	40	16	1	4	33	42	49	3	1	-0.4	.257	.349	.357	-.106	.254	.345	.351	.245	5.9	87-C	3		

Breakout: 20% Improve: 43% Collapse: 28% Attrition: 24%   Comparables: Jeff Horn, Matt Tupman, Brad King, Michel Hernandez

Hanigan has a good batting eye and fine defensive skills (he was near the top of his leagues in throwing out runners), but at 27 he's fated to be a backup. Unfortunately for him, the Reds have Dave Ross and Javier Valentin under contract for 2008, so advancement will require a trade or an injury.

Scott Hatteberg — 1B

Bats: L Throws: R Height: 6' 1" Weight: 210 Born: December 14, 1969 Age: 38

YEAR	TEAM	LVL	AGE	PA	R	2B	3B	HR	RBI	BB	SO	SB	CS	EqBRR	AVG	OBP	SLG	MLVr	EqAVG	EqOBP	EqSLG	EqA	VORP	DEFENSE	
2005	OAK	MLB	35	523	52	19	0	7	59	51	54	0	1	-0.7	.256	.334	.343	-.109	.263	.349	.354	.252	-3.5	49-1B	-2
2006	CIN	MLB	36	539	62	28	0	13	51	74	41	2	2	-2.3	.289	.389	.436	.114	.281	.384	.424	.285	16.9	122-1B	2
2007	CIN	MLB	37	417	50	27	1	10	47	49	35	0	0	0.4	.310	.394	.474	.194	.301	.391	.468	.298	25.1	86-1B	1
2008	CIN	MLB	38	278	36	15	0	7	34	32	26	1	1	-0.7	.285	.368	.440	.057	.281	.364	.433	.274	10.8	68-1B	-3

Breakout: 12% Improve: 42% Collapse: 36% Attrition: 37%   Comparables: J. T. Snow, Dave Bergman, Mark Grace, Rusty Staub

Last year saw Scott Hatteberg post career highs in batting average, slugging percentage, and EqA. Sadly, there's an illusion at hand produced by his home park (Hatteberg picks up 80 points of isolated power at the GABP) and his shrinking playing time against lefties (ten percent of his plate appearances came against portsiders last year, down from 17 percent in 2006). Hatteberg will need that sort of hocus pocus to fight off Joey Votto's advance upon the first base job, but his best trick would be convincing Dusty Baker that he's the second coming of Eric Karros.

Norris Hopper CF

Bats: R   Throws: R   Height: 5' 10"   Weight: 210   Born: March 24, 1979   Age: 29

YEAR	TEAM	LVL	AGE	PA	R	2B	3B	HR	RBI	BB	SO	SB	CS	EqBRR	AVG	OBP	SLG	MLVr	EqAVG	EqOBP	EqSLG	EqA	VORP	DEFENSE			
2005	CHT	AA	26	487	70	15	4	1	37	27	38	25	7	-0.9	.310	.354	.368	.007	.261	.298	.313	.219	-27.2	59-RF	1	28-CF	2
2006	LOU	AAA	27	410	47	11	3	0	26	20	25	25	7	1.6	.347	.378	.392	.166	.320	.354	.370	.261	2.4	56-LF	1	15-CF	2
2006	CIN	MLB	27	47	6	1	0	1	5	6	4	2	2	-0.6	.359	.435	.462	.284	.359	.435	.462	.306	3.4				
2007	CIN	MLB	28	335	51	14	2	0	14	20	33	14	6	1.9	.329	.371	.388	.054	.331	.377	.399	.271	12.6	46-CF	-1	13-LF	2
2008	CIN	MLB	29	354	44	13	2	0	25	22	32	11	4	0.7	.288	.334	.342	-.133	.284	.330	.337	.236	0.4	85-CF	2		

Breakout: 10%   Improve: 26%   Collapse: 46%   Attrition: 31%   Comparables: Alex Sanchez, Aaron Ledesma, John Wehner, Jim Holt

Last year, Hopper made one of the headiest plays you'll ever see. After a vicious diving collision between Hopper and Freel knocked the latter out cold, Hopper had the presence of mind to slide the ball into Freel's glove, getting the out. Aside from that, he's just a fifth outfielder with wheels whose value will diminish significantly once the team no longer needs a caddy for Ken Griffey. As for those gaudy major league rate stats, they're all batting average, and that's all BABIP (.367 in 2007, higher in 2006), though some of that is speed as Hopper at least has the good sense to put more than half of his balls in play on the ground and to run like hell when he does.

Keltavious Jones OF

Bats: L   Throws: L   Height: 5' 9"   Weight: 170   Born: September 21, 1985   Age: 22

YEAR	TEAM	LVL	AGE	PA	R	2B	3B	HR	RBI	BB	SO	SB	CS	EqBRR	AVG	OBP	SLG	MLVr	EqAVG	EqOBP	EqSLG	EqA	VORP	DEFENSE			
2006	RDS	Rk	20	94	20	4	1	0	2	12	15	6	1	1.9	.256	.372	.333	.080	.205	.287	.289	.212	-15.7				
2007	BIL	Rk	21	179	31	11	2	3	25	13	21	7	4	-0.8	.318	.381	.471	.203	.239	.284	.350	.222	-17.2	17-LF	-5	11-CF	0
2007	DYT	A	21	92	10	7	1	0	8	4	23	1	0	0.3	.212	.272	.318	-.163	.172	.209	.264	.152	-12.8	18-LF	0		
2008	CIN	MLB	22	341	32	17	2	3	24	21	73	9	4	0.9	.222	.276	.319	-.312	.219	.273	.314	.201	-15.2	82-LF	-1		

Breakout: 32%   Improve: 50%   Collapse: 28%   Attrition: 17%   Comparables: Joe Holden, Robert Felmy, Dennis Malave, Michael Basse

If you Google "Keltavious," all you're going to get is Jones; like Jhonny Peralta, his is a name made for search engines. A 27th-round pick out of Darton College in 2006, Jones doesn't do any one thing well, but seems to have a knack for playing the game. Scouts call him "heady" rather than toolsy. At his height, he could use another head.

Jeff Keppinger INF

Bats: R   Throws: R   Height: 6' 0"   Weight: 180   Born: April 21, 1980   Age: 28

YEAR	TEAM	LVL	AGE	PA	R	2B	3B	HR	RBI	BB	SO	SB	CS	EqBRR	AVG	OBP	SLG	MLVr	EqAVG	EqOBP	EqSLG	EqA	VORP	DEFENSE			
2005	NOR	AAA	25	278	40	15	3	3	29	16	13	5	1	0.8	.337	.377	.455	.252	.307	.351	.420	.270	14.7	52-2B	8		
2006	NOR	AAA	26	366	36	13	0	2	26	28	21	0	4	-0.3	.300	.353	.359	.105	.287	.341	.349	.243	6.3	54-2B	5	12-LF	1
2006	OMA	AAA	26	142	21	6	1	2	17	12	9	0	0	-1.2	.354	.407	.465	.287	.318	.369	.426	.278	9.7	16-2B	-4		
2006	KCA	MLB	26	67	11	2	0	2	8	5	6	0	0	-0.1	.267	.323	.400	-.090	.271	.338	.407	.260	0.0	12-3B	0		
2007	LOU	AAA	27	261	31	15	1	2	18	23	14	1	1	-1.1	.368	.424	.469	.343	.336	.391	.448	.293	23.3	19-3B	-1	19-2B	3
2007	CIN	MLB	27	276	39	16	2	5	32	24	12	2	1	1.4	.332	.400	.477	.230	.326	.397	.479	.302	22.8	44-SS	-1		
2008	CIN	MLB	28	514	65	28	2	7	52	41	31	5	2	0.0	.305	.364	.418	.036	.301	.360	.411	.267	23.1	121-SS	4		

Breakout: 9%   Improve: 28%   Collapse: 37%   Attrition: 10%   Comparables: Mark Loretta, Cookie Rojas, Placido Polanco, George Kell

A natural second baseman on a team that already has Brandon Phillips, Keppinger ran with his first major playing time at shortstop, holding his own with the glove while delivering beyond all expectations with the bat. If that collapse rate seems high, it's more an acknowledgment that another .330 batting average is unlikely, rather than a repudiation of Keppinger's skills. Given Dusty Baker's affinity for the Neifis of the world, there's reason to worry that the label "offensive shortstop" will doom Keppinger in his new manager's eyes.

Devin Mesoraco C

Bats: R   Throws: R   Height: 6' 1"   Weight: 200   Born: June 19, 1988   Age: 20

YEAR	TEAM	LVL	AGE	PA	R	2B	3B	HR	RBI	BB	SO	SB	CS	EqBRR	AVG	OBP	SLG	MLVr	EqAVG	EqOBP	EqSLG	EqA	VORP	DEFENSE	
2007	RDS	Rk	19	155	16	4	0	1	8	15	26	2	0	-2.1	.219	.310	.270	-.139	.167	.231	.208	.135	-46.9	27-C	-2
2008	CIN	MLB	20	474	26	18	1	5	34	30	123	6	2	-0.6	.189	.245	.267	-.455	.187	.242	.263	.162	-27.8	112-C	-3

Breakout: 70%   Improve: 74%   Collapse: 23%   Attrition: 8%   Comparables: Brandon Snyder, Edgar Cruz, Mike Nixon, Tommy Arko

After taking Mesoraco with the fifteenth overall pick in June, the Reds started every description of his talents with the word "plus." Others aren't as sold on him, describing him as a late first-round talent drafted on scarcity and organizational need. In his professional debut in the Gulf Coast League, Mesoraco showed none of the plus power the Reds trumpeted, but he was limited by hand injuries. He might have been over-drafted, but he's still an impressive talent and was the best high school catcher available in last year's draft.

Brandon Phillips   2B

Bats: R   Throws: R   Height: 6' 0"   Weight: 195   Born: June 28, 1981   Age: 27

YEAR	TEAM	LVL	AGE	PA	R	2B	3B	HR	RBI	BB	SO	SB	CS	EqBRR	AVG	OBP	SLG	MLVr	EqAVG	EqOBP	EqSLG	EqA	VORP	DEFENSE	
2005	BUF	AAA	24	518	79	24	1	15	46	39	90	7	5	-2.2	.256	.326	.409	-.059	.228	.294	.362	.228	-3.2	109-SS	3
2006	CIN	MLB	25	587	65	28	1	17	75	35	88	25	2	3.0	.276	.324	.427	-.020	.271	.320	.416	.263	22.6	136-2B	-9
2007	CIN	MLB	26	702	107	26	6	30	94	33	109	32	8	1.5	.288	.331	.485	.088	.284	.330	.488	.277	37.2	153-2B	14
2008	CIN	MLB	27	629	83	31	3	20	75	39	99	20	4	0.7	.274	.325	.444	-.019	.271	.322	.437	.260	22.4	147-2B	4

Breakout: 16% Improve: 39% Collapse: 22% Attrition: 12%   Comparables: Carlos Garcia, Ty Wigginton, Dan Uggla, Dave Concepcion

Someday, Wayne Krivsky is going to tell his grandkids that he was the guy who saved Brandon Phillips's career. Once out of the Indian's system, Phillips began showing signs of the guy who was so good he was mentioned ahead of Grady Sizemore when they were traded together to Cleveland. That ship has sailed—Phillips will be 27 in June and had a 109/33 K/BB ratio last year, a regression from his first season in Cincy—but as a good defensive second baseman with power and speed, he should be an asset to the organization for his three remaining team-controlled years. Lest anyone go too crazy about his 30/30 achievement, we'd suggest a moratorium on comparisons between Phillips and Joe Morgan until Phillips can crack a .340 OBP.

Dave Ross   C

Bats: R   Throws: R   Height: 6' 2"   Weight: 240   Born: March 19, 1977   Age: 31

YEAR	TEAM	LVL	AGE	PA	R	2B	3B	HR	RBI	BB	SO	SB	CS	EqBRR	AVG	OBP	SLG	MLVr	EqAVG	EqOBP	EqSLG	EqA	VORP	DEFENSE	
2005	PIT	MLB	28	119	9	8	0	3	15	6	24	0	0	-0.3	.222	.263	.380	-.187	.222	.267	.389	.229	-1.1	31-C	5
2005	SDN	MLB	28	19	2	0	1	0	0	0	4	0	0	0.5	.353	.389	.471	.282	.333	.368	.444	.281	1.9		
2006	CIN	MLB	29	296	37	15	1	21	52	37	75	0	0	-1.3	.255	.353	.579	.215	.246	.346	.560	.299	22.6	70-C	5
2007	CIN	MLB	30	348	32	10	0	17	39	30	92	0	0	-1.3	.203	.271	.399	-.198	.196	.270	.395	.228	-3.0	94-C	11
2008	CIN	MLB	31	214	23	10	0	10	30	20	51	1	0	-0.6	.235	.310	.448	-.071	.232	.307	.441	.251	6.1	54-C	2

Breakout: 19% Improve: 42% Collapse: 28% Attrition: 43%   Comparables: Ramon Castro, Tim Laudner, Rich Rowland, Sal Fasano

Ross's 2007 was as bad as his 2006 was good. A late-season concussion kept him out for the better part of August, and he looked shaky even after returning. Ross's defensive problems keep him from being more than a timeshare backstop with the potential to have an occasional hot month at the plate.

Drew Stubbs   CF

Bats: R   Throws: R   Height: 6' 4"   Weight: 200   Born: October 4, 1984   Age: 23

YEAR	TEAM	LVL	AGE	PA	R	2B	3B	HR	RBI	BB	SO	SB	CS	EqBRR	AVG	OBP	SLG	MLVr	EqAVG	EqOBP	EqSLG	EqA	VORP	DEFENSE	
2006	BIL	Rk	21	252	39	7	3	6	24	32	64	19	4	0.9	.252	.368	.400	.063	.195	.271	.288	.204	-29.6	52-CF	6
2007	DYT	A	22	575	93	29	5	12	43	69	142	23	15	-7.1	.270	.364	.421	.140	.210	.289	.324	.216	-24.3	125-CF	6
2008	CIN	MLB	23	580	67	30	4	13	53	54	167	17	8	0.9	.227	.304	.374	-.183	.224	.301	.368	.231	-4.0	136-CF	-1

Breakout: 53% Improve: 75% Collapse: 8%   Attrition: 13%   Comparables: Rick Asadoorian, Chip Ambres, Michael Rosamond, Choo Freeman

Yet another of the athletic Texan outfielders in the Reds organization, Stubbs is likely the team's center fielder of the future. That's not meant as an insult to Bruce's or Hamilton's skills in the middle pasture, just an acknowledgment that Stubbs's glove could probably play at GABP right now. His bat's not yet ready for prime time, however. His patience and long swing make for a total package that compares to Mike Cameron in the unlikely best-case scenario.

Chris Valaika   SS

Bats: R   Throws: R   Height: 6' 1"   Weight: 200   Born: August 14, 1985   Age: 22

YEAR	TEAM	LVL	AGE	PA	R	2B	3B	HR	RBI	BB	SO	SB	CS	EqBRR	AVG	OBP	SLG	MLVr	EqAVG	EqOBP	EqSLG	EqA	VORP	DEFENSE	
2006	BIL	Rk	20	315	58	22	4	8	60	24	61	2	2	1.3	.324	.387	.520	.321	.230	.271	.361	.217	-10.2	65-SS	-4
2007	DYT	A	21	331	38	20	3	10	56	17	72	1	4	-4.3	.307	.353	.493	.250	.231	.269	.377	.220	-4.3	71-SS	-10
2007	SAR	A+	21	241	26	9	1	2	23	13	42	0	3	-1.6	.253	.310	.332	-.113	.217	.267	.290	.192	-12.0	50-SS	-1
2008	CIN	MLB	22	611	54	34	2	13	63	36	149	4	3	0.0	.234	.286	.373	-.213	.230	.283	.367	.220	-1.1	143-SS	-6

Breakout: 41% Improve: 64% Collapse: 16%   Attrition: 7%   Comparables: Tommy Davis, Chad Spann, Aaron Herr, Van Pope

A 2006 third-round pick, Valaika hit well enough in the Midwest League, but his bat balked when he was promoted to High-A Sarasota. That's understandable for someone in his second pro season, but Valaika will play 2008 as an "old" 22-year-old. He was moved across the keystone to play second base in Hawaii this winter, which could mark the beginning of the end of his career at short.

Javier Valentin   C   Bats: S   Throws: R   Height: 5' 10"   Weight: 215   Born: September 19, 1975   Age: 32

YEAR	TEAM	LVL	AGE	PA	R	2B	3B	HR	RBI	BB	SO	SB	CS	EqBRR	AVG	OBP	SLG	MLVr	EqAVG	EqOBP	EqSLG	EqA	VORP	DEFENSE
2005	CIN	MLB	29	254	36	11	0	14	50	30	37	0	0	-0.4	.281	.362	.520	.209	.273	.357	.514	.294	20.8	58-C -2
2006	CIN	MLB	30	201	24	6	1	8	27	13	29	0	0	0.3	.269	.313	.441	-.027	.259	.308	.427	.253	4.5	35-C 3
2007	CIN	MLB	31	265	19	21	0	2	34	19	25	0	0	-2.7	.276	.328	.387	-.064	.269	.327	.380	.249	5.7	53-C -8
2008	CIN	MLB	32	208	23	11	0	6	27	18	25	1	0	-0.6	.269	.333	.424	-.036	.266	.330	.417	.255	7.1	52-C -3

Breakout: 18% Improve: 41% Collapse: 35% Attrition: 36%   Comparables: Jim Essian, Joe Nolan, Ben Molina, Bob Stinson

Javier Valentin is still coming down off of his offensive explosion in 2005. To the Reds' credit, they didn't lose their heads when it happened and think they had a superstar on their hands. Valentin remains a decent hitter for a backup catcher. He's not a good receiver anymore, but he's far from an embarrassment. In short, he's a useful spare part.

Joey Votto   1B   Bats: L   Throws: R   Height: 6' 3"   Weight: 220   Born: September 10, 1983   Age: 24

YEAR	TEAM	LVL	AGE	PA	R	2B	3B	HR	RBI	BB	SO	SB	CS	EqBRR	AVG	OBP	SLG	MLVr	EqAVG	EqOBP	EqSLG	EqA	VORP	DEFENSE
2005	SAR	A+	21	529	64	23	2	17	83	52	122	4	5	-1.8	.256	.330	.425	.055	.213	.278	.348	.218	-32.2	105-1B 1
2006	CHT	AA	22	590	85	46	2	22	77	78	109	24	7	-6.9	.319	.408	.547	.386	.302	.385	.541	.310	55.5	134-1B 10
2007	LOU	AAA	23	580	74	21	2	22	92	70	110	17	10	-5.3	.294	.381	.478	.222	.277	.361	.471	.285	26.1	90-1B 8 34-LF 4
2007	CIN	MLB	23	89	11	7	0	4	17	5	15	1	0	-2.6	.321	.360	.548	.249	.310	.356	.548	.301	6.7	15-1B 1
2008	CIN	MLB	24	590	86	31	2	26	88	62	114	12	4	-0.5	.278	.357	.494	.103	.275	.353	.486	.283	24.6	138-1B 6

Breakout: 20% Improve: 47% Collapse: 13% Attrition: 13%   Comparables: Tino Martinez, Eric Karros, J. T. Snow, Kevin Barker

It is said that the specter of Hee Seop Choi now haunts the upper deck of the Great American Ball Park, trying to warn Joey Votto about how Dusty Baker killed his career. The parallels—big, young, foreign (Votto's Canadian), power-and-patience first baseman challenging aging all-American veteran who can't hit same-handed pitching—aren't lost on us. Votto has a few advantages over Choi, specifically the lack of a language barrier, sufficient athleticism to play a credible left field at Louisville last season, and the aggression (moreso than the actual speed) to swipe a few bases in the minors, even if he gets caught a bit too often. That last element, while not necessarily smart baseball, could be particularly endearing to his new manager, who played the game in the go-go '70s and '80s.

PITCHERS

Bronson Arroyo   Bats: R   Throws: R   Height: 6' 5"   Weight: 195   Born: February 24, 1977   Age: 31

YEAR	TEAM	LVL	AGE	W	L	SV	G	GS	IP	H	BB	SO	HR	GB%	BABIP	STUFF	WHIP	ERA	PERA	EqERA	EqH9	EqBB9	EqSO9	EqHR9	VORP	SN/WX
2005	BOS	MLB	28	14	10	0	35	32	205¹	213	54	100	22	40.1%	.281	5	1.30	4.52	3.92	4.41	8.5	2.3	4.2	0.9	18.7	2.90
2006	CIN	MLB	29	14	11	0	35	35	240²	222	64	184	31	39.9%	.274	18	1.19	3.29	3.44	3.12	7.7	2.0	6.2	1.0	64.9	7.35
2007	CIN	MLB	30	9	15	0	34	34	210²	232	63	156	28	37.6%	.317	13	1.40	4.23	4.28	3.81	8.9	2.2	6.1	1.0	30.7	4.25
2008	CIN	MLB	31	11	10	0	29	29	185	194	53	131	26	42.2%	.292	11	1.34	4.37	4.50	4.34	9.2	2.4	5.6	1.2	25.0	4.10

Breakout: 5% Improve: 22% Collapse: 40% Attrition: 15%   Comparables: John Thomson, Mark Clark, Jim Lonborg, Pat Dobson

The Arroyo the Reds got last year was a little more like the pitcher the Red Sox thought they were giving up in the Wily Mo Peña trade. In retrospect, Arroyo's breakout 2006 was "hit lucky"—his batting average on balls in play was about 29 points lower than the league average, while in 2007 it regressed to some 12 or so points above average. Aside from the hits, his other peripherals were largely steady last year. There's an unavoidable similarity here to another lanky, guitar-playing right-hander, former White Sox ace Jack McDowell, whose career folded after he turned

31. Fortunately for Reds fans, Arroyo wasn't worked anywhere near as hard as the Stickfigure frontman was early in his career. Arroyo was signed through 2010 before last season and should serve as a league-average innings-eater for the term of the contract.

Homer Bailey

Bats: R Throws: R Height: 6' 4" Weight: 205 Born: May 3, 1986 Age: 22

YEAR	TEAM	LVL	AGE	W	L	SV	G	GS	IP	H	BB	SO	HR	GB%	BABIP	STUFF	WHIP	ERA	PERA	EqERA	EqH9	EqBB9	EqSO9	EqHR9	VORP	SN/WX
2005	DYT	A	19	8	4	0	28	21	103²	89	62	125	5	49.3%	.332	13	1.46	4.43	6.71	7.90	10.1	7.9	7.0	1.1	-23.0	—
2006	SAR	A+	20	3	5	0	13	13	70²	49	22	79	6	44.8%	.247	8	1.01	3.33	5.02	6.44	8.1	4.2	6.0	1.6	-6.1	—
2006	CHT	AA	20	7	1	0	13	13	68¹	50	28	77	1	52.4%	.298	39	1.15	1.59	3.82	2.84	8.0	4.3	7.0	0.3	19.4	—
2007	LOU	AAA	21	6	3	0	12	12	67¹	49	32	59	4	46.5%	.254	13	1.20	3.08	3.80	4.73	7.0	4.6	5.7	0.8	6.3	—
2007	CIN	MLB	21	4	2	0	9	9	45¹	43	28	28	3	47.3%	.294	9	1.57	5.76	3.74	5.24	7.6	4.7	5.1	0.6	-1.4	0.63
2008	CIN	MLB	22	6	8	0	32	20	114²	114	69	92	16	44.8%	.292	2	1.60	5.30	5.30	5.32	8.7	4.9	6.4	1.2	3.2	1.10

Breakout: 25% Improve: 52% Collapse: 25% Attrition: 32%   Comparables: Gil Meche, Dennis Blair, Jon Garland, Jim Clancy

It's been around for less than 50 innings at the major league level, but Bailey's Ebby Calvin LaLoosh impression is already starting to wear thin. In the movie, by the time "Nuke" reached the big leagues, he'd experienced some life lessons and gained some maturity. Bailey, on the other hand, appears disinterested to coaches and indifferent to opposing players—not the attitude you want to see from someone who still has a lot to learn about the craft of pitching. It's too soon to declare him the latest Texas schoolboy bust, but 2007 was a disappointment for a prospect who looked like he had the pure stuff to take the league by storm.

Matt Belisle

Bats: R Throws: R Height: 6' 3" Weight: 230 Born: June 6, 1980 Age: 28

YEAR	TEAM	LVL	AGE	W	L	SV	G	GS	IP	H	BB	SO	HR	GB%	BABIP	STUFF	WHIP	ERA	PERA	EqERA	EqH9	EqBB9	EqSO9	EqHR9	VORP	SN/WX
2005	CIN	MLB	25	4	8	1	60	5	85²	101	26	59	11	53.8%	.330	-9	1.48	4.41	5.01	4.78	9.8	2.4	5.5	1.1	3.5	0.60
2006	CIN	MLB	26	2	0	0	30	2	40	43	19	26	5	50.0%	.306	-9	1.55	3.60	4.80	3.57	9.1	3.6	5.4	0.9	9.0	0.39
2007	CIN	MLB	27	8	9	0	30	30	177²	212	43	125	26	43.1%	.336	7	1.44	5.32	4.86	4.79	9.8	1.8	5.9	1.2	7.7	1.70
2008	CIN	MLB	28	9	10	0	37	23	154²	174	44	107	20	47.0%	.311	5	1.41	4.51	4.73	4.51	9.8	2.3	5.5	1.1	17.5	2.90

Breakout: 12% Improve: 48% Collapse: 14% Attrition: 15%   Comparables: John Burkett, Danny Cox, Doc Medich, Carl Pavano

Major league teams keep guys like Belisle around with a big sign over their heads that says "break glass in case of emergency." Unfortunately for all involved, the Reds' emergency last year was that they needed a number-three starter. After a strong April, Belisle got lit up like a Christmas tree, allowing 26 homers from May to September, 17 of them at the Great American Ball Park. Whether or not he's still in the rotation come Opening Day will be a litmus test for the organization's off-season moves.

Bill Bray

Bats: L Throws: L Height: 6' 3" Weight: 220 Born: June 5, 1983 Age: 25

YEAR	TEAM	LVL	AGE	W	L	SV	G	GS	IP	H	BB	SO	HR	GB%	BABIP	STUFF	WHIP	ERA	PERA	EqERA	EqH9	EqBB9	EqSO9	EqHR9	VORP	SN/WX
2005	POT	A+	22	1	0	3	8	0	12²	8	3	18	1	44.8%	.250	10	0.87	2.13	4.56	4.09	8.2	3.3	8.2	1.6	1.8	—
2005	NWO	AAA	22	1	4	2	23	0	21¹	23	9	25	3	39.1%	.351	-7	1.50	5.07	7.16	7.78	11.0	4.1	7.8	1.4	-4.8	—
2006	NWO	AAA	23	4	1	5	21	0	31²	26	9	45	5	41.3%	.300	13	1.12	4.04	5.41	4.80	8.7	3.0	9.9	1.8	2.7	—
2006	WAS	MLB	23	1	1	0	19	0	23	24	9	16	2	50.0%	.314	-3	1.43	3.91	4.42	3.97	9.1	3.2	6.0	0.8	4.2	0.41
2006	CIN	MLB	23	2	1	2	29	0	27²	33	9	23	3	40.7%	.345	1	1.52	4.22	4.75	4.82	10.0	2.6	6.8	1.0	2.9	0.69
2007	LOU	AAA	24	1	2	0	18	0	19	19	6	29	1	49.0%	.383	16	1.32	4.26	4.86	5.79	10.1	3.4	10.1	1.0	-0.4	—
2007	CIN	MLB	24	3	3	1	19	0	14¹	16	5	14	1	43.2%	.357	8	1.47	6.29	3.87	5.52	9.2	2.5	8.0	0.6	-0.4	0.01
2008	CIN	MLB	25	2	2	4	51	1	47¹	46	17	45	5	43.8%	.305	9	1.34	4.13	4.09	4.14	8.6	2.9	7.5	1.0	8.1	0.70

Breakout: 47% Improve: 71% Collapse: 19% Attrition: 23%   Comparables: Jim Crawford, Denny Neagle, Steve Wilson, Bill Lee

Unlike Gary Majewski, with whom he was packaged in the Austin Kearns trade, Bray wasn't injured when he came to the Reds from the Nationals, but the shoulder problems he suffered coming out of spring training last year only reinforced the feeling that the trade was a disaster. Bray's stuff looked strong when he returned to the ballclub in August, even if the results were a tad ugly. He still has the highest ceiling of any of the lefty relief prospects the Reds have on hand.

Jared Burton

Bats: R   Throws: R   Height: 6' 5"   Weight: 230   Born: June 2, 1981   Age: 27

YEAR	TEAM	LVL	AGE	W	L	SV	G	GS	IP	H	BB	SO	HR	GB%	BABIP	STUFF	WHIP	ERA	PERA	EqERA	EqH9	EqBB9	EqSO9	EqHR9	VORP	SN/WX
2005	STO	A+	24	4	4	24	52	0	55¹	44	20	67	2	41.3%	.302	0	1.16	2.60	4.36	4.38	7.5	4.7	6.5	0.7	7.0	—
2006	MID	AA	25	6	5	1	53	0	74²	71	27	66	7	45.5%	.306	-19	1.32	4.12	5.34	5.32	9.5	4.0	5.5	1.3	2.2	—
2007	LOU	AAA	26	1	0	1	10	0	14	11	4	13	0	61.1%	.306	9	1.07	0.64	3.63	1.46	8.0	2.9	6.6	0.0	5.7	—
2007	CIN	MLB	26	4	2	0	47	0	43	28	22	36	2	45.7%	.232	11	1.16	2.51	2.45	2.68	5.2	3.9	7.0	0.4	13.3	1.22
2008	CIN	MLB	27	2	2	2	47	0	49	47	25	40	5	45.1%	.292	-1	1.46	4.39	4.44	4.43	8.4	4.1	6.6	0.9	6.8	0.50

Breakout: 11%   Improve: 27%   Collapse: 47%   Attrition: 17%   Comparables: Mike Garman, Tom Davey, Jeff Nelson, Bill Wertz

Burton is the other Rule 5 pick (after Josh Hamilton) that stuck in Cincinnati last season. Some are suspicious of the injuries that kept him in minor league rehab assignments much of the first half of the season, but regardless of their legitimacy, those assignments paid dividends when the coaches at Louisville got Burton to throw his slider more often, rather than over-relying on his good cut fastball. Adjustments made, Burton was lights-out in the second half, and finished the season as the Reds' second-most effective reliever.

Todd Coffey

Bats: R   Throws: R   Height: 6' 5"   Weight: 255   Born: September 9, 1980   Age: 27

YEAR	TEAM	LVL	AGE	W	L	SV	G	GS	IP	H	BB	SO	HR	GB%	BABIP	STUFF	WHIP	ERA	PERA	EqERA	EqH9	EqBB9	EqSO9	EqHR9	VORP	SN/WX
2005	CIN	MLB	24	4	1	1	57	0	58	84	11	26	5	53.8%	.371	-16	1.64	4.50	6.09	5.15	12.2	1.6	3.6	0.8	2.4	0.56
2006	CIN	MLB	25	6	7	8	81	0	78	85	26	60	7	51.8%	.321	5	1.42	3.46	4.17	3.33	9.3	2.5	6.3	0.7	19.8	2.59
2007	LOU	AAA	26	2	0	1	19	0	27	17	5	25	0	56.3%	.254	12	0.81	1.33	2.76	2.08	5.9	2.1	6.2	0.0	10.2	—
2007	CIN	MLB	26	2	1	0	58	0	51	70	19	43	12	58.9%	.358	-20	1.75	5.82	8.05	6.06	11.2	2.8	6.9	1.9	-2.0	-0.55
2008	CIN	MLB	27	3	3	2	58	0	61²	68	18	41	7	52.6%	.309	-3	1.40	4.03	4.37	4.06	9.6	2.4	5.3	0.9	10.7	0.90

Breakout: 36%   Improve: 63%   Collapse: 21%   Attrition: 28%   Comparables: Antonio Alfonseca, Steve Crawford, Chris Reitsma, Steve Woodard

Todd Coffey parlayed a weight-loss program and a scruffy, sprint-in-from-the-bullpen personality into cult hero status last year. As the quirky relievers of yesteryear will tell you, the rituals and hustle may win you fans, but you do have to register the occasional out to keep them. Coffey, a dedicated groundballista, had gopherball problems at home in 2007, surrendering nine big flies in fewer than 29 innings at the GABP. The Reds signed him to a fairly generous extension last April, so despite those troubles, he'll be given every chance to make this year's bullpen.

Jonathan Coutlangus

Bats: L   Throws: L   Height: 6' 1"   Weight: 185   Born: October 21, 1980   Age: 27

YEAR	TEAM	LVL	AGE	W	L	SV	G	GS	IP	H	BB	SO	HR	GB%	BABIP	STUFF	WHIP	ERA	PERA	EqERA	EqH9	EqBB9	EqSO9	EqHR9	VORP	SN/WX
2005	SJO	A+	24	4	0	3	50	0	77	64	29	79	3	55.9%	.318	-5	1.21	3.04	4.95	4.83	8.9	5.1	5.6	0.7	5.9	—
2006	CHT	AA	25	1	3	9	49	0	63	40	32	56	0	59.3%	.250	3	1.14	2.86	3.53	4.50	6.4	5.1	5.2	0.2	7.3	—
2007	LOU	AAA	26	2	0	0	9	0	11¹	14	7	14	3	57.6%	.393	-34	1.86	6.37	16.56	12.19	13.9	6.1	8.7	3.5	-7.5	—
2007	CIN	MLB	26	4	2	0	64	0	41	38	27	38	3	50.0%	.315	8	1.59	4.39	4.01	3.89	7.8	5.0	7.6	0.6	5.3	0.16
2008	CIN	MLB	27	2	2	2	46	0	38²	40	23	32	4	49.3%	.312	-4	1.62	4.83	5.05	4.88	8.9	4.9	6.7	0.8	3.0	0.20

Breakout: 17%   Improve: 38%   Collapse: 37%   Attrition: 40%   Comparables: Pedro A. Martinez, Len Whitehouse, Gene Walter, Gary Lavelle

Hasn't this guy taken enough abuse because of his last name already? Did you come here expecting some sophomoric sex joke rather than a mature discussion of his near-sidearm delivery or his fastball/slider mix? Did you think we'd giggle like Beavis instead of pointing out that his future as an effective LOOGY is imperiled only by spotty control, and that if he could find the strike zone more consistently, he might be good enough against righties to earn a full setup spot? Shame on you.

Johnny Cueto

Bats: R   Throws: R   Height: 5' 10"   Weight: 198   Born: February 15, 1986   Age: 22

YEAR	TEAM	LVL	AGE	W	L	SV	G	GS	IP	H	BB	SO	HR	GB%	BABIP	STUFF	WHIP	ERA	PERA	EqERA	EqH9	EqBB9	EqSO9	EqHR9	VORP	SN/WX
2006	DYT	A	20	8	1	0	14	14	76¹	52	15	82	5	53.4%	.254	4	0.88	2.60	5.61	5.07	8.9	3.8	5.6	1.8	3.9	—
2006	SAR	A+	20	7	2	0	12	12	61	48	23	61	6	37.0%	.268	-2	1.16	3.54	6.42	5.80	9.4	5.1	5.6	1.8	-1.2	—
2007	SAR	A+	21	4	5	0	14	14	78¹	72	21	72	3	47.4%	.304	10	1.19	3.33	4.78	5.23	9.2	3.6	5.2	0.9	3.0	—
2007	CHT	AA	21	6	3	0	10	10	61	52	11	77	6	37.2%	.324	26	1.03	3.10	4.74	4.32	8.8	2.0	7.6	1.4	8.3	—
2007	LOU	AAA	21	2	1	0	4	4	22	22	2	21	2	34.4%	.323	20	1.09	2.05	5.13	3.10	10.2	1.3	6.6	1.3	5.6	—
2008	*CIN*	*MLB*	*22*	*8*	*9*	*0*	*26*	*26*	*150*	*160*	*54*	*122*	*25*	*40.7%*	*.299*	*14*	*1.42*	*4.83*	*5.07*	*4.77*	*9.3*	*2.9*	*6.5*	*1.4*	*13.0*	*2.60*

Breakout: 19% Improve: 49% Collapse: 18% Attrition: 14%   *Comparables: John Stephens, Juan Peña, Dicky Gonzalez, Anibal Sanchez*

Cueto hopscotched three levels in 2007, which is a pretty good indication of how high the Reds are on the young right-hander. He has a plus slider, clean mechanics, and a fastball that gets up into the mid-90s. Since he's under-sized, there are questions about him holding up to a starter's workload, but he's been able to counter those concerns with solid command and efficiency and had enough left in the tank at the end of last season to throw another 31 innings in winter ball. He could break into the big-league rotation out of spring training.

Aaron Harang

Bats: R   Throws: R   Height: 6' 7"   Weight: 275   Born: May 9, 1978   Age: 30

YEAR	TEAM	LVL	AGE	W	L	SV	G	GS	IP	H	BB	SO	HR	GB%	BABIP	STUFF	WHIP	ERA	PERA	EqERA	EqH9	EqBB9	EqSO9	EqHR9	VORP	SN/WX
2005	CIN	MLB	27	11	13	0	32	32	211²	217	51	163	22	41.1%	.311	19	1.27	3.83	3.83	3.66	8.6	2.0	6.3	0.9	38.9	4.85
2006	CIN	MLB	28	16	11	0	36	35	234¹	242	56	216	28	42.8%	.326	26	1.27	3.76	3.89	3.66	8.8	1.8	7.5	0.9	50.2	6.11
2007	CIN	MLB	29	16	6	0	34	34	231²	213	52	218	28	43.0%	.292	30	1.14	3.73	3.23	3.14	7.4	1.7	7.8	1.0	53.8	6.11
2008	*CIN*	*MLB*	*30*	*13*	*10*	*0*	*31*	*31*	*204*	*202*	*52*	*176*	*26*	*43.7%*	*.296*	*21*	*1.24*	*3.74*	*3.95*	*3.72*	*8.6*	*2.1*	*6.9*	*1.1*	*42.6*	*6.00*

Breakout: 5%   Improve: 37% Collapse: 26% Attrition: 6%   *Comparables: Freddy Garcia, John Candelaria, Don Newcombe, Andy Benes*

Harang stands out on the Reds' pitching staff like a stripper at a James Dobson rally—the one attractive option in a big homely pile of hurlers. Harang's hardly a looker, but winning 16 games for one of the worst teams in baseball is an accomplishment, and he's managed to maintain excellent peripherals to go with those impressive win totals. A late-bloomer on a bad team, he's managed to avoid attention, but he's an ideal anchor to build a young rotation around.

Sam LeCure

Bats: R   Throws: R   Height: 6' 1"   Weight: 190   Born: May 4, 1984   Age: 24

YEAR	TEAM	LVL	AGE	W	L	SV	G	GS	IP	H	BB	SO	HR	GB%	BABIP	STUFF	WHIP	ERA	PERA	EqERA	EqH9	EqBB9	EqSO9	EqHR9	VORP	SN/WX
2005	BIL	Rk	21	5	1	0	13	6	41¹	43	15	44	2	51.3%	.366	-17	1.40	3.27	8.65	7.56	13.0	7.6	4.3	1.4	-7.3	—
2006	SAR	A+	22	7	12	0	27	27	141¹	130	46	115	12	40.9%	.290	-24	1.25	3.44	6.65	6.23	10.5	4.6	4.3	1.6	-8.8	—
2007	CHT	AA	23	7	5	0	21	21	110	119	46	104	12	45.4%	.347	-16	1.50	4.17	7.18	5.77	11.2	4.4	5.7	1.6	-1.9	—
2008	*CIN*	*MLB*	*24*	*5*	*10*	*0*	*31*	*21*	*125²*	*151*	*63*	*86*	*24*	*42.7%*	*.314*	*-6*	*1.70*	*6.18*	*6.41*	*6.11*	*10.5*	*4.1*	*5.5*	*1.7*	*-6.7*	*0.10*

Breakout: 21% Improve: 47% Collapse: 24% Attrition: 11%   *Comparables: Rhett Parrott, Brian Sikorski, Kevin McGehee, Ryan Nye*

The Filthy LeCure doesn't have the same ceiling as the big arms in the system, but he is a more polished product. He also has a unique background as he sat out his junior year in college due to academic problems, but that may have been a blessing in disguise, as the Reds got a fresh arm out of the college game. LeCure is not big, and he lacks that one big pitch to get scouts excited, but he mixes his pitches well, throws strikes, and should be a solid back of the ro-tation option by 2009.

Bobby Livingston

Bats: L   Throws: L   Height: 6' 3"   Weight: 205   Born: September 3, 1982   Age: 25

YEAR	TEAM	LVL	AGE	W	L	SV	G	GS	IP	H	BB	SO	HR	GB%	BABIP	STUFF	WHIP	ERA	PERA	EqERA	EqH9	EqBB9	EqSO9	EqHR9	VORP	SN/WX
2005	SAN	AA	22	8	4	0	18	18	116¹	103	27	78	7	50.6%	.282	1	1.12	2.86	4.27	4.72	8.4	3.2	4.0	0.9	10.4	—
2005	TAC	AAA	22	6	2	0	10	10	51²	53	15	41	2	49.1%	.317	6	1.32	4.70	4.60	6.38	9.9	3.0	5.1	0.6	-4.2	—
2006	TAC	AAA	23	8	11	0	23	22	135¹	165	36	69	18	45.8%	.328	-30	1.49	4.60	7.17	6.36	11.7	2.9	3.2	1.7	-10.6	—
2007	LOU	AAA	24	3	4	0	17	16	104¹	123	17	63	7	54.0%	.340	-3	1.34	3.80	5.50	5.22	11.3	1.8	3.8	0.9	4.2	—
2007	CIN	MLB	24	3	3	0	10	10	56¹	77	8	27	8	43.5%	.342	-2	1.51	5.28	5.25	4.68	10.9	1.1	4.1	1.1	2.5	0.83
2008	*CIN*	*MLB*	*25*	*6*	*9*	*0*	*40*	*21*	*130¹*	*162*	*37*	*66*	*20*	*47.5%*	*.313*	*-8*	*1.52*	*5.38*	*5.53*	*5.37*	*10.8*	*2.3*	*4.0*	*1.3*	*2.9*	*1.10*

Breakout: 19% Improve: 48% Collapse: 27% Attrition: 23%   *Comparables: Eddie Priest, Andrew Lorraine, Jeff Ballard, Mike Bacsik*

The Reds were shocked—shocked!—to learn that Livingston, a pitcher placed on waivers by the Mariners, had a labrum that was in less-than-mint condition. It remains to be seen what will be left of his career after a pit stop on Tim Kremchek's operating table; although labrum surgery isn't the death sentence it once was, Livingston's star was on the wane before the injury.

Gary Majewski

Bats: R   Throws: R   Height: 6' 1"   Weight: 220   Born: February 26, 1980   Age: 28

YEAR	TEAM	LVL	AGE	W	L	SV	G	GS	IP	H	BB	SO	HR	GB%	BABIP	STUFF	WHIP	ERA	PERA	EqERA	EqH9	EqBB9	EqSO9	EqHR9	VORP	SN/WX
2005	WAS	MLB	25	4	4	1	79	0	86	80	37	50	2	47.2%	.288	5	1.36	2.93	3.56	3.56	8.3	3.5	4.7	0.2	19.7	3.07
2006	WAS	MLB	26	3	2	0	46	0	55¹	49	25	34	4	55.9%	.262	-3	1.34	3.58	3.46	3.56	7.6	3.6	5.0	0.6	12.7	0.07
2006	CIN	MLB	26	1	2	0	19	0	15	30	4	9	1	55.6%	.492	-34	2.27	8.40	13.24	10.43	17.8	1.8	4.9	0.6	-3.7	-1.67
2007	LOU	AAA	27	1	1	4	38	0	38²	33	15	30	2	55.5%	.292	-12	1.24	3.95	4.45	4.89	8.7	4.1	5.4	0.8	2.8	—
2007	CIN	MLB	27	0	4	0	32	0	23	43	3	10	3	54.1%	.421	-34	2.00	8.22	10.26	9.00	15.7	0.8	3.9	1.2	-6.3	-1.43
2008	CIN	MLB	28	2	2	2	41	0	43²	49	16	27	4	50.5%	.309	-9	1.49	4.42	4.68	4.46	9.8	3.0	4.9	0.9	5.3	0.40

Breakout: 42% Improve: 62% Collapse: 24% Attrition: 33%   Comparables: Adrian Devine, Matt Whiteside, Dale Murray, Joe Grahe

The front office would much rather Reds fans remember their getting Brandon Phillips for table scraps or grabbing Jeff Keppinger in an equally minor deal, but the swap that brought Majewski to the Queen City might be the deal most emblematic of recent Reds history. Majewski may or may not have been injured when he came over from Jim Bowden's Nationals, but the mere thought of being snookered by Ol' Leatherpants had the Cincy media in a lather. More than a year after his shoulder injury came to light, there's no sign of when or if Majewski will ever get his effectiveness back.

Matthew Maloney

Bats: L   Throws: L   Height: 6' 4"   Weight: 220   Born: January 16, 1984   Age: 24

YEAR	TEAM	LVL	AGE	W	L	SV	G	GS	IP	H	BB	SO	HR	GB%	BABIP	STUFF	WHIP	ERA	PERA	EqERA	EqH9	EqBB9	EqSO9	EqHR9	VORP	SN/WX
2005	BAT	A-	21	2	1	0	8	8	37	38	15	36	2	31.7%	.364	-16	1.43	3.89	8.59	8.80	12.0	7.6	4.1	1.8	-10.9	—
2006	LWD	A	22	16	9	0	27	27	168¹	120	73	180	5	46.2%	.267	9	1.15	2.03	5.51	5.41	8.9	6.4	5.3	0.9	3.2	—
2007	REA	AA	23	9	7	0	21	21	125²	117	45	115	13	43.5%	.300	-9	1.29	3.94	5.65	6.18	9.7	3.9	5.7	1.5	-7.7	—
2007	CHT	AA	23	2	2	0	4	4	28	17	3	39	4	39.3%	.241	27	0.71	2.57	3.73	3.71	6.4	1.4	8.4	2.0	5.6	—
2007	LOU	AAA	23	2	1	0	3	3	17	10	6	23	2	45.9%	.235	16	0.94	3.18	3.75	3.94	6.2	3.4	9.6	1.7	3.0	—
2008	PHI	MLB	24	7	8	0	22	22	125¹	129	56	99	21	41.1%	.290	9	1.48	4.98	5.17	4.95	9.0	3.7	6.4	1.4	9.5	1.90

Breakout: 38% Improve: 69% Collapse: 7% Attrition: 12%   Comparables: J. A. Happ, Micah Bowie, Ed Yarnall, Rob Henkel

Acquired from the Phillies for Kyle Lohse at the trading deadline, Maloney could pay some quick dividends for the Reds, although the payments won't be huge. Maloney's one of those classic finesse left-handers who only throws in the upper 80s, but pounds the strike zone with it, setting up hitters for his changeup and slider. While that's not the most exciting style in the world, Maloney is exceedingly good at it and will likely get his chance at some point in 2008.

Marcus McBeth

Bats: R   Throws: R   Height: 6' 2"   Weight: 195   Born: August 23, 1980   Age: 27

YEAR	TEAM	LVL	AGE	W	L	SV	G	GS	IP	H	BB	SO	HR	GB%	BABIP	STUFF	WHIP	ERA	PERA	EqERA	EqH9	EqBB9	EqSO9	EqHR9	VORP	SN/WX
2005	KNC	A	24	1	2	1	16	0	19²	20	13	21	2	29.8%	.340	-14	1.68	5.03	9.74	8.10	12.4	8.6	5.9	2.2	-4.6	—
2006	MID	AA	25	3	2	25	45	0	54¹	43	20	65	4	42.9%	.287	2	1.16	2.50	4.06	3.52	7.5	3.9	7.2	1.0	12.4	—
2007	SAC	AAA	26	1	0	5	8	0	10	7	3	6	2	43.3%	.185	-15	1.00	1.80	4.32	2.79	6.5	2.8	3.7	1.9	3.0	—
2007	LOU	AAA	26	1	1	12	30	0	31²	33	7	29	2	39.0%	.323	-4	1.26	2.56	4.70	4.31	9.8	2.3	5.7	0.9	4.5	—
2007	CIN	MLB	26	3	2	0	23	0	19²	22	7	17	2	28.6%	.345	2	1.47	5.94	4.16	4.87	8.9	2.7	7.1	0.9	0.1	-0.19
2008	CIN	MLB	27	2	2	3	41	1	41²	41	17	32	7	37.5%	.280	-4	1.40	4.55	4.69	4.49	8.7	3.4	6.1	1.3	5.1	0.50

Breakout: 22% Improve: 40% Collapse: 38% Attrition: 39%   Comparables: Darrel Akerfelds, Floyd Chiffer, Juan Acevedo, Bob Priddy

Converted to pitching from the outfield, Marcus McBeth might actually one of the fastest players in the organization—he was a kick returner for South Carolina before going pro in baseball. Like many a late convert to the mound he has good velocity, but unlike most he has a fantastic changeup, which has translated to odd spurts of dominance in the minors despite the fact that his breaking ball is below average. He should be a bigger part of the bullpen in 2008.

Eric Milton

Bats: L   Throws: L   Height: 6' 3"   Weight: 220   Born: August 4, 1975   Age: 32

YEAR	TEAM	LVL	AGE	W	L	SV	G	GS	IP	H	BB	SO	HR	GB%	BABIP	STUFF	WHIP	ERA	PERA	EqERA	EqH9	EqBB9	EqSO9	EqHR9	VORP	SN/WX
2005	CIN	MLB	29	8	15	0	34	34	186¹	237	52	123	40	33.9%	.317	-19	1.55	6.47	6.10	6.44	10.2	2.2	5.1	1.8	-24.3	-0.06
2006	CIN	MLB	30	8	8	0	26	26	152²	163	42	90	29	32.6%	.275	-6	1.34	5.19	4.42	4.69	8.6	2.1	4.7	1.4	10.2	2.20
2007	CIN	MLB	31	0	4	0	6	6	31¹	39	9	18	4	28.4%	.321	1	1.53	5.18	4.40	4.86	9.5	2.2	4.6	1.1	0.1	0.03
2008	CIN	MLB	32	4	5	0	23	11	74²	88	20	44	14	36.8%	.298	-8	1.45	5.47	5.53	5.37	10.3	2.2	4.7	1.6	1.9	0.60

Breakout: 18%   Improve: 46%   Collapse: 34%   Attrition: 43%   Comparables: Greg Swindell, Mike McCormick, Doyle Alexander, James Baldwin

If Majewski/Kearns was the signature trade of the 21st-century Reds, here's the signature signing. The Reds had money to spend after the 2004 season, and by golly, they were going to spend it. They'd have been better off pocketing the cash, burning it, or spending it on the next Jay Bruce. Heck, the next Bruce Vilanch would have been a better investment than Milton (and no, he didn't write that quip). Elbow surgery last June brought an early end to Milton's time with the Reds. Any future applicants for his services should have distant outfield fences and some patience for rehab.

Tyler Pelland

Bats: R   Throws: L   Height: 6' 0"   Weight: 198   Born: October 9, 1983   Age: 24

YEAR	TEAM	LVL	AGE	W	L	SV	G	GS	IP	H	BB	SO	HR	GB%	BABIP	STUFF	WHIP	ERA	PERA	EqERA	EqH9	EqBB9	EqSO9	EqHR9	VORP	SN/WX
2005	SAR	A+	21	5	8	0	30	15	102¹	103	63	103	5	43.5%	.359	-3	1.62	4.05	7.76	7.03	11.1	8.9	5.3	1.1	-14.0	—
2006	CHT	AA	22	9	5	0	28	28	142	144	89	107	11	42.7%	.331	-15	1.64	3.99	7.97	7.18	11.3	6.6	4.7	1.4	-22.0	—
2007	CHT	AA	23	5	4	2	35	5	66	63	32	71	6	51.1%	.328	-11	1.44	3.95	5.80	6.43	9.6	4.9	6.4	1.3	-5.8	—
2007	LOU	AAA	23	1	1	0	19	0	23²	17	7	27	1	55.9%	.308	11	1.01	3.04	3.51	4.37	7.1	3.2	7.5	0.8	3.1	—
2008	CIN	MLB	24	3	5	2	25	7	59²	64	39	48	8	46.1%	.312	-5	1.72	5.44	5.82	5.44	9.3	5.3	6.4	1.1	1.1	0.40

Breakout: 43%   Improve: 73%   Collapse: 9%   Attrition: 5%   Comparables: Joey Eischen, Steve Dixon, Ricardo Jordan, Aaron Fultz

A shift to the bullpen precipitated a sharp drop in Pelland's walk rate, one that might have been sharp enough to salvage his prospects for a major league career. With a fastball/curve repertoire that's murder on left-handers, he's well positioned for a specialist role in the bigs.

Elizardo Ramirez

Bats: L   Throws: R   Height: 6' 0"   Weight: 190   Born: January 28, 1983   Age: 25

YEAR	TEAM	LVL	AGE	W	L	SV	G	GS	IP	H	BB	SO	HR	GB%	BABIP	STUFF	WHIP	ERA	PERA	EqERA	EqH9	EqBB9	EqSO9	EqHR9	VORP	SN/WX
2005	LOU	AAA	22	7	7	0	21	21	131¹	150	18	82	14	53.1%	.319	-2	1.28	3.77	4.99	4.71	10.2	1.7	3.9	1.2	12.3	—
2005	CIN	MLB	22	0	3	0	6	4	22¹	33	10	9	5	42.7%	.341	-32	1.93	8.48	9.17	9.00	12.1	3.5	3.1	2.0	-7.7	-0.50
2006	LOU	AAA	23	0	1	0	4	4	20	22	2	19	2	24.2%	.333	8	1.20	4.05	5.84	5.68	11.4	1.4	6.2	1.4	-0.2	—
2006	CIN	MLB	23	4	9	0	21	19	104	123	29	69	14	45.4%	.323	4	1.46	5.37	4.88	5.35	9.8	2.1	5.3	1.0	1.0	0.79
2007	LOU	AAA	24	4	3	0	12	12	65	71	19	44	4	52.1%	.325	-3	1.38	3.74	5.34	4.94	10.5	3.0	4.4	0.9	4.5	—
2007	CIN	MLB	24	0	2	0	4	3	16¹	20	8	8	5	40.4%	.294	-29	1.71	7.73	8.42	7.31	10.1	3.9	4.5	2.8	-3.1	-0.26
2008	TEX	MLB	25	4	7	0	38	15	97²	123	37	52	15	47.8%	.320	-11	1.63	5.94	5.59	5.74	10.7	3.1	4.3	1.4	-3.3	0.20

Breakout: 15%   Improve: 33%   Collapse: 29%   Attrition: 30%   Comparables: Luis de los Santos, Dicky Gonzalez, Julio Santana, Mariano Rivera

One could say Easy E was rushed to the majors, but, on the other hand, what was his ceiling? Sometimes described as a control specialist, Ramirez has neither outstanding peripherals nor a consistent out pitch. To add to his troubles, he lost time in 2007 to a recurrence of shoulder tendonitis. He signed a minor league deal with the Rangers.

Brad Salmon

Bats: L   Throws: R   Height: 6' 4"   Weight: 225   Born: January 3, 1980   Age: 28

YEAR	TEAM	LVL	AGE	W	L	SV	G	GS	IP	H	BB	SO	HR	GB%	BABIP	STUFF	WHIP	ERA	PERA	EqERA	EqH9	EqBB9	EqSO9	EqHR9	VORP	SN/WX
2005	CHT	AA	25	3	8	4	38	0	72²	66	31	71	3	49.8%	.326	-4	1.33	3.34	4.78	4.97	9.0	4.6	5.8	0.8	4.7	—
2005	LOU	AAA	25	0	0	0	9	0	16¹	14	5	8	2	59.3%	.231	-22	1.17	3.31	4.02	3.52	7.6	3.5	2.9	1.2	3.5	—
2006	CHT	AA	26	2	1	2	16	0	23¹	18	16	24	0	55.6%	.300	4	1.47	2.73	4.24	3.63	8.1	6.9	6.0	0.4	4.9	—
2006	LOU	AAA	26	5	1	3	39	0	57¹	36	27	72	3	39.7%	.273	15	1.10	2.36	3.83	4.05	6.8	5.1	8.6	0.8	9.2	—
2007	LOU	AAA	27	2	2	4	37	0	43	41	17	40	3	50.8%	.319	-9	1.35	3.56	5.38	4.91	9.6	4.0	6.2	0.9	3.1	—
2007	CIN	MLB	27	0	1	0	26	0	24	22	10	22	3	39.7%	.292	7	1.33	4.13	3.83	3.42	7.6	3.4	7.6	1.1	4.9	-0.29
2008	CIN	MLB	28	2	2	2	44	1	43²	44	22	35	5	44.0%	.299	-3	1.49	4.56	4.71	4.57	8.7	4.0	6.5	0.9	5.1	0.50

Breakout: 13%   Improve: 27%   Collapse: 40%   Attrition: 35%   Comparables: Rodney Myers, Tim Worrell, Mike James, Jerrod Riggan

Salmon's a power reliever who held his own in an extended tryout with the big league club last year. His value is limited by his vulnerability to lefty batters—the splitter he worked on last season to keep them off-balance was only moderately effective. A right-handed relief specialist seems like a luxury the Cincy roster can't afford.

Alexander Smit

Bats: L | Throws: L | Height: 6' 3" | Weight: 210 | Born: October 2, 1985 | Age: 22

YEAR	TEAM	LVL	AGE	W	L	SV	G	GS	IP	H	BB	SO	HR	GB%	BABIP	STUFF	WHIP	ERA	PERA	EqERA	EqH9	EqBB9	EqSO9	EqHR9	VORP	SN/WX
2005	BLT	A	19	1	9	0	14	10	49²	58	28	54	9	41.3%	.345	-32	1.73	5.98	15.71	13.18	14.5	7.8	6.3	3.5	-35.1	—
2005	ELZ	Rk	19	6	1	3	21	0	45²	25	12	86	3	43.2%	.314	21	0.81	1.97	7.65	6.55	10.7	7.3	9.2	1.8	-3.6	—
2006	BLT	A	20	7	2	0	34	13	108²	77	53	141	6	37.0%	.297	1	1.20	2.99	6.88	7.15	9.5	7.9	7.1	1.6	-15.6	—
2007	FTM	A+	21	1	4	1	18	8	50²	62	26	38	4	38.5%	.347	-27	1.74	5.86	9.13	9.91	12.8	6.6	4.1	1.6	-22.2	—
2007	DYT	A	21	2	2	0	5	5	22²	19	8	19	1	40.6%	.295	-8	1.19	1.19	6.73	5.79	10.6	6.3	3.9	1.4	-0.4	—
2007	SAR	A+	21	0	2	0	4	3	17	12	8	19	0	44.2%	.308	13	1.18	3.71	4.18	6.89	7.5	5.7	6.9	0.6	-2.3	—
2008	CIN	MLB	22	3	7	0	27	13	80¹	94	61	59	16	39.7%	.313	-14	1.93	6.77	7.14	6.68	10.2	6.2	5.8	1.7	-9.2	-0.50

Breakout: 45% Improve: 70% Collapse: 14% Attrition: 14%   Comparables: Ryan Rowland-Smith, Daniel Christensen, Juan Cedeno, Dan Cevette

Wayne Krivsky got his big Dutch lefty back from his former employers when he swiped Smit from the Twins on a waiver claim. Smit was available because he'd lost the strike zone in the Florida State League. He's been known to struggle with his mechanics, but has posted some pretty sweet strikeout rates with a deceptive low-90s fastball. He projects as a reliever.

Mike Stanton

Bats: L | Throws: L | Height: 6' 1" | Weight: 215 | Born: June 2, 1967 | Age: 41

YEAR	TEAM	LVL	AGE	W	L	SV	G	GS	IP	H	BB	SO	HR	GB%	BABIP	STUFF	WHIP	ERA	PERA	EqERA	EqH9	EqBB9	EqSO9	EqHR9	VORP	SN/WX
2005	NYA	MLB	38	1	2	0	28	0	14	17	6	12	1	37.0%	.364	-6	1.64	7.07	5.13	7.07	10.3	3.9	7.7	0.6	-2.1	-0.29
2005	WAS	MLB	38	2	1	0	30	0	27²	31	9	14	2	46.3%	.322	-15	1.45	3.57	4.79	4.72	10.1	2.7	4.4	0.7	3.4	1.10
2006	WAS	MLB	39	3	5	0	56	0	44¹	47	21	30	1	43.1%	.333	-1	1.53	4.47	4.13	4.12	9.5	3.7	5.6	0.2	7.3	0.31
2006	SFN	MLB	39	4	2	8	26	0	23¹	23	6	18	1	43.5%	.328	9	1.24	3.09	3.91	2.91	9.6	2.1	6.6	0.4	7.7	1.30
2007	CIN	MLB	40	1	3	0	69	0	57²	75	18	40	6	37.0%	.359	-6	1.61	5.93	5.45	5.28	10.7	2.3	5.9	0.8	-0.5	0.89
2008	CIN	MLB	41	2	2	2	48	0	46²	53	16	30	6	43.7%	.309	-11	1.47	4.62	4.64	4.64	9.9	2.8	5.2	1.0	4.6	0.40

Breakout: 23% Improve: 50% Collapse: 27% Attrition: 41%   Comparables: Jeff Fassero, Harry Gumbert, Jose Mesa, Mike Timlin

Stanton's now on the veteran lefty job-security plan, which makes him as indestructible as a vampire, even after posting a 5.93 ERA at the age of 40. Given his $3 million contract for 2008 and the fact that he's only 74 games shy of Jesse Orosco's record for career appearances, it's unlikely Stanton will just slip off into the night, but that doesn't mean the Reds should be paying so much for his extremely specialized services.

Daryl Thompson

Bats: R | Throws: R | Height: 6' 1" | Weight: 183 | Born: November 2, 1985 | Age: 22

YEAR	TEAM	LVL	AGE	W	L	SV	G	GS	IP	H	BB	SO	HR	GB%	BABIP	STUFF	WHIP	ERA	PERA	EqERA	EqH9	EqBB9	EqSO9	EqHR9	VORP	SN/WX
2005	SAV	A	19	2	3	0	11	11	53²	46	24	48	3	47.4%	.293	-5	1.30	3.35	6.94	6.80	10.6	7.2	4.4	1.4	-6.0	—
2006	RDS	Rk	20	0	0	0	5	4	14¹	10	4	16	1	40.0%	.321	-4	0.99	2.55	10.83	7.20	12.6	6.3	7.2	3.6	-1.8	—
2007	DYT	A	21	5	0	0	5	5	28	16	2	24	1	34.2%	.208	7	0.64	0.96	3.92	3.24	6.8	2.2	4.0	1.1	6.6	—
2007	SAR	A+	21	9	5	0	22	22	105	106	31	97	19	34.8%	.301	-50	1.30	3.77	10.11	7.23	11.5	4.1	5.5	3.3	-16.9	—
2008	CIN	MLB	22	6	10	0	32	22	129	150	58	89	31	37.3%	.293	-5	1.60	6.13	6.45	5.96	10.1	3.6	5.5	2.1	-5.1	0.30

Breakout: 31% Improve: 62% Collapse: 11% Attrition: 7%   Comparables: Scott Mathieson, Calvin Medlock, Jensen Lewis, Jack Cressend

Thompson was the pitcher in the Kearns trade who had his shoulder surgery *before* coming to the Reds. He's bounced back nicely and was young for his levels last year, but his extreme fly-ball tendencies and league-leading 19 homers in the pitcher-friendly Florida State League have to give one pause.

Philippe-Alexandre Valiquette

Bats: L   Throws: L   Height: 6' 0"   Weight: 175   Born: February 14, 1987   Age: 21

YEAR	TEAM	LVL	AGE	W	L	SV	G	GS	IP	H	BB	SO	HR	GB%	BABIP	STUFF	WHIP	ERA	PERA	EqERA	EqH9	EqBB9	EqSO9	EqHR9	VORP	SN/WX
2005	BIL	Rk	18	2	1	0	7	3	21	23	10	18	1	41.9%	.367	-25	1.57	6.43	9.05	11.65	12.7	9.0	3.2	1.6	-11.4	—
2005	DYT	A	18	2	5	0	19	16	64¹	81	44	42	3	57.0%	.368	-24	1.94	6.30	9.85	10.83	13.7	9.1	3.1	1.1	-32.4	—
2006	DYT	A	19	2	4	0	12	9	37²	52	21	24	5	44.9%	.362	-71	1.96	7.50	22.11	19.80	17.7	9.6	2.7	3.6	-47.3	—
2007	BIL	Rk	20	3	1	3	11	0	40²	31	11	29	0	48.8%	.267	-13	1.03	1.77	4.51	5.89	7.4	5.2	2.5	0.5	-1.2	—
2007	DYT	A	20	1	2	0	7	0	10²	17	2	8	1	38.1%	.400	-54	1.78	6.73	14.26	14.90	17.7	3.7	2.8	1.9	-10.0	—
2008	CIN	MLB	21	2	5	0	27	8	62	79	42	25	14	44.1%	.298	-33	1.95	7.75	7.52	7.74	11.1	5.6	3.2	1.9	-15.8	-1.20

Breakout: 40%   Improve: 65%   Collapse: 17%   Attrition: 15%   Comparables: Eric O'Flaherty, Dave Bigham, Paul Mildren, Dave Giberti

Montreal native Valiquette was on his third go-round at Dayton last year, having started his pro career there in 2005, quit baseball over his struggles there in mid-2006, and returned there after being convinced to rejoin the organization in 2007. He still hasn't solved the Midwest League, but he's likely to keep on getting chances to do so. That's how valuable lefties who can touch 95 mph with their fastball are.

Sean Watson

Bats: R   Throws: R   Height: 6' 2"   Weight: 220   Born: July 24, 1985   Age: 22

YEAR	TEAM	LVL	AGE	W	L	SV	G	GS	IP	H	BB	SO	HR	GB%	BABIP	STUFF	WHIP	ERA	PERA	EqERA	EqH9	EqBB9	EqSO9	EqHR9	VORP	SN/WX
2006	BIL	Rk	20	0	0	1	7	4	23²	16	5	19	0	46.3%	.246	-8	0.91	1.55	4.54	5.57	8.1	3.9	3.4	0.4	0.1	—
2006	DYT	A	20	1	2	0	10	0	14	22	5	16	2	41.7%	.444	-63	1.93	9.00	27.94	21.60	20.8	6.2	5.4	3.9	-20.8	—
2007	DYT	A	21	5	2	0	13	13	71²	58	13	85	7	45.5%	.309	-10	0.99	1.88	7.89	5.86	11.4	4.0	6.3	2.5	-1.7	—
2007	SAR	A+	21	4	4	0	14	10	54²	54	21	50	8	41.2%	.303	-25	1.37	5.43	8.69	7.97	10.9	5.1	5.3	2.7	-13.1	—
2008	CIN	MLB	22	5	9	0	30	19	112¹	135	56	77	24	42.6%	.310	-7	1.70	6.43	6.61	6.33	10.5	4.1	5.5	1.8	-9.2	-0.20

Breakout: 44%   Improve: 71%   Collapse: 13%   Attrition: 8%   Comparables: Andy Rush, Jensen Lewis, Jeff Yoder, Claudio Vargas

Watson was a closer in college, so concern over his ERA going up about three and a half runs after his move from Low-A to High-A should be tempered by the understanding that he was moving into uncharted territory in terms of workload. The good news is that the starting experiment seems to be over; this season, Watson will be back in the bullpen, where he can focus on only his fastball and curve, both of which are plus pitches that could get him to the big leagues soon.

Dave Weathers

Bats: R   Throws: R   Height: 6' 3"   Weight: 235   Born: September 25, 1969   Age: 38

YEAR	TEAM	LVL	AGE	W	L	SV	G	GS	IP	H	BB	SO	HR	GB%	BABIP	STUFF	WHIP	ERA	PERA	EqERA	EqH9	EqBB9	EqSO9	EqHR9	VORP	SN/WX
2005	CIN	MLB	35	7	4	15	73	0	77²	71	29	61	7	52.3%	.283	4	1.29	3.94	3.39	3.74	7.4	2.9	6.2	0.8	11.6	2.59
2006	CIN	MLB	36	4	4	12	67	0	73²	61	34	50	12	46.5%	.236	-9	1.29	3.54	3.52	2.97	6.7	3.4	5.5	1.2	18.9	2.57
2007	CIN	MLB	37	2	6	33	70	0	77²	67	27	48	4	38.3%	.268	7	1.21	3.59	2.77	3.14	6.7	2.6	5.0	0.3	18.5	3.19
2008	CIN	MLB	38	2	4	20	38	0	46	48	19	27	6	43.9%	.284	-15	1.47	4.48	4.75	4.47	9.1	3.5	4.7	1.1	5.9	0.80

Breakout: 7%   Improve: 19%   Collapse: 70%   Attrition: 38%   Comparables: Ted Power, Jose Mesa, Bill Campbell, Al Benton

It took him seventeen years and 824 appearances in the majors, but Weathers finally became a full-season closer in 2007. At 37, he was the oldest player ever to collect more than 30 saves for the first time. That the Reds didn't ship him out amid the increased interest his "proven closer" status invoked was something of a missed opportunity, particularly as the addition of Francisco Cordero knocks Weathers back into his more familiar setup role.

Travis Wood

Bats: R   Throws: L   Height: 5' 11"   Weight: 166   Born: February 6, 1987   Age: 21

YEAR	TEAM	LVL	AGE	W	L	SV	G	GS	IP	H	BB	SO	HR	GB%	BABIP	STUFF	WHIP	ERA	PERA	EqERA	EqH9	EqBB9	EqSO9	EqHR9	VORP	SN/WX
2005	BIL	Rk	18	2	0	0	6	4	24²	15	13	22	0	36.9%	.234	1	1.13	1.82	5.62	4.35	6.5	9.6	3.0	0.4	2.9	—
2006	DYT	A	19	10	5	0	27	27	140	108	56	133	14	37.9%	.265	-33	1.17	3.66	8.30	7.70	10.2	6.7	4.7	2.7	-27.5	—
2007	SAR	A+	20	3	2	0	12	12	46¹	49	27	54	6	37.1%	.350	-5	1.64	4.86	10.13	9.36	12.0	7.4	7.2	2.4	-17.3	—
2008	CIN	MLB	21	4	8	0	28	18	102²	113	72	87	22	38.2%	.302	-5	1.80	6.30	6.81	6.15	9.6	5.7	6.7	1.9	-5.8	0.00

Breakout: 51%   Improve: 73%   Collapse: 12%   Attrition: 10%   Comparables: Chuck Tiffany, Jason Miller, Alexander Smit, Paul Byrd

A second-round pick in 2005, Wood was shut down with shoulder tendonitis last year after pitching just 46 innings. He's a lefty, he just turned 21, and even with the tendonitis, he maintained a respectable strikeout rate at High-A

Sarasota. Nonetheless, some Reds officials have already begun comparing Wood to former first-round bust Chris Gruler.

LINEOUTS

Hitters

PLAYER	TEAM	LVL	AGE	PA	R	2B	3B	HR	RBI	BB	SO	SB-CS	EqBRR	AVG/OBP/SLG	MLVr	EqAVG/EqOBP/EqSLG	EqA	VORP
INF J. Castro	CIN	MLB	35	98	5	5	0	0	5	4	21	0-0	-0.5	.180/.211/.236	-.541	.178/.216/.233	.149	-9.4
UT B. Coats*	IOW	AAA	25	508	81	21	3	11	59	44	74	18-2	3.7	.303/.363/.435	.057	.266/.327/.386	.256	-5.0
	CIN	MLB	25	38	2	4	0	0	2	3	15	0-0	-0.4	.206/.263/.324	-.315	.206/.263/.324	.208	-2.0
SS P. Janish	CHT	AA	24	391	46	21	2	1	20	50	54	10-3	-0.3	.244/.358/.330	-.066	.214/.314/.295	.225	-8.5
	LOU	AAA	24	227	20	8	·1	3	19	14	31	2-0	-0.3	.221/.278/.317	-.210	.225/.277/.333	.217	-5.7
C C. Tatum	SAR	A+	24	231	29	15	0	10	39	9	41	0-1	-1.3	.320/.348/.525	.254	.277/.307/.455	.258	9.2
	CHT	AA	24	194	21	10	1	2	22	17	49	0-1	-1.1	.231/.299/.335	-.164	.205/.263/.307	.196	-10.6

If you squint, **Juan Castro** looks a little bit like Neifi Perez. If Castro's on the Opening Day roster for the Reds, we'll know Dusty's squinting again. ⊘ A toolsy outfielder with some speed, **Buck Coats** was shipped off to Toronto, where he could be the 25th man on the roster. ⊘ The Reds took **Jerry Gil**, a cannon-armed shortstop, and turned him into a cannon-armed outfielder. He promptly blew out the elbow on that cannon and missed 2007. ⊘ Slick-fielding shortstop **Paul Janish** had a hard time hitting right-handed pitching in both Double- and Triple-A. Since most pitchers in baseball are righties, that's not promising. ⊘ After a great professional debut in late 2006, **Milton Loo** ranked among the Reds' top-ten prospects, but he spent 2007 on the suspended list and has told the team he's retired. The Reds are still holding out hope that he'll change his mind. ⊘ **Craig Tatum** had a nice batting-average-driven half-season in Sarasota, but came back to earth at Double-A and in the Arizona Fall League.

Pitchers

PLAYER	TEAM	LVL	AGE	W	L	SV	IP	H	BB	SO	HR	GB%	BABIP	STUFF	WHIP	ERA	PERA	EqERA	EqH9	EqBB9	EqSO9	EqHR9	VORP
P. Dumatrait*	LOU	AAA	25	10	6	0	125	114	49	76	10	43.6%	.269	-10	1.30	3.53	4.59	4.88	8.5	3.8	3.8	1.1	9.7
	CIN	MLB	25	0	4	0	18	39	12	9	6	37.8%	.458	-83	2.83	15.00	23.06	19.29	17.8	4.8	4.3	2.4	-17.8
R. Gardner	SAR	A+	25	5	1	0	43²	29	9	25	1	60.9%	.217	0	0.87	1.65	3.28	3.24	6.0	2.8	2.8	0.4	10.9
	CHT	AA	25	2	1	0	34²	27	8	33	1	54.3%	.283	16	1.01	1.82	3.41	3.27	7.6	2.5	5.7	0.5	8.5
	LOU	AAA	25	4	5	0	64²	82	20	41	10	46.2%	.348	-39	1.58	5.70	10.02	8.59	13.0	3.4	4.1	2.1	-19.5
E. Guardado*	CIN	MLB	36	0	0	0	13²	16	4	8	2	22.4%	.304	-15	1.46	7.23	4.47	6.28	8.8	1.9	5.0	1.3	-1.8
R. Ramirez	SAR	A+	24	5	2	1	73¹	64	25	86	5	47.1%	.319	0	1.21	4.05	5.72	6.30	9.7	4.7	7.3	1.4	-5.1
	CHT	AA	24	5	1	1	31¹	30	12	35	3	38.8%	.338	-9	1.34	4.60	5.83	5.59	9.9	4.0	6.8	1.6	0.0
	LOU	AAA	24	1	0	0	14²	7	6	16	0	53.1%	.226	13	0.88	0.00	0.17	0.00	4.7	4.1	7.4	0.0	8.3
K. Saarloos	LOU	AAA	28	0	2	0	41	47	9	28	3	51.4%	.331	-14	1.37	3.95	5.48	5.31	11.1	2.3	4.4	0.9	1.3
	CIN	MLB	28	1	5	0	42²	54	19	27	8	55.9%	.324	-22	1.71	7.17	6.13	6.50	10.2	3.2	5.1	1.4	-7.3
P. Viola*	DYT	A	24	3	1	2	43¹	29	17	49	3	44.9%	.257	-14	1.06	1.87	6.28	5.89	8.6	6.9	5.6	1.7	-1.2
	SAR	A+	24	0	1	2	20	14	7	28	0	38.3%	.298	16	1.05	0.90	3.80	1.89	7.6	4.3	8.5	0.5	7.8
	CHT	AA	24	0	0	2	19	12	6	17	2	47.9%	.182	-6	0.95	0.95	3.44	1.89	5.7	3.3	5.2	1.4	7.8

Lefty **Phil Dumatrait** had a nice second go-round at Triple-A, although it was driven by an extremely low BABIP. Called up in August, he posted the highest ERA (minimum 15 IP) by a Reds pitcher in 100 years. Undeterred, the Pirates picked him off waivers after the World Series. ⊘ Sinkerballer **Richie Gardner** was a top prospect in 2004, when he won 13 games in his first full professional season, but in 2005, shoulder surgery erased his status. He finally put it all back together last year, making for a nice feel-good story, even though the comeback stalled out in Louisville. ⊘ After elbow surgery cut his 2006 season short, **Eddie Guardado** made it back to the majors in August last year and was greeted with fireworks—he allowed ten runs in his first five innings of work, but a scoreless September earned him an incentive-laden $2-million deal with the Rangers. ⊘ **Carlos Guevara** was snatched away by the Marlins in the Rule 5 draft; he's a short, righty reliever with a flair for strikeouts and a screwball that keeps lefties off-balance. ⊘ **Ramon Ramirez**, not to be confused with the Rockies' reliever, is a short righty who has put up some big strikeout numbers in the minors, but scouts are less than enthralled with him. ⊘ In last year's annual we said a pitcher with **Kirk Saarloos**'s K/BB ratios (career 1.31) was "walking a tightrope"; after getting traded to Cincinnati, he fell off. ⊘ **Pedro Viola** is a late-blooming lefty out of the Dominican Republic. He was old for his levels last year, but he tore through them like a man who knew the clock was ticking.

MANAGER: DUSTY BAKER

YEAR	TEAM	W-L	Pythag +/−	Avg PC	100+ P	120+ P	QS	BQS	REL	REL w Zero R	IBB	Subs	PH	PH Avg	PH HR	SB2	CS2	SB3	CS3	SAC Att	SAC %	POS SAC	Squeeze	Swing	In Play
2005	CHN	79-83	-1	97.7	80	10	88	4	457	284	48	49	240	.195	2	60	34	5	3	93	74.2%	42	2	123	105
2006	CHN	66-96	-3	91.9	57	7	55	5	542	357	44	40	270	.216	5	107	41	13	5	117	71.8%	56	7	145	117

When Jerry Narron was fired before Independence Day last year, there wasn't a dry eye in the house. Although some accused Narron of being too easygoing, the ax fell because the Reds were horrific, and it's easier for the GM to fire one manager than 25 players, or himself. Strategically, the change from Narron to interim manager Pete Mackanin wasn't much of a change at all; the main difference was that the latter featured a quicker hook with his starting pitchers. Incoming manager Dusty Baker has a notoriously slow hook, but otherwise figures to be more aggressive in his tactics across the board—he's as big a fan of the bunt as you'll find, and he loves to mix and match with relievers, hunting for a hot hand. The big question is how the veteran-friendly Baker will integrate the young talent the farm system will be placing in his care.

Cleveland Indians

Even if you're on the right track, you'll get run over if you just sit there.
—WILL ROGERS

Over the course of the current decade, the Indians have ridden an extraordinary rollercoaster, lurching from a Central Division dynasty, through rebuilding, to contention, down to a quick one-year retooling, and back up once again to contention. That ride might have reached its apex last year as the Indians won 96 games, their first AL Central title since 2001, and came within one game of the World Series. At the end of the coming season, the Cleveland coaster could take its final plunge, the door to an era of opportunity slamming irrevocably shut.

The Indians' wild ride began in November of 2001, when Mark Shapiro replaced ten-year incumbent John Hart as general manager. The Tribe was coming off its sixth AL Central title in seven years, but it was an aging, expensive team that was finding it increasingly difficult to fend off the White Sox, who won the division in 2000, and a young, resurgent Twins team. In an effort to reduce both age and payroll, Shapiro's first move that winter was to ship All-Star second baseman Roberto Alomar and ballast to the Mets for outfielder Matt Lawton, who had been one of those Twins just four months earlier, and prospects. The move saved the team $2.5 million in salary and made them nearly four year's younger at Alomar's spot on the roster. Unfortunately, the payroll savings were quickly erased by the decision to sign free agent infielder Ricky Gutierrez to fill the hole at second base. A more legitimate reduction was achieved by allowing veteran outfielders Kenny Lofton and Juan Gonzalez to leave as free agents, with Lawton replacing Gonzalez in right field and a 24-year-old Mil-

ton Bradley replacing Lofton in center, but the savings were still not sufficient to drop the Indians out of the top ten in payroll.

In June of 2002, Shapiro found his team scuffling with a 33-35 record despite being burdened with baseball's ninth-highest player payroll. Given that the players primarily responsible for both the payroll and the performance were on the down-slopes of their careers, Shapiro did the only reasonable thing he could have done; he rolled up his sleeves, picked up his snickersnee, and commenced paring. In the process, he began sculpting the team that would return Cleveland to the postseason last year. On June 27, 2002, Shapiro made a deal that would shape the franchise's future by sending staff ace Bartolo Colon and young right-hander Tim Drew to the Montreal Expos for first baseman Lee Stevens and a trio of prospects—infielder Brandon Phillips, lefty Cliff Lee, and center fielder Grady Sizemore. In July, veteran southpaw Chuck Finley was dealt to the Cardinals for two prospects, one of whom grew up to be Coco Crisp. As the trading deadline approached, relievers Paul Shuey and Ricardo Rincon were spun off to the Dodgers and A's, respectively. At season's end, first baseman Jim Thome and injury-plagued starter Charles Nagy exited via free agency, clearing $14 million of salary off Cleveland's books. The final, crowning transaction in Shapiro's dismantling came that December: in a trade with the Rangers (run by Hart), Shapiro exchanged punchless catcher Einar Diaz, Diaz's seven-figure salary, and Ryan Drese, a right-hander who had posted a 6.55 ERA in 23 starts 2002, for righty Aaron

---

INDIANS PROSPECTUS

2007 record: 96-66; First place, AL Central; Lost to Red Sox in Championship Series

Pythagenport record: 92-70

Runs scored per game: 5.01 (6th in AL)

Runs allowed per game: 4.35 (3rd in AL)

Team EqA: .260 (8th in AL)

2007 Batters Age: 28.5 (2nd youngest in AL)

2007 Pitchers Age: 28.9 (4th oldest in AL)

Ballpark: Jacobs Field; Slight hitter's park; Park Factor of 1.013

2007: Mark Shapiro's rebuilding reaches fruition only to fall a game short of the World Series.

2008: Put up or shut up time for the Tribe.

Myette and first baseman Travis Hafner. When the dust settled, Shapiro had acquired a franchise cornerstone in Sizemore, an undervalued power bat in Hafner, and had dropped the payroll not only out of the top ten, but out of the top 20 (see Table 1).

Shapiro made these moves with confidence in part because of his experience in the team's minor league operations dating back to 1993. That experience helped him develop not only a good eye for prospects (witness the acquisitions of Sizemore, Hafner, and Crisp), but also a first-hand knowledge of the homegrown talent working its way up through the Indians' system. That talent began to emerge midway through the 2003 season when Victor Martinez, an international free agent signed out of Venezuela in 1996, began taking over at catcher. Crisp supplanted the cranky, injury-prone Bradley in center in August of that year; Bradley was subsequently flipped to the Dodgers in a deal that fetched minor league outfielder Franklin Gutierrez, who emerged in right field in 2007. Lawton was traded after the 2004 season, thereby allowing Crisp to move to left and opening up center for Sizemore, who had emerged from Tribe finishing school in July of that year. Another international signee, Dominican Jhonny Peralta was a bust while subbing at shortstop for an injured Omar Vizquel in 2003 at the tender age of 21, but returned ready in 2005 after Vizquel had departed as a free agent. Catcher-turned-first baseman Ryan Garko, a 2003 third-round pick, made incumbent gatekeeper Ben Broussard, himself a nifty Shapiro pickup from the Reds in 2002, expendable just as he reached his arbitration years by claiming the position in August of 2006. Garko's arrival also allowed Shapiro to flip Broussard's platoon partner, veteran lefty-killer Eduardo Perez, to the Mariners for infield prospect Asdrubal Cabrera, who claimed second base in August of last year.

Despite the transition of 1998 first-round pick C. C. Sabathia from solid starter to Cy Young Award winner on Shapiro's watch, the Indians have been less successfull rebuilding their pitching staff, which has had a high rate of annual turnover. Indians bullpens have varied wildly, as bullpens are wont to do, from the utter debacle of 2006 to last year's successful unit built around 2003 free-talent find Rafael Betancourt and farm-raised lefty Rafael Perez. The starting rotation has been more consistent as a unit (see Table 2), but lining up a stable supporting cast behind Sabathia has been a bumpy ride. In the four seasons between the departure of Colon and the arrival of Fausto Carmona last year, 14 other pitchers made seven or more starts for the Tribe as the team searched fruitlessly for a reliable number-two starter. Their search was briefly rewarded in 2005,

Table 1. The Cuyahoga Diet Plan: Indians player payroll, 1995–2007

Year	Record	Payroll	MLB Rank	% Of MLB Avg
1995	**100-44**	**$37,937,835**	**8**	**112**
1996	**99-62**	**$48,107,360**	**4**	**141**
1997	86-75	$56,802,460	4	141
1998	89-73	$60,800,166	4	143
1999	**97-65**	**$72,978,462**	**6**	**147**
2000	90-72	$75,880,771	8	137
2001	**91-71**	**$93,152,001**	**5**	**143**
2002	74-88	$78,909,449	9	117
2003	68-94	$48,584,834	26	69
2004	80-82	$34,319,300	27	50
2005	93-69	$41,502,500	26	57
2006	78-84	$56,031,500	25	72
2007	**96-66**	**$61,673,267**	**23**	**75**

Bold indicates AL Central champions.

when Kevin Millwood led the AL with a 2.86 ERA, and Lee won 18 games on a 3.79 ERA in 202 innings, but the former promptly fled for Texas lucre, and the latter regressed in 2006 and pitched his way off the team last year. Otherwise, the results have been middling to poor, with the only consistent presence behind Sabathia being the ground-balling Jake Westbrook, who has been steady, if unexceptional over the last five seasons.

That changed last year as Carmona, who had made a significant contribution to the bullpen's struggles in 2006, emerged as a dominant sinker-balling number two, or even 1A, behind Sabathia. Of course, Carmona's rise occurred almost by accident, as he had been sent to Triple-A Buffalo on May 1 to make room for Lee, who was coming off the DL, only to be yanked back three days later when Westbrook went down with an oblique injury. Carmona's development bodes well for the future. Even though Sabathia has been in the Indians' rotation since Hart was the GM, he won't reach his 27th birthday until late July. Having a young pair of aces would greatly improve the Indians' outlook in the coming seasons, but although Shapiro bought out Sabathia's arbitration years with a pair of multi-year deals, Sabathia's latest deal expires at the end of the 2008 season. If the Indians can retain him, he and Carmona could combine to be the core of the team's rotation until well into the next decade. If Sabathia leaves, they will be back to square one, this time with Carmona taking the place of Sabathia as staff anchor. That's the best-case scenario; as good as Carmona was in 2007, the chances of his reproducing Sabathia's consistency and durability are small.

Even with the rotation and bullpen on a steadier footing than they have been in recent seasons, emerg-

Table 2. As We Go Up We Go Down: Indians starters and relievers, 2003–2007

Year	Starters' SNLVAR	AL Rank	Relievers' WXRL	AL Rank
2003	16.3	10	6.185	8
2004	16.7	9	5.602	11
2005	20.9	5	12.506	3
2006	20.1	3	-1.533	13
2007	21.0	4	13.517	2

ing weaknesses in the lineup may moot that progress. Only two of last year's regulars, Sizemore and Martinez, had seasons that ranked well above average for their positions. Elsewhere, Garko is an unexceptional hitter for a first baseman. Cabrera is a fine glove, but unlikely to be much more than a break-even prospect on offense. Peralta, having been maddeningly inconsistent, appears to be settling down at a level well below what he showed in his breakout 2005 season.

More problematically, the trade that sent Crisp along with reliever David Riske and backup catcher Josh Bard to the Red Sox following the 2005 season has proven to be a bust. Kelly Shoppach, obtained in the deal, has emerged as one of the most productive backup catchers in the game, but the primary target of the deal, third base prospect Andy Marte, has failed to develop, forcing the Indians to return to the defensively maladroit Casey Blake at the hot corner. At 33, Blake is the oldest of the Indians' regulars and has reached the dangerous age at which players of his modest offensive talents begin to slide. His versatility as a four-corners fill-in is an asset, but the Indians have had to rely on him as a regular, which has been problematic. Furthermore, the loss of Crisp has left the outfield corners, generally a primary source of production, in the hands of an assortment of platoon players such as righties Gutierrez, Jason Michaels, and Ben Francisco, and lefty David Dellucci. Crisp may not be an ideal corner outfield regular, and he's had his struggles in Boston, some of which were injury-related, but the current solution looks desperate in comparison.

Perhaps most troubling, however, is the charging decline of designated hitter Travis Hafner, who had been the team's most productive hitter from 2004 to 2006.

Heading for his 31st birthday, it is possible that Hafner doesn't have another of those seasons in him. Pronk's patience will be the strut that continues to carry him as the rest of his game fails. Still, it seems increasingly likely that in making last summer's decision to extend his contract through 2012 at an average salary of more than $11 million over the next five years (with an option for 2013), the Indians made precisely the same kind of deal, with the same kind of player, at the same point in his career, as the Yankees did with Jason Giambi, only Hafner's decline is likely to be steeper.

Given the impact of Hafner's contract on the team's strictly controlled budget, the Tribe should have thought twice before committing nearly $60 million to a player who may soon have all the impact of an Indian of the cigar store variety. Hafner was ice cold at the time the deal was made in July—from May through August, Hafner batted .237/.358/.403 before reviving in September only to go cold again in the playoffs—and it would have made much more sense for the Indians simply to have exercised his $8.05-million option for 2008 so as to have another year's worth of performance on which to base the value of a contract extension.

It would be tragic if the deal with Hafner cost the Indians the financial flexibility to retain Sabathia or prevented them from addressing their offensive weaknesses at the corner positions. The core of a very good team exists in Cleveland, one that could, with a little work, surpass 2007's 96 wins sometime in the next several years. As currently constructed, the Indians have two studs in the rotation, a deep, talented, and mostly young bullpen, and offensive strength up the middle. They just need some significant complementary parts, and they need them now. That makes the Tribe's quiet winter—in which the only trade was one for utility infielder Jamey Carroll and the only free agent signing was of Japanese reliever Masahide Kobayashi—all the more troubling. With the other powers of the American League improving from within (Boston, New York) or without (division rival Detroit), the door to the Indians' new era of opportunity could close. For now, however, it remains ajar, as it will for as long as Sabathia remains in the fold.

HITTERS

Mike Aubrey   1B   Bats: L   Throws: L   Height: 6' 0"   Weight: 195   Born: April 15, 1982   Age: 26

YEAR	TEAM	LVL	AGE	PA	R	2B	3B	HR	RBI	BB	SO	SB	CS	EqBRR	AVG	OBP	SLG	MLVr	EqAVG	EqOBP	EqSLG	EqA	VORP	DEFENSE	
2005	AKR	AA	23	119	17	5	1	4	20	7	18	1	0	-0.1	.283	.336	.462	.110	.252	.303	.421	.252	-0.8	24-1B	1
2007	KIN	A+	25	59	15	5	0	5	11	6	7	0	0	-0.9	.400	.492	.800	.937	.340	.407	.698	.347	10.5		
2007	AKR	AA	25	221	22	11	0	7	34	10	35	0	0	0.6	.248	.290	.403	-.077	.225	.261	.378	.217	-11.3	31-1B	-2
2008	*CLE*	*MLB*	*26*	*313*	*32*	*14*	*1*	*11*	*44*	*19*	*61*	*2*	*1*	*-0.3*	*.249*	*.302*	*.417*	*-.086*	*.246*	*.301*	*.432*	*.255*	*-0.9*	*76-1B*	*1*

Breakout: 32% Improve: 58% Collapse: 22% Attrition: 18%   Comparables: Jim Spencer, Kevin Garner, Stan Royer, Vince Faison

Arguably the most frustrating prospect in baseball, Aubrey is a career .301/.375/.501 hitter in the minors, but has only played 107 games over the last three years due to a never-ending string of injuries. He now has chronic back problems, constant hamstring issues, and is perpetually mixing in random ailments such as oblique strains and extensive bouts of deja vu, in which he relives the sensation of having a never-ending string of injuries. He can rake, but at this point there's no reason to think he's ever going to perform for the Indians.

Josh Barfield   2B   Bats: R   Throws: R   Height: 6' 0"   Weight: 190   Born: December 17, 1982   Age: 25

YEAR	TEAM	LVL	AGE	PA	R	2B	3B	HR	RBI	BB	SO	SB	CS	EqBRR	AVG	OBP	SLG	MLVr	EqAVG	EqOBP	EqSLG	EqA	VORP	DEFENSE	
2005	POR	AAA	22	578	74	25	1	15	72	52	108	20	5	1.0	.310	.370	.450	.117	.269	.325	.389	.252	11.7	135-2B	-14
2006	SDN	MLB	23	578	72	32	3	13	58	30	81	21	5	2.3	.280	.318	.423	-.002	.288	.327	.435	.266	21.8	139-2B	-2
2007	CLE	MLB	24	444	53	19	3	3	50	14	90	14	5	4.0	.243	.270	.324	-.271	.249	.281	.341	.220	-13.6	114-2B	-2
2008	*CLE*	*MLB*	*25*	*467*	*53*	*22*	*2*	*10*	*49*	*26*	*82*	*12*	*4*	*0.9*	*.260*	*.305*	*.394*	*-.105*	*.258*	*.304*	*.408*	*.251*	*5.0*	*110-2B*	*-1*

Breakout: 27% Improve: 54% Collapse: 22% Attrition: 21%   Comparables: Terry Shumpert, Pat Kelly, Shawon Dunston, Juan Uribe

Going into the season, Barfield was an impressive young hitter moving to a home park much friendlier to hitters than the one he left behind. By mid-August he was out of a job. Despite the park, Barfield never got his bat going and was usurped by Asdrubal Cabrera, who now seems to be the better answer at second base in the minds of Cleveland officials. That puts Barfield in limbo, as there is little room on a major league bench for an infielder who can't play on the left side. Chances are someone will want to give him another shot because of his age and minor league credentials, but if Cleveland deals him now, they'll be selling low.

Brian Barton   OF   Bats: R   Throws: R   Height: 6' 3"   Weight: 187   Born: April 25, 1982   Age: 26

YEAR	TEAM	LVL	AGE	PA	R	2B	3B	HR	RBI	BB	SO	SB	CS	EqBRR	AVG	OBP	SLG	MLVr	EqAVG	EqOBP	EqSLG	EqA	VORP	DEFENSE			
2005	LKC	A	23	160	31	14	1	4	32	18	21	7	2	0.6	.414	.506	.624	.696	.296	.369	.458	.284	7.0	25-RF	-1		
2005	KIN	A+	23	273	42	15	6	3	32	34	57	13	8	-0.9	.274	.404	.435	.178	.223	.320	.345	.234	-3.9	32-CF	3	23-LF	0
2006	KIN	A+	24	359	56	16	3	13	57	39	83	26	3	3.4	.308	.410	.515	.348	.240	.321	.419	.264	5.5	24-CF	-3	21-RF	1
2006	AKR	AA	24	171	32	5	0	6	26	13	26	15	5	-1.5	.351	.415	.503	.366	.325	.380	.494	.297	15.9	23-CF	2		
2007	AKR	AA	25	461	56	18	2	9	59	41	99	20	9	-4.1	.314	.416	.440	.223	.255	.343	.381	.257	-2.7	72-RF	-3	14-CF	-1
2007	BUF	AAA	25	96	9	3	0	1	7	7	18	1	1	0.2	.264	.333	.333	-.098	.239	.302	.307	.214	-3.5	22-CF	-3		
2008	*SLN*	*MLB*	*26*	*549*	*68*	*25*	*3*	*11*	*55*	*45*	*123*	*19*	*6*	*0.7*	*.256*	*.329*	*.385*	*-.106*	*.255*	*.329*	*.400*	*.254*	*4.8*	*129-RF*	*2*		

Breakout: 15% Improve: 39% Collapse: 27% Attrition: 14%   Comparables: Chris Denorfia, Mike Zywica, Wonderful Monds, T.J. Bohn

The Cardinals made Barton the best position player taken in this winter's Rule 5 draft. Based on his age and skill set, the resulting big-league promotion should simply accelerate what should be a pretty nice career as a bench outfielder. Barton is among the smartest people in the game; he completed a degree in aerospace engineering at Miami, but turned down a high-paying job with Boeing to give this baseball thing a shot. There were some whispered concerns about Barton's makeup during the year, but they amounted to little more than an ugly reminder that, even more than half a century after Jackie Robinson, there remains a small segment of the baseball community that is unable to accept intelligent black players.

Casey Blake   4C   Bats: R   Throws: R   Height: 6' 2"   Weight: 210   Born: August 23, 1973   Age: 34

YEAR	TEAM	LVL	AGE	PA	R	2B	3B	HR	RBI	BB	SO	SB	CS	EqBRR	AVG	OBP	SLG	MLVr	EqAVG	EqOBP	EqSLG	EqA	VORP	DEFENSE	
2005	CLE	MLB	31	583	72	32	1	23	58	43	116	4	5	-0.3	.241	.308	.438	-.024	.249	.325	.462	.266	4.4	133-RF	8
2006	CLE	MLB	32	456	63	20	1	19	68	45	93	6	0	-1.0	.282	.356	.479	.109	.280	.363	.487	.293	22.4	93-RF	2
2007	CLE	MLB	33	662	81	36	4	18	78	54	123	4	5	0.3	.270	.339	.437	.037	.272	.346	.461	.274	17.6	134-3B	-8
2008	CLE	MLB	34	496	58	26	2	15	67	43	95	4	2	-0.4	.264	.334	.433	-.002	.262	.333	.449	.272	9.8	117-3B	-1

Breakout: 9%   Improve: 37%   Collapse: 28%   Attrition: 20%   Comparables: Doug DeCinces, Tim Wallach, Matt Williams, Todd Zeile

Casey Blake might not be an impact player, but that doesn't mean he's not incredibly valuable. You know he's going to hit around 20 bombs and draw about 50 walks, but what makes him integral is his versatility. Need someone to fill an outfield job? Blake's your man. Third base prospect Andy Marte still struggling to do anything well? Blake prevents the position from becoming a black hole. This sort of player is always underappreciated.

Jordan Brown   1B   Bats: L   Throws: L   Height: 6' 0"   Weight: 205   Born: December 18, 1983   Age: 24

YEAR	TEAM	LVL	AGE	PA	R	2B	3B	HR	RBI	BB	SO	SB	CS	EqBRR	AVG	OBP	SLG	MLVr	EqAVG	EqOBP	EqSLG	EqA	VORP	DEFENSE	
2005	MHV	A-	21	79	15	1	0	3	7	3	7	2	1	1.3	.253	.291	.387	-.036	.234	.253	.325	.193	-11.9	14-LF	0
2006	KIN	A+	22	533	71	26	7	15	87	51	59	4	0	-1.4	.290	.362	.469	.203	.254	.312	.414	.251	-6.7	111-LF	5
2007	AKR	AA	23	558	85	36	2	11	76	63	56	11	2	-5.0	.333	.421	.484	.307	.298	.376	.445	.287	27.4	92-1B	0
2008	CLE	MLB	24	582	69	31	3	11	64	45	81	7	3	-0.5	.271	.332	.403	-.039	.268	.331	.418	.264	2.1	136-1B	0

Breakout: 16%   Improve: 42%   Collapse: 21%   Attrition: 5%   Comparables: Matt Franco, Ryan McGuire, Jamie Dismuke, Mike Lamb

In 2006, Brown was the Carolina League MVP, and last year, he won Eastern League honors. One would think that would make him a big-time prospect, but it doesn't. He's a first baseman without a lot of power, and nobody is quite sure what to do with players like this. In a perfect world, he would be some kind of Mark Grace or Lyle Overbay type, but of the last 20 guys in the minors we could have said that about, the only ones who panned out were Mark Grace and Lyle Overbay.

Asdrubal Cabrera   2B/SS   Bats: S   Throws: R   Height: 6' 0"   Weight: 170   Born: November 13, 1985   Age: 22

YEAR	TEAM	LVL	AGE	PA	R	2B	3B	HR	RBI	BB	SO	SB	CS	EqBRR	AVG	OBP	SLG	MLVr	EqAVG	EqOBP	EqSLG	EqA	VORP	DEFENSE	
2005	WIS	A	19	228	26	12	3	4	30	30	32	2	6	-5.7	.318	.407	.474	.281	.265	.341	.405	.253	7.5	28-2B	-1
2005	SBR	A+	19	244	31	15	6	1	26	15	47	3	1	0.9	.284	.325	.418	-.066	.218	.254	.314	.196	-11.2	54-SS	-2
2006	BUF	AAA	20	211	26	11	0	1	14	8	39	5	4	1.0	.263	.295	.337	-.131	.246	.279	.319	.213	-5.7	52-SS	-7
2006	TAC	AAA	20	233	27	12	2	3	22	24	51	7	5	-2.3	.236	.323	.360	-.070	.214	.293	.335	.222	-4.4	60-SS	5
2007	AKR	AA	21	425	78	23	3	8	54	45	42	23	7	2.4	.310	.383	.454	.189	.279	.347	.420	.271	22.6	90-SS	-5
2007	CLE	MLB	21	186	30	9	2	3	22	17	29	0	0	2.3	.283	.354	.421	.048	.285	.363	.443	.281	7.6	36-2B	6
2008	CLE	MLB	22	625	74	33	4	9	58	49	102	15	7	1.7	.264	.325	.384	-.081	.261	.324	.398	.257	11.5	146-SS	1

Breakout: 32%   Improve: 60%   Collapse: 12%   Attrition: 8%   Comparables: D'Angelo Jimenez, Ralph Milliard, Jhonny Peralta, Alfredo Griffin

In a great trade that looks better every day, the Indians acquired Cabrera from Seattle in June 2006 for a guy who now spends his time in a suit talking about baseball on TV. Like most Mariners prospects, Cabrera was rushed through the Seattle system at a breakneck pace, not standing still long enough to make an impression. Still, what we saw during his big-league debut last year was very real. Cabrera is the best defensive shortstop on the Indians; exactly how the team will sort that out won't be decided until spring training, but Cabrera will be starting somewhere in the middle infield, and he'll be damn good.

Shin-Soo Choo   OF

Bats: L   Throws: L   Height: 5' 11"   Weight: 205   Born: July 13, 1982   Age: 25

YEAR	TEAM	LVL	AGE	PA	R	2B	3B	HR	RBI	BB	SO	SB	CS	EqBRR	AVG	OBP	SLG	MLVr	EqAVG	EqOBP	EqSLG	EqA	VORP	DEFENSE			
2005	TAC	AAA	22	502	73	21	5	11	54	69	97	20	10	-2.1	.282	.382	.431	.127	.247	.339	.374	.251	-7.4	112-LF	14		
2006	TAC	AAA	23	427	71	21	3	13	48	45	73	26	4	3.3	.323	.394	.499	.330	.295	.362	.468	.290	18.1	50-LF	-3	30-RF	-5
2006	CLE	MLB	23	167	23	11	3	3	22	18	46	5	3	0.2	.295	.373	.473	.138	.299	.386	.500	.297	8.4	29-RF	1		
2007	BUF	AAA	24	238	34	11	2	3	26	21	40	10	3	1.6	.260	.328	.375	-.056	.243	.307	.371	.244	-8.0	31-LF	-1		
2007	CLE	MLB	24	20	5	0	0	0	5	2	5	0	1	-0.1	.294	.350	.294	-.124	.294	.350	.294	.228	-0.8				
2008	CLE	MLB	25	347	43	16	2	6	34	30	74	10	3	0.8	.254	.322	.377	-.103	.251	.321	.390	.255	-1.9	84-LF	2		

Breakout: 16% Improve: 39% Collapse: 31% Attrition: 18%   Comparables: Armando Rios, Troy O'Leary, Oreste Marrero, Marvin Benard

Quick lesson: when the first thing you're told about a hitting prospect is that he has a great throwing arm, that's not a good sign. Choo has—had?—a great throwing arm. Unfortunately, he needed Tommy John surgery at the end of last season and will miss a good portion of 2008, hence the indeterminate state of his major asset. That's not to say he has no other skills—he runs well and can hit a little bit—but in the end, he's no more than an extra outfielder.

Trevor Crowe   CF

Bats: S   Throws: R   Height: 6' 0"   Weight: 190   Born: November 17, 1983   Age: 24

YEAR	TEAM	LVL	AGE	PA	R	2B	3B	HR	RBI	BB	SO	SB	CS	EqBRR	AVG	OBP	SLG	MLVr	EqAVG	EqOBP	EqSLG	EqA	VORP	DEFENSE			
2005	MHV	A-	21	58	9	2	1	1	6	6	8	4	3	-0.2	.255	.345	.392	.050	.204	.259	.278	.183	-8.1	12-CF	-1		
2005	LKC	A	21	199	18	8	2	0	23	18	25	7	5	-2.3	.258	.327	.326	-.099	.208	.261	.251	.177	-16.9	37-CF	2		
2006	KIN	A+	22	273	51	15	2	4	31	48	46	29	6	3.2	.329	.449	.470	.360	.266	.375	.384	.278	9.8	59-CF	-11		
2006	AKR	AA	22	176	20	7	2	1	13	20	24	16	6	-1.4	.234	.318	.325	-.086	.212	.290	.308	.222	-8.3	22-CF	2		
2007	AKR	AA	23	589	87	26	4	5	50	62	71	28	9	0.1	.259	.341	.353	-.051	.231	.306	.324	.229	-17.2	99-CF	8	26-RF	-1
2008	CLE	MLB	24	590	70	26	4	5	46	53	101	23	8	1.1	.245	.316	.337	-.171	.242	.315	.350	.243	-7.4	138-CF	-3		

Breakout: 44% Improve: 65% Collapse: 12% Attrition: 13%   Comparables: Shaun Boyd, Chris Magruder, Tony Gwynn, McKay Christensen

Crowe looked like one of the better pure leadoff men in the minors entering the year, but failed to get his average above the Mendoza line until late June. He was quite good from then on, hitting .314/.384/.428 after the break. Crowe's biggest weakness is his defense; his range is somewhat limited for an everyday center fielder, and this isn't the 1980s so his bat won't carry a corner spot. That makes him a tweener, and that's not a good thing to be if you want to start in the major leagues.

David Dellucci   OF

Bats: L   Throws: L   Height: 5' 11"   Weight: 195   Born: October 31, 1973   Age: 34

YEAR	TEAM	LVL	AGE	PA	R	2B	3B	HR	RBI	BB	SO	SB	CS	EqBRR	AVG	OBP	SLG	MLVr	EqAVG	EqOBP	EqSLG	EqA	VORP	DEFENSE			
2005	TEX	MLB	31	518	97	17	5	29	65	76	121	5	3	2.3	.251	.367	.513	.146	.250	.376	.526	.302	28.1	43-LF	-3		
2006	PHI	MLB	32	301	41	14	5	13	39	28	62	1	3	-1.7	.292	.369	.530	.215	.288	.365	.527	.295	17.7	31-LF	0	21-RF	-3
2007	CLE	MLB	33	199	25	11	2	4	20	17	40	2	1	0.1	.230	.296	.382	-.147	.233	.307	.398	.247	-3.4	42-LF	6		
2008	CLE	MLB	34	181	24	8	1	6	24	21	39	2	1	0.2	.249	.342	.428	-.005	.247	.341	.444	.276	4.2	46-LF	-1		

Breakout: 16% Improve: 36% Collapse: 39% Attrition: 45%   Comparables: Jim King, Pat Mullin, Ray Lankford, Al Zarilla

The Indians signed Dellucci to a three-year deal prior to last season, and they're hoping that the next two are far better than the first. He was constantly injured in 2007, the knockout blow being a torn hamstring that was severe enough to require surgery and cost him nearly all of the second half of the season. History tells us that, if healthy, he should be a solidly productive corner outfielder that you only have to bench against lefties, but he now has that giant "if" hanging over his head.

Ben Francisco   OF

Bats: R   Throws: R   Height: 6' 1"   Weight: 190   Born: October 23, 1981   Age: 26

YEAR	TEAM	LVL	AGE	PA	R	2B	3B	HR	RBI	BB	SO	SB	CS	EqBRR	AVG	OBP	SLG	MLVr	EqAVG	EqOBP	EqSLG	EqA	VORP	DEFENSE			
2005	AKR	AA	23	352	45	19	7	7	46	24	59	15	4	-1.3	.307	.357	.474	.176	.270	.319	.423	.256	0.3	38-RF	-2	31-LF	-1
2006	BUF	AAA	24	579	80	32	4	17	59	45	72	25	5	3.0	.278	.345	.454	.108	.260	.325	.442	.267	18.0	38-CF	0	34-RF	-3
2007	BUF	AAA	25	425	60	27	2	12	51	36	66	22	8	-2.5	.318	.382	.496	.231	.296	.358	.479	.286	29.9	45-CF	-5	29-LF	4
2007	CLE	MLB	25	66	10	5	0	3	12	3	19	0	2	-1.8	.274	.303	.500	.063	.274	.303	.532	.266	0.9	11-LF	1		
2008	CLE	MLB	26	515	67	30	3	14	65	37	91	16	5	0.5	.273	.329	.438	.005	.271	.328	.454	.273	10.5	121-LF	-1		

Breakout: 19% Improve: 44% Collapse: 16% Attrition: 12%   Comparables: Mickey Brantley, Craig Monroe, Reggie Sanders, Jackie Brandt

More of an organizational player than anything else, Francisco was having the best season of his minor league career when he finally got the call and hit a game-winning home run in his major league debut. Then the Indians acquired Kenny Lofton and that was the end of that. In another organization, Francisco would have an opportunity to stick as an extra outfielder, but this is the wrong organization to be in if that's your ceiling, as there is a large group of guys already in line.

Ryan Garko — 1B

Bats: R Throws: R Height: 6' 2" Weight: 225 Born: January 2, 1981 Age: 27

YEAR	TEAM	LVL	AGE	PA	R	2B	3B	HR	RBI	BB	SO	SB	CS	EqBRR	AVG	OBP	SLG	MLVr	EqAVG	EqOBP	EqSLG	EqA	VORP	DEFENSE			
2005	BUF	AAA	24	520	75	25	3	19	77	44	92	1	3	-1.2	.303	.384	.498	.197	.274	.349	.448	.273	15.6	63-1B	-2	55-C	-8
2006	BUF	AAA	25	437	43	18	0	15	59	45	67	4	5	-4.0	.247	.352	.420	.055	.235	.331	.414	.260	0.4	85-1B	5		
2006	CLE	MLB	25	209	28	12	0	7	45	14	37	0	0	-1.4	.292	.359	.470	.105	.295	.365	.492	.293	8.0	45-1B	-1		
2007	CLE	MLB	26	541	62	29	1	21	61	34	94	0	1	-8.8	.289	.359	.483	.152	.293	.364	.506	.294	27.8	118-1B	0		
2008	CLE	MLB	27	554	67	29	1	21	80	45	101	3	2	-1.6	.272	.343	.461	.056	.270	.342	.477	.283	13.6	130-1B	2		

Breakout: 19% Improve: 48% Collapse: 17% Attrition: 9%　Comparables: Eric Karros, Earl Williams, Paul Konerko, Doug Rader

The Indians cleared out the first base job for Garko in 2007, and while he performed admirably, he still seems like a placeholder until something better comes along. He's hardly a liability, but he's also kind of a generic first baseman in terms of batting average and power. He'll be around for a long time, but he'll always seem like Plan B.

Jared Goedert — INF

Bats: R Throws: R Height: 6' 1" Weight: 180 Born: May 25, 1985 Age: 23

YEAR	TEAM	LVL	AGE	PA	R	2B	3B	HR	RBI	BB	SO	SB	CS	EqBRR	AVG	OBP	SLG	MLVr	EqAVG	EqOBP	EqSLG	EqA	VORP	DEFENSE	
2006	MHV	A-	21	264	31	14	2	3	27	19	28	1	0	0.8	.269	.328	.382	.087	.224	.274	.339	.212	-16.7	62-3B	6
2007	LKC	A	22	205	44	10	0	16	51	35	29	0	1	0.2	.364	.475	.715	.707	.295	.392	.538	.312	23.5	32-3B	-2
2007	KIN	A+	22	149	23	9	0	4	23	23	25	1	0	-0.8	.256	.369	.424	.111	.215	.309	.346	.237	-2.1	30-2B	2
2008	CLE	MLB	23	390	39	19	1	9	43	34	81	3	1	-0.2	.243	.312	.380	-.123	.241	.311	.394	.248	0.2	93-3B	2

Breakout: 16% Improve: 45% Collapse: 18% Attrition: 7%　Comparables: Steve Goodell, Rob Grable, Elston Hansen, Donnie Murphy

Goedert's eye-popping numbers at Lake County in the first two months of last season are inflated by the fact that he was pretty old for his league and playing his home games in a bandbox. What he did after his promotion to High-A was tempered by the fact that he was nursing a sore shoulder. He's definitely some kind of prospect, as he can play third or second base, understands the value of a walk, and has some pop, but we won't really know what kind until he's in a more age-appropriate league and settles in at one position.

Franklin Gutierrez — RF

Bats: R Throws: R Height: 6' 2" Weight: 180 Born: February 21, 1983 Age: 25

YEAR	TEAM	LVL	AGE	PA	R	2B	3B	HR	RBI	BB	SO	SB	CS	EqBRR	AVG	OBP	SLG	MLVr	EqAVG	EqOBP	EqSLG	EqA	VORP	DEFENSE			
2005	AKR	AA	22	426	70	25	2	11	42	30	77	14	4	3.8	.261	.322	.423	.021	.229	.286	.371	.231	-9.3	82-CF	-5		
2005	BUF	AAA	22	75	10	6	2	0	7	6	13	2	2	-1.5	.254	.320	.403	-.078	.221	.289	.368	.223	-1.7	16-CF	3		
2006	BUF	AAA	23	413	63	27	0	9	38	49	84	13	8	-2.0	.278	.373	.433	.122	.262	.355	.420	.269	15.7	56-CF	4	18-LF	2
2006	CLE	MLB	23	141	21	9	0	1	8	3	28	0	0	1.5	.272	.288	.360	-.201	.274	.295	.370	.229	-3.6	24-RF	-2		
2007	BUF	AAA	24	138	29	7	0	4	16	8	20	7	3	-1.3	.341	.384	.488	.245	.315	.360	.469	.282	7.1	15-RF	-1	13-CF	4
2007	CLE	MLB	24	301	41	13	2	13	36	21	77	8	3	0.4	.266	.318	.472	.047	.268	.324	.502	.277	8.3	64-RF	0		
2008	CLE	MLB	25	370	49	19	2	12	47	28	76	10	3	0.8	.268	.331	.449	.016	.265	.330	.465	.276	8.8	89-RF	1		

Breakout: 37% Improve: 63% Collapse: 17% Attrition: 20%　Comparables: Lou Clinton, Felipe Alou, Steve Brye, Corey Hart

After starting the year at Buffalo, Gutierrez was promoted into a right field platoon with Trot Nixon, then assumed a larger share of the job as injuries slowed Nixon in the season's final two months. The platoon arrangement is the ideal one for Gutierrez, who is an MVP candidate against left-handers (.330/.366/.553) but against righties appears to be capable of little more than an occasional bit of power (.232/.292/.429). The Indians seem to understand his limitations and are hoping that Dellucci can remain healthy enough to keep Gutierrez from having to face his own kind.

Travis Hafner — DH

Bats: L   Throws: R   Height: 6' 3"   Weight: 240   Born: June 3, 1977   Age: 31

YEAR	TEAM	LVL	AGE	PA	R	2B	3B	HR	RBI	BB	SO	SB	CS	EqBRR	AVG	OBP	SLG	MLVr	EqAVG	EqOBP	EqSLG	EqA	VORP	DEFENSE	
2005	CLE	MLB	28	578	94	42	0	33	108	79	123	0	0	-1.9	.305	.408	.595	.408	.314	.426	.632	.345	68.9		
2006	CLE	MLB	29	563	100	31	1	42	117	100	111	0	0	-1.8	.308	.439	.659	.518	.304	.442	.663	.357	79.7		
2007	CLE	MLB	30	659	80	25	2	24	100	102	115	1	1	-0.3	.266	.385	.451	.132	.262	.388	.464	.296	30.7	10-1B	0
2008	CLE	MLB	31	636	92	30	1	28	97	91	127	2	1	-1.2	.274	.383	.490	.159	.272	.382	.508	.305	34.6	149-DH	

Breakout: 3%   Improve: 24%   Collapse: 36%   Attrition: 11%   Comparables: Boog Powell, Carlos Delgado, Fred McGriff, Kent Hrbek

Concerned about Hafner's huge drop in production last year? You should be. Look at his age and look at those comps. Kent Hrbek? Washed up at 32. Boog Powell? Cooked by 31. Travis Hafner has those dreaded old-player skills, and once they start going downhill, they tend to simply pick up speed. The fact that the Indians owe him more than $57 million through 2012 could turn into a nightmare.

Wes Hodges — 3B

Bats: R   Throws: R   Height: 6' 2"   Weight: 180   Born: September 14, 1984   Age: 23

YEAR	TEAM	LVL	AGE	PA	R	2B	3B	HR	RBI	BB	SO	SB	CS	EqBRR	AVG	OBP	SLG	MLVr	EqAVG	EqOBP	EqSLG	EqA	VORP	DEFENSE	
2007	KIN	A+	22	450	60	22	3	15	71	44	90	0	0	-0.3	.288	.367	.473	.199	.238	.302	.387	.240	1.4	98-3B	-12
2008	CLE	MLB	23	505	48	26	2	12	53	38	140	3	2	-0.2	.234	.297	.377	-.159	.232	.296	.390	.240	-5.7	119-3B	-9

Breakout: 27%   Improve: 55%   Collapse: 20%   Attrition: 10%   Comparables: Tripper Johnson, Brent Clevlen, Mike Bell, Gabe Alvarez

With his successful full-season debut, Hodges has officially overtaken the disappointing Andy Marte for the organization's title of Third Baseman of the Future. While Hodges will never be confused with Scott Rolen in the field, he's good enough to stay at third base and looks like an offensive powerhouse with all of those secondary skills like power and walks that make us all warm and fuzzy inside. ETA: 2009.

Kenny Lofton — LF

Bats: L   Throws: L   Height: 5' 11"   Weight: 190   Born: May 31, 1967   Age: 41

YEAR	TEAM	LVL	AGE	PA	R	2B	3B	HR	RBI	BB	SO	SB	CS	EqBRR	AVG	OBP	SLG	MLVr	EqAVG	EqOBP	EqSLG	EqA	VORP	DEFENSE	
2005	PHI	MLB	38	406	67	15	5	2	36	32	41	22	3	3.7	.335	.392	.420	.160	.329	.389	.413	.289	28.7	84-CF	7
2006	LAN	MLB	39	522	79	15	12	3	41	45	42	32	5	1.6	.301	.360	.403	.043	.300	.362	.406	.277	26.1	107-CF	-11
2007	TEX	MLB	40	363	62	16	3	7	23	39	28	21	4	1.1	.303	.380	.438	.110	.309	.391	.462	.300	24.2	76-CF	-6
2007	CLE	MLB	40	196	24	9	3	0	15	17	23	2	3	-0.5	.283	.344	.370	-.041	.292	.359	.380	.258	0.3	43-LF	2
2008	CLE	MLB	41	363	50	15	4	3	33	34	34	13	4	0.8	.277	.346	.382	-.039	.274	.345	.396	.269	5.4	87-CF	-3

Breakout: 4%   Improve: 34%   Collapse: 35%   Attrition: 29%   Comparables: Enos Slaughter, B. J. Surhoff, Paul Molitor, Wade Boggs

The fact that Lofton has played for ten teams in the past seven years, bookended by his second and third stints in Cleveland, became an unlikely gag in a shipping company commercial last summer. While Lofton may be moving around a lot, he's not being passed around by second division teams; he's made the playoffs in 11 of the last 13 years. Lofton may be turning 41 in May, but he still runs well, can still get on base, and has even developed a reputation as a clubhouse leader. A late bloomer, he didn't get a big-league job until he was 25, but as a career .299/.372/.423 hitter with 2,428 hits and 622 stolen bases (15th all-time), he just might have had an outside shot at the Hall of Fame had he gotten going a bit sooner.

Andy Marte — 3B

Bats: R   Throws: R   Height: 6' 1"   Weight: 190   Born: October 21, 1983   Age: 24

YEAR	TEAM	LVL	AGE	PA	R	2B	3B	HR	RBI	BB	SO	SB	CS	EqBRR	AVG	OBP	SLG	MLVr	EqAVG	EqOBP	EqSLG	EqA	VORP	DEFENSE	
2005	RIC	AAA	21	460	51	26	2	20	74	64	83	0	3	-6.9	.275	.372	.506	.182	.247	.343	.446	.271	22.2	108-3B	10
2005	ATL	MLB	21	66	3	2	1	0	4	7	13	0	1	-0.5	.140	.227	.211	-.520	.140	.227	.211	.147	-7.5	15-3B	-7
2006	BUF	AAA	22	394	49	23	0	15	46	34	81	1	0	-1.6	.261	.322	.451	.057	.244	.307	.437	.255	10.4	91-3B	9
2006	CLE	MLB	22	178	20	15	1	5	23	13	38	0	0	-0.1	.226	.287	.421	-.151	.228	.298	.438	.250	-2.5	49-3B	3
2007	BUF	AAA	23	379	47	17	1	16	60	21	64	0	0	0.3	.267	.309	.457	.028	.246	.286	.439	.245	6.4	84-3B	7
2007	CLE	MLB	23	60	3	4	0	1	8	2	9	0	0	0.1	.193	.233	.316	-.388	.193	.233	.351	.195	-4.0	15-3B	-3
2008	CLE	MLB	24	452	45	23	1	15	62	35	91	2	1	-0.8	.244	.305	.415	-.087	.241	.304	.431	.255	3.0	107-3B	2

Breakout: 39%   Improve: 56%   Collapse: 18%   Attrition: 15%   Comparables: Edwin Encarnacion, Russ Davis, Willis Otanez, Cole Liniak

Oh, how the mighty have fallen. Once the pride of the Atlanta system, Marte has been reduced to Triple-A filler. As it turns out, he just isn't that good, a pure miss from a scouting and player development standpoint. If you look at his numbers, you'll see that Marte was never blow-you-away great in the first place. Since coming to Cleveland, he's gotten a little bit bigger, a little bit stiffer, and a whole lot worse. While some in the organization are still holding out hope for him, their numbers are shrinking.

Victor Martinez — C · Bats: S · Throws: R · Height: 6' 2" · Weight: 195 · Born: December 23, 1978 · Age: 29

YEAR	TEAM	LVL	AGE	PA	R	2B	3B	HR	RBI	BB	SO	SB	CS	EqBRR	AVG	OBP	SLG	MLVr	EqAVG	EqOBP	EqSLG	EqA	VORP	DEFENSE
2005	CLE	MLB	26	622	73	33	0	20	80	63	78	0	1	-2.7	.305	.378	.475	.201	.312	.392	.500	.306	52.9	138-C -1
2006	CLE	MLB	27	652	82	37	0	16	93	71	78	0	0	-5.7	.316	.391	.465	.182	.315	.397	.473	.302	47.8	126-C -14 19-1B -4
2007	CLE	MLB	28	645	78	40	0	25	114	62	76	0	0	-1.8	.301	.374	.505	.218	.298	.376	.524	.305	55.0	116-C 5 25-1B -4
2008	CLE	MLB	29	603	75	32	1	18	86	62	74	2	1	-1.8	.293	.369	.457	.110	.290	.368	.474	.293	31.7	141-C -2

Breakout: 7% Improve: 28% Collapse: 28% Attrition: 14% Comparables: Ted Simmons, Earl Battey, Thurman Munson, Joe Torre

Everyone knows Martinez is a great hitter, but few talk about the transformation he's undergone defensively. It wasn't so long ago that it was just assumed that Martinez would eventually move to first base because of his deficiencies behind the plate. Now, while he's still not Johnny Bench back there, he's not bad, either. Martinez blocks balls well, has soft hands, and threw out 32 percent of opposing basestealers last year, which was the fourth-best rate in the American League (behind only Joe Mauer, Kenji Johjima, and Gerald Laird). At $17 million for the next three years, Martinez is an absolute bargain.

Matthew McBride — C · Bats: R · Throws: R · Height: 6' 2" · Weight: 215 · Born: May 23, 1985 · Age: 23

YEAR	TEAM	LVL	AGE	PA	R	2B	3B	HR	RBI	BB	SO	SB	CS	EqBRR	AVG	OBP	SLG	MLVr	EqAVG	EqOBP	EqSLG	EqA	VORP	DEFENSE
2006	MHV	A-	21	211	24	12	0	4	31	16	22	5	2	-1.0	.272	.355	.402	.146	.233	.290	.347	.223	-8.5	26-C -6
2007	LKC	A	22	474	66	35	2	8	66	38	54	1	0	0.6	.283	.348	.432	.080	.233	.285	.350	.223	-10.5	84-C -11
2008	CLE	MLB	23	509	47	29	1	8	54	30	83	4	3	-0.1	.242	.293	.363	-.178	.240	.292	.376	.235	-3.9	120-C -7

Breakout: 43% Improve: 62% Collapse: 19% Attrition: 9% Comparables: Rob Johnson, Eli Marrero, Ryan Doumit, Jake Fox

The Indians were pretty excited about McBride as an offensive catching prospect, but his full-season debut left a lot to be desired. He's a good contact hitter who slices a lot of doubles into the gap, but the good things to say about him end there, as he was old for his level, doesn't have a ton of power, and could use a more patient approach. An optimist would say McBride could end up as a good backup, but a pessimist would point out that he's not a terribly good defender, either.

Jason Michaels — OF · Bats: R · Throws: R · Height: 6' 0" · Weight: 205 · Born: May 4, 1976 · Age: 32

YEAR	TEAM	LVL	AGE	PA	R	2B	3B	HR	RBI	BB	SO	SB	CS	EqBRR	AVG	OBP	SLG	MLVr	EqAVG	EqOBP	EqSLG	EqA	VORP	DEFENSE
2005	PHI	MLB	29	343	54	16	2	4	31	44	45	3	3	-1.3	.304	.399	.415	.142	.301	.395	.419	.287	17.6	61-CF 9
2006	CLE	MLB	30	548	77	32	1	9	55	43	101	9	5	2.0	.267	.326	.391	-.083	.270	.337	.400	.258	-1.7	115-LF -6
2007	CLE	MLB	31	295	43	11	1	7	39	20	50	3	4	-0.8	.270	.324	.397	-.045	.275	.334	.423	.258	0.4	55-LF 5 13-RF -1
2008	CLE	MLB	32	247	30	11	1	5	27	22	42	3	2	0.3	.267	.337	.402	-.035	.264	.336	.417	.266	2.6	61-LF 1

Breakout: 25% Improve: 49% Collapse: 33% Attrition: 28% Comparables: Jeffrey Hammonds, Brady Clark, Mike Huff, Mike McCormick

A platoon outfielder, Michaels still hits lefties pretty well (.287/.359/.441 in 2007; .300/.382/.460 career), but he's been unable to replicate the success he found with the Phillies. We can forgive a fluctuating batting average, but plummeting walk rates are always confusing. It's hard to say that a guy's eye has gotten worse, but the alternative is that pitchers just don't fear him anymore.

Beau Mills   **1B**   Bats: L   Throws: R   Height: 6' 3"   Weight: 220   Born: August 15, 1986   Age: 21

YEAR	TEAM	LVL	AGE	PA	R	2B	3B	HR	RBI	BB	SO	SB	CS	EqBRR	AVG	OBP	SLG	MLVr	EqAVG	EqOBP	EqSLG	EqA	VORP	DEFENSE		
2007	MHV	A-	20	33	5	2	0	0	1	3	7	0	0	0.2	.179	.303	.250	-.230	.133	.212	.233	.119	-8.1			
2007	LKC	A	20	198	32	12	1	5	36	14	38	0	0	0.6	.271	.333	.435	.051	.219	.266	.350	.214	-6.4	22-3B	-2	16-1B 1
2007	KIN	A+	20	48	7	6	0	1	5	4	8	0	0	0.2	.275	.375	.500	.236	.233	.292	.419	.246	-0.3			
2008	CLE	MLB	21	566	47	32	2	10	59	33	145	4	3	0.3	.221	.272	.349	-.248	.218	.271	.361	.220	-19.3	133-3B	-2	

Breakout: 56% Improve: 73% Collapse: 20% Attrition: 13%   Comparables: Kevin Witt, Johnny Woodard, Chris Duncan, Corey Myers

Some believed that Mills was the most dangerous hitter in the 2007 draft. While at perennial NAIA powerhouse Lewis-Clark State, Mills put up numbers normally associated with video games, batting .458/.556/1.033 with 38 home runs, 100 runs scored and 123 RBI—in just 62 games. He's a bit of an all-or-nothing slugger and isn't very good at first base defensively, but some within the organization see Hafner-esque potential here.

Trot Nixon   **RF**   Bats: L   Throws: L   Height: 6' 2"   Weight: 210   Born: April 11, 1974   Age: 34

YEAR	TEAM	LVL	AGE	PA	R	2B	3B	HR	RBI	BB	SO	SB	CS	EqBRR	AVG	OBP	SLG	MLVr	EqAVG	EqOBP	EqSLG	EqA	VORP	DEFENSE	
2005	BOS	MLB	31	470	64	29	1	13	67	53	59	2	1	-0.9	.275	.357	.446	.070	.274	.367	.454	.286	15.1	106-RF	9
2006	BOS	MLB	32	452	59	24	0	8	52	60	55	0	2	-0.4	.268	.374	.395	-.002	.264	.377	.397	.276	8.0	100-RF	8
2007	CLE	MLB	33	354	30	17	0	3	31	44	59	0	0	-2.0	.251	.342	.336	-.114	.251	.348	.347	.252	-4.2	75-RF	-9
2008	CLE	MLB	34	267	29	12	0	5	30	34	41	1	1	-0.6	.249	.347	.375	-.065	.247	.346	.389	.264	-0.1	66-RF	-2

Breakout: 17% Improve: 41% Collapse: 29% Attrition: 36%   Comparables: Willard Marshall, J. T. Snow, Richie Hebner, Walt Moryn

After a decade with the Red Sox, Nixon moved to Cleveland on a one-year deal and promptly proved that he's pretty much done, posting career lows in numerous offensive categories when nursing an assortment of injuries. Nixon always needed a platoon partner to hit the left-handers for him, but now he can't hit righties, either. He does have some on-base skills, and his résumé will get him another chance, but his prime is now five years in his rearview mirror, and in this one objects are actually further away than they appear.

Jhonny Peralta   **SS**   Bats: R   Throws: R   Height: 6' 1"   Weight: 195   Born: May 28, 1982   Age: 26

YEAR	TEAM	LVL	AGE	PA	R	2B	3B	HR	RBI	BB	SO	SB	CS	EqBRR	AVG	OBP	SLG	MLVr	EqAVG	EqOBP	EqSLG	EqA	VORP	DEFENSE	
2005	CLE	MLB	23	570	82	35	4	24	78	58	128	0	2	-1.1	.292	.366	.520	.230	.300	.383	.546	.310	51.8	137-SS	13
2006	CLE	MLB	24	632	84	28	3	13	68	56	152	0	1	-2.6	.257	.323	.385	-.105	.258	.332	.395	.254	10.5	145-SS	25
2007	CLE	MLB	25	647	87	27	1	21	72	61	146	4	4	-3.0	.270	.341	.430	.030	.271	.348	.450	.274	26.3	149-SS	12
2008	CLE	MLB	26	597	72	28	2	18	74	59	133	5	3	-0.6	.266	.342	.432	.012	.264	.341	.448	.275	23.8	140-SS	6

Breakout: 16% Improve: 48% Collapse: 18% Attrition: 9%   Comparables: Bobby Crosby, Chris Speier, Mike Cuddyer, Clete Boyer

After a great 2005 and an awful 2006, Peralta arrived at a happy medium last year. This version of Peralta is likely the real deal, as it was almost an exact match for his career numbers. He attributed his rebound last year to laser eye surgery, but it's too bad there's no medical procedure that will help his range at shortstop. The Indians insist that he's staying put, but it seems like a forgone conclusion that he'll eventually have to move to second or third, an impression only made stronger by the emergence of Asdrubal Cabrera. Still, as a middle infielder with patience and good power, Peralta's a valuable part of this team.

Josh Rodriguez   **INF**   Bats: R   Throws: R   Height: 6' 0"   Weight: 175   Born: December 18, 1984   Age: 23

YEAR	TEAM	LVL	AGE	PA	R	2B	3B	HR	RBI	BB	SO	SB	CS	EqBRR	AVG	OBP	SLG	MLVr	EqAVG	EqOBP	EqSLG	EqA	VORP	DEFENSE	
2006	MHV	A-	21	175	26	11	4	4	24	14	33	2	0	-0.2	.268	.337	.465	.195	.216	.273	.377	.223	-4.8	41-SS	-7
2007	KIN	A+	22	568	84	20	9	20	82	68	95	21	8	-2.5	.262	.351	.460	.136	.216	.290	.369	.232	-4.5	123-SS	-8
2008	CLE	MLB	23	598	61	28	4	12	57	48	146	13	6	0.5	.226	.291	.359	-.197	.224	.290	.372	.235	-3.0	140-SS	-6

Breakout: 33% Improve: 56% Collapse: 19% Attrition: 11%   Comparables: Tony Manahan, Tyler Greene, Brent Lillibridge, Joe Jester

A second-round pick out of Rice in 2006, Rodriguez's numbers in his full-season debut last year might not impress when taken as a whole, but he came on strong late in the season, hitting .287/.372/.513 after the All-Star break, including 10 home runs in August alone. The bad news is that he's not really a shortstop. The good news is that some think he has Jeff Kent–level potential as a second baseman. We'll see if the Indians are smart enough to hold on to Kent II, having yielded the original for one year of Matt Williams back in the last century.

Kelly Shoppach   C

Bats: R | Throws: R | Height: 6' 0" | Weight: 220 | Born: April 29, 1980 | Age: 28

YEAR	TEAM	LVL	AGE	PA	R	2B	3B	HR	RBI	BB	SO	SB	CS	EqBRR	AVG	OBP	SLG	MLVr	EqAVG	EqOBP	EqSLG	EqA	VORP	DEFENSE
2005	PAW	AAA	25	432	60	16	0	26	75	46	116	0	0	-0.3	.253	.352	.507	.120	.231	.322	.454	.264	14.0	83-C 7
2006	BUF	AAA	26	87	11	8	0	4	9	6	25	0	1	-1.4	.282	.356	.538	.235	.253	.322	.506	.272	5.1	21-C 2
2006	CLE	MLB	26	120	7	6	0	3	16	8	45	0	0	-1.7	.245	.297	.382	-.170	.248	.305	.404	.244	-0.6	32-C 4
2007	CLE	MLB	27	177	26	13	0	7	30	11	56	0	0	0.0	.261	.310	.472	.030	.262	.316	.488	.270	8.3	47-C 3
2008	CLE	MLB	28	281	29	13	1	11	36	24	85	1	1	-0.5	.231	.305	.414	-.099	.229	.304	.429	.255	4.6	69-C 3

Breakout: 21% Improve: 42% Collapse: 34% Attrition: 38%   Comparables: Nelson Santovenia, Todd Pratt, Hank Foiles, John Russell

It's hard to find a backup catcher this good. Hell, it's hard to find a *starting* catcher this good. Shoppach makes a lot of outs, but half of his hits go for extra bases, and he's a very good defender. If there's a problem it's that he's in the wrong organization. He'll have to wait out his team-control years to move elsewhere and blossom as a starter.

Grady Sizemore   CF

Bats: L | Throws: L | Height: 6' 2" | Weight: 200 | Born: August 2, 1982 | Age: 25

YEAR	TEAM	LVL	AGE	PA	R	2B	3B	HR	RBI	BB	SO	SB	CS	EqBRR	AVG	OBP	SLG	MLVr	EqAVG	EqOBP	EqSLG	EqA	VORP	DEFENSE
2005	CLE	MLB	22	706	111	37	11	22	81	52	132	22	10	4.5	.289	.348	.484	.151	.300	.367	.517	.296	44.4	153-CF -10
2006	CLE	MLB	23	751	134	53	11	28	76	78	153	22	6	7.0	.290	.375	.533	.224	.290	.381	.543	.310	69.1	157-CF 5
2007	CLE	MLB	24	748	118	34	5	24	78	101	155	33	10	7.2	.277	.390	.462	.163	.280	.398	.486	.304	53.8	156-CF -5
2008	CLE	MLB	25	671	103	35	6	25	90	76	131	20	6	2.9	.277	.367	.488	.132	.274	.365	.506	.301	38.0	156-CF -3

Breakout: 14% Improve: 41% Collapse: 13% Attrition: 6%   Comparables: Ray Lankford, Barry Bonds, Bobby Murcer, Lloyd Moseby

For a moment, let's ignore that Sizemore is great. His 2007 season is also just plain weird. His walk rate grew dramatically for the second straight season, and he established a new career high in stolen bases by 50 percent, but he also struck out at the highest rate of his career, and his extra-base-hit rate dropped considerably. His PECOTA projection is a logical approximation of his skills, but would you really be surprised if he hit .260? .310? Would it be silly to expect 25 home runs from him yet not shocking if he slugged 36? There are so many directions Sizemore can go from here that his future is largely unpredictable, but whichever way he goes, he'll be good.

Brad Snyder   RF

Bats: L | Throws: L | Height: 6' 3" | Weight: 200 | Born: May 25, 1982 | Age: 26

YEAR	TEAM	LVL	AGE	PA	R	2B	3B	HR	RBI	BB	SO	SB	CS	EqBRR	AVG	OBP	SLG	MLVr	EqAVG	EqOBP	EqSLG	EqA	VORP	DEFENSE	
2005	KIN	A+	23	241	36	10	2	6	28	24	64	12	1	0.4	.278	.365	.431	.112	.216	.282	.335	.224	-9.7	47-CF -1	
2005	AKR	AA	23	337	56	21	5	16	54	25	94	5	3	-0.9	.280	.345	.539	.220	.240	.301	.464	.256	0.3	37-RF 5	17-LF 0
2006	AKR	AA	24	594	86	28	5	18	72	62	158	20	2	2.0	.270	.351	.446	.135	.239	.315	.412	.256	-7.2	124-RF 7	
2007	BUF	AAA	25	303	41	12	3	10	35	36	91	12	0	2.0	.263	.355	.448	.081	.232	.320	.414	.262	-3.1	69-RF -6	
2008	CLE	MLB	26	293	35	14	1	9	34	27	84	9	2	0.3	.239	.314	.403	-.093	.237	.313	.417	.260	-0.8	71-RF 1	

Breakout: 30% Improve: 52% Collapse: 25% Attrition: 23%   Comparables: Steve Hosey, Greg Blosser, Vince Faison, Dave Krynzel

Snyder was a first-round pick in 2003, and while he missed much of the 2007 season with a broken thumb, he has yet to address the one aspect of his game that has kept him out of the majors—his alarming strikeout rate. Snyder has a ton of tools, and you could live with his strikeouts if he was going to pound out 30 home runs a year, but he doesn't have that much power and is likely on his way to one of those Quadruple-A career paths.

Nick Weglarz   LF

Bats: L | Throws: L | Height: 6' 3" | Weight: 215 | Born: December 16, 1987 | Age: 20

YEAR	TEAM	LVL	AGE	PA	R	2B	3B	HR	RBI	BB	SO	SB	CS	EqBRR	AVG	OBP	SLG	MLVr	EqAVG	EqOBP	EqSLG	EqA	VORP	DEFENSE
2005	BNC	Rk	17	166	22	11	0	2	13	17	42	2	1	-1.7	.231	.313	.347	-.097	.169	.223	.227	.142	-50.1	40-RF -8
2007	LKC	A	19	532	75	28	0	23	82	82	129	1	1	-1.4	.276	.395	.497	.229	.224	.323	.378	.248	-13.7	103-LF -11
2008	CLE	MLB	20	619	60	29	1	15	61	65	179	4	3	-0.3	.214	.301	.357	-.189	.212	.300	.370	.238	-18.4	145-LF -3

Breakout: 33% Improve: 63% Collapse: 17% Attrition: 3%   Comparables: Dernell Stenson, Mike Whitlock, Nick Johnson, Michael Hall

Weglarz is a big, slow, unathletic Canadian who missed nearly all of 2006 with a broken bone in his hand. Now the good part: he can really hit. In his full-season debut last year, Weglarz proved to be far less raw than expected, showing a fantastic approach at the plate and a truckload of power. Defensively, he's limited to left field at this point, and that could soon shift to just first base, but he's a pretty intriguing young slugger.

Matt Whitney   **1B**   Bats: R   Throws: R   Height: 6' 4"   Weight: 200   Born: February 13, 1984   Age: 24

YEAR	TEAM	LVL	AGE	PA	R	2B	3B	HR	RBI	BB	SO	SB	CS	EqBRR	AVG	OBP	SLG	MLVr	EqAVG	EqOBP	EqSLG	EqA	VORP	DEFENSE	
2005	LKC	A	21	319	38	7	0	6	27	34	64	0	3	-3.5	.242	.332	.332	-.091	.187	.256	.242	.169	-26.7	55-3B	6
2006	KIN	A+	22	391	40	20	2	10	39	41	131	0	2	-3.2	.206	.294	.362	-.104	.177	.246	.303	.187	-26.9	84-3B	-10
2007	LKC	A	23	326	52	19	0	16	64	31	62	0	1	0.2	.308	.377	.542	.293	.244	.304	.407	.245	-4.3	62-1B	-9
2007	KIN	A+	23	251	43	11	0	16	49	22	59	1	0	0.1	.288	.347	.549	.275	.237	.287	.440	.247	-2.8	44-1B	-1
2008	WAS	MLB	24	572	50	25	1	19	70	45	156	3	1	-0.9	.225	.289	.389	-.193	.225	.289	.397	.232	-8.1	134-1B	1

Breakout: 46% Improve: 71% Collapse: 14% Attrition: 9%   Comparables: Tagg Bozied, Doug Hecker, Corey Smith, Joe Mather

A first-round pick in 2002, Whitney blew out his knee in a pick-up basketball game prior to the 2003 season and wasn't the same until his shocking resurgence last year, when he led all Indians minor leaguers with 32 home runs, which impressed the Nationals enough for them to select him in the Rule 5 draft. As a 24-year-old first baseman who has never played above A-Ball, his chances of sticking are slim, but they're a lot better than they were 12 months ago.

PITCHERS

Rafael Betancourt   Bats: R   Throws: R   Height: 6' 2"   Weight: 200   Born: April 29, 1975   Age: 33

YEAR	TEAM	LVL	AGE	W	L	SV	G	GS	IP	H	BB	SO	HR	GB%	BABIP	STUFF	WHIP	ERA	PERA	EqERA	EqH9	EqBB9	EqSO9	EqHR9	VORP	SN/WX
2005	CLE	MLB	30	4	3	1	54	0	67²	57	17	73	5	35.2%	.295	28	1.09	2.79	3.34	3.29	7.9	2.3	9.5	0.7	19.9	1.14
2006	CLE	MLB	31	3	4	3	50	0	56²	52	11	48	7	25.6%	.280	10	1.11	3.81	3.12	3.41	7.3	1.6	7.0	0.9	13.2	1.62
2007	CLE	MLB	32	5	1	3	68	0	79¹	51	9	80	4	29.0%	.242	35	0.76	1.48	2.14	1.73	5.4	0.9	8.4	0.5	39.8	6.85
2008	CLE	MLB	33	3	3	7	47	0	55	51	13	53	7	33.2%	.288	13	1.15	3.31	3.18	3.18	7.9	1.9	7.7	1.1	16.1	1.50

Breakout: 11% Improve: 33% Collapse: 44% Attrition: 16%   Comparables: Keith Foulke, Trevor Hoffman, John Wetteland, Tom Henke

According to Adjusted Runs Prevented, Betancourt was the top relief pitcher in the American League last year. While his low-90s velocity isn't normally considered "closer stuff," his ability to locate his fastball perfectly (primarily on the low outside corner) makes him very effective. There are a number of good relievers in Cleveland who should be closing instead of Joe Borowski, and Betancourt leads the pack.

Joe Borowski   Bats: R   Throws: R   Height: 6' 2"   Weight: 225   Born: May 4, 1971   Age: 37

YEAR	TEAM	LVL	AGE	W	L	SV	G	GS	IP	H	BB	SO	HR	GB%	BABIP	STUFF	WHIP	ERA	PERA	EqERA	EqH9	EqBB9	EqSO9	EqHR9	VORP	SN/WX
2005	CHN	MLB	34	0	0	0	11	0	11	12	1	11	5	48.6%	.233	-8	1.18	6.55	8.40	7.15	9.5	0.8	7.9	4.0	-1.3	-0.19
2005	TBA	MLB	34	1	5	0	32	0	35¹	26	11	16	3	49.1%	.217	-9	1.05	3.82	2.77	3.41	6.0	2.9	3.9	0.8	7.5	1.04
2006	FLO	MLB	35	3	3	36	72	0	69²	63	33	64	7	34.6%	.284	7	1.38	3.74	3.67	3.66	7.6	3.5	7.3	0.8	14.6	2.82
2007	CLE	MLB	36	4	5	45	69	0	65²	77	17	58	9	35.8%	.342	-1	1.43	5.07	4.89	4.95	9.9	2.0	7.1	1.2	4.1	2.78
2008	CLE	MLB	37	3	5	30	45	0	51²	55	16	41	6	40.3%	.307	-1	1.37	4.21	4.14	4.07	9.2	2.5	6.3	1.1	8.3	1.40

Breakout: 33% Improve: 56% Collapse: 25% Attrition: 21%   Comparables: Cal Eldred, Steve Reed, Giovanni Carrara, Ted Power

As weird as it is that Joe Borowski somehow held onto the closer job all of last year despite posting an ERA over 5.00, it's even weirder that the Indians brought him back to close again this year. Here at BP, we often have internal arguments over the concept of "closer mentality," with some of us believing that a certain mindset is required to succeed in the role, and others believing that if a pitcher can get it done in the seventh or eighth inning, he can get it done in the ninth. If the former group represents the conservative point of view in this debate, Eric Wedge would seem to be to the right of Reagan, quite possibly to the detriment of his team.

Paul Byrd

Bats: R   Throws: R   Height: 6' 1"   Weight: 190   Born: December 3, 1970   Age: 37

YEAR	TEAM	LVL	AGE	W	L	SV	G	GS	IP	H	BB	SO	HR	GB%	BABIP	STUFF	WHIP	ERA	PERA	EqERA	EqH9	EqBB9	EqSO9	EqHR9	VORP	SN/WX
2005	ANA	MLB	34	12	11	0	31	31	204¹	216	28	102	22	39.6%	.290	8	1.19	3.74	4.09	4.27	9.3	1.2	4.4	0.9	35.4	4.10
2006	CLE	MLB	35	10	9	0	31	31	179	232	38	88	26	41.3%	.322	-5	1.51	4.88	5.08	5.37	10.3	1.7	4.0	1.1	-0.5	1.98
2007	CLE	MLB	36	15	8	0	31	31	192¹	239	28	88	27	40.1%	.313	-5	1.39	4.59	5.03	4.69	10.3	1.1	3.8	1.2	18.9	2.51
2008	CLE	MLB	37	6	7	0	29	17	115¹	144	24	52	17	42.8%	.312	-10	1.46	5.19	4.95	5.02	10.8	1.7	3.6	1.3	5.6	1.30

Breakout: 9%   Improve: 35%   Collapse: 43%   Attrition: 38%   Comparables: Vern Law, Dick Donovan, Hal Brown, Kevin Tapani

It's a pretty simple formula for Byrd: don't walk anybody and get some help from the defense. That gets him a little success here and there, and nothing more is really expected of him. The Indians picked up his 2008 option for $8 million, and in today's market, that might be a bargain for a guy who reliably gives you six innings (which he did in 23 of 31 starts last year) and keeps the team in the ball game.

Fausto Carmona

Bats: R   Throws: R   Height: 6' 4"   Weight: 220   Born: December 7, 1983   Age: 24

YEAR	TEAM	LVL	AGE	W	L	SV	G	GS	IP	H	BB	SO	HR	GB%	BABIP	STUFF	WHIP	ERA	PERA	EqERA	EqH9	EqBB9	EqSO9	EqHR9	VORP	SN/WX
2005	AKR	AA	21	6	5	0	14	14	90²	100	20	57	7	57.4%	.312	-12	1.32	4.07	6.58	6.44	11.9	3.1	3.3	1.1	-7.6	—
2005	BUF	AAA	21	7	4	0	13	12	83	76	15	49	10	53.5%	.261	0	1.10	3.25	4.13	3.79	8.2	2.2	3.7	1.3	15.7	—
2006	BUF	AAA	22	1	3	0	6	5	27¹	28	8	28	2	49.4%	.342	2	1.33	5.65	5.74	8.77	10.9	3.2	7.0	1.1	-9.1	—
2006	CLE	MLB	22	1	10	0	38	7	74²	88	31	58	9	60.1%	.346	1	1.59	5.42	5.33	5.06	9.9	3.5	6.5	1.0	3.8	-0.91
2007	CLE	MLB	23	19	8	0	32	32	215	199	61	137	16	64.8%	.282	21	1.21	3.06	3.46	3.00	8.0	2.3	5.4	0.6	64.0	6.85
2008	CLE	MLB	24	12	9	0	29	29	183²	197	62	123	15	58.0%	.310	14	1.41	4.13	4.05	4.11	9.2	2.7	5.4	0.7	27.9	4.40

Breakout: 5%   Improve: 27%   Collapse: 38%   Attrition: 13%   Comparables: Scott Erickson, Brad Penny, Mel Stottlemyre, Jim Kaat

Last year we said that Carmona could succeed as a starter if only the Indians would give him the opportunity. It still took an injury to Jake Westbrook for Carmona to get that chance, but there's no looking back now. He's basically Chien-Ming Wang with better stuff, and his strikeout rate grew throughout the season. If he turns out to be a better pitcher than C. C. Sabathia for the remainder of the decade, we won't be shocked.

Aaron Fultz

Bats: L   Throws: L   Height: 6' 0"   Weight: 210   Born: September 4, 1973   Age: 34

YEAR	TEAM	LVL	AGE	W	L	SV	G	GS	IP	H	BB	SO	HR	GB%	BABIP	STUFF	WHIP	ERA	PERA	EqERA	EqH9	EqBB9	EqSO9	EqHR9	VORP	SN/WX
2005	PHI	MLB	31	4	0	0	62	0	72¹	47	23	54	6	41.2%	.212	8	0.97	2.24	2.77	2.65	5.9	2.6	6.2	0.8	23.5	0.62
2006	PHI	MLB	32	3	1	0	66	1	71¹	80	28	62	7	38.7%	.349	5	1.51	4.54	4.54	4.40	9.5	3.0	7.2	0.8	9.4	0.48
2007	CLE	MLB	33	4	3	0	49	0	37	31	18	28	2	36.9%	.274	3	1.32	2.92	3.21	2.65	7.0	3.9	6.3	0.5	12.5	0.19
2008	CLE	MLB	34	2	2	2	47	0	46	46	19	36	5	41.2%	.294	-2	1.41	4.07	4.01	3.97	8.6	3.4	6.2	0.9	8.1	0.70

Breakout: 10%   Improve: 28%   Collapse: 48%   Attrition: 19%   Comparables: Ricardo Rincon, Ron Mahay, Jerry Don Gleaton, Dennis Cook

Signed on the cheap, Fultz was assigned the job of getting left-handers out, and he did it well, depending mostly on his fastball/changeup combination. The Indians were happy to pick up his cheap 2008 option, as chances are he'll do it again.

Masahide Kobayashi

Bats: R   Throws: R   Height: 6' 0"   Weight: 195   Born: May 24, 1974   Age: 34

YEAR	TEAM	LVL	AGE	W	L	SV	G	GS	IP	H	BB	SO	HR	GB%	BABIP	STUFF	WHIP	ERA	PERA	EqERA	EqH9	EqBB9	EqSO9	EqHR9	VORP	SN/WX
2005	CHB	JP	31	2	2	29	46	0	45¹	49	9	33	6	—	.295	-17	1.28	2.58	6.43	4.39	11.4	2.4	5.3	1.5	5.5	—
2006	CHB	JP	32	6	2	34	53	0	53²	49	8	48	4	—	.296	1	1.06	2.68	4.23	3.93	8.9	2.0	6.4	1.1	9.3	—
2007	CHB	JP	33	2	7	27	49	0	47¹	53	12	35	4	—	.318	-18	1.37	3.62	5.32	6.07	10.2	3.1	5.1	1.2	-2.4	—
2008	CLE	MLB	34	2	3	10	34	0	39²	46	13	27	5	45.2%	.316	-8	1.48	4.94	4.74	4.81	9.9	2.7	5.4	1.1	2.9	0.40

Breakout: 26%   Improve: 49%   Collapse: 31%   Attrition: 38%   Comparables: Ken Sanders, Dyar Miller, Dave Schmidt, Dick Drago

The Indians made their second dip into the pool of Japanese talent during the offseason by signing Kobayashi, one of the top closers in Nippon Professional Baseball history, to a two-year deal. While Kobayashi is on the downward slope of his career, he should be yet another fine bullpen arm. Unlike many Japanese hurlers who depend on finesse and control, Kobayashi is more of a power pitcher, as both his low-90s splitter and hard slider are above-average offerings. Plus, there's always his Keyser Soze connection to add a little intimidation.

Aaron Laffey

Bats: L   **Throws:** L   **Height:** 6' 0"   **Weight:** 170   **Born:** April 15, 1985   **Age:** 23

YEAR	TEAM	LVL	AGE	W	L	SV	G	GS	IP	H	BB	SO	HR	GB%	BABIP	STUFF	WHIP	ERA	PERA	EqERA	EqH9	EqBB9	EqSO9	EqHR9	VORP	SN/WX
2005	LKC	A	20	7	7	1	25	23	142¹	123	52	69	5	68.9%	.268	-19	1.23	3.23	5.63	6.46	9.5	5.9	1.6	0.9	-11.7	—
2006	KIN	A+	21	4	1	1	10	4	41²	38	6	24	0	70.8%	.284	-4	1.07	2.18	4.19	5.31	9.5	2.3	2.8	0.2	1.3	—
2006	AKR	AA	21	8	3	0	19	19	112²	121	33	61	9	61.6%	.320	-19	1.37	3.53	6.86	5.94	11.6	3.7	3.0	1.3	-3.8	—
2007	AKR	AA	22	4	1	0	6	6	35	29	7	24	2	61.7%	.262	5	1.03	2.31	3.93	4.32	8.1	2.4	4.1	0.8	4.7	—
2007	BUF	AAA	22	9	3	0	16	15	96¹	89	23	75	5	63.6%	.293	16	1.16	3.08	4.04	4.00	8.9	2.5	5.1	0.7	16.4	—
2007	CLE	MLB	22	4	2	0	9	9	49¹	54	12	25	2	64.5%	.323	11	1.34	4.56	4.03	4.56	9.7	2.1	4.4	0.4	6.7	0.83
2008	*CLE*	*MLB*	*23*	*9*	*9*	*0*	*43*	*27*	*159¹*	*179*	*58*	*88*	*13*	*57.7%*	*.310*	*0*	*1.48*	*4.58*	*4.38*	*4.57*	*9.7*	*2.9*	*4.4*	*0.7*	*15.1*	*2.70*

Breakout: 30% Improve: 59% Collapse: 17% Attrition: 20%   *Comparables: Dave Stieb, John Mitchell, Mel Stottlemyre, Dick Ellsworth*

Laffey finished the year in the rotation when Cleveland decided they'd had just about enough of Cliff Lee, and he was . . . functional. A classic, undersized left-hander who gets a ton of groundballs, Laffey's not some big prospect with a lot of projection, but what he is should still be of some value to a big-league staff as either a long reliever or back-end starter.

Juan Lara

Bats: R   **Throws:** L   **Height:** 6' 2"   **Weight:** 190   **Born:** January 26, 1981   **Age:** 27

YEAR	TEAM	LVL	AGE	W	L	SV	G	GS	IP	H	BB	SO	HR	GB%	BABIP	STUFF	WHIP	ERA	PERA	EqERA	EqH9	EqBB9	EqSO9	EqHR9	VORP	SN/WX
2005	KIN	A+	24	0	1	0	26	0	42¹	40	15	46	4	61.3%	.316	-23	1.30	4.04	7.22	7.43	11.4	5.2	5.9	1.7	-7.4	—
2005	AKR	AA	24	1	2	5	18	0	23²	27	14	16	1	51.9%	.342	-25	1.73	4.56	7.90	7.84	12.2	7.4	3.5	0.9	-5.2	—
2006	AKR	AA	25	4	2	7	40	0	46²	32	21	48	2	55.2%	.254	-3	1.15	2.73	4.01	4.00	7.2	5.0	5.8	0.6	8.0	—
2006	BUF	AAA	25	1	1	1	13	0	15²	17	3	15	1	63.0%	.356	-4	1.32	2.96	6.27	5.14	12.2	2.6	6.4	1.3	0.7	—
2007	BUF	AAA	26	4	3	2	52	0	58	53	27	50	3	50.0%	.307	-7	1.38	3.88	4.55	4.95	8.8	4.5	5.6	0.6	4.1	—
2008	*CLE*	*MLB*	*27*	*3*	*3*	*1*	*27*	*4*	*50²*	*56*	*28*	*36*	*6*	*50.0%*	*.313*	*-6*	*1.64*	*5.18*	*5.01*	*5.09*	*9.5*	*4.4*	*5.8*	*1.0*	*2.3*	*0.40*

Breakout: 31% Improve: 61% Collapse: 24% Attrition: 17%   *Comparables: Pedro Martinez, Fernando Figueroa, Bryan Eversgerd, Jose Rodriguez*

A left-hander with plus velocity and an outstanding slider, Lara was expected to have been in the big leagues by now, but he was disappointing at Triple-A in 2007, turning in merely a good season. Lara was in a very serious motorcycle accident in the Dominican Republic over the winter, and his long-term outlook is currently unknown.

Cliff Lee

Bats: L   **Throws:** L   **Height:** 6' 3"   **Weight:** 190   **Born:** August 30, 1978   **Age:** 29

YEAR	TEAM	LVL	AGE	W	L	SV	G	GS	IP	H	BB	SO	HR	GB%	BABIP	STUFF	WHIP	ERA	PERA	EqERA	EqH9	EqBB9	EqSO9	EqHR9	VORP	SN/WX
2005	CLE	MLB	26	18	5	0	32	32	202	194	52	143	22	36.2%	.282	15	1.22	3.79	4.09	4.20	8.9	2.3	6.2	1.0	37.2	4.66
2006	CLE	MLB	27	14	11	0	33	33	200²	224	58	129	29	33.9%	.300	5	1.41	4.39	4.37	4.41	8.9	2.4	5.3	1.1	20.0	2.95
2007	BUF	AAA	28	1	3	0	8	8	41	32	25	50	1	45.8%	.298	26	1.39	3.51	3.98	4.43	7.5	5.8	8.0	0.4	5.3	—
2007	CLE	MLB	28	5	8	0	20	16	97¹	112	36	66	17	37.4%	.304	-13	1.52	6.29	5.56	6.23	9.6	2.9	5.5	1.4	-9.3	0.22
2008	*CLE*	*MLB*	*29*	*6*	*7*	*0*	*31*	*17*	*107²*	*117*	*42*	*77*	*15*	*39.0%*	*.301*	*1*	*1.47*	*5.06*	*4.77*	*4.88*	*9.3*	*3.1*	*5.8*	*1.3*	*7.3*	*1.40*

Breakout: 12% Improve: 40% Collapse: 26% Attrition: 23%   *Comparables: Don Carman, Denny Lemaster, Jarrod Washburn, Bud Daley*

Cliff Lee's extreme fly-ball rate always flirted with danger, and when danger flirted back last summer it seemed to shatter Lee's confidence. He still has the same stuff that made him successful in the past, but he'll need to learn to trust it again. Rumors have had him on the trading block, but they might have been generated by his agent, who wants to see his client get another rotation job and another payday.

Jensen Lewis

Bats: R   **Throws:** R   **Height:** 6' 3"   **Weight:** 195   **Born:** May 16, 1984   **Age:** 24

YEAR	TEAM	LVL	AGE	W	L	SV	G	GS	IP	H	BB	SO	HR	GB%	BABIP	STUFF	WHIP	ERA	PERA	EqERA	EqH9	EqBB9	EqSO9	EqHR9	VORP	SN/WX
2005	MHV	A-	21	4	2	0	13	11	59	58	11	59	6	52.0%	.317	-36	1.17	3.20	10.08	7.82	13.0	4.5	4.3	3.0	-11.9	—
2006	KIN	A+	22	7	6	0	21	20	108¹	110	29	94	11	40.5%	.313	-30	1.29	4.00	7.94	7.88	11.9	3.8	5.1	2.1	-24.3	—
2006	AKR	AA	22	1	2	0	7	7	39²	41	12	44	4	41.4%	.356	1	1.35	3.90	7.86	7.20	12.1	3.9	6.9	1.5	-6.2	—
2007	AKR	AA	23	2	0	1	24	0	39	27	13	49	2	39.6%	.287	13	1.03	1.85	3.89	3.75	7.5	3.8	8.5	0.8	7.4	—
2007	BUF	AAA	23	1	0	1	10	0	13	5	4	12	1	31.3%	.133	4	0.69	1.38	2.56	2.08	3.5	2.8	6.2	0.7	5.1	—
2007	CLE	MLB	23	1	1	0	26	0	29¹	26	10	34	1	36.3%	.329	28	1.23	2.15	3.04	2.40	7.5	2.7	9.3	0.3	11.4	0.63
2008	*CLE*	*MLB*	*24*	*3*	*2*	*3*	*43*	*1*	*47*	*45*	*20*	*42*	*5*	*40.2%*	*.296*	*6*	*1.39*	*4.06*	*4.01*	*3.93*	*8.3*	*3.5*	*7.1*	*1.0*	*9.2*	*0.80*

Breakout: 45% Improve: 71% Collapse: 14% Attrition: 29%   *Comparables: Jim Donohue, Dave Beard, Esteban Yan, Eduardo Rodriguez*

No more than decent as a starter in the minors, Lewis was moved to the bullpen last year and took off, all but assuring that his days in the bus leagues are over with a strong big-league debut. His stuff doesn't come close to matching his numbers. He has average velocity and a nice changeup, but what makes him so good is his deception. His motion naturally hides the ball from hitters until near the point of release, which adds a virtual three to five miles per hour to his pitches. It's a nice little trick, and not one you can necessarily teach.

Scott Lewis — Bats: S — Throws: L — Height: 6' 0" — Weight: 185 — Born: September 26, 1983 — Age: 24

YEAR	TEAM	LVL	AGE	W	L	SV	G	GS	IP	H	BB	SO	HR	GB%	BABIP	STUFF	WHIP	ERA	PERA	EqERA	EqH9	EqBB9	EqSO9	EqHR9	VORP	SN/WX
2006	KIN	A+	22	3	3	0	27	26	115[1]	84	28	123	3	43.4%	.277	20	0.97	1.49	4.22	3.57	8.4	3.3	6.5	0.6	23.3	—
2007	AKR	AA	23	7	9	0	27	25	134[2]	135	34	121	13	37.2%	.320	-7	1.25	3.67	5.88	5.20	10.5	3.0	5.9	1.5	5.5	—
2008	CLE	MLB	24	6	7	0	27	17	106[2]	122	43	75	16	39.8%	.312	2	1.55	5.23	5.14	5.02	9.9	3.3	5.7	1.3	5.3	1.30

Breakout: 17% Improve: 46% Collapse: 24% Attrition: 18%   Comparables: Casey Fossum, Ron Bryant, Randy Wolf, Ted Lilly

After winning the somewhat fictional minor league ERA title in 2006, Lewis pitched at the more age-appropriate Double-A level last year and people started to calm down about him. Then again, scouts were never all that high on him in the first place, as his fastball doesn't get out of the mid 80s, leaving him to get by solely on outstanding command. Imagine Jeremy Sowers, only with even less heat. You're not so excited anymore, are you?

Chuck Lofgren — Bats: L — Throws: L — Height: 6' 4" — Weight: 215 — Born: January 29, 1986 — Age: 22

YEAR	TEAM	LVL	AGE	W	L	SV	G	GS	IP	H	BB	SO	HR	GB%	BABIP	STUFF	WHIP	ERA	PERA	EqERA	EqH9	EqBB9	EqSO9	EqHR9	VORP	SN/WX
2005	LKC	A	19	5	5	0	18	18	93	73	43	89	6	43.7%	.279	-3	1.25	2.81	6.67	5.47	9.6	7.3	4.7	1.5	1.1	—
2006	KIN	A+	20	17	5	0	25	25	139	108	54	125	5	38.0%	.276	14	1.17	2.33	4.88	5.14	8.7	4.9	5.2	0.9	6.4	—
2007	AKR	AA	21	12	7	0	26	26	146[1]	153	68	123	14	43.1%	.321	-8	1.51	4.37	6.76	6.27	10.7	5.0	5.2	1.4	-10.1	—
2008	CLE	MLB	22	6	9	0	24	24	126	146	80	85	19	41.3%	.315	-2	1.79	6.09	6.00	5.85	10.0	5.1	5.5	1.4	-5.9	0.30

Breakout: 30% Improve: 62% Collapse: 11% Attrition: 12%   Comparables: Chris Seddon, Jarrod Washburn, Ben Van Ryn, Aaron Myette

One of the most misunderstood things about prospects is that they're rarely already good enough. Rather, they have to continually get better as they climb the ladder to the major leagues. If they don't, you get something like Chuck Lofgren. His 2007 season was a disappointment that left a lot of people scratching their heads, but not because he pitched worse than he did in 2006; he just didn't get any better, and because the level of competition was harder, his performance regressed. He's still a solid prospect, he's just not as shiny as he once was.

Thomas Mastny — Bats: R — Throws: R — Height: 6' 6" — Weight: 225 — Born: February 4, 1981 — Age: 27

YEAR	TEAM	LVL	AGE	W	L	SV	G	GS	IP	H	BB	SO	HR	GB%	BABIP	STUFF	WHIP	ERA	PERA	EqERA	EqH9	EqBB9	EqSO9	EqHR9	VORP	SN/WX
2005	KIN	A+	24	7	3	2	29	11	88	78	26	94	4	57.4%	.320	-7	1.18	2.35	5.74	4.93	10.4	4.3	5.6	0.9	5.7	—
2005	AKR	AA	24	1	1	0	5	3	20[2]	18	5	18	0	32.3%	.290	0	1.11	2.17	4.41	4.34	9.6	3.4	4.8	0.5	2.6	—
2006	AKR	AA	25	0	1	1	12	1	24[1]	15	8	30	0	60.7%	.254	10	0.95	1.12	3.28	3.00	6.4	3.8	7.1	0.4	6.9	—
2006	BUF	AAA	25	2	1	0	24	0	38[2]	25	16	46	0	46.7%	.278	17	1.07	2.59	3.56	3.47	6.9	4.5	8.2	0.2	8.6	—
2006	CLE	MLB	25	0	1	5	15	0	16[1]	17	8	14	1	50.0%	.348	0	1.53	5.52	4.19	4.96	8.8	3.9	7.2	0.6	1.0	0.09
2007	CLE	MLB	26	7	2	2	51	0	57[2]	63	32	52	6	43.8%	.345	1	1.65	4.68	5.29	4.42	9.6	4.4	7.6	0.9	7.9	0.60
2008	CLE	MLB	27	3	2	2	45	0	54	54	25	46	5	46.9%	.304	3	1.46	4.19	4.09	4.12	8.5	3.8	6.9	0.9	9.1	0.70

Breakout: 30% Improve: 47% Collapse: 27% Attrition: 24%   Comparables: Paul Shuey, Jeff Nelson, Brad Arnsberg, Rick Bauer

Mastny is no more than that extra bullpen arm, nor will he ever be any more than that, but that's certainly more than was ever expected of him. A lower-round pick whose claim to fame is being the greatest pitcher in the history of Furman University, Mastny doesn't have much in the way of stuff, but he throws a sinker and uses his height to add even more of a downhill plane to the pitch, and that's good enough to be that extra arm that everyone is looking for.

Adam Miller

| | | | | | | | | | | | | Bats: R | | Throws: R | | Height: 6' 4" | | Weight: 200 | | Born: November 26, 1984 | | Age: 23 |

YEAR	TEAM	LVL	AGE	W	L	SV	G	GS	IP	H	BB	SO	HR	GB%	BABIP	STUFF	WHIP	ERA	PERA	EqERA	EqH9	EqBB9	EqSO9	EqHR9	VORP	SN/WX
2005	KIN	A+	20	2	4	0	12	12	59²	76	17	45	5	47.7%	.376	-25	1.56	4.82	9.58	10.28	14.5	4.4	3.5	1.6	-26.9	—
2006	AKR	AA	21	15	6	0	26	24	153²	129	43	157	9	55.6%	.301	16	1.12	2.76	4.84	4.75	9.3	3.4	6.1	1.0	13.4	—
2007	BUF	AAA	22	5	4	0	19	11	65¹	68	21	68	4	53.6%	.346	8	1.36	4.82	5.33	6.21	10.4	3.3	6.9	0.9	-4.2	—
2008	CLE	MLB	23	5	5	0	24	13	86	94	37	69	8	50.2%	.323	9	1.51	4.84	4.55	4.76	9.4	3.5	6.5	0.9	6.8	1.20

Breakout: 46% Improve: 73% Collapse: 15% Attrition: 24%   Comparables: Kevin Gross, Colby Lewis, J.D. Martin, Cesar Carrillo

Although his talent is undeniable, Miller has become a frustration. Last year, for the second time in three years, he missed considerable time due to elbow issues (call it soreness, call it inflammation, call it unreliability), and the Tommy John surgery he's been avoiding now seems less like a possibility and more like an inevitability. That's a shame, because Miller's pretty much everything you look for in a power pitcher. He's tall, throws in the mid 90s, has a wipeout slider, and pitches with a fearless arrogance that teams love to see. He looked good in the Arizona Fall League and could get a look as a reliever this year as a way to get him to the big leagues in a quicker (and safer) manner.

Edward Mujica

| | | | | | | | | | | | | Bats: R | | Throws: R | | Height: 6' 2" | | Weight: 220 | | Born: May 10, 1984 | | Age: 24 |

YEAR	TEAM	LVL	AGE	W	L	SV	G	GS	IP	H	BB	SO	HR	GB%	BABIP	STUFF	WHIP	ERA	PERA	EqERA	EqH9	EqBB9	EqSO9	EqHR9	VORP	SN/WX
2005	KIN	A+	21	1	0	14	25	0	26	17	2	32	3	40.3%	.241	7	0.73	2.08	4.66	3.91	7.8	2.0	6.7	2.0	4.3	—
2005	AKR	AA	21	2	1	10	27	0	34¹	36	5	33	2	44.7%	.351	-1	1.20	2.89	5.76	4.75	11.9	2.4	5.6	0.9	2.9	—
2006	AKR	AA	22	1	0	8	12	0	19²	11	9	17	0	54.0%	.229	2	1.04	0.00	3.43	1.50	6.0	5.5	5.0	0.0	8.2	—
2006	BUF	AAA	22	3	1	5	22	0	32¹	31	5	29	1	37.9%	.333	7	1.12	2.52	4.37	3.94	10.0	1.8	6.1	0.6	5.5	—
2006	CLE	MLB	22	0	1	0	10	0	18¹	25	0	12	1	24.6%	.387	10	1.36	2.95	4.69	3.00	11.5	0.5	5.5	0.5	6.3	-0.24
2007	BUF	AAA	23	2	1	14	34	0	37²	35	9	44	4	35.0%	.333	2	1.17	5.01	5.21	6.17	9.8	2.6	8.2	1.5	-2.2	—
2007	CLE	MLB	23	0	0	0	10	0	13	19	2	7	3	29.4%	.340	-23	1.62	8.31	7.71	8.10	12.2	1.4	4.1	2.0	-3.7	-0.00
2008	CLE	MLB	24	3	3	5	50	3	57	60	16	44	8	37.0%	.297	2	1.33	4.23	4.19	4.06	9.1	2.3	6.2	1.3	9.1	1.00

Breakout: 55% Improve: 81% Collapse: 8% Attrition: 16%   Comparables: Manny Sarmiento, Edwin Nuñez, Ryan Kohlmeier, Jorge Julio

Yet another power arm with a fastball/slider combination, Mujica has everything it takes to be in the majors with one exception—the ability to retire lefties. At Triple-A Buffalo last year, left-handers hit .304/.367/.522 off the Venezuelan, while righties could only manage a meager .194/.216/.264. This is the danger with pitchers who have a low-three-quarters delivery—opposite-handed hitters just see the ball too early and too well. Insert requisite Chad Bradford reference here.

Rafael Perez

| | | | | | | | | | | | | Bats: L | | Throws: L | | Height: 6' 3" | | Weight: 185 | | Born: May 15, 1982 | | Age: 26 |

YEAR	TEAM	LVL	AGE	W	L	SV	G	GS	IP	H	BB	SO	HR	GB%	BABIP	STUFF	WHIP	ERA	PERA	EqERA	EqH9	EqBB9	EqSO9	EqHR9	VORP	SN/WX
2005	KIN	A+	23	8	5	0	14	14	77²	54	32	48	6	65.7%	.213	-17	1.11	3.36	4.90	5.77	7.5	5.5	2.8	1.3	-1.3	—
2005	AKR	AA	23	4	3	1	15	8	66²	53	12	46	5	61.1%	.245	-7	0.97	1.75	4.29	4.35	8.6	2.5	3.8	1.0	8.3	—
2006	AKR	AA	24	4	5	0	12	12	67¹	53	22	53	3	61.2%	.267	0	1.12	2.82	4.27	4.76	8.2	3.9	4.5	0.7	5.8	—
2006	BUF	AAA	24	0	3	0	13	0	27¹	20	8	33	0	71.0%	.303	15	1.03	2.66	3.48	4.78	7.5	3.1	7.9	0.3	2.4	—
2006	CLE	MLB	24	0	0	0	18	0	12¹	10	6	15	2	60.0%	.250	14	1.30	4.39	3.12	3.29	5.9	4.0	9.2	1.3	2.3	0.11
2007	BUF	AAA	25	3	3	0	8	7	46²	53	11	31	3	52.3%	.347	-4	1.37	3.66	5.63	6.07	11.3	2.5	4.4	0.8	-2.2	—
2007	CLE	MLB	25	1	2	1	44	0	60²	41	15	62	5	54.7%	.237	25	0.92	1.78	2.42	2.04	5.5	1.9	8.3	0.7	25.3	3.14
2008	CLE	MLB	26	4	4	3	54	4	74¹	71	28	57	6	53.0%	.294	4	1.34	3.78	3.59	3.76	8.3	3.1	6.2	0.7	16.1	1.50

Breakout: 22% Improve: 42% Collapse: 32% Attrition: 22%   Comparables: Bill Scherrer, Ed Vande Berg, Paul Assenmacher, Gene Walter

Yet another power arm in the bullpen, Perez didn't join the big league squad until late May, then pitched so well that the club wondered why they had waited so long to make the call. Perez is more than a little like Carmona, as he comes at hitters with a mid-90s sinker and then makes them look foolish with a hard, biting slider out of the zone. The Indians pen is really a great thing until you get to Joe Borowski; it's like eating a remarkable meal at the best restaurant in town and having a Twinkie for dessert.

C. C. Sabathia

Bats: L   Throws: L   Height: 6' 7"   Weight: 290   Born: July 21, 1980   Age: 27

YEAR	TEAM	LVL	AGE	W	L	SV	G	GS	IP	H	BB	SO	HR	GB%	BABIP	STUFF	WHIP	ERA	PERA	EqERA	EqH9	EqBB9	EqSO9	EqHR9	VORP	SN/WX
2005	CLE	MLB	24	15	10	0	31	31	196²	185	62	161	19	50.1%	.294	22	1.26	4.03	4.20	4.36	8.9	2.9	7.3	0.9	32.8	4.48
2006	CLE	MLB	25	12	11	0	28	28	192²	182	44	172	17	46.6%	.301	32	1.17	3.22	3.19	3.44	7.6	1.9	7.4	0.7	46.5	5.99
2007	CLE	MLB	26	19	7	0	34	34	241	238	37	209	20	47.6%	.316	32	1.14	3.21	3.49	3.30	8.6	1.2	7.3	0.7	65.2	6.54
2008	CLE	MLB	27	15	8	0	32	32	215	210	53	179	20	46.8%	.299	24	1.22	3.51	3.38	3.45	8.4	2.0	6.7	0.8	47.6	6.90

Breakout: 18%   Improve: 50%   Collapse: 22%   Attrition: 14%   Comparables: Andy Benes, Don Drysdale, Mark Gubicza, Freddy Garcia

On a per-inning basis, Sabathia was pretty much the exact same pitcher last year that he was in 2006. The difference was that, after carefully keeping Sabathia's innings-pitched totals below 200 through his age-25 season, the team worked the 26-year-old *hard* last year, to a point that almost seemed dangerous. Sabathia eclipsed the 250-inning mark during the ALCS, and it was evident to everybody watching that Sabathia was just plain out of gas in the postseason. The 87 pitches Sabathia threw in a loss to Detroit on July 5 represented his lowest single-game total on the year; he reached 100 pitches in all but seven starts, and went to 110 or more 12 times. All of that work earned Sabathia the Cy Young award and got the Tribe into the playoffs for the first time in six years, but this year the team might want to consider easing up on the hefty lefty.

Jeremy Sowers

Bats: L   Throws: L   Height: 6' 1"   Weight: 180   Born: May 17, 1983   Age: 25

YEAR	TEAM	LVL	AGE	W	L	SV	G	GS	IP	H	BB	SO	HR	GB%	BABIP	STUFF	WHIP	ERA	PERA	EqERA	EqH9	EqBB9	EqSO9	EqHR9	VORP	SN/WX
2005	KIN	A+	22	8	3	0	13	13	71¹	60	19	75	5	54.9%	.291	-1	1.11	2.78	5.63	5.20	10.0	4.0	5.5	1.3	2.8	—
2005	AKR	AA	22	5	1	0	13	13	82¹	74	9	70	8	49.0%	.288	3	1.01	2.08	5.08	4.15	9.9	1.8	4.9	1.3	11.9	—
2006	BUF	AAA	23	9	1	0	15	15	97²	78	29	54	1	53.5%	.263	14	1.10	1.39	3.59	2.72	8.2	3.4	3.5	0.2	28.6	—
2006	CLE	MLB	23	7	4	0	14	14	88¹	85	20	35	10	49.2%	.257	4	1.19	3.57	3.37	3.17	7.7	1.9	3.4	0.9	23.0	2.78
2007	CLE	MLB	24	1	6	0	13	13	67¹	84	21	24	10	40.9%	.310	-20	1.56	6.42	5.80	6.25	10.5	2.4	2.9	1.3	-4.7	0.40
2007	BUF	AAA	24	4	5	0	15	15	96²	112	24	61	6	49.0%	.329	-3	1.41	4.10	5.13	5.93	10.6	2.5	3.9	0.8	-3.5	—
2008	CLE	MLB	25	7	9	0	26	26	131²	159	46	66	18	46.1%	.312	-3	1.56	5.45	5.13	5.31	10.4	2.8	4.0	1.2	2.1	1.20

Breakout: 10%   Improve: 41%   Collapse: 35%   Attrition: 19%   Comparables: Chris George, Tim Drew, Allen Watson, Brian Anderson

Sowers' 2006 performance was a lie. That shouldn't surprise anyone; when your strikeout rate is the same as your ERA, something has to give. Last year, Sowers got hit hard for the first time in his life, and the logical, yet dangerous conclusion he reached was that if he stopped throwing strikes, the guys with the lumber in their hands would stop hitting him so hard. That's a common self-diagnosis that comes with the side effect of falling behind in counts and thus having to throw even more hittable strikes. The Indians believe that Sowers straightened some things out in the minors during the second half, learning not only to trust his stuff, as the scouts say, but also to accept the fact that he's a command-and-control pitcher who isn't going to put up goose eggs every time out. They still feel he has rotation potential, they just don't have an opening in the rotation anymore.

Jake Westbrook

Bats: R   Throws: R   Height: 6' 3"   Weight: 200   Born: September 29, 1977   Age: 30

YEAR	TEAM	LVL	AGE	W	L	SV	G	GS	IP	H	BB	SO	HR	GB%	BABIP	STUFF	WHIP	ERA	PERA	EqERA	EqH9	EqBB9	EqSO9	EqHR9	VORP	SN/WX
2005	CLE	MLB	27	15	15	0	34	34	210²	218	56	119	19	61.8%	.291	8	1.30	4.49	4.46	5.36	9.7	2.4	5.0	0.8	12.2	3.06
2006	CLE	MLB	28	15	10	0	32	32	211¹	247	55	109	15	62.4%	.326	13	1.43	4.17	4.22	4.11	9.8	2.2	4.4	0.6	35.6	5.02
2007	CLE	MLB	29	6	9	0	25	25	152	159	55	93	13	55.7%	.310	11	1.41	4.32	4.30	4.31	9.1	3.0	5.2	0.8	21.8	3.27
2008	CLE	MLB	30	10	10	0	29	29	173¹	199	58	103	15	56.2%	.318	7	1.48	4.60	4.40	4.58	9.9	2.7	4.8	0.7	16.5	3.20

Breakout: 17%   Improve: 54%   Collapse: 18%   Attrition: 12%   Comparables: Dick Ruthven, Dennis Lamp, Mike LaCoss, Mel Stottlemyre

Westbrook is something like a younger Paul Byrd. All he has to do is keep throwing sinkers and changeups for strikes, get a little help from his defense and some runs to work with, and everything works out just fine. Whether that's worth $31 million for the next three years is worthy of a debate, but an abdominal strain that cost him six weeks last year is the only knock against his health record in the last four seasons, and sometimes dependable can be as valuable as good.

LINEOUTS

Hitters

PLAYER	TEAM	LVL	AGE	PA	R	2B	3B	HR	RBI	BB	SO	SB-CS	EqBRR	AVG/OBP/SLG	MLVr	EqAVG/EqOBP/EqSLG	EqA	VORP
OF J. Cooper*	BUF	AAA	26	395	60	26	8	10	51	51	81	9-2	3.2	.260/.357/.472	.113	.243/.335/.456	.273	5.0
2B A. Davis#	LKC	A	22	583	95	23	8	6	41	74	113	22-11	1.0	.266/.367/.380	.029	.212/.296/.301	.214	-21.9
OF J. Drennen*	KIN	A+	20	565	72	25	2	13	77	53	104	6-6	-1.3	.254/.336/.391	.013	.208/.273/.317	.205	-43.6
3B K. Ginter	BUF	AAA	31	449	50	15	1	15	62	63	68	3-3	-0.3	.247/.364/.415	.043	.232/.342/.397	.261	11.8
INF C. Gomez	BAL	MLB	36	185	17	10	1	1	16	10	20	1-2	-3.2	.302/.339/.391	-.012	.310/.350/.399	.258	3.2
	CLE	MLB	36	55	4	2	0	0	5	0	6	0-0	0.4	.283/.278/.321	-.236	.283/.278/.321	.209	-1.8
1B S. Head*	KIN	A+	23	447	73	29	0	13	61	40	71	5-0	0.0	.251/.336/.426	.058	.210/.275/.349	.220	-24.7
	AKR	AA	23	106	13	9	0	3	18	8	18	1-0	0.3	.276/.330/.459	.086	.253/.302/.434	.252	-0.8
1B R. Mulhern	BUF	AAA	26	527	67	36	2	16	76	40	133	1-3	-3.6	.290/.350/.475	.131	.256/.314/.446	.258	4.8
2B L. Rivas	BUF	AAA	27	465	58	17	3	11	43	42	69	13-7	-0.7	.263/.341/.400	-.001	.243/.316/.388	.246	8.3
SS C. Rivero	LKC	A	19	490	59	26	0	7	62	47	84	1-2	-2.8	.261/.332/.369	-.045	.213/.271/.289	.195	-23.6
2B M. Rouse*	CLE	MLB	27	76	7	1	0	0	4	7	20	1-1	0.1	.119/.200/.134	-.723	.121/.213/.136	.096	-10.6
	BUF	AAA	27	79	11	4	1	0	3	9	8	1-1	0.6	.277/.368/.369	.013	.254/.346/.343	.249	1.4
C W. Toregas	AKR	AA	24	324	36	16	0	6	39	27	45	3-1	-1.3	.250/.317/.370	-.075	.228/.288/.334	.223	-9.0

Jason Cooper is a one-dimensional outfielder, and that one dimension, power, seems to be winking out of existence. After four consecutive seasons at Triple-A Buffalo in 2007, and with a fifth likely, he's no more than an insurance policy, but we bet he knows where to find the best wings. ⊘ **Adam Davis** is a switch-hitter who can get on base and run well, which just might be enough to give him some kind of career. ⊘ **John Drennen**'s prospect status took a huge hit with a disappointing 2007. As a guy who projects as a corner outfielder, he needs to pick up the pace offensively. ⊘ Last year, **Keith Ginter** spent his second straight season at Triple-A without getting a call. He'll be Boston's insurance policy in 2008. ⊘ Every year, someone is going to need an extra who can play shortstop, and they're going to call **Chris Gomez**, even though he's getting near the end. This winter that someone was new Pirates GM (and former Indians executive) Neal Huntington. ⊘ **Stephen Head** had a bit of a rebound in 2007, but as he's supposed to be a slugging first baseman, it wasn't enough. ⊘ After hitting 32 home runs in 2005, **Ryan Mulhern** was unable to top half of that total in either of the last two years, and at 27, that's pretty much the end of that. ⊘ A one-time starter for the Twins, **Luis Rivas** toiled away at Triple-A last year while getting passed by Asdrubal Cabrera. He might have a better shot with the Pirates, not that he really deserves one. ⊘ Shortstop **Carlos Rivero** is notable for being young and loaded with tools, but he has a long way to go to convert them into baseball skills. ⊘ **Mike Rouse** made the Opening Day roster last year, but after going 8-for-67, he lost the utility job, never to return. ⊘ **Wyatt Toregas** is one of the better defensive catchers in the minors and has just enough bat to profile as a future backup.

Pitchers

PLAYER	TEAM	LVL	AGE	W	L	SV	IP	H	BB	SO	HR	GB%	BABIP	STUFF	WHIP	ERA	PERA	EqERA	EqH9	EqBB9	EqSO9	EqHR9	VORP
M. Koplove	BUF	AAA	30	4	2	14	54	49	22	44	3	50.3%	.297	-8	1.31	2.50	4.56	3.38	8.9	4.1	5.5	0.7	12.5
J. Martin	AKR	AA	24	2	3	0	42^1	42	16	23	4	50.3%	.281	-24	1.37	4.26	5.65	5.80	9.6	4.0	3.1	1.3	-0.9
M. Miller	BUF	AAA	35	0	1	1	37^1	25	21	36	4	52.6%	.247	-5	1.23	2.90	4.40	4.33	6.6	5.6	6.4	1.5	5.0
S. Nottingham*	AKR	AA	22	9	12	0	149	157	59	96	11	38.3%	.315	-14	1.45	4.77	5.76	6.57	10.3	4.3	3.8	1.1	-15.2
R. Santos*	AKR	AA	24	8	3	2	96	80	30	85	10	44.6%	.264	-17	1.15	2.72	4.85	4.67	8.4	3.5	5.6	1.5	9.4
B. Slocum	BUF	AAA	26	2	2	0	26	21	16	28	3	46.6%	.257	6	1.42	4.15	4.99	5.19	7.6	5.9	6.9	1.4	1.2
S. Smith	BUF	AAA	23	9	7	0	133^1	130	58	90	16	39.7%	.289	-20	1.41	4.25	5.90	5.36	9.5	4.4	4.4	1.6	3.4
J. Stanford*	BUF	AAA	30	5	1	0	87^2	84	34	60	8	44.0%	.292	-13	1.35	4.10	5.27	5.27	9.3	3.9	4.4	1.2	3.1
	CLE	MLB	30	1	1	0	26^1	32	7	16	1	46.2%	.341	2	1.48	4.79	4.34	4.72	10.1	2.0	5.1	0.3	2.0
S. Tseng	KIN	A+	22	6	9	0	140	130	47	92	10	38.0%	.287	-26	1.26	4.05	6.49	7.06	10.6	4.8	3.3	1.5	-20.1
N. Wagner	LKC	A	23	1	4	11	44	41	11	49	3	40.7%	.330	-19	1.18	3.68	6.28	6.35	10.9	4.1	5.7	1.4	-3.3
	KIN	A+	23	0	0	0	24	17	6	18	2	54.4%	.227	-22	0.96	3.00	4.99	5.06	8.0	3.8	4.2	1.7	1.3

After nine years in Arizona's system, **Mike Koplove** needed just one with Cleveland to prove that he's not much more than a Triple-A arm. He'll prove it to the Dodgers this spring. ⊘ Right-hander **J.D. Martin** constantly teases the organization with his talents, only to frustrate them with his elbow problems. Dropped from the roster and brought back on a minor league deal, he may be on his last chance with Cleveland. ⊘ Side-armer **Matt Miller** once had a steady job in the Cleveland bullpen, but he's now 36 and has been passed by the plethora of young relievers in the system. ⊘ **Shawn Nottingham** is a fringy lefty whose lack of velocity started to catch up to him at Double-A last year. Curiously, the poor of Sherwood Forest were all throwing in the mid-90s. ⊘ Southpaw **Reid Santos** also has fringy stuff, but his breaking ball has been good enough for him to have some success as a reliever, and teams always need lefties. ⊘ Left-hander **Tony Sipp** was one of the best relief prospects in the system before he missed all of 2007 recovering from Tommy John surgery. ⊘ After reaching the majors at the end of 2006, **Brian Slocum** missed the majority of 2007 with elbow problems, but he pitched well in Venezuela this winter and will serve as a Triple-A insurance policy this year. ⊘ A right-hander who has been slowly moving up the ladder, **Sean Smith** reached Triple-A in his sixth professional season, but bumped his head on his ceiling in the process. ⊘ **Jason Stanford** spent most of the year at Triple-A Buffalo, but made a pair of emergency starts and some garbage-time relief appearances for the Tribe before getting "designated for assignment," which is a baseball term for, "we are done with you." ⊘ A big-budget signing out of Taiwan, **Sung-Wei Tseng** held his own in the Carolina League during his stateside debut, but scouts were left wondering why he was worth 300 grand. ⊘ **Neil Wagner** is a prospect because he packs some serious heat and strikes guys out, but he's still looking for a second pitch.

MANAGER: ERIC WEDGE

YEAR	TEAM	W-L	Pythag +/−	Avg PC	100+ P	120+ P	QS	BQS	REL	REL w Zero R	IBB	Subs	PH	PH Avg	PH HR	SB2	CS2	SB3	CS3	SAC Att	SAC %	POS SAC	Squeeze	Swing	In Play
2005	CLE	93-69	-5	96.7	72	0	83	12	409	281	20	33	87	.213	0	55	30	6	5	54	72.2%	38	0	126	97
2006	CLE	78-84	-12	97.4	81	2	77	14	379	221	35	26	97	.232	2	50	19	5	4	44	68.2%	27	0	121	87
2007	CLE	96-66	4	95.9	69	1	89	10	395	248	42	58	116	.272	4	66	40	6	1	43	74.4%	30	0	136	98

Maybe we should refer to Wedge as flexibly inflexible. He used his bench and his bullpen more than ever last year, but those units were also more talented than ever, especially the relief corps. Still, it was his handling of the bullpen that was so perplexing. Wedge got the best out of an ever-changing unit that was constantly being bolstered by talented youngsters from Buffalo, yet never showed any willingness to change closers, even when Borowski was at his worst. That certainly seemed like a mistake, but we don't have any guarantee that someone else would have done better, and in the end, it wasn't Borowski who cost the team the pennant. The problem with judging Wedge for his devotion to Borowski is that, while the numbers might tell us that someone else could have done a better job in the role, we don't know what was going on in the team's internal meetings, or how the organization's pitching coaches advised Wedge as far as the use of the team's young arms.

That brings us to a larger point. There's a lot more that goes into certain managerial decisions than simply choosing the player with the highest statistical probability of success. The manager has to maximize each individual player's probability of success as well, and only by doing that can he properly maximize his team's chances. Sometimes that requires using less-optimal players in certain roles, because of their mental or emotional disposition toward the type of work involved or because of other players' disposition against it. As outsiders, and by that we mean anyone not employed by the team, we are generally unqualified to pass judgment on that aspect of a manager's performance. In Wedge's case, using Borowski as the closer may have been a better use of the personalities on his roster than saving one of his better relievers for that role while using Borowski in the often even more crucial seventh and eighth innings. It certainly seemed to work out last year.

Colorado Rockies

Last year, the Rockies taught us something extremely simple—that today's game is being played in a competitive environment so dynamic that almost every team in the National League has reason to look to the future with equal measures of hope and faith. In such an environment, our existing archetypes of big and small market, have and have-not, small ball and Moneyball have little bearing. Rather the task at hand is, quite simply, to build the best ballclub one can, which is exactly what the Rockies did. For humbling us with this lovely lesson, we owe the Colorado Rockies, a franchise which few, if any, had argued was one of the great examples of perceptive organizational management in the game, a tremendous debt.

Another lesson we learned from the 2007 Rockies is that the odds are not guarantees. With little more than two weeks left in the season, the Rockies bounded back from virtual elimination by winning 13 of their last 14 games to pass the rest of a crowded National League wild-card field and force a play-in game against the Padres, which they also won in dramatic fashion. By Nate Silver's calculations, that run was one of the five greatest regular-season comebacks in baseball history. As Silver pointed out on Baseball Prospectus.com, the Rockies "were never, not for one day, greater than even-money to make the playoffs until they actually did . . . in fact, they were never higher than 34 percent."

In the playoffs, the Rockies extended their winning streak to 21 of 22 games by sweeping their way past the Phillies and Diamondbacks into the World Series, only to be swept themselves by the Red Sox. That postseason performance was a continuation of the team's habit of blowing hot and cold throughout the season.

With the offense struggling early, the Rockies opened the 2007 season with a weak 18-27 run. They then snapped off the sort of streak for which they are now famous, racking up 20 wins in their next 27 games to get back above .500. Then they slumped again, losing eight straight at one point and dropping to 39-43 after the first day of July, only to rally again, winning five of six to pull even at the All-Star break and going 37-29 through September 15. At that point the Rockies were 76-72, 6½ games behind in the NL West, 4½ games back and in the wild-card standings, and in fourth place in both races. Then began their 13-1 run.

What you might lose in all of that in-season *Sturm und Drang* is that the Rockies didn't just outplay their competition over the final two weeks of the season, they outplayed them all year long. Take a look at the three sets of standings in Table 1, which contains the actual NL West finish as well as the standings sorted by both straightforward Pythagenport records determined by run differential and Clay Davenport's more involved Third-Order Wins, which first adjust runs scored and allowed according to their component parts (hits, walks, etc.), then make further adjustments for strength of schedule. The wild comeback that took place in late September wasn't so much an upset as a correction—the Rockies were the best team in the division.

What makes that so surprising is that in the 14-year history of the franchise, the Rockies had finished better than third in the division just once, that coming all the way back in 1995, and had finished no better than fourth in the nine seasons leading up to last year. One reason for this protracted futility is that throughout the franchise's history, and particularly since current gen-

Table 1. Westing (by Musket and Sextant)

Actual		Pythagenport		Third-Order Wins	
D'backs	90-72	Rockies	91.4-71.7	Rockies	90.2-72.8
Rockies	90-73	Padres	89.5-73.5	Dodgers	87.3-74.7
Padres	89-74	Dodgers	81.8-80.2	Padres	84.6-78.4
Dodgers	82-89	D'backs	78.9-83.1	Giants	78.2-83.8
Giants	71-91	Giants	77.1-84.9	D'backs	77.8-84.2

eral manager Dan O'Dowd took the helm just before the end of the 1999 season, the team had searched for ways to win in Denver's altitude. This was something of a fool's errand because the club had always been reliably stronger at home. In the Rockies' first 14 years of existence, they had a .543 winning percentage in Denver, which works out to a 44-37 record in a season's worth of home games. Their real problems came on the road, where the team had played at a much more feeble .387 clip, which translates to just 31 road wins a year. A 75-win team seemed like this franchise's birthright.

Despite this split, the Rockies' efforts to build a team that could win in Denver's thin air played out like yet another over-long Dan Simmons novel on mankind's learning to adapt or die. Whether it was the Blake Street Bombers of their previous wild-card season of 1995—a team that scored nearly 500 runs at home but just 300 on the road—or the great changeup experiment of 2001 that made starters Mike Hampton and Denny Neagle very wealthy men only to watch them get rocked as Rockies, the team's hunger for a magic formula that would allow it to exploit its unique environment only seemed to get in the way of more basic concerns such as player development or building a ballclub good enough to win the one place it never had: on the road.

Such attempts to exploit his environment having failed, O'Dowd chose instead to exploit the marketplace. Absorbing the true lesson of *Moneyball*, O'Dowd identified team defense as an area in which arbitrage-driven analysis might yield low- or modest-cost improvements that would have a much larger impact on the fortunes of his club than the size of the investment might suggest. Billy Beane tried this himself, but whereas Beane wound up spending buckets of money on Mark Kotsay, O'Dowd found more cost-effective solutions, pulling together parts from different sources to plug in at the key up-the-middle positions. Last year's rookie sensation, shortstop Troy Tulowitzki, actually came first, when the Rockies picked him in the first round of the 2005 draft. While some worried about Tulo's size at short, his plus arm and other gifts made him a short-list candidate for Gold Glove consideration in his first full season in The Show last year. At the major league level, O'Dowd's defensive upgrades began in

2006 with a pair of low-profile trades that added second baseman Kaz Matsui and catcher Yorvit Torrealba, neither of whom is all that valuable offensively. The following offseason, O'Dowd added center fielder Willy Taveras in a five-player deal with the Astros. Taveras lacks the power and patience to be a great regular, but with his plus range in center and a stronger arm than you'll find on the shoulder of your typical speed guy, he's tremendously valuable in the field, especially when covering Coors Field's expansive middle pasture.

That quartet formed the foundation of an exceptional defense that improved the club's play both home and abroad. Last year's Rockies were tied for seventh in MLB and sixth in the NL in Defensive Efficiency, both rakings representing all-time bests for the franchise. As impressive as that might be, the Rockies' defense was actually much better still—playing defense at altitude isn't any easier than pitching at such heights, particularly given Coors Field's massive outfield. Indeed, the Rockies' team defense has traditionally rated among the very worst in the majors. Adjusting for the park's effect by using James Click's Park-Adjusted Defensive Efficiency (or PADE), last year's Rockies were actually the second-best defensive unit in baseball, rating just a hair behind the Red Sox team that beat them in the World Series. That rating reflects the excellence of homegrown players such as Tulowitzki, left fielder Matt Holliday, and veteran first baseman Todd Helton, each of whom is among the best at his respective position, as well as O'Dowd's low-cost defense-first imports, Taveras, Matsui, and Torrealba.

The defensive virtues of those six men allowed the Rockies to reap benefits from the very different risks taken at the remaining positions in the lineup. A lot of organizations would look at third baseman Garrett Atkins and right fielder Brad Hawpe and see two guys who started out at first base and should have stayed there. In part due to their long-term commitment to Helton, the Rockies have instead worked extensively with both to make them as close to playable at their respective positions as possible. Atkins and Hawpe are both still terrible defenders by major league standards, but their patient approach at the plate helps their bats play in any park.

Having a defense that could support fielders as limited as Atkins and Hawpe allowed the Rockies to build an offense that could support the weaker offensive contributions of their slick-fielding imports. Most teams couldn't or wouldn't want to rely on Taveras and Matsui in the top two spots in the lineup, but with Taveras reaching base at a .367 clip thanks to his major league–leading 54 infield hits (including an MLB-best 37 bunt hits), and five patient sluggers backing that pair, the Rockies offense rose up to sixth in the league in Equivalent Average. Better still, the team's .264 EqA set a franchise record and marked the first time in team history that the Rockies had finished above the base average of .260. Although last year's team slugged only .395 on the road, they drew walks in profusion, finishing an uncharacteristic first in the league in unintentional freebies. That's a skill that carries over in any park, and it made for a lineup that generated franchise road records in OBP (.336) and runs scored per nine innings (4.7), resulting in another high-water mark, a franchise-best 39-42 road record. The greatest Rockies lineup in franchise history wasn't the club's previous wild-card playoff entry from the high-offense '90s, it was this team's attack, built around the homegrown quintet of Holliday, Helton, Tulowitzki, Hawpe, and Atkins.

While the strategic synergy between offense and defense created a better blend of Rockies position-player talent, the Rockies also benefited from the synergistic effects of that defense on their bullpen, the outstanding performance of which recalled the unit's contribution to the franchise's mid-'90s run at relevance and their one previous playoff appearance. Like defense, relief pitching is an area in which a team can make considerable improvements without necessarily breaking the bank. That is in part due to the ability of the manager and pitching coach to manipulate the roles and workloads of those pitchers, as Clint Hurdle did midseason by flip-flopping closer Brian Fuentes and flame-throwing set-up man Manny Corpas following the struggles of the former. Fuentes and Corpas headed a pen that had both depth and talent thanks to the fine work the team got out of scrapheap finds both young and old. That said, it's likely that the Rox got more than a little lucky with guys such as Matt Herges, LaTroy Hawkins, early season addition Jorge Julio, and 2006 holdover Jeremy Affeldt. A former starter who came over in the Taveras deal, young Taylor Buchholz could give the team a third quality reliever, but the Rockies are going to have to show continuing clairvoyance to find the next crew of bit players to support that Big Three. As many disappointed contenders can tell you, that's not as easy as it sounds.

Injuries to Aaron Cook, Jason Hirsh, and Rodrigo Lopez and the continuing handicap of the team's home environment prevented last year's Rockies rotation from generating much excitement beyond emerging lefty ace Jeff Francis, but this was less a problem than an excuse for Hurdle to keep turning to his superior bullpen. More than a third of the Rockies' total innings in 2007 were thrown by a relief unit that posted a Fair Runs Allowed mark of 4.18, good for ninth-best in the majors. In contrast, the rotation posted a modest Support-Neutral Lineup-adjusted Value Above Replacement mark of 17.0, which was only 19th in the majors. Of course, that was another franchise record. Taken together, the entire pitching staff actually ranked fourth in the National League in park-adjusted runs allowed; the park will always to disguise it, but the Rockies' pitching was an asset last year.

Having gotten to the World Series, repeating won't be easy, not with the Dodgers throwing even more money at their problems, the Padres cannily retooling in their way, and a talented Diamondbacks team expecting its young talent to come into its own. The challenge the Rockies face in convincing a pitcher of any note to come pitch in their big park is probably one the franchise will never fully overcome. Happily, O'Dowd doesn't need to go shopping for a starter as both Ubaldo Jimenez and Franklin Morales showed that they have exceptional stuff while making their contributions to the Rockies' late-season kick. If they build on those performances while both Cook and Hirsh come back healthy, Jeff Francis might find himself fronting the strongest rotation in franchise history.

Having salvaged his career with a team that understood his value, Matsui cashed in with a three-year deal with Houston. Replacing his glove won't be easy, but finding an adequate second baseman should be, particularly given the low offensive standard O'Dowd will be working from at one of his defense-first positions. Fellow free-agent Torreabla has returned to the fold, but could lose a good chunk of his playing time to homegrown backstop Chris Iannetta. Looking further down the road, center-field prospect Dexter Fowler is the outstanding in-house talent who might someday claim the job in the majors, making Taveras a short-term fix and expendable once he starts getting expensive.

With homegrown and cost-controlled talent everywhere else, the Rockies are built to last. As much as last season's breakthrough might have seemed like a Cinderella story, the Rockies have finally arrived, not as some sort of peculiarly adapted mile-high construction, but as an organization that has put together all of the working parts necessary to create a well-balanced ballclub that can contend at any elevation.

HITTERS

Garrett Atkins — 3B

Bats: R Throws: R Height: 6' 3" Weight: 215 Born: December 12, 1979 Age: 28

YEAR	TEAM	LVL	AGE	PA	R	2B	3B	HR	RBI	BB	SO	SB	CS	EqBRR	AVG	OBP	SLG	MLVr	EqAVG	EqOBP	EqSLG	EqA	VORP	DEFENSE
2005	COL	MLB	25	573	62	31	1	13	89	45	72	0	2	-1.1	.287	.347	.426	.034	.275	.337	.414	.261	13.4	133-3B -12
2006	COL	MLB	26	695	117	48	1	29	120	79	76	4	0	0.5	.329	.409	.556	.328	.313	.396	.528	.314	62.7	155-3B -15
2007	COL	MLB	27	684	83	35	1	25	111	67	96	3	1	-1.8	.301	.367	.486	.143	.290	.361	.477	.288	34.8	146-3B -16
2008	COL	MLB	28	647	90	37	1	25	100	65	85	6	2	-1.1	.301	.373	.501	.161	.277	.352	.467	.280	29.5	151-3B -9

Breakout: 4% Improve: 31% Collapse: 31% Attrition: 6%   Comparables: Ken McMullen, Mike Lowell, Travis Fryman, Todd Zeile

Because of the Rockies' low profile prior to their September surge, Atkins might seem like a rising star, but at 28, he's a finished product, an above-average hitter and mediocre, though improving, defender. His durability and home park give him counting stats that will make him expensive in arbitration. All of this makes him a better trade property than building block.

Jeff Baker — UT

Bats: R Throws: R Height: 6' 2" Weight: 210 Born: June 21, 1981 Age: 27

YEAR	TEAM	LVL	AGE	PA	R	2B	3B	HR	RBI	BB	SO	SB	CS	EqBRR	AVG	OBP	SLG	MLVr	EqAVG	EqOBP	EqSLG	EqA	VORP	DEFENSE	
2005	CSP	AAA	24	248	40	16	1	10	41	16	44	3	1	1.9	.303	.348	.513	.083	.260	.302	.437	.252	6.6	57-3B -7	
2005	COL	MLB	24	43	6	4	0	1	4	5	12	0	0	-0.1	.211	.302	.395	-.152	.184	.279	.342	.217	-0.8		
2006	CSP	AAA	25	538	71	30	4	20	108	46	110	7	1	-0.4	.305	.369	.508	.154	.266	.326	.451	.267	7.5	119-RF -12	
2006	COL	MLB	25	58	13	7	2	5	21	1	14	2	0	0.2	.368	.379	.825	.699	.351	.362	.789	.354	10.8		
2007	COL	MLB	26	159	17	2	2	4	12	13	40	0	0	-1.0	.222	.296	.347	-.227	.217	.296	.343	.223	-5.1	11-1B 0	10-RF 0
2008	COL	MLB	27	180	25	10	1	8	28	15	39	2	1	-0.1	.283	.347	.504	.107	.261	.327	.470	.269	7.2		

Breakout: 36% Improve: 60% Collapse: 24% Attrition: 36%   Comparables: Ryan Ludwick, Ozzie Timmons, Sam Bowens, Mark Smith

Baker may have spent most of last year in the majors, but doing so derailed his progress as he made just 186 plate appearances all season, serving primarily as a pinch-hitter. Then again, with the team set at the corners, that's the role in which he's most likely to remain, though he could slip into the vacancy at second base after getting a look there in the instructional league. As a reserve, he could enjoy a long career.

Clint Barmes — UT

Bats: R Throws: R Height: 6' 0" Weight: 210 Born: March 6, 1979 Age: 29

YEAR	TEAM	LVL	AGE	PA	R	2B	3B	HR	RBI	BB	SO	SB	CS	EqBRR	AVG	OBP	SLG	MLVr	EqAVG	EqOBP	EqSLG	EqA	VORP	DEFENSE
2005	COL	MLB	26	377	55	19	1	10	46	16	36	6	4	2.1	.289	.330	.434	.013	.276	.320	.425	.254	13.6	78-SS -2
2006	COL	MLB	27	535	57	26	4	7	56	22	72	5	4	2.9	.220	.264	.335	-.304	.214	.257	.326	.204	-20.5	120-SS -8
2007	CSP	AAA	28	477	68	20	6	11	44	22	52	8	6	-0.4	.299	.364	.451	.008	.258	.320	.394	.247	11.3	87-SS 18
2007	COL	MLB	28	39	5	3	0	0	1	1	13	0	0	1.3	.216	.237	.297	-.398	.216	.237	.297	.179	-2.3	
2008	COL	MLB	29	472	53	25	3	10	53	24	60	8	3	0.9	.268	.315	.409	-.088	.247	.297	.382	.233	4.3	112-SS 1

Breakout: 26% Improve: 50% Collapse: 28% Attrition: 23%   Comparables: Brian Dallimore, Rob Mummau, Keith Johnson, Chris Snopek

Barmes' decline is right there with that of Pat Listach, who at least won the Rookie of the Year award in his one good season. Barmes was never ticketed to be a starting shortstop, and the emergence of Tulowitzki hastened his ride into oblivion. He's slated to be the utility infielder this year.

Jamey Carroll — INF

Bats: R Throws: R Height: 5' 9" Weight: 170 Born: February 18, 1974 Age: 34

YEAR	TEAM	LVL	AGE	PA	R	2B	3B	HR	RBI	BB	SO	SB	CS	EqBRR	AVG	OBP	SLG	MLVr	EqAVG	EqOBP	EqSLG	EqA	VORP	DEFENSE	
2005	WAS	MLB	31	358	44	8	1	0	22	34	55	3	4	0.5	.251	.333	.284	-.160	.260	.341	.295	.232	-5.2	48-2B 2	27-SS 0
2006	COL	MLB	32	534	84	23	5	5	36	56	66	10	12	-3.6	.300	.377	.404	.044	.290	.371	.387	.263	18.2	101-2B 29	
2007	COL	MLB	33	268	45	9	1	2	22	28	34	6	2	2.8	.225	.317	.300	-.248	.219	.314	.294	.225	-7.6	48-2B 7	
2008	CLE	MLB	34	170	19	6	1	1	13	17	26	4	2	0.4	.247	.329	.320	-.169	.244	.328	.332	.244	0.0	44-2B 4	

Breakout: 24% Improve: 44% Collapse: 34% Attrition: 44%   Comparables: Jeff Reboulet, Scott Fletcher, Alex Grammas, Ivan DeJesus Sr.

Carroll's listed at 5-foot-10, which would be a stretch even in a Match.com profile. He's about ten percent worse than you'd like your utility infielder to be, lacking as he does some bat, some speed, some left-handedness, and the ability to play an acceptable shortstop. The Indians traded for him anyway.

Dexter Fowler — CF

Bats: S Throws: R Height: 6' 4" Weight: 173 Born: March 22, 1986 Age: 22

YEAR	TEAM	LVL	AGE	PA	R	2B	3B	HR	RBI	BB	SO	SB	CS	EqBRR	AVG	OBP	SLG	MLVr	EqAVG	EqOBP	EqSLG	EqA	VORP	DEFENSE	
2005	CAS	Rk	19	252	43	10	4	4	23	27	73	18	6	1.3	.273	.357	.409	-.013	.177	.240	.255	.175	-45.2	57-CF	0
2006	ASH	A	20	458	92	31	6	8	46	43	79	43	23	0.6	.296	.373	.462	.150	.233	.293	.357	.226	-10.9	97-CF	-2
2007	MOD	A+	21	299	43	7	5	2	23	44	64	20	11	-0.6	.273	.397	.367	.066	.227	.332	.301	.232	-6.9	61-CF	-1
2008	COL	MLB	22	358	44	15	3	4	28	30	85	17	6	1.8	.249	.317	.352	-.174	.229	.299	.329	.222	-6.6	86-CF	-1

Breakout: 31% Improve: 61% Collapse: 19% Attrition: 6%   Comparables: Sheldon Fulse, Aron Weston, Rashad Eldridge, Dwight Maness

Fowler's 2007 season came to a brutal end when a wall viciously attacked his wrist, breaking a bone. He's an interesting package with very good speed, a willingness to work counts, well-regarded baseball smarts, and a knack for impressing observers, but an utter lack of power limits his upside. He didn't show well in the Arizona Fall League. That, combined with the glut of outfielders high in the system, means he's at least a full season away from cracking the big-league roster.

Hector Gomez — SS

Bats: R Throws: R Height: 6' 1" Weight: 157 Born: March 5, 1988 Age: 20

YEAR	TEAM	LVL	AGE	PA	R	2B	3B	HR	RBI	BB	SO	SB	CS	EqBRR	AVG	OBP	SLG	MLVr	EqAVG	EqOBP	EqSLG	EqA	VORP	DEFENSE			
2006	CAS	Rk	18	221	24	9	4	5	35	11	26	5	3	-4.5	.327	.364	.485	.205	.248	.268	.367	.217	-5.8	25-SS	-5	21-3B	-1
2006	TRI	A-	18	48	4	3	0	0	6	0	14	0	1	-0.2	.244	.255	.311	-.125	.196	.191	.239	.123	-9.9	11-SS	-1		
2007	ASH	A	19	576	89	34	8	11	61	29	120	20	10	-1.4	.266	.309	.421	-.057	.208	.242	.324	.194	-30.2	121-SS	-1		
2008	COL	MLB	20	620	65	37	6	10	58	27	122	14	8	0.9	.254	.289	.394	-.166	.234	.272	.367	.216	-4.2	145-SS	0		

Breakout: 55% Improve: 78% Collapse: 4% Attrition: 8%   Comparables: Hector Made, Eduardo Nuñez, Teuris Olivares, Arquimedez Pozo

While Gomez's numbers might not blow you away, scouts are crazy about the kid. He's long, rangy, and ultra-athletic, projecting as a well-above-average defensive shortstop with power and speed. He's still very rough around the edges and needs to refine nearly every part of his game, especially his approach at the plate, but this is a high-ceiling talent who could be an elite prospect at this time next year. He's a classic high-risk/high-reward type.

Brad Hawpe — RF

Bats: L Throws: L Height: 6' 3" Weight: 205 Born: June 22, 1979 Age: 29

YEAR	TEAM	LVL	AGE	PA	R	2B	3B	HR	RBI	BB	SO	SB	CS	EqBRR	AVG	OBP	SLG	MLVr	EqAVG	EqOBP	EqSLG	EqA	VORP	DEFENSE	
2005	COL	MLB	26	351	38	10	3	9	47	43	70	2	2	-0.4	.262	.350	.403	-.011	.248	.339	.396	.259	2.9	79-RF	2
2006	COL	MLB	27	575	67	33	6	22	84	74	123	5	5	-3.5	.293	.383	.515	.197	.276	.370	.487	.290	32.0	134-RF	4
2007	COL	MLB	28	606	80	33	4	29	116	81	137	0	2	-4.3	.291	.387	.539	.233	.277	.380	.524	.304	37.4	137-RF	-16
2008	COL	MLB	29	470	69	25	3	20	73	62	97	3	2	-0.7	.283	.379	.513	.169	.261	.357	.478	.282	17.9	111-RF	-5

Breakout: 9% Improve: 25% Collapse: 33% Attrition: 20%   Comparables: Paul O'Neill, Pete Ward, Dwight Evans, Trot Nixon

Like Atkins, Hawpe is less a young stud and more a player who arrived late and is peaking quickly, but he's more valuable than Atkins because the Rockies aren't deep in the outfield or from the left side. An awkward outfielder, Hawpe compensates for his lack of range with a howitzer of an arm. Remember, he was a first baseman until Todd Helton's contract forced him into the pasture.

Todd Helton — 1B

Bats: L Throws: L Height: 6' 2" Weight: 210 Born: August 20, 1973 Age: 34

YEAR	TEAM	LVL	AGE	PA	R	2B	3B	HR	RBI	BB	SO	SB	CS	EqBRR	AVG	OBP	SLG	MLVr	EqAVG	EqOBP	EqSLG	EqA	VORP	DEFENSE	
2005	COL	MLB	31	626	92	45	2	20	79	106	80	3	0	-1.4	.320	.445	.534	.352	.297	.426	.507	.322	58.3	140-1B	16
2006	COL	MLB	32	649	94	40	5	15	81	91	64	3	2	-2.4	.302	.404	.476	.186	.285	.391	.449	.294	31.1	142-1B	-6
2007	COL	MLB	33	682	86	42	2	17	91	116	74	0	1	-5.0	.320	.434	.494	.277	.303	.425	.476	.316	51.9	148-1B	12
2008	COL	MLB	34	542	86	31	2	15	75	81	62	5	2	-1.2	.309	.415	.488	.217	.285	.390	.455	.293	24.1	127-1B	3

Breakout: 2% Improve: 28% Collapse: 37% Attrition: 20%   Comparables: Wally Joyner, John Olerud, Keith Hernandez, Mike Hargrove

For all the talk of his decline, Helton was second in the NL in on-base percentage last year and one of the dozen most productive hitters in the league. His contract, which guarantees him just shy of $69 million through 2011, is almost starting to look reasonable. He's become an underrated player, and he's critical to this team's chances.

Matt Holliday   LF

Bats: R   Throws: R   Height: 6' 4"   Weight: 235   Born: January 15, 1980   Age: 28

YEAR	TEAM	LVL	AGE	PA	R	2B	3B	HR	RBI	BB	SO	SB	CS	EqBRR	AVG	OBP	SLG	MLVr	EqAVG	EqOBP	EqSLG	EqA	VORP	DEFENSE	
2005	COL	MLB	25	526	68	24	7	19	87	36	79	14	3	-3.6	.307	.361	.505	.176	.291	.347	.485	.285	30.2	120-LF	4
2006	COL	MLB	26	667	119	45	5	34	114	47	110	10	5	-2.3	.326	.387	.586	.333	.312	.375	.566	.310	56.8	149-LF	7
2007	COL	MLB	27	713	120	50	6	36	137	63	126	11	4	2.8	.340	.405	.607	.404	.327	.397	.597	.325	75.0	153-LF	12
2008	COL	MLB	28	635	105	39	4	29	108	54	107	13	4	0.2	.318	.383	.555	.267	.294	.361	.517	.295	35.2	148-LF	1

Breakout: 0%   Improve: 21%   Collapse: 31%   Attrition: 8%   Comparables: Ivan Calderon, Jermaine Dye, Carlos Lee, Marty Cordova

Holliday was only robbed of the MVP award if you narrow the discussion to him and Jimmy Rollins. Compared to the whole field, he was around the fourth-most valuable player in the league. Holliday has had a classic career arc that peaked at 27 last year (like most of this lineup, he's older than you think). With more defensive value, a higher peak, and better indicators than Hawpe and Atkins, Holliday is a keeper until free agency arrives after the 2010 season.

Chris Iannetta   C

Bats: R   Throws: R   Height: 6' 0"   Weight: 225   Born: April 8, 1983   Age: 25

YEAR	TEAM	LVL	AGE	PA	R	2B	3B	HR	RBI	BB	SO	SB	CS	EqBRR	AVG	OBP	SLG	MLVr	EqAVG	EqOBP	EqSLG	EqA	VORP	DEFENSE	
2005	MOD	A+	22	312	51	17	3	11	58	45	61	1	2	-3.0	.276	.381	.490	.128	.207	.301	.351	.228	-5.6	68-C	-4
2005	TUL	AA	22	70	7	3	1	2	11	8	15	0	0	0.2	.233	.329	.417	-.025	.197	.286	.393	.231	-0.9	14-C	0
2006	TUL	AA	23	185	38	10	2	11	26	24	26	1	0	-0.5	.321	.418	.622	.450	.280	.368	.547	.304	19.2	37-C	-2
2006	CSP	AAA	23	180	23	12	1	3	22	24	29	0	0	-3.3	.351	.447	.503	.308	.299	.391	.448	.292	14.4	36-C	3
2006	COL	MLB	23	93	12	4	0	2	10	13	17	0	1	0.2	.260	.370	.390	-.023	.247	.359	.364	.258	1.3	22-C	-2
2007	CSP	AAA	24	63	8	3	0	1	7	7	6	0	0	-0.3	.296	.397	.407	.006	.255	.359	.345	.255	1.1	14-C	0
2007	COL	MLB	24	234	22	8	3	4	27	29	58	0	0	-1.4	.218	.330	.350	-.157	.209	.326	.352	.244	0.2	55-C	0
2008	COL	MLB	25	344	45	17	2	11	45	37	66	2	1	-0.6	.271	.357	.454	.046	.250	.336	.423	.261	11.6	83-C	1

Breakout: 21%   Improve: 48%   Collapse: 25%   Attrition: 27%   Comparables: Ben Petrick, A. J. Hinch, Tim Laudner, Pat Corrales

Yell all you want, but if a player doesn't hit .200, he can't keep his job, no matter what else he's doing. Clint Hurdle, who knows a bit about how young players can scuffle, was fairly patient last year with his rookie catcher; Iannetta was the starter through about mid-May and had a share of the job up through the All-Star break. One challenge Iannetta faced was his lineup spot. It's not easy batting eighth in the NL and getting pitched around much of the time. He batted .190/.296/.306 in the eight hole, but .237/.375/.424 with a better contact rate batting seventh. He also hit much better after being recalled in late August: .348/.434/.565 in 53 PA. Even with Torrealba back, Iannetta should be the starter in 2008.

Joe Koshansky   1B

Bats: L   Throws: L   Height: 6' 4"   Weight: 225   Born: May 26, 1982   Age: 26

YEAR	TEAM	LVL	AGE	PA	R	2B	3B	HR	RBI	BB	SO	SB	CS	EqBRR	AVG	OBP	SLG	MLVr	EqAVG	EqOBP	EqSLG	EqA	VORP	DEFENSE	
2005	ASH	A	23	525	92	31	1	36	103	53	122	6	6	-3.3	.291	.373	.603	.285	.222	.286	.416	.239	-12.5	115-1B	-1
2005	TUL	AA	23	48	5	3	0	2	12	2	15	0	0	-0.2	.267	.292	.467	.007	.200	.229	.400	.205	-3.1	12-1B	1
2006	TUL	AA	24	573	84	28	0	31	109	64	134	3	2	-1.9	.284	.371	.526	.211	.246	.322	.445	.262	6.0	125-1B	8
2007	CSP	AAA	25	569	79	30	2	21	99	67	128	4	3	-2.1	.295	.380	.490	.085	.253	.339	.418	.263	5.7	130-1B	-13
2007	COL	MLB	25	15	0	1	0	0	2	2	5	0	0	0.0	.083	.200	.167	-.692	.083	.200	.167	.133	-1.8		
2008	COL	MLB	26	517	62	25	1	20	76	55	126	4	2	-0.7	.258	.339	.452	.002	.238	.320	.422	.253	2.5	122-1B	-1

Breakout: 19%   Improve: 48%   Collapse: 26%   Attrition: 12%   Comparables: Brian Daubach, Larry Broadway, Dan Johnson, Damon Minor

The slugging Koshansky was productive, if uninspiring, in a full year at Triple-A Colorado Springs. He can't play anywhere but first base, so only a trade will get him more than occasional cups of coffee in the majors. With a job, he'd be Paul Sorrento.

Kazuo Matsui　2B

Bats: S　Throws: R　Height: 5' 10"　Weight: 185　Born: October 23, 1975　Age: 32

YEAR	TEAM	LVL	AGE	PA	R	2B	3B	HR	RBI	BB	SO	SB	CS	EqBRR	AVG	OBP	SLG	MLVr	EqAVG	EqOBP	EqSLG	EqA	VORP	DEFENSE	
2005	NYN	MLB	29	295	31	9	4	3	24	14	43	6	1	1.4	.255	.300	.352	-.135	.257	.300	.364	.238	-0.7	63-2B	1
2006	NYN	MLB	30	139	10	6	0	1	7	6	19	2	0	0.8	.200	.235	.269	-.429	.198	.239	.260	.170	-8.7	31-2B	3
2006	CSP	AAA	30	129	26	4	0	3	16	9	20	3	1	0.9	.278	.328	.391	-.092	.248	.295	.342	.228	-1.2	26-SS	-1
2006	COL	MLB	30	126	22	6	3	2	19	10	27	8	1	1.1	.345	.392	.504	.243	.327	.381	.487	.305	12.9	20-2B	5
2007	COL	MLB	31	453	84	24	6	4	37	34	69	32	4	6.2	.288	.342	.405	-.018	.280	.339	.401	.268	16.9	96-2B	14
2008	HOU	MLB	32	355	43	14	4	4	28	25	57	15	4	1.6	.259	.313	.369	-.152	.262	.316	.376	.243	5.6	85-2B	-2

Breakout: 11% Improve: 25% Collapse: 38% Attrition: 27%　　　Comparables: Sandy Alomar, Horace Clarke, U.L. Washington, Vince Coleman

It's hard to not see Matsui's 2007 season as an altitude-induced fluke. His .249/.304/.333 performance on the road was much closer to his major league career averages than his .330/.381/.482 line at Coors. Still, he provided lineup balance, excellent basestealing, and had better range than Carroll. Those things had value, but they don't represent a career renaissance. The Astros, who signed him to a three-year deal, will be disappointed.

Daniel Mayora　2B

Bats: R　Throws: R　Height: 5' 11"　Weight: 145　Born: July 27, 1985　Age: 22

YEAR	TEAM	LVL	AGE	PA	R	2B	3B	HR	RBI	BB	SO	SB	CS	EqBRR	AVG	OBP	SLG	MLVr	EqAVG	EqOBP	EqSLG	EqA	VORP	DEFENSE			
2005	CAS	Rk	19	168	20	12	1	1	14	9	36	4	3	-2.9	.265	.325	.377	-.120	.182	.220	.258	.152	-29.4	28-3B	-4	12-SS	-2
2006	TRI	A-	20	312	40	19	2	5	30	23	70	8	4	3.1	.304	.375	.442	.274	.219	.271	.333	.211	-17.8	60-SS	0	12-2B	-1
2007	ASH	A	21	571	88	42	1	14	78	41	124	26	9	3.9	.310	.366	.477	.136	.234	.282	.357	.224	-12.1	118-2B	3		
2008	COL	MLB	22	593	62	32	3	11	59	35	142	15	6	1.1	.251	.301	.381	-.164	.231	.284	.355	.219	-5.5	139-2B	2		

Breakout: 34% Improve: 52% Collapse: 21% Attrition: 10%　　　Comparables: Gregorio Petit, Luis Guance, Ramon Nuñez, Teuris Olivares

Hector Gomez's double-play partner in the Sally League, Mayora is considerably older and a far more refined product. He profiles as a middle infielder who can hit second in the lineup, as he's shown an ability to hit for average with a bit of power. Do take some caution with players at Asheville, however, as the Tourists play in one of the better hitting parks in the minors; on the road, Mayora hit .267/.320/.337.

Chris Nelson　SS

Bats: R　Throws: R　Height: 5' 11"　Weight: 176　Born: September 3, 1985　Age: 22

YEAR	TEAM	LVL	AGE	PA	R	2B	3B	HR	RBI	BB	SO	SB	CS	EqBRR	AVG	OBP	SLG	MLVr	EqAVG	EqOBP	EqSLG	EqA	VORP	DEFENSE	
2005	ASH	A	19	349	51	13	3	3	38	25	88	7	4	-0.2	.241	.304	.330	-.195	.188	.235	.255	.163	-29.8	67-SS	-10
2006	ASH	A	20	517	69	38	1	11	76	32	101	14	2	-0.7	.260	.313	.416	-.016	.206	.246	.329	.200	-25.5	109-SS	-19
2007	MOD	A+	21	600	97	42	7	19	99	55	92	27	5	3.3	.289	.358	.503	.200	.239	.298	.396	.245	6.4	129-SS	-15
2008	COL	MLB	22	627	76	37	4	14	67	42	123	20	6	0.7	.262	.316	.413	-.087	.241	.297	.385	.236	6.9	147-SS	-10

Breakout: 43% Improve: 66% Collapse: 10% Attrition: 9%　　　Comparables: Shaun Boyd, Troy Tulowitzki, Chris Burke, Royce Clayton

Getting Nelson with the ninth overall pick in the 2004 draft seemed like a steal at the time. Then he made 66 errors and drew 57 walks in two Sally League seasons. At best, he's a utility infielder in the majors, and it's an open question as to whether he can climb the three levels to become even that. His 2007 line is a California League mirage.

Seth Smith　OF

Bats: L　Throws: L　Height: 6' 3"　Weight: 215　Born: September 30, 1982　Age: 25

YEAR	TEAM	LVL	AGE	PA	R	2B	3B	HR	RBI	BB	SO	SB	CS	EqBRR	AVG	OBP	SLG	MLVr	EqAVG	EqOBP	EqSLG	EqA	VORP	DEFENSE			
2005	MOD	A+	22	585	87	45	6	9	72	44	115	5	3	0.3	.300	.353	.458	.050	.228	.275	.337	.211	-36.9	106-RF	-8	17-CF	-5
2006	TUL	AA	23	582	79	46	4	15	71	51	74	4	4	0.8	.294	.361	.483	.146	.256	.314	.421	.252	-3.3	107-RF	-8		
2007	CSP	AAA	24	505	68	32	6	17	82	39	73	7	3	-1.1	.317	.381	.528	.159	.273	.337	.455	.272	11.1	96-RF	6	21-CF	-3
2008	COL	MLB	25	523	67	32	4	14	69	42	88	7	3	0.3	.283	.345	.457	.039	.261	.325	.426	.257	6.0	123-RF	-1		

Breakout: 20% Improve: 57% Collapse: 20% Attrition: 16%　　　Comparables: Jacob Cruz, David Murphy, Brant Brown, Matt Franco

The Forrest Gump of Rocktober, Smith tripled over the head of Padres center fielder Brady Clark in the sixth inning of Game 163 and subsequently scored a tie-breaking run. He then blooped a double down the left-field line to give the Rockies a lead they wouldn't relinquish in the decisive Game Four of the NLCS. When not being a hero, he's a decent lefty-hitting platoon corner/fourth outfielder on a team with no need for that skill set.

Ryan Spilborghs — CF

Bats: R Throws: R Height: 6'1" Weight: 190 Born: September 5, 1979 Age: 28

YEAR	TEAM	LVL	AGE	PA	R	2B	3B	HR	RBI	BB	SO	SB	CS	EqBRR	AVG	OBP	SLG	MLVr	EqAVG	EqOBP	EqSLG	EqA	VORP	DEFENSE			
2005	TUL	AA	25	301	52	23	3	6	54	42	49	10	3	2.7	.341	.435	.525	.380	.281	.372	.438	.282	10.0	28-LF	5	22-RF	0
2005	CSP	AAA	25	253	49	23	5	5	30	22	53	7	3	-0.9	.339	.405	.551	.269	.260	.321	.424	.256	0.0	29-RF	-5	25-LF	0
2006	CSP	AAA	26	306	50	20	1	5	34	30	49	8	2	1.1	.338	.400	.476	.188	.293	.355	.421	.275	6.1	40-LF	4	27-CF	0
2006	COL	MLB	26	186	26	6	3	4	21	14	30	5	2	0.0	.287	.337	.431	.002	.275	.330	.407	.260	4.6	19-CF	0	11-RF	-2
2007	CSP	AAA	27	145	25	7	1	5	17	18	19	4	3	-0.1	.323	.410	.516	.196	.278	.366	.460	.281	5.2	19-LF	-1		
2007	COL	MLB	27	300	40	14	1	11	51	28	45	4	1	-0.4	.299	.363	.485	.137	.290	.359	.481	.290	16.5	36-CF	-4	14-RF	-2
2008	COL	MLB	28	314	47	17	2	8	40	30	52	7	3	0.5	.300	.369	.467	.107	.277	.347	.435	.270	11.2	76-CF	-1		

Breakout: 11% Improve: 37% Collapse: 34% Attrition: 23%   Comparables: Gary Ward, Mike Huff, Dave Gallagher, Steve Henderson

The Rockies mint fourth outfielders, and when Willy Taveras' legs gave him trouble last year, this one was a solid substitute at the plate and passable in center. Spilborghs is an excellent caddy for Hawpe in right field, a lefty-killer who plays the corners well.

Ian Stewart — 3B

Bats: L Throws: R Height: 6'3" Weight: 205 Born: April 5, 1985 Age: 23

YEAR	TEAM	LVL	AGE	PA	R	2B	3B	HR	RBI	BB	SO	SB	CS	EqBRR	AVG	OBP	SLG	MLVr	EqAVG	EqOBP	EqSLG	EqA	VORP	DEFENSE	
2005	MOD	A+	20	499	83	32	7	17	86	52	113	2	2	2.0	.274	.353	.497	.081	.210	.277	.364	.222	-11.7	106-3B	0
2006	TUL	AA	21	528	75	41	7	10	71	50	103	3	8	-2.9	.268	.351	.452	.065	.232	.301	.387	.237	0.8	113-3B	18
2007	CSP	AAA	22	474	72	23	2	15	65	49	92	11	2	3.4	.304	.379	.478	.076	.263	.337	.413	.264	16.6	105-3B	-13
2007	COL	MLB	22	46	3	4	0	1	9	1	17	0	0	0.0	.209	.261	.372	-.268	.209	.261	.349	.208	-1.5		
2008	COL	MLB	23	601	83	36	3	18	80	56	124	10	4	0.9	.284	.355	.466	.069	.262	.334	.435	.263	16.8	141-3B	1

Breakout: 44% Improve: 74% Collapse: 7% Attrition: 8%   Comparables: Scott Moore, Dee Brown, Gabe Gross, Dave McCarty

The idea that Stewart was going to slide to second base for 2008 was ill-conceived given a team built around contact pitchers and defense; Stewart's only so-so at third base and couldn't handle the keystone in an instructional league. His home-run power hasn't come, hurting his perceived value. However, he's 80 percent of Atkins right now for ten percent of the cost, and he'll be a better player than Atkins by 2010 at 25 percent of the cost. He's young enough to locate his power stroke and be even better than that.

Cory Sullivan — CF

Bats: L Throws: L Height: 6'0" Weight: 180 Born: August 20, 1979 Age: 28

YEAR	TEAM	LVL	AGE	PA	R	2B	3B	HR	RBI	BB	SO	SB	CS	EqBRR	AVG	OBP	SLG	MLVr	EqAVG	EqOBP	EqSLG	EqA	VORP	DEFENSE			
2005	COL	MLB	25	424	64	15	4	4	30	28	83	12	3	2.5	.294	.343	.386	-.020	.281	.332	.378	.254	8.6	71-CF	-4	17-LF	1
2006	COL	MLB	26	443	47	26	10	2	30	32	100	10	6	-2.7	.267	.321	.402	-.079	.257	.313	.384	.245	3.9	94-CF	-3		
2007	CSP	AAA	27	228	29	9	3	1	21	18	44	4	3	-0.7	.262	.324	.350	-.228	.221	.283	.298	.202	-11.8	50-CF	-6		
2007	COL	MLB	27	153	19	6	1	2	14	9	25	2	0	0.9	.286	.336	.386	-.056	.279	.333	.379	.254	2.9	29-CF	2		
2008	COL	MLB	28	358	43	17	4	5	34	28	67	8	3	0.5	.266	.328	.392	-.090	.245	.309	.366	.235	0.2	86-CF	0		

Breakout: 19% Improve: 42% Collapse: 38% Attrition: 28%   Comparables: Jason Conti, Adam Shabala, Don Landrum, Mark Budzinski

Does Sullivan make four or five center fielders on the Rockies better than anything the Marlins ran out there in 2007? It's easy to lose count. Sullivan is another extra outfielder, more speedy than savvy, and he lost most of his playing time to Taveras. Arbitration-eligible this winter, the Rockies could save a million bucks or so by non-tendering Sullivan and using Sean Barker or Seth Smith in his place.

Willy Taveras — CF

Bats: R Throws: R Height: 6'0" Weight: 160 Born: December 25, 1981 Age: 26

YEAR	TEAM	LVL	AGE	PA	R	2B	3B	HR	RBI	BB	SO	SB	CS	EqBRR	AVG	OBP	SLG	MLVr	EqAVG	EqOBP	EqSLG	EqA	VORP	DEFENSE	
2005	HOU	MLB	23	635	82	13	4	3	29	25	103	34	11	3.8	.291	.325	.341	-.087	.292	.328	.347	.244	4.9	142-CF	16
2006	HOU	MLB	24	587	83	19	5	1	30	34	88	33	9	6.6	.278	.333	.338	-.118	.281	.337	.343	.248	5.1	123-CF	22
2007	COL	MLB	25	408	64	13	2	2	24	21	55	33	9	0.7	.320	.367	.382	.015	.318	.366	.388	.269	16.4	79-CF	4
2008	COL	MLB	26	431	64	16	4	2	34	25	56	26	6	1.9	.303	.350	.380	-.042	.279	.329	.354	.245	5.5	102-CF	5

Breakout: 14% Improve: 29% Collapse: 39% Attrition: 25%   Comparables: David Hulse, Eric Yelding, Brian Hunter, Alex Sanchez

Groin and quad injuries limited Taveras to 97 games in 2007. When healthy, he was a critical part of the Rockies' performance, giving them a true defensive center fielder—a great one, actually—for the first time in franchise history.

His glove, along with that of Tulowitzki, knocked enough runs off the board to make the soft-throwing Rockies staff an effective one. Taveras has been working this offseason to improve his conditioning with an eye toward staying in the lineup. If healthy, he's a down-ballot MVP candidate thanks to his speed-driven batting average and Gold Glove-quality defense in center.

Yorvit Torrealba C   Bats: R   Throws: R   Height: 5' 11"   Weight: 200   Born: July 19, 1978   Age: 29

YEAR	TEAM	LVL	AGE	PA	R	2B	3B	HR	RBI	BB	SO	SB	CS	EqBRR	AVG	OBP	SLG	MLVr	EqAVG	EqOBP	EqSLG	EqA	VORP	DEFENSE	
2005	SFN	MLB	26	105	18	8	0	1	7	9	25	1	0	0.2	.226	.301	.344	-.175	.223	.305	.362	.236	-0.5	24-C	3
2005	SEA	MLB	26	119	14	4	0	2	8	7	25	0	0	0.6	.241	.293	.333	-.202	.255	.319	.368	.242	-0.9	36-C	1
2006	COL	MLB	27	241	23	16	3	7	43	11	49	4	3	-0.7	.247	.293	.439	-.095	.237	.283	.415	.236	0.4	60-C	6
2007	COL	MLB	28	443	47	22	1	8	47	34	73	2	1	0.4	.255	.323	.376	-.115	.249	.320	.370	.243	4.6	104-C	6
2008	COL	MLB	29	243	26	11	1	4	27	17	42	3	1	-0.2	.263	.323	.381	-.118	.242	.304	.355	.227	0.7	60-C	3

Breakout: 15% Improve: 36% Collapse: 38% Attrition: 41%   Comparables: Gary Bennett, Joe Girardi, Alberto Castillo, Ed Fitz Gerald

When Iannetta spit the bit, this career backup inherited his playing time behind the plate. Like Matsui, Torrealba was a humidor hero, batting just .212/.292/.326 away from Denver. He didn't even throw as well as he usually does. Back with the Rockies, he should revert to a backup role, while being cheered wildly for his heroics last October.

Troy Tulowitzki SS   Bats: R   Throws: R   Height: 6' 3"   Weight: 205   Born: October 10, 1984   Age: 23

YEAR	TEAM	LVL	AGE	PA	R	2B	3B	HR	RBI	BB	SO	SB	CS	EqBRR	AVG	OBP	SLG	MLVr	EqAVG	EqOBP	EqSLG	EqA	VORP	DEFENSE	
2005	MOD	A+	20	105	17	6	0	4	14	9	18	1	0	0.3	.266	.343	.457	-.003	.206	.267	.330	.207	-3.8	19-SS	0
2006	TUL	AA	21	485	75	34	2	13	61	46	71	6	5	-4.1	.291	.370	.473	.144	.253	.320	.411	.253	14.7	102-SS	-7
2006	COL	MLB	21	108	15	2	0	1	6	10	25	3	0	1.6	.240	.318	.292	-.251	.229	.308	.281	.219	-1.7	25-SS	-1
2007	COL	MLB	22	682	104	33	5	24	99	57	130	7	6	-0.2	.291	.359	.479	.112	.283	.355	.477	.280	37.8	152-SS	25
2008	COL	MLB	23	593	83	33	4	19	80	50	100	10	4	0.5	.292	.358	.479	.099	.269	.337	.447	.267	28.3	139-SS	11

Breakout: 29% Improve: 50% Collapse: 20% Attrition: 10%   Comparables: Denis Menke, Larry Parrish, Ron Hansen, Ken McMullen

It's rare for a rookie to dominate his position defensively the way Tulowitzki did last year. By any metric, Tulo was the best defensive shortstop in baseball in 2007. He isn't fast, just effective with a good first step, lateral quickness, and an excellent arm. At the plate, he had a big home/road split, but even his road line of .256/.327/.393 would have been worth a starting job when coupled with his defense. Just 23, he's a coming star.

Eric Young Jr. 2B   Bats: S   Throws: R   Height: 5' 10"   Weight: 180   Born: May 25, 1985   Age: 23

YEAR	TEAM	LVL	AGE	PA	R	2B	3B	HR	RBI	BB	SO	SB	CS	EqBRR	AVG	OBP	SLG	MLVr	EqAVG	EqOBP	EqSLG	EqA	VORP	DEFENSE	
2005	CAS	Rk	20	264	48	7	7	3	25	35	52	25	10	-0.9	.301	.404	.438	.130	.205	.280	.274	.204	-27.3	54-2B	1
2006	ASH	A	21	569	92	28	6	5	49	67	75	87	31	2.6	.295	.391	.409	.109	.237	.313	.328	.234	-8.7	117-2B	7
2007	MOD	A+	22	613	113	29	11	8	63	46	105	73	18	0.2	.291	.359	.430	.098	.241	.296	.343	.235	-10.6	126-2B	6
2008	COL	MLB	23	643	93	31	7	6	50	49	121	62	18	2.5	.268	.331	.379	-.102	.247	.312	.353	.241	3.3	150-2B	5

Breakout: 42% Improve: 72% Collapse: 14% Attrition: 11%   Comparables: Denny Hocking, Elliot Johnson, Chone Figgins, Alfredo Amezaga

There's just not enough here. Young is a second baseman with terrific speed and little else. That spike in his K/BB last year (from 1.12 in 2006 to 2.28) is a warning sign given his age and experience. His dad started later, but was always an on-base machine with great indicators and put off utility work until age 37. For Junior, utility work is likely his ceiling.

PITCHERS

Jeremy Affeldt

Bats: L   Throws: L   Height: 6' 4"   Weight: 225   Born: June 6, 1979   Age: 29

YEAR	TEAM	LVL	AGE	W	L	SV	G	GS	IP	H	BB	SO	HR	GB%	BABIP	STUFF	WHIP	ERA	PERA	EqERA	EqH9	EqBB9	EqSO9	EqHR9	VORP	SN/WX
2005	KCA	MLB	26	0	2	0	49	0	49²	56	29	39	3	53.7%	.331	2	1.71	5.25	4.31	5.44	8.8	4.9	6.5	0.5	-3.3	1.36
2006	KCA	MLB	27	4	6	0	27	9	70	71	42	28	9	49.8%	.265	-20	1.61	5.91	4.26	5.47	7.8	4.9	3.2	1.0	-3.2	0.11
2006	COL	MLB	27	4	2	1	27	0	27¹	31	13	20	4	54.3%	.307	-14	1.61	6.92	4.71	6.52	9.0	3.4	5.6	0.9	-3.6	0.25
2007	COL	MLB	28	4	3	0	75	0	59	47	33	46	3	53.2%	.277	7	1.36	3.51	3.30	3.53	7.1	4.3	6.6	0.5	13.6	-0.65
2008	COL	MLB	29	2	2	2	50	0	48	49	25	34	5	51.6%	.295	-5	1.53	4.65	4.21	4.58	8.3	4.0	6.0	0.8	7.3	0.60

Breakout: 26% Improve: 53% Collapse: 30% Attrition: 34%   Comparables: Greg Cadaret, Jay Powell, C. J. Nitkowski, Dennys Reyes

Despite his big breaking ball, Affeldt is miscast as a specialist. If you look past his opposing hitters' slash stats, you'll see that, of the 150 righties he didn't intentionally pass, Affeldt struck out 19.3 percent, walked 8.6 percent, and allowed homers to just 2, which are roughly the same percentages he had against lefties. The variability of where batted balls land can swing relievers splits around in any given year, so it's important to look at those three defense-independent rates to see what batters are actually doing against them.

Taylor Buchholz

Bats: R   Throws: R   Height: 6' 4"   Weight: 220   Born: October 13, 1981   Age: 26

YEAR	TEAM	LVL	AGE	W	L	SV	G	GS	IP	H	BB	SO	HR	GB%	BABIP	STUFF	WHIP	ERA	PERA	EqERA	EqH9	EqBB9	EqSO9	EqHR9	VORP	SN/WX
2005	ROU	AAA	23	6	0	0	20	14	76²	79	27	45	14	47.8%	.285	-32	1.38	4.81	6.38	5.68	9.8	3.5	3.7	1.9	-0.6	—
2006	ROU	AAA	24	1	3	0	7	7	44	47	17	37	2	42.6%	.345	0	1.45	4.91	5.74	7.08	11.3	4.0	5.8	0.7	-6.7	—
2006	HOU	MLB	24	6	10	0	22	19	113	107	34	77	21	45.5%	.258	-6	1.25	5.89	4.24	5.83	8.2	2.3	5.5	1.5	-3.6	1.40
2007	COL	MLB	25	6	5	0	41	8	93²	105	20	61	8	46.3%	.329	7	1.33	4.23	4.28	4.40	10.0	1.7	5.6	0.7	16.1	0.93
2008	COL	MLB	26	4	5	1	40	7	82²	94	24	54	11	47.2%	.309	1	1.42	4.96	4.38	4.82	9.3	2.3	5.6	1.1	10.1	1.20

Breakout: 25% Improve: 47% Collapse: 24% Attrition: 26%   Comparables: Eddie Fisher, Bob Heffner, Chris Reitsma, Rick White

Despite a high ERA, Buchholz was settling into the rotation in place of an injured Rodrigo Lopez in late May when Lopez came off the DL to reclaim his spot. Sent to the bullpen, he was terrific thereafter, posting a 2.32 ERA and 5.2 K/UIBB in 42 2/3 innings, including three high-leverage appearances during the season-ending 14-1 stretch. He's a stealth closer candidate should Manny Corpas falter.

Aaron Cook

Bats: R   Throws: R   Height: 6' 3"   Weight: 215   Born: February 8, 1979   Age: 29

YEAR	TEAM	LVL	AGE	W	L	SV	G	GS	IP	H	BB	SO	HR	GB%	BABIP	STUFF	WHIP	ERA	PERA	EqERA	EqH9	EqBB9	EqSO9	EqHR9	VORP	SN/WX
2005	COL	MLB	26	7	2	0	13	13	83¹	101	16	24	8	60.6%	.307	-2	1.40	3.67	4.22	3.55	9.7	1.5	2.4	0.8	15.7	2.48
2006	COL	MLB	27	9	15	0	32	32	212²	242	55	92	17	58.6%	.308	8	1.40	4.23	4.02	4.01	9.4	2.0	3.6	0.6	40.6	4.58
2007	COL	MLB	28	8	7	0	25	25	166	178	44	61	15	59.5%	.290	2	1.34	4.12	4.22	4.56	9.5	2.1	3.2	0.7	25.3	2.85
2008	COL	MLB	29	7	9	0	23	23	135²	166	36	55	15	56.8%	.312	0	1.49	4.94	4.56	4.87	10.0	2.1	3.5	0.9	15.7	2.70

Breakout: 10% Improve: 27% Collapse: 41% Attrition: 23%   Comparables: Jim Barr, Al Fitzmorris, Bob Shaw, Jake Westbrook

Cook has one of the lowest strikeout rates in baseball, and was thus the biggest beneficiary of the Rockies' improved defense in 2007. The 12-point drop in team BABIP was reflected in his decreased batting average against. With his ability to control the running game and get double plays, Cook can survive like this for a while. Having given him a new four-year, $36.4 million extension that runs through 2011, the Rockies are banking on it.

Manny Corpas

Bats: R   Throws: R   Height: 6' 3"   Weight: 170   Born: December 3, 1982   Age: 25

YEAR	TEAM	LVL	AGE	W	L	SV	G	GS	IP	H	BB	SO	HR	GB%	BABIP	STUFF	WHIP	ERA	PERA	EqERA	EqH9	EqBB9	EqSO9	EqHR9	VORP	SN/WX
2005	MOD	A+	22	3	2	2	47	0	69	83	14	52	2	60.9%	.362	-15	1.41	3.78	5.51	5.37	11.3	3.1	3.7	0.6	1.6	—
2006	TUL	AA	23	2	1	19	34	0	36²	22	4	35	0	63.0%	.247	12	0.72	0.99	3.06	2.94	6.7	1.6	6.1	0.3	10.0	—
2006	COL	MLB	23	1	2	0	35	0	32¹	36	8	27	3	45.5%	.344	9	1.36	3.62	4.49	3.19	9.9	2.0	7.3	0.9	9.2	0.20
2007	COL	MLB	24	4	2	19	78	0	78	63	20	58	6	58.4%	.263	14	1.06	2.08	2.97	2.14	7.3	2.0	6.4	0.6	31.8	4.16
2008	COL	MLB	25	4	4	12	60	0	64¹	64	21	47	6	53.1%	.296	6	1.33	3.65	3.49	3.62	8.2	2.6	6.3	0.7	17.1	1.70

Breakout: 3% Improve: 14% Collapse: 64% Attrition: 21%   Comparables: Rusty Meacham, Steve Olin, Ryan Madson, Rawly Eastwick

Corpas didn't pitch every single day down the stretch, it just seemed that way. Corpas's sinking fastball, which he used to generate a ton of groundballs, is his only above-average pitch, so the chances that his walk rate will jump as hitters learn to lay off it is significant. Long term, he's a set-up man.

Sam Deduno

Bats: R   Throws: R   Height: 6' 1"   Weight: 156   Born: July 2, 1983   Age: 24

YEAR	TEAM	LVL	AGE	W	L	SV	G	GS	IP	H	BB	SO	HR	GB%	BABIP	STUFF	WHIP	ERA	PERA	EqERA	EqH9	EqBB9	EqSO9	EqHR9	VORP	SN/WX
2005	ASH	A	22	8	8	0	20	20	89^2	82	65	110	9	54.5%	.346	-9	1.64	5.62	9.44	10.11	10.8	10.9	6.3	2.0	-37.9	—
2006	MOD	A+	23	5	8	0	27	26	146^1	121	92	167	3	63.6%	.315	21	1.46	4.80	5.07	6.52	8.1	7.4	5.9	0.5	-14.2	—
2007	TUL	AA	24	5	8	0	21	21	124	120	66	121	13	60.4%	.310	-7	1.50	5.44	6.63	8.25	10.2	5.9	6.1	1.4	-34.4	—
2008	COL	MLB	24	5	8	0	27	19	107^1	118	83	80	12	55.5%	.318	-2	1.87	6.27	5.65	6.10	9.0	6.1	6.3	0.9	-2.0	0.50

Breakout: 56% Improve: 78% Collapse: 10% Attrition: 23%   Comparables: Denny Bautista, Anastacio Martinez, Jose Oyervidez, Mike MacDougal

This lanky Dominican got caught in an identity mix-up last spring and was unable to leave the D.R. in time for spring training. He never did catch up, struggling with his command all season despite leading the Texas League in strikeouts. He has three pitches, including a very good curve. If he can just find the strike zone, he'll reach the majors.

Josh Fogg

Bats: R   Throws: R   Height: 6' 0"   Weight: 205   Born: December 13, 1976   Age: 31

YEAR	TEAM	LVL	AGE	W	L	SV	G	GS	IP	H	BB	SO	HR	GB%	BABIP	STUFF	WHIP	ERA	PERA	EqERA	EqH9	EqBB9	EqSO9	EqHR9	VORP	SN/WX
2005	PIT	MLB	28	6	11	0	34	28	169^1	196	53	85	27	41.1%	.301	-19	1.47	5.05	5.89	5.91	10.4	2.6	4.2	1.4	-0.9	1.74
2006	COL	MLB	29	11	9	0	31	31	172	206	60	93	24	43.5%	.319	-5	1.55	5.49	5.13	5.33	10.0	2.7	4.4	1.0	4.6	1.47
2007	COL	MLB	30	10	9	0	30	29	165^2	194	59	94	23	41.1%	.313	-4	1.53	4.94	5.55	5.12	10.2	2.7	4.8	1.1	13.4	2.31
2008	COL	MLB	31	6	8	0	20	20	114	135	36	65	18	44.2%	.307	3	1.50	5.27	4.89	5.05	9.7	2.5	4.9	1.2	11.3	2.00

Breakout: 20% Improve: 52% Collapse: 25% Attrition: 35%   Comparables: Jim Colborn, James Baldwin, Lew Burdette, Richard Dotson

You can't even call Josh Fogg an innings guy. In 179 career starts, he's averaged 5 2/3 innings per start, exactly what he averaged last year. He doesn't have great control, or miss a lot of bats, or throw a ton of groundballs. His primary asset is that he stays off the DL, and how hard is that when you're throwing junk for 90 pitches a night?

Jeff Francis

Bats: L   Throws: L   Height: 6' 5"   Weight: 205   Born: January 8, 1981   Age: 27

YEAR	TEAM	LVL	AGE	W	L	SV	G	GS	IP	H	BB	SO	HR	GB%	BABIP	STUFF	WHIP	ERA	PERA	EqERA	EqH9	EqBB9	EqSO9	EqHR9	VORP	SN/WX
2005	COL	MLB	24	14	12	0	33	33	183^2	228	70	128	26	38.8%	.349	-3	1.62	5.68	5.74	5.42	10.3	3.1	5.7	1.2	0.1	1.00
2006	COL	MLB	25	13	11	0	32	32	199	187	69	117	18	46.1%	.276	14	1.29	4.16	3.45	3.90	7.8	2.6	4.8	0.7	35.5	4.18
2007	COL	MLB	26	17	9	0	34	34	215^1	234	63	165	25	46.3%	.321	17	1.38	4.22	4.64	4.08	9.7	2.3	6.5	0.9	42.7	5.37
2008	COL	MLB	27	11	10	0	30	30	185^1	204	59	132	23	45.6%	.309	16	1.42	4.48	4.28	4.31	9.0	2.5	6.1	1.0	31.5	4.80

Breakout: 13% Improve: 42% Collapse: 17% Attrition: 12%   Comparables: Denny Neagle, Jerry Reuss, Pete Schourek, Frank Viola

Whether emboldened by the improved defense, the squishy baseballs, or simple maturity, Francis came after hitters last year, posting the best walk rate and Stuff score of his career. His loose mechanics and reasonable pitch counts keep him healthy, too. His ERA will always run high because of his home park, but he's one of the top 15 starters in the NL.

Brian Fuentes

Bats: L   Throws: L   Height: 6' 4"   Weight: 230   Born: August 9, 1975   Age: 32

YEAR	TEAM	LVL	AGE	W	L	SV	G	GS	IP	H	BB	SO	HR	GB%	BABIP	STUFF	WHIP	ERA	PERA	EqERA	EqH9	EqBB9	EqSO9	EqHR9	VORP	SN/WX
2005	COL	MLB	29	2	5	31	78	0	74^1	59	34	91	6	41.4%	.305	26	1.25	2.91	3.32	2.62	6.7	3.7	9.6	0.7	21.8	5.37
2006	COL	MLB	30	3	4	30	66	0	65^1	50	26	73	8	35.5%	.266	19	1.16	3.45	3.13	2.84	6.3	3.0	8.9	0.9	19.8	2.18
2007	COL	MLB	31	3	5	20	64	0	61^1	46	23	56	6	36.7%	.248	13	1.13	3.08	3.11	3.36	6.6	2.9	7.6	0.7	15.0	0.39
2008	COL	MLB	32	3	4	18	54	0	52^2	48	23	52	6	41.1%	.293	12	1.35	3.75	3.64	3.62	7.5	3.4	8.4	0.9	12.8	1.60

Breakout: 7% Improve: 23% Collapse: 42% Attrition: 12%   Comparables: Jason Christiansen, Joe Page, Roberto Hernandez, Arthur Rhodes

Ten days in June put a damper on Fuentes' season, as he allowed half of the runs he would allow all season over five appearances from June 22 through July 1. Whether pitching through an injury—he pitched just one more inning before hitting the DL on July 13 with a strained left lat muscle—or just having a bad stretch, Fuentes blew four straight saves and allowed 13 runs, 10 hits, and three walks in just 3⅓ innings, losing the closer job to Manny Corpas in the process. Before that he was awesome—1.89 ERA in 33⅓ innings—and as the primary set-up man after his mid-August return he was just as good: 1.52 ERA in 23⅔ innings. He'll remain in that set-up role in 2008 and deliver more of the same.

LaTroy Hawkins

Bats: R   Throws: R   Height: 6' 5"   Weight: 215   Born: December 21, 1972   Age: 35

YEAR	TEAM	LVL	AGE	W	L	SV	G	GS	IP	H	BB	SO	HR	GB%	BABIP	STUFF	WHIP	ERA	PERA	EqERA	EqH9	EqBB9	EqSO9	EqHR9	VORP	SN/WX
2005	CHN	MLB	32	1	4	4	21	0	19	18	7	13	4	46.7%	.255	-13	1.32	3.32	5.19	4.34	8.7	2.9	5.8	1.9	2.6	-0.48
2005	SFN	MLB	32	1	4	2	45	0	37¹	40	17	30	3	46.7%	.325	-3	1.53	4.10	4.68	4.34	9.6	3.6	6.5	0.7	4.9	-0.07
2006	BAL	MLB	33	3	2	0	60	0	60¹	73	15	27	4	46.6%	.325	-9	1.46	4.48	4.19	4.03	10.0	2.1	3.7	0.6	10.8	1.81
2007	COL	MLB	34	2	5	0	62	0	55¹	52	16	29	6	62.8%	.269	-7	1.23	3.42	3.67	3.17	8.3	2.3	4.5	0.8	15.9	0.27
2008	NYA	MLB	35	2	2	1	44	0	48¹	56	17	26	5	52.2%	.310	-14	1.50	4.76	4.66	4.81	10.1	2.9	4.4	0.9	3.5	0.30

Breakout: 5%   Improve: 16%   Collapse: 60%   Attrition: 28%   Comparables: Dale Murray, Antonio Alfonseca, David Weathers, Phil Regan

After contemplating retirement during the offseason and posting an 8.59 ERA in the first three weeks of the 2007 season, Hawkins landed on the DL with a sore forearm. When he returned in late May, he was a different pitcher, posting a 2.63 ERA and serving as the right-handed set-up man for most of the second half. A spike in his ground-ball rate combined with the stellar Colorado defense played a large part. Hawkins doesn't have the stuff he had five years ago, and his ERA could double at any time, particularly if his ground-ball rate reverts. Even if it doesn't, moving back to the American League, where he'll have Derek Jeter behind him in place of Troy Tulowitzki, doesn't bode well.

Matt Herges

Bats: L   Throws: R   Height: 6' 0"   Weight: 210   Born: April 1, 1970   Age: 38

YEAR	TEAM	LVL	AGE	W	L	SV	G	GS	IP	H	BB	SO	HR	GB%	BABIP	STUFF	WHIP	ERA	PERA	EqERA	EqH9	EqBB9	EqSO9	EqHR9	VORP	SN/WX
2005	TUC	AAA	35	1	2	0	26	0	28²	39	8	29	3	49.4%	.434	-10	1.64	3.14	7.72	5.06	13.5	3.0	6.8	1.0	1.6	—
2005	SFN	MLB	35	1	1	0	21	0	21	23	7	6	2	46.8%	.292	-28	1.43	4.71	4.69	4.87	9.7	2.7	2.2	0.9	2.1	0.14
2006	FLO	MLB	36	2	3	0	66	0	71	94	28	36	5	47.9%	.353	-14	1.72	4.31	5.71	5.35	11.5	3.1	4.2	0.5	3.3	-0.95
2007	CSP	AAA	37	2	1	1	32	0	35¹	24	10	33	2	52.7%	.247	9	0.96	1.27	2.93	1.87	5.9	2.9	6.7	0.5	14.0	—
2007	COL	MLB	37	5	1	0	35	0	48²	34	15	30	4	48.6%	.217	3	1.01	2.96	2.55	2.96	5.9	2.4	5.2	0.7	15.6	1.93
2008	COL	MLB	38	2	2	2	33	0	36¹	43	14	20	5	46.7%	.308	-14	1.54	4.84	4.74	4.68	9.6	3.0	4.7	1.1	5.0	0.40

Breakout: 19%   Improve: 40%   Collapse: 37%   Attrition: 34%   Comparables: Mike Maddux, Jim Hearn, Jack Sanford, Jerry Staley

Herges was the Rockies' best reliever in the postseason, tossing seven shutout innings, including a dominant, strike-out-the-side performance in Game Two of the World Series. In 11⅓ post-season innings over 10 appearances, Herges' career ERA is 0.00. Does that make him clutch, or do you have to be famous for that?

Jason Hirsh

Bats: R   Throws: R   Height: 6' 8"   Weight: 250   Born: February 20, 1982   Age: 26

YEAR	TEAM	LVL	AGE	W	L	SV	G	GS	IP	H	BB	SO	HR	GB%	BABIP	STUFF	WHIP	ERA	PERA	EqERA	EqH9	EqBB9	EqSO9	EqHR9	VORP	SN/WX
2005	CCH	AA	23	13	8	0	29	29	172¹	137	42	165	12	45.4%	.277	9	1.04	2.87	4.71	4.62	8.8	3.4	6.3	1.1	16.8	—
2006	ROU	AAA	24	13	2	0	23	23	137¹	94	51	118	5	40.8%	.245	21	1.06	2.10	3.53	3.41	7.1	3.8	5.8	0.5	31.5	—
2006	HOU	MLB	24	3	4	0	9	9	44²	48	22	29	11	32.2%	.264	-16	1.57	6.04	6.21	6.07	9.2	3.7	5.3	2.0	-1.8	0.68
2007	COL	MLB	25	5	7	0	19	19	112¹	103	48	75	18	32.7%	.258	0	1.34	4.81	4.10	4.43	7.8	3.2	5.5	1.3	13.2	1.43
2008	COL	MLB	26	7	8	0	23	23	127¹	133	53	88	19	39.5%	.289	10	1.46	4.95	4.52	4.73	8.5	3.3	5.9	1.2	15.9	2.70

Breakout: 14%   Improve: 40%   Collapse: 34%   Attrition: 18%   Comparables: Steve Renko, Tommy Greene, Aaron Harang, Jason Johnson

Hirsh is built a bit like Jason Jennings, for whom he was acquired from the Astros. The key difference between the two isn't physical, but aerial; Hirsh is a fly-ball pitcher (career 0.60 G/F), whereas Jennings is a ground-ball pitcher (career 1.42 G/F). That makes a big difference in a place like Coors Field. Hirsh missed six weeks of 2007 with a broken right fibula suffered when J. J. Hardy lined a ball off his shin. He's expected to be healthy and back in the rotation by spring training.

Ubaldo Jimenez

Bats: R   **Throws:** R   **Height:** 6' 4"   **Weight:** 200   **Born:** January 22, 1984   **Age:** 24

YEAR	TEAM	LVL	AGE	W	L	SV	G	GS	IP	H	BB	SO	HR	GB%	BABIP	STUFF	WHIP	ERA	PERA	EqERA	EqH9	EqBB9	EqSO9	EqHR9	VORP	SN/WX
2005	MOD	A+	21	5	3	0	14	14	72¹	61	40	78	5	38.7%	.311	10	1.40	3.98	5.50	5.48	8.4	7.0	5.8	1.1	0.9	—
2005	TUL	AA	21	2	5	0	12	11	63	58	31	53	12	30.9%	.264	-18	1.41	5.43	8.39	7.92	10.0	6.3	5.3	2.6	-14.4	—
2006	TUL	AA	22	9	2	0	13	13	73²	49	40	86	2	43.2%	.287	34	1.22	2.46	4.43	3.72	7.9	6.1	7.9	0.4	13.6	—
2006	CSP	AAA	22	5	2	0	13	13	78¹	74	43	64	7	43.2%	.300	4	1.50	5.07	4.97	5.68	8.4	5.3	5.2	1.1	-0.7	—
2007	CSP	AAA	23	8	5	0	19	19	103	110	62	89	9	47.6%	.341	7	1.67	5.85	5.60	6.48	9.6	5.8	6.0	0.9	-9.7	—
2007	COL	MLB	23	4	4	0	15	15	82	70	37	68	10	47.7%	.262	16	1.30	4.28	3.73	4.45	7.4	3.5	6.9	1.0	9.9	1.80
2008	COL	MLB	24	8	10	0	28	28	149¹	153	80	116	19	46.7%	.298	11	1.56	5.10	4.69	4.91	8.4	4.2	6.6	1.0	15.7	2.80

Breakout: 27%   **Improve:** 51%   **Collapse:** 15%   **Attrition:** 22%   **Comparables:** Tony Armas Jr., Mark Hutton, Matt Clement, Ron Darling

Part of a talent pipeline from Latin America that also produced Panamanian Manny Corpas and Venezuelan Franklin Morales, Dominican Jimenez gave the Rockies' rotation a needed power arm after the All-Star break last year. Despite loads of experience—120 minor league starts—he remains raw and unable to command his breaking ball at all. Don't look at his 2.25 post-season ERA, look at the 13 walks in 16 innings spread out over three starts. He hadn't actually mastered Triple-A when the Rockies promoted him, and there's a very good chance he'll find himself back there this year.

Jorge Julio

Bats: R   **Throws:** R   **Height:** 6' 1"   **Weight:** 225   **Born:** March 3, 1979   **Age:** 29

YEAR	TEAM	LVL	AGE	W	L	SV	G	GS	IP	H	BB	SO	HR	GB%	BABIP	STUFF	WHIP	ERA	PERA	EqERA	EqH9	EqBB9	EqSO9	EqHR9	VORP	SN/WX
2005	BAL	MLB	26	3	5	0	67	0	71²	76	24	58	14	39.7%	.294	-14	1.41	5.90	5.28	5.90	9.2	2.9	7.0	1.6	-4.5	-0.56
2006	NYN	MLB	27	1	2	1	18	0	21¹	21	10	33	4	51.9%	.354	16	1.45	5.07	5.93	6.33	9.7	3.8	11.4	1.7	-1.2	-0.19
2006	ARI	MLB	27	1	2	15	44	0	44²	31	25	55	6	38.5%	.245	19	1.25	3.83	3.16	3.35	5.9	4.3	9.7	1.0	10.5	1.36
2007	FLO	MLB	28	0	2	0	10	0	9¹	18	11	6	2	42.5%	.432	-45	3.11	12.58	16.13	14.81	14.8	7.8	5.2	1.7	-8.4	-1.87
2007	COL	MLB	28	0	3	0	58	0	52²	50	20	50	6	56.0%	.317	10	1.33	3.93	4.14	3.86	8.6	3.0	8.2	0.9	10.4	0.56
2008	COL	MLB	29	3	3	3	51	0	58¹	56	26	55	6	47.4%	.302	11	1.40	4.23	3.87	4.13	7.9	3.4	8.0	0.9	12.4	1.00

Breakout: 54%   **Improve:** 78%   **Collapse:** 7%   **Attrition:** 20%   **Comparables:** Kyle Farnsworth, Dan Miceli, Bobby Ayala, Edwin Nuñez

It's probably not a good sign if you post an ERA of 3.93 in 52 2/3 innings and your team leaves you off of its playoff roster. Julio was used in a wide variety of roles after the Rockies and Marlins swapped assumed head cases (with Byung-Hyun Kim heading to Florida) and was intermittently effective. He throws hard enough to accidentally have a sub-2.00 ERA and 30 saves some random season, which would add several years to the end of his career.

Ching-Lung Lo

Bats: R   **Throws:** R   **Height:** 6' 6"   **Weight:** 190   **Born:** August 20, 1985   **Age:** 22

YEAR	TEAM	LVL	AGE	W	L	SV	G	GS	IP	H	BB	SO	HR	GB%	BABIP	STUFF	WHIP	ERA	PERA	EqERA	EqH9	EqBB9	EqSO9	EqHR9	VORP	SN/WX
2005	ASH	A	19	7	9	0	24	24	121	148	38	91	23	49.4%	.334	-69	1.54	5.65	12.43	10.83	13.6	5.4	3.2	3.4	-60.8	—
2006	MOD	A+	20	10	5	0	27	25	155²	179	54	128	14	51.7%	.340	-16	1.50	5.39	6.97	7.71	11.2	4.6	4.0	1.5	-34.2	—
2007	TUL	AA	21	8	8	0	26	26	139²	162	66	87	20	53.5%	.328	-36	1.63	5.60	9.09	8.48	12.2	5.4	3.7	1.9	-40.7	—
2008	COL	MLB	22	4	9	0	27	20	106	145	68	54	21	49.2%	.332	-18	2.01	7.93	7.12	7.52	11.1	5.0	4.3	1.6	-17.3	-1.10

Breakout: 34%   **Improve:** 67%   **Collapse:** 13%   **Attrition:** 10%   **Comparables:** Jose Espinal, Willis Roberts, Juan Castillo, Aaron Dean

This Taiwanese bonus baby keeps moving forward without making tangible progress. Lo has drop-and-drive mechanics, but lacks the leg strength to be a power pitcher. Still, as a ground-ball pitcher, he fits the Rockies' current setup well and could be a serviceable midseason replacement if he's able to improve his command and secondary pitches.

Rodrigo Lopez

Bats: R   **Throws:** R   **Height:** 6' 1"   **Weight:** 185   **Born:** December 14, 1975   **Age:** 32

YEAR	TEAM	LVL	AGE	W	L	SV	G	GS	IP	H	BB	SO	HR	GB%	BABIP	STUFF	WHIP	ERA	PERA	EqERA	EqH9	EqBB9	EqSO9	EqHR9	VORP	SN/WX
2005	BAL	MLB	29	15	12	0	35	35	209¹	232	63	118	28	44.0%	.294	-1	1.41	4.90	4.80	5.06	9.5	2.7	4.8	1.1	8.0	3.81
2006	BAL	MLB	30	9	18	0	36	29	189	234	59	136	32	44.8%	.333	-3	1.55	5.90	5.53	5.56	10.2	2.6	6.0	1.3	-2.0	1.43
2007	COL	MLB	31	5	4	0	14	14	79¹	83	21	43	11	48.7%	.288	1	1.31	4.43	4.31	4.58	9.2	2.1	4.7	1.1	10.9	1.53
2008	COL	MLB	32	5	6	0	25	14	92	105	28	56	14	45.7%	.302	0	1.45	5.13	4.65	4.93	9.3	2.4	5.2	1.2	10.3	1.50

Breakout: 19%   **Improve:** 49%   **Collapse:** 21%   **Attrition:** 33%   **Comparables:** Ruben Gomez, Russ Meyer, Marty Pattin, Jack Kramer

Clint Hurdle issued the fourth-most intentional walks in the majors last year, which means you have to consider the IBB column when evaluating his pitchers. Nearly 40 percent of Lopez's 21 walks allowed were intentional, meaning his true K/BB ratio was better than 3-to-1, and his walk rate was below two per nine innings. That would have been a nice hook for his free agent pitch this winter, but two surgeries on his arm—to repair a torn flexor tendon and his ulnar collateral ligament—will keep him out until 2009.

Franklin Morales

Bats: L   Throws: L   Height: 6' 0"   Weight: 170   Born: January 24, 1986   Age: 22

YEAR	TEAM	LVL	AGE	W	L	SV	G	GS	IP	H	BB	SO	HR	GB%	BABIP	STUFF	WHIP	ERA	PERA	EqERA	EqH9	EqBB9	EqSO9	EqHR9	VORP	SN/WX
2005	ASH	A	19	8	4	1	21	15	96^1	73	48	108	6	54.9%	.295	5	1.26	3.08	6.04	5.70	8.5	7.6	5.6	1.3	-0.9	—
2006	MOD	A+	20	10	9	0	27	26	154^2	126	89	179	9	54.5%	.310	15	1.39	3.68	5.58	5.76	8.4	7.1	6.3	1.1	-2.5	—
2007	TUL	AA	21	3	4	0	17	17	95^2	77	45	77	8	47.6%	.270	1	1.27	3.48	5.22	5.07	8.6	5.4	5.1	1.1	5.1	—
2007	CSP	AAA	21	2	0	0	3	3	17	20	13	16	1	41.3%	.422	14	1.94	3.71	8.83	5.79	12.9	8.4	7.7	0.6	-0.3	—
2007	COL	MLB	21	3	2	0	8	8	39^1	34	14	26	2	57.0%	.283	22	1.22	3.44	3.17	3.23	7.6	2.8	5.5	0.5	11.1	1.32
2008	COL	MLB	22	7	10	0	37	25	132^1	149	83	96	16	49.9%	.318	1	1.75	5.70	5.38	5.48	9.2	4.9	6.2	1.0	5.7	1.50

Breakout: 9%   Improve: 27%   Collapse: 42%   Attrition: 27%   Comparables: Horacio Estrada, Wade Blasingame, Alberto Blanco, Dallas Braden

Injuries to Cook, Hirsh, and Lopez forced the Rockies to advance Morales a bit too quickly, giving him just two ineffective weeks in Triple-A before putting him in the rotation down the stretch. He didn't pitch poorly, but he was a bit overmatched in the postseason. He needs at least another half season in the minors to work on commanding his mid-90s fastball and developing his off-speed pitches.

Juan Morillo

Bats: R   Throws: R   Height: 6' 3"   Weight: 190   Born: November 5, 1983   Age: 24

YEAR	TEAM	LVL	AGE	W	L	SV	G	GS	IP	H	BB	SO	HR	GB%	BABIP	STUFF	WHIP	ERA	PERA	EqERA	EqH9	EqBB9	EqSO9	EqHR9	VORP	SN/WX
2005	ASH	A	21	1	3	0	7	7	33^2	40	13	43	2	55.8%	.409	-1	1.57	4.54	9.39	9.85	14.3	6.4	6.7	1.3	-13.4	—
2005	MOD	A+	21	6	5	0	20	20	112^1	107	65	101	10	52.7%	.319	-5	1.53	4.41	6.23	6.77	9.1	7.3	4.6	1.3	-13.3	—
2006	TUL	AA	22	12	8	0	27	27	140	128	80	132	13	47.9%	.307	-1	1.49	4.63	6.52	6.79	10.1	6.2	6.0	1.3	-16.8	—
2007	TUL	AA	23	6	4	0	46	0	57^1	44	27	59	2	46.4%	.282	6	1.24	2.36	4.37	4.02	8.0	5.2	6.5	0.5	9.4	—
2007	CSP	AAA	23	0	1	0	7	0	9^2	7	4	12	0	39.1%	.304	9	1.13	3.71	3.11	3.86	6.8	3.9	8.7	0.0	1.8	—
2007	COL	MLB	23	0	0	0	4	0	3^2	3	1	3	1	27.3%	.200	-4	1.09	9.73	4.54	9.82	7.4	2.5	7.4	2.5	-1.4	-0.04
2008	COL	MLB	24	3	4	1	31	4	55^1	61	36	44	8	45.2%	.314	-4	1.76	5.77	5.60	5.48	9.0	5.2	6.7	1.2	2.5	0.30

Breakout: 44%   Improve: 71%   Collapse: 15%   Attrition: 12%   Comparables: Grant Balfour, Craig House, Francisco Cordero, Emiliano Giron

The Rockies' decision to convert the flame-throwing Morillo to relief last year paid off, as the Dominican adapted well to shorter outings, improving all of his rate stats and staying healthy in the new role. While the Rockies have many relief options, Morillo is the one with the best chance to be a dominant short man given his high-90s fastball and good slider. He should arrive in the majors for good this summer.

Ramon Ortiz

Bats: R   Throws: R   Height: 6' 0"   Weight: 175   Born: May 23, 1973   Age: 35

YEAR	TEAM	LVL	AGE	W	L	SV	G	GS	IP	H	BB	SO	HR	GB%	BABIP	STUFF	WHIP	ERA	PERA	EqERA	EqH9	EqBB9	EqSO9	EqHR9	VORP	SN/WX
2005	CIN	MLB	32	9	11	0	30	30	171^1	206	51	96	34	44.9%	.312	-19	1.50	5.36	5.97	5.53	10.0	2.4	4.6	1.7	-3.4	1.33
2006	WAS	MLB	33	11	16	0	33	33	190^2	230	64	104	31	41.3%	.311	-11	1.54	5.57	5.86	5.68	10.4	2.6	4.5	1.3	-2.6	2.38
2007	MIN	MLB	34	4	4	0	28	10	91	112	15	44	12	44.6%	.313	-11	1.40	5.14	4.98	5.05	10.2	1.3	4.0	1.2	6.4	0.72
2007	COL	MLB	34	1	0	0	10	0	13	15	7	7	4	45.5%	.289	-36	1.69	7.62	9.20	7.82	9.9	4.3	5.0	2.8	-1.9	-0.03
2008	COL	MLB	35	3	3	1	28	5	55^1	69	16	29	9	45.8%	.315	-12	1.54	5.50	5.06	5.28	10.2	2.3	4.4	1.2	4.4	0.50

Breakout: 21%   Improve: 44%   Collapse: 32%   Attrition: 48%   Comparables: Frank Lary, Hank Borowy, Willie Blair, Vern Ruhle

Ortiz's career is a pretty good data point for why a player would lie about his age. Had the Angels known in 1995 that Ortiz was 22 rather than 19, they most likely would have passed on him, and prospect hounds wouldn't have regarded his 225 strikeouts in 181 innings in the Midwest League as impressive knowing he was 24 years old at the time. Without that chance and that hype, Ortiz wouldn't have made nearly $16 million over the last nine years. That's a pretty big incentive to roll back the odometer. At 35 and with ERAs above five in three straight years, he's about done.

Ramon Ramirez

Bats: R   Throws: R   Height: 5' 11"   Weight: 190   Born: August 31, 1981   Age: 26

YEAR	TEAM	LVL	AGE	W	L	SV	G	GS	IP	H	BB	SO	HR	GB%	BABIP	STUFF	WHIP	ERA	PERA	EqERA	EqH9	EqBB9	EqSO9	EqHR9	VORP	SN/WX
2005	TRN	AA	23	6	5	0	15	15	89	79	35	82	10	44.4%	.284	-11	1.28	3.84	5.87	6.07	9.3	4.9	5.3	1.6	-4.2	—
2005	COH	AAA	23	1	3	0	6	6	27	32	9	26	3	48.1%	.382	-4	1.52	5.33	6.78	6.48	11.5	3.6	6.5	1.4	-2.4	—
2005	TUL	AA	23	2	1	0	9	3	25¹	27	8	23	6	41.0%	.300	-30	1.38	5.34	10.43	8.87	11.7	4.4	6.0	3.2	-8.1	—
2006	COL	MLB	24	4	3	0	61	0	67²	58	27	61	5	41.3%	.285	14	1.26	3.46	3.08	3.26	7.0	3.0	7.3	0.5	18.8	0.89
2007	CSP	AAA	25	4	0	0	25	0	27²	18	16	35	2	50.8%	.258	17	1.23	2.27	3.34	3.29	5.6	5.3	8.9	0.7	7.0	—
2007	COL	MLB	25	2	2	0	22	0	17¹	21	6	15	2	35.7%	.380	-6	1.56	8.32	5.77	7.94	11.1	2.6	7.4	1.1	-4.0	-0.10
2008	COL	MLB	26	2	2	2	49	0	49²	46	24	42	6	42.5%	.281	4	1.41	4.35	4.00	4.20	7.6	3.8	7.2	1.0	9.6	0.80

Breakout: 41% Improve: 66% Collapse: 19% Attrition: 22%   Comparables: Bobby Castillo, Jim Ray, Trevor Hoffman, Travis Phelps

Elbow and forearm problems carved up Ramirez's 2007 season, but his 8.31 ERA is deceptive; he allowed runs in just five of his 22 big-league appearances last year, but when he was bad, he was awful. Ramirez pitched well enough during a six-week stay at Colorado Springs to indicate that he can help a team when he's healthy; he might inherit Hawkins' innings this year.

Greg Reynolds

Bats: R   Throws: R   Height: 6' 7"   Weight: 225   Born: July 3, 1985   Age: 22

YEAR	TEAM	LVL	AGE	W	L	SV	G	GS	IP	H	BB	SO	HR	GB%	BABIP	STUFF	WHIP	ERA	PERA	EqERA	EqH9	EqBB9	EqSO9	EqHR9	VORP	SN/WX
2006	MOD	A+	21	2	1	0	11	11	48¹	51	14	29	1	57.2%	.316	-6	1.35	3.37	4.84	5.00	9.8	4.0	2.6	0.6	3.0	—
2007	TUL	AA	22	4	1	0	8	8	50²	32	9	35	2	53.5%	.213	16	0.81	1.42	3.16	2.83	6.2	2.3	4.2	0.6	14.7	—
2008	COL	MLB	22	8	8	0	22	22	129²	137	48	68	13	53.7%	.288	7	1.43	4.58	4.13	4.52	8.6	2.9	4.5	0.8	18.6	3.10

Breakout: 1% Improve: 18% Collapse: 60% Attrition: 16%   Comparables: Justin Wayne, Jon Garland, Brett Myers, Roy Halladay

The second overall pick in 2006, Reynolds got off to a fantastic start at Double-A last year before his shoulder started bothering him. It eventually required arthroscopic surgery, but according to everyone involved, it wasn't as serious as it sounds, and Reynolds is expected to make a full recovery for 2008. After a year in which guys such as Jimenez and Morales stepped forward as future rotation stalwarts, Reynolds is kind of the organization's forgotten man. Don't make that mistake. If he really is healthy, he's a ground-ball machine who throws a low- to mid-90s fastball with both sink and a downward plane because of his height. In a perfect world, he could become something like Chien-Ming Wang.

Ryan Speier

Bats: R   Throws: R   Height: 6' 7"   Weight: 210   Born: July 24, 1979   Age: 28

YEAR	TEAM	LVL	AGE	W	L	SV	G	GS	IP	H	BB	SO	HR	GB%	BABIP	STUFF	WHIP	ERA	PERA	EqERA	EqH9	EqBB9	EqSO9	EqHR9	VORP	SN/WX
2005	CSP	AAA	25	2	2	6	45	0	52¹	70	18	45	2	52.6%	.407	-8	1.68	4.99	5.91	4.97	11.7	3.4	5.3	0.5	3.5	—
2005	COL	MLB	25	2	1	0	22	0	24²	26	13	10	0	48.3%	.310	-18	1.58	3.64	3.70	3.96	8.6	4.3	3.2	0.0	2.8	-0.36
2007	CSP	AAA	27	1	4	33	50	0	49¹	47	23	40	3	47.3%	.308	-7	1.42	4.38	4.21	4.62	8.1	4.4	5.5	0.6	5.3	—
2007	COL	MLB	27	3	1	0	20	0	18	20	8	13	1	43.6%	.358	-4	1.56	4.00	5.33	4.32	10.8	3.8	6.5	0.5	4.2	0.25
2008	COL	MLB	28	3	3	4	53	2	54	63	28	36	7	47.6%	.320	-9	1.68	5.40	5.17	5.20	9.5	4.1	5.8	1.0	4.3	0.50

Breakout: 18% Improve: 32% Collapse: 43% Attrition: 14%   Comparables: Toby Borland, Chad Paronto, Al Levine, Brandon Puffer

After missing 2006 following surgery to repair a torn labrum, Speier came back last year as essentially the same pitcher—a ground-ball guy who doesn't have enough command or stuff to sustain a high-leverage role in a major league bullpen. You can't be Steve Reed if you walk a man every other inning.

Pedro Strop

Bats: S   Throws: R   Height: 6' 0"   Weight: 160   Born: June 13, 1985   Age: 23

YEAR	TEAM	LVL	AGE	W	L	SV	G	GS	IP	H	BB	SO	HR	GB%	BABIP	STUFF	WHIP	ERA	PERA	EqERA	EqH9	EqBB9	EqSO9	EqHR9	VORP	SN/WX
2006	ASH	A	21	2	1	0	11	0	13²	10	5	13	3	37.1%	.226	-22	1.14	4.77	11.19	9.00	9.8	5.7	4.9	4.9	-4.2	—
2006	CAS	Rk	21	1	0	0	11	0	13	9	2	22	1	53.8%	.320	11	0.85	2.08	6.02	3.97	9.5	3.2	8.7	1.6	2.0	—
2007	MOD	A+	22	5	2	7	48	0	54²	43	29	75	4	46.2%	.322	5	1.32	4.28	6.10	6.24	9.6	6.8	7.9	1.1	-3.5	—
2008	COL	MLB	23	2	4	1	24	6	53	55	47	46	8	46.0%	.305	-5	1.93	6.11	5.97	5.80	8.5	7.0	7.4	1.2	0.6	0.20

Breakout: 35% Improve: 61% Collapse: 23% Attrition: 14%   Comparables: Harvey Garcia, Matt Elliott, Gabriel Ozuna, Manny Barrios

Strop was a career .212/.276/.298 hitter as a shortstop, which is all the explanation you need for why he's now in the pitcher section. In his first full season on the mound, Strop was darn good at High-A, limiting Cal League hitters to a

.215 average with a high strikeout rate. Strop is a bit undersized, but he has two-plus pitches with a 92 to 95 mph fastball and a hard slider. If he refines his control, he projects as a late-inning, high-leverage reliever.

Casey Weathers

Bats: R   Throws: R   Height: 6' 1"   Weight: 205   Born: June 10, 1985   Age: 23

YEAR	TEAM	LVL	AGE	W	L	SV	G	GS	IP	H	BB	SO	HR	GB%	BABIP	STUFF	WHIP	ERA	PERA	EqERA	EqH9	EqBB9	EqSO9	EqHR9	VORP	SN/WX
2007	ASH	A	22	0	1	2	13	0	13²	6	7	19	2	53.6%	.160	5	0.95	4.60	5.09	6.39	5.0	7.1	7.1	2.1	-1.1	—
2008	COL	MLB	23	4	6	1	34	12	90	92	65	72	12	46.6%	.297	-2	1.74	5.75	5.28	5.50	8.3	5.7	6.8	1.1	3.9	0.80

Breakout: NA   Improve: NA   Collapse: NA   Attrition: NA   Comparables: Dustin Hermanson, Chris Macca, Royce Ring, Mike Zimmerman

In recent years, every draft has had that one college closer that teams hope can move quickly and pay some early dividends. Last June, Weathers was that guy and was taken with the eighth overall pick by Colorado. His fastball sits between 95 and 97 mph and touches 99, and he throws his slider harder than some big leaguers can throw their fastball. He's a monster who could give the Rockies that pure shutdown closer that the organization has been looking for since forever.

LINEOUTS

Hitters

PLAYER	TEAM	LVL	AGE	PA	R	2B	3B	HR	RBI	BB	SO	SB-CS	EqBRR	AVG/OBP/SLG	MLVr	EqAVG/EqOBP/EqSLG	EqA	VORP
UT S. Barker	CSP	AAA	27	285	52	23	2	6	46	14	65	13-5	1.5	.330/.373/.502	.123	.259/.305/.403	.248	-5.3
C E. Bellorin	CSP	AAA	25	244	38	18	0	9	45	16	27	1-0	-2.4	.326/.369/.529	.151	.284/.328/.455	.270	12.0
CF S. Finley*	COL	MLB	42	102	9	3	0	1	2	8	4	0-0	-0.3	.181/.245/.245	-.471	.172/.245/.237	.159	-8.1
SS J. Herrera#	TUL	AA	22	573	65	24	4	3	40	36	68	18-12	-1.9	.257/.315/.338	-.134	.227/.275/.300	.203	-23.3
2B J. Nix	CSP	AAA	24	483	80	33	2	11	58	31	79	24-8	4.0	.292/.342/.451	-.035	.251/.301/.395	.244	3.1
2B O. Quintanilla*	CSP	AAA	25	393	54	30	4	3	43	31	65	3-1	2.6	.319/.380/.454	.057	.272/.333/.391	.255	12.6
	COL	MLB	25	75	6	4	0	0	5	5	15	0-0	0.7	.229/.280/.286	-.335	.214/.267/.271	.183	-3.7

Hamstring problems cut **Sean Barker**'s 2007 season short. Non-tendered in December, he could be a decent fifth outfielder in a different organization. ⊘ Catch-and-throw backup catching prospect **Edwin Bellorin** strained a hamstring in his MLB debut last year and immediately went on the DL. ⊘ Even with three awful years behind him, **Steve Finley** wants to keep playing and was chasing a job in December. He must be traveling by bus, because airport metal detectors would have called attention to the fork sticking out of his back. ⊘ **Jonathan Herrera** isn't going to hit enough to keep a starting job, but he has the speed and glove to be a backup up the middle. ⊘ The Rockies' lack of second-base options could be a boon for **Jayson Nix**, who played well at Colorado Springs and for Team USA last year. ⊘ **Omar Quintanilla** has good hands and a functioning batting eye. He would be a more useful utility infielder than Barmes.

Pitchers

PLAYER	TEAM	LVL	AGE	W	L	SV	IP	H	BB	SO	HR	GB%	BABIP	STUFF	WHIP	ERA	PERA	EqERA	EqH9	EqBB9	EqSO9	EqHR9	VORP
D. Bautista	CSP	AAA	26	3	2	0	64²	54	31	63	1	52.8%	.306	13	1.31	2.92	3.55	3.14	7.3	4.6	6.7	0.3	17.2
	COL	MLB	26	2	1	0	8²	18	4	8	0	37.1%	.529	-32	2.54	12.41	14.16	14.54	18.7	3.1	7.3	0.0	-5.8
D. Clarke	TUL	AA	26	1	1	0	11	5	1	16	2	40.0%	.167	10	0.55	1.64	3.78	2.79	5.6	1.9	9.3	2.8	3.0
E. Dessens	MIL	MLB	36	1	1	0	15	24	3	12	3	51.9%	.420	-18	1.80	6.60	9.68	9.82	14.1	1.2	6.8	1.8	-6.1
	COL	MLB	36	1	1	0	19	21	9	10	3	47.1%	.286	-16	1.58	7.58	5.06	6.86	9.2	3.7	4.1	1.4	-2.9
B. Hynick	MOD	A+	22	16	5	0	182¹	170	31	136	13	46.8%	.285	-4	1.10	2.52	5.11	4.56	9.9	2.7	3.8	1.1	19.4
T. Martin*	COL	MLB	37	0	0	0	25²	32	9	10	4	46.4%	.304	-26	1.60	4.90	5.93	4.85	10.7	2.8	3.5	1.4	3.4
J. Newman*	CSP	AAA	25	3	2	0	62	73	30	49	3	40.0%	.354	-7	1.66	4.06	5.23	4.99	10.1	4.5	5.3	0.6	4.2
M. Redman*	ATL	MLB	33	0	4	0	21²	38	11	13	4	31.5%	.410	-44	2.26	11.61	12.93	14.10	15.3	3.6	4.8	1.6	-15.1
	COL	MLB	33	2	0	0	19²	21	6	14	2	42.2%	.306	9	1.37	3.20	4.22	3.20	9.2	2.3	5.9	0.9	5.2
E. Rogers	ASH	A	21	7	4	0	117²	125	42	90	6	49.3%	.327	-10	1.42	3.75	6.14	6.27	10.5	5.3	3.4	1.0	-8.0

Denny Bautista has allowed just 11 homers in 194⅓ innings over the last two years. Maybe he's getting there. If so, the Tigers might have pulled off a steal in getting him for Jose Capellan. ⊘ The huge (6-foot-8, 235 pounds) **Darren**

Clarke was non-tendered in December after throwing just 94⅓ innings over the past four seasons. ⊘ The Rockies were so desperate for arms in August that they claimed **Elmer Dessens** off waivers. He was lousy and is now, appropriately enough, a Pirate. ⊘ The Rockies pushed **Brandon Hynick** to the Cal League, and he responded with a 4.0 K/BB. As a command guy, however, his upside his limited. ⊘ Veteran LOOGY **Tom Martin** hasn't gotten lefties out since 2003. After being released in July, he's most likely done. ⊘ Changeup artist **Josh Newman** has impressive numbers, but his stuff is that of a swingman or long reliever, and he hasn't been handled like a prospect. ⊘ The Rockies signed **Mark Redman** to a minor league deal in late August, then won all three starts they were forced to give him down the stretch; it helped that they scored 26 runs in those games. ⊘ Converted infielder **Esmil Rogers** held his own in the Sally League in his first full season of pitching.

MANAGER: CLINT HURDLE

YEAR	TEAM	W-L	Pythag +/−	Avg PC	100+ P	120+ P	QS	BQS	REL	REL w Zero R	IBB	Subs	PH	PH Avg	PH HR	SB2	CS2	SB3	CS3	SAC Att	SAC %	POS SAC	Squeeze	Swing	In Play
2005	COL	67-95	-2	94.2	52	1	63	6	459	283	54	61	272	.224	4	61	26	4	5	123	71.5%	52	3	142	116
2006	COL	76-86	-5	95.8	56	2	74	11	498	310	81	34	259	.214	6	80	44	4	3	162	73.5%	64	0	145	111
2007	COL	90-73	-2	90.5	51	0	74	5	529	348	61	52	283	.216	4	98	31	2	0	124	66.9%	37	2	142	104

Any time a team projected to finish last goes to the World Series, the manager gets a significant portion of the credit. In this case, Clint Hurdle deserves praise for trusting Manny Corpas in a high-leverage slot, for being flexible with the roles in his bullpen, and for working a number of young starters into the mix on the fly; remember, the Rockies lost their third, fourth, and fifth starters over the summer. Hurdle had an easier time with the offense. All five of his big bats in the middle of the lineup played at least 152 games, making it easier to work around injuries at second base and in center field. The challenge this year will be to maintain the flexibility that was so beneficial to last year's run and to allow Chris Iannetta, Juan Morillo, and perhaps Jayson Nix to claim roles as contributors.

Detroit Tigers

This is how fairy tales really end. Cinderella may have landed her prince, but the story sort of glosses over the "happily ever after" part. At some point during the honeymoon she must have realized that she and the prince barely knew each other, that they came from totally different socioeconomic backgrounds, and that there was never going to be peace when they visited her family for the holidays.

The Tigers were the Cinderella story of 2006, a team that rose from the ashes of a 119-loss season just three years earlier to win 95 games and the AL pennant. That Tigers team delivered the greatest three-year improvement in winning percentage of any team in 90 years. Though they fell in the World Series to the Cardinals, who won the Comedy—er, National League Central with all of 83 wins, the Tigers went into the offseason optimistic about the future and secure in the knowledge that virtually the entire team was under contract to defend their pennant in 2007.

Unfortunately, happily ever after wasn't happy enough. The 2007 Tigers won 88 games, a perfectly respectable showing which would have earned them another playoff spot if only they'd had the foresight to insist on switching leagues in place of the Brewers nine years earlier. Instead, after the heady rush of success the year before, the team seemed like a disappointment, finishing second to the resurgent Indians in the AL Central and heading home to count the post-season "Frank TV" promos.

There was no reason to be disappointed. Baseball isn't the stock market; win totals don't appreciate steadily over time. The Tigers' dizzying ascent up the standings made it almost impossible for them to con-

> ## TIGERS PROSPECTUS
>
> **2007 record:** 88-74; Second place, AL Central
>
> **Pythagenport record:** 89-73
>
> **Runs scored per game:** 5.48 (2nd in AL)
>
> **Runs allowed per game:** 4.92 (9th in AL)
>
> **Team EqA:** .271 (2nd in AL)
>
> **2007 Batters Age:** 31.5 (Oldest in AL)
>
> **2007 Pitchers Age:** 28.4 (7th youngest in AL)
>
> **Ballpark:** Comerica Park; Neutral Park; Park Factor of 1.005
>
> **2007:** The bill for the DL time the pitchers avoided in 2006 comes due.
>
> **2008:** Dombrowski has pushed his chips to the middle of the table, it's up to the team to cash them in.

tinue, or even sustain, their improvement. The "Plexiglas Principle" is a time-honored baseball maxim which states that teams that improve dramatically from one year to the next have a strong tendency to regress the following year. In that context, an eight-game drop-off seems like a perfectly reasonable breather after a 52-game rise over three years.

In another way, the Tigers had every reason to hope for better in 2007, because they avoided the trap that ensnares most teams that are dizzy with sudden success. Convinced they have hit upon the right formula, teams that rise from obscurity overnight are typically loathe to make changes to their roster, seemingly unaware that they're setting themselves up to get nailed by the dual forces of aging and regression to the mean. Winners of 75 games the year before, the 2002 Angels went 99-63 and won a World Series, then spent the offseason trying to keep the roster intact. They snapped back to 77 games in 2003.

The Tigers didn't wait even three weeks after their World Series loss to send a signal that they were not about to rest on their laurels. On November 10, 2006, they sent three pitching prospects to the Yankees for slugger Gary Sheffield, reuniting Sheffield with his manager and general manager from the 1997 world champion Florida Marlins. By any reasonable expectation, the acquisition worked. At age 38, Sheffield's power was down from his peak years, but he continued to take his walks, thus infusing the Tiger lineup with the one ingredient it lacked the year before. Coupled with a ridiculous career year from right fielder Magglio Ordoñez and a big breakout from 26-year-old center fielder Curtis Granderson, Sheffield helped the Tigers jump from 12th to 3rd in the American League in on-base percentage and score 65 more runs than in the preceding pennant-winning year.

Offense wasn't the Tigers' problem in 2007. Rather, Detroit missed the playoffs because its pitching staff leaked runs faster than its offense could pour them in. The Tigers allowed 122 more runs than they did with virtually the same cast of characters in 2006. That last part was the problem—whereas the Tigers were proactive about improving their offense, they stood pat on the pitching, thus allowing regression to the mean to take hold of the staff. It wasn't that Detroit's pitching staff slumped in 2007, but that it was unusually effective and unusually healthy the year before. The top four starters in the Tigers' rotation—Kenny Rogers, Justin Verlander, Jeremy Bonderman, and Nate Robertson—made 129 starts in 2006 and spent not a single day on the disabled list. In fact, the 2006 Tigers only placed a pitcher on the DL three times: closer Todd Jones was out two weeks with a pulled hamstring in April, fifth starter Mike Maroth missed two months with bone chips in his elbow, and non-entity Roman Colon was shelved in August with a herniated disc in his neck. The health of the staff made up for the lack of a true number-one starter. Verlander led the 2006 rotation with a 3.63 ERA while the team as a whole finished only slightly higher with a 3.84 ERA, the best mark in either league. Of the 13 pitchers who threw 40 or more innings for Detroit in 2006, only Zach Miner had an ERA above 4.21.

It is one hell of a balancing act to lead the majors in ERA without a single dominant starter, and in 2007, the Tigers fell off the wire. Part of the problem was that the Tigers staff was highly polarized in age with the hoary Rogers (42) and Jones (39) on one end and the fuzzy-cheeked Verlander and Bonderman (both 24) on the other. Pitchers are a fragile lot in general, but they're most vulnerable to injury at the beginnings and ends of their careers, something the Tigers learned firsthand last year. Rogers missed most of the season with first a blood clot in his shoulder and then elbow inflammation. Bonderman tried to pitch through a sore elbow and put up an 8.23 ERA in his final ten starts before being shut down in early September. Ace set-up man Joel Zumaya (22) snapped a tendon in his finger in early May, missed over three months, and was not particularly effective on his return. The injuries forced the Tigers to resort to contingency plans they had not needed to pursue in 2006, including giving Chad Durbin a major role on the staff and forcing rookies Andrew Miller and Jair Jurrjens into the rotation before they were ready. Bonderman's injury was particularly

painful, because he was supposed to join Verlander to give the Tigers a pair of young aces that would propel the otherwise average pitching staff forward. The staff as a whole complied by being decidedly average, but without both of the expected aces up front, that's all it was.

The irony is that the offense, which was aging to begin with, improved with the addition of Sheffield, who instantly became the oldest hitter on the team. Irony may be too strong a word: in general, older players are better players because bad old players retire, whereas young players frequently earn playing time based on the hope that they will be good one day, even if they're not now. With that in mind, it's okay to reinforce your lineup with a 38-year-old if he's a Hall of Fame–caliber hitter, but going forward, the age distribution for the Tigers is a concern. While old hitters are generally good hitters, they're also hitters on the decline, and both are true of the men in the Tigers' lineup. The average age of the Tigers' hitters last year, weighted by plate appearances, was 31.5, the third-oldest in the majors and the oldest in the American League.

The Tigers thus entered the offseason in a very dangerous position. Their offense's window of excellence is quickly closing, and their pitching staff relies on young pitchers who might still be two or three years from their peak. Many general managers would be tempted to rely on hope as a strategy in such a situation, trusting that the starting pitchers would improve enough to paper over any decline by the offense and thus keep the team in the playoff chase for the foreseeable future. The Tigers' Dave Dombrowski is not one of those GMs.

Deciding that the team as constructed was just good enough to finish in second place, Dombrowski sprang into action. Just days after the World Series ended, he traded Jurrjens and minor league center fielder Gorkys Hernandez, both top prospects, to the Braves for shortstop Edgar Renteria. The swap allows incumbent shortstop Carlos Guillen, whose chronic knee injuries have diminished his range afield, to shift to first base, thereby improving the defense at both positions while simultaneously upgrading the lineup by inserting Renteria in place of departing gatekeeper Sean Casey.

As stirring as that deal may have been, it was merely an appetizer for the biggest transaction of the Winter Meetings. On December 5, Dombrowski sent Miller and outfielder Cameron Maybin, the Tigers' first-round picks from 2006 and 2005, respectively, backup catcher Mike Rabelo, and three pitching prospects to the Marlins in exchange for third baseman Miguel Cabrera and lefty Dontrelle Willis. It's not often that a team trades four of its top five prospects (2007 first-rounder Rick

Porcello is the last man standing) in the span of one off-season, but then, it's rare that a team trades for another team's best hitter and pitcher simultaneously, particularly when the players in question are a superstar slugger and a former Rookie of the Year and Cy Young runner-up. It's especially rare for a team to add two such players and actually get *younger*. Willis is 26, while Cabrera doesn't turn 25 until April, making him the youngest hitter in the Detroit lineup (Granderson is the only Tiger regular who hadn't started school by the time Cabrera was born).

What made that trade possible wasn't simply that the Tigers were willing to mortgage their future for the present, it was that they had Miller and Maybin to trade in the first place. For this, they can thank the other 29 teams for following the commissioner's "suggested" slot bonus amounts for draft pick, and owner Mike Ilitch's willingness to tell Selig where he can stick his suggestions. (What's Selig going to do? Retroactively take away the 2005 All-Star Game?) Following the slot recommendations only serves to lower the price on draft picks if everyone plays along. When a few teams do not, the rest get played for suckers. It's no surprise that the Red Sox and Yankees have gamed the draft to select premier talents that drop because of signability issues, but the Tigers have been just as aggressive in the draft the last few years, and drafting ahead of Boston and New York, they've had their pick of the litter.

Maybin dropped to the tenth pick in 2005 and the Tigers signed him for $2.65 million, more than any of the players drafted fifth through eighth received. The following year, Miller was thought to be the favorite to go first overall, but his perceived bonus demands allowed the Tigers to draft him with the sixth pick; they signed him to a major league contract for more money than any other player from that year's first round. Last June, high school pitching phenom Porcello was considered the best player available after top overall pick David Price, but only the Tigers were willing to meet the demands of his agent, Scott Boras, and landed him with the 26th pick and a major league deal for a guaranteed $7 million.

The Tigers are a medium-market team, and medium-market teams can't afford to operate with large-market payrolls, but they absolutely can afford to impersonate a large-market franchise in the draft. To their credit, the Tigers are one of the few teams willing to take that approach. Between Maybin and Miller, the Tigers spent about $4 million over slot. Two years later, they've cashed them in for two years each of Cabrera and Willis, each of whom would easily draw tens of millions on the open market. If Cabrera and Willis leave as free agents, the Tigers will likely get four draft picks in return, picks they can use to repeat the cycle all over again.

Even with Cabrera taking over for 31-year-old Brandon Inge at third base, the additions of the 32-year-old Renteria and 33-year-old outfielder Jacque Jones, acquired from the Cubs for utilityman Omar Infante, and the passing of time guarantee that the projected lineup for this season will be even older than last year's. But oh, what a lineup! Cabrera, Guillen, Granderson, and Ordoñez each posted a .300 or better EqA in either 2006 or 2007, and Renteria, Sheffield, and Polanco were all at .288 or better last season. The rotation should benefit from the addition of Willis even if he doesn't reverse his recent slide. Willis has taken the ball at least 34 times and thrown more than 200 innings in each of the last three seasons, and that has value by itself. Better yet, the Marlins defense, which had the second-worst defensive efficiency in the majors last year, did Willis no favors. Simply replacing that defense with the Tigers' (even if both aggregations include Cabrera's questionable work at the hot corner) should help Willis to a league-average season or better if he regains his previous form.

The bill for all of this comes due in 2010, when the only Tigers still under contract will be Granderson, Bonderman, and Verlander, all three under team control (albeit at arbitration prices), a 34-year-old Guillen, and a 36-year-old Ordoñez. Following this winter's wheeling and dealing, the Tigers' farm system is now, aside from Porcello, among the most barren in the game. For all of Dombrowski's wizardry in recent years, even his magic may not keep the Tigers from another rebuilding phase.

Still, the Tigers will worry about the future in the future. As Leo Durocher said, "Don't save your pitcher for tomorrow; tomorrow it might rain." The Tigers had a team with a chance to contend now and have done everything in their power to maximize that chance. For the next two years, at least, their chances look awfully good. This fairy tale may yet have the happiest of endings.

HITTERS

Sean Casey — 1B

Bats: L Throws: R Height: 6' 4" Weight: 235 Born: July 2, 1974 Age: 33

YEAR	TEAM	LVL	AGE	PA	R	2B	3B	HR	RBI	BB	SO	SB	CS	EqBRR	AVG	OBP	SLG	MLVr	EqAVG	EqOBP	EqSLG	EqA	VORP	DEFENSE	
2005	CIN	MLB	31	587	75	32	0	9	58	48	48	2	0	0.9	.312	.371	.423	.120	.307	.368	.423	.279	22.5	130-1B	0
2006	PIT	MLB	32	244	30	15	0	3	29	23	22	0	0	-1.8	.296	.377	.408	.069	.291	.373	.408	.277	5.5	52-1B	-3
2006	DET	MLB	32	196	17	7	0	5	30	10	21	0	1	-1.5	.245	.286	.364	-.221	.242	.291	.368	.227	-8.0	46-1B	-4
2007	DET	MLB	33	496	40	30	1	4	54	39	42	2	2	-2.1	.296	.353	.393	.012	.298	.361	.405	.268	9.6	111-1B	-6
2008	DET	MLB	33	314	33	15	1	5	36	23	31	2	1	-0.7	.275	.330	.380	-.069	.275	.333	.397	.257	1.2	76-1B	-2

Breakout: 13% Improve: 31% Collapse: 36% Attrition: 39%   Comparables: Hal Morris, Larry Biittner, Ed Kranepool, Larry Sheets

Despite a .393 SLG and .097 ISO, Casey tied for seventh in the AL in intentional walks last year with 11. Of the nine players ahead of or tied with him on that list, the only one who slugged below .450 or had an ISO below .180 was Ichiro Suzuki, who hit for a .351 average. Casey spent the year batting in front of low-OBP right-handed hitters such as Brandon Inge, Craig Monroe, and Marcus Thames, making the relative gap between him and the next guy fairly wide. Casey could last a very long time as a pinch-hitter, but his future managers would be ill-advised to play match-ups with him; he's had a reverse split in four of the last five seasons and posted an 891 OPS against lefties in the fifth.

Brent Clevlen — OF

Bats: R Throws: R Height: 6' 2" Weight: 190 Born: October 27, 1983 Age: 24

YEAR	TEAM	LVL	AGE	PA	R	2B	3B	HR	RBI	BB	SO	SB	CS	EqBRR	AVG	OBP	SLG	MLVr	EqAVG	EqOBP	EqSLG	EqA	VORP	DEFENSE			
2005	LAK	A+	21	568	77	28	4	18	102	65	118	14	5	2.5	.302	.387	.484	.241	.245	.322	.391	.250	-9.1	128-RF	4		
2006	ERI	AA	22	451	47	17	0	11	45	47	138	6	2	0.9	.230	.313	.357	-.060	.219	.295	.339	.226	-25.0	100-RF	1		
2006	DET	MLB	22	42	9	1	2	3	6	2	15	0	0	-0.9	.282	.317	.641	.270	.282	.317	.641	.303	4.0				
2007	TOL	AAA	23	366	33	14	5	7	36	39	113	4	4	-1.7	.220	.304	.360	-.080	.218	.298	.372	.233	-6.3	57-CF	0	31-RF	1
2008	DET	MLB	24	452	46	20	3	11	50	38	133	6	3	0.1	.231	.299	.378	-.157	.232	.301	.395	.245	-6.3	107-RF	-1		

Breakout: 33% Improve: 65% Collapse: 14% Attrition: 15%   Comparables: Chad Alexander, Gary Mota, Jason Michaels, Mike Mallory

Clevlen's tasty cup of coffee in 2006 obscured the fact that he was overmatched at Double-A, striking out in more than a third of his at-bats without the power to justify that rate. The same thing happened at Triple-A, where he scuffled both before and after spending time on the DL with a broken finger. Clevlen has power and can play some defense, so he could eventually be the short end of a platoon.

Curtis Granderson — CF

Bats: L Throws: R Height: 6' 1" Weight: 185 Born: March 16, 1981 Age: 27

YEAR	TEAM	LVL	AGE	PA	R	2B	3B	HR	RBI	BB	SO	SB	CS	EqBRR	AVG	OBP	SLG	MLVr	EqAVG	EqOBP	EqSLG	EqA	VORP	DEFENSE	
2005	TOL	AAA	24	503	79	29	13	15	65	48	129	22	6	3.7	.290	.359	.515	.230	.241	.313	.442	.261	10.4	105-CF	10
2005	DET	MLB	24	174	18	6	3	8	20	10	43	1	1	-1.1	.272	.314	.494	.087	.283	.337	.528	.286	7.9	36-CF	11
2006	DET	MLB	25	679	90	31	9	19	68	66	174	8	5	1.8	.260	.335	.438	-.012	.260	.343	.447	.272	22.7	147-CF	20
2007	DET	MLB	26	676	122	38	23	23	74	52	141	26	1	6.1	.302	.361	.552	.260	.305	.367	.580	.315	67.3	144-CF	25
2008	DET	MLB	27	635	88	32	8	21	80	58	143	15	5	2.1	.267	.339	.467	.054	.268	.341	.488	.286	26.2	148-CF	10

Breakout: 10% Improve: 40% Collapse: 23% Attrition: 8%   Comparables: Andy Van Slyke, Mike Davis, Mack Jones, Lloyd Moseby

Granderson has improved his ability to attack the ball in the zone and drive it—as indicated by his increased batting average, contact rate, and power—but as good a hitter as he's become, he simply has to be platooned. His career .202/.265/.366 line against lefties includes strikeouts in 30 percent of his plate appearances and a 4.7 K/BB, the latter being nearly twice his ratio against righties. Granderson's not improving against lefties, either, posting a miserable 494 OPS against portsiders in 2007. An MVP candidate 75 percent of the time is a good player, but that doesn't mean he gets a pass for the other quarter.

Carlos Guillen   SS-1B

Bats: S   Throws: R   Height: 6' 1"   Weight: 215   Born: September 30, 1975   Age: 32

YEAR	TEAM	LVL	AGE	PA	R	2B	3B	HR	RBI	BB	SO	SB	CS	EqBRR	AVG	OBP	SLG	MLVr	EqAVG	EqOBP	EqSLG	EqA	VORP	DEFENSE	
2005	DET	MLB	29	361	48	15	4	5	23	24	45	2	3	-1.1	.320	.368	.434	.138	.331	.388	.456	.290	24.5	71-SS -3	
2006	DET	MLB	30	622	100	41	5	19	85	71	87	20	9	2.4	.320	.400	.519	.274	.319	.407	.526	.314	66.3	138-SS 1	
2007	DET	MLB	31	630	86	35	9	21	102	55	93	13	8	-0.6	.296	.357	.502	.175	.299	.365	.524	.296	45.0	120-SS -10	20-1B 1
2008	DET	MLB	32	610	89	32	5	17	80	57	88	13	6	0.7	.293	.362	.465	.110	.293	.364	.486	.294	37.8	143-SS -3	

Breakout: 7%   Improve: 36%   Collapse: 22%   Attrition: 5%   Comparables: Ken Caminiti, Roberto Alomar, Ken Boyer, David Segui

For all the talk about his bad knees and the decision to move him to first base to keep his bat in the lineup, Guillen has missed just 20 games over the past two seasons. He's also stolen 33 bases and hit 14 triples, neither of which suggests bum wheels. The trade for shortstop Edgar Renteria, who effectively replaces Casey in the lineup, helps the Tigers because Casey is such a replaceable commodity, not because Guillen is that bad or injury-prone a shortstop.

Gorkys Hernandez   CF

Bats: R   Throws: R   Height: 6' 0"   Weight: 175   Born: September 7, 1987   Age: 20

YEAR	TEAM	LVL	AGE	PA	R	2B	3B	HR	RBI	BB	SO	SB	CS	EqBRR	AVG	OBP	SLG	MLVr	EqAVG	EqOBP	EqSLG	EqA	VORP	DEFENSE
2006	TGR	Rk	18	217	41	9	2	5	23	10	27	20	4	1.0	.327	.356	.463	.277	.269	.292	.394	.238	-1.3	49-CF -2
2007	WMI	A	19	533	84	25	5	4	50	36	69	54	11	10.2	.293	.344	.391	.091	.238	.280	.316	.220	-24.0	119-CF 1
2008	ATL	MLB	20	611	72	28	5	5	44	33	99	33	11	2.5	.256	.298	.352	-.204	.254	.296	.360	.230	-3.5	143-CF 2

Breakout: 31% Improve: 62% Collapse: 14% Attrition: 7%   Comparables: Carlos Gomez, Jesus Tavarez, Willy Taveras, Juan Piniella

Hernandez was one of the two big prizes sent to Atlanta in the Renteria trade. He put on a show in the Midwest League last year in his full-season debut, earning league MVP honors. Call us picky, but we'd like to see him do something more than just catch every fly ball hit in his direction and run like the wind. There's little reason to think Hernandez will ever develop much power, so he'll need to work on a more patient approach to project as a leadoff man. He has a high upside, but not without some risk.

Michael Hollimon   2B

Bats: S   Throws: R   Height: 6' 1"   Weight: 185   Born: June 14, 1982   Age: 26

YEAR	TEAM	LVL	AGE	PA	R	2B	3B	HR	RBI	BB	SO	SB	CS	EqBRR	AVG	OBP	SLG	MLVr	EqAVG	EqOBP	EqSLG	EqA	VORP	DEFENSE	
2005	ONE	A-	23	313	66	13	10	13	53	48	76	8	3	-1.4	.277	.389	.559	.314	.209	.295	.370	.234	-3.5	67-SS 6	
2006	WMI	A	24	537	69	29	13	15	54	77	124	19	5	-0.9	.278	.386	.501	.290	.224	.314	.401	.252	9.7	123-SS 7	
2007	ERI	AA	25	552	91	34	8	14	76	64	121	17	6	5.7	.282	.371	.478	.157	.251	.331	.427	.264	19.4	93-2B 9	30-SS -1
2008	DET	MLB	26	512	58	26	5	12	53	50	143	10	4	1.2	.228	.307	.391	-.127	.229	.309	.409	.254	5.6	121-2B 4	

Breakout: 19% Improve: 45% Collapse: 25% Attrition: 15%   Comparables: Brooks Conrad, Craig Kuzmic, Keith Ginter, Chris Clapinski

Hollimon has always been behind the eight-ball. Once one of the best high school players in the country, he opted to go the college route, struggled at Texas, transferred, and finished his amateur career at Oral Roberts. All of that time wasted in college meant he was just a few days short of his 23rd birthday when he was drafted. He'll be 26 this year and probably still needs some minor league seasoning. He's a hit-first, field-later second baseman, with enough power and patience to be of some value.

Omar Infante   UT

Bats: R   Throws: R   Height: 6' 0"   Weight: 180   Born: December 26, 1981   Age: 26

YEAR	TEAM	LVL	AGE	PA	R	2B	3B	HR	RBI	BB	SO	SB	CS	EqBRR	AVG	OBP	SLG	MLVr	EqAVG	EqOBP	EqSLG	EqA	VORP	DEFENSE	
2005	DET	MLB	23	434	36	28	2	9	43	16	73	8	0	0.9	.222	.254	.367	-.238	.228	.270	.390	.231	-7.4	67-2B -4	44-SS 2
2006	DET	MLB	24	245	35	11	4	4	25	14	45	3	2	0.4	.277	.325	.415	-.048	.275	.332	.423	.261	5.5	34-2B 6	
2007	DET	MLB	25	178	24	6	1	2	17	9	29	4	1	1.3	.271	.307	.355	-.140	.279	.318	.382	.247	-0.1	14-2B 0	
2008	ATL	MLB	26	252	30	12	2	6	26	17	38	6	1	0.3	.261	.315	.401	-.105	.259	.313	.409	.249	5.8	62-2B 1	

Breakout: 17% Improve: 46% Collapse: 29% Attrition: 27%   Comparables: Eddie Bressoud, Rich Aurilia, Chuck Cottier, Alex Gonzalez

It's hard to believe Infante slugged .449 and drew 40 walks as a 22-year-old, but he did. Now, he's an extra, and a good one with a little pop against lefties and no worse than an average glove at three infield positions. The Braves picked him up from the Cubs in a minor trade after the Tigers sent him to Chicago for Jacque Jones. He should serve as a helpful platoon partner for Kelly Johnson and caddy for Chipper Jones.

Brandon Inge — 3B

Bats: R   Throws: R   Height: 5′ 11″   Weight: 190   Born: May 19, 1977   Age: 31

YEAR	TEAM	LVL	AGE	PA	R	2B	3B	HR	RBI	BB	SO	SB	CS	EqBRR	AVG	OBP	SLG	MLVr	EqAVG	EqOBP	EqSLG	EqA	VORP	DEFENSE	
2005	DET	MLB	28	694	75	31	9	16	72	63	140	7	6	-3.4	.261	.330	.419	-.002	.271	.349	.446	.273	13.7	158-3B	16
2006	DET	MLB	29	601	83	29	2	27	83	43	128	7	4	-1.6	.253	.313	.463	-.022	.252	.319	.470	.267	9.4	156-3B	26
2007	DET	MLB	30	577	64	25	2	14	71	47	150	9	2	0.2	.236	.312	.376	-.129	.240	.321	.401	.254	-3.3	147-3B	15
2008	DET	MLB	31	488	56	23	3	14	58	42	115	7	3	-0.1	.245	.316	.407	-.080	.245	.318	.426	.261	5.4	115-3B	5

Breakout: 22% Improve: 50% Collapse: 29% Attrition: 24%   Comparables: Max Alvis, Butch Hobson, Travis Fryman, Jim Fregosi

Swing! Inge's strikeout rate has nearly doubled over four years, going from one every 6.4 plate appearances in 2004, when he batted .287/.340/.453, to one every 3.8 in 2007. His defense at third base remains exceptional, but it's all that is keeping him a viable starter as his bat deteriorates. The Tigers' trade activity, most notably the acquisition of Miguel Cabrera, leaves Inge's status up in the air; he could be a utility player, as he was in 2004, or he could be a third baseman elsewhere.

Matt Joyce — RF

Bats: L   Throws: R   Height: 6′ 2″   Weight: 185   Born: August 3, 1984   Age: 23

YEAR	TEAM	LVL	AGE	PA	R	2B	3B	HR	RBI	BB	SO	SB	CS	EqBRR	AVG	OBP	SLG	MLVr	EqAVG	EqOBP	EqSLG	EqA	VORP	DEFENSE	
2005	ONE	A-	20	283	51	10	4	4	45	30	29	9	5	2.3	.331	.397	.453	.237	.254	.305	.344	.231	-20.9	60-RF	7
2006	WMI	A	21	530	75	30	5	11	86	56	70	5	4	3.1	.258	.338	.415	.103	.213	.278	.347	.217	-32.6	105-RF	7
2007	ERI	AA	22	514	61	33	3	17	70	51	127	4	6	-1.0	.257	.333	.454	.048	.228	.298	.409	.241	-13.0	112-RF	3
2008	DET	MLB	23	567	57	28	3	13	64	46	138	5	3	1.1	.230	.295	.374	-.168	.231	.297	.391	.241	-13.9	133-RF	-1

Breakout: 41% Improve: 67% Collapse: 17% Attrition: 6%   Comparables: Kevin Burford, Ryan Church, Doug Deeds, Jeremy Dodson

Joyce didn't get his batting average over .200 last year until mid-June, but once he did, he hit .304 with gap power the rest of the way. He'll probably never be enough of a hitter to play every day, but he's left-handed, has a little bit of juice in his bat, and is an outstanding defensive player. Those ingredients could be enough for a decade or so of bench play.

Jeffrey Larish — 1B

Bats: L   Throws: R   Height: 6′ 2″   Weight: 200   Born: October 11, 1982   Age: 25

YEAR	TEAM	LVL	AGE	PA	R	2B	3B	HR	RBI	BB	SO	SB	CS	EqBRR	AVG	OBP	SLG	MLVr	EqAVG	EqOBP	EqSLG	EqA	VORP	DEFENSE	
2005	ONE	A-	22	79	16	3	0	6	13	13	6	0	0	0.4	.297	.430	.625	.460	.261	.354	.478	.283	6.1	16-1B	3
2006	LAK	A+	23	552	76	34	2	18	65	81	101	9	7	-5.1	.258	.379	.460	.176	.224	.328	.402	.254	-4.1	131-1B	-2
2007	ERI	AA	24	556	71	25	2	28	101	87	108	6	2	-1.1	.267	.390	.515	.220	.238	.351	.452	.278	14.7	120-1B	4
2008	DET	MLB	25	540	65	24	2	16	63	63	122	6	3	-0.2	.238	.333	.396	-.070	.238	.335	.414	.265	-1.1	127-1B	5

Breakout: 20% Improve: 43% Collapse: 24% Attrition: 13%   Comparables: Ben Broussard, Ryan Langerhans, Kory Casto, Bo Dodson

Larish moved up a level in 2007 and did everything just as well, showing good power and the kind of ratios that suggest extreme patience. Note the walks and strikeouts; many players see a big drop-off in their K/BB ratio when they hit Double-A, so it's a mark in Larish's favor that his was steady. There's little here aside from the bat, however, and Larish can't move to the outfield, so he'll have to keep raking, particularly as he's now blocked at first base by Carlos Guillen, who's signed through 2011.

Cameron Maybin — OF

Bats: R   Throws: R   Height: 6′ 4″   Weight: 205   Born: April 4, 1987   Age: 21

YEAR	TEAM	LVL	AGE	PA	R	2B	3B	HR	RBI	BB	SO	SB	CS	EqBRR	AVG	OBP	SLG	MLVr	EqAVG	EqOBP	EqSLG	EqA	VORP	DEFENSE	
2006	WMI	A	19	445	59	20	6	9	69	50	116	27	7	-0.2	.304	.387	.457	.257	.211	.283	.333	.223	-18.4	87-CF	-2
2007	LAK	A+	20	350	58	14	5	10	44	43	83	25	6	2.4	.304	.393	.486	.250	.237	.321	.405	.259	3.8	69-CF	-1
2007	ERI	AA	20	26	9	1	0	4	8	6	6	0	0	0.0	.400	.538	1.050	1.209	.333	.462	.999	.412	8.6		
2007	DET	MLB	20	53	8	3	0	1	2	3	21	5	0	1.0	.143	.208	.265	-.527	.143	.208	.245	.187	-3.8		
2008	FLO	MLB	21	513	75	27	5	14	55	56	131	23	7	1.4	.256	.342	.436	-.015	.256	.341	.446	.271	18.1	121-CF	0

Breakout: 60% Improve: 90% Collapse: 2% Attrition: 5%   Comparables: Austin Kearns, Michael Cuddyer, Dee Brown, Chip Ambres

For an organization that does so much so well, the Tigers mishandled Maybin, rushing him to Detroit when he was just weeks removed from the Florida State League. In the majors, Maybin was well over his head in every aspect of the game, and that performance may cause him to be underrated in 2008. Maybin remains a complete box of tools, needing only to refine his skills, particularly his pitch recognition, to become a star. The Marlins are desperate for a center fielder, but need to resist the urge to repeat the Tigers' mistake; Maybin needs a full year in the minors to work on identifying and hitting breaking balls.

Magglio Ordoñez   **RF**   Bats: R   Throws: R   Height: 6' 0"   Weight: 215   Born: January 28, 1974   Age: 34

YEAR	TEAM	LVL	AGE	PA	R	2B	3B	HR	RBI	BB	SO	SB	CS	EqBRR	AVG	OBP	SLG	MLVr	EqAVG	EqOBP	EqSLG	EqA	VORP	DEFENSE
2005	DET	MLB	31	343	38	17	0	8	46	30	35	0	0	-2.2	.302	.359	.436	.107	.310	.375	.460	.291	14.4	76-RF -2
2006	DET	MLB	32	646	82	32	1	24	104	45	87	1	4	-4.4	.298	.350	.477	.106	.297	.356	.483	.283	27.6	142-RF -12
2007	DET	MLB	33	678	117	54	0	28	139	76	79	4	1	-1.8	.363	.434	.595	.500	.365	.441	.621	.352	87.8	137-RF -5
2008	DET	MLB	34	590	83	35	1	19	88	59	75	5	2	-1.4	.306	.376	.485	.170	.307	.379	.507	.305	31.1	138-RF -8

Breakout: 2%   Improve: 22%   Collapse: 31%   Attrition: 8%   Comparables: Pedro Guerrero, Jim Rice, Joe Torre, Dusty Baker

Last year was a season right out of Ordoñez's White Sox peak, with some extra hits falling in to nab him a batting title as a bonus. Given his solid peripherals, still-present tools, and renewed health, Ordoñez could go on to a very long, late second peak along the lines of Moises Alou's second act. Credit the Tigers, who were criticized long and loud for this contract when it was signed; they got it right.

Neifi Perez   **SS/2B**   Bats: S   Throws: R   Height: 6' 0"   Weight: 175   Born: June 2, 1973   Age: 35

YEAR	TEAM	LVL	AGE	PA	R	2B	3B	HR	RBI	BB	SO	SB	CS	EqBRR	AVG	OBP	SLG	MLVr	EqAVG	EqOBP	EqSLG	EqA	VORP	DEFENSE
2005	CHN	MLB	32	609	59	33	1	9	54	18	47	8	4	1.9	.274	.298	.383	-.091	.270	.295	.379	.234	7.4	120-SS 21 18-2B -2
2006	CHN	MLB	33	246	27	13	1	2	24	5	21	0	1	1.3	.254	.266	.343	-.254	.250	.265	.339	.206	-7.6	37-2B 4 15-SS -1
2006	DET	MLB	33	70	4	1	0	0	5	3	4	1	0	0.4	.200	.235	.215	-.554	.203	.250	.219	.164	-6.0	13-2B 4
2007	DET	MLB	34	71	5	3	0	1	6	4	8	0	0	-0.3	.172	.221	.266	-.487	.172	.232	.266	.171	-5.6	12-SS -3
2008	DET	MLB	35	104	7	4	0	1	10	3	10	1	0	0.0	.218	.247	.285	-.378	.218	.249	.298	.187	-5.6	29-SS 0

Breakout: 26%   Improve: 34%   Collapse: 52%   Attrition: 52%   Comparables: Alfredo Griffin, Paul Popovich, Juan Castro, Luis Sojo

Last year, Perez famously became the first player to test positive three times for amphetamine usage, earning an 80-day suspension for the third violation. He claims to have used an unprescribed amphetamine to control his attention deficit and hyperactivity disorder, and that the repeat offenses were the result of multiple tests in a short period of time that all covered the same usage. Perez is also famous for not having posted an on-base percentage over .300 since 2001. Now a free agent, his prospects for continuing his career are bad.

Placido Polanco   **2B**   Bats: R   Throws: R   Height: 5' 10"   Weight: 195   Born: October 10, 1975   Age: 32

YEAR	TEAM	LVL	AGE	PA	R	2B	3B	HR	RBI	BB	SO	SB	CS	EqBRR	AVG	OBP	SLG	MLVr	EqAVG	EqOBP	EqSLG	EqA	VORP	DEFENSE
2005	PHI	MLB	29	173	26	7	0	3	20	12	9	0	0	1.0	.316	.376	.418	.121	.310	.370	.418	.276	8.7	26-2B 4
2005	DET	MLB	29	378	58	20	2	6	36	21	16	4	3	2.3	.338	.386	.461	.215	.352	.405	.485	.305	30.0	81-2B 4
2006	DET	MLB	30	495	58	18	1	4	52	17	27	1	2	-1.3	.295	.329	.364	-.100	.296	.335	.371	.247	7.9	106-2B 18
2007	DET	MLB	31	641	105	36	3	9	67	37	30	7	3	0.6	.341	.388	.458	.207	.348	.399	.480	.303	49.0	135-2B 22
2008	DET	MLB	32	546	69	27	2	5	53	32	29	6	3	0.0	.305	.353	.402	.021	.306	.356	.420	.275	22.3	128-2B 8

Breakout: 8%   Improve: 31%   Collapse: 36%   Attrition: 8%   Comparables: Glenn Beckert, Steve Sax, Mark Loretta, Johnny Ray

If this were *Baseball Prospectus 1975*, we'd probably be obsessed with the fact that Polanco had 200 hits and made no errors last year. We know better now. We know to look at rate stats and advanced metrics and range-based defensive models. Nevertheless, the pairing of 200 hits and no errors is a rare feat, a credit to Polanco's ability to make hard contact and to his good hands at second base. He's just the third player, along with Juan Pierre in 2006 and B. J. Surhoff in 1999, to turn the trick. Moreover, his season holds up when you consider everything else as well; that 8.6 WARP was 12th in the AL, and his 20 FRAA was fifth in the league.

Mike Rabelo   C   Bats: S   Throws: R   Height: 6' 1"   Weight: 200   Born: January 17, 1980   Age: 28

YEAR	TEAM	LVL	AGE	PA	R	2B	3B	HR	RBI	BB	SO	SB	CS	EqBRR	AVG	OBP	SLG	MLVr	EqAVG	EqOBP	EqSLG	EqA	VORP	DEFENSE		
2005	ERI	AA	25	314	33	18	1	2	26	18	42	0	1	-0.5	.273	.334	.365	-.029	.240	.295	.328	.217	-7.5	53-C	2	14-1B -1
2006	ERI	AA	26	242	31	13	1	6	28	19	38	2	1	0.6	.277	.361	.432	.134	.257	.328	.422	.258	7.8	54-C	6	
2006	TOL	AAA	26	153	19	12	0	3	22	11	33	1	1	0.4	.270	.333	.423	.111	.268	.327	.435	.262	5.8	37-C	-2	
2007	DET	MLB	27	185	14	10	2	1	18	6	41	0	0	-2.4	.256	.300	.357	-.163	.263	.307	.371	.238	0.4	44-C	-1	
2008	FLO	MLB	28	299	29	15	1	5	32	20	60	2	1	-0.3	.246	.308	.370	-.169	.246	.308	.379	.235	3.3	73-C	-1	

Breakout: 11% Improve: 41% Collapse: 36% Attrition: 33%   Comparables: Buck Rodgers, Matt Walbeck, Javier Valentin, Geronimo Gil

The Tigers were one of three teams, along with the Indians and Nationals, to use just two catchers last season, marking the third straight year the Tigers had turned that particular trick. Rabelo inherited Vance Wilson's playing time and performed serviceably, throwing out 28 percent of attempted basestealers. As a switch-hitter who can hit .260 with some doubles, he'll be around for a while as a kind of poor man's Johnny Estrada and could find himself starting for the Marlins this year.

Ryan Raburn   UT   Bats: R   Throws: R   Height: 6' 0"   Weight: 185   Born: April 17, 1981   Age: 27

YEAR	TEAM	LVL	AGE	PA	R	2B	3B	HR	RBI	BB	SO	SB	CS	EqBRR	AVG	OBP	SLG	MLVr	EqAVG	EqOBP	EqSLG	EqA	VORP	DEFENSE		
2005	TOL	AAA	24	524	62	22	4	19	64	45	109	8	3	2.4	.253	.323	.437	.027	.230	.300	.399	.241	1.8	96-2B	-2	
2006	TOL	AAA	25	512	68	29	4	20	79	51	120	16	4	1.9	.275	.352	.490	.233	.264	.340	.487	.281	15.9	73-LF	1	32-2B -3
2007	TOL	AAA	26	373	60	21	3	17	64	51	73	12	4	2.6	.292	.394	.540	.358	.282	.380	.545	.308	37.2	45-CF	11	39-LF -1
2007	DET	MLB	26	148	28	12	2	4	27	8	33	3	0	2.0	.304	.340	.507	.167	.307	.347	.533	.296	9.8	10-RF	1	
2008	DET	MLB	27	555	72	28	3	19	72	52	128	14	4	0.9	.256	.330	.441	-.004	.256	.332	.461	.277	13.3	130-LF	-1	

Breakout: 11% Improve: 36% Collapse: 29% Attrition: 9%   Comparables: Scott Hairston, Brent Cookson, Pat Lennon, Darren Burton

Recast as an outfielder who can play some second base, Raburn had his best year with the bat last year and was a key spare part for the Tigers in August. With his power and speed, he projects as an excellent bench player who can cover four positions and be used as both a pinch-hitter and pinch-runner, the latter a key for a team that is slow at five lineup spots. He'd make a good platoon partner for Granderson.

Ivan Rodriguez   C   Bats: R   Throws: R   Height: 5' 9"   Weight: 195   Born: November 30, 1971   Age: 36

YEAR	TEAM	LVL	AGE	PA	R	2B	3B	HR	RBI	BB	SO	SB	CS	EqBRR	AVG	OBP	SLG	MLVr	EqAVG	EqOBP	EqSLG	EqA	VORP	DEFENSE
2005	DET	MLB	33	525	71	33	5	14	50	11	93	7	3	-0.9	.276	.290	.444	-.023	.282	.307	.470	.263	18.3	117-C 10
2006	DET	MLB	34	580	74	28	4	13	69	26	86	8	3	0.9	.300	.332	.437	.016	.299	.339	.445	.269	22.0	118-C 15
2007	DET	MLB	35	515	50	31	3	11	63	9	96	2	2	-2.0	.281	.294	.420	-.064	.287	.304	.443	.252	12.3	118-C 9
2008	DET	MLB	36	303	30	15	2	6	36	11	52	3	1	-0.3	.266	.294	.389	-.125	.267	.296	.407	.244	4.0	74-C 3

Breakout: 6% Improve: 27% Collapse: 40% Attrition: 40%   Comparables: Mike Heath, Joe Girardi, Steve Garvey, Bill Skowron

We think of Pudge as being durable, but he's caught 130 games or more just once since 1999 (doing so with the Marlins in 2003). His legendary arm may be slipping a bit as well; the 68 attempts against him last year tied his high since 1999, the 47 steals he allowed were his most since 1993, and his 31 percent throwout rate, though still above average, was the lowest of his career. Given where his offense has gone—39 unintentional walks since 2004 and sub-.300 OBPs twice in three years—he's now an average player at best. He's also a 36-year-old backstop who has been catching in the major leagues since he was 19.

Gary Sheffield   DH   Bats: R   Throws: R   Height: 6' 0"   Weight: 215   Born: November 18, 1968   Age: 39

YEAR	TEAM	LVL	AGE	PA	R	2B	3B	HR	RBI	BB	SO	SB	CS	EqBRR	AVG	OBP	SLG	MLVr	EqAVG	EqOBP	EqSLG	EqA	VORP	DEFENSE
2005	NYA	MLB	36	675	104	27	0	34	123	78	76	10	2	1.5	.291	.379	.512	.223	.297	.393	.536	.314	47.5	124-RF -3
2006	NYA	MLB	37	166	22	5	0	6	25	13	16	5	1	-0.1	.298	.355	.450	.079	.295	.361	.463	.286	7.0	19-RF -1
2007	DET	MLB	38	593	107	20	1	25	75	84	71	22	5	4.9	.265	.378	.462	.126	.270	.388	.491	.303	30.4	
2008	DET	MLB	39	414	66	19	2	15	54	53	51	17	4	0.7	.274	.372	.460	.102	.274	.374	.481	.302	21.1	99-DH

Breakout: 8% Improve: 50% Collapse: 17% Attrition: 20%   Comparables: Dwight Evans, Moises Alou, Brian Downing, Edgar Martinez

Sheffield was awful down the stretch last season; his .178/.312/.254 over the last two months was a big part of why the Tigers' offense struggled over that time. He's well into his decline, having not hit .300 or gotten on base at a .400

clip in four years and not slugged .500 in two. It's not unreasonable to suggest that the Tigers would be better off DHing Miguel Cabrera and playing Brandon Inge at third base, thereby saving more runs on defense than they'd otherwise gain on offense by replacing Inge's bat with Sheffield's. Then again, there's the matter of the $28 million owed Sheffield through 2009.

Chris Shelton 1B Bats: R Throws: R Height: 6' 0" Weight: 215 Born: June 26, 1980 Age: 28

YEAR	TEAM	LVL	AGE	PA	R	2B	3B	HR	RBI	BB	SO	SB	CS	EqBRR	AVG	OBP	SLG	MLVr	EqAVG	EqOBP	EqSLG	EqA	VORP	DEFENSE	
2005	TOL	AAA	25	211	34	19	0	8	39	25	33	0	2	0.6	.331	.417	.569	.442	.306	.389	.530	.305	18.4	31-1B	1
2005	DET	MLB	25	431	61	22	3	18	59	34	87	0	0	1.8	.299	.360	.510	.208	.309	.377	.545	.308	28.2	83-1B	3
2006	DET	MLB	26	412	50	16	4	16	47	34	107	1	2	-1.3	.273	.340	.466	.049	.274	.347	.482	.279	9.5	102-1B	-5
2006	TOL	AAA	26	129	20	6	2	3	14	18	37	1	0	-0.4	.266	.372	.440	.189	.227	.333	.427	.266	0.7	24-1B	-2
2007	TOL	AAA	27	594	75	31	1	14	65	83	141	4	2	-1.1	.269	.381	.420	.160	.257	.363	.422	.275	14.3	128-1B	2
2008	TEX	MLB	28	506	60	25	2	17	63	55	127	4	2	-0.5	.251	.338	.431	-.006	.248	.338	.442	.274	4.8	119-1B	1

Breakout: 5% Improve: 35% Collapse: 28% Attrition: 16%   Comparables: Scott Mcclain, Andy Phillips, Todd Trafton, Josh Willingham

A year after providing league-average offense in 373 AB, Shelton didn't spend a single day in Detroit. Note that Sean Casey didn't match Shelton's .269 EqA in 2006 in either of his two seasons (one partial) with the Tigers. Sometimes, it's all about perception. Shelton was dealt to the Rangers in December and is expected to slot into a first-base platoon with subsequent acquisition Ben Broussard.

Scott Sizemore 2B Bats: R Throws: R Height: 6' 0" Weight: 185 Born: January 4, 1985 Age: 23

YEAR	TEAM	LVL	AGE	PA	R	2B	3B	HR	RBI	BB	SO	SB	CS	EqBRR	AVG	OBP	SLG	MLVr	EqAVG	EqOBP	EqSLG	EqA	VORP	DEFENSE	
2006	ONE	A-	21	333	49	15	4	3	37	32	47	7	5	-1.5	.327	.394	.435	.252	.267	.326	.370	.244	12.6	63-SS	-8
2007	WMI	A	22	530	78	33	5	4	48	73	60	16	10	-2.1	.265	.376	.390	.118	.216	.306	.316	.225	-14.0	113-2B	-12
2008	DET	MLB	23	595	64	32	4	6	49	52	102	11	6	1.1	.241	.311	.350	-.164	.241	.314	.366	.243	-0.2	139-2B	-7

Breakout: 38% Improve: 66% Collapse: 13% Attrition: 7%   Comparables: Danny Garcia, Joe Jester, Rich Aurilia, Jarrett Hoffpauir

An infield tweener, Sizemore is a second baseman by trade, but the Tigers are trying very hard to have him stick at shortstop. They had him play the position in the Arizona Fall League, and he performed passably. A polished hitter without any standout tools, Sizemore is fairly close to a finished product and is most likely going to end up as a good-hitting utilityman, like Raburn.

Marcus Thames LF Bats: R Throws: R Height: 6' 2" Weight: 220 Born: March 6, 1977 Age: 31

YEAR	TEAM	LVL	AGE	PA	R	2B	3B	HR	RBI	BB	SO	SB	CS	EqBRR	AVG	OBP	SLG	MLVr	EqAVG	EqOBP	EqSLG	EqA	VORP	DEFENSE			
2005	TOL	AAA	28	314	53	18	3	22	56	41	59	4	1	-1.7	.340	.427	.679	.620	.313	.398	.623	.332	37.7	31-LF	-3	23-RF	-4
2005	DET	MLB	28	118	11	2	0	7	16	9	38	0	0	0.4	.196	.263	.411	-.179	.200	.280	.419	.239	-2.9	17-LF	-1		
2006	DET	MLB	29	390	61	20	2	26	60	37	92	1	1	-3.2	.256	.333	.549	.134	.253	.338	.561	.294	19.7	45-LF	-7		
2007	DET	MLB	30	284	37	15	0	18	54	13	72	2	1	-0.2	.242	.278	.498	-.009	.243	.285	.521	.265	4.1	31-LF	-1	22-1B	-2
2008	DET	MLB	31	435	55	20	1	22	71	39	104	4	1	-0.5	.251	.321	.480	.029	.251	.323	.502	.281	10.2	103-LF	-4		

Breakout: 16% Improve: 40% Collapse: 29% Attrition: 12%   Comparables: Ron Kittle, Gus Zernial, Dave Kingman, Glenn Davis

Thames has one skill: he hits lefties. In Jacque Jones, the Tigers have acquired a player who complements Thames perfectly by doing everything well *except* hit lefties. As a platoon, they could prove to be the most productive left fielder in the AL next year, save for Manny Ramirez. Thames has shown more patience in the past than he did last year, so that wretched OBP should climb in 2008.

PITCHERS

Yorman Bazardo

Bats: R   Throws: R   Height: 6' 2"   Weight: 220   Born: July 11, 1984   Age: 23

YEAR	TEAM	LVL	AGE	W	L	SV	G	GS	IP	H	BB	SO	HR	GB%	BABIP	STUFF	WHIP	ERA	PERA	EqERA	EqH9	EqBB9	EqSO9	EqHR9	VORP	SN/WX
2005	CAR	AA	20	8	7	0	19	19	108¹	108	36	73	12	56.8%	.294	-19	1.33	3.99	6.72	6.70	10.4	3.8	3.8	1.8	-12.0	—
2005	SAN	AA	20	3	1	0	6	6	33²	38	11	26	4	41.3%	.343	-1	1.45	4.27	7.12	5.93	11.3	4.5	4.7	1.8	-1.1	—
2006	SAN	AA	21	6	5	0	25	25	138¹	144	45	80	10	43.3%	.309	-10	1.37	3.65	5.62	5.50	10.4	3.7	3.3	1.1	1.4	—
2007	TOL	AAA	22	10	6	0	23	21	136²	134	43	69	8	54.0%	.292	-6	1.29	3.75	4.95	5.77	9.8	3.3	3.2	0.9	-2.4	—
2007	DET	MLB	22	2	1	0	11	2	23²	19	5	15	2	47.9%	.243	8	1.01	2.28	3.02	2.66	6.8	1.5	5.3	0.8	8.8	0.32
2008	DET	MLB	23	5	8	0	36	16	111	132	44	49	15	49.6%	.303	-12	1.59	5.50	5.34	5.55	10.4	3.2	3.7	1.2	-0.5	0.60

Breakout: 11% Improve: 42% Collapse: 25% Attrition: 14%   Comparables: Ramon Garcia, Albert Bustillos, Ramon Morel, Chien-Ming Wang

A nice below-the-radar pickup by Dave Dombrowski, Bazardo was acquired last spring in exchange for Jeff Frazier, a toolsy outfield prospect who failed to hit at Double-A at age 24. Bazardo uses a low-90s fastball and average curve and change to get groundballs, but he lacks an out pitch, which limits both his strikeouts and his projectability. The exodus of prospects from this system bodes well for Bazardo.

Jeremy Bonderman

Bats: R   Throws: R   Height: 6' 2"   Weight: 220   Born: October 28, 1982   Age: 25

YEAR	TEAM	LVL	AGE	W	L	SV	G	GS	IP	H	BB	SO	HR	GB%	BABIP	STUFF	WHIP	ERA	PERA	EqERA	EqH9	EqBB9	EqSO9	EqHR9	VORP	SN/WX
2005	DET	MLB	22	14	13	0	29	29	189	199	57	145	21	48.4%	.313	19	1.35	4.57	4.60	4.76	9.4	2.7	6.8	0.9	19.8	3.93
2006	DET	MLB	23	14	8	0	34	34	214	214	64	202	18	50.3%	.323	33	1.30	4.08	4.08	4.43	9.2	2.5	8.1	0.7	39.8	5.33
2007	DET	MLB	24	11	9	0	28	28	174¹	193	48	145	23	49.6%	.323	11	1.38	5.01	4.88	5.19	9.8	2.2	6.9	1.1	10.1	2.44
2008	DET	MLB	25	12	9	0	29	29	188	188	53	153	20	47.7%	.299	22	1.28	4.00	3.83	4.05	8.7	2.3	6.7	1.0	30.5	4.80

Breakout: 44% Improve: 75% Collapse: 7%   Attrition: 11%   Comparables: Alex Fernandez, Larry Dierker, Bret Saberhagen, Brett Myers

Bonderman's disappointing season was really a disappointing final ten starts as he slowly succumbed to a sore elbow. The injury appears to have begun affecting his performance in July. For the first four months of the season, he had his usual poor luck with balls in play, but his peripherals were fine. Starting July 24, his walk rate doubled, his strike percentage dropped, his home run rate and HR/FB rate doubled and his K/BB dropped from 4.0 to barely 1.5. Bonderman simply had less command of less effective stuff for six weeks before being shut down in early September. All signs point to a full recovery in 2008.

Tim Byrdak

Bats: L   Throws: L   Height: 5' 11"   Weight: 195   Born: October 31, 1973   Age: 34

YEAR	TEAM	LVL	AGE	W	L	SV	G	GS	IP	H	BB	SO	HR	GB%	BABIP	STUFF	WHIP	ERA	PERA	EqERA	EqH9	EqBB9	EqSO9	EqHR9	VORP	SN/WX
2005	OTT	AAA	31	3	2	11	37	0	38²	23	15	44	4	41.8%	.218	3	0.98	2.09	3.62	3.47	5.9	4.2	7.7	1.2	8.6	—
2005	BAL	MLB	31	0	1	1	41	0	26²	27	21	31	1	51.3%	.351	23	1.80	4.04	4.57	4.23	8.5	6.8	9.8	0.3	2.9	0.74
2006	BAL	MLB	32	1	0	0	16	0	7	14	8	2	2	53.1%	.429	-74	3.14	12.86	22.58	16.71	16.7	9.0	2.6	2.6	-5.3	-0.05
2007	TOL	AAA	33	1	0	0	17	0	24¹	22	8	30	3	41.9%	.339	4	1.23	2.59	6.08	4.03	10.1	3.6	8.9	1.6	3.9	—
2007	DET	MLB	33	3	0	1	39	0	45	38	26	49	3	42.3%	.310	16	1.42	3.20	3.58	4.30	7.4	4.5	8.8	0.6	6.8	0.79
2008	DET	MLB	34	2	3	2	44	1	46²	46	26	42	5	45.9%	.302	-1	1.53	4.54	4.60	4.56	8.5	4.5	7.4	1.0	5.0	0.50

Breakout: 37% Improve: 61% Collapse: 18% Attrition: 26%   Comparables: Moe Burtschy, Doug Creek, Scott Sauerbeck, Pedro Borbon

Well, if this isn't the darndest thing. After having Byrdak, who'd been used as a specialist by the Orioles for a year and change, dropped in his lap, Jim Leyland proceeded to use him as a multiple-inning lefty. Byrdak went multiple innings in 22 of his 39 outings, tossed at least two innings nine times, and went four no-hit innings against the Royals on September 21. It may not last—he's never been this effective against righties—but you have to like Leyland's approach.

Jose Capellan

Bats: R   Throws: R   Height: 6' 4"   Weight: 235   Born: January 13, 1981   Age: 27

YEAR	TEAM	LVL	AGE	W	L	SV	G	GS	IP	H	BB	SO	HR	GB%	BABIP	STUFF	WHIP	ERA	PERA	EqERA	EqH9	EqBB9	EqSO9	EqHR9	VORP	SN/WX
2005	NAS	AAA	24	5	3	6	36	12	90²	88	42	76	4	44.0%	.319	1	1.43	3.87	4.53	4.52	9.0	4.5	5.4	0.5	10.3	—
2005	MIL	MLB	24	1	1	0	17	0	15²	17	5	14	1	35.4%	.372	7	1.40	2.87	4.59	3.60	10.2	2.4	7.8	0.6	3.6	-0.49
2006	MIL	MLB	25	4	2	0	61	0	71²	65	31	58	11	35.3%	.274	-3	1.34	4.39	3.95	3.70	7.6	3.3	6.5	1.2	11.2	1.94
2007	NAS	AAA	26	3	2	1	17	3	28	23	14	22	1	45.2%	.275	-7	1.32	3.86	3.86	5.60	7.6	4.6	5.3	0.3	0.0	—
2007	MIL	MLB	26	0	2	0	7	0	12	10	6	8	2	39.5%	.229	-7	1.33	4.50	3.45	3.55	6.4	3.6	5.7	1.4	1.9	-0.47
2007	DET	MLB	26	0	1	0	10	0	14	18	3	12	5	36.2%	.310	-22	1.50	6.43	10.53	9.64	11.6	1.9	7.1	3.2	-3.9	-0.05
2008	COL	MLB	27	2	2	1	40	0	44²	47	18	31	6	42.4%	.289	-3	1.45	4.61	4.32	4.45	8.5	3.2	5.9	1.2	7.1	0.60

Breakout: 28% Improve: 57% Collapse: 30% Attrition: 35%   Comparables: Amaury Telemaco, Dave Stevens, Antonio Alfonseca, Wayne Rosenthal

Capellan has been vocally unhappy about role changes and demotions during his career, but when given a chance to pitch, he doesn't take advantage. His fastball doesn't move enough to get major league hitters out consistently, so you end up with a pitcher who can miss bats (7.1 K/9) but whose mistakes go a long way (1.6 HR/9). Capellan was traded to Colorado for Denny Bautista, which is a pretty lousy career move, all things considered.

Eulogio de la Cruz

Bats: R   Throws: R   Height: 5' 11"   Weight: 175   Born: March 12, 1984   Age: 24

YEAR	TEAM	LVL	AGE	W	L	SV	G	GS	IP	H	BB	SO	HR	GB%	BABIP	STUFF	WHIP	ERA	PERA	EqERA	EqH9	EqBB9	EqSO9	EqHR9	VORP	SN/WX
2005	LAK	A+	21	4	3	5	40	10	95²	66	36	97	5	58.4%	.250	-6	1.07	3.39	5.21	6.78	8.4	5.7	5.5	1.1	-10.8	—
2006	ERI	AA	22	5	6	2	38	12	105¹	103	45	87	3	56.1%	.324	0	1.41	3.43	5.06	5.27	9.8	5.0	4.7	0.6	3.6	—
2007	ERI	AA	23	4	5	0	11	11	66	54	19	57	5	62.9%	.274	3	1.11	3.41	4.59	5.37	8.8	3.3	5.7	1.2	1.5	—
2007	TOL	AAA	23	3	0	0	22	1	38¹	41	18	25	0	46.3%	.350	-10	1.54	3.52	5.75	5.50	11.3	5.0	4.5	0.3	0.4	—
2007	DET	MLB	23	0	0	0	6	0	6²	10	4	5	1	78.3%	.409	-35	2.10	6.72	11.13	12.79	14.2	5.7	7.1	1.4	-3.7	-0.00
2008	FLO	MLB	24	4	5	1	30	8	74²	79	37	50	6	53.9%	.309	-4	1.57	4.77	5.10	5.07	9.5	4.0	5.2	0.8	4.2	0.70

Breakout: 50% Improve: 74% Collapse: 15% Attrition: 17%   Comparables: Ramiro Mendoza, Carlos Valdez, Cory Lidle, Juan Rincon

If you squint, you can almost see Francisco Rodriguez in de la Cruz, a small Dominican righty with high-90s heat and a sharp breaking ball. Rodriguez gets more movement and velocity, however, which is a difference worth tens of millions of dollars over time. De la Cruz was part of the big Marlins deal and, given the situation in Florida, could end up as their top righty reliever this season.

Chad Durbin

Bats: S   Throws: R   Height: 6' 2"   Weight: 200   Born: December 3, 1977   Age: 30

YEAR	TEAM	LVL	AGE	W	L	SV	G	GS	IP	H	BB	SO	HR	GB%	BABIP	STUFF	WHIP	ERA	PERA	EqERA	EqH9	EqBB9	EqSO9	EqHR9	VORP	SN/WX
2005	NWO	AAA	27	4	5	0	26	20	115¹	121	48	99	24	43.8%	.300	-38	1.47	5.78	7.31	7.02	10.2	4.2	5.5	2.3	-17.0	—
2006	TOL	AAA	28	11	8	0	28	28	185	169	46	149	17	42.3%	.283	-5	1.16	3.11	5.25	5.05	9.6	2.9	5.3	1.4	10.6	—
2007	DET	MLB	29	8	7	1	36	19	127²	133	49	66	21	46.3%	.274	-20	1.43	4.72	5.07	4.64	9.0	3.0	4.3	1.4	13.5	2.27
2008	PHI	MLB	30	3	4	1	27	6	59²	68	21	38	11	44.0%	.295	-9	1.49	5.31	5.52	5.27	9.8	2.9	5.2	1.6	2.5	0.40

Breakout: 17% Improve: 30% Collapse: 45% Attrition: 42%   Comparables: Jason Simontacchi, Paul Mitchell, Dave Telgheder, Jae Weong Seo

Move along, nothing to see here. Forced into the rotation by Kenny Rogers' injuries, Durbin held his spot for much of the first half thanks to the Tigers' defense and nothing else. From May 1 through June 19, he had an ERA of 3.49 despite walking 24 and striking out 23. He's entirely a product of good fortune on balls in play and not likely to ever throw 127 innings in a major league season again. Signed by the Phillies after being non-tendered, he's unlikely to get as much help from his new set of fielders.

Jason Grilli

Bats: R   Throws: R   Height: 6' 5"   Weight: 225   Born: November 11, 1976   Age: 31

YEAR	TEAM	LVL	AGE	W	L	SV	G	GS	IP	H	BB	SO	HR	GB%	BABIP	STUFF	WHIP	ERA	PERA	EqERA	EqH9	EqBB9	EqSO9	EqHR9	VORP	SN/WX
2005	TOL	AAA	28	12	9	0	28	28	167¹	170	58	120	21	51.7%	.294	-17	1.36	4.09	6.00	6.02	10.1	3.9	4.7	1.5	-7.2	—
2005	DET	MLB	28	1	1	0	3	2	16	14	6	5	1	46.2%	.265	-9	1.25	3.38	3.74	3.68	8.0	3.7	3.1	0.6	4.2	0.35
2006	DET	MLB	29	2	3	0	51	0	62	61	25	31	6	48.8%	.279	-13	1.39	4.21	4.41	4.43	8.9	3.4	4.3	0.7	10.8	0.08
2007	DET	MLB	30	5	3	0	57	0	79²	81	32	62	5	45.6%	.315	6	1.42	4.74	4.03	4.93	8.9	3.1	6.4	0.6	6.8	0.33
2008	DET	MLB	31	3	3	2	40	1	57	59	25	37	6	46.8%	.296	-7	1.47	4.53	4.43	4.59	9.1	3.5	5.4	0.9	6.3	0.60

Breakout: 34% Improve: 54% Collapse: 28% Attrition: 32%   Comparables: Matt Karchner, Paul Reuschel, Mike Dejean, George Frazier

A decade removed from being the fourth overall pick in the 1997 draft, Grilli had his best year as a pro, settling down after a lousy start to be a stalwart in the Tigers' bullpen. He did not pitch in many high-leverage situations, nor did he pitch well consistently, but he was durable, threw strikes, and kept the ball in the park. While Durbin's ERA outpaced his performance, Grilli's went the other way. He can be the seventh-inning guy this season.

Todd Jones

| | | | | | | | | | | | | | Bats: L | | Throws: R | | Height: 6' 3" | | Weight: 230 | | Born: April 24, 1968 | | Age: 40 |

YEAR	TEAM	LVL	AGE	W	L	SV	G	GS	IP	H	BB	SO	HR	GB%	BABIP	STUFF	WHIP	ERA	PERA	EqERA	EqH9	EqBB9	EqSO9	EqHR9	VORP	SN/WX
2005	FLO	MLB	37	1	5	40	68	0	73	61	14	62	2	54.8%	.294	24	1.03	2.10	2.64	2.35	6.9	1.8	6.9	0.2	24.9	4.83
2006	DET	MLB	38	2	6	37	62	0	64	70	11	28	4	55.7%	.297	-6	1.27	3.94	3.95	4.52	9.8	1.4	3.7	0.6	12.2	2.30
2007	DET	MLB	39	1	4	38	63	0	61¹	64	23	33	3	47.8%	.299	-6	1.42	4.26	3.87	4.13	9.0	3.0	4.4	0.4	11.6	3.05
2008	DET	MLB	40	3	5	22	53	0	59	65	18	33	6	49.3%	.299	-11	1.40	4.34	4.18	4.43	9.5	2.5	4.6	0.9	6.5	1.00

Breakout: 6%　Improve: 24%　Collapse: 47%　Attrition: 33%　　　　Comparables: Steve Reed, Doug Brocail, Kent Tekulve, Dennis Lamp

By notching his 300th career save in September, Jones slid in behind Jose Mesa as the second-worst pitcher to ever reach that mark. He remains an unimpressive closer, surviving by keeping the ball down as much as possible. More than a quarter of his walks allowed the past two years have been intentional, including six last year. Regardless, he skirts the edge and could implode any minute now.

Jair Jurrjens

| | | | | | | | | | | | | | Bats: R | | Throws: R | | Height: 6' 1" | | Weight: 160 | | Born: January 29, 1986 | | Age: 22 |

YEAR	TEAM	LVL	AGE	W	L	SV	G	GS	IP	H	BB	SO	HR	GB%	BABIP	STUFF	WHIP	ERA	PERA	EqERA	EqH9	EqBB9	EqSO9	EqHR9	VORP	SN/WX
2005	WMI	A	19	12	6	0	26	26	142²	132	36	108	5	56.7%	.300	8	1.18	3.41	5.61	6.06	10.6	3.9	4.0	0.9	-6.4	—
2006	LAK	A+	20	5	0	0	12	12	73²	53	10	59	4	54.8%	.239	11	0.86	2.09	4.17	4.54	8.2	2.3	4.3	1.1	7.9	—
2006	ERI	AA	20	4	3	0	12	12	67¹	71	21	53	7	51.7%	.327	-4	1.37	3.35	7.05	5.85	11.2	3.9	4.7	1.6	-1.7	—
2007	ERI	AA	21	7	5	0	19	19	112²	112	31	94	7	49.3%	.314	10	1.27	3.19	5.35	4.69	10.5	3.2	5.3	1.0	10.5	—
2007	DET	MLB	21	3	1	0	7	7	30²	24	11	13	4	37.1%	.217	-3	1.14	4.69	3.47	4.25	7.0	3.0	3.6	1.2	4.2	0.68
2008	ATL	MLB	22	8	10	0	39	26	149¹	164	56	97	23	42.7%	.296	0	1.47	5.04	5.29	5.35	9.6	3.0	5.2	1.3	5.8	1.60

Breakout: 9%　Improve: 32%　Collapse: 39%　Attrition: 20%　　　　Comparables: Jose Martinez, Jose Parra, Felipe Lira, Dicky Gonzalez

The Tigers sent Jair Jurrjens to Atlanta with Gorkys Hernandez for Edgar Renteria in a trade as notable for the names involved as for the players. For such a young pitcher, Jurrjens has very good control of his three pitches, among them a low-90s fastball. The sore shoulder that interrupted his time in Detroit isn't expected to affect him this year. Look for him to be up by midseason and establish himself as a mid-rotation starter.

Macay McBride

| | | | | | | | | | | | | | Bats: L | | Throws: L | | Height: 5' 11" | | Weight: 210 | | Born: October 24, 1982 | | Age: 25 |

YEAR	TEAM	LVL	AGE	W	L	SV	G	GS	IP	H	BB	SO	HR	GB%	BABIP	STUFF	WHIP	ERA	PERA	EqERA	EqH9	EqBB9	EqSO9	EqHR9	VORP	SN/WX
2005	MIS	AA	22	3	1	0	6	3	24²	21	12	16	2	64.0%	.264	-15	1.34	3.64	5.29	5.24	8.5	5.2	3.6	1.2	0.9	—
2005	RIC	AAA	22	1	5	2	25	1	43²	49	22	47	5	45.4%	.376	-5	1.62	4.32	7.87	7.03	11.8	5.7	7.3	1.4	-6.3	—
2005	ATL	MLB	22	1	0	1	23	0	14	18	7	22	0	43.6%	.486	14	1.79	5.79	5.93	7.71	12.2	3.9	11.6	0.0	-2.4	1.08
2006	ATL	MLB	23	4	1	1	71	0	56²	53	32	46	2	48.2%	.307	8	1.50	3.65	3.67	4.13	8.1	4.4	6.7	0.3	9.9	1.19
2007	RIC	AAA	24	1	2	0	7	5	23	26	7	24	3	40.3%	.338	-4	1.43	3.13	6.65	5.16	11.1	3.2	6.8	1.6	1.1	—
2007	ATL	MLB	24	1	0	0	18	0	15	14	15	17	1	40.5%	.317	16	1.93	3.60	4.96	5.17	8.0	7.5	9.2	0.6	0.8	0.18
2007	DET	MLB	24	0	1	0	20	0	17²	19	10	13	3	42.1%	.302	-18	1.64	6.10	6.14	6.11	9.7	4.6	6.1	1.5	-0.4	0.07
2008	DET	MLB	25	2	2	1	32	1	35¹	37	20	29	4	44.5%	.309	-2	1.59	5.16	4.91	5.20	9.1	4.6	6.8	1.0	1.6	0.20

Breakout: 22%　Improve: 43%　Collapse: 27%　Attrition: 39%　　　　Comparables: Jorge De La Rosa, Ted Bowsfield, Jerry Stephenson, Phil Hennigan

It just seems like a waste to take a live arm like McBride's and turn him into a specialist at such a young age, but that's what the Braves did. An early season spate of wildness cost him his roster spot, however, and he was sent to Detroit for Wil Ledezma in June. Just 25, he'll battle Byrdak and Seay for a spot in the Tigers pen this spring. There's upside here.

Andrew Miller

Bats: L   Throws: L   Height: 6' 6"   Weight: 210   Born: May 21, 1985   Age: 23

YEAR	TEAM	LVL	AGE	W	L	SV	G	GS	IP	H	BB	SO	HR	GB%	BABIP	STUFF	WHIP	ERA	PERA	EqERA	EqH9	EqBB9	EqSO9	EqHR9	VORP	SN/WX
2006	DET	MLB	21	0	1	0	8	0	10^1	8	10	6	0	69.7%	.242	-1	1.74	6.12	4.17	7.59	6.8	7.6	5.1	0.0	-2.0	-0.04
2007	LAK	A+	22	1	4	0	7	7	41^1	43	15	28	1	65.2%	.313	-5	1.40	3.49	5.17	5.59	9.8	4.7	3.5	0.5	0.0	—
2007	ERI	AA	22	2	0	0	4	4	30^2	22	5	24	2	75.9%	.250	16	0.88	0.59	3.98	1.63	7.8	2.0	5.2	1.0	12.2	—
2007	DET	MLB	22	5	5	0	13	13	64	73	39	56	8	50.7%	.333	9	1.75	5.63	6.03	5.76	9.9	4.8	7.0	1.1	-0.6	0.80
2008	FLO	MLB	23	10	11	0	30	30	167^1	166	81	143	14	53.5%	.310	14	1.48	4.52	4.72	4.81	8.9	3.9	6.5	0.7	13.4	2.80

Breakout: 37% Improve: 64% Collapse: 14% Attrition: 18%   Comparables: Mike Pelfrey, Adam Loewen, Jerry Reuss, B. J. Wallace

As good a job as the Tigers have done of picking players in the draft in recent years, their handling of them has been suspect. Maybin, completely unready, was rushed to cover a problem in left field. Similarly, Miller was bounced around the system like a piñata, going from the draft to the Florida State League to the majors in 2006 and then pitching at four different levels in 2007. It's not that he was ineffective in the minors; it's just that you can't really develop much other than your flying habits when you change teams as often as Miller did last year. Miller still has all the tools that made him arguably the top pitcher in the 2006 draft class and just needs a full season in one place— it's called "Triple-A"—to work on his mechanics, command, and secondary pitches. Given that development times, the Marlins could have the Josh Beckett of their next championship team here.

Zach Miner

Bats: R   Throws: R   Height: 6' 3"   Weight: 200   Born: March 12, 1982   Age: 26

YEAR	TEAM	LVL	AGE	W	L	SV	G	GS	IP	H	BB	SO	HR	GB%	BABIP	STUFF	WHIP	ERA	PERA	EqERA	EqH9	EqBB9	EqSO9	EqHR9	VORP	SN/WX
2005	MIS	AA	23	0	1	1	4	2	16^2	21	5	18	0	64.0%	.429	-1	1.56	4.31	6.64	7.20	13.8	3.6	6.6	0.0	-2.7	—
2005	RIC	AAA	23	2	7	0	17	17	89^1	97	45	63	6	51.4%	.320	-3	1.59	4.23	6.35	5.86	11.1	5.5	4.5	0.8	-2.3	—
2005	TOL	AAA	23	3	1	0	6	6	34^1	28	20	20	4	59.0%	.245	-4	1.40	2.36	5.21	3.41	8.0	6.3	3.7	1.4	7.7	—
2006	TOL	AAA	24	6	0	0	9	9	51^2	43	21	40	2	57.9%	.287	7	1.25	2.81	4.71	4.57	9.1	4.8	5.4	0.6	5.2	—
2006	DET	MLB	24	7	6	0	27	16	93	100	32	59	11	49.2%	.305	-3	1.42	4.84	4.90	5.20	9.8	3.0	5.5	1.0	9.6	1.51
2007	TOL	AAA	25	1	4	0	11	8	51^2	43	22	33	4	55.1%	.257	-14	1.26	4.87	4.64	6.70	8.4	4.3	4.1	1.1	-5.9	—
2007	DET	MLB	25	3	4	0	34	1	53^2	56	22	34	3	58.5%	.315	-1	1.45	3.02	4.09	3.57	9.2	3.2	5.3	0.5	13.7	0.32
2008	DET	MLB	26	3	4	1	38	5	65^1	70	29	40	6	53.2%	.303	-7	1.52	4.69	4.59	4.80	9.4	3.7	5.0	0.8	5.9	0.70

Breakout: 14% Improve: 41% Collapse: 32% Attrition: 29%   Comparables: Vince Colbert, Joe Grahe, Sergio Mitre, Dave Weathers

With the loss of Kenny Rogers and the failure of anyone to step up to take his place in the rotation, the Tigers bullpen had a lot more low-leverage innings to fill last season. Miner, along with Durbin and Grilli, picked them up. Like Grilli, Miner kept the ball down on the way to an effective season, posting a 2.3 G/F ratio and allowing just 14 extra-base hits in 232 opponent plate appearances. Miner was also effective with runners on, stranding 24 of the 30 he inherited. Of the Tigers' three garbagemen, Miner has the most upside.

Rick Porcello

Bats: R   Throws: R   Height: 6' 5"   Weight: 195   Born: December 27, 1988   Age: 20

YEAR	TEAM	LVL	AGE	W	L	SV	G	GS	IP	H	BB	SO	HR	GB%	BABIP	STUFF	WHIP	ERA	PERA	EqERA	EqH9	EqBB9	EqSO9	EqHR9	VORP	SN/WX
2008	DET	MLB	19	6	11	0	27	27	136	161	109	82	22	45.8%	.312	-11	1.98	6.79	6.86	6.73	10.3	6.5	5.0	1.4	-18.0	-1.00

Breakout: NA Improve: NA Collapse: NA Attrition: NA   Comparables: Jon Garland, Kurt Miller, Clint Everts, Sam Marsonek

Rather than let the commissioner's office bonus suggestions dictate their future, the Tigers nabbed the best high school pitcher in the draft all the way down at number 27 and paid far over slot to sign him, committing to a major league deal worth about $7 million. It was the third-straight year the Tigers had gone over slot in the first round. Porcello works in the mid-90s, peaking at 98 mph throws both a slider and curve, and has ace potential.

Nate Robertson

Bats: R   Throws: L   Height: 6' 2"   Weight: 225   Born: September 3, 1977   Age: 30

YEAR	TEAM	LVL	AGE	W	L	SV	G	GS	IP	H	BB	SO	HR	GB%	BABIP	STUFF	WHIP	ERA	PERA	EqERA	EqH9	EqBB9	EqSO9	EqHR9	VORP	SN/WX
2005	DET	MLB	27	7	16	0	32	32	196^2	202	65	122	28	52.0%	.285	0	1.36	4.48	4.68	5.00	9.0	3.0	5.4	1.2	13.3	3.29
2006	DET	MLB	28	13	13	0	32	32	208^2	206	67	137	29	48.0%	.281	6	1.31	3.84	4.54	4.20	8.9	2.7	5.7	1.2	42.4	5.61
2007	DET	MLB	29	9	13	0	30	30	177^2	199	63	119	22	46.6%	.315	3	1.47	4.76	5.02	4.78	9.8	2.8	5.5	1.1	19.6	2.78
2008	DET	MLB	30	10	10	0	28	28	172^2	181	59	114	20	47.6%	.295	9	1.39	4.42	4.38	4.46	9.2	2.8	5.4	1.0	20.3	3.50

Breakout: 18% Improve: 55% Collapse: 16% Attrition: 16%   Comparables: Kenny Rogers, Chris Hammond, Atlee Hammaker, Brian Bohanon

Over the past four seasons, Robertson has been remarkably consistent at a level just below average, with his ERA moving in tune with his BABIP as his rates have stayed mostly unchanged. Baseball Prospectus alum Gary Huckabay used to write about pitchers who needed to lop one walk per nine innings off of their line to reach a higher level. Robertson is the best example in the book right now; he's a walk-per-nine from signing a six-year, $100 million contract in two years. Robertson spent some time on the DL last year with a tired arm, but that doesn't seem to have been an injury as much as a euphemistic way of saying, "He's not pitching well and we don't know why."

Fernando Rodney

Bats: R   Throws: R   Height: 5' 11"   Weight: 220   Born: March 18, 1977   Age: 31

YEAR	TEAM	LVL	AGE	W	L	SV	G	GS	IP	H	BB	SO	HR	GB%	BABIP	STUFF	WHIP	ERA	PERA	EqERA	EqH9	EqBB9	EqSO9	EqHR9	VORP	SN/WX
2005	DET	MLB	28	2	3	9	39	0	44	39	17	42	5	41.1%	.291	13	1.27	2.86	3.98	2.72	8.0	3.6	8.4	1.0	13.9	0.71
2006	DET	MLB	29	7	4	7	63	0	71²	51	34	65	6	58.4%	.238	10	1.19	3.51	3.25	4.27	6.4	4.0	7.7	0.6	12.3	2.22
2007	DET	MLB	30	2	6	1	48	0	50²	46	21	54	5	49.0%	.306	13	1.32	4.26	3.73	4.30	7.7	3.3	8.4	0.9	6.6	0.39
2008	DET	MLB	31	3	2	4	48	0	54²	49	23	50	5	49.3%	.288	8	1.32	3.73	3.62	3.81	7.8	3.4	7.5	0.8	11.7	1.00

Breakout: 21% Improve: 57% Collapse: 18% Attrition: 11%   Comparables: Darren Holmes, Hoyt Wilhelm, Steve Farr, Aurelio Lopez

Around August of last year, if you'd seen a headline announcing "Rodney placed on DL with polio," it wouldn't have been a surprise. The big righty was on and off the list with forearm and shoulder problems all year long, and never showed the command of the changeup that made him a postseason star in 2006. With Zumaya out for a while, the Tigers need Rodney missing bats in the eighth inning. He's expected to be healthy in the spring.

Kenny Rogers

Bats: L   Throws: L   Height: 6' 1"   Weight: 190   Born: November 10, 1964   Age: 43

YEAR	TEAM	LVL	AGE	W	L	SV	G	GS	IP	H	BB	SO	HR	GB%	BABIP	STUFF	WHIP	ERA	PERA	EqERA	EqH9	EqBB9	EqSO9	EqHR9	VORP	SN/WX
2005	TEX	MLB	40	14	8	0	30	30	195¹	205	53	87	15	46.8%	.291	10	1.32	3.46	3.75	3.33	8.7	2.4	3.9	0.6	41.4	3.95
2006	DET	MLB	41	17	8	0	34	33	204	195	62	99	23	50.1%	.265	3	1.26	3.84	4.12	4.33	8.7	2.6	4.2	0.9	40.6	5.24
2007	DET	MLB	42	3	4	0	11	11	63	65	25	36	8	50.2%	.282	-2	1.43	4.43	4.52	4.83	8.8	3.1	4.7	1.1	5.6	0.82
2008	DET	MLB	43	3	4	0	16	9	57²	62	22	33	6	50.3%	.295	-7	1.46	4.66	4.56	4.73	9.4	3.1	4.7	1.0	7.4	0.90

Breakout: 13% Improve: 42% Collapse: 51% Attrition: 59%   Comparables: Jeff Fassero, Joe Niekro, Jamie Moyer, Warren Spahn

Another injury case, Rogers missed three months following surgery to remove a blood clot in his shoulder, then five weeks with a sore elbow. When he did pitch, he was basically the same guy who picked up Cy Young votes in 2006, not that those were deserved. He's back in Detroit on a one-year deal, but at 43, he's not a good bet to stay in the rotation all season, for both health and performance reasons.

Bobby Seay

Bats: L   Throws: L   Height: 6' 2"   Weight: 235   Born: June 20, 1978   Age: 30

YEAR	TEAM	LVL	AGE	W	L	SV	G	GS	IP	H	BB	SO	HR	GB%	BABIP	STUFF	WHIP	ERA	PERA	EqERA	EqH9	EqBB9	EqSO9	EqHR9	VORP	SN/WX
2005	CSP	AAA	27	1	0	3	17	0	22²	23	10	24	2	36.5%	.356	-2	1.45	2.38	4.71	3.27	9.0	4.1	6.5	0.8	5.7	—
2005	COL	MLB	27	0	0	0	17	0	11²	18	8	11	3	43.6%	.429	-28	2.14	8.46	13.87	10.32	13.5	5.6	7.9	2.4	-2.4	-0.39
2006	TOL	AAA	28	1	2	0	24	1	24²	25	6	14	3	44.8%	.313	-35	1.28	4.83	6.91	7.77	11.0	2.9	3.7	2.0	-5.3	—
2006	DET	MLB	28	0	0	0	14	0	15¹	14	9	12	1	36.2%	.295	-2	1.50	6.47	4.48	6.46	8.2	4.7	6.5	0.6	-0.7	0.03
2007	DET	MLB	29	3	0	1	58	0	46¹	38	15	38	1	39.8%	.289	16	1.14	2.33	2.87	2.36	7.3	2.6	6.9	0.2	18.9	2.30
2008	DET	MLB	30	2	2	3	54	0	47²	48	19	38	5	44.5%	.298	0	1.40	4.04	4.09	4.07	8.8	3.2	6.5	0.9	8.4	0.70

Breakout: 30% Improve: 57% Collapse: 16% Attrition: 19%   Comparables: Jim Poole, Mike Myers, Rich Monteleone, Scott Radinsky

Like Grilli, Seay has found a home in Detroit years after losing his status as a first-round pick. Seay served as the lefty specialist last year and did well in the role, striking out almost one of every four lefty batters he faced and doing his best work with runners on base and on little rest. He can be very good in this job for a while.

Dallas Trahern

Bats: R   Throws: R   Height: 6' 3"   Weight: 190   Born: November 29, 1985   Age: 22

YEAR	TEAM	LVL	AGE	W	L	SV	G	GS	IP	H	BB	SO	HR	GB%	BABIP	STUFF	WHIP	ERA	PERA	EqERA	EqH9	EqBB9	EqSO9	EqHR9	VORP	SN/WX
2005	WMI	A	19	7	11	0	26	26	156	158	50	66	9	62.8%	.286	-23	1.33	3.58	6.69	6.87	11.3	4.7	1.6	1.3	-19.2	—
2006	LAK	A+	20	6	11	0	25	25	144¹	129	41	86	9	65.7%	.269	-14	1.18	3.31	5.84	6.12	10.1	4.1	2.9	1.3	-7.5	—
2007	ERI	AA	21	12	6	0	26	26	162²	177	51	92	12	60.8%	.317	-12	1.40	3.87	6.64	6.02	11.7	3.7	3.5	1.1	-6.8	—
2008	FLO	MLB	22	7	10	0	25	25	137¹	168	64	66	15	55.9%	.319	-6	1.69	5.62	6.03	5.96	10.9	3.7	3.7	1.0	-5.8	0.40

Breakout: 18% Improve: 51% Collapse: 18% Attrition: 11%   Comparables: Chance Douglass, Tim Dillard, David Pauley, Scott Randall

Trahern is a performance prospect who advance through the Tigers' system by throwing a sinker in the 88 to 91 mph range and getting a bunch of groundballs with it. That's his only MLB-ready pitch, and as you see above, he doesn't miss many bats. Triple-A will be a test. Trahern was sent to the Marlins as part of the Cabrera/Willis deal; their infield defense will not help his career prospects.

Virgil Vasquez

Bats: R   Throws: R   Height: 6' 3"   Weight: 205   Born: June 7, 1982   Age: 26

YEAR	TEAM	LVL	AGE	W	L	SV	G	GS	IP	H	BB	SO	HR	GB%	BABIP	STUFF	WHIP	ERA	PERA	EqERA	EqH9	EqBB9	EqSO9	EqHR9	VORP	SN/WX
2005	LAK	A+	23	4	1	0	8	8	47	52	7	31	6	44.0%	.322	-33	1.26	4.21	9.25	8.03	13.2	2.9	3.1	2.5	-10.9	—
2005	ERI	AA	23	2	8	0	15	15	83²	93	14	53	10	31.9%	.310	-26	1.28	5.27	6.38	8.10	11.0	2.5	3.3	1.6	-21.3	—
2006	ERI	AA	24	7	12	0	27	27	173²	174	50	129	21	41.9%	.302	-28	1.29	3.74	6.72	5.74	10.4	3.6	4.3	1.8	-2.5	—
2007	TOL	AAA	25	12	5	0	25	25	155	139	33	127	18	36.2%	.280	-8	1.11	3.48	5.15	5.05	9.3	2.3	5.5	1.6	8.8	—
2007	DET	MLB	25	0	1	0	5	3	16²	27	5	7	7	41.2%	.328	-61	1.92	8.62	16.90	11.88	14.0	2.2	3.2	3.8	-4.9	-0.28
2008	DET	MLB	26	5	8	0	33	16	110¹	130	37	60	19	40.7%	.300	-8	1.51	5.60	5.44	5.53	10.3	2.7	4.5	1.6	-0.4	0.60

Breakout: 36% Improve: 70% Collapse: 13% Attrition: 22%   Comparables: Mark DiFelice, Tim Wakefield, Travis Harper, Matt Wise

Like Trahern, Vasquez's prospect status is based more on what he's done than what he's done it with. A sinker/slider guy, Vasquez has some of the best command in the minor leagues with a career K/BB of 3.3. With Miller, Jurrjens, and Trahern gone, this spring may be his best chance to earn a major league job.

Justin Verlander

Bats: R   Throws: R   Height: 6' 5"   Weight: 200   Born: February 20, 1983   Age: 25

YEAR	TEAM	LVL	AGE	W	L	SV	G	GS	IP	H	BB	SO	HR	GB%	BABIP	STUFF	WHIP	ERA	PERA	EqERA	EqH9	EqBB9	EqSO9	EqHR9	VORP	SN/WX
2005	LAK	A+	22	9	2	0	13	13	86	70	19	104	3	45.7%	.338	18	1.03	1.67	5.43	4.01	10.3	3.8	6.8	0.9	13.1	—
2005	ERI	AA	22	2	0	0	7	7	32²	11	7	32	1	43.4%	.135	18	0.55	0.28	2.85	1.76	2.9	2.6	5.6	0.6	13.1	—
2005	DET	MLB	22	0	2	0	2	2	11¹	15	5	7	1	48.8%	.350	-3	1.76	7.17	6.62	7.15	11.9	4.0	5.6	0.8	-2.0	-0.13
2006	DET	MLB	23	17	9	0	30	30	186	187	60	124	21	42.6%	.297	13	1.33	3.63	4.61	3.86	9.4	2.8	5.9	0.9	47.5	6.15
2007	DET	MLB	24	18	6	0	32	32	201²	181	67	183	20	42.7%	.281	25	1.23	3.66	3.64	3.60	7.7	2.6	7.3	0.8	45.9	5.57
2008	DET	MLB	25	13	10	0	31	31	200¹	193	67	161	22	43.3%	.289	20	1.30	3.93	3.87	3.95	8.4	2.7	6.6	1.0	34.7	5.30

Breakout: 8% Improve: 38% Collapse: 28% Attrition: 12%   Comparables: Josh Beckett, Kevin Millwood, Don Newcombe, Bill Singer

What's most intriguing about Verlander is that he's still working on commanding his stuff. On nights like June 12 of last year, when he no-hit the Brewers, you wonder how anyone ever touches him; his fastball edges up near 100 and his breaking ball has Bugs Bunny action. Even that night, he walked four men, and that's where you can see the improvement coming as he harnesses his stuff and gets better at throwing it for strikes. Verlander closed the year striking out 63 and walking 18 in his last 67⅔ innings, providing a taste of what is yet to come. The over/under on Cy Young Awards is 2 1/2.

Joel Zumaya

Bats: R   Throws: R   Height: 6' 3"   Weight: 210   Born: November 9, 1984   Age: 23

YEAR	TEAM	LVL	AGE	W	L	SV	G	GS	IP	H	BB	SO	HR	GB%	BABIP	STUFF	WHIP	ERA	PERA	EqERA	EqH9	EqBB9	EqSO9	EqHR9	VORP	SN/WX
2005	ERI	AA	20	8	3	0	18	18	107¹	71	52	143	8	40.7%	.276	30	1.15	2.77	4.60	4.67	7.3	6.0	8.0	1.1	10.0	—
2005	TOL	AAA	20	1	2	0	8	8	44	30	24	56	2	37.6%	.289	41	1.23	2.66	4.22	3.54	7.3	6.0	8.6	0.7	9.3	—
2006	DET	MLB	21	6	3	1	62	0	83¹	56	42	97	6	34.9%	.254	39	1.18	1.94	2.94	2.13	6.0	4.2	9.5	0.5	36.5	5.01
2007	DET	MLB	22	2	3	1	28	0	33²	23	17	27	3	37.1%	.217	5	1.19	4.27	2.89	3.89	5.7	3.9	6.5	0.8	6.3	0.90
2008	DET	MLB	23	4	3	3	47	3	67¹	55	31	62	7	39.8%	.265	11	1.27	3.62	3.40	3.66	7.2	3.7	7.5	0.9	15.6	1.40

Breakout: 12% Improve: 35% Collapse: 42% Attrition: 19%   Comparables: Chad Cordero, Mark Clear, Gregg Olson, Joey McLaughlin

Zumaya's career has thus far been a string of bizarre ailments, starting with his "Guitar Hero"-related forearm strain during the 2006 postseason, then a ruptured tendon in the middle finger of his right hand last year, and most recently and tragically a career-threatening shoulder injury suffered last October when a 50-pound box landed on him while he was moving his belongings ahead of the California wildfires. Zumaya started the 2007 season poorly, with 13 walks in 17 ⅓ innings. After returning from his finger injury, he posted a 4.96 ERA and just 10 strikeouts in 16⅓ innings. As exciting as he was in 2006, he'll be two years and a surgery removed from that pitcher the next time he takes the mound. Lower your expectations accordingly.

LINEOUTS

Hitters

PLAYER	TEAM	LVL	AGE	PA	R	2B	3B	HR	RBI	BB	SO	SB-CS	EqBRR	AVG/OBP/SLG	MLVr	EqAVG/EqOBP/EqSLG	EqA	VORP
INF T. Giarratano '08	DET	MLB	25	102	10	5	1	1	8	7	20	3-1	0.2	.229/.288/.325	-.245	.229/.290/.340	.228	-1.2
1B M. Hessman	TOL	AAA	29	498	71	24	2	31	101	64	153	6-11	-3.1	.254/.356/.540	.266	.253/.348/.546	.290	43.1
	DET	MLB	29	57	7	0	0	4	12	5	17	0-0	-0.3	.235/.298/.471	-.024	.235/.298/.490	.265	0.8
SS C. Iorg	LAK	A+	21	19	0	2	0	0	5	1	5	0-0	-0.1	.278/.316/.389	-.010	.222/.263/.333	.203	-1.1
LF T. Perez*	TOL	AAA	32	540	76	39	1	13	69	35	47	13-6	-5.1	.309/.356/.472	.229	.294/.340/.474	.276	17.8
	DET	MLB	32	96	12	9	2	0	13	6	6	1-1	0.3	.389/.427/.533	.431	.393/.438/.539	.330	10.7
LF W. Ramirez	LAK	A+	21	343	48	7	4	10	41	20	86	28-6	5.7	.273/.315/.414	.018	.236/.276/.379	.233	-17.6
	ERI	AA	21	133	15	3	1	2	14	8	38	6-2	-0.5	.215/.273/.306	-.271	.195/.242/.285	.188	-15.0
SS R. Santiago#	TOL	AAA	27	402	40	19	4	3	30	16	61	8-9	-4.6	.263/.309/.362	-.040	.247/.289/.358	.222	-2.7
	DET	MLB	27	74	10	5	1	0	7	1	10	3-0	-0.1	.284/.324/.388	-.055	.299/.338/.403	.266	2.6
CF C. Thomas*	ERI	AA	23	599	97	30	6	8	53	59	110	18-11	-3.0	.280/.359/.405	.043	.249/.318/.369	.241	-1.5
C V. Wilson '08	DET	MLB	35	51	4	2	0	1	5	2	10	0-0	-0.1	.229/.276/.329	-.262	.230/.278/.344	.219	-1.1

Tony Giarratano's comeback from knee surgery was ended by a torn right labrum suffered early in spring training that cost him the entire 2007 season. ⊘ Low-OBP slugger **Mike Hessman** hit a buck-sixty-five in '06 and still kept his job as the Mud Hens' third baseman. He even got a cup of coffee in Detroit. He'll get a couple more without ever sticking. ⊘ The Tigers gave shortstop **Cale Iorg** nearly $1.5 million as a sixth-round pick last June, hoping that his impressive skills haven't atrophied following a two-year mission for the Mormon church in Portugal. ⊘ **Timo Perez** doesn't have the speed to be a good fourth outfielder anymore, unless hitting .389 is his replacement skill. (It's not.) ⊘ Moved to left field last year, **Wilkin Ramirez** did not reestablish himself as a prospect. Although reaching Double-A at 21 is mildly promising, he just can't hit. ⊘ **Ramon Santiago** has exactly *one* major-league walk in each of the last three seasons. Yes, that's the most interesting thing about him. ⊘ **Clete Thomas** is a speedy center fielder with enough skills to be a bench player. He does many things well, but nothing especially well. ⊘ Save for three rehab games at Triple-A, **Vance Wilson** missed the entire 2007 season with first a torn muscle in his right forearm, then an elbow injury that required Tommy John surgery. He's expected to enter spring training as the backup catcher.

Pitchers

PLAYER	TEAM	LVL	AGE	W	L	SV	IP	H	BB	SO	HR	GB%	BABIP	STUFF	WHIP	ERA	PERA	EqERA	EqH9	EqBB9	EqSO9	EqHR9	VORP
B. Badenhop	LAK	A+	24	10	6	0	135¹	130	34	78	5	58.4%	.287	-6	1.21	3.13	4.51	4.95	8.8	3.4	2.9	0.8	9.3
	ERI	AA	24	2	0	0	18²	8	3	12	1	63.6%	.119	8	0.59	1.44	2.72	2.45	3.9	2.0	3.9	1.0	6.4
C. Lambert	SFD	AA	24	0	2	0	26¹	24	8	17	5	34.6%	.250	-22	1.22	3.42	6.91	5.25	9.4	3.8	3.8	2.6	0.9
	MEM	AAA	24	1	4	0	57²	74	29	50	10	41.3%	.372	-30	1.79	7.49	8.94	8.84	11.9	4.9	6.1	1.8	-19.8
A. Lopez	TOL	AAA	32	3	5	26	53²	46	11	58	5	34.0%	.293	1	1.06	2.35	4.42	4.24	8.8	2.1	7.2	1.2	7.7
	DET	MLB	32	0	0	1	17¹	18	6	7	2	47.5%	.281	-18	1.38	5.20	4.60	4.67	8.8	2.6	3.1	1.0	1.5
C. Rapada*	IOW	AAA	26	7	2	17	55¹	55	25	50	4	50.0%	.345	-4	1.45	3.58	4.98	4.24	9.2	4.6	6.5	0.9	7.7
J. Tata	TOL	AAA	25	4	5	0	82²	67	28	50	8	49.4%	.240	-11	1.15	3.05	4.33	4.44	8.0	3.4	3.9	1.4	10.2
	DET	MLB	25	1	1	0	14	16	8	8	1	30.4%	.341	-13	1.71	7.71	6.10	7.43	10.8	4.7	4.7	0.7	-2.8

Sent to the Marlins in the big Cabrera/Willis deal, **Burke Badenhop** is a highly polished product with outstanding command of a sinker/slider combination that should be good enough for a back-of-the-rotation job when all is said and done. ⊘ The booty for Mike Maroth, **Chris Lambert** is back-end roster filler, another in a long line of weak Cardinals' first-round picks. ⊘ **Aquilino Lopez** can still pitch well in 20-pitch bursts and could be a pseudo-Zumaya until the real one comes back. ⊘ The player-to-be-named-later for Craig Monroe, side-arming southpaw **Clay Rapada** was being used as a closer in the Cubs' system. He'll be a specialist in the majors and could arrive later this season. ⊘ A shoulder problem at the start of last year limited **Jordan Tata** to 96⅔ innings. He remains a decent swingman prospect who doesn't throw as hard as his 6-foot-6, 220-pound frame makes it look like he should.

MANAGER: JIM LEYLAND

YEAR	TEAM	W-L	Pythag +/−	Avg PC	100+ P	120+ P	QS	BQS	REL	REL w Zero R	IBB	Subs	PH	PH Avg	PH HR	SB2	CS2	SB3	CS3	SAC Att	SAC %	POS SAC	Squeeze	Swing	In Play
2006	DET	95-67	-2	94.0	68	2	83	9	390	238	35	51	81	.222	2	49	32	11	6	60	75.0%	44	2	151	116
2007	DET	88-74	-2	94.8	65	1	66	4	441	261	41	67	77	.246	2	86	25	16	4	42	73.8%	30	5	157	127

Leyland didn't get as much praise last year as he did in 2006, but he may have done a better job. Injuries, not much of a problem the year before, tore apart his pitching staff and forced him to get by with the 13th, 14th, and 15th men in the preseason mix. To his credit, he became more matchup-centric without Joel Zumaya and Fernando Rodney, using Bobby Seay to get lefties. Leyland also adjusted to a much-improved offense by dropping from second in the AL in sac bunts to 12th. When you add in the leader-of-men qualities that we can't quantify very well, but that Leyland is often praised for having, you get a manager who is valuable in both the dugout and the clubhouse, a rare combination.

Florida Marlins

You know the scenario. A market hungry for a major league team finally gets its wish only to have its enthusiasm ground down by losing seasons, a lousy venue, and the team's tendency to make horrendously ill-advised trades. Soon attendance is only a fraction of what it was in the team's inaugural season. To make matters worse, a local stadium initiative that had political support and a solid financial plan (as far as these things go), fails because of the team's intransigence. No local white knight rides to the rescue to shore up the franchise's fortunes, no civic-minded sports fan with lots of cash and a love of the game (and profits) who could symbolically represent the relationship between the community and the ballclub. Instead, that relationship continues to erode as the blighted hometown nine—those left behind after the team's stars are dealt to legitimately operated franchises—cash checks paid to them by a carpetbagger installed via the web of connections that form the exclusive assemblage known as "the lords of the game."

This scenario has played itself out in Miami over the last decade, but it is hardly unique to the present day. A half-century ago, the same thing happened in Kansas City. Following the 1954 season, the other AL team owners, after much dickering, approved the sale of the Philadelphia Athletics by the Mack family to Arnold Johnson. Johnson was a business associate of Yankee co-owners Del Webb and Dan Topping and, at the time of the sale, held the deed to Yankee Stadium while also owning the home park of the Yankees' top farm club, the Kansas City Blues. That setup was designed by the three men the year before to prevent the city of Kansas City from purchasing Blues Stadium and leasing it to

---

MARLINS PROSPECTUS

2007 record: 71-91; Fifth place, NL East

Pythagenport record: 72-90

Runs scored per game: 4.88 (6th in NL)

Runs allowed per game: 5.50 (16th in NL)

Team EqA: .270 (3rd in NL)

2007 Batters Age: 27.0 (Youngest in NL)

2007 Pitchers Age: 26.4 (Youngest in NL)

Ballpark: Dolphin Stadium; Slight pitcher's park; Park Factor of .982

2007: A great bullpen is of little use when your big bats can't out-slug your crumbling starting pitching and brutal defense.

2008: Now losing at a ballpark near you, Country Hanley and the Fish.

---

someone other than Johnson who might offer to bring a major league team to Missouri. Thus, Johnson was the only A's bidder who had a stadium in hand. Contingent to officially taking over the A's, Johnson was instructed to sell both parks, notionally severing his baseball ties to Topping and Webb, though the degree to which he complied with regards to Yankee Stadium remains murky. Upon taking control, Johnson moved the team to Kansas City and into the now city-owned Blues Stadium and effectively operated the franchise for the benefit of the Yankees. During his six years as owner of the Athletics, Johnson couldn't even hold up the pretense of being an independent owner, constantly dealing his best players to New York in trades that helped perpetuate the Yankee dynasty while lining Johnson's pockets with the cash that accompanied Yankee castoffs on their way to Missouri. To many observers, then and now, it appeared as though Kansas City was still the Yankees' top farm club.

In their way, the Marlins have had to live with that sort of ownership fixing twice over. After breaking the bank to assemble the 1997 world champions, original Marlins owner/robber baron Wayne Huizenga ordered the team's best players sold off that winter, and unloaded the team itself after the 1998 season. Given the state of the club at that point, it seems a convenient fiction that the man who bought the team, former Yankees minority owner John Henry, was in it for the long haul. Henry had aspired to full ownership control of a major league team for almost a decade and Huizenga's deflowered Marlins merely provided entry into that exclusive fraternity.

A year after Henry bought the Marlins, another former Yankees minority owner, Jeffrey Loria, purchased a 24 percent stake in the Montreal Expos. Loria, too, had long aspired to full major league ownership and quickly began increasing his stake in the team through repeated cash calls—to afford "stars" such as Hideki Irabu and Lee Stevens—eventually reducing the local co-owners to a mere 6 percent share, a gambit that prompted a racketeering suit against both Loria and the commissioner (the suit was subsequently settled out of court before it could do any damage). Loria also began maneuvering the team for relocation by demanding a new ballpark, then sabotaging the plans for the new park by squabbling over funding and then letting the lease option on the site expire. He also ran down the team within its market by eliminating local television and English-language radio broadcasts of the team's games, thereby torpedoing any chance of preserving the team's fan base.

As things reached their nadir in Montreal, and with the industry issuing its empty threat of contraction, Loria and Henry collaborated with Major League Baseball to solve yet another of the game's ownership problems in Boston, where, after failing to secure a new stadium deal of their own, the Red Sox had been put up for sale by the Jean R. Yawkey Trust, which had taken control of the team in 1992. In early 2002 MLB, representing the other 29 owners, including Henry, bought the Expos from Loria for $120 million plus a $38.5 million loan for the remaining cost of the Marlins. Henry then sold the Marlins to Loria at a practical loss—$158.5 million after buying them for $158 million—absorbing three years of inflation for the privilege of having MLB accept his group's bid on the Red Sox. It was a pre-cooked solution; MLB signed off on the deal before Henry and Loria even had a chance to sign it. It's had precisely the desired effects. Under baseball's collective ownership, the Expos continued to disenfranchise the remnants of their fan base and were finally moved to Washington, D.C., for the 2005 season. Once again independently owned, the team will open a brand-new ballpark this season. Under Henry's ownership, the Red Sox have remained in Fenway Park and metamorphosed from a star-crossed provincial team into a 21st-century dynasty able to rival the Yankees both on the field and in the marketplace.

Given those accomplishments, the state of the Marlins amounts to little more than collateral damage, though Loria did get an unanticipated championship for his troubles, thanks in no small part to the leavings of Dave Dombrowski and some quick work by manager Jack McKeon as an in-season fixer. However, Loria's GM, Larry Beinfest, imported from Montreal along with most of the rest of the Expos front office, deserves

credit for shoring up the 2003 rotation by adding Dontrelle Willis and Mark Redman in deals with consenting adults, as well as nabbing Carl Pavano from the game's new wards of the state—and his old club—the Expos.

Despite that ring, there are some admittedly glib similarities between the shenanigans that birthed the Kansas City A's and the Washington Nationals. However, the Arnold Johnson of the present-day scenario, Loria, wasn't just operating a Potemkin franchise in Montreal for the benefit of one other team, he was serving as a franchise killer for the benefit of the industry at large. Having capitalized on their brief window of opportunity in 2003—no small thing, that—the Lorians got down to the business of running a second franchise into the ground in Florida by distributing almost all of the Marlins' name talent about the leagues, lowering payroll to near the minimum, kibitzing about the team's need for new stadium, and threatening to move the franchise to Pocatello, Idaho, or the like.

Over the past three seasons, the club's player transactions have had a Kansas City A's quality to them. While it is admittedly impossible to prove that he could have done better, Beinfest's returns on his wares after tearing down the second Marlins championship team haven't been particularly inspiring (see Table 1), and with Beinfest moving up into the position of team president at the conclusion of the 2007 season, new GM Michael Hill has merely picked up where his predecessor and boss left off. Indeed, Hill's first swap was perhaps the most bitter pill to swallow as it sent third baseman Miguel Cabrera and ace Dontrelle Willis, the last remaining members of the 2003 championship roster, to Dombrowski's contending Tigers. What hurts most is not just the loss of the team's two signature talents, but the fact that Willis just turned 26 and Cabrera won't be 25 until April; established stars that young are the sort of players a team like the Marlins should be building around, not dumping.

Summing up the transactions in Table 1, for five lineup regulars and an ace who'd won a title together in 2003, the Marlins have received a superstar in Hanley Ramirez, one still-healthy and genuinely good starting pitcher prospect in Gaby Hernandez, a goodly amount of replacement-level pitching, and some cost savings. That is not the makings of the next Marlins championship squad. Though it might be partially ascribed to a more difficult trading environment, it amounts to no better than what Dombrowski got when he had to tear down 1997 World Series champions even more hastily at the behest of Huizenga. Of course, that summary leaves out blue-chip center fielder Cameron Maybin and left-hander Adam Miller, but the weakness of the

Table 1. Fishmongering

Year	Outbound	Fresh Fish	Result?
2005	RHPs Josh Beckett and Guillermo Mota, 3B Mike Lowell	SS Hanley Ramirez, RHPs Anibal Sanchez, Harvey Garcia, and Jesus Delgado	A cost-saving push
	1B Carlos Delgado and cash	1B Mike Jacobs, RHP Yusmeiro Petit, INF Grant Psomas	~$27 million in savings
	2B Luis Castillo	RHPs Travis Bowyer, Scott Tyler	Roster slurry; a complete loss
	C Paul Lo Duca	RHP Gaby Hernandez, OF Dante Brinkley	Hernandez has upside, then and now
	CF Juan Pierre	RHPs Ricky Nolasco and Sergio Mitre, LHP Renyel Pinto	Being charitable, a wash that everybody lost
2006	RHP Chris Resop	RHP Kevin Gregg	Resop broke down; Gregg added "closer" to his utility pitcher résumé
	LHPs Jason Vargas, Adam Bostick	RHPs Henry Owens, Matt Lindstrom	Some added value in the pen
2007	RHP Yusmeiro Petit	RHP Jorge Julio	Spontaneous combustion
	3B Miguel Cabrera, LHP Dontrelle Willis	CF Cameron Maybin, C Mike Rabelo, LHP Adam Miller, RHPs Eulogio De La Cruz, Dallas Trahern, and Burke Badenhop	Wait and see

major league roster may yet visit new horrors upon the team in the wake of the Cabrera/Willis deal. Manager Fredi Gonzalez has said that Maybin has a shot to fill the team's opening in center this year, but the kid hasn't really proven himself above A-ball yet. Miller hasn't done much better in the minors, but it's even more likely that he will be similarly sucked into the vacuum that is the Marlins' rotation. In both cases, the premature opportunity would put a huge dent in the unready prospects' futures, thereby greatly diminishing the team's return for their two stars.

When Huizenga had the team torn down after the 1997 championship, it was to make it an affordable proposition for an ill-fated bid to buy the ballclub and build a new stadium by a group led by team president Don Smiley. This time around, the motivations are generally supposed to be the same—except that the Lorians claim they want to set down roots. After five years of dickering over a stadium, are they really any closer? Could the franchise destroyers actually become franchise builders?

Perhaps they can, as the latest development in the stadium deal machinations that have been percolating for years might prove decisive. In mid-December, local political leadership in the Miami city commission and the Miami-Dade County commission considered the components of a new deal that proposes that the team lay out more cash up front but spend less overall, while the county would pay more in tourist tax revenues to make a proposed stadium built on the site of the Orange Bowl a done deal (see Table 2). This new deal could close the long-debated and strangely persistent "funding gap" of $30 million that had been carried over from stadium proposal to stadium proposal over the years, all while the price tag on the project escalated from $325 million to $490 million. The Lorians have always insisted that this funding gap be closed with

someone else's money, the usual target for log-rolling being the understandably intractable state legislature. In 2005, with the stadium initiative stalled on this very point, the Marlins started threatening to relocate to San Antonio or wherever else they might find a pliable local government not too squeamish about cutting a stadium deal with a group that would have burned two other, larger cities willing to pay hundreds of millions of dollars to construct a stadium for them. Unsurprisingly, they did not find municipalities desperate to take them in and seemed forced to cut a deal to stay in southern Florida. In addition to closing that gap, this latest initiative may depend upon the absence of any state money to make it happen.

The good news, such as it is, is that the Marlins have finally expressed a willingness to make do with the Orange Bowl site if that's what it takes to achieve a stadium deal. The city would build a parking garage, the Marlins would absorb any cost overruns, and the county would own the $525 million stadium. And yes, it would have a retractable roof, because if the Brewers can have a ballpark with a moon roof it doesn't need, then by comparison, the Marlins simply gots to have one. This might be a case of the carpetbaggers finally choosing to be good actors, or a bottom-line realization that nobody else will give the Lorians a stadium during a time when state and local governments are being pinched by a nationwide economic downturn. Should all this be achievable, the new stadium could reasonably be expected to open in 2011.

In the meantime, back in the old park, the Marlins actually have a few things going for them. Last year, their lineup ranked among the league's best, behind only those of the division rival Mets and Phillies. Even after dealing away Cabrera, there are still assets in place—Ramirez is an MVP-caliber hitter and second baseman Dan Uggla, right fielder Jeremy Hermida, and left fielder

Table 2. Building the Fish Palace

Source	2/07 Proposal	12/07 Proposal
Budget	$490 million	$525 million
City	$108 million	$121 million in tourist tax revenue
County	$145 million in bonded tax revenues	$199 million in tourist tax revenue
	$162 million in bonds repaid by the team through gate receipts and concession sales	$50 million "General Obligation Fund"
Lorians	$45 million up front $162 million in bond repayments	$155 million up front
Total	**$460 million**	**$525 million**
Balance	($30 million short)	Even Steven

Josh Willingham all would be outstanding contributors to an eight-cylinder offense, and there's reason to hope that first baseman Mike Jacobs will improve entering his age-27 season. The problem is that this isn't a young group; with the exception of Hermida and Ramirez, the Marlins' hitters are already into their peak seasons and thus are better described as useful complementary players than as budding superstars along the lines of Han-Ram, who stands alone as the future of the franchise. Then again, the fact that Cabrera will be suiting up in someone else's uniform prior to his 25th birthday is a cold reminder that even Ramirez's Fish Clock is already a third of the way toward striking its free agency alarm.

A more urgent issue is that, shorn of Cabrera and with Hill having non-tendered incumbent backstop Miguel Olivo, the lineup now lacks not only a major league-ready center fielder, but also remotely adequate replacements at third base and catcher. Given the organization's almost ludicrous inability to find a center fielder since trading Juan Pierre to the Cubs after the 2005 season, the additional vacancies should be cause for considerable alarm as they leave the lineup just five men deep. The fact that the front office has been talking up Mike Rabelo, the backup catcher acquired in the deal with Detroit, as a possible starter behind the plate should provide damning evidence that fielding an also-ran in the International League would suit ownership's purposes just fine if it didn't handicap their chances for a new stadium.

The pitching staff, meanwhile, is still trying to pick up the pieces from the disappointments that came with the initial wave of hurler help acquired and/or promoted in 2006 after the last big tear-down. Of that year's two young pitching stars, Josh Johnson is already lost for the season following August 2007 Tommy John surgery, and Anibal Sanchez is unlikely to be ready by Opening Day as he continues to recover from a labrum injury that also resulted in his filing a grievance against the team alleging that he was demoted to the minors after suffering the injury. That leaves the team with Scott Olsen, Sergio Mitre, and whatever other willing bodies can mark time until Gaby Hernandez and the cadre of starters who were yesterday's Jupiter Hammerheads become tomorrow's Miami Marlins.

You can invest hope and faith in the organization's Fish-finding formula, but so far, the results aren't all that promising, and only underscore the essential unpredictability of young pitching as a commodity. Add in the off-the-rack qualities of the lineup beyond Hanley Ramirez's nascent superstardom, and you've got a team on which Ramirez might be the only genuinely important working part to build around for the new stadium's 2011 opening. Then again, getting that new stadium might be just what it takes to get the Lorians to strive for stability. If so, Miami might yet join Boston and Washington, D.C., as a winner in the Great Franchise Swaperoo Caper of 2002. If so, Loria may no longer be dogged by the ghost of Arnold Johnson, but rather than of Johnson's equally controversial, but far more successful successor, Charlie Finley, the owner-operator who steered the A's from joke to juggernaut.

HITTERS

Reggie Abercrombie			CF							Bats: R	Throws: R		Height: 6' 3"		Weight: 220		Born: July 15, 1980			Age: 27	

YEAR	TEAM	LVL	AGE	PA	R	2B	3B	HR	RBI	BB	SO	SB	CS	EqBRR	AVG	OBP	SLG	MLVr	EqAVG	EqOBP	EqSLG	EqA	VORP	DEFENSE	
2005	JUP	A+	24	321	51	12	3	15	45	14	87	19	6	2.1	.274	.317	.485	.191	.234	.270	.413	.235	-4.4	73-CF	5
2005	CAR	AA	24	197	28	7	2	10	23	11	40	7	5	-0.3	.253	.315	.483	.080	.214	.264	.412	.227	-4.3	46-CF	2
2006	FLO	MLB	25	281	39	12	2	5	24	18	78	6	5	-2.1	.212	.271	.333	-.264	.219	.277	.352	.217	-10.7	67-CF	1
2007	ABQ	AAA	26	379	71	23	9	17	55	11	95	41	6	2.5	.323	.361	.584	.189	.258	.296	.478	.269	3.0	74-RF	-13
2007	FLO	MLB	26	80	16	3	0	2	5	2	22	7	1	2.3	.197	.238	.316	-.358	.211	.250	.329	.216	-3.0	14-CF	4
2008	HOU	MLB	27	428	53	22	3	15	53	20	112	30	8	1.3	.250	.294	.435	-.105	.252	.296	.443	.254	6.2	102-CF	-4

Breakout: 38% Improve: 58% Collapse: 20% Attrition: 23%　　　　Comparables: Charlton Jimerson, Gerald Williams, Chris Jones, Nick Gorneault

Given an audition as the Marlins' starting center fielder in 2006, the toolsy Abercrombie played poorly and lost the job by midseason. In May of last year, he got a second chance in a platoon role; he failed, again. There's room for him on a roster as a pinch-runner and defensive replacement—he can run like the wind—but he should only start a couple times a month. The Astros snagged Abercrombie off of waivers in October, and he'll try to snag a spot as Michael Bourn's understudy. If Bourn is only an echo of a major league hitter, then Abercrombie is the fossil of that echo, the after-image of the shadow of something that wasn't quite there in the first place.

Alfredo Amezaga **UT** Bats: S Throws: R Height: 5' 10" Weight: 180 Born: January 16, 1978 Age: 30

YEAR	TEAM	LVL	AGE	PA	R	2B	3B	HR	RBI	BB	SO	SB	CS	EqBRR	AVG	OBP	SLG	MLVr	EqAVG	EqOBP	EqSLG	EqA	VORP	DEFENSE			
2005	IND	AAA	27	211	28	12	2	1	12	17	27	14	7	-2.4	.341	.398	.443	.208	.303	.361	.404	.266	11.9	21-SS	1	14-2B	2
2006	FLO	MLB	28	378	43	9	3	3	19	33	46	20	12	0.3	.260	.332	.332	-.117	.268	.340	.348	.243	-0.5	60-CF	0	14-2B	2
2007	FLO	MLB	29	448	46	14	9	2	30	35	52	13	7	-1.5	.263	.324	.358	-.090	.276	.339	.381	.252	2.9	72-CF	0	14-SS	-2
2008	FLO	MLB	30	382	47	15	4	2	29	32	48	11	4	1.0	.262	.328	.348	-.153	.263	.327	.356	.240	3.5	91-CF	0		

Breakout: 13% Improve: 30% Collapse: 39% Attrition: 27%   Comparables: John Moses, Quinton McCracken, Dave Collins, Jose Macias

This former Angels prospect had never played the outfield until doing so in Triple-A in 2005 as a member of the Pirates organization. Since then, he's led the Marlins in defensive innings in center field. It should come as no surprise, then, that he's been part of the massive defensive problems plaguing the Marlins; he's slightly below average out there with a mediocre arm. If Amezaga could hit, you'd forgive that, but he hits like the fifth infielder he really is. If returned to that role, he'd be a valuable bench player, but that might have to wait until Cameron Maybin is ready.

Robert Andino **SS** Bats: R Throws: R Height: 6' 0" Weight: 170 Born: April 25, 1984 Age: 24

YEAR	TEAM	LVL	AGE	PA	R	2B	3B	HR	RBI	BB	SO	SB	CS	EqBRR	AVG	OBP	SLG	MLVr	EqAVG	EqOBP	EqSLG	EqA	VORP	DEFENSE	
2005	CAR	AA	21	570	63	30	0	5	48	37	111	22	7	-1.3	.269	.324	.357	-.067	.233	.279	.319	.212	-17.9	124-SS	-1
2005	FLO	MLB	21	50	4	4	0	0	1	5	8	1	0	0.1	.159	.245	.250	-.411	.159	.245	.250	.176	-2.8	14-SS	-5
2006	ABQ	AAA	22	549	70	18	6	8	46	33	100	13	11	-1.8	.255	.303	.363	-.209	.221	.266	.318	.204	-20.8	113-SS	6
2007	ABQ	AAA	23	644	85	25	13	13	50	40	129	21	13	-3.9	.278	.322	.428	-.131	.237	.283	.368	.225	-5.3	136-SS	-13
2008	FLO	MLB	24	576	61	27	5	9	53	36	121	14	5	0.9	.246	.296	.367	-.196	.246	.295	.376	.230	4.2	135-SS	-6

Breakout: 40% Improve: 68% Collapse: 12% Attrition: 19%   Comparables: Edwin Diaz, Dan Cey, Eric Owens, Tony Manahan

Andino's power boost last year is probably real, the result of his reaching physical maturity. That puts him in the picture should the Marlins tire of Hanley Ramirez's "defense" and move their star to the outfield. Andino has a strong defensive reputation built around an excellent arm and would be viable at shortstop even if he only managed a .250 EqA. He'll have a starting job somewhere in 2010.

Aaron Boone **INF** Bats: R Throws: R Height: 6' 2" Weight: 200 Born: March 9, 1973 Age: 35

YEAR	TEAM	LVL	AGE	PA	R	2B	3B	HR	RBI	BB	SO	SB	CS	EqBRR	AVG	OBP	SLG	MLVr	EqAVG	EqOBP	EqSLG	EqA	VORP	DEFENSE	
2005	CLE	MLB	32	565	61	19	1	16	60	35	92	9	3	-0.8	.243	.299	.378	-.121	.250	.316	.396	.250	-2.6	139-3B	2
2006	CLE	MLB	33	392	50	19	1	7	46	27	62	5	4	-1.8	.251	.314	.370	-.146	.254	.323	.380	.245	-5.8	96-3B	-12
2007	FLO	MLB	34	228	27	11	0	5	28	21	41	2	0	0.7	.286	.388	.423	.126	.291	.392	.444	.297	10.9	44-1B	-4
2008	WAS	MLB	35	209	24	9	1	5	25	17	35	2	1	-0.1	.255	.327	.401	-.088	.255	.327	.409	.253	3.6	53-3B	-4

Breakout: 19% Improve: 41% Collapse: 36% Attrition: 39%   Comparables: Bob Kennedy, Charlie Hayes, Scott Brosius, Chuck Hinton

Boone was having one of his better seasons and had moved into a semi-regular role in June when knee pain pushed him to the DL. He never returned, finally undergoing arthroscopic surgery in August. He's expected to be fully recovered by the spring, which he'll spend with the Nationals, who signed him to a one-year, $1 million deal.

Joe Borchard   **OF**   Bats: S   Throws: R   Height: 6' 4"   Weight: 230   Born: November 25, 1978   Age: 29

YEAR	TEAM	LVL	AGE	PA	R	2B	3B	HR	RBI	BB	SO	SB	CS	EqBRR	AVG	OBP	SLG	MLVr	EqAVG	EqOBP	EqSLG	EqA	VORP	DEFENSE		
2005	CHR	AAA	26	550	69	20	0	29	67	50	143	6	4	0.8	.263	.335	.480	.068	.237	.308	.429	.251	-5.2	109-RF	-2	13-CF -2
2006	FLO	MLB	27	261	30	7	1	10	28	28	66	0	2	-0.7	.230	.322	.400	-.065	.235	.326	.413	.253	-0.8	37-RF	1	
2007	ABQ	AAA	28	93	19	3	0	8	28	15	12	1	2	-0.2	.355	.452	.711	.531	.312	.409	.610	.327	11.3	15-LF	-2	
2007	FLO	MLB	28	202	20	9	0	4	19	21	60	4	0	0.7	.196	.287	.313	-.257	.197	.292	.315	.220	-7.5	31-RF	3	
2008	ATL	MLB	29	146	17	5	1	6	20	15	35	2	1	-0.1	.249	.328	.431	-.051	.247	.326	.440	.258	4.9	38-RF	-2	

Breakout: 35% Improve: 55% Collapse: 33% Attrition: 51%   Comparables: Eduardo Perez, Joe Vitiello, Mike Young, Dave Clark

If nothing else, over the past two years the Marlins have provided final verdicts on some players making their final appeals for major league status. They let Abercrombie fail, and they did the same with Borchard, making him the starting right fielder last year and watching him hit .203/.293/.347 through mid-May. He started just six times after May 10 and was designated for assignment on August 8. Verdict: Borchard can't play in the majors. Still, the Braves signed him to a minor league deal and attached a spring training invite to see for themselves.

Miguel Cabrera   **3B**   Bats: R   Throws: R   Height: 6' 4"   Weight: 240   Born: April 18, 1983   Age: 25

YEAR	TEAM	LVL	AGE	PA	R	2B	3B	HR	RBI	BB	SO	SB	CS	EqBRR	AVG	OBP	SLG	MLVr	EqAVG	EqOBP	EqSLG	EqA	VORP	DEFENSE		
2005	FLO	MLB	22	685	106	43	2	33	116	64	125	1	0	-0.1	.323	.385	.561	.370	.326	.391	.575	.321	68.5	124-LF	-14	27-3B 1
2006	FLO	MLB	23	676	112	50	2	26	114	86	108	9	6	-3.6	.339	.430	.568	.443	.341	.433	.572	.335	78.7	151-3B	4	
2007	FLO	MLB	24	680	91	38	2	34	119	79	127	2	1	-4.0	.320	.401	.565	.377	.320	.404	.579	.326	71.4	147-3B	6	
2008	DET	MLB	25	657	96	36	2	28	104	67	113	5	2	-1.2	.300	.376	.515	.202	.301	.378	.538	.310	47.8	153-3B	2	

Breakout: 2% Improve: 22% Collapse: 33% Attrition: 3%   Comparables: Cal Ripken, Kent Hrbek, Greg Luzinski, Chris Brown

Different defensive metrics serve different purposes. Our Fielding Runs Above Average is strongest in terms of comparing performances across eras or levels, but it can produce different results than the others, which seem unanimous in their condemnation of Cabrera's work in the field. Even if he can't play defense, Cabrera is an MVP candidate every year thanks to his bat. Using Bill James's similarity scores, which don't adjust for era, Cabrera's top statistical comp at every age has been Hank Aaron, and if the visual doesn't work very well, the numbers don't lie—he's in the early stages of a Hall of Fame career. Moving to the Tigers changes nothing for him, save the possibility that he'll spend some time at DH or even first base. Concerns about his weight are overblown; if he was ripped, they'd say other things about him.

Brett Carroll   **OF**   Bats: R   Throws: R   Height: 6' 0"   Weight: 190   Born: October 3, 1982   Age: 25

YEAR	TEAM	LVL	AGE	PA	R	2B	3B	HR	RBI	BB	SO	SB	CS	EqBRR	AVG	OBP	SLG	MLVr	EqAVG	EqOBP	EqSLG	EqA	VORP	DEFENSE		
2005	GRB	A	22	449	57	28	1	18	54	17	108	10	10	-2.3	.243	.296	.447	-.012	.190	.224	.326	.182	-45.7	76-RF	2	20-CF 2
2006	JUP	A+	23	244	31	12	1	8	30	18	48	9	3	0.1	.241	.324	.417	.112	.216	.283	.387	.233	-11.0	52-RF	-4	
2006	CAR	AA	23	280	29	15	3	9	30	18	62	4	1	-1.3	.231	.303	.422	.029	.222	.283	.420	.240	-1.9	46-CF	5	27-RF 1
2007	CAR	AA	24	117	9	13	0	3	12	12	20	0	2	-2.5	.270	.359	.490	.169	.252	.325	.447	.262	1.0	21-RF	2	
2007	ABQ	AAA	24	346	60	21	6	19	70	18	69	0	4	-0.1	.314	.361	.597	.200	.269	.317	.506	.271	10.9	39-RF	3	34-CF 1
2007	FLO	MLB	24	53	10	1	0	0	2	3	15	0	0	0.7	.184	.231	.204	-.528	.184	.231	.204	.134	-5.2			
2008	FLO	MLB	25	533	55	29	3	16	66	35	123	5	4	0.4	.237	.297	.408	-.145	.237	.296	.418	.240	-0.8	125-RF	-1	

Breakout: 25% Improve: 50% Collapse: 14% Attrition: 18%   Comparables: Ray Sadler, Mike Vento, Tyrone Woods, Andy Bevins

The lack of real prospects in the Marlins' system allowed Carroll, a tenth-round pick in 2004, to advance rapidly despite not hitting anywhere at any time. The second he did hit, the Fish pushed him to the majors, where he flopped in a September tryout. When you're a nominal tools guy and you go 0-for-6 stealing bases, it's a bad sign. Carroll is Abercrombie with less natural ability.

Chris Coghlan　2B

Bats: L　Throws: R　Height: 6' 1"　Weight: 190　Born: June 18, 1985　Age: 23

YEAR	TEAM	LVL	AGE	PA	R	2B	3B	HR	RBI	BB	SO	SB	CS	EqBRR	AVG	OBP	SLG	MLVr	EqAVG	EqOBP	EqSLG	EqA	VORP	DEFENSE	
2006	JAM	A-	21	111	14	5	1	0	12	13	9	5	2	-0.7	.298	.373	.372	.111	.245	.309	.316	.227	-4.2	19-3B	-2
2007	GRB	A	22	360	60	26	4	10	64	47	43	19	4	1.6	.325	.419	.534	.331	.261	.341	.409	.265	12.4	75-2B	5
2007	JUP	A+	22	148	17	5	3	2	18	15	19	5	1	2.1	.200	.277	.331	-.130	.212	.277	.341	.221	-5.2	31-2B	6
2008	FLO	MLB	23	598	75	36	5	8	53	56	97	19	7	1.4	.254	.326	.384	-.112	.255	.325	.393	.250	12.5	140-2B	7

Breakout: 28%　Improve: 67%　Collapse: 15%　Attrition: 4%　　Comparables: Scott Pratt, Mitch Maier, Dan Cholowsky, Jason Romano

A third baseman in college, Coghlan has been learning second base for a year, and the early returns have been good enough to keep him at the keystone, the position he played in last year's Futures Game after raking in the Sally League. He was less successful after a promotion to the High-A Florida State League, but an injury may be to blame for that. With his solid on-base skills and improving defense at second, Coghlan is sort of the anti-Uggla.

Alejandro De Aza　CF

Bats: L　Throws: L　Height: 6' 0"　Weight: 174　Born: April 11, 1984　Age: 24

YEAR	TEAM	LVL	AGE	PA	R	2B	3B	HR	RBI	BB	SO	SB	CS	EqBRR	AVG	OBP	SLG	MLVr	EqAVG	EqOBP	EqSLG	EqA	VORP	DEFENSE			
2005	JUP	A+	21	554	75	24	9	3	37	58	87	34	17	-2.3	.286	.370	.394	.157	.245	.318	.344	.237	-7.1	53-CF	3	49-LF	-2
2006	CAR	AA	22	266	40	12	2	2	16	21	46	27	10	1.0	.278	.346	.374	.061	.261	.321	.370	.250	0.5	51-CF	-3		
2007	FLO	MLB	23	158	14	8	2	0	8	6	37	2	0	0.8	.229	.261	.313	-.290	.234	.271	.317	.210	-5.7	34-CF	-3		
2008	FLO	MLB	24	350	45	18	3	6	32	29	67	13	4	1.5	.260	.324	.390	-.103	.261	.323	.400	.252	6.5	84-CF	0		

Breakout: 33%　Improve: 54%　Collapse: 22%　Attrition: 27%　　Comparables: Ty Cline, Mickey Rivers, Dave Martinez, Herm Winningham

Even prospect hounds were scratching their heads when the Marlins tabbed De Aza as their Opening Day center fielder last year, but a .354 batting average in March combined with the absence of better ideas elevated De Aza from organizational player to major leaguer during spring training. It was sort of working—De Aza was hitting an empty .313 a week into the season—when a sore ankle, later discovered to be a broken ankle, sat him down for four months. He's not a starter in the majors, but then teams shouldn't give guys jobs because some singles fall in during exhibition season.

Matt Dominguez　3B

Bats: R　Throws: R　Height: 6' 2"　Weight: 180　Born: August 28, 1989　Age: 18

YEAR	TEAM	LVL	AGE	PA	R	2B	3B	HR	RBI	BB	SO	SB	CS	EqBRR	AVG	OBP	SLG	MLVr	EqAVG	EqOBP	EqSLG	EqA	VORP	DEFENSE	
2007	JAM	A-	17	38	3	2	0	1	4	1	12	0	0	-0.1	.189	.211	.324	-.300	.162	.184	.270	.131	-10.2		
2008	FLO	MLB	18	507	32	19	2	5	38	30	142	9	4	0.1	.192	.243	.276	-.446	.193	.242	.282	.172	-30.0	120-3B	-2

Breakout: NA　Improve: NA　Collapse: NA　Attrition: NA　　Comparables: Corey Smith, Brandon Wood, Trevor Plouffe, Josh Murray

The Marlins took one of the five-best high school hitters available in last year's draft with the 12th overall pick, snagging this third baseman out of Chatsworth, California. Dominguez's professional debut was a write-off; what you want to note is that he didn't turn 18 until the season was almost over, making him an incredibly young prospect. His glove is considered above-average, and his bat is expected to provide more power than average.

Jeremy Hermida　RF

Bats: L　Throws: R　Height: 6' 3"　Weight: 210　Born: January 30, 1984　Age: 24

YEAR	TEAM	LVL	AGE	PA	R	2B	3B	HR	RBI	BB	SO	SB	CS	EqBRR	AVG	OBP	SLG	MLVr	EqAVG	EqOBP	EqSLG	EqA	VORP	DEFENSE	
2005	CAR	AA	21	507	77	29	2	18	63	111	89	23	2	3.7	.293	.457	.518	.366	.253	.402	.452	.303	26.4	113-RF	1
2005	FLO	MLB	21	47	9	2	0	4	11	6	12	2	0	0.5	.293	.383	.634	.434	.293	.383	.634	.331	6.1		
2006	FLO	MLB	22	348	37	19	1	5	28	33	70	4	1	-0.5	.251	.332	.368	-.073	.253	.336	.373	.253	-0.2	78-RF	-8
2007	FLO	MLB	23	484	54	32	1	18	63	47	105	3	4	-3.8	.296	.369	.501	.210	.304	.379	.525	.300	27.3	111-RF	1
2008	FLO	MLB	24	532	80	31	2	19	71	68	106	9	3	-0.4	.284	.380	.485	.135	.285	.378	.497	.296	28.7	125-RF	0

Breakout: 27%　Improve: 56%　Collapse: 19%　Attrition: 15%　　Comparables: Ben Grieve, Clint Hurdle, Steve Kemp, Mel Hall

One of the positives to emerge from the Marlins' disappointing 2007 season was that Hermida finally stayed in the lineup and finally hit. From July 1 on, Hermida hit .339/.403/.559 while missing just one game. He hit both lefties and righties, showed off a good arm in right field, and established himself as the team's number-three hitter. Still just 24, he could make the All-Star team this year.

Mike Jacobs 1B

Bats: L Throws: R Height: 6' 3" Weight: 215 Born: October 30, 1980 Age: 27

YEAR	TEAM	LVL	AGE	PA	R	2B	3B	HR	RBI	BB	SO	SB	CS	EqBRR	AVG	OBP	SLG	MLVr	EqAVG	EqOBP	EqSLG	EqA	VORP	DEFENSE	
2005	BIN	AA	24	482	66	37	2	25	93	35	94	1	2	-1.4	.321	.376	.589	.375	.285	.338	.525	.286	28.0	52-1B 1	41-C -12
2005	NYN	MLB	24	112	19	7	0	11	23	10	22	0	0	-0.3	.310	.375	.710	.520	.310	.375	.730	.343	14.9	27-1B -5	
2006	FLO	MLB	25	520	54	37	1	20	77	45	105	3	0	-0.7	.262	.325	.473	.065	.266	.330	.482	.277	12.2	111-1B -3	
2007	FLO	MLB	26	460	57	27	2	17	54	31	101	1	2	-1.7	.265	.317	.458	.042	.271	.328	.481	.271	10.5	101-1B -10	
2008	FLO	MLB	27	551	66	31	2	24	85	47	117	4	1	-0.9	.262	.329	.476	.020	.263	.328	.487	.271	16.7	129-1B -5	

Breakout: 7% Improve: 39% Collapse: 29% Attrition: 9% Comparables: Tino Martinez, Dave Revering, Paul Sorrento, Greg Walker

It's easy to point to the thumb injury Jacobs sustained on April 20 as the reason for his falloff last season. After missing six days to rest it, though, he went on a 7-for-18 tear with four extra-base hits and hit .275/.310/.500 between suffering the injury and being placed on the DL on May 17. After he returned on June 23, Jacobs batted just .261/.306/.448. It seems the time off, not the injury itself, is what messed him up, as his walk rate and K/BB were the problem, not his contact or power. With his job safe entering his age-27 season, he seems like a good bet to have his best year.

Todd Linden OF

Bats: S Throws: R Height: 6' 3" Weight: 220 Born: June 30, 1980 Age: 28

YEAR	TEAM	LVL	AGE	PA	R	2B	3B	HR	RBI	BB	SO	SB	CS	EqBRR	AVG	OBP	SLG	MLVr	EqAVG	EqOBP	EqSLG	EqA	VORP	DEFENSE	
2005	FRE	AAA	25	415	81	25	4	30	80	62	97	6	2	1.8	.321	.437	.682	.568	.274	.383	.577	.314	35.1	86-RF -4	
2005	SFN	MLB	25	187	20	8	0	4	13	10	54	3	0	0.3	.216	.280	.333	-.224	.215	.278	.337	.217	-6.8	36-RF 0	
2006	FRE	AAA	26	221	31	11	3	5	23	29	44	5	0	2.0	.278	.385	.449	.157	.251	.351	.408	.271	1.6	41-RF 4	
2006	SFN	MLB	26	89	15	4	2	2	5	9	20	1	0	0.9	.273	.356	.455	.079	.269	.360	.449	.281	3.4	15-LF 0	
2007	SFN	MLB	27	60	6	1	0	0	3	5	23	0	0	0.3	.182	.250	.200	-.505	.182	.250	.200	.143	-5.8		
2007	FLO	MLB	27	144	15	7	1	1	8	14	36	4	0	0.0	.271	.347	.364	-.032	.281	.361	.375	.268	3.4	13-LF -2	
2008	FLO	MLB	28	190	25	9	1	6	23	20	49	3	1	0.2	.254	.342	.436	-.017	.254	.341	.447	.269	6.8		

Breakout: 31% Improve: 49% Collapse: 24% Attrition: 40% Comparables: Gabe Gross, Ron Swoboda, Duke Carmel, Danny Goodwin

There's no mystery here. Todd Linden didn't make it because Todd Linden wasn't very good. He slugged .500 in the PCL just once, hit .280 there just once, and for some reason, the Giants kept acting as if he were Justin Upton. As long as Hermida and Willingham stay healthy, there's no role for Linden in Florida.

Miguel Olivo C

Bats: R Throws: R Height: 6' 0" Weight: 220 Born: July 15, 1978 Age: 29

YEAR	TEAM	LVL	AGE	PA	R	2B	3B	HR	RBI	BB	SO	SB	CS	EqBRR	AVG	OBP	SLG	MLVr	EqAVG	EqOBP	EqSLG	EqA	VORP	DEFENSE	
2005	TAC	AAA	26	99	13	4	1	3	21	7	19	8	1	0.0	.233	.293	.400	-.135	.209	.263	.363	.229	-3.2	15-C 1	
2005	SEA	MLB	26	157	14	4	0	5	18	4	49	1	1	-0.7	.151	.172	.276	-.554	.153	.185	.293	.149	-14.8	46-C -2	
2005	SDN	MLB	26	124	16	7	1	4	16	4	31	6	1	-1.7	.304	.341	.487	.196	.313	.350	.522	.297	11.1	32-C 0	
2006	FLO	MLB	27	452	52	22	3	16	58	9	103	2	3	-0.5	.263	.287	.440	-.046	.267	.291	.448	.248	5.9	111-C 6	
2007	FLO	MLB	28	469	43	20	4	16	60	14	123	3	2	0.6	.237	.262	.405	-.155	.242	.271	.422	.233	0.3	111-C 2	
2008	KCA	MLB	29	312	29	15	2	8	39	11	75	5	2	0.0	.241	.273	.388	-.180	.236	.270	.399	.232	-1.8	76-C 1	

Breakout: 25% Improve: 48% Collapse: 25% Attrition: 35% Comparables: Ned Yost, Jason LaRue, Jeff Newman, Jim Hegan

Not that the Marlins aren't taking 2008 seriously, but they didn't bother to tender Olivo a contract. That meant cutting loose someone who last year caught 122 games, threw out about a third of opposing basestealers, and slugged a respectable .405. There are warts there, but when a team's payroll is going to be less than 20 percent of its revenue sharing receipts, they can afford to go to arbitration with their starting catcher. The Royals should consider that Olivo would make a better platoon half (843 career OPS vs. LHP; 620 vs. RHP) than full-timer.

Hanley Ramirez SS

Bats: R Throws: R Height: 6' 3" Weight: 200 Born: December 23, 1983 Age: 24

YEAR	TEAM	LVL	AGE	PA	R	2B	3B	HR	RBI	BB	SO	SB	CS	EqBRR	AVG	OBP	SLG	MLVr	EqAVG	EqOBP	EqSLG	EqA	VORP	DEFENSE	
2005	PME	AA	21	519	66	21	7	6	52	39	62	26	13	3.0	.271	.335	.385	.000	.239	.300	.343	.228	-4.3	109-SS 2	
2006	FLO	MLB	22	700	119	46	11	17	59	56	128	51	15	11.2	.292	.353	.480	.150	.300	.362	.494	.291	54.9	150-SS 3	
2007	FLO	MLB	23	706	125	48	6	29	81	52	95	51	14	1.7	.332	.386	.562	.367	.344	.400	.595	.324	89.5	146-SS -7	
2008	FLO	MLB	24	672	113	42	6	21	86	59	92	38	10	3.3	.306	.371	.501	.162	.307	.370	.513	.298	59.7	156-SS 3	

Breakout: 24% Improve: 50% Collapse: 22% Attrition: 8% Comparables: Jim Fregosi, Carney Lansford, Paul Molitor, Andy Carey

It's hard to recall the last time a player led his league in VORP and was neither a mainstream nor stathead MVP candidate, but that was the case for Ramirez last year. The catch is that VORP doesn't take into account a player's defense, and Ramirez's work at shortstop was so bad that it knocked him down to about the eighth-best player in the league. He's a star and a stud; he's just one who's on a fast track to the outfield. Think Derek Jeter without the rings or the reputation. Now think about future MVP awards.

John Raynor OF Bats: R Throws: R Height: 6' 2" Weight: 185 Born: January 4, 1984 Age: 24

YEAR	TEAM	LVL	AGE	PA	R	2B	3B	HR	RBI	BB	SO	SB	CS	EqBRR	AVG	OBP	SLG	MLVr	EqAVG	EqOBP	EqSLG	EqA	VORP	DEFENSE			
2006	JAM	A-	22	223	36	8	4	4	21	17	51	21	2	3.6	.286	.356	.427	.148	.223	.278	.350	.228	-15.8	28-CF	3	15-RF	1
2007	GRB	A	23	526	110	28	8	13	57	66	98	54	8	7.8	.333	.429	.519	.333	.249	.331	.387	.259	-7.3	106-LF	-2		
2008	FLO	MLB	24	578	77	31	6	12	52	54	146	28	8	1.9	.248	.325	.403	-.093	.249	.325	.412	.257	4.4	135-LF	0		

Breakout: 34% Improve: 59% Collapse: 12% Attrition: 9%   Comparables: Steve Martin, Reid Gorecki, Richard Barnwell, Brian Barton

Raynor earned South Atlantic League MVP honors last year, but there are reasons to be skeptical of his performance. A ninth-round pick in 2006 out of UNC Wilmington, Raynor didn't turn pro until after his senior year, so most of his Sally League competition was two to four years younger than he was. He's certainly shown more talent than expected—he can fly, play center field, and has a line-drive bat—but we want to see him pick on kids his own size before we believe.

Cody Ross OF Bats: R Throws: L Height: 5' 9" Weight: 205 Born: December 23, 1980 Age: 27

YEAR	TEAM	LVL	AGE	PA	R	2B	3B	HR	RBI	BB	SO	SB	CS	EqBRR	AVG	OBP	SLG	MLVr	EqAVG	EqOBP	EqSLG	EqA	VORP	DEFENSE			
2005	LVG	AAA	24	448	79	21	4	22	63	49	103	4	2	-0.8	.267	.348	.509	.028	.225	.299	.415	.245	-9.5	58-RF	-1	47-CF	-4
2006	LOU	AAA	25	64	11	1	0	3	6	13	12	0	2	0.0	.340	.484	.540	.500	.294	.438	.490	.310	6.9				
2006	FLO	MLB	25	279	30	11	1	11	37	22	61	0	1	-0.6	.212	.284	.396	-.149	.216	.288	.408	.238	-5.7	25-RF	-2	23-LF	-2
2007	FLO	MLB	26	197	35	19	0	12	39	20	38	2	0	1.6	.335	.411	.653	.529	.337	.416	.663	.348	28.8	27-CF	-4	12-RF	2
2008	FLO	MLB	27	302	41	17	1	14	44	30	64	3	1	0.0	.270	.349	.493	.082	.271	.348	.505	.283	17.1	73-CF	-2		

Breakout: 15% Improve: 41% Collapse: 27% Attrition: 18%   Comparables: Joe Charboneau, Bubba Trammell, Jeffrey Leonard, Ivan Calderon

As Ross bounced around the last few seasons—he was traded twice and sold once in 26 months—his status took a hit as the perception of him changed from prospect to journeyman. That's a bit unfair. He's not going to hit .335 again, but he had more development left in him than might have been thought. He's a bit fringy as a center fielder, but is the only one of the Marlins' non-Maybin candidates with any chance of hitting, so he should play.

Matt Treanor C Bats: R Throws: R Height: 6' 0" Weight: 210 Born: March 3, 1976 Age: 32

YEAR	TEAM	LVL	AGE	PA	R	2B	3B	HR	RBI	BB	SO	SB	CS	EqBRR	AVG	OBP	SLG	MLVr	EqAVG	EqOBP	EqSLG	EqA	VORP	DEFENSE	
2005	FLO	MLB	29	154	10	8	0	0	13	16	28	0	0	-0.6	.201	.301	.261	-.273	.201	.301	.254	.200	-4.5	41-C	-2
2006	FLO	MLB	30	185	12	6	1	2	14	19	34	0	1	-0.7	.229	.328	.318	-.164	.234	.332	.323	.236	-2.8	49-C	6
2007	FLO	MLB	31	198	16	7	1	4	19	19	29	0	0	-0.9	.269	.357	.392	.021	.275	.362	.415	.273	8.2	50-C	-6
2008	FLO	MLB	32	204	19	8	1	3	19	20	33	1	1	-0.6	.239	.325	.346	-.175	.240	.324	.354	.235	2.1	51-C	-1

Breakout: 17% Improve: 36% Collapse: 44% Attrition: 44%   Comparables: Greg Olson, Al Evans, Larry Cox, Mickey Grasso

We're contractually obligated to remind you that Treanor is married to volleyball star Misty May. (The enforcing clause in that contract states that if we don't, Treanor will come to one of our events wearing his wife's work clothes. No one wants that.) Treanor is a catch-and-throw backup who will play a bit more this season now that Mike Rabelo is the nominal starter.

Dan Uggla 2B Bats: R Throws: R Height: 5' 11" Weight: 200 Born: March 11, 1980 Age: 28

YEAR	TEAM	LVL	AGE	PA	R	2B	3B	HR	RBI	BB	SO	SB	CS	EqBRR	AVG	OBP	SLG	MLVr	EqAVG	EqOBP	EqSLG	EqA	VORP	DEFENSE			
2005	TEN	AA	25	569	88	33	3	21	87	52	103	15	8	0.6	.297	.378	.502	.217	.253	.322	.441	.260	20.5	93-2B	-18	10-SS	-2
2006	FLO	MLB	26	683	105	26	7	27	90	48	123	6	6	1.4	.282	.339	.480	.115	.289	.346	.491	.281	39.1	148-2B	22		
2007	FLO	MLB	27	728	113	49	3	31	88	68	167	2	1	2.4	.245	.326	.479	.066	.251	.333	.503	.282	29.8	155-2B	13		
2008	FLO	MLB	28	627	83	34	3	25	88	58	132	7	3	0.9	.260	.336	.470	.022	.261	.335	.481	.273	31.7	146-2B	7		

Breakout: 15% Improve: 42% Collapse: 26% Attrition: 11%   Comparables: Jim Morrison, Travis Fryman, Max Alvis, Gary Gaetti

Last year, Uggla wore down in September for the second straight season. Given that he's missed just 11 games over those two years, it seems clear that he needs a few more days off throughout the summer. His approach changed a bit last year, as he worked deeper counts and emphasized power at the cost of contact. The value of his offense was about the same, however. As with Cabrera, our defensive system may be overly generous to him, as the consensus has him being below average and a candidate to move to third base.

Josh Willingham   **LF**   Bats: R   Throws: R   Height: 6' 2"   Weight: 215   Born: February 17, 1979   Age: 29

YEAR	TEAM	LVL	AGE	PA	R	2B	3B	HR	RBI	BB	SO	SB	CS	EqBRR	AVG	OBP	SLG	MLVr	EqAVG	EqOBP	EqSLG	EqA	VORP	DEFENSE
2005	ABQ	AAA	26	279	56	14	3	19	54	47	54	5	1	0.2	.324	.455	.676	.448	.273	.396	.542	.316	29.3	58-C -8
2006	FLO	MLB	27	573	62	28	2	26	74	54	109	2	0	-5.6	.277	.356	.496	.162	.283	.361	.511	.296	27.8	122-LF -15
2007	FLO	MLB	28	604	75	32	4	21	89	66	122	8	1	1.5	.265	.364	.463	.124	.272	.373	.484	.294	26.9	132-LF -22
2008	FLO	MLB	29	589	85	30	3	23	82	69	117	7	2	-0.6	.271	.365	.482	.096	.271	.364	.494	.289	28.0	138-LF -13

Breakout: 12%   Improve: 37%   Collapse: 26%   Attrition: 9%   Comparables: Jermaine Dye, Ellis Burks, Tom Brunansky, Jesse Barfield

Like Jacobs, Willingham is a fair complementary player for a team that gets plenty of production from its stars. Unfortunately, that team is not the Marlins. Willingham was a little more interesting as a part-time catcher, but he hasn't gone behind the plate since April of 2006. His defense in left field isn't good, but it seems like our system is blaming him for all the plays Cabrera and Uggla didn't make.

PITCHERS

Daniel Barone   Bats: R   Throws: R   Height: 6' 2"   Weight: 185   Born: April 24, 1983   Age: 25

YEAR	TEAM	LVL	AGE	W	L	SV	G	GS	IP	H	BB	SO	HR	GB%	BABIP	STUFF	WHIP	ERA	PERA	EqERA	EqH9	EqBB9	EqSO9	EqHR9	VORP	SN/WX
2005	GRB	A	22	2	2	1	12	6	39¹	35	10	29	4	38.0%	.272	-31	1.15	4.12	6.71	6.82	10.0	4.5	3.1	2.1	-4.6	—
2005	JAM	A-	22	2	0	2	9	0	19²	14	4	17	1	49.1%	.245	-19	0.91	0.46	5.24	2.65	7.9	4.2	3.2	1.6	5.6	—
2006	GRB	A	23	4	0	0	9	6	49¹	36	9	60	1	41.3%	.292	12	0.92	2.38	4.62	4.91	8.8	3.3	6.3	0.6	3.4	—
2006	JUP	A+	23	3	5	0	17	8	73	84	18	57	9	48.3%	.333	-46	1.40	4.32	9.71	8.91	13.0	3.7	4.0	2.5	-24.2	—
2006	CAR	AA	23	1	0	0	3	2	20²	13	6	13	1	41.4%	.211	2	0.94	1.78	3.24	2.84	6.2	3.3	3.8	0.9	5.8	—
2007	CAR	AA	24	1	3	0	13	13	74²	68	18	60	7	46.0%	.290	-7	1.15	3.86	5.10	5.14	9.5	2.6	4.8	1.4	3.6	—
2007	ABQ	AAA	24	7	0	0	10	10	61²	60	14	31	6	46.4%	.274	-3	1.20	4.08	3.94	4.18	8.4	2.2	3.3	0.9	9.5	—
2007	FLO	MLB	24	1	3	0	16	6	41	50	19	18	11	41.4%	.295	-36	1.68	5.71	7.37	5.75	9.7	3.5	3.8	2.2	-2.8	0.27
2008	FLO	MLB	25	6	9	0	50	20	134	154	52	79	22	43.4%	.301	-10	1.53	5.44	5.79	5.64	10.3	3.1	4.6	1.4	-1.1	0.60

Breakout: 15%   Improve: 44%   Collapse: 24%   Attrition: 13%   Comparables: Jeff Karstens, Trey Hodges, Brandon Knight, Greg Perschke

A better story than pitcher, Barone is an organizational guy who followed in his grandfather's footsteps by reaching the majors. While moving out of the bullpen has been good for him, there's little chance that his fringe stuff will be enough for him to hold a job.

Armando Benitez   Bats: R   Throws: R   Height: 6' 4"   Weight: 260   Born: November 3, 1972   Age: 35

YEAR	TEAM	LVL	AGE	W	L	SV	G	GS	IP	H	BB	SO	HR	GB%	BABIP	STUFF	WHIP	ERA	PERA	EqERA	EqH9	EqBB9	EqSO9	EqHR9	VORP	SN/WX
2005	SFN	MLB	32	2	3	19	30	0	30	25	16	23	5	31.8%	.247	-9	1.37	4.50	4.50	4.91	7.7	4.3	6.4	1.5	1.5	0.65
2006	SFN	MLB	33	4	2	17	41	0	38¹	39	21	31	6	32.8%	.303	-5	1.57	3.52	5.27	3.32	9.2	4.3	6.6	1.2	10.7	0.03
2007	SFN	MLB	34	0	3	9	19	0	17¹	17	9	18	3	43.1%	.304	5	1.50	4.68	4.71	4.00	8.5	4.0	8.5	1.5	2.3	-0.08
2007	FLO	MLB	34	2	5	0	36	0	33	32	20	39	5	33.3%	.338	8	1.55	5.73	4.40	6.55	7.6	4.5	9.4	1.3	-6.3	-1.30
2008	FLO	MLB	35	2	3	4	41	0	47	46	26	44	7	37.3%	.297	-4	1.53	4.86	5.34	5.01	8.8	4.4	7.2	1.3	2.7	0.30

Breakout: 18%   Improve: 32%   Collapse: 35%   Attrition: 26%   Comparables: Turk Farrell, Tim Stoddard, Stan Bahnsen, Ray Moore

The Fish took Benitez off of the Giants' hands at midseason, when the Florida pen was in flux. He was mostly used to set up Kevin Gregg, with mixed results. Benitez's problems with the long ball mean he will always have fans holding their breath when he's on the mound. A free agent, Benitez is unlikely to land a high-leverage job.

Marcos Carvajal

Bats: R   Throws: R   Height: 6' 4"   Weight: 175   Born: August 19, 1984   Age: 23

YEAR	TEAM	LVL	AGE	W	L	SV	G	GS	IP	H	BB	SO	HR	GB%	BABIP	STUFF	WHIP	ERA	PERA	EqERA	EqH9	EqBB9	EqSO9	EqHR9	VORP	SN/WX
2005	COL	MLB	20	0	2	0	39	0	53	52	21	47	8	51.3%	.301	15	1.38	5.09	4.28	4.39	8.1	3.2	7.1	1.2	4.1	-0.17
2006	MNT	AA	21	2	2	0	39	0	72	66	39	69	7	41.6%	.292	-16	1.46	3.88	7.00	6.31	10.3	5.5	5.8	1.6	-5.3	—
2007	BIN	AA	22	5	10	0	28	22	119	120	63	92	13	43.9%	.298	-20	1.54	5.22	5.88	6.90	9.2	5.4	4.4	1.5	-16.9	—
2008	FLO	MLB	23	4	6	0	35	12	84²	97	54	56	14	42.0%	.306	-15	1.77	6.36	6.65	6.62	10.1	5.1	5.1	1.4	-9.9	-0.50

Breakout: 19%   Improve: 41%   Collapse: 22%   Attrition: 14%   Comparables: Jesus Colome, Pasqual Coco, Carlos Marmol, Jose Ventura

Just 23 years old, Carvajal has been the property of seven different organizations, including the Brewers for just a few hours and, since September 12, the Marlins, who claimed him when the Mets waived him. The Mets' attempt to make him a starter didn't go very well, so look for him to return to the bullpen this year. He throws hard and is young enough to still have considerable potential.

Hector Correa

Bats: R   Throws: R   Height: 6' 3"   Weight: 165   Born: March 18, 1988   Age: 20

YEAR	TEAM	LVL	AGE	W	L	SV	G	GS	IP	H	BB	SO	HR	GB%	BABIP	STUFF	WHIP	ERA	PERA	EqERA	EqH9	EqBB9	EqSO9	EqHR9	VORP	SN/WX
2006	MRL	Rk	18	1	2	0	10	5	41¹	38	15	38	1	48.7%	.316	1	1.29	1.75	8.06	6.21	12.7	7.0	4.3	1.4	-2.3	—
2007	GRB	A	19	1	5	0	8	8	31	55	16	20	7	39.3%	.436	-85	2.29	9.29	29.14	23.45	21.0	8.2	2.8	4.3	-50.2	—
2007	JAM	A-	19	6	2	0	11	11	58²	61	13	83	5	43.4%	.384	13	1.26	3.22	9.34	6.97	13.4	3.9	7.5	2.3	-7.7	—
2008	FLO	MLB	20	4	9	0	20	20	97²	128	59	76	20	42.5%	.344	-6	1.91	7.32	7.81	7.53	11.7	4.8	6.0	1.8	-20.0	-1.40

Breakout: 78%   Improve: 91%   Collapse: 3%   Attrition: 12%   Comparables: Johann Lopez, John Lloyd, Ervin Santana, Dave Doorneweerd

The Marlins felt as though Correa could handle a full-season assignment at age 19. Not quite. He washed out of Low-A Greensboro, but he was the talk of the New York–Penn League once he found his groove again in extended spring training. Long and lanky, Correa has a ton of upside, with many feeling that the mid-90s velocity he occasionally shows now will become a more regular occurrence with more seasoning. Throw in a biting slider, and he is still a high-ceiling prospect, although he's not far off the floor right now.

Lee Gardner

Bats: R   Throws: R   Height: 6' 0"   Weight: 220   Born: January 16, 1975   Age: 33

YEAR	TEAM	LVL	AGE	W	L	SV	G	GS	IP	H	BB	SO	HR	GB%	BABIP	STUFF	WHIP	ERA	PERA	EqERA	EqH9	EqBB9	EqSO9	EqHR9	VORP	SN/WX
2005	DUR	AAA	30	4	3	15	48	0	52	56	15	35	8	59.6%	.302	-26	1.37	3.29	5.34	4.35	9.2	3.3	4.2	1.6	6.9	—
2006	TOL	AAA	31	5	5	30	58	0	61	46	17	45	3	52.3%	.249	-9	1.03	2.95	3.80	4.45	7.8	3.2	4.9	0.8	7.2	—
2007	FLO	MLB	32	3	4	2	62	0	74¹	72	18	52	2	44.5%	.304	19	1.21	1.94	2.71	1.87	7.2	1.8	5.7	0.2	28.9	1.92
2008	FLO	MLB	33	3	3	4	47	0	53²	57	17	34	5	46.5%	.302	-7	1.38	4.08	4.36	4.29	9.5	2.5	4.9	0.8	7.9	0.70

Breakout: 5%   Improve: 16%   Collapse: 54%   Attrition: 24%   Comparables: Bill Landrum, Jerry Reed, Dale Mohorcic, Matt Herges

This Triple-A veteran—he reached that level in 2000 and has pitched there in parts of eight straight seasons—was the random veteran reliever of 2007. It almost didn't happen; Gardner was up and down throughout the first three months of the season, making three separate trips to Albuquerque. Finally, he came up for good on June 30 and was nearly unhittable from that day on, posting a 0.78 ERA in 46 1/3 innings with 33 strikeouts, eight walks, and just one homer allowed. It was a peak season, not to be repeated.

Kevin Gregg

Bats: R   Throws: R   Height: 6' 6"   Weight: 240   Born: June 20, 1978   Age: 30

YEAR	TEAM	LVL	AGE	W	L	SV	G	GS	IP	H	BB	SO	HR	GB%	BABIP	STUFF	WHIP	ERA	PERA	EqERA	EqH9	EqBB9	EqSO9	EqHR9	VORP	SN/WX
2005	SLC	AAA	27	3	1	0	7	6	34²	36	10	36	2	46.4%	.362	15	1.33	3.89	4.33	4.05	9.2	3.0	6.8	0.5	5.7	—
2005	ANA	MLB	27	1	2	0	33	2	64¹	70	29	52	8	47.1%	.316	-3	1.52	5.04	5.36	5.23	9.6	4.0	7.1	1.0	3.6	-0.26
2006	ANA	MLB	28	3	4	0	32	3	78¹	88	21	71	10	35.4%	.335	10	1.39	4.14	4.82	4.38	9.9	2.2	7.6	1.0	11.5	0.17
2007	FLO	MLB	29	0	5	32	74	0	84	63	40	87	7	29.7%	.264	20	1.23	3.54	2.79	3.00	5.7	3.5	8.4	0.6	19.8	3.51
2008	FLO	MLB	30	3	5	18	50	0	62²	61	29	60	7	39.0%	.306	4	1.43	4.20	4.60	4.36	8.6	3.7	7.4	0.9	8.5	1.10

Breakout: 13%   Improve: 34%   Collapse: 41%   Attrition: 20%   Comparables: Don Robinson, Todd Worrell, Dick Radatz, Dave Burba

Last year had to be Gregg's most enjoyable professional season. After four years with the Angels in which he pitched low-leverage relief—his Leverage score never rose above 0.81 and he was never among the top-five relievers on the team in the category—Gregg was given a shot at the closer role in May and never let it go. To hold it, he'll need to be better about throwing strikes; a career-high walk rate was the only red flag in his 2007 season.

Gaby Hernandez

Bats: R   Throws: R   Height: 6' 3"   Weight: 215   Born: May 21, 1986   Age: 22

YEAR	TEAM	LVL	AGE	W	L	SV	G	GS	IP	H	BB	SO	HR	GB%	BABIP	STUFF	WHIP	ERA	PERA	EqERA	EqH9	EqBB9	EqSO9	EqHR9	VORP	SN/WX
2005	HAG	A	19	6	1	0	18	18	92²	59	30	99	4	48.3%	.243	16	0.96	2.43	5.19	5.22	8.2	5.4	5.4	1.0	3.3	—
2005	SLU	A+	19	2	5	0	10	10	42¹	48	10	32	1	40.0%	.367	-4	1.37	5.74	6.83	8.29	12.3	4.0	3.6	0.7	-11.4	—
2006	JUP	A+	20	9	7	0	21	20	120	120	35	115	7	44.7%	.330	0	1.29	3.68	6.73	6.92	11.4	4.2	5.2	1.2	-15.8	—
2007	CAR	AA	21	9	11	0	28	28	153²	144	56	113	14	39.5%	.282	-10	1.30	4.22	5.38	6.03	9.5	3.7	4.1	1.3	-7.1	—
2008	FLO	MLB	22	6	9	0	23	23	127	144	58	80	20	40.5%	.302	0	1.59	5.57	5.92	5.77	10.1	3.7	4.9	1.4	-2.7	0.70

Breakout: 28% Improve: 61% Collapse: 15% Attrition: 13%   Comparables: Chad Durbin, Bob Wolcott, Tony Armas Jr., Sean Douglass

Hernandez lost a little ground at Double-A, which you might expect given that he's more of a pitcher than a power arm. With four good pitches, including a low-90s fastball, he's projectable as a mid-rotation starter, it's just going to take a little while for him to adapt to each new level.

Josh Johnson

Bats: L   Throws: R   Height: 6' 7"   Weight: 230   Born: January 31, 1984   Age: 24

YEAR	TEAM	LVL	AGE	W	L	SV	G	GS	IP	H	BB	SO	HR	GB%	BABIP	STUFF	WHIP	ERA	PERA	EqERA	EqH9	EqBB9	EqSO9	EqHR9	VORP	SN/WX
2005	CAR	AA	21	12	4	0	26	26	139²	139	50	113	4	53.1%	.325	9	1.35	3.87	5.09	5.67	10.2	4.0	4.7	0.6	-1.0	—
2005	FLO	MLB	21	0	0	0	4	1	12¹	11	10	10	0	41.2%	.333	12	1.70	3.66	4.48	3.86	8.5	6.9	6.9	0.0	2.5	0.32
2006	FLO	MLB	22	12	7	0	31	24	157	136	68	133	14	48.0%	.284	26	1.30	3.10	3.48	3.29	7.5	3.4	7.0	0.7	40.2	4.54
2007	FLO	MLB	23	0	3	0	4	4	15²	26	12	14	1	50.0%	.481	0	2.43	7.45	9.34	9.77	13.8	5.7	7.5	0.6	-7.3	-0.19
2008	FLO	MLB	24	6	5	1	26	13	93²	91	39	90	7	49.6%	.315	17	1.39	3.77	4.15	3.97	8.6	3.4	7.4	0.7	19.3	2.20

Breakout: 31% Improve: 66% Collapse: 14% Attrition: 14%   Comparables: Lee Smith, Kameron Loe, Gil Meche, Pete Vuckovich

A strained forearm followed Johnson from 2006 into 2007, and while he was eventually activated by the Marlins, he was never quite right and landed back on the DL after just four starts. While rehabbing, he blew out his elbow and will miss most of 2008 following Tommy John surgery. It will be at least 2009 before he's relevant again; the good news is that he'll be just 25 at that point.

Logan Kensing

Bats: R   Throws: R   Height: 6' 1"   Weight: 185   Born: July 3, 1982   Age: 25

YEAR	TEAM	LVL	AGE	W	L	SV	G	GS	IP	H	BB	SO	HR	GB%	BABIP	STUFF	WHIP	ERA	PERA	EqERA	EqH9	EqBB9	EqSO9	EqHR9	VORP	SN/WX
2005	CAR	AA	23	4	1	0	7	7	39²	35	14	33	4	50.4%	.267	-5	1.23	3.17	5.95	5.00	9.5	4.0	4.8	1.8	2.4	—
2006	ABQ	AAA	24	1	1	2	13	0	18	11	5	18	2	60.5%	.220	6	0.89	3.00	3.25	3.24	5.9	2.7	7.0	1.1	4.4	—
2006	FLO	MLB	24	1	3	1	36	0	37²	30	19	45	6	30.9%	.282	15	1.30	4.54	3.94	4.06	6.9	3.8	9.8	1.2	5.7	-0.09
2007	FLO	MLB	25	3	0	0	9	0	13¹	11	7	13	0	32.4%	.306	14	1.35	1.35	2.93	1.32	6.6	4.0	7.9	0.0	6.7	0.60
2008	FLO	MLB	25	3	3	2	36	3	51	49	24	49	6	40.7%	.298	6	1.42	4.18	4.53	4.34	8.5	3.7	7.3	1.0	7.8	0.70

Breakout: 12% Improve: 34% Collapse: 46% Attrition: 22%   Comparables: Chad Orvella, Marty Pattin, Jim York, Joe Decker

Kensing returned from September 2006 Tommy John surgery last year to set himself up as a key member of the Marlins' 2008 bullpen. He has power stuff that translates well to the pen, and in limited work over two seasons, he's struck out 52 men in 47 innings. Along with Matt Lindstrom, Henry Owens, and Taylor Tankersley, he could be part of an effective, low-cost bullpen in Florida this year.

Byung-Hyun Kim

Bats: R   Throws: R   Height: 5' 9"   Weight: 175   Born: January 19, 1979   Age: 29

YEAR	TEAM	LVL	AGE	W	L	SV	G	GS	IP	H	BB	SO	HR	GB%	BABIP	STUFF	WHIP	ERA	PERA	EqERA	EqH9	EqBB9	EqSO9	EqHR9	VORP	SN/WX
2005	COL	MLB	26	5	12	0	40	22	148	156	71	115	17	43.0%	.320	3	1.54	4.86	4.61	4.40	8.7	3.9	6.3	1.0	13.3	0.64
2006	COL	MLB	27	8	12	0	27	27	155	179	61	129	18	43.4%	.350	13	1.55	5.57	5.08	5.40	10.0	3.1	6.9	0.9	4.9	1.71
2007	ARI	MLB	28	0	1	0	2	2	2²	11	2	3	1	37.5%	.714	-137	4.88	23.33	45.83	40.50	37.1	6.8	10.1	3.4	-7.1	-0.42
2007	COL	MLB	28	1	2	0	3	1	6	6	4	2	2	36.4%	.235	-44	1.67	10.50	7.21	9.95	8.5	4.3	2.8	2.8	-2.8	-0.51
2007	FLO	MLB	28	9	5	0	23	19	109²	114	62	102	17	43.2%	.313	5	1.60	5.41	4.78	5.02	8.1	4.2	7.5	1.3	-4.4	1.35
2008	FLO	MLB	29	6	7	0	31	16	108²	109	49	92	13	43.4%	.302	5	1.45	4.54	4.87	4.74	9.0	3.6	6.5	1.0	10.2	1.70

Breakout: 36% Improve: 61% Collapse: 15% Attrition: 26%   Comparables: Bobby Castillo, Tom Gordon, Juan Guzman, Dan Spillner

Completing the trio of assumed head cases to pitch for the Marlins last year, Kim was acquired for Jorge Julio in the middle of April, waived after the trading deadline, and re-signed three weeks later. That teams persist in using him as a starter is bizarre; he throws too many pitches to work deep into games and struggles against lefties. A team that uses him to get righties out in the seventh inning will be pleased.

Matt Lindstrom

Bats: R   Throws: R   Height: 6' 4"   Weight: 210   Born: February 11, 1980   Age: 28

YEAR	TEAM	LVL	AGE	W	L	SV	G	GS	IP	H	BB	SO	HR	GB%	BABIP	STUFF	WHIP	ERA	PERA	EqERA	EqH9	EqBB9	EqSO9	EqHR9	VORP	SN/WX
2005	BIN	AA	25	2	5	0	35	10	73¹	90	55	58	11	55.6%	.345	-41	1.98	5.40	11.12	10.23	12.3	9.1	4.2	2.0	-34.0	—
2006	SLU	A+	26	1	0	2	11	0	18²	14	7	16	2	68.6%	.250	-23	1.15	2.47	6.61	5.62	9.6	5.1	5.1	2.2	-0.0	—
2006	BIN	AA	26	2	4	11	35	0	40²	42	14	54	2	54.7%	.392	-3	1.39	3.81	7.23	6.50	12.5	4.2	8.5	0.8	-3.6	—
2007	FLO	MLB	27	3	4	0	71	0	67	66	21	62	2	48.0%	.333	23	1.31	3.09	3.02	3.03	7.8	2.4	7.6	0.3	14.9	1.59
2008	FLO	MLB	28	2	2	2	41	0	46	48	21	39	4	48.5%	.318	1	1.48	4.25	4.65	4.47	9.3	3.6	6.5	0.7	6.2	0.50

Breakout: 30% Improve: 53% Collapse: 32% Attrition: 38%   Comparables: Frank Reberger, Alan Hargesheimer, Heathcliff Slocumb, Billy Muffett

Mets fans watching their bullpen disintegrate over the last three weeks of last season no doubt ground their teeth at the thought of Lindstrom pitching well a thousand miles to the south after having been dealt away prior to the season along with Henry Owens for Jason Vargas and Adam Bostick. Lindstrom was one of the few Marlins relievers not to get a crack at the closer job before Gregg snagged it. He did not enter a single game in a save situation in the ninth inning. Despite never getting to be the big cheese, Lindstrom pitched well as the eighth-inning guy until Benitez arrived, and as the seventh-inning righty thereafter. He has a closer's fastball and slider and should eventually get a chance in that role somewhere.

Justin Miller

Bats: R   Throws: R   Height: 6' 2"   Weight: 200   Born: August 27, 1977   Age: 30

YEAR	TEAM	LVL	AGE	W	L	SV	G	GS	IP	H	BB	SO	HR	GB%	BABIP	STUFF	WHIP	ERA	PERA	EqERA	EqH9	EqBB9	EqSO9	EqHR9	VORP	SN/WX
2005	SYR	AAA	27	3	1	2	28	4	50¹	39	14	56	3	46.6%	.283	12	1.05	2.33	3.69	3.23	7.4	3.0	7.4	0.8	12.5	—
2006	CHB	JP	28	0	1	0	12	0	11²	18	10	11	3	0.0%	.385	-48	2.39	10.77	22.15	18.82	14.7	9.8	6.5	3.3	-16.2	—
2007	ABQ	AAA	29	0	0	6	11	0	12	9	4	20	0	50.0%	.346	12	1.08	1.50	3.41	3.09	7.7	3.1	10.8	0.0	3.3	—
2007	FLO	MLB	29	5	0	0	62	0	61²	53	24	74	5	44.1%	.314	25	1.25	3.65	2.99	3.41	6.8	2.8	9.5	0.7	12.5	1.18
2008	FLO	MLB	30	3	3	4	46	1	56²	52	25	55	7	42.7%	.292	5	1.36	4.22	4.30	4.43	8.2	3.6	7.5	1.0	7.4	0.70

Breakout: 34% Improve: 67% Collapse: 20% Attrition: 18%   Comparables: Rich DeLucia, Tom Sturdivant, Mike Hartley, Wes Stock

Miller came back from Japan last year to have the best season of his career and even moved into the Marlins' set-up role late in the season. Perhaps best known for his heavily tattooed body, Miller put the needle to batters last year, posting a 4.0 K/UIBB ratio. He brought his struggles against lefty batters (.324/.390/.544) back with him, though, so long-term success may elude him unless he's handled carefully.

Sergio Mitre

Bats: R   Throws: R   Height: 6' 3"   Weight: 225   Born: February 16, 1981   Age: 27

YEAR	TEAM	LVL	AGE	W	L	SV	G	GS	IP	H	BB	SO	HR	GB%	BABIP	STUFF	WHIP	ERA	PERA	EqERA	EqH9	EqBB9	EqSO9	EqHR9	VORP	SN/WX
2005	IOW	AAA	24	5	6	0	13	13	70²	72	22	55	5	62.9%	.313	3	1.33	4.33	4.51	4.59	9.3	3.1	5.0	0.8	7.5	—
2005	CHN	MLB	24	2	5	0	21	7	60¹	62	23	37	11	68.3%	.268	-17	1.41	5.37	5.25	5.31	9.1	3.1	4.9	1.6	0.5	0.40
2006	FLO	MLB	25	1	5	0	15	7	41	44	20	31	7	53.0%	.303	-9	1.56	5.71	5.52	5.62	9.1	3.7	6.0	1.3	-1.5	0.18
2007	FLO	MLB	26	5	8	0	27	27	149	180	41	80	9	61.8%	.338	15	1.48	4.65	3.90	4.39	9.3	2.0	4.5	0.5	7.9	1.65
2008	FLO	MLB	27	7	8	0	29	19	122	137	41	68	10	57.3%	.311	-1	1.46	4.51	4.75	4.82	10.0	2.7	4.3	0.7	9.4	1.90

Breakout: 14% Improve: 42% Collapse: 35% Attrition: 28%   Comparables: John Doherty, Dennis Lamp, Mike Morgan, Chien-Ming Wang

The "Under the Knife" MVP for 2007, Mitre opened the season rehabbing the sore shoulder that cut his 2006 short. He then tore a blister in his third start, suffered a strained hamstring in May, and was shut down in September as a precautionary measure after he fell apart in the second half, posting an 8.62 ERA with more walks than strikeouts in his last 10 starts, only one of which was quality. With all the physical problems, a move to the bullpen seems inevitable.

Ricky Nolasco

Bats: R Throws: R Height: 6' 2" Weight: 220 Born: December 13, 1982 Age: 25

YEAR	TEAM	LVL	AGE	W	L	SV	G	GS	IP	H	BB	SO	HR	GB%	BABIP	STUFF	WHIP	ERA	PERA	EqERA	EqH9	EqBB9	EqSO9	EqHR9	VORP	SN/WX
2005	WTN	AA	22	14	3	0	27	27	161²	151	46	173	13	46.2%	.320	5	1.22	2.89	5.81	4.70	10.3	3.3	6.5	1.4	14.6	—
2006	FLO	MLB	23	11	11	0	35	22	140	157	41	99	20	41.0%	.319	1	1.41	4.82	4.89	5.13	9.6	2.2	5.8	1.2	6.7	2.78
2007	FLO	MLB	24	1	2	0	5	4	21¹	26	9	11	3	39.7%	.343	-10	1.64	5.49	4.73	5.56	9.1	3.2	4.0	1.2	-2.6	0.05
2008	FLO	MLB	25	3	3	1	24	5	51²	56	17	40	6	43.4%	.307	2	4.80	4.69	9.6	2.6	6.0	1.1	6.5	0.70

Breakout: 41% Improve: 61% Collapse: 22% Attrition: 46%   Comparables: Dick Pole, Mike Williams, Rod Nichols, Matt Ginter

Nolasco won a spot in the rotation in the spring, but outside of four starts in May, was unable to claim it due to the world's worst case of elbow inflammation, which ended the major league portion of his season that month (several attempts at rehab went nowhere). Nolasco had velocity, if not much else, in an Arizona Fall League stint. The Marlins need some of their young starters to actually hold up to a starter's workload, especially given how many good true relievers they have.

Scott Olsen

Bats: L Throws: L Height: 6' 5" Weight: 215 Born: January 12, 1984 Age: 24

YEAR	TEAM	LVL	AGE	W	L	SV	G	GS	IP	H	BB	SO	HR	GB%	BABIP	STUFF	WHIP	ERA	PERA	EqERA	EqH9	EqBB9	EqSO9	EqHR9	VORP	SN/WX
2005	CAR	AA	21	6	4	0	14	14	80¹	75	27	94	7	52.1%	.343	10	1.27	3.92	6.21	6.00	10.5	3.9	7.2	1.5	-3.2	—
2005	FLO	MLB	21	1	1	0	5	4	20¹	21	10	21	5	40.0%	.291	17	1.52	3.99	6.05	5.66	8.7	3.9	8.3	2.2	-0.9	0.54
2006	FLO	MLB	22	12	10	0	31	31	180²	160	75	166	23	46.6%	.285	23	1.30	4.03	3.83	4.27	7.7	3.3	7.6	1.1	24.3	4.70
2007	FLO	MLB	23	10	15	0	33	33	176²	226	85	133	29	40.2%	.354	-5	1.76	5.81	5.80	5.95	10.0	3.5	6.1	1.3	-23.1	-0.13
2008	FLO	MLB	24	7	8	0	33	19	123²	130	53	101	15	45.7%	.309	6	1.48	4.77	5.08	4.99	9.4	3.4	6.2	1.1	7.9	1.60

Breakout: 33% Improve: 56% Collapse: 26% Attrition: 27%   Comparables: Bill Travers, Frank Viola, Bob Owchinko, Randy Lerch

The informed-outsider position we generally take at Baseball Prospectus holds that the nonplaying characteristics of a player are both opaque to the outsider—filtered as they are through the media, which has a larger stake in a good story than the truth—and secondary to that player's applied skills. We evaluate performers without regard to their personality, focusing almost exclusively on their on-field performance. At the extremes, however, nonplaying factors have to come into consideration. Olsen, who has repeatedly had run-ins with his teammates, his superiors, and law enforcement, exists at one of those extremes. Whatever physical talent he possesses—and his 2007 statistics notwithstanding, he has considerable talent—comes packaged with an inability to interact positively with the people around him on a consistent basis. Olsen's boorishness may wash out as he matures, or it may wash him out of the major leagues entirely. Even an informed outsider can see that.

Henry Owens

Bats: R Throws: R Height: 6' 3" Weight: 230 Born: April 23, 1979 Age: 29

YEAR	TEAM	LVL	AGE	W	L	SV	G	GS	IP	H	BB	SO	HR	GB%	BABIP	STUFF	WHIP	ERA	PERA	EqERA	EqH9	EqBB9	EqSO9	EqHR9	VORP	SN/WX
2005	SLU	A+	26	2	5	4	38	1	54¹	49	24	74	2	43.8%	.351	1	1.34	3.15	6.74	7.33	11.0	6.6	7.7	1.0	-9.0	—
2006	BIN	AA	27	2	2	20	37	0	40¹	19	10	74	1	42.4%	.281	29	0.72	1.57	3.29	3.62	6.5	3.1	10.4	0.5	8.2	—
2007	FLO	MLB	28	2	0	4	22	0	23	19	10	16	3	37.5%	.232	-1	1.26	1.96	2.92	1.85	5.9	3.3	5.5	1.1	7.8	1.05
2008	FLO	MLB	29	3	3	6	40	2	50²	48	24	46	5	42.0%	.296	2	1.42	4.28	4.50	4.48	8.4	3.9	7.0	0.9	6.1	0.70

Breakout: 26% Improve: 46% Collapse: 31% Attrition: 26%   Comparables: Tim Worrell, Hector Mercado, Jerry Johnson, Mike James

Owens had just moved into the closer job in the first week of May when a sore shoulder effectively ended his 2007 season. Owens made a brief return in June, but otherwise spent three months resting and rehabbing to no avail. Shoulder surgery ended the dream in September, leaving both his short- and long-term futures up in the air. Check back in 2009.

Renyel Pinto

Bats: L   Throws: L   Height: 6' 4"   Weight: 215   Born: July 8, 1982   Age: 25

YEAR	TEAM	LVL	AGE	W	L	SV	G	GS	IP	H	BB	SO	HR	GB%	BABIP	STUFF	WHIP	ERA	PERA	EqERA	EqH9	EqBB9	EqSO9	EqHR9	VORP	SN/WX
2005	WTN	AA	22	10	3	0	22	21	129²	101	58	123	3	52.1%	.300	20	1.23	2.71	4.24	4.17	8.1	4.8	5.6	0.5	18.9	—
2005	IOW	AAA	22	1	2	0	6	6	22²	31	24	24	3	46.5%	.452	-6	2.42	9.52	11.96	13.92	13.5	10.1	6.8	1.3	-19.7	—
2006	ABQ	AAA	23	8	2	0	18	18	95¹	82	47	96	8	49.2%	.297	12	1.36	3.41	4.56	3.88	7.9	4.8	6.6	1.0	17.7	—
2006	FLO	MLB	23	0	0	1	27	0	29²	20	27	36	3	45.7%	.258	27	1.58	3.03	3.67	2.97	5.9	6.8	9.8	0.9	7.4	0.30
2007	FLO	MLB	24	2	4	1	57	0	58²	45	32	56	7	37.7%	.271	10	1.31	3.68	3.41	3.14	6.3	4.2	8.2	0.9	12.4	0.97
2008	FLO	MLB	25	3	3	3	45	2	52¹	47	30	49	5	44.2%	.292	3	1.48	4.05	4.52	4.23	8.0	4.6	7.3	0.8	8.3	0.80

Breakout: 10%   Improve: 29%   Collapse: 51%   Attrition: 27%   Comparables: Sammy Stewart, Jeff Jones, Neal Cotts, Chuck McElroy

How could a team with as many power arms and as many young, strong bats as the Marlins had last year lose so many games? A combination of a wretched defense and a poor, injury-prone rotation is the answer, but man, do the Marlins have the makings of a nasty bullpen in 2008. Pinto was often used to get out of jams last year, inheriting runners in more than 40 percent of his appearances and stranding 30 of the 38 he inherited. The shoulder strain that sent him to the DL in August didn't affect him in September as he didn't allow a run or an inherited runner to score in any of his eight outings that month.

Anibal Sanchez

Bats: R   Throws: R   Height: 6' 0"   Weight: 180   Born: February 27, 1984   Age: 24

YEAR	TEAM	LVL	AGE	W	L	SV	G	GS	IP	H	BB	SO	HR	GB%	BABIP	STUFF	WHIP	ERA	PERA	EqERA	EqH9	EqBB9	EqSO9	EqHR9	VORP	SN/WX
2005	WIL	A+	21	6	1	0	14	14	78²	53	24	95	7	47.9%	.253	8	0.98	2.40	5.12	4.70	8.2	4.3	6.5	1.6	6.9	—
2005	PME	AA	21	3	5	0	11	11	57¹	53	16	63	5	46.5%	.322	8	1.20	3.46	5.90	5.96	10.3	3.7	6.5	1.2	-2.1	—
2006	CAR	AA	22	3	6	0	15	15	85	82	27	92	7	48.2%	.319	4	1.28	3.18	5.56	5.75	10.1	3.3	6.4	1.3	-1.4	—
2006	FLO	MLB	22	10	3	0	18	17	114¹	90	46	72	9	43.5%	.243	21	1.19	2.83	3.00	2.84	6.6	3.2	5.2	0.6	36.2	4.81
2007	FLO	MLB	23	2	1	0	6	6	30	43	19	14	3	46.6%	.367	-10	2.07	4.80	6.45	4.31	11.2	4.6	3.7	0.9	2.3	0.38
2008	FLO	MLB	24	4	4	0	22	9	69	72	31	51	8	45.6%	.300	0	1.49	4.59	5.03	4.79	9.3	3.6	5.6	1.0	6.7	1.00

Breakout: 8%   Improve: 19%   Collapse: 49%   Attrition: 37%   Comparables: Jim Nelson, Vern Law, Dick Selma, Bob Mahoney

All of the Marlins' top five starters in 2006 saw their ERAs rise in 2007. Three of the five—Sanchez, Johnson, and Nolasco—went from 63 combined starts to 14. The other two, Olsen and Willis, saw their combined ERA go from 3.94 to 5.47. Now, Billy Martin is dead, so we can't blame him. Joe Girardi, however, is very much alive and seems to have escaped detection by getting himself fired in advance of this carnage. It's facile to say "Girardi broke his pitchers," because pitchers get hurt for all kinds of reasons, but when the aftermath is this dramatic, more questions should be asked. Sanchez, who despite his no-hitter was well over his head as a major leaguer in 2006, was demoted last May and later diagnosed with a torn labrum, the timing of which resulted in a dispute between Sanchez and the team as to whether he should have been placed on the major league DL rather than sent down. He might be ready for spring training, but he's not likely to be at all effective this year.

Brett Sinkbeil

Bats: R   Throws: R   Height: 6' 2"   Weight: 170   Born: December 26, 1984   Age: 23

YEAR	TEAM	LVL	AGE	W	L	SV	G	GS	IP	H	BB	SO	HR	GB%	BABIP	STUFF	WHIP	ERA	PERA	EqERA	EqH9	EqBB9	EqSO9	EqHR9	VORP	SN/WX
2006	GRB	A	21	1	1	0	8	8	39¹	45	14	32	5	54.4%	.339	-34	1.51	5.06	12.11	9.64	14.1	6.1	3.9	3.0	-14.7	—
2006	JAM	A-	21	2	0	0	5	5	22²	14	8	22	1	52.8%	.260	-2	0.99	1.22	7.19	4.67	9.3	7.3	5.2	2.1	1.8	—
2007	JUP	A+	22	6	4	0	14	14	79	82	14	49	8	53.8%	.297	-26	1.22	3.42	6.61	6.69	10.7	2.7	3.2	2.0	-8.8	—
2008	FLO	MLB	23	6	10	0	23	23	125²	156	55	61	21	50.7%	.310	-10	1.68	6.15	6.54	6.43	11.1	3.5	3.7	1.5	-11.5	-0.30

Breakout: 33%   Improve: 61%   Collapse: 19%   Attrition: 16%   Comparables: Jamie Arnold, Beau Hale, Chris Bootcheck, Brent Knackert

The Marlins' top pick in 2006, Sinkbeil's full-season debut was marred by elbow and back problems. If he can stay healthy, he projects as a mid-rotation type, as he has outstanding command of a good sinker (yes, really) and a plus slider. As a result, he gets tons of groundballs, but when you are a college product in A-ball, scouts want to see more missed bats before they get too excited.

Taylor Tankersley

Bats: L   Throws: L   Height: 6' 1"   Weight: 220   Born: March 7, 1983   Age: 25

YEAR	TEAM	LVL	AGE	W	L	SV	G	GS	IP	H	BB	SO	HR	GB%	BABIP	STUFF	WHIP	ERA	PERA	EqERA	EqH9	EqBB9	EqSO9	EqHR9	VORP	SN/WX
2005	GRB	A	22	2	7	0	12	12	66	74	25	63	12	41.9%	.326	-47	1.50	5.18	13.07	11.29	13.7	6.4	4.7	3.4	-34.8	—
2005	JUP	A+	22	1	0	0	4	4	24	21	9	19	1	41.8%	.308	-1	1.25	3.38	5.17	5.48	8.9	5.5	3.8	0.8	0.3	—
2006	CAR	AA	23	4	1	6	22	0	28²	11	14	40	0	49.1%	.229	22	0.89	0.96	2.73	2.30	4.3	4.9	8.6	0.3	10.0	—
2006	FLO	MLB	23	2	1	3	49	0	41	33	26	46	4	46.7%	.305	20	1.44	2.85	3.78	2.66	7.1	4.9	9.3	0.9	13.0	2.13
2007	FLO	MLB	24	6	1	1	67	0	47¹	42	29	49	4	39.5%	.322	15	1.50	4.00	3.90	3.50	7.4	4.9	8.9	0.8	8.3	1.41
2008	FLO	MLB	25	2	2	3	48	1	46¹	42	25	47	4	41.8%	.297	7	1.44	3.98	4.36	4.15	8.0	4.3	7.8	0.8	8.2	0.70

Breakout: 27% Improve: 46% Collapse: 26% Attrition: 24%   Comparables: Chuck McElroy, Neal Cotts, Sean Runyan, Kent Mercker

Tankersley's been touted as a closer in the making, and he has the stuff for it, but between nagging shoulder problems and more-than-nagging command issues, he was a disaster in the first half of 2007. After a two-week vacation in Albuquerque—can you imagine a better motivator?—he channeled Billy Wagner the rest of the way: 24 1/3 IP, 33 K, 12 UIBB, 1.48 ERA. Whether he gets the saves in 2008 or not, he'll be the best pitcher in this ridiculously deep bullpen.

Rick Vanden Hurk

Bats: R   Throws: R   Height: 6' 5"   Weight: 195   Born: May 22, 1985   Age: 23

YEAR	TEAM	LVL	AGE	W	L	SV	G	GS	IP	H	BB	SO	HR	GB%	BABIP	STUFF	WHIP	ERA	PERA	EqERA	EqH9	EqBB9	EqSO9	EqHR9	VORP	SN/WX
2007	CAR	AA	22	2	2	0	9	9	53²	42	21	61	5	37.2%	.294	11	1.17	3.52	5.07	4.89	8.7	4.0	7.1	1.4	3.9	—
2007	ABQ	AAA	22	2	0	0	2	2	12	6	4	14	3	42.3%	.130	11	0.83	2.25	3.51	2.38	4.8	3.2	8.7	2.4	4.0	—
2007	FLO	MLB	22	4	6	0	18	17	81²	94	48	82	15	31.3%	.354	6	1.74	6.83	5.98	6.18	9.3	4.4	8.2	1.5	-11.3	0.14
2008	FLO	MLB	23	8	10	1	37	24	144¹	140	74	137	21	37.8%	.296	10	1.48	4.78	5.18	4.93	8.6	4.1	7.3	1.3	9.9	2.00

Breakout: 34% Improve: 65% Collapse: 8% Attrition: 22%   Comparables: Ruben Quevedo, Ugueth Urbina, Fernando Cabrera, Ervin Santana

The tall Dutchman moved into third place in wins for pitchers born in the Netherlands last year, passing Win Remmerswaal. Up next, Rynie Wolters with 19, and just beyond that, Bert Blyleven with a mere 287. Vanden Hurk signed at age 17 and, despite being a starter his entire career, had never thrown more than 58 innings in a season before 2007. Tommy John surgery cost him nearly all of 2005 and 2006, and while he has a high-90s fastball, the rest of his repertoire—a curve and a changeup—is a work in progress.

Chris Volstad

Bats: R   Throws: R   Height: 6' 7"   Weight: 190   Born: September 23, 1986   Age: 21

YEAR	TEAM	LVL	AGE	W	L	SV	G	GS	IP	H	BB	SO	HR	GB%	BABIP	STUFF	WHIP	ERA	PERA	EqERA	EqH9	EqBB9	EqSO9	EqHR9	VORP	SN/WX
2005	JAM	A-	18	3	2	0	7	7	38	43	11	29	0	59.1%	.344	-3	1.42	2.13	6.84	7.16	12.1	5.8	2.8	0.6	-5.7	—
2006	GRB	A	19	11	8	0	26	26	152	161	36	99	12	61.4%	.314	-27	1.30	3.08	7.82	7.35	12.2	4.2	2.7	1.9	-25.5	—
2007	JUP	A+	20	8	9	0	21	20	126	152	37	93	8	56.8%	.345	-11	1.50	4.50	7.22	7.67	12.2	4.0	4.0	1.3	-27.0	—
2007	CAR	AA	20	4	2	0	7	7	42²	41	10	25	4	53.9%	.276	-2	1.19	3.16	5.16	4.91	9.8	2.5	3.1	1.3	3.1	—
2008	FLO	MLB	21	7	12	0	28	28	156²	189	69	80	20	53.7%	.314	-4	1.64	5.61	5.96	5.92	10.7	3.5	3.9	1.1	-5.9	0.60

Breakout: 45% Improve: 78% Collapse: 8% Attrition: 8%   Comparables: Kyle Waldrop, Jake Dittler, Dustin Moseley, Todd Ritchie

Volstad is a finesse pitcher trapped in the body of a power pitcher. At 6-foot-7, he's physically intimidating, but what comes out of his hand is not. He's a strike-thrower (which is a rare for a pitcher his size, especially a young one) who lives off an average-velocity fastball that he can sink, run, and locate at will, as well as an above-average curveball. His numbers don't pop out at you, and it's hard to throw a lot of projection on him, but he should be a rotation stalwart by 2009.

Dontrelle Willis

Bats: L   Throws: L   Height: 6' 4"   Weight: 225   Born: January 12, 1982   Age: 26

YEAR	TEAM	LVL	AGE	W	L	SV	G	GS	IP	H	BB	SO	HR	GB%	BABIP	STUFF	WHIP	ERA	PERA	EqERA	EqH9	EqBB9	EqSO9	EqHR9	VORP	SN/WX
2005	FLO	MLB	23	22	10	0	34	34	236¹	213	55	170	11	46.8%	.290	32	1.13	2.63	2.96	2.90	7.5	1.9	5.9	0.4	65.2	8.58
2006	FLO	MLB	24	12	12	0	34	34	223¹	234	83	160	21	49.2%	.316	16	1.42	3.87	4.36	4.02	9.1	2.9	5.9	0.8	40.5	5.41
2007	FLO	MLB	25	10	15	0	35	35	205¹	241	87	146	29	49.1%	.329	3	1.60	5.17	4.79	4.75	9.0	3.1	5.8	1.1	0.7	1.99
2008	DET	MLB	26	11	11	0	31	31	194	212	70	119	21	49.4%	.302	8	1.45	4.55	4.54	4.60	9.5	2.9	5.0	1.0	19.3	3.60

Breakout: 9% Improve: 34% Collapse: 30% Attrition: 10%   Comparables: Jerry Reuss, Jim Abbott, Joe Kennedy, Dave LaPoint

Despite moving to the superior American League, Willis could see his ERA drop considerably in 2008. The reason is that he was victimized by the worst defense in the National League last season, allowing a .329 batting average on balls in play, surrendering a whopping 194 singles and doubles allowed to right-handed batters in 820 plate appearances. Left-side defenders Cabrera, Ramirez, and Willingham cost Willis at least a half-run of ERA more than average fielders would have, perhaps more. Willis isn't the All-Star pitcher he looked like in his peak year of 2005. He's also not a 5.00 ERA guy, and with the massive upgrades almost everywhere behind him, Willis, more than anyone else, may end up the biggest winner in the winter's biggest trade.

LINEOUTS

Hitters

PLAYER		TEAM	LVL	AGE	PA	R	2B	3B	HR	RBI	BB	SO	SB-CS	EqBRR	AVG/OBP/SLG	MLVr	EqAVG/EqOBP/EqSLG	EqA	VORP
CF	G. Burns*	GRB	A	20	468	70	21	4	7	54	40	122	39-6	1.2	.280/.347/.401	.013	.207/.263/.289	.204	-31.9
UT	J. Gall	ABQ	AAA	29	456	75	28	3	13	58	38	49	10-4	-3.7	.300/.362/.477	.022	.255/.316/.407	.251	-6.0
OF	K. Harvey	JUP	A+	23	469	52	16	3	12	55	34	100	6-3	-2.5	.238/.301/.376	-.003	.211/.268/.347	.215	-31.9
C	P. Hoover	ABQ	AAA	31	105	11	7	1	4	21	7	18	0-1	-0.3	.292/.333/.510	.012	.250/.295/.458	.253	2.9
OF	J. Miller	CAR	AA	22	473	54	26	2	14	58	55	127	12-5	-0.8	.261/.354/.438	.088	.237/.318/.405	.252	4.2
UT	E. Reed*	ABQ	AAA	26	332	54	10	12	0	20	17	58	30-3	9.0	.285/.323/.397	-.167	.242/.283/.343	.233	-10.4
		FLO	MLB	26	21	3	0	0	0	0	1	6	1-0	0.3	.100/.143/.100	-.861	.100/.143/.100	.000	-3.2
UT	J. Wood	FLO	MLB	37	127	11	6	0	3	26	8	38	0-0	0.1	.239/.286/.368	-.166	.239/.291/.376	.232	-1.8

Greg Burns may be the fastest man in an organization loaded with speed. He improved in a second stint in the Sally League and is young enough to develop into a fourth outfielder. ⊘ Triple-A mainstay **John Gall** continued grinding away last year, hitting a soft .300. ⊘ The Marlins' second-round pick in 2005, **Kris Harvey** has been the same undisciplined hitter in the pros that he was in college, just without the power. He'll eventually try pitching to save his career. ⊘ Catch-and-throw backup catcher **Paul Hoover** is third in line for playing time following the dismissal of Miguel Olivo. ⊘ Another toolsy Marlins prospect, **Jai Miller** hit for the first time ever at Double-A last year and was added to the 40-man roster. He's not a threat to make the majors. ⊘ **Eric Reed** couldn't hold off De Aza for the center-field job in the spring, and now is a long shot to even have Jason Tyner's career. ⊘ Thirty-seven-year-old **Jason Wood** threw a 1-2-3 inning at the Braves on June 29, which is interesting only because Wood is an infielder.

Pitchers

PLAYER	TEAM	LVL	AGE	W	L	SV	IP	H	BB	SO	HR	GB%	BABIP	STUFF	WHIP	ERA	PERA	EqERA	EqH9	EqBB9	EqSO9	EqHR9	VORP
J. Delgado	CAR	AA	23	5	7	1	93²	97	45	75	6	56.6%	.317	-15	1.52	4.80	6.11	6.80	10.7	4.8	4.6	1.0	-11.8
N. Field	ABQ	AAA	31	6	6	11	46¹	37	17	45	6	40.6%	.250	-3	1.17	3.50	3.72	3.61	6.8	3.4	6.5	1.1	10.5
H. Garcia	CAR	AA	23	2	2	0	24¹	21	17	25	3	43.9%	.286	-8	1.56	4.07	7.21	6.45	9.7	6.9	6.4	2.0	-2.1
	ABQ	AAA	23	4	1	1	48	59	22	45	9	44.5%	.355	-22	1.69	6.19	7.68	6.70	11.1	4.4	6.3	1.7	-5.7
	FLO	MLB	23	0	1	0	12¹	14	7	15	3	39.4%	.379	12	1.62	4.39	7.40	4.50	9.8	4.5	10.5	2.2	1.9
C. Martinez	CAR	AA	25	1	1	0	21¹	21	5	18	2	32.4%	.292	-17	1.22	3.38	5.34	6.00	9.9	2.6	4.7	1.3	-0.9
S. Nestor	CAR	AA	22	2	4	1	75	65	41	86	5	44.8%	.319	-3	1.41	4.44	5.64	6.37	9.6	5.5	6.9	1.0	-6.0
E. Ramirez*	SAC	AAA	31	3	0	2	21¹	18	2	11	0	50.7%	.261	-4	0.94	1.27	2.78	2.11	7.2	1.3	3.4	0.0	8.3
	ABQ	AAA	31	2	1	1	21²	27	4	10	3	49.4%	.329	-26	1.43	3.73	6.35	4.43	11.5	2.2	3.1	1.3	2.6
C. Seddon*	CAR	AA	23	3	6	0	68²	65	25	58	6	48.9%	.306	-11	1.31	4.32	5.76	5.97	10.1	3.8	5.1	1.3	-2.6
	MNT	AA	23	3	4	0	71	71	23	40	7	53.3%	.302	-24	1.32	4.94	6.73	6.89	10.9	3.6	3.3	1.6	-9.0
	FLO	MLB	23	0	2	0	17¹	29	5	10	2	40.0%	.380	-17	1.96	8.84	5.82	8.55	11.7	1.8	4.1	0.9	-8.1
R. Tucker	JUP	A+	20	5	8	0	138¹	142	46	104	6	48.4%	.319	2	1.36	3.71	5.79	5.85	10.4	4.4	4.1	1.0	-3.5
R. Wolf	ABQ	AAA	24	4	3	2	47¹	54	17	23	5	61.4%	.314	-28	1.50	3.42	5.34	4.53	10.1	3.5	3.2	1.0	5.4
	FLO	MLB	24	0	1	0	12¹	24	3	6	4	50.0%	.392	-53	2.27	11.71	13.57	12.51	14.5	1.3	4.0	2.6	-8.2
M. Zarate	JUP	A+	24	2	2	1	26	19	11	20	1	45.8%	.265	-10	1.15	2.42	4.48	3.91	7.4	5.5	4.7	0.8	4.3
	CAR	AA	24	0	1	1	25²	14	9	32	2	59.0%	.207	6	0.89	1.40	3.36	3.20	5.7	3.6	7.5	1.1	6.7
	ABQ	AAA	24	2	0	0	34	29	12	23	2	40.6%	.278	-6	1.21	2.38	3.54	2.41	7.2	3.5	4.5	0.5	11.9

Another arm received from Boston in the Hanley Ramirez/Josh Beckett deal, Venezuelan righty **Jesus Delgado** throws hard and has a decent curve, but his lack of polish has most seeing him as a reliever in the end. ⊘ **Nate Field** throws strikes, which makes him a reasonable candidate to put up decent numbers in Shea Stadium now that he's signed with the Mets. ⊘ **Harvey Garcia** lost some of his buzz last year by struggling at Double-A and Triple-A while many other Marlins relievers pitched well. ⊘ **Carlos Martinez** returned from Tommy John surgery last year and pitched poorly. Like Garcia, he has become something of a forgotten man. ⊘ **Scott Nestor** is a big reliever with a big fastball, who recorded some big strikeout totals at Double-A but also a big walk rate. Sometimes, you don't want everything to be big. ⊘ **Erasmo Ramirez** made a cameo as a lefty specialist last year and could help most teams in that role thanks to excellent control. ⊘ With their rotation in shambles late last year, the Marlins had to call on soft-tossing **Chris Seddon** for four September starts. The results were disastrous. ⊘ Right-hander **Ryan Tucker** has the best arm strength in the system, with a fastball that sits in the mid-90s and touches 97 mph, but scouts project him as a reliever in the end due to his lack of command or any usable secondary offering. ⊘ Like Seddon, **Ross Wolf** was asked to perform tasks above his pay grade last year and was found wanting. He needs to be perfect to survive with his mediocre stuff. ⊘ Organizational arm **Mauro Zarate** moved from the Florida State League to the National League in four months, his fastball/slider combination proving effective. Impressed, the Padres claimed him off waivers after the season.

MANAGER: FREDI GONZALEZ

YEAR	TEAM	W-L	Pythag +/−	Avg PC	100+ P	120+ P	QS	BQS	REL	REL w Zero R	IBB	Subs	PH	PH Avg	PH HR	SB2	CS2	SB3	CS3	SAC Att	SAC %	POS SAC	Squeeze	Swing	In Play
2007	FLO	71-91	0	91.0	50	3	48	11	560	375	60	54	284	.213	7	83	25	22	7	92	78.3%	24	4	135	90

We didn't learn a lot about Fredi Gonzalez in 2007. He inherited a bunch of pitchers who may have been worked too hard, or at least to their maximum stress point, by his predecessor, and the failure of those pitchers to approach expectations defined the season. One thing we did like was Gonzalez's flexibility in the bullpen, where he adapted to changing availability well, assembling and reassembling an effective relief corps on a weekly basis. He correctly identified Hanley Ramirez as his best hitter and attempted to use him in the third slot in the order for about a month, then later switched to Jeremy Hermida in that role. Gonzalez also showed a Piniella-esque knack for letting the guys who can run run, and stopping everyone else: four Marlins had eight or more steal attempts, and they went 79-for-102 on the bases. The rest of the team only tried 37 times, many of those blown hit-and-runs.

Houston Astros

Although organizational management in the major leagues is trending toward an almost technocratic thoroughness, there are still those rare holdouts that take their cue from Frank Sinatra and do it their way. Consider the Astros, one of the last franchises to have what you might consider an old-school owner/operator in Drayton McLane. Whether it's been overvaluing the contributions of franchise (though not necessarily fan) favorites such as catcher Brad Ausmus and shortstop Adam Everett, or reducing the team's 2007 season to a farewell parade for one of the greatest Astros of all time, this is one outfit in which things get done in accordance to the wishes—or caprices—of the owner.

McLane's inconsistency and shortsightedness have been the butt of criticism going back to his earliest days with the team, leading to rebukes not merely in the pages of books like this one, but even at the hands of Whitey Herzog. In his *You're Missin' a Great Game*, Herzog expressed disbelief over the fact that McLane failed to anticipate arbitration-related salary hikes. The Astros were forced to trade two lineup cornerstones, center fielder Steve Finley and third baseman Ken Caminiti, when they became arbitration eligible after the 1994 season in part because the team's payroll was larded up with the then-monster contracts McLane had given to free agent pitchers Greg Swindell and Doug Drabek upon taking over the team prior to the 1993 season. Wrote Herzog, "He could have seen it coming and made allowances, but from everything I hear, the whole thing caught him by surprise! . . . How could an otherwise smart man mess up *that* bad?"

Since just before the Finley/Caminiti trade, the man providing advice on how to avoid such mistakes has been the franchise's gray eminence, team president Tal Smith. While Smith has the benefit of a half-century of industry experience, it seems strange that among the accomplishments listed most prominently in his official team bio are the installation of AstroTurf in the Astrodome and the inclusion of a hill in deepest center field at Minute Maid Park. Not only is the positive value of these achievements not universally accepted, but their prominence serves to obscure Smith's most distinguishing characteristic: he's a survivor in a front office in which not many execs survive. Not even success has spared Houston managers or general managers from McLane's ax. From the decision after his first season in possession of the team to fire Art Howe for not doing better than a third-place finish behind the hundred-win Braves and Giants in the old seven-team NL West, to running off former Manager of the Year Larry Dierker after four division titles in five years—essentially for not keeping some of the key Killer B's happy—to last season's decision to ax general manager Tim Purpura in August for merely following orders instead of finding a miraculous solution to the inevitable implosion of a team built around a used-up Craig Biggio, the franchise's operations on McLane's watch have been characterized by a remarkably bloody-minded turnover. Joining Purpura at the wall in August was manager Phil Garner; whatever else may be said about Scrap Iron, he was widely credited for his work in helping guide the team to the NL wild card in 2004 and its first-ever NL pennant in 2005.

This front-office turnover has contributed to a fundamental disconnect between the aspiration to contend and what appears to be the preferred means of doing so. Rather than focus on how to contend through

---

ASTROS PROSPECTUS

2007 record: 73-89; Fourth place, NL Central

Pythagenport record: 72-90

Runs scored per game: 4.46 (13th in NL)

Runs allowed per game: 5.02 (12th in NL)

Team EqA: .257 (10th in NL)

2007 Batters Age: 31.9 (2nd oldest in NL)

2007 Pitchers Age: 30.8 (5th oldest in NL)

Ballpark: Minute Maid Park; Slight pitcher's park; Park Factor of .984

2007: Biggio's Viking funeral results in just the second losing season on Drayton McLane's watch.

2008: Ed Wade's win-now strategy is so crazy it just might work.

improving the personnel in the lineup, the Astros have instead operated for years on the assumption that certain players were building blocks because they liked them, not because of what they actually contributed on the field. When the players in question are Biggio and Jeff Bagwell in their primes, that's fine; when they are Ausmus, Everett, or a completely cooked Biggio, the term "building block" is robbed of its meaning.

Given this mentality, it was really no surprise that the Astros turned 2007 into a supersized Viking funeral for legitimate franchise great Biggio, complete with a team-level self-immolation, and with little but the ashes left to show for it at the end. While there is no doubt that the Astros saw themselves as a contending ballclub entering the 2007 season, they operated on the assumption that they could contend with a lineup that included demonstrably ineffective players because they had won the wild card twice before with them. What they failed to recognize was that the lineups thus encumbered only made it to the playoffs because those teams had Roger Clemens and Andy Pettitte in the rotation alongside remaining ace Roy Oswalt. The team assumed that employing Biggio was a key component to contending, and when they failed to recognize that this had stopped being the case at least a year earlier, they lost sight of the impossible contradiction between trying to win, and trying to win with Biggio and their other punchless standbys.

Singling out the Biggio example is to risk overstating it, when it is instead the most obvious symptom of an organization that has long been averting its collective gaze from the future. Despite a farm system that has ranked among the game's worst for years, the franchise had successfully avoided reckoning with the unpleasantness to come in its wild-card years. The declining standards of the NL Central inspired ongoing delusions of grandeur even as the team struggled to play .500 ball in 2006. Last year's meltdown was a necessary reminder that tomorrow had already come, and it didn't bring a good Astros team with it.

With the franchise in apparent ruin, and Purpura out of a job, McLane and Smith found themselves at a crossroads as they began their search for a new general manager. Some of the men interviewed for the position were frank in discussing how miserable the Astros' situation was, which apparently wasn't what the Texas tycoon or his factotum wanted to hear. And so, instead of hiring someone with an extensive player development background to overhaul the organization from top to bottom, or some progressive ivy league wunderkind cranked out of the front offices of Boston, Cleveland, or Oakland, the Astros hired the man who told them that the good times didn't have to come to an end, and that if contention with Biggio had been a pipe dream, contention without him was immediately possible. Sometimes, a good interview makes all the difference.

The pied piper who landed the job, Ed Wade, was an unlikely candidate for a comeback, but in this industry, unlikely comebacks happen in the boardroom even more often than on the diamond. The former Phillies GM was nobody's first choice for resurrection. His relatively slender résumé showed Wade to be a product of a franchise with an unrepentant reliance on cronyism, the architect of a big-league team noted for its reliable non-achievement, and the instigator of merely modest (but measurable) improvements in player development for a farm system that had nowhere to go but up when he took over the team after the 1997 season. Add in what became an almost laughable penchant for overpaying for relief help on the free agent market and managing to lose almost every major swap he'd ever swung, and it would seem nearly impossible to believe that there was something in Wade's past that would make him a great choice to relaunch the Astros into the playoff picture. Truth be told, there wasn't, but that isn't what mattered. What mattered was that Wade told McLane he thought the Astros could win now. The crazy part is, it might not be such a bad idea.

Why not make a banzai run? It's actually an inspired decision reflecting an understanding of the competitive ecology of a National League—and especially a NL Central Division—that is devoid of real titans, as evidenced by the Rockies' run to the World Series. Only two teams in the league won 90 games last year and 85 victories have been enough to claim the Central in each of the last two seasons. What's more, the Astros key big-ticket veterans—Oswalt, first baseman Lance Berkman, and left fielder Carlos Lee—are all in their thirties and locked in for years to come at prices that make them nearly untradeable. In an environment in which not many teams are parting with their blue-chip talent (witness the Dan Haren trade or the absence of a Johan Santana exchange), it isn't all that likely that the Astros could have gotten much for their stars anyway.

In contrast, consider what blasting down to the foundations would have involved. There's very little talent in the pipeline; the Astros' house is effectively built on quicksand. Stripping the team bare would mean season after season of terrible baseball, as it would be years before a rebuilt, fully functioning farm system could become the platform for any future success in Houston. The Astros player development system was once notable for being among the first to truly exploit Venezuela as a pool of talent, but 10 to 15 years later, everybody's throwing money around Latin America. What had been a relatively cheap private reserve has become another area in which the Astros' scouting isn't particularly exceptional. Perhaps most significantly, a long-term plan is pointless in this organization, because nobody—except for McLane and Smith—is going to be here long enough to enjoy the benefits.

Charged with fulfilling his sunny vision of the present, Wade got busy quickly, essentially dealing closer Brad Lidge, outfielder Luke Scott, and three of the system's best remaining arms (Troy Patton, Matt Albers, and Juan Gutierrez) to get former D'back Jose Valverde to close, former Phillie farmhand Michael Bourn to play center and leadoff, and former Oriole Miguel Tejada to give the team its best-hitting shortstop since Dickie Thon was unhurt. While pawning off the system's best nearly ready young pitchers only deepens the shadows of the club's medium-term picture two or three years from now, there's a logic to the moves that works for the here and now. Valverde has pitched in another tough park for pitchers without going through Lidge's epic struggles, and he'll be under team control for a year longer than Lidge would have been. Tejada is the sort of hitter who should provide two or three wins of difference over Everett in the lineup, and concerns over Tejada's declining range at short were somewhat compensated for by the decision to bring in second baseman Kazuo Matsui from the Rockies on a three-year deal. Matsui will disabuse those who believe he's turned the corner as a hitter, but he will provide slick glove work. Similarly, whether or not you believe in Bourn's on-base abilities, last year's leadoff men got aboard at a .309 clip, a mark Bourn should be able to top. Also, starting Bourn in center pushes Hunter Pence to right and thus upgrades the team's outfield defense. Add in the likelihood that rookie J. R. Towles will take over the majority of the playing time behind the plate, and the Astros' lineup should be able to pick up some ground while also fronting a better overall defensive unit. An increased reliance on Towles would also effectively remove the last of the team's ineffective troika from the lineup following Biggio's retirement and Wade's non-tendering of Everett in the wake of the Tejada acquisition.

Given those improvements to the lineup, the team's immediate fortune remains to be made on the pitching side of the equation. For the Astros to really make a run at the division, the key will be sorting out who's going to fill the nine or ten spots between Oswalt and Valverde on the pitching staff. Some of the obvious bits can be discerned—they're stuck with homer-prone 41-year-old Woody Williams, lefty starter Wandy Rodriguez took a large step forward last year, and relief additions such as journeymen Doug Brocail and Chad Paronto and trade acquisitions Oscar Villarreal and Geoff Geary should provide a frisson of veteran utility to the Opening Day bullpen.

Beyond scraping up vets like Brocail and Paronto out of the low end of the free agent market, the team's real hope for assembling a better pitching staff might be reflected in the decision to promote Dewey Robinson, the organization's pitching development director, to pitching coach; if there's a pitcher in the Astros' system that is remotely close to being ready for the major leagues, Robinson will both know about him and have already worked with him. Robinson previously received credit for putting Brad Lidge back together again, and while the list of pitching coaches who have been credited as geniuses has an almost perfect one-for-one relationship with the list of men who have been pitching coaches, there's reason to invest some hope in Robinson's ability to provide manager Cecil Cooper with some assistance in sorting out who's going to occupy the last two slots in the rotation and three or four bullpen jobs.

While contention might sound like a tall order, keep in mind the low bar for success. None of the National League playoff teams from the last two seasons had a rotation as good as those Astros wild-card teams from a few years ago; instead, many of them relied on an ace, a few innings eaters, and a deep bullpen. It worked for last year's Rockies, and while the 2008 Astros will have to rely on scrapheap pickups in the pen, where do you think the 2007 Rockies found LaTroy Hawkins or Matt Herges? If contention in the NL requires little more than a winning record, Wade can justifiably claim that his activity might have put his team in that vicinity. The organization's player development program will still need to be restarted at some point, but given that Wade was a man who already didn't appear to have any tomorrows in the game, he can afford to leave that for later.

HITTERS

Josh Anderson   CF

Bats: L   Throws: R   Height: 6' 2"   Weight: 195   Born: August 10, 1982   Age: 25

YEAR	TEAM	LVL	AGE	PA	R	2B	3B	HR	RBI	BB	SO	SB	CS	EqBRR	AVG	OBP	SLG	MLVr	EqAVG	EqOBP	EqSLG	EqA	VORP	DEFENSE		
2005	CCH	AA	22	573	67	17	9	1	26	29	80	50	19	-1.2	.282	.329	.355	-.054	.243	.288	.306	.217	-25.0	125-CF	5	
2006	CCH	AA	23	610	83	26	4	3	50	27	73	43	13	-0.3	.308	.349	.385	.022	.270	.301	.338	.232	-11.8	117-CF	-17	
2007	ROU	AAA	24	564	64	17	6	2	43	32	75	40	8	2.1	.273	.325	.341	-.137	.241	.291	.303	.221	-36.4	55-RF	-2	38-CF 1
2007	HOU	MLB	24	75	10	3	0	0	11	5	6	1	1	0.0	.358	.413	.403	.181	.373	.434	.418	.304	4.8	15-CF	-3	
2008	ATL	MLB	25	557	69	20	5	1	35	29	80	35	8	1.4	.266	.309	.332	-.206	.264	.307	.338	.231	-5.7	131-CF	-4	

Breakout: 31% Improve: 52% Collapse: 21% Attrition: 20%   Comparables: Kerry Robinson, Jerry Owens, Alex Sanchez, Rich Thompson

The fastest way to unwarranted playing time is to hit a small-sample .350 in your MLB debut. Anderson hit .358 despite not being anything like that kind of hitter; in fact, he can't hit at all and will put up an empty .280 at best, an empty .240 at worst. His speed and defense make him viable as a fifth outfielder. Acquired by the Braves as a holding pattern until they picked up a starting center fielder, Anderson is dubious insurance against a Mark Kotsay injury; their own Gregor Blanco is a better version of the same player.

Brad Ausmus   C

Bats: R   Throws: R   Height: 5' 11"   Weight: 190   Born: April 14, 1969   Age: 39

YEAR	TEAM	LVL	AGE	PA	R	2B	3B	HR	RBI	BB	SO	SB	CS	EqBRR	AVG	OBP	SLG	MLVr	EqAVG	EqOBP	EqSLG	EqA	VORP	DEFENSE	
2005	HOU	MLB	36	451	35	19	0	3	47	51	48	5	3	-2.1	.258	.351	.331	-.073	.254	.349	.332	.246	7.7	120-C	8
2006	HOU	MLB	37	502	37	16	1	2	39	45	71	3	1	-1.2	.230	.308	.285	-.265	.231	.311	.285	.217	-17.5	125-C	5
2007	HOU	MLB	38	397	38	16	3	3	25	37	74	6	1	-0.8	.235	.318	.324	-.187	.241	.327	.338	.240	-1.3	100-C	5
2008	HOU	MLB	39	170	15	5	1	1	13	16	31	3	1	-0.3	.225	.303	.291	-.294	.227	.305	.297	.212	-2.5	44-C	1

Breakout: 15% Improve: 28% Collapse: 46% Attrition: 58%   Comparables: Elston Howard, Tony Peña, Bob Boone, Sherm Lollar

He's just *so* bad. Ausmus' defense doesn't come close to making up for his utter lack of offense. He has been killing the Astros for the better part of five years, and yet they keep bringing him back, largely because he's popular, quotable, and experienced. How Cecil Cooper divides the playing time behind the plate between Ausmus and J. R. Towles will be one of the earliest indicators of his facility as a major league manager. Optimism isn't warranted.

Lance Berkman   1B

Bats: S   Throws: L   Height: 6' 1"   Weight: 220   Born: February 10, 1976   Age: 32

YEAR	TEAM	LVL	AGE	PA	R	2B	3B	HR	RBI	BB	SO	SB	CS	EqBRR	AVG	OBP	SLG	MLVr	EqAVG	EqOBP	EqSLG	EqA	VORP	DEFENSE		
2005	HOU	MLB	29	565	76	34	1	24	82	91	72	4	1	-3.5	.293	.411	.524	.301	.285	.405	.520	.315	47.1	83-1B	-1	32-LF -3
2006	HOU	MLB	30	646	95	29	0	45	136	98	106	3	2	-2.7	.315	.420	.621	.440	.310	.416	.614	.338	70.1	102-1B	1	34-RF -2
2007	HOU	MLB	31	668	95	24	2	34	102	94	125	7	3	-3.6	.278	.386	.510	.210	.282	.393	.526	.310	42.1	118-1B	8	25-RF 0
2008	HOU	MLB	32	639	99	30	2	30	99	93	110	7	2	-1.4	.281	.389	.515	.185	.283	.392	.524	.306	42.0	149-1B	2	

Breakout: 5% Improve: 30% Collapse: 30% Attrition: 8%   Comparables: Eddie Murray, Chili Davis, Gil Hodges, Carlos Delgado

One of the strangest stories of last season was Berkman's power outage in the first two months. He hit one double in his first 189 at-bats and just six homers in that time, slugging .339 through June 3. There was no injury, no radical change in approach, just a complete lack of power for two months. That was his low point; he hit .298/.388/.597 after June 3, and can be expected to be himself—and a full-time first baseman—in 2008.

Craig Biggio   2B

Bats: R   Throws: R   Height: 5' 11"   Weight: 185   Born: December 14, 1965   Age: 42

YEAR	TEAM	LVL	AGE	PA	R	2B	3B	HR	RBI	BB	SO	SB	CS	EqBRR	AVG	OBP	SLG	MLVr	EqAVG	EqOBP	EqSLG	EqA	VORP	DEFENSE	
2005	HOU	MLB	39	651	94	40	1	26	69	37	90	11	1	2.6	.264	.325	.468	.067	.262	.322	.471	.271	29.6	132-2B	-3
2006	HOU	MLB	40	607	79	33	0	21	62	40	84	3	2	1.7	.246	.306	.422	-.075	.247	.307	.425	.251	8.3	118-2B	-11
2007	HOU	MLB	41	555	68	31	3	10	50	23	112	4	3	-0.5	.251	.285	.381	-.159	.257	.294	.397	.237	-6.7	104-2B	-17

Biggio didn't need 3,000 hits to be a Hall of Famer. His long run of greatness and MVP-caliber peak qualified him for the honor by the end of 2005. He fell off a cliff in 2006, so much so that he was clearly unqualified to be a regular last season. The Astros started him anyway and paid a severe price, but Biggio reached his milestone. That was supposedly "for the fans," but any time a team puts individual accomplishment, or worse, a statistic, ahead of team goals, it sends the wrong message. Respect Biggio's body of work and the good things he does off the field, but remember that, like Pete Rose, he played too long while chasing a number.

Eric Bruntlett UT

Bats: R   Throws: R   Height: 6' 0"   Weight: 190   Born: March 29, 1978   Age: 30

YEAR	TEAM	LVL	AGE	PA	R	2B	3B	HR	RBI	BB	SO	SB	CS	EqBRR	AVG	OBP	SLG	MLVr	EqAVG	EqOBP	EqSLG	EqA	VORP	DEFENSE			
2005	HOU	MLB	27	121	19	5	2	4	14	10	25	7	2	0.0	.220	.292	.413	-.095	.220	.298	.440	.253	1.3	11-CF	4		
2006	HOU	MLB	28	136	11	8	0	0	10	13	21	3	1	0.0	.277	.351	.345	-.077	.275	.353	.333	.251	2.0	16-SS	1		
2007	ROU	AAA	29	262	31	10	4	1	21	31	36	13	4	2.1	.278	.365	.370	-.012	.243	.332	.326	.242	-3.2	34-CF	5	12-SS	-1
2007	HOU	MLB	29	165	16	5	0	0	14	20	27	6	3	-0.5	.246	.346	.283	-.176	.257	.358	.293	.240	-1.4	39-SS	-3		
2008	PHI	MLB	30	379	48	18	3	4	30	40	63	14	5	0.8	.252	.336	.357	-.133	.248	.334	.349	.243	4.1	91-SS	-4		

Breakout: 15%   Improve: 45%   Collapse: 25%   Attrition: 31%   Comparables: Jose Flores, Pete Coachman, Chris Sexton, Dick Tracewski

Bruntlett is a useful bench player, providing average or better defense at six positions, pinch-runner's speed, and a willingness to draw walks. You wouldn't want him to play regularly because his defense doesn't really carry his offense at any single position, but as a Swiss-Army-knife reserve, he helps a good manager win games. Traded with Brad Lidge, he'll have the same job in Philadelphia, where he will get most of his playing time as a defensive replacement in the outfield.

Chris Burke 2B/OF

Bats: R   Throws: R   Height: 5' 11"   Weight: 180   Born: March 11, 1980   Age: 28

YEAR	TEAM	LVL	AGE	PA	R	2B	3B	HR	RBI	BB	SO	SB	CS	EqBRR	AVG	OBP	SLG	MLVr	EqAVG	EqOBP	EqSLG	EqA	VORP	DEFENSE			
2005	HOU	MLB	25	359	49	19	2	5	26	23	62	11	6	0.2	.248	.309	.368	-.107	.248	.309	.376	.240	-4.4	72-LF	-2		
2006	HOU	MLB	26	413	58	23	1	9	40	27	77	11	1	1.6	.276	.347	.418	.016	.279	.348	.420	.272	15.3	38-2B	-2	32-CF	2
2007	HOU	MLB	27	363	39	19	2	6	28	27	52	9	3	-1.2	.229	.304	.357	-.180	.237	.313	.374	.243	-5.6	34-2B	-3	22-CF	-2
2008	ARI	MLB	28	374	50	21	3	9	40	29	55	10	3	0.5	.271	.339	.430	-.016	.261	.329	.410	.256	8.6	90-2B	-2		

Breakout: 23%   Improve: 47%   Collapse: 31%   Attrition: 22%   Comparables: Mark Ellis, Pat Kelly, Joel Youngblood, Steve Lombardozzi

If after 2004, the Astros had embarked on a project to drive Chris Burke's value as far down as possible, they wouldn't have done anything differently. The biggest loser in Biggio's pursuit of his 3,000th hit, Burke was jerked between second base and all three outfield positions, which clearly affected his offense and thus made it harder to justify playing him at all. He would have been better off spending three full seasons at the keystone in Triple-A Round Rock. Traded to Arizona, he's blocked again, this time by Orlando Hudson, and still has to prove he can hit even enough to justify a bench spot.

Collin DeLome OF

Bats: L   Throws: R   Height: 6' 2"   Weight: 195   Born: December 18, 1985   Age: 22

YEAR	TEAM	LVL	AGE	PA	R	2B	3B	HR	RBI	BB	SO	SB	CS	EqBRR	AVG	OBP	SLG	MLVr	EqAVG	EqOBP	EqSLG	EqA	VORP	DEFENSE			
2007	TCV	A-	21	273	31	17	6	6	28	23	65	9	2	0.3	.300	.374	.494	.226	.225	.281	.383	.229	-11.2	33-CF	-7	11-LF	-2
2008	HOU	MLB	22	553	55	31	5	12	53	40	150	11	5	0.8	.221	.283	.375	-.223	.223	.285	.383	.226	-6.5	130-CF	-1		

Breakout: 26%   Improve: 51%   Collapse: 19%   Attrition: 12%   Comparables: Steve Murphy, Jeremy Dodson, K.C Gillum, Mark Little

Last year, the Astros lost their top-two draft picks to free agent compensation. On Drayton McLane's orders, they toed the line on signing bonuses to their third- and fourth-round picks. All of which made DeLome, their fifth-round selection, the prize of their 2007 draft class. He's a toolsy outfielder with good speed and some lefty pop whose stats mean nothing given his combination of age and level.

Mitch Einertson OF

Bats: R   Throws: R   Height: 5' 10"   Weight: 178   Born: April 4, 1986   Age: 22

YEAR	TEAM	LVL	AGE	PA	R	2B	3B	HR	RBI	BB	SO	SB	CS	EqBRR	AVG	OBP	SLG	MLVr	EqAVG	EqOBP	EqSLG	EqA	VORP	DEFENSE			
2005	LEX	A	19	422	52	19	1	7	45	52	99	5	4	-2.3	.234	.353	.352	-.044	.187	.275	.275	.193	-40.1	39-LF	-5	35-CF	-7
2006	LEX	A	20	469	51	25	1	12	62	31	77	6	2	-2.1	.211	.276	.359	-.128	.185	.230	.301	.179	-54.5	78-LF	6	28-CF	-3
2007	SLM	A+	21	496	68	40	3	11	87	35	75	5	4	0.5	.305	.365	.482	.230	.257	.302	.402	.243	1.8	65-CF	-7	33-LF	3
2008	HOU	MLB	22	545	51	31	2	12	57	36	117	5	3	-0.1	.236	.293	.379	-.191	.239	.295	.386	.231	-4.9	128-CF	0		

Breakout: 46%   Improve: 74%   Collapse: 11%   Attrition: 12%   Comparables: Damon Hollins, Steve Gibralter, Willie Romero, Ronnie Hall

In 2004, Einertson had the best debut of any 2004 draftee, tying the Appalachian League record with 24 home runs in just 63 games. That was followed by two horrible years in the Sally League as Einertson dealt with some personal issues. Back-to-back showings like that at Low-A are often enough to warrant a write-off, but Einertson was one of the comeback stories of 2007, winning the Carolina League batting title and earning MVP honors. He's no longer a true power hitter, and his lack of athleticism limits him to left, but he's back to the point of looking like a guy who could reach the majors, as opposed to a candidate for the "Whatever Happened To?" files.

Adam Everett   **SS**   Bats: R   Throws: R   Height: 6' 0"   Weight: 170   Born: February 2, 1977   Age: 31

YEAR	TEAM	LVL	AGE	PA	R	2B	3B	HR	RBI	BB	SO	SB	CS	EqBRR	AVG	OBP	SLG	MLVr	EqAVG	EqOBP	EqSLG	EqA	VORP	DEFENSE	
2005	HOU	MLB	28	595	58	27	2	11	54	26	103	21	7	2.6	.248	.290	.364	-.145	.247	.289	.372	.233	2.5	146-SS	3
2006	HOU	MLB	29	566	52	28	6	6	59	34	71	9	6	-0.7	.239	.290	.352	-.204	.240	.292	.354	.226	-8.7	142-SS	20
2007	HOU	MLB	30	236	18	11	1	2	15	14	31	4	2	-1.7	.232	.281	.318	-.271	.237	.289	.324	.214	-7.0	59-SS	5
2008	MIN	MLB	31	265	23	10	1	3	23	13	41	5	2	0.4	.233	.275	.320	-.272	.235	.279	.337	.219	-4.3	65-SS	3

Breakout: 19%   Improve: 42%   Collapse: 39%   Attrition: 37%   Comparables: Frank Duffy, Greg Pryor, Joe McEwing, Alvaro Espinoza

Everett remains wildly underrated due to the lack of appreciation for his defensive work, which is almost unmatched. He was on his way to another Gold Glove–caliber season last year when he collided with Carlos Lee while chasing a popup in short left field against the A's on June 14. The broken fibula he suffered cost him three months. Everett was non-tendered after the season (a brutal decision, even after the acquisition of Miguel Tejada) and signed with the Twins, for whom he'll do what he's always done.

Josh Flores   **OF**   Bats: R   Throws: R   Height: 6' 0"   Weight: 195   Born: November 18, 1985   Age: 22

YEAR	TEAM	LVL	AGE	PA	R	2B	3B	HR	RBI	BB	SO	SB	CS	EqBRR	AVG	OBP	SLG	MLVr	EqAVG	EqOBP	EqSLG	EqA	VORP	DEFENSE			
2005	GRV	Rk	19	269	49	12	5	8	25	16	57	20	6	1.7	.335	.384	.520	.349	.207	.243	.297	.184	-58.8	35-LF	-2	21-CF	-2
2006	LEX	A	20	526	81	19	2	11	35	33	107	28	6	3.8	.253	.313	.371	-.031	.204	.248	.299	.193	-40.4	107-CF	-9		
2007	SLM	A+	21	276	49	16	6	5	30	23	47	25	5	2.6	.325	.392	.500	.314	.264	.318	.409	.257	4.5	53-CF	-5		
2007	CCH	AA	21	219	29	8	3	2	12	18	40	14	0	3.6	.219	.284	.323	-.215	.193	.252	.294	.206	-16.5	54-CF	-6		
2008	HOU	MLB	22	554	60	23	4	8	43	34	127	26	7	1.8	.237	.289	.347	-.241	.239	.291	.354	.226	-6.6	130-CF	-1		

Breakout: 49%   Improve: 77%   Collapse: 11%   Attrition: 10%   Comparables: Kenny Kelly, Andre King, Scott Hunter, Decomba Conner

Another of the Astros' burners, Flores had a hot streak to kick off the year at High-A Salem before being slapped down by the Texas League. When looking at this kind of player's profile, the important things to consider are his contact rate, walk rate, and power. Flores doesn't walk enough or slug enough to justify his strikeouts, which aren't a byproduct of patience or power but an indication that he can't hit.

Mike Lamb   **3B**   Bats: L   Throws: R   Height: 6' 1"   Weight: 190   Born: August 9, 1975   Age: 32

YEAR	TEAM	LVL	AGE	PA	R	2B	3B	HR	RBI	BB	SO	SB	CS	EqBRR	AVG	OBP	SLG	MLVr	EqAVG	EqOBP	EqSLG	EqA	VORP	DEFENSE			
2005	HOU	MLB	29	349	41	13	5	12	53	22	65	1	1	-1.3	.236	.284	.419	-.088	.234	.284	.425	.242	-3.0	48-1B	-5	12-3B	2
2006	HOU	MLB	30	421	70	22	3	12	45	35	55	2	4	-0.7	.307	.361	.475	.147	.303	.360	.472	.282	16.9	56-1B	-4	28-3B	3
2007	HOU	MLB	31	353	45	14	2	11	40	36	45	0	0	1.6	.289	.366	.453	.114	.290	.371	.471	.290	16.0	46-3B	-2	25-1B	2
2008	MIN	MLB	32	263	29	13	2	5	32	22	41	1	1	0.0	.265	.329	.403	-.048	.267	.333	.425	.266	4.4	65-3B	-1		

Breakout: 8%   Improve: 26%   Collapse: 37%   Attrition: 30%   Comparables: Dick Sisler, Irv Noren, Glenn Adams, Catfish Metkovich

Lamb has reached the "professional hitter" portion of his career, during which he will get work by virtue of being a left-handed batter who can keep his average above .280 and his OPS in the 800s. That's not to denigrate him; Lamb hits for average, draws a few walks, has a little pop, plays the corners passably, and doesn't expect 500 at-bats. The Twins, who have gotten nothing from third base since Corey Koskie left, signed him to a two-year, $6.6 million deal. It's a good fit.

Carlos Lee — LF

Bats: R Throws: R Height: 6' 2" Weight: 240 Born: June 20, 1976 Age: 32

YEAR	TEAM	LVL	AGE	PA	R	2B	3B	HR	RBI	BB	SO	SB	CS	EqBRR	AVG	OBP	SLG	MLVr	EqAVG	EqOBP	EqSLG	EqA	VORP	DEFENSE	
2005	MIL	MLB	29	688	85	41	0	32	114	57	87	13	4	-4.0	.265	.324	.487	.092	.261	.322	.489	.275	24.6	158-LF	0
2006	MIL	MLB	30	435	60	18	0	28	81	38	39	12	2	-1.1	.286	.347	.549	.202	.282	.346	.549	.300	27.2	95-LF	-14
2006	TEX	MLB	30	260	42	19	1	9	35	20	26	7	0	0.0	.322	.369	.525	.222	.313	.369	.524	.306	20.0	48-LF	-7
2007	HOU	MLB	31	697	93	43	1	32	119	53	63	10	5	-4.1	.303	.354	.528	.208	.307	.360	.546	.301	42.5	152-LF	-15
2008	HOU	MLB	32	636	88	36	2	27	100	51	68	12	3	-0.9	.291	.348	.499	.108	.293	.351	.508	.288	32.7	149-LF	-10

Breakout: 9% Improve: 40% Collapse: 27% Attrition: 7%   Comparables: Kevin McReynolds, Dante Bichette, Eric Karros, Dave Henderson

The problem with the six-year, $100-million contract the Astros signed Lee to prior to last season is that, even if he keeps doing Carlos Lee things, he's not good enough to be the highest-paid player on a championship team, and he'll be the highest-paid Astro over the final four years of the deal. Lee's durability leads to excellent counting stats, for which he's being paid. However, he uses a ton of outs—at least 422 in each of the past five seasons—while playing poor defense, which gives still more outs to the opposition. Those two things kill his actual value. RBI are nice; wins are nicer, and Lee doesn't produce enough of them.

Mark Loretta — INF

Bats: R Throws: R Height: 6' 0" Weight: 185 Born: August 14, 1971 Age: 36

YEAR	TEAM	LVL	AGE	PA	R	2B	3B	HR	RBI	BB	SO	SB	CS	EqBRR	AVG	OBP	SLG	MLVr	EqAVG	EqOBP	EqSLG	EqA	VORP	DEFENSE			
2005	SDN	MLB	33	463	54	16	1	3	38	45	34	8	4	-5.6	.280	.360	.347	-.006	.292	.370	.366	.265	10.8	101-2B	-7		
2006	BOS	MLB	34	703	75	33	0	5	59	49	63	4	1	-2.0	.285	.345	.361	-.093	.282	.349	.361	.254	12.3	132-2B	-14		
2007	HOU	MLB	35	511	52	23	2	4	41	44	41	1	2	-4.6	.287	.352	.372	-.025	.294	.363	.386	.263	9.8	54-SS	-3	22-2B	-4
2008	HOU	MLB	36	290	30	13	1	3	27	26	26	2	1	-0.9	.268	.339	.357	-.118	.270	.341	.363	.247	7.8	71-2B	-6		

Breakout: 4% Improve: 28% Collapse: 49% Attrition: 45%   Comparables: Dick Groat, Bill Russell, Cookie Rojas, Willie Randolph

Loretta will warrant a bench job as long as he raps out good contact rates and .280 batting averages. However, the steep decline in his range and loss of the power he had at his peak make him a substandard starting second baseman, and it's likely that he'll end up as an at least part-time starter for the Astros this year, because it's unlikely that Kaz Matsui will both stay healthy and play well all season long.

Tommy Manzella — SS

Bats: R Throws: R Height: 6' 2" Weight: 190 Born: April 16, 1983 Age: 25

YEAR	TEAM	LVL	AGE	PA	R	2B	3B	HR	RBI	BB	SO	SB	CS	EqBRR	AVG	OBP	SLG	MLVr	EqAVG	EqOBP	EqSLG	EqA	VORP	DEFENSE	
2005	TCV	A-	22	233	24	6	4	0	18	9	40	5	3	-1.0	.232	.260	.295	-.226	.170	.190	.219	.115	-54.8	45-SS	-3
2006	LEX	A	23	387	50	22	1	7	43	33	80	16	8	-4.0	.275	.340	.408	.073	.225	.276	.330	.214	-11.4	90-SS	5
2007	SLM	A+	24	251	28	13	0	0	24	19	30	5	2	-0.4	.238	.305	.296	-.175	.199	.250	.238	.167	-20.7	55-SS	1
2007	CCH	AA	24	254	35	12	3	1	15	19	40	10	2	2.2	.289	.343	.382	.013	.258	.307	.348	.235	0.2	58-SS	1
2008	HOU	MLB	25	495	42	19	3	3	36	26	102	11	5	0.5	.226	.270	.301	-.343	.228	.273	.306	.199	-11.6	117-SS	2

Breakout: 37% Improve: 55% Collapse: 22% Attrition: 16%   Comparables: Derek Henderson, Jim Byrd, Kurt Ehmann, Tim Bogar

There's an old saying about the ease of finding good-field/no-hit players: "Shake a tree, and ten gloves fall out." One of them would be a Tommy Manzella model. The starting shortstop on Tulane's College World Series team in 2005, Manzella could play defense in the majors right now, it's just that he'd hit about .175 with no secondary skills. John McDonald's career path is Manzella's upside, but he's unlikely to ever reach the majors.

Eric Munson — C

Bats: L Throws: R Height: 6' 3" Weight: 220 Born: October 3, 1977 Age: 30

YEAR	TEAM	LVL	AGE	PA	R	2B	3B	HR	RBI	BB	SO	SB	CS	EqBRR	AVG	OBP	SLG	MLVr	EqAVG	EqOBP	EqSLG	EqA	VORP	DEFENSE			
2005	DUR	AAA	27	425	67	22	0	25	71	38	81	1	1	-3.4	.285	.351	.539	.177	.255	.321	.482	.269	10.5	90-1B	-10		
2006	HOU	MLB	28	156	10	6	0	5	19	11	32	0	0	-1.6	.199	.269	.348	-.272	.199	.269	.355	.216	-5.9	31-C	-1		
2007	ROU	AAA	29	201	28	18	0	7	26	24	34	1	1	-0.2	.283	.368	.509	.198	.257	.342	.469	.276	11.2	32-C	0	15-1B	2
2007	HOU	MLB	29	150	14	4	0	4	15	16	15	0	0	0.7	.235	.313	.356	-.147	.237	.320	.374	.246	0.4	34-C	-5		
2008	MIL	MLB	30	306	34	14	0	11	41	31	56	1	1	-0.8	.251	.331	.435	-.040	.251	.329	.438	.259	9.9	74-C	-6		

Breakout: 27% Improve: 51% Collapse: 24% Attrition: 21%   Comparables: Tony Clark, Charles Johnson, Tyler Houston, Travis Lee

Phil Garner's decision to make Eric Munson his backup catcher was inspired, as Munson—a lefty power bat without defensive skills—was the perfect complement to Ausmus. Unfortunately, Munson stopped hitting for power, slugging .352 over his two years in Houston. He has signed with the Brewers, and while it's tempting to say that he'd be a good backup to Jason Kendall for the same reasons, it's not clear that Munson still possesses the bat to fill that role.

Hunter Pence — OF

Bats: R   Throws: R   Height: 6′ 4″   Weight: 210   Born: April 13, 1983   Age: 25

YEAR	TEAM	LVL	AGE	PA	R	2B	3B	HR	RBI	BB	SO	SB	CS	EqBRR	AVG	OBP	SLG	MLVr	EqAVG	EqOBP	EqSLG	EqA	VORP	DEFENSE			
2005	LEX	A	22	341	59	14	3	25	60	38	53	8	3	-0.7	.338	.413	.652	.521	.260	.323	.474	.267	14.9	42-CF	-5	27-LF	-2
2005	SLM	A+	22	171	24	8	1	6	30	18	37	1	2	2.4	.305	.374	.490	.251	.237	.297	.372	.229	-2.6	28-CF	-2		
2006	CCH	AA	23	592	97	31	8	28	95	60	109	17	4	1.9	.283	.357	.533	.224	.245	.311	.453	.262	1.6	105-RF	5	20-CF	-2
2007	ROU	AAA	24	106	17	11	1	3	21	10	15	2	0	0.3	.326	.387	.558	.351	.292	.355	.510	.295	8.5	18-CF	4		
2007	HOU	MLB	24	484	57	30	9	17	69	26	95	11	5	-0.4	.322	.360	.539	.252	.329	.370	.561	.305	40.5	93-CF	5	13-RF	2
2008	HOU	MLB	25	567	81	30	4	23	82	44	110	13	4	0.9	.285	.344	.495	.090	.288	.346	.504	.284	31.6	133-CF	4		

Breakout: 19%   Improve: 53%   Collapse: 12%   Attrition: 13%   Comparables: Luis Matos, Glenn Braggs, Charlie Spikes, George Hendrick

Six weeks spent on the DL with a broken right wrist cost Pence a shot at the Rookie of the Year award. Even with that, his debut was a success, albeit one with some flaws. There's just no way to spin his K/BB numbers, which reflect a see-ball/hit-ball approach that withered a bit against good breaking pitches. Pence struck out in about one of every four at-bats against righties. His second-half, post-wrist numbers—.293/.348/.464—are a better portrayal of where he is as a hitter than his overall line.

Humberto Quintero — C

Bats: R   Throws: R   Height: 5′ 9″   Weight: 215   Born: August 2, 1979   Age: 28

YEAR	TEAM	LVL	AGE	PA	R	2B	3B	HR	RBI	BB	SO	SB	CS	EqBRR	AVG	OBP	SLG	MLVr	EqAVG	EqOBP	EqSLG	EqA	VORP	DEFENSE	
2005	ROU	AAA	25	205	23	13	0	8	31	10	30	2	1	0.9	.288	.327	.482	.077	.254	.284	.420	.240	1.6	46-C	6
2005	HOU	MLB	25	57	6	1	0	1	8	1	10	0	0	0.2	.185	.200	.259	-.484	.182	.196	.255	.134	-4.6	14-C	-1
2006	ROU	AAA	26	322	39	21	2	4	37	19	48	4	0	0.5	.298	.352	.425	.109	.267	.315	.395	.248	5.2	78-C	7
2006	HOU	MLB	26	22	2	2	0	0	2	1	3	0	0	0.2	.333	.364	.429	.106	.333	.364	.429	.275	1.1		
2007	ROU	AAA	27	188	22	12	1	5	22	4	21	0	2	-1.6	.333	.355	.497	.216	.296	.319	.453	.258	8.9	45-C	9
2007	HOU	MLB	27	57	2	2	0	0	1	2	13	0	0	-1.4	.226	.281	.264	-.343	.226	.281	.264	.188	-2.4	17-C	1
2008	HOU	MLB	28	240	23	13	1	5	28	12	39	2	1	-0.3	.262	.306	.392	-.131	.265	.309	.400	.240	4.6	60-C	5

Breakout: 27%   Improve: 55%   Collapse: 27%   Attrition: 19%   Comparables: Yamid Haad, Vance Wilson, Chris Coste, Ruben Rodriguez

Quintero is more or less what the Astros think Ausmus is, a defense-first catcher with a strong arm and good mechanics behind the plate. Quintero's arm is a true deterrent: thieves were just 9-for-28 against him at Triple-A last year. His bat would be comparable to, or maybe a bit worse than Ausmus's, but the overall package would be better. With Ausmus back, Quintero will return to Triple-A and wait.

Max Sapp — C

Bats: L   Throws: R   Height: 6′ 2″   Weight: 220   Born: February 21, 1988   Age: 20

YEAR	TEAM	LVL	AGE	PA	R	2B	3B	HR	RBI	BB	SO	SB	CS	EqBRR	AVG	OBP	SLG	MLVr	EqAVG	EqOBP	EqSLG	EqA	VORP	DEFENSE	
2006	TCV	A-	18	189	20	9	0	1	20	22	37	0	0	-3.7	.229	.317	.301	-.055	.187	.259	.257	.178	-28.9	27-C	0
2007	LEX	A	19	359	25	23	0	2	32	38	70	0	0	-3.6	.241	.330	.333	-.108	.194	.265	.262	.183	-26.2	49-C	-5
2008	HOU	MLB	20	403	27	17	1	4	31	37	94	1	1	-1.5	.208	.284	.294	-.336	.210	.286	.299	.198	-12.6	96-C	-3

Breakout: 59%   Improve: 75%   Collapse: 20%   Attrition: 6%   Comparables: Scott Heard, Jared Abruzzo, Marcus Jensen, Mark Johnson

The Astros' first-round pick in 2006, Sapp was supposed to make the Ausmus debate moot. Now, he's just trying to escape the Sally League. Sapp was drafted for his power, but has just three homers and a .095 ISO as a pro. He's been young for his leagues, and you have to wonder if some of his problem is overcoaching. Last year, Sapp was hitting over .300 with an OBP above .400 in May, which would be valuable even without much power, but the team wanted him to be more aggressive at the plate, and he fell apart from there. He's too young to give up on, but with so little talent in the Astros' system, there will be a disproportionate focus on his development.

Luke Scott   OF

Bats: L   Throws: R   Height: 6' 0"   Weight: 210   Born: June 25, 1978   Age: 30

YEAR	TEAM	LVL	AGE	PA	R	2B	3B	HR	RBI	BB	SO	SB	CS	EqBRR	AVG	OBP	SLG	MLVr	EqAVG	EqOBP	EqSLG	EqA	VORP	DEFENSE			
2005	ROU	AAA	27	449	69	25	4	31	87	43	96	2	2	-1.9	.286	.363	.603	.318	.249	.318	.519	.276	12.7	86-LF	13	11-RF	1
2005	HOU	MLB	27	89	6	4	2	0	4	9	23	1	1	-0.1	.188	.270	.288	-.320	.188	.270	.287	.194	-5.9	17-LF	-2		
2006	ROU	AAA	28	381	63	15	1	20	63	52	66	6	1	-1.9	.299	.400	.541	.352	.275	.368	.506	.298	20.1	82-LF	6		
2006	HOU	MLB	28	249	31	19	6	10	37	30	43	2	1	-1.4	.336	.426	.621	.478	.332	.422	.617	.340	29.9	45-LF	-1		
2007	HOU	MLB	29	425	49	28	5	18	64	53	95	3	1	0.2	.255	.351	.504	.123	.256	.357	.526	.295	17.6	90-RF	9		
2008	BAL	MLB	30	398	51	20	2	16	56	43	91	4	1	0.0	.252	.336	.458	.024	.249	.337	.472	.280	8.4	95-RF	-1		

Breakout: 2%   Improve: 23%   Collapse: 36%   Attrition: 16%   Comparables: Jeromy Burnitz, Dan Pasqua, Franklin Stubbs, Geoff Jenkins

A brutal April weighed down Scott's stat line all season, so his good year was a bit overlooked. He was also killed by Minute Maid Park; his road line was .305/.400/.593. Traded to Baltimore in the Tejada deal, he should be the Orioles' platoon left fielder at the very least and capable of repeating his 2007 value at a low price for a couple of years. He's already 30, so there's not much upside left.

J. R. Towles   C

Bats: R   Throws: R   Height: 6' 2"   Weight: 195   Born: February 11, 1984   Age: 24

YEAR	TEAM	LVL	AGE	PA	R	2B	3B	HR	RBI	BB	SO	SB	CS	EqBRR	AVG	OBP	SLG	MLVr	EqAVG	EqOBP	EqSLG	EqA	VORP	DEFENSE	
2005	LEX	A	21	193	35	14	2	5	23	16	29	11	7	-1.3	.346	.436	.549	.421	.279	.340	.430	.263	8.4	36-C	0
2006	LEX	A	22	321	39	19	2	12	55	21	46	13	5	-1.9	.317	.382	.525	.318	.260	.305	.422	.251	6.8	58-C	3
2007	SLM	A+	23	115	14	3	2	0	11	12	15	3	5	-0.9	.200	.339	.278	-.156	.184	.278	.245	.191	-7.8	26-C	0
2007	CCH	AA	23	257	47	12	2	11	49	23	35	9	4	0.9	.324	.425	.551	.402	.292	.373	.509	.295	23.7	46-C	-3
2007	ROU	AAA	23	50	5	0	0	0	2	4	7	2	4	-1.3	.279	.354	.279	-.164	.250	.327	.250	.198	-1.7	12-C	-2
2007	HOU	MLB	23	44	9	5	0	1	12	3	1	0	1	-0.3	.375	.432	.575	.468	.375	.432	.550	.323	5.8	11-C	1
2008	HOU	MLB	24	474	61	25	3	13	55	35	77	12	6	1.4	.268	.334	.433	-.024	.270	.337	.441	.265	20.0	112-C	-1

Breakout: 32%   Improve: 61%   Collapse: 11%   Attrition: 9%   Comparables: A. J. Hinch, Phil Avlas, Raul Ibañez, Joe Randa

Before getting too crazy about Towles' season, remember that he was getting owned by the Carolina League in May when a suspension opened up a job at Double-A Corpus Christi. He tore up the Texas League and eventually made it all the way to Houston for a few weeks. Towles' buzz is the result of spending his age-21 and -22 seasons in the Sally League and two good months in Double-A. As much as the Astros need to replace Ausmus, they also need to be realistic about their in-house alternatives.

Ty Wigginton   3B

Bats: R   Throws: R   Height: 6' 0"   Weight: 225   Born: October 11, 1977   Age: 30

YEAR	TEAM	LVL	AGE	PA	R	2B	3B	HR	RBI	BB	SO	SB	CS	EqBRR	AVG	OBP	SLG	MLVr	EqAVG	EqOBP	EqSLG	EqA	VORP	DEFENSE			
2005	IND	AAA	27	328	53	18	0	14	52	45	56	8	5	-1.0	.293	.390	.507	.237	.266	.363	.461	.281	21.8	51-3B	2		
2005	PIT	MLB	27	171	20	9	1	7	25	14	30	0	1	-3.1	.258	.324	.465	.058	.258	.327	.477	.270	4.8	34-3B	-10		
2006	TBA	MLB	28	486	55	25	1	24	79	32	97	4	3	-2.9	.275	.330	.498	.074	.278	.339	.515	.284	20.5	38-1B	-2	38-2B	4
2007	TBA	MLB	29	417	47	21	0	16	49	28	73	1	4	-2.1	.275	.329	.458	.038	.285	.341	.501	.280	11.2	36-2B	-6	29-3B	-4
2007	HOU	MLB	29	187	24	12	0	6	18	13	40	2	0	0.5	.284	.342	.462	.085	.286	.348	.482	.285	7.7	43-3B	-1		
2008	HOU	MLB	30	480	60	25	1	19	72	41	88	4	2	-0.9	.273	.340	.471	.041	.276	.343	.480	.276	23.6	113-3B	-5		

Breakout: 14%   Improve: 37%   Collapse: 33%   Attrition: 16%   Comparables: Doug Rader, Sean Berry, Mike Blowers, Morgan Ensberg

Like a lot of guys who spend their careers on bad teams, Wigginton is a platoon player who has gotten too much playing time. Partnered with a lefty bat at third base, he'd be a useful cog on a winning team. Playing every day, his struggles against righties hurt the offense, and he's not nearly enough of a glove man to make up for that. With Mike Lamb in Minnesota, Wigginton is in line to be the Astros' full-time third baseman, exacerbating their lineup's OBP issues.

PITCHERS

Matt Albers

Bats: L   Throws: R   Height: 6' 0"   Weight: 205   Born: January 20, 1983   Age: 25

YEAR	TEAM	LVL	AGE	W	L	SV	G	GS	IP	H	BB	SO	HR	GB%	BABIP	STUFF	WHIP	ERA	PERA	EqERA	EqH9	EqBB9	EqSO9	EqHR9	VORP	SN/WX
2005	SLM	A+	22	8	12	0	28	27	148²	161	62	146	15	55.1%	.349	-26	1.50	4.66	9.04	8.55	12.9	5.9	5.1	1.8	-41.7	—
2006	CCH	AA	23	10	2	0	19	19	116¹	96	47	95	4	53.5%	.277	13	1.23	2.17	4.24	3.96	8.2	4.4	4.9	0.6	20.3	—
2006	ROU	AAA	23	2	1	0	4	4	25²	24	10	26	2	40.2%	.304	11	1.35	3.93	6.10	5.16	10.7	4.4	7.1	1.2	1.1	—
2006	HOU	MLB	23	0	2	0	4	2	15	17	7	11	1	45.8%	.356	-1	1.60	6.00	5.30	6.28	10.7	3.8	6.3	0.6	-0.2	-0.12
2007	ROU	AAA	24	2	3	0	9	9	53	50	22	43	6	53.8%	.301	-1	1.36	3.74	5.09	5.07	8.9	4.2	5.8	1.3	2.9	—
2007	HOU	MLB	24	4	11	0	31	18	110²	127	50	71	18	49.5%	.313	-15	1.60	5.85	5.51	5.64	9.5	3.4	5.3	1.4	-4.6	1.81
2008	BAL	MLB	25	4	6	0	31	11	83²	92	39	52	10	49.2%	.304	-4	1.56	5.03	4.83	4.90	9.4	3.8	5.3	1.0	5.5	0.90

Breakout: 36% Improve: 54% Collapse: 24% Attrition: 37%   Comparables: Mark Portugal, Fred Talbot, Buster Narum, Bob Wickman

In another organization, Albers wouldn't be considered much of a prospect and would likely have spent last year working at Triple-A, but the Astros just don't have much in their system, so Albers jumped from Double-A to the majors in a year, getting just 13 passable starts at Triple-A in between. He has a major league fastball and curve, but lacks command or good mechanics. Shipped to Baltimore in the Tejada deal, he will probably be an overmatched fifth starter for the Orioles this year.

Brandon Backe

Bats: R   Throws: R   Height: 6' 0"   Weight: 195   Born: April 5, 1978   Age: 30

YEAR	TEAM	LVL	AGE	W	L	SV	G	GS	IP	H	BB	SO	HR	GB%	BABIP	STUFF	WHIP	ERA	PERA	EqERA	EqH9	EqBB9	EqSO9	EqHR9	VORP	SN/WX
2005	HOU	MLB	27	10	8	0	26	25	149¹	151	67	97	19	43.1%	.288	-3	1.46	4.76	5.18	5.19	9.5	3.7	5.4	1.1	10.4	2.61
2006	HOU	MLB	28	3	2	0	8	8	43	43	18	19	4	38.3%	.275	-2	1.42	3.77	4.23	3.56	8.8	3.1	3.8	0.8	10.6	1.28
2007	HOU	MLB	29	3	1	0	5	5	28²	27	11	11	4	43.4%	.245	-5	1.33	3.76	3.90	3.41	7.8	2.8	3.4	1.2	5.9	0.77
2008	HOU	MLB	30	3	5	0	24	12	74¹	81	32	47	11	42.6%	.296	-7	1.52	5.12	5.57	5.40	9.8	3.4	5.1	1.3	2.0	0.60

Breakout: 8% Improve: 22% Collapse: 54% Attrition: 44%   Comparables: Steve Mura, Geremi Gonzalez, Charlie Bishop, Mike Bielecki

Backe has made just 13 starts over the last two seasons due to Tommy John surgery. In those 13 games, he struck out 30 and walked 29. Three six-inning quality starts at the end of last season gave rise to the notion that Backe's, uh, back, but he struck out eight in 18 innings and, having faced the Pirates, the late-September Cardinals, and the Braves, only beat one major league lineup. When healthy and at his best, he was a fourth starter, so the idea that he'll be a sufficient number-two behind Roy Oswalt this year is addled.

Brian Bogusevic

Bats: L   Throws: L   Height: 6' 3"   Weight: 215   Born: February 18, 1984   Age: 24

YEAR	TEAM	LVL	AGE	W	L	SV	G	GS	IP	H	BB	SO	HR	GB%	BABIP	STUFF	WHIP	ERA	PERA	EqERA	EqH9	EqBB9	EqSO9	EqHR9	VORP	SN/WX
2005	TCV	A-	21	0	2	3	13	0	21¹	30	9	17	2	56.4%	.368	-62	1.83	7.61	18.82	17.28	18.4	8.6	2.7	3.2	-21.7	—
2006	TCV	A-	22	0	0	0	3	3	11¹	10	5	6	1	60.5%	.250	-44	1.35	4.05	13.17	14.00	13.0	9.0	2.0	4.0	-8.4	—
2006	LEX	A	22	2	5	0	17	17	70	76	24	60	6	52.9%	.330	-36	1.43	4.76	9.21	9.64	13.1	5.6	4.0	1.9	-27.2	—
2007	SLM	A+	23	9	7	0	21	21	114¹	133	39	91	7	43.8%	.359	-22	1.50	4.02	8.37	7.62	13.3	5.1	4.4	1.4	-22.0	—
2007	CCH	AA	23	1	1	0	6	6	24¹	29	14	17	1	34.1%	.350	-16	1.77	7.41	7.22	9.53	11.9	6.4	4.0	0.8	-9.9	—
2008	HOU	MLB	24	4	9	0	20	20	100¹	128	63	59	17	43.5%	.326	-13	1.90	6.98	7.48	7.35	11.5	5.0	4.7	1.5	-18.7	-1.20

Breakout: 41% Improve: 76% Collapse: 10% Attrition: 17%   Comparables: Joe Saunders, Trey Moore, Mike Matthews, Scott Christman

A first-round pick in 2005, Bogusevic is yet another of this system's many disappointments. Injured throughout much of his junior year leading up to the draft, Bogusevic has never returned to the form he showed at Tulane. His fastball now sits in the 88 to 90 mph range, two or three ticks below his college days. There was a small minority that wanted to make him an outfielder rather than a pitcher, but there has been no talk of moving him yet.

Dave Borkowski

Bats: R   Throws: R   Height: 6' 1"   Weight: 230   Born: February 7, 1977   Age: 31

YEAR	TEAM	LVL	AGE	W	L	SV	G	GS	IP	H	BB	SO	HR	GB%	BABIP	STUFF	WHIP	ERA	PERA	EqERA	EqH9	EqBB9	EqSO9	EqHR9	VORP	SN/WX
2005	OTT	AAA	28	10	10	0	29	28	182²	217	38	104	18	47.7%	.327	-12	1.40	4.33	6.08	5.88	11.4	2.5	3.5	1.1	-5.3	—
2006	HOU	MLB	29	3	2	0	40	0	71	70	23	52	8	49.1%	.292	1	1.31	4.69	4.08	4.50	8.9	2.6	6.2	0.9	9.9	0.59
2007	HOU	MLB	30	5	3	1	64	0	71²	76	34	63	8	45.1%	.329	0	1.53	5.15	4.58	5.15	9.0	3.6	7.2	0.9	1.2	0.85
2008	HOU	MLB	31	2	2	2	38	0	48	50	18	33	6	46.0%	.295	-6	1.41	4.35	4.69	4.64	9.4	3.0	5.5	1.0	5.3	0.40

Breakout: 38% Improve: 57% Collapse: 26% Attrition: 33%   Comparables: Cal McLish, Masao Kida, Rodney Myers, Tyler Walker

For two seasons, Borkowski has occupied the second-lowest rung in the Astros bullpen. He pitches when they trail, or when the game is in extra innings, or occasionally when they're ahead by a bunch or if a starter gets pulled early. It's a bit unusual for one guy to hold that job for two straight years, and even Borkowski started getting some holds late last year. Still, he's a replacement-level talent with no upside.

Juan Gutierrez

Bats: R   Throws: R   Height: 6' 3"   Weight: 200   Born: July 14, 1983   Age: 24

YEAR	TEAM	LVL	AGE	W	L	SV	G	GS	IP	H	BB	SO	HR	GB%	BABIP	STUFF	WHIP	ERA	PERA	EqERA	EqH9	EqBB9	EqSO9	EqHR9	VORP	SN/WX
2005	LEX	A	21	9	5	0	22	21	120²	106	43	100	10	45.7%	.287	-24	1.23	3.21	7.16	6.93	10.6	6.0	3.9	1.8	-15.2	—
2006	CCH	AA	22	8	4	0	20	20	103	94	34	106	10	41.5%	.288	4	1.24	3.06	5.23	4.42	9.4	3.7	6.4	1.3	12.8	—
2007	ROU	AAA	23	5	10	0	26	25	156	154	63	108	17	48.6%	.295	-7	1.39	4.15	4.95	5.18	9.0	4.0	4.8	1.2	7.0	—
2007	HOU	MLB	23	1	1	0	7	3	21¹	25	6	16	3	32.4%	.338	2	1.45	5.92	5.00	5.48	10.1	2.1	6.3	1.3	0.1	-0.07
2008	ARI	MLB	24	5	8	0	35	20	113¹	126	53	76	19	45.3%	.299	-3	1.58	5.51	5.39	5.38	9.5	3.8	5.6	1.4	4.5	1.20

Breakout: 15% Improve: 44% Collapse: 24% Attrition: 16%   Comparables: Rodrigo Lopez, Jose Paniagua, Ricardo Rodriguez, Felix Diaz

Dealt to the Diamondbacks in the Jose Valverde trade, Gutierrez relies mainly on a sinking fastball in the low 90s to get groundballs. His other pitches are just passable, and his command of everything needs work. The rapid development of someone like Fausto Carmona is the model, but the D'backs would be happy to just get a good year from him in middle relief.

Jason Jennings

Bats: L   Throws: R   Height: 6' 2"   Weight: 235   Born: July 17, 1978   Age: 29

YEAR	TEAM	LVL	AGE	W	L	SV	G	GS	IP	H	BB	SO	HR	GB%	BABIP	STUFF	WHIP	ERA	PERA	EqERA	EqH9	EqBB9	EqSO9	EqHR9	VORP	SN/WX
2005	COL	MLB	26	6	9	0	20	20	122	130	62	75	11	49.9%	.306	5	1.57	5.02	4.26	4.71	8.5	4.1	4.9	0.7	6.4	1.24
2006	COL	MLB	27	9	13	0	32	32	212	206	85	142	17	45.4%	.295	18	1.37	3.78	3.62	3.44	8.2	3.1	5.5	0.6	50.8	5.68
2007	HOU	MLB	28	2	9	0	19	18	99	119	34	71	19	38.5%	.327	-11	1.55	6.45	5.88	6.17	10.1	2.6	6.0	1.6	-8.2	0.74
2008	HOU	MLB	29	6	7	0	29	18	115	119	43	79	14	42.9%	.290	2	1.41	4.45	4.87	4.71	9.2	3.0	5.5	1.1	11.6	1.90

Breakout: 14% Improve: 39% Collapse: 27% Attrition: 24%   Comparables: Joey Hamilton, Jim Clancy, Doyle Alexander, Joey Jay

Just erase 2007 and start over. Jennings was a durable ground-ball machine for the Rockies, but he missed 15 starts and got the ball in the air more than ever before for the Astros. Diagnosed with tendonitis in his right elbow after just two starts and treated with six weeks of rehab, Jennings came back and pitched progressively worse, then was shut down in August with a torn flexor tendon in the same spot. He underwent surgery and hit the market as a broken free agent, and remained unsigned as we went to press. He's not a bad gamble for an NL team with a good middle infield.

Brad Lidge

Bats: R   Throws: R   Height: 6' 5"   Weight: 210   Born: December 23, 1976   Age: 31

YEAR	TEAM	LVL	AGE	W	L	SV	G	GS	IP	H	BB	SO	HR	GB%	BABIP	STUFF	WHIP	ERA	PERA	EqERA	EqH9	EqBB9	EqSO9	EqHR9	VORP	SN/WX
2005	HOU	MLB	28	4	4	42	70	0	70²	58	23	103	5	48.8%	.349	34	1.15	2.29	3.88	3.06	8.6	2.8	10.9	0.7	22.1	4.62
2006	HOU	MLB	29	1	5	32	78	0	75	69	36	104	10	47.4%	.335	17	1.40	5.28	4.44	5.24	8.5	3.6	10.5	1.0	3.6	0.81
2007	HOU	MLB	30	5	3	19	66	0	67	54	30	88	9	45.5%	.300	20	1.25	3.36	3.68	3.44	7.1	3.4	10.1	1.1	15.0	2.13
2008	PHI	MLB	31	4	4	17	53	0	60²	53	24	65	7	45.9%	.291	14	1.27	3.54	3.70	3.56	7.6	3.3	8.6	1.0	14.5	1.70

Breakout: 31% Improve: 60% Collapse: 19% Attrition: 8%   Comparables: Kyle Farnsworth, Roberto Hernandez, Lee Smith, Ben Wade

As expected, Lidge bounced back from his poor 2006 to be one of the best relievers in the game again last year. The thing is, his rates have shown very little variation over the past three seasons seen above. His BABIP allowed dropped 30 points last year, all of which went to his ERA, but he didn't actually pitch much differently in 2006 than in the two stronger years surrounding it. Dealt to Philadelphia, Lidge will find his new home park no more forgiving of his fly-ball tendencies than Minute Maid was.

Trever Miller

| | | | | Bats: R | | Throws: L | | Height: 6' 3" | | Weight: 200 | | Born: May 29, 1973 | | | Age: 35 |

YEAR	TEAM	LVL	AGE	W	L	SV	G	GS	IP	H	BB	SO	HR	GB%	BABIP	STUFF	WHIP	ERA	PERA	EqERA	EqH9	EqBB9	EqSO9	EqHR9	VORP	SN/WX
2005	TBA	MLB	32	2	2	0	61	0	44¹	45	29	35	4	43.0%	.333	1	1.67	4.06	5.34	4.36	8.7	5.8	7.1	0.8	5.2	-0.90
2006	HOU	MLB	33	2	3	1	70	0	50²	42	13	56	7	34.3%	.282	19	1.09	3.02	3.54	2.68	7.5	2.0	9.1	1.1	17.0	1.65
2007	HOU	MLB	34	0	0	1	76	0	46¹	45	23	46	6	37.7%	.302	4	1.47	4.86	4.24	4.28	8.0	3.7	8.0	1.1	4.4	0.46
2008	HOU	MLB	35	2	2	4	51	0	45²	43	20	41	5	38.7%	.291	1	1.38	4.03	4.43	4.25	8.5	3.5	7.2	1.0	6.8	0.60

Breakout: 12% Improve: 29% Collapse: 43% Attrition: 24% — Comparables: Pedro Borbon, Dennis Cook, Ron Mahay, Willie Hernandez

It's been a pretty good second act for Miller, who after the 2000 season was cut loose by the Dodgers, then his fourth organization in five years. He had a 5.43 ERA in 162 major league innings at that point, a 10.47 mark in 2000, and seemed like a good candidate for law school. After two more organizations over the next two years, Miller popped up in Toronto at the beginning of 2003 and hasn't looked back, posting a 3.93 ERA in 346 appearances as a lefty specialist for the Jays, Rays, and 'Stros. There are hundreds of pitchers in this book who have some dismissive comment beneath their statistics; a handful of them will have Miller's future.

Brian Moehler

| | | | | Bats: R | | Throws: R | | Height: 6' 3" | | Weight: 235 | | Born: December 31, 1971 | | | Age: 36 |

YEAR	TEAM	LVL	AGE	W	L	SV	G	GS	IP	H	BB	SO	HR	GB%	BABIP	STUFF	WHIP	ERA	PERA	EqERA	EqH9	EqBB9	EqSO9	EqHR9	VORP	SN/WX
2005	FLO	MLB	33	6	12	0	37	25	158¹	198	42	95	16	46.4%	.349	0	1.52	4.55	5.22	4.55	10.7	2.2	5.0	0.9	13.4	2.65
2006	FLO	MLB	34	7	11	0	29	21	122	164	38	58	19	46.8%	.340	-22	1.66	6.57	6.61	6.97	11.6	2.4	3.9	1.3	-16.5	0.21
2007	HOU	MLB	35	1	4	1	42	0	59²	67	17	36	8	53.9%	.304	-8	1.41	4.07	4.53	3.90	9.4	2.1	5.1	1.0	10.2	-0.01
2008	HOU	MLB	36	3	3	2	37	2	60²	67	18	33	6	48.4%	.300	-11	1.41	4.20	4.69	4.48	9.9	2.4	4.3	0.9	7.2	0.70

Breakout: 34% Improve: 63% Collapse: 18% Attrition: 37% — Comparables: Terry Leach, Roger Craig, Mike Maddux, Ted Power

Hey, remember when scuffing a baseball was considered the height of cheating in baseball? You know, all the way back in 1999 when nobody was paying attention to that other stuff? Moehler's use of sandpaper to help his breaking ball earned him notoriety, a suspension, and a nickname. Nearly a decade later, just one of those persists, as Scuffy's attempt to gain an advantage seems almost quaint in the post–Mitchell Report era. Moehler is a replacement-level pitcher who serves as little more than a jumping-off point for a story.

Bud Norris

| | | | | Bats: R | | Throws: R | | Height: 6' 0" | | Weight: 195 | | Born: March 2, 1985 | | | Age: 23 |

YEAR	TEAM	LVL	AGE	W	L	SV	G	GS	IP	H	BB	SO	HR	GB%	BABIP	STUFF	WHIP	ERA	PERA	EqERA	EqH9	EqBB9	EqSO9	EqHR9	VORP	SN/WX
2006	TCV	A-	21	2	0	2	15	3	38²	28	13	46	1	44.6%	.305	-9	1.07	3.77	6.72	8.82	10.2	6.6	5.8	1.4	-11.7	—
2007	LEX	A	22	2	8	0	22	22	96²	85	41	117	8	49.2%	.321	-9	1.30	4.75	7.09	7.87	10.5	6.3	6.5	1.6	-21.4	—
2007	SLM	A+	22	1	0	0	1	1	6	4	1	2	0	63.2%	.211	-13	0.83	1.50	3.57	3.38	6.8	3.4	1.7	0.0	1.3	—
2008	HOU	MLB	23	4	9	0	29	19	109	119	77	83	17	46.7%	.307	-7	1.80	6.21	6.74	6.58	9.8	5.6	6.1	1.4	-11.5	-0.50

Breakout: 40% Improve: 69% Collapse: 12% Attrition: 11% — Comparables: Aaron Cames, Rob Steinert, Tom LaRosa, Matt Lorenzo

Norris is one of the few bright spots in baseball's worst minor league system. A sixth-round pick in 2006, Norris surprised scouts last year when he started putting his fastball in the 93 to 95 mph range and touching 97 while also missing bats with a hammer curve. Some see him as a reliever due to his size and lack of a changeup, but the Astros will take anything they can get right now.

Roy Oswalt

| | | | | Bats: R | | Throws: R | | Height: 6' 0" | | Weight: 185 | | Born: August 29, 1977 | | | Age: 30 |

YEAR	TEAM	LVL	AGE	W	L	SV	G	GS	IP	H	BB	SO	HR	GB%	BABIP	STUFF	WHIP	ERA	PERA	EqERA	EqH9	EqBB9	EqSO9	EqHR9	VORP	SN/WX
2005	HOU	MLB	27	20	12	0	35	35	241²	243	48	184	18	51.2%	.310	26	1.20	2.94	3.98	3.48	9.4	1.6	6.3	0.7	65.1	7.69
2006	HOU	MLB	28	15	8	0	33	32	220²	220	38	166	18	50.4%	.310	28	1.17	2.98	3.73	3.07	9.1	1.3	6.4	0.7	72.4	7.52
2007	HOU	MLB	29	14	7	0	33	32	212	221	60	154	14	54.4%	.311	27	1.33	3.18	3.60	3.05	8.7	2.1	6.0	0.5	59.8	6.71
2008	HOU	MLB	30	13	10	0	30	30	199²	205	50	138	19	50.8%	.296	14	1.27	3.62	4.13	3.86	9.2	2.0	5.5	0.9	37.0	5.60

Breakout: 2% Improve: 13% Collapse: 41% Attrition: 13% — Comparables: Frank Lary, Doug Drabek, Joaquin Andujar, Larry Jackson

In an article published on BaseballProspectus.com the day after Oswalt signed his five-year, $73 million contract extension in August 2006, Joe Sheehan wrote: "Oswalt is likely to spend his ages 29-31 seasons much as Mike Mussina did: pitching for a depleted team getting further from its peak, one that doesn't support him with defense or runs, and seeing his win-loss records separate from the quality of his pitching." That still sounds right, although Oswalt's contract, which has four years and $58 million left on it, now seems like a huge bargain. He's a threat to win a Cy Young Award every year.

Troy Patton

Bats: S Throws: L Height: 6' 1" Weight: 185 Born: September 3, 1985 Age: 22

YEAR	TEAM	LVL	AGE	W	L	SV	G	GS	IP	H	BB	SO	HR	GB%	BABIP	STUFF	WHIP	ERA	PERA	EqERA	EqH9	EqBB9	EqSO9	EqHR9	VORP	SN/WX
2005	LEX	A	19	5	2	0	15	15	78²	59	20	94	3	55.3%	.306	25	1.00	1.94	5.44	5.08	9.5	4.5	6.3	0.9	3.9	—
2005	SLM	A+	19	1	4	0	10	9	41	34	8	38	2	43.9%	.291	13	1.02	2.63	4.96	4.50	9.5	3.2	4.8	1.0	4.4	—
2006	SLM	A+	20	7	7	0	19	19	101	92	37	102	4	45.7%	.318	13	1.28	2.94	5.66	6.60	10.3	4.7	5.9	0.9	-10.3	—
2006	CCH	AA	20	2	5	0	8	8	45	48	13	37	6	36.1%	.327	1	1.36	4.40	6.59	6.59	10.8	3.4	4.9	1.7	-4.7	—
2007	CCH	AA	21	6	6	0	16	16	102¹	96	33	69	10	43.7%	.278	-6	1.26	2.99	5.26	4.36	9.3	3.7	3.9	1.3	13.4	—
2007	ROU	AAA	21	4	2	0	8	8	49	44	11	25	5	40.0%	.264	0	1.12	4.59	3.85	5.06	7.9	2.2	3.4	1.1	2.9	—
2007	HOU	MLB	21	0	2	0	3	2	12²	10	4	8	3	30.0%	.194	10	1.11	3.54	3.81	3.38	6.1	2.0	5.4	2.0	2.4	0.17
2008	BAL	MLB	22	6	11	0	26	26	141²	167	62	75	25	41.2%	.298	-3	1.61	5.94	5.66	5.67	10.1	3.6	4.5	1.6	-4.4	0.60

Breakout: 8% Improve: 29% Collapse: 39% Attrition: 11% Comparables: Abe Alvarez, Jarrod Washburn, Andrew Lorraine, Bob Wolcott

Like Albers and Gutierrez, Patton was rushed to the majors as the Astros adjusted to an injury-riddled, post–Clemens/Pettitte world. Patton has the most talent of all the pitchers the Astros traded away this winter, but seems to have recurring shoulder problems that, combined with his age, are a huge red flag. The Orioles need to think about the long term and would be wise to manage Patton's innings carefully for the next year or two.

Felipe Paulino

Bats: R Throws: R Height: 6' 2" Weight: 180 Born: October 5, 1983 Age: 24

YEAR	TEAM	LVL	AGE	W	L	SV	G	GS	IP	H	BB	SO	HR	GB%	BABIP	STUFF	WHIP	ERA	PERA	EqERA	EqH9	EqBB9	EqSO9	EqHR9	VORP	SN/WX
2005	LEX	A	21	1	1	0	7	5	24¹	21	6	30	2	48.4%	.328	0	1.11	1.85	7.01	5.75	11.5	4.4	6.6	1.8	-0.3	—
2005	TCV	A-	21	2	2	1	13	2	30²	21	11	34	2	47.4%	.253	-14	1.04	3.81	7.16	7.92	9.4	6.8	5.0	2.2	-6.4	—
2006	SLM	A+	22	9	7	0	27	26	126	119	59	91	13	45.2%	.285	-37	1.41	4.36	8.16	7.64	11.1	5.9	4.1	2.1	-25.1	—
2007	CCH	AA	23	6	9	0	22	21	112	103	49	110	6	39.0%	.307	9	1.36	3.62	4.98	5.67	9.3	4.8	6.1	0.8	-0.8	—
2007	HOU	MLB	23	2	1	0	5	3	19	22	7	11	5	49.3%	.283	-13	1.53	7.11	6.29	6.41	9.6	2.7	4.6	2.3	-2.3	0.27
2008	HOU	MLB	24	5	9	0	38	20	119	125	63	91	18	43.6%	.297	-2	1.57	5.27	5.74	5.56	9.4	4.2	6.1	1.3	0.6	0.80

Breakout: 39% Improve: 66% Collapse: 12% Attrition: 13% Comparables: Javier De La Hoya, Jorge DePaula, Manny Aybar, Ramon Ramirez

This big Dominican is the best prospect remaining in the Astros' system, and while he has just one season above A-ball, he may well find himself in the rotation come April. Paulino throws a mid-90s fastball and hard breaking stuff and has the kind of size that lets you project a big workload onto him. He even improved upon moving up to Double-A last year. He's a legitimate mid-rotation prospect.

Chad Qualls

Bats: R Throws: R Height: 6' 5" Weight: 225 Born: August 17, 1978 Age: 29

YEAR	TEAM	LVL	AGE	W	L	SV	G	GS	IP	H	BB	SO	HR	GB%	BABIP	STUFF	WHIP	ERA	PERA	EqERA	EqH9	EqBB9	EqSO9	EqHR9	VORP	SN/WX
2005	HOU	MLB	26	6	4	0	77	0	79²	73	23	60	7	59.6%	.292	4	1.21	3.27	4.06	3.89	8.7	2.5	6.4	0.8	15.5	1.98
2006	HOU	MLB	27	7	3	0	81	0	88²	76	28	56	10	60.5%	.266	-3	1.17	3.75	3.78	3.63	8.0	2.6	5.4	1.0	21.8	2.93
2007	HOU	MLB	28	6	5	5	79	0	82²	84	25	78	10	57.7%	.335	12	1.32	3.05	4.35	2.91	9.0	2.4	8.2	1.0	25.3	3.61
2008	ARI	MLB	29	3	3	5	58	0	65²	70	23	48	6	54.8%	.311	1	1.41	3.99	4.11	3.99	9.1	2.8	6.1	0.8	13.4	1.10

Breakout: 8% Improve: 25% Collapse: 41% Attrition: 15% Comparables: Mike Timlin, Mark Eichhorn, Braden Looper, Tim Crabtree

Qualls has had a persistent backward split over his last three seasons, making him valuable as a second "lefty" or, more importantly, as a pitcher who can be used for complete or multiple innings. Throw in a propensity for getting groundballs, and you have a very valuable reliever. Sent to Arizona in the Valverde deal, Qualls will be part of a deep pen that has no clear closer candidate, but he'd be wasted in a 65-inning role.

Chad Reineke

Bats: R   Throws: R   Height: 6' 6"   Weight: 210   Born: April 9, 1982   Age: 26

YEAR	TEAM	LVL	AGE	W	L	SV	G	GS	IP	H	BB	SO	HR	GB%	BABIP	STUFF	WHIP	ERA	PERA	EqERA	EqH9	EqBB9	EqSO9	EqHR9	VORP	SN/WX
2005	LEX	A	23	10	8	4	42	11	102¹	84	49	108	5	52.7%	.312	-11	1.30	3.52	6.75	6.91	10.2	7.6	5.3	1.2	-12.5	—
2006	SLM	A+	24	6	5	0	17	17	99	82	29	87	5	52.9%	.275	-5	1.12	3.00	4.93	5.81	9.1	3.8	4.9	1.1	-2.2	—
2006	CCH	AA	24	1	3	0	15	4	44¹	33	26	45	3	45.6%	.264	5	1.34	3.06	4.84	4.43	8.0	6.4	6.4	0.9	5.3	—
2007	ROU	AAA	25	5	5	0	32	16	100	99	52	95	7	38.0%	.332	5	1.51	4.68	4.98	5.93	9.3	5.1	6.7	0.8	-3.5	—
2008	HOU	MLB	26	3	5	1	24	10	71¹	73	41	58	9	42.8%	.299	-1	1.58	5.09	5.49	5.40	9.1	4.5	6.4	1.1	1.6	0.50

Breakout: 32% Improve: 61% Collapse: 14% Attrition: 25%   Comparables: Marcus Moore, Dennis Sarfate, Jon Leicester, Jimmy Journell

Reineke has been frustrating in that the Astros have tried hard to develop him as a starter, but his changeup has never come around, and last year he pitched much better in relief, a role that will likely become permanent for him this year. He's built like a power pitcher, and his slider is definitely a power pitch, but his fastball is no more than average, so his future is likely no more than middle relief.

Wandy Rodriguez

Bats: S   Throws: L   Height: 5' 11"   Weight: 160   Born: January 18, 1979   Age: 29

YEAR	TEAM	LVL	AGE	W	L	SV	G	GS	IP	H	BB	SO	HR	GB%	BABIP	STUFF	WHIP	ERA	PERA	EqERA	EqH9	EqBB9	EqSO9	EqHR9	VORP	SN/WX
2005	ROU	AAA	26	4	2	0	8	8	46¹	43	16	48	7	40.6%	.300	4	1.27	3.69	5.67	4.60	9.4	3.6	6.9	1.7	4.8	—
2005	HOU	MLB	26	10	10	0	25	22	128²	135	53	80	19	46.1%	.294	-13	1.46	5.52	5.89	6.15	10.0	3.5	5.3	1.3	-1.8	1.26
2006	ROU	AAA	27	2	2	0	5	5	26¹	32	13	13	2	43.6%	.333	-28	1.72	6.90	8.10	9.62	12.6	5.2	3.0	1.1	-10.9	—
2006	HOU	MLB	27	9	10	0	30	24	135²	154	63	98	17	47.5%	.329	-3	1.60	5.64	5.76	6.23	10.4	3.7	6.1	1.0	-4.3	0.96
2007	HOU	MLB	28	9	13	0	31	31	182²	179	62	158	22	43.6%	.299	19	1.32	4.58	3.87	4.47	8.2	2.6	7.1	1.0	18.9	4.01
2008	HOU	MLB	29	7	9	0	32	20	133¹	136	51	101	17	44.4%	.295	5	1.40	4.56	4.87	4.84	9.2	3.0	6.0	1.1	11.3	2.10

Breakout: 29% Improve: 59% Collapse: 18% Attrition: 20%   Comparables: Casey Fossum, Al Jackson, Ramon Ortiz, Dave Koslo

Look past the ERA and the record: Rodriguez took a huge leap forward last season, as you can see by the translated rates above. Just a year after suffering a midseason demotion, Rodriguez established himself as a credible third starter. He's not pitch-efficient, and as a small, high-effort hurler—a bit like Ted Lilly in some ways—he's not going to be an innings guy, but within his limits, he'll be valuable.

Chris Sampson

Bats: R   Throws: R   Height: 6' 1"   Weight: 190   Born: May 23, 1978   Age: 30

YEAR	TEAM	LVL	AGE	W	L	SV	G	GS	IP	H	BB	SO	HR	GB%	BABIP	STUFF	WHIP	ERA	PERA	EqERA	EqH9	EqBB9	EqSO9	EqHR9	VORP	SN/WX
2005	CCH	AA	27	4	12	4	32	19	150	147	19	92	11	56.6%	.288	-11	1.11	3.12	5.18	5.52	10.5	2.1	3.7	1.1	1.2	—
2006	ROU	AAA	28	12	3	4	27	18	125	110	14	68	12	59.9%	.250	-9	0.99	2.52	3.98	4.59	8.6	1.3	3.3	1.2	13.7	—
2006	HOU	MLB	28	2	1	0	12	3	34	25	5	15	3	55.0%	.212	1	0.88	2.12	2.57	2.67	6.4	1.1	3.7	0.8	12.9	1.34
2007	HOU	MLB	29	7	8	0	24	19	121²	138	30	51	20	48.2%	.294	-13	1.38	4.59	5.02	4.24	9.5	1.9	3.6	1.4	16.4	2.24
2008	HOU	MLB	30	5	7	0	36	13	99²	113	26	44	12	50.2%	.293	-11	1.39	4.54	4.94	4.85	10.2	2.0	3.5	1.1	8.0	1.40

Breakout: 8% Improve: 33% Collapse: 44% Attrition: 30%   Comparables: Fernando Arroyo, Elmer Dessens, Jerry Staley, Bob Tewksbury

Drafted by the Astros as a shortstop in 1999, Sampson retired after a poor pro debut in Low-A and became a coach at a Dallas-area community college. After a few years of throwing batting practice to his team, he tried out for the Astros as a pitcher in 2003 and landed a minor league contract, restarting his playing career. Sampson made his major league debut in 2006 and became part of the Astros rotation last year, but he's a better story than pitcher. A command specialist, he needs to be perfect to survive; last year he had four starts in which he didn't strike out anyone and two others with just one whiff. A sprained right UCL all but ended his season in July, but his good fortune was already starting to run out at the time of the injury, as he had posted a 6.86 ERA over his last seven starts. The massive exportation of starting pitching from Houston creates an opportunity for him to win another job in March, but he won't hold on to it for long.

Dennis Sarfate

Bats: R   Throws: R   Height: 6' 4"   Weight: 225   Born: April 9, 1981   Age: 27

YEAR	TEAM	LVL	AGE	W	L	SV	G	GS	IP	H	BB	SO	HR	GB%	BABIP	STUFF	WHIP	ERA	PERA	EqERA	EqH9	EqBB9	EqSO9	EqHR9	VORP	SN/WX
2005	HUN	AA	24	9	9	0	24	24	130	120	59	110	13	42.5%	.292	-18	1.38	3.88	5.67	5.36	8.9	4.8	4.8	1.6	3.2	—
2006	NAS	AAA	25	10	7	0	34	21	125¹	125	78	117	7	51.6%	.340	7	1.62	3.67	6.37	5.73	10.7	6.3	6.4	0.8	-1.7	—
2006	MIL	MLB	25	0	0	0	8	0	8¹	9	4	11	0	30.4%	.391	8	1.56	4.34	4.18	4.32	9.7	3.2	10.8	0.0	1.6	0.05
2007	NAS	AAA	26	2	7	4	45	1	61²	61	47	68	6	55.4%	.362	4	1.75	4.52	7.30	6.23	10.4	7.7	8.1	1.1	-3.9	—
2007	HOU	MLB	26	1	0	0	7	0	8¹	5	1	14	0	62.5%	.333	8	0.72	1.08	2.22	1.12	6.8	1.1	11.2	0.0	4.5	0.44
2008	BAL	MLB	27	3	4	3	46	4	53²	55	40	48	5	49.0%	.317	-3	1.77	4.96	5.30	4.79	8.8	6.2	7.4	0.9	4.1	0.50

Breakout: 34%   Improve: 61%   Collapse: 17%   Attrition: 15%   Comparables: Justin Kaye, Brad Salmon, Brian Bowles, Ryan Braun

Thanks to the Tejada deal, Safarte is the fourth Oriole in this chapter. A fastball/slider guy, Safarte may have found a home as a relief pitcher. His lack of command of either pitch led the Brewers to give up on him late last year, but he was fantastic for the Astros in what amounted to garbage time in September and now possesses a 25/5 K/BB in 16 2/3 MLB innings. He could be the bat-missing righty the O's need in the late innings.

Woody Williams

Bats: R   Throws: R   Height: 6' 0"   Weight: 200   Born: August 19, 1966   Age: 41

YEAR	TEAM	LVL	AGE	W	L	SV	G	GS	IP	H	BB	SO	HR	GB%	BABIP	STUFF	WHIP	ERA	PERA	EqERA	EqH9	EqBB9	EqSO9	EqHR9	VORP	SN/WX
2005	SDN	MLB	38	9	12	0	28	28	159²	174	51	106	24	36.3%	.299	-5	1.41	4.85	5.06	5.06	9.5	2.6	5.4	1.4	3.1	2.17
2006	SDN	MLB	39	12	5	0	25	24	145¹	152	35	72	21	37.8%	.275	-4	1.29	3.65	4.71	4.28	9.6	1.9	4.1	1.2	27.3	3.59
2007	HOU	MLB	40	8	15	0	33	31	188	216	53	101	35	41.8%	.292	-12	1.43	5.27	5.22	4.87	9.5	2.1	4.5	1.5	10.4	2.42
2008	HOU	MLB	41	5	7	0	25	16	106¹	121	31	54	16	42.7%	.290	-10	1.43	4.84	5.30	5.09	10.1	2.3	4.0	1.4	6.1	1.30

Breakout: 6%   Improve: 39%   Collapse: 28%   Attrition: 39%   Comparables: Danny Darwin, Rick Reuschel, Rip Sewell, Joe Niekro

It was an interesting little experiment, this combination of a fly-ball pitcher who typically gives up loads of power to right-handed batters and the Crawford Boxes in left field at Minute Maid Park. Thirty-five homers later, we learned that if a team is bad enough, they'll put up with whatever they get from a pitcher who never turns the ball down. Williams is due another $6 million this year. This is not going to end well.

LINEOUTS

Hitters

PLAYER		TEAM	LVL	AGE	PA	R	2B	3B	HR	RBI	BB	SO	SB-CS	EqBRR	AVG/OBP/SLG	MLVr	EqAVG/EqOBP/EqSLG	EqA	VORP
RF	E. Iorg	SLM	A+	24	177	35	12	4	5	24	14	36	14-2	-0.1	.296/.350/.512	.243	.236/.282/.406	.243	-5.9
UT	O. Palmeiro*	HOU	MLB	38	122	12	3	0	0	6	16	8	0-1	0.6	.233/.342/.262	-.224	.233/.347/.262	.225	-3.4
OF	J. Parraz	LEX	A	22	530	69	28	3	14	76	47	89	33-10	0.0	.281/.364/.446	.122	.227/.292/.354	.229	-25.0
SS	C. Ransom	ROU	AAA	31	563	75	35	0	28	90	52	131	21-5	2.6	.260/.333/.497	.095	.237/.307/.454	.262	17.3
		HOU	MLB	31	46	9	2	0	1	3	9	9	0-0	0.3	.229/.413/.371	.045	.229/.413/.371	.289	1.9

Outfielder **Eli Iorg** has plenty of talent, but Tommy John surgery cost him most of the 2007 season. That and a Mormon mission before he turned pro have made him a 25-year-old who still hasn't reached Double-A. ⊘ **Orlando Palmiero** has hit .252 or less in three of the past four seasons and has lost most of his speed. Despite his good eye at the plate, the free agent might be done. ⊘ Outfielder **Jordan Parraz** is a little old for his level, but he has a well-rounded set of skills and an outside chance of developing into an intriguing power/speed package. ⊘ **Cody Ransom** has good hands and enough bat to stick as a utility infielder in the majors. He'll go to camp with the Yankees.

Pitchers

PLAYER	TEAM	LVL	AGE	W	L	SV	IP	H	BB	SO	HR	GB%	BABIP	STUFF	WHIP	ERA	PERA	EqERA	EqH9	EqBB9	EqSO9	EqHR9	VORP
J. Barthmaier	CCH	AA	23	2	9	0	90	116	44	73	11	51.8%	.365	-32	1.78	6.20	9.44	9.75	13.2	5.5	4.9	1.6	-38.7
P. Estrada	ROU	AAA	24	1	8	8	70¹	72	42	69	6	48.6%	.333	-5	1.62	5.12	5.37	6.56	9.3	5.5	6.6	0.9	-7.5
M. McLemore*	ROU	AAA	26	0	1	0	52	34	35	52	2	31.6%	.246	15	1.33	2.77	3.51	3.66	5.7	6.3	6.8	0.5	11.1
	HOU	MLB	26	3	0	0	35	38	18	35	5	20.6%	.327	4	1.60	3.86	5.06	4.00	9.2	3.8	8.2	1.2	5.8
F. Nieve	ROU	AAA	24	1	3	0	21²	30	15	13	1	30.3%	.397	-18	2.07	6.22	8.86	9.15	13.7	6.9	4.1	0.5	-7.8
C. Park	NWO	AAA	34	4	4	0	51²	64	16	49	9	44.7%	.364	-10	1.55	5.57	8.56	7.36	12.5	3.2	7.0	1.9	-9.3
	ROU	AAA	34	2	10	0	84	100	24	70	18	47.7%	.323	-29	1.48	6.21	7.35	8.27	10.8	2.8	5.7	2.2	-24.5
	NYN	MLB	34	0	1	0	4	6	2	4	2	28.6%	.333	-42	2.00	15.75	17.24	18.00	13.5	4.5	9.0	4.5	-4.6
S. Randolph*	ROU	AAA	33	10	2	4	52	23	22	78	5	39.2%	.200	21	0.87	1.90	2.93	2.88	4.5	4.1	9.9	1.1	15.1
	HOU	MLB	33	0	1	0	13¹	21	17	22	4	21.1%	.531	-8	2.85	12.18	21.45	16.88	14.9	10.1	13.5	2.7	-10.4

A highly regarded prospect a year ago, **Jimmy Barthmaier** crashed and burned at Double-A last year as he continued to struggle to find a secondary pitch to go with his low-90s fastball. The Pirates have picked him up off waivers. ⊘ Closer prospect **Paul Estrada** couldn't follow up on his big 2006 in Double-A, as control problems once again got the better of him in his Triple-A debut. ⊘ Two years removed from shoulder surgery, lefty **Mark McLemore** reached the majors last year and survived. He's a sleeper in the crowded, unpleasant scrum for the Astros' fifth-starter slot. ⊘ **Fernando Nieve** just missed making the Opening Day roster, then blew out his elbow a month later in Triple-A. He'll be coming back from Tommy John surgery this year. ⊘ The Astros took a flier on **Chan Ho Park** after the Mets released him in June and were rewarded with 18 home runs in 84 innings at Triple-A Round Rock. He's done. ⊘ **Stephen Randolph** had arguably the most random good year of any pitcher in baseball last year, with a 3.6 K/BB and 23 hits allowed in 52 innings at Round Rock. This from a pitcher who typically walks six or more per nine innings. It screams fluke, particularly as he walked 17 in 13 1/3 across four stints with the big club last year.

MANAGER: CECIL COOPER

YEAR	TEAM	W-L	Pythag +/−	Avg PC	100+ P	120+ P	QS	BQS	REL	REL w Zero R	IBB	Subs	PH	PH Avg	PH HR	SB2	CS2	SB3	CS3	SAC Att	SAC %	POS SAC	Squeeze	Swing	In Play
2007	HOU	15-16	0	92.2	10	0	16	0	88	57	14	24	60	.265	0	11	5	2	1	16	81.2%	9	0	20	12

Phil Garner got a lot of credit for "leading" the Astros to a 48-26 finish in 2004, then to the World Series in his first full season as the team's skipper. However, watching the games, one got the impression that the Astros won in spite of Scrap Iron, whose roster assembly, player usage, and tactical acumen were all lacking. The moment the talent couldn't overcome his flaws, the team spiraled downward. Firing him was inevitable, and the end came on August 27, with bench coach Cecil Cooper being named interim manager. With all due respect to Cooper, Drayton McLane's decision to retain him as manager for 2008 is dubious at best. Cooper's entire managerial résumé consists of two desultory seasons as manager of the Triple-A Indianapolis Indians, with whom he went 130-156 and made no notable impression. In his month at the helm of the Astros last year, Cooper didn't strike anyone as a tactical savant or tremendous leader of men. When Cooper was tabbed to take over, Bud Selig let it be known that he wanted him to have a chance at the job beyond the end of the season, and McLane, always looking to please Selig, made it happen. Were Cooper a dynamo, that might have been excusable, but it appears he's no better or worse than any of a dozen other candidates. The process of picking a top administrator in a $200 million business should be treated with more care than this.

Kansas City Royals

The circus has left town. The traveling carnival ("Witness the Worst Baseball Team on Earth!") has finally packed up from Kansas City, headed out for Pittsburgh, or Houston, or San Francisco. The Royals, for so long the laughingstock of the major leagues, are now just another baseball team.

You would be forgiven for thinking otherwise—the Royals had the worst record in the majors in 2005, the second-worst in 2006, and the third-worst in 2007—but don't be misled by the product on the field. Since Dayton Moore was hired as general manager two years ago, the Royals have become focused on the process, not the product. As Moore learned from his years with the Braves, successful teams do not allow short-term results to disrupt the long-term process of building a winning organization.

Under previous GM Allard Baird, the Royals were not just consistently bad, they were embarrassing. Above all, they were unprofessional. First basemen would get drilled in the back by throws from the right fielders. Outfielders would drop routine fly balls with two outs in the ninth to snatch defeat from victory. The team burned through pitching coaches like they were Spinal Tap drummers. Manager Tony Muser found out he was fired from a beat writer. His successor, Tony Peña, resigned at the end of a road trip as there was a subpoena awaiting him in Kansas City to appear in court regarding his role in breaking up his neighbors' marriage.

The contrast in administrations is jarring. Virtually every decision the Royals have made during Moore's tenure has been made deliberately, thoughtfully, and, dare we say it, professionally. It helps that the Glass family, the owners who previously could not go a week without interfering with front-office decisions, have given Moore the keys to the car and thus far resisted asking for them back. Not once since Moore took over has the organization given off a whiff of panic.

The idea is to stand back and let Moore build Atlanta Midwest. Seventeen years after John Schuerholz left Kansas City for Atlanta, launching one of the longest runs of sustained dominance in sports history, new corporate ownership, a new GM, and what is likely Bobby Cox's final season have brought the end of the Braves' dynasty. Moore hopes to bring things full circle by founding a new dynasty in Kansas City based on the principles he learned from Schuerholz:

1. Everything starts with a player development machine

When the Braves won the World Series in 1995, all but two of their regulars (first baseman Fred McGriff and center fielder Marquis Grissom) had been signed and developed by the organization. Of the seven pitchers to start a game for the Braves that year, only Greg Maddux had begun his major league career elsewhere. When the Braves won their final divisional title ten years later, the only member of the starting lineup who had spent a day with another team was catcher Johnny Estrada, and he was in the process of losing his job to the home-grown Brian McCann. Though the rotation was not as pure, homegrown pitchers started more than half the team's games.

Player development stands at the core of almost everything the Royals have done in the past two years. Last year, they were one of just two organizations with seven minor league teams (a total the Braves had for years before corporate belt-tightening forced them to downsize). Last summer, they were the surprise team of the international signing season, handing out six-figure

---

ROYALS PROSPECTUS

2007 record: 69-93, Fifth place, AL Central

Pythagenport record: 74-88

Runs scored per game: 4.36 (13th in AL)

Runs allowed per game: 4.80 (7th in AL)

Team EqA: .241 (14th in AL)

2007 Batters Age: 28.5 (3rd youngest in AL)

2007 Pitchers Age: 26.4 (2nd youngest in AL)

Ballpark: Kauffman Stadium; Slight hitter's park; Park Factor of 1.026

2007: Dayton Moore accomplishes first goal: avoiding another 100-loss season.

2008: The long march back to respectability continues.

Table 1. The Meek Shall Inherit the Earth

Braves				Royals			
Year	Pick	Player	Pos	Year	Pick	Player	Pos
1985	14	Tommy Greene	RHP	2002	6	Zack Greinke	RHP
1986	5	Kent Mercker	LHP	2003	5	Chris Lubanski	OF
1987	6	Derek Lilliquist	LHP	2004	14	Billy Butler	OF
1988	3	Steve Avery	LHP	2005	2	Alex Gordon	3B
1989	2	Tyler Houston	C	2006	1	Luke Hochevar	RHP
1990	1	Chipper Jones	SS	2007	2	Mike Moustakas	SS
1991	2	Mike Kelly	OF	2008	3	To Be Determined	

bonuses to five different players from Latin America, players they plan to develop at the team's brand-new Dominican academy.

Like the Braves, whom it's easy to forget were also very bad for a very long time, the Royals have had the benefit of hoarding draft picks at the top of the first round. Both teams will have had six top-six picks over a seven year span. As Table 1 shows, the Royals appear to have done at least as well with their picks as the Braves did. (Especially when you consider the Braves traded Tommy Greene to the Phillies for scraps.)

2. Pitching is priority number one

In 1990, the Braves lost 97 games with a pitching staff that allowed the most runs in the National League. In 1991, the Braves ranked third in the league in runs allowed. Starting in 1992, they would allow the fewest runs in the league for 11 straight years.

In 2006, the Royals allowed the most runs in the American League—the ninth straight year that they ranked in the AL's bottom four. During the offseason, Moore signed starter Gil Meche and traded erratic reliever Ambiorix Burgos to the Mets for right-hander Brian Bannister. At the time, both moves were widely panned by both scouts and analysts, but Meche and Bannister gave the Royals two starters with more than 162 innings pitched and ERAs under four, matching the team's total over the previous seven years. Despite playing in a good hitters' park, the Royals improved to eighth in the 14-team AL in runs allowed.

3. To improve the pitching, improve the defense

The 1991 Braves surrendered 177 fewer runs than the year before, but their pitchers had very little to do with it. Relative to the league, the Braves' strikeout rate and propensity to give up homers was almost unchanged from 1990, but the team's defensive efficiency—its rate of converting balls in play into outs—leapt from a major league-worst .688 in 1990 to an NL-leading .727, marking the greatest one-season improvement by any team since 1981.

The Braves' breakthrough was the result of an Extreme Makeover: Glove Edition. Terry Pendleton replaced the anvil-esque Jim Presley at third base. Shortstop Rafael Belliard and second baseman Mark Lemke took playing time up the middle away from Andres Thomas and Jeff Treadway. Sid Bream was brought in to man first base. Otis Nixon roamed center field in place of a gimpy Dale Murphy. At five positions, the Braves had replaced the incumbent with a dramatically better fielder.

The Royals have not undergone as drastic a defensive makeover, but they did make a few key upgrades in addition to continuing to favor Mark Grudzielanek's superior glove over Esteban German's potentially superior bat at second base. After a breakout season at the plate as the club's third baseman in 2006, Mark Teahen was moved to right field to make room for top prospect Alex Gordon. Though Gordon struggled at the plate and in the field early in the year, by season's end the move had improved the defense at both positions. By then, center fielder Joey Gathright, who had been acquired the previous summer, had returned from the minors and rounded out a strong defensive outfield by settling into left. Most notably, a week before the 2007 season began, Moore traded a pitching prospect who was coming off Tommy John surgery to Atlanta for good-field/no-hit shortstop Tony Peña Jr., banishing no-field/no-hit former Rookie of the Year Angel Berroa to the minors in the process. As a result, the Royals, who had the worst park-adjusted defensive efficiency in baseball in both 2004 and 2005 and the third-worst in 2006, improved to a respectable 17th in the majors last year.

4. If you know what you're doing, it's okay to be bold

Prior to the 1991 season, the Braves signed Terry Pendleton to a four-year contract. Pendleton was 30, had a career OBP of .308, and had hit .230/.277/.324 the year before. If this signing happened today, it would cause the baseball blogosphere to tilt off its axis and careen into the sun.

In 1991, Pendleton won the NL MVP award. In 1992, he finished second. Never mind whether or not Pendleton deserved the award, how often does a player have the best year of his career the year *after* he becomes a free agent? It happened for the Royals with Gil Meche, whom they signed to a universally mocked five-year, $55 million contract last winter, a deal that now looks like a bargain.

The Royals were not oblivious to Meche's negatives, such as the shoulder surgery that cost him two full seasons, his 4.65 career ERA compiled while pitching his home games in pitcher-friendly Safeco Field, or the fact that many scouts pegged him as a number-three starter at best. Still, they took the risk because, at 28, Meche was the youngest free agent available and had the best stuff on the market not only that winter, but—outside of potential belle of the ball Carlos Zambrano, who wound up signing an extension with the Cubs during the season anyway—the following winter as well.

The Royals also saw room for improvement in Meche's mechanics. In spring training, pitching coach Bob McClure altered Meche's delivery, having him land on the toes of his front foot instead of his heel. Meche claimed the change helped him throw more strikes with his off-speed pitches, and backed it up by dropping his walk rate nearly 40 percent.

The Royals hit a home run with Meche's contract because they got input from a number of sources—the scouts who gave the thumbs-up to the quality of his stuff despite inconsistent results, the pitching coach who thought he could mold him into a better pitcher, and the doctors who signed off on his medical history (Meche tied for the league lead in starts and exceeded his previous innings high by 30)—and because they had a GM who trusted his sources and his own gut instincts enough to pull the trigger. Going forward, the organizational process that led to the decision to sign Meche is likely to benefit the Royals more than Meche himself.

5. Character matters

"Character" is an utterly meaningless term when used, as it so often is, as a crutch to explain why a particular player or team has exceeded expectations. Why bother trying to determine how the pennant-winning Colorado Rockies won games when you can simply extol their moral virtues? Still, not all players are willing to do the work necessary to squeeze every ounce of production from their talents.

The Royals entered the 2006 season with three relievers who had the arm strength to throw in the mid-to-upper 90s, but didn't use the velocity to its fullest potential. So, Moore cleaned house. Mike MacDougal was traded at the deadline for a pair of prospects, one of

whom, righty starter Daniel Cortes, is now one of the top three prospects in the organization. Andy Sisco was traded last winter for first baseman Ross Gload, who's useful as bench players go. Burgos was traded for Bannister, who throws nearly ten miles per hour slower, but has actually bothered to learn how to pitch.

Just as important as knowing who to trade for is knowing who to trade away. The Braves were legendary for their uncanny ability to distinguish the prospects who would make it from the ones who wouldn't and trade the latter before anyone else figured it out. Mac-Dougal mustered a 6.80 ERA last season, but at least he survived the year in the White Sox' bullpen; Sisco pitched his way to Triple-A by the end of May. Burgos was shut down in June with elbow trouble that necessitated Tommy John surgery.

6. Trust in your players

When a true lights-out closer was not available, the Braves were comfortable giving the job to a rookie unknown (Greg McMichael, Kerry Ligtenberg). When putative closer Octavio Dotel started the year on the disabled list, it took only a week before the Royals decided that Joakim Soria, a Rule 5 pick who had never before pitched above A-ball, was the best man for the job. Few teams would trust the ninth inning to a pitcher making his fourth major league appearance, but it worked for the Royals on April 10, and most days after that.

On paper, Moore's methods seem swell: copy the Braves' blueprint for success, achieve the same level of success. Rinse, lather, repeat. Obviously, it's not that simple.

For one, baseball teams today are a lot smarter than they were 15 or 20 years ago. Teams have significantly more information available to them and are much more willing to use that information to their advantage. The most prepared man in the room in 1991 would be a middle-of-the-pack GM today.

As high as the bar for GMs has been set, it's higher still in the AL Central, where the Tigers and Indians are keen on building elite farm systems, something which the Twins have been benefiting from for years. The only team in the division that's weak down on the farm is the White Sox, and they won a World Series two years ago.

Moreover, what made the Braves' success so impressive was that it was really an act in two parts. The last ten years of the streak were a testament to the most prolific farm system in baseball, but the Braves owe their three straight pennants from 1991 to 1993 as much to their ability to sign and trade for the right veteran players as to their ability to develop their own. Atlanta went to the World Series in 1991 by complementing a homegrown core with the mishmash of veterans they signed (Pendleton, Bream, Belliard, left fielder Lonnie Smith, and closer Juan Berenguer) or traded for (Nixon, starter Charlie Leibrandt, and reliever Alejandro Peña). It was several years before the Braves would start regularly reloading their roster from within.

Even if the Royals do a spectacular job of signing and developing amateur talent under Moore, the earliest they can expect those players to start paying dividends is 2011, when last year's second-overall pick, shortstop Mike Moustakas, will be 22 years old. In the short term, the Royals can not win on homegrown talent alone, nor do they expect to, judging from an offseason in which the Royals were players for free agents from center

fielders Torii Hunter and Andruw Jones to pitchers Hiroki Kuroda and Carlos Silva. In the end, Moore landed outfielder Jose Guillen and capitalized on new manager Trey Hillman's experience in the Japanese leagues by bringing set-up man Yasuhiko Yabuta across the Pacific. Moore also outbid the Yankees for lefty reliever Ron Mahay and pounced on catcher Miguel Olivo when the Marlins cut him.

None of those players is likely to contribute to the Royals' next playoff team, but they could help Kansas City factor into a pennant race before the decade is out as complementary pieces to the real team building that is targeting the decade to come. Even if Moore's methods pay off, the Royals won't win 14 division titles in a row, but they might win two or three, which is two or three more than Kansas City has seen in a generation.

HITTERS

Angel Berroa   SS   Bats: R   Throws: R   Height: 6' 0"   Weight: 195   Born: January 27, 1978   Age: 30

YEAR	TEAM	LVL	AGE	PA	R	2B	3B	HR	RBI	BB	SO	SB	CS	EqBRR	AVG	OBP	SLG	MLVr	EqAVG	EqOBP	EqSLG	EqA	VORP	DEFENSE
2005	KCA	MLB	27	652	68	21	5	11	55	18	108	7	5	2.7	.270	.305	.375	-.108	.277	.320	.393	.247	8.6	156-SS -5
2006	KCA	MLB	28	503	45	18	1	9	54	14	88	3	1	-0.3	.234	.259	.333	-.332	.235	.267	.337	.210	-17.4	127-SS -16
2007	KCA	MLB	29	13	0	0	0	0	1	0	4	0	1	0.0	.091	.167	.091	-.864	.091	.167	.091	.000	-2.8	
2007	OMA	AAA	29	352	47	17	0	8	40	25	44	2	2	-5.8	.300	.364	.433	.070	.269	.330	.388	.253	10.0	67-SS 5
2008	KCA	MLB	30	343	31	15	1	6	35	16	57	4	1	-0.3	.250	.300	.360	-.170	.250	.290	.370	.240	0.0	83-SS -3

Breakout: 35% Improve: 57% Collapse: 19% Attrition: 26%   Comparables: Rafael Ramirez, Orlando Miller, Gus Polidor, Hector Torres

You can't fault his attitude; Berroa handled the rare indignity of being optioned to Triple-A while on a multi-year contract about as well as could be expected. Of course, the reason the indignity is so rare is that teams rarely give out contracts as ill-considered as the four-year deal Berroa signed after his Rookie of the Year season. Going into the offseason, Berroa had the second-highest 2008 salary ($4.75 million, second only to Gil Meche) on the team, but his major league career appears to be in its death throes.

Craig Brazell   1B   Bats: L   Throws: R   Height: 6' 3"   Weight: 210   Born: May 10, 1980   Age: 28

YEAR	TEAM	LVL	AGE	PA	R	2B	3B	HR	RBI	BB	SO	SB	CS	EqBRR	AVG	OBP	SLG	MLVr	EqAVG	EqOBP	EqSLG	EqA	VORP	DEFENSE
2005	NOR	AAA	25	187	22	11	2	6	28	13	32	2	0	-1.5	.249	.301	.439	.010	.231	.285	.416	.240	-5.7	21-LF -7
2006	JAX	AA	26	448	56	26	1	21	91	19	94	1	0	0.8	.247	.283	.463	.092	.238	.270	.460	.245	-5.2	73-1B 4
2007	WIC	AA	27	120	15	5	0	7	15	11	19	0	0	-0.4	.349	.408	.587	.429	.306	.364	.505	.293	10.2	
2007	OMA	AAA	27	455	68	33	0	32	76	20	83	0	1	-3.7	.307	.337	.605	.288	.274	.305	.546	.278	22.0	57-1B -8
2008	KCA	MLB	28	551	56	30	1	20	82	32	119	2	1	-1.1	.260	.300	.440	-.060	.250	.300	.450	.270	1.7	129-1B 1

Breakout: 21% Improve: 50% Collapse: 30% Attrition: 19%   Comparables: Eddie Robinson, Drew Denson, Eric Karros, Todd Trafton

Some Royals fans were apoplectic about Brazell's lack of opportunity with the team last season given that he led the minors with 38 homers and the Royals had a need for a first baseman. They would do well to remember that the franchise record-holder for homers in the minors, Chris Hatcher (46 in 1998), went 1-for-15 in a callup that September, never played in the majors again, and was out of baseball at age 33. Slow Triple-A sluggers in their late 20s do not become prospects simply because they hit a bunch of home runs. They do head off to Japan, however, which is exactly where Brazell is rumored to be going.

Emil Brown — OF

Bats: R   Throws: R   Height: 6' 2"   Weight: 210   Born: December 29, 1974   Age: 33

YEAR	TEAM	LVL	AGE	PA	R	2B	3B	HR	RBI	BB	SO	SB	CS	EqBRR	AVG	OBP	SLG	MLVr	EqAVG	EqOBP	EqSLG	EqA	VORP	DEFENSE			
2005	KCA	MLB	30	609	75	31	5	17	86	48	108	10	1	-3.2	.286	.349	.455	.090	.293	.363	.479	.292	25.9	126-RF	-14		
2006	KCA	MLB	31	601	77	41	2	15	81	59	95	6	3	0.1	.287	.358	.457	.067	.287	.365	.469	.288	20.6	82-LF	-1	47-RF	4
2007	KCA	MLB	32	397	44	13	1	6	62	24	71	12	2	3.5	.257	.300	.347	-.189	.259	.307	.364	.242	-9.0	68-LF	3	17-RF	2
2008	OAK	MLB	33	384	42	17	2	8	43	30	68	7	2	0.1	.256	.316	.386	-.100	.259	.321	.411	.260	-0.2	92-LF	-3		

Breakout: 7% Improve: 26% Collapse: 38% Attrition: 24%   Comparables Gary Ward, Larry Herndon, Cesar Cedeño, Gino Cimoli

When historians look back at the train wreck that was the turn-of-the-century Kansas City Royals, they can wax poetic on the flubs, errors, and general incompetence of the organization from top to bottom, or they can simply point out that Emil Brown led the team in RBI . . . for *three straight years*. Brown was a revelation as a 30-year-old minor league free agent; two years of arbitration later, he was an expensive albatross. Such is the fleeting nature of uncovering free talent—soon enough, it's no longer free and it's no longer talent. Veteran minor leaguers such as Brown who finally get their major league shot have typically been around long enough that they reach their decline phase and salary arbitration simultaneously. The Royals finally wised up and non-tendered Brown in December. He signed a one-year deal with the A's.

John Buck — C

Bats: R   Throws: R   Height: 6' 3"   Weight: 220   Born: July 7, 1980   Age: 27

YEAR	TEAM	LVL	AGE	PA	R	2B	3B	HR	RBI	BB	SO	SB	CS	EqBRR	AVG	OBP	SLG	MLVr	EqAVG	EqOBP	EqSLG	EqA	VORP	DEFENSE	
2005	KCA	MLB	25	430	40	21	1	12	47	23	94	2	2	-1.2	.242	.287	.389	-.142	.246	.301	.405	.242	2.2	112-C	-1
2006	KCA	MLB	26	409	37	21	1	11	50	26	84	0	2	-2.3	.245	.306	.396	-.146	.245	.312	.406	.247	-1.0	106-C	-1
2007	KCA	MLB	27	399	41	18	0	18	48	36	92	0	1	-0.1	.222	.308	.429	-.086	.223	.313	.449	.261	7.8	104-C	3
2008	KCA	MLB	27	315	29	15	1	9	40	25	69	1	1	-0.7	.240	.310	.400	-.110	.230	.310	.410	.260	3.4	76-C	-1

Breakout: 33% Improve: 52% Collapse: 31% Attrition: 38%   Comparables: Todd Pratt, Charles Johnson, Randy Knorr, John Bateman

For the first two months of the 2007 season, Buck was a candidate for Breakout of the Year. He made some alterations to his swing in spring training, incorporating a timing mechanism with his front foot, and on June 4th was hitting .288/.383/.600 with ten homers in just 40 games. The Royals, apparently channeling the wisdom of the Allard Baird years, then became concerned that the new approach impaired Buck's ability to hit with men on base (for the year, he hit just .183 with five home runs when runners were on), so they had Buck return to his old approach. Soon enough, he couldn't hit in any situation, going .185/.264/.333 the rest of the way. Repeat step one without step two, and the raw material for a true, sustained breakout is still there.

Billy Butler — DH

Bats: R   Throws: R   Height: 6' 1"   Weight: 240   Born: April 18, 1986   Age: 22

YEAR	TEAM	LVL	AGE	PA	R	2B	3B	HR	RBI	BB	SO	SB	CS	EqBRR	AVG	OBP	SLG	MLVr	EqAVG	EqOBP	EqSLG	EqA	VORP	DEFENSE			
2005	HDS	A+	19	430	70	30	2	25	91	42	80	0	0	-1.6	.348	.419	.636	.360	.259	.321	.449	.262	16.3	40-3B	-7	34-LF	-7
2005	WIC	AA	19	119	14	9	0	5	19	7	18	0	0	-0.8	.313	.353	.527	.242	.268	.311	.464	.259	1.2	25-LF	-6		
2006	WIC	AA	20	535	82	33	1	15	96	41	67	1	0	-4.7	.331	.388	.499	.252	.291	.339	.439	.270	11.4	95-RF	-1	20-LF	-1
2007	OMA	AAA	21	256	40	10	1	13	46	43	32	1	0	-3.8	.291	.412	.542	.296	.256	.375	.483	.296	11.0	25-LF	-2	22-1B	-3
2007	KCA	MLB	21	360	38	23	2	8	52	27	55	0	0	-1.5	.292	.347	.447	.063	.291	.353	.463	.280	11.6				
2008	KCA	MLB	22	626	77	34	2	18	85	54	97	3	2	-1.5	.290	.350	.460	.080	.280	.350	.470	.290	20.1	146-DH			

Breakout: 41% Improve: 71% Collapse: 10% Attrition: 7%   Comparables: Marc Newfield, Greg Luzinski, Gary Carter, Paul Konerko

Standardized testing has proven that Butler fields at a first-grade level, but, man, can he hit. Just the third Royal ever to bat 300 times in a season at age 21 or younger (joining Clint Hurdle and George Brett), Butler's rookie numbers were the best of the bunch. The Royals still hold out hope he can learn to play first base and dispatched him to the Caribbean to start a remedial course in winter ball. They're just postponing the inevitable—Butler should be one of the three best designated hitters in the league in two years.

Shane Costa — OF

Bats: L   Throws: R   Height: 6' 0"   Weight: 190   Born: December 12, 1981   Age: 26

YEAR	TEAM	LVL	AGE	PA	R	2B	3B	HR	RBI	BB	SO	SB	CS	EqBRR	AVG	OBP	SLG	MLVr	EqAVG	EqOBP	EqSLG	EqA	VORP	DEFENSE			
2005	WIC	AA	23	316	37	18	2	8	43	24	23	5	1	1.9	.282	.349	.448	.097	.255	.317	.404	.252	-4.2	59-LF	-9	12-RF	0
2005	KCA	MLB	23	88	13	2	0	2	7	5	11	0	0	0.1	.235	.287	.333	-.226	.237	.299	.338	.223	-3.1	19-LF	-4		
2006	OMA	AAA	24	224	35	12	4	10	29	13	25	4	0	0.3	.342	.398	.593	.447	.309	.359	.539	.301	16.5	37-RF	3	13-LF	-2
2006	KCA	MLB	24	252	23	20	1	3	23	6	29	2	0	0.4	.274	.304	.405	-.115	.272	.308	.413	.250	0.4	35-RF	0	18-CF	-1
2007	OMA	AAA	25	267	46	20	3	5	14	26	20	8	2	0.6	.326	.402	.502	.263	.288	.363	.445	.282	9.1	37-RF	3		
2007	KCA	MLB	25	109	13	6	1	0	12	5	23	0	1	-0.2	.223	.257	.301	-.356	.225	.266	.304	.194	-7.7	11-LF	1		
2008	KCA	MLB	26	342	41	21	2	6	39	23	41	6	2	0.2	.280	.330	.420	-.020	.270	.330	.430	.280	4.0	82-RF	1		

Breakout: 46% Improve: 64% Collapse: 15% Attrition: 22%   Comparables: Al Woods, Bill Buckner, Daryl Sconiers, Jerry Lynch

The existence of the Quadruple-A player has yet to be definitively established, but Costa is certainly a point in its favor. Over the last two years, he has hit .334/.400/.541 in the minors, with a 1.2 strikeout-to-walk ratio. With the Royals over the same span, he's hit .259/.290/.374 with a 4.7 K:BB ratio. The performance metrics are there for a late-career blossoming in the Raul Ibañez mold, but like Ibañez, Costa will probably have to leave the womb to find success.

David DeJesus — CF

Bats: L   Throws: L   Height: 6' 0"   Weight: 185   Born: December 20, 1979   Age: 28

YEAR	TEAM	LVL	AGE	PA	R	2B	3B	HR	RBI	BB	SO	SB	CS	EqBRR	AVG	OBP	SLG	MLVr	EqAVG	EqOBP	EqSLG	EqA	VORP	DEFENSE			
2005	KCA	MLB	25	523	69	31	6	9	56	42	76	5	5	0.5	.293	.359	.445	.100	.302	.376	.469	.289	25.5	115-CF	-3		
2006	KCA	MLB	26	552	83	36	7	8	56	43	70	6	3	4.4	.295	.364	.446	.069	.294	.369	.451	.284	23.2	62-LF	2	55-CF	2
2007	KCA	MLB	27	703	101	29	9	7	58	64	83	10	4	2.3	.260	.351	.372	-.060	.263	.357	.391	.266	12.0	152-CF	-12		
2008	KCA	MLB	28	558	71	28	5	8	53	47	72	7	4	1.3	.270	.350	.400	-.020	.270	.340	.410	.280	9.8	131-CF	-3		

Breakout: 16% Improve: 47% Collapse: 18% Attrition: 16%   Comparables: Darin Erstad, Mark Kotsay, Bill Virdon, Eddie Milner

So much for the notion that career years happen at age 27. DeJesus stayed healthy for a full season for the first time in 2007, but a 40-point dip in his batting average on balls in play dropped his overall average 35 points. Fortunately, he was able to maintain his on-base numbers by getting hit with a franchise-record 23 pitches and improving his overall plate discipline. Unfortunately, the dip in BABIP alone doesn't explain his 74-point drop in slugging. The average should bounce back, and the discipline is a good sign, but the Royals have to ask if he still represents a long-term solution coming off his worst major league season at age 28. If they decide he doesn't, DeJesus's favorable contract should make him one of the team's most tradeable commodities.

Joey Gathright — OF

Bats: L   Throws: R   Height: 5' 10"   Weight: 170   Born: April 27, 1981   Age: 27

YEAR	TEAM	LVL	AGE	PA	R	2B	3B	HR	RBI	BB	SO	SB	CS	EqBRR	AVG	OBP	SLG	MLVr	EqAVG	EqOBP	EqSLG	EqA	VORP	DEFENSE	
2005	DUR	AAA	24	260	46	10	5	1	18	29	47	31	8	2.4	.305	.388	.407	.077	.272	.353	.360	.264	4.2	50-CF	-6
2005	TBA	MLB	24	218	29	7	3	0	13	10	39	20	5	2.8	.276	.316	.340	-.128	.290	.340	.355	.257	2.3	58-CF	2
2006	TBA	MLB	25	182	25	6	0	0	13	20	30	12	3	2.2	.201	.305	.240	-.378	.204	.316	.237	.220	-7.9	50-CF	7
2006	KCA	MLB	25	263	34	6	3	1	28	22	45	10	6	-1.7	.262	.332	.328	-.182	.265	.344	.332	.246	-2.1	66-CF	1
2007	OMA	AAA	26	277	44	10	4	0	25	43	24	25	8	0.5	.341	.457	.422	.257	.300	.415	.366	.290	15.1	54-CF	3
2007	KCA	MLB	26	261	28	8	0	0	19	20	36	9	8	-1.3	.307	.371	.342	-.032	.319	.386	.350	.259	0.6	59-LF	7
2008	KCA	MLB	27	296	42	9	3	0	19	27	41	16	5	1.3	.280	.350	.340	-.090	.280	.350	.340	.270	1.0	72-CF	1

Breakout: 24% Improve: 52% Collapse: 26% Attrition: 22%   Comparables: Alex Sanchez, Chris Duffy, David Hulse, Lance Johnson

For the first time in his career, Gathright showed he might have more to offer a baseball team than just his speed. In Omaha to start the year, he finally got the memo that a man with his speed should endeavor to reach base by any means necessary, resulting in a much-improved walk rate and a .457 OBP. After a midseason promotion, he played the little-man role to the hilt, attempting a bunt in 12.3 percent of his plate appearances, the second-highest rate in baseball behind Willy Taveras. Slotted into left field in deference to DeJesus, his defense was excellent as usual last year, but, even with the improved approach at the plate, he'll never have the bat to carry the position. Fortunately, with Jose Guillen on hand, he won't have to.

Esteban German — UT

Bats: R   Throws: R   Height: 5' 9"   Weight: 195   Born: January 26, 1978   Age: 30

YEAR	TEAM	LVL	AGE	PA	R	2B	3B	HR	RBI	BB	SO	SB	CS	EqBRR	AVG	OBP	SLG	MLVr	EqAVG	EqOBP	EqSLG	EqA	VORP	DEFENSE			
2005	OKL	AAA	27	564	103	27	6	5	68	65	74	43	6	5.9	.313	.400	.423	.145	.273	.353	.369	.265	15.6	74-3B	-6	14-SS	1
2006	KCA	MLB	28	331	44	18	5	3	34	40	49	7	3	-0.7	.326	.422	.459	.218	.327	.429	.469	.312	26.5	21-3B	-2	19-2B	-4
2007	KCA	MLB	29	405	49	15	6	4	37	43	60	11	7	-1.5	.264	.351	.376	-.049	.270	.361	.400	.266	5.1	46-2B	-9	32-3B	-5
2008	KCA	MLB	30	434	60	21	3	5	38	44	66	14	4	0.7	.280	.360	.390	-.020	.270	.350	.400	.280	10.0	103-2B	-8		

Breakout: 19% Improve: 47% Collapse: 26% Attrition: 21%   Comparables: Kevin Seitzer, Ryan Freel, Jeff Frye, Tony Taylor

In 2007 German proved that, while 2006 was a career year, it was not a fluke. This is who he is: a player who gets on base (career .373 OBP) and is capable of playing second, third, and the outfield equally poorly. The Royals would prefer to keep him in the supersub role, where he makes for one of the best bench players in baseball, but they could do worse than to hold their nose and let German start at the keystone in a post-Grudzielanek future.

Ross Gload — 1B

Bats: L   Throws: L   Height: 6' 1"   Weight: 190   Born: April 5, 1976   Age: 32

YEAR	TEAM	LVL	AGE	PA	R	2B	3B	HR	RBI	BB	SO	SB	CS	EqBRR	AVG	OBP	SLG	MLVr	EqAVG	EqOBP	EqSLG	EqA	VORP	DEFENSE	
2005	CHR	AAA	29	263	45	22	1	15	45	22	37	0	1	-0.8	.364	.416	.657	.547	.329	.384	.586	.318	30.1	37-1B	5
2005	CHA	MLB	29	44	2	2	0	0	5	2	9	0	0	-0.2	.167	.205	.214	-.570	.171	.227	.220	.136	-5.2		
2006	CHA	MLB	30	167	22	8	2	3	18	6	15	6	0	-1.5	.327	.354	.462	.099	.325	.360	.461	.288	8.6	28-1B	1
2007	KCA	MLB	31	346	37	22	3	7	51	16	39	2	2	-0.3	.288	.318	.441	-.001	.289	.324	.459	.267	5.7	76-1B	0
2008	KCA	MLB	32	363	44	21	2	8	48	23	44	3	1	-0.6	.300	.340	.450	.050	.290	.340	.460	.280	8.3	87-1B	0

Breakout: 23% Improve: 60% Collapse: 16% Attrition: 20%   Comparables: Dane Iorg, Lee Maye, Dick Sisler, Hal Morris

When Gload is on the bench, as he was to start the season last year, his ability to hit for average, drive the balls into the gaps, and hit lefties as well as righties (if not better; in 150 plate appearances, he's a lifetime .345 hitter against southpaws) makes him a strong asset. As a starting first baseman, as he was for much of 2007 due to Ryan Shealy's inability to stay healthy, his lack of secondary skills makes him a strong asset to the opposing team. The Royals are hoping a better candidate will emerge to force Gload back to the pines.

Alex Gordon — 3B

Bats: L   Throws: R   Height: 6' 1"   Weight: 220   Born: February 10, 1984   Age: 24

YEAR	TEAM	LVL	AGE	PA	R	2B	3B	HR	RBI	BB	SO	SB	CS	EqBRR	AVG	OBP	SLG	MLVr	EqAVG	EqOBP	EqSLG	EqA	VORP	DEFENSE			
2006	WIC	AA	22	576	111	39	1	29	101	72	113	22	3	7.2	.325	.427	.588	.427	.284	.373	.505	.300	52.3	119-3B	8		
2007	KCA	MLB	23	600	60	36	4	15	60	41	137	14	4	-1.1	.247	.314	.411	-.082	.248	.319	.431	.259	3.1	128-3B	-1	17-1B	-2
2008	KCA	MLB	24	551	75	34	3	18	73	51	113	16	5	0.7	.270	.350	.470	.070	.260	.340	.480	.290	19.6	129-3B	1		

Breakout: 45% Improve: 67% Collapse: 11% Attrition: 14%   Comparables: Eric Chavez, Mel Hall, Hank Blalock, Mike Jorgensen

There's no way to sugarcoat it: Alex Gordon's rookie season was a disappointment. Turns out, the top prospect in the land was not ready for the major leagues at the start of the year after all. Through June 4, he was hitting .172/.287/.278 with all of eight RBI. That the Royals declined to send Gordon back to the minors for a refresher is puzzling given that 1) a demotion would have delayed his free agency by a year and 2) the same move resurrected Mark Teahen's career the year before. Long-term, there's little reason to worry. Gordon hit .284/.328/.477 the rest of the way, numbers similar to a pair of 23-year-old rookie third basemen, Mark Teixeira (.259/.331/.480) and Chipper Jones (.265/.353/.450). Gordon may not match their performance going forward, but he also plays a better third base than either of them. The hype returns this year.

Mark Grudzielanek — 2B

Bats: R   Throws: R   Height: 6' 1"   Weight: 200   Born: June 30, 1970   Age: 38

YEAR	TEAM	LVL	AGE	PA	R	2B	3B	HR	RBI	BB	SO	SB	CS	EqBRR	AVG	OBP	SLG	MLVr	EqAVG	EqOBP	EqSLG	EqA	VORP	DEFENSE	
2005	SLN	MLB	35	563	64	30	3	8	59	26	81	8	6	0.3	.294	.334	.407	.025	.292	.335	.410	.257	16.0	130-2B	10
2006	KCA	MLB	36	586	85	32	4	7	52	28	69	3	2	1.4	.297	.331	.409	-.041	.297	.338	.413	.261	18.2	126-2B	6
2007	KCA	MLB	37	486	70	32	3	6	51	23	60	1	2	1.5	.302	.346	.426	.040	.306	.352	.443	.273	18.1	107-2B	-5
2008	KCA	MLB	38	329	34	19	1	4	35	15	41	2	1	0.1	.280	.310	.380	-.100	.270	.310	.390	.250	3.1	79-2B	-2

Breakout: 13% Improve: 35% Collapse: 33% Attrition: 39%   Comparables: Alvin Dark, Pete Suder, Jeff Cirillo, Lou Piniella

The rare free agent signed by Baird who actually panned out, Grudzielanek is as reliable as a Honda Accord and just as exciting. He's a .300 hitter (.300 on the nose as a member of the Royals) who makes contact, hits doubles, and plays a sure-handed second base (he's made just ten errors in the last two years). Even Hondas break down, however, and Grudzielanek had surgery on his left knee twice between March and July of last year, reducing his range afield. With Grudzielanek in his walk year and due to turn 38 at the end of June, the Royals should look for a decent trade-in at the deadline.

Justin Huber			1B										Bats: R		Throws: R		Height: 6' 2"		Weight: 205		Born: July 1, 1982				Age: 26

YEAR	TEAM	LVL	AGE	PA	R	2B	3B	HR	RBI	BB	SO	SB	CS	EqBRR	AVG	OBP	SLG	MLVr	EqAVG	EqOBP	EqSLG	EqA	VORP	DEFENSE
2005	WIC	AA	23	396	68	22	3	16	74	51	70	7	3	-2.6	.343	.432	.570	.449	.287	.374	.488	.294	24.2	67-1B -11
2005	OMA	AAA	23	131	19	6	1	7	23	16	33	3	0	1.2	.274	.374	.531	.198	.243	.331	.461	.273	2.6	32-1B -2
2005	KCA	MLB	23	85	6	3	0	0	6	5	20	0	0	-0.3	.218	.271	.256	-.370	.221	.282	.260	.192	-6.1	16-1B -4
2006	OMA	AAA	24	398	47	22	2	15	44	40	94	2	2	-3.3	.278	.358	.480	.154	.252	.327	.445	.264	2.5	68-LF -2 29-1B -7
2007	OMA	AAA	25	318	39	13	1	18	68	20	48	1	0	-0.6	.276	.336	.517	.120	.247	.303	.465	.261	2.7	29-1B -4 23-LF 3
2007	KCA	MLB	25	10	2	0	0	0	0	0	2	0	0	-0.1	.100	.100	.100	-.985	.100	.100	.100	.000	-2.2	
2008	KCA	MLB	25	382	42	18	1	12	51	32	84	3	1	-0.5	.250	.320	.420	-.050	.250	.320	.430	.270	0.9	91-1B -4

Breakout: 27% Improve: 60% Collapse: 18% Attrition: 18%   Comparables: Jose Malave, Alejandro Freire, Victor Diaz, Sherman Obando

The Royals' treatment of Huber since they traded for him in 2004 is a model of how not to handle a prospect. The Royals moved Huber from catcher to first base, called him up for three weeks in May 2006 but gave him all of 11 plate appearances, buried him back in Omaha, tried him in left field, moved him back to first base, and most recently made him a quasi-platoon player in Triple-A. Lost in all of the position switches is the fact that Huber can hit. He'll get the opportunity to show it eventually as, despite all the mileage, he'll still be just 25 when the season begins.

Jason LaRue			C										Bats: R		Throws: R		Height: 5' 11"		Weight: 205		Born: March 19, 1974				Age: 34

YEAR	TEAM	LVL	AGE	PA	R	2B	3B	HR	RBI	BB	SO	SB	CS	EqBRR	AVG	OBP	SLG	MLVr	EqAVG	EqOBP	EqSLG	EqA	VORP	DEFENSE
2005	CIN	MLB	31	422	38	27	0	14	60	41	101	0	0	-0.3	.260	.355	.452	.089	.255	.348	.453	.276	23.2	104-C -1
2006	CIN	MLB	32	230	22	5	0	8	21	27	51	1	0	-1.0	.194	.317	.346	-.197	.187	.307	.332	.230	-4.3	57-C 7
2007	KCA	MLB	33	195	14	9	0	4	13	17	66	1	0	-0.5	.148	.240	.272	-.461	.149	.249	.280	.189	-13.0	54-C 4
2008	SLN	MLB	34	151	14	6	0	4	18	14	38	1	0	-0.4	.220	.310	.368	-.183	.219	.310	.383	.238	2.1	40-C 0

Breakout: 38% Improve: 56% Collapse: 28% Attrition: 57%   Comparables: Ron Tingley, Cal Neeman, Mike DiFelice, Kelly Stinnett

The lowest batting averages of the lively ball era (min: 160 AB):

1. Ray Oyler, 1968: .135
2. Chris Bando, 1985: .139
3. Vic Harris, 1972: .140
4. Jose Oliva, 1995: .142
5. Jason LaRue, 2007: .148

A torrid September (he hit .227!) kept LaRue from ranking second on this list. You would think a team that has a 26-year-old catcher who started the year on fire would play him as much as possible over a 34-year-old backstop in the last year of his contract who is struggling to hit his wife's weight. You're obviously not Buddy Bell. Having returned to the weaker league by signing with the Cardinals, LaRue's a sure bet to get that average back over .170.

Mario Lisson			3B										Bats: R		Throws: R		Height: 6' 2"		Weight: 193		Born: May 31, 1984				Age: 24

YEAR	TEAM	LVL	AGE	PA	R	2B	3B	HR	RBI	BB	SO	SB	CS	EqBRR	AVG	OBP	SLG	MLVr	EqAVG	EqOBP	EqSLG	EqA	VORP	DEFENSE
2005	BUR	A	21	324	57	15	4	6	36	53	68	23	4	3.2	.250	.386	.408	.143	.208	.320	.328	.240	-4.6	58-3B 5
2006	BUR	A	22	551	67	30	2	13	73	65	109	41	11	3.8	.263	.368	.421	.192	.218	.300	.346	.235	-9.6	120-3B 5
2007	WIL	A+	23	524	72	27	3	8	61	41	93	23	9	2.4	.285	.348	.408	.059	.234	.284	.334	.219	-14.5	109-3B 14
2008	KCA	MLB	24	590	61	30	2	10	55	46	146	19	6	0.9	.230	.300	.350	-.190	.230	.300	.360	.250	-10.4	138-3B 8

Breakout: 52% Improve: 76% Collapse: 11% Attrition: 9%   Comparables: Juan Espinal, Enrique Cruz, Jose Fernandez, Chin-Feng Chen

The Royals have jacked up their presence in Latin America, a good thing since the Venezuelan Lisson might be the best international hitter they've signed since Carlos Febles, which is damning to all involved. Lisson was added to the 40-man roster this winter after a fine season in Wilmington, but he turns 24 in May and has yet to reach Double-A. A very good glove gives him a shot as a utility infielder, but let's not get crazy with expectations here.

Chris Lubanski LF Bats: L   Throws: L   Height: 6' 3"   Weight: 206   Born: March 24, 1985   Age: 23

YEAR	TEAM	LVL	AGE	PA	R	2B	3B	HR	RBI	BB	SO	SB	CS	EqBRR	AVG	OBP	SLG	MLVr	EqAVG	EqOBP	EqSLG	EqA	VORP	DEFENSE		
2005	HDS	A+	20	581	91	38	6	28	116	38	131	14	1	-0.7	.301	.349	.554	.077	.223	.265	.386	.226	-15.4	121-CF	-18	
2006	WIC	AA	21	613	93	34	11	15	70	72	112	11	7	-0.1	.282	.369	.475	.142	.245	.322	.410	.255	-6.5	107-LF	-15	25-CF -3
2007	WIC	AA	22	274	33	14	3	9	34	28	43	3	5	-0.4	.295	.361	.490	.172	.257	.318	.433	.255	-0.5	58-LF	-2	
2007	OMA	AAA	22	190	20	6	1	6	22	16	48	0	3	-0.3	.208	.273	.363	-.276	.188	.250	.335	.199	-16.0	49-LF	5	
2008	KCA	MLB	23	542	59	29	3	14	63	45	124	7	4	0.8	.250	.310	.410	-.090	.240	.310	.420	.260	-3.9	127-LF	-1	

Breakout: 58%   Improve: 75%   Collapse: 7%   Attrition: 8%   Comparables: Gabe Gross, Dee Brown, Trot Nixon, Lloyd Moseby

If 2007 was a make-or-break year for Lubanski, the Royals were calling for a cleanup on aisle five. Returning to Double-A because of a roster crunch in Omaha, Lubanski avoided his typical slow start, but his numbers went backward after he was promoted in the second half. An outfielder with nearly two full seasons in Double-A under his belt should hit better than .208 in his first crack at Triple-A. Lubanski's best asset is still his birth date, but that's the funny thing about youth: it's not a quality that ages very well. Lubanski was left off the 40-man roster over the winter, as strong an indictment as there is for a former first-round pick.

Mitch Maier OF Bats: L   Throws: R   Height: 6' 2"   Weight: 210   Born: June 30, 1982   Age: 26

YEAR	TEAM	LVL	AGE	PA	R	2B	3B	HR	RBI	BB	SO	SB	CS	EqBRR	AVG	OBP	SLG	MLVr	EqAVG	EqOBP	EqSLG	EqA	VORP	DEFENSE		
2005	HDS	A+	23	227	42	26	1	8	32	12	43	6	1	1.4	.336	.370	.583	.193	.252	.282	.421	.242	-4.8	41-RF	6	
2005	WIC	AA	23	342	55	21	5	7	49	15	47	10	3	4.2	.255	.289	.416	-.068	.220	.257	.356	.212	-15.4	76-CF	-5	
2006	WIC	AA	24	603	95	35	7	14	92	41	96	13	12	0.9	.306	.357	.473	.141	.265	.308	.411	.247	7.0	114-CF	6	20-RF 4
2007	OMA	AAA	25	596	75	29	5	14	62	33	89	7	2	1.3	.279	.320	.428	-.036	.246	.288	.385	.234	-7.2	82-CF	15	31-RF 1
2008	KCA	MLB	26	505	49	29	3	9	54	27	94	7	3	1.1	.250	.290	.380	-.160	.240	.290	.390	.250	-7.9	119-CF	-2	

Breakout: 35%   Improve: 57%   Collapse: 21%   Attrition: 22%   Comparables: Midre Cummings, Luke Wilcox, Pat Watkins, Brian Buchanan

Maier is a solid Triple-A player: solid power, solid average, solid defense, solid contact ability. Unfortunately, being merely solid in Triple-A means that you're likely to get eaten alive in the majors. How Maier hits in his next 50 major league plate appearances could determine whether he winds up with a ten-year career as a fourth outfielder, or spends the next decade bussing around the minors. No pressure, kid.

Mike Moustakas SS Bats: L   Throws: R   Height: 6' 0"   Weight: 195   Born: September 11, 1988   Age: 19

YEAR	TEAM	LVL	AGE	PA	R	2B	3B	HR	RBI	BB	SO	SB	CS	EqBRR	AVG	OBP	SLG	MLVr	EqAVG	EqOBP	EqSLG	EqA	VORP	DEFENSE
2007	IDA	Rk	18	47	6	4	1	0	10	4	8	0	0	-0.3	.293	.383	.439	.144	.209	.277	.302	.193	-5.1	
2008	KCA	MLB	19	581	43	30	3	7	52	37	151	11	5	0.3	.224	.277	.327	-.265	.220	.274	.336	.216	-12.8	136-SS -4

Breakout: NA   Improve: NA   Collapse: NA   Attrition: NA   Comparables: Sean Burroughs, B. J. Upton, Derek Jeter, Felipe Lopez

Moustakas was older than most high school draftees—he turned 19 a month after signing—and the Royals may be the only organization that thinks he can handle shortstop—but the lad can hit: .577 with a California prep-record 24 homers as a senior. The best-case scenario is that Moustakas evolves into an offense-minded second baseman in the Chase Utley mold. He's already the best hitting prospect in the organization.

Tony Peña Jr. SS Bats: R   Throws: R   Height: 6' 2"   Weight: 180   Born: March 23, 1981   Age: 27

YEAR	TEAM	LVL	AGE	PA	R	2B	3B	HR	RBI	BB	SO	SB	CS	EqBRR	AVG	OBP	SLG	MLVr	EqAVG	EqOBP	EqSLG	EqA	VORP	DEFENSE
2005	RIC	AAA	24	526	49	25	4	5	40	21	113	17	15	-2.5	.249	.285	.347	-.206	.224	.261	.313	.197	-22.7	134-SS 14
2006	RIC	AAA	25	319	38	12	4	1	23	12	56	12	3	4.8	.282	.312	.359	-.038	.258	.289	.338	.223	-4.1	81-SS 0
2006	ATL	MLB	25	46	12	2	0	1	3	2	10	0	0	0.1	.227	.261	.341	-.273	.227	.261	.341	.204	-1.3	
2007	KCA	MLB	26	536	58	25	7	2	47	10	78	5	6	-3.1	.267	.284	.356	-.198	.273	.294	.375	.229	-7.6	144-SS 13
2008	KCA	MLB	27	402	39	18	3	3	35	14	68	7	3	0.9	.260	.290	.350	-.200	.250	.280	.360	.230	-2.5	96-SS 5

Breakout: 55%   Improve: 69%   Collapse: 23%   Attrition: 33%   Comparables: Craig Robinson, Rob Picciolo, Pat Meares, Damaso Garcia

If the Royals are copying the early-'90s Atlanta Braves, Peña is their Rafael Belliard. He is a genuinely excellent short-stop, ranking sixth in the majors in FRAA, but his bat is strictly minor league. What the Royals seem to have missed is that Belliard never had to bat even 400 times in a season for the Braves, as he shared shortstop with Jeff Blauser on a team with platoons at five positions. Peña is a decent stopgap until the Royals find a real solution at shortstop, but the bill for his acquisition is about to come due. Eric Cordier, the young pitcher the Royals traded to the Braves for Peña, is expected back from Tommy John surgery this season. They may yet regret that deal.

Reggie Sanders OF

Bats: R Throws: R Height: 6' 1" Weight: 205 Born: December 1, 1967 Age: 40

YEAR	TEAM	LVL	AGE	PA	R	2B	3B	HR	RBI	BB	SO	SB	CS	EqBRR	AVG	OBP	SLG	MLVr	EqAVG	EqOBP	EqSLG	EqA	VORP	DEFENSE	
2005	SLN	MLB	37	329	49	14	2	21	54	28	75	14	1	0.5	.271	.340	.546	.201	.269	.338	.548	.298	23.1	71-LF	-1
2006	KCA	MLB	38	358	45	23	1	11	49	28	86	7	7	-2.0	.246	.304	.425	-.106	.246	.313	.436	.252	-3.4	68-RF	10
2007	KCA	MLB	39	85	12	7	0	2	11	11	15	0	1	-0.9	.315	.412	.493	.259	.319	.424	.514	.317	6.0		
2008	KCA	MLB	40	141	18	8	0	5	20	15	29	2	1	-0.2	.260	.340	.440	.010	.250	.340	.450	.280	2.7	37-RF	1

Breakout: 23% Improve: 53% Collapse: 31% Attrition: 38%   Comparables: Hank Sauer, Ken Griffey, Walker Cooper, Bob Thurman

Health is a skill, and what little of it Sanders ever had disappeared as he approached his forties. Sanders was hitting .367 when he tore his left hamstring on May 2. He returned in mid-July, but lasted just two weeks before tearing the hamstring again just two days before the trading deadline. In 2006, the Royals nearly had a trade worked out that would have sent Sanders to the Yankees, but Sanders pulled a muscle before the Royals could get him out of town. Instead, the team wound up paying $10 million over two years for 112 games and 13 home runs. It's no wonder the Royals moved the similarly fragile Octavio Dotel at the first chance they got (naturally, Dotel strained his shoulder a week after he was traded to Atlanta). Sanders can still hit when he's healthy, so he might catch on with a contending team that needs a stick off the bench and has an excellent health plan.

Ryan Shealy 1B

Bats: R Throws: R Height: 6' 5" Weight: 240 Born: August 29, 1979 Age: 28

YEAR	TEAM	LVL	AGE	PA	R	2B	3B	HR	RBI	BB	SO	SB	CS	EqBRR	AVG	OBP	SLG	MLVr	EqAVG	EqOBP	EqSLG	EqA	VORP	DEFENSE	
2005	CSP	AAA	25	468	85	30	2	26	88	41	81	4	0	-0.2	.328	.393	.601	.309	.281	.340	.498	.284	21.6	101-1B	2
2005	COL	MLB	25	104	14	7	0	2	16	13	22	1	0	-0.8	.330	.413	.473	.234	.308	.394	.462	.299	7.4	17-1B	-1
2006	CSP	AAA	26	248	37	16	1	15	55	20	34	0	0	-1.5	.284	.351	.568	.186	.253	.315	.502	.274	7.3	44-1B	4
2006	KCA	MLB	26	210	29	10	1	7	36	15	50	1	1	-1.2	.280	.338	.451	.014	.277	.343	.461	.274	3.2	52-1B	-7
2007	OMA	AAA	27	139	14	7	0	7	24	15	28	0	0	-2.0	.262	.345	.492	.085	.236	.317	.447	.261	0.9	16-1B	-2
2007	KCA	MLB	27	189	18	6	0	3	21	13	53	0	0	-2.7	.221	.286	.308	-.292	.222	.295	.316	.216	-9.7	48-1B	1
2008	KCA	MLB	28	259	27	13	1	9	36	21	58	2	0	-0.7	.250	.320	.430	-.050	.250	.310	.440	.270	0.5	64-1B	-2

Breakout: 27% Improve: 54% Collapse: 24% Attrition: 33%   Comparables: Earl Williams, Pete Incaviglia, Butch Huskey, Wes Helms

The Royals have blamed a chronically lame hamstring for Shealy's troubles last year because it's considered impo-lite to publicly state that the problem with your starting first baseman is that he can't catch up with a fastball. Shealy put up some monster numbers in some very favorable ballparks up and down the Rockies' system, which disguised the fact that he was old for his leagues and has a long swing. The Royals want to give Billy Butler every opportunity to win the first base job, so either Shealy hits right out of the gate or he starts the itinerant portion of his career.

Michael Stodolka 1B

Bats: L Throws: L Height: 6' 2" Weight: 210 Born: September 24, 1981 Age: 26

YEAR	TEAM	LVL	AGE	PA	R	2B	3B	HR	RBI	BB	SO	SB	CS	EqBRR	AVG	OBP	SLG	MLVr	EqAVG	EqOBP	EqSLG	EqA	VORP	DEFENSE	
2006	HDS	A+	24	513	81	33	2	11	67	78	103	4	3	1.6	.284	.396	.449	.071	.220	.320	.345	.239	-16.6	79-1B	-6
2007	WIC	AA	25	460	69	27	1	12	59	73	91	4	0	1.7	.291	.409	.462	.205	.258	.363	.411	.275	10.0	86-1B	-5
2008	KCA	MLB	26	398	44	22	1	8	42	46	99	4	2	0.1	.250	.340	.380	-.080	.240	.330	.390	.270	-2.4	95-1B	-2

Breakout: 33% Improve: 63% Collapse: 17% Attrition: 28%   Comparables: Gabe Gross, Joey Fernandez, Kevin Garner, Monty Fariss

Rick Ankiel, eat your heart out. Stodolka was the fourth pick in the 2000 draft, but after six years of ineffectual pitch-ing interrupted by Tommy John surgery, the left-hander was moved to first base in the 2005 instructional league. Two years later, he has a lifetime .402 OBP and was named the best defensive first baseman in the Texas League last year. He's not really a prospect—his upside looks something like Ross Gload's career—but a major league debut appears more likely than not. You have to appreciate the effort; the Royals did, re-signing him as a minor league free agent with an invite to spring training.

Mike Sweeney — DH

Bats: R   Throws: R   Height: 6' 3"   Weight: 225   Born: July 22, 1973   Age: 34

YEAR	TEAM	LVL	AGE	PA	R	2B	3B	HR	RBI	BB	SO	SB	CS	EqBRR	AVG	OBP	SLG	MLVr	EqAVG	EqOBP	EqSLG	EqA	VORP	DEFENSE
2005	KCA	MLB	31	514	63	39	0	21	83	33	61	3	0	0.4	.300	.347	.517	.191	.303	.357	.539	.300	34.8	48-1B -2
2006	KCA	MLB	32	252	23	15	0	8	33	28	48	2	0	-0.6	.258	.349	.438	-.002	.252	.353	.439	.278	6.1	
2007	KCA	MLB	33	289	26	15	1	7	38	17	29	0	0	1.0	.260	.315	.404	-.080	.259	.316	.422	.254	-0.5	
2008	KCA	MLB	34	290	31	16	1	8	41	21	41	2	1	-0.5	.270	.330	.430	-.020	.260	.320	.440	.270	5.4	71-DH

Breakout: 14% Improve: 42% Collapse: 30% Attrition: 28%   Comparables: Jeff Conine, Orlando Cepeda, Tom Paciorek, Frank Thomas

The career of the best Royals player of the post-Brett era looks like it will end with a whimper, not a bang. Sweeney can still hit lefties when he's healthy, and should land on someone's bench, but his time in Kansas City is almost certainly over. When judging the incompetence of the previous administration in Kansas City, it's important to remember that Allard Baird reportedly worked out a trade in 2005 that would have sent Sweeney to the Angels in exchange for, among others, Casey Kotchman; the deal was nixed by ownership. In Kansas City, they blame Glass in case of emergency.

Mark Teahen — RF

Bats: L   Throws: R   Height: 6' 3"   Weight: 210   Born: September 6, 1981   Age: 26

YEAR	TEAM	LVL	AGE	PA	R	2B	3B	HR	RBI	BB	SO	SB	CS	EqBRR	AVG	OBP	SLG	MLVr	EqAVG	EqOBP	EqSLG	EqA	VORP	DEFENSE
2005	KCA	MLB	23	491	60	29	4	7	55	40	107	7	2	4.5	.246	.309	.376	-.118	.250	.323	.389	.250	-1.8	123-3B 4
2006	OMA	AAA	24	98	14	8	4	2	14	19	12	0	0	0.9	.380	.500	.658	.716	.333	.455	.593	.349	17.7	21-3B -2
2006	KCA	MLB	24	439	70	21	7	18	69	40	85	10	0	4.2	.290	.357	.517	.151	.289	.364	.528	.302	27.9	105-3B 6
2007	KCA	MLB	25	608	78	31	8	7	60	55	127	13	5	3.1	.285	.353	.410	.014	.286	.359	.423	.273	11.9	130-RF 22
2008	KCA	MLB	26	539	71	30	4	11	62	51	108	11	4	1.4	.280	.350	.430	.020	.270	.340	.440	.280	9.7	127-RF 8

Breakout: 24% Improve: 52% Collapse: 18% Attrition: 14%   Comparables: Carlos May, Bob Skinner, Michael Tucker, Mark Whiten

Ladies and gentlemen, your WARP leader on offense for the 2007 Royals. Do you know how hard it is to find a right fielder capable of hitting .285 with seven homers? That's one more than backup infielder Jason Smith! Teahen's power outage has to concern the Royals. On the one hand, he was returning from off-season surgery on his throwing labrum. On the other hand, the arm surgery did not prevent Teahen from tying the franchise record for baserunner kills with 17. Power in a young player is generally not a fluke, so the 18 homers in 109 games at age 24 will manifest itself again sooner or later.

PITCHERS

John Bale

Bats: L   Throws: L   Height: 6' 4"   Weight: 220   Born: May 22, 1974   Age: 34

YEAR	TEAM	LVL	AGE	W	L	SV	G	GS	IP	H	BB	SO	HR	GB%	BABIP	STUFF	WHIP	ERA	PERA	EqERA	EqH9	EqBB9	EqSO9	EqHR9	VORP	SN/WX
2005	HRO	JP	31	2	1	24	51	0	53²	44	16	72	9	—	.282	8	1.12	3.18	4.20	4.26	7.8	3.0	9.2	1.4	7.5	—
2006	HRO	JP	32	1	2	6	30	5	43	45	11	46	5	—	.331	1	1.30	2.93	5.57	4.20	10.4	3.1	7.5	1.3	6.3	—
2007	KCA	MLB	33	1	1	0	26	0	40	45	17	42	1	49.6%	.393	19	1.55	4.05	4.23	3.83	9.7	3.4	8.6	0.2	8.9	-0.10
2008	KCA	MLB	34	2	2	3	44	0	50¹	52	19	44	5	47.1%	.319	6	1.41	4.21	4.06	4.01	8.8	3.0	7.4	0.8	8.3	0.70

Breakout: 23% Improve: 54% Collapse: 21% Attrition: 23%   Comparables: Lance Painter, Paul Assenmacher, Trever Miller, Jerry Don Gleaton

After being signed out of Japan to a two-year deal, Bale had a shoulder strain that necessitated three separate rehab assignments before he finally made his return debut stateside in mid-July. From that point on, he was a key member of the bullpen as a rare left-handed long reliever, the large platoon split that characterized his pre-Japan career having disappeared. By year's end, the Royals were contemplating moving Bale to the rotation for 2008. Given his strong peripherals, it's not as crazy as it sounds.

Brian Bannister

Bats: R   Throws: R   Height: 6' 2"   Weight: 210   Born: February 28, 1981   Age: 27

YEAR	TEAM	LVL	AGE	W	L	SV	G	GS	IP	H	BB	SO	HR	GB%	BABIP	STUFF	WHIP	ERA	PERA	EqERA	EqH9	EqBB9	EqSO9	EqHR9	VORP	SN/WX
2005	BIN	AA	24	9	4	0	18	18	109	91	27	94	11	49.2%	.278	-6	1.08	2.56	4.57	3.84	8.1	3.3	4.7	1.3	19.7	—
2005	NOR	AAA	24	4	1	0	8	8	45¹	48	13	48	0	45.9%	.369	19	1.35	3.18	5.06	5.23	11.1	3.3	7.2	0.2	1.7	—
2006	NOR	AAA	25	3	3	0	6	6	30²	34	5	24	4	41.4%	.319	-9	1.29	3.87	6.28	5.90	10.6	1.9	5.0	1.9	-1.0	—
2006	NYN	MLB	25	2	1	0	8	6	38	34	22	19	4	43.0%	.252	-4	1.47	4.26	4.04	3.92	7.8	4.4	3.9	0.9	6.8	1.02
2007	KCA	MLB	26	12	9	0	27	27	165	156	44	77	15	42.5%	.264	8	1.21	3.87	3.36	3.69	7.8	2.1	3.9	0.8	34.9	4.55
2008	KCA	MLB	27	6	8	0	21	21	116²	136	42	59	15	45.0%	.304	0	1.52	5.19	4.91	4.93	9.9	2.9	4.2	1.1	6.3	1.60

Breakout: 4%   Improve: 13%   Collapse: 55%   Attrition: 22%   Comparables: John Farrell, Dick Tidrow, Mike Thurman, Brian Moehler

Bannister is a *cum laude* graduate of USC; his post-game quotes are delivered with an eloquence that would make Curt Schilling jealous. While on the DL with the Mets in 2006, he made several appearances on the Mets' post-game show as an analyst, even though he had made all of eight career major league appearances. He owns a photography studio and his work has appeared in the *New York Times*. In Gil Meche's words, "I have never met a guy as smart as him in baseball." Intelligence may have split the atom and put a man on the moon, but it can't sustain a .264 BABIP. What it can do is sustain a pitcher's ability to pitch above his God-given talent. Bannister showed the ability to adjust last year, dropping his cutter in favor of a revamped curveball in spring training. He's likely to go through some tough times in 2008, but if he can stay one step ahead of the hitters, he'll avoid being a one-year wonder

Ryan Braun

Bats: R   Throws: R   Height: 6' 1"   Weight: 220   Born: July 29, 1980   Age: 27

YEAR	TEAM	LVL	AGE	W	L	SV	G	GS	IP	H	BB	SO	HR	GB%	BABIP	STUFF	WHIP	ERA	PERA	EqERA	EqH9	EqBB9	EqSO9	EqHR9	VORP	SN/WX
2006	WIC	AA	25	1	6	10	26	0	40²	30	16	58	2	48.9%	.322	16	1.14	2.24	4.28	3.52	8.0	4.2	9.2	0.7	8.9	—
2006	OMA	AAA	25	0	2	3	17	0	25¹	23	13	22	0	52.7%	.324	-2	1.43	2.15	4.15	3.75	8.6	5.2	5.6	0.4	4.9	—
2006	KCA	MLB	25	0	1	0	9	0	10²	13	3	6	2	40.5%	.333	-18	1.50	6.73	5.59	6.10	10.5	2.6	5.2	1.7	-0.7	-0.34
2007	OMA	AAA	26	2	2	9	23	0	33	19	12	36	1	54.7%	.247	17	0.94	1.09	3.01	2.70	6.0	3.9	8.1	0.3	9.7	—
2007	KCA	MLB	26	2	0	0	26	0	39¹	46	22	24	4	51.1%	.333	-17	1.73	6.64	5.20	6.75	9.7	4.3	4.9	0.9	-5.5	0.02
2008	KCA	MLB	27	2	3	2	37	1	46²	48	22	35	4	49.3%	.304	0	1.49	4.65	4.25	4.48	8.7	3.8	6.3	0.8	5.4	0.50

Breakout: 46%   Improve: 69%   Collapse: 14%   Attrition: 29%   Comparables: John Montague, Rodney Myers, D.J. Carrasco, Pete Mikkelsen

For the last time, this is not the Brewers' third baseman; for one thing, this Braun can probably play a better third base. Stop us if you've heard this before: he's a strong-armed reliever with a good slider and nothing left to prove in the minors, but got hammered in four separate stints in the majors because of struggles with command. Going forward, he's a cheap back-of-the-bullpen option with some upside.

Billy Buckner

Bats: R   Throws: R   Height: 6' 2"   Weight: 215   Born: August 27, 1983   Age: 24

YEAR	TEAM	LVL	AGE	W	L	SV	G	GS	IP	H	BB	SO	HR	GB%	BABIP	STUFF	WHIP	ERA	PERA	EqERA	EqH9	EqBB9	EqSO9	EqHR9	VORP	SN/WX
2005	BUR	A	21	3	7	0	11	11	60¹	66	17	60	9	50.0%	.322	-26	1.38	3.88	9.88	8.54	12.5	4.3	5.5	2.9	-17.2	—
2005	HDS	A+	21	5	6	0	17	17	94	105	46	92	10	58.4%	.357	-8	1.61	5.36	7.03	7.35	10.7	6.3	5.0	1.5	-16.7	—
2006	HDS	A+	22	7	1	0	16	16	90¹	92	47	85	6	56.6%	.328	0	1.54	3.90	6.53	5.56	10.3	6.7	5.0	1.2	0.4	—
2006	WIC	AA	22	5	3	0	13	13	75²	78	39	63	7	57.1%	.308	-4	1.56	4.67	6.24	6.00	10.1	5.5	4.9	1.2	-3.2	—
2007	OMA	AAA	23	9	7	0	27	15	104²	108	26	83	11	48.9%	.319	-3	1.28	3.78	5.39	4.96	10.3	2.6	5.6	1.2	7.0	—
2007	KCA	MLB	23	1	2	0	7	5	34	37	16	17	5	41.8%	.308	-12	1.56	5.29	5.99	5.17	10.1	4.0	4.6	1.4	2.9	0.23
2008	ARI	MLB	24	4	6	0	31	14	86¹	98	42	56	14	48.0%	.305	-6	1.62	5.43	5.55	5.30	9.7	3.9	5.4	1.3	4.5	0.90

Breakout: 23%   Improve: 61%   Collapse: 13%   Attrition: 18%   Comparables: Ricky Stone, Jamie McAndrew, Ryan Nye, Rocky Biddle

Buckner is a polished collegiate pitcher with an excellent curveball that he can throw for strikes and good sink on his fastball. The downside is that his velocity is just average, and he doesn't offer much projection. He got passing marks in his major league debut if you consider a "D" a passing grade. Swapped to Arizona for infielder Alberto Callaspo, Buckner should be a cheap back-of-the-rotation option for the Snakes.

Daniel Cortes

Bats: R   Throws: R   Height: 6' 5"   Weight: 205   Born: March 4, 1987   Age: 21

YEAR	TEAM	LVL	AGE	W	L	SV	G	GS	IP	H	BB	SO	HR	GB%	BABIP	STUFF	WHIP	ERA	PERA	EqERA	EqH9	EqBB9	EqSO9	EqHR9	VORP	SN/WX
2005	BRI	Rk	18	1	4	0	15	7	38¹	44	13	38	2	52.6%	.375	-25	1.49	5.17	10.56	10.38	14.5	8.6	3.3	1.8	-16.1	—
2006	BUR	A	19	1	2	0	7	7	35	40	17	30	7	27.0%	.317	-60	1.63	6.69	24.86	18.84	16.0	8.2	4.1	5.3	-42.2	—
2006	KAN	A	19	3	9	0	20	19	107²	109	38	96	6	41.4%	.324	-8	1.37	4.03	6.81	7.36	11.0	5.5	4.1	1.4	-18.9	—
2007	WIL	A+	20	8	8	0	24	24	123	102	45	120	7	39.4%	.293	2	1.20	3.07	6.23	6.12	10.3	5.2	5.7	1.3	-6.2	—
2008	KCA	MLB	21	5	11	0	32	22	126	155	85	84	22	39.6%	.323	-9	1.90	7.00	6.68	6.54	10.5	5.4	5.6	1.6	-15.2	-0.90

Breakout: 35% Improve: 57% Collapse: 22% Attrition: 15%   Comparables: Fernando Cabrera, Anthony Swarzak, Chad Durbin, Ken Ray

Widely seen as a throw-in (with Tyler Lumsden being the primary acquisition) in the trade that sent Mike MacDougal to the White Sox, Cortes emerged last season in High-A Wilmington, bumping his fastball into the mid-90s, which in turn added more separation with his 12-to-6 curveball. Cortes was dominant down the stretch, posting a 0.77 ERA in his last eight starts, and should start the year at Double-A. At just 21, he's the Royals' best pitching prospect after Luke Hochevar.

Kyle Davies

Bats: R   Throws: R   Height: 6' 2"   Weight: 205   Born: September 9, 1983   Age: 24

YEAR	TEAM	LVL	AGE	W	L	SV	G	GS	IP	H	BB	SO	HR	GB%	BABIP	STUFF	WHIP	ERA	PERA	EqERA	EqH9	EqBB9	EqSO9	EqHR9	VORP	SN/WX
2005	RIC	AAA	21	5	2	0	13	13	73¹	66	34	62	6	41.7%	.299	10	1.36	3.44	5.11	4.30	9.1	5.1	5.6	0.9	9.7	—
2005	ATL	MLB	21	7	6	0	21	14	87²	98	49	62	8	35.4%	.321	6	1.68	4.93	5.29	5.46	9.9	4.5	5.8	0.8	3.4	1.07
2006	ATL	MLB	22	3	7	0	14	14	63¹	90	33	51	14	38.2%	.369	-16	1.94	8.39	8.94	8.77	12.1	3.9	6.5	1.7	-18.2	-0.24
2007	ATL	MLB	23	4	8	0	17	17	86	92	44	59	12	42.6%	.300	-4	1.58	5.76	5.30	6.15	9.4	4.0	5.7	1.1	-5.1	0.87
2007	KCA	MLB	23	3	7	0	11	11	50	63	26	40	10	35.3%	.338	-11	1.78	6.66	7.33	7.06	10.6	4.1	6.5	1.8	-7.2	0.06
2008	KCA	MLB	24	4	6	0	25	13	83²	95	43	61	11	43.6%	.315	0	1.64	5.73	5.34	5.43	9.6	4.1	6.1	1.2	-0.5	0.40

Breakout: 44% Improve: 66% Collapse: 21% Attrition: 31%   Comparables: Fred Talbot, Herm Wehmeier, Ken Cloude, Colby Lewis

Davies put up terrible numbers for the second straight year in 2007, but this time he didn't have the alibi of a torn groin muscle, something which should excuse his 2006 season purely on principle. Davies has an option year left, so a Triple-A refresher might be in order, but as a 24-year-old with four average pitches, he was definitely worth eight innings of Octavio Dotel's career.

Jorge de la Rosa

Bats: L   Throws: L   Height: 6' 1"   Weight: 210   Born: April 5, 1981   Age: 27

YEAR	TEAM	LVL	AGE	W	L	SV	G	GS	IP	H	BB	SO	HR	GB%	BABIP	STUFF	WHIP	ERA	PERA	EqERA	EqH9	EqBB9	EqSO9	EqHR9	VORP	SN/WX
2005	MIL	MLB	24	2	2	0	38	0	42¹	48	38	42	1	52.3%	.382	16	2.03	4.47	6.17	5.23	10.9	7.4	8.3	0.2	2.8	-0.11
2006	HUN	AA	25	3	1	0	6	6	30	31	3	23	1	47.3%	.341	4	1.13	2.40	4.68	4.94	10.9	1.3	4.6	0.7	2.0	—
2006	MIL	MLB	25	2	2	0	18	3	30¹	32	22	31	4	43.5%	.333	4	1.78	8.32	5.23	7.39	8.8	5.4	8.0	0.9	-8.6	0.27
2006	KCA	MLB	25	3	4	0	10	10	48²	49	32	36	10	41.4%	.279	-1	1.66	5.17	5.48	4.62	8.1	5.5	6.3	1.7	4.1	0.97
2007	KCA	MLB	26	8	12	0	26	23	130	160	53	82	20	41.2%	.329	-13	1.64	5.82	6.08	5.76	10.5	3.3	5.2	1.3	-0.5	1.31
2008	KCA	MLB	27	3	6	0	30	11	75	88	35	52	10	44.1%	.323	-4	1.64	5.63	5.32	5.33	10.0	3.7	5.8	1.2	0.5	0.50

Breakout: 26% Improve: 55% Collapse: 24% Attrition: 40%   Comparables: Mike Kekich, Alex Kellner, Jeriome Robertson, Bob Hendley

Nine starts into the 2007 season, de la Rosa looked like he had swapped arms with David Wells, pitching to contact (just 12 walks and 30 K's in 58 innings) and generally getting guys out (3.59 ERA). He reverted to form after that, surrendering 42 walks and 15 homers in 72 innings the rest of the way and posting an ERA a staggering four runs higher. As we wrote last year, de la Rosa's future is likely as a power reliever. As such, even a slight uptick in his velocity and command could pay huge dividends.

Brandon Duckworth

Bats: R   Throws: R   Height: 6' 1"   Weight: 215   Born: January 23, 1976   Age: 32

YEAR	TEAM	LVL	AGE	W	L	SV	G	GS	IP	H	BB	SO	HR	GB%	BABIP	STUFF	WHIP	ERA	PERA	EqERA	EqH9	EqBB9	EqSO9	EqHR9	VORP	SN/WX
2005	ROU	AAA	29	8	6	0	20	19	115	138	37	89	17	43.7%	.344	-22	1.52	4.62	7.36	6.69	11.8	3.3	5.0	1.6	-12.9	—
2005	HOU	MLB	29	0	1	0	7	2	16¹	24	7	10	4	43.3%	.364	-45	1.90	11.04	14.35	13.79	14.4	3.4	5.2	2.3	-10.0	-0.47
2006	IND	AAA	30	8	3	0	12	12	74	67	23	57	4	55.2%	.292	5	1.22	2.43	4.90	4.10	9.7	3.6	5.2	0.8	11.3	—
2006	KCA	MLB	30	1	5	0	10	8	45²	62	24	27	3	46.6%	.376	-6	1.88	6.11	6.19	6.60	11.4	4.4	5.0	0.6	-4.9	0.28
2007	KCA	MLB	31	3	5	1	26	3	46²	51	23	21	3	45.8%	.298	-16	1.59	4.63	4.21	5.29	8.9	3.8	3.6	0.6	1.5	-0.19
2008	KCA	MLB	32	2	3	1	24	5	47²	56	20	28	6	46.5%	.318	-10	1.60	5.57	5.11	5.32	10.1	3.4	4.9	1.0	0.4	0.20

Breakout: 34% Improve: 61% Collapse: 20% Attrition: 46%   Comparables: Bruce Dal Canton, Hank Wyse, Sean Lowe, Juan Acevedo

Duckworth is the pitching equivalent of a White Castle hamburger: cheap, consistent, and not very good. His lifetime 20-31 record and 5.37 ERA is a very nice career for a player who was never drafted. He was still on the roster as we went to press; apparently the Royals have an intractable case of the munchies.

Jimmy Gobble

Bats: L   Throws: L   Height: 6' 3"   Weight: 200   Born: July 19, 1981   Age: 26

YEAR	TEAM	LVL	AGE	W	L	SV	G	GS	IP	H	BB	SO	HR	GB%	BABIP	STUFF	WHIP	ERA	PERA	EqERA	EqH9	EqBB9	EqSO9	EqHR9	VORP	SN/WX
2005	OMA	AAA	23	2	7	0	12	12	58¹	76	21	45	8	43.8%	.360	-21	1.66	6.64	7.57	8.51	12.1	3.6	4.9	1.5	-17.8	—
2005	KCA	MLB	23	1	1	0	28	4	53²	64	30	38	9	35.6%	.329	-9	1.75	5.70	5.96	5.00	9.5	4.8	6.2	1.3	0.3	0.94
2006	KCA	MLB	24	4	6	2	60	6	84	95	29	80	12	39.6%	.339	4	1.48	5.14	4.67	4.76	9.2	2.9	7.9	1.1	6.4	-0.24
2007	KCA	MLB	25	4	1	1	74	0	53²	56	23	50	6	36.1%	.342	4	1.47	3.02	4.79	3.61	9.3	3.4	7.9	1.0	13.0	1.69
2008	KCA	MLB	26	3	3	3	62	0	59¹	56	23	53	6	41.2%	.294	9	1.34	3.80	3.77	3.59	8.1	3.1	7.5	1.0	12.9	1.10

Breakout: 47% Improve: 70% Collapse: 11% Attrition: 18%   Comparables: Neal Cotts, Kyle Farnsworth, Jorge Julio, Mike Stanton

Washed out left-handed starting pitchers need not distress, there's always room for a LOOGY. After toying with a side-arm delivery in the spring, Gobble started to mix it in against left-handers in game-situations in May and June, corresponding to an improvement in his strikeout-to-walk ratio (1.22 before May 20th, 2.79 afterwards.) Still, Gobble was not quite as effective in that role last year as his ERA suggests; he allowed eight more inherited runners to score than would have been expected. Situational work may not be glamorous, but Gobble has as much job security as anyone on the team.

Zack Greinke

Bats: R   Throws: R   Height: 6' 2"   Weight: 185   Born: October 21, 1983   Age: 24

YEAR	TEAM	LVL	AGE	W	L	SV	G	GS	IP	H	BB	SO	HR	GB%	BABIP	STUFF	WHIP	ERA	PERA	EqERA	EqH9	EqBB9	EqSO9	EqHR9	VORP	SN/WX
2005	KCA	MLB	21	5	17	0	33	33	183	233	53	114	23	40.1%	.340	9	1.56	5.80	5.13	5.26	10.0	2.5	5.3	1.0	-7.0	1.70
2006	WIC	AA	22	8	3	0	18	17	105	96	27	94	12	44.0%	.297	-3	1.17	4.37	5.00	5.56	9.1	3.0	5.4	1.4	0.4	—
2007	KCA	MLB	23	7	7	1	52	14	122	122	36	106	12	32.6%	.321	15	1.30	3.69	3.99	3.48	8.7	2.4	7.3	0.9	30.1	5.27
2008	KCA	MLB	24	6	8	2	44	15	121	124	38	99	14	39.0%	.302	12	1.34	4.27	4.06	4.02	8.7	2.5	6.8	1.1	18.9	2.50

Breakout: 23% Improve: 57% Collapse: 17% Attrition: 13%   Comparables: Don Sutton, Ralph Terry, Frank Pastore, Reggie Cleveland

Modern medicine has saved the careers of legions of pitchers through use of a scalpel, but it may have saved the career of the Royals' potential ace without one, thanks instead to a combination of medication and the Royals' refreshingly enlightened approach to the depression and social anxiety that caused Greinke to take some time away from baseball in 2006. Greinke's approach on the mound last year was very different from that of his rookie season; he threw much harder, routinely in the mid-to-upper 90s, but relied almost exclusively on his fastball and plus-plus curveball while almost abandoning his changeup. The Royals are understandably reluctant to push Greinke too hard, but he's already halfway to free agency, so they need to take the gloves off now. If the Royals can get him to re-deploy the slow stuff that made him so good as a rookie and combine it with last year's power stuff, he could be a Cy Young candidate.

Rowdy Hardy

Bats: L   Throws: L   Height: 6' 4"   Weight: 170   Born: October 26, 1982   Age: 25

YEAR	TEAM	LVL	AGE	W	L	SV	G	GS	IP	H	BB	SO	HR	GB%	BABIP	STUFF	WHIP	ERA	PERA	EqERA	EqH9	EqBB9	EqSO9	EqHR9	VORP	SN/WX
2006	IDA	Rk	23	5	3	0	15	15	80²	79	5	52	4	60.0%	.293	-20	1.05	2.81	5.62	5.27	10.4	2.3	2.3	1.4	2.6	—
2007	WIL	A+	24	15	5	1	26	22	167	144	16	91	6	56.3%	.273	-6	0.96	2.48	4.98	5.07	10.3	2.0	2.7	0.9	8.6	—
2008	KCA	MLB	25	5	10	0	35	18	118	166	35	33	17	52.5%	.329	-19	1.70	6.51	5.96	6.23	12.0	2.4	2.3	1.2	-12.3	-0.50

Breakout: 4% Improve: 19% Collapse: 45% Attrition: 19%   Comparables: David Cassidy, Don Vidmar, Dennis Wiseman, Chris Begg

Hardy received as much attention as any prospect in the Royals' system last year, and not just because "Rowdy Hardy" sounds like the sidekick to "Rocky Cherry" in the script for *Boogie Nights 2*. Hardy is a left-hander who keeps the ball down and has impeccable control; he has nearly as many wins (20) as walks (21) in his pro career. He'd be a nice prospect if he could hit 86 miles per hour on the radar gun, but he only hits 83 on a good day, which is why the Royals got him as an undrafted fifth-year senior. He's already 25, has yet to reach Double-A, and his ERA was 1.81 runs worse after the All-Star Break than before. Root for him, but don't bet on him.

Luke Hochevar   Bats: R   Throws: R   Height: 6' 5"   Weight: 205   Born: September 15, 1983   Age: 24

YEAR	TEAM	LVL	AGE	W	L	SV	G	GS	IP	H	BB	SO	HR	GB%	BABIP	STUFF	WHIP	ERA	PERA	EqERA	EqH9	EqBB9	EqSO9	EqHR9	VORP	SN/WX
2006	BUR	A	22	0	1	0	4	4	15	8	2	16	2	39.5%	.167	-3	0.67	1.20	6.03	4.61	7.9	2.6	5.3	3.3	1.5	—
2007	WIC	AA	23	3	6	0	17	16	94	110	26	94	13	40.4%	.350	-16	1.45	4.69	7.42	7.41	11.8	3.3	6.3	1.8	-17.8	—
2007	OMA	AAA	23	1	3	0	10	10	58	53	21	44	11	40.7%	.259	-12	1.28	5.12	5.85	5.89	9.0	3.6	5.2	2.0	-1.8	—
2007	KCA	MLB	23	0	1	0	4	1	12²	11	4	5	1	64.3%	.250	-4	1.18	2.13	3.49	2.13	7.1	2.8	3.6	0.7	4.5	0.05
2008	KCA	MLB	24	5	9	0	33	18	124	143	52	80	19	44.0%	.310	-1	1.57	5.62	5.31	5.30	9.8	3.3	5.4	1.3	1.2	0.80

Breakout: 39%   Improve: 67%   Collapse: 17%   Attrition: 12%   Comparables: Kris Benson, Jason Young, Chris Bootcheck, Dewon Brazelton

A first-round pick really shouldn't be written off as a bust after striking out nearly three times as many hitters as he walked in the high minors and making his major league debut in his first full professional season. Unfortunately, Hochevar is criticized not for who he is, but for who he isn't. The Royals drafted Hochevar when they could (and should, as people said at the time) have drafted Andrew Miller or Tim Lincecum, to say nothing of Joba Chamberlain or even high schooler Clayton Kershaw. Hochevar should settle in as a consistent, if homer-prone, number-three starter. The Royals could have done worse, but they should have done better.

Gil Meche   Bats: R   Throws: R   Height: 6' 3"   Weight: 220   Born: September 8, 1978   Age: 29

YEAR	TEAM	LVL	AGE	W	L	SV	G	GS	IP	H	BB	SO	HR	GB%	BABIP	STUFF	WHIP	ERA	PERA	EqERA	EqH9	EqBB9	EqSO9	EqHR9	VORP	SN/WX
2005	SEA	MLB	26	10	8	0	29	26	143¹	153	72	83	18	40.8%	.296	-8	1.57	5.09	5.50	5.89	9.6	4.5	5.2	1.1	-1.8	1.42
2006	SEA	MLB	27	11	8	0	32	32	186²	183	84	156	24	45.1%	.298	11	1.43	4.48	4.53	4.79	8.5	3.8	7.1	1.1	18.0	3.44
2007	KCA	MLB	28	9	13	0	34	34	216	218	62	156	22	47.6%	.301	17	1.30	3.67	3.84	3.68	8.5	2.3	6.0	0.9	47.1	5.26
2008	KCA	MLB	29	10	11	0	29	29	177¹	187	67	130	19	45.5%	.305	14	1.43	4.55	4.33	4.32	9.0	3.0	6.1	0.9	21.4	3.70

Breakout: 15%   Improve: 58%   Collapse: 15%   Attrition: 14%   Comparables: Vicente Padilla, Roger Pavlik, Bill Singer, Pete Vuckovich

In 1987, Danny Jackson finished 9-18 for the Royals despite an above-average 4.02 ERA. Even though he had the lowest run support in the American League that year, Jackson was labeled a pitcher who just didn't "know how to win," and the Royals shipped him to Cincinnati for Kurt Stillwell that winter. In 1988, Jackson won 23 games for the Reds. Nineteen years later, Gil Meche went 9-13 for the Royals despite a stellar 3.67 ERA, but by August the papers in Kansas City had changed his name to "Gil Meche, who has the lowest run support of any American League starter" (although Carlos Silva nipped him for last place at season's end). Meche's record was properly recognized as an anomaly in what was universally considered a triumphant first season with the Royals, and he was named the team's Pitcher of the Year by the local media. We've come a long way, baby.

Neal Musser   Bats: L   Throws: L   Height: 6' 1"   Weight: 235   Born: August 25, 1980   Age: 27

YEAR	TEAM	LVL	AGE	W	L	SV	G	GS	IP	H	BB	SO	HR	GB%	BABIP	STUFF	WHIP	ERA	PERA	EqERA	EqH9	EqBB9	EqSO9	EqHR9	VORP	SN/WX
2005	NOR	AAA	24	6	11	0	24	24	123²	140	52	89	12	47.0%	.331	-16	1.55	5.02	6.97	7.15	11.4	4.7	4.7	1.2	-19.5	—
2006	TUC	AAA	25	1	3	0	8	7	36	44	24	18	4	40.2%	.328	-23	1.89	5.50	8.41	7.68	11.6	6.6	2.9	1.3	-7.9	—
2006	WIC	AA	25	6	3	2	18	11	83	80	48	67	12	38.7%	.294	-24	1.54	4.99	7.01	7.22	9.8	6.2	4.9	1.9	-13.9	—
2007	OMA	AAA	26	4	1	8	32	0	55¹	32	11	47	1	44.8%	.226	18	0.78	0.49	2.66	1.56	5.7	2.1	6.1	0.2	23.3	—
2007	KCA	MLB	26	0	1	0	17	0	24²	32	14	19	5	34.9%	.346	-16	1.86	4.37	8.36	5.18	11.5	4.4	6.3	1.8	3.7	-0.25
2008	KCA	MLB	27	1	2	2	39	0	33¹	36	17	23	4	42.1%	.302	-9	1.59	5.05	4.97	4.76	9.2	4.2	5.8	1.1	2.9	0.20

Breakout: 37%   Improve: 58%   Collapse: 26%   Attrition: 45%   Comparables: Jason Christiansen, Ken Patterson, Sid Monge, Bob MacDonald

Musser did not surrender an earned run in Triple-A until August 12, but in five separate stints with the Royals, he surrendered the same number of hits and more walks in less than half the innings. His season ended with a broken finger when he learned that you can't take out post-game frustrations on the quality furniture they have in Kansas City; it's not like that cheap junk in Omaha. Musser gives the Royals a decent third option from the left side, so long as he's not miscast as a LOOGY; left-handers hit more than 100 points higher against him than right-handers at both levels.

Leo Nuñez

Bats: R   Throws: R   Height: 6' 1"   Weight: 165   Born: August 14, 1983   Age: 24

YEAR	TEAM	LVL	AGE	W	L	SV	G	GS	IP	H	BB	SO	HR	GB%	BABIP	STUFF	WHIP	ERA	PERA	EqERA	EqH9	EqBB9	EqSO9	EqHR9	VORP	SN/WX
2005	KCA	MLB	21	3	2	0	41	0	53²	73	18	32	9	37.8%	.354	-14	1.70	7.54	6.62	6.75	11.1	3.0	5.2	1.4	-10.5	-0.57
2006	WIC	AA	22	1	2	3	15	0	21²	18	12	22	3	47.4%	.278	-3	1.42	4.25	6.20	5.49	8.7	5.9	6.4	1.8	0.2	—
2006	OMA	AAA	22	2	2	5	23	0	38²	37	13	33	5	35.7%	.299	-7	1.31	2.12	5.48	3.28	9.3	3.5	5.8	1.5	9.2	—
2006	KCA	MLB	22	0	0	0	7	0	13¹	15	5	7	2	45.5%	.317	-10	1.50	4.74	5.72	4.26	9.9	3.6	5.0	1.4	2.2	0.04
2007	WIC	AA	23	1	0	0	6	5	20²	10	6	13	1	45.5%	.167	-3	0.77	0.87	2.97	1.86	4.2	3.3	3.7	0.5	8.0	—
2007	OMA	AAA	23	1	2	0	5	4	23	16	4	19	3	38.5%	.213	11	0.87	2.74	3.29	3.18	6.4	2.0	5.6	1.2	6.1	—
2007	KCA	MLB	23	2	4	0	13	6	43²	44	10	37	8	34.8%	.288	8	1.24	3.91	4.31	3.89	8.4	1.8	7.0	1.6	8.5	0.83
2008	KCA	MLB	24	3	5	1	31	8	67²	73	23	48	10	39.8%	.300	1	1.43	5.07	4.67	4.77	9.2	2.7	5.9	1.3	5.4	0.80

Breakout: 11%   Improve: 29%   Collapse: 45%   Attrition: 37%   Comparables: Steve Ridzik, Joe Presko, Kazuhito Tadano, Carl Erskine

This rail-thin strike-thrower had his wrist broken by a line drive in spring training, then was traded to Oakland for Milton Bradley after the outfielder had been designated for assignment in June, only to have the trade rescinded when Bradley announced he had strained an oblique muscle (the injury miraculously healed with a strict regimen of San Diego sun). It was just as well for the Royals, as Nuñez came up in July as an emergency starter and pitched well enough to take a half-dozen turns in the rotation, then slotted into the bullpen in September and struck out 16 against just two walks in 10 1/3 innings. Between his being rushed to the majors at age 21 three years ago and the variety of minor injuries he's suffered since, Nuñez remains a bit of an enigma to the Royals. Whatever his role, he's a major league pitcher; Billy Beane's no dummy.

Joel Peralta

Bats: R   Throws: R   Height: 5' 11"   Weight: 190   Born: March 23, 1976   Age: 32

YEAR	TEAM	LVL	AGE	W	L	SV	G	GS	IP	H	BB	SO	HR	GB%	BABIP	STUFF	WHIP	ERA	PERA	EqERA	EqH9	EqBB9	EqSO9	EqHR9	VORP	SN/WX
2005	SLC	AAA	29	4	1	10	19	0	20	11	6	18	0	34.0%	.216	3	0.85	2.70	2.71	3.26	4.2	2.8	5.6	0.0	5.0	—
2005	ANA	MLB	29	1	0	0	28	0	34²	28	14	30	6	34.7%	.239	1	1.21	3.89	3.83	3.63	7.0	3.6	7.5	1.6	7.1	0.84
2006	KCA	MLB	30	1	3	1	64	0	73²	74	17	57	10	32.0%	.299	3	1.24	4.40	3.76	3.80	8.2	2.0	6.5	1.1	13.4	0.76
2007	KCA	MLB	31	1	3	1	62	0	87²	93	19	66	9	37.6%	.318	5	1.28	3.80	4.01	3.63	9.0	1.8	6.2	0.9	20.0	0.90
2008	KCA	MLB	32	3	3	3	53	0	65	68	19	46	8	39.2%	.293	-1	1.33	4.14	4.05	3.89	8.9	2.3	5.9	1.1	11.5	1.00

Breakout: 15%   Improve: 44%   Collapse: 32%   Attrition: 21%   Comparables: Barry Manuel, Cliff Politte, David Cortes, Dyar Miller

In last year's book, we pointed out that Peralta's repertoire had led to huge platoon splits; in his career, left-handers had batted 92 points higher than right-handers against him with a 346-point advantage in OPS. Last season, Peralta unveiled a cut fastball he worked on during winter ball, and left-handed hitters actually hit worse (.248/.299/.456) than right-handers (.290/.322/.449). Sometimes, it really is that simple. Peralta throws enough strikes with enough stuff to remain a valuable middle-innings asset at pre-arbitration prices.

Odalis Perez

Bats: L   Throws: L   Height: 6' 0"   Weight: 225   Born: June 11, 1977   Age: 31

YEAR	TEAM	LVL	AGE	W	L	SV	G	GS	IP	H	BB	SO	HR	GB%	BABIP	STUFF	WHIP	ERA	PERA	EqERA	EqH9	EqBB9	EqSO9	EqHR9	VORP	SN/WX
2005	LVG	AAA	28	1	0	0	4	4	14²	14	4	11	1	40.0%	.302	-1	1.22	4.29	3.54	3.77	7.5	2.5	4.4	0.6	2.9	—
2005	LAN	MLB	28	7	8	0	19	19	108²	109	28	74	13	48.1%	.292	6	1.26	4.55	4.32	4.91	9.1	2.1	5.7	1.1	8.2	2.04
2006	LAN	MLB	29	4	4	0	20	8	59¹	89	13	33	9	50.2%	.372	-18	1.72	6.83	7.32	7.28	12.7	1.7	4.6	1.2	-9.4	-0.52
2006	KCA	MLB	29	2	4	0	12	12	67	80	18	48	9	42.9%	.332	8	1.46	5.64	4.46	5.06	9.5	2.2	5.8	1.0	1.9	0.68
2007	KCA	MLB	30	8	11	0	26	26	137¹	178	50	64	14	46.3%	.341	-7	1.66	5.57	5.64	5.57	10.9	2.9	3.9	0.9	2.4	1.14
2008	KCA	MLB	31	5	8	0	31	18	114²	142	39	61	14	47.1%	.323	-6	1.58	5.43	5.14	5.16	10.6	2.7	4.4	1.0	2.8	1.00

Breakout: 23%   Improve: 60%   Collapse: 20%   Attrition: 27%   Comparables: Darren Oliver, Dave LaPoint, Alex Kellner, John Cerutti

Maybe he really wasn't tanking to get out of LA; maybe he just started to suck. Perez filled the rotation slot vacated by Mark Redman and responded with an equally replacement-level performance. His main contribution to the Royals was in bringing along a pair of pitching prospects, including the next player, as the price for taking him off the Dodgers' hands. Weak free-agent market or no, it's non-tender time.

Julio Pimentel

Bats: R   Throws: R   Height: 6′ 1″   Weight: 190   Born: December 14, 1985   Age: 22

YEAR	TEAM	LVL	AGE	W	L	SV	G	GS	IP	H	BB	SO	HR	GB%	BABIP	STUFF	WHIP	ERA	PERA	EqERA	EqH9	EqBB9	EqSO9	EqHR9	VORP	SN/WX
2005	VRO	A+	19	8	10	0	26	24	124	149	43	105	9	55.0%	.374	-17	1.55	5.08	8.99	9.08	13.5	5.5	4.2	1.4	-41.4	—
2006	HDS	A+	20	2	1	2	12	0	22^1	21	10	26	3	47.7%	.323	-1	1.40	3.26	6.98	4.43	9.7	5.8	6.2	2.2	2.6	—
2006	VRO	A+	20	3	8	2	30	9	74^1	85	45	77	4	46.9%	.387	-9	1.75	5.71	8.32	9.18	12.2	7.9	5.8	1.1	-26.1	—
2007	WIL	A+	21	12	4	0	27	22	152^2	145	43	73	8	61.5%	.275	-23	1.23	2.65	6.24	5.83	11.1	4.2	2.1	1.1	-3.4	—
2008	KCA	MLB	22	4	10	0	33	19	113^2	160	69	39	16	53.8%	.335	-25	2.00	7.37	6.99	7.04	12.0	4.8	2.8	1.3	-21.3	-1.50

Breakout: 11%   Improve: 37%   Collapse: 30%   Attrition: 14%   Comparables: *Yoel Hernandez, Nibaldo Acosta, Duaner Sanchez, Francisco Gamez*

In 2006, 158 of the batters Pimentel faced in his 97 innings either walked or struck out. In 2007, he produced the same two outcomes just 116 times in 153 innings. If the pitcher who learns to take a few miles per hour off his mid-90s heater, allowing him to get more sink on the pitch while controlling it better, is a cliché, Pimentel is either "a stitch in time saves nine," or "those who do not remember the past are condemned to repeat it." Now that Pimentel has shown the skills of both a power pitcher and a ground-ball pitcher, the Royals hope he can figure out how to do both at once.

David Riske

Bats: R   Throws: R   Height: 6′ 2″   Weight: 180   Born: October 23, 1976   Age: 31

YEAR	TEAM	LVL	AGE	W	L	SV	G	GS	IP	H	BB	SO	HR	GB%	BABIP	STUFF	WHIP	ERA	PERA	EqERA	EqH9	EqBB9	EqSO9	EqHR9	VORP	SN/WX
2005	CLE	MLB	28	3	4	1	58	0	72^2	55	15	48	11	43.0%	.214	-3	0.96	3.09	3.36	3.39	6.9	1.9	5.8	1.3	17.9	0.20
2006	BOS	MLB	29	0	1	0	8	0	9^2	8	3	5	2	43.8%	.207	-9	1.14	3.71	3.54	2.61	6.1	2.6	4.4	1.7	2.6	-0.05
2006	CHA	MLB	29	1	1	0	33	0	34^1	32	14	23	4	36.7%	.272	-5	1.34	3.94	3.90	3.67	7.9	3.4	5.8	0.8	7.6	0.05
2007	KCA	MLB	30	1	4	4	65	0	69^2	61	27	52	8	43.1%	.273	2	1.26	2.45	3.56	2.08	7.4	3.1	6.2	1.0	27.7	1.11
2008	MIL	MLB	31	3	3	4	50	0	58	57	21		8	42.4%	.283	-3	1.35	3.96	4.39	3.99	8.8	2.7	5.8	1.2	10.5	0.90

Breakout: 6%   Improve: 12%   Collapse: 70%   Attrition: 18%   Comparables: *Roy Lee Jackson, Mark Williamson, Tom Gorman, Dave Tobik*

Riske is a rare breed: a consistent middle reliever. He's had an ERA under 4.00 for five straight years and, while last year's 2.45 ERA was an anomaly, he should continue to provide above-average performance. This makes it all the more puzzling that the Royals agreed to put a clause in his contract that turned his 2008 season into a player option when Riske appeared in his 60th game in 2007. Handed that decision, Riske put himself back on the market, as well he should have given the size of his new deal with the Brewers (a minimum of $13 million over three years). Young players frequently give teams a club option in exchange for guaranteed financial security in the years before free agency, but it's unclear what benefits teams get when the shoe is on the other foot.

Carlos Rosa

Bats: R   Throws: R   Height: 6′ 1″   Weight: 185   Born: September 24, 1984   Age: 23

YEAR	TEAM	LVL	AGE	W	L	SV	G	GS	IP	H	BB	SO	HR	GB%	BABIP	STUFF	WHIP	ERA	PERA	EqERA	EqH9	EqBB9	EqSO9	EqHR9	VORP	SN/WX
2006	BUR	A	144	8	6	0	24	24	138^2	121	54	102	6	51.5%	.288	-21	1.27	2.54	7.33	6.59	11.1	6.7	3.5	1.4	-12.6	—
2006	HDS	A+	144	0	1	0	3	3	11^2	20	4	13	1	42.9%	.526	-40	2.14	7.23	13.73	13.50	17.7	5.1	5.9	1.7	-9.4	—
2007	WIL	A+	145	2	1	0	4	4	23	18	3	15	0	57.7%	.254	2	0.91	0.39	4.00	2.57	9.0	2.1	3.4	0.4	7.1	—
2007	WIC	AA	145	6	6	1	21	17	97	101	43	70	8	50.8%	.317	-14	1.48	4.36	6.00	5.66	10.3	5.1	4.4	1.1	-0.6	—
2008	KCA	MLB	23	4	8	0	33	16	104^2	124	64	52	6	76.0%	.327	-10	1.79	5.45	5.25	5.43	10.1	4.9	4.2	0.5	-0.6	0.50

Breakout: 36%   Improve: 53%   Collapse: 24%   Attrition: 16%   Comparables: *Sean Stidfole, Jerome Williams, Gerson Mercedes, Rafael Perez*

Since returning from Tommy John surgery in 2005, Rosa has emerged as the team's best Latin American prospect. He pitched through a pulled oblique muscle for part of last year, which brought down his numbers, but he has good control of a three-pitch mix and is positioned to get a callup at midseason should any of the incumbent starters falter. Long-term, he's a number-four starter.

Joakim Soria

Bats: R   Throws: R   Height: 6' 3"   Weight: 185   Born: May 18, 1984   Age: 24

YEAR	TEAM	LVL	AGE	W	L	SV	G	GS	IP	H	BB	SO	HR	GB%	BABIP	STUFF	WHIP	ERA	PERA	EqERA	EqH9	EqBB9	EqSO9	EqHR9	VORP	SN/WX
2005	MCD	MX	21	5	0	0	30	5	66¹	75	31	60	7	39.2%	.352	8	1.60	4.48	5.30	4.50	9.1	4.8	7.5	1.1	7.8	—
2006	FTW	A	22	1	0	0	7	0	11¹	5	2	11	1	48.4%	.207	-9	0.63	2.43	4.50	4.50	5.4	3.6	4.5	2.7	1.2	—
2006	MCD	MX	22	0	0	15	39	0	37	37	11	30	2	49.6%	.325	1	1.30	3.89	4.13	4.38	8.0	3.4	6.6	0.7	5.0	—
2007	KCA	MLB	23	2	3	17	62	0	69	46	19	75	3	41.1%	.256	33	0.94	2.48	2.32	2.58	5.6	2.2	8.8	0.4	26.4	4.77
2008	KCA	MLB	24	4	4	15	68	0	76	63	28	82	6	43.1%	.288	23	1.20	3.26	3.01	3.11	7.1	3.0	9.0	0.7	20.3	2.20

Breakout: 19% Improve: 49% Collapse: 28% Attrition: 19%   Comparables: Scott Williamson, Bruce Sutter, Huston Street, Brian Fisher

Rule 5 picks are supposed to be the toolsy outfielders or raw pitchers. You're not supposed to be able to grab a major league–ready closer like Soria with an excellent cut fastball, a deceptive changeup, and the poise that comes from pitching in the Mexican leagues. By Adjusted Runs Prevented, Soria was the seventh-best reliever in the majors last year. He has a history as a starting pitcher and the stuff to match, but the Royals are loath to mess with success. In the pen, his fastball has Rivera-level potential. Indeed, left-handers hit just .167/.217/.229 against him last year.

Blake Wood

Bats: R   Throws: R   Height: 6' 4"   Weight: 225   Born: August 8, 1985   Age: 22

YEAR	TEAM	LVL	AGE	W	L	SV	G	GS	IP	H	BB	SO	HR	GB%	BABIP	STUFF	WHIP	ERA	PERA	EqERA	EqH9	EqBB9	EqSO9	EqHR9	VORP	SN/WX
2006	IDA	Rk	20	3	1	0	12	12	52²	50	15	46	1	45.4%	.341	-9	1.25	4.48	6.15	7.24	10.8	5.1	3.5	0.8	-8.4	—
2007	BUR	A	21	2	1	0	7	7	35²	32	14	26	3	38.5%	.276	-19	1.29	3.03	8.42	6.30	11.1	6.9	3.0	2.1	-2.3	—
2008	KCA	MLB	22	4	9	0	28	18	102	135	71	55	19	42.0%	.327	-19	2.01	7.40	7.27	6.89	11.2	5.6	4.5	1.7	-17.7	-1.20

Breakout: 14% Improve: 40% Collapse: 31% Attrition: 11%   Comparables: Shawn Chacon, Todd Wellemeyer, Joaquin Benoit, Ryan Baerlocher

Wood fell to the third round in the 2006 draft after shin splints led to a disappointing junior year at Georgia Tech. He then missed the first half of the 2007 season with back problems. When healthy, he mixes a mid-90s fastball with a very effective changeup, and he was healthy in the Hawaii Winter League, striking out 57 batters in 33 innings. The numbers aren't much to look at now, but he could move very quickly.

Matt Wright

Bats: R   Throws: R   Height: 6' 4"   Weight: 250   Born: March 13, 1982   Age: 26

YEAR	TEAM	LVL	AGE	W	L	SV	G	GS	IP	H	BB	SO	HR	GB%	BABIP	STUFF	WHIP	ERA	PERA	EqERA	EqH9	EqBB9	EqSO9	EqHR9	VORP	SN/WX
2005	MIS	AA	23	6	8	1	17	14	84	101	37	63	7	52.5%	.351	-26	1.64	6.11	8.16	8.80	12.5	4.9	4.3	1.4	-26.9	—
2006	MIS	AA	24	7	3	0	15	14	89¹	74	28	84	3	48.3%	.310	15	1.14	2.22	4.38	3.90	9.0	3.5	5.9	0.7	15.2	—
2006	RIC	AAA	24	3	5	0	10	10	48²	57	29	34	6	49.7%	.338	-24	1.78	5.79	9.34	8.39	11.9	6.5	4.7	1.8	-13.6	—
2007	OMA	AAA	25	10	5	0	28	21	137¹	142	40	98	21	43.5%	.292	-19	1.33	4.06	5.82	5.15	10.0	3.0	4.9	1.6	6.6	—
2008	KCA	MLB	26	4	7	0	25	14	89¹	109	41	52	13	45.3%	.317	-7	1.66	6.01	5.64	5.68	10.4	3.6	4.9	1.3	-3.2	0.20

Breakout: 27% Improve: 57% Collapse: 16% Attrition: 17%   Comparables: Doug Brocail, Tim Worrell, Allen Levrault, Shawn Sedlacek

An unheralded member of the mass migration from Atlanta to Kansas City, Wright signed as a minor league free agent and, courtesy of an improved changeup, had a nice year in Triple-A Omaha. Though he looks for all the world like a future member of the Quadruple-A All-Stars, the Royals re-signed him. They know from painful experience that they could do a lot worse as emergency starters go.

Yasuhiko Yabuta

Bats: R   Throws: R   Height: 6' 0"   Weight: 190   Born: June 9, 1973   Age: 35

YEAR	TEAM	LVL	AGE	W	L	SV	G	GS	IP	H	BB	SO	HR	GB%	BABIP	STUFF	WHIP	ERA	PERA	EqERA	EqH9	EqBB9	EqSO9	EqHR9	VORP	SN/WX
2005	CHB	JP	32	7	4	2	51	0	55²	42	13	54	7	—	.236	-2	0.99	3.07	4.23	4.41	7.9	2.8	7.2	1.4	6.7	—
2006	CHB	JP	33	4	2	1	47	0	55	43	26	48	3	—	.258	-1	1.25	2.62	4.02	4.27	7.3	5.5	6.2	0.7	7.8	—
2007	CHB	JP	34	4	6	4	58	0	62²	64	10	45	5	—	.292	-9	1.18	2.73	4.20	4.04	9.0	2.0	4.9	1.0	10.8	—
2008	KCA	MLB	35	2	3	2	43	0	49²	54	20	32	6	45.0%	.302	-9	1.50	4.81	4.56	4.58	9.3	3.3	5.3	1.0	4.5	0.40

Breakout: 13% Improve: 35% Collapse: 44% Attrition: 28%   Comparables: Jerry Reed, Donne Wall, Harry Dorish, Don Elston

The principle that mediocre starters sometimes become excellent relievers applies in Japan, too. Yabuta's career blossomed in 2004 after a move to the pen, where he relies on a good fastball-forkball mix. As a group, Japanese relievers have been much more successful stateside than their compatriot hitters and starting pitchers. Just since

2004, Akinori Otsuka, Hideki Okajima, and Takashi Saito have all been tremendous pickups. Yabuta should replace David Riske in the setup role with similar results, which would make signing Yabuta for a less than a third of the guaranteed money the White Sox gave Scott Linebrink a steal.

LINEOUTS

Hitters

PLAYER	TEAM	LVL	AGE	PA	R	2B	3B	HR	RBI	BB	SO	SB-CS	EqBRR	AVG/OBP/SLG	MLVr	EqAVG/EqOBP/EqSLG	EqA	VORP
INF M. Aviles	OMA	AAA	26	581	78	27	6	17	77	30	59	5-5	-1.3	.296/.332/.463	.051	.261/.298/.414	.243	12.7
SS J. Bianchi	BUR	A	20	403	43	19	0	2	36	25	72	15-4	0.7	.247/.296/.315	-.076	.203/.244/.251	.175	-33.9
OF J. Dickerson*	BUR	A	20	466	50	23	2	3	43	38	76	26-13	1.5	.289/.354/.375	.121	.235/.289/.309	.214	-33.9
2B J. Johnson#	WIL	A+	21	307	28	11	2	1	31	41	49	4-7	-3.2	.252/.354/.321	-.069	.206/.291/.257	.193	-18.5
C P. Phillips	OMA	AAA	30	224	21	7	0	2	14	17	25	0-0	-1.1	.238/.294/.302	-.301	.230/.284/.294	.204	-9.9
OF D. Robinson#	BUR	A	19	449	42	11	3	2	26	32	100	34-7	3.7	.243/.299/.300	-.095	.198/.245/.251	.181	-45.1
SS A. Sanchez '08	KCA	MLB	24	84	7	3	0	0	6	5	11	1-0	0.2	.238/.283/.304	-.278	.233/.280/.312	.211	-2.2
SS J. Smith*	TOR	MLB	29	56	7	1	1	0	4	3	22	0-0	0.5	.212/.268/.269	-.384	.212/.268/.269	.183	-3.7
	KCA	MLB	29	89	9	2	1	6	14	3	29	0-0	-1.1	.188/.213/.447	-.253	.190/.225/.488	.234	-2.4
C M. Tupman*	OMA	AAA	27	344	21	16	0	1	32	36	34	2-2	-6.5	.281/.361/.344	-.079	.248/.328/.300	.228	-5.4

Mike Aviles is a free-swinging, lefty-mashing utility-infielder type, but without the glove to handle shortstop, his major league career is likely to be brief and intermittent. ⊘ **Jeff Bianchi** was the disappointment of the year in the Royals' farm system; finally healthy following shoulder surgery, the former second-round pick failed to hit .250 in A-ball after tearing up Rookie ball in 40 games across 2005 and 2006. The Royals gave him a mulligan and sent him to the Hawaiian Winter League, where he hit a flat .284/.338/.365. A rebound will come quick or not at all. ⊘ **Joseph Dickerson** was a fourth-round pick out of high school in 2005 and has hit right around the league average at every level. He currently profiles as a fourth-outfielder type, but he's got plenty of time to change that projection either way. ⊘ **Joshua Johnson** is Esteban German with less power, if that's possible. It probably isn't, so unless he figures out a way to muscle the ball into the gaps, he isn't going to have much of a career. ⊘ **Paul Phillips** has appeared in just 58 major league games over the last four years, is now 31, and stopped hitting even Triple-A pitching two years ago. He was designated for assignment in December. ⊘ **Derrick Robinson** was a fourth-round pick in 2006 who was lured away from a football scholarship with supplemental first-round money. The fastest player in that year's draft, his game is all speed as his bat is purely theoretical at this point. ⊘ **Angel Sanchez** has an outstanding glove, but a questionable bat. Missing all of 2007 due to shoulder surgery didn't help with the latter. ⊘ **Jason Smith** was picked up off waivers in July and clubbed six homers in 85 at-bats as a backup infielder. The Royals need an offense-minded shortstop to back up Tony Peña, but despite major league power, Smith's career .261 OBP won't cut it. That's just part of the reason he's been with five organizations in the last three years. ⊘ If there's a silver lining to the Jason LaRue Experience, it's that the Royals have decided they can get the same performance from a homegrown player at minimum wage. **Matt Tupman** bats left-handed and will take a walk, but we're talking strictly poor man's Paul Bako territory here.

Pitchers

PLAYER	TEAM	LVL	AGE	W	L	SV	IP	H	BB	SO	HR	GB%	BABIP	STUFF	WHIP	ERA	PERA	EqERA	EqH9	EqBB9	EqSO9	EqHR9	VORP
D. Christensen*	WIC	AA	23	3	15	0	140²	173	56	99	23	42.5%	.346	-43	1.63	6.20	9.20	8.07	12.3	4.6	4.2	2.2	-35.5
D. Duffy*	ROY	Rk	18	2	3	0	37¹	24	17	63	0	44.6%	.333	33	1.10	1.45	5.68	6.06	8.0	7.7	7.2	0.6	-1.7
L. Hudson	OMA	AAA	30	0	1	0	9	11	4	14	2	48.0%	.391	9	1.67	5.00	9.65	9.00	12.0	4.0	11.0	2.0	-3.4
D. Hughes*	WIC	AA	25	6	2	1	108	98	45	77	5	39.5%	.284	-1	1.32	3.08	4.48	4.33	8.5	4.6	4.2	0.7	14.7
B. Johnson	WIL	A+	22	9	6	1	131²	119	33	80	7	48.8%	.280	-20	1.15	3.28	5.93	6.09	10.7	3.8	3.1	1.2	-6.3
T. Lumsden*	OMA	AAA	0	9	6	0	119¹	141	59	74	11	46.0%	.346	-18	1.68	5.88	7.20	7.91	11.8	5.0	4.3	1.1	-28.3
J. Plummer	WIC	AA	23	5	6	11	79	65	16	90	13	37.7%	.264	-11	1.03	3.08	4.84	4.48	8.1	2.5	7.2	2.0	9.5

Daniel Christensen is a crafty lefty who fell apart when he reached Double-A, was foisted upon the Tigers after the season as the player-to-be-named-later in the Roman Colon deal. The Tigers promptly outrighted him, rather optimistically, to Triple-A. ⊘ **Daniel Duffy** was drafted in the third round last year out of an obscure California high school, then opened eyes with 63 strikeouts in 37 innings in Rookie ball. He's a lefty who throws in the low 90s with a very good curve. If he stays healthy, he'll get a much longer comment next year. ⊘ The Royals went into spring training last year relying on **Luke Hudson** to be their third starter, but he made only one start before shoulder surgery ended his season. He's a longshot to make a full recovery, and he wasn't that good before he got hurt. ⊘ Upon returning from Tommy John surgery last year, **Dusty Hughes** jumped to Double-A for the first time, then capped a solid year by being named pitcher of the year in the Arizona Fall League. A short left-hander with a funky delivery, he should be getting the acceptance letter from the Fraternity of LOOGYs any day now. ⊘ Like Julio Pimentel, **Blake Johnson** was acquired from the Dodgers as an incentive for taking on Odalis Perez's contract, but it was a bad bribe. Johnson has excellent command of average stuff, and the attrition rate for A-ball pitchers of that description is enormous. ⊘ **Tyler Lumsden** was supposed to be the prize of the Mike MacDougal trade, but was awful in every way last season. The Royals added him to the 40-man roster anyway, because he's left-handed and, um, throws with his left hand. ⊘ **Jarod Plummer** was acquired in a minor deal with the Dodgers two years ago, and since then he has 208 strikeouts against just 40 walks. He's tall and throws hard but is exceedingly homer-prone. He should have a future somewhere, likely in Petco Park.

MANAGER: BUDDY BELL

YEAR	TEAM	W-L	Pythag +/−	Avg PC	100+ P	120+ P	QS	BQS	REL	REL w Zero R	IBB	Subs	PH	PH Avg	PH HR	SB2	CS2	SB3	CS3	SAC Att	SAC %	POS SAC	Squeeze	Swing	In Play
2005	KCA	43-69	1	88.5	25	0	32	6	308	174	17	15	95	.183	1	32	12	2	2	40	77.5%	29	2	72	61
2006	KCA	62-100	1	89.8	46	5	46	10	473	241	40	32	91	.250	1	55	30	10	4	76	68.4%	48	2	110	81
2007	KCA	69-93	-4	92.1	47	1	63	3	447	255	54	36	117	.170	2	72	41	6	3	61	67.2%	41	1	139	101

The last two times the Royals needed a new manager, the organization's search for a replacement was done publicly and the candidates for the job were all familiar names. With uncanny precision, the team then honed in on the candidate with the shortest track record of success, ergo Tony Peña and Buddy Bell. The process after Bell announced he was stepping down could not have been more different. The search for a new manager was conducted discreetly, to the degree that no one even knew that Trey Hillman was even under consideration until he had already been offered the job.

Hillman appears to be an excellent choice. Having led the previously hapless Nippon Ham Fighters to consecutive Japan Series and one championship in his five years with the club, Hillman has the unique distinction of being neither a recycled manager with a history of failure, nor a new manager without the requisite experience. The Fighters reached the 2007 Japan Series despite finishing last in virtually every offensive category, including runs scored. That raises concerns that Hillman might have smuggled back a super-aggressive speed-and-defense brand of baseball in his luggage, but the Fighters won the Japan Series in 2006 with a much more potent offense only to lose their two best hitters to retirement and free agency. Hillman's ability to win in both seasons and his public statements since taking the Royals job suggest that he understands the need to tailor his style to the talents of his team. Having achieved success in a foreign land while speaking a foreign language and learning a foreign culture, Hillman is unlikely to have any problems with a team on which the most challenging player to communicate with might be Zack Greinke.

Los Angeles Angels

If you want your baseball to be played by fleet-footed athletes with sweet-swings and strong throwing arms, the Angels are your team. Add Mike Scioscia, a thoughtful, articulate, and tactically aggressive manager well-regarded from his days as the regular catcher across town with the Dodgers, and rooting for them becomes easier still. However, the Angels aren't merely more athletic than your average bear, they're also one of the best-run organizations in the game today. When Arte Moreno bought the defending world champion Angels from Disney five years ago, it was expected that the Angels would continue their new-found winning ways, and at least to some extent, they have, winning their division in three of the last four years.

Last year, the Angels jumped out to a 5 1/2-game lead in the American League West by June 1. Although they made things interesting by falling back to only a game up on the Mariners three weeks into July, and again a month later in August, they put the M's away before Labor Day with a three-game sweep in Seattle. The future offers more of the same: with both the A's and Rangers in full rebuild mode and the Mariners flirting with mediocrity, the short-stack AL West should belong to Moreno's minions for at least the next year or two and perhaps much longer.

There are few areas in which the Angels aren't doing things well. Their farm system is humming, and their immediate future is pretty sunny due in no small part to the many players that system has produced who are already up and established with the big club. Second baseman Howie Kendrick looks like a future All-Star and batting champion. First baseman Casey Kotchman won't be a great player, but he's already a very good one.

Jered Weaver, Ervin Santana, and Joe Saunders all have their virtues as starting pitchers, and while none of them is likely to grow up to be an ace, the Angels have already grown one in John Lackey as well as one of the game's best closers in Francisco Rodriguez. Further hope for the immediate future is invested in shortstop Erick Aybar, third baseman Brandon Wood, first baseman Kendry Morales, and perhaps also outfielder Terry Evans.

However, the Angels are far from being a merely farm-dependent franchise. Moreno has been more than willing to open his checkbook to bring in premium talent from the free-agent market, most notably superstar Vladimir Guerrero, who was reeled in with a five-year, $70 million deal following the 2003 season. Powered by the financial success that comes from delivering a winner to a huge, supportive market and providing that audience with an improved (if not new) venue, the Angels have come to resemble the self-perpetuating powerhouses of the AL East, the Yankees and the Red Sox, at least in the broad strokes.

That, right there, is the problem. A passing resemblance to someone might impress your friends, and it might get you in trouble in a police lineup, but it's not the same as being the real thing. In 2007, as in 2004, the Angels were quickly swept by the Red Sox in the ALDS, while 2005 saw them squeak past the Yankees, only to lose the ALCS to the White Sox in five games. Despite all that they have going for them, the Angels are in danger of perpetually settling for division titles and brief appearances in the postseason, when the real stakes are higher. The Angels are confronted with the same challenge that former old-school favorites, the Twins, failed to meet earlier this decade, and that the Moneyball A's never successfully solved: the building of a ballclub with enough talent to win multiple post-season series.

In October, seven-year incumbent general manager Bill Stoneman stepped down to take an advisory role with the organization, passing the GM job on to former director of player development Tony Reagins. Reagins has to set the bar higher. He got off to a decent start this winter by signing center fielder Torii Hunter, the team's biggest free-agent pickup since they snagged Guerrero, but while Hunter's contract exceeds Guerrero's in total dollars, he isn't a pickup of the same caliber. Rather, Hunter is an improvement on the margins, a correction of the previous winter's mistake of throwing money at Gary Matthews Jr. What's more, Hunter wasn't even the best center fielder available; that would have been Andruw Jones, who will man the position across town for Scioscia's old club after signing a much shorter contract for roughly the same average salary as Hunter. The Angels need to make more drastic improvements to their team. This year's Hot Stove League didn't boast a full panoply of great free agents at every position, making it all the more strange that the Angels seemed to excuse themselves with unseemly haste from bidding on the one truly great player who would have best fit their needs, Alex Rodriguez.

Beyond the open market, some premium talent did get bandied about in trade talk, notably the Marlins' young star slugger Miguel Cabrera and the Twins' world-class ace Johan Santana. Despite a bevy of talent in their farm system, the Angels lost the Cabrera sweepstakes to the Tigers, who it was generally agreed had an inferior collection of talent to offer Florida. As for the Santana talks, the Angels never seemed to be a serious part of the conversation. Instead, Reagins picked up moderately useful fourth starter Jon Garland from the White Sox for shortstop Orlando Cabrera in an exchange of players entering their walk years.

That failure to significantly improve the ballclub was a troubling early indication that Reagins may share Stoneman's most glaring weakness. Like the Twins under GM Terry Ryan, the Angels under Stoneman and now Reagins have held on to too many prospects for too long, only to watch their value plummet as it turns out that they aren't really as good as they were cracked up to be. Consider some of the Angels' current crop of highly touted homegrown products. Wood's trade value has already peaked, as he's shifted from shortstop to third base while continuing to struggle to make consistent contact. Aybar is pure aggression in spikes; at the plate, on the bases, or in the field, he's consistently daring to do the impossible—and failing. Any suggestion that he might be a star now seems like a stretch, and his

growing up to be the new Alfredo Griffin would be one of the happier possible outcomes. Kotchman is a talented defensive first baseman, but lacks the power associated with his position. Jeff Mathis has been touted for years as a premium catching prospect, but catch-and-throw guys who don't hit are a dime a dozen. A bad third season in the majors put a major dent in Ervin Santana's prospects; he remains a pitcher with promise, but is no longer seen as future ace material. Alone among the club's most recent crop of kids, Kendrick possesses true top-shelf production potential. If he can stay healthy, he could be the one who delivers.

The crime here isn't that the Angels' system has cranked out prospects who have turned out to be something less than expected; that happens. The problem is that the team has been tardy in identifying which of their kids will and won't deliver on their potential and, correspondingly, debilitatingly slow about trading those less likely to deliver before their weaknesses become obvious. Yes, an attempt to trade Santana and Aybar for All-Star shortstop Miguel Tejada in 2006 was quashed by the caprices of Baltimore boss Peter Angelos, but that attempt remains distressingly singular in the team's recent history. The Halos have still more good prospects on the way up—notably catcher Hank Conger and righty Nick Adenhart—but their farm system is heavily stocked with guys who can't beat out the solidly average collection of players that currently occupy much of the roster. As a result, failing to flip those youngsters for players who would improve that talent core only leaves the farm's prospective value unharvested. The contrast with the Braves, who have proven consistently willing to peddle their oft-touted farm talent, and who have rarely come to regret it, could not be greater.

Looking forward, the challenge for Reagins won't be to win the increasingly weak AL West. Instead, his responsibility must be to leverage his team's assets to reach the same level as the best teams in the league. That will require more than throwing a lot of money at an outfielder simply because he's better than Gary Matthews Jr. and more than getting a starting pitcher of Jon Garland's caliber. It will require having the wisdom to cut the cord to some of the prospects the organization has cultivated and perhaps too-jealously treasured. The price of failure will be a fate no different than that of the post-Ryan Twins, who missed their opportunity to build a championship ballclub and have since watched helplessly as other teams in their division have improved and passed them. Ultimately, the willingness to settle for the simple goal of just being good enough will leave a team short of even that.

Angels on the Basepaths

In some regards, the Angels' offense represents a perfect antithesis of the so-called "Moneyball" approach. It doesn't rely on the grim, grinding, actuarial certainty of walks, home runs, and the wearing down of pitchers by working deep counts. Rather, the Angels' offense is heavily dependent on hitting for average and aggressive baserunning. Manager Mike Scioscia is matter-of-fact about his tactics, acknowledging that he's quite aware of the percentages, and if they add up to around 75 percent or better on a given opportunity, he lets fly. That's hardly the basepath-banzai approach of Whitey Herzog's old Cardinal quads. In fact, Scioscia's methods make "old school" seem every bit as coolly calculated as anything sabermetric heroes Billy Beane or Earl Weaver have been accused of.

Another curious aspect of the Angels' attack is that the bulk of the value derived from the team's baserunning doesn't come from baserunning's most easily recognized component, basestealing. The Angels ranked second in the league in steals last year, but their 71.6 percent success rate fell short of the league average of 73.2 percent, and well short of Scioscia's decision-making 75 percent. As a result, the Angels' steal attempts resulted in a net loss of nearly eight runs, which ranked them a dreadful 26th in the majors in Equivalent Stolen Base Runs (EqSBR). The stolen base may well be a fundamental element of Mike Scioscia's tactical playbook, but nobody understands better than Scioscia that his team will have to be more efficient on the bases moving forward. Making this a difficult proposition will be the exchange of two of his more reliable basestealing weapons from a year ago, Reggie Willits and Orlando Cabrera,

for Torii Hunter, a career 68 percent base thief, and Erick Aybar, who has been running his way into outs throughout his career.

Stealing fewer bases won't make the Angels a station-to-station team, however, as the Angels excelled at taking the extra base in nearly every other situation. Taking stolen bases out of the equation, the Angels were the second-best team in baseball last year at taking the extra base, generating more than ten and a half runs that way, a total second only to that of the Dodgers (see Table 1). Practically speaking, that means that nobody in the American League was better than the Angels when it came to exploiting opposing defenses to pick up that extra base on a ball in play (or one that gets by the catcher), which is the ideal complementary skill to the team's hitting approach, which emphasizes putting balls in play. Some teams believe that a walk is as good as a hit; the Angels are not one of them, and this is why.

Table 1. All Your Base Are Belong to Us: Leading teams, total EqBRR, 2007

Team	EqBRR	Team	EqBRR-EqSBR
Phillies	14.8	Dodgers	14.4
Dodgers	12.8	**Angels**	**10.6**
Rangers	9.5	Rangers	9.5
Mets	8.5	Royals	7.7
Devil Rays	6.3	Padres	5.4
Tigers	4.7	Devil Rays	4.9
Twins	4.5	Brewers	3.9
D'backs	2.8	Indians	3.0
Angels	**2.6**	D'backs	2.9
Brewers	2.2	Tigers	2.6

HITTERS

Garret Anderson   **LF**   Bats: L   Throws: L   Height: 6' 3"   Weight: 225   Born: June 30, 1972   Age: 36

YEAR	TEAM	LVL	AGE	PA	R	2B	3B	HR	RBI	BB	SO	SB	CS	EqBRR	AVG	OBP	SLG	MLVr	EqAVG	EqOBP	EqSLG	EqA	VORP	DEFENSE
2005	LAA	MLB	33	603	68	34	1	17	96	23	84	1	1	-3.1	.283	.308	.435	.001	.288	.323	.454	.265	11.0	102-LF -6
2006	LAA	MLB	34	588	63	28	2	17	85	38	95	1	0	-0.6	.280	.323	.433	-.015	.277	.328	.439	.265	9.0	91-LF 7
2007	LAA	MLB	35	450	67	31	1	16	80	27	54	1	0	0.8	.297	.336	.492	.137	.298	.341	.516	.288	22.1	82-LF -3
2008	LAA	MLB	36	469	52	28	1	13	70	27	65	2	1	-0.6	.279	.321	.440	-.002	.276	.321	.459	.268	7.9	111-LF -4

Breakout: 15%   Improve: 43%   Collapse: 20%   Attrition: 24%   Comparables: Dante Bichette, Dave Parker, B. J. Surhoff, Brian Jordan

Would you believe that Anderson posted the fourth-highest EqA of his career in 2007? At his peak, Anderson was an above-average left fielder. That peak ended four years ago, and he's now part of the Angels' problem—not getting enough runners on base. Just three players in the history of baseball with 7,000 or more career plate appearances walked less frequently than Anderson has—Garry Templeton, Ozzie Guillen, and Bill Buckner. Anderson may have to DH a lot more with Torii Hunter in center and Gary Matthews fighting for playing time in left. As a barely adequate offensive left fielder, Anderson would be a below-average DH.

Erick Aybar   SS

Bats: S   Throws: R   Height: 5' 10"   Weight: 170   Born: January 14, 1984   Age: 24

YEAR	TEAM	LVL	AGE	PA	R	2B	3B	HR	RBI	BB	SO	SB	CS	EqBRR	AVG	OBP	SLG	MLVr	EqAVG	EqOBP	EqSLG	EqA	VORP	DEFENSE	
2005	ARK	AA	21	590	101	29	10	9	54	29	51	49	23	-3.2	.303	.350	.445	.084	.260	.305	.386	.243	8.7	133-SS	-8
2006	SLC	AAA	22	368	63	20	3	6	45	21	36	32	18	-1.5	.283	.327	.413	-.067	.245	.285	.364	.227	-2.6	80-SS	-9
2006	LAA	MLB	22	40	5	1	1	0	2	0	8	1	0	0.7	.250	.250	.325	-.337	.250	.250	.325	.199	-1.2		
2007	LAA	MLB	23	211	18	5	1	1	19	10	32	4	4	-0.5	.237	.279	.289	-.311	.249	.293	.301	.207	-10.3	36-2B	-2
2008	LAA	MLB	24	295	35	13	2	3	27	16	36	15	5	1.2	.261	.306	.358	-.151	.259	.305	.374	.247	1.5	72-SS	-1

Breakout: 46%   Improve: 65%   Collapse: 12%   Attrition: 26%   Comparables: Donnie Hill, Brian Roberts, Bip Roberts, Cesar Izturis

Aybar has steadily lost 25 points off his average at each level, so there's a limit as to how valuable he will be as an everyday player. His speed and glove make him a very good extra infielder, but he'd be better off getting 500 plate appearances in Triple-A than 150 in the AL this year. The trade of Orlando Cabrera puts him in a battle with Maicer Izturis for the starting shortstop job, a battle that will come down to how many singles Aybar hits in March. These are the professionals, folks.

Peter Bourjos   CF

Bats: R   Throws: R   Height: 6' 1"   Weight: 175   Born: March 31, 1987   Age: 21

YEAR	TEAM	LVL	AGE	PA	R	2B	3B	HR	RBI	BB	SO	SB	CS	EqBRR	AVG	OBP	SLG	MLVr	EqAVG	EqOBP	EqSLG	EqA	VORP	DEFENSE	
2006	ORM	Rk	19	279	42	16	7	5	28	22	67	13	5	-0.2	.292	.354	.472	.232	.206	.249	.317	.195	-33.2	62-CF	4
2007	CDR	A	20	270	37	9	6	5	29	20	53	19	9	-2.2	.274	.335	.426	.110	.217	.267	.340	.217	-13.0	61-CF	0
2008	LAA	MLB	21	332	30	14	3	3	23	18	86	11	5	1.0	.223	.269	.318	-.293	.220	.268	.332	.214	-11.6	80-CF	1

Breakout: 42%   Improve: 62%   Collapse: 15%   Attrition: 14%   Comparables: Kenny Kelly, Rich Stuart, Willy Taveras, Joshua Flores

After starting the year as a stealth prospect with a strong defensive reputation, Bourjos had his 2007 season cleaved by a ruptured left ring finger. The injury cost him two months of playing time and any chance of advancing past Low-A. The lost time hurt; while the tools are still there, he's now behind on the age/level matrix. Despite the PECOTA comp above, his long-term outlook is more fourth outfielder than Willy Taveras.

Matt Brown   3B

Bats: R   Throws: R   Height: 6' 0"   Weight: 200   Born: August 8, 1972   Age: 35

YEAR	TEAM	LVL	AGE	PA	R	2B	3B	HR	RBI	BB	SO	SB	CS	EqBRR	AVG	OBP	SLG	MLVr	EqAVG	EqOBP	EqSLG	EqA	VORP	DEFENSE			
2005	RCU	A+	32	547	68	39	4	12	65	40	125	4	5	-3.7	.262	.329	.432	-.078	.201	.256	.317	.196	-28.8	119-3B	5		
2006	ARK	AA	33	576	77	41	3	19	79	47	108	7	6	-0.9	.293	.362	.495	.145	.252	.310	.424	.250	14.2	128-3B	-9		
2007	SLC	AAA	34	442	69	30	2	19	60	45	106	5	9	-5.0	.276	.358	.509	.060	.239	.320	.434	.253	13.1	59-3B	3	20-LF	0
2008	LAA	MLB	35	301	27	15	1	7	36	24	81	3	2	-0.2	.223	.289	.365	-.194	.220	.289	.381	.236	-5.7	73-3B	-2		

Breakout: 27%   Improve: 43%   Collapse: 34%   Attrition: 39%   Comparables: Jason Wood, Rick Schu, Pedro Swann, Shane Halter

The need to move Brandon Wood off of shortstop last year sent Brown, who had been playing to Wood's right on their way up the ladder and isn't a terrible third baseman, all around the field. As a result, Brown played first, second, and the outfield corners for Triple-A Salt Lake while turning in his typical offensive performance. He's loosely comparable to Robb Quinlan, whose job he could take as soon as midsummer.

Orlando Cabrera   SS

Bats: R   Throws: R   Height: 5' 9"   Weight: 185   Born: November 2, 1974   Age: 33

YEAR	TEAM	LVL	AGE	PA	R	2B	3B	HR	RBI	BB	SO	SB	CS	EqBRR	AVG	OBP	SLG	MLVr	EqAVG	EqOBP	EqSLG	EqA	VORP	DEFENSE	
2005	LAA	MLB	30	587	70	28	3	8	57	38	50	21	2	2.2	.257	.309	.365	-.115	.264	.326	.384	.256	12.6	137-SS	4
2006	LAA	MLB	31	675	95	45	1	9	72	51	58	27	3	8.7	.282	.335	.404	-.035	.284	.344	.416	.273	29.5	147-SS	-3
2007	LAA	MLB	32	701	101	35	1	8	86	44	64	20	4	4.1	.301	.345	.397	.016	.310	.357	.420	.276	31.7	150-SS	13
2008	CHA	MLB	33	570	68	27	2	7	50	40	53	14	4	1.3	.269	.323	.372	-.096	.265	.322	.376	.252	8.1	134-SS	1

Breakout: 4%   Improve: 24%   Collapse: 51%   Attrition: 14%   Comparables: Eric Young, Phil Garner, Johnny Temple, Luis Aparicio

Cabrera turned in a second consecutive good year in 2007, with nearly identical offensive numbers and slightly better defense that was, if not Gold Glove–caliber (he won his second), at least above average. His contact rate and speed are both stable, so he should be just as valuable this year. He's a significant upgrade for the White Sox at shortstop and could add five homers in their bandbox of a ballpark.

Hank Conger — C

Bats: S   Throws: R   Height: 6' 0"   Weight: 205   Born: January 29, 1988   Age: 20

YEAR	TEAM	LVL	AGE	PA	R	2B	3B	HR	RBI	BB	SO	SB	CS	EqBRR	AVG	OBP	SLG	MLVr	EqAVG	EqOBP	EqSLG	EqA	VORP	DEFENSE	
2006	ANG	Rk	18	76	11	3	4	1	11	7	11	1	0	0.2	.319	.382	.522	.299	.222	.263	.333	.203	-11.0		
2007	CDR	A	19	320	33	20	0	11	48	21	48	9	4	-3.3	.290	.336	.472	.185	.233	.274	.368	.224	-7.4	68-C	-8
2008	LAA	MLB	20	372	30	19	1	6	38	20	75	7	3	-0.4	.231	.274	.342	-.246	.229	.274	.357	.223	-7.7	89-C	-4

Breakout: 42% Improve: 60% Collapse: 23% Attrition: 5%   Comparables: Jarrod Saltalamacchia, Ryan Luzinski, Javier Valentin, Ryan Doumit

Like Bourjos, Conger lost part of last season to an injury, in his case a back problem in June and July. Conger's a big guy who, while displaying a decent arm (he caught 21 percent of basestealers) and defensive skills, is going to progress through the system because of his bat. His size and the value of that bat mean that he will always be in danger of being moved out from behind the plate. Until that happens, he'll be one of the five best catching prospects in the game.

Bradley Coon — OF

Bats: L   Throws: L   Height: 6' 0"   Weight: 175   Born: December 11, 1982   Age: 25

YEAR	TEAM	LVL	AGE	PA	R	2B	3B	HR	RBI	BB	SO	SB	CS	EqBRR	AVG	OBP	SLG	MLVr	EqAVG	EqOBP	EqSLG	EqA	VORP	DEFENSE			
2005	ORM	Rk	22	254	42	7	3	0	18	28	47	19	7	-1.2	.300	.381	.359	.069	.209	.269	.239	.180	-50.5	38-LF	3	12-CF	-2
2006	CDR	A	23	555	79	18	8	0	29	75	82	55	21	2.6	.278	.382	.352	.086	.227	.314	.298	.230	-19.5	116-CF	7		
2007	RCU	A+	24	326	44	13	2	3	27	21	48	31	9	2.7	.258	.311	.344	-.163	.210	.254	.272	.193	-26.4	70-CF	0		
2007	ARK	AA	24	258	37	8	4	1	17	23	36	25	12	-2.0	.301	.372	.385	.048	.263	.325	.336	.238	-2.3	57-CF	2		
2008	LAA	MLB	25	543	62	20	4	2	33	40	107	33	11	2.2	.243	.302	.311	-.232	.240	.302	.325	.233	-12.5	128-CF	0		

Breakout: 55% Improve: 77% Collapse: 11% Attrition: 13%   Comparables: Quincy Foster, Chip Glass, Sebastien Boucher, Kennard Bibbs

This old-for-his-levels flyer is coming fast enough to project as an extra outfielder in 2009. The one thing holding him back is the fact that his contact rate is lousy for a player with so little power, and pitchers at the higher levels may just start coming right after him. You can already see a decrease in his walk rate as he jumped through the Cal and Texas leagues last year. Coon's speed translates well on the field—he plays center well and has decent stolen base percentages.

Terry Evans — RF

Bats: R   Throws: R   Height: 6' 3"   Weight: 205   Born: January 19, 1982   Age: 26

YEAR	TEAM	LVL	AGE	PA	R	2B	3B	HR	RBI	BB	SO	SB	CS	EqBRR	AVG	OBP	SLG	MLVr	EqAVG	EqOBP	EqSLG	EqA	VORP	DEFENSE			
2005	PMB	A+	23	425	34	16	1	8	47	29	110	12	6	-1.2	.221	.285	.330	-.131	.189	.243	.286	.182	-46.6	103-RF	-14		
2006	PMB	A+	24	263	43	10	1	15	45	20	50	21	1	3.5	.311	.373	.550	.387	.277	.331	.512	.287	11.9	41-RF	4	18-CF	1
2006	SFD	AA	24	84	13	4	0	7	20	3	21	5	1	0.4	.307	.369	.640	.418	.269	.318	.538	.286	3.6	21-RF	1		
2006	ARK	AA	24	213	48	9	2	11	22	18	56	11	6	0.1	.309	.385	.553	.274	.244	.307	.456	.258	5.2	44-CF	1		
2007	SLC	AAA	25	507	70	40	4	15	75	26	119	24	9	1.0	.316	.352	.512	.091	.256	.294	.426	.247	-6.8	59-RF	3	46-CF	-2
2007	LAA	MLB	25	13	3	0	0	1	2	2	4	0	0	0.0	.091	.231	.364	-.381	.091	.231	.364	.203	-1.0				
2008	LAA	MLB	26	469	48	24	2	12	56	26	128	14	5	0.7	.237	.284	.380	-.175	.235	.284	.396	.240	-9.0	111-RF	-2		

Breakout: 12% Improve: 37% Collapse: 34% Attrition: 19%   Comparables: Scott Krause, Mike Hill, Nick Gorneault, Barry Wesson

Whatever Evans did between the end of 2005 and the start of 2006, it stuck in 2007. Evans brings line-drive power and decent speed; the difference between him and Coon is that Coon's skills would play better coming off the bench, whereas Evans is going to have to hit enough to be a starter to hold on to a roster spot. There's not a lot of reason to think he can hold a job given his 4.0 K/BB at the upper levels. There's no opening for him in 2008.

Chone Figgins — UT

Bats: S   Throws: R   Height: 5' 8"   Weight: 180   Born: January 22, 1978   Age: 30

YEAR	TEAM	LVL	AGE	PA	R	2B	3B	HR	RBI	BB	SO	SB	CS	EqBRR	AVG	OBP	SLG	MLVr	EqAVG	EqOBP	EqSLG	EqA	VORP	DEFENSE			
2005	LAA	MLB	27	720	113	25	10	8	57	64	101	62	17	10.2	.290	.352	.397	.025	.301	.371	.422	.283	30.4	48-3B	1	44-CF	5
2006	LAA	MLB	28	683	93	23	8	9	62	65	100	52	16	9.9	.267	.336	.376	-.083	.270	.347	.384	.265	14.2	92-CF	0	31-3B	-8
2007	LAA	MLB	29	503	81	24	6	3	58	51	81	41	12	6.4	.330	.393	.432	.172	.343	.410	.455	.304	36.2	95-3B	-7		
2008	LAA	MLB	30	547	83	24	5	6	44	57	82	33	9	3.5	.284	.359	.393	.002	.281	.359	.410	.281	15.8	129-3B	-4		

Breakout: 9% Improve: 36% Collapse: 20% Attrition: 8%   Comparables: Don Buford, Bip Roberts, Jose Offerman, Vince Coleman

The broken fingers Figgins suffered in spring training cost him the season's first month and may have affected him in its second. Figgins was batting just .133/.212/.211 on May 29 and was benched both that day and the next against the Mariners. When he returned, he went 3-for-4 and never looked back, batting .381/.438/.489 the rest of the way. Overall, Figgins' 2006 and 2007 seasons average to his career norms; the balls that didn't fall in two years ago did so last year, and then some. Figgins played just three positions last year, and was the when-healthy regular at one—third base—for the first time in his career. Although the Angels' need for power will probably force Figgins back into a utility role this year with Wood taking over at third, Figgins will still play 140 games in that role.

Vladimir Guerrero   RF   Bats: R   Throws: R   Height: 6' 3"   Weight: 235   Born: February 9, 1976   Age: 32

YEAR	TEAM	LVL	AGE	PA	R	2B	3B	HR	RBI	BB	SO	SB	CS	EqBRR	AVG	OBP	SLG	MLVr	EqAVG	EqOBP	EqSLG	EqA	VORP	DEFENSE		
2005	LAA	MLB	29	594	95	29	2	32	108	61	48	13	1	-3.6	.317	.394	.565	.358	.320	.405	.586	.331	63.8	115-RF	-1	
2006	LAA	MLB	30	665	92	34	1	33	116	50	68	15	5	-0.8	.329	.382	.552	.310	.327	.386	.560	.315	63.9	122-RF	-10	
2007	LAA	MLB	31	660	89	45	1	27	125	71	62	2	3	-2.3	.324	.403	.547	.348	.322	.406	.564	.322	62.6	105-RF	-8	
2008	LAA	MLB	32	625	89	37	1	21	99	51	63	7	2	-0.7	.310	.370	.495	.176	.307	.369	.517	.301	33.2	146-RF	-7	

Breakout: 5%   Improve: 16%   Collapse: 34%   Attrition: 9%   Comparables: Bob Watson, Joe Torre, Dave Winfield, George Hendrick

Vlad's slipping a bit, mostly because his body is slowly breaking down, forcing him into more DH time and limiting his defensive value. His arm remains one of the best in the game, but he doesn't cover ground as well as he used to, and his baserunning speed is all but gone. He's just 32 years old, and his skills at the plate are completely intact, so the question is less about whether he's done and more about what the next phase of his career will look like. Our guess is 1970s Frank Robinson, with fewer walks and more longevity.

Maicer Izturis   INF   Bats: S   Throws: R   Height: 5' 8"   Weight: 165   Born: September 12, 1980   Age: 27

YEAR	TEAM	LVL	AGE	PA	R	2B	3B	HR	RBI	BB	SO	SB	CS	EqBRR	AVG	OBP	SLG	MLVr	EqAVG	EqOBP	EqSLG	EqA	VORP	DEFENSE		
2005	LAA	MLB	24	210	18	8	4	1	15	17	21	9	3	0.5	.246	.306	.346	-.157	.255	.325	.356	.246	-0.5	31-3B	-2	24-SS -2
2006	LAA	MLB	25	399	64	21	3	5	44	38	35	14	6	3.8	.293	.365	.412	.042	.296	.376	.425	.280	13.9	79-3B	-8	
2007	LAA	MLB	26	374	47	17	2	6	51	33	39	7	1	1.8	.289	.349	.405	.024	.294	.359	.426	.277	13.0	51-3B	0	35-2B -3
2008	LAA	MLB	27	454	62	23	3	5	43	44	48	12	4	1.5	.284	.355	.397	.001	.281	.355	.415	.276	13.5	108-3B	-2	

Breakout: 18%   Improve: 53%   Collapse: 16%   Attrition: 12%   Comparables: Jerry Browne, Tom Herr, Brian Roberts, Tito Fuentes

Izturis is a terrific bench player, able to pinch-hit at the start or end of an inning, pinch-run, play three positions well enough to not hurt you, and start without costing you much compared to the regular. He even switch-hits, although he's not great from the right side. The Cabrera trade opens up a role as the team's shortstop, although it's more likely that he'll start 60 percent of the team's games while backing up both Aybar and Wood at short and third, respectively and battling Figgins for playing time at the latter.

Howie Kendrick   2B   Bats: R   Throws: R   Height: 5' 10"   Weight: 200   Born: July 12, 1983   Age: 24

YEAR	TEAM	LVL	AGE	PA	R	2B	3B	HR	RBI	BB	SO	SB	CS	EqBRR	AVG	OBP	SLG	MLVr	EqAVG	EqOBP	EqSLG	EqA	VORP	DEFENSE		
2005	RCU	A+	21	304	69	23	6	12	47	14	42	13	4	-2.1	.384	.421	.638	.545	.301	.330	.479	.275	19.5	59-2B	3	
2005	ARK	AA	21	204	35	20	2	7	42	6	20	12	4	2.7	.342	.382	.579	.358	.297	.333	.500	.281	15.4	46-2B	2	
2006	SLC	AAA	22	312	57	25	6	13	62	12	48	11	3	0.5	.369	.408	.631	.442	.323	.359	.561	.304	35.8	59-2B	7	
2006	LAA	MLB	22	283	25	21	1	4	30	9	44	6	0	0.9	.285	.314	.416	-.053	.283	.320	.423	.261	5.0	39-1B	6	25-2B 2
2007	LAA	MLB	23	353	55	24	2	5	39	9	61	5	4	2.3	.322	.347	.450	.119	.330	.358	.476	.281	19.3	85-2B	-5	
2008	LAA	MLB	24	499	60	31	2	12	63	18	83	9	3	0.9	.286	.320	.438	.001	.283	.320	.457	.269	15.8	118-2B	1	

Breakout: 8%   Improve: 32%   Collapse: 37%   Attrition: 12%   Comparables: Josh Barfield, Andy Carey, Rennie Stennett, Ken Boyer

Kendrick has been compared favorably to all manner of high-average, moderate-power right-handed hitters. To have a career, though, Kendrick is going to have to improve his contact rate or his discipline, because his major league career 7.5 K/UIBB ratio is not acceptable. It's also not improving; he walked less and struck out more last year than in his rookie season of 2006. Of 280 MLB players with at least 300 plate appearances last year, just five saw fewer pitches per plate appearance than Kendrick did. Caveat: Vladimir Guerrero was tied with Kendrick at 3.23 P/PA.

Casey Kotchman — 1B

Bats: L   Throws: L   Height: 6' 3"   Weight: 215   Born: February 22, 1983   Age: 25

YEAR	TEAM	LVL	AGE	PA	R	2B	3B	HR	RBI	BB	SO	SB	CS	EqBRR	AVG	OBP	SLG	MLVr	EqAVG	EqOBP	EqSLG	EqA	VORP	DEFENSE	
2005	SLC	AAA	22	417	62	23	1	10	58	43	40	0	2	-0.8	.289	.372	.441	-.009	.245	.321	.372	.242	-7.2	89-1B	-1
2005	LAA	MLB	22	143	16	5	0	7	22	15	18	1	1	-0.4	.278	.352	.484	.134	.282	.366	.508	.294	7.2	15-1B	0
2006	LAA	MLB	23	88	6	2	0	1	6	7	13	0	1	-0.7	.152	.221	.215	-.600	.154	.233	.218	.146	-11.7	22-1B	2
2007	LAA	MLB	24	508	64	37	3	11	68	53	43	2	4	-6.1	.296	.372	.467	.156	.301	.383	.499	.298	26.2	117-1B	10
2008	LAA	MLB	25	462	57	27	1	10	60	45	49	2	2	-1.0	.289	.363	.433	.066	.286	.363	.453	.285	13.1	109-1B	6

Breakout: 35% Improve: 60% Collapse: 15% Attrition: 17%   Comparables: Sean Casey, Ed Kranepool, Travis Lee, Bruce Bochte

At 24, Wally Joyner batted .290/.348/.457 producing a .282 EqA and tacked on 10 fielding runs above average for a WARP of 6.5. Kotchman played a little less than Joyner did, but everything else is basically right in line, and should continue to be so as Kotchman plays through his peak. He's very valuable to this Angels team, which needs all the OBP it can get.

Jeff Mathis — C

Bats: R   Throws: R   Height: 6' 0"   Weight: 200   Born: March 31, 1983   Age: 25

YEAR	TEAM	LVL	AGE	PA	R	2B	3B	HR	RBI	BB	SO	SB	CS	EqBRR	AVG	OBP	SLG	MLVr	EqAVG	EqOBP	EqSLG	EqA	VORP	DEFENSE	
2005	SLC	AAA	22	479	78	26	3	21	73	42	85	4	3	1.6	.276	.340	.499	.003	.232	.291	.409	.240	1.2	94-C	1
2006	SLC	AAA	23	417	62	33	3	5	45	26	75	3	1	2.4	.289	.333	.430	-.029	.251	.293	.380	.234	-1.5	83-C	2
2006	LAA	MLB	23	63	9	2	0	2	6	7	14	0	0	-0.1	.145	.238	.291	-.463	.148	.254	.296	.195	-4.7	15-C	-3
2007	SLC	AAA	24	273	39	14	2	5	26	17	45	3	1	1.7	.244	.295	.376	-.257	.210	.264	.329	.206	-12.2	58-C	6
2007	LAA	MLB	24	195	24	12	0	4	23	15	49	0	1	-0.9	.211	.276	.351	-.237	.212	.285	.371	.230	-3.6	53-C	0
2008	LAA	MLB	25	386	37	20	1	8	44	26	79	3	2	0.4	.235	.291	.368	-.179	.233	.291	.384	.238	-1.1	92-C	1

Breakout: 39% Improve: 59% Collapse: 23% Attrition: 33%   Comparables: Gil Hodges, Andy Etchebarren, Randy Hundley, Eli Marrero

Sometimes, players peak at a young age. We notice it when a rookie has his career year, earns an award or two, and never quite reaches that level again. It happens in the minor leagues, too. Mathis appears to have peaked at age 20, in the California League. Despite playing in good hitters' parks since, Mathis hasn't hit .300 or slugged .500 in four seasons, and his underlying indicators have fallen off the charts since 2005. Bobby Wilson is the same age as Mathis and has outplayed him for two years straight, so Mathis's ability to hold on to even the backup role is in doubt. PECOTA's top comp is weirdly optimistic.

Gary Matthews Jr. — OF

Bats: S   Throws: R   Height: 6' 3"   Weight: 225   Born: August 25, 1974   Age: 33

YEAR	TEAM	LVL	AGE	PA	R	2B	3B	HR	RBI	BB	SO	SB	CS	EqBRR	AVG	OBP	SLG	MLVr	EqAVG	EqOBP	EqSLG	EqA	VORP	DEFENSE			
2005	TEX	MLB	30	526	72	25	5	17	55	47	90	9	2	-0.4	.255	.320	.436	-.025	.255	.331	.448	.270	11.3	95-CF	-2	21-RF	2
2006	TEX	MLB	31	690	102	44	6	19	79	58	99	10	7	-0.9	.313	.371	.495	.164	.308	.373	.498	.294	50.0	139-CF	-6		
2007	LAA	MLB	32	579	79	26	3	18	72	55	102	18	4	3.5	.252	.323	.419	-.033	.254	.332	.442	.270	15.8	129-CF	12		
2008	LAA	MLB	33	500	66	25	3	13	64	46	85	9	4	0.7	.274	.342	.428	.012	.271	.342	.447	.276	15.4	118-CF	-2		

Breakout: 16% Improve: 38% Collapse: 24% Attrition: 21%   Comparables: Jerry Mumphrey, Turner Ward, Gary Ward, Fred Valentine

The 60 points of batting average that Matthews gained in 2006 disappeared last year—looks like they weren't the product of maturity after all—and with them went Matthews' claim to being an everyday center fielder. His five-year, $50-million contract remains, however, as does his reputation as a glove man, so he'll be playing more than he deserves to for some time to come. He helps your fantasy team more than he does the Angels. Torii Hunter pushes him to a corner, most likely left, where his bat is wholly inadequate.

Kendry Morales · 1B · Bats: S · Throws: R · Height: 6' 1" · Weight: 225 · Born: June 20, 1983 · Age: 25

YEAR	TEAM	LVL	AGE	PA	R	2B	3B	HR	RBI	BB	SO	SB	CS	EqBRR	AVG	OBP	SLG	MLVr	EqAVG	EqOBP	EqSLG	EqA	VORP	DEFENSE	
2005	RCU	A+	22	100	18	3	0	5	17	6	11	0	0	1.0	.344	.400	.544	.309	.269	.310	.419	.250	-0.1	15-1B	-2
2005	ARK	AA	22	301	47	12	0	17	54	17	43	2	0	1.1	.306	.349	.530	.203	.262	.306	.457	.259	3.3	60-1B	0
2006	SLC	AAA	23	273	41	13	1	12	52	14	40	0	3	0.2	.320	.359	.520	.162	.279	.315	.457	.259	5.2	50-1B	-5
2006	LAA	MLB	23	215	21	10	1	5	22	17	28	1	1	-2.3	.234	.293	.371	-.198	.231	.298	.379	.235	-7.3	51-1B	4
2007	SLC	AAA	24	275	42	20	1	5	37	15	30	0	2	-3.5	.341	.385	.486	.135	.293	.338	.422	.260	5.4	42-1B	-4
2007	LAA	MLB	24	126	12	10	0	4	15	6	21	0	1	-2.6	.294	.333	.479	.114	.297	.341	.508	.282	5.0	14-1B	2
2008	LAA	MLB	25	429	45	23	1	12	59	25	63	2	1	-0.7	.274	.321	.424	-.028	.271	.320	.443	.264	4.6	102-1B	3

Breakout: 22% Improve: 55% Collapse: 16% Attrition: 16%   Comparables: Tony Perez, Robin Jennings, Aramis Ramirez, Rob Cosby

In the long term, Morales may end up being just a very good pinch-hitter. He will hit for average without drawing enough walks or having enough power to be an everyday first baseman or DH. He's been stronger from the left side in his career; that won't help him take at-bats from Kotchman, but it should make him viable as the inexpensive big half of a DH platoon this year and next, or would if Garret Anderson wasn't being squeezed out of the outfield picture.

Mike Napoli · C · Bats: R · Throws: R · Height: 6' 0" · Weight: 210 · Born: October 31, 1981 · Age: 26

YEAR	TEAM	LVL	AGE	PA	R	2B	3B	HR	RBI	BB	SO	SB	CS	EqBRR	AVG	OBP	SLG	MLVr	EqAVG	EqOBP	EqSLG	EqA	VORP	DEFENSE	
2005	ARK	AA	23	541	96	22	2	31	99	88	140	12	4	-1.3	.237	.372	.508	.146	.202	.327	.417	.260	10.1	103-C	4
2006	SLC	AAA	24	90	12	6	0	3	10	8	29	1	1	-0.5	.244	.344	.436	-.036	.213	.300	.375	.234	-0.8	17-C	2
2006	LAA	MLB	24	325	47	13	0	16	42	51	90	2	3	-1.1	.228	.360	.455	.039	.231	.372	.473	.287	13.0	80-C	2
2007	LAA	MLB	25	263	40	11	1	10	34	33	63	5	2	1.8	.247	.351	.443	.044	.253	.363	.475	.287	13.8	68-C	-3
2008	LAA	MLB	26	326	40	14	1	12	40	43	84	5	2	-0.1	.233	.344	.417	-.028	.230	.344	.435	.276	10.9	79-C	-1

Breakout: 21% Improve: 49% Collapse: 31% Attrition: 27%   Comparables: Bobby Estalella, Mickey Tettleton, Jim Pagliaroni, Darren Daulton

Despite being just 26, Napoli is a fully formed baseball player unlikely to develop much beyond what he already is. It's a nice package, a catcher with good secondary skills who throws out better than one of every four basestealers. Because of Napoli, Mathis's failure to develop doesn't sting quite as much.

Chris Pettit · OF · Bats: R · Throws: R · Height: 6' 0" · Weight: 193 · Born: August 15, 1984 · Age: 23

YEAR	TEAM	LVL	AGE	PA	R	2B	3B	HR	RBI	BB	SO	SB	CS	EqBRR	AVG	OBP	SLG	MLVr	EqAVG	EqOBP	EqSLG	EqA	VORP	DEFENSE			
2006	ORM	Rk	21	272	41	25	3	7	54	31	48	5	1	1.1	.336	.445	.566	.542	.241	.315	.396	.248	-9.7	34-LF	1	13-CF	1
2007	CDR	A	22	266	47	24	1	9	41	23	41	17	4	2.7	.346	.429	.579	.495	.285	.348	.469	.281	9.3	37-LF	-1	14-CF	-1
2007	RCU	A+	22	307	54	20	2	9	54	36	48	13	3	5.3	.309	.395	.502	.252	.255	.330	.401	.258	-2.5	32-LF	-3	31-CF	-2
2008	LAA	MLB	23	615	71	38	3	14	71	47	142	15	6	1.3	.253	.319	.406	-.071	.250	.319	.424	.261	1.8	144-LF	0		

Breakout: 24% Improve: 53% Collapse: 18% Attrition: 6%   Comparables: Mark Quinn, Adam Riggs, Marty Cordova, Aldo Pecorilli

It was no surprise that the 22-year-old Petit raked in Low-A despite being a 19th-round pick in 2006. What was surprising was that scouts began to buy into his skills, especially when he continued to produce at High-A. Petit is a bit of a tweener—limited defensively to a corner, while lacking the raw power one expects from those positions—but scouts are convinced he'll hit, and convinced he'll get there, which is more than you can say for most players selected 582nd overall.

Robb Quinlan · 1B · Bats: R · Throws: R · Height: 6' 1" · Weight: 215 · Born: March 17, 1977 · Age: 31

YEAR	TEAM	LVL	AGE	PA	R	2B	3B	HR	RBI	BB	SO	SB	CS	EqBRR	AVG	OBP	SLG	MLVr	EqAVG	EqOBP	EqSLG	EqA	VORP	DEFENSE			
2005	LAA	MLB	28	143	17	8	0	5	14	7	26	0	1	-0.5	.231	.273	.403	-.148	.235	.287	.417	.238	-2.4	27-3B	-2		
2006	LAA	MLB	29	244	28	11	1	9	32	7	28	2	1	-0.1	.321	.344	.491	.150	.323	.352	.504	.289	12.5	43-1B	3	15-3B	-2
2007	LAA	MLB	30	194	21	9	0	3	21	14	27	3	2	-1.7	.247	.304	.348	-.167	.254	.318	.373	.241	-4.3	26-1B	2		
2008	LAA	MLB	31	168	18	9	0	4	21	10	25	2	1	-0.3	.270	.320	.403	-.061	.268	.319	.421	.259	1.6	43-1B	0		

Breakout: 21% Improve: 41% Collapse: 38% Attrition: 35%   Comparables: Greg Colbrunn, Ricky Jordan, Art Schult, Matt Mieske

Pat Tabler with more Scrabble value. What people think Jeff Conine was. Conor Jackson's downside. Kevin Youkilis without the walks. The right-handed Ross Gload. Two-thirds of Kevin Seitzer. Shea Hillenbrand with better people skills. Melvin Mora minus the speed, defense, peak, and quintuplets.

Juan Rivera — RF

Bats: R   Throws: R   Height: 6' 2"   Weight: 205   Born: July 3, 1978   Age: 29

YEAR	TEAM	LVL	AGE	PA	R	2B	3B	HR	RBI	BB	SO	SB	CS	EqBRR	AVG	OBP	SLG	MLVr	EqAVG	EqOBP	EqSLG	EqA	VORP	DEFENSE			
2005	LAA	MLB	27	376	46	17	1	15	59	23	44	1	9	-3.4	.271	.316	.454	.030	.282	.337	.483	.267	4.9	33-LF	1	26-RF	-3
2006	LAA	MLB	28	494	65	27	0	23	85	33	59	0	4	-1.5	.310	.362	.525	.218	.312	.369	.544	.302	33.5	53-LF	10	27-RF	-3
2007	SLC	AAA	29	65	4	8	0	0	17	3	6	0	0	-0.2	.262	.292	.393	-.226	.230	.262	.328	.204	-3.6				
2007	LAA	MLB	29	44	3	1	0	2	8	1	4	0	0	0.1	.279	.295	.442	-.029	.279	.295	.442	.249	0.4				
2008	LAA	MLB	29	359	38	20	0	11	53	24	47	1	1	-0.8	.280	.331	.440	.015	.277	.331	.459	.273	7.6	86-LF	-2		

Breakout: 15% Improve: 41% Collapse: 26% Attrition: 14%   Comparables: Rondell White, Rip Repulski, Wes Covington, Gene Green

The Case Against Winter Ball, Exhibit K: Juan Rivera broke his left leg in December of 2006 while playing for Oriente in Venezuela. After a career year in 2006, he missed all of 2007 save some scattered at-bats in September. The injury cost the Angels a DH—they would get a .257/.315/.391 line from the position, even with Vladimir Guerrero hitting there 40 times—and figures to cost Rivera at least a couple million dollars in lost earnings this offseason. That's a hefty price to pay for playing some extra baseball.

Sean Rodriguez — UT

Bats: R   Throws: R   Height: 6' 1"   Weight: 198   Born: April 26, 1985   Age: 23

YEAR	TEAM	LVL	AGE	PA	R	2B	3B	HR	RBI	BB	SO	SB	CS	EqBRR	AVG	OBP	SLG	MLVr	EqAVG	EqOBP	EqSLG	EqA	VORP	DEFENSE			
2005	CDR	A	20	546	86	29	3	14	45	78	85	27	11	-2.5	.250	.371	.422	.081	.204	.301	.334	.228	-9.4	84-SS	3	15-CF	4
2006	RCU	A+	21	523	78	29	5	24	77	47	124	15	3	-0.5	.301	.377	.545	.280	.246	.306	.436	.256	16.0	113-SS	18		
2006	ARK	AA	21	79	16	5	0	5	9	11	18	0	3	-2.7	.354	.462	.662	.576	.279	.380	.544	.298	9.2	19-SS	1		
2007	ARK	AA	22	587	84	31	2	17	73	54	132	15	8	-2.8	.254	.345	.423	.022	.223	.299	.368	.234	-1.4	125-SS	8		
2008	LAA	MLB	23	622	66	33	2	14	69	53	155	13	6	0.3	.231	.304	.376	-.149	.229	.304	.392	.247	3.6	145-SS	8		

Breakout: 30% Improve: 58% Collapse: 17% Attrition: 6%   Comparables: Tony Manahan, Adam Piatt, Jay Canizaro, Josh Barfield

The Angels have never fully committed to the idea that Rodriguez is a shortstop, giving him occasional time in center field and having him play a number of positions in the Arizona Fall League. His 2006 line looks like a Rancho Cucamonga mirage, so developing him as a utilityman to eventually replace Chone Figgins is a better idea than hoping he makes enough contact to be a major league infielder.

Hainley Statia — SS

Bats: S   Throws: R   Height: 5' 10"   Weight: 160   Born: January 19, 1986   Age: 22

YEAR	TEAM	LVL	AGE	PA	R	2B	3B	HR	RBI	BB	SO	SB	CS	EqBRR	AVG	OBP	SLG	MLVr	EqAVG	EqOBP	EqSLG	EqA	VORP	DEFENSE	
2005	RCU	A+	19	112	12	2	0	1	8	5	13	6	3	-0.8	.245	.286	.292	-.388	.213	.241	.250	.171	-9.8	22-2B	2
2005	ORM	Rk	19	308	44	17	6	2	41	23	40	12	10	-3.7	.300	.360	.426	.132	.215	.256	.287	.186	-31.7	65-SS	10
2006	CDR	A	20	480	68	31	1	1	38	52	54	23	15	-1.0	.297	.379	.384	.133	.245	.312	.322	.226	-4.4	107-SS	5
2006	RCU	A+	20	70	8	2	1	0	8	8	7	1	1	0.3	.300	.386	.367	.040	.242	.314	.306	.224	-1.0	15-SS	2
2007	RCU	A+	21	609	86	27	7	3	74	48	79	29	8	0.5	.288	.344	.379	-.029	.237	.285	.305	.213	-19.3	132-SS	22
2008	LAA	MLB	22	599	60	27	3	2	44	38	97	14	6	1.4	.250	.300	.321	-.218	.247	.299	.335	.228	-5.4	140-SS	12

Breakout: 52% Improve: 73% Collapse: 8% Attrition: 15%   Comparables: Jonathan Herrera, Hanley Frias, Ramon Santiago, Maicer Izturis

One reason to shift Rodriguez into a utilty role is that he's about to be caught from behind by this guy. Statia may be the best glove man of the Angels' many shortstop prospects, although his bat is well behind what Aybar was doing at a similar age. If you don't hit for power in the Cal League, you probably won't ever hit for power, which leaves a decent average, plate discipline, speed, and that glove as his assets. Not bad.

Reggie Willits — OF

Bats: S   Throws: R   Height: 5' 11"   Weight: 185   Born: May 30, 1981   Age: 27

YEAR	TEAM	LVL	AGE	PA	R	2B	3B	HR	RBI	BB	SO	SB	CS	EqBRR	AVG	OBP	SLG	MLVr	EqAVG	EqOBP	EqSLG	EqA	VORP	DEFENSE			
2005	ARK	AA	24	561	75	23	6	2	46	54	78	40	14	2.0	.304	.377	.388	.053	.260	.331	.333	.244	-4.1	79-CF	-6	34-RF	5
2006	SLC	AAA	25	437	85	18	4	3	39	77	50	31	15	0.0	.327	.448	.426	.181	.283	.401	.369	.280	20.3	75-CF	4	19-LF	2
2006	LAA	MLB	25	58	12	1	0	0	2	11	10	4	3	-0.1	.267	.411	.289	-.053	.273	.429	.295	.266	0.8	13-CF	0		
2007	LAA	MLB	26	518	74	20	1	0	34	69	83	27	8	-1.3	.293	.391	.344	.017	.304	.406	.365	.284	15.2	58-LF	10	26-CF	0
2008	LAA	MLB	27	379	52	15	2	3	29	42	58	15	5	1.2	.269	.354	.354	-.068	.266	.353	.370	.267	2.6	91-LF	2		

Breakout: 16% Improve: 43% Collapse: 32% Attrition: 32%   Comparables: Stan Javier, Billy North, Jason McDonald, Lee Tinsley

It's not easy to sustain a walk rate like Willits's with so little power. As you look at his 2007 season, you see evidence that pitchers started coming at him a bit more as time went by. He didn't handle it well, striking out much more in the second half (18.6 percent of his plate appearances vs. 13.8 percent of his first-half PAs) and walking less (12.3 percent, down from 13.6 percent). Willits' whole game is walks and speed, so look for him to return to a fourth-outfielder role in 2008, especially given the Angels' crowded outfield/DH situation.

Brandon Wood — 3B

Bats: R   Throws: R   Height: 6' 3"   Weight: 185   Born: March 2, 1985   Age: 23

YEAR	TEAM	LVL	AGE	PA	R	2B	3B	HR	RBI	BB	SO	SB	CS	EqBRR	AVG	OBP	SLG	MLVr	EqAVG	EqOBP	EqSLG	EqA	VORP	DEFENSE	
2005	RCU	A+	20	595	109	51	4	43	115	48	128	7	3	4.3	.321	.383	.672	.442	.244	.297	.483	.260	26.2	123-SS	-4
2006	ARK	AA	21	522	74	42	4	25	83	54	149	19	3	2.3	.276	.355	.552	.194	.234	.303	.465	.264	20.3	115-SS	10
2007	SLC	AAA	22	488	73	27	1	23	77	45	120	10	1	3.7	.272	.338	.497	.006	.236	.303	.427	.254	8.8	73-3B -1	32-SS -1
2007	LAA	MLB	22	33	2	1	0	1	3	0	12	0	0	0.0	.152	.152	.273	-.623	.152	.152	.273	.102	-4.0		
2008	LAA	MLB	23	555	62	30	2	20	75	43	147	11	3	0.4	.245	.306	.429	-.068	.242	.306	.448	.263	10.9	130-SS	2

Breakout: 33% Improve: 59% Collapse: 19% Attrition: 13%   Comparables: Scott Moore, Ron Hansen, Ryan Braun, Willie Greene

Wood's unholy 2005 season may be his undoing, as his perfectly acceptable work at young ages since then has all seemed relatively disappointing. There's no question that his contact rate is a concern, although he did make some strides in that area last year. Throw in a successful shift to third base, and he has developed reasonably well for a high-school draftee. All that's left to be done is to let Wood play at the major league level, be patient with his problems against breaking stuff, and let him develop into a second-level star.

PITCHERS

Nick Adenhart

Bats: R   Throws: R   Height: 6' 3"   Weight: 185   Born: August 24, 1986   Age: 21

YEAR	TEAM	LVL	AGE	W	L	SV	G	GS	IP	H	BB	SO	HR	GB%	BABIP	STUFF	WHIP	ERA	PERA	EqERA	EqH9	EqBB9	EqSO9	EqHR9	VORP	SN/WX
2006	CDR	A	19	10	2	0	16	16	106	84	26	99	2	52.5%	.283	19	1.04	1.95	5.00	5.21	9.3	4.3	4.5	0.7	4.0	—
2006	RCU	A+	19	5	2	0	9	9	52	51	16	46	1	57.8%	.331	18	1.29	3.81	5.20	5.55	10.3	4.2	4.6	0.6	0.3	—
2007	ARK	AA	20	10	8	0	26	26	153	158	65	116	7	51.8%	.332	10	1.46	3.65	6.24	5.77	11.1	5.0	4.8	0.7	-2.6	—
2008	LAA	MLB	21	6	10	0	25	25	134²	166	76	75	15	48.7%	.328	-3	1.80	6.02	5.94	5.94	10.6	4.5	4.6	1.0	-7.8	0.20

Breakout: 14% Improve: 45% Collapse: 24% Attrition: 14%   Comparables: Dustin McGowan, Ryan Kibler, Dustin Moseley, Shane Loux

The Angels drafted Adenhart in the 14th round in 2004 after news that he needed Tommy John surgery allowed him to slip down that far. The gamble paid off; Adenhart is the team's top prospect, holding his own in the Texas League despite not turning 21 until August. There were some signs of struggle, as you can see from the rates above as well as the 17 hit batsmen not listed. Look for him to be a key late-season addition to the Angels' rotation and effective right from the start.

Jose Arredondo

Bats: R   Throws: R   Height: 6' 0"   Weight: 175   Born: March 30, 1984   Age: 24

YEAR	TEAM	LVL	AGE	W	L	SV	G	GS	IP	H	BB	SO	HR	GB%	BABIP	STUFF	WHIP	ERA	PERA	EqERA	EqH9	EqBB9	EqSO9	EqHR9	VORP	SN/WX
2005	ORM	Rk	21	5	0	0	15	13	68²	76	20	60	4	50.2%	.355	-29	1.40	4.19	8.88	8.47	13.3	6.2	3.0	1.6	-18.0	—
2006	RCU	A+	22	5	6	0	15	15	90	62	35	115	4	39.4%	.299	23	1.08	2.30	4.70	4.28	8.0	5.2	7.4	0.9	11.7	—
2006	ARK	AA	22	2	3	0	11	11	60¹	80	22	48	8	45.9%	.367	-23	1.70	6.59	8.32	8.63	12.7	4.1	4.7	1.7	-19.3	—
2007	ARK	AA	23	0	1	10	23	0	25	16	12	28	2	40.3%	.246	4	1.12	2.52	4.15	4.56	6.8	5.3	7.2	1.1	2.7	—
2007	RCU	A+	23	2	4	4	28	0	35	46	11	34	5	46.6%	.387	-40	1.63	6.43	10.25	11.08	14.2	4.3	5.1	2.0	-19.3	—
2008	LAA	MLB	24	3	4	1	26	6	58¹	68	36	40	8	44.8%	.320	-10	1.77	6.02	6.00	5.89	10.0	4.9	5.7	1.2	-3.4	-0.10

Breakout: 46% Improve: 73% Collapse: 13% Attrition: 14%   Comparables: Gabriel Ozuna, Jean Machi, Juan Padilla, Beltran Perez

This hard-throwing Dominican made his long-awaited move to the bullpen last year, but the season was more notable for his behavior than his pitching. Arredondo was suspended, then demoted to the Cal League after throwing a tantrum upon being taken out of a game. The step backward made it a lost year, so forget the lines above, remember the high-90s heat, and see what he does starting at Triple-A Salt Lake this year. Like Adenhart, he could be in Anaheim by August.

Chris Bootcheck

| | | | | | | | | | | | | | Bats: R | | Throws: R | | Height: 6' 5" | | Weight: 200 | | Born: October 24, 1978 | | Age: 29 |

YEAR	TEAM	LVL	AGE	W	L	SV	G	GS	IP	H	BB	SO	HR	GB%	BABIP	STUFF	WHIP	ERA	PERA	EqERA	EqH9	EqBB9	EqSO9	EqHR9	VORP	SN/WX
2005	SLC	AAA	26	7	4	0	21	21	116¹	144	50	90	13	43.8%	.366	-11	1.67	5.42	6.00	5.79	10.7	4.2	4.7	1.1	-2.4	—
2005	LAA	MLB	26	0	1	1	5	2	18²	19	4	8	1	37.3%	.277	-2	1.29	3.37	3.42	3.32	8.5	1.9	3.8	0.5	4.9	0.30
2006	SLC	AAA	27	4	3	1	40	5	65²	84	34	43	10	46.7%	.351	-43	1.81	6.76	9.26	8.95	12.3	5.3	4.3	1.8	-22.8	—
2006	LAA	MLB	27	0	1	0	7	0	10¹	16	9	7	3	36.8%	.382	-39	2.42	10.49	16.38	13.50	14.4	7.2	6.3	2.7	-5.2	0.11
2007	LAA	MLB	28	3	3	0	51	0	77¹	81	24	56	7	44.7%	.318	2	1.37	4.77	4.10	4.46	8.9	2.5	6.0	0.8	7.8	0.51
2008	LAA	MLB	29	2	2	1	38	0	50¹	55	20	36	5	45.1%	.310	-2	1.48	4.52	4.53	4.45	9.3	3.2	5.9	0.9	6.2	0.50

Breakout: 47% Improve: 70% Collapse: 15% Attrition: 42%   Comparables: Mike Dyer, Bill Sampen, Sean Lowe, John Montague

Here's a good example of a low-leverage reliever: not once all season was Bootcheck asked to protect a lead of four runs or fewer after the sixth inning. Of his 51 appearances, 35 saw him enter a game the Angels were losing. The only Angel reliever to post a lower leverage score than Bootcheck's 0.69 was Hector Carrasco. For an 11th man, Bootcheck is pretty good, posting average rates. The big righty can do this job for a while.

Jason Bulger

| | | | | | | | | | | | | | Bats: R | | Throws: R | | Height: 6' 4" | | Weight: 215 | | Born: December 6, 1978 | | Age: 29 |

YEAR	TEAM	LVL	AGE	W	L	SV	G	GS	IP	H	BB	SO	HR	GB%	BABIP	STUFF	WHIP	ERA	PERA	EqERA	EqH9	EqBB9	EqSO9	EqHR9	VORP	SN/WX
2005	TUC	AAA	26	3	6	4	56	0	56	50	27	55	3	51.6%	.320	-1	1.38	3.54	4.37	4.75	8.5	4.6	6.3	0.7	5.0	—
2005	ARI	MLB	26	1	0	0	9	0	10	14	5	9	1	32.4%	.406	-8	1.90	5.40	7.09	5.40	12.6	3.6	7.2	0.9	0.3	0.22
2006	SLC	AAA	27	2	2	4	27	0	34¹	30	15	44	0	53.4%	.353	11	1.32	4.75	4.15	5.40	8.6	4.3	8.6	0.3	0.7	—
2007	SLC	AAA	28	5	2	10	49	0	52²	51	24	81	4	51.2%	.392	21	1.42	3.76	4.73	4.18	9.1	4.4	10.5	0.7	8.2	—
2007	LAA	MLB	28	0	0	0	6	0	6¹	5	3	8	0	57.1%	.357	6	1.26	2.86	3.40	3.18	7.9	4.8	11.1	0.0	2.2	-0.03
2008	LAA	MLB	29	3	3	7	53	3	55	51	29	60	3	49.2%	.323	16	1.44	3.87	3.80	3.87	7.9	4.2	9.0	0.5	10.4	1.10

Breakout: 45% Improve: 72% Collapse: 11% Attrition: 17%   Comparables: Jim Gott, Mike MacDougal, Tim Stoddard, Jim Kern

The longer Bulger stays at Triple-A, the better he looks, with steadily improving strikeout rates and K/BB numbers. He has allowed seven homers in three Pacific Coast League seasons, and one in 18 major league innings against 18 strikeouts. It's probably time to find out for sure if he's a major league pitcher. Like Heath Bell or Al Reyes, Bulger just needs an opportunity, one he's not going to get in this organization.

Bartolo Colon

| | | | | | | | | | | | | | Bats: R | | Throws: R | | Height: 5' 11" | | Weight: 245 | | Born: May 24, 1973 | | Age: 35 |

YEAR	TEAM	LVL	AGE	W	L	SV	G	GS	IP	H	BB	SO	HR	GB%	BABIP	STUFF	WHIP	ERA	PERA	EqERA	EqH9	EqBB9	EqSO9	EqHR9	VORP	SN/WX
2005	LAA	MLB	32	21	8	0	33	33	222²	215	43	157	26	42.1%	.285	17	1.16	3.48	3.82	3.76	8.6	1.7	6.2	1.0	49.1	6.70
2006	LAA	MLB	33	1	5	0	10	10	56¹	71	11	31	11	42.2%	.316	-9	1.46	5.12	6.13	5.88	10.8	1.6	4.6	1.6	-1.7	0.20
2007	LAA	MLB	34	6	8	0	19	18	99¹	132	29	76	15	42.3%	.364	-4	1.62	6.34	6.45	6.41	11.3	2.3	6.3	1.4	-8.9	0.45
2008	LAA	MLB	35	5	6	0	26	14	92¹	104	26	62	12	43.1%	.309	1	1.41	4.77	4.59	4.67	9.6	2.3	5.5	1.1	8.2	1.40

Breakout: 24% Improve: 44% Collapse: 23% Attrition: 39%   Comparables: Pete Harnisch, Mike Garcia, Joe Dobson, Alex Kellner

Ah, karma. Colon got Johan Santana's Cy Young Award in 2005, then missed 40 starts over the next two seasons, posting a 5.90 ERA when he did pitch. Everything hurt last year—ankle, back, triceps, elbow, shoulder—and of course there's the question of how much his weight played into those problems. All of that said, Colon came off the DL in September to get 25 groundballs in his last two starts, a glimpse of the pitcher he is when healthy. He's well worth a flier in a tight pitching market, and is likely to be one of the top three bargains of the winter.

Kelvim Escobar

| | | | | | | | | | | | | | Bats: R | | Throws: R | | Height: 6' 1" | | Weight: 230 | | Born: April 11, 1976 | | Age: 32 |

YEAR	TEAM	LVL	AGE	W	L	SV	G	GS	IP	H	BB	SO	HR	GB%	BABIP	STUFF	WHIP	ERA	PERA	EqERA	EqH9	EqBB9	EqSO9	EqHR9	VORP	SN/WX
2005	LAA	MLB	29	3	2	1	16	7	59²	45	21	63	4	46.8%	.273	33	1.11	3.02	3.03	3.22	6.8	3.2	9.4	0.6	17.2	2.59
2006	LAA	MLB	30	11	14	0	30	30	189¹	192	50	147	17	46.4%	.311	23	1.28	3.61	4.01	4.10	9.1	2.2	6.7	0.7	33.9	4.83
2007	LAA	MLB	31	18	7	0	30	30	195²	182	66	160	11	44.4%	.304	31	1.27	3.40	3.30	3.29	7.8	2.7	6.8	0.5	49.9	6.25
2008	LAA	MLB	32	11	9	0	29	29	181¹	183	63	144	18	45.1%	.303	17	1.36	4.07	4.02	4.02	8.7	2.8	6.6	0.9	27.4	4.50

Breakout: 3% Improve: 27% Collapse: 34% Attrition: 13%   Comparables: Burt Hooton, Jack Morris, Early Wynn, Andy Messersmith

Escobar has made $36 million in his career, is guaranteed $18.5 million more, and has thrown 200 innings exactly once. One way or another, he misses three to five starts a year, and he usually needs to be babied in the 30 he makes. Last year a stretch in which he averaged 104 pitches a start over 20 starts seemed to leave him with nothing left for September (7.99 ERA). That doesn't sound like abuse—it isn't abuse—but it may be that Escobar needs to work in the 95-to-100 pitch range to get through a season. The need to carefully control his workload makes him a good fit for the Angels and their deep bullpen.

John Lackey

Bats: R   Throws: R   Height: 6' 6"   Weight: 235   Born: October 23, 1978   Age: 29

YEAR	TEAM	LVL	AGE	W	L	SV	G	GS	IP	H	BB	SO	HR	GB%	BABIP	STUFF	WHIP	ERA	PERA	EqERA	EqH9	EqBB9	EqSO9	EqHR9	VORP	SN/WX
2005	LAA	MLB	26	14	5	0	33	33	209	208	71	199	13	46.0%	.328	36	1.33	3.44	4.09	3.76	9.0	3.1	8.5	0.5	49.1	5.50
2006	LAA	MLB	27	13	11	0	33	33	217²	203	72	190	14	44.8%	.304	32	1.26	3.56	3.55	3.74	8.2	2.8	7.4	0.5	47.1	5.43
2007	LAA	MLB	28	19	9	0	33	33	224	219	52	179	18	45.6%	.302	28	1.21	3.01	3.49	3.10	8.2	1.9	6.6	0.7	60.7	6.94
2008	LAA	MLB	29	13	9	0	31	31	201	199	62	166	17	45.5%	.303	22	1.30	3.77	3.71	3.73	8.5	2.5	6.8	0.8	38.4	5.70

Breakout: 4%   Improve: 32%   Collapse: 24%   Attrition: 13%   Comparables: Gaylord Perry, Len Barker, Aaron Sele, Freddy Garcia

Lackey has assumed Mike Mussina's old position as one of the best pitchers in baseball, but one whose traditional stats don't quite represent his full value. Lackey's third-place finish in the Cy Young voting last year was the first time he'd even received votes. He's never won 20 games or had an ERA below 3.00, but he racks up innings, keeps the ball in the park, and gets a little better every season. His 6.2 K/BB down the stretch may be a harbinger of many more Cy Young votes to come.

Dustin Moseley

Bats: R   Throws: R   Height: 6' 4"   Weight: 215   Born: December 26, 1981   Age: 26

YEAR	TEAM	LVL	AGE	W	L	SV	G	GS	IP	H	BB	SO	HR	GB%	BABIP	STUFF	WHIP	ERA	PERA	EqERA	EqH9	EqBB9	EqSO9	EqHR9	VORP	SN/WX
2005	SLC	AAA	23	4	6	0	17	17	82¹	102	30	38	11	48.7%	.327	-25	1.60	5.03	5.79	5.40	10.2	3.6	2.6	1.4	1.8	—
2006	SLC	AAA	24	13	8	0	26	26	149¹	164	51	114	18	52.7%	.318	-14	1.44	4.71	6.12	5.90	10.5	3.5	5.0	1.4	-4.7	—
2006	LAA	MLB	24	1	0	0	3	2	11	22	2	3	3	37.5%	.432	-69	2.18	9.00	20.09	13.94	18.3	1.7	2.6	2.6	-3.8	-0.33
2007	LAA	MLB	25	4	3	0	46	8	92	97	27	50	7	48.8%	.307	-1	1.35	4.40	4.01	3.94	9.1	2.4	4.7	0.7	15.5	1.26
2008	LAA	MLB	26	3	4	1	34	5	61²	72	22	36	7	47.8%	.314	-7	1.52	5.01	4.87	4.96	10.0	2.9	4.8	1.0	3.6	0.50

Breakout: 21%   Improve: 45%   Collapse: 24%   Attrition: 39%   Comparables: Dick Pole, Sergio Mitre, Jerry Johnson, Matt Belisle

Moseley was a ground-ball machine in the first half, with a better than two-to-one groundball-to-flyball ratio above and a 2.60 ERA to match. After that, his GB/FB ratio was just 1.25, and he doesn't have the stuff to survive that as his 6.13 ERA and .468 SLG allowed in the second half proved. Moseley's more suited to starting than relieving, but the addition of Jon Garland, a comparable pitcher, cuts off his opportunity to do so.

Darren Oliver

Bats: R   Throws: L   Height: 6' 2"   Weight: 200   Born: October 6, 1970   Age: 37

YEAR	TEAM	LVL	AGE	W	L	SV	G	GS	IP	H	BB	SO	HR	GB%	BABIP	STUFF	WHIP	ERA	PERA	EqERA	EqH9	EqBB9	EqSO9	EqHR9	VORP	SN/WX
2005	IOW	AAA	34	0	3	0	3	3	13¹	28	5	10	3	46.4%	.500	-81	2.48	13.53	23.13	20.43	20.4	3.6	4.4	2.2	-20.3	—
2005	TUC	AAA	34	1	0	0	4	4	18¹	33	3	8	3	56.6%	.411	-40	1.97	6.39	12.24	8.83	16.6	2.1	2.6	1.6	-6.2	—
2006	NYN	MLB	35	4	1	0	45	0	81	70	21	60	13	49.8%	.248	-1	1.12	3.44	3.69	3.32	7.6	2.0	6.1	1.3	21.0	1.36
2007	LAA	MLB	36	3	1	0	61	0	64¹	58	23	51	5	48.0%	.283	6	1.26	3.78	3.19	3.82	7.2	2.7	6.4	0.7	11.5	1.23
2008	LAA	MLB	37	2	2	2	41	0	45²	51	15	32	5	45.8%	.315	-4	1.44	4.44	4.44	4.38	9.5	2.6	5.8	0.9	5.6	0.50

Breakout: 27%   Improve: 55%   Collapse: 27%   Attrition: 26%   Comparables: Mike Myers, Rich Rodriguez, Alan Embree, Joe Hoerner

Mike Scioscia did a nice job of adjusting to Oliver in-season, getting him out of the specialist role for which he was ill-suited, and into something that fit his skills better; Oliver has never dominated lefties and has neither the mechanics nor the repertoire of a LOOGY. Through June 24, Oliver averaged about two-thirds of an inning and less than four batters faced per appearance, but after that, he went at least an inning in 31 of 34 outings, averaging nearly six batters (and four outs) per outing. In a related story, Oliver had a 2.66 ERA and 3.5 K/BB in those 34 appearances.

Chris Resop

Bats: R   Throws: R   Height: 6' 3"   Weight: 215   Born: November 4, 1982   Age: 25

YEAR	TEAM	LVL	AGE	W	L	SV	G	GS	IP	H	BB	SO	HR	GB%	BABIP	STUFF	WHIP	ERA	PERA	EqERA	EqH9	EqBB9	EqSO9	EqHR9	VORP	SN/WX
2005	CAR	AA	22	3	2	24	43	0	49	47	16	56	2	50.7%	.331	4	1.29	2.57	5.31	4.09	10.6	3.7	7.2	0.8	7.4	—
2005	FLO	MLB	22	2	0	0	15	0	17	22	9	15	1	27.3%	.404	-7	1.82	8.47	6.21	8.64	11.3	4.3	7.6	0.5	-6.0	-0.03
2006	ABQ	AAA	23	4	0	2	40	0	49	49	15	43	4	46.4%	.315	-5	1.31	3.86	4.30	4.07	8.7	3.0	5.5	0.9	8.3	—
2006	FLO	MLB	23	1	2	0	21	0	21¹	26	16	10	1	39.2%	.342	-16	1.97	3.38	6.37	3.98	11.1	6.2	4.0	0.4	5.1	-0.13
2007	SLC	AAA	24	1	3	0	27	0	45¹	50	16	39	4	37.9%	.333	-7	1.46	4.57	4.49	4.93	9.1	3.4	5.7	0.8	3.4	—
2008	*ATL*	*MLB*	*25*	*2*	*2*	*1*	*31*	*3*	*40²*	*43*	*16*	*30*	*5*	*42.3%*	*.298*	*-2*	*1.42*	*4.25*	*4.74*	*4.52*	*9.1*	*3.1*	*5.9*	*1.1*	*6.8*	*0.60*

Breakout: 24%   Improve: 44%   Collapse: 31%   Attrition: 37%   Comparables: Bo McLaughlin, Matt Ginter, Gaylord Perry, Jose Paniagua

Coming to the Angels is a Catch-22 for young relief pitchers. The Angels tend to turn prospects into players, and pitching in Angel Stadium in front of a generally good defense helps you look good. On the other hand, opportunities can be hard to come by. Resop was picked up for Kevin Gregg a year ago and didn't pitch well enough at Triple-A to break out from the crowd. Keep in mind that he's a converted infielder who was mishandled badly by the Marlins; just 25, there's time for him to use his low-90s fastball and good curve to have a career.

Francisco Rodriguez

Bats: R   Throws: R   Height: 6' 0"   Weight: 180   Born: January 7, 1982   Age: 26

YEAR	TEAM	LVL	AGE	W	L	SV	G	GS	IP	H	BB	SO	HR	GB%	BABIP	STUFF	WHIP	ERA	PERA	EqERA	EqH9	EqBB9	EqSO9	EqHR9	VORP	SN/WX
2005	LAA	MLB	23	2	5	45	66	0	67¹	45	32	91	7	46.2%	.259	28	1.14	2.67	3.17	2.67	6.1	4.1	10.4	0.9	22.9	5.62
2006	LAA	MLB	24	2	3	47	69	0	73	52	28	98	6	40.2%	.288	33	1.10	1.73	3.09	1.88	6.8	3.3	10.3	0.6	33.4	7.30
2007	LAA	MLB	25	5	2	40	64	0	67¹	50	34	90	3	45.6%	.309	32	1.25	2.81	2.98	2.78	6.6	4.0	10.1	0.4	22.6	4.26
2008	*LAA*	*MLB*	*26*	*5*	*5*	*38*	*62*	*0*	*69²*	*52*	*32*	*89*	*5*	*42.0%*	*.292*	*31*	*1.20*	*2.78*	*2.81*	*2.74*	*6.4*	*3.7*	*10.6*	*0.6*	*21.4*	*3.60*

Breakout: 19%   Improve: 40%   Collapse: 40%   Attrition: 9%   Comparables: Ugueth Urbina, Mark Littell, Scott Garrelts, Juan Rincon

The changeup he added two years ago solved his problems with lefty batters and makes him entertaining in a Pedro-at-his-peak way when all three of his pitches are working. Pay no attention to the bouncing ERA, and note that his Stuff scores, which reflect his underlying performance, remain constant. Rodriguez will eventually hold the career saves record, and given the Angels' run context most years, he may get a shot at Bobby Thigpen's single-season mark of 57.

Ervin Santana

Bats: R   Throws: R   Height: 6' 2"   Weight: 160   Born: December 12, 1982   Age: 25

YEAR	TEAM	LVL	AGE	W	L	SV	G	GS	IP	H	BB	SO	HR	GB%	BABIP	STUFF	WHIP	ERA	PERA	EqERA	EqH9	EqBB9	EqSO9	EqHR9	VORP	SN/WX
2005	ARK	AA	22	5	1	0	7	7	39	34	15	32	2	36.3%	.288	5	1.26	2.31	4.71	3.79	8.6	4.8	5.0	0.8	7.2	—
2005	SLC	AAA	22	1	0	0	3	3	19¹	19	2	17	2	33.3%	.315	16	1.09	4.20	3.93	4.82	8.2	1.4	5.8	1.0	1.6	—
2005	LAA	MLB	22	12	8	0	23	23	133²	139	47	99	17	35.7%	.300	12	1.39	4.64	4.81	4.91	9.2	3.1	6.5	1.1	11.9	2.92
2006	LAA	MLB	23	16	8	0	33	33	204	181	70	141	21	38.6%	.272	16	1.23	4.28	3.72	4.24	7.9	2.9	6.0	0.9	30.2	4.12
2007	SLC	AAA	24	2	1	0	5	5	32¹	39	10	32	4	43.4%	.380	8	1.52	5.02	6.18	5.23	10.7	3.2	7.0	1.2	1.3	—
2007	LAA	MLB	24	7	14	0	28	26	150	174	58	126	26	36.9%	.327	-4	1.55	5.76	5.81	5.72	9.8	3.0	6.9	1.5	-4.2	1.51
2008	*LAA*	*MLB*	*25*	*9*	*9*	*0*	*27*	*27*	*154*	*160*	*56*	*119*	*19*	*39.5%*	*.299*	*15*	*1.40*	*4.56*	*4.42*	*4.46*	*8.9*	*2.9*	*6.4*	*1.1*	*17.2*	*3.00*

Breakout: 34%   Improve: 66%   Collapse: 7%   Attrition: 11%   Comparables: Bob Welch, Melido Perez, Ramon Martinez, Ian Snell

Much has been made of Santana's home/road splits, which look stark from an ERA standpoint (career: 3.14 at home, 7.14 on the road). A major factor behind that is the fact that he allows homers about 2½ times more often away from Angels Stadium. On the other hand, his strikeout and walk rates at different locations don't differ very much and his BABIPs are abnormal in both places (.268 at home, .328 on the road). How much of this is noise, and how much is a real effect? It's very hard to tease that out from the stats, but we can say that the real effect is almost certainly less than the ERA gap. Santana struggled in the first half of last year, but pitched better after spending a month at Salt Lake after the All-Star break. After returning he posted a 39/16 K/BB in 40 innings and had a very good relief outing in the Division Series at Fenway Park. Don't forget about him, as he's a strong sleeper.

Joe Saunders

Bats: L   Throws: L   Height: 6' 3"   Weight: 210   Born: June 16, 1981   Age: 27

YEAR	TEAM	LVL	AGE	W	L	SV	G	GS	IP	H	BB	SO	HR	GB%	BABIP	STUFF	WHIP	ERA	PERA	EqERA	EqH9	EqBB9	EqSO9	EqHR9	VORP	SN/WX
2005	ARK	AA	24	7	4	0	18	18	105²	107	32	80	9	52.3%	.308	-12	1.32	3.49	5.58	5.81	10.0	4.0	4.6	1.2	-2.2	—
2005	SLC	AAA	24	3	3	0	9	9	55	65	21	29	3	54.9%	.341	-10	1.56	4.58	4.72	6.08	9.8	3.7	3.0	0.5	-2.8	—
2006	SLC	AAA	25	10	4	0	21	20	135²	117	38	97	12	53.6%	.268	4	1.15	2.66	3.98	3.21	8.0	2.9	4.7	1.0	34.3	—
2006	LAA	MLB	25	7	3	0	13	13	70²	71	29	51	6	48.0%	.307	11	1.42	4.71	4.32	5.00	9.1	3.6	6.3	0.7	4.8	2.13
2007	SLC	AAA	26	4	7	0	14	14	86¹	89	20	84	10	44.7%	.319	11	1.26	5.11	4.15	5.17	8.6	2.3	6.5	1.1	4.2	—
2007	LAA	MLB	26	8	5	0	18	18	107¹	129	34	69	11	45.8%	.334	8	1.52	4.45	4.87	4.28	10.1	2.5	5.3	0.9	14.8	1.72
2008	LAA	MLB	27	8	9	0	25	25	138¹	157	50	91	15	47.1%	.315	8	1.50	4.88	4.77	4.82	9.7	2.9	5.4	1.0	9.5	2.10

Breakout: 12% Improve: 41% Collapse: 26% Attrition: 11%   Comparables: Scott Karl, Paul Splittorff, Woodie Fryman, Chris Welsh

All things considered, Santana is a better bet to contribute than Saunders is. The former first-round pick is back-of-rotation fodder, a lefty who doesn't miss enough bats to be dangerous while lacking pinpoint control. He's actually reminiscent of Oliver, who had a similar skill set at the same age. Oliver has pitched 1,500 innings of 4.93 ERA ball in the major leagues, for which he's been paid $30 million, so while Saunders isn't a star in the making, he should do all right for himself.

Scot Shields

Bats: R   Throws: R   Height: 6' 1"   Weight: 180   Born: July 22, 1975   Age: 32

YEAR	TEAM	LVL	AGE	W	L	SV	G	GS	IP	H	BB	SO	HR	GB%	BABIP	STUFF	WHIP	ERA	PERA	EqERA	EqH9	EqBB9	EqSO9	EqHR9	VORP	SN/WX
2005	LAA	MLB	29	10	11	7	78	0	91²	66	37	98	5	55.5%	.270	29	1.12	2.75	2.89	3.26	6.3	3.6	9.3	0.5	25.3	4.52
2006	LAA	MLB	30	7	7	2	74	0	87²	70	24	84	8	53.7%	.270	21	1.07	2.87	3.03	2.80	7.1	2.3	8.1	0.7	29.1	3.73
2007	LAA	MLB	31	4	5	2	71	0	77	62	33	77	7	46.6%	.278	14	1.23	3.86	3.32	3.66	6.8	3.4	8.3	0.8	14.8	2.70
2008	LAA	MLB	32	3	3	5	54	0	62²	58	26	59	5	49.1%	.301	10	1.34	3.72	3.63	3.71	7.9	3.3	7.8	0.7	13.1	1.20

Breakout: 14% Improve: 32% Collapse: 43% Attrition: 11%   Comparables: Jeff Montgomery, Jason Isringhausen, Hoyt Wilhelm, Dave Smith

The late spring-training decision to commit to Shields through 2010 with a three-year contract extension was questionable at the time given the pitcher's workload from 2003 to 2006. It looked worse by the end of the year, as Shields stumbled to the finish giving up more walks and fly balls than he had in years. His overall performance and value were still within his normal range, but when you combine the statistical trends with how he looked in the second half—brutal—there's a lot to worry about. Justin Speier may take the eighth inning away from him this year.

Justin Speier

Bats: R   Throws: R   Height: 6' 4"   Weight: 205   Born: November 6, 1973   Age: 34

YEAR	TEAM	LVL	AGE	W	L	SV	G	GS	IP	H	BB	SO	HR	GB%	BABIP	STUFF	WHIP	ERA	PERA	EqERA	EqH9	EqBB9	EqSO9	EqHR9	VORP	SN/WX
2005	TOR	MLB	31	3	2	0	65	0	66²	48	15	56	10	34.7%	.216	8	0.95	2.56	3.00	2.55	6.2	2.0	7.3	1.2	23.0	0.96
2006	TOR	MLB	32	2	0	0	58	0	51¹	47	21	55	5	31.7%	.300	17	1.32	3.16	3.73	2.94	8.0	3.3	8.8	0.7	16.1	1.35
2007	LAA	MLB	33	2	3	0	51	0	50	36	12	47	6	38.5%	.240	14	0.96	2.88	2.80	2.68	5.9	2.0	7.7	1.1	16.0	1.95
2008	LAA	MLB	34	3	2	3	53	0	56²	52	19	49	7	37.0%	.277	6	1.24	3.68	3.61	3.59	7.8	2.7	7.1	1.1	12.2	1.10

Breakout: 9% Improve: 20% Collapse: 62% Attrition: 13%   Comparables: Moe Drabowsky, Steve Reed, Jay Howell, Trevor Hoffman

Of course, Speier will need to stay healthy to take the eighth inning away from Shields. Speier missed two and a half months last season with a viral infection and was pitching on a sprained knee at the end of the year. When on the mound, he was nasty, throwing everything for strikes and avoiding the longball problems that have plagued him in the past. Speier has been on the DL in four of the past six seasons, never with anything devastating, but just enough to make him a little unreliable.

Rich Thompson

Bats: R   Throws: R   Height: 6' 1"   Weight: 180   Born: July 1, 1984   Age: 24

YEAR	TEAM	LVL	AGE	W	L	SV	G	GS	IP	H	BB	SO	HR	GB%	BABIP	STUFF	WHIP	ERA	PERA	EqERA	EqH9	EqBB9	EqSO9	EqHR9	VORP	SN/WX
2005	RCU	A+	21	6	8	3	42	15	121¹	132	53	92	20	42.6%	.307	-43	1.53	5.27	7.77	7.14	10.7	5.8	3.7	2.2	-18.8	—
2006	ARK	AA	22	3	4	10	42	0	66	52	27	60	13	35.1%	.235	-24	1.20	5.18	5.47	5.97	7.5	4.4	5.5	2.4	-2.6	—
2007	ARK	AA	23	2	3	0	21	3	49¹	34	14	50	5	42.6%	.240	3	0.97	2.01	4.13	3.66	7.1	3.3	6.4	1.3	10.1	—
2007	SLC	AAA	23	3	0	1	16	0	24²	17	6	32	2	44.1%	.278	25	0.93	2.19	3.00	2.52	5.8	2.5	9.0	0.7	8.6	—
2008	LAA	MLB	23	3	3	2	27	4	56	56	24	46	9	40.1%	.282	3	1.42	4.60	4.72	4.45	8.5	3.4	6.8	1.5	6.5	0.80

Breakout: 52% Improve: 79% Collapse: 7% Attrition: 15%   Comparables: Mark Worrell, Brad Clontz, Leo Torres, Alfredo Gonzalez

An Australian hurler who took a while to find success, Thompson cruised through the Angels' system in 2007, dominating at Double- and Triple-A before getting hammered in his brief appearance in the majors. With a low-90s fastball that touches 94 mph and a very good curve, he has everything it takes to be an effective reliever, but big-league hitters took advantage of his tendency to work up in the zone by smashing four home runs off of him in less than seven innings. He's better than that.

Jordan Walden   Bats: R   Throws: R   Height: 6' 4"   Weight: 180   Born: November 16, 1987   Age: 20

YEAR	TEAM	LVL	AGE	W	L	SV	G	GS	IP	H	BB	SO	HR	GB%	BABIP	STUFF	WHIP	ERA	PERA	EqERA	EqH9	EqBB9	EqSO9	EqHR9	VORP	SN/WX
2007	ORM	Rk	19	1	1	0	15	15	64¹	49	17	63	3	57.2%	.272	-1	1.03	3.08	5.49	6.63	8.7	5.3	4.2	1.1	-6.4	—
2008	LAA	MLB	20	5	9	0	22	22	111²	132	75	56	14	50.5%	.311	-10	1.86	6.49	6.18	6.44	10.2	5.4	4.2	1.1	-12.7	-0.50

Breakout: 18% Improve: 59% Collapse: 18% Attrition: 13%   Comparables: Blake Johnson, Nick Adenhart, Jamie Arnold, Yovani Gallardo

Going into 2006, Walden was the best high school pitcher in the country, a big Texan right-hander with a fastball in the upper 90s. A case of draftitis and some messy mechanics dropped that pitch into the low 90s, but didn't drop his bonus demands, so nobody drafted him until the Angels took him in the 12th round, subsequently treating him like a draft-and-follow, happily handing him a cool million when the velocity returned during a year at a junior college. Walden was touching 98 mph during his pro debut and could end up as yet another one of scouting director Eddie Bane's late-round gambles that pays off huge.

Jered Weaver   Bats: R   Throws: R   Height: 6' 7"   Weight: 205   Born: October 4, 1982   Age: 25

YEAR	TEAM	LVL	AGE	W	L	SV	G	GS	IP	H	BB	SO	HR	GB%	BABIP	STUFF	WHIP	ERA	PERA	EqERA	EqH9	EqBB9	EqSO9	EqHR9	VORP	SN/WX
2005	RCU	A+	22	4	1	0	7	7	33	25	7	49	3	29.7%	.314	20	0.97	3.82	4.75	6.37	8.5	3.3	8.5	1.2	-2.5	—
2005	ARK	AA	22	3	3	0	8	8	43	43	19	46	5	31.5%	.314	6	1.44	3.98	6.78	6.28	10.5	5.6	7.0	1.6	-2.9	—
2006	SLC	AAA	23	6	1	0	12	11	77¹	63	10	93	7	32.6%	.308	33	0.95	2.10	3.80	2.75	8.2	1.5	8.4	1.1	22.8	—
2006	LAA	MLB	23	11	2	0	19	19	123	94	33	105	15	31.8%	.239	28	1.03	2.56	3.03	2.35	6.6	2.3	7.2	1.0	46.5	5.11
2007	LAA	MLB	24	13	7	0	28	28	161	178	45	115	17	37.7%	.319	13	1.39	3.91	4.20	3.82	9.1	2.2	5.8	0.9	29.1	4.15
2008	LAA	MLB	25	11	9	0	28	28	174	181	54	128	21	38.6%	.297	16	1.35	4.32	4.25	4.21	8.9	2.5	6.1	1.1	23.3	3.90

Breakout: 3% Improve: 20% Collapse: 49% Attrition: 14%   Comparables: Dick Hall, Brett Tomko, Doc Medich, Scott Sanderson

Now that we're a couple of years past the hype, is it okay to wonder if this is all there is? Weaver is a fly-ball pitcher who doesn't miss bats and whose ERA would be a run higher if he pitched for about 24 other teams. He's brutal at holding runners (30 steals in 35 attempts in two years) and, most damning, he hasn't improved since coming into the league. If he ends up being a slightly less annoying version of his big brother Jeff, that's valuable; however, the Angels thought they were getting an ace, and that pitcher hasn't made an appearance.

LINEOUTS

Hitters

PLAYER	TEAM	LVL	AGE	PA	R	2B	3B	HR	RBI	BB	SO	SB-CS	EqBRR	AVG/OBP/SLG	MLVr	EqAVG/EqOBP/EqSLG	EqA	VORP
C R. Budde	SLC	AAA	27	177	21	12	0	4	28	18	27	2-2	-2.7	.295/.367/.449	.010	.261/.333/.401	.256	4.7
LF N. Gorneault	SLC	AAA	28	533	82	24	1	19	59	58	108	17-8	-1.5	.261/.346/.437	-.069	.223/.306/.373	.238	-19.6
RF N. Haynes*	SLC	AAA	27	198	33	9	6	4	32	22	36	14-7	0.2	.386/.462/.579	.433	.287/.371/.443	.280	11.6
	LAA	MLB	27	48	10	0	1	0	1	3	11	1-2	-0.1	.267/.313/.311	-.193	.267/.312/.311	.205	-1.7
C B. Johnson	DNV	Rk	20	115	13	2	0	1	12	9	22	3-2	-0.5	.282/.351/.330	.042	.215/.263/.252	.177	-17.6
D. McPherson '08	LAA	MLB	27	226	24	11	1	10	33	17	77	3-1	0.1	.225/.287/.433	-.110	.223/.286/.452	.254	1.2
INF A. Morrissey	ARK	AA	26	599	85	27	2	9	50	92	131	12-7	-6.5	.263/.396/.383	.060	.230/.346/.335	.246	2.7
RF T. Murphy#	SLC	AAA	27	337	36	18	6	4	32	23	67	15-10	-1.0	.270/.323/.407	-.144	.233/.287/.350	.221	-9.5
	LAA	MLB	27	39	2	1	0	0	2	0	9	0-0	-0.6	.184/.205/.211	-.588	.184/.205/.211	.103	-4.7
OF A. Norman	ANG	Rk	22	202	40	4	10	0	33	19	19	12-1	2.2	.362/.440/.500	.376	.262/.312/.369	.242	-13.1
3B F. Sandoval#	ARK	AA	24	563	84	32	6	11	72	67	78	21-11	0.3	.305/.392/.468	.195	.269/.347/.411	.265	23.8
C B. Wilson	ARK	AA	24	204	24	9	0	6	27	22	26	5-3	-1.9	.271/.348/.420	.034	.239/.309/.375	.237	0.1
	SLC	AAA	24	141	15	13	1	3	22	8	18	1-0	1.2	.295/.336/.477	-.005	.256/.298/.421	.247	2.2

Ryan Budde has never been a regular at Triple-A, much less a threat to hold a job in the majors. His first good partial year with the bat doesn't change that. ⊘ Perhaps frustrated by being stuck at Triple-A, **Nick Gorneault** stalled out last year. Claimed off of waivers by the Rangers after the season, he was subsequently non-tendered. ⊘ Oft-injured **Nathan Haynes** returned from independent ball to make his major league debut last year. He could be a decent extra outfielder, not that the Angels need one. ⊘ Not to be confused with the Mets outfielder, the disgraced sprinter, or the Elizabethan playwright, this **Ben Johnson** is a catcher with some speed and pop, but not much glove. He's at least two injured players away from the dream. ⊘ Ex-prospect **Dallas McPherson** missed last season after back surgery and was non-tendered in December. Though he never developed much in the way of plate judgment or defense, if the surgery hasn't sapped his lefty power, he represents an interesting salvage project, though he'd be a role player at best. ⊘ Veteran minor league infielder **Adam Morrissey** was very un-Angelic at Triple-A last year, walking 92 times and striking out 131. ⊘ Their added outfield depth will keep the Angels from having to call on **Tommy Murphy** this year. He might have been a bench player back when teams carried nine or ten pitchers, but he's not good enough now. ⊘ UCLA product **Anthony Norman**'s Player of the Year award in the Arizona League would have looked better if the AZL wasn't a step down in competition from the Pac-10. He's no prospect. ⊘ **Freddy Sandoval**'s shot at a career ended when Wood moved to third base in front of him. With his glove and line-drive bat, he can be a cheap stopgap for some team during the next four years. ⊘ **Bobby Wilson** keeps hitting for average, making him a good bet to be the backup catcher in place of Mathis by the end of the year.

Pitchers

PLAYER	TEAM	LVL	AGE	W	L	SV	IP	H	BB	SO	HR	GB%	BABIP	STUFF	WHIP	ERA	PERA	EqERA	EqH9	EqBB9	EqSO9	EqHR9	VORP
M. Anton*	ANG	Rk	22	5	3	0	61²	58	15	82	2	53.7%	.357	-15	1.18	3.21	8.17	7.91	12.7	5.3	5.5	1.5	-13.4
J. Bachanov '08	LAA	MLB	19	4	11	0	118	165	90	51	25	46.2%	.329	-25	2.16	8.50	8.23	8.24	12.0	6.1	3.6	1.9	-36.8
B. Browning*	CDR	A	22	9	4	8	74	54	26	74	2	64.6%	.269	-9	1.08	2.80	5.17	5.51	8.3	6.1	4.5	0.8	0.7
N. Green	ARK	AA	22	10	8	0	178¹	164	32	107	17	39.8%	.267	-8	1.10	3.68	4.71	5.25	9.2	2.3	3.5	1.3	6.5
M. Gwyn	SLC	AAA	29	2	1	15	57	68	17	54	5	54.9%	.380	-1	1.49	3.79	5.40	3.98	10.8	3.0	6.6	1.0	9.8
J. Haynes	CDR	A	21	5	6	0	94	98	41	75	3	54.0%	.326	-12	1.48	3.06	7.43	6.92	11.7	7.5	3.3	1.0	-11.8
G. Jones	SLC	AAA	30	4	2	3	53²	68	14	39	7	48.9%	.367	-19	1.53	4.86	6.27	5.65	11.1	2.6	5.1	1.4	-0.3
	LAA	MLB	30	0	0	0	8²	10	5	5	2	51.6%	.276	-27	1.73	6.21	6.67	6.00	9.0	4.0	5.0	2.0	-0.2
W. Madrigal	CDR	A	23	5	4	20	61	44	23	75	3	56.1%	.293	-8	1.10	2.07	5.99	5.37	9.0	6.6	6.2	1.4	1.3
S. O'Sullivan	CDR	A	19	10	7	0	158¹	136	40	125	6	55.2%	.279	0	1.11	2.22	5.45	5.80	9.3	4.7	3.2	1.1	-3.2
M. Tobin	ANG	Rk	19	2	0	0	28¹	17	7	32	1	60.9%	.254	3	0.85	0.95	5.81	4.24	8.1	5.4	4.6	1.5	3.5
	ORM	Rk	19	2	1	0	28	23	7	23	0	51.9%	.299	0	1.07	3.21	5.22	5.62	9.4	5.2	3.4	0.4	-0.1

Lefty **Michael Anton** led the Arizona League in strikeouts, not wholly impressive given that he came out of the Virginia Military Institute. Check back when he faces some challenging competition. ⊘ The Angels top pick last June, righty **Jon Bachanov** is a high-reward/high-risk teenager with a rocket arm and questionable mechanics and makeup. ⊘ Another over-aged prospect, **Barret Browning**'s success relieving in the Midwest League doesn't tell us much about a guy who came from the Atlantic Coast Conference. His poetry, on the other hand, is quite insightful. ⊘ Not to be confused with the journeyman infielder, this **Nick Green** impressed enough with his pinpoint control at Double-A to get added to the 40-man roster this winter. It's cheaper than paying Carlos Silva. ⊘ Last year, minor league veteran **Marcus Gwyn** turned a nice run at Salt Lake into a line in *The Baseball Encyclopedia*. Unfortunately, it was ugly (11.81 ERA) and will be his only one. ⊘ **Jeremy Haynes** is a raw, but extremely promising, draft-and-follow right-hander with a good fastball and an even better curve. He's still figuring out what to do with both. ⊘ For the third straight season, **Greg Jones** got a cup of coffee in the majors and was hammered. He's off the 40-man roster, finally. ⊘ Outfielder-turned-closer **Warner Madrigal** pitched well in the Midwest League, then was lost to the Rangers through minor league free agency. ⊘ Young **Sean O'Sullivan** owned the Midwest League, but he's a command guy without a great out pitch, which limits his upside. ⊘ Like Adenhart, **Mason Tobin** was a late-round steal for the Angels. He used a mid-90s fastball and excellent changeup to wow in his first pro season.

MANAGER: MIKE SCIOSCIA

YEAR	TEAM	W-L	Pythag +/−	Avg PC	100+ P	120+ P	QS	BQS	REL	REL w Zero R	IBB	Subs	PH	PH Avg	PH HR	SB2	CS2	SB3	CS3	SAC Att	SAC %	POS SAC	Squeeze	Swing	In Play
2005	LAA	95-67	0	97.2	76	1	93	7	377	246	24	49	90	.234	1	149	47	12	8	65	66.1%	42	3	171	137
2006	LAA	89-73	4	97.3	83	2	86	11	380	231	27	50	101	.171	4	123	45	23	6	42	73.8%	29	2	189	154
2007	LAA	94-68	4	97.4	85	0	85	2	396	245	22	31	101	.250	2	118	47	20	8	48	66.7%	31	3	170	142

Mike Scioscia is managing a team in transition, one that has gotten older and slower since the Angels' speed/contact approach peaked in 2004. He is not adapting, as the decline in the Angels' stolen-base percentage—while remaining the league leader in attempts—shows. With Torii Hunter and Brandon Wood in line to pick up playing time that belonged to Reggie Willits and Chone Figgins, the team could be even slower in 2008. Scioscia is going to have to get away from what's worked for him in the past and do a better job of matching his strategy to his personnel. The same applies in the bullpen, which Scioscia did not run well last year, initially shoehorning lefty Darren Oliver into an ill-fitting specialist role and then failing to react quickly enough to Scot Shields' decline. For the first time in his career, Scioscia is faced with the need to change. The Angels will probably win the West regardless of how he handles the challenge, but his management style should provide an interesting subtext to the team's 2008 season.

Los Angeles Dodgers

The drama never ends. Just as the Dodgers began their 2004 NL West title defense with a hot start that devolved into a disappointing season characterized by injuries, acrimony, and an organizational shakeup, so too did they follow their 2006 wild card–winning campaign with one of squandered promise, rancor, and insecurity. Once the model of stability, the Los Angeles Dodgers have become a daily soap opera under the ownership of Frank Mc-Court, who assumed control of the team prior to the 2004 season. This has happened despite the fact that the team possesses a wealth of organizational resources and a promising long-range forecast.

For the 2007 Dodgers, the turmoil began in November 2006, when right fielder J. D. Drew, on the advice of his agent, Scott Boras, opted out of the final three years of his five-year, $55 million deal after repeatedly hinting he would stay. The injury-prone Drew's decision, which came on the heels of a rare healthy season in which he'd led the team in RBI while tying first baseman Nomar Garciaparra for the team lead in home runs, caught general manager Ned Colletti off guard. The 2006 Dodgers had finished 15th in the league in homers and the loss of Drew's bat was too much for the GM to bear. Colletti quickly re-signed the similarly injury-prone Garciaparra to a public-relations-minded, two-year, $18.5 million deal. He did this despite the readiness of first-base prospect James Loney, who'd led all of the minor leagues in batting average in 2006 before hitting .323/.373/.726 after a late-season promotion prompted, fittingly, by a Garciaparra injury.

That chain of events cast the die for the 2007 team, as Colletti spent the year placing obstacles in the paths of the organization's enviable collection of blue-chip prospects. The day after Garciaparra agreed to terms, the team announced a stupefying five-year, $44 million deal with Juan Pierre, thus blocking 22-year-old Matt Kemp in center field. Kemp and 25-year-old Andre Ethier were further crowded in the outfield corners by the signing of 39-year-old left fielder Luis Gonzalez. In the rotation, the additions of free agents Jason Schmidt (three years, $47 million) and Randy Wolf (one year, $8 million) exiled 22-year-old Chad Billingsley to the bull-pen.

Loney, Kemp, Ethier and Billingsley—all well-regarded prospects—had each made promising, if uneven, debuts in 2006, but belt-and-suspenders man Colletti felt compelled to sign the veterans as insurance for the youngsters. The bitter irony is that it was those five free agents—who, due to injuries and ineffectiveness, netted a mere 12.0 WARP3 at the hefty price of more than $42 million—who needed to be bailed out by the team's young talent, not the other way around.

The absurdity of the situation was best captured by the team's third-base quagmire. Twenty-five-year-old Wilson Betemit, the Opening Day starter, quickly wore out his welcome with an early slump. The team then briefly turned the reins over to top prospect Andy LaRoche, but he was soon crowded out by fellow rookie Tony Abreu, a second-base prospect with a much lower ceiling. Abreu then lost the job to Garciaparra, who was pushed back across the diamond when Loney hit his way into the lineup in June; Abreu was subsequently accused by Colletti of faking an abdominal injury to avoid a demotion. When Garciaparra took his annual trip to the disabled list in August, both LaRoche and Abreu (who wasn't faking) were also out with injuries, and Betemit was wearing Yankee pinstripes following a

---

DODGERS PROSPECTUS

2007 record: 82-80; Fourth place, NL West

Pythagenport record: 82-80

Runs scored per game: 4.54 (10th in NL)

Runs allowed per game: 4.49 (6th in NL)

Team EqA: .256 (11th in NL)

2007 Batters Age: 30.2 (7th oldest in NL)

2007 Pitchers Age: 31.2 (3rd oldest in NL)

Ballpark: Dodger Stadium; Slight hitter's park; Park Factor of 1.010

2007: Colletti buries kids, team starts strong but skids.

2008: The more things change, the more they stay the same.

deadline trade. The Dodgers were thus reduced to picking Shea Hillenbrand off the scrap heap and inserting him in the lineup until Garciaparra returned.

Despite this self-defeating pattern, the Dodgers spent much of the 2007 season as serious contenders in the hyper-competitive NL West. They held first place for 68 days, more than any NL West team save for the division-winning Diamondbacks, sitting atop the division from mid-April to early June and then again in the latter half of July. The turning point may have come on July 19, when the team woke up with the National League's best record at 54-41. That night, the Mets bombed starter Derek Lowe for ten runs in three innings, handing the Dodgers a 13-9 loss. Three days later, Lowe tweaked his groin during a rare relief appearance. Though he made his next start, Lowe was a different pitcher over his final 11 starts, yielding a 4.76 ERA and 12 of the 20 homers he allowed on the season.

That July 19 loss touched off a 6-18 skid that sent the Dodgers—by then featuring replacement-level hacks Mark Hendrickson and Brett Tomko in the rotation instead of the injured Schmidt, Wolf, or lefty Hong-Chih Kuo (all done for the year)—tumbling into fourth place. While the team continued to battle for the wild card in August, a 1-10 September bellyflop ended those hopes. The Dodgers's 28-39 record after July 19 was the third-worst in the NL, outdone only by the sorry performances of the Pirates and Marlins.

That stretch of futility hammered a nail in the coffin of Grady Little's tenure as Dodger manager while providing further evidence of Colletti's distrust for the youth movement. Veterans Gonzalez and second baseman Jeff Kent groused to the press about the younger players, criticizing their professionalism (Kent) and bemoaning lost playing time (Gonzalez), exposing a generational rift that suggested that Little had lost control of the clubhouse. Colletti responded via a poison-pen Bill Plaschke column in the *L.A. Times*, declaring his willingness to trade said youngsters, particularly Kemp, whose occasional baserunning gaffes drew disproportionate attention (Kemp was above average at advancing on hits and ground outs according to our new baserunning statistic, EqBRR). Soon, rumors of a deal sending Kemp and Clayton Kershaw—perhaps the minors' top pitching prospect—to the Twins for lefty ace Johan Santana burned through the grapevine. When that rumor fizzled, both prospects' names surfaced in potential deals for Marlins third baseman Miguel Cabrera and Orioles starter Erik Bedard. At this writing, Colletti hasn't pulled the trigger, but Dodger fans live in fear of his drunk-with-a-gun act when it comes to their highly regarded neophytes.

As for Little, other than the clubhouse culture, it's unclear to which of his failures were his own rather than the results of organizational mandates. Saddled with a collection of mismatched parts, he struggled to make them fit. Beyond third base, where five players made between 17 and 41 starts, the outfield saw its four principals' playing time vary inversely to their productivity as measured by Marginal Lineup Value rate and defensive performance: Pierre (162 starts, -.080 MLVr, 89 Fielding Rate), Gonzalez (126, .069, 98), Ethier (117, .086, 104), Kemp (66, .271, 96). While it's unlikely that Kemp would have sustained the .396 BABIP which drove his .342/.373/.521 performance, Little didn't grant him a single start in center field, thus limiting his team's ability to find out. Little wrote Kemp and Ethier into in the starting lineup together just 26 times all season.

By the end of September, a weary Little was said to have been wavering about returning to fulfill the final year of his deal. Before Little's return was even publicly questioned, Colletti surreptitiously interviewed Joe Girardi to replace him. Soon after that news leaked, Girardi accepted the Yankees job, and Colletti swooped in to hire the ousted Joe Torre while negotiating a buyout of Little's contract. Torre's efforts to integrate youngsters Robinson Cano, Melky Cabrera, Chien-Ming Wang, Phil Hughes, and Joba Chamberlain into the Yankees' mix over the past few years suggest that shifting gears from a superstar-laden lineup to a younger one more in need of nurturing won't be an entirely foreign proposition for the new Dodger manager, though Torre is not immune to the seductive virtues of veteran experience.

Colletti has reason to look over his own shoulder as well. The machinations behind the managerial coup recall the surprise ouster of Colletti's predecessor Paul DePodesta after the 2005 season, hinting that the GM himself could be on the hot seat. Indeed, the Dodgers possess within their ranks two highly regarded GM candidates in assistant GMs Kim Ng and Logan White, the latter responsible for one of the top collections of homegrown talent in the game. Word that Colletti and White had clashed over the team's willingness to trade prospects such as Kershaw further exposes Colletti's win-now mindset, serving as a reminder of the danger that he represents to the organization. In his defense, the youngsters Colletti has dealt thus far have yet to amount to much beyond a couple of months when starter Edwin Jackson and catcher Dioner Navarro, both now with the Tampa Bay Rays, resembled actual major leaguers.

Ironically, the man who has suppressed the playing time of hitting prospects Loney, Kemp, Ethier, and LaRoche now faces the challenge of improving an offense that made sub-par showings last year in every key category except on-base percentage, where its .337 ranked sixth in the National League. The 2007 Dodgers were tenth in the NL in scoring (4.54 runs/game), eleventh in Equivalent Average (.256), thirteenth in slugging (.406), fourteenth in home runs (129), and dead last in isolated power (.131). Among the primary offenders were Colletti signings Pierre, who had a typically counterproductive season, and Garciaparra, who suffered through yet another underwhelming, injury-marred season.

Not that the lineup doesn't have its strengths, particularly catcher Russell Martin (not coincidentally, a homegrown prospect), who led the team in VORP while winning All-Star and Gold Glove honors in just his second season. Martin has also filled the emotional void left by the departures of fan favorites Paul Lo Duca and Eric Gagné by becoming the face of the franchise. Every other asset comes with caveats. Kent rebounded from a down 2006 to finish second on the team in VORP but is a liability in the field, and at 40 years old, an injury risk as well. Despite his sweet swing, Loney has below-average power for a first baseman; he needs to bat .300 to truly help, though he's shown the ability to do so. Should Kemp remain in Dodger blue, he might provide 25- to 30-home-run power, but his free-swinging ways could keep his OBP below .350. To this mix the Dodgers have added free agent center fielder Andruw Jones, who is coming off a season in which he hit .222/.311/.413, all three career lows. Still, the 26 homers Jones hit last year would have led his new team, and his stellar defense (13 fielding runs above average) was roughly three wins better than that of Pierre (-17 FRAA).

The drawback to the Jones signing is that rather than having him replace Pierre entirely, the team plans to simply move the incumbent to left field, which would only raise the offensive bar further beyond Pierre's reach while negating Jones' defensive contribution. Colletti's reluctance to fully acknowledge the Pierre signing as a mistake suggests that he's still wary of his young talent and incapable of recognizing a sunk cost. Signing Jones to a two-year, $36.2 million deal doesn't allow him to tear up the doozy he gave Pierre the year before, but rather than sink the cost to help the club, Colletti plans to keep running Pierre out there, indifferent to the fact that such a move further marginalizes Ethier and Kemp, the latter of whom will apparently play center field only over Colletti's dead body. If anything, the signing increases the likelihood that one of those two youngsters will be traded. This scenario is repeated at third base, where Garciaparra's punchless performance and 83 Fielding Rate at the hot corner last year weren't enough to drop him below LaRoche on the organizational depth chart. Nomar will open this season as the starting third baseman despite the fact that the abortive pursuits of Alex Rodriguez, Mike Lowell, and the aforementioned Cabrera suggest the team is hardly sold on his services.

One area that does need external reinforcement is the rotation, which finished seventh in the league in SNLVAR. Only the top three spots are spoken for. Brad Penny avoided the physical and mental pitfalls which hampered his second-half performance in 2006 to emerge as the staff ace in 2007. Entering the final year of a three-year, $25.5 million deal, Penny remains the most positive remnant of DePodesta's regime. Despite his late-season struggles, fellow DePodesta pickup Lowe remains a reliable innings-eater and then some. Billingsley emerged as the team's top starter in the second half of 2007 after escaping the bullpen in late June and is well on his way to fulfilling his front-of-the-rotation promise. It's unclear, however, how much the Dodgers can expect from Schmidt (who underwent surgery for a torn labrum in June), Kuo (who had bone chips removed in late July), and late-season pickup Esteban Loaiza. All three offer modest returns if they can overcome their injury woes; none is anywhere close to a lock to do so. Kershaw is at least a year away, and nobody from the upper minors appears ready to help in more than a relief role.

The bullpen remains a strength, having finished fourth in the league in WXRL and second in Adjusted Runs Prevented last year. For all of the concerns about Torre's overreliance on his top relievers in New York, he has more to work with here. Righty Jonathan Broxton is a reliably imposing set-up man, and Joe Beimel offers Torre the true lefty set-up man that he hasn't had since Mike Stanton's initial departure from the Bronx. Rookie Jonathan Meloan may be along to augment the corps at some point, as well, further reducing Torre's need to ride Scott Proctor as hard as he did in New York. Topping things off, Takashi Saito, who made a mere $1.3 million in 2007, is dollar-for-dollar the game's best closer.

Indeed, for all of the instability fostered by the McCourt regime—not to mention the owner's undercapitalized purchase of the club—the Dodgers are on very solid footing financially. The team has led the league in attendance for four straight years, with a franchise record of 3,857,036 turning out in 2007, while their $108.5 million payroll ranked sixth in the majors, falling well below the luxury tax threshold. As a result, *Forbes'* 2007 estimates placed the Dodgers fourth among the thirty teams in revenues ($211 million) and second in operating income ($27.5 million). McCourt has shared that wealth with Dodger fans by pouring more than $130 million into the first four phases of a six-phase renovation of Dodger Stadium that includes replacing every seat in the ballpark, installing box seats, and doubling the number of concession stands and restroom facilities to stay abreast of modern ballpark amenities.

Money may be the team's big advantage within the division. As enviable as the Dodgers' young talent base is, the Diamondbacks and Rockies both boast bright prospects of their own. The Dodgers can afford to outspend those teams (not to mention the Padres), but there's no point in doing so if it simply means more big-money contracts for players such as Pierre, who do little more than block the blue-chippers, or trades for mediocrities such as Hendrickson. The Dodgers hold the best hand in the division. Their biggest handicap is the man playing it.

HITTERS

Tony Abreu — INF

Bats: S Throws: R Height: 5' 11" Weight: 200 Born: November 13, 1984 Age: 23

YEAR	TEAM	LVL	AGE	PA	R	2B	3B	HR	RBI	BB	SO	SB	CS	EqBRR	AVG	OBP	SLG	MLVr	EqAVG	EqOBP	EqSLG	EqA	VORP	DEFENSE			
2005	VRO	A+	20	421	54	23	7	4	43	15	56	14	10	-0.5	.327	.356	.452	.165	.271	.298	.387	.234	2.8	83-2B	5		
2005	JAX	AA	20	102	10	3	2	0	9	4	21	0	2	-0.6	.250	.284	.323	-.174	.216	.245	.289	.176	-7.2	20-2B	-4		
2006	JAX	AA	21	509	66	24	3	6	55	33	69	8	4	2.5	.287	.343	.392	.110	.269	.319	.387	.247	8.2	110-2B	-1		
2007	LVG	AAA	22	253	48	22	5	2	18	14	34	5	0	0.6	.355	.399	.517	.221	.302	.348	.447	.276	14.9	24-2B	-1	17-SS	-6
2007	LAN	MLB	22	178	19	14	1	2	17	7	21	0	0	0.3	.271	.309	.404	-.069	.273	.315	.424	.255	1.3	22-3B	3	13-2B	3
2008	LAN	MLB	23	469	56	27	3	7	49	27	65	7	3	1.0	.279	.326	.408	-.062	.277	.324	.412	.251	12.5	111-2B	3		

Breakout: 22% Improve: 47% Collapse: 17% Attrition: 14%   Comparables: Tito Fuentes, Ronny Cedeño, Luis Rivas, Juan Castro

The heir apparent to Jeff Kent at second base, Abreu offers a limited upside; he hits for average, but lacks a great batting eye, power, or the speed to be a stolen-base threat. In early July, he suffered what was believed to be a lower abdominal strain and cried foul when he was demoted rather than disabled. That prompted Ned Colletti, who publicly questioned the veracity of his injury, to place Abreu on the inactive list. Though Abreu finally returned to action one contentious month later, off-season surgery confirmed he'd suffered a sports hernia. No word on whether Colletti sent a note of apology.

Josh Bell — 3B

Bats: S Throws: R Height: 6' 3" Weight: 205 Born: November 13, 1986 Age: 21

YEAR	TEAM	LVL	AGE	PA	R	2B	3B	HR	RBI	BB	SO	SB	CS	EqBRR	AVG	OBP	SLG	MLVr	EqAVG	EqOBP	EqSLG	EqA	VORP	DEFENSE	
2006	OGD	Rk	19	276	45	17	3	12	53	23	72	4	0	2.6	.308	.367	.544	.252	.208	.250	.346	.204	-22.8	51-3B	-9
2007	GRL	A	20	438	65	21	3	15	62	39	109	5	1	0.0	.289	.354	.470	.212	.219	.275	.365	.220	-10.6	88-3B	-17
2007	SBR	A+	20	79	4	2	1	2	9	3	19	0	0	-0.4	.173	.203	.307	-.454	.158	.177	.303	.143	-8.6	17-3B	-3
2008	LAN	MLB	21	574	51	28	2	14	61	37	161	6	3	0.1	.223	.276	.362	-.254	.221	.273	.365	.214	-12.2	135-3B	-13

Breakout: 40% Improve: 57% Collapse: 17% Attrition: 9%   Comparables: Elvis Corporan, Jose Lopez, Terry Jones, Ryan Balfe

Bell offers monster power from both sides of the plate. Alas, while his pitch recognition is good, his long swing results in too many strikeouts. In his full-season debut, the Ks stayed while his Isolated Power dipped, the result of moving from a tremendous offensive environment to the most pitcher-friendly league in baseball. Things went no better in the field as sloppy footwork and a strong but erratic arm led to 35 errors and an .859 fielding percentage. Still, the Dodgers plan to give him every opportunity to improve before moving him off the hot corner.

Ivan DeJesus Jr. — SS

Bats: R Throws: R Height: 5' 11" Weight: 182 Born: May 1, 1987 Age: 21

YEAR	TEAM	LVL	AGE	PA	R	2B	3B	HR	RBI	BB	SO	SB	CS	EqBRR	AVG	OBP	SLG	MLVr	EqAVG	EqOBP	EqSLG	EqA	VORP	DEFENSE	
2005	OGD	Rk	18	81	4	1	0	0	3	6	18	3	3	-0.7	.208	.296	.222	-.437	.145	.198	.158	.070	-21.0	16-SS	-5
2006	CGA	A	19	563	65	17	2	1	44	63	85	16	5	-1.0	.277	.361	.327	.025	.229	.296	.270	.208	-22.0	114-SS	0
2007	SBR	A+	20	502	69	22	3	4	52	57	64	11	6	-0.6	.287	.371	.381	.054	.240	.313	.312	.226	-6.4	115-SS	-22
2008	LAN	MLB	21	583	55	25	2	3	41	49	97	11	5	0.2	.243	.310	.313	-.244	.241	.307	.317	.219	-2.6	137-SS	-7

Breakout: 41% Improve: 60% Collapse: 22% Attrition: 8%   Comparables: Oscar Robles, Paul Kelly, Mike Bell, Brent Abernathy

Yes, this is the son of the former major league shortstop whom the Cubs traded to Philadelphia for Larry Bowa and Ryne Sandberg. Coincidentally, Ned Colletti's first major league job was as a media director for the Cubs in the wake of that 1982 trade. The younger DeJesus generates rave reviews for his glovework and has shown excellent on-base skills and a compact, line-drive swing, but his greatest value could be as a constant reminder to Colletti about the value of trading mediocre veterans for prospects rather than the other way around.

Blake DeWitt — 3B

Bats: L Throws: R Height: 5' 11" Weight: 175 Born: August 20, 1985 Age: 22

YEAR	TEAM	LVL	AGE	PA	R	2B	3B	HR	RBI	BB	SO	SB	CS	EqBRR	AVG	OBP	SLG	MLVr	EqAVG	EqOBP	EqSLG	EqA	VORP	DEFENSE			
2005	CGA	A	19	522	61	31	3	11	65	34	79	0	1	-3.8	.283	.333	.428	.087	.225	.264	.335	.204	-21.6	110-3B	-12		
2006	VRO	A+	20	478	61	18	1	18	61	45	79	8	5	-5.1	.268	.339	.442	.101	.233	.296	.388	.238	-1.1	90-2B	-3	16-3B	2
2006	JAX	AA	20	112	6	1	0	1	6	8	21	0	1	-0.3	.183	.241	.221	-.324	.190	.241	.229	.147	-11.0	24-3B	0		
2007	SBR	A+	21	361	48	29	2	8	46	20	42	2	3	-0.9	.298	.338	.466	.129	.247	.282	.375	.222	-3.7	79-3B	2		
2007	JAX	AA	21	187	20	13	1	6	20	7	26	0	1	-0.4	.281	.306	.466	.118	.256	.278	.450	.242	3.7	43-3B	8		
2008	LAN	MLB	22	642	62	35	2	15	76	39	108	4	3	-0.5	.255	.302	.395	-.139	.253	.300	.399	.236	3.2	150-3B	4		

Breakout: 45% Improve: 64% Collapse: 12% Attrition: 7%   Comparables: Scott Hodges, Brent Butler, Mike Robertson, Adam Lind

After a failed attempt to convert to second base and a horrific late-season stint at Double-A Jacksonville in 2006, this 2004 first-rounder returned to High-A as a third baseman. After a slow start, DeWitt hit his way back to Jacksonville by early July. Once there, he showed why scouts are enamored of his bat speed and smooth swing mechanics by hitting for average and decent power, but his ability to make consistent contact continues to hamper the development of his plate discipline. There's been a lot of water under the bridge since DeWitt was considered the best high school hitter in the draft, but he's young enough to still amount to something.

Andre Ethier — OF

Bats: L Throws: L Height: 6' 2" Weight: 210 Born: April 10, 1982 Age: 26

YEAR	TEAM	LVL	AGE	PA	R	2B	3B	HR	RBI	BB	SO	SB	CS	EqBRR	AVG	OBP	SLG	MLVr	EqAVG	EqOBP	EqSLG	EqA	VORP	DEFENSE			
2005	MID	AA	23	572	104	30	3	18	80	48	93	1	4	3.1	.319	.385	.497	.243	.273	.337	.431	.264	5.9	69-LF	3	46-RF	7
2006	LVG	AAA	24	103	15	4	3	1	12	14	16	2	1	0.2	.349	.447	.500	.296	.295	.388	.432	.287	4.3	20-RF	-1		
2006	LAN	MLB	24	441	50	20	7	11	55	34	77	5	5	0.9	.308	.365	.477	.162	.309	.367	.478	.287	19.1	99-LF	-6		
2007	LAN	MLB	25	505	50	32	2	13	64	46	68	0	4	-1.1	.284	.350	.452	.086	.279	.349	.455	.275	13.8	87-RF	2	34-LF	3
2008	LAN	MLB	26	493	64	27	2	14	64	45	81	4	2	0.2	.286	.354	.453	.051	.283	.351	.458	.274	16.6	116-RF	0		

Breakout: 17% Improve: 44% Collapse: 24% Attrition: 18%   Comparables: Lee Thomas, Terry Whitfield, Ryan Langerhans, Terrence Long

A belated diagnosis of acromioclavicular joint inflammation and rotator cuff damage might excuse both the September slump that took the shine off Ethier's otherwise stellar rookie season and his slow start in 2007, but the reality is that his rookie line was propped up by an unsustainable .347 BABIP and the drop to a league-average .293 took a bite out of his production. Furthermore, his seemingly improved walk rate was inflated by 12 intentional passes, ten while batting seventh or eighth. As a corner outfielder, Ethier isn't a tremendous asset at his current level of production, something Ned Colletti will undoubtedly be reminded of as he shops Ethier in the wake of the Andruw Jones signing. Ethier's cheap and just entering his prime—not thrilling, but nice, as Mel Brooks would say.

Rafael Furcal — SS

Bats: S Throws: R Height: 5' 9" Weight: 195 Born: October 24, 1977 Age: 30

YEAR	TEAM	LVL	AGE	PA	R	2B	3B	HR	RBI	BB	SO	SB	CS	EqBRR	AVG	OBP	SLG	MLVr	EqAVG	EqOBP	EqSLG	EqA	VORP	DEFENSE	
2005	ATL	MLB	27	689	100	31	11	12	58	62	78	46	10	6.5	.284	.348	.429	.065	.283	.349	.436	.278	42.5	147-SS	23
2006	LAN	MLB	28	736	113	32	9	15	63	73	98	37	13	-0.6	.300	.369	.445	.115	.299	.371	.444	.283	46.9	153-SS	6
2007	LAN	MLB	29	642	87	23	4	6	47	55	68	25	6	4.6	.270	.333	.355	-.090	.272	.339	.360	.252	11.8	135-SS	17
2008	LAN	MLB	30	613	87	25	5	8	53	58	71	25	6	2.0	.280	.350	.389	-.045	.278	.347	.393	.262	23.8	143-SS	8

Breakout: 9% Improve: 32% Collapse: 31% Attrition: 16%   Comparables: Omar Vizquel, Tony Fernandez, Harold Reynolds, Maury Wills

A late-March ankle sprain cost Furcal the first nine games of the season and was still a factor in September, when he was further hampered by a bulging disc. He hit just .205/.253/.250 in those bookend months while playing in about half of the Dodgers' games. During the other four months of the season, he hit .290/.356/.387—still well short of his recent power production—and didn't homer until June 17. Entering the final year of his contract, Furcal will earn $13 million plus a $4 million balloon payment. If healthy, he can produce enough to be worth the money, but with Chin-Lung Hu apparently ready, the Dodgers find themselves blocking another prospect at great expense.

Nomar Garciaparra — 3B/1B

Bats: R Throws: R Height: 6' 0" Weight: 190 Born: July 23, 1973 Age: 34

YEAR	TEAM	LVL	AGE	PA	R	2B	3B	HR	RBI	BB	SO	SB	CS	EqBRR	AVG	OBP	SLG	MLVr	EqAVG	EqOBP	EqSLG	EqA	VORP	DEFENSE			
2005	CHN	MLB	31	247	28	12	0	9	30	12	24	0	0	-0.2	.283	.320	.452	.044	.275	.315	.441	.260	8.8	33-3B	-5	23-SS	-4
2006	LAN	MLB	32	523	82	31	2	20	93	42	30	3	0	-1.6	.303	.367	.505	.199	.299	.364	.502	.295	27.6	114-1B	-8		
2007	LAN	MLB	33	466	39	17	0	7	59	31	41	3	1	-0.7	.283	.328	.371	-.067	.283	.333	.376	.250	0.8	64-1B	-7	40-3B	-6
2008	LAN	MLB	34	388	45	19	1	8	48	27	35	3	1	-0.5	.283	.337	.411	-.037	.281	.334	.415	.256	7.8	93-1B	-5		

Breakout: 7% Improve: 29% Collapse: 45% Attrition: 26% Comparables: Bill Madlock, Vic Power, Frank Malzone, Ray Knight

Sentimentality and damage control over the loss of J. D. Drew prompted Garciaparra's two-year, $18.5 million return to L.A., but like most sequels, *Nomar in Dodger Blue 2: Replacement-Level Boogaloo* wound up more costly and less compelling than the original. After blocking James Loney at first base for three months, Garciaparra was shifted to third, where he was a defensive liability, hastened the exit of the capable Wilson Betemit, and prevented Andy LaRoche from getting a big-league foothold. Worse, though he avoided the DL until a mid-August calf injury, Garciaparra hit as though something wasn't right all year, his power drastically reduced but his reputation for clutch goodness upheld by a .373/.443/.436 performance with runners in scoring position. A smart GM might have eaten half of Garciaparra's 2008 salary and returned him to the AL to DH, but on Ned Colletti's team he enters 2008 still blocking LaRoche.

Luis Gonzalez — LF

Bats: L Throws: R Height: 6' 2" Weight: 210 Born: September 3, 1967 Age: 40

YEAR	TEAM	LVL	AGE	PA	R	2B	3B	HR	RBI	BB	SO	SB	CS	EqBRR	AVG	OBP	SLG	MLVr	EqAVG	EqOBP	EqSLG	EqA	VORP	DEFENSE	
2005	ARI	MLB	37	672	90	37	0	24	79	78	90	4	1	-3.5	.271	.366	.459	.117	.261	.358	.450	.281	26.5	147-LF	1
2006	ARI	MLB	38	668	93	52	2	15	73	69	58	0	1	2.0	.271	.352	.444	.040	.262	.344	.430	.269	11.3	146-LF	-1
2007	LAN	MLB	39	526	70	23	2	15	68	56	56	6	2	-0.2	.278	.359	.433	.069	.278	.362	.443	.279	16.1	111-LF	-1
2008	LAN	MLB	40	349	42	16	1	8	41	37	39	4	1	-0.4	.262	.342	.399	-.060	.260	.339	.403	.257	3.6	84-LF	-2

Breakout: 3% Improve: 35% Collapse: 41% Attrition: 32% Comparables: B. J. Surhoff, Jeff Conine, Wade Boggs, Carl Yastrzemski

Luis Gonzalez was symbolic of the 2007 Dodgers' season. Despite his history with the Diamondbacks, Gonzalez's problematic defense and fading power—the latter slightly obscured by Chase Field's friendly hitting environment—made him easy to dismiss once the burgeoning youth brigade took hold in Arizona. The Dodgers, possessed of a youth brigade of their own, preferred to add Gonzalez's veteran herbs and spices to their recipe via a one-year, $7.35 million contract. His arrival displaced Andre Ethier in left field, which in turn forestalled the arrival of Matt Kemp, but those problems were masked as Gonzo hit a robust .294/.384/.471 while helping the Dodgers assemble the league's best first-half record. However, both Gonzalez (.251/.316/.368) and the team faded in the second half as the youthful D'backs sprinted to the division title. Meanwhile, Gonzalez had the gall to complain about losing playing time to Ethier, apparently unaware that his value has all but dried up.

Chin-Lung Hu — SS

Bats: R Throws: R Height: 5' 11" Weight: 190 Born: February 2, 1984 Age: 24

YEAR	TEAM	LVL	AGE	PA	R	2B	3B	HR	RBI	BB	SO	SB	CS	EqBRR	AVG	OBP	SLG	MLVr	EqAVG	EqOBP	EqSLG	EqA	VORP	DEFENSE			
2005	VRO	A+	21	505	80	29	1	8	56	19	40	23	6	1.2	.313	.347	.430	.110	.263	.295	.366	.233	1.2	114-SS	14		
2006	JAX	AA	22	556	71	20	2	5	34	49	63	11	5	1.0	.254	.326	.334	-.011	.238	.303	.329	.225	-6.7	119-SS	-1		
2007	JAX	AA	23	356	56	30	5	6	34	26	33	12	4	1.6	.329	.380	.508	.332	.296	.341	.477	.279	27.7	77-SS	6		
2007	LVG	AAA	23	200	33	10	1	8	28	6	18	3	4	-1.3	.318	.337	.505	.063	.271	.291	.432	.241	5.4	26-SS	-1	17-2B	3
2007	LAN	MLB	23	31	5	0	1	2	5	0	8	0	0	1.0	.241	.241	.517	-.044	.233	.233	.500	.241	0.7				
2008	LAN	MLB	24	609	72	33	3	11	64	34	70	12	4	1.5	.274	.319	.403	-.085	.272	.316	.407	.247	17.1	142-SS	4		

Breakout: 25% Improve: 51% Collapse: 22% Attrition: 12% Comparables: Angel Berroa, Carlos Garcia, Eddy Diaz, Jose Ortiz

Already considered the best defensive shortstop in the minors, this Taiwanese pixie broke out with the bat in 2007 thanks to a more aggressive approach at the plate. After he lit up Southern League pitching and won MVP honors in the Futures Game, Hu's hit parade continued in Las Vegas. The question is whether that performance, comprised of a repeat-level improvement and an altitude-driven showing, was real or a fluke. The power may be illusory, but Hu has the bat speed and hand-eye coordination to sustain a .300 average with lots of doubles and few walks or strikeouts, giving the Dodgers a dirt-cheap, major league–ready shortstop to replace Furcal possibly as soon as the trading deadline.

Matt Kemp — OF

Bats: R Throws: R Height: 6' 2" Weight: 230 Born: September 23, 1984 Age: 23

YEAR	TEAM	LVL	AGE	PA	R	2B	3B	HR	RBI	BB	SO	SB	CS	EqBRR	AVG	OBP	SLG	MLVr	EqAVG	EqOBP	EqSLG	EqA	VORP	DEFENSE			
2005	VRO	A+	20	454	76	21	4	27	90	25	92	23	6	0.8	.306	.349	.569	.292	.251	.290	.461	.255	9.4	66-CF	-2	34-RF	-2
2006	JAX	AA	21	224	38	15	2	7	34	20	38	11	2	-1.3	.327	.402	.528	.403	.312	.379	.540	.308	24.0	44-CF	2		
2006	LVG	AAA	21	202	37	14	6	3	36	17	26	14	3	1.1	.368	.428	.560	.371	.319	.376	.497	.298	17.9	36-CF	3		
2006	LAN	MLB	21	166	30	7	1	7	23	9	53	6	0	2.0	.253	.289	.448	-.053	.248	.289	.438	.256	3.2	20-CF	-6		
2007	LVG	AAA	22	174	32	16	3	4	20	10	26	9	2	2.7	.329	.374	.540	.186	.284	.331	.469	.276	4.6	18-RF	4	18-CF	0
2007	LAN	MLB	22	311	47	12	5	10	42	16	66	10	5	-0.5	.342	.373	.521	.271	.345	.379	.541	.304	23.4	69-RF	-4		
2008	LAN	MLB	23	489	73	28	4	19	71	34	96	17	5	1.5	.296	.349	.505	.123	.294	.346	.510	.287	27.2	116-RF	-1		

Breakout: 18% Improve: 49% Collapse: 29% Attrition: 15%   Comparables: Derek Bell, Todd Hollandsworth, Pedro Muñoz, Corey Hart

No player represents the disconnect between the tremendous assets the Dodgers control and their willingness to utilize them better than Kemp, whom PECOTA showed as having significantly more upside than any under-25 center fielder besides Grady Sizemore and Chris Young a year ago. The Dodgers could be forgiven for wanting Kemp to start the year in Triple-A after he hit just .202/.233/.275 following his seven-homers-in-15-games debut in 2006. Instead, they blocked him in center with Juan Pierre and squeezed him into a right field job-share. They then let him languish in Las Vegas for six extra weeks after rehabbing an early-season shoulder injury. (Kemp "mildly" separated his right shoulder by colliding with the Plexiglas scoreboard the Dodgers brilliantly had installed on the right field wall in place of padding.) After he returned, Kemp posted the second-best MLVr on the team, but still couldn't shake the part-time role. Kemp's game lacks polish, but he drew disproportionate criticism as the team collapsed in the second half. The flashpoint of a Jeff Kent outburst, he's become potential trade fodder in Ned Colletti's cringeworthy quest to acquire veteran moxie at the expense of blue-chip talent, and has been further blocked from his natural position by the Andruw Jones signing. A great deal about the future of this team can be learned simply from whether or not he's still a Dodger when you read this.

Jeff Kent — 2B

Bats: R Throws: R Height: 6' 2" Weight: 210 Born: March 7, 1968 Age: 40

YEAR	TEAM	LVL	AGE	PA	R	2B	3B	HR	RBI	BB	SO	SB	CS	EqBRR	AVG	OBP	SLG	MLVr	EqAVG	EqOBP	EqSLG	EqA	VORP	DEFENSE	
2005	LAN	MLB	37	637	100	36	0	29	105	72	85	6	2	1.1	.289	.377	.512	.242	.290	.377	.522	.303	52.5	137-2B	-6
2006	LAN	MLB	38	473	61	27	3	14	68	55	69	1	2	-2.4	.292	.385	.477	.179	.291	.383	.473	.295	32.8	99-2B	10
2007	LAN	MLB	39	562	78	36	1	20	79	57	61	1	3	-1.4	.302	.375	.500	.208	.301	.377	.511	.299	40.3	121-2B	-9
2008	LAN	MLB	40	443	60	26	1	17	69	48	54	3	2	-1.0	.287	.368	.493	.130	.285	.365	.498	.289	32.1	105-2B	-2

Breakout: 9% Improve: 36% Collapse: 29% Attrition: 16%   Comparables: Cal Ripken, Moises Alou, Jeff Conine, Graig Nettles

Even at 39, Kent remained a force to be reckoned with in 2007, finishing second among all second basemen in MLVr, and second among Dodger hitters in VORP. Unlike 2006 he avoided the DL, though a hamstring strain at the end of July cooled him off from an especially torrid streak (.447/.500/.737 that month). The only knock on his season was his exposure of the team's age-based clubhouse rift by criticizing the professionalism of some of the team's youngsters, which, in turn, raised the ugly memory of Kent's 2005 feud with Milton Bradley. No, he won't make your list of Historical Figures You'd Invite to Dinner, but his ticket to Cooperstown is increasingly validated with every passing season, and at $9 million he's a bargain if he can approach his 2007 production.

Andy LaRoche — 3B

Bats: R Throws: R Height: 6' 1" Weight: 215 Born: September 13, 1983 Age: 24

YEAR	TEAM	LVL	AGE	PA	R	2B	3B	HR	RBI	BB	SO	SB	CS	EqBRR	AVG	OBP	SLG	MLVr	EqAVG	EqOBP	EqSLG	EqA	VORP	DEFENSE	
2005	VRO	A+	21	271	54	14	1	21	51	19	38	6	1	2.8	.333	.380	.651	.469	.278	.321	.532	.283	23.0	55-3B	-3
2005	JAX	AA	21	264	41	12	0	9	43	32	54	2	2	-0.8	.273	.367	.445	.150	.240	.322	.408	.252	5.7	58-3B	-3
2006	JAX	AA	22	277	42	13	0	9	46	41	32	6	3	-0.9	.309	.419	.483	.348	.298	.397	.489	.304	28.0	60-3B	4
2006	LVG	AAA	22	230	35	14	1	10	35	32	32	3	2	-2.8	.322	.400	.550	.267	.283	.357	.502	.288	18.7	52-3B	5
2007	LVG	AAA	23	311	55	18	1	18	48	39	42	2	2	0.8	.309	.399	.589	.271	.269	.357	.504	.290	23.9	64-3B	1
2007	LAN	MLB	23	115	16	5	0	1	10	20	24	2	1	0.8	.226	.365	.312	-.111	.217	.365	.293	.250	-0.8	27-3B	0
2008	LAN	MLB	24	463	66	23	1	19	67	51	76	5	2	0.2	.280	.364	.485	.105	.277	.362	.490	.286	25.6	110-3B	3

Breakout: 20% Improve: 54% Collapse: 11% Attrition: 11%   Comparables: Denis Menke, Dwight Evans, Ron Swoboda, Darnell Coles

A staple of our recent top prospect lists, LaRoche rode a roller coaster in 2007. Coming off surgery to repair a torn labrum in his left shoulder, he hit just .235/.309/.367 at Las Vegas before being recalled to replace the benched

Wilson Betemit in early May. Batting seventh or eighth, LaRoche had little chance to show what he could do, as he was frequently pitched around; within a couple of weeks, the team turned to Tony Abreu. Back in Vegas, LaRoche bopped 12 homers in July, but was sidelined by shoulder and back problems and thus missed his opening when Nomar Garciaparra hit the DL in August, an injury that delayed LaRoche's return until September. LaRoche profiles as a genuine blue-chipper with a great batting eye, 20-plus–homer power, and solid defense, but the Dodgers keep throwing obstacles in his path. It would surprise no one if he were in a different organization by the time you read this.

Mike Lieberthal   C   Bats: R   Throws: R   Height: 6' 0"   Weight: 195   Born: January 18, 1972   Age: 36

YEAR	TEAM	LVL	AGE	PA	R	2B	3B	HR	RBI	BB	SO	SB	CS	EqBRR	AVG	OBP	SLG	MLVr	EqAVG	EqOBP	EqSLG	EqA	VORP	DEFENSE	
2005	PHI	MLB	33	443	48	25	0	12	47	35	35	0	0	-1.3	.263	.336	.418	.011	.253	.327	.416	.259	16.1	113-C	-4
2006	PHI	MLB	34	230	22	14	0	9	36	8	19	0	0	-2.1	.273	.316	.469	.025	.269	.311	.458	.261	7.1	54-C	7
2007	LAN	MLB	35	82	6	2	0	1	4	4	11	0	0	-0.2	.234	.280	.260	-.346	.234	.280	.260	.185	-3.6	19-C	0
2008	LAN	MLB	36	97	8	4	0	2	10	5	11	0	0	-0.3	.247	.295	.353	-.216	.245	.292	.357	.219	0.0	27-C	1

Breakout: 11% Improve: 26% Collapse: 50% Attrition: 48%   Comparables: John Flaherty, Clyde McCullough, Del Crandall, Ray Murray

Like Randy Wolf, Lieberthal departed Philadelphia as a free agent to sign a one-year deal with his hometown team. Unlike his phellow Phil, Lieberthal stayed healthy in 2007. His problem was Energizer Bunny Russell Martin, whose 143 starts left Lieberthal with just 17, including just four between July 3 and September 5. It couldn't have helped the backup's cause that the team went just 3-14 in those starts, no doubt due in part to the cobwebs that had accumulated on Lieberthal's bat. On the other hand, a year away from the grind may have helped Lieberthal's assorted owies heal. A career .310/.381/.510 hitter against lefties, he could contribute to a team with a less durable backstop.

James Loney   1B   Bats: L   Throws: L   Height: 6' 3"   Weight: 220   Born: May 7, 1984   Age: 24

YEAR	TEAM	LVL	AGE	PA	R	2B	3B	HR	RBI	BB	SO	SB	CS	EqBRR	AVG	OBP	SLG	MLVr	EqAVG	EqOBP	EqSLG	EqA	VORP	DEFENSE			
2005	JAX	AA	21	572	74	31	2	11	65	59	87	1	4	-1.6	.284	.357	.419	.107	.245	.309	.379	.239	-12.4	130-1B	10		
2006	LVG	AAA	22	406	64	33	2	8	67	32	34	9	5	2.0	.380	.426	.546	.363	.330	.374	.484	.293	27.9	77-1B	4		
2006	LAN	MLB	22	111	20	6	5	4	18	8	10	1	0	0.6	.284	.342	.559	.209	.284	.342	.569	.299	6.5	25-1B	-4		
2007	LVG	AAA	23	261	28	19	1	1	32	25	48	2	1	-2.4	.279	.345	.382	-.129	.235	.303	.329	.224	-11.3	33-1B	1	22-RF	2
2007	LAN	MLB	23	375	41	18	4	15	67	28	48	0	1	-0.8	.331	.381	.538	.295	.327	.381	.547	.310	30.7	87-1B	-5		
2008	LAN	MLB	24	624	81	37	3	18	84	54	89	6	3	0.1	.290	.353	.461	.065	.287	.350	.466	.275	21.9	146-1B	1		

Breakout: 28% Improve: 53% Collapse: 13% Attrition: 7%   Comparables: Chris Chambliss, Jim Spencer, Gus Bell, Tony Horton

Instead of Kemp, it was Loney who began 2007 in Triple-A. Blocked by the PR-driven return of Nomar Garciaparra at first base and squeezed out of the already congested right field situation in spring training, Loney languished in Las Vegas until an early-June Garciaparra slump necessitated his recall. Loney had already shown himself ready to take over the first base job in 2006, and responded to his recall by hitting .440 through the end of the month to push Nomar across the diamond; he never relinquished his hold on the position. At the plate, Loney's trademark is excellent plate coverage. While his overall power numbers took a step forward in 2007, the reality was more feast or famine; in June and September he slugged over .700, in July and August less than .400. Afield, Loney impressed some observers, but neither his Davenport numbers nor ones from alternative defensive metrics such as Revised Zone Rating backed those observations. Still, the first base job is now his, and, while he probably won't beat his 90th percentile PECOTA projection again, he'll hit well enough to be an asset.

Russell Martin   C   Bats: R   Throws: R   Height: 5' 10"   Weight: 210   Born: February 15, 1983   Age: 25

YEAR	TEAM	LVL	AGE	PA	R	2B	3B	HR	RBI	BB	SO	SB	CS	EqBRR	AVG	OBP	SLG	MLVr	EqAVG	EqOBP	EqSLG	EqA	VORP	DEFENSE	
2005	JAX	AA	22	505	83	17	1	9	61	78	69	15	7	-1.1	.311	.430	.423	.248	.270	.377	.378	.272	21.3	112-C	1
2006	LVG	AAA	23	91	14	9	0	0	9	13	11	0	2	0.4	.297	.389	.419	.056	.263	.352	.355	.252	1.7	22-C	4
2006	LAN	MLB	23	468	65	26	4	10	65	45	57	10	5	0.3	.282	.355	.436	.062	.280	.355	.435	.274	18.5	113-C	6
2007	LAN	MLB	24	620	87	32	3	19	87	67	89	21	9	-2.2	.293	.374	.469	.155	.296	.380	.486	.294	46.1	140-C	9
2008	LAN	MLB	25	514	75	26	2	13	63	57	75	14	4	0.5	.284	.370	.439	.058	.282	.367	.444	.280	29.9	121-C	7

Breakout: 14% Improve: 44% Collapse: 19% Attrition: 17%   Comparables: Thurman Munson, Craig Biggio, Ray Fosse, Todd Zeile

Martin took another great leap forward last year, improving his power, plate discipline, and defense on the way to leading NL catchers in VORP, WARP, and caught-stealing percentage and winning a Gold Glove. He was almost too good, as his 1,254 innings behind the plate—a single-season total surpassed only by Jason Kendall in the past decade—likely led to a .259/.330/.395 September slump. Durable as Martin may be, former catcher Grady Little should have eased off the throttle. Joe Torre's shown a decent ability to modulate Jorge Posada's usage to avoid late-season burnout; expect him to take a stronger hand here, and for Martin to spend the next few years battling Brian McCann for the title of the league's best catcher. PECOTA likes McCann more based on his body type, power, and ability to hit for average, but Martin's speed, defense, and durability ain't hay, and he's out-WARPed his Atlanta rival by two wins over the past two years.

Preston Mattingly   **2B**   Bats: R   Throws: R   Height: 6' 3"   Weight: 205   Born: August 28, 1987   Age: 20

YEAR	TEAM	LVL	AGE	PA	R	2B	3B	HR	RBI	BB	SO	SB	CS	EqBRR	AVG	OBP	SLG	MLVr	EqAVG	EqOBP	EqSLG	EqA	VORP	DEFENSE
2006	DGR	Rk	18	199	22	12	3	1	29	9	39	12	3	2.2	.290	.322	.403	.126	.226	.250	.332	.205	-21.8	30-SS -9
2007	GRL	A	19	437	42	12	7	3	40	22	119	11	3	0.0	.210	.251	.297	-.218	.176	.211	.251	.154	-49.1	72-2B -11 17-SS -12
2008	LAN	MLB	20	510	41	23	3	6	39	25	137	12	5	0.9	.207	.248	.303	-.393	.205	.246	.306	.184	-21.8	120-2B -14

Breakout: 52% Improve: 70% Collapse: 18% Attrition: 6%   Comparables: Ian Desmond, Dave Kelton, Damian Rolls, Tim Lemon

Finding out that Preston Mattingly isn't a shortstop (.773 fielding percentage in 18 games there last year) wasn't a big surprise to anyone in the Dodgers organization. Finding out that he isn't much of a hitter, either, was. The spitting image of his dad, the new Dodger hitting coach, but significantly bigger, Mattingly was a first-round pick in 2006 because of his bat. In his first full professional season, that bat, which produced a ridiculously pathetic .157/.204/.196 line after the All-Star break, was nowhere to be found.

Lucas May   **C**   Bats: R   Throws: R   Height: 6' 0"   Weight: 190   Born: October 24, 1984   Age: 23

YEAR	TEAM	LVL	AGE	PA	R	2B	3B	HR	RBI	BB	SO	SB	CS	EqBRR	AVG	OBP	SLG	MLVr	EqAVG	EqOBP	EqSLG	EqA	VORP	DEFENSE
2005	CGA	A	20	416	46	14	2	9	53	16	92	5	2	0.7	.229	.267	.345	-.173	.180	.207	.261	.150	-42.6	46-SS -8 25-LF -3
2006	CGA	A	21	497	76	27	9	18	82	35	130	14	2	1.9	.273	.332	.493	.199	.220	.266	.393	.228	-25.2	48-LF -4 34-RF -3
2007	SBR	A+	22	554	81	25	3	25	89	36	107	5	7	-5.1	.256	.313	.465	.044	.210	.256	.366	.210	-19.9	76-C -6
2008	LAN	MLB	23	566	49	26	2	15	64	31	143	7	3	0.1	.218	.267	.361	-.274	.217	.265	.365	.211	-12.8	133-C -4

Breakout: 35% Improve: 52% Collapse: 27% Attrition: 11%   Comparables: Giuseppe Chiaramonte, Matt Carson, Dustan Mohr, Bryan Bogle

In the grand tradition of Joe Ferguson and Russell Martin, the Dodgers have attempted to make a catcher out of the strong-armed May, who was drafted in 2003 as a shortstop, then shifted to the outfield in 2005 before donning the tools of ignorance last year. Behind the plate, May's a work in progress; he threw out 30 percent of runners but was charged with 31 passed balls (!) in 78 games. At the plate, he has power when he connects, but contact and strike zone judgment are not-so-trivial problems he'll have to overcome.

Xavier Paul   **OF**   Bats: L   Throws: R   Height: 6' 0"   Weight: 200   Born: February 25, 1985   Age: 23

YEAR	TEAM	LVL	AGE	PA	R	2B	3B	HR	RBI	BB	SO	SB	CS	EqBRR	AVG	OBP	SLG	MLVr	EqAVG	EqOBP	EqSLG	EqA	VORP	DEFENSE
2005	VRO	A+	20	330	42	15	3	7	41	32	81	1	5	-4.4	.247	.328	.392	-.015	.207	.278	.332	.210	-24.7	53-LF -2
2006	VRO	A+	21	520	62	23	3	13	49	38	114	22	15	0.0	.285	.343	.430	.103	.244	.295	.380	.232	-18.7	114-RF -14
2007	JAX	AA	22	482	64	21	2	11	50	48	112	17	9	-1.6	.291	.366	.429	.165	.254	.322	.386	.248	3.5	95-CF -6
2008	LAN	MLB	23	542	63	26	2	12	59	46	136	16	7	1.2	.250	.318	.388	-.125	.248	.315	.392	.243	2.3	127-CF -2

Breakout: 29% Improve: 61% Collapse: 18% Attrition: 5%   Comparables: Richard Brown, Jacob Cruz, Jon Saffer, Brandon Jones

Once thought to be among the team's top ten prospects, this toolsy 2003 fourth-rounder is only now rebounding from his stock's slippage. Relentless tinkering with his swing caused him to struggle at Vero Beach, but he made solid gains upon repeating the level, and barely missed a beat when adapting from that hitter-friendly environment to pitcher-friendly Jacksonville. Though his power remains a work in progress, Paul's plate discipline improved dramatically, from one unintentional walk every 15.3 plate appearances in 2006 to one every 10.3 in 2007. Defensively, he combines above-average speed with the strongest arm in the system, tools he'll need so long as his bat isn't up to carrying a corner spot.

Juan Pierre — CF

Bats: L Throws: L Height: 5' 11" Weight: 180 Born: August 14, 1977 Age: 30

YEAR	TEAM	LVL	AGE	PA	R	2B	3B	HR	RBI	BB	SO	SB	CS	EqBRR	AVG	OBP	SLG	MLVr	EqAVG	EqOBP	EqSLG	EqA	VORP	DEFENSE
2005	FLO	MLB	27	718	96	19	13	2	47	41	45	57	17	10.4	.276	.326	.354	-.059	.285	.336	.372	.256	12.9	155-CF -20
2006	CHN	MLB	28	750	87	32	13	3	40	32	38	58	20	4.5	.292	.330	.388	-.051	.290	.329	.388	.254	18.0	161-CF -12
2007	LAN	MLB	29	729	96	24	8	0	41	33	37	64	15	11.6	.293	.331	.353	-.080	.300	.340	.363	.256	16.2	158-CF -17
2008	LAN	MLB	30	607	83	23	7	0	43	32	34	37	10	3.3	.290	.332	.357	-.115	.287	.330	.360	.247	7.7	142-CF -9

Breakout: 9% Improve: 32% Collapse: 28% Attrition: 16% Comparables: Lance Johnson, Luis Polonia, Tony Womack, Eric Owens

If Pierre's five-year, $44 million deal wasn't the worst contract in the history of history, it still ranks among the dumbest of last winter given the Dodgers' possession of a leadoff hitter (Rafael Furcal) and a highly regarded and nearly ready center-field prospect (Matt Kemp). Ned Colletti could have done less harm by donating Pierre's salary to the Baby Harp Seal Clubbers of North America than by making a needlessly lengthy investment in a liability at the plate and afield whose sole asset, his speed, is sure to decline now that he's on the wrong side of 30. As bad as Pierre was, his season would have looked worse if not for a strong final two months (.277/.312/.330 through July, .325/.369/.399 thereafter), and even that was all batting average. The Andruw Jones signing won't mitigate this mistake; shunting Pierre to left field raises the offensive bar even further above Pierre's head while stealing still more playing time from less expensive and more able hitters and fielders. Put simply, Pierre's an impediment to winning, and Colletti needs to sink this cost before the task falls to his successor.

Anthony Raglani — OF

Bats: L Throws: L Height: 6' 2" Weight: 215 Born: April 6, 1983 Age: 25

YEAR	TEAM	LVL	AGE	PA	R	2B	3B	HR	RBI	BB	SO	SB	CS	EqBRR	AVG	OBP	SLG	MLVr	EqAVG	EqOBP	EqSLG	EqA	VORP	DEFENSE	
2005	VRO	A+	22	491	82	20	5	19	77	60	98	9	2	1.7	.289	.383	.496	.226	.236	.320	.403	.253	-8.6	54-LF 0	47-RF -1
2006	VRO	A+	23	74	10	4	1	1	7	10	10	0	1	-0.5	.317	.419	.460	.271	.277	.373	.415	.273	1.9	13-LF -1	
2006	JAX	AA	23	386	49	25	0	9	40	44	88	6	2	1.1	.244	.339	.399	.084	.236	.321	.408	.254	-5.4	56-LF -1	31-RF -2
2007	JAX	AA	24	545	76	24	5	21	68	85	139	9	7	-6.0	.248	.369	.461	.175	.229	.338	.427	.264	0.1	126-LF 4	
2008	LAN	MLB	25	550	70	27	2	19	72	68	138	8	3	0.2	.245	.343	.431	-.029	.243	.340	.436	.265	9.2	129-LF -3	

Breakout: 33% Improve: 59% Collapse: 18% Attrition: 10% Comparables: Ryan Langerhans, Jason Cooper, Tracy Sanders, John Jensen

Raglani has joined the ranks of the Three True Outcomes heroes, as 45 percent of his plate appearances ended in a homer, walk, or strikeout in 2007. Repeating at Jacksonville, Raglani rediscovered the power he'd shown in 2005 while upping his walk rate. Alas, the flip side of his newfound patience was his increased strikeout rate and its impact on his batting average, though some of the latter may be due to Jacksonville's pitcher-friendly park (Raglani hit .222/.330/.413 at home and .273/.406/.506 on the road). With little speed and average defense, he'll go only as far as his bat will take him.

Mark Sweeney — PH

Bats: L Throws: L Height: 6' 1" Weight: 215 Born: October 26, 1969 Age: 38

YEAR	TEAM	LVL	AGE	PA	R	2B	3B	HR	RBI	BB	SO	SB	CS	EqBRR	AVG	OBP	SLG	MLVr	EqAVG	EqOBP	EqSLG	EqA	VORP	DEFENSE	
2005	SDN	MLB	35	267	31	12	1	8	40	40	58	4	0	0.1	.294	.395	.466	.228	.305	.404	.491	.313	19.5	38-1B -1	
2006	SFN	MLB	36	291	32	15	2	5	37	28	50	0	1	-2.8	.251	.330	.382	-.077	.248	.328	.376	.247	-2.9	45-1B 4	13-LF -2
2007	SFN	MLB	37	107	18	8	0	2	10	13	18	2	0	0.9	.256	.368	.411	.027	.256	.374	.422	.283	4.0		
2007	LAN	MLB	37	34	2	1	0	0	3	1	11	0	0	0.1	.273	.294	.303	-.238	.273	.294	.303	.206	-0.8		
2008	LAN	MLB	38	80	10	4	0	2	10	8	15	1	0	-0.1	.256	.339	.415	-.048	.254	.336	.419	.259	2.3	24-DH	

Breakout: 14% Improve: 34% Collapse: 44% Attrition: 49% Comparables: Wally Joyner, Tim McCarver, George Crowe, Elmer Valo

From being implicated in Barry Bonds's failed amphetamine test, to witnessing Bonds' 756th homer, to climbing past Smoky Burgess and Manny Mota into second on the all-time pinch-hit list, to being catapulted into a playoff hunt and making a crucial, game-ending baserunning mistake, it certainly was an eventful year for Sweeney. With 163 career pinch hits, Sweeney's unlikely to catch Lenny Harris' record 212, but because of his career .271/.364/.404 line in that role, he'll find work.

Wilson Valdez — INF

Bats: R   Throws: R   Height: 5' 11"   Weight: 160   Born: May 20, 1978   Age: 30

YEAR	TEAM	LVL	AGE	PA	R	2B	3B	HR	RBI	BB	SO	SB	CS	EqBRR	AVG	OBP	SLG	MLVr	EqAVG	EqOBP	EqSLG	EqA	VORP	DEFENSE			
2005	POR	AAA	27	175	14	5	3	1	15	15	27	8	0	1.9	.245	.310	.335	-.221	.214	.272	.289	.208	-8.2	43-SS	1		
2005	SEA	MLB	27	133	9	5	1	0	8	6	25	2	2	-0.6	.198	.235	.254	-.442	.210	.258	.266	.176	-9.3	39-SS	-3		
2006	LVG	AAA	28	599	94	24	1	6	53	56	52	26	17	-1.4	.297	.366	.381	-.033	.257	.323	.331	.232	1.4	112-SS	3		
2007	LAN	MLB	29	80	12	2	1	0	7	4	12	1	0	2.2	.216	.263	.270	-.364	.216	.262	.270	.189	-4.3				
2007	LVG	AAA	29	411	81	19	1	4	29	43	34	14	6	3.3	.343	.413	.435	.116	.293	.364	.373	.264	18.3	58-SS	-2	12-2B	0
2008	LAN	MLB	30	501	60	18	2	3	38	45	57	14	5	1.7	.262	.331	.331	-.170	.259	.328	.335	.235	3.5	118-SS	1		

Breakout: 24% Improve: 46% Collapse: 24% Attrition: 23%   Comparables: Jose Mota, Andy Stankiewicz, Ivan DeJesus Sr., Johnny Paredes

A smaller mystery of the Colletti regime is the Dodgers' fascination with this particular futilityman. Yes, he's a speedy slap-hitter who's developed a bit of plate discipline, but 28-year-olds in Triple-A are organizational fodder, not 40-man roster material. Still, the Dodgers protected him after the 2006 season, and their man-crush blossomed when he tore up the Grapefruit League last spring. Valdez made the club when Rafael Furcal began the year on the DL, but, surprise, he didn't rediscover his spring mojo until returning to Las Vegas. He clung to the 40-man like a barnacle until Colletti sold him to the Kia Tigers in South Korea. Yeah, that was worth losing Wesley Wright in the Rule 5 draft.

Delwyn Young — OF

Bats: S   Throws: R   Height: 5' 10"   Weight: 210   Born: June 30, 1982   Age: 26

YEAR	TEAM	LVL	AGE	PA	R	2B	3B	HR	RBI	BB	SO	SB	CS	EqBRR	AVG	OBP	SLG	MLVr	EqAVG	EqOBP	EqSLG	EqA	VORP	DEFENSE			
2005	JAX	AA	23	406	52	25	1	16	62	27	86	1	3	-2.6	.296	.346	.499	.215	.259	.300	.450	.253	11.9	88-2B	-14		
2005	LVG	AAA	23	170	23	12	0	4	14	8	35	0	0	0.8	.325	.361	.475	.056	.272	.306	.389	.239	1.9	36-2B	3		
2006	LVG	AAA	24	583	76	42	1	18	98	42	104	3	4	-1.0	.273	.326	.457	-.015	.240	.290	.410	.239	-14.2	89-RF	-9	34-LF	-6
2007	LVG	AAA	25	537	107	54	5	17	97	38	105	4	3	-0.5	.337	.384	.571	.254	.287	.335	.492	.279	18.8	52-LF	-6	51-RF	-3
2007	LAN	MLB	25	36	4	1	1	2	3	2	5	1	0	0.2	.382	.417	.647	.569	.382	.417	.647	.349	5.8				
2008	LAN	MLB	26	558	64	33	2	19	81	36	118	5	2	0.1	.268	.318	.451	-.026	.266	.316	.456	.258	11.2	131-RF	-3		

Breakout: 15% Improve: 42% Collapse: 21% Attrition: 18%   Comparables: Roosevelt Brown, Jeff Baker, Todd Benzinger, Keith Williams

This stocky hacker did nothing but paste the ball during his third go-round in Las Vegas, setting a modern PCL record for doubles and offering hope that he may yet avoid a Quadruple-A fate. Most notably, he pounded lefties to a .365/.405/.609 tune after hitting just .198/.235/.325 against them in 2006 and made a strong showing during his brief taste of action with the Dodgers. Slow, unathletic, and lacking in versatility, Young is a less-than-ideal candidate for the bench; his best-case scenario involves a trade to an AL club for whom he can DH.

PITCHERS

James Adkins

Bats: L   Throws: L   Height: 6' 5"   Weight: 195   Born: November 26, 1985   Age: 22

YEAR	TEAM	LVL	AGE	W	L	SV	G	GS	IP	H	BB	SO	HR	GB%	BABIP	STUFF	WHIP	ERA	PERA	EqERA	EqH9	EqBB9	EqSO9	EqHR9	VORP	SN/WX
2007	GRL	A	21	0	1	0	11	11	26	17	10	30	1	60.9%	.254	0	1.04	2.42	5.12	4.63	7.3	6.6	5.4	1.2	2.5	—
2008	LAN	MLB	22	5	8	0	28	18	104	111	85	78	13	52.3%	.308	-8	1.89	5.90	6.50	6.17	9.3	6.5	5.9	1.1	-5.3	0.10

Breakout: 3% Improve: 13% Collapse: 54% Attrition: 16%   Comparables: C. J. Nitkowski, Nate Bump, Joshua Sullivan, Darrin Paxton

As if attempting to prove that they scout more than just high-ceiling high school arms, the Dodgers spent a 2007 supplemental first-round pick on Atkins, your classic polished college left-hander. Atkins pitched very well at Low-A after signing, but that's not a huge shock as he was older than most of the league, has quality off-speed stuff, and throws strikes. He also has a fastball that rarely gets out of the 80s, causing scouts to question whether or not he has enough pure stuff to remain effective as he moves up the ladder.

Joe Beimel

Bats: L　Throws: L　Height: 6' 3"　Weight: 215　Born: April 19, 1977　Age: 31

YEAR	TEAM	LVL	AGE	W	L	SV	G	GS	IP	H	BB	SO	HR	GB%	BABIP	STUFF	WHIP	ERA	PERA	EqERA	EqH9	EqBB9	EqSO9	EqHR9	VORP	SN/WX
2005	DUR	AAA	28	1	2	0	48	0	52²	58	21	36	3	59.3%	.322	-16	1.50	3.93	4.77	4.83	9.5	4.3	4.3	0.7	4.3	—
2005	TBA	MLB	28	0	0	0	7	0	11	15	4	3	1	43.2%	.326	-26	1.73	3.27	5.77	3.27	11.5	3.3	2.5	0.8	3.0	0.02
2006	LAN	MLB	29	2	1	2	62	0	70	70	21	30	7	58.2%	.274	-10	1.30	2.96	3.51	2.79	8.1	2.3	3.5	0.8	20.9	2.44
2007	LAN	MLB	30	4	2	1	83	0	67¹	63	24	39	1	49.3%	.297	6	1.29	3.88	3.02	3.49	7.9	2.7	5.0	0.1	14.0	2.20
2008	LAN	MLB	31	2	2	2	54	0	50¹	55	20	27	5	50.6%	.297	-14	1.48	4.30	4.67	4.53	9.6	3.2	4.3	0.8	5.8	0.50

Breakout: 7%　Improve: 18%　Collapse: 56%　Attrition: 28%　　　　Comparables: John O'Donoghue, Juan Agosto, Graeme Lloyd, Dave Tomlin

Having showed adequate contrition over the late-night bar incident that cost him the 2006 postseason, Beimel was welcomed back into the fold and rewarded the Dodgers with another strong year as the set-up man, stifling lefties (.188/.240/.250) while faring adequately enough against righties (.294/.366/.379) to avoid the LOOGY trap. Rising ERA to the contrary, his Fair Run Average fell slightly, from 3.39 to 3.33, proving he was actually more effective at stranding inherited runners than in 2006.

Chad Billingsley

Bats: R　Throws: R　Height: 6' 1"　Weight: 245　Born: July 29, 1984　Age: 23

YEAR	TEAM	LVL	AGE	W	L	SV	G	GS	IP	H	BB	SO	HR	GB%	BABIP	STUFF	WHIP	ERA	PERA	EqERA	EqH9	EqBB9	EqSO9	EqHR9	VORP	SN/WX
2005	JAX	AA	20	13	6	0	28	26	146	116	50	162	12	47.3%	.284	14	1.14	3.51	5.17	5.22	9.0	3.8	6.9	1.4	5.5	—
2006	LVG	AAA	21	6	3	0	13	13	70	57	32	78	7	47.8%	.289	19	1.27	3.99	4.34	4.37	7.7	4.4	7.4	1.2	9.3	—
2006	LAN	MLB	21	7	4	0	18	16	90	92	58	59	7	49.8%	.313	15	1.67	3.90	4.74	3.90	9.0	5.1	5.5	0.6	17.0	2.68
2007	LAN	MLB	22	12	5	0	43	20	147	131	64	141	15	43.4%	.299	25	1.33	3.31	3.61	2.88	7.7	3.4	8.0	0.9	40.7	4.62
2008	LAN	MLB	23	8	8	1	36	20	142²	136	61	128	16	44.9%	.296	15	1.38	3.96	4.32	4.13	8.4	3.4	7.1	0.9	23.7	3.30

Breakout: 2%　Improve: 17%　Collapse: 59%　Attrition: 18%　　　　Comparables: Jaret Wright, Barry Latman, Jim Clancy, Pete Smith

After a mixed bag in his rookie season and the free-agent signings of Jason Schmidt and Randy Wolf, the Dodgers decided to start Billingsley's sophomore season in the bullpen, a defensible strategy in terms of limiting the 22-year-old's innings. Working as the seventh-inning setup man, Billingsley struggled in April, then found his groove. Entering the rotation upon Jason Schmidt's demise in late June, he outpitched his rotation mates in the second half, putting up a 3.38 ERA with a 101/48 K/UIBB ratio in 112 innings. Lowering his walk rate and generating more groundballs remain on Billingsley's to-do list, but he ranks with any of the Dodgers' other blue-chip youngsters.

Jonathan Broxton

Bats: R　Throws: R　Height: 6' 4"　Weight: 290　Born: June 16, 1984　Age: 24

YEAR	TEAM	LVL	AGE	W	L	SV	G	GS	IP	H	BB	SO	HR	GB%	BABIP	STUFF	WHIP	ERA	PERA	EqERA	EqH9	EqBB9	EqSO9	EqHR9	VORP	SN/WX
2005	JAX	AA	21	5	3	5	33	13	96²	79	31	107	4	45.1%	.307	15	1.14	3.16	4.53	4.76	9.1	3.6	6.8	0.7	8.1	—
2005	LAN	MLB	21	1	0	0	14	0	13²	13	12	22	0	15.2%	.419	14	1.83	5.91	5.18	7.07	9.6	7.1	11.6	0.0	-3.0	-0.13
2006	LAN	MLB	22	4	1	3	68	0	76¹	61	33	97	7	41.3%	.303	33	1.23	2.60	3.24	2.57	7.0	3.3	9.8	0.7	26.2	2.30
2007	LAN	MLB	23	4	4	2	83	0	82	69	25	99	6	48.3%	.312	33	1.15	2.85	3.09	2.98	7.5	2.3	9.7	0.6	23.6	2.81
2008	LAN	MLB	24	4	3	7	68	0	73	61	27	80	6	46.0%	.292	21	1.20	2.95	3.24	3.09	7.4	2.9	8.7	0.7	21.5	1.90

Breakout: 25%　Improve: 52%　Collapse: 22%　Attrition: 13%　　　　Comparables: Scott Elarton, Charlie Kerfeld, Lance McCullers, Brian Fisher

Possibly the heaviest player in the majors after any given meal, "the Ox" once again did a fine job as the Dodger bullpen's beast of burden, blowing hitters away with his high-90s heat and hard slider while rating as one of the majors' top set-up men. As superhuman as he may seem, Broxton's not indestructible; he faded down the stretch due to overuse. In ten appearances from September 6 to 19, he put up an 11.05 ERA and allowed five of his six homers and a .794 SLG. Grady Little, in one of his worst moments, dismissed both that stretch and Broxton's own complaints of arm soreness. Joe Torre will do better.

Scott Elbert

Bats: L   Throws: L   Height: 6' 2"   Weight: 190   Born: August 13, 1985   Age: 22

YEAR	TEAM	LVL	AGE	W	L	SV	G	GS	IP	H	BB	SO	HR	GB%	BABIP	STUFF	WHIP	ERA	PERA	EqERA	EqH9	EqBB9	EqSO9	EqHR9	VORP	SN/WX
2005	CGA	A	19	8	5	0	25	24	115	83	57	128	8	48.6%	.269	1	1.22	2.66	6.20	5.22	8.5	7.7	5.7	1.6	4.2	—
2006	VRO	A+	20	5	5	0	17	15	83¹	57	41	97	4	46.8%	.275	19	1.18	2.38	4.63	4.13	7.1	6.2	6.5	0.9	12.5	—
2006	JAX	AA	20	6	4	0	11	11	62	40	44	76	11	32.9%	.254	1	1.35	3.63	8.35	6.43	8.5	7.2	7.9	3.1	-5.2	—
2007	JAX	AA	21	0	1	0	3	3	14	6	10	24	0	26.1%	.261	13	1.14	3.86	3.34	4.85	5.5	6.9	10.4	0.0	1.1	—
2008	LAN	MLB	22	5	7	0	18	18	96	84	69	104	13	38.9%	.290	18	1.59	4.80	5.22	4.95	7.7	5.8	8.6	1.2	7.7	1.50

Breakout: 25% Improve: 43% Collapse: 27% Attrition: 26%   Comparables: Cole Hamels, Lance Dickson, Jim Parque, Dick Weik

The 17th pick of the 2004 draft, this power lefty made our top prospect list at number 32 last year and appeared poised for bigger things after tossing five no-hit innings in his second start of 2007. Alas, a bout of shoulder soreness led to surgery in June to remove scar tissue from his labrum, a relatively minor procedure that should clear up the problem. When healthy, Elbert misses lots of bats with a 91 to 94 mph fastball and a sharp, devastating curveball, but a lack of consistency in his delivery and a tendency to overthrow cause control problems that he'll need to iron out as he works his way back.

Mark Hendrickson

Bats: L   Throws: L   Height: 6' 9"   Weight: 240   Born: June 23, 1974   Age: 34

YEAR	TEAM	LVL	AGE	W	L	SV	G	GS	IP	H	BB	SO	HR	GB%	BABIP	STUFF	WHIP	ERA	PERA	EqERA	EqH9	EqBB9	EqSO9	EqHR9	VORP	SN/WX
2005	TBA	MLB	31	11	8	0	31	31	178¹	227	49	89	24	45.7%	.329	-8	1.55	5.91	5.50	5.84	10.6	2.4	4.3	1.1	-12.8	0.79
2006	TBA	MLB	32	4	8	0	13	13	89²	81	34	51	10	48.6%	.258	8	1.28	3.81	3.33	3.56	7.0	3.2	4.7	0.9	18.6	2.55
2006	LAN	MLB	32	2	7	0	18	12	75	92	28	48	7	50.0%	.336	3	1.60	4.68	4.86	4.81	10.2	2.8	5.2	0.7	4.8	0.48
2007	LAN	MLB	33	4	8	0	39	15	122²	142	29	92	15	48.0%	.335	5	1.39	5.21	4.45	4.85	9.7	1.7	6.2	1.0	5.1	1.16
2008	LAN	MLB	34	5	6	1	35	11	90²	101	27	59	11	46.6%	.305	-4	1.40	4.70	4.79	4.92	9.7	2.4	5.2	1.1	7.9	1.20

Breakout: 18% Improve: 47% Collapse: 29% Attrition: 28%   Comparables: Dennis Rasmussen, Bill Krueger, Mike Smithson, John Halama

Thanks to Hendrickson's 1.30 ERA in 27 2/3 innings through May 2, the Dodgers labored under the illusion that he was an adequate stopgap for their banged-up rotation. Despite his absorbing more beatings than the Bayonne Bleeder the rest of the way (6.35 ERA), they couldn't be convinced otherwise. Hendrickson handles lefties well and generates the peripherals of a pitcher with an ERA closer to 4.00 than 5.00, but he tilts strongly toward the bullpen in his splits (3.17 Fair Run Average, compared to 6.52 as a starter). Put simply, he serves up too many meatballs to be trusted outside of middle relief, especially with a line-drive rate nearly double the league average.

D. J. Houlton

Bats: R   Throws: R   Height: 6' 4"   Weight: 225   Born: August 12, 1979   Age: 28

YEAR	TEAM	LVL	AGE	W	L	SV	G	GS	IP	H	BB	SO	HR	GB%	BABIP	STUFF	WHIP	ERA	PERA	EqERA	EqH9	EqBB9	EqSO9	EqHR9	VORP	SN/WX
2005	LAN	MLB	25	6	9	0	35	19	129	145	52	90	21	38.3%	.317	-16	1.53	5.16	6.31	5.77	10.4	3.3	5.8	1.5	-1.1	1.32
2006	LVG	AAA	26	9	11	0	29	29	162¹	180	60	132	25	37.4%	.318	-23	1.48	5.61	6.31	6.76	10.1	3.6	5.2	1.7	-20.4	—
2007	LVG	AAA	27	6	4	0	23	19	106	106	39	92	12	35.6%	.306	2	1.37	3.65	4.19	3.71	7.9	3.5	5.7	1.1	22.4	—
2007	LAN	MLB	27	0	2	0	18	0	28	28	7	21	5	36.5%	.291	0	1.25	4.18	4.51	4.00	8.7	2.0	6.7	1.7	4.3	0.20
2008	LAN	MLB	28	4	6	2	29	10	78¹	86	32	57	14	39.5%	.299	-4	1.50	5.21	5.54	5.33	9.7	3.2	5.7	1.5	3.1	0.70

Breakout: 23% Improve: 48% Collapse: 26% Attrition: 23%   Comparables: Dave Swartzbaugh, Shane Bowers, Jim Coates, Adam Bernero

A Rule 5 pick from the Astros, Houlton spent all of 2005 on the big-league roster, but his shaky performance mandated further minor league seasoning. Las Vegas is a particularly rough place for a fly-baller to iron things out, but Houlton improved command of his 88 to 90 mph fastball last year and took a solid step forward, boosting his K/PA by 10 percent and cutting his home run rate by 25 percent. Those gains held up during a pair of second-half stints with the Dodgers. He should get a shot at a middle-relief job with the big club this year.

Eric Hull

Bats: R　**Throws:** R　**Height:** 5′ 11″　**Weight:** 185　**Born:** December 3, 1979　**Age:** 28

YEAR	TEAM	LVL	AGE	W	L	SV	G	GS	IP	H	BB	SO	HR	GB%	BABIP	STUFF	WHIP	ERA	PERA	EqERA	EqH9	EqBB9	EqSO9	EqHR9	VORP	SN/WX
2005	JAX	AA	25	7	7	3	27	18	117	105	44	117	9	45.6%	.303	-10	1.27	3.38	5.77	5.50	10.0	4.2	6.1	1.4	1.2	—
2006	LVG	AAA	26	2	4	2	44	2	73¹	54	43	78	6	44.4%	.271	3	1.33	4.19	4.22	4.99	6.9	5.6	7.2	1.0	4.8	—
2007	LVG	AAA	27	4	3	11	49	0	65²	59	26	81	3	47.9%	.348	21	1.29	2.74	3.70	2.98	7.8	3.8	8.8	0.6	18.4	—
2007	LAN	MLB	27	0	0	0	5	0	6²	4	3	5	0	36.8%	.222	2	1.05	4.03	2.15	3.86	5.1	3.9	6.4	0.0	1.4	-0.00
2008	LAN	MLB	28	3	3	4	27	4	53	49	29	51	5	44.3%	.294	7	1.45	4.09	4.40	4.27	8.0	4.3	7.6	0.9	8.4	0.90

Breakout: 33%　**Improve:** 57%　**Collapse:** 22%　**Attrition:** 14%　　**Comparables:** Mike Ignasiak, Matt Duff, Doug Bair, Jason Frasor

Not to be confused with Eric Stults, this 2002 amateur free agent signing out of the University of Portland plodded his way through the system as an organizational soldier until 2006, when he was shifted to the bullpen with Triple-A Las Vegas. Pitching exclusively in relief last year, he drew notice by surviving the thin air of the PCL while the rest of the staff was getting hammered. His deceptive delivery and ability to generate groundballs have earned him a spot on the 40-man roster, but whether or not they'll earn him a shot at the 25-man remains to be seen.

Clayton Kershaw

Bats: L　**Throws:** L　**Height:** 6′ 3″　**Weight:** 210　**Born:** March 19, 1988　**Age:** 20

YEAR	TEAM	LVL	AGE	W	L	SV	G	GS	IP	H	BB	SO	HR	GB%	BABIP	STUFF	WHIP	ERA	PERA	EqERA	EqH9	EqBB9	EqSO9	EqHR9	VORP	SN/WX
2006	DGR	Rk	18	2	0	1	10	8	37	28	5	54	0	51.5%	.357	31	0.89	1.95	5.54	5.52	11.3	3.5	7.8	0.6	0.3	—
2007	GRL	A	19	7	5	0	20	20	97¹	72	50	134	5	49.3%	.310	14	1.25	2.77	6.52	6.37	8.9	8.5	7.0	1.4	-7.1	—
2007	JAX	AA	19	1	2	0	5	5	24²	17	17	29	4	41.0%	.236	19	1.38	3.64	6.12	6.17	7.3	6.6	6.9	2.3	-1.5	—
2008	LAN	MLB	20	6	10	0	24	24	127¹	126	104	119	19	44.2%	.303	6	1.81	5.60	6.30	5.77	8.7	6.5	7.4	1.3	-1.4	0.80

Breakout: 32%　**Improve:** 67%　**Collapse:** 15%　**Attrition:** 10%　　**Comparables:** Scott Kazmir, Homer Bailey, Kerry Wood, Boof Bonser

Ladies and gentlemen, start your superlatives. Picked seventh overall in the 2006 draft, this Dallas native stepped to the fore as the top pitching prospect in the minors last year by manhandling the Midwest League thanks to a combination of size and stuff that scouts have called "once in a generation," comparing him to Scott Kazmir, but bigger and with cleaner mechanics. Though Kershaw did pitch poorly in a few A-ball starts, he skipped all the way to Double-A in August. While his results at the higher level were uneven, the teenager continued to missed plenty of bats; that'll happen when you have a 93 to 95 mph fastball that can touch 97, a plus curveball, and a rapidly improving changeup. A true number-one starter in the making, Kershaw will start the year in Double-A Jacksonville; his performance, not his age, will dictate his timetable.

Hong-Chih Kuo

Bats: L　**Throws:** L　**Height:** 6′ 1″　**Weight:** 235　**Born:** July 23, 1981　**Age:** 26

YEAR	TEAM	LVL	AGE	W	L	SV	G	GS	IP	H	BB	SO	HR	GB%	BABIP	STUFF	WHIP	ERA	PERA	EqERA	EqH9	EqBB9	EqSO9	EqHR9	VORP	SN/WX
2005	VRO	A+	23	1	1	0	11	3	26	19	10	42	2	45.3%	.340	15	1.12	2.08	6.49	4.50	9.8	6.1	9.4	1.6	2.7	—
2005	JAX	AA	23	1	1	3	17	0	28¹	22	11	44	1	48.4%	.350	20	1.17	1.91	4.89	3.60	9.7	4.3	10.1	0.7	5.6	—
2006	LVG	AAA	24	4	3	1	23	9	53¹	52	22	63	5	45.7%	.356	6	1.39	3.05	5.54	4.62	10.0	4.3	8.3	1.1	5.3	—
2006	LAN	MLB	24	1	5	0	28	5	59²	54	33	71	3	45.8%	.347	29	1.46	4.22	3.78	4.14	8.1	4.3	10.0	0.5	9.9	1.04
2007	LVG	AAA	25	0	1	0	7	5	20	18	8	28	2	41.3%	.364	19	1.30	3.60	4.60	3.86	8.7	3.9	10.1	1.0	3.6	—
2007	LAN	MLB	25	1	4	0	8	6	30¹	35	14	27	3	33.7%	.344	5	1.62	7.43	4.81	6.89	9.5	3.4	7.2	0.9	-6.5	0.07
2008	LAN	MLB	26	3	4	2	38	7	64²	60	31	65	8	41.1%	.297	10	1.40	4.28	4.37	4.46	8.1	3.8	7.9	1.0	10.3	1.10

Breakout: 36%　**Improve:** 54%　**Collapse:** 27%　**Attrition:** 21%　　**Comparables:** Grant Jackson, Marcelino Lopez, Rich Garces, Greg Cadaret

When healthy, this Taiwanese power lefty can pump gas in the mid- to high-90s and generate eye-popping strikeout numbers. Alas, he's rarely healthy. With two Tommy Johns on his résumé already, Kuo was shut down by shoulder inflammation at the end of spring training, delaying his 2007 arrival until mid-May. He hinted at his promise during a brief trial as the fifth starter, but struggled with command before being sidelined again for surgery to remove bone chips from his elbow. Continued soreness prevented his return. Kuo remains an enigma, tantalizing but frustrating.

Hideki Kuroda

Bats: R Throws: R Height: 6' 0" Weight: 190 Born: February 10, 1975 Age: 33

YEAR	TEAM	LVL	AGE	W	L	SV	G	GS	IP	H	BB	SO	HR	GB%	BABIP	STUFF	WHIP	ERA	PERA	EqERA	EqH9	EqBB9	EqSO9	EqHR9	VORP	SN/WX
2005	HRO	JP	30	15	11	0	28	27	203²	173	42	161	17	—	.257	17	1.06	3.14	3.26	3.39	7.4	2.2	5.2	0.7	47.6	—
2006	HRO	JP	31	13	6	1	26	25	189¹	169	21	144	12	—	.280	22	1.00	1.85	3.64	2.97	8.7	1.4	5.4	0.7	52.3	—
2007	HRO	JP	32	12	8	0	26	26	179²	176	42	123	20	—	.285	-1	1.21	3.56	4.73	4.56	9.4	2.5	4.8	1.2	19.6	—
2008	LAN	MLB	33	10	9	0	25	25	159²	166	45	104	19	45.9%	.290	8	1.32	4.12	4.38	4.30	9.1	2.3	5.1	1.0	23.3	3.70

Breakout: 3% Improve: 22% Collapse: 37% Attrition: 11%   Comparables: Ray Scarborough, Joaquin Andujar, Elmer Dessens, Ray Herbert

One year into a four-year deal with the cellar-dwelling Hiroshima Carp, Kuroda opted out to head stateside, and the Dodgers outbid the Mariners and others for his services with a three-year, $35.3 million contract. While he's not Daisuke Matsuzaka, Kuroda is a well-regarded power pitcher with a big-game reputation and a broad arsenal that includes a low- to mid-90s fastball that he locates well to both sides of the plate, a slider, a forkball and a ishuutoa. He generates a ton of groundballs, which should enable him to eat innings behind Brad Penny, Derek Lowe, and Billingsley while serving as insurance in the case of injury or ineffectiveness on the part of Jason Schmidt, Esteban Loaiza, or Hong Chih Kuo.

Esteban Loaiza

Bats: R Throws: R Height: 6' 3" Weight: 215 Born: December 31, 1971 Age: 36

YEAR	TEAM	LVL	AGE	W	L	SV	G	GS	IP	H	BB	SO	HR	GB%	BABIP	STUFF	WHIP	ERA	PERA	EqERA	EqH9	EqBB9	EqSO9	EqHR9	VORP	SN/WX
2005	WAS	MLB	33	12	10	0	34	34	217	227	55	173	18	45.8%	.322	22	1.30	3.77	4.28	4.22	9.6	2.1	6.6	0.8	39.4	5.24
2006	OAK	MLB	34	11	9	0	26	26	154²	179	40	97	17	43.0%	.320	9	1.42	4.89	4.45	5.11	9.6	2.1	5.2	0.9	11.9	2.24
2007	OAK	MLB	35	1	0	0	2	2	14²	10	4	5	1	23.4%	.196	3	0.95	1.84	2.49	1.88	5.7	2.5	3.1	0.6	6.8	0.62
2007	LAN	MLB	35	1	4	0	5	5	22²	26	16	15	9	25.0%	.270	-27	1.85	8.33	10.68	8.61	9.4	5.5	5.5	3.1	-5.9	-0.29
2008	LAN	MLB	36	4	5	0	24	10	71¹	78	25	48	10	40.8%	.299	-4	1.44	4.72	5.01	4.87	9.6	2.8	5.4	1.3	6.5	1.00

Breakout: 13% Improve: 38% Collapse: 38% Attrition: 41%   Comparables: Kevin Appier, Jim Hearn, Kevin Gross, Mike Bielecki

Though a spate of injuries—trapezius, neck, knee—kept Loaiza from making his 2007 debut until August 22, Billy Beane's decision to cut bait just two starts after his return came as a surprise. Loaiza was spotty after switching from Oakland green to Dodger blue, but his track record and $6.5 million price tag (plus a $7.5 million option for 2009) make him a more palatable back-of-the-rotation option than Hendrickson or Tomko. Another season along the lines of his modest 2005 and 2006 campaigns seems attainable and would rank his acquisition among Ned Colletti's better moves.

Derek Lowe

Bats: R Throws: R Height: 6' 6" Weight: 230 Born: June 1, 1973 Age: 35

YEAR	TEAM	LVL	AGE	W	L	SV	G	GS	IP	H	BB	SO	HR	GB%	BABIP	STUFF	WHIP	ERA	PERA	EqERA	EqH9	EqBB9	EqSO9	EqHR9	VORP	SN/WX
2005	LAN	MLB	32	12	15	0	35	35	222	223	55	146	28	64.4%	.286	6	1.25	3.61	4.34	4.55	9.1	2.0	5.4	1.1	22.5	3.83
2006	LAN	MLB	33	16	8	0	35	34	218	221	55	123	14	67.9%	.293	19	1.27	3.63	3.38	3.58	8.4	1.9	4.6	0.5	49.3	6.60
2007	LAN	MLB	34	12	14	0	33	32	199¹	194	59	147	20	66.3%	.292	20	1.27	3.88	3.57	3.88	8.2	2.3	6.2	0.8	30.5	4.52
2008	LAN	MLB	35	9	9	0	26	26	160²	169	50	108	13	58.9%	.305	10	1.37	4.12	4.21	4.41	9.3	2.5	5.3	0.7	21.0	3.50

Breakout: 6% Improve: 27% Collapse: 31% Attrition: 20%   Comparables: Rick Reuschel, Jerry Reuss, Mike Morgan, Gaylord Perry

Lowe's first missed start in five and a half years marked a turning point in the Dodger season. Ten games above .500 and atop the NL West prior to Lowe's missed turn, the team had fallen to third place by the next time Lowe took the ball. Having tweaked his groin in a one-inning relief stint, eventually leading to the missed start, Lowe clearly wasn't the same pitcher over the final six weks, yielding a 4.76 ERA and 12 of the 20 homers he allowed on the year (a pace of 1.7 HR/9IP). Still, the Dodgers are playing with house money on the once-ridiculed four-year, $36 million deal he was given by Paul DePodesta after Lowe's unimpressive 2004; according to our 2007 MORP calculations, his performance as a Dodger thus far has been worth more than $44.8 million

James Zeil McDonald

Bats: L　Throws: R　Height: 6' 5"　Weight: 195　Born: October 19, 1984　Age: 23

YEAR	TEAM	LVL	AGE	W	L	SV	G	GS	IP	H	BB	SO	HR	GB%	BABIP	STUFF	WHIP	ERA	PERA	EqERA	EqH9	EqBB9	EqSO9	EqHR9	VORP	SN/WX
2006	CGA	A	21	5	10	0	30	22	142	119	65	146	15	46.3%	.290	-32	1.30	3.99	8.11	7.59	10.1	7.1	5.2	2.5	-26.8	—
2007	SBR	A+	22	6	7	0	16	15	82	79	21	104	8	36.5%	.355	4	1.22	3.95	6.19	5.38	10.6	3.7	7.3	1.5	1.8	—
2007	JAX	AA	22	7	2	0	10	10	52²	42	16	64	5	43.6%	.298	16	1.10	1.71	4.73	3.44	8.5	3.3	7.4	1.4	11.9	—
2008	LAN	MLB	23	6	9	0	31	20	123	133	58	100	23	40.3%	.297	3	1.54	5.48	5.79	5.61	9.5	3.7	6.4	1.6	0.8	0.90

Breakout: 25%　Improve: 48%　Collapse: 24%　Attrition: 12%　　Comparables: Duff Brumley, Garrett Stephenson, Scott Mathieson, Dennis Tankersley

Drafted as a pitcher in 2002, converted to the outfield in 2004, then back to the mound in 2006, James Zeil McDonald took a bigger step forward than any other player in the organization in 2007. No statistical fluke, McDonald's was a real performance from a very real pitching prospect; he's tall, throws hard, has an outstanding curveball, and his funky delivery makes all of his pitches that much harder to hit.

Jonathan Meloan

Bats: R　Throws: R　Height: 6' 3"　Weight: 230　Born: July 11, 1984　Age: 23

YEAR	TEAM	LVL	AGE	W	L	SV	G	GS	IP	H	BB	SO	HR	GB%	BABIP	STUFF	WHIP	ERA	PERA	EqERA	EqH9	EqBB9	EqSO9	EqHR9	VORP	SN/WX
2005	OGD	Rk	20	0	2	1	16	6	39	30	18	54	4	55.4%	.306	-6	1.23	3.69	8.32	6.61	10.1	8.9	6.0	2.3	-3.5	—
2006	CGA	A	21	1	1	1	12	0	23	9	7	41	2	61.1%	.212	20	0.70	1.57	4.50	3.98	5.8	4.9	9.7	1.8	3.7	—
2006	VRO	A+	21	1	0	0	4	3	18¹	15	4	27	2	67.9%	.346	16	1.05	2.49	6.18	4.96	9.9	3.3	8.8	2.2	1.2	—
2007	JAX	AA	22	5	2	19	35	0	45¹	24	18	70	3	46.5%	.256	21	0.93	2.19	3.56	3.61	6.2	4.0	9.6	1.1	9.4	—
2007	LVG	AAA	22	2	0	1	14	0	21¹	12	9	21	2	46.4%	.189	8	0.99	1.69	2.68	2.01	3.6	3.6	6.4	0.8	8.9	—
2007	LAN	MLB	22	0	0	0	5	0	7¹	8	8	7	1	36.4%	.350	7	2.18	11.10	7.50	9.82	9.8	8.6	8.6	1.2	-4.2	-0.08
2008	LAN	MLB	23	3	3	6	43	3	49¹	41	30	48	6	43.6%	.269	4	1.45	4.25	4.53	4.42	7.4	4.9	7.8	1.1	7.2	0.80

Breakout: 40%　Improve: 60%　Collapse: 18%　Attrition: 16%　　Comparables: Jim Miller, David Riske, P.J. Bevis, Chris Ray

Discovered by Logan White while he was scouting James Loney, this 2005 fifth-rounder was handled with kid gloves even as he shot through the system, tossing only 91 innings across four levels through his first two seasons. Working more regularly in 2007, Meloan avoided the elbow issues which hampered him in 2006, continuing to dominate both lefties (.174 average against) and righties (.144) with his 92 to 94 mph fastball and monstrous spike curveball. While his cup of coffee with the Dodgers didn't go well, it's notable that the two weeks he languished without an appearance coincided with Grady Little's attempt to make Jonathan Broxton's arm fall off. Expect Meloan to be in the mix for a bullpen slot out of spring training.

Justin Orenduff

Bats: R　Throws: R　Height: 6' 2"　Weight: 205　Born: May 27, 1983　Age: 25

YEAR	TEAM	LVL	AGE	W	L	SV	G	GS	IP	H	BB	SO	HR	GB%	BABIP	STUFF	WHIP	ERA	PERA	EqERA	EqH9	EqBB9	EqSO9	EqHR9	VORP	SN/WX
2005	VRO	A+	22	5	3	0	12	12	60¹	35	26	81	3	36.9%	.256	20	1.01	2.24	4.64	5.16	7.1	6.4	7.6	1.0	2.6	—
2005	JAX	AA	22	5	2	0	14	13	66¹	59	24	65	6	29.7%	.305	-7	1.25	4.07	5.91	6.22	9.9	4.1	5.9	1.5	-4.1	—
2006	JAX	AA	23	4	2	0	10	10	50	40	19	54	4	29.6%	.286	0	1.18	3.42	5.50	6.41	9.5	3.9	6.6	1.4	-4.2	—
2007	JAX	AA	24	8	5	0	27	23	109	112	45	113	16	38.0%	.328	-36	1.44	4.21	7.91	6.66	10.9	4.3	6.3	2.2	-11.9	—
2008	LAN	MLB	25	5	7	0	25	15	93²	97	45	78	17	36.9%	.294	3	1.52	5.18	5.56	5.28	9.1	3.9	6.6	1.5	3.9	1.00

Breakout: 43%　Improve: 74%　Collapse: 10%　Attrition: 17%　　Comparables: Boof Bonser, Jonathan Papelbon, Jason Bell, James Baldwin

After a season cut short by surgery to repair his biceps tendon, this 2004 supplemental first-rounder made a solid return. Still, it's clear he wasn't all the way back as his fastball sat at 88 to 90 instead of 90 to 92, his homer rate spiked more than 60 percent relative to his previous go-rounds in Jacksonville, and hitters caught up to him the second time through the order after getting a look at his wares (.314/.369/.577 as compared to .220/.315/.382 the first time through). His ceiling is as a number-three or -four starter, but he'll need to show that he's back on track in 2008, or risk getting lost in the shuffle.

Brad Penny

Bats: R   Throws: R   Height: 6' 4"   Weight: 260   Born: May 24, 1978   Age: 30

YEAR	TEAM	LVL	AGE	W	L	SV	G	GS	IP	H	BB	SO	HR	GB%	BABIP	STUFF	WHIP	ERA	PERA	EqERA	EqH9	EqBB9	EqSO9	EqHR9	VORP	SN/WX
2005	LAN	MLB	27	7	9	0	29	29	175¹	185	41	122	17	48.4%	.307	15	1.29	3.90	4.40	4.10	9.7	1.9	5.8	0.9	29.6	4.43
2006	LAN	MLB	28	16	9	0	34	33	189	206	54	148	19	45.3%	.327	19	1.38	4.33	4.24	4.01	9.3	2.2	6.5	0.8	32.8	4.56
2007	LAN	MLB	29	16	4	0	33	33	208	199	73	135	9	50.6%	.306	27	1.31	3.03	3.37	2.87	8.2	2.7	5.6	0.4	61.7	7.25
2008	LAN	MLB	30	9	9	0	26	26	159²	173	55	112	18	47.9%	.307	10	1.42	4.29	4.66	4.48	9.5	2.7	5.5	1.0	20.9	3.40

Breakout: 2%   Improve: 9%   Collapse: 52%   Attrition: 14%   Comparables: Livan Hernandez, Jaime Navarro, Chris Bosio, Dave Lemanczyk

After starting the 2006 All-Star game, Penny's second-half ERA of 6.25 prompted questions about the state of his shoulder, mechanics, conditioning, and attitude. He provided reassuring answers to all of them in 2007, battling Jake Peavy for the title of league's best starter with a 10-1, 2.39 ERA first-half showing, and curbing his second-half pitfalls by pitching to contact and thus decreasing his pitches per plate appearance by 10 percent. The result was a respectable 3.84 second-half ERA. Though the concurrent erosion of his strikeout and walk rates might generate concern, Penny's increased reliance on his sinker helped him cut his home run rate by more than half to lead all ERA qualifiers. As he enters the final year of the three-year, $25.5 million extension, the staff ace remains another feather in the deposed DePodesta's cap.

Scott Proctor

Bats: R   Throws: R   Height: 6' 1"   Weight: 195   Born: January 2, 1977   Age: 31

YEAR	TEAM	LVL	AGE	W	L	SV	G	GS	IP	H	BB	SO	HR	GB%	BABIP	STUFF	WHIP	ERA	PERA	EqERA	EqH9	EqBB9	EqSO9	EqHR9	VORP	SN/WX
2005	COH	AAA	28	6	1	14	35	1	42²	47	11	54	8	42.7%	.368	-7	1.36	4.22	7.54	5.49	11.2	3.0	8.7	2.1	0.5	—
2005	NYA	MLB	28	1	0	0	29	1	44²	46	17	36	10	30.6%	.271	-13	1.41	6.04	5.22	5.87	8.4	3.3	6.8	1.8	-3.4	-0.34
2006	NYA	MLB	29	6	4	1	83	0	102¹	89	33	89	12	34.8%	.273	9	1.19	3.52	3.50	3.33	7.5	2.7	7.3	1.0	28.2	1.83
2007	NYA	MLB	30	2	5	0	52	0	54¹	53	29	37	8	26.7%	.280	-15	1.51	3.81	4.72	4.07	8.3	4.2	5.5	1.3	9.1	0.23
2007	LAN	MLB	30	3	0	0	31	0	32	25	15	27	4	37.0%	.247	3	1.25	3.38	3.33	3.31	6.3	3.6	6.9	1.1	7.0	0.73
2008	LAN	MLB	31	3	3	3	51	0	59	59	25	47	8	36.7%	.287	-3	1.42	4.48	4.71	4.62	8.7	3.4	6.4	1.2	6.7	0.60

Breakout: 13%   Improve: 30%   Collapse: 42%   Attrition: 28%   Comparables: John Wyatt, Al Reyes, Mike Armstrong, Dave Tobik

The development of a reliable curveball turned Proctor into a go-to guy in the Yankee bullpen in 2006, when he led the league in appearances and relief innings. His early 2007 troubles with the strike zone suggested the Yankees had overextended him, but their staff's disarray and Proctor's gamer attitude kept Joe Torre calling his number. The Yankees cut bait before he could fall apart on their watch, trading him back to the Dodgers (who drafted him in 1998) for Wilson Betemit. Slotted into the number-two righty set-up role vacated by Chad Billingsley, Proctor acquitted himself well after some early hiccups, but the history of relievers worked this hard in consecutive years isn't a pretty one. Bet on Torre to ride him hard anyway.

Takashi Saito

Bats: L   Throws: R   Height: 6' 2"   Weight: 200   Born: February 14, 1970   Age: 38

YEAR	TEAM	LVL	AGE	W	L	SV	G	GS	IP	H	BB	SO	HR	GB%	BABIP	STUFF	WHIP	ERA	PERA	EqERA	EqH9	EqBB9	EqSO9	EqHR9	VORP	SN/WX
2005	YKO	JP	35	3	4	0	21	16	106	111	29	93	12	—	.306	4	1.32	3.82	5.29	4.78	10.4	2.9	6.1	1.0	8.9	—
2006	LAN	MLB	36	6	2	24	72	0	78¹	48	23	107	3	36.8%	.280	41	0.91	2.07	2.35	2.32	5.7	2.3	10.0	0.3	33.6	5.47
2007	LAN	MLB	37	2	1	39	63	0	64¹	33	13	78	5	48.6%	.207	34	0.72	1.40	2.10	1.43	4.6	1.6	9.3	0.7	32.0	5.76
2008	LAN	MLB	38	4	6	39	44	2	58	49	19	61	6	42.4%	.284	15	1.18	2.99	3.20	3.12	7.4	2.7	8.4	0.9	18.8	2.90

Breakout: 32%   Improve: 41%   Collapse: 35%   Attrition: 14%   Comparables: Rollie Fingers, Al Worthington, Larry Andersen, John Smoltz

With all the hype, mystery, and occasional disappointment surrounding the likes of Daisuke Matsuzaka and Kei Igawa, it's still a marvel that Saito went from imported curio to ninth-inning lock so rapidly. Last year, he proved his stateside debut was no fluke by leading the NL in WXRL and improving his already stellar strikeout-to-walk ratio. Righties had no chance against his 93 mph heat and killer slider, batting just .114/.177/.152 against him, while lefties hit a comparatively robust .186/.240/.319. Don't think managers didn't notice; they pinch-hit often enough that he wound up facing more lefties than righties. Saito's only black mark was a bout of shoulder soreness that limited him to just one appearance in the latter half of July, though the presence of closer-in-waiting Jonathan Broxton helped mitigate that and should continue to provide insurance against Saito's advancing age. Every team should be so lucky as to have such a late-inning tandem.

Jason Schmidt

Bats: R   Throws: R   Height: 6' 4"   Weight: 210   Born: January 29, 1973   Age: 35

YEAR	TEAM	LVL	AGE	W	L	SV	G	GS	IP	H	BB	SO	HR	GB%	BABIP	STUFF	WHIP	ERA	PERA	EqERA	EqH9	EqBB9	EqSO9	EqHR9	VORP	SN/WX
2005	SFN	MLB	32	12	7	0	29	29	172	160	85	165	16	40.4%	.306	21	1.42	4.40	4.23	4.66	8.4	4.0	7.8	0.8	17.5	3.00
2006	SFN	MLB	33	11	9	0	32	32	213^1	189	80	180	21	38.5%	.283	24	1.26	3.59	3.67	3.58	8.0	2.9	7.0	0.8	49.4	5.89
2007	LAN	MLB	34	1	4	0	6	6	25^2	32	14	22	4	37.5%	.341	-2	1.79	6.30	5.96	6.26	10.2	4.0	6.9	1.3	-3.5	0.24
2008	LAN	MLB	35	4	5	0	22	11	75^2	75	33	66	11	39.0%	.296	5	1.43	4.57	4.82	4.72	8.7	3.5	6.9	1.2	8.9	1.20

Breakout: 13% Improve: 26% Collapse: 43% Attrition: 43%   Comparables: Cal Eldred, Rick Helling, Diego Segui, Dwight Gooden

Though clearly diminished from his 2003/2004 heyday, Schmidt rebounded strongly enough from a mediocre 2005 for his three-year, $47 million deal with the Dodgers to draw praise in these quarters. Further reassurance came via the green light from incoming director of medical services Stan Conte, who was intimately familiar with Schmidt's shoulder from their days with the Giants. Alas, by mid-April, Schmidt's troubling lack of velocity prompted an MRI and a lengthy stay on the DL. He survived less than two weeks upon returning, and exploratory surgery in late June revealed the Torn Labrum Platter Deluxe with all the trimmings, including an inflamed bursa and a frayed biceps tendon. While the Dodgers expect him to recover, Schmidt may be in for rough sledding until he rebuilds his arm strength, and even that's no guarantee of a return to his established form.

Rudy Seanez

Bats: R   Throws: R   Height: 6' 0"   Weight: 225   Born: October 20, 1968   Age: 39

YEAR	TEAM	LVL	AGE	W	L	SV	G	GS	IP	H	BB	SO	HR	GB%	BABIP	STUFF	WHIP	ERA	PERA	EqERA	EqH9	EqBB9	EqSO9	EqHR9	VORP	SN/WX
2005	SDN	MLB	36	7	1	0	57	0	60^1	49	22	84	4	37.9%	.338	31	1.18	2.69	3.62	3.09	8.0	3.1	10.6	0.6	17.3	1.65
2006	BOS	MLB	37	2	1	0	41	0	46^2	51	26	48	6	31.2%	.336	6	1.65	4.82	4.83	4.69	8.8	4.5	8.4	0.9	4.0	-1.16
2006	SDN	MLB	37	1	2	0	8	0	6^1	7	6	6	2	38.1%	.263	-8	2.05	5.71	8.41	5.14	9.0	6.4	6.4	2.6	0.2	-0.85
2007	LAN	MLB	38	6	3	1	73	0	76	78	27	73	10	39.1%	.324	8	1.38	3.79	4.42	3.43	8.8	2.7	8.1	1.1	16.6	0.77
2008	LAN	MLB	39	2	3	4	41	0	48^1	49	18	43	6	39.7%	.303	1	1.38	4.31	4.49	4.47	8.8	3.0	7.1	1.1	6.3	0.60

Breakout: 11% Improve: 29% Collapse: 44% Attrition: 29%   Comparables: Don McMahon, Al Worthington, Doug Jones, Greg Harris

Twenty-one years after being drafted by the Indians and on his third go-round with the Dodgers, ol' Traction Action—or was that Transaction Action?—set career highs in appearances, innings pitched, and strikeouts in 2007. As his leverage score (0.89) indicates, he wasn't doing much heavy lifting; 24 appearances came with the team down one to three runs, seven came when up one to three runs, and 23 came when the margin was greater than four runs in either direction. After umpteen trips to the DL and a wait on the unemployment line, Seanez wasn't in a position to complain.

David Wells

Bats: L   Throws: L   Height: 6' 3"   Weight: 250   Born: May 20, 1963   Age: 45

YEAR	TEAM	LVL	AGE	W	L	SV	G	GS	IP	H	BB	SO	HR	GB%	BABIP	STUFF	WHIP	ERA	PERA	EqERA	EqH9	EqBB9	EqSO9	EqHR9	VORP	SN/WX
2005	BOS	MLB	42	15	7	0	30	30	184	220	21	107	21	49.9%	.324	12	1.31	4.45	4.45	4.18	10.0	1.0	5.1	0.9	25.1	3.64
2006	BOS	MLB	43	2	3	0	8	8	47	64	8	24	10	48.9%	.333	-9	1.53	4.98	6.32	5.17	11.1	1.3	4.2	1.7	2.0	0.64
2006	SDN	MLB	43	1	2	0	5	5	28^1	33	4	14	1	52.0%	.327	9	1.31	3.50	4.39	4.00	11.0	1.0	4.3	0.3	7.7	1.04
2007	SDN	MLB	44	5	8	0	22	22	118^2	156	33	63	17	43.9%	.344	-12	1.59	5.53	6.79	5.88	11.8	2.2	4.6	1.2	0.7	1.53
2007	LAN	MLB	44	4	1	0	7	7	38^2	45	9	19	5	48.5%	.313	-1	1.40	5.12	4.84	4.78	10.0	1.9	4.3	1.2	2.5	0.32
2008	LAN	MLB	45	7	10	0	33	22	138	173	39	82	19	47.7%	.327	-6	1.53	5.12	5.53	5.31	11.0	2.2	4.7	1.2	4.2	1.50

Breakout: 16% Improve: 44% Collapse: 27% Attrition: 27%   Comparables: Jim Kaat, Gaylord Perry, Jamie Moyer, Charlie Hough

Boomer's late-2006 trade from Boston to San Diego's more favorable environs appeared to give Wells a new lease on life. Back in the sand last year, he was a league-average inning muncher through mid-July, making nine quality starts out of 18 for a 4.15 ERA. Then four consecutive bombings convinced the Padres that he was done. Wells conceded the possibility, but after a few weeks of rest and rehab, he reemerged as a Dodger and pitched better than his ERA would indicate. A full year of Wells is probably out of the question, but a budget version of Roger Clemens' typical midseason return could help somebody. He's indicated that he'll retire, but then so did Clemens.

Chris Withrow

Bats: R Throws: R Height: 6' 3" Weight: 195 Born: April 1, 1989 Age: 19

YEAR	TEAM	LVL	AGE	W	L	SV	G	GS	IP	H	BB	SO	HR	GB%	BABIP	STUFF	WHIP	ERA	PERA	EqERA	EqH9	EqBB9	EqSO9	EqHR9	VORP	SN/WX
2007	DGR	Rk	18	0	0	0	6	4	9	5	4	13	0	36.4%	.333	8	1.00	5.00	5.68	8.22	7.0	8.2	7.0	0.0	-2.2	—
2008	LAN	MLB	19	3	10	1	27	20	103	128	93	67	22	44.4%	.318	-23	2.14	8.13	8.41	8.38	10.9	7.2	5.1	1.9	-33.0	-2.40

Breakout: NA Improve: NA Collapse: NA Attrition: NA   Comparables: Chaz Roe, Brandon Erbe, Matt Cain, Jerome Williams

The Dodgers' first-round pick last June, Withrow is everything the Dodgers like in a young arm. He has size, athleticism, and smooth mechanics and already sits in the low-90s with his fastball. Like most teenage hurlers, his secondary stuff needs improvement, but he's got enough going for him right now to succeed at Low-A this year while he works on those pitches.

Randy Wolf

Bats: L Throws: L Height: 5' 10" Weight: 200 Born: August 22, 1976 Age: 31

YEAR	TEAM	LVL	AGE	W	L	SV	G	GS	IP	H	BB	SO	HR	GB%	BABIP	STUFF	WHIP	ERA	PERA	EqERA	EqH9	EqBB9	EqSO9	EqHR9	VORP	SN/WX
2005	PHI	MLB	28	6	4	0	13	13	80	87	26	61	14	36.8%	.312	-1	1.41	4.39	6.25	4.81	10.3	2.7	6.5	1.5	10.1	1.41
2006	PHI	MLB	29	4	0	0	12	12	56²	63	33	44	13	39.0%	.305	-11	1.69	5.56	6.33	5.34	9.3	4.4	6.3	1.7	1.1	0.97
2007	LAN	MLB	30	9	6	0	18	18	102²	110	39	94	10	42.9%	.334	24	1.45	4.73	4.26	4.20	9.0	2.8	7.5	0.8	12.1	1.55
2008	SDN	MLB	31	4	4	0	24	11	75²	75	29	55	9	41.6%	.284	0	1.37	4.19	4.83	4.81	8.9	3.2	5.7	1.1	8.8	1.20

Breakout: 17% Improve: 45% Collapse: 32% Attrition: 39%   Comparables: Denny Lemaster, Juan Pizarro, John Curtis, Luis Tiant

His decade in the Phillies' organization having come to a close, Wolf spurned multi-year offers to sign a one-year, $8 million deal with his hometown team. The move paid off initially (six quality starts in his first 11 with a 3.41 ERA and 3.6 K/BB ratio), but shoulder inflammation possibly related to the mechanical adjustments made upon returning from his 2005 Tommy John surgery soon cost him velocity, and the rest of his season wasn't so pretty (two quality starts out of seven with a 7.12 ERA, 1.2 K/BB ratio, and a second half spent rehabbing). While Wolf's long-term prognosis is still favorable, the fact that he has thrown just 376 big-league innings over the past four years has him back on a one-year deal in San Diego, this time at half the price (though it could grow to $9 million via incentives).

Wesley Wright

Bats: R Throws: L Height: 5' 11" Weight: 160 Born: January 28, 1985 Age: 23

YEAR	TEAM	LVL	AGE	W	L	SV	G	GS	IP	H	BB	SO	HR	GB%	BABIP	STUFF	WHIP	ERA	PERA	EqERA	EqH9	EqBB9	EqSO9	EqHR9	VORP	SN/WX
2005	CGA	A	20	1	5	1	30	0	60²	38	33	68	2	50.7%	.252	4	1.17	1.93	5.36	5.30	7.2	8.2	5.6	0.9	1.8	—
2006	VRO	A+	21	3	3	0	26	0	42	29	23	51	0	42.4%	.302	18	1.24	1.50	4.39	3.58	7.2	7.2	6.9	0.2	8.5	—
2006	JAX	AA	21	1	1	1	15	0	21	14	11	28	2	42.9%	.273	9	1.19	4.71	5.59	7.78	8.2	5.5	8.2	1.8	-4.8	—
2007	JAX	AA	22	6	2	2	30	1	61¹	45	31	68	4	47.8%	.275	4	1.24	2.50	4.20	3.66	7.5	4.9	6.6	1.1	12.7	—
2007	LVG	AAA	22	1	2	0	14	1	16²	28	18	18	4	40.0%	.511	-27	2.75	9.16	21.00	17.02	15.8	10.6	7.6	2.3	-19.4	—
2008	HOU	MLB	23	3	5	2	27	7	58²	59	45	48	8	42.4%	.295	-8	1.76	5.69	6.24	6.02	9.0	6.1	6.6	1.2	-2.8	0.00

Breakout: 25% Improve: 52% Collapse: 24% Attrition: 14%   Comparables: Steve Dixon, Huck Flener, Mike Bumatay, Colin Young

Once again, this undersized southpaw consolidated his gains at a level he'd been introduced to the year before, but struggled upon being promoted further. That's not a horrible thing; the Dodgers challenged Wright, and merely reaching Triple-A at age 22 suggests promise. Wright's fastball reaches the low 90s with good late movement, and he also has a deceptive delivery and an above-average curveball. The control issues that have resulted from his tendency to overthrow were enough for the Dodgers to leave him off the 40-man roster, and he was claimed by the Astros in the Rule 5 draft.

LINEOUTS

Hitters

PLAYER	TEAM	LVL	AGE	PA	R	2B	3B	HR	RBI	BB	SO	SB-CS	EqBRR	AVG/OBP/SLG	MLVr	EqAVG/EqOBP/EqSLG	EqA	VORP
3B P. Baez	DGR	Rk	19	229	35	14	2	3	39	17	40	3-1	2.9	.274/.341/.408	.118	.209/.253/.308	.195	-34.6
C A. Ellis	JAX	AA	26	430	59	22	2	8	57	60	61	1-4	-2.4	.269/.382/.409	.145	.245/.344/.383	.257	9.8
1/3 S. Hillenbrand	LAA	MLB	31	204	19	5	0	3	22	5	18	0-2	-1.4	.254/.275/.325	-.254	.260/.284/.337	.211	-9.9
	LAN	MLB	31	74	6	0	2	1	9	2	12	0-1	-0.2	.243/.257/.343	-.260	.243/.257/.343	.204	-3.7
OF J. Hoffmann	SBR	A+	22	495	67	22	7	9	81	47	70	19-7	-1.9	.309/.378/.455	.191	.258/.316/.368	.243	-11.9
INF R. Martinez	LVG	AAA	34	18	6	1	0	0	2	4	1	0-0	0.6	.357/.500/.429	.270	.286/.444/.357	.301	1.0
	LAN	MLB	34	147	10	4	0	0	27	11	15	1-0	0.7	.194/.248/.225	-.468	.194/.253/.225	.175	-11.9
SS J. Pedroza#	SBR	A+	20	16	1	0	0	0	1	3	2	1-1	0.0	.250/.400/.250	-.091	.231/.375/.231	.233	-0.4
	OGD	Rk	20	239	33	18	1	8	40	14	44	4-4	-2.8	.360/.413/.569	.378	.241/.280/.377	.226	-2.3
OF J. Repko '08	LAN	MLB	27	190	24	9	1	5	21	15	38	5-1	0.7	.250/.322/.406	-0.095	.248/.319/.410	.252	3.5
PH O. Saenz	LAN	MLB	36	132	9	5	0	4	18	16	25	0-0	-0.5	.191/.295/.345	-.221	.193/.303/.367	.241	-3.4

Though his GCL stats didn't blow anyone away, the Dodgers adore **Pedro Baez**, a raw, toolsy 19-year-old with plus power (he homered off a rehabbing Pedro Martinez), a strong arm, and excellent range at third. ⊘ A defensively sound backstop who's made glacial progress up the organizational ladder, **A. J. Ellis** outslugged his OBP last year for the first time as a pro. ⊘ **Shea Hillenbrand** bounced from the Angels through the Padres' system to the Dodgers, but hit nowhere. Beyond synthesizing carbon dioxide so that somewhere a tree may grow, it's unclear what value he provides and it's probably not worth the headache to find out. ⊘ Like Ellis, former NHL draftee **Jamie Hoffman** is a grinder who, because of his limited power, has made slow progress despite excellent bat control and defense. ⊘ A serviceable enough utilityman who's generally not a Neifi-esque embarrassment with the stick, **Ramon Martinez** nonetheless spent most of the year below the Mendoza Line, thus wearing out his welcome in L.A. ⊘ The younger, less polished brother of 2005 third-rounder Sergio (since traded to Tampa Bay), **Jamie Pedroza** has a bat that may carry him to the majors, but he'll have to find a new defensive home. ⊘ After missing much of 2006 with a high ankle sprain, **Jason Repko** tore his hamstring so severely during spring training that it cost him the 2007 season, then was shut down during the fall instructional league season after re-injuring the ankle. ⊘ **Olmedo Saenz** enjoyed three good years for the Dodgers, but The Killer Tomato's luck ran out in 2007, as Grady Little couldn't find the at-bats to keep him fresh. Here's hoping he finds an NL manager who can put him to work.

Pitchers

PLAYER	TEAM	LVL	AGE	W	L	SV	IP	H	BB	SO	HR	GB%	BABIP	STUFF	WHIP	ERA	PERA	EqERA	EqH9	EqBB9	EqSO9	EqHR9	VORP
B. Akin	JAX	AA	25	1	2	2	68	64	42	91	3	45.7%	.365	10	1.56	4.37	5.80	6.30	10.1	6.0	8.1	0.7	-5.0
	LVG	AAA	25	1	2	0	14¹	15	8	19	1	55.6%	.424	13	1.61	5.03	5.60	5.40	10.1	5.4	10.1	0.7	0.3
M. Alexander	JAX	AA	26	5	1	5	67¹	54	35	81	11	36.8%	.272	-23	1.32	4.41	6.45	5.88	8.5	5.2	7.3	2.4	-2.0
	LVG	AAA	26	0	0	0	12	17	19	14	1	23.7%	.432	-1	3.00	14.25	11.67	15.75	12.0	14.2	7.5	0.8	-13.5
M. Alvarez	SBR	A+	23	7	10	0	107²	123	48	103	11	45.5%	.362	-27	1.59	5.60	7.70	8.49	11.6	5.7	5.0	1.5	-32.0
A. Bastardo*	SBR	A+	23	6	5	0	69	73	25	73	8	39.3%	.351	-15	1.42	4.57	7.28	6.60	11.3	4.8	5.9	1.8	-6.8
Y. Brazoban	LVG	AAA	27	0	0	3	13²	6	3	14	2	38.7%	.138	12	0.66	1.97	2.50	2.03	3.4	2.0	7.4	1.4	5.3
R. Hernandez	CLE	MLB	42	3	1	0	26	33	16	18	2	47.8%	.356	-16	1.88	6.23	6.16	6.92	11.1	4.8	5.9	0.7	-4.0
	LAN	MLB	42	0	2	0	20¹	26	9	13	3	44.4%	.348	-19	1.72	6.65	6.39	6.53	10.9	3.5	5.2	1.3	-2.7
G. Miller*	JAX	AA	22	1	2	1	48	46	43	65	2	55.1%	.370	16	1.85	4.69	6.46	7.33	10.0	8.5	7.9	0.8	-9.0
	LVG	AAA	22	1	1	0	28²	19	46	32	1	55.2%	.290	25	2.26	7.84	5.92	9.11	5.5	15.0	7.8	0.3	-10.8
D. Rondon	DGR	Rk	20	7	2	1	65	68	4	59	1	56.0%	.358	1	1.11	2.77	6.21	6.13	12.6	2.5	3.8	0.8	-3.2
E. Stults*	LVG	AAA	27	5	7	0	89¹	134	36	81	12	41.7%	.422	-18	1.90	7.56	8.06	7.77	12.7	3.9	6.1	1.3	-21.2
	LAN	MLB	27	1	4	0	38²	50	17	30	5	43.5%	.363	-3	1.73	5.81	6.35	5.59	11.2	3.3	6.5	1.2	-0.7
R. Troncoso	SBR	A+	24	3	1	7	26	18	3	30	0	65.2%	.286	8	0.81	1.04	3.42	3.24	6.8	1.8	6.1	0.4	6.6
	JAX	AA	24	7	3	7	52	52	18	39	3	64.0%	.314	-17	1.35	3.12	5.16	4.47	10.1	3.7	4.3	0.9	6.1
C. Tsao	LAN	MLB	26	0	1	0	24²	18	8	16	3	40.3%	.217	-2	1.05	4.37	2.87	3.70	5.9	2.6	5.5	1.1	4.0
C. Wade	SBR	A+	24	7	0	6	66	50	17	67	6	40.0%	.262	-9	1.02	2.45	4.47	3.34	7.4	3.5	5.4	1.3	15.6
	JAX	AA	24	0	0	1	33	22	11	33	3	41.3%	.233	2	1.00	1.36	3.25	2.14	6.1	3.2	5.6	0.8	13.0

After a big leap forward in 2006, **Brian Akin** continued to miss bats last year, but paired that with some unsightly walk rates. Still, his ability to keep the ball on the ground could help him run the Las Vegas gauntlet. ⊘ The organization's Minor League Pitcher of the Year in 2006, **Mark Alexander** struggled with his control and was hit in 2007, fumbling his shot at an audition in L.A. ⚾ A converted third-baseman with a power arm, **Mario Alvarez** was added to the 40-man roster in the offseason because his velocity might attract some Rule 5 interest, but he still has a ways to go. ⚾ **Alberto Bastardo** is a small lefty with surprising velocity and good command who might end up in the majors as a reliever. ⚾ No sooner had **Yhency Brazoban** returned from Tommy John surgery than he was felled by the torn labrum all too common to post-TJers. He could resurface in the second half of 2008, or he could be finished. ⚾ When Earl Weaver said that the hitters will tell you when a pitcher is done, he was referring to in-game situations, but the jury appears to have rendered a verdict on **Roberto Hernandez's** career as well. ⚾ **Greg Miller**'s descent from teenage top prospect to Dalkowskian nightmare is the kind of macabre tale told around campfires. His walk rate is surreal, but he throws heat with his left arm, so the Dodgers will continue trying to salvage his career. ⚾ Sure, it was only the Gulf Coast League, but **Daigoro Rondon**'s eye-popping K/BB ratio and homer rate make this 20-year-old Dominican worth following. ⚾ The return to Sin City didn't go too well for **Eric Stults**; he was rocked to a .414/.472/.680 tune at Cashman Field, and while he held PCL hitters to just .263/.308/.369 elsewhere, he's little more than a soft-tossing organizational soldier at this point. ⚾ A late bloomer who spent three years in the Dominican Summer League, **Ramon Troncoso** is a strike-throwing machine who can touch 96 mph with his fastball, and his secondary stuff continues to improve as he climbs the ladder. ⚾ Labrum and rotator cuff woes kept **Chin-Hui Tsao** from fulfilling his promise in Colorado, and, after a strong start with the Dodgers, his shoulder troubles returned to wreck yet another season. ⚾ A bit of a sleeper in the system, late-blooming **Cory Wade** thrived in a bullpen role in 2007 thanks to his 91 to 93 mph fastball and pinpoint control. He has an outside shot to reach Dodger Stadium this year.

MANAGER: GRADY LITTLE

YEAR	TEAM	W-L	Pythag +/-	Avg PC	100+ P	120+ P	QS	BQS	REL	REL w Zero R	IBB	Subs	PH	PH Avg	PH HR	SB2	CS2	SB3	CS3	SAC Att	SAC %	POS SAC	Squeeze	Swing	In Play
2006	LAN	88-74	0	91.6	54	1	75	4	454	278	34	58	285	.195	7	116	42	12	5	86	76.7%	27	2	157	125
2007	LAN	82-80	0	91.9	42	0	72	4	482	317	40	73	271	.249	10	115	44	22	4	89	65.2%	27	10	142	126

Grady Little's second year in L.A. didn't go as well as his first, culminating in a buyout of the final year of his contract rather than a playoff berth. After doing an excellent job of integrating several rookies into the lineup in 2006, Little was saddled with a motley collection of free agents by the front office, and thus struggled to find playing time for the team's top young talents (so much so that team MLVr leaders Matt Kemp and James Loney got just 686 plate appearances between them). Little tried to compensate for the punchless vets by keeping his team active on the basepaths—they were second in stolen-base attempts, first in hit-and-runs—to no avail. As for the pitching staff, Little again had to deal with a slew of injuries in the rotation, forcing him to lean heavily on his strong bullpen—too heavily, perhaps; in what might have been the most damning moment of his tenure, Little wore out Jonathan Broxton while refusing to believe that the Ox's late-season struggles were workload-related. Little's fate was sealed when his efforts to work the kids into the lineup created an age-based clubhouse rift that spilled over into the press toward season's end as the team collapsed and the disenchanted Little withdrew. Judging by his public reaction to the backroom machinations involving Joe Torre, Little appeared relieved to be relieved. Coupled with his painful exit from Boston, it would be a surprise if he ever took another major league managerial position.

Milwaukee Brewers

In 2007, the Brewers finished with the franchise's first winning record since 1992 and came closer to reaching the postseason than any Brewers squad since their 1982 pennant winners. Forget the nitpicking, the second-guessing, and the agony of their near-miss—that statement alone marks this past season as a watershed moment for the team. At last, the Brewers emerged from the shadows of the Selig era, those final humiliating years paying off in a homegrown bounty of frontline talent that rocketed the club into contention and should be capable of keeping them there for the foreseeable future.

That last point is important, for it lessens the sting of a season that, as promising as it was, had a bittersweet ending. After a modest 7-6 start, the Brewers zoomed out to a 25-11 record and held an eight-game NL Central lead by May 12. Though they would remain in first place until mid-August, they were no juggernaut. The team quickly fell back to earth after that initial burst, losing 12 out of 15 and, after a scorching June, stumbling badly in July and August with a 20-34 record over those two months. The Cubs caught them on the first day of August and, while the two teams were separated by more than two games for a total of just seven days over the final two months, the Brewers would hold a share of first place for only nine days after the Cubs first passed them on August 17, and no days after September 12. When the smoke cleared, Milwaukee had fallen two games short of the second playoff appearance in franchise history.

That the Brewers finished above .500 was not surprising; the team finished 81-81 in 2005, their first year under the ownership of Mark Attanasio. The nucleus of young talent assembled by general manager Doug Melvin (on the job since the 2002 postseason) and

scouting director Jack Zduriencik (in place since 2000), particularly the addition of 2002 first-round pick Prince Fielder, offered hope that the Brewers could surpass that showing in 2006. Instead, injuries set the team back that year. Ace Ben Sheets lost about half a season to shoulder woes, while three-quarters of the starting infield—second baseman Rickie Weeks, shortstop J. J. Hardy, and third baseman Corey Koskie—was done for the year by the end of July. The 2006 Brewers lost 20.5 percent of their payroll to the disabled list, a crippling blow to a small-market team with aspirations of contention, and finished a disappointing 75-87.

Still, the outlook for 2007 was sanguine. The Cardinals had captured the division in 2006 and won an unlikely World Championship, but did so with a weak 83-78 regular-season record and had executed a questionable plan in the offseason that decimated their rotation. With the recovery of their key players (with the exception of Koskie, whose post-concussion syndrome may end his career) and the potential for major in-season upgrades via two top prospects, starting pitcher Yovani Gallardo and third baseman Ryan Braun, the Brewers were poised to contend. PECOTA projected them to finish 86-76 and beat out the much-improved Cubs (85-77; score that a direct hit) in a race that appeared wide open.

Much of what needed to go right for the Brewers to win did so, particularly on offense. Fielder cracked 50 home runs, hit .288/.395/.618, and emerged as an MVP candidate in his second full season. Hardy returned with a vengeance, emerging as an offensive force in the first half. Perennial prospect Corey Hart asserted his hold on the right-field job by hitting a robust .295/.353/.539, banishing to the dustbin of history the lame pop-star references that had shadowed him. Braun, the team's 2005 first-round pick and the 12th-ranked prospect on last year's Baseball Prospectus Top 100 Prospects list, arrived in late May and opened up a can of Whoop-Ass on opposing pitchers, hitting .324/.370/ .634 with 34 homers. As a result, the Brewers finished fifth in the NL in scoring with 4.94 runs per game. The injury situation was also relatively rosy, as the team lost just 15.8 percent of its payroll to the DL, dropping from seventh in the majors to 14th, with 51 percent of the money and 35 percent of the days lost attributable to Koskie; Sheets was the only other player whose absence totaled more than $1 million of lost salary.

If so much went right, what went wrong? In short, the rotation, which appeared to be one of the game's deepest at the start of the season, fell apart. That put a strain on the bullpen, which had much less depth, and the problems of both units were exacerbated by the porous defense behind them. Through their May 12 high point, the Brewers allowed just 3.89 runs per game, fourth-best in the NL; the rest of the way they yielded 5.05 runs per game, which was tenth-best in the league. The offense dipped slightly after that date (from 5.14 runs per game to 4.89), but the team's real problems were on the other side of the ball.

For the third season in a row, Sheets missed significant time; he was limited to six starts in the second half due to finger and hamstring injuries. Working in the first year of the four-year, $42 million deal that had lured him away from the world champion Cardinals, Jeff Suppan posted a 5.19 ERA after May 12, while David Bush (4.93) and Claudio Vargas (5.92) did little to help. Number-two starter Chris Capuano was the emblem of the team's futility—not only did he put up a 6.08 ERA after May 12, eventually losing his spot in the rotation, but the Brewers lost *every single game* in which he appeared after that date, 22 in total.

The rotation nonetheless maintained a semblance of respectability thanks to Gallardo. The team's 2004 second-round choice ranked 14th on our top prospect list last year, profiling as a number-two starter (and thus mitigating the litany of injuries that have derailed 2004 first-rounder, Mark Rogers). Making his major league debut on June 18 and forcing his way into the rotation for good a month later, Gallardo finished second on the team in SNLVAR (3.6), despite throwing just 110 1/3 innings, and posted a 3.67 ERA. Second-year hurler Carlos Villanueva spent most of the year in the bullpen, but his 1.8 SNLVAR in just six starts outdid Vargas (1.5) and nearly equaled the contributions of Capuano (2.0) and Bush (2.2); taking his relief contribution (1.9 WXRL) into account, Villanueva was the team's third most-valuable pitcher behind Sheets (4.0) and Gallardo (3.8).

As a whole, the rotation ranked ninth in the league in SNLVAR (18.3) and tenth in innings pitched (5.76 per start). The bullpen didn't fare much better, finishing tenth in WXRL (8.8) and 12th in Adjusted Runs Prevented (-1.1). In the latter case, the late-inning combo of Francisco Cordero and Derrick Turnbow was largely dependable, but manager Ned Yost's orthodox adherence to the use of situational lefties, principally Brian Shouse, appears to have been detrimental.

FRA stands for Fair Run Average, which accounts for the baserunners relievers inherit and bequeath. Looking at that column in Table 1, it's apparent that Yost didn't have a great deal to work with among his middle relievers. His LOOGY addiction exacerbated the problem. All of the relievers save for swing-man Carlos Villanueva and mop-up man Chris Spurling averaged less than an inning per appearance. Only 50 right-handed relievers averaged less than an inning per game in 2007, and average of 1.7 per team. Counting deadline addition Linebrink as one third of a season, the Brewers exactly doubled the major league average in that department. The reason was Yost's unhealthy addiction to playing matchups with Shouse, who averaged less than two-thirds of an inning per appearance last year. In games in which Yost called upon Shouse, the Brewers were seven wins under .500, the worst of any Brewers reliever of significance (Spurling's far worse mark is the result of his being used primarily for mop-up work).

Table 1. The Middle Will Not Hold

Pitcher	G	IP	WXRL	LEV	FRA	Tm W-L
Francisco Cordero	66	63.1	3.220	1.87	3.25	56-10
Derrick Turnbow	77	68.0	2.752	1.60	4.96	49-28
Carlos Villanueva	59	79.1	1.906	1.09	5.26	28-25
Scott Linebrink	27	25.1	-0.294	1.06	4.54	12-15
Brian Shouse	73	47.2	1.132	0.99	2.52	33-40
Matt Wise	56	53.2	1.286	0.97	4.50	30-26
Chris Spurling	49	50.0	0.625	0.78	6.47	18-31

All statistics for relief appearances only.

At the base of the team's pitching woes were its defensive problems. The Brewers finished 13th in the league in Defensive Efficiency, their rate of converting balls in play into outs. Adjusting for their environment via James Click's Park-Adjusted Defensive Efficiency methodology (using a park factor specific to defensive efficiency rather than to runs scored or homers), they finished 15th in the league and 28th in the majors. According to Click's work, a one percent difference in PADE is worth 13 runs, or 1.3 wins, over the course of a season. The Brewers' defensive deficiency on balls in play was 3.44 percent below average, thus Milwaukees' iron gloves cost them 44.7 runs, or nearly 4.5 wins.

That deficiency has multiple sources, but the main culprit lies in the team's most visible personnel asset, its homegrown infield. Numerous systems—Clay Davenport's Translations, David Pinto's Probabilistic Model of Range, Baseball Information Solutions' Plus/Minus rating, Dan Fox's Simple Fielding Runs—show the otherwise fab four to be well below average as a defensive unit, with Hardy the only one breaking into the black in some metrics. Focusing on the Davenport numbers, which are derived from traditional defensive statistics, as well as a the observation-based Plus/Minus numbers (which we can convert into runs using the Linear Weights marginal value of turning a single into an out of 0.74 runs) we get the results in Table 2.

Table 2. The Quartet of Clank

Player	FRAA	+/-
1B Fielder	-13	-11.1
2B Weeks	-13	-12.6
SS Hardy	4	5.2
3B Braun	-27	-30.4
Infield Total	-49	-48.9

That's not a pretty picture, particularly in the case of Braun and Weeks, who played 112 and 115 games respectively at key defensive positions. Those weren't the team's only defensive shortcomings, either. Last winter Melvin decided that Bill Hall, a utilityman from 2003 to 2005 and the team's regular shortstop after Hardy went down to injury in 2006, would take over from Brady Clark in center field; Hall finished with -12 FRAA. Catcher Johnny Estrada, acquired via trade from Arizona, displaced incumbent Damian Miller but threw out just 13 percent of stolen base attempts, finishing with -9 FRAA.

To address some of these issues, Estrada was traded to the Mets over the winter for reliever Guillermo Mota, but his replacement, free agent Jason Kendall, doesn't represent an upgrade on either side of the ball (-15 FRAA between the A's and Cubs last year). As for the rest of the defense, Melvin and company went into the winter with an array of options to consider, some—such as moving Weeks to center and upgrading at second—admittedly more far-fetched than others. Melvin toyed with bringing in a new third baseman during the Winter Meetings, but after coming up empty on deals for players such as Scott Rolen, Hank Blalock, and Tadahito Iguchi, he instead signed center fielder Mike Cameron to a $7 million deal with a $10 million option for 2009.

That course of action represents an upgrade in center (though not an immediate one, as Cameron must first serve a 25-game suspension for testing positive for a banned stimulant), but it remains to be seen how it will impact the rest of the team. Moving Hall to left field would raise the bar for his offensive production following a year in which he was apparently pressing at the plate to make up for his defensive woes. Moving him to third base, with Braun taking over left field, is another option. Hall doesn't have a ton of experience at the hot corner, but he's posted an FRAA Rate2 of 100 (exactly average) in 84 career games there and would almost certainly represent a defensive upgrade. The major hitch with that scenario is that Braun in left would be blocking last year's first-round pick, Matt LaPorta, who is already blocked at first base by Fielder. Charitably described as defensively challenged, LaPorta is attempting to learn left in time for a potential late-2008 arrival. Perhaps the team could petition its former owner for a return to the AL so that one of their defensive liabilities could DH.

As for the rest of the challenges facing Melvin, his surplus of starting pitchers makes him a popular man with his fellow GMs. A full year of Gallardo and a healthy Sheets, however unlikely the latter might be, could provide major improvement. As could establishing Villanueva and rookie Manny Parra in the rotation (the latter pitched well in a 26 1/3-inning cup of coffee), thus relegating Capuano, Bush, and/or Vargas to trade fodder.

The bullpen is more of a challenge. Cordero departed via a four-year, $46 million deal with the Reds. Linebrink, acquired from the Padres in a questionable deal that cost the team pitching prospect Will Inman as well as LOOGY Joe Thatcher, signed a cringe-inducing four-year, $19 million deal with the White Sox, netting the Brewers a draft pick for their troubles.

The veterans that have been imported to help replace Cordero and Linebrink don't necessarily inspire confidence. While snagging Eric Gagné for a one-year, $10 million deal might be considered a coup, his lengthy injury history and dismal late-season performance in Boston (6.75 ERA, -1.4 WXRL) classify the signing as a high-risk, high-reward venture. Elsewhere, Mota was awful after returning from a suspension for performance-enhancing drug use in June (5.76 ERA, -0.4 WXRL). Salomon Torres, acquired from Pittsburgh in December for a pair of minor league relievers, wasn't much better (5.47 ERA, -0.1 WXRL) in a season that saw him lose his job as closer at the end of May and battle elbow problems thereafter (at this writing he's hinting at retirement). The one-year contract handed Quadruple-A LOOGY Randy Choate merely feeds Ned Yost's situational relief habit.

Former Royal David Riske (2.45 ERA, 1.1 WXRL) is a more promising addition, but he'll cost the team $13 million over three-years, a price that could increase should he serve time as the team's closer, a not unlikely scenario given Gagné's fragility. Still, it's good to see that Attanasio has shown a willingness to increase the payroll to augment the Brewers' ability to contend. The team's Opening Day payroll rose from $57.6 million in 2006 to $71.0 million in 2007, and coming off a season in which they set a franchise record for attendance (2,869,144), they needn't be shy about going higher.

It took the exit of Bud Selig and his family for the Brewers to get back on their feet, but after more than a decade of wandering in a bleak wilderness of mediocrity, the franchise finally has hope and faith. Even better, they have what every club, small- or large-market, craves: a nucleus of young blue-chip talent under club control. Windows of opportunity like this one don't open by accident; they are a product of years of good decision making. If Melvin can tap the team's resources, both financial and developmental, while dealing from strength to patch the team's few holes, the Brewers may well outdo last year's club and write a new chapter in the history of Milwaukee baseball.

HITTERS

Ryan Braun 3B Bats: R Throws: R Height: 6' 2" Weight: 200 Born: November 17, 1983 Age: 24

YEAR	TEAM	LVL	AGE	PA	R	2B	3B	HR	RBI	BB	SO	SB	CS	EqBRR	AVG	OBP	SLG	MLVr	EqAVG	EqOBP	EqSLG	EqA	VORP	DEFENSE
2005	WVA	A	21	166	21	16	2	8	35	9	34	2	4	-1.6	.355	.396	.645	.540	.244	.279	.449	.240	2.9	34-3B -5
2006	BRV	A+	22	260	34	12	2	7	37	23	54	14	4	0.1	.274	.346	.438	.156	.241	.302	.392	.246	1.6	58-3B -4
2006	HUN	AA	22	257	42	19	1	15	40	21	46	12	0	1.4	.303	.367	.589	.386	.289	.346	.583	.308	30.0	57-3B -15
2007	NAS	AAA	23	134	28	12	0	10	22	15	11	4	3	0.0	.342	.418	.701	.620	.314	.388	.636	.324	21.4	29-3B 1
2007	MIL	MLB	23	492	91	26	6	34	97	29	112	15	5	0.8	.324	.370	.634	.404	.325	.374	.653	.326	57.2	106-3B -24
2008	MIL	MLB	24	678	111	40	4	39	117	60	137	16	6	0.8	.300	.367	.575	.251	.300	.365	.579	.307	60.6	158-3B -14

Breakout: 30% Improve: 60% Collapse: 9% Attrition: 5%   Comparables: Tony Conigliaro, Alex Rodriguez, Del Ennis, Eric Chavez

The Hebrew Hammer made a major impact in his debut, leading the league in slugging percentage (even with a phantom 0-for-10 to give him the minimum number of plate appearances), setting an all-time rookie record in that category, and beating out Colorado's Troy Tulowitzki for Rookie of the Year honors. Yet his season was not an unalloyed triumph. In a division decided by two games, the tardiness of Braun's promotion (and that of starter Yovani Gallardo) may have been a difference-maker, and if that wasn't, Braun's godawful defense certainly was. By any available methodology, Braun's bad hands and throwing problems made him off-the-charts brutal in the field, costing the team 20 to 30 runs and contributing to their ranking 28th in Park-Adjusted Defensive Efficiency. Moving him to an outfield corner is an option, but would complicate the pending arrival of last year's first-round draft pick, Matt LaPorta. This isn't an easy problem to solve.

Lorenzo Cain OF Bats: R Throws: R Height: 6' 2" Weight: 185 Born: April 13, 1986 Age: 22

YEAR	TEAM	LVL	AGE	PA	R	2B	3B	HR	RBI	BB	SO	SB	CS	EqBRR	AVG	OBP	SLG	MLVr	EqAVG	EqOBP	EqSLG	EqA	VORP	DEFENSE	
2006	WVA	A	20	603	91	36	4	6	60	58	104	34	11	2.5	.307	.384	.425	.184	.250	.311	.345	.235	-23.0	123-RF 8	
2007	BRV	A+	21	533	67	21	3	2	44	37	97	24	9	2.9	.276	.338	.344	.008	.239	.294	.310	.217	-35.1	84-RF 8	36-CF 1
2008	MIL	MLB	22	572	61	27	3	5	41	40	126	19	7	1.4	.237	.297	.330	-.248	.237	.295	.332	.219	-16.8	134-RF -1	

Breakout: 21% Improve: 52% Collapse: 24% Attrition: 12%   Comparables: Garey Ingram, Darren Burton, Joe McEwing, Steve Moss

Cain had an outstanding full-season debut in 2006, but took a step backward when promoted to High-A last season. The Florida State League is certainly a more difficult environment in which to put up big numbers than the Sally League, but the promotion is not the lone explanation for Cain's struggles. Cain's biggest problem is plate discipline; he doesn't take enough bad pitches or swing at enough good ones. That's one of the hardest adjustments to make for a player, but if Cain can do that, his physical tools can carry him to a starting job in the major leagues.

Craig Counsell   INF   Bats: L   Throws: R   Height: 6' 0"   Weight: 175   Born: August 21, 1970   Age: 37

YEAR	TEAM	LVL	AGE	PA	R	2B	3B	HR	RBI	BB	SO	SB	CS	EqBRR	AVG	OBP	SLG	MLVr	EqAVG	EqOBP	EqSLG	EqA	VORP	DEFENSE		
2005	ARI	MLB	34	670	85	34	4	9	42	78	69	26	7	4.6	.256	.350	.375	-.029	.250	.345	.371	.259	15.4	138-2B	17	
2006	ARI	MLB	35	415	56	14	4	4	30	31	47	15	8	-1.6	.255	.327	.347	-.146	.252	.324	.346	.238	-0.6	81-SS	20	
2007	MIL	MLB	36	334	31	12	2	3	24	41	47	4	2	-1.0	.220	.323	.309	-.205	.223	.331	.322	.238	-7.3	33-3B	6	22-2B -1
2008	MIL	MLB	37	180	20	7	1	1	14	19	26	4	1	0.1	.237	.323	.323	-.210	.237	.320	.325	.228	-0.3	46-2B	2	

Breakout: 13% Improve: 24% Collapse: 37% Attrition: 48%   Comparables: Floyd Baker, Bill Russell, Jeff Reboulet, Keith Lockhart

Three years ago, we slammed the Twins for doling out a two-year, $2.05 million deal to replacement-level futility-man Juan Castro, but that contract pales in comparison to the two-year, $6 million deal handed to Counsell after the 2006 season by Brewers GM Doug Melvin. The deal even contains a poison-pill clause; if traded, Counsell's $3.4 million club option for 2009 becomes a $2.8 million player option. Counsell's the anti-Braun; he can pick it at three infield positions, but despite patience at the plate, his subzero offense negates that minimal value.

Joe Dillon   4C   Bats: R   Throws: R   Height: 6' 2"   Weight: 215   Born: August 2, 1975   Age: 32

YEAR	TEAM	LVL	AGE	PA	R	2B	3B	HR	RBI	BB	SO	SB	CS	EqBRR	AVG	OBP	SLG	MLVr	EqAVG	EqOBP	EqSLG	EqA	VORP	DEFENSE		
2005	ABQ	AAA	29	425	80	21	1	24	72	57	59	11	1	-0.3	.360	.459	.631	.438	.303	.395	.519	.313	45.4	74-3B	10	17-LF -1
2005	FLO	MLB	29	39	6	1	0	1	1	1	8	0	0	0.4	.167	.211	.278	-.436	.162	.205	.270	.146	-3.0			
2007	NAS	AAA	31	378	69	28	2	20	73	50	34	6	1	1.7	.317	.405	.605	.426	.283	.372	.540	.307	39.8	53-3B	5	17-LF -1
2007	MIL	MLB	31	82	12	8	2	0	10	5	14	0	0	-0.1	.342	.390	.500	.260	.342	.390	.500	.304	6.7			
2008	MIL	MLB	32	467	71	27	2	18	66	56	66	6	2	-0.2	.286	.376	.501	.150	.286	.373	.504	.295	30.3	111-3B	4	

Breakout: 27% Improve: 53% Collapse: 14% Attrition: 14%   Comparables: Edgar Martinez, Russ Morman, Bob Brenly, Emil Brown

A natural third baseman who was drafted by the Royals back in 1997, this longtime minor league thumper (.296/.380/.524 career) parlayed his versatility into a late-season utility role with the Brewers; he even went 8-for-20 as a pinch-hitter. He won't sustain his scorching performance, but a four-corner backup who plays a little second base as well while providing pop off the bench is more than worthy of a roster spot.

Alcides Escobar   SS   Bats: R   Throws: R   Height: 6' 1"   Weight: 155   Born: December 16, 1986   Age: 21

YEAR	TEAM	LVL	AGE	PA	R	2B	3B	HR	RBI	BB	SO	SB	CS	EqBRR	AVG	OBP	SLG	MLVr	EqAVG	EqOBP	EqSLG	EqA	VORP	DEFENSE
2005	WVA	A	18	562	80	25	8	2	36	20	90	30	13	-1.2	.271	.305	.362	-.072	.214	.239	.280	.181	-40.3	120-SS -3
2006	BRV	A+	19	386	47	9	1	2	33	19	56	28	8	5.0	.257	.296	.306	-.109	.227	.261	.272	.198	-24.7	79-SS -12
2007	BRV	A+	20	283	37	8	3	0	25	7	35	18	10	0.4	.325	.345	.377	.101	.281	.301	.330	.223	-1.7	61-SS -2
2007	HUN	AA	20	245	27	5	4	1	28	11	36	4	3	-2.0	.283	.314	.354	-.063	.251	.277	.312	.204	-7.8	59-SS 2
2008	MIL	MLB	21	574	53	21	4	2	35	14	87	23	8	2.0	.241	.262	.306	-.345	.240	.260	.308	.194	-15.7	135-SS -1

Breakout: 16% Improve: 39% Collapse: 38% Attrition: 7%   Comparables: Joaquin Arias, Wilton Guerrero, William Bergolla, Pedro Lopez

Escobar is a mixed bag. He's a good prospect, but may also be a tad overrated. On the plus side, he hit for average at Double-A as a 20-year-old and is one of the better defensive shortstops in the minors. On the other hand, he has absolutely no power, there's little reason to believe any is coming, and he rarely walks. That makes him a defensive-oriented shortstop who bats seventh or eighth in the majors. Valuable? Yes. Special? No.

Johnny Estrada   C   Bats: S   Throws: R   Height: 5' 11"   Weight: 215   Born: June 27, 1976   Age: 32

YEAR	TEAM	LVL	AGE	PA	R	2B	3B	HR	RBI	BB	SO	SB	CS	EqBRR	AVG	OBP	SLG	MLVr	EqAVG	EqOBP	EqSLG	EqA	VORP	DEFENSE
2005	ATL	MLB	29	383	31	26	0	4	39	20	38	0	0	-4.2	.261	.303	.367	-.112	.256	.300	.369	.234	3.2	93-C 7
2006	ARI	MLB	30	443	43	26	0	11	71	13	40	0	0	-1.3	.302	.328	.444	.028	.292	.318	.430	.259	14.3	103-C -3
2007	MIL	MLB	31	464	40	25	0	10	54	12	43	0	0	-2.5	.278	.296	.403	-.088	.277	.297	.407	.243	7.7	108-C -9
2008	NYN	MLB	32	273	21	14	0	5	31	9	27	1	1	-1.0	.258	.287	.367	-.205	.261	.290	.382	.225	2.7	67-C -2

Breakout: 6% Improve: 24% Collapse: 44% Attrition: 44%   Comparables: Toby Hall, Bengie Molina, Tom Pagnozzi, Ray Fosse

Acquired in the Doug Davis deal, Estrada supplanted Damian Miller as the Brewers' starting backstop last year, but was a thorough disappointment. A 22-point drop in BABIP spelled the difference between a useful season at the plate and lousy one, and that's before factoring in his throwing troubles (only 13 percent caught stealing). Those shortcomings may have been related to a bone spur in his elbow and torn cartilage in his left knee, both surgically repaired over the winter. Not explained by the injuries were complaints that Estrada clashed with pitching coach Mike Maddux and members of the pitching staff. Sent to the Mets for Guillermo Mota in a swap of unwanteds on the eve of the Jason Kendall signing, Estrada found himself in a crowded catching situation following the Mets' acquisition of Brian Schneider and was subsequently non-tendered. He'll soon be on his fifth team in four years.

Prince Fielder 1B Bats: L Throws: R Height: 6' 0" Weight: 260 Born: May 9, 1984 Age: 24

YEAR	TEAM	LVL	AGE	PA	R	2B	3B	HR	RBI	BB	SO	SB	CS	EqBRR	AVG	OBP	SLG	MLVr	EqAVG	EqOBP	EqSLG	EqA	VORP	DEFENSE
2005	NAS	AAA	21	441	68	21	0	28	86	54	93	8	5	-4.0	.291	.388	.569	.311	.254	.342	.484	.278	15.8	91-1B -8
2005	MIL	MLB	21	62	2	4	0	2	10	2	17	0	0	-0.1	.288	.306	.458	.039	.288	.306	.441	.256	2.0	
2006	MIL	MLB	22	648	82	35	1	28	81	59	125	7	2	-2.0	.271	.347	.483	.098	.269	.346	.479	.282	20.0	150-1B -2
2007	MIL	MLB	23	681	109	35	2	50	119	90	121	2	2	-2.7	.288	.395	.618	.374	.284	.395	.626	.329	69.1	150-1B -14
2008	MIL	MLB	24	653	106	34	1	38	111	82	121	7	2	-0.9	.287	.384	.560	.242	.287	.381	.564	.308	49.3	152-1B -5

Breakout: 21% Improve: 58% Collapse: 17% Attrition: 7%   Comparables: Boog Powell, Kent Hrbek, John Mayberry, Jose Canseco

Having already emerged as the friendly face of the franchise's resurgence, Fielder gained even more prominence during the Brewers' hot start, gracing the cover of the country's two major sports magazines. More importantly, he far outdistanced his rookie performance, providing the team with MVP-level production for under $500,000 while supplanting Willie Mays as the youngest player ever to belt 50 homers in a season. For all of that, Fielder's third-place finish in the NL MVP voting overestimates his contribution; he ranked 34th in WARP due to defense that fell off dramatically from 2006. In tandem with his unique physique, that rates as a concern going forward. Note PECOTA's long-range forecast: the careers of the four men above didn't have a second act.

Mat Gamel 3B Bats: L Throws: R Height: 6' 0" Weight: 205 Born: July 26, 1985 Age: 22

YEAR	TEAM	LVL	AGE	PA	R	2B	3B	HR	RBI	BB	SO	SB	CS	EqBRR	AVG	OBP	SLG	MLVr	EqAVG	EqOBP	EqSLG	EqA	VORP	DEFENSE
2005	HEL	Rk	19	216	34	15	2	5	37	12	49	7	4	-3.5	.327	.375	.497	.237	.208	.240	.300	.182	-25.3	38-3B -8
2006	WVA	A	20	555	65	28	5	17	88	52	81	9	2	-3.0	.288	.359	.469	.189	.236	.292	.379	.233	-3.2	108-3B -6
2007	BRV	A+	21	534	78	37	8	9	60	58	98	14	7	-4.6	.300	.378	.472	.260	.261	.333	.425	.262	21.8	112-3B -25
2008	MIL	MLB	22	629	74	37	4	14	68	56	142	11	4	0.0	.250	.319	.406	-.099	.250	.317	.409	.247	7.7	147-3B -12

Breakout: 34% Improve: 61% Collapse: 10% Attrition: 6%   Comparables: Brandon Moss, Laynce Nix, Scott Hodges, Ron Lockett

If you thought Ryan Braun was a bad fielder, get a load of Gamel, a fourth-round 2005 pick who made 53 errors and fielded .826 last year. As bad as his hands and footwork may be, the Brewers think his problems are correctable, so they don't plan to move him yet. At the plate, the story is happier; Gamel offers very good contact skills, decent plate discipline, and plus power. He ran off a 33-game hitting streak at High-A Brevard County and won MVP honors in the Hawaii Winter Baseball League. His future likely lies beyond Milwaukee, but he'll start 2008 in Double-A Huntsville.

Cole Gillespie OF Bats: R Throws: R Height: 6' 1" Weight: 205 Born: June 20, 1984 Age: 24

YEAR	TEAM	LVL	AGE	PA	R	2B	3B	HR	RBI	BB	SO	SB	CS	EqBRR	AVG	OBP	SLG	MLVr	EqAVG	EqOBP	EqSLG	EqA	VORP	DEFENSE	
2006	HEL	Rk	22	233	49	12	1	8	31	40	34	18	4	4.4	.344	.464	.548	.484	.259	.352	.393	.266	0.4	27-LF -1	16-CF -1
2007	BRV	A+	23	522	75	25	3	12	62	72	95	16	8	1.2	.267	.378	.420	.164	.235	.333	.381	.253	-10.0	122-LF 4	
2008	MIL	MLB	24	604	83	33	3	17	65	71	132	18	7	1.5	.253	.346	.424	-.026	.253	.343	.427	.266	10.1	141-LF -2	

Breakout: 28% Improve: 63% Collapse: 9% Attrition: 8%   Comparables: Chris Snopek, Jeremy Giambi, Anthony Raglani, Nolan Reimold

A third-round 2006 pick from NCAA champion Oregon State, Gillespie enjoyed an excellent pro debut that year, finishing in the top five in the Pioneer League in all three slash stats. Last year, he skipped right to the High-A Florida State League, where, after a rough start, he hit an impressive .332/.426/.491 over the final two months of the season. Though he offers a smooth line-drive swing and a patient approach at the plate, Gillespie has just average power potential, a problem seeing as a weak arm places the onus on him to produce as a left fielder.

Tony Graffanino   2B/3B   Bats: R   Throws: R   Height: 6' 1"   Weight: 190   Born: June 6, 1972   Age: 36

YEAR	TEAM	LVL	AGE	PA	R	2B	3B	HR	RBI	BB	SO	SB	CS	EqBRR	AVG	OBP	SLG	MLVr	EqAVG	EqOBP	EqSLG	EqA	VORP	DEFENSE			
2005	KCA	MLB	33	217	29	5	2	3	18	22	28	3	1	2.3	.298	.377	.393	.062	.309	.395	.420	.289	8.6	19-2B	-4	15-3B	-1
2005	BOS	MLB	33	200	39	12	1	4	20	9	23	4	1	3.4	.319	.355	.457	.122	.319	.365	.476	.289	11.9	48-2B	-3		
2006	KCA	MLB	34	250	34	16	0	5	32	25	31	3	4	-1.4	.268	.346	.409	-.033	.267	.354	.415	.264	3.1	25-3B	1	11-1B	-2
2006	MIL	MLB	34	261	34	17	3	2	27	20	37	2	0	1.2	.280	.345	.403	-.004	.280	.345	.403	.263	9.0	55-2B	-13		
2007	MIL	MLB	35	260	34	8	0	9	30	24	44	0	1	-0.6	.238	.315	.390	-.101	.235	.318	.391	.247	-0.9	27-2B	-1	22-3B	0
2008	MIL	MLB	36	187	21	8	1	4	21	16	29	2	1	0.0	.253	.322	.389	-.114	.253	.320	.392	.243	3.5	48-2B	-4		

Breakout: 9%   Improve: 23%   Collapse: 57%   Attrition: 49%   Comparables: Billy Hitchcock, Don Hoak, Greg Pryor, Jim Davenport

For a utilityman, Graffanino has always provided a reasonable amount of lumber to go with the leather, but as the short half of a platoon with Craig Counsell last year—at third before Ryan Braun's promotion, then at second when Rickie Weeks went down—he was dreadful save for a .380/.429/.740 June. His season ended when he tore his meniscus and ACL in early August, knocking him out of action until next summer and putting a damper on his marketability as a free agent this winter.

Gabe Gross   OF   Bats: L   Throws: R   Height: 6' 3"   Weight: 210   Born: October 21, 1979   Age: 28

YEAR	TEAM	LVL	AGE	PA	R	2B	3B	HR	RBI	BB	SO	SB	CS	EqBRR	AVG	OBP	SLG	MLVr	EqAVG	EqOBP	EqSLG	EqA	VORP	DEFENSE			
2005	SYR	AAA	25	449	64	29	4	6	46	52	83	14	2	1.3	.297	.380	.438	.100	.265	.347	.392	.264	-0.4	58-LF	0	38-RF	3
2005	TOR	MLB	25	102	11	4	1	1	7	10	21	1	1	-0.4	.250	.324	.348	-.137	.253	.340	.352	.245	-1.8	16-RF	1	11-LF	1
2006	MIL	MLB	26	252	42	15	0	9	38	36	60	1	0	2.5	.274	.382	.476	.151	.269	.380	.466	.294	15.7	29-CF	0	14-LF	3
2007	NAS	AAA	27	90	13	3	2	4	10	14	14	2	0	0.0	.355	.456	.605	.552	.312	.411	.571	.328	11.8				
2007	MIL	MLB	27	210	28	12	2	7	24	25	37	3	1	1.6	.235	.329	.437	-.017	.236	.333	.451	.270	2.9	32-RF	1		
2008	MIL	MLB	28	239	36	12	2	8	28	31	46	4	1	0.5	.267	.366	.467	.073	.267	.363	.470	.283	12.5				

Breakout: 22%   Improve: 47%   Collapse: 23%   Attrition: 32%   Comparables: Roger Repoz, Len Gabrielson, Duane Walker, Jeromy Burnitz

Slowed by a hamstring strain in spring training, Gross spent the better part of the first four months of the season as the forgotten man in the Brewers' outfield. Through July 20, he drew just 106 PA and hit a meager .202/.321/.382. A month in Nashville helped him find his stroke, and he returned to hit .266/.337/.489 over the final six weeks of the season. Given his 2006 performance and all-around skills as a fourth outfielder, Gross was underutilized. If nothing else, he could fit into a low-cost platoon arrangement in left field now that Geoff Jenkins has departed.

Tony Gwynn Jr.   CF   Bats: L   Throws: R   Height: 6' 0"   Weight: 190   Born: October 4, 1982   Age: 25

YEAR	TEAM	LVL	AGE	PA	R	2B	3B	HR	RBI	BB	SO	SB	CS	EqBRR	AVG	OBP	SLG	MLVr	EqAVG	EqOBP	EqSLG	EqA	VORP	DEFENSE			
2005	HUN	AA	22	601	83	21	5	1	41	76	75	34	15	-1.4	.271	.370	.338	-.028	.228	.315	.290	.222	-22.6	130-CF	-8		
2006	NAS	AAA	23	494	73	21	5	4	42	42	84	30	11	3.1	.300	.360	.396	.064	.265	.322	.358	.243	-0.7	91-CF	7	11-LF	-1
2006	MIL	MLB	23	80	5	2	1	0	4	2	15	3	1	-0.3	.260	.275	.312	-.274	.260	.275	.312	.210	-2.5	15-CF	1		
2007	NAS	AAA	24	138	19	3	3	0	13	9	14	4	3	-1.0	.286	.336	.357	-.090	.252	.304	.315	.219	-4.1	27-CF	1		
2007	MIL	MLB	24	135	13	3	2	0	10	12	24	8	1	1.0	.260	.326	.317	-.161	.262	.333	.320	.245	0.1	17-CF	-5		
2008	MIL	MLB	25	243	30	10	2	2	18	21	39	8	2	0.7	.251	.321	.344	-.176	.251	.319	.347	.235	-0.2	60-CF	0		

Breakout: 32%   Improve: 49%   Collapse: 31%   Attrition: 25%   Comparables: Tom Goodwin, McKay Christensen, Trey Beamon, Dave May

On a team whose best player is the son of another former All-Star, Gwynn's pedigree garners him more attention than his talent merits. While he's got speed to burn, his minimal on-base skills and total lack of pop don't add up to a major league regular; he's more suited to working in the exciting fields of defensive replacement and pinch-hitting. His .310/.370/.405 line in 46 career plate appearances in the latter role—not to mention the career-defining RBI triple that started the spectacular crash of his father's former team last September—suggests he's more likely to be the next Orlando Palmeiro than the next Tony Gwynn Sr.

Bill Hall — CF

Bats: R Throws: R Height: 6' 0" Weight: 210 Born: December 28, 1979 Age: 28

YEAR	TEAM	LVL	AGE	PA	R	2B	3B	HR	RBI	BB	SO	SB	CS	EqBRR	AVG	OBP	SLG	MLVr	EqAVG	EqOBP	EqSLG	EqA	VORP	DEFENSE
2005	MIL	MLB	25	546	69	39	6	17	62	39	103	18	6	-0.9	.291	.342	.495	.153	.289	.341	.501	.284	36.3	56-SS 6 49-3B 0
2006	MIL	MLB	26	608	101	39	4	35	85	63	162	8	9	-5.3	.270	.345	.553	.189	.269	.348	.554	.292	44.3	124-SS -17
2007	MIL	MLB	27	503	59	35	0	14	63	40	128	4	5	-2.0	.254	.315	.425	-.044	.258	.322	.439	.258	6.7	115-CF -12
2008	MIL	MLB	28	454	61	27	2	19	66	40	106	8	3	0.0	.267	.335	.482	.042	.267	.332	.485	.274	23.7	108-CF -6

Breakout: 13% Improve: 46% Collapse: 24% Attrition: 13% Comparables: Dave Henderson, Wally Post, Brian Jordan, Ellis Burks

Add Bill Hall to the list of players who might have brought a NL Central crown to Milwaukee if he had had a better season. Coming off an excellent 2006 as J. J. Hardy's fill-in, Hall shed his jack-of-all-trades role to become the team's starting center fielder. Ill-suited to the defensive demands of the position—late jumps and poor instincts led to "creative" routes to the ball—his troubles in the field likely contributed to his slow start at the plate. A sprained ankle on July 5 which cruelly ended a four-week hot streak didn't help, and he hit just .224/.275/.385 after returning from the DL. Despite Doug Melvin's reluctance to move Hall again, the combination of his versatility and the team's defensive woes made it inevitable. Following the Mike Cameron signing, the question is whether Hall will move to third base (with Braun taking left field) or take over left himself, which might be a stretch given his offensive capabilities.

J. J. Hardy — SS

Bats: R Throws: R Height: 6' 2" Weight: 190 Born: August 19, 1982 Age: 25

YEAR	TEAM	LVL	AGE	PA	R	2B	3B	HR	RBI	BB	SO	SB	CS	EqBRR	AVG	OBP	SLG	MLVr	EqAVG	EqOBP	EqSLG	EqA	VORP	DEFENSE
2005	MIL	MLB	22	427	46	22	1	9	50	44	48	0	0	1.1	.247	.327	.384	-.055	.241	.324	.377	.247	9.4	106-SS -1
2006	MIL	MLB	23	139	13	5	0	5	14	10	23	1	1	-1.4	.242	.295	.398	-.123	.244	.302	.394	.240	0.4	29-SS 4
2007	MIL	MLB	24	638	89	30	1	26	80	40	73	2	3	-1.0	.277	.323	.463	.043	.278	.329	.475	.270	26.4	143-SS 2
2008	MIL	MLB	25	525	62	27	1	17	66	39	63	3	2	-0.4	.273	.329	.441	-.016	.273	.327	.444	.260	22.7	123-SS 2

Breakout: 22% Improve: 43% Collapse: 27% Attrition: 19% Comparables: Kevin Elster, Bob Aspromonte, Joe Crede, Rico Petrocelli

Hardy bounced back from his 2006 ankle injury, emerging as an offensive force amid the Brewers' opening run and one of the team's few bright spots on defense. He hit .304/.350/.567 though the end of May while battling Prince Fielder for the league lead in homers, but like most of his teammates, he cooled down considerably thereafter; his .261/.308/.403 the rest of the way suggests he'll have to either improve his plate discipline or hit .300 to contribute. Nonetheless, while playing just his second full season out of the last four, Hardy surpassed his 75th percentile PECOTA projection, offering hope that he can recover the development time he's lost to injuries. An asset at his current level, Hardy should continue to make gains as he enters his prime years.

Corey Hart — RF

Bats: R Throws: R Height: 6' 6" Weight: 215 Born: March 24, 1982 Age: 26

YEAR	TEAM	LVL	AGE	PA	R	2B	3B	HR	RBI	BB	SO	SB	CS	EqBRR	AVG	OBP	SLG	MLVr	EqAVG	EqOBP	EqSLG	EqA	VORP	DEFENSE
2005	NAS	AAA	23	489	85	29	9	17	69	48	88	31	7	3.6	.308	.377	.536	.265	.267	.330	.461	.273	9.7	71-RF 6 29-LF 1
2005	MIL	MLB	23	63	9	2	1	2	7	6	11	2	0	1.0	.193	.270	.368	-.224	.193	.270	.368	.228	-1.5	11-CF -1
2006	NAS	AAA	24	115	19	10	1	4	21	12	25	11	2	0.8	.320	.391	.560	.368	.275	.345	.490	.291	4.3	17-LF -3
2006	MIL	MLB	24	256	32	13	2	9	33	17	58	5	8	-3.3	.283	.328	.468	.060	.284	.332	.479	.264	4.2	30-RF 1 19-LF -1
2007	MIL	MLB	25	566	86	33	9	24	81	36	99	23	7	2.1	.295	.353	.539	.212	.299	.357	.558	.301	39.2	97-RF 17 26-CF -2
2008	MIL	MLB	26	571	92	33	5	26	83	51	103	22	6	1.7	.288	.358	.528	.160	.288	.355	.531	.295	35.5	134-RF 7

Breakout: 32% Improve: 61% Collapse: 8% Attrition: 8% Comparables: Sammy Sosa, Wes Chamberlain, Cliff Floyd, Joe Carter

On a team whose young, homegrown infield grabs most of the attention, Hart's the not-so-trivial answer to the question of which Brewer was the most valuable in 2007. Seven seasons after being drafted and three after making his big-league debut, Hart finally spent a full year in the majors, and the results weren't too shabby. He hit for average and power, stole bases, played great defense, and wound up leading the team in WARP (9.0). Going forward, he could stand to walk more often; his OBP is propped up by 13 HBPs. In the field, Hart's fast and has a good first step and better instincts than Bill Hall, in whose domain both Hart and the none-too-fleet Geoff Jenkins snagged a lot of balls last year; Hart's performance suggests he might be able to handle center on a full-time basis, which would make his bat even more of an asset.

Hernan Iribarren — 2B

Bats: L   Throws: R   Height: 6' 1"   Weight: 180   Born: June 29, 1984   Age: 24

YEAR	TEAM	LVL	AGE	PA	R	2B	3B	HR	RBI	BB	SO	SB	CS	EqBRR	AVG	OBP	SLG	MLVr	EqAVG	EqOBP	EqSLG	EqA	VORP	DEFENSE	
2005	WVA	A	21	560	72	15	8	4	48	51	99	38	15	1.3	.290	.360	.379	.054	.228	.284	.296	.211	-25.4	121-2B	-4
2006	BRV	A+	22	455	50	12	4	2	50	39	57	19	15	-3.5	.319	.376	.384	.163	.279	.332	.341	.238	3.7	104-2B	-3
2007	HUN	AA	23	542	72	23	12	4	53	44	109	18	16	-0.5	.307	.363	.430	.137	.268	.318	.387	.244	8.8	118-2B	5
2008	MIL	MLB	24	619	75	29	7	6	44	48	123	20	8	2.7	.257	.317	.364	-.154	.257	.314	.367	.237	5.3	145-2B	-1

Breakout: 23% Improve: 55% Collapse: 19% Attrition: 7%   Comparables: Danny Richar, Trent Oeltjen, Hector Luna, Jermaine Clark

"Second-base prospect" is, almost by definition, an oxymoron. The players who fit that description are generally not athletic enough for shortstop and not good enough at the plate to carry a corner position. Even carrying that stigma, this undrafted free agent out of Venezuela has had a decent go stateside, hitting .323/.382/.436 in four minor league seasons. As that line suggests, Iribarren is a quick-wristed contact hitter who doesn't have much power or plate discipline. He has speed, but as those caught-stealing numbers attest, little idea of how to use it. Iribarren is blocked by Rickie Weeks, but the incumbent's fragility and defensive shortcomings leave the door ajar.

Geoff Jenkins — LF

Bats: L   Throws: R   Height: 6' 1"   Weight: 210   Born: July 21, 1974   Age: 33

YEAR	TEAM	LVL	AGE	PA	R	2B	3B	HR	RBI	BB	SO	SB	CS	EqBRR	AVG	OBP	SLG	MLVr	EqAVG	EqOBP	EqSLG	EqA	VORP	DEFENSE	
2005	MIL	MLB	30	618	87	42	1	25	86	56	138	0	0	-1.3	.292	.375	.513	.231	.288	.371	.515	.300	41.1	140-RF	5
2006	MIL	MLB	31	555	62	26	1	17	70	56	129	4	1	1.5	.271	.357	.434	.048	.269	.355	.428	.274	14.6	125-RF	-2
2007	MIL	MLB	32	464	45	24	2	21	64	32	116	2	2	-0.6	.255	.319	.471	.029	.254	.321	.478	.268	8.9	109-LF	9
2008	PHI	MLB	33	339	43	16	1	16	57	28	78	3	1	-0.5	.269	.336	.485	.050	.264	.334	.475	.271	11.4	82-LF	-3

Breakout: 12% Improve: 37% Collapse: 31% Attrition: 37%   Comparables: Mike Easler, Lee Stevens, Walt Moryn, Henry Rodriguez

You have to feel for Jenkins. The longtime fan favorite and former first-round pick played out the final year of his contract with the Brewers as a pricey platoon player on a team headed for better times than he'd endured over the last decade. That isn't to say Jenkins had a great year. Though his power rebounded from his 2006 dip, he posted his lowest on-base percentage since his rookie year, and even that was inflated by ten intentional walks. Furthermore, the simultaneous spike in his strikeout rate (the second-highest of his career) and drop in BABIP (.301, lowest of any full season) strongly suggest slowing bat speed. He caught on as the strong side of a platoon in the Phillies' outfield.

Matt LaPorta — LF

Bats: R   Throws: R   Height: 6' 2"   Weight: 212   Born: January 8, 1985   Age: 23

YEAR	TEAM	LVL	AGE	PA	R	2B	3B	HR	RBI	BB	SO	SB	CS	EqBRR	AVG	OBP	SLG	MLVr	EqAVG	EqOBP	EqSLG	EqA	VORP	DEFENSE	
2007	HEL	Rk	22	28	4	1	0	2	4	1	8	0	0	0.0	.259	.286	.519	.060	.185	.214	.333	.179	-4.7		
2007	WVA	A	22	102	18	8	0	10	27	7	22	0	1	-0.4	.318	.392	.750	.609	.250	.304	.543	.274	3.1	17-LF	3
2008	MIL	MLB	23	555	50	28	2	19	69	44	141	5	3	-0.5	.237	.303	.415	-.124	.237	.301	.418	.242	-2.4	130-LF	0

Breakout: NA Improve: NA Collapse: NA Attrition: NA   Comparables: Todd Dunn, Conor Jackson, Xavier Nady, Brian Anderson

Considered the top power hitter entering the 2006 draft, LaPorta slipped to the 14th round after a strained oblique wrecked his junior season and chose to return to school rather than sign with Boston. A banner senior season catapulted him to a surprisingly high seventh-overall pick by the Brewers and a $2 million bonus. Blocked by Prince Fielder at first base, LaPorta has been shifted to left field, a position he's never played before. He's Ron Kittle–level bad out there, and will likely never be more than merely acceptable. Much closer to big-league ready is his bat, as he showed in his brief Sally League stint and in a dominating postseason in which he went 7-for-14 with 13 total bases. LaPorta will likely start the year at Double-A and stands a very good chance of being the first hitter from the 2007 draft to reach the majors.

Kevin Mench   OF

Bats: R   Throws: R   Height: 6' 0"   Weight: 215   Born: January 7, 1978   Age: 30

YEAR	TEAM	LVL	AGE	PA	R	2B	3B	HR	RBI	BB	SO	SB	CS	EqBRR	AVG	OBP	SLG	MLVr	EqAVG	EqOBP	EqSLG	EqA	VORP	DEFENSE			
2005	TEX	MLB	27	615	71	33	3	25	73	50	68	4	3	0.7	.264	.328	.469	.039	.263	.337	.482	.276	14.9	110-LF	-3	35-RF	-5
2006	TEX	MLB	28	349	36	18	1	12	50	23	42	1	0	0.2	.284	.338	.459	.023	.278	.340	.457	.274	9.2	55-RF	2	15-LF	-4
2006	MIL	MLB	28	133	9	6	1	1	18	4	17	0	0	0.2	.230	.248	.317	-.336	.232	.250	.320	.196	-9.3	32-LF	-1		
2007	MIL	MLB	29	308	39	20	3	8	37	16	21	3	1	1.2	.267	.305	.441	-.030	.269	.312	.451	.261	2.6	42-LF	-6	25-RF	3
2008	MIL	MLB	30	313	40	18	1	10	41	23	33	3	1	0.1	.274	.331	.452	.000	.274	.328	.455	.263	8.5	76-LF	-3		

Breakout: 25%   Improve: 52%   Collapse: 23%   Attrition: 26%   Comparables: Shane Spencer, Tracy Jones, Ron Jackson, Matt Mieske

The Brewers entered last season with a perfectly conceived left-field platoon of righty Mench (career .305/.361/.563 vs. lefties, .255/.310/.420 vs. righties) and lefty Jenkins (career .242/.313/.408 vs. lefties, .288/.358/.525 vs. righties). Unfortunately, while Jenkins only faced lefties in 15 percent of his plate appearances, Mench wound up facing his own kind 46 percent of the time, including in 14 of 21 starts in right field at Corey Hart's expense. That was all the more detrimental because, while Mr. Big Head did his usual damage against lefties (.314/.343/.558), he was worse than ever against righties (.212/.261/.303). This from a guy who spent the spring griping about deserving to be an everyday player. Designated for assignment in December, Mench should have a new audience for such complaints by the time you read this.

Damian Miller   C

Bats: R   Throws: R   Height: 6' 3"   Weight: 220   Born: October 13, 1969   Age: 38

YEAR	TEAM	LVL	AGE	PA	R	2B	3B	HR	RBI	BB	SO	SB	CS	EqBRR	AVG	OBP	SLG	MLVr	EqAVG	EqOBP	EqSLG	EqA	VORP	DEFENSE	
2005	MIL	MLB	35	431	50	25	1	9	43	37	94	0	1	-0.6	.273	.340	.413	.025	.268	.336	.416	.262	17.0	103-C	0
2006	MIL	MLB	36	376	34	28	0	6	38	33	86	0	0	-1.0	.251	.322	.390	-.089	.248	.320	.390	.250	2.0	95-C	-1
2007	MIL	MLB	37	206	19	9	0	4	24	14	39	1	0	0.5	.237	.296	.349	-.192	.238	.301	.351	.232	-1.3	50-C	4
2008	MIL	MLB	38	155	12	6	0	3	17	12	32	1	0	-0.4	.219	.282	.329	-.288	.219	.280	.331	.207	-2.7	41-C	1

Breakout: 5%   Improve: 15%   Collapse: 63%   Attrition: 60%   Comparables: Elston Howard, Tony Peña, Joe Girardi, Jim Hegan

Buried on the bench by the acquisition of Johnny Estrada, Miller nonetheless enjoyed an uncharacteristically hot first half (.312/.356/.462) while seeing spot duty. Alas, the hits stopped falling in (.161/.238/.237 in the second half), though he still managed to throw out more baserunners than Estrada despite starting less than half as often. At this writing, he's still looking to catch on for 2008.

Brad Nelson   1B/OF

Bats: L   Throws: R   Height: 6' 2"   Weight: 220   Born: December 23, 1982   Age: 25

YEAR	TEAM	LVL	AGE	PA	R	2B	3B	HR	RBI	BB	SO	SB	CS	EqBRR	AVG	OBP	SLG	MLVr	EqAVG	EqOBP	EqSLG	EqA	VORP	DEFENSE			
2005	HUN	AA	22	238	27	8	1	6	38	26	42	1	2	-0.2	.293	.370	.428	.107	.249	.318	.380	.242	-5.7	53-LF	2		
2005	NAS	AAA	22	331	50	16	2	7	39	45	74	4	5	-1.6	.253	.359	.399	-.020	.220	.316	.338	.231	-14.8	54-LF	-4	13-RF	1
2006	HUN	AA	23	332	47	14	1	6	39	63	62	6	3	-0.7	.264	.401	.392	.153	.251	.377	.399	.278	7.7	65-1B	4		
2006	NAS	AAA	23	152	22	10	0	3	17	18	36	4	3	-1.3	.215	.316	.362	-.125	.197	.289	.348	.223	-7.8	34-1B	1		
2007	NAS	AAA	24	445	54	23	1	20	65	31	98	9	6	0.1	.263	.317	.470	.021	.235	.289	.419	.241	-8.4	55-1B	2	19-RF	-1
2008	MIL	MLB	25	514	63	24	2	15	60	57	119	11	4	0.5	.245	.331	.408	-.079	.245	.329	.411	.254	2.6	121-1B	1		

Breakout: 35%   Improve: 66%   Collapse: 12%   Attrition: 6%   Comparables: Kevin Barker, Paul Carey, Dernell Stenson, Jason Cooper

Five years ago, Brad Nelson was the top offensive prospect in the Brewers' system, but that was so five years ago. Since then, he's been hurt a lot and effective little. He was toiling away in almost complete obscurity before some signs of life at Triple-A in 2007 got him placed on the 40-man. His kind of power from the left side should equal some kind of bench career at the very least, and some work in the outfield and third base last year could help make him a solid four-corners reserve.

Lou Palmisano   C

Bats: R   Throws: R   Height: 6' 0"   Weight: 200   Born: September 16, 1982   Age: 25

YEAR	TEAM	LVL	AGE	PA	R	2B	3B	HR	RBI	BB	SO	SB	CS	EqBRR	AVG	OBP	SLG	MLVr	EqAVG	EqOBP	EqSLG	EqA	VORP	DEFENSE	
2005	BRV	A+	22	475	47	16	7	5	49	34	65	3	1	-2.1	.255	.314	.359	-.035	.214	.266	.312	.198	-26.0	88-C	4
2006	HUN	AA	23	393	39	17	1	4	37	48	65	2	0	1.0	.241	.338	.334	-.023	.226	.314	.337	.234	-5.4	96-C	-3
2007	HUN	AA	24	421	49	22	1	11	63	57	80	8	2	-1.5	.256	.368	.419	.091	.233	.330	.388	.256	6.6	97-C	-5
2008	MIL	MLB	25	358	39	16	1	7	37	35	71	4	1	-0.3	.235	.317	.366	-.164	.235	.315	.369	.237	3.3	86-C	-1

Breakout: 23%   Improve: 45%   Collapse: 27%   Attrition: 15%   Comparables: Eric Christopherson, Mike Durant, Danny Ardoin, Bill Haselman

A third-round pick in 2003, Palmisano was once considered among the top catching prospects in all of the minors, but his stock plunged with his hitting performance as he rose through the ranks. A torrid start to his repeat appearance at Double-A Huntsville last year (.315/.426/.475 through June) helped restore some hope, though he tailed off badly (.175/.293/.344) the rest of the way. Regarded as the best defensive backstop in the organization, Palmisano has enough secondary offensive skills that he could one day join the International Brotherhood of Backup Catchers.

Vinny Rottino   UT

Bats: R   Throws: R   Height: 6' 0"   Weight: 210   Born: April 7, 1980   Age: 28

YEAR	TEAM	LVL	AGE	PA	R	2B	3B	HR	RBI	BB	SO	SB	CS	EqBRR	AVG	OBP	SLG	MLVr	EqAVG	EqOBP	EqSLG	EqA	VORP	DEFENSE				
2005	HUN	AA	25	516	63	20	6	6	52	40	68	2	1	0.8	.296	.351	.403	.046	.252	.298	.354	.228	-4.8	62-3B	-4	22-C	-3
2006	NAS	AAA	26	452	55	25	2	7	42	40	74	12	7	2.6	.314	.379	.440	.171	.281	.342	.400	.260	16.5	80-3B	2	15-C	1
2007	NAS	AAA	27	430	59	17	3	12	53	37	58	15	9	-3.8	.289	.363	.446	.095	.257	.329	.403	.254	10.5	56-C	3	18-RF	1
2008	MIL	MLB	28	401	47	19	2	9	43	33	67	10	4	0.5	.257	.323	.393	-.105	.257	.320	.396	.247	5.4	96-C	1		

Breakout: 13%   Improve: 46%   Collapse: 25%   Attrition: 17%   Comparables: Josh Rabe, Brad Seitzer, Virgil Chevalier, Scooter Tucker

The first Racine native ever to play for the Brewers, this undrafted free agent has clawed his way up the organizational ladder by virtue of his gap power and versatility. The bulk of Rottino's playing time has been at third base, but he can play all four corners and since 2003 has dabbled in catching. Last year, the organization upped the ante, having him spend more time behind the plate than anywhere else. Rottino did a solid job, nabbing 35 percent of base thieves. Though he'll draw consideration as Jason Kendall's backup, the reluctance of most managers to be creative when deploying their reserve catchers suggests he'd be more valuable as 25th man who can provide flexibility.

Angel Salome   C

Bats: R   Throws: R   Height: 5' 7"   Weight: 195   Born: June 8, 1986   Age: 22

YEAR	TEAM	LVL	AGE	PA	R	2B	3B	HR	RBI	BB	SO	SB	CS	EqBRR	AVG	OBP	SLG	MLVr	EqAVG	EqOBP	EqSLG	EqA	VORP	DEFENSE	
2005	WVA	A	19	126	15	7	1	4	21	8	17	1	0	1.1	.254	.302	.432	.007	.200	.238	.342	.196	-7.6	15-C	-1
2005	HEL	Rk	19	175	34	17	0	8	50	15	16	6	2	-0.4	.415	.469	.673	.758	.297	.337	.442	.265	16.2	19-C	-7
2006	WVA	A	20	467	63	31	2	10	85	39	63	7	3	-0.7	.292	.349	.447	.151	.240	.287	.359	.227	-8.2	76-C	1
2007	BRV	A+	21	276	33	20	0	6	53	12	32	1	0	0.2	.318	.341	.465	.215	.285	.308	.431	.255	9.3	38-C	-12
2008	MIL	MLB	22	298	32	16	1	7	34	18	49	3	1	0.0	.263	.308	.404	-.111	.263	.306	.407	.242	5.0	73-C	-3

Breakout: 25%   Improve: 47%   Collapse: 23%   Attrition: 12%   Comparables: Tommy Eason, Raul Gonzalez, Bengie Molina, Brook Fordyce

This Bronx-raised Dominican rates as the Brewers' top catching prospect. Solid at the plate, he draws raves for his work ethic and arm strength. The rest of his defensive game is a work in progress, however, so much so that it raises questions about where else a 5-foot-7, 195-pound fireplug can play. Progress was in limited supply last year, as Salome missed the first month of the season recuperating from a broken ankle, then drew a 50-game suspension after the results of his performance-enhancing drug test came back positive in late July. Once he gets back into the swing of things, he's likely to find himself in Double-A.

Rickie Weeks   2B

Bats: R   Throws: R   Height: 6' 0"   Weight: 205   Born: September 13, 1982   Age: 25

YEAR	TEAM	LVL	AGE	PA	R	2B	3B	HR	RBI	BB	SO	SB	CS	EqBRR	AVG	OBP	SLG	MLVr	EqAVG	EqOBP	EqSLG	EqA	VORP	DEFENSE	
2005	NAS	AAA	22	249	43	14	9	12	48	28	51	10	1	0.1	.320	.435	.655	.544	.284	.385	.564	.315	27.6	54-2B	-11
2005	MIL	MLB	22	414	56	13	2	13	42	40	96	15	2	-2.9	.239	.333	.394	-.041	.235	.329	.396	.260	9.7	94-2B	-12
2006	MIL	MLB	23	413	73	15	3	8	34	30	92	19	5	1.8	.279	.363	.404	.022	.282	.362	.414	.276	18.5	90-2B	-4
2007	MIL	MLB	24	506	87	21	6	16	36	78	116	25	2	4.7	.235	.374	.433	.055	.235	.377	.439	.292	26.1	110-2B	-14
2008	MIL	MLB	25	501	79	24	4	16	55	59	105	18	5	1.2	.265	.368	.454	.059	.265	.365	.457	.284	27.2	118-2B	-6

Breakout: 21%   Improve: 44%   Collapse: 17%   Attrition: 17%   Comparables: Joe Foy, Frank Bolling, Mark Teahen, Andre Rodgers

For the third year in a row, Weeks was dogged by a hand injury. After missing the final two months of 2006 following surgery to repair a torn tendon in his right wrist, he began 2007 battling the injury's aftereffects. He wasn't horrible during the first two months (.243/.345/.432), but pain caused by the breakup of scar tissue compromised his bat control and generated fears of a cascade injury, sending him to the DL at the end of May. Out of sync upon returning (.149/.292/.223 over a six-week span), Weeks was briefly sent down in early August to regain his stroke. His return ten days later provided a glimpse of the amazing potential his injuries have concealed as he hit .273/.442/.553 with 11 homers through the end of the season. For the first time since 2004, Weeks isn't spending the offseason rehabbing from surgery. Weeks's defensive shortcomings might tempt another team to move him, but the Brewers will settle for having him healthy for an entire season.

PITCHERS

Greg Aquino

Bats: R   Throws: R   Height: 6' 1"   Weight: 190   Born: January 11, 1978   Age: 30

YEAR	TEAM	LVL	AGE	W	L	SV	G	GS	IP	H	BB	SO	HR	GB%	BABIP	STUFF	WHIP	ERA	PERA	EqERA	EqH9	EqBB9	EqSO9	EqHR9	VORP	SN/WX
2005	ARI	MLB	27	0	1	1	35	0	31¹	42	17	34	7	44.0%	.385	-16	1.88	7.76	9.22	8.53	11.7	4.3	8.8	2.0	-9.4	0.22
2006	ARI	MLB	28	2	0	0	42	0	48¹	54	24	51	8	49.6%	.348	2	1.61	4.47	5.99	4.50	9.9	3.9	8.6	1.3	6.2	0.53
2007	NAS	AAA	29	3	2	7	35	0	38²	26	19	45	2	61.1%	.273	12	1.16	2.33	3.62	3.38	6.8	4.8	8.2	0.5	9.2	—
2007	MIL	MLB	29	0	1	0	15	0	14	13	5	12	2	42.9%	.282	2	1.29	4.50	3.56	5.02	7.5	2.5	6.9	1.3	0.2	-1.26
2008	BAL	MLB	30	2	2	2	47	0	47	48	22	41	6	46.9%	.305	2	1.48	4.50	4.47	4.36	8.7	3.9	7.4	1.1	6.1	0.50

Breakout: 35% Improve: 69% Collapse: 12% Attrition: 18%   Comparables: Turk Wendell, Vicente Romo, Danny Frisella, Wes Stock

Acquired from Arizona in the Doug Davis/Johnny Estrada deal, Aquino beat out Jose Capellan for the final bullpen spot last spring, but the decision wasn't worth the ensuing headache. Capellan groused about being sent down and was eventually traded to Detroit, while Aquino spent the summer in Nashville after a rehab stint for a forearm strain, an afterthought rather than the potential solution to the team's late-summer bullpen woes that Capellan might have been. Aquino has a bit of upside, but he still has to trim that walk rate. He was claimed off waivers by the Orioles.

Zach Braddock

Bats: L   Throws: L   Height: 6' 4"   Weight: 230   Born: August 23, 1987   Age: 20

YEAR	TEAM	LVL	AGE	W	L	SV	G	GS	IP	H	BB	SO	HR	GB%	BABIP	STUFF	WHIP	ERA	PERA	EqERA	EqH9	EqBB9	EqSO9	EqHR9	VORP	SN/WX
2006	HEL	Rk	18	2	2	0	14	8	39¹	32	31	30	3	46.9%	.269	-27	1.61	5.52	9.22	9.95	10.2	12.2	3.1	2.0	-15.3	—
2007	WVA	A	19	3	1	0	10	9	47	28	15	68	1	44.4%	.276	42	0.91	1.15	4.25	2.79	7.3	4.9	7.9	0.6	13.1	—
2008	MIL	MLB	20	5	8	0	30	19	110²	106	92	113	14	46.0%	.310	7	1.79	5.33	6.02	5.42	8.5	6.3	8.0	1.1	1.7	0.90

Breakout: 23% Improve: 44% Collapse: 35% Attrition: 13%   Comparables: Bill Pulsipher, Jose Silva, Jake Peavy, Blake Hawksworth

The grandson of "Cinderella Man" boxer Jim Braddock, Zach is an 18th-round draft-and-follow from 2005 who underwent Tommy John surgery while still in high school. Young Braddock was fashioning a storybook season of his own when shoulder tendonitis derailed him in June. Nonetheless, his projectable body and the sinking action on his low-90s fastball make him a sleeper worth following.

Steve Bray

Bats: R   Throws: R   Height: 6' 1"   Weight: 193   Born: December 22, 1980   Age: 27

YEAR	TEAM	LVL	AGE	W	L	SV	G	GS	IP	H	BB	SO	HR	GB%	BABIP	STUFF	WHIP	ERA	PERA	EqERA	EqH9	EqBB9	EqSO9	EqHR9	VORP	SN/WX
2005	HDS	A+	24	3	1	9	26	0	34²	37	8	39	9	29.3%	.311	-33	1.30	4.93	8.07	6.54	10.5	3.4	6.0	3.1	-3.3	—
2005	WIC	AA	24	1	1	0	20	0	30²	38	11	40	3	40.2%	.417	-9	1.60	4.40	8.53	8.56	13.2	4.9	8.6	1.3	-9.0	—
2006	HUN	AA	25	5	4	1	29	2	63²	57	7	57	4	38.0%	.301	-1	1.01	2.71	4.34	3.97	9.5	1.4	5.5	1.1	10.7	—
2006	NAS	AAA	25	2	0	0	21	0	21¹	11	4	18	3	33.3%	.143	-2	0.71	1.28	3.06	2.14	5.1	2.1	5.6	1.7	8.1	—
2007	NAS	AAA	26	5	2	1	42	3	77²	59	26	73	4	37.0%	.272	12	1.09	1.62	3.63	2.34	7.5	3.3	6.8	0.6	26.4	—
2008	MIL	MLB	27	4	4	3	23	7	60¹	59	25	52	9	37.1%	.287	6	1.39	4.22	4.62	4.22	8.7	3.2	6.8	1.3	9.4	1.20

Breakout: 18% Improve: 38% Collapse: 43% Attrition: 18%   Comparables: Shawn Kohn, Jeff Bajenaru, Frank Funk, Dan Miceli

Originally drafted by Milwaukee back in 2000, Bray went the college route instead and was drafted by the Royals in 2003 only to be recaptured by the Brewers in the minor league portion of the 2005 Rule 5 draft. Since then, he's led the life of an organizational soldier, but organizational soldiers who post eye-popping K/BB ratios while the big-league bullpen is imploding deserve some love, don't they? Bray's fastball tops out at only 90 mph, but he has excellent command and can throw both his slider and changeup for strikes. The thinning of Milwaukee's bullpen may offer him an opening; better late than never.

David Bush

| | | | | Bats: R | | Throws: R | | Height: 6' 2" | | Weight: 210 | | Born: November 9, 1979 | | Age: 28 |

YEAR	TEAM	LVL	AGE	W	L	SV	G	GS	IP	H	BB	SO	HR	GB%	BABIP	STUFF	WHIP	ERA	PERA	EqERA	EqH9	EqBB9	EqSO9	EqHR9	VORP	SN/WX
2005	SYR	AAA	25	2	2	0	9	9	55	65	9	40	6	49.2%	.343	-2	1.35	4.42	5.73	5.26	11.2	2.1	4.7	1.2	1.9	—
2005	TOR	MLB	25	5	11	0	25	24	136¹	142	29	75	20	46.5%	.282	-2	1.25	4.49	4.75	4.80	9.3	1.9	4.9	1.2	16.2	2.62
2006	MIL	MLB	26	12	11	0	34	32	210	201	38	166	26	48.7%	.289	21	1.14	4.41	3.61	3.93	8.2	1.4	6.5	1.0	30.9	4.12
2007	MIL	MLB	27	12	10	0	33	31	186¹	217	44	134	27	45.6%	.324	7	1.40	5.12	4.76	4.50	9.6	1.8	6.0	1.2	13.0	2.67
2008	MIL	MLB	28	10	10	0	27	27	168¹	181	41	119	22	45.9%	.300	13	1.32	4.31	4.54	4.37	9.5	1.8	5.5	1.1	21.1	3.60

Breakout: 11% Improve: 50% Collapse: 17% Attrition: 14%   Comparables: LaMarr Hoyt, Jon Lieber, Dick Bosman, John Burkett

Bush appeared poised for a breakout after posting the best strikeout-to-walk ratio among NL ERA qualifiers in 2006; PECOTA envisioned his 2007 ERA to be around 4.00. Instead, everything went in the opposite direction: his strikeout rate went down, his walk rate went up, he generated fewer grounders and more fly balls, and was burned by an increased BABIP (thanks, porous infield defense) and the highest rate of fly balls becoming home runs on the team. Topping it off, his career-long pattern of struggling at the start of games continued—opposing hitters ripped him at a .350/.390/.540 pace in the first frame. For all of that, Bush remains a low-cost inning-muncher who still provides reason to hope that his ERA can catch up to his peripherals.

Chris Capuano

| | | | | Bats: L | | Throws: L | | Height: 6' 2" | | Weight: 220 | | Born: August 19, 1978 | | Age: 29 |

YEAR	TEAM	LVL	AGE	W	L	SV	G	GS	IP	H	BB	SO	HR	GB%	BABIP	STUFF	WHIP	ERA	PERA	EqERA	EqH9	EqBB9	EqSO9	EqHR9	VORP	SN/WX
2005	MIL	MLB	26	18	12	0	35	35	219	212	91	176	31	40.4%	.292	6	1.38	3.99	4.91	4.35	8.9	3.4	6.7	1.3	31.5	4.03
2006	MIL	MLB	27	11	12	0	34	34	221¹	229	47	174	29	41.5%	.303	18	1.25	4.03	3.96	3.62	8.8	1.6	6.4	1.0	41.1	4.86
2007	MIL	MLB	28	5	12	0	29	25	150	170	54	132	20	45.1%	.339	12	1.49	5.10	4.78	4.78	9.4	2.7	7.3	1.1	6.3	2.02
2008	MIL	MLB	29	8	8	0	23	23	134	140	47	109	18	43.5%	.304	14	1.39	4.51	4.77	4.57	9.3	2.7	6.3	1.2	15.3	2.60

Breakout: 5% Improve: 39% Collapse: 28% Attrition: 21%   Comparables: Kenny Rogers, Donovan Osborne, Nate Robertson, Gary Peters

Won-lost record to the contrary, Capuano pitched better in 2006 than in 2005 thanks to improved control. In 2007, he appeared to be building on those gains amid the Brewers' hot start, going 5-0 with a 2.31 ERA through May 7, but he must have befouled an ancient burial ground at that point, because the Brewers lost every one of his remaining 22 games. Poor run support and a groin pull that sidelined him for four weeks played a part, but Capuano's 6.08 ERA and 1.5 HR/9 suggest he wasn't entirely blameless. Despite the skid, numerous teams professed interest over the winter; given the Brewers' rotation depth, he's as good a bet as any to be dealt.

Francisco Cordero

| | | | | Bats: R | | Throws: R | | Height: 6' 2" | | Weight: 235 | | Born: May 11, 1975 | | Age: 33 |

YEAR	TEAM	LVL	AGE	W	L	SV	G	GS	IP	H	BB	SO	HR	GB%	BABIP	STUFF	WHIP	ERA	PERA	EqERA	EqH9	EqBB9	EqSO9	EqHR9	VORP	SN/WX
2005	TEX	MLB	30	3	1	37	69	0	69	61	30	79	5	45.0%	.316	25	1.32	3.39	3.38	3.17	7.2	3.7	9.6	0.6	16.8	3.49
2006	TEX	MLB	31	7	4	6	49	0	48²	48	16	54	5	43.8%	.341	18	1.32	4.80	3.79	4.38	8.2	2.7	9.1	0.7	6.5	-0.94
2006	MIL	MLB	31	3	1	16	28	0	26²	20	16	30	2	36.4%	.290	23	1.35	1.69	3.32	1.37	6.8	4.8	9.2	0.7	12.9	1.72
2007	MIL	MLB	32	0	4	44	66	0	63¹	52	18	86	4	42.3%	.322	34	1.11	2.99	2.86	2.92	7.1	2.1	10.0	0.6	18.6	3.22
2008	CIN	MLB	33	4	6	40	57	0	64	57	25	68	7	42.8%	.297	14	1.28	3.45	3.71	3.44	7.8	3.2	8.5	0.9	14.6	2.60

Breakout: 22% Improve: 38% Collapse: 37% Attrition: 7%   Comparables: Roberto Hernandez, Eric Plunk, Jay Howell, Jeff Russell

Cordero had no trouble staying in the groove he found after arriving from Texas in 2006. He dominated hitters with his high-90s heat, posting career-best strikeout and walk rates; among NL closers only Takashi Saito had a better K/BB ratio, and among relievers with 60 or more innings pitched, only Juan Cruz and Carlos Marmol struck out more men per nine innings. Cordero expressed a desire to return, and the Brewers bid competitively, but he wound up taking a four-year, $46 million deal with the Reds. Those looking for sour grapes in small sample sizes can take heart: as a Brewer, Cordero put up a 1.08 ERA in Miller Park, 5.40 elsewhere.

Yovani Gallardo

| | | | | | | | | | | | | | | Bats: R | | Throws: R | | Height: 6' 1" | | Weight: 210 | | Born: February 27, 1986 | | Age: 22 |

YEAR	TEAM	LVL	AGE	W	L	SV	G	GS	IP	H	BB	SO	HR	GB%	BABIP	STUFF	WHIP	ERA	PERA	EqERA	EqH9	EqBB9	EqSO9	EqHR9	VORP	SN/WX
2005	WVA	A	19	8	3	1	26	18	121¹	100	51	110	5	52.9%	.297	1	1.24	2.75	6.00	5.78	9.5	6.6	4.3	1.0	-2.1	—
2006	BRV	A+	20	6	3	0	13	13	77¹	54	23	103	4	58.8%	.298	32	1.00	2.10	4.75	4.54	8.3	4.2	7.8	1.0	8.2	—
2006	HUN	AA	20	5	2	0	13	13	77	50	28	85	2	42.6%	.268	39	1.01	1.64	3.43	3.25	7.0	3.8	6.9	0.5	18.8	—
2007	NAS	AAA	21	8	3	0	13	13	77²	53	28	110	4	43.7%	.295	51	1.04	2.90	3.42	3.72	7.1	3.5	9.8	0.6	15.7	—
2007	MIL	MLB	21	9	5	0	20	17	110¹	103	37	101	8	40.2%	.305	41	1.27	3.67	3.19	3.28	7.6	2.5	7.5	0.6	25.1	3.80
2008	MIL	MLB	22	11	10	0	29	29	175¹	162	69	177	18	44.2%	.302	28	1.32	3.88	4.05	3.96	8.2	3.0	7.9	0.9	29.9	4.60

Breakout: 7%   Improve: 32%   Collapse: 34%   Attrition: 18%   Comparables: Jeremy Bonderman, Pete Broberg, Denny McLain, Gary Bell

Phil Hughes and Tim Lincecum may have gotten the headlines last year, but Gallardo also belongs in the discussion of the game's top young pitchers. Called up in June, this 2004 second-round pick showed polish well beyond his years, missing bats, limiting homers, and dramatically outpitching his rotation mates the rest of the way. He surrendered more than four runs just three times, all in a four-start span, and if you disregard that 11-run avalanche in Colorado, his ERA falls to just 2.82. If there's a concern, it's that Felix Hernandez was the only 21-year-old in Organized Baseball last year to throw more than Gallardo's 188 combined innings and, as Gallardo moves forward in the rotation this year, the temptation to ride his arm will only increase.

Zach Jackson

| | | | | | | | | | | | | | | Bats: L | | Throws: L | | Height: 6' 5" | | Weight: 220 | | Born: May 13, 1983 | | Age: 25 |

YEAR	TEAM	LVL	AGE	W	L	SV	G	GS	IP	H	BB	SO	HR	GB%	BABIP	STUFF	WHIP	ERA	PERA	EqERA	EqH9	EqBB9	EqSO9	EqHR9	VORP	SN/WX
2005	DUN	A+	22	8	1	0	10	10	59¹	56	6	48	3	59.8%	.301	-1	1.05	2.88	4.95	5.64	10.1	2.2	4.1	1.0	-0.2	—
2005	NHP	AA	22	4	3	0	9	9	54	57	12	43	3	53.8%	.338	-1	1.28	4.00	5.56	6.06	10.8	3.1	4.4	0.9	-2.5	—
2005	SYR	AAA	22	4	4	0	8	8	47¹	61	21	33	3	48.1%	.379	-6	1.73	5.14	6.98	7.36	12.3	4.9	4.5	0.8	-8.6	—
2006	NAS	AAA	23	4	6	0	18	18	107²	106	44	58	11	51.2%	.286	-19	1.40	4.11	6.09	5.77	10.2	4.2	3.5	1.3	-1.9	—
2006	MIL	MLB	23	2	2	0	8	7	38¹	48	14	22	6	47.1%	.323	-6	1.62	5.40	6.01	5.31	10.6	2.8	4.6	1.2	0.0	-0.06
2007	NAS	AAA	24	11	10	0	29	28	169²	184	64	123	13	49.4%	.333	-2	1.46	4.45	5.81	5.97	10.7	3.8	5.1	0.9	-6.5	—
2008	MIL	MLB	25	4	7	0	25	16	95	111	45	63	13	48.0%	.319	-4	1.64	5.59	5.86	5.71	10.4	3.6	5.2	1.2	-1.7	0.50

Breakout: 24%   Improve: 50%   Collapse: 19%   Attrition: 18%   Comparables: Trevor Miller, Alex Graman, Heath Murray, Travis Miller

Jackson made seven starts for the Brewers in 2006, but he spent all of 2007 in Triple-A without getting the call. That says pretty much all you need to know about his standing within the organization. Jackson is the perfect example of why going the safe route in the draft is often no more likely to produce a useful major leaguer than taking some raw, high-ceiling tools guy. Being high on polish but low on stuff will get a pitcher only so far. Sometimes that draftee will turn into a back-of-the-rotation starter, but quite often he turns into Zach Jackson.

Jeremy Jeffress

| | | | | | | | | | | | | | Bats: R | | Throws: R | | Height: 6' 0" | | Weight: 175 | | Born: September 21, 1987 | | Age: 20 |

YEAR	TEAM	LVL	AGE	W	L	SV	G	GS	IP	H	BB	SO	HR	GB%	BABIP	STUFF	WHIP	ERA	PERA	EqERA	EqH9	EqBB9	EqSO9	EqHR9	VORP	SN/WX
2006	BRR	Rk	18	2	5	0	13	4	33	30	25	37	0	68.0%	.316	-11	1.67	6.00	7.35	10.16	9.9	11.3	3.8	0.6	-15.7	—
2007	WVA	A	19	9	5	0	18	18	86¹	62	44	95	8	45.5%	.263	0	1.23	3.13	6.28	6.60	8.4	7.3	5.8	1.8	-8.5	—
2008	MIL	MLB	20	5	9	0	24	24	118	117	107	105	17	44.7%	.298	1	1.90	6.10	6.60	6.21	8.8	6.9	7.0	1.3	-7.4	0.00

Breakout: 40%   Improve: 65%   Collapse: 17%   Attrition: 11%   Comparables: Scott Elbert, Dan Serafini, Eduardo Morlan, Don Levinski

Bongloads in the basement rec room or radar guns on a big league mound—the choice of which to light up is apparently a tough one for Jeffress. The 16th pick of the 2006 draft out of a Virginia high school, Jeffress has drawn comparisons to Dwight Gooden for his triple-digit velocity, athleticism, and smooth delivery, but the Gooden connection took on a darker dimension last August. Nearing the end of a fine season at West Virginia, Jeffress drew a 50-game suspension for testing positive for a "drug of abuse" (reported to be marijuana), then flunked a club-administered whiz quiz during the Arizona Fall League. While that latter doesn't count as a second strike and only subjects him to discipline by the Brewers, Jeffress has already jeopardized his future while turning the whispers about his makeup into snickers. With the suspension, he's likely out of action until June; hopefully he can sort out his priorities and return his focus to his smoking fastball rather than his smoking.

Ray King

Bats: L　　Throws: L　　Height: 6' 1"　　Weight: 240　　Born: January 15, 1974　　Age: 34

YEAR	TEAM	LVL	AGE	W	L	SV	G	GS	IP	H	BB	SO	HR	GB%	BABIP	STUFF	WHIP	ERA	PERA	EqERA	EqH9	EqBB9	EqSO9	EqHR9	VORP	SN/WX
2005	SLN	MLB	31	4	4	0	77	0	40	46	16	23	4	49.6%	.323	-17	1.55	3.38	6.12	4.50	10.9	3.3	5.0	0.9	7.3	-1.11
2006	COL	MLB	32	1	4	1	67	0	44²	56	21	23	6	52.6%	.352	-24	1.72	4.43	6.54	5.06	11.2	3.8	4.4	1.1	4.9	0.01
2007	WAS	MLB	33	1	1	0	55	0	33²	31	18	18	5	40.5%	.252	-20	1.43	4.54	4.57	4.24	7.9	4.0	4.5	1.3	4.6	0.69
2007	MIL	MLB	33	0	0	0	12	0	6	6	3	7	1	50.0%	.333	6	1.50	6.00	5.07	6.00	9.0	4.5	9.0	1.5	-0.0	0.04
2008	WAS	MLB	34	1	2	1	39	0	34¹	38	17	22	4	45%	.299	-15	1.57	4.82	5.37	5.21	9.6	4.0	5.1	1.1	2.1	0.20

Breakout: 12% Improve: 30% Collapse: 44% Attrition: 30%　　　　Comparables: Terry Mathews, Jim Brower, Jim Poole, Rodney Myers

The portly portsider returned to Milwaukee in September for his second tour of duty following a swap for Andrew Lefave, winner of the Sally League batting title. Despite the declining peripherals, King stills handles lefties (.187/.276/.347), but managers don't have much trouble countering with righty hitters, who beat the tar out of him (.311/.407/.568) in an equal number of plate appearances last year. Supposedly down 20 pounds thanks to off-season diet and conditioning efforts, he re-signed with Washington on a minor league deal.

Scott Linebrink

Bats: R　　Throws: R　　Height: 6' 2"　　Weight: 200　　Born: August 4, 1976　　Age: 31

YEAR	TEAM	LVL	AGE	W	L	SV	G	GS	IP	H	BB	SO	HR	GB%	BABIP	STUFF	WHIP	ERA	PERA	EqERA	EqH9	EqBB9	EqSO9	EqHR9	VORP	SN/WX
2005	SDN	MLB	28	8	1	1	73	0	73²	55	23	70	4	39.5%	.270	23	1.06	1.83	2.85	2.27	6.8	2.6	7.9	0.5	27.4	3.71
2006	SDN	MLB	29	7	4	2	73	0	75²	70	22	68	9	40.4%	.289	8	1.22	3.57	4.06	3.77	8.8	2.3	7.5	1.0	18.9	3.99
2007	SDN	MLB	30	3	3	1	44	0	45	41	14	25	9	39.7%	.234	-17	1.22	3.80	4.50	3.43	8.1	2.4	4.8	1.8	9.8	2.07
2007	MIL	MLB	30	2	3	0	27	0	25¹	27	11	25	3	50.7%	.343	7	1.50	3.56	4.72	4.38	9.1	3.3	8.4	1.1	2.7	-0.29
2008	CHA	MLB	31	3	3	3	51	0	58²	61	20	43	8	43.0%	.293	-3	1.38	4.29	4.10	4.00	8.8	2.8	5.9	1.2	10.1	0.80

Breakout: 12% Improve: 30% Collapse: 44% Attrition: 17%　　　　Comparables: Dave Veres, T.J. Mathews, Roy Lee Jackson, Dave Tobik

Few GMs are more savvy about bullpen assembly than Kevin Towers, so it was telling when the Padres' GM put Linebrink on the market and cashed him in for a trio of Brewer pitching prospects. If the doubling of Linebrink's home run rate and ERA from 2005 to 2006 didn't suggest which way his trend arrows pointed, the further collapse of his peripherals in 2007 certainly did. He wasn't much help to the Brewers, but he stopped the bleeding just enough to sucker the White Sox into gifting him with a four-year, $19 million deal that, in a home run haven like U.S. Cellular Park, appears destined to earn a spot in the *Big Book of Bad Bullpen Ideas*.

Seth McClung

Bats: R　　Throws: R　　Height: 6' 6"　　Weight: 260　　Born: February 7, 1981　　Age: 27

YEAR	TEAM	LVL	AGE	W	L	SV	G	GS	IP	H	BB	SO	HR	GB%	BABIP	STUFF	WHIP	ERA	PERA	EqERA	EqH9	EqBB9	EqSO9	EqHR9	VORP	SN/WX
2005	TBA	MLB	24	7	11	0	34	17	109¹	106	62	92	20	35.7%	.274	-9	1.55	6.59	5.01	6.27	7.9	4.9	7.1	1.5	-15.4	0.49
2006	TBA	MLB	25	6	12	6	39	15	103	120	68	59	14	38.7%	.316	-14	1.83	6.29	5.58	5.91	9.3	5.4	4.7	1.0	-7.3	0.41
2007	DUR	AAA	26	1	5	5	40	0	58²	38	43	68	3	50.4%	.259	17	1.38	1.99	4.40	3.58	7.0	7.2	7.8	0.7	12.4	—
2007	NAS	AAA	26	2	0	0	5	3	19	14	5	25	2	50.0%	.293	18	1.00	1.42	3.89	2.04	7.6	2.5	9.7	1.0	7.0	—
2007	MIL	MLB	26	0	1	0	14	0	12	11	5	11	0	55.9%	.333	7	1.33	3.75	3.19	6.00	7.5	3.0	7.5	0.0	-1.1	0.01
2008	MIL	MLB	27	3	4	4	41	5	58¹	52	38	55	6	44.4%	.290	2	1.54	4.57	4.76	4.69	8.0	4.9	7.4	0.9	5.7	0.70

Breakout: 40% Improve: 59% Collapse: 22% Attrition: 23%　　　　Comparables: Colter Bean, Chad Ricketts, Rick Huisman, Brad Salmon

McClung can dial it into the high 90s, but inconsistent mechanics have led to command issues that have generated stats so ugly it's a wonder they actually print. Having failed as a starter, he found some success working out of the bullpen; as a set-up man in Durham, he held batters to a .179 average, prompting the Brewers to take a flier on him when they had to deal Grant Balfour. Yes, it's a small sample size, but McClung's walk rate plummeted after the trade, suggesting that the instruction of Mike Maddux and company ("The rose goes in the front, big guy . . .") may be the key to unlocking his potential.

Derek Miller

Bats: L   Throws: L   Height: 6' 0"   Weight: 195   Born: November 8, 1981   Age: 26

YEAR	TEAM	LVL	AGE	W	L	SV	G	GS	IP	H	BB	SO	HR	GB%	BABIP	STUFF	WHIP	ERA	PERA	EqERA	EqH9	EqBB9	EqSO9	EqHR9	VORP	SN/WX
2005	HEL	Rk	23	1	1	1	9	6	36	31	4	35	4	44.2%	.276	-29	0.97	2.75	6.94	7.20	10.5	3.3	3.9	2.4	-5.3	—
2005	WVA	A	23	2	1	0	8	7	36	35	10	27	3	31.8%	.311	-25	1.25	3.50	7.20	6.03	11.2	4.9	3.2	1.7	-1.5	—
2006	WVA	A	24	8	2	0	18	18	93¹	93	34	105	6	41.3%	.347	-16	1.36	3.58	8.02	7.03	12.3	5.8	5.8	1.6	-12.8	—
2006	BRV	A+	24	1	3	0	9	7	46¹	39	19	43	2	41.9%	.303	-2	1.26	3.90	5.45	6.53	9.4	5.4	5.0	0.9	-4.3	—
2007	BRV	A+	25	4	4	0	17	17	94²	89	25	75	10	46.4%	.276	-33	1.20	3.71	6.74	7.21	10.5	3.7	4.4	1.9	-15.9	—
2007	HUN	AA	25	6	2	0	11	11	68	58	16	65	10	44.0%	.276	-11	1.09	3.18	5.70	4.95	9.2	2.5	5.8	2.1	4.6	—
2008	MIL	MLB	26	5	9	0	35	18	116²	141	55	77	22	42.4%	.313	-10	1.68	6.28	6.52	6.33	10.7	3.6	5.2	1.7	-9.9	-0.30

Breakout: 27% Improve: 55% Collapse: 18% Attrition: 18%   Comparables: Rob Kell, Mario Ramos, Steven Bondurant, Bryan Ward

Miller was chosen as a draft-and-follow out of the University of Vermont in 2004 following Tommy John surgery, and has put up superficially good stats at every stop since. The caveat is that he's always been old for his level, and isn't exactly on the fast track; one can almost conjure up an image of Matthew McConaughey's character from *Dazed and Confused*: "That's what I love about these A-Ball hitters. I get older, they stay the same age." With excellent command of a low-90s fastball and a plus slider, he could take advantage of the system's thinning out and earn a look in the bullpen.

Manny Parra

Bats: L   Throws: L   Height: 6' 3"   Weight: 200   Born: October 30, 1982   Age: 25

YEAR	TEAM	LVL	AGE	W	L	SV	G	GS	IP	H	BB	SO	HR	GB%	BABIP	STUFF	WHIP	ERA	PERA	EqERA	EqH9	EqBB9	EqSO9	EqHR9	VORP	SN/WX
2005	HUN	AA	22	5	6	0	16	16	91	111	21	86	4	59.0%	.374	8	1.45	3.96	5.88	5.79	11.9	2.8	5.6	0.8	-1.8	—
2006	BRV	A+	23	1	3	0	15	14	54²	47	32	61	4	53.1%	.319	-3	1.46	2.99	7.34	7.23	10.3	7.8	6.5	1.5	-8.6	—
2006	HUN	AA	23	3	0	0	6	6	31²	26	8	29	0	54.0%	.370	12	1.09	2.88	3.85	5.02	8.8	2.8	5.7	0.3	1.8	—
2007	HUN	AA	24	7	3	0	13	13	80²	70	26	81	2	48.7%	.315	19	1.19	2.68	4.25	4.16	9.2	3.3	6.1	0.5	12.1	—
2007	NAS	AAA	24	3	1	0	4	4	26	15	7	25	1	46.3%	.230	24	0.85	1.73	2.81	2.84	5.3	2.8	6.8	0.4	7.8	—
2007	MIL	MLB	24	0	1	0	9	2	26¹	25	12	26	1	36.8%	.338	19	1.41	3.76	3.40	3.67	8.0	3.3	8.0	0.3	4.4	-0.09
2008	MIL	MLB	25	7	8	1	40	20	131²	134	62	114	13	46.9%	.313	9	1.49	4.66	4.79	4.79	9.1	3.6	6.8	0.9	10.7	1.80

Breakout: 11% Improve: 33% Collapse: 33% Attrition: 21%   Comparables: Joe Saunders, C. J. Nitkowski, Dean Stone, Scott Ruffcorn

A 2001 draft-and-follow, this hard-throwing lefty has been derailed by shoulder woes so frequently that last season was just the second time he's topped 100 innings. After finally clearing Huntsville (where he'd spent parts of every season since 2004), he tossed a perfect game in his second PCL start and soon found himself in the Brewer bullpen. A broken thumb ended his season just as he stepped in to patch the rotation, but he'll compete for a spot there this spring. With a 92 to 95 mph fastball, a sinker, and a big curve, he'll miss plenty of bats.

Luis Peña

Bats: R   Throws: R   Height: 6' 5"   Weight: 200   Born: January 10, 1983   Age: 25

YEAR	TEAM	LVL	AGE	W	L	SV	G	GS	IP	H	BB	SO	HR	GB%	BABIP	STUFF	WHIP	ERA	PERA	EqERA	EqH9	EqBB9	EqSO9	EqHR9	VORP	SN/WX
2005	BRV	A+	22	2	6	0	15	12	76	72	28	51	6	59.8%	.297	-26	1.32	4.26	7.29	7.44	11.0	5.6	3.2	1.7	-13.4	—
2006	BRV	A+	23	4	6	1	23	11	65	68	33	59	6	51.8%	.339	-26	1.55	4.43	9.30	7.76	12.3	7.0	5.0	1.9	-13.4	—
2007	BRV	A+	24	5	0	6	16	0	21²	14	7	27	1	65.4%	.271	3	0.97	2.07	4.35	3.60	7.7	4.5	7.7	0.9	4.4	—
2007	HUN	AA	24	0	4	12	35	0	46²	36	14	42	1	58.0%	.273	0	1.07	2.89	3.73	3.83	7.9	3.0	5.2	0.4	8.8	—
2008	MIL	MLB	25	3	5	2	26	7	61²	67	35	43	6	53.2%	.311	-6	1.65	5.04	5.45	5.20	9.7	4.3	5.4	0.9	2.4	0.50

Breakout: 33% Improve: 60% Collapse: 13% Attrition: 15%   Comparables: Edwin Almonte, Jeff McCurry, Monte Mansfield, Roman Colon

This Venezuelan spent seven years as a minor league starter and moved up the organizational ladder at the glacial pace of two years per level. Moved to the bullpen full time last year, he took a major leap forward; his fastball touched 99 mph in the Southern League playoffs. Doug Melvin likes his arm and considered him a sleeper in the closer battle prior to the acquisition of Gagné, comparing Peña to the Rockies' Manny Corpas. Stay tuned.

Ben Sheets

Bats: R Throws: R Height: 6' 1" Weight: 220 Born: July 18, 1978 Age: 29

YEAR	TEAM	LVL	AGE	W	L	SV	G	GS	IP	H	BB	SO	HR	GB%	BABIP	STUFF	WHIP	ERA	PERA	EqERA	EqH9	EqBB9	EqSO9	EqHR9	VORP	SN/WX
2005	MIL	MLB	26	10	9	0	22	22	156²	142	25	141	19	38.9%	.281	24	1.07	3.33	3.56	3.82	8.2	1.3	7.3	1.0	32.1	4.12
2006	MIL	MLB	27	6	7	0	17	17	106	105	11	116	9	42.5%	.342	45	1.09	3.82	3.32	3.48	8.7	0.8	9.0	0.7	24.0	3.24
2007	MIL	MLB	28	12	5	0	24	24	141¹	138	37	106	17	37.9%	.287	18	1.24	3.82	3.43	3.17	7.8	1.9	6.2	1.0	31.4	4.08
2008	MIL	MLB	29	9	7	0	24	24	145¹	145	36	122	18	41.4%	.295	20	1.24	3.93	4.08	3.97	8.9	1.9	6.5	1.1	25.2	3.80

Breakout: 2% Improve: 30% Collapse: 33% Attrition: 14%   Comparables: Alex Fernandez, Turk Farrell, Larry Christenson, Curt Schilling

The great baseball scout Roseanne Roseannadanna said it best about Sheets: "It's always something." For the third year in a row, assorted maladies prevented the Brewers' nominal ace from pitching a full season. Sheets found a groove in the first half, at one point making nine quality starts out of ten on his way to a 3.41 ERA. Alas, a torn tendon sheath in his middle finger and a strained hamstring limited him to six second-half starts and a 5.68 ERA; the franchise's best pitcher could do little more than watch his team's playoff hopes melt away. Entering the final season of a four-year, $38.5 million deal, Sheets's no-trade clause no longer applies to eight teams; the Brewers may put him on the market if they don't think they can sign him.

Brian Shouse

Bats: L Throws: L Height: 5' 11" Weight: 185 Born: September 26, 1968 Age: 39

YEAR	TEAM	LVL	AGE	W	L	SV	G	GS	IP	H	BB	SO	HR	GB%	BABIP	STUFF	WHIP	ERA	PERA	EqERA	EqH9	EqBB9	EqSO9	EqHR9	VORP	SN/WX
2005	TEX	MLB	36	3	2	0	64	0	53¹	55	18	35	7	54.2%	.291	-10	1.37	5.23	4.15	5.30	8.3	3.0	5.6	1.0	-2.0	0.15
2006	TEX	MLB	37	0	0	0	6	0	4¹	6	1	3	1	37.5%	.333	-9	1.62	4.19	6.53	3.86	11.6	1.9	5.8	1.9	1.0	-0.29
2006	MIL	MLB	37	1	3	2	59	0	34	34	17	20	3	53.2%	.292	-11	1.50	3.97	4.53	3.44	8.7	4.0	4.8	0.8	6.9	0.36
2007	MIL	MLB	38	1	1	1	73	0	47²	46	14	32	0	57.5%	.313	9	1.26	3.02	2.94	2.98	7.8	2.2	5.6	0.0	12.4	1.13
2008	MIL	MLB	39	2	2	3	44	0	39	42	13	23	4	52.8%	.300	-11	1.40	4.12	4.30	4.26	9.6	2.5	4.7	0.8	5.3	0.50

Breakout: 16% Improve: 35% Collapse: 46% Attrition: 30%   Comparables: Buddy Groom, Chris Hammond, Terry Leach, Tom Burgmeier

Not to pick on Shouse, but if you're looking for a brief sermon on the evils of the LOOGY, look no further. Yes, his 2.52 Fair Run Average led the Brewers and was one of only two on the team under 4.50 (Francisco Cordero's 3.25 being the other), but in games in which Ned Yost called upon Shouse, the team was 33-40. By comparison, the Brewers were at least three games above .500 in the set of games pitched by every other reliever who threw at least 26 innings with the club, and 50-39 in the games in which Shouse didn't pitch. Like most LOOGYs, Shouse wound up facing more righties—against whom he was predictably less effective (.295/.358/.337, vs. .214/.264/.262 against lefties). His presence contributed to the fact that all of the team's key relievers save for Carlos Villanueva averaged less than an inning per appearance.

Chris Spurling

Bats: R Throws: R Height: 6' 6" Weight: 240 Born: June 28, 1977 Age: 31

YEAR	TEAM	LVL	AGE	W	L	SV	G	GS	IP	H	BB	SO	HR	GB%	BABIP	STUFF	WHIP	ERA	PERA	EqERA	EqH9	EqBB9	EqSO9	EqHR9	VORP	SN/WX
2005	DET	MLB	28	3	4	0	56	0	70²	58	22	26	8	47.9%	.229	-17	1.13	3.44	3.42	3.67	7.2	2.8	3.3	0.9	14.8	1.28
2006	TOL	AAA	29	1	4	5	49	0	66²	61	10	34	4	50.9%	.281	-17	1.07	2.04	4.51	4.18	9.5	1.9	3.3	0.9	9.5	—
2006	DET	MLB	29	0	0	0	9	0	11¹	13	4	4	2	39.0%	.282	-25	1.50	3.19	6.13	3.27	10.6	3.3	3.3	1.6	3.7	-0.08
2006	MIL	MLB	29	0	0	0	7	0	10	12	4	3	3	38.5%	.250	-37	1.60	7.20	6.65	6.10	9.6	2.6	2.6	2.6	-1.3	0.00
2007	NAS	AAA	30	2	0	0	10	0	16	19	2	9	1	57.9%	.327	-10	1.31	1.69	4.95	2.93	11.2	1.2	3.5	0.6	4.5	—
2007	MIL	MLB	30	2	1	0	49	0	50	63	14	28	6	51.4%	.328	-12	1.54	4.68	4.93	4.73	10.2	2.1	4.6	0.9	1.9	0.63
2008	MIL	MLB	31	2	2	1	34	0	37¹	42	11	20	5	47.6%	.293	-13	1.40	4.39	4.67	4.47	10.0	2.3	4.1	1.1	4.8	0.40

Breakout: 28% Improve: 49% Collapse: 38% Attrition: 36%   Comparables: Tom Buskey, Brian Meadows, Steve Crawford, Cecil Upshaw

Cleanup on aisle five! A few years removed from being a mainstay of the pre–Leyland Tiger bullpen, Spurling has become the Brewers' mop-and-bucket man. Only five pitchers who threw at least 50 relief innings last year had lower leverage scores than Spurling's 0.78. That's a grim lot, but Spurling's poor performance in dealing with inherited baserunners (11 out of 22 scored, fluffing his Fair Run Average up to 6.47) suggests he was lucky to have even that job.

Jeff Suppan

| | | | | | | | | | | | | | | | | | | Bats: R | Throws: R | Height: 6' 2" | Weight: 220 | Born: January 2, 1975 | Age: 33 |

YEAR	TEAM	LVL	AGE	W	L	SV	G	GS	IP	H	BB	SO	HR	GB%	BABIP	STUFF	WHIP	ERA	PERA	EqERA	EqH9	EqBB9	EqSO9	EqHR9	VORP	SN/WX
2005	SLN	MLB	30	16	10	0	32	32	194¹	206	63	114	24	47.7%	.298	-1	1.38	3.57	5.12	4.78	9.9	2.7	4.9	1.1	27.5	4.28
2006	SLN	MLB	31	12	7	0	32	32	190	207	69	104	21	47.5%	.299	3	1.45	4.12	4.69	4.60	9.6	2.8	4.5	0.9	27.0	4.35
2007	MIL	MLB	32	12	12	0	34	34	206²	243	68	114	18	47.8%	.329	10	1.50	4.62	4.40	4.12	9.6	2.5	4.6	0.7	23.0	3.04
2008	MIL	MLB	33	8	9	0	25	25	145²	165	49	80	19	48.2%	.301	0	1.47	4.84	5.11	4.94	10.1	2.5	4.3	1.1	9.8	2.20

Breakout: 7% Improve: 36% Collapse: 38% Attrition: 21% Comparables: Chris Bosio, Mark Gubicza, Aaron Sele, Milt Pappas

Suppan parlayed a stellar 2006 postseason into a four-year, $42 million contract, but the deal didn't make much sense for the pitching-rich/cash-poor Brewers. While he can certainly eat innings, Suppan's low strikeout rate makes him extremely reliant on his fielders and thus a poor fit for a defense that yielded the sixth-highest BABIP in the majors. After a hot start (2.62 ERA through May 5), Suppan put up a 5.22 ERA the rest of the way, surrendering more hits than any NL pitcher save for Livan Hernandez. With Graig Nettles, Ozzie Smith, and Roberto Alomar behind him, he'd stand a chance.

Derrick Turnbow

| | | | | | | | | | | | | | | | | | | Bats: R | Throws: R | Height: 6' 3" | Weight: 210 | Born: January 25, 1978 | Age: 30 |

YEAR	TEAM	LVL	AGE	W	L	SV	G	GS	IP	H	BB	SO	HR	GB%	BABIP	STUFF	WHIP	ERA	PERA	EqERA	EqH9	EqBB9	EqSO9	EqHR9	VORP	SN/WX
2005	MIL	MLB	27	7	1	39	69	0	67¹	49	24	64	5	51.1%	.249	18	1.08	1.74	2.99	2.17	6.6	3.0	7.9	0.7	26.2	4.64
2006	MIL	MLB	28	4	9	24	64	0	56¹	56	39	69	8	44.8%	.336	9	1.69	6.87	5.22	7.18	8.7	5.3	9.8	1.1	-12.8	-1.24
2007	MIL	MLB	29	4	5	1	77	0	68	44	46	84	4	48.1%	.261	28	1.32	4.63	2.82	4.13	5.4	5.2	9.7	0.5	8.7	2.75
2008	MIL	MLB	30	2	3	4	48	0	53	48	34	58	5	46.9%	.311	8	1.54	4.56	4.65	4.71	8.0	4.9	8.6	0.8	5.4	0.40

Breakout: 22% Improve: 43% Collapse: 24% Attrition: 19% Comparables: Charlie Hough, Todd Jones, Joe Boever, Jeff Schwarz

After a horrendous 2006 in which he lost the closer job, Turnbow salvaged a modicum of dignity last year as the top set-up man for his replacement, Cordero. Though wild (among NL pitchers with at least 60 innings, none walked hitters more frequently) and inconsistent (ERAs under 3.00 in three months, above 6.00 in the other three), he held opponents to a .183 batting average while cutting his home run rate in half. He was brutal when forced to cope with inherited runners (12 out of 14 scored) and continued the self-defeating habit of abandoning his slider at times, reverting to an all-fastball repertoire.

Claudio Vargas

| | | | | | | | | | | | | | | | | | | Bats: R | Throws: R | Height: 6' 3" | Weight: 230 | Born: June 19, 1978 | Age: 30 |

YEAR	TEAM	LVL	AGE	W	L	SV	G	GS	IP	H	BB	SO	HR	GB%	BABIP	STUFF	WHIP	ERA	PERA	EqERA	EqH9	EqBB9	EqSO9	EqHR9	VORP	SN/WX
2005	NWO	AAA	27	2	2	0	5	5	28	24	12	35	4	41.1%	.308	13	1.29	4.18	5.23	4.85	8.7	4.2	8.3	1.7	2.2	—
2005	WAS	MLB	27	0	3	0	4	4	12²	22	7	5	4	29.6%	.360	-77	2.29	9.21	18.70	15.63	15.6	4.3	3.6	2.8	-7.0	-0.16
2005	ARI	MLB	27	9	6	0	21	19	119²	124	40	90	21	37.6%	.290	-1	1.37	4.81	4.81	4.48	8.7	2.7	6.0	1.5	9.9	1.90
2006	ARI	MLB	28	12	10	0	31	30	167²	185	52	123	27	41.5%	.300	4	1.41	4.83	4.52	4.55	9.1	2.3	5.8	1.2	13.4	2.68
2007	MIL	MLB	29	11	6	1	29	23	134¹	153	54	107	23	36.2%	.319	-1	1.54	5.09	5.04	4.48	9.2	3.0	6.5	1.4	8.6	1.55
2008	MIL	MLB	30	5	7	1	28	16	104¹	113	40	78	16	40.1%	.300	1	1.46	4.98	5.24	5.01	9.6	2.9	5.8	1.3	6.6	1.30

Breakout: 11% Improve: 34% Collapse: 27% Attrition: 24% Comparables: Jason Johnson, James Baldwin, Shawn Boskie, Jae Weong Seo

After moving from the hitters' haven of Chase Field to neutral Miller Park, Vargas gave a standout performance for a fifth starter over the first four months of 2007, putting up a 4.30 ERA and striking out 7.6 per nine. Then the airplane landed, specifically a Boeing-like 7.67 ERA over the final two months that, in conjunction with a late-August back injury, cost him a spot in the rotation. Long balls were the problem; among NL pitchers with at least 100 innings, only seven surrendered them more frequently, and Vargas's extreme fly-ball tendencies suggest that wasn't a fluke. Given the crowded back end of the Brewer rotation, Vargas is probably the first who should be shopped.

Carlos Villanueva

Bats: R   Throws: R   Height: 6' 3"   Weight: 215   Born: November 28, 1983   Age: 24

YEAR	TEAM	LVL	AGE	W	L	SV	G	GS	IP	H	BB	SO	HR	GB%	BABIP	STUFF	WHIP	ERA	PERA	EqERA	EqH9	EqBB9	EqSO9	EqHR9	VORP	SN/WX
2005	BRV	A+	21	8	1	0	21	21	112¹	78	32	124	11	41.6%	.252	-8	0.98	2.32	5.69	4.56	8.7	4.6	6.1	1.9	11.2	—
2005	HUN	AA	21	1	3	0	4	4	20²	21	9	14	3	30.0%	.277	-20	1.45	7.39	7.09	9.47	9.9	4.7	3.8	2.4	-8.2	—
2006	HUN	AA	22	4	5	0	11	10	62¹	60	14	59	6	48.6%	.303	0	1.19	3.77	5.66	6.14	10.1	2.5	5.7	1.5	-3.5	—
2006	NAS	AAA	22	7	1	0	11	9	66²	42	26	61	6	41.4%	.210	14	1.03	2.72	3.68	3.43	6.6	3.9	6.1	1.1	15.2	—
2006	MIL	MLB	22	2	2	0	10	6	53²	43	11	39	8	44.7%	.230	19	1.01	3.69	3.07	2.98	6.6	1.5	6.0	1.2	14.1	1.42
2007	MIL	MLB	23	8	5	1	59	6	114¹	101	53	99	16	37.7%	.272	5	1.35	3.94	3.71	3.26	7.2	3.5	7.1	1.2	23.1	3.70
2008	MIL	MLB	24	4	5	2	43	7	86	85	40	72	12	41.2%	.289	2	1.44	4.72	4.94	4.77	8.8	3.5	6.6	1.3	7.9	0.90

Breakout: 6%   Improve: 21%   Collapse: 60%   Attrition: 29%   Comparables: Steve Dunning, Wayne Simpson, Todd Van Poppel, Mudcat Grant

Though Villanueva's 2006 performance suggested he could hold down a rotation spot, the Brewers' pitching depth forced him to the bullpen to start 2007. The results were mixed: a solid first half (2.83 ERA, 2.3 K/BB), was followed by a 9.67 ERA through the end of August before Claudio Vargas's back injury pressed him into the rotation. While Villanueva's peripherals didn't support the 2.10 ERA he put up in five September starts, his performance still suggested he could have outpitched the likes of Vargas, Bush, or Capuano over a full season. He'll compete for the opportunity to prove that this year.

Matt Wise

Bats: R   Throws: R   Height: 6' 4"   Weight: 195   Born: November 18, 1975   Age: 32

YEAR	TEAM	LVL	AGE	W	L	SV	G	GS	IP	H	BB	SO	HR	GB%	BABIP	STUFF	WHIP	ERA	PERA	EqERA	EqH9	EqBB9	EqSO9	EqHR9	VORP	SN/WX
2005	MIL	MLB	29	4	4	1	49	0	64¹	37	25	62	6	41.9%	.190	13	0.96	3.36	2.53	3.51	5.0	3.0	7.6	0.8	14.3	1.45
2006	MIL	MLB	30	5	6	0	40	0	44¹	45	14	27	6	46.9%	.289	-9	1.33	3.86	4.23	4.09	8.8	2.5	5.1	1.0	5.9	0.80
2007	MIL	MLB	31	3	2	1	56	0	53²	61	17	43	5	36.6%	.337	4	1.45	4.19	4.19	4.28	9.4	2.3	6.6	0.8	5.3	1.29
2008	NYN	MLB	32	3	2	3	42	0	50¹	49	17	35	6	40.9%	.281	-4	1.32	3.91	4.38	4.37	8.8	2.7	5.7	1.0	7.6	0.60

Breakout: 12%   Improve: 32%   Collapse: 36%   Attrition: 24%   Comparables: Roy Lee Jackson, Ron Taylor, Ernie Johnson, Donne Wall

Wise came back from the surgery to correct an irritated nerve in his elbow that ended his 2006 season to share seventh-inning duties with Carlos Villanueva, often pitching only a fraction of an inning because of Ned Yost's insistence on using Shouse. The reduced workload didn't seem to help; like Villanueva, Wise's performance collapsed late in the year. There may have been extenuating circumstances for Wise, however, as after he hit Reds infielder Pedro Lopez in the face with a pitch on July 25, he posted a 10.45 ERA while allowing 34 baserunners in 10 1/3 innings. Wise's overall peripherals were still better than in 2006, suggesting he can be part of a productive bullpen; he'll get that chance with the Mets.

LINEOUTS

Hitters

PLAYER		TEAM	LVL	AGE	PA	R	2B	3B	HR	RBI	BB	SO	SB-CS	EqBRR	AVG/OBP/SLG	MLVr	EqAVG/EqOBP/EqSLG	EqA	VORP
OF	D. Anderson*	HUN	AA	26	46	12	7	2	1	11	0	10	1-3	-0.8	.444/.444/.756	.896	.261/.261/.543	.251	1.7
		NAS	AAA	26	415	57	28	3	4	36	28	89	16-5	-2.0	.273/.324/.395	-.065	.242/.294/.350	.230	-20.2
2B	C. Crabbe#	NAS	AAA	24	541	84	23	9	9	38	67	70	17-14	-3.7	.287/.377/.435	.104	.254/.343/.390	.256	14.5
OF	D. Ford	WVA	A	21	254	48	15	4	5	33	23	56	31-10	2.3	.335/.398/.504	.302	.226/.281/.343	.225	-9.1
		BRV	A+	21	317	46	7	1	4	27	35	67	36-6	5.3	.231/.317/.308	-.103	.201/.280/.272	.217	-22.5
OF	C. Gindl*	HEL	Rk	18	231	40	22	3	5	42	20	38	4-4	-2.0	.372/.420/.580	.479	.255/.300/.387	.238	-11.2
3B	T. Green*	WVA	A	20	460	68	29	2	14	86	51	65	0-5	-4.2	.327/.406/.516	.323	.265/.332/.409	.256	14.9
OF	B. Katin	HUN	AA	24	508	72	24	0	24	94	41	163	3-2	-1.0	.258/.329/.471	.101	.232/.292/.430	.246	-9.6
C	J. Lucroy	HEL	Rk	21	253	35	18	2	4	39	16	37	0-3	-4.8	.342/.383/.487	.254	.248/.285/.340	.214	-11.4
OF	L. Nix*	NAS	AAA	26	386	60	20	1	24	74	31	104	5-0	0.3	.268/.329/.539	.149	.244/.303/.481	.267	12.2
C	M. Rivera	NAS	AAA	30	382	37	15	0	19	61	24	71	5-5	-4.9	.215/.270/.421	-.179	.217/.267/.393	.225	-7.2

Though he spent most of the year at Triple-A Nashville, **Drew Anderson**'s quest for the glory of fourth outfielderdom took a significant hit due to his eroding plate discipline. ⊘ A switch-hitter with good on-base skills, **Callix Crabbe** is a 5-foot-7 water bug who enjoyed a modest breakout in the power department at Nashville. Chosen in the Rule 5 draft by the Padres, he can play third and the outfield as well as second. ⊘ Considered the fastest player in the organization, **Darren Ford** used blazing speed and gap power to break out of the Sally League last year, but he struggled upon promotion to High-A Brevard County, likely earning him a return ticket to start the 2008 season. ⊘ A 2007 fifth-round Florida prepster, the 5-foot-9, 185-pound **Caleb Gindl** doesn't fit the image of a player who drew draft consideration as a hitter and a pitcher, but he made an impressive pro debut, winning the Pioneer League batting title as an 18-year-old playing against 21-year-olds. ⊘ **Taylor Green** was the Brewers' Minor League Player of the Year based on a big season at Low-A, but scouts love his effort and hard-nosed playing style far more than they love his tools. ⊘ A college teammate of Ryan Braun's at Miami, **Brendan Katin** is a lumberjack—big and powerful, but with a long swing that makes him prone to strikeouts. Too prone, probably, as whiffing in 32 percent of his plate appearances will likely keep him from The Show. ⊘ A third-round 2007 pick out of Lousiana-Lafayette, **Jonathan Lucroy** reinforced the opinion that he was the second-best offensive catcher in last year's crop behind only Matt Wieters by tearing up the Pioneer League with such conviction that he'll likely skip to the Florida State League to start 2008. ⊘ After missing the first six weeks of the 2007 season with an oblique strain, **Laynce Nix** hit for plenty of power at Nashville, but continued to show the lackluster plate discipline that has limited him to the Quadruple-A realm. He also comes up six points shy of "Callix Crabbe" as a Scrabble score. ⊘ Once the Brewers shed their Chad Moeller fetish in 2006, **Mike Rivera** stepped in as Damian Miller's backup and hit .268/.325/.458, but the acquisition of Johnny Estrada that winter forced him to spend last year in Nashville.

Pitchers

PLAYER	TEAM	LVL	AGE	W	L	SV	IP	H	BB	SO	HR	GB%	BABIP	STUFF	WHIP	ERA	PERA	EqERA	EqH9	EqBB9	EqSO9	EqHR9	VORP
C. Cody*	WMI	A	23	5	5	0	91^1	70	15	92	1	57.6%	.296	10	0.93	1.77	4.76	4.50	9.3	3.6	5.0	0.6	9.5
	BRV	A+	23	2	1	0	20	18	6	23	2	38.9%	.314	-3	1.20	3.60	7.35	6.00	11.0	4.0	7.0	2.0	-0.8
R. Dickey	NAS	AAA	32	13	6	0	169^1	159	60	119	18	54.7%	.286	-7	1.29	3.72	5.02	4.95	9.2	3.6	4.9	1.2	11.4
M. DiFelice	HUN	AA	30	6	1	0	66^2	50	6	60	3	44.3%	.264	10	0.84	1.62	3.37	2.60	7.8	1.2	5.5	0.7	20.8
	NAS	AAA	30	4	2	0	58	45	9	63	6	43.5%	.273	24	0.93	3.10	3.61	3.83	7.5	1.6	7.7	1.1	11.1
T. Dillard	NAS	AAA	23	8	4	0	133	167	37	62	13	54.8%	.339	-23	1.53	4.74	6.99	6.13	12.3	2.9	3.1	1.1	-7.3
S. Hammond*	HUN	AA	25	7	9	1	142	163	43	109	19	43.1%	.334	-40	1.45	4.69	8.31	7.49	12.2	3.3	4.5	2.0	-27.5
M. Rogers '08	MIL	MLB	22	3	8	0	942	93	108	95	7	49.8%	.329	-5	2.12	7.06	6.79	7.44	8.8	8.6	7.8	0.7	-15.3
M. Stetter*	NAS	AAA	26	1	0	1	14^2	8	5	19	1	58.1%	.250	13	0.88	4.29	3.01	5.27	5.9	3.3	9.2	0.7	0.5
	MIL	MLB	26	1	0	0	5	2	2	4	0	41.7%	.182	5	0.80	3.60	2.13	3.60	3.6	3.6	7.2	0.0	1.3

The Tigers' eighth-round pick from 2006, **Chris Cody** was an underwhelming return for pouting reliever Jose Capellan. Though Cody's dominated two leagues thus far, he's been old for his level both times. As an undersized lefty soft-tosser, he's got the deck stacked against him. ⊘ Banished from the majors after giving up six homers in his lone 2006 start, **R. A. Dickey** returned to Triple-A in 2007 to hone his knuckleball and earned PCL Pitcher of the Year honors after putting up a 2.70 ERA from June onward. With the Brewers not feeling experimental, Dickey signed a minor league deal with Minnesota after the season and was subsequently picked in the Rule 5 draft by Seattle. ⊘ **Mark DiFelice**, not to be confused with veteran backup catcher Mike, returned to Organized Baseball after spending the better part of two years in the independent Atlantic League. Though on the wrong side of 30, he's still a strike-throwing machine, which might get him a look in spring training. ⊘ Lacking great stuff, the knock on otherwise well-regarded sinkerballer **Tim Dillard**—the son of former major league utilityman Steve Dillard—had always been his inability to miss bats. It caught up to him in Nashville, sending his peripherals plunging through the floor. ⊘ **Steve Hammond** tore through three levels in his first two years of pro ball and was considered by some to be the organization's top lefty-pitching prospect ahead of Manny Parra, but a case of gopheritis took hold at Double-A Huntsville last year before he settled into a late-season groove. ⊘ The fifth overall pick in the 2004 draft, **Mark Rogers** already faced command and mechanics issues when he was shelved by shoulder woes in the second half of 2006. Labrum surgery cost him all of 2007, and he'll have to tackle his other problems as well on his way back. ⊘ Sore-armed LOOGY candidates are a dime a dozen, but unlike many of the Brewers' other overage pitching suspects, **Mitch Stetter** did see time with the big club. Still, he's battling Randy Choate on a depth chart that's hardly worthy of the name.

MANAGER: NED YOST

YEAR	TEAM	W-L	Pythag +/−	Avg PC	100+ P	120+ P	QS	BQS	REL	REL w Zero R	IBB	Subs	PH	PH Avg	PH HR	SB2	CS2	SB3	CS3	SAC Att	SAC %	POS SAC	Squeeze	Swing	In Play
2005	MIL	81-81	-3	99.5	86	4	87	11	395	238	52	43	255	.245	6	68	30	11	3	97	68.0%	41	5	135	100
2006	MIL	75-87	5	94.6	67	3	77	13	427	257	34	20	235	.267	4	60	33	10	4	84	69.1%	20	1	134	96
2007	MIL	83-79	-1	94.1	56	3	75	12	492	305	37	50	253	.224	6	86	25	9	4	75	80.0%	22	1	125	100

In his five years at the helm in Milwaukee, Ned Yost has overseen the Brewers' slow and sometimes painful journey from laughingstock to contender. Those two types of teams generally require different skill sets from their manager. The former requires patience, teaching, and nurturing, as the skipper oversees the development of young ballplayers while waiting out the bad times; the latter requires the more traditional ability to use the roster to the best tactical advantage to give the team the best opportunity to win. The odd thing about Yost is that his contending team is actually younger than the deadwood-laden squad of vets he inherited in 2003. That's created a difficult balancing act he has yet to master, as seen in the patience he showed Hardy and Weeks through injuries and extended slumps, to the detriment of the offense and thus the team's playoff hopes. As a result, Yost's suitability for the next phase of the team's journey was called into question as the Brewers squandered their fast start. Particularly scrutinized was his handling of a deep pitching staff; the numbers above place him solidly in the middle of the pack overall, but he came under fire early in the season for overreliance on his bullpen, with a chorus of "I-told-you-sos" echoing through Miller Park as Carlos Villanueva, Matt Wise, and Derrick Turnbow flamed out in the second half (Yost is most definitely *not* popular among the fan base). Not only did the team share the major league lead with 16 blown three-run leads—a total ranking among the 25 highest since 1959—but 12 of those came after July 28. Despite that ugly figure, the near-miss, and the criticism surrounding it, Yost has the enthusiastic backing of Mark Attanasio and Doug Melvin, and will return for the final year of his contract.

Minnesota Twins

After general manager Andy MacPhail departed for the Chicago Cubs during baseball's 1994 labor stoppage, Terry Ryan took over as GM of a Twins club that bore little resemblance to the scrappy, youth-oriented, budget-conscious model that we have come to be familiar with today. A clunky, aging squad whose best years had come—with world championships in 1987 and 1991—and gone, the Twins that Ryan inherited were desperately trying to extend their competitive window by one or two more seasons in order to delay the slow and painful process of rebuilding. They had a pair of good young players who were already starting to get more expensive via arbitration in second baseman Chuck Knoblauch and starter Scott Erickson. They had one highly paid, extremely popular, and perennially overrated superstar in center fielder Kirby Puckett, who a year earlier had signed a five-year, $30 million contract extension, one of the richest deals in the game at the time. Mostly, though, they had become a sort of hospice for players with local ties who were nearing the end of their careers, such as first baseman Kent Hrbek, designated hitter Dave Winfield, and Winfield's successor, Paul Molitor.

The Twins' payroll in 1994 was $27.6 million, pocket change now but middle-of-the-road by the standards of the day, yet it was not paying for winning baseball. When Ryan took over, the Twins were coming off consecutive losing seasons and heading in the wrong direction. Barely a decade old, their domed stadium had been upstaged by newer, fancier facilities such as SkyDome, with its state-of-the-art retractable roof, and the new wave of open-air throwbacks that had begun with Camden Yards, Jacobs Field, and the Ballpark at Arlington. The Metrodome never seemed to bother Min-

nesotans up to that point, particularly when 3 million of them packed the park in 1988 to see the Twins defend their first championship, but suddenly it seemed unconscionable that residents of the Twin Cities, who might be lucky to have 60 nights of nice weather out of the whole year, should spend one of those nights indoors. Most teams experienced a decline in attendance following the strike, but the Twins dropped down to dead last in the American League in 1995, barely surpassing the million-fan mark.

Then, disaster struck. Puckett hadn't had any trouble hitting pitchers in spring training in 1996, but he woke up on March 28 with severely blurred vision in his right eye. It was soon revealed that he had glaucoma, and that his sight had been diminished below the minimum level which might allow a human being to hit a 95-mile-per-hour fastball. After some last-ditch surgical attempts failed to resolve the problem, Puckett announced his retirement in July without having played a single regular season game. The Twins actually improved that year—their 78-84 record would be the closest they'd come to the .500 mark until 2001—but for all intents and purposes, they were playing out the clock, Puckett's sudden retirement having removed any joy from the endeavor.

Absent Puckett or many other assets beyond Knoblauch—Erickson proved to be little more than a league-average innings-eater and was dealt to the Orioles in July of 1995, his walk year—the Twins continued to lose, and the fans continued to find better things to do with their summer evenings. As a result, Ryan and owner Carl Pohlad began paring the payroll down to the league minimum, trading Knoblauch to the Yankees after the 1997 season, and allowing the team's other expensive veterans to leave as free agents or declining to replace them with more of the same after they retired. As a result, the average age of the Twins' position players plummeted from 29.9 in 1998 to 26.9 in 1999, while the age of the pitchers went from 28.6 to 26.3.

Looking back now, it seems that Puckett's retirement had liberated the Twins. Much as they put it off, rebuilding was necessary, and thanks to Ryan, who had been working in the team's player development department since taking over as scouting director in 1987, the Twins' farm system was rich with young talent. Ryan had always drafted well, landing a couple of quality major leaguers in nearly every draft, but while the major league team was contending, or at least pretending to, the Twins had a bad habit of either failing to sign their draft picks or parting ways with them before they'd had the chance to establish themselves. In addition to the players who didn't sign listed in Table 1, left-hander Denny Neagle was traded for a single (albeit very valuable) season of John Smiley, righty Todd Ritchie was released, and catcher Damian Miller was lost to the Diamondbacks in the 1997 expansion draft. The Twins' new, small-budget identity would not permit such wastes of resources.

Table 1. Key Twins Draft Picks, 1987–1998

1987: Willie Banks, Mark Guthire, Bret Boone (did not sign)
1988: Pat Mahomes, Aaron Sele (did not sign)
1989: Chuck Knoblauch, Denny Neagle, Scott Erickson, Marty Cordova
1990: Todd Ritchie, Rich Becker, Damian Miller, Eddie Guardado
1991: LaTroy Hawkins, Brad Radke, Matt Lawton
1992: Dan Serafini
1993: Torii Hunter, Jason Varitek (did not sign), Javier Valentin
1994: Todd Walker, A. J. Pierzynski, David Dellucci (did not sign), Corey Koskie
1995: Mark Redman, Doug Mientkiewicz
1996: Travis Lee (declared free agent after Twins failed to tender contract), Jacque Jones
1997: Michael Cuddyer, Matt LeCroy, J. C. Romero
1998: J. J. Putz (did not sign)

Just as the commissioner's office was lobbing empty threats of contraction at the Twins, who turned in their eighth-straight losing season in 2000, Ryan's young charges coalesced, resurrecting the franchise with an 85-win season in 2001 and division titles in 2002, 2003, 2004 and 2006. As is typically the case, the wins brought back the fans; Twins' attendance has steadily improved over the last seven years, with increases in six of those seven seasons, topping out at just shy of 2.3 million last year. Although Ryan rarely delved into the free-agent market—resigning Shannon Stewart after the 2003 season was the most prominent exception, and an unremarkable one at that—the team gradually ramped up its payroll to retain its homegrown stars. By 2007, the

Twins' payroll had reached $71 million, still a bit below the league median, but hardly befitting of the cheapskate image that Pohlad has engendered.

Having built and sustained a winning team at low cost in this era of extravagant payrolls and financial haves and have-nots, Ryan could be seen as one of the original "Moneyball" general managers. The description isn't a perfect fit; Ryan was never particularly adept at identifying players from the freely available talent pool, and while he ascended to the job ahead of Billy Beane, Beane's A's beat Ryan's Twins to the postseason by two years. Yet when it came to understanding players' actual values within the marketplace, the goal at the heart of the Moneyball philosophy, Ryan excelled.

In *Baseball Between the Numbers*, we explored the relationship between team success and its revenues, the key finding being that the relationship between wins and revenues is not particularly linear, as teams receive a big, all-or-nothing boost from reaching the playoffs. In doing so, we were able to estimate the value of a regular season win at about $750,000 and the value of a playoff appearance at $29 million. So how much money was Ryan making, or losing, for the Twins based on these estimates?

In order to determine this, we have to make a handful of adjustments. First, we need to adjust all of the dollars involved to 2007 terms in order to allow our analysis to measure all 13 years of Ryan's tenure equally. Typical revenue growth in baseball is about 8 percent per year, but it's been a little bit more rapid than that since *Baseball Between the Numbers* was written in 2005, so we'll set the value of a regular season win at $900,000 and the value of a playoff appearance at $35 million. Having adjusted those benchmarks, we need to adjust the Twins' payroll expenditures to 2007 terms, which can be accomplished by simply prorating the team's salaries based on the growth in the average league payroll since the year in question (Knoblauch's $6 million salary in 1997, for example, becomes $12.4 million in 2007 MLB dollars). Secondly, we need to figure out just where to start counting wins toward a team's marginal revenues. VORP figures that a team full of replacement-level players making the league minimum would win about 45 games, so we'll give Ryan credit for any wins above that 45-win threshold. Finally, we need to subtract the league minimum salaries from the payroll, since that is money that a team is obligated to spend at least 25 times over, regardless of what sort of club they want to field. Having done all of that, we get the basic profit/loss data in Table 2.

All told, we estimate that the Twins spent about $579 million in marginal payroll (in 2007 dollars) over the course of Ryan's tenure, while generating about $541

Table 2. Marginal Payroll and Marginal Revenue under Terry Ryan (1995-2007, in 2007 MLB Dollars)

Year	Record	Marginal Revenue	Marginal Payroll	Profit/Loss
1995	56-88*	$16,200,000	$57,807,000	($41,607,000)
1996	78-84	$29,700,000	$47,035,000	($17,335,000)
1997	68-94	$20,700,000	$46,496,000	($25,796,000)
1998	70-92	$22,500,000	$45,152,000	($22,652,000)
Subtotal	('95-'98)	$89,100,000	$196,490,000	($107,390,000)
1999	63-97	$16,200,000	$19,439,000	($3,239,000)
2000	69-93	$21,600,000	$15,702,000	$5,898,000
2001	85-77	$36,000,000	$24,356,000	$11,644,000
Subtotal	('99-'01)	$73,800,000	$59,497,000	$14,303,000
2002	94-67+	$79,100,000	$43,274,000	$35,826,000
2003	90-72+	$75,500,000	$54,968,000	$20,532,000
2004	92-70+	$77,300,000	$54,217,000	$23,083,000
2005	83-79	$34,200,000	$53,300,000	($19,100,000)
2006	96-66+	$80,900,000	$56,388,000	$24,512,000
2007	79-83	$30,600,000	$60,800,000	($30,200,000)
Subtotal	('02-'07)	$377,600,000	$322,947,000	$54,653,000
Total	**('95-'07)**	**$540,500,000**	**$578,934,000**	**($38,434,000)***

*Revenue estimate adjusted upward for shortened season.   + Made Playoffs

million in marginal revenues, resulting in a small net loss that roughly matches the price of two years of Barry Zito's contract. However, this does not tell the whole story. The team hemorrhaged money in the first several years of Ryan's term, but once he had the chance to purge the books and start anew, they became one of the more efficient operations in baseball. As per the subtotals in Table 2, we can break Ryan's term into three periods:

• **The Legacy Years (1995-1998)** During this period, the Twins were weighed down by quite a few undesirable contracts, most of them left over from MacPhail's regime. This is a snapshot of a team at its least efficient, spending a decent amount on salary without a winning record to show for it. Few teams can operate profitably under such conditions, and we estimate that the Twins cost themselves the equivalent of $100 million during this period.

• **The Rebuilding Years (1999-2001)** Following the 1998 payroll purge, Ryan was able to stop the bleeding and return the team to a break even, or even a slightly profitable state. It's not that the Twins were playing great baseball—they were a bad team in 1999 and 2000, and relying on too many players of the Ron Coomer/Denny Hocking variety—but they were spending barely more than the league minimum, and it doesn't take much to turn a profit under such conditions.

• **The Competitive Years (2002-2007)** Even as payroll ramped up, these were the most profitable years of

Ryan's regime as the Twins made the playoffs in four of these six seasons. Still, in the two seasons when the team fell short of the postseason, its marginal income was substantially negative. What Ryan had done was raise the stakes: payroll was low enough to permit a substantial profit when the team reached the postseason, but high enough to enable a substantial loss when it didn't.

We can also allocate the Twins' profits and losses to individual players by dividing the team's marginal revenues according to the percentage of the team's total VORP that each player produced. For example, catcher Joe Mauer was responsible for a VORP of 66.9 in 2006, which was 13.7 percent of the team total of 488.8. He is therefore assigned 13.7 percent of the team's estimated marginal revenues of $80.9 million, or slightly more than $11 million. By adding these numbers together for each season and subtracting the players' adjusted salaries, we can determine which players contributed the most to the Twins' bottom line under Ryan's tenure (Table 3a).

Seven of the players in Table 3a were originally signed or drafted by the Twins, while the other three (Santana, Guerrier, and Lohse) were acquired before they'd played a game in the major leagues. Although it is hardly a shocking revelation, this illustrates the fact that the most profitable players are those a team brings up through its own farm system. Still, even that profit center can have its limits, as we see from the ten most costly players from Ryan's tenure listed in Table 3b.

Puckett's place atop Table 3b is largely the result of the career-ending illness he suffered early in his $30

Table 3a: Most Profitable Twins 1995-2007 (in 2007 MLB dollars)

Player	VORP	Marginal Revenue	Marginal Salary	Profit/Loss
Johan Santana	393.0	$56,229,000	$27,828,000	$28,401,000
Joe Mauer	144.0	$19,341,000	$3,455,000	$15,886,000
A. J. Pierzynski	79.0	$12,312,000	$150,000	$12,162,000
Corey Koskie	175.9	$22,996,000	$11,151,000	$11,845,000
Juan Rincon	91.2	$13,578,000	$2,383,000	$11,195,000
J. C. Romero	66.5	$11,404,000	$1,718,000	$9,687,000
Justin Morneau	95.1	$13,701,000	$4,212,000	$9,489,000
Francisco Liriano	52.0	$8,586,000	$30,000	$8,556,000
Matt Guerrier	73.2	$8,276,000	$47,000	$8,229,000
Kyle Lohse	92.4	$13,696,000	$6,218,000	$7,478,000

Table 3b: Least Profitable Twins 1995-2007 (in 2007 MLB dollars)

Player	VORP	Marginal Revenue	Marginal Salary	Profit/Loss
Kirby Puckett	40.5	$3,587,000	$31,984,000	($28,397,000)
Rick Aguilera	76.4	$6,096,000	$30,831,000	($24,735,000)
Torii Hunter	178.4	$25,550,000	$46,192,000	($20,642,000)
Brad Radke	489.0	$52,057,000	$72,603,000	($20,546,000)
Paul Molitor	63.5	$4,600,000	$20,195,000	($15,595,000)
Chuck Knoblauch	223.0	$17,333,000	$31,775,000	($14,442,000)
Shannon Stewart	34.1	$5,688,000	$18,856,000	($13,168,000)
Terry Steinbach	18.0	$1,474,000	$12,591,000	($11,117,000)
Joe Mays	121.6	$10,688,000	$21,439,000	($10,751,000)
Rick Reed	49.8	$8,778,000	$17,274,000	($8,496,000)

million contract, but otherwise there is a lesson to be learned: loyalty comes at a price. Once a homegrown players reaches his free-agent years, he's no more cost-effective than any other free agent of equal ability raised outside of the system. Thus, hanging on to homegrown players too long, particularly when those players are not contributing to a playoff club, can be damaging. Knoblauch, for all the good he did for the franchise, comes out as a net negative under this analysis because by the time that Ryan inherited him in 1995, he was already commanding inflated, free agent-level salaries, while the team was posting losing records. Likewise, rotation stalwart Brad Radke and center fielder Torii Hunter wind up in the red, although the latter would do better if we used a measure like WARP that accounted for his value on defense.

Ryan stepped down from his post as the Twins GM at the end of the 2007 season, taking a position as senior adviser to his former assistant, new GM Bill Smith. Assuming Smith was paying attention, there are three distinct lessons he should take from Ryan's tenure. First, as we just alluded to, smaller market clubs in particular cannot afford to be homers; in the words of Hall of Fame GM Branch Rickey, it is better to give up on a player a year too early than a year too late. On that front, the team's decision to let Hunter leave as a free

agent when he was only becoming more expensive as he entered his decline years was almost certainly the right decision. Second, spending a little more to field a playoff-caliber team can be more profitable than fielding a replacement-level team that is living off the scraps of revenue sharing money, but, and this is the third lesson, that extra profit comes with extra risk; if the team spends a little more but fails to make the playoffs, it can end up having to write off a substantial loss.

It is this third lesson that has the most significant implications for Smith's career going forward, because the Twins are presently in a position from which it is not quite clear if they can compete for a playoff spot or not. The team's indecision as to what to do with ace Johan Santana in the final year of his contract is a symptom of this. Similarly, where Smith has made moves, he is in danger of splitting the proverbial baby. Letting Hunter go and trading for outfielder Delmon Young are consistent with a rebuilding effort. On the other hand, signing players such as shortstop Adam Everett and third baseman Mike Lamb, who have some marginal value but are probably not good enough to help a team into the playoffs on their own, seems like an effort to win in the near-term.

Terry Ryan leaves the general manager job with a proud legacy. Though the club suffered its first losing season since 2000 last year, it is in much better shape than when he took the job. The Wisconsin-born Ryan's most important characteristic, however, might have been his Midwestern humility. Ryan was not too proud to shepherd the Twins through some lean years in 1999 and 2000, because he knew the team's core competencies in scouting and development could lead the team back to the promised land. The Twins have some chance of competing in 2008 if Santana stays with the club, fellow lefty Francisco Liriano progresses well in his rehab from Tommy John surgery, and Young has a breakout season, but with powerhouses Detroit and Cleveland in their division, the most likely scenario is that they'll end up close to the .500 mark. If that is the case, Smith may regret getting started on the rebuilding process a year too late.

HITTERS

Jason Bartlett — SS
Bats: R Throws: R Height: 6' 0" Weight: 185 Born: October 30, 1979 Age: 28

YEAR	TEAM	LVL	AGE	PA	R	2B	3B	HR	RBI	BB	SO	SB	CS	EqBRR	AVG	OBP	SLG	MLVr	EqAVG	EqOBP	EqSLG	EqA	VORP	DEFENSE	
2005	ROC	AAA	25	269	41	10	2	5	33	29	34	2	2	1.4	.332	.405	.459	.205	.297	.368	.418	.277	17.6	60-SS	4
2005	MIN	MLB	25	252	33	10	1	3	16	21	37	4	0	1.3	.241	.316	.335	-.162	.244	.328	.353	.246	1.6	65-SS	12
2006	ROC	AAA	26	250	42	23	3	1	20	10	28	6	3	-0.4	.306	.336	.443	.116	.281	.312	.421	.253	9.2	57-SS	3
2006	MIN	MLB	26	372	44	18	2	2	32	22	46	10	5	0.7	.306	.364	.390	.005	.312	.375	.397	.274	16.2	99-SS	-6
2007	MIN	MLB	27	570	75	20	7	5	43	50	73	23	3	6.1	.265	.339	.361	-.084	.275	.353	.385	.267	14.7	135-SS	9
2008	TBA	MLB	28	535	66	25	4	6	45	43	71	12	5	1.4	.261	.327	.368	-.100	.264	.332	.387	.258	11.6	126-SS	1

Breakout: 13% Improve: 34% Collapse: 33% Attrition: 14% Comparables: Ivan DeJesus Sr., Mike Bordick, Alan Bannister, Joey Amalfitano

For the third year in a row, Bartlett completely fell apart in September, bringing his career line in the month to .205/.280/.246. It's possible that this is statistical noise, and just as possible that he needs conditioning and strength work to get through a full season as a major league shortstop. For the other five months of the season, Bartlett is a league-average hitter and an underrated defender. Traded to the Rays in the Delmon Young deal, he will help stabilize Tampa Bay's infield defense.

Joe Benson — CF
Bats: R Throws: R Height: 6' 1" Weight: 205 Born: March 5, 1988 Age: 20

YEAR	TEAM	LVL	AGE	PA	R	2B	3B	HR	RBI	BB	SO	SB	CS	EqBRR	AVG	OBP	SLG	MLVr	EqAVG	EqOBP	EqSLG	EqA	VORP	DEFENSE	
2006	TWI	Rk	18	221	30	11	5	5	28	21	41	9	10	-3.2	.260	.335	.444	.163	.207	.262	.355	.207	-27.0	45-CF	1
2007	BLT	A	19	507	73	18	8	5	38	49	124	18	16	1.3	.255	.347	.368	.034	.207	.279	.296	.205	-30.0	106-CF	-5
2008	MIN	MLB	20	575	57	26	5	7	43	39	157	15	9	3.3	.226	.285	.335	-.238	.227	.289	.353	.229	-13.8	135-CF	-1

Breakout: 76% Improve: 87% Collapse: 2% Attrition: 7% Comparables: Darren Burton, Austin Jackson, Cody Ross, Scott Hunter

The Twins' second-round pick in 2006, Benson held his own at Beloit last year; that increased strikeout rate is a by-product of his attempts to work the count. Benson has plus tools across the board, but his raw power and speed haven't translated into on-field results thus far. Both his hitting and fielding mechanics need work, but he has as much upside as any hitter in the system.

Alexi Casilla — 2B/SS
Bats: S Throws: R Height: 5' 9" Weight: 180 Born: July 20, 1984 Age: 23

YEAR	TEAM	LVL	AGE	PA	R	2B	3B	HR	RBI	BB	SO	SB	CS	EqBRR	AVG	OBP	SLG	MLVr	EqAVG	EqOBP	EqSLG	EqA	VORP	DEFENSE			
2005	CDR	A	20	347	62	11	3	3	17	29	31	47	12	1.7	.325	.392	.409	.153	.273	.325	.345	.245	4.2	41-SS	2	35-2B	0
2006	FTM	A+	21	359	56	12	6	0	33	30	36	31	6	8.5	.331	.390	.406	.211	.292	.345	.368	.259	10.1	43-2B	1	36-SS	-3
2006	NBR	AA	21	199	28	10	1	1	13	18	20	19	4	0.6	.294	.375	.382	.107	.267	.338	.358	.255	4.5	45-SS	4		
2007	ROC	AAA	22	365	53	13	1	3	20	34	50	24	12	-0.9	.269	.345	.344	-.048	.246	.320	.332	.235	-0.2	41-SS	-10	41-2B	-4
2007	MIN	MLB	22	204	15	5	1	0	9	9	29	11	1	1.3	.222	.256	.259	-.408	.234	.271	.271	.207	-10.9	48-2B	-3		
2008	MIN	MLB	23	585	72	23	5	2	40	39	79	31	10	2.0	.264	.317	.340	-.154	.265	.321	.358	.250	4.0	137-2B	-6		

Breakout: 34% Improve: 69% Collapse: 12% Attrition: 11% Comparables: Alejandro Machado, Anderson Hernandez, Maicer Izturis, Nelson Liriano

When the Twins traded Luis Castillo to the Mets, they created space for an inferior version of the same player in Casilla. Casilla has very little power and is thus reliant on making contact, working walks, and his speed. A switch-hitter, he also shares Castillo's preference for batting from the right side. The 50 walks he drew in the minors will be 25 to 30 in the majors, forcing him to hit .300 to carry a job, but he was clearly overmatched after his call-up. The addition of Adam Everett may allow the Twins to start Casilla at Triple-A, which would be best for all parties.

Michael Cuddyer — RF

Bats: R   Throws: R   Height: 6' 2"   Weight: 220   Born: March 27, 1979   Age: 29

YEAR	TEAM	LVL	AGE	PA	R	2B	3B	HR	RBI	BB	SO	SB	CS	EqBRR	AVG	OBP	SLG	MLVr	EqAVG	EqOBP	EqSLG	EqA	VORP	DEFENSE		
2005	MIN	MLB	26	470	55	25	3	12	42	41	93	3	4	-3.8	.263	.330	.422	-.006	.265	.343	.439	.268	8.0	90-3B	-8	18-RF 1
2006	MIN	MLB	27	635	102	41	5	24	109	62	130	6	0	-1.4	.284	.362	.504	.144	.281	.367	.515	.300	36.3	138-RF	-13	
2007	MIN	MLB	28	623	87	28	5	16	81	64	107	5	0	-1.0	.276	.356	.433	.055	.284	.369	.467	.290	18.4	138-RF	0	
2008	MIN	MLB	29	601	76	31	3	17	78	60	112	6	2	-0.5	.269	.346	.437	.028	.271	.351	.461	.284	14.0	141-RF	-3	

Breakout: 10% Improve: 42% Collapse: 22% Attrition: 7%   Comparables: Benny Agbayani, Jermaine Dye, Leon Roberts, Gary Matthews

Cuddyer has improved his raw walk total in every season of his career, which reflects his increased playing time, but also his maturity as a hitter. He's also become a good right fielder with a strong arm. The problem is that he isn't a good enough hitter to bat third or fourth on a contending team, though Ron Gardenhire hit him in one of those two spots 97 times last year. If Delmon Young hits well enough to push Cuddyer to sixth, that helps. If Mike Lamb takes 150 at-bats from Cuddyer against the Justin Verlanders of the world, that does, too.

Torii Hunter — CF

Bats: R   Throws: R   Height: 6' 2"   Weight: 225   Born: July 18, 1975   Age: 32

YEAR	TEAM	LVL	AGE	PA	R	2B	3B	HR	RBI	BB	SO	SB	CS	EqBRR	AVG	OBP	SLG	MLVr	EqAVG	EqOBP	EqSLG	EqA	VORP	DEFENSE	
2005	MIN	MLB	29	416	63	24	1	14	56	34	65	23	7	2.3	.269	.337	.452	.053	.273	.349	.467	.282	19.1	90-CF	-6
2006	MIN	MLB	30	611	86	21	2	31	98	45	108	12	6	0.5	.278	.336	.490	.073	.279	.344	.506	.285	32.6	139-CF	7
2007	MIN	MLB	31	650	94	45	1	28	107	40	101	18	9	-1.0	.287	.334	.505	.128	.295	.346	.539	.291	39.2	148-CF	1
2008	LAA	MLB	32	586	79	32	1	20	86	42	94	17	5	0.3	.284	.339	.461	.060	.281	.339	.481	.284	24.1	137-CF	-2

Breakout: 10% Improve: 46% Collapse: 21% Attrition: 12%   Comparables: Ellis Burks, Jermaine Dye, Jim Rice, Bob Cerv

Hunter is a fun player to watch. He seems to love the game and wants to be involved in getting African American kids to love it, too. He's just not a good gamble at $18 million a season for the next five years, which is what the Angels will be paying him. He's losing speed and range, and a two-year spike in batting average has masked the decline of his plate discipline. Should Hunter regress to his career .271, and he should, it will leave the Angels with another .320 OBP in the middle of their lineup, and Hunter does not have the power to support that. All the good-guyness in the world won't make paying $18 million to a .260/.310/.425 left fielder any fun in 2011.

Jason Kubel — LF

Bats: L   Throws: R   Height: 6' 0"   Weight: 210   Born: May 25, 1982   Age: 26

YEAR	TEAM	LVL	AGE	PA	R	2B	3B	HR	RBI	BB	SO	SB	CS	EqBRR	AVG	OBP	SLG	MLVr	EqAVG	EqOBP	EqSLG	EqA	VORP	DEFENSE	
2006	ROC	AAA	24	134	18	7	2	4	22	12	23	2	0	-0.1	.283	.343	.475	.150	.267	.328	.475	.276	3.3	22-RF	-4
2006	MIN	MLB	24	235	23	8	0	8	26	12	45	2	0	-0.4	.241	.279	.386	-.207	.239	.283	.390	.233	-6.0	23-LF	-2
2007	MIN	MLB	25	466	49	31	2	13	65	41	79	5	0	-3.4	.273	.335	.450	.039	.280	.348	.483	.285	13.5	79-LF	2
2008	MIN	MLB	26	475	58	28	3	14	65	40	84	8	2	-0.8	.275	.337	.449	.034	.276	.342	.474	.283	14.5	112-LF	-1

Breakout: 33% Improve: 66% Collapse: 17% Attrition: 20%   Comparables: Norm Miller, Lee Thomas, Willie Montañez, Paul O'Neill

Kubel still hasn't recovered from missing the 2005 season after a devastating knee injury. Through 2004, Kubel had walked 177 times and struck out 193 as a pro. Since then, he's walked 65 times and struck out 147, striking out 60 percent more frequently than he did before the injury. He's just not the same type of hitter, much less the same caliber. It's as if he's lost either his confidence or his sense of the strike zone. A .341/.418/.553 showing over the last two months of last season provides cause for cautious optimism, but his contact rate remains at a career low.

Joe Mauer   C   Bats: L   Throws: R   Height: 6' 5"   Weight: 215   Born: April 19, 1983   Age: 25

YEAR	TEAM	LVL	AGE	PA	R	2B	3B	HR	RBI	BB	SO	SB	CS	EqBRR	AVG	OBP	SLG	MLVr	EqAVG	EqOBP	EqSLG	EqA	VORP	DEFENSE
2005	MIN	MLB	22	554	61	26	2	9	55	61	64	13	1	0.6	.294	.372	.411	.077	.295	.383	.418	.287	34.3	111-C 11
2006	MIN	MLB	23	608	86	36	4	13	84	79	54	8	3	1.2	.347	.429	.507	.325	.342	.433	.512	.326	66.9	119-C 8
2007	MIN	MLB	24	471	62	27	3	7	60	57	51	7	1	0.7	.293	.382	.426	.100	.299	.394	.448	.296	30.2	88-C 10
2008	MIN	MLB	25	560	79	29	3	9	62	62	61	10	3	0.3	.295	.375	.420	.072	.296	.380	.443	.291	30.4	131-C 11

Breakout: 10% Improve: 31% Collapse: 36% Attrition: 9%   *Comparables: Bruce Bochte, Mark Grace, Carlos May, Mike Hargrove*

Since making Joe Mauer their starting catcher in April of 2004, the Twins have played 648 games; Mauer has played 415. That's a problem, and it's not going away until the Twins pick a new position for their franchise player. That he's an excellent catcher isn't the point; the Twins need his bat in the lineup 150 times a season, and they need Mauer to develop into the guy he was in 2006, but with more power. None of that will happen until he's a third baseman or left fielder. His recurring leg injuries are a flashing red sign that he should be moved.

Justin Morneau   1B   Bats: L   Throws: R   Height: 6' 4"   Weight: 225   Born: May 15, 1981   Age: 27

YEAR	TEAM	LVL	AGE	PA	R	2B	3B	HR	RBI	BB	SO	SB	CS	EqBRR	AVG	OBP	SLG	MLVr	EqAVG	EqOBP	EqSLG	EqA	VORP	DEFENSE
2005	MIN	MLB	24	543	62	23	4	22	79	44	94	0	2	-0.3	.239	.304	.437	-.050	.241	.315	.450	.261	0.1	129-1B -8
2006	MIN	MLB	25	661	97	37	1	34	130	53	93	3	3	-1.8	.321	.375	.559	.283	.320	.381	.568	.314	52.0	152-1B 11
2007	MIN	MLB	26	668	84	31	3	31	111	64	91	1	1	-2.8	.271	.343	.492	.108	.277	.354	.524	.294	28.8	142-1B 16
2008	MIN	MLB	27	637	77	33	2	24	99	56	96	3	2	-1.1	.271	.339	.465	.055	.273	.343	.491	.286	19.0	149-1B 6

Breakout: 7% Improve: 36% Collapse: 27% Attrition: 3%   *Comparables: Kent Hrbek, Greg Walker, Dave Revering, Carlos Delgado*

The difference between being the MVP and being a guy who finishes 20th in the balloting is about 30 singles, which is what Morneau lost between 2006 and 2007. Well, that and having the guy in front of him put up a .429 OBP and play 140 games. It's hard to say for sure what Morneau is, given that he's had three widely disparate seasons since 2005. The power is real, and it seems that he's traded some walks for it (more than 15 percent of his walks the last two years came via the opposing manager's fingers), but his strikeouts haven't increased. He could have another 2006 in him, but it's more likely that he'll hit .290 with 40 or more homers, which will do just fine.

Chris Parmelee   OF   Bats: L   Throws: L   Height: 6' 1"   Weight: 200   Born: February 24, 1988   Age: 20

YEAR	TEAM	LVL	AGE	PA	R	2B	3B	HR	RBI	BB	SO	SB	CS	EqBRR	AVG	OBP	SLG	MLVr	EqAVG	EqOBP	EqSLG	EqA	VORP	DEFENSE
2006	TWI	Rk	18	179	29	7	4	8	32	23	47	3	3	-1.6	.279	.369	.532	.328	.217	.289	.410	.240	-15.0	30-RF -3 10-1B 0
2007	BLT	A	19	501	56	23	5	15	70	46	137	8	4	0.2	.239	.313	.414	.031	.196	.257	.325	.203	-44.1	103-RF -11
2008	MIN	MLB	20	581	51	30	5	13	56	44	181	8	5	0.7	.212	.275	.360	-.233	.213	.278	.379	.230	-22.1	136-RF -1

Breakout: 52% Improve: 79% Collapse: 11% Attrition: 3%   *Comparables: Michael Hall, Jay Bruce, John Drennen, Bronson Sardinha*

The Twins' first-round pick in 2006, Parmelee stands out among the organization's outfield prospects as the rare bomber in a field of burners. While his glove work in right field has been a pleasant surprise, his bat has disappointed, with the high strikeout totals of a slugger, but the production of a tweener. His body and swing are built for power, so patience is warranted as he heads to—gulp—the Florida State League.

Trevor Plouffe   SS   Bats: R   Throws: R   Height: 6' 1"   Weight: 175   Born: June 15, 1986   Age: 22

YEAR	TEAM	LVL	AGE	PA	R	2B	3B	HR	RBI	BB	SO	SB	CS	EqBRR	AVG	OBP	SLG	MLVr	EqAVG	EqOBP	EqSLG	EqA	VORP	DEFENSE
2005	BLT	A	19	532	58	18	0	13	60	50	78	8	4	-2.0	.223	.300	.345	-.141	.195	.256	.288	.189	-31.1	123-SS -11
2006	FTM	A+	20	524	60	26	4	4	45	58	93	8	5	-1.5	.246	.333	.347	-.010	.215	.291	.311	.214	-15.7	93-SS 0 23-3B -3
2007	NBR	AA	21	555	75	37	2	9	50	38	89	12	7	-1.8	.274	.326	.410	.001	.244	.291	.376	.232	0.2	121-SS -12
2008	MIN	MLB	22	621	59	33	2	9	58	43	123	11	5	0.4	.237	.294	.353	-.193	.239	.298	.372	.238	-1.2	145-SS -7

Breakout: 52% Improve: 77% Collapse: 11% Attrition: 9%   *Comparables: Pokey Reese, J. J. Hardy, Jason Romano, Corey Smith*

For an organization that finds so many prizes later in the draft, the Twins have had a distinct lack of success in the first round of late. Since Mauer in 2001, the only first-round picks they've made that are likely to produce MLB value are pitchers Glen Perkins and Matt Garza, the latter of whom is now a Ray. Plouffe was their first pick in 2004, and had his best season yet last year, but it still featured a .326 OBP and 32 errors, and he doesn't have outstanding range.

Nick Punto   INF   Bats: S   Throws: R   Height: 5' 9"   Weight: 185   Born: November 8, 1977   Age: 30

YEAR	TEAM	LVL	AGE	PA	R	2B	3B	HR	RBI	BB	SO	SB	CS	EqBRR	AVG	OBP	SLG	MLVr	EqAVG	EqOBP	EqSLG	EqA	VORP	DEFENSE			
2005	MIN	MLB	27	439	45	18	4	4	26	36	86	13	8	1.1	.239	.301	.335	-.192	.245	.318	.351	.237	-6.7	63-2B	-1	27-SS	0
2006	MIN	MLB	28	524	73	21	7	1	45	47	68	17	5	0.6	.290	.352	.373	-.055	.291	.361	.380	.267	9.1	86-3B	-5	17-SS	-2
2007	MIN	MLB	29	536	53	18	4	1	25	55	90	16	6	-0.6	.210	.291	.271	-.331	.221	.308	.293	.221	-27.1	93-3B	1	24-SS	2
2008	MIN	MLB	30	407	44	15	4	2	30	37	68	11	4	0.7	.238	.309	.321	-.207	.240	.313	.338	.239	-3.9	97-3B	1		

Breakout: 18% Improve: 42% Collapse: 31% Attrition: 32%   Comparables: Al Newman, Walt Weiss, Len Randle, Julio Cruz

To Ron Gardenhire's credit, he did try to minimize Punto's role last year once he realized the 2006 version wasn't walking through that door. He dropped Punto to the bottom of the lineup part of the time starting in May, and all the time by late June. He then tried to give Brian Buscher the third-base job in August, but Buscher played poorly and then picked up a disabling infection. After Casilla also failed to perform, Punto picked up playing time once again. With the additions of Mike Lamb and Brendan Harris, Punto should be reduced to a utility infielder, a role he can fill ably.

Mike Redmond   C   Bats: R   Throws: R   Height: 5' 11"   Weight: 200   Born: May 5, 1971   Age: 37

YEAR	TEAM	LVL	AGE	PA	R	2B	3B	HR	RBI	BB	SO	SB	CS	EqBRR	AVG	OBP	SLG	MLVr	EqAVG	EqOBP	EqSLG	EqA	VORP	DEFENSE	
2005	MIN	MLB	34	159	17	9	0	1	26	6	14	0	0	-1.8	.311	.350	.392	.025	.315	.363	.404	.269	7.3	42-C	3
2006	MIN	MLB	35	191	20	13	0	0	23	4	19	0	0	-1.1	.339	.363	.411	.065	.343	.374	.433	.282	9.4	43-C	5
2007	MIN	MLB	36	298	23	13	0	1	38	18	23	0	0	-2.5	.294	.346	.353	-.057	.304	.357	.374	.261	6.4	54-C	6
2008	MIN	MLB	37	208	17	11	0	1	22	12	18	0	0	-0.8	.274	.322	.356	-.117	.276	.327	.375	.249	2.4	52-C	1

Breakout: 8%   Improve: 20% Collapse: 49% Attrition: 43%   Comparables: Don Slaught, Rick Cerone, Joe Girardi, Sandy Alomar

Given all the time Mauer missed last year, Redmond was a godsend, posting another good OBP and playing good defense. He's not the Practically Perfect Backup Catcher, but he may be the best one not named in the Mitchell Report. The strained ligaments in the knuckle of his left ring finger that cut his season short aren't expected to affect him this year.

Ben Revere   CF   Bats: L   Throws: R   Height: 5' 9"   Weight: 175   Born: May 3, 1988   Age: 20

YEAR	TEAM	LVL	AGE	PA	R	2B	3B	HR	RBI	BB	SO	SB	CS	EqBRR	AVG	OBP	SLG	MLVr	EqAVG	EqOBP	EqSLG	EqA	VORP	DEFENSE	
2007	TWI	Rk	19	216	46	6	10	0	29	13	20	21	9	1.6	.325	.388	.461	.277	.264	.299	.383	.238	-2.2	49-CF	5
2008	MIN	MLB	20	565	58	27	10	3	42	29	114	19	9	2.8	.246	.289	.352	-.198	.248	.293	.371	.236	-8.0	133-CF	0

Breakout: 30% Improve: 57% Collapse: 20% Attrition: 5%   Comparables: Duane Singleton, Adrian Cardenas, Jason Pridie, Johnny Damon

Revere was widely considered a reach for the Twins when they selected him with the 28th pick in the 2007 draft. The small, slightly built speedster from Kentucky was projected as a second-rounder or sandwich pick and was derided as a signability selection by a penurious organization. It has worked out thus far, as Revere has played well in short-season ball in his pro debut. With his profile, however, he'll have to work hard to keep from having the bat knocked out of his hands at higher levels. His speed and defense both play and project well.

Denard Span   CF   Bats: L   Throws: L   Height: 6' 0"   Weight: 195   Born: February 27, 1984   Age: 24

YEAR	TEAM	LVL	AGE	PA	R	2B	3B	HR	RBI	BB	SO	SB	CS	EqBRR	AVG	OBP	SLG	MLVr	EqAVG	EqOBP	EqSLG	EqA	VORP	DEFENSE	
2005	FTM	A+	21	212	38	3	3	1	19	22	25	13	4	-1.7	.339	.410	.403	.225	.284	.348	.342	.248	2.3	47-CF	-7
2005	NBR	AA	21	304	47	6	5	0	26	22	41	10	8	0.0	.285	.355	.345	.003	.253	.316	.311	.222	-7.4	65-CF	-4
2006	NBR	AA	22	597	80	16	6	2	45	40	78	24	11	-0.4	.285	.340	.349	.007	.260	.311	.322	.227	-13.5	128-CF	-1
2007	ROC	AAA	23	548	59	20	7	3	55	40	90	25	14	2.3	.267	.323	.355	-.071	.245	.300	.338	.226	-13.5	133-CF	18
2008	MIN	MLB	24	547	64	20	7	1	39	36	92	21	8	2.4	.263	.315	.340	-.158	.265	.319	.358	.246	-2.3	128-CF	-1

Breakout: 51% Improve: 74% Collapse: 8%   Attrition: 14%   Comparables: Tony Gwynn Jr., Tom Goodwin, Del Unser, David Miller

Skeptical about Revere? Here is a good reason to be, as the Twins' first-round pick from 2003 continues to frustrate, failing to develop the leadoff skills the organization had hoped to see. Span's raw speed hasn't made him a good center fielder, either. Still, he hit well in the second half last year at Triple-A Rochester, and with the center-field job for the Twins wide open, he could find himself in the major leagues this spring. There is not much reason to believe he can be more than an extra outfielder.

Jason Tyner OF — Bats: L — Throws: L — Height: 6' 1" — Weight: 180 — Born: April 23, 1977 — Age: 31

YEAR	TEAM	LVL	AGE	PA	R	2B	3B	HR	RBI	BB	SO	SB	CS	EqBRR	AVG	OBP	SLG	MLVr	EqAVG	EqOBP	EqSLG	EqA	VORP	DEFENSE			
2005	ROC	AAA	28	591	81	18	2	1	36	48	57	18	6	4.9	.286	.351	.334	-.092	.254	.319	.298	.225	-16.3	93-CF	-11	31-LF	0
2005	MIN	MLB	28	60	8	1	1	0	5	4	4	2	0	0.7	.321	.367	.375	.037	.327	.383	.382	.279	2.2	10-LF	0		
2006	ROC	AAA	29	352	52	14	5	0	22	25	39	8	2	1.2	.329	.379	.405	.148	.302	.352	.387	.264	11.4	77-CF	0		
2006	MIN	MLB	29	232	29	5	2	0	18	11	18	4	2	2.8	.312	.345	.353	-.079	.315	.353	.356	.254	1.2	32-LF	10	17-CF	1
2007	MIN	MLB	30	328	42	14	2	1	22	16	26	8	3	3.1	.286	.331	.355	-.091	.301	.348	.384	.258	-0.5	35-LF	7	16-RF	0
2008	MIN	MLB	31	261	28	9	2	0	19	16	27	5	2	0.8	.265	.314	.326	-.176	.266	.319	.344	.238	-3.9	64-LF	2		

Breakout: 22% Improve: 34% Collapse: 41% Attrition: 36% — Comparables: Jose Tartabull, Eric Owens, Russ Snyder, Duane Kuiper

The Twins' inability to find enough major league position players because of a combination of penury, draft incompetence, and stasis forces them to take perfectly good bench players and call them regulars. Although Tyner finally hit his first MLB homer last year, he has no business starting 60 games, and he damn sure has no business starting 15 of them at DH.

PITCHERS

Scott Baker — Bats: R — Throws: R — Height: 6' 4" — Weight: 210 — Born: September 19, 1981 — Age: 26

YEAR	TEAM	LVL	AGE	W	L	SV	G	GS	IP	H	BB	SO	HR	GB%	BABIP	STUFF	WHIP	ERA	PERA	EqERA	EqH9	EqBB9	EqSO9	EqHR9	VORP	SN/WX
2005	ROC	AAA	23	5	8	0	22	22	134²	123	26	107	15	36.6%	.280	5	1.11	3.01	4.35	3.86	8.6	2.3	5.1	1.2	24.4	—
2005	MIN	MLB	23	3	3	0	10	9	53²	48	14	32	5	35.1%	.265	12	1.16	3.35	3.51	3.61	8.1	2.4	5.3	0.9	13.5	1.68
2006	ROC	AAA	24	5	4	0	12	12	84¹	77	25	68	4	42.4%	.303	10	1.21	2.68	4.62	3.99	9.5	3.3	5.4	0.7	14.1	—
2006	MIN	MLB	24	5	8	0	16	16	83¹	114	16	62	17	34.8%	.355	-8	1.56	6.37	6.73	6.62	11.4	1.6	6.2	1.6	-7.1	0.10
2007	ROC	AAA	25	3	2	1	7	6	42²	34	4	41	3	48.3%	.279	20	0.89	3.16	3.68	4.31	8.4	1.1	6.6	0.9	5.7	—
2007	MIN	MLB	25	9	9	0	24	23	143²	162	29	102	15	36.6%	.329	15	1.33	4.26	4.52	4.21	9.8	1.6	5.9	1.0	25.8	3.29
2008	MIN	MLB	26	8	9	0	25	25	146¹	161	36	102	18	39.7%	.306	13	1.34	4.44	4.40	4.51	9.6	2.0	5.5	1.1	16.3	2.90

Breakout: 17% Improve: 49% Collapse: 19% Attrition: 13% — Comparables: Brett Tomko, Chad Ogea, Doc Medich, David Bush

The 2007 Twins featured a Buscher and a Baker, but no Candlestick Maker. Shame, that. A Brad Radke wannabe, Baker bounced back from a brutal 2006 to reclaim a rotation spot in May, keeping his home run rate under control long enough to be an above-average starter and even throw a near no-hitter against the Royals. While he's prone to the occasional disastrous start, he'll be a roughly league-average third starter this year.

Nick Blackburn — Bats: R — Throws: R — Height: 6' 4" — Weight: 230 — Born: February 24, 1982 — Age: 26

YEAR	TEAM	LVL	AGE	W	L	SV	G	GS	IP	H	BB	SO	HR	GB%	BABIP	STUFF	WHIP	ERA	PERA	EqERA	EqH9	EqBB9	EqSO9	EqHR9	VORP	SN/WX
2005	FTM	A+	23	7	5	0	15	15	93²	95	16	55	5	56.1%	.302	-19	1.18	3.36	5.78	6.42	10.9	3.0	2.6	1.1	-7.5	—
2005	NBR	AA	23	2	4	0	7	7	49	35	10	27	1	45.6%	.239	1	0.92	1.84	3.34	4.00	7.0	2.8	2.8	0.4	8.0	—
2006	NBR	AA	24	7	8	0	30	19	132¹	141	37	81	11	46.5%	.310	-26	1.35	4.43	6.11	6.27	10.8	3.5	3.3	1.3	-9.1	—
2007	NBR	AA	25	3	1	0	8	7	38	36	7	18	1	54.5%	.267	-9	1.13	3.08	3.57	5.40	8.2	2.1	2.3	0.5	0.9	—
2007	ROC	AAA	25	7	3	0	17	17	110²	96	12	57	7	52.2%	.255	4	0.98	2.11	3.62	3.40	8.3	1.3	3.2	0.8	25.9	—
2007	MIN	MLB	25	0	2	0	6	0	11²	19	2	8	2	38.6%	.405	-24	1.80	7.69	10.05	10.32	14.3	1.6	5.6	1.6	-4.2	-0.56
2008	MIN	MLB	26	4	7	0	34	13	101²	126	31	41	14	46.8%	.309	-15	1.55	5.80	5.48	5.94	10.8	2.5	3.2	1.2	-5.5	0.00

Breakout: 17% Improve: 41% Collapse: 35% Attrition: 18% — Comparables: Dennis Wiseman, Brady Raggio, Mike Ziegler, Nap Robinson

Not shown above is Blackburn's terrific stint in the Arizona Fall League (1.64 ERA, 20/2 K/BB in 22 innings). He showed very good command of his three-pitch assortment in Phoenix, impressing observers by retaining the improvements that had elevated him from organizational arm to prospect in 2007. His low strikeout rate stems from the lack of a true out pitch and is a real concern that will likely relegate him to being a fourth or fifth starter, and even then only after a period of adjustment.

Boof Bonser

Bats: R   Throws: R   Height: 6' 4"   Weight: 260   Born: October 14, 1981   Age: 26

YEAR	TEAM	LVL	AGE	W	L	SV	G	GS	IP	H	BB	SO	HR	GB%	BABIP	STUFF	WHIP	ERA	PERA	EqERA	EqH9	EqBB9	EqSO9	EqHR9	VORP	SN/WX
2005	ROC	AAA	23	11	9	0	28	28	160¹	153	57	168	22	39.8%	.312	-1	1.31	3.99	5.50	5.27	9.4	3.9	7.1	1.5	5.5	—
2006	ROC	AAA	24	6	4	0	14	14	86¹	68	35	83	4	38.3%	.272	16	1.20	2.82	4.23	4.41	8.2	4.4	6.4	0.7	10.8	—
2006	MIN	MLB	24	7	6	0	18	18	100¹	104	24	84	18	43.2%	.299	9	1.28	4.22	4.43	4.06	8.8	2.0	7.0	1.4	17.8	2.36
2007	MIN	MLB	25	8	12	0	31	30	173	199	65	136	27	46.6%	.323	-2	1.53	5.10	5.60	5.40	9.9	3.0	6.5	1.4	7.3	2.27
2008	MIN	MLB	26	8	9	0	33	22	147	155	55	108	17	43.8%	.302	7	1.42	4.64	4.58	4.74	9.2	3.0	5.8	1.1	12.2	2.30

Breakout: 21% Improve: 52% Collapse: 19% Attrition: 20%   Comparables: Aaron Harang, Ryan Rupe, Doc Medich, Danny Cox

Here's an analytical mystery. In 2006, Bonser had no platoon split of note. In 2007, his strikeout and walk rates were essentially the same against both lefties and righties, and his home run rate was slightly worse against lefties, but still not troublesome. However, when lefties put the ball in play against him, they hit .401, while righties hit only .231. That kind of BABIP split is out of context with the rest of his line and cries out for an explanation better than "randomness." The Twins didn't have a dramatically better defense on one side of the field, so that's not the answer. One facet of the defense-independent pitching theory is that pitchers who do not have a bare minimum of ability to suppress hits on balls in play wash out either in the minors or quickly upon reaching the majors. Bonser held major league lefties to a .289 BABIP in a much smaller sample 2006, but if it turns out that he either can't or has lost his ability to keep lefties from getting hits, he's not going to last long.

David Bromberg

Bats: L   Throws: R   Height: 6' 5"   Weight: 230   Born: September 14, 1987   Age: 20

YEAR	TEAM	LVL	AGE	W	L	SV	G	GS	IP	H	BB	SO	HR	GB%	BABIP	STUFF	WHIP	ERA	PERA	EqERA	EqH9	EqBB9	EqSO9	EqHR9	VORP	SN/WX
2006	TWI	Rk	18	3	3	0	10	10	50	42	18	31	2	49.0%	.267	-14	1.20	2.70	6.31	6.49	9.2	6.5	2.3	1.7	-4.3	—
2007	ELZ	Rk	19	9	0	0	13	11	58¹	45	32	81	4	54.9%	.320	-1	1.32	2.78	10.46	7.57	11.9	11.7	6.5	2.5	-9.6	—
2008	MIN	MLB	20	3	9	0	22	22	97²	104	112	81	14	47.4%	.314	-14	2.21	7.29	7.46	7.42	9.3	9.4	6.6	1.3	-18.9	-1.50

Breakout: 19% Improve: 37% Collapse: 32% Attrition: 11%   Comparables: Jeremy Haynes, Larry Barnes, Jon Huber, John Rocker

In a system filled with precise control artists, Bromberg, a raw power arm, is the exception. A 32nd-round pick in 2005, Bromberg has yet to pitch in a full-season league, but he took a major step forward in 2007, winning Appalachian League Pitcher of the Year honors. His best pitch is a low-90s sinker, and his height makes the pitch even more difficult to hit because of the added downward angle. He's still got a long way to go when it comes to command and secondary stuff, but scouts are intrigued by him.

Jesse Crain

Bats: R   Throws: R   Height: 6' 1"   Weight: 205   Born: July 5, 1981   Age: 26

YEAR	TEAM	LVL	AGE	W	L	SV	G	GS	IP	H	BB	SO	HR	GB%	BABIP	STUFF	WHIP	ERA	PERA	EqERA	EqH9	EqBB9	EqSO9	EqHR9	VORP	SN/WX
2005	MIN	MLB	24	12	5	1	75	0	79²	61	29	25	6	50.4%	.222	-13	1.13	2.71	3.17	3.10	6.8	3.2	2.8	0.7	23.1	3.84
2006	MIN	MLB	25	4	5	1	68	0	76²	79	18	60	6	56.7%	.309	12	1.27	3.52	3.55	3.36	8.6	2.0	6.5	0.6	21.1	0.59
2007	MIN	MLB	26	1	2	0	18	0	16¹	19	4	10	4	48.2%	.294	-25	1.41	5.52	6.59	8.82	9.9	2.2	5.0	2.2	-5.2	-0.06
2008	MIN	MLB	26	3	2	2	39	1	49²	50	15	33	4	50.1%	.293	-1	1.31	3.77	3.79	3.93	8.8	2.5	5.3	0.8	10.1	0.80

Breakout: 21% Improve: 43% Collapse: 27% Attrition: 20%   Comparables: Jack Cressend, Randy Moffitt, Matt Whiteside, Max Leon

Crain's stuff was lacking at the start of the season. That prompted an MRI and a very ugly diagnosis: a torn rotator cuff *and* a torn labrum. Surgery to repair both injuries was deemed successful, and there is happy talk about Crain being ready for spring training, but given the severity of the injuries, he's most likely to be available at midseason and intermittently effective, at best.

Brian Duensing

Bats: L   Throws: L   Height: 5' 11"   Weight: 195   Born: February 22, 1983   Age: 25

YEAR	TEAM	LVL	AGE	W	L	SV	G	GS	IP	H	BB	SO	HR	GB%	BABIP	STUFF	WHIP	ERA	PERA	EqERA	EqH9	EqBB9	EqSO9	EqHR9	VORP	SN/WX
2005	ELZ	Rk	22	4	3	0	12	9	50¹	49	16	55	4	58.3%	.326	-24	1.29	2.33	11.21	8.60	14.6	8.6	4.3	2.4	-12.6	—
2006	BLT	A	23	2	3	0	11	11	70	68	14	55	3	52.9%	.314	-17	1.17	2.96	6.28	5.95	11.3	3.8	3.5	1.3	-2.4	—
2006	FTM	A+	23	2	5	0	7	7	40²	47	8	33	4	50.4%	.352	-25	1.37	4.25	9.20	9.09	13.8	3.1	4.4	2.1	-13.5	—
2006	NBR	AA	23	1	2	0	10	9	49¹	51	18	30	6	57.4%	.304	-28	1.41	3.67	6.97	7.00	10.6	4.4	3.4	1.8	-7.0	—
2007	NBR	AA	24	4	1	0	9	9	50²	47	7	38	2	43.8%	.288	9	1.07	2.66	3.76	4.01	8.6	1.8	4.4	0.5	8.7	—
2007	ROC	AAA	24	11	5	0	19	19	116²	115	30	86	13	50.8%	.299	-12	1.24	3.24	5.76	5.25	10.2	2.8	4.9	1.5	4.2	—
2008	MIN	MLB	25	5	9	0	30	18	112	138	46	61	15	46.9%	.319	-9	1.63	5.78	5.73	5.89	10.7	3.3	4.3	1.2	-5.2	0.20

Breakout: 16%   Improve: 51%   Collapse: 24%   Attrition: 15%   Comparables: Scott Schoeneweis, Cory Vance, Eddie Priest, Mike Myers

The Twins mass-produce command pitchers who have 10 percent less stuff than would get anyone particularly excited about them. Loosely speaking, Duensing is what you get if you make Blackburn throw lefty and give him a slider. A Nebraska product, Duensing has had more consistent success through the system than Blackburn, but right now the two are essentially even. If teams still used swingmen, platooning the pair in the fifth-starter slot would be a neat tactic that would break both into the majors effectively while giving the Twins a small competitive edge. Anybody remember when managers showed initiative?

Matt Garza

Bats: R   Throws: R   Height: 6' 4"   Weight: 185   Born: November 11, 1983   Age: 24

YEAR	TEAM	LVL	AGE	W	L	SV	G	GS	IP	H	BB	SO	HR	GB%	BABIP	STUFF	WHIP	ERA	PERA	EqERA	EqH9	EqBB9	EqSO9	EqHR9	VORP	SN/WX
2005	BLT	A	21	3	3	0	10	10	56	53	15	64	5	46.7%	.338	2	1.21	3.54	7.27	6.10	11.5	4.1	6.7	1.8	-2.7	—
2006	FTM	A+	22	5	1	0	8	8	44	27	11	53	3	46.8%	.231	12	0.86	1.43	4.11	4.25	6.8	3.4	6.4	1.3	6.3	—
2006	NBR	AA	22	6	2	0	10	10	57	40	14	68	2	39.9%	.271	25	0.95	2.53	3.59	4.61	7.2	3.0	7.1	0.7	6.0	—
2006	ROC	AAA	22	3	1	0	5	5	34	20	7	33	1	51.8%	.235	29	0.79	1.85	3.12	2.90	6.4	2.3	6.7	0.6	9.3	—
2006	MIN	MLB	22	3	6	0	10	9	50	62	23	38	6	37.4%	.346	6	1.70	5.76	5.55	5.51	10.3	3.7	6.4	0.9	0.8	0.65
2007	ROC	AAA	23	4	6	0	16	16	92²	93	31	95	5	42.6%	.341	16	1.35	3.62	5.22	5.24	10.4	3.4	6.9	0.7	3.5	—
2007	MIN	MLB	23	5	7	0	16	15	83	96	32	67	8	47.7%	.351	13	1.54	3.69	5.29	4.67	10.2	3.1	6.8	0.9	11.3	2.00
2008	TBA	MLB	24	10	12	0	31	31	175²	187	70	144	19	45.7%	.315	16	1.46	4.59	4.61	4.29	9.3	3.2	6.6	1.0	16.1	3.10

Breakout: 33%   Improve: 71%   Collapse: 10%   Attrition: 17%   Comparables: Joe Coleman, Kevin Gross, Milt Pappas, Kip Wells

It would be a stretch to say that the Twins traded Garza because he didn't fit their organizational personality; they did get Delmon Young for him, after all. However, Garza's expressed displeasure with the team—over pitch selection and roster decisions—certainly made him a top candidate to be sent away. The right-hander works off a mid-90s fastball, and while he relies heavily on it, he has good breaking stuff as well, and his command has become a strength over the past two seasons. He's going to be a story this year, maybe even an All-Star.

Matt Guerrier

Bats: R   Throws: R   Height: 6' 3"   Weight: 195   Born: August 2, 1978   Age: 29

YEAR	TEAM	LVL	AGE	W	L	SV	G	GS	IP	H	BB	SO	HR	GB%	BABIP	STUFF	WHIP	ERA	PERA	EqERA	EqH9	EqBB9	EqSO9	EqHR9	VORP	SN/WX
2005	MIN	MLB	26	0	3	0	43	0	71²	71	24	46	6	48.9%	.293	1	1.33	3.39	4.17	3.73	9.0	3.0	5.7	0.8	18.1	0.44
2006	MIN	MLB	27	1	0	1	39	1	69²	78	21	37	9	47.1%	.305	-10	1.42	3.36	4.51	3.37	9.3	2.5	4.5	1.0	18.3	0.77
2007	MIN	MLB	28	2	4	1	73	0	88	71	21	68	9	48.2%	.253	10	1.05	2.35	3.06	2.16	6.9	1.9	6.4	0.9	36.8	2.46
2008	MIN	MLB	29	3	3	3	54	0	66¹	69	21	48	7	46.7%	.301	-1	1.35	3.88	4.12	3.98	9.1	2.6	5.7	0.9	12.0	1.00

Breakout: 3%   Improve: 12%   Collapse: 66%   Attrition: 22%   Comparables: Chuck Taylor, Tim Burke, Luis Aloma, Brian Holton

Injuries to Crain and Dennys Reyes gave Guerrier an opportunity to move out of his no-leverage role into something a bit meatier, and he responded by missing more bats than ever before on his way to a career year. The extra work he earned caught up to him down the stretch, as he allowed six homers in his final 21 appearances. Look for him to regress a little this year, while still being an effective seventh-inning reliever.

Bobby Korecky

Bats: R   Throws: R   Height: 5' 11"   Weight: 180   Born: September 16, 1979   Age: 28

YEAR	TEAM	LVL	AGE	W	L	SV	G	GS	IP	H	BB	SO	HR	GB%	BABIP	STUFF	WHIP	ERA	PERA	EqERA	EqH9	EqBB9	EqSO9	EqHR9	VORP	SN/WX
2006	NBR	AA	26	1	2	5	16	0	25¹	30	13	14	1	45.6%	.337	-31	1.71	3.23	6.69	6.85	11.4	5.7	2.7	0.8	-3.3	—
2006	ROC	AAA	26	5	3	8	34	0	51	52	16	28	4	52.2%	.280	-28	1.33	3.35	5.37	5.73	10.2	3.5	3.3	1.1	-0.7	—
2007	ROC	AAA	27	5	6	35	66	0	85	80	34	71	5	52.2%	.311	-11	1.34	3.71	4.98	5.47	9.7	4.1	5.6	0.8	1.1	—
2008	MIN	MLB	28	3	5	3	23	7	57¹	64	26	35	6	49.4%	.309	-9	1.58	5.18	5.08	5.36	9.8	3.8	4.9	10	0.9	0.30

Breakout: 30% Improve: 58% Collapse: 22% Attrition: 20%   Comparables: J. J. Trujillo, Spike Lundberg, Matt Stevens, Mark Guerra

Korecky has been groomed as a closer by two organizations now, but minor league closers generally don't become major league closers. With pedestrian rates at every level, Korecky doesn't have any kind of track record of dominance, or any one pitch that makes you think he could be a high-leverage guy in the majors. He's a top-15 pick in your International League fantasy draft because he'll probably spend the season there.

Francisco Liriano

Bats: L   Throws: L   Height: 6' 2"   Weight: 200   Born: October 26, 1983   Age: 24

YEAR	TEAM	LVL	AGE	W	L	SV	G	GS	IP	H	BB	SO	HR	GB%	BABIP	STUFF	WHIP	ERA	PERA	EqERA	EqH9	EqBB9	EqSO9	EqHR9	VORP	SN/WX
2005	NBR	AA	21	3	5	0	13	13	76²	70	26	92	6	60.4%	.335	13	1.25	3.64	5.91	5.96	10.3	4.5	7.1	1.2	-2.7	—
2005	ROC	AAA	21	9	2	0	14	14	91	56	24	112	4	55.1%	.259	47	0.88	1.78	3.01	3.28	6.0	3.0	8.4	0.5	21.9	—
2005	MIN	MLB	21	1	2	0	6	4	23²	19	7	33	4	47.2%	.306	22	1.10	5.70	4.44	5.73	8.2	2.9	11.0	1.6	0.3	0.25
2006	MIN	MLB	22	12	3	1	28	16	121	89	32	144	9	57.1%	.285	49	1.00	2.16	2.73	2.27	6.5	2.3	9.5	0.6	51.0	5.09
2008	MIN	MLB	24	6	5	1	34	11	94²	78	34	103	6	51.4%	.293	26	1.18	3.00	3.01	3.12	7.2	3.0	8.5	0.6	29.2	3.10

Breakout: 22% Improve: 47% Collapse: 28% Attrition: 18%   Comparables: Francisco Rodriguez, Bruce Sutter, Sammy Ellis, Byung-Hyun Kim

Tommy John surgery in November 2006 meant no pitching in 2007 for Liriano, who instead spent the year rehabbing. He started long tossing in August and throwing lightly from a mound in October with an eye toward being ready to go for spring training. Liriano was the best pitcher in baseball for a brief stretch in 2006, but expecting that kind of performance in his first year back is folly. The Twins should be happy with 150 innings of league-average work, providing a base for 2009 and beyond.

Jeff Manship

Bats: R   Throws: R   Height: 6' 0"   Weight: 165   Born: January 16, 1985   Age: 23

YEAR	TEAM	LVL	AGE	W	L	SV	G	GS	IP	H	BB	SO	HR	GB%	BABIP	STUFF	WHIP	ERA	PERA	EqERA	EqH9	EqBB9	EqSO9	EqHR9	VORP	SN/WX
2007	BLT	A	22	7	1	0	13	13	77²	51	9	77	4	59.2%	.241	1	0.77	1.51	4.63	3.95	8.0	2.8	4.7	1.3	12.5	—
2007	FTM	A+	22	8	5	0	13	13	71¹	77	25	59	5	49.1%	.326	-13	1.43	3.16	6.91	6.75	11.3	4.7	4.7	1.4	-8.3	—
2008	MIN	MLB	23	7	12	0	27	27	149¹	176	73	88	20	49.1%	.313	-2	1.66	5.72	5.72	5.85	10.3	4.0	4.7	1.2	-6.2	0.50

Breakout: 7% Improve: 32% Collapse: 34% Attrition: 14%   Comparables: Terric McFarlin, Reynol Mendoza, Kyle Yates, Jose Mieses

The line of Twins pitching prospects never seems to end, with Manship near the top of the list. Manship is a slight right-hander with a fastball/curveball combination and outstanding control drafted out of Notre Dame in the 14th round in 2006. He destroyed the Midwest League last year, but the competition there was probably a small step down from the Big East, and he came back to earth in the Florida State League. Manship carries just 165 pounds on a six-foot frame, so durability is his primary concern.

Jose Mijares

Bats: L   Throws: L   Height: 6' 0"   Weight: 230   Born: October 29, 1984   Age: 23

YEAR	TEAM	LVL	AGE	W	L	SV	G	GS	IP	H	BB	SO	HR	GB%	BABIP	STUFF	WHIP	ERA	PERA	EqERA	EqH9	EqBB9	EqSO9	EqHR9	VORP	SN/WX
2005	BLT	A	20	6	3	2	20	6	54¹	43	40	78	6	51.7%	.330	9	1.53	4.31	8.93	7.43	10.4	9.8	8.8	2.2	-9.4	—
2006	FTM	A+	21	3	5	0	27	5	63	52	27	77	10	42.6%	.301	-23	1.25	3.57	9.34	7.41	10.7	5.9	7.2	3.1	-11.0	—
2007	NBR	AA	22	5	3	9	46	0	61	40	48	75	7	47.3%	.243	6	1.44	3.54	5.12	4.55	6.7	7.9	7.7	1.5	6.9	—
2008	MIN	MLB	23	3	4	2	27	6	55²	51	47	52	7	41.9%	.287	-4	1.75	5.29	5.59	5.35	8.0	6.9	7.3	1.2	0.8	0.30

Breakout: 27% Improve: 60% Collapse: 19% Attrition: 13%   Comparables: Radhames Dykhoff, Adam Butler, Joel Barreto, Carlos Chavez

There are scouts who believe that Mijares could close based on his stuff alone—it's hard to find a lefty with a mid-90s fastball and wipeout slider. There are some issues here, though. Mijares may be listed at 230 pounds, but it's not a good 230, as he's just plain out of shape, which is never a good sign for a player in his early twenties. His attitude is also a concern, as it seems that he doesn't like baseball as much as he's simply good at it. He'll either make the commitment or be a waste of talent in a few years.

Eduardo Morlan

Bats: R Throws: R Height: 6' 2" Weight: 178 Born: March 1, 1986 Age: 22

YEAR	TEAM	LVL	AGE	W	L	SV	G	GS	IP	H	BB	SO	HR	GB%	BABIP	STUFF	WHIP	ERA	PERA	EqERA	EqH9	EqBB9	EqSO9	EqHR9	VORP	SN/WX
2005	BLT	A	19	4	4	0	10	10	51¹	39	31	55	5	39.3%	.266	6	1.36	4.39	7.13	6.45	9.1	7.9	6.0	2.0	-4.2	—
2005	ELZ	Rk	19	2	0	0	4	4	22	6	6	30	0	52.4%	.146	18	0.55	0.82	5.37	3.93	4.4	6.4	5.4	0.5	3.4	—
2006	BLT	A	20	5	5	2	28	18	106	78	38	125	6	36.1%	.281	-4	1.09	2.29	6.41	5.26	9.6	6.1	6.2	1.6	3.4	—
2007	FTM	A+	21	4	3	18	41	0	65²	55	17	92	7	28.8%	.314	4	1.10	3.15	6.23	5.25	9.8	3.6	8.7	2.0	2.3	—
2008	TBA	MLB	22	3	5	4	25	7	60	61	35	58	10	36.2%	.301	5	1.58	5.29	5.44	4.86	8.9	4.7	7.8	1.6	1.8	0.40

Breakout: 40% Improve: 54% Collapse: 24% Attrition: 11%   Comparables: David Riske, Dan Miceli, Miguel A. Martinez, Eddy Rodriguez

Set loose in the bullpen last year, Morlan established himself as one of the top relief prospects in the game. His classic combo of a high-90s fastball and sharp slider marks him as a closer candidate, and escaping to a reliever-poor organization in Tampa Bay via the Garza/Young trade puts him on the fast track to the majors. He still has some work to do on his mechanics and controlling his emotions, both critical traits for high-leverage relievers.

Joe Nathan

Bats: R Throws: R Height: 6' 4" Weight: 220 Born: November 22, 1974 Age: 33

YEAR	TEAM	LVL	AGE	W	L	SV	G	GS	IP	H	BB	SO	HR	GB%	BABIP	STUFF	WHIP	ERA	PERA	EqERA	EqH9	EqBB9	EqSO9	EqHR9	VORP	SN/WX
2005	MIN	MLB	30	7	4	43	69	0	70	46	22	94	5	37.5%	.270	33	0.97	2.70	2.80	3.01	6.4	2.8	10.4	0.7	22.9	4.38
2006	MIN	MLB	31	7	0	36	64	0	68¹	38	16	95	3	38.0%	.246	41	0.79	1.58	2.15	1.82	4.9	1.9	9.9	0.4	34.5	6.58
2007	MIN	MLB	32	4	2	37	68	0	71²	54	19	77	4	43.2%	.282	31	1.02	1.88	2.66	1.90	6.6	2.2	8.9	0.5	32.9	5.08
2008	MIN	MLB	33	4	5	41	53	0	59²	49	18	63	5	40.4%	.278	17	1.12	2.80	2.84	2.87	7.1	2.5	8.3	0.8	18.7	3.30

Breakout: 7% Improve: 23% Collapse: 52% Attrition: 5%   Comparables: Brendan Donnelly, Tom Henke, Arthur Rhodes, Eric Plunk

Morlan won't be succeeding Nathan, but someone will, as the Twins seem unlikely to spend market price on one of the top closers in the game and Nathan will be a free agent after the season. There's less speculation about a Nathan trade than there is about a Santana deal, but the fungibility of relievers and the aura that surrounds closers make Nathan the better trade chit. Besides, Nathan is 33 and saw his strikeout rate take a nasty left turn last season.

Pat Neshek

Bats: S Throws: R Height: 6' 3" Weight: 205 Born: September 4, 1980 Age: 27

YEAR	TEAM	LVL	AGE	W	L	SV	G	GS	IP	H	BB	SO	HR	GB%	BABIP	STUFF	WHIP	ERA	PERA	EqERA	EqH9	EqBB9	EqSO9	EqHR9	VORP	SN/WX
2005	NBR	AA	24	6	4	24	55	0	82¹	69	21	95	9	42.4%	.297	-11	1.09	2.19	5.41	4.15	9.4	3.4	6.8	1.6	11.9	—
2006	ROC	AAA	25	6	2	14	33	0	60	41	14	87	7	50.8%	.276	14	0.92	1.95	4.42	3.07	7.9	2.7	9.9	1.6	15.7	—
2006	MIN	MLB	25	4	2	0	32	0	37	23	6	53	6	32.9%	.236	31	0.78	2.19	2.67	1.98	5.7	1.5	10.2	1.2	16.2	1.46
2007	MIN	MLB	26	7	2	0	74	0	70¹	44	27	74	7	35.4%	.233	18	1.01	2.94	2.65	2.94	5.4	3.1	8.7	0.9	21.9	3.57
2008	MIN	MLB	27	3	3	5	58	0	61²	53	23	63	6	38.7%	.283	14	1.22	3.34	3.40	3.41	7.5	3.0	8.0	0.9	15.0	1.40

Breakout: 11% Improve: 24% Collapse: 39% Attrition: 20%   Comparables: Dennis Higgins, Matt Turner, Scott Dohmann, Trevor Hoffman

More so than Guerrier, Neshek reacted badly to overwork last year after proving to be the best non-Nathan reliever in the Twins' bullpen. The side-armer threw in six straight games over seven days coming out of the All-Star break and wasn't the same after that; he'd posted a 1.49 ERA and 60/13 K/UIBB in 48 1/3 innings through that stretch, but a 6.14 ERA and 14/9 K/UIBB in his 22 innings after it. A winter of rest should do him wonders, but Ron Gardenhire has to watch his usage patterns in 2008, because he broke two of his best pitchers last year.

Glen Perkins

Bats: L Throws: L Height: 5' 11" Weight: 200 Born: March 2, 1983 Age: 25

YEAR	TEAM	LVL	AGE	W	L	SV	G	GS	IP	H	BB	SO	HR	GB%	BABIP	STUFF	WHIP	ERA	PERA	EqERA	EqH9	EqBB9	EqSO9	EqHR9	VORP	SN/WX
2005	FTM	A+	22	3	2	0	10	9	55	41	13	66	2	43.5%	.295	15	0.98	2.13	4.72	4.31	8.8	3.9	6.8	0.8	6.9	—
2005	NBR	AA	22	4	4	0	14	14	79	80	35	67	4	40.2%	.326	-1	1.46	4.90	6.29	6.85	10.8	5.6	4.7	0.8	-9.9	—
2006	NBR	AA	23	4	11	0	23	23	117²	109	45	131	11	36.8%	.320	-5	1.31	3.92	6.14	6.17	10.1	4.6	6.8	1.4	-6.8	—
2007	MIN	MLB	24	0	0	0	19	0	28²	23	12	20	2	40.7%	.273	2	1.22	3.14	3.46	3.00	7.3	3.7	6.0	0.7	9.2	0.45
2008	MIN	MLB	25	2	3	1	29	3	47	48	24	39	5	39.9%	.301	-1	1.52	4.83	4.84	4.91	8.9	4.2	6.5	1.0	3.9	0.40

Breakout: 35% Improve: 52% Collapse: 29% Attrition: 41%   Comparables: Tug McGraw, Frank Bertaina, Kent Peterson, Gene Pentz

Shunted to the bullpen so that Twins fans could enjoy the Sidney Ponson era, Perkins went down with a strained shoulder muscle in May. After nearly four months of rest and rehab, he returned to the bullpen. If healthy, he's exactly what he was a year ago: a mid-rotation starter who throws strikes with an above-average fastball and curve. No team in the majors has more legitimate rotation starters than the Twins do.

Yohan Piño

Bats: R   Throws: R   Height: 6' 3"   Weight: 158   Born: December 26, 1983   Age: 24

YEAR	TEAM	LVL	AGE	W	L	SV	G	GS	IP	H	BB	SO	HR	GB%	BABIP	STUFF	WHIP	ERA	PERA	EqERA	EqH9	EqBB9	EqSO9	EqHR9	VORP	SN/WX
2005	ELZ	Rk	21	9	2	0	12	12	67²	68	13	64	3	48.0%	.325	-24	1.20	3.72	9.09	8.94	14.3	6.0	3.4	1.5	-19.4	—
2006	BLT	A	22	14	2	3	42	7	94¹	69	20	99	4	45.5%	.257	-13	0.95	1.91	5.00	4.64	8.8	3.8	5.1	1.2	9.1	—
2007	FTM	A+	23	4	3	0	19	9	67²	47	17	64	2	37.9%	.251	7	0.95	1.73	3.79	3.13	7.1	3.4	5.5	0.7	17.4	—
2007	NBR	AA	23	2	4	0	9	8	47¹	57	9	40	6	41.2%	.357	-11	1.40	5.14	7.50	6.75	12.3	2.5	5.3	1.8	-5.6	—
2008	MIN	MLB	24	5	8	0	27	17	106¹	123	43	70	16	40.8%	.309	-2	1.56	5.43	5.48	5.47	10.1	3.3	5.2	1.4	0.1	0.70

Breakout: 19% Improve: 44% Collapse: 21% Attrition: 6%   Comparables: Nelson Cruz, Rodrigo Lopez, Juan Mateo, Cha Seung Baek

Piño is one of several Twins pitchers who struggled upon promotion to Double-A last year. In his case, it wasn't a huge surprise. He's tall and skinny and just doesn't have much in the way of stuff; his fastball sits in the mid to upper 80s and he spins a merely decent curve. What separates him from most is his outstanding command. Unfortunately, even with precise location, you still need a little giddy-up to get it by big-league hitters.

Jay Rainville

Bats: R   Throws: R   Height: 6' 3"   Weight: 230   Born: October 16, 1985   Age: 22

YEAR	TEAM	LVL	AGE	W	L	SV	G	GS	IP	H	BB	SO	HR	GB%	BABIP	STUFF	WHIP	ERA	PERA	EqERA	EqH9	EqBB9	EqSO9	EqHR9	VORP	SN/WX
2005	BLT	A	19	8	2	0	16	16	88¹	83	27	77	14	29.1%	.276	-25	1.25	3.77	8.99	6.72	11.2	4.6	4.7	3.1	-9.5	—
2005	FTM	A+	19	4	3	0	9	9	54	54	6	35	7	40.3%	.278	-13	1.11	2.67	7.44	6.23	11.3	2.3	3.0	2.5	-3.3	—
2007	FTM	A+	21	9	11	0	27	26	142¹	145	31	110	9	37.0%	.308	-7	1.24	3.29	5.56	5.78	10.3	3.1	4.2	1.2	-2.7	—
2008	MIN	MLB	22	7	11	0	26	26	148	175	58	88	26	37.5%	.305	-1	1.57	5.85	5.79	5.85	10.3	3.2	4.7	1.6	-6.2	0.50

Breakout: 18% Improve: 59% Collapse: 24% Attrition: 9%   Comparables: Josh Banks, Jensen Lewis, Sam LeCure, Chad Ogea

After missing all of 2006 following shoulder surgery, Rainville bounced back strong last year, nearly matching his 2005 campaign. His big curve came back more easily than his fastball did, and it's the progression of the latter pitch, which sat in the low 90s with good sinking action before the surgery, that will determine whether he moves back up prospect lists.

Dennys Reyes

Bats: R   Throws: L   Height: 6' 3"   Weight: 245   Born: April 19, 1977   Age: 31

YEAR	TEAM	LVL	AGE	W	L	SV	G	GS	IP	H	BB	SO	HR	GB%	BABIP	STUFF	WHIP	ERA	PERA	EqERA	EqH9	EqBB9	EqSO9	EqHR9	VORP	SN/WX
2005	SDN	MLB	28	3	2	0	36	1	43²	57	32	35	3	67.3%	.378	-5	2.04	5.15	7.31	6.70	11.9	6.1	6.7	0.6	-3.1	-0.42
2006	MIN	MLB	29	5	0	0	66	0	50²	35	15	49	3	72.3%	.254	25	0.99	0.89	2.53	1.46	5.8	2.6	8.4	0.5	26.5	2.14
2007	MIN	MLB	30	2	1	0	50	0	29¹	34	21	21	1	67.4%	.375	-2	1.88	3.99	5.59	4.08	10.4	6.0	6.0	0.3	5.5	0.09
2008	MIN	MLB	31	2	2	2	45	0	41¹	39	24	34	2	59.1%	.308	-2	1.53	3.76	4.08	3.96	8.3	4.8	6.4	0.3	7.2	0.70

Breakout: 21% Improve: 46% Collapse: 25% Attrition: 15%   Comparables: Terry Forster, Jay Powell, Kelly Wunsch, Ray King

Soreness in his left elbow ended Reyes's 2007 season in August, and the diagnosis of a triceps tear and bone chips leaves his availability for this year in question. He did not have surgery over the offseason, so there will be uncertainty until he starts throwing in February. Given that he's had just one good year in the last eight, it's not worth losing any sleep over him.

Juan Rincon

Bats: R   Throws: R   Height: 5' 11"   Weight: 210   Born: January 23, 1979   Age: 29

YEAR	TEAM	LVL	AGE	W	L	SV	G	GS	IP	H	BB	SO	HR	GB%	BABIP	STUFF	WHIP	ERA	PERA	EqERA	EqH9	EqBB9	EqSO9	EqHR9	VORP	SN/WX
2005	MIN	MLB	26	6	6	0	75	0	77	63	30	84	2	49.5%	.313	33	1.21	2.45	3.22	3.13	7.6	3.5	9.6	0.2	23.4	3.37
2006	MIN	MLB	27	3	1	1	75	0	74¹	76	24	65	2	52.5%	.344	20	1.35	2.91	3.64	3.47	8.9	2.7	7.6	0.2	20.6	3.20
2007	MIN	MLB	28	3	3	0	63	0	59²	65	28	49	9	49.5%	.311	-12	1.56	5.13	5.33	5.34	9.2	3.7	6.7	1.3	0.7	0.37
2008	MIN	MLB	29	3	3	3	49	0	55¹	55	21	47	4	48.7%	.309	5	1.37	3.84	3.84	3.99	8.6	3.2	6.7	0.6	10.7	0.90

Breakout: 25% Improve: 54% Collapse: 18% Attrition: 10%   Comparables: Jack Baldschun, Marc Wilkins, Mel Rojas, Hal Reniff

The steady degradation in Rincon's peripherals—you can ski down those Stuff scores—finally showed up in his ERA last season. Gardenhire banished Rincon to the depths of the pen in July, after which the righty went six weeks without getting so much as a hold opportunity. There's been no whiff of a health problem; in fact, Rincon pitched winter ball to, as he put it, "eat up some innings" following his lowest workload in five years. It'd be more encouraging if he was hurt; now, he just looks like a pitcher on his way out of the league.

Tyler Robertson

Bats: L   Throws: L   Height: 6' 5"   Weight: 220   Born: December 23, 1987   Age: 20

YEAR	TEAM	LVL	AGE	W	L	SV	G	GS	IP	H	BB	SO	HR	GB%	BABIP	STUFF	WHIP	ERA	PERA	EqERA	EqH9	EqBB9	EqSO9	EqHR9	VORP	SN/WX
2006	TWI	Rk	18	4	2	0	11	10	48^1	54	15	54	2	48.2%	.380	3	1.43	4.30	9.52	8.19	13.7	6.0	5.3	1.8	-11.7	—
2007	BLT	A	19	9	5	1	18	16	102^1	87	33	123	3	58.6%	.324	20	1.17	2.29	6.39	5.73	10.8	5.9	6.0	0.9	-1.2	—
2008	MIN	MLB	20	6	11	0	26	26	134	163	90	97	15	50.8%	.340	0	1.88	5.97	6.35	6.08	10.6	5.5	5.7	1.0	-8.8	0.10

Breakout: 24% Improve: 52% Collapse: 24% Attrition: 11%   Comparables: Dennys Reyes, Michael Bowden, Bill Pulsipher, Jonathon Niese

The Twins held Robertson back in extended spring training to begin 2007, but when their Low-A franchise needed another arm, he went to Beloit and was one of the league's best pitchers during his three-month-plus tenure. He's big and physical, with plus control of an average fastball and a very good slider, but some wonder how well that combination will play as he moves up.

Johan Santana

Bats: L   Throws: L   Height: 6' 0"   Weight: 210   Born: March 13, 1979   Age: 29

YEAR	TEAM	LVL	AGE	W	L	SV	G	GS	IP	H	BB	SO	HR	GB%	BABIP	STUFF	WHIP	ERA	PERA	EqERA	EqH9	EqBB9	EqSO9	EqHR9	VORP	SN/WX
2005	MIN	MLB	26	16	7	0	33	33	231^2	180	45	238	22	40.9%	.265	41	0.97	2.87	2.91	3.02	6.9	1.7	8.9	0.8	73.0	7.64
2006	MIN	MLB	27	19	6	0	34	34	233^2	186	47	245	24	41.8%	.273	41	1.00	2.77	2.81	2.80	6.6	1.7	8.8	0.8	79.6	8.38
2007	MIN	MLB	28	15	13	0	33	33	219	183	52	235	33	39.5%	.275	26	1.07	3.33	3.48	3.30	7.2	1.9	8.9	1.4	57.7	6.30
2008	MIN	MLB	29	15	9	0	33	33	227	197	62	230	25	41.3%	.284	30	1.14	3.32	3.28	3.39	7.6	2.2	8.0	1.0	54.5	7.50

Breakout: 4% Improve: 31% Collapse: 19% Attrition: 3%   Comparables: Floyd Bannister, Mickey Lolich, Tom Seaver, Billy Pierce

There's nothing wrong with Johan Santana. His rates last year were all in line with his career norms. The main difference between 2007 and the years before it was that a few more fly balls found the seats last year. That's going to happen from time to time; when it happens to the best pitcher in baseball, it means that in that one particular season he's merely the fifth-best pitcher in baseball. There's much more variance in the year-to-year performance of baseball players than is commonly acknowledged, which leads many to overreact to what is quite often just statistical noise. Santana is in the last year of his contract; the Twins opted not to trade him during the winter, but he's a lock to be dealt by the deadline if the Twins are out of contention. Re-signing him is apparently not an option, but Santana remains the only pitcher in baseball worth the gamble of a six-year contract.

Carlos Silva

Bats: R   Throws: R   Height: 6' 4"   Weight: 245   Born: April 23, 1979   Age: 29

YEAR	TEAM	LVL	AGE	W	L	SV	G	GS	IP	H	BB	SO	HR	GB%	BABIP	STUFF	WHIP	ERA	PERA	EqERA	EqH9	EqBB9	EqSO9	EqHR9	VORP	SN/WX
2005	MIN	MLB	26	9	8	0	27	27	188^1	212	9	71	25	50.5%	.295	-2	1.17	3.44	4.79	4.22	10.5	0.5	3.5	1.2	38.4	4.02
2006	MIN	MLB	27	11	15	0	36	31	180^1	246	32	70	38	45.6%	.320	-28	1.54	5.94	6.55	6.21	11.2	1.5	3.3	1.7	-7.6	1.34
2007	MIN	MLB	28	13	14	0	33	33	202	229	36	89	20	48.3%	.304	3	1.31	4.19	4.24	4.19	9.6	1.4	3.7	0.9	35.5	4.97
2008	SEA	MLB	29	8	10	0	25	25	148^1	184	31	67	19	48.7%	.315	-1	1.45	4.97	4.98	4.87	10.9	1.7	3.5	1.1	7.0	1.90

Breakout: 18% Improve: 47% Collapse: 28% Attrition: 21%   Comparables: Bill Wegman, Carl Pavano, Bobby Jones, Jim Barr

When a pitcher who *isn't* the best in baseball gives up a few more homers, he becomes an unmitigated disaster. That was Silva in 2006, when he lost command of his sinking fastball, allowing fly balls and walks at the highest rates of his Twins career. He pitched better in last year, but we're still talking about someone who rides the knife edge of survival. His decision to sign with the Mariners, who by home park, defensive personnel, and schedule routinely provide the safest route for pitchers of any team in the AL, is either notably self-aware or blindly lucky. In either case, he's not a good bet to survive the four years of his contract.

Kevin Slowey

Bats: R   Throws: R   Height: 6' 3"   Weight: 195   Born: May 4, 1984   Age: 24

YEAR	TEAM	LVL	AGE	W	L	SV	G	GS	IP	H	BB	SO	HR	GB%	BABIP	STUFF	WHIP	ERA	PERA	EqERA	EqH9	EqBB9	EqSO9	EqHR9	VORP	SN/WX
2005	BLT	A	21	3	2	0	13	9	64¹	42	8	69	4	37.8%	.242	14	0.78	2.24	4.23	4.24	7.5	2.4	6.1	1.3	8.7	—
2006	FTM	A+	22	4	2	0	14	14	89	52	9	99	2	42.5%	.230	29	0.69	1.01	3.35	3.52	6.5	1.8	6.0	0.5	19.5	—
2006	NBR	AA	22	4	3	0	9	9	59²	50	13	52	6	39.4%	.265	2	1.06	3.19	4.64	4.45	8.4	2.7	4.9	1.4	7.2	—
2007	ROC	AAA	23	10	5	0	20	20	133²	110	18	107	4	43.3%	.277	28	0.96	1.88	3.33	2.88	8.1	1.5	5.3	0.4	38.7	—
2007	MIN	MLB	23	4	1	0	13	11	66²	82	11	47	16	30.1%	.297	-8	1.40	4.72	5.88	5.01	10.0	1.3	5.5	2.1	5.4	1.09
2008	MIN	MLB	24	9	10	1	39	26	158²	163	37	108	22	37.8%	.285	7	1.26	4.22	4.17	4.27	9.0	1.9	5.4	1.2	21.4	3.40

Breakout: 14% Improve: 35% Collapse: 37% Attrition: 18%   Comparables: Mike Mussina, John Fulgham, Bryan Rekar, Jeff Russell

Pitchers who rely on something other than really great pitches usually need some adjustment time as they move up from one level to the next. Like eight other guys listed above, Slowey has more command than stuff, and he allowed 13 homers in his first seven MLB starts, which chased him back to Triple-A in June. Upon his return in September, he allowed three homers in six appearances, and just one in his four starts. More notably, he did not walk a batter in any of those starts. He's an extreme fly-ball pitcher who is going to give up 30 to 35 homers a year without walking even that many men and will be a very valuable mid-rotation starter. Finding a true center fielder would help him a lot. Think Bob Tewksbury.

Oswaldo Sosa

Bats: R   Throws: R   Height: 6' 2"   Weight: 187   Born: September 19, 1985   Age: 22

YEAR	TEAM	LVL	AGE	W	L	SV	G	GS	IP	H	BB	SO	HR	GB%	BABIP	STUFF	WHIP	ERA	PERA	EqERA	EqH9	EqBB9	EqSO9	EqHR9	VORP	SN/WX
2005	ELZ	Rk	19	6	5	0	12	11	56¹	59	21	40	4	69.6%	.307	-43	1.42	4.96	11.24	12.12	14.5	9.6	1.9	2.1	-30.6	—
2006	BLT	A	20	9	7	0	20	20	117²	102	36	95	1	59.5%	.296	8	1.18	2.76	5.42	5.80	10.0	5.3	3.7	0.5	-2.3	—
2006	FTM	A+	20	4	1	0	6	6	34²	23	18	27	1	52.7%	.241	4	1.20	2.11	4.43	4.83	7.1	6.5	4.0	0.6	2.7	—
2007	FTM	A+	21	5	5	0	19	19	105	94	36	82	2	51.9%	.296	11	1.24	2.23	4.60	3.79	9.1	4.5	4.3	0.5	19.6	—
2007	NBR	AA	21	1	4	0	9	9	48	45	22	35	4	52.4%	.293	-5	1.40	4.50	5.65	6.00	9.2	5.0	4.4	1.2	-2.0	—
2008	MIN	MLB	22	6	11	0	26	26	139²	163	88	79	15	50.5%	.316	-6	1.79	5.93	5.96	6.09	10.2	5.1	4.5	1.0	-9.6	0.00

Breakout: 5% Improve: 29% Collapse: 41% Attrition: 11%   Comparables: Wascar Serrano, Pedro Liriano, Rene Miniel, Ivan Arteaga

Sosa was among the league leaders in ERA at High-A Fort Myers, but he was met with some adversity upon his promotion to Double-A, which, as with Piño, wasn't a huge surprise. Sosa's fastball is above average in every way—from velocity, to movement, to location—but he has yet to find much consistency with his breaking stuff, and it's hard to find success at the upper levels without a second pitch. Even if he doesn't find it, he should still be good enough to relieve.

Anthony Swarzak

Bats: R   Throws: R   Height: 6' 3"   Weight: 195   Born: September 10, 1985   Age: 22

YEAR	TEAM	LVL	AGE	W	L	SV	G	GS	IP	H	BB	SO	HR	GB%	BABIP	STUFF	WHIP	ERA	PERA	EqERA	EqH9	EqBB9	EqSO9	EqHR9	VORP	SN/WX
2005	BLT	A	19	9	5	0	18	18	91¹	81	32	101	7	49.2%	.318	9	1.24	4.04	6.73	7.00	10.6	5.0	6.3	1.6	-12.4	—
2005	FTM	A+	19	3	4	0	10	10	59	72	11	55	3	44.7%	.379	8	1.41	3.66	7.96	6.71	14.1	3.4	4.9	1.1	-6.3	—
2006	FTM	A+	20	11	7	0	27	27	145¹	131	60	131	8	40.2%	.300	-1	1.32	3.29	6.20	5.54	10.3	5.6	4.9	1.2	0.9	—
2007	NBR	AA	21	5	4	0	15	14	86¹	78	23	76	6	33.6%	.304	12	1.17	3.23	4.68	4.35	9.0	3.1	5.6	1.0	11.2	—
2008	MIN	MLB	22	6	9	0	30	21	128¹	144	61	89	20	37.1%	.306	0	1.59	5.40	5.59	5.41	9.8	3.9	5.5	1.4	1.1	1.00

Breakout: 10% Improve: 33% Collapse: 28% Attrition: 18%   Comparables: Josh Banks, Chad Ogea, John Wasdin, Aaron Myette

By dint of the alphabet, we've saved the best Twins' pitching prospect for last. Like the others, Swarzak has good command, but he has ace stuff, with a fastball that gets up to 95 mph, a good curve, and changeup. Now the bad news: Swarzak served a 50-game suspension last season after testing positive for a "drug of abuse." It's notable that the Twins, a fairly conservative organization, seem to think that the righty's problems are behind him. The suspension also saved Swarzak about 60 innings at age 21, not a small consideration. He'll be up later this year, and fronting the rotation in 2010.

LINEOUTS

Hitters

PLAYER	TEAM	LVL	AGE	PA	R	2B	3B	HR	RBI	BB	SO	SB-CS	EqBRR	AVG/OBP/SLG	MLVr	EqAVG/EqOBP/EqSLG	EqA	VORP
3B B. Buscher*	NBR	AA	26	284	37	19	1	7	37	31	30	2-2	-3.8	.308/.391/.478	.218	.278/.354/.448	.276	17.8
	ROC	AAA	26	147	21	7	0	7	22	13	11	1-0	-0.7	.311/.374/.523	.266	.293/.354/.511	.292	13.6
	MIN	MLB	26	94	8	1	0	2	10	10	16	1-0	-2.6	.244/.323/.329	-.174	.247/.333/.333	.244	-1.4
2B B. Dinkelman*	BLT	A	23	278	48	16	6	7	21	30	34	10-0	0.6	.283/.373/.488	.240	.233/.304/.390	.247	0.8
	FTM	A+	23	292	56	7	4	6	21	36	43	8-3	-1.7	.255/.361/.389	.073	.224/.318/.358	.241	-1.0
LF L. Ford	ROC	AAA	30	139	14	12	0	2	17	17	30	2-1	-1.2	.262/.353/.410	.045	.244/.331/.390	.253	-2.0
	MIN	MLB	30	130	13	6	0	3	14	11	24	3-1	0.1	.233/.315/.362	-.148	.243/.331/.391	.255	-1.9
DH G. Jones*	ROC	AAA	26	446	57	32	3	13	70	32	83	2-2	-0.3	.280/.334/.473	.113	.263/.315/.459	.264	3.8
	MIN	MLB	26	84	7	2	1	2	5	6	20	1-1	-0.4	.208/.262/.338	-.299	.224/.286/.395	.234	-4.7
C/1 M. LeCroy	ROC	AAA	31	281	12	12	0	3	25	26	48	0-0	-1.8	.194/.281/.279	-.279	.204/.284/.300	.208	-13.4
3B M. Macri	TUL	AA	25	298	46	23	0	11	33	20	58	4-4	-0.9	.298/.349/.502	.178	.265/.309/.434	.252	9.5
	ROC	AAA	25	50	5	1	0	3	6	3	13	0-0	0.2	.213/.260/.426	-.116	.191/.240/.404	.216	-2.5
RF D. McDonald	COH	AAA	28	304	39	17	4	2	41	31	64	14-5	2.5	.315/.382/.431	.175	.264/.334/.390	.258	-2.6
	ROC	AAA	28	252	32	12	2	5	32	19	35	19-2	1.8	.277/.339/.415	.041	.257/.315/.407	.261	-2.6
C J. Morales#	ROC	AAA	24	411	42	25	1	2	37	30	44	1-4	-6.1	.311/.366/.399	.088	.282/.336/.377	.247	10.1
INF L. Rodriguez#	MIN	MLB	27	173	18	5	1	2	12	12	14	1-0	1.5	.219/.281/.303	-.302	.227/.292/.331	.223	-7.7
INF M. Tolbert#	ROC	AAA	25	477	65	24	7	6	53	37	56	11-3	4.1	.293/.353/.427	.090	.271/.329/.416	.261	15.9

Brian Buscher came over in the Triple-A phase of the 2006 Rule 5 draft and had a career year before stalling in the majors. He's not a prospect, and even a bench role is unlikely after the Twins' winter additions. ⊘ Non-drafted free-agent **Brian Dinkelman** played well for a second straight season, although an experiment in the outfield was mostly unproductive. At 24, he can't afford a bad year. ⊘ A second straight poor season chased fan favorite **Lew Ford** to the minors, and then to Japan's Hanshin Tigers. ⊘ Rochester veteran **Garrett Jones** sipped a cup of bitter coffee in what was probably his only shot at making an impression in the majors. Guys who can't field have to be monsters with the bat, and he's not. ⊘ As a third catcher and platoon DH, **Matt LeCroy** would be worth the roster spot. He might be worth one in the NL if the team had a lefty first baseman who needed some platoon protection, say the Pirates with Adam LaRoche. ⊘ Injury-prone infielder **Matt Macri** came over from the Rockies in exchange for Ramon Ortiz. He's never played 100 games in a season and has been tried all over the infield when healthy. Until he completes a season, there's nothing here. ⊘ **Darnell McDonald** has extra-outfielder skills and seems to be improving as a hitter late in his career. The Twins will need someone to stand out in center field, so why not him? ⊘ Converted infielder **Jose Morales** is now a switch-hitting catcher with a good arm. He has no place to play unless the Twins move Mauer. ⊘ **Luis Rodriguez** is a generic utility infielder who was claimed off waivers by the Padres immediately after last season. He can't play short, which limits his career options. ⊘ Second baseman **Matt Tolbert** gets high marks for his defense and has enough line-drive pop and speed to warrant a look in spring training.

Pitchers

PLAYER	TEAM	LVL	AGE	W	L	SV	IP	H	BB	SO	HR	GB%	BABIP	STUFF	WHIP	ERA	PERA	EqERA	EqH9	EqBB9	EqSO9	EqHR9	VORP
B. Bass	ROC	AAA	25	7	3	1	103¹	96	24	80	8	57.1%	.290	-6	1.16	3.49	4.67	4.81	9.4	2.5	5.1	1.0	8.5
A. Burnett	BLT	A	19	9	8	0	155	140	38	117	9	49.7%	.285	-14	1.15	3.02	6.55	6.35	10.6	4.7	3.1	1.5	-11.2
C. Cali*	ROC	AAA	28	5	1	1	47²	42	14	28	1	55.9%	.295	-9	1.17	2.45	3.97	3.98	9.0	3.1	4.0	0.4	7.7
	MIN	MLB	28	0	1	0	21	22	16	14	2	53.6%	.299	-9	1.81	4.71	5.39	4.22	8.9	5.9	5.5	0.8	3.0
J. DePaula	ROC	AAA	24	12	5	2	83²	66	27	63	8	65.6%	.262	-16	1.11	2.90	4.41	4.42	8.1	3.4	5.1	1.3	10.1
	MIN	MLB	24	0	1	0	20	30	10	8	5	56.4%	.352	-55	2.00	8.55	12.74	10.53	13.3	4.1	3.2	2.3	-6.7
S. Ponson	MIN	MLB	30	2	5	0	37²	54	17	23	7	53.6%	.359	-22	1.88	6.92	9.38	8.20	12.5	3.6	5.1	1.7	-5.8
K. Waldrop	FTM	A+	21	7	5	0	92²	90	24	57	3	56.3%	.304	-2	1.23	3.40	5.28	5.64	10.2	3.7	3.4	0.8	-0.4
	NBR	AA	21	3	6	0	59	74	19	33	7	52.8%	.332	-25	1.58	5.34	8.18	7.88	12.2	3.5	3.1	1.6	-14.2

Brian Bass earned his ticket out of the Royals' organization with a poor 2006 season that featured a suspension. He's on the Twins' 40-man, although it's hard to see a role for him in the Land of 10,000 Pitchers. ⊘ The Twins have brought right-hander **Alex Burnett** along slowly with good results. He's a performance prospect so far and a good one. The Florida State League should be a good test. ⊘ Ex-Cardinals closer prospect **Carmen Cali** filled in during the Twins' injury woes and walked more men than he struck out. He's roster fodder. ⊘ Not the former Yankees prospect, this **Julio DePaula** climbed another rung last year on the strength of a plus changeup. He needs more than that to make an impact. ⊘ **Sidney Ponson** is an awful pitcher who had no business being in the major leagues last year. The decision to blow seven starts on him was simply incompetent. ⊘ The rare bit of bad news in Pitcherland, **Kyle Waldrop** couldn't handle a promotion to Double-A and landed back in the Florida State League. The former first-round pick is now caught behind the team's crop of command prospects.

MANAGER: RON GARDENHIRE

YEAR	TEAM	W-L	Pythag +/−	Avg PC	100+ P	120+ P	QS	BQS	REL	REL w Zero R	IBB	Subs	PH	PH Avg	PH HR	SB2	CS2	SB3	CS3	SAC Att	SAC %	POS SAC	Squeeze	Swing	In Play
2005	MIN	83-79	-1	92.1	45	0	84	14	396	273	38	35	104	.259	2	85	39	17	4	70	60.0%	40	3	141	116
2006	MIN	96-66	2	90.1	43	0	71	5	421	287	25	35	93	.143	2	88	36	13	6	59	52.5%	28	0	177	146
2007	MIN	79-83	-1	93.8	47	0	75	5	436	291	33	40	102	.250	1	94	29	18	1	55	61.8%	29	4	161	134

Partition the blame however you care to, but Gardenhire has been a key member of the management team that has chosen to break camp two years in a row with dead weight all over the roster. Two years ago, it was the left side of the infield; last year, it was the back of the rotation. Gardenhire's preferences—experience and defense—are getting in the way of a team that is loaded with young talent and struggles to score runs. In 2007, Gardenhire did not adjust well to the problems his pitchers had, shifting too much of the workload to Neshek and Guerrier and paying a price as both lost effectiveness later in the year. In a division that includes two of the league's best teams, Gardenhire can't punt the first six weeks before getting his best team on the field, and he can't leave himself naked in the last six by burning out his bullpen.

New York Mets

That vague, crepuscular time, the time of regrets that resemble hopes,
of hopes that resemble regrets, when youth has passed
but old age has not yet arrived.
—IVAN TURGENEV, from *Fathers and Sons*

For the Mets, "that vague, crepuscular time" was early 2007, when they enjoyed a fleeting period of success while attempting to finish up business left over from 2006, a season in which they were the favorite to win the National League pennant but were dispatched from the National League Championship Series by a clearly inferior Cardinals team. Youth *had* passed, but throughout the warmer months of last summer, it seemed as though the Mets could delay the arrival of old age by getting a head start and simply outrunning it. In the end, the decay of age proved to be faster.

The version of the Mets that won 97 games in 2006 was old. Yes, it had two of the best young players in the game in shortstop Jose Reyes and third baseman David Wright, plus one more star on the good side of 30 in center fielder Carlos Beltran, but at most other positions the Mets favored what you might call "senior veterans," players from the 35-and-over crowd, most of whom were retained for the 2007 season. Catcher Paul Lo Duca turned 35 last April. First baseman Carlos Delgado turned 35 in June. Second baseman Jose Valentin was 37, and was backed up by 37-year-old Damion Easley, an offseason pickup. Another new addition, left fielder Moises Alou, a player who trouble staying healthy when he was 25, turned 41 on July 7. Right fielder Shawn Green was only 34, but the rapid decline of his skills following the 2002 season made him an honorary 35-year-old in the minds of most observers.

METS PROSPECTUS

2007 record: 88-74; Second place, NL East

Pythagenport record: 86-76

Runs scored per game: 4.96 (4th in NL)

Runs allowed per game: 4.63 (7th in NL)

Team EqA: .273 (2nd in NL)

2007 Batters Age: 31.1 (3rd oldest in NL)

2007 Pitchers Age: 31.9 (Oldest in NL)

Ballpark: Shea Stadium; Pitcher's park; Park Factor of .959

2007: Mets suffer second-worst September fall in baseball history, break hip.

2008: They won't blow another late-season lead, because they won't have another late-season lead.

Those hitters were mere babes compared to the old-timers who populated the pitching staff; the Mets pitchers were the only ones in the majors drinking Geritol instead of Gatorade. The 2006 staff was among the 20 oldest aggregations of pitchers in major league history (Table 1), and much of the group also returned for the 2007 encore. Tom Glavine was 41 last year. Orlando Hernandez, while listed at 41, probably won't see 45 again, though there is no way of knowing for sure without cutting him open and counting the rings. The great Pedro Martinez was 35 and was scheduled to miss most of the season rehabbing from surgery to repair a torn rotator cuff. Closer Billy Wagner turned 36 in July. Honorary 35-year-old Chan Ho Park, also 34, was given a chance to make the team in case the starting rotation's relative tyros—John Maine (26) and Oliver Perez (25)—proved to too immature and began eating the paste and hiding each other's propeller beanies.

As it turned out, the expanded roles given to Maine and Perez dropped the Mets staff out of the historic range in Table 1, down to an average age of 31.8, which still made them the second-oldest pitching staff in the majors last year. Altogether, the Mets' roster just missed being the oldest in the business in 2007 (Table 2).

As we wrote in last year's book, having an old team doesn't necessarily mean having a bad one. Six of the eight oldest teams in Table 1, and 11 of the 20 listed, won 90 games or more, including the 2006 Mets. That

Table 1. Geritolball—Oldest Pitching Staffs: Pitchers weighted by total batters faced

Rank	Year	Team	Age	Record
1	2005	Yankees	34.63	95-67
2	2003	Yankees	34.13	101-61
3	2005	Red Sox	34.12	95-67
4	1935	Braves	33.58	38-115
5	2002	Yankees	33.53	103-58
6	1988	Astros	33.47	82-80
7	1945	Cubs	33.43	98-56
8	2004	Yankees	33.40	101-61
9	1983	Angels	33.30	70-92
10	1947	Pirates	33.29	62-92
11	1945	Reds	33.25	61-93
12	1989	Astros	33.20	86-76
13	1999	Mets	33.20	97-66
14	1944	Pirates	33.18	90-63
15	2004	Mets	33.14	71-91
16	1947	Phillies	33.13	62-92
17	2006	Mets	33.01	97-65
18	2004	Red Sox	33.01	98-64
19	2002	D'Backs	32.97	98-64
20	1931	Dodgers	32.96	79-73

Table 2. Age-Enhanced Ballclubs of 2007 (weighted by playing time)

Oldest Hitters 2007		Oldest Pitchers 2007		Oldest Roster 2007	
Giants	33.55	Red Sox	31.92	Yankees	31.51
Astros	31.89	**Mets**	**31.90**	**Mets**	**31.48**
Tigers	31.53	Yankees	31.75	Astros	31.36
Yankees	31.22	Padres	31.58	Red Sox	31.29
Mets	**31.12**	Dodgers	31.19	Padres	30.92

said, older teams run an increased risk of injury or sudden erosion of skill, and that risk compounds with each additional elder added to the ranks. This is true if the players are coming off good or great seasons, if they are perennial All-Stars, or are just earning time toward their pension. Age doesn't care what a player did last year; past accomplishments are unable to slow the forward march of time that carries an athlete toward his competitive demise.

The 2007 Mets hit the ground running. At the quarter pole, they were 26-14, a pace for 105 wins. By the end of that month, they had a 4½ game lead on the second-place Braves. Yet, the worms were already at work. Carlos Delgado opened the season in a fugue state, batting .188/.262/.280 in April with just one home run that month. Though he recovered somewhat, his post-April averages of .274/.348/.489 fell short of the .282/.390/.558 career rates he carried into the season. In addition, he was neutered by Shea Stadium (.225/.313/.368) and southpaws (.267/.318/.386). Valentin, re-signed by the Mets after a fluky last-gasp season, didn't hit and then

broke his leg, disappearing for good on July 20. Alou was productive, but vanished from May 12 to July 27 with a strained left quadriceps. Green got off to a good start but was carried by the team during midsummer, batting .237/.280/.360 from May through July. This led to countless (and appropriate) efforts to replace him with Lastings Milledge. Ironically, Green recovered some of his old pizzazz down the stretch, batting .350/.438/.487 in a platoon role. For but one month, Paul Lo Duca's bat was completely limp (in May the catcher hit .393/.441/.488).

Despite the age, infirmity, and Jose Reyes's quiet last two months (.240/.311/.364), it wasn't the offense that gave out. Over the fateful final two weeks of the season, the offense actually improved. Through September 15, the Mets had hit .273/.341/.430 and scored 4.8 runs per game, thereafter the team averaged 6.2 runs per game on rates of .298/.360/.452. Rather it was the pitching staff that slowly unraveled over the course of the season. In April, Mets pitching allowed 3.5 runs a game; in May, it was 4.0; in June, 4.4; in July, 4.9; in August, 5.1; and September, 5.7. Over the disastrous final 17 games of the season, the Mets allowed 6.76 runs per game. Pedro Martinez returned on September 3 and pitched well, but lacked stamina; Orlando Hernandez missed most of May and made just one start and three abbreviated relief appearances in September; Tom Glavine's ERA after May was 5.03. John Maine brought an ERA of 2.92 into August, but from then until his heroic final start of the season (he and two relievers one-hit the Marlins in the Mets' penultimate game) it was 7.06; he may have been suffering from a bad hip or was simply gassed. Oliver Perez looked to be having his most consistent season in years through July (2.84 ERA), but after that, he reverted to his formless form with a 4.86 ERA.

For these reasons, the Mets were an inconsistent team. They played sub-.500 baseball at midsummer, but only the Phillies took advantage of New York's downturn, and even in their case, it wasn't enough to threaten the Mets' lead (see Table 3). The Mets emerged from their midsummer's malaise still holding a three-game lead over the Phillies, who gained just one game on the Mets over the month of August despite sweeping a four-game series from them as the month drew to a close. The Braves went 13-15 that month and fell to 6 1/2 games out.

Thus did the Mets arrive at the fatal month of September. Before the wheels came off mid-month, it seemed safe for them to print up their postseason tickets. In the 30 games preceding September 12, the Mets were 19-11 (.633); through the first 11 games of September they were 9-2. With 17 games left to play, the Mets

Table 3. It Could Have Happened Then: NL East combined records in June and July

Team	W	L	PCT
Phillies	30	23	.566
Braves	26	28	.481
Mets	25	29	.463
Nationals	24	28	.461
Marlins	23	30	.434

had a record of 83-62 and a seven-game lead on the second-place Phillies in the NL East. The Mets had the pennant won; their odds of reaching the playoffs were 99.8 percent. Even if they played one game under .500 the rest of the way, they would finish with a record of 91-71, which would mean that the Phillies would have to go 16-1 to beat them.

In the end, the Mets didn't make the Phillies work nearly that hard. Stumbling to a 5-12 finish, the Mets watched helplessly as Philadelphia went 13-4 to steal the division title on the final day of the season. To paraphrase our resident oddsmaker, Nate Silver, it was the second biggest choke job in baseball history, ranking behind that of the 1995 Angels. The Phamous Phillie Phlop of 1964 doesn't come anywhere close.

The magnitude of the collapse didn't mean that it should have been unexpected. The Mets reserved their losing for the end of the season, but their weaknesses could easily have manifested themselves earlier, and in a sense they did—over the final three-quarters of the season they were just a little over .500 at 62-60, including a 4-13 stretch in June that was a game worse than their September collapse. The only thing that kept them in first place as long as they were was the weakness of the competition. The Phillies played at only a 92-win pace over those final two-thirds of the season; if they warmed to a 100-win pace, the Mets would have finished seven games out.

When age caught up to the Mets, they lacked the depth to react. This was due in part to some of general manager Omar Minaya's winter moves. The bullpen, a problem all season long (18th in the majors in WXRL), could have used Heath Bell, Royce Ring, Henry Owens, and Matt Lindstrom, all dealt for players who combined to make 30 plate appearances and pitch 11 1/3 innings for the 2007 Mets. The trade of starter Brian Bannister for reliever Ambiorix Burgos, while more understandable, also backfired in a large way. Simultaneously, the Mets' farm failed to answer the call. Former Royal and current reclamation project Ruben Gotay played well after taking over second base for Valentin and Easley, but outfielder Carlos Gomez proved to have been badly rushed when taking over for the injured Endy Chavez, who him-

self had taken over for the fragile Alou. Milledge, long billed as a coming star, didn't impress when given the opportunity and finished the season as Green's platoon partner. Fomer first-round pick Mike Pelfrey failed to contribute a quality start in 10 of 13 tries. The depletion of the rotation ultimately forced the Mets to spend two crucial late September starting assignments on replacement-level veteran Brian Lawrence and rookie Phil Humber. The farm's only success was side-arming reliever Joe Smith. Unfortunately, Randolph pushed him hard in the first half (40 games through the break), and the Mets were forced to demote Smith at the end of July just so he could take some time off.

Then there was the truly bizarre manner in which Randolph kept going back to Guillermo Mota (-0.437 WXRL). Mota's performance-enhancing-drug suspension, handed down while he was still a free agent, should have made him persona non grata with the club. Instead, it somehow made him its most popular reliever, at least with the manager and general manager; the fans were another matter. Publicly unstinting in their praise of Mota, both Randolph and Minaya refused to bail out on the veteran reliever, even when he was bailing out on them. In that light, the November trade that sent Mota to the Milwaukee Brewers in exchange for catcher Johnny Estrada, who was subsequently non-tendered, must be looked upon as an act of self-preservation. In announcing the trade, Minaya could have borrowed one of Samuel L. Jackson's lines from *Pulp Fiction:* "I was sitting here eating my muffin and drinking my coffee . . . when I had what alcoholics refer to as a moment of clarity."

Minaya's other off-season moves suggest that he has not yet had another of those moments. He re-signed reserve catcher Ramon Castro to a two-year deal, but given the subsequent acquisitions of Estrada and Brian Schneider, looks to keep Castro's bat in a reserve role. The day before the Mota deal, second baseman Luis Castillo was signed to a four-year contract, and although Castillo played reasonably well after his July 30 acquisition from Minnesota, his offensive value is on the wane due to his declining baserunning game, only moderate patience, and almost complete lack of power (career slugging percentage of .358, career isolated power of .064). He can hit .300-worth of singles, but that's increasingly all, and he'll be less likely to do even that in the final years of his contract. In dealing the supremely talented Milledge to the Nationals for a redundant and unproductive catcher like Schneider and an inferior outfielder in Ryan Church, Minaya incredibly sacrificed one of the few prospects the team had who offered the possibility of stardom for players who make the Mets young*er* at catcher and right field without making them *young* (Schneider is 31, Church 29).

The Mets endured a shocking last-minute disappointment in 2007. Unable or unwilling to undertake a needed rebuilding of their aging roster, the Mets will suffer more disappointment in 2008, only this year it will start on Opening Day.

HITTERS

Moises Alou   LF

Bats: R   Throws: R   Height: 6' 3"   Weight: 225   Born: July 3, 1966   Age: 41

YEAR	TEAM	LVL	AGE	PA	R	2B	3B	HR	RBI	BB	SO	SB	CS	EqBRR	AVG	OBP	SLG	MLVr	EqAVG	EqOBP	EqSLG	EqA	VORP	DEFENSE			
2005	SFN	MLB	39	490	67	21	3	19	63	56	43	5	1	-0.7	.321	.400	.518	.299	.318	.398	.525	.314	42.1	65-LF	-4	46-RF	-5
2006	SFN	MLB	40	378	52	25	1	22	74	28	31	2	1	-1.1	.301	.352	.571	.257	.300	.354	.566	.303	27.9	73-RF	1		
2007	NYN	MLB	41	360	51	19	1	13	49	27	30	3	0	0.5	.341	.392	.524	.327	.347	.400	.543	.319	32.6	78-LF	-3		
2008	NYN	MLB	41	377	53	21	1	12	57	33	35	8	1	-0.7	.307	.368	.484	.135	.312	.372	.504	.295	20.8	90-LF	-4		

Breakout: 15% Improve: 31% Collapse: 44% Attrition: 40%   Comparables: Dave Winfield, Brian Downing, Paul Molitor, Carlton Fisk

As has been the case since the president's daddy lived in the White House, Alou was highly productive when healthy. This time, shoulder and quadriceps problems limited him to barely more than half a season. Now in his 40s, Alou's career line brings on some feelings of melancholy. Even a conservative estimate has him missing at least 400 games due to injury—including a full season in his prime—not to mention all of the games that he played at less than 100 percent. In a different, injury-free universe, he'd be a borderline Hall of Fame candidate. The Mets picked up his 2008 option, and once again, when he's healthy, he'll hit—Alou's body will end his career before his bat does.

Chip Ambres   OF

Bats: R   Throws: R   Height: 6' 1"   Weight: 230   Born: December 19, 1979   Age: 28

YEAR	TEAM	LVL	AGE	PA	R	2B	3B	HR	RBI	BB	SO	SB	CS	EqBRR	AVG	OBP	SLG	MLVr	EqAVG	EqOBP	EqSLG	EqA	VORP	DEFENSE			
2005	PAW	AAA	25	332	47	20	3	10	50	47	64	19	5	2.5	.294	.401	.495	.220	.261	.364	.435	.281	15.1	42-CF	-8	24-LF	1
2005	KCA	MLB	25	167	25	8	0	4	9	16	32	3	2	-0.9	.241	.323	.379	-.086	.245	.335	.392	.254	0.1	20-LF	-4	18-CF	0
2006	OMA	AAA	26	213	19	8	1	3	15	22	41	2	4	-3.2	.203	.284	.305	-.272	.184	.259	.279	.186	-22.2	23-LF	1	21-CF	2
2007	NWO	AAA	27	504	80	23	0	21	71	71	107	7	0	1.4	.274	.379	.475	.150	.248	.349	.433	.274	5.9	106-LF	6		
2008	NYN	MLB	28	435	55	20	2	13	50	52	96	11	3	0.1	.242	.337	.409	-.070	.245	.341	.425	.265	9.3	103-LF	-2		
2008	SDN	MLB	28	435	53	19	2	13	48	53	102	10	3	0.1	.237	.334	.398	-.092	.244	.341	.426	.265	9.4	103-LF	-2		

Breakout: 23% Improve: 58% Collapse: 26% Attrition: 24%   Comparables: Scott Bryant, Gabe Alvarez, Adam Hyzdu, Brian Banks

A first-round pick nearly a decade ago, Ambres has become one of those Triple-A floaters, most recently landing a 2008 invite to Padres camp on a minor league deal. He's not without some skills: he has some power, is judicious in his pitch selection, runs well, and is a good defender. Yet Ambres continues to toil away in the minors. We're not saying he should be a star. Heck, we're not even saying he should start, but there's a good number of reserve outfielders in the big leagues who aren't as good.

Marlon Anderson   PH

Bats: L   Throws: R   Height: 5' 11"   Weight: 200   Born: January 6, 1974   Age: 34

YEAR	TEAM	LVL	AGE	PA	R	2B	3B	HR	RBI	BB	SO	SB	CS	EqBRR	AVG	OBP	SLG	MLVr	EqAVG	EqOBP	EqSLG	EqA	VORP	DEFENSE			
2005	NYN	MLB	31	260	31	9	0	7	19	18	45	6	1	-0.5	.264	.316	.391	-.045	.263	.318	.390	.252	3.3	18-1B	1	16-2B	2
2006	WAS	MLB	32	239	31	13	2	5	23	18	41	2	4	-0.2	.274	.331	.423	.015	.282	.340	.444	.265	6.1	26-2B	-2		
2006	LAN	MLB	32	73	12	3	2	7	15	7	8	2	2	0.0	.375	.431	.813	.800	.375	.431	.812	.370	13.6	13-LF	-2		
2007	LAN	MLB	33	29	3	0	0	0	2	3	5	1	0	-0.7	.231	.310	.231	-.324	.231	.310	.231	.206	-1.1				
2007	NYN	MLB	33	77	14	7	0	3	25	5	12	3	1	-0.2	.319	.355	.551	.277	.333	.377	.580	.311	7.0				
2008	NYN	MLB	34	158	21	8	1	4	21	17	27	3	1	0.2	.264	.346	.430	-.011	.268	.349	.447	.273	7.3				

Breakout: 30% Improve: 42% Collapse: 38% Attrition: 38%   Comparables: Tommy McCraw, Gates Brown, Bob Skinner, Max Venable

Picked off the scrap heap at midseason after the Dodgers released him, Anderson was brought on to serve as a left-handed bat off the bench. As he did for the Dodgers in September 2006, he shined in that role, delivering key hit after key hit and serving as one of the few bright spots for the Mets in the second half. Signed to a cheap two-year deal after the season, there's no reason for him not to be the next incarnation of ex-Met Lenny Harris, but with enough pop to be useful. If only you could bottle the quality that allows a poor starter like Anderson or Daryle Ward to become a superior bench player.

Carlos Beltran — CF

Bats: S Throws: R Height: 6' 1" Weight: 205 Born: April 24, 1977 Age: 31

YEAR	TEAM	LVL	AGE	PA	R	2B	3B	HR	RBI	BB	SO	SB	CS	EqBRR	AVG	OBP	SLG	MLVr	EqAVG	EqOBP	EqSLG	EqA	VORP	DEFENSE	
2005	NYN	MLB	28	650	83	34	2	16	78	56	96	17	6	5.4	.266	.330	.414	.010	.267	.333	.422	.263	17.7	146-CF	9
2006	NYN	MLB	29	617	127	38	1	41	116	95	99	18	3	4.1	.275	.388	.594	.332	.278	.392	.600	.326	68.5	132-CF	21
2007	NYN	MLB	30	636	93	33	3	33	112	69	111	23	2	4.3	.276	.353	.525	.195	.282	.362	.549	.307	51.1	138-CF	11
2008	NYN	MLB	31	608	92	32	2	27	92	71	102	14	3	1.5	.276	.363	.501	.121	.280	.367	.522	.296	44.0	142-CF	5

Breakout: 11% Improve: 36% Collapse: 26% Attrition: 5%   Comparables: Tom Tresh, Ray Lankford, Carl Everett, Roger Maris

Beltran drove the Mets at both ends of the season. In April, he hit .356/.412/.663 to get the team off to a great start. As the Mets collapsed, Beltran tried his best to keep the team afloat, mashing 14 home runs and driving in 50 runs over the season's final two months. He struggled in between, batting .228/.314/.415. from May through July as various ailments took their toll, including an oblique strain that sent him to the DL in late July. Beltran may never live up to the contract he signed three years ago, but he's still an impact player capable of carrying a team and arguably one of the top ten players in baseball's weaker league.

Mike Carp — 1B

Bats: L Throws: R Height: 6' 2" Weight: 215 Born: June 30, 1986 Age: 22

YEAR	TEAM	LVL	AGE	PA	R	2B	3B	HR	RBI	BB	SO	SB	CS	EqBRR	AVG	OBP	SLG	MLVr	EqAVG	EqOBP	EqSLG	EqA	VORP	DEFENSE	
2005	HAG	A	19	375	49	12	1	19	63	35	96	2	2	-2.8	.249	.358	.476	.156	.201	.275	.356	.219	-20.6	77-1B	-3
2006	SLU	A+	20	573	69	27	1	17	88	51	107	2	1	-2.1	.287	.379	.450	.204	.253	.326	.409	.256	0.1	134-1B	7
2007	BIN	AA	21	412	55	16	0	11	48	39	75	2	1	0.6	.251	.337	.387	-.009	.228	.303	.356	.234	-14.9	95-1B	-6
2008	NYN	MLB	22	465	47	21	1	13	54	41	101	3	2	-0.6	.239	.316	.388	-.137	.242	.319	.404	.247	-0.9	110-1B	0

Breakout: 34% Improve: 63% Collapse: 18% Attrition: 4%   Comparables: Jon Tucker, Steve Cox, Ryan Klesko, Justin Morneau

In an organization light on prospects, Carp was seen as one of the golden boys coming off of an impressive showing in the Florida State League. *Splat!* A big, unathletic first baseman, Carp needs his bat to carry him to the big leagues, but his swing is what scouts call "slider speed," and he can't do anything against lefties. The jump to Double-A can make or break a prospect, and it might just have broken Mike Carp.

Luis Castillo — 2B

Bats: S Throws: R Height: 5' 11" Weight: 190 Born: September 12, 1975 Age: 32

YEAR	TEAM	LVL	AGE	PA	R	2B	3B	HR	RBI	BB	SO	SB	CS	EqBRR	AVG	OBP	SLG	MLVr	EqAVG	EqOBP	EqSLG	EqA	VORP	DEFENSE	
2005	FLO	MLB	29	524	72	12	4	4	30	65	32	10	7	-1.8	.301	.391	.374	.097	.310	.402	.389	.281	23.8	114-2B	13
2006	MIN	MLB	30	652	84	22	6	3	49	56	58	25	11	-1.2	.296	.358	.370	-.042	.300	.369	.384	.268	21.2	140-2B	-16
2007	MIN	MLB	31	384	54	11	3	0	18	29	28	9	4	4.9	.304	.356	.352	-.037	.318	.375	.376	.268	8.2	82-2B	-11
2007	NYN	MLB	31	231	37	8	2	1	20	24	17	10	2	4.5	.296	.371	.372	.032	.310	.388	.385	.280	9.5	48-2B	-8
2008	NYN	MLB	32	526	74	16	4	0	32	51	40	16	5	1.6	.290	.361	.341	-.084	.294	.365	.355	.258	17.6	124-2B	-7

Breakout: 4% Improve: 27% Collapse: 43% Attrition: 11%   Comparables: Maury Wills, Steve Sax, Mark McLemore, Bip Roberts

Acquired from the Twins at the trading deadline for a couple of mediocre-at-best prospects, Castillo was exactly what the Mets thought he would be, because, if anything, he's highly predictable. In the last five years, he's never hit less than .291 or more than .314, his on-base percentage has only ranged from .358 to .381, and he's never had a slugging percentage more than 12 points above his OBP (typically it's below his OBP). In November, the Mets signed Castillo to a four-year extension worth $25 million. That might seem like a head-scratcher, but given their second base situation since Edgardo Alfonzo left, it's exactly that consistency that they're paying for.

Ramon Castro   C

Bats: R   Throws: R   Height: 6' 3"   Weight: 255   Born: March 1, 1976   Age: 32

YEAR	TEAM	LVL	AGE	PA	R	2B	3B	HR	RBI	BB	SO	SB	CS	EqBRR	AVG	OBP	SLG	MLVr	EqAVG	EqOBP	EqSLG	EqA	VORP	DEFENSE	
2005	NYN	MLB	29	240	26	16	0	8	41	25	58	1	0	-0.8	.244	.321	.435	.006	.244	.322	.445	.265	9.1	65-C	1
2006	NYN	MLB	30	144	13	7	0	4	12	15	40	0	0	-1.2	.238	.322	.389	-.083	.238	.326	.397	.254	1.0	34-C	3
2007	NYN	MLB	31	157	24	6	0	11	31	10	39	0	0	-3.2	.285	.331	.556	.200	.294	.344	.580	.303	13.1	37-C	-2
2008	NYN	MLB	32	251	30	12	0	12	37	24	63	2	1	-0.8	.249	.324	.463	-.015	.252	.328	.482	.270	13.1	62-C	-1

Breakout: 14%   Improve: 33%   Collapse: 35%   Attrition: 29%   Comparables: Gene Oliver, Charles Johnson, Lance Parrish, Bruce Bochy

Castro had his best season with the bat in 2007. In his three seasons with the Mets, he's smacked 23 home runs in roughly a full season of play (479 at-bats). In this catching-deprived world, there are less productive backstops with starting jobs, and the Mets will keep Castro in an understudy role to one of them: new acquisition Brian Schneider.

Endy Chavez   OF

Bats: L   Throws: L   Height: 6' 0"   Weight: 165   Born: February 7, 1978   Age: 30

YEAR	TEAM	LVL	AGE	PA	R	2B	3B	HR	RBI	BB	SO	SB	CS	EqBRR	AVG	OBP	SLG	MLVr	EqAVG	EqOBP	EqSLG	EqA	VORP	DEFENSE				
2005	NWO	AAA	27	101	11	4	0	1	4	10	7	6	1	-0.1	.253	.330	.333	-.150	.256	.323	.322	.239	-1.6	22-CF	1			
2005	PHI	MLB	27	118	17	3	3	0	10	4	13	2	1	0.1	.215	.243	.299	-.346	.218	.252	.309	.195	-6.7	13-CF	1			
2006	NYN	MLB	28	390	48	22	5	4	42	24	44	12	3	0.1	.306	.348	.431	.074	.308	.353	.440	.276	15.3	35-RF	1	29-CF	6	
2007	NYN	MLB	29	165	20	7	2	1	17	9	16	5	2	1.3	.287	.325	.380	-.045	.298	.340	.391	.256	1.3	22-LF	1	11-RF	1	
2008	NYN	MLB	30	187	23	7	2	1	15	13	20	5	2	0.5	.282	.334	.362	-.108	.286	.338	.377	.250	3.3	48-LF	2			

Breakout: 16%   Improve: 35%   Collapse: 40%   Attrition: 36%   Comparables: Gene Richards, Milt Thompson, Jason Tyner, Roger Cedeño

One of the surprising heroes of the 2006 season (especially the postseason), Chavez went back to being Endy Chavez this year, serving as a decent reserve outfielder before a severe hamstring injury in June all but wiped out the remainder of his season. Chavez could warm benches for another five years or so, but he'll never have a season like 2006 again.

Carlos Delgado   1B

Bats: L   Throws: R   Height: 6' 3"   Weight: 240   Born: June 25, 1972   Age: 36

YEAR	TEAM	LVL	AGE	PA	R	2B	3B	HR	RBI	BB	SO	SB	CS	EqBRR	AVG	OBP	SLG	MLVr	EqAVG	EqOBP	EqSLG	EqA	VORP	DEFENSE	
2005	FLO	MLB	33	616	81	41	3	33	115	72	121	0	0	-2.7	.301	.399	.582	.393	.303	.399	.601	.329	62.7	136-1B	-12
2006	NYN	MLB	34	618	89	30	2	38	114	74	120	0	0	0.4	.265	.361	.548	.221	.268	.363	.554	.305	35.2	139-1B	-11
2007	NYN	MLB	35	607	71	30	0	24	87	52	118	4	0	-7.3	.258	.333	.448	.039	.264	.340	.465	.277	15.5	136-1B	10
2008	NYN	MLB	36	491	63	24	1	21	75	48	91	4	1	-1.2	.265	.344	.471	.041	.269	.347	.490	.280	19.0	116-1B	-4

Breakout: 5%   Improve: 17%   Collapse: 46%   Attrition: 24%   Comparables: Luke Easter, Mo Vaughn, Boog Powell, Fred McGriff

Last year was Delgado's age-35 season, but he looked more like 45. Coming off elbow and wrist surgery over the winter, Delgado developed a sore neck in spring training, and during the season he hyper-extended his left knee, strained a hip, then finished the season with a fractured hand. Even if healthy, Delgado needs a platoon partner and another ballpark—he has struggled at Shea Stadium in both seasons as a Met. After a dreadful April, Delgado shaped up enough to hit .274/.348/.489 the rest of the way. Those numbers are below average for a NL first baseman, but unless Delgado moves into a more favorable environment, they would seem to be his best-case scenario for the near term. This from a player who is going to cost the Mets $20 million this year: $16 million for the final year of his contract and, barring some sort of miracle return to form, $4 million to buy out his 2009 option at the end of the year and make him go away.

Damion Easley   INF

Bats: R   Throws: R   Height: 5' 11"   Weight: 195   Born: November 11, 1969   Age: 38

YEAR	TEAM	LVL	AGE	PA	R	2B	3B	HR	RBI	BB	SO	SB	CS	EqBRR	AVG	OBP	SLG	MLVr	EqAVG	EqOBP	EqSLG	EqA	VORP	DEFENSE				
2005	FLO	MLB	35	304	37	19	1	9	30	26	47	4	1	1.6	.240	.312	.419	-.018	.243	.315	.442	.262	7.7	36-2B	-1	24-SS	-1	
2006	ARI	MLB	36	220	24	6	1	9	28	21	30	1	1	-0.8	.233	.323	.418	-.069	.226	.317	.405	.251	2.4	23-SS	-4	14-3B	-4	
2007	NYN	MLB	37	218	24	6	0	10	26	19	35	0	1	1.1	.280	.358	.466	.127	.286	.364	.484	.288	11.0	37-2B	4			
2008	NYN	MLB	38	153	17	6	0	5	20	13	25	1	1	-0.1	.253	.326	.417	-.071	.256	.330	.434	.259	5.7	40-2B	-1			

Breakout: 16%   Improve: 35%   Collapse: 40%   Attrition: 43%   Comparables: Hank Bauer, Phil Garner, Chris Speier, George Hendrick

Easley was plugged in as the starting second baseman when Jose Valentin was out with an early-season knee injury. After slipping back into his utility role upon Valentin's return, Easley put up his best numbers in a decade then missed the last six weeks of the season with an ankle injury. Easley now has the dubious honor of being the only player to be part of the two greatest collapses in baseball history, the 1995 Angels and the 2007 Mets, but at least this time around Easley was on the DL at the moment of truth, making him more of a bystander than a culprit. Like much of the 2007 Mets bench, Easley has already re-signed with the team.

Nick Evans — 1B

Bats: R Throws: R Height: 6' 2" Weight: 180 Born: January 30, 1986 Age: 22

YEAR	TEAM	LVL	AGE	PA	R	2B	3B	HR	RBI	BB	SO	SB	CS	EqBRR	AVG	OBP	SLG	MLVr	EqAVG	EqOBP	EqSLG	EqA	VORP	DEFENSE			
2005	BRO	A-	19	245	30	11	3	6	33	17	34	0	1	-0.7	.252	.302	.407	.022	.190	.228	.297	.171	-48.0	56-1B	-3		
2005	KNG	Rk	19	68	11	7	0	6	22	4	17	1	0	-1.1	.344	.382	.734	.605	.215	.250	.415	.226	-6.4	11-1B	1		
2006	HAG	A	20	565	55	33	3	15	67	45	99	2	0	-2.0	.254	.320	.419	.061	.207	.258	.337	.204	-42.6	127-1B	-9		
2007	SLU	A+	21	440	65	25	1	15	54	53	64	3	0	0.1	.286	.374	.476	.210	.251	.333	.429	.265	4.9	101-1B	3		
2008	NYN	MLB	22	457	45	23	1	11	52	37	92	3	1	-0.6	.238	.303	.380	-.170	.241	.307	.395	.238	-4.3	108-1B	2		

Breakout: 38% Improve: 61% Collapse: 12% Attrition: 11%   Comparables: Ozzie Timmons, Tom Evans, Nick Leach, Juan Tejeda

This year's version of Mike Carp, Evans is a young slugger who put up some impressive numbers in the Florida State League last year. Evans has a unique skill set in that he has plus power, draws plenty of walks, yet also has a manageable strikeout rate. As with Carp, it won't mean a thing if his swing is exposed in Double-A, where the men are separated from the boys.

Carlos Gomez — OF

Bats: R Throws: R Height: 6' 2" Weight: 175 Born: December 4, 1985 Age: 22

YEAR	TEAM	LVL	AGE	PA	R	2B	3B	HR	RBI	BB	SO	SB	CS	EqBRR	AVG	OBP	SLG	MLVr	EqAVG	EqOBP	EqSLG	EqA	VORP	DEFENSE				
2005	HAG	A	19	539	75	13	6	8	48	32	88	64	24	2.7	.275	.331	.376	.000	.219	.260	.291	.202	-49.8	59-RF	-7	53-CF	6
2006	BIN	AA	20	486	53	24	8	7	48	27	97	41	9	0.8	.281	.350	.423	.120	.262	.319	.407	.259	7.4	115-CF	11		
2007	NWO	AAA	21	157	24	8	2	2	13	15	23	17	4	2.2	.286	.363	.414	.045	.248	.325	.376	.255	0.6	35-CF	6		
2007	NYN	MLB	21	139	14	3	0	2	12	8	27	12	3	1.3	.232	.288	.304	-.258	.242	.302	.331	.238	-4.4	20-LF	2	15-RF	-1
2008	NYN	MLB	22	299	38	13	3	5	26	19	57	22	5	1.2	.253	.310	.371	-.160	.257	.313	.386	.249	1.1	73-CF	0		

Breakout: 37% Improve: 62% Collapse: 14% Attrition: 16%   Comparables: David Green, Willie Cañate, Luis Matos, Bill Russell

Pressed into duty when Moises Alou went down (didn't see that coming!), Gomez was more exciting than good. While Gomez is a high-ceiling prospect with a ton of talent and amazing speed, it was apparent that he wasn't ready for the big leagues. Worse, a strained hamstring and broken hand cost him the majority of the season at an age and stage that was crucial to his development. Between Alou's injuries and his own, Gomez lost a year of progress that should have been made in the minors.

Ruben Gotay — 2B

Bats: S Throws: R Height: 5' 11" Weight: 190 Born: December 25, 1982 Age: 25

YEAR	TEAM	LVL	AGE	PA	R	2B	3B	HR	RBI	BB	SO	SB	CS	EqBRR	AVG	OBP	SLG	MLVr	EqAVG	EqOBP	EqSLG	EqA	VORP	DEFENSE	
2005	KCA	MLB	22	317	32	14	2	5	29	22	51	2	2	0.8	.227	.288	.344	-.211	.235	.304	.365	.237	-7.1	76-2B	0
2005	WIC	AA	22	122	22	8	0	3	15	12	13	0	2	0.5	.245	.320	.400	-.045	.234	.303	.369	.228	-0.7	25-2B	-1
2006	OMA	AAA	23	374	45	16	2	9	43	26	67	7	1	-1.4	.264	.322	.404	-.026	.236	.290	.373	.233	-3.9	80-2B	-14
2006	NOR	AAA	23	169	19	12	1	3	21	10	29	4	5	-2.6	.266	.317	.416	.099	.258	.305	.426	.244	3.9	37-2B	-4
2007	NWO	AAA	24	98	12	7	1	2	13	14	14	1	1	-0.4	.256	.367	.439	.063	.229	.337	.398	.258	2.1	17-2B	0
2007	NYN	MLB	24	211	25	12	0	4	24	16	42	3	3	-1.1	.295	.351	.421	.062	.305	.364	.442	.272	8.0	33-2B	-6
2008	NYN	MLB	25	228	27	12	1	5	27	20	38	4	1	0.2	.261	.329	.408	-.071	.264	.333	.425	.260	9.6	57-2B	-1

Breakout: 34% Improve: 53% Collapse: 29% Attrition: 29%   Comparables: Billy Smith, Darrel Chaney, Carlos Guillen, Jason Bates

Gotay was another contestant in the pre–Luis Castillo game of second base musical chairs. He performed well enough, but it's hard to see much of a future for him. If you can't play on the left side of the infield, which Gotay can't, then you have to be an everyday player, and Gotay can't be that either, because another thing he can't do is hit left-handers. Sadly, he's more suited for the Island of Misfit Toys than a championship-caliber big-league roster.

Shawn Green — RF/1B

Bats: L Throws: L Height: 6' 4" Weight: 205 Born: November 10, 1972 Age: 35

YEAR	TEAM	LVL	AGE	PA	R	2B	3B	HR	RBI	BB	SO	SB	CS	EqBRR	AVG	OBP	SLG	MLVr	EqAVG	EqOBP	EqSLG	EqA	VORP	DEFENSE			
2005	ARI	MLB	32	656	87	37	4	22	73	62	95	8	4	-0.7	.286	.355	.477	.134	.277	.348	.472	.280	29.4	115-RF	5	35-CF	-3
2006	ARI	MLB	33	462	59	22	3	11	51	37	64	4	4	-0.6	.283	.348	.429	.024	.276	.344	.421	.263	7.0	96-RF	-5	11-1B	0
2006	NYN	MLB	33	126	14	9	0	4	15	8	18	0	0	-0.2	.257	.325	.442	.011	.265	.333	.460	.271	2.0	28-RF	-4		
2007	NYN	MLB	34	490	62	30	1	10	46	37	62	11	1	0.6	.291	.352	.430	.074	.300	.362	.450	.284	16.8	103-RF	-10	11-1B	-1
2008	NYN	MLB	35	332	42	17	1	6	41	27	45	7	2	-0.1	.279	.342	.407	-.037	.282	.346	.424	.264	9.0	80-RF	-3		

Breakout: 12% Improve: 27% Collapse: 36% Attrition: 36%   Comparables: Ken Griffey Sr., Jim Northrup, Lee Maye, Claudell Washington

Green got off to great start last year, hitting .355/.412/.538 in April, but that only confused the Mets' outfield situation as they tried to figure out what to do with Lastings Milledge. By May, he was pretty much back to being Shawn Green: intermittently healthy, and only intermittently productive. Green had another hot streak down the stretch, but hit a dreadful .237/.280/.360 from May through July. His four-year peak ended five years ago, and he hasn't slugged .500 since. Combine that with Green's age and the fact that he's a defensive liability everywhere but first base, and he has little use other than as a lefty bat off the bench.

Brett Harper — 1B

Bats: L Throws: R Height: 6' 4" Weight: 185 Born: July 31, 1981 Age: 26

YEAR	TEAM	LVL	AGE	PA	R	2B	3B	HR	RBI	BB	SO	SB	CS	EqBRR	AVG	OBP	SLG	MLVr	EqAVG	EqOBP	EqSLG	EqA	VORP	DEFENSE			
2005	SLU	A+	23	264	35	11	1	20	60	21	64	0	1	-2.0	.280	.337	.586	.299	.231	.284	.479	.254	0.3	47-1B	-5		
2005	BIN	AA	23	256	37	11	0	16	42	26	85	0	0	0.0	.273	.352	.533	.220	.226	.301	.443	.252	-1.4	51-1B	0		
2006	BIN	AA	24	75	8	7	0	0	8	7	19	1	0	-0.6	.338	.427	.446	.302	.224	.316	.299	.225	-3.9	18-1B	1		
2007	BIN	AA	25	517	69	25	0	24	88	34	119	2	0	-0.1	.296	.350	.500	.201	.263	.311	.451	.260	5.8	31-1B	-4	20-LF	-3
2008	NYN	MLB	26	533	53	24	1	21	74	40	150	2	1	-0.9	.238	.300	.421	-.122	.241	.303	.438	.247	4.2				

Breakout: 12% Improve: 37% Collapse: 34% Attrition: 19%   Comparables: Chris Fick, Scott Cepicky, Jay Gainer, Ryan Mulhern

Two years ago, Harper led all Mets minor leaguers with 36 home runs. He then missed nearly all of 2006 with a severe shoulder injury. Healthy again in 2007, Harper put up some decent numbers and took a stab at left field, but he turns 27 this summer, so it's hard to think of him as any real kind of prospect.

Ben Johnson — OF

Bats: R Throws: R Height: 6' 1" Weight: 220 Born: June 18, 1981 Age: 27

YEAR	TEAM	LVL	AGE	PA	R	2B	3B	HR	RBI	BB	SO	SB	CS	EqBRR	AVG	OBP	SLG	MLVr	EqAVG	EqOBP	EqSLG	EqA	VORP	DEFENSE			
2005	POR	AAA	24	472	79	27	0	25	83	51	88	6	1	0.7	.312	.394	.558	.321	.273	.347	.476	.281	16.7	64-RF	-1	42-CF	-10
2005	SDN	MLB	24	88	10	8	1	3	13	11	23	0	2	-1.8	.213	.310	.467	.019	.227	.322	.507	.269	0.6				
2006	POR	AAA	25	227	35	11	1	7	22	23	55	7	1	-0.1	.263	.344	.434	.055	.239	.313	.403	.254	1.3	42-CF	-2		
2006	SDN	MLB	25	135	19	5	2	4	12	14	36	3	0	-0.7	.250	.333	.425	.008	.258	.346	.458	.279	3.5	19-LF	4	12-CF	3
2007	NWO	AAA	26	218	26	10	0	2	12	25	36	3	1	-0.8	.271	.364	.356	-.047	.242	.332	.321	.238	-7.7	31-RF	0	17-CF	0
2007	NYN	MLB	26	30	2	1	0	0	1	2	11	0	0	-0.4	.185	.233	.222	-.492	.185	.233	.222	.156	-3.0				
2008	NYN	MLB	27	223	26	10	1	6	26	22	49	3	1	-0.1	.245	.327	.400	-.098	.248	.330	.416	.257	3.7	56-RF	0		

Breakout: 20% Improve: 42% Collapse: 32% Attrition: 22%   Comparables: Adam Piatt, Bill McCarthy, Marcus Thames, Chris Aguila

Johnson had his chance with the Padres a couple of years ago, but his window for a big-league career has probably shut, especially after a broken ankle cost him much of 2007. A few years back, Johnson looked like a late bloomer who was finally turning his unquestioned athletic ability into real baseball skills, but now he's pretty much one of those guys who will spend the next few years on the bubble, spending most of his time in Triple-A while getting called up to plug a roster hole here and there.

Paul Lo Duca — C

Bats: R Throws: R Height: 5' 10" Weight: 205 Born: April 12, 1972 Age: 36

YEAR	TEAM	LVL	AGE	PA	R	2B	3B	HR	RBI	BB	SO	SB	CS	EqBRR	AVG	OBP	SLG	MLVr	EqAVG	EqOBP	EqSLG	EqA	VORP	DEFENSE	
2005	FLO	MLB	33	496	45	23	1	6	57	34	31	4	3	-2.4	.283	.334	.380	-.002	.288	.339	.389	.257	16.3	116-C	-5
2006	NYN	MLB	34	551	80	39	1	5	49	24	38	3	0	-1.5	.318	.355	.428	.095	.322	.359	.439	.277	27.2	114-C	-6
2007	NYN	MLB	35	488	46	18	1	9	54	24	33	2	0	-2.1	.272	.311	.378	-.081	.279	.320	.394	.252	9.2	109-C	-4
2008	WAS	MLB	36	296	30	13	1	4	31	17	22	2	1	-0.7	.278	.323	.373	-.117	.278	.323	.381	.242	7.3	72-C	-2

Breakout: 2% Improve: 21% Collapse: 42% Attrition: 40%   Comparables: Joe Girardi, Mike Redmond, Jerry Grote, Mike Heath

Lo Duca has to hit .300 to have a good year, because he doesn't have much in the way of power or patience. In 2007 he lost 46 points off his 2006 average, leaving him virtually naked on the field. That extends to Lo Duca's glove as well; he's error-prone and doesn't throw out many runners. Mix in assorted injuries, some unfriendly press for off-field issues in 2006, and the team's historic collapse in 2007, and it wasn't exactly how the Brooklyn-born Lo Duca would have wanted his Mets career to have ended. A one-year deal has taken him down I-95 to Washington, where he'll replace current Mets backstop Brian Schneider.

Fernando Martinez   **OF**   Bats: L   Throws: R   Height: 6' 0"   Weight: 185   Born: October 10, 1988   Age: 19

YEAR	TEAM	LVL	AGE	PA	R	2B	3B	HR	RBI	BB	SO	SB	CS	EqBRR	AVG	OBP	SLG	MLVr	EqAVG	EqOBP	EqSLG	EqA	VORP	DEFENSE
2006	HAG	A	17	211	24	14	2	5	28	15	36	7	4	-3.9	.333	.389	.505	.340	.264	.308	.396	.243	1.3	43-CF -5
2006	SLU	A+	17	130	18	4	2	5	11	6	24	1	1	-0.4	.193	.254	.387	-.124	.205	.252	.377	.214	-5.7	27-CF -1
2007	BIN	AA	18	259	32	11	1	4	21	20	51	3	4	-2.8	.271	.336	.377	-.010	.242	.300	.342	.221	-6.2	57-CF -16
2008	NYN	MLB	19	313	29	15	1	4	26	21	67	4	3	0.0	.236	.291	.338	-.250	.239	.294	.352	.219	-4.3	76-CF -1

Breakout: 27%   Improve: 54%   Collapse: 27%   Attrition: 7%   Comparables: Rafael Alvarez, Alex Fernandez, Ruben Cruz, Jhonny Perez

The bloom came off the rose a bit in 2007 as Martinez didn't do much at Double-A before getting shut down at the end of June with a hand injury. There are plenty of mitigating factors here, the largest of which is his age; there were plenty of players drafted out of high school last June who are older. For Martinez to even hold his own at Double-A at his age was an impressive feat. If there's any actual bad news here, it's that he's clearly not much of a center fielder, so the bar for his bat has to be set higher. Time and potential are still on his side in the biggest of ways.

Lastings Milledge   **OF**   Bats: R   Throws: R   Height: 6' 0"   Weight: 205   Born: April 5, 1985   Age: 23

YEAR	TEAM	LVL	AGE	PA	R	2B	3B	HR	RBI	BB	SO	SB	CS	EqBRR	AVG	OBP	SLG	MLVr	EqAVG	EqOBP	EqSLG	EqA	VORP	DEFENSE		
2005	SLU	A+	20	269	48	15	0	4	22	19	41	18	13	0.6	.302	.385	.418	.166	.257	.321	.357	.235	-1.1	59-CF -5		
2005	BIN	AA	20	214	33	17	0	4	24	14	47	11	5	-3.1	.337	.392	.487	.277	.260	.315	.383	.246	0.8	41-CF -5		
2006	NOR	AAA	21	367	52	21	4	7	36	43	67	13	10	0.1	.277	.388	.440	.250	.269	.372	.449	.280	22.2	54-CF 2	21-LF 1
2006	NYN	MLB	21	185	14	7	2	4	22	12	39	1	2	-0.3	.241	.310	.380	-.118	.246	.314	.383	.241	-3.8	23-RF -3	21-LF 1
2007	NWO	AAA	22	43	9	1	0	1	5	2	12	5	0	1.2	.333	.372	.436	.139	.231	.279	.333	.239	-1.9			
2007	NYN	MLB	22	206	27	9	1	7	29	13	42	3	2	-1.2	.272	.341	.446	.069	.283	.351	.473	.278	6.4	25-RF -2	13-CF 2
2008	WAS	MLB	23	380	57	20	2	13	50	30	71	15	4	1.1	.289	.358	.478	.094	.288	.358	.488	.287	22.2	91-RF 1		

Breakout: 48%   Improve: 76%   Collapse: 12%   Attrition: 18%   Comparables: Rondell White, Dwight Evans, Ron Swoboda, Darryl Motley

Milledge has spent the last couple of years being too good for the minors, not having an every-day opportunity in the majors, or getting hurt. All of that has made a lot of people forget that he is a truly massive talent, some of which began to show itself by the end of 2007. Unmoved, Omar Minaya dealt Milledge to Washington in the offseason, netting only catcher Brian Schneider and outfielder Ryan Church in return. We know Milledge isn't exactly the ideal clubhouse citizen, but the only way to explain that deal is to say there was something else going on with Milledge that we don't know about. He is expected to play center for the Nats, and should be good enough in the field to be a very valuable bat at the position.

Jose Reyes   **SS**   Bats: S   Throws: R   Height: 6' 1"   Weight: 200   Born: June 11, 1983   Age: 25

YEAR	TEAM	LVL	AGE	PA	R	2B	3B	HR	RBI	BB	SO	SB	CS	EqBRR	AVG	OBP	SLG	MLVr	EqAVG	EqOBP	EqSLG	EqA	VORP	DEFENSE
2005	NYN	MLB	22	733	99	24	17	7	58	27	78	60	15	8.8	.273	.300	.386	-.072	.275	.306	.393	.251	22.1	158-SS -9
2006	NYN	MLB	23	703	122	30	17	19	81	53	81	64	17	5.0	.300	.354	.487	.161	.305	.361	.500	.293	58.8	147-SS -19
2007	NYN	MLB	24	765	119	36	12	12	57	77	78	78	21	8.8	.280	.354	.421	.058	.295	.371	.451	.285	46.2	160-SS 6
2008	NYN	MLB	25	698	110	34	9	14	70	56	74	60	14	4.6	.290	.350	.438	.028	.294	.353	.456	.282	44.5	162-SS 0

Breakout: 25%   Improve: 50%   Collapse: 17%   Attrition: 7%   Comparables: Cristian Guzman, Roberto Alomar, Barry Larkin, Jimmy Rollins

Reyes took a lot of blame for the Mets' late-season collapse, and for good reason—he hit just .205/.279/.333 in September. There's no specific explanation for it; he wasn't hurt, he wasn't getting pitched any differently, it was just one of those things, a sentiment supported by his unlucky .220 BABIP for the month. Looking at the eleven months of Reyes's career that preceded that one, we expect he'll be just fine. The question is what type of player will he be? He wasn't able to repeat his 2006 power surge last year, but he continued to improve his walk rate and developed into the best basestealer the game has seen since the thieving heyday of the 1980s. Reyes won't turn 25 until June, so his skills are still coalescing; more important, they're also still improving.

Jose Valentin   2B

Bats: S   Throws: R   Height: 5' 10"   Weight: 190   Born: October 12, 1969   Age: 38

YEAR	TEAM	LVL	AGE	PA	R	2B	3B	HR	RBI	BB	SO	SB	CS	EqBRR	AVG	OBP	SLG	MLVr	EqAVG	EqOBP	EqSLG	EqA	VORP	DEFENSE		
2005	LAN	MLB	35	184	17	4	2	2	14	31	38	3	1	-0.6	.170	.326	.265	-.239	.170	.326	.265	.227	-7.2	25-3B	-2	18-LF -1
2006	NYN	MLB	36	432	56	24	3	18	62	37	71	6	2	-0.6	.271	.330	.490	.095	.273	.335	.490	.280	23.6	86-2B	17	
2007	NYN	MLB	37	183	18	11	1	3	18	15	28	2	1	0.3	.241	.302	.373	-.130	.242	.308	.394	.244	-0.8	42-2B	0	
2008	NYN	MLB	38	183	20	9	1	5	21	17	30	2	1	-0.1	.240	.312	.395	-.133	.243	.316	.411	.248	4.2	47-2B	-1	

Breakout: 15% Improve: 30% Collapse: 43% Attrition: 43%   Comparables: Phil Garner, Ruben Sierra, Ron Cey, Alan Trammell

A happy solution to the Mets' second-base problem in 2006, Valentin was brought back for 2007 despite his age, injury history, and inconsistent record. He missed all of May with a partially torn tendon in his knee and, just three weeks after his return, was lost for the year with a broken leg. The good news is that the injuries kept his $4.3 million option from vesting. Valentin is 38 and coming off an injury-shortened year in which he did nothing offensively. However, if he's healthy, his strong 2006 showing should earn him a shot with a team trying to see if the underrated player behind the .243 career batting average can still come out and play.

David Wright   3B

Bats: R   Throws: R   Height: 6' 0"   Weight: 215   Born: December 20, 1982   Age: 25

YEAR	TEAM	LVL	AGE	PA	R	2B	3B	HR	RBI	BB	SO	SB	CS	EqBRR	AVG	OBP	SLG	MLVr	EqAVG	EqOBP	EqSLG	EqA	VORP	DEFENSE	
2005	NYN	MLB	22	657	99	42	1	27	102	72	113	17	7	5.0	.306	.388	.523	.288	.309	.392	.541	.312	57.4	159-3B	4
2006	NYN	MLB	23	661	96	40	5	26	116	66	113	20	5	2.2	.311	.381	.531	.278	.314	.385	.536	.311	54.3	152-3B	-2
2007	NYN	MLB	24	711	113	42	1	30	107	94	115	34	5	2.5	.325	.416	.546	.372	.335	.428	.577	.338	81.1	158-3B	7
2008	NYN	MLB	25	688	119	40	3	31	105	85	111	21	5	1.1	.305	.395	.540	.251	.309	.399	.562	.319	69.3	160-3B	0

Breakout: 9% Improve: 40% Collapse: 17% Attrition: 3%   Comparables: Ron Santo, Cal Ripken, Jeff Bagwell, Jim Ray Hart

The Mets' plummet cost them more than a postseason berth, it cost them some individual hardware, as well. David Wright might have walked away with the NL MVP had Jimmy Rollins's Phillies not unseated his Mets on the final day of the season. As it was, Wright probably deserved it anyway. What doesn't he do well? He hits for average, draws walks, hits for power, steals bases, plays good defense. The really scary part is trying to find something he's not getting better at. Just 24, Wright is coming off three straight superstar-level years, and in 2007 he set career highs in nearly every offensive category. He's just getting warmed up.

PITCHERS

Adam Bostick

Bats: L   Throws: L   Height: 6' 1"   Weight: 235   Born: March 17, 1983   Age: 25

YEAR	TEAM	LVL	AGE	W	L	SV	G	GS	IP	H	BB	SO	HR	GB%	BABIP	STUFF	WHIP	ERA	PERA	EqERA	EqH9	EqBB9	EqSO9	EqHR9	VORP	SN/WX
2005	JUP	A+	22	4	5	0	17	17	91¹	95	36	94	7	38.1%	.351	-13	1.43	3.84	7.75	7.37	11.7	6.0	5.4	1.6	-15.6	—
2005	CAR	AA	22	4	3	0	9	9	44¹	42	25	39	3	47.0%	.310	-4	1.51	4.67	6.34	6.92	10.0	6.0	5.1	1.1	-5.9	—
2006	CAR	AA	23	8	7	0	22	22	115¹	100	67	109	7	42.2%	.301	3	1.45	3.52	5.58	5.83	9.1	5.8	5.7	1.1	-2.8	—
2006	ABQ	AAA	23	1	2	0	5	5	27²	39	13	30	4	42.0%	.432	-5	1.91	4.63	9.96	7.96	13.8	4.8	7.3	1.7	-6.8	—
2007	NWO	AAA	24	6	7	0	21	20	97	106	45	91	20	46.7%	.327	-30	1.56	5.66	8.23	7.25	10.8	4.7	6.8	2.3	-16.6	—
2008	NYN	MLB	25	4	6	0	25	14	87	89	50	69	12	42.0%	.297	-1	1.60	5.22	5.84	5.77	9.2	4.6	6.4	1.2	-0.1	0.50

Breakout: 42% Improve: 65% Collapse: 13% Attrition: 19%   Comparables: Matt Riley, Dennis Moeller, Jason Miller, Mike Judd

Acquired last winter from the Marlins, Bostick spent all of 2007 at Triple-A proving to the Mets that there is little reason for him to ever pitch above that level. He has consistently put up solid strikeout numbers in the minors, but he depends more on deception than stuff, and his upper-80s fastball will only get him so far in the end. He'll get a chance at some point somewhere.

Ambiorix Burgos

Bats: R   Throws: R   Height: 6' 3"   Weight: 245   Born: April 19, 1984   Age: 24

YEAR	TEAM	LVL	AGE	W	L	SV	G	GS	IP	H	BB	SO	HR	GB%	BABIP	STUFF	WHIP	ERA	PERA	EqERA	EqH9	EqBB9	EqSO9	EqHR9	VORP	SN/WX
2005	KCA	MLB	21	3	5	2	59	0	63¹	60	31	65	6	47.5%	.321	24	1.44	3.98	3.96	3.55	7.7	4.3	8.8	0.7	11.6	0.55
2006	KCA	MLB	22	4	5	18	68	1	73¹	83	37	72	16	44.3%	.335	-6	1.64	5.53	6.35	5.40	9.4	4.2	8.2	1.7	1.2	-1.34
2007	NYN	MLB	23	1	0	0	17	0	23²	17	9	19	3	30.9%	.222	6	1.10	3.42	3.12	3.38	6.4	3.0	6.8	1.1	5.2	0.02
2008	NYN	MLB	24	2	2	2	38	0	42¹	36	19	38	4	39.8%	.267	7	1.29	3.43	4.00	3.82	7.6	3.6	7.2	0.9	10.2	0.80

Breakout: 37%   Improve: 62%   Collapse: 21%   Attrition: 28%   Comparables: Edwin Nuñez, Esteban Yan, Carlos Castillo, Dave Beard

While the Royals got a nice year from their half of the Burgos/Brian Bannister trade, the Mets didn't fare nearly as well. A pure power arm, Burgos pitched well enough in the majors early in the year, but was demoted twice, then developed a sore elbow while with New Orleans in June. The joint only got worse when he tried to return, leading to Tommy John surgery in late August. He'll miss the 2008 season.

Pedro Feliciano

Bats: L   Throws: L   Height: 5' 10"   Weight: 190   Born: August 25, 1976   Age: 31

YEAR	TEAM	LVL	AGE	W	L	SV	G	GS	IP	H	BB	SO	HR	GB%	BABIP	STUFF	WHIP	ERA	PERA	EqERA	EqH9	EqBB9	EqSO9	EqHR9	VORP	SN/WX
2005	FKU	JP	28	3	2	0	37	0	37	30	13	36	5	—	.250	-7	1.16	3.89	4.60	4.98	7.9	3.9	7.1	1.6	2.4	—
2006	NYN	MLB	29	7	2	0	64	0	60¹	56	20	54	4	52.0%	.310	16	1.26	2.09	3.64	2.25	8.6	2.5	7.3	0.6	25.2	1.27
2007	NYN	MLB	30	2	2	2	78	0	64	47	31	61	3	57.9%	.257	17	1.22	3.09	2.92	3.43	6.4	3.6	7.8	0.4	15.4	2.09
2008	NYN	MLB	31	3	2	5	61	0	56¹	52	25	45	4	51.4%	.288	1	1.35	3.43	4.01	3.90	8.2	3.5	6.5	0.6	11.3	1.00

Breakout: 10%   Improve: 29%   Collapse: 50%   Attrition: 23%   Comparables: Ricardo Rincon, Steve Mingori, Windy McCall, Tom Hilgendorf

Now that Feliciano has comfortably settled into the lefty situational job, he's actually proven that he can handle more. Sure, he's deadly against the forces of *los zurdos* (who hit .168/.273/.211 against Feliciano in 2007), but he's also quite effective against right-handers (.221/.325/.371 last year), giving Willie Randolph the option of leaving him in the game when the hitters due up are mostly left-handed, as opposed to only left-handed. Pitchers like this don't get paid a ton and don't get a lot of attention, but teams love having them.

Tom Glavine

Bats: L   Throws: L   Height: 6' 0"   Weight: 205   Born: March 25, 1966   Age: 42

YEAR	TEAM	LVL	AGE	W	L	SV	G	GS	IP	H	BB	SO	HR	GB%	BABIP	STUFF	WHIP	ERA	PERA	EqERA	EqH9	EqBB9	EqSO9	EqHR9	VORP	SN/WX
2005	NYN	MLB	39	13	13	0	33	33	211¹	227	61	105	12	49.9%	.308	12	1.36	3.54	4.28	4.06	9.9	2.4	4.2	0.5	42.4	5.40
2006	NYN	MLB	40	15	7	0	32	32	198	202	62	131	22	46.7%	.299	11	1.33	3.82	4.40	4.17	9.3	2.5	5.6	0.9	37.1	4.98
2007	NYN	MLB	41	13	8	0	34	34	200¹	219	64	89	23	44.1%	.293	-3	1.41	4.45	4.88	4.48	9.9	2.5	3.9	1.0	28.1	5.57
2008	ATL	MLB	42	5	6	0	26	15	96	114	33	45	12	45.8%	.307	-14	1.53	5.10	5.47	5.45	10.4	2.8	3.8	1.1	3.3	0.90

Breakout: 0%   Improve: 7%   Collapse: 58%   Attrition: 48%   Comparables: Kenny Rogers, Warren Spahn, Jamie Moyer, Jerry Koosman

The lingering memory from Tom Glavine's 2007 campaign should have been his 300th win. Instead, Glavine's season will always be associated with his start against the lowly Marlins in the final game of the season; he gave up seven runs in one third of an inning to drive the final nail into the Mets' coffin. In his five years with the Mets, Glavine was often good but never great, serving as more of a consistently healthy innings-eater than a true stopper. The Mets, who signed Glavine entering his age-37 season, shouldn't have expected more. The Braves, who brought him back to Atlanta on a one-year, $8-million deal, should expect less.

Deolis Guerra

Bats: R   Throws: R   Height: 6' 5"   Weight: 200   Born: April 17, 1989   Age: 19

YEAR	TEAM	LVL	AGE	W	L	SV	G	GS	IP	H	BB	SO	HR	GB%	BABIP	STUFF	WHIP	ERA	PERA	EqERA	EqH9	EqBB9	EqSO9	EqHR9	VORP	SN/WX
2006	HAG	A	17	6	7	0	17	17	81	59	37	64	3	48.2%	.259	7	1.19	2.22	5.71	4.74	8.8	7.1	3.8	1.1	6.5	—
2007	SLU	A+	18	2	6	0	21	20	89²	80	25	66	9	50.7%	.274	-4	1.17	4.01	5.89	6.01	9.3	3.8	4.0	1.9	-3.7	—
2008	NYN	MLB	19	4	8	0	29	16	101¹	120	52	54	21	45.9%	.294	-15	1.69	6.16	6.91	6.77	10.6	4.1	4.2	1.8	-10.5	-0.50

Breakout: 11%   Improve: 30%   Collapse: 40%   Attrition: 22%   Comparables: Hugo Pivaral, Jerome Williams, Craig Anderson, Mike Kusiewicz

Guerra is kind of the pitching version of Mets' outfield prospect Fernando Martinez; he's so young that simply being able to perform admirably at an advanced level is a tremendous accomplishment. If you really want to play the "what have you done for me lately" game, however, he falls a bit flat. Yes, he's huge and still a teenager. Yes, he throws pretty hard—at times. Yes, he shows the signs of a solid breaking ball. Yes, his changeup could become a plus pitch. Yes, there are very few pitchers with Guerra's kind of promise. Right now, however, the gap between what he is and what he could be is enormous.

Aaron Heilman

| | | | | Bats: R | | Throws: R | | Height: 6' 5" | | Weight: 225 | | Born: November 12, 1978 | | Age: 29 | |

YEAR	TEAM	LVL	AGE	W	L	SV	G	GS	IP	H	BB	SO	HR	GB%	BABIP	STUFF	WHIP	ERA	PERA	EqERA	EqH9	EqBB9	EqSO9	EqHR9	VORP	SN/WX
2005	NYN	MLB	26	5	3	5	53	7	108	87	37	106	6	47.4%	.290	26	1.15	3.17	3.37	3.55	7.7	2.9	8.3	0.5	25.9	3.25
2006	NYN	MLB	27	4	5	0	74	0	87	73	28	73	5	47.6%	.286	16	1.16	3.62	3.21	3.80	7.7	2.5	7.1	0.4	20.6	3.27
2007	NYN	MLB	28	7	7	1	81	0	86	72	20	63	8	48.1%	.256	8	1.07	3.03	3.09	3.52	7.2	1.8	6.1	0.7	19.4	0.60
2008	NYN	MLB	29	4	3	4	58	0	67¹	64	22	51	6	47.7%	.287	3	1.27	3.47	3.86	3.93	8.5	2.6	6.1	0.7	13.8	1.20

Breakout: 12% Improve: 36% Collapse: 33% Attrition: 13%   Comparables: Lerrin LaGrow, Tim Burke, Greg McMichael, Mike Henneman

For the last three years, Heilman has been a darn good reliever, and that sort of consistency out of the pen is rare. The problem is that Aaron Heilman is unhappy. He wants to start, but the Mets value him too much as in the bullpen to make a change. If the Mets could find a team that wants Heilman as a starter and is willing to offer corresponding value in a trade, they'd listen. Given Heilman's plunging strikeout rate and impending salary arbitration, they'd better.

Orlando Hernandez

| | | | | Bats: R | | Throws: R | | Height: 6' 2" | | Weight: 220 | | Born: October 11, 1965 | | Age: 42 | |

YEAR	TEAM	LVL	AGE	W	L	SV	G	GS	IP	H	BB	SO	HR	GB%	BABIP	STUFF	WHIP	ERA	PERA	EqERA	EqH9	EqBB9	EqSO9	EqHR9	VORP	SN/WX
2005	CHA	MLB	39	9	9	1	24	22	128¹	137	50	91	18	40.0%	.306	-1	1.46	5.12	5.82	5.60	10.0	3.6	6.3	1.2	6.9	1.41
2006	ARI	MLB	40	2	4	0	9	9	45²	52	20	52	8	32.8%	.373	17	1.58	6.11	6.45	5.89	10.4	3.5	9.5	1.4	-0.4	0.75
2006	NYN	MLB	40	9	7	0	20	20	116²	103	41	112	14	36.8%	.287	24	1.23	4.09	3.85	4.17	8.0	2.7	7.9	0.9	19.4	3.37
2007	NYN	MLB	41	9	5	0	27	24	147²	109	64	128	23	39.7%	.228	11	1.17	3.72	3.51	3.48	6.5	3.4	7.3	1.3	31.7	4.63
2008	NYN	MLB	42	6	5	0	23	15	98	90	37	79	13	38.7%	.271	5	1.29	4.08	4.40	4.53	8.2	3.1	6.5	1.1	13.7	2.00

Breakout: 8% Improve: 32% Collapse: 23% Attrition: 46%   Comparables: Charlie Hough, Early Wynn, Phil Niekro, Don McMahon

For most of last year, the magic was back. Hernandez, now somewhere between 40 and 60 years old, was changing speeds with aplomb, snapping off curves, and using his deception to maximum advantage. Then, at the end of August, his foot started hurting, and that was that. Hernandez made just one start in September, was rocked, and didn't reappear until the final week of the season. Restricted to the pen, he made three appearances but didn't pitch more than an inning and a third in any of them. Following offseason bunion surgery, Hernandez will be back in the rotation in 2008. Though he'll pitch well at times, he won't make it all the way through the season. Still, half a season of Hernandez is better than none—the team just has to be prepared for the other half.

Philip Humber

| | | | | Bats: R | | Throws: R | | Height: 6' 4" | | Weight: 225 | | Born: December 21, 1982 | | Age: 25 | |

YEAR	TEAM	LVL	AGE	W	L	SV	G	GS	IP	H	BB	SO	HR	GB%	BABIP	STUFF	WHIP	ERA	PERA	EqERA	EqH9	EqBB9	EqSO9	EqHR9	VORP	SN/WX
2005	SLU	A+	22	2	6	0	14	14	70¹	74	18	65	6	45.2%	.340	-21	1.31	4.99	7.60	7.88	11.8	4.2	4.7	1.6	-15.6	—
2006	SLU	A+	23	3	1	0	7	7	38¹	24	9	36	4	53.4%	.211	-5	0.87	2.36	4.85	4.58	7.4	3.3	5.1	2.0	4.0	—
2006	BIN	AA	23	2	2	0	6	6	34	25	10	36	4	41.9%	.239	4	1.03	2.91	4.82	4.41	8.0	3.6	6.1	1.7	4.3	—
2007	NWO	AAA	24	11	9	0	25	25	139	129	44	120	21	42.1%	.278	-8	1.24	4.27	5.11	4.92	8.8	3.2	6.0	1.6	10.1	—
2007	NYN	MLB	24	0	0	0	3	1	7	9	2	2	1	28.6%	.296	-29	1.57	7.71	5.50	7.36	11.0	2.5	2.5	1.2	-1.5	-0.17
2008	NYN	MLB	25	6	7	0	31	16	112¹	112	45	82	15	41.5%	.282	3	1.39	4.55	4.99	5.05	8.9	3.2	5.8	1.2	8.3	1.60

Breakout: 26% Improve: 59% Collapse: 16% Attrition: 21%   Comparables: John Patterson, Greg Gohr, Alan Benes, Jaret Wright

In 2006, Humber made an impressive return from Tommy John surgery, showing good command of a three-pitch mix and leaving scouts awfully impressed. Last year, he simply wasn't as good and left those same scouts scratching their heads. It wasn't that he was awful, but he wasn't throwing as hard, his curveball and changeup both went from very good to merely good, and no one could figure out why. If anything, he should have improved as he was further removed from the surgery. Humber now projects as a back-end starter, and the Mets aren't exactly drooling over the thought of adding him to the 2008 rotation.

Eddie Kunz

| | Bats: R | Throws: R | Height: 6' 5" | Weight: 250 | Born: April 8, 1986 | Age: 22 |

YEAR	TEAM	LVL	AGE	W	L	SV	G	GS	IP	H	BB	SO	HR	GB%	BABIP	STUFF	WHIP	ERA	PERA	EqERA	EqH9	EqBB9	EqSO9	EqHR9	VORP	SN/WX
2007	BRO	A-	21	0	1	5	12	0	12	8	8	9	0	82.4%	.242	-16	1.33	6.75	5.60	10.45	7.8	9.6	3.5	0.9	-5.6	—
2008	NYN	MLB	22	4	7	0	42	12	97	98	94	47	8	63.3%	.283	-29	1.98	6.74	6.64	7.88	9.1	7.8	3.9	0.7	-19.9	-1.80

Breakout: 51% Improve: 76% Collapse: 7% Attrition: 16%   Comparables: Nick Webber, Jesus Yepez, Jack Egbert, Don Levinsk

While teams like the crosstown Yankees have been spending big money to sign draft picks who fall to them due to other teams' concerns about their signability, the Mets have been conservative with their picks of late. Kunz was their top selection in 2007, and, while he was a reasonable choice at the 42nd overall pick, there were probably 42 better players available who would have cost a little more. That's money the Mets have and should be willing to spend to bolster their poor minor league system. Kunz is hardly the answer there. He's a big reliever who throws hard, which is nice, but he fell out of favor with his college team in the postseason, and that's never a good sign.

John Maine

| | Bats: R | Throws: R | Height: 6' 4" | Weight: 200 | Born: May 8, 1981 | Age: 27 |

YEAR	TEAM	LVL	AGE	W	L	SV	G	GS	IP	H	BB	SO	HR	GB%	BABIP	STUFF	WHIP	ERA	PERA	EqERA	EqH9	EqBB9	EqSO9	EqHR9	VORP	SN/WX
2005	OTT	AAA	24	6	11	0	23	23	128¹	128	42	111	13	41.3%	.307	-4	1.33	4.56	5.38	5.92	9.9	3.7	5.7	1.1	-4.2	—
2005	BAL	MLB	24	2	3	0	10	8	40	39	24	24	8	44.4%	.248	-12	1.58	6.30	5.33	6.15	8.1	5.0	5.0	1.5	-4.4	0.14
2006	NOR	AAA	25	3	5	0	10	10	56¹	55	20	48	2	52.3%	.317	7	1.34	3.53	4.27	4.94	8.9	3.8	5.4	0.7	4.0	—
2006	NYN	MLB	25	6	5	0	16	15	90	69	33	71	15	40.9%	.225	8	1.13	3.60	3.57	3.64	6.9	2.8	6.6	1.3	19.3	2.38
2007	NYN	MLB	26	15	10	0	32	32	191	168	75	180	23	39.3%	.283	23	1.27	3.91	3.80	3.90	7.8	3.0	7.9	1.0	33.3	5.44
2008	NYN	MLB	27	9	8	0	32	22	147	137	60	127	17	41.6%	.285	13	1.34	4.03	4.47	4.48	8.4	3.3	6.9	1.0	20.1	3.10

Breakout: 11% Improve: 39% Collapse: 30% Attrition: 21%   Comparables: Ron Darling, Charlie Lea, Brandon Duckworth, Danny Darwin

Maine was the Mets' best starter for most of the year. Then crunch time came, and he crumpled like a cheap suit. It wasn't the pressure that got to Maine, it was the innings. Maine threw just 152 innings in 2006 with an injury time-out in the middle. In 2005 he went boom after about 160 frames. Before that, his season high was 148. Last year, Maine took every turn in order for the first four months, got to 132 1/3 innings, and ran out of gas. Worse, the tank was being drained with an SUV's thirst because Maine's left hip troubled him from spring training, worsening as the year went on. Prior to his near no-hit gem on the penultimate day of the season, which was likely all adrenalin, Maine posted a 7.06 ERA over ten consecutive starts beginning on August 4. It's enough to make one wonder if he's capable of doing what he did for the season's first four months (12-5, 2.92 ERA) over a full season. If he can, he's a front-of-the-rotation pitcher.

Pedro Martinez

| | Bats: R | Throws: R | Height: 5' 11" | Weight: 180 | Born: October 25, 1971 | Age: 36 |

YEAR	TEAM	LVL	AGE	W	L	SV	G	GS	IP	H	BB	SO	HR	GB%	BABIP	STUFF	WHIP	ERA	PERA	EqERA	EqH9	EqBB9	EqSO9	EqHR9	VORP	SN/WX
2005	NYN	MLB	33	15	8	0	31	31	217	159	47	208	19	40.9%	.253	35	0.95	2.82	2.89	3.05	6.8	1.8	8.0	0.8	64.8	7.57
2006	NYN	MLB	34	9	8	0	23	23	132²	108	39	137	19	37.1%	.266	24	1.11	4.48	3.54	4.51	7.3	2.2	8.4	1.1	15.4	3.11
2007	NYN	MLB	35	3	1	0	5	5	28	33	7	32	0	32.2%	.393	29	1.43	2.57	4.07	3.41	10.2	1.9	9.3	0.0	7.1	1.00
2008	NYN	MLB	36	8	5	0	21	21	120	106	35	109	14	39.0%	.274	21	1.17	3.37	3.77	3.74	7.9	2.3	7.3	1.0	27.3	3.70

Breakout: 15% Improve: 52% Collapse: 26% Attrition: 22%   Comparables: Don Sutton, Tom Seaver, Mike Mussina, Mike Jackson

Tracking Pedro Martinez's slow recovery from rotator-cuff surgery was a parallel occupation to following the Mets for most of the 2007 season. Leading up to his September return, the local papers provided daily updates on his progress and nearly blow-by-blow accounts of every time he took the mound to test the ol' ball and socket. His stuff will never be what it was in his heyday, but even back when he was arguably the best peak-period pitcher in history, his command was top-drawer and he was crafty as all hell. That part of his game is still there, and that's enough for him to be successful. Chances are good that he'll be worth what he's going to be paid in the last year of his contract.

Guillermo Mota

| | | | | | | Bats: R | | Throws: R | | Height: 6' 6" | | Weight: 210 | | Born: July 25, 1973 | | | Age: 34 |

YEAR	TEAM	LVL	AGE	W	L	SV	G	GS	IP	H	BB	SO	HR	GB%	BABIP	STUFF	WHIP	ERA	PERA	EqERA	EqH9	EqBB9	EqSO9	EqHR9	VORP	SN/WX
2005	FLO	MLB	31	2	2	2	56	0	67	65	32	60	5	42.0%	.314	5	1.45	4.70	3.90	4.81	8.2	3.9	7.2	0.7	1.8	1.44
2006	CLE	MLB	32	1	3	0	34	0	37²	45	19	27	9	29.9%	.313	-24	1.70	6.21	6.68	5.92	9.7	4.3	5.9	1.9	-2.0	-0.18
2006	NYN	MLB	32	3	0	0	18	0	18	10	5	19	2	47.7%	.190	18	0.83	1.00	2.37	1.00	5.0	2.0	8.5	1.0	10.0	0.83
2007	NYN	MLB	33	2	2	0	52	0	59¹	63	18	47	8	44.8%	.299	-4	1.37	5.77	4.51	5.49	9.2	2.2	6.5	1.2	-0.8	-0.44
2008	MIL	MLB	34	2	2	2	40	0	47²	50	19	37	6	41.9%	.301	-5	1.46	4.77	4.88	4.86	9.4	3.1	6.1	1.2	3.7	0.30

Breakout: 24%   Improve: 45%   Collapse: 33%   Attrition: 32%   Comparables: Turk Farrell, Mark Guthrie, Stan Bahnsen, Roger Mason

Mota missed the first two months of the season while serving a suspension for performance-enhancing substances. When he returned he wasn't very good, but he's big and throws hard and usually throws strikes. This combination proved too big a temptation for Willie Randolph to resist, and he kept going back to Mota looking for results that ultimately proved to be chimerical. The impact was large—when talking about the team's collapse, Randolph put the blame squarely on the players rather than himself, but his handling of Mota makes him just as culpable. The Brewers have similarly succumbed to Mota's siren song, shipping Johnny Estrada to the Mets for him; Ned Yost might even let him set up for Eric Gagné.

Kevin Mulvey

| | | | | | | Bats: R | | Throws: R | | Height: 6' 1" | | Weight: 195 | | Born: May 26, 1985 | | | Age: 23 |

YEAR	TEAM	LVL	AGE	W	L	SV	G	GS	IP	H	BB	SO	HR	GB%	BABIP	STUFF	WHIP	ERA	PERA	EqERA	EqH9	EqBB9	EqSO9	EqHR9	VORP	SN/WX
2006	BIN	AA	21	0	1	0	3	3	13	10	5	10	1	61.1%	.257	-3	1.15	1.38	5.11	3.97	8.7	4.8	4.8	1.6	2.0	—
2007	BIN	AA	22	11	10	0	26	26	151²	145	43	110	4	55.7%	.305	13	1.24	3.32	3.99	4.89	8.6	3.1	4.3	0.4	11.6	—
2008	NYN	MLB	23	8	9	0	24	24	143²	147	54	84	13	50.7%	.288	7	1.40	4.41	4.65	5.02	9.2	3.0	4.7	0.8	11.1	2.30

Breakout: 11%   Improve: 46%   Collapse: 31%   Attrition: 18%   Comparables: Marc Valdes, Jay Tibbs, Dave Stieb, Richie Gardner

The Mets' top pick out of Villanova in 2006, Mulvey made his full-season debut in Double-A last year and more than held his own, finishing in the Eastern League's top five in ERA. As exciting as that might make him sound, he's just not that good. He's not much more than a generic right-hander who throws strikes with a selection of average pitches and offers little in the way of projection. He'll be at Triple-A this year and will probably be toward the front of the queue for a call-up as an emergency starter, but he's no future stalwart.

Carlos Muñiz

| | | | | | | Bats: R | | Throws: R | | Height: 6' 1" | | Weight: 180 | | Born: March 12, 1981 | | | Age: 27 |

YEAR	TEAM	LVL	AGE	W	L	SV	G	GS	IP	H	BB	SO	HR	GB%	BABIP	STUFF	WHIP	ERA	PERA	EqERA	EqH9	EqBB9	EqSO9	EqHR9	VORP	SN/WX
2005	HAG	A	24	3	4	14	30	0	37²	37	19	43	6	41.9%	.326	-38	1.49	4.77	13.10	10.68	13.6	8.3	6.2	3.3	-17.1	—
2005	SLU	A+	24	3	0	0	14	0	17	13	9	19	3	42.2%	.250	-23	1.29	5.82	9.04	9.42	9.4	8.2	6.3	3.1	-6.1	—
2006	SLU	A+	25	4	3	31	48	0	49¹	39	18	45	5	36.0%	.254	-30	1.16	3.12	6.11	6.15	9.1	5.0	4.8	2.0	-2.8	—
2007	BIN	AA	26	2	4	23	44	0	58²	43	17	62	2	34.4%	.266	6	1.02	2.45	3.31	3.81	6.6	3.1	6.4	0.6	11.7	—
2008	NYN	MLB	27	3	4	4	27	4	55²	53	27	43	9	36.6%	.269	-4	1.43	4.80	5.07	5.32	8.6	3.8	6.1	1.4	2.7	0.40

Breakout: 36%   Improve: 58%   Collapse: 24%   Attrition: 12%   Comparables: Judd Songster, Nick Mattioni, Scott Proctor, David Lee

Muñiz had a great season as the Mets' Double-A closer in 2007, but he's not a great prospect. He's a bit of a late-bloomer who gets by on a plus slider; his fastball is average at best. There is a long history of pitchers of this type putting up impressive minor league numbers and struggling in the bigs. Muñiz was called up for the final week of the season, but only pitched twice. Bouncing up and down between the minors and majors seems to be his destiny.

Jonathon Niese

| | | | | | | Bats: L | | Throws: L | | Height: 6' 3" | | Weight: 190 | | Born: October 27, 1986 | | | Age: 21 |

YEAR	TEAM	LVL	AGE	W	L	SV	G	GS	IP	H	BB	SO	HR	GB%	BABIP	STUFF	WHIP	ERA	PERA	EqERA	EqH9	EqBB9	EqSO9	EqHR9	VORP	SN/WX
2006	HAG	A	19	11	9	0	25	25	123	121	62	132	7	51.4%	.342	-9	1.49	3.95	8.91	8.54	12.5	7.8	5.5	1.5	-33.7	—
2007	SLU	A+	20	11	7	0	27	27	134¹	151	31	110	9	50.4%	.346	-6	1.36	4.29	6.78	7.18	11.8	3.4	4.7	1.3	-21.4	—
2008	NYN	MLB	21	7	10	0	26	26	141²	166	66	87	20	46.6%	.313	0	1.64	5.55	6.21	6.16	10.5	3.8	4.9	1.2	-5.8	0.50

Breakout: 43%   Improve: 76%   Collapse: 5%   Attrition: 11%   Comparables: Mike Kusiewicz, Andy Van Hekken, Derrick Van Dusen, Michael Hinckley

Niese is the best left-handed prospect in the organization, which says more about the system than it does about Niese's talent. His best pitch is his curveball, his average-velocity sinker is solid enough, and he doesn't allow a lot of walks, but he gives up too many hits and doesn't have that one go-to swing-and-miss offering to depend on when he needs it. Double-A could prove to be problematic.

Robert Parnell

Bats: R Throws: R Height: 6' 3" Weight: 180 Born: September 8, 1984 Age: 23

YEAR	TEAM	LVL	AGE	W	L	SV	G	GS	IP	H	BB	SO	HR	GB%	BABIP	STUFF	WHIP	ERA	PERA	EqERA	EqH9	EqBB9	EqSO9	EqHR9	VORP	SN/WX
2005	BRO	A-	20	2	3	0	15	14	73	48	29	67	1	66.0%	.246	1	1.05	1.73	5.45	5.31	8.0	7.2	3.8	0.7	2.0	—
2006	HAG	A	21	5	10	0	18	18	93²	84	40	84	7	56.8%	.295	-22	1.33	4.06	7.84	8.10	11.1	6.6	4.4	1.8	-22.2	—
2007	SLU	A+	22	3	3	0	12	12	55¹	56	22	62	0	64.9%	.364	17	1.41	3.25	5.73	5.07	11.1	5.3	6.9	0.4	2.9	—
2007	BIN	AA	22	5	5	0	17	17	88²	98	38	74	9	46.8%	.327	-14	1.53	4.77	6.40	6.43	10.4	4.5	5.1	1.5	-7.9	—
2008	NYN	MLB	23	6	9	0	30	20	122¹	134	70	85	16	49.2%	.308	-3	1.67	5.52	6.11	6.17	9.8	4.6	5.6	1.1	-5.4	0.30

Breakout: 24% Improve: 52% Collapse: 17% Attrition: 11%   Comparables: Rett Johnson, Steven Wolf, Curt Leskanic, Nelson Figueroa

There's a lot to like about Parnell, including low- to mid-90s velocity and a solid slider, but he's pretty rough around the edges. He doesn't have much of a changeup, his fastball is pretty straight, and his command is spotty. He's got the talent to get to the big leagues, but it will likely come with a move to the bullpen.

Mike Pelfrey

Bats: R Throws: R Height: 6' 7" Weight: 215 Born: January 14, 1984 Age: 24

YEAR	TEAM	LVL	AGE	W	L	SV	G	GS	IP	H	BB	SO	HR	GB%	BABIP	STUFF	WHIP	ERA	PERA	EqERA	EqH9	EqBB9	EqSO9	EqHR9	VORP	SN/WX
2006	SLU	A+	22	2	1	0	4	4	22²	17	2	26	1	64.7%	.327	18	0.86	1.62	5.20	4.00	10.5	2.0	7.5	1.0	3.2	—
2006	BIN	AA	22	4	2	0	12	12	66¹	60	26	77	2	49.7%	.347	20	1.30	2.72	5.61	4.76	10.7	4.8	7.4	0.6	5.5	—
2006	NYN	MLB	22	2	1	0	4	4	21¹	25	12	13	1	49.3%	.353	-1	1.73	5.49	6.19	6.20	11.1	4.4	5.3	0.4	-0.0	0.15
2007	NWO	AAA	23	3	6	0	14	14	74	74	26	56	6	58.7%	.306	3	1.35	4.01	4.75	4.62	9.2	3.5	5.1	0.9	7.8	—
2007	NYN	MLB	23	3	8	0	15	13	72²	85	39	45	6	50.2%	.338	0	1.71	5.57	5.85	5.72	10.6	4.1	5.2	0.7	-0.2	0.29
2008	NYN	MJLB	24	9	9	1	36	25	150²	152	68	104	13	51.4%	.296	4	1.46	4.32	4.82	4.89	9.1	3.6	5.5	0.8	13.3	2.50

Breakout: 36% Improve: 70% Collapse: 17% Attrition: 24%   Comparables: Jason Young, Paul Wilson, Jon Garland, Kyle Peterson

The Mets went into the 2007 season expecting a big contribution from Pelfrey. They didn't get it. He has a fantastic fastball that gets into the mid-90s and features a ton of natural sink, and he commands it well. The problem is that you need more than one pitch to get big-league hitters out, and Pelfrey is still looking for something else to throw. His slider is flat, and his changeup is about as deceptive as Milton Berle in drag. If something else doesn't come along, he'll never be the star most thought he would be.

Oliver Perez

Bats: L Throws: L Height: 6' 3" Weight: 215 Born: August 15, 1981 Age: 26

YEAR	TEAM	LVL	AGE	W	L	SV	G	GS	IP	H	BB	SO	HR	GB%	BABIP	STUFF	WHIP	ERA	PERA	EqERA	EqH9	EqBB9	EqSO9	EqHR9	VORP	SN/WX
2005	PIT	MLB	23	7	5	0	20	20	103	102	70	97	23	32.9%	.297	-9	1.67	5.85	7.18	6.28	9.2	5.7	7.9	2.0	-4.4	0.58
2006	IND	AAA	24	1	3	0	6	6	32¹	28	11	34	6	33.7%	.275	-13	1.21	5.61	7.65	8.19	9.7	3.9	7.3	2.7	-8.5	—
2006	PIT	MLB	24	2	10	0	15	15	76	88	51	61	13	32.5%	.336	-3	1.83	6.63	5.86	6.75	9.4	5.0	6.4	1.3	-12.4	0.27
2006	NOR	AAA	24	1	2	0	4	4	19²	18	12	26	4	44.7%	.333	4	1.56	6.09	10.77	9.35	10.4	6.7	9.9	3.1	-7.2	—
2006	NYN	MLB	24	1	3	0	7	7	36²	41	17	41	7	30.8%	.358	12	1.58	6.38	7.11	6.62	10.7	3.8	9.4	1.5	-1.9	0.40
2007	NYN	MLB	25	15	10	0	29	29	177	153	79	174	22	35.2%	.278	22	1.31	3.56	3.84	4.16	7.7	3.4	8.1	1.1	24.0	3.98
2008	NYN	MLB	26	8	8	0	23	23	138	124	63	133	17	37.1%	.283	21	1.35	4.22	4.58	4.67	8.0	3.7	7.7	1.1	16.8	2.80

Breakout: 35% Improve: 62% Collapse: 13% Attrition: 18%   Comparables: Tim Lollar, Denny Neagle, Arthur Rhodes, Don Robinson

Perez showed some of his old form last year, bringing to mind his first full season in Pittsburgh when he was one of the more intriguing young arms around, but overall he was maddeningly inconsistent. He allowed two or fewer earned runs in 16 of his 29 starts, but allowed five or more runs in nine others. Perez's mechanics have a lot of working parts, and the team is stuck with the difficult choice often faced with pitchers like this: If you straighten him out, does he lose his at-times dominating stuff?

Scott Schoeneweis

Bats: L   Throws: L   Height: 6' 0"   Weight: 190   Born: October 2, 1973   Age: 34

YEAR	TEAM	LVL	AGE	W	L	SV	G	GS	IP	H	BB	SO	HR	GB%	BABIP	STUFF	WHIP	ERA	PERA	EqERA	EqH9	EqBB9	EqSO9	EqHR9	VORP	SN/WX
2005	TOR	MLB	31	3	4	1	80	0	57	54	25	43	2	60.1%	.297	6	1.39	3.32	3.81	3.67	8.5	3.8	6.6	0.3	12.9	0.69
2006	TOR	MLB	32	2	2	1	55	0	37¹	39	16	18	3	57.9%	.295	-21	1.47	6.51	4.55	6.25	9.2	3.8	4.2	0.8	-1.2	0.06
2006	CIN	MLB	32	2	0	3	16	0	14¹	9	8	11	1	60.0%	.205	4	1.19	0.63	2.65	0.61	4.9	4.3	6.1	0.6	8.6	0.95
2007	NYN	MLB	33	0	2	2	70	0	59	62	28	41	8	53.4%	.300	-13	1.53	5.03	5.16	5.19	9.3	3.7	5.8	1.2	2.1	0.59
2008	NYN	MLB	34	2	2	3	52	0	48¹	49	21	31	4	52.5%	.295	-9	1.44	4.05	4.43	4.65	9.1	3.5	5.1	0.6	5.7	0.50

Breakout: 22% Improve: 43% Collapse: 27% Attrition: 25%   Comparables: Steve Kline, Darold Knowles, Jamie Easterly, Steve Barber

Despite the fact that he had pitched well in only one of the previous three seasons, the Mets signed Schoeneweis to a three-year contract following the 2006 campaign. He responded by making it one in four. A sinker/slider pitcher who gets plenty of groundballs, Schoeneweis is murder on lefties, but right-handers hit .292/.364/.466 against him on his career and .316/.390/.574 in 2007. That makes him no more than a LOOGY, and LOOGYs don't deserve three-year contracts. Further complicating matters were post-season headlines connecting Schoeneweis to a sham Florida pharmacy that was involved in steroid shipments.

Aaron Sele

Bats: R   Throws: R   Height: 6' 3"   Weight: 220   Born: June 25, 1970   Age: 38

YEAR	TEAM	LVL	AGE	W	L	SV	G	GS	IP	H	BB	SO	HR	GB%	BABIP	STUFF	WHIP	ERA	PERA	EqERA	EqH9	EqBB9	EqSO9	EqHR9	VORP	SN/WX
2005	SEA	MLB	35	6	12	0	21	21	116	147	41	53	18	41.3%	.326	-21	1.62	5.66	7.09	6.43	11.5	3.2	4.1	1.4	-3.4	1.70
2006	LVG	AAA	36	3	0	0	5	5	29	25	5	28	1	45.8%	.296	23	1.03	2.48	3.29	2.83	7.5	1.9	6.3	0.3	8.8	—
2006	LAN	MLB	36	8	6	0	28	15	103¹	120	30	57	11	46.4%	.315	0	1.45	4.53	4.46	4.41	9.7	2.2	4.5	0.9	12.2	1.84
2007	NYN	MLB	37	3	2	0	34	0	53²	78	21	29	5	46.5%	.397	-21	1.84	5.36	8.29	6.53	13.6	3.2	4.8	0.9	0.7	0.63
2008	NYN	MLB	38	2	2	1	25	2	45	53	15	23	5	46.2%	.307	-16	1.51	4.58	5.35	5.12	10.5	2.8	4.1	1.0	3.3	0.30

Breakout: 32% Improve: 45% Collapse: 24% Attrition: 33%   Comparables: Rick White, Ron Kline, Jim Hearn, Jack Sanford

When the Mets signed Sele to a minor league deal prior to spring training, he said he'd retire if he didn't make the team. He then posted an ERA over six in the Grapefruit League, but the Mets took him north anyway. Sele spent 2007 in the Mets' bullpen as the team's official blowout pitcher; 20 of his 34 appearances saw him enter the game with his team either up or down by a minimum of four runs. In the latter case, all he ever seemed to do was dig a deeper hole.

Joe Smith

Bats: R   Throws: R   Height: 6' 2"   Weight: 215   Born: March 22, 1984   Age: 24

YEAR	TEAM	LVL	AGE	W	L	SV	G	GS	IP	H	BB	SO	HR	GB%	BABIP	STUFF	WHIP	ERA	PERA	EqERA	EqH9	EqBB9	EqSO9	EqHR9	VORP	SN/WX
2006	BRO	A-	22	0	1	9	17	0	20	10	3	28	0	60.5%	.233	5	0.65	0.45	4.22	3.93	6.4	3.4	6.9	0.5	3.4	—
2006	BIN	AA	22	0	2	0	10	0	12²	12	11	12	1	54.3%	.344	-4	1.89	5.90	9.36	8.44	11.8	11.0	5.9	1.7	-3.4	—
2007	NYN	MLB	23	3	2	0	54	0	44¹	48	21	45	3	62.9%	.354	13	1.56	3.45	5.09	3.65	9.9	3.7	8.5	0.6	10.6	0.55
2008	NYN	MLB	24	3	2	2	44	2	55²	51	25	49	3	55.8%	.298	9	1.36	3.18	3.85	3.64	8.2	3.6	7.0	0.5	14.2	1.30

Breakout: 27% Improve: 49% Collapse: 37% Attrition: 18%   Comparables: Ryan Wagner, Vicente Padilla, Terry Adams, Al McBean

A 2006 draftee who entered last year with just those 33 innings of professional experience, Smith earned a job in the Mets bullpen with an outstanding spring training performance, then performed admirably when he was used correctly. As a right-handed sidewinder, Smith is a solid ROOGY. Left-handed batters hit .298/.411/.447 against him in 2007, and there's no reason to expect that to change. Chad Bradford is the model here, but the Mets had Bradford for the one season in which he actually had success against lefties, so they have yet to fully understand Smith's utility.

Jorge Sosa

Bats: R   Throws: R   Height: 6' 2"   Weight: 175   Born: April 28, 1977   Age: 31

YEAR	TEAM	LVL	AGE	W	L	SV	G	GS	IP	H	BB	SO	HR	GB%	BABIP	STUFF	WHIP	ERA	PERA	EqERA	EqH9	EqBB9	EqSO9	EqHR9	VORP	SN/WX
2005	ATL	MLB	28	13	3	0	44	20	134	122	64	85	12	37.1%	.269	2	1.39	2.55	3.83	2.89	7.9	3.9	5.2	0.8	41.3	4.99
2006	ATL	MLB	29	3	10	3	26	13	87^1	105	32	58	20	37.3%	.310	-24	1.57	5.46	6.20	5.87	10.0	2.7	5.4	1.8	-3.4	-0.95
2006	SLN	MLB	29	0	1	1	19	0	30^2	33	8	17	10	35.2%	.247	-27	1.34	5.28	6.57	5.28	9.4	2.1	4.7	2.6	2.7	0.07
2007	NWO	AAA	30	4	0	0	5	5	32	29	4	29	1	49.5%	.326	27	1.03	1.13	3.48	2.40	8.7	1.5	6.6	0.3	10.7	—
2007	NYN	MLB	30	9	8	0	42	14	112^2	109	41	69	10	41.0%	.284	2	1.33	4.47	3.79	4.38	8.5	2.8	5.2	0.7	14.7	2.45
2008	NYN	MLB	31	4	4	1	35	8	74	75	27	48	10	40.9%	.281	-6	1.37	4.33	4.86	4.81	9.1	2.9	5.2	1.2	8.5	1.00

Breakout: 10%   Improve: 28%   Collapse: 46%   Attrition: 33%   Comparables: Greg Harris, Jesse Jefferson, Paul Foytack, Paul Byrd

Signed as an insurance policy, Sosa forced his way back to the majors by allowing just four earned runs over 32 innings in his first five starts at Triple-A. He then began his Mets career with quality starts in five of his first seven outings before falling back to earth and being sent to the bullpen. He's a decent arm who should stick in the majors. What the Mets do over the remainder of the offseason will dictate whether Sosa is a league-average back-end starter, or a league-average middle reliever this year.

Jason Vargas

Bats: L   Throws: L   Height: 6' 0"   Weight: 215   Born: February 2, 1983   Age: 25

YEAR	TEAM	LVL	AGE	W	L	SV	G	GS	IP	H	BB	SO	HR	GB%	BABIP	STUFF	WHIP	ERA	PERA	EqERA	EqH9	EqBB9	EqSO9	EqHR9	VORP	SN/WX
2005	GRB	A	22	4	1	0	5	5	33^2	16	10	33	1	35.4%	.188	9	0.77	0.80	4.08	3.00	5.1	4.8	4.8	0.9	8.7	—
2005	JUP	A+	22	2	3	0	9	9	55^1	47	14	60	6	36.8%	.287	-7	1.10	3.42	6.30	6.14	9.7	4.1	6.0	2.0	-2.9	—
2005	CAR	AA	22	1	0	0	3	3	19	13	7	25	3	41.9%	.256	17	1.05	2.84	5.87	4.24	7.9	4.2	8.5	2.6	2.6	—
2005	FLO	MLB	22	5	5	0	17	13	73^2	71	31	59	4	32.5%	.302	21	1.38	4.03	3.51	3.91	7.8	3.3	6.3	0.5	10.8	1.76
2006	ABQ	AAA	23	3	6	0	13	13	69	98	28	51	11	37.6%	.395	-33	1.83	7.43	10.44	9.47	13.7	4.2	4.9	1.8	-27.4	—
2006	FLO	MLB	23	1	2	0	12	5	43	50	30	25	9	33.1%	.299	-19	1.86	7.33	6.60	7.54	9.5	5.2	4.6	1.6	-10.8	-0.54
2007	NWO	AAA	24	9	7	0	24	24	125	141	44	108	14	36.9%	.339	-6	1.48	4.97	5.83	6.16	10.5	3.5	5.9	1.2	-7.5	—
2007	NYN	MLB	24	0	1	0	2	2	10^1	17	2	4	4	26.7%	.317	-51	1.84	12.23	14.21	14.73	13.1	1.6	3.3	3.3	-7.0	-0.27
2008	NYN	MLB	25	5	7	0	25	14	95	105	40	69	16	36.9%	.299	-2	1.52	5.46	5.89	5.99	9.9	3.4	5.8	1.5	-2.4	0.30

Breakout: 36%   Improve: 61%   Collapse: 16%   Attrition: 25%   Comparables: Steve Rosenberg, Jason Miller, Bob Sykes, Brad Havens

Vargas was a big surprise for the Marlins in 2005, not only because he reached the majors, but because he pitched pretty well once he got there. Since then, he's done very little. Scouts never trusted his stuff much in the first place; he's one of those lefty battlers who throws strikes and changes speeds and keeps guys off balance, but he's just not fooling enough hitters.

Billy Wagner

Bats: L   Throws: L   Height: 5' 11"   Weight: 205   Born: July 25, 1971   Age: 36

YEAR	TEAM	LVL	AGE	W	L	SV	G	GS	IP	H	BB	SO	HR	GB%	BABIP	STUFF	WHIP	ERA	PERA	EqERA	EqH9	EqBB9	EqSO9	EqHR9	VORP	SN/WX
2005	PHI	MLB	33	4	3	38	75	0	77^2	45	20	87	6	44.4%	.218	29	0.84	1.51	2.46	2.11	5.4	2.1	8.9	0.7	30.8	3.75
2006	NYN	MLB	34	3	2	40	70	0	72^1	59	21	94	7	53.9%	.308	30	1.11	2.24	3.50	2.78	7.8	2.3	10.1	0.8	26.0	5.95
2007	NYN	MLB	35	2	2	34	66	0	68^1	55	22	80	6	40.4%	.290	27	1.13	2.64	3.17	2.75	7.3	2.5	9.4	0.8	22.2	3.75
2008	NYN	MLB	36	4	5	40	59	0	58^2	47	20	61	6	43.6%	.270	13	1.15	2.77	3.29	3.11	7.2	2.8	8.3	0.9	18.3	2.90

Breakout: 13%   Improve: 20%   Collapse: 53%   Attrition: 7%   Comparables: Mike Remlinger, Paul Assenmacher, Jim Brewer, Tug McGraw

Wagner is still one of the best closers around, but as he gets into his late 30s the Mets are going to have to deal with the fact that his mechanics and Father Time are both taking their toll. Back spasms plagued Wagner for much of the second half of the season, often leaving him ineffective or unavailable, and the Mets never found a dependable backup plan. They'll need one this year.

LINEOUTS

Hitters

PLAYER		TEAM	LVL	AGE	PA	R	2B	3B	HR	RBI	BB	SO	SB-CS	EqBRR	AVG/OBP/SLG	MLVr	EqAVG/EqOBP/EqSLG	EqA	VORP
C	S. Alomar	NWO	AAA	41	156	15	8	1	4	29	8	24	1-0	-1.7	.292/.323/.444	.020	.255/.288/.407	.240	0.8
		NYN	MLB	41	22	1	1	0	0	0	0	3	0-0	0.0	.136/.136/.182	-.763	.136/.136/.182	.000	-3.0
SS	J. Coronado#	BIN	AA	21	346	31	7	2	1	15	31	84	7-3	0.9	.212/.284/.257	-.293	.188/.256/.233	.173	-28.3
C	M. DiFelice	NWO	AAA	38	272	37	9	0	7	38	20	61	0-1	-1.7	.282/.339/.403	-.019	.252/.309/.360	.233	-0.8
		NYN	MLB	38	47	1	2	1	0	5	2	12	0-0	-0.2	.250/.311/.350	-.142	.268/.326/.366	.248	0.2
INF	A. Hernandez#	NWO	AAA	24	597	84	28	5	5	42	31	82	16-9	0.5	.301/.339/.397	-.012	.266/.303/.354	.231	1.3
INF	M. Kiger	BIN	AA	27	484	75	27	4	10	50	75	92	16-7	-0.5	.312/.432/.478	.305	.272/.383/.433	.287	32.8
		NWO	AAA	27	40	5	1	0	1	2	7	16	0-0	-0.1	.121/.275/.242	-.464	.121/.275/.242	.188	-3.7
UT	D. Newhan*	NWO	AAA	33	196	27	12	3	7	30	20	28	7-4	-1.8	.347/.413/.572	.429	.310/.378/.517	.299	20.2
		NYN	MLB	33	83	9	1	1	1	6	8	19	2-0	1.2	.203/.289/.284	-.296	.203/.298/.284	.215	-2.9
C	F. Peña	SAV	A	17	399	26	12	0	5	30	24	76	1-1	-7.6	.210/.263/.283	-.288	.171/.213/.227	.133	-52.3
3B	F. Tatis	NWO	AAA	32	572	90	31	5	21	67	62	103	8-6	0.4	.276/.359/.485	.130	.245/.327/.434	.262	19.4

In case you missed it, **Sandy Alomar Jr.** really did play last year, spending most of the season in the minor leagues' oldest catching platoon with **Mike DiFelice**. ⊘ **Jose Coronado** is an outstanding defensive shortstop who can't hit his way out of a paper bag. There was a time when the majors had room for players like this; we are not currently in that time. ⊘ **Anderson Hernandez** is a middle infielder with speed who can slap singles with the best of them, but offers little else. He still has a shot at some kind of utility career. ⊘ **Mark Kiger** led the Eastern League with a .432 on-base percentage, but he'll be 28 in May and can't play shortstop at the big-league level. His unique feat of making his only major league appearances in the postseason is unlikely to be sullied. ⊘ **David Newhan** has made a career out of putting up gaudy batting averages at Triple-A only to disappoint in the majors. ⊘ **Francisco Peña** has daddy Tony's defensive chops, but he's got a long way to go with the bat. The good news is that he played the entire year in a full-season league at the tender age of 17. ⊘ In case you haven't figured out that the 2007 roster of the Triple-A New Orleans Zephyrs was not just pathetic, but hilariously so, we offer up **Fernando Tatis** as our next piece of evidence.

Pitchers

PLAYER	TEAM	LVL	AGE	W	L	SV	IP	H	BB	SO	HR	GB%	BABIP	STUFF	WHIP	ERA	PERA	EqERA	EqH9	EqBB9	EqSO9	EqHR9	VORP
J. Adkins	NWO	AAA	29	2	4	5	65¹	71	17	44	8	41.7%	.315	-20	1.35	4.00	5.32	4.97	9.9	2.7	4.5	1.3	4.4
W. Collazo*	NWO	AAA	27	6	5	4	98²	91	19	69	5	53.8%	.300	5	1.11	2.46	3.86	3.48	8.7	2.0	4.9	0.6	21.9
	NYN	MLB	27	0	0	0	5²	7	5	0	0	45.5%	.318	-45	2.12	6.32	7.05	6.75	11.8	6.8	0.0	0.0	-0.4
M. Devaney	BIN	AA	24	6	9	0	104	105	43	71	11	40.7%	.298	-25	1.42	4.85	5.96	6.03	9.6	4.5	4.1	1.6	-4.6
B. Lawrence	CSP	AAA	31	0	2	0	19²	32	5	10	3	53.9%	.403	-32	1.88	8.68	10.15	10.31	14.7	2.9	3.4	1.5	-9.6
	NWO	AAA	31	8	3	0	85	88	9	57	6	42.0%	.313	10	1.14	3.81	4.10	4.54	9.6	1.2	4.6	0.8	9.6
	NYN	MLB	31	1	2	0	29	43	13	18	4	43.0%	.382	-17	1.93	6.83	9.43	7.71	13.8	3.5	5.5	1.3	-3.2
S. Moviel	MTS	Rk	19	0	2	0	40	45	11	37	2	54.0%	.355	-26	1.40	3.38	10.16	9.99	14.6	5.7	3.8	1.9	-16.2
D. Owen	BRO	A-	20	9	1	0	72¹	51	12	69	0	59.3%	.268	19	0.87	1.49	4.35	3.80	8.9	3.1	4.5	0.4	12.8
B. Rustich	BRO	A-	22	2	0	2	12²	4	1	11	2	51.6%	.069	-15	0.39	2.13	5.54	5.73	5.7	1.6	4.1	4.1	-0.2
D. Sanchez '08	NYN	MLB	28	3	3	2	55	51	21	40	5	47.7%	.279	0	1.32	3.60	4.03	4.08	8.3	3.1	5.9	0.8	10.4
L. Urdaneta	BIN	AA	27	1	1	3	22²	26	8	12	1	48.1%	.325	-29	1.50	4.76	5.34	5.82	10.4	3.7	2.9	0.8	-0.5
	NWO	AAA	27	1	0	6	12¹	12	2	2	3	44.7%	.214	-42	1.14	5.85	5.06	5.84	8.0	1.5	0.7	2.2	-0.3
D. Williams*	NWO	AAA	28	3	4	0	61¹	58	13	38	11	39.9%	.257	-12	1.16	3.96	5.14	4.85	8.6	2.1	4.1	1.8	4.9
	NYN	MLB	28	0	1	0	4¹	12	5	2	2	31.8%	.526	-120	3.92	23.02	33.94	31.15	24.9	8.3	4.2	4.2	-8.2

Jon Adkins doesn't do any one thing well enough to get him out of Triple-A, and shouldn't be expecting any miracles now that he's 30. ⊘ **Willie Collazo** had a very good year at Triple-A and made his big-league debut in September, though he might have wished he was back in New Orleans. He could have a future as a LOOGY. ⊘ **Mike Devaney** is a former college star who has found a modicum of success at Double-A thanks to a very good slow curveball. Unfortunately, his mid-80s fastball will make getting to the big leagues a struggle. ⊘ **Brian Lawrence** made five starts for the Mets when he replaced Jorge Sosa in the rotation and one more in September. The Mets lost five of them. He's nothing more than a strike-thrower at this point. ⊘ A second-round pick last June, **Scott Moviel** is a 6-foot-11 teenager who already throws in the low 90s. Two years from now, everyone will either know his name or have forgotten about him completely. ⊘ **Dylan Owen** had a 1.43 ERA in his pro debut, but there's a reason 632 players were selected before him in June: he's a short righty with weak stuff who succeeds on command and moxie. ⊘ After spending six years proving that he can't hit, **Corey Ragsdale** was finally convinced to take his cannon arm to the mound. He's raw as sushi, but he does throw hard. ⊘ **Brant Rustich** never put up good numbers in college, but scouts found it hard to ignore a six-foot-six behemoth who can get it into the mid-90s. He looked awfully good after signing. ⊘ One of the Mets better bullpen arms in 2006, **Duaner Sanchez** had surgery in April to repair a fracture in his right shoulder, and, while he insisted he'd return to the mound last year, that didn't happen. He'll be healthy for 2008, but we won't know if he'll be the same pitcher until he takes the mound. ⊘ **Lino Urdaneta** pitched one inning for the Mets last year and is unlikely to pitch another. ⊘ There was a time when **Dave Williams** was a fringe lefty starter. Now he's a fringe lefty reliever.

MANAGER: WILLIE RANDOLPH

YEAR	TEAM	W-L	Pythag +/−	Avg PC	100+ P	120+ P	QS	BQS	REL	REL w Zero R	IBB	Subs	PH	PH Avg	PH HR	SB2	CS2	SB3	CS3	SAC Att	SAC %	POS SAC	Squeeze	Swing	In Play
2005	NYN	83-79	-7	97.3	73	4	93	9	392	250	43	65	220	.291	5	121	34	31	6	94	73.4%	39	1	129	104
2006	NYN	97-65	5	96.0	79	1	78	4	473	330	39	32	246	.187	3	119	33	27	2	105	73.3%	38	1	127	101
2007	NYN	88-74	1	99.0	83	4	84	0	499	319	40	36	264	.228	3	168	37	32	7	103	74.8%	32	2	145	114

Considering that Willie Randolph spent nine years at the Joe Torre Managerial Finishing School, it should come as no surprise that there are many similarities between the two skippers. When the Mets won the East in 2006, Randolph was praised for being a calm and quiet leader. When the Mets struggled in 2007, he was condemned for being indifferent, emotionless, and inattentive. More specific criticisms also line up with those leveled at Torre during his Yankee tenure, among them the inability to trust young talent. Lastings Milledge never got the chance he deserved in New York in part because Randolph disapproved of his flashy ways. Then there was Philip Humber's start on September 26, which came on 15 days' rest because Randolph had let the rookie waste away unused in the bullpen only to call on him to make a crucial start with his team in freefall—does that ever work? Like Torre, Randolph's handling of the bullpen also came under frequent fire last year as, other than having Aaron Heilman and Billy Wagner pitching the eighth and ninth innings when the Mets were ahead, Randolph was constantly flip-flopping roles and workloads, making it difficult for his other relievers to pitch with much consistency. Despite those faults, Randolph is not a bad manager. As is usually the case, he got too much credit for the 2006 team's postseason run while shouldering too much blame for the 2007 collapse. Despite much of the public calling for his head during and after the collapse, Minaya brought him back; hiring someone to manage in New York is risky business, and sometimes it's better to have the devil you know.

New York Yankees

In retrospect, 2007 was a transitional season for the Yankees despite 94 wins and a wild-card berth. Just as 1996 through 2001 (or, more aptly, 1993 through 2003) is recognized as a distinct epoch in Yankees history, so too will the 2004 to 2007 period be noted as an era of its own, the rump years in which a fallen dynasty tried to get back on its feet and, at least by its own standards, failed. If the Yankees' decision-makers are correct in their estimation of their new-found bounty of homegrown pitchers, 2007 will have been the last year of a cycle of relative frustration that began in the winter of 2003.

Too much has already been made of the post-2003 decline of Yankees' pitching, so we'll just hit the key notes: After the team's World Series loss to the Marlins, Roger Clemens, Andy Pettitte, and David Wells moved on by various motivations and means, and the Yankee farm offered nothing in the way of rearmament. In the winter prior to the 2004 season, the organization's top pitching prospects according to Baseball America were, in order of promise, Ramon Ramirez (Triple-A), Jorge DePaula (Double-A), Edwardo Sierra (Low-A), Chien-Ming Wang (Double-A), Scott Proctor (Triple-A), Danny Borrell (Triple-A), Matt DeSalvo (Low-A), Sean Henn (High-A), Mark Phillips (High-A), Jose Garcia (High-A),

Jose Valdez (High-A), Brad Halsey (Double-A), Jason Stephens (Rookie), Tyler Clippard (Rookie), Ben Julianel (Low-A), and Mike Knox (High-A). It did not take a seer's perception of the future to know that the makings of the next great Yankees rotation were not to be found within the organization. Even if some of the tyro hurlers did exceed expectations, they were unlikely to do it in time to help the Yankees defend their pennant.

Help wasn't to be found outside of the organization either. The Yankees of 2004 to 2007 were in the exact same bind that the organization had been in exactly 20 years earlier: poor to non-existent drafting (the latter due to picks lost to free-agent compensation) had led them to rely on the free agent market for a pitching boost, and for that matter, a lineup boost as well. Unlike position players, however, not enough top pitchers made it to market each winter to meet the staff's needs. Thus did the Yankees end up as proud owners of Carl Pavano and Jaret Wright, just as they had Andy Hawkins and Dave LaPoint a generation before.

The Yankees had been one of the worst drafting teams in baseball for years, if not decades. Aside from the brief period that produced Andy Pettitte, Jorge Posada (both from the 1990 draft), Mariano Rivera (a

---

YANKEES PROSPECTUS

2007 record: 94-68; Second place, AL East; Lost to Indians in Division Series

Pythagenport record: 98-64

Runs scored per game: 5.98 (1st in AL)

Runs allowed per game: 4.80 (8th in AL)

Team EqA: .280 (1st in AL)

2007 Batters Age: 31.2 (2nd oldest in AL)

2007 Pitchers Age: 31.8 (2nd oldest in AL)

Ballpark: Yankee Stadium; Neutral park; Park Factor of 1.007

2007: The end of the end of an era despite a 12th-straight playoff berth for Uncle Joe.

2008: Farmer Joe wakes to the dawn of a new day, ready to cultivate a rich crop of young arms.

non-drafted free agent, also 1990), and Derek Jeter (1992 draft), the farm had always finished a distant third when it came to player procurement: free-agent signings and trading for veterans were always the top items on the agenda. Outside of that fab four, the few players that emerged from the system were used as trade fodder. The rare exceptions came in the years when the Yankees couldn't buy their way into contention—1984, when Don Mattingly, Mike Pagliarulo, and others were given a chance to play after the team was an early casualty of the Detroit Tigers' 35-5 start; 1989 to 1991, when the team was flat-lining, leading to opportunities for players such as Roberto Kelly, Kevin Maas, Pat Kelly, and Jim Leyritz. Even during the years in which Jeter, Rivera, Pettitte, and Posada established themselves, they were outliers; far more prospects headed out of town than got a chance to play in pinstripes. If the organization had to pick between a fresh-faced Mike Lowell and an aging Scott Brosius, there was never any doubt as to who they would choose.

As former Yankees manager Casey Stengel once said, "Anything you can't do well and don't enjoy you generally fall behind in." The Yankees didn't enjoy making prospects since they really weren't all that interested in using them, and thus very few turned out well. The malaise spread from the top down. The scouting staff knew their signees weren't wanted, the player development staff knew it, and the players knew it, so there was a sense of futility in the pursuit of a promotion that was never going to come. Yankees farmhands would openly acknowledge that they were playing to catch the eye of other organizations. The Yankees didn't even bother to use the regional sports network money that began flowing their way in the late 1980s to offer hard-to-sign draftees a chance to get rich instead of go to college—why waste money on kids when you could spend it on Terry Mulholland?

General manager Brian Cashman was perhaps the first Yankee executive to recognize that if the team persisted on that course, it would not only fail to win, but would exhaust its seemingly endless reserves of cash in stockpiling dead-armed pitchers and their inevitable replacements. As a result, the Yankee organization, led by Cashman, decided for the first time during more than 30 years of Steinbrenner ownership to stop the madness. Cashman convinced ownership to instead focus the team's resources on the farm system, but the Yankees' player development program didn't turn around overnight on Cashman's say-so. It took some time.

With one very significant exception, the Yankees'

2004 draft has thus far proved unremarkable. That exception was first-round pick Phil Hughes, a blue-chip pitching prospect whose selection was a major success that must have emboldened the Yankees' youth mavens. In a sense 2005 wasn't much better. The Yankees blew their first-round choice on shortstop C. J. Henry, who was quickly proven a bust, though to the team's credit they immediately recognized this fact and flipped him to Philadelphia as the primary "prospect" in the Bobby Abreu deal. Second- and third-round picks J. B. Cox and Brett Gardner have proven to be C-grade prospects at best. The Yanks pulled off a coup in the eighth round, however, prying Texan high school outfielder Austin Jackson away from a college basketball scholarship with a record bonus for that round. Jackson took a great leap forward as a prospect in 2007 and has nearly usurped Jose Tabata (an international signee from the same year) as the team's top outfield prospect. Also on the plus side, they picked up promising starter Alan Horne in the 11th round. Horne will start the 2008 season in Triple-A and could find himself working as a spot starter or reliever for the big club before the year is out.

In 2006, the Yankees hit the mother lode. Choosing to emphasize pitching, the team selected and signed 15 hurlers. Two of them, first-round pick Ian Kennedy and supplemental first-round pick Joba Chamberlain, have already had an impact at the major league level. Chamberlain caused a sensation as a late-season addition to the bullpen last year and has been inked in as a member of the 2008 rotation. Kennedy actually supplanted Mike Mussina briefly at the end of last season and currently lurks as a sixth starter should an injury to one of the top five reopen the door. Several other pitchers from that draft may be useful major leaguers in the future, including George Kontos, Dellin Betances, and Daniel McCutchen.

This past offseason presented the Yankees with a crisis similar to the one they faced following the 2003 World Series, but this time the results were different. Roger Clemens again rode off into the sunset, this time likely to stay. Andy Pettitte declined his player option and threatened retirement (though he ultimately relented and returned on a one-year, $16 million deal equivalent to his option price). Though under contract for another year, Mike Mussina looked nearly as done as Clemens in the last quarter of the 2007 season. Carl Pavano was still trying to break Bret Saberhagen's major league record for days spent on the disabled list. Japanese import Kei Igawa was a major bust, and the bevy of C-grade prospects the Yankees had used as spot starters early in the season had failed to impress. Yet, this time the Yankees did not hunt after free-agent dreck such as Carlos Silva, and they balked at trading their newfound pitching bounty even for so august a veteran hurler as 29-year-old multiple-Cy-Young-Award-winner Johan Santana. They remained committed to their young hurlers.

If the organization's resolve holds through the season (though the Santana talks have reportedly cooled, the threat of a deal continues to lurk in the shadows), then the 2007 season will have marked the end of the desperate clutching after veteran pitching that characterized the Yankees' post-2003 period and George Steinbrenner's ownership as a whole. Say good-bye to the likes of Kevin Brown, Jon Lieber, Javier Vazquez, Esteban Loaiza, Orlando Hernandez II, Randy Johnson, Jaret Wright, Carl Pavano, Shawn Chacon, Aaron Small, Darrell May, Tim Redding, Al Leiter II, Cory Lidle, Sidney Ponson, Roger Clemens II, and the rest of the flotsam that wandered through in the days when the Yankees' pursuit of pitching was, at its most basic level, lazy and cowardly, as if the team was too frightened of failure to make their own wine by planting grapes and instead stuffed some discarded rinds into a bottle, shook well, and pretended the results were champagne.

It is only fitting that this new age begins with a separation from manager Joe Torre. It's not that Torre has grown too old to manage effectively, though he did seem out of touch in his handling of Alex Rodriguez in 2006 and his pitching staff in 2007, particularly during the postseason in both cases. It's just that not all managers are suitable for all occasions. Torre was the right man for 1996, when the Yankees had a largely veteran team that simply needed to be put together in the right order and receive the proper encouragement, something Torre could provide as the avuncular alternative to the overly intense Buck Showalter. That's no slight of Torre either; there have been many managers who were too obtuse to win even when the organization served up a winning team on a silver platter. Torre knew how to use what he had if he had it, but he was not a builder.

This is what differentiates Torre from his National League counterpart and two-time World Series rival Bobby Cox. Cox has eagerly embraced young players over the years, building a legacy of establishing newbies that stretches from Dale Murphy to Kelly Johnson and will likely continue this year with Yunel Escobar. That's not Joe Torre. When it comes to personnel, Torre isn't particularly a creative manager. Improvising and dealing with unknowns seems to unsettle the sense of stability that, at least as far as the culture of the clubhouse is concerned, is his greatest strength. This makes Torre

a dicey proposition when it comes to establishing young talent, as the prospect-rich Dodgers are about to find out. His greatest weakness, however, is an inability to trust young pitchers.

Torre leaves the Yankees having presided over the emergence of just two pitchers of lasting impact, Mariano Rivera (whose potential as a reliever had been made clear in the 1995 American League Division Series under Showalter) and Chien-Ming Wang. The names of two middle relievers, Ramiro Mendoza and Scott Proctor, can also be inscribed on Torre's monument, and if one wants to bend far backward, so can those of Cuban veterans Orlando Hernandez and Jose Contreras. That's a notably short list for twelve years' residency. True, the Yankees were not exactly flooding Torre's inbox with high-quality pitching prospects, but of the few worthwhile young hurlers who did pass under Torre's nose, just as many were passed over only to find success elsewhere, including Ted Lilly, Jake Westbrook, Joe Borowski, and Jim Mecir. This failure to establish young pitchers stretches over Torre's entire 26-year career as a major league manager with the Mets, Braves, Cardinals, and Yankees. Reaching all the way back to 1977, the only significant names that can be added to those above are Jeff Reardon, Neil Allen, and Steve Bedrosian. Even the best young pitchers have a very high attrition rate, but his is a very small list for a quarter century of managing, and it's unevenly skewed toward relief pitchers and the early 1990s Cardinals.

Torre's track record made him a problematic manager for the forthcoming youth movement in the Bronx. Neither the front office nor the pitchers themselves could ever be certain of his commitment to Phil Hughes, Joba Chamberlain, and Ian Kennedy as starters, but they could be certain that any young pitchers who were force-fed to the bullpen would either be burned out in a matter of weeks or, more likely, ignored completely. Enter Joe Girardi, who now becomes the mentor to *Yankees: The Next Generation*.

Girardi comes to the Yankees a year removed from winning the NL Manager of the Year Award for skippering a very young Florida Marlins team to an unlikely, and ultimately ill-fated, run at contention. Given his experience with both that team and his relative proximity to his days handling young pitchers from 60 feet away, Girardi is expected to have a far more nurturing approach than his former skipper. While his Marlins year contained some rough patches when it came to handling that young staff (particularly an inexplicable incident in which he brought 22-year-old Josh Johnson back into a game after a long rain delay), Girardi has gone out of his way this winter to say that he's learned from his errors, emphasizing that his pitchers will have their confidence bolstered and their workloads carefully monitored.

Yet even if Girardi does succeed in making Hughes and pals the first great homegrown pitching trio in Yankees history, the mission will only be half done. The roster of position players is rapidly aging, and with few intriguing players on the farm, the team risks finding itself in a similar position to that of the San Francisco Giants last year, having a roster bifurcated between position players in their mid- to late 30s and pitchers in their early 20s. In spite of their newfound emphasis on the farm, the Yankees still haven't learned how to draft and educate hitters and fielders. Perhaps that will come next. If not, the Carl Pavano of the upcoming offseason may carry a bat.

HITTERS

Bobby Abreu   RF

Bats: L   Throws: R   Height: 6' 0"   Weight: 210   Born: March 11, 1974   Age: 34

YEAR	TEAM	LVL	AGE	PA	R	2B	3B	HR	RBI	BB	SO	SB	CS	EqBRR	AVG	OBP	SLG	MLVr	EqAVG	EqOBP	EqSLG	EqA	VORP	DEFENSE
2005	PHI	MLB	31	719	104	37	1	24	102	117	134	31	9	-1.8	.286	.405	.474	.212	.276	.398	.468	.303	47.1	154-RF -17
2006	PHI	MLB	32	438	61	25	2	8	65	91	86	20	4	3.8	.277	.427	.434	.167	.270	.424	.421	.308	25.5	95-RF -5
2006	NYA	MLB	32	248	37	16	0	7	42	33	52	10	2	1.5	.330	.419	.507	.298	.330	.427	.515	.326	23.5	50-RF 2
2007	NYA	MLB	33	699	123	40	5	16	101	84	115	25	8	0.1	.283	.369	.445	.102	.288	.381	.473	.295	27.9	149-RF -2
2008	NYA	MLB	34	581	91	28	3	15	69	81	105	18	6	1.2	.276	.378	.435	.082	.276	.382	.454	.298	19.0	136-RF -6

Breakout: 11% Improve: 36% Collapse: 22% Attrition: 13%   Comparables: Carl Yastrzemski, Kenny Lofton, Brian Giles, Enos Slaughter

Abreu endured a miserable first two months last season. The lingering effects of the strained oblique muscle that sidelined him in spring training might have played a part, but that doesn't account for the way he lost control of the strike zone in May, walking just once in 81 plate appearances from April 28 to May 19 despite a career rate of 6.3 PA/BB. By the end of that month, Abreu was hitting .228/.313/.289 with just two home runs. He turned things around thereafter, batting .309/.396/.520 with 14 homers after May 31 and convincing the Yankees to pick up his 2008 option. Still, Abreu registered the lowest full-season on-base and slugging percentages of his career and managed just one home run off a left-handed pitcher all year. As a defender, he goes back on the ball with all the enthusiasm of a Roman convict being herded toward the lions' den. Given the thin winter market, re-upping Abreu was the right thing to do, but next winter's bidders might want to think of him as a platoon DH rather than a starting right fielder.

Wilson Betemit   INF

Bats: S   Throws: R   Height: 6' 3"   Weight: 230   Born: November 2, 1981   Age: 26

YEAR	TEAM	LVL	AGE	PA	R	2B	3B	HR	RBI	BB	SO	SB	CS	EqBRR	AVG	OBP	SLG	MLVr	EqAVG	EqOBP	EqSLG	EqA	VORP	DEFENSE	
2005	ATL	MLB	23	274	36	12	4	4	20	22	55	1	3	-1.1	.305	.359	.435	.113	.300	.357	.441	.272	12.0	48-3B -6	15-SS -1
2006	ATL	MLB	24	219	30	16	0	9	29	19	57	2	1	-0.3	.281	.344	.497	.136	.281	.347	.492	.283	12.4	23-3B 0	10-SS 0
2006	LAN	MLB	24	193	19	7	0	9	24	17	45	1	0	-1.6	.241	.306	.437	-.056	.237	.306	.422	.252	0.5	44-3B -5	
2007	LAN	MLB	25	192	22	8	0	10	26	32	49	0	0	-0.8	.231	.359	.474	.084	.226	.359	.477	.288	7.9	39-3B -5	
2007	NYA	MLB	25	92	11	4	0	4	24	6	33	0	0	0.1	.226	.278	.417	-.139	.229	.289	.446	.249	-0.7		
2008	NYA	MLB	26	265	31	13	1	9	36	27	69	2	1	-0.2	.255	.333	.437	-.006	.256	.336	.456	.275	8.5	65-3B -1	

Breakout: 18% Improve: 49% Collapse: 20% Attrition: 25%   Comparables: Ron Jackson, Bob Chance, Mike Epstein, Russ Morman

Wilson Betemit might have been more aptly named Wilson Betamax. Like that 1970s technology, Betemit is a potentially useful appliance that has failed to find acceptance in the marketplace. This is partially due to his having been stuck behind better or more expensive players—specifically Chipper Jones, Nomar Garciaparra, and Alex Rodriguez—but also in part because of his limitations. He's a switch-hitter who doesn't hit switched (.232/.281/.353 career batting righty) and can play all over the field, but doesn't excel anywhere. If you're in need of a platoon solution to keep you above replacement level at one of the infield corners, he's quite valuable, as his lefty swing has a bit of pop (career .268/.347/.464, 22.6 AB/HR). As a reserve, he's the sort of luxury the Yankees have tried to win without this decade. Given their situation at first base, it's good that they've given in.

Melky Cabrera   CF

Bats: S   Throws: L   Height: 5' 11"   Weight: 200   Born: August 11, 1984   Age: 23

YEAR	TEAM	LVL	AGE	PA	R	2B	3B	HR	RBI	BB	SO	SB	CS	EqBRR	AVG	OBP	SLG	MLVr	EqAVG	EqOBP	EqSLG	EqA	VORP	DEFENSE	
2005	TRN	AA	20	464	57	22	3	10	60	28	72	11	2	1.5	.275	.322	.411	.052	.245	.291	.366	.231	-8.5	103-CF	12
2005	COH	AAA	20	112	15	3	0	3	17	9	15	2	0	1.3	.248	.309	.366	-.122	.225	.288	.333	.221	-3.9	14-CF	1
2006	COH	AAA	21	135	19	6	2	4	24	10	9	3	1	-0.3	.385	.430	.566	.525	.361	.407	.566	.326	19.8	27-CF	-3
2006	NYA	MLB	21	525	75	26	2	7	50	56	60	12	5	2.0	.280	.360	.390	-.013	.281	.369	.398	.272	7.8	112-LF	5
2007	NYA	MLB	22	612	66	24	8	8	73	43	68	13	5	0.2	.273	.327	.391	-.055	.279	.337	.414	.263	9.8	120-CF 15 16-LF 0	
2008	NYA	MLB	23	573	75	26	4	10	61	44	70	14	5	1.0	.283	.342	.404	-.013	.284	.345	.422	.273	14.0	134-CF	6

Breakout: 36% Improve: 57% Collapse: 17% Attrition: 10%   Comparables: Carlos Beltran, Coco Crisp, Pete Rose, Brian McRae

Cabrera's season was shaped like a camel, low on both ends with a hump in the middle. In April and May, he batted .224/.284/.306. From June through August, he hit .325/.375/.482. That production, combined with Cabrera's defense—which features just average range for a center fielder, but a terrific throwing arm—seemed to herald the arrival of a major new talent. Then came September. For the second year in a row, Cabrera's bat went into hibernation on Labor Day. He hit .180/.236/.220 in the final month. The aggregate is still a bit soft for a starting center fielder, and while it's apparent that Cabrera has the ability to be greater than that, whether he will find the consistency required is more a matter of faith than science.

Robinson Cano   2B

Bats: L   Throws: R   Height: 6' 0"   Weight: 205   Born: October 22, 1982   Age: 25

YEAR	TEAM	LVL	AGE	PA	R	2B	3B	HR	RBI	BB	SO	SB	CS	EqBRR	AVG	OBP	SLG	MLVr	EqAVG	EqOBP	EqSLG	EqA	VORP	DEFENSE	
2005	COH	AAA	22	114	19	8	3	4	24	6	13	0	0	1.5	.333	.368	.574	.351	.306	.342	.519	.287	10.0	21-2B	1
2005	NYA	MLB	22	551	78	34	4	14	62	16	68	1	3	-0.9	.297	.320	.458	.058	.305	.338	.479	.275	21.6	129-2B	-2
2006	NYA	MLB	23	508	62	41	1	15	78	18	54	5	2	-3.3	.342	.365	.525	.252	.342	.371	.535	.303	49.1	113-2B	14
2007	NYA	MLB	24	669	93	41	7	19	97	39	85	4	5	-2.2	.306	.353	.488	.158	.310	.361	.514	.292	40.5	157-2B	28
2008	NYA	MLB	25	613	78	36	3	15	82	33	77	6	3	-0.1	.299	.340	.455	.066	.299	.344	.475	.282	31.1	143-2B	9

Breakout: 10% Improve: 37% Collapse: 29% Attrition: 5%   Comparables: Carlos Baerga, George Brett, Chris Brown, Al Oliver

In all three of his major league seasons, Cano has hit far better after the All-Star break than before. His career pre-break rates are .295/.327/.440; after the break, he's hit .330/.361/.508. If he ever gets hot early, he'll win a batting title. That inconsistency is the only complaint about Cano, and it exists because he doesn't walk much. Without walks, there are no saving graces when he slumps, just outs. That said, he's still in the uphill phase of his career, and 2007 brought improvements both in selectivity, as he saw fractionally more pitchers per pate appearance, and in the field, where he has improved to the point that he can fairly be called underrated. Someday, when discussing the best keystone men in the history of the Yankees, we may mention Cano along with Tony Lazzeri and Joe Gordon.

Francisco Cervelli   C

Bats: R   Throws: R   Height: 6' 1"   Weight: 170   Born: March 6, 1986   Age: 22

YEAR	TEAM	LVL	AGE	PA	R	2B	3B	HR	RBI	BB	SO	SB	CS	EqBRR	AVG	OBP	SLG	MLVr	EqAVG	EqOBP	EqSLG	EqA	VORP	DEFENSE	
2006	STA	A-	20	157	21	10	0	2	16	13	30	0	0	-0.6	.309	.397	.426	.339	.238	.306	.343	.230	-3.9	36-C	0
2007	TAM	A+	21	348	34	24	2	2	32	36	59	4	3	-3.8	.279	.387	.397	.117	.239	.328	.355	.242	1.0	88-C	8
2008	NYA	MLB	22	348	31	19	1	5	35	26	79	3	2	-0.6	.235	.304	.347	-.184	.235	.308	.362	.239	-1.3	84-C	5

Breakout: 27% Improve: 55% Collapse: 22% Attrition: 15%   Comparables: Omar Fuentes, Max Ramirez, Justin Huber, Javier Cardona

An unheralded signing out of Venezuela from 2003, Cervelli started 2007 hot, but cooled rapidly after May. He has doubles power, some sense of the strike zone, and is apparently fearless as he's been hit by 24 pitches in 155 career games. Solid on defense, Cervelli will be a starter rather than a career backup if he can develop a little more home run power.

Colin Curtis   OF

Bats: L   Throws: L   Height: 6' 0"   Weight: 190   Born: February 1, 1985   Age: 23

YEAR	TEAM	LVL	AGE	PA	R	2B	3B	HR	RBI	BB	SO	SB	CS	EqBRR	AVG	OBP	SLG	MLVr	EqAVG	EqOBP	EqSLG	EqA	VORP	DEFENSE	
2006	STA	A-	21	177	25	9	2	1	18	12	19	4	5	-3.1	.302	.362	.403	.259	.256	.301	.354	.225	-5.3	41-CF	-4
2007	TAM	A+	22	281	37	9	2	5	26	29	43	4	4	-3.3	.298	.378	.412	.137	.256	.330	.360	.242	-6.7	45-LF	1
2007	TRN	AA	22	262	32	10	1	3	15	17	47	1	1	1.3	.242	.298	.329	-.142	.218	.267	.300	.197	-22.9	54-LF	5
2008	NYA	MLB	23	624	62	31	3	8	60	43	122	8	6	0.6	.245	.301	.353	-.177	.245	.304	.368	.237	-14.1	146-LF	0

Breakout: 47% Improve: 71% Collapse: 14% Attrition: 5%   Comparables: Shane Costa, Mike Darr, Richard Brown, Andre Ethier

Though it's a lovely place to see a ballgame, Trenton is where Yankee hitting prospects go to die. The cold wind off the Delaware River retards hitting and aids pitchers. That helps account for Curtis's drop-off upon reaching Double-A, but it doesn't necessarily restore his status as a prospect. A fourth-round pick in 2006, Curtis is the kind of polished college product who is what he is without much room for development. What he is right now is a fourth outfielder, as he may not have the range to play center and may not hit with enough thump to justify a corner spot.

Johnny Damon — OF

Bats: L   Throws: L   Height: 6' 2"   Weight: 205   Born: November 5, 1973   Age: 34

YEAR	TEAM	LVL	AGE	PA	R	2B	3B	HR	RBI	BB	SO	SB	CS	EqBRR	AVG	OBP	SLG	MLVr	EqAVG	EqOBP	EqSLG	EqA	VORP	DEFENSE			
2005	BOS	MLB	31	688	117	35	6	10	75	53	69	18	1	5.2	.316	.366	.439	.112	.316	.376	.450	.293	40.4	139-CF	6		
2006	NYA	MLB	32	671	115	35	5	24	80	67	85	25	10	5.6	.285	.359	.482	.118	.287	.368	.498	.293	42.3	122-CF	-14		
2007	NYA	MLB	33	605	93	27	2	12	63	66	79	27	3	7.0	.270	.351	.396	-.007	.275	.362	.415	.279	17.8	42-CF	4	30-LF	0
2008	NYA	MLB	34	534	76	25	3	11	59	55	69	15	4	1.8	.278	.355	.417	.023	.278	.359	.436	.283	17.3	126-CF	-3		

Breakout: 15%   Improve: 42%   Collapse: 23%   Attrition: 19%   Comparables: Kenny Lofton, Ken Griffey, Enos Slaughter, Andy Van Slyke

Damon illustrates the hazard of relying on players who are only moderately powerful and moderately patient, but goose their numbers by hitting for a good average: batting averages fluctuate. We've seen this kind of off-year from Damon before in 2001 and 2003, but the temptation here is to interpret 2007's malaise as the manifestation of transient injuries rather than age or the player's historic inconsistency. Indeed, Damon hit .296/.364/.450 in the second half after getting some love from his chiropractor, a body-saving move to left field (a pre-chiropractic stint as the team's primary DH paid no dividends), and a few extra days off. Damon still has his speed and, despite his lack of arm, is a better defensive left fielder than Hideki Matsui, but he's signed through 2009, which puts the Yankees in a bit of a bind. Melky Cabrera is the future in center, and anything less than Damon's best hitting won't be of much benefit in left or at DH. The moral of the story is that giving four-year contracts to 32-year-olds without good secondary skills is rarely a good idea.

Shelley Duncan — 1B/OF

Bats: R   Throws: R   Height: 6' 5"   Weight: 215   Born: September 29, 1979   Age: 28

YEAR	TEAM	LVL	AGE	PA	R	2B	3B	HR	RBI	BB	SO	SB	CS	EqBRR	AVG	OBP	SLG	MLVr	EqAVG	EqOBP	EqSLG	EqA	VORP	DEFENSE			
2005	TRN	AA	25	606	86	28	2	34	92	56	140	3	2	-3.1	.240	.323	.490	.131	.215	.290	.428	.244	-11.3	136-1B	-16		
2006	TRN	AA	26	394	47	24	0	19	61	34	77	3	1	-1.1	.256	.327	.487	.184	.244	.307	.469	.263	4.5	53-1B	2	16-LF	0
2007	SWB	AAA	27	387	58	18	1	25	79	45	82	2	2	0.0	.295	.380	.577	.356	.280	.362	.569	.305	32.7	19-1B	-1	12-LF	-1
2007	NYA	MLB	27	83	16	1	0	7	17	8	20	0	0	-0.2	.257	.329	.554	.165	.260	.341	.575	.298	4.4				
2008	NYA	MLB	28	460	51	19	1	21	70	39	112	3	1	-0.5	.239	.309	.439	-.054	.239	.312	.459	.266	3.1	109-1B	-3		

Breakout: 12%   Improve: 32%   Collapse: 29%   Attrition: 22%   Comparables: Nick Esasky, Ryan Ludwick, Roy Sievers, Craig Wilson

This 2001 second-rounder always had power, but his low batting averages seemed to preclude big-league effectiveness. Enjoying his best minor league season with Triple-A Scranton last year, Duncan was called up in late July in a desperate attempt to inject some life into the Yankees' moribund DH situation. He blasted three home runs in his first five games, becoming an instant fan favorite for his bruising, maniacal celebrations. Nonetheless, Joe Torre quickly relegated him to the bench. As a regular, Duncan might hit like a poor man's Steve Balboni, with a lot of strikeouts and a troubling platoon split (last year he batted .303/.378/.606 against southpaws, but just .220/.289/.512 against righties, albeit in a small sample). Still, he could be a much-needed lefty-killer in the Yankees' first base/DH rotation and an occasional platoon partner for Bobby Abreu in right field.

Brett Gardner — OF

Bats: L   Throws: L   Height: 5' 10"   Weight: 180   Born: August 24, 1983   Age: 24

YEAR	TEAM	LVL	AGE	PA	R	2B	3B	HR	RBI	BB	SO	SB	CS	EqBRR	AVG	OBP	SLG	MLVr	EqAVG	EqOBP	EqSLG	EqA	VORP	DEFENSE			
2005	STA	A-	21	335	62	9	1	5	32	39	49	19	3	5.7	.284	.377	.376	.175	.221	.288	.274	.209	-35.7	67-CF	4		
2006	TAM	A+	22	278	46	12	5	0	22	43	51	30	7	6.5	.323	.433	.418	.270	.255	.357	.351	.262	3.7	48-CF	2	12-LF	1
2006	TRN	AA	22	251	41	4	3	0	13	27	39	28	5	4.0	.272	.352	.318	.014	.253	.327	.294	.243	-6.2	51-CF	2		
2007	TRN	AA	23	241	43	14	5	0	17	33	32	18	4	2.9	.300	.392	.419	.179	.271	.354	.391	.271	7.0	50-CF	0		
2007	SWB	AAA	23	207	37	4	3	1	9	21	43	21	3	4.7	.260	.343	.331	-.054	.239	.317	.315	.242	-5.1	42-CF	8		
2008	NYA	MLB	24	483	58	17	4	3	31	44	100	25	7	2.4	.239	.312	.316	-.209	.239	.315	.330	.242	-6.7	114-CF	1		

Breakout: 21%   Improve: 38%   Collapse: 34%   Attrition: 16%   Comparables: Michael Bourn, Michael Basse, Mike Curry, Scott Sollmann

Gardner has some things going for him—excellent speed, good range in the outfield, some patience, and the ability to hit for a respectable average. The thing that will keep him on a major league bench as opposed to the starting lineup is a complete, total, absolute lack of power. This is a guy who managed an isolated power of .037 *in the Arizona Fall League.* You can't get much more powerless than that—it's like failing to hit home runs in zero gravity. If Gardner suddenly shows the ability to hit .330, it might change things, but his best hope right now is to have a general manager fall in love with him the way Ed Wade fell in love with Michael Bourn, a not dissimilar player. As Kevin Goldstein said last year, "Twenty years ago, Brett Gardner would have been the next Rudy Law. No one wants the next Rudy Law anymore."

Jason Giambi DH

Bats: L   Throws: R   Height: 6' 3"   Weight: 235   Born: January 8, 1971   Age: 37

YEAR	TEAM	LVL	AGE	PA	R	2B	3B	HR	RBI	BB	SO	SB	CS	EqBRR	AVG	OBP	SLG	MLVr	EqAVG	EqOBP	EqSLG	EqA	VORP	DEFENSE	
2005	NYA	MLB	34	545	74	14	0	32	87	108	109	0	0	-0.5	.271	.440	.535	.330	.280	.455	.569	.346	50.7	63-1B	-9
2006	NYA	MLB	35	579	92	25	0	37	113	110	106	2	0	-6.0	.253	.413	.558	.281	.250	.418	.564	.329	47.4	54-1B	-10
2007	NYA	MLB	36	303	31	8	0	14	39	40	66	1	0	-3.5	.236	.356	.433	.028	.238	.363	.452	.283	7.3	14-1B	-3
2008	NYA	MLB	37	300	40	10	0	15	44	46	67	2	1	-1.0	.235	.363	.453	.049	.235	.367	.473	.293	11.0	73-DH	

Breakout: 6%   Improve: 28%   Collapse: 48%   Attrition: 29%   Comparables: Frank Thomas, Willie McCovey, Jose Canseco, Cliff Johnson

Giambi had a good April, but was quickly handicapped by bone spurs in his left heel. No sooner did orthotics ease his pain than he popped the plantar fascia in the foot while jogging the bases after a home run in Toronto in late May. Out of the lineup until August, Giambi went on a short-lived tear after coming off the DL, but quickly went so cold that polar bears took refuge in his boxer-briefs. From May 1 until the end of the season, Giambi batted .192/.333/.389. For this performance, Giambi earned a cool $21 million, the same amount the Yankees will pay him in 2008 before the inevitable buyout of his 2009 option (at a cost of $5 million). Given their outfield/DH logjam, the Yankees have to hope that the former MVP can mount a comeback while playing first base, something that seems unlikely given that he fields with all the agility of a mastodon drowning in the La Brea Tar Pits. Giambi was an underrated contributor in 2005 and 2006, but it remains to be seen if he can get all his parts moving in the same direction again.

Mitchell Hilligoss 3B

Bats: L   Throws: R   Height: 6' 1"   Weight: 195   Born: June 17, 1985   Age: 23

YEAR	TEAM	LVL	AGE	PA	R	2B	3B	HR	RBI	BB	SO	SB	CS	EqBRR	AVG	OBP	SLG	MLVr	EqAVG	EqOBP	EqSLG	EqA	VORP	DEFENSE			
2006	STA	A-	21	297	40	8	1	2	36	24	47	12	2	1.9	.292	.357	.352	.180	.244	.296	.302	.216	-18.0	35-3B	5	30-SS	1
2007	CSC	A	22	559	83	35	4	4	53	33	65	35	7	8.9	.310	.352	.415	.127	.255	.290	.338	.224	-11.0	98-3B	10	20-SS	1
2008	NYA	MLB	23	603	60	28	3	4	49	34	109	16	6	1.3	.248	.292	.326	-.226	.248	.295	.341	.228	-12.2	141-3B	10		

Breakout: 33%   Improve: 61%   Collapse: 19%   Attrition: 8%   Comparables: Kevin Howard, Fernando Cortez, Tim Flannelly, Sean Gamble

Hilligoss briefly became a boldface name last summer when he hit in 38 straight games, a Sally League record. Unfortunately, it doesn't signify much. A contact hitter who can hit doubles and singles in his sleep, Hilligoss lacks the power or patience to carry third base, as his six home runs in 789 professional at-bats suggest. Were he a second baseman or a shortstop, as he was in college, he'd be a more intriguing prospect. For now, he's just a guy who had a nice year in the low minors, and who will have to add a new wrinkle if he wants to be more.

Austin Jackson OF

Bats: R   Throws: R   Height: 6' 1"   Weight: 185   Born: February 1, 1987   Age: 21

YEAR	TEAM	LVL	AGE	PA	R	2B	3B	HR	RBI	BB	SO	SB	CS	EqBRR	AVG	OBP	SLG	MLVr	EqAVG	EqOBP	EqSLG	EqA	VORP	DEFENSE	
2006	CSC	A	19	611	90	24	5	4	47	61	151	37	12	4.6	.260	.340	.346	.007	.205	.269	.277	.198	-43.8	125-CF	-14
2007	CSC	A	20	266	33	16	1	3	25	24	59	19	6	-1.0	.260	.336	.374	.004	.210	.271	.300	.205	-16.4	56-CF	-1
2007	TAM	A+	20	284	53	15	6	10	34	22	48	13	5	0.9	.345	.398	.566	.414	.299	.349	.510	.288	23.1	63-CF	7
2008	NYA	MLB	21	629	68	31	4	11	59	45	159	20	8	1.7	.235	.294	.363	-.182	.235	.297	.379	.242	-7.3	147-CF	0

Breakout: 44%   Improve: 74%   Collapse: 8%   Attrition: 5%   Comparables: Pat Bryant, Dwight Maness, Cody Ross, Charlie Fermaint

Jackson was just plodding along last year in his third professional season when Charleston hitting coach Greg Colbrunn completely overhauled his swing. Colbrunn helped Jackson adopt a more open stance, so he wasn't a one-eyed hitter, as well as shorten his swing so his bat had a quicker trip through the zone. Promoted to High-A Tampa after the fix, Austin became Action Jackson, the hard work paying off in a dominating half-season in which he hit more home runs at Tampa than he had in his previous 918 professional at-bats. Jackson will have to show that his great leap forward was something more than a fluke, but the boost in power suggests that what he showed after his promotion was the result of more than a few extra singles falling in (a suggestion supported by his Hawaiian Winter Baseball ISO of .218). If he can keep this up at higher levels, questions about whether his bat will play in a corner should he fail to master center field will become moot.

Derek Jeter — SS

Bats: R   Throws: R   Height: 6' 3"   Weight: 195   Born: June 26, 1974   Age: 34

YEAR	TEAM	LVL	AGE	PA	R	2B	3B	HR	RBI	BB	SO	SB	CS	EqBRR	AVG	OBP	SLG	MLVr	EqAVG	EqOBP	EqSLG	EqA	VORP	DEFENSE	
2005	NYA	MLB	31	752	122	25	5	19	70	77	117	14	5	0.7	.309	.389	.450	.173	.318	.407	.474	.305	59.6	153-SS	11
2006	NYA	MLB	32	715	118	39	3	14	97	69	102	34	5	1.2	.343	.417	.483	.276	.344	.424	.492	.320	80.5	145-SS	7
2007	NYA	MLB	33	714	102	39	4	12	73	56	100	15	8	2.4	.322	.388	.452	.180	.329	.398	.477	.300	53.3	147-SS	-5
2008	NYA	MLB	34	637	89	30	3	8	64	55	94	13	4	0.5	.297	.365	.407	.040	.298	.369	.425	.283	31.7	149-SS	-4

Breakout: 1%   Improve: 15%   Collapse: 44%   Attrition: 11%   Comparables: Julio Franco, Dick Groat, Paul Molitor, Mark Loretta

On the surface, it was another typical Jeter season, with rates right on his career marks. However, while he never went on the DL or sat out more than one game in a row, the strain of playing every day seemed to tell a little more than it did when he was younger. Particularly troublesome was a sore right knee that struck in August, dramatically slowing Jeter on defense and weakening his ability to drive the ball. While Jeter never hit less than .301 in any month, he became more of a singles hitter, grounded into a career high in double plays, and was caught stealing more often while stealing fewer bases. It says something when even the Gold Glove voters, who confer something like tenure on anointed winners, notice that you look like you're carrying a piano on your back when going after grounders and give the award to someone else. For years, Jeter's offense has made him a net positive at shortstop despite his defense. The second half of 2007, taken together with his age, suggests that the day of reckoning has finally arrived.

Hideki Matsui — LF

Bats: L   Throws: R   Height: 6' 2"   Weight: 230   Born: June 12, 1974   Age: 34

YEAR	TEAM	LVL	AGE	PA	R	2B	3B	HR	RBI	BB	SO	SB	CS	EqBRR	AVG	OBP	SLG	MLVr	EqAVG	EqOBP	EqSLG	EqA	VORP	DEFENSE			
2005	NYA	MLB	31	703	108	45	3	23	116	63	78	2	2	0.9	.305	.367	.496	.196	.312	.383	.523	.306	43.8	111-LF	1	25-CF	-4
2006	NYA	MLB	32	201	32	9	0	8	29	27	23	1	0	-0.5	.302	.393	.494	.208	.300	.398	.494	.308	13.3	32-LF	5		
2007	NYA	MLB	33	633	100	28	4	25	103	73	73	4	2	2.3	.285	.367	.488	.160	.288	.375	.516	.302	32.4	109-LF	-9		
2008	NYA	MLB	34	561	79	28	2	18	83	63	67	4	2	0.1	.286	.367	.465	.111	.287	.371	.485	.297	23.7	132-LF	-7		

Breakout: 10%   Improve: 39%   Collapse: 26%   Attrition: 10%   Comparables: Ryan Klesko, Larry Walker, Paul O'Neill, Cliff Floyd

It was a wildly streaky season for Matsui, who was hampered by injuries in both April (hamstring) and September (knee) and ice cold in both months as a result. In between he hit .309/.370/.526, though still mixing torrid spells with periods of pointlessness. In spite of the roller-coaster highs and lows, the end result was still within a hairs-breadth of Matsui's typical numbers—even at his most inconsistent, he's consistent. Between Damon's availability to play left and Matsui's right knee (which underwent arthroscopic surgery over the winter), Matsui will enter the season as the primary DH. That's not a bad thing; Matsui is a fundamentally sound outfielder with a decent arm and quick release, but the rag-armed Damon has much better range and is less likely to take a wrong turn on his way to the ball. There were rumors over the offseason of the Yankees asking Matsui to waive his no-trade clause so as to ease their outfield/DH logjam. While they would do well to reduce the age of their roster, a return to form by Damon is less likely than more of the same from Matsui.

Doug Mientkiewicz — 1B

Bats: L   Throws: R   Height: 6' 2"   Weight: 205   Born: June 19, 1974   Age: 34

YEAR	TEAM	LVL	AGE	PA	R	2B	3B	HR	RBI	BB	SO	SB	CS	EqBRR	AVG	OBP	SLG	MLVr	EqAVG	EqOBP	EqSLG	EqA	VORP	DEFENSE	
2005	NYN	MLB	31	313	36	13	0	11	29	32	39	0	1	-0.2	.240	.322	.407	-.033	.236	.321	.411	.253	-0.0	76-1B	-5
2006	KCA	MLB	32	360	37	24	2	4	43	35	50	3	0	-1.2	.283	.359	.411	.005	.284	.368	.419	.280	6.2	82-1B	-6
2007	NYA	MLB	33	192	26	12	0	5	24	16	23	0	0	-0.3	.277	.349	.440	.057	.279	.358	.455	.280	5.8	51-1B	1
2008	NYA	MLB	34	219	24	12	1	5	28	22	30	1	0	-0.4	.260	.338	.400	-.041	.260	.342	.417	.269	1.9	55-1B	-2

Breakout: 22%   Improve: 42%   Collapse: 35%   Attrition: 34%   Comparables: Sid Bream, Greg Brock, Matt Franco, Willard Marshall

The Great Mientkiewicz, who has been dining out on his 2001 Gold Glove like Tommy Tutone on Jenny's phone number, was batting .226/.292/.379 on June 2 when a collision with Mike Lowell broke his wrist and put him on the shelf until September. When he returned, he batted .429/.510/.619 in 51 plate appearances, giving his overall numbers a frisson of respectability and earning his way into the lineup for the playoffs in which he went hitless. A free agent at this writing, Minky's future, if any, should be limited to a Dave Bergman–esque 90 games as a defensive sub and spot starter for a team with an unusually capacious bench.

Juan Miranda — 1B

Bats: L Throws: L Height: 6' 0" Weight: 220 Born: April 25, 1983 Age: 25

YEAR	TEAM	LVL	AGE	PA	R	2B	3B	HR	RBI	BB	SO	SB	CS	EqBRR	AVG	OBP	SLG	MLVr	EqAVG	EqOBP	EqSLG	EqA	VORP	DEFENSE	
2007	TAM	A+	24	293	35	17	3	9	50	29	60	1	0	-2.0	.264	.348	.464	.134	.230	.304	.409	.249	-4.6	66-1B	-3
2007	TRN	AA	24	227	29	17	2	7	46	23	46	0	1	0.1	.265	.352	.480	.170	.239	.316	.443	.259	1.1	28-1B	-5
2008	NYA	MLB	25	564	59	32	3	16	76	47	142	3	3	-0.2	.237	.306	.407	-.102	.237	.309	.425	.256	-4.2	132-1B	-3

Breakout: 31% Improve: 65% Collapse: 19% Attrition: 8% Comparables: Nick Delvecchio, Tony Derosso, Luis Antonio Jimenez, Karim Garcia

Cuban defector Miranda's not much of a prospect, but he takes a spot here because New York's first base situation is as wide-open as it was on May 2, 1939, the day Lou Gehrig asked out of the lineup. Anyone short of Gehrig might get a shot at playing time there this year. There's an old joke about a guy who borrowed a friend's car and then wrecked it. "Where did you park my car?" the owner says. "Between Fifth and Eighth," comes the answer. "*Where* between Fifth and Eighth?" "*All the way* between Fifth and Eighth." Miranda's age is all the way between 24 and 26, and the smart money is on the latter. Any age in that range suggests little in the way of further development. That's unfortunate because, though Miranda has some home-run pop, he has limited patience and needs to be platooned. Move along; nothing to see here.

Jose Molina — C

Bats: R Throws: R Height: 6' 2" Weight: 245 Born: June 3, 1975 Age: 33

YEAR	TEAM	LVL	AGE	PA	R	2B	3B	HR	RBI	BB	SO	SB	CS	EqBRR	AVG	OBP	SLG	MLVr	EqAVG	EqOBP	EqSLG	EqA	VORP	DEFENSE	
2005	ANA	MLB	30	203	14	4	0	6	25	13	41	2	0	0.0	.228	.286	.348	-.200	.232	.302	.365	.236	-1.2	53-C	12
2006	ANA	MLB	31	245	18	17	0	4	22	9	49	1	0	-1.4	.240	.273	.369	-.234	.239	.278	.374	.228	-4.8	67-C	8
2007	ANA	MLB	32	131	9	8	0	0	10	3	30	2	1	-1.0	.224	.242	.288	-.388	.226	.250	.290	.186	-6.6	37-C	1
2007	NYA	MLB	32	71	9	5	0	1	9	2	13	0	0	-1.1	.318	.333	.439	.072	.318	.333	.470	.274	3.9	19-C	3
2008	NYA	MLB	33	170	14	8	0	3	18	9	36	2	1	-0.5	.240	.284	.346	-.218	.240	.288	.361	.229	-1.0	44-C	3

Breakout: 35% Improve: 50% Collapse: 37% Attrition: 45% Comparables: Javy Lopez, Mike Difelice, Bob Melvin, Ebba St. Claire

Molina's struggles with Anaheim over the first half of the season stretched even Mike Scioscia's tolerance for this good-field, no-hit catcher. The Yankees found that one team's trash is another's treasure given their lack of even a replacement-level backup for Jorge Posada. In other words, Mike Napoli is to Jose Molina as Jose Molina is to Wil Nieves. Molina even had a nice small-sample hot streak after arriving in New York. Re-signed to a two-year deal, Molina is an acceptable backup given the very limited population of quality reserves at his position.

Jesus Montero — C

Bats: R Throws: R Height: 6' 4" Weight: 225 Born: November 28, 1989 Age: 18

YEAR	TEAM	LVL	AGE	PA	R	2B	3B	HR	RBI	BB	SO	SB	CS	EqBRR	AVG	OBP	SLG	MLVr	EqAVG	EqOBP	EqSLG	EqA	VORP	DEFENSE	
2007	YAN	Rk	17	123	13	6	0	3	19	12	18	0	0	-2.4	.280	.366	.421	.147	.221	.282	.336	.216	-9.8	21-C	-5
2008	NYA	MLB	18	250	14	10	0	4	23	15	50	0	0	-0.7	.208	.260	.303	-.337	.209	.263	.316	.201	-9.7	62-C	-7

Breakout: 28% Improve: 41% Collapse: 42% Attrition: 9% Comparables: Aramis Ramirez, Tom Maleski, Adam Coe, Dmitri Young

This hulking teenager, the recipient of a $2-million signing bonus in 2006, has spectacular, Roy Hobbs shattering-the-clock power. He's also a miserable catcher, having thrown out just three of 32 attempted basestealers last year. The Yankees are still wrestling with whether he'll learn the position with time or just has no aptitude for it, but they're going to put off the decision for as long as possible so as to give Montero every chance to make it as a backstop. What's certain is that he's already huge and terrifically slow, as his seven double plays in 107 at-bats in his professional debut last year suggest. As such, his future is limited to one of three positions: catcher, first base, or ornamental fountain.

Andy Phillips — INF

Bats: R Throws: R Height: 6' 0" Weight: 210 Born: April 6, 1977 Age: 31

YEAR	TEAM	LVL	AGE	PA	R	2B	3B	HR	RBI	BB	SO	SB	CS	EqBRR	AVG	OBP	SLG	MLVr	EqAVG	EqOBP	EqSLG	EqA	VORP	DEFENSE			
2005	COH	AAA	28	340	60	14	1	22	54	36	61	2	0	2.4	.300	.379	.573	.326	.272	.350	.517	.291	27.8	28-3B	3	26-1B	1
2005	NYA	MLB	28	41	7	4	0	1	4	1	13	0	0	0.1	.150	.171	.325	-.499	.154	.195	.308	.158	-3.9				
2006	NYA	MLB	29	263	30	11	3	7	29	15	56	3	2	0.1	.240	.281	.394	-.186	.239	.289	.403	.237	-7.5	60-1B	-3		
2007	SWB	AAA	30	283	37	11	2	11	36	32	43	2	1	-0.4	.301	.382	.494	.254	.283	.360	.490	.288	22.7	30-2B	-3	16-1B	-3
2007	NYA	MLB	30	207	27	7	1	2	25	12	26	0	3	-1.9	.292	.338	.373	-.044	.299	.348	.397	.257	-0.2	48-1B	-4		
2008	CIN	MLB	31	452	55	20	2	15	59	41	77	4	2	-0.2	.264	.334	.438	-.019	.261	.331	.431	.259	9.0	107-1B	1		

Breakout: 18% Improve: 36% Collapse: 40% Attrition: 25%   Comparables: Russ Morman, Craig Worthington, Marty Cordova, John Ramos

Last year was another snake-bit season for a player whose timing is always off. Beaten out for a platoon job at first base by Josh Phelps due in part to a family emergency which shortened his spring training, Phillips was recalled in June and seemed like he might finally be establishing himself when a pitch broke his wrist, shelving him for the last month of the season. Phillips turns 31 in April; the bloom is off this late bloomer. In 519 career plate appearances (or something like a full season), Phillips has hit .253/.294/.384. The Reds signed him to a minor league deal, but the days of thinking of him as a potential starting first baseman should be over.

Jorge Posada — C

Bats: S Throws: R Height: 6' 2" Weight: 205 Born: August 17, 1971 Age: 36

YEAR	TEAM	LVL	AGE	PA	R	2B	3B	HR	RBI	BB	SO	SB	CS	EqBRR	AVG	OBP	SLG	MLVr	EqAVG	EqOBP	EqSLG	EqA	VORP	DEFENSE	
2005	NYA	MLB	33	546	67	23	0	19	71	66	94	1	0	-2.0	.262	.352	.430	.044	.266	.366	.448	.284	26.4	122-C	-3
2006	NYA	MLB	34	544	65	27	2	23	93	64	96	3	0	-5.5	.278	.375	.494	.154	.277	.381	.503	.302	38.0	118-C	9
2007	NYA	MLB	35	589	91	42	1	20	90	74	98	2	0	-7.6	.338	.426	.543	.384	.339	.433	.565	.337	73.4	124-C	-4
2008	NYA	MLB	36	525	74	28	1	19	78	66	91	4	1	-1.9	.287	.380	.479	.151	.288	.384	.500	.306	37.1	124-C	-3

Breakout: 7% Improve: 34% Collapse: 26% Attrition: 12%   Comparables: Chili Davis, J. T. Snow, Carlton Fisk, Alan Ashby

It was a superlative season, but it would be a mistake to assume it means that Posada can play forever. Think of Dwight Evans, who busted out career highs in all three rates (.305/.417/.569) as a 35-year-old in 1987, or Chili Davis, who had back-to-back .300 seasons at 34 and 35. In neither case did the player's strong age-35 showing alter their course toward obsolescence, nor the rate at which they traveled it. This very likely applies to Posada as well, but due to an imbalance of supply and demand in the backstop market, the Yankees were obligated to re-sign Podada for four years if they wanted to stay out of the Johnny Estrada aisle at Wal-Mart. If they can get two years of the four at 75 percent of Posada's 2007 value, it will be money well spent.

Alex Rodriguez — 3B

Bats: R Throws: R Height: 6' 3" Weight: 225 Born: July 27, 1975 Age: 32

YEAR	TEAM	LVL	AGE	PA	R	2B	3B	HR	RBI	BB	SO	SB	CS	EqBRR	AVG	OBP	SLG	MLVr	EqAVG	EqOBP	EqSLG	EqA	VORP	DEFENSE	
2005	NYA	MLB	29	715	124	29	1	48	130	91	139	21	6	-0.4	.321	.421	.610	.448	.331	.438	.646	.351	91.0	157-3B	-3
2006	NYA	MLB	30	674	113	26	1	35	121	90	139	15	4	-0.3	.290	.392	.523	.234	.288	.398	.531	.314	51.6	145-3B	-16
2007	NYA	MLB	31	708	143	31	0	54	156	95	120	24	4	5.2	.314	.422	.645	.489	.315	.427	.676	.354	96.6	149-3B	3
2008	NYA	MLB	32	684	120	34	2	36	116	94	130	23	4	0.4	.294	.401	.550	.280	.295	.405	.574	.333	63.3	159-3B	-2

Breakout: 7% Improve: 29% Collapse: 17% Attrition: 5%   Comparables: Frank Robinson, Mike Schmidt, Willie McCovey, George Brett

Last year was the best offensive season of Alex Rodriguez's career, narrowly eclipsing his excellent 2000 (.343 EqA) and 2005 (.351 EqA) campaigns. He not only led the majors in value over replacement with an astounding 96.6, but had the 17th best non-Bonds VORP total since 1959. The Yankees re-signed him to a ten-year contract not so much because A-Rod is going to be supplying that kind of punch at 41, but because (a) he should be plenty good for the bulk of the contract, hitting enough to carry first base if his defense wilts at the hot corner; (b) because, as with Posada, the absence of plausible alternatives on the farm and on the market forced their hand; and (c) they should make a lot of dough as Rodriguez proceeds to shatter a good number of records, including Bonds's home run mark. In pure baseball terms, the Yankees probably rooked themselves, but they won't start to regret it until Rodriguez is in his late 30s.

Damon Sublett   2B

Bats: L   **Throws:** R   **Height:** 6' 1"   **Weight:** 190   **Born:** September 22, 1985   **Age:** 22

YEAR	TEAM	LVL	AGE	PA	R	2B	3B	HR	RBI	BB	SO	SB	CS	EqBRR	AVG	OBP	SLG	MLVr	EqAVG	EqOBP	EqSLG	EqA	VORP	DEFENSE
2007	STA	A-	21	300	43	19	3	8	53	43	47	10	4	0.2	.326	.426	.531	.487	.280	.360	.449	.281	34.8	64-2B -9
2008	NYA	MLB	22	605	68	34	2	12	66	56	128	11	6	0.5	.249	.322	.391	-.088	.250	.326	.408	.261	9.6	141-2B -13

Breakout: 6%   **Improve:** 27%   **Collapse:** 39%   **Attrition:** 2%   **Comparables:** Daniel Dorn, Scott Hairston, Phil Dauphin, Joe Randa

A seventh-round pick out of Wichita State last June, Sublett is a polished hitter with a patient approach who mashed in the New York-Penn League in his pro debut; a lot of collegiate types can do that last bit, but it doesn't mean much unless they can do it again at a higher level. Offense will be key for Sublett, because he doesn't look to be much more than an average fielder. More important, Sublett won't be able to get to the majors until he can find someone to take over his lease.

Jose Tabata   OF

Bats: R   **Throws:** R   **Height:** 5' 11"   **Weight:** 160   **Born:** August 12, 1988   **Age:** 19

YEAR	TEAM	LVL	AGE	PA	R	2B	3B	HR	RBI	BB	SO	SB	CS	EqBRR	AVG	OBP	SLG	MLVr	EqAVG	EqOBP	EqSLG	EqA	VORP	DEFENSE
2005	YAN	00	16	173	30	5	1	3	25	15	14	22	6	0.6	.314	.382	.417	.194	.261	.316	.360	.244	-56.0	
2006	CSC	A	17	363	50	22	1	5	51	30	66	15	5	-0.4	.298	.377	.420	.187	.246	.303	.351	.232	-14.6	68-RF 1
2007	TAM	A+	18	456	56	16	2	5	54	33	70	15	7	-1.4	.307	.371	.392	.107	.265	.322	.348	.239	-12.8	85-RF -12
2008	NYA	MLB	19	529	51	24	2	4	42	30	101	13	6	0.4	.245	.293	.330	-.220	.246	.297	.344	.228	-18.5	125-RF 1

Breakout: 23%   **Improve:** 48%   **Collapse:** 27%   **Attrition:** 7%   **Comparables:** Rafael Alvarez, Raul Gonzalez, Ruben Cruz, Rene Capellan

Tabata has been held back by hand injuries the last two seasons, so we're not any closer to figuring out exactly what he's capable of. He seems to be able to hit for a good average, even when hurt, but power and plate judgment haven't arrived yet, and it's not clear if that's attributable to his youth, the injuries, his approach, his talent, or some combination of the above. To borrow Casey Stengel's evaluation of an earlier Yankees outfield prospect, Tabata has it in his body to be great. Until he gets healthy, we won't know for sure if his body will let that greatness out.

PITCHERS

Chris Britton

Bats: R   **Throws:** R   **Height:** 6' 3"   **Weight:** 280   **Born:** December 16, 1982   **Age:** 25

YEAR	TEAM	LVL	AGE	W	L	SV	G	GS	IP	H	BB	SO	HR	GB%	BABIP	STUFF	WHIP	ERA	PERA	EqERA	EqH9	EqBB9	EqSO9	EqHR9	VORP	SN/WX
2005	FRD	A+	22	6	0	6	46	0	78²	47	23	110	5	50.0%	.264	8	0.89	1.60	4.32	3.36	7.1	4.1	7.8	1.2	17.3	—
2006	BAL	MLB	23	0	2	1	52	0	53²	46	17	41	4	34.4%	.268	9	1.17	3.35	2.91	3.29	6.8	2.6	6.3	0.7	14.2	0.50
2007	SWB	AAA	24	4	2	8	37	0	57¹	51	14	58	3	37.9%	.310	6	1.13	2.51	3.99	3.95	8.7	2.6	6.8	0.8	10.0	—
2007	NYA	MLB	24	0	1	0	11	0	12²	9	4	5	2	33.3%	.179	-17	1.03	3.54	2.86	3.46	5.5	2.8	3.5	1.4	3.5	-0.14
2008	NYA	MLB	25	3	3	3	51	2	56	55	22	42	7	39.3%	.282	-1	1.37	4.26	4.28	4.22	8.5	3.2	6.1	1.2	8.1	0.80

Breakout: 8%   **Improve:** 30%   **Collapse:** 42%   **Attrition:** 12%   **Comparables:** Dave Borkowski, Bill Simas, Andrew Brown, Brent Stentz

Britton is young and had a useful rookie year for the O's, so when Brian Cashman acquired him for Jaret Wright, it was a major steal, getting something for an expensive corpse. It soon became apparent that the Yankees were satisfied with winning half the battle by ridding themselves of Wright, and didn't care much about making use of Britton. The rotund reliever put up good numbers at Triple-A Scranton, but failed to stick in the bigs despite the team's unsettled bullpen. Rumor had it that Britton was unpopular with Torre, that his stuff failed to impress, and that his 20-stone build was a turnoff. Whatever the reason, to paraphrase Billy Preston, nothing for nothing leaves nothing. In order to get something, the Yankees need give Britton an honest shot at this year's pen.

Brian Bruney

Bats: R   **Throws:** R   **Height:** 6' 3"   **Weight:** 245   **Born:** February 17, 1982   **Age:** 26

YEAR	TEAM	LVL	AGE	W	L	SV	G	GS	IP	H	BB	SO	HR	GB%	BABIP	STUFF	WHIP	ERA	PERA	EqERA	EqH9	EqBB9	EqSO9	EqHR9	VORP	SN/WX
2005	ARI	MLB	23	1	3	12	47	0	46	56	35	51	6	41.7%	.385	3	1.98	7.43	7.38	7.58	10.7	6.0	8.9	1.2	-10.2	-0.61
2006	NYA	MLB	24	1	1	0	19	0	20²	14	15	25	1	34.7%	.271	20	1.40	0.87	3.39	0.89	6.2	6.2	10.2	0.4	12.0	0.51
2007	NYA	MLB	25	3	2	0	58	0	50	44	37	39	5	33.6%	.285	-1	1.60	4.68	4.48	4.50	7.6	5.9	6.5	0.9	6.2	-0.23
2008	NYA	MLB	26	2	1	1	27	0	29²	27	19	27	4	38.9%	.285	0	1.54	4.60	4.67	4.55	8.0	5.1	7.3	1.1	3.9	0.30

Breakout: 40% **Improve:** 60% **Collapse:** 30% **Attrition:** 47%   **Comparables:** Jeff Jones, Francisco Cordero, Seth McClung, Bill Simas

Bruney did the Yankees a major service last year by pitching so badly in July that the team was forced to rush Joba Chamberlain up in his place. Prior to that fateful month, Bruney had pitched 33 innings for the big club with a 1.91 ERA, keeping runs off the board with his strikeouts and heavy fastball (just five of 24 hits went for extra bases). Still, he walked 23 and that wildness made the Yankees reluctant to trust him with a lead. Three weeks in the minors didn't do him any good. Assuming that his late-season struggles don't hint at a physical or psychological problem, the hard-throwing Bruney can still be an asset.

Joba Chamberlain

Bats: R   **Throws:** R   **Height:** 6' 2"   **Weight:** 230   **Born:** September 23, 1985   **Age:** 22

YEAR	TEAM	LVL	AGE	W	L	SV	G	GS	IP	H	BB	SO	HR	GB%	BABIP	STUFF	WHIP	ERA	PERA	EqERA	EqH9	EqBB9	EqSO9	EqHR9	VORP	SN/WX
2007	TAM	A+	21	4	0	0	7	7	40	25	11	51	0	62.5%	.287	35	0.90	2.03	3.75	3.82	7.6	3.8	8.2	0.3	7.0	—
2007	TRN	AA	21	4	2	0	8	7	40¹	32	15	66	4	54.2%	.364	35	1.17	3.35	6.56	5.09	10.4	4.3	11.2	1.5	2.0	—
2007	SWB	AAA	21	1	0	0	3	1	8	5	1	18	0	20.0%	.500	6	0.75	0.00	0.21	0.00	12.8	1.4	14.2	0.0	3.9	—
2007	NYA	MLB	21	2	0	1	19	0	24	12	6	34	1	38.0%	.229	24	0.71	0.38	2.11	1.12	4.5	1.9	10.1	0.4	14.0	1.85
2008	NYA	MLB	22	9	6	1	65	15	145²	126	55	162	12	45.5%	.302	26	1.24	3.39	3.33	3.40	7.5	3.0	9.1	0.7	33.7	4.10

Breakout: 5% **Improve:** 21% **Collapse:** 41% **Attrition:** 13%   **Comparables:** Tom Griffin, Dave Boswell, Curt Simmons, Roger Clemens

Chamberlain had one of the best debuts of any player in history, going 11 games and 14⅓ innings before allowing a run, and an unearned run at that. Later he became a key figure in Joe Torre's downfall when a biblical plague of midges descended on Chamberlain during Game Two of the ALDS—Torre took no action. Unnerved, Chamberlain blew the lead via wild pitches, and the manager's essential passivity was fatally exposed. It was a heady beginning for the chunky 21-year-old Nebraskan from the Winnebago tribe who had begun the season pitching for High-A Tampa. He'll now take his pinpoint high-90s stuff and amazing corkscrew slider to the starting rotation, where he'll mix in the plus curve and changeup he rarely used out of the pen. Expectations could not possibly be higher.

Roger Clemens

Bats: R   **Throws:** R   **Height:** 6' 4"   **Weight:** 235   **Born:** August 4, 1962   **Age:** 45

YEAR	TEAM	LVL	AGE	W	L	SV	G	GS	IP	H	BB	SO	HR	GB%	BABIP	STUFF	WHIP	ERA	PERA	EqERA	EqH9	EqBB9	EqSO9	EqHR9	VORP	SN/WX
2005	HOU	MLB	42	13	8	0	32	32	211¹	151	62	185	11	50.9%	.248	38	1.01	1.87	2.75	2.46	6.6	2.4	7.2	0.5	80.2	9.37
2006	HOU	MLB	43	7	6	0	19	19	113¹	89	29	102	7	50.0%	.271	39	1.04	2.30	2.87	2.66	7.2	2.0	7.5	0.5	42.1	4.84
2007	NYA	MLB	44	6	6	0	18	17	99	99	31	68	9	48.4%	.298	13	1.31	4.18	3.97	4.50	8.6	2.5	5.7	0.8	13.8	2.52
2008	NYA	MLB	45	7	6	0	19	19	107	112	44	74	12	48.0%	.299	3	1.45	4.43	4.51	4.43	9.0	3.4	5.7	1.0	12.6	2.10

Breakout: 0% **Improve:** 24% **Collapse:** 35% **Attrition:** 46%   **Comparables:** Phil Niekro, Hoyt Wilhelm, Tommy John, Nolan Ryan

The Rocket seems likely to be retired for real this time. When the Yankees lured Clemens away from his rocking chair with a pro-rated $28 million, the legend had gone 38-18 with a 2.40 ERA and 505 strikeouts in 539 innings since turning 40. The team was hoping for more age-defying excellence and, in a sense, got it; Clemens was a better-than-average starter, something of a miracle for a 44-year-old. Still, the old magic was gone. He struggled with groin and hamstring pulls and, most troublingly, a balky ligament in his pitching elbow. His heater lost still more zip, bringing his strikeouts down accordingly, and when his location and splitter weren't sharp, he had no plan B. Clemens may yet have some pitching left, but given his crumbling superstructure and high price tag, there seems little point in trying to wring any more out of him.

Tyler Clippard

Bats: R   Throws: R   Height: 6' 4"   Weight: 170   Born: February 14, 1985   Age: 23

YEAR	TEAM	LVL	AGE	W	L	SV	G	GS	IP	H	BB	SO	HR	GB%	BABIP	STUFF	WHIP	ERA	PERA	EqERA	EqH9	EqBB9	EqSO9	EqHR9	VORP	SN/WX
2005	TAM	A+	20	10	9	0	26	25	147¹	118	34	169	12	39.3%	.296	7	1.03	3.18	5.57	5.22	9.3	3.8	6.3	1.6	5.5	—
2006	TRN	AA	21	12	10	0	28	28	166	118	55	175	14	44.4%	.258	6	1.04	3.36	5.25	5.80	8.9	4.1	6.5	1.4	-3.3	—
2007	SWB	AAA	22	4	4	0	14	14	69¹	82	35	55	7	34.8%	.354	-13	1.69	4.16	7.93	6.99	11.9	5.2	5.3	1.4	-9.9	—
2007	NYA	MLB	22	3	1	0	6	6	27	29	17	18	6	39.3%	.277	-8	1.70	6.33	6.71	6.00	9.3	5.0	5.7	2.0	-1.1	0.25
2007	TRN	AA	22	2	1	0	6	6	26²	22	12	28	5	29.6%	.266	-5	1.27	5.39	8.03	8.25	9.8	4.9	7.1	2.6	-7.1	—
2008	WAS	MLB	23	5	9	0	36	22	119	128	63	86	21	38.3%	.292	-5	1.60	5.67	6.01	6.02	9.4	4.3	5.9	1.5	-3.5	0.40

Breakout: 27% Improve: 63% Collapse: 19% Attrition: 15%   Comparables: Scott Mathieson, Mike Johnson, Kevin Correia, Mike Meyers

Clippard got called up from Triple-A in May when the rotation was in disarray and beat the Mets at Shea in his major league debut while confidently stomping and snorting about on the mound. He struggled after that and was sent back down, but the worst was yet to come, as he completely lost his command, earning a further demotion to Double-A Trenton. He was only moderately better there. Command is the name of the game for Clippard, as his fastball doesn't light up radar guns. Clippard's future is very much in doubt, but he'll have more opportunity to work things out in the Nationals' system now that he's been exchanged for reliever Jonathan Albaladejo, turning the Yankee Clippard back into regular old Ty Clip.

Matt DeSalvo

Bats: R   Throws: R   Height: 6' 0"   Weight: 170   Born: September 11, 1980   Age: 27

YEAR	TEAM	LVL	AGE	W	L	SV	G	GS	IP	H	BB	SO	HR	GB%	BABIP	STUFF	WHIP	ERA	PERA	EqERA	EqH9	EqBB9	EqSO9	EqHR9	VORP	SN/WX
2005	TRN	AA	24	9	5	0	25	24	149	106	67	151	8	54.2%	.268	13	1.16	3.02	4.40	4.66	7.4	5.6	5.8	0.9	14.1	—
2006	TRN	AA	25	5	4	0	16	16	78¹	80	59	52	7	46.3%	.305	-25	1.78	5.76	9.71	10.54	12.1	9.0	3.8	1.6	-37.5	—
2006	COH	AAA	25	1	6	0	11	8	38²	47	34	30	4	55.6%	.355	-19	2.12	7.77	10.60	11.97	12.2	9.4	5.1	1.5	-25.0	—
2007	SWB	AAA	26	9	5	0	20	20	113¹	92	56	102	4	44.5%	.285	19	1.31	2.70	4.04	3.89	7.8	4.9	5.9	0.5	20.7	—
2007	NYA	MLB	26	1	3	0	7	6	27²	34	18	10	2	36.9%	.320	-17	1.88	6.17	5.96	6.43	10.6	5.1	2.9	0.6	-1.7	0.02
2008	NYA	MLB	27	4	6	0	33	15	89	100	63	59	12	45.0%	.310	-14	1.82	6.28	6.07	6.26	9.7	5.7	5.4	1.2	-8.6	-0.40

Breakout: 21% Improve: 45% Collapse: 23% Attrition: 29%   Comparables: Chris Brock, Derek Brandow, Chris Fussell, Mike Judd

Another graduate of the Fabian school of pitching, DeSalvo doesn't have the stuff to challenge hitters so he has to beat them with smarts and precision. That precision deserted him in 2006; and though he made something of a recovery at Scranton last year, his walk rate was still too high for a pitcher with his stuff and approach, and that proved to be his downfall in the majors. Interesting stat: just 4.6 percent of the fly balls DeSalvo gave up in the majors left the park (league average is about 11 percent).

Kyle Farnsworth

Bats: R   Throws: R   Height: 6' 4"   Weight: 235   Born: April 14, 1976   Age: 32

YEAR	TEAM	LVL	AGE	W	L	SV	G	GS	IP	H	BB	SO	HR	GB%	BABIP	STUFF	WHIP	ERA	PERA	EqERA	EqH9	EqBB9	EqSO9	EqHR9	VORP	SN/WX
2005	DET	MLB	29	1	1	6	46	0	42²	29	20	55	1	46.9%	.295	33	1.15	2.32	2.92	2.61	6.5	4.4	10.5	0.2	15.2	2.22
2005	ATL	MLB	29	0	0	10	26	0	27¹	15	7	32	4	37.1%	.193	23	0.80	1.98	2.68	2.03	5.1	2.0	9.1	1.4	10.7	2.06
2006	NYA	MLB	30	3	6	6	72	0	66	62	28	75	8	37.3%	.314	15	1.36	4.36	4.06	4.30	8.2	3.5	9.4	0.9	10.5	1.92
2007	NYA	MLB	31	2	1	0	64	0	60	60	27	48	9	30.2%	.288	-10	1.45	4.80	4.65	4.87	8.6	3.5	6.5	1.3	4.8	1.14
2008	NYA	MLB	32	3	2	3	47	0	53	48	21	51	6	38.0%	.286	9	1.29	3.71	3.67	3.68	7.8	3.2	7.9	1.0	11.4	1.00

Breakout: 30% Improve: 65% Collapse: 19% Attrition: 12%   Comparables: Eric Plunk, Mike Trombley, Jeff Russell, Stan Belinda

Perhaps all you need to know about Farnsworth is his high fly-ball rate. What goes up must come down, a law of nature that readily applies to baseballs. Sometimes, in fact quite often when Farnsworth is pitching, the baseballs come down on the wrong side of the fence. Farnsworth throws very hard, but very straight. Hitters know this, and they time that magnificent fastball and launch it straight to hell. This is not an ideal quality for a set-up man, which Torre insisted Farnsworth was from approximately April 2006 until the moment Joba Chamberlain arrived, a tacit admission that he was wrong and that the fans, who convulsively boo "Farnsworthless's" every appearance, were right. In Torre's favor, there really were no other good options and he had to play the hand he was dealt. As for Farnsworth, he's an overpaid trash-time pitcher, albeit one with unusually good velocity for that role.

Sean Henn

Bats: R   Throws: L   Height: 6' 4"   Weight: 225   Born: April 23, 1981   Age: 27

YEAR	TEAM	LVL	AGE	W	L	SV	G	GS	IP	H	BB	SO	HR	GB%	BABIP	STUFF	WHIP	ERA	PERA	EqERA	EqH9	EqBB9	EqSO9	EqHR9	VORP	SN/WX
2005	TRN	AA	24	2	1	0	4	4	25¹	16	9	21	1	54.7%	.238	9	0.99	0.71	3.57	1.96	6.3	4.3	4.7	0.8	9.3	—
2005	COH	AAA	24	5	5	0	16	16	86¹	79	27	64	5	47.8%	.306	5	1.23	3.23	4.16	4.44	8.4	3.4	4.8	0.7	10.4	—
2006	COH	AAA	25	3	1	0	18	6	42²	44	20	33	1	53.1%	.341	-3	1.52	4.05	5.18	4.85	9.9	5.3	5.1	0.5	3.3	—
2007	NYA	MLB	26	2	2	0	29	1	36²	44	27	28	6	40.7%	.328	-16	1.94	7.11	7.36	7.71	10.4	5.8	6.3	1.4	-8.0	0.07
2007	SWB	AAA	26	1	3	0	16	3	33¹	29	9	30	1	47.4%	.308	3	1.14	3.24	3.60	4.18	8.4	2.8	5.8	0.6	5.1	—
2008	NYA	MLB	27	2	2	1	39	1	43	43	21	31	5	44.1%	.290	-6	1.50	4.72	4.56	4.73	8.7	4.1	5.8	1.0	4.2	0.30

Breakout: 50% Improve: 66% Collapse: 16% Attrition: 38%   Comparables: Drew Hall, Jack O'Connor, Hank Aguirre, Francisco Cordero

Henn beat out Ron Villone to be the lefty long reliever out of camp, but couldn't keep the job for long. The question is whether he lacks the ability to pitch in the majors, or if Torre simply burned him out early. Henn pitched fairly well in April, but Torre used him 12 times in the space of 23 games. Henn's 15 innings pitched for the month put him on a 90-inning pace, but his control deserted him after the first 12 1/3, leading to an early-May demotion. He was relentlessly pounded during various recall opportunities. As a 27-year-old southpaw with decent velocity, he'll get several thousand other chances.

Alan Horne

Bats: R   Throws: R   Height: 6' 4"   Weight: 195   Born: January 5, 1983   Age: 25

YEAR	TEAM	LVL	AGE	W	L	SV	G	GS	IP	H	BB	SO	HR	GB%	BABIP	STUFF	WHIP	ERA	PERA	EqERA	EqH9	EqBB9	EqSO9	EqHR9	VORP	SN/WX
2006	TAM	A+	23	6	9	0	28	26	122¹	105	61	122	10	43.7%	.293	-17	1.36	4.86	6.83	7.66	10.0	6.6	5.4	1.6	-25.0	—
2007	TRN	AA	24	12	4	0	27	27	153¹	149	57	165	10	50.8%	.341	6	1.34	3.11	6.26	5.62	11.0	4.2	7.1	1.0	-0.3	—
2008	NYA	MLB	25	7	8	0	32	19	121¹	136	64	88	16	45.7%	.314	-1	1.65	5.58	5.46	5.55	9.7	4.3	5.9	1.2	-1.5	0.60

Breakout: 28% Improve: 67% Collapse: 14% Attrition: 22%   Comparables: Oscar Muñoz, Erik Schullstrom, Garr Finnvold, Sean Douglass

Horne was hot stuff coming out of high school; the Indians made him their first-round pick in the 2001 draft, but lost him to college. Four years later, his stock had cooled, and the Yankees got him in the 11th round. In between, he pitched for three different schools and had Tommy John surgery. In two professional seasons, he's worked his way around to being hot stuff again, posting a terrific strikeout rate and showing decent control with low-90s stuff and three off-speed pitches. Caveats: no pitcher is quite as good as he looks at Trenton thanks to Old Man Delaware; Horne's mechanics aren't the cleanest in the world and he already has one surgery on his record; and he was gassed at the end of the season and put up a 6.00 ERA in the final month. Those matters aside, Horne would be on the cusp of a major league job in most organizations, but with the Yankees' depth of pitching prospects he's just another arm and could wind up in the pen before he gets a chance to start.

Philip Hughes

Bats: R   Throws: R   Height: 6' 5"   Weight: 220   Born: June 24, 1986   Age: 22

YEAR	TEAM	LVL	AGE	W	L	SV	G	GS	IP	H	BB	SO	HR	GB%	BABIP	STUFF	WHIP	ERA	PERA	EqERA	EqH9	EqBB9	EqSO9	EqHR9	VORP	SN/WX
2005	CSC	A	19	7	1	0	12	12	68²	46	16	72	1	49.4%	.269	27	0.90	1.97	4.38	4.62	7.6	4.2	5.2	0.6	6.6	—
2005	TAM	A+	19	2	0	0	5	4	17²	8	4	21	0	45.9%	.222	16	0.68	3.05	3.55	4.50	5.1	3.4	6.2	0.6	2.0	—
2006	TAM	A+	20	2	3	0	5	5	30²	19	2	30	0	51.9%	.247	28	0.70	1.79	3.28	3.58	7.2	1.3	5.5	0.3	6.2	—
2006	TRN	AA	20	10	3	0	21	21	116¹	73	32	138	5	52.8%	.266	39	0.90	2.25	3.95	3.94	7.8	3.4	7.5	0.8	19.4	—
2007	SWB	AAA	21	4	1	0	5	5	28²	16	8	28	0	62.3%	.235	27	0.84	2.20	2.74	3.04	5.4	3.0	6.8	0.3	7.6	—
2007	NYA	MLB	21	5	3	0	13	13	72²	64	29	58	8	37.8%	.272	21	1.28	4.46	3.67	4.46	7.6	3.2	6.6	1.0	9.0	1.53
2008	NYA	MLB	22	10	8	0	27	27	152	146	65	129	16	43.8%	.294	19	1.39	4.42	4.14	4.43	8.3	3.5	6.9	1.0	16.5	3.00

Breakout: 13% Improve: 40% Collapse: 25% Attrition: 16%   Comparables: Pete Broberg, Jaret Wright, Jim Nash, Storm Davis

The team's spring vow that Hughes would get a full year in the sticks lasted only as long as the Opening Day rotation, or about three weeks. What followed was disappointing only in the context of the great expectations raised by the 2004 first-round pick's extraordinary minor league record: 275 innings, 170 hits, 66 walks, 311 strikeouts, 2.03 ERA. In Hughes's second big-league start, he no-hit the Rangers for 6 1/3 innings, and the impossible seemed to be true: the Yankees had actually produced a pitching ace. Then his hamstring went "twang." Thanks to a severe ankle sprain suffered during rehab, Hughes next appeared in August. Just one of six August starts was quality, and it was theorized that Hughes's various leg injuries were sapping his velocity. September was better (2.73 ERA in five starts), and he was dominant in his Game Three ALDS relief appearance against the Indians. It was an uneven year, but the future remains bright.

Kei Igawa

Bats: L   Throws: L   Height: 6' 1"   Weight: 73   Born: July 13, 1979   Age: 28

YEAR	TEAM	LVL	AGE	W	L	SV	G	GS	IP	H	BB	SO	HR	GB%	BABIP	STUFF	WHIP	ERA	PERA	EqERA	EqH9	EqBB9	EqSO9	EqHR9	VORP	SN/WX
2005	HNS	JP	25	13	9	0	27	27	172¹	199	60	145	23	—	.321	-6	1.50	3.87	6.14	5.68	10.9	3.6	5.7	1.2	-1.4	—
2006	HAN	JP	26	14	9	0	29	29	209	180	49	194	17	—	.282	17	1.10	2.97	4.22	4.23	8.8	2.8	6.7	0.9	29.8	—
2007	SWB	AAA	27	5	4	0	11	11	68¹	68	15	71	10	36.1%	.320	-1	1.22	3.69	6.27	5.23	10.3	2.4	7.1	2.0	2.6	—
2007	NYA	MLB	27	2	3	0	14	12	67²	76	37	53	15	31.1%	.299	-17	1.67	6.25	7.09	6.25	9.7	4.4	6.5	2.0	-3.5	0.13
2008	NYA	MLB	28	5	6	1	33	13	90¹	98	38	67	14	38.1%	.303	-1	1.51	5.16	5.09	5.07	9.4	3.4	6.1	1.4	4.4	0.90

Breakout: 19% Improve: 48% Collapse: 26% Attrition: 37%   Comparables: Casey Fossum, Mike Matthews, Joel Bennett, Kevin Foster

The arm that launched a thousand baseballs, Igawa gave up 25 home runs in 136 innings split between the majors and minors last year. In both places, Igawa showed an ability to get batters to swing and miss, but when hitters wouldn't chase pitches off the plate, he'd either walk them or serve up a meatball. Igawa showed good control in Japan and walked less than two batters per nine innings at Scranton, so his performance screams of another too-nervous-for-New York scenario in which the ravenous, man-eating Yankee Stadium crowds unnerved the new hurler by threatening to do unnatural things to kittens during his windup. Igawa was so thoroughly brutal that a comeback seems unlikely, but in pitching a turnaround is often a small adjustment away. The Yankees have Igawa under contract until 2011, so there's plenty of time for experimentation.

Jeffrey Karstens

Bats: R   Throws: R   Height: 6' 3"   Weight: 185   Born: September 24, 1982   Age: 25

YEAR	TEAM	LVL	AGE	W	L	SV	G	GS	IP	H	BB	SO	HR	GB%	BABIP	STUFF	WHIP	ERA	PERA	EqERA	EqH9	EqBB9	EqSO9	EqHR9	VORP	SN/WX
2005	TRN	AA	22	12	11	0	28	27	169	192	42	147	16	47.7%	.344	-13	1.38	4.15	6.89	6.87	11.9	3.4	4.9	1.4	-21.4	—
2006	TRN	AA	23	6	0	0	11	11	74²	54	14	67	4	46.9%	.248	11	0.92	2.30	4.03	3.99	8.4	2.4	5.3	0.9	12.5	—
2006	COH	AAA	23	5	5	0	14	14	73²	80	30	48	9	35.6%	.303	-24	1.50	4.30	6.53	6.27	10.2	4.4	4.1	1.7	-5.2	—
2006	NYA	MLB	23	2	1	0	8	6	42²	40	10	16	6	33.1%	.238	-4	1.17	3.79	3.61	3.74	7.9	1.9	3.1	1.0	8.6	0.86
2007	SWB	AAA	24	3	0	0	6	5	31	25	9	27	2	37.5%	.271	11	1.10	1.74	3.77	2.43	7.9	3.0	5.8	0.9	10.5	—
2007	NYA	MLB	24	1	4	0	7	3	14²	27	9	5	4	31.8%	.390	-70	2.45	11.02	16.10	15.26	15.3	4.7	2.9	2.3	-11.2	-0.65
2008	NYA	MLB	25	4	5	0	31	10	82	96	36	48	15	40.2%	.299	-12	1.60	6.01	5.77	5.90	10.1	3.5	4.8	1.6	-4.8	-0.10

Breakout: 33% Improve: 60% Collapse: 18% Attrition: 18%   Comparables: Jason Ryan, Tim Scott, Jamie Brown, Eric Schmitt

Karstens won the fifth-starter job in spring training, but a stiff elbow delayed his debut until late April. He was hammered. In his second start of the season, Julio Lugo lined a ball off of Karstens's right leg, breaking it and sending him to the 60-day DL. Karstens returned in August to serve as a long man out of the pen, was hammered again and shipped back to Scranton. His low strikeout rates and fly-ball tendencies make him an unlikely candidate for any kind of sustained success, and he has been surpassed by younger pitchers of greater promise.

Ian Kennedy

Bats: R   Throws: R   Height: 6' 0"   Weight: 190   Born: December 19, 1984   Age: 23

YEAR	TEAM	LVL	AGE	W	L	SV	G	GS	IP	H	BB	SO	HR	GB%	BABIP	STUFF	WHIP	ERA	PERA	EqERA	EqH9	EqBB9	EqSO9	EqHR9	VORP	SN/WX
2007	TAM	A+	22	6	1	0	11	10	63	39	22	72	2	35.7%	.266	26	0.97	1.29	4.24	2.82	7.5	4.8	7.5	0.7	16.8	—
2007	TRN	AA	22	5	1	0	9	9	48²	27	17	57	2	41.8%	.234	27	0.90	2.59	3.54	3.86	6.5	3.9	7.9	0.6	8.6	—
2007	SWB	AAA	22	1	1	0	6	6	34²	25	11	34	2	43.8%	.267	22	1.04	2.07	3.72	2.78	7.2	3.3	6.7	0.8	10.1	—
2007	NYA	MLB	22	1	0	0	3	3	19	13	9	15	1	26.4%	.231	19	1.16	1.89	2.70	2.84	5.7	3.8	6.6	0.5	6.7	0.68
2008	NYA	MLB	23	9	7	0	38	25	141	129	68	120	16	38.7%	.282	11	1.40	4.24	4.19	4.21	7.9	3.9	6.9	1.0	19.8	3.00

Breakout: 1% Improve: 10% Collapse: 67% Attrition: 15%   Comparables: Gary Nolan, Barry Zito, Chuck Estrada, Dave Morehead

Like Chamberlain, Kennedy shot through the minors after being drafted in 2006's first round. Though derided for not having stuff that breaks the sound barrier, Kennedy knows how to use what he has. His strikeout rates are those of a man with a much better fastball, his control is strong (but could still get better), and he keeps the ball in the ballpark, with just seven home runs allowed in 168 career innings. With a drinking bird windup reminiscent of Mike Mussina working from the stretch, he may be on the verge of a similar career.

Jeff Marquez

| | | | | | | | | | | | | | | Bats: R | Throws: R | Height: 6' 2" | Weight: 175 | Born: August 10, 1984 | Age: 23 |

YEAR	TEAM	LVL	AGE	W	L	SV	G	GS	IP	H	BB	SO	HR	GB%	BABIP	STUFF	WHIP	ERA	PERA	EqERA	EqH9	EqBB9	EqSO9	EqHR9	VORP	SN/WX
2005	CSC	A	20	9	13	0	27	27	139²	138	61	107	4	0.0%	.300	-6	1.42	3.41	6.67	6.71	11.0	7.0	3.4	0.8	-14.7	—
2006	TAM	A+	21	7	5	0	18	17	92²	102	29	82	4	57.5%	.351	-9	1.42	3.61	7.13	8.04	12.6	4.5	4.8	1.0	-22.1	—
2007	TRN	AA	22	15	9	0	27	27	155¹	166	44	94	11	52.8%	.304	-13	1.35	3.65	6.12	6.28	11.3	3.3	3.5	1.1	-10.9	—
2008	NYA	MLB	23	6	9	0	31	22	127¹	164	58	59	17	52.3%	.324	-12	1.74	6.26	6.02	6.29	11.1	3.7	3.8	1.2	-12.0	-0.40

Breakout: 28% Improve: 56% Collapse: 17% Attrition: 11%   Comparables: Dan Perkins, Nate Bump, Aaron Cook, Bob Wickman

Marquez was the Yankees' supplemental-round pick in the 2004 draft. He throws a sinking fastball and, given his declining strikeout rates, seems to want to take the Chien-Ming Wang path to success. It's a grand idea but for two problems: his ground-ball rate took a step back last year, and there's only one Wang. Marquez will be among the team's starting prospects to be considered for the major league pen this spring, but will likely start the season in the Triple-A rotation.

Mike Mussina

| | | | | | | | | | | | | | | Bats: L | Throws: R | Height: 6' 2" | Weight: 190 | Born: December 8, 1968 | Age: 39 |

YEAR	TEAM	LVL	AGE	W	L	SV	G	GS	IP	H	BB	SO	HR	GB%	BABIP	STUFF	WHIP	ERA	PERA	EqERA	EqH9	EqBB9	EqSO9	EqHR9	VORP	SN/WX
2005	NYA	MLB	36	13	8	0	30	30	179²	199	47	142	23	45.2%	.328	15	1.37	4.41	4.84	4.41	9.7	2.4	7.0	1.1	22.9	3.39
2006	NYA	MLB	37	15	7	0	32	32	197¹	184	35	172	22	42.6%	.285	28	1.11	3.51	3.48	3.76	8.2	1.5	7.4	0.9	44.9	5.07
2007	NYA	MLB	38	11	10	0	28	27	152	188	35	91	14	43.5%	.348	6	1.47	5.15	5.21	5.36	10.9	1.9	5.1	0.9	11.0	2.63
2008	NYA	MLB	39	9	8	0	25	25	149²	164	40	101	18	44.7%	.305	8	1.36	4.54	4.38	4.53	9.5	2.2	5.5	1.1	15.2	2.80

Breakout: 12% Improve: 48% Collapse: 28% Attrition: 18%   Comparables: Jim Bunning, Bert Blyleven, Jack Morris, Don Sutton

Last year in this space we wrote that the Yankees took a good risk in turning Mussina's one-year option into a discounted two-year extension. Not all good risks pay off. Like Clemens, Mussina saw his velocity drop and his strikeout rate go with it and, after a torn hamstring limited him to two starts in April, it took a while to catch up. After a stretch of 12 mostly good starts beginning in June (3.54 ERA in 73 2/3 innings), the wheels came off on August 16 against Detroit. Mussina was bombed so badly in that start and his next two that it shook his confidence and that of his manager, who pulled him from the rotation in favor of rookie Ian Kennedy. Veterans have to work hard to lose their standing with Torre, but the skipper only returned Moose to the rotation when Clemens's elbow forced the move and opted not to start him with the team facing elimination in the ALDS. As he's signed through this year, new manager Joe Girardi is obligated to give him a chance to turn back the clock, but success seems unlikely.

Ross Ohlendorf

| | | | | | | | | | | | | | | Bats: R | Throws: R | Height: 6' 4" | Weight: 235 | Born: August 8, 1982 | Age: 25 |

YEAR	TEAM	LVL	AGE	W	L	SV	G	GS	IP	H	BB	SO	HR	GB%	BABIP	STUFF	WHIP	ERA	PERA	EqERA	EqH9	EqBB9	EqSO9	EqHR9	VORP	SN/WX
2005	SBN	A	22	11	10	0	27	26	157	181	48	144	10	59.6%	.357	-18	1.46	4.53	7.57	8.14	12.5	4.5	4.8	1.4	-39.3	—
2006	TEN	AA	23	10	8	0	27	27	177²	180	29	125	13	48.7%	.317	-5	1.18	3.30	5.34	4.85	10.4	2.0	4.2	1.2	13.4	—
2007	SWB	AAA	24	3	3	0	21	9	66¹	86	24	48	7	47.3%	.369	-29	1.66	5.02	8.48	7.19	12.9	3.8	4.8	1.5	-10.8	—
2007	NYA	MLB	24	0	0	0	6	0	6¹	5	2	9	1	53.3%	.286	6	1.11	2.86	3.67	2.84	7.1	2.8	9.9	1.4	2.2	0.14
2008	NYA	MLB	25	3	4	1	26	7	63	79	24	37	9	48.9%	.324	-10	1.62	5.94	5.66	5.93	10.8	3.1	4.7	1.3	-4.0	-0.10

Breakout: 35% Improve: 52% Collapse: 24% Attrition: 23%   Comparables: Ryan Basner, Travis Thompson, Rick White, Eric Thompson

The key prospect received for Randy Johnson, this Princeton product struggled as a starter in Triple-A but, after a time out due to a bad back, improved when he took his sinking fastball to the bullpen. Ohlendorf showed improved velocity in relief, but his breaking pitches are still in the research and development phase, which puts him at a disadvantage against lefties. Nonetheless, his September call-up was good enough to get him added to the postseason roster, and he stands a good chance of making a wide-open bullpen in spring training.

Andy Pettitte

Bats: L   Throws: L   Height: 6' 5"   Weight: 225   Born: June 15, 1972   Age: 36

YEAR	TEAM	LVL	AGE	W	L	SV	G	GS	IP	H	BB	SO	HR	GB%	BABIP	STUFF	WHIP	ERA	PERA	EqERA	EqH9	EqBB9	EqSO9	EqHR9	VORP	SN/WX
2005	HOU	MLB	33	17	9	0	33	33	222¹	188	41	171	17	51.8%	.272	29	1.03	2.39	3.22	2.97	7.9	1.5	6.4	0.7	72.1	8.56
2006	HOU	MLB	34	14	13	0	36	35	214¹	238	70	178	27	51.4%	.333	14	1.44	4.20	5.06	4.66	10.1	2.6	6.9	1.0	30.3	4.15
2007	NYA	MLB	35	15	9	0	36	34	215¹	238	69	141	16	49.5%	.329	15	1.43	4.05	4.43	4.35	9.8	2.6	5.6	0.6	36.8	5.44
2008	NYA	MLB	36	12	8	0	28	28	176	187	60	117	18	49.0%	.300	8	1.40	4.22	4.29	4.23	9.2	2.8	5.4	0.9	23.9	4.00

Breakout: 9%   Improve: 37%   Collapse: 25%   Attrition: 17%   Comparables: Kenny Rogers, Mark Langston, Frank Tanana, Bruce Hurst

Pettitte stayed healthy all last season despite occasional back spasms and pitched well, his best stretch coming in his first ten starts after the All-Star break (8-1, 2.79 ERA, 7.7 K/9), fueling the Yankees' second-half run for the wild card. He struggled after that, but it was only his final start that pushed his season ERA over 4.00. Pettitte also had some rotten luck on balls in play, but you would expect that from a lefty ground-ball pitcher performing in front of Derek Jeter. Pettitte's performances have always outpaced his stuff; having returned to the Yankees just in time to save them from overbidding on Johan Santana, he should have another year of gutty pitching in him.

Edwar Ramirez

Bats: R   Throws: R   Height: 6' 3"   Weight: 155   Born: March 28, 1981   Age: 27

YEAR	TEAM	LVL	AGE	W	L	SV	G	GS	IP	H	BB	SO	HR	GB%	BABIP	STUFF	WHIP	ERA	PERA	EqERA	EqH9	EqBB9	EqSO9	EqHR9	VORP	SN/WX
2006	TAM	A+	25	4	1	3	19	0	30¹	14	6	47	0	32.8%	.241	24	0.66	1.20	3.19	2.89	5.8	2.9	9.0	0.3	8.4	—
2007	TRN	AA	26	3	0	1	9	0	16²	6	8	33	1	56.0%	.208	16	0.84	0.54	3.41	1.69	5.1	5.1	11.2	1.1	7.0	—
2007	SWB	AAA	26	1	0	6	25	0	40	20	14	69	0	43.3%	.308	37	0.85	0.90	3.05	1.96	6.4	3.7	10.8	0.2	14.8	—
2007	NYA	MLB	26	1	1	1	21	0	21	24	14	31	6	36.4%	.383	-1	1.86	8.14	10.20	9.00	10.7	5.1	11.6	2.6	-5.3	-0.73
2008	NYA	MLB	27	4	3	7	58	1	60²	48	31	76	7	39.0%	.292	23	1.31	3.61	3.58	3.58	6.9	4.2	10.2	1.0	13.5	1.30

Breakout: 70%   Improve: 91%   Collapse: 3%   Attrition: 12%   Comparables: John Wetteland, David Riske, Mark Clear, Bryan Harvey

Plucked off of the independent leagues in 2006, Ramirez puts up stunning strikeout rates with an otherworldly changeup, but despite striking out the side in his major league debut, he proved rather hitable in the big leagues as he struggled with his control, leading to an approach that took all the guesswork out of hitting. "Changeup" is just another word for "fat fastball with nothing on it." When the batter knows it's coming or the location is off, that otherwordly changeup reaches other worlds, as seen by Ramirez's frightening home run rate. Obviously a pitcher who can get so many batters to swing and miss has something going for him, but Ramirez needs to add another wrinkle.

Darrell Rasner

Bats: R   Throws: R   Height: 6' 3"   Weight: 210   Born: January 13, 1981   Age: 27

YEAR	TEAM	LVL	AGE	W	L	SV	G	GS	IP	H	BB	SO	HR	GB%	BABIP	STUFF	WHIP	ERA	PERA	EqERA	EqH9	EqBB9	EqSO9	EqHR9	VORP	SN/WX
2005	HAR	AA	24	6	7	0	27	26	150¹	150	29	96	10	52.5%	.297	-9	1.19	3.59	4.93	5.15	9.8	2.7	3.3	1.0	6.9	—
2005	WAS	MLB	24	0	1	0	5	1	7¹	5	2	4	0	30.4%	.227	-3	0.95	3.70	2.60	3.52	5.9	2.3	4.7	0.0	1.3	-0.03
2006	COH	AAA	25	4	0	0	10	10	58²	60	11	47	4	44.3%	.316	6	1.22	2.78	4.61	4.18	9.6	2.2	5.1	1.0	8.8	—
2006	NYA	MLB	25	3	1	0	6	3	20¹	18	5	11	2	40.9%	.254	0	1.13	4.43	3.38	4.05	7.7	2.2	4.5	0.9	3.7	0.84
2007	NYA	MLB	26	1	3	0	6	6	24²	29	8	11	4	41.1%	.294	-14	1.50	4.01	5.63	5.04	9.7	2.5	3.6	1.4	2.1	0.47
2008	NYA	MLB	27	3	4	0	22	8	60¹	71	21	30	8	45.8%	.303	-10	1.52	5.24	5.12	5.22	10.2	2.8	4.1	1.2	1.7	0.50

Breakout: 9%   Improve: 34%   Collapse: 42%   Attrition: 48%   Comparables: Curt Barclay, Gary Waslewski, Steve Comer, Dick Pole

Twice in two years, Rasner had a chance to claim a spot in the Yankees' rotation derailed by injuries. He opened last year as the team's number-five starter in place of the injured Jeff Karstens, but blisters hampered his effectiveness, and in his sixth and final start a comebacker fractured his finger. The only indication Rasner has given that he can't be a useful back of the rotation pitcher or long man is that he hasn't been able to stay out of the infirmary. As with Karstens, he'll have to wait his turn for another chance, possibly with another team.

Mariano Rivera

								Bats: R		Throws: R		Height: 6' 2"		Weight: 185		Born: November 29, 1969		Age: 38	

YEAR	TEAM	LVL	AGE	W	L	SV	G	GS	IP	H	BB	SO	HR	GB%	BABIP	STUFF	WHIP	ERA	PERA	EqERA	EqH9	EqBB9	EqSO9	EqHR9	VORP	SN/WX
2005	NYA	MLB	35	7	4	43	71	0	78¹	50	18	80	2	55.9%	.239	37	0.87	1.38	2.23	2.15	5.3	2.0	8.7	0.2	32.2	5.15
2006	NYA	MLB	36	5	5	34	63	0	75	61	11	55	3	57.7%	.269	22	0.96	1.80	2.74	1.96	7.2	1.2	6.3	0.4	34.9	5.33
2007	NYA	MLB	37	3	4	30	67	0	71¹	68	12	74	4	53.0%	.327	28	1.12	3.16	3.29	3.03	8.3	1.3	8.6	0.5	22.4	3.70
2008	NYA	MLB	38	5	4	29	53	0	60²	54	15	51	4	53.0%	.286	10	1.13	2.69	2.72	2.74	7.7	2.0	6.9	0.6	22.6	3.00

Breakout: 19% Improve: 43% Collapse: 36% Attrition: 19%   Comparables: Larry Andersen, Stu Miller, John Smoltz, Rollie Fingers

The by-acclamation Greatest Closer of All Time had a few rough patches last year. Though he was still quite good on the whole, including posting his highest strikeout rate since 1996, he wasn't the automatic closing machine of years past. Rivera has made a career of bearing his cut fastball in on hitters (especially lefties), jamming them and breaking their bats. He scrapped less lumber in 2007 as the cutter didn't seem to have the same bite, leading to more line drives and a career-high BABIP. Whether this was an expression of age or an aberration isn't clear, but the Yankees re-signed Rivera through his age-40 season, so they'll find out.

Humberto Sanchez

								Bats: R		Throws: R		Height: 6' 6"		Weight: 230		Born: May 28, 1983		Age: 25	

YEAR	TEAM	LVL	AGE	W	L	SV	G	GS	IP	H	BB	SO	HR	GB%	BABIP	STUFF	WHIP	ERA	PERA	EqERA	EqH9	EqBB9	EqSO9	EqHR9	VORP	SN/WX
2005	ERI	AA	22	3	5	0	15	11	64²	72	27	65	10	49.2%	.346	-22	1.53	5.56	8.91	8.27	11.9	5.3	5.8	2.2	-17.1	—
2006	ERI	AA	23	5	3	0	11	11	71	47	27	86	2	51.8%	.281	28	1.04	1.77	3.77	3.31	7.0	4.5	7.4	0.6	16.6	—
2006	TOL	AAA	23	5	3	0	9	9	51¹	50	20	43	2	41.1%	.327	5	1.37	3.87	5.60	5.87	10.6	4.5	5.7	0.6	-1.4	—
2008	NYA	MLB	25	3	3	0	18	7	51²	51	27	44	6	45.4%	.303	6	1.52	4.78	4.66	4.78	8.6	4.3	6.9	1.0	4.7	0.70

Breakout: 31% Improve: 56% Collapse: 23% Attrition: 30%   Comparables: Jim Britton, Gary Kroll, Roger Salkeld, Pete Vuckovich

This portly pitcher was plundered from the Tigers in the Gary Sheffield deal, but by the time he actually pitches for the Yankees, they may need to take him on *Antiques Roadshow* to see what they got. Previously a hard thrower who got by on his fastball and slider, Sanchez was never good at staying healthy and had missed the last month of the 2006 season with an inflamed elbow. In spring training, that inflammation returned and soon he was going under for Tommy John surgery, which the Yankees hope will solve things. Losing a few pounds wouldn't hurt his recovery; the Yankees will get to see how many Twinkies went into the rehab when spring training convenes.

Jose Veras

								Bats: R		Throws: R		Height: 6' 5"		Weight: 235		Born: October 20, 1980		Age: 27	

YEAR	TEAM	LVL	AGE	W	L	SV	G	GS	IP	H	BB	SO	HR	GB%	BABIP	STUFF	WHIP	ERA	PERA	EqERA	EqH9	EqBB9	EqSO9	EqHR9	VORP	SN/WX
2005	OKL	AAA	24	3	5	24	57	0	61²	63	33	72	4	48.5%	.366	6	1.56	3.79	5.37	4.47	9.9	5.1	7.7	0.8	7.3	—
2006	COH	AAA	25	5	3	21	50	0	59	49	19	68	3	46.5%	.311	8	1.15	2.44	3.88	3.43	7.8	3.4	7.5	0.8	13.9	—
2006	NYA	MLB	25	0	0	1	12	0	11	8	5	6	2	31.3%	.200	-14	1.18	4.09	3.88	3.48	7.0	4.4	5.2	1.7	2.4	0.22
2007	SWB	AAA	26	2	0	4	12	0	16	17	7	17	1	57.4%	.348	-7	1.50	4.50	6.11	5.87	10.6	4.1	7.0	0.6	-0.5	—
2007	NYA	MLB	26	0	0	2	9	0	9¹	6	7	7	0	40.7%	.222	-1	1.39	5.81	2.70	5.59	5.6	5.6	5.6	0.0	0.2	0.37
2008	NYA	MLB	27	3	3	3	41	2	47¹	48	24	39	5	46.8%	.303	-1	1.50	4.66	4.52	4.69	8.7	4.0	6.7	0.9	4.4	0.50

Breakout: 16% Improve: 32% Collapse: 44% Attrition: 32%   Comparables: Jim Britton, Brad Arnsberg, Paul Shuey, George Witt

Veras missed most of the season after having bone chips removed from his elbow, but made it back to pitch for the Yankees in September and even snuck onto the postseason roster. Veras has struck out 417 in 439 1/3 minor league innings, but has always been loose with his control, a problem that he made progress on in 2006, but that reasserted itself postsurgery. If the wildness was merely rust, he should get a long look for the pen.

Luis Vizcaino

								Bats: R		Throws: R		Height: 5' 11"		Weight: 210		Born: August 6, 1974		Age: 33	

YEAR	TEAM	LVL	AGE	W	L	SV	G	GS	IP	H	BB	SO	HR	GB%	BABIP	STUFF	WHIP	ERA	PERA	EqERA	EqH9	EqBB9	EqSO9	EqHR9	VORP	SN/WX
2005	CHA	MLB	30	6	5	0	65	0	70	74	29	43	8	45.9%	.303	-11	1.47	3.73	5.40	4.16	10.1	3.8	5.5	0.9	15.2	0.29
2006	ARI	MLB	31	4	6	0	70	0	65¹	51	29	72	8	46.7%	.274	17	1.22	3.58	3.41	2.91	6.8	3.5	9.0	1.0	18.5	2.17
2007	NYA	MLB	32	8	2	0	77	0	75¹	66	43	62	6	37.0%	.282	4	1.46	4.30	3.67	3.97	7.4	4.4	6.7	0.7	12.0	2.08
2008	COL	MLB	33	3	3	2	50	0	56	60	26	45	7	43.7%	.307	-1	1.52	4.77	4.43	4.59	8.7	3.6	6.9	1.1	7.7	0.70

Breakout: 5% Improve: 21% Collapse: 49% Attrition: 25%   Comparables: John Wyatt, Turk Wendell, Greg Harris, Don McMahon

Worked hard and hit hard early (7.27 ERA in his first 25 games), Vizcaino soon settled down and became one of the club's more reliable relievers, striking out 49 in 49 1/3 innings with a 2.74 ERA from June on. Vizcaino was especially tough on righty hitters, holding them to .213/.318/.354 after something of a reverse split on his career. On his way to a career high in appearances, Vizcaino did wear down with a bit of TIFS (Torre-Induced Fatigue Syndrome), complaining of a sore shoulder in September. Though he appeared to be uncustomarily wild last year, his numbers were inflated by a league-leading 11 intentional walks. Having traded places with fellow free agent LaTroy Hawkins, he'll be better for the Rockies than the man he replaces will be for the Yankees.

Chien-Ming Wang

Bats: R **Throws: R** **Height: 6' 3"** **Weight: 225** **Born: March 31, 1980** **Age: 28**

YEAR	TEAM	LVL	AGE	W	L	SV	G	GS	IP	H	BB	SO	HR	GB%	BABIP	STUFF	WHIP	ERA	PERA	EqERA	EqH9	EqBB9	EqSO9	EqHR9	VORP	SN/WX
2005	COH	AAA	25	2	1	0	6	6	34	40	6	21	4	66.1%	.333	-8	1.35	4.24	5.72	4.83	11.1	2.3	4.0	1.4	2.7	—
2005	NYA	MLB	25	8	5	0	18	17	116¹	113	32	47	9	65.3%	.270	7	1.25	4.02	3.61	4.07	8.2	2.4	3.5	0.6	16.8	2.14
2006	NYA	MLB	26	19	6	1	34	33	218	233	52	76	12	63.8%	.293	9	1.31	3.63	3.99	3.75	9.7	2.1	3.1	0.5	54.6	5.68
2007	NYA	MLB	27	19	7	0	30	30	199¹	199	59	104	9	58.4%	.298	18	1.29	3.70	3.66	3.70	8.8	2.4	4.5	0.4	48.5	5.96
2008	NYA	MLB	28	11	9	0	29	29	178¹	200	59	95	14	58.3%	.308	5	1.45	4.37	4.34	4.47	9.7	2.7	4.3	0.7	19.0	3.50

Breakout: 4% Improve: 19% Collapse: 34% Attrition: 15%   Comparables: Jake Westbrook, Dennis Lamp, Kevin Brown, Dave Goltz

Surviving an early hamstring pull, which kept him on the DL until late April and likely cost him a 20-win season, and a split fingernail that troubled him from May on, Wang was largely consistent with what he's done before. The only difference was a slight slippage in his signature ground-ball rate and an accompanying rise in strikeouts as, from time to time, Wang chose to emphasize his slider rather than his sinker. This resulted in six starts of six or more strikeouts, topping out at 10 against the Mets on June 17. The only blemishes on his season were his two horrific starts against the Indians in the ALDS—12 runs allowed in 5 2/3 IP. Assuming those starts were largely the result of nerves and good Cleveland hitting, there's no reason not to expect more consistency from Wang in 2008.

Chase Wright

Bats: L **Throws: L** **Height: 6' 2"** **Weight: 205** **Born: February 8, 1983** **Age: 25**

YEAR	TEAM	LVL	AGE	W	L	SV	G	GS	IP	H	BB	SO	HR	GB%	BABIP	STUFF	WHIP	ERA	PERA	EqERA	EqH9	EqBB9	EqSO9	EqHR9	VORP	SN/WX
2005	CSC	A	22	10	4	0	25	24	144	128	69	110	10	49.4%	.289	-20	1.37	3.75	7.04	7.24	10.1	7.5	3.4	1.5	-22.4	—
2006	TAM	A+	23	12	3	0	37	14	119	95	43	100	1	57.0%	.281	7	1.16	1.89	4.43	3.83	8.6	4.9	4.4	0.3	21.2	—
2007	SWB	AAA	24	8	3	1	15	14	85¹	79	42	40	7	49.8%	.265	-16	1.42	4.01	5.07	5.53	8.6	4.9	2.9	1.1	0.6	—
2007	NYA	MLB	24	2	0	0	3	2	10	12	6	8	5	36.4%	.250	-40	1.80	7.20	16.56	9.90	10.8	4.5	6.3	4.5	-1.4	0.02
2007	TRN	AA	24	5	2	0	10	10	59²	55	21	41	8	59.9%	.273	-23	1.27	3.62	7.09	5.60	10.5	4.1	4.4	2.0	0.0	—
2008	NYA	MLB	25	5	7	0	34	16	103	124	61	47	16	48.3%	.305	-21	1.80	6.28	6.28	6.24	10.5	4.8	3.7	1.4	-9.7	-0.40

Breakout: 15% Improve: 39% Collapse: 28% Attrition: 14%   Comparables: Scott Mullen, Scott Forster, Shawn Bryant, John Courtright

Few prospects have gone up and down the pop charts faster than Wright. Called up after just two Double-A starts, Wright won his first start against the Indians and made history in his second. In the third inning of his April 22 start at Fenway Park, he gave up consecutive home runs to Manny Ramirez, J. D. Drew, Mike Lowell, and Jason Varitek, becoming just the second AL hurler ever to surrender four straight taters. Naturally, he was sent down. Wright continued to pitch poorly and was demoted again to Trenton. He'll have to show massive improvement with his control to reclaim the Yankees' affections.

LINEOUTS

Hitters

PLAYER	TEAM	LVL	AGE	PA	R	2B	3B	HR	RBI	BB	SO	SB-CS	EqBRR	AVG/OBP/SLG	MLVr	EqAVG/EqOBP/EqSLG	EqA	VORP
SS R. Corona#	TAM	A+	20	460	56	17	3	3	37	51	65	22-6	1.3	.271/.356/.352	.007	.233/.310/.317	.229	-6.4
	TRN	AA	20	163	19	6	0	0	6	18	30	7-2	0.6	.221/.315/.264	-.209	.196/.278/.238	.192	-10.7
SS A. Gonzalez	TRN	AA	24	125	18	10	1	0	16	10	14	1-1	0.9	.330/.385/.440	.225	.295/.347/.402	.261	6.1
	SWB	AAA	24	426	44	21	10	1	35	24	49	11-5	1.6	.247/.300/.362	-.094	.228/.278/.354	.222	-7.4
C W. Nieves	SWB	AAA	29	98	5	1	2	1	8	6	10	1-0	-0.4	.256/.306/.344	-.102	.242/.293/.330	.222	-2.4
	NYA	MLB	29	66	6	4	0	0	8	2	9	0-0	-0.1	.164/.190/.230	-.605	.164/.190/.230	.127	-6.4
3B B. Suttle#	YAN	Rk	21	9	1	0	0	0	1	1	2	0-0	0.0	.125/.222/.125	-.501	.125/.222/.125	.059	-3.9

That Delaware river breeze also got **Reegie Corona**, who showed good patience last year but failed to hit at the higher level. Capable of playing second or short, his future is as an infield reserve with disproportionate popularity due to the scoreboard-led "Ree-gie! Ree-gie!" chants whenever he comes to bat in home games. ⊘ The Yankees signed **Kelvin DeLeon** out of the Dominican Republic in July, gaining another potential slugger who can't get into an R-rated movie. He's completely raw as a baseball talent, but as far as tools go, he's got the whole Craftsman gift set. He'll begin forging his legend in the Gulf Coast League this summer. If things don't work out, the Yankees plan to multiply him by 1.8 then subtract 459.67 to transform him into his more primitive brother, Fahrenheit Escobar. ⊘ **Alberto Gonzalez**, the shortstop that some have nicknamed "The Attorney General," began the year at Triple-A, but headed back down a level for a refresher on the strike zone before his September call-up. His glove will inspire someone to give him a shot at some point. His bat is off of the Rey Sanchez shelf—better than Tony Peña Jr.'s, but that's all. ⊘ It took some spectacularly pollyannaish, panglossian thinking to conclude that **Wil Nieves** could hit well enough to be of any service to a major league team. He can't. ⊘ A switch-hitting third baseman the Yankees signed as a sophomore-eligible out of Texas, **Brad Suttle** is a slick fielder with solid hitting skills who could move quickly, although he lacks the power normally associated with the position.

Pitchers

PLAYER	TEAM	LVL	AGE	W	L	SV	IP	H	BB	SO	HR	GB%	BABIP	STUFF	WHIP	ERA	PERA	EqERA	EqH9	EqBB9	EqSO9	EqHR9	VORP
T. Beam	SWB	AAA	26	4	3	3	47²	51	10	45	6	49.0%	.333	-12	1.28	3.58	6.08	5.00	10.6	2.2	6.4	1.6	3.0
D. Betances	STA	A-	19	1	2	0	25	24	17	29	0	44.6%	.369	12	1.64	3.60	7.91	6.97	11.8	10.0	6.1	0.4	-3.2
A. Brackman '08	NYA	MLB	22	7	11	0	151	182	81	89	24	46.7%	.314	-5	1.74	6.42	6.15	6.37	10.4	4.4	4.8	1.4	-16.1
M. Dunn*	CSC	A	22	12	5	0	144²	136	45	138	14	40.1%	.316	-28	1.25	3.42	8.21	7.51	12.1	5.1	5.1	1.9	-25.7
M. Gardner	TRN	AA	26	3	5	2	81¹	72	30	66	1	64.4%	.301	-1	1.25	2.88	4.48	4.68	9.4	4.0	5.0	0.2	7.9
G. Kontos	TAM	A+	22	4	6	0	94	95	30	101	15	44.4%	.321	-39	1.33	4.02	10.50	8.52	12.4	4.5	6.8	3.0	-26.4
D. McCutchen	TAM	A+	24	11	2	0	101	86	21	67	7	45.8%	.272	-14	1.06	2.50	5.45	4.43	9.8	3.2	3.9	1.4	11.3
	TRN	AA	24	3	2	0	41	30	12	36	2	43.4%	.259	10	1.02	2.41	3.99	3.55	8.1	3.3	5.7	0.7	8.7
S. Patterson	TRN	AA	28	4	2	2	74¹	45	15	91	1	32.4%	.254	27	0.81	1.09	3.10	2.80	6.6	2.4	7.9	0.3	22.0
C. Pavano	NYA	MLB	31	1	0	0	11¹	12	2	4	1	52.5%	.282	-6	1.24	4.78	3.83	5.73	9.0	1.6	3.3	0.8	0.5
D. Robertson	CSC	A	22	5	2	3	47	25	15	67	0	65.3%	.253	18	0.85	0.77	4.00	2.74	7.0	4.9	7.8	0.4	13.6
	TAM	A+	22	3	1	1	33¹	18	15	37	0	58.4%	.237	16	0.99	1.08	3.75	3.03	6.1	5.8	7.0	0.3	8.5
R. Villone*	SWB	AAA	37	0	1	1	23²	21	10	27	0	48.4%	.350	9	1.31	1.90	4.06	3.18	8.7	4.4	7.5	0.0	6.1
	NYA	MLB	37	0	0	0	42¹	36	18	25	5	36.9%	.250	-10	1.28	4.26	3.84	3.92	7.4	3.5	5.0	1.1	8.1
K. Whelan	TAM	A+	23	2	0	0	28	11	12	28	2	40.3%	.141	6	0.82	1.93	3.66	3.42	4.4	5.5	5.8	1.4	6.4
	TRN	AA	23	4	2	4	54¹	34	42	68	2	41.1%	.269	23	1.40	2.98	4.77	4.17	7.2	8.2	8.3	0.7	7.9
S. White	SWB	AAA	26	6	4	1	91²	85	32	55	3	44.3%	.293	4	1.28	3.34	4.24	4.66	8.8	3.5	3.8	0.5	9.1

The Yankees used 18 different relief pitchers in 2007—not counting lone relief appearances by Roger Clemens, Andy Pettitte, and Mike Mussina—and yet never once called on **T. J. Beam**, who spent the entire year on the 40-man roster. Those five home runs he allowed in 18 major league innings in 2006 must have made quite an impression. ⊘ Brooklyn teen **Dellin Betances** fell to the eighth round in 2006 because he seemed committed to college. The Yankees gave him $1 million to pass up playing quarters with coeds, which, when you think about it, is a lot to give up even for a million. His fastball sits in the mid-90s and might get faster with physical maturity and better mechanics, and he can bend a superior curve. He was shut down with minor elbow pain, but it was purely precautionary; he'll start at Low-A Charleston. ⊘ **Andrew Brackman** was the Yankees' number-one pick in 2007 even though it was widely rumored that he was injured. Indeed, he underwent Tommy John surgery in August and won't be back until 2009, when he's 23. Brackman is crazy tall (6-foot-11) and has great stuff; In 2009, he'll still be tall, but the other thing might not be there anymore. ⊘ **Michael Dunn** discovered that if you bat .160/.269/.225 as an outfielder you have to either go home or learn to pitch. Since converting in 2006, he's shown good control and low-90s stuff, but probably profiles best as a reliever. ⊘ Reliever **Michael Gardner** is a sinker/slider guy with a very low, almost sidearm release point who keeps the ball on the ground and has had some success at Double-A. He's 27 and doesn't have any projection, but the Padres took a flier on him in the Rule-5 draft, where they've found success before with picks such as fellow reliever Kevin Cameron. ⊘ The fifth-round pick from New York's terrific 2006 draft, **George Kontos** throws in the low 90s and has better control than his college career suggested. What's scary is his high fly-ball rate and concomitantly lush number of home runs allowed. ⊘ Another 2006 pick (13th round), **Daniel McCutchen** lost time to a performance-enhancing drug suspension last year. He's a hardish thrower with a solid, diving curveball. Given the organization's glut of pitching prospects, he's likely headed for the bullpen. ⊘ A ninth-round pick in 2006, **Mark Melancon** is a hard thrower who lost last season to Tommy John surgery. He's reportedly still throwing hard in rehab. If healthy, he could move very quickly. ⊘ Not the former Yankee farmhand who went on to star in *Gilmore Girls,* this **Scott Patterson** is a 28-year-old, 6-foot-6 righty the Yanks plucked out of the independent leagues in 2006. His Double-A numbers recall those of fellow indy-league grad Edwar Ramirez, but his stuff is purely average, as he gets by on the deception and angles on his low-90s fastball, which is unlikely to work in the bigs. ⊘ The Yankees' default Opening Day starter in 2007, **Carl Pavano** made just one more start before a DL stint and Tommy John surgery. Curiously, the Yankees' pitching-rich farm system may be his legacy, as GM Brian Cashman has been hoarding pitching prospects ever since an empty cupboard forced him to bid on Mr. Glass. ⊘ A member of the class of 2006 (someone with the Yankees should take that draft out and have it framed), **Dave Robertson** has a fastball-slider combo that batters can't touch, but they don't always have to before they see four balls. Robertson will be an intriguing bullpen option as soon as he can refine his control. ⊘ In a pleasantly unexpected twist, **Ron Villone** was passed over last spring for a younger rival, but after being talked into a minor league deal, he was back in the bigs by mid-May. He pitched decently at first but, keeping to a career-long pattern, slowed in the second half, in part due to a bad back. A free agent, he'll get another shot. ⊘ Picked up in the Gary Sheffield trade, **Kevin Whelan** throws very hard and very wild. The Yankees need all the bullpen help they can get, but Whelan walked nearly seven men per nine innings at Trenton. ⊘ Drafted back in 2003, **Steven White** has always had promise, but also every injury known to man and some that aren't. It's long since time to try him in the bullpen.

MANAGER: JOE TORRE

YEAR	TEAM	W-L	Pythag +/-	Avg PC	100+ P	120+ P	QS	BQS	REL	REL w Zero R	IBB	Subs	PH	PH Avg	PH HR	SB2	CS2	SB3	CS3	SAC Att	SAC %	POS SAC	Squeeze	Swing	In Play
2005	NYA	95-67	5	95.8	74	8	78	5	417	240	25	58	94	.244	2	67	20	17	7	43	65.1%	28	0	148	119
2006	NYA	97-65	1	90.7	44	1	74	8	488	297	41	79	106	.231	0	121	30	18	4	50	68.0%	33	0	140	99
2007	NYA	94-68	-5	90.8	39	0	75	9	522	326	33	33	98	.221	1	113	35	10	5	52	78.9%	39	1	190	145

Los Angeles Dodgers, you've gotten an unflappable manager. Unless he's developed an Ahab complex when it comes to showing up the Steinbrenners, Torre is going to be very patient. He has the forbearance of a man who knows he's been very lucky and will be playing with the house's money for the rest of his life. In fact, he can be excessively patient, especially when it comes to sticking with a declining veteran—Torre could have the next Mike Schmidt at Triple-A, and he would still give Nomar Garciaparra just one more week to find his stroke at third base. Returning to the National League should not mean that Torre will let his heretofore repressed small-ball desires run wild. Torre has never been a big fan of the bunt. However, he just might run himself out of an inning or two. He is very aware of the double play on offense and, when not using the straight steal, will often put on the hit-and-run, though ironically that will sometimes result in strikeout/caught-stealing or lineout double plays. He likes players who walk. He loves reserve catchers who can't hit. On a team with a shaky bullpen, he'll find his one favorite and wear him out, but with a deep pen like L.A.'s, he'll find the right roles for his relievers and never deviate from the formula. In short, if the Dodgers are ready to win, they'll win under Torre. If Torre has to make decisions, like choosing between Garciaparra and Andy LaRoche at the hot corner or figuring out how to distribute playing time between Matt Kemp, Juan Pierre, and Andre Ethier in the outfield corners, chances are they won't.

MANAGER: JOE GIRARDI

YEAR	TEAM	W-L	Pythag +/−	Avg PC	100+ P	120+ P	QS	BQS	REL	REL w Zero R	IBB	Subs	PH	PH Avg	PH HR	SB2	CS2	SB3	CS3	SAC Att	SAC %	POS SAC	Squeeze	Swing	In Play
2006	FLO	78-84	-2	94.9	74	3	86	9	436	270	58	96	247	.242	4	95	50	13	6	103	73.8%	42	4	145	104

New Yankee skipper Joe Girardi has a grand total of one season of managerial experience, the one show above in which he won the NL Manager of the Year award for leading a gutted Marlins team through a surprisingly competitive season. Conflicts with ownership and criticisms that he abused his young starting pitchers haunt him from that stint, but Girardi claims to have learned from his mistakes. Given the Yankees' crop of young starters and Hank Steinbrenner's offseason emergence to fill the ownership void created by his father, he'll have his chance to prove it.

Oakland Athletics

It hardly mattered now; it was, in fact, a fine and enviable madness,
this delusion that all questions have answers, and nothing is beyond reach.
—LARRY NIVEN AND JERRY POURNELLE, *The Mote in God's Eye*

Cycling from success to failure has been the lot of every franchise in the history of baseball, but few have experienced more extreme peaks and valleys than the Athletics. Third all-time behind the Yankees and Cardinals in world championships with nine, the A's have also endured 28 seasons in which their winning percentage dipped below .400. Desperate lurches from absolute failure to success and back have characterized the franchise's fortunes from its very inception, as Connie Mack's original Philadelphia team alternated between two different dynasties (six pennants and three titles in the 13 years spanning 1902 to 1914, then three more pennants and a pair of titles from 1929 to 1931) and the ignominy of fielding some of the worst teams of all time, including the 1916 squad which posted the worst winning percentage in major league history at .235.

Mack's successes were based on intelligence and canny scouting, his failures a product of his dubious finances. The stars of his second dynasty—Hall of Famers Jimmie Foxx, Lefty Grove, Al Simmons, and Mickey Cochrane—were scattered around the league once they became unaffordable, but as the minor leagues were brought entirely under the control of the major league teams, Mack discovered that he was unable to repeat his successes in player development a third time. It took another twenty years, but Mack and his sons finally sold and scrammed after the 1954 season. In their wake, the team was moved to Kansas City.

Insurance-sales magnate Charlie Finley purchased the infamous Kansas City A's and moved them to Oak-

land, a market which failed to reward even his best teams with deserving attendance. Mack's formula of player development–based success despite restricted financial means was nonetheless repeated on Finley's watch, as the franchise boomed with farm-driven successes in the period between the creation of the amateur draft and the abolishment of the reserve clause. The Big Green Machine won three consecutive championships wrapped in five division titles from 1971 to 1975, achieving the game's last real dynasty before the late-'90s Yankees. These accomplishments were followed by another wipeout when the reserve clause finally fell, bringing about free agency. Anticipating the effect of scarcity upon the market should only a select group of players become free agents at any one time, Finley proposed that all players be made free agents after every season, thus creating market inefficiencies that would make free agents more affordable for someone of his means. Finley's financial limitations were brought home to him with a vengeance when commissioner Bowie Kuhn helped squash that suggestion while also taking it upon himself to prevent Finley from selling his soon-to-be-free agents to other teams in order to derive some benefit from the dynasty he had created before it completely collapsed. As a result, stars such as ace Catfish Hunter, slugger Reggie Jackson, fireman Rollie Fingers, and team captain Sal Bando scattered to the winds, and the A's again became one of baseball's worst teams.

Finley's franchise would briefly bob back to relevance with Billyball in 1980 and '81, as maverick man-

---

ATHLETICS PROSPECTUS

2007 record: 76-86; Third place, AL West

Pythagenport record: 79-83

Runs scored per game: 4.57 (11th in AL)

Runs allowed per game: 4.68 (6th in AL)

Team EqA: .262 (6th in AL)

2007 Batters Age: 29.4 (6th youngest in AL)

2007 Pitchers Age: 27.1 (2nd youngest in AL)

Ballpark: McAfee Coliseum; Strong pitcher's park; Park Factor of .948

2007: Somewhere, Joe Morgan is gloating.

2008: Rebuilding begins in earnest.

---

ager Billy Martin did his usual make-then-flake act that kept him hopping from franchise to franchise, turning around yet another moribund team with aggressive in-game tactics, some inspired retreading of seemingly useless veterans, and a few career-altering workloads for his starting pitchers. The timing was convenient; Finley was desperate to sell, and the team's 83-win season in Martin's first year at the helm allowed Finley to hook Levi Strauss chairman and heir Walter Haas, who bought the team prior to Martin's second season.

Life under Haas was strikingly similar to what had gone before. As with nearly all of Martin's previous rejuvenation projects, the A's went back into the ditch in 1982 after only one strike-aided playoff appearance. From that wreckage Haas's son-in-law and then-team president Sandy Alderson slowly emerged as the team's top executive. At a time when Bill James was writing his Baseball Abstracts and sabermetrics was gaining broad public dissemination, Alderson and took to the spirit of the '80s by using analysis (and analysts) to supplement his team's scouting and inform his player acquisitions. Relying equally on improved player development, canny free agent choices, and some inspired trades that were bought low and sold high, Alderson assembled the Bash Brothers teams that from 1988 to 1992 produced four AL West titles, three pennants, and a championship. Unfortunately, Haas's declining health, the club's related financial limitations, and an ill-advised tendency to retain too many veteran players on the downsides of their careers in an attempt to mount one last pennant push for Haas helped send the organization into the doldrums yet again. Unproductive trades of first one Bash Brother and then the other scattered the team's stars around the game once again.

Billy Beane succeeded Alderson as general manager after the 1997 season, and it was from that last trough that Beane and his crew lifted the A's back into contention for their latest run at prominence. Under Beane, the so-called "Moneyball" A's struggled against—you guessed it—financial limitations by using new and improved approaches in performance analysis to assemble a contending ballclub that delivered five playoff appearances in eight years while working around an almost constant, adaptive roster turnover. In the context of the short-stack AL West and wild-card playoff format, however, it remains to be seen if Beane's legacy will be that of a more creative and durable brand of Billyball—and as title-free—or of a piece with the achievements of Alderson, Finley, and Mack.

On some level, the A's did a better job of retooling on the cheap in the last decade than ever before; the only player who was on both the first and last playoff teams in the A's most recent run was third baseman Eric Chavez. By avoiding long-term commitments—or trading them away before they became onerous—the A's were able to move lightly from one set of circumstances to the next, exploiting market inefficiencies from one offseason to the next, constantly mutating into whatever shape the team had to take to mount a challenge. It was only by being so relentlessly adaptive that the A's were able to keep up with the self-sustaining engines of financial and on-field success in Boston and New York as long as they did. They were less successful in applying those approaches to their player development program, however, which is part of the reason why the A's have now found themselves at the end of their latest cycle of success.

What went wrong? The new climbdown is a product of two major setbacks. First, there's the unhappy fact that the players tabbed to be the stars of the current iteration of the club have fallen short of expectations, almost to a man. A major reason is that injuries have seriously deflected the anticipated career trajectories of Chavez, shortstop Bobby Crosby, and starter Rich Harden. They also hobbled the team's top rookie of a year ago, outfielder Travis Buck, as well as closer Huston Street. Imports from outside fared little better in remaining game-ready. Two-thirds of last year's projected starting outfield, Mark Kotsay and Milton Bradley, also broke down, as did single-season DH rental Mike Piazza and right-hander Esteban Loaiza. The team's problems with keeping its players healthy have been simmering for years, but they finally boiled over last year as the club tied its record for players placed on the DL with 22, leading to a few understandable firings and an off-season organizational "health conference." The amount of progress that can be made overnight was underscored by the subsequent sobering announcements that Chavez was progressing a little more slowly than expected from his latest round of surgeries, and that both Chad Gaudin and Justin Duchscherer—two-fifths of the projected 2008 rotation—were both going to have to recover from injuries received in camp. For all of the high marks the organization has gotten in so many other areas over the years, the A's are playing catch-up not just in the areas of diagnosis and rehab, but also in preventive maintenance, or "prehab."

A more fundamental problem, however, has been the farm system, which has failed to supply the depth and breadth of talent that the club has needed to fuel its continuing competitiveness. This is a reflection of the fact that the A's are playing in a more competitive talent-acquisition environment than they were ten years ago. As a result, there are rivals at every level of organizational operations, from big-league acquisitions, to the draft, to international player acquisition and development, to free-talent pickups via waivers, the minor league free agent market, and the Rule 5 draft. The Dominican Republic used to be a place where the A's had a considerable advantage in scouting and signings, but now they are merely one of a crowd of teams pawing prospects on the island.

The A's obtained several solid big-league ballplayers in the 2002 to 2004 drafts, including Street, the team's top hitter in Nick Swisher, rotation stalwart Joe Blanton, catcher of the present and future Kurt Suzuki, and outfielders Andre Ethier and Mark Teahen, both of whom established themselves after being traded away. That's a good yield, but given that the A's averaged seven of the top hundred picks in each of those three drafts, it's not a great one. Matters get dodgier when you look at the last three drafts, as the number of Oakland picks in the top hundred has declined, while the team's ability to get reinforcements from those classes has been hampered by the organization's return to a broader spread of talent from high schools as well as colleges. However necessary the changes may have been, the simple fact is that those younger draftees are further away from The Show, and much of what the organization's upper levels had to contribute is already there.

On the free-talent side of things, swiping slugger DH Jack Cust from the Padres made for a lovely story last year, but it also reflected how much less frequently teams find "surprises" like Cust these days. Where once the A's seemed to conjure up key contributors—such as six-figure free agent flyers Olmedo Saenz, Matt Stairs, Gil Heredia, and Scott Hatteberg—out of thin air, finding quality free talent is no longer quite so easy, which makes replacing the team's increasingly injured core of star talent that much more difficult. Stairs and Saenz have had long careers, but there are doubts about Cust, and there's even less reason to get worked up about last year's waiver-claim find, Lenny DiNardo.

Where Beane's genius perhaps shined brightest was in trades, particularly his smaller exchanges for players such as Gaudin and Cust, and his add-ons to larger deals, such as second baseman Mark Ellis and late righty Cory Lidle, both of whom came over as throw-ins in the three-way deal that brought Johnny Damon over from the Royals. Beane's strength in this area continues to be a source of optimism, as he got power lefty Jerry Blevins from the Cubs for used-up backstop Jason Kendall last summer. This winter, Beane struck two major deals, sending Swisher to the White Soz for two premium pitching prospects and acquiring a compelling six-player package from Arizona for Haren. Several of the players added are young enough and good enough to be part of the next great A's team. If Carlos Gonzalez delivers, the deals would automatically be seen as successful, but the other players picked up could all enjoy productive careers in the major leagues, and any one of them might be "the other guy" who adds that little bit of extra luster to Beane's reputation.

What's different about the A's decline this time around is that it was preceded, rather than followed, by an ownership change. A group headed by real-estate tycoon Lewis Wolff bought the A's at the start of the 2005 season. The combined dedication of the Wolff group and Beane's fellow travelers in the front office, joined by skipper Bob Geren, appears poised to break the franchise's historical cycle. Then again, another of the franchise's historical patterns could reemerge if a legally required environmental impact study determines that the site of the team's prospective new park in Fremont impinges on a neighboring protected wetland. If Fremont doesn't work out, it won't be easy to find another site as close to San Jose without offending Bud Selig's officious sensibilities about what is "Giants territory," and the Wolff group might be forced to break its commitment to stay in the Bay Area. Yet, wherever the A's end up, it seems that Wolff has the money to afford operating a team, which means the A's might actually be in the business of a long-term, structured rebuild, one that combines their business model and team-building strategy with some cash, and could ultimately deliver both a new stadium and a replenished franchise.

The A's situation is made that much more fluid by the possibility of pending room to maneuver on payroll. Mark Ellis is in his walk year, and the club's 2009 options on Harden and lefty reliever Alan Embree lack even so much as a buyout clause. All totaled, more than $18 million could come off of the books after 2008. Some of that will be eaten up by arbitration-related raises, of course (Blanton, Gaudin, and Street were eligible this winter after earning close to the league minimum in 2007), but the savings helps create that much more freedom of action for the A's to invest, should the blend of the Arizona package and players such as Harden, Buck, and Street coalesce quickly, perhaps by 2009 or 2010. Indeed, because Oakland's rebuilding was prompted in part by the fragility of star players who are still part of the organization, the A's aren't the typical depleted team in the initial stages of a rebuild. There's always the possibility that Chavez and Harden will renter the ranks of the best players in the league, joining forces with the rest to return the A's to contention ahead of schedule.

If Beane and company can indeed restore the team's

fortunes, it would be the first time an Athletics' administration accomplished the feat since Mack himself built his second, briefly great ballclub in the late 1920s. It's Beane's charge to deliver his own second act through the same methods that produced his initial success: hard work, research, adaptability, and a keen eye for market inefficiencies. Few major league executives, if any, are as well-equipped to adapt to the game's more rigorous competitive ecology and deliver. If Beane can do that, he will have delivered a more lasting victory over the franchise's cyclical legacy of success and failure.

HITTERS

Daric Barton   1B

Bats: L   Throws: R   Height: 6' 0"   Weight: 225   Born: August 16, 1985   Age: 22

YEAR	TEAM	LVL	AGE	PA	R	2B	3B	HR	RBI	BB	SO	SB	CS	EqBRR	AVG	OBP	SLG	MLVr	EqAVG	EqOBP	EqSLG	EqA	VORP	DEFENSE			
2005	STO	A+	19	361	60	16	2	8	52	62	49	0	1	-0.9	.318	.438	.469	.253	.246	.353	.341	.251	-4.2	58-1B	-10		
2005	MID	AA	19	249	38	20	1	5	37	35	30	1	1	-1.3	.316	.410	.491	.270	.273	.364	.435	.278	8.2	54-1B	-10		
2006	SAC	AAA	20	180	25	6	4	2	22	32	26	1	0	1.6	.259	.389	.395	.105	.233	.359	.353	.260	-1.2	36-1B	0		
2007	SAC	AAA	21	604	84	38	5	9	70	78	69	3	4	-4.2	.293	.389	.438	.173	.263	.358	.403	.267	9.2	111-1B	10	16-3B	-3
2007	OAK	MLB	21	84	16	9	0	4	8	10	11	1	0	0.4	.347	.429	.639	.545	.366	.452	.718	.375	12.2	18-1B	-2		
2008	OAK	MLB	22	646	82	38	4	13	73	74	83	5	3	-0.1	.273	.360	.425	.038	.277	.366	.453	.288	18.2	151-1B	1		

Breakout: 44%   Improve: 73%   Collapse: 8%   Attrition: 11%   Comparables: Jeremy Hermida, Carlos May, Carlos Peña, Mark Kotsay

As if Dan Haren wasn't enough, the Athletics also pilfered Barton from the Cardinals in the Mark Mulder deal, giving them one of the minor league's better pure hitters and their First Baseman of the Future. Barton's not the standard slugger one normally associates with the position; he's a batting-average and on-base machine with just enough juice in his bat to put up .300/.400/.500 seasons annually starting this year.

Rob Bowen   C

Bats: S   Throws: R   Height: 6' 3"   Weight: 225   Born: February 24, 1981   Age: 27

YEAR	TEAM	LVL	AGE	PA	R	2B	3B	HR	RBI	BB	SO	SB	CS	EqBRR	AVG	OBP	SLG	MLVr	EqAVG	EqOBP	EqSLG	EqA	VORP	DEFENSE	
2005	ROC	AAA	24	303	38	13	2	6	25	37	68	0	2	-2.1	.267	.366	.401	.011	.238	.333	.366	.244	2.9	63-C	4
2006	SDN	MLB	25	110	22	5	0	3	13	13	26	0	1	-0.6	.245	.339	.394	-.035	.255	.355	.426	.270	1.8	22-C	0
2007	SDN	MLB	26	98	12	8	0	2	11	13	28	1	2	-0.5	.268	.371	.439	.098	.280	.388	.476	.287	5.0	23-C	-3
2007	CHN	MLB	26	36	3	1	0	0	2	4	13	0	0	0.1	.065	.167	.097	-.835	.065	.167	.097	.000	-5.7		
2007	OAK	MLB	26	54	6	1	0	2	5	10	20	0	0	0.2	.279	.415	.442	.174	.286	.434	.452	.313	4.3	15-C	-2
2008	OAK	MLB	27	282	29	13	1	7	31	32	74	2	1	-0.3	.234	.326	.384	-.099	.238	.332	.410	.262	5.9	69-C	-1

Breakout: 56%   Improve: 71%   Collapse: 19%   Attrition: 33%   Comparables: Mickey Tettleton, Ben Davis, Fran Healy, Stan Lopata

He's a trav'lin' man, and he's made a lot of stops all over the world, but we're not sure if he owns the heart of a lovely girl in every port. Bowen went from San Diego to Oakland in 2007, with a brief layover in the north side of Chicago. He's a strikeout machine (101 in 341 career plate appearances), but he makes up for it with some walks, occasional power, and good defense, or at least enough of each to make him a solid backup. The A's seem pretty comfortable with him backing up Kurt Suzuki this year in what will be the latter's first full major league season.

Corey Brown   OF

Bats: L   Throws: L   Height: 6' 2"   Weight: 190   Born: November 26, 1985   Age: 22

YEAR	TEAM	LVL	AGE	PA	R	2B	3B	HR	RBI	BB	SO	SB	CS	EqBRR	AVG	OBP	SLG	MLVr	EqAVG	EqOBP	EqSLG	EqA	VORP	DEFENSE			
2007	VAN	A-	21	256	31	18	4	11	48	37	77	5	3	-3.1	.268	.379	.545	.314	.193	.273	.364	.220	-17.8	36-CF	2	17-RF	-4
2008	OAK	MLB	22	540	47	29	3	10	53	46	167	8	5	0.0	.206	.277	.343	-.254	.209	.281	.366	.228	-14.6	127-CF	-2		

Breakout: 39%   Improve: 65%   Collapse: 19%   Attrition: 11%   Comparables: Joe Hamilton, Mike Meggers, Nolan Reimold, Dustin Majewski

One of Oakland's two first-round supplemental picks last June, Brown is a typical A's draftee in that he's a college player from a well-established program (Oklahoma State), but an atypical selection in that he's far from polished. A high-upside type with power, speed, and plenty of walks, Brown also has a disturbingly high strikeout rate, which continued in his pro debut and was the thing that kept scouts from loving him, as opposed to merely liking him.

Travis Buck   OF

Bats: L   Throws: R   Height: 6' 2"   Weight: 225   Born: November 18, 1983   Age: 24

YEAR	TEAM	LVL	AGE	PA	R	2B	3B	HR	RBI	BB	SO	SB	CS	EqBRR	AVG	OBP	SLG	MLVr	EqAVG	EqOBP	EqSLG	EqA	VORP	DEFENSE		
2005	KNC	A	21	144	17	13	0	1	22	19	19	3	1	0.2	.341	.427	.472	.286	.289	.361	.406	.270	2.8	31-RF	0	
2006	STO	A+	22	145	24	17	3	3	26	14	18	2	1	1.2	.349	.400	.603	.477	.285	.331	.500	.281	5.3	34-LF	2	
2006	MID	AA	22	238	32	22	1	4	22	22	39	9	1	1.5	.302	.376	.472	.158	.263	.328	.410	.260	-0.9	50-LF	6	
2007	OAK	MLB	23	334	41	22	5	7	34	39	66	4	1	-0.3	.288	.377	.474	.161	.301	.395	.521	.312	17.8	57-RF	0	14-LF 0
2008	OAK	MLB	24	497	64	32	3	12	63	49	91	7	3	0.1	.278	.353	.447	.058	.282	.359	.477	.290	17.2	117-RF	2	

Breakout: 20% Improve: 50% Collapse: 16% Attrition: 13%   Comparables: Mel Hall, Bruce Bochte, Norm Miller, Ben Grieve

Last year, Buck was the surprise winner of a starting outfield job during spring training and had a pretty darn impressive rookie campaign that was derailed by constant injuries, as boo-boos on his wrist, thumb, hamstring, and elbow kept him out of the lineup at various times during the season. The good news is that what you saw in 2007 was very real—Buck can hit for average and get on base at a high frequency, but whether that will be enough to make up for his lacking the power normally associated with a corner outfielder has yet to be determined.

Eric Chavez   3B

Bats: L   Throws: R   Height: 6' 1"   Weight: 230   Born: December 7, 1977   Age: 30

YEAR	TEAM	LVL	AGE	PA	R	2B	3B	HR	RBI	BB	SO	SB	CS	EqBRR	AVG	OBP	SLG	MLVr	EqAVG	EqOBP	EqSLG	EqA	VORP	DEFENSE	
2005	OAK	MLB	27	694	92	40	1	27	101	58	129	6	0	3.2	.269	.329	.466	.056	.274	.343	.487	.284	26.2	151-3B	7
2006	OAK	MLB	28	576	74	24	2	22	72	84	100	3	0	-3.1	.241	.351	.435	-.001	.243	.361	.448	.283	12.9	130-3B	23
2007	OAK	MLB	29	379	43	21	2	15	46	34	76	4	2	-2.8	.240	.306	.446	-.039	.251	.322	.488	.272	4.7	87-3B	0
2008	OAK	MLB	30	437	50	21	1	15	57	46	81	4	2	-0.5	.244	.326	.421	-.044	.248	.332	.449	.272	10.5	104-3B	3

Breakout: 6% Improve: 37% Collapse: 30% Attrition: 14%   Comparables: Wayne Gross, Sid Bream, Corey Koskie, Don Mincher

After playing hurt all year, Chavez saw his 2007 season come to a merciful conclusion at the end of July. Since then, he's been living an episode of *House*, undergoing three separate surgical procedures: first, right shoulder surgery to repair a damaged tendon and some labrum problems; second, the big one, a procedure to repair a bulging disk in his back; finally, in the interest of symmetry, doctors cut open his other shoulder to clean up some frayed tissue. The only thing certain about Chavez's future now is that the A's will be giving him $34 million dollars over the next three years.

Bobby Crosby   SS

Bats: R   Throws: R   Height: 6' 3"   Weight: 215   Born: January 12, 1980   Age: 28

YEAR	TEAM	LVL	AGE	PA	R	2B	3B	HR	RBI	BB	SO	SB	CS	EqBRR	AVG	OBP	SLG	MLVr	EqAVG	EqOBP	EqSLG	EqA	VORP	DEFENSE	
2005	OAK	MLB	25	371	66	25	4	9	38	35	54	0	0	3.2	.276	.346	.456	.078	.280	.361	.482	.288	21.3	83-SS	8
2006	OAK	MLB	26	398	42	12	0	9	40	36	76	8	1	0.8	.229	.298	.338	-.245	.229	.306	.346	.235	-4.1	92-SS	-5
2007	OAK	MLB	27	374	40	16	0	8	31	23	62	10	2	1.7	.226	.278	.341	-.246	.237	.294	.364	.233	-6.0	91-SS	1
2008	OAK	MLB	28	336	37	15	1	6	35	28	57	8	2	0.4	.247	.315	.368	-.130	.251	.320	.393	.255	7.1	81-SS	0

Breakout: 29% Improve: 57% Collapse: 21% Attrition: 26%   Comparables: Glenn Hoffman, Scott Leius, Bill Pecota, Andre Rodgers

Crosby's season ended two days before Chavez's did when he took a Justin Speier pitch off his wrist. The healing of the broken joint was complicated by fluid buildup, and he never returned. That makes three straight seasons in which Crosby has been unable to reach the century mark in games played, and let's face it, his rookie year was a bit overrated in the first place; 22 home runs from a rookie shortstop is great, but outside of his power, he struggled at the plate (.239/.319/.426 with 141 Ks). Over the past two seasons, he's cut down on the strikeouts and everything else as well, hitting .228/.288/.339 in 833 plate appearances. When the A's gave him a five-year extension after 2004 to buy away his arbitration years, it seemed to make sense, but all they've gotten for their money thus far is way too much Marco Scutaro.

Jack Cust — DH

Bats: L Throws: R Height: 6' 1" Weight: 230 Born: January 16, 1979 Age: 29

YEAR	TEAM	LVL	AGE	PA	R	2B	3B	HR	RBI	BB	SO	SB	CS	EqBRR	AVG	OBP	SLG	MLVr	EqAVG	EqOBP	EqSLG	EqA	VORP	DEFENSE
2005	SAC	AAA	26	600	95	28	1	19	75	115	153	2	4	-3.8	.257	.402	.438	.125	.228	.363	.378	.264	-2.5	75-LF -10
2006	POR	AAA	27	591	97	23	0	30	77	143	124	0	3	-2.2	.293	.467	.549	.429	.267	.434	.508	.324	47.3	117-LF -17
2007	POR	AAA	28	100	17	7	0	9	20	19	29	0	0	0.2	.300	.430	.725	.598	.259	.390	.630	.327	10.2	14-LF -2
2007	OAK	MLB	28	507	61	18	1	26	82	105	164	0	2	-3.9	.256	.408	.504	.223	.267	.426	.550	.329	32.6	43-RF -3
2008	OAK	MLB	29	548	72	20	1	21	70	102	151	1	1	-1.4	.239	.383	.438	.066	.242	.389	.467	.302	20.4	129-DH

Breakout: 12% Improve: 28% Collapse: 31% Attrition: 13%   Comparables: Jim Thome, Jason Thompson, Mike Epstein, Randy Milligan

Once upon a time, Jack Cust finally got his chance to play. He hit a bunch of home runs, drew a truckload of walks, and stat-heads around the world squealed with glee at the success of their hero. Then they realized that there was no way in H-E-double-hockey-sticks that a player with his strikeout rate could ever hit anything approaching .256 again. Then the Mitchell Report provided evidence that he was dumb enough to actually write checks when getting himself involved in alleged nefarious activities. And not everyone lived happily ever after. The end.

Mark Ellis — 2B

Bats: R Throws: R Height: 5' 11" Weight: 190 Born: June 6, 1977 Age: 31

YEAR	TEAM	LVL	AGE	PA	R	2B	3B	HR	RBI	BB	SO	SB	CS	EqBRR	AVG	OBP	SLG	MLVr	EqAVG	EqOBP	EqSLG	EqA	VORP	DEFENSE
2005	OAK	MLB	28	486	76	21	5	13	52	44	51	1	3	-3.0	.316	.384	.477	.206	.323	.399	.501	.304	36.2	109-2B 13
2006	OAK	MLB	29	500	64	25	1	11	52	40	76	4	0	3.0	.249	.319	.385	-.124	.252	.327	.397	.257	7.2	119-2B 15
2007	OAK	MLB	30	642	84	33	3	19	76	44	94	9	4	-1.5	.276	.336	.441	.036	.290	.353	.485	.284	23.9	148-2B 30
2008	OAK	MLB	31	592	69	30	3	14	70	50	85	6	3	0.1	.263	.332	.412	-.033	.267	.338	.439	.273	19.0	139-2B 11

Breakout: 12% Improve: 41% Collapse: 32% Attrition: 9%   Comparables: John Valentin, Edgardo Alfonzo, Denis Menke, Phil Garner

A second baseman who hits for a decent average, draws a fair share of walks, shows above average power for the position, and plays mistake-free defense, Ellis is one of the more underappreciated members of the team. If "solid but unspectacular" could only be used to describe one player, Ellis might be the guy. Picking up his $5 million option for 2008 was a no-brainer.

Jack Hannahan — 3B

Bats: L Throws: R Height: 6' 2" Weight: 205 Born: March 4, 1980 Age: 28

YEAR	TEAM	LVL	AGE	PA	R	2B	3B	HR	RBI	BB	SO	SB	CS	EqBRR	AVG	OBP	SLG	MLVr	EqAVG	EqOBP	EqSLG	EqA	VORP	DEFENSE	
2005	TOL	AAA	25	269	31	15	0	4	28	25	58	6	3	0.5	.269	.342	.382	-.003	.246	.319	.350	.238	-0.1	51-3B 3	
2006	TOL	AAA	26	494	59	27	0	9	62	61	114	9	6	-5.0	.282	.379	.412	.176	.257	.352	.405	.267	18.2	50-2B -3	40-3B 5
2007	TOL	AAA	27	417	56	20	1	13	63	76	92	5	5	-2.1	.295	.422	.476	.317	.274	.398	.471	.299	36.4	35-2B 2	20-3B 7
2007	OAK	MLB	27	169	16	12	0	3	24	21	39	1	0	-0.5	.278	.369	.424	.069	.289	.387	.458	.296	6.5	41-3B 0	
2008	OAK	MLB	28	551	64	26	2	13	62	67	125	6	3	-0.5	.250	.345	.399	-.036	.254	.351	.426	.275	13.5	129-3B 2	

Breakout: 19% Improve: 46% Collapse: 24% Attrition: 23%   Comparables: Ed Bouchee, Jon Nunnally, Brad Tyler, Graig Nettles

When the A's ran out of infielders last year, they traded one of their Quadruple-A outfielders to Detroit for Quadruple-A infielder Hannahan, who was wasting his age-27 season by having a career year at Triple-A Toledo. The A's inserted him at third base, where he out-produced the tattered remains of Eric Chavez. This year, "Home Run" Hannahan will be the insurance policy, and with Chavez penciled back in as the starter, the A's are making sure their premiums are paid.

Javier Herrera — OF

Bats: R Throws: R Height: 5' 10" Weight: 205 Born: April 9, 1985 Age: 23

YEAR	TEAM	LVL	AGE	PA	R	2B	3B	HR	RBI	BB	SO	SB	CS	EqBRR	AVG	OBP	SLG	MLVr	EqAVG	EqOBP	EqSLG	EqA	VORP	DEFENSE
2005	KNC	A-	20	422	70	18	2	13	62	47	110	26	5	-0.2	.275	.374	.444	.121	.215	.294	.350	.231	-11.4	88-CF -4
2007	STO	A+	22	279	45	17	0	9	39	19	60	11	7	-1.4	.274	.337	.448	.050	.224	.273	.355	.217	-9.7	46-CF -4
2007	MID	AA	22	79	13	5	0	3	13	4	13	1	0	0.1	.254	.316	.451	.014	.233	.287	.411	.243	-0.9	
2008	OAK	MLB	23	376	36	18	1	8	37	23	96	9	4	0.3	.227	.284	.354	-.217	.231	.288	.377	.235	-6.3	90-CF -1

Breakout: 38% Improve: 58% Collapse: 23% Attrition: 10%   Comparables: Jackson Melian, Melvin Mora, Franklin Gutierrez, Tony Alvarez

Herrera has always had as many raw tools as anyone in the system, but he hasn't exactly endeared himself to the organization with the effort he's made to apply them. He missed all of 2006 recovering from Tommy John surgery, but the team expected him back much sooner and was displeased with his rehab efforts. Healthy last year, Herrera reached Double-A, but he's made little progress on his overly aggressive approach at the plate and is still largely coasting on his athleticism. There's still breakout potential in him, but it won't happen unless he supplements his natural ability with some man-made hard work.

Dan Johnson — 1B — Bats: L — Throws: R — Height: 6' 2" — Weight: 225 — Born: August 10, 1979 — Age: 28

YEAR	TEAM	LVL	AGE	PA	R	2B	3B	HR	RBI	BB	SO	SB	CS	EqBRR	AVG	OBP	SLG	MLVr	EqAVG	EqOBP	EqSLG	EqA	VORP	DEFENSE	
2005	SAC	AAA	25	217	36	17	0	8	41	32	24	0	1	-3.7	.324	.424	.549	.388	.285	.381	.478	.293	12.3	43-1B	0
2005	OAK	MLB	25	434	54	21	0	15	58	50	52	0	1	-1.9	.275	.355	.451	.086	.280	.369	.476	.291	14.5	99-1B	-2
2006	SAC	AAA	26	209	34	13	1	7	44	32	27	0	1	-1.4	.314	.426	.523	.391	.284	.390	.483	.300	13.2	38-1B	7
2006	OAK	MLB	26	331	30	13	1	9	37	40	45	0	0	-1.4	.234	.323	.381	-.131	.234	.332	.390	.256	-5.5	80-1B	15
2007	OAK	MLB	27	495	53	20	1	18	62	72	77	0	0	-0.2	.236	.349	.418	-.005	.246	.366	.453	.284	8.0	96-1B	-10
2008	OAK	MLB	28	497	57	23	1	15	64	66	72	1	1	-1.2	.254	.355	.416	.003	.258	.361	.443	.283	10.5	117-1B	-1

Breakout: 20% Improve: 39% Collapse: 24% Attrition: 16%   Comparables: John Mayberry, Ed Bouchee, John Olerud, Greg Brock

Oakland's primary first baseman for the majority of 2007, Johnson's poor performance helped usher in the Daric Barton era. Johnson's primary abilities are the two things Oakland loves—he can hit some home runs and draw some walks—but he doesn't do enough of either to make up for all of his other deficiencies. The A's are trying to find him a new home, but haven't gotten a lot of interest.

Mark Kotsay — CF — Bats: L — Throws: L — Height: 6' 0" — Weight: 205 — Born: December 2, 1975 — Age: 32

YEAR	TEAM	LVL	AGE	PA	R	2B	3B	HR	RBI	BB	SO	SB	CS	EqBRR	AVG	OBP	SLG	MLVr	EqAVG	EqOBP	EqSLG	EqA	VORP	DEFENSE	
2005	OAK	MLB	29	629	75	35	1	15	82	40	51	5	5	-2.3	.280	.325	.421	-.001	.287	.342	.437	.267	15.2	132-CF	-7
2006	OAK	MLB	30	558	57	29	3	7	59	44	55	6	3	-4.4	.275	.332	.386	-.078	.278	.343	.395	.260	9.8	117-CF	-13
2007	OAK	MLB	31	226	20	14	0	1	20	19	20	1	1	-0.4	.214	.279	.296	-.311	.221	.292	.309	.212	-9.8	53-CF	-1
2008 2008	ATL	MLB	32	261	28	11	1	3	26	23	24	2	1	-0.4	.258	.325	.358	-.147	.256	.323	.365	.238		2.564-CF	-2

Breakout: 11% Improve: 34% Collapse: 37% Attrition: 40%   Comparables: Joe Orsulak, Danny Heep, Gus Bell, Willard Marshall

The 2007 season was the one in which Mark Kotsay's back troubles became chronic. Limited to just 56 games in which his production at the plate would only have been above-average for a pitcher, Kotsay finally shut it down in August in order to begin focusing on 2008. It's an interesting strategy, as for the first time in three years Kotsay was "healthy" enough to actually work out during the winter. The A's were optimistic that his off-season conditioning program would add enough strength to give them some return on the $8 million they owed him for 2008, but were still willing to eat most of that money to ship him to Atlanta, where he'll be the starting center fielder.

Kevin Melillo — 2B — Bats: L — Throws: R — Height: 5' 10" — Weight: 195 — Born: May 14, 1982 — Age: 26

YEAR	TEAM	LVL	AGE	PA	R	2B	3B	HR	RBI	BB	SO	SB	CS	EqBRR	AVG	OBP	SLG	MLVr	EqAVG	EqOBP	EqSLG	EqA	VORP	DEFENSE			
2005	KNC	A	23	342	47	18	3	8	36	53	40	10	4	0.6	.286	.399	.457	.181	.238	.331	.378	.252	4.4	64-2B	-10		
2005	STO	A+	23	104	21	7	1	9	23	12	18	2	0	-0.3	.400	.471	.800	.915	.312	.375	.613	.323	14.2	21-2B	-3		
2005	MID	AA	23	147	33	10	0	7	34	14	23	9	2	1.6	.282	.347	.519	.180	.242	.306	.432	.258	3.1	32-2B	-1		
2006	MID	AA	24	581	73	31	3	12	73	68	98	14	7	-5.8	.280	.367	.426	.062	.242	.320	.366	.244	2.1	130-2B	-16		
2007	SAC	AAA	25	443	63	27	6	10	55	54	100	8	7	-5.1	.262	.355	.442	.087	.235	.328	.403	.252	8.5	87-2B	3	11-3B	-1
2008	OAK	MLB	26	461	51	23	3	10	49	47	103	8	3	0.3	.233	.314	.378	-.129	.237	.319	.403	.256	5.0	109-2B	-5		

Breakout: 25% Improve: 51% Collapse: 18% Attrition: 14%   Comparables: Jason Grabowski, Aaron Guiel, Brad Tyler, Brooks Conrad

Melillo spent his second straight year at Triple-A last year. Despite missing some time with a wrist injury, he was what he's always been—a younger version of Mark Ellis without the defensive chops. The Athletics opted for the real thing and picked up Ellis's option, which means Melillo gets to enjoy Sacramento for another year.

Jermaine Mitchell · OF

Bats: L   Throws: L   Height: 6' 0"   Weight: 200   Born: November 2, 1984   Age: 23

YEAR	TEAM	LVL	AGE	PA	R	2B	3B	HR	RBI	BB	SO	SB	CS	EqBRR	AVG	OBP	SLG	MLVr	EqAVG	EqOBP	EqSLG	EqA	VORP	DEFENSE			
2006	VAN	A-	21	163	23	7	2	3	23	22	27	14	6	-0.6	.362	.460	.507	.500	.255	.337	.379	.252	3.8	32-CF	-1		
2007	KNC	A	22	513	79	20	5	8	58	74	115	24	8	2.1	.288	.390	.413	.150	.214	.303	.308	.222	-32.4	54-RF	4	45-CF	-5
2008	OAK	MLB	23	593	64	25	5	6	43	57	162	17	8	1.6	.230	.307	.330	-.204	.233	.312	.352	.240	-10.9	139-CF	0		

Breakout: 34% Improve: 63% Collapse: 21% Attrition: 14%   Comparables: Ben Copeland, Mike Neill, Claudio Liverziani, Freddy May

Mitchell had a nice full-season debut at Kane County last year, showing a patient approach at the plate as well as good speed and some center-field skills. He's a good athlete but a little raw as a baseball player, and because he was a little old for a Low-A player, many wonder if he'll hit enough in the end. The A's used to avoid this kind of high-risk player, but that's no longer the case. Every system needs athletes, even if only a few of them work out.

Donnie Murphy · INF

Bats: R   Throws: R   Height: 5' 10"   Weight: 185   Born: March 10, 1983   Age: 25

YEAR	TEAM	LVL	AGE	PA	R	2B	3B	HR	RBI	BB	SO	SB	CS	EqBRR	AVG	OBP	SLG	MLVr	EqAVG	EqOBP	EqSLG	EqA	VORP	DEFENSE			
2005	WIC	AA	22	235	33	13	1	10	32	13	32	1	1	-1.8	.313	.362	.523	.252	.273	.322	.458	.264	10.8	29-2B	4	20-SS	2
2005	KCA	MLB	22	88	4	5	0	1	8	9	23	0	1	-0.9	.156	.241	.260	-.443	.158	.253	.250	.175	-7.3	24-2B	-4		
2006	WIC	AA	23	395	57	25	1	14	45	19	65	6	3	1.2	.249	.300	.437	-.054	.217	.256	.377	.215	-11.7	87-2B	-5		
2007	SAC	AAA	24	199	31	19	2	3	22	17	44	4	2	0.6	.326	.388	.509	.311	.254	.320	.424	.257	6.5	39-SS	2		
2007	OAK	MLB	24	132	21	8	0	6	21	10	35	1	0	-0.6	.220	.290	.441	-.090	.231	.305	.487	.267	2.3	30-SS	0		
2008	OAK	MLB	25	394	38	21	1	10	49	24	85	5	2	-0.1	.239	.295	.392	-.139	.243	.300	.418	.251	5.3	94-SS	0		

Breakout: 30% Improve: 58% Collapse: 20% Attrition: 19%   Comparables: Bret Boone, Nick Green, Cole Liniak, Tucker Ashford

Purchased out of the Royals' system, Murphy was another guy pressed into duty last year when the left side of the infield began to crumble. While Murphy hit only .220 for the big club, he surprised everyone by showing off some power, with 14 of his 26 hits going for extra bases. After weighing those 118 big-league at-bats against six years of minor league data and scouting reports, we regret to announce that the .220 average is real, but the power is not.

Cliff Pennington · SS

Bats: S   Throws: R   Height: 5' 11"   Weight: 185   Born: June 15, 1984   Age: 24

YEAR	TEAM	LVL	AGE	PA	R	2B	3B	HR	RBI	BB	SO	SB	CS	EqBRR	AVG	OBP	SLG	MLVr	EqAVG	EqOBP	EqSLG	EqA	VORP	DEFENSE	
2005	KNC	A	21	334	49	15	0	3	29	39	47	25	6	3.9	.276	.364	.359	-.004	.230	.301	.297	.221	-8.7	65-SS	-3
2006	STO	A+	22	202	36	7	0	2	21	24	35	7	1	3.6	.203	.302	.277	-.289	.181	.262	.236	.182	-15.6	43-SS	-6
2007	STO	A+	23	333	50	17	3	6	36	43	54	9	2	-0.4	.255	.348	.399	-.014	.207	.288	.312	.216	-10.4	66-SS	6
2007	MID	AA	23	314	41	13	2	2	21	38	35	8	2	2.9	.251	.343	.336	-.095	.220	.304	.300	.221	-8.1	64-SS	6
2008	OAK	MLB	24	613	60	29	4	6	48	52	110	13	5	1.2	.225	.294	.328	-.232	.229	.299	.350	.234	-4.6	143-SS	2

Breakout: 59% Improve: 75% Collapse: 11% Attrition: 12%   Comparables: Russ Adams, Shawn Livsey, Adam Everett, Greg Norton

Pennington is a gritty, gutsy grinder. In fact, the only "g"-word he's missing is "good." As a switch-hitter with excellent fundamentals, lots of energy, above-average speed, and soft hands in the field, he might have value as a utility man, but he just hasn't hit enough to provide any evidence that he was worth the A's first-round pick in 2005.

Gregorio Petit · INF

Bats: R   Throws: R   Height: 5' 10"   Weight: 160   Born: December 10, 1984   Age: 23

YEAR	TEAM	LVL	AGE	PA	R	2B	3B	HR	RBI	BB	SO	SB	CS	EqBRR	AVG	OBP	SLG	MLVr	EqAVG	EqOBP	EqSLG	EqA	VORP	DEFENSE			
2005	KNC	A	20	318	55	10	4	9	33	26	44	8	2	3.8	.289	.349	.446	.097	.238	.286	.367	.226	-4.5	41-2B	-6	28-SS	1
2006	STO	A+	21	576	71	25	7	8	63	38	96	22	13	-3.0	.256	.310	.378	-.098	.206	.250	.306	.193	-34.9	75-2B	5	61-SS	-7
2007	MID	AA	22	299	33	14	0	4	31	25	44	3		-0.6	.306	.366	.403	.070	.271	.327	.359	.244	5.4	63-SS	4		
2007	SAC	AAA	22	260	20	12	0	2	28	16	48	1	2	-2.2	.277	.327	.353	-.087	.249	.298	.316	.217	-4.3	57-SS	11		
2008	OAK	MLB	23	545	46	22	2	5	44	33	103	11	5	0.3	.234	.284	.317	-.259	.238	.289	.339	.224	-8.3	128-SS	0		

Breakout: 33% Improve: 58% Collapse: 19% Attrition: 9%   Comparables: Luis Maza, Juan Ciriaco, Pedro Lopez, Teuris Olivares

Petit has been playing shortstop one level ahead of Pennington and has proven to be the better prospect. Offensively the two are very similar; Petit might be a slightly better hitter, but like Pennington, he doesn't offer much in the way of secondary skills. What separates Petit from the pack is his defense; he is the best glove man in the system and is equally adept at second, third, or shortstop. The A's have been trying for years to develop versatile players to save them roster spots, and Petit is on pace to be the first one to actually work out.

Mike Piazza **DH** Bats: R Throws: R Height: 6' 3" Weight: 215 Born: September 4, 1968 Age: 39

YEAR	TEAM	LVL	AGE	PA	R	2B	3B	HR	RBI	BB	SO	SB	CS	EqBRR	AVG	OBP	SLG	MLVr	EqAVG	EqOBP	EqSLG	EqA	VORP	DEFENSE
2005	NYN	MLB	36	442	41	23	0	19	62	41	67	0	0	-2.6	.251	.326	.452	.045	.249	.326	.463	.268	19.8	91-C -6
2006	SDN	MLB	37	439	39	19	1	22	68	34	66	0	0	-3.6	.283	.342	.501	.153	.294	.353	.523	.294	26.7	79-C -16
2007	OAK	MLB	38	329	33	17	1	8	44	18	61	0	0	-2.2	.275	.313	.414	-.041	.287	.328	.453	.267	2.5	
2008	OAK	MLB	39	294	29	16	1	10	43	21	56	1	1	-1.1	.255	.310	.426	-.058	.259	.315	.454	.265	7.1	72-DH

Breakout: 7% Improve: 26% Collapse: 42% Attrition: 37%   Comparables: Ellis Burks, Andre Dawson, Tony Perez, Jeff Conine

After striking gold with a one-year DH deal for Frank Thomas in 2006, the A's struck pyrite with Piazza last year, as the former catcher missed almost two months with a shoulder injury, didn't hit, was outshined by Jack Cust, cleared waivers, didn't go anywhere because nobody wanted him, and wound up benched so that the A's could work Barton into the lineup while still showcasing Johnson for a possible trade. Piazza may have been the best offensive catcher in the history of the game, but at age 39, he's done.

Danny Putnam **OF** Bats: L Throws: L Height: 5' 10" Weight: 200 Born: September 17, 1982 Age: 25

YEAR	TEAM	LVL	AGE	PA	R	2B	3B	HR	RBI	BB	SO	SB	CS	EqBRR	AVG	OBP	SLG	MLVr	EqAVG	EqOBP	EqSLG	EqA	VORP	DEFENSE			
2005	STO	A+	22	594	97	37	3	15	100	66	92	1	3	-2.4	.307	.388	.479	.163	.238	.309	.355	.233	-22.5	102-LF	-4	25-RF	0
2006	STO	A+	23	46	7	2	0	1	9	6	8	0	0	0.0	.375	.457	.500	.434	.268	.348	.366	.254	0.5				
2006	MID	AA	23	254	33	13	2	8	37	23	37	2	1	-1.4	.244	.317	.427	-.049	.217	.281	.370	.226	-12.8	32-LF	-1	25-RF	1
2007	MID	AA	24	57	9	7	1	2	15	5	4	1	2	-0.8	.327	.386	.615	.412	.302	.351	.566	.291	4.6	11-LF	-2		
2007	SAC	AAA	24	193	14	11	1	1	17	17	41	2	2	-3.5	.216	.302	.310	-.244	.197	.276	.283	.196	-15.7	21-RF	2	14-LF	0
2007	OAK	MLB	24	31	3	0	0	1	2	3	11	0	0	-0.1	.214	.290	.321	-.261	.214	.290	.321	.214	-1.2				
2008	OAK	MLB	25	330	28	16	1	5	33	26	66	2	1	-0.4	.226	.290	.339	-.226	.229	.295	.361	.232	-9.3	80-LF	-1		

Breakout: 27% Improve: 58% Collapse: 23% Attrition: 19%   Comparables: Jason Grove, Dan Peltier, Bobby Malek, Daren Epley

Putnam is a typical specimen of a college type who hits a bunch but scouts don't love him because he's short, thick, and doesn't have enough power for the positions (left field, first base) to which his meager athleticism limits him. Further hindering Putnam is an inability to stay healthy, though that's been more the result of bad luck than bad genes; after missing a large chunk of the 2006 season to a knee injury, a pitch broke his hand last year. He's on the verge of being passed by younger and better prospects, and can't afford to miss more time this year.

Tony Recker **C** Bats: R Throws: R Height: 6' 2" Weight: 225 Born: August 29, 1983 Age: 24

YEAR	TEAM	LVL	AGE	PA	R	2B	3B	HR	RBI	BB	SO	SB	CS	EqBRR	AVG	OBP	SLG	MLVr	EqAVG	EqOBP	EqSLG	EqA	VORP	DEFENSE
2005	VAN	A-	21	169	16	8	0	5	18	16	40	0	0	-0.6	.233	.315	.387	.022	.179	.243	.269	.171	-26.1	38-C 3
2006	KNC	A	22	453	52	24	3	14	57	42	115	5	5	-5.2	.287	.358	.464	.174	.218	.276	.361	.219	-12.1	93-C 1
2007	STO	A+	23	244	39	17	2	13	47	27	48	2	0	-3.2	.319	.402	.609	.429	.259	.331	.472	.276	12.2	53-C -2
2007	MID	AA	23	219	16	12	0	4	20	17	63	0	1	0.2	.204	.269	.323	-.267	.186	.245	.279	.177	-17.7	55-C -12
2008	OAK	MLB	24	447	32	20	1	10	48	30	127	3	1	-1.0	.209	.267	.332	-.284	.212	.272	.355	.219	-11.3	106-C -2

Breakout: 32% Improve: 56% Collapse: 23% Attrition: 6%   Comparables: Brad Cresse, Dan Conway, Aaron McNeal, Giuseppe Chiaramonte

"A Tale of Two Seasons," starring Tony Recker. First half of 2007: 1,000-plus OPS at High-A; Second half: sub-600 OPS at Double-A. Reality? Probably somewhere in between. Recker has power and patience to be sure, but he also has a long swing that will probably always suppress his batting average. That's the offensive profile of a future backup, but his defense still has a long way to go for him to have value in that role.

Richie Robnett   OF

Bats: L   Throws: L   Height: 5' 10"   Weight: 200   Born: September 17, 1983   Age: 24

YEAR	TEAM	LVL	AGE	PA	R	2B	3B	HR	RBI	BB	SO	SB	CS	EqBRR	AVG	OBP	SLG	MLVr	EqAVG	EqOBP	EqSLG	EqA	VORP	DEFENSE			
2005	STO	A+	21	519	77	30	0	20	74	56	151	8	4	-1.9	.243	.324	.440	-.077	.194	.264	.326	.205	-39.6	99-RF	8	13-CF	-1
2006	STO	A+	22	307	46	8	2	11	38	35	73	4	3	1.2	.266	.358	.434	.075	.214	.292	.344	.224	-9.6	38-CF	2	28-RF	-4
2007	MID	AA	23	532	74	39	2	18	75	34	130	4	3	-2.1	.269	.318	.466	.049	.237	.280	.406	.235	-5.6	63-CF	-4	44-RF	-4
2007	SAC	AAA	23	39	6	0	0	0	1	4	16	0	0	0.1	.152	.263	.152	-.579	.118	.231	.118	.096	-5.8				
2008	OAK	MLB	24	562	51	27	3	13	62	41	160	6	3	0.3	.220	.280	.361	-.217	.223	.285	.385	.234	-13.4	132-RF	-2		

Breakout: 41% Improve: 64% Collapse: 14% Attrition: 12%   Comparables: Jeff Liefer, Dee Brown, Jason Cooper, Dustin Majewski

Four years after being selected in the first round of the 2004 draft, Robnett has proven two things: he can hit for power, and he strikes out far too much for that to really matter. He hasn't totally stunk, and he'll be at Triple-A next year, so he's on pace to reach the majors, but it's hard to see him as more than a fourth outfielder.

Marco Scutaro   INF

Bats: R   Throws: R   Height: 5' 10"   Weight: 185   Born: October 30, 1975   Age: 32

YEAR	TEAM	LVL	AGE	PA	R	2B	3B	HR	RBI	BB	SO	SB	CS	EqBRR	AVG	OBP	SLG	MLVr	EqAVG	EqOBP	EqSLG	EqA	VORP	DEFENSE			
2005	OAK	MLB	29	423	48	22	3	9	37	36	48	5	2	1.5	.247	.310	.391	-.092	.251	.325	.413	.257	6.3	74-SS	3	30-2B	3
2006	OAK	MLB	30	423	52	21	6	5	41	50	66	5	1	1.3	.266	.350	.397	-.032	.269	.362	.414	.275	14.7	64-SS	-9	34-2B	3
2007	OAK	MLB	31	379	49	13	0	7	41	35	40	2	1	0.0	.260	.332	.361	-.095	.275	.350	.391	.262	2.5	39-SS	-3	33-3B	-6
2008	TOR	MLB	32	364	42	16	2	7	36	36	51	3	2	0.0	.257	.334	.383	-.073	.256	.335	.387	.258	6.5	87-SS	-3		

Breakout: 13% Improve: 35% Collapse: 35% Attrition: 23%   Comparables: Denis Menke, Kevin Seitzer, Rick Burleson, Edgardo Alfonzo

Every year it's the same: Scutaro enters the year as a backup infielder, somebody (usually Bobby Crosby) suffers some kind of big injury that makes Scutaro an everyday player, and Scutaro performs well enough that nobody notices the change (Crosby 2005-7: .243/.307/.377; Scutaro 2005-7: .257/.331/.384). This year he'll do it for the Blue Jays, as Oakland dealt him to Toronto in the offseason for a pair of fringy minor league arms on the assumption that Donnie Murphy can turn the same trick at a cheaper price.

Chris Snelling   OF

Bats: L   Throws: L   Height: 5' 10"   Weight: 205   Born: December 3, 1981   Age: 26

YEAR	TEAM	LVL	AGE	PA	R	2B	3B	HR	RBI	BB	SO	SB	CS	EqBRR	AVG	OBP	SLG	MLVr	EqAVG	EqOBP	EqSLG	EqA	VORP	DEFENSE			
2005	TAC	AAA	23	291	50	17	2	8	46	36	43	2	3	-1.7	.370	.452	.553	.529	.317	.395	.468	.298	18.5	41-RF	-3	11-LF	0
2005	SEA	MLB	23	35	4	2	0	1	1	5	2	0	2	-0.8	.276	.382	.448	.137	.276	.400	.448	.275	0.6				
2006	TAC	AAA	24	290	36	13	1	5	39	31	60	4	2	0.4	.216	.326	.340	-.104	.198	.297	.319	.222	-17.4	31-RF	2		
2006	SEA	MLB	24	119	14	6	1	3	6	13	38	2	1	0.6	.250	.360	.427	.023	.263	.377	.474	.292	3.2	26-RF	-5		
2007	WAS	MLB	25	61	6	1	1	1	7	9	11	0	1	0.0	.204	.361	.327	-.093	.204	.371	.327	.253	-1.1	14-LF	0		
2007	OAK	MLB	25	25	4	0	0	0	0	5	4	0	0	-1.4	.350	.480	.350	.209	.350	.480	.350	.316	1.9				
2008	PHI	MLB	26	274	33	13	1	7	31	30	57	3	1	0.0	.245	.339	.398	-.077	.241	.337	.390	.253	2.3	67-LF	-2		

Breakout: 15% Improve: 38% Collapse: 37% Attrition: 29%   Comparables: Dave Bergman, Tom Evans, Aaron Guiel, Jim Gosger

For years, we've written about how Snelling can really hit, but is always hurt. Indeed, Snelling missed most of 2007 with a deep knee bruise. The problem is that he's no longer hitting. When the A's waived him after the season, the Rays picked him up, then sold him to the Phillies less than month later. Having been the property of six teams in a twelve-month span, he's officially become a journeyman.

Shannon Stewart   LF

Bats: R   Throws: R   Height: 5' 11"   Weight: 210   Born: February 25, 1974   Age: 34

YEAR	TEAM	LVL	AGE	PA	R	2B	3B	HR	RBI	BB	SO	SB	CS	EqBRR	AVG	OBP	SLG	MLVr	EqAVG	EqOBP	EqSLG	EqA	VORP	DEFENSE	
2005	MIN	MLB	31	599	69	27	3	10	56	34	73	7	5	-4.3	.274	.323	.388	-.055	.280	.337	.405	.259	1.4	123-LF	3
2006	MIN	MLB	32	190	21	5	1	2	21	14	19	3	1	0.3	.293	.347	.368	-.070	.297	.358	.372	.261	0.6	32-LF	2
2007	OAK	MLB	33	630	79	22	1	12	48	47	60	11	3	2.0	.290	.345	.394	-.002	.306	.366	.427	.278	11.3	129-LF	9
2008	OAK	MLB	34	435	48	18	2	6	46	32	47	6	3	-0.2	.271	.328	.374	-.085	.275	.334	.399	.261	1.5	103-LF	1

Breakout: 12% Improve: 29% Collapse: 39% Attrition: 27%   Comparables: Brady Clark, Jay Payton, Harvey Kuenn, Brian Jordan

Prior to last season, if you had to bet on which Athletics players would be healthy enough to play 146 games, would you have placed money on Shannon Stewart? After four years of foot problems, Stewart signed a relatively cheap contract with the A's and, while everyone else was getting hurt around him, became the everyday left fielder. That was a good thing for Stewart, not so much for the A's, as he played pretty much the way you'd expect an aging Shannon Stewart to play. Given his résumé, the healthy season likely bought him a few more years in the majors, but they won't come in Oakland.

Kurt Suzuki   C   Bats: R   Throws: R   Height: 6' 0"   Weight: 205   Born: October 4, 1983   Age: 24

YEAR	TEAM	LVL	AGE	PA	R	2B	3B	HR	RBI	BB	SO	SB	CS	EqBRR	AVG	OBP	SLG	MLVr	EqAVG	EqOBP	EqSLG	EqA	VORP	DEFENSE
2005	STO	A+	21	523	85	26	5	12	65	63	61	5	3	-0.5	.277	.378	.440	.058	.216	.301	.329	.223	-12.3	103-C -6
2006	MID	AA	22	444	64	26	1	7	55	58	50	5	3	-0.5	.285	.392	.415	.093	.247	.342	.363	.250	6.3	87-C 3
2007	SAC	AAA	23	240	32	9	0	3	27	21	41	0	0	-0.6	.280	.351	.365	-.018	.254	.322	.333	.235	-1.3	43-C 3
2007	OAK	MLB	23	248	27	13	0	7	39	24	39	0	0	-0.9	.249	.327	.408	-.046	.261	.343	.450	.275	7.1	60-C 0
2008	OAK	MLB	24	448	42	21	1	7	46	38	70	3	1	-0.3	.240	.311	.352	-.163	.243	.316	.375	.247	1.7	106-C 2

Breakout: 25%   Improve: 45%   Collapse: 27%   Attrition: 23%   Comparables: A. J. Hinch, Charlie Moore, Glenn Borgmann, Jerry Grote

When the A's finally found a way to get rid of the grisly remains of Jason Kendall (and somehow get a decent prospect for him, to boot), Suzuki became the starting catcher, a position he will likely retain for some time. What you saw in his first 68 big-league games is real in the sense that he should be good for 10 to 15 home runs a year and a healthy walk rate, but based on his scouting reports and minor league track record, his batting average is more likely to be in the .280 range. Still, that makes him one of the better-hitting catchers in the American League.

Nick Swisher   OF   Bats: S   Throws: L   Height: 6' 0"   Weight: 215   Born: November 25, 1980   Age: 27

YEAR	TEAM	LVL	AGE	PA	R	2B	3B	HR	RBI	BB	SO	SB	CS	EqBRR	AVG	OBP	SLG	MLVr	EqAVG	EqOBP	EqSLG	EqA	VORP	DEFENSE
2005	OAK	MLB	24	522	66	32	1	21	74	55	110	0	1	0.0	.236	.322	.446	-.008	.240	.335	.468	.273	6.7	115-RF -5 13-1B -1
2006	OAK	MLB	25	672	106	24	2	35	95	97	152	1	2	-1.6	.254	.372	.493	.122	.255	.381	.510	.301	28.1	78-1B 2 73-LF 11
2007	OAK	MLB	26	659	84	36	1	22	78	100	131	3	2	0.7	.262	.381	.455	.120	.272	.397	.493	.306	31.5	54-CF -5 46-RF 5
2008	CHA	MLB	27	633	91	30	1	31	93	88	137	3	2	-0.6	.265	.373	.501	.150	.262	.372	.506	.301	27.4	148-RF -1

Breakout: 18%   Improve: 54%   Collapse: 9%   Attrition: 8%   Comparables: Mark Teixeira, Jeff Burroughs, Bob Allison, Bobby Kielty

All of the talk about how Swisher is going to become a better hitter is both misguided and unnecessary. Swisher's 35 home runs in 2006 already make him seem like a bit of an outlier, and his career batting average in the minors was .261, but as he's likely to hit 25-plus homers a year while drawing 100 walks, can play all three outfield positions and first base, and plays the game as hard as anyone in baseball. In trading for Swisher, the White Sox acquired an incredibly valuable pull hitter perfectly suited to their home park who is locked up through 2012.

PITCHERS

Andrew Bailey   Bats: R   Throws: R   Height: 6' 3"   Weight: 220   Born: May 31, 1984   Age: 24

YEAR	TEAM	LVL	AGE	W	L	SV	G	GS	IP	H	BB	SO	HR	GB%	BABIP	STUFF	WHIP	ERA	PERA	EqERA	EqH9	EqBB9	EqSO9	EqHR9	VORP	SN/WX
2006	VAN	A-	22	2	5	0	13	10	58	39	20	53	2	44.7%	.240	-7	1.02	2.02	5.35	5.96	8.4	5.8	4.2	1.1	-2.1	—
2007	KNC	A	23	1	4	0	11	10	51	42	22	74	6	45.4%	.321	-10	1.25	3.35	9.87	8.57	11.6	7.7	7.7	2.8	-13.9	—
2007	STO	A+	23	3	4	0	11	11	66	56	31	72	8	40.7%	.312	-2	1.32	3.82	7.24	5.84	9.9	6.3	6.3	1.9	-1.5	—
2008	OAK	MLB	24	5	10	0	24	24	122¹	136	89	84	20	41.2%	.303	-6	1.84	6.48	6.53	6.50	9.8	5.8	5.8	1.5	-16.3	-0.70

Breakout: 27%   Improve: 50%   Collapse: 19%   Attrition: 9%   Comparables: Corey Thurman, Ryan Vogelsong, Ryan Baerlocher, Bart Evans

A sixth-round pick in 2006, Bailey dominated in the lower levels of the A's system last year, but he's not as good as his numbers might suggest. Bailey spent a full four years in college, due in part to having Tommy John surgery during that span, and as a 23-year-old last year, he was *supposed* to dominate the Midwest League, which is largely populated by players are two to four years younger. The Athletics tend to have one or two guys like this at their Kane

County affiliate every year, and while some turn out like Joe Blanton, most turn out like Stephen Bondurant and Brad Knox. There's a reason you haven't heard of those last two guys.

Joe Blanton

Bats: R Throws: R Height: 6' 3" Weight: 250 Born: December 11, 1980 Age: 27

YEAR	TEAM	LVL	AGE	W	L	SV	G	GS	IP	H	BB	SO	HR	GB%	BABIP	STUFF	WHIP	ERA	PERA	EqERA	EqH9	EqBB9	EqSO9	EqHR9	VORP	SN/WX
2005	OAK	MLB	24	12	12	0	33	33	201¹	178	67	116	23	44.8%	.252	6	1.22	3.53	4.10	3.98	8.4	3.0	5.1	1.0	44.4	5.64
2006	OAK	MLB	25	16	12	0	32	31	194¹	241	58	107	17	44.5%	.341	7	1.54	4.82	5.11	5.10	10.7	2.5	4.7	0.7	19.7	2.90
2007	OAK	MLB	26	14	10	0	34	34	230	240	40	140	16	48.6%	.304	19	1.22	3.95	3.67	3.92	9.1	1.4	5.1	0.6	46.3	5.87
2008	OAK	MLB	27	11	10	0	29	29	184²	206	51	110	19	47.7%	.305	10	1.39	4.40	4.45	4.48	9.8	2.2	5.0	0.9	19.0	3.50

Breakout: 8% Improve: 38% Collapse: 22% Attrition: 14% Comparables: Chris Bosio, Danny Cox, Bobby Jones, Dick Bosman

Is Blanton underrated or overrated? He will always give up a good number of hits—he just doesn't have the stuff to miss very many bats—but he only issues about one walk per game, and because he doesn't go deep into counts, he goes deep into the games. He also never misses a turn on the bump. A pitcher who can consistently give you 200-plus innings of average- to slightly above-average performance, as Blanton can, is enormously valuable. He might be too overrated to be underrated, but in the minds of those who think he's the former, he's actually the latter.

Jerry Blevins

Bats: L Throws: L Height: 6' 6" Weight: 185 Born: September 6, 1983 Age: 24

YEAR	TEAM	LVL	AGE	W	L	SV	G	GS	IP	H	BB	SO	HR	GB%	BABIP	STUFF	WHIP	ERA	PERA	EqERA	EqH9	EqBB9	EqSO9	EqHR9	VORP	SN/WX
2005	PEO	A	21	3	7	14	48	2	76¹	75	38	96	6	41.0%	.369	-10	1.48	5.54	8.24	8.73	11.7	6.8	7.4	1.6	-23.0	—
2006	DAY	A+	22	0	1	1	8	0	11²	18	4	9	0	47.6%	.450	-48	1.96	8.84	10.85	13.50	17.1	5.4	3.6	0.0	-8.8	—
2006	BOI	A-	22	1	2	0	16	0	22¹	27	8	19	3	53.2%	.333	-54	1.58	6.11	13.28	15.49	14.6	6.2	3.5	3.1	-22.3	—
2007	DAY	A+	23	1	0	6	15	0	23²	13	5	32	0	65.4%	.260	21	0.76	0.38	3.22	1.61	6.0	2.8	8.1	0.4	9.9	—
2007	TEN	AA	23	2	2	3	23	0	29¹	23	8	37	1	43.2%	.319	14	1.06	1.54	3.98	2.57	8.7	2.9	7.7	0.6	9.4	—
2007	MID	AA	23	1	3	1	17	0	21²	18	5	29	2	45.1%	.348	12	1.06	3.32	4.77	5.49	9.2	2.7	9.2	1.4	0.2	—
2007	OAK	MLB	23	0	1	0	6	0	4²	8	2	3	1	10.0%	.368	-39	2.14	9.57	10.33	12.60	14.4	3.6	5.4	1.8	-3.0	-0.21
2008	OAK	MLB	24	3	4	3	35	4	61	64	25	49	8	42.0%	.305	3	1.46	4.79	4.86	4.82	9.2	3.3	6.8	1.2	4.2	0.50

Breakout: 67% Improve: 89% Collapse: 3% Attrition: 10% Comparables: Robert Dodd, Dave Richards, Luke Anderson, Anthony Shumaker

Well, at least Oakland got something for putting up with three years of Jason Kendall. Blevins began the minor league portion of his year as a generic arm in the Cubs' system and ended it by striking out 20 men in nine shutout innings in the Pacific Coast League playoffs to emerge as the best lefty reliever in the Oakland system, after which he made his major league debut. The 6-foot-6 Blevins has a heavy fastball in the low- to mid-90s which he supplements with a changeup. He's not going to close in the majors, but he could be a key part of the Oakland bullpen as early as this year.

Dallas Braden

Bats: L Throws: L Height: 6' 1" Weight: 185 Born: August 13, 1983 Age: 24

YEAR	TEAM	LVL	AGE	W	L	SV	G	GS	IP	H	BB	SO	HR	GB%	BABIP	STUFF	WHIP	ERA	PERA	EqERA	EqH9	EqBB9	EqSO9	EqHR9	VORP	SN/WX
2005	STO	A+	21	6	0	0	7	7	43²	31	11	64	4	42.4%	.314	30	0.96	2.68	4.34	3.79	7.1	3.6	8.3	1.3	8.1	—
2005	MID	AA	21	9	5	0	16	16	97	104	32	71	5	46.9%	.337	3	1.40	3.90	5.34	5.08	10.3	4.3	4.4	0.8	5.1	—
2006	ATH	Rk	22	2	0	0	6	6	21²	12	3	36	0	48.6%	.364	17	0.71	0.85	4.86	3.18	8.5	3.7	9.0	0.5	4.6	—
2006	STO	A+	22	2	0	0	3	3	13	12	5	17	3	27.3%	.300	-8	1.31	6.23	9.78	9.00	10.5	5.2	7.5	3.8	-4.5	—
2007	MID	AA	23	1	0	0	2	2	12	5	3	13	2	38.5%	.125	11	0.67	2.25	3.48	3.27	4.1	3.3	7.4	2.5	2.8	—
2007	SAC	AAA	23	2	3	0	11	11	64	51	18	74	4	44.0%	.292	31	1.08	2.95	3.54	3.71	7.6	2.7	8.0	0.7	13.2	—
2007	OAK	MLB	23	1	8	0	20	14	72¹	91	26	55	9	39.4%	.347	-5	1.62	6.72	5.98	7.15	11.0	2.8	6.2	1.1	-11.7	0.17
2008	OAK	MLB	24	8	9	1	38	24	145	149	55	114	17	42.6%	.301	11	1.41	4.64	4.50	4.71	9.0	3.1	6.7	1.0	10.8	2.10

Breakout: 48% Improve: 73% Collapse: 10% Attrition: 21% Comparables: Jose Rosado, Sterling Hitchcock, Kevin Rogers, Pete Richert

Braden is a left-hander with a vicious changeup. Those two things are enough to torture minor league hitters, but the majors require a little more in the way of stuff. While Braden's major league ERA was downright awful last year, striking out 55 batters in your first 72 1/3 big-league innings is no easy feat, and he should be able to find some success over time as he gains big-league experience. With the A's rotation in flux, he'll get that chance.

Andrew Brown

| | | | | | | Bats: R | | | Throws: R | | | Height: 6' 6" | | | Weight: 230 | | Born: February 17, 1981 | | | Age: 27 |

YEAR	TEAM	LVL	AGE	W	L	SV	G	GS	IP	H	BB	SO	HR	GB%	BABIP	STUFF	WHIP	ERA	PERA	EqERA	EqH9	EqBB9	EqSO9	EqHR9	VORP	SN/WX
2005	BUF	AAA	24	4	2	4	49	0	69²	52	19	81	7	38.1%	.269	6	1.02	3.36	3.80	4.13	7.2	3.0	7.9	1.1	10.7	—
2006	BUF	AAA	25	5	4	5	39	0	62	52	36	53	5	46.4%	.276	-8	1.42	2.61	5.40	4.12	8.5	6.1	5.5	1.2	9.7	—
2006	CLE	MLB	25	0	0	0	9	0	10	6	8	7	0	39.3%	.214	0	1.40	3.60	2.84	3.60	4.5	6.3	6.3	0.0	2.7	-0.17
2007	POR	AAA	26	2	3	0	32	0	35²	26	15	43	3	47.7%	.274	10	1.15	2.77	3.39	3.53	6.1	4.0	8.3	1.0	8.2	—
2007	OAK	MLB	26	3	3	0	33	0	41²	38	17	43	1	44.3%	.333	20	1.32	4.53	3.49	4.17	8.3	3.3	8.6	0.2	6.6	-0.05
2008	OAK	MLB	27	3	3	3	57	0	57¹	53	25	50	5	44.7%	.288	7	1.35	3.87	3.91	3.94	8.1	3.5	7.3	0.8	10.6	0.80

Breakout: 29% Improve: 46% Collapse: 29% Attrition: 20%   *Comparables: Bill Wertz, Aaron Heilman, Matt Turner, Kevin Gregg*

Brown has arguably been good enough to pitch in a major league bullpen for years, but he never quite endeared himself to the Indians or Padres, the latter of whom passed him off on Oakland after half a year in exchange for Milton Bradley. Brown has consistently allowed less than a hit per inning while striking out more than a batter per, which is a quick and easy indication that he's got what it takes to succeed. A big right-hander with power stuff, he's no trick pitcher, so there's no reason for him not to continue hitting both sides of that equation in the future.

Trevor Cahill

| | | | | | | Bats: R | | | Throws: R | | | Height: 6' 3" | | | Weight: 195 | | Born: March 1, 1988 | | | Age: 20 |

YEAR	TEAM	LVL	AGE	W	L	SV	G	GS	IP	H	BB	SO	HR	GB%	BABIP	STUFF	WHIP	ERA	PERA	EqERA	EqH9	EqBB9	EqSO9	EqHR9	VORP	SN/WX
2007	KNC	A	19	11	4	0	20	19	105¹	85	40	117	3	58.3%	.308	13	1.19	2.74	6.28	5.99	9.9	6.8	5.5	0.9	-3.8	—
2008	OAK	MLB	20	6	10	0	25	25	130²	146	110	91	13	53.0%	.321	-3	1.95	6.02	6.43	6.15	9.8	6.7	5.9	0.9	-11.1	-0.20

Breakout: 19% Improve: 50% Collapse: 29% Attrition: 7%   *Comparables: Don Levinski, Yovani Gallardo, Hayden Penn, Frankie Rodriguez*

Fans who don't necessarily understand that *Moneyball* was about exploiting marketplace inefficiencies, not about any specific set of rules for running a ballclub, gasped in horror when the A's used their top pick in 2006 on a high school pitcher. Turns out the kid is pretty good, as he was one of the top pitchers in the Midwest League during his professional debut. He's got a good fastball, an excellent curve, and a developing changeup, and he's probably smarter than a lot of those college kids, as he turned down Dartmouth to sign with the A's.

Kiko Calero

| | | | | | | Bats: R | | | Throws: R | | | Height: 6' 1" | | | Weight: 205 | | Born: January 9, 1975 | | | Age: 33 |

YEAR	TEAM	LVL	AGE	W	L	SV	G	GS	IP	H	BB	SO	HR	GB%	BABIP	STUFF	WHIP	ERA	PERA	EqERA	EqH9	EqBB9	EqSO9	EqHR9	VORP	SN/WX
2005	OAK	MLB	30	4	1	1	58	0	55²	45	18	52	6	37.3%	.260	13	1.13	3.23	3.55	3.29	7.6	3.0	8.2	1.0	15.7	1.35
2006	OAK	MLB	31	3	2	2	70	0	58	50	24	67	4	33.3%	.317	24	1.28	3.41	3.40	3.32	7.6	3.5	9.6	0.6	17.3	2.40
2007	OAK	MLB	32	1	5	1	46	0	40²	46	21	31	3	33.6%	.350	-8	1.65	5.75	5.30	5.62	10.1	4.3	6.3	0.7	0.8	0.21
2008	OAK	MLB	33	2	2	3	39	0	43²	43	20	38	4	39.0%	.304	4	1.44	4.25	4.33	4.28	8.7	3.6	7.4	0.9	5.7	0.50

Breakout: 15% Improve: 46% Collapse: 34% Attrition: 19%   *Comparables: Jim Hughes, Don McMahon, Kerry Ligtenberg, Turk Wendell*

Calero had two strong seasons as a situational reliever for Oakland, but everything came crashing down in 2007 as shoulder problems plagued him throughout the year. When he's healthy, his slider is a shutdown pitch against righties. Oakland gave him a one-year deal over the winter to see if he can get back to his old ways.

Santiago Casilla

| | | | | | | Bats: R | | | Throws: R | | | Height: 6' 0" | | | Weight: 200 | | Born: June 25, 1980 | | | Age: 28 |

YEAR	TEAM	LVL	AGE	W	L	SV	G	GS	IP	H	BB	SO	HR	GB%	BABIP	STUFF	WHIP	ERA	PERA	EqERA	EqH9	EqBB9	EqSO9	EqHR9	VORP	SN/WX
2005	MID	AA	25	0	0	6	10	0	16²	9	9	30	1	56.7%	.286	15	1.08	1.08	4.38	3.07	6.8	6.8	11.7	0.6	4.1	—
2005	SAC	AAA	25	3	6	20	44	0	48¹	45	20	73	6	43.2%	.358	7	1.35	4.47	5.62	6.20	9.8	4.2	10.2	1.4	-3.0	—
2006	SAC	AAA	26	2	0	4	25	0	33¹	25	10	32	2	45.7%	.264	1	1.06	3.26	3.37	4.09	6.8	3.0	6.3	0.8	5.5	—
2007	SAC	AAA	27	2	1	3	22	0	24	18	14	29	1	54.2%	.304	14	1.33	4.13	3.95	4.70	7.4	5.5	8.6	0.4	2.3	—
2007	OAK	MLB	27	3	1	2	46	0	50²	43	23	52	6	33.6%	.276	9	1.30	4.44	3.67	3.98	7.3	3.5	8.3	1.0	8.5	1.00
2008	OAK	MLB	28	3	3	3	54	0	57²	53	26	51	6	39.3%	.286	6	1.37	4.06	4.02	4.11	8.0	3.7	7.5	0.9	8.5	0.80

Breakout: 30% Improve: 52% Collapse: 24% Attrition: 24%   *Comparables: Shawn Hillegas, Tim Scott, Michael Wuertz, Larry Sherry*

Three years ago, Casilla was "Jairo Garcia" and one of the better young relief pitchers in the minors. Then his birth certificate turned up, and he became a prospect who was old for his level and had some command issues. Casilla's still a pure power bullpen arm with a mid-90s fastball and wipeout slider who could pick up some saves if Huston

Street is unavailable, but he needs to provide the organization with a little more confidence that he'll throw strikes if called upon.

Lenny DiNardo

Bats: L   Throws: L   Height: 6' 4"   Weight: 190   Born: September 19, 1979   Age: 28

YEAR	TEAM	LVL	AGE	W	L	SV	G	GS	IP	H	BB	SO	HR	GB%	BABIP	STUFF	WHIP	ERA	PERA	EqERA	EqH9	EqBB9	EqSO9	EqHR9	VORP	SN/WX
2005	PAW	AAA	25	6	3	0	23	22	108²	109	35	93	7	67.2%	.328	6	1.32	3.15	4.87	4.78	9.6	3.6	5.6	0.8	9.3	—
2005	BOS	MLB	25	0	1	0	8	1	14²	13	5	15	1	66.7%	.308	15	1.23	1.84	3.09	3.00	7.2	3.0	8.4	0.6	3.6	-0.01
2006	BOS	MLB	26	1	2	0	13	6	39	61	20	17	6	59.9%	.379	-34	2.08	7.85	9.27	8.29	13.3	4.5	3.8	1.2	-8.0	-0.22
2007	OAK	MLB	27	8	10	0	35	20	131¹	136	50	59	13	58.2%	.295	-10	1.42	4.11	4.62	4.79	9.3	3.1	3.9	0.9	12.9	2.24
2008	OAK	MLB	28	4	4	0	27	8	71¹	83	30	37	7	55.3%	.311	-9	1.58	5.17	5.14	5.33	10.2	3.4	4.4	0.9	0.5	0.30

Breakout: 20% Improve: 41% Collapse: 33% Attrition: 45%   Comparables: Dave Otto, Paul Kilgus, Scott Schoeneweis, John Curtis

Fool me once, shame on you, fool me twice . . . that's the story with DiNardo, who throws a sinker and a slider. He tries to get hitters to chase the slider by breaking it off the plate, which worked for a while, but once the scouting reports got out, everyone just sat on the sinker, which has a ton of drop but never gets out of the mid-80s, and bashed it around. As a result, his ERA nearly doubled after the All-Star break last year. Though the A's brought him back for 2008, he's no more than an extra arm.

Justin Duchscherer

Bats: R   Throws: R   Height: 6' 3"   Weight: 205   Born: November 19, 1977   Age: 30

YEAR	TEAM	LVL	AGE	W	L	SV	G	GS	IP	H	BB	SO	HR	GB%	BABIP	STUFF	WHIP	ERA	PERA	EqERA	EqH9	EqBB9	EqSO9	EqHR9	VORP	SN/WX
2005	OAK	MLB	27	7	4	5	65	0	85²	67	19	85	7	44.0%	.274	27	1.00	2.21	3.15	2.82	7.5	2.1	8.9	0.7	30.0	3.26
2006	OAK	MLB	28	2	1	9	53	0	55²	52	9	51	4	39.9%	.304	21	1.10	2.91	3.11	2.93	8.0	1.3	7.8	0.7	19.6	3.57
2007	OAK	MLB	29	3	3	0	17	0	16¹	18	8	13	3	51.9%	.313	-12	1.59	4.97	5.77	4.86	9.7	3.8	6.5	1.6	1.8	0.00
2008	OAK	MLB	30	3	2	3	44	0	51¹	49	15	43	5	45.3%	.289	8	1.24	3.45	3.57	3.50	8.4	2.4	7.0	0.9	11.7	1.00

Breakout: 12% Improve: 33% Collapse: 33% Attrition: 10%   Comparables: Jay Howell, Robb Nen, Bill Campbell, Rick Aguilera

One of Oakland's more resilient bullpen arms, Duchscherer suffered through a lost season in 2007. After pitching hurt throughout the first half, he finally gave up the ghost in July and went under the knife for hip surgery. His raw stuff is somewhat similar to DiNardo's, but all of his pitches come out a full grade higher because of impeccable command. Duchscherer has always wanted to start and might get that chance to do so this year.

Alan Embree

Bats: L   Throws: L   Height: 6' 2"   Weight: 190   Born: January 23, 1970   Age: 38

YEAR	TEAM	LVL	AGE	W	L	SV	G	GS	IP	H	BB	SO	HR	GB%	BABIP	STUFF	WHIP	ERA	PERA	EqERA	EqH9	EqBB9	EqSO9	EqHR9	VORP	SN/WX
2005	BOS	MLB	35	1	4	1	43	0	37²	42	11	30	8	41.3%	.309	-13	1.41	7.64	5.45	7.17	9.3	2.6	6.9	1.7	-8.3	-0.96
2005	NYA	MLB	35	1	1	0	24	0	14¹	20	3	8	2	44.6%	.353	-22	1.60	7.55	5.90	8.40	11.4	1.8	4.8	1.2	-4.9	-0.50
2006	SDN	MLB	36	4	3	0	73	0	52¹	50	15	53	4	44.4%	.319	17	1.24	3.27	3.79	3.81	9.0	2.2	8.3	0.7	13.4	1.40
2007	OAK	MLB	37	1	2	17	68	0	68	67	19	51	5	34.6%	.304	6	1.26	3.97	3.63	3.72	8.6	2.3	6.3	0.7	15.2	3.33
2008	OAK	MLB	38	3	3	12	46	0	44²	46	13	32	5	42.4%	.295	-3	1.32	4.09	4.08	4.14	9.1	2.3	6.0	1.0	6.7	0.80

Breakout: 33% Improve: 54% Collapse: 13% Attrition: 30%   Comparables: Dennis Cook, Kent Mercker, Grant Jackson, Bob Patterson

Embree has now fashioned a 14-year career out of being able to get left-handers out and being good enough against the other side that he can be more than just a situational reliever. When Street went down in mid-May, Embree got the closer job based on his experience and acquitted himself well. Even late into his 30s, Embree still has a low-90s fastball and a sharp slider; he should be an important part of the Oakland bullpen again this year.

Chad Gaudin

Bats: R   Throws: R   Height: 5' 10"   Weight: 180   Born: March 24, 1983   Age: 25

YEAR	TEAM	LVL	AGE	W	L	SV	G	GS	IP	H	BB	SO	HR	GB%	BABIP	STUFF	WHIP	ERA	PERA	EqERA	EqH9	EqBB9	EqSO9	EqHR9	VORP	SN/WX
2005	SYR	AAA	22	9	8	0	23	23	150¹	140	35	113	12	45.8%	.296	10	1.16	3.35	4.19	4.08	8.7	2.7	4.8	0.9	23.9	—
2006	SAC	AAA	23	3	0	0	4	4	24¹	14	8	26	0	56.1%	.255	23	0.91	0.37	2.76	3.13	5.5	3.5	7.4	0.0	6.3	—
2006	OAK	MLB	23	4	2	2	55	0	64	51	42	36	3	40.1%	.251	3	1.45	3.09	3.40	3.14	6.7	5.6	4.9	0.4	19.3	1.59
2007	OAK	MLB	24	11	13	0	34	34	199¹	205	100	154	21	51.1%	.310	8	1.53	4.43	4.88	4.57	9.1	4.0	6.4	1.0	24.3	3.77
2008	OAK	MLB	25	10	10	0	41	26	176¹	174	76	131	18	48.3%	.292	10	1.42	4.26	4.34	4.35	8.7	3.5	6.2	0.9	20.3	3.40

Breakout: 19% Improve: 58% Collapse: 17% Attrition: 16%   Comparables: Richard Dotson, Ray Culp, Ryan Dempster, Blue Moon Odom

Gaudin always put up gaudy numbers in the minor leagues, but scouts saw him as a short right-hander with a good slider and little more. He finally got his shot in 2007, and the results were so-so. While he had a league-average ERA, when you allow more than 200 hits and have a triple-figure walk total, your future isn't especially bright. Complicating that future is off-season hip surgery that has his early-2008 availability in question.

Rich Harden — Bats: L — Throws: R — Height: 6' 1" — Weight: 190 — Born: November 30, 1981 — Age: 26

YEAR	TEAM	LVL	AGE	W	L	SV	G	GS	IP	H	BB	SO	HR	GB%	BABIP	STUFF	WHIP	ERA	PERA	EqERA	EqH9	EqBB9	EqSO9	EqHR9	VORP	SN/WX
2005	OAK	MLB	23	10	5	0	22	19	128	93	43	121	7	43.7%	.257	42	1.06	2.53	2.98	3.17	6.9	3.0	8.4	0.4	40.7	5.14
2006	OAK	MLB	24	4	0	0	9	9	46²	31	26	49	5	43.5%	.241	29	1.22	4.24	3.14	3.94	5.7	4.7	9.1	0.8	9.2	1.35
2007	OAK	MLB	25	1	2	0	7	4	25²	18	11	27	3	38.7%	.254	24	1.13	2.45	3.34	2.22	6.7	3.7	9.2	1.1	10.0	1.06
2008	OAK	MLB	26	5	4	1	24	11	81	67	34	82	7	43.5%	.277	23	1.23	3.34	3.33	3.40	7.2	3.4	8.5	0.8	22.5	2.40

Breakout: 16% Improve: 39% Collapse: 34% Attrition: 14%   Comparables: Scott Williamson, Ugueth Urbina, Dave Righetti, Mark Littell

After breaking into the Oakland rotation in late July of 2003, Harden made 63 starts over the next two and a half seasons, but has managed just 13 more over the last two. In 2006 he was sidelined by a strained elbow ligament, in 2007 his shoulder was the problem, and the A's trainers have yet to find any kind of long-term solution for either ailment. It's sad business, as before the injuries struck, Harden was a kid with a mid-90s fastball and a devastating changeup. That probably doesn't matter much anymore. Pitching is an unnatural act, and throwing 100 or more pitches in a day at maximum effort is even more so. For whatever reason, some bodies just can't handle it. The A's would obviously love to have Harden as a part of the 2008 rotation, but they're not especially counting on it.

Dan Haren — Bats: R — Throws: R — Height: 6' 5" — Weight: 220 — Born: September 17, 1980 — Age: 27

YEAR	TEAM	LVL	AGE	W	L	SV	G	GS	IP	H	BB	SO	HR	GB%	BABIP	STUFF	WHIP	ERA	PERA	EqERA	EqH9	EqBB9	EqSO9	EqHR9	VORP	SN/WX
2005	OAK	MLB	24	14	12	0	34	34	217	212	53	163	26	47.1%	.290	15	1.22	3.73	4.51	4.41	9.3	2.2	6.8	1.0	39.5	5.24
2006	OAK	MLB	25	14	13	0	34	34	223	224	45	176	31	45.4%	.292	16	1.21	4.12	3.89	4.10	8.4	1.7	6.6	1.1	41.4	5.29
2007	OAK	MLB	26	15	9	0	34	34	222²	214	55	192	24	45.4%	.292	23	1.21	3.07	3.66	3.35	8.3	1.9	7.0	1.0	56.4	6.26
2008	ARI	MLB	27	13	10	0	31	31	202	197	53	175	25	46.5%	.293	25	1.24	3.78	3.73	3.74	8.3	2.1	7.2	1.0	43.3	6.20

Breakout: 18% Improve: 49% Collapse: 17% Attrition: 13%   Comparables: Curt Schilling, Pete Vuckovich, Freddy Garcia, Fergie Jenkins

Oakland's rebuilding process began in December with the trade of Haren to Arizona for a cornucopia of prospects. Oakland definitely sold high; Haren is generally seen as one of the top starting pitchers in baseball, but he's run out of gas toward the end of each of the last two seasons, and pitching in McAfee Coliseum masked his biggest weakness—giving up big fly balls. As a big-time home-run park, Arizona's Chase Field could prove to be troublesome for Haren, but pitching in the weaker league and not having to worry about those pesky designated hitters should make it a wash in the end.

Shane Komine — Bats: R — Throws: R — Height: 5' 9" — Weight: 180 — Born: October 18, 1980 — Age: 27

YEAR	TEAM	LVL	AGE	W	L	SV	G	GS	IP	H	BB	SO	HR	GB%	BABIP	STUFF	WHIP	ERA	PERA	EqERA	EqH9	EqBB9	EqSO9	EqHR9	VORP	SN/WX
2005	MID	AA	24	2	1	0	5	5	31¹	27	7	33	5	47.6%	.286	5	1.09	3.16	5.52	4.40	8.8	3.1	6.9	2.2	3.8	—
2006	SAC	AAA	25	11	8	0	24	22	140	145	38	116	13	42.7%	.319	0	1.31	4.05	5.04	4.92	9.7	2.8	5.5	1.1	10.1	—
2007	SAC	AAA	26	5	12	0	23	23	133	143	46	99	21	45.7%	.313	-22	1.42	4.87	6.65	6.10	10.5	3.6	5.3	1.7	-6.9	—
2008	OAK	MLB	27	4	6	0	29	11	82¹	97	33	47	13	43.1%	.305	-10	1.58	5.67	5.68	5.69	10.3	3.3	4.8	1.5	-3.2	0.10

Breakout: 12% Improve: 37% Collapse: 39% Attrition: 38%   Comparables: Jody Treadwell, Evan Thomas, Ed Hobaugh, Tim Redding

It's impossible not to root for Komine. His listed height of 5-foot-9 is generous, he's a Tommy John survivor, and he was one of the greatest pitchers in college baseball history (Komine was almost solely responsible for putting the Nebraska program back on the map). Unfortunately, he's not a great pitcher. He has a hellacious curveball, but that's about it; his fastball is a little slow and a lot straight, and he just doesn't have the command to set up big-league hitters. His best hope is to stick in middle relief. If every athlete had his makeup, the world would be a better place.

Ruddy Lugo

Bats: R   Throws: R   Height: 6' 0"   Weight: 190   Born: May 22, 1980   Age: 28

YEAR	TEAM	LVL	AGE	W	L	SV	G	GS	IP	H	BB	SO	HR	GB%	BABIP	STUFF	WHIP	ERA	PERA	EqERA	EqH9	EqBB9	EqSO9	EqHR9	VORP	SN/WX
2005	MNT	AA	25	1	1	2	26	0	40¹	25	23	48	1	46.0%	.242	11	1.19	1.12	3.76	3.62	6.3	6.0	7.2	0.5	8.2	—
2006	TBA	MLB	26	2	4	0	64	0	85	75	37	48	4	43.2%	.272	3	1.32	3.81	3.11	3.56	6.9	3.6	4.7	0.4	18.7	0.87
2007	DUR	AAA	27	2	1	0	11	0	14²	12	12	7	0	56.5%	.267	-15	1.63	1.84	4.80	4.05	8.1	8.1	2.7	0.0	2.3	—
2007	TBA	MLB	27	2	0	0	11	0	10²	17	13	8	2	45.0%	.405	-22	2.81	9.25	11.77	9.53	12.7	9.5	5.6	1.6	-4.0	-0.48
2007	SAC	AAA	27	3	0	10	17	0	20	5	7	22	0	75.6%	.125	17	0.60	0.45	2.31	1.86	2.3	3.3	7.9	0.0	8.0	—
2007	OAK	MLB	27	4	0	0	27	0	37²	31	24	26	1	51.3%	.273	3	1.46	4.30	3.39	3.79	7.1	5.0	5.7	0.2	7.0	0.44
2008	OAK	MLB	28	2	2	2	44	0	48¹	47	27	33	4	48.1%	.287	-6	1.52	4.37	4.49	4.48	8.5	4.4	5.8	0.7	5.5	0.40

Breakout: 16% Improve: 34% Collapse: 33% Attrition: 27%   Comparables: Bruce Dal Canton, Hector Carrasco, Don Stanhouse, Steve Ridzik

Lugo has always been a bit of a mystery and source of frustration to the teams that have employed him, as his scouting reports are far better than his numbers. His fastball sits in the low 90s and touches 95, and he mixes in a nifty curveball, but he just doesn't get as many outs as one would expect given his stuff. The primary reason is a lack of control, as he often finds himself forced into fastball counts, and when hitters know it's coming, they can hit it. Now that Lugo's in his late 20s, there's little reason to think he's just going to suddenly "get it."

Jay Marshall

Bats: L   Throws: L   Height: 6' 5"   Weight: 185   Born: February 25, 1983   Age: 25

YEAR	TEAM	LVL	AGE	W	L	SV	G	GS	IP	H	BB	SO	HR	GB%	BABIP	STUFF	WHIP	ERA	PERA	EqERA	EqH9	EqBB9	EqSO9	EqHR9	VORP	SN/WX
2005	GRF	Rk	22	2	0	6	29	0	43¹	35	7	43	3	60.3%	.274	-30	0.97	2.70	5.92	6.57	9.2	4.1	3.6	1.7	-4.0	—
2006	WNS	A+	23	5	1	4	58	0	62	46	8	44	2	71.7%	.254	-7	0.87	1.02	3.89	2.88	8.1	2.1	4.0	0.8	17.0	—
2007	OAK	MLB	24	1	2	0	51	0	42	50	22	18	3	60.4%	.320	-26	1.71	6.43	5.41	6.59	10.2	4.0	3.6	0.6	-5.3	-0.42
2008	OAK	MLB	25	2	2	1	34	1	39²	40	16	21	3	57.2%	.286	-8	1.42	4.26	4.03	4.46	8.9	3.3	4.4	0.6	4.8	0.40

Breakout: 40% Improve: 67% Collapse: 14% Attrition: 38%   Comparables: Jim Crawford, Kevin Saucier, George Culver, Brian Maxcy

Claimed by the A's in the 2006 Rule 5 draft, Marshall was coming off a season in which left-handed hitters in the Carolina League did almost nothing against him (.096 with no walks and 87 of their 94 outs coming via a strikeout or groundball), but the difference between High-A and the majors is the difference between Pong and PlayStation 3. Big-league lefties hit .296 against the sidewinder last year, but despite his struggles, they managed only four extra-base hits and no home runs off him in 71 at-bats, while his ground-ball percentage remained outstanding. Marshall had an eventful winter as the Red Sox picked him off waivers when the A's tried to slip him through, only to have Oakland return the favor, reclaiming him, then outrighting him to Triple-A, where they hope he'll be able to build on his major league experience and work toward a return engagement with the big club.

Dan Meyer

Bats: R   Throws: L   Height: 6' 3"   Weight: 210   Born: July 3, 1981   Age: 26

YEAR	TEAM	LVL	AGE	W	L	SV	G	GS	IP	H	BB	SO	HR	GB%	BABIP	STUFF	WHIP	ERA	PERA	EqERA	EqH9	EqBB9	EqSO9	EqHR9	VORP	SN/WX
2005	SAC	AAA	24	2	8	0	19	17	89	101	43	63	15	39.1%	.313	-27	1.62	5.36	6.88	6.94	10.4	4.7	4.4	1.8	-12.6	—
2006	SAC	AAA	25	3	3	0	10	10	49¹	63	20	29	10	37.7%	.329	-43	1.69	5.13	9.59	7.47	11.9	4.0	3.6	2.5	-9.8	—
2007	SAC	AAA	26	8	2	0	21	21	115¹	103	51	105	12	39.0%	.297	5	1.34	3.28	4.92	4.00	8.8	4.4	6.6	1.2	19.2	—
2007	OAK	MLB	26	0	2	0	6	3	16¹	20	9	11	2	23.7%	.327	-22	1.78	8.83	5.59	9.87	9.9	4.2	5.2	1.0	-8.2	-0.51
2008	OAK	MLB	26	4	6	0	31	14	85	91	42	59	13	37.3%	.295	-5	1.57	5.59	5.40	5.61	9.4	4.0	5.9	1.3	-2.4	0.20

Breakout: 32% Improve: 57% Collapse: 25% Attrition: 29%   Comparables: David West, Pete Falcone, Tim Lollar, Art Mahaffey

Billy Beane is an outstanding general manager, easily one of the best around. However, he's developed an almost cult-like following in some circles, and each of his moves is typically accompanied by undiscriminating praise from his devotees, anointing it as further proof of his genius. Is he a genius? Maybe, but it's important to note that he's not perfect. Exhibit One: Dan Meyer. Meyer was supposed to be the big prize in the Tim Hudson deal, but he's spent the last three years in Triple-A Sacramento struggling to stay healthy. Last year, Meyer experienced a bit of a comeback, and he will compete for a back-of-the-rotation job this spring, but as good as the Mark Mulder deal was, that's how bad the Tim Hudson deal turned out.

Henry Rodriguez

Bats: R   Throws: R   Height: 6' 1"   Weight: 175   Born: February 25, 1987   Age: 21

YEAR	TEAM	LVL	AGE	W	L	SV	G	GS	IP	H	BB	SO	HR	GB%	BABIP	STUFF	WHIP	ERA	PERA	EqERA	EqH9	EqBB9	EqSO9	EqHR9	VORP	SN/WX
2006	ATH	Rk	19	5	2	1	15	4	43	46	50	59	1	57.9%	.441	-8	2.23	7.53	16.49	14.94	15.5	20.7	6.6	1.7	-32.5	—
2007	KNC	A	20	6	8	0	20	18	99²	75	58	106	2	50.6%	.300	15	1.33	3.07	6.58	6.22	9.3	10.0	5.3	0.8	-5.6	—
2008	OAK	MLB	21	3	7	0	22	16	79	87	98	56	8	50.2%	.318	-22	2.33	7.88	7.73	8.12	9.6	10.0	6.0	1.0	-23.0	-2.10

Breakout: 23% Improve: 47% Collapse: 32% Attrition: 22%   Comparables: Juan Morillo, Don Levinski, Corey Avrard, Abel Gomez

Rodriguez has arguably the strongest arm in the A's system. During his stateside debut in 2006, he hit triple-digits on the radar gun, but also walked more than one batter per inning. The Oakland coaching staff has worked hard to get Rodriguez to accept the fact that a mid-90s pitch with some idea of where it's going is better than a wild 99-mph heater, and he made great strides by applying the philosophy in 2007, more than halving his 2006 walk rate. He's still a high-risk/high-upside guy, but to make a play on the old basketball cliché, you can't teach velocity.

James Simmons

Bats: R   Throws: R   Height: 6' 3"   Weight: 205   Born: September 29, 1986   Age: 21

YEAR	TEAM	LVL	AGE	W	L	SV	G	GS	IP	H	BB	SO	HR	GB%	BABIP	STUFF	WHIP	ERA	PERA	EqERA	EqH9	EqBB9	EqSO9	EqHR9	VORP	SN/WX
2007	MID	AA	20	0	0	0	13	2	29²	36	8	23	2	46.8%	.369	-5	1.48	3.94	6.72	6.33	12.3	3.3	4.7	1.0	-2.2	—
2008	OAK	MLB	21	5	9	0	42	17	124¹	163	53	62	18	49.2%	.329	-12	1.73	6.32	6.30	6.40	11.5	3.4	4.2	1.3	-14.1	-0.80

Breakout: 18% Improve: 50% Collapse: 25% Attrition: 13%   Comparables: Adam Miller, Randy Knoll, Matt Belisle, Daniel Ehler

Oakland's first-round pick in the 2007 draft, Simmons was arguably the most polished pitcher available, but he's much more than just a finesse pitcher who makes up for substandard stuff with outstanding location. His command is exceptional, but he also has a low-90s fastball than can reach 94 mph when he dials it up, a very good changeup, and a decent slider. His ceiling is probably mid-rotation starter, but he could reach it quickly.

Huston Street

Bats: R   Throws: R   Height: 6' 0"   Weight: 195   Born: August 2, 1983   Age: 24

YEAR	TEAM	LVL	AGE	W	L	SV	G	GS	IP	H	BB	SO	HR	GB%	BABIP	STUFF	WHIP	ERA	PERA	EqERA	EqH9	EqBB9	EqSO9	EqHR9	VORP	SN/WX
2005	OAK	MLB	21	5	1	23	67	0	78¹	53	26	72	3	44.2%	.253	36	1.01	1.72	2.81	2.29	6.6	3.0	8.3	0.4	33.3	4.36
2006	OAK	MLB	22	4	4	37	69	0	70²	64	13	67	4	39.4%	.303	28	1.09	3.31	2.89	3.50	7.5	1.5	7.9	0.5	19.7	3.26
2007	OAK	MLB	23	5	2	16	48	0	50	35	12	63	5	43.5%	.259	27	0.94	2.88	2.70	3.35	6.2	1.9	9.4	0.9	13.1	2.23
2008	OAK	MLB	24	6	4	19	60	2	77¹	61	19	88	6	43.6%	.282	31	1.03	2.62	2.51	2.67	6.9	2.0	9.7	0.8	25.2	3.00

Breakout: 45% Improve: 67% Collapse: 12% Attrition: 17%   Comparables: Rafael Soriano, Byung-Hyun Kim, Rod Beck, Bruce Sutter

Street missed more than two months of last season with an irritated nerve in his right elbow. If you think that sounds painful, it is, but the good news is that there was no serious damage in the joint. The other good news is that, when he was healthy, he was having his best season as a pro, allowing less than a baserunner per inning. If the Oakland rebuilding continues, Street is on the short list of high-end talent who could bring back impressive prospects in a trade.

Brad Ziegler

Bats: R   Throws: R   Height: 6' 4"   Weight: 190   Born: October 10, 1979   Age: 28

YEAR	TEAM	LVL	AGE	W	L	SV	G	GS	IP	H	BB	SO	HR	GB%	BABIP	STUFF	WHIP	ERA	PERA	EqERA	EqH9	EqBB9	EqSO9	EqHR9	VORP	SN/WX
2005	STO	A+	25	9	7	0	24	24	141	166	20	144	13	50.3%	.365	-7	1.32	4.66	6.00	6.42	11.3	2.5	5.3	1.3	-11.9	—
2005	MID	AA	25	2	1	0	4	4	21	27	4	20	1	52.2%	.394	-3	1.48	6.86	6.77	8.38	13.0	2.8	6.1	0.9	-6.0	—
2006	MID	AA	26	9	6	0	23	22	141²	151	37	88	17	45.9%	.307	-21	1.33	3.38	5.95	4.78	10.3	3.1	3.6	1.6	12.0	—
2006	SAC	AAA	26	0	1	0	4	4	21¹	32	5	11	3	41.3%	.387	-33	1.75	5.97	10.23	9.15	14.2	2.7	3.2	1.8	-7.8	—
2007	MID	AA	27	4	0	1	15	0	23²	19	4	18	0	62.5%	.275	-2	0.97	1.14	3.26	3.13	7.4	2.0	4.3	0.4	6.3	—
2007	SAC	AAA	27	8	3	1	35	0	54²	46	14	44	0	64.6%	.297	8	1.10	2.96	3.41	4.01	8.0	2.6	5.7	0.2	9.1	—
2008	OAK	MLB	28	3	4	2	24	6	57	62	22	33	6	52.9%	.300	-5	1.46	4.60	4.67	4.72	9.6	3.1	4.9	0.9	4.8	0.70

Breakout: 34% Improve: 61% Collapse: 21% Attrition: 23%   Comparables: Mike Cather, Talley Haines, Daryl Irvine, Brian Schmack

Signed out of the independent leagues, Ziegler has always put up solid minor league numbers, but was seen more as an organizational arm than anything else, a pitcher with a great changeup who could throw strikes but lacked any kind of projection. Minor league pitching coordinator Ron Romanick saw him as an ideal candidate for a conversion to sidearming, and Ziegler proved him right, getting tons of groundballs at both Double- and Triple-A. The A's hope they've created the next Chad Bradford; if so, Ziegler would be reunited in Oakland with Romanick, now the team's bullpen coach.

LINEOUTS

Hitters

PLAYER		TEAM	LVL	AGE	PA	R	2B	3B	HR	RBI	BB	SO	SB-CS	EqBRR	AVG/OBP/SLG	MLVr	EqAVG/EqOBP/EqSLG	EqA	VORP
3B	J. Baisley	MID	AA	24	442	60	22	3	11	46	29	84	4-1	0.7	.257/.308/.408	-.055	.225/.269/.364	.220	-11.4
C	J. Brown	SAC	AAA	27	390	46	22	1	14	58	47	74	0-0	-8.8	.276/.364/.469	.156	.250/.338/.427	.265	13.7
OF	J. DaVanon#	ARI	MLB	33	33	5	2	0	0	1	5	8	1-1	0.1	.154/.303/.231	-.368	.154/.303/.231	.207	-2.7
		OAK	MLB	33	71	9	1	1	0	5	7	19	0-0	1.6	.238/.310/.286	-.260	.258/.338/.306	.236	-2.2
OF	C. Denorfia '08	OAK	MLB	27	85	10	4	0	2	9	7	14	2-0	0.2	.261/.326/.388	-.077	.265/.331/.414	.265	1.4
1B	S. Doolittle*	VAN	A-	20	57	6	3	0	0	4	9	10	0-0	-0.5	.283/.421/.348	.132	.220/.316/.260	.215	-6.8
		KNC	A	20	222	23	10	0	4	29	24	40	1-0	-1.1	.233/.320/.347	-.065	.186/.257/.276	.188	-22.2
INF	J. Furmaniak	SAC	AAA	27	490	70	18	2	15	51	49	105	21-8	-4.7	.292/.373/.450	.162	.265/.343/.416	.267	21.0
C	L. Powell#	MID	AA	25	256	46	9	2	11	39	36	40	1-0	-1.6	.292/.391/.502	.229	.259/.350/.446	.277	13.7
INF	J. Sellers	STO	A+	21	495	72	25	4	4	37	46	69	11-4	0.3	.274/.350/.378	-.025	.225/.288/.304	.211	-18.9
		MID	AA	21	51	2	1	0	0	3	3	10	2-0	0.4	.156/.224/.178	-.557	.170/.235/.191	.156	-6.5
1B	J. Stokes	SAC	AAA	25	68	10	0	0	5	11	9	23	0-0	0.0	.186/.294/.441	-.096	.167/.275/.383	.227	-2.6
OF	M. Sulentic*	KNC	A	19	222	14	6	0	1	16	13	37	2-0	-1.1	.175/.234/.218	-.382	.167/.212/.205	.120	-36.6
		VAN	A-	19	324	41	19	2	4	40	42	79	2-5	-5.5	.261/.362/.388	.075	.201/.272/.294	.195	-51.2
OF	K. Thompson	SWB	AAA	27	319	39	18	3	5	37	42	56	24-8	0.2	.281/.382/.427	.149	.261/.358/.419	.274	12.3

Third baseman **Jeff Baisley** led the Midwest League in total bases in 2006, but he flopped at Double-A last year and is already 25. ⊘ When it comes to **Jeremy Brown**, the A's might not be selling jeans, but nobody's buying the idea that he's much of a ballplayer anymore, either. ⊘ Off-season shoulder surgery delayed the start of **Jeff DaVanon**'s 2007 season until July. After 33 plate appearances, the D'backs decided he was done, and after claiming him off waivers in August, the A's were apparently compelled to agree. He has signed a minor league deal with the Padres. ⊘ The A's nabbed **Chris Denorfia** in a strange trade last April, picking him up three weeks after he underwent Tommy John surgery with the understanding that he wouldn't be ready to wear the green and gold until 2008. If he's fully recovered, there's no reason for him not to be a good bench outfielder with a solid bat. ⊘ A supplemental first-round pick last June, **Sean Doolittle** is an outstanding defensive first baseman with a picture-perfect swing, but he has yet to prove anything as a professional. ⊘ **J. J. Furmaniak** deserved the opportunity Donnie Murphy got last year at least as much as Murphy did. ⊘ **Landon Powell** has star-level skills as a catcher, but he can't stay in shape and suffered the second severe knee injury of his brief career in 2007. ⊘ **Justin Sellers** is a nifty little shortstop with no single overwhelming skill, but he can defend the position well and sometimes that's enough. ⊘ **Jason Stokes** has ridiculous power, but a never-ending string of injuries has limited him to a grand total of 97 games in the last three years combined. ⊘ After an impressive pro debut in 2006, **Matt Sulentic**'s bat went on vacation last year, and nobody's sure where it went. ⊘ After toiling away in the Yankees' system for nearly eight years, **Kevin Thompson** looked like he'd get a chance at being a bench outfielder in Oakland, but he'll now hope for that chance in Pittsburgh, as the Pirates grabbed him when the A's tried to pass him through waivers.

Pitchers

PLAYER	TEAM	LVL	AGE	W	L	SV	IP	H	BB	SO	HR	GB%	BABIP	STUFF	WHIP	ERA	PERA	EqERA	EqH9	EqBB9	EqSO9	EqHR9	VORP
R. Flores*	SAC	AAA	27	1	2	1	36^1	38	17	26	4	38.5%	.301	-22	1.52	2.73	5.35	5.94	9.4	4.5	4.7	1.2	-1.4
	OAK	MLB	27	0	2	0	17^2	16	12	15	2	27.8%	.275	0	1.58	3.56	4.31	3.44	7.9	5.4	6.9	1.0	3.7
J. Gray	MID	AA	25	2	0	3	12^1	7	2	12	0	72.4%	.250	11	0.73	0.00	3.04	1.64	5.7	2.5	6.5	0.0	4.8
	SAC	AAA	25	2	4	12	55	58	22	45	2	59.8%	.339	-6	1.45	4.09	5.10	5.08	10.3	4.0	5.8	0.5	3.0
C. Lewis	SAC	AAA	27	8	3	0	95^2	70	23	97	8	51.6%	.256	25	0.97	1.88	3.34	2.82	6.9	2.4	7.1	1.0	28.6
	OAK	MLB	27	0	2	0	37^2	44	14	23	7	37.7%	.308	-23	1.54	6.45	6.48	6.45	10.3	2.9	5.0	1.7	-3.0
M. Madsen	STO	A+	24	1	2	0	24	21	9	20	1	46.2%	.317	-3	1.25	3.75	5.90	4.95	10.4	5.4	4.9	0.9	1.4
	MID	AA	24	5	2	0	65^1	51	26	69	2	39.9%	.310	22	1.18	2.76	4.19	3.75	8.1	4.5	6.9	0.4	12.3
	SAC	AAA	24	5	1	0	58^1	54	30	40	8	41.4%	.267	-11	1.44	5.09	5.63	6.02	8.8	5.0	4.7	1.5	-2.6
V. Mazzaro	STO	A+	20	9	12	0	153^2	159	71	115	13	54.5%	.319	-16	1.50	5.33	7.23	7.33	11.2	6.1	3.8	1.3	-26.2
C. Robertson	SAC	AAA	28	4	1	2	39^1	43	21	40	3	38.9%	.367	-3	1.63	4.35	6.65	6.75	11.2	5.5	7.5	1.0	-4.6
D. Shafer	MID	AA	25	0	0	8	23^2	19	8	21	1	42.0%	.273	-7	1.14	2.28	3.73	3.09	7.3	3.9	5.4	0.8	6.5
	SAC	AAA	25	1	1	0	34^2	37	24	23	8	40.4%	.282	-39	1.76	7.78	9.26	10.09	10.1	6.5	4.6	2.5	-16.5
J. Windsor	SAC	AAA	24	5	3	0	56^2	67	25	41	3	45.7%	.360	-3	1.62	5.40	6.27	6.71	11.4	4.4	5.0	0.7	-6.6

A small lefty with a good changeup, **Ron Flores** has spent the last three years bouncing between Triple-A and the majors, and now he'll likely do the same in the Cardinals' organization, where he'll be re-united with his brother Randy. ⊘ Right-hander **Jeff Grey** is a strike-throwing reliever with good velocity but little in the way of secondary offerings. ⊘ **Colby Lewis** has two things going for him: he's big, and he can really bring it. That can be enough in the minors, but as he learned last year, you need a second pitch in the major leagues, and Lewis doesn't really have one. Radar gun readings will get Lewis plenty of looks, starting with one from the Royals, who picked him off waivers over the offseason. ⊘ Finesse righty **Mike Madsen** finally had his lack of knockout stuff catch up to him at Triple-A last year; he could reach the big leagues as a middle reliever on moxie alone. ⊘ Despite pedestrian numbers, the A's still have high hopes for **Vince Mazzarro**, a raw power arm who gets plenty of groundballs with his sinker/slider combination. ⊘ Traded to Arizona with Dan Haren, righty **Connor Robertson** doesn't have a ton of stuff, but he's found success with one of the more deceptive deliveries around. ⊘ Acquired from the Reds for Kirk Saarloos after the 2006 season, promising reliever **David Shafer** ran into control problems at Triple-A Sacramento last year. ⊘ After tying for the minor league lead with 17 wins in 2006, finesse righty **Jason Windsor** made ten disappointing starts at Triple-A last year before undergoing shoulder surgery.

MANAGER: BOB GEREN

YEAR	TEAM	W-L	Pythag +/−	Avg PC	100+ P	120+ P	QS	BQS	REL w REL	Zero R	IBB	Subs	PH	PH Avg	PH HR	SB2	CS2	SB3	CS3	SAC Att	SAC %	POS SAC	Squeeze	Swing	In Play
2007	OAK	76-86	-3	95.8	69	2	80	6	445	276	60	33	64	.175	0	51	17	1	3	31	58.1%	16	1	134	86

It is a nearly impossible task to form any conclusions about Bob Geren's ability as a major league manager based on a single season. Injuries robbed him of both of his left-side infielders at midseason, took his closer for two months, prevented him from ever having a reliable fourth or fifth starter, and forced him to use 17 different outfielders over the course of the year. In other words, he was too busy plugging all the leaks to implement any kind of discernable managerial plan. In some ways, Geren's A's were still a classic Oakland team offensively, as they drew the second-most walks and attempted the fewest steals in all of baseball, but still wound up 11th in the AL in runs scored. Even there, it's difficult to say whether or not the lack of running was the result of Geren's decision-making or simply the fact that there was nobody on the team who could steal a base. Geren worked the few reliable starters he had hard, as both Dan Haren and Joe Blanton topped 220 innings, but was that the slow hook part of his managerial style, or simply a side effect of the fact that, with Street and Duchscherer on the DL, the only reliever he could consistently depend on was Embree? There's still a whole lot we don't know about Geren. Some people were turned off by his unemotional demeanor last year, but that might be just what the team needs as it enters a rebuilding process for the first time in a decade.

Philadelphia Phillies

A Global jet airliner, en route from London to New York on an uneventful afternoon in the year 1961, but now reported overdue and missing, and by now searched for on land, sea, and air by anguished human beings fearful of what they'll find. But you and I know where she is, you and I know what's happened. So if some moment, any moment, you hear the sound of jet engines flying atop the overcast, engines that sound searching and lost, engines that sound desperate, shoot up a flare or do something. That would be Global 33 trying to get home—from the Twilight Zone.
—ROD SERLING, "The Odyssey of Flight 33," *The Twilight Zone,* 1961

Like flight Global 33, the Phillies have been lost in the Twilight Zone for a long time. It would be a mistake to focus too much on the team's late-season comeback to win last year's NL East title. It was a wonderful moment in baseball history, but ultimately it was a fluke that says little about the franchise's potential to compete going forward and much more about the incompetence with which the Mets are run. The Phillies remain a conservative organization, one in stasis. In fact, they've done a better job of running in place than any team in recent history.

In 2000, the Phillies went 65-97 and broke up their team, trading away pitchers Curt Schilling and Andy Ashby, infielders Desi Relaford and Mickey Morandini, outfielder Ron Gant, waiving first baseman Rico Brogna, and firing manager Terry Francona. They received little of lasting value in these deals, but the next year, under new manager Larry Bowa, they had a marvelous turnaround, going 86-76.

And that was it. Every year since then, the Phillies' win total has remained in the 80s. Despite a foundation strong enough to win better than half their games in most seasons, the Phillies haven't been able to take the next step forward. Incredibly enough, they haven't fallen either. Remaining in suspended animation like

> ## PHILLIES PROSPECTUS
>
> **2007 record:** 89-73; First place, NL East; Lost to Rockies in Division Series
>
> **Pythagenport record:** 88-74
>
> **Runs scored per game:** 5.51 (1st in NL)
>
> **Runs allowed per game:** 5.07 (13th in NL)
>
> **Team EqA:** .276 (1st in NL)
>
> **2007 Batters Age:** 29.3 (8th youngest in NL)
>
> **2007 Pitchers Age:** 31.1 (4rd oldest in NL)
>
> **Ballpark:** Citizens Bank Park; Slight hitter's park; Park Factor of 1.020
>
> **2007:** The Phillies consistent mediocrity is enough for them to slip past the collapsing Mets.
>
> **2008:** Given the absence of a dominant team in the division, there's no reason they can't pull the same trick again.

that for seven seasons is highly unusual. The Phillies are only the second team in the expansion era to be so ordinary for so long, the first being the Red Sox, who won 80-something games for seven straight years between their 1967 and 1975 pennants (Table 1).

Some of that stagnation is related to a conservative spending strategy; the transfer from Veterans Stadium to Citizens Bank Park hasn't turned the Phillies into big spenders, nor has the team's monopoly on the country's fourth-largest metropolitan area (after New York, Los Angeles, and Chicago). In fact, relative to the league, the Phillies' spending trended downward in the late 1990s, and after a brief peak in conjunction with the opening of the new ballpark, has again begun a steady descent (Table 2).

The organization has been a conservative drafter as well. You can't fault any team whose current roster boasts a quartet of first-round hits, as the Phillies' does in second baseman Chase Utley, left fielder Pat Burrell, and starters Brett Myers and Cole Hamels, but cadging talent out of the later rounds has been a problem. Since Ed Wade took over as general manager following the 1997 season, the Phillies have found just one player of any impact in the later rounds of the draft; that player is literally a big one, first baseman Ryan Howard, who

**Table 1. The Odyssey of Flight 33:
Teams stuck in the 80-something win zone**

Team	Streak	First	Last	W	Avg W	G	Pct
Phillies	**7**	**2001**	**2007**	**600**	**86**	**1133**	**.530**
Red Sox	7	1968	1974	603	86	1127	.535
Braves	6	1961	1966	512	85	964	.531
Yankees	5*	1971	1975	417	83	808	.516
Tigers	5*	1978	1982	427	85	809	.528
Padres	4	2004	2007	346	87	649	.533
Blue Jays	4	1998	2001	335	84	648	.517
Dodgers	4	1969	1972	346	87	640	.541
White Sox	4	2001	2004	333	83	648	.514
Mets	4	1969	1973	331	83	641	.516
Reds	4	1984	1988	346	87	646	.536
Red Sox	4	1988	1991	344	86	648	.531

*W-L record during strike seasons extrapolated from winning percentage.

Table 2. The City of Brotherly Cheap

Year	W-L	Payroll	MLB Rank	% of MLB Avg
1995	69-75	$30,555,945	19	90
1996	67-95	$34,314,500	14	100
1997	68-94	$36,656,500	18	91
1998	75-87	$36,297,500	21	85
1999	77-85	$31,692,500	23	64
2000	65-97	$47,308,000	20	85
2001	86-76	$41,663,833	24	64
2002	80-81	$57,954,999	17	86
2003	86-76	$70,780,000	15	100
2004*	86-76	$92,919,167	5	135
2005	88-74	$95,522,000	4	131
2006	85-77	$88,273,333	12	114
2007	89-73	$89,428,213	13	108

*Indicates first year of Citizens Bank Park.

came in the fifth round of the 2001 draft. Otherwise, the list of eventual major leaguers drafted by the Phillies after the first round under Wade has thus far been limited to Eric Valent (1998, first-round supplemental), Jason Michaels (1998, 4th round), Ryan Madson (1998, 9th), Geoff Geary (1998, 15th), Nick Punto (1998, 21st), Marlon Byrd (1999, 10th), Taylor Buchholz (2000, 6th), Chris Roberson (2001, 9th), Zach Segovia (2002, 2nd), Scott Mathieson (2002, 17th), Michael Bourn (2003, 4th), Kyle Kendrick (2003, 7th), Joe Bisenius (2004, 12th), and Mike Zagurski (2005, 12th). Half of those fourteen players—outfielder Roberson and pitchers Kendrick, Madson, Mathieson, Zagurski, Bisenius, and Segovia—remain in the organization, but none is likely to have much positive impact on the team. Geary and Bourne were just traded this winter for closer Brad Lidge and utility infielder Eric Bruntlett. Most of the others were dealt in trades that have had no lasting influence on the team's fortunes, the most significant being Buchholz who was half of the lure in a trade for the previous Astros closer, Billy Wagner.

Taking a closer look at the team's recent drafts shows a continuing lack of impact talent, though there's still time for that evaluation to change. Taking outfielder Greg Golson with 2004's first-round pick was almost certainly a misjudgment, but that year's second-, third-, and fourth-round picks—catcher Jason Jaramillo, pitcher J. A. Happ, and catcher Lou Marson, respectively—may yet prove to be useful reserve or complementary players. The Phillies had no first-round pick in 2005 because they signed center fielder Kenny Lofton away from the Yankees. The Yankees used that pick, the seventeenth overall, on shortstop C. J. Henry, who the Phillies later acquired in the Bobby Abreu trade, only to have him fail to develop. Philadelphia's second-round

pick that year, third baseman Mike Costanzo, was the final piece of the Lidge deal this winter. Right-hander Kyle Drabek, the team's first-round pick from 2006, has been a bust so far, and though later picks such as shortstop Jason Donald may eventually break through, there are once again no stars in the making. Similarly, while the team has been quite active in the international arena, they favor quantity over quality, and thus rarely have much to show for their efforts.

There is an element of bad luck here, but also some outright terrible player shuffling on the major league level. Since becoming general manager in November 2005, Pat Gillick has made few quality moves to shore up the franchise. Getting Freddy Garcia was, on paper, a sharp move, as it appeared to give the team a desperately needed reliable starter a cut above Jon Lieber and Jamie Moyer to go with the youthful and sometimes erratic Brett Myers and Cole Hamels. Alas, neither Garcia's rotator cuff nor his labrum could hold up his end of the bargain. The trade of pitching prospects Andy Baldwin and Andrew Barb to the Mariners for Moyer in August 2006 has worked out better despite Moyer's move from one of best parks to pitch in to one of the worst. Outfielder Jayson Werth was an astute free agent signing, and third baseman Greg Dobbs a surprisingly effective waiver claim pick-up. The rest, however, has been awful.

Giving a three-year contract to the 38-year-old Tom Gordon and asking him to close was overreaching, and flipping outfielder Jason Michaels to Cleveland for veteran lefty reliever Arthur Rhodes was a complete loss. Free agent infielder Abraham Nuñez has been the worst thing to happen to Philadelphia since the Navy yards closed up. Starter Vicente Padilla was given away for a reliever who was quickly released. Acquiring outfielder David Dellucci in a trade with the Rangers cost the

Phillies little in terms of prospects but was an incongruous move given that Dellucci had nowhere to play for the first half of the 2006 season, then left as a free agent. The Bobby Abreu trade was an outright giveaway. The trade of lefty Rheal Cormier to the Reds brought pitcher Justin Germano, who was subsequently waived and claimed by the Padres, where he developed into a useful starting candidate. Gillick weirdly brought Curacaon wiener-smasher Randall Simon back to the majors in September, 2006, buying him from the Rangers. Third baseman Wes Helms, catcher Rod Barajas, and pitchers Adam Eaton and Antonio Alfonseca were all overvalued as free agents prior to last season.

The in-season moves Gillick made last year to help prop up the Phillies' playoff bid were largely good, but it will be years before we know if any the prospects dealt away will haunt the team, though it's unlikely, given the organizations player-development problems and, as the saying goes, flags fly forever. The decision to sign 41-year-old relief relic Jose Mesa was a sentimental choice that didn't pay off, but lefty J. C. Romero proved to have something left after he was cut by the Red Sox, second baseman Tadahito Iguchi was acquired just in the nick of time after Chase Utley went down with a broken hand, and Kyle Lohse helped shore up a sinking rotation.

Heading into the last season before his announced retirement, Gillick has not pulled off the blockbuster deal that would give the 2008 Phillies a real chance to be his final monument in the game. That said, despite being in a minor key, most of the changes the Phillies have made have been beneficial. The addition of Lidge solves the team's closer problems of a year ago, allows Myers to return to the rotation where he belongs, and eases the demands on Gordon's aging arm. Letting center fielder Aaron Rowand leave for San Francisco prevented the team from making a bad contract commitment. Shifting to center, Shane Victorino becomes a much greater asset than he was in right, and the two-year deal given to free agent Geoff Jenkins should give the team a solid platoon of Jenkins and Werth in right.

Appropriately, most of Gillick's works will end with him. Though he signed manager Charlie Manuel to a two-year contract extension with a club option for 2010, Romero is signed through 2010 (with a 2011 club option), and Utley is signed through 2013, Gillick didn't proffer too many other long-term contracts. Burrell, Lidge, Moyer, Helms, and Gordon are free to depart (or be bought out) at the end of 2008, while Myers, Eaton, and Jenkins are up (or eligible for buyout) at the end of 2009. Jimmy Rollins' contract stretches to 2010 with a 2011 option, but Gillick inherited that one from Wade.

It thus appears that the Phillies have reached the breaking point. Something's got to give and give soon. As to which way their fortunes will fall, let's return to those teams from Table 1, who were stuck like the Phillies in the 80-something-win Twilight Zone. The Global 33 list is one of the more optimistic groups you can find. Many of those teams were just a player away (see Table 3).

Table 3. The Boundaries Are That of the Imagination

Team	Streak	Last	What Happened Next?
Phillies	**7**	**2007**	**?**
Red Sox	7	1974	1975 AL Champions
Braves	6	1966	Under .500 in 1967, .500 in 1968, 1969 NL West Champs
Yankees	5	1975	1976 AL Champions, 1977 and 1978 World Champions
Tigers	5	1982	92 wins in 1983, 1984 World Champions
Padres	4	2007	?
Blue Jays	4	2001	Still on the same treadmill, with the occasional sub-80-win season
Dodgers	4	1972	95 wins in 1973, 1974 NL Champions
White Sox	4	2004	2005 World Champions
Mets	4	1973	1973 NL Champs, then back to irrelevance
Reds	4	1988	Under .500 in 1989, 1990 World Champions
Red Sox	4	1991	Three losing seasons before re-emerging as a mediocre AL East Champ in 1995, also won 1988 and 1990 titles in a weak AL East

That most of these teams were ultimately successful suggests that, for a team stuck in the 80-win strata, success is only an adjustment away. The 1974 Red Sox more or less simultaneously received Jim Rice, Fred Lynn, and Rick Burleson, who the following year helped them to overcome long-term deficiencies in pitching and defense; they also had a lot of luck, outplaying their Pythagorean projection by seven games in 1975. The Yankees replaced hopeless manager Bill Virdon with strategic genius Billy Martin and made a series of canny trades to bring in Willie Randolph, Dock Ellis, Mickey Rivers, Oscar Gamble, and Ed Figueroa to bolster their core. Detroit took off as their pitching staff improved in the early 1980s, climaxing with the addition of fireman Willie Hernandez for the 1984 season. By 1974, the Dodgers had finished installing the Steve Garvey/Davey Lopes/Ron Cey/Bill Russell infield that would drive them for so many years. The 2005 White Sox jumped from 11th in the league in ERA to first with a reconfigured defense. The 1990 Reds were relieved of Pete Rose by the commissioner, and replaced him with a more adept manager in Lou Piniella, who was able to stabilize the lineup, rotation, and bullpen in ways that Rose could not.

This history argues that the Phillies are not building, but their division title does not mean they have arrived. Rather, they have reached the precipice. They can either take a step forward or fall backward. Nothing stays in stasis forever. Arrival will come with the 90- and 100-win seasons which are within their grasp. The core of this team—Howard, Rollins, Utley—is peaking now; two years from now may be too late. In a weak division, with the stage set, all the Phillies need is that one transformative move, the one that boosts their offense from very good to great, or more optimally, changes their pitching staff from weak to strong. The clock is ticking, but they don't seem to be in a hurry, and by the time they get re-organized with a new general manager and a more aggressive plan, Global 33 may finally have run out of fuel.

HITTERS

Rod Barajas   C   Bats: R   Throws: R   Height: 6' 2"   Weight: 230   Born: September 5, 1975   Age: 32

YEAR	TEAM	LVL	AGE	PA	R	2B	3B	HR	RBI	BB	SO	SB	CS	EqBRR	AVG	OBP	SLG	MLVr	EqAVG	EqOBP	EqSLG	EqA	VORP	DEFENSE
2005	TEX	MLB	29	449	53	24	0	21	60	26	70	0	0	-2.1	.254	.306	.466	-.011	.252	.315	.480	.268	16.4	115-C 7
2006	TEX	MLB	30	371	49	20	0	11	41	17	51	0	0	-0.3	.256	.298	.410	-.139	.253	.303	.415	.247	0.6	93-C 1
2007	PHI	MLB	31	146	16	8	0	4	10	21	24	0	1	-0.4	.230	.352	.393	-.038	.221	.349	.393	.261	3.4	34-C 4
2008	PHI	MLB	32	217	23	11	0	8	29	18	36	1	0	-0.5	.245	.316	.433	-.072	.241	.314	.424	.251	6.2	54-C 0

Breakout: 21% Improve: 45% Collapse: 36% Attrition: 30%   Comparables: Gus Triandos, Joe Oliver, Jody Davis, Charles Johnson

Barajas was signed just in case Carlos Ruiz failed, but Ruiz would have had to fail like the Hindenberg to be worthy of replacement by a player with career .240/.282/.410 rates. Barajas was the Opening Day starter, but his bat didn't justify further playing time; all he hit was the bench, the DL with a strained groin, and finally the free agent market when the Phillies declined his option. Unsigned at press time, Barajas is best suited to be a reserve catcher, a role in which his occasional home-run power would distinguish him from the usual catch-and-throw guys.

Quintin Berry   OF   Bats: L   Throws: L   Height: 6' 1"   Weight: 165   Born: November 21, 1984   Age: 23

YEAR	TEAM	LVL	AGE	PA	R	2B	3B	HR	RBI	BB	SO	SB	CS	EqBRR	AVG	OBP	SLG	MLVr	EqAVG	EqOBP	EqSLG	EqA	VORP	DEFENSE
2006	BAT	A-	21	247	34	2	2	0	13	25	51	19	4	3.8	.219	.314	.248	-.098	.176	.250	.199	.168	-56.8	57-CF -7
2007	LWD	A	22	581	86	19	4	3	44	61	85	55	18	3.0	.312	.395	.386	.187	.261	.329	.320	.240	-7.6	91-CF 1 32-LF 0
2008	PHI	MLB	23	583	67	18	4	1	32	46	122	34	11	2.3	.235	.302	.291	-.290	.232	.300	.285	.213	-18.6	137-CF 0

Breakout: 20% Improve: 44% Collapse: 33% Attrition: 11%   Comparables: Vincent Blue, Mike Curry, Endy Chavez, Joey Gathright

There's a lot to like about Berry, but it comes with some projection issues. He's a good hitter who makes consistent contact, is a burner on the base paths, and can play all three outfield positions, although his arm is a bit lacking. He's also 23 years old, doesn't have any power or project to have any, and has only gotten it done in A-ball. In the end, he's probably a very nice extra outfielder, which will make him a good comp for the only other "Quint" in major league history, Quinton McCracken.

Michael Bourn   OF   Bats: L   Throws: R   Height: 5' 11"   Weight: 180   Born: December 27, 1982   Age: 25

YEAR	TEAM	LVL	AGE	PA	R	2B	3B	HR	RBI	BB	SO	SB	CS	EqBRR	AVG	OBP	SLG	MLVr	EqAVG	EqOBP	EqSLG	EqA	VORP	DEFENSE
2005	REA	AA	22	614	80	18	8	6	44	63	123	38	12	1.3	.268	.348	.364	-.000	.237	.313	.322	.232	-15.2	78-CF 11 52-RF 2
2006	REA	AA	23	361	62	5	6	4	26	36	67	30	4	7.1	.274	.350	.365	.044	.254	.324	.347	.250	-2.4	78-CF 2
2006	SWB	AAA	23	174	34	5	7	1	15	20	33	15	1	4.8	.283	.368	.428	.145	.261	.345	.405	.274	5.0	27-CF 1
2007	PHI	MLB	24	133	29	3	3	1	6	13	21	18	1	3.9	.277	.348	.378	-.035	.277	.353	.378	.280	6.0	24-LF 0
2008	HOU	MLB	25	166	23	6	2	2	13	17	29	9	2	1.1	.259	.338	.365	-.115	.261	.340	.372	.255	3.4	43-CF -2

Breakout: 21% Improve: 39% Collapse: 33% Attrition: 35%   Comparables: Herm Winningham, Curtis Goodwin, Milt Cuyler, Steve Finley

One man's trash is Ed Wade's treasure. The Phillies looked at Bourn and saw a pinch-runner and a defensive replacement for Pat Burrell. Current Astros general manager Wade, who drafted Bourn in 2003, looks at him and sees a starting center fielder, and dealt Brad Lidge to get him. The Phillies had it right. As Houston's leadoff hitter, Bourne will steal some bases and run down the odd fly ball in the gaps, but acceptable offense will prove to be a bridge too far.

Pat Burrell   **LF**   Bats: R   Throws: R   Height: 6' 4"   Weight: 235   Born: October 10, 1976   Age: 31

YEAR	TEAM	LVL	AGE	PA	R	2B	3B	HR	RBI	BB	SO	SB	CS	EqBRR	AVG	OBP	SLG	MLVr	EqAVG	EqOBP	EqSLG	EqA	VORP	DEFENSE
2005	PHI	MLB	28	669	78	27	1	32	117	99	160	0	0	-7.5	.281	.389	.504	.218	.271	.381	.495	.300	41.2	146-LF -13
2006	PHI	MLB	29	567	80	24	1	29	95	98	131	0	0	-5.0	.258	.388	.502	.176	.250	.383	.491	.300	27.5	109-LF 1
2007	PHI	MLB	30	598	77	26	0	30	97	114	120	0	0	-0.9	.256	.400	.502	.200	.254	.401	.511	.313	34.5	114-LF -16
2008	PHI	MLB	31	477	71	23	1	25	74	81	108	2	1	-1.7	.263	.392	.518	.178	.259	.389	.508	.303	28.1	113-LF -7

Breakout: 10% Improve: 39% Collapse: 21% Attrition: 23%   Comparables: Tim Salmon, Randy Milligan, Andre Thornton, Morgan Ensberg

Burrell isn't exactly a park-effect fraud, but Citizens Bank Park sure doesn't hurt him. Over the last three years, Pat the Bat has hit .284/.414/.545 at home against .249/.370/.462 on the road. Not every hitter can take advantage of CBP to the degree that Burrell does, so his ability to do so is valuable to the Phillies, but his defense in left is poor enough that he gives a good deal of that value back when he puts on a glove. Burrell's in his walk year, and the Phillies will be trying hard to move him.

Adrian Cardenas   **INF**   Bats: L   Throws: R   Height: 6' 0"   Weight: 185   Born: October 10, 1987   Age: 20

YEAR	TEAM	LVL	AGE	PA	R	2B	3B	HR	RBI	BB	SO	SB	CS	EqBRR	AVG	OBP	SLG	MLVr	EqAVG	EqOBP	EqSLG	EqA	VORP	DEFENSE
2006	PHL	Rk	18	177	22	5	4	2	21	17	28	13	3	1.0	.318	.384	.442	.253	.256	.311	.356	.240	2.9	41-SS -3
2007	LWD	A	19	564	70	30	2	9	79	47	80	19	7	1.4	.295	.354	.417	.148	.246	.295	.339	.226	-11.0	123-2B -3
2008	PHI	MLB	20	639	67	32	3	10	59	42	114	19	8	0.6	.250	.302	.363	-.187	.246	.300	.355	.227	-0.6	149-2B 0

Breakout: 27% Improve: 52% Collapse: 26% Attrition: 5%   Comparables: Hank Blalock, Nate Spears, Paul Kelly, Brent Abernathy

Drafted in the supplemental first round in 2006 after a standout high school career in Miami, Cardenas had a very successful full-season debut last year. After a slow April, he raked over the final four months, showing good plate judgment for a teen and beginning to display the power that will be his calling card. Already shifted from shortstop to second base, Cardenas may eventually move to third or left field because of his poor defense, the presence of Chase Utley, or both. That decision is awhile away, as is Cardenas. For now he remains the top position playing prospect in the Phillies' organization and a possible future impact player at the keystone. For a possible upside, think Ray Durham minus the stolen bases.

Michael Costanzo   **3B**   Bats: L   Throws: R   Height: 6' 3"   Weight: 215   Born: September 9, 1983   Age: 24

YEAR	TEAM	LVL	AGE	PA	R	2B	3B	HR	RBI	BB	SO	SB	CS	EqBRR	AVG	OBP	SLG	MLVr	EqAVG	EqOBP	EqSLG	EqA	VORP	DEFENSE
2005	BAT	A-	21	323	47	17	3	11	50	35	89	0	1	-1.4	.274	.356	.473	.209	.194	.255	.316	.196	-32.8	68-3B 3
2006	CLR	A+	22	593	72	33	1	14	81	74	133	3	2	-2.5	.258	.364	.411	.104	.225	.316	.365	.240	-0.1	131-3B -2
2007	REA	AA	23	595	92	29	1	27	86	75	157	2	0	1.0	.270	.368	.490	.177	.245	.333	.447	.269	25.6	134-3B 4
2008	BAL	MLB	24	608	63	28	2	18	75	58	177	4	2	-0.3	.231	.309	.393	-.118	.229	.310	.405	.251	-1.4	142-3B -3

Breakout: 34% Improve: 61% Collapse: 16% Attrition: 5%   Comparables: Jason Grabowski, Jason Cooper, Chris Haas, Larry Broadway

Born in Philadelphia and the Phillies' top pick in 2005, Costanzo made a great story as the organization's Third Baseman of the Future. That's over now, as he was traded twice over the winter, going first to Houston in the Lidge deal, then to Baltimore as part of the package that netted Miguel Tejada. Costanzo has a ton of power, but has been held back by his Brobdingnagian strikeout rate and high error totals at the hot corner. If he can fix the latter, he could be enough of a hitter to start, but if has to move to a less challenging position, his future will be limited.

Chris Coste   C   Bats: R   Throws: R   Height: 6' 1"   Weight: 215   Born: February 4, 1973   Age: 35

YEAR	TEAM	LVL	AGE	PA	R	2B	3B	HR	RBI	BB	SO	SB	CS	EqBRR	AVG	OBP	SLG	MLVr	EqAVG	EqOBP	EqSLG	EqA	VORP	DEFENSE			
2005	SWB	AAA	32	562	73	26	1	20	89	40	85	3	4	-7.1	.292	.351	.466	.112	.265	.321	.420	.255	17.1	91-3B	2	26-1B	0
2006	SWB	AAA	33	161	12	8	0	2	14	9	28	1	1	0.4	.177	.236	.272	-.332	.204	.256	.313	.197	-13.4	25-1B	5	12-C	1
2006	PHI	MLB	33	213	25	14	0	7	32	10	31	0	0	-0.4	.328	.376	.505	.233	.323	.371	.490	.293	16.5	49-C	-6		
2007	REA	AA	34	116	14	5	0	5	31	5	13	0	0	0.0	.287	.319	.472	.095	.257	.284	.422	.242	1.1	19-C	2		
2007	OTT	AAA	34	102	8	5	0	0	10	10	14	0	0	0.5	.233	.317	.289	-.158	.220	.304	.275	.208	-6.9	16-1B	3		
2007	PHI	MLB	34	137	15	3	0	5	22	4	20	0	0	0.7	.279	.311	.419	-.039	.279	.316	.434	.256	3.6	27-C	0		
2008	PHI	MLB	35	192	19	8	0	5	24	10	31	1	1	-0.4	.259	.306	.393	-.133	.255	.304	.385	.234	1.8	49-C	-1		

Breakout: 16% Improve: 33% Collapse: 44% Attrition: 52%   Comparables: Jamie Burke, Barry Lyons, Randy Knorr, John Flaherty

Charlie Manuel's Crash Davis, Coste was in the minors long enough to have done the breaking-in-Nuke LaLoosh thing with Lefty Grove. The Phillies regarded his unexpected 2006 breakthrough with appropriate skepticism and returned him to the minors to start 2007, then busted him all the way down to Double-A after an early call-up. At age 35, Coste won't have much of a shelf life, but if he beats out Jason Jaramillo for the reserve catcher spot this year, he'll provide a bit of sock and the versatility to play either infield corner in an emergency.

Greg Dobbs   3B   Bats: L   Throws: R   Height: 6' 1"   Weight: 205   Born: July 2, 1978   Age: 29

YEAR	TEAM	LVL	AGE	PA	R	2B	3B	HR	RBI	BB	SO	SB	CS	EqBRR	AVG	OBP	SLG	MLVr	EqAVG	EqOBP	EqSLG	EqA	VORP	DEFENSE			
2005	TAC	AAA	27	208	27	9	0	3	22	14	22	5	2	-2.1	.321	.367	.416	.114	.285	.327	.373	.247	-1.3	31-1B	-2		
2005	SEA	MLB	27	154	8	7	1	1	20	9	25	1	0	-0.6	.246	.288	.331	-.213	.250	.301	.336	.227	-3.8				
2006	TAC	AAA	28	421	60	19	3	9	55	37	58	14	5	-0.4	.314	.375	.451	.220	.285	.342	.423	.266	19.9	42-3B	-3	30-1B	4
2007	PHI	MLB	29	358	45	20	4	10	55	29	67	3	0	1.1	.272	.330	.451	.029	.267	.330	.450	.269	10.0	46-3B	-6	11-1B	0
2008	PHI	MLB	29	255	32	13	2	8	34	21	42	4	1	0.1	.268	.331	.444	-.013	.264	.329	.435	.260	7.9	63-3B	-2		

Breakout: 24% Improve: 42% Collapse: 35% Attrition: 31%   Comparables: Steve Lyons, Mike Lamb, Jerry Lynch, Roy Howell

Dobbs has some legitimate value as a pinch-hitter, having hit .292/.350/.528 in 100 career pinch-hit plate appearances. He did fairly well pinch-hitting and spot starting in the first half of last year, but when Wes Helms proved once again that he's best suited to a bench role, Dobbs began to slip into the lineup more and more often. By season's end, Dobbs had started more games at third base (57) than either Helms (53) or Abraham Nuñez (51), but he too was exposed as a starter, both offensively and defensively, and hit just .253/.339/.364 in the second half. Given the alternatives, the Phillies picked the right man. That was resourcefulness; going into the 2008 season with the same options is negligence.

Jason Donald   SS   Bats: R   Throws: R   Height: 6' 1"   Weight: 190   Born: September 4, 1984   Age: 23

YEAR	TEAM	LVL	AGE	PA	R	2B	3B	HR	RBI	BB	SO	SB	CS	EqBRR	AVG	OBP	SLG	MLVr	EqAVG	EqOBP	EqSLG	EqA	VORP	DEFENSE	
2006	BAT	A-	21	243	33	14	2	1	24	23	42	12	1	2.3	.263	.347	.362	.102	.213	.280	.303	.212	-19.3	58-SS	-4
2007	LWD	A	22	238	41	9	3	4	30	29	39	2	5	0.4	.310	.409	.447	.289	.256	.335	.357	.243	4.4	52-SS	1
2007	CLR	A+	22	336	48	22	5	8	41	35	70	3	2	-1.6	.300	.386	.491	.264	.250	.328	.430	.260	14.0	79-SS	-6
2008	PHI	MLB	23	620	73	35	4	13	66	53	140	9	4	0.8	.257	.327	.405	-.083	.252	.324	.396	.248	16.0	145-SS	-1

Breakout: 33% Improve: 64% Collapse: 11% Attrition: 6%   Comparables: Mike Edwards, Tony Manahan, Joe Jester, Adam Piatt

Drafted out of the University of Arizona with the Phillies' third-round pick in 2006, Donald has some extra pop for a middle infielder. Given his good hands and terrific arm, he could play a bit of third base someday. His bat took a major leap forward last year after a less-than-stellar college career. He'll have to consolidate those gains in Double-A this season to prove that he deserves consideration as more than a utility player.

Greg Golson — OF

Bats: R · Throws: R · Height: 6' 0" · Weight: 190 · Born: September 17, 1985 · Age: 22

YEAR	TEAM	LVL	AGE	PA	R	2B	3B	HR	RBI	BB	SO	SB	CS	EqBRR	AVG	OBP	SLG	MLVr	EqAVG	EqOBP	EqSLG	EqA	VORP	DEFENSE	
2005	LWD	A	19	409	51	19	8	4	27	26	106	25	9	1.5	.264	.322	.389	.037	.199	.241	.295	.188	-33.0	89-CF	-8
2006	LWD	A	20	419	56	15	4	7	31	19	107	23	7	1.4	.220	.258	.333	-.136	.187	.215	.280	.170	-42.8	92-CF	-7
2006	CLR	A+	20	174	31	11	2	6	17	11	53	7	3	0.8	.264	.324	.472	.129	.222	.276	.407	.232	-2.6	37-CF	0
2007	CLR	A+	21	449	66	27	3	12	52	21	124	25	8	0.8	.285	.322	.450	.104	.225	.262	.384	.225	-13.9	98-CF	-4
2007	REA	AA	21	158	20	5	2	3	16	2	49	5	0	1.4	.242	.255	.359	-.199	.208	.222	.318	.187	-12.8	34-CF	1
2008	PHI	MLB	22	604	63	30	4	16	61	28	168	21	8	1.9	.231	.272	.384	-.226	.227	.270	.376	.220	-9.2	141-CF	-1

Breakout: 57% Improve: 69% Collapse: 12% Attrition: 14% Comparables: Dante Powell, Josh Burrus, Jason Repko, Timmie Morrow

On a pure tools level, Golson is among the most talented players in baseball. He's a plus-plus runner, has considerable raw power, can cover a ton of ground in center field, and has a rocket arm—and none of that means a damn thing because his ability to recognize pitches falls somewhere between that of Jose Feliciano and Stevie Wonder, as evidenced by his 49 strikeouts against just two walks in 37 games at Double-A last year. He's young enough that he deserves plenty of chances, but he's so far away from turning a corner that the odds are stacked against him.

Brad Harman — SS

Bats: R · Throws: R · Height: 6' 1" · Weight: 175 · Born: November 19, 1985 · Age: 22

YEAR	TEAM	LVL	AGE	PA	R	2B	3B	HR	RBI	BB	SO	SB	CS	EqBRR	AVG	OBP	SLG	MLVr	EqAVG	EqOBP	EqSLG	EqA	VORP	DEFENSE			
2005	LWD	A	19	472	63	23	1	11	58	45	89	5	11	-3.1	.303	.380	.442	.235	.235	.295	.334	.215	-7.2	78-SS	-12	26-2B	-7
2006	CLR	A+	20	482	59	19	1	2	25	48	102	6	2	1.0	.241	.322	.305	-.100	.207	.280	.267	.194	-25.7	111-SS	-15		
2007	CLR	A+	21	499	63	26	5	13	62	40	105	1	1	-1.6	.281	.341	.449	.127	.242	.298	.402	.242	3.1	110-2B	2	11-SS	4
2008	PHI	MLB	22	555	59	30	2	15	63	43	130	5	2	0.4	.246	.309	.406	-.120	.242	.306	.398	.240	8.1	130-2B	-4		

Breakout: 47% Improve: 66% Collapse: 11% Attrition: 8% Comparables: Jose Bautista, Robinson Chirinos, Ramon Castro, Marco Scutaro

Aussie Harman is no defensive kangaroo, but if he can continue to hit with power he should have a major league future as a second baseman. The catch is that Harman repeated the Florida State League last year and needs to show that he can continue to produce after making the jump to Double-A this year. The Phillies are seemingly set forever in the middle infield with Rollins and Utley, but with like Harman and Donald coming along, they might someday have better infield alternates than Abraham Nuñez and his immediate forebear, Tomas Perez.

Wes Helms — 3B/1B

Bats: R · Throws: R · Height: 6' 4" · Weight: 220 · Born: May 12, 1976 · Age: 32

YEAR	TEAM	LVL	AGE	PA	R	2B	3B	HR	RBI	BB	SO	SB	CS	EqBRR	AVG	OBP	SLG	MLVr	EqAVG	EqOBP	EqSLG	EqA	VORP	DEFENSE			
2005	MIL	MLB	29	188	18	13	1	4	24	14	30	0	1	-1.7	.298	.356	.458	.132	.293	.351	.467	.280	8.8	20-3B	1	13-1B	1
2006	FLO	MLB	30	278	30	19	5	10	47	21	55	0	4	-4.7	.329	.390	.575	.387	.333	.391	.580	.316	26.3	49-1B	-3	10-3B	0
2007	PHI	MLB	31	308	21	19	0	5	39	19	62	0	0	-0.8	.246	.297	.368	-.159	.244	.300	.366	.234	-5.1	49-3B	-7	11-1B	-2
2008	PHI	MLB	32	184	21	11	1	6	26	14	34	1	1	-0.7	.275	.336	.458	.019	.271	.333	.449	.264	7.8	47-3B	-2		

Breakout: 13% Improve: 37% Collapse: 37% Attrition: 43% Comparables: Lamar Johnson, Walt Dropo, Art Schult, Bob Oliver

As a reserve for the Brewers and Marlins in 2005 and 2006, Helms hit an impressive .316/.376/.527 in 466 plate appearances. Given their gaping hole at the hot corner, the Phillies figured they'd give Helms a chance to put up those numbers over the course of a single season as a starter. What they didn't consider was that nearly 50 percent of those plate appearances came against lefties (by comparison, 30 percent of Jimmy Rollins' 2007 PAs came against lefties). See, lefties are the guys Helms can actually hit. Righties are a whole other ballgame, as Helms proved by hitting .221/.261/.313 against them last year. He's useful as the short end of a platoon with Dobbs, but the Phillies would have a better chance of contending if they, y'know, got a third baseman.

Ryan Howard — 1B

Bats: L   Throws: L   Height: 6' 4"   Weight: 255   Born: November 19, 1979   Age: 28

YEAR	TEAM	LVL	AGE	PA	R	2B	3B	HR	RBI	BB	SO	SB	CS	EqBRR	AVG	OBP	SLG	MLVr	EqAVG	EqOBP	EqSLG	EqA	VORP	DEFENSE	
2005	SWB	AAA	25	257	38	19	0	16	54	39	66	0	0	-2.4	.371	.467	.690	.679	.263	.370	.545	.304	18.7	57-1B	-4
2005	PHI	MLB	25	348	52	17	2	22	63	33	100	0	1	-1.1	.288	.356	.567	.262	.277	.348	.559	.298	23.7	80-1B	5
2006	PHI	MLB	26	704	104	25	1	58	149	108	181	0	0	-3.1	.313	.425	.659	.492	.301	.415	.634	.341	81.5	157-1B	-13
2007	PHI	MLB	27	648	94	26	0	47	136	107	199	1	0	-4.8	.268	.392	.584	.304	.257	.386	.573	.317	53.6	138-1B	-5
2008	PHI	MLB	28	638	100	26	1	44	122	91	175	2	1	-1.7	.273	.381	.574	.242	.268	.379	.562	.306	42.7	149-1B	-4

Breakout: 1%   Improve: 31%   Collapse: 43%   Attrition: 14%   Comparables: Mike Epstein, Cecil Fielder, Calvin Pickering, Mo Vaughn

Howard's PECOTA comparables suggest the system doesn't expect him to have a long battery life, a reflection of his late start and old-player skills. Still, Howard is a better hitter than any of those guys and is going to be fun while he lasts given his prodigious home runs and strikeouts. Only May's quadriceps injury kept the big man from topping 50 home runs again, though he still managed to break Adam Dunn's single-season strikeout record. For sheer entertainment value, Howard is a modern analogue to Babe Ruth.

Tadahito Iguchi — 2B

Bats: R   Throws: R   Height: 5' 10"   Weight: 200   Born: December 4, 1974   Age: 33

YEAR	TEAM	LVL	AGE	PA	R	2B	3B	HR	RBI	BB	SO	SB	CS	EqBRR	AVG	OBP	SLG	MLVr	EqAVG	EqOBP	EqSLG	EqA	VORP	DEFENSE	
2005	CHA	MLB	30	581	74	25	6	15	71	47	114	15	5	-1.4	.278	.342	.438	.043	.279	.351	.452	.278	24.8	129-2B	-8
2006	CHA	MLB	31	627	97	24	0	18	67	59	110	11	5	-2.9	.281	.352	.422	-.001	.276	.355	.423	.271	25.5	135-2B	-12
2007	CHA	MLB	32	377	45	17	4	6	31	44	65	8	1	2.5	.251	.340	.382	-.073	.250	.347	.398	.267	6.4	88-2B	-1
2007	PHI	MLB	32	156	22	10	0	3	12	13	23	6	1	0.1	.304	.361	.442	.095	.307	.368	.445	.288	8.5	30-2B	6
2008	SDN	MLB	33	488	63	22	3	10	48	50	83	9	3	0.3	.265	.344	.401	-.051	.272	.352	.429	.269	20.9	115-2B	-5

Breakout: 15%   Improve: 42%   Collapse: 28%   Attrition: 17%   Comparables: Bobby Avila, Randy Velarde, Phil Garner, Jerry Priddy

Though you can find his picture in the dictionary next to "generic second baseman," Iguchi meant a lot more than that to the Phillies after Chase Utley broke his hand in late July. Quickly obtained from the White Sox, Iguchi batted .301/.357/.425 in Utley's stead, saving the Phils from a month of starts by Honest Abe Nuñez. Utley made a quick return, and Iguchi, his job done, spent the last month pinch-hitting. Iguchi signed a one-year, $3.85 million contract with the Padres, where he'll be a modest upgrade.

Jason Jaramillo — C

Bats: S   Throws: R   Height: 6' 0"   Weight: 200   Born: October 9, 1982   Age: 25

YEAR	TEAM	LVL	AGE	PA	R	2B	3B	HR	RBI	BB	SO	SB	CS	EqBRR	AVG	OBP	SLG	MLVr	EqAVG	EqOBP	EqSLG	EqA	VORP	DEFENSE	
2005	LWD	A	22	496	46	28	4	8	63	44	72	2	3	-4.5	.304	.368	.438	.211	.245	.296	.345	.222	-8.5	102-C	-10
2006	REA	AA	23	364	35	25	1	6	39	32	55	0	1	-1.9	.248	.320	.388	.011	.229	.294	.370	.231	-4.1	81-C	1
2007	OTT	AAA	24	496	52	13	4	6	56	50	79	0	1	-2.3	.271	.350	.361	.018	.255	.331	.352	.243	3.1	108-C	-8
2008	PHI	MLB	25	368	35	17	1	7	42	30	65	1	1	-0.8	.250	.316	.374	-.148	.246	.313	.366	.234	3.3	88-C	-3

Breakout: 21%   Improve: 46%   Collapse: 29%   Attrition: 31%   Comparables: Josh Bard, Koyie Hill, Buck Rodgers, Sean Mulligan

The gap between starting catchers and their backups has become so severe that teams with a secondary backstop of any quality have a real tactical advantage. Underqualified to start, Jaramillo is overqualified to be a backup by the standards of Wil Nieves or Paul Bako. He's a good defender, and though he won't hit with any real impact, he's more than an automatic out.

Lou Marson — C

Bats: R   Throws: R   Height: 6' 1"   Weight: 200   Born: June 26, 1986   Age: 22

YEAR	TEAM	LVL	AGE	PA	R	2B	3B	HR	RBI	BB	SO	SB	CS	EqBRR	AVG	OBP	SLG	MLVr	EqAVG	EqOBP	EqSLG	EqA	VORP	DEFENSE	
2005	BAT	A-	19	252	25	11	3	5	25	27	52	0	1	-1.4	.245	.329	.391	.042	.183	.244	.274	.173	-37.2	55-C	-6
2006	LWD	A	20	410	44	16	5	4	39	49	82	4	0	-1.5	.243	.343	.351	.040	.202	.280	.295	.204	-21.1	100-C	10
2007	CLR	A+	21	457	68	24	1	7	63	52	80	3	1	-0.1	.288	.373	.407	.124	.249	.327	.363	.246	3.3	106-C	4
2008	PHI	MLB	22	474	50	22	1	9	48	45	105	5	2	-0.4	.242	.319	.367	-.156	.238	.317	.359	.234	3.2	112-C	2

Breakout: 46%   Improve: 71%   Collapse: 14%   Attrition: 10%   Comparables: Pat Cline, Pee-Wee Lopez, Alberto Castillo, John Roskos

"Lou Marson" just sounds like a catcher's name, a hard-nosed, bruised-knuckles catcher who runs the team from behind the plate, but even if it turns out that Marson likes cucumber sandwiches on hot days and knows all the words to "I'm Called Little Buttercup," he still has the makings of a fine major league catcher. The question is whether he will hit enough to start. The Phillies believe he will, but 2007 was the first year he showed any kind of offensive proficiency beyond the ability to draw walks. Stay tuned for early results from Double-A; if Marson keeps hitting he'll be pressing Carlos Ruiz in short order.

Abraham Nuñez — INF

Bats: S Throws: R Height: 5' 11" Weight: 190 Born: March 16, 1976 Age: 32

YEAR	TEAM	LVL	AGE	PA	R	2B	3B	HR	RBI	BB	SO	SB	CS	EqBRR	AVG	OBP	SLG	MLVr	EqAVG	EqOBP	EqSLG	EqA	VORP	DEFENSE			
2005	SLN	MLB	29	467	64	13	2	5	44	37	63	0	1	2.1	.285	.343	.361	-.029	.284	.344	.364	.250	5.9	81-3B	9	15-2B	-2
2006	PHI	MLB	30	369	42	10	2	2	32	41	58	1	0	1.3	.211	.303	.273	-.299	.205	.302	.264	.205	-18.2	70-3B	2		
2007	PHI	MLB	31	287	24	10	1	0	16	30	48	2	0	0.2	.234	.318	.282	-.245	.230	.319	.282	.220	-9.4	66-3B	8		
2008	PHI	MLB	32	170	16	5	1	1	12	16	27	2	1	0.0	.237	.310	.287	-.280	.234	.308	.281	.204	-4.5	44-3B	2		

Breakout: 16% Improve: 35% Collapse: 48% Attrition: 42% Comparables: Al Newman, Wayne Tolleson, Wilson Delgado, Jose Vizcaino

Make it stop. Nuñez has hit .221/.277/.310 in 656 plate appearances over the past two seasons, most of that playing time coming in 120 starts at third base. That's not complacency, that's suicide. Since 1900, just five players have had lower slugging percentages relative to the league average in as many or more career PAs as Nuñez has had (2,802)—Bill Bergen, Dal Maxvill, Rabbit Warstler, Rey Ordoñez, and Tommy Thevenow. Only the last ever spent any time starting at the hot corner (for a team managed by Hall of Fame third baseman Pie Traynor, no less). The Phillies declined their option on Nuñez, making him a free agent. Someone will bite given his reputation for solid glovework, but benches are too short these days to carry a player who's only valuable in the field.

Jimmy Rollins — SS

Bats: S Throws: R Height: 5' 8" Weight: 175 Born: November 27, 1978 Age: 29

YEAR	TEAM	LVL	AGE	PA	R	2B	3B	HR	RBI	BB	SO	SB	CS	EqBRR	AVG	OBP	SLG	MLVr	EqAVG	EqOBP	EqSLG	EqA	VORP	DEFENSE	
2005	PHI	MLB	26	732	115	38	11	12	54	47	71	41	6	6.1	.290	.338	.431	.051	.281	.333	.430	.270	42.2	153-SS	-9
2006	PHI	MLB	27	758	127	45	9	25	83	57	80	36	4	6.9	.277	.334	.478	.072	.273	.331	.472	.279	45.2	154-SS	4
2007	PHI	MLB	28	778	139	38	20	30	94	49	85	41	6	7.2	.296	.344	.531	.188	.295	.346	.538	.297	66.1	160-SS	9
2008	PHI	MLB	29	691	102	37	8	20	79	51	73	29	6	3.2	.291	.346	.472	.069	.286	.344	.462	.277	42.8	161-SS	2

Breakout: 9% Improve: 32% Collapse: 26% Attrition: 5% Comparables: Brian Roberts, Ray Durham, Bert Campaneris, Don Buford

Rollins won last year's NL MVP award, but on a per-game basis his offense was a cut below that of the game's top hitters. He wasn't even the league's most productive shortstop—that was Hanley Ramirez. Still, he was always there, setting a record for most plate appearances in a season, and is without a doubt one of the most visually dynamic players in the game. Add in his key role on a Cinderella team, and that he was the only one of that team's three MVP candidates not to lose any time to injury, and it's not surprising that he was crowned. Fun Stat: Most home runs in a season with 20 or more triples: Willie Mays 35 in 1957; Jim Bottomley 31 in 1929; J-Roll 30 in 2007. Chances are we just saw Rollins' peak, and while he has several good seasons ahead of him, he won't be mentioned in the same breath as Mays again.

Aaron Rowand — CF

Bats: R Throws: R Height: 6' 0" Weight: 200 Born: August 29, 1977 Age: 30

YEAR	TEAM	LVL	AGE	PA	R	2B	3B	HR	RBI	BB	SO	SB	CS	EqBRR	AVG	OBP	SLG	MLVr	EqAVG	EqOBP	EqSLG	EqA	VORP	DEFENSE	
2005	CHA	MLB	27	640	77	30	5	13	69	32	116	16	5	3.5	.270	.329	.407	-.029	.271	.338	.419	.265	14.9	150-CF	4
2006	PHI	MLB	28	445	59	24	3	12	47	18	76	10	4	1.7	.262	.321	.425	-.040	.262	.318	.429	.257	8.8	101-CF	5
2007	PHI	MLB	29	684	105	45	0	27	89	47	119	6	3	2.1	.309	.374	.515	.225	.308	.375	.525	.302	52.0	153-CF	5
2008	SFN	MLB	30	537	67	30	3	15	68	34	91	8	3	0.5	.279	.337	.444	.006	.277	.337	.459	.269	23.4	126-CF	-2

Breakout: 8% Improve: 29% Collapse: 35% Attrition: 11% Comparables: Mike Devereaux, Bob Kennedy, Rip Repulski, Gary Ward

What's the bigger mind-bender, that the Giants thought they needed Rowand or that Rowand thought he needed the Giants? After signing a five-year deal with the team that set the major league record for old, Rowand said that the financial security offered by the contract is what sealed the deal. Fair enough, but he gave up the promise of the rising Phillies for what will probably be a career-length sojourn in the second division. For their part, the Giants acquired the age-30 through age-34 seasons of a player who is more likely to hit as he did in 2005 and 2006 (.267/.326/.414) than he did in 2004 (.310/.361/.544) or 2007. Rowand is still a good glove, but by the time the Giants are ready to compete, he might not be that anymore either.

Carlos Ruiz C

Bats: R Throws: R Height: 5' 10" Weight: 200 Born: January 22, 1979 Age: 29

YEAR	TEAM	LVL	AGE	PA	R	2B	3B	HR	RBI	BB	SO	SB	CS	EqBRR	AVG	OBP	SLG	MLVr	EqAVG	EqOBP	EqSLG	EqA	VORP	DEFENSE	
2005	SWB	AAA	26	388	50	25	9	4	40	30	48	4	5	-1.5	.300	.354	.458	.113	.269	.325	.410	.253	10.7	55-C	3
2006	SWB	AAA	27	423	56	25	0	16	69	42	56	4	3	0.7	.307	.389	.505	.296	.293	.370	.497	.294	38.4	78-C	7
2006	PHI	MLB	27	78	5	1	1	3	10	5	8	0	0	-0.5	.261	.316	.435	-.033	.257	.312	.429	.256	1.4	19-C	-1
2007	PHI	MLB	28	429	42	29	2	6	54	42	49	6	1	0.2	.259	.340	.396	-.037	.254	.338	.396	.260	13.0	101-C	5
2008	PHI	MLB	29	389	46	20	2	9	47	34	49	5	2	-0.2	.270	.341	.413	-.038	.266	.338	.404	.255	12.9	93-C	3

Breakout: 10% Improve: 32% Collapse: 37% Attrition: 24%   Comparables: Jerry Grote, Michael Barrett, Jim Sundberg, Joe Azcue

The average NL catcher hit .257/.318/.394 last year, so Ruiz's mediocre season still put the Phils slightly ahead of the pack. Their advantage would have been greater had Ruiz only done what we might expect a right-handed batter to do against lefty pitchers. Last year, the average NL righty batted .281/.351/.447 against southpaws, while Ruiz hit .189/.265/.311 in 104 plate appearances against them, a split that's very likely to improve this year. Ruiz was fine in the field last year, displaying an accurate arm. He's an asset for now, but given his late arrival in the major leagues, he's not going to grow from this point beyond the aforementioned correction.

Chase Utley 2B

Bats: L Throws: R Height: 6' 1" Weight: 185 Born: December 17, 1978 Age: 29

YEAR	TEAM	LVL	AGE	PA	R	2B	3B	HR	RBI	BB	SO	SB	CS	EqBRR	AVG	OBP	SLG	MLVr	EqAVG	EqOBP	EqSLG	EqA	VORP	DEFENSE	
2005	PHI	MLB	26	628	93	39	6	28	105	69	109	16	3	0.4	.291	.376	.540	.256	.283	.368	.532	.304	54.8	135-2B	-4
2006	PHI	MLB	27	739	131	40	4	32	102	63	132	15	4	5.8	.309	.379	.527	.244	.304	.375	.518	.302	65.2	152-2B	-9
2007	PHI	MLB	28	613	104	48	5	22	103	50	89	9	1	2.6	.332	.410	.566	.376	.333	.411	.578	.331	68.8	130-2B	4
2008	PHI	MLB	29	638	102	36	4	27	94	64	100	10	3	1.3	.298	.377	.522	.193	.294	.375	.511	.299	51.1	149-2B	-1

Breakout: 5% Improve: 25% Collapse: 33% Attrition: 6%   Comparables: Will Clark, Lou Whitaker, Bobby Murcer, Rusty Greer

The reason that Chase Utley is even cooler than you think: in his first major league exposure, 439 plate appearances split over the 2003 and 2004 seasons, he batted .257/.313/.436, drawing just 25 unintentional walks. That's a pace for about 40 walks in a 700-plate appearance season. His minor league rates were a little better, but with a discount applied for the greater difficulties of major league pitching, it was safe to conclude, yes, that's all there is. Almost magically, Utley became more selective, seeing more pitches per plate appearance and upping his walk rate. In 2004 he hit .200 against lefties, in 2005 he hit .219. Again, he got better, hitting over .300 against them in both '06 and '07. This is the rare player who actually grew on the job. The only blemish on his season was a month missed after a John Lannan pitch broke his hand. He should be an MVP candidate again in 2008.

Shane Victorino OF

Bats: S Throws: R Height: 5' 9" Weight: 180 Born: November 30, 1980 Age: 27

YEAR	TEAM	LVL	AGE	PA	R	2B	3B	HR	RBI	BB	SO	SB	CS	EqBRR	AVG	OBP	SLG	MLVr	EqAVG	EqOBP	EqSLG	EqA	VORP	DEFENSE			
2005	SWB	AAA	24	559	93	25	16	18	70	51	74	17	9	2.6	.310	.377	.534	.266	.279	.345	.475	.277	32.1	120-CF	17		
2006	PHI	MLB	25	462	70	19	8	6	46	24	54	4	3	0.0	.287	.346	.414	.017	.286	.343	.414	.262	12.1	61-CF	8	17-RF	2
2007	PHI	MLB	26	510	78	23	3	12	46	37	62	37	4	3.3	.281	.347	.423	.027	.283	.351	.436	.281	17.1	102-RF	11		
2008	PHI	MLB	27	513	75	24	4	13	56	39	63	22	5	1.6	.283	.345	.437	.012	.279	.343	.428	.268	13.8	121-RF	10		

Breakout: 15% Improve: 32% Collapse: 28% Attrition: 14%   Comparables: Coco Crisp, R.J. Reynolds, Dave Collins, Billy Hatcher

With the departure of Rowand, Victorino returns to center field, where he excelled defensively in 2006. His bat also plays better in the middle pasture; he's underpowered for right, but his overall 2007 performance was in line with what the average NL center fielder hit last year (.273/.336/.426). Victorino might be a bit better than that; he was hitting .284/.351/.430 last year before a calf injury cost him three weeks in August and limited his playing time in September. Playing on one leg, he hit just .255/.308/.362 in 53 scattered plate appearances, dragging down his overall numbers.

Jayson Werth RF

Bats: R Throws: R Height: 6' 4" Weight: 210 Born: May 20, 1979 Age: 29

YEAR	TEAM	LVL	AGE	PA	R	2B	3B	HR	RBI	BB	SO	SB	CS	EqBRR	AVG	OBP	SLG	MLVr	EqAVG	EqOBP	EqSLG	EqA	VORP	DEFENSE			
2005	LAN	MLB	26	395	46	22	2	7	43	48	114	11	2	2.3	.234	.338	.374	-.049	.237	.341	.386	.262	3.2	39-LF	2	33-RF	4
2007	PHI	MLB	28	304	43	11	3	8	49	44	73	7	1	1.0	.298	.404	.459	.192	.295	.406	.465	.306	18.3	50-RF	5	14-LF	2
2008	PHI	MLB	29	275	41	12	2	8	30	38	67	6	2	0.5	.260	.367	.437	.032	.256	.365	.428	.276	8.2	67-RF	4		

Breakout: 13% Improve: 32% Collapse: 33% Attrition: 38%   Comparables: Mike Huff, Damon Mashore, Dustan Mohr, Jason Michaels

Wrist problems only shelved Werth for a month last year, an accomplishment given that the joint ruined his 2005 and caused him to miss all of 2006. When he played, he toasted lefties the way he had back in 2004, hitting .375/.467/.591 against them. He's not the same hitter against righties, as he struck out in more than a third of his at-bats against them, but he did maintain his willingness to take a walk against the same-handed. This year, Werth will form a platoon with Geoff Jenkins, assuming he can stay off the DL. That caveat would be gratuitous with a lot of players, but in Werth's case it's absolutely necessary.

PITCHERS

Antonio Alfonseca

Bats: R   Throws: R   Height: 6' 5"   Weight: 250   Born: April 16, 1972   Age: 36

YEAR	TEAM	LVL	AGE	W	L	SV	G	GS	IP	H	BB	SO	HR	GB%	BABIP	STUFF	WHIP	ERA	PERA	EqERA	EqH9	EqBB9	EqSO9	EqHR9	VORP	SN/WX
2005	FLO	MLB	33	1	1	0	33	0	27¹	29	14	16	2	62.8%	.342	-12	1.54	4.95	5.12	4.91	9.5	4.6	4.9	0.7	1.1	-0.05
2006	TEX	MLB	34	0	0	0	19	0	16	23	7	5	3	51.6%	.345	-41	1.88	5.63	8.39	5.87	12.3	3.5	2.9	1.8	0.9	0.45
2007	PHI	MLB	35	5	2	8	61	0	49²	65	27	24	3	53.3%	.344	-19	1.85	5.43	5.61	5.36	11.1	4.1	4.1	0.5	1.6	-0.10
2008	PHI	MLB	36	2	2	2	36	0	39¹	47	18	20	4	52.8%	.318	-19	1.65	4.87	5.27	4.94	10.4	3.8	4.2	0.8	2.6	0.20

Breakout: 27% Improve: 43% Collapse: 28% Attrition: 35%   Comparables: Lee Guetterman, Hugh Casey, Scott Erickson, Mike Myers

It's rare that a guy who has been stamped with the closer label is so completely defrocked that teams avoid the temptation to put him back in the ninth-inning role, but the eight saves that Alfonseca registered in 2007 were his first since 2002. The Phillies turned to him more in desperation than out of respect for his résumé, but Alfonseca isn't fooling anyone, and hasn't for years. His strikeout-to-walk ratio is essentially even, and lefties have *moidalized* him over the past two seasons to the tune of a .393 average. A free agent at press time, he should stay that way; there's little reason to doubt that a randomly selected farmhand could do better.

Carlos Carrasco

Bats: R   Throws: R   Height: 6' 3"   Weight: 180   Born: March 21, 1987   Age: 21

YEAR	TEAM	LVL	AGE	W	L	SV	G	GS	IP	H	BB	SO	HR	GB%	BABIP	STUFF	WHIP	ERA	PERA	EqERA	EqH9	EqBB9	EqSO9	EqHR9	VORP	SN/WX
2005	LWD	A	18	1	7	0	13	13	62²	78	28	46	11	43.5%	.333	-49	1.69	7.03	15.66	13.67	14.9	7.3	3.1	3.6	-47.3	—
2005	BAT	A-	18	0	3	0	4	4	15¹	29	5	12	8	34.9%	.389	-84	2.22	13.53	40.08	34.59	31.2	8.4	3.4	16.9	-34.5	—
2006	LWD	A	19	12	6	0	26	26	159¹	103	65	159	6	50.4%	.254	13	1.06	2.26	5.36	5.35	8.3	6.3	5.0	1.0	3.8	—
2007	CLR	A+	20	6	2	0	12	12	69²	49	22	53	8	47.4%	.222	-8	1.02	2.84	5.73	4.65	8.1	4.4	4.4	2.2	6.5	—
2007	REA	AA	20	6	4	0	14	13	70¹	65	46	49	9	37.2%	.273	-16	1.58	4.86	7.27	6.72	9.6	6.9	4.1	1.8	-8.2	—
2008	PHI	MLB	21	5	9	0	30	20	112²	127	75	71	24	41.3%	.287	-14	1.79	6.47	6.84	6.37	9.8	5.5	5.1	1.9	-8.5	-0.20

Breakout: 25% Improve: 46% Collapse: 31% Attrition: 19%   Comparables: Rafael Rodriguez, Victor Santos, Calvin Maduro, Tony Armas Jr.

Carrasco is generally considered the top arm in the Phillies' system, but despite reaching Double-A as a 20-year-old, he's not an elite-level prospect. Rather, he's something less than the sum of his parts. He boasts two above-average pitches (fastball, curve), one outstanding one (changeup), and good command, but his strikeout rates don't foretell of a future beyond that of a solid, mid-rotation innings-eater.

Clay Condrey

Bats: R   Throws: R   Height: 6' 3"   Weight: 215   Born: November 19, 1975   Age: 32

YEAR	TEAM	LVL	AGE	W	L	SV	G	GS	IP	H	BB	SO	HR	GB%	BABIP	STUFF	WHIP	ERA	PERA	EqERA	EqH9	EqBB9	EqSO9	EqHR9	VORP	SN/WX
2005	SWB	AAA	29	7	8	0	25	24	132¹	159	29	74	13	52.4%	.330	-15	1.42	4.15	5.86	5.47	11.2	2.6	3.4	1.1	1.8	—
2006	SWB	AAA	30	4	2	6	39	0	51¹	41	15	28	1	57.2%	.267	-11	1.10	1.94	4.02	3.47	8.7	3.5	3.5	0.4	11.1	—
2006	PHI	MLB	30	2	2	0	21	0	28²	35	9	16	3	48.5%	.352	-9	1.53	3.14	5.40	3.33	11.0	2.7	5.0	1.0	8.2	0.03
2007	OTT	AAA	31	1	0	1	10	0	22	19	5	10	0	51.5%	.288	-11	1.09	2.45	3.23	3.15	7.7	2.7	3.2	0.0	5.4	—
2007	PHI	MLB	31	5	0	2	39	0	50	61	16	27	4	47.8%	.331	-9	1.56	5.04	4.77	5.12	10.1	2.5	4.6	0.7	2.9	1.61
2008	PHI	MLB	32	2	2	2	38	0	44¹	52	15	22	5	50.4%	.305	-16	1.51	4.76	5.04	4.80	10.2	2.8	3.9	1.1	3.7	0.30

Breakout: 22% Improve: 36% Collapse: 35% Attrition: 32%   Comparables: Danny Kolb, Mike Barlow, Johnny Hetki, Jeff Tam

Condrey has minor groundball tendencies and major line-drive tendencies; his pitches up get smoked, particularly by lefties, who have career rates of .309/.381/.472 against him. Batters hit about .720 on line drives, so being above-average in that department is about as encouraging as leading the league in cholesterol.

J. D. Durbin

Bats: R   Throws: R   Height: 6' 0"   Weight: 210   Born: February 24, 1982   Age: 26

YEAR	TEAM	LVL	AGE	W	L	SV	G	GS	IP	H	BB	SO	HR	GB%	BABIP	STUFF	WHIP	ERA	PERA	EqERA	EqH9	EqBB9	EqSO9	EqHR9	VORP	SN/WX
2005	ROC	AAA	23	5	5	0	22	19	104	97	51	90	8	48.5%	.309	5	1.42	4.33	5.05	5.20	8.9	5.3	5.7	0.8	4.3	—
2006	ROC	AAA	24	4	3	0	16	16	89	67	50	81	3	42.0%	.270	20	1.31	2.33	4.41	3.80	7.9	6.1	6.1	0.5	16.6	—
2007	OTT	AAA	25	2	4	0	10	10	59^1	67	21	44	9	40.8%	.322	-22	1.48	4.55	7.04	6.11	10.6	3.7	4.8	2.1	-3.2	—
2007	PHI	MLB	25	6	5	1	18	10	64^2	71	36	39	6	51.4%	.314	-4	1.65	5.15	4.75	5.37	9.2	4.3	5.1	0.7	0.8	0.56
2008	PHI	MLB	26	3	4	1	23	9	65^2	72	33	43	9	46.4%	.301	-6	1.59	5.26	5.43	5.29	9.5	4.2	5.3	1.2	2.6	0.50

Breakout: 19%   Improve: 58%   Collapse: 21%   Attrition: 41%   Comparables: Ryan Jensen, Ryan Bowen, Rich Robertson, Justin Miller

Once a top prospect, Durbin's profile had fallen by the start of the 2007 season to the point at which he was worth a waiver flier but not the resulting roster spot. The property of four teams over the span of about three weeks, Durbin was waived by the Twins at the end of spring training, then claimed and designated for assignment in quick succession by the D'backs, Red Sox, and Phillies. The game could have gone on indefinitely, but by the time the Phillies DFA'd J. D., the list of intrigued general managers had finally been exhausted. With the Phils' rotation in disarray in June, the whirling Durbin spun again and landed in the Show. He had four quality starts in his first seven tries, including a shutout in San Diego, but a 20.25 ERA in three September starts put an end to the experiment. Durbin is young enough that there is still some hope for him, especially if he can trim his walk rate.

Adam Eaton

Bats: R   Throws: R   Height: 6' 2"   Weight: 200   Born: November 23, 1977   Age: 30

YEAR	TEAM	LVL	AGE	W	L	SV	G	GS	IP	H	BB	SO	HR	GB%	BABIP	STUFF	WHIP	ERA	PERA	EqERA	EqH9	EqBB9	EqSO9	EqHR9	VORP	SN/WX
2005	SDN	MLB	27	11	5	0	24	22	128^2	140	44	100	14	41.3%	.319	9	1.43	4.27	4.73	4.80	9.5	2.8	6.3	1.0	8.0	2.26
2006	TEX	MLB	28	7	4	0	13	13	65	78	24	43	11	37.7%	.324	-4	1.57	5.12	5.77	4.76	10.1	3.1	5.6	1.4	6.4	0.71
2007	PHI	MLB	29	10	10	0	30	30	161^2	192	71	97	30	40.5%	.318	-17	1.63	6.29	6.31	6.19	10.1	3.3	5.1	1.5	-9.7	0.65
2008	PHI	MLB	30	6	7	0	29	19	116^2	132	44	78	19	42.3%	.303	-2	1.51	5.18	5.45	5.14	9.9	3.1	5.4	1.4	6.1	1.40

Breakout: 22%   Improve: 59%   Collapse: 18%   Attrition: 19%   Comparables: Andy Hawkins, James Baldwin, Ray Burris, Josh Fogg

One of baseball's enduring mysteries is what teams see in Adam Eaton. His last sustained bout of good pitching came in the first three months of the 2005 season. Before that, you can pick out some select spots. June 2004 was pretty good. July 2003 had its moments. June 2001 was okay. Every once in awhile, Eaton dials it up and delivers a few strong starts. The rest of the time, he gets pounded. Even in 2003, his most consistent season, he was average at best. You can't even say he's a league-average innings-eater because he's neither league-average nor durable. The Phillies will spend more than $16 million on their 1996 first-round pick before they get to bid adieu to him for the second time.

Freddy Garcia

Bats: R   Throws: R   Height: 6' 4"   Weight: 260   Born: June 10, 1976   Age: 32

YEAR	TEAM	LVL	AGE	W	L	SV	G	GS	IP	H	BB	SO	HR	GB%	BABIP	STUFF	WHIP	ERA	PERA	EqERA	EqH9	EqBB9	EqSO9	EqHR9	VORP	SN/WX
2005	CHA	MLB	29	14	8	0	33	33	228	225	60	146	26	50.4%	.285	11	1.25	3.87	4.41	4.24	9.3	2.4	5.8	1.0	45.7	5.07
2006	CHA	MLB	30	17	9	0	33	33	216^1	228	48	135	32	41.8%	.285	6	1.28	4.54	4.23	4.31	8.9	1.8	5.2	1.2	32.3	3.71
2007	PHI	MLB	31	1	5	0	11	11	58	74	19	50	12	38.9%	.363	-1	1.60	5.90	7.23	6.09	11.1	2.5	7.3	1.7	-0.1	0.51
2008	PHI	MLB	32	6	6	0	27	15	100	109	27	69	14	45.0%	.299	3	1.36	4.43	4.64	4.43	9.5	2.3	5.5	1.2	14.8	1.90

Breakout: 14%   Improve: 51%   Collapse: 24%   Attrition: 27%   Comparables: Don Robinson, Danny Cox, Len Barker, Chris Bosio

It seemed like a good idea at the time. Wanting to win now, the Phillies dealt pitching prospects Gio Gonzalez and Gavin Floyd to the White Sox for Garcia, who had been a reliable starter for most of the decade. Unfortunately, Chief broke down after 11 starts and when the Phillies tried to fix him up they found out he was like an iPod: no user-serviceable parts. After failing to find his velocity in rehab, Garcia was sent back to the factory with a frayed rotator cuff and a torn labrum. He's expected to be out until June or July this year, and may remain a free agent until then, when teams in the pennant race can bid on a presumably fully operational hurler.

Geoff Geary

Bats: R   Throws: R   Height: 6' 0"   Weight: 180   Born: August 26, 1976   Age: 31

YEAR	TEAM	LVL	AGE	W	L	SV	G	GS	IP	H	BB	SO	HR	GB%	BABIP	STUFF	WHIP	ERA	PERA	EqERA	EqH9	EqBB9	EqSO9	EqHR9	VORP	SN/WX
2005	PHI	MLB	28	2	1	0	40	0	58	54	21	42	5	46.7%	.287	0	1.29	3.72	3.88	4.53	8.4	3.0	5.9	0.8	6.9	0.11
2006	PHI	MLB	29	7	1	1	81	0	91¹	103	20	60	6	51.5%	.331	9	1.35	2.96	4.01	3.08	9.6	1.7	5.5	0.5	27.6	1.84
2007	OTT	AAA	30	2	1	0	14	0	25	28	1	21	0	41.8%	.354	7	1.16	2.52	3.72	3.75	10.1	0.8	5.6	0.0	4.9	—
2007	PHI	MLB	30	3	2	0	57	0	67¹	72	25	38	8	52.7%	.308	-13	1.44	4.41	4.77	5.40	9.2	2.8	4.9	0.9	0.3	0.73
2008	HOU	MLB	31	3	3	2	50	0	57²	62	18	34	5	48.4%	.296	-8	1.38	4.04	4.41	4.32	9.6	2.5	4.7	0.8	8.3	0.70

Breakout: 22%   Improve: 39%   Collapse: 36%   Attrition: 28%   Comparables: Rick Lysander, Johnny Hetki, Ken Sanders, Dave Smith

Generic Geoff Geary appeared to have cemented a place in the Phillies' bullpen over the last few seasons, but an 11.57 ERA in nine mid-June appearances last year got him sent down. He returned at the end of July and posted a 3.18 ERA from there until the end of the season, but missed the playoffs due to a strained elbow. Citizens Bank Park was a real problem for him last year, as he posted a 6.06 ERA at home versus 2.86 on the road, but that's not his problem now that he's been shipped to Houston as part of the payment for Brad Lidge. His new bandbox home is slightly more forgiving.

Tom Gordon

Bats: R   Throws: R   Height: 5' 10"   Weight: 200   Born: November 18, 1967   Age: 40

YEAR	TEAM	LVL	AGE	W	L	SV	G	GS	IP	H	BB	SO	HR	GB%	BABIP	STUFF	WHIP	ERA	PERA	EqERA	EqH9	EqBB9	EqSO9	EqHR9	VORP	SN/WX
2005	NYA	MLB	37	5	4	2	79	0	80²	59	29	69	8	51.8%	.238	12	1.09	2.57	2.91	2.58	6.2	3.1	7.4	0.8	26.6	3.27
2006	PHI	MLB	38	3	4	34	59	0	59¹	53	22	68	9	46.9%	.293	17	1.26	3.34	3.61	2.80	7.4	2.8	9.1	1.2	17.1	3.39
2007	PHI	MLB	39	3	2	6	44	0	40	40	13	32	7	49.6%	.292	-3	1.33	4.73	4.53	4.28	8.6	2.5	6.8	1.4	5.3	1.27
2008	PHI	MLB	40	2	2	6	36	0	40²	41	15	31	6	46.9%	.287	-5	1.37	4.26	4.41	4.28	8.7	3.0	6.2	1.2	5.9	0.60

Breakout: 9%   Improve: 21%   Collapse: 51%   Attrition: 37%   Comparables: Stu Miller, Doug Bair, Ellis Kinder, Al Worthington

What a wonderful, variegated career. Gordon started out long enough ago that his initial Royals teammates included Bill Buckner and Gene Garber, both of whom first reached the majors in 1969. He's been a starter, a middleman, a set-up man, and a closer. He's been a White Sock and a Cub, a Red Sock and a Yankee, a Stephen King book and a resulting anecdote in *The Curse of the Bambino*. Somehow in all that, he's never managed to pitch in the World Series, in part because of his role in reversing the Curse in 2004. Gordon still has as a wicked curveball, but every so often snapping one off snaps off his elbow, or his rotator cuff, the latter of which shelved him from May through July of last year, during which time he lost the closer job to Brett Myers. The Phillies will pay him $6.5 million to be 40, watch Brad Lidge close, and then be bought out of his 2009 option.

Cole Hamels

Bats: L   Throws: L   Height: 6' 3"   Weight: 190   Born: December 27, 1983   Age: 24

YEAR	TEAM	LVL	AGE	W	L	SV	G	GS	IP	H	BB	SO	HR	GB%	BABIP	STUFF	WHIP	ERA	PERA	EqERA	EqH9	EqBB9	EqSO9	EqHR9	VORP	SN/WX
2005	CLR	A+	21	2	0	0	3	3	16	7	7	18	0	40.0%	.212	14	0.88	2.25	3.62	4.40	4.4	6.3	6.3	0.6	1.9	—
2005	REA	AA	21	2	0	0	3	3	19	10	12	19	2	42.2%	.190	17	1.16	2.37	4.66	4.24	5.8	7.9	5.8	1.6	2.6	—
2006	CLR	A+	22	1	1	0	4	4	20	16	9	29	0	53.1%	.327	19	1.25	1.80	4.91	5.30	9.2	5.8	8.2	0.5	0.6	—
2006	SWB	AAA	22	2	0	0	3	3	23	10	1	36	0	39.0%	.244	21	0.48	0.39	2.54	1.74	6.1	0.9	10.0	0.0	8.9	—
2006	PHI	MLB	22	9	8	0	23	23	132¹	117	48	145	19	41.7%	.298	32	1.25	4.08	3.57	3.81	7.4	2.7	8.8	1.1	23.1	3.43
2007	PHI	MLB	23	15	5	0	28	28	183¹	163	43	177	25	44.2%	.282	29	1.12	3.39	3.37	3.14	7.5	1.8	8.1	1.1	48.8	5.16
2008	PHI	MLB	24	13	8	0	29	29	190¹	173	55	176	23	44.0%	.282	27	1.19	3.45	3.61	3.45	7.9	2.4	7.5	1.0	45.7	6.20

Breakout: 19%   Improve: 37%   Collapse: 22%   Attrition: 9%   Comparables: Jon Matlack, Dennis Bennett, Greg Swindell, Johnny Antonelli

An ace in the making, Hamels has yet to overcome the dual hurdles of health and consistency to realize his full potential. Last year he turned in a quality start a little over half the time, which isn't bad but falls short of the elite level (Jamie Moyer had a similar success rate, as did Barry Zito). On any given day, Hamels might give up five runs on nine hits in six innings, as he did on April 14, or allow just one run in a complete game while striking out 15, as he did in his next start on April 21. He missed a month beginning in mid-August due to a strained left elbow. Add in the injuries of previous years, and it's clear the crucible of Hamels' early career will be staying on the mound long enough for that consistency to come.

J. A. Happ

Bats: L   Throws: L   Height: 6' 6"   Weight: 200   Born: October 19, 1982   Age: 25

YEAR	TEAM	LVL	AGE	W	L	SV	G	GS	IP	H	BB	SO	HR	GB%	BABIP	STUFF	WHIP	ERA	PERA	EqERA	EqH9	EqBB9	EqSO9	EqHR9	VORP	SN/WX
2005	LWD	A	22	4	4	0	14	12	72¹	57	26	70	3	46.5%	.278	-3	1.15	2.37	5.61	5.60	9.0	5.9	4.7	1.0	0.0	—
2006	CLR	A+	23	3	7	0	13	13	80¹	63	19	77	9	47.5%	.255	-17	1.02	2.81	5.99	6.03	9.4	3.5	5.3	2.1	-3.4	—
2006	REA	AA	23	6	2	0	12	12	74¹	58	29	81	2	41.2%	.298	19	1.17	2.67	4.57	4.79	8.9	4.7	6.7	0.5	6.1	—
2007	OTT	AAA	24	4	6	0	24	24	118¹	118	62	117	12	33.6%	.335	-5	1.52	5.02	5.90	6.57	9.6	5.3	6.6	1.4	-12.0	—
2008	PHI	MLB	25	4	5	0	28	12	81	83	44	68	14	38.5%	.293	0	1.56	5.45	5.55	5.41	8.9	4.4	6.8	1.5	1.9	0.60

Breakout: 32% Improve: 63% Collapse: 19% Attrition: 28%   Comparables: Tim Birtsas, Matt Kinney, Bill Butler, Renie Martin

For the first three years of his career, Happ never posted an ERA above 2.81 at any level, but as a tall lefty with average-at-best velocity who got by on location and changing speeds, he was seen as a pitcher whose style wouldn't play well against more advanced hitters. The rubber hit the road in 2007, though some elbow soreness didn't help matters. He looks like no more than a back-of-the-rotation starter or middle reliever.

Kyle Kendrick

Bats: R   Throws: R   Height: 6' 3"   Weight: 190   Born: August 26, 1984   Age: 23

YEAR	TEAM	LVL	AGE	W	L	SV	G	GS	IP	H	BB	SO	HR	GB%	BABIP	STUFF	WHIP	ERA	PERA	EqERA	EqH9	EqBB9	EqSO9	EqHR9	VORP	SN/WX
2005	BAT	A-	20	5	4	0	14	14	91¹	94	22	70	7	53.9%	.309	-39	1.27	3.75	8.27	8.77	11.8	5.1	2.8	2.3	-27.1	—
2005	LWD	A	20	0	3	0	5	5	22²	38	10	11	2	37.2%	.400	-68	2.11	9.12	17.15	17.53	18.9	7.6	1.4	1.9	-25.2	—
2006	LWD	A	21	3	2	0	7	7	46²	34	15	54	0	51.7%	.291	16	1.06	2.14	5.04	5.31	9.3	5.1	6.0	0.4	1.3	—
2006	CLR	A+	21	9	7	0	21	20	130²	117	37	79	15	40.9%	.260	-38	1.18	3.53	6.90	6.30	10.3	4.1	3.0	2.2	-9.0	—
2007	REA	AA	22	4	7	0	12	12	81¹	82	18	50	3	51.7%	.307	3	1.23	3.21	4.71	5.35	10.2	2.6	3.7	0.6	2.1	—
2007	PHI	MLB	22	10	4	0	20	20	121	129	25	49	16	47.4%	.285	1	1.27	3.87	4.29	3.67	9.1	1.6	3.6	1.1	27.1	3.19
2008	PHI	MLB	23	9	11	0	29	29	163²	197	51	78	27	47.5%	.301	-3	1.52	5.35	5.56	5.35	10.5	2.6	3.9	1.4	4.1	1.70

Breakout: 7% Improve: 31% Collapse: 37% Attrition: 23%   Comparables: Paul Quantrill, Joe Roa, Paul Menhart, Jason Dickson

Kendrick saved the Phillies last year. With Freddy Garcia checking out of the rotation in early June, and Jon Lieber about to do likewise, Kendrick checked in and gave the team 13 quality starts in 20 tries. He should get his medal now, because as long as his strikeout rate stays as low as it is, there won't be too many more reasons to honor him. Another thing that won't happen again: a slightly above-average rate of line drives allowed (21 percent) yielding a below-average batting average on balls in play (.285).

Jon Lieber

Bats: L   Throws: R   Height: 6' 2"   Weight: 240   Born: April 2, 1970   Age: 38

YEAR	TEAM	LVL	AGE	W	L	SV	G	GS	IP	H	BB	SO	HR	GB%	BABIP	STUFF	WHIP	ERA	PERA	EqERA	EqH9	EqBB9	EqSO9	EqHR9	VORP	SN/WX
2005	PHI	MLB	35	17	13	0	35	35	218¹	223	41	149	33	47.1%	.285	4	1.21	4.21	4.50	4.41	9.3	1.5	5.6	1.3	30.1	4.15
2006	PHI	MLB	36	9	11	0	27	27	168	196	24	100	27	44.7%	.309	2	1.31	4.93	4.54	4.73	9.6	1.1	4.9	1.2	13.6	2.67
2007	PHI	MLB	37	3	6	0	14	12	78	91	22	54	7	45.2%	.336	14	1.45	4.73	4.46	4.71	9.9	2.2	5.9	0.7	7.7	1.04
2008	PHI	MLB	38	4	5	0	22	10	73²	88	16	42	11	45.6%	.311	-5	1.41	4.89	5.02	4.89	10.4	1.8	4.6	1.2	6.4	1.00

Breakout: 18% Improve: 35% Collapse: 32% Attrition: 40%   Comparables: Bryn Smith, Don Larsen, Rick Mahler, Sonny Siebert

On June 9, Lieber shutout the Royals on three hits, walking none, and striking out 11. It was an outlier in a stretch of six starts in which he was tagged for 28 runs in 36 innings. Those six were also his last starts of the season, as a ruptured tendon in his right foot ended his season as of June 20. Lieber has been injured in three of his four seasons since missing all of 2003 following Tommy John surgery, and at 38, his chances of staying healthy aren't increasing. He still has his fine control, walking just 1.7 per nine innings over the last two seasons, so he still has value if he can stay healthy, but that's a very big "if."

Kyle Lohse

Bats: R   Throws: R   Height: 6' 2"   Weight: 210   Born: October 4, 1978   Age: 29

YEAR	TEAM	LVL	AGE	W	L	SV	G	GS	IP	H	BB	SO	HR	GB%	BABIP	STUFF	WHIP	ERA	PERA	EqERA	EqH9	EqBB9	EqSO9	EqHR9	VORP	SN/WX
2005	MIN	MLB	26	9	13	0	31	30	178²	211	44	86	22	45.6%	.316	-3	1.43	4.18	5.72	4.59	10.9	2.3	4.4	1.1	30.9	3.75
2006	MIN	MLB	27	2	5	0	22	8	63²	80	25	46	8	39.0%	.350	-7	1.65	7.06	5.96	6.79	10.7	3.3	6.1	1.0	-6.7	-0.44
2006	CIN	MLB	27	3	5	0	12	11	63	70	19	51	7	49.3%	.341	16	1.41	4.57	4.37	4.16	9.5	2.3	6.8	0.9	9.5	1.45
2007	CIN	MLB	28	6	12	0	21	21	131²	143	33	80	16	37.3%	.307	9	1.34	4.58	3.99	4.26	8.7	1.9	5.1	0.9	11.6	2.16
2007	PHI	MLB	28	3	0	0	13	11	61	64	24	42	6	42.9%	.315	8	1.44	4.72	4.41	4.45	9.0	3.0	5.8	0.7	7.2	1.42
2008	*PHI*	*MLB*	*29*	*8*	*8*	*0*	*24*	*24*	*138*	*157*	*42*	*90*	*21*	*45.0%*	*.305*	*6*	*1.44*	*4.86*	*5.06*	*4.85*	*9.9*	*2.5*	*5.2*	*1.3*	*11.5*	*2.30*

Breakout: 12%   Improve: 42%   Collapse: 33%   Attrition: 21%   Comparables: *Stan Bahnsen, Jaime Navarro, Jeff Suppan, Jim Clancy*

Like Popeye the Sailor Man, Lohse am what he am, and that's all that he am, a fourth or fifth starter who can deliver a league-average ERA in a good year and something not too far below that in a bad one. When the Phillies picked him up on July 30, their rotation was in such dire shape that they just needed him to make it to the stadium without getting hurt. He barely managed that, leaving his first Phils start in the second inning with a bruised forearm, but he was quality in five of his next ten starts. A courted free agent as we go to press, Lohse will be the canary in the coal mine for whoever signs him. If a team is asking more of Lohse than to be a decent presence at the back of their rotation, there's likely a gas leak in their offices.

Ryan Madson

Bats: L   Throws: R   Height: 6' 6"   Weight: 200   Born: August 28, 1980   Age: 27

YEAR	TEAM	LVL	AGE	W	L	SV	G	GS	IP	H	BB	SO	HR	GB%	BABIP	STUFF	WHIP	ERA	PERA	EqERA	EqH9	EqBB9	EqSO9	EqHR9	VORP	SN/WX
2005	PHI	MLB	24	6	5	0	78	0	87	84	25	79	11	49.0%	.312	4	1.25	4.14	4.60	4.61	9.1	2.4	7.6	1.1	9.7	0.91
2006	PHI	MLB	25	11	9	2	50	17	134¹	176	50	99	20	44.7%	.364	-10	1.68	5.70	6.46	5.84	11.2	2.9	6.1	1.1	-1.0	1.26
2007	REA	AA	26	0	0	0	2	0	3	3	0	4	0	42.9%	.429	2	1.00	0.00	0.80	0.00	11.6	0.0	11.6	0.0	1.4	—
2007	PHI	MLB	26	2	2	1	38	0	56	48	23	43	5	49.1%	.269	7	1.27	3.05	3.21	2.68	7.1	3.2	6.3	0.8	17.7	1.64
2008	*PHI*	*MLB*	*27*	*3*	*3*	*2*	*38*	*2*	*56*	*60*	*20*	*41*	*7*	*47.6%*	*.302*	*-1*	*1.41*	*4.33*	*4.61*	*4.35*	*9.3*	*2.9*	*6.0*	*1.1*	*8.0*	*0.70*

Breakout: 24%   Improve: 52%   Collapse: 27%   Attrition: 32%   Comparables: *Rick Bauer, Travis Harper, Bill Gogolewski, Gary Glover*

One of the stranger stats of the year: lefty batters hit .170/.308/.284 off of Madson, in large part due to a unreal .206 BABIP. That helped him to something of a rebound year after his much-lobbied-for transfer to the starting rotation in 2006 was a miserable failure. It was all fun and games until Madson got hurt, landing on the DL in July with a shoulder strain and never coming back. The good luck against lefties won't hold up, even if Madson's arm does, but he should continue to be a serviceable, changeup-oriented middle reliever.

Jose Mesa

Bats: R   Throws: R   Height: 6' 3"   Weight: 235   Born: May 22, 1966   Age: 42

YEAR	TEAM	LVL	AGE	W	L	SV	G	GS	IP	H	BB	SO	HR	GB%	BABIP	STUFF	WHIP	ERA	PERA	EqERA	EqH9	EqBB9	EqSO9	EqHR9	VORP	SN/WX
2005	PIT	MLB	39	2	8	27	55	0	56²	61	26	37	7	46.6%	.318	-15	1.54	4.76	5.18	4.89	9.5	3.6	5.2	1.1	4.5	-1.17
2006	COL	MLB	40	1	5	1	79	0	72¹	73	35	39	9	47.2%	.288	-14	1.49	3.86	4.56	3.31	8.7	3.8	4.6	1.0	17.7	0.93
2007	DET	MLB	41	1	1	0	16	0	11²	19	6	9	3	43.2%	.400	-51	2.14	12.31	14.02	14.66	14.7	3.9	6.2	2.3	-8.3	-0.47
2007	PHI	MLB	41	1	2	1	40	0	39	34	19	20	6	47.3%	.241	-22	1.36	5.54	3.74	6.47	6.9	3.6	4.2	1.1	-6.0	0.28
2008	*PHI*	*MLB*	*42*	*2*	*2*	*1*	*37*	*0*	*43*	*47*	*20*	*23*	*6*	*46.9%*	*.289*	*-22*	*1.56*	*5.30*	*5.18*	*5.38*	*9.6*	*3.9*	*4.3*	*1.2*	*1.0*	*0.10*

Breakout: 26%   Improve: 73%   Collapse: 15%   Attrition: 32%   Comparables: *Roberto Hernandez, Mike Morgan, Jeff Fassero, Jim Kaat*

Referencing Pat Gillick's stint as general manager of the Mariners in the 2006 edition of this book we wrote, "Those who forget Jose Mesa are condemned to repeat him." It's sadly predictable truths about human nature like that one that have allowed Joe Table to become one of just 13 pitchers in major league history to appear in over 1,000 games. He really doesn't have anything left to offer, but there is always another GM who prefers to watch a veteran get his head beat in than give a youngster a chance.

Jamie Moyer

Bats: L   Throws: L   Height: 6' 0"   Weight: 185   Born: November 18, 1962   Age: 45

YEAR	TEAM	LVL	AGE	W	L	SV	G	GS	IP	H	BB	SO	HR	GB%	BABIP	STUFF	WHIP	ERA	PERA	EqERA	EqH9	EqBB9	EqSO9	EqHR9	VORP	SN/WX
2005	SEA	MLB	42	13	7	0	32	32	200	225	52	102	23	38.0%	.301	1	1.39	4.28	4.88	4.56	10.0	2.3	4.5	1.0	27.8	3.67
2006	SEA	MLB	43	6	12	0	25	25	160	179	44	82	25	38.7%	.296	-6	1.39	4.39	4.94	4.50	9.6	2.3	4.4	1.3	20.6	2.67
2006	PHI	MLB	43	5	2	0	8	8	51¹	49	7	26	8	50.3%	.255	5	1.09	4.04	3.34	3.78	7.6	1.0	4.1	1.2	9.3	1.20
2007	PHI	MLB	44	14	12	0	33	33	199¹	222	66	133	30	41.6%	.311	2	1.44	5.01	4.85	4.91	9.4	2.5	5.6	1.2	14.0	3.24
2008	*PHI*	*MLB*	*45*	*7*	*6*	*0*	*20*	*20*	*114¹*	*129*	*35*	*69*	*16*	*46.9%*	*.302*	*1*	*1.42*	*4.25*	*4.79*	*4.24*	*9.8*	*2.5*	*4.9*	*1.2*	*18.4*	*2.70*

Breakout: 52%   Improve: 66%   Collapse: 34%   Attrition: 48%   Comparables: Phil Niekro, Tommy John, Hoyt Wilhelm, Satchel Paige

How old is Moyer? So old that PECOTA figures his only peers are two knuckleballers, a guy who liked to say that his surgically repaired left arm was 20 years younger than he was, and a victim of the color line who was a Rookie of the Year candidate at 41 and pitched three scoreless innings at 58. Wouldja believe Moyer had the third-highest strike-out rate of his career last year, trailing only those of 1987 and 1998? He also had his highest walk rate since 2000. That's right, folks: Moyer has been around so long he's actually wrapped around and restarted as a power pitcher (not really). That's not to say Moyer didn't show signs of the inevitable last year: his season began with a string of seven consecutive quality starts, but thereafter he posted a 5.65 ERA as he lost consistency. When he was good, he was very good. When he was bad, it was time to warm up the TiVo and watch an old Hitchcock film. Moyer probably has more of the same in him in this, the last year of his contract. The real question is when the injury termites will finally start gnawing.

Brett Myers

Bats: R   Throws: R   Height: 6' 4"   Weight: 220   Born: August 17, 1980   Age: 27

YEAR	TEAM	LVL	AGE	W	L	SV	G	GS	IP	H	BB	SO	HR	GB%	BABIP	STUFF	WHIP	ERA	PERA	EqERA	EqH9	EqBB9	EqSO9	EqHR9	VORP	SN/WX
2005	PHI	MLB	24	13	8	0	34	34	215¹	193	68	208	31	47.7%	.282	18	1.21	3.72	4.22	3.85	8.3	2.6	7.9	1.3	41.6	4.89
2006	PHI	MLB	25	12	7	0	31	31	198	194	63	189	29	47.1%	.307	21	1.30	3.91	4.00	3.64	8.3	2.5	7.8	1.1	40.7	5.42
2007	PHI	MLB	26	5	7	21	51	3	68²	61	27	83	9	48.4%	.308	19	1.27	4.32	3.66	3.86	7.6	3.0	9.6	1.0	12.2	1.40
2008	*PHI*	*MLB*	*27*	*9*	*6*	*0*	*23*	*23*	*136*	*130*	*45*	*125*	*16*	*47.2%*	*.297*	*24*	*1.29*	*3.83*	*4.04*	*3.85*	*8.3*	*2.8*	*7.4*	*1.0*	*28.8*	*3.80*

Breakout: 18%   Improve: 39%   Collapse: 31%   Attrition: 14%   Comparables: Ralph Branca, Rollie Fingers, Gary Bell, Kyle Farnsworth

In 2005 and 2006 combined, Myers started 65 games, pitching 413 1/3 innings while allowing 387 hits, 131 walks, striking out 397, and posting a 3.81 ERA. Despite that, it took just three 2007 starts for the Phillies to decide that Myers could do more for them as a closer. Save for two months lost to a right shoulder strain, he did well in the role, saving 21 games in 24 opportunities while striking out 64 in 53 1/3 innings. Still, it took only the availability of Brad Lidge for the Phillies to move him back to the rotation, which is where he belongs. The growth that Myers had shown as a starter over 2005 and 2006, if continued, would make him more productive than all but the very best closers in the game. Finding a reliever who can deliver the equivalent of four extra wins over the course of a season is easier than finding a starter with the potential to add five or six.

Josh Outman

Bats: L   Throws: L   Height: 6' 1"   Weight: 180   Born: September 14, 1984   Age: 23

YEAR	TEAM	LVL	AGE	W	L	SV	G	GS	IP	H	BB	SO	HR	GB%	BABIP	STUFF	WHIP	ERA	PERA	EqERA	EqH9	EqBB9	EqSO9	EqHR9	VORP	SN/WX
2005	BAT	A-	20	2	1	0	11	4	29¹	23	14	31	1	58.0%	.278	-8	1.26	2.76	6.56	7.66	9.1	8.4	4.4	1.5	-5.7	—
2006	LWD	A	21	14	6	0	27	27	155¹	119	75	161	5	47.4%	.288	7	1.25	2.96	6.44	6.46	10.0	7.4	5.4	1.0	-12.5	—
2007	CLR	A+	22	10	4	0	20	18	117¹	104	54	117	7	47.9%	.306	5	1.35	2.46	6.34	4.49	10.1	6.0	6.0	1.2	12.9	—
2007	REA	AA	22	2	3	0	7	7	42	38	23	34	5	42.1%	.280	-6	1.45	4.50	6.61	6.75	9.5	5.8	5.1	1.6	-4.9	—
2008	*PHI*	*MLB*	*23*	*5*	*9*	*0*	*33*	*20*	*116¹*	*129*	*83*	*88*	*20*	*44.8%*	*.307*	*-8*	*1.83*	*6.08*	*6.60*	*6.04*	*9.7*	*5.9*	*6.1*	*1.5*	*-5.3*	*0.20*

Breakout: 15%   Improve: 34%   Collapse: 32%   Attrition: 15%   Comparables: Josh Kalinowski, Daniel Haigwood, Michael Mimbs, Charlie Manning

If he gets off to a good start this year, Outman will give the Phillies one more option than they had in 2007, when they had to Kyle up their rotation to make it through the season. A southpaw with a low-90s fastball, a slider, and a change, Outman has more strikeout ability than your average Tom, Dick, or Kendrick, but as with many young lefties, he has yet to refine his control. Until he does, he won't be truly worthy of his name.

J. C. Romero

Bats: S   Throws: L   Height: 5' 11"   Weight: 205   Born: June 4, 1976   Age: 32

YEAR	TEAM	LVL	AGE	W	L	SV	G	GS	IP	H	BB	SO	HR	GB%	BABIP	STUFF	WHIP	ERA	PERA	EqERA	EqH9	EqBB9	EqSO9	EqHR9	VORP	SN/WX
2005	MIN	MLB	29	4	3	0	68	0	57	50	39	48	6	57.9%	.277	5	1.56	3.47	4.66	3.92	7.7	6.0	7.2	0.9	9.5	0.78
2006	ANA	MLB	30	1	2	0	65	0	48¹	57	28	31	3	57.8%	.344	-12	1.76	6.71	5.44	6.94	10.5	4.9	5.4	0.6	-7.9	0.11
2007	BOS	MLB	31	1	0	1	23	0	20	24	15	11	2	55.9%	.338	-12	1.95	3.15	7.67	3.86	11.6	6.3	4.8	1.0	6.5	0.60
2007	PHI	MLB	31	1	2	0	51	0	36¹	15	25	31	1	64.7%	.169	19	1.10	1.24	2.19	1.27	3.6	5.6	7.4	0.3	18.8	2.22
2008	PHI	MLB	32	2	2	2	49	0	45	44	28	35	4	54.0%	.296	-8	1.59	4.45	4.70	4.55	8.5	5.1	6.3	0.8	4.8	0.40

Breakout: 15% Improve: 33% Collapse: 46% Attrition: 37%   Comparables: Greg Cadaret, Willie Banks, Darold Knowles, Lance Painter

Romero seemed to be trending downward over the last few seasons, so it's hard to fault the Red Sox for cutting bait as soon as they did. The problem with using a pitcher whose control is as poor as Romero's as a match-up lefty is that he's so likely to issue a walk that you don't know if he'll end up facing the hitter you wanted him to or the Vlad Guerrero-type that's due up next. The other problem with using Romero specifically as a match-up lefty is that he's useful against right-handed hitters, and such use fails to exploit his more valuable ability to work whole innings. All of that said, Romero was indeed successful in shutting down lefties when he did pitch to them last year, holding them to .208/.333/.312 with no home runs. The Phillies re-signed him to a three-year, $12 million deal with a club option for 2011. This was perhaps a bit overzealous, but given the state of their bullpen and the free agent market, their importunate reaction is understandable.

Joe Savery

Bats: L   Throws: L   Height: 6' 3"   Weight: 215   Born: November 4, 1985   Age: 22

YEAR	TEAM	LVL	AGE	W	L	SV	G	GS	IP	H	BB	SO	HR	GB%	BABIP	STUFF	WHIP	ERA	PERA	EqERA	EqH9	EqBB9	EqSO9	EqHR9	VORP	SN/WX
2007	WPT	A-	21	2	3	0	7	7	26¹	22	13	22	0	51.9%	.272	-6	1.33	2.74	5.21	5.18	8.9	6.7	3.3	0.4	1.1	—
2008	PHI	MLB	22	6	11	0	26	26	133	160	87	74	23	47.5%	.309	-12	1.85	6.54	6.81	6.55	10.5	5.4	4.5	1.5	-13.3	-0.40

Breakout: NA Improve: NA Collapse: NA Attrition: NA   Comparables: Corey Lee, Joe Saunders, Michael Pasqualicchio, Wade Leblanc

The Phillies' first-round pick in 2007, Savery was a two-way star at Rice who played first base and hit cleanup when not pitching, but as a left-handed power arm, his professional future was always on the mound. Considered a sure-fire top ten pick entering the spring, Savery slipped to 19th because of some shoulder soreness, but he was impressive in his pro debut, with all three of his pitches (fastball, slider, changeup) grading out as average to plus. The Phillies were impressed enough to send him to the Arizona Fall League with just 26 innings of pro experience, which suggests that his timetable could be accelerated.

Michael Zagurski

Bats: L   Throws: L   Height: 6' 0"   Weight: 225   Born: January 27, 1983   Age: 25

YEAR	TEAM	LVL	AGE	W	L	SV	G	GS	IP	H	BB	SO	HR	GB%	BABIP	STUFF	WHIP	ERA	PERA	EqERA	EqH9	EqBB9	EqSO9	EqHR9	VORP	SN/WX
2005	BAT	A-	22	3	4	0	15	8	45	47	15	43	2	41.2%	.341	-27	1.38	4.60	8.08	10.04	12.2	6.5	3.8	1.7	-18.6	—
2006	LWD	A	23	4	4	1	42	0	56	46	22	75	0	53.9%	.341	5	1.21	3.54	6.30	6.60	11.5	6.4	7.6	0.4	-5.1	—
2007	CLR	A+	24	0	0	5	12	0	16¹	6	4	30	0	56.0%	.261	15	0.61	1.10	3.14	3.00	5.4	3.6	10.2	0.0	4.3	—
2007	PHI	MLB	24	1	0	0	25	0	21¹	25	11	21	3	44.1%	.349	-1	1.69	5.92	5.43	5.24	9.7	3.6	8.1	1.2	0.2	-0.41
2008	PHI	MLB	25	2	2	2	37	1	36²	36	19	35	4	44.1%	.306	4	1.51	4.64	4.69	4.69	8.5	4.3	7.6	1.0	5.0	0.40

Breakout: 45% Improve: 71% Collapse: 13% Attrition: 34%   Comparables: Neal Cotts, Grant Jackson, Steve Baker, Gerry Arrigo

The Phillies really did run the gamut of pitching last year, from Alfredo Alfonseca to Michael Zagurski. Built like a fire hydrant, Zags is the exemplar of how bad things got in the Phillies' pen last year. After climbing all the way from High-A to the majors, he did a fine job of holding down lefties (.216/.286/.216), but was blown away by righties, who turned into Rogers Hornsby against him (.340/.431/.620 in 58 PA). He then injured his right hamstring in August, prompting season-ending surgery. Zagurski doesn't throw hard and gets some groundballs, but he's going to need more, because even LOOGYs end up facing more righties than lefties in their quixotic role. Still, he could get another shot as the team's second lefty after Romero.

LINEOUTS

Hitters

PLAYER	TEAM	LVL	AGE	PA	R	2B	3B	HR	RBI	BB	SO	SB-CS	EqBRR	AVG/OBP/SLG	MLVr	EqAVG/EqOBP/EqSLG	EqA	VORP
OF T. Bohn	MIS	AA	27	101	15	3	0	1	6	14	23	3-0	1.9	.224/.337/.294	-.114	.195/.297/.264	.207	-8.5
	RIC	AAA	27	170	20	8	0	1	14	21	41	8-4	-1.0	.241/.343/.317	-.085	.231/.325/.313	.234	-7.8
C T. D'Arnaud	PHL	Rk	18	151	18	3	0	4	20	4	23	4-2	1.0	.241/.278/.348	-.099	.185/.204/.267	.152	-38.7
SS F. Galvis#	WPT	A-	17	156	20	5	1	0	7	10	20	9-4	-0.3	.203/.255/.252	-.249	.197/.234/.245	.164	-26.3
C P. Laforest*	POR	AAA	29	354	53	6	0	29	72	54	92	2-0	0.0	.230/.347/.544	.142	.204/.319/.478	.271	12.6
RF C. Roberson#	OTT	AAA	27	509	64	21	3	4	48	31	57	19-9	-0.9	.266/.313/.350	-.064	.246/.291/.338	.224	-14.7
	PHI	MLB	27	29	6	0	0	0	1	1	4	2-0	0.8	.286/.310/.286	-.229	.286/.310/.286	.228	-0.4
OF J. Slayden*	CLR	A+	24	500	71	24	4	14	73	60	96	7-1	-0.6	.287/.376/.458	.195	.247/.329/.410	.258	-2.0
OF M. Spencer*	WPT	A-	21	198	21	10	0	9	26	11	46	3-3	-2.3	.263/.320/.469	.182	.220/.258/.387	.220	-20.3

T. J. Bohn sailed through the winter on the Phils' 40-man roster as a placeholder for someone with promise. ⊘ Many thought **Travis D'Arnaud** was the best high school catcher in the 2007 draft. A talented defender, he's expected to develop above-average power, but he's still very raw. ⊘ **Freddy Galvis** is toolsy, but completely unformed. Already a very strong defender, his bat is as yet nonexistent, but he's young enough that it could develop to the point at which he'd be a viable major leaguer regular. ⊘ A Quebec native drafted by the Expos, **Pierre-Luc "Pete" LaForest** is baseball's man without a country. He's also baseball's man without a clue when it comes to making consistent contact, which is why, despite a bit of home run pop, he's on the fringe. ⊘ Organizational soldier **Chris Roberson** has some speed, but his bat is so light that he's not even qualified to be a fifth outfielder in the majors. ⊘ **Jeremy Slayden** has had decent results with the bat the last two years, but when you're a 24-year-old college hitter playing in A-ball, that's expected. He'll be a proud member of the Union of Concerned Fourth Outfielders. ⊘ **Matthew Spencer** has big-time power but is an all-or-nothing hitter with a big swing and a bigger strikeout rate.

Pitchers

PLAYER	TEAM	LVL	AGE	W	L	SV	IP	H	BB	SO	HR	GB%	BABIP	STUFF	WHIP	ERA	PERA	EqERA	EqH9	EqBB9	EqSO9	EqHR9	VORP
A. Bastardo*	LWD	A	21	9	0	0	91²	63	42	98	3	40.3%	.259	17	1.15	1.86	5.01	4.15	8.0	6.6	5.5	0.8	13.3
J. Bisenius	OTT	AAA	24	3	4	0	46	52	31	41	5	37.1%	.370	-16	1.80	5.48	7.71	6.96	11.0	6.8	5.9	1.5	-6.5
F. Castro*	REA	AA	22	2	0	1	16²	12	6	24	0	39.5%	.316	16	1.08	2.69	3.76	4.02	8.0	4.0	9.8	0.0	2.8
	OTT	AAA	22	5	5	1	58¹	53	33	47	7	36.4%	.289	-12	1.48	4.01	5.25	5.53	8.1	5.4	5.1	1.6	0.4
	PHI	MLB	22	0	0	0	12	9	13	14	2	41.4%	.259	12	1.83	6.00	4.97	5.25	6.8	8.2	9.8	1.5	0.1
K. Drabek	LWD	A	19	5	1	0	54	50	23	46	9	55.8%	.266	-25	1.35	4.33	9.52	8.31	11.0	6.2	4.2	3.0	-14.4
J. Ennis	OTT	AAA	27	4	4	1	88	90	32	83	7	49.8%	.339	-6	1.39	3.38	5.09	4.82	9.5	3.6	6.2	1.1	7.3
A. Garcia	REA	AA	26	0	2	7	17¹	16	1	19	1	44.9%	.319	7	0.98	3.12	4.24	4.41	9.9	1.1	7.2	1.1	2.2
	OTT	AAA	26	1	5	4	59²	63	20	42	7	46.7%	.304	-26	1.39	5.13	5.11	5.70	9.0	3.3	4.3	1.5	-0.7
E. Garcia	LWD	A	19	4	9	0	113²	119	32	83	10	45.9%	.311	-21	1.33	4.12	7.56	7.75	11.9	4.5	3.3	1.8	-24.1
Y. Hernandez	OTT	AAA	27	1	3	5	29²	33	14	16	0	61.9%	.327	-18	1.58	3.94	4.18	4.50	9.0	4.5	3.0	0.3	3.7
	PHI	MLB	27	0	0	0	15¹	20	1	13	2	45.3%	.353	5	1.37	5.29	4.81	5.17	10.9	0.6	6.9	1.1	1.2
J. Mateo	SEA	MLB	29	1	0	0	12	12	5	4	0	34.9%	.279	-17	1.42	3.75	3.07	2.92	8.0	2.9	2.9	0.0	2.8
	REA	AA	29	1	0	0	16	14	1	14	2	30.4%	.279	-3	0.94	2.81	4.92	3.68	9.2	1.2	5.5	1.8	3.1
	TAC	AAA	29	3	1	12	34¹	25	2	29	3	44.8%	.237	11	0.79	0.79	2.75	1.32	5.8	0.8	5.8	1.1	16.2
S. Mathieson '08	PHI	MLB	24	3	5	0	72¹	82	41	56	15	40%	.302	-9	1.69	6.41	6.46	6.35	9.9	4.7	6.2	1.8	-6.2
D. Naylor	WPT	A-	21	8	6	0	93¹	78	28	97	3	45.4%	.310	-1	1.14	3.28	6.09	6.36	10.5	4.8	5.1	1.1	-6.8
F. Rosario	CLR	A+	26	0	0	0	13¹	9	5	16	1	42.4%	.258	-5	1.05	4.06	5.16	5.84	8.0	5.1	7.3	1.5	-0.3
	PHI	MLB	26	0	3	1	26¹	34	13	25	3	34.1%	.397	-1	1.78	5.48	6.73	5.40	11.1	3.7	7.8	1.0	1.4
B. Sanches	OTT	AAA	28	2	3	16	47¹	57	8	52	5	41.3%	.382	-6	1.37	4.76	6.19	6.55	11.5	1.8	7.3	1.4	-4.8
	PHI	MLB	28	1	1	0	14²	13	12	9	6	39.1%	.179	-24	1.70	5.51	8.07	6.60	7.2	6.0	4.8	3.6	-1.2
Z. Segovia	REA	AA	24	5	3	0	57²	65	22	30	4	43.8%	.321	-21	1.51	4.84	6.67	6.71	11.4	4.2	2.9	1.0	-6.6
	OTT	AAA	24	1	9	0	77¹	99	28	22	8	46.3%	.320	-36	1.64	6.05	6.56	7.11	11.1	3.6	1.4	1.4	-12.5
M. Smith*	OTT	AAA	28	2	1	1	17¹	13	7	16	2	56.3%	.250	-8	1.16	2.60	3.96	3.18	6.9	3.7	5.8	1.6	4.6

Antonio Bastardo had a good year in the Sally League last year. He's a smallish lefty with a good arm and a low-90s fastball, but his secondary stuff needs work. ⊘ **Joe Bisenius** made the Phils' Opening Day roster last year, but only as a seat-warmer for an injured veteran. He's your standard low-90s fastball/slider reliever, or he was until his command took a giant step backward at Triple-A Ottawa. ⊘ Finally off the Rule 5 merry-go-round, **Fabio Castro** yo-yo'd between the majors and the minors last year. He's a little guy with big velocity who has LOOGY potential at the very least—in 52 plate appearances against him, big-league lefties have just three hits, all singles. ⊘ Doug's son and the Phils' 2006 first-round pick, **Kyle Drabek** underwent Tommy John surgery last June, which helped explain his poor performance up to that point. ⊘ **John Ennis** was another minor league vet hauled in by the Phils' desperation dragnet. He is a man of spots, not stuff. ⊘ Once traded by the Yankees for Armando Benitez, **Anderson Garcia** was a pre-season waiver claim from the Orioles who made it up for a moment last July; 27 in March, he has yet to master Triple-A. ⊘ **Edgar Garcia** has as good an arm as anyone in the Phillies' system but has problems staying in shape and/or caring. ⊘ **Yoel Hernandez** was released by the Phillies in October. Injuries and a lack of accomplishment limit him to the big league fringe. ⊘ Veteran Mariner **Julio Mateo** was charged with assaulting his wife in May, flipped to the Phillies in July, sent to Double-A and forgotten about, released in December, pleaded guilty and avoided jail time later that month, and is now fair game for any team looking to sign a pitcher of his sterling character. ⊘ A 17th-round pick back in 2002, **Scott Mathieson** made it up to the majors in 2006, got bombed, and went under the knife for Tommy John surgery. He only managed a few rehab innings at the end of last year. Before the operation he could throw his fastball through a fully bloated politician. ⊘ The Phillies' Australian scouting program almost seems to be more prolific than their domestic operation. **Drew Naylor** has a good fastball and a decent curve, but probably is best suited to the bullpen. ⊘ Purchased from the Blue Jays in April, **Francisco Rosario**'s injury problems continued as he missed more than two months of last season with right shoulder inflammation. His iffy control and fly-ball habits suggest that he's no more than filler, preferably in a starting role. ⊘ **Brian Sanches**'s fastball rarely gets out of 80s, so he relies on off-speed pitches. The problem is that he has no control, so when he falls behind, batters hit his weak fastball over the moon. ⊘ The Phils' second-round pick in 2002, **Zach Segovia** was Tommy Johned in 2003 and his velocity has never been the same. He made last year's Opening Day roster, stuck around for one pounding, then posted a negative strikeout-to-walk ratio in the minors. ⊘ Part of the weak payoff from the Yankees for Bobby Abreu, **Matt Smith** underwent Tommy John surgery in July. It's going to be difficult for him to reestablish his tenuous hold on a big-league job when he returns.

MANAGER: CHARLIE MANUEL

YEAR	TEAM	W-L	Pythag +/-	Avg PC	100+ P	120+ P	QS	BQS	REL	REL w Zero R	IBB	Subs	PH	PH Avg	PH HR	SB2	CS2	SB3	CS3	SAC Att	SAC %	POS SAC	Squeeze	Swing	In Play
2005	PHI	88-74	-2	93.1	58	3	80	8	441	281	51	46	263	.233	4	99	26	17	1	92	67.4%	25	0	111	83
2006	PHI	85-77	-1	92.9	56	2	68	7	500	323	63	77	296	.209	3	87	25	5	0	82	69.5%	28	0	105	69
2007	PHI	89-73	1	92.8	55	1	72	8	498	310	62	121	262	.230	9	126	18	11	2	85	76.5%	26	1	146	113

Early last year, the Phillies record dropped to 3-9 after an 8-1 loss to the Mets on April 17. That night, Charlie Manuel's postgame press conference went off the tracks when a local radio talk-show host pushed Manuel as to whether he was hard enough or angry enough with his team, presumably operating on the theory that yelling at grown men somehow motivates them to exceed the limits of their own talent. If a fierce bit of irony, Manuel nearly thrashed his interlocutor, which was not a disproportionate response: the ignoramus was simultaneously impugning Manuel's job performance and manhood by saying his players didn't take him seriously, while advancing an explanation for the Phillies' early struggles which was completely nonsensical. Six months later, the Phillies had won a division title without any histrionics, Manuel finished second in the Manager of the Year balloting and was rewarded with a two-year contract extension with a club option for a third. That said, it's not surprising that an uninformed observer would miss the subtleties of Manuel's approach. He's not a hyperactive tactician; he's not big on one-run strategies and bunts infrequently for a National League manager, though he was more aggressive on the bases last year, both with straight steals and the hit and run. With the league's best lineup two years running, it would have been counterproductive for him to do more. His grasp of pitching is less sure. His most significant decision, moving Brett Myers to the bullpen, was hasty to say the least, but it is unlikely that he made it without front office oversight and approval.

Pittsburgh Pirates

The Pittsburgh Pirates haven't been a losing team forever. It just seems that way. The Pirates have had 15 consecutive losing seasons and are on the brink of making some ignominious history. With another sub-.500 season, they will tie the major league record for most consecutive losing seasons, which was set by the Philadelphia Phillies from 1933 to 1948.

If the Pirates do indeed plunge feet first into the record, they will at least do so with new leadership. After years of being extremely patient with their general managers and other front-office types, the Nutting family, which quietly assumed principal ownership of the franchise sometime earlier this decade—true to the family's rather secretive nature, an official announcement was never made—decided to shake things up before, during, and after the 2007 season.

It all started in January when Bob Nutting took over as the principal owner, or "control person" as the Pirates put it, gently nudging his predecessor Kevin McClatchy to the side and, eventually, all but out of the organization. Displacing McClatchy as the face of the franchise was a rather gutsy move. After all, McClatchy, a newspaper heir from Sacramento, overcame steep odds by putting together an ownership group that bought the Pirates from a public/private consortium in 1996 and kept the team from leaving Pittsburgh. It was also McClatchy who, after a ballot referendum was shot down by voters by a 3-1 margin, was still able to land public funding for the construction of PNC Park, a jewel of a ballpark on the Allegheny River. The new park opened in 2001 and is clearly the one thing the franchise has done right in the last decade and a half. Though McClatchy remains on the club's board of directors, he announced at the All-Star break that he

PIRATES PROSPECTUS
2007 record: 68-94; Sixth place, NL Central
Pythagenport record: 69-93
Runs scored per game: 4.47 (12th in NL)
Runs allowed per game: 5.22 (14th in NL)
Team EqA: .254 (12th in NL)
2007 Batters Age: 27.7 (3rd youngest in NL)
2007 Pitchers Age: 27.4 (2nd youngest in NL)
Ballpark: PNC Park; Neutral Park; Park Factor of .993
2007: At long last, some change in the front office.
2008: Meet the new bosses. Year One: same old losses.

would step down from his post as chief executive officer at the end of the 2007 season.

In early September, McClatchy was replaced as CEO by Frank Coonelly, who had been Major League Baseball's vice president and general counsel for labor. Less than a week before Coonelly came aboard, general manager Dave Littlefield was finally dismissed after six mostly fruitless years that were marked by a string of awful free agent signings and poor drafts. The last straw came at the July 31 non-waiver trading deadline when Littlefield stunned everyone in baseball by acquiring right-hander Matt Morris from San Francisco. It wasn't just that Morris had registered a 7.94 ERA in his last eight starts with the Giants while hitters raked him at a .386/.419/.614 clip, but that Littlefield agreed to pay all of the $13.7 million left on Morris's contract, which runs through the end of the 2008 season, and also gave up two middling prospects in outfielder Rajai Davis and left-hander Steven MacFarland. Morris didn't fare much better with the Pirates, posting a 6.10 ERA in 11 starts while serving up an opponents' line of .315/.377/.468.

Neal Huntington, a special assistant to Cleveland Indians GM Mark Shapiro, was hired as Littlefield's replacement during the final week of the season. Huntington's first order of business was to fire manager Jim Tracy, scouting director Ed Creech, and director of player development Brian Graham.

Tracy had led the Los Angeles Dodgers to the 2004 National League West title, but compiled a horrendous 135-189 record in two seasons with the Pirates. He never seemed to make a connection with his players, who then completely quit on him in the final three weeks of last season after Littlefield was fired. Not only did Tracy's charges fail to run out groundballs and hustle in the field, but they arrived late for stretching and batting practice without facing disciplinary action from the manager. The last straw for Coonelly came on the final day of the season, when only two Pirates bothered to stand on the top step of the dugout for the playing of God Bless America during the seventh-inning stretch.

On the player development side, Creech had a series of poor drafts, but to be fair, Littlefield often meddled in the selections, most notably when he overruled Creech's decision to draft B. J. Upton with the first overall pick in 2002, selecting Bryan Bullington instead. Bullington is now 27 and has logged just 18 1/3 innings in the major leagues. Under Graham's watch, the Pirates developed a number of useful pitchers, most notably left-handed starters Tom Gorzelanny, Paul Maholm, and Zach Duke, right-hander Ian Snell, and closer Matt Capps. However, the organization has not produced an impact hitter since signing third baseman Aramis Ramirez out of the Dominican Republic in 1995. Ramirez made his major league debut three years later as a 19-year-old, but was shipped to the Cubs in a cost-cutting trade during the 2003 season.

Just as when Littlefield did when he replaced Cam Bonifay midway through 2001, Huntington is promising to build the Pirates through scouting and player development. As a low-revenue franchise that relies on revenue sharing to make a profit and has penny-pinching owners in the Nuttings—they can't help it, they're newspaper people, and no other business knows more about cutting costs—the Pirates have no choice but to develop young, cost-effective players if they are to have any chance of ever being competitive. Huntington also promises to take a systematic approach to building the organization. That is certainly a welcome change, since the Littlefield administration seemed to shift its philosophy once every 15 minutes.

Meanwhile, Coonelly has made it clear that he is a no-nonsense guy. Just three weeks of watching the 2007 Pirates mail it in while Tracy twisted in the wind was enough to make the new boss's stomach turn. Thus, Coonelly is preaching accountability on all levels. That too is a welcome change, as Littlefield never seemed to admit or learn from his numerous personnel blunders, including trading pitcher Chris Young for Matt Herges, losing Bronson Arroyo on waivers, and not only trading for Randall Simon, but later bringing him back as a free agent. Meanwhile, Tracy appeared to be in denial that he had ever made a wrong decision or lost his clubhouse during his brief tenure as the Pirates' manager.

While scouting, player development, and accountability sound like a good formula for pulling the Pirates from the clutches of perpetual losing, it will not be that simple. The Pirates lack star-caliber talent beyond left fielder Jason Bay, and even he had a subpar season in 2007 while being dragged down by a sore knee and the malaise that comes with enduring one's fourth season on a treadmill to nowhere. The club leader in Value Over Replacement was second baseman Freddy Sanchez, whose 27.5 VORP ranked 88th in the major leagues.

Snell and Gorzlanny showed the potential to be a potent one-two punch in the starting rotation last season, and Capps, who was promoted from his set-up role on June 1, has the makings of a top-flight closer. However, the rest of the roster consists primarily of league-average players or those dipping dangerously close to replacement level. The farm system also is devoid of first-rate talent beyond first baseman/outfielder Steven Pearce, third baseman Neil Walker, and center fielder Andrew McCutchen, and only McCutchen has a better than 50/50 chance of stardom.

Furthermore, the new Pirates' management team comes with plenty of questions about its acumen. All who know Coonelly say he is a brilliant man. The *New York Sun*'s Tim Marchman called him "the most powerful man in baseball that no one knows." Coonelly played in large part in accomplishing the seemingly impossible task of negotiating a labor peace without a work stoppage in 2006. However, Coonelly is also the man who devised MLB's slotting system for draft picks. While Coonelly insists he will be willing to pay above slot for the Pirates' picks, his reputation as the MLB executive responsible for yelling at clubs who overspent for draft picks precedes him, and that casts doubt over whether the Pirates will begin spending top dollar for amateur talent. Nutting has shown no inclination to spend money over the years as the Pirates have been in the bottom third in the major leagues in payroll in 11 of the 12 seasons since McClatchy and the Nuttings bought the team. The exception was in PNC Park's inaugural season of 2001, when the Pirates moved up to 18th among the 30 teams, but all that got them was 100 losses.

Huntington worked for one of baseball's best GMs in Shapiro and has experience both as an office-type in his roles of assistant GM and farm director and as a field-type in his duties as a special assignment scout, but he comes to the Pirates with a slightly damaged reputation, as he moved downward in the Indians' hierarchy from assistant GM to special assistant to make room for whiz kid Chris Antonetti. Huntington says he wanted out of the office because he missed evaluating talent. Indians insiders say Huntington lost influence after Milton Bradley, whom the team acquired on Huntington's recommendation, left the organization during the final week of spring training in 2004 following a memorable on-field meltdown and subsequent $62 cab ride from Kissimmee to Winter Haven.

Huntington's first major moves after firing Tracy, Creech, and Graham wer to replace them with manager John Russell, scouting director Greg Smith, and farm director Kyle Stark. Russell was the Pirates' third-base coach from 2003 to 2005 and returned to the organization just a hair more than two years after being fired by Littlefield along with the rest of the coaching staff on the final day of the 2005 season. While the new regime argues that Russell's dismissal should be disregarded because it came under the old regime, bringing him back with a promotion and a substantial raise is still tough for the Pirates to sell to their increasingly cynical fans. In fairness to Russell, he was well respected by both the veterans and youngsters on the Pirates during his coaching stint, and he has had success as a skipper down on the farm, especially at the Triple-A level. Russell was named Minor League Manager of the Year by Baseball America in 2002 after leading Edmonton, at that time the Twins' Triple-A affiliate, to the Pacific Coast League title, and was selected by his peers as International League Manager of the Year in 2006 after guiding Scranton/Wilkes-Barre, at that time the Phillies' Triple-A club, to the playoffs.

As for Huntington's new lieutenants overseeing the farm system, Smith was Detroit's scouting director from 1997 to 2004, but, like Huntington, had since been bumped down to special assistant to the GM. As scouting director, Smith was responsible for the Tigers drafting such players as Justin Verlander, Curtis Granderson, Joel Zumaya, and Brandon Inge, but also picked first-round busts in Matt Anderson, Eric Munson, Matt Wheatland, Kenny Baugh, and Kyle Sleeth. Stark is just 29, but gained a wide range of experience during his four years with the Indians, including overseeing international scouting and doing advance scouting. While he developed an outstanding reputation during his time with Cleveland, this also marks the first time he will be in a position of power. In fact, outside of Smith, none of the Pirates' new hires have experience in their current positions at the major league level.

Nutting is admittedly not a baseball man and is trusting this group to restore dignity to a once-proud franchise that has turned into a laughingstock. The Pirates shouldn't lose 100 games this season, but they seem like a lock to tie the Phillies' record with their 16th consecutive losing season. More compelling will be the action off the field, as this new and untested management team attempts to move the franchise in the right direction for the first time since a young, lithe Barry Bonds patrolled left field in Three Rivers Stadium.

HITTERS

Jose Bautista | **3B** | Bats: R　Throws: R　Height: 6' 0"　Weight: 195　Born: October 19, 1980　Age: 27

YEAR	TEAM	LVL	AGE	PA	R	2B	3B	HR	RBI	BB	SO	SB	CS	EqBRR	AVG	OBP	SLG	MLVr	EqAVG	EqOBP	EqSLG	EqA	VORP	DEFENSE		
2005	ALT	AA	24	507	63	27	1	23	90	48	101	7	3	-3.4	.283	.364	.503	.232	.254	.328	.453	.266	22.2	113-3B -12		
2005	PIT	MLB	24	31	3	1	0	0	1	3	7	1	0	-1.2	.143	.226	.179	-.557	.143	.226	.179	.138	-3.2			
2006	IND	AAA	25	119	12	9	0	2	9	14	19	2	1	-1.2	.277	.370	.426	.169	.265	.353	.431	.273	6.1	23-3B -1		
2006	PIT	MLB	25	469	58	20	3	16	51	46	110	2	4	-2.7	.235	.335	.420	-.033	.239	.335	.428	.262	4.4	47-CF 2	30-3B -4	
2007	PIT	MLB	26	614	75	36	2	15	63	68	101	6	3	-2.8	.254	.339	.414	-.014	.258	.346	.430	.270	9.1	119-3B -11	15-RF -3	
2008	PIT	MLB	27	553	68	29	2	18	71	55	102	6	2	-0.8	.260	.340	.440	-.010	.250	.340	.450	.280	17.6	130-3B -5		

Breakout: 34%　Improve: 60%　Collapse: 20%　Attrition: 16%　　　　Comparables: Steve Buechele, Gary Gaetti, Doug Decinces, Craig Worthington

Because of their lack of resources, bad teams are often forced to stretch complementary players into starting roles. Bautista doesn't have enough power to be a true corner infielder, strikes out far too often, and is too inconsistent defensively at third base. He does, however, have enough pop, speed, and versatility to be a valuable utility player, as he is capable of playing every position on the diamond except pitcher and catcher. As such, 2006's usage (57 games in center, 33 at third, 25 in right, six in left, two at second) makes more sense than 2007's (126 games at third, 23 in the outfield). The value of a versatile player with a mediocre bat is that he can prevent a team from having to sink all the way down to replacement level when an injury occurs. Parking that player at one position emphasizes his weaknesses over his strengths.

Jason Bay — LF

Bats: R Throws: R Height: 6' 2" Weight: 205 Born: September 20, 1978 Age: 29

YEAR	TEAM	LVL	AGE	PA	R	2B	3B	HR	RBI	BB	SO	SB	CS	EqBRR	AVG	OBP	SLG	MLVr	EqAVG	EqOBP	EqSLG	EqA	VORP	DEFENSE			
2005	PIT	MLB	26	707	110	44	6	32	101	95	142	21	1	5.0	.306	.402	.559	.347	.303	.400	.566	.326	72.7	134-LF	15	25-CF	-2
2006	PIT	MLB	27	689	101	29	3	35	109	102	156	11	2	1.3	.286	.396	.532	.257	.283	.395	.526	.314	49.7	155-LF	20		
2007	PIT	MLB	28	614	78	25	2	21	84	59	141	4	1	-2.0	.247	.327	.418	-.034	.250	.333	.436	.268	3.9	138-LF	-6		
2008	PIT	MLB	29	582	85	28	3	25	82	74	127	9	2	0.4	.270	.360	.490	.100	.260	.360	.490	.300	26.1	136-LF	0		

Breakout: 15% Improve: 43% Collapse: 18% Attrition: 10%   Comparables: Greg Vaughn, Dwight Evans, Derrek Lee, Bob Allison

Bay's 2007 season took a turn for the worse in June, and he was never able to pull out of the freefall, hitting just .209/.292/.358 over the season's final four months. The primary culprits appeared to be his knees. Bay had minor surgery on his left knee following the 2006 season. Compensating for that weak left knee in early 2007 resulted in tendonitis in his right knee, which robbed him of his speed on the bases, range in the outfield, and power at the plate. That his walk rate also fell dramatically is a concern, but the feeling here is that the poor season was an aberration. After finally being able to rest those knees this offseason, Bay should bounce back in 2008, provided he isn't beaten down mentally by another season of losing in Pittsburgh.

Brian Bixler — SS

Bats: R Throws: R Height: 6' 1" Weight: 195 Born: October 22, 1982 Age: 25

YEAR	TEAM	LVL	AGE	PA	R	2B	3B	HR	RBI	BB	SO	SB	CS	EqBRR	AVG	OBP	SLG	MLVr	EqAVG	EqOBP	EqSLG	EqA	VORP	DEFENSE			
2005	HIC	A	22	557	74	23	2	9	50	38	134	21	10	0.2	.281	.343	.388	.033	.210	.257	.285	.189	-34.5	125-SS	-8		
2006	LYN	A+	23	317	46	16	2	5	33	35	58	18	7	1.6	.303	.402	.434	.207	.256	.332	.377	.251	7.8	71-SS	-7		
2006	ALT	AA	23	253	36	13	1	3	19	16	57	6	2	2.2	.301	.363	.407	.135	.247	.302	.351	.232	-0.7	56-SS	-7		
2007	IND	AAA	24	556	77	23	10	5	51	54	131	28	4	6.8	.274	.368	.396	.076	.249	.336	.383	.259	14.9	111-SS	-7	15-2B	3
2008	PIT	MLB	25	514	62	25	4	7	43	39	121	17	5	1.8	.250	.320	.370	-.150	.250	.320	.380	.250	9.7	121-SS	-3		

Breakout: 30% Improve: 63% Collapse: 16% Attrition: 17%   Comparables: Eric Owens, Jed Hansen, Tony Manahan, Freddie Bynum

A second-round draft pick out of Eastern Michigan in 2004, Bixler has been living up to his pedigree more with each passing year and was among the top shortstops in the International League last season. Bixler has good speed and plays solid defense, but he continually posts high strikeout numbers, leading to concern that major league pitchers could have their way with him. With Jack Wilson staying in Pittsburgh, Bixler is likely headed back to Triple-A to start the season. At his age, it's likely that he is what he is.

Jose Castillo — INF

Bats: R Throws: R Height: 6' 0" Weight: 210 Born: March 19, 1981 Age: 27

YEAR	TEAM	LVL	AGE	PA	R	2B	3B	HR	RBI	BB	SO	SB	CS	EqBRR	AVG	OBP	SLG	MLVr	EqAVG	EqOBP	EqSLG	EqA	VORP	DEFENSE			
2005	PIT	MLB	24	398	49	16	3	11	53	23	59	2	3	-1.8	.268	.307	.416	-.033	.266	.309	.421	.249	5.6	95-2B	-2		
2006	PIT	MLB	25	562	54	25	0	14	65	32	98	6	4	0.7	.253	.299	.382	-.136	.251	.299	.381	.236	-0.1	139-2B	-19		
2007	PIT	MLB	26	230	18	18	1	0	24	6	48	0	0	-0.3	.244	.270	.335	-.254	.245	.274	.336	.209	-8.1	28-3B	4	14-2B	-5
2008	FLO	MLB	27	206	21	10	1	5	23	11	39	2	1	-0.1	.258	.303	.394	-.137	.258	.302	.403	.237	3.8	52-2B	-3		

Breakout: 39% Improve: 54% Collapse: 32% Attrition: 38%   Comparables: Mel Roach, George Arias, Bobby Wine, Billy Ripken

After Castillo's subpar 2006, Jim Tracy asked him to show up to spring training in better shape. Castillo did as told, but nevertheless lost his second base job in spring training to an infield shuffle that saw batting champ Freddy Sanchez move to the keystone with Jose Bautista taking Sanchez's place at third base. As a result, Castillo was buried to the point that he became the Pirates' forgotten man. Released in December, Castillo has enough raw ability to salvage his career and should benefit from a new start with the Marlins.

Brad Corley — OF

Bats: R Throws: R Height: 6' 2" Weight: 198 Born: December 28, 1983 Age: 24

YEAR	TEAM	LVL	AGE	PA	R	2B	3B	HR	RBI	BB	SO	SB	CS	EqBRR	AVG	OBP	SLG	MLVr	EqAVG	EqOBP	EqSLG	EqA	VORP	DEFENSE			
2005	WPT	A-	21	287	29	10	6	4	35	16	56	3	7	-3.1	.279	.331	.408	.099	.212	.247	.307	.184	-49.0	33-RF	-3	30-CF	0
2006	HIC	A	22	575	87	32	2	16	100	18	109	9	3	1.1	.281	.323	.438	.108	.229	.257	.356	.210	-38.1	131-RF	-11		
2007	LYN	A+	23	518	73	36	4	14	89	14	99	3	2	-1.7	.285	.319	.462	.075	.231	.253	.376	.213	-31.8	107-RF	-4		
2007	ALT	AA	23	39	3	2	0	0	4	0	6	1	0	-0.9	.256	.256	.308	-.256	.231	.231	.282	.173	-3.8				
2008	PIT	MLB	24	545	48	29	2	11	58	18	130	5	3	0.2	.240	.270	.370	-.240	.240	.270	.380	.220	-17.2	128-RF	0		

Breakout: 50% Improve: 73% Collapse: 13% Attrition: 9%   Comparables: Ryan Long, Matt Carson, Jeffrey Frazier, Al Benjamin

Corley is appealing to scouts because he has a power bat and an arm strong enough that it allowed him to double as a closer at Mississippi State. However, his horrible strikeout-to-walk ratio scares off statistical analysts. The disturbing part is Corley does not feel the lack of walks is a hindrance to his development, a theory which will be tested this year at Double-A.

Humberto Cota — C

Bats: R Throws: R Height: 6' 0" Weight: 220 Born: February 7, 1979 Age: 29

YEAR	TEAM	LVL	AGE	PA	R	2B	3B	HR	RBI	BB	SO	SB	CS	EqBRR	AVG	OBP	SLG	MLVr	EqAVG	EqOBP	EqSLG	EqA	VORP	DEFENSE	
2005	PIT	MLB	26	320	29	20	1	7	43	17	80	0	0	-0.2	.242	.285	.387	-.128	.240	.284	.389	.233	1.5	77-C	-1
2006	PIT	MLB	27	110	5	1	0	0	5	8	26	0	0	-0.4	.190	.248	.200	-.516	.190	.248	.200	.145	-10.4	28-C	-1
2007	IND	AAA	28	104	9	6	0	0	9	7	8	2	0	-0.5	.284	.330	.347	-.044	.260	.308	.312	.226	-2.1	23-C	-2
2007	PIT	MLB	28	18	1	1	0	0	3	2	2	0	0	0.0	.286	.389	.357	.013	.286	.389	.357	.282	0.7		
2008	PIT	MLB	29	149	12	7	0	2	15	9	25	1	0	-0.3	.250	.300	.340	-.230	.240	.290	.350	.230	-0.2	39-C	-1

Breakout: 45% Improve: 60% Collapse: 27% Attrition: 39%   Comparables: Dave Van Gorder, Mike Matheny, Ray Fosse, Robert Machado

Cota was considered the Pirates' catcher of the future at the turn of the century, but was blocked by Jason Kendall, who signed a six-year, $60 million contract following the 2000 season. Kendall has been gone from Pittsburgh for three years now, but Cota's window of opportunity closed in a matter of weeks in 2006 when he began the season as the Pirates' starting catcher, only to lose the job to Ronny Paulino before April was over. Now 29, Cota's role is that of a Triple-A backstop waiting for an emergency to arise in the major leagues.

Jason Delaney — 1B/LF

Bats: R Throws: R Height: 6' 3" Weight: 215 Born: November 9, 1982 Age: 25

YEAR	TEAM	LVL	AGE	PA	R	2B	3B	HR	RBI	BB	SO	SB	CS	EqBRR	AVG	OBP	SLG	MLVr	EqAVG	EqOBP	EqSLG	EqA	VORP	DEFENSE			
2005	WPT	A-	22	221	19	8	0	0	13	19	33	2	2	-0.7	.213	.281	.254	-.224	.162	.211	.191	.112	-66.2	35-RF	-4	17-LF	0
2006	HIC	A	23	518	64	27	3	9	75	56	79	5	5	-6.1	.300	.379	.432	.193	.246	.310	.361	.233	-19.1	116-LF	-19		
2007	LYN	A+	24	296	39	16	3	9	44	38	52	2	1	-2.6	.340	.432	.536	.389	.264	.345	.418	.267	4.8	45-1B	-5	19-LF	-1
2007	ALT	AA	24	262	25	10	0	7	35	38	52	0	0	-2.3	.265	.370	.404	.070	.238	.336	.374	.251	-2.9	29-1B	-4	21-LF	1
2008	PIT	MLB	25	570	54	27	1	9	61	53	123	4	2	-1.2	.250	.320	.360	-.170	.240	.320	.360	.240	-8.0	134-LF	-3		

Breakout: 37% Improve: 68% Collapse: 15% Attrition: 14%   Comparables: Eric Battersby, Eric Nielsen, Darren Stumberger, T.J. Bohn

Delaney has shown the ability to hit for average both at Boston College and during his first two full seasons of professional baseball. However, his mediocre power makes him a less than a blue-chip prospect as a first baseman/left fielder. He might make it to the major leagues as a front-office type, though, as he holds a degree in finance and aspires to be a club president or general manager if the playing thing doesn't pan out. If he doesn't flash more power in his second stint at Double-A this year, he might want to start working on the résumé.

Ryan Doumit — RF/C

Bats: S Throws: R Height: 6' 1" Weight: 220 Born: April 3, 1981 Age: 27

YEAR	TEAM	LVL	AGE	PA	R	2B	3B	HR	RBI	BB	SO	SB	CS	EqBRR	AVG	OBP	SLG	MLVr	EqAVG	EqOBP	EqSLG	EqA	VORP	DEFENSE			
2005	IND	AAA	24	188	41	11	0	12	35	16	36	1	3	0.2	.345	.415	.630	.501	.305	.372	.551	.301	20.6	35-C	-2		
2005	PIT	MLB	24	257	25	13	1	6	35	11	48	2	1	-0.7	.255	.324	.398	-.034	.258	.320	.412	.254	6.1	48-C	2		
2006	PIT	MLB	25	178	15	9	0	6	17	15	42	0	0	-0.6	.208	.322	.389	-.113	.212	.320	.397	.252	-2.2	23-1B	-2	10-C	0
2007	PIT	MLB	26	279	33	19	2	9	32	22	59	1	2	-1.3	.274	.341	.472	.085	.279	.348	.486	.279	11.1	35-RF	-3	25-C	-4
2008	PIT	MLB	27	277	35	16	1	10	37	22	55	3	2	-0.1	.270	.340	.460	.020	.260	.340	.470	.280	11.7	68-C	-2		

Breakout: 26% Improve: 55% Collapse: 26% Attrition: 28%   Comparables: Jason Varitek, Ben Davis, Harry Chiti, John Orsino

Doumit has plenty of value as a switch-hitting catcher with power. As an outfielder, though, he's just another guy with adequate pop for a corner man but little else to distinguish him. Unfortunately, the Pirates don't seem trust his defense behind the plate and are convinced his future is in the outfield. Doumit has been plagued by a variety of injuries throughout his career and cannot be counted on to stay healthy for 162 games.

Chris Duffy — CF

Bats: L   Throws: L   Height: 5' 9"   Weight: 180   Born: April 20, 1980   Age: 28

YEAR	TEAM	LVL	AGE	PA	R	2B	3B	HR	RBI	BB	SO	SB	CS	EqBRR	AVG	OBP	SLG	MLVr	EqAVG	EqOBP	EqSLG	EqA	VORP	DEFENSE	
2005	IND	AAA	25	340	55	13	7	7	31	16	57	17	9	2.1	.308	.358	.464	.140	.279	.324	.426	.257	9.3	71-CF	-3
2005	PIT	MLB	25	136	22	4	2	1	9	7	22	2	2	0.0	.341	.385	.429	.180	.349	.397	.437	.286	8.2	28-CF	3
2006	IND	AAA	26	118	18	7	2	2	19	10	13	13	3	2.2	.349	.415	.509	.413	.327	.390	.514	.309	12.9	24-CF	1
2006	PIT	MLB	26	348	46	14	3	2	18	19	71	26	1	5.7	.255	.317	.338	-.164	.256	.317	.338	.249	3.8	76-CF	-5
2007	PIT	MLB	27	270	31	11	3	3	22	21	43	13	4	0.7	.249	.313	.357	-.140	.258	.327	.379	.251	-0.1	60-CF	7
2008	PIT	MLB	28	295	40	13	3	3	25	19	48	13	3	1.5	.280	.330	.390	-.080	.270	.330	.390	.260	8.1	72-CF	3

Breakout: 23% Improve: 40% Collapse: 34% Attrition: 37%   Comparables: David Hulse, Milt Thompson, Russ Snyder, Lance Johnson

Duffy has plenty of speed, is a good base stealer, and can go gap-to-gap to chase down fly balls with just about anybody in the game. However, he has two fatal flaws: a lack of plate discipline, which makes him an ineffective leadoff hitter, and an inability to stay healthy. As Duffy will be 28 in April, his window of opportunity as a starter has all but shut; his future looks to be that of a fourth or fifth outfielder.

Brad Eldred — 1B/RF

Bats: R   Throws: R   Height: 6' 5"   Weight: 275   Born: July 12, 1980   Age: 27

YEAR	TEAM	LVL	AGE	PA	R	2B	3B	HR	RBI	BB	SO	SB	CS	EqBRR	AVG	OBP	SLG	MLVr	EqAVG	EqOBP	EqSLG	EqA	VORP	DEFENSE			
2005	ALT	AA	24	93	22	6	0	13	27	8	25	1	1	0.0	.333	.387	.869	.809	.306	.362	.753	.338	15.3	19-1B	-1		
2005	IND	AAA	24	214	31	13	1	15	48	14	57	4	0	-0.5	.282	.336	.590	.254	.260	.313	.541	.283	9.6	37-1B	2		
2005	PIT	MLB	24	208	23	9	0	12	27	13	77	1	1	-2.3	.221	.279	.458	-.061	.222	.280	.466	.250	-1.2	46-1B	-7		
2007	IND	AAA	26	342	37	10	2	15	45	20	90	9	3	-1.6	.209	.275	.399	-.116	.201	.258	.385	.222	-18.4	45-1B	2	27-RF	-3
2007	PIT	MLB	26	47	3	1	0	2	3	1	16	0	0	0.0	.109	.128	.261	-.692	.109	.128	.261	.067	-6.9				
2008	CHA	MLB	27	405	45	16	1	21	61	29	121	8	3	-0.5	.225	.288	.445	-.091	.222	.287	.449	.254	-4.2	97-1B	1		

Breakout: 48% Improve: 76% Collapse: 7% Attrition: 11%   Comparables: Juan Diaz, Scott Morgan, Bucky Jacobsen, Mike Busch

Eldred has as much raw power as anyone in the game, but his pure uppercut swing has more holes than Joe Elliott's jeans, and International League pitchers have had no trouble finding them. Despite his massive size, Eldred runs fairly well and proved to be passable in right field last season after spending his whole career at first base. A truly dull team, the Pirates would be much more fun to watch if they gave Eldred 500 at-bats to see if he could hit 50 home runs before striking out for the 200th time. Instead, they designated him for assignment to make room for infielder Josh Wilson.

Shelby Ford — 2B

Bats: S   Throws: R   Height: 6' 3"   Weight: 190   Born: December 15, 1984   Age: 23

YEAR	TEAM	LVL	AGE	PA	R	2B	3B	HR	RBI	BB	SO	SB	CS	EqBRR	AVG	OBP	SLG	MLVr	EqAVG	EqOBP	EqSLG	EqA	VORP	DEFENSE	
2006	HIC	A	21	249	43	16	3	6	27	14	51	4	3	-2.3	.265	.329	.444	.110	.216	.259	.358	.211	-9.0	54-2B	6
2007	LYN	A+	22	413	64	26	7	5	55	34	68	14	0	5.2	.281	.360	.433	.096	.231	.291	.364	.233	-6.0	88-2B	-5
2008	PIT	MLB	23	483	54	32	5	6	43	30	101	9	3	1.1	.250	.310	.390	-.140	.250	.300	.400	.250	5.4	114-2B	-1

Breakout: 60% Improve: 83% Collapse: 8% Attrition: 13%   Comparables: Gookie Dawkins, Shawn Livsey, Elliot Johnson, Tony Giarratano

Ford draws high marks for his feel for the game, which is fitting for someone who grew up as the son of a high school coach. The Pirates' third-round pick from Oklahoma State in 2006 hits for average, has slightly above-average pop for a middle infielder, and is solid defensively. Ford, who will start this season at Double-A, is unlikely to be a star, but could be a decent major-league regular.

Cesar Izturis — SS

Bats: S   Throws: R   Height: 5' 9"   Weight: 190   Born: February 10, 1980   Age: 28

YEAR	TEAM	LVL	AGE	PA	R	2B	3B	HR	RBI	BB	SO	SB	CS	EqBRR	AVG	OBP	SLG	MLVr	EqAVG	EqOBP	EqSLG	EqA	VORP	DEFENSE	
2005	LAN	MLB	25	478	48	19	2	2	31	25	51	8	8	-1.7	.257	.302	.322	-.166	.261	.307	.328	.221	-4.4	104-SS	8
2006	LAN	MLB	26	129	10	7	1	1	12	7	6	1	3	-0.8	.252	.302	.353	-.163	.252	.308	.353	.224	-4.4	28-3B	0
2006	CHN	MLB	26	79	4	2	0	0	6	5	8	0	1	-0.2	.233	.282	.260	-.360	.233	.282	.260	.183	-4.6	18-SS	-1
2007	CHN	MLB	27	207	15	11	0	0	8	13	16	3	0	1.8	.246	.298	.304	-.248	.241	.296	.293	.212	-4.2	51-SS	-7
2007	PIT	MLB	27	130	16	3	2	0	8	6	3	3	3	-0.7	.276	.310	.333	-.163	.276	.315	.333	.220	-2.8	23-SS	2
2008	SLN	MLB	28	264	23	8	1	0	21	17	19	3	2	0.1	.251	.304	.299	-.268	.250	.304	.311	.212	-1.8	65-SS	-1

Breakout: 29% Improve: 44% Collapse: 41% Attrition: 32%   Comparables: Felix Fermin, Larry Milbourne, Ted Kubiak, Tom Veryzer

In Jim Tracy's never-ending quest to transform the 2007 Pirates into the 2004 Dodger team that he led to the NL West title, he convinced general manager Dave Littlefield to acquire Izturis from the Cubs in July. The plan was for the Pirates to trade decent-hitting, slick-fielding Jack Wilson to open up shortstop for the light-hitting, slick-fielding Izturis. Fortunately for the Pirates, that did not happen. Wilson is still in Pittsburgh, while Tracy, Littlefield, and Izturis, the last of whom signed a one-year deal with the Cardinals in November, are long gone.

Adam LaRoche   1B   Bats: L   Throws: L   Height: 6' 3"   Weight: 185   Born: November 6, 1979   Age: 28

YEAR	TEAM	LVL	AGE	PA	R	2B	3B	HR	RBI	BB	SO	SB	CS	EqBRR	AVG	OBP	SLG	MLVr	EqAVG	EqOBP	EqSLG	EqA	VORP	DEFENSE
2005	ATL	MLB	25	502	53	28	0	20	78	39	87	0	2	-1.9	.259	.320	.455	.034	.256	.317	.458	.264	7.9	114-1B -6
2006	ATL	MLB	26	557	89	38	1	32	90	55	128	0	2	-0.5	.285	.354	.561	.240	.286	.357	.563	.303	33.3	130-1B 11
2007	PIT	MLB	27	632	71	42	0	21	88	62	131	1	1	-1.8	.272	.345	.458	.070	.274	.351	.470	.280	19.6	146-1B 0
2008	PIT	MLB	28	571	69	33	1	24	87	57	110	3	2	-1.1	.270	.350	.480	.060	.260	.340	.490	.290	18.7	134-1B 0

Breakout: 17% Improve: 47% Collapse: 21% Attrition: 16%   Comparables: Paul Sorrento, Greg Walker, J. T. Snow, Tino Martinez

After years of either trading away hitters in the primes of their careers or allowing them to leave as free agents, the Pirates excited their fans a month before spring training by trading for 27-year-old LaRoche following his breakout season with the Braves. While LaRoche ended up having a decent year, he bombed early as he hit .191/.306/.325 through his first 47 games. LaRoche, who went on to hit .303/.361/.510 over his final 107 games, admittedly pressed when asked to be a star for the first time in his career and figures to be more relaxed and productive this season.

Andrew McCutchen   CF   Bats: R   Throws: R   Height: 5' 11"   Weight: 170   Born: October 10, 1986   Age: 21

YEAR	TEAM	LVL	AGE	PA	R	2B	3B	HR	RBI	BB	SO	SB	CS	EqBRR	AVG	OBP	SLG	MLVr	EqAVG	EqOBP	EqSLG	EqA	VORP	DEFENSE
2006	HIC	A	19	503	77	20	4	14	62	42	91	22	7	1.4	.291	.356	.446	.172	.236	.286	.361	.226	-12.9	113-CF -7
2006	ALT	AA	19	87	12	4	0	3	12	8	20	1	1	-0.2	.308	.379	.474	.251	.266	.333	.418	.258	2.0	
2007	ALT	AA	20	498	70	20	3	10	48	44	83	17	1	3.6	.258	.327	.383	-.032	.232	.294	.355	.233	-12.0	116-CF 9
2007	IND	AAA	20	72	7	4	0	1	5	4	11	4	3	1.0	.313	.347	.418	.104	.284	.319	.373	.239	0.5	15-CF 0
2008	PIT	MLB	21	627	72	30	3	11	60	46	110	18	6	1.3	.250	.310	.380	-.140	.250	.310	.390	.250	3.3	146-CF 0

Breakout: 48% Improve: 70% Collapse: 9% Attrition: 8%   Comparables: Lastings Milledge, Pokey Reese, Shaun Boyd, Grady Sizemore

After a strong showing in major league camp during spring training, McCutchen was jumped from Low-A up to Double-A to begin the 2007 season. The Florida, native struggled to adjust to the cold weather in the Eastern League, and his bat never really heated up until July. Thus, his strong finish after a late-season promotion to Triple-A was heartening. McCutchen has plus-power potential and speed with outstanding range in center field and remains the one Pirates prospect with definite star potential.

Nate McLouth   OF   Bats: L   Throws: R   Height: 5' 11"   Weight: 185   Born: October 28, 1981   Age: 26

YEAR	TEAM	LVL	AGE	PA	R	2B	3B	HR	RBI	BB	SO	SB	CS	EqBRR	AVG	OBP	SLG	MLVr	EqAVG	EqOBP	EqSLG	EqA	VORP	DEFENSE		
2005	IND	AAA	23	455	64	20	3	5	39	39	58	34	8	4.3	.297	.364	.401	.053	.269	.334	.361	.255	-8.0	73-LF 7	27-CF 0	
2005	PIT	MLB	23	120	20	6	0	5	12	3	20	2	0	2.5	.257	.305	.450	.006	.255	.303	.464	.262	3.3	19-CF -2		
2006	PIT	MLB	24	297	50	16	2	7	16	18	59	10	1	4.5	.233	.293	.385	-.158	.236	.295	.395	.244	-1.0	39-CF -3	19-RF -4	
2007	PIT	MLB	25	382	62	21	3	13	38	39	77	22	1	3.4	.258	.351	.459	.068	.261	.357	.477	.293	21.7	55-CF 2	12-LF -2	
2008	PIT	MLB	26	410	58	23	3	12	47	35	70	18	4	1.5	.270	.340	.450	.010	.260	.340	.450	.280	15.2	98-CF 1		

Breakout: 31% Improve: 72% Collapse: 15% Attrition: 24%   Comparables: Rick Miller, Al Pilarcik, Tony Tarasco, Max Venable

McLouth doesn't do any one thing great, but does enough important things well, including hitting the ball out of the park and being a high-percentage base stealer. Playing regularly for most of the second half, McLouth dispelled the idea he would be exposed by major league pitchers in regular duty by hitting .270/.369/.506 in 75 games beginning on June 30. McLouth is likely ticketed for a career as a fourth outfielder, but should be one of the best given his ability to provide above-average offense off the bench.

Nyjer Morgan CF

Bats: L   Throws: L   Height: 6' 0"   Weight: 170   Born: July 2, 1980   Age: 27

YEAR	TEAM	LVL	AGE	PA	R	2B	3B	HR	RBI	BB	SO	SB	CS	EqBRR	AVG	OBP	SLG	MLVr	EqAVG	EqOBP	EqSLG	EqA	VORP	DEFENSE			
2005	LYN	A+	25	277	36	12	3	0	24	11	40	24	10	0.8	.286	.328	.357	-.049	.238	.265	.288	.201	-17.0	57-CF	0		
2006	LYN	A+	26	274	43	7	3	0	22	20	40	38	11	3.4	.303	.390	.360	.090	.262	.322	.311	.237	-5.3	58-CF	3		
2006	ALT	AA	26	244	39	6	5	1	10	15	28	21	11	-0.5	.306	.359	.393	.114	.281	.329	.366	.245	-4.2	37-LF	6	15-CF	0
2007	IND	AAA	27	184	30	4	2	0	10	15	28	26	7	3.7	.305	.374	.354	.051	.277	.344	.331	.254	0.4	32-CF	1		
2007	PIT	MLB	27	118	15	3	4	1	7	9	19	7	3	-1.1	.299	.359	.430	.083	.308	.373	.439	.278	5.8	25-CF	7		
2008	PIT	MLB	27	341	45	13	4	2	24	21	55	22	6	1.9	.270	.320	.350	-.150	.260	.320	.360	.250	2.4	82-CF	5		

Breakout: 26% Improve: 49% Collapse: 24% Attrition: 30%   Comparables: Kerry Robinson, Rich Thompson, Steve Bieser, David Hulse

Making his major league debut as a September call-up despite missing most of the season at Triple-A Indianapolis due to thumb surgery, Morgan was one of the few bright spots for the Pirates in the season's final month as he sparked the big-league lineup with speed from the leadoff spot and made a series of spectacular catches in center field. Morgan spent four years as a junior hockey player in western Canada, so he isn't a kid and has likely reached his upside, which is less than he showed in the majors last year considering his unsustainable .356 BABIP, but he will arrive at spring training as the favorite to win the center field job.

Xavier Nady RF

Bats: R   Throws: R   Height: 6' 2"   Weight: 210   Born: November 14, 1978   Age: 29

YEAR	TEAM	LVL	AGE	PA	R	2B	3B	HR	RBI	BB	SO	SB	CS	EqBRR	AVG	OBP	SLG	MLVr	EqAVG	EqOBP	EqSLG	EqA	VORP	DEFENSE			
2005	SDN	MLB	26	356	40	15	2	13	43	22	67	2	1	-0.1	.261	.321	.439	.041	.270	.331	.463	.270	8.7	33-1B	0	27-CF	-8
2006	NYN	MLB	27	292	37	15	1	14	40	19	51	2	1	-0.8	.264	.326	.487	.084	.267	.329	.496	.277	9.5	69-RF	-3		
2006	PIT	MLB	27	220	20	13	0	3	23	11	34	1	2	0.1	.300	.352	.409	.029	.299	.350	.412	.261	2.6	27-1B	4	26-RF	0
2007	PIT	MLB	28	470	55	23	1	20	72	23	101	3	1	1.0	.278	.330	.476	.076	.281	.334	.491	.279	15.0	84-RF	-7		
2008	PIT	MLB	29	449	55	24	2	16	65	29	86	4	2	-0.4	.280	.340	.470	.040	.280	.340	.470	.280	15.2	107-RF	-6		

Breakout: 26% Improve: 57% Collapse: 15% Attrition: 14%   Comparables: Wes Chamberlain, Larry Parrish, Rick Reichardt, Rip Repulski

At age 29, Nady has passed the expiration date for reaching major league stardom. He has become a useful player with moderate power, but his refusal to take a walk and his average-at-best defense in right field limit his opportunities to start to second-division clubs. His BABIP-inflated average figures to take a hit this season as it regresses to the mean, but he still profiles as a top-flight reserve if he can escape Pittsburgh and hook up with a contender. Such a move would also benefit the Pirates by freeing up right field for Steve Pearce.

Ronny Paulino C

Bats: R   Throws: R   Height: 6' 2"   Weight: 245   Born: April 21, 1981   Age: 27

YEAR	TEAM	LVL	AGE	PA	R	2B	3B	HR	RBI	BB	SO	SB	CS	EqBRR	AVG	OBP	SLG	MLVr	EqAVG	EqOBP	EqSLG	EqA	VORP	DEFENSE	
2005	ALT	AA	24	184	24	6	0	6	20	15	30	3	0	2.1	.292	.350	.435	.127	.260	.317	.391	.248	2.7	40-C	3
2005	IND	AAA	24	302	49	18	2	13	42	26	48	3	0	1.4	.315	.372	.538	.274	.285	.344	.485	.282	20.9	63-C	3
2006	PIT	MLB	25	481	37	19	0	6	55	34	79	0	0	-2.3	.310	.360	.394	.033	.306	.360	.392	.265	16.4	119-C	0
2007	PIT	MLB	26	494	56	25	0	11	55	33	79	2	2	-0.9	.263	.314	.389	-.086	.267	.322	.407	.251	8.1	122-C	-1
2008	PIT	MLB	27	373	42	18	1	9	44	29	61	5	1	-0.4	.270	.330	.410	-.070	.260	.330	.410	.260	12.2	89-C	1

Breakout: 30% Improve: 46% Collapse: 27% Attrition: 29%   Comparables: Ramon Hernandez, Ray Fosse, Harry Chiti, Dan Walters

As big of a surprise as Paulino was in 2006, when he came up from the minor leagues in mid-April and seized the starting catcher's job, he was that much of a disappointment in 2007. Paulino's work habits last year were poor and he regressed both at the plate and behind it. Most of his regression on offense, however, was due to a 47-point dip in batting average, as he actually hit for more power and saw very little change in his walk rate. There's still potential here if Paulino can improve his worth ethic and get his average and his defense to rebound.

Steve Pearce
1B/RF   Bats: R   Throws: R   Height: 5' 11"   Weight: 200   Born: April 13, 1983   Age: 25

YEAR	TEAM	LVL	AGE	PA	R	2B	3B	HR	RBI	BB	SO	SB	CS	EqBRR	AVG	OBP	SLG	MLVr	EqAVG	EqOBP	EqSLG	EqA	VORP	DEFENSE			
2005	WPT	A-	22	312	48	26	0	7	52	35	43	2	4	0.6	.301	.381	.474	.277	.235	.295	.351	.223	-23.9	69-1B	2		
2006	HIC	A	23	179	35	13	1	12	38	15	32	1	3	2.7	.288	.363	.606	.389	.229	.289	.470	.250	-0.1	39-1B	3		
2006	LYN	A+	23	377	48	27	1	14	60	34	65	7	5	-2.0	.265	.348	.482	.161	.231	.294	.418	.243	-6.6	86-1B	3		
2007	LYN	A+	24	85	19	4	1	11	24	8	13	2	0	1.0	.347	.412	.867	.824	.282	.329	.705	.320	11.0	18-1B	-2		
2007	ALT	AA	24	335	57	27	2	14	72	33	45	7	2	0.3	.334	.400	.586	.422	.301	.361	.530	.300	25.6	78-1B	7		
2007	IND	AAA	24	131	18	9	1	6	17	6	12	5	0	2.0	.320	.366	.557	.333	.301	.344	.553	.300	10.1	20-1B	0		
2007	PIT	MLB	24	73	13	5	1	0	6	5	12	2	1	0.5	.294	.342	.397	.000	.294	.342	.397	.259	0.9	15-RF	-1		
2008	PIT	MLB	25	556	67	31	2	18	75	43	98	9	4	0.6	.270	.330	.440	-.020	.260	.330	.450	.270	10.3	130-1B	2		

Breakout: 20% Improve: 53% Collapse: 20% Attrition: 21%   Comparables: Gene Schall, Jason Lane, Shane Spencer, Bubba Trammell

Pearce has hit ever since being drafted out of high school by the Pirates in the eighth-round in 2005. He had one of the best seasons in the minor leagues in 2007, beginning the year in High-A, ending it in the major leagues, and hitting a combined .333/.394/.622 on the way up. Pearce does not look the part of an athlete with his short, stocky build, but he stole 16 bases in 19 attempts last season and quickly made the conversion from first baseman to right fielder in Triple-A. He did not tear up the majors as a September call-up, but was not overmatched either and has the look of a productive middle-of-the-order hitter.

Jamie Romak
OF   Bats: R   Throws: R   Height: 6' 2"   Weight: 220   Born: September 30, 1985   Age: 22

YEAR	TEAM	LVL	AGE	PA	R	2B	3B	HR	RBI	BB	SO	SB	CS	EqBRR	AVG	OBP	SLG	MLVr	EqAVG	EqOBP	EqSLG	EqA	VORP	DEFENSE			
2005	DNV	Rk	19	145	25	10	1	7	27	14	38	2	1	0.4	.274	.368	.540	.338	.189	.255	.318	.196	-25.4	31-RF	-2		
2006	ROM	A	20	420	55	26	2	16	68	59	102	3	1	0.2	.247	.369	.471	.210	.207	.300	.376	.237	-16.9	94-RF	-9		
2007	HIC	A	21	84	16	4	0	5	15	9	24	0	2	-0.4	.275	.393	.551	.301	.219	.301	.425	.243	-1.5	17-RF	3		
2007	LYN	A+	21	355	49	21	1	15	45	55	90	2	2	-1.3	.252	.380	.483	.167	.208	.313	.380	.241	-12.6	55-LF	-9	18-RF	-1
2008	PIT	MLB	22	483	47	25	1	14	55	49	134	3	2	-0.4	.220	.310	.390	-.160	.220	.310	.390	.250	-6.1	114-RF	-1		

Breakout: 43% Improve: 74% Collapse: 17% Attrition: 7%   Comparables: Kala Kaaihue, Mike Glendenning, Benji Simonton, John Donati

Romak was the other guy acquired from Atlanta along with Adam LaRoche in the January 2007 trade that sent closer Mike Gonzalez and shortstop prospect Brent Lillibridge to the Braves. Romak has as much raw power as any Pirates' prospect, but the operative word is raw, as his amateur experience was limited while growing up in Ontario. He has no speed and is subpar defensively, but his willingness to take a walk only enhances his power potential. Romak will begin this season at Double-A and that should begin to tell whether he has a legitimate chance to play in the major leagues.

Freddy Sanchez
2B   Bats: R   Throws: R   Height: 5' 10"   Weight: 185   Born: December 21, 1977   Age: 30

YEAR	TEAM	LVL	AGE	PA	R	2B	3B	HR	RBI	BB	SO	SB	CS	EqBRR	AVG	OBP	SLG	MLVr	EqAVG	EqOBP	EqSLG	EqA	VORP	DEFENSE			
2005	PIT	MLB	27	492	54	26	4	5	35	27	36	2	2	-3.4	.291	.336	.400	.015	.291	.337	.406	.258	11.9	54-3B	5	44-2B	-3
2006	PIT	MLB	28	632	85	53	2	6	85	31	52	3	2	1.2	.344	.378	.473	.207	.342	.377	.467	.292	43.3	92-3B	16	27-SS	2
2007	PIT	MLB	29	653	77	42	4	11	81	32	76	0	1	-2.6	.304	.343	.442	.072	.308	.349	.455	.277	27.5	142-2B	-8		
2008	PIT	MLB	30	598	70	37	3	10	68	35	60	4	2	-0.4	.300	.340	.430	.010	.290	.340	.440	.270	25.0	140-2B	-2		

Breakout: 11% Improve: 33% Collapse: 25% Attrition: 6%   Comparables: Frank Malzone, Joe Randa, Billy Moran, George Kell

Sanchez did not match his breakout 2006 season in 2007, but he proved that the batting crown he won in his first year as a full-time player wasn't necessarily a fluke. Sanchez missed most of spring training with a knee injury, but returned to play in the final three games, which is all the former minor league shortstop needed to make the transition to full-time duty at second, where his gap power profiles better. The one minor red flag was Sanchez's slightly increased strikeout rate, as pitchers found his weaknesses and attacked them; that will bear watching. Even more so than Jason Bay, Sanchez experienced his breakout somewhat late in his professional life, which means his decline should arrive sooner than most.

Neil Walker   **3B**   Bats: S   Throws: R   Height: 6' 3"   Weight: 210   Born: September 10, 1985   Age: 22

YEAR	TEAM	LVL	AGE	PA	R	2B	3B	HR	RBI	BB	SO	SB	CS	EqBRR	AVG	OBP	SLG	MLVr	EqAVG	EqOBP	EqSLG	EqA	VORP	DEFENSE	
2005	HIC	A	19	518	78	33	2	12	68	20	71	7	4	2.4	.301	.332	.452	.119	.240	.263	.354	.210	-17.5	80-C	0
2006	LYN	A+	20	294	32	22	1	3	35	19	41	3	5	-2.4	.284	.345	.409	.075	.248	.294	.372	.227	-2.1	53-C	-1
2007	ALT	AA	21	490	77	30	3	13	66	53	73	9	4	1.7	.288	.362	.462	.152	.258	.327	.418	.259	16.1	113-3B	-6
2007	IND	AAA	21	69	7	3	0	0	0	2	13	1	1	-0.8	.203	.261	.250	-.338	.185	.232	.231	.148	-6.9	17-3B	-3
2008	PIT	MLB	22	619	71	38	2	15	72	43	105	8	4	0.9	.270	.320	.420	-.060	.260	.320	.430	.260	13.5	145-3B	-4

Breakout: 69%   Improve: 86%   Collapse: 4%   Attrition: 5%   Comparables: Troy Tulowitzki, Antone Williamson, Matt Moses, Mike Bell

The Pirates moved Walker from catcher to third base on the first day of spring training last year, reducing his long-term value. As a switch-hitter with power potential, Walker was one of the best catching prospects in the game. He is still a top prospect, but his power is not appreciably better than that of most third basemen. Walker made a relatively smooth transition to the hot corner at Triple-A and will put the finishing touches on his game there this year before getting a chance to move into the starting lineup in 2009.

Jack Wilson   **SS**   Bats: R   Throws: R   Height: 6' 0"   Weight: 195   Born: December 29, 1977   Age: 30

YEAR	TEAM	LVL	AGE	PA	R	2B	3B	HR	RBI	BB	SO	SB	CS	EqBRR	AVG	OBP	SLG	MLVr	EqAVG	EqOBP	EqSLG	EqA	VORP	DEFENSE	
2005	PIT	MLB	27	639	60	24	7	8	52	31	58	7	3	-1.3	.257	.299	.363	-.124	.256	.300	.364	.233	3.9	153-SS	19
2006	PIT	MLB	28	594	70	27	1	8	35	33	65	4	3	-1.5	.273	.316	.370	-.108	.273	.318	.368	.241	4.6	127-SS	4
2007	PIT	MLB	29	535	67	29	2	12	56	38	46	2	5	0.6	.296	.350	.440	.074	.300	.356	.455	.276	24.8	128-SS	22
2008	PIT	MLB	30	504	55	25	2	9	52	31	51	4	2	0.0	.270	.320	.390	-.090	.270	.320	.400	.260	13.4	119-SS	6

Breakout: 22%   Improve: 46%   Collapse: 20%   Attrition: 17%   Comparables: Greg Pryor, Eddie Kasko, Pat Meares, Tim Foli

Typical of the old Pirate regime's proclivity for changing its mind more often than the wind changes direction, Littlefield spent most of 2007 trying to trade Wilson despite the fact that the three-year, $20.2 million contract extension he had given Wilson prior to the 2006 season had only just taken effect. Wilson wound up staying put when a deadline deal with Detroit fell through. That proved to be fortuitous, as Wilson was in the process of replicating his 2004 career year, raising his OPS a second straight season, and playing his usual above-average defense. With Jimmy Rollins, Jose Reyes, Hanley Ramirez, and now Troy Tulowitzki around, Wilson will never be an All-Star again, but the Bucs could do a lot worse at shortstop.

PITCHERS

Tony Armas   Bats: R   Throws: R   Height: 6' 3"   Weight: 225   Born: April 29, 1978   Age: 30

YEAR	TEAM	LVL	AGE	W	L	SV	G	GS	IP	H	BB	SO	HR	GB%	BABIP	STUFF	WHIP	ERA	PERA	EqERA	EqH9	EqBB9	EqSO9	EqHR9	VORP	SN/WX
2005	WAS	MLB	27	7	7	0	19	19	101¹	100	54	59	16	38.0%	.268	-15	1.51	4.98	5.38	5.29	8.8	4.4	4.8	1.4	5.2	1.71
2006	WAS	MLB	28	9	12	0	30	30	154	167	64	97	19	41.0%	.307	-1	1.50	5.03	4.93	5.21	9.4	3.2	5.2	1.0	5.8	2.80
2007	PIT	MLB	29	4	5	0	31	15	97	111	38	73	18	38.1%	.314	-12	1.54	6.03	5.16	5.44	9.0	2.9	6.1	1.5	-3.9	0.43
2008	PIT	MLB	30	4	6	1	30	10	82¹	90	32	56	11	41.4%	.302	-3	1.48	4.92	5.19	5.11	9.5	3.2	5.6	1.1	4.9	0.90

Breakout: 23%   Improve: 47%   Collapse: 27%   Attrition: 25%   Comparables: Bob Milacki, Ron Kline, Moe Drabowsky, Ralph Branca

The Pirates signed Armas just two weeks before the beginning of spring training last year in the hope that he could be a veteran stabilizer in their young starting rotation. Instead, he found himself in the pen by the end of May and spent the next two months mopping up. Though he put together an impressive 12 innings in July in that role, and had more forgivable results in a second stint in the rotation in August and early September, Armas's arm is pretty much shot after two shoulder operations. He would be best utilized in shorter relief stints.

Olivo Astacio

Bats: R   Throws: R   Height: 6' 5"   Weight: 190   Born: July 28, 1984   Age: 23

YEAR	TEAM	LVL	AGE	W	L	SV	G	GS	IP	H	BB	SO	HR	GB%	BABIP	STUFF	WHIP	ERA	PERA	EqERA	EqH9	EqBB9	EqSO9	EqHR9	VORP	SN/WX
2006	WPT	A-	21	2	3	9	22	0	28	16	15	39	0	57.8%	.267	10	1.11	3.54	5.59	7.40	7.4	9.2	7.0	0.4	-4.9	—
2007	HIC	A	22	1	1	11	30	0	48¹	39	28	71	0	41.6%	.358	17	1.39	3.54	5.73	6.07	9.4	8.2	8.0	0.4	-2.2	—
2007	LYN	A+	22	0	1	1	7	0	15¹	14	12	19	3	38.5%	.306	-10	1.70	8.24	12.81	13.85	11.1	10.4	7.6	3.5	-11.9	—
2008	PIT	MLB	23	2	5	2	25	7	57²	57	54	53	6	43.5%	.312	-5	1.91	6.06	6.35	6.37	8.5	7.7	7.6	0.9	-5.0	-0.20

Breakout: 50% Improve: 68% Collapse: 19% Attrition: 9%   Comparables: Craig Dingman, Todd Schmitt, Mike Nicolas, Danny Mota

Astacio signed with the Pirates after being released by the Cubs following the 2005 season and has worked his way up to the 40-man roster. His 95 mph fastball blew hitters away in the low minors, but whether that will continue to work when he makes the jump to Double-A this year remains to be seen, but his size and arm strength make him intriguing. Typical control caveats apply.

Jonah Bayliss

Bats: R   Throws: R   Height: 6' 2"   Weight: 200   Born: August 13, 1980   Age: 27

YEAR	TEAM	LVL	AGE	W	L	SV	G	GS	IP	H	BB	SO	HR	GB%	BABIP	STUFF	WHIP	ERA	PERA	EqERA	EqH9	EqBB9	EqSO9	EqHR9	VORP	SN/WX
2005	WIC	AA	24	1	2	8	30	0	57	43	26	63	5	32.4%	.273	2	1.21	2.84	4.82	4.01	7.7	5.7	7.1	1.2	9.1	—
2005	KCA	MLB	24	0	0	0	11	0	11²	7	4	10	2	25.0%	.167	6	0.94	4.62	2.68	3.65	4.4	2.9	7.3	1.5	1.5	-0.02
2006	IND	AAA	25	3	3	23	46	0	58¹	37	28	67	4	41.3%	.248	7	1.12	2.17	4.12	3.44	6.9	5.1	7.7	1.0	13.2	—
2006	PIT	MLB	25	1	1	0	11	0	14²	13	11	15	1	38.1%	.316	11	1.64	4.29	3.63	3.45	6.9	5.7	8.0	0.6	2.8	0.01
2007	PIT	MLB	26	4	3	0	39	0	37²	51	18	29	8	27.7%	.355	-25	1.83	8.36	7.75	8.22	11.0	3.5	6.3	1.6	-11.3	0.65
2007	IND	AAA	26	3	2	0	16	0	21²	23	10	17	5	30.0%	.295	-40	1.52	7.05	8.88	9.86	10.3	4.7	5.1	3.0	-9.9	—
2008	PIT	MLB	27	1	1	2	24	0	24²	25	13	19	4	36.4%	.287	-7	1.51	4.98	5.14	5.16	8.8	4.2	6.2	1.2	1.7	0.10

Breakout: 36% Improve: 65% Collapse: 20% Attrition: 51%   Comparables: Dave Stevens, Jeff Jones, Darrel Akerfelds, Al Osuna

Bayliss has the makings of an effective middle or set-up reliever given his 95 mph fastball and late-breaking slider. However, he fatigued after being used heavily in the first two months of 2007 (30 games) and began leaving too many pitches up in the strike zone, forcing the Pirates to demote him in late June. Though he continued to struggle in Triple-A, it would be unwise to write Bayliss off. Still, he needs a strong spring to get back on track.

Bryan Bullington

Bats: R   Throws: R   Height: 6' 4"   Weight: 220   Born: September 30, 1980   Age: 27

YEAR	TEAM	LVL	AGE	W	L	SV	G	GS	IP	H	BB	SO	HR	GB%	BABIP	STUFF	WHIP	ERA	PERA	EqERA	EqH9	EqBB9	EqSO9	EqHR9	VORP	SN/WX
2005	IND	AAA	24	9	5	0	18	18	109¹	104	26	82	11	53.8%	.290	-2	1.19	3.38	4.89	4.92	9.6	2.8	4.9	1.2	7.6	—
2007	IND	AAA	26	11	9	0	26	26	150²	146	59	89	10	46.4%	.297	-8	1.36	4.00	4.87	5.11	9.2	4.0	3.8	1.0	7.7	—
2007	PIT	MLB	26	0	3	0	5	3	17	24	5	7	3	51.6%	.350	-20	1.71	5.29	7.11	5.40	11.9	2.2	3.8	1.6	0.2	0.04
2008	PIT	MLB	27	5	7	0	33	18	102	119	41	54	13	48.0%	.307	-10	1.57	5.24	5.54	5.49	10.1	3.3	4.3	1.1	1.5	0.70

Breakout: 14% Improve: 45% Collapse: 38% Attrition: 13%   Comparables: Jeremy Guthrie, Chris Bootcheck, Jason Grilli, Todd Van Poppel

If nothing else, Bullington has shown perseverance since being drafted out of Ball State with the first overall pick in 2002. Despite being labeled a bust and having fans continually question why the Pirates chose him, Bullington bounced back last season after sitting out 2006 because of shoulder surgery, finishing the year in the majors and delivering two solid starts in September. He's never going to be a star, but he could fashion a career as a back-of-the-rotation starter.

Sean Burnett

Bats: L   Throws: L   Height: 6' 1"   Weight: 195   Born: September 17, 1982   Age: 25

YEAR	TEAM	LVL	AGE	W	L	SV	G	GS	IP	H	BB	SO	HR	GB%	BABIP	STUFF	WHIP	ERA	PERA	EqERA	EqH9	EqBB9	EqSO9	EqHR9	VORP	SN/WX
2006	IND	AAA	23	8	11	0	25	24	120	136	46	46	13	46.5%	.301	-45	1.52	5.18	7.62	7.78	11.7	4.3	2.2	1.6	-26.9	—
2007	IND	AAA	24	4	5	0	15	15	70¹	83	39	31	4	48.2%	.336	-19	1.74	4.48	6.69	6.37	11.4	5.7	2.6	0.8	-5.6	—
2008	PIT	MLB	25	3	7	0	26	13	80¹	105	48	31	13	46.8%	.316	-27	1.90	6.91	7.20	7.22	11.3	4.9	3.1	1.3	-14.2	-1.00

Breakout: 20% Improve: 52% Collapse: 32% Attrition: 25%   Comparables: Chris Roberts, Marc Valdes, Ben Christensen, Scott Christman

The Pirates' first-round draft pick in 2000, Burnett hasn't been the same since throwing 118 pitches to complete a 10-hit shutout of the Montreal Expos in San Juan on July 9, 2004 when he was just 21. He underwent Tommy John surgery later that year, a shoulder operation the following summer, and has spent the last three years rehabbing and trying to put his career back together at Triple-A. His chances of reclaiming his career keep growing slimmer, but it isn't for lack of effort.

Matt Capps

Bats: R   Throws: R   Height: 6' 2"   Weight: 245   Born: September 3, 1983   Age: 24

YEAR	TEAM	LVL	AGE	W	L	SV	G	GS	IP	H	BB	SO	HR	GB%	BABIP	STUFF	WHIP	ERA	PERA	EqERA	EqH9	EqBB9	EqSO9	EqHR9	VORP	SN/WX
2005	HIC	A	21	3	4	14	35	0	53²	47	5	39	0	54.9%	.297	-10	0.97	2.51	4.43	4.53	9.4	2.5	3.2	0.4	5.7	—
2005	ALT	AA	21	0	2	7	17	0	20	21	1	26	2	51.7%	.339	13	1.10	2.70	6.15	5.60	12.2	1.0	8.2	1.5	0.0	—
2006	PIT	MLB	22	9	1	1	85	0	80²	81	12	56	12	43.4%	.292	2	1.15	3.79	3.55	3.54	8.1	1.1	5.6	1.2	17.3	0.74
2007	PIT	MLB	23	4	7	18	76	0	79	64	16	64	5	34.1%	.266	21	1.01	2.28	2.45	2.22	6.2	1.4	6.7	0.6	29.7	4.10
2008	PIT	MLB	24	4	4	13	63	0	70¹	68	15	54	8	40.1%	.283	8	1.17	3.20	3.47	3.32	8.4	1.7	6.3	0.9	19.4	1.90

Breakout: 6%   Improve: 29%   Collapse: 43%   Attrition: 16%   Comparables: Edwin Nuñez, Bobby Thigpen, Rod Beck, Brian Fisher

Capps was promoted from set-up man to closer on June 1 and made a seamless transition. He has everything you would want in a closer: excellent stuff, outstanding poise, and the ability to pound the strike zone. Capps should blossom into one of the game's top closers as he gains experience, though it would help if his team gave him a few more leads. The only concern is that Jim Tracy used Capps 161 times combined in his age-22 and -23 seasons.

Shawn Chacon

Bats: R   Throws: R   Height: 6' 3"   Weight: 220   Born: December 23, 1977   Age: 30

YEAR	TEAM	LVL	AGE	W	L	SV	G	GS	IP	H	BB	SO	HR	GB%	BABIP	STUFF	WHIP	ERA	PERA	EqERA	EqH9	EqBB9	EqSO9	EqHR9	VORP	SN/WX
2005	COL	MLB	27	1	7	0	13	12	72²	69	36	39	7	38.5%	.283	2	1.44	4.09	3.88	3.42	7.6	3.9	4.3	0.7	13.7	1.30
2005	NYA	MLB	27	7	3	0	14	12	79	66	30	40	7	42.5%	.240	8	1.22	2.85	3.39	2.64	7.0	3.3	4.4	0.7	25.0	3.23
2006	NYA	MLB	28	5	3	0	17	11	63	77	36	35	11	33.9%	.313	-23	1.79	7.00	6.79	7.65	10.4	4.6	4.6	1.4	-13.1	-0.01
2006	PIT	MLB	28	2	3	0	9	9	46	47	27	27	12	36.2%	.261	-18	1.61	5.48	5.73	5.32	8.0	4.4	4.8	2.1	-1.0	0.65
2007	PIT	MLB	29	5	4	1	64	4	96	95	48	79	9	45.9%	.317	7	1.49	3.94	3.89	3.20	7.9	3.8	6.8	0.7	20.9	2.14
2008	PIT	MLB	30	3	4	2	40	3	62²	66	28	45	8	42.5%	.296	-6	1.50	4.69	5.06	4.87	9.0	3.7	5.9	1.1	5.5	0.60

Breakout: 12% Improve: 35% Collapse: 41% Attrition: 30%   Comparables: Ralph Branca, Moe Drabowsky, Barry Latman, Larry Sherry

Chacon lost out to Armas in a spring training competition to be the fifth starter, but proceeded to have one of his best seasons while working out of the bullpen. Starting the season as the long man, Chacon eventually worked his way into a set-up role and excelled. It was only the second season in Chacon's career in which he had pitched more than a handful of games in relief. The last came with the Rockies in 2004, when he had 35 saves but an unsightly 7.11 ERA. Having matured over the intervening years, he's much better suited to relieving now.

David Davidson

Bats: L   Throws: L   Height: 6' 1"   Weight: 187   Born: April 23, 1984   Age: 24

YEAR	TEAM	LVL	AGE	W	L	SV	G	GS	IP	H	BB	SO	HR	GB%	BABIP	STUFF	WHIP	ERA	PERA	EqERA	EqH9	EqBB9	EqSO9	EqHR9	VORP	SN/WX
2005	HIC	A	21	1	2	0	10	2	19¹	16	21	23	4	40.8%	.273	-14	1.92	9.79	16.40	17.61	11.2	16.4	6.5	4.1	-20.4	—
2005	WPT	A-	21	1	1	0	5	4	17	14	8	23	0	61.5%	.359	7	1.29	3.18	8.19	8.10	12.8	8.8	6.8	0.7	-3.7	—
2006	HIC	A	22	2	1	0	27	0	56¹	39	21	72	2	58.3%	.294	2	1.07	1.93	5.55	5.18	9.1	5.9	6.8	0.9	2.3	—
2006	ALT	AA	22	1	1	0	10	1	11²	8	10	13	0	52.6%	.237	10	1.61	2.41	5.02	4.22	7.6	9.3	6.8	0.0	1.6	—
2007	ALT	AA	23	3	1	2	39	0	59²	44	30	55	3	58.2%	.261	-3	1.24	4.22	4.26	5.53	7.4	5.2	5.7	0.8	0.4	—
2008	PIT	MLB	24	2	4	1	31	4	55¹	59	35	39	6	51.8%	.308	-10	1.70	5.48	5.63	5.83	9.3	5.3	5.7	0.9	-1.5	0.00

Breakout: 65% Improve: 84% Collapse: 8% Attrition: 11%   Comparables: J. C. Romero, Adam Gardner, Carlos Vasquez, David Sanders

The Canadian kid with the redundant name has emerged as a prospect now that he has finally gotten healthy. Shoulder problems limited him to a combined 62 1/3 innings over his first three professional seasons, but a fine 2006 season earned him a spot on the 40-man roster, and he made his major league debut last September. His above-average curveball ties up lefties, and that gives him a shot to at least have a career as a LOOGY.

Zach Duke

Bats: L   Throws: L   Height: 6' 2"   Weight: 220   Born: April 19, 1983   Age: 25

YEAR	TEAM	LVL	AGE	W	L	SV	G	GS	IP	H	BB	SO	HR	GB%	BABIP	STUFF	WHIP	ERA	PERA	EqERA	EqH9	EqBB9	EqSO9	EqHR9	VORP	SN/WX
2005	IND	AAA	22	12	3	0	16	16	108	108	23	66	8	53.0%	.302	4	1.21	2.92	4.72	4.17	9.9	2.5	3.9	0.9	15.8	—
2005	PIT	MLB	22	8	2	0	14	14	84²	79	23	58	3	50.4%	.303	32	1.20	1.81	3.50	2.35	8.7	2.4	5.8	0.3	32.7	3.96
2006	PIT	MLB	23	10	15	0	34	34	215¹	255	68	117	17	54.4%	.336	12	1.50	4.47	4.41	4.39	9.8	2.5	4.5	0.6	28.5	3.80
2007	PIT	MLB	24	3	8	0	20	19	107¹	161	25	41	14	52.5%	.374	-16	1.73	5.54	7.11	6.04	12.6	1.8	3.4	1.1	-3.4	0.66
2008	*PIT*	*MLB*	*25*	*4*	*5*	*0*	*25*	*13*	*80²*	*97*	*25*	*43*	*9*	*51.3%*	*.317*	*-4*	*1.51*	*4.77*	*5.26*	*5.00*	*10.4*	*2.5*	*4.4*	*1.0*	*6.3*	*1.00*

Breakout: 13%   Improve: 36%   Collapse: 42%   Attrition: 31%   Comparables: Charlie Leibrandt, Scott Karl, Tom Morgan, Bruce Ruffin

Duke's downfall came on the first day of spring training in 2006, when new pitching coach Jim Colborn decided to tinker with his pitching mechanics. It seemed like a bad idea considering Duke's 1.81 ERA in 14 starts as a rookie in 2005, and it was. Duke has yet to regain that rookie form and missed a large chunk of last season with a sore elbow. He's too young to give up on, but he's now a cautionary tale of the evils of overcoaching.

Tom Gorzelanny

Bats: L   Throws: L   Height: 6' 2"   Weight: 220   Born: July 12, 1982   Age: 25

YEAR	TEAM	LVL	AGE	W	L	SV	G	GS	IP	H	BB	SO	HR	GB%	BABIP	STUFF	WHIP	ERA	PERA	EqERA	EqH9	EqBB9	EqSO9	EqHR9	VORP	SN/WX
2005	ALT	AA	22	8	5	0	23	23	129²	114	46	124	6	47.7%	.306	10	1.23	3.26	4.83	4.83	9.1	4.5	5.4	0.8	10.0	—
2006	IND	AAA	23	6	5	0	16	16	99	67	27	94	4	48.2%	.254	23	0.95	2.36	3.57	3.79	7.4	3.2	6.6	0.7	18.2	—
2006	PIT	MLB	23	2	5	0	11	11	61²	50	31	40	3	51.6%	.264	16	1.31	3.79	2.85	3.64	6.3	3.8	5.2	0.4	12.1	1.76
2007	PIT	MLB	24	14	10	0	32	32	201²	214	68	135	18	43.5%	.311	18	1.40	3.88	3.78	3.38	8.4	2.5	5.6	0.7	42.6	5.15
2008	*PIT*	*MLB*	*25*	*9*	*10*	*0*	*27*	*27*	*165*	*174*	*61*	*116*	*19*	*44.7%*	*.301*	*12*	*1.43*	*4.44*	*4.79*	*4.63*	*9.1*	*3.1*	*5.8*	*1.0*	*18.1*	*3.20*

Breakout: 2%   Improve: 12%   Collapse: 58%   Attrition: 13%   Comparables: Scott Karl, Alex Kellner, Justin Thompson, Noah Lowry

Amidst the disappointment of another awful Pirates season was the emergence of Gorzelanny in 2007 as one baseball's better young pitchers. A rare power left-hander, Gorzo has a live fastball, an outstanding slider, and he's gaining a feel for setting hitters up and pitching to their weaknesses. Add in outstanding mound presence and a killer instinct, and all the pieces are there for him to continue to develop as a top-of-the-rotation starter.

John Grabow

Bats: L   Throws: L   Height: 6' 2"   Weight: 205   Born: November 4, 1978   Age: 29

YEAR	TEAM	LVL	AGE	W	L	SV	G	GS	IP	H	BB	SO	HR	GB%	BABIP	STUFF	WHIP	ERA	PERA	EqERA	EqH9	EqBB9	EqSO9	EqHR9	VORP	SN/WX
2005	PIT	MLB	26	2	3	0	63	0	52	46	25	42	6	47.7%	.276	-7	1.37	4.85	4.28	5.33	8.2	3.9	6.8	1.1	0.7	0.99
2006	PIT	MLB	27	4	2	0	72	0	69²	68	30	66	7	52.5%	.323	9	1.41	4.13	3.80	3.82	8.0	3.3	7.6	0.8	13.0	1.25
2007	PIT	MLB	28	3	2	1	63	0	51²	56	19	42	6	52.4%	.325	1	1.45	4.53	4.02	3.88	8.6	2.7	6.6	1.0	6.9	0.76
2008	*PIT*	*MLB*	*29*	*2*	*2*	*4*	*51*	*0*	*48*	*49*	*19*	*39*	*4*	*49.4%*	*.307*	*2*	*1.42*	*4.03*	*4.39*	*4.25*	*8.8*	*3.3*	*6.6*	*0.8*	*7.5*	*0.60*

Breakout: 17%   Improve: 44%   Collapse: 27%   Attrition: 28%   Comparables: Mike Myers, C. J. Nitkowski, Scott Ruskin, Chuck McElroy

When he throws strikes and attacks the hitter, Grabow can look as good as any left-handed reliever in the game. At other times, he fails to locate his pitches and begins to nibble. Grabow pitched last season with bone chips in his elbow, but was able to gut it out after spending most of April on the DL. He decided against having surgery over the winter, so the condition of his elbow will bear watching in spring training.

Yoslan Herrera

Bats: R   Throws: R   Height: 6' 2"   Weight: 200   Born: April 28, 1981   Age: 27

YEAR	TEAM	LVL	AGE	W	L	SV	G	GS	IP	H	BB	SO	HR	GB%	BABIP	STUFF	WHIP	ERA	PERA	EqERA	EqH9	EqBB9	EqSO9	EqHR9	VORP	SN/WX
2007	ALT	AA	26	6	9	0	25	25	128²	151	38	70	11	44.8%	.326	-26	1.47	4.69	6.63	6.40	11.6	3.3	3.0	1.3	-10.8	—
2008	*PIT*	*MLB*	*27*	*4*	*8*	*0*	*26*	*15*	*91¹*	*120*	*35*	*40*	*15*	*43.7%*	*.320*	*-17*	*1.70*	*6.48*	*6.62*	*6.74*	*11.4*	*3.2*	*3.6*	*1.4*	*-11.2*	*-0.60*

Breakout: 14%   Improve: 43%   Collapse: 36%   Attrition: 25%   Comparables: Juan Figueroa, Albert Bustillos, Roland Delamaza, Oscar Alvarez

Once pioneers in procuring talent from Latin America, the Pirates have an abysmal record of signing players from that part of the world in recent years. Thus, they were quite proud when they signed Herrera, a Cuban defector, to a three-year, $1.92 million major league contract in December 2006. He hadn't pitched competitively since 2004 and it showed as he struggled to get his fastball above the mid-80s at Double-A last season, lost confidence in the pitch, and resorted to throwing his curveball almost exclusively. Right now, he looks like a colossal bust.

Paul Maholm

Bats: L   Throws: L   Height: 6' 2"   Weight: 230   Born: June 25, 1982   Age: 26

YEAR	TEAM	LVL	AGE	W	L	SV	G	GS	IP	H	BB	SO	HR	GB%	BABIP	STUFF	WHIP	ERA	PERA	EqERA	EqH9	EqBB9	EqSO9	EqHR9	VORP	SN/WX
2005	ALT	AA	23	6	2	0	16	16	81²	73	26	75	5	63.7%	.308	-1	1.21	3.19	4.94	4.86	9.2	4.1	5.2	1.0	6.1	—
2005	IND	AAA	23	1	1	0	6	6	35²	40	12	21	2	55.5%	.325	-10	1.46	3.53	5.71	6.06	11.0	3.9	3.6	0.8	-1.7	—
2005	PIT	MLB	23	3	1	0	6	6	41¹	31	17	26	2	58.2%	.242	17	1.16	2.18	3.11	2.25	6.8	3.4	5.2	0.4	15.7	1.94
2006	PIT	MLB	24	8	10	0	30	30	176	202	81	117	19	55.2%	.334	7	1.61	4.76	5.00	4.49	9.7	3.6	5.5	0.9	20.7	3.09
2007	PIT	MLB	25	10	15	0	29	29	177²	204	49	105	22	54.9%	.323	5	1.42	5.01	4.35	4.84	9.2	2.1	5.0	1.0	7.4	2.17
2008	PIT	MLB	26	8	10	0	26	26	153	173	53	97	17	52.3%	.312	8	1.47	4.59	4.99	4.83	9.8	2.8	5.2	0.9	13.1	2.60

Breakout: 11% Improve: 39% Collapse: 29% Attrition: 11%   Comparables: Bruce Hurst, Scott Karl, Joe Kennedy, Jim Kaat

Maholm gets by more on guile than stuff. He lacks a dominant pitch and succeeds by mixing up his arsenal and throwing strikes. Maholm also is quite adept at inducing groundballs with runners on base, which helps make up for the fact he allows a lot of batters to reach. When he's not throwing strikes and is leaving the ball up in the zone, he's in big trouble. Maholm rose into the role of the third starter last year, but is really more of a four.

Damaso Marte

Bats: L   Throws: L   Height: 6' 2"   Weight: 210   Born: February 14, 1975   Age: 33

YEAR	TEAM	LVL	AGE	W	L	SV	G	GS	IP	H	BB	SO	HR	GB%	BABIP	STUFF	WHIP	ERA	PERA	EqERA	EqH9	EqBB9	EqSO9	EqHR9	VORP	SN/WX
2005	CHA	MLB	30	3	4	4	66	0	45¹	45	33	54	5	40.7%	.342	21	1.72	3.77	5.97	4.30	9.4	6.5	10.6	1.0	8.2	1.15
2006	PIT	MLB	31	1	7	0	75	0	58¹	51	31	63	5	40.1%	.326	14	1.41	3.70	3.57	3.94	7.3	4.1	8.6	0.6	9.3	-0.05
2007	PIT	MLB	32	2	0	0	65	0	45¹	32	18	51	2	43.2%	.280	27	1.10	2.38	2.53	2.58	5.8	3.0	9.1	0.4	15.7	1.23
2008	PIT	MLB	33	2	2	4	49	0	43¹	39	22	45	4	41.9%	.299	10	1.40	3.69	4.07	3.85	7.8	4.2	8.5	0.8	8.4	0.80

Breakout: 14% Improve: 39% Collapse: 34% Attrition: 16%   Comparables: Randy Myers, Jesse Orosco, Don McMahon, Jim Gott

Marte can be death to left-handed batters with his low-90s fastball and sharp-breaking slider; he throws with a crossfire motion that makes it appear as though the ball is coming at them from somewhere behind their right ear. Marte also handles right-handers well, making him more valuable than the standard-issue LOOGY. Best of all for the Bucs, Marte took a pay cut after the 2005 season in order to have two club-option years tacked on to his contract, so the Pirates have him under control at a below-market salary this year. His option for 2009 triples his salary to $6 million, which could make him a candidate to be moved at the this year's trading deadline.

Matt Morris

Bats: R   Throws: R   Height: 6' 5"   Weight: 215   Born: August 9, 1974   Age: 33

YEAR	TEAM	LVL	AGE	W	L	SV	G	GS	IP	H	BB	SO	HR	GB%	BABIP	STUFF	WHIP	ERA	PERA	EqERA	EqH9	EqBB9	EqSO9	EqHR9	VORP	SN/WX
2005	SLN	MLB	30	14	10	0	31	31	192²	209	37	117	22	50.5%	.303	6	1.28	4.11	4.66	5.17	9.9	1.6	5.0	1.0	18.3	2.94
2006	SFN	MLB	31	10	15	0	33	33	207²	218	63	117	22	47.7%	.291	7	1.35	4.98	4.32	4.84	9.2	2.3	4.6	0.8	16.0	3.13
2007	SFN	MLB	32	7	7	0	21	21	136²	162	39	73	12	49.9%	.325	8	1.47	4.35	4.71	4.93	10.2	2.2	4.5	0.7	11.3	2.21
2007	PIT	MLB	32	3	4	0	11	11	62	78	22	29	6	49.6%	.338	-3	1.61	6.10	4.88	5.57	10.0	2.7	4.0	0.7	-3.0	0.33
2008	PIT	MLB	33	6	9	0	22	22	127¹	152	37	68	16	48.0%	.312	1	1.48	5.02	5.23	5.27	10.3	2.4	4.4	1.0	5.3	1.50

Breakout: 8% Improve: 44% Collapse: 31% Attrition: 24%   Comparables: Jim Lonborg, Mark Gubicza, Walt Terrell, Bob Forsch

Dave Littlefield made more than his share of dumb trades during his six-year tenure as Pirates general manager, but none caused more head-scratching than his deadline deal to acquire Morris from the Giants while also taking on the remaining $13.7 million on his contract. Morris is a real pro, but as his stuff has continued to decline, he's been reduced to flipping one curveball after another in an attempt to deceive hitters. He's also the Pirates' highest paid player.

Daniel Moskos

Bats: R   Throws: L   Height: 6' 1"   Weight: 210   Born: April 28, 1986   Age: 22

YEAR	TEAM	LVL	AGE	W	L	SV	G	GS	IP	H	BB	SO	HR	GB%	BABIP	STUFF	WHIP	ERA	PERA	EqERA	EqH9	EqBB9	EqSO9	EqHR9	VORP	SN/WX
2007	SCO	A-	21	0	0	1	11	0	12²	19	6	13	1	42.2%	.409	-42	1.97	4.25	15.37	11.12	17.5	7.1	4.8	2.4	-6.9	—
2008	PIT	MLB	22	4	10	0	36	19	113¹	138	79	68	18	46.6%	.320	-16	1.91	6.64	7.04	6.91	10.6	5.8	4.9	1.3	-15.5	-1.00

Breakout: NA Improve: NA Collapse: NA Attrition: NA   Comparables: Jacob Marceaux, Greg Whiteman, Derick Grigsby, Cesar Ramos

Never has a first-round draft pick caused Pirates fans more consternation than the selection of Moskos out of Clemson with the fourth overall pick last year. Most fans wanted the Pirates to choose highly touted Georgia Tech catcher Josh Wieters, whom the Orioles took with the next pick, instead of Moskos. Moskos's excellent slider makes him a candidate to be a fine set-up man, but his willingness to accept slot money seemed to be what made him most attractive to the Pirates.

Luis Muñoz

Bats: R   Throws: R   Height: 6' 2"   Weight: 150   Born: January 10, 1982   Age: 26

YEAR	TEAM	LVL	AGE	W	L	SV	G	GS	IP	H	BB	SO	HR	GB%	BABIP	STUFF	WHIP	ERA	PERA	EqERA	EqH9	EqBB9	EqSO9	EqHR9	VORP	SN/WX
2005	WPT	A-	23	6	3	0	16	13	78	69	22	46	8	48.2%	.261	-64	1.17	3.81	10.44	10.27	12.6	6.0	1.9	3.2	-31.8	—
2006	HIC	A	24	6	2	0	16	14	85¹	82	20	55	5	51.6%	.294	-33	1.20	3.28	6.60	6.81	11.3	4.1	2.7	1.5	-9.9	—
2006	LYN	A+	24	4	3	0	11	11	66²	66	29	36	4	38.0%	.291	-21	1.44	3.81	6.63	6.52	10.9	5.5	2.7	1.2	-6.1	—
2007	ALT	AA	25	12	5	0	25	23	136	130	32	89	11	43.4%	.284	-11	1.19	3.63	4.97	5.22	9.6	2.7	3.9	1.2	5.4	—
2007	IND	AAA	25	2	1	0	3	3	17¹	22	4	16	2	41.8%	.392	-1	1.50	3.12	8.17	6.19	12.9	2.8	6.2	1.7	-1.0	—
2008	PIT	MLB	26	4	8	0	28	16	98¹	126	42	49	18	43.1%	.315	-16	1.71	6.41	6.71	6.62	11.1	3.6	4.1	1.5	-10.9	-0.50

Breakout: 17% Improve: 46% Collapse: 30% Attrition: 17%   *Comparables: Jose Martinez, Mario Brito, Tony Peguero, Pasqual Coco*

Muñoz went by the name Reynaldo Reyes when the Pirates signed him out of the Dominican Republic in 2000, but his real name and birthdate were revealed in the spring of 2002 after the U.S. began cracking down on false visas in the wake of the 2001 terrorist attacks. Luiz Muñoz turned out to be 2½ years older than Reynaldo Reyes. Since then, he's made a slow climb with a pedestrian sinker/slider combination, but made enough of an impression in Double-A last season to be placed on the 40-man roster in October.

Franquelis Osoria

Bats: R   Throws: R   Height: 6' 0"   Weight: 205   Born: September 12, 1981   Age: 26

YEAR	TEAM	LVL	AGE	W	L	SV	G	GS	IP	H	BB	SO	HR	GB%	BABIP	STUFF	WHIP	ERA	PERA	EqERA	EqH9	EqBB9	EqSO9	EqHR9	VORP	SN/WX
2005	LVG	AAA	23	6	4	9	40	0	55	63	13	35	3	66.3%	.347	-7	1.38	2.62	4.27	2.68	9.4	2.3	3.9	0.5	17.4	—
2005	LAN	MLB	23	0	2	0	24	0	29²	28	8	15	3	61.5%	.278	-10	1.21	3.94	4.29	4.13	8.9	2.2	4.4	1.0	4.1	0.51
2006	LVG	AAA	24	2	2	2	44	0	51	81	21	28	2	56.5%	.407	-31	2.00	4.41	8.44	6.34	14.3	4.2	3.3	0.5	-4.1	—
2006	LAN	MLB	24	0	2	0	12	0	17²	27	9	13	4	50.8%	.397	-30	2.04	7.12	11.37	8.31	13.5	4.2	6.2	2.1	-2.3	0.02
2007	IND	AAA	25	2	5	11	39	0	54²	51	19	33	3	62.6%	.284	-15	1.28	2.63	4.29	4.33	8.3	3.3	3.7	0.7	7.6	—
2007	PIT	MLB	25	0	2	0	25	0	28¹	33	8	13	3	51.5%	.306	-13	1.45	4.77	4.41	4.34	9.3	2.2	3.7	0.9	2.7	-0.04
2008	PIT	MLB	26	3	3	2	64	0	59²	70	21	29	5	54.6%	.311	-13	1.51	4.41	4.82	4.68	10.1	2.9	3.9	0.7	6.0	0.50

Breakout: 26% Improve: 53% Collapse: 22% Attrition: 20%   *Comparables: Julian Tavarez, Danny Patterson, Clay Carroll, Beau Kemp*

Osoria is a true one-pitch pitcher as he throws sinker after sinker after sinker. He was born with six fingers on his right hand, which helps give him a unique grip on the pitch. When he keeps it low, he's moderately effective, and when he doesn't, he's likely to find himself back in Triple-A. Quadruple-A status looks to be his limit.

Juan Perez

Bats: R   Throws: L   Height: 6' 0"   Weight: 175   Born: September 3, 1978   Age: 29

YEAR	TEAM	LVL	AGE	W	L	SV	G	GS	IP	H	BB	SO	HR	GB%	BABIP	STUFF	WHIP	ERA	PERA	EqERA	EqH9	EqBB9	EqSO9	EqHR9	VORP	SN/WX
2006	NOR	AAA	27	0	1	0	43	0	63²	65	34	55	4	44.4%	.337	-8	1.57	2.85	5.82	4.68	9.8	5.7	5.7	1.1	6.1	—
2007	IND	AAA	28	3	2	2	40	0	55²	52	25	63	5	46.4%	.322	-5	1.38	4.69	5.26	6.08	9.3	4.4	7.6	1.2	-2.8	—
2007	PIT	MLB	28	0	0	0	17	0	12¹	14	8	10	2	46.2%	.324	-3	1.78	4.39	5.86	4.38	9.5	5.1	6.6	1.5	1.1	-0.12
2008	PIT	MLB	29	2	3	4	52	3	48	51	28	40	5	45.6%	.314	-4	1.62	4.74	5.39	4.94	9.1	4.8	6.9	0.9	3.7	0.40

Breakout: 21% Improve: 47% Collapse: 31% Attrition: 27%   *Comparables: Allen McDill, Gino Minutelli, Jesus Sanchez, Julio Santana*

Perez is pushing 30 and has yet to gain a foothold in the major leagues. Still, he is a left-handed pitcher who has shown the ability to get left-handed hitters out from time to time over the course of his career, which means he'll have plenty of opportunities to establish himself as a journeyman LOOGY.

Matt Peterson

Bats: R   Throws: R   Height: 6' 4"   Weight: 220   Born: February 11, 1982   Age: 26

YEAR	TEAM	LVL	AGE	W	L	SV	G	GS	IP	H	BB	SO	HR	GB%	BABIP	STUFF	WHIP	ERA	PERA	EqERA	EqH9	EqBB9	EqSO9	EqHR9	VORP	SN/WX
2005	ALT	AA	23	11	9	0	27	26	143²	156	74	87	19	42.4%	.304	-38	1.60	5.51	8.12	8.61	10.9	6.4	3.1	1.9	-43.4	—
2006	ALT	AA	24	6	6	0	31	17	112²	115	47	83	10	41.8%	.322	-30	1.44	5.05	7.53	7.53	11.6	5.1	4.3	1.4	-21.5	—
2007	ALT	AA	25	4	2	29	51	0	63²	50	27	56	4	37.6%	.284	-6	1.21	1.98	4.67	2.97	8.3	4.7	5.8	0.9	16.9	—
2008	PIT	MLB	26	2	5	2	23	6	53²	61	33	36	7	39.8%	.311	-12	1.75	5.93	6.21	6.16	9.8	5.1	5.5	1.1	-3.1	-0.10

Breakout: 27% Improve: 51% Collapse: 30% Attrition: 24%   *Comparables: Jonathan Searles, David Lundquist, David Manning, Jared Burton*

If Peterson knew in 2004 what he knows now, he would have bought in Altoona instead of renting. Back then, he was a highly regarded prospect whom the Pirates had acquired from the Mets at the trading deadline along with Ty Wigginton for Kris Benson and Jeff Keppinger. Save for three games at Triple-A at the tail end of 2007, he's been in Double-A ever since. Peterson may have finally put Altoona behind him, however, by swapping starting for closing, a role in which he excelled.

Brian Rogers — Bats: R — Throws: R — Height: 6' 4" — Weight: 190 — Born: July 17, 1982 — Age: 25

YEAR	TEAM	LVL	AGE	W	L	SV	G	GS	IP	H	BB	SO	HR	GB%	BABIP	STUFF	WHIP	ERA	PERA	EqERA	EqH9	EqBB9	EqSO9	EqHR9	VORP	SN/WX
2005	LAK	A+	22	4	1	2	52	1	65²	50	21	65	2	51.1%	.284	-6	1.08	2.05	5.05	4.13	9.2	4.9	5.4	0.8	9.3	—
2006	ERI	AA	23	3	2	1	37	0	64¹	49	14	69	7	45.8%	.268	-6	0.98	2.39	4.54	3.79	8.0	2.7	6.5	1.7	11.9	—
2007	IND	AAA	24	2	1	2	48	0	65	50	32	65	1	56.1%	.292	11	1.26	3.05	3.62	3.90	7.4	4.8	6.6	0.3	11.8	—
2008	PIT	MLB	25	3	4	5	41	6	58²	59	30	46	5	49.5%	.303	0	1.51	4.19	4.67	4.41	8.7	4.2	6.4	0.7	8.5	1.00

Breakout: 21% Improve: 51% Collapse: 22% Attrition: 15% — Comparables: Scott Henderson, Will Cunnane, Ryan Speier, Tom Mastny

One of the few times Jim Tracy showed a pulse during his two seasons as Pirates manager came last May 26 in Cincinnati. In that game, Tracy came charging out to the mound to remove Rogers after the righty reliever had given up home runs to each of the first two batters he faced. Rogers was sent back to Triple-A after the game and did not return to the major leagues despite not allowing another home run all year. After the season, he was designated for assignment to make room for waiver pickup Ty Taubenheim. Thanks, skip.

Romulo Sanchez — Bats: R — Throws: R — Height: 6' 6" — Weight: 208 — Born: April 28, 1984 — Age: 24

YEAR	TEAM	LVL	AGE	W	L	SV	G	GS	IP	H	BB	SO	HR	GB%	BABIP	STUFF	WHIP	ERA	PERA	EqERA	EqH9	EqBB9	EqSO9	EqHR9	VORP	SN/WX
2005	HIC	A	21	3	3	0	10	10	53²	59	19	24	5	53.3%	.312	-39	1.45	4.69	8.56	9.00	11.9	5.7	1.1	1.9	-17.8	—
2005	ALT	AA	21	1	0	0	2	2	10	11	4	5	2	51.4%	.281	-27	1.50	3.60	9.03	6.00	11.0	5.0	2.0	3.0	-0.4	—
2006	HIC	A	22	0	3	4	21	3	40	51	18	28	4	54.5%	.343	-51	1.73	7.20	11.90	12.88	14.4	6.7	2.7	2.2	-29.4	—
2007	ALT	AA	23	6	3	1	40	0	57²	43	17	52	8	49.4%	.232	-18	1.04	2.81	4.67	4.69	7.6	3.2	5.5	1.9	5.6	—
2007	PIT	MLB	23	1	0	0	16	0	18	16	8	11	2	50.9%	.280	-7	1.33	5.00	3.88	4.24	7.4	3.7	5.3	1.1	1.7	-0.01
2008	PIT	MLB	24	2	3	2	50	2	52¹	59	26	33	7	47.7%	.302	-13	1.61	5.26	5.75	5.48	9.7	4.1	5.1	1.2	0.7	0.10

Breakout: 37% Improve: 70% Collapse: 15% Attrition: 13% — Comparables: Jose Garcia, Duaner Sanchez, Carlos Martinez, Talley Haines

Sanchez was released by the Los Angeles Dodgers in 2003 after two seasons in the Venezuelan Summer League. Picked up off the scrapheap by the Pirates, he reached the major leagues last August. Sanchez throws extremely hard, though he isn't always sure where the ball is going. If he gains command of his heater and adds a reliable second pitch, something he will work on at Triple-A to begin this season, he could be a future closer. If not, it's back to the Beta Quadrant.

Ian Snell — Bats: R — Throws: R — Height: 5' 11" — Weight: 190 — Born: October 30, 1981 — Age: 26

YEAR	TEAM	LVL	AGE	W	L	SV	G	GS	IP	H	BB	SO	HR	GB%	BABIP	STUFF	WHIP	ERA	PERA	EqERA	EqH9	EqBB9	EqSO9	EqHR9	VORP	SN/WX
2005	IND	AAA	23	11	3	0	18	18	112	90	23	104	14	43.4%	.255	5	1.01	3.70	4.24	4.81	8.1	2.4	6.3	1.4	9.0	—
2005	PIT	MLB	23	1	2	0	15	5	42	43	24	34	5	38.5%	.311	1	1.60	5.14	5.34	5.44	9.4	4.8	6.8	1.1	0.7	0.21
2006	PIT	MLB	24	14	11	0	32	32	186	198	74	169	29	44.4%	.327	12	1.46	4.74	4.50	4.35	8.7	3.1	7.4	1.2	21.5	3.49
2007	PIT	MLB	25	9	12	0	32	32	208	209	68	177	22	46.5%	.315	24	1.33	3.76	3.70	3.43	8.1	2.5	7.1	0.9	42.8	5.31
2008	PIT	MLB	26	10	10	0	28	28	174²	177	60	143	18	45.3%	.303	19	1.36	4.07	4.36	4.26	8.8	2.9	6.7	0.9	25.6	4.10

Breakout: 7% Improve: 33% Collapse: 35% Attrition: 15% — Comparables: Lynn McGlothen, Adam Eaton, Joel Pineiro, Pat Hentgen

Snell established himself as a top-notch young starter last season. The only hiccup came when the Pirates suddenly had the goofy idea of turning him into a curveball pitcher, resulting in a five-game losing streak coming out of the All-Star break. Scouts worry that the lithe Snell will eventually break down under the stress of throwing 95 mph fastballs and sharp sliders, but he is a well-conditioned athlete who has never had an arm problem. He is definitely a rising star.

Salomon Torres

Bats: R   Throws: R   Height: 5' 11"   Weight: 210   Born: March 11, 1972   Age: 36

YEAR	TEAM	LVL	AGE	W	L	SV	G	GS	IP	H	BB	SO	HR	GB%	BABIP	STUFF	WHIP	ERA	PERA	EqERA	EqH9	EqBB9	EqSO9	EqHR9	VORP	SN/WX
2005	PIT	MLB	33	5	5	3	78	0	94²	76	36	55	7	51.4%	.246	-1	1.18	2.76	3.32	3.31	7.2	3.1	4.9	0.7	23.7	1.68
2006	PIT	MLB	34	3	6	12	94	0	93¹	98	38	72	6	57.6%	.329	9	1.46	3.28	3.83	3.52	8.6	3.1	6.3	0.5	20.8	4.62
2007	PIT	MLB	35	2	4	12	56	0	52²	57	17	45	7	49.1%	.325	1	1.41	5.46	4.27	5.00	8.7	2.3	7.0	1.0	0.7	-0.06
2008	MIL	MLB	36	3	3	8	47	0	54	55	22	40	6	49.5%	.298	-5	1.42	4.29	4.47	4.41	9.0	3.1	5.8	0.9	6.4	0.70

Breakout: 14%   Improve: 26%   Collapse: 51%   Attrition: 33%   Comparables: Mike Marshall, Dave Giusti, Scott Kamieniecki, Elmer Dessens

Torres filled in admirably as the closer when Mike Gonzalez was injured at the end of 2006, but struggled when given the job at the start of last season and yielded to the inevitable ascension of Matt Capps in June. Back in his customary set-up role, Torres battled elbow problems throughout much of the final four months of the season, no doubt due in large part to appearing in 256 games from 2004 to 2006, more than any major league reliever in that span. Torres had been a revelation since returning from a five-year retirement in 2002, but the odometer on his right arm has rolled over. Shipped to Milwaukee, he'll serve as a set-up man to closer Derrick Turnbow.

John Van Benschoten

Bats: R   Throws: R   Height: 6' 4"   Weight: 225   Born: April 14, 1980   Age: 28

YEAR	TEAM	LVL	AGE	W	L	SV	G	GS	IP	H	BB	SO	HR	GB%	BABIP	STUFF	WHIP	ERA	PERA	EqERA	EqH9	EqBB9	EqSO9	EqHR9	VORP	SN/WX
2007	IND	AAA	27	10	7	0	19	19	109	98	51	79	8	47.8%	.286	0	1.37	2.56	4.98	3.74	8.8	4.7	4.8	1.1	20.9	—
2007	PIT	MLB	27	0	7	0	11	9	39	55	29	26	4	39.2%	.381	-13	2.15	10.15	7.14	9.66	11.2	5.5	5.5	0.9	-20.0	-0.54
2008	PIT	MLB	28	4	7	0	35	15	99	104	52	69	11	45.0%	.298	-5	1.57	5.32	5.30	5.60	9.1	4.4	5.7	1.0	0.2	0.50

Breakout: 51%   Improve: 73%   Collapse: 13%   Attrition: 24%   Comparables: Mike Drumright, Jeremy Guthrie, Sean Lowe, John Burke

The Pirates surprised many by drafting Van Benschoten as a pitcher in the first round in 2001 despite the fact that he'd led college baseball with 31 home runs at Kent State that spring. That decision doesn't look any better today—he has as many homers as wins in the majors, going 1-10 with an 8.78 ERA in 67 2/3 innings. Three shoulder surgeries in 2004 and 2005, including one on his labrum, derailed Van Benschoten's career, and it looks like he might never get back on track.

LINEOUTS

Hitters

	PLAYER	TEAM	LVL	AGE	PA	R	2B	3B	HR	RBI	BB	SO	SB-CS	EqBRR	AVG/OBP/SLG	MLVr	EqAVG/EqOBP/EqSLG	EqA	VORP
UT	Y. de Caster	IND	AAA	27	477	55	25	1	9	54	58	95	13-8	-0.8	.280/.380/.413	.122	.264/.357/.412	.269	9.2
SS	B. Friday	SCO	A-	21	176	31	10	1	2	13	10	33	6-4	0.0	.295/.371/.410	.177	.244/.291/.354	.222	-2.7
SS	J. Guzman#	ALT	AA	25	183	19	13	0	2	25	5	20	7-0	1.5	.310/.333/.421	.071	.282/.298/.379	.243	2.4
UT	J. Keel	HIC	A	22	400	63	23	1	17	56	56	79	5-2	2.3	.261/.386/.494	.206	.206/.307/.378	.240	-1.4
OF	Q. Latimore	PIR	Rk	18	196	29	9	2	3	17	16	25	13-4	1.7	.257/.352/.386	.083	.198/.255/.291	.193	-35.7
OF	J. Pacheco	HIC	A	24	514	97	25	5	27	99	41	71	18-7	0.9	.315/.372/.566	.334	.255/.302/.438	.252	-2.8
1B	J. Phelps	NYA	MLB	29	88	8	2	0	2	12	6	19	0-0	0.7	.263/.330/.363	-.098	.262/.337/.363	.248	-0.3
		PIT	MLB	29	95	13	4	2	5	19	14	23	0-0	-0.9	.351/.463/.649	.586	.351/.469/.688	.374	15.3
OF	P. Powell#	LYN	A+	23	561	71	16	7	0	29	56	94	67-17	3.0	.241/.325/.303	-.157	.198/.266/.250	.197	-48.2

There are worse utility players in the major leagues than **Yurendell de Caster**, who can hit for some average and power while playing all over the field, but he is still waiting for an extended major-league shot. He'll try anew in Nationals camp as a non-roster invitee. ⊘ **Brian Friday** was a two-time All-American at Rice, but didn't bring along his college batting eye for his professional debut last summer. ⊘ **Javier Guzman** was dropped off the 40-man roster in spring training, missed the first half of the season following knee surgery, then had a fine second half to register a small blip on the prospect radar once again. ⊘ **Jared Keel** was set to become a park ranger until the Pirates drafted him out of Troy State in the 31st round in 2006. He has since opened eyes by flashing power and warning fans not to feed the bears. ⊘ **Quincy Latimore** is all projection at this point in his career, but his power/speed potential is quite intriguing. ⊘ **Jonel Pacheco** tore up the Low-A Sally League last season, but he was also 24 and in his sixth professional season. ⊘ **Josh Phelps**'s major league career was resurrected when he made the Yankees out of spring training as a Rule 5 draftee then started raking after the Pirates claimed him off waivers in June, but he is strictly a bench player at this point. ⊘ The diminutive **Pedro Powell** has led the High-A Carolina League in stolen bases in each of the past two seasons, but speed is of little use when your OBP is barely above .300.

Pitchers

PLAYER	TEAM	LVL	AGE	W	L	SV	IP	H	BB	SO	HR	GB%	BABIP	STUFF	WHIP	ERA	PERA	EqERA	EqH9	EqBB9	EqSO9	EqHR9	VORP
R. Belisario	LYN	A+	24	0	3	4	34¹	38	13	19	5	57.5%	.297	-50	1.49	4.46	8.69	7.11	11.4	5.1	2.6	2.6	-5.3
	ALT	AA	24	1	0	0	24²	23	14	21	4	46.1%	.275	-24	1.50	3.28	7.49	5.32	9.5	5.7	4.9	2.3	0.7
K. Bloom*	LYN	A+	24	9	12	0	129	144	57	90	14	36.1%	.320	-45	1.56	5.51	8.46	8.30	11.6	6.0	3.5	2.1	-34.8
K. Bouknight	ALT	AA	28	11	6	0	138²	135	36	83	12	49.9%	.289	-16	1.23	3.83	5.38	5.51	9.9	3.0	3.6	1.3	1.3
	IND	AAA	28	1	1	0	18	19	8	12	3	36.2%	.302	-21	1.50	4.50	7.93	6.48	10.3	4.3	4.3	2.2	-1.6
D. Brazelton	OMA	AAA	27	0	4	0	19	24	8	14	3	44.4%	.362	-25	1.68	7.11	9.33	9.35	13.0	4.2	5.2	1.6	-7.2
	ALT	AA	27	5	5	0	86²	88	17	52	5	40.9%	.314	-5	1.21	3.53	5.21	4.98	10.5	2.4	3.7	0.9	5.4
J. Chavez	IND	AAA	23	3	3	2	80¹	94	17	65	4	39.2%	.353	-4	1.38	3.92	5.09	5.68	11.0	2.2	5.2	0.7	-0.7
T. Redmond	LYN	A+	22	7	12	0	142²	151	32	95	13	40.8%	.312	-29	1.28	4.54	6.47	7.04	10.7	3.4	3.3	1.7	-21.2
	ALT	AA	22	1	1	0	17¹	15	3	12	2	35.2%	.250	3	1.04	3.12	4.65	3.78	8.6	2.2	4.3	1.6	3.4
J. Sharpless	IND	AAA	26	1	5	3	64¹	61	39	69	10	34.4%	.307	-18	1.56	4.34	7.11	6.34	9.6	5.9	7.2	2.1	-5.0
D. Welker	SCO	A-	21	2	2	0	30²	29	10	27	2	52.9%	.325	-15	1.27	2.35	8.45	5.76	11.9	5.4	4.3	2.2	-0.4
S. Youman*	IND	AAA	27	4	6	0	82¹	94	36	61	3	44.8%	.350	2	1.58	4.70	5.46	5.97	10.8	4.4	4.8	0.6	-3.2
	PIT	MLB	27	3	5	0	57¹	65	23	29	5	42.3%	.326	-6	1.53	5.97	4.19	5.37	8.9	3.1	4.1	0.8	-2.1

Ronald Belisario is a Venezuelan reliever whom the Pirates added to their 40-man roster in the offseason. That means they like him, though scouts with other teams aren't exactly sure why. ⊘ **Kyle Bloom** has shown flashes of being a good pitcher during his three straight seasons in the Carolina League, and left-handers have been known to be, ahem, late bloomers. ⊘ **Kip Bouknight** was a college star at South Carolina, but after seven pro seasons in four organizations he's still having trouble sticking in Triple-A. ⊘ **Dewon Brazelton** showed flashes of brilliance at Double-A last season, but the one-time phenom with the bad knees didn't come close to getting a chance to improve upon his 8-25 career major league record. ⊘ **Jesse Chavez** throws hard for a little guy, but as with many hard throwers, he doesn't always know where the ball is going. ⊘ **Todd Redmond** performed well at Low-A by spotting his fastball and off-speed pitches, but that strategy didn't work so well in High-A last year. ⊘ **Josh Sharpless** posted ridiculous strikeout totals coming up through the minors, but major league hitters have thus far been able to lay off his sliders in the dirt. ⊘ The Pirates' second-round draft pick last year out of Arkansas, **Duke Welker** pitched well in his pro debut and projects as a potential third starter. ⊘ **Shane Youman** beat the odds by rising from the 43rd round of the draft in 2001 to pitch in the major leagues, converting from relief to starting along the way, but he lacks the stuff to stick. He was nonetheless plucked off of waivers by the Phillies.

MANAGER: JIM TRACY

YEAR	TEAM	W-L	Pythag +/-	Avg PC	100+ P	120+ P	QS	BQS	REL	REL w Zero R	IBB	Subs	PH	PH Avg	PH HR	SB2	CS2	SB3	CS3	SAC Att	SAC %	POS SAC	Squeeze	Swing	In Play
2005	LAN	71-91	-2	92.0	55	6	73	12	457	278	34	62	298	.231	4	54	33	4	2	81	70.4%	19	3	132	95
2006	PIT	67-95	-3	94.5	58	2	67	6	503	313	62	35	261	.227	5	63	18	5	3	87	71.3%	32	3	113	81
2007	PIT	68-94	0	92.6	48	1	73	9	495	289	55	35	238	.231	9	62	27	6	2	84	71.4%	22	4	112	86

Jim Tracy came to the Pirates after the 2005 season with high hopes. One year removed from managing the Dodgers to a division title, Tracy believed he could turn around a franchise that hadn't had a winning season since 1992. Instead, Tracy's two-year tenure in Pittsburgh was a disaster, as the Pirates went 67-95 in 2006, the same record they had under Lloyd McClendon in 2005, and 68-94 in 2007. Throw in the Dodgers' 71-91 finish in 2005, and Tracy's record over the past three seasons is an ugly 206-280 (.424). Tracy is a wonderful man with a warm personality, but he never connected with many of his players. Few loved him or hated him; most viewed him with indifference. Likewise, Tracy's stewardship of the team betrayed a certain indifference, as he did nothing strategically to stand out from the crowd.

John Russell, who was the Pirates' third base coach from 2003 to 2005 under McClendon, was hired to replace Tracy after spending the past two seasons managing Philadelphia's Triple-A farm club. Russell is a quiet man noted for his no-nonsense approach. He drew high marks as a minor league manager despite a 666-667 record over ten seasons. Of course, after 15 years of losing, exhuming John McGraw might not be enough to jump-start such a moribund franchise.

St. Louis Cardinals

*I point out to you a lesson from over-machined societies . . . the devices themselves
condition the users to employ each other the way they employ machines.*
—**FRANK HERBERT,** *God Emperor of Dune*

General Manager Walt Jocketty was fired by the Cardinals at the conclusion of the 2007 season, the organization's first losing season of the millennium. Despite the dismissal, Jocketty will go down as one of the great executives in the history of the franchise that effectively invented the front office structure as we know it today. In Jocketty's 13 years at the helm, his charges made seven playoff appearances, winning six division titles, two pennants, and a world title, making his regime an unqualified success.

It's important to remember the state of the Cardinals' organization when Jocketty took over after the 1994 season. At that point, the Cards had just completed their seventh straight season of mediocrity, stretching back to the meltdown of Whitey Herzog's fleet feet approach following the team's 1987 World Series loss. Joe Torre eventually replaced Herzog as manager in the later half of 1990, but his four full seasons at the helm weren't notable for any particular wasted greatness or unrealized ambition; they were merely as nondescript as those that came before them. The Cardinals' one area of strength under Torre was their outfield. By 1993, the team had assembled a strong foursome in the homegrown Ray Lankford, Bernard Gilkey, and Brian Jordan, and the imported Mark Whiten.

Jocketty tried to leverage that outfield depth to repair the club's innumerable problems, but the first-time GM showed his greenness when first Whiten and then Gilkey were dealt for negligible returns. The former director of baseball administration for the A's did better

---

CARDINALS PROSPECTUS

2007 record: 78-84; Third place, NL Central

Pythagenport record: 71-91

Runs scored per game: 4.48 (11th in NL)

Runs allowed per game: 5.12 (11th in NL)

Team EqA: .260 (8th in NL)

2007 Batters Age: 30.7 (4th oldest in NL)

2007 Pitchers Age: 29.7 (7th oldest in NL)

Ballpark: Busch Stadium; Slight pitcher's park; Park Factor of .973

2007: A late-season surge by an injury-riddled team isn't enough to defend the division title.

2008: With Jocketty gone, the Cards find themselves in limbo between rebuilding and retooling.

---

cutting deals with his old boss, Oakland GM Sandy Alderson. Having lured Tony La Russa away from the scuffling post-Bash Brother A's after the 1995 season, Jocketty added a number of players his new manager was quite familiar with, including right-hander Todd Stottlemyre and closer Dennis Eckersley, both of whom were obtained for "prospects" who never came back to haunt the team. That would become a hallmark of Jocketty's tenure. As the inspired tandem of off-season deals that brought in pitcher Darryl Kile and center fielder Jim Edmonds for the 2000 season illustrated, Jocketty had a knack for dealing bulk (in the case of the Kile trade) or entirely replaceable talent (the Edmonds deal) to acquire quality. He also developed an almost-incredible track record as a crunchtime-deal GM who would consistently find a way to add that missing piece or two despite a sparsely populated cupboard from which to deal. Whether the quarry was big game—Mark McGwire in '97, Will Clark in '00, Scott Rolen and Chuck Finley in '02, Larry Walker in '04—or relative small fry—second baseman Ronnie Belliard and right-hander Jeff Weaver in '06—Jocketty's care in addressing and fixing his club's problems in-season was a strength most teams would do well to mimic.

In the same way that it's important to remember where the Cardinals were when Jocketty arrived, it's informative to consider where he's left them. A comparison to the conclusion of Herzog's reign as manager and general manager is particularly instructive. Herzog's teams slowly burned out waiting for that one last comeback season from dominating-when-healthy starting pitchers such as John Tudor and Joe Magrane and hoping to hit Jack Clark-like paydirt with retread sluggers such as Bob Horner and Pedro Guerrero. As Herzog's teams got older and more fragile, their potential to contend became more tenuous. As a larger portion of the roster—and payroll—was devoted to unreliable players, the team had less maneuverability to bring in topshelf help from outside. If this sounds familiar, it should. It isn't hard to see Guerrero in Scott Rolen or Tudor in Chris Carpenter and recognize the way in which relying too heavily on damaged goods can lead to the limited means that force a GM to settle for filler pickups such as Tom Brunansky or Juan Encarnacion.

Jocketty reportedly chafed against these limitations, preferring to repair his team's holes by spending money he was not allowed to spend. Perhaps taking his cue from Alderson, Jocketty also tended to work hand-inglove with La Russa. While that sort of relationship between manager and general manager might seem ideal, managers tend to be focused on their immediate needs on the major league squad, while the general manager needs to take his organization's farm system and longterm view into account. The Cards' farm system did not make great progress during Jocketty's reign, and this too would become an area of friction, as the eventual solution imposed on him from above was to bring in management consultant Jeff Luhnow to overhaul the club's player development program following the 2003 season, further limiting the GM's freedom of action.

It would have been close to impossible for the Cards' system to have been any worse than it was in the years running up to the decision to bring in Luhnow, but the system's improvement in the years since has been real nonetheless. Still, the fact that Luhnow was a baseball outsider was a source of friction as Jocketty refused to cooperate with him. When Luhnow was promoted to replace one of Jocketty's aides following the 2006 season, increasing his reach to the scouting department, the decreasing scope of the GM's power was made obvious. These frustrations added up, and, in the end, it appears the mounting in-house tension got to be too much for ownership to continue turning a blind eye.

After a brief, aggressive flirtation with Indians Assistant GM Chris Antonetti was rebuffed, the Cardinals decided on the path of least resistance, promoting Jocketty's Assistant GM, John Mozeliak, from an interim role to the full monty. Mozeliak's ability to work with both La Russa and Luhnow was critical to his hiring, and La Russa's willingness to work with Mozeliak dictated his decision to remain with the organization after it fired the man who had brought him in. Exactly how the power will balance out remains to be seen, but we have contemporary examples of GMs who diplomatically work around competing in-house interests (such as the Yankees' Brian Cashman) and who butt up against them (think Ned Colletti of the Dodgers).

Those power struggles were what ultimately led to Jocketty's dismissal, but it's still worth noting that Jocketty's approach seemed to promise increasingly limited returns. Though they went on to win the World Series, the Birds only made the playoffs in 2006 through stunningly incapable intradivision competition. With that last desperate run, the old foundation of Cardinals contention—which had at its four corners superstar Albert Pujols and the fragile trio of Edmonds, Rolen, and Carpenter—finally crumbled.

As a result, some hard decisions had to be made this winter. To the credit of Mozeliak, La Russa, Luhnow, and whoever else has a seat at the table, the Cards didn't shrink from the challenge. Trading Edmonds and Rolen and allowing shortstop David Eckstein to leave as a free agent might seem an embittering break from the transient glory of 2006, but those decisions were of a piece with the happily abrupt end of right-hander Kip Wells's Cardinals career via free agency. The value that any one of those veterans is likely to provide in 2008 will be marginal at best, and breaking with the lot is a symptom of a general repositioning of the franchise. Rather than building on a foundation of Pujols and a mostly veteran cast of increasingly fragile supporting players, the new-look Cardinals are attempting to rebuild that foundation around Pujols and collection of homegrown players who have some upside. It's still a slender bet, but as the Cubs and Brewers are the teams to beat in the Central—neither a lock to win 90 games—the Cardinals could still thrust themselves into contention midseason should they be able to hover around .500 in the early going.

The initial challenge will be to integrate the kids. If they're ready, the Cards won't have to deal with the ignominy of slumming around with the Pirates in the second division. Their front rank of potential plug-ins already has experience at Double-A or higher: Colby Rasmus, Cody Haerther, and Joe Mather in the outfield, Brendan Ryan and perhaps Tyler Greene at short, Jarrett Hoffpauir at second, Bryan Anderson behind the plate, and right-handers Chris Perez, Mark Worrell, and Kyle McClellan for the bullpen. While Rasmus and perhaps Anderson are the only ones with significant star potential, all of them should be in a position to make it up and contribute at some point during the 2007 season, and the placeholders penciled into the lineup in their places—guys like second baseman Adam Kennedy, shortstop Cesar Izturis, and outfielder Skip Schumaker—don't deserve a lot of loyalty, should they fail to produce.

The farm system provided one significant addition to the lineup last year via the almost miraculous repurposing of Rick Ankiel. Generally speaking, it's only failed position players who find a career renaissance by going to the mound, not the other way around. Ankiel's transition from a blue-chip pitching prospect to Tunguska-level wipeout to a legitimate major league power bat is effectively without modern precedent. His amazing return to prospectdom was perhaps overshadowed by Josh Hamilton's equally improbable and dramatic rise to the majors with the Reds, as well as some doping allegations that dated back to his pitching days, but Ankiel's the guy who hit 43 home runs between Triple-A and the majors last year. It isn't hard to envision the Cardinals' lineup getting southpaw power from all three of its outfield slots with Ankiel, Rasmus, and Chris Duncan playing regularly from right to left by June. Wrap that group around Pujols, and you can see the Cards doing some real damage in the division.

The decision to trade Rolen had been a long time coming. Rolen's increasingly noisy feuding with La Russa was petty and pointless and merely distracted from the more fundamental problem, which was that age and injury had reduced Rolen to something less than a star-caliber hitter. Rather than keep him on in the hope that he'd go back to hitting like the Rolen of old, Mozeliak swapped hot-corner problems with the Blue Jays, sending Rolen to Toronto for fellow third baseman Troy Glaus. Doing so has all sorts of upside, both short- and long-term; Glaus is younger, has been more reliably productive at the plate despite an even more checkered injury history, and is only guaranteed through 2008 (with a 2009 player option), potentially freeing the Cards to explore their options with the money saved by dealing Rolen, who is signed through 2010.

An even larger gamble is being made in the rotation, again. Can La Russa and pitching coach Dave Duncan fashion one from a mixed bag not much unlike last year's collection of retreads? Mark Mulder's recovery from his latest shoulder surgery could find him throwing off of a mound by spring training, but Carpenter may not be ready until after the All-Star break, and it remains to be seen if either will be effective. That leaves La Russa and Duncan to fill in the rotation behind Adam Wainwright with four men from a group that includes veterans Looper, Joel Pineiro, and Todd Wellemeyer, and farm products Anthony Reyes and Brad Thompson. That's not a hopeless collection; Duncan has been known to have success reatreading veteran journeymen and worked some of that magic with mid-season additions Pineiro and Wellemeyer last year. But with the exception of Reyes, who still has time to deliver on his fading promise, these are the sort pitchers you want to have backing up your rotation, not filling it.

All of that adds up to a weird sort of ballclub. The Cardinals are closer to rebuilding than contending, but in a way they're not doing either. Lacking the quality to commit to the former and the star power to force the latter, they're stalling, keeping their options open by the competitive standards of the pathetic NL Central. Should the off-season effort to restore order in the front office pay off, Mozeliak might be able to establish a happy middle ground that integrates La Russa's demands for veteran add-ons and Luhnow's homegrown goodies, allowing for a new house of Cards to be placed on a foundation of Pujols, Rasmus, Ankiel, and Wainwright. That's something less than what they had before, but for a team that was supposed to have little going for it in player development, it would make for a remarkable turnaround.

HITTERS

Bryan Anderson   C

| | | | | | | | | Bats: L | Throws: R | Height: 6' 1" | Weight: 200 | Born: December 16, 1986 | Age: 21 |

YEAR	TEAM	LVL	AGE	PA	R	2B	3B	HR	RBI	BB	SO	SB	CS	EqBRR	AVG	OBP	SLG	MLVr	EqAVG	EqOBP	EqSLG	EqA	VORP	DEFENSE
2005	JCY	Rk	18	176	28	8	1	6	36	15	29	6	1	0.2	.331	.383	.513	.286	.224	.263	.304	.203	-20.5	36-C -7
2006	QUD	A	19	431	50	29	3	3	51	42	66	2	6	-3.8	.302	.377	.417	.192	.247	.307	.354	.229	-3.1	89-C -7
2007	SFD	AA	20	431	51	15	1	6	53	32	77	0	1	-3.5	.298	.350	.388	.039	.263	.309	.349	.232	-2.3	99-C -7
2008	SLN	MLB	21	491	46	24	2	8	52	34	96	4	2	-0.4	.255	.307	.370	-.165	.254	.307	.385	.236	5.5	116-C -4

Breakout: 42% Improve: 66% Collapse: 14% Attrition: 2%   Comparables: Pee-Wee Lopez, Jason Belcher, Cody Haerther, Dioner Navarro

In something of a surprise, the Cardinals had Anderson skip High-A and move straight to the Texas League, where he hit for average and little else. Holding your own as a 20-year-old catcher in the Texas League is notable, but the excitement over Anderson is based largely on his ability to slap line drives, and his contact rate is low for hitter of that type. He hasn't shown power, and he has catcher's speed and average defensive skills. The end result is likely to be a Paul Lo Duca/A. J. Pierzynski-type of player in the majors.

Rick Ankiel   OF

Bats: L   Throws: L   Height: 6' 1"   Weight: 210   Born: July 19, 1979   Age: 28

YEAR	TEAM	LVL	AGE	PA	R	2B	3B	HR	RBI	BB	SO	SB	CS	EqBRR	AVG	OBP	SLG	MLVr	EqAVG	EqOBP	EqSLG	EqA	VORP	DEFENSE			
2005	QUD	A	25	223	33	10	1	11	45	27	37	0	0	-0.1	.270	.368	.514	.235	.221	.296	.421	.247	-4.8	23-RF	-2		
2005	SFD	AA	25	146	18	7	0	10	30	10	29	0	0	-2.4	.243	.295	.515	.076	.206	.260	.419	.228	-6.5	24-RF	-2		
2007	MEM	AAA	27	423	62	15	3	32	89	25	90	4	3	-1.4	.267	.314	.568	.184	.240	.286	.514	.263	14.7	86-CF	-8	10-RF	1
2007	SLN	MLB	27	190	31	8	1	11	39	13	41	1	0	0.2	.285	.328	.535	.161	.292	.339	.556	.297	10.9	22-RF	2	16-CF	-5
2008	SLN	MLB	28	610	74	26	2	30	101	45	130	5	2	-0.2	.257	.315	.474	-.009	.256	.315	.493	.267	20.9	143-CF	-5		

Breakout: 25% Improve: 52% Collapse: 20% Attrition: 14%   Comparables: Eric Munson, Geoff Jenkins, Brooks Kieschnick, Jose Cruz, Jr.

Back up three steps from *The Rick Ankiel Story* and take a look at Rick Ankiel, baseball player. At 28, he's a low-contact, high-power lefty bat who can play a plus corner or an average center field. Think Russell Branyan minus walks and plus a little defense. The thing most in his favor is that his unique career path makes him a "younger" 28 developmentally; because he has so few pro at-bats, you can expect him to still have some growth left, and he's in a range of production in which even a little improvement—such as cutting his strikeout rate while adding average and OBP—will be worth tens of millions of dollars.

Allen Craig   3B

Bats: R   Throws: R   Height: 6' 2"   Weight: 190   Born: July 18, 1984   Age: 23

YEAR	TEAM	LVL	AGE	PA	R	2B	3B	HR	RBI	BB	SO	SB	CS	EqBRR	AVG	OBP	SLG	MLVr	EqAVG	EqOBP	EqSLG	EqA	VORP	DEFENSE			
2006	SCO	A-	21	201	21	13	0	4	29	13	28	0	0	0.0	.257	.325	.400	.128	.219	.269	.350	.215	-12.1	34-3B	-7		
2007	PMB	A+	22	468	77	25	2	21	77	35	79	8	3	-4.4	.312	.370	.530	.336	.275	.329	.476	.273	28.6	83-3B	-6	15-1B	0
2007	SFD	AA	22	25	5	2	0	3	3	1	6	0	0	0.0	.292	.320	.750	.500	.292	.320	.750	.327	4.1				
2008	SLN	MLB	23	534	58	27	1	15	69	34	101	7	3	-0.7	.260	.312	.416	-.091	.258	.312	.432	.251	9.0	126-3B	-5		

Breakout: 19% Improve: 40% Collapse: 25% Attrition: 14%   Comparables: Russ Davis, Andy Hartung, Kevin Kouzmanoff, Kevin Haverbusch

Craig had a breakout season in 2007, but there are reasons to believe that it still might not be enough to establish him as a prospect. He's a gifted hitter with the ability to hit for both average and power, but he was a little bit older than most of the players in the Florida State League last year, his overly aggressive approach might catch up to him at the higher levels, and he doesn't really have a true defensive home. He's more of a guy to keep an eye on than one with a projectable future right now.

Chris Duncan   LF

Bats: L   Throws: R   Height: 6' 5"   Weight: 230   Born: May 5, 1981   Age: 27

YEAR	TEAM	LVL	AGE	PA	R	2B	3B	HR	RBI	BB	SO	SB	CS	EqBRR	AVG	OBP	SLG	MLVr	EqAVG	EqOBP	EqSLG	EqA	VORP	DEFENSE			
2005	MEM	AAA	24	500	57	21	2	21	73	63	104	1	3	-3.2	.265	.358	.469	.108	.230	.316	.401	.247	-6.2	99-1B	-4	17-RF	-3
2006	MEM	AAA	25	206	23	11	0	7	31	25	53	1	2	-1.2	.271	.359	.448	.133	.246	.330	.421	.257	0.1	27-RF	-1	14-LF	-6
2006	SLN	MLB	25	314	60	11	3	22	43	30	69	0	0	1.2	.293	.363	.589	.292	.294	.366	.591	.313	24.8	37-LF	-1	16-RF	1
2007	SLN	MLB	26	432	51	20	0	21	70	55	123	2	1	2.9	.259	.354	.480	.108	.263	.363	.503	.292	17.3	84-LF	-4		
2008	SLN	MLB	27	450	59	21	1	21	68	53	107	3	1	-0.2	.261	.351	.479	.059	.259	.351	.497	.283	19.0	107-LF	-3		

Breakout: 20% Improve: 43% Collapse: 19% Attrition: 18%   Comparables: Ryan Klesko, Carlos Peña, Boog Powell, David Ortiz

Duncan's numbers might have looked better had he not gutted out an infected knee in June. After aggravating the problem on May 26, he picked up a double, a homer, and 14 strikeouts against no walks in 28 at-bats over the next three weeks. Once healthy again, he was one of the team's best hitters, going .269/.388/.492 from June 14 until a sports hernia ended his season in September. A big guy who is a bit awkward, Duncan may need to move to the AL and DH to remain a regular, though to his credit, he's improved to "acceptable" in left field.

David Eckstein   SS   Bats: R   Throws: R   Height: 5' 7"   Weight: 175   Born: January 20, 1975   Age: 33

YEAR	TEAM	LVL	AGE	PA	R	2B	3B	HR	RBI	BB	SO	SB	CS	EqBRR	AVG	OBP	SLG	MLVr	EqAVG	EqOBP	EqSLG	EqA	VORP	DEFENSE	
2005	SLN	MLB	30	713	90	26	7	8	61	58	44	11	8	-0.6	.294	.363	.395	.059	.294	.362	.404	.268	32.9	150-SS	7
2006	SLN	MLB	31	552	68	18	1	2	23	31	41	7	6	-2.2	.292	.350	.344	-.067	.299	.355	.349	.250	8.5	117-SS	12
2007	SLN	MLB	32	484	58	23	0	3	31	24	22	10	1	-1.8	.309	.356	.382	.018	.320	.367	.405	.277	20.7	107-SS	-10
2008	TOR	MLB	33	451	49	20	2	3	36	26	32	6	2	-0.2	.274	.326	.352	-.117	.273	.327	.355	.247	4.8	107-SS	-2

Breakout: 3%   Improve: 21%   Collapse: 54%   Attrition: 23%   Comparables: Felix Millan, Roberto Peña, Rey Sanchez, Cookie Rojas

If OBP is life, as we often insist, then why wouldn't we love Eckstein? He has a career mark of .351 and was at .350 or better in all three of his Cardinals seasons. For a shortstop, that's well above average, and if you're hitting .290 and getting plunked 15 times a year, you can get away with walking just once a week or so. Ecksteisn real shortcomings have been durability and range; he missed 45 games last year with back problems, and 39 the year prior with various ailments. A marginal physical talent at his best, he's not good enough to play if he's hurt. He signed a one-year deal with the Blue Jays, who would be best served by making him the fifth infielder and letting John McDonald and his +20 glove start at shortstop.

Jim Edmonds   CF   Bats: L   Throws: L   Height: 6' 1"   Weight: 210   Born: June 27, 1970   Age: 38

YEAR	TEAM	LVL	AGE	PA	R	2B	3B	HR	RBI	BB	SO	SB	CS	EqBRR	AVG	OBP	SLG	MLVr	EqAVG	EqOBP	EqSLG	EqA	VORP	DEFENSE	
2005	SLN	MLB	35	567	88	37	1	29	89	91	139	5	5	0.4	.263	.385	.533	.250	.260	.383	.539	.306	44.2	129-CF	22
2006	SLN	MLB	36	408	52	18	0	19	70	53	101	4	0	-0.1	.257	.350	.471	.079	.256	.352	.471	.285	20.0	90-CF	-3
2007	SLN	MLB	37	411	39	15	2	12	53	41	75	0	2	-1.8	.252	.325	.403	-.053	.256	.334	.421	.261	4.9	94-CF	-6
2008	SDN	MLB	38	250	27	10	1	9	33	28	54	2	1	-0.6	.240	.327	.415	-.081	.247	.334	.444	.264	9.8	62-CF	-4

Breakout: 9%   Improve: 29%   Collapse: 45%   Attrition: 44%   Comparables: Fred Lynn, John Vander Wal, Ken Griffey Sr., Tino Martinez

The 2007 Cardinals were victimized by injuries, some predictable, some not. Edmonds belonged to the first group, as his 37-going-on-50 body continued to break down, taking his productivity with it. Back and leg problems have sapped both his power and his range in center, turning him into a liability. The Padres' plan to play him in center in spacious Petco Park is misguided; Edmonds needs a sinecure, a corner spot in a small outfield that will spare his body, or a DH job that will allow him to rest his weary bones. He's unlikely to play 100 games or crack a .270 EqA as a center fielder.

Juan Encarnacion   RF   Bats: R   Throws: R   Height: 6' 3"   Weight: 215   Born: March 8, 1976   Age: 32

YEAR	TEAM	LVL	AGE	PA	R	2B	3B	HR	RBI	BB	SO	SB	CS	EqBRR	AVG	OBP	SLG	MLVr	EqAVG	EqOBP	EqSLG	EqA	VORP	DEFENSE			
2005	FLO	MLB	29	563	59	27	3	16	76	41	104	6	5	-1.6	.287	.349	.447	.118	.292	.354	.467	.279	21.2	125-RF	-10		
2006	SLN	MLB	30	598	74	25	5	19	79	30	86	6	5	-1.8	.278	.317	.443	.003	.279	.318	.445	.260	8.8	111-RF	5	25-CF	-7
2007	SLN	MLB	31	307	43	17	1	9	47	18	43	2	2	-0.6	.283	.324	.445	.029	.291	.336	.472	.272	5.0	69-RF	-12		
2008	SLN	MLB	32	331	40	15	1	9	45	23	51	4	2	0.0	.275	.328	.428	-.035	.273	.328	.445	.261	8.0	80-RF	-3		

Breakout: 21%   Improve: 46%   Collapse: 31%   Attrition: 30%   Comparables: Bob Kennedy, Larry Herndon, Barry Bonnell, Mike McCormick

In one of the most devastating flukes in baseball history, Encarnacion's season, and possibly his career, came to an end on August 31 in Houston. While the veteran was waiting in the on-deck circle to pinch-hit during the sixth inning of the Cardinals' game against the Reds, he was struck by a foul ball off the bat of Aaron Miles. The impact crushed his left eye socket and damaged his optic nerve, leaving him with severely impaired vision in the eye. Signed through the end of 2008, the well-regarded Encarnacion will attempt a comeback as his vision allows. Here's hoping he succeeds.

Cody Haerther   OF   Bats: L   Throws: R   Height: 6' 1"   Weight: 205   Born: July 14, 1983   Age: 24

YEAR	TEAM	LVL	AGE	PA	R	2B	3B	HR	RBI	BB	SO	SB	CS	EqBRR	AVG	OBP	SLG	MLVr	EqAVG	EqOBP	EqSLG	EqA	VORP	DEFENSE	
2005	PMB	A+	21	192	29	8	7	8	30	17	31	8	3	0.9	.318	.380	.584	.435	.267	.323	.477	.270	4.1	16-LF	0
2005	SFD	AA	21	219	30	10	1	10	37	9	44	0	1	-0.6	.298	.333	.500	.171	.255	.289	.442	.243	-2.9	30-LF	-4
2006	SFD	AA	22	452	56	27	3	11	52	37	59	3	4	-2.7	.277	.336	.437	.047	.241	.294	.382	.232	-17.1	92-LF	-9
2007	SFD	AA	23	162	22	13	0	5	28	16	31	0	0	-0.6	.289	.377	.486	.207	.260	.333	.418	.260	0.1	30-LF	-4
2008	SLN	MLB	24	192	21	9	1	5	23	14	38	2	1	0.1	.257	.315	.400	-.109	.256	.315	.416	.247	1.0	49-LF	-1

Breakout: 18%   Improve: 47%   Collapse: 24%   Attrition: 8%   Comparables: Richard Brown, Tony Longmire, Chris Richard, Jason Grove

A wrist injury that eventually required surgery kept Haerther from patching the Cards' injury-riddled outfield last year. He did come back to play well for Double-A Springfield at the end of the season, sparking hope that he'll regain his prospect status. The lost year put him behind Ankiel on the depth chart, but Haerther's youth, plate discipline, and contact ability make him a better bet in the medium term.

Jarrett Hoffpauir — 2B

Bats: R   Throws: R   Height: 5' 9"   Weight: 165   Born: June 18, 1983   Age: 25

YEAR	TEAM	LVL	AGE	PA	R	2B	3B	HR	RBI	BB	SO	SB	CS	EqBRR	AVG	OBP	SLG	MLVr	EqAVG	EqOBP	EqSLG	EqA	VORP	DEFENSE	
2005	QUD	A	22	256	27	16	1	2	28	21	14	5	1	-1.6	.313	.376	.419	.158	.268	.318	.366	.240	1.9	60-2B	5
2005	PMB	A+	22	265	23	10	1	0	19	32	26	11	5	-2.1	.257	.346	.310	-.035	.220	.299	.267	.209	-13.1	61-2B	-1
2006	SFD	AA	23	460	55	20	1	7	46	54	41	8	6	-1.4	.249	.345	.359	-.066	.242	.323	.341	.237	-1.8	117-2B	-3
2007	SFD	AA	24	236	23	16	0	7	33	26	18	3	1	-2.5	.345	.420	.527	.383	.311	.380	.478	.295	22.2	54-2B	7
2007	MEM	AAA	24	225	27	10	0	4	24	29	21	2	3	-2.7	.300	.394	.416	.134	.269	.363	.378	.262	7.9	40-2B	-2
2008	SLN	MLB	25	486	53	24	1	7	47	46	50	7	3	-0.5	.264	.339	.373	-.096	.263	.339	.388	.254	12.7	115-2B	1

Breakout: 19%   Improve: 48%   Collapse: 21%   Attrition: 13%   Comparables: Keith Luuloa, David Fisher, Joe Lis, Jason Hardtke

A fantastic two months as a Springfield repeater elevated Hoffpauir from organizational soldier to prospect. While comparisons to Eckstein are facile, they also ring true, from their shared lack of size to their college pedigrees to their approaches at the plate. Hoffpauir is unlikely to be able to make the transition to shortstop, however, so his chance for a career comes down to sustaining a .280 average in the majors. If he can do that, it would be enough to make him an average second baseman with his walks and good hands, which would also make him a good value until arbitration hits.

Adam Kennedy — 2B

Bats: L   Throws: R   Height: 6' 1"   Weight: 195   Born: January 10, 1976   Age: 32

YEAR	TEAM	LVL	AGE	PA	R	2B	3B	HR	RBI	BB	SO	SB	CS	EqBRR	AVG	OBP	SLG	MLVr	EqAVG	EqOBP	EqSLG	EqA	VORP	DEFENSE	
2005	LAA	MLB	29	460	49	23	0	2	37	29	64	19	4	-0.8	.300	.354	.370	.006	.312	.374	.390	.276	17.6	123-2B	4
2006	LAA	MLB	30	503	50	26	6	4	55	39	72	16	10	-3.2	.273	.334	.384	-.073	.276	.344	.395	.258	10.9	127-2B	-6
2007	SLN	MLB	31	306	27	9	1	3	18	22	33	6	2	-1.9	.219	.282	.290	-.303	.223	.291	.306	.213	-13.1	71-2B	0
2008	SLN	MLB	32	260	28	10	2	3	23	19	32	7	2	0.1	.254	.313	.344	-.190	.253	.313	.358	.234	2.1	64-2B	0

Breakout: 11%   Improve: 28%   Collapse: 43%   Attrition: 34%   Comparables: Rob Wilfong, Denny Doyle, Chuck Hiller, Ramon Martinez

Playing Hoffpauir would involve recognizing Kennedy as a sunk cost. A remarkably consistent player prior to last year, Kennedy had his worst season at age 31 and is signed for both 2009 and 2010 at a cost of $7.5 million. With a thousand games at second base under his belt and almost all of his value tied up in his bat speed and legs, the sudden decline isn't surprising. While a dead-cat bounce is likely, he's no better than a replacement-level player and a drag on the roster.

Peter Kozma — SS

Bats: R   Throws: R   Height: 6' 0"   Weight: 170   Born: April 11, 1988   Age: 20

YEAR	TEAM	LVL	AGE	PA	R	2B	3B	HR	RBI	BB	SO	SB	CS	EqBRR	AVG	OBP	SLG	MLVr	EqAVG	EqOBP	EqSLG	EqA	VORP	DEFENSE	
2007	JCY	Rk	19	120	16	8	0	2	9	12	21	3	2	-1.4	.264	.350	.396	.092	.198	.258	.288	.187	-14.8	27-SS	-2
2007	BAT	A-	19	28	1	0	1	0	2	1	7	1	1	-0.3	.148	.179	.222	-.465	.148	.179	.222	.111	-8.6		
2008	SLN	MLB	20	543	42	22	3	4	38	33	132	13	6	0.5	.203	.255	.283	-.407	.202	.255	.294	.186	-19.2	128-SS	-5

Breakout: 65%   Improve: 80%   Collapse: 12%   Attrition: 7%   Comparables: Mike Moschetti, Jason Camilli, Andre Montgomery, Ryan Jaroncyk

The Cardinals raised some eyebrows when they selected Kozma with the 18th overall pick last June. Positional scarcity played into the selection, as neither the high school nor college classes offered much in the way of up-the-middle players. Kozma looked pretty good in his pro debut, and that's what he is—pretty good. He's a fine defender with good contact skills, but while he's highly polished for a teenager and could move up quickly, his small frame and lack of any true plus-plus tools or skills will prevent him from being an impact player.

Ryan Ludwick — OF

Bats: R Throws: L Height: 6' 3" Weight: 220 Born: July 13, 1978 Age: 29

YEAR	TEAM	LVL	AGE	PA	R	2B	3B	HR	RBI	BB	SO	SB	CS	EqBRR	AVG	OBP	SLG	MLVr	EqAVG	EqOBP	EqSLG	EqA	VORP	DEFENSE			
2005	BUF	AAA	26	213	27	10	2	4	16	17	48	0	1	-0.3	.191	.272	.330	-.299	.174	.249	.305	.191	-15.6	35-CF	-1	18-RF	-1
2005	CLE	MLB	26	48	8	0	0	4	5	7	13	0	1	-0.5	.220	.333	.512	.103	.225	.354	.525	.285	1.4				
2006	TOL	AAA	27	571	81	34	2	28	80	48	167	2	6	-3.9	.266	.342	.506	.231	.250	.324	.500	.273	15.8	92-RF	2	18-LF	1
2007	MEM	AAA	28	121	27	8	0	8	36	10	20	1	1	-0.3	.340	.380	.642	.498	.308	.352	.589	.308	10.5	21-LF	2		
2007	SLN	MLB	28	339	42	22	0	14	52	26	72	4	4	-3.1	.267	.339	.479	.087	.277	.350	.505	.282	10.9	37-LF	2	29-RF	-2
2008	SLN	MLB	29	375	47	19	1	17	57	34	86	3	2	-0.2	.256	.331	.475	.017	.254	.331	.493	.274	13.4	90-LF	-1		

Breakout: 16% Improve: 43% Collapse: 25% Attrition: 20%   Comparables: Pete Incaviglia, Craig Wilson, Wally Post, Dave Henderson

Save for 2005 when he suffered a broken wrist, Ludwick has never not hit, so it isn't a surprise that when forced into the Cardinals' lineup last year, he was a credible fourth outfielder. As the organization's outfield depth is heavily left-handed, there should be plenty of opportunities for him and his power to help. Bonus: he plays much better defense than most of his competition. He'll lose some batting average, but remain valuable.

Aaron Miles — 2B

Bats: S Throws: R Height: 5' 8" Weight: 185 Born: December 15, 1976 Age: 31

YEAR	TEAM	LVL	AGE	PA	R	2B	3B	HR	RBI	BB	SO	SB	CS	EqBRR	AVG	OBP	SLG	MLVr	EqAVG	EqOBP	EqSLG	EqA	VORP	DEFENSE			
2005	COL	MLB	28	347	37	12	3	2	28	8	38	4	2	3.4	.281	.306	.355	-.138	.271	.298	.345	.225	-2.5	69-2B	7		
2006	SLN	MLB	29	471	48	20	5	2	30	38	42	2	1	0.4	.263	.324	.347	-.129	.261	.326	.341	.238	1.4	73-2B	-4	33-SS	2
2007	SLN	MLB	30	449	55	16	1	2	32	25	40	2	1	2.6	.290	.328	.348	-.098	.298	.340	.363	.250	2.7	67-2B	-10	34-SS	-5
2008	SLN	MLB	31	316	30	10	2	1	25	17	31	4	1	0.3	.265	.307	.321	-.227	.263	.307	.333	.221	-0.2	77-2B	-3		

Breakout: 7% Improve: 24% Collapse: 49% Attrition: 29%   Comparables: Garry Templeton, Jose Vizcaino, Rey Sanchez, Duane Kuiper

One of the Cards' problems last year was having way too many guys like Miles who have just one skill. Miles's skill is hitting for average, but it's an empty average as he doesn't hit for any power and isn't especially patient at the plate. He also can't play shortstop and doesn't have good speed. Miles has to bat .320 to help you; otherwise he's pushing you away from contention.

Yadier Molina — C

Bats: R Throws: R Height: 5' 11" Weight: 220 Born: July 13, 1982 Age: 25

YEAR	TEAM	LVL	AGE	PA	R	2B	3B	HR	RBI	BB	SO	SB	CS	EqBRR	AVG	OBP	SLG	MLVr	EqAVG	EqOBP	EqSLG	EqA	VORP	DEFENSE	
2005	SLN	MLB	22	421	36	15	1	8	49	23	30	2	3	-3.5	.252	.295	.358	-.140	.251	.297	.362	.228	-0.4	108-C	16
2006	SLN	MLB	23	461	29	26	0	6	49	26	41	1	2	-4.2	.216	.274	.321	-.287	.219	.276	.328	.209	-19.7	117-C	14
2007	SLN	MLB	24	396	30	15	0	6	40	34	43	1	1	-2.3	.275	.340	.368	-.056	.281	.349	.375	.257	9.4	97-C	15
2008	SLN	MLB	25	320	29	14	1	5	37	23	32	2	1	-1.0	.263	.322	.371	-.132	.262	.322	.385	.242	6.7	77-C	8

Breakout: 33% Improve: 52% Collapse: 27% Attrition: 34%   Comparables: Michael Barrett, Tom Nieto, Carlos Hernandez, Bruce Benedict

That the NL Gold Glove voters gave last year's catching award to Russell Martin rather than Molina is right up there with the time they awarded Rafael Palmeiro after he'd played just 28 games in the field. The only possible explanation is to acknowledge that the award has nothing to do with defensive performance. Molina is the best defensive catcher in baseball and has an arm that changes the way Cardinals opponents play the game. He should have three Gold Glove awards, and he's still waiting for his first. The voting pool for the award is destroying the credibility of what should be a great honor, and should be drained posthaste.

Albert Pujols — 1B

Bats: R Throws: R Height: 6' 3" Weight: 230 Born: January 16, 1980 Age: 28

YEAR	TEAM	LVL	AGE	PA	R	2B	3B	HR	RBI	BB	SO	SB	CS	EqBRR	AVG	OBP	SLG	MLVr	EqAVG	EqOBP	EqSLG	EqA	VORP	DEFENSE	
2005	SLN	MLB	25	700	129	38	2	41	117	97	65	16	2	3.6	.330	.430	.609	.482	.322	.423	.607	.341	89.0	152-1B	-10
2006	SLN	MLB	26	634	119	33	1	49	137	92	50	7	2	2.5	.331	.431	.671	.548	.328	.431	.668	.354	85.4	140-1B	19
2007	SLN	MLB	27	679	99	38	1	32	103	99	58	2	6	-1.6	.327	.429	.568	.406	.333	.436	.586	.336	72.1	150-1B	23
2008	SLN	MLB	28	662	120	37	2	32	115	94	60	8	2	-0.3	.327	.427	.577	.370	.326	.427	.599	.335	73.1	154-1B	9

Breakout: 11% Improve: 46% Collapse: 16% Attrition: 4%   Comparables: Jeff Bagwell, Albert Belle, Eddie Murray, Orlando Cepeda

Speaking of tarnished awards, Pujols was jobbed out of last year's NL MVP honors. He led the NL in WARP, thanks in part to his Gold Glove-caliber defense at first base. When September dawned, the Cardinals were stronger contenders than the Rockies and right there with the Phillies. Pujols hit .386/.486/.625 that month, as clutch a performance as you'll find. So why wasn't he a candidate in the voters' eyes? Because his teammates played terribly, while those of Matt Holliday and Jimmy Rollins played well. When the Cards were losing 12 of 13, Pujols was trying to carry them, batting .372/.453/.628. He was every bit the September player the other two were, but he didn't have the Phillies' bullpen or the Rockies' defense on his side. That, and not the performance of the players involved, is why Pujols was an afterthought and why the current thinking of the voting pool on the major awards is so flawed as to completely invalidate them.

Colby Rasmus — CF

Bats: L Throws: L Height: 6' 2" Weight: 195 Born: August 11, 1986 Age: 21

YEAR	TEAM	LVL	AGE	PA	R	2B	3B	HR	RBI	BB	SO	SB	CS	EqBRR	AVG	OBP	SLG	MLVr	EqAVG	EqOBP	EqSLG	EqA	VORP	DEFENSE	
2005	JCY	Rk	18	244	47	16	5	7	27	21	73	13	3	3.6	.296	.362	.514	.223	.173	.222	.274	.170	-54.5	58-CF	-1
2006	QUD	A	19	341	49	22	3	11	50	29	55	17	5	0.4	.310	.373	.512	.317	.256	.308	.426	.254	5.5	73-CF	-7
2006	PMB	A+	19	225	22	4	5	5	35	27	35	11	3	-0.6	.254	.351	.404	.114	.222	.307	.364	.239	-3.5	51-CF	-8
2007	SFD	AA	20	556	93	37	3	29	72	70	108	18	3	0.3	.275	.381	.551	.287	.243	.335	.484	.279	27.5	120-CF	-1
2008	SLN	MLB	21	620	80	32	4	21	77	62	130	21	6	1.1	.245	.327	.437	-.049	.244	.327	.454	.266	19.4	145-CF	-1

Breakout: 33% Improve: 70% Collapse: 4% Attrition: 4%   Comparables: Chris Lubanski, Dee Brown, Willie Greene, Carlos Beltran

The shining star of an otherwise dim player development system, Rasmus owned the Texas League last year as a 20-year-old. Credit the Cards for letting him play out the season in Springfield rather than rushing him to the majors as their season spun out of control. He's not a Pujols-caliber hitter—he'll hit .280 rather than .320—but his power has come on like gangbusters and, most importantly, he's a true center fielder. The trade of Edmonds opens center for him less than three years after he was drafted, but he's never played above Double-A, so a bad spring and six weeks at Louisville wouldn't hurt. He projects as Edmonds, but with less defense.

Scott Rolen — 3B

Bats: R Throws: R Height: 6' 4" Weight: 240 Born: April 4, 1975 Age: 33

YEAR	TEAM	LVL	AGE	PA	R	2B	3B	HR	RBI	BB	SO	SB	CS	EqBRR	AVG	OBP	SLG	MLVr	EqAVG	EqOBP	EqSLG	EqA	VORP	DEFENSE	
2005	SLN	MLB	30	223	28	12	1	5	28	25	28	1	2	-1.4	.235	.323	.383	-.070	.236	.327	.395	.249	-0.6	55-3B	11
2006	SLN	MLB	31	594	94	48	1	22	95	56	69	7	4	0.7	.296	.369	.518	.210	.298	.370	.525	.301	36.6	137-3B	21
2007	SLN	MLB	32	441	55	24	2	8	58	37	56	5	3	1.9	.265	.331	.398	-.038	.272	.339	.418	.264	4.1	106-3B	17
2008	TOR	MLB	33	462	55	26	2	13	59	38	67	4	2	0.0	.263	.328	.430	-.017	.261	.329	.435	.268	8.5	109-3B	-1

Breakout: 7% Improve: 38% Collapse: 38% Attrition: 15%   Comparables: Mike Lowell, Matt Williams, Cal Ripken, Kevin Young

Rolen has lost two of the last three seasons to injuries, including shoulder problems that killed his power last year. When healthy, he was on a Hall of Fame career path; now he's a 33-year-old with a bad body and three $12 million years left on his contract. Dealt to Toronto straight up for Troy Glaus, Rolen might have escaped his spat with his manager, but now he'll be playing on turf. He'll be up and down, as his body allows, for the rest of his career, though his defensive stats still look good, which is surprising given his health problems.

Brendan Ryan — SS

Bats: R Throws: R Height: 6' 2" Weight: 195 Born: March 26, 1982 Age: 26

YEAR	TEAM	LVL	AGE	PA	R	2B	3B	HR	RBI	BB	SO	SB	CS	EqBRR	AVG	OBP	SLG	MLVr	EqAVG	EqOBP	EqSLG	EqA	VORP	DEFENSE			
2005	PMB	A+	23	207	29	17	0	1	16	15	20	8	1	1.5	.303	.355	.410	.145	.263	.310	.358	.238	1.5	47-SS	7		
2005	SFD	AA	23	174	28	8	1	2	9	15	19	6	0	1.7	.273	.343	.377	-.007	.237	.302	.340	.231	-1.5	42-SS	1		
2006	SFD	AA	24	47	6	1	0	0	3	3	6	1	1	0.1	.302	.348	.326	-.072	.273	.319	.295	.218	-0.5	10-SS	1		
2006	MEM	AAA	24	27	4	0	0	1	6	1	3	1	0	0.7	.154	.185	.269	-.520	.269	.296	.385	.242	-0.3				
2007	MEM	AAA	25	353	55	9	5	1	15	25	39	17	6	4.8	.272	.328	.341	-.126	.240	.295	.302	.217	-9.4	76-SS	6		
2007	SLN	MLB	25	199	30	9	0	4	12	15	19	7	0	2.1	.289	.347	.406	.017	.294	.355	.411	.275	8.2	19-SS	2	17-3B	4
2008	SLN	MLB	26	512	61	20	3	3	39	35	58	17	5	2.0	.268	.322	.348	-.159	.267	.322	.361	.241	8.4	121-SS	8		

Breakout: 32% Improve: 56% Collapse: 18% Attrition: 14%   Comparables: Stu Cole, Eddie Kasko, Matt Howard, Mark DeRosa

Ryan is a career .264 hitter at Triple-A, a .279 hitter at Double-A, and a .312 hitter at High-A. Given that trend, let's go ahead and assume that last year's major league line was a fluke, the result of six weeks and 120 plate appearances selected from the same bin that guys like Dwayne Hosey once shopped at. Ryan is an adequate replacement for Aaron Miles, but nothing more, no matter how he wears his socks or how dirty his uniform gets.

Skip Schumaker OF

Bats: L   Throws: R   Height: 5' 10"   Weight: 195   Born: February 3, 1980   Age: 28

YEAR	TEAM	LVL	AGE	PA	R	2B	3B	HR	RBI	BB	SO	SB	CS	EqBRR	AVG	OBP	SLG	MLVr	EqAVG	EqOBP	EqSLG	EqA	VORP	DEFENSE			
2005	MEM	AAA	25	487	66	24	3	7	34	29	54	14	3	5.7	.287	.330	.402	-.024	.250	.288	.347	.226	-12.6	107-CF	10		
2006	MEM	AAA	26	403	47	13	3	3	27	23	48	11	4	1.2	.306	.348	.382	.051	.275	.314	.345	.235	-3.5	89-CF	3		
2006	SLN	MLB	26	60	3	1	0	1	2	5	6	2	1	-0.4	.185	.254	.259	-.428	.185	.254	.259	.182	-5.0				
2007	MEM	AAA	27	264	34	16	0	7	31	27	37	2	3	-2.2	.306	.382	.466	.190	.278	.354	.423	.268	11.1	46-CF	-6		
2007	SLN	MLB	27	188	19	12	2	2	19	8	20	1	1	-1.7	.333	.358	.458	.150	.341	.369	.483	.290	10.1	14-LF	-3	13-RF	-2
2008	SLN	MLB	28	383	42	17	2	5	39	25	51	6	2	0.0	.272	.322	.375	-.119	.271	.322	.390	.245	4.6	92-CF	0		

Breakout: 16% Improve: 35% Collapse: 39% Attrition: 28%   Comparables: George Vukovich, Larry Biittner, Jim Holt, Quinn Mack

Like Ankiel and Ludwick, organizational soldier Schumaker was pressed into major league action by injuries to others last year. Like Ryan, he rode a batting-average spike to semi-regular playing time. Like a hundred other guys, he's a marginal fifth outfielder who doesn't do enough to stay in the roster unless he's hitting .330.

Scott Spiezio UT

Bats: S   Throws: R   Height: 6' 2"   Weight: 215   Born: September 21, 1972   Age: 35

YEAR	TEAM	LVL	AGE	PA	R	2B	3B	HR	RBI	BB	SO	SB	CS	EqBRR	AVG	OBP	SLG	MLVr	EqAVG	EqOBP	EqSLG	EqA	VORP	DEFENSE			
2005	SEA	MLB	32	51	2	1	0	1	1	4	18	0	0	0.0	.064	.137	.149	-.816	.087	.176	.174	.038	-8.6				
2006	SLN	MLB	33	321	44	15	4	13	52	37	66	1	0	0.4	.272	.366	.496	.151	.275	.369	.500	.296	16.3	25-LF	-3	23-3B	0
2007	SLN	MLB	34	257	31	14	0	4	31	27	40	0	1	-2.7	.269	.354	.386	-.011	.275	.362	.396	.268	3.4	21-3B	2	12-RF	-3
2008	SLN	MLB	35	235	28	11	1	6	29	24	40	1	1	-0.4	.259	.340	.413	-.046	.258	.340	.429	.264	7.1	59-DH			

Breakout: 12% Improve: 39% Collapse: 39% Attrition: 43%   Comparables: J. T. Snow, Richie Hebner, Charlie Hayes, Eduardo Perez

Twenty-three years ago, Commissioner Peter Ueberroth tried to run players caught up in a cocaine scandal out of the game, and the sordid tales that emerged from that era were considered one of the game's darkest moments. Today, with the focus on performance-enhancing drugs, a player can quietly excuse himself to enter rehab for a month, as Spiezio did toward the end of last year, without bringing fire and brimstone down upon his head. He'll be a valuable four-corners bench player again in this year.

So Taguchi OF

Bats: R   Throws: R   Height: 5' 10"   Weight: 170   Born: July 2, 1969   Age: 38

YEAR	TEAM	LVL	AGE	PA	R	2B	3B	HR	RBI	BB	SO	SB	CS	EqBRR	AVG	OBP	SLG	MLVr	EqAVG	EqOBP	EqSLG	EqA	VORP	DEFENSE			
2005	SLN	MLB	35	424	45	21	2	8	53	20	62	11	2	3.0	.288	.322	.412	.010	.286	.323	.415	.259	9.8	36-RF	1	31-LF	0
2006	SLN	MLB	36	361	46	19	1	2	31	32	48	11	3	2.6	.266	.335	.351	-.100	.270	.342	.351	.251	0.2	41-LF	3	40-CF	-5
2007	SLN	MLB	37	340	48	15	0	3	30	23	32	7	4	-1.2	.290	.350	.368	-.029	.303	.364	.384	.262	5.5	43-CF	-2	24-LF	0
2008	PHI	MLB	38	181	22	8	1	2	17	14	21	5	1	0.2	.273	.335	.364	-.111	.269	.332	.357	.244	1.5	46-CF	-5		

Breakout: 12% Improve: 29% Collapse: 43% Attrition: 40%   Comparables: Lee Lacy, Eric Young, Willie McGee, Hank Bauer

Taguchi has lost enough steps in the outfield to make him a marginal bench player. He can no longer play a credible center field, and you'd like your extra corner men to have either more pop or more speed than he does. Released in December, Taguchi was signed by the Phillies, who will use him as a defensive replacement for Pat Burrell and an off-day center fielder for Shane Victorino. They could have done better.

PITCHERS

Chris Carpenter

Bats: R   Throws: R   Height: 6' 6"   Weight: 230   Born: April 27, 1975   Age: 33

YEAR	TEAM	LVL	AGE	W	L	SV	G	GS	IP	H	BB	SO	HR	GB%	BABIP	STUFF	WHIP	ERA	PERA	EqERA	EqH9	EqBB9	EqSO9	EqHR9	VORP	SN/WX
2005	SLN	MLB	30	21	5	0	33	33	241²	204	51	213	18	55.3%	.285	33	1.06	2.83	3.28	3.44	8.0	1.8	7.4	0.7	67.8	8.56
2006	SLN	MLB	31	15	8	0	32	32	221²	194	43	184	21	55.2%	.278	29	1.07	3.09	3.21	3.22	7.7	1.5	6.9	0.8	67.8	7.35
2008	SLN	MLB	33	5	4	0	20	13	84¹	83	22	63	7	52.1%	.294	12	1.24	3.55	3.86	3.93	8.7	2.1	6.2	0.7	20.1	2.20

Breakout: 10% Improve: 29% Collapse: 43% Attrition: 35%   Comparables: Tex Hughson, Orel Hershiser, Andy Pettitte, Tommy John

Hey, here's an idea: don't give a pitcher with a sketchy health record what amounts to a three-year contract extension for $50 million that doesn't kick in for two more years. Leapin' lizards, there's 400 innings to be navigated! Giving Carpenter's a five-year contract was a ridiculous idea in December 2006, and looked worse when the righty blew out his elbow just six innings into it. He didn't have Tommy John surgery until July and will miss most of the 2008 season. The contract leaves the Cardinals spending tens of millions of dollars they would not have had to spend if they had just waited.

Randy Flores

| | | | | Bats: L | | Throws: L | | Height: 6' 0" | | Weight: 190 | | Born: July 31, 1975 | | | Age: 32 |

YEAR	TEAM	LVL	AGE	W	L	SV	G	GS	IP	H	BB	SO	HR	GB%	BABIP	STUFF	WHIP	ERA	PERA	EqERA	EqH9	EqBB9	EqSO9	EqHR9	VORP	SN/WX
2005	SLN	MLB	29	3	1	1	50	0	41²	37	13	43	5	41.7%	.302	10	1.20	3.45	4.16	4.87	8.4	2.7	8.6	1.1	3.3	0.70
2006	SLN	MLB	30	1	1	0	65	0	41²	49	22	40	5	41.4%	.355	-5	1.70	5.61	5.76	6.17	10.4	4.0	7.7	0.9	-1.0	1.07
2007	SLN	MLB	31	3	0	1	70	0	55	71	15	47	2	44.7%	.383	11	1.56	4.25	4.76	4.79	11.0	2.1	7.0	0.3	5.0	-0.48
2008	SLN	MLB	32	2	2	3	48	0	45¹	47	16	34	4	45.4%	.306	-1	1.39	4.22	4.50	4.65	9.2	2.9	6.3	0.8	5.2	0.50

Breakout: 31% Improve: 58% Collapse: 16% Attrition: 31%   Comparables: Arnold Earley, Tom Hilgendorf, Mike Muñoz, Buddy Groom

The overall stat lines for relief pitchers in the era of specialization don't mean much. Here are the important numbers for Flores, one of the Cards' two LOOGYs: .385 OBP allowed to lefties (mostly because he struck out just 14 percent of them) and .343 OBP by the first batter he faced. Oh, and he allowed a whopping 19 of 34 inherited runners to score. He had a lousy year, much worse than his ERA and ratios indicate. He's just not dominant enough to be a specialist.

Ryan Franklin

| | | | | Bats: R | | Throws: R | | Height: 6' 3" | | Weight: 190 | | Born: March 5, 1973 | | | Age: 35 |

YEAR	TEAM	LVL	AGE	W	L	SV	G	GS	IP	H	BB	SO	HR	GB%	BABIP	STUFF	WHIP	ERA	PERA	EqERA	EqH9	EqBB9	EqSO9	EqHR9	VORP	SN/WX
2005	SEA	MLB	32	8	15	0	32	30	190²	212	62	93	28	42.1%	.289	-10	1.44	5.10	5.42	5.30	9.9	2.9	4.3	1.3	11.5	2.90
2006	PHI	MLB	33	1	5	0	46	0	53	59	17	25	10	48.1%	.278	-22	1.43	4.58	4.98	4.02	9.1	2.5	3.9	1.5	7.9	0.10
2006	CIN	MLB	33	5	2	0	20	0	24¹	27	17	18	3	48.7%	.343	-7	1.81	4.81	6.06	5.01	10.0	5.8	6.2	1.2	1.5	-0.36
2007	SLN	MLB	34	4	4	1	69	0	80	70	11	44	8	49.4%	.251	2	1.01	3.04	2.99	2.81	7.4	1.0	4.6	0.8	24.3	3.01
2008	SLN	MLB	35	3	3	2	48	0	58¹	65	17	31	7	46.1%	.293	-12	1.39	4.35	4.77	4.78	9.7	2.4	4.4	1.0	5.8	0.50

Breakout: 10% Improve: 31% Collapse: 43% Attrition: 39%   Comparables: Eddie Fisher, Rick White, Jim Konstanty, Dan Osinski

An industry that gives a player once suspended for performance-enhancing drug use a two-year, $10 million contract while at the same time sinking $30 million into a study designed to investigate the severity of such abuse among players has enough issues to keep a team of psychoanalysts in business for decades. Franklin was helped last year by an extremely low opponent's batting average on balls in play (.249), although he also posted career-low walk and home run rates. This year, his ERA should jump by a run, maybe more.

Jaime Garcia

| | | | | Bats: L | | Throws: L | | Height: 6' 1" | | Weight: 200 | | Born: July 8, 1986 | | | Age: 21 |

YEAR	TEAM	LVL	AGE	W	L	SV	G	GS	IP	H	BB	SO	HR	GB%	BABIP	STUFF	WHIP	ERA	PERA	EqERA	EqH9	EqBB9	EqSO9	EqHR9	VORP	SN/WX
2006	QUD	A	19	5	4	0	13	13	77²	67	18	80	1	64.1%	.313	22	1.10	2.91	5.33	5.80	10.3	4.2	5.1	0.5	-1.5	—
2006	PMB	A+	19	5	4	0	12	12	77¹	84	16	51	3	60.8%	.337	3	1.30	3.85	6.02	5.93	11.7	3.3	3.3	0.9	-2.5	—
2007	SFD	AA	20	5	9	0	18	18	103¹	93	45	97	14	59.3%	.295	-2	1.34	3.75	6.19	5.57	9.4	4.9	5.9	1.8	0.3	—
2008	SLN	MLB	21	7	9	0	31	21	130²	142	64	87	14	55.1%	.309	3	1.57	4.82	5.41	5.32	9.5	4.0	5.6	0.9	5.7	1.50

Breakout: 32% Improve: 59% Collapse: 19% Attrition: 14%   Comparables: Mike Hampton, Jimmy Anderson, Alberto Blanco, Odalis Perez

Teams are still wondering how Garcia slipped to the 22nd round of the 2005 draft, because he's become the top starting-pitching prospect in the Cardinals organization. He has a monster curveball and a very good sinker. He also has a weird combination of a better-than-two-to-one groundball-to-flyball ratio and a problem with the long ball. Elbow problems shut him down for the second half of the season, but he didn't need surgery and is expected to be at full strength for 2008.

Jason Isringhausen

| | | | | | | | | Bats: R | | Throws: R | | Height: 6' 3" | | Weight: 230 | | Born: September 7, 1972 | | | Age: 35 |

YEAR	TEAM	LVL	AGE	W	L	SV	G	GS	IP	H	BB	SO	HR	GB%	BABIP	STUFF	WHIP	ERA	PERA	EqERA	EqH9	EqBB9	EqSO9	EqHR9	VORP	SN/WX
2005	SLN	MLB	32	1	2	39	63	0	59	43	27	51	4	52.4%	.247	10	1.19	2.14	3.13	2.30	6.8	3.7	7.1	0.6	22.0	3.72
2006	SLN	MLB	33	4	8	33	59	0	58¹	47	38	52	10	44.5%	.247	-2	1.46	3.55	4.41	3.39	7.3	5.1	7.3	1.4	14.1	1.06
2007	SLN	MLB	34	4	0	32	63	0	65¹	42	28	54	4	46.4%	.215	13	1.07	2.48	2.46	2.67	5.3	3.2	6.7	0.5	21.7	4.20
2008	SLN	MLB	35	3	4	21	46	0	52¹	48	26	39	5	46.5%	.277	-5	1.43	4.05	4.46	4.46	8.1	4.2	6.3	0.9	6.8	1.00

Breakout: 4%   Improve: 8%   Collapse: 80%   Attrition: 19%   Comparables: Don McMahon, Turk Lown, Jim Gott, Dan Miceli

Isringhausen got his command back after a tough 2006 that was worse than his ERA suggested. The degenerative hip problem that messed up his mechanics that season was fixed by surgery, allowing him to once again get on top of his pitches, especially his good curve. His numbers last year were helped along by an unusually low .213 BABIP, which was even lower than his typical .240s figure. Izzy's stuff isn't dominant, and he's at the point at which he'll probably have an ERA under 3.00 or over 5.00, but never in-between. As with Rolen, he's most valuable to the Cards as a trade chip.

Tyler Johnson

| | | | | | | | | Bats: S | | Throws: L | | Height: 6' 2" | | Weight: 180 | | Born: June 7, 1981 | | | Age: 27 |

YEAR	TEAM	LVL	AGE	W	L	SV	G	GS	IP	H	BB	SO	HR	GB%	BABIP	STUFF	WHIP	ERA	PERA	EqERA	EqH9	EqBB9	EqSO9	EqHR9	VORP	SN/WX
2005	MEM	AAA	24	2	1	7	57	0	59	51	26	77	6	45.1%	.328	5	1.31	4.27	4.78	5.17	8.6	4.4	8.7	1.1	2.7	—
2006	SLN	MLB	25	2	4	0	56	0	36¹	33	23	37	5	41.0%	.301	5	1.54	4.96	5.00	4.75	8.2	5.0	8.5	1.0	3.3	0.07
2007	SLN	MLB	26	1	1	0	55	0	38	31	16	24	4	41.3%	.235	-6	1.24	4.03	3.24	3.66	6.6	3.2	5.3	0.9	6.9	0.26
2008	SLN	MLB	27	2	2	2	50	0	43²	41	20	33	5	42.5%	.277	-2	1.40	3.99	4.36	4.39	8.1	3.9	6.3	0.9	6.8	0.60

Breakout: 19%   Improve: 44%   Collapse: 34%   Attrition: 26%   Comparables: Mike Stanton, Drew Hall, Pete Filson, Al Osuna

It can sometimes be hard to discern the roles Tony La Russa has assigned his relievers, but it seemed clear which of his two lefties he valued more highly last year. Flores made just 27 of his 70 appearances (39 percent) with the Cards trailing. Johnson, however, came into 33 of 55 games (60 percent) with his team behind. Johnson is more a true specialist due to his big-breaking curve and tough arm angle. He struck out 19 percent of the lefty batters he faced last year and 23 percent of them on his career.

Braden Looper

| | | | | | | | | Bats: R | | Throws: R | | Height: 6' 3" | | Weight: 235 | | Born: October 28, 1974 | | | Age: 33 |

YEAR	TEAM	LVL	AGE	W	L	SV	G	GS	IP	H	BB	SO	HR	GB%	BABIP	STUFF	WHIP	ERA	PERA	EqERA	EqH9	EqBB9	EqSO9	EqHR9	VORP	SN/WX
2005	NYN	MLB	30	4	7	28	60	0	59¹	65	22	27	7	54.4%	.282	-21	1.47	3.95	4.99	4.75	9.6	3.0	3.6	1.0	4.8	-0.21
2006	SLN	MLB	31	9	3	0	69	0	73¹	76	20	41	3	52.2%	.317	3	1.31	3.56	3.76	3.77	9.3	2.1	4.8	0.4	19.1	1.59
2007	SLN	MLB	32	12	12	0	31	30	175	183	51	87	22	44.4%	.281	-1	1.34	4.94	4.24	4.62	8.9	2.2	4.2	1.0	14.8	3.74
2008	SLN	MLB	33	5	7	0	32	14	98²	112	30	47	12	46.8%	.296	-10	1.43	4.82	5.13	5.29	9.9	2.5	4.0	1.1	5.0	1.00

Breakout: 5%   Improve: 24%   Collapse: 53%   Attrition: 28%   Comparables: Brett Tomko, Walt Terrell, Aaron Sele, Dock Ellis

The experiment with starting Looper last year was a success, as he stayed in the rotation most of the season and was a league-average starter. One key was his relative effectiveness against lefty batters, who usually tattoo him but managed just a .326 OBP against him last year. Eighteen of Looper's 30 starts were quality starts, although he tired late in the season, posting a 8.14 ERA in his last four. The decreases in his groundball and strikeout rates, however, are warning signs of a coming problem.

Mike Maroth

| | | | | | | | | Bats: L | | Throws: L | | Height: 6' 0" | | Weight: 190 | | Born: August 17, 1977 | | | Age: 30 |

YEAR	TEAM	LVL	AGE	W	L	SV	G	GS	IP	H	BB	SO	HR	GB%	BABIP	STUFF	WHIP	ERA	PERA	EqERA	EqH9	EqBB9	EqSO9	EqHR9	VORP	SN/WX
2005	DET	MLB	27	14	14	0	34	34	209	235	51	115	30	47.6%	.306	-3	1.37	4.74	5.27	5.30	10.1	2.2	4.9	1.2	10.0	1.97
2006	DET	MLB	28	5	2	0	13	9	53²	64	16	24	11	42.0%	.291	-20	1.49	4.19	6.65	4.67	10.7	2.6	3.8	1.7	10.0	1.44
2007	DET	MLB	29	5	2	0	13	13	78¹	97	33	28	15	44.7%	.314	-32	1.66	5.06	8.04	5.86	11.4	3.5	3.2	1.8	5.0	0.55
2007	SLN	MLB	29	0	5	0	14	7	38	71	17	23	11	43.5%	.411	-68	2.32	10.66	17.39	16.25	15.8	3.2	5.0	2.3	-31.1	-0.89
2008	SLN	MLB	30	3	4	0	27	7	59	71	21	31	8	45.2%	.309	-12	1.54	5.15	5.74	5.59	10.5	2.9	4.5	1.2	1.1	0.40

Breakout: 36%   Improve: 61%   Collapse: 16%   Attrition: 43%   Comparables: Curt Young, Neal Heaton, Wayne Garland, Joe Mays

Last season, the Cardinals traded for, claimed, or signed Todd Wellemeyer, Troy Percival, Tomo Ohka, Joel Pineiro, and Maroth. If you knew nothing else about their season, you would still be able to diagnose precisely what the problem was. Percival and Pineiro sort of worked out, but the Cards lost 12 of the 14 games in which Maroth pitched. He just didn't have enough stuff to survive his first major injury, and is likely done as a relevant pitcher.

Clayton Mortensen

Bats: R   Throws: R   Height: 6' 4"   Weight: 180   Born: April 10, 1985   Age: 23

YEAR	TEAM	LVL	AGE	W	L	SV	G	GS	IP	H	BB	SO	HR	GB%	BABIP	STUFF	WHIP	ERA	PERA	EqERA	EqH9	EqBB9	EqSO9	EqHR9	VORP	SN/WX
2007	QUD	A	22	0	2	0	10	10	40¹	44	8	45	2	62.6%	.372	-17	1.29	3.13	9.01	7.83	14.3	4.3	5.7	1.4	-8.3	—
2007	BAT	A-	22	1	1	0	6	4	20¹	13	11	23	0	74.5%	.283	8	1.18	1.77	4.99	3.63	7.3	7.8	5.7	0.5	3.8	—
2008	SLN	MLB	23	5	8	0	27	18	106²	124	62	65	9	59.0%	.325	-5	1.74	5.37	5.99	5.98	10.2	4.8	5.1	0.7	-2.8	0.40

Breakout: 26% Improve: 59% Collapse: 18% Attrition: 15%   Comparables: Jeffrey Marquez, Lance Broadway, Joshua Sullivan, Chris Ray

Few college pitchers saw their stock rise faster last spring than Mortensen, whose sinker seems to defy physics at times. That's not to say that it travels backward in time (some guy in Korea has that pitch), but that its drop is amazingly hard. He continued to dazzle in his professional debut posting a GB/FB rate better than 3-to-1 while also striking out more than a batter per inning. The only caveat is that he spent a full four years in college, so he opens the season as a 23-year-old with limited experience, but solid upside.

Mark Mulder

Bats: L   Throws: L   Height: 6' 6"   Weight: 215   Born: August 5, 1977   Age: 30

YEAR	TEAM	LVL	AGE	W	L	SV	G	GS	IP	H	BB	SO	HR	GB%	BABIP	STUFF	WHIP	ERA	PERA	EqERA	EqH9	EqBB9	EqSO9	EqHR9	VORP	SN/WX
2005	SLN	MLB	27	16	8	0	32	32	205	212	70	111	19	61.1%	.299	4	1.38	3.64	4.85	4.43	9.8	2.9	4.6	0.8	37.0	5.30
2006	SLN	MLB	28	6	7	0	17	17	93¹	124	35	50	19	56.8%	.339	-28	1.70	7.14	8.11	7.95	12.0	2.9	4.5	1.7	-14.9	0.22
2007	SLN	MLB	29	0	3	0	3	3	11	22	7	3	4	35.4%	.419	-88	2.64	12.27	24.61	20.03	18.3	5.2	2.6	3.5	-9.6	-0.61
2008	SLN	MLB	30	2	4	0	20	7	53¹	67	22	27	7	50.3%	.322	-15	1.66	5.71	6.17	6.26	10.9	3.4	4.3	1.1	-3.4	0.00

Breakout: 31% Improve: 54% Collapse: 19% Attrition: 52%   Comparables: Stan Williams, Bill Laskey, Rob Bell, Mike Harkey

The Cardinals should be ashamed of themselves for putting Mulder on the mound last year when he had no business anywhere near one. Mulder faced 59 batters and struck out three of them, and he hasn't seen a fifth inning since June 15, 2006, which was only seven starts ago. He needed additional surgery on his shoulder in September, but it was less extensive than the operation on his rotator cuff a year earlier. He is expected to be healthy for spring training, but even when healthy, he was declining, so there's not much here.

Troy Percival

Bats: R   Throws: R   Height: 6' 3"   Weight: 240   Born: August 9, 1969   Age: 38

YEAR	TEAM	LVL	AGE	W	L	SV	G	GS	IP	H	BB	SO	HR	GB%	BABIP	STUFF	WHIP	ERA	PERA	EqERA	EqH9	EqBB9	EqSO9	EqHR9	VORP	SN/WX
2005	DET	MLB	35	1	3	8	26	0	25	19	11	20	7	28.4%	.185	-12	1.20	5.76	4.54	5.26	6.3	3.9	6.7	2.1	-0.2	-0.73
2007	SLN	MLB	37	3	0	0	34	1	40	24	10	36	3	33.7%	.208	21	0.85	1.80	2.22	1.82	5.2	1.8	7.5	0.7	18.2	1.29
2008	TBA	MLB	38	2	2	3	41	0	47²	44	17	42	7	35.5%	.272	1	1.28	4.06	4.02	3.73	8.0	3.0	7.1	1.3	7.5	0.70

Breakout: 4% Improve: 22% Collapse: 67% Attrition: 22%   Comparables: Don McMahon, Lee Smith, Russ Springer, Trevor Hoffman

There's a lesson here for Mark Prior, Rich Harden, and so many other pitchers who spend their lives bouncing from the DL to rehab assignments and back. Sometimes just taking a year off allows the arm to heal. Percival hadn't thrown a pitch in anger since July of 2005, but came out of retirement in June to pitch well in very low-leverage relief (18 of his 34 appearances came with the Cards leading or trailing by more than four runs). The Rays signed him to a two-year contract for a base of $8 million and a raft of incentives. He's not 1.80-ERA good, but he doesn't have to be at that price.

Chris Perez

Bats: R   Throws: R   Height: 6' 4"   Weight: 225   Born: July 1, 1985   Age: 23

YEAR	TEAM	LVL	AGE	W	L	SV	G	GS	IP	H	BB	SO	HR	GB%	BABIP	STUFF	WHIP	ERA	PERA	EqERA	EqH9	EqBB9	EqSO9	EqHR9	VORP	SN/WX
2006	QUD	A	22	2	0	12	25	0	29	20	19	32	0	53.4%	.296	7	1.34	1.86	6.30	5.25	8.6	10.5	5.6	0.4	0.9	—
2007	SFD	AA	23	2	0	27	39	0	40²	17	28	62	3	29.7%	.200	31	1.11	2.43	3.96	3.26	4.7	7.2	10.0	0.9	10.1	—
2007	MEM	AAA	23	0	1	8	15	0	14	6	13	15	2	58.6%	.160	13	1.36	4.50	4.27	4.26	4.3	9.2	7.8	1.4	1.9	—
2008	SLN	MLB	22	3	4	5	23	7	56²	33	62	70	4	41.9%	.238	14	1.68	3.97	4.69	4.34	5.1	9.1	10.3	0.6	7.7	1.10

Breakout: 11% Improve: 22% Collapse: 47% Attrition: 17%   Comparables: Russ Ortiz, Mitch Williams, Kevin Whelan, Brian Bruney

In his first full season, Perez staked his claim to the Cardinals' closer job after Izzy's contract is up at the end of the 2008 season. With a good spring training, he might end up with a big-league apprenticeship this year. Perez's stuff is classic closer: a mid-90s fastball and a slider that is among the best in the minor leagues. Of course, he has some control problems. The good news is that, when you limit opposing hitters to a .130 average, as Perez did last year, a few walks here and there don't matter much.

Joel Pineiro

Bats: R   Throws: R   Height: 6' 1"   Weight: 200   Born: September 25, 1978   Age: 29

YEAR	TEAM	LVL	AGE	W	L	SV	G	GS	IP	H	BB	SO	HR	GB%	BABIP	STUFF	WHIP	ERA	PERA	EqERA	EqH9	EqBB9	EqSO9	EqHR9	VORP	SN/WX
2005	SEA	MLB	26	7	11	0	30	30	189	224	56	107	23	46.0%	.326	-2	1.48	5.62	5.77	5.96	10.8	2.7	5.1	1.1	2.3	1.42
2006	SEA	MLB	27	8	13	1	40	25	165²	209	64	87	23	48.3%	.331	-17	1.65	6.35	6.38	6.65	11.0	3.3	4.5	1.2	-14.4	0.63
2007	BOS	MLB	28	1	1	0	31	0	34	41	14	20	3	54.9%	.325	-15	1.62	5.03	5.43	5.24	10.7	3.1	4.7	0.8	3.0	-0.36
2007	SLN	MLB	28	6	4	0	11	11	63²	69	12	40	11	47.8%	.296	3	1.27	3.96	4.97	3.79	9.6	1.5	5.5	1.5	12.7	1.68
2008	SLN	MLB	29	4	5	1	32	10	82¹	90	25	49	10	49.0%	.297	-3	1.39	4.35	4.76	4.79	9.5	2.5	5.0	1.0	9.5	1.20

Breakout: 36% Improve: 61% Collapse: 20% Attrition: 32%   Comparables: Dick Drago, Dennis Martinez, Art Ditmar, Jim McGlothlin

This doesn't end well. Pineiro was picked up after the Sox designated him for assignment in July, and he immediately turned into Curt Schilling, walking 12 men and allowing 11 homers in 11 starts for the Cards. The team, in turn, signed him to a two-year deal. Again, Pineiro was literally free talent four months prior, and based on 63 2/3 innings of pitching unlike anything he'd done in years, the Cards handed over $13 million. When the control reverts, so does the ERA. Hijinks ensue.

Anthony Reyes

Bats: R   Throws: R   Height: 6' 2"   Weight: 230   Born: October 16, 1981   Age: 26

YEAR	TEAM	LVL	AGE	W	L	SV	G	GS	IP	H	BB	SO	HR	GB%	BABIP	STUFF	WHIP	ERA	PERA	EqERA	EqH9	EqBB9	EqSO9	EqHR9	VORP	SN/WX
2005	MEM	AAA	23	7	6	0	23	23	128²	105	34	136	13	36.3%	.283	15	1.08	3.64	3.89	4.22	7.6	2.7	7.0	1.1	18.7	—
2005	SLN	MLB	23	1	1	0	4	1	13¹	6	4	12	2	37.1%	.129	14	0.75	2.71	2.27	2.63	4.0	2.6	7.2	1.3	4.2	0.28
2006	MEM	AAA	24	6	1	0	13	13	84	70	11	82	9	42.0%	.270	14	0.96	2.57	3.82	3.51	7.9	1.5	6.4	1.3	19.0	—
2006	SLN	MLB	24	5	8	0	17	17	85¹	84	34	72	17	37.0%	.289	-1	1.38	5.06	5.28	4.80	8.9	3.1	7.0	1.6	9.8	1.92
2007	MEM	AAA	25	1	1	0	6	6	38²	27	11	33	4	46.1%	.245	14	0.98	2.79	3.43	2.97	6.4	3.0	6.2	1.2	10.6	—
2007	SLN	MLB	25	2	14	0	22	20	107¹	108	43	74	16	36.2%	.284	-3	1.41	6.04	4.65	5.80	8.6	3.1	5.7	1.2	-6.9	0.41
2008	SLN	MLB	26	6	7	0	30	17	114²	111	42	83	15	39.3%	.277	7	1.33	4.32	4.60	4.69	8.5	3.0	6.1	1.1	13.3	2.00

Breakout: 21% Improve: 51% Collapse: 25% Attrition: 19%   Comparables: Eric Gagné, Paul Moskau, Rick Helling, Steve Renko

Assigning wins and losses to pitchers is an archaic practice. What makes it problematic is that the people making decisions for $200 million businesses used said archaic practice to guide them. Reyes opened last year with seven starts in which he went five or six innings and allowed four or fewer runs, work for which he was assigned a record of 0-6. His ERA of 5.08 was actually good for a fifth starter, but the Cards had scored eight runs total in those seven games, and Walter Johnson wouldn't have been better than 3-4 with that support. With the pressure of "oh-and" rising, Reyes struggled in his next two outings and was sent to Memphis so that retread Todd Wellemeyer could start for a while. Reyes returned for two bad starts and one good one when Looper got hurt in June, dropping to 0-10 in a rain-shortened game in which he threw five good innings and his teammates got shut out for the fifth time in his 12 starts; he was again demoted. Wellemeyer watched his new teammates score 48 runs in his first six starts, and won every one. Reyes returned in July and was okay over seven starts (4.25 ERA, 25/12 K/BB, 2-3), but a sore shoulder limited him down the stretch. When healthy, Reyes is a command guy with third-starter stuff, same as he was a year ago. The only reason he was demoted was the Cards' offensive incompetence and the front office's inability to separate his work from his teammates' work. In the 21st century, with all of the information available, this kind of thing shouldn't happen.

Russ Springer

Bats: R   Throws: R   Height: 6' 4"   Weight: 225   Born: November 7, 1968   Age: 39

YEAR	TEAM	LVL	AGE	W	L	SV	G	GS	IP	H	BB	SO	HR	GB%	BABIP	STUFF	WHIP	ERA	PERA	EqERA	EqH9	EqBB9	EqSO9	EqHR9	VORP	SN/WX
2005	HOU	MLB	36	4	4	0	62	0	59	49	21	54	9	40.5%	.253	-1	1.19	4.73	4.09	5.09	7.7	2.9	7.6	1.4	1.9	0.76
2006	HOU	MLB	37	1	1	0	72	0	59²	46	16	46	10	28.7%	.222	0	1.04	3.47	3.36	3.02	6.8	2.1	6.3	1.4	17.0	0.62
2007	SLN	MLB	38	8	1	0	76	0	66	41	19	66	3	32.0%	.242	28	0.91	2.18	2.26	2.44	5.3	2.2	8.3	0.4	25.1	2.17
2008	SLN	MLB	39	3	2	4	50	0	54¹	49	17	45	6	36.4%	.274	4	1.20	3.60	3.71	3.93	7.8	2.6	6.9	0.9	10.4	1.00

Breakout: 8% Improve: 20% Collapse: 48% Attrition: 25%   Comparables: Don McMahon, Trevor Hoffman, Al Worthington, Lee Smith

Almost all of the Cardinals' relievers had extremely low BABIPs last year, which was a big reason for the pen's success, or rather, defense and good luck were the reasons. Springer allowed just three homers despite a 0.6 GB/FB ratio, which helped, but he won't do that again. Last year's Cardinals staff was lousy with pitchers who just had everything break their way for a year, and the team still won only 79 games; that, more than any other reason, is why the Cardinals will be a fourth-place team in 2008.

Brad Thompson

													Bats: R		Throws: R		Height: 6' 1"		Weight: 190		Born: January 31, 1982		Age: 26

YEAR	TEAM	LVL	AGE	W	L	SV	G	GS	IP	H	BB	SO	HR	GB%	BABIP	STUFF	WHIP	ERA	PERA	EqERA	EqH9	EqBB9	EqSO9	EqHR9	VORP	SN/WX
2005	SLN	MLB	23	4	0	1	40	0	55	46	15	29	5	59.7%	.243	-5	1.11	2.95	3.45	3.83	7.7	2.2	4.3	0.8	11.5	1.59
2006	MEM	AAA	24	2	0	0	14	5	42¹	36	6	33	3	60.8%	.282	4	1.00	2.14	3.69	3.12	8.0	1.6	5.1	0.9	11.1	—
2006	SLN	MLB	24	1	2	0	43	1	56²	58	20	32	4	56.9%	.298	-4	1.38	3.33	4.21	3.56	9.2	2.7	4.7	0.6	15.0	0.72
2007	SLN	MLB	25	8	6	0	44	17	129¹	157	40	53	23	50.8%	.301	-28	1.52	4.73	6.34	5.05	10.5	2.4	3.6	1.5	9.0	2.24
2008	SLN	MLB	26	3	4	1	32	6	65¹	72	20	29	7	51.1%	.290	-11	1.41	4.29	4.87	4.73	9.7	2.5	3.8	1.0	8.0	0.90

Breakout: 17% Improve: 34% Collapse: 42% Attrition: 38%   Comparables: Johnny Kucks, Tom Murphy, Jimmy Jones, Ray Crone

Strikeout rate is more consistent from year to year than ERA, and thus a better indicator of future performance, because it's a better indicator of the quality of a pitcher's pitches. Thompson's 5.1 K/9 in 2006 was a flashing red light that his ERA would be rising sharply, which is exactly what it did. Throw in a lack of command and an unusually low home run rate bound to regress, and Thompson's 2007 season was as predictable as they come. He's a fringe swingman.

Adam Wainwright

													Bats: R		Throws: R		Height: 6' 7"		Weight: 230		Born: August 30, 1981		Age: 26

YEAR	TEAM	LVL	AGE	W	L	SV	G	GS	IP	H	BB	SO	HR	GB%	BABIP	STUFF	WHIP	ERA	PERA	EqERA	EqH9	EqBB9	EqSO9	EqHR9	VORP	SN/WX
2005	MEM	AAA	23	10	10	0	29	29	182	204	51	147	18	46.8%	.333	0	1.40	4.40	5.35	5.35	10.3	2.9	5.1	1.1	4.8	—
2006	SLN	MLB	24	2	1	3	61	0	75	64	22	72	6	49.8%	.290	20	1.15	3.12	3.27	3.01	7.7	2.3	8.0	0.6	24.3	2.84
2007	SLN	MLB	25	14	12	0	32	32	202	212	70	136	13	49.6%	.311	21	1.40	3.70	3.93	3.76	9.1	2.6	5.7	0.5	39.8	5.85
2008	SLN	MLB	26	10	10	0	38	24	164¹	171	56	114	16	48.4%	.301	9	1.38	4.14	4.56	4.56	9.1	2.8	5.8	0.8	20.4	3.30

Breakout: 3% Improve: 25% Collapse: 39% Attrition: 16%   Comparables: Doc Medich, John Lackey, Bobby Jones, Aaron Harang

With Isringhausen healthy, the Cardinals converted their championship closer back to starting—Wainwright was drafted and developed as a starter before spending 2006 in the pen—giving him his first crack at a major league rotation. The big righty with the bigger curve was on the brink of being pulled from the rotation after a May 15 shelling that left his ERA at 6.34 and his K/BB nearly even, but with few better options, the Cards stuck with him, and his command improved from that point forward and took everything else with it: 110/48 K/BB in 158 innings, nearly 6 1/2 innings per start, and a 2.96 ERA. Thirteen of his final 16 starts were quality outings. Wainwright's about as good as he's going to be, which is a number-two starter in the NL.

Todd Wellemeyer

													Bats: R		Throws: R		Height: 6' 3"		Weight: 225		Born: August 30, 1978		Age: 29

YEAR	TEAM	LVL	AGE	W	L	SV	G	GS	IP	H	BB	SO	HR	GB%	BABIP	STUFF	WHIP	ERA	PERA	EqERA	EqH9	EqBB9	EqSO9	EqHR9	VORP	SN/WX
2005	IOW	AAA	26	3	2	0	12	12	53²	47	25	48	2	37.0%	.300	9	1.34	3.02	4.03	3.88	8.1	4.4	5.6	0.5	9.7	—
2005	CHN	MLB	26	2	1	1	22	0	32¹	32	22	32	7	48.9%	.305	-4	1.67	6.13	7.05	6.61	9.5	5.7	8.3	2.0	-3.1	0.41
2006	FLO	MLB	27	0	2	0	18	0	21¹	20	13	17	1	44.6%	.317	1	1.55	5.49	3.94	4.98	7.9	4.6	6.6	0.4	0.9	-0.37
2006	KCA	MLB	27	1	2	1	28	0	57	48	37	37	5	52.3%	.265	3	1.49	3.63	3.72	3.36	6.9	5.4	5.6	0.6	14.0	0.42
2007	KCA	MLB	28	0	1	0	12	0	15²	25	11	9	4	41.3%	.362	-46	2.30	10.32	11.99	11.34	13.0	5.4	4.3	2.2	-8.3	-0.23
2007	SLN	MLB	28	3	2	0	20	11	63²	52	29	51	7	42.2%	.259	8	1.27	3.11	3.43	3.78	7.0	3.5	6.7	1.0	10.8	1.50
2008	SLN	MLB	29	3	3	1	30	4	58¹	56	29	43	6	44.7%	.285	-2	1.47	4.39	4.80	4.81	8.4	4.2	6.2	0.9	6.5	0.70

Breakout: 22% Improve: 43% Collapse: 30% Attrition: 35%   Comparables: Tom Griffin, Frank Wills, Dave Sisler, Willie Banks

In one of the stranger sequences of the year, the Cards claimed Wellemeyer, a journeyman who's never shown any control, off waivers from the Royals and stuck him in the rotation a week later. He made eight starts, allowed 24 runs in 36 1/3 innings, and ended up on the DL with a sprained elbow. He did pitch well after returning in late-August, however, including two good starts in September, so he'll be in the mix for a starting job this year. He shouldn't be; despite a big ERA split, he didn't pitch that much better as a starter, and got hurt while trying.

Kip Wells

| | | | | | | | | Bats: R | | Throws: R | | Height: 6′ 3″ | | Weight: 205 | | Born: April 21, 1977 | | Age: 31 | |

YEAR	TEAM	LVL	AGE	W	L	SV	G	GS	IP	H	BB	SO	HR	GB%	BABIP	STUFF	WHIP	ERA	PERA	EqERA	EqH9	EqBB9	EqSO9	EqHR9	VORP	SN/WX
2005	PIT	MLB	28	8	18	0	33	33	182	186	99	132	23	45.3%	.300	-1	1.57	5.09	5.25	5.75	9.2	4.4	5.9	1.1	-3.2	2.64
2006	PIT	MLB	29	1	5	0	7	7	36¹	46	18	16	3	52.3%	.344	-12	1.76	6.69	5.77	6.31	10.6	4.0	3.8	0.8	-3.0	0.14
2006	TEX	MLB	29	1	0	0	2	2	8	15	3	4	0	54.5%	.455	-25	2.25	6.75	10.06	8.22	16.4	3.5	4.7	0.0	-0.5	0.14
2007	SLN	MLB	30	7	17	0	34	26	162²	186	78	122	19	49.5%	.329	2	1.62	5.70	5.34	5.95	9.9	3.7	6.2	1.0	-9.4	0.70
2008	COL	MLB	31	5	7	0	28	14	100²	115	47	72	13	48.5%	.317	1	1.61	5.37	5.00	5.17	9.3	3.7	6.1	1.1	8.4	1.40

Breakout: 29% Improve: 62% Collapse: 22% Attrition: 32%   Comparables: Bill Voiselle, Doyle Alexander, Andy Hawkins, Stan Bahnsen

There were the elements of a Dave Duncan tent revival here—a pitcher coming off surgery who had some success in his past, but had lost his way prior to getting hurt—but Wells just didn't have enough stuff to work with, and his command has never been a strong suit. He signed a one-year deal with Colorado; if he gets a little better in his second year past surgery, the Rockies' defense could make him a reasonable fifth starter.

LINEOUTS

Hitters

PLAYER	TEAM	LVL	AGE	PA	R	2B	3B	HR	RBI	BB	SO	SB-CS	EqBRR	AVG/OBP/SLG	MLVr	EqAVG/EqOBP/EqSLG	EqA	VORP
3B B. Barden	TUC	AAA	26	329	36	9	2	2	25	31	56	2-3	-0.5	.269/.355/.336	-.144	.234/.319/.297	.221	-6.9
	SLN	MLB	26	25	6	1	0	0	0	2	4	0-0	0.6	.217/.280/.261	-.350	.217/.280/.261	.187	-1.3
C G. Bennett	SLN	MLB	35	170	12	7	0	2	17	8	16	1-1	0.4	.252/.286/.335	-.218	.258/.296/.348	.226	-2.6
3B R. Branyan*	SDN	MLB	31	146	16	5	1	7	19	21	48	1-0	-1.1	.197/.322/.426	-.046	.207/.336/.463	.275	1.6
	PHI	MLB	31	9	2	0	0	2	5	0	6	0-0	0.0	.222/.222/.889	.428	.222/.222/.889	.318	1.1
	SLN	MLB	31	39	4	0	0	1	2	7	15	0-0	-0.3	.188/.333/.281	-.238	.188/.333/.281	.228	-1.3
INF M. Cairo	NYA	MLB	33	121	12	7	0	0	10	8	19	8-1	-0.5	.252/.308/.318	-.209	.255/.316/.321	.243	-1.2
	SLN	MLB	33	72	8	2	2	0	5	3	5	2-1	-0.2	.254/.296/.343	-.187	.269/.310/.358	.235	-1.6
SS T. Greene	SFD	AA	23	247	41	17	2	8	25	16	62	10-2	1.9	.244/.309/.448	.011	.220/.273/.396	.234	-1.5
1B M. Hamilton*	PMB	A+	22	244	31	12	0	13	49	20	48	1-0	1.4	.290/.348/.520	.271	.254/.310/.469	.264	3.9
	SFD	AA	22	276	32	15	0	6	41	24	54	1-1	0.0	.250/.318/.383	-.058	.226/.287/.345	.222	-14.2
OF J. Mather	SFD	AA	24	272	48	17	0	18	46	29	32	4-0	-0.1	.303/.387/.607	.401	.271/.346/.521	.293	15.8
	MEM	AAA	24	288	32	10	1	13	31	23	51	6-0	0.4	.241/.329/.443	-.001	.218/.300/.397	.245	-8.2
C K. Stinnett	LVG	AAA	37	113	10	2	0	3	10	9	22	0-0	-1.0	.196/.268/.304	-.429	.194/.265/.291	.193	-6.6
	SLN	MLB	37	87	7	3	0	1	5	5	22	0-0	-0.1	.159/.207/.232	-.555	.159/.216/.232	.136	-8.0
OF P. Wilson	SLN	MLB	32	68	6	3	0	1	5	4	17	2-1	-0.8	.219/.265/.313	-.308	.219/.265/.312	.197	-3.9

Claimed off waivers from the Diamondbacks last August, third baseman **Brian Barden** has doubles pop, but can't play the middle infield well enough to stick as a utility guy. ⊘ **Gary Bennett** is a generic backup catcher who throws very poorly for a player who's on the roster for his defense. Signed by the Dodgers to back up Russell Martin, he's a more logical fit than he was caddying for defense-first Yadier Molina in St. Louis. ⊘ **Russell Branyan** continues to bounce around the league playing the corners and delivering the Three True Outcomes in poor proportion. At his current pace, he'll have passed through a third of the organizations in baseball by year's end. ⊘ Another August pickup, **Miguel Cairo** made some starts at third base after injuries ended Rolen's season early yet again. He still can't hit. ⊘ Knee problems hampered 2005 first-rounder **Tyler Greene** last year, and he underwent season-ending surgery in July. That won't help his unimpressive work at shortstop. ⊘ The Cards' second-round pick in 2006, first baseman **Mark Hamilton** sustained his strike-zone management but not his power after a midseason move to Double-A last year. ⊘ **Joe Mather** had a career year last year in his seventh pro season, but the 24-year-old outfielder reverted to form after a promotion to Triple-A and still projects as nothing more than bench help. ⊘ Backup catcher **Kelly Stinnett** retired and unretired twice last year to the yawns of a disinterested nation. He's made $6.4 million in his career. ⊘ **Preston Wilson** was killing the Cardinals when he hit the DL with a knee injury in May. He never returned, undergoing microfracture surgery in June that ended his season. Wilson hasn't been a good player since 2003 and will have a hard time even finding an invite to spring training.

Pitchers

PLAYER	TEAM	LVL	AGE	W	L	SV	IP	H	BB	SO	HR	GB%	BABIP	STUFF	WHIP	ERA	PERA	EqERA	EqH9	EqBB9	EqSO9	EqHR9	VORP
M. Boggs	SFD	AA	23	11	7	0	152¹	167	62	117	15	51.6%	.325	-16	1.50	3.84	6.64	6.80	11.0	4.6	4.6	1.3	-19.2
B. Hawksworth	MEM	AAA	24	4	13	0	129²	150	41	88	24	46.8%	.317	-32	1.47	5.27	7.01	6.23	10.5	3.2	4.6	2.0	-8.7
T. Herron	QUD	A	20	10	7	1	137¹	123	26	130	7	52.2%	.309	-12	1.09	3.74	6.57	7.38	11.2	4.0	4.5	1.4	-23.1
K. Jimenez	MEM	AAA	26	2	3	1	39²	46	11	34	2	66.4%	.358	-1	1.44	2.72	4.84	3.96	10.5	2.8	5.8	0.7	7.1
	SLN	MLB	26	3	0	0	42	56	17	24	2	45.1%	.362	-14	1.74	7.50	5.79	7.29	11.6	3.0	4.9	0.4	-8.7
K. McClellan	PMB	A+	23	4	1	0	29	22	4	24	0	54.9%	.272	1	0.90	1.24	3.71	2.70	8.1	2.4	4.7	0.3	8.6
	SFD	AA	23	2	0	0	30²	24	6	30	2	58.5%	.275	2	0.98	2.35	3.95	3.81	8.3	2.5	6.4	1.0	5.6
M. McCormick	PMB	A+	23	0	0	0	3	2	0	2	0	42.9%	.286	2	0.67	0.00	1.46	0.00	7.7	0.0	3.9	0.0	1.4
J. Motte	PMB	A+	25	1	0	3	10	7	1	6	0	63.6%	.219	-15	0.80	0.90	3.01	3.48	6.1	1.7	2.6	0.0	2.4
	SFD	AA	25	3	3	8	49	36	22	63	3	41.1%	.308	12	1.18	2.20	4.78	3.68	8.4	5.1	8.8	0.8	9.4
C. Narveson*	MEM	AAA	25	3	2	0	45²	41	21	35	6	32.6%	.276	-8	1.36	5.71	4.90	6.02	8.1	4.6	5.4	1.5	-2.0
T. Norrick*	PMB	A+	23	11	9	0	165¹	134	73	134	11	41.5%	.267	-9	1.25	3.59	5.74	5.57	9.1	5.8	4.7	1.3	0.5
A. Ottavino	PMB	A+	21	12	8	0	143¹	130	63	128	10	50.1%	.296	-8	1.35	3.08	6.63	6.03	10.2	5.8	5.3	1.4	-6.1
M. Parisi	MEM	AAA	24	8	13	0	165	192	65	111	21	48.3%	.334	-18	1.56	4.91	6.48	5.97	10.7	3.9	4.6	1.4	-6.4
M. Worrell	MEM	AAA	24	3	2	4	67	58	25	66	6	42.9%	.299	1	1.24	3.09	4.08	3.51	7.7	3.5	6.8	0.9	15.5

Mitch Boggs is moving up a level per year without dominating any of them. A fastball/slider righty, he needs a third pitch to be a real starting prospect. ⊘ Three years removed from labrum surgery, **Blake Hawksworth** finally reached Triple-A last season and was ineffective all year long. ⊘ **Tyler Herron** has been brought along slowly since being a supplemental first-round pick in 2005. He is the best of a good crop of pitchers low in the system and features a low-90s fastball and very good command. ⊘ Organizational soldier **Kelvin Jimenez** reached the majors the old-fashioned way: by being on the 40-man roster when the big-league team needed an arm. He's not a major league pitcher. ⊘ One of the key arms in the 2006 championship bullpen, **Josh Kinney** suffered a torn UCL last March, underwent Tommy John surgery, and missed the season. A broken arm suffered during rehab pushed his return back to midseason. ⊘ Returning after nearly two years lost to elbow surgeries, righty **Kyle McClellan** picked up velocity and command as a reliever last year and had his best season. ⊘ Injury problems, including shoulder woes last year, have limited hard-throwing **Mark McCormick** to 28 pro starts since he was a first-round pick in 2005. Until he stays off the DL for a full year, he's a myth. ⊘ Converted catcher **Jason Motte** used a mid-90s fastball to dominate the Texas League last year in just his second season on the mound. If his secondary pitches develop, he could be a factor in the major league bullpen as soon as 2009. ⊘ Shoulder and knee problems put another detour on **Chris Narveson**'s long comeback trail last year; he was ineffective when he was able to take the mound. ⊘ **Tyler Norrick** put up good stats in the Florida State League last year despite unimpressive stuff and merits notice as a performance prospect. ⊘ Norrick's teammate **Adam Ottavino** didn't pitch as well, but rates more highly because of his low-90s fastball and good slider. ⊘ **Mike Parisi** is an undersized right-hander with decent stuff who could end up as a reliable middle reliever. ⊘ Righty **Mark Worrell** has spent time as a closer in the minors without being a top prospect. The Cards added him to the 40-man roster over the winter, and he should show up on the 25-man during the season. He's not related to Herzog-era Cards closer Todd.

MANAGER: TONY La RUSSA

YEAR	TEAM	W-L	Pythag +/-	Avg PC	100+ P	120+ P	QS	BQS	REL w REL	Zero R	IBB	Subs	PH	PH Avg	PH HR	SB2	CS2	SB3	CS3	SAC Att	SAC %	POS SAC	Squeeze	Swing	In Play
2005	SLN	100-62	0	96.6	62	1	92	6	436	298	27	78	265	.226	6	69	28	13	4	104	74.0%	47	15	173	145
2006	SLN	83-78	1	92.7	55	2	74	5	468	294	35	69	271	.235	7	53	26	6	5	93	76.3%	32	4	135	110
2007	SLN	78-84	8	89.7	44	2	68	4	515	339	25	56	315	.296	5	50	26	6	3	93	73.1%	31	1	140	121

For all of the times the word "genius" has been used to describe Tony La Russa during his career, it looks more and more like he's just like a lot of managers: he won when he had the horses, and only when he had the horses. Last year, the staff ace of the 2006 world champions made one star, two other stars aged in a hurry, and no amount of batting the pitcher eighth—which La Russa did for the final two months of the season supposedly to get more men on base in front of third-place hitter Albert Pujols—could put Humpty Dumpty back together again. La Russa hastened his team's demise by dumping Anthony Reyes based on his win total, setting up the brief, disastrous Mike Maroth Era. It will be interesting to see what happens with Jocketty gone; will the new front office force La Russa to have stronger benches and give him the power arms in the bullpen he's been doing without? Like a jockey looking for a mount, La Russa just needs the right talent under him to get that g-word going for him again.

San Diego Padres

One strike away. That's how close the Padres were to clinching their third straight post-season berth last year. Needing just one win to clinch the wild card on the penultimate day of the regular season in Milwaukee, San Diego carried a 3-2 lead into the bottom of the ninth against the Brewers, whom they'd eliminated from the postseason the night before. Manager Bud Black called upon all-time saves leader Trevor Hoffman to take the Padres home. Hoffman got them two-thirds of the way there by striking out Prince Fielder and Laynce Nix, but surrendered a double to Corey Hart in between. Facing pinch-hitter Tony Gwynn Jr.—the irony police were late to the scene—Hoffman got the count to 2-2 before Gwynn lined a game-tying triple to right field. The Padres wound up losing in 11 innings, unable to close the one-game gap behind the division-leading Diamondbacks but entering the season's final day remained one game ahead of the hard-charging Rockies and the two teams still alive in the NL East, the Mets and Phillies.

Opting to save ace Jake Peavy for a potential tiebreaker, Black sent journeyman Brett Tomko to the hill for Game 162. Tomko carried a 4-2 lead into the fifth inning but combined with reliever Cla Meredith to surrender four runs in that frame, and the Brewers pulled away for an 11-6 win. The Phillies claimed the NL East by winning while the Mets lost, which eliminated New York from the wild card as well. In Denver, the Rockies and Diamondbacks played a taught 1-1 game through seven and a half innings only to score five combined runs in the final frame. When the dust cleared, the Rockies had won 4-3, forcing the Padres to travel to

Coors Field for a one-game playoff to determine the wild card.

The Padres fell behind 3-0 early in the playoff—Peavy wasn't sharp—but they stormed back with a five-run third against Rockies starter Josh Fogg. Peavy couldn't hold the lead, and departed in the seventh trailing 6-5. A Brian Giles double helped the Pads knot the game back up in the eighth, and the do-or-die contest carried into the 13th inning, when Scott Hairston smacked a two-run homer off Jorge Julio to give the Padres the lead. Again Black called on Hoffman to put his team in the postseason, and again Hoffman failed, surrendering consecutive extra-base hits, the last of which, a Matt Holliday triple, tied the game and put the season-ending run on third base with none out. Hoffman then intentionally walked Todd Helton to get to the light-hitting Jamey Carroll, who had pinch-run for starting third baseman Garrett Atkins in the seventh. Carroll lifted a fly ball to right. Holliday tagged up at third and tried to beat Brian Giles's throw with a face-first slide around catcher Michael Barrett. Replays suggested that Holliday never touched the plate, but home-plate umpire Tim McClelland called him safe, and the Padres' season was over.

It was a stunning end for San Diego, and a historic one. According to Baseball Prospectus's Postseason Odds Report, the Padres had a 90.6 percent chance of making the playoffs after eliminating the Brewers in Milwaukee. According to oddsmeister Clay Davenport, no team ever blew a chance so good so quickly.

That the fates were against San Diego became clear a week before the end of the season when, during the fi-

---

PADRES PROSPECTUS

2007 record: 89-74; Third place, NL West

Pythagenport record: 89-74

Runs scored per game: 4.55 (9th in NL)

Runs allowed per game: 4.09 (1st in NL)

Team EqA: .260 (7th in NL)

2007 Batters Age: 30.3 (6th oldest in NL)

2007 Pitchers Age: 31.6 (2nd oldest in NL)

Ballpark: Petco Park; Extreme pitcher's park; Park Factor of 0.910

2007: The all-time saves leader blows two of the biggest of his career and the Padres experience the fastest collapse in baseball history.

2008: A stop-gap season full of stop-gap players leaves the Pads stopped in the gap.

nal game of a three-game sweep at the hands of the visiting Rockies on September 23, the Padres lost two-thirds of their starting outfield. In the sixth inning of the 7-3 loss, left fielder Milton Bradley accidentally stepped on center fielder Mike Cameron's right hand while the two chased down what became an inside-the-park home run. Cameron sustained a torn ligament and a fracture, effectively ending his season. One inning later, Bradley's season ended even more bizarrely when he tore his anterior cruciate ligament while being restrained by Black during an argument with first-base umpire Mike Winters. The volatile, ever-controversial Bradley later charged that he was baited by Winters, a charge upheld by the commissioner's office, which found that the umpire had crossed the line in using a profanity directed at Bradley and suspended Winters for the season—a pyrrhic victory, at best.

That the Padres' season could hinge on a mere handful of plays wasn't all that surprising, at least from PECOTA's point of view. Before the season, the system foresaw them finishing with an 86-76 record that placed them second in the NL West, two games behind the Diamondbacks, but was enough to win the wild card by one game over the Cubs and two over the Mets. That projection wasn't far off, but the components of that projection were skewed to a certain degree by the fact that Petco Park, though always an extreme pitchers park, rated a .910 Park Factor, the 16th-lowest ever. As a result, the offense fell 35 runs shy of its projected 776, while the pitching staff surpassed its projection by 60 runs, allowing a league-low 666. Indeed, the offense was third in the league in walks, but still finished an abysmal 15th in on-base percentage (.322), and seventh in the NL in isolated power (.160) but a mere 12th in slugging percentage (.411). While the Padres' park-adjusted EqA was a dead-average .260, good for seventh in the league, the team was only ninth in actual runs scored.

Among the individual hitters, first baseman Adrian Gonzalez built on his breakout 2006, but he was the team's most productive hitter and his 38.4 VORP was just 28th in the league. The next highest-ranked Padre was shortstop Khalil Greene (57th with 23.0 VORP), whose abysmal plate discipline (.291 OBP and 128/29 K/UIBB) kept him four runs shy of his PECOTA projection. Again, most of the lineup fell significantly short of its PECOTAs, including Cameron (6.2 runs shy), Giles (19.1), and off-season additions Kevin Kouzmanoff at third (17.2) and Marcus Giles at second (29.8 runs short, and well below replacement level). Not all of that can be blamed on Petco. Giles the Elder missed a month with a

bone bruise in his right knee and failed to recapture the power he had lost in 2006. Despite a hot start (.327/.376/.459 in April), Giles the Younger made Atlanta's non-tender decision look prophetic, as oblique and knee injuries held him to just .199/.283/.273 the rest of the way, leading to Geoff Blum getting the vast majority of the starts at second base in the second half. Inversely, Kouzmanoff, acquired from Cleveland for Giles's keystone predecessor Josh Barfield, started horrendously (.138/.190/.234 through May 15), but heated up thereafter (.310/.364/.514). Still, his value over the final four and a half months was largely negated by his abysmal defense (-26 FRAA).

Forced to make trades in-season to bolster the offense, general manager Kevin Towers delivered modest upgrades. Bradley was acquired from Oakland at the end of June for minor league relief suspect Andrew Brown and hit .313/.414/.590 with 11 homers, but was limited to 42 games by his usual litany of injuries. He nonetheless finished fifth on the team in VORP (19.0). Hairston was acquired from Arizona at the deadline for minor league reliever Leo Rosales; he hit .287/.337/.644 in 95 plate appearances while filling in for Bradley in left field, but an oblique strain cost him a month as well. Despite the injuries, that duo played a major role in helping the team increase its scoring from 4.3 runs per game before the All-Star break to 4.8 after.

Less robust was the contribution of Barrett, acquired from the Cubs in June for backup catcher Rob Bowen and minor league outfielder Kyler Burke. Barrett hit just .226/.235/.286 for a -7.1 VORP, and his defense (-3 FRAA) did little to counter incumbent Josh Bard's weak work (-13 FRAA). Barrett also missed three weeks in August with concussion-like symptoms. Other pickups—third baseman Morgan Ensberg, utilityman Rob Mackowiak, and outfielders Brady Clark and Jose Cruz Jr.—made negligible contributions, though they cost the Pads almost nothing in terms of blood and treasure.

The pitchers, meanwhile, led the major leagues in both starter and reliever win expectancy categories, finishing with 25.0 SNLVAR and 15.7 WXRL for a combined total of 40.7 that dusted the field, with the Red Sox (37.5) and Diamondbacks (34.6) the closest competitors. Unanimous NL Cy Young Award winner Jake Peavy bounced back from a subpar 2006 to lead the majors with 9.1 SNLVAR and win the pitching triple crown by leading the NL in wins (19), ERA (2.45), and strikeouts (240). Chris Young placed ninth in the NL at 6.0 SNLVAR and was even more untouchable than Peavy for nearly half the season, putting up a 1.08 ERA from May 1 to July 24 before oblique and back troubles wrecked his final two months. Forty-one-year-old Greg Maddux, despite finishing with an ERA below the park-adjusted league average for the first time since 1987, still ranked 15th in the league in SNLVAR at 5.4. The rest of the rotation was more problematic. Clay Hensley pitched through a sore shoulder only to discover he'd torn his labrum. David Wells was released at midseason after four consecutive bombings. Rookie Justin Germano turned in quality starts in eight of his first nine games after joining the rotation in early May, but fizzled from there, eventually losing his spot in September.

In the bullpen, Hoffman finished just 21st in WXRL (2.89) due to late-season struggles which saw him put up a 5.06 ERA after August 1 and blow five of his last 19 save opportunities, including the final pair that cost the Padres the postseason. The rest of the pen, however, was a testament to Towers's budget-minded creativity. Heath Bell was acquired from the Mets in the offseason for reliever Jon Adkins, outfielder Ben Johnson, and a broken Happy Meal prize; he finished second in the league in WXRL (5.66) while leading all major league relievers in innings and strikeouts. Despite declining peripherals, Scott Linebrink provided 2.07 WXRL before being traded to Milwaukee at the deadline for three pitching prospects, the most ready of whom, Joe Thatcher, did solid LOOGY work over the final two months. Forty-year-old medical marvel Doug Brocail, Cla Meredith (stolen from the Red Sox in 2006's Doug Mirabelli return-to-sender), Justin Hampson (plucked off the waiver wire after the 2006 season), and Kevin Cameron (a Rule 5 pick) also made solid contributions while serving as reminders that strong bullpens can be assembled without exorbitant expenditures.

Looking forward, the Padres are a team in transition. Gonzalez, Peavy, and Young are the only three Padres signed beyond 2008, but with those two dominant starting pitchers, San Diego already has a head start toward building its next playoff team, particularly given the parity in the NL these days. The team has second- and third-base prospects on the way in Matt Antonelli and Chase Headley, both of whom had strong showings at Double-A San Antonio last year, Greene and Bard under team control through 2009, and Kouzmanoff, Hairston, and most of the bullpen after Hoffman are under control beyond that. However, old-timers such as Brian Giles, Maddux, and Hoffman don't seem likely to be a part of the team's next post-season run. The hope appears to be that the Padres can establish Antonelli and Headley later this season. Then, after the team's veterans head off to market or to pasture, they'll make a big free agent splash over the winter by signing a slugging outfielder, a strong third starter, or a dominant closer to

make a serious run in 2009. For 2008, however, Towers appears to be biding his time, patching a team that had the second oldest pitching staff in the league (31.6) and the sixth-oldest lineup (30.3) with a series of one-year deals for veteran stop-gaps.

Jim Edmonds was acquired from St. Louis for minor league third baseman David Freese. Entering his walk year, Edmonds is supposed to slot into center field and help fill the sizable offensive void left by the free agency departures of Cameron and Bradley, but he's coming off his worst season in years, has always been injury-prone, and will be 38 in June. Tadahito Iguchi, 33, arrives on a one-year, $3.85 million deal to play second until Antonelli is ready. Barrett was accidentally retained; the Padres offered the Type-A free agent arbitration, expecting him to decline and net them two extra drafts picks by signing somewhere else. Instead, Barrett's down year (-2.1 VORP) curbed his desire to enter the market, and he accepted arbitration, forcing a one-year, $3.5 million deal. In the rotation, Maddux returns for $10 million this year. Towers also took fliers on a pair of considerably less durable pitchers. Randy Wolf, who did promising work for the Dodgers in the first half of last year before being shut down by shoulder inflammation, was signed to an incentive-based one-year deal for $4.75 million, while San Diego native Mark Prior, who missed all of 2007 after undergoing shoulder surgery, signed an incentive-based deal for a mere $1 million. Towers' most significant move this winter, and the only one that will impact roster beyond this year, was extending Jake Peavy's contract. Already signed for a ridiculously below-market $6 million in 2008 and $8 million in 2009, Peavy agreed to a three-year, $52 million extension with a $22 million club option for 2013, which measured against the current market is closer to Carlos Silva money than the sort of exhorbitant contract the more comparable Johan Santana is likely to land.

The problem with the 2009 plan is that, among the four NL West contenders (the Giants need not apply), the Padres have the least favorable combination of finances and young talent. Headley and Antonelli are future major league regulars, but are much longer shots for stardom, and while the Padres' farm system has improved considerably since Grady Fuson took over as vice president of scouting and player development two years ago, it still ranked a lowly 28th in Kevin Goldstein's Organizational Rankings a year ago. Meanwhile, the Dodgers, Diamondbacks, and Rockies are all bursting with blue-chip youngsters. Part of the Padres' plan has been to stockpile compensation picks as their free agents depart. Last year they had five supplemental first-round picks and eight of the first 87 overall picks. This year they'll have two more supplemental first-rounders following the departures of Brocail and, eventually, Cameron. Next year they hope to have still more as Giles, Edmonds, Iguchi, and perhaps Maddux and Hoffman find new homes, though the backfired arbitration offer to Barrett might put a hitch in their swing. Still, all of those picks, even if well used, will need time to develop into useful major leaguers. In the meantime, the Padres still lag behind their rivals, as even Headley and Antonelli have combined for just eight games about Double-A. More troublingly, while it would seem to be a no-brainer to try to move the stone-gloved Kouzmanoff to an outfield corner to make room for the sure-handed Headley, it was Headley who was seen taking fly balls in left field at Petco in January (Antonelli, incidentally, was brought in for fly balls in center).

As for the divison's financial picture, the Dodgers' attendance, revenue, and payroll put them in a class by themselves. The Padres, Rockies, and Diamondbacks ranked 24th through 26th in Opening Day payroll last year, but while the Rox and D'backs are loaded with homegrown talent earning six-figure salaries, the Padres have no such luxury. To make matters worse, while San Diego has consistently outdrawn its small-market rivals, Forbes.com's 2007 estimates placed the Padres second to last in all of baseball in operating income ($5.2 million). Lacking financial brawn, the Padres are going to need organizational brains to remain competitive in their division, as ever. The Peavy contract was a major step in the right direction, as is a pending extension for Towers (his contract expires after this season), but until their stockpile of draft picks matures, the team's near miss last year will haunt them.

HITTERS

Matt Antonelli — 2B

Bats: R Throws: R Height: 6' 0" Weight: 203 Born: April 8, 1985 Age: 23

YEAR	TEAM	LVL	AGE	PA	R	2B	3B	HR	RBI	BB	SO	SB	CS	EqBRR	AVG	OBP	SLG	MLVr	EqAVG	EqOBP	EqSLG	EqA	VORP	DEFENSE	
2006	EUG	A-	21	245	38	12	1	0	22	46	31	9	1	-0.4	.286	.426	.360	.169	.236	.350	.296	.244	-2.2	43-3B	-2
2007	LEL	A+	22	406	89	14	4	14	54	53	58	18	6	1.8	.314	.409	.499	.294	.259	.341	.396	.260	11.5	75-2B	-2
2007	SAN	AA	22	223	34	11	1	7	24	30	36	10	3	-2.0	.294	.395	.476	.294	.271	.359	.443	.281	13.3	48-2B	-11
2008	SDN	MLB	23	653	86	30	5	12	58	77	123	19	7	0.9	.252	.344	.387	-.079	.259	.352	.414	.267	23.8	152-2B	-5

Breakout: 35% Improve: 60% Collapse: 12% Attrition: 5%   Comparables: Tim Hummel, Tony Manahan, Aaron Hill, Shaun Boyd

Padres prospects come through some very good hitting environments, which makes evaluating them problematic; keep that in mind throughout this chapter. Antonelli was the 17th overall pick in 2006, and is a line-drive hitter whose work-the-count approach is a good fit for Petco. He played third in college, but with an organizational logjam at the hot corner, the Pads have tried to make him a second baseman. So far he's survived, but his defense is a work in progress, with a good arm and lateral range, but problems on the pivot.

Josh Bard — C

Bats: S Throws: R Height: 6' 3" Weight: 210 Born: March 30, 1978 Age: 30

YEAR	TEAM	LVL	AGE	PA	R	2B	3B	HR	RBI	BB	SO	SB	CS	EqBRR	AVG	OBP	SLG	MLVr	EqAVG	EqOBP	EqSLG	EqA	VORP	DEFENSE	
2005	CLE	MLB	27	95	6	4	0	1	9	9	11	0	0	-0.9	.193	.266	.277	-.345	.198	.280	.272	.201	-3.9	25-C	1
2006	BOS	MLB	28	21	2	1	0	0	0	3	3	0	0	-0.2	.278	.381	.333	-.063	.278	.381	.333	.262	0.4		
2006	SDN	MLB	28	263	28	19	0	9	40	27	39	1	0	-0.6	.338	.406	.537	.364	.351	.420	.550	.328	29.7	55-C	0
2007	SDN	MLB	29	443	42	27	2	5	51	50	58	0	1	-4.2	.285	.364	.404	.065	.298	.380	.425	.283	22.5	102-C	-13
2008	SDN	MLB	30	443	52	24	1	7	50	48	59	3	2	-1.4	.286	.364	.409	.010	.294	.372	.438	.278	26.7	105-C	-5

Breakout: 7% Improve: 31% Collapse: 35% Attrition: 16%   Comparables: Chad Kreuter, Jim Sundberg, Mitch Meluskey, Michael Barrett

The power Bard showed in 2006 was a fluke. Everything else is a skill, making him a very valuable property—a switch-hitting catcher with real on-base skills. That he started 33 games in the middle of the order last year is a reflection of the Padres' problems assembling a lineup, not an endorsement of his bat. That he allowed 121 stolen bases in 108 games (7.6 percent caught stealing) is not an endorsement of his arm, but there's some evidence that Pads pitchers share the blame, especially Chris Young, on whom basestealers went a perfect 44-0 in their attempts last year. Bard threw out 33.6 percent of thieves in his career prior joining the Padres.

Michael Barrett   C   Bats: R   Throws: R   Height: 6' 3"   Weight: 210   Born: October 22, 1976   Age: 31

YEAR	TEAM	LVL	AGE	PA	R	2B	3B	HR	RBI	BB	SO	SB	CS	EqBRR	AVG	OBP	SLG	MLVr	EqAVG	EqOBP	EqSLG	EqA	VORP	DEFENSE	
2005	CHN	MLB	28	477	48	32	3	16	61	40	61	0	3	-0.8	.276	.345	.479	.120	.269	.340	.479	.276	28.3	115-C	-9
2006	CHN	MLB	29	418	54	25	3	16	53	33	41	0	1	-2.8	.307	.368	.517	.209	.299	.362	.507	.293	31.3	96-C	-14
2007	CHN	MLB	30	231	23	9	0	9	29	17	36	2	2	-2.1	.256	.307	.427	-.056	.249	.304	.426	.248	5.0	53-C	-4
2007	SDN	MLB	30	136	6	8	0	0	12	2	21	0	0	-1.9	.226	.235	.286	-.385	.235	.250	.288	.179	-7.1	32-C	-3
2008	SDN	MLB	31	279	26	13	1	6	32	20	39	1	1	-0.7	.248	.306	.380	-.159	.255	.313	.406	.243	6.4	68-C	-5

Breakout: 9%   Improve: 29%   Collapse: 42%   Attrition: 30%   Comparables: Don Leppert, Joe Oliver, Brian Johnson, Javy Lopez

Note to all red asses: your job security is entirely tied to your performance, and your act gets old fast when you stop hitting. In the first half of last season, Barrett had significant problems making contact with anything other than Carlos Zambrano's face and was promptly shipped to San Diego, where the only thing he hit was the disabled list following an August concussion. Barrett surprised the Padres by accepting arbitration, and thus starts the year as Bard's backup. He's a strong candidate to be traded should his bat returns.

Kyle Blanks   1B   Bats: R   Throws: R   Height: 6' 6"   Weight: 281   Born: September 11, 1986   Age: 21

YEAR	TEAM	LVL	AGE	PA	R	2B	3B	HR	RBI	BB	SO	SB	CS	EqBRR	AVG	OBP	SLG	MLVr	EqAVG	EqOBP	EqSLG	EqA	VORP	DEFENSE	
2006	FTW	A	19	359	41	20	0	10	52	36	79	2	0	-0.1	.292	.382	.455	.249	.233	.304	.363	.235	-11.5	51-1B	-2
2007	LEL	A+	20	531	94	31	4	24	100	44	98	11	2	-0.7	.301	.380	.540	.293	.246	.309	.422	.253	-2.5	59-1B	-1
2008	SDN	MLB	21	590	62	29	2	17	69	47	138	8	3	-0.2	.237	.306	.397	-.143	.244	.313	.425	.250	4.1	138-1B	-2

Breakout: 22%   Improve: 59%   Collapse: 12%   Attrition: 4%   Comparables: Richie Sexson, Butch Huskey, Jermaine Dye, Joel Guzman

Weighing 280 pounds at age 21 isn't guaranteed to kill a player's career, but it is a problem to be managed. Blanks shot up over three bills while out with an injury in 2006, and is always going to be fighting his weight, but he has terrific power, is surprisingly dexterous around first base, and is a smart baserunner—he stole 11 bases last year and has an 84 percent success rate on the bases in his young career. He also has an excellent contact rate for a big slugger, which is a good indicator of his true offensive potential. All of that is enough to make him a real prospect if he can stay in playing shape.

Geoff Blum   INF   Bats: S   Throws: R   Height: 6' 3"   Weight: 205   Born: April 26, 1973   Age: 35

YEAR	TEAM	LVL	AGE	PA	R	2B	3B	HR	RBI	BB	SO	SB	CS	EqBRR	AVG	OBP	SLG	MLVr	EqAVG	EqOBP	EqSLG	EqA	VORP	DEFENSE				
2005	SDN	MLB	32	252	26	13	1	5	22	24	28	3	2	-0.2	.241	.321	.375	-.065	.251	.331	.399	.253	1.7	26-3B	6	18-2B	-1
2005	CHA	MLB	32	99	6	2	1	1	3	4	15	0	1	-0.4	.200	.232	.274	-.430	.202	.250	.277	.173	-8.4				
2006	SDN	MLB	33	299	27	17	1	4	34	17	51	0	1	-0.1	.254	.293	.366	-.151	.262	.303	.382	.238	-2.7	43-SS	5	22-3B	-1
2007	SDN	MLB	34	370	34	21	1	5	33	32	52	0	0	1.1	.252	.319	.367	-.098	.261	.332	.383	.252	1.2	54-2B	-2		
2008	HOU	MLB	35	201	19	10	1	4	23	16	30	1	1	-0.3	.249	.311	.377	-.153	.251	.313	.384	.239	3.1	51-2B	-5		

Breakout: 23%   Improve: 42%   Collapse: 36%   Attrition: 46%   Comparables: Vance Law, Thomas Howard, Bill Mazeroski, Charlie Hayes

Marcus Giles' fragility and limp bat left the Padres with no choice but to make Blum their semiregular second baseman down the stretch last year. It didn't work out that badly; Blum posted a .341 OBP from July 15, when he more or less became a regular, through the end of the season. He'll be back in a utility role with the Astros this year, with his best opportunity for more coming as a lefty foil for Ty Wigginton at third base.

Milton Bradley   OF   Bats: S   Throws: R   Height: 6' 0"   Weight: 225   Born: April 15, 1978   Age: 30

YEAR	TEAM	LVL	AGE	PA	R	2B	3B	HR	RBI	BB	SO	SB	CS	EqBRR	AVG	OBP	SLG	MLVr	EqAVG	EqOBP	EqSLG	EqA	VORP	DEFENSE	
2005	LAN	MLB	27	315	49	14	1	13	38	25	47	6	1	-3.0	.290	.350	.484	.164	.289	.354	.500	.290	20.7	71-CF	7
2006	OAK	MLB	28	405	53	14	2	14	52	51	65	10	2	0.5	.276	.370	.447	.082	.280	.383	.468	.296	17.9	90-RF	-4
2007	OAK	MLB	29	75	6	4	0	2	7	8	14	2	1	-0.8	.292	.373	.446	.125	.312	.400	.500	.308	4.2	14-CF	-3
2007	SDN	MLB	29	169	31	5	1	11	30	23	27	3	1	-1.1	.313	.414	.590	.421	.329	.432	.650	.350	19.0	36-LF	3
2008	TEX	MLB	30	407	61	19	2	16	56	44	76	7	2	-0.1	.283	.364	.476	.118	.279	.364	.488	.296	17.9	97-LF	-1

Breakout: 5%   Improve: 31%   Collapse: 27%   Attrition: 12%   Comparables: Willie Crawford, Mark Whiten, Chili Davis, Bobby Bonilla

Bradley has reached the point at which his temperament isn't the worst thing about him. Rather, it's his inability to stay on the field that limits his value. Barring rehab assignments, he hasn't played 100 games in a season since 2004 and has cracked 110 games just once since 2002. When healthy, he's a championship-caliber corner outfielder; he's just never healthy. He'll help the Rangers for as long as his body will allow.

Mike Cameron — CF

Bats: R Throws: R Height: 6' 2" Weight: 200 Born: January 8, 1973 Age: 35

YEAR	TEAM	LVL	AGE	PA	R	2B	3B	HR	RBI	BB	SO	SB	CS	EqBRR	AVG	OBP	SLG	MLVr	EqAVG	EqOBP	EqSLG	EqA	VORP	DEFENSE	
2005	NYN	MLB	32	343	47	23	2	12	39	29	85	13	1	1.7	.273	.342	.477	.123	.273	.342	.494	.287	17.8	67-RF	-6
2006	SDN	MLB	33	634	88	34	9	22	83	71	142	25	9	0.0	.268	.355	.482	.135	.282	.369	.509	.296	39.8	138-CF	9
2007	SDN	MLB	34	651	88	33	6	21	78	67	160	18	5	3.8	.242	.328	.431	.003	.257	.345	.466	.278	20.4	146-CF	-3
2008	MIL	MLB	35	502	76	28	4	21	68	55	114	14	4	0.9	.269	.356	.493	.093	.269	.353	.496	.286	27.8	118-CF	-3

Breakout: 14% Improve: 42% Collapse: 24% Attrition: 28%   Comparables: Ron Gant, Reggie Sanders, Eric Davis, Sam Chapman

There was muted reaction to the news that Cameron, one of the game's nice guys, would be suspended for the first 25 games of the 2008 season after twice testing positive for a banned stimulant. The lack of outrage reinforces the notion that the drugs-in-baseball story is about personalities more than anything else. Cameron struggled to find an employer before finally settling for a one-year deal with the Brewers, which had more to do with the depth of the off-season center-field pool than his suspension. At 35 and in decline, he's a risky investment.

Morgan Ensberg — 3B

Bats: R Throws: R Height: 6' 2" Weight: 220 Born: August 26, 1975 Age: 32

YEAR	TEAM	LVL	AGE	PA	R	2B	3B	HR	RBI	BB	SO	SB	CS	EqBRR	AVG	OBP	SLG	MLVr	EqAVG	EqOBP	EqSLG	EqA	VORP	DEFENSE	
2005	HOU	MLB	29	624	86	30	3	36	101	85	119	6	7	-3.4	.283	.388	.557	.302	.280	.385	.560	.309	53.7	145-3B	9
2006	HOU	MLB	30	495	67	17	1	23	58	101	96	1	4	-3.2	.235	.396	.463	.125	.234	.397	.462	.296	19.0	108-3B	2
2007	HOU	MLB	31	259	36	10	0	8	31	31	48	0	1	-1.1	.232	.323	.384	-.103	.238	.333	.390	.254	-1.6	55-3B	-2
2007	SDN	MLB	31	65	11	3	0	4	8	7	19	0	0	-0.5	.224	.308	.483	.021	.241	.323	.534	.283	1.8	10-3B	2
2008	SDN	MLB	32	277	38	11	1	12	38	42	57	2	1	-0.5	.249	.368	.457	.051	.256	.377	.489	.292	18.7	68-3B	0

Breakout: 21% Improve: 48% Collapse: 27% Attrition: 33%   Comparables: Andre Thornton, John Jaha, Wayne Gross, Gary Roenicke

As good as Ensberg has been at times, the Astros were right to cut his playing time last season as his low batting average and lack of power rendered him useless. Flipped to the Padres for a player-to-be-named, Ensberg arrived in San Diego just in time to watch Kevin Kouzmanoff get hot and secure the third base job. Non-tendered over the winter, Ensberg can help a number of teams as a platoon player at third base, but he needs a manager willing to suffer his batting average.

Brian Giles — RF

Bats: L Throws: L Height: 5' 10" Weight: 205 Born: January 20, 1971 Age: 37

YEAR	TEAM	LVL	AGE	PA	R	2B	3B	HR	RBI	BB	SO	SB	CS	EqBRR	AVG	OBP	SLG	MLVr	EqAVG	EqOBP	EqSLG	EqA	VORP	DEFENSE			
2005	SDN	MLB	34	674	92	38	8	15	83	119	64	13	5	-2.2	.301	.423	.483	.297	.314	.435	.513	.327	55.9	136-RF	2	15-CF	-3
2006	SDN	MLB	35	717	87	37	1	14	83	104	60	9	4	-1.0	.263	.374	.397	.050	.274	.385	.414	.283	17.7	155-RF	-14		
2007	SDN	MLB	36	552	72	27	2	13	51	64	61	4	6	1.3	.271	.361	.416	.058	.287	.379	.452	.283	11.2	117-RF	-8		
2008	SDN	MLB	37	493	64	23	2	11	56	61	55	6	2	-0.2	.268	.362	.405	-.011	.276	.371	.433	.277	15.4	116-RF	-4		

Breakout: 3% Improve: 28% Collapse: 35% Attrition: 23%   Comparables: Enos Slaughter, Gene Woodling, Mark Grace, Luis Gonzalez

Petco isn't helping him, of course, but Giles's power decline has more to do with his advancing age than his tough hitting environment. Combine that outage with his loss of range afield and the change in how he's being pitched now that he's shown less power, and he looks like a spare part rather than a key offensive cog.

Marcus Giles — 2B

Bats: R Throws: R Height: 5' 8" Weight: 175 Born: May 18, 1978 Age: 30

YEAR	TEAM	LVL	AGE	PA	R	2B	3B	HR	RBI	BB	SO	SB	CS	EqBRR	AVG	OBP	SLG	MLVr	EqAVG	EqOBP	EqSLG	EqA	VORP	DEFENSE	
2005	ATL	MLB	27	654	104	45	4	15	63	64	108	16	3	5.0	.291	.365	.461	.142	.289	.364	.466	.288	41.1	143-2B	8
2006	ATL	MLB	28	626	87	32	2	11	60	62	105	10	5	3.2	.262	.341	.387	-.040	.265	.346	.392	.260	14.5	129-2B	3
2007	SDN	MLB	29	476	52	19	3	4	39	44	82	10	3	5.5	.229	.304	.317	-.202	.243	.321	.340	.239	-8.7	104-2B	7
2008	COL	MLB	30	514	68	26	3	11	55	49	78	11	3	0.9	.274	.348	.418	-.014	.252	.328	.390	.251	10.5	121-2B	0

Breakout: 15% Improve: 36% Collapse: 40% Attrition: 25%   Comparables: Charlie Neal, John Castino, Dick Green, Ron Belliard

After a strong start, Giles went straight downhill all year long, batting .199/.283/.273 after April and losing a piece of the second-base job to Blum along the way. He's always battling injuries of some type—oblique, hip, and knee problems were on the menu in 2007—and seems to be simply unable to handle the physical demands of playing second on an everyday basis. He signed a minor league deal with the Rockies and will get a shot at the second-base job.

Adrian Gonzalez 1B
Bats: L   Throws: L   Height: 6' 2"   Weight: 220   Born: May 8, 1982   Age: 26

YEAR	TEAM	LVL	AGE	PA	R	2B	3B	HR	RBI	BB	SO	SB	CS	EqBRR	AVG	OBP	SLG	MLVr	EqAVG	EqOBP	EqSLG	EqA	VORP	DEFENSE		
2005	OKL	AAA	23	368	61	17	1	18	65	32	44	0	0	-2.3	.338	.399	.561	.378	.296	.352	.488	.285	18.4	82-1B	3	
2005	TEX	MLB	23	162	17	7	1	6	17	10	37	0	0	-0.2	.227	.272	.407	-.168	.224	.280	.429	.242	-2.8			
2006	SDN	MLB	24	631	83	38	1	24	82	52	113	0	1	-3.9	.304	.362	.500	.204	.313	.372	.518	.300	32.8	148-1B	19	
2007	SDN	MLB	25	720	101	46	3	30	100	65	140	0	0	0.3	.282	.347	.502	.166	.294	.362	.534	.300	38.4	161-1B	14	
2008	SDN	MLB	26	647	84	34	2	28	99	58	117	4	2	-0.9	.281	.348	.492	.090	.289	.356	.526	.291	36.9	151-1B	8	

Breakout: 16% Improve: 49% Collapse: 20% Attrition: 8%   Comparables: Kent Hrbek, Justin Morneau, Mo Vaughn, Rico Brogna

In some ways, Gonzalez's last two years look a lot like Derrek Lee's age-24 and -25 seasons, but just a little bit better across the board. Lee added speed and 30 walks a year to his game; Gonzalez is unlikely to do the former, but the latter is within his reach. Both players can save 15 to 20 runs a year on defense while hitting .300 with power. Gonzalez is a very underrated player and the most valuable Padre after Jake Peavy.

Khalil Greene SS
Bats: R   Throws: R   Height: 5' 11"   Weight: 195   Born: October 21, 1979   Age: 28

YEAR	TEAM	LVL	AGE	PA	R	2B	3B	HR	RBI	BB	SO	SB	CS	EqBRR	AVG	OBP	SLG	MLVr	EqAVG	EqOBP	EqSLG	EqA	VORP	DEFENSE	
2005	SDN	MLB	25	476	51	30	2	15	70	25	93	5	0	-0.6	.250	.296	.431	-.022	.257	.303	.450	.259	15.5	115-SS	-11
2006	SDN	MLB	26	460	56	26	2	15	55	39	87	5	1	0.0	.245	.320	.427	-.020	.255	.329	.450	.268	14.2	111-SS	6
2007	SDN	MLB	27	659	89	44	3	27	97	32	128	4	0	1.7	.254	.291	.468	-.000	.265	.305	.502	.272	23.0	153-SS	-7
2008	SDN	MLB	28	592	68	33	2	22	82	41	111	6	2	0.2	.253	.310	.443	-.062	.261	.318	.474	.264	28.5	139-SS	-2

Breakout: 14% Improve: 43% Collapse: 29% Attrition: 12%   Comparables: Tony Batista, Jim Morrison, Max Alvis, Jeff Kent

Last year, Greene became the only player in major league history to play 75 percent or more of his games at shortstop while posting an OBP under .300 and picking up 70 or more extra-base hits. In fact, he's the only one to do all of that and have more than 60 extra-base hits. Greene has made a conscious decision to pull the ball and hit for power at the expense of contact, but his actual value is largely unchanged as a result. What those robust home-run and RBI totals will do is make him more expensive. Our system doesn't do his defense justice; it's very good.

Scott Hairston LF
Bats: R   Throws: R   Height: 6' 0"   Weight: 200   Born: May 25, 1980   Age: 28

YEAR	TEAM	LVL	AGE	PA	R	2B	3B	HR	RBI	BB	SO	SB	CS	EqBRR	AVG	OBP	SLG	MLVr	EqAVG	EqOBP	EqSLG	EqA	VORP	DEFENSE				
2005	TUC	AAA	25	237	45	8	3	16	40	21	40	3	0	2.1	.311	.384	.608	.278	.263	.326	.493	.277	6.0	31-LF	4	16-CF	-3
2006	TUC	AAA	26	440	83	22	1	26	81	52	78	3	0	0.7	.323	.407	.591	.370	.287	.367	.530	.302	27.4	85-LF	1		
2007	ARI	MLB	27	199	21	13	1	3	16	19	37	2	0	-1.1	.222	.301	.358	-.191	.216	.299	.364	.235	-5.4	43-LF	5		
2007	SDN	MLB	27	95	16	5	1	8	20	7	18	0	0	0.0	.287	.337	.644	.353	.302	.358	.698	.331	9.2	20-LF	-2		
2008	SDN	MLB	28	378	49	18	2	17	53	35	75	4	1	0.2	.258	.332	.469	.013	.266	.340	.501	.280	16.7	91-LF	1		

Breakout: 18% Improve: 49% Collapse: 22% Attrition: 16%   Comparables: Jeffrey Leonard, Richard Hidalgo, Jeffrey Hammonds, Bubba Trammell

Tossed aside by the Diamondbacks at last year's trading deadline, Hairston had two walk-off homers and three other huge blasts for the Padres over the final two months, including a tie-breaking shot in the 13th inning of Game 163. He'd be a legend in San Diego if not for Trevor Hoffman's meltdown 20 minutes later. Heroics aside, Hairston has never been able to make enough contact to keep a job in the majors. The Pads' thin outfield offers him the best chance he'll ever have at a career, as he'll enter spring training as the starting left fielder.

Chase Headley 3B

Bats: S   Throws: R   Height: 6' 2"   Weight: 195   Born: May 9, 1984   Age: 24

YEAR	TEAM	LVL	AGE	PA	R	2B	3B	HR	RBI	BB	SO	SB	CS	EqBRR	AVG	OBP	SLG	MLVr	EqAVG	EqOBP	EqSLG	EqA	VORP	DEFENSE
2005	EUG	A-	21	259	29	14	3	6	33	34	48	1	1	0.9	.268	.375	.441	.159	.199	.282	.307	.207	-21.0	57-3B -10
2006	LEL	A+	22	571	79	33	0	12	73	74	96	4	5	-1.8	.291	.389	.434	.144	.237	.321	.353	.238	0.1	124-3B -17
2007	SAN	AA	23	522	82	38	5	20	78	74	114	1	0	-1.0	.330	.437	.580	.538	.255	.356	.474	.285	35.1	118-3B 2
2007	SDN	MLB	23	21	1	1	0	0	0	2	4	0	0	0.0	.222	.333	.278	-.213	.222	.333	.278	.224	-0.6	
2008	SDN	MLB	24	560	58	26	3	15	64	58	140	4	2	-0.2	.231	.315	.390	-.140	.238	.323	.417	.252	8.4	131-3B -5

Breakout: 18% Improve: 48% Collapse: 16% Attrition: 10%   Comparables: Tom Evans, Matt Craig, Rey Noriega, Troy Cameron

The Texas League's player of the year in 2007 could be the Padres' 2008 third baseman by the time you read this. The power he showed last year may have been a bit of a peak; he's more of an OBP/doubles hitter without speed. Last year's comparison to Bill Mueller still holds. As well as Kouzmanoff played last season, Headley is the better player and a better fit for Petco's big gaps.

Nick Hundley C

Bats: R   Throws: R   Height: 6' 1"   Weight: 210   Born: September 8, 1983   Age: 24

YEAR	TEAM	LVL	AGE	PA	R	2B	3B	HR	RBI	BB	SO	SB	CS	EqBRR	AVG	OBP	SLG	MLVr	EqAVG	EqOBP	EqSLG	EqA	VORP	DEFENSE
2005	EUG	A-	21	184	30	7	1	7	22	33	35	1	0	-0.4	.250	.391	.453	.185	.184	.297	.291	.214	-15.4	40-C -4
2005	FTW	A	21	42	2	2	0	0	5	4	9	0	0	0.3	.222	.310	.278	-.186	.184	.238	.211	.150	-5.0	
2006	FTW	A	22	248	29	19	0	8	44	25	45	1	1	-0.5	.274	.355	.474	.224	.229	.294	.386	.236	-1.3	57-C 5
2006	LEL	A+	22	200	18	13	0	3	23	20	44	1	1	-0.8	.278	.357	.403	.036	.227	.291	.337	.220	-5.0	41-C -3
2007	SAN	AA	23	422	55	23	1	20	72	42	74	0	2	0.8	.247	.324	.475	.134	.224	.292	.429	.245	3.9	93-C 2
2008	SDN	MLB	24	397	37	17	1	11	45	37	95	2	1	-0.2	.219	.296	.369	-.210	.225	.303	.394	.237	3.5	95-C 2

Breakout: 28% Improve: 58% Collapse: 19% Attrition: 15%   Comparables: Creighton Gubanich, Eric Helfand, Joe Depastino, Kevin Brown

No relation to the other catching Hundleys, Nick is making steady progress toward being a low-average, high-power backup catcher in the make of Mark Parent, Tim Laudner, and Sal Fasano. His good throwing arm—he nailed 36 percent of thieves last season—and solid catcher's body complete the package.

Kevin Kouzmanoff 3B

Bats: R   Throws: R   Height: 6' 1"   Weight: 210   Born: July 25, 1981   Age: 26

YEAR	TEAM	LVL	AGE	PA	R	2B	3B	HR	RBI	BB	SO	SB	CS	EqBRR	AVG	OBP	SLG	MLVr	EqAVG	EqOBP	EqSLG	EqA	VORP	DEFENSE
2005	KIN	A+	23	287	47	20	4	12	58	24	51	3	1	-2.0	.339	.401	.591	.447	.274	.321	.464	.266	14.5	55-3B 2
2006	AKR	AA	24	276	46	19	1	15	55	23	34	2	3	-1.4	.389	.449	.660	.655	.363	.415	.633	.339	51.0	54-3B 4
2006	BUF	AAA	24	115	22	9	0	7	20	10	12	2	1	-0.2	.353	.409	.647	.517	.333	.391	.627	.330	18.8	19-3B 5
2006	CLE	MLB	24	61	4	2	0	3	11	5	12	0	0	-0.3	.214	.279	.411	-.195	.218	.295	.418	.244	-1.4	
2007	SDN	MLB	25	534	57	30	2	18	74	32	94	1	0	-1.9	.275	.329	.457	.066	.288	.343	.493	.284	18.6	125-3B -24
2008	SDN	MLB	26	549	70	29	3	20	79	39	97	5	2	-0.4	.280	.337	.473	.046	.289	.345	.505	.282	32.7	129-3B -6

Breakout: 5% Improve: 29% Collapse: 27% Attrition: 5%   Comparables: Tony Perez, Kevin Mitchell, Larry Parrish, Chris Brown

Kouzmanoff had the inverse of Marcus Giles's year, with a 354 OPS in April and a strong season afterwards, hitting .309/.362/.511 from May 10 on. Even at that, he's a flawed player who rarely walks, doesn't hit righties, and can't play defense. As a platoon corner guy in a better park for his game, he might work. Headley will pass him by midseason, if the Padres haven't just gone ahead and traded him by then.

Jason Lane OF

Bats: R   Throws: L   Height: 6' 2"   Weight: 220   Born: December 22, 1976   Age: 31

YEAR	TEAM	LVL	AGE	PA	R	2B	3B	HR	RBI	BB	SO	SB	CS	EqBRR	AVG	OBP	SLG	MLVr	EqAVG	EqOBP	EqSLG	EqA	VORP	DEFENSE	
2005	HOU	MLB	28	561	65	34	4	26	78	32	105	6	2	-3.3	.267	.316	.499	.098	.264	.314	.503	.273	20.6	126-RF -7	
2006	HOU	MLB	29	345	44	10	0	15	45	49	75	1	2	1.7	.201	.318	.392	-.125	.201	.322	.396	.252	-6.0	75-RF 2	
2007	ROU	AAA	30	214	37	15	0	9	41	23	26	2	1	0.3	.319	.393	.546	.333	.289	.363	.508	.294	12.6	38-RF -7	
2007	HOU	MLB	30	192	18	5	0	8	27	16	30	1	1	-1.4	.178	.257	.349	-.295	.185	.267	.369	.220	-9.1	29-CF 2	14-RF 4
2008	NYA	MLB	31	321	35	14	1	11	43	28	61	4	1	-0.2	.232	.305	.403	-.113	.232	.308	.420	.257	-0.6	78-RF0	

Breakout: 22% Improve: 46% Collapse: 31% Attrition: 32%   Comparables: Jermaine Dye, Bubba Trammell, Chris Cron, Ernie Young

Desperate for any outfielders the last week of the season after Cameron, Bradley, and Mackowiak were all lost to injury, the Padres dealt for Lane, who was at the end of his second straight lost season for the Astros. Once one of our favorites, Lane is now just a guy who can't hit; the Yankees signed him to a minor league deal anyway.

Rob Mackowiak   UT

Bats: L   Throws: R   Height: 5' 11"   Weight: 195   Born: June 20, 1976   Age: 32

YEAR	TEAM	LVL	AGE	PA	R	2B	3B	HR	RBI	BB	SO	SB	CS	EqBRR	AVG	OBP	SLG	MLVr	EqAVG	EqOBP	EqSLG	EqA	VORP	DEFENSE			
2005	PIT	MLB	29	512	57	21	3	9	58	43	100	8	4	-1.2	.272	.337	.389	-.011	.271	.337	.392	.255	8.6	50-3B	1	32-CF	-2
2006	CHA	MLB	30	290	31	12	1	5	23	28	59	5	2	-1.1	.290	.365	.404	.005	.286	.368	.409	.275	10.0	49-CF	-3	11-RF	-1
2007	CHA	MLB	31	268	34	11	2	6	36	23	53	3	1	2.0	.278	.354	.418	.019	.281	.360	.443	.279	6.1	48-LF	-6	10-RF	0
2007	SDN	MLB	31	61	6	3	0	0	2	3	18	1	0	1.1	.196	.262	.250	-.391	.196	.262	.250	.181	-4.2				
2008	WAS	MLB	32	194	24	8	1	3	20	17	38	3	1	0.2	.265	.336	.388	-.083	.264	.336	.395	.253	4.0	49-LF	-1		

Breakout: 15% Improve: 31% Collapse: 42% Attrition: 44%   Comparables: Russ Snyder, Todd Hollandsworth, Milt Thompson, Pat Sheridan

The Padres brought in a lot of players in 2007 who won't be with them in 2008. Look back at the last couple of pages: Bradley, Ensberg, Marcus Giles, Lane. They tried to let Barrett leave, but he wouldn't go. Mackowiak was another late-season pickup for the bench, but he went down with a sports hernia in September. He'll serve in a utility role for the Nationals this year, and is a good fit for their heavily right-handed team.

Colt Morton   C

Bats: R   Throws: R   Height: 6' 5"   Weight: 230   Born: April 10, 1982   Age: 26

YEAR	TEAM	LVL	AGE	PA	R	2B	3B	HR	RBI	BB	SO	SB	CS	EqBRR	AVG	OBP	SLG	MLVr	EqAVG	EqOBP	EqSLG	EqA	VORP	DEFENSE	
2005	FTW	A	23	265	27	15	0	10	46	35	57	0	0	-2.7	.261	.362	.464	.172	.220	.302	.379	.239	-1.4	59-C	-5
2005	LEL	A+	23	113	19	4	0	9	19	14	30	0	1	-1.4	.323	.407	.646	.452	.242	.319	.455	.261	3.9	23-C	-4
2006	LEL	A+	24	222	30	15	0	5	22	36	44	0	1	-2.3	.227	.374	.398	.020	.188	.308	.317	.225	-6.2	45-C	3
2006	MOB	AA	24	152	15	10	0	6	21	11	44	0	0	-1.1	.266	.329	.468	.152	.248	.303	.447	.254	4.2	37-C	2
2007	SAN	AA	25	116	17	3	0	6	19	15	34	0	0	-2.1	.266	.383	.489	.266	.235	.330	.439	.267	3.9	20-C	2
2008	SDN	MLB	26	171	17	7	0	7	22	18	48	1	0	-0.5	.216	.308	.398	-.153	.222	.315	.425	.251	3.6	44-C	0

Breakout: 32% Improve: 60% Collapse: 19% Attrition: 18%   Comparables: Eric Wedge, David Ross, Michael Johnson, Jeff Bailey

Shoulder surgery made 2007 a lost year for Morton, who was lapped by Hundley while he rehabbed. The two are similar players, but Morton has a bit more power. His appearance in the majors—he spent September on the roster and got one at-bat—was more about him being on the 40-man roster than earning the call-up. The Padres like the way he catches, and his power seemed to come back after the surgery, so he adds to the deep stable of Pads back-stops.

PITCHERS

Heath Bell

Bats: R   Throws: R   Height: 6' 3"   Weight: 225   Born: September 29, 1977   Age: 30

YEAR	TEAM	LVL	AGE	W	L	SV	G	GS	IP	H	BB	SO	HR	GB%	BABIP	STUFF	WHIP	ERA	PERA	EqERA	EqH9	EqBB9	EqSO9	EqHR9	VORP	SN/WX
2005	NOR	AAA	27	1	0	6	13	2	26²	15	5	29	1	63.5%	.233	17	0.75	1.69	2.84	2.92	5.8	2.2	7.3	0.4	7.4	—
2005	NYN	MLB	27	1	3	0	42	0	46²	56	13	43	3	47.7%	.373	6	1.48	5.59	5.22	6.31	11.2	2.4	7.7	0.6	-2.0	-0.01
2006	NOR	AAA	28	3	3	12	30	0	35¹	27	8	56	1	54.5%	.356	29	1.00	1.28	3.61	2.94	8.0	2.7	10.2	0.5	10.0	—
2006	NYN	MLB	28	0	0	0	22	0	37	51	11	35	6	53.3%	.398	-5	1.68	5.11	8.54	6.94	13.1	2.3	8.2	1.3	-0.6	0.29
2007	SDN	MLB	29	6	4	2	81	0	93²	60	30	102	3	60.5%	.259	38	0.96	2.02	2.40	2.15	5.9	2.4	9.1	0.3	39.7	5.66
2008	SDN	MLB	30	4	3	6	54	0	61¹	54	22	61	4	53.4%	.298	13	1.24	2.97	3.55	3.50	8.0	3.0	7.8	0.6	15.8	1.40

Breakout: 30% Improve: 66% Collapse: 13% Attrition: 8%   Comparables: Steve Karsay, Mike Timlin, Greg McMichael, Jay Howell

Take a pitcher with good stuff and a home-run problem, put him in a park fly balls don't leave, and watch the fun. Bell allowed a homer every 7 2/3 innings prior to last season, then gave up one every 31 IP last year. Like Rafael Be-tancourt, Bell pounds the strike zone with a plus fastball he locates well and relies on heavily. The only concern is that he was worked heavily last year. He's the top in-house candidate to supplant Trevor Hoffman if Hoffman's late-season decline continues.

Doug Brocail

Bats: L   Throws: R   Height: 6' 5"   Weight: 250   Born: May 16, 1967   Age: 41

YEAR	TEAM	LVL	AGE	W	L	SV	G	GS	IP	H	BB	SO	HR	GB%	BABIP	STUFF	WHIP	ERA	PERA	EqERA	EqH9	EqBB9	EqSO9	EqHR9	VORP	SN/WX
2005	TEX	MLB	38	5	3	1	61	0	73¹	90	34	61	2	48.6%	.373	9	1.69	5.53	4.73	5.21	10.2	4.0	7.1	0.2	0.1	-0.29
2006	SDN	MLB	39	2	2	0	25	0	28¹	27	8	19	1	46.7%	.299	-1	1.24	4.77	3.41	5.40	8.9	2.2	5.4	0.3	2.7	0.35
2007	SDN	MLB	40	5	1	0	67	0	76²	66	24	43	8	44.0%	.243	-5	1.17	3.05	3.32	3.59	7.4	2.3	4.8	0.9	16.3	1.75
2008	HOU	MLB	41	2	3	2	45	0	53²	55	19	33	6	45.5%	.286	-11	1.37	4.25	4.38	4.56	9.2	2.8	4.9	0.9	6.0	0.50

Breakout: 10% Improve: 41% Collapse: 33% Attrition: 35%   Comparables: Jose Mesa, Mike Timlin, Ron Reed, Al Benton

Brocail's 2007 ERA is a mirage produced by pitching in the best environment for pitchers in the game, and even with that adavantage he still allowed eight homers and had a mediocre K/BB ratio. His comeback from heart disease and angioplasty is a nice story, but let's not confuse the narrative with the pitching. The Astros signed Brocail to a one-year deal, paying $2.5 million for an ERA over 5.00.

Kevin Cameron

Bats: R   Throws: R   Height: 6' 1"   Weight: 180   Born: December 15, 1979   Age: 28

YEAR	TEAM	LVL	AGE	W	L	SV	G	GS	IP	H	BB	SO	HR	GB%	BABIP	STUFF	WHIP	ERA	PERA	EqERA	EqH9	EqBB9	EqSO9	EqHR9	VORP	SN/WX
2005	NBR	AA	25	6	2	6	43	0	79¹	76	27	60	8	55.3%	.280	-29	1.30	2.72	6.01	5.83	10.1	4.4	4.2	1.4	-1.8	—
2006	ROC	AAA	26	6	4	9	40	0	66	53	26	65	2	57.2%	.278	4	1.20	3.00	4.08	4.57	8.3	4.3	6.4	0.4	7.2	—
2007	SDN	MLB	27	2	0	0	48	0	58	55	36	50	0	50.3%	.322	15	1.57	2.79	3.73	3.51	8.5	4.7	7.2	0.2	13.3	1.39
2008	SDN	MLB	28	2	2	2	34	0	43¹	43	22	34	3	50.2%	.303	-3	1.50	4.20	4.76	4.94	9.0	4.3	6.2	0.6	4.1	0.30

Breakout: 11% Improve: 27% Collapse: 56% Attrition: 36%   Comparables: Horacio Piña, Rodney Myers, Brandon Puffer, Marc Valdes

A Rule 5 pick out of the Twins' system, Cameron was the ultimate low-leverage pitcher last year, making just one appearance all season with the Padres leading by less than four runs, and entering just four games with the score tied. That's a twelfth man. He has a good fastball and all the control of a 17-year-old boy at his first spring break in Daytona.

Joshua Geer

Bats: R   Throws: R   Height: 6' 3"   Weight: 190   Born: June 2, 1983   Age: 25

YEAR	TEAM	LVL	AGE	W	L	SV	G	GS	IP	H	BB	SO	HR	GB%	BABIP	STUFF	WHIP	ERA	PERA	EqERA	EqH9	EqBB9	EqSO9	EqHR9	VORP	SN/WX
2005	FTW	A	22	1	1	0	5	5	29²	29	9	23	3	54.3%	.302	-18	1.28	4.24	7.24	7.27	11.1	4.5	4.2	2.1	-4.8	—
2005	EUG	A-	22	2	3	1	7	6	31²	35	4	25	5	52.2%	.286	-54	1.23	3.69	10.83	7.76	12.5	3.4	0.7	3.7	-6.4	—
2006	FTW	A	23	6	2	0	12	11	72¹	72	13	46	3	51.9%	.307	-21	1.18	3.12	6.35	6.03	11.3	3.6	2.6	1.3	-3.0	—
2006	LEL	A+	23	7	4	0	15	15	89²	116	16	56	7	50.4%	.354	-28	1.48	4.94	7.66	8.16	13.2	2.9	2.9	1.4	-23.2	—
2007	SAN	AA	24	16	6	0	26	26	171¹	163	27	102	9	49.0%	.287	0	1.11	3.20	4.54	4.94	9.7	2.1	3.5	0.8	11.8	—
2008	SDN	MLB	25	6	9	0	31	19	122¹	144	40	58	18	46.7%	.299	-11	1.50	5.44	5.95	6.27	10.7	2.7	3.7	1.3	-6.9	0.10

Breakout: 13% Improve: 37% Collapse: 30% Attrition: 17%   Comparables: Mike Ferry, Gary Wilson, Bill King, Mike Mathile

Geer might not have the raw talent that many of the recent pitchers out of Rice do, but at least he's been able to stay healthy. He's a control pitcher with an upper-80s fastball, a solid curve, and a very good changeup whose success comes from his ability to locate all of his pitches at will. Coming off a season in which he led the Texas League in wins and ERA, he projects as an innings-eater at the very least.

Justin Germano

Bats: R   Throws: R   Height: 6' 3"   Weight: 205   Born: August 6, 1982   Age: 25

YEAR	TEAM	LVL	AGE	W	L	SV	G	GS	IP	H	BB	SO	HR	GB%	BABIP	STUFF	WHIP	ERA	PERA	EqERA	EqH9	EqBB9	EqSO9	EqHR9	VORP	SN/WX
2005	POR	AAA	22	7	6	0	19	19	112	111	32	100	13	44.6%	.311	4	1.28	3.70	5.11	4.99	9.5	2.9	5.8	1.3	7.1	—
2005	LOU	AAA	22	3	2	0	8	8	49¹	62	5	38	7	46.3%	.359	1	1.36	4.02	6.44	5.59	11.6	1.3	4.8	1.5	0.1	—
2006	LOU	AAA	23	8	6	0	19	18	117²	124	22	67	11	53.1%	.309	-15	1.25	3.69	6.06	5.84	10.8	2.3	3.7	1.4	-2.8	—
2006	SWB	AAA	23	2	0	0	6	6	38	40	2	25	2	60.5%	.322	6	1.11	2.84	4.92	4.79	11.1	1.0	4.3	0.8	3.2	—
2007	POR	AAA	24	4	0	0	5	5	32	23	3	20	0	57.1%	.237	18	0.81	1.69	2.38	2.20	5.2	1.1	4.1	0.3	12.4	—
2007	SDN	MLB	24	7	10	0	26	23	133¹	133	40	78	14	50.9%	.282	5	1.30	4.46	4.17	4.57	8.9	2.3	5.0	0.9	13.1	2.71
2008	SDN	MLB	25	7	7	0	34	17	123	128	37	73	13	49.9%	.289	0	1.34	4.04	4.67	4.70	9.4	2.5	4.6	0.9	13.5	2.10

Breakout: 20% Improve: 44% Collapse: 31% Attrition: 22%   Comparables: Paul Thormodsgard, Tommy Boggs, Chris Reitsma, Sean Bergman

Waived by the Phillies in spring training, Germano landed back in San Diego, his original organization, and spent most of the year as the fifth starter. Even in Petco, Germano needs to be perfect to survive, and his performance valences tracked his control: a 3.5 K/BB in his first nine starts led to a 2.67 ERA; a 1.5 K/BB in his next 14 yielded a 5.93 ERA and got him booted from the rotation. The signings of Randy Wolf and Mark Prior bode ill for his future in San Diego.

Justin Hampson

Bats: L　Throws: L　Height: 6' 1"　Weight: 200　Born: May 24, 1980　Age: 28

YEAR	TEAM	LVL	AGE	W	L	SV	G	GS	IP	H	BB	SO	HR	GB%	BABIP	STUFF	WHIP	ERA	PERA	EqERA	EqH9	EqBB9	EqSO9	EqHR9	VORP	SN/WX
2005	CSP	AAA	25	5	13	0	27	26	144¹	167	71	93	18	48.1%	.317	-18	1.65	5.99	5.64	6.26	9.5	4.7	3.8	1.2	-10.3	—
2006	CSP	AAA	26	8	4	0	31	13	121¹	121	39	95	10	44.9%	.314	-3	1.32	3.34	4.51	4.40	8.9	3.2	5.1	1.0	15.6	—
2006	COL	MLB	26	1	0	0	5	1	12	19	5	9	3	31.1%	.381	-23	2.00	7.50	10.61	8.03	13.1	2.9	5.8	2.2	-1.3	-0.22
2007	POR	AAA	27	1	1	0	10	0	12²	12	8	12	3	34.2%	.273	-11	1.57	3.54	6.21	4.15	7.6	5.5	6.2	2.1	2.1	—
2007	SDN	MLB	27	2	3	0	39	0	53¹	48	16	34	1	48.2%	.288	10	1.20	2.70	3.16	2.77	8.1	2.4	5.5	0.2	17.4	0.84
2008	SDN	MLB	28	2	2	2	36	0	37¹	37	16	25	4	44.7%	.282	-9	1.40	3.89	4.73	4.50	8.9	3.5	5.2	0.9	5.6	0.40

Breakout: 23%　Improve: 42%　Collapse: 33%　Attrition: 40%　　　　Comparables: Fred Scherman, Bob Smith, Don Hood, John Cummings

A command lefty, Hampson rode the shuttle to Triple-A Portland last season more because of roster machinations than his own performance. A starter in the Rockies' system, his effectiveness out of the bullpen last season positions him as the non-specialist lefty this year, especially if Joe Thatcher takes the LOOGY spot.

Clay Hensley

Bats: R　Throws: R　Height: 5' 11"　Weight: 190　Born: August 31, 1979　Age: 28

YEAR	TEAM	LVL	AGE	W	L	SV	G	GS	IP	H	BB	SO	HR	GB%	BABIP	STUFF	WHIP	ERA	PERA	EqERA	EqH9	EqBB9	EqSO9	EqHR9	VORP	SN/WX
2005	POR	AAA	25	2	2	0	15	14	90¹	63	22	71	8	58.4%	.228	10	0.94	2.99	3.29	3.49	6.4	2.5	5.1	1.0	19.9	—
2005	SDN	MLB	25	1	1	0	24	1	47²	33	17	28	0	56.3%	.234	8	1.05	1.70	2.45	2.28	6.1	2.9	4.8	0.2	16.8	1.97
2006	SDN	MLB	26	11	12	0	37	29	187	174	76	122	15	55.5%	.285	11	1.34	3.71	4.14	4.09	8.9	3.2	5.6	0.7	40.8	5.39
2007	POR	AAA	27	2	7	0	13	13	71	102	34	50	10	53.3%	.374	-24	1.92	6.72	8.13	8.32	12.2	4.5	4.6	1.4	-21.2	—
2007	SDN	MLB	27	2	3	0	13	9	50	62	32	30	5	50.3%	.341	-11	1.88	6.84	6.75	7.30	11.3	4.9	5.1	0.9	-7.9	-0.10
2008	SDN	MLB	28	5	6	1	31	15	95	100	44	59	10	50.8%	.295	-7	1.51	4.65	5.33	5.42	9.5	3.9	4.9	0.9	3.7	0.90

Breakout: 10%　Improve: 37%　Collapse: 28%　Attrition: 31%　　　　Comparables: Chuck Rainey, Mark Bomback, Bob Chesnes, Denny Harriger

The staff savior in 2006, Hensley was never right in 2007 and was eventually diagnosed with a torn labrum. He elected to not have surgery and is rehabbing the injury with an eye toward making the rotation this year. As with Germano, he may be supplanted by the winter imports. Hensley wasn't gifted with great stuff before he got hurt, so expecting him to pitch effectively through a weakened shoulder is folly.

Trevor Hoffman

Bats: R　Throws: R　Height: 6' 0"　Weight: 215　Born: October 13, 1967　Age: 40

YEAR	TEAM	LVL	AGE	W	L	SV	G	GS	IP	H	BB	SO	HR	GB%	BABIP	STUFF	WHIP	ERA	PERA	EqERA	EqH9	EqBB9	EqSO9	EqHR9	VORP	SN/WX
2005	SDN	MLB	37	1	6	43	60	0	57²	52	12	54	3	37.8%	.299	19	1.11	2.96	2.98	3.49	7.7	1.7	7.4	0.5	11.2	3.69
2006	SDN	MLB	38	0	2	46	65	0	63	48	13	50	6	33.2%	.236	12	0.97	2.14	2.92	2.45	7.1	1.6	6.6	0.7	25.7	6.00
2007	SDN	MLB	39	4	5	42	61	0	57¹	49	15	44	2	33.0%	.278	14	1.12	2.98	2.78	3.26	7.4	2.0	6.4	0.3	15.6	2.89
2008	SDN	MLB	40	3	5	37	35	0	41	40	11	30	5	36.8%	.279	-5	1.25	3.78	4.23	4.34	8.9	2.2	5.7	1.2	7.2	1.40

Breakout: 3%　Improve: 10%　Collapse: 65%　Attrition: 37%　　　　Comparables: Steve Reed, Art Fowler, Ellis Kinder, Mike Timlin

When your changeup is your best pitch, the end comes when you can't throw your fastball hard enough to create some differentiation between the two offerings. That's where Hoffman was at the end of last season; his fastball sat in the low 80s and was often elevated, leading to the two blown saves that sent the Padres home for October. His overall stat line reveals little decline, and it's worth remembering that in the three weeks prior to those last two outings he had thrown seven scoreless innings with eight strikeouts and one walk. Still, even if it doesn't come this year, the end is in sight for the future first-ballot Hall of Famer.

Will Inman

Bats: R   Throws: R   Height: 6′ 0″   Weight: 200   Born: February 6, 1987   Age: 21

YEAR	TEAM	LVL	AGE	W	L	SV	G	GS	IP	H	BB	SO	HR	GB%	BABIP	STUFF	WHIP	ERA	PERA	EqERA	EqH9	EqBB9	EqSO9	EqHR9	VORP	SN/WX
2005	HEL	Rk	18	6	0	1	13	5	45	29	11	58	5	55.9%	.250	9	0.89	2.00	6.60	4.82	8.4	5.3	5.5	2.7	3.2	—
2006	WVA	A	19	10	2	0	23	20	110	75	24	134	3	42.6%	.279	32	0.90	1.72	4.68	3.77	8.4	3.8	6.3	0.8	19.9	—
2007	BRV	A+	20	4	3	0	13	13	78²	56	23	98	4	42.9%	.287	34	1.00	1.72	4.81	3.58	8.7	4.1	7.8	1.0	15.8	—
2007	HUN	AA	20	1	5	0	8	8	39²	38	16	42	7	53.6%	.316	0	1.36	5.44	8.45	7.61	10.8	4.2	6.4	2.7	-8.2	—
2007	SAN	AA	20	3	3	0	7	7	41	33	19	40	6	26.1%	.267	8	1.27	4.17	6.25	6.03	8.9	5.3	6.3	1.9	-1.8	—
2008	SDN	MLB	21	9	9	0	26	26	151²	144	69	135	20	40.1%	.287	17	1.40	4.29	5.05	4.88	8.6	3.8	6.9	1.2	13.0	2.70

Breakout: 21% Improve: 62% Collapse: 19% Attrition: 14%   Comparables: Kyle Davies, Matt Riley, Frankie Rodriguez, Luke Prokopec

On paper, Inman looks like an elite pitching prospect. Just 20 years old, he has reached Double-A, and has a career ERA of 2.53 with 373 strikeouts in 317 innings. Like most Padres pitching prospects, however, Inman relies more on finesse than stuff; his only plus pitch is his fastball, and that's notable more for his outstanding command of it than its 88 to 91 mph velocity. Scouts aren't terribly impressed, which is why the Brewers had to throw in two other players along with Inman in order to fetch a good middle reliever in Scott Linebrink. Inman met with some adversity for the first time in his career at Double-A last year, and he'll need to make some adjustments to project as a starter in the long term.

Wade LeBlanc

Bats: L   Throws: L   Height: 6′ 3″   Weight: 202   Born: August 7, 1984   Age: 23

YEAR	TEAM	LVL	AGE	W	L	SV	G	GS	IP	H	BB	SO	HR	GB%	BABIP	STUFF	WHIP	ERA	PERA	EqERA	EqH9	EqBB9	EqSO9	EqHR9	VORP	SN/WX
2006	FTW	A	21	4	1	0	7	7	32¹	31	10	27	1	46.8%	.303	-9	1.28	2.24	6.28	4.76	10.8	5.4	3.8	1.0	2.6	—
2006	EUG	A-	21	1	0	0	7	3	21¹	19	6	20	0	39.0%	.339	-9	1.18	4.27	5.87	7.13	11.2	5.1	4.6	0.5	-3.0	—
2007	LEL	A+	22	6	5	0	16	16	92	72	17	90	5	42.0%	.275	12	0.97	2.64	3.92	4.21	7.5	2.7	5.1	0.8	13.5	—
2007	SAN	AA	22	7	3	0	12	11	57¹	48	19	55	8	45.9%	.267	-5	1.17	3.46	5.82	5.16	9.1	4.0	6.2	1.9	2.6	—
2008	SDN	MLB	23	8	9	0	24	24	141¹	142	56	97	19	41.5%	.282	7	1.40	4.49	5.12	5.14	9.1	3.3	5.4	1.2	9.0	2.10

Breakout: 18% Improve: 42% Collapse: 33% Attrition: 14%   Comparables: Garrett Olson, Alan Embree, Casey Fossum, Tom Gorzelanny

LeBlanc is another pitcher who leaves hitters shaking their heads in frustration without lighting up the radar gun. Although his fastball rarely touches 90 mph, it's a good enough pitch to set up his changeup, which is an absolute monster and among the best in the minor leagues. He's moving quickly through the system and could get a look toward the end of the season, but his ceiling is third or fourth starter.

Wil Ledezma

Bats: L   Throws: L   Height: 6′ 4″   Weight: 210   Born: January 21, 1981   Age: 27

YEAR	TEAM	LVL	AGE	W	L	SV	G	GS	IP	H	BB	SO	HR	GB%	BABIP	STUFF	WHIP	ERA	PERA	EqERA	EqH9	EqBB9	EqSO9	EqHR9	VORP	SN/WX
2005	TOL	AAA	24	5	3	0	11	10	51	52	27	44	3	46.5%	.320	2	1.55	5.29	5.85	6.75	10.4	5.8	5.8	0.8	-6.0	—
2005	DET	MLB	24	2	4	0	10	10	49²	61	24	30	10	44.4%	.317	-23	1.71	7.06	7.19	8.46	10.6	4.1	5.2	1.6	-14.4	-0.79
2006	TOL	AAA	25	4	3	0	12	12	71²	60	23	66	6	39.4%	.295	4	1.17	2.53	5.12	4.29	9.1	3.7	6.4	1.2	9.5	—
2006	DET	MLB	25	3	3	0	24	7	60¹	60	23	39	5	36.5%	.286	1	1.38	3.58	4.04	4.15	8.8	3.1	5.3	0.6	12.6	1.00
2007	DET	MLB	26	3	1	0	23	0	35²	38	26	24	4	42.2%	.312	-7	1.79	4.79	5.68	5.09	9.4	5.9	5.6	1.0	2.6	-0.05
2007	ATL	MLB	26	0	2	0	12	0	9¹	12	4	7	1	58.8%	.344	-18	1.71	7.74	5.31	9.00	10.8	2.7	6.3	0.9	-4.0	-0.23
2007	SDN	MLB	26	0	0	0	9	1	14¹	20	8	16	2	33.3%	.429	-3	1.95	6.29	9.09	7.71	12.9	4.5	9.6	1.3	-1.9	0.11
2008	SDN	MLB	27	2	2	1	34	2	48¹	46	23	39	5	43.2%	.286	-1	1.42	4.07	4.68	4.71	8.6	4.0	6.4	0.9	5.7	0.50

Breakout: 42% Improve: 60% Collapse: 23% Attrition: 37%   Comparables: Jack O'Connor, Kenny Rogers, Joe Beimel, Drew Hall

Lanky, long-armed and frustrating as hell, Ledezma was twice dealt for other left-handed relievers last year, a sign that he's not filling the need for his teams. Using him as a starter hasn't worked either, as his ERA and ratios are worse when he opens the game. His live arm means he'll keep getting chances, and there are worse places for a guy to try to pull it together than San Diego, but he could still be two teams from finding himself.

Greg Maddux

Bats: R   Throws: R   Height: 6' 0"   Weight: 180   Born: April 14, 1966   Age: 42

YEAR	TEAM	LVL	AGE	W	L	SV	G	GS	IP	H	BB	SO	HR	GB%	BABIP	STUFF	WHIP	ERA	PERA	EqERA	EqH9	EqBB9	EqSO9	EqHR9	VORP	SN/WX
2005	CHN	MLB	39	13	15	0	35	35	225	239	36	136	29	55.1%	.299	5	1.22	4.24	4.51	4.49	9.7	1.3	5.0	1.1	28.6	4.10
2006	CHN	MLB	40	9	11	0	22	22	136¹	153	23	81	14	52.1%	.313	12	1.29	4.69	4.31	4.76	10.0	1.3	5.0	0.8	14.0	1.90
2006	LAN	MLB	40	6	3	0	12	12	73²	66	14	36	6	55.0%	.263	13	1.09	3.30	2.93	3.34	7.4	1.5	4.1	0.6	18.7	2.51
2007	SDN	MLB	41	14	11	0	34	34	198	221	25	104	14	53.8%	.315	16	1.24	4.14	3.94	4.03	9.8	0.9	4.5	0.6	35.7	5.42
2008	SDN	MLB	42	6	6	0	24	15	101	113	19	49	10	51.4%	.298	-6	1.31	4.07	4.65	4.76	10.2	1.6	3.8	0.9	11.9	1.80

Breakout: 7%   Improve: 18%   Collapse: 44%   Attrition: 50%   Comparables: Dennis Martinez, Warren Spahn, Don Sutton, David Wells

Maddux has 347 career wins. No pitcher born since 1921 has won 360 games, and no pitcher born since 1887 has won 365. If Cal Ripken Jr. wasn't a unanimous Hall of Fame selection, perhaps no one will ever be, but you have to wonder about people who would deny themselves the honor of voting for Greg Maddux for the Hall of Fame. With 2 2/3 strategically relocated innings, Maddux would have a 20-year streak of 200-inning seasons (he threw 199 1/3 in 2002). While he's no longer a Cy Young contender, he keeps piling up league-average seasons for winning teams. Look for more of the same this year.

Cla Meredith

Bats: R   Throws: R   Height: 6' 0"   Weight: 180   Born: June 4, 1983   Age: 25

YEAR	TEAM	LVL	AGE	W	L	SV	G	GS	IP	H	BB	SO	HR	GB%	BABIP	STUFF	WHIP	ERA	PERA	EqERA	EqH9	EqBB9	EqSO9	EqHR9	VORP	SN/WX
2005	PME	AA	22	1	0	9	12	0	15	5	3	12	0	75.0%	.143	7	0.53	0.00	0.31	0.00	3.2	2.6	4.5	0.0	8.7	—
2005	PAW	AAA	22	2	5	10	40	0	48¹	63	12	42	6	55.9%	.370	-17	1.55	5.59	7.50	6.85	12.7	3.0	5.6	1.4	-6.2	—
2006	PAW	AAA	23	0	0	0	8	0	13	16	5	14	1	68.3%	.395	-13	1.62	5.54	7.18	8.03	12.4	4.4	7.3	1.5	-3.3	—
2006	POR	AAA	23	3	0	2	24	0	32	26	4	24	2	66.3%	.264	3	0.94	1.41	3.10	1.72	6.9	1.4	4.9	0.9	13.5	—
2006	SDN	MLB	23	5	1	0	45	0	50²	30	6	37	3	70.0%	.199	19	0.71	1.07	2.21	1.46	5.7	0.9	6.2	0.5	27.9	3.76
2007	SDN	MLB	24	5	6	0	80	0	79²	94	17	59	6	72.2%	.348	6	1.39	3.50	4.81	4.29	10.8	1.6	6.4	0.7	13.0	0.47
2008	SDN	MLB	25	4	3	3	58	3	76¹	74	19	49	5	61.7%	.288	1	1.22	3.06	3.61	3.65	8.8	2.1	5.0	0.5	19.2	1.70

Breakout: 25%   Improve: 55%   Collapse: 26%   Attrition: 22%   Comparables: Roger McDowell, Bill Castro, Brad Clontz, Brad Thompson

Meredith's ERA jumped last year on the heels of a BABIP correction (.344 in 2007 vs. .199 in 2006), and a completely fluky homer-per-fly ball rate. Meredith allowed six homers despite a 5.8 GB/FB ratio, which is not going to happen again. He still needs to work on lefty batters, who see him well enough to create problems (17 strikeouts in 144 plate appearances, versus 42 in 198 for righties). Acquiring Bard and Meredith for Doug Mirabelli may have been the best move of Kevin Towers' substantial career.

Jake Peavy

Bats: R   Throws: R   Height: 6' 1"   Weight: 180   Born: May 31, 1981   Age: 27

YEAR	TEAM	LVL	AGE	W	L	SV	G	GS	IP	H	BB	SO	HR	GB%	BABIP	STUFF	WHIP	ERA	PERA	EqERA	EqH9	EqBB9	EqSO9	EqHR9	VORP	SN/WX
2005	SDN	MLB	24	13	7	0	30	30	203	162	50	216	18	46.0%	.281	38	1.04	2.88	3.11	3.14	7.1	2.0	8.7	0.8	53.1	6.53
2006	SDN	MLB	25	11	14	0	32	32	202¹	187	62	215	23	39.8%	.307	30	1.23	4.09	4.14	4.23	8.8	2.4	8.9	1.0	39.2	5.86
2007	SDN	MLB	26	19	6	0	34	34	223¹	169	68	240	13	45.4%	.279	47	1.06	2.54	2.79	2.67	6.8	2.3	9.0	0.5	77.0	9.07
2008	SDN	MLB	27	15	8	0	31	31	212²	179	60	223	20	44.3%	.285	32	1.13	2.98	3.40	3.44	7.6	2.4	8.2	0.8	52.3	7.20

Breakout: 11%   Improve: 36%   Collapse: 29%   Attrition: 6%   Comparables: Melido Perez, Don Sutton, Dennis Leonard, Tom Seaver

Peavy was obnoxiously consistent in the best year of his career, going exactly seven innings in 20 of his starts, allowing four or more runs just six times, and throwing between 95 and 118 pitches in every outing. With his talent and home park, he could win a few more Cy Young awards. The contract extension that takes him through 2012, worth at least $52 million, is a small risk because the Pads had Peavy signed through 2009 already and a lot can happen in two years. The price, however, is low enough to make the risk tolerable.

Will Startup

| | | | | Bats: L | | | Throws: L | | Height: 6' 0" | | Weight: 195 | | Born: August 4, 1984 | | | Age: 23 |

YEAR	TEAM	LVL	AGE	W	L	SV	G	GS	IP	H	BB	SO	HR	GB%	BABIP	STUFF	WHIP	ERA	PERA	EqERA	EqH9	EqBB9	EqSO9	EqHR9	VORP	SN/WX
2005	ROM	A	20	3	2	5	25	0	38	31	6	30	3	40.9%	.262	-17	0.97	2.37	5.47	5.73	9.3	3.3	3.5	1.6	-0.5	—
2006	MIS	AA	21	3	0	4	16	0	25¹	18	6	29	0	48.4%	.300	23	0.96	0.72	3.29	1.93	7.7	2.7	7.3	0.0	9.5	—
2006	RIC	AAA	21	5	2	0	30	0	42¹	45	11	38	3	42.6%	.341	0	1.33	3.42	5.34	4.76	10.4	2.9	5.9	1.1	3.7	—
2007	RIC	AAA	22	3	2	1	43	0	49¹	39	18	49	3	29.3%	.286	5	1.16	2.19	3.98	3.28	7.9	3.7	6.8	0.8	12.0	—
2007	POR	AAA	22	0	0	0	14	0	19¹	13	11	16	2	25.5%	.208	-4	1.24	4.66	3.23	4.50	4.9	4.9	5.4	0.9	2.4	—
2008	SDN	MLB	23	3	3	3	24	5	52¹	47	24	42	6	36.0%	.269	2	1.35	3.86	4.54	4.42	8.2	3.8	6.3	1.1	8.0	1.00

Breakout: 20% Improve: 33% Collapse: 50% Attrition: 22%   Comparables: Mike Cosgrove, Sean Spencer, Jaime Cerda, Randy Beam

The closer on Georgia's College World Series team in 2004, Startup had been relieving but rarely closing in the Braves' system before coming to San Diego with Ledezma for Royce Ring. Startup doesn't have the power stuff you'd like to see in a high-leverage reliever, which limits his eventual upside, but he pitched well in the Arizona Fall League and could make the Pads' roster as a seventh-inning guy this spring.

Tim Stauffer

| | | | | Bats: R | | | Throws: R | | Height: 6' 1" | | Weight: 205 | | Born: June 2, 1982 | | | Age: 26 |

YEAR	TEAM	LVL	AGE	W	L	SV	G	GS	IP	H	BB	SO	HR	GB%	BABIP	STUFF	WHIP	ERA	PERA	EqERA	EqH9	EqBB9	EqSO9	EqHR9	VORP	SN/WX
2005	POR	AAA	23	3	5	0	13	13	75¹	90	17	64	5	45.1%	.362	6	1.42	5.14	5.79	6.43	11.7	2.4	5.5	0.8	-6.5	—
2005	SDN	MLB	23	3	6	0	15	14	81	92	29	49	10	41.8%	.312	-4	1.49	5.33	5.40	5.56	10.1	2.9	5.0	1.1	-0.2	0.66
2006	POR	AAA	24	7	12	0	28	26	153¹	199	52	89	20	43.4%	.349	-31	1.64	5.53	7.26	7.19	11.7	3.4	3.5	1.6	-26.3	—
2007	POR	AAA	25	8	5	0	25	20	130²	147	36	96	12	45.4%	.328	1	1.40	4.34	4.40	4.77	9.1	2.7	4.8	1.0	12.2	—
2007	SDN	MLB	25	0	1	0	2	2	7²	15	6	6	5	28.1%	.370	-71	2.74	21.04	23.62	23.62	16.9	5.6	6.8	5.6	-12.6	-0.50
2008	SDN	MLB	26	5	7	0	25	15	97¹	106	37	61	13	43.0%	.294	-5	1.47	5.11	5.58	5.87	9.9	3.2	4.9	1.2	-1.4	0.50

Breakout: 45% Improve: 69% Collapse: 11% Attrition: 29%   Comparables: Brian Powell, Bob Wolcott, Fred Talbot, Scott Klingenbeck

"Stauffer's, nothing comes closer to homer." He's been dinged 15 times in 94 2/3 career innings, including five in two hideous appearances last year. The fourth overall pick in the 2003 draft, Stauffer has never lived up to that billing. Shoulder surgery right after the draft may have altered his career path, but however he got here, he's now a fringe talent, and if a fringe pitcher can't make it in Petco . . .

Joe Thatcher

| | | | | Bats: L | | | Throws: L | | Height: 6' 2" | | Weight: 203 | | Born: April 10, 1981 | | | Age: 27 |

YEAR	TEAM	LVL	AGE	W	L	SV	G	GS	IP	H	BB	SO	HR	GB%	BABIP	STUFF	WHIP	ERA	PERA	EqERA	EqH9	EqBB9	EqSO9	EqHR9	VORP	SN/WX
2006	WVA	A	25	1	3	10	26	0	29	28	6	42	2	63.5%	.366	-14	1.17	2.48	7.79	7.01	12.6	3.9	7.7	1.8	-4.0	—
2006	BRV	A+	25	3	1	2	16	0	30	12	9	32	1	60.6%	.162	-2	0.70	0.30	3.29	3.41	4.0	3.7	5.6	0.6	7.1	—
2007	HUN	AA	26	1	0	0	14	0	16¹	11	2	20	0	45.7%	.294	15	0.80	0.55	3.17	1.80	7.8	1.8	7.8	0.0	6.3	—
2007	NAS	AAA	26	2	1	1	24	0	21²	19	7	33	0	56.6%	.373	21	1.20	2.07	3.90	2.95	9.3	3.0	10.1	0.0	6.3	—
2007	POR	AAA	26	1	0	0	8	0	8²	10	1	11	0	68.0%	.400	9	1.26	1.03	4.08	4.15	10.4	1.0	8.3	0.0	1.4	—
2007	SDN	MLB	26	2	2	0	22	0	21	13	6	16	1	54.8%	.197	9	0.90	1.29	2.17	2.42	5.2	2.0	6.0	0.4	7.6	0.38
2008	SDN	MLB	27	3	2	4	64	1	54	49	18	47	4	50.4%	.290	7	1.25	3.19	3.72	3.75	8.2	2.8	6.8	0.7	12.9	1.20

Breakout: 13% Improve: 28% Collapse: 46% Attrition: 14%   Comparables: Fred Scherman, Travis Miller, Gary Lucas, Scott Stewart

If Startup does get setup work, he should be paired with this guy. Thatcher was an independent league find by the Brewers in 2005, and part of the Linebrink trade at last year's deadline. He's a side-armer with a big slider, and is most certainly a LOOGY-in-training rather than a closer candidate. The Padres have often gone without a left-hander in the pen, but Thatcher and Hampson should give them two good ones this year.

Mike Thompson

Bats: R | Throws: R | Height: 6' 4" | Weight: 200 | Born: November 6, 1980 | Age: 27

YEAR	TEAM	LVL	AGE	W	L	SV	G	GS	IP	H	BB	SO	HR	GB%	BABIP	STUFF	WHIP	ERA	PERA	EqERA	EqH9	EqBB9	EqSO9	EqHR9	VORP	SN/WX
2005	MOB	AA	24	6	6	0	18	18	114²	116	27	68	6	46.8%	.307	-6	1.25	3.22	4.60	4.89	9.4	2.7	3.2	0.9	8.4	—
2005	POR	AAA	24	4	2	0	9	9	60	58	13	25	6	49.0%	.268	-9	1.18	3.15	4.19	3.51	8.8	2.2	2.4	1.1	13.1	—
2006	POR	AAA	25	6	1	0	13	13	69	69	20	41	4	46.2%	.300	-1	1.29	3.78	4.29	4.23	8.9	3.0	3.7	0.7	10.0	—
2006	SDN	MLB	25	4	5	0	19	16	92	103	30	35	13	50.5%	.288	-18	1.45	4.99	5.71	5.70	10.4	2.6	3.2	1.2	4.5	1.20
2007	POR	AAA	26	4	11	0	23	22	132²	171	40	71	19	46.4%	.332	-24	1.59	6.24	5.97	6.48	10.4	2.9	3.4	1.5	-13.0	—
2007	SDN	MLB	26	0	1	0	7	0	15²	19	7	5	2	43.3%	.321	-31	1.66	6.88	6.22	8.44	10.7	3.4	2.8	1.1	-5.0	-0.52
2008	PIT	MLB	27	4	6	0	30	11	89	113	31	39	12	47.2%	.316	-15	1.62	5.88	5.98	6.17	11.0	2.9	3.6	1.2	-5.4	-0.10

Breakout: 13% Improve: 44% Collapse: 35% Attrition: 22%   Comparables: Gary Wilson, Jim Brower, Jason Roach, Nic Ungs

After spending much of 2006 in the rotation, Thompson opened last year as the long man, allowed runs in five straight April outings, and was almost never heard from again. He got hammered at Triple-A Portland after his demotion and was repeatedly passed over as the Padres shuffled through their options at the back of the rotation. He lacks an out pitch, which limits his potential. The Pirates signed him to a minor league deal.

Brett Tomko

Bats: R | Throws: R | Height: 6' 1" | Weight: 220 | Born: April 7, 1973 | Age: 35

YEAR	TEAM	LVL	AGE	W	L	SV	G	GS	IP	H	BB	SO	HR	GB%	BABIP	STUFF	WHIP	ERA	PERA	EqERA	EqH9	EqBB9	EqSO9	EqHR9	VORP	SN/WX
2005	SFN	MLB	32	8	15	1	33	30	190²	205	57	114	20	40.3%	.301	5	1.37	4.48	4.64	4.74	9.7	2.4	4.9	0.9	19.3	2.41
2006	LAN	MLB	33	8	7	0	44	15	112¹	123	29	76	17	39.6%	.300	-5	1.35	4.73	4.16	4.63	8.8	1.9	5.4	1.2	8.4	1.05
2007	LAN	MLB	34	2	11	0	33	15	104	124	42	79	13	43.8%	.338	-2	1.60	5.80	5.10	5.74	10.0	3.0	6.2	1.0	-6.7	-0.29
2007	SDN	MLB	34	2	1	0	7	4	27¹	25	6	26	5	43.2%	.274	16	1.13	4.62	3.99	4.23	8.1	1.6	7.8	1.6	3.7	0.49
2008	SDN	MLB	35	5	5	1	33	11	90	93	29	63	11	42.8%	.291	-3	1.34	4.21	4.81	4.84	9.4	2.6	5.4	1.1	9.3	1.30

Breakout: 17% Improve: 47% Collapse: 26% Attrition: 38%   Comparables: Bobby Witt, Tim Wakefield, Don Robinson, Steve Trachsel

Tomko wants to be a starter, and he's a reasonable back-end guy with some long-ball issues, but he's also a classic candidate for a switch to the pen as he works off a good fastball and not much else. He had 33 strikeouts and just seven walks allowed in 29 2/3 relief innings last year and his K/BB out of the pen in 2006 was 29/9 in 29 2/3 IP. The home-run problem persists, but he does seem to be more effective in shorter stints. He was still a free agent as we went to press.

Chris Young

Bats: R | Throws: R | Height: 6' 10" | Weight: 260 | Born: May 25, 1979 | Age: 29

YEAR	TEAM	LVL	AGE	W	L	SV	G	GS	IP	H	BB	SO	HR	GB%	BABIP	STUFF	WHIP	ERA	PERA	EqERA	EqH9	EqBB9	EqSO9	EqHR9	VORP	SN/WX
2005	TEX	MLB	26	12	7	0	31	31	164²	162	45	137	19	34.2%	.294	20	1.26	4.26	3.67	3.87	8.0	2.4	7.1	0.9	24.1	3.56
2006	SDN	MLB	27	11	5	0	31	31	179¹	134	69	164	28	27.8%	.232	15	1.13	3.46	3.61	3.49	7.0	3.0	7.5	1.3	45.8	6.50
2007	SDN	MLB	28	9	8	0	30	30	173	118	72	167	10	30.3%	.246	38	1.10	3.12	2.70	3.26	6.1	3.2	8.0	0.5	45.8	6.00
2008	SDN	MLB	29	9	7	0	23	23	140	120	53	131	17	34.5%	.270	20	1.23	3.73	4.13	4.25	7.8	3.1	7.3	1.1	22.0	3.50

Breakout: 0% Improve: 19% Collapse: 39% Attrition: 22%   Comparables: Rick Sutcliffe, Andy Benes, Blake Stein, Steve Renko

While Young's work over the past two years has been impressive, it's fair to consider the warts. First, he's as well-suited to his home park as any player in baseball, an extreme fly-ball pitcher playing in a huge yard. Second, his 6-foot-10 body has been a problem for him, with trunk problems—back in '06, oblique in '07—that have now kept him under 180 innings in every season of his career, and he did not pitch well at all after the latter injury (33 walks and six homers allowed in 54 1/3 innings). He's good, but because of those shortcomings, he's not a star.

LINEOUTS

Hitters

PLAYER	TEAM	LVL	AGE	PA	R	2B	3B	HR	RBI	BB	SO	SB-CS	EqBRR	AVG/OBP/SLG	MLVr	EqAVG/EqOBP/EqSLG	EqA	VORP
C M. Canham*	EUG	A-	22	133	20	4	1	2	18	11	35	5-2	1.2	.293/.379/.397	.110	.194/.242/.250	.165	-20.6
OF Y. Carvajal	PDR	Rk	18	114	27	13	0	1	22	10	22	5-0	0.7	.340/.404/.500	.286	.226/.272/.340	.217	-12.4
OF B. Clark	LAN	MLB	34	66	7	4	0	0	5	6	11	1-2	-0.5	.224/.308/.293	-.239	.224/.318/.293	.207	-3.6
	SDN	MLB	34	57	6	1	2	0	6	8	7	0-1	-0.6	.306/.404/.408	.129	.306/.404/.408	.283	2.5
1B C. Cooper	LEL	A+	22	528	83	32	4	10	78	56	87	4-4	-3.3	.317/.397/.469	.235	.262/.330/.380	.249	-3.5
SS A. Cumberland*	PDR	Rk	18	95	16	2	1	0	7	7	9	6-1	-0.2	.318/.389/.365	.060	.222/.263/.256	.179	-14.0
3B D. Freese	LEL	A+	24	592	104	31	6	17	96	69	99	6-1	2.2	.302/.400/.489	.254	.248/.329/.387	.252	10.7
LF C. Huffman	LEL	A+	22	371	63	19	2	15	76	42	56	0-1	0.4	.307/.402/.522	.307	.252/.332/.407	.257	-1.9
	SAN	AA	22	197	28	4	1	7	28	22	44	0-0	0.4	.269/.362/.431	.157	.244/.321/.407	.254	-2.5
CF C. Hunter*	FTW	A	19	549	53	20	2	7	58	47	78	8-9	-5.4	.282/.344/.373	.065	.229/.282/.302	.203	-28.9
OF D. Macias*	SAN	AA	24	391	43	15	5	8	50	51	53	5-8	-3.6	.251/.355/.399	.086	.227/.320/.363	.238	-3.0
	POR	AAA	24	131	14	6	1	2	11	21	25	3-1	-1.5	.282/.397/.409	.094	.252/.366/.369	.266	3.0
OF P. McAnulty*	POR	AAA	26	265	25	12	1	4	31	29	47	0-2	-4.3	.262/.347/.373	-.067	.230/.316/.332	.228	-11.9
	SDN	MLB	26	43	5	1	0	1	5	3	10	0-0	0.1	.200/.256/.300	-.339	.200/.256/.300	.189	-2.6
1B B. Myrow*	POR	AAA	30	414	61	31	4	13	73	56	74	1-0	-4.7	.354/.440/.579	.483	.299/.387/.501	.305	30.1
INF O. Robles*	POR	AAA	31	113	9	5	3	0	11	8	9	0-1	-0.9	.284/.330/.392	-.054	.252/.301/.340	.225	-0.7
	SDN	MLB	31	33	0	0	0	0	2	2	4	0-0	0.0	.231/.286/.231	-.353	.250/.300/.250	.204	-1.7
LF T. Sledge*	SDN	MLB	30	233	22	9	0	7	23	27	60	1-2	-1.6	.210/.310/.360	-.144	.221/.326/.392	.249	-4.8
2B C. Stansberry	POR	AAA	25	548	83	33	3	14	75	70	95	10-10	-2.6	.273/.370/.446	.089	.242/.339/.401	.257	14.1
	SDN	MLB	25	10	1	0	0	0	1	0	3	0-0	0.1	.286/.375/.286	-.079	.250/.333/.250	.223	0.1

Mitch Canham has only been catching for three years, which means physically he's a very young 23. The Pads' supplemental first-round pick has a good approach at the plate and, as the catcher for back-to-back College World Series teams, has major intangibles points. ⊘ The Padres' long drought in finding Latin American talent might end with **Yefri Carvajal**, a teenage outfielder with outstanding hitting skills but not much else in the way of tools. ⊘ Padres fans won't remember **Brady Clark** fondly, as the outfielder's defensive miscues in Game 163 were key to their team's loss. He's lost too many steps to be a viable backup center fielder. ⊘ It's hard to take a first-base prospect seriously when he slugs .469 in the California League, and it's not like **Craig Cooper** brings speed or defense to the table. ⊘ **Drew Cumberland** was one the Pads' quintet of supplemental first-round picks last year. He has terrific speed that played well in his pro debut, but there are questions about his arm and range at shortstop. ⊘ **David Freese** was traded to the Cardinals for Jim Edmonds in December. His power and plate discipline make him a strong third-base prospect. ⊘ A left fielder because he has to be, **Chad Huffman** earned a promotion to Double-A last year and saw his contact rate and power numbers dip precipitously. He has to hit his way to the majors, so this is a critical year for him. ⊘ Burner **Cedric Hunter** followed up a big debut with a raw performance in the Midwest League. Just 20, he has to get back to the highly skilled game he showed in 2006. ⊘ **Drew Macias** draws walks and plays good defense, skills that would make him a solid fourth outfielder in the majors perhaps as soon as this year. ⊘ Bad-bodied **Paul McAnulty** has yet to show well in three cups of San Diego coffee. Despite this, he still looks like a serviceable pinch-hitter and spare outfielder who would provide good on-base skills. ⊘ **Brian Myrow** is in a similar bind, with a .413 career OBP in the minors and a .324 mark despite a .167 average in the majors. He's a lousy defensive infielder as well. ⊘ The Dodgers fished **Oscar Robles** out of the Mexican League in 2005 and got some solid utility work out of him. He hasn't hit since, but he's still clinging to the Padres' 40-man roster. ⊘ Like Lane, **Terrmel Sledge** was a BP favorite after he hit fairly well as a Last Expo in 2004, but injuries big and small have held him back, and when he has played he's been unproductive. He signed a two-year deal with the Nippon Ham Fighters. ⊘ Waiver claim **Craig Stansberry** had his best season as a pro last year, but the signing of Tadahito Iguchi puts a crimp in his shot at the second-base job this spring. Stansberry might still be the better option, even before considering his salary.

Pitchers

PLAYER	TEAM	LVL	AGE	W	L	SV	IP	H	BB	SO	HR	GB%	BABIP	STUFF	WHIP	ERA	PERA	EqERA	EqH9	EqBB9	EqSO9	EqHR9	VORP
M. Buschmann	LEL	A+	23	12	6	0	149¹	153	26	115	9	53.7%	.325	-5	1.20	2.89	5.19	4.75	10.2	2.7	4.0	1.0	12.9
C. Carrillo	POR	AAA	23	0	2	0	15²	22	14	8	2	51.7%	.364	-24	2.29	8.60	9.42	9.98	11.7	8.2	2.9	1.2	-7.4
J. Cassel	POR	AAA	26	7	14	0	156²	203	42	117	13	58.0%	.369	2	1.56	3.91	5.39	5.32	10.8	2.7	5.0	0.9	4.8
	SDN	MLB	26	1	1	0	22²	30	5	11	1	43.2%	.363	-2	1.54	3.96	5.80	4.22	12.2	1.7	4.2	0.4	4.4
E. Frieri	FTW	A	21	1	2	0	64²	48	23	65	4	36.0%	.273	-16	1.10	2.64	6.19	5.20	9.1	6.3	4.7	1.6	2.5
	LEL	A+	21	1	0	1	21²	11	6	27	1	33.3%	.233	17	0.78	1.24	3.57	2.33	5.6	3.7	7.4	0.9	7.0
S. Garrison*	BRV	A+	20	8	4	0	104²	105	28	74	6	47.1%	.296	-8	1.27	3.44	5.83	7.07	10.7	3.7	3.8	1.2	-16.0
	LEL	A+	20	2	3	0	42	32	6	28	2	45.8%	.238	7	0.90	2.79	3.48	4.32	6.7	2.2	3.0	0.6	5.9
M. Latos	EUG	A-	19	1	4	0	56¹	58	22	74	1	47.3%	.399	2	1.42	3.84	8.40	8.22	13.7	7.0	5.9	0.8	-13.4
W. Lopez	FTW	A	23	1	0	0	30	34	2	17	2	66.3%	.327	-40	1.20	3.30	7.79	6.39	13.5	2.5	2.1	1.8	-2.2
	LEL	A+	23	2	1	3	20²	35	1	19	3	58.7%	.444	-41	1.74	6.09	13.98	10.80	18.2	1.5	4.9	2.0	-10.6
C. Ramos*	SAN	AA	23	13	9	0	163²	153	43	90	15	44.9%	.271	-17	1.20	3.41	5.33	5.34	9.7	3.2	3.2	1.3	4.3
N. Schmidt*	FTW	A	21	0	1	0	7	8	6	6	0	31.8%	.364	-10	2.00	6.43	10.39	11.12	12.7	14.3	3.2	0.0	-3.5
J. Wells	POR	AAA	25	3	7	9	92²	107	48	87	9	41.2%	.366	-7	1.67	5.24	5.53	5.61	9.7	4.8	6.3	1.1	-0.1

Right-hander **Matt Buschmann** proved able to handle the Cal League in 2007 with his average-fastball/plus-slider combo. He turns 24 before the 2008 season begins and doesn't offer much projection. ⊘ **Cesar Carrillo** suffered another lost year in 2007, making five awful appearances before Tommy John surgery put him on the shelf. He can't be considered a prospect any longer. ⊘ **Jack Cassel**'s specialty is keeping the ball on the ground, but he doesn't miss enough bats for it to matter much. The Astros signed him anyway. ⊘ Right-hander **Ernesto Frieri** thrived in a bullpen role last year and gained some velocity on his fastball, but his secondary stuff still lags behind. ⊘ **Steve Garrison** is left-handed and throws 90 mph, but was less than impressive in the Florida State League before being traded to the Padres in the Linebrink deal. Just 21, there's time for him to figure it out. ⊘ A 2006 draft-and-follow out of a Florida high school, **Matt Latos** signed just before last year's draft and owned the Northwest League in his pro debut with a fastball that touched 96 mph at times. He might be the Padres' top pitching prospect. ⊘ A former Yankee prospect whom the Padres signed out of Nicaragua, righty **Wilton Lopez** is a sinker specialist who pounds the strike zone. ⊘ **Cesar Ramos** has put up good ERAs and remained healthy while pitching in tough environments, but his lack of stuff (reflected by his lousy strikeout rates) makes him more suspect than prospect. ⊘ The Padres have had some downright awful luck with their top draft picks. That continued with **Nick Schmidt**, their first-round pick last June, who lasted seven innings before his elbow popped and required Tommy John surgery. He won't pitch again until 2009. Like many Padres prospects, he's more of a moxie guy than a velocity guy, despite his size. ⊘ **Jared Wells** has always had one of the better arms in the Padres' system, but he's never made the transition from thrower to pitcher and is running out of time.

MANAGER: BUD BLACK

YEAR	TEAM	W-L	Pythag +/−	Avg PC	100+ P	120+ P	QS	BQS	REL	REL w Zero R	IBB	Subs	PH	PH Avg	PH HR	SB2	CS2	SB3	CS3	SAC Att	SAC %	POS SAC	Squeeze	Swing	In Play
2007	SDN	89-74	-1	90.1	47	0	89	7	485	340	48	22	273	.187	3	50	16	5	7	88	72.7%	28	1	114	89

Having inherited a largely veteran roster, Bud Black didn't have much chance to make his mark during his rookie season. While critics can point to two losses in the last three games of the season as evidence of failure, Black had his Hall of Fame closer on the mound with a lead in both contests, so it's hard to argue against his tactics. He rolled with the trade-deadline turmoil in which a popular pitcher, Scott Linebrink, was sent away at the same time his entire bench was rebuilt. Coming from the Angels, Black was unfazed by the fact that his four best relievers for most of the year were all right-handed, but he also worked in lefty Joe Thatcher in September when that option presented itself. Black will continue to preside over a collection of position players ill-suited to its home ballpark this year, so how he addresses the Padres' need to emphasize outfield defense, on-base percentage, and doubles will determine his success as a manager.

San Francisco Giants

I guess it's better to be booed than not noticed at all.
—VON HAYES, maligned Phillies outfielder

Typically when a franchise player reaches the end of his run with his team, there is an outpouring of affection from both his hometown fans and those around the game who want to honor what the player has accomplished over the preceding decade or two. Barry Bonds's departure from the Giants, however, was met with more of a quiet sigh of relief that it was all over. This, despite his having hit .312/.477/.666 with 586 home runs in his 14 seasons with the team. That same deafening silence followed Bonds's record-breaking 756th career home run, as the baseball world was overcome with a mix of emotions ranging from anger and embarrassment to reserved admiration. Even Bonds's indictment on perjury charges in November failed to elicit much reaction as it was, ironically, upstaged by the Mitchell Report.

Despite the collective shrug, Bonds's departure from the Giants is a major event for the franchise, whether or not they care to recognize it as such. The Giants have relied on Bonds as heavily as any baseball team has ever relied on any one player. During Bonds's 14 years in San Francisco, the Giants made the playoffs four times, and in each case, they very well might have missed the postseason had they not had Bonds in the lineup (see Table 1).

Simply put, the Giants' strategy over the years has been to cobble together a league-average roster and hope that Bonds would be enough to put them over the top. Baseball is not typically a sport in which a single player can dominate, so it's a testament to Bonds's abilities that this strategy actually worked on those four occasions. In recent years, however, this has not been the case. The Barry Bonds of 2006 and 2007 was still a very good player (20th and 11th in the NL in VORP, respectively), but he was no longer the player who could carry his team into the playoffs on his back. He's also going to be 44 years old in July, so even if the Giants had decided to bring him back for yet another season (and even if he had not been indicted), the bridge to a future without Barry Bonds was one the Giants were going to have to cross sooner rather than later.

To learn more about what Bonds's departure will mean to the Giants, let's take a look at what has happened in the past to other teams that have lost a player who was such an integral part of both their identity and their on-field success. Since the beginning of the free agency era in 1975, there have been 26 players other than Bonds who played with a single team for at least ten consecutive seasons, accumulated at least 100 WARP during their time with that team, and averaged at least a 6.0 WARP per season during that time. Table 2 lists those 26 players along with their cumulative WARP totals and the year and method of their departure from the team in question. Bonds's WARP total for the Giants (161.2) would rank second on this list.

Some of the teams that appear in Table 2 actually lost multiple players in a short span of time. The Tigers lost Lou Whitaker (123.3 WARP) and Alan Trammell (122.8) to retirement in consecutive years. The same was true for the Brewers, who lost Paul Molitor (102.2) to free agency and Robin Yount (136.0) to retirement, and the Braves, who lost Tom Glavine (105.4) and Greg Maddux

---

GIANTS PROSPECTUS

2007 record: 71-91; Fifth place, NL West

Pythagenport record: 77-85

Runs scored per game: 4.22 (15th in NL)

Runs allowed per game: 4.44 (5th in NL)

Team EqA: .247 (16th in NL)

2007 Batters Age: 33.6 (Oldest in NL)

2007 Pitchers Age: 27.6 (3rd youngest in NL)

Ballpark: AT&T Park; Neutral Park; Park Factor of .995

2007: The circus was no fun, but it left wins behind in each town it visited.

2008: Removing Bonds' shadow sheds light on a horribly run last-place team.

Table 1. It's a Wonderful Life

Year	Actual Record	Bonds's WARP	Record w/o Bonds	Closest Contender
1997	90-72	11.1	79-83	Dodgers 88-74
2000	97-65	12.0	85-77	Dodgers 86-76
2002	95-66	14.4	81-80	Dodgers 92-70
2003	100-61	13.4	86-76	Dodgers 85-77

WARP: Wins Above Replacement Player

Table 2. Why Not Take All of Me:
Franchise players of the free agency era

Player	Team	WARP-3	Last Year	Departed by?
Cal Ripken	BAL	169.4	2001	Retirement
Mike Schmidt	PHI	160.0	1989	Retirement
Carl Yastrzemski	BOS	140.6	1983	Retirement
George Brett	KCA	137.2	1993	Retirement
Robin Yount	MIL	136.0	1993	Retirement
Jeff Bagwell	HOU	135.4	2005	Retirement
Pete Rose	CIN	128.5	1978	Free Agency
Tony Gwynn	SDN	124.1	2001	Retirement
Phil Niekro	ATL	123.7	1983	Free Agency
Lou Whitaker	DET	123.3	1995	Retirement
Alan Trammell	DET	122.8	1996	Retirement
Barry Larkin	CIN	122.2	2004	Retirement
Johnny Bench	CIN	120.8	1983	Retirement
Bob Gibson	SLN	120.0	1975	Retirement
Frank Thomas	CHA	118.4	2005	Free Agency
Roger Clemens	BOS	116.2	1996	Free Agency
Dwight Evans	BOS	114.1	1990	Free Agency
Ryne Sandberg	CHN	113.8	1997	Retirement
Ozzie Smith	SLN	110.9	1996	Retirement
Wade Boggs	BOS	109.4	1992	Free Agency
Greg Maddux	ATL	108.0	2003	Free Agency
Bernie Williams	NYA	106.3	2006	Retirement
Tom Glavine	ATL	105.4	2002	Free Agency
Ken Griffey Jr.	SEA	104.3	1999	Trade
Jim Palmer	BAL	103.0	1984	Retirement
Paul Molitor	MIL	102.2	1992	Free Agency

(108.0) to free agency, each pair having consecutive-season departures. The Tigers and Brewers went into prolonged tailspins after these losses, as did the Royals after the retirement of George Brett (137.2), and the Orioles after Cal Ripken stood down (169.4). The Braves' record streak of post-season appearances ended in the third year after the departures of Glavine and Maddux. On the other hand, the Red Sox returned to the World Series three years after losing Carl Yastrzemski (140.6) as did the Phillies four years after losing Mike Schmidt (160.0), while the Mariners won 116 games two years after trading Ken Griffey Jr. (104.3).

Looking at the performance of those teams in aggregate, some general patterns begin to emerge. In Chart 1, we've plotted a ten-year window around the departure of the franchise player, starting four years before the

player's last year with the club (L-4) and ending five years afterwards (L+5). What we see is a noticeable and somewhat predictable decline in the quality of the team, as measured by their average number of regular season wins (all seasons are prorated to 162 games). However, the decline comes not as a sudden drop coinciding with the player's departure, but rather in the form of a prolonged and steady decline. The average team was only about a win-and-a-half worse in their first season without their franchise player than in their final season with him, but was a full eight wins worse than they had been five years earlier. In other words, the team had already begun to suffer the consequences of its franchise player's diminishing skills before his actual departure.

The Barry Bonds Giants are an extreme example of this trend, as their record declined by a whopping 29 wins over Bonds's final five seasons with the team. More disturbing than this pattern of team decline echoing player decline, however, is what happens after the franchise player departs. Rather than bouncing back quickly, the average team instead suffers through an extended malaise, posting a record two wins *worse* five years after the player's departure than in the first year without the player. Thus the most problematic aspect of the departure of a franchise player is not the immediate impact of the departure so much as the prolonged hangover effect it seems to produce.

This suggests that teams with franchise players tend to become dependent on those players to the detriment of the rest of the team. As those players age, the teams typically become focused on assembling one more winner around their signature player, which often means putting together an expensive, veteran team and abandoning any sort of long-term planning or team-building. Indeed, in quite a number of these cases, the departure of the player coincided with the departure of the general manager. Harry Dalton left the Brewers just a year before Molitor. Haywood Sullivan was quick to follow Yastrzemski out the door in Boston. It now appears as though the departures of Glavine and Maddux from the Braves were a precursor to John Schuerholz stepping down. Some of these GMs were fine evaluators of talent, especially Schuerholz and Dalton, but others were one-trick ponies whose fate was tied to that of their star.

The Giants have been particularly vulnerable to this mentality, as GM Brian Sabean has always focused on finding veteran complements to Bonds, rather than building from the ground up. In terms of their overall organizational strength, from their 25-man roster on down to their rookie-ball clubs, the Giants have quite possibly the weakest group of players in baseball. A

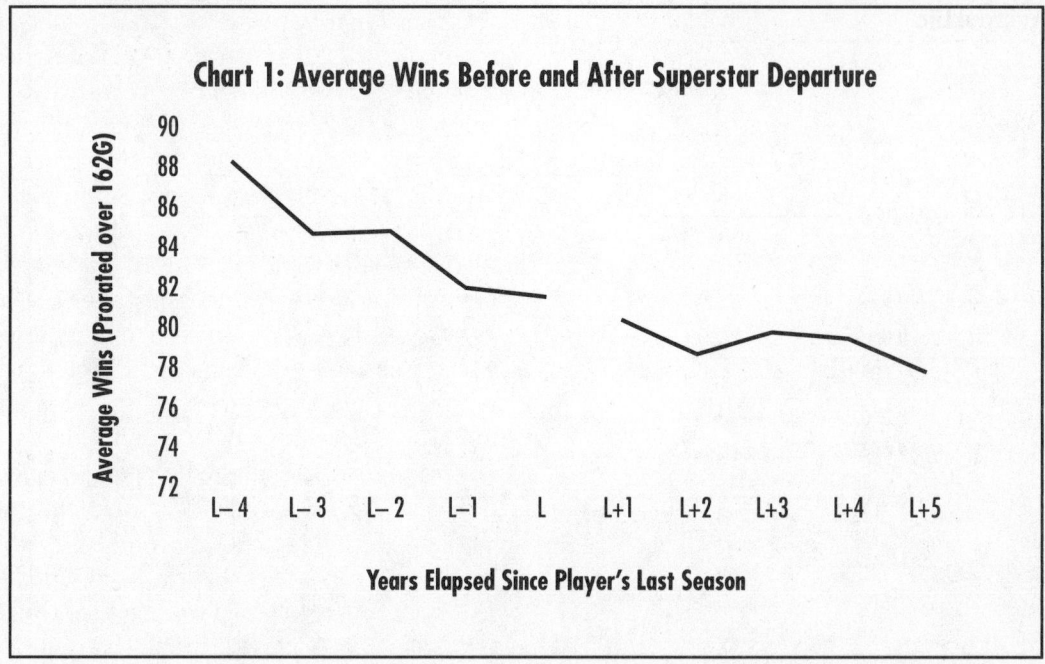

Chart 1: Average Wins Before and After Superstar Departure

Y-axis: Average Wins (Prorated over 162G)

X-axis values: L–4, L–3, L–2, L–1, L, L+1, L+2, L+3, L+4, L+5

X-axis label: Years Elapsed Since Player's Last Season

year ago, in a PECOTA-driven measure of long-term organizational depth the Giants ranked 29th out of the 30 major league clubs, ahead of only the Pirates, and with right-hander Tim Lincecum having graduated to the major leagues, there are no first-tier prospects left on the farm.

With the end clearly in sight for Bonds ever since he missed nearly all of the 2005 season due to a knee injury, Sabean's tendency seems to have been to placate Giants fans by means of a few symbolic big-ticket free agent signings, most notably lefty Barry Zito a year ago, based on the assumption that San Franciscans will turn out for their beautiful ballpark by the Bay so long as the Giants make some pretense of contention. AT&T Park is indeed an asset for the Giants, but not the immutable one that it might seem. Yes, it has been at or near sell-out capacity since the opening in 2000, but the Giants have also had Bonds on their roster that entire time, most of which he spent chasing two of the most revered records in the game.

History suggests that teams can expect an unusually sharp decline in attendance after losing a franchise player. Using our list of 26 franchise players from Table 2, we can also look at what happened to their teams' per-game attendance after those players left the roster (Chart 2). One adjustment is necessary: because attendance has tended to increase steadily over time, we've prorate each team's attendance relative to the league average, then adjust it to a baseline average of 30,000 fans per game.

This pattern repeats the steady decline of win-loss record seen in Chart 1, but at a steeper slope. The de-

parture of a franchise player brings with it an immediate loss of about 1,750 fans per game, or about 145,000 fans per season, but once again, things are worse in the second and third years without the player, with the team down about 2,750 fans per game (or 220,000 fans per season). Those are merely the decreases compared to the last year of the player's tenure with the club, at which point his drawing power, per Chart 2, has already atrophied. If we compare the teams' attendance two years after the player's departure to the L-2 year, when the superstar was closer to his peak, the decline is on the order of 3,500 fans per game, or 275,000 fans per season. The magnitude of these declines is several times sharper than what would be expected based on the relatively modest decline in team quality alone.

There is not a lot of good news here for the Giants. Ordinarily, we would advocate a standard three- to five-year rebuilding plan designed around trading what favorable veteran contracts the team has for prospects and writing off a couple of seasons, but the Giants do not really have any veteran contracts that can be considered assets, and their organizational depth is so poor, particularly on the offensive side, that playing the kids could produce some truly embarrassing results.

The long-term fix, naturally, will depend on reorienting the team's approach to the amateur draft. Since Sabean took over as GM in 1997, the Giants have tilted very heavily toward pitching in the draft, and relatively heavily toward "safe" college selections with modest upside. They have mined a couple of star pitchers out of this effort in Tim Lincecum and Matt Cain, as well as several other quality major league arms such as Noah

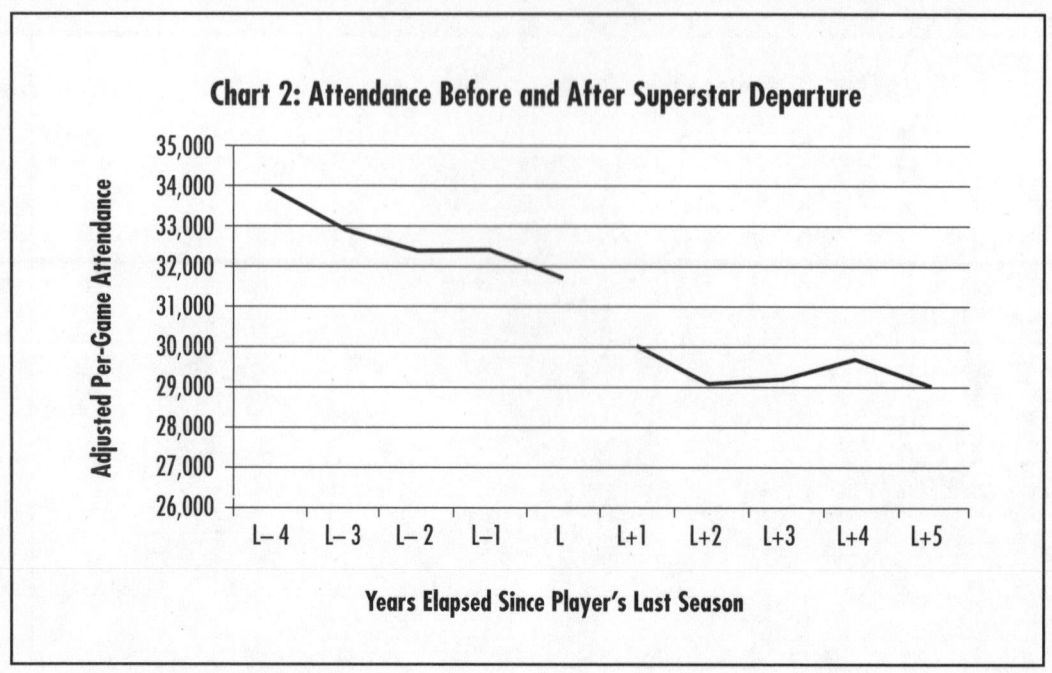

Chart 2: Attendance Before and After Superstar Departure

Adjusted Per-Game Attendance

Years Elapsed Since Player's Last Season

Lowry and the since-dealt Boof Bonser and Scott Line-brink. On the other hand, they have not drafted a single quality major league position player during Sabean's term. The last Giants position-player draft picks to have played at least 500 games in the major leagues were outfielder Chris Singleton and infielder Bill Mueller, both of whom were drafted in 1993; the last position player the Giants drafted that went on to appear on an All-Star team was Royce Clayton, hardly anyone's idea of a true All-Star, and he was selected in *1988*.

The good news is that the Giants may already have changed their philosophy. Just two years after having none of the top-100 picks due to Sabean's free agent habit, the Giants had six first-round selections in 2007 as a result of MLB's liberal compensation-pick rules. Five of those six picks were high school players, and four of the six were position players, both departures from their usual way of doing business. The Giants will ultimately need the depth provided by lower-risk college picks as well, but in the post-Bonds universe, greater priority must be given to high-upside high school picks, to whom same-age college picks can be added three or four years later.

As for what to do with the major league squad until those players arrive, the Giants appear to be following a piece of advice that we originally gave them in our "Offseason Plans" series on BaseballProspectus.com in November. That advice was to orient their position player roster around defense. The strategy is roughly analogous to the "Princeton Offense" in college basketball in which a team attempts to dictate the tempo of its games and keep them low-scoring in the hope of forg-

ing a few upsets, rather than trying to win the shootouts in which it knows it can't compete. The team's only big move over the winter was to sign Aaron Rowand, which gives them three outfielders—from left to right: Dave Roberts, Rowand, and Randy Winn—who each have legitimate center-field-quality range. They also re-upped ageless Gold Glover Omar Vizquel, whose bat seems to have retired, but whose glove might play forever.

That outfield alignment has the potential to be a particularly important asset given the size of AT&T Park's pastures. Moreover, it may result in their pitchers posting artificially low ERAs, thereby increasing their trade value. That sort of defense-first approach, which also comes with some speed—the three outfielders, Vizquel, and lead-gloved second baseman Ray Durham combined to go 76 for 95 (80 percent) on the bases last year—helps give the team a bit of a scrappy, blue-collar identity that stands in sharp contrast to the bloated, self-impressed image projected by Bonds. That may not necessarily fit with the Anchor Steam-and-camembert stereotype of San Francisco fans, but it ought to achieve its goal of providing plenty of close, well-played ballgames.

This strategy is not likely to produce a winning record for the Giants, particularly not in the NL West, which is emerging as the deepest division in baseball, but the two pillars of this plan—the Princeton Offense for now, high-upside position-player draft picks for later—are the team's best hopes to move out beyond under Bonds's long shadow. With a little bit of luck and a lot of patience, the Giants can become a robust and competitive baseball team again, instead of a one-man traveling circus.

HITTERS

Rich Aurilia INF

Bats: R   Throws: R   Height: 6' 1"   Weight: 190   Born: September 2, 1971   Age: 36

YEAR	TEAM	LVL	AGE	PA	R	2B	3B	HR	RBI	BB	SO	SB	CS	EqBRR	AVG	OBP	SLG	MLVr	EqAVG	EqOBP	EqSLG	EqA	VORP	DEFENSE			
2005	CIN	MLB	33	468	61	23	2	14	68	37	67	2	0	0.2	.282	.338	.444	.069	.278	.338	.450	.272	20.4	62-2B	4	27-SS	1
2006	CIN	MLB	34	481	61	25	1	23	70	34	51	3	0	-0.1	.300	.349	.518	.169	.292	.344	.506	.287	27.4	40-3B	-1	37-1B	2
2007	SFN	MLB	35	358	40	19	2	5	33	22	45	0	0	0.1	.252	.304	.368	-.140	.254	.308	.376	.239	-4.7	41-1B	2	20-3B	0
2008	SFN	MLB	36	252	29	13	1	6	32	20	32	2	1	-0.2	.267	.329	.417	-.055	.265	.329	.430	.259	8.3	62-1B	1		

Breakout: 11% Improve: 39% Collapse: 34% Attrition: 45%   Comparables: Ken Boyer, Joe Randa, Bill Madlock, Brooks Robinson

Let's get this out of the way: the Giants are just lousy with veterans who would make fairly good reserves, but whom they treat as regulars. Aurilia's a serviceable platoon cornerman who can pretend to play the middle infield for innings at a time, but he was signed to be the regular first baseman after the 2006 season. He hit the DL in June having started two-thirds of the Giants' games and hit .236/.278/.346. When he got healthy, he was dropped right back into the lineup, and played just as often. Naturally, he's signed for 2008, too.

Barry Bonds LF

Bats: L   Throws: L   Height: 6' 2"   Weight: 240   Born: July 24, 1964   Age: 43

YEAR	TEAM	LVL	AGE	PA	R	2B	3B	HR	RBI	BB	SO	SB	CS	EqBRR	AVG	OBP	SLG	MLVr	EqAVG	EqOBP	EqSLG	EqA	VORP	DEFENSE	
2005	SFN	MLB	40	52	8	1	0	5	10	9	6	0	0	-0.1	.286	.404	.667	.466	.262	.385	.643	.330	6.5	11-LF	-1
2006	SFN	MLB	41	493	74	23	0	26	77	115	51	3	0	-0.4	.270	.454	.545	.352	.256	.445	.520	.334	46.6	99-LF	-6
2007	SFN	MLB	42	477	75	14	0	28	66	132	54	5	0	-2.0	.276	.480	.565	.422	.261	.475	.549	.353	55.2	94-LF	-6
2008	SFN	MLB	43	475	76	22	0	20	70	103	63	4	1	-1.4	.248	.419	.478	.162	.246	.420	.494	.304	24.8	112-LF	-7

Breakout: 6% Improve: 6% Collapse: 62% Attrition: 52%   Comparables: Carlton Fisk, Carl Yastrzemski, Tony Perez, Dave Winfield

Even if you take Bonds's intentional walks away, wiping those plate appearances clean off his record, he's still one of the 30 best hitters in the game. He costs his team a few runs in the field and on the bases, but not enough to sink his value. Without the DH as a crutch (save for a spattering of interleague contests), he's started 115 and 110 games in the field the past two years, so you have to figure he'd be able to DH at least that much, and most likely a lot more. How many AL teams wouldn't improve by five wins by signing Bonds, even allowing for some decline? Of course, that's just the on-field analysis. Bonds is under indictment for perjury in the BALCO case, and while plenty of players have endured legal proceedings—admittedly for "lesser" crimes such as spousal abuse, assault, and weapons possession, nothing as severe as lying to the witch-hunters—and played on, unaffected, Bonds is a special case for two decades' worth of reasons we'd need another entire book to properly explore. If you focus on his performance, however, you realize that he can help any team win a World Series. There's a lot of circus a team can endure if there's a parade at the end of it.

Manny Burriss SS

Bats: S   Throws: R   Height: 6' 0"   Weight: 170   Born: January 17, 1985   Age: 23

YEAR	TEAM	LVL	AGE	PA	R	2B	3B	HR	RBI	BB	SO	SB	CS	EqBRR	AVG	OBP	SLG	MLVr	EqAVG	EqOBP	EqSLG	EqA	VORP	DEFENSE	
2006	SLO	A-	21	293	50	8	2	1	27	27	22	35	11	6.1	.307	.384	.366	.141	.257	.315	.306	.229	-6.0	59-SS	-1
2007	AUG	A	22	405	64	14	4	0	38	28	49	51	15	3.8	.321	.374	.381	.109	.264	.306	.312	.227	-5.3	86-SS	-2
2007	SJO	A+	22	160	23	2	0	0	8	12	20	17	3	2.4	.165	.237	.180	-.532	.174	.229	.188	.161	-17.7	35-SS	-4
2008	SFN	MLB	23	603	76	21	5	1	35	37	82	60	17	2.9	.254	.304	.316	-.244	.252	.305	.326	.233	0.8	141-SS	-3

Breakout: 52% Improve: 79% Collapse: 9% Attrition: 8%   Comparables: Mike Metcalfe, Wylie Campbell, Shawn Livsey, Freddie Bynum

Burriss runs very well and has the kind of slappy approach at the plate that should lead to Juan Pierre–like .300 batting averages. The California League owned him last year, however, to the point that he had to be sent down to the Sally League. While his line at Augusta is nice, it makes him a 23-year-old who hasn't gotten to High-A yet. His speed and glove will get him to the majors; they just won't get him playing time once there.

Rajai Davis   CF

Bats: R   Throws: R   Height: 5' 11"   Weight: 195   Born: October 19, 1980   Age: 27

YEAR	TEAM	LVL	AGE	PA	R	2B	3B	HR	RBI	BB	SO	SB	CS	EqBRR	AVG	OBP	SLG	MLVr	EqAVG	EqOBP	EqSLG	EqA	VORP	DEFENSE			
2005	ALT	AA	24	561	82	22	5	4	34	43	76	45	9	8.8	.281	.351	.369	.035	.250	.314	.332	.238	-10.1	115-CF	2		
2006	IND	AAA	25	417	53	17	1	2	21	27	59	45	13	6.9	.283	.335	.348	.015	.264	.316	.337	.240	-5.5	75-CF	5	17-LF	-1
2007	IND	AAA	26	239	31	12	4	4	30	21	25	27	9	-2.4	.318	.384	.469	.233	.294	.357	.453	.282	8.1	26-LF	1	26-CF	5
2007	PIT	MLB	26	57	6	2	1	0	2	7	3	5	2	-1.0	.271	.357	.354	-.034	.292	.375	.375	.268	1.5				
2007	SFN	MLB	26	162	26	9	1	1	7	14	25	17	4	3.4	.282	.363	.380	.007	.296	.375	.401	.279	7.2	33-CF	5		
2008	SFN	MLB	27	415	58	20	3	4	32	31	55	31	7	1.9	.274	.335	.375	-.096	.272	.335	.387	.259	8.6	99-CF	3		

Breakout: 22% Improve: 49% Collapse: 21% Attrition: 22%   Comparables: Jamal Strong, Trenidad Hubbard, James Mouton, Jacob Brumfield

This former Pirate prospect who came over in the Matt Morris deal at last year's deadline excited fantasy players and Giants fans alike by stealing 17 bases in two months after his arrival in San Francisco. His true level is more fourth outfielder than starter, owing to a strikeout rate that will keep his on-base percentage in the .330s. With the arrival of Aaron Rowand in center, Davis is in a four-man fight for playing time in left.

Ray Durham   2B

Bats: S   Throws: R   Height: 5' 8"   Weight: 190   Born: November 30, 1971   Age: 36

YEAR	TEAM	LVL	AGE	PA	R	2B	3B	HR	RBI	BB	SO	SB	CS	EqBRR	AVG	OBP	SLG	MLVr	EqAVG	EqOBP	EqSLG	EqA	VORP	DEFENSE	
2005	SFN	MLB	33	560	67	33	0	12	62	48	59	6	3	3.0	.290	.356	.429	.081	.288	.355	.433	.275	25.1	128-2B	-6
2006	SFN	MLB	34	555	79	30	7	26	93	51	61	7	2	1.5	.293	.360	.538	.219	.292	.361	.541	.301	47.9	129-2B	-15
2007	SFN	MLB	35	528	56	21	2	11	71	53	75	10	2	-0.4	.218	.295	.343	-.213	.217	.299	.352	.235	-10.5	115-2B	-16
2008	SFN	MLB	36	300	35	14	2	7	35	29	42	5	2	0.0	.250	.327	.390	-.106	.249	.327	.403	.252	8.9	73-2B	-6

Breakout: 8% Improve: 28% Collapse: 48% Attrition: 41%   Comparables: Roberto Alomar, Luis Alicea, Jay Bell, Mike Bordick

The two-year contract to which the Giants signed Durham after the 2006 season made no sense given that his 2006 homer total screamed "fluke" and was paired with a defense only slightly stronger than "I thought it was flaxseed oil." That said, Durham's disastrous 2007 season amounted to 30 missing singles and 10 missing doubles with just a few additional strikeouts in the mix, so it, too, was fluky. His average will bounce back; his defense, however, is deadly to a pitching staff that was 11th in the league in strikeouts last year.

Pedro Feliz   3B

Bats: R   Throws: R   Height: 6' 1"   Weight: 210   Born: April 27, 1975   Age: 33

YEAR	TEAM	LVL	AGE	PA	R	2B	3B	HR	RBI	BB	SO	SB	CS	EqBRR	AVG	OBP	SLG	MLVr	EqAVG	EqOBP	EqSLG	EqA	VORP	DEFENSE			
2005	SFN	MLB	30	615	69	30	4	20	81	38	102	0	2	-0.1	.250	.295	.422	-.061	.247	.296	.428	.247	-1.2	69-LF	-4	66-3B	5
2006	SFN	MLB	31	644	75	35	5	22	98	33	112	1	1	-1.1	.244	.281	.428	-.110	.243	.283	.424	.241	-8.2	155-3B	10		
2007	SFN	MLB	32	590	61	28	2	20	72	29	70	2	2	-4.6	.253	.290	.418	-.096	.255	.295	.433	.246	-2.7	136-3B	15		
2008	SFN	MLB	33	423	42	21	2	11	55	23	59	2	1	-0.7	.260	.302	.409	-.119	.258	.302	.422	.243	5.7	101-3B	3		

Breakout: 21% Improve: 47% Collapse: 28% Attrition: 25%   Comparables: Ed Sprague, Gary Gaetti, Charlie Hayes, Matt Williams

As frustrating a player as Feliz is, you can't argue that he's fooling anyone. He's had the same season three years in a row, showing durability, a low batting average, a walk a week, 20 homers, and good defense. If he's batting seventh for you and you're not paying a lot of money and you get OBP from everywhere else . . . well, he's still only a three-win player. He was fourth on the Giants in WARP3 last year and two of those four, Feliz and Bonds, aren't coming back. Send in your season-ticket renewal checks today!

Kevin Frandsen   2B

Bats: R   Throws: R   Height: 6' 0"   Weight: 180   Born: May 24, 1982   Age: 26

YEAR	TEAM	LVL	AGE	PA	R	2B	3B	HR	RBI	BB	SO	SB	CS	EqBRR	AVG	OBP	SLG	MLVr	EqAVG	EqOBP	EqSLG	EqA	VORP	DEFENSE			
2005	SJO	A+	23	335	57	22	3	2	40	26	22	13	11	-3.7	.351	.429	.467	.340	.283	.344	.378	.252	9.2	60-2B	-5	14-SS	-2
2005	NRW	AA	23	142	22	8	0	2	20	4	14	7	3	1.5	.287	.336	.395	.055	.265	.305	.371	.238	0.3	26-2B	2		
2005	FRE	AAA	23	98	18	10	1	2	16	2	5	1	1	-1.5	.351	.378	.543	.315	.305	.320	.484	.267	6.0	20-2B	0		
2006	FRE	AAA	24	328	46	25	3	3	30	12	30	7	4	-1.8	.304	.358	.440	.124	.272	.318	.405	.250	7.2	46-2B	3	12-3B	-2
2006	SFN	MLB	24	102	12	4	0	2	7	3	14	0	1	-0.2	.215	.284	.323	-.265	.223	.284	.319	.207	-3.6	19-2B	-5		
2007	FRE	AAA	25	83	13	5	0	1	7	9	6	4	2	1.4	.403	.506	.522	.560	.348	.451	.449	.317	9.1	10-2B	0		
2007	SFN	MLB	25	296	26	12	1	5	31	21	24	4	3	-0.9	.269	.331	.379	-.065	.273	.337	.390	.254	2.9	38-2B	-5	15-SS	-2
2008	SFN	MLB	26	343	41	17	2	4	32	19	30	8	3	0.3	.281	.336	.382	-.080	.279	.336	.394	.254	10.3	83-2B	-2		

Breakout: 21% Improve: 43% Collapse: 26% Attrition: 24%   Comparables: Doug Flynn, Billy Ripken, Placido Polanco, Gary Sutherland

Given a regular second-base job, Frandsen would play near-adequate defense and hit .270 with some doubles and not enough walks, making $400,000 for his trouble. Even an average year from Durham wouldn't return $7 million more in value than that because of the 10-15 runs he gives away on defense. Remember that the next time someone tries to tell you that Barry Bonds's salary was handicapping the Giants.

Ryan Klesko   **1B**   Bats: L   Throws: L   Height: 6' 3"   Weight: 220   Born: June 12, 1971   Age: 37

YEAR	TEAM	LVL	AGE	PA	R	2B	3B	HR	RBI	BB	SO	SB	CS	EqBRR	AVG	OBP	SLG	MLVr	EqAVG	EqOBP	EqSLG	EqA	VORP	DEFENSE
2005	SDN	MLB	34	520	61	19	1	18	58	75	80	3	4	-3.0	.248	.358	.418	.062	.259	.369	.444	.280	12.3	103-LF -1
2006	SDN	MLB	35	6	0	1	0	0	2	2	0	0	0	0.0	.750	.833	1.000	1.946	.750	.833	.999	.742	3.0	
2007	SFN	MLB	36	411	51	27	3	6	44	46	68	5	1	0.8	.260	.344	.401	-.019	.261	.350	.408	.268	5.5	90-1B 6
2008	SFN	MLB	37	283	36	15	1	6	33	32	47	5	2	-0.2	.269	.354	.411	-.018	.267	.355	.424	.270	7.9	69-1B 1

Breakout: 22%   Improve: 48%   Collapse: 30%   Attrition: 40%   Comparables: Dale Long, John Olerud, John Vander Wal, Tino Martinez

Klesko's return from shoulder surgery last year went reasonably well. If that seems generous given his season line, remember that a .344 OBP is to the Giants what seeing a minus sign is to the Spears family. Klesko's numbers declined in the second half as nagging injuries killed his power and limited his playing time, but when healthy, he's a viable platoon first baseman or DH. He was a free agent as we went to press.

Justin Knoedler   **C**   Bats: R   Throws: R   Height: 6' 2"   Weight: 215   Born: July 17, 1980   Age: 27

YEAR	TEAM	LVL	AGE	PA	R	2B	3B	HR	RBI	BB	SO	SB	CS	EqBRR	AVG	OBP	SLG	MLVr	EqAVG	EqOBP	EqSLG	EqA	VORP	DEFENSE
2005	FRE	AAA	24	327	35	19	1	4	32	26	61	5	5	-0.1	.272	.345	.387	-.062	.237	.302	.336	.223	-5.6	77-C 4
2006	NRW	AA	25	76	7	6	0	1	8	4	24	1	1	0.1	.211	.263	.338	-.095	.208	.260	.319	.198	-4.2	21-C -2
2006	FRE	AAA	25	261	32	13	4	4	27	22	58	4	0	1.8	.253	.319	.395	-.051	.228	.290	.359	.229	-4.5	63-C -1
2007	FRE	AAA	26	336	44	30	2	7	42	26	78	7	1	-1.6	.288	.346	.470	.092	.250	.307	.421	.253	6.1	78-C 4
2008	OAK	MLB	27	313	29	16	1	6	32	20	78	5	2	0.3	.230	.285	.355	-.212	.233	.289	.378	.236	-2.5	76-C 0

Breakout: 29%   Improve: 50%   Collapse: 24%   Attrition: 16%   Comparables: Paul Hoover, Chad Moeller, Josh Paul, A. J. Hinch

Catch-and-throw guy Guillermo Rodriguez got the call to back up Bengie Molina when Eliezer Alfonzo went down with a knee injury last year. It was a curious choice given that Knoedler had been up for brief stretches in both 2005 and 2006, and was having a good year at Triple-A Fresno. Knoedler is just a backup, but seeing as he has a little more bat than glove, he would seem to pair well with a Randomly Generated Molina. He'll go to camp with the A's, who may better appreciate his skills.

Fred Lewis   **OF**   Bats: L   Throws: R   Height: 6' 2"   Weight: 190   Born: December 9, 1980   Age: 27

YEAR	TEAM	LVL	AGE	PA	R	2B	3B	HR	RBI	BB	SO	SB	CS	EqBRR	AVG	OBP	SLG	MLVr	EqAVG	EqOBP	EqSLG	EqA	VORP	DEFENSE	
2005	NRW	AA	24	594	79	28	7	7	47	69	124	30	13	1.5	.273	.361	.396	.087	.244	.327	.357	.245	-1.9	63-CF -5	62-LF 1
2006	FRE	AAA	25	517	85	20	11	12	56	68	105	18	8	5.2	.276	.375	.453	.144	.248	.342	.416	.265	1.1	85-LF 0	20-CF -1
2007	FRE	AAA	26	191	31	8	6	8	32	19	36	9	1	2.4	.292	.366	.550	.247	.262	.335	.488	.282	10.0	23-CF -4	18-LF 0
2007	SFN	MLB	26	180	34	6	2	3	19	19	32	5	1	0.3	.287	.374	.408	.058	.293	.383	.433	.289	6.0	23-RF 1	13-LF 1
2008	SFN	MLB	27	287	39	13	3	6	29	29	58	10	3	1.1	.262	.342	.409	-.046	.260	.343	.422	.266	7.1	70-LF -1	

Breakout: 16%   Improve: 38%   Collapse: 27%   Attrition: 28%   Comparables: Rick Miller, Pat Kelly, Ted Wood, Larry Harlow

Lewis has generally been old for his levels, which accounts for the lack of buzz surrounding him despite his multiple 30-steal seasons, occasionally good batting averages, and athletic build. After coming off of the DL on June 30 following an oblique injury, he was killing in a part-time role for the big club, posting a .417 OBP over 28 games, but a roster crunch pushed him to the minors in early August, where he was stuck until the season's final week. He's better than Davis, but in ways that require a full season to appreciate. As with Durham and Frandsen, there's just no way the difference between Lewis and Rowand was worth the investment in the veteran, as it's not entirely clear who the better player is between them.

Bengie Molina　　　**C**　　　　Bats: R　　Throws: R　　Height: 5' 11"　　Weight: 225　　Born: July 20, 1974　　Age: 33

YEAR	TEAM	LVL	AGE	PA	R	2B	3B	HR	RBI	BB	SO	SB	CS	EqBRR	AVG	OBP	SLG	MLVr	EqAVG	EqOBP	EqSLG	EqA	VORP	DEFENSE
2005	LAA	MLB	30	449	45	17	0	15	69	27	41	0	2	-5.4	.295	.336	.446	.076	.303	.351	.471	.281	24.1	97-C -2
2006	TOR	MLB	31	458	44	20	1	19	57	19	47	1	1	-4.0	.284	.319	.467	.008	.280	.322	.471	.268	15.5	96-C -7
2007	SFN	MLB	32	517	38	19	1	19	81	15	53	0	0	-3.5	.276	.298	.433	-.042	.277	.304	.440	.253	14.4	123-C 5
2008	SFN	MLB	33	407	39	18	1	12	56	19	42	2	1	-1.6	.278	.316	.426	-.056	.276	.316	.441	.255	14.8	97-C -3

Breakout: 9%　Improve: 34%　Collapse: 35%　Attrition: 25%　　　　Comparables: Sandy Alomar, Darrin Fletcher, Terry Steinbach, Bob Boone

Molina has 152 career walks; Bonds walked 132 times last year. Nothing against Molina, who had another year off the factory line, but his was another "what's the point?" signing. He did exactly what he could be expected to do, but no one came to the park to see him, he didn't make the Giants good, and he cost millions of dollars. Replacing him with a combination of Knoedler and Rodriguez might have dropped the team's 71 wins to a mere 70. Of course, that's all because of Bonds's salary again.

Nick Noonan　　　**2B**　　　　Bats: L　　Throws: R　　Height: 6' 0"　　Weight: 180　　Born: May 4, 1989　　Age: 19

YEAR	TEAM	LVL	AGE	PA	R	2B	3B	HR	RBI	BB	SO	SB	CS	EqBRR	AVG	OBP	SLG	MLVr	EqAVG	EqOBP	EqSLG	EqA	VORP	DEFENSE
2007	GIA	Rk	18	224	33	11	4	3	40	12	20	18	3	1.6	.316	.357	.451	.199	.233	.256	.335	.206	-23.6	20-2B -3 17-SS 4
2008	SFN	MLB	19	528	43	24	2	4	40	24	98	16	6	0.3	.226	.263	.311	-.343	.224	.264	.321	.200	-15.2	124-2B 0

Breakout: 33%　Improve: 54%　Collapse: 27%　Attrition: 8%　　　　Comparables: Rob Valido, Brent Butler, Chris Smith, Trevor Plouffe

A supplemental first-round pick last year, Noonan was one of the best pure high school hitters in the draft and would have drawn a million-dollar bonus if he played a more premium position; he just doesn't have the skills to play shortstop, but he can really hit, has some power and runs well. The Giants think he has All-Star potential.

Dan Ortmeier　　　**OF/1B**　　　　Bats: S　　Throws: L　　Height: 6' 4"　　Weight: 215　　Born: May 11, 1981　　Age: 27

YEAR	TEAM	LVL	AGE	PA	R	2B	3B	HR	RBI	BB	SO	SB	CS	EqBRR	AVG	OBP	SLG	MLVr	EqAVG	EqOBP	EqSLG	EqA	VORP	DEFENSE
2005	NRW	AA	24	575	85	23	6	20	79	48	115	35	12	3.3	.274	.360	.463	.172	.247	.322	.420	.259	-2.2	124-RF -3
2006	NRW	AA	25	189	17	9	1	2	11	17	38	7	4	-1.4	.251	.328	.353	.058	.241	.311	.341	.232	-3.6	34-CF -6
2006	FRE	AAA	25	283	37	14	3	6	33	16	40	8	6	-1.1	.244	.293	.389	-.111	.219	.264	.355	.212	-11.5	45-CF -10 16-LF 1
2007	FRE	AAA	26	342	39	19	1	10	54	27	63	16	2	-0.4	.262	.333	.430	-.014	.234	.303	.390	.247	-9.8	36-LF 2 17-RF 3
2007	SFN	MLB	26	167	20	7	4	6	16	7	41	2	1	0.5	.287	.317	.497	.094	.288	.323	.519	.281	6.1	19-1B 1 10-LF 2
2008	SFN	MLB	27	466	55	23	3	11	51	33	95	16	5	1.0	.251	.311	.398	-.123	.249	.312	.411	.250	2.2	110-RF 1

Breakout: 22%　Improve: 55%　Collapse: 21%　Attrition: 19%　　　　Comparables: Shawn Garrett, Pete Whisenant, Bobby Brown, Kenny Kelly

Ortmeier is roughly analogous to Todd Linden, if only Linden had never really hit at Triple-A and had come up at a time when the Giants didn't really have to worry about a player's production in order to play him, but could just run anyone out there. From August 10 through September 22, Ortmeier started 20 times (delivering three walks and 20 strikeouts in 90 plate appearances) while Fred Lewis bided his time in Triple-A, a state of affairs that defies description. Can we use "Sabean" as a verb yet?

Dave Roberts　　　**OF**　　　　Bats: L　　Throws: L　　Height: 5' 10"　　Weight: 180　　Born: May 31, 1972　　Age: 36

YEAR	TEAM	LVL	AGE	PA	R	2B	3B	HR	RBI	BB	SO	SB	CS	EqBRR	AVG	OBP	SLG	MLVr	EqAVG	EqOBP	EqSLG	EqA	VORP	DEFENSE
2005	SDN	MLB	33	480	65	19	10	8	38	53	59	23	12	1.6	.275	.356	.428	.095	.290	.371	.459	.283	20.9	100-CF -16
2006	SDN	MLB	34	566	80	18	13	2	44	51	61	49	6	5.2	.293	.360	.393	.038	.306	.373	.416	.289	22.2	108-LF 12 11-CF 2
2007	SFN	MLB	35	442	61	17	9	2	23	42	66	31	5	7.1	.260	.331	.364	-.089	.263	.339	.377	.261	8.6	84-CF 3
2008	SFN	MLB	36	361	52	14	6	3	27	32	47	21	4	1.9	.278	.345	.382	-.065	.276	.346	.395	.264	10.5	87-CF 1

Breakout: 6%　Improve: 31%　Collapse: 37%　Attrition: 29%　　　　Comparables: Al Bumbry, Kenny Lofton, Otis Nixon, Lance Johnson

In 2006, Roberts played mostly left field, batted 566 times, and made 121 starts. In 2007, Roberts played mostly center field, batted 442 times, and made 94 starts. That drop in availability was entirely predictable on the day the Giants signed him in December 2006. Rowand's arrival pushes Roberts back to left field where he's caught in a scrum with Davis, Lewis, Ortmeier, and Nate Schierholtz. Roberts is 36 and owed another $13 million through 2009, by the way.

Marcus Sanders 2B

Bats: R Throws: R Height: 6' 0" Weight: 160 Born: August 25, 1985 Age: 22

YEAR	TEAM	LVL	AGE	PA	R	2B	3B	HR	RBI	BB	SO	SB	CS	EqBRR	AVG	OBP	SLG	MLVr	EqAVG	EqOBP	EqSLG	EqA	VORP	DEFENSE	
2005	AUG	A	19	504	86	19	4	5	40	69	90	57	9	9.5	.300	.407	.400	.185	.235	.321	.310	.238	-5.2	107-SS	-6
2006	SJO	A+	20	246	39	9	1	0	17	25	43	24	5	3.1	.213	.302	.265	-.249	.174	.244	.219	.181	-22.6	50-SS	-7
2007	AUG	A	21	346	53	17	3	0	26	46	56	29	6	5.8	.264	.372	.342	.014	.214	.302	.273	.217	-15.7	80-2B	-15
2008	SFN	MLB	22	402	43	17	2	2	25	36	84	18	5	1.3	.224	.300	.302	-.288	.222	.300	.312	.221	-5.6	96-2B	-6

Breakout: 33% Improve: 57% Collapse: 16% Attrition: 14%   Comparables: Chris Phillips, Elinton Jasco, Brian Benefield, Mike McCoy

Multiple shoulder surgeries have sent Sanders's once-promising career off the rails, pushing him off of shortstop to second base and taking away what little power he once had. He still runs well and has a disciplined approach that helps him reach base, but that lack of power will chip away at his OBP as he ascends, as pitchers begin to challenge him. Having had no success above the Sally League at age 22, he needs to have a big season this year.

Nate Schierholtz RF

Bats: L Throws: R Height: 6' 2" Weight: 215 Born: February 15, 1984 Age: 24

YEAR	TEAM	LVL	AGE	PA	R	2B	3B	HR	RBI	BB	SO	SB	CS	EqBRR	AVG	OBP	SLG	MLVr	EqAVG	EqOBP	EqSLG	EqA	VORP	DEFENSE	
2005	SJO	A+	21	548	83	37	8	15	86	32	132	5	7	2.7	.319	.363	.514	.255	.227	.266	.361	.214	-31.9	108-RF	-4
2006	NRW	AA	22	510	55	25	7	14	54	27	81	8	3	0.4	.270	.325	.443	.191	.261	.308	.441	.256	0.2	112-RF	-18
2007	FRE	AAA	23	439	67	31	7	16	68	17	58	10	4	1.3	.333	.365	.560	.311	.295	.328	.504	.279	18.1	98-RF	6
2007	SFN	MLB	23	117	9	5	3	0	10	2	19	3	1	1.3	.304	.316	.402	-.032	.306	.325	.414	.259	1.0	26-RF	-2
2008	SFN	MLB	24	580	70	35	5	15	73	28	98	10	4	1.3	.281	.321	.449	-.013	.279	.321	.464	.263	13.4	136-RF	1

Breakout: 24% Improve: 58% Collapse: 13% Attrition: 15%   Comparables: Nic Jackson, Rico Brogna, Matt Cepicky, Josh Kroeger

So if Ortmeier is the post-Bonds version of Linden, Schierholtz is the new Lance Niekro. With 125 walks and 66 home runs in roughly 2,200 minor league plate appearances, Scheirholtz has the perfect combination of hackery and middling power to serve as Niekro's heir. That two-walk, no-homer cup of coffee last year was just a tease, folks; there's more to come! Tip for the Giants: aim that cloning ray at Matt Cain and Tim Lincecum, not your failed outfield prospects.

Eugenio Velez UT

Bats: S Throws: R Height: 6' 1" Weight: 160 Born: May 16, 1982 Age: 26

YEAR	TEAM	LVL	AGE	PA	R	2B	3B	HR	RBI	BB	SO	SB	CS	EqBRR	AVG	OBP	SLG	MLVr	EqAVG	EqOBP	EqSLG	EqA	VORP	DEFENSE			
2005	LNS	A	23	254	25	11	3	4	34	9	40	7	5	0.5	.285	.311	.406	.018	.238	.256	.344	.204	-10.0	63-2B	-10		
2006	AUG	A	24	508	90	29	20	14	90	34	81	64	15	0.4	.315	.369	.557	.388	.262	.302	.449	.259	16.1	64-2B	-3	31-SS	-3
2007	NRW	AA	25	411	55	17	9	1	25	26	66	49	17	0.1	.298	.344	.399	.153	.272	.313	.380	.247	1.6	44-CF	-7	29-2B	-7
2007	SFN	MLB	25	13	5	0	2	0	2	2	3	4	0	1.6	.273	.385	.636	.369	.273	.385	.636	.351	2.7				
2008	SFN	MLB	26	467	59	23	7	5	39	25	90	41	12	1.5	.261	.304	.386	-.145	.259	.305	.398	.249	6.3	111-2B	-4		

Breakout: 22% Improve: 47% Collapse: 27% Attrition: 14%   Comparables: Fernando Ramsey, John Patterson, Alfredo Amezaga, Ramon Caraballo

As a Blue Jays prospect, Velez stole 11 bases in 24 attempts in three seasons. In two seasons since being taken by the Giants in the 2005 Rule 5 draft, he has 118 steals in 150 attempts. The Jays are noted for not running in the low minors, but that split seems absurd. Velez has been old for his leagues, never walks, and spent most of 2007 learning the outfield with mediocre results, so don't get too excited. He's a utility player in the making, not the new Luis Castillo.

Angel Villalona 3B

Bats: R Throws: R Height: 6' 3" Weight: 200 Born: August 13, 1990 Age: 17

YEAR	TEAM	LVL	AGE	PA	R	2B	3B	HR	RBI	BB	SO	SB	CS	EqBRR	AVG	OBP	SLG	MLVr	EqAVG	EqOBP	EqSLG	EqA	VORP	DEFENSE	
2007	GIA	Rk	16	224	40	12	3	5	37	15	42	1	1	1.4	.285	.344	.450	.148	.204	.233	.313	.183	-36.1	48-3B	-5
2008	SFN	MLB	17	498	40	26	3	8	46	29	97	7	3	0.3	.216	.264	.340	-.309	.214	.264	.351	.209	-15.1	118-3B	-3

Breakout: 68% Improve: 100% Collapse: 0% Attrition: 0%   Comparables: Angel Castillo, Willy Aybar, Andruw Jones, Luke Prokopec

The youngest player to be included in the 13-year run of the Baseball Prospectus annual, Villalona draws comparisons to Albert Pujols despite having just 237 professional plate appearances and no memory of the Cold War. Miguel Cabrera, Manny Ramirez, Frank Thomas . . . pick your comp, because Villalona has the complete package of hitting tools: power, bat speed, pitch recognition, and a plan at the plate. He'll be a first baseman or perhaps a corner out-fielder before he reaches the majors, but so what? There's a chance Villalona will play in the Cal League this year before he turns 18. The sky is the limit like it's been for no other prospect perhaps since Alex Rodriguez was drafted.

Omar Vizquel — SS

Bats: S   Throws: R   Height: 5' 9"   Weight: 175   Born: April 24, 1967   Age: 41

YEAR	TEAM	LVL	AGE	PA	R	2B	3B	HR	RBI	BB	SO	SB	CS	EqBRR	AVG	OBP	SLG	MLVr	EqAVG	EqOBP	EqSLG	EqA	VORP	DEFENSE	
2005	SFN	MLB	38	651	66	28	4	3	45	56	58	24	10	-4.3	.271	.341	.350	-.064	.273	.343	.358	.251	14.3	145-SS	11
2006	SFN	MLB	39	659	88	22	10	4	58	56	51	24	7	-1.0	.295	.361	.389	.016	.295	.361	.391	.270	28.0	145-SS	-3
2007	SFN	MLB	40	575	54	18	3	4	51	44	48	14	6	0.5	.246	.305	.316	-.214	.250	.313	.326	.228	-9.1	136-SS	11
2008	SFN	MLB	41	317	33	10	2	2	26	24	26	13	3	-0.1	.248	.306	.318	-.242	.246	.306	.328	.227	0.0	77-SS	2

Breakout: 11% Improve: 38% Collapse: 35% Attrition: 36%   Comparables: Ozzie Smith, Minnie Minoso, Wade Boggs, Craig Biggio

Last year the 40-year-old Vizquel lost 40 singles he couldn't afford to lose, the first sign that perhaps he won't play forever. He'll get some of them back in this year, but not enough to make him an asset, especially since you can expect his nearly nonexistent power to keep fading and taking his walks with it. The Giants re-signed him for his glove, but he also counts toward their collection of old, expensive players who can't hit. It's not quite Bonds's climb up the home run charts, but San Fran fans can look forward to Omar becoming the all-time leader in games played at short when he he surpasses fellow Venezuelan Luis Aparicio about two weeks into the season.

Randy Winn — OF

Bats: S   Throws: R   Height: 6' 2"   Weight: 195   Born: June 9, 1974   Age: 34

YEAR	TEAM	LVL	AGE	PA	R	2B	3B	HR	RBI	BB	SO	SB	CS	EqBRR	AVG	OBP	SLG	MLVr	EqAVG	EqOBP	EqSLG	EqA	VORP	DEFENSE			
2005	SEA	MLB	31	436	46	25	1	6	37	37	53	12	6	-0.3	.275	.342	.391	-.002	.289	.364	.421	.275	7.5	90-LF	10		
2005	SFN	MLB	31	247	39	22	5	14	26	11	38	7	5	-0.9	.359	.391	.680	.567	.358	.392	.698	.337	38.3	55-CF	9		
2006	SFN	MLB	32	635	82	34	5	11	56	48	63	10	8	-0.4	.262	.324	.396	-.062	.264	.327	.398	.251	0.8	74-RF	12	50-CF	1
2007	SFN	MLB	33	653	73	42	1	14	65	44	85	15	3	0.3	.300	.353	.445	.090	.302	.358	.458	.283	26.4	97-RF	1	32-CF	0
2008	SFN	MLB	34	511	66	28	3	10	60	37	65	9	4	0.2	.293	.348	.429	.015	.291	.349	.443	.270	17.6	120-RF	1		

Breakout: 10% Improve: 32% Collapse: 30% Attrition: 20%   Comparables: Jerry Mumphrey, Dave Philley, Willie McGee, Devon White

The best two months of Winn's career, August and September 2005, will end up costing the Giants more than $28 million over four years for a player who, at his best, is maybe one win better than the alternatives (sound familiar?). Winn has a limited no-trade clause for the rest of his deal, and while he's a good fourth outfielder, he's a marginal starter, especially on a corner. Winn, Roberts, and Rowand are all taking playing time from Lewis and Davis, inexpensive players who are broadly comparable, potentially better, and tens of millions of dollars cheaper. The Giants have made decisions like that all across the roster, while feeding the idea that it was Barry Bonds's $16 million—a bargain in both theoretical and real terms—standing in the way of their plans. No franchise has wasted more money on marginal upgrades. This is a diseased organization that needs a complete and thorough cleansing, from the owner's box on down.

PITCHERS

Travis Blackley

Bats: L   Throws: L   Height: 6' 3"   Weight: 200   Born: November 4, 1982   Age: 25

YEAR	TEAM	LVL	AGE	W	L	SV	G	GS	IP	H	BB	SO	HR	GB%	BABIP	STUFF	WHIP	ERA	PERA	EqERA	EqH9	EqBB9	EqSO9	EqHR9	VORP	SN/WX
2006	SAN	AA	23	8	11	0	25	25	144²	139	45	100	18	38.8%	.283	-23	1.28	4.06	5.88	6.12	9.6	3.6	4.1	1.7	-7.8	—
2007	FRE	AAA	24	10	8	0	28	28	162¹	156	68	121	21	41.1%	.293	-12	1.38	4.66	5.52	5.29	9.3	4.2	5.3	1.4	5.2	—
2007	SFN	MLB	24	0	0	0	2	2	8²	10	5	5	2	46.7%	.296	-20	1.73	7.24	7.23	7.27	10.4	4.2	5.2	2.1	-1.3	-0.02
2008	PHI	MLB	25	5	7	0	31	15	101	116	47	66	20	41.8%	.296	-9	1.61	5.88	6.13	5.81	10.0	3.8	5.2	1.7	-2.2	0.40

Breakout: 14% Improve: 46% Collapse: 19% Attrition: 14%   Comparables: Lance Painter, Jorge DePaula, Rigo Beltran, Horacio Estrada

Two healthy seasons removed from shoulder surgery, Blackley isn't the same pitcher who owned the Texas League at age 20, as he lacks the dominant stuff that marked his rise. His moderate success caught the eye of the Phillies, who selected him in the Rule 5 draft. Given the wide-open back of Phils' rotation, Blackley has an opportunity to stick as the high-powered Philly offense just needs its pitchers to take the ball and survive five innings.

Madison Bumgarner

Bats: R   Throws: L   Height: 6' 4"   Weight: 215   Born: August 1, 1989   Age: 18

YEAR	TEAM	LVL	AGE	W	L	SV	G	GS	IP	H	BB	SO	HR	GB%	BABIP	STUFF	WHIP	ERA	PERA	EqERA	EqH9	EqBB9	EqSO9	EqHR9	VORP	SN/WX
2008	SFN	MLB	18	3	11	0	23	23	104	148	89	46	23	46.2%	.334	-31	2.27	8.59	9.57	9.19	12.5	7.2	3.6	1.9	-36.7	-3.30

Breakout: NA   Improve: NA   Collapse: NA   Attrition: NA   Comparables: Trever Miller, Scott Elarton, Brian Barber, Jacob McGee

As a 6-foot-5 left-hander with a mid-90s fastball, Bumgarner is the rarest of rare, which is why he was the tenth overall pick in June. He might have gone higher if not for his delivery; not only is it sloppy, but he has a low, three-quarters release which limits his ability to spin a good breaking ball and could give him trouble against right-handers down the road. Nonetheless, the raw materials where just too good to pass up.

Matt Cain

Bats: R   Throws: R   Height: 6' 3"   Weight: 235   Born: October 1, 1984   Age: 23

YEAR	TEAM	LVL	AGE	W	L	SV	G	GS	IP	H	BB	SO	HR	GB%	BABIP	STUFF	WHIP	ERA	PERA	EqERA	EqH9	EqBB9	EqSO9	EqHR9	VORP	SN/WX
2005	FRE	AAA	20	10	5	0	26	26	145²	118	73	176	22	32.7%	.280	19	1.31	4.39	5.12	5.14	8.1	4.9	8.0	1.6	7.0	—
2005	SFN	MLB	20	2	1	0	7	7	46¹	24	19	30	4	29.5%	.160	27	0.93	2.33	2.34	2.49	4.4	3.3	5.2	0.8	17.0	2.12
2006	SFN	MLB	21	13	12	0	32	31	190²	157	87	179	18	38.6%	.272	35	1.28	4.15	3.41	3.90	7.3	3.5	7.6	0.7	34.9	4.76
2007	SFN	MLB	22	7	16	0	32	32	200	173	79	163	14	41.0%	.285	32	1.26	3.65	3.35	3.46	7.6	3.1	6.9	0.6	47.6	6.46
2008	SFN	MLB	23	10	10	0	27	27	168²	156	66	142	18	40.9%	.283	21	1.32	3.93	4.27	4.29	8.1	3.3	7.0	0.9	25.6	4.10

Breakout: 8%   Improve: 23%   Collapse: 46%   Attrition: 15%   Comparables: John Smoltz, Tony Armas Jr., Andy Benes, Ryan Dempster

Take this with a grain of small-sample salt, but over his last dozen starts covering 77 innings, Cain struck out 74 against just 15 unintentional walks; that's one strikeout shy of a 5-to-1 ratio, which is up in Pedro Martinez territory. Cain threw more than two-thirds of his pitches for strikes over that stretch. The problem is that he might be one of the five best pitchers in baseball the next few years and still be saddled with 7-16 records; three of the last four losses he suffered came in quality starts, and it's not as though the Giants' offense got better over the winter. If you can get 3:2 on a headline of "Giants Pitcher Assaults General Manager" at some point this year, take it.

Vinnie Chulk

Bats: R   Throws: R   Height: 6' 2"   Weight: 195   Born: December 19, 1978   Age: 29

YEAR	TEAM	LVL	AGE	W	L	SV	G	GS	IP	H	BB	SO	HR	GB%	BABIP	STUFF	WHIP	ERA	PERA	EqERA	EqH9	EqBB9	EqSO9	EqHR9	VORP	SN/WX
2005	TOR	MLB	26	0	1	0	62	0	72	68	26	39	9	43.8%	.269	-13	1.31	3.88	4.27	4.13	8.5	3.2	4.8	1.0	13.7	1.94
2006	SYR	AAA	27	3	2	1	19	0	32	20	14	43	4	50.7%	.239	11	1.06	2.25	4.28	2.90	6.4	4.6	9.0	1.7	9.3	—
2006	TOR	MLB	27	1	0	0	20	0	24	29	5	18	4	42.7%	.325	-5	1.42	5.25	5.52	5.55	10.4	1.8	6.3	1.1	0.5	0.04
2006	SFN	MLB	27	0	3	0	28	0	22¹	17	15	25	2	43.9%	.278	12	1.43	5.25	3.75	4.84	6.9	5.2	9.3	0.8	2.1	0.08
2007	SFN	MLB	28	5	4	0	57	0	53	53	14	41	3	32.7%	.318	11	1.26	3.57	3.59	3.44	8.8	2.1	6.5	0.5	12.8	0.59
2008	SFN	MLB	29	2	2	3	45	0	50	49	17	38	6	41.3%	.290	1	1.33	3.82	4.32	4.17	8.6	2.9	6.3	0.9	9.3	0.70

Breakout: 20%   Improve: 44%   Collapse: 32%   Attrition: 26%   Comparables: T.J. Mathews, Vicente Romo, Jack Cressend, Ricky Bottalico

The other guy in 2006's Shea Hillenbrand trade, Chulk pitched well in an ill-defined role for most of last season before picking up set-up innings for a while after the All-Star break. Circulatory problems possibly related to his use of chewing tobacco ended his season in August, but he's expected to make a comeback in spring training. His upside is set-up man, but in the Giants' deep pen, he's more likely to resume a low-leverage existence.

Kevin Correia

Bats: R   Throws: R   Height: 6' 3"   Weight: 205   Born: August 24, 1980   Age: 27

YEAR	TEAM	LVL	AGE	W	L	SV	G	GS	IP	H	BB	SO	HR	GB%	BABIP	STUFF	WHIP	ERA	PERA	EqERA	EqH9	EqBB9	EqSO9	EqHR9	VORP	SN/WX
2005	FRE	AAA	24	3	2	7	31	3	46	50	23	35	6	40.5%	.310	-27	1.59	6.07	6.40	8.16	10.5	4.8	4.8	1.5	-12.2	—
2005	SFN	MLB	24	2	5	0	16	11	58¹	61	31	44	12	37.3%	.293	-14	1.58	4.63	6.62	5.02	9.6	4.4	6.3	1.9	5.2	0.79
2006	SFN	MLB	25	2	0	0	48	0	69²	64	22	57	5	35.7%	.291	13	1.23	3.49	3.45	3.21	8.2	2.4	6.7	0.5	19.9	1.83
2007	SFN	MLB	26	4	7	0	59	8	101²	94	40	80	9	46.7%	.284	11	1.32	3.45	3.54	3.04	7.9	3.0	6.5	0.7	26.9	1.79
2008	SFN	MLB	27	3	4	2	39	4	67	66	25	48	7	43.6%	.286	-1	1.37	4.04	4.53	4.42	8.7	3.2	5.9	1.0	10.0	1.00

Breakout: 6%   Improve: 21%   Collapse: 54%   Attrition: 41%   Comparables: Carlos Reyes, Ron Schueler, Vicente Romo, Dave Stewart

Correia was effective out of the pen all of last year and, like Chulk, saw his role change as pitchers around him flailed and failed. Given a crack at the rotation in September, he showed well, with a 2.81 ERA, three quality starts, and four others that were short on length but not effectiveness. There's an important caveat that also applies to Cain's strong finish: the Giants ducked most of the league's good lineups down the stretch. Correia has a better than 2-to-1 K/BB over the last two seasons, and is certainly one of the 120 best starting pitchers in baseball. The Giants could do worse.

Dan Giese

Bats: R   Throws: R   Height: 6' 3"   Weight: 200   Born: May 19, 1977   Age: 31

YEAR	TEAM	LVL	AGE	W	L	SV	G	GS	IP	H	BB	SO	HR	GB%	BABIP	STUFF	WHIP	ERA	PERA	EqERA	EqH9	EqBB9	EqSO9	EqHR9	VORP	SN/WX
2005	SWB	AAA	28	3	4	2	26	0	38	51	1	28	9	40.4%	.339	-34	1.37	5.68	9.05	8.41	13.0	0.8	4.8	2.5	-11.0	—
2006	REA	AA	29	1	2	1	23	0	36	27	14	27	5	52.4%	.232	-28	1.14	2.50	5.98	4.50	8.7	4.8	4.5	2.2	3.9	—
2006	SWB	AAA	29	2	2	0	25	0	35¹	46	4	33	3	40.2%	.394	-14	1.42	3.08	8.37	7.24	14.5	1.7	6.4	1.4	-5.9	—
2007	FRE	AAA	30	3	1	2	47	0	73¹	65	10	76	2	42.2%	.318	22	1.02	2.82	3.35	3.82	8.4	1.5	7.4	0.4	14.0	—
2007	SFN	MLB	30	0	2	0	8	0	9¹	8	2	7	4	57.1%	.174	-9	1.07	4.84	6.32	4.82	6.8	1.9	6.8	3.9	1.1	-0.05
2008	NYA	MLB	31	3	3	4	43	3	50¹	54	13	38	7	44.4%	.299	0	1.32	4.36	4.29	4.33	9.3	2.1	6.1	1.3	6.8	0.8

Breakout: 41% Improve: 64% Collapse: 19% Attrition: 29%   Comparables: Willie Fraser, Tim Crews, Blas Minor, Ron Rightnowar

One of the feel-good stories of last season, Giese got a September call-up nearly a decade after being drafted and a little more than two years after briefly quitting baseball and working as a used-car salesman. The minor league journeyman lives by spotting mediocre stuff, but has had some absurd stat lines over the years, including that K/BB ratio in Triple-A in 2005 seen above. He'll be in camp with the Yankees, who seem to be collecting second-chancers with wild peripherals and do enough shuffling at the back end of their pen to provide hope for Giese. He's maybe ten percent worse than LaTroy Hawkins.

Brad Hennessey

Bats: R   Throws: R   Height: 6' 2"   Weight: 200   Born: February 7, 1980   Age: 28

YEAR	TEAM	LVL	AGE	W	L	SV	G	GS	IP	H	BB	SO	HR	GB%	BABIP	STUFF	WHIP	ERA	PERA	EqERA	EqH9	EqBB9	EqSO9	EqHR9	VORP	SN/WX
2005	FRE	AAA	25	4	2	0	11	11	67²	75	22	46	7	49.3%	.315	-9	1.43	5.18	5.70	5.83	10.5	3.3	4.3	1.1	-1.6	—
2005	SFN	MLB	25	5	8	0	21	21	118¹	127	52	64	15	49.4%	.294	-8	1.51	4.64	5.39	4.92	9.8	3.7	4.5	1.1	10.4	2.53
2006	SFN	MLB	26	5	6	1	34	12	99¹	92	42	42	12	44.7%	.256	-13	1.35	4.26	4.21	4.21	8.2	3.3	3.6	1.0	13.6	1.32
2007	SFN	MLB	27	4	5	19	69	0	68¹	66	23	40	7	47.1%	.281	-4	1.30	3.43	3.92	3.07	8.4	2.5	5.1	0.8	18.6	1.97
2008	SFN	MLB	28	2	4	7	35	1	47²	51	18	27	5	46.9%	.293	-11	1.45	4.41	4.95	4.85	9.4	3.2	4.6	0.9	5.1	0.50

Breakout: 12% Improve: 27% Collapse: 45% Attrition: 40%   Comparables: Jeff Shaw, Bob Priddy, Clyde King, Charlie Williams

As a converted starter with no dominant pitch who struggles to miss bats, Hennessey was never going to hold the closer role for long. "For long" turned out to be about 14 weeks, as Brian Wilson came along to claim the job in September. The Giants have too many guys like Hennessey—failed starters best-suited for multi-inning work—coming out of their pen and not enough fire-breathers. Hennessey won't have 19 saves the rest of his career.

Steve Kline

Bats: R   Throws: L   Height: 6' 1"   Weight: 230   Born: August 22, 1972   Age: 35

YEAR	TEAM	LVL	AGE	W	L	SV	G	GS	IP	H	BB	SO	HR	GB%	BABIP	STUFF	WHIP	ERA	PERA	EqERA	EqH9	EqBB9	EqSO9	EqHR9	VORP	SN/WX
2005	BAL	MLB	32	2	4	0	67	0	61	59	30	36	11	57.1%	.262	-22	1.44	4.28	5.13	4.68	8.4	4.4	5.3	1.5	4.8	-0.83
2006	SFN	MLB	33	4	3	1	72	0	51²	53	26	33	3	49.1%	.318	-6	1.53	3.66	4.44	3.93	9.5	3.9	5.4	0.5	10.6	1.56
2007	SFN	MLB	34	1	2	2	68	0	46	58	18	17	2	51.4%	.322	-17	1.65	4.70	4.63	4.50	10.5	2.8	3.0	0.4	5.3	1.03
2008	SFN	MLB	35	2	2	2	44	0	40²	44	17	21	3	50.4%	.296	-16	1.49	4.33	4.70	4.83	9.4	3.5	4.3	0.7	3.9	0.30

Breakout: 19% Improve: 39% Collapse: 44% Attrition: 29%   Comparables: Mike Myers, Joe Gibbon, Steve Barber, Dave Roberts

Last year, Kline went from striking out about 20 percent of the lefty batters he faced to about ten percent, which rendered him essentially useless. Slash stats bounce around based on what happens to balls in play, but if a specialist isn't whiffing 15 percent of his same-side guys, he has a real problem. Kline actually walked just one less left-hander than he struck out. That's bad.

Tim Lincecum

Bats: L Throws: R Height: 5' 11" Weight: 170 Born: June 15, 1984 Age: 24

YEAR	TEAM	LVL	AGE	W	L	SV	G	GS	IP	H	BB	SO	HR	GB%	BABIP	STUFF	WHIP	ERA	PERA	EqERA	EqH9	EqBB9	EqSO9	EqHR9	VORP	SN/WX
2006	SJO	A+	22	2	0	0	6	6	27	13	12	48	3	50.0%	.246	25	0.93	2.00	4.72	3.96	6.5	5.4	10.1	1.8	4.6	—
2007	FRE	AAA	23	4	0	0	5	5	31	12	11	46	0	53.6%	.218	29	0.74	0.29	2.46	1.23	4.3	3.4	9.8	0.3	14.2	—
2007	SFN	MLB	23	7	5	0	24	24	146¹	122	65	150	12	48.1%	.292	35	1.28	4.00	3.31	3.91	7.3	3.4	8.5	0.7	26.5	3.86
2008	SFN	MLB	24	8	8	0	23	23	140²	120	59	133	13	46.0%	.279	26	1.27	3.58	3.82	3.95	7.5	3.5	7.8	0.8	28.3	4.00

Breakout: 14% Improve: 34% Collapse: 30% Attrition: 24%   Comparables: Billy Loes, Rich Harden, Tom Gordon, Al Downing

As you're evaluating Lincecum's rookie season, remember that he went from the Pac-10 to the NL in less than a year and made just 13 minor league starts—posting PlayStation stats—along the way. His high-90s heat and 13-to-6 curve (12-to-6 doesn't do it justice) made MLB hitters look ridiculous at times. At other times, he couldn't command either pitch and walked the park, passing four or more hitters in nine of his starts. Like the other young Giants, he settled down toward the end of the year, with a 2.9 K/UIBB ratio in his last seven outings. He has big-leap potential and could very well be the best pitcher in the NL this year . . . and go 12-10.

Noah Lowry

Bats: R Throws: L Height: 6' 2" Weight: 205 Born: October 10, 1980 Age: 27

YEAR	TEAM	LVL	AGE	W	L	SV	G	GS	IP	H	BB	SO	HR	GB%	BABIP	STUFF	WHIP	ERA	PERA	EqERA	EqH9	EqBB9	EqSO9	EqHR9	VORP	SN/WX
2005	SFN	MLB	24	13	13	0	33	33	204²	193	76	172	21	42.1%	.295	18	1.31	3.78	4.10	4.03	8.5	3.0	6.9	0.9	36.5	4.86
2006	SFN	MLB	25	7	10	0	27	27	159¹	166	56	84	21	38.3%	.288	-1	1.39	4.75	4.62	4.56	9.2	2.7	4.4	1.0	17.7	4.12
2007	SFN	MLB	26	14	8	0	26	26	156	155	87	87	12	47.6%	.295	9	1.55	3.92	4.31	4.01	8.7	4.3	4.8	0.6	26.6	3.65
2008	SFN	MLB	27	5	8	0	28	16	106²	114	45	66	12	45.6%	.298	-2	1.49	4.72	5.15	5.17	9.4	3.6	5.1	0.9	6.7	1.40

Breakout: 4% Improve: 15% Collapse: 58% Attrition: 34%   Comparables: Darren Oliver, Damian Moss, Chris Haney, Neal Heaton

Through 2005, Lowry looked like the real thing, a strikeout/fly-ball lefty with big breaking stuff good enough to fool many of the people much of the time. He looked like Doug Davis, or even Mark Mulder. Since then, he's been fragile, hittable, and wild. The generous dimensions of AT&T Park are the only things standing between him and an ERA higher than Mike Tyson's credit score. The entire package looks like a pitcher who worked at max effort in his early 20s and is left without much to give.

Randy Messenger

Bats: R Throws: R Height: 6' 6" Weight: 240 Born: August 13, 1981 Age: 26

YEAR	TEAM	LVL	AGE	W	L	SV	G	GS	IP	H	BB	SO	HR	GB%	BABIP	STUFF	WHIP	ERA	PERA	EqERA	EqH9	EqBB9	EqSO9	EqHR9	VORP	SN/WX
2005	ABQ	AAA	23	4	2	7	39	0	48²	46	17	35	5	57.3%	.287	-15	1.29	3.88	4.55	4.70	8.6	3.5	4.5	1.0	4.6	—
2005	FLO	MLB	23	0	0	0	29	0	37	39	30	29	5	48.7%	.312	-4	1.86	5.35	5.57	4.97	8.8	6.4	6.2	1.2	0.3	-0.40
2006	FLO	MLB	24	2	7	0	59	0	60¹	72	24	45	8	41.5%	.337	-11	1.59	5.67	5.23	5.98	10.1	3.1	6.0	1.0	-3.0	-0.76
2007	FLO	MLB	25	1	1	0	23	0	23²	27	9	12	0	45.1%	.351	-5	1.52	2.66	3.55	2.28	9.1	3.0	4.2	0.0	8.2	0.18
2007	SFN	MLB	25	1	3	1	37	0	40²	58	12	22	4	48.4%	.378	-16	1.72	5.09	6.68	5.36	12.5	2.2	4.7	0.9	3.6	-0.87
2008	SFN	MLB	26	2	3	2	37	1	48¹	54	17	29	5	47.0%	.306	-6	1.46	4.22	4.77	4.65	9.8	3.0	5.0	0.8	6.4	0.50

Breakout: 24% Improve: 45% Collapse: 29% Attrition: 38%   Comparables: Antonio Alfonseca, Todd Coffey, Brad Rigby, Dan Wheeler

Last August, inanimate objects continued their long winning streak against angry pitchers when Messenger, upset about losing a game, punched a plastic cart and broke his left hand, putting himself on the shelf for a month. It should have been six weeks: a rusty Messenger allowed 13 runs on 19 hits in six innings across seven outings at the end of the season. He throws enough strikes to be a viable fourth guy in the pen.

Pat Misch

Bats: R Throws: L Height: 6' 2" Weight: 170 Born: August 18, 1981 Age: 26

YEAR	TEAM	LVL	AGE	W	L	SV	G	GS	IP	H	BB	SO	HR	GB%	BABIP	STUFF	WHIP	ERA	PERA	EqERA	EqH9	EqBB9	EqSO9	EqHR9	VORP	SN/WX
2005	NRW	AA	23	4	2	0	9	9	61¹	63	7	43	7	45.1%	.306	-10	1.14	3.52	5.75	5.17	10.5	1.8	3.7	1.6	2.7	—
2005	FRE	AAA	23	3	9	0	19	19	102	135	40	69	18	42.9%	.357	-38	1.72	6.35	8.99	8.40	12.7	4.0	4.2	1.9	-29.6	—
2006	NRW	AA	24	5	4	0	18	17	103	95	24	79	7	48.5%	.294	-5	1.16	2.27	5.30	4.24	9.9	3.0	4.4	1.2	14.1	—
2006	FRE	AAA	24	4	2	0	10	10	65²	74	11	57	7	42.7%	.342	3	1.30	4.00	5.52	5.05	10.8	1.9	5.8	1.3	3.8	—
2007	FRE	AAA	25	2	5	1	34	6	66²	54	19	74	4	49.4%	.313	17	1.09	2.29	3.77	3.75	8.1	2.9	8.1	0.7	12.8	—
2007	SFN	MLB	25	0	4	0	18	4	40¹	47	12	26	3	44.9%	.338	0	1.46	4.24	4.75	4.54	10.2	2.3	5.4	0.7	5.4	0.06
2008	SFN	MLB	26	3	3	2	40	5	54²	56	19	38	6	47.0%	.294	-1	1.36	4.01	4.49	4.41	9.0	2.9	5.7	0.9	9.1	0.90

Breakout: 30% Improve: 55% Collapse: 28% Attrition: 33%   Comparables: Scott Bailes, Bud Daley, Scott Downs, Ricky Horton

Misch is Noah Lowry without the good years, more or less. Another low-ceiling college draftee by the Giants, Misch took well to a move to the bullpen last year, although he's not your typical starter-to-reliever conversion. A command southpaw with a good changeup, Misch, like a lot of guys, is qualified for a job that doesn't exist anymore: swingman. There are probably 60 pitchers in this book who could make 15 starts and 40 relief appearances at just below league-average performance. All they need is a time machine.

Scott Munter

Bats: R   Throws: R   Height: 6' 6"   Weight: 260   Born: March 7, 1980   Age: 28

YEAR	TEAM	LVL	AGE	W	L	SV	G	GS	IP	H	BB	SO	HR	GB%	BABIP	STUFF	WHIP	ERA	PERA	EqERA	EqH9	EqBB9	EqSO9	EqHR9	VORP	SN/WX
2005	SFN	MLB	25	2	0	0	45	0	38²	40	12	11	1	64.4%	.298	-18	1.34	2.56	4.02	3.75	9.8	2.8	2.5	0.2	8.7	0.85
2006	NRW	AA	26	1	4	1	28	0	40	45	15	22	1	65.9%	.336	-29	1.50	4.73	5.89	7.05	11.4	4.4	2.9	0.5	-6.0	—
2006	SFN	MLB	26	0	1	0	27	0	22²	30	18	7	1	59.0%	.392	-34	2.12	8.72	8.32	9.00	12.9	6.9	3.0	0.4	-6.5	0.00
2007	FRE	AAA	27	1	6	1	48	0	58¹	62	24	14	3	63.2%	.288	-33	1.48	4.17	4.78	4.72	9.6	4.1	1.3	0.7	5.4	—
2007	SFN	MLB	27	1	1	0	12	0	10²	14	4	4	0	63.2%	.412	-23	1.69	4.21	5.98	4.66	13.0	2.8	3.7	0.0	2.0	-0.23
2008	SFN	MLB	28	2	3	1	39	3	47²	56	23	17	3	59.7%	.309	-24	1.65	5.03	5.37	5.69	10.3	4.0	2.9	0.5	0.2	0.10

Breakout: 27%   Improve: 49%   Collapse: 31%   Attrition: 26%   Comparables: Todd Williams, Greg Booker, Ron Rightnowar, Joe Winkelsas

Munter illustrates the point that a great sinker that gets pounded into the ground isn't always enough. His fantastic ground-ball rates are paired with more walks than strikeouts—59 passes and 41 whiffs above Double-A in his career. He's a free agent, and while that one pitch is nasty, there's little evidence that it will be enough to make him a major league reliever.

Russ Ortiz

Bats: R   Throws: R   Height: 6' 1"   Weight: 220   Born: June 5, 1974   Age: 34

YEAR	TEAM	LVL	AGE	W	L	SV	G	GS	IP	H	BB	SO	HR	GB%	BABIP	STUFF	WHIP	ERA	PERA	EqERA	EqH9	EqBB9	EqSO9	EqHR9	VORP	SN/WX
2005	ARI	MLB	31	5	11	0	22	22	115	147	65	46	18	37.8%	.319	-27	1.84	6.89	6.68	6.77	10.6	4.5	3.2	1.3	-18.3	-1.09
2006	ARI	MLB	32	0	5	0	6	6	22²	27	22	21	3	40.6%	.369	9	2.16	7.53	8.06	8.18	11.0	7.8	7.8	1.2	-5.1	-0.10
2006	BAL	MLB	32	0	3	0	20	5	40¹	59	18	23	15	34.0%	.336	-59	1.91	8.49	13.67	10.38	12.5	3.9	5.1	3.0	-11.6	-0.82
2007	SFN	MLB	33	2	3	0	12	8	49	57	20	27	4	44.1%	.327	-4	1.55	5.51	5.19	5.55	10.2	3.1	4.8	0.7	1.0	0.65
2008	SFN	MLB	34	2	3	0	19	5	41¹	47	17	24	6	43.2%	.299	-15	1.54	5.25	5.78	5.69	10.0	3.4	4.7	1.3	0.3	0.20

Breakout: 53%   Improve: 66%   Collapse: 19%   Attrition: 48%   Comparables: Kent Mercker, Jim Slaton, Bob Johnson, Craig Swan

"Near . . . far . . . whereeeeeeeeever you are, I believe that my contract goes oooooooonnnnnn." Ortiz will miss the 2008 season following Tommy John surgery, denying us the chance to see him pitch for four other teams while still being paid by the Diamondbacks, whose four-year, $33 million deal with Ortiz runs through the end of the season. Those of you annoyed that we've put a Céline Dion song in your head should note that the composition in question is from a movie in which a large, expensive item filled with food broke apart and sunk quickly without being used much. Apology accepted.

Sergio Romo

Bats: R   Throws: R   Height: 5' 11"   Weight: 185   Born: March 4, 1983   Age: 25

YEAR	TEAM	LVL	AGE	W	L	SV	G	GS	IP	H	BB	SO	HR	GB%	BABIP	STUFF	WHIP	ERA	PERA	EqERA	EqH9	EqBB9	EqSO9	EqHR9	VORP	SN/WX
2005	SLO	A-	22	7	1	0	15	14	68²	70	9	65	7	43.7%	.321	-39	1.15	2.75	9.60	7.39	13.5	3.7	4.0	2.7	-11.1	—
2006	AUG	A	23	10	2	4	31	10	103	78	19	95	9	36.4%	.255	-31	0.94	2.53	5.74	5.30	9.1	3.3	4.4	2.0	3.1	—
2007	SJO	A+	24	6	2	9	41	0	66¹	35	15	106	4	35.2%	.267	19	0.75	1.36	3.75	3.13	6.6	3.3	9.4	1.0	16.5	—
2008	SFN	MLB	25	3	5	5	27	6	63²	61	26	53	10	37.9%	.280	5	1.37	4.20	4.85	4.51	8.4	3.5	6.9	1.3	8.4	1.10

Breakout: 40%   Improve: 62%   Collapse: 20%   Attrition: 13%   Comparables: Heath Haynes, Santos Hernandez, Bo Donaldson, Chris Demaria

It's tempting to call Romo a performance prospect, but there are holes in the performance, most notably his combination of age and level. A real 24-year-old prospect in the California league would be, well, a 24-year-old prospect in the Eastern League. The Giants' refusal to promote him in-season twice is worrisome. Romo has excellent command of decent stuff; pitchers like that usually have a moment of truth at Double-A, so stay tuned.

Jonathan Sanchez

Bats: L Throws: L Height: 6' 2" Weight: 165 Born: November 19, 1982 Age: 25

YEAR	TEAM	LVL	AGE	W	L	SV	G	GS	IP	H	BB	SO	HR	GB%	BABIP	STUFF	WHIP	ERA	PERA	EqERA	EqH9	EqBB9	EqSO9	EqHR9	VORP	SN/WX
2005	AUG	A	22	5	7	0	25	25	125²	122	39	166	8	47.5%	.373	-4	1.28	4.08	7.32	7.13	11.7	5.4	7.0	1.4	-18.2	—
2006	NRW	AA	23	2	1	2	13	3	31²	14	9	46	0	49.2%	.250	27	0.74	1.15	2.95	3.45	5.3	3.5	9.1	0.3	6.9	—
2006	FRE	AAA	23	2	2	0	6	6	23¹	13	13	28	1	38.9%	.235	18	1.13	3.90	3.27	4.30	5.1	5.1	7.8	0.4	3.3	—
2006	SFN	MLB	23	3	1	0	27	4	40	39	23	33	2	36.0%	.306	4	1.55	4.95	4.16	5.27	8.6	4.4	6.6	0.4	1.0	0.23
2007	FRE	AAA	24	0	0	0	6	3	20²	15	8	27	0	36.7%	.306	20	1.11	2.17	3.23	2.70	7.2	3.6	9.4	0.0	6.4	—
2007	SFN	MLB	24	1	5	0	33	4	52	57	28	62	8	43.4%	.374	8	1.63	5.88	6.42	5.82	10.1	4.2	10.2	1.2	-0.1	0.41
2008	SFN	MLB	25	3	4	2	34	7	67	61	31	67	6	43.5%	.302	15	1.37	3.95	4.27	4.33	8.0	3.9	8.3	0.8	12.2	1.30

Breakout: 47% Improve: 69% Collapse: 14% Attrition: 25%   Comparables: Tug McGraw, Grant Jackson, Pete Richert, Dick Stigman

At the start of 2006, Sanchez was a 23-year-old coming off an impressive season in the Sally League, prone to fighting his command and mechanics but otherwise very talented. That season the Giants jerked him around between Double-A and the majors and between starting and relieving, resulting in a season broken into four stints with three teams in two roles with no more than eight weeks spent in any one place. Last year was more of the same, minus Double-A, but plus a recurring oblique injury. If there is a plan to all of this, it's well concealed. The Giants still don't know what they want him to be, and while making up their minds they've wasted two years of Sanchez's career. No one mishandling a million-dollar asset this badly should be allowed to keep their job.

Henry Sosa

Bats: R Throws: R Height: 6' 2" Weight: 185 Born: July 28, 1985 Age: 22

YEAR	TEAM	LVL	AGE	W	L	SV	G	GS	IP	H	BB	SO	HR	GB%	BABIP	STUFF	WHIP	ERA	PERA	EqERA	EqH9	EqBB9	EqSO9	EqHR9	VORP	SN/WX
2006	GIA	Rk	20	2	1	0	9	6	32²	20	12	41	3	48.0%	.246	-20	0.99	3.91	10.51	8.89	9.9	7.2	5.8	4.8	-9.6	—
2007	AUG	A	21	6	0	1	13	10	62	30	25	61	2	46.6%	.193	13	0.89	0.73	4.19	2.96	5.9	5.9	5.1	0.8	16.0	—
2007	SJO	A+	21	5	5	0	14	14	63²	66	36	78	8	41.2%	.349	-5	1.60	4.38	9.03	7.58	11.8	7.1	6.9	1.9	-12.5	—
2008	SFN	MLB	22	5	9	0	29	19	112²	116	76	86	18	42.7%	.289	-4	1.70	5.56	6.32	5.98	9.0	5.7	6.3	1.4	-2.7	0.50

Breakout: 19% Improve: 41% Collapse: 26% Attrition: 13%   Comparables: Winston Abreu, Juan Cruz, Fernando Hernandez, Felix Rodriguez

Brought to you by the "Where Did He Come From?" files, Sosa entered last year as just another generic strong-armed thrower and ended it as the top pitching prospect in the Giants organization. With a fastball that sits in the low to mid 90s and touches 98 mph, he can dominate on his heater alone, but he also features a power curve that flashes plus at times. Like many young arms, his control lags behind his stuff, but he's one of the few arms in the system with big-time upside.

Jack Taschner

Bats: L Throws: L Height: 6' 3" Weight: 210 Born: April 21, 1978 Age: 30

YEAR	TEAM	LVL	AGE	W	L	SV	G	GS	IP	H	BB	SO	HR	GB%	BABIP	STUFF	WHIP	ERA	PERA	EqERA	EqH9	EqBB9	EqSO9	EqHR9	VORP	SN/WX
2005	FRE	AAA	27	3	0	10	44	0	49¹	30	24	62	3	46.9%	.250	17	1.10	1.64	3.45	2.14	6.0	4.7	8.4	0.8	17.8	—
2005	SFN	MLB	27	2	0	0	24	0	22²	15	13	19	0	30.2%	.242	11	1.24	1.59	2.73	1.99	6.0	4.8	6.8	0.0	8.8	0.58
2006	FRE	AAA	28	6	7	14	45	0	49	49	17	68	5	43.1%	.389	8	1.35	3.67	5.95	4.73	10.4	3.5	9.7	1.2	4.4	—
2006	SFN	MLB	28	0	1	0	24	0	19¹	31	7	15	4	28.6%	.380	-29	1.97	8.39	9.24	10.71	13.3	2.6	6.0	1.7	-9.7	-0.17
2007	SFN	MLB	29	3	1	0	63	0	50	44	29	51	4	34.8%	.303	10	1.48	5.40	3.72	4.94	7.6	4.4	8.3	0.7	1.7	0.44
2008	SFN	MLB	30	2	2	3	38	1	38²	37	20	35	4	39.3%	.300	2	1.47	4.51	4.77	4.92	8.4	4.3	7.6	0.9	3.8	0.30

Breakout: 34% Improve: 44% Collapse: 29% Attrition: 36%   Comparables: Paul Spoljaric, Yorkis Perez, Arnold Earley, Mickey Mahler

An odd BABIP split hides the fact that Taschner has been pretty effective against hitters on both sides of the plate over his career, striking out 20.1 percent of righties and 19.4 percent of lefties. That BABIP quirk—lefties hit .377 off of him on balls in play last year—cost him a set-up job. Taschner doesn't need to be limited to LOOGY status, but lefty relievers who throw complete or multiple innings are another species of pitcher that has been forced into extinction.

Brian Wilson

Bats: R　Throws: R　Height: 6' 1"　Weight: 205　Born: March 16, 1982　Age: 26

YEAR	TEAM	LVL	AGE	W	L	SV	G	GS	IP	H	BB	SO	HR	GB%	BABIP	STUFF	WHIP	ERA	PERA	EqERA	EqH9	EqBB9	EqSO9	EqHR9	VORP	SN/WX
2005	AUG	A	23	5	1	13	26	0	33	23	7	30	0	70.7%	.253	-11	0.91	0.82	4.15	3.64	7.3	3.6	4.2	0.3	6.5	—
2005	NRW	AA	23	0	0	8	15	0	15²	6	5	22	0	50.0%	.200	14	0.70	0.57	2.91	1.88	4.4	3.8	8.2	0.0	5.9	—
2005	FRE	AAA	23	1	1	0	9	0	11¹	8	8	13	0	29.0%	.276	11	1.42	3.98	3.95	5.91	6.8	6.8	7.6	0.0	-0.4	—
2006	FRE	AAA	24	1	3	7	24	0	28¹	20	14	30	2	51.4%	.269	4	1.21	2.88	4.01	3.42	7.2	5.1	7.2	1.0	6.4	—
2006	SFN	MLB	24	2	3	1	31	0	30	32	21	23	1	45.8%	.344	-2	1.77	5.40	4.87	5.40	9.6	5.4	6.3	0.3	1.1	0.09
2007	FRE	AAA	25	1	2	11	31	0	34¹	24	24	37	0	44.9%	.276	15	1.40	2.10	3.85	3.74	6.7	6.4	7.5	0.3	7.0	—
2007	SFN	MLB	25	1	2	6	24	0	23²	16	7	18	1	56.7%	.227	11	0.97	2.28	2.36	2.28	5.7	2.3	6.5	0.4	9.4	1.71
2008	SFN	MLB	26	3	3	6	50	1	51²	47	25	41	3	50.6%	.284	2	1.37	3.68	4.04	4.11	7.9	4.0	6.6	0.6	10.0	0.90

Breakout: 5%　Improve: 30%　Collapse: 43%　Attrition: 20%　　　Comparables: Jack Lamabe, Hal Reniff, Jack Baldschun, Darren Dreifort

It has to be frustrating for a pitcher like Sanchez to see Wilson get promoted from Triple-A and slotted right into a defined role. Wilson became the set-up man just three outings after joining the big club and was made the closer a month later. The power righty with a big-time fastball and good slider still hasn't conquered his control problems, so despite a low ERA and good walk rate in his seven weeks in the majors, skepticism is warranted. God only knows what he'll do this year.

Barry Zito

Bats: L　Throws: L　Height: 6' 4"　Weight: 210　Born: May 13, 1978　Age: 30

YEAR	TEAM	LVL	AGE	W	L	SV	G	GS	IP	H	BB	SO	HR	GB%	BABIP	STUFF	WHIP	ERA	PERA	EqERA	EqH9	EqBB9	EqSO9	EqHR9	VORP	SN/WX
2005	OAK	MLB	27	14	13	0	35	35	228¹	185	89	171	26	42.2%	.249	14	1.20	3.86	3.91	4.22	7.7	3.5	6.6	1.0	41.1	5.46
2006	OAK	MLB	28	16	10	0	34	34	221	211	99	151	27	40.0%	.287	8	1.40	3.83	4.36	3.77	8.2	3.9	5.9	1.0	49.9	6.07
2007	SFN	MLB	29	11	13	0	34	33	196²	182	83	131	24	41.1%	.267	7	1.35	4.53	3.80	4.22	7.8	3.2	5.5	1.0	24.7	4.22
2008	SFN	MLB	30	9	9	0	26	26	158	152	62	117	17	43.6%	.284	13	1.36	4.01	4.45	4.38	8.5	3.3	6.1	0.9	23.2	3.70

Breakout: 7%　Improve: 36%　Collapse: 29%　Attrition: 16%　　　Comparables: Chuck Finley, Vinegar Bend Mizell, Kevin Gross, Darryl Kile

The killer thing about the seven-year, $119 million contract the Giants lavished on Zito isn't just the price tag for a pitcher who isn't an ace. No, the punch to the gut is that six months after the contract was executed, Zito was the number-three starter on the team, and has no shot of ranking higher in the rotation for the duration of the deal. Having a durable innings-eater is a benefit; it's just not worth breaking the bank when the strength of your organization is two young starting pitchers who might be true number-ones. It's not all bad: Zito's durability and good career start combine to make him among the next in line—behind former teammate Tim Hudson and essentially even with Roy Oswalt—to make a run at 300 wins.

LINEOUTS

Hitters

PLAYER		TEAM	LVL	AGE	PA	R	2B	3B	HR	RBI	BB	SO	SB-CS	EqBRR	AVG/OBP/SLG	MLVr	EqAVG/EqOBP/EqSLG	EqA	VORP
C	E. Alfonzo	FRE	AAA	28	66	9	6	0	3	10	1	8	0-0	-0.4	.297/.308/.531	.127	.266/.277/.469	.249	1.7
		SFN	MLB	28	67	5	2	1	1	6	2	23	0-2	-2.1	.250/.284/.359	-.196	.250/.284/.359	.211	-1.8
OF	J. Bowker*	NRW	AA	23	587	79	35	6	22	90	41	103	3-7	-2.9	.307/.363/.523	.377	.287/.335/.505	.280	26.9
SS	C. Culberson	GIA	Rk	18	187	32	8	5	1	16	19	38	19-1	4.8	.286/.374/.416	.145	.203/.258/.279	.197	-27.3
2B	T. Denker	SBR	A+	21	461	65	27	3	10	57	48	65	8-2	-0.8	.294/.369/.450	.154	.243/.308/.366	.239	-1.0
1B	T. Ishikawa*	SJO	A+	23	222	35	15	1	13	34	19	78	0-0	-1.7	.268/.342/.551	.292	.196/.257/.402	.225	-10.9
		NRW	AA	23	192	17	3	1	3	17	17	48	0-0	-0.5	.214/.292/.295	-.155	.199/.266/.278	.187	-18.2
OF	E. Martinez-Esteve	SJO	A+	23	91	5	5	0	0	8	9	13	0-0	-0.7	.207/.286/.268	-.281	.190/.253/.238	.163	-11.2
		NRW	AA	23	147	10	2	1	1	10	12	33	2-1	-0.5	.239/.306/.291	-.118	.221/.284/.272	.196	-13.6
PH	L. Niekro	FRE	AAA	28	158	21	8	2	5	20	12	32	0-1	-1.1	.301/.354/.490	.148	.264/.321/.438	.257	1.7
C	G. Rodriguez	FRE	AAA	29	119	15	6	0	1	16	11	8	1-0	0.6	.243/.319/.330	-.199	.257/.331/.324	.241	-0.4
		SFN	MLB	29	98	10	6	0	1	14	10	17	0-1	-1.5	.253/.327/.356	-.109	.256/.337/.349	.243	0.6
1B	P. Sandoval#	SJO	A+	20	423	56	33	5	11	52	16	52	3-1	0.8	.287/.312/.476	.150	.241/.262/.387	.220	-8.1
CF	C. Timpner*	FRE	AAA	24	437	51	11	4	6	39	37	68	9-11	-3.0	.301/.363/.395	.026	.265/.329/.351	.236	-0.2

Catcher **Eliezer Alfonzo** tore ligaments in his left knee and missed three months while having it scoped. Meanwhile, Guillermo Rodriguez claimed the backup role with the big club. Apparently, an injury *can* cost you your job. ⌀ After two poor seasons in the Cal League, the Giants promoted **John Bowker** to the Eastern League for 2007. Apparently he had sent his bat ahead to Connecticut after the 2004 season, because he found it again at Double-A. He's an inferior version of Schierholtz, and unlikely to build on his progress. ⌀ A shortstop in name only, 2007 supplemental first-round pick **Charlie Culberson** will be a second or third baseman soon, but he has an interesting set of secondary skills if not the sharpest tools. ⌀ **Travis Denker** is a small second baseman picked up from the Dodgers in exchange for a few weeks of Mark Sweeney's time. He doesn't do much other than hit, and he's not a power guy, so his future could come down to what he does in Double-A this year. ⌀ First baseman **Travis Ishikawa** is no longer a prospect, as the only place he's ever hit is the Cal League, and his sub-.310 career OBP in Double-A invalidates those numbers. ⌀ Similarly, **Eddy Martinez-Esteve** did not bounce back from 2006 shoulder surgery and is now a 24-year-old who has never hit above the Cal League. ⌀ An empty .300 in the PCL is an empty .250 in the NL, and so ends **Lance Niekro**'s career. He never adapted his approach. ⌀ Veteran catch-and-throw guy **Guillermo Rodriguez** was just standing there when Alfonzo hurt his knee, and became a part of the pension plan for his trouble. He seems to have established himself ahead of Alfonzo and could stick in the majors for a while. ⌀ Free-swinging **Pablo Sandoval** has been bounced from catcher to third to first and back behind the plate in his four professional seasons and hit last year for just the second time in that span, albeit with lousy perihperals. He's 21, but it's still not clear what the Giants have here. ⌀ **Clay Timpner** had his best offensive season last year, but it was really just a hot start followed by a slow fade. His good glove in center field was a ticket to the majors prior to the Rowand signing. Yes, the Giants lead the world in fifth outfielders.

Pitchers

PLAYER	TEAM	LVL	AGE	W	L	SV	IP	H	BB	SO	HR	GB%	BABIP	STUFF	WHIP	ERA	PERA	EqERA	EqH9	EqBB9	EqSO9	EqHR9	VORP
J. Martinez	SJO	A+	24	10	10	0	162²	172	36	151	11	50.3%	.348	-9	1.28	4.26	6.42	6.56	11.8	3.4	5.1	1.1	-15.4
O. Matos	NRW	AA	22	5	0	4	56	50	21	43	3	38.7%	.288	-12	1.27	2.89	4.80	4.56	9.3	4.1	4.7	0.8	6.2
P. Oseguera*	SJO	A+	23	10	6	0	157²	145	35	132	10	50.2%	.303	-5	1.14	3.54	5.12	5.55	9.7	3.2	4.4	1.1	0.8
K. Pichardo	SJO	A+	21	2	3	3	46²	37	17	71	2	40.2%	.361	15	1.16	3.08	5.04	6.54	9.3	4.9	8.9	0.8	-4.5
	NRW	AA	21	2	2	2	21	14	16	16	2	41.5%	.250	-9	1.43	3.86	5.56	5.12	7.4	7.9	4.7	1.4	1.0
K. Pucetas	AUG	A	22	15	4	1	145¹	124	21	104	7	54.7%	.270	-7	1.00	1.86	5.02	4.48	9.7	2.8	3.3	1.0	16.3
B. Sadler	FRE	AAA	25	3	2	6	42¹	36	35	59	5	37.0%	.333	15	1.68	5.96	6.18	7.20	8.8	7.9	10.1	1.4	-7.1
B. Snyder*	AUG	A	21	16	5	1	151	128	32	145	12	44.5%	.282	-9	1.06	2.09	5.88	5.13	10.1	3.6	4.9	1.5	7.1
C. Tanner*	AUG	A	19	12	8	0	135¹	147	44	104	5	58.7%	.345	-4	1.41	3.59	7.52	6.97	13.0	5.2	3.8	0.9	-17.5
E. Threets*	FRE	AAA	25	3	1	1	54²	46	35	40	4	57.8%	.276	-7	1.48	3.46	4.69	4.53	7.8	6.3	5.1	0.9	6.1
M. Valdez '08	SFN	MLB	26	1	2	0	23	23	13	17	2	44.2%	.292	-3	1.57	4.97	5.35	5.45	8.7	4.9	6.1	0.9	1.5
T. Walker	FRE	AAA	31	1	2	7	23	25	10	23	5	43.7%	.308	-17	1.52	4.70	7.18	5.16	9.9	4.0	6.8	2.4	1.1
	SFN	MLB	31	2	0	0	14¹	12	4	9	0	35.0%	.308	7	1.12	1.26	3.11	1.42	8.5	2.1	5.7	0.0	7.4
T. Wilding	SJO	A+	22	4	2	12	60¹	38	19	71	4	48.6%	.245	-1	0.95	2.54	4.21	4.31	6.9	4.2	6.6	1.1	8.1
	NRW	AA	22	1	1	0	17²	23	8	15	1	43.9%	.415	-22	1.75	4.58	10.18	8.22	14.7	5.3	5.9	1.2	-4.5

Lefty **Joseph Martinez** is a Boston College product with a marginal prospect profile who just keeps taking the ball and throwing strikes. As with many pitchers like this, Double-A will be the crucible. ⌀ Hard-throwing **Osiris Matos** has a fastball, slider, and forkball, all of which scouts like, but the fall-off in his strikeout rate last year at Double-A Connecticut is a bad sign. ⌀ Hampered by injuries at UCLA, **Paul Oseguera** was one of the best pitchers in the Cal League in his first full pro season. Long-term, he looks more like a reliever than a starter. ⌀ Small righty **Kelvin Pichardo** moved to the bullpen last year and had success with a fastball/slider combination. His command deserts him at times, but he could be a high-leverage reliever two years down the road. ⌀ Southpaw **Kevin Pucetas** led the minor leagues in ERA for an Augusta team that had a very strong rotation. He's a command pitcher, however, so it's hard to get excited about him. ⌀ The Giants have moved reliever **Billy Sadler** along slowly, but he seemed ready at the end of 2006. Command problems haunted him at Triple-A last year, and with so many arms at the upper levels, he'll have trouble breaking through. ⌀ **Ben Snyder** joined Sosa and Pucetas by posting excellent numbers on that Augusta team. Like Pucetas, Snyder is more performance than projection. ⌀ Left-hander **Clayton Tanner** doesn't have a ton in the way of pure stuff, but he has a fastball that's average or slightly better and an outstanding feel for his craft; he could move quickly as a back-of-the-rotation type. ⌀ Lefty **Erick Threets** is huge, fragile, and throws very hard. If he can stay healthy, he can make the Giants this year. For a team with so many soft-tossers, he'd be a godsend. ⊘ **Merkin Valdez**'s prospect status had already taken a hit before a torn UCL at the end of 2006 pushed him into Tommy John surgery and out of the 2007 season. He's rehabbing this spring. ⊘ **Tyler Walker** returned from Tommy John surgery to make 15 effective appearances for the Giants last year. He'll be in the mix to set up Wilson this spring. ⊘ Reliever **Taylor Wilding**'s strong season at High-A San Jose was something of a surprise, and he did not show well after a brief promotion to Double-A Connecticut.

MANAGER: BRUCE BOCHY

YEAR	TEAM	W-L	Pythag +/−	Avg PC	100+ P	120+ P	QS	BQS	REL	REL w Zero R	IBB	Subs	PH	PH Avg	PH HR	SB2	CS2	SB3	CS3	SAC Att	SAC %	POS SAC	Squeeze	Swing	In Play
2005	SDN	82-80	6	94.4	59	2	75	7	456	295	45	72	274	.209	4	94	36	4	6	97	74.2%	36	0	141	118
2006	SDN	88-74	1	95.8	66	5	83	9	475	320	63	82	258	.260	8	111	26	12	4	79	74.7%	19	1	157	114
2007	SFN	71-91	-6	98.8	78	8	78	7	495	310	41	83	261	.268	5	106	29	13	2	94	71.3%	31	4	145	115

Bochy took over a team for which wins and losses were secondary in 2007, making it difficult to evaluate his performance. It didn't help that he was managing a team that was woefully underqualified to play National League baseball games, stocked as it was with slow, aging defenders and young pitchers fighting their command. Still, Bochy showed some of the same in-game deficiencies that frustrated Padres fans, particularly on offense, as he was very slow to exercise tactical leverage via pinch-hitters or pinch-runners, often failing to gain the platoon advantage or replace poor batters in high-leverage situations with his team trailing. Bochy's primary responsibility, though, was to manage the clubhouse amid the circus that followed Barry Bonds around all season. It would have been more difficult had the team been better, so perhaps he caught a break. With his best player gone and most of the roster a year closer to dead, 2008 promises to be much less fun for Bochy, who won't have the clowns and elephants distracting the crowds. Then again, the crowds may follow the entertainment out of town.

Seattle Mariners

Last year we said that the Mariners had constructed themselves in such a way that anything short of a run at contention could signal the start of a disastrous period for the franchise, but with their budget expanded above the $100 million mark, contend is exactly what the Mariners did. Ironically, that could prove to be disastrous in its own way, as it merely perpetuated the win-now attitude of a team that's quite simply not good enough to win now after having ultimately failed to win last year.

By the time manager Mike Hargrove resigned from his post on July 1 of last year, Seattle was only one game behind Detroit for the wild card and four games behind the Angels in the AL West. During their first eight weeks under Hargrove's successor, bench coach John McLaren, the Mariners went 28-20 to build a three-game wild-card lead over the Yankees and pull within a single, slender game of the Angels in their division. At the end of that run, the M's were 20 games over .500 and had a 59 percent chance of making it to the postseason according to Clay Davenport's Playoff Odds Report.

Then it all fell apart. The breakdown, which ran from the end of August to mid-September, saw the Mariners lose 15 of 17, with series sweeps at the hands of the Angels and Blue Jays, and was capped by series losses to their closest competitors for the wild card, the Yankees and Tigers. During this season-wrecking stretch, virtually every piece of the Mariners' team took its turn misfiring, and they were outscored by a total of 69 to 119. By the time the dust settled, the Yankees and Tigers had both pulled ahead in the wild-card race, and the Angels had extended their lead in the West to 9 1/2 games. For all intents and purposes, Seattle's season was over.

> ## MARINERS PROSPECTUS
>
> **2007 record:** 88-74; Second place, AL West
>
> **Pythagenport record:** 79-83
>
> **Runs scored per game:** 4.90 (7th in AL)
>
> **Runs allowed per game:** 5.02 (10th in AL)
>
> **Team EqA:** .264 (5th in AL)
>
> **2007 Batters Age:** 30.5 (6th oldest in AL)
>
> **2007 Pitchers Age:** 28.6 (6th oldest in AL)
>
> **Ballpark:** Safeco Park; Pitcher's Park; Park Factor of .959
>
> **2007:** The M's attempt to be the AL's answer to the Diamondbacks ends with another Bavasi-led collapse.
>
> **2008:** Unlike the D'backs, the M's are old and more likely to repeat their 2007 Pythagenport record than their actual one.

Despite that collapse, the Mariners' 2007 season was a success. The team exceeded expectations by recording its first winning season since 2003, halted the erosion of ticket sales over that span (Table 1), and subsequently implemented the franchise's first major ticket-price increases since 2002. The team also extended its cable contract for a reported $450 million over ten years. The annual average of that deal puts the Mariners' among the elite in the sport in terms of cable income; according to *Forbes*, the Dodgers' identical 2006 total of $45 million in local media revenues—which included radio and local broadcast rights—was the fourth-highest in baseball at the time.

The M's September swoon reflected least favorably on their general manager, Bill Bavasi. Bavasi's career has been marked by his inability to take his teams to the playoffs, and late-season collapses in particular, ever since the California Angels suffered the worst collapse in major league history in his second year as that team's GM. On August 20, 1995, the Angels held a 9 1/2-game lead in both the AL West and wild-card races, boasting a 99.988 percent chance of making the playoffs according to our Postseason Odds Report. Ironically, their collapse was made complete when they lost a one-game playoff to the Mariners, giving Seattle its first taste of the baseball postseason and setting in motion a sea change in the history of the franchise. In 1997, Bavasi's Angels again tangled with the Mariners for the AL West lead in August, but a 10-15 September sank their hopes. The next year, Bavasi's squad held a slim lead over Texas in the West as late as September 15, but won just four of their final 13 games, including a three-game sweep at the hands of the Rangers, and again finished out of the pic-

Table 1. Mariner Ticket Sales, 2001–2007

Year	Record	Tickets Sold	AL Rank
2001	114-46	3,507,326	1st
2002	93-69	3,542,938	1st
2003	93-69	3,268,509	2nd
2004	63-99	2,940,731	3rd
2005	69-93	2,725,459	4th
2006	78-84	2,481,165	6th
2007	88-74	2,672,223	6th

ture. In 1996 and 1999, the latter Bavasi's final season with the club, the Angels finished dead last.

Bavasi had come up through the Angels front office along the player development track prior to taking the top job in January 1994. His tenure as GM was marked by strong drafts and a good farm system, but also by limited budgets. During most of his time running the team, the Angels were in the lower half of the league in payroll, often in the lower third. Perhaps more problematically, the few times that the purse strings were loosened for Bavasi to sign top free agents, the results weren't pretty (Exhibit 1: Mo Vaughn). Bavasi's farm products were thus counted on not only to keep the team winning, but to keep the payroll down. Three years after Bavasi departed, the Angels won the World Series with a core of talent he had developed.

Bavasi has been unable to cry poor in Seattle, as the Mariners have had one of the top five payrolls in the American League in each of his four years with the team. He's made more big-money free agent splashes, but the deals he has handed out have run the gamut from surprisingly good—the once-ridiculed deal for third baseman Adrian Beltre and last year's inexpensive flier on outfielder Jose Guillen—to the truly lousy—$50 million for first baseman Richie Sexson and $8 million-plus for one dreadful year of starter Jeff Weaver. As a result, the Mariners' results have lagged behind their payroll.

The team's resulting lack of direction appeared to influence the decision of coveted Japanese pitcher Hiroki Kuroda to sign with the Dodgers rather than the M's. Bavasi's reaction to the Kuroda snub was to sign former Twins right-hander Carlos Silva, one of the most extreme contact-and-control pitchers in the major leagues, to a four-year, $48 million deal. The addition of Silva was intended to shore up one of the team's greatest weaknesses, its lack of depth in the rotation. As Table 2 shows, the 68 starts the Mariners received last year from starters other than Felix Hernandez, Miguel Batista, or Jarrod Washburn produced only one win more than would be expected from a crew of replacement-level pitchers; most of that damage being done by Weaver and Horacio Ramirez, who combined for 47

starts with an ERA of 6.58. By Starters' Fair Runs Allowed (FRA), a measure that separates the contributions of starting pitchers from those of the relievers who follow them, the Mariners' rotation ranked among the worst four in the majors, hardly what you'd expect from a team with a $100 million payroll.

Table 2. The Worst Five 2007 Starting Rotations, by SNLVAR

Team	Top 3 SNLVAR	Top 3 GS	Others' SNLVAR	Starters' FRA	Rank
Marlins	4.9	81	-0.4	6.50	30
Rays	12.8	96	0.7	5.55	26
Mariners	**12.0**	**94**	**1.0**	**5.58**	**27**
Pirates	12.6	93	1.8	5.40	24
Cardinals	11.6	79	2.0	5.59	28

While Silva will be better than Weaver by default, he's unlikely to be the solution to the Mariners' rotation problems. Over his career, Silva has been rather effective (4.31 career ERA) for a pitcher who doesn't strike anyone out (3.8 K/9), but he enjoyed a sizeable home-field advantage in Minnesota (4.26 RA in the Metrodome against 5.26 RA on the road). While Safeco is a pitcher-friendly park, no one knows if Silva will glean the same advantage from his new home. The high upside of this acquisition is another league-average innings-eater in the rotation, which is enough to cause some serious sticker shock—is this all that $48 million buys these days?

The Silva signing continues a pattern going back to the acquisitions of Washburn, Batista, and Ramirez of selecting low-strikeout "contact" pitchers who stay around the plate and count on their team's defense to get their outs for them. Looking at the Mariners' offense, we see a similar pattern. The 2007 Mariners were last in the majors in walks by a large margin, and were also the third-hardest team in the majors to strike out. That latter ranking would likely be higher if not for the strikeout-increasing effects of Safeco—the Mariners struck out in only 13 percent of their plate appearances on the road, which would have been the lowest rate in the majors if it had been duplicated at home. This high-contact approach might have some benefits, as the Mariners finished third in baseball in batting average last year and led the American League in reaching base on errors, but the downsides are a league-high in double plays batted into and the fourth-worst isolated power in the league. What's most puzzling about this method of team building is that, if the Mariners have identified contact hitters as a good fit for their high-strikeout ballpark, wouldn't it follow that contact pitchers would be a bad fit?

This same lack of thought can be seen in the team's defensive makeup. If you're going to have a pitching staff that relies on the defense, it would follow that you'd assemble an excellent defense. Instead, the Mariners ranked second to last in the American League and 27th in the majors in park-adjusted defensive efficiency last year. Watching corner outfielders Raul Ibañez and Jose Guillen go after fly balls last year was like watching kids play Pin the Tail on the Donkey at a birthday party. Adam Jones should be a vast improvement over Guillen in right field this year, but in all other regards the 2007 defense has been returned intact. The Mariners will soon be forced to confront the reality that their touted infield defense is springing leaks.

As befits a team of such mediocrity, the Mariners will face the challenge this year of balancing the development of their prospects against the organization's desire to contend. Thanks to an aggressive promotion policy, Seattle has three well-regarded prospects who have already proven themselves at Triple-A. The team cleared right field for Jones by buying out Guillen's option, but fellow outfielder Wladimir Balentien and catcher Jeff Clement will have to fight established veterans for their opportunities; the team thus far appears unwilling to make the sort of commitment to either that might require it to endure their rookie struggles in full-time roles. The ironic truth about this win-now attitude is that if the Mariners don't exhibit more patience, they not only won't win now, they won't win in the future either. This is especially true in the case of the prospects named above, as the players blocking them—Ibañez and/or Sexson and thirty-something catcher Kenji Johjima—will almost certainly not be part of the next great Mariners team.

Conversely, there is the example of Brandon Morrow, who was rushed to the majors last year to fill a middle relief role. Morrow is a pitcher who needs to improve in a number of areas; he has a fine fastball, but his other offerings are inconsistent, and the list of successful major leaguers who walk more than six batters per nine innings is nonexistent. He's unlikely to develop pitching 60 innings per year out of the bullpen, however, and would likely benefit from not having to make his mistakes at the major league level. Yet once again, allowing the prospect the best chance to fulfill his potential might mean sacrificing immediate results at the major league level, and the Mariners appear unwilling to do that.

Development or damn the torpedoes? It's a tough call. Playing in a four-team division in the wild-card era, contention never looks too far away, and with the A's rebuilding and the Rangers still in their 21st century funk, the Mariners have a window through which they could slip into the playoffs if the Angels slip up. At the same time, they don't have the talent to run with the big dogs in the league, and it would take a pretty major slip up for the Angels to let the M's get by them. The first winning season after a long stretch of losing is often a pleasant surprise, but just because the M's lucked into contention last year doesn't mean they should expect to contend again in 2008. It won't be long before reality sets in.

HITTERS

| Wladimir Balentien | | | RF | | | | | | | | | | Bats: R | | Throws: R | | Height: 6' 2" | | Weight: 190 | | Born: July 2, 1984 | | | Age: 23 |

YEAR	TEAM	LVL	AGE	PA	R	2B	3B	HR	RBI	BB	SO	SB	CS	EqBRR	AVG	OBP	SLG	MLVr	EqAVG	EqOBP	EqSLG	EqA	VORP	DEFENSE	
2005	SBR	A+	21	539	76	38	8	25	93	33	160	9	2	-0.9	.291	.338	.553	.174	.215	.256	.390	.222	-17.0	74-CF -10	
2006	SAN	AA	22	522	76	23	1	22	82	70	140	14	7	-0.7	.230	.337	.435	.051	.208	.302	.384	.241	-18.9	94-RF -2	20-CF 2
2007	TAC	AAA	23	544	77	24	4	24	84	54	105	15	4	2.8	.291	.362	.509	.226	.264	.334	.472	.276	13.2	106-RF -7	
2008	SEA	MLB	23	534	58	26	2	17	65	46	147	10	4	0.5	.233	.302	.405	-.114	.236	.305	.430	.257	-2.9	126-RF 1	

Breakout: 25% Improve: 49% Collapse: 21% Attrition: 14%   Comparables: Yamil Benitez, Edgard Clemente, Justin Huber, Jose Malave

Balentien is unlikely to ever displace Curacao's favorite baseball-playing son—by the time Andruw Jones was his age, he had already hit 80 major league homers and played in two World Series—but he's certainly made a case that he's ready to play in the big leagues. Last year, he gave back some of the gains in plate discipline that he made in 2006, but his overall game continued to improve, this time with a substantial reduction in his strikeout rate. It remains to be seen if the team will clear some of its first-base/outfield logjam to make room for him.

Adrian Beltre   3B

Bats: R   Throws: R   Height: 5' 11"   Weight: 220   Born: April 7, 1979   Age: 29

YEAR	TEAM	LVL	AGE	PA	R	2B	3B	HR	RBI	BB	SO	SB	CS	EqBRR	AVG	OBP	SLG	MLVr	EqAVG	EqOBP	EqSLG	EqA	VORP	DEFENSE	
2005	SEA	MLB	26	650	69	36	1	19	87	38	108	3	1	-1.5	.255	.303	.413	-.059	.264	.322	.436	.261	5.9	150-3B	-2
2006	SEA	MLB	27	681	88	39	4	25	89	47	118	11	5	-1.5	.268	.328	.465	.032	.274	.340	.484	.278	19.9	152-3B	9
2007	SEA	MLB	28	639	87	41	2	26	99	38	104	14	2	-1.0	.276	.319	.482	.078	.286	.335	.522	.288	28.6	145-3B	-1
2008	SEA	MLB	29	625	76	34	2	21	89	42	106	10	3	-0.1	.268	.322	.445	-.002	.271	.325	.473	.275	18.6	146-3B	0

Breakout: 14% Improve: 44% Collapse: 20% Attrition: 5%   Comparables: Gary Gaetti, Sean Berry, Doug Rader, Charlie Hayes

Adrian Beltre's 2007 season was pretty much a repeat of his 2006. The consistency is welcome, as is the fact that he won his first Gold Glove—his reputation at the hot corner has been golden for his entire career, even if some defensive metrics aren't big fans. After a few years of teeth-gnashing and clothes-rending by the writerly classes, the market seems to have caught up to Beltre's contract—$12 million per year for the tail end of his peak doesn't seem so unreasonable when 34-year-old Mike Lowell will be making the same for the next three years.

Yuniesky Betancourt   SS

Bats: R   Throws: R   Height: 5' 10"   Weight: 190   Born: January 31, 1982   Age: 26

YEAR	TEAM	LVL	AGE	PA	R	2B	3B	HR	RBI	BB	SO	SB	CS	EqBRR	AVG	OBP	SLG	MLVr	EqAVG	EqOBP	EqSLG	EqA	VORP	DEFENSE	
2005	SAN	AA	23	239	25	10	3	5	20	9	18	12	7	-0.1	.273	.301	.410	.001	.256	.287	.383	.231	0.8	51-SS	-2
2005	TAC	AAA	23	194	13	9	6	2	30	6	14	7	5	-1.5	.295	.323	.443	.046	.258	.280	.387	.224	0.3	48-SS	17
2005	SEA	MLB	23	228	24	11	5	1	15	11	24	1	3	0.2	.256	.296	.370	-.134	.269	.319	.389	.242	0.1	52-SS	-4
2006	SEA	MLB	24	584	68	28	6	8	47	17	54	11	8	0.8	.289	.310	.403	-.071	.297	.326	.424	.255	13.6	154-SS	-9
2007	SEA	MLB	25	559	72	38	2	9	67	15	48	5	4	0.5	.289	.308	.418	-.025	.302	.324	.452	.263	16.2	147-SS	-4
2008	SEA	MLB	26	518	55	27	3	7	52	20	48	9	4	1.0	.271	.302	.387	-.112	.274	.305	.411	.250	9.6	122-SS	3

Breakout: 20% Improve: 43% Collapse: 28% Attrition: 12%   Comparables: Rafael Ramirez, Tim Foli, Rennie Stennett, Bill Russell

Betancourt is poetry in motion. He may not be the fastest shortstop, but he has a gun for an arm and the type of balance and body control that convince you he must be a hell of a dancer—his feet always seem to be directly underneath his center of gravity. However, defensive metrics don't dig his kind of poetry, looking at his performance and reacting with a collective "meh." In an analog world, we'd be tapping the control panel to make sure none of the dials are stuck. As a hitter, he's platoon material. He sees southpaws well but wilts against righties (career .284/.323/.452 against LHPs, .283/.302/.390 against RHPs), and has almost completely eliminated walks from his offensive repertoire. When you take only 12 unintentional passes in a full season, you'd better be doing a heck of a lot of hitting, running, and fielding to make up for it. Betancourt isn't quite at that point.

Ben Broussard   1B

Bats: L   Throws: L   Height: 6' 2"   Weight: 220   Born: September 24, 1976   Age: 31

YEAR	TEAM	LVL	AGE	PA	R	2B	3B	HR	RBI	BB	SO	SB	CS	EqBRR	AVG	OBP	SLG	MLVr	EqAVG	EqOBP	EqSLG	EqA	VORP	DEFENSE	
2005	CLE	MLB	28	505	59	30	5	19	68	32	98	2	2	-3.7	.255	.307	.464	.020	.261	.321	.490	.272	9.2	117-1B	-6
2006	CLE	MLB	29	288	44	14	0	13	46	17	58	0	1	-0.6	.321	.361	.519	.219	.321	.368	.528	.300	18.3	65-1B	-1
2006	SEA	MLB	29	177	17	7	0	8	17	9	45	2	0	0.7	.238	.282	.427	-.132	.241	.294	.438	.252	-1.3		
2007	SEA	MLB	30	264	27	10	0	7	29	17	50	2	0	-1.1	.275	.330	.404	-.017	.286	.345	.429	.271	4.5	38-1B	-3
2008	TEX	MLB	31	253	30	12	1	9	34	18	51	2	1	-0.2	.270	.327	.446	.009	.267	.327	.457	.272	5.5	62-1B	-2

Breakout: 20% Improve: 47% Collapse: 31% Attrition: 31%   Comparables: Gordy Coleman, Dave Parker, Mike Lamb, Leon Durham

Broussard's hopes for regular playing time in 2007 were largely extinguished by the offseason acquisition of Jose Vidro, only to be revived when Richie Sexson's plate approach turned into "blindfolded kid swinging at piñata." Unfortunately, Broussard wasn't able to seize the opportunity; his power went AWOL, and his defensive value remained nil. Dealt to Texas in December, he's likely to end up in a first-base platoon with Tigers cast-off Chris Shelton.

Jamie Burke   C

Bats: R   Throws: R   Height: 6' 0"   Weight: 225   Born: September 24, 1971   Age: 36

YEAR	TEAM	LVL	AGE	PA	R	2B	3B	HR	RBI	BB	SO	SB	CS	EqBRR	AVG	OBP	SLG	MLVr	EqAVG	EqOBP	EqSLG	EqA	VORP	DEFENSE			
2005	CHR	AAA	33	414	50	22	1	10	53	36	53	1	3	-0.7	.265	.350	.416	.011	.238	.317	.378	.242	3.0	45-3B	-6	45-C	2
2006	OKL	AAA	34	399	46	21	1	10	49	22	41	0	0	0.0	.278	.323	.422	.036	.251	.292	.396	.235	0.8	53-C	-2	21-3B	1
2007	SEA	MLB	35	129	19	8	0	1	12	7	17	0	1	-0.2	.301	.363	.398	.052	.319	.384	.434	.282	6.3	36-C	-4		
2008	SEA	MLB	36	154	13	7	0	2	16	9	22	1	0	-0.2	.237	.290	.338	-.220	.239	.293	.359	.230	-1.4	40-C	-1		

Breakout: 14% Improve: 35% Collapse: 46% Attrition: 59%   Comparables: John Marzano, John Flaherty, Rick Cerone, Ray Murray

With more than 4,500 career minor league plate appearances to his credit, Burke is a testament to persistence. He gives you a little more on-base ability than the average backup catcher and the added utility of being an emergency corner infielder. Having a journeyman like Burke around in 2006 might have kept the M's from rushing their catching prospects up the ladder. Ironically, his fate this year will depend on whether the team views one of those prospects, Jeff Clement, as a catcher who can DH or as a DH who can catch.

Yung Chi Chen   2B

Bats: R   Throws: R   Height: 5' 11"   Weight: 170   Born: July 13, 1983   Age: 24

YEAR	TEAM	LVL	AGE	PA	R	2B	3B	HR	RBI	BB	SO	SB	CS	EqBRR	AVG	OBP	SLG	MLVr	EqAVG	EqOBP	EqSLG	EqA	VORP	DEFENSE			
2005	WIS	A	21	549	77	27	7	7	80	37	76	15	6	-1.0	.292	.339	.416	.079	.245	.282	.351	.220	-10.7	77-3B	5	35-2B	1
2006	SBR	A+	22	309	49	17	3	5	48	22	40	21	7	-0.3	.342	.388	.478	.274	.281	.321	.400	.255	7.6	61-2B	-3		
2006	SAN	AA	22	174	22	9	2	3	22	18	23	5	3	1.0	.295	.365	.443	.169	.261	.326	.405	.254	4.4	34-2B	1		
2007	TAC	AAA	23	18	2	2	0	0	3	0	3	1	1	-0.7	.333	.294	.467	.044	.250	.222	.438	.219	-0.5				
2008	SEA	MLB	24	94	9	5	0	1	9	6	18	2	1	0.2	.241	.290	.352	-.199	.244	.293	.374	.238	-0.6	27-2B	1		

Breakout: 21% Improve: 44% Collapse: 35% Attrition: 21%   Comparables: Felix Escalona, Issmael Salas, Ed Renteria, Ryan Lane

Chen lost last season to a dislocated shoulder; fortunately for him, 2007 wasn't kind to any of the Mariners' high-level infield prospects, so his place in line hasn't been usurped. A rakish stint in the Arizona Fall League reaffirmed what we already knew—he's a utility type who'll go as far as that batting average and a hint of gap power can take him.

Jeff Clement   C

Bats: L   Throws: R   Height: 6' 1"   Weight: 210   Born: August 21, 1983   Age: 24

YEAR	TEAM	LVL	AGE	PA	R	2B	3B	HR	RBI	BB	SO	SB	CS	EqBRR	AVG	OBP	SLG	MLVr	EqAVG	EqOBP	EqSLG	EqA	VORP	DEFENSE	
2005	WIS	A	21	127	17	5	0	6	20	12	25	1	2	-2.6	.319	.386	.522	.318	.256	.307	.410	.243	2.0	20-C	-2
2006	SAN	AA	22	70	7	6	1	2	10	7	8	0	0	-0.2	.288	.386	.525	.313	.262	.343	.475	.280	4.2	12-C	0
2006	TAC	AAA	22	272	23	10	0	4	32	16	53	0	2	-3.0	.257	.321	.347	-.077	.237	.294	.321	.215	-7.5	36-C	0
2007	TAC	AAA	23	530	76	35	3	20	80	61	88	0	2	1.2	.275	.370	.497	.203	.248	.340	.454	.273	23.8	74-C	-5
2007	SEA	MLB	23	19	4	1	0	2	3	3	3	0	0	0.0	.375	.474	.813	.910	.375	.474	.812	.397	4.5		
2008	SEA	MLB	24	572	61	30	1	16	72	51	116	2	2	-0.6	.249	.323	.410	-.060	.252	.327	.436	.266	12.1	134-C	-1

Breakout: 27% Improve: 58% Collapse: 17% Attrition: 15%   Comparables: Eric Munson, Todd Helton, Trot Nixon, Adrian Gonzalez

Clement absolutely slaughtered left-handed pitching in Tacoma last year (10 HR, .358 ISO), but scouts believe that he was beating up on soft-tossing Triple-A lefties, making that performance something he's unlikely to be able to repeat in the Show. This is reflected in his PECOTA projection—one improvement that has been made to PECOTA this year is a new sensitivity to platoon data, in this case making it aware of Clement's more pedestrian results against righties (.261/.348/.433) and thus producing a projection that might otherwise seem underwhelming given his composite 2007 statistics. That projection is still above average for a catcher, but while Clement's bat may be ready for the majors, his defense behind the plate remains a work in progress. It will be interesting to see if the Mariners go the on-the-job training route by making him Johjima's caddy in the varsity, shift him defensively to get his bat into the lineup, or send him back down to the PCL for further defensive seasoning.

Jose Guillen   RF

Bats: R   Throws: R   Height: 6' 0"   Weight: 195   Born: May 17, 1976   Age: 32

YEAR	TEAM	LVL	AGE	PA	R	2B	3B	HR	RBI	BB	SO	SB	CS	EqBRR	AVG	OBP	SLG	MLVr	EqAVG	EqOBP	EqSLG	EqA	VORP	DEFENSE	
2005	WAS	MLB	29	611	81	32	2	24	76	31	102	1	1	-1.8	.283	.338	.479	.137	.289	.340	.497	.284	26.8	132-RF	7
2006	WAS	MLB	30	268	28	15	1	9	40	15	48	1	0	0.9	.216	.276	.398	-.168	.220	.276	.411	.238	-6.6	61-RF	10
2007	SEA	MLB	31	658	84	28	2	23	99	41	118	5	1	-0.8	.290	.353	.460	.116	.303	.368	.502	.296	28.0	144-RF	-15
2008	KCA	MLB	32	497	60	25	2	16	68	30	83	4	2	-0.4	.279	.334	.445	.027	.274	.331	.457	.273	7.8	117-RF	-4

Breakout: 11% Improve: 35% Collapse: 34% Attrition: 18%   Comparables: Dan Ford, Rondell White, Del Ennis, Gary Ward

Guillen's 2007 season made for a nice comeback story until it was reported that he had bought performance-enhancing drugs from the Florida-based Signature Pharmacy. Prior to the revelation, Guillen was hailed in Seattle as a clutchy, vocal clubhouse leader, who'd apparently gotten over the rage issues that plagued him with the Angels and Nationals. He even earned some Don Baylor-type respect by setting the franchise's single-season record for times hit by a pitch. After it came to light that he'd ordered a steady diet of anabolic steroids and growth hormones from 2002 to 2005, the Mariners politely declined his 2008 option. The Royals snapped him up with a three-year, $36 million contract, despite the 15-game suspension the league has levied against him for a "non-analytic positive." Guillen's grievance against that suspension will likely set the ground rules for the punishment of players accused of PED use in the Mitchell Report and elsewhere, but who haven't failed a drug test.

Raul Ibañez   LF

Bats: L   Throws: R   Height: 6' 2"   Weight: 220   Born: June 2, 1972   Age: 36

YEAR	TEAM	LVL	AGE	PA	R	2B	3B	HR	RBI	BB	SO	SB	CS	EqBRR	AVG	OBP	SLG	MLVr	EqAVG	EqOBP	EqSLG	EqA	VORP	DEFENSE	
2005	SEA	MLB	33	690	92	32	2	20	89	71	99	9	4	-0.5	.280	.355	.436	.085	.291	.375	.464	.289	29.1	53-LF	2
2006	SEA	MLB	34	699	103	33	5	33	123	65	115	2	4	-1.6	.289	.353	.516	.171	.293	.365	.537	.299	37.8	156-LF	0
2007	SEA	MLB	35	636	80	35	5	21	105	53	97	0	0	-0.7	.291	.351	.480	.141	.303	.366	.521	.299	31.3	126-LF	-17
2008	SEA	MLB	36	550	69	28	2	17	79	50	86	3	2	-0.6	.277	.345	.451	.050	.280	.348	.480	.285	16.8	129-LF	-9

Breakout: 10% Improve: 27% Collapse: 30% Attrition: 19%   Comparables: Paul O'Neill, Larry Walker, B. J. Surhoff, Dave Parker

A red-hot streak to end the year (combined .357/.423/.634 in August and September with 15 homers) salvaged what had been an ugly season for Ibañez. There's no telling if he had a similar revitalization in the field, but overall, it looked as though his feet had been staked to the Safeco turf. On Ibañez's wishlist for 2008: a platoon partner (he hit just .256/.294/.356 against lefties last year while wrecking righties by going .305/.371/.528), and more time at a less demanding position such as first base or DH.

Charlton Jimerson   OF

Bats: R   Throws: R   Height: 6' 3"   Weight: 210   Born: September 22, 1979   Age: 28

YEAR	TEAM	LVL	AGE	PA	R	2B	3B	HR	RBI	BB	SO	SB	CS	EqBRR	AVG	OBP	SLG	MLVr	EqAVG	EqOBP	EqSLG	EqA	VORP	DEFENSE			
2005	CCH	AA	25	467	67	24	3	16	44	29	145	27	10	-1.9	.259	.317	.442	.029	.202	.260	.360	.217	-31.6	98-RF	-9	13-CF	4
2006	ROU	AAA	26	501	56	27	6	18	45	23	183	28	8	3.9	.247	.287	.445	-.020	.192	.230	.368	.209	-40.2	77-RF	10	40-CF	1
2007	WTN	AA	27	361	54	18	3	23	73	29	117	30	9	-0.9	.276	.346	.565	.265	.239	.300	.497	.268	12.6	73-CF	4		
2007	TAC	AAA	27	71	7	4	1	2	7	5	22	5	1	-0.5	.308	.357	.492	.211	.212	.268	.379	.237	-2.1	15-CF	1		
2008	SEA	MLB	28	349	37	17	2	11	40	21	123	17	5	0.8	.222	.275	.388	-.191	.224	.277	.413	.243	-3.9	84-CF	-1		

Breakout: 36% Improve: 57% Collapse: 22% Attrition: 32%   Comparables: Darren Blakely, Scott Wade, Jacques Landry, Chris Hatcher

Analytically, there's not much to like about Jimerson, a player who posted a merely good season as a 27-year-old in Double-A while striking out in about a third of his plate appearances, more than four times as often as he walked. That said, Jimerson's reportedly a great guy who's overcome a lot of adversity in his life, so we'd still like to see him grab a fifth-outfielder slot and keep it long enough to qualify for a major league pension. Some players are just worth rooting for.

Kenji Johjima — C

Bats: R Throws: R Height: 6' 0" Weight: 200 Born: June 8, 1976 Age: 32

YEAR	TEAM	LVL	AGE	PA	R	2B	3B	HR	RBI	BB	SO	SB	CS	EqBRR	AVG	OBP	SLG	MLVr	EqAVG	EqOBP	EqSLG	EqA	VORP	DEFENSE	
2005	FKU	JP	29	444	70	22	4	24	57	33	32	3	4	—	.309	.360	.557	.330	.288	.349	.453	.275	22.9		
2006	SEA	MLB	30	542	61	25	1	18	76	20	46	3	1	-2.8	.291	.332	.451	.039	.297	.343	.470	.278	24.0	131-C	1
2007	SEA	MLB	31	513	52	29	0	14	61	15	41	0	2	-3.9	.287	.322	.433	.020	.300	.337	.472	.274	22.2	125-C	15
2008	SEA	MLB	32	420	43	20	1	8	51	21	38	2	2	-1.1	.274	.319	.395	-.070	.277	.322	.420	.259	10.1	100-C	5

Breakout: 34% Improve: 70% Collapse: 17% Attrition: 21%   Comparables: Manny Sanguillen, Del Crandall, Brian Harper, Paul Lo Duca

Scouts don't consider Johjima to be one of the better-throwing catchers in the majors, but last year he led the American League in runners caught stealing with 40 and was second behind Joe Mauer in percentage of thieves caught (46.5). Some credit manager John McLaren, then the team's bench coach, for working on Johjima's throwing mechanics in spring training, but Johjima's improved record behind the plate, with decreased numbers of errors and passed balls, seems to indicate that better communication with his pitchers played a part as well (or a better relationship with official scorers). Along with Ichiro Suzuki and Jose Vidro, Johjima is part of an ongoing experiment with low strikeout hitters in whiff-enhancing Safeco Field. Those three, along with Jose Lopez and Betancourt, are among the fifteen most difficult American Leaguers to strike out.

Rob Johnson — C

Bats: R Throws: R Height: 6' 1" Weight: 200 Born: July 22, 1983 Age: 24

YEAR	TEAM	LVL	AGE	PA	R	2B	3B	HR	RBI	BB	SO	SB	CS	EqBRR	AVG	OBP	SLG	MLVr	EqAVG	EqOBP	EqSLG	EqA	VORP	DEFENSE	
2005	WIS	A	21	335	41	19	1	9	51	20	31	10	3	-0.7	.272	.319	.430	.051	.236	.271	.367	.221	-7.5	75-C	1
2005	SBR	A+	21	86	15	3	0	2	12	10	14	2	0	0.4	.314	.381	.443	.110	.247	.310	.315	.236	-1.6	19-C	2
2006	TAC	AAA	22	359	28	9	4	4	33	13	74	14	7	-0.1	.231	.261	.318	-.252	.208	.236	.290	.182	-27.1	71-C	3
2007	TAC	AAA	23	465	57	26	0	6	40	39	62	7	7	-0.6	.268	.331	.372	-.059	.245	.307	.348	.228	-4.4	68-C	-4
2008	SEA	MLB	24	430	39	17	1	5	40	27	81	8	4	0.6	.233	.284	.323	-.252	.236	.287	.344	.224	-8.7	102-C	0

Breakout: 38% Improve: 58% Collapse: 20% Attrition: 14%   Comparables: Mike Durant, Josh Paul, Joe Perona, Koyie Hill

We're beginning to wonder if Johnson is a fugitive from justice in one or more jurisdictions of the Southern League. Why else would the Mariners insist that he not see any time at Double-A, no matter how badly his bat suffered at Triple-A Tacoma? Johnson will likely get his third tour of the Pacific Coast League this season, the upside being that if he ever solves the league well enough to convince people he can hit, his reward will be to come to the majors as either Johjima's or Clement's backup.

Adam Jones — OF

Bats: R Throws: R Height: 6' 2" Weight: 200 Born: August 1, 1985 Age: 22

YEAR	TEAM	LVL	AGE	PA	R	2B	3B	HR	RBI	BB	SO	SB	CS	EqBRR	AVG	OBP	SLG	MLVr	EqAVG	EqOBP	EqSLG	EqA	VORP	DEFENSE			
2005	SBR	A+	19	315	43	20	5	8	46	29	64	4	5	-0.2	.295	.374	.494	.155	.228	.294	.374	.231	-0.5	64-SS	-8		
2005	SAN	AA	19	257	33	10	3	7	20	22	48	9	4	0.3	.298	.365	.461	.204	.260	.324	.416	.256	9.3	59-SS	-4		
2006	TAC	AAA	20	416	69	19	4	16	62	28	78	13	4	2.9	.287	.345	.484	.190	.262	.315	.460	.263	14.0	83-CF	-1	12-RF	1
2006	SEA	MLB	20	76	6	4	0	1	8	2	22	3	1	-0.4	.216	.237	.311	-.405	.219	.250	.301	.194	-4.1	22-CF	5		
2007	TAC	AAA	21	469	75	27	6	25	84	36	106	8	7	1.5	.314	.382	.586	.402	.281	.347	.533	.289	36.3	93-CF	9		
2007	SEA	MLB	21	71	16	2	1	2	4	4	21	2	1	2.1	.246	.300	.400	-.099	.262	.324	.462	.267	-0.2	13-LF	-1		
2008	SEA	MLB	22	622	79	34	4	21	81	48	150	12	5	1.9	.266	.329	.449	.014	.269	.333	.478	.279	21.4	145-CF	0		

Breakout: 37% Improve: 64% Collapse: 20% Attrition: 8%   Comparables: Steve Hosey, Chet Lemon, Larry Hisle, Jack Clark

Jones's bat made the Leap at Triple-A last year, and there's a good argument to be made that he was ready to play in the majors as of mid-May. It's a little less well-known that his conversion to the outfield from shortstop has worked out beyond anyone's expectations, as he was considered one of the best defensive outfielders in the minors. Jones is one of the reasons why, when Jose Guillen made pouty faces about getting a contract extension, the Mariners gave him a smile, a handshake, and bid him farewell. What is less clear is why the M's called Jones up in early August only to let him rust on the bench; he started just 17 of the team's last 56 games.

Jose Lopez — 2B

Bats: R   Throws: R   Height: 6' 0"   Weight: 200   Born: November 24, 1983   Age: 24

YEAR	TEAM	LVL	AGE	PA	R	2B	3B	HR	RBI	BB	SO	SB	CS	EqBRR	AVG	OBP	SLG	MLVr	EqAVG	EqOBP	EqSLG	EqA	VORP	DEFENSE	
2005	TAC	AAA	21	194	29	19	0	5	31	8	25	2	3	-1.5	.319	.354	.505	.229	.286	.316	.449	.255	8.1	44-2B	-5
2005	SEA	MLB	21	203	18	19	0	2	25	6	25	4	2	-1.7	.247	.282	.379	-.150	.262	.303	.406	.246	-1.2	50-2B	1
2006	SEA	MLB	22	655	78	28	8	10	79	26	80	5	2	-2.1	.282	.319	.405	-.058	.290	.332	.426	.262	18.3	148-2B	-11
2007	SEA	MLB	23	561	58	17	2	11	62	20	64	2	3	-3.2	.252	.284	.355	-.189	.265	.301	.384	.235	-9.7	139-2B	5
2008	SEA	MLB	24	544	54	26	2	10	58	24	67	5	3	-0.3	.262	.299	.379	-.133	.265	.302	.403	.246	4.8	128-2B	1

Breakout: 18% Improve: 37% Collapse: 29% Attrition: 16%   Comparables: Bill Mazeroski, Mark Lewis, Davey Johnson, Ken Reitz

After April, it was all downhill last year for Lopez, who turned in one of the worst second halves in the entire American League (.213/.238/.281). While he is insulated somewhat by the fact that the organization's infield prospects as a whole had poor seasons, Lopez could soon find himself facing challenges from Bloomquist, Chen, or Tug Hulett, the last of whom was acquired from the Rangers in the Ben Broussard trade. Thanks to a contract extension signed in April, the M's are on the hook for more sub-.300 OBP hi-jinks through 2010 whether Lopez plays or not.

Jeremy Reed — CF

Bats: L   Throws: L   Height: 6' 0"   Weight: 200   Born: June 15, 1981   Age: 27

YEAR	TEAM	LVL	AGE	PA	R	2B	3B	HR	RBI	BB	SO	SB	CS	EqBRR	AVG	OBP	SLG	MLVr	EqAVG	EqOBP	EqSLG	EqA	VORP	DEFENSE			
2005	SEA	MLB	24	544	61	33	3	3	45	48	74	12	11	-2.2	.254	.322	.352	-.108	.269	.346	.379	.253	-2.0	131-CF	8		
2006	SEA	MLB	25	229	27	6	5	6	17	11	31	2	3	0.6	.217	.260	.377	-.257	.224	.273	.400	.227	-6.5	57-CF	-1		
2007	TAC	AAA	26	628	92	37	5	13	64	47	73	14	9	-3.3	.300	.354	.452	.135	.270	.323	.418	.255	-1.2	91-LF	-7	17-CF	3
2007	SEA	MLB	26	17	2	0	1	0	0	0	3	0	0	-0.2	.176	.176	.294	-.524	.176	.176	.294	.135	-1.6				
2008	SEA	MLB	27	561	65	29	4	8	58	41	79	11	5	1.0	.265	.321	.385	-.085	.268	.325	.409	.260	3.5	132-CF	2		

Breakout: 36% Improve: 62% Collapse: 11% Attrition: 17%   Comparables: Scott Podsednik, Kevin Reese, Mike Rodriguez, Darrell Whitmore

The last time someone needed a change of scenery this badly, Dorothy was clicking her ruby slippers together and saying "there's no place like home." Reed managed to stay healthy and hit well at Tacoma last year, but there was no interest from the big club, save for a token call-up once rosters expanded in September. Now that the expectations have receded, what remains is still a ballplayer of some value—a league-average bat, doubles power, decent speed, and a legitimate center-field glove. There are teams that could use such a player, but none of them are in the Pacific Northwest.

Michael Saunders — OF

Bats: L   Throws: R   Height: 6' 4"   Weight: 205   Born: November 19, 1986   Age: 21

YEAR	TEAM	LVL	AGE	PA	R	2B	3B	HR	RBI	BB	SO	SB	CS	EqBRR	AVG	OBP	SLG	MLVr	EqAVG	EqOBP	EqSLG	EqA	VORP	DEFENSE			
2005	EVE	A-	18	228	24	13	3	7	39	27	74	2	7	-2.8	.270	.361	.474	.166	.180	.254	.293	.186	-40.5	52-RF	-2		
2006	WIS	A	19	416	48	10	8	4	39	48	103	22	7	1.4	.240	.329	.345	-.013	.199	.272	.293	.206	-27.8	68-CF	-3	23-RF	-4
2007	HDS	A+	20	507	91	25	4	14	77	60	116	27	10	0.9	.299	.392	.473	.108	.230	.311	.353	.238	-7.5	52-CF	-4	33-RF	-3
2007	WTN	AA	20	60	8	1	2	1	7	7	20	2	1	-0.2	.288	.373	.442	.151	.189	.271	.340	.216	-2.9	11-CF	1		
2008	SEA	MLB	21	620	64	27	3	10	50	53	182	19	8	1.9	.223	.293	.334	-.229	.225	.296	.355	.234	-16.1	145-CF	-1		

Breakout: 45% Improve: 78% Collapse: 11% Attrition: 6%   Comparables: Rod Myers, Shin-Soo Choo, Todd Dunwoody, Jimmy White

A big outfielder out of British Columbia, Saunders is a power/speed threat who has drawn walks consistently at every level, rare for a high school athlete who didn't focus on baseball until going pro. Since he only turned 21 in November, he should repeat at Double-A West Tennessee, but given the franchise's promotion patterns, it wouldn't be a shock to see him at Triple-A or higher in 2008.

Richie Sexson — 1B

Bats: R   Throws: R   Height: 6' 8"   Weight: 235   Born: December 29, 1974   Age: 33

YEAR	TEAM	LVL	AGE	PA	R	2B	3B	HR	RBI	BB	SO	SB	CS	EqBRR	AVG	OBP	SLG	MLVr	EqAVG	EqOBP	EqSLG	EqA	VORP	DEFENSE	
2005	SEA	MLB	30	656	99	36	1	39	121	89	167	1	1	-2.7	.263	.369	.541	.233	.275	.389	.577	.318	45.8	148-1B	17
2006	SEA	MLB	31	663	75	40	0	34	107	64	154	1	1	-3.2	.264	.338	.504	.103	.269	.350	.524	.292	24.9	147-1B	15
2007	SEA	MLB	32	491	58	21	0	21	63	51	100	1	0	-2.3	.205	.295	.399	-.140	.214	.308	.437	.255	-7.1	112-1B	11
2008	SEA	MLB	33	475	55	21	0	19	69	52	112	2	1	-1.2	.245	.333	.433	-.018	.248	.336	.461	.276	7.0	112-1B	4

Breakout: 11% Improve: 25% Collapse: 32% Attrition: 23%   Comparables: Cecil Fielder, Dale Murphy, Jose Canseco, Deron Johnson

If you ever wonder what those collapse rates PECOTA gives out are about, here's a good example. Last year, Sexson's collapse rate was 34 percent, which meant he had a 34 percent chance of losing 20 percent or more of his offensive value. He did that and more. There was no redeeming feature of Sexson's performance last year—he didn't hit better in the second half, as he has throughout his career; he didn't mash lefties; he wasn't better on the road. He could probably use a fresh start, and the team could use the first-base slot to get Ibañez out of the outfield. Unfortunately, Sexson is anchored in place by the $14 million he's due in this, the final year of his contract.

Ichiro Suzuki   **CF**   Bats: L   Throws: R   Height: 5′ 9″   Weight: 170   Born: October 22, 1973   Age: 34

YEAR	TEAM	LVL	AGE	PA	R	2B	3B	HR	RBI	BB	SO	SB	CS	EqBRR	AVG	OBP	SLG	MLVr	EqAVG	EqOBP	EqSLG	EqA	VORP	DEFENSE		
2005	SEA	MLB	31	739	111	21	12	15	68	48	66	33	8	4.0	.303	.350	.436	.096	.313	.368	.461	.289	34.3	158-RF	22	
2006	SEA	MLB	32	752	110	20	9	9	49	49	71	45	2	7.3	.322	.370	.416	.088	.327	.382	.424	.292	46.4	119-RF	-3	38-CF 5
2007	SEA	MLB	33	736	111	22	7	6	68	49	77	37	8	6.8	.351	.396	.431	.205	.367	.416	.458	.308	63.5	151-CF	15	
2008	SEA	MLB	34	579	80	22	5	4	45	34	58	19	5	2.1	.304	.346	.384	-.017	.307	.350	.408	.271	14.7	136-CF	0	

Breakout: 0%   Improve: 9%   Collapse: 58%   Attrition: 11%   Comparables: Lance Johnson, Matty Alou, Frank Baumholtz, Lou Brock

Suzuki was given a five-year, $90 million extension last in July, which grants him a luxurious amount of time to go after a number of franchise records. If he stays healthy, Julio Cruz's career stolen base mark is virtually guaranteed to go down in 2008, as is Edgar Martinez's record for career singles, and Martinez's marks in hits and runs scored could be within reach before the end of the extension. There's little question that M's fans will enjoy having Ichiro around in 2008 and 2009, the question is how they'll feel when he's getting paid $17 million a year in 2011 and 2012. Speed players age well, and part of Suzuki's appeal is the idea that he's holding back further reserves of talent—who wouldn't love to see him in the home run derby, for example?—but that's a sizeable bet to place on anyone's age-37 and -38 seasons.

Carlos Triunfel   **SS**   Bats: R   Throws: R   Height: 5′ 11″   Weight: 175   Born: February 27, 1990   Age: 18

YEAR	TEAM	LVL	AGE	PA	R	2B	3B	HR	RBI	BB	SO	SB	CS	EqBRR	AVG	OBP	SLG	MLVr	EqAVG	EqOBP	EqSLG	EqA	VORP	DEFENSE	
2007	WIS	A	17	164	18	8	2	0	14	5	23	4	8	0.0	.309	.342	.388	.092	.247	.273	.312	.197	-5.8	40-SS	-1
2007	HDS	A+	17	225	32	10	2	0	22	12	31	3	4	-2.6	.288	.333	.356	-.158	.231	.266	.278	.185	-11.6	49-SS	1
2008	SEA	MLB	18	439	33	16	2	1	28	14	71	8	6	1.1	.232	.259	.286	-.347	.235	.262	.304	.196	-15.9	104-SS	-2

Breakout: 55%   Improve: 74%   Collapse: 19%   Attrition: 6%   Comparables: Luis Rivas, Jose Lopez, Donovan Solano, Maicer Izturis

Wanna feel old? Carlos Triunfel was born in the 1990s. So for anyone wondering where his power is, give him a break, he's a minor! Triunfel was the youngest player in the Midwest League, then got promoted to High-A and was the youngest player at that level. The scouts are convinced that his power will come, but no one is quite sure if, once he fills out to gain that power, he will still be a shortstop. He should probably repeat the Cal League this year, but that wouldn't quite jibe with the organization's Darwinian prospect promotion schedule.

Matt Tuiasosopo   **3B**   Bats: R   Throws: R   Height: 6′ 2″   Weight: 210   Born: May 10, 1986   Age: 22

YEAR	TEAM	LVL	AGE	PA	R	2B	3B	HR	RBI	BB	SO	SB	CS	EqBRR	AVG	OBP	SLG	MLVr	EqAVG	EqOBP	EqSLG	EqA	VORP	DEFENSE		
2005	WIS	A	19	464	72	21	3	6	45	44	96	8	5	-3.4	.276	.359	.386	.057	.226	.289	.316	.212	-12.1	76-SS	-23	
2006	SBR	A+	20	253	31	14	0	1	34	14	58	5	6	-1.2	.306	.359	.379	.040	.227	.267	.286	.189	-12.4	39-SS	-5	15-3B 1
2006	SAN	AA	20	241	16	4	0	1	10	20	64	2	1	0.3	.185	.259	.218	-.425	.167	.229	.190	.130	-29.9	56-3B	-13	
2007	WTN	AA	21	548	74	27	5	9	57	76	113	4	8	-2.5	.260	.371	.404	.077	.236	.334	.371	.251	7.2	127-3B	-2	
2008	SEA	MLB	22	625	59	27	2	8	55	58	159	7	4	0.4	.229	.306	.331	-.206	.232	.309	.352	.237	-10.0	146-3B	-9	

Breakout: 50%   Improve: 73%   Collapse: 11%   Attrition: 8%   Comparables: Michael Cuddyer, Corey Smith, Joe Lawrence, Benji Gil

Baby Tui's performance gained a new wrinkle upon repeating Double-A as he added both walks and power, but lost some batting average. His minor league record has been such a hodgepodge that it's difficult to see how all these ingredients will gel into a major league ballplayer, but he's young and currently blocked at the major league level, so there's still time to see how it all shakes out.

Jose Vidro　DH

Bats: S　　Throws: R　　Height: 5' 11"　　Weight: 195　　Born: August 27, 1974　　Age: 33

YEAR	TEAM	LVL	AGE	PA	R	2B	3B	HR	RBI	BB	SO	SB	CS	EqBRR	AVG	OBP	SLG	MLVr	EqAVG	EqOBP	EqSLG	EqA	VORP	DEFENSE
2005	WAS	MLB	30	347	38	21	2	7	32	31	30	0	0	-2.7	.275	.339	.424	.055	.279	.344	.438	.272	13.2	74-2B	-8
2006	WAS	MLB	31	511	52	26	1	7	47	41	48	1	0	-0.6	.289	.348	.395	.011	.297	.357	.403	.268	17.3	102-2B	-4
2007	SEA	MLB	32	625	78	26	0	6	59	63	57	0	0	-0.2	.314	.381	.394	.090	.328	.400	.423	.293	24.4	
2008	SEA	MLB	33	506	54	24	1	5	50	45	51	2	1	-1.0	.282	.346	.373	-.048	.284	.350	.396	.266	9.8	119-DH

Breakout: 1%　Improve: 24%　Collapse: 38%　Attrition: 21%　　　Comparables: Tom Herr, David Segui, Kevin Seitzer, Red Schoendienst

Despite low expectations, Vidro's first year in Seattle was anything but horrible. In fact, the second baseman-turned-DH hit so well at Safeco (.330/.397/.403) you'd think the building had been designed with him in mind. Vidro blistered the ball from the All-Star break through the end of August, hitting .370/.437/.481 during that span. The main complaint at the time of the trade—that Vidro, while a valuable bat as an infielder, is nowhere near as valuable as a full-time DH—is still completely valid. Should his 2007 .337 BABIP regress, there isn't going to be much left to say in his favor.

PITCHERS

Cha Seung Baek

Bats: R　　Throws: R　　Height: 6' 4"　　Weight: 220　　Born: May 29, 1980　　Age: 28

YEAR	TEAM	LVL	AGE	W	L	SV	G	GS	IP	H	BB	SO	HR	GB%	BABIP	STUFF	WHIP	ERA	PERA	EqERA	EqH9	EqBB9	EqSO9	EqHR9	VORP	SN/WX
2005	TAC	AAA	25	8	8	0	25	21	113²	147	36	73	19	47.8%	.340	-43	1.61	6.41	8.37	8.54	12.6	3.2	4.0	1.8	-34.4	—
2006	TAC	AAA	26	12	4	0	24	24	147²	133	37	103	17	49.6%	.269	-8	1.15	3.00	4.51	4.20	8.5	2.6	4.5	1.4	22.0	—
2006	SEA	MLB	26	4	1	0	6	6	34¹	26	13	23	6	44.1%	.208	7	1.14	3.67	3.52	3.44	6.4	3.2	5.8	1.3	7.9	1.20
2007	TAC	AAA	27	1	1	0	6	6	31	33	10	18	1	40.6%	.314	0	1.39	3.19	3.81	3.73	8.6	3.2	3.7	0.3	6.5	—
2007	SEA	MLB	27	4	3	0	14	12	73¹	87	14	49	6	36.1%	.328	13	1.38	5.16	3.94	4.97	9.4	1.4	5.3	0.7	2.8	0.88
2008	SEA	MLB	28	4	6	0	29	12	84²	96	27	50	11	43.7%	.304	-6	1.45	4.98	4.92	4.86	10.0	2.6	4.6	1.2	4.4	0.90

Breakout: 19%　Improve: 45%　Collapse: 32%　Attrition: 39%　　　Comparables: Doug Brocail, Bryan Rekar, Lerrin LaGrow, Joe Moeller

It was a golden opportunity: in late May, the Mariners' underperforming fourth and fifth starters, Horacio Ramirez and Jeff Weaver, were both on the DL. Baek had stepped into the rotation in place of Felix Hernandez in late April, had a respectable 4.60 ERA, and was seemingly poised to seize a rotation spot. Then the wheels fell off: Baek posted an ERA of 8.02 over his next four starts before being shut down with shoulder tendonitis. You only get so many missed opportunities in a career, and Baek may have filled his allotment with that one. In nine years as a pro, he's exceeded 130 innings in a season exactly once.

Miguel Batista

Bats: R　　Throws: R　　Height: 6' 1"　　Weight: 195　　Born: February 19, 1971　　Age: 37

YEAR	TEAM	LVL	AGE	W	L	SV	G	GS	IP	H	BB	SO	HR	GB%	BABIP	STUFF	WHIP	ERA	PERA	EqERA	EqH9	EqBB9	EqSO9	EqHR9	VORP	SN/WX
2005	TOR	MLB	34	5	8	31	71	0	74²	80	27	54	9	46.8%	.302	-5	1.43	4.10	4.71	4.68	9.4	3.1	6.2	1.0	9.5	0.78
2006	ARI	MLB	35	11	8	0	34	33	206¹	231	84	110	18	52.8%	.316	6	1.53	4.58	4.54	4.48	9.6	3.2	4.4	0.7	25.2	3.43
2007	SEA	MLB	36	16	11	0	33	32	193	209	85	133	18	45.3%	.315	10	1.52	4.29	4.29	4.13	8.7	3.4	5.6	0.8	25.0	4.36
2008	SEA	MLB	37	7	10	0	42	22	148²	168	60	96	16	47.6%	.314	-5	1.53	4.87	4.94	4.79	9.9	3.3	5.0	1.0	7.6	1.80

Breakout: 8%　Improve: 29%　Collapse: 36%　Attrition: 31%　　　Comparables: Joe Niekro, Bob Buhl, Tom Candiotti, Bob Lemon

Batista is hailed as a renaissance man because he writes poetry and crime novels, has recently been attempting to make like Kenny G on the alto saxophone, and he pitches a little bit, too. His peripherals have been shaky for awhile, and that's never promising for a pitcher in his late 30s, but he keeps getting by on guile and a steady diet of sinkers and cutters. His margin of error is tiny, but so long as he can take the ball every fifth day, he has value.

Tony Butler

Bats: L   Throws: L   Height: 6' 7"   Weight: 205   Born: November 18, 1987   Age: 20

YEAR	TEAM	LVL	AGE	W	L	SV	G	GS	IP	H	BB	SO	HR	GB%	BABIP	STUFF	WHIP	ERA	PERA	EqERA	EqH9	EqBB9	EqSO9	EqHR9	VORP	SN/WX
2006	EVE	A-	18	1	2	0	9	9	42	23	25	52	2	42.1%	.233	22	1.14	2.79	5.92	6.06	7.1	9.6	6.3	1.5	-1.8	—
2007	WIS	A	19	4	7	0	20	18	85¹	78	46	73	10	45.0%	.292	-41	1.45	4.75	11.20	10.22	11.8	9.4	3.9	3.0	-35.3	—
2008	SEA	MLB	20	3	10	0	22	22	100	107	99	65	10	42.5%	.306	-15	2.05	7.60	6.64	7.64	9.3	8.1	5.1	0.9	-21.8	-2.10

Breakout: 36% Improve: 71% Collapse: 11% Attrition: 11%   Comparables: Jonathan Figueroa, Chuck Lofgren, Tony DeJesus, Jon-Michael Nickerson

At 6-foot-7, Butler has a lot to keep track of in his delivery, and consistent mechanics and good command have eluded him thus far. His results at Wisconsin last year weren't promising, nor was the fact that he missed more than a month with a "tired arm." Still, a big lefty with a legit fastball will get plenty of time to develop, and Butler is only 20 years old. In the meantime, unless he can get his breaking ball over for strikes, things could get ugly at High-A High Desert this year.

Ryan Feierabend

Bats: L   Throws: L   Height: 6' 3"   Weight: 190   Born: August 22, 1985   Age: 22

YEAR	TEAM	LVL	AGE	W	L	SV	G	GS	IP	H	BB	SO	HR	GB%	BABIP	STUFF	WHIP	ERA	PERA	EqERA	EqH9	EqBB9	EqSO9	EqHR9	VORP	SN/WX
2005	SBR	A+	19	8	7	0	29	29	150²	186	51	122	16	44.6%	.368	-10	1.57	3.88	7.14	6.15	11.6	4.7	3.9	1.5	-8.5	—
2006	SAN	AA	20	9	12	0	28	28	153	156	55	127	16	38.7%	.317	-3	1.38	4.29	6.29	6.67	10.5	4.1	5.1	1.5	-16.7	—
2006	SEA	MLB	20	0	1	0	4	2	17	15	7	11	3	40.0%	.235	14	1.29	3.71	3.82	3.06	7.1	3.1	5.1	1.5	4.5	0.19
2007	TAC	AAA	21	6	4	0	19	19	108¹	131	33	70	9	39.2%	.349	3	1.51	3.99	5.41	5.09	10.5	3.0	4.4	0.9	5.9	—
2007	SEA	MLB	21	1	6	0	13	9	49¹	73	23	27	10	37.4%	.371	-25	1.95	8.03	10.10	8.75	12.7	3.7	4.7	1.9	-12.2	-0.22
2008	SEA	MLB	22	6	10	0	39	23	135¹	163	57	81	22	40.9%	.313	-7	1.63	5.88	5.86	5.70	10.5	3.4	4.7	1.5	-6.5	0.20

Breakout: 45% Improve: 70% Collapse: 12% Attrition: 14%   Comparables: Andrew Lorraine, Chris Seddon, Ross Grimsley, Adam Pettyjohn

Feierabend's fly-ball tendencies played well enough at Triple-A Tacoma, but in the big leagues he got punished for them, badly. Right-handed batters facing him morphed into Alex Rodriguez, hitting .366/.421/.640 against the hapless southpaw. Still, Feierabend's only 22 years old, so he has time to prove that his poise and control can overcome his middling assortment of pitches.

Sean Green

Bats: R   Throws: R   Height: 6' 6"   Weight: 230   Born: April 20, 1979   Age: 29

YEAR	TEAM	LVL	AGE	W	L	SV	G	GS	IP	H	BB	SO	HR	GB%	BABIP	STUFF	WHIP	ERA	PERA	EqERA	EqH9	EqBB9	EqSO9	EqHR9	VORP	SN/WX
2005	SAN	AA	26	0	1	14	21	0	24¹	17	8	18	1	67.1%	.225	-17	1.03	2.96	3.66	5.24	6.4	4.0	4.4	0.8	0.9	—
2005	TAC	AAA	26	4	2	1	33	0	49¹	40	29	44	1	63.6%	.287	2	1.40	3.65	4.21	4.86	8.0	5.6	5.8	0.4	3.8	—
2006	TAC	AAA	27	4	1	5	15	0	24	18	11	12	0	64.8%	.265	-12	1.21	2.25	3.55	2.86	7.0	4.5	3.3	0.0	6.7	—
2006	SEA	MLB	27	0	0	0	24	0	32	34	13	15	2	59.6%	.305	-14	1.47	4.50	4.40	4.35	9.3	3.5	4.1	0.6	5.5	-0.04
2007	TAC	AAA	28	2	1	1	10	0	17²	13	8	10	0	74.1%	.250	-12	1.19	2.03	2.92	2.60	5.7	4.2	3.6	0.0	5.8	—
2007	SEA	MLB	28	5	2	0	64	0	68	77	34	53	2	63.1%	.369	7	1.63	3.84	4.41	3.78	9.6	4.1	6.6	0.3	13.6	1.12
2008	SEA	MLB	29	2	3	2	52	0	57	60	26	40	3	60.4%	.315	-5	1.51	4.12	4.27	4.13	9.3	3.7	5.4	0.5	7.6	0.60

Breakout: 13% Improve: 48% Collapse: 35% Attrition: 30%   Comparables: Rich Loiselle, Jose Jimenez, Mike Fetters, Tom Davey

During the first half of last season, Green looked like proof of the adage that if you don't have an effective middle reliever, you can always find one. Prior to the All-Star break, he had a healthy strikeout rate and a 2-to-1 K/UIBB ratio, and it looked like the M's had found a righty set-up man. Then in the second half, his strikeouts declined, his ratio retreated, and his ERA nearly doubled. Green could be a useful situational right-hander, especially when the team needs a quick double play—his limited sinker/slider repertoire has only one purpose: to make hitters beat the ball into the ground—but lefty batters seem perfectly content to lay off his pitches and take their walks.

Felix Hernandez

Bats: R   Throws: R   Height: 6' 3"   Weight: 230   Born: April 8, 1986   Age: 22

YEAR	TEAM	LVL	AGE	W	L	SV	G	GS	IP	H	BB	SO	HR	GB%	BABIP	STUFF	WHIP	ERA	PERA	EqERA	EqH9	EqBB9	EqSO9	EqHR9	VORP	SN/WX
2005	TAC	AAA	19	9	4	0	19	14	88	62	48	100	3	56.6%	.277	47	1.25	2.25	3.83	3.17	7.1	5.2	7.5	0.4	22.2	—
2005	SEA	MLB	19	4	4	0	12	12	84¹	61	23	77	5	67.7%	.257	63	1.00	2.67	2.78	2.98	6.5	2.4	8.2	0.6	28.1	3.09
2006	SEA	MLB	20	12	14	0	31	31	191	195	60	176	23	58.7%	.315	38	1.34	4.52	4.25	4.65	8.8	2.7	7.8	1.0	22.1	3.70
2007	SEA	MLB	21	14	7	0	30	30	190¹	209	53	165	20	61.5%	.338	30	1.37	3.93	4.24	3.76	9.1	2.2	7.2	1.0	36.4	4.33
2008	SEA	MLB	22	11	10	0	28	28	177	186	56	146	12	57.4%	.323	22	1.37	3.97	3.98	3.97	9.2	2.6	6.4	0.6	27.0	4.30

Breakout: 16% Improve: 45% Collapse: 16% Attrition: 8%   Comparables: Jeremy Bonderman, Don Drysdale, Larry Dierker, Bert Blyleven

Having taken the majors by storm upon his arrival in August 2005, King Felix has a whiff of disappointment about him after two fairly average seasons, but it's important to remember that he won't be 22 until after the season starts. Among his comparables above, all but Bonderman experienced performance spikes in their age-22 seasons. Given Hernandez's fearsome stuff, strong peripherals, and swollen BABIP last year, there's every reason to expect a breakout, but even if his performance is closer to that underwhelming PECOTA line, he'll remain one of the best young starters in the game. The only cause for concern is the elbow tightness that caused him to miss a few weeks early last season.

Jonathan Huber Bats: R   Throws: R   Height: 6' 2"   Weight: 195   Born: July 7, 1981   Age: 26

YEAR	TEAM	LVL	AGE	W	L	SV	G	GS	IP	H	BB	SO	HR	GB%	BABIP	STUFF	WHIP	ERA	PERA	EqERA	EqH9	EqBB9	EqSO9	EqHR9	VORP	SN/WX
2005	SAN	AA	24	7	8	0	26	26	148	159	49	112	11	45.8%	.326	-11	1.41	4.74	5.99	6.95	10.6	4.3	4.6	1.1	-20.2	—
2006	SAN	AA	25	0	3	11	21	0	24	30	4	19	0	53.1%	.395	-13	1.42	4.88	5.53	6.35	12.3	2.0	4.8	0.4	-1.9	—
2006	TAC	AAA	25	3	1	12	29	0	41²	46	10	38	3	48.4%	.350	-4	1.36	2.62	5.48	4.12	10.8	2.5	6.2	0.9	6.5	—
2006	SEA	MLB	25	2	1	0	16	0	16²	10	6	11	0	55.1%	.213	4	0.96	1.08	2.17	2.12	4.8	3.2	5.3	0.0	8.3	0.80
2007	TAC	AAA	26	1	4	5	24	1	33¹	43	9	28	5	50.9%	.358	-23	1.56	7.57	6.15	9.17	10.7	2.6	5.5	1.6	-13.6	—
2007	SEA	MLB	26	0	0	0	9	0	11¹	13	4	8	1	60.0%	.353	-4	1.50	4.78	5.11	4.35	10.5	3.5	6.1	0.9	1.3	0.31
2008	SEA	MLB	26	2	2	2	33	2	39²	43	16	29	4	50.5%	.312	-3	1.47	4.54	4.46	4.50	9.5	3.3	5.7	0.8	4.6	0.40

Breakout: 47% Improve: 66% Collapse: 19% Attrition: 39%   Comparables: Warren Hacker, Peter Munro, Matt Belisle, Jim York

The main thing Huber has going for him is the power of a good first impression. Toward the end of 2006, he got some time in the Mariners bullpen to show how well he had taken to his conversion to relief and delivered 16 2/3 strong innings. Having lost much of last season to a recurrence of elbow trouble, however, that first impression has faded and Huber now looks a lot more like a fungible minor league reliever. He has neither stats nor stuff; the opportunity to make another good impression might be hard to come by.

Mark Lowe Bats: R   Throws: R   Height: 6' 3"   Weight: 190   Born: June 7, 1983   Age: 25

YEAR	TEAM	LVL	AGE	W	L	SV	G	GS	IP	H	BB	SO	HR	GB%	BABIP	STUFF	WHIP	ERA	PERA	EqERA	EqH9	EqBB9	EqSO9	EqHR9	VORP	SN/WX
2005	WIS	A	22	6	6	0	22	22	103²	107	49	72	12	48.4%	.295	-46	1.50	5.47	9.07	9.33	11.6	6.5	3.4	2.3	-37.6	—
2006	SBR	A+	23	1	0	2	13	2	29¹	14	11	46	0	60.0%	.233	19	0.86	1.86	3.44	4.71	5.3	4.4	8.5	0.3	2.8	—
2006	SAN	AA	23	0	2	4	11	0	16	14	3	14	1	50.0%	.289	-2	1.06	2.25	4.15	3.60	9.0	2.4	5.4	0.6	3.3	—
2006	SEA	MLB	23	1	0	0	15	0	18²	12	9	20	1	47.7%	.262	18	1.13	1.93	2.96	2.04	6.1	4.1	9.7	0.5	8.6	1.63
2007	SEA	MLB	24	0	0	0	4	0	2²	2	3	3	1	0.0%	.167	3	1.88	6.67	6.42	6.00	6.0	9.0	9.0	3.0	-0.3	0.14
2008	SEA	MLB	25	2	2	1	29	3	37¹	37	21	32	4	40.4%	.300	-3	1.56	4.85	4.98	4.71	8.7	4.7	6.6	1.1	3.3	0.30

Breakout: 43% Improve: 69% Collapse: 21% Attrition: 39%   Comparables: Don Cooper, Franklyn German, Jesus Colome, Sean Douglass

Prior to the microfracture elbow surgery Mark Lowe had before last season, his calling card was a mid-90s fastball with good life that made him ideal for relief work. The radar-gun readings were still good when Lowe returned from the DL at the end of July, but he only lasted four appearances before elbow pain stopped him cold. While reports said he was throwing without pain again over the offseason, doing so under game conditions is a completely different animal.

Kameron Mickolio Bats: R   Throws: R   Height: 6' 9"   Weight: 256   Born: May 10, 1984   Age: 24

YEAR	TEAM	LVL	AGE	W	L	SV	G	GS	IP	H	BB	SO	HR	GB%	BABIP	STUFF	WHIP	ERA	PERA	EqERA	EqH9	EqBB9	EqSO9	EqHR9	VORP	SN/WX
2006	EVE	A-	22	1	0	4	21	0	32²	34	7	26	1	67.3%	.324	-29	1.27	2.80	6.59	6.21	11.8	4.3	3.4	0.9	-2.0	—
2007	WTN	AA	23	3	1	2	18	0	29²	24	12	27	0	39.0%	.300	-2	1.21	1.82	3.78	3.54	8.0	4.2	5.5	0.3	6.4	—
2007	TAC	AAA	23	3	3	1	14	0	24	19	10	28	3	45.2%	.276	7	1.21	3.75	4.03	4.50	6.8	3.8	7.9	1.5	2.9	—
2008	SEA	MLB	24	3	5	2	27	6	62	67	31	48	7	47.1%	.313	-1	1.57	4.94	5.06	4.84	9.4	4.0	6.1	1.1	3.5	0.60

Breakout: 18% Improve: 50% Collapse: 24% Attrition: 7%   Comparables: Ben Ford, Chad Ricketts, Brent Stentz, Aaron Small

An 18th-round pick last year out of Utah Valley State, Mickolio has only been pitching for the last four years. Not only did he not take the mound for the first time until he was nearly 18, but his home state of Montana doesn't have any organized high school baseball, so his experience in the sport in general is extremely limited. At 6-foot-9 and nearly 260 pounds, he's as intimidating as a pitcher can get, and he's already made great strides since signing by adding velocity to his fastball, which now touches 96 mph, while also developing a slider that projects as a plus pitch. He has a long way to go when it comes to throwing strikes and smoothing out his mechanics, but tuck his name away as a deep sleeper.

Brandon Morrow

Bats: R   Throws: R   Height: 6' 3"   Weight: 190   Born: July 26, 1984   Age: 23

YEAR	TEAM	LVL	AGE	W	L	SV	G	GS	IP	H	BB	SO	HR	GB%	BABIP	STUFF	WHIP	ERA	PERA	EqERA	EqH9	EqBB9	EqSO9	EqHR9	VORP	SN/WX
2007	SEA	MLB	22	3	4	0	60	0	63¹	56	50	66	3	36.6%	.329	26	1.67	4.12	3.89	3.66	7.3	6.2	8.4	0.4	12.6	2.35
2008	SEA	MLB	23	3	3	2	39	2	54	47	32	55	5	40.2%	.291	9	1.46	3.98	4.09	3.89	7.6	4.9	8.0	0.8	10.4	0.90

Breakout: 20% Improve: 41% Collapse: 32% Attrition: 31%   Comparables: Dave Cole, Armando Benitez, Ed Whitson, Roger Moret

So Brandon Morrow got to spend his first full season as a pro in the major leagues, coming out of the bullpen as a contender. What could be better? Maybe if he had a more committed relationship with the strike zone prior to becoming a major leaguer, that would've been nice. Morrow was not one of those "so polished he doesn't need any instruction" college prospects. He returned to starting in winter ball and should probably be sent back to the minors, as a starter, to work on his control at the start of the season. We'll soon find out if the Mariners have the discipline to do that, or if they'll continue to sacrifice Morrow's development to fill a short-term hole in the bullpen.

Eric O'Flaherty

Bats: L   Throws: L   Height: 6' 2"   Weight: 195   Born: February 5, 1985   Age: 23

YEAR	TEAM	LVL	AGE	W	L	SV	G	GS	IP	H	BB	SO	HR	GB%	BABIP	STUFF	WHIP	ERA	PERA	EqERA	EqH9	EqBB9	EqSO9	EqHR9	VORP	SN/WX
2005	WIS	A	20	4	4	13	45	0	69²	73	30	51	2	54.0%	.324	-18	1.48	3.74	6.44	6.57	11.2	5.8	3.6	0.7	-6.6	—
2006	SBR	A+	21	0	1	1	16	0	28¹	31	6	33	1	60.5%	.417	2	1.32	3.52	7.48	5.70	13.7	3.4	6.8	0.8	-0.3	—
2006	SAN	AA	21	2	2	7	25	0	39	45	15	36	0	56.4%	.391	1	1.54	1.15	6.63	3.93	12.6	4.5	6.0	0.3	6.4	—
2006	SEA	MLB	21	0	0	0	15	0	11	18	6	6	2	40.0%	.381	-31	2.18	4.09	10.10	7.94	13.5	4.8	4.8	1.6	-1.7	-0.42
2007	SEA	MLB	22	7	1	0	56	0	52¹	45	20	36	1	46.3%	.280	9	1.24	4.47	2.86	3.91	6.8	3.1	5.6	0.2	8.2	0.64
2008	SEA	MLB	23	2	3	2	53	1	53¹	53	21	44	4	47.8%	.306	5	1.38	4.10	3.88	4.08	8.7	3.3	6.5	0.6	7.5	0.70

Breakout: 28% Improve: 57% Collapse: 27% Attrition: 25%   Comparables: Nelson Briles, Vicente Padilla, Bob Miller, Rick Baldwin

O'Flaherty justified the rush to bring him to the majors in 2006 by brutalizing left-handed batters last year (.183/.278/.204) and doing surprisingly well against righties (.277/.354/.376). The Walla Walla native wore down in the second half, but if he can show more durability this year, he might make George Sherrill expendable.

John Parrish

Bats: L   Throws: L   Height: 5' 11"   Weight: 210   Born: November 26, 1977   Age: 30

YEAR	TEAM	LVL	AGE	W	L	SV	G	GS	IP	H	BB	SO	HR	GB%	BABIP	STUFF	WHIP	ERA	PERA	EqERA	EqH9	EqBB9	EqSO9	EqHR9	VORP	SN/WX
2005	BAL	MLB	27	1	0	0	14	0	17¹	19	17	25	1	52.3%	.429	17	2.08	3.12	6.91	3.78	10.3	9.2	12.4	0.5	5.0	-0.15
2007	BAL	MLB	29	2	2	0	45	0	41²	41	33	36	2	50.0%	.312	7	1.78	5.40	4.41	5.02	8.4	6.1	6.9	0.4	1.5	-0.71
2007	SEA	MLB	29	0	0	0	8	0	10¹	22	4	5	0	69.6%	.489	-39	2.52	6.99	11.85	8.71	18.3	3.5	4.4	0.0	-1.3	-0.12
2008	SEA	MLB	30	1	2	1	34	0	35¹	40	22	31	2	52.5%	.350	-4	1.76	5.05	5.31	5.02	10.0	5.1	6.8	0.6	1.2	0.10

Breakout: 29% Improve: 67% Collapse: 22% Attrition: 39%   Comparables: Bill Landrum, J. C. Romero, Jamie Easterly, Jack Hamilton

Seattle dealt disappointing minor league outfielder Sebastien Boucher to Baltimore for equally disappointing reliever John Parrish last August. Parrish made eight appearances for the M's, all in losses save for his second outing in which he was charged with the tying runs, yet still earned a hold because his runners scored after he had been removed from the game. Non-tendered in December, he's likely to have a new dance partner lined up by spring training despite his poor control and past elbow surgeries because it's hard to give up on a lefty who can bring it in the 90s.

J. J. Putz

Bats: R   Throws: R   Height: 6' 5"   Weight: 250   Born: February 22, 1977   Age: 31

YEAR	TEAM	LVL	AGE	W	L	SV	G	GS	IP	H	BB	SO	HR	GB%	BABIP	STUFF	WHIP	ERA	PERA	EqERA	EqH9	EqBB9	EqSO9	EqHR9	VORP	SN/WX
2005	SEA	MLB	28	6	5	1	64	0	60	58	23	45	8	56.1%	.286	-5	1.35	3.60	4.44	3.92	8.4	3.3	6.5	1.2	10.9	0.74
2006	SEA	MLB	29	4	1	36	72	0	78¹	59	13	104	4	52.2%	.311	41	0.92	2.30	2.73	2.48	7.1	1.4	10.1	0.5	32.6	5.64
2007	SEA	MLB	30	6	1	40	68	0	71²	37	13	82	6	44.2%	.201	30	0.70	1.38	2.05	1.51	4.2	1.4	8.8	0.8	36.6	7.42
2008	SEA	MLB	31	4	5	41	62	0	67¹	56	18	72	5	47.7%	.291	20	1.10	2.81	2.77	2.76	7.3	2.2	8.3	0.7	20.0	3.40

Breakout: 15% Improve: 33% Collapse: 41% Attrition: 12%   Comparables: Bryan Harvey, Robb Nen, Jeff Nelson, Tom Henke

The pride of Trenton, Michigan (well, after Mary Lynn Rajskub, who plays Chloe on *24*), Putz was the best reliever in baseball last year according to WXRL. His transformation from a middling relief prospect with a great fastball to a relentless, dominating closer is one of the best stories in the game, but there are a couple of reasons for caution. First, his BABIP was freakishly low last year (second lowest in the majors among pitchers who'd thrown 50 or more innings). Second, his season was bracketed by arm troubles (elbow tightness in March, triceps soreness in September). The arm trouble could turn into something more serious down the road. The BABIP is almost guaranteed to correct itself immediately.

Horacio Ramirez

Bats: L   Throws: L   Height: 6' 1"   Weight: 210   Born: November 24, 1979   Age: 28

YEAR	TEAM	LVL	AGE	W	L	SV	G	GS	IP	H	BB	SO	HR	GB%	BABIP	STUFF	WHIP	ERA	PERA	EqERA	EqH9	EqBB9	EqSO9	EqHR9	VORP	SN/WX
2005	ATL	MLB	25	11	9	0	33	32	202¹	214	67	80	31	50.1%	.282	-18	1.39	4.63	5.20	5.07	9.5	2.8	3.4	1.4	17.5	3.34
2006	ATL	MLB	26	5	5	0	14	14	76¹	85	31	37	6	54.7%	.312	1	1.52	4.48	4.52	4.64	9.5	3.2	4.0	0.6	9.2	2.22
2007	SEA	MLB	27	8	7	0	20	20	98	139	42	40	13	49.7%	.351	-27	1.85	7.16	7.01	7.65	11.7	3.4	3.4	1.2	-22.8	-0.55
2008	SEA	MLB	28	3	5	0	24	10	67²	83	26	31	8	50.6%	.314	-14	1.61	5.45	5.43	5.39	10.7	3.2	3.6	1.1	-1.1	0.30

Breakout: 31%   Improve: 46%   Collapse: 29%   Attrition: 44%   Comparables: Jimmy Anderson, Frank Baumann, Mike Kekich, Paul Kilgus

When you say that a pitcher who finished the season with a 7.16 ERA was "lucky," it's usually meant as a platitude on the order of "at least you have your health" or "you could be living in war-torn central Africa right now," but we mean it literally. Ramirez finished the 2007 season with an 8-7 record, one game over .500, when by all rights he should have been about six games under. By our account, that made him the sixth-luckiest pitcher in baseball behind Paul Byrd, Chien Ming Wang, C. C. Sabathia, Justin Verlander, and Josh Beckett—you'll note, none of those other guys had an ERA in the sevens. Like the others, Ramirez was the beneficiary of some of the best run support in the league, which boosted his win totals; unlike the others, he did precious little to merit the support, managing only five quality starts in twenty chances.

Juan Ramirez

Bats: R   Throws: R   Height: 6' 3"   Weight: 175   Born: August 16, 1988   Age: 19

YEAR	TEAM	LVL	AGE	W	L	SV	G	GS	IP	H	BB	SO	HR	GB%	BABIP	STUFF	WHIP	ERA	PERA	EqERA	EqH9	EqBB9	EqSO9	EqHR9	VORP	SN/WX
2007	EVE	A-	18	3	7	0	15	15	75¹	61	43	73	3	47.0%	.272	-7	1.38	4.30	6.92	9.27	9.5	8.7	3.5	1.2	-27.3	—
2008	SEA	MLB	19	3	10	0	22	22	101¹	119	104	56	17	44.8%	.305	-26	2.20	8.37	7.81	8.31	10.3	8.4	4.3	1.5	-32.1	-3.00

Breakout: 33%   Improve: 59%   Collapse: 23%   Attrition: 12%   Comparables: Rafael Rodriguez, Jermaine Van Buren, Chris Gambs, Hal Garrett

One member of the Mariners' organization claims that Ramirez is the second-best pitcher to ever come out of their Venezuelan program, Felix Hernandez being the first. After winning Venezuela Summer League Pitcher of the Year honors in 2006, Ramirez's stateside debut showed that he has plenty of upside and plenty of work to be done. He throws a mid-90s fastball and a hammer curve, and if he can improve his command during his full-season debut this year, he'll be rocketing up everyone's prospect charts.

Chris Reitsma

Bats: R   Throws: R   Height: 6' 5"   Weight: 235   Born: December 31, 1977   Age: 30

YEAR	TEAM	LVL	AGE	W	L	SV	G	GS	IP	H	BB	SO	HR	GB%	BABIP	STUFF	WHIP	ERA	PERA	EqERA	EqH9	EqBB9	EqSO9	EqHR9	VORP	SN/WX
2005	ATL	MLB	27	3	6	15	76	0	73¹	79	14	42	3	53.8%	.310	3	1.27	3.93	3.61	4.21	9.4	1.6	4.7	0.4	12.9	0.64
2006	ATL	MLB	28	1	2	8	27	0	28	46	8	13	7	52.5%	.364	-42	1.93	8.68	9.98	9.10	13.3	2.1	3.6	1.8	-8.4	-0.23
2007	SEA	MLB	29	0	2	0	26	0	23²	37	9	11	3	47.4%	.382	-34	1.94	7.59	7.41	8.14	12.6	3.0	3.7	1.1	-6.9	-0.85
2008	SEA	MLB	30	1	1	1	23	0	26²	34	8	14	3	50.0%	.328	-15	1.56	5.29	5.24	5.21	11.2	2.4	4.0	1.0	0.2	0.00

Breakout: 41%   Improve: 56%   Collapse: 17%   Attrition: 43%   Comparables: Dallas Green, Brian Meadows, Tom Morgan, Don Wengert

Reitsma had a second season in a row ruined by elbow surgery last year. It was initially thought that he might have a career-threatening degenerative condition, but reports after surgery were much more positive, indicating that his primary problem might have been scar tissue, rather than arthritis. Unswayed, Reitsma's record provides no clue as to why he's been so coveted throughout his career, but after playing the $700,000 buyout on his $2.7 million option, the Mariners signed him to a minor league deal, apparently determined to find out.

Robert Rohrbaugh

Bats: R　Throws: L　Height: 6' 2"　Weight: 195　Born: December 28, 1983　Age: 24

YEAR	TEAM	LVL	AGE	W	L	SV	G	GS	IP	H	BB	SO	HR	GB%	BABIP	STUFF	WHIP	ERA	PERA	EqERA	EqH9	EqBB9	EqSO9	EqHR9	VORP	SN/WX
2005	EVE	A-	21	5	2	0	14	12	68	68	18	71	7	47.4%	.335	-33	1.26	3.84	10.03	8.95	13.0	5.7	4.6	2.8	-20.6	—
2006	SBR	A+	22	7	1	0	10	9	55¹	43	8	47	2	50.0%	.270	9	0.93	1.47	4.06	3.20	8.3	2.3	4.4	0.7	13.5	—
2006	SAN	AA	22	5	5	0	14	14	85²	87	27	64	9	49.1%	.310	-10	1.34	3.80	6.01	5.24	10.4	3.6	4.6	1.5	3.2	—
2007	WTN	AA	23	7	5	0	15	15	85	84	21	62	5	38.1%	.304	1	1.24	3.28	4.51	4.41	9.4	2.6	4.1	0.9	10.8	—
2007	TAC	AAA	23	6	3	0	13	13	85¹	84	26	49	10	31.3%	.278	-5	1.29	2.95	4.32	3.33	8.2	3.0	3.8	1.3	21.1	—
2008	SEA	MLB	24	5	10	0	33	20	124¹	151	51	66	21	40.9%	.308	-11	1.62	5.94	5.91	5.76	10.6	3.3	4.2	1.5	-6.7	0.10

Breakout: 4%　Improve: 25%　Collapse: 48%　Attrition: 16%　　Comparables: Steve Wojciechowski, Eddie Guardado, Mike Vavrek, Larry Thomas

Rohrbaugh is another lefty finesse type, big on control and "pitchability," but not so big with the fastball, which sits in the high 80s. While there's something appealing about guys who get it done on guile and cojones, the successes are few and far between, so the odds are against him being John Halama, much less Jamie Moyer. On the depth chart he's stuck behind fellow spelling challenge Ryan Feierabend—who profiles much the same way and is younger, to boot.

Ryan Rowland-Smith

Bats: L　Throws: L　Height: 6' 3"　Weight: 205　Born: January 26, 1983　Age: 25

YEAR	TEAM	LVL	AGE	W	L	SV	G	GS	IP	H	BB	SO	HR	GB%	BABIP	STUFF	WHIP	ERA	PERA	EqERA	EqH9	EqBB9	EqSO9	EqHR9	VORP	SN/WX
2005	SAN	AA	22	6	7	0	33	17	122	133	51	102	7	41.4%	.349	-6	1.51	4.35	6.25	7.02	10.8	5.4	5.1	0.9	-17.4	—
2006	SAN	AA	23	1	3	4	23	1	41²	38	18	48	2	46.1%	.333	2	1.36	2.84	4.87	5.18	9.2	4.7	7.2	0.7	1.9	—
2007	TAC	AAA	24	3	4	1	25	0	41²	35	22	50	2	38.9%	.320	14	1.37	3.67	3.93	4.57	7.4	5.0	8.3	0.7	4.7	—
2007	SEA	MLB	24	1	0	0	26	0	38²	39	15	42	4	35.2%	.354	15	1.40	3.95	4.10	3.92	8.3	3.0	8.8	0.9	6.4	0.20
2008	SEA	MLB	25	2	3	2	40	2	50	48	23	48	5	41.0%	.305	7	1.42	4.31	4.24	4.22	8.4	3.8	7.5	0.9	7.4	0.70

Breakout: 35%　Improve: 65%　Collapse: 13%　Attrition: 26%　　Comparables: Steve Wilson, Sean Runyan, Grant Jackson, Neal Cotts

Purportedly the first player in major league history with a hyphenated last name, Aussie Rowland-Smith spent the last two years in the bullpen, but was working on a conversion back to starting in winter ball. The lefty has a broad enough assortment of pitches to make it work and figures to start the season in Tacoma to see if it does.

George Sherrill

Bats: L　Throws: L　Height: 6' 0"　Weight: 225　Born: April 19, 1977　Age: 31

YEAR	TEAM	LVL	AGE	W	L	SV	G	GS	IP	H	BB	SO	HR	GB%	BABIP	STUFF	WHIP	ERA	PERA	EqERA	EqH9	EqBB9	EqSO9	EqHR9	VORP	SN/WX
2005	TAC	AAA	28	1	3	7	22	0	23²	19	6	38	0	52.8%	.358	21	1.05	2.28	4.04	3.80	9.7	3.0	10.5	0.0	4.3	—
2005	SEA	MLB	28	4	3	0	29	0	19	13	7	24	3	40.0%	.250	16	1.05	5.21	3.47	5.30	6.3	3.4	10.1	1.4	-0.0	0.94
2006	SEA	MLB	29	2	4	1	72	0	40	30	27	42	0	33.3%	.303	23	1.43	4.28	3.13	4.05	6.5	5.6	8.8	0.0	7.7	1.35
2007	SEA	MLB	30	2	0	3	73	0	45²	28	17	56	4	29.6%	.250	24	0.99	2.36	2.45	2.12	5.0	2.9	9.3	0.8	18.2	1.63
2008	SEA	MLB	31	3	3	7	64	0	52	42	23	62	5	37.0%	.291	18	1.25	3.44	3.32	3.35	7.1	3.6	9.3	0.9	13.1	1.20

Breakout: 23%　Improve: 51%　Collapse: 22%　Attrition: 8%　　Comparables: Brian Fuentes, Dave LaRoche, Damaso Marte, Arthur Rhodes

Long an underrated lefty specialist, Sherrill hinted at something more in 2007 by holding right-handed hitters to a sterling .212/.284/.303 line. Given the small sample (76 plate appearances) and the fact that the 31-year-old lefty had consistently shown a large platoon split in his twenties, the wisest course might be to accept last year as a fluke and deal him while his value is highest. Despite the number of other lefty relievers in the organization, that's a tougher decision to make than it might seem; LOOGYs who can actually do their job are far from commonplace.

Chris Tillman

Bats: R　Throws: R　Height: 6' 5"　Weight: 195　Born: April 15, 1988　Age: 20

YEAR	TEAM	LVL	AGE	W	L	SV	G	GS	IP	H	BB	SO	HR	GB%	BABIP	STUFF	WHIP	ERA	PERA	EqERA	EqH9	EqBB9	EqSO9	EqHR9	VORP	SN/WX
2006	EVE	A-	18	1	3	0	5	5	19¹	25	15	29	4	48.0%	.477	-23	2.09	8.01	37.04	24.37	21.1	14.5	9.2	5.9	-28.6	—
2007	WIS	A	19	1	4	0	8	8	33	31	13	34	1	43.3%	.316	-4	1.33	3.55	6.69	9.00	10.9	6.8	4.7	0.9	-11.0	—
2007	HDS	A+	19	6	7	0	20	20	102²	107	48	105	12	40.4%	.332	-3	1.51	5.26	6.68	7.46	10.0	5.7	5.3	1.6	-20.2	—
2008	SEA	MLB	20	5	12	0	26	26	130	160	95	94	22	42.8%	.331	-8	1.96	7.16	7.15	6.97	10.8	6.0	5.6	1.6	-25.1	-1.70

Breakout: 49%　Improve: 75%　Collapse: 5%　Attrition: 8%　　Comparables: Kris Honel, Chris Seelbach, Gaby Hernandez, Carlos Carrasco

Tillman's minor league ERAs are a little deceptive. For one thing, 27 unearned runs were scored on him between two levels last year, which is a high total even in the bus leagues. On the other hand, the tall right-hander finished the season as the youngest pitcher in the hitter's paradise that is the Cal League. The Mariners love his makeup, his mid-90s heat, and his improving command, "Improving" being the key word—he still uncorked 13 wild pitches and hit 12 batters last year, so he's far from a finished product.

Jarrod Washburn

Bats: L   Throws: L   Height: 6' 1"   Weight: 190   Born: August 13, 1974   Age: 33

YEAR	TEAM	LVL	AGE	W	L	SV	G	GS	IP	H	BB	SO	HR	GB%	BABIP	STUFF	WHIP	ERA	PERA	EqERA	EqH9	EqBB9	EqSO9	EqHR9	VORP	SN/WX
2005	LAA	MLB	30	8	8	0	29	29	177¹	184	51	94	19	41.2%	.296	6	1.33	3.20	4.67	3.52	9.5	2.7	4.8	1.0	47.7	5.64
2006	SEA	MLB	31	8	14	0	31	31	187	198	55	103	25	40.8%	.284	1	1.35	4.67	4.30	4.58	8.9	2.4	4.6	1.0	20.6	3.05
2007	SEA	MLB	32	10	15	0	32	32	193²	201	67	114	23	38.6%	.291	4	1.38	4.32	3.98	4.10	8.2	2.7	4.8	1.0	24.8	3.45
2008	SEA	MLB	33	8	10	0	25	25	148²	168	49	85	20	42.1%	.299	1	1.45	4.91	4.92	4.78	9.9	2.7	4.5	1.2	8.3	2.10

Breakout: 4%   Improve: 23%   Collapse: 40%   Attrition: 24%   Comparables: Larry Gura, Mike Flanagan, Floyd Bannister, Charlie Leibrandt

That sound you heard was Washburn's fastball slowing down to the point at which there isn't enough separation left between it and his changeup to fool people. Or rather, it wasn't actual the slowing of the fastball that you were hearing, but the deafening cannonade of the 16 homers Washburn allowed in the second half. That total was tied for second-most in the American League behind Washburn's rotation-mate Jeff Weaver. Washburn joins Batista and free agent Carlos Silva to give the M's a trifecta of mediocre inning-eaters behind Felix Hernandez.

Jeff Weaver

Bats: R   Throws: R   Height: 6' 5"   Weight: 200   Born: August 22, 1976   Age: 31

YEAR	TEAM	LVL	AGE	W	L	SV	G	GS	IP	H	BB	SO	HR	GB%	BABIP	STUFF	WHIP	ERA	PERA	EqERA	EqH9	EqBB9	EqSO9	EqHR9	VORP	SN/WX
2005	LAN	MLB	28	14	11	0	34	34	224	220	43	157	35	42.4%	.278	4	1.17	4.22	4.60	4.43	9.0	1.6	5.8	1.4	27.0	4.20
2006	LAA	MLB	29	3	10	0	16	16	88²	114	21	62	18	40.3%	.332	-11	1.52	6.29	6.84	6.75	11.2	1.9	5.9	1.6	-9.2	-0.22
2006	SLN	MLB	29	5	4	0	15	15	83¹	99	26	45	16	43.6%	.305	-14	1.50	5.19	6.15	5.29	10.5	2.4	4.4	1.5	7.0	1.51
2007	SEA	MLB	30	7	13	0	27	27	146²	190	35	80	23	37.1%	.334	-12	1.53	6.20	5.67	5.92	10.4	1.9	4.5	1.4	-9.7	1.30
2008	SEA	MLB	31	7	9	0	23	23	135²	159	35	79	20	41.9%	.307	2	1.43	5.06	5.00	4.92	10.3	2.1	4.5	1.3	5.6	1.70

Breakout: 28%   Improve: 59%   Collapse: 22%   Attrition: 26%   Comparables: Ray Burris, Brett Tomko, Ismael Valdez, James Baldwin

Trolling the off-season pitching market is often like last-minute Christmas shopping. You talk yourself into things. Fifteen minutes before the mall closes, you find yourself in the DVD section of one of the big stores, and *Navy Seals* finds its way into your hands. It's not that you know someone who wants *Navy Seals*, it's not even that you like the movie yourself, it's just there, and it's on sale, and it's got Charlie Sheen. Jeff Weaver is the *Navy Seals* of pitchers. Weaver always seems to put it together for a month or so each season, a stretch of starts that will later result in some GM talking himself into signing him. In 2006, to the Cardinals' great delight, that month was October. Last year, it was June. Just remember that if you give them Weaver, your fan base might fake some enthusiasm, but they'll be looking for a gift receipt, hoping that he can be returned.

Sean White

Bats: R   Throws: R   Height: 6' 4"   Weight: 215   Born: April 25, 1981   Age: 27

YEAR	TEAM	LVL	AGE	W	L	SV	G	GS	IP	H	BB	SO	HR	GB%	BABIP	STUFF	WHIP	ERA	PERA	EqERA	EqH9	EqBB9	EqSO9	EqHR9	VORP	SN/WX
2005	MYR	A+	24	9	3	0	18	18	97	112	29	65	5	63.2%	.346	-22	1.45	3.71	7.09	6.75	12.4	4.4	3.0	1.1	-10.9	—
2005	MIS	AA	24	2	5	0	8	8	50¹	43	18	33	2	60.0%	.272	-6	1.21	4.12	4.38	5.63	8.4	3.9	3.7	0.8	-0.2	—
2006	MIS	AA	25	5	6	1	21	16	102¹	124	43	73	3	56.0%	.359	-8	1.64	4.41	6.45	6.80	12.1	4.3	4.1	0.6	-12.9	—
2007	TAC	AAA	26	1	1	0	2	2	10²	11	2	7	0	48.6%	.314	7	1.21	2.52	3.51	3.38	8.4	1.7	4.2	0.0	2.6	—
2007	SEA	MLB	26	1	1	0	15	0	35¹	35	20	16	2	52.9%	.284	-14	1.56	5.61	4.07	5.20	7.7	4.5	3.7	0.5	-1.4	-0.25
2008	SEA	MLB	27	2	3	0	21	4	49	56	23	28	5	54.1%	.313	-11	1.61	5.18	5.09	5.17	10.0	3.8	4.4	0.9	0.7	0.20

Breakout: 38%   Improve: 59%   Collapse: 24%   Attrition: 48%   Comparables: Mike Fetters, Steve Shields, Peter Munro, Heathcliff Slocumb

Sean White is a local product, which is probably what got the Mariners interested enough to take a Rule 5 flier on him prior to last season, even though he was neither particularly young nor particularly accomplished. His low-90s two-seam fastball has given White strong ground-ball rates in the minors, but all of his other indicators are pretty bad. Having served his season on the 25-man roster (half of it on the DL with biceps tendonitis), he'll be fighting for a spot this year. If he makes the team, he probably won't be the best right-handed sinker-balling reliever named Sean with a colorful, five-letter last name on the staff.

LINEOUTS

Hitters

PLAYER	TEAM	LVL	AGE	PA	R	2B	3B	HR	RBI	BB	SO	SB-CS	EqBRR	AVG/OBP/SLG	MLVr	EqAVG/EqOBP/EqSLG	EqA	VORP
UT W. Bloomquist	SEA	MLB	29	188	28	3	0	2	13	10	35	7-5	0.0	.277/.321/.329	-.137	.297/.342/.360	.243	-1.7
OF D. Carroll	MRN	Rk	18	238	39	9	6	0	24	27	56	27-11	-0.1	.323/.415/.428	.280	.194/.255/.259	.184	-49.9
OF G. Halman	WIS	A	19	202	26	5	0	4	15	8	77	15-7	-0.4	.182/.234/.273	-.297	.147/.184/.215	.126	-31.6
	EVE	A-	19	265	37	19	1	16	37	21	85	16-8	-4.3	.307/.371/.597	.387	.197/.239/.365	.206	-27.6
1B B. LaHair*	TAC	AAA	24	606	79	46	2	12	81	49	126	0-1	-0.3	.275/.332/.431	.039	.247/.304/.395	.241	-10.3
3B A. Liddi	WIS	A	18	451	41	28	3	8	52	36	123	5-4	-3.2	.240/.308/.385	-.010	.200/.254/.311	.196	-27.5
3B M. Mangini*	EVE	A-	21	93	12	4	0	2	9	13	18	3-0	0.8	.291/.398/.418	.166	.214/.290/.274	.210	-8.9
	HDS	A+	21	69	7	1	2	2	8	6	21	1-0	-0.6	.226/.304/.403	-.186	.188/.257/.344	.205	-3.1
C A. Moore	HDS	A+	23	491	74	30	3	22	102	41	84	1-0	1.3	.307/.371/.543	.173	.244/.297/.414	.246	4.7
1B M. Morse	TAC	AAA	25	324	48	26	0	6	39	26	47	5-3	-1.5	.309/.368/.460	.184	.283/.341/.427	.266	14.7
	SEA	MLB	25	20	1	2	0	0	3	1	4	0-0	-0.1	.444/.500/.556	.684	.444/.500/.556	.367	3.6
DH C. Peguero*	WIS	A	20	321	35	21	6	9	50	16	97	4-3	-1.9	.263/.315/.465	.118	.198/.240/.347	.198	-28.5

"Now with 34 percent less **Willie Bloomquist!**" may not have gotten serious consideration as the Mariners' team slogan for 2007, but it was still good news for their fans. ⊘ A third-round pick last June, **Danny Carroll** has a quick bat, an advanced approach for a teenager, and ideal makeup. His ability to play center field, or lack thereof, will be the key to his future. ⊘ Dutch outfielder **Greg Halman** is one to watch, even though he's extremely raw, as his 162 strikeouts last year will attest. ⊘ **Bryan LaHair** snuck into the Mariners' prospect picture in 2006 by wrapping up his first season above A-ball with a .327/.393/.525 showing in 230 plate appearances in the PCL, but just as quietly snuck out last year with a weak full-season showing there. ⊘ The key word with **Alex Liddi** is "projectable." A teenage signing out of Italy, he's pretty far away from the majors, but he's a sleeper. ⊘ A left-handed bat drafted last year out of Oklahoma State, **Matt Mangini** is a fairly polished hitter with wood-bat experience, but he's not considered likely to stick at third. ⊘ You temper your enthusiasm when a 23-year-old puts up big power numbers in the California League, especially when that guy is a catcher who might not have the skills to stay behind the plate like **Adam Moore**. We'll know more once he's in Double-A. ⊘ As utilitymen go, **Michael Morse** is a tweener—he doesn't have the defensive skill to back up the middle infield positions or the power to hold down even the short-side of a platoon at one of the corners. What that leaves, particularly on a team that already has Willie Bloomquist, is not much. ⊘ Six-foot-five **Carlos Peguero** has a truckload of power from the left side, but that won't do him any good if he can't curb his ridiculous strikeout rate.

Pitchers

PLAYER	TEAM	LVL	AGE	W	L	SV	IP	H	BB	SO	HR	GB%	BABIP	STUFF	WHIP	ERA	PERA	EqERA	EqH9	EqBB9	EqSO9	EqHR9	VORP
P. Aumont '08	SEA	MLB	19	4	12	0	124²	164	113	67	23	46.1%	.328	-24	2.21	8.13	8.22	7.96	11.5	7.4	4.2	1.7	-37.2
C. Jimenez*	TAC	AAA	22	2	1	2	25²	28	12	23	2	41.0%	.329	-7	1.56	3.50	4.59	5.47	8.9	4.1	5.8	0.7	0.4
J. Thomas*	WTN	AA	23	4	9	0	119¹	147	61	100	11	44.8%	.372	-21	1.74	5.51	8.12	7.83	12.2	5.1	4.8	1.4	-27.9
J. Woerman	WTN	AA	24	7	7	0	144¹	119	68	124	8	45.5%	.282	3	1.30	3.74	4.50	4.98	8.1	4.7	5.0	0.9	9.5
J. Woods*	TAC	AAA	25	5	7	1	114²	151	42	79	17	43.5%	.364	-32	1.68	6.90	7.85	7.81	11.9	3.7	4.7	1.7	-26.6
	SEA	MLB	25	0	0	0	10²	9	7	4	1	35.1%	.222	-15	1.59	5.89	3.41	5.56	6.4	4.8	3.2	0.8	-1.1

The eleventh overall pick in the 2007 draft, francophone **Phillippe Aumont** is a big guy (6-foot-7, 220 pounds) with a big fastball (96 mph). He's also a bit of a project, even for a high school pitcher. ⊘ A stress fracture in his elbow sidelined lefty **Cesar Jimenez** in spring training last year, but he came back strong enough at Triple-A Tacoma and in the Venezuelan Winter League that he should be in the mix for this year's bullpen. ⊘ After an impressive full-season debut in 2006, southpaw **Justin Thomas** became quite hittable last year at Double-A, where his control regressed. ⊘ After dominating at the lower levels as a reliever, **Joe Woerman** was converted to starting at Double-A and continued to succeed with his fastball/slider mix. ⊘ It seems there was a reason **Jake Woods** wound up on waivers in the first place. Since the Mariners have a younger, more promising version of the same pitcher in Ryan Feierabend, Woods was deemed expendable, and is now off the 40-man roster.

MANAGER: JOHN McLAREN

YEAR	TEAM	W-L	Pythag +/−	Avg PC	100+ P	120+ P	QS	BQS	REL	REL w Zero R	IBB	Subs	PH	PH Avg	PH HR	SB2	CS2	SB3	CS3	SAC Att	SAC %	POS SAC	Squeeze	Swing	In Play
2007	SEA	43-41	4	96.5	43	3	36	7	247	141	19	30	53	.260	2	35	12	5	3	20	80.0%	16	1	88	70

Many were puzzled when Mike Hargrove resigned in July with his team 12 games over .500 and winners of nine out of their last ten. The manager had been a regular on the hot seat and only then had his perch started to cool. While Hargrove's reasons for resigning were deeply personal, he might also have had the sense that the team's success wasn't sustainable—the Mariners were barely outscoring the opposition. New boss John McLaren was strategically the same as the old boss. Part of that was due to the deep bullpen McLaren inherited, complete with two quality lefties with which to play matchups. After 15 years as part of Lou Piniella's coaching entourage, McLaren returned to Seattle last year as Hargrove's bench coach and stumbled into his first chance to manage in the big leagues at 55 years old. For 2008, he's assembled a coaching staff so absurdly veteran (bench coach Jim Riggleman, 55, third base coach Sam Perlozzo, 57, pitching coach Mel Stottlemyre, 66) it sounds like the setup for a long-delayed *Grumpy Old Men* sequel. Relatability is key to a manager succeeding in the clubhouse; self-inflicting a generation gap is a good way to ensure that 25 post-teens think of you more as a fussy grandmother than a leader of men. McLaren already had one minor clubhouse rebellion to face down when Adam Jones was promoted, so reuniting the cast of *Going My Way* may prove to have been a misjudgment.

Tampa Bay Rays

On November 28, 2007, the Rays traded outfielders Delmon Young and Jason Pridie and infielder Brendan Harris to the Twins for pitchers Matt Garza and Eduardo Morlan and shortstop Jason Bartlett. That trade might prove to be the most important moment in the history of the Tampa Bay franchise, not because of the caliber of the players involved—although it is unusual to see young players as talented as Young and Garza swapped for one another—but because the deal represents the largest step yet in the Rays' slow but sure transition from team-building to contention.

In the first two years of his tenure as general manager, Tampa Bay's Andrew Friedman focused primarily on collecting assets without much regard to how those assets might actually fit together on the field. Hence, the rather asymmetrical distribution of talent in the Rays organization in recent years, which featured a deep group of outfielders, a thinner group of infielders, and very little pitching depth at all. In trading Young, however, Friedman knowingly gave up the best player in the deal for two other very good young players who will help correct that imbalance, thereby making the Rays more of a real baseball team rather than a random assemblage of talented youngsters.

Of the players received from the Twins, the one who drew most of the headlines is the 24-year-old right-hander Garza, who should emerge from a season split between Minnesota and Rochester to be the Rays' third starter behind Scott Kazmir and James Shields. However, Bartlett, the other major leaguer acquired in the deal, has the potential to be just as integral to the Rays' success. That's because he should vastly improve the Rays' middle infield defense, which will further improve the fortunes of the Rays' pitching staff.

Indeed, it's on the defensive side of the ledger that a team constructed of ill-fitting parts often shows its cracks. The Rays' defense showed a lot of cracks in 2007, allowing 71 runs to slip through according to our Fielding Runs Above Average metric (FRAA). In other words, they allowed 71 more runs to score over the course of the season than an average defense would have, or nearly one extra run every other game. Consider the effects of that upon the ERAs of their pitchers; ace Scott Kazmir posted a 3.48 ERA last year, but with a merely average defense behind him, he might have flirted with something in the twos.

The middle infield was the focal point of the Rays' defensive problems, as they sifted through Ben Zobrist, B. J. Upton, Brendan Harris, Ty Wigginton, Josh Wilson, and Jorge Velandia at second base and shortstop. Collectively, the Rays were 56 runs below average between those two middle infield positions, and lost another 16 runs to Akinori Iwamura's awkward defense at third base. Together that's -72 FRAA, evidence that the rest of the team's defense was essentially average as a unit.

With Bartlett solidifying shortstop, Iwamura moving to the keystone to clear room for top prospect Evan Longoria at third, and former center fielder Rocco Baldelli slated to replace Young's poor range in right field, things are looking much better for 2008. In fact, based on PECOTA's forecasts for the team's eight projected positional regulars, the Rays might actually have an above-average defense next season (Table 1).

The projection in Table 1 is a bit optimistic. Longoria's glove is not as highly regarded by scouts as it is by

---

RAYS PROSPECTUS

2007 record: 66-96; Fifth place, AL East

Pythagenport record: 66-96

Runs scored per game: 4.83 (8th in AL)

Runs allowed per game: 5.83 (14th in AL)

Team EqA: .266 (4th in AL)

2007 Batters Age: 26.5 (Youngest in AL)

2007 Pitchers Age: 26.8 (Youngest in AL)

Ballpark: Tropicana Field; Slight pitchers's park; Park Factor of .984

2007: Yet another last-place finish for an increasingly talented, but increasingly imbalanced team.

2008: Still young but no longer Young, the new-look Rays swap potential for pitching and learn how to win.

Table 1. Exorcizing the Rays' Defense

	2007 (Actual)		2008 (Projected)	
Position	Primary Players	FRAA	Primary Players	FRAA
C	Dioner Navarro	-7	Navarro	-1
1B	Carlos Peña	+14	Peña	+4
2B	Brendan Harris, B. J. Upton, Josh Wilson, Ty Wigginton	-28	Iwamura*	-13
3B	Akinori Iwamura	-16	Evan Longoria	+12
SS	Harris, Wilson, Ben Zobrist	-28	Jason Bartlett	+5
LF	Carl Crawford	+4	Crawford	+4
CF	Upton, Delmon Young, Elijah Dukes	-5	Upton	-5
RF	Young, Jonny Gomes	-5	Rocco Baldelli*	+10
	Total	**-71**	**Total**	**+16**

*Projection updated to reflect position change

FRAA and PECOTA, and the chances of the injury-plagued Baldelli being healthy enough to spend most of the year in the outfield are very slim. Table 1 also doesn't ration any playing time to mediocre defenders such as Cliff Floyd and Johnny Gomes, who are slated for a DH platoon, but are sure to find their way into the outfield on occasion, even without the need that another Baldelli injury would create. Even so, the Rays' defense is almost guaranteed to improve by the mere dint of eliminating unhappy experiments such as Upton and Wigginton at second base and Young in center. If they can get merely average defensive performances from Longoria and their right fielders, the Rays would still improve their defense by 65 runs, or 6 1/2 wins.

Add to that defensive improvement the addition of Garza atop the organization's waves of pitching prospects (Jacob McGee, Jeff Niemann, Wade Davis, and 2007's top overall draft pick David Price are just the first), and the Rays are well positioned to deduct radically from their major league-worst 944 runs allowed last year. Even if the kids have their growing pains, the Rays stand to gain a lot of ground simply from addition by subtraction. Excluding Kazmir and Shields, the rest of the Rays' pitchers combined for a 6.31 ERA last year, given the talent of their pitching prospects, it's unthinkable that they could be worse.

The boost that improved defense should give to the Rays' starters will in turn help their bullpen. While the organization's lopsided roster construction has not prioritized the bullpen, the unit's 6.16 ERA last year—one of the worst marks in baseball history—was inexcusable. However, the problem was compounded by a team defense that turned outs into hits and therefore reduced the pitch-efficiency of its starters. That in turn

forced the bullpen into action early and often, and the Rays churned through relievers as a result; no fewer than 14 different Rays made ten or more relief appearances last year. If the defense can help the starters be more efficient, the gains could reverberate throughout the pitching staff and be exponential rather than linear.

There's also a notion that a good defense could not only help the team's young pitchers to spare their arms, but could also boost their self-confidence. A pitcher can develop an awful lot of bad habits if he doesn't trust his defense to make the necessary plays to help him through his performance, but is the opposite true? Is there any evidence that teams with good defenses do a better job of developing young arms?

To address this question, we need to follow three steps. First, we need to identify some young pitching staffs to study. Second, we need to identify the quality of the defenses behind those pitching staffs. Third, we need to measure and compare the development of those pitching staffs while pitching in front of those defenses.

For the first step, we will define a young pitching staff as one on which the average age of the pitchers, weighting for innings pitched, is less than 27 years old. There are typically three to five teams that meet this criterion each season (last year those teams were Tampa Bay, Oakland, and Florida). In searching for teams that fit that description, however, we immediately run in to a methodological quirk, which is that pitching staffs that are young one year tend also to be young the next. For example, the Mariners' pitching staff was under 27 for seven consecutive seasons between 1984 and 1990. Thus, so as not to overweigh the impact of any one set of pitchers, we have restricted participation in our study to one pitching staff per team in any five-year period. When forced to choose from among several pitching staffs from a given team, we have chosen the one with the lowest average age. For example, the 1978 Cardinals' staff (average age 25.3) gets the nod over the team's 1977 (25.7) and 1979 (26.4) squads. The study covers all pitching staffs from 1977 through 2003; we cut things off after 2003 because more recent staffs are still in the process of developing, thus making their results inconclusive.

After eliminating the overlapping examples, we arrived at a total of 49 staffs. For step two, we divided those pitching staffs into quartiles based on their teams' cumulative FRAA over a five-year period starting with the year in which the team qualified for the study. For the 1990 Orioles, for example, we look at their FRAA between 1990 and 1994, which totaled +88 (easily qualifying them for the top quartile). The 49 pitching staffs

Table 2. Young Pitching Staffs, with Team FRAA

Top Quartile (Good Defense)				Bottom Quartile (Poor Defense)			
Team	Year	Age	FRAA	Team	Year	Age	FRAA
DET	1980	25.6	+207	HOU	1991	26.4	-64
BAL	1978	26.6	+133	ATL	1989	25.4	-72
CHA	1990	24.9	+123	TBA	2003	26.5	-84
MON	1977	26.9	+103	MIL	1986	26.1	-85
SLN	1978	25.3	+100	PIT	1997	25.7	-85
PIT	1988	26.2	+99	SEA	1979	25.5	-85
CHA	2002	25.8	+91	DET	1998	26.6	-93
BAL	1990	26.2	+88	SDN	1993	26.6	-102
KCA	2000	25.8	+78	CHN	1977	26.9	-102
MIL	1977	24.1	+60	BOS	1984	25.8	-124
DET	2003	25.3	+46	MON	1999	25.5	-128
TOR	1979	25.5	+42	CLE	1979	26.7	-219

Middle Quartiles (Average Defense)							
Team	Year	Age	FRAA	Team	Year	Age	FRAA
MIN	2000	26.6	+28	CIN	1980	26	-19
CLE	2003	26.3	+18	MIN	1978	26.5	-21
CIN	1985	26.4	+17	MIN	1995	25.7	-27
MIN	1983	26.3	+11	OAK	1983	26.9	-28
OAK	1978	25.3	+10	MON	1994	26.2	-28
NYN	1979	26.5	+10	HOU	1977	24.9	-31
PHI	1990	26.5	+3	CAL	1978	26.6	-31
CHN	1990	26.1	+0	NYN	1985	24.7	-36
HOU	1997	26.9	+0	CLE	1991	26.8	-38
TEX	1986	26.4	-3	FLO	1998	24.5	-45
SEA	1987	25.9	-13	CHA	1980	24.7	-46
SDN	1977	26	-19	KCA	1985	26.1	-62
				LAN	1981	26.2	-62

sorted by FRAA into their respective quartiles are listed in Table 2.

The top quartile of teams, those with strong defenses, includes a number of success stories. Four of the twelve teams (the 1978 Orioles, 1980 Tigers, 1982 Cardinals, and 2002 White Sox) won the World Series within five years of qualifying for our study, while most of the others turned out to be competitive. By contrast, most of the bottom quartile teams remained stuck in neutral, with the notable exception of the 1989 Braves, who started out having a very poor defense (-53 in 1989 and -85 in 1990), but ended up having a pretty good one by the end of their cycle (+20 in 1991 and +42 in 1992).*

For step three, we can track the progress of each team's pitching staff over a five-year period. Our measuring stick will be defense-neutral earned run average (DERA), which adjusts a pitcher's performance for park and league effects as well as for the quality of his de-

---

*See the Kansas City Royals essay for more on the defense of those Braves teams.

fense. That last adjustment allows us to evaluate the underlying skills of the pitching staff itself and thus levels the playing field between the staffs that pitched in front of good defenses and those that pitched in front of poor defenses.

The cumulative DERAs of each of the three groups in Table 2 in each of the five years being studied (the year listed for each team in Table 2 being Year 1) can be found in Table 3 and have been plotted on Chart 1. As you can see, we do find some meaningful patterns in the data. The teams in the top quartile (those with the best defenses) started out with a 4.72 DERA in Year 1, but had lowered it to 4.39 in Year 4, and 4.44 in Year 5, a roughly 30-point improvement. By contrast, the teams with poor defenses did not experience any improvement; in fact, they saw their DERA tick upward by Year 5. Meanwhile, the teams with average defenses demonstrated a milder improvement, as might be expected from any young pitching staff, amounting to about 10 points of DERA.

Table 3. Development of Young Pitching Staffs, by FRAA Quartile

Quartile	DERA				
	Year 1	Year 2	Year 3	Year 4	Year 5
Good Defense	4.72	4.58	4.53	4.39	4.44
Average Defense	4.57	4.54	4.46	4.46	4.49
Poor Defense	4.49	4.52	4.41	4.46	4.61

Could the patterns we're seeing here be explained by other phenomenon? Certainly. It may be that teams that are well-run enough to invest in good defenses are better at team building in general, and therefore do a better job of constructing a young pitching staff and managing that pitching staff over the period of our study. It could even be that DERA is unable to fully remove all of the effects of team defense from a pitchers' performance. What's more, the sample sizes are fairly small, so any result should be taken with a grain of salt. Nevertheless, the pattern does conform to common sense as it supports the notion that a strong defense provides a boost to the development of a young pitching staff, with effects on the order of 20 to 30 points of long-term ERA.

It isn't surprising that a smart team like the Rays has figured this out. If they do indeed get their run prevention in order, they have quite a bright future. Their offense, which is just as young as the pitching staff, improved substantially last season, upping its OBP from .314 to .336, and there is more help on the way in the form of Longoria, shortstop Reid Brignac, and the top

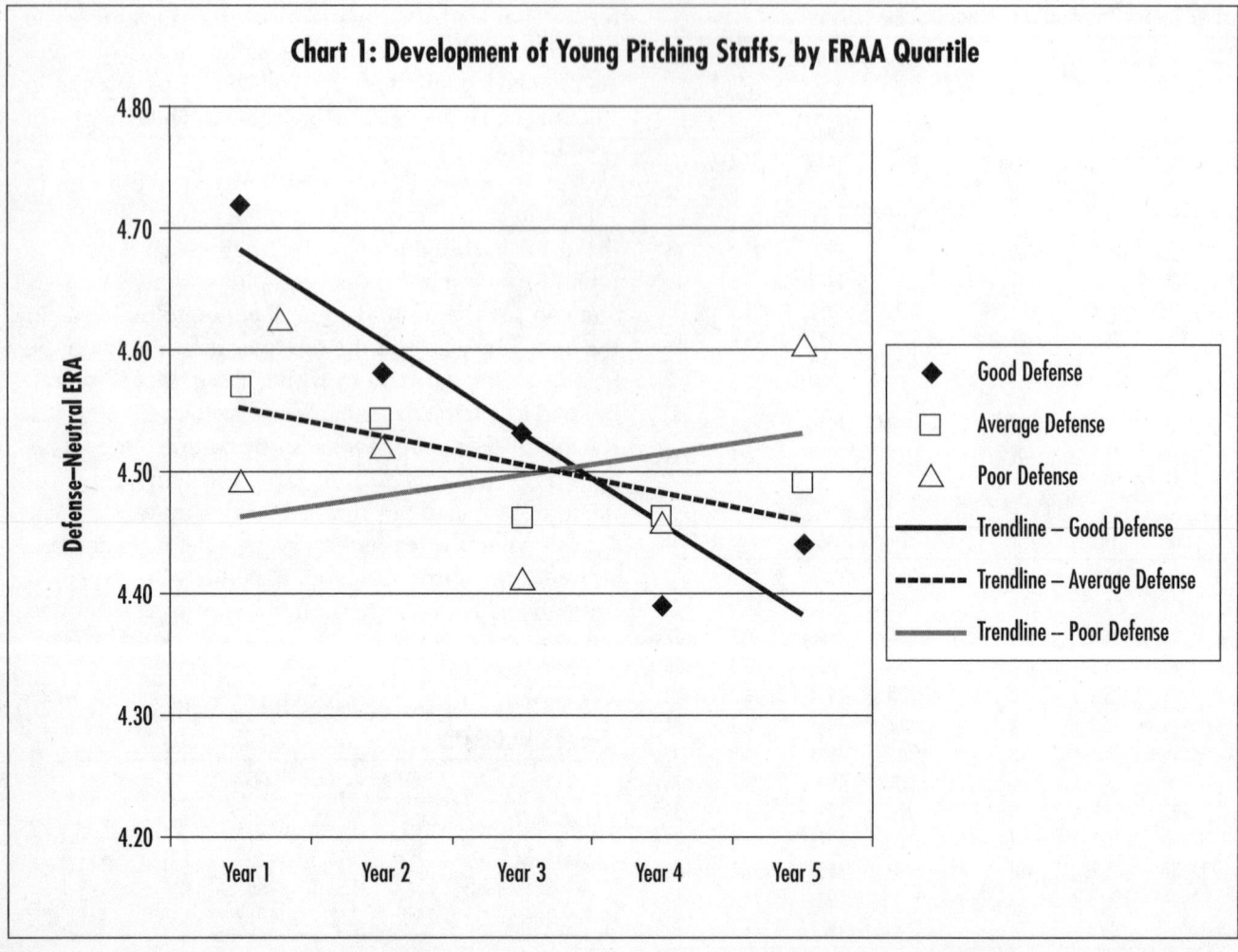

Chart 1: Development of Young Pitching Staffs, by FRAA Quartile

pick in this June's draft, which could turn into Vanderbilt slugger Pedro Alvarez. Youngsters such as Upton and catcher Dioner Navarro, whose numbers bumped up sharply after the All-Star break last season, may also have further room for growth. The only position at which the Rays don't appear to have a potential long-term star, or at least a long-term starter, is second base, though that hole could move to shortstop if Brignac were to take over at the keystone. It will also be interesting to see if, as the defense improves their pitchers' performances, they find themselves trading high on their own pitchers rather than acquiring additional arms in the seasons to come.

Is it far-fetched to think that the Rays could compete next season? Probably, but only because of the league and the division in which they play. While the Rays might contend were they in the NL Central, everyone but the Red Sox, Yankees, Indians, Tigers, and Angels could well be shut out of the American League race next season. However, the .500 mark is a very achievable near-term goal, and the Rays only have room to grow

thereafter. How the Tampa Bay market reacts to a winner remains to be seen, but the Rays have cited the turnarounds of the NFL's Buccaneers and the NHL's Lightning as favorable precedents, and have ambitiously already drawn up plans for a new bayside ballpark.

As such, their focus remains beyond 2008, and youngsters such as Longoria, Brignac, and Price will not be rushed to the major leagues until and unless their ability demands it, which in Longoria's case, it already has. Not only does Tampa Bay have a ton of young talent, but because the organization tended to draft high school players before turning to collegians more recently, a lot of that talent is developing on the same schedule: Upton, Kazmir, Shields, Garza, Navarro, Price, Longoria, Brignac, Carl Crawford, and David Price will all be between the ages of 22 and 26 this season. In terms of their overall long-term talent, the Rays are the envy of all but a handful of clubs in baseball, and this year for the first time, that talent may start to congeal into a very interesting baseball team.

HITTERS

Rocco Baldelli — OF

Bats: R | Throws: R | Height: 6′ 4″ | Weight: 200 | Born: September 25, 1981 | Age: 26

YEAR	TEAM	LVL	AGE	PA	R	2B	3B	HR	RBI	BB	SO	SB	CS	EqBRR	AVG	OBP	SLG	MLVr	EqAVG	EqOBP	EqSLG	EqA	VORP	DEFENSE	
2006	TBA	MLB	24	387	59	24	6	16	57	14	70	10	1	2.0	.302	.339	.533	.171	.305	.346	.551	.300	33.1	86-CF	1
2007	TBA	MLB	25	150	16	6	0	5	12	9	35	4	1	0.8	.204	.268	.358	-.260	.213	.282	.375	.231	-4.9	18-CF	4
2008	TBA	MLB	26	350	45	18	3	12	45	21	71	8	2	0.9	.268	.321	.452	.007	.272	.326	.475	.277	13.0	84-CF	5

Breakout: 28% Improve: 57% Collapse: 20% Attrition: 13%   Comparables: Brian Jordan, Wes Chamberlain, Jeffrey Leonard, Tommie Agee

Apparently "Baldelli" is Italian for injured. After losing all of 2005 to knee and elbow surgery and almost half of 2006 to hamstring problems, Baldelli's leg issues took a turn for the worse last year as his hamstring problems became chronic and he twice reinjured himself while on a rehab assignment. That left him available for only 35 games and healthy for none of them. It's hard to have much optimism about his future, which is a heartbreaking thing to say about a player who was once a prodigious young talent. Fortunately for the Rays, they're swimming in prodigious young talent these days.

Reid Brignac — SS

Bats: L | Throws: R | Height: 6′ 3″ | Weight: 180 | Born: January 16, 1986 | Age: 22

YEAR	TEAM	LVL	AGE	PA	R	2B	3B	HR	RBI	BB	SO	SB	CS	EqBRR	AVG	OBP	SLG	MLVr	EqAVG	EqOBP	EqSLG	EqA	VORP	DEFENSE	
2005	SWM	A	19	565	77	29	2	15	61	40	131	5	5	-2.8	.264	.319	.416	.006	.219	.262	.340	.206	-19.2	124-SS	-20
2006	VIS	A+	20	455	82	26	3	21	83	35	82	12	6	0.7	.326	.382	.557	.327	.261	.309	.451	.258	18.5	97-SS	-8
2006	MNT	AA	20	121	18	6	2	3	16	7	31	3	0	-0.7	.300	.355	.473	.228	.250	.298	.446	.256	4.0	28-SS	-5
2007	MNT	AA	21	596	91	30	5	17	81	55	94	15	5	1.9	.260	.328	.433	.057	.234	.294	.396	.242	4.5	126-SS	8
2008	TBA	MLB	22	619	65	31	3	16	68	44	131	11	4	1.0	.235	.292	.386	-.153	.238	.297	.406	.247	5.3	145-SS	-2

Breakout: 33% Improve: 65% Collapse: 16% Attrition: 7%   Comparables: Brandon Phillips, Sean Rodriguez, Pokey Reese, Kelly Johnson

Brignac entered last season as a blue-chip prospect coming off a California League MVP season, but his showing at Double-A left much to be desired. There was a silver lining, however, as he made great strides defensively. Many of the scouts who believed a move to third would be inevitable now think Brignac can stay in the middle infield as a defender with average range who makes the play on every ball he gets to. Combine that with a projection for 25-plus home runs annually, and he's still pretty special.

Raul Casanova — C

Bats: S | Throws: R | Height: 6′ 0″ | Weight: 235 | Born: August 23, 1972 | Age: 35

YEAR	TEAM	LVL	AGE	PA	R	2B	3B	HR	RBI	BB	SO	SB	CS	EqBRR	AVG	OBP	SLG	MLVr	EqAVG	EqOBP	EqSLG	EqA	VORP	DEFENSE	
2005	CHR	AAA	32	255	25	13	0	13	42	20	29	0	0	-0.7	.266	.325	.489	.067	.256	.316	.453	.261	9.4	59-C	-1
2007	DUR	AAA	34	153	14	9	0	5	21	12	32	0	0	-1.4	.291	.346	.461	.105	.268	.325	.444	.261	6.4	37-C	-4
2007	TBA	MLB	34	89	12	1	1	6	11	7	17	0	0	-0.3	.253	.315	.519	.082	.256	.326	.577	.295	5.2	19-C	-2
2008	TBA	MLB	35	213	18	8	0	6	27	15	45	0	0	-0.8	.242	.298	.377	-.151	.245	.303	.397	.244	1.3	54-C	-4

Breakout: 9% Improve: 24% Collapse: 48% Attrition: 44%   Comparables: Mandy Romero, Alan Ashby, Jerry McNertney, Walt Dropo

After getting a grand total of five big-league plate appearances over the preceding four seasons, Casanova got semi-regular time as Tampa's backup catcher last year and slugged over .500. Despite that, his defensive shortcomings demonstrated why he wasn't getting much playing time in the first place, and Tampa designated him for assignment, not once but twice, properly identifying that slugging percentage as a small-sample fluke.

Carl Crawford — LF

Bats: L | Throws: L | Height: 6′ 2″ | Weight: 215 | Born: August 5, 1981 | Age: 26

YEAR	TEAM	LVL	AGE	PA	R	2B	3B	HR	RBI	BB	SO	SB	CS	EqBRR	AVG	OBP	SLG	MLVr	EqAVG	EqOBP	EqSLG	EqA	VORP	DEFENSE	
2005	TBA	MLB	23	687	101	33	15	15	81	27	84	46	8	1.4	.301	.331	.469	.103	.314	.352	.500	.294	37.6	142-LF	8
2006	TBA	MLB	24	652	89	20	16	18	77	37	85	58	9	6.2	.305	.348	.482	.113	.309	.359	.496	.297	41.1	144-LF	2
2007	TBA	MLB	25	624	93	37	9	11	80	32	112	50	10	5.4	.315	.355	.466	.131	.329	.371	.503	.300	38.0	134-LF	4
2008	TBA	MLB	26	622	91	31	8	12	65	35	91	35	8	3.0	.299	.343	.447	.061	.303	.348	.470	.289	22.0	145-LF	4

Breakout: 11% Improve: 32% Collapse: 25% Attrition: 7%   Comparables: Bill White, Ralph Garr, Darin Erstad, Bake McBride

Crawford just gets a little bit better every year. Last year his power, walk rate, strikeout rate, and success rate on the bases all took slight downward turns, but yet another increase in batting average—Crawford has upped his average in every one of his major league seasons—combined with a league-wide decrease in offense to give him career highs in our adjusted total-offense metrics EqA and MLVr. His excitement-to-production ratio is high, meaning he's a little bit overrated, but he's still well above average, relatively young, and has a good shot at ending up as good as everyone thinks he is.

Elijah Dukes — OF

Bats: R Throws: R Height: 6' 2" Weight: 250 Born: June 26, 1984 Age: 24

YEAR	TEAM	LVL	AGE	PA	R	2B	3B	HR	RBI	BB	SO	SB	CS	EqBRR	AVG	OBP	SLG	MLVr	EqAVG	EqOBP	EqSLG	EqA	VORP	DEFENSE			
2005	MNT	AA	21	498	73	21	5	18	73	45	83	19	9	-2.0	.287	.355	.478	.174	.246	.307	.422	.249	6.0	79-CF	-7	24-LF	-4
2006	DUR	AAA	22	334	58	15	5	10	50	44	47	9	4	1.9	.293	.401	.488	.245	.275	.379	.477	.292	16.5	39-LF	-6	26-RF	0
2007	TBA	MLB	23	220	27	3	2	10	21	33	44	2	4	-1.2	.190	.318	.391	-.131	.203	.336	.440	.261	-2.5	38-CF	-5		
2008	WAS	MLB	24	407	60	18	2	17	55	45	71	10	3	0.7	.272	.358	.473	.074	.271	.359	.483	.284	23.2	97-CF	-4		

Breakout: 38% Improve: 61% Collapse: 19% Attrition: 17%   Comparables: Austin Kearns, Dwight Evans, Charlie Spikes, Ron Swoboda

Talented. Troublesome. Powerful. Angry. Fast. Confrontational. Exciting. Rebellious. Toolsy. Thuggish. Star potential. Criminal record. Balancing the two sides of Elijah Dukes is now Washington's problem, and they gave up a decent young lefty in Glenn Gibson for the privilege. They most likely gave up something for nothing, but the outside chance that they can somehow rein Dukes in and turn the deal into the steal of the century was just too tempting to resist.

Jonny Gomes — DH

Bats: R Throws: R Height: 6' 1" Weight: 225 Born: November 22, 1980 Age: 27

YEAR	TEAM	LVL	AGE	PA	R	2B	3B	HR	RBI	BB	SO	SB	CS	EqBRR	AVG	OBP	SLG	MLVr	EqAVG	EqOBP	EqSLG	EqA	VORP	DEFENSE			
2005	DUR	AAA	24	202	34	13	0	14	46	30	44	7	1	-2.2	.321	.446	.660	.510	.289	.406	.584	.327	19.4	23-LF	-4	22-RF	-5
2005	TBA	MLB	24	407	61	13	6	21	54	39	113	9	5	0.1	.282	.372	.534	.238	.297	.392	.580	.318	31.3	33-RF	-3	13-LF	1
2006	TBA	MLB	25	461	53	21	1	20	59	61	116	1	5	-4.3	.216	.325	.431	-.075	.218	.334	.445	.266	-0.4				
2007	TBA	MLB	26	394	48	20	2	17	49	35	126	12	4	0.8	.244	.322	.460	.005	.255	.336	.501	.282	7.9	29-RF	-1	21-LF	1
2008	TBA	MLB	27	477	67	22	2	23	68	57	130	12	5	0.1	.246	.346	.480	.065	.250	.352	.504	.294	18.1	113-DH			

Breakout: 25% Improve: 54% Collapse: 11% Attrition: 10%   Comparables: Rob Deer, Dwight Evans, Andre Thornton, Bob Robertson

We now know that Gomes's 2005 rookie season was not a true representation of his skills. He has just one mode at the plate: wait for a pitch to drive, and when it comes, swing for the fences. He makes no adjustments and no apologies for that. He's a one-dimensional player who will hit some home runs and draw some walks, but not nearly enough of either to make up for his low batting averages, high strikeout rates, and poor defense. Still, he'll get regular work next year as a part-time DH and by filling the inevitable hole in the outfield when Rocco Baldelli breaks again.

Joel Guzman — 3B

Bats: R Throws: R Height: 6' 6" Weight: 250 Born: November 24, 1984 Age: 23

YEAR	TEAM	LVL	AGE	PA	R	2B	3B	HR	RBI	BB	SO	SB	CS	EqBRR	AVG	OBP	SLG	MLVr	EqAVG	EqOBP	EqSLG	EqA	VORP	DEFENSE			
2005	JAX	AA	20	496	63	31	2	16	75	42	128	7	3	-2.2	.287	.351	.475	.180	.239	.294	.415	.244	7.9	92-SS	-2	18-3B	-3
2006	LVG	AAA	21	352	44	16	2	11	55	26	72	9	5	-2.7	.297	.353	.464	.058	.259	.312	.414	.251	-3.9	39-LF	1	24-1B	1
2006	LAN	MLB	21	23	2	0	0	0	3	3	2	0	0	0.0	.211	.348	.211	-.295	.211	.348	.211	.214	-1.2				
2006	DUR	AAA	21	92	7	5	0	4	9	4	23	0	0	0.0	.193	.228	.386	-.212	.182	.217	.352	.188	-6.2	12-3B	-4	12-LF	-1
2007	DUR	AAA	22	445	44	17	2	16	64	23	117	9	2	2.4	.242	.281	.408	-.102	.227	.264	.388	.226	-8.2	73-3B	0	11-1B	-1
2007	TBA	MLB	22	39	5	1	2	0	4	2	10	0	0	-0.5	.243	.282	.378	-.180	.243	.282	.378	.226	-0.6				
2008	TBA	MLB	23	541	52	24	2	15	64	34	139	10	3	-0.3	.233	.285	.380	-.177	.236	.289	.399	.241	-6.5	127-3B	-6		

Breakout: 36% Improve: 61% Collapse: 21% Attrition: 5%   Comparables: Butch Huskey, Wilson Betemit, Wes Helms, Jose Leon

There was a time, not so long ago, when Joel Guzman was considered a stud. Signed in 2001 as a 16-year-old and given the largest bonus of any Latin American prospect in history, Guzman was a 6-foot-4, 200-pound wunderkind with as much upside as anyone in the game. That youth and size worked against him, however, as he wasn't done growing. Now 6-foot-6 and somewhere around 250, he's too big to play short, is barely passable at third, and with the bulk came a loss of bat speed and therefore production. He's a perfect example of how projections can go wrong.

Brendan Harris INF

Bats: R   Throws: R   Height: 6' 1"   Weight: 200   Born: August 26, 1980   Age: 27

YEAR	TEAM	LVL	AGE	PA	R	2B	3B	HR	RBI	BB	SO	SB	CS	EqBRR	AVG	OBP	SLG	MLVr	EqAVG	EqOBP	EqSLG	EqA	VORP	DEFENSE
2005	NWO	AAA	24	519	67	22	4	13	81	40	77	9	5	-2.8	.270	.329	.417	-.014	.236	.289	.366	.227	-7.1	81-2B 2 42-3B 2
2006	NWO	AAA	25	257	37	14	0	5	32	26	56	3	2	1.4	.283	.379	.416	.128	.259	.344	.384	.257	6.9	34-3B 2 14-SS -2
2006	WAS	MLB	25	36	3	2	0	0	2	3	3	0	0	-0.1	.250	.333	.313	-.148	.250	.333	.312	.233	-0.2	
2006	LOU	AAA	25	165	22	14	1	5	28	14	29	2	0	1.6	.324	.384	.534	.348	.309	.370	.530	.304	18.2	20-3B -3
2007	TBA	MLB	26	576	72	35	3	12	59	42	96	4	1	0.6	.286	.343	.434	.040	.296	.359	.466	.283	25.2	85-SS -12 46-2B -12
2008	MIN	MLB	27	585	64	30	3	12	67	43	105	6	2	0.1	.263	.322	.399	-.067	.265	.326	.421	.263	14.1	137-SS -1

Breakout: 14% Improve: 35% Collapse: 30% Attrition: 13%   Comparables: Mark Lewis, Ty Wigginton, Clete Boyer, Michael Young

Brendan Harris always hit in the minors, but he had never been given a proper opportunity to establish himself in the majors until last year, and even that came only after Ben Zobrist's continued offensive failures. Lo and behold, Harris hit in the majors as well, but his limited range in the field continued to be a problem. Sent to Minnesota in the Delmon Young deal, he will compete with the inversely talented Adam Everett for the starting shortstop job. Which one would *you* want behind a young pitching staff?

Akinori Iwamura 3B/2B

Bats: L   Throws: R   Height: 5' 9"   Weight: 175   Born: February 9, 1979   Age: 29

YEAR	TEAM	LVL	AGE	PA	R	2B	3B	HR	RBI	BB	SO	SB	CS	EqBRR	AVG	OBP	SLG	MLVr	EqAVG	EqOBP	EqSLG	EqA	VORP	DEFENSE
2005	YKL	JP	26	611	83	31	4	30	102	63	146	6	3	—	.319	.390	.555	.304	.257	.336	.407	.261	10.4	
2006	YKL	JP	27	621	84	27	2	32	77	70	128	8	1	—	.311	.389	.544	.292	.278	.362	.434	.279	27.3	
2007	TBA	MLB	28	559	82	21	10	7	34	58	114	12	8	1.3	.285	.359	.411	.035	.300	.378	.449	.285	15.3	118-3B -10
2008	TBA	MLB	29	562	70	25	5	11	53	57	121	9	4	0.9	.253	.332	.389	-.071	.257	.337	.408	.266	8.4	132-3B -6

Breakout: 94% Improve: 95% Collapse: 3% Attrition: 13%   Comparables: Billy Klaus, Grady Hatton, Mike Cubbage, Marcus Giles

As expected, Iwamura's power in Japan—106 home runs in his last three years for Yakult—didn't translate to the States, but his solid hitting skills, patient approach, and very good defense did. He'll be moving to second base this year in order to accommodate top prospect Evan Longoria, which only increases his value, as without the power, his offensive skill set is more suited to the keystone.

John Jaso C

Bats: L   Throws: R   Height: 6' 2"   Weight: 205   Born: September 19, 1983   Age: 24

YEAR	TEAM	LVL	AGE	PA	R	2B	3B	HR	RBI	BB	SO	SB	CS	EqBRR	AVG	OBP	SLG	MLVr	EqAVG	EqOBP	EqSLG	EqA	VORP	DEFENSE
2005	SWM	A	21	386	61	25	1	14	50	42	53	3	1	1.4	.307	.383	.515	.269	.255	.319	.417	.255	9.6	27-C 2
2006	VIS	A+	22	406	58	22	0	10	55	31	48	1	2	-1.5	.309	.362	.451	.122	.253	.298	.368	.232	-2.1	21-C -4
2007	MNT	AA	23	450	62	24	2	12	71	59	49	2	2	-0.9	.316	.408	.484	.293	.285	.369	.444	.283	29.5	68-C 1
2008	TBA	MLB	24	463	48	23	1	10	51	39	72	3	2	-0.2	.251	.317	.381	-.108	.254	.322	.401	.256	4.8	110-C -3

Breakout: 10% Improve: 35% Collapse: 28% Attrition: 10%   Comparables: Doug Radziewicz, Rusty Greer, Jamie Dismuke, Andy Barkett

At this point, there is no doubt that Jaso can hit; he's exceeded a .300 batting average in each of the last four seasons. All of the questions about him concern his defense. He's a below-average catcher, and a slow recovery from rotator cuff surgery had him playing the position only part time in 2007. As strong as his bat may be, it doesn't profile well enough for first base, the only other position he can play, so this year's showing at Triple-A Durham will be key.

Desmond Jennings CF

Bats: R   Throws: R   Height: 6' 2"   Weight: 180   Born: October 30, 1986   Age: 21

YEAR	TEAM	LVL	AGE	PA	R	2B	3B	HR	RBI	BB	SO	SB	CS	EqBRR	AVG	OBP	SLG	MLVr	EqAVG	EqOBP	EqSLG	EqA	VORP	DEFENSE
2006	PRI	Rk	19	246	48	10	1	4	20	22	39	32	5	4.1	.277	.360	.390	.067	.199	.254	.261	.195	-47.4	54-CF -4
2007	CGA	A	20	448	75	21	5	9	37	45	53	45	15	1.9	.315	.401	.465	.268	.261	.329	.375	.250	3.7	84-CF 3
2008	TBA	MLB	21	507	56	22	3	5	36	35	95	22	9	1.7	.235	.294	.327	-.228	.238	.299	.344	.234	-10.0	119-CF 0

Breakout: 33% Improve: 57% Collapse: 20% Attrition: 6%   Comparables: Marc Lewis, Noah Hall, Dax Jones, Willie Cañate

Jennings just might be the next big thing. Going into the season, he was a raw athlete who was loaded with athletic gifts but offered little in the way of baseball skills, but one could argue that no player in baseball took a larger step forward in 2007. He projects as a leadoff man who can hit 20 home runs, steal 50 bags, reach base at a .400 or so clip, and play an outstanding center. If you start talking about him now, you'll look smart, because chances are good that he'll be on everyone's lips a year from now.

Evan Longoria   **3B**   Bats: R   Throws: R   Height: 6' 2"   Weight: 180   Born: October 7, 1985   Age: 22

YEAR	TEAM	LVL	AGE	PA	R	2B	3B	HR	RBI	BB	SO	SB	CS	EqBRR	AVG	OBP	SLG	MLVr	EqAVG	EqOBP	EqSLG	EqA	VORP	DEFENSE	
2006	VIS	A+	20	128	22	8	0	8	28	13	19	1	1	-0.5	.327	.402	.618	.444	.272	.336	.500	.283	8.5	22-3B	3
2006	MNT	AA	20	109	14	5	0	6	19	1	20	2	1	0.1	.267	.266	.486	.098	.257	.257	.495	.251	3.1	25-3B	9
2007	MNT	AA	21	447	78	21	0	21	76	51	81	4	0	1.2	.307	.403	.528	.334	.281	.362	.490	.292	35.5	96-3B	9
2007	DUR	AAA	21	128	19	8	0	5	19	22	29	0	0	0.0	.269	.398	.490	.202	.257	.383	.486	.299	10.8	27-3B	-3
2008	TBA	MLB	22	638	83	31	2	25	87	58	130	6	3	0.2	.266	.339	.459	.042	.270	.344	.482	.285	25.4	149-3B	12

Breakout: 18% Improve: 41% Collapse: 21% Attrition: 6%   Comparables: Paul Konerko, Tony Conigliaro, Bob Bailey, Cal Ripken

The best prospect in the American League, Longoria will most likely be the Rays' starting third baseman on Opening Day. He was just drafted in 2006, but the Rays aren't rushing him in the least—he's ready. There are no real weaknesses in Longoria's game. He's a .300 hitter with a ton of power and a very good approach at the plate. You could knock his defense a bit, but that would be more to say he's dependable with average range as opposed to a Gold Glove candidate. He's an immediate contender for Rookie of the Year honors and should be in the running for much larger awards down the line.

Dioner Navarro   **C**   Bats: S   Throws: R   Height: 5' 9"   Weight: 205   Born: February 9, 1984   Age: 24

YEAR	TEAM	LVL	AGE	PA	R	2B	3B	HR	RBI	BB	SO	SB	CS	EqBRR	AVG	OBP	SLG	MLVr	EqAVG	EqOBP	EqSLG	EqA	VORP	DEFENSE	
2005	LVG	AAA	21	286	31	12	0	6	29	38	24	2	2	-1.9	.266	.366	.390	-.101	.255	.344	.352	.250	3.6	64-C	2
2005	LAN	MLB	21	199	21	9	0	3	14	20	21	0	0	-2.0	.273	.354	.375	.012	.273	.357	.375	.260	7.6	49-C	-1
2006	LAN	MLB	22	86	5	2	0	2	8	11	18	1	0	0.1	.280	.372	.387	.028	.267	.360	.360	.261	3.1	22-C	-5
2006	TBA	MLB	22	216	23	7	0	4	20	20	33	1	1	-1.2	.244	.316	.342	-.191	.246	.326	.351	.240	-2.6	53-C	1
2007	TBA	MLB	23	434	46	19	2	9	44	33	67	3	1	-0.5	.227	.286	.356	-.216	.234	.297	.384	.239	-4.0	108-C	-3
2008	TBA	MLB	24	394	39	18	1	8	43	34	55	4	1	-0.6	.242	.311	.366	-.142	.246	.316	.385	.249	2.6	94-C	-1

Breakout: 32% Improve: 53% Collapse: 17% Attrition: 23%   Comparables: Biff Pocoroba, Butch Wynegar, Buck Rodgers, Mike Scioscia

During the first half of the 2007 season, Dioner hit more like Jamie Navarro, but the Rays stuck with him—not that they had much of a choice—and in the second half, he was one of the more productive catchers in the league, batting .285/.340/.475 after the break. He's a strange hitter in that he hits junk, using his excellent hand-eye coordination to turn on hanging curveballs or take hard sliders the other way, but his bat is a little slow, leaving him behind on good fastballs. It's hard to see him putting up an 815 OPS over the course of a season, but it's easy to see him being productive enough to be in the middle of the pack among starting catchers.

Greg Norton   **DH**   Bats: S   Throws: R   Height: 6' 1"   Weight: 205   Born: July 6, 1972   Age: 35

YEAR	TEAM	LVL	AGE	PA	R	2B	3B	HR	RBI	BB	SO	SB	CS	EqBRR	AVG	OBP	SLG	MLVr	EqAVG	EqOBP	EqSLG	EqA	VORP	DEFENSE			
2005	CHR	AAA	32	381	57	19	1	17	56	47	67	0	2	-2.1	.285	.374	.503	.181	.255	.344	.453	.271	19.9	42-3B	-3	10-1B	1
2006	TBA	MLB	33	335	47	15	0	17	45	35	69	1	5	-2.4	.296	.374	.520	.205	.300	.386	.541	.304	20.9	24-RF	-5	20-1B	-3
2007	TBA	MLB	34	240	25	9	0	4	23	37	55	1	1	-1.4	.243	.358	.347	-.082	.251	.375	.372	.269	-0.7				
2008	TBA	MLB	35	223	25	10	1	6	27	28	48	1	1	-0.6	.242	.341	.394	-.055	.245	.347	.414	.270	4.7	56-DH			

Breakout: 20% Improve: 41% Collapse: 37% Attrition: 43%   Comparables: J. T. Snow, Jerry Hairston, Kevin Millar, Champ Summers

Norton had some value in 2006 thanks to a fluky year and his ability to play all four corners. Last year he snapped back to reality, as offseason knee surgery limited his defensive versatility and offensive value, leaving him a part-time DH whose only tangible skill was the semiregular ability to coax a walk. There's no room for a player like this on a young, developing team, or even an old, developed team. The Rays released him at the end of the year.

Josh Paul   C   Bats: R   Throws: R   Height: 6' 1"   Weight: 210   Born: May 19, 1975   Age: 33

YEAR	TEAM	LVL	AGE	PA	R	2B	3B	HR	RBI	BB	SO	SB	CS	EqBRR	AVG	OBP	SLG	MLVr	EqAVG	EqOBP	EqSLG	EqA	VORP	DEFENSE	
2005	LAA	MLB	30	40	4	1	0	2	4	2	9	0	0	0.2	.189	.231	.378	-.287	.194	.256	.389	.221	-1.1	12-C	0
2006	TBA	MLB	31	165	15	9	0	1	8	14	39	1	2	-0.6	.260	.327	.342	-.161	.264	.340	.354	.243	-1.5	46-C	-3
2007	TBA	MLB	32	115	8	3	0	1	9	6	30	1	0	0.5	.190	.234	.248	-.483	.202	.252	.260	.181	-8.0	32-C	1
2008	TBA	MLB	33	121	10	4	0	1	10	10	27	1	1	-0.1	.216	.284	.303	-.288	.219	.288	.318	.219	-3.0	33-C	0

Breakout: 49% Improve: 57% Collapse: 29% Attrition: 42%   Comparables: Phil Roof, Dixie Howell, Mike Roarke, Mike DiFelice

Paul was Navarro's primary backup in 2007, but never threatened the starter's job during the latter's slow first half because of his own offensive shortcomings and a hyper-extended elbow suffered in a home plate collision in late May that put him on the shelf for a couple of months. Simply being able to catch has kept him in the majors for nine years, and someone will give him at least a spring training invite.

Carlos Peña   1B   Bats: L   Throws: L   Height: 6' 2"   Weight: 215   Born: May 17, 1978   Age: 30

YEAR	TEAM	LVL	AGE	PA	R	2B	3B	HR	RBI	BB	SO	SB	CS	EqBRR	AVG	OBP	SLG	MLVr	EqAVG	EqOBP	EqSLG	EqA	VORP	DEFENSE	
2005	TOL	AAA	27	309	43	17	1	12	45	45	65	3	4	-4.2	.311	.424	.525	.370	.276	.385	.475	.292	17.9	63-1B	-3
2005	DET	MLB	27	295	37	9	0	18	44	31	95	0	1	0.0	.235	.325	.477	.048	.242	.340	.508	.283	8.0	48-1B	-1
2006	COH	AAA	28	462	65	17	0	19	66	63	89	4	0	-1.3	.260	.370	.454	.171	.249	.353	.452	.281	13.2	86-1B	-5
2006	BOS	MLB	28	37	3	2	0	1	3	4	10	0	0	-0.7	.273	.351	.424	.002	.273	.351	.424	.270	0.5		
2007	TBA	MLB	29	612	99	29	1	46	121	103	142	1	0	-1.7	.282	.411	.627	.404	.289	.424	.669	.350	68.5	138-1B	14
2008	TBA	MLB	30	639	92	27	1	33	99	91	148	3	1	-1.3	.259	.372	.500	.140	.263	.377	.525	.308	30.6	149-1B	4

Breakout: 7% Improve: 30% Collapse: 22% Attrition: 10%   Comparables: Carlos Delgado, Fred McGriff, Mike Epstein, Jim Gentile

Scouts always loved Peña, and his numbers in the minors always warmed the hearts of analysts as well. Last year, in his seventh big-league season, it all came together. In the American League, only Alex Rodriguez hit more home runs than Peña, who started the year as a non-roster invitee and ended it in possession of several single-season franchise records. Whether Peña can repeat that monster season at age 30 is anyone's guess; even PECOTA is confused, listing among his top four comps two perennial MVP candidates and two one-dimensional sluggers who had just one big year each, though his actual projection is certainly encouraging. As Agent Rogersz says in *Repo Man*, "It happens sometimes. People just explode."

Fernando Perez   CF   Bats: S   Throws: R   Height: 6' 1"   Weight: 195   Born: April 23, 1983   Age: 25

YEAR	TEAM	LVL	AGE	PA	R	2B	3B	HR	RBI	BB	SO	SB	CS	EqBRR	AVG	OBP	SLG	MLVr	EqAVG	EqOBP	EqSLG	EqA	VORP	DEFENSE	
2005	SWM	A	22	594	93	17	13	6	48	58	80	57	17	3.7	.289	.361	.406	.075	.239	.297	.338	.229	-16.4	128-CF	10
2006	VIS	A+	23	641	123	19	9	4	56	78	134	33	16	-4.4	.307	.398	.397	.103	.233	.313	.309	.226	-18.6	129-CF	8
2007	MNT	AA	24	476	84	24	10	8	33	76	104	32	18	-1.8	.308	.423	.481	.302	.257	.364	.422	.273	20.2	99-CF	9
2008	TBA	MLB	25	535	65	21	6	6	38	52	129	22	7	2.3	.238	.315	.346	-.164	.241	.320	.363	.250	-1.5	126-CF	0

Breakout: 22% Improve: 42% Collapse: 26% Attrition: 11%   Comparables: Donzell McDonald, Tim Raines Jr., Sebastien Boucher, Chris Latham

In another system, Fernando Perez would attract more attention, but in an organization as loaded as Tampa's he's gotten lost in the shuffle. While he's a little old for his level—giving up four full years for an Ivy League education can do that—the Columbia grad runs well, plays a good center, and posts leadoff-worthy on-base percentages. There's no real room for him with the big club right now, however, so this season at Triple-A may serve more as a showcase for other teams than his own.

Jason Pridie   OF   Bats: L   Throws: R   Height: 6' 1"   Weight: 190   Born: October 9, 1983   Age: 24

YEAR	TEAM	LVL	AGE	PA	R	2B	3B	HR	RBI	BB	SO	SB	CS	EqBRR	AVG	OBP	SLG	MLVr	EqAVG	EqOBP	EqSLG	EqA	VORP	DEFENSE			
2005	MNT	AA	21	104	15	4	2	3	8	8	29	5	1	-0.5	.213	.275	.394	-.128	.188	.243	.344	.204	-6.7	25-CF	-2		
2006	MNT	AA	22	503	39	11	4	5	34	31	93	16	5	-0.9	.230	.281	.304	-.146	.217	.261	.303	.201	-33.3	126-CF	-4		
2007	MNT	AA	23	300	42	16	7	4	27	14	45	14	7	-0.6	.290	.331	.441	.099	.261	.293	.408	.241	0.7	36-CF	3	27-LF	3
2007	DUR	AAA	23	274	47	16	4	10	39	22	47	12	3	0.0	.318	.375	.539	.275	.296	.349	.514	.291	21.7	61-CF	8		
2008	MIN	MLB	24	578	65	30	8	10	60	32	115	16	6	1.3	.255	.300	.397	-.111	.257	.304	.419	.254	2.6	135-CF	-2		

Breakout: 46% Improve: 75% Collapse: 8% Attrition: 10%   Comparables: Terrence Long, Mitch Maier, Nic Jackson, Jason Repko

Consistently inconsistent, Pridie's minor league career has been marked by good seasons, bad seasons, and the occasional injury. Last year was his best yet, however, and included a very impressive second half showing in Triple-A. He has speed, some hitting skills, and gap power, and having been sent to the Twins in the Young deal, will now be one of many candidates trying to fill the crater-size hole left by the departure of Torii Hunter.

Ryan Royster — LF

Bats: R Throws: R Height: 6' 2" Weight: 210 Born: July 25, 1986 Age: 21

YEAR	TEAM	LVL	AGE	PA	R	2B	3B	HR	RBI	BB	SO	SB	CS	EqBRR	AVG	OBP	SLG	MLVr	EqAVG	EqOBP	EqSLG	EqA	VORP	DEFENSE			
2005	PRI	Rk	18	203	30	8	0	12	37	13	48	6	0	0.8	.246	.300	.481	.032	.161	.201	.269	.151	-62.9	25-LF	-2	19-RF	-5
2006	HUD	A-	19	249	20	15	1	8	29	9	65	5	2	0.0	.247	.286	.424	.110	.212	.245	.356	.205	-37.7	56-LF	-9		
2007	CGA	A	20	518	90	31	4	30	98	36	121	17	5	-4.9	.329	.380	.601	.445	.245	.288	.445	.249	-8.1	104-LF	6		
2008	TBA	MLB	21	566	54	28	2	16	63	31	165	10	4	-0.4	.227	.273	.380	-.200	.230	.278	.399	.235	-15.6	133-LF	-1		

Breakout: 43% Improve: 63% Collapse: 15% Attrition: 7%   Comparables: Matt Kemp, Jason Fransz, Aaron McNeal, Troy Hughes

Royster seemed to come out of nowhere last year. A fifth-round pick out of an Oregon high school in 2004, he spent three years in short-season ball before the Rays felt he was prepared for a full-season league last year. Boy, was he ready! He nearly won the Sally League Triple Crown while leading the circuit in home runs, slugging, and total bases. He's still a little rough around the edges and needs to tighten his approach, but that was the kind of performance that can't be denied.

Justin Ruggiano — OF

Bats: R Throws: R Height: 6' 2" Weight: 205 Born: April 12, 1982 Age: 26

YEAR	TEAM	LVL	AGE	PA	R	2B	3B	HR	RBI	BB	SO	SB	CS	EqBRR	AVG	OBP	SLG	MLVr	EqAVG	EqOBP	EqSLG	EqA	VORP	DEFENSE			
2005	VRO	A+	23	280	47	15	4	9	37	28	65	16	5	0.5	.310	.400	.517	.294	.236	.312	.408	.251	-4.6	47-RF	-7	18-CF	-1
2005	JAX	AA	23	185	23	10	1	6	29	17	56	8	3	0.6	.342	.422	.528	.411	.223	.297	.410	.244	-5.1	20-LF	-1	15-RF	2
2006	MNT	AA	24	130	25	14	3	4	27	19	29	4	4	-1.3	.333	.442	.630	.562	.270	.372	.568	.303	11.0	27-RF	0		
2006	JAX	AA	24	346	51	18	3	9	45	46	74	10	5	-1.3	.260	.367	.435	.181	.252	.347	.443	.274	6.3	64-RF	-5		
2007	DUR	AAA	25	546	78	29	2	20	73	53	151	26	11	0.3	.309	.386	.502	.232	.246	.325	.439	.263	2.5	74-RF	-2	40-LF	3
2008	TBA	MLB	26	526	63	25	3	15	59	46	144	15	6	1.2	.242	.315	.405	-.087	.246	.320	.425	.262	-0.4	124-RF	-1		

Breakout: 14% Improve: 43% Collapse: 20% Attrition: 20%   Comparables: Prentice Redman, Jason Bay, Jody Hurst, Mark Little

Something of an organizational player entering last year, Ruggiano had a breakout season in Triple-A, but that only upgraded him to marginal prospect. He has some athleticism and power, but also a date of birth and high strikeout rate that make it difficult to see him as an everyday outfielder. He'll return to Triple-A this year and wait for Baldelli to get hurt.

B. J. Upton — CF

Bats: R Throws: R Height: 6' 3" Weight: 185 Born: August 21, 1984 Age: 23

YEAR	TEAM	LVL	AGE	PA	R	2B	3B	HR	RBI	BB	SO	SB	CS	EqBRR	AVG	OBP	SLG	MLVr	EqAVG	EqOBP	EqSLG	EqA	VORP	DEFENSE			
2005	DUR	AAA	20	631	98	36	6	18	74	78	127	44	13	0.8	.303	.392	.490	.192	.269	.357	.438	.278	37.9	130-SS	-18		
2006	DUR	AAA	21	470	72	18	4	8	41	65	89	46	17	1.0	.269	.374	.394	.074	.251	.353	.383	.265	17.5	84-SS	-7	18-3B	-3
2006	TBA	MLB	21	189	20	5	0	1	10	13	40	11	3	0.4	.246	.302	.291	-.291	.249	.312	.289	.224	-7.6	46-3B	-10		
2007	TBA	MLB	22	548	86	25	1	24	82	65	154	22	8	3.8	.300	.386	.508	.229	.311	.402	.552	.317	46.9	75-CF	3	47-2B	-8
2008	TBA	MLB	23	575	88	28	3	18	67	67	133	30	9	1.4	.270	.358	.446	.059	.274	.364	.468	.294	28.5	135-CF	-5		

Breakout: 24% Improve: 55% Collapse: 23% Attrition: 10%   Comparables: Chet Lemon, Jhonny Peralta, Rick Monday, Sixto Lezcano

Last year, the Rays finally gave up hoping that Upton would develop enough defensive consistency to be an infielder, and by taking that pressure off his back, they finally allowed his talent to shine through. Upton not only took to center field with aplomb, but delivered a 20/20 season despite losing a month to a quadriceps strain. If he went 30/30 this year we wouldn't be surprised in the least, but if he hit .300 again, we would be. You just can't hit for a consistent average when you strike out nearly once every three at-bats.

Delmon Young RF Bats: R Throws: R Height: 6' 3" Weight: 215 Born: September 14, 1985 Age: 22

YEAR	TEAM	LVL	AGE	PA	R	2B	3B	HR	RBI	BB	SO	SB	CS	EqBRR	AVG	OBP	SLG	MLVr	EqAVG	EqOBP	EqSLG	EqA	VORP	DEFENSE		
2005	MNT	AA	19	370	59	13	4	20	71	25	66	25	8	0.8	.336	.386	.582	.418	.294	.337	.525	.288	21.0	78-RF	-11	
2005	DUR	AAA	19	234	33	13	3	6	28	4	33	7	4	-0.9	.285	.303	.447	-.028	.256	.275	.401	.228	-7.4	50-RF	-8	
2006	DUR	AAA	20	370	50	22	4	8	59	15	65	22	4	-0.9	.316	.341	.474	.162	.293	.319	.460	.272	7.8	83-RF	-6	
2006	TBA	MLB	20	131	16	9	1	3	10	1	24	2	2	-1.5	.317	.336	.476	.094	.320	.344	.504	.280	5.2	28-RF	-3	
2007	TBA	MLB	21	681	65	38	0	13	93	26	127	10	3	0.4	.288	.316	.408	-.043	.300	.330	.437	.265	5.7	129-RF	-1	28-CF -6
2008	MIN	MLB	22	615	77	35	3	17	84	29	105	14	4	0.2	.294	.329	.458	.048	.295	.333	.483	.282	19.4	144-RF	-3	

Breakout: 40% Improve: 64% Collapse: 18% Attrition: 10% Comparables: Tommy Davis, Vladimir Guerrero, Rocco Baldelli, Larry Parrish

The Marlins/Tigers blockbuster aside, the Delmon Young deal was of a sort you rarely see in baseball. Teams are generally nervous about trading young talent of this pedigree for fear of looking very, very dumb a few years down the road. Yes Young's moody, yes he's overly aggressive at the plate, yes his power hasn't come as expected, but he's also still just 22 and regarded by scouts as one of the best young hitters around. Rays officials are hoping against hope that he fails to live up to PECOTA's Vladimir Guerrero comp (a comparison scouts have made as well) as he heads north to the land of 10,000 lakes.

Ben Zobrist SS Bats: S Throws: R Height: 6' 3" Weight: 200 Born: May 26, 1981 Age: 27

YEAR	TEAM	LVL	AGE	PA	R	2B	3B	HR	RBI	BB	SO	SB	CS	EqBRR	AVG	OBP	SLG	MLVr	EqAVG	EqOBP	EqSLG	EqA	VORP	DEFENSE	
2005	LEX	A	24	310	45	17	2	2	32	47	35	16	5	-2.5	.304	.415	.413	.177	.244	.333	.317	.242	0.1	63-SS	8
2005	SLM	A+	24	180	25	12	1	3	13	37	17	2	1	-1.6	.333	.475	.496	.434	.282	.402	.403	.288	14.0	36-SS	5
2006	CCH	AA	25	381	57	25	6	3	30	55	46	9	5	-3.2	.327	.434	.473	.304	.285	.381	.417	.281	26.9	79-SS	3
2006	DUR	AAA	25	82	12	3	1	0	6	10	9	4	1	-1.0	.304	.400	.377	.114	.271	.370	.343	.262	2.8	18-SS	-6
2006	TBA	MLB	25	198	10	6	2	2	18	10	26	2	3	-0.8	.224	.260	.311	-.358	.227	.270	.315	.202	-9.7	50-SS	2
2007	DUR	AAA	26	276	42	14	2	7	22	43	38	8	3	0.8	.279	.403	.455	.173	.260	.378	.445	.288	19.9	52-SS	4
2007	TBA	MLB	26	105	8	2	0	1	9	3	21	2	0	0.6	.155	.184	.206	-.654	.167	.204	.219	.144	-11.6	26-SS	-6
2008	TBA	MLB	27	360	43	17	2	4	30	37	56	6	3	0.2	.249	.333	.358	-.111	.252	.339	.376	.259	7.0	86-SS	0

Breakout: 30% Improve: 53% Collapse: 23% Attrition: 25% Comparables: Chris Clapinski, Carlos Guillen, D'Angelo Jimenez, Turner Ward

While he's made it pretty clear that he's doesn't deserve a starting shortstop job, Zobrist is still a fundamentally sound defender with good on-base skills who will likely fill Josh Wilson's bench spot next year, but do it better.

PITCHERS

Grant Balfour Bats: R Throws: R Height: 6' 2" Weight: 190 Born: December 30, 1977 Age: 30

YEAR	TEAM	LVL	AGE	W	L	SV	G	GS	IP	H	BB	SO	HR	GB%	BABIP	STUFF	WHIP	ERA	PERA	EqERA	EqH9	EqBB9	EqSO9	EqHR9	VORP	SN/WX
2007	HUN	AA	29	0	0	2	8	0	11¹	8	4	21	0	50.0%	.381	11	1.06	2.39	3.97	3.38	9.3	3.4	11.0	0.0	2.6	—
2007	NAS	AAA	29	1	1	5	24	0	32	17	11	47	2	39.7%	.254	26	0.88	1.69	3.01	2.40	6.0	3.6	9.9	0.6	10.7	—
2007	TBA	MLB	29	1	0	0	22	0	22	26	16	27	1	46.7%	.455	20	1.91	6.14	5.36	5.40	10.0	5.8	10.4	0.4	-0.4	-0.36
2008	TBA	MLB	30	2	2	3	47	0	46	45	29	55	4	43.4%	.343	12	1.61	4.98	4.86	4.72	8.7	5.2	9.6	0.8	2.4	0.20

Breakout: 54% Improve: 80% Collapse: 11% Attrition: 16% Comparables: Doug Bair, Arnold Earley, Joe Boever, Scott Sauerbeck

Now resigned to journeyman status, Balfour missed most of 2005 and 2006 recovering first from Tommy John surgery then repairs to a torn labrum *and* rotator cuff. Finally back in action last year, he dominated in the minors for the Brewers before coming over to Tampa Bay in a deadline deal for perennial disappointment Seth McClung. Whether or not Balfour still has it or not is debatable; his velocity is now no more than average, but he still has that good curveball. The Rays brought him back for 2008 in the hope that his second year back from surgery will be a better one.

Shawn Camp

Bats: R   Throws: R   Height: 6' 1"   Weight: 200   Born: November 18, 1975   Age: 32

YEAR	TEAM	LVL	AGE	W	L	SV	G	GS	IP	H	BB	SO	HR	GB%	BABIP	STUFF	WHIP	ERA	PERA	EqERA	EqH9	EqBB9	EqSO9	EqHR9	VORP	SN/WX
2005	OMA	AAA	29	3	6	1	21	7	67²	71	22	42	9	48.6%	.300	-22	1.37	3.86	5.28	5.06	9.4	3.2	3.8	1.4	3.8	—
2005	KCA	MLB	29	1	4	0	29	0	49	69	13	28	4	56.3%	.369	-10	1.67	6.43	5.42	6.48	11.2	2.3	4.9	0.7	-8.8	-1.39
2006	TBA	MLB	30	7	4	4	75	0	75	93	19	53	9	57.4%	.357	-4	1.49	4.68	5.39	4.81	10.5	2.2	6.2	1.0	7.8	0.75
2007	TBA	MLB	31	0	3	0	50	0	40	63	18	36	7	57.4%	.438	-19	2.03	7.20	9.12	7.30	12.6	3.5	7.3	1.5	-6.3	-0.86
2007	DUR	AAA	31	0	1	4	12	0	15¹	13	2	16	0	61.0%	.325	14	0.98	1.18	3.69	1.88	8.8	1.3	6.9	0.0	5.9	—
2008	TBA	MLB	32	2	2	2	36	0	40	47	13	27	4	52.7%	.325	-6	1.50	4.83	4.83	4.54	10.4	2.7	5.4	1.0	2.6	0.20

Breakout: 43% Improve: 70% Collapse: 16% Attrition: 35%   Comparables: Chuck Taylor, Ken Burkhart, Matt Whiteside, Travis Driskill

At least Camp was resilient last year; he made 50 appearances by the end of July before being mercifully sent back to the minors. Even in an organization desperate for bullpen arms, Camp is probably not going to get another chance, and the only reason he got such an extended one in the first place was that there was simply nobody else available.

Wade Davis

Bats: R   Throws: R   Height: 6' 5"   Weight: 220   Born: September 7, 1985   Age: 22

YEAR	TEAM	LVL	AGE	W	L	SV	G	GS	IP	H	BB	SO	HR	GB%	BABIP	STUFF	WHIP	ERA	PERA	EqERA	EqH9	EqBB9	EqSO9	EqHR9	VORP	SN/WX
2005	HUD	A-	19	7	4	0	15	15	86	75	23	97	5	56.1%	.320	-6	1.14	2.72	7.84	7.29	11.6	5.6	5.1	1.9	-13.2	—
2006	SWM	A	20	7	12	0	27	27	146²	124	64	165	5	50.1%	.330	8	1.29	3.02	7.11	6.62	10.9	7.4	6.1	1.1	-13.6	—
2007	VRO	A+	21	3	0	0	13	13	78¹	54	21	88	5	50.0%	.268	20	0.96	1.84	4.30	3.53	7.3	3.7	6.8	1.3	16.4	—
2007	MNT	AA	21	7	3	0	14	14	80	74	30	81	3	50.7%	.333	18	1.30	3.15	5.03	5.47	10.1	3.9	6.2	0.6	1.1	—
2008	TBA	MLB	22	7	10	0	26	26	141²	161	77	105	17	48.7%	.322	6	1.68	5.59	5.63	5.29	10.0	4.4	6.0	1.1	-3.2	0.80

Breakout: 21% Improve: 47% Collapse: 29% Attrition: 16%   Comparables: Jason Bell, Rod Henderson, Curt Lyons, Adam Miller

Davis is one of the true studs in the Rays' system, and some in the organization think he's their best, better even than last year's number-one overall draft pick David Price. Davis is a pure power pitcher with a big frame, a big fastball in the mid-90s, and a hammer curve that grades out even better than the heater. His command is average, and his changeup is spotty, but he's young, has room for improvement, and projects as a well-above-average starter with All-Star possibilities.

Scott Dohmann

Bats: R   Throws: R   Height: 6' 1"   Weight: 200   Born: February 13, 1978   Age: 30

YEAR	TEAM	LVL	AGE	W	L	SV	G	GS	IP	H	BB	SO	HR	GB%	BABIP	STUFF	WHIP	ERA	PERA	EqERA	EqH9	EqBB9	EqSO9	EqHR9	VORP	SN/WX
2005	CSP	AAA	27	2	1	1	34	0	39	41	16	53	5	41.3%	.375	5	1.46	4.38	5.71	4.34	9.9	4.1	8.9	1.2	5.2	—
2005	COL	MLB	27	2	1	0	32	0	31	33	19	35	6	33.7%	.325	5	1.68	6.10	5.66	5.40	8.8	4.8	9.1	1.7	-0.9	-0.21
2006	COL	MLB	28	1	1	1	27	0	24²	26	15	22	4	36.5%	.324	-5	1.66	6.19	5.35	5.76	9.0	4.7	7.2	1.1	-0.8	0.22
2006	KCA	MLB	28	1	3	0	21	0	23²	33	18	22	5	49.3%	.412	-14	2.15	7.97	11.31	8.87	12.5	6.9	8.5	1.6	-4.6	-0.91
2007	DUR	AAA	29	4	1	5	37	0	48²	37	13	48	2	46.9%	.282	8	1.03	2.03	3.74	3.20	8.0	2.8	6.8	0.6	12.0	—
2007	TBA	MLB	29	3	0	0	31	0	32²	29	18	26	3	41.3%	.310	3	1.44	3.30	3.65	2.84	7.1	4.5	6.8	0.9	8.7	1.12
2008	TBA	MLB	30	2	2	2	49	0	49	51	24	43	6	42.0%	.310	0	1.52	4.71	4.83	4.36	9.1	4.0	7.1	1.1	4.4	0.30

Breakout: 32% Improve: 49% Collapse: 23% Attrition: 22%   Comparables: Turk Wendell, John Wyatt, Mike Hartley, Larry Sherry

Unlike some of the other organizational arms who got a chance in last year's bullpen, Dohmann actually acquitted himself pretty well. He's no great shakes, mind you, but he's one of those guys with a fastball, a slider, and a pretty good idea of what to do with them, which gives him between one and three more tools than most of the dreck Tampa threw out there last year.

Gary Glover

Bats: R   Throws: R   Height: 6' 5"   Weight: 225   Born: December 3, 1976   Age: 31

YEAR	TEAM	LVL	AGE	W	L	SV	G	GS	IP	H	BB	SO	HR	GB%	BABIP	STUFF	WHIP	ERA	PERA	EqERA	EqH9	EqBB9	EqSO9	EqHR9	VORP	SN/WX
2005	NAS	AAA	28	6	4	1	17	16	92	91	29	75	9	46.3%	.305	1	1.30	3.03	4.67	4.15	9.1	3.2	5.2	1.0	14.0	—
2005	MIL	MLB	28	5	4	0	15	11	64²	74	20	58	10	43.1%	.339	3	1.45	5.56	5.96	5.97	10.5	2.6	7.4	1.4	-1.0	0.75
2006	YOM	JP	29	5	7	0	20	18	96	125	23	63	13	—	.349	-26	1.54	4.97	8.04	7.38	12.5	2.9	4.7	1.5	-17.6	—
2007	TBA	MLB	30	6	5	2	67	0	77¹	87	27	51	12	39.6%	.314	-14	1.47	4.89	4.55	4.04	8.7	2.8	5.4	1.4	7.4	0.68
2008	TBA	MLB	31	2	3	2	31	2	45	50	17	32	6	42.5%	.308	-5	1.47	4.84	4.77	4.49	9.7	3.0	5.7	1.1	3.2	0.30

Breakout: 38% Improve: 59% Collapse: 25% Attrition: 41%   Comparables: Doug Brocail, Bill Dawley, Edwin Nuñez, Steve Crawford

Stop us if you've heard this one before: Glover is a righty in his early 30s who was bouncing around from team to team before lading in the Rays' bullpen last year. Because Glover was simply bad, as opposed to awful, he led the team in relief appearances and innings and got a one-year deal for a return engagement. He has enough stuff to be a decent bullpen arm, but a tendency to work up in the zone and give up too many extra-base hits has always been his downfall, and at his age, that's not going to change.

Jason Hammel

Bats: R   Throws: R   Height: 6' 6"   Weight: 220   Born: September 2, 1982   Age: 25

YEAR	TEAM	LVL	AGE	W	L	SV	G	GS	IP	H	BB	SO	HR	GB%	BABIP	STUFF	WHIP	ERA	PERA	EqERA	EqH9	EqBB9	EqSO9	EqHR9	VORP	SN/WX
2005	MNT	AA	22	8	2	0	12	12	81¹	70	19	76	5	43.6%	.300	11	1.09	2.66	4.30	3.84	8.5	2.8	5.5	1.1	14.7	—
2005	DUR	AAA	22	3	2	0	10	10	54²	57	27	48	8	45.0%	.306	-1	1.54	4.11	5.98	5.37	9.2	5.2	5.5	1.6	1.3	—
2006	DUR	AAA	23	5	9	0	24	24	127¹	133	36	117	11	47.8%	.335	-1	1.33	4.25	5.37	5.70	9.9	3.2	6.0	1.2	-1.4	—
2006	TBA	MLB	23	0	6	0	9	9	44	61	21	32	7	42.9%	.375	-8	1.86	7.77	7.31	7.42	11.5	3.9	6.2	1.2	-8.4	-0.27
2007	DUR	AAA	24	4	5	0	13	13	76¹	61	28	75	3	50.7%	.283	19	1.17	3.42	4.01	4.35	8.3	3.7	6.6	0.6	10.0	—
2007	TBA	MLB	24	3	5	0	24	14	85	100	40	64	12	41.4%	.333	-6	1.64	6.14	5.06	5.00	9.2	3.6	6.2	1.3	-1.7	0.91
2008	TBA	MLB	25	6	8	0	33	18	116¹	127	50	86	14	44.5%	.310	3	1.52	5.05	5.02	4.73	9.6	3.5	6.0	1.1	4.8	1.20

Breakout: 27% Improve: 59% Collapse: 16% Attrition: 19%   Comparables: Alan Benes, Dan Wright, Tommy Greene, Steve Trachsel

For the second straight season, Hammel pitched very well at Triple-A, then got shelled in the big leagues. Can the dreaded Quadruple-A label be far off? Though his stuff is above average, Hammel is primarily a strike-thrower, and once big-league hitters started smacking those strikes around a bit, he became too careful and began falling behind in counts, which forced him to throw fatter strikes, which got smacked around, and so forth. There's still some talent here, but he'll need to make some adjustments for it to pay off.

Jeremy Hellickson

Bats: R   Throws: R   Height: 6' 1"   Weight: 185   Born: April 8, 1987   Age: 21

YEAR	TEAM	LVL	AGE	W	L	SV	G	GS	IP	H	BB	SO	HR	GB%	BABIP	STUFF	WHIP	ERA	PERA	EqERA	EqH9	EqBB9	EqSO9	EqHR9	VORP	SN/WX
2006	HUD	A-	19	4	3	0	15	14	77	55	16	96	3	55.8%	.280	10	0.92	2.45	6.25	5.94	9.7	4.6	6.1	1.8	-2.5	—
2007	CGA	A	20	13	3	0	21	21	111¹	87	34	106	7	44.2%	.273	0	1.09	2.67	5.68	5.12	9.5	4.8	4.9	1.3	5.2	—
2008	TBA	MLB	21	5	10	0	33	22	126¹	154	78	80	22	44.5%	.319	-10	1.83	6.46	6.67	6.03	10.7	5.0	5.1	1.6	-13.3	-0.60

Breakout: 11% Improve: 37% Collapse: 32% Attrition: 12%   Comparables: Ricky Nolasco, Gaby Hernandez, Carey Paige, Ryan Hawblitzel

Hellickson took an extra year to make his full-season debut, as his home state of Iowa isn't exactly known for producing polished talent, but he turned out to be just that in 2007, showing outstanding command and control of a low-90s fastball that is currently his bread and butter pitch (both his curveball and changeup are more usable than good). Between that and his size, it's hard to see future stardom in him, but only an injury will keep him from getting to the big leagues.

J. P. Howell

Bats: L   Throws: L   Height: 6' 0"   Weight: 180   Born: April 25, 1983   Age: 25

YEAR	TEAM	LVL	AGE	W	L	SV	G	GS	IP	H	BB	SO	HR	GB%	BABIP	STUFF	WHIP	ERA	PERA	EqERA	EqH9	EqBB9	EqSO9	EqHR9	VORP	SN/WX
2005	HDS	A+	22	3	1	0	8	8	46	33	24	48	2	68.7%	.274	14	1.24	1.96	4.35	4.01	6.5	6.5	5.5	0.6	7.5	—
2005	WIC	AA	22	2	0	0	3	3	18	12	5	23	2	63.4%	.256	16	0.94	2.50	4.30	3.31	7.2	3.9	8.3	1.7	4.1	—
2005	OMA	AAA	22	3	1	0	7	7	37²	40	19	29	1	56.6%	.355	4	1.56	4.06	4.85	5.05	9.8	4.8	4.8	0.3	2.2	—
2005	KCA	MLB	22	3	5	0	15	15	72²	73	39	54	9	54.1%	.299	8	1.54	6.19	4.42	5.74	7.8	4.6	6.4	1.0	-7.9	0.05
2006	OMA	AAA	23	3	2	0	8	8	36²	39	14	33	3	61.1%	.360	0	1.46	4.72	5.77	5.35	10.7	4.0	6.1	1.1	0.9	—
2006	DUR	AAA	23	5	3	0	10	10	55¹	53	15	49	2	49.4%	.333	15	1.23	2.61	4.48	3.55	9.4	3.2	6.0	0.5	11.5	—
2006	TBA	MLB	23	1	3	0	8	8	42¹	52	14	33	4	46.7%	.366	13	1.56	5.11	5.23	5.01	10.5	2.8	6.8	0.9	3.5	0.91
2007	DUR	AAA	24	7	8	0	21	21	128	110	34	145	16	54.3%	.295	3	1.13	3.38	5.31	5.53	9.2	2.8	7.8	1.6	0.9	—
2007	TBA	MLB	24	1	6	0	10	10	51	69	21	49	8	46.2%	.381	4	1.76	7.59	6.04	6.88	10.4	3.2	7.5	1.3	-11.5	0.03
2008	TBA	MLB	25	8	10	1	40	26	152²	158	60	130	15	49.2%	.313	13	1.42	4.55	4.42	4.30	9.1	3.2	6.8	0.9	14.5	2.50

Breakout: 55% Improve: 81% Collapse: 5% Attrition: 11%   Comparables: Tom Underwood, Ken Holtzman, Jim O'Toole, Casey Fossum

Howell has struck out more than a batter per inning during his minor league career, but he's now been given 33 big-league starts and has a 6.34 ERA to show for it. He's a classic Quadruple-A pitcher, as his combination of an excellent curve but below-average velocity just doesn't work in the big leagues. Major league hitters can lay off a good breaking ball, and if you have nothing else to back it up, they're going to work the count, sit dead red, and hit you hard.

Edwin Jackson

Bats: R   Throws: R   Height: 6' 3"   Weight: 210   Born: September 9, 1983   Age: 24

YEAR	TEAM	LVL	AGE	W	L	SV	G	GS	IP	H	BB	SO	HR	GB%	BABIP	STUFF	WHIP	ERA	PERA	EqERA	EqH9	EqBB9	EqSO9	EqHR9	VORP	SN/WX
2005	JAX	AA	21	6	4	0	11	11	62	52	18	44	7	47.7%	.249	-12	1.13	3.48	5.55	6.14	9.1	3.4	4.0	1.9	-3.3	—
2005	LVG	AAA	21	3	7	0	12	11	55¹	76	37	33	13	37.6%	.339	-35	2.04	8.63	9.50	10.10	11.4	6.1	3.3	2.2	-27.2	—
2005	LAN	MLB	21	2	2	0	7	6	28²	31	17	13	2	33.0%	.293	-13	1.67	6.27	4.98	6.83	9.6	4.7	3.7	0.6	-4.6	0.06
2006	DUR	AAA	22	3	7	5	22	13	73¹	84	35	66	7	47.6%	.352	-13	1.63	5.54	6.85	7.84	10.9	5.1	5.8	1.3	-17.4	—
2006	TBA	MLB	22	0	0	0	23	1	36¹	42	25	27	2	52.1%	.348	2	1.84	5.45	4.89	6.08	9.5	5.6	6.1	0.5	-2.4	-0.59
2007	TBA	MLB	23	5	15	0	32	31	161	195	88	128	19	46.0%	.349	4	1.76	5.76	5.03	5.27	9.3	4.2	6.3	1.0	-8.4	1.47
2008	TBA	MLB	24	5	8	0	29	18	112¹	123	56	85	13	48.2%	.317	4	1.59	5.33	5.20	5.04	9.6	4.1	6.1	1.0	0.6	0.80

Breakout: 36% Improve: 61% Collapse: 24% Attrition: 32%   Comparables: Matt Keough, Herm Wehmeier, Jaret Wright, Livan Hernandez

It's been more than four years since Jackson was one of the top pitching prospects in the game and out-pitched Randy Johnson in his big-league debut on his 20th birthday. He's done little since, and remains one of the game's mysteries. He still flashes mid-90s heat and a hard slider with two-plane break, and he still has flashes of greatness, like his four-hit shutout against Texas in August. Considering his youth and stuff, the Rays can afford to give him some more chances, but their rotation is going to get crowded fast, so his time to make good is running out.

Scott Kazmir

Bats: L   Throws: L   Height: 6' 0"   Weight: 190   Born: January 24, 1984   Age: 24

YEAR	TEAM	LVL	AGE	W	L	SV	G	GS	IP	H	BB	SO	HR	GB%	BABIP	STUFF	WHIP	ERA	PERA	EqERA	EqH9	EqBB9	EqSO9	EqHR9	VORP	SN/WX
2005	TBA	MLB	21	10	9	0	32	32	186	172	100	174	12	41.6%	.316	39	1.46	3.77	3.96	3.97	7.9	4.8	8.2	0.5	29.4	4.46
2006	TBA	MLB	22	10	8	0	24	24	144²	132	52	163	15	42.7%	.314	43	1.27	3.23	3.41	3.20	7.4	3.0	9.3	0.8	38.7	4.80
2007	TBA	MLB	23	13	9	0	34	34	206²	196	89	239	18	43.8%	.339	40	1.38	3.48	3.54	3.22	7.5	3.4	9.4	0.8	47.2	5.51
2008	TBA	MLB	24	12	9	0	29	29	189¹	168	77	194	17	43.8%	.297	31	1.29	3.58	3.63	3.33	7.8	3.3	8.3	0.8	40.7	5.70

Breakout: 23% Improve: 45% Collapse: 11% Attrition: 6%   Comparables: Curt Simmons, Johnny Antonelli, Jon Matlack, Al Downing

Last year was when we stopped talking about Scott Kazmir as a potential ace, because he simply started pitching like one. He's going to get even better. He went over 200 innings for the first time in his career last year, but showed no signs of fatigue, putting up a 2.39 ERA after the All-Star break and striking out 45 over 31 innings in his last five starts. He's a real ace now, and a potential Cy Young candidate.

Chris Mason

Bats: R   Throws: R   Height: 6' 0"   Weight: 185   Born: July 1, 1984   Age: 24

YEAR	TEAM	LVL	AGE	W	L	SV	G	GS	IP	H	BB	SO	HR	GB%	BABIP	STUFF	WHIP	ERA	PERA	EqERA	EqH9	EqBB9	EqSO9	EqHR9	VORP	SN/WX
2005	SWM	A	22	1	0	0	10	0	18²	17	5	16	0	50.9%	.321	-5	1.18	1.44	5.18	6.06	10.5	3.9	4.4	0.6	-0.8	—
2005	HUD	A-	22	1	1	2	9	0	15	11	8	14	0	57.9%	.306	-9	1.27	2.40	6.29	5.11	8.8	9.5	3.6	0.7	0.7	—
2006	VIS	A+	23	12	10	0	28	27	152¹	177	44	111	17	53.6%	.330	-34	1.45	5.03	8.02	7.76	12.2	4.0	3.6	1.9	-33.1	—
2007	MNT	AA	24	15	4	0	28	28	161¹	147	44	136	7	52.1%	.300	13	1.18	2.57	4.64	4.08	9.6	2.9	5.0	0.7	25.3	—
2008	TBA	MLB	23	6	10	0	33	23	138²	175	58	78	18	50.9%	.328	-5	1.67	5.80	5.85	5.46	11.0	3.4	4.5	1.2	-6.1	0.30

Breakout: 16% Improve: 43% Collapse: 30% Attrition: 13%   Comparables: Mitch Talbot, Ricky Stone, Ryan Hawblitzel, Lance Broadway

Mason led the Southern League in wins and ERA in 2007 and finished fourth in strikeouts, but he just doesn't compare to the elite arms in the Rays' system. As a pitcher, he's something of an artist as he keeps the ball down and hitters off balance by adding and subtracting to his fastball in order to set up a very good changeup and keeps all of his pitches in the strike zone. In other organizations, he'd project as a fourth or fifth starter, but given the coming flood of arms in this one, he'll be forced to the bullpen.

Jacob McGee

Bats: L   Throws: L   Height: 6' 3"   Weight: 190   Born: August 6, 1986   Age: 21

YEAR	TEAM	LVL	AGE	W	L	SV	G	GS	IP	H	BB	SO	HR	GB%	BABIP	STUFF	WHIP	ERA	PERA	EqERA	EqH9	EqBB9	EqSO9	EqHR9	VORP	SN/WX
2005	HUD	A-	18	5	4	0	15	14	76²	64	23	89	4	41.3%	.316	7	1.13	3.64	7.44	7.36	11.1	6.1	5.3	1.7	-12.2	—
2006	SWM	A	19	7	9	0	26	26	134	103	65	171	7	44.9%	.311	9	1.25	2.96	7.07	6.51	10.0	8.0	6.9	1.5	-11.3	—
2007	VRO	A+	20	5	4	0	21	21	116²	86	39	145	8	43.1%	.289	23	1.07	2.93	4.75	4.79	8.0	4.5	7.7	1.3	9.6	—
2007	MNT	AA	20	3	2	0	5	5	23¹	19	13	30	2	42.5%	.316	21	1.37	4.25	6.02	5.57	9.4	5.6	8.1	1.3	0.1	—
2008	TBA	MLB	21	6	9	0	31	21	128	134	75	115	18	42.3%	.314	9	1.63	5.19	5.47	4.84	9.2	4.8	7.2	1.3	4.2	1.30

Breakout: 33% Improve: 65% Collapse: 15% Attrition: 14%   Comparables: Terrell Wade, Kyle Davies, Bruce Chen, Pat Mahomes

McGee is one of the system's elite arms, and you don't need more than two hands to count the number of left-handers who can match his velocity, which reaches 96 mph nearly every time out. His lack of secondary stuff could hinder his development as a starter, but there are no plans to move him right now. Still, the organization certainly needs some bullpen help, and McGee has closer possibilities.

Jeff Niemann

Bats: R Throws: R Height: 6' 9" Weight: 280 Born: February 28, 1983 Age: 25

YEAR	TEAM	LVL	AGE	W	L	SV	G	GS	IP	H	BB	SO	HR	GB%	BABIP	STUFF	WHIP	ERA	PERA	EqERA	EqH9	EqBB9	EqSO9	EqHR9	VORP	SN/WX
2005	VIS	A+	22	0	1	0	5	5	20¹	12	10	28	3	38.6%	.220	15	1.08	3.99	4.75	5.21	5.7	6.2	7.6	1.9	0.8	—
2005	MNT	AA	22	0	1	0	6	3	10¹	7	5	14	0	45.8%	.292	5	1.17	4.37	3.76	7.71	7.7	4.8	8.7	0.0	-2.2	—
2006	MNT	AA	23	5	5	0	14	14	77²	56	29	84	6	45.7%	.255	6	1.10	2.68	4.89	4.25	8.4	3.9	6.8	1.4	10.8	—
2007	DUR	AAA	24	12	6	0	25	25	131	144	46	123	13	42.8%	.342	-9	1.45	3.98	6.99	6.27	11.6	3.7	6.3	1.3	-9.1	—
2008	TBA	MLB	25	5	8	0	26	18	108²	123	54	85	15	44.4%	.321	3	1.62	5.61	5.57	5.26	9.9	4.0	6.3	1.2	-2.1	0.50

Breakout: 33% Improve: 60% Collapse: 16% Attrition: 19% Comparables: John Patterson, Jeff Juden, Todd Van Poppel, Mark Redman

Last year, for the first time in his professional career, Niemann stayed healthy for the majority of a season. Unfortunately, he didn't pitch especially well. It seems the Rice product's constant injuries have had a negative effect on his stuff. He's still going to be a big-league starter, but his star has dimmed greatly since the Rays made him the fourth overall pick in the 2004 draft.

Chad Orvella

Bats: R Throws: R Height: 5' 11" Weight: 195 Born: October 1, 1980 Age: 27

YEAR	TEAM	LVL	AGE	W	L	SV	G	GS	IP	H	BB	SO	HR	GB%	BABIP	STUFF	WHIP	ERA	PERA	EqERA	EqH9	EqBB9	EqSO9	EqHR9	VORP	SN/WX
2005	MNT	AA	24	0	0	9	16	0	25	15	6	29	0	42.6%	.250	15	0.84	0.36	2.98	1.54	5.8	2.7	6.9	0.4	10.5	—
2005	TBA	MLB	24	3	3	1	37	0	50	47	23	43	4	34.6%	.299	6	1.38	3.60	3.67	4.06	7.8	3.9	7.2	0.7	6.8	0.81
2006	DUR	AAA	25	4	0	1	27	0	38¹	31	9	55	2	37.1%	.337	23	1.05	1.89	3.88	3.47	8.2	2.7	9.7	0.7	8.6	—
2006	TBA	MLB	25	1	5	0	22	0	24¹	36	20	17	6	37.8%	.370	-26	2.30	7.41	11.02	8.64	11.9	6.8	5.8	1.8	-6.5	-0.77
2007	DUR	AAA	26	3	3	20	42	0	52	39	19	53	6	42.6%	.250	-8	1.12	3.12	4.49	4.32	7.7	3.6	6.8	1.4	7.1	—
2007	TBA	MLB	26	0	2	0	10	0	8	18	10	6	3	43.6%	.417	-65	3.50	14.63	21.38	19.80	15.3	8.1	5.4	2.7	-10.8	-0.95
2008	TBA	MLB	27	2	3	3	53	0	51	53	25	42	7	41.5%	.299	-4	1.53	5.11	5.03	4.75	9.1	4.1	6.6	1.3	2.1	0.20

Breakout: 62% Improve: 75% Collapse: 11% Attrition: 15% Comparables: Luis Vizcaino, Mike Crudale, Brad Clontz, Lee Gronkiewicz

In the spring of 2006, Orvella went into camp with an honest shot at the Rays' closer job. Now, he's drifting toward the fringes of the organization. One statistic really pops out when looking at Orvella's record: in 201 2/3 minor league innings, he's walked only 45 batters; in 82 1/3 major league frames, he's issued 53 free passes. That's called pitching scared, and it's how ERAs end up in the double-digits and prospects are quickly forgotten.

David Price

Bats: L Throws: L Height: 6' 6" Weight: 225 Born: August 26, 1985 Age: 22

YEAR	TEAM	LVL	AGE	W	L	SV	G	GS	IP	H	BB	SO	HR	GB%	BABIP	STUFF	WHIP	ERA	PERA	EqERA	EqH9	EqBB9	EqSO9	EqHR9	VORP	SN/WX
2008	TBA	MLB	22	6	12	0	27	27	147²	177	79	95	20	46.9%	.322	-1	1.73	6.22	6.04	5.88	10.5	4.4	5.2	1.2	-13.8	-0.30

Breakout: NA Improve: NA Collapse: NA Attrition: NA Comparables: Mark Mulder, Paul Wilson, Mark Prior, Dewon Brazelton

The first overall pick last June, Price is believed to be a superior talent to former Tiger/current Marlins prospect Andrew Miller, another big, power college lefty who was considered the top talent in the 2006 draft. Price doesn't have as much juice on his fastball as Miller, but he has plenty, his slider is better, and his command is head and shoulders above Miller's. He could move very quickly and be a rotation stalwart alongside Kazmir, James Shields, and Matt Garza by 2009.

Al Reyes

Bats: R Throws: R Height: 6' 1" Weight: 210 Born: April 10, 1970 Age: 38

YEAR	TEAM	LVL	AGE	W	L	SV	G	GS	IP	H	BB	SO	HR	GB%	BABIP	STUFF	WHIP	ERA	PERA	EqERA	EqH9	EqBB9	EqSO9	EqHR9	VORP	SN/WX
2005	SLN	MLB	35	4	2	3	65	0	62²	38	20	67	5	36.8%	.231	24	0.93	2.15	2.73	2.36	5.8	2.7	9.0	0.7	23.2	2.72
2007	TBA	MLB	37	2	4	26	61	0	60²	49	21	70	13	21.7%	.248	5	1.15	4.89	3.43	4.08	5.9	2.7	9.0	1.8	5.6	2.56
2008	TBA	MLB	38	3	4	21	41	0	49¹	43	15	51	7	31.5%	.272	11	1.18	3.72	3.61	3.38	7.6	2.6	8.3	1.4	10.1	1.50

Breakout: 30% Improve: 55% Collapse: 22% Attrition: 17% Comparables: Bob Patterson, Troy Percival, Russ Springer, Aurelio Lopez

Reyes's peripherals were far superior to his ERA last year and far more reflective of his closer status. The problem for the Rays is that Reyes is a temporary fix; he'll be 37 in the season's second week, and by the time they're any good (and that's not too far away), he'll be pushing 40. The Rays almost dealt Reyes at last year's trading deadline, but they picked up his option for 2008, possibly in search of four more good months out of the pen and some better offers in July.

Jae Kuk Ryu

Bats: R   Throws: R   Height: 6' 3"   Weight: 220   Born: May 30, 1983   Age: 25

YEAR	TEAM	LVL	AGE	W	L	SV	G	GS	IP	H	BB	SO	HR	GB%	BABIP	STUFF	WHIP	ERA	PERA	EqERA	EqH9	EqBB9	EqSO9	EqHR9	VORP	SN/WX
2005	WTN	AA	22	11	8	0	27	27	169²	154	49	133	12	47.2%	.295	-4	1.20	3.34	5.06	4.97	9.4	3.3	4.6	1.2	10.8	—
2006	IOW	AAA	23	8	8	0	24	23	139	123	51	114	12	52.1%	.282	4	1.25	3.24	4.30	3.95	8.2	3.6	5.3	1.1	24.6	—
2006	CHN	MLB	23	0	1	0	10	1	15	23	6	17	7	40.4%	.381	-21	1.93	8.40	16.31	10.91	13.2	2.9	8.6	3.4	-3.6	-0.56
2007	DUR	AAA	24	5	4	0	14	14	71¹	67	21	67	5	51.9%	.305	6	1.23	4.04	4.89	5.64	9.8	3.1	6.3	0.9	-0.3	—
2007	TBA	MLB	24	1	2	0	17	0	23¹	31	11	14	2	50.6%	.367	-17	1.80	7.34	6.06	6.26	11.0	3.9	5.1	0.8	-3.5	-0.70
2008	TBA	MLB	25	4	6	0	34	10	86	97	36	60	11	48.5%	.314	-2	1.54	5.21	5.14	4.90	9.9	3.4	5.7	1.1	2.1	0.60

Breakout: 33% Improve: 59% Collapse: 23% Attrition: 24%   Comparables: Vicente Padilla, Rodrigo Lopez, Juan Dominguez, John Stephens

Since being lured out of his native South Korea as a teenager with a seven-figure contract from the Cubs, Ryu has become best known for the April 2003 incident in which he purposely knocked an osprey from its perch with a ball, ultimately killing the bird and earning himself a demotion, a lot of bad press, and a few death threats. At this point, that may be his legacy. Back in the day, when Ryu's age began with a one instead of a two, he could dial up low- to mid-90s fastballs, but he's never been the same since some 2004 elbow problems and is now reduced to being a finesse pitcher without enough finesse. Karma's a bitch.

Juan Salas

Bats: R   Throws: R   Height: 6' 2"   Weight: 230   Born: November 7, 1978   Age: 29

YEAR	TEAM	LVL	AGE	W	L	SV	G	GS	IP	H	BB	SO	HR	GB%	BABIP	STUFF	WHIP	ERA	PERA	EqERA	EqH9	EqBB9	EqSO9	EqHR9	VORP	SN/WX
2005	VIS	A+	26	2	1	1	25	0	38¹	30	18	47	6	45.3%	.279	-10	1.25	3.52	5.69	5.05	7.3	6.1	6.6	2.0	2.2	—
2005	MNT	AA	26	1	0	0	15	0	22	25	12	18	2	54.2%	.333	-23	1.68	3.68	7.85	6.64	11.5	5.8	4.4	1.3	-2.3	—
2006	MNT	AA	27	3	0	14	23	0	34¹	13	14	52	0	56.1%	.197	24	0.79	0.00	2.69	2.43	4.6	4.1	9.2	0.3	11.7	—
2006	DUR	AAA	27	1	1	3	27	0	28²	15	11	33	3	44.1%	.185	4	0.92	1.60	3.28	2.22	4.8	3.8	7.3	1.3	10.6	—
2006	TBA	MLB	27	0	0	0	8	0	10	13	3	8	1	43.2%	.343	-4	1.60	5.40	4.21	5.73	9.8	2.5	5.7	0.8	-0.2	0.08
2007	TBA	MLB	28	1	1	1	34	0	36¹	36	17	26	7	31.7%	.259	-12	1.49	3.72	4.23	3.43	7.1	3.4	5.5	1.6	5.2	0.02
2008	TBA	MLB	29	2	2	2	42	0	45²	44	23	38	6	40.5%	.285	-2	1.45	4.53	4.63	4.18	8.4	4.0	6.6	1.2	5.1	0.40

Breakout: 20% Improve: 44% Collapse: 31% Attrition: 36%   Comparables: Steve Montgomery, Dave Tobik, Mike Armstrong, Dan Naulty

In many ways, Salas is still learning on the job, which can be tough when you're 29 years old. A converted third baseman, he didn't start pitching until the end of 2004. He has one excellent pitch, a mid-90s fastball with plenty of movement, but everything else is still a work in progress, including his slider and his command. He could have late-inning possibilities with just a small amount of improvement in those last two areas.

James Shields

Bats: R   Throws: R   Height: 6' 4"   Weight: 215   Born: December 20, 1981   Age: 26

YEAR	TEAM	LVL	AGE	W	L	SV	G	GS	IP	H	BB	SO	HR	GB%	BABIP	STUFF	WHIP	ERA	PERA	EqERA	EqH9	EqBB9	EqSO9	EqHR9	VORP	SN/WX
2005	MNT	AA	23	7	5	0	17	16	109¹	95	31	104	6	50.5%	.318	10	1.15	2.80	4.45	4.02	8.7	3.2	5.6	1.0	17.7	—
2006	DUR	AAA	24	3	2	0	10	10	61¹	60	6	64	3	53.3%	.352	25	1.08	2.65	4.25	4.29	9.7	1.3	7.1	0.8	8.3	—
2006	TBA	MLB	24	6	8	0	21	21	124²	141	38	104	18	43.8%	.334	13	1.44	4.84	4.76	4.43	9.4	2.5	7.0	1.2	14.6	2.17
2007	TBA	MLB	25	12	8	0	31	31	215	202	36	184	28	45.3%	.287	22	1.11	3.85	3.11	3.14	7.0	1.3	6.9	1.1	45.4	5.76
2008	TBA	MLB	26	11	10	0	29	29	184²	194	49	147	22	45.3%	.306	19	1.31	4.30	4.20	4.02	9.2	2.1	6.4	1.1	23.2	3.90

Breakout: 7%   Improve: 27% Collapse: 33% Attrition: 17%   Comparables: Danny Haren, Jim Bunning, Tom Bradley, Dustin Hermanson

Shields is the exception among all of the young pitchers who have made it to Tampa Bay only to fail. His approach illustrates the difference between command and control; sure, he throws all three of his solid pitches for strikes (control), but he also works all four quadrants of the zone (command) and seems to put every pitch exactly where he wants it and exactly where the hitter doesn't. Lost in his fine performance last year was the team's intelligent decision to shut him down after 215 innings with nothing left to play for. That's proof that the Rays are not only thinking about the future, but that they just plain get it.

Andy Sonnanstine

Bats: L   Throws: R   Height: 6' 3"   Weight: 185   Born: March 18, 1983   Age: 25

YEAR	TEAM	LVL	AGE	W	L	SV	G	GS	IP	H	BB	SO	HR	GB%	BABIP	STUFF	WHIP	ERA	PERA	EqERA	EqH9	EqBB9	EqSO9	EqHR9	VORP	SN/WX
2005	SWM	A	22	10	4	0	18	18	116²	103	11	103	10	44.6%	.281	-10	0.98	2.54	5.92	5.33	10.7	2.0	4.9	1.7	3.0	—
2005	VIS	A+	22	4	1	0	10	10	64	71	7	75	5	34.4%	.375	13	1.22	3.80	5.39	5.03	10.8	2.1	6.4	1.1	3.7	—
2006	MNT	AA	23	15	8	0	28	28	185¹	151	34	153	15	45.0%	.276	-2	1.00	2.67	4.84	4.67	9.3	2.1	5.1	1.4	17.3	—
2007	DUR	AAA	24	6	4	0	11	11	71	60	13	66	8	47.8%	.275	7	1.03	2.66	4.56	4.03	8.9	2.0	6.3	1.5	11.7	—
2007	TBA	MLB	24	6	10	0	22	22	130²	151	26	97	18	39.9%	.333	9	1.35	5.85	4.23	4.77	8.9	1.6	6.1	1.2	0.2	1.24
2008	TBA	MLB	25	8	9	0	25	25	143²	161	37	101	19	42.9%	.310	13	1.38	4.80	4.60	4.48	9.8	2.1	5.7	1.2	10.3	2.20

Breakout: 23% Improve: 57% Collapse: 23% Attrition: 14%   Comparables: Francisco Barrios, Bob Sebra, Reggie Cleveland, Bill Laskey

Take Shields, add even more control, but a little less command and stuff, and you have Sonnanstine. He knows he's going to get hit because he just doesn't have the stuff to miss enough bats, but he doesn't complicate things by walking anybody and thus avoids the trap that Hammel and Orvella have fallen into. He has some value as a back-of-the-rotation starter for now, but he'll soon be pushed out by the young arms.

Brian Stokes

Bats: R   Throws: R   Height: 6' 1"   Weight: 210   Born: September 7, 1979   Age: 28

YEAR	TEAM	LVL	AGE	W	L	SV	G	GS	IP	H	BB	SO	HR	GB%	BABIP	STUFF	WHIP	ERA	PERA	EqERA	EqH9	EqBB9	EqSO9	EqHR9	VORP	SN/WX
2005	MNT	AA	25	4	6	0	16	16	93¹	82	28	70	8	40.9%	.277	-12	1.18	3.47	4.78	4.50	8.6	3.3	4.3	1.5	10.5	—
2006	DUR	AAA	26	7	7	0	29	23	133	134	49	103	8	48.0%	.312	-4	1.38	4.13	4.84	5.54	9.3	3.9	4.9	0.8	0.9	—
2006	TBA	MLB	26	1	0	0	5	4	24	31	9	15	2	41.2%	.363	1	1.67	4.88	5.18	4.50	10.5	3.0	5.2	0.8	3.2	0.75
2007	TBA	MLB	27	2	7	0	59	0	62¹	90	25	35	11	49.8%	.366	-31	1.83	7.08	7.23	6.25	11.2	3.1	4.5	1.6	-7.5	-1.26
2008	NYN	MLB	28	2	2	1	30	0	37¹	37	16	25	4	45.9%	.285	-6	1.41	4.11	4.69	4.62	8.9	3.3	5.4	0.9	5.7	0.4

Breakout: 29% Improve: 58% Collapse: 26% Attrition: 45%   Comparables: Sean Lowe, Ken Tatum, Bob Priddy, Jon Adkins

An undrafted free agent, Stokes has already beaten the odds by reaching the big leagues. Unfortunately, his nine-year relationship with the Rays came to an end when he was sold to the Mets, which couldn't have amounted to much considering how poorly Stokes pitched last year. He'll be lucky to come anywhere close to making 59 big-league appearances in a season again.

Mitch Talbot

Bats: R   Throws: R   Height: 6' 2"   Weight: 200   Born: October 17, 1983   Age: 24

YEAR	TEAM	LVL	AGE	W	L	SV	G	GS	IP	H	BB	SO	HR	GB%	BABIP	STUFF	WHIP	ERA	PERA	EqERA	EqH9	EqBB9	EqSO9	EqHR9	VORP	SN/WX
2005	SLM	A+	21	8	11	0	27	27	151¹	169	46	100	15	58.1%	.316	-37	1.42	4.34	8.15	8.41	12.6	4.5	2.9	1.7	-41.1	—
2006	CCH	AA	22	6	4	1	18	17	90	94	29	96	4	52.5%	.360	13	1.37	3.40	5.69	6.18	11.1	3.7	6.8	0.7	-5.3	—
2006	MNT	AA	22	4	3	0	10	10	66	51	18	59	2	51.8%	.277	18	1.05	1.91	4.05	3.56	8.6	3.0	5.5	0.6	13.8	—
2007	DUR	AAA	23	13	9	0	29	29	161	169	59	124	13	56.0%	.326	-8	1.42	4.53	6.32	6.40	11.0	3.8	5.2	1.1	-13.1	—
2008	TBA	MLB	24	4	7	0	27	16	98²	122	45	64	12	52.0%	.334	-3	1.69	5.87	5.78	5.57	10.8	3.8	5.2	1.1	-5.9	0.00

Breakout: 34% Improve: 63% Collapse: 14% Attrition: 17%   Comparables: Bob Wickman, Ricky Stone, Shane Reynolds, Sean Bergman

Talbot is something of a lost soul in the Rays system because of all the high-upside arms around him, but he's a solid prospect in his own right. He lives primarily off his fastball/changeup combination; both are solid pitches that he commands well, but his lack of a plus breaking ball was his downfall at Triple-A last year. His future is in relief anyway, so the need for a third pitch won't be as much of an issue going forward.

Dan Wheeler

Bats: R   Throws: R   Height: 6' 3"   Weight: 220   Born: December 10, 1977   Age: 30

YEAR	TEAM	LVL	AGE	W	L	SV	G	GS	IP	H	BB	SO	HR	GB%	BABIP	STUFF	WHIP	ERA	PERA	EqERA	EqH9	EqBB9	EqSO9	EqHR9	VORP	SN/WX
2005	HOU	MLB	27	2	3	3	71	0	73¹	53	19	69	7	38.6%	.250	17	0.98	2.21	3.04	2.40	6.8	2.1	7.8	0.9	26.7	3.34
2006	HOU	MLB	28	3	5	9	75	0	71¹	58	24	68	5	38.3%	.279	20	1.15	2.52	3.08	2.64	7.3	2.6	7.8	0.5	26.0	3.88
2007	HOU	MLB	29	1	4	11	45	0	49²	46	13	56	8	37.3%	.306	15	1.19	5.07	4.00	4.56	8.0	2.0	9.5	1.3	4.9	1.17
2007	TBA	MLB	29	0	5	0	25	0	25	28	10	26	3	40.5%	.347	4	1.52	5.76	3.91	5.93	8.2	3.0	7.9	1.0	-3.3	0.19
2008	TBA	MLB	30	3	4	9	59	0	67²	70	23	60	9	40.4%	.307	4	1.37	4.38	4.39	4.05	9.1	2.8	7.1	1.2	8.3	0.80

Breakout: 16% Improve: 39% Collapse: 41% Attrition: 15%   Comparables: Scott Sullivan, Guillermo Mota, Mike Trombley, Alejandro Peña

After back-to-back excellent years with the Astros, Wheeler was given some save opportunities early in 2007 when Brad Lidge struggled. After experiencing some struggles of his own, he wound up back with the team that drafted him in exchange for Ty Wigginton. Wheeler's walk and strikeout rates were better than ever last year, but he suddenly became more hittable, especially when it came to giving up the long ball. It's a coin toss as to whether or not that was a one-year fluke or a cause for concern. The Rays have the time to find out.

Jay Witasick

Bats: R   Throws: R   Height: 6' 4"   Weight: 250   Born: August 28, 1972   Age: 35

YEAR	TEAM	LVL	AGE	W	L	SV	G	GS	IP	H	BB	SO	HR	GB%	BABIP	STUFF	WHIP	ERA	PERA	EqERA	EqH9	EqBB9	EqSO9	EqHR9	VORP	SN/WX
2005	COL	MLB	32	0	4	0	32	0	35²	27	12	40	2	55.9%	.287	25	1.09	2.52	2.70	2.45	6.1	2.7	8.8	0.5	11.4	0.91
2005	OAK	MLB	32	1	1	1	28	0	27²	26	17	33	2	47.4%	.324	21	1.55	3.25	4.84	4.88	8.8	5.5	10.4	0.7	2.7	0.19
2006	OAK	MLB	33	1	0	0	20	0	22²	25	21	23	3	45.5%	.349	10	2.03	6.74	7.13	6.55	9.8	8.2	8.6	1.2	-1.7	0.21
2007	OAK	MLB	34	1	0	0	16	0	15	14	9	10	1	31.1%	.295	-3	1.53	3.60	4.52	3.14	8.8	5.0	5.7	0.6	4.0	-0.38
2007	TBA	MLB	34	0	0	0	20	0	16¹	17	18	8	1	41.8%	.308	-14	2.14	6.63	4.90	5.94	8.1	8.6	3.8	0.5	-2.0	-0.21
2008	TBA	MLB	35	1	2	1	31	0	33¹	34	20	27	4	46.0%	.302	-7	1.59	4.94	4.87	4.67	8.9	4.8	6.6	1.0	1.6	0.10

Breakout: 14% Improve: 33% Collapse: 29% Attrition: 21%   Comparables: Jim Kern, Mike Fetters, Doug Henry, Tim Stoddard

In his 15 years of professional baseball, Witasick has now donned the uniforms of 23 different teams. After being used sparingly by the A's, he was released in June and landed in Tampa Bay, where elbow troubles limited his availability and effectiveness. He's been released, so his closet should get a little more crowded this year.

LINEOUTS

Hitters

	PLAYER	TEAM	LVL	AGE	PA	R	2B	3B	HR	RBI	BB	SO	SB-CS	EqBRR	AVG/OBP/SLG	MLVr	EqAVG/EqOBP/EqSLG	EqA	VORP
1B	W. Bankston	DUR	AAA	23	426	46	23	1	15	59	25	88	2-0	-1.1	.238/.282/.418	-.090	.224/.265/.408	.232	-15.7
2B	E. Johnson#	DUR	AAA	23	524	56	17	6	11	45	43	139	16-6	-1.7	.207/.285/.341	-.201	.197/.271/.333	.214	-21.7
C	M. McCormick	HUD	A-	20	270	35	20	1	8	44	27	66	3-5	-0.6	.276/.352/.469	.215	.231/.292/.397	.234	-0.8
OF	S. Pedroza*	VRO	A+	23	465	59	27	4	22	70	43	95	1-2	-6.5	.286/.368/.539	.254	.246/.320/.468	.267	6.4
C	S. Riggans	DUR	AAA	26	133	10	9	1	4	16	4	30	0-3	-2.0	.281/.333/.471	.091	.268/.311/.472	.259	5.7
SS	J. Wilson	WAS	MLB	26	25	3	0	0	0	0	5	6	0-0	0.0	.053/.280/.053	-.637	.053/.280/.053	.121	-2.9
		TBA	MLB	26	285	25	15	3	2	24	12	51	6-2	-1.8	.251/.291/.354	-.191	.264/.309/.383	.243	-2.7

Wes Bankston is a guy with a lot of power and an inability to stay healthy. The Rays tried to pass him through waivers at the end of the year, but the A's snagged him. ⊘ Athletic second baseman **Elliot Johnson** had a big year at Double-A in 2006, but crashed and burned at Triple-A Durham last season. ⊘ Drafted as a shortstop in the fifth round in 2005, **Mike McCormick** was converted to catcher last year and was impressive both offensively and defensively. ⊘ The Rays tried to make **Sergio Pedroza** a catcher in 2007, but it didn't go so well; he's now a one-dimensional slugger without a defensive home. ⊘ **Shawn Riggans** used to profile as a potential offense-first catcher, but he missed most of 2007 with elbow problems and will turn 28 this year, so his window is closing. ⊘ The Rays picked **Josh Wilson** up off of waivers in May and gave him semiregular work at short and second out of desperation more than anything else. Waived at end of the season, he was claimed by the Pirates.

Pitchers

PLAYER	TEAM	LVL	AGE	W	L	SV	IP	H	BB	SO	HR	GB%	BABIP	STUFF	WHIP	ERA	PERA	EqERA	EqH9	EqBB9	EqSO9	EqHR9	VORP
J. Butler	CGA	A	22	5	1	0	77¹	63	20	54	3	71.3%	.268	-9	1.07	2.33	5.22	5.05	9.4	4.3	3.3	0.9	4.1
	VRO	A+	22	4	3	0	49¹	51	21	34	9	55.1%	.292	-40	1.46	4.93	11.10	8.72	11.4	5.8	3.9	3.3	-15.0
J. Gonzalez*	VRO	A+	24	5	6	1	91¹	81	34	93	6	51.4%	.310	-12	1.26	2.86	5.54	5.29	9.3	4.9	6.0	1.3	2.9
J. Houser*	MNT	AA	22	5	4	0	103²	88	39	90	10	39.1%	.276	-10	1.22	3.65	5.16	5.67	8.9	3.8	5.0	1.5	-0.8
C. Medlock	CHT	AA	24	2	2	2	47²	35	5	59	3	40.0%	.288	15	0.84	2.64	3.49	3.40	7.6	1.4	7.6	1.0	11.0
	LOU	AAA	24	2	1	0	16	17	14	17	0	30.4%	.370	5	1.94	5.63	6.50	7.20	10.8	8.4	7.2	0.0	-2.7
	DUR	AAA	24	2	0	0	15²	9	9	8	2	35.4%	.167	-24	1.15	3.44	4.01	4.70	5.9	5.3	2.9	1.8	1.5
E. Meek	MNT	AA	24	2	1	1	67	74	34	69	2	53.9%	.385	-3	1.61	4.30	7.04	6.67	12.6	5.5	6.5	0.6	-7.1
J. Ridgway*	DUR	AAA	26	2	3	4	64²	54	30	67	8	49.4%	.284	-12	1.30	3.06	5.62	4.45	8.9	4.6	7.0	1.6	7.8
J. Seo	DUR	AAA	30	9	4	0	97²	98	14	64	8	43.4%	.303	-3	1.15	3.68	5.13	5.16	10.5	1.7	4.4	1.1	4.4
	TBA	MLB	30	3	4	0	52	84	16	28	11	39.0%	.390	-31	1.92	8.13	9.74	9.00	13.0	2.4	4.5	1.9	-18.4
J. Switzer*	DUR	AAA	27	0	0	1	33	26	8	23	0	47.9%	.283	1	1.03	0.82	3.51	2.12	8.5	2.7	4.9	0.3	11.5
	TBA	MLB	27	0	2	0	19	27	7	13	2	30.9%	.385	-16	1.79	8.05	5.80	6.98	11.2	2.8	5.6	0.9	-4.3
W. Townsend	CGA	A	24	6	10	0	102²	91	53	92	16	47.5%	.273	-53	1.40	5.08	9.92	9.48	11.1	7.6	4.5	3.0	-37.6

A second-round pick in 2006, **Josh Butler** is a big righty with a heavy sinker that generates tons of groundballs. ⊘ Lefty **Jino Gonzalez** is a sinker/slider specialist who found success in the High-A bullpen, but is already 25. ⊘ Once a highly regarded prospect, southpaw **James Houser** was having an impressive comeback campaign at Double-A last year before he drew a 50-game suspension for taking performance enhancers. ⊘ One of two arms received from the Reds for Jorge Cantu, diminutive righty **Calvin Medlock** has averaged over a strikeout per inning in the minors thanks to his plus changeup and surprisingly solid fastball. He could compete for a bullpen job this year. ⊘ A right-hander whose fastball can get into the mid-90s, **Evan Meek** continued to makes progress last year after being released by the Twins two years ago because of a case of the yips. The Pirates took him in December's Rule 5 draft. ⊘ We imagine **Jeff Ridgway** is dying for just one more chance to pitch in the big leagues in order to lower his career ERA of 189.00 (his minor league mark is just 3.58). ⊘ Rather than hoping for a non-roster invite this spring, **Jae Seo** signed a $1.5 billion deal to return to his native South Korea and pitch for the Kia Tigers, joining Hee-Seop Choi as the Tigers' prodigal sons. Sure, $1.5 billion won is worth "only" $1.6 million U.S., but it's still several times what he'd be making on a minor league deal, and he'll be earning it at home. ⊘ **Jon Switzer** is a left-hander who, like so many in the system, has dominated at Triple-A and, shall we say, not dominated in the majors. ⊘ **Wade Townsend** showed some signs of life last year for the first time since his full-season debut in 2004, but he'll turn 25 during spring training, which means it was probably a case of too little, too late.

MANAGER: JOE MADDON

YEAR	TEAM	W-L	Pythag +/−	Avg PC	100+ P	120+ P	QS	BQS	REL	REL w Zero R	IBB	Subs	PH	PH Avg	PH HR	SB2	CS2	SB3	CS3	SAC Att	SAC %	POS SAC	Squeeze	Swing	In Play
2006	TBA	61-101	-3	93.0	49	1	62	5	444	228	39	68	80	.225	1	109	45	24	7	64	54.7%	32	4	153	112
2007	TBA	66-96	0	97.1	80	0	69	12	483	258	31	16	80	.159	1	114	43	16	4	48	70.8%	33	4	129	92

It's unfair to judge Maddon by his won/loss record, as he has yet to be given the talent to compete, especially on the pitching side of the ledger. He is firmly entrenched in the Rays' future, however, a notion supported by the team's off-season moves. Maddon wants to lead a young, talented, cohesive unit, so Elijah Dukes and Delmon Young, both young and talented but obstacles to cohesion, had to go. This gave Maddon not only the team chemistry he desired, but also the flexibility to begin the transformation of his roster from an interesting collection of players to an actual team with set positions, something further established by the off-season decision to permanently lock B. J. Upton in center by moving Akinori Iwamura to second and installing future star Evan Longoria at third. That he got a much-needed young arm with something to prove in the bargain didn't hurt.

Texas Rangers

There's a dirty secret down in Texas. At a time when baseball claims to be busting attendance records like buttons off a fat man's pants, the Rangers' is trending downwards. That should be no surprise. Attendance is the product of winning, and the Rangers have had one winning season in the last eight. They last made the playoffs in 1999, concluding a brief flurry of three October appearances at the end of that decade under late manager Johnny Oates.

This dry spell is more the rule than the exception for the Rangers. The franchise has spent much of its life as either an investment or a toy rather than as a baseball team, and it has shown in the inattention and, at times, outright ineptitude the team's various owners have displayed when it comes to putting a quality product on the field. The franchise began its life when an expansion team was awarded to a Washington, D.C., investment group headed by former Air Force general Elwood Quesada. Quesada was quickly frustrated by the team's financial losses. When Quesada complained that the team had lost $250,000 in its inaugural season of 1961, recently retired White Sox owner Bill Veeck observed, "Quesada has every reason to be worried about losing a quarter of a million dollars in his first season. If he were doing his job right he'd have lost five million!" Veeck's words would not be heeded by Quesada or any of the team's subsiquent owners.

After just two predictably awful seasons of expansion-quality baseball, Quesada sold out to his ownership partners James Johnston, James Lemon, and George Bunker, blaming the press, an unsupportive business community, and lower-than-expected attendance for his failures. New chairman Johnston hired former big-league outfielder George Selkirk to run the

RANGERS PROSPECTUS

2007 record: 75-87; Fourth place, AL West

Pythagenport record: 78-84

Runs scored per game: 5.04 (5th in AL)

Runs allowed per game: 5.21 (11th in AL)

Team EqA: .257 (9th in AL)

2007 Batters Age: 29.9 (7th youngest in AL)

2007 Pitchers Age: 28.3 (6th youngest in AL)

Ballpark: Rangers Ballpark in Arlington; Neutral park; Park Factor of 1.005

2007: Their merely adequate second half felt like a great accomplishment.

2008: Small-time fixes won't solve big-time problems, and there's still no pitching.

club, and Selkirk, in turn, traded for Mets first baseman Gil Hodges, naming him manager. With Johnston leaving the management of his baseball team to these baseball men, the team then known as the Senators began to steadily improve. Unfortunately, Johnston died of cancer in 1967, and Lemon promptly sold out for $9 million to Robert E. "Bob" Short, the former owner of the NBA's Los Angeles Lakers.

The Lakers had played in Short's home town of Minneapolis when he purchased the team, but he didn't hesitate to relocate them. Having purchased the Lakers for $300,000 in 1957, he sold them in 1965 for $5.5 million. Washington fans were understandably concerned. "I did not buy the Washington team to move it," Short said. More prophetic was his assessment at his inaugural press conference. "The team now probably isn't worth what I paid for it," Short said, "but nobody ever lost money selling a big league baseball franchise." Short named himself general manager and went on to consummate some amazingly horrific trades in a misguided attempt to attract fans with familiar names, the best example being the 1970 deal that brought in washed-up former 30-game winner and malcontent Denny McLain along with some of the Tigers' other unwanteds in exchange for the left side of the infield and the number-two starter on Detroit's next contending club. Short spent his first three years as owner running down the fans, the market, his parking concession, his lease, and anything else he could think of. Finally, he presented the Lords of Baseball with an ultimatum: Allow him to move the team to Texas or, as a fellow owner told *The Sporting News*, "he would go to court and take us down with him." Permission was granted, and the team moved to Arlington for the 1972 season.

In its first two years in Texas, the team lost 100 games and failed to outdraw its Washington peak. After the second Texas season, with his five-year window to depreciate his investment in the team closing, Short sold out, though not before pulling one more publicity stunt by infamously rushing high school pitching phenom David Clyde to the majors just weeks after the 1973 draft.

In 1974, under new owner Brad Corbett, a plastic piping millionaire, the franchise had its first good year since rookie manager Ted Williams' 1969 Senators club shocked baseball with an 86-76 record. In going 84-76, Billy Martin's first Rangers squad outplayed its Pythagorean projection of 79-81. First baseman Mike Hargrove won the Rookie of the Year award. Right fielder Jeff Burroughs won the MVP award. As the Pythagorean projection hinted, however, the Rangers were quickly back under .500, with Martin's inevitable firing in his second season turning the team over to a long series of nonentities. Despite featuring four such skippers, the 1977 season remains one of the best in franchise history. The team's 94-68 record has only been surpassed once in franchise history, by Oates's 1998 division champions who went 95-67. The '77 team didn't hit much, but through a series of trades and free agent signings, Corbett and general manager Dan O'Brien had assembled a starting rotation of Gaylord Perry, Bert Blyleven, Doyle Alexander, and Dock Ellis. The 1977 Rangers missed the league lead in staff ERA by four one-hundredths of a run.

Though the Rangers' attendance perked up, ranking in the league's top five from 1974 through 1976, and continued to rise through 1979, the increase was slow relative to overall league growth and the team's attendance rankings began to recede. Most significantly, attendance was not keeping pace with Corbett's spending. An early and enthusiastic free agent bidder, Corbett dove headfirst into the market following the 1976 season. He gave 35-year-old shortstop Bert Campaneris a five-year contract, authorized signing DH Richie Zisk to a ten-year contract, and re-signed Blyleven to a six-year deal with an additional 16 years of deferred payments. There was no guiding strategy to his signings, however, and by 1979, the club was in debt. Corbett received a cash infusion by diluting the team's stock and inviting new partners to buy in, but early in 1980, when Corbett tried to re-sign 29-year-old catcher Jim Sundberg to a 16-year contract that included $3 million for six years of playing and $2.1 million for a ten-year post-retirement personal-services contract, one of those new partners, oilman Eddie Chiles, balked. Not long after, Corbett sold out to the 70-year-old Chiles.

Chiles presided over five years of poorly attended also-rans, followed by three years of poorly attended excitement under first-time manager Bobby Valentine. The Rangers hit franchise attendance highs in 1986 and 1987, but sales were still sluggish compared to the league as a whole. Still the team was finally profitable. However, Chiles was pushing 80 and his oil business was going through a rough patch. As early as 1986, if not sooner, he was looking for a buyer.

It took time and some false starts, including a flirtation with Tampa Bay money, before Chiles was finally able to sell prior to the 1989 season. As Chiles headed out the door, he said, "This baseball team needs a new stadium. To be successful, it's got to have one, and I don't have the muscle to do it. It's got to be somebody with very deep pockets." It was telling then that the group that bought the Rangers from Chiles, an investment syndicate headed by the future president of the United States, George W. Bush, bought not only the team and Arlington Stadium, but 120 acres of land surrounding the Rangers home park.

In April, 1991, three months after residents of Arlington had voted in favor of a half-cent sales tax to pay for ballpark construction, the Texas legislature voted into existence the Arlington Sports Facilities Development Authority, granting it the power of eminent domain. Though a government agency, the ASFDA cooperated with the Rangers in effecting land transfers from independent owners on the edges of those 120 acres, thereby annexing those properties to the ballpark site. As columnist Nicholas Kristof put it in the *New York Times* in 2002, "As part of the deal, the city would even confiscate land so that the Rangers owners could engage in real estate speculation." The Rangers would give lowball offers to landholders adjacent to the site. When the landholders refused, the ASFDA would condemn the land. This practice led to several lawsuits.

To the Bush group, the acquisition of the Rangers wasn't about the team itself as much as about the related real estate speculation. In 1990, Bush told the *Fort Worth Star-Telegram*, "The idea of making a land play, absolutely, to plunk the field down in the middle of a big piece of land, that's kind of always been the strategy." According to the Rangers' media guide, when leveraged buyout millionaire and owner of the NHL's Dallas Stars Thomas Hicks purchased the club from the Bush group in June 1998 for $250 million, roughly three times what the Bush group paid for the team, he acquired the ballclub, the lease to the new publicly funded Ballpark at Arlington (which is actually more of a deeply discounted mortgage, which the Rangers are slowly paying off), and 270 acres of land, more than double the property the Bush group had initially bought from Chiles.

Bush, who would become governor of Texas in 1994, didn't have deep pockets when his group bought the Rangers, but he did in the wake of his group's land grab and stadium deal. As Mark S. Rosentraub wrote in *Major League Losers: The Real Cost of Sports and Who's Paying for It*, "Governor George Bush of Texas paid $606,000 for a share of the Texas Rangers [Bush owned roughly two percent of the team] and then sold his interest in the team for approximately $15 million. The value of the Texas Rangers increased as a direct result of a $130+ million tax subsidy received by Governor Bush and his partners."

Despite the fact that the club had become a real estate business that happened to have a baseball team instead of the other way around, the tail end of the Bush era proved to be the franchise's lone period of sustained success. The Rangers did need a new ballpark (publicly financed or otherwise). Arlington Stadium had come into the world in 1965 as Turnpike Stadium, the home of the Texas League's Dallas-Fort Worth Spurs. Though renovated several times, it lacked amenities and revenue-generating extras such as luxury suites, and had the majority of its seats located in the outfield. When the Ballpark at Arlington finally opened in 1994, the Rangers jumped from sixth to third in American League attendance. The beautiful new park and the ensuing Oates-led playoff teams would help the Rangers stay in the top five—for a while. In 1996, Oates's second season at the helm and the team's third season in their new park, the Rangers won 90 games for just the second time in team history and made their first playoff appearance. They would go on to make two more in the following three years, but all three times they faced the dynastic Yankees in the Division Series and lost, winning just the first game of the first series in 1996.

All too soon it was over. In 2000, the Rangers' pitching crashed with a historic season in which the team allowed nearly six runs per game. Their total of 974 runs allowed that year was the 12th-highest of all time and the third-highest (after the 1996 Tigers and 1999 Rockies) since 1939. The 2001 and 2003 pitching staffs were nearly as bad, and the 2002 staff was only slightly better. The team's third-place, 89-73 showing under second-year skipper Buck Showalter in 2004 proved to be a fluke, yielding to more mediocrity.

Recent Rangers GMs have proven to be poor assessors of talent, particularly John Hart, who was the architect of the great Indians teams of the 1990s, but lost his way in Texas from 2001 to 2005. Sadly, current GM Jon Daniels has not shown an ability to reverse that

trend. In the recent past, the Rangers have executed one huge steal of a trade when then-GM Doug Melvin got a young Michael Young from the Blue Jays in return for righty Esteban Loaiza in 2000, but otherwise have made it their business to give away talent. Trading current Reds ace Aaron Harang for aging infielder Randy Velarde that same year was a crippling mistake that was recently reinforced by Daniels' signature disaster, the January 2006 deal that sent first baseman Adrian Gonzalez and Chris Young, now the Padres' best hitter and number-two starter, respectively, to San Diego for since-injured thirtysomething reliever Akinori Otsuka and the exorable Adam Eaton. First basemen Travis Hafner and Carlos Peña, infielders Edwin Encarnacion and Esteban German, and pitcher Justin Duchscherer are just some of the other talented players who have been frittered away by the team in recent years, and that doesn't count the delusional deal that sent closer Francisco Cordero to Milwaukee for two months of Carlos Lee amid a losing season, or the team's remarkable ability to turn Alex Rodriguez into the Nationals' leftovers via a pair of similarly self-inflicted cuts.

The 2007 season seemed destined to be the Rangers' worst since the early 1970s, as the club posted a record of 19-35 in the first two months. Though the team rebounded to play better than .500 baseball (56-52) over the remaining four months of the season, even then the offense, pitching staff, and defense were average at best. The Rangers made few moves in the offseason to change their situation. The principal transactions were a trade for slugging center fielder Josh Hamilton, whose career was salvaged by the Reds last year, the signing of perpetually injured free agent outfielder Milton Bradley, and a pair of minor deals that have set up a first-base platoon of Ben Broussard and Chris Shelton. The rotation remains the same, with no likely ace, no number-twos, just a bunch of four-fives. The bullpen remains the same with the exception of Japanese free agent Kaz Fukumori, who is not expected to have a large impact. Though last year's deadline trade of first baseman Mark Teixeira to Atlanta brought in several interesting prospects, none will have an impact in the short term outside of catcher Jarrod Saltalamacchia, who has been charged with the unenviable task of replacing Teixeira in the lineup.

The team's hopes for offensive improvement thus rest on a collection of rehab cases, including Hamilton, Bradley, and third baseman Hank Blalock, who hit .313/.405/.656 last September after coming back from surgery to have a rib removed to solve a nerve problem in his shoulder. If Blalock can continue his comeback, if Hamilton and Bradley can be happy, healthy, productive members of the team, if Saltalamacchia can deliver on his promise, if the first-base platoon proves productive, and if second baseman Ian Kinsler and shortstop Michael Young continue to give the team the best punch it has ever received from its double-play combo, the Rangers will score a lot of runs. Given the franchise's epidemic inability to assemble a pitching staff, however, they still won't win, even if all of those tickets hit the jackpot.

That sort of off-season strategy has been par for the course under Hicks, who is already the longest-serving owner in franchise history. Hicks' policy toward high-priced acquisitions has bordered on the strange. In 2001, Hicks stunned baseball by wildly overbidding his closest competitor to sign Alex Rodriguez to a 10-year, $252 million deal. The next winter he gave Chan Ho Park $65 million for five years. The latter deal was a straightforward mistake, while the first imprisoned the team by its sheer magnitude, and since then the Rangers have shied away from the high end of the market, instead remaining happy to bid on mid- to low-end types such as pitcher Pedro Astacio, catcher Rod Barajas, and outfielders David Dellucci, Gary Matthews Jr., and Brian Jordan, or players coming off of injuries such as Bradley and closer Eric Gagné.

As a result, the Rangers' payroll, which had steadily increased during Hicks' early tenure and topped out over $100 million during Rodriguez's time in Texas, remains among the smallest in the majors, proof that little has changed for the franchise. Hicks dumped Rodriguez on the Yankees prior to the 2004 season and the Rangers' payroll dropped by nearly half that offseason, to $55.1 million. Though it has slowly risen since, the $68.3 million spent in 2007 was far below the payroll's Rodriguez-era peak, and ranked a mere 20th in the majors behind those of the A's and Twins, two small market, old-park teams. That's extraordinary for a team that has the massive Dallas-Fort Worth-Arlington market, the fourth-largest in the country, to itself. A short-term retrenchment would be understandable, but Hicks has now kept his wallet holstered for three years going on four.

This is not surprising. Beyond civic duty, Hicks doesn't have a huge motivation to spend. While the Rangers have certainly increased in value since his purchase, worth $365 million in 2007 according to *Forbes*, it is only the 17th-most-valuable franchise in the majors and is growing slowly. While a championship would bring the team a momentary cash windfall and increase its value somewhat, there is no chance of making the kind of short-term killing that the Bush group did. After more than 40 years, the Rangers have finally matured as a vehicle for big profits. Now all that is left is the tawdry business of running a baseball team. The ownership that wants the Rangers for *that* reason will be the first in team history, but they have yet to present themselves.

HITTERS

Elvis Andrus SS Bats: R Throws: R Height: 6' 0" Weight: 185 Born: August 26, 1988 Age: 19

YEAR	TEAM	LVL	AGE	PA	R	2B	3B	HR	RBI	BB	SO	SB	CS	EqBRR	AVG	OBP	SLG	MLVr	EqAVG	EqOBP	EqSLG	EqA	VORP	DEFENSE
2006	ROM	A	17	478	67	25	4	3	50	36	91	23	15	-0.4	.265	.324	.362	.015	.217	.262	.297	.193	-25.1	104-SS -10
2007	MYR	A+	18	440	59	20	3	3	37	44	88	25	7	1.8	.244	.330	.335	-.074	.201	.269	.278	.198	-25.1	98-SS 1
2007	BAK	A+	18	123	19	2	0	2	12	10	19	15	8	-2.1	.300	.369	.373	.010	.248	.303	.310	.220	-2.2	28-SS -1
2008	TEX	MLB	19	616	64	27	4	5	40	40	139	26	12	2.1	.232	.287	.321	-.252	.230	.286	.329	.222	-11.6	144-SS -1

Breakout: 60% Improve: 84% Collapse: 11% Attrition: 4%   Comparables: Dennis Abreu, Luis Rivas, Marcos Vechionacci, Danny Klassen

Loaded with tools and playing in a full-season league at age 17, Andrus was the darling of the Braves' system in 2006, but by last year's deadline he was headed to Texas in the Mark Teixeira deal. The problem is that Andrus is just not a good hitter. He is, however, an outstanding defensive player. We'd say he'll never bat at the top of a lineup, but this is the organization that led off Wayne Tolleson and Curtis Wilkerson.

Joaquin Arias SS Bats: R Throws: R Height: 6' 1" Weight: 165 Born: September 21, 1984 Age: 23

YEAR	TEAM	LVL	AGE	PA	R	2B	3B	HR	RBI	BB	SO	SB	CS	EqBRR	AVG	OBP	SLG	MLVr	EqAVG	EqOBP	EqSLG	EqA	VORP	DEFENSE
2005	FRI	AA	20	526	65	23	8	5	56	17	46	20	10	0.0	.315	.335	.423	.060	.273	.298	.375	.234	4.9	117-SS -1
2006	OKL	AAA	21	525	56	14	10	4	49	19	64	26	10	-1.6	.268	.296	.361	-.110	.241	.268	.332	.212	-15.7	122-SS -5
2008	TEX	MLB	23	96	9	4	1	1	7	3	14	3	1	0.3	.241	.269	.325	-.273	.238	.269	.333	.216	-2.1	27-SS 0

Breakout: 23% Improve: 40% Collapse: 30% Attrition: 18%   Comparables: Sergio Nuñez, Nelson Samboy, Jesus Merchan, Oscar Materano

When the Rangers traded Alex Rodriguez to the Yankees in early 2004, they had their choice of one of two athletic infielders in the Yankees' system. The Rangers chose Arias, passing on Robinson Cano. Whoops. Arias has always been high on tools and low on performance, the kind of guy who blows you away in batting practice and fielding drills, but bores you once the game starts. That he missed nearly all of last season due to shoulder problems didn't help matters.

Hank Blalock　　　　**3B**　　　　Bats: L　　Throws: R　　Height: 6' 1"　　Weight: 200　　Born: November 21, 1980　　Age: 27

YEAR	TEAM	LVL	AGE	PA	R	2B	3B	HR	RBI	BB	SO	SB	CS	EqBRR	AVG	OBP	SLG	MLVr	EqAVG	EqOBP	EqSLG	EqA	VORP	DEFENSE	
2005	TEX	MLB	24	705	80	34	0	25	92	51	132	1	0	-1.3	.263	.318	.431	-.029	.262	.328	.441	.264	11.0	155-3B	-4
2006	TEX	MLB	25	646	76	26	3	16	89	51	98	1	0	-1.6	.266	.325	.401	-.093	.260	.328	.404	.255	0.0	120-3B	-11
2007	TEX	MLB	26	232	32	16	3	10	33	21	38	4	1	1.8	.293	.358	.543	.213	.296	.366	.573	.310	16.9	38-3B	-1
2008	TEX	MLB	27	455	55	22	2	15	62	41	80	5	2	-0.4	.263	.332	.437	.000	.260	.331	.449	.272	10.4	108-3B	-2

Breakout: 19%　Improve: 42%　Collapse: 27%　Attrition: 18%　　　　Comparables: Pete Ward, Scott Cooper, Chad Tracy, Jack Howell

Last year, for the first time in three seasons, Blalock actually hit up to his capabilities, smacking doubles all over the park, hitting a home run every five games or so, and keeping his batting average around .300. He even hit southpaws and on the road, two things he had never done in the past. Unfortunately, he played in just 58 games due to a strange surgery in which doctors removed a rib that was pressing on some nerves that were causing ongoing arm soreness. Blalock kept hitting when he returned, and is still pretty young, so let's call the glass half full.

Brandon Boggs　　　　**CF**　　　　Bats: S　　Throws: R　　Height: 6' 0"　　Weight: 190　　Born: January 9, 1983　　Age: 25

YEAR	TEAM	LVL	AGE	PA	R	2B	3B	HR	RBI	BB	SO	SB	CS	EqBRR	AVG	OBP	SLG	MLVr	EqAVG	EqOBP	EqSLG	EqA	VORP	DEFENSE			
2005	CLN	A	22	363	54	16	2	13	51	50	69	14	6	-0.5	.246	.353	.437	.078	.196	.284	.340	.220	-23.4	50-LF	5	24-CF	-4
2006	BAK	A+	23	327	48	20	4	8	37	40	63	13	4	-0.6	.261	.352	.444	.069	.209	.287	.356	.228	-10.0	64-CF	-10	10-LF	-1
2007	BAK	A+	24	108	17	9	1	4	17	14	28	5	1	-0.1	.250	.361	.500	.129	.208	.303	.406	.249	-3.2	17-LF	1		
2007	FRI	AA	24	429	69	21	4	19	55	70	103	10	4	2.5	.266	.385	.508	.208	.231	.342	.433	.270	13.5	93-CF	-8		
2008	TEX	MLB	25	545	62	27	3	14	55	59	152	13	5	1.0	.220	.308	.381	-.143	.217	.308	.391	.250	-4.8	128-CF	0		

Breakout: 23%　Improve: 53%　Collapse: 24%　Attrition: 11%　　　　Comparables: Kevin Belcher, Pat Bryant, David Cook, Rob Lukachyk

There's a whole lot to like about Boggs; he's a great athlete, a fine center fielder, has pop in his bat, and draws walks. There's also a whole lot not to like about Boggs, as he's already 25 years old, does most of his damage against lefties, and strikes out like he has an incentive in his contract to do so. Still, as a switch-hitter with defensive skills and pop, he should be able to carve out a career on the bench.

Julio Borbon　　　　**CF**　　　　Bats: L　　Throws: L　　Height: 6' 1"　　Weight: 190　　Born: February 20, 1986　　Age: 22

YEAR	TEAM	LVL	AGE	PA	R	2B	3B	HR	RBI	BB	SO	SB	CS	EqBRR	AVG	OBP	SLG	MLVr	EqAVG	EqOBP	EqSLG	EqA	VORP	DEFENSE	
2007	SPO	A-	21	31	1	0	0	0	2	2	3	3	1	-1.4	.172	.226	.172	-.535	.167	.194	.167	.107	-9.9		
2008	TEX	MLB	22	560	46	21	3	4	43	34	133	15	7	0.2	.217	.268	.295	-.327	.214	.268	.303	.203	-25.6	131-CF	-3

Breakout: NA　Improve: NA　Collapse: NA　Attrition: NA　　　　Comparables: Paul Ottavinia, Jason Fitzgerald, Jacob Cruz, Jason Tyner

Borbon was considered by most to be the top pure center fielder coming out of college in last June's draft, which really just means that that last year's group of college center fielders stunk. Borbon has serious speed and an excellent feel for contact, but he hit just seven home runs in his college career, and his swing-at-anything approach prevents him from fitting in well as a leadoff man. Considered a late-first round talent, he dropped to 35th overall because teams shied away from dealing with his agent, Scott Boras. Boras was unable to secure a big bonus for his client, but nonetheless got him a big-league deal that put him on the 40-man roster.

Jason Botts — DH

Bats: S   Throws: R   Height: 6' 5"   Weight: 250   Born: July 26, 1980   Age: 27

YEAR	TEAM	LVL	AGE	PA	R	2B	3B	HR	RBI	BB	SO	SB	CS	EqBRR	AVG	OBP	SLG	MLVr	EqAVG	EqOBP	EqSLG	EqA	VORP	DEFENSE
2005	OKL	AAA	24	589	93	31	7	25	102	67	152	2	4	-5.3	.286	.375	.522	.217	.244	.325	.443	.261	1.5	81-LF -11
2006	OKL	AAA	25	259	43	19	1	13	39	31	61	6	0	1.0	.309	.398	.582	.416	.268	.354	.522	.297	13.6	24-LF 2 18-1B -2
2006	TEX	MLB	25	60	8	4	0	1	6	8	18	0	0	-0.6	.220	.317	.360	-.207	.204	.317	.327	.238	-1.4	
2007	OKL	AAA	26	459	69	36	4	13	78	81	102	0	1	0.6	.320	.436	.545	.405	.259	.381	.460	.293	17.7	48-LF -2
2007	TEX	MLB	26	190	19	8	1	2	14	19	59	1	0	0.3	.240	.326	.335	-.168	.247	.340	.361	.252	-4.0	24-LF 4
2008	TEX	MLB	27	508	59	26	2	15	62	57	140	4	2	-0.5	.242	.331	.416	-.044	.239	.331	.427	.267	3.6	120-LF 0

Breakout: 5%   Improve: 35%   Collapse: 31%   Attrition: 20%   Comparables: Jon Knott, Damon Minor, Jason Jones, Scott McClain

Once again last year, Botts put up big, big numbers at Triple-A only to turn into a pumpkin once Texas gave him a shot at the big leagues. At 27 years old, Botts is no longer a prospect, but a classic Quadruple-A hitter. He could be huge in Japan one day.

Marlon Byrd — OF

Bats: R   Throws: R   Height: 6' 0"   Weight: 235   Born: August 30, 1977   Age: 30

YEAR	TEAM	LVL	AGE	PA	R	2B	3B	HR	RBI	BB	SO	SB	CS	EqBRR	AVG	OBP	SLG	MLVr	EqAVG	EqOBP	EqSLG	EqA	VORP	DEFENSE
2005	WAS	MLB	27	244	20	15	2	2	26	18	47	5	1	-2.5	.264	.318	.380	-.045	.267	.322	.396	.256	1.8	43-LF 5
2006	NWO	AAA	28	179	20	9	0	7	29	16	31	3	1	-1.9	.271	.363	.465	.158	.252	.333	.428	.265	4.9	17-CF 4 14-RF -2
2006	WAS	MLB	28	228	28	8	1	5	18	22	47	3	3	0.8	.223	.317	.350	-.152	.232	.325	.374	.244	-3.1	45-CF -3
2007	OKL	AAA	29	195	29	15	2	6	32	13	30	3	2	1.1	.358	.415	.568	.458	.322	.379	.514	.301	14.6	17-RF 1 12-LF 1
2007	TEX	MLB	29	454	60	17	8	10	70	29	88	5	3	2.9	.307	.355	.459	.104	.314	.364	.487	.289	21.2	56-CF -10 35-RF 8
2008	TEX	MLB	30	432	53	22	3	11	51	30	82	5	3	0.3	.275	.331	.429	-.004	.271	.331	.440	.269	8.2	103-CF -3

Breakout: 8%   Improve: 27%   Collapse: 33%   Attrition: 16%   Comparables: Shane Spencer, Benny Agbayani, Derek Bell, Dante Bichette

Signed as an extra body prior to the season, Byrd was waived by the Rangers shortly after Opening Day. Fortunately for them, there were no takers. Byrd went down to Triple-A Oklahoma until May and ended up being extremely valuable by filling in admirably after Kenny Lofton was traded to Cleveland. Defensively, Byrd doesn't have the range for center field any more, nor the offensive prowess to play every day in a corner, but his performance last year might have salvaged a career for him as a bench outfielder.

Frank Catalanotto — LF

Bats: L   Throws: R   Height: 6' 0"   Weight: 195   Born: April 27, 1974   Age: 34

YEAR	TEAM	LVL	AGE	PA	R	2B	3B	HR	RBI	BB	SO	SB	CS	EqBRR	AVG	OBP	SLG	MLVr	EqAVG	EqOBP	EqSLG	EqA	VORP	DEFENSE
2005	TOR	MLB	31	475	56	29	5	8	59	37	53	0	2	-3.2	.301	.367	.451	.117	.303	.377	.462	.290	20.3	85-LF 6
2006	TOR	MLB	32	499	56	36	2	7	56	52	37	1	3	-2.7	.300	.376	.439	.085	.297	.382	.441	.286	17.4	86-LF 3
2007	TEX	MLB	33	377	52	20	4	11	44	28	37	2	1	-0.5	.260	.337	.444	.010	.267	.348	.477	.280	7.3	55-LF -1 11-1B -2
2008	TEX	MLB	34	351	46	18	2	7	41	32	38	2	2	-0.4	.284	.357	.422	.036	.280	.357	.432	.279	8.2	84-LF -2

Breakout: 16%   Improve: 37%   Collapse: 32%   Attrition: 33%   Comparables: Jim Northrup, Dale Mitchell, Mike Kingery, Gene Woodling

Signed to a three-year deal prior to last season, Catalanotto had issues with biceps tendonitis and a groin injury, which cost him a third of the 2007 season and pushed his production well below expectations. Frankie the Cat is a solid player, but as an aging corner outfielder who can only play against right-handers and doesn't have a ton of power, he has limited value to a rebuilding team.

Nelson Cruz — RF

Bats: R   Throws: R   Height: 6' 3"   Weight: 225   Born: July 1, 1980   Age: 28

YEAR	TEAM	LVL	AGE	PA	R	2B	3B	HR	RBI	BB	SO	SB	CS	EqBRR	AVG	OBP	SLG	MLVr	EqAVG	EqOBP	EqSLG	EqA	VORP	DEFENSE
2005	HUN	AA	24	286	45	19	0	16	54	31	71	10	3	-2.5	.306	.388	.577	.347	.260	.332	.496	.280	9.6	65-RF -6
2005	NAS	AAA	24	246	33	13	0	11	27	30	62	9	4	0.6	.269	.382	.490	.167	.238	.340	.421	.264	0.9	53-RF 7
2006	NAS	AAA	25	423	68	22	1	20	73	42	100	17	6	2.4	.302	.378	.528	.283	.265	.337	.475	.277	11.9	86-RF 5
2006	TEX	MLB	25	138	15	3	0	6	22	7	32	1	0	-0.2	.223	.261	.385	-.260	.217	.261	.372	.218	-5.1	35-RF 2
2007	OKL	AAA	26	187	32	9	1	15	45	21	34	1	2	0.8	.352	.428	.698	.660	.317	.394	.628	.328	23.0	44-RF 0
2007	TEX	MLB	26	332	35	15	2	9	34	21	87	2	4	-0.9	.235	.287	.384	-.177	.239	.298	.407	.238	-10.8	69-RF 7 13-LF -1
2008	TEX	MLB	27	404	50	20	2	16	56	33	101	8	2	0.1	.256	.323	.453	.001	.253	.323	.465	.274	5.4	96-RF 1

Breakout: 25%   Improve: 59%   Collapse: 19%   Attrition: 14%   Comparables: Dave Henderson, Bubba Trammell, Pete Incaviglia, Ken Hunt

Over the last two seasons, Cruz has hit 35 home runs and slugged .580 at Triple-A, but he's been given two sizable opportunities with the Rangers and proven each time that he's probably yet another Quadruple-A talent. Cruz is just too much of a hacker and a chaser at the plate, and once big league pitchers realized that, they stopped giving him anything to hit.

Chris Davis			3B										Bats: L		Throws: R		Height: 6' 3"		Weight: 210		Born: March 17, 1986		Age: 22		
YEAR	TEAM	LVL	AGE	PA	R	2B	3B	HR	RBI	BB	SO	SB	CS	EqBRR	AVG	OBP	SLG	MLVr	EqAVG	EqOBP	EqSLG	EqA	VORP	DEFENSE		
2006	SPO	A-	20	280	38	18	1	15	42	23	65	2	3	-2.2	.277	.343	.534	.226	.218	.270	.402	.228	-24.2	33-LF	-6	29-1B -3
2007	BAK	A+	21	418	69	28	3	24	93	22	123	3	3	-1.6	.298	.340	.573	.246	.228	.263	.433	.233	-0.5	90-3B	-1	
2007	FRI	AA	21	124	21	7	0	12	25	13	27	0	0	-1.2	.294	.371	.688	.453	.252	.323	.568	.291	10.9	29-3B	-3	
2008	TEX	MLB	22	557	51	28	2	20	71	35	171	3	2	-0.4	.220	.274	.401	-.176	.218	.274	.411	.236	-10.6	131-3B	-3	

Breakout: 27% Improve: 55% Collapse: 24% Attrition: 8%   Comparables: Jose Oliva, David Ortiz, Russell Branyan, Tate Seefried

One of the real breakout players in the Rangers' minor league system last year, Davis put to rest any concerns about his California League showing in the first half being a league-based fluke when he was even better following a promotion to Double-A. One of the top power prospects around, Davis's future will be dictated by what he doesn't do: make much contact or play good defense. His defensive struggles have been attributed to a foot problem. If he can stay on the left side of the infield, his upside falls somewhere between Dean Palmer and Troy Glaus.

Victor Diaz			RF										Bats: R		Throws: R		Height: 6' 0"		Weight: 200		Born: December 10, 1981		Age: 26		
YEAR	TEAM	LVL	AGE	PA	R	2B	3B	HR	RBI	BB	SO	SB	CS	EqBRR	AVG	OBP	SLG	MLVr	EqAVG	EqOBP	EqSLG	EqA	VORP	DEFENSE		
2005	NOR	AAA	23	184	30	11	0	10	34	14	47	6	2	0.6	.300	.353	.541	.298	.259	.315	.482	.269	4.4	25-1B	1	11-RF 0
2005	NYN	MLB	23	313	41	17	3	12	38	30	82	6	2	-0.2	.257	.329	.468	.076	.254	.329	.473	.272	10.1	74-RF	-4	
2006	NOR	AAA	24	411	30	16	0	8	38	25	99	5	5	-6.3	.224	.276	.330	-.117	.218	.271	.337	.208	-29.2	82-RF	-9	
2007	OKL	AAA	25	299	39	15	2	14	65	21	81	3	0	0.3	.321	.371	.546	.306	.253	.304	.458	.261	0.0	27-LF	-4	15-RF -2
2007	TEX	MLB	25	108	13	4	0	9	25	1	33	0	0	-0.3	.240	.259	.538	-.003	.240	.266	.558	.267	1.7	18-RF	-1	
2008	HOU	MLB	26	381	44	17	2	16	56	27	102	6	2	-0.3	.253	.309	.452	-.053	.255	.312	.461	.259	6.6	91-RF	-4	

Breakout: 33% Improve: 62% Collapse: 17% Attrition: 22%   Comparables: Edgard Clemente, Tony Armas Sr., Mario Encarnacion, Yurendell de Caster

Like Botts and Cruz, Diaz is now in the latter portion of his 20s, has proven that he can mash at Triple-A, but has done little in his big-league opportunities. Sure, he hit nine home runs in 104 at-bats last year, but that was hardly enough to mitigate his one walk and 33 strikeouts. Released in November, Diaz hooked on with the Astros via a minor league deal and will compete for a bench-job in camp.

German Duran			2B										Bats: R		Throws: R		Height: 5' 10"		Weight: 185		Born: August 3, 1984		Age: 23		
YEAR	TEAM	LVL	AGE	PA	R	2B	3B	HR	RBI	BB	SO	SB	CS	EqBRR	AVG	OBP	SLG	MLVr	EqAVG	EqOBP	EqSLG	EqA	VORP	DEFENSE		
2005	SPO	A-	20	274	36	17	2	4	33	18	56	6	4	3.1	.262	.313	.393	-.023	.194	.234	.291	.175	-36.1	56-SS	3	
2006	BAK	A+	21	503	81	31	2	13	72	35	89	15	9	-8.0	.284	.331	.446	.061	.229	.269	.358	.218	-10.3	49-SS	-14	44-2B 7
2007	FRI	AA	22	529	81	32	5	22	84	34	77	11	2	-1.4	.300	.352	.525	.214	.266	.311	.462	.264	22.2	124-2B	2	
2008	TEX	MLB	23	566	58	31	3	14	62	30	117	10	4	0.1	.246	.290	.395	-.140	.243	.289	.405	.243	0.8	133-2B	-3	

Breakout: 39% Improve: 57% Collapse: 15% Attrition: 7%   Comparables: Trace Coquillette, Josh Barfield, Brian Barden, Donnie Murphy

Duran's 2007 performance was another shocker. He entered the year as a nondescript middle infielder and finished it in the Texas League's top five in eight offensive categories. Duran's greatest strength is his lack of weaknesses; he's a decent hitter with decent power and decent defensive skills, but doesn't excel in any one of those areas. He's going to get some work at third base and the outfield at Triple-A in order to give him some versatility.

Jerry Hairston Jr.   UT

Bats: R   Throws: R   Height: 5' 10"   Weight: 185   Born: May 29, 1976   Age: 32

YEAR	TEAM	LVL	AGE	PA	R	2B	3B	HR	RBI	BB	SO	SB	CS	EqBRR	AVG	OBP	SLG	MLVr	EqAVG	EqOBP	EqSLG	EqA	VORP	DEFENSE			
2005	CHN	MLB	29	430	51	25	2	4	30	31	46	8	9	2.2	.261	.336	.368	-.056	.260	.335	.375	.245	1.0	43-CF	-2	37-2B	-1
2006	CHN	MLB	30	92	8	3	0	0	4	4	14	3	0	0.3	.207	.253	.244	-.438	.202	.247	.238	.176	-6.0	17-2B	-3		
2006	TEX	MLB	30	100	17	3	1	0	6	9	20	2	2	-0.2	.205	.286	.261	-.400	.207	.296	.264	.199	-7.4	16-LF	2		
2007	TEX	MLB	31	184	22	7	0	3	16	11	24	5	1	1.5	.189	.249	.289	-.406	.196	.260	.304	.210	-11.8	15-CF	2	12-2B	2
2008	TEX	MLB	32	166	16	7	1	2	14	10	25	4	2	0.5	.235	.293	.334	-.223	.232	.292	.342	.229	-4.2	43-CF	1		

Breakout: 38%   Improve: 54%   Collapse: 38%   Attrition: 38%   Comparables: Keith Miller, Jerry Morales, Jerry Coleman, Gus Gil

For two straight years, Hairston has failed to post either an on-base or slugging percentage above .300. Last year, his problems were compounded by back issues and a strained rib cage. A free agent at press time, Hairston will likely get a shot with someone just for the sake of roster flexibility, which is the advantage of being able to play six positions.

Ian Kinsler   2B

Bats: R   Throws: R   Height: 6' 0"   Weight: 200   Born: June 22, 1982   Age: 26

YEAR	TEAM	LVL	AGE	PA	R	2B	3B	HR	RBI	BB	SO	SB	CS	EqBRR	AVG	OBP	SLG	MLVr	EqAVG	EqOBP	EqSLG	EqA	VORP	DEFENSE	
2005	OKL	AAA	23	597	102	28	2	23	94	53	89	19	5	3.8	.274	.348	.464	.071	.238	.304	.397	.245	3.6	126-2B	-1
2006	TEX	MLB	24	474	65	27	1	14	55	40	64	11	4	0.7	.286	.347	.454	.036	.282	.351	.457	.279	24.3	117-2B	-2
2007	TEX	MLB	25	566	96	22	2	20	61	62	83	23	2	5.8	.263	.355	.441	.042	.267	.364	.468	.291	27.8	129-2B	5
2008	TEX	MLB	26	595	82	29	3	19	72	55	91	20	6	1.0	.267	.341	.441	.023	.264	.341	.452	.280	22.5	139-2B	2

Breakout: 25%   Improve: 57%   Collapse: 15%   Attrition: 9%   Comparables: Khalil Greene, Davey Johnson, Ken McMullen, Don Money

A drop in batting average meant that Kinsler's 2007 wasn't much more valuable on a pure statistical level than his 2006 showing, but he drew more walks and turned some of his doubles into home runs, which projects far better for his future than mere batting average, which can fluctuate pretty wildly while having little to do with a player's skill. A closer look at Kinsler's season tells two different stories: In April he hit nine home runs, one every 10.8 plate appearances; he went deep once every 42.6 PA the rest of the season. A stress fracture sidelined Kinsler for a month starting in late June, at which point he was hitting .241/.334/.452. When he returned, he showed less power than before, but more strongly resembled the more rounded hitter he had been in 2006 by going .288/.379/.428. PECOTA thinks the version of Kinsler we'll see this year will more strongly resemble that of the first half. Either way, the Rangers are trying to sign him to a long-term deal.

Gerald Laird   C

Bats: R   Throws: R   Height: 6' 1"   Weight: 225   Born: November 13, 1979   Age: 28

YEAR	TEAM	LVL	AGE	PA	R	2B	3B	HR	RBI	BB	SO	SB	CS	EqBRR	AVG	OBP	SLG	MLVr	EqAVG	EqOBP	EqSLG	EqA	VORP	DEFENSE	
2005	OKL	AAA	25	317	51	12	4	17	55	28	61	12	2	-1.2	.310	.380	.562	.311	.272	.334	.484	.279	18.2	72-C	9
2005	TEX	MLB	25	42	7	2	0	1	4	2	7	0	0	-0.1	.225	.262	.350	-.263	.231	.286	.359	.222	-0.9	11-C	0
2006	TEX	MLB	26	260	46	20	1	7	22	12	54	3	1	0.1	.296	.332	.473	.051	.292	.336	.475	.276	12.2	66-C	6
2007	TEX	MLB	27	448	48	18	3	9	47	30	103	6	2	2.2	.224	.278	.349	-.251	.228	.287	.374	.231	-7.5	112-C	11
2008	TEX	MLB	28	323	35	15	2	9	36	22	72	5	2	0.3	.242	.299	.397	-.123	.239	.299	.407	.248	2.9	78-C	4

Breakout: 20%   Improve: 42%   Collapse: 31%   Attrition: 31%   Comparables: Jim Hegan, Bobby Hughes, Ray Fosse, Ray Katt

Laird's last two seasons followed a familiar pattern: a catcher has a really good season as a backup, one that seems out of line with his expected performance, gets a starting job, and goes back to hitting as poorly as he did in the first place. It wasn't the first time it had happened, and it won't be the last. Laird can settle in as the backup once again now that the Rangers have Jarrod Saltalamacchia, but if he tries to impress the pitchers in the bullpen with his reminiscences of the golden summer of 2006, he'll quickly find out they've heard it all before.

John Mayberry Jr.   RF

Bats: R   Throws: R   Height: 6' 6"   Weight: 230   Born: December 21, 1983   Age: 24

YEAR	TEAM	LVL	AGE	PA	R	2B	3B	HR	RBI	BB	SO	SB	CS	EqBRR	AVG	OBP	SLG	MLVr	EqAVG	EqOBP	EqSLG	EqA	VORP	DEFENSE			
2005	SPO	A-	21	302	51	16	0	11	26	26	71	7	3	1.2	.253	.341	.438	.070	.191	.254	.299	.194	-52.0	60-RF	-9		
2006	CLN	A	22	533	77	26	4	21	77	59	117	9	3	-0.6	.268	.358	.479	.205	.220	.293	.388	.238	-19.8	90-RF	-3	25-LF	0
2007	BAK	A+	23	277	47	15	1	16	45	28	64	9	1	2.3	.230	.314	.496	.026	.183	.256	.367	.219	-19.3	58-RF	2		
2007	FRI	AA	23	271	35	10	0	14	38	20	62	7	1	2.8	.241	.307	.453	-.005	.212	.267	.384	.227	-14.7	68-RF	-2		
2008	TEX	MLB	24	547	56	26	2	17	62	40	156	10	4	0.5	.220	.283	.384	-.183	.217	.283	.394	.238	-15.9	128-RF	0		

Breakout: 49%   Improve: 71%   Collapse: 17%   Attrition: 13%   Comparables: Chad Mottola, Todd Dunn, J. J. Davis, Tim Costo

Mayberry was a surprise first-round pick in 2005, and thus far the naysayers have been right. Mayberry has tons of raw power but not much in the way of pure hitting skills, and though he's a good athlete for his size, his transition from first base to right field has been spotty. This year could be a make-or-break year for him; he'll either prove that he's a future big leaguer or be branded with the minor league slugger label.

Travis Metcalf   3B

Bats: R   Throws: R   Height: 6' 3"   Weight: 215   Born: August 17, 1982   Age: 25

YEAR	TEAM	LVL	AGE	PA	R	2B	3B	HR	RBI	BB	SO	SB	CS	EqBRR	AVG	OBP	SLG	MLVr	EqAVG	EqOBP	EqSLG	EqA	VORP	DEFENSE	
2005	BAK	A+	22	566	80	32	7	22	94	49	129	8	2	0.3	.291	.358	.513	.147	.224	.281	.376	.228	-8.2	132-3B	3
2006	FRI	AA	23	477	51	16	2	8	37	45	112	9	7	-1.7	.221	.298	.325	-.235	.189	.255	.279	.187	-34.0	116-3B	-8
2007	FRI	AA	24	226	38	18	0	7	34	21	44	2	1	1.0	.280	.345	.475	.116	.246	.305	.409	.249	3.4	54-3B	5
2007	OKL	AAA	24	70	2	3	0	0	6	7	17	0	0	0.0	.148	.232	.197	-.603	.145	.229	.194	.141	-8.1	18-3B	5
2007	TEX	MLB	24	181	25	12	1	5	21	13	41	0	1	0.0	.255	.307	.435	-.060	.256	.312	.450	.259	0.8	49-3B	2
2008	TEX	MLB	25	491	44	24	2	10	52	36	128	5	3	0.2	.224	.285	.354	-.215	.222	.285	.363	.229	-11.2	116-3B	2

Breakout: 36%   Improve: 59%   Collapse: 15%   Attrition: 13%   Comparables: Ed Smith, Joe Dillon, Jim Deschaine, Sean McNally

Metcalf got some third base time when Blalock went down, but he didn't do much to establish himself, making his 2005 breakout campaign look more like a product of the supercharged California League than anything else. Metcalf's best tool is his average power, but his overly aggressive approach prevents him from tapping into it enough, and he's no more than an average fielder. If he has any future, it's as a bench player.

David Murphy   OF

Bats: L   Throws: L   Height: 6' 4"   Weight: 215   Born: October 18, 1981   Age: 26

YEAR	TEAM	LVL	AGE	PA	R	2B	3B	HR	RBI	BB	SO	SB	CS	EqBRR	AVG	OBP	SLG	MLVr	EqAVG	EqOBP	EqSLG	EqA	VORP	DEFENSE			
2005	PME	AA	23	535	71	25	4	14	75	46	83	13	6	-1.2	.275	.337	.430	.065	.242	.303	.383	.239	-3.4	129-CF	-22		
2006	PME	AA	24	184	22	17	1	3	25	11	29	4	2	-0.2	.273	.315	.436	.072	.249	.288	.405	.237	-0.8	41-CF	-2		
2006	PAW	AAA	24	366	45	23	5	8	44	45	53	3	3	-0.7	.267	.355	.447	.117	.247	.333	.425	.262	9.5	61-CF	-11	15-RF	-3
2007	PAW	AAA	25	444	50	20	5	9	47	41	68	8	1	-0.8	.280	.347	.423	.058	.259	.324	.410	.256	8.2	51-CF	-12	32-LF	3
2007	TEX	MLB	25	110	16	12	1	2	14	7	19	0	0	0.2	.340	.382	.534	.297	.343	.391	.569	.319	9.9	11-LF	1		
2008	TEX	MLB	26	563	67	30	3	13	64	44	103	8	3	0.4	.263	.322	.410	-.053	.259	.321	.421	.261	4.5	132-CF	1		

Breakout: 31%   Improve: 57%   Collapse: 17%   Attrition: 13%   Comparables: Jacob Cruz, Gabe Gross, Darrell Whitmore, Larry Bigbie

Acquired from Boston in the Gagné deal, Murphy was given a full-time job for the last six weeks of the season, during which he hit like the player he wishes he was instead of the player he actually is. A career .273/.343/.407 hitter in the minors, there is absolutely no evidence whatsoever that his .340 run was real. That said, he's a guy who can play all three outfield positions extremely well and hit enough to be a valuable bench player for the next decade.

Max Ramirez   C

Bats: R   Throws: R   Height: 5' 11"   Weight: 170   Born: October 11, 1984   Age: 23

YEAR	TEAM	LVL	AGE	PA	R	2B	3B	HR	RBI	BB	SO	SB	CS	EqBRR	AVG	OBP	SLG	MLVr	EqAVG	EqOBP	EqSLG	EqA	VORP	DEFENSE	
2005	DNV	Rk	20	278	45	19	0	8	47	31	41	1	2	-4.3	.347	.424	.527	.482	.249	.306	.328	.222	-9.8	27-C	1
2006	LKC	A	21	161	19	6	1	4	26	30	27	0	0	-0.9	.307	.435	.465	.297	.246	.354	.373	.263	4.0	17-C	-3
2006	ROM	A	21	326	50	17	0	9	37	54	72	2	0	-0.5	.285	.408	.449	.268	.228	.328	.352	.244	0.0	36-C	-4
2007	KIN	A+	22	342	46	20	0	12	62	53	63	1	0	-2.9	.303	.418	.505	.331	.251	.348	.409	.267	11.9	65-C	-1
2007	BAK	A+	22	138	16	10	0	4	20	21	39	1	0	-1.5	.307	.420	.500	.279	.218	.319	.361	.243	-0.4	24-C	0
2008	TEX	MLB	23	501	47	22	1	11	50	50	138	3	1	-1.2	.231	.311	.359	-.158	.228	.311	.368	.243	-1.6	118-C	-3

Breakout: 11%   Improve: 37%   Collapse: 31%   Attrition: 17%   Comparables: Bob Henley, George Kottaras, Felix Colon, Gabriel Martinez

While Ramirez has yet to get out of A-ball, he's already been traded twice for big leaguers, going from Atlanta to Cleveland in 2006 for Bob Wickman, and moving to Texas last year in the Kenny Lofton deal. He's one of the top offensive catchers in the minors, having shown an ability to hit for average with decent power and plenty of walks, but his defense remains a large enough question mark for some to wonder if he can stay behind the plate and where his future lies if he can't.

Jarrod Saltalamacchia   **1B**   Bats: S   Throws: R   Height: 6' 4"   Weight: 195   Born: May 2, 1985   Age: 23

YEAR	TEAM	LVL	AGE	PA	R	2B	3B	HR	RBI	BB	SO	SB	CS	EqBRR	AVG	OBP	SLG	MLVr	EqAVG	EqOBP	EqSLG	EqA	VORP	DEFENSE		
2005	MYR	A+	20	529	70	35	1	19	81	57	99	4	2	0.6	.314	.394	.519	.330	.260	.323	.411	.254	13.7	93-C -11		
2006	MIS	AA	21	377	30	18	1	9	39	55	71	0	1	-2.2	.230	.353	.380	.077	.222	.332	.381	.253	4.6	80-C 2		
2007	MIS	AA	22	94	18	7	0	6	13	13	17	2	0	-1.2	.309	.404	.617	.484	.277	.362	.566	.306	10.4	20-C 1		
2007	ATL	MLB	22	153	11	6	0	4	12	10	28	0	0	-1.4	.284	.333	.411	.004	.286	.340	.421	.264	4.4	21-C -1	12-1B -2	
2007	TEX	MLB	22	176	28	7	1	7	21	9	47	0	0	1.1	.251	.290	.431	-.095	.253	.295	.446	.250	1.1	23-1B -7	21-C -4	
2008	TEX	MLB	23	460	54	24	1	16	61	40	96	3	1	-0.7	.269	.337	.447	.025	.266	.337	.458	.276	15.1	109-C -5		

Breakout: 47% Improve: 69% Collapse: 15% Attrition: 18%   Comparables: Mark Bailey, Butch Wynegar, Dale Sveum, Gary Carter

Ignore the sub-par showing; Saltalamacchia is still a future star. He was pressed into an extremely difficult situation last year, as he was first blocked at his primary position in Atlanta, then had to replace the best hitter on a team mired in a disappointing season after being traded to Texas. He'll get a chance to settle in behind the plate this year, so we should get a better idea as to his true performance level. Salty is no great shakes defensively, but he's good enough, and his bat will more than make up for it, as he'll be one of the few catchers from whom you can expect a .280-plus batting average and 25 home runs annually.

Sammy Sosa   **DH**   Bats: R   Throws: R   Height: 6' 0"   Weight: 230   Born: November 12, 1968   Age: 39

YEAR	TEAM	LVL	AGE	PA	R	2B	3B	HR	RBI	BB	SO	SB	CS	EqBRR	AVG	OBP	SLG	MLVr	EqAVG	EqOBP	EqSLG	EqA	VORP	DEFENSE	
2005	BAL	MLB	36	424	39	15	1	14	45	39	84	1	1	-3.2	.221	.295	.376	-.153	.225	.309	.396	.245	-7.6	66-RF	0
2007	TEX	MLB	38	454	53	24	1	21	92	34	112	0	0	-3.3	.252	.311	.468	-.006	.254	.319	.489	.272	7.0	15-RF	2
2008	TEX	MLB	39	282	32	16	1	12	42	26	70	0	0	-1.2	.255	.327	.469	.027	.252	.326	.481	.277	8.3	69-DH	

Breakout: 26% Improve: 61% Collapse: 17% Attrition: 46%   Comparables: Tony Perez, Ellis Burks, Andres Galarraga, Hank Sauer

For Sosa to play as well as he did last season after more than a year away from the game made for a pretty remarkable comeback, but that isn't the same as saying he was actually good. The rise and fall of Sosa's plate discipline has had far more to do with how pitchers have approached him than with his own selectivity. Sosa twice drew more than 100 walks in a season earlier in the decade, but that was because pitchers came nowhere near the strike zone against him. He didn't lose the ability to control the strike zone after that; he just wasn't as scary. Throughout it all, he's been the same hacker he ever was. Sosa wants a job in 2008, and chances are, someone will give it to him, but there are more versatile players out there who can deliver the same production for much less dough.

Taylor Teagarden   **C**   Bats: R   Throws: R   Height: 6' 1"   Weight: 200   Born: December 21, 1983   Age: 24

YEAR	TEAM	LVL	AGE	PA	R	2B	3B	HR	RBI	BB	SO	SB	CS	EqBRR	AVG	OBP	SLG	MLVr	EqAVG	EqOBP	EqSLG	EqA	VORP	DEFENSE	
2005	SPO	A-	21	122	23	5	4	7	16	23	32	1	1	0.4	.281	.426	.635	.443	.214	.328	.447	.267	7.1	20-C	-1
2007	BAK	A+	23	364	75	25	0	20	67	65	89	2	1	-1.4	.315	.448	.606	.470	.242	.360	.454	.281	20.4	29-C	1
2007	FRI	AA	23	115	19	3	0	7	16	10	39	0	0	0.6	.294	.357	.529	.220	.202	.267	.394	.228	-2.5	14-C	-2
2008	TEX	MLB	24	502	55	21	3	16	57	56	163	4	2	-0.1	.216	.311	.392	-.127	.214	.310	.402	.252	-0.7	118-DH	

Breakout: 16% Improve: 38% Collapse: 30% Attrition: 11%   Comparables: Mike Napoli, Jeff Bailey, Danny Peoples, Eddy Furniss

A frustrating prospect, Teagarden has been a Three True Outcomes hero with 34 home runs, 107 walks, and 167 strikeouts in 147 minor league games, but he lost nearly all of 2006 to Tommy John surgery, and continuing elbow soreness limited him to part-time duty behind the plate last year. When Teagarden is behind the dish, he's one of the top defensive catchers around. If he can stay there, he's Mickey Tettleton with defensive chops.

Ramon Vazquez   INF

Bats: L   Throws: R   Height: 5' 11"   Weight: 170   Born: August 21, 1976   Age: 31

YEAR	TEAM	LVL	AGE	PA	R	2B	3B	HR	RBI	BB	SO	SB	CS	EqBRR	AVG	OBP	SLG	MLVr	EqAVG	EqOBP	EqSLG	EqA	VORP	DEFENSE			
2005	BUF	AAA	28	92	13	3	1	0	4	7	16	1	1	-0.3	.214	.275	.274	-.356	.190	.253	.250	.171	-7.0	16-SS	3		
2005	BOS	MLB	28	66	6	2	0	0	4	3	14	0	0	-0.3	.197	.234	.230	-.488	.200	.250	.233	.164	-5.3				
2006	BUF	AAA	29	123	19	2	1	2	11	22	27	2	1	0.0	.242	.377	.343	-.001	.220	.352	.330	.250	1.5	14-SS	-1		
2006	CLE	MLB	29	77	11	2	0	1	8	6	18	0	0	1.5	.209	.267	.284	-.385	.212	.280	.288	.208	-4.4	11-3B	-2		
2007	OKL	AAA	30	161	27	10	2	2	13	24	27	3	1	0.5	.258	.375	.409	.050	.231	.348	.373	.261	4.1	21-SS	7	13-2B	1
2007	TEX	MLB	30	345	42	13	3	8	28	29	72	1	0	0.2	.230	.300	.373	-.171	.236	.312	.397	.249	-5.0	61-3B	6	13-SS	2
2008	TEX	MLB	31	288	32	12	2	4	25	29	60	3	2	0.5	.243	.324	.359	-.129	.240	.323	.368	.249	0.4	70-3B	2		

Breakout: 32% Improve: 60% Collapse: 25% Attrition: 38%   Comparables: Billy Klaus, Joe Koppe, Fred Hatfield, Bobby Morgan

Last year, Vazquez ended up with the most major league playing time he's had since 2003 thanks to the rash of injuries that hit the Rangers' infield. That's his value: he can play all over the place and he's better than Jerry Hairston. It was enough to fetch him another one-year deal for 2008.

John Whittleman   3B

Bats: L   Throws: R   Height: 6' 2"   Weight: 195   Born: February 11, 1987   Age: 21

YEAR	TEAM	LVL	AGE	PA	R	2B	3B	HR	RBI	BB	SO	SB	CS	EqBRR	AVG	OBP	SLG	MLVr	EqAVG	EqOBP	EqSLG	EqA	VORP	DEFENSE	
2006	CLN	A	19	530	56	21	3	9	43	60	97	7	6	-1.8	.227	.313	.343	-.054	.184	.255	.282	.186	-39.1	119-3B	-18
2007	CLN	A	20	406	56	25	1	14	57	63	91	5	3	0.4	.271	.382	.476	.233	.217	.310	.370	.240	-1.2	84-3B	-5
2007	BAK	A+	20	129	18	9	0	3	15	23	33	0	3	-2.1	.240	.372	.413	.027	.202	.318	.339	.229	-1.6	29-3B	-2
2008	TEX	MLB	21	598	52	28	2	12	56	58	160	5	4	-0.1	.215	.293	.341	-.223	.212	.293	.350	.228	-15.2	140-3B	-7

Breakout: 47% Improve: 68% Collapse: 14% Attrition: 7%   Comparables: Andy Fox, Joey Votto, Chris Haas, Bo Dodson

Sometimes, all you need is a second chance. A second-round pick in 2005, Whittleman did next to nothing at Low-A Clinton in 2006, but began to put things together last year, showing solid power and a very good approach. Unfortunately, that's unlikely to be enough, as he's a poor third baseman with limited range who is coming off back-to-back 34-error seasons. Whittleman took a big step forward, but like Joe McDoakes, he's still behind the eight ball.

Brad Wilkerson   1B/OF

Bats: L   Throws: L   Height: 6' 0"   Weight: 205   Born: June 1, 1977   Age: 31

YEAR	TEAM	LVL	AGE	PA	R	2B	3B	HR	RBI	BB	SO	SB	CS	EqBRR	AVG	OBP	SLG	MLVr	EqAVG	EqOBP	EqSLG	EqA	VORP	DEFENSE			
2005	WAS	MLB	28	661	76	42	7	11	57	84	147	8	10	-6.7	.248	.351	.405	.032	.253	.358	.421	.268	13.2	84-CF	-3	32-LF	0
2006	TEX	MLB	29	365	56	15	2	15	44	37	116	3	2	1.0	.222	.306	.422	-.134	.218	.311	.424	.253	-5.3	75-LF	-2		
2007	TEX	MLB	30	389	54	17	1	20	62	43	107	4	1	-0.4	.234	.319	.467	-.011	.237	.329	.491	.278	6.2	52-1B	-4	31-LF	3
2008	TEX	MLB	31	365	47	17	2	14	47	42	96	5	2	0.1	.238	.330	.438	-.021	.235	.330	.449	.272	4.3	88-LF	0		

Breakout: 26% Improve: 50% Collapse: 26% Attrition: 29%   Comparables: Roger Repoz, Pete Ward, Willie Smith, Daryl Boston

In case you haven't figured it out, the Alfonso Soriano trade didn't work out too well for the Rangers. Wilkerson was supposed to be the big prize, but shoulder problems and a variety of leg ailments have sapped his skills, leaving him a low-average/high-power guy who is rarely healthy enough to play anywhere but first base. Meanwhile, in the two seasons since the deal, Soriano has hit 79 home runs, stolen 60 bases, scored 216 runs, and recorded 41 outfield assists (after years of fighting the Rangers to stay at second base). There's no crying in baseball, but if you want to anyway, Wilkerson is the spilt milk.

Mike Young   SS

Bats: R   Throws: R   Height: 6' 1"   Weight: 200   Born: October 19, 1976   Age: 31

YEAR	TEAM	LVL	AGE	PA	R	2B	3B	HR	RBI	BB	SO	SB	CS	EqBRR	AVG	OBP	SLG	MLVr	EqAVG	EqOBP	EqSLG	EqA	VORP	DEFENSE	
2005	TEX	MLB	28	732	114	40	5	24	91	58	91	5	2	0.1	.331	.385	.513	.255	.330	.395	.527	.312	71.8	153-SS	-18
2006	TEX	MLB	29	748	93	52	3	14	103	48	96	7	3	-0.4	.314	.356	.459	.086	.310	.359	.460	.282	46.0	154-SS	23
2007	TEX	MLB	30	692	80	37	1	9	94	47	107	13	3	0.0	.315	.366	.418	.069	.322	.376	.440	.285	38.1	146-SS	7
2008	TEX	MLB	31	626	76	33	3	11	69	43	90	10	3	-0.4	.289	.340	.411	-.001	.286	.340	.422	.270	23.0	146-SS	1

Breakout: 2% Improve: 18% Collapse: 47% Attrition: 7%   Comparables: Jeff Cirillo, Dave Concepcion, Alvin Dark, Derek Jeter

Young needed a .349/.399/.457 second half and a .362 average in September to get his fifth-straight 200-hit season, but that streak has made him considerably overrated, especially if he's not going to hit 20 home runs a year anymore. He's still a very good player, but when the face of the franchise is a guy who's merely one of the top five players in the league at his position but is still going to be paid $16 million a year into the latter portion of his 30s, it underscores the dysfunction inherent in the franchise.

PITCHERS

Blake Beavan
Bats: R   Throws: R   Height: 6' 6"   Weight: 200   Born: January 17, 1989   Age: 19

YEAR	TEAM	LVL	AGE	W	L	SV	G	GS	IP	H	BB	SO	HR	GB%	BABIP	STUFF	WHIP	ERA	PERA	EqERA	EqH9	EqBB9	EqSO9	EqHR9	VORP	SN/WX
2008	TEX	MLB	19	4	12	0	26	26	125	171	104	60	27	47.3%	.327	-26	2.20	8.41	8.12	8.02	11.7	6.9	3.9	1.9	-36.9	-3.00

Breakout: NA   Improve: NA   Collapse: NA   Attrition: NA   Comparables: Kurt Miller, Chaz Roe, Jon Garland, Gil Meche

The Rangers' first-round pick last June, Beavan is a local product who played high school baseball just 15 minutes from Arlington. He's a tall right-hander who absolutely pounds the strike zone with a low- to mid-90s fastball; in his senior year, he recorded 124 strikeouts in 66 innings with just four walks. The downside is a violent delivery and a low arm angle that hampers his secondary stuff. Some see starter, some see closer.

Joaquin Benoit
Bats: R   Throws: R   Height: 6' 3"   Weight: 220   Born: July 26, 1977   Age: 30

YEAR	TEAM	LVL	AGE	W	L	SV	G	GS	IP	H	BB	SO	HR	GB%	BABIP	STUFF	WHIP	ERA	PERA	EqERA	EqH9	EqBB9	EqSO9	EqHR9	VORP	SN/WX
2005	TEX	MLB	27	4	4	0	32	9	87	69	38	78	9	31.9%	.251	15	1.23	3.72	3.12	3.43	6.2	3.7	7.6	0.8	18.0	1.92
2006	TEX	MLB	28	1	1	0	56	0	79²	68	38	85	5	38.5%	.296	20	1.33	4.86	3.20	4.94	6.9	3.8	8.7	0.4	5.9	0.19
2007	TEX	MLB	29	7	4	6	70	0	82	68	28	87	6	38.6%	.297	25	1.17	2.85	3.10	2.85	7.1	2.7	8.7	0.7	27.2	3.52
2008	TEX	MLB	30	4	4	6	60	0	71¹	65	30	73	8	40.3%	.295	11	1.32	4.04	3.74	3.92	7.8	3.4	8.3	1.0	13.2	1.20

Breakout: 17%   Improve: 41%   Collapse: 23%   Attrition: 7%   Comparables: Rick Aguilera, Kyle Farnsworth, Brian Fuentes, Roberto Hernandez

The Rangers have been giving chances to Benoit since 2001, and it's only over the last two years that he's finally made good on them. Benoit always had a nasty fastball/slider combination, but control issues and the lack of a third pitch limited him as a starter. As a reliever, he's gained more confidence with his pure power stuff, and is now a fine option to close when needed. In appreciation for all of those chances, Benoit showed some rare loyalty by sticking with Texas for two years and $6 million.

Scott Feldman
Bats: L   Throws: R   Height: 6' 5"   Weight: 210   Born: February 7, 1983   Age: 25

YEAR	TEAM	LVL	AGE	W	L	SV	G	GS	IP	H	BB	SO	HR	GB%	BABIP	STUFF	WHIP	ERA	PERA	EqERA	EqH9	EqBB9	EqSO9	EqHR9	VORP	SN/WX
2005	FRI	AA	22	1	2	14	46	0	61	43	23	41	3	63.4%	.237	-10	1.08	2.36	3.71	3.54	6.4	4.8	4.0	0.8	12.8	—
2006	OKL	AAA	23	2	2	4	23	0	27	20	9	24	2	53.3%	.254	-2	1.07	2.00	3.72	3.42	6.8	3.4	5.8	1.0	6.4	—
2006	TEX	MLB	23	0	2	0	36	0	41¹	42	10	30	4	60.3%	.306	5	1.26	3.92	3.76	3.70	8.3	2.0	6.1	0.7	9.5	-0.01
2007	OKL	AAA	24	1	1	2	21	0	30	28	12	24	1	51.1%	.303	-9	1.33	4.50	4.11	5.90	8.7	4.0	5.6	0.3	-1.0	—
2007	TEX	MLB	24	1	2	0	29	0	39	44	32	19	3	58.0%	.308	-15	1.95	5.77	5.64	5.45	9.5	6.4	4.1	0.7	0.5	-0.42
2008	TEX	MLB	25	2	3	1	43	2	52	52	26	34	4	55.4%	.293	-5	1.49	4.32	4.05	4.31	8.5	4.1	5.4	0.7	7.6	0.70

Breakout: 23%   Improve: 49%   Collapse: 24%   Attrition: 28%   Comparables: Jay Powell, Jim Hannan, Ron Willis, Tom Hausman

A 30th-round pick in 2003, Feldman is now the only 886th overall pick to ever reach the majors. He's a side-armer and comes with the usual good things (tons of groundballs) and bad things (doesn't miss many bats, opposite-handed hitters hit him hard) that the delivery entails. He has spent the last two years splitting time between Triple-A and the majors, and unless he's possessed by the benevolent ghost of Dan Quisenberry, there's no reason to expect a great leap forward.

Neftali Feliz

Bats: R   Throws: R   Height: 6' 3"   Weight: 180   Born: May 2, 1988   Age: 20

YEAR	TEAM	LVL	AGE	W	L	SV	G	GS	IP	H	BB	SO	HR	GB%	BABIP	STUFF	WHIP	ERA	PERA	EqERA	EqH9	EqBB9	EqSO9	EqHR9	VORP	SN/WX
2006	BRA	Rk	18	0	2	2	11	5	29¹	20	14	42	0	51.9%	.346	23	1.17	4.02	6.48	7.43	10.2	8.6	7.8	0.4	-4.7	—
2007	SPO	A-	19	0	2	0	8	1	15	13	12	27	2	48.4%	.393	8	1.67	3.60	16.31	10.80	14.7	13.1	9.3	3.9	-6.8	—
2007	DNV	Rk	19	2	0	0	8	7	27¹	18	12	28	0	50.7%	.273	-2	1.10	1.98	6.18	5.91	8.9	9.3	4.2	0.8	-0.7	—
2008	TEX	MLB	20	3	6	0	24	15	78	87	85	63	12	49.9%	.321	-15	2.20	7.06	7.19	6.80	9.5	9.0	6.5	1.3	-11.5	-0.80

Breakout: 39% Improve: 61% Collapse: 19% Attrition: 4%   Comparables: Mark Rogers, Darwin Peguero, Chi-Hung Cheng, Manny Tejada

Feliz was probably not the best-known prospect received from Atlanta in the Teixeira trade, but he might prove to be the best. As a 19-year-old who already pumps out fastballs in the upper 90s, Feliz has recorded 97 strikeouts while allowing just 51 hits in 71 1/3 innings as a pro, and (pardon the mangled metaphor) his ceiling is through the roof. He still needs better command and a more consistent slider, but the number of teenage arms with this kind of upside can be counted on one hand.

Frank Francisco

Bats: R   Throws: R   Height: 6' 2"   Weight: 235   Born: September 11, 1979   Age: 28

YEAR	TEAM	LVL	AGE	W	L	SV	G	GS	IP	H	BB	SO	HR	GB%	BABIP	STUFF	WHIP	ERA	PERA	EqERA	EqH9	EqBB9	EqSO9	EqHR9	VORP	SN/WX
2006	FRI	AA	26	0	0	0	13	0	14	10	4	22	1	41.9%	.300	14	1.00	1.93	3.78	2.63	7.2	3.3	9.9	0.7	4.5	—
2006	TEX	MLB	26	0	1	0	8	0	7¹	8	2	6	2	50.0%	.273	-4	1.36	4.93	5.08	4.70	8.2	2.3	7.0	2.3	0.9	-0.00
2007	TEX	MLB	27	1	1	0	59	0	59¹	57	38	49	3	38.5%	.320	8	1.60	4.55	4.09	4.55	8.2	5.2	6.8	0.5	7.2	1.56
2008	TEX	MLB	28	3	3	2	51	0	56¹	53	29	48	6	42.1%	.291	1	1.45	4.32	4.14	4.20	8.1	4.2	6.9	0.9	8.6	0.70

Breakout: 26% Improve: 44% Collapse: 28% Attrition: 24%   Comparables: Hector Mercado, Hal Reniff, Bill Kelso, Ron Villone

After losing most of the last two years to elbow surgery, Francisco still has days when his plus fastball/slider mix is lights out, but more often than not, there aren't enough strikes coming out of his hand. The Rangers have brought him back in the hope that the cliché of control being the last thing to come back after Tommy John surgery will prove true.

Kaz Fukumori

Bats: R   Throws: R   Height: 5' 11"   Weight: 170   Born: August 4, 1976   Age: 31

YEAR	TM	LVL	AGE	W	L	SV	G	GS	IP	H	BB	SO	HR	GB%	BABIP	STUFF	WHIP	ERA	PERA	EQERA	EQH9	EQBB9	EQSO9	EQHR9	VORP	WXRL
2005	RAK	JPL	28	4	3	11	49	0	63	75	24	36	5	—	.314	-19	1.57	3.57	5.11	4.15	9.8	4.2	3.9	0.9	9.8	—
2006	RAK	JPL	29	0	3	21	50	0	58	50	27	55	2	—	.289	6	1.33	2.17	4.11	3.67	7.8	5.3	6.6	0.5	12.1	—
2007	RAK	JPL	30	4	2	17	34	0	36	44	17	33	1	—	.377	-3	1.69	4.75	5.92	6.29	11.0	5.5	6.6	0.5	-2.6	—
2008	TEX	MLB	31	2	3	9	31	0	37²	40	21	28	4	46.7%	.308	-8	1.62	4.85	4.80	4.72	9.1	4.7	5.9	0.9	3.3	0.40

Breakout: 20% Improve: 42% Collapse: 32% Attrition: 33%   Comparables: Hal Jeffcoat, Dave Jolly, Yorkis Perez, Scott Eyre

The Rangers dipped their pinky toe into the wading pool section of Japanese baseball talent this offseason by signing Fukumori to a cheap two-year deal. He's past 30 and coming off a season in which he put up a 4.75 ERA in Japan, but he's been better than that in the past. He's not going to dominate, as he's more of a moxie kind of guy who mixes things up with an upper-80s fastball, two distinct breaking balls, and a good changeup, but he'll likely be of some value working out of the Rangers' pen.

Kason Gabbard

Bats: L   Throws: L   Height: 6' 3"   Weight: 205   Born: April 8, 1982   Age: 26

YEAR	TEAM	LVL	AGE	W	L	SV	G	GS	IP	H	BB	SO	HR	GB%	BABIP	STUFF	WHIP	ERA	PERA	EqERA	EqH9	EqBB9	EqSO9	EqHR9	VORP	SN/WX
2005	PME	AA	23	9	11	0	27	25	132²	128	65	96	10	55.9%	.298	-14	1.45	4.61	6.26	7.07	10.1	6.2	3.9	1.1	-19.3	—
2006	PME	AA	24	9	2	0	13	13	73¹	51	25	68	4	61.8%	.242	4	1.04	2.59	4.18	4.61	7.6	4.1	5.4	0.9	7.5	—
2006	PAW	AAA	24	1	7	0	9	8	51¹	51	26	48	8	64.4%	.321	-13	1.51	5.28	8.58	7.74	10.9	5.8	6.6	2.4	-10.8	—
2006	BOS	MLB	24	1	3	0	7	4	25²	24	16	15	0	61.3%	.304	6	1.56	3.50	3.69	3.28	8.0	5.5	5.1	0.0	6.3	0.86
2007	PAW	AAA	25	7	2	0	14	14	75	66	25	64	10	61.1%	.271	-9	1.21	3.24	5.31	4.16	8.8	3.4	5.7	1.8	11.4	—
2007	BOS	MLB	25	4	0	0	7	7	41	28	18	29	3	53.5%	.225	15	1.12	3.73	3.16	3.66	6.4	3.7	6.2	0.7	10.4	1.15
2007	TEX	MLB	25	2	1	0	8	8	40¹	40	23	26	5	56.7%	.292	-2	1.56	5.58	5.04	5.03	8.7	4.6	5.5	1.1	1.8	0.42
2008	TEX	MLB	26	5	7	0	30	16	98²	107	51	65	10	52.9%	.308	-3	1.61	5.15	4.91	5.06	9.3	4.3	5.4	0.9	4.7	1.10

Breakout: 15% Improve: 40% Collapse: 35% Attrition: 32%   Comparables: Joe Saunders, Dean Stone, Rich Wortham, Mike Madden

Gabbard exceeded his ability in seven starts for Boston last summer, creating some trade value for the Sox. After coming to Texas in the Gagné swap, he pitched like most scouts expected him to, getting plenty of groundouts, but not much else. Gabbard is a mismatched platypus of a pitcher, a finesse guy without plus control, but his sinker is good enough for fifth starter-dom. In a testament to how over-the-top the game's love of relief pitching has become, Gabbard finished tied for fifth in the AL in shutouts—with one.

Armando Galarraga

Bats: R   Throws: R   Height: 6' 4"   Weight: 180   Born: January 15, 1982   Age: 26

YEAR	TEAM	LVL	AGE	W	L	SV	G	GS	IP	H	BB	SO	HR	GB%	BABIP	STUFF	WHIP	ERA	PERA	EqERA	EqH9	EqBB9	EqSO9	EqHR9	VORP	SN/WX
2005	POT	A+	23	3	4	0	14	14	80	69	23	79	7	47.1%	.287	-10	1.15	2.48	5.97	5.32	9.8	4.2	5.1	1.5	2.2	—
2005	HAR	AA	23	3	4	0	13	13	76¹	80	21	58	10	41.1%	.314	-24	1.32	5.19	6.71	7.27	10.6	3.6	4.2	1.8	-12.9	—
2006	FRI	AA	24	1	6	0	9	9	41	56	13	38	5	53.3%	.398	-23	1.68	5.49	9.69	9.71	14.0	3.8	5.7	1.7	-17.4	—
2007	FRI	AA	25	9	6	0	23	22	127²	122	47	114	14	45.5%	.308	-13	1.32	4.02	6.51	5.63	10.5	4.4	5.8	1.5	-0.4	—
2007	OKL	AAA	25	2	2	0	4	4	24²	23	11	21	1	44.7%	.293	6	1.38	4.74	4.10	5.11	8.4	4.0	5.8	0.4	1.3	—
2007	TEX	MLB	25	0	0	0	3	1	8²	8	7	6	2	40.7%	.250	-8	1.73	6.21	6.06	5.19	8.3	6.2	6.2	2.1	-0.1	-0.11
2008	TEX	MLB	26	4	8	0	35	14	100²	121	55	65	17	45.8%	.317	-12	1.76	6.52	6.12	6.27	10.3	4.5	5.2	1.5	-9.8	-0.40

Breakout: 24% Improve: 55% Collapse: 20% Attrition: 15%   Comparables: Isabel Giron, Frank Campos, Sun-Woo Kim, Wilton Chavez

Another disappointing product of the Alfonso Soriano trade, Galarraga missed much of 2006 with shoulder issues, and while he had a bit of a bounce-back last year, he will enter the season as a 26-year-old with just seven games of experience above Double-A. Still, Galarraga flashes a couple of plus pitches at times with his fastball/slider combination, and could end up with a decent bullpen career.

Matt Harrison

Bats: L   Throws: L   Height: 6' 5"   Weight: 205   Born: August 16, 1985   Age: 22

YEAR	TEAM	LVL	AGE	W	L	SV	G	GS	IP	H	BB	SO	HR	GB%	BABIP	STUFF	WHIP	ERA	PERA	EqERA	EqH9	EqBB9	EqSO9	EqHR9	VORP	SN/WX
2005	ROM	A	19	12	7	0	27	27	167	151	30	118	17	43.1%	.270	-23	1.08	3.23	6.60	6.30	10.4	3.6	3.1	2.1	-11.2	—
2006	MYR	A+	20	8	4	0	13	13	81	77	16	60	6	50.2%	.297	-1	1.15	3.11	5.90	5.23	10.5	2.9	4.2	1.5	3.0	—
2006	MIS	AA	20	3	4	0	13	12	77	83	17	54	6	43.8%	.314	0	1.30	3.62	5.71	5.74	10.8	2.4	4.0	1.3	-1.1	—
2007	MIS	AA	21	5	7	0	20	20	116²	118	34	78	6	49.5%	.309	3	1.30	3.39	4.78	4.92	9.8	3.1	3.8	0.8	8.3	—
2008	TEX	MLB	22	7	10	0	24	24	135	165	54	68	21	47.9%	.310	-3	1.62	5.81	5.48	5.63	10.4	3.3	4.1	1.4	-2.8	0.80

Breakout: 15% Improve: 46% Collapse: 30% Attrition: 6%   Comparables: Billy Traber, Zach Jackson, Justin Thompson, Randey Dorame

Acquired in the Teixeira deal, Harrison was generally considered the top lefty in the Braves' system, which is why the Rangers took him knowing he was suffering from the shoulder soreness which ultimately prevented him from pitching for the remainder of the season. He was healthy enough to pitch in the Arizona Fall League and did quite well. There is a disconnect here, as Harrison has a power arsenal but confounds scouts with an inability to miss many bats. Still, he's young and has plenty of time to work out the kinks; some within the organization think he could be the steal of the deal.

Eric Hurley

Bats: R   Throws: R   Height: 6' 4"   Weight: 195   Born: September 17, 1985   Age: 22

YEAR	TEAM	LVL	AGE	W	L	SV	G	GS	IP	H	BB	SO	HR	GB%	BABIP	STUFF	WHIP	ERA	PERA	EqERA	EqH9	EqBB9	EqSO9	EqHR9	VORP	SN/WX
2005	CLN	A	19	12	6	0	28	28	155¹	135	59	152	11	38.7%	.300	5	1.25	3.77	6.16	6.04	9.8	5.3	5.4	1.4	-6.7	—
2006	BAK	A+	20	5	6	0	18	18	100²	92	32	106	12	41.5%	.308	-8	1.24	4.13	5.91	6.58	9.2	4.2	5.5	1.9	-10.3	—
2006	FRI	AA	20	3	1	0	6	6	37²	21	11	31	4	44.2%	.189	19	0.86	1.94	3.53	2.86	5.5	3.4	5.2	1.3	10.6	—
2007	FRI	AA	21	7	2	0	15	14	88²	71	27	76	13	38.2%	.247	-6	1.10	3.25	5.37	5.20	8.5	3.7	5.4	1.9	3.6	—
2007	OKL	AAA	21	4	7	0	13	13	73¹	65	28	59	13	35.9%	.255	-5	1.27	4.91	5.11	5.75	8.1	3.6	5.5	1.9	-1.2	—
2008	TEX	MLB	22	6	9	0	21	21	114¹	127	55	76	23	39.1%	.289	0	1.58	5.97	5.61	5.67	9.5	3.9	5.4	1.8	-2.8	0.60

Breakout: 14% Improve: 44% Collapse: 25% Attrition: 18%   Comparables: Aaron Myette, Buddy Carlyle, John Wasdin, Josh Banks

Hurley is seen by many as the top prospect in the Rangers' organization, but that's only because *somebody* had to be. Hurley has size and a solid three-pitch mix, but he has always struggled against left-handers and didn't exactly blow anyone away at Triple-A. He's still a very good prospect, but his ceiling is no higher than a solid third-starter/innings-eater. The good news is that players like this are worth $10-12 million a year on the open market.

Kasey Kiker

Bats: L   Throws: L   Height: 5' 10"   Weight: 170   Born: November 19, 1987   Age: 20

YEAR	TEAM	LVL	AGE	W	L	SV	G	GS	IP	H	BB	SO	HR	GB%	BABIP	STUFF	WHIP	ERA	PERA	EqERA	EqH9	EqBB9	EqSO9	EqHR9	VORP	SN/WX
2006	SPO	A-	18	0	7	0	16	15	52	44	35	51	5	45.6%	.291	-16	1.52	4.15	8.66	8.87	9.5	10.5	4.6	2.4	-16.2	—
2007	CLN	A	19	7	4	0	20	20	96[1]	84	41	112	10	39.2%	.318	-20	1.30	2.90	10.73	7.70	12.4	7.9	6.2	2.7	-17.7	—
2008	TEX	MLB	20	4	9	0	23	23	110	132	92	79	21	41.1%	.319	-10	2.03	7.04	7.20	6.64	10.3	6.9	5.8	1.7	-14.0	-0.70

Breakout: 33% Improve: 73% Collapse: 8% Attrition: 13%   Comparables: Travis Wood, Brian Barber, John Danks, Bobby Seay

The Rangers' first-round pick in 2006, Kiker put up some impressive totals in his pro debut, but despite a quality fastball that sits in the low 90s and a power curve that is equally effective, he has some things working against him; he's short, has a violent delivery, does not have a changeup, and needs to throw more strikes. That combination usually adds up to a future in the bullpen, but with Kiker's raw stuff that's not necessarily a bad thing.

Wes Littleton

Bats: R   Throws: R   Height: 6' 2"   Weight: 210   Born: September 2, 1982   Age: 25

YEAR	TEAM	LVL	AGE	W	L	SV	G	GS	IP	H	BB	SO	HR	GB%	BABIP	STUFF	WHIP	ERA	PERA	EqERA	EqH9	EqBB9	EqSO9	EqHR9	VORP	SN/WX
2005	FRI	AA	22	2	3	3	48	0	81[2]	93	24	71	9	56.0%	.354	-21	1.43	3.97	6.81	5.45	11.3	4.0	5.4	1.6	1.2	—
2006	FRI	AA	23	3	0	3	17	0	27[2]	13	7	25	1	64.3%	.174	5	0.74	0.66	2.85	1.98	4.0	2.6	5.3	0.7	11.0	—
2006	TEX	MLB	23	2	1	1	33	0	36[1]	23	13	17	2	70.8%	.204	-2	0.99	1.74	2.46	1.56	5.2	3.1	4.2	0.5	17.8	1.58
2007	OKL	AAA	24	0	1	2	23	0	32[1]	31	8	21	5	59.4%	.277	-21	1.21	5.02	5.18	5.70	9.3	2.7	4.5	1.8	-0.3	—
2007	TEX	MLB	24	3	2	2	35	0	48	48	16	24	6	56.2%	.275	-13	1.33	4.31	4.15	3.75	8.4	2.6	4.1	1.1	9.3	0.40
2008	TEX	MLB	25	2	2	2	44	0	47	47	18	29	4	54.7%	.287	-5	1.37	3.98	3.81	3.95	8.6	3.1	5.0	0.8	9.5	0.70

Breakout: 17% Improve: 33% Collapse: 40% Attrition: 23%   Comparables: Brad Thompson, Brad Clontz, Jose Paniagua, Chuck Seelbach

Littleton profiles as the premise for a political metaphor, a right-handed side-armer who can get lefties out. The problem is that with his weak stuff he doesn't get them, or anyone, out consistently enough. You think there'd be a role for a pitcher like this, the reverse-righty groundball specialist, but the Rangers haven't found one yet.

Kameron Loe

Bats: R   Throws: R   Height: 6' 7"   Weight: 240   Born: September 10, 1981   Age: 26

YEAR	TEAM	LVL	AGE	W	L	SV	G	GS	IP	H	BB	SO	HR	GB%	BABIP	STUFF	WHIP	ERA	PERA	EqERA	EqH9	EqBB9	EqSO9	EqHR9	VORP	SN/WX
2005	OKL	AAA	23	2	1	0	5	5	28[1]	32	10	23	5	46.2%	.314	-8	1.48	5.09	6.38	6.00	10.3	3.7	5.0	1.7	-1.2	—
2005	TEX	MLB	23	9	6	1	48	8	92	89	31	45	7	60.2%	.272	-1	1.30	3.42	3.42	3.47	7.7	2.9	4.1	0.6	17.4	1.35
2006	OKL	AAA	24	1	2	1	13	3	22[1]	32	13	21	3	58.8%	.392	-29	2.04	9.37	9.80	11.69	13.3	5.6	6.0	1.6	-15.1	—
2006	TEX	MLB	24	3	6	0	15	15	78[1]	105	22	34	10	52.2%	.331	-9	1.62	5.86	5.36	5.71	10.8	2.2	3.6	1.0	-0.0	0.62
2007	TEX	MLB	25	6	11	0	28	23	136	162	56	78	13	56.0%	.325	-3	1.60	5.36	5.07	5.99	10.1	3.2	4.7	0.9	-3.6	0.82
2008	TEX	MLB	26	5	7	0	30	15	99[2]	117	39	56	10	54.0%	.318	-5	1.57	5.25	4.83	5.18	10.1	3.2	4.6	0.9	3.1	0.90

Breakout: 34% Improve: 56% Collapse: 20% Attrition: 35%   Comparables: Jim Beattie, Lerrin LaGrow, Mark Clark, Jose Silva

Loe's bread and butter pitch is his sinker, which is made even more effective by his height, but he's maddeningly inconsistent. Last year he made seven starts in which he allowed one or fewer earned runs, but was also rocked for six or more runs seven times. It's a sad fact of life: if you can't miss bats consistently—and Loe can't—you can't be consistently successful.

Michael Main

Bats: R   Throws: R   Height: 6' 2"   Weight: 170   Born: December 14, 1988   Age: 19

YEAR	TEAM	LVL	AGE	W	L	SV	G	GS	IP	H	BB	SO	HR	GB%	BABIP	STUFF	WHIP	ERA	PERA	EqERA	EqH9	EqBB9	EqSO9	EqHR9	VORP	SN/WX
2007	SPO	A-	18	2	0	0	5	5	15[1]	14	7	18	1	46.3%	.325	-2	1.37	4.71	8.74	9.69	11.8	7.6	4.8	2.1	-5.9	—
2007	RNG	Rk	18	0	1	0	5	5	12[2]	9	6	16	1	36.7%	.276	5	1.18	1.42	9.82	4.50	10.8	9.0	5.4	3.6	1.2	—
2008	TEX	MLB	19	4	10	0	24	24	109	137	102	66	23	45.6%	.319	-21	2.19	8.13	7.85	7.76	10.8	7.7	4.9	1.8	-29.0	-2.20

Breakout: NA Improve: NA Collapse: NA Attrition: NA   Comparables: Brian Barber, Clint Everts, Corey Avrard, Jermaine Van Buren

Another first-round pick last June, Main actually showed better stuff in his pro debut than he did during his senior year of high school. One of the best athletes in the draft (some had him on the board as the top high school outfielder in the nation), Main sits at 92 to 94 mph with his fastball, touches 96, already has an above-average curve, and has mechanics that are smooth and fluid. With Beavan, Feliz, and Main, the Rangers' Low-A pitching staff will be one of the best around this year.

Brandon McCarthy

Bats: R   Throws: R   Height: 6' 7"   Weight: 200   Born: July 7, 1983   Age: 24

YEAR	TEAM	LVL	AGE	W	L	SV	G	GS	IP	H	BB	SO	HR	GB%	BABIP	STUFF	WHIP	ERA	PERA	EqERA	EqH9	EqBB9	EqSO9	EqHR9	VORP	SN/WX
2005	CHR	AAA	22	7	7	0	20	19	119¹	104	32	130	16	40.8%	.292	16	1.14	3.92	4.63	4.61	8.5	3.1	7.4	1.5	12.2	—
2005	CHA	MLB	22	3	2	0	12	10	67	62	17	48	13	37.6%	.251	13	1.18	4.03	4.62	3.97	8.5	2.3	6.3	1.6	13.6	1.56
2006	CHA	MLB	23	4	7	0	53	2	84²	77	33	69	17	39.3%	.260	-4	1.30	4.68	4.39	4.09	7.7	3.3	6.9	1.6	14.1	1.05
2007	TEX	MLB	24	5	10	0	23	22	101²	111	48	59	9	37.8%	.307	0	1.56	4.87	4.49	4.96	9.1	3.7	4.7	0.8	6.5	1.88
2008	TEX	MLB	24	5	6	0	27	13	87²	92	36	61	12	41.0%	.292	1	1.45	4.88	4.60	4.71	8.9	3.4	5.7	1.2	8.5	1.30

Breakout: 16% Improve: 39% Collapse: 35% Attrition: 28%   Comparables: Dick Woodson, Arnie Portocarrero, Glenn Abbott, Wayne Simpson

Thinking that they needed help now rather than later, the Rangers traded their top left-hander, John Danks, to the White Sox for McCarthy prior to last season. McCarthy then spent the year proving that he's just not as good as his minor league numbers suggested. His fastball has no more than average velocity, his arm angle makes him susceptible to left-handed hitters, and as a fly-ball pitcher, he's a horrible match for the Rangers' home park. McCarthy performed better than Danks in 2007, but in the long term Danks will prove to be the better pitcher.

Kevin Millwood

Bats: R   Throws: R   Height: 6' 4"   Weight: 230   Born: December 24, 1974   Age: 33

YEAR	TEAM	LVL	AGE	W	L	SV	G	GS	IP	H	BB	SO	HR	GB%	BABIP	STUFF	WHIP	ERA	PERA	EqERA	EqH9	EqBB9	EqSO9	EqHR9	VORP	SN/WX
2005	CLE	MLB	30	9	11	0	30	30	192	182	52	146	20	47.2%	.286	20	1.22	2.86	4.09	3.51	8.9	2.5	6.7	0.9	50.4	5.69
2006	TEX	MLB	31	16	12	0	34	34	215	228	53	157	23	46.0%	.311	18	1.31	4.52	3.85	4.26	8.7	2.0	6.1	0.8	32.9	4.12
2007	TEX	MLB	32	10	14	0	31	31	172²	213	67	123	19	47.8%	.343	4	1.62	5.16	5.56	5.50	10.5	3.1	5.9	0.9	5.7	1.57
2008	TEX	MLB	33	9	9	0	26	26	152¹	165	52	105	17	48.6%	.306	9	1.42	4.61	4.35	4.50	9.3	2.8	5.6	1.0	16.7	3.00

Breakout: 13% Improve: 50% Collapse: 24% Attrition: 21%   Comparables: Jim Clancy, Gaylord Perry, Kevin Gross, Mike Torrez

Millwood had the worst season of his career in 2007. The Rangers are still on the hook with him for three more years and hope it was just a bump in the road, as he was pitching through a hamstring issue early in the season and a respiratory infection later on, continuing his history of pitching through minor problems. Apart from his hits-allowed ratio, Millwood's rates remained respectable last year, and his BABIP was significantly inflated, so don't be shocked if he comes back strong.

Akinori Otsuka

Bats: R   Throws: R   Height: 6' 0"   Weight: 210   Born: January 13, 1972   Age: 36

YEAR	TEAM	LVL	AGE	W	L	SV	G	GS	IP	H	BB	SO	HR	GB%	BABIP	STUFF	WHIP	ERA	PERA	EqERA	EqH9	EqBB9	EqSO9	EqHR9	VORP	SN/WX
2005	SDN	MLB	33	2	8	1	66	0	62²	55	34	60	3	52.8%	.302	13	1.42	3.59	3.63	3.98	7.7	4.4	7.7	0.4	9.2	1.53
2006	TEX	MLB	34	2	4	32	63	0	59²	53	11	47	3	52.9%	.294	18	1.07	2.11	2.83	2.48	7.4	1.6	6.8	0.5	23.9	2.67
2007	TEX	MLB	35	2	1	4	34	0	32¹	26	9	23	0	56.6%	.271	9	1.11	2.51	2.48	2.73	6.5	2.2	5.7	0.0	11.8	1.57
2008	TEX	MLB	36	2	2	6	39	0	43¹	42	16	34	4	52.5%	.291	1	1.32	3.64	3.54	3.59	8.2	3.1	6.3	0.8	10.0	1.00

Breakout: 12% Improve: 31% Collapse: 45% Attrition: 13%   Comparables: Dave Smith, Roberto Hernandez, Clay Carroll, Al Worthington

Otsuka was having his second consecutive strong season with the Rangers when he pulled out of a game on July 1 with a sore forearm, never to return to the active roster. At one point it was thought that he'd require Tommy John surgery, but that never transpired, and by November, the Rangers were talking about how Otsuka had resumed throwing and looked good. A little more than one month later they non-tendered him, so perhaps the question should have been, "Looking good relative to what?"

Vicente Padilla

Bats: R   Throws: R   Height: 6' 2"   Weight: 220   Born: September 27, 1977   Age: 30

YEAR	TEAM	LVL	AGE	W	L	SV	G	GS	IP	H	BB	SO	HR	GB%	BABIP	STUFF	WHIP	ERA	PERA	EqERA	EqH9	EqBB9	EqSO9	EqHR9	VORP	SN/WX
2005	PHI	MLB	27	9	12	0	27	27	147	146	74	103	22	46.7%	.284	-6	1.50	4.71	5.42	4.85	9.1	4.2	5.8	1.3	13.2	2.81
2006	TEX	MLB	28	15	10	0	33	33	200	206	70	156	21	45.2%	.310	18	1.38	4.50	4.09	4.30	8.5	2.9	6.5	0.8	29.2	4.19
2007	TEX	MLB	29	6	10	0	23	23	120¹	146	50	71	16	47.0%	.323	-10	1.63	5.76	5.81	6.25	10.3	3.3	4.8	1.2	-6.8	0.62
2008	TEX	MLB	30	6	8	0	30	19	118²	130	49	84	14	46.8%	.309	2	1.51	4.93	4.74	4.78	9.4	3.4	5.7	1.1	9.3	1.70

Breakout: 25% Improve: 56% Collapse: 19% Attrition: 18%   Comparables: Doyle Alexander, Stan Bahnsen, Joey Hamilton, Bobby Witt

Having received a three-year, $33 million deal after the 2006 season, Padilla, like Millwood, had the worst season of his career in 2007, missing a third of the campaign with a sore arm and pitching quite poorly when available. In

2002 and 2003, Padilla went over 200 innings and then got hurt and was ineffective for a couple of seasons. In 2006, Padilla threw 200 innings and then was hurt and ineffective the next year. See the pattern yet?

John Rheinecker

Bats: L   Throws: L   Height: 6' 2"   Weight: 230   Born: May 29, 1979   Age: 29

YEAR	TEAM	LVL	AGE	W	L	SV	G	GS	IP	H	BB	SO	HR	GB%	BABIP	STUFF	WHIP	ERA	PERA	EqERA	EqH9	EqBB9	EqSO9	EqHR9	VORP	SN/WX
2005	SAC	AAA	26	4	0	0	7	7	45²	29	14	24	0	58.0%	.213	6	0.94	1.77	2.75	3.30	5.4	3.1	3.1	0.2	11.2	—
2006	OKL	AAA	27	4	5	0	15	15	93	93	24	68	5	58.3%	.319	9	1.26	2.52	4.67	4.01	9.9	2.7	5.0	0.7	15.1	—
2006	TEX	MLB	27	4	6	0	21	13	70²	104	19	28	6	58.8%	.371	-14	1.74	5.86	6.56	5.90	12.6	2.4	3.4	0.7	2.9	1.04
2007	OKL	AAA	28	4	2	0	9	9	58	59	12	30	4	59.4%	.299	-1	1.22	3.57	4.39	4.47	9.6	2.2	3.5	0.8	6.8	—
2007	TEX	MLB	28	4	3	0	23	7	50¹	61	28	40	9	57.4%	.329	-16	1.77	5.37	6.70	6.49	10.2	4.4	6.5	1.6	-3.7	-0.26
2008	TEX	MLB	29	4	6	0	42	12	87¹	102	33	50	9	56.1%	.316	-8	1.54	4.95	4.77	4.87	10.0	3.1	4.6	0.9	6.1	1.00

Breakout: 28% Improve: 58% Collapse: 25% Attrition: 38%   Comparables: John O'Donoghue, Danny Coombs, Paul Splittorff, Chris Hammond

After busting out in the Oakland system, Rheinecker missed most of the 2005 season with a mysterious finger injury and was was downright awful after coming to the Rangers in 2006. He missed the first two months of 2007 with back troubles, and upon returning to the starting rotation in the second half, was awful once again (6.21 ERA). He finally found some success after moving to the pen in late August, striking out 15 in 12 2/3 innings while allowing just four runs. Rheinecker is your classic crafty lefty, with deception in his delivery and a darting fastball that gives lefty batters fits. Despite some ugly overall numbers, he just might have a future as a LOOGY.

Rob Tejeda

Bats: R   Throws: R   Height: 6' 3"   Weight: 230   Born: March 24, 1982   Age: 26

YEAR	TEAM	LVL	AGE	W	L	SV	G	GS	IP	H	BB	SO	HR	GB%	BABIP	STUFF	WHIP	ERA	PERA	EqERA	EqH9	EqBB9	EqSO9	EqHR9	VORP	SN/WX
2005	SWB	AAA	23	2	0	0	5	5	28¹	21	13	28	0	32.9%	.300	19	1.20	2.23	3.59	3.42	7.2	5.1	6.5	0.3	6.4	—
2005	PHI	MLB	23	4	3	0	26	13	85²	67	51	72	5	36.3%	.270	19	1.38	3.57	3.82	3.78	7.5	5.0	7.0	0.5	17.7	2.77
2006	OKL	AAA	24	6	2	0	15	15	80	61	42	79	7	42.0%	.265	10	1.29	3.15	4.45	3.93	7.5	5.1	6.7	1.1	14.0	—
2006	TEX	MLB	24	5	5	0	14	14	73²	83	32	40	10	38.6%	.307	-5	1.56	4.27	4.95	4.28	9.3	3.7	4.5	1.1	10.1	1.60
2007	TEX	MLB	25	5	9	0	19	19	95¹	110	60	69	17	36.1%	.317	-15	1.78	6.61	6.61	6.96	9.7	4.9	5.8	1.6	-12.9	-0.29
2008	TEX	MLB	26	3	4	0	23	10	65	69	35	48	9	39.1%	.300	-3	1.60	5.39	5.09	5.18	9.0	4.5	6.0	1.2	2.4	0.60

Breakout: 27% Improve: 57% Collapse: 26% Attrition: 43%   Comparables: John Miller, Jaret Wright, Joaquin Benoit, Seth McClung

Tejeda began last season with seven shutout innings against the Red Sox, but it was all downhill from there, as hitters were slugging .499 against him before he was mercifully sent down. Tejeda has always had a big fastball, but his secondary pitches are lacking, and his tendency to work too high in the zone has contributed to his downfall. He was one of the top pitchers in the Domincan Winter League, but he'll still enter spring training on the outside looking in.

Edison Volquez

Bats: R   Throws: R   Height: 6' 0"   Weight: 200   Born: July 3, 1983   Age: 24

YEAR	TEAM	LVL	AGE	W	L	SV	G	GS	IP	H	BB	SO	HR	GB%	BABIP	STUFF	WHIP	ERA	PERA	EqERA	EqH9	EqBB9	EqSO9	EqHR9	VORP	SN/WX
2005	BAK	A+	22	5	4	0	11	11	66²	64	12	77	9	49.2%	.327	4	1.14	4.18	6.34	6.30	10.5	2.8	6.4	1.8	-4.7	—
2005	FRI	AA	22	1	5	0	10	10	58²	58	17	49	6	47.2%	.306	1	1.28	4.14	5.49	5.53	9.6	3.9	5.2	1.3	0.4	—
2005	TEX	MLB	22	0	4	0	6	3	12²	25	10	11	3	42.3%	.458	-35	2.76	14.17	18.27	18.23	16.2	6.8	7.4	2.0	-13.1	-0.89
2006	OKL	AAA	23	6	6	0	21	21	120²	86	72	130	9	46.2%	.270	22	1.31	3.22	4.29	4.42	7.1	5.8	7.3	0.9	14.9	—
2006	TEX	MLB	23	1	6	0	8	8	33¹	52	17	15	7	43.5%	.366	-31	2.07	7.30	10.20	8.18	13.1	4.4	3.8	1.6	-5.0	-0.12
2007	BAK	A+	24	0	4	0	7	7	35¹	27	20	38	4	40.9%	.267	-2	1.33	7.14	5.65	8.54	7.7	6.9	5.8	1.7	-10.7	—
2007	FRI	AA	24	8	1	0	11	11	58¹	46	19	62	9	45.8%	.253	-2	1.11	3.55	5.44	4.80	8.4	3.8	6.8	2.0	4.8	—
2007	OKL	AAA	24	6	1	0	8	8	51	25	21	66	0	45.9%	.238	44	0.90	1.41	2.64	2.19	4.9	4.0	9.1	0.2	18.7	—
2007	TEX	MLB	24	2	1	0	6	6	34	34	15	29	4	37.9%	.309	15	1.44	4.50	4.47	4.24	8.5	3.4	7.1	1.1	4.6	0.54
2008	CIN	MLB	24	8	9	0	29	29	145¹	137	73	136	20	42.3%	.289	16	1.44	4.57	4.73	4.55	8.2	4.1	7.5	1.2	16.2	2.90

Breakout: 35% Improve: 67% Collapse: 12% Attrition: 18%   Comparables: Chan Ho Park, Kelvim Escobar, Gary Bell, Ernie Broglio

After struggling tremendously in his auditions the last two years, Volquez was sent all the way back down to High-A to regain his confidence. It was a big risk, but it worked. By the time Volquez was back in Triple-A, he was absolutely dominant, and he found his first taste of success in the big leagues with two quality starts in six September attempts. He was subsequently dealt to the Reds for Josh Hamilton in what basically amounts to an "I'll give you my talented guy who could go backward at any minute and you give me yours" trade.

C. J. Wilson

Bats: L   Throws: L   Height: 6' 1"   Weight: 215   Born: November 18, 1980   Age: 27

YEAR	TEAM	LVL	AGE	W	L	SV	G	GS	IP	H	BB	SO	HR	GB%	BABIP	STUFF	WHIP	ERA	PERA	EqERA	EqH9	EqBB9	EqSO9	EqHR9	VORP	SN/WX
2005	FRI	AA	24	0	4	0	12	12	44²	51	14	43	7	55.1%	.349	-25	1.45	4.43	8.07	8.19	11.5	4.2	6.0	2.0	-11.7	—
2005	TEX	MLB	24	1	7	1	24	6	48	63	18	30	5	60.9%	.360	-13	1.69	6.94	5.95	6.65	11.2	3.4	5.5	1.0	-7.0	-0.23
2006	TEX	MLB	25	2	4	1	44	0	44¹	39	18	43	7	52.8%	.274	6	1.29	4.06	3.94	4.03	7.3	3.4	8.1	1.2	7.5	0.19
2007	TEX	MLB	26	2	1	12	66	0	68¹	50	33	63	4	49.2%	.266	15	1.21	3.03	3.03	2.91	6.2	3.8	7.7	0.5	21.0	2.34
2008	TEX	MLB	27	3	3	8	59	0	58	56	26	51	5	50.9%	.303	5	1.41	4.07	3.93	4.00	8.3	3.7	7.1	0.8	10.7	1.00

Breakout: 27% Improve: 57% Collapse: 23% Attrition: 15%   Comparables: Sparky Lyle, Steve Kline, J. C. Romero, Paul Spoljaric

When Gagné got traded and Otsuka got hurt, Wilson got his first shot at closing and did well enough to enter spring training as the leading candidate for the game-ending role this year. Wilson relies primarily on a 92 to 94 mph fastball and a very hard slider that registers in the mid to upper 80s. He's absolute hell against left-handed hitters, who went 11-for-98 (.112) against him with 39 strikeouts last year, but righties reached base against him at a .381 clip, a rate which will have to decrease if he's going to keep the closer job.

Jamey Wright

Bats: R   Throws: R   Height: 6' 5"   Weight: 205   Born: December 24, 1974   Age: 33

YEAR	TEAM	LVL	AGE	W	L	SV	G	GS	IP	H	BB	SO	HR	GB%	BABIP	STUFF	WHIP	ERA	PERA	EqERA	EqH9	EqBB9	EqSO9	EqHR9	VORP	SN/WX
2005	COL	MLB	30	8	16	0	34	27	171¹	201	81	101	22	54.0%	.322	-9	1.65	5.46	5.46	5.68	9.7	3.8	4.8	1.1	-7.1	0.67
2006	SFN	MLB	31	6	10	0	34	21	156	167	64	79	16	58.9%	.303	-4	1.48	5.19	5.07	5.17	9.9	3.3	4.4	0.8	10.0	1.73
2007	TEX	MLB	32	4	5	0	20	9	77	72	41	39	6	55.3%	.283	-3	1.47	3.62	4.19	3.77	8.1	4.4	4.4	0.7	17.1	1.71
2008	TEX	MLB	33	3	4	0	25	8	68¹	80	32	36	7	53.3%	.312	-13	1.64	5.41	5.12	5.32	10.0	3.9	4.3	1.0	1.1	0.40

Breakout: 13% Improve: 39% Collapse: 43% Attrition: 42%   Comparables: Don Cardwell, Omar Olivares, Mike LaCoss, Pete Vuckovich

Wright missed two months with an ailing shoulder, which allowed him to post a career-best ERA by limiting him to 77 innings. Wright also walked more men than he struckout, which proved that ERA was a fluke. Hoping the fluke can sustain a little longer, the Rangers signed him to a minor league deal in December.

LINEOUTS

Hitters

PLAYER	TEAM	LVL	AGE	PA	R	2B	3B	HR	RBI	BB	SO	SB-CS	EqBRR	AVG/OBP/SLG	MLVr	EqAVG/EqOBP/EqSLG	EqA	VORP
OF E. Beltre*	RSX	Rk	17	145	20	3	3	5	13	12	44	6-3	2.2	.208/.310/.400	-.001	.172/.233/.299	.183	-31.5
	RNG	Rk	17	99	19	3	4	4	15	8	21	3-2	-1.4	.310/.388/.583	.373	.220/.265/.374	.220	-8.0
1B N. Gold	OKL	AAA	27	522	74	25	1	26	103	40	104	0-0	1.2	.292/.347/.516	.185	.265/.319/.472	.269	11.8
PR F. Guzman#	OKL	AAA	26	610	92	22	8	4	34	62	88	56-14	8.6	.269/.348/.363	-.059	.237/.315/.322	.239	-13.9
SS M. Lemon*	CLN	A	19	535	62	26	6	3	38	56	100	12-14	-5.9	.261/.353/.364	.047	.208/.282/.298	.205	-22.0
C G. Quiroz	OKL	AAA	25	278	22	16	0	6	33	15	52	0-0	-1.7	.266/.307/.398	-.090	.238/.281/.362	.221	-5.2
	TEX	MLB	25	11	1	1	0	0	2	1	2	0-0	0.0	.400/.455/.500	.442	.400/.455/.500	.333	1.6
C C. Santana	SPO	A-	18	26	1	2	0	1	4	0	6	0-0	-0.2	.320/.346/.520	.206	.231/.231/.385	.203	-2.5
	RNG	Rk	18	117	20	7	3	3	15	12	27	3-3	-1.8	.302/.427/.531	.344	.215/.288/.346	.218	-7.2

Acquired from the Red Sox in the Eric Gagné deal, Dominican outfielder **Engel Beltre** Humperdinck is just 17 and loaded with tools. If he was an American, he'd have been a surefire first-round pick in June. ⌀ First baseman **Nate Gold** has hit 60 home runs in the last two years, but he turns 28 in June and mashing balls out of Triple-A parks seems to be his ceiling and his destiny. ⌀ Outfielder **Freddy Guzman** has never done much consistently other than run fast. He was dealt to the Tigers in the off-season swap for Chris Shelton. ⌀ The son of Chet, shortstop **Marcus Lemon** is a good defender with a patient approach, which is enough for him to be classified as a sleeper by some. ⌀ Once seen as the Blue Jays' Catcher of the Future, **Guillermo Quiroz** has struggled through four straight injury-plagued seasons and will try to stick in Baltimore this spring. ⊘ The Rangers' organization is very excited about teenager **Christian Santana**, an athletic catcher with plenty of raw power.

Pitchers

PLAYER	TEAM	LVL	AGE	W	L	SV	IP	H	BB	SO	HR	GB%	BABIP	STUFF	WHIP	ERA	PERA	EqERA	EqH9	EqBB9	EqSO9	EqHR9	VORP
F. Cruceta	OKL	AAA	26	3	0	1	65²	38	40	70	2	48.8%	.225	21	1.19	3.01	3.14	3.88	5.3	5.7	7.3	0.4	12.4
T. Diamond '08	TEX	MLB	25	2	2	0	38	36	27	33		42.9%	.291	1	1.65	5.11	4.96	4.94	8.1	5.9	7.1	1.0	2.8
W. Eyre	TEX	MLB	28	4	6	1	68	78	32	42	8	47.0%	.321	-14	1.62	5.16	5.22	5.16	9.8	3.7	5.2	1.1	4.1
F. German	OKL	AAA	27	2	2	7	59¹	44	46	72	5	42.8%	.285	16	1.52	3.49	4.90	4.58	7.3	7.4	8.7	0.9	6.5
D. Herrera*	FRI	AA	22	5	2	0	52¹	43	20	64	3	49.6%	.339	10	1.20	3.79	5.26	5.67	9.6	4.5	8.4	0.8	-0.4
B. Jones*	ROM	A	20	5	0	3	48²	38	12	46	1	45.2%	.276	3	1.03	2.96	4.35	4.63	8.1	3.8	4.6	0.6	4.8
	CLN	A	20	4	1	0	26²	23	12	29	3	47.9%	.290	-9	1.31	2.70	9.67	7.25	11.3	7.7	5.2	2.8	-4.1
L. Mendoza	FRI	AA	23	15	4	0	148²	145	48	93	11	47.5%	.294	-12	1.30	3.93	5.38	5.86	10.0	3.8	3.6	1.0	-4.0
	TEX	MLB	23	1	0	0	16	13	4	7	1	54.9%	.250	-1	1.06	2.25	2.96	2.30	6.9	2.3	3.4	0.6	6.8
A. Murray*	OKL	AAA	25	3	3	5	52²	42	25	51	2	54.5%	.292	8	1.27	3.07	3.85	3.75	7.7	4.6	6.8	0.5	10.3
	TEX	MLB	25	1	2	0	28	25	15	18	6	39.3%	.235	-16	1.43	4.50	4.54	4.03	7.1	4.0	5.3	1.9	3.7
Z. Phillips*	CLN	A	20	11	7	0	151²	139	43	157	6	55.1%	.333	-3	1.20	2.91	7.22	6.66	12.0	5.5	5.2	1.2	-14.6
O. Poveda	CLN	A	19	11	4	0	125²	94	32	120	10	43.6%	.262	-11	1.00	2.79	6.54	6.24	9.7	5.0	4.6	2.1	-7.5
	BAK	A+	19	1	2	0	28	27	13	33	4	37.7%	.324	15	1.43	5.14	7.24	7.36	10.2	6.0	6.7	2.1	-5.0
J. Rupe	OKL	AAA	24	2	2	0	37	39	14	20	4	46.3%	.302	-15	1.43	4.62	6.02	5.56	10.3	4.0	3.7	1.3	0.2
B. White*	FRI	AA	28	2	0	2	48²	48	26	64	4	44.6%	.361	2	1.52	4.44	6.87	6.46	10.8	5.9	8.4	1.2	-4.4
	TEX	MLB	28	2	0	0	9¹	8	7	9	1	45.8%	.304	8	1.61	4.84	5.50	4.15	8.3	6.2	8.3	1.0	1.3
M. Wood	OKL	AAA	27	9	3	0	97²	83	21	73	7	53.6%	.273	13	1.06	3.22	3.67	4.05	8.0	2.2	5.2	0.8	16.1
	TEX	MLB	27	3	2	0	50²	68	15	25	9	48.9%	.331	-25	1.64	5.33	6.99	6.35	11.3	2.3	4.1	1.6	-1.8

Right-hander **Francisco Cruceta** has always had lights-out stuff and little idea of what to do with it. This spring, the Tigers will become the fifth team to try to help with the latter. ⊘ The tenth overall pick in the 2004 draft, **Thomas Diamond** was lined up for a big-league debut at some point in 2007, but he missed the entire year following Tommy John surgery. He could be back at some point in 2008. ⊘ **Willie Eyre** didn't pitch well enough in his rookie year of 2006 to justify another turn in the majors, but he made the Rangers' roster anyway, didn't especially pitch well again, then went down with Tommy John surgery in late August. He'll likely miss all of 2008. ⊘ A 260-pound right-hander with mid-90s heat, **Franklyn German** once drew comparisons to Lee Smith, but he's never come close to mastering the strike zone or Smith's Louisiana accent. ⊘ Shipped to Cincy in the Josh Hamilton deal, lefty **Daniel Herrera** is one of the smallest pitchers around at 5-foot-8 and 145 pounds. He has LOOGY potential. ⊘ Another part of the bounty for Teixeira, 2005 first-round pick **Beau Jones** is a power lefty who has been a bit slow to develop due to control issues, but scouts still love his arm. ⊘ A former prospect with the Red Sox who had all but fallen off the radar, right-hander **Luis Mendoza** had a surprising rebound at Double-A last year and got a big-league look. He projects as a middle reliever. ⊘ **A. J. Murray** is an oft-injured left-hander who has yet to establish himself, which is a shame, as the A in his name stands for Arlington. ⊘ **Zach Phillips** had an excellent season at Low-A last year, but other than being a left-hander with a plus curveball, he lacks anything that would lead to a big projection. ⊘ Venezuelan **Omar Poveda** is a long, skinny righty with excellent control of a three-pitch mix; he profiles as a rotation regular. ⊘ Right-hander **Josh Rupe** has big-league potential and a complete inability to stay healthy. ⊘ **Bill White** is a big lefty with power stuff who has never been able to control the strike zone often enough to make good use of it. ⊘ **Mike Wood** is no more than an extra arm, a crafty right-hander who doesn't have much in the way of stuff, but throws strikes and changes speed well. He refused an outright assignment in December and later signed with the Yomiuri Giants. *Sayonara, zetsubô sensei!*

MANAGER: RON WASHINGTON ————————————————

YEAR	TEAM	W-L	Pythag +/−	Avg PC	100+ P	120+ P	QS	BQS	REL	REL w Zero R	IBB	Subs	PH	PH Avg	PH HR	SB2	CS2	SB3	CS3	SAC Att	SAC %	POS SAC	Squeeze	Swing	In Play
2007	TEX	75-87	-3	89.8	43	0	48	5	467	290	38	64	89	.215	4	76	23	12	2	82	69.5%	54	1	121	101

Washington's first year as a major league manager was a nightmare. The team was hampered by injuries all year. Mark Teixeira and Kenny Lofton got dealt. Triple-A sluggers Jason Botts and Nelson Cruz proved to be no more than Triple-A sluggers. On the mound, only Kevin Millwood topped 150 innings (barely, at 172 2/3) or 23 starts, while the team's top two relievers, Eric Gagné and Akinori Otsuka, got dealt and hurt, respectively. Still, Washington only made things worse by trying to bring small ball to a park designed for big ball. His laid-back approach also had some accusing him of losing control of his clubhouse, which seemed to be a popular accusation lobbed at managers last year. Washington didn't have much to work with, but with nothing to lose he failed to show much ingenuity.

Toronto Blue Jays

J. P. Ricciardi was hired as the general manager of the Blue Jays on November 14, 2001. While his Jays have been moderately successful, finishing above .500 in three of his six years, they have never been a factor in a pennant race. They have finished above third place in the AL East just once, which availed them not as they still lost the wild card by seven games to the Tigers. Their overall record under Ricciardi is a losing one, 481-490. Unless Ricciardi's charges make their first post-season appearance of his tenure this season, there is no reason for him to celebrate a seventh anniversary in the office.

Ricciardi came into the job claiming that he could compete with the AL East's monsters on a relatively low payroll, but just three years later, after a frustrating 2004 season that featured injuries to ace Roy Halladay, first baseman Carlos Delgado, and outfielders Vernon Wells and Frank Catalanotto, Ricciardi shifted gears and convinced owner Ted Rogers to push the payroll upward, garnering a commitment of $210 million for the 2005 through 2007 season. The ill-considered signing of third baseman Corey Koskie that winter was followed by $102 million committed to pitchers B. J. Ryan and A. J. Burnett, a trade for Troy Glaus and the $33 million left on his contract to replace Koskie at third, and the signing of designated hitter Frank Thomas to an $18 million deal. Contract extensions worth $190 million were lavished on Wells, Halladay, and moderately productive first baseman Lyle Overbay.

The Jays' payroll jumped from $45 million in 2005 to $72 million in '06 and $82 million last year. It will be above $90 million in 2008. While much of this is merely keeping up with the Joneses—the Jays remain in the middle of the payroll pack league-wide, and are plow-ing increases in central-fund revenue back into their roster—that's likely to be cold comfort as the payroll doubles over a three-year period, while the number of post-season games played remains constant. The increased payroll hasn't produced a postseason berth. Only in 2006, when the Jays went 87-75, was their record one that might have made them a playoff team in any season. Rogers is seeing more of his money go out the door, without any additional games being played in the stadium that now bears his name.

Ricciardi's decisions came to a head this season, after which the Jays' roster is likely to look a lot different. Acquiring Scott Rolen from the Cardinals for Troy Glaus has the Jays fixed up at third base through 2010, but it's a fix as expensive as it is risky. Thomas's deal is supposed to end by then; although his 2010 option vests with 376 plate appearances this season, given his injury history that is no sure thing. Catcher Gregg Zaun, who quietly adds wins each year, will also be a free agent after the season. Most importantly, Burnett can opt out of his deal at the end of the year, and as long as his arm is attached to his shoulder, he will. Those four players were good for 15.5 wins above replacement last year, a quarter of the team total. It is difficult to replace that much production all at once, even if their departure also frees up a large chunk of the payroll.

That brings us to the other area in which Ricciardi has failed to impress, the one that makes it hard for the Jays to suffer that kind of talent exodus. In part because of poor returns from Ricciardi's first several drafts, the Blue Jays have very little talent in the top half of their farm system. The entire organization includes just one of the top-100 prospects in baseball, outfielder Travis

---

BLUE JAYS PROSPECTUS

2007 record: 83-79; Third place, AL East

Pythagenport record: 87-75

Runs scored per game: 4.65 (10th in AL)

Runs allowed per game: 4.31 (2nd in AL)

Team EqA: .253 (11th in AL)

2007 Batters Age: 31.0 (3rd oldest in AL)

2007 Pitchers Age: 27.9 (5th youngest in AL)

Ballpark: Rogers Centre; Neutral Park; Park Factor of .999

2007: Despite encouraging signs from their young starting pitchers, the Blue Jays return to their third-place perch.

2008: In a make-or-break season for the Ricciardi regime, the Jays continue to neither make nor break.

Snider, and he is a 2006 draftee who will play A-ball in 2008. Of the other top prospects in the organization, most are 2007 draftees who won't be factors at the major league level until 2010. The Jays have drafted better of late, but the void in their system was created by questionable decisions in the 2002 to 2005 drafts, a run of poor drafting that climaxed when the Jays took pitcher Ricky Romero ahead of shortstop Troy Tulowitzki with the sixth pick in the 2005 draft, a move almost universally criticized on draft day, long before Tulowitzki emerged as rookie star on a pennant-winning club. This lack of homegrown help creates an enormous amount of pressure to win with the current roster; there are no reinforcements coming.

The team's roster reflects that development gap. Of the players likely to make notable contributions to the 2008 Blue Jays, only second baseman Aaron Hill and right-hander Shawn Marcum are products of Ricciardi-era drafts. Less significant contributions can be expected from Ricciardi draftees Adam Lind, who will fight for the left-field job, and pitchers Casey Janssen and Jesse Litsch. Those five players combined for 18.1 WARP last year. If you'd like, you can call Overbay a farm product, as he was acquired from Milwaukee in exchange for a package built around Ricciardi-drafted hurlers David Bush and Zach Jackson, but that brings up the question of which team actually won that trade. In addition to their poor drafts, the Ricciardi Jays have done virtually nothing internationally in terms of player acquisitions and development. Ricciardi's failure to populate his roster with homegrown players was what forced him to ask Rogers for the payroll increases so that he could fill it with expensive imports. Should they lose a quarter of the roster's marginal value next winter, they will have no hope of contending in the American League for the immediate future.

This offseason has shown the value of player development around the league, as the teams with the deepest farm systems have been able to leverage their prospects to acquire top-tier established talent or have had the wherewithal to pass on expensive veterans, confident that their systems would soon produce comparable talent at a fraction of the price. While that is the direction in which the best-run teams in the game are moving, the Jays' roster is like something out of the 1980s, a team of expensive older players brought together in an effort to win a championship right now. The most productive system products on the roster are from the previous regime, which drafted or signed Wells, Halladay, right fielder Alex Rios, and starter Dustin McGowan, not to mention Orlando Hudson, who begat Glaus via trade from Arizona. The 2008 Blue Jays are more former GM Gord Ash's Jays supplemented by Ted Rogers' dollars than they are a team built by J. P. Ricciardi.

The importance of the 2008 season to this franchise is why Toronto's offseason was so very disappointing. With a team that's still clearly not quite good enough, the best players Ricciardi was able to acquire were a pair of utility infielders in Marco Scutaro and David Eckstein. The Jays also retained immobile 40-year-old free agent platoon slugger Matt Stairs. Thus, an 83-79 team that finished 13 games behind in its division and 11 games out of a playoff spot, going into what should be its last, best shot at contention this decade, will return with essentially the same roster. That's not good enough, not when the Tigers are aggressively adding Hall of Fame hitters, the Yankees and Red Sox are both rebuilding their rosters with some of the game's top prospects, and the Angels are spending money liberally in what has become baseball's weakest division. The buy-in for the postseason in the American League is 92 wins—no AL playoff team has won fewer since 2003—and nothing about the 2008 Blue Jays suggests that they have any hope of being nine wins better than they were a year ago.

What could they have done? Well, here you run into the problem created by the commitments of the past few seasons. The easiest team to improve is one that has a mix of great players and great big holes. The Tigers, for example, added Miguel Cabrera and Edgar Renteria, who replace Brandon Inge and Sean Casey. The combined gain there is seven or eight wins. Dontrelle Willis is a two-win upgrade in the rotation as well, given how bad the back end of the Tigers' rotation was last year.

The Blue Jays don't have gaping lineup holes. Shortstop John McDonald is their worst-hitting regular, but he is actually an acceptable player because of his Gold Glove-caliber defense, defense that takes on added importance when played behind the Jays' groundball-throwing rotation. The Jays have average to average-plus players at almost every lineup spot, with left field being a potential question mark coming off a season in which Reed Johnson was hurt and Lind didn't hit. Then again, Stairs could well fill the bill out there. The Blue Jays enter the season with four solid starting pitchers and a number of decent candidates for the fifth spot, all pitching in front of a defense that was, as much as anything else in Toronto, responsible for whatever success they had last season. The bullpen, even without Ryan (who lost last year to Tommy John surgery), was very good in 2007, and should be bolstered by his return this year.

For all of Ricciardi's poor decisions, he has the sixth-best team in the league. On the other hand, it's a team devoid of superstars. Not a single player on the Blue Jays produced a WARP of 7.0 last season. Each of the AL playoff teams had at least two, with the Indians, Red Sox, and Yankees having at least three. You need stars, or star-caliber seasons, to win, and it's not clear where the Blue Jays are supposed to get theirs. Wells is paid like a star, but his career-high WARP was 6.5 back in 2003, and that was his only season as a six-win player. Even conceding that the WARP system underrates his defense relative to other defensive measurements, Wells has had just two star-caliber seasons in his career. Halladay's star seems to be fading as he enters his early 30s. A full-season version of Burnett might be a star, but that animal has only been seen twice in nine years. Rolen has posted a WARP above 8.0 in five of the last seven seasons, but only one of those came in the last three years since injuries have ground him down, which is a large part of the reason that he's no longer a Cardinal. The Jays three other highest-paid players—Thomas, Ryan, and Overbay—have just one seven-WARP season (Ryan's 2006) in the 21st century. That leaves just Rios, who reached 6.0 WARP for the first time last year and is entering his age-27 season.

The organizational commitment to players below the star level all but ties Ricciardi's hands. While Glaus and Thomas and Zaun may not be stars, they are good enough to produce four to six wins in a full season. Improving upon that through the trade or free-agent markets requires the acquisition of one of the best players in the game, which means spending massive doses of young talent or cash. We know the Jays don't have the former, and using the latter last winter would not have helped them much. Spending upwards of $12 million a season on past-prime center fielders or mid-rotation starters is a road to nowhere, and Ricciardi, to his credit, correctly avoided doing so.

The best ways for Ricciardi to make up ground on the teams ahead of him in the AL would be to add another great starting pitcher, or a top-tier left fielder. Yet, the Jays were never players in the sweepstakes for Twins ace Johan Santana, and judging from the A's return on their ace, Toronto wouldn't have had what it took to land Dan Haren, either. The best package the Jays might have assembled would have been Snider, Lind, and some long-term options like teenage outfielder Yohermyn Chavez or a 2007 draft pick as a player to be named later. Perhaps Marcum, Romero, or lefty David Purcey would have had trade value, but only as a third- or fourth-best player in a deal. Given their chips, the Jays would not have been able to pick up an impact starting pitcher.

Could a subset of that pool bring back an impact hitter to play left field that was enough of an upgrade on Lind or Stairs to make a deal worthwhile? Using the return the A's got on Nick Swisher as a guideline, a trade for an outfielder would probably have required dealing Snider and at least two other players. There aren't many players like Swisher available, and the Jays' lack of depth in prospects makes it hard to acquire them short of trading their best. It's worth inquiring about, say, the Reds' Adam Dunn, but the combination of price and expected performance makes a deal unlikely.

Put simply, the Jays have painted themselves into a corner. They're good enough to see themselves as contenders. However, they are chasing what are probably the five best teams in baseball. They have no holes that have to be filled by Opening Day. They also have no way of making their team five games better with one transaction. They have some young talent, just not enough to form the sort of core around which a run of success can be built. They are spending money, but spending money isn't enough when the best players in the game are being locked up without ever reaching the market.

Some of these problems are outside the Jays' purview. However, the lack of talent in the system and the large contract commitments to Rolen, Overbay, Ryan, and Wells, players who aren't pushing the team toward a championship, can be laid at the feet of Ricciardi. He has assembled a good but not great team, one likely to win between 80 and 87 games for the fourth time in five years, one whose season will again end on the last Sunday in September. As the sun sets on Game 162, with no Game 163 coming, Ted Rogers will have to ask himself: What am I paying for?

HITTERS

Russ Adams INF

Bats: L Throws: R Height: 6' 1" Weight: 195 Born: August 30, 1980 Age: 27

YEAR	TEAM	LVL	AGE	PA	R	2B	3B	HR	RBI	BB	SO	SB	CS	EqBRR	AVG	OBP	SLG	MLVr	EqAVG	EqOBP	EqSLG	EqA	VORP	DEFENSE	
2005	TOR	MLB	24	545	68	27	5	8	63	50	57	11	2	1.8	.256	.325	.383	-.083	.256	.335	.389	.260	13.0	123-SS -23	
2006	SYR	AAA	25	179	21	9	3	0	15	17	23	3	2	-0.8	.311	.374	.404	.109	.280	.346	.373	.254	4.9	37-2B -1	
2006	TOR	MLB	25	280	31	14	1	3	28	22	41	1	2	-2.2	.219	.282	.319	-.320	.218	.289	.319	.214	-10.1	37-2B -1	31-SS -5
2007	SYR	AAA	26	484	62	23	2	11	54	41	57	3	3	-0.2	.262	.333	.401	-.010	.243	.310	.391	.242	3.9	99-2B -12	
2007	TOR	MLB	26	69	14	3	0	2	12	7	14	2	1	-1.4	.233	.313	.383	-.131	.237	.328	.441	.264	-0.5	14-3B -6	
2008	TOR	MLB	27	538	58	27	3	9	53	43	79	6	3	0.2	.249	.314	.374	-.122	.248	.316	.378	.247	2.1	126-2B -11	

Breakout: 25% Improve: 52% Collapse: 20% Attrition: 18% Comparables: Kevin Nicholson, Cass Michaels, Chris Speier, Roy Howell

Not that Adams had played well enough to keep his job coming into 2007, but signing Royce Clayton to replace him didn't exactly change the Jays' outlook much. Last year, Adams didn't play well enough at Triple-A to warrant a call-up when Clayton spit the bit, only reaching the majors as an extra infielder in August when injuries ran rampant. As a lefty batter who can draw some walks and play shortstop passably, he makes a decent utility infielder.

Kevin Ahrens 3B

Bats: S Throws: R Height: 6' 1" Weight: 190 Born: April 26, 1989 Age: 19

YEAR	TEAM	LVL	AGE	PA	R	2B	3B	HR	RBI	BB	SO	SB	CS	EqBRR	AVG	OBP	SLG	MLVr	EqAVG	EqOBP	EqSLG	EqA	VORP	DEFENSE	
2007	BLJ	Rk	18	192	19	6	0	3	21	25	47	3	0	-1.7	.230	.339	.321	-.043	.178	.259	.236	.173	-39.8	24-3B -3	11-SS -1
2008	TOR	MLB	19	513	36	21	2	6	40	35	156	8	4	-0.3	.198	.256	.291	-.363	.197	.258	.294	.193	-27.5	121-3B -4	

Breakout: 63% Improve: 72% Collapse: 15% Attrition: 8% Comparables: Corey Smith, Dmitri Young, Brandon Wood, Pokey Reese

Ahrens rose up draft boards throughout the spring, and by the time the draft rolled around, he was generally seen as the top high-school player in Texas. Drafted as a shortstop, he's already been moved to third base, which will work just fine as Ahrens is a switch-hitter with plus power from both sides and a great arm. Ignore the poor numbers in his pro debut; another powerful switch-hitting third baseman named Chipper Jones hit .229/.321/.271 in his Gulf Coast League debut.

J. P. Arencibia C

Bats: R Throws: R Height: 6' 1" Weight: 210 Born: January 5, 1986 Age: 22

YEAR	TEAM	LVL	AGE	PA	R	2B	3B	HR	RBI	BB	SO	SB	CS	EqBRR	AVG	OBP	SLG	MLVr	EqAVG	EqOBP	EqSLG	EqA	VORP	DEFENSE
2007	AUB	A-	21	249	31	17	1	3	25	14	56	0	0	-0.4	.254	.309	.377	.011	.209	.245	.319	.191	-27.9	54-C 0
2008	TOR	MLB	22	435	33	23	2	7	40	21	123	3	2	-0.1	.215	.258	.329	-.302	.214	.259	.333	.205	-15.3	103-C 2

Breakout: 55% Improve: 66% Collapse: 19% Attrition: 15% Comparables: David Parrish, Sammy Serrano, Todd Jennings, Jake Fox

Arencibia began last year as one of the top college position players on the draft board, but a disappointing junior year dropped him to the bottom half of the first round. He's an offense-oriented catcher with good hitting skills and gap power. Despite a whopping 18 passed balls in short-season play, his defense is at least average and should be enough to allow him to start in the big leagues.

Robinzon Diaz C

Bats: R Throws: R Height: 5' 11" Weight: 210 Born: September 19, 1983 Age: 24

YEAR	TEAM	LVL	AGE	PA	R	2B	3B	HR	RBI	BB	SO	SB	CS	EqBRR	AVG	OBP	SLG	MLVr	EqAVG	EqOBP	EqSLG	EqA	VORP	DEFENSE
2005	DUN	A+	21	414	47	17	6	1	65	15	28	5	2	-1.8	.294	.325	.376	-.009	.245	.274	.321	.204	-15.4	84-C 0
2006	DUN	A+	22	447	59	21	1	3	44	20	37	8	1	-2.7	.306	.341	.383	.055	.267	.299	.345	.227	-5.1	88-C 1
2007	NHP	AA	23	319	33	17	1	3	30	11	16	5	0	-1.2	.316	.344	.409	.072	.282	.307	.367	.238	1.5	49-C -4
2007	SYR	AAA	23	69	4	3	0	1	10	1	6	0	0	0.1	.338	.358	.431	.128	.303	.324	.379	.244	1.5	16-C -1
2008	TOR	MLB	24	378	35	17	2	2	33	12	35	4	2	-0.4	.264	.291	.341	-.197	.262	.293	.345	.224	-5.5	90-C -2

Breakout: 24% Improve: 44% Collapse: 27% Attrition: 11% Comparables: Einar Diaz, Humberto Quintero, Wil Nieves, Brayan Peña

Six years into his pro career, the Dominican Diaz finally escaped A-ball and continued slapping singles all over the diamond. There's nothing here beyond an average, but Diaz's high contact rate gives him a shot at sustaining an empty .300 in the majors. That and his good defense would make him an average catcher. September surgery to repair a fractured hamate bone in his left hand would be worrisome if he had power to lose.

Troy Glaus   3B   Bats: R   Throws: R   Height: 6' 5"   Weight: 240   Born: August 3, 1976   Age: 31

YEAR	TEAM	LVL	AGE	PA	R	2B	3B	HR	RBI	BB	SO	SB	CS	EqBRR	AVG	OBP	SLG	MLVr	EqAVG	EqOBP	EqSLG	EqA	VORP	DEFENSE
2005	ARI	MLB	28	634	78	29	1	37	97	84	145	4	2	0.0	.258	.363	.522	.182	.250	.356	.513	.292	37.5	141-3B -11
2006	TOR	MLB	29	634	105	27	0	38	104	86	134	3	2	0.0	.252	.355	.513	.104	.246	.358	.512	.292	29.3	133-3B 11
2007	TOR	MLB	30	456	60	19	1	20	62	61	102	0	1	-4.3	.262	.366	.473	.104	.265	.375	.501	.298	20.5	104-3B 3
2008	SLN	MLB	31	489	65	22	1	21	71	67	99	3	1	-1.0	.258	.364	.472	.071	.257	.364	.491	.288	27.3	115-3B 0

Breakout: 11%   Improve: 36%   Collapse: 25%   Attrition: 18%   Comparables: Morgan Ensberg, Bobby Bonilla, Cecil Fielder, Tim Salmon

Despite not being healthy for single day all last year, Glaus played exactly as well when able to take the field as he did in 2006. It was the 40 additional missed games, rather than any performance lapse, that trimmed his value, but he'll be back on grass in St. Louis, and his new manager, Tony La Russa, has plenty of experience handling fragile veterans. He has so many nagging problems with his legs that even a winter's rest won't fix them.

Aaron Hill   2B   Bats: R   Throws: R   Height: 5' 11"   Weight: 195   Born: March 21, 1982   Age: 26

YEAR	TEAM	LVL	AGE	PA	R	2B	3B	HR	RBI	BB	SO	SB	CS	EqBRR	AVG	OBP	SLG	MLVr	EqAVG	EqOBP	EqSLG	EqA	VORP	DEFENSE
2005	SYR	AAA	23	168	22	11	0	5	18	4	17	2	0	0.9	.301	.339	.468	.075	.272	.308	.411	.250	4.6	39-SS -1
2005	TOR	MLB	23	407	49	25	3	3	40	34	41	2	1	-0.9	.274	.342	.385	-.037	.276	.352	.397	.265	7.3	32-3B 3 20-2B 5
2006	TOR	MLB	24	606	70	28	3	6	50	42	66	5	2	1.3	.291	.349	.386	-.047	.289	.353	.389	.263	18.7	103-2B 25 49-SS -10
2007	TOR	MLB	25	657	87	47	2	17	78	41	102	4	3	0.1	.291	.333	.459	.054	.295	.343	.486	.280	27.1	158-2B 2
2008	TOR	MLB	26	593	66	33	3	11	63	40	79	5	3	-0.1	.271	.325	.405	-.048	.270	.326	.409	.260	12.0	139-2B 5

Breakout: 8%   Improve: 29%   Collapse: 33%   Attrition: 5%   Comparables: Buddy Bell, Ron Hunt, Davey Johnson, Bill Mazeroski

If Adams' 2007 season effectively ended his career, Hill's performance last year raised his to a new level. Hill made a concerted effort to drive the ball more, trading some walks for a ton of power and, overall, more productivity. He's a more valuable player than indicated above; in zone-based systems, his defense was worth 15 to 25 runs above average. His peak is going to be very impressive, starting now.

Brian Jeroloman   C   Bats: L   Throws: R   Height: 6' 0"   Weight: 195   Born: May 10, 1985   Age: 23

YEAR	TEAM	LVL	AGE	PA	R	2B	3B	HR	RBI	BB	SO	SB	CS	EqBRR	AVG	OBP	SLG	MLVr	EqAVG	EqOBP	EqSLG	EqA	VORP	DEFENSE
2006	AUB	A-	21	169	27	10	1	0	21	26	38	0	0	0.1	.241	.363	.326	.073	.196	.292	.277	.203	-17.3	32-C 3
2007	DUN	A+	22	382	32	14	0	3	39	85	57	0	0	-2.9	.259	.421	.338	.084	.225	.376	.301	.257	3.0	92-C -6
2008	TOR	MLB	23	396	37	18	1	5	33	52	90	2	1	-0.8	.222	.327	.322	-.182	.221	.328	.326	.241	-2.5	95-C -1

Breakout: 29%   Improve: 49%   Collapse: 29%   Attrition: 14%   Comparables: Pete Gonzalez, Mark Johnson, Cory Dunlap, Eric Albright

That stat line isn't a misprint. Last year, in 382 plate-appearances, Jeroloman drew 85 walks, resulting in an on-base percentage 162 points above his batting average. That said, the ability to draw walks is the sum of his offensive abilities. Combine that with above-average defensive skills and you have a guy who should be a decent backup at a position at which it's hard to find even that.

Reed Johnson   LF   Bats: R   Throws: R   Height: 5' 10"   Weight: 180   Born: December 8, 1976   Age: 31

YEAR	TEAM	LVL	AGE	PA	R	2B	3B	HR	RBI	BB	SO	SB	CS	EqBRR	AVG	OBP	SLG	MLVr	EqAVG	EqOBP	EqSLG	EqA	VORP	DEFENSE
2005	TOR	MLB	28	439	55	21	6	8	58	22	82	5	6	0.4	.269	.332	.412	-.020	.272	.341	.424	.262	3.6	66-LF 7 28-RF 0
2006	TOR	MLB	29	517	86	34	2	12	49	33	81	8	2	0.2	.317	.388	.477	.173	.315	.390	.486	.302	32.5	72-LF 4 28-RF 5
2007	TOR	MLB	30	307	31	13	2	2	14	16	56	4	2	-0.5	.236	.305	.320	-.230	.245	.315	.343	.233	-11.7	56-LF 5
2008	TOR	MLB	31	385	43	19	3	6	38	24	70	4	2	0.1	.261	.322	.385	-.086	.260	.324	.389	.253	-2.3	92-LF 2

Breakout: 10%   Improve: 24%   Collapse: 43%   Attrition: 28%   Comparables: Peanuts Lowrey, Billy Hatcher, Jay Payton, Danny Bautista

A herniated disk in the season's second week ruined Johnson's year. He was vocal about demanding playing time when he returned in July, then backed up his argument by hitting .232/.302/.307 with two steals through the end of the season. He's a fourth outfielder, a good one, and should return to that role this year.

Adam Lind — LF

Bats: L Throws: L Height: 6' 2" Weight: 195 Born: July 17, 1983 Age: 24

YEAR	TEAM	LVL	AGE	PA	R	2B	3B	HR	RBI	BB	SO	SB	CS	EqBRR	AVG	OBP	SLG	MLVr	EqAVG	EqOBP	EqSLG	EqA	VORP	DEFENSE	
2005	DUN	A+	21	554	80	42	4	12	84	49	77	2	1	1.0	.313	.375	.487	.226	.260	.318	.413	.252	-4.8	119-LF	-13
2006	NHP	AA	22	378	43	24	0	19	71	25	87	2	1	-5.1	.310	.357	.543	.321	.274	.320	.500	.275	11.6	78-LF	-5
2006	SYR	AAA	22	137	20	7	0	5	18	23	18	1	0	0.9	.394	.496	.596	.594	.355	.456	.564	.349	18.5	33-LF	6
2006	TOR	MLB	22	65	8	8	0	2	8	5	12	0	0	-1.0	.367	.415	.600	.464	.356	.415	.610	.338	8.4		
2007	SYR	AAA	23	190	20	8	2	6	28	14	42	0	0	-0.8	.299	.353	.471	.140	.280	.332	.463	.271	4.2	38-LF	-2
2007	TOR	MLB	23	311	34	14	0	11	46	16	65	1	2	0.7	.238	.278	.400	-.167	.243	.288	.424	.240	-7.9	73-LF	7
2008	TOR	MLB	24	473	54	26	2	16	64	35	97	3	1	-0.5	.267	.324	.443	-.003	.265	.325	.448	.268	5.4	112-LF	3

Breakout: 20% Improve: 42% Collapse: 26% Attrition: 20%   Comparables: Steve Whitaker, Curtis Granderson, Jim King, Luis Gonzalez

Lind didn't have an argument for holding onto his playing time after Johnson's return. He was batting .230/.274/.383 as Johnson's replacement in left. The obvious solution—a platoon—was problematic within the parameters of a 12-man pitching staff, the lack of an everyday shortstop, and the need to spot Troy Glaus a day or two a week. All that, and Matt Stairs, too! Lind should be the regular left fielder this year, but both Johnson and Stairs are still around, so he's not going to be handed the job. His lousy September (.273/.298/.473) didn't help his case.

John McDonald — SS

Bats: R Throws: R Height: 5' 11" Weight: 185 Born: September 24, 1974 Age: 33

YEAR	TEAM	LVL	AGE	PA	R	2B	3B	HR	RBI	BB	SO	SB	CS	EqBRR	AVG	OBP	SLG	MLVr	EqAVG	EqOBP	EqSLG	EqA	VORP	DEFENSE			
2005	DET	MLB	30	78	10	3	1	0	4	5	12	1	1	-0.1	.260	.308	.329	-.165	.264	.321	.333	.230	-0.4	17-SS	3		
2005	TOR	MLB	30	106	8	3	0	0	12	6	12	5	0	-0.8	.290	.340	.323	-.114	.293	.350	.326	.258	2.7	25-SS	3		
2006	TOR	MLB	31	286	35	7	3	3	23	16	41	7	2	1.5	.223	.271	.308	-.349	.222	.279	.307	.212	-10.4	75-SS	1		
2007	TOR	MLB	32	353	32	20	2	1	31	11	48	7	2	0.4	.251	.279	.333	-.254	.258	.290	.357	.228	-7.8	89-SS	13	10-3B	4
2008	TOR	MLB	33	188	18	8	1	1	15	9	26	5	1	0.2	.246	.288	.330	-.228	.244	.290	.334	.226	-2.1	48-SS	3		

Breakout: 23% Improve: 44% Collapse: 37% Attrition: 43%   Comparables: Claude Corbitt, Ivan DeJesus, Sr., Chris Gomez, Tim Foli

McDonald may be the rare player whose defense is so good that he can keep a job despite being one of the worst hitters in baseball. His hands are among the best in the game, and he has sneaky-good lateral range. Those who think Derek Jeter can play shortstop should watch Yankees-Jays games and carefully compare the two. McDonald is particularly valuable to the Blue Jays, who feature a groundball-centric pitching staff. The Jays can even gain on the margins by finding a bat to play shortstop when fly-baller Shaun Marcum starts, although David Eckstein is decidedly not that player. Eckstein should not play ahead of McDonald; when he does, the Jays will be hurting themselves.

Lyle Overbay — 1B

Bats: L Throws: L Height: 6' 2" Weight: 235 Born: January 28, 1977 Age: 31

YEAR	TEAM	LVL	AGE	PA	R	2B	3B	HR	RBI	BB	SO	SB	CS	EqBRR	AVG	OBP	SLG	MLVr	EqAVG	EqOBP	EqSLG	EqA	VORP	DEFENSE	
2005	MIL	MLB	28	622	80	34	1	19	72	78	98	1	0	-0.6	.276	.367	.449	.118	.269	.363	.447	.282	23.6	143-1B	10
2006	TOR	MLB	29	640	82	46	1	22	92	55	96	5	3	-3.8	.312	.372	.508	.185	.307	.375	.512	.299	36.3	140-1B	-7
2007	TOR	MLB	30	476	49	30	2	10	44	47	78	2	0	-0.3	.240	.315	.391	-.114	.242	.324	.411	.256	-3.6	109-1B	6
2008	TOR	MLB	31	505	60	27	1	14	62	50	85	3	2	-0.9	.265	.341	.423	-.003	.264	.342	.428	.271	5.0	119-1B	2

Breakout: 7% Improve: 37% Collapse: 25% Attrition: 15%   Comparables: Travis Lee, Greg Brock, Bruce Bochte, Sid Bream

Overbay wasn't having a good season when, on June 3, the White Sox' John Danks hit him on the right hand with a pitch, breaking bones. He went to the DL hitting .256/.332/.464, basically down a hit a week, which happens. Overbay came back after the All-Star break and seemed fine, starting the second half with a six-game hitting streak. From there, he fell apart, going .201/.276/.304 the rest of the way. He indicated late in the season that the hand still bothered him, so give him a mulligan and expect him to return to his acceptable established level this year.

Ryan Patterson　　　　OF　　　　Bats: R　Throws: R　Height: 5' 11"　Weight: 205　Born: May 2, 1983　Age: 25

YEAR	TEAM	LVL	AGE	PA	R	2B	3B	HR	RBI	BB	SO	SB	CS	EqBRR	AVG	OBP	SLG	MLVr	EqAVG	EqOBP	EqSLG	EqA	VORP	DEFENSE			
2005	AUB	A-	22	306	52	23	4	13	65	21	53	5	2	2.6	.339	.386	.595	.469	.246	.281	.423	.239	-0.7	36-CF	-4	15-LF	-1
2006	DUN	A+	23	380	65	25	0	19	69	20	61	2	4	-1.9	.288	.327	.520	.202	.251	.288	.455	.248	-3.7	62-LF	-9	15-CF	-1
2006	NHP	AA	23	205	19	14	1	6	20	13	50	2	0	-0.2	.257	.310	.439	.072	.238	.286	.413	.240	-6.3	40-LF	-3		
2007	NHP	AA	24	475	53	27	0	18	68	23	102	1	4	-4.0	.267	.302	.448	.021	.240	.272	.411	.230	-16.0	57-RF	2	40-LF	-7
2008	TOR	MLB	25	560	53	28	2	19	75	30	145	4	3	-0.1	.237	.281	.408	-.142	.236	.282	.413	.241	-10.8	131-LF	0		

Breakout: 28% Improve: 56% Collapse: 20% Attrition: 12%　　　　Comparables: Dee Haynes, Stefan Bailie, Steve Gibralter, David Gibralter

The wheels fell off Patterson's bus last year, as the problems he showed making contact in his first taste of Double-A persisted. He can still hit a ball a long way, but that rarely happened last season. Without any notable speed or defense, Patterson is left trying to hit his way to the majors, and he's not that kind of prospect.

Alex Rios　　　　RF　　　　Bats: R　Throws: R　Height: 6' 5"　Weight: 195　Born: February 18, 1981　Age: 27

YEAR	TEAM	LVL	AGE	PA	R	2B	3B	HR	RBI	BB	SO	SB	CS	EqBRR	AVG	OBP	SLG	MLVr	EqAVG	EqOBP	EqSLG	EqA	VORP	DEFENSE			
2005	TOR	MLB	24	519	71	23	6	10	59	28	101	14	9	0.0	.262	.306	.397	-.091	.264	.317	.411	.251	-3.6	118-RF	10		
2006	TOR	MLB	25	498	68	33	6	17	82	35	89	15	6	-0.7	.302	.349	.516	.149	.299	.353	.524	.294	29.0	108-RF	9		
2007	TOR	MLB	26	711	114	43	7	24	85	55	103	17	4	1.7	.297	.354	.498	.149	.301	.363	.527	.299	38.9	140-RF	2	18-CF	0
2008	TOR	MLB	27	637	88	36	6	20	83	49	108	16	5	1.4	.280	.339	.468	.066	.279	.341	.473	.284	16.0	149-RF	3		

Breakout: 13% Improve: 38% Collapse: 20% Attrition: 5%　　　　Comparables: Garry Maddox, Al Cowens, Moises Alou, Roberto Kelly

Rios's groundball-to-flyball ratios by season: 2.42, 1.46, 0.91, 0.87. His early-career struggles were a problem of approach, rather than a lack of talent, and the race to get off of his bandwagon—led by our own Joe Sheehan—was hasty. Rios improved his contact rate last season and may have a bit more power in him, so there's still upside. The Jays' chances of catching one of the two monsters in the AL East are predicated in part on Rios stepping up and becoming an MVP candidate.

Ryan Roberts　　　　UT　　　　Bats: R　Throws: R　Height: 5' 11"　Weight: 190　Born: September 19, 1980　Age: 27

YEAR	TEAM	LVL	AGE	PA	R	2B	3B	HR	RBI	BB	SO	SB	CS	EqBRR	AVG	OBP	SLG	MLVr	EqAVG	EqOBP	EqSLG	EqA	VORP	DEFENSE			
2005	DUN	A+	24	192	33	9	0	9	35	24	27	6	1	0.7	.287	.380	.506	.234	.243	.326	.420	.262	5.2	40-2B	-2		
2005	NHP	AA	24	399	54	19	3	15	44	55	94	5	1	1.3	.272	.379	.479	.222	.243	.342	.429	.268	16.0	90-2B	-11		
2006	SYR	AAA	25	403	44	28	1	10	49	30	86	5	3	-1.5	.273	.330	.439	.061	.255	.311	.422	.252	9.1	76-2B	7		
2007	SYR	AAA	26	399	46	16	1	12	47	55	85	1	2	-3.5	.249	.355	.409	.027	.235	.335	.402	.258	9.9	33-3B	-6	31-2B	-2
2008	TEX	MLB	27	427	44	19	1	11	46	41	105	4	2	-0.5	.235	.313	.384	-.120	.233	.313	.394	.251	0.3	101-2B	-4		

Breakout: 14% Improve: 40% Collapse: 23% Attrition: 15%　　　　Comparables: Keith Ginter, Jason Maxwell, Marshall McDougall, Trace Coquillette

Roberts completed his slide from middle-infield prospect to utility guy by playing eight positions at Triple-A Syracuse last season, including two cameos behind the plate. With enough bat to warrant a roster spot, Roberts could be valuable to the Rangers, who signed him to a minor league deal and typically carry 12 and sometimes 13 pitchers. Their deep pool of candidates for outfield spots, however, will push him to the minors again.

Sergio Santos　　　　SS　　　　Bats: R　Throws: R　Height: 6' 2"　Weight: 240　Born: July 4, 1983　Age: 24

YEAR	TEAM	LVL	AGE	PA	R	2B	3B	HR	RBI	BB	SO	SB	CS	EqBRR	AVG	OBP	SLG	MLVr	EqAVG	EqOBP	EqSLG	EqA	VORP	DEFENSE	
2005	TUC	AAA	21	532	55	21	3	12	68	34	108	2	2	0.6	.239	.288	.367	-.291	.202	.244	.304	.187	-30.4	124-SS	-17
2006	SYR	AAA	22	509	48	24	1	5	38	24	96	1	3	0.7	.214	.254	.299	-.273	.198	.239	.291	.175	-34.6	127-SS	-3
2007	NHP	AA	23	483	63	34	2	20	62	43	97	2	0	-1.6	.250	.325	.477	.081	.226	.292	.435	.248	9.4	108-SS	9
2007	SYR	AAA	23	50	4	2	0	0	4	1	10	2	0	-0.3	.191	.204	.234	-.484	.170	.184	.234	.137	-6.0	13-SS	1
2008	TOR	MLB	24	542	47	29	2	12	60	32	130	4	2	-0.2	.225	.274	.364	-.220	.224	.276	.368	.225	-6.4	127-SS	1

Breakout: 50% Improve: 64% Collapse: 13% Attrition: 15%　　　　Comparables: Clay Bellinger, Brennan King, Mike Bell, Keith Reed

Roberts' exodus creates hope for Santos, who isn't going to be a major league shortstop but may have enough secondary skills and physical tools to be a fifth infielder. Santos played some third base in the Arizona Fall League, which given his size should be a more natural spot for him. With two brutal years at Triple-A in his past, he needs to show he can play at that level before he becomes a viable utility option for the big club.

Travis Snider RF Bats: L Throws: L Height: 5' 11" Weight: 245 Born: February 2, 1988 Age: 20

YEAR	TEAM	LVL	AGE	PA	R	2B	3B	HR	RBI	BB	SO	SB	CS	EqBRR	AVG	OBP	SLG	MLVr	EqAVG	EqOBP	EqSLG	EqA	VORP	DEFENSE	
2006	PUL	Rk	18	226	36	12	1	11	41	30	47	6	3	0.1	.325	.412	.567	.380	.221	.288	.363	.229	-21.9	43-RF	1
2007	LNS	A	19	517	72	35	7	16	93	49	129	3	10	-1.7	.313	.377	.525	.312	.217	.275	.368	.220	-27.7	108-RF	-21
2008	TOR	MLB	20	604	60	34	3	17	65	45	181	6	4	1.2	.228	.288	.392	-.158	.227	.289	.396	.238	-17.0	141-RF	-1

Breakout: 54% Improve: 72% Collapse: 13% Attrition: 1%   Comparables: Jay Bruce, Dee Brown, Austin Kearns, Billy Butler

Look, it's not a failed infield prospect! The top guy in the Jays' system, Snider has terrific power and an idea of what he's doing at the plate. Arizona Fall League stats have to be taken with a grain of salt, but when a 19-year-old hits .316 with walks and power, it's notable because of the age and experience of his competition. Snider will be an adequate corner outfielder who rakes, comparable to peak Brian Giles. His ETA is 2009.

Matt Stairs 1B/LF Bats: L Throws: R Height: 5' 9" Weight: 215 Born: February 27, 1968 Age: 40

YEAR	TEAM	LVL	AGE	PA	R	2B	3B	HR	RBI	BB	SO	SB	CS	EqBRR	AVG	OBP	SLG	MLVr	EqAVG	EqOBP	EqSLG	EqA	VORP	DEFENSE			
2005	KCA	MLB	37	466	55	26	1	13	66	60	69	1	2	-2.7	.275	.373	.444	.109	.280	.386	.460	.294	19.8	58-1B	-4	11-RF	-2
2006	KCA	MLB	38	261	31	14	0	8	32	31	52	0	0	-0.2	.261	.352	.429	.000	.260	.360	.439	.279	5.6				
2006	TEX	MLB	38	88	6	4	0	3	11	6	22	0	0	0.7	.210	.273	.370	-.268	.200	.273	.350	.215	-3.5				
2006	DET	MLB	38	44	5	3	0	2	8	3	12	0	0	-0.1	.244	.295	.463	-.063	.244	.311	.439	.256	0.3				
2007	TOR	MLB	39	405	58	28	1	21	64	44	66	2	1	-2.5	.289	.368	.549	.233	.289	.375	.578	.313	29.5	37-1B	-1	32-LF	0
2008	TOR	MLB	40	346	49	20	1	16	58	39	62	2	1	-0.8	.276	.361	.511	.153	.275	.362	.517	.300	16.8	83-DH			

Breakout: 18% Improve: 57% Collapse: 17% Attrition: 24%   Comparables: Brian Downing, Ron Fairly, Edgar Martinez, Gene Woodling

Stairs reversed what seemed like a fade into oblivion last year with his best season since he was a regular with the A's. He even played 600 innings in the field without hurting himself or those around him, which may be a bigger surprise than his .297 EqA. A new two-year deal will take him through age 41; how much he plays will depend on the health and performance of Lind, Overbay, and Frank Thomas.

Curtis Thigpen C Bats: R Throws: R Height: 5' 11" Weight: 190 Born: April 19, 1983 Age: 25

YEAR	TEAM	LVL	AGE	PA	R	2B	3B	HR	RBI	BB	SO	SB	CS	EqBRR	AVG	OBP	SLG	MLVr	EqAVG	EqOBP	EqSLG	EqA	VORP	DEFENSE			
2005	LNS	A	22	352	41	18	2	5	35	54	34	5	0	0.9	.287	.397	.413	.161	.242	.333	.343	.244	0.6	58-C	5		
2005	NHP	AA	22	157	18	8	0	4	15	9	19	0	0	0.9	.284	.340	.426	.102	.257	.310	.375	.238	0.7	30-C	6		
2006	NHP	AA	23	373	49	25	5	5	36	52	61	5	1	-1.8	.259	.370	.421	.138	.240	.341	.407	.263	11.1	73-C	-4		
2006	SYR	AAA	23	56	3	3	0	1	9	2	9	0	1	-0.4	.264	.304	.377	-.065	.245	.286	.340	.210	-1.3	14-C	-4		
2007	SYR	AAA	24	202	20	10	0	3	20	17	23	1	0	-0.4	.285	.348	.391	.016	.260	.318	.365	.242	1.0	39-C	-10		
2007	TOR	MLB	24	110	13	5	0	0	11	8	17	2	0	0.8	.238	.294	.287	-.295	.240	.303	.290	.216	-3.8	14-C	3	11-1B	0
2008	TOR	MLB	25	246	25	13	1	4	25	21	40	2	1	-0.1	.244	.312	.369	-.136	.243	.314	.373	.245	-0.4	61-C	0		

Breakout: 27% Improve: 47% Collapse: 29% Attrition: 32%   Comparables: Charlie Moore, Jerry Grote, Brook Fordyce, Jerry May

The shape of Thigpen's performance is a bit different from that of Robinzon Diaz's, but the two end up in about the same place. Thigpen, however, gets higher marks for his defense, particularly for working with pitchers. A job-sharing arrangement with Gregg Zaun is likely this year, with Thigpen having an opportunity to win the job if his bat comes around. As you can see, the first few drafts of the J. P. Ricciardi era, which focused on collegians, were wildly unproductive. We praised the approach at the time, but as Rany Jazayerli has noted, there's not much edge in drafting collegians any longer, and very little sense in emphasizing one subset of players over another.

Frank Thomas — DH

Bats: R   Throws: R   Height: 6' 5"   Weight: 275   Born: May 27, 1968   Age: 40

YEAR	TEAM	LVL	AGE	PA	R	2B	3B	HR	RBI	BB	SO	SB	CS	EqBRR	AVG	OBP	SLG	MLVr	EqAVG	EqOBP	EqSLG	EqA	VORP	DEFENSE
2005	CHA	MLB	37	124	19	3	0	12	26	16	31	0	0	-0.9	.219	.315	.590	.146	.214	.323	.602	.298	7.4	
2006	OAK	MLB	38	559	77	11	0	39	114	81	81	0	0	-3.4	.270	.381	.545	.224	.272	.390	.563	.317	41.3	
2007	TOR	MLB	39	624	63	30	0	26	95	81	94	0	0	-4.2	.277	.377	.480	.142	.280	.385	.509	.304	31.5	
2008	TOR	MLB	40	425	52	20	0	20	69	58	68	2	1	-2.3	.257	.362	.485	.105	.256	.364	.490	.296	19.1	101-DH

Breakout: 5%   Improve: 27%   Collapse: 33%   Attrition: 29%   Comparables: Edgar Martinez, Fred McGriff, Dave Winfield, Mike Schmidt

Any doubt that Frank Thomas would go into the Hall of Fame ended last year. He hit his 500th career home run, had his second straight big season late in his career, and was not only unscathed by the Mitchell Report, he was the only active player to voluntarily speak with the commission. In conjunction with his performance in front of Congress in 2005, Thomas is almost certain to benefit from a halo effect as a perceived "clean" player, something the steroid-obsessed voting pool will use to push him into Cooperstown. Not that he needs the push: he has been qualified since about 1997 or so. Let's just hope that it's his all-time great peak, not his position on PEDs, that drives the discussion about his career.

Vernon Wells — CF

Bats: R   Throws: R   Height: 6' 1"   Weight: 225   Born: December 8, 1978   Age: 29

YEAR	TEAM	LVL	AGE	PA	R	2B	3B	HR	RBI	BB	SO	SB	CS	EqBRR	AVG	OBP	SLG	MLVr	EqAVG	EqOBP	EqSLG	EqA	VORP	DEFENSE
2005	TOR	MLB	26	678	78	30	3	28	97	47	86	8	3	-1.1	.269	.320	.463	.028	.269	.330	.475	.274	23.3	152-CF -7
2006	TOR	MLB	27	677	91	40	5	32	106	54	90	17	4	1.2	.303	.357	.542	.200	.300	.361	.550	.304	58.9	146-CF -10
2007	TOR	MLB	28	642	85	36	4	16	80	49	89	10	4	1.5	.245	.304	.402	-.115	.249	.313	.425	.255	2.6	143-CF -3
2008	TOR	MLB	29	609	79	32	3	21	82	51	88	9	3	0.3	.270	.333	.454	.028	.269	.334	.458	.277	18.4	142-CF -5

Breakout: 18%   Improve: 50%   Collapse: 20%   Attrition: 8%   Comparables: Carlos Lee, Ivan Calderon, Kevin Mench, Jason Lane

Say, is it okay to point out that Vernon Wells isn't a star? In six seasons as a full-time player, he's had two EqAs above .266, and while his defense is good, it's not good enough to make that kind of hitter into one of the best players in the game. Wells's plate-discipline indicators have been remarkably consistent; in some years, he has the singles and doubles fall in, in others he doesn't. The contract that pays him $126 million from now through 2014 will overpay him considerably on the back end.

Gregg Zaun — C

Bats: S   Throws: R   Height: 5' 10"   Weight: 190   Born: April 14, 1971   Age: 37

YEAR	TEAM	LVL	AGE	PA	R	2B	3B	HR	RBI	BB	SO	SB	CS	EqBRR	AVG	OBP	SLG	MLVr	EqAVG	EqOBP	EqSLG	EqA	VORP	DEFENSE
2005	TOR	MLB	34	512	61	18	1	11	61	73	70	2	3	-2.0	.251	.355	.373	-.041	.251	.366	.378	.267	14.0	122-C -3
2006	TOR	MLB	35	339	39	19	0	12	40	41	42	0	2	-1.6	.272	.363	.462	.070	.266	.366	.465	.285	15.3	61-C -2
2007	TOR	MLB	36	391	43	24	1	10	52	51	55	0	0	-2.3	.242	.341	.411	-.038	.242	.349	.428	.273	12.5	94-C -7
2008	TOR	MLB	37	281	31	14	0	7	33	33	42	1	1	-0.8	.251	.343	.402	-.036	.250	.344	.406	.266	6.9	69-C -3

Breakout: 12%   Improve: 42%   Collapse: 21%   Attrition: 31%   Comparables: Alan Ashby, Ernie Whitt, Rick Dempsey, Chad Kreuter

The Practically Perfect Backup Catcher just grinds on. A decade after earning that moniker, Zaun continues to put up good OBPs, show some pop, and play so-so defense. A switch-hitter with that profile is valuable; indeed, 2008 will be the former journeyman's fifth season with the Jays. The biggest problem is his playing time; he's led the Jays in innings caught in three of the last four seasons, making it hard to justify the "B" in PPBC.

PITCHERS

Jeremy Accardo

Bats: R   Throws: R   Height: 6' 2"   Weight: 190   Born: December 18, 1981   Age: 26

YEAR	TEAM	LVL	AGE	W	L	SV	G	GS	IP	H	BB	SO	HR	GB%	BABIP	STUFF	WHIP	ERA	PERA	EqERA	EqH9	EqBB9	EqSO9	EqHR9	VORP	SN/WX
2005	FRE	AAA	23	2	0	3	25	0	32¹	25	10	30	0	47.7%	.287	7	1.08	1.95	3.29	2.67	7.4	3.3	5.9	0.3	9.9	—
2005	SFN	MLB	23	1	5	0	28	0	29²	26	9	16	2	41.8%	.255	-6	1.18	3.94	3.25	3.90	7.5	2.4	4.2	0.6	5.0	-0.02
2006	SFN	MLB	24	1	3	3	38	0	40¹	38	11	40	2	43.2%	.321	17	1.21	4.91	3.33	4.87	8.4	2.0	8.0	0.4	3.9	0.54
2006	TOR	MLB	24	1	1	0	27	0	28²	38	9	14	5	44.2%	.337	-27	1.64	5.96	7.36	6.26	11.9	2.6	4.3	1.3	0.5	-0.92
2007	TOR	MLB	25	4	4	30	64	0	67¹	51	24	57	4	49.0%	.251	15	1.11	2.14	2.99	2.55	7.0	2.8	7.0	0.5	26.2	3.22
2008	TOR	MLB	26	4	4	20	56	0	62¹	57	22	52	6	49.2%	.284	5	1.27	3.58	3.38	3.70	7.9	2.9	6.5	0.8	16.2	1.90

Breakout: 15% Improve: 39% Collapse: 25% Attrition: 12%   Comparables: Mike Henneman, Rawly Eastwick, Bob Wickman, Randy St. Claire

Fantasy baseball will drive you absolutely nuts. B. J. Ryan establishes himself as among the best closers in baseball, then blows out his elbow 15 minutes into last season. If you had him, tough; those saves will now be passed around at random. For the Jays, Accardo, an afterthought in the process of discarding Shea Hillenbrand in 2006, opened the season with 21 shutout innings through May 24, by which time he was the closer. His stuff isn't dominant, and even if Ryan isn't back, he'll be in danger of losing the job to Casey Janssen.

A. J. Burnett

Bats: R   Throws: R   Height: 6' 4"   Weight: 230   Born: January 3, 1977   Age: 31

YEAR	TEAM	LVL	AGE	W	L	SV	G	GS	IP	H	BB	SO	HR	GB%	BABIP	STUFF	WHIP	ERA	PERA	EqERA	EqH9	EqBB9	EqSO9	EqHR9	VORP	SN/WX
2005	FLO	MLB	28	12	12	0	32	32	209	184	79	198	12	59.8%	.304	34	1.26	3.44	3.29	3.99	7.5	3.1	7.8	0.5	30.5	4.57
2006	TOR	MLB	29	10	8	0	21	21	135²	138	39	118	14	52.9%	.317	25	1.30	3.98	4.21	4.18	9.0	2.4	7.4	0.8	25.3	3.05
2007	TOR	MLB	30	10	8	0	25	25	165²	131	66	176	23	55.8%	.262	23	1.19	3.75	3.95	3.75	7.4	3.2	8.9	1.2	37.5	4.30
2008	TOR	MLB	31	12	8	0	28	28	183¹	164	67	163	16	53.3%	.287	21	1.26	3.64	3.33	3.76	7.7	3.0	6.9	0.8	38.0	5.60

Breakout: 19% Improve: 55% Collapse: 18% Attrition: 15%   Comparables: Matt Clement, Chris Carpenter, Jack Morris, Roger Clemens

Burnett made 46 starts in the first two years of his five-year, $55 million deal. With an opt-out clause waiting to be exercised at the end of this season and hundreds of millions of dollars of extra money floating around the game, look for Burnett to pitch through the minor injuries this season. That should work for the Jays, who have every reason to maximize the short-term value of their players this year. Burnett was badly mismanaged by Gibbons throughout 2007, and spent six weeks on the DL not long after a three-start stretch of 125, 117, and 130 pitches. After coming back, Gibbons had him throw 110, 115, 114, 120, 124, and 119, all for a team going nowhere fast. Those extra pitches will be needed this year; if Burnett does pull up lame, Gibbons will have no defense.

Brett Cecil

Bats: R   Throws: L   Height: 6' 3"   Weight: 220   Born: July 2, 1986   Age: 21

YEAR	TEAM	LVL	AGE	W	L	SV	G	GS	IP	H	BB	SO	HR	GB%	BABIP	STUFF	WHIP	ERA	PERA	EqERA	EqH9	EqBB9	EqSO9	EqHR9	VORP	SN/WX
2007	AUB	A-	20	1	0	0	14	13	49²	36	11	56	1	58.3%	.278	13	0.95	1.27	4.57	3.60	8.4	3.6	5.4	0.8	10.0	—
2008	TOR	MLB	21	8	8	0	32	21	131¹	143	58	80	16	56.6%	.300	0	1.53	4.57	4.70	4.64	9.4	3.6	4.8	1.1	14.2	2.50

Breakout: 2% Improve: 18% Collapse: 59% Attrition: 16%   Comparables: Zach Duke, Keith Heberling, Scott Downs, LaTroy Hawkins

Because Cecil is a big, physical left-hander with a low-90s fastball, above-average slider, and solid changeup, scouts are understandably optimistic about his ability to start, despite his having been a closer for most of his college days. If his pro debut is any indication, his future is quite bright; some are already wondering how he slid all the way down to the compensation round in last year's draft.

Gustavo Chacin

Bats: L   Throws: L   Height: 5' 11"   Weight: 195   Born: December 4, 1980   Age: 27

YEAR	TEAM	LVL	AGE	W	L	SV	G	GS	IP	H	BB	SO	HR	GB%	BABIP	STUFF	WHIP	ERA	PERA	EqERA	EqH9	EqBB9	EqSO9	EqHR9	VORP	SN/WX
2005	TOR	MLB	24	13	9	0	34	34	203	213	70	121	20	40.3%	.304	9	1.39	3.72	4.66	4.21	9.5	3.1	5.3	0.8	39.3	4.98
2006	TOR	MLB	25	9	4	0	17	17	87¹	90	38	47	19	37.5%	.261	-21	1.47	5.05	5.72	4.81	8.9	3.7	4.6	1.8	8.7	1.47
2007	TOR	MLB	26	2	1	0	5	5	27¹	29	7	11	6	41.8%	.250	-16	1.32	5.60	5.94	5.67	9.7	2.0	3.3	2.0	1.5	0.35
2008	TOR	MLB	27	3	3	0	18	7	51	60	19	29	9	43.7%	.302	-11	1.55	5.48	5.25	5.45	10.1	3.1	4.5	1.5	1.7	0.40

Breakout: 9% Improve: 28% Collapse: 38% Attrition: 56%   Comparables: Dave Hamilton, Art Ceccarelli, Mike Kekich, Scott Bailes

The charade that Chacin is important to the Jays' rotation should be just about over by now. The soft-tossing lefty maxed out his effort in 2005 by making 34 starts and posting a 3.72 ERA. That he's made just 22 starts around three DL stints, allowed a home run every 4 2/3 innings, and posted a 1.29 K/BB since then is as surprising as a Baseball Prospectus writer starting a simile he can't find an end for. September shoulder surgery is supposed to have him healthy this year, but the best way for the Jays to use him would be to trade him after the first time he goes six innings.

Scott Downs

| | | | | Bats: L | | Throws: L | | Height: 6' 2" | | Weight: 190 | | Born: March 17, 1976 | | | Age: 32 |

YEAR	TEAM	LVL	AGE	W	L	SV	G	GS	IP	H	BB	SO	HR	GB%	BABIP	STUFF	WHIP	ERA	PERA	EqERA	EqH9	EqBB9	EqSO9	EqHR9	VORP	SN/WX
2005	SYR	AAA	29	2	3	0	7	7	39¹	45	3	35	5	53.7%	.339	6	1.22	4.81	5.48	5.40	11.0	1.2	5.9	1.5	0.8	—
2005	TOR	MLB	29	4	3	0	26	13	94	93	34	75	12	53.9%	.289	6	1.35	4.31	4.51	4.55	8.8	3.2	7.0	1.1	12.2	1.88
2006	TOR	MLB	30	6	2	1	59	5	77	73	30	61	9	56.4%	.287	2	1.34	4.09	4.11	4.04	8.3	3.3	6.8	1.0	14.8	0.80
2007	TOR	MLB	31	4	2	1	81	0	58	47	24	57	3	61.1%	.291	19	1.22	2.17	3.36	2.40	7.7	3.4	8.3	0.5	24.0	2.26
2008	TOR	MLB	32	3	2	4	56	0	52	49	20	44	5	54.7%	.293	3	1.31	3.60	3.49	3.74	8.1	3.1	6.6	0.8	12.0	1.10

Breakout: 21% Improve: 42% Collapse: 29% Attrition: 26%   Comparables: Trever Miller, Mike Myers, Gary Lavelle, Windy McCall

When we talk about pitchers moving to the bullpen and thriving by using smaller repertoires in shorter outings, we are generally talking about righties who take on setup and closer roles. Downs, however, followed a similar path as a southpaw, resurrecting his career by lowering his ERA for four straight seasons. He struck out one of every four lefty batters he faced last year, a career high that made him one of the best specialists in the league. Since his last start on August 18, 2006, Downs has a 1.96 ERA.

Jason Frasor

| | | | | Bats: R | | Throws: R | | Height: 5' 10" | | Weight: 170 | | Born: August 9, 1977 | | | Age: 30 |

YEAR	TEAM	LVL	AGE	W	L	SV	G	GS	IP	H	BB	SO	HR	GB%	BABIP	STUFF	WHIP	ERA	PERA	EqERA	EqH9	EqBB9	EqSO9	EqHR9	VORP	SN/WX
2005	TOR	MLB	27	3	5	1	67	0	74²	67	28	62	8	50.9%	.294	6	1.27	3.25	4.24	3.73	8.4	3.5	7.7	0.9	18.3	2.88
2006	SYR	AAA	28	3	1	1	18	0	20²	21	13	33	1	60.9%	.444	18	1.68	4.01	7.84	6.50	12.0	7.0	11.5	1.0	-1.8	—
2006	TOR	MLB	28	3	2	0	51	0	50	47	17	51	8	43.4%	.291	9	1.28	4.32	4.12	3.91	8.0	2.8	8.5	1.2	10.3	0.72
2007	TOR	MLB	29	1	5	3	51	0	57	47	23	59	3	47.5%	.289	18	1.23	4.58	3.28	4.40	7.5	3.1	8.5	0.5	9.4	0.72
2008	TOR	MLB	30	3	3	4	53	0	60	56	25	57	7	47.4%	.297	6	1.35	4.03	3.85	4.09	8.1	3.4	7.5	1.0	11.2	1.00

Breakout: 19% Improve: 56% Collapse: 18% Attrition: 10%   Comparables: Mike Marshall, Darren Holmes, Don Elston, Steve Farr

Frasor was given the first shot at the closer job after Ryan went down, but as is often the case with that position, early failure is long-term doom. A badly blown save on April 28 against the Rangers marked the last time Frasor would pitch in a save situation until September, but his Stuff score for the season was actually better than Accardo's. For the past two years, Frasor's numbers with runners in scoring position have been lousy, driving up his ERA and inherited-runners figures. Whatever he's doing wrong in those situations, he's running out of chances to fix it.

Lee Gronkiewicz

| | | | | Bats: R | | Throws: R | | Height: 5' 11" | | Weight: 185 | | Born: August 21, 1978 | | | Age: 29 |

YEAR	TEAM	LVL	AGE	W	L	SV	G	GS	IP	H	BB	SO	HR	GB%	BABIP	STUFF	WHIP	ERA	PERA	EqERA	EqH9	EqBB9	EqSO9	EqHR9	VORP	SN/WX
2005	NHP	AA	26	2	0	24	38	0	38¹	24	10	45	2	50.0%	.253	4	0.89	1.41	3.65	2.86	6.7	3.4	7.0	0.8	10.6	—
2005	SYR	AAA	26	0	1	6	28	0	28¹	21	13	26	3	48.7%	.247	-6	1.20	2.23	4.09	3.42	6.8	5.1	6.2	1.0	6.4	—
2006	SYR	AAA	27	2	3	17	41	0	44¹	47	8	33	4	44.1%	.316	-15	1.25	3.27	5.16	4.50	10.3	2.1	4.7	1.3	5.1	—
2007	NHP	AA	28	3	2	11	24	0	30	31	4	37	3	50.0%	.394	9	1.17	1.80	5.76	3.29	10.9	2.0	8.2	1.6	7.0	—
2007	SYR	AAA	28	3	1	2	23	1	44²	38	6	46	4	41.1%	.272	6	0.98	2.82	3.61	4.17	7.5	1.4	6.6	1.2	7.2	—
2008	BOS	MLB	29	4	4	4	29	5	61¹	62	18	45	7	43.6%	.291	4	1.31	3.93	3.90	3.96	8.6	2.5	6.1	1.0	12.4	1.40

Breakout: 12% Improve: 45% Collapse: 21% Attrition: 18%   Comparables: Brian Holton, Julio Navarro, Tim Crews, Will Cunnane

At some point, the body of work has to mean something. If Gronkiewicz had a name like "Jarred Sharp" he might have been a prospect. Instead he's just a guy with a 2.48 ERA in 402 1/3 minor league innings in which he's struck out 421 against 111 walks. Isolate Triple-A, and you get a 2.85 ERA in 117 innings, and 105/27 K/BB. Like Heath Bell or Al Reyes, Gronkiewicz deserves a chance to fail in the majors, but that chance will have to come with the Red Sox, with whom he's signed a minor league deal.

Roy Halladay

Bats: R   Throws: R   Height: 6' 6"   Weight: 225   Born: May 14, 1977   Age: 31

YEAR	TEAM	LVL	AGE	W	L	SV	G	GS	IP	H	BB	SO	HR	GB%	BABIP	STUFF	WHIP	ERA	PERA	EqERA	EqH9	EqBB9	EqSO9	EqHR9	VORP	SN/WX
2005	TOR	MLB	28	12	4	0	19	19	141²	118	18	108	11	61.6%	.264	34	0.96	2.41	2.96	2.60	7.5	1.2	6.8	0.7	53.3	6.02
2006	TOR	MLB	29	16	5	0	32	32	220	208	34	132	19	58.9%	.279	21	1.10	3.19	3.36	3.24	8.3	1.3	5.2	0.7	68.0	6.45
2007	TOR	MLB	30	16	7	0	31	31	225¹	232	48	139	15	54.8%	.304	19	1.24	3.72	4.04	4.11	9.6	1.7	5.3	0.6	50.6	6.69
2008	TOR	MLB	31	14	10	0	32	32	215	225	49	131	21	55.8%	.293	10	1.27	3.85	3.65	3.99	9.0	1.9	4.8	0.9	40.1	6.00

Breakout: 5%   Improve: 27%   Collapse: 34%   Attrition: 7%   Comparables: Scott Erickson, Rick Reuschel, Dave Goltz, Kevin Brown

Some of the contract extensions teams have signed pitchers to over the last three years look criminal compared to the money being handed out to inferior arms on the open market. Halladay, one of the ten best starters in the AL, will average $13.3 million from 2008 to 2010, which is about 60 percent of what he'd have gotten for twice as long if he had been a free agent this winter. Halladay is an extreme ground-ball pitcher whose strikeout rate doesn't reflect how dominant he can be. If the Jays go with McDonald and Hill behind him, he could have another Cy Young-caliber season.

Casey Janssen

Bats: R   Throws: R   Height: 6' 4"   Weight: 205   Born: September 17, 1981   Age: 26

YEAR	TEAM	LVL	AGE	W	L	SV	G	GS	IP	H	BB	SO	HR	GB%	BABIP	STUFF	WHIP	ERA	PERA	EqERA	EqH9	EqBB9	EqSO9	EqHR9	VORP	SN/WX
2005	LNS	A	23	4	0	0	7	7	46	27	4	38	0	59.2%	.231	15	0.67	1.37	3.35	3.43	6.0	1.7	4.3	0.2	10.1	—
2005	DUN	A+	23	6	1	0	10	10	59²	46	12	51	2	54.3%	.275	3	0.97	2.26	4.25	4.05	8.1	3.4	4.4	0.7	9.2	—
2005	NHP	AA	23	3	3	0	9	9	43	49	4	47	3	54.8%	.383	6	1.23	2.93	6.36	6.05	12.6	1.6	6.3	1.2	-1.9	—
2006	SYR	AAA	24	1	5	0	9	9	42¹	47	8	32	3	55.9%	.336	-4	1.31	4.92	5.50	5.90	10.9	2.3	5.0	1.1	-1.3	—
2006	TOR	MLB	24	6	10	0	19	17	94	103	21	44	12	54.0%	.285	-4	1.32	5.07	4.44	5.15	9.3	1.8	3.9	1.0	6.1	1.19
2007	TOR	MLB	25	2	3	6	70	0	72²	67	20	39	4	48.9%	.276	1	1.20	2.35	3.60	2.83	8.6	2.3	4.6	0.5	26.8	2.63
2008	TOR	MLB	26	4	3	3	45	3	63	66	20	39	6	52.2%	.294	-4	1.35	4.02	3.84	4.16	9.0	2.6	4.9	0.9	12.8	1.20

Breakout: 16%   Improve: 41%   Collapse: 32%   Attrition: 16%   Comparables: Jose Santiago, Matt Morris, Adrian Devine, Cecil Upshaw

In addition to four ground-balling starters, the Jays have a number of relievers who keep the ball down. Janssen's a big guy who could start for a number of teams, and pitched well in a set-up role most of last year despite a strikeout rate low enough to inspire concern. The Jays' depth in the bullpen was a big reason for their 83-79 record last season. Collectively, you have to expect some regression, particularly from Janssen, who will reprise his setup role this year.

Brandon League

Bats: R   Throws: R   Height: 6' 3"   Weight: 190   Born: March 16, 1983   Age: 25

YEAR	TEAM	LVL	AGE	W	L	SV	G	GS	IP	H	BB	SO	HR	GB%	BABIP	STUFF	WHIP	ERA	PERA	EqERA	EqH9	EqBB9	EqSO9	EqHR9	VORP	SN/WX
2005	SYR	AAA	22	4	4	0	19	10	63	78	18	35	7	56.4%	.333	-24	1.52	5.71	6.52	7.02	11.4	3.2	3.4	1.2	-9.3	—
2005	TOR	MLB	22	1	0	0	20	0	35²	42	20	17	8	56.9%	.298	-28	1.74	6.55	8.84	7.56	11.1	5.4	4.3	1.9	-3.7	0.08
2006	SYR	AAA	23	3	2	8	31	1	54²	57	15	43	0	78.4%	.343	2	1.33	2.16	4.63	3.96	10.4	3.2	5.2	0.2	9.1	—
2006	TOR	MLB	23	1	2	1	33	0	42²	34	9	29	3	76.5%	.244	8	1.01	2.53	2.78	3.32	6.6	1.7	5.6	0.6	12.1	0.54
2007	TOR	MLB	24	0	0	0	14	0	11²	19	7	7	1	59.1%	.429	-30	2.23	6.15	11.86	8.18	15.5	4.9	4.9	0.8	-0.1	-0.17
2008	TOR	MLB	25	2	3	1	35	3	47¹	49	22	32	4	59.3%	.304	-6	1.51	4.52	4.27	4.71	8.9	3.9	5.3	0.7	6.2	0.60

Breakout: 32%   Improve: 65%   Collapse: 15%   Attrition: 32%   Comparables: Ryan Wagner, Jim Acker, George Culver, Jim Hannan

Shoulder problems ruined League's season, killing his velocity and pushing him to the disabled list for most of the year. Rest and rehab, rather than surgery, was the chosen course; the results (12 baserunners in five September innings) didn't inspire confidence. He also pitched through an oblique problem during the season. A power ground-baller when healthy, League now has just one effective, healthy season in the last three, and it's an open question as to whether he'll be healthy to start 2008.

Jesse Litsch

Bats: R   Throws: R   Height: 6' 1"   Weight: 195   Born: March 9, 1985   Age: 23

YEAR	TEAM	LVL	AGE	W	L	SV	G	GS	IP	H	BB	SO	HR	GB%	BABIP	STUFF	WHIP	ERA	PERA	EqERA	EqH9	EqBB9	EqSO9	EqHR9	VORP	SN/WX
2005	PUL	Rk	20	5	1	0	11	11	65²	51	10	67	6	55.7%	.268	-16	0.93	2.74	6.85	6.13	9.8	4.8	3.6	2.2	-3.2	—
2006	DUN	A+	21	6	6	0	16	15	89¹	94	8	81	5	58.6%	.333	5	1.14	3.54	5.47	5.57	11.0	1.7	4.8	1.1	0.3	—
2006	NHP	AA	21	3	4	0	12	12	69¹	85	13	54	6	53.3%	.367	-10	1.42	5.08	8.05	8.03	13.3	2.6	4.5	1.5	-16.7	—
2007	NHP	AA	22	7	2	0	10	10	61¹	51	14	46	5	55.9%	.253	5	1.06	2.35	3.79	3.98	7.2	2.5	4.4	1.2	11.0	—
2007	SYR	AAA	22	1	0	0	2	2	15	12	3	10	0	64.4%	.279	13	1.00	1.80	2.99	2.51	6.9	1.9	4.4	0.0	4.9	—
2007	TOR	MLB	22	7	9	0	20	20	111	116	36	50	14	49.9%	.279	-5	1.37	3.81	5.03	4.49	9.6	2.7	3.8	1.2	18.7	2.99
2008	TOR	MLB	23	9	11	0	29	29	163	179	54	93	22	49.8%	.293	4	1.43	4.80	4.52	4.87	9.4	2.7	4.5	1.2	14.6	2.90

Breakout: 15% Improve: 47% Collapse: 24% Attrition: 25%   Comparables: Justin Germano, Rod Bolton, Ramon Garcia, Paul Quantrill

Another of the Jays' four ground-ball starters, Litsch jumped from the Florida State League to Toronto in less than a year on the strength of his pinpoint command. His stuff is the worst of the four, and there's very little chance that he will repeat his 2007 ERA this year. He pitched in good fortune last year; consider that in his last three starts of the season, against the Red Sox, Yankees and Devil Rays, Litsch walked eight and struck out just five, yet allowed just three runs in 20 1/3 frames. He's the right-handed Chacin.

Shaun Marcum

Bats: R   Throws: R   Height: 6' 0"   Weight: 185   Born: December 14, 1981   Age: 26

YEAR	TEAM	LVL	AGE	W	L	SV	G	GS	IP	H	BB	SO	HR	GB%	BABIP	STUFF	WHIP	ERA	PERA	EqERA	EqH9	EqBB9	EqSO9	EqHR9	VORP	SN/WX
2005	NHP	AA	23	7	1	0	9	9	53¹	44	10	40	5	44.2%	.265	-2	1.01	2.53	4.48	3.51	8.3	2.6	4.1	1.3	11.3	—
2005	SYR	AAA	23	6	4	0	18	18	103²	112	18	90	17	43.4%	.309	-9	1.25	4.95	5.86	5.75	10.3	2.1	5.7	1.8	-1.6	—
2006	SYR	AAA	24	4	0	0	18	5	52¹	48	9	60	6	49.6%	.316	5	1.09	3.45	5.06	4.41	9.4	2.0	7.9	1.7	6.5	—
2006	TOR	MLB	24	3	4	0	21	14	78¹	87	38	65	14	36.8%	.313	-5	1.60	5.06	5.97	4.73	9.7	4.0	7.0	1.4	9.4	1.69
2007	TOR	MLB	25	12	6	1	38	25	159	149	49	122	27	42.4%	.271	-4	1.25	4.13	4.78	4.14	8.7	2.5	6.5	1.5	31.1	4.38
2008	TOR	MLB	26	7	8	1	35	18	123¹	130	42	90	18	43.1%	.294	3	1.39	4.59	4.41	4.60	9.1	2.8	5.7	1.3	15.2	2.30

Breakout: 8% Improve: 36% Collapse: 27% Attrition: 25%   Comparables: Jose Acevedo, Frank Castillo, Eric Gagné, Adam Eaton

The difference between Litsch and Marcum is that Marcum displayed his good command in the majors, using it to post above-average rates. The small right-hander has posted amazing K/BB numbers in the pros, and pitched passably in a half-season in the bigs in 2006. He's the one non-ground ball pitcher in the rotation, and like command pitchers of his ilk, will battle his home run rate. He's closer to Paul Byrd than Josh Towers, however.

Dustin McGowan

Bats: R   Throws: R   Height: 6' 3"   Weight: 220   Born: March 24, 1982   Age: 26

YEAR	TEAM	LVL	AGE	W	L	SV	G	GS	IP	H	BB	SO	HR	GB%	BABIP	STUFF	WHIP	ERA	PERA	EqERA	EqH9	EqBB9	EqSO9	EqHR9	VORP	SN/WX
2005	DUN	A+	23	0	1	0	5	5	21	21	5	20	2	49.2%	.311	-18	1.24	4.29	7.19	7.85	11.3	3.9	4.9	2.0	-4.6	—
2005	NHP	AA	23	0	2	0	6	6	35	35	10	33	6	43.3%	.309	-13	1.29	3.34	7.68	6.03	10.9	3.7	5.5	2.3	-1.5	—
2005	TOR	MLB	23	1	3	0	13	7	45¹	49	17	34	7	46.3%	.309	-2	1.46	6.36	5.67	6.60	9.6	3.4	6.6	1.2	-4.3	0.21
2006	SYR	AAA	24	4	5	1	23	13	84	77	39	86	7	55.2%	.303	-1	1.38	4.39	5.22	5.69	8.9	4.9	6.7	1.1	-0.8	—
2006	TOR	MLB	24	1	2	0	16	3	27¹	35	25	22	2	43.6%	.363	-5	2.20	7.25	7.25	8.68	11.2	7.4	6.8	0.6	-8.5	-0.14
2007	SYR	AAA	25	0	2	0	5	5	22	16	9	29	0	52.9%	.333	21	1.14	1.64	3.33	3.00	7.3	3.9	9.0	0.0	6.1	—
2007	TOR	MLB	25	12	10	0	27	27	169²	146	61	144	14	53.8%	.276	24	1.22	4.08	3.57	4.09	8.0	2.9	7.1	0.8	34.0	4.29
2008	TOR	MLB	26	10	9	0	27	27	164	159	66	134	19	49.9%	.292	15	1.37	4.39	3.99	4.48	8.4	3.3	6.4	1.0	21.5	3.60

Breakout: 23% Improve: 55% Collapse: 13% Attrition: 17%   Comparables: Dock Ellis, Roger Pavlik, Freddy Garcia, Dick Ruthven

The Jays spent two years trying to ruin McGowan, and they nearly succeeded. After the right-hander underwent Tommy John surgery in 2004, the organization rushed him back to the majors, then proceeded to bounce him from level to level and role to role for two years, culminating with a start on August 21, 2005, in which he was left in to allow 12 runs to the Tigers. It was an inexplicable mismanagement of a key resource. Last year, however, the Jays got out of his way and were rewarded, as McGowan used his fastball and slider to establish himself, finally, as a mid-rotation starter. He has the most upside of the Jays' younger arms, good enough to lower his ERA and raise his strikeout rate this year.

You might argue that last year's Blue Jays were comparable to the 2006 Twins in that both teams started slowly with poorly chosen veteran rotations, then got a boost when the kids came up to pitch. Litsch, Marcum, and Mc-

Gowan all entered the Jay's rotation in a two-week period in May. Starting May 15, the day of Litsch's first start, the Jays went 67-57. This year, all three will start the year in the rotation, and there's some more depth behind them.

David Purcey

Bats: L   Throws: L   Height: 6' 5"   Weight: 235   Born: April 22, 1982   Age: 26

YEAR	TEAM	LVL	AGE	W	L	SV	G	GS	IP	H	BB	SO	HR	GB%	BABIP	STUFF	WHIP	ERA	PERA	EqERA	EqH9	EqBB9	EqSO9	EqHR9	VORP	SN/WX
2005	DUN	A+	23	5	4	0	21	21	94¹	80	56	116	8	50.4%	.319	-3	1.44	3.63	7.82	7.48	10.2	8.6	6.8	1.7	-16.9	—
2005	NHP	AA	23	4	3	0	8	8	43	32	25	45	2	46.9%	.275	15	1.33	2.93	4.92	4.93	8.0	7.3	6.1	0.7	2.9	—
2006	NHP	AA	24	4	5	0	16	16	88	101	44	81	9	43.1%	.351	-20	1.65	5.63	8.86	8.44	12.2	5.8	5.3	1.6	-25.6	—
2006	SYR	AAA	24	2	7	0	12	12	51²	49	38	45	7	51.6%	.290	-14	1.70	5.45	7.29	8.57	9.3	7.7	5.7	1.8	-16.3	—
2007	NHP	AA	25	3	5	0	11	11	62	67	16	55	4	43.5%	.344	0	1.34	5.37	5.21	6.86	10.2	2.9	5.5	0.9	-8.3	—
2008	TOR	MLB	26	4	7	0	25	17	94	105	62	69	15	44.5%	.309	-9	1.78	6.43	5.94	6.38	9.7	5.4	5.8	1.5	-7.8	-0.20

Breakout: 39% Improve: 65% Collapse: 10% Attrition: 26%   Comparables: Rob Henkel, Sean Henn, Chris Clemons, Mark Redman

This monstrous lefty was making strides in harnessing his stuff when a strained elbow set him down for the year. The former first-round pick is now 26 and has made just a dozen appearances above Double-A. For the Jays, it's more about whether Purcey can build some trade value that they can leverage at the deadline, rather than if he'll eventually help them on the field. His size, velocity, and handedness mean that he'll always have backers.

Ricky Romero

Bats: R   Throws: L   Height: 6' 1"   Weight: 200   Born: November 6, 1984   Age: 23

YEAR	TEAM	LVL	AGE	W	L	SV	G	GS	IP	H	BB	SO	HR	GB%	BABIP	STUFF	WHIP	ERA	PERA	EqERA	EqH9	EqBB9	EqSO9	EqHR9	VORP	SN/WX
2005	DUN	A+	20	1	0	0	8	8	30²	36	7	22	2	46.7%	.330	-15	1.40	3.81	7.24	6.00	12.7	3.7	3.3	1.3	-1.2	—
2006	DUN	A+	21	2	1	0	10	10	58	48	14	61	5	41.8%	.291	6	1.07	2.48	5.20	4.05	8.9	3.5	5.7	1.7	9.2	—
2006	NHP	AA	21	2	7	0	12	12	67	65	26	41	7	47.7%	.282	-22	1.36	5.10	5.99	7.32	9.8	4.6	3.3	1.6	-12.0	—
2007	NHP	AA	22	3	6	0	18	18	88¹	98	51	80	9	45.6%	.340	-10	1.69	4.89	7.13	6.99	10.6	6.0	5.6	1.5	-12.9	—
2008	TOR	MLB	23	5	9	0	22	22	116²	130	75	78	19	45.1%	.301	-6	1.76	6.29	5.92	6.24	9.6	5.3	5.2	1.5	-7.3	0.10

Breakout: 26% Improve: 58% Collapse: 23% Attrition: 13%   Comparables: Jeff Granger, Dan Serafini, Chris George, Noah Lowry

Maybe it's unfair to keep pointing out what a franchise-altering decision it was, but Troy Tulowitzki, who the Jays should have taken with the sixth pick in the 2005 draft, might have pushed them into contention last year. Instead, they had Romero battling shoulder problems and walking five men per nine in Double-A. Romero's young enough that there's still reason for optimism, but it's increasingly likely that his future is in the bullpen because of his lack of a third pitch.

B. J. Ryan

Bats: L   Throws: L   Height: 6' 6"   Weight: 260   Born: December 28, 1975   Age: 32

YEAR	TEAM	LVL	AGE	W	L	SV	G	GS	IP	H	BB	SO	HR	GB%	BABIP	STUFF	WHIP	ERA	PERA	EqERA	EqH9	EqBB9	EqSO9	EqHR9	VORP	SN/WX
2005	BAL	MLB	29	1	4	36	69	0	70¹	54	26	100	4	45.7%	.321	37	1.14	2.43	3.25	2.61	7.4	3.3	10.8	0.5	24.9	3.36
2006	TOR	MLB	30	2	2	38	65	0	72¹	42	20	86	3	39.0%	.245	37	0.86	1.37	2.32	1.81	5.4	2.5	9.6	0.4	37.4	5.97
2007	TOR	MLB	31	0	2	3	5	0	4¹	7	4	3	1	33.3%	.353	-38	2.54	12.56	12.56	15.43	13.5	7.7	5.8	1.9	-4.1	-1.33
2008	TOR	MLB	32	4	4	14	48	2	58¹	47	22	67	5	42.8%	.286	20	1.18	2.96	2.85	3.03	6.9	3.1	9.0	0.8	18.1	2.10

Breakout: 10% Improve: 45% Collapse: 29% Attrition: 10%   Comparables: Roberto Hernandez, Lee Smith, Eric Plunk, Arthur Rhodes

Ryan was the cause for controversy last year when, after an elbow injury ended his season in April, it was discovered that the Jays had known about it in March but issued misleading statements about it being a back problem. Regardless, he missed all but two weeks, undergoing Tommy John surgery in May. He's expected to be back for spring training. The track record of relievers coming back from UCL surgery is excellent, so he should be effective, though his workload might be reduced.

Brian Tallet

Bats: L   Throws: L   Height: 6' 7"   Weight: 220   Born: September 21, 1977   Age: 30

YEAR	TEAM	LVL	AGE	W	L	SV	G	GS	IP	H	BB	SO	HR	GB%	BABIP	STUFF	WHIP	ERA	PERA	EqERA	EqH9	EqBB9	EqSO9	EqHR9	VORP	SN/WX
2005	BUF	AAA	27	6	5	0	22	17	97²	98	25	61	17	40.7%	.271	-28	1.26	4.05	5.41	5.09	9.1	2.9	3.9	1.9	5.2	—
2006	SYR	AAA	28	1	2	3	20	0	25	32	10	21	4	44.6%	.368	-38	1.68	5.76	10.76	8.49	13.1	4.2	5.4	2.3	-7.5	—
2006	TOR	MLB	28	3	0	0	44	1	54¹	45	31	37	5	41.1%	.272	0	1.40	3.81	4.08	3.68	7.5	5.1	6.1	0.7	13.2	1.46
2007	TOR	MLB	29	2	4	0	48	0	62¹	49	28	54	1	41.9%	.277	17	1.24	3.47	3.11	3.61	7.2	3.6	7.1	0.1	16.0	-0.09
2008	TOR	MLB	30	2	2	2	45	0	47	47	21	37	6	43.2%	.292	-4	1.44	4.51	4.33	4.55	8.7	3.6	6.2	1.2	6.9	0.50

Breakout: 19% Improve: 37% Collapse: 32% Attrition: 27%   Comparables: Matt Thornton, Dan Plesac, Lerrin LaGrow, Ted Power

The injury to Ryan created a roster spot that Tallet filled ably, although it wasn't exactly a glamour role. Often working multiple innings, tallet made the majority of his appearances (32 of 48) with the team behind, and from July 7 through the end of the season, the Jays went 2-20 in games in which he appeared. His home run rate was a fluke, as he's not a ground-ball pitcher; expect his ERA to rise accordingly.

Ty Taubenheim

Bats: R   Throws: R   Height: 6' 6"   Weight: 250   Born: November 17, 1982   Age: 25

YEAR	TEAM	LVL	AGE	W	L	SV	G	GS	IP	H	BB	SO	HR	GB%	BABIP	STUFF	WHIP	ERA	PERA	EqERA	EqH9	EqBB9	EqSO9	EqHR9	VORP	SN/WX
2005	BRV	A+	22	10	2	0	16	16	106	86	26	75	7	45.4%	.262	-15	1.06	2.63	5.44	4.86	9.3	4.0	3.4	1.4	7.6	—
2005	HUN	AA	22	2	6	0	11	11	64	64	24	44	7	44.2%	.305	-18	1.38	4.36	5.80	5.92	9.4	4.1	3.8	1.8	-2.1	—
2006	SYR	AAA	23	2	4	0	18	14	75¹	75	18	48	9	49.4%	.287	-17	1.24	2.88	5.69	3.99	9.8	2.8	4.1	1.7	12.5	—
2006	TOR	MLB	23	1	5	0	12	7	35	40	18	26	5	47.1%	.315	-6	1.66	4.89	5.69	5.25	9.8	4.2	6.0	1.0	2.1	0.52
2007	NHP	AA	24	2	1	0	5	5	31¹	21	11	29	2	48.1%	.244	12	1.02	2.01	3.63	2.76	6.4	4.0	5.8	0.9	9.2	—
2007	SYR	AAA	24	4	7	0	19	16	89	107	33	73	12	45.9%	.344	-27	1.57	6.37	7.69	7.55	11.5	3.7	5.3	1.8	-18.4	—
2008	PIT	MLB	25	4	7	0	32	13	96¹	112	42	61	14	33.2%	.310	-6	1.59	5.53	5.87	5.74	10.0	3.6	5.2	1.2	-1.3	0.40

Breakout: 16% Improve: 55% Collapse: 21% Attrition: 14%   Comparables: Gary Knotts, Tim Worrell, Steve Olsen, Kevin Gregg

Despite his size, Taubenheim does not have a power game, instead getting by with what you might call "National League stuff." This becomes relevant now that the Pirates, who contrary to popular belief do still exist, have claimed him off waivers. The big righty becomes part of a scrum for the last rotation spot in Pittsburgh and, failing that, could stick as the long man in a thin bullpen. If it turns out he actually has International League stuff, you can doodle over that PECOTA line above.

Josh Towers

Bats: R   Throws: R   Height: 6' 1"   Weight: 190   Born: February 26, 1977   Age: 31

YEAR	TEAM	LVL	AGE	W	L	SV	G	GS	IP	H	BB	SO	HR	GB%	BABIP	STUFF	WHIP	ERA	PERA	EqERA	EqH9	EqBB9	EqSO9	EqHR9	VORP	SN/WX
2005	TOR	MLB	28	13	12	0	33	33	208²	237	29	112	24	45.0%	.306	8	1.27	3.71	4.59	4.49	10.1	1.2	4.8	1.0	35.2	4.24
2006	SYR	AAA	29	5	5	0	15	15	101	121	11	76	12	48.3%	.345	-14	1.31	4.01	6.95	6.05	12.0	1.4	4.9	1.6	-4.7	—
2006	TOR	MLB	29	2	10	0	15	12	62	93	17	35	17	40.4%	.347	-39	1.77	8.42	10.04	9.67	12.9	2.3	4.8	2.2	-18.9	-0.73
2007	TOR	MLB	30	5	10	0	25	15	107	129	22	76	18	44.9%	.326	-10	1.41	5.38	6.36	6.26	11.1	1.6	6.0	1.5	-0.5	0.48
2008	TOR	MLB	31	4	5	0	23	10	77	89	19	46	11	46.7%	.305	-3	1.39	4.94	4.58	4.98	10.0	2.0	4.7	1.3	7.0	1.00

Breakout: 40% Improve: 58% Collapse: 22% Attrition: 40%   Comparables: Vern Ruhle, Brian Lawrence, Dick Bosman, Randy Gumpert

Towers' problems with the long ball—even as he becomes less of a fly-ball pitcher—make him ill-suited to relief work. The decision to yank him from the rotation after four starts last April when he sported a 5.3 K/BB was something shy of inspired. He bounced back and forth between roles all season and was non-tendered in December. He remains unsigned as we go to press, but there's not $48 million worth of difference between him and Carlos Silva, that's for sure.

Jamie Vermilyea

Bats: R   Throws: R   Height: 6' 4"   Weight: 195   Born: February 10, 1982   Age: 26

YEAR	TEAM	LVL	AGE	W	L	SV	G	GS	IP	H	BB	SO	HR	GB%	BABIP	STUFF	WHIP	ERA	PERA	EqERA	EqH9	EqBB9	EqSO9	EqHR9	VORP	SN/WX
2005	NHP	AA	23	3	3	1	27	4	65²	67	16	52	5	56.4%	.318	-15	1.26	2.60	5.67	4.25	10.6	3.3	4.4	1.1	8.9	—
2005	SYR	AAA	23	3	0	0	16	4	35¹	49	11	24	6	55.9%	.364	-34	1.70	5.61	9.29	8.45	13.1	3.5	4.4	1.9	-10.5	—
2006	SYR	AAA	24	6	7	1	25	17	114¹	129	28	64	9	62.6%	.323	-17	1.38	3.87	5.63	5.43	10.8	2.8	3.4	1.1	2.0	—
2007	SYR	AAA	25	2	2	1	25	1	43¹	39	20	32	4	59.8%	.280	-17	1.36	4.16	4.90	4.93	8.4	4.5	4.7	1.3	3.1	—
2008	TOR	MLB	26	3	4	1	28	5	60¹	65	25	33	6	56.2%	.296	-9	1.49	4.53	4.45	4.67	9.3	3.3	4.3	0.9	7.5	0.90

Breakout: 30% Improve: 57% Collapse: 22% Attrition: 21%   Comparables: Chris Young, Justin Huisman, Carlos Hines, Jeff Tam

It's never interesting when a rookie gets his head handed to him and retreats back to the minors. It is interesting when one throws three shutout innings and disappears. Vermilyea is an owner of a career ERA of 0.00 and the same walk rate, as well as a great sinker that plunges like the housing market. He did that twice and still couldn't stick. He's a one-trick pony, but until someone solves the trick, maybe he should get to keep playing it.

Brian Wolfe

Bats: R   Throws: R   Height: 6' 3"   Weight: 220   Born: January 29, 1980   Age: 28

YEAR	TEAM	LVL	AGE	W	L	SV	G	GS	IP	H	BB	SO	HR	GB%	BABIP	STUFF	WHIP	ERA	PERA	EqERA	EqH9	EqBB9	EqSO9	EqHR9	VORP	SN/WX
2005	BRV	A+	25	1	1	8	18	0	22²	19	8	22	0	73.8%	.311	-3	1.19	0.79	5.20	2.79	9.8	5.6	5.1	0.5	6.0	—
2005	HUN	AA	25	3	1	0	16	0	24	32	8	19	1	58.6%	.373	-22	1.67	3.38	6.77	5.64	12.5	3.6	4.4	0.8	-0.1	—
2006	DUN	A+	26	1	4	0	5	5	24²	33	3	17	3	56.8%	.357	-36	1.49	5.95	9.65	10.72	13.9	2.4	3.2	2.4	-12.9	—
2006	NHP	AA	26	1	3	0	24	2	42	54	15	34	5	44.6%	.350	-41	1.64	5.79	8.72	8.70	12.9	4.2	4.5	1.8	-13.9	—
2007	SYR	AAA	27	2	0	0	17	0	26	18	6	23	1	46.5%	.243	7	0.92	1.04	2.89	1.78	6.0	2.5	5.7	0.7	10.7	—
2007	TOR	MLB	27	3	1	0	38	0	45¹	36	9	22	5	56.0%	.231	-7	0.99	2.98	3.32	3.35	7.5	1.7	4.2	1.0	13.5	0.40
2008	TOR	MLB	28	2	2	1	31	0	35	38	12	20	4	51.5%	.293	-11	1.42	4.55	4.28	4.68	9.4	2.8	4.5	1.1	5.0	0.30

Breakout: 26% Improve: 59% Collapse: 23% Attrition: 38%   Comparables: Mike Lincoln, John Verhoeven, Scott Winchester, Chris Spurling

Yet another groundballer, the big journeyman had a career year in 2007 that screams fluke and was helped along by a .228 BABIP in the majors. Wolfe had one of the biggest platoon splits you'll ever see, allowing a 356 OPS against righties and a 1023 OPS against lefties, calling to mind the stranger seasons of Todd Frohwirth and Steve Reed. There's no reason to expect him to come close to that performance ever again.

LINEOUTS

Hitters

PLAYER		TEAM	LVL	AGE	PA	R	2B	3B	HR	RBI	BB	SO	SB-CS	EqBRR	AVG/OBP/SLG	MLVr	EqAVG/EqOBP/EqSLG	EqA	VORP
OF	Y. Chavez	BLJ	Rk	18	203	29	12	2	6	21	20	50	7-2	0.8	.301/.389/.494	.290	.204/.266/.333	.208	-36.8
C	S. Fasano	SYR	AAA	35	163	18	4	0	8	14	6	33	1-0	-1.2	.262/.337/.455	.066	.250/.313/.453	.262	5.2
		TOR	MLB	35	49	5	3	0	1	4	2	19	0-0	0.5	.178/.229/.311	-.420	.178/.229/.311	.183	-2.8
RF	J. Griffin*	SYR	AAA	27	551	69	28	4	26	83	59	144	4-0	0.9	.252/.330/.488	.090	.238/.314/.474	.268	4.1
UT	J. Inglett*	BUF	AAA	29	455	45	15	9	4	57	40	62	7-12	-4.4	.253/.327/.367	-.071	.233/.304/.351	.229	-5.3
INF	H. Luna	BUF	AAA	27	350	39	18	0	6	35	21	48	4-4	0.2	.251/.297/.362	-.128	.231/.275/.343	.213	-8.2
		SYR	AAA	27	79	15	7	1	2	8	9	14	0-0	0.6	.343/.443/.567	.432	.309/.405/.574	.325	11.2
INF	R. Olmedo#	SYR	AAA	26	373	32	12	1	1	26	28	53	7-5	-0.1	.290/.345/.341	-.051	.263/.318/.313	.226	-2.2
		TOR	MLB	26	54	6	4	0	0	1	2	9	0-0	1.6	.216/.245/.294	-.388	.216/.245/.294	.182	-3.0
2B	J. Tolisano#	BLJ	Rk	18	211	35	5	0	10	33	26	40	7-1	2.1	.246/.336/.437	.107	.178/.246/.293	.191	-37.6

Venezuelan teenager **Yohermyn Chavez** is a raw outfielder with tremendous power and a right-field arm, but his bat will have to be his ticket to the big leagues. ⊘ **Sal Fasano** has become something of a minor celebrity among the usually faceless ranks of backup catchers. This has more to do with the fact that he looks like Snuffleupagus wearing a Thurman Munson costume and talks like one of *Saturday Night Live*'s Super Fans than with his occasional power and solid defensive reputation. ⊘ A non-roster invitee with the Dodgers, former first-round pick **John-Ford Griffin** has a career line of .304/.370/.696 in 27 plate appearances. As with Vermilyea, there's considerable evidence he's not quite that good. ⊘ Thirty-year-old Triple-A roster fodder **Joe Inglett** occupies a spot on the 40-man roster, while Vermilyea and Griffin were removed from it. That's the sort of inexplicable roster management the Jays have repeated time and again during Ricciardi's tenure as GM. ⊘ It seems like so long ago that **Hector Luna** was doing Geromimo Peña-like things for the Cardinals, but it was merely two seasons back. Weight gain erased his range and the Jays' infield depth will make it hard for him to get back to the majors. ⊘ **Ray Olmedo** neither hits nor fields as well as John McDonald, making him a marginal utility infielder, and useless in an organization with eight guys better than him. ⊘ A second-round pick last June, second baseman **John Tolisano** led the Gulf Coast League with 10 home runs, although he sells out his ability to hit for average by swinging for power.

Pitchers

PLAYER	TEAM	LVL	AGE	W	L	SV	IP	H	BB	SO	HR	GB%	BABIP	STUFF	WHIP	ERA	PERA	EqERA	EqH9	EqBB9	EqSO9	EqHR9	VORP
J. Banks	SYR	AAA	24	12	10	0	169	192	24	101	22	46.8%	.307	-19	1.28	4.63	5.55	5.14	10.3	1.6	3.7	1.6	8.4
	TOR	MLB	24	0	0	0	7^1	11	2	2	1	41.9%	.345	-35	1.77	7.40	7.87	7.36	13.5	2.5	2.5	1.2	-1.2
K. Ginley	LNS	A	20	7	6	0	121^2	142	41	129	11	46.0%	.378	-40	1.50	4.73	11.17	10.84	14.3	6.3	5.2	2.3	-59.0
J. Machi	NHP	AA	24	2	4	2	81^2	68	24	56	8	50.0%	.251	-22	1.13	3.53	4.16	4.33	7.4	3.2	4.0	1.4	11.1
D.Romero'08	TOR	MLB	25	3	3	0	47	50	18	34	6	51.1%	.302	0	1.44	4.66	4.39	4.75	9.1	3.2	5.6	1.1	6.5
T. Thorpe	NHP	AA	26	5	4	10	56^2	46	29	55	5	28.2%	.277	-10	1.32	4.60	4.68	5.27	7.6	5.3	5.9	1.3	2.0

Yet another Jays hurler with more command than stuff, **Josh Banks** has been a rotation stalwart at Syracuse for two seasons. He's 10 percent worse than Josh Towers, but will get a shot to fill in for injuries in 2008. ⊘ **Kyle Ginley** stands out in this system because of his plus fastball and poor command. It's a nice change of pace, which come to think of it is something Ginley might want to work on in the Florida State League. He will become a reliever before long. ⊘ Smallish right-hander **Jean Machi** has a very good fastball and little else, but he's close to getting a look in the major league bullpen. ⊘ **Davis Romero** missed the entire 2007 season following surgery to repair a torn labrum. The slight Panamanian lefty can't be expected to return to the majors until 2009, if ever. ⊘ Massive right-hander **Tracy Thorpe** is entering his eighth year in the Toronto system. His fastball/slider combination gets good grades from scouts, but command troubles and inconsistency have held him back.

MANAGER: JOHN GIBBONS

YEAR	TEAM	W-L	Pythag +/−	Avg PC	100+ P	120+ P	QS	BQS	REL	REL w Zero R	IBB	Subs	PH	PH Avg	PH HR	SB2	CS2	SB3	CS3	SAC Att	SAC %	POS SAC	Squeeze	Swing	In Play
2005	TOR	80-82	-9	90.6	45	1	76	8	432	278	29	59	144	.306	3	58	32	13	2	32	65.6%	20	2	157	118
2006	TOR	87-75	0	90.2	54	2	63	9	480	282	56	59	112	.240	2	53	26	12	7	25	64.0%	16	3	164	140
2007	TOR	83-79	-4	96.7	70	9	80	11	420	266	34	54	138	.226	4	47	16	9	6	43	76.7%	33	4	124	98

John Gibbons is a terrible handler of starting pitchers. From what appear to be intentional attempts to break an already-fragile A. J. Burnett, to the way he contributed to Dustin McGowan's trip through the wilderness, to riding Roy Halladay well past 120 pitches in four of five starts late last summer, Gibbons shows no recognition of the fact that starting pitchers have limits. Keep in mind that Gibbons handled his starters this way in a season in which he had a deep, effective pool of relievers and nothing on the line. If either of those things change this year, we could see a science experiment in Toronto. Gibbons was notable for using B. J. Ryan more aggressively than the average closer, but when Ryan went down, he stuck to a one-inning model with Jeremy Accardo. On the whole, Gibbons is a net negative for the Blue Jays because of the risks he takes with the team's top asset, its starting rotation.

Washington Nationals

Among the variety of terms floating in the alphabet soup of these pages, one that often comes up without explanation is "free talent." It's shorthand, of course—nobody plays for free, and no player transaction is truly free. Whether it's the scouting resources involved in picking amateur draftees, finding untapped international talent, sifting through minor league free agents for that low-end add-on, or turning up a find in the Rule 5 draft or off the waiver wire, or the money spent signing anyone from those amateur players to a big-ticket free agent, there's a cost, in dollars, flesh, and opportunities. As measured against the gross scales of a multi-billion-dollar industry, however, some of these methods amount to getting something for *almost* nothing. Not every team has the same range of options, and those whose options are limited can help themselves by exploiting the pool of players who cost very little and are freely available to all 30 teams, players we refer to as free talent.

After three years of being managed by the Conspiracy of the 29 as wards of the industry in Montreal and Puerto Rico, and being operated day-to-day by general manager Omar Minaya as something of a résumé-padding caretaker, the newly christened Nationals were about as moribund as a franchise could be as they moved into the nation's capital. Minaya peddled off premium up-the-middle talents such as center fielder Grady Sizemore, infielders Brandon Phillips and Orlando Cabrera, and catcher Michael Barrett, as well as pitchers Javier Vazquez, Chris Young, Cliff Lee, and Carl Pavano. Not every deal Minaya made turned out badly; getting outfielder Ryan Church and infielder Maicer Izturis from the Indians for reliever Scott Stewart worked out; Vazquez yielded first baseman Nick Johnson, out-

> ## NATIONALS PROSPECTUS
>
> **2007 record:** 73-89; Fourth place, NL East
>
> **Pythagenport record:** 70-92
>
> **Runs scored per game:** 4.15 (16th in NL)
>
> **Runs allowed per game:** 4.83 (10th in NL)
>
> **Team EqA:** .254 (13th in NL)
>
> **2007 Batters Age:** 28.3 (6th youngest in NL)
>
> **2007 Pitchers Age:** 27.9 (4th youngest in NL)
>
> **Ballpark:** Robert F. Kennedy Memorial Stadium; Strong pitcher's park; Park Factor of .946
>
> **2007:** Deft free-talent pickups and Acta-vision lift the Nats out of last place.
>
> **2008:** More of the same, but with more upside and a new ballpark.

fielder Juan Rivera, and LOOGY Randy Choate, and Choate turned into right-handed starter John Patterson in a deal the Diamondbacks won't be celebrating in any of their official histories. Adding set-up man Jon Rauch from the White Sox for a rental of Carl Everett worked nicely enough as Minaya's final deal of note before he skipped out before the final season in Montreal had even ended to take up the reins with the Mets. Still, the Expos under Minaya had been in the business of Expo-rting talent to their owners, the other 29 teams.

Nothing drove that bitter truth home better than the ignominy of not even being allowed to offer superstar slugger Vladimir Guerrero arbitration so that the team could get compensatory draft picks following his certain departure via free agency. Still, Minaya somehow found the funding to give slowing second sacker Jose Vidro an irresponsible $30 million extension during his final spring on the job, a move which only served to compromise what little financial freedom the team did have. As a result of all of this, the cupboard was relatively bare when the team arrived in D.C. That left new GM Jim Bowden and his hard-working skeleton crew in scouting and player development to re-stock the organization with almost as much totality as if they were kick-starting an expansion team.

There are essentially four ways of adding talent to a major league roster. There are the draft picks and amateur international free agents developed on the farm, major league players acquired via trade, premium major league free agents, and the aforementioned free talent pickups. The Nats only got out from under MLB's thumb at the end of the 2006 season, when a group led by local real estate developer Ted Lerner finally purchased the D.C. fiefdom from its suzerain lords. As a result, the franchise is only entering its second full year as an independent entity, completing its second offseason with any real freedom of action, and still shy of its second fully funded amateur draft. Given the Nationals' relatively limited means, big-ticket free agents have been almost entirely out of the question thus far, the lone exception being shortstop Cristian Guzman who was signed to an unlikely four-year, $16.8 million contract during Bowden's first month on the job. Similarly, the Nationals' farm system has been running on empty at its upper levels. That has left Bowden with just two means of filling his big-league roster: trades to add quality, and Dumpster diving to add quantity.

In both respects, he's had some remarkable successes. In 2005 he was able to acquire outfielder Austin Kearns and infielder Felipe Lopez for less value in trade than similar talents would have cost on the free agent market. Additional trades for top prospects such as outfielders Lastings Milledge and Elijah Dukes, or even the fading luster of slugging prodigy Wily Mo Peña, have given the Nationals young, major league-ready, cost-controlled talents more quickly and more efficiently than they could have been procured via the draft and at the marginal cost of repurposed leftovers such as Church and catcher Brian Schneider, and extra arms such as Glenn Gibson and Emiliano Fruto. The potential upside of these sorts of deals, and what that can mean for making the Nationals a better ballclub overnight, cannot be overstated.

In the meantime, the Nats have had to fill out their roster with other team's leavings or generally unwanted ballplayers. Take a look at Table 1, basically a napkin-level exercise that sorts every player on the Nats' 2007 roster who had 100 or more at bats or pitched 30 or more innings according to the provenance of the player and compares them on an equal scale using their 2007 wins above replacement-level as converted from VORP, SNLVAR and WXRL.

The players in bold have been added on Bowden's watch. The bolded numbers in parentheses are the totals contributed by Bowden's acquisitions. The free talent is made up of guys who were signed to deals worth less than a million dollars, and who were freely available to all 30 teams before joining the Nats. Missing from this table is Guzman, the club's one free agent of note; he chipped in an unexpected 1.6 wins' worth of offensive value before getting hurt, again.

What's especially remarkable about the list of players in Table 1 is both the sheer quantity *and* quality of the free talent. Every team has its lacunae waiting to be filled, but the Nats effectively peopled last year's pitching staff and lineup with free talent, finding the right side of their infield, their catcher of the future, and chunks of their rotation and bullpen. Those players delivered the sort of value for which most teams spend millions, but nobody on the right side of Table 1 had a base compensation of more than $850,000 last year. For the baseball equivalent of "negligible," the Nats added value from a source most teams either see as too picked-over or an area for reinforcing their Triple-A affiliates.

How did they leverage this sort of ballplayer into the small upset of avoiding the hundred-loss season so many analysts expected of them heading into 2007? A major reason was that in addition to moving past their caretaker days in the front office, the Nats finally worked up the nerve to excuse Frank Robinson from the dugout and pick a prospect of a different sort, Mets' third-base coach Manny Acta, to be their new manager. To call the selection a revelation would be an understatement.

Whether it was a matter of necessity mothering invention or just a natural gift for in-game tactics, Acta demonstrated a superb ability to identify what scrap-heap finds could and couldn't do, and set them to work accordingly. Consider his work with the pitching staff—despite the absence of a single reliable or established

Table 1. Washington Wizardry: 2007 Player Contributions, in Wins

Traded For	Wins	Drafted	Wins	Free Talent	Wins	Free Talent	Wins
M. Chico	2.9	C. Cordero	3.6	**Dm. Young**	3.6	**T. Redding**	2.8
J. Rauch	2.9	S. Hill	3.2	**S. Rivera**	2.6	**R. Belliard**	2.1
R. Church	2.2	J. Bergmann	3.2	**J. Colome**	1.7	**M. Bowie**	1.2
A. Kearns	1.3	**R. Zimmerman**	2.4	**M. Bacsik**	1.2	**J. Hanrahan**	.7
W. Peña	.9	**J. Lannan**	.9	**R. King**	.7	**J. Simontacchi**	.5
J. Patterson	.4	L. Ayala	.7	**D. Jimenez**	.5	**J. Flores**	.1
N. Logan	.1	C. Schroder	.5	**L. Speigner**	.1	**T. Batista**	.1
F. Lopez	.0	B. Schneider	.2	**J. Williams**	.0	**W. Abreu**	-.1
R. Langerhans	-.2			**B. Traber**	-.3	**R. Fick**	-.8
TOTAL	10.5 (5.0)		14.7 (3.3)		16.7		

starting pitcher, Acta and pitching coach Randy St. Claire coaxed their oft-patched rotation to a 21st-place finish in staff SNLVAR, better than the Reds, Cardinals, Phillies, Pirates, Rangers, and Mariners, all teams that went into the season thinking they had full stables of expensive workhorses and/or quality prospects. One reason for that success was that Acta and St. Claire did an outstanding job of hooking their cast of kids and castoffs early while refraining from making their lives difficult by trying to manage around them with gambits like the intentional walk, a Robinson standby. Instead, Acta provided assistance through on-field manipulation such as aggressively shifting his defense far more often and effectively than most; given the mountains of information that is available through scouting reports and ball-in-play data, it finally appeared as if a manager was employing that information on an inning-by-inning and nightly basis, not as a matter of managerial discretion, but of survival.

After getting what he could out of his starters, Acta would reliably turn to his pen early and often, so much so that the Nats' rotation faced fewer batters than any other in baseball. Acta's bullpen really had only two known quantities in closer Chad Cordero and set-up giant Rauch, but he managed to get value out of discards such as Saul Rivera and Jesus Colome in middle relief, and Ray King and Micah Bowie in situational chores. They were all employed with a remarkable regularity, as Rivera and Rauch pitched in more than half the team's game played, and both Cordero and Colome would likely have done the same but for absences due to family and injury, respectively. While they pitched with remarkable regularity, they rarely pitched for very long; collectively the Nats relievers who pitched more than 40 innings were asked to face a batter a second time in a game on just six occasions for a whopping 14 PA. It's unclear if such heavy game workloads are sustainable or not, but if ever there was a pen that took an active day-to-day role in the team's fortunes as a unit, it was this one, which generated the fifth-best WXRL mark in baseball.

Acta provided additional tactical value in areas we can measure less well. His aggressive bullpen usage was aided in-game with well-constructed double-switches. When using relievers that often, you want to keep the pitcher's slot from coming up in-game as much as possible, and with a player like the lead-gloved Dmitri Young in the lineup, switching in a better fielder at first base added a certain routine elegance to his exchanges. Young would complete less than half of his starts at first, a remarkable but instructive reflection of Acta's brand of always-active in-game management. That,

however, was just one element of the basic principle: Acta always kept his bench involved in ballgames; everybody played, not just in the blowouts. Whether it was Rule 5 pick catcher Jesus Flores, or Tony Batista and D'Angelo Jimenez regularly being called upon to pinch-hit, or outfielder Ryan Langerhans getting swapped into games no matter how long his slump lasted, *everybody* played. There was no room for a dead spot on this roster. He didn't despair over anyone's utility, and he didn't get locked in to riding the hot hand; he'd already sorted out what everyone was for and found ways to keep everyone in those roles. Few managers have been as successful in keeping their entire rosters active to positive purpose while using so many discards and journeymen.

Despite these many positives, this is still a losing baseball team, and the men in charge are not without their flaws. As he did while GM of the Reds, Bowden became a bit too enamored with his own genius and recommitted to some of his free-talent finds. Belliard went from being a cheap late-winter pickup to somebody rewarded with a two-year $3.5 million deal. That's not much by baseball standards, but it moves into the area of paying market price for a merely adequate ballplayer. More egregiously, Young was rewarded with a two-year $10 million extension. Then again Young is seen as a prospective mentor for Milledge and Dukes (the latter of whom was a teammate of Young's little brother Delmon in Tampa Bay) and provides a working example of an African American ballplayer who has dealt with off-field difficulties and managed to overcome them to salvage his career.

Despite perhaps settling on the right side of the infield, Bowden has been as aggressive as ever in digging up better in-game weapons for Acta to use off of the bench. Low-cost free agents Rob Mackowiak and Willie Harris have considerable experience with pinchhitting and playing almost every position on the diamond, and Harris adds a measure of speed that was missing on last year's bench. Bowden has just as reliably explored adding talent through the Rule 5 draft, most recently picking up outfielder Garrett Guzman from the Twins and slugger Matt Whitney from the Indians.

Better news is that Bowden may soon no longer have to be such an efficient scrounger, as he is increasingly going to have the benefit of staffing his ballclub with players selected by scouting director Dana Brown and his crew. Recent top picks such as outfielders Christopher Marrero and Justin Maxwell and left-hander Ross Detwiler could be ready to play in the majors in 2009, and they represent just the cream of a series of already-promising crops.

With the move to the club's new ballpark this spring, the foundations are in place. The Nationals are going to be the best team in the National League East, not in 2008, not overnight, and not by sneaking up on anyone, but they're in the act of becoming, slowly assembling star-level talent through the draft as well as through trades, supplementing that base of talent with other people's junk and putting it to good use, relying on a front office that has shown considerable moxie, intelligence, and ambition, and guided on the field by a manager who's not merely a babysitter or a media attraction. Stay tuned, because the next four years should be all sorts of fun.

HITTERS

Ron Belliard   2B   Bats: R   Throws: R   Height: 5' 8"   Weight: 195   Born: April 7, 1975   Age: 33

YEAR	TEAM	LVL	AGE	PA	R	2B	3B	HR	RBI	BB	SO	SB	CS	EqBRR	AVG	OBP	SLG	MLVr	EqAVG	EqOBP	EqSLG	EqA	VORP	DEFENSE
2005	CLE	MLB	30	587	71	36	1	17	78	35	72	2	2	-1.1	.284	.325	.450	.057	.292	.342	.474	.277	24.5	139-2B 14
2006	CLE	MLB	31	379	43	21	0	8	44	21	45	2	0	0.9	.291	.337	.420	.000	.292	.345	.434	.270	15.9	87-2B 0
2006	SLN	MLB	31	211	20	9	1	5	23	15	36	0	3	-1.6	.237	.295	.371	-.166	.237	.299	.366	.226	-3.1	50-2B -2
2007	WAS	MLB	32	557	57	35	1	11	58	34	72	3	0	0.8	.290	.332	.427	.038	.300	.345	.445	.274	20.6	113-2B 10
2008	WAS	MLB	33	497	55	27	1	11	59	33	62	4	2	-0.5	.282	.332	.417	-.038	.281	.332	.425	.258	18.1	117-2B 1

Breakout: 6%   Improve: 34%   Collapse: 35%   Attrition: 17%   Comparables: Bill Mazeroski, Joe Randa, Frank Malzone, Johnny Logan

Never mind the braids or the weird tongue tics, Belliard is adequacy in cleats. A beneficiary of the Nats' rush to retain some of the filler ballplayers with whom they had success last year, Belliard will earn $3.5 million combined for his age-33 and -34 seasons, which is less than he made in 2006 alone, but still probably more than he's worth. From metric to metric there's not a lot of agreement on his value in the field, but he's always enjoyed a pretty good reputation for turning the deuce.

Mike Burgess   OF   Bats: L   Throws: L   Height: 5' 11"   Weight: 195   Born: October 20, 1988   Age: 19

YEAR	TEAM	LVL	AGE	PA	R	2B	3B	HR	RBI	BB	SO	SB	CS	EqBRR	AVG	OBP	SLG	MLVr	EqAVG	EqOBP	EqSLG	EqA	VORP	DEFENSE
2007	VER	A-	18	81	10	1	1	3	10	10	23	1	1	-0.5	.286	.383	.457	.193	.219	.296	.356	.227	-7.5	18-RF -1
2007	NAT	Rk	18	154	22	6	3	8	32	25	37	1	2	-1.7	.336	.442	.617	.507	.222	.312	.407	.249	-7.5	33-RF -4
2008	WAS	MLB	19	515	45	21	2	10	45	46	145	7	4	0.1	.208	.283	.327	-.295	.208	.283	.334	.211	-21.7	121-RF 1

Breakout: 8%   Improve: 23%   Collapse: 55%   Attrition: 6%   Comparables: Thomas Hickman, Chris Parmelee, Michael Hall, Xavier Paul

Burgess had as much power as anybody in the 2007 draft, but some wondered if he had enough pure hitting skills to tap into it. Stop wondering. Burgess' pro debut was an eye opener, as he showed a solid approach while leading the Gulf Coast League in OBP and slugging before moving up to the New York-Penn League, where he barely missed a step. He's a stud, and many teams are going to regret passing on him.

Kory Casto   4C   Bats: L   Throws: R   Height: 6' 1"   Weight: 195   Born: December 8, 1981   Age: 26

YEAR	TEAM	LVL	AGE	PA	R	2B	3B	HR	RBI	BB	SO	SB	CS	EqBRR	AVG	OBP	SLG	MLVr	EqAVG	EqOBP	EqSLG	EqA	VORP	DEFENSE	
2005	POT	A+	23	594	86	36	4	22	90	84	98	6	3	-0.9	.290	.394	.510	.267	.236	.322	.399	.251	10.5	131-3B 17	
2006	HAR	AA	24	590	84	24	6	20	80	81	104	6	5	2.7	.272	.379	.468	.199	.253	.350	.441	.275	30.4	89-3B 7	47-LF 6
2007	COH	AAA	25	472	56	20	2	11	55	54	106	4	4	-2.9	.246	.334	.384	-.013	.231	.315	.378	.242	2.5	59-3B -10	46-LF 0
2007	WAS	MLB	25	57	1	2	0	0	3	2	17	0	0	0.1	.130	.158	.167	-.741	.130	.158	.167	.000	-9.1	10-LF -1	
2008	WAS	MLB	26	516	59	25	2	15	62	54	112	5	2	0.2	.244	.326	.410	-.087	.244	.326	.418	.255	6.9	122-3B 0	

Breakout: 34%   Improve: 56%   Collapse: 17%   Attrition: 20%   Comparables: Jason Grabowski, Kevin Barker, Graig Nettles, Paul Carey

Setting aside Casto's flop in his brief trial last spring, his future was more secure at the hot corner than in the outfield even before the Nats started acquiring other teams' outfield prospects. Of course, he's not about to start taking time away from Ryan Zimmerman, and he wouldn't represent an upgrade to another team unless it has a gaping hole at the hot corner. If he can adapt to coming off the bench, he could be a four-corners reserve of modest value. Casto gets top marks for his work ethic, so his chances of sticking in such a role are good.

Ryan Church · OF

Bats: L   Throws: L   Height: 6' 1"   Weight: 190   Born: October 14, 1978   Age: 29

YEAR	TEAM	LVL	AGE	PA	R	2B	3B	HR	RBI	BB	SO	SB	CS	EqBRR	AVG	OBP	SLG	MLVr	EqAVG	EqOBP	EqSLG	EqA	VORP	DEFENSE			
2005	WAS	MLB	26	301	41	15	3	9	42	24	70	3	2	-1.6	.287	.353	.466	.154	.295	.359	.485	.286	15.4	37-LF	1	15-RF	3
2006	WAS	MLB	27	230	22	17	1	10	35	26	60	6	1	0.2	.276	.366	.526	.215	.284	.373	.543	.308	18.5	41-CF	-2	11-RF	-1
2007	WAS	MLB	28	530	57	43	1	15	70	49	107	3	2	1.7	.272	.349	.464	.104	.282	.360	.489	.288	22.2	81-LF	7	37-CF	5
2008	NYN	MLB	29	420	56	24	2	16	59	44	94	5	2	-0.2	.268	.349	.472	.054	.271	.353	.492	.283	21.3	100-LF	0		

Breakout: 19% Improve: 48% Collapse: 24% Attrition: 12%   Comparables: Geoff Jenkins, Jimmie Hall, Jim Edmonds, Bill Howerton

Church finally got the regular playing time he's long deserved last year, so now we know just what he's capable of. As a dead pull-hitter, he won't be hurt by leaving RFK via the Lastings Milledge trade, but it seems unlikely that Shea's similarly damp air and deep fences will be much of an improvement over a full season. His throwing arm is supposed to be something, but he didn't do much with it in left field last year; it will be interesting to see if the move to right will yield some results. If he's your third-best outfielder, that's a good outfield, but the problem for the Mets is that it's unclear how often Moises Alou will be in the other corner.

Ian Desmond · SS

Bats: R   Throws: R   Height: 6' 2"   Weight: 185   Born: September 20, 1985   Age: 22

YEAR	TEAM	LVL	AGE	PA	R	2B	3B	HR	RBI	BB	SO	SB	CS	EqBRR	AVG	OBP	SLG	MLVr	EqAVG	EqOBP	EqSLG	EqA	VORP	DEFENSE	
2005	SAV	A	19	320	37	10	2	4	23	13	60	20	6	2.8	.247	.291	.334	-.134	.194	.224	.260	.165	-29.1	72-SS	0
2005	POT	A+	19	248	37	13	3	3	15	21	53	13	6	1.8	.256	.325	.384	-.040	.207	.261	.304	.199	-12.1	54-SS	-6
2006	POT	A+	20	408	50	20	2	9	45	29	79	14	8	0.7	.244	.313	.384	-.017	.212	.261	.339	.207	-14.7	89-SS	-14
2006	HAR	AA	20	132	8	4	1	0	3	5	35	4	1	-0.2	.182	.214	.231	-.398	.169	.202	.218	.135	-15.9	36-SS	-7
2007	POT	A+	21	536	69	30	4	13	45	57	99	27	11	-7.1	.264	.357	.432	.118	.218	.290	.354	.228	-7.0	127-SS	1
2008	WAS	MLB	22	613	61	31	3	12	58	43	145	18	7	0.9	.225	.286	.355	-.242	.225	.286	.362	.224	-1.5	143-SS	-4

Breakout: 51% Improve: 73% Collapse: 12% Attrition: 8%   Comparables: Ryan Lane, Josh Barfield, Gookie Dawkins, Kelly Dransfeldt

Desmond has been touted as the next big thing longer than Gretchen Mol, and with results that are as reliably disappointing. However, last year's progress at High-A Potomac is encouraging, even though it was his third pass through the circuit. Desmond is filling out, and his physical gifts are delivering better results in the field. He's not the blue-chipper some expected, but he's making slow progress toward becoming a decent shortstop in a world in which people are relying on punchless types such as Adam Everett and John McDonald.

Robert Fick · 1B/C

Bats: L   Throws: R   Height: 6' 1"   Weight: 200   Born: March 15, 1974   Age: 34

YEAR	TEAM	LVL	AGE	PA	R	2B	3B	HR	RBI	BB	SO	SB	CS	EqBRR	AVG	OBP	SLG	MLVr	EqAVG	EqOBP	EqSLG	EqA	VORP	DEFENSE			
2005	SDN	MLB	31	260	25	10	2	3	30	26	33	0	2	0.6	.265	.340	.365	-.022	.275	.351	.389	.259	2.9	22-1B	3	21-C	-3
2006	WAS	MLB	32	141	14	4	0	2	9	10	24	1	1	-0.8	.266	.324	.344	-.120	.271	.333	.341	.239	-1.1	19-C	-5		
2007	WAS	MLB	33	221	24	6	1	2	16	19	42	0	1	1.3	.234	.309	.305	-.211	.245	.323	.332	.232	-8.0	43-1B	-5		
2008	SDN	MLB	34	105	10	4	0	2	11	11	20	1	0	0.0	.243	.325	.358	-.157	.250	.332	.383	.250	1.4	29-1B	0		

Breakout: 37% Improve: 48% Collapse: 40% Attrition: 53%   Comparables: Danny Heep, Harry Spilman, Tito Francona, Dick Phillips

Fick got more playing time than expected as a defensive replacement at first base thanks to Manny Acta's double switches, which would always get the journeyman at-bats while flinging the pitcher's slot somewhere furthest from the inning at hand. That was probably the best possible role for Fick, but alas, the salad days have come to an end, as he has signed a minor league deal with the Padres.

Jesus Flores · C

Bats: R   Throws: R   Height: 6' 1"   Weight: 185   Born: October 26, 1984   Age: 23

YEAR	TEAM	LVL	AGE	PA	R	2B	3B	HR	RBI	BB	SO	SB	CS	EqBRR	AVG	OBP	SLG	MLVr	EqAVG	EqOBP	EqSLG	EqA	VORP	DEFENSE	
2005	HAG	A	20	337	34	18	0	7	42	12	90	2	2	-0.9	.216	.250	.339	-.223	.176	.199	.265	.141	-38.8	70-C	-5
2006	SLU	A+	21	480	66	32	0	21	70	28	127	2	0	-1.2	.266	.335	.487	.174	.240	.293	.442	.250	8.9	102-C	10
2007	WAS	MLB	22	197	21	9	0	4	25	14	48	0	1	-0.5	.244	.310	.361	-.130	.251	.320	.369	.239	0.8	44-C	2
2008	WAS	MLB	23	255	29	13	1	10	35	18	60	3	1	-0.3	.258	.320	.448	-.035	.258	.321	.457	.262	11.6	63-C	0

Breakout: 53% Improve: 77% Collapse: 13% Attrition: 32%   Comparables: Todd Hundley, Dave Duncan, Andy Etchebarren, John Bateman

For all of the talk that the Rule 5 draft isn't yielding the same sort of goodies that it used to, there are lovely counter-examples like Flores. The Nats should be able to look forward to reaping the benefits of his fluidity as a receiver and his potent throwing arm for years to come. He already pulls the ball with some power, so he should be a good match for the new park's slightly shallower power alleys. If he isn't sharing the playing time behind the plate with Paul Lo Duca, a return to the minors for a couple of months of full-time play would probably help him start hitting right-handers with more authority. It's within his power to push the veteran to the bench before the end of the season and get named to an All-Star team within the next four.

Esmailyn Gonzalez   SS   Bats: S   Throws: R   Height: 5' 11"   Weight: 175   Born: September 21, 1989   Age: 18

YEAR	TEAM	LVL	AGE	PA	R	2B	3B	HR	RBI	BB	SO	SB	CS	EqBRR	AVG	OBP	SLG	MLVr	EqAVG	EqOBP	EqSLG	EqA	VORP	DEFENSE	
2007	NAT	Rk	17	131	13	3	2	0	11	19	18	4	2	-1.3	.245	.382	.311	-.003	.191	.288	.243	.192	-19.1	30-SS	1
2008	WAS	MLB	18	244	21	9	1	1	13	21	43	6	3	0.3	.202	.279	.266	-.384	.201	.279	.272	.191	-8.8	60-SS	1

Breakout: 45% Improve: 58% Collapse: 22% Attrition: 10%   Comparables: Osvaldo Martinez, Jorge Velandia, Jimmy Rollins, Justin Jacobs

The Dominican Gonzalez was Washington's big plunge into the Latin American talent pool, but the $1.4 million player had a subpar pro debut. Scouts love his defense, but they have serious questions about his ability to ever hit enough to be an everyday player. The optimists point to his high walk rate and low strikeout rate and see potential.

Cristian Guzman   SS   Bats: S   Throws: R   Height: 6' 0"   Weight: 195   Born: March 21, 1978   Age: 30

YEAR	TEAM	LVL	AGE	PA	R	2B	3B	HR	RBI	BB	SO	SB	CS	EqBRR	AVG	OBP	SLG	MLVr	EqAVG	EqOBP	EqSLG	EqA	VORP	DEFENSE	
2005	WAS	MLB	27	492	39	19	6	4	31	25	76	7	4	-2.7	.219	.260	.314	-.271	.221	.264	.321	.203	-14.7	129-SS	-9
2007	WAS	MLB	29	192	31	6	6	2	14	15	21	2	0	2.8	.328	.380	.466	.208	.341	.396	.497	.309	16.4	42-SS	-5
2008	WAS	MLB	30	234	26	9	2	2	20	16	32	4	1	0.6	.257	.310	.345	-.192	.257	.310	.352	.229	2.8	58-SS	-3

Breakout: 5% Improve: 16% Collapse: 61% Attrition: 36%   Comparables: Wayne Tolleson, Dennis Hocking, Mike Ramsey, Aaron Miles

Between time lost to a hamstring strain and a subsequent thumb injury, there was just enough in Guzman's come-back from a season lost to shoulder surgery to inspire hope. Although he looked a bit stiff at shortstop in his return, he made much more solid contact at the plate, a nice change from his slappier tendencies of yore. Don't get too carried away—he's hit well over a full season exactly once in his career, and that was in his age-23 season back in 2001. It's not inconceivable that he'll be part of an adequate three-headed setup in the middle infield, but that hardly salvages his four-year deal, which was a mistake from the day it was signed and will finally expire after this season.

Nick Johnson   1B   Bats: L   Throws: L   Height: 6' 3"   Weight: 225   Born: September 19, 1978   Age: 29

YEAR	TEAM	LVL	AGE	PA	R	2B	3B	HR	RBI	BB	SO	SB	CS	EqBRR	AVG	OBP	SLG	MLVr	EqAVG	EqOBP	EqSLG	EqA	VORP	DEFENSE	
2005	WAS	MLB	26	547	66	35	3	15	74	80	87	3	8	-3.0	.289	.408	.479	.253	.296	.413	.503	.308	34.2	122-1B	20
2006	WAS	MLB	27	628	100	46	0	23	77	110	99	10	3	-1.5	.290	.428	.520	.317	.298	.435	.538	.331	51.0	142-1B	11
2008	WAS	MLB	29	520	80	26	1	18	70	81	83	6	2	-0.7	.283	.402	.477	.160	.282	.403	.486	.303	30.9	122-1B	6

Breakout: 7% Improve: 23% Collapse: 30% Attrition: 10%   Comparables: Mike Epstein, Kent Hrbek, Jason Thompson, John Mayberry

Recovering from his third operation on the leg he broke in a nasty collision with Austin Kearns at the tail end of 2006, Johnson is supposed to be ready to go this spring and has reportedly lost weight and toned up his previously Hrbekian build. The Nats multi-year commitment to Comrade Dmitri at first base should put Nick the Stick in somebody else's double-knits as soon as he proves he's healthy enough to hit. The problem is getting value for him; he's owed $11 million over the next two years, and his fragility doesn't help make that sort of financial commitment look like a good risk to most clubs. Reuniting him with the Yankees would perhaps be too perfect a match—a club that can afford to take a chance and has an obvious need at his position.

Austin Kearns — RF

Bats: R   Throws: R   Height: 6' 4"   Weight: 225   Born: May 20, 1980   Age: 28

YEAR	TEAM	LVL	AGE	PA	R	2B	3B	HR	RBI	BB	SO	SB	CS	EqBRR	AVG	OBP	SLG	MLVr	EqAVG	EqOBP	EqSLG	EqA	VORP	DEFENSE	
2005	LOU	AAA	25	123	24	15	1	7	21	11	30	0	0	1.0	.342	.407	.685	.551	.268	.339	.580	.298	8.6	26-RF	0
2005	CIN	MLB	25	448	62	26	1	18	67	48	107	0	0	1.6	.240	.333	.452	.036	.238	.330	.456	.270	9.0	101-RF	8
2006	CIN	MLB	26	368	53	21	1	16	50	35	85	7	1	0.3	.274	.351	.492	.111	.269	.348	.485	.285	15.7	84-RF	11
2006	WAS	MLB	26	261	33	12	1	8	36	41	50	2	3	-0.5	.250	.381	.429	.088	.259	.388	.453	.290	7.8	55-RF	5
2007	WAS	MLB	27	674	84	35	1	16	74	71	106	2	2	1.0	.266	.355	.411	.035	.276	.366	.432	.277	12.6	154-RF	17
2008	WAS	MLB	28	564	76	29	2	20	75	63	104	6	2	0.0	.270	.359	.457	.052	.269	.360	.466	.280	19.9	132-RF	6

Breakout: 10% Improve: 48% Collapse: 16% Attrition: 13%   Comparables: Bob Allison, Mike Cuddyer, Josh Willingham, Glenn Braggs

Some might be disappointed that Kearns never blossomed into something more, but he's your basic nifty non-star ballplayer—athletic and finally durable, a plus defender in right, and a hitter with solid pop and on-base skills. The new park should give him a few more homers, but leaving Cincy cost him at least a hundred points of slugging on contact, and that isn't coming back as long as he's a Nat. If he stays at this level, picking up his $10 million option in 2010 would be a mistake, but the team's newly acquired crowd in the outfield makes him a solid bartering chip should everyone else pan out.

Ryan Langerhans — OF

Bats: L   Throws: L   Height: 6' 3"   Weight: 205   Born: February 20, 1980   Age: 28

YEAR	TEAM	LVL	AGE	PA	R	2B	3B	HR	RBI	BB	SO	SB	CS	EqBRR	AVG	OBP	SLG	MLVr	EqAVG	EqOBP	EqSLG	EqA	VORP	DEFENSE				
2005	ATL	MLB	25	373	48	22	3	8	42	37	75	0	2	2.9	.267	.348	.426	.048	.264	.346	.429	.268	8.0	43-LF	5	40-RF	-2
2006	ATL	MLB	26	369	46	16	3	7	28	50	91	1	2	1.7	.241	.350	.378	-.051	.239	.350	.382	.259	-0.8	79-LF	4	13-CF	2
2007	ATL	MLB	27	52	3	1	0	0	1	6	16	0	1	-0.4	.068	.192	.091	-.786	.068	.192	.091	.000	-9.2	13-LF	-1		
2007	WAS	MLB	27	187	24	6	2	6	22	22	63	3	0	0.1	.198	.296	.370	-.173	.205	.306	.398	.249	-2.1	29-CF	2	13-LF	0
2008	WAS	MLB	28	124	14	6	1	4	14	14	33	2	1	0.1	.235	.327	.412	-.089	.234	.327	.420	.255	2.9	33-LF	1		

Breakout: 46% Improve: 55% Collapse: 30% Attrition: 52%   Comparables: Doug Frobel, Danny Goodwin, Ricky Ledee, Duke Carmel

Langerhans' 2007 was one of those years in which a cold start led to pressing, engendering a cycle of failure he never really escaped. That savage overcorrection squashed any suggestion that Langerhans is more than a potentially good fourth outfielder, which frees him up to provide the Nats with some utility as a lefty bat to spot in their righty-heavy outfield.

Nook Logan — CF

Bats: S   Throws: R   Height: 6' 2"   Weight: 180   Born: November 28, 1979   Age: 28

YEAR	TEAM	LVL	AGE	PA	R	2B	3B	HR	RBI	BB	SO	SB	CS	EqBRR	AVG	OBP	SLG	MLVr	EqAVG	EqOBP	EqSLG	EqA	VORP	DEFENSE	
2005	DET	MLB	25	356	47	12	5	1	17	21	52	23	6	1.3	.258	.305	.335	-.166	.268	.326	.350	.248	-1.0	99-CF	17
2006	WAS	MLB	26	99	13	3	1	1	8	6	20	2	1	-0.2	.300	.337	.389	-.013	.311	.347	.400	.264	2.5	25-CF	-5
2007	WAS	MLB	27	350	39	18	4	0	21	19	86	23	5	1.7	.265	.304	.345	-.150	.277	.320	.372	.249	1.1	85-CF	4
2008	WAS	MLB	28	238	28	10	3	2	18	16	49	11	3	0.9	.254	.307	.348	-.195	.254	.308	.354	.234	0.9	59-CF	2

Breakout: 19% Improve: 36% Collapse: 43% Attrition: 41%   Comparables: Cecil Espy, David Hulse, Wilbur Howard, Lee Tinsley

A good fielder but not a great one, Logan is an example of a fifth outfielder stretched into full-time duty in the absence of a real regular center fielder. His performance for the Nats last year was the spitting image of his 2005 season for the similarly unfortunate Tigers. Logan is also an interesting test case for whether or not a fringe guy named in the Mitchell Report is going to be able to survive a doping accusation given that his tepid performance has him barely hanging on as it is. Whether he used or not, he's never had any power; his offensive game consists of legging out grounders to the left side and hitting a few soft liners, giving his batted balls all the loft of an already-dead quail.

Felipe Lopez   **SS/2B**   Bats: S   Throws: R   Height: 6' 1"   Weight: 185   Born: May 12, 1980   Age: 28

YEAR	TEAM	LVL	AGE	PA	R	2B	3B	HR	RBI	BB	SO	SB	CS	EqBRR	AVG	OBP	SLG	MLVr	EqAVG	EqOBP	EqSLG	EqA	VORP	DEFENSE			
2005	CIN	MLB	25	648	97	34	5	23	85	57	111	15	7	0.4	.291	.352	.486	.156	.289	.352	.495	.286	45.8	134-SS	-12		
2006	CIN	MLB	26	394	55	14	1	9	30	47	66	23	6	0.8	.268	.355	.394	-.018	.262	.354	.382	.266	14.9	82-SS	-5		
2006	WAS	MLB	26	320	43	13	2	2	22	34	60	21	6	2.7	.281	.362	.365	-.007	.292	.375	.375	.274	12.9	68-SS	-11		
2007	WAS	MLB	27	671	70	25	6	9	50	53	109	24	9	-3.2	.245	.308	.352	-.144	.260	.323	.376	.248	0.2	104-SS	-12	42-2B	6
2008	WAS	MLB	28	639	87	28	5	11	59	62	102	23	6	1.2	.271	.344	.396	-.055	.270	.344	.403	.262	24.2	149-SS	-3		

Breakout: 18%   Improve: 42%   Collapse: 24%   Attrition: 10%   Comparables: U.L. Washington, Bump Wills, Carlos Guillen, Orlando Hudson

Lopez is one of the worst shortstops around when it comes to making it to the bag to turn the double play, and his arm might be politely described as scattershot after he led the league in throwing errors from his position (not that having Dmitri Young rooted in place at first base helped any). If he's hitting, you can put up with his defensive shortcomings, but Lopez is really only an adequate hitter, even for a middle infielder. Last spring's experiment with moving him to second made sense, but it started from the assumption that you'd want to play Guzman regularly at short; that's the sort of decision tree that could use pruning.

Christopher Marrero   **OF**   Bats: R   Throws: R   Height: 6' 3"   Weight: 210   Born: July 2, 1988   Age: 19

YEAR	TEAM	LVL	AGE	PA	R	2B	3B	HR	RBI	BB	SO	SB	CS	EqBRR	AVG	OBP	SLG	MLVr	EqAVG	EqOBP	EqSLG	EqA	VORP	DEFENSE	
2006	NAT	Rk	17	91	10	9	0	0	16	8	19	0	0	1.5	.309	.374	.420	.195	.214	.264	.298	.199	-21.5	21-LF	-2
2007	HAG	A	18	243	31	14	0	14	53	14	39	0	4	-0.1	.293	.337	.545	.235	.233	.269	.405	.226	-10.7	35-LF	-7
2007	POT	A+	18	290	40	11	3	9	35	32	63	0	0	-4.0	.259	.338	.431	.083	.217	.283	.357	.223	-16.8	53-LF	-5
2008	WAS	MLB	19	616	53	30	2	15	65	42	139	2	3	-0.3	.231	.285	.368	-.224	.230	.285	.375	.220	-15.6	144-LF	-3

Breakout: 36%   Improve: 62%   Collapse: 21%   Attrition: 5%   Comparables: Marc Newfield, Corey Smith, Danny Clyburn, Austin Kearns

Marrero has the same kind of game-breaking power as Wily Mo Peña, but he has a much better approach at the plate. That he hit High-A pitching at age 18 last year reinforced the perception that he was one of the best high school hitters available in the 2006 draft. Having nabbed him with the 15th overall pick that year after a poor senior season dropped his status, the Nats may have a steal on their hands. He spent the majority of his time in instructional league taking reps at first base, making it obvious that he's being groomed as the long-term solution at the position.

Justin Maxwell   **OF**   Bats: R   Throws: R   Height: 6' 5"   Weight: 225   Born: November 6, 1983   Age: 24

YEAR	TEAM	LVL	AGE	PA	R	2B	3B	HR	RBI	BB	SO	SB	CS	EqBRR	AVG	OBP	SLG	MLVr	EqAVG	EqOBP	EqSLG	EqA	VORP	DEFENSE			
2006	VER	A-	22	306	36	11	3	4	33	27	61	20	5	2.4	.269	.346	.376	.100	.218	.279	.318	.216	-29.1	50-CF	-7	21-LF	1
2006	SAV	A	22	68	8	2	2	1	7	8	23	1	0	0.8	.172	.294	.328	-.138	.148	.235	.279	.173	-7.2				
2007	HAG	A	23	244	51	12	2	14	40	26	57	14	3	2.9	.301	.389	.579	.361	.243	.314	.436	.261	5.0	36-CF	0		
2007	POT	A+	23	260	35	13	0	13	43	24	65	21	5	1.1	.263	.338	.491	.169	.225	.285	.403	.243	-2.9	54-CF	-1		
2007	WAS	MLB	23	27	5	0	0	2	5	1	8	0	0	0.1	.269	.296	.500	.064	.269	.296	.500	.264	1.2				
2008	WAS	MLB	24	570	70	27	3	18	65	46	160	29	9	1.2	.238	.305	.408	-.130	.238	.305	.416	.250	5.5	134-CF	0		

Breakout: 39%   Improve: 62%   Collapse: 15%   Attrition: 13%   Comparables: Lyle Mouton, Jim Kavourias, Craig Monroe, Joe Mather

You can't really call Maxwell a sleeper; he's always had tremendous potential, and if not for his problems with injuries, he'd have shown up on prospect lists sooner and ranked higher. Finally healthy enough to play a full season last year, he delivered on the power-speed package the Nats anticipated when they picked him in the fourth round of the 2005 draft. After crushing A-ball pitching, he initially struggled upon his promotion to High-A, but rebounded with a good finish, bopping 11 homers in his last 27 games. The Nats responded by calling the local kid from suburban Olney, Maryland, up at the tail end of the season to give him a taste of major league life, then shipping him off to the AFL for extra seasoning. He's still a bit raw at the plate and is always going to strike out a lot, but it won't be long before he's pushing for a spot in an already crowded outfield.

Wily Mo Peña — OF

Bats: R Throws: R Height: 6' 3" Weight: 245 Born: January 23, 1982 Age: 26

YEAR	TEAM	LVL	AGE	PA	R	2B	3B	HR	RBI	BB	SO	SB	CS	EqBRR	AVG	OBP	SLG	MLVr	EqAVG	EqOBP	EqSLG	EqA	VORP	DEFENSE			
2005	CIN	MLB	23	335	42	17	0	19	51	20	116	2	1	-1.1	.254	.304	.492	.057	.252	.302	.503	.268	9.5	46-RF	-1	22-CF	-3
2006	BOS	MLB	24	305	36	15	2	11	42	20	91	0	1	1.2	.300	.348	.487	.105	.296	.351	.493	.286	14.3	32-RF	0	22-CF	1
2007	BOS	MLB	25	172	18	9	1	5	17	14	58	0	1	-1.1	.218	.291	.385	-.176	.213	.291	.394	.234	-4.3	23-RF	-2	10-LF	-2
2007	WAS	MLB	25	145	24	4	0	8	22	8	36	2	0	0.8	.293	.352	.504	.180	.301	.359	.526	.298	8.7	31-LF	-3		
2008	WAS	MLB	26	316	42	15	1	16	49	27	85	3	1	0.0	.270	.341	.501	.081	.270	.341	.511	.282	15.9	77-LF	-2		

Breakout: 34% Improve: 60% Collapse: 20% Attrition: 27%   Comparables: Pete Incaviglia, Craig Wilson, Hensley Meulens, Andres Galarraga

Bless Jim Bowden; not all of us have the courage to be unapologetic creatures of habit. His desire to trade for Peña a second time didn't cost the Nats much (Emiliano Fruto to get the older, less talented Chris Carter to flip to Boston with cash for Peña). The same thing that makes Wily Mo exciting is the same thing he's always had going for him: Hulk-smash power, pure and simple. The problem is deciding whether or not he's worth playing every day, because as the Sox found out, part-time play can produce problems for a guy with a swing this long. The Incaviglia comp seems about right, but it remains to be seen if Peña will get enough at-bats playing in an outfield that also includes Kearns, Milledge, and Dukes.

Brian Schneider — C

Bats: L Throws: R Height: 6' 1" Weight: 195 Born: November 26, 1976 Age: 31

YEAR	TEAM	LVL	AGE	PA	R	2B	3B	HR	RBI	BB	SO	SB	CS	EqBRR	AVG	OBP	SLG	MLVr	EqAVG	EqOBP	EqSLG	EqA	VORP	DEFENSE	
2005	WAS	MLB	28	408	38	20	1	10	44	29	48	1	0	-1.0	.268	.330	.409	.014	.271	.334	.423	.263	16.0	103-C	9
2006	WAS	MLB	29	455	30	18	0	4	55	38	67	2	2	-2.7	.256	.320	.329	-.153	.259	.326	.335	.235	-4.9	112-C	2
2007	WAS	MLB	30	477	33	21	1	6	54	56	56	0	0	-1.8	.235	.326	.336	-.139	.241	.335	.352	.248	2.4	118-C	1
2008	NYN	MLB	31	289	27	13	1	4	28	28	39	2	1	-0.8	.242	.319	.345	-.185	.246	.323	.359	.235	3.3	71-C	0

Breakout: 14% Improve: 36% Collapse: 33% Attrition: 40%   Comparables: Brent Mayne, Ron Hassey, Greg Olson, Toby Atwell

Now that Mike Matheny's out of the game, Schneider's name comes up in the discussion of the game's toughest catchers. This might be a corollary of Nichols' Law of Catcher Defense (a catcher's defensive rep is inversely related to his ability to hit). Not that Schneider doesn't deserve credit for handling the hammering that catching entails, but it's not like Mike Piazza didn't take his lumps catching more than 1,600 games. Shipped to the Mets with Church for Lastings Milledge, Schneider is expected to split the catching chores with Ramon Castro. The Mets are talking up his valuable intangibles, but they'll reap what they sow: intangible value.

Josh Whitesell — 1B

Bats: L Throws: L Height: 6' 3" Weight: 220 Born: April 14, 1982 Age: 26

YEAR	TEAM	LVL	AGE	PA	R	2B	3B	HR	RBI	BB	SO	SB	CS	EqBRR	AVG	OBP	SLG	MLVr	EqAVG	EqOBP	EqSLG	EqA	VORP	DEFENSE	
2005	POT	A+	23	474	59	32	2	18	66	74	125	1	1	-4.4	.293	.416	.524	.321	.220	.323	.386	.248	-7.7	86-1B	-2
2006	HAR	AA	24	467	47	11	0	19	56	53	125	2	6	-6.8	.264	.354	.433	.114	.244	.326	.405	.252	-1.5	84-1B	-2
2007	HAR	AA	25	487	78	23	1	21	74	87	107	6	2	1.4	.284	.425	.512	.284	.255	.383	.463	.294	24.2	87-1B	-3
2008	WAS	MLB	26	485	59	20	1	19	64	63	126	4	2	-0.8	.243	.348	.433	-.020	.243	.348	.441	.269	10.9	115-1B	-2

Breakout: 20% Improve: 42% Collapse: 27% Attrition: 15%   Comparables: Paul Carey, Eddy Furniss, Ben Broussard, Brian Daubach

A fly-ball hitter with some pop, Whitesell hit right-handers with authority last year (.300/.451/.546), but after repeating Double-A at his age, he can't really be called a prospect. Having both him and Rule 5 pick Matt Whitney on the 40-man roster might seem a bit strange, but if anybody can deal the two starting first basemen in front of them in one season, it's Jim Bowden. Barring that sort of hyperactive miracle, Whitesell's trade fodder at best.

Dmitri Young — 1B

Bats: S Throws: R Height: 6' 2" Weight: 220 Born: October 11, 1973 Age: 34

YEAR	TEAM	LVL	AGE	PA	R	2B	3B	HR	RBI	BB	SO	SB	CS	EqBRR	AVG	OBP	SLG	MLVr	EqAVG	EqOBP	EqSLG	EqA	VORP	DEFENSE			
2005	DET	MLB	31	508	61	25	3	21	72	29	100	1	0	0.1	.271	.325	.471	.067	.276	.340	.497	.282	19.0	29-1B	-1	16-LF	1
2006	DET	MLB	32	184	19	4	1	7	23	11	39	1	1	-1.3	.250	.293	.407	-.141	.247	.299	.424	.246	-2.4				
2007	WAS	MLB	33	508	57	38	1	13	74	44	74	0	0	-2.8	.320	.378	.491	.233	.328	.390	.514	.307	35.6	99-1B	-6		
2008	WAS	MLB	34	363	46	20	1	12	54	32	61	2	1	-1.0	.292	.356	.468	.081	.292	.357	.477	.280	18.3	87-1B	-3		

Breakout: 12% Improve: 38% Collapse: 38% Attrition: 18%   Comparables: David Segui, Joe Torre, Rondell White, Bob Watson

Baseball loves its little dramas of redemption and rebirth, so Young joins an honored tradition of veterans cut too quickly (by a team that needed him, no less) who prove they have something left in the tank after all. The problem remains one of leagues (and the weird failure of so many AL teams to employ DHs at DH), as Young plays first base with all of the nimble grace of a mailbox. That might not seem so bad at first blush—Jason Giambi *wishes* he was a mailbox—but have you ever seen one stretch to scoop up a parcel? The deal Young was rewarded with in the offseason (two years plus a playing time-driven vesting option for 2010) was more than a little crazy given his age, girth, and the very short list of suitors for his services.

Ryan Zimmerman **3B**   Bats: R   Throws: R   Height: 6' 2"   Weight: 210   Born: September 28, 1984   Age: 23

YEAR	TEAM	LVL	AGE	PA	R	2B	3B	HR	RBI	BB	SO	SB	CS	EqBRR	AVG	OBP	SLG	MLVr	EqAVG	EqOBP	EqSLG	EqA	VORP	DEFENSE
2005	HAR	AA	20	252	40	20	0	9	32	15	34	1	5	-0.3	.326	.371	.528	.290	.289	.333	.464	.266	15.2	53-3B 2
2005	WAS	MLB	20	62	6	10	0	0	6	3	12	0	0	0.0	.397	.419	.569	.550	.397	.419	.552	.330	9.3	12-3B 4
2006	WAS	MLB	21	682	84	47	3	20	110	61	120	11	8	-1.5	.287	.351	.471	.123	.294	.361	.484	.285	26.9	155-3B 17
2007	WAS	MLB	22	722	99	43	5	24	91	61	125	4	1	1.4	.266	.330	.458	.057	.276	.342	.484	.281	23.9	160-3B 23
2008	WAS	MLB	23	666	92	42	3	24	95	58	110	8	3	0.3	.291	.355	.490	.109	.291	.356	.500	.286	41.0	155-3B 12

Breakout: 28%   Improve: 57%   Collapse: 16%   Attrition: 3%   Comparables: Ken McMullen, Don Money, Bob Bailey, Larry Parrish

Of the 33 double plays turned (but not started) by all major league third basemen last year, Zim turned seven, the most in a single season in our database, which reaches back to 1959. That was a reflection of Manny Acta's aggressiveness in every phase of the game, as the skipper played the shift on lefty pull hitters more than any manager of recent memory, a gambit which paid off in part because of Zimmerman's shortstop-level athleticism. Six of those DPs were 4-5-3s (three hit by Ryan Howard, two by Carlos Delgado, and one by Adam Dunn); the last was a 6-5-3 hit into by Barry Bonds. Zim isn't perfect—he could do better charging bunts—but he's already among the best gloves at the hot corner in the game today, and he has the gifts to become one of the game's all-time greats in the field. Oh, and he can hit a bit too, although last season's struggles against right-handers involved a few too many weakly pulled grounders (and far too many GIDPs of his own) to give him a free pass on the step down from his rookie year. He spreads his fly balls around, so his new home's closer power alleys could make for a performance spike, as RFK doubles become Nationals Park souvenirs.

PITCHERS

Luis Ayala   Bats: R   Throws: R   Height: 6' 2"   Weight: 185   Born: January 12, 1978   Age: 30

YEAR	TEAM	LVL	AGE	W	L	SV	G	GS	IP	H	BB	SO	HR	GB%	BABIP	STUFF	WHIP	ERA	PERA	EqERA	EqH9	EqBB9	EqSO9	EqHR9	VORP	SN/WX
2005	WAS	MLB	27	8	7	1	68	0	71	75	14	40	7	43.3%	.316	-5	1.25	2.66	4.64	3.34	9.9	1.7	4.8	0.9	18.8	2.22
2007	WAS	MLB	29	2	2	1	44	0	42¹	43	12	28	5	39.3%	.297	-3	1.30	3.19	4.14	3.38	8.9	2.1	5.5	1.1	11.3	0.70
2008	WAS	MLB	30	2	2	3	38	0	43	47	13	27	6	43.2%	.292	-9	1.39	4.17	4.83	4.47	9.6	2.5	5.0	1.2	5.9	0.50

Breakout: 8%   Improve: 20%   Collapse: 61%   Attrition: 31%   Comparables: John Frascatore, Travis Harper, Jose Bautista, Dave Smith

After missing 2006 following elbow surgery possibly brought on by pitching in the World Baseball Classic (what, you've already forgotten about that epic contest?), Ayala made his comeback in late June of last year. While he wasn't the middle-innings iceman he'd been before the injury, he still provided value as one of the Nats' cast of thousands in the pen. The one thing that he probably would rather have left on the surgeon's table is his tendency to make a few too many mistakes up in the zone, especially against right-handers.

Mike Bacsik   Bats: L   Throws: L   Height: 6' 3"   Weight: 190   Born: November 11, 1977   Age: 30

YEAR	TEAM	LVL	AGE	W	L	SV	G	GS	IP	H	BB	SO	HR	GB%	BABIP	STUFF	WHIP	ERA	PERA	EqERA	EqH9	EqBB9	EqSO9	EqHR9	VORP	SN/WX
2005	SWB	AAA	27	7	10	0	30	27	160¹	184	41	112	23	45.7%	.319	-22	1.40	4.55	6.37	6.09	10.9	3.0	4.5	1.6	-8.1	—
2006	TUC	AAA	28	11	0	0	28	10	87²	81	19	57	8	46.3%	.286	-7	1.15	2.79	4.21	3.27	8.6	2.3	4.2	1.1	21.4	—
2007	COH	AAA	29	1	3	0	9	5	36	40	6	28	6	46.5%	.327	-17	1.28	4.00	8.04	6.27	11.7	1.9	5.2	2.2	-2.5	—
2007	WAS	MLB	29	5	8	0	29	20	118	141	29	45	26	42.5%	.283	-36	1.44	5.11	6.56	5.80	10.4	1.8	3.3	1.9	3.2	1.16
2008	WAS	MLB	30	3	5	0	27	24	67¹	81	20	34	12	44.4%	.300	-14	1.50	5.22	5.77	5.57	10.6	2.4	4.0	1.5	1.5	0.40

Breakout: 18%   Improve: 42%   Collapse: 40%   Attrition: 38%   Comparables: Donne Wall, Jason Simontacchi, Dave Telgheder, Scott Aldred

David Pinto's work on pitchers' fielding support suggests that Bacsik received much more help from the other eight guys on the diamond last year than most moundsmen; among the others at the top of the list were Chien-Ming Wang, Jeremy Guthrie, and Brian Bannister, and those last two are certainly pitchers who will be entering 2008 with a lot of question marks. The Nats understood what they got out of the soft-tossing southpaw as one of their coalition of the willing used to people the pitching staff, thanked him for his time, and only re-signed him to a minor league deal with an invitation to camp. If he shows up in a ballpark near you, you'll either see some great defense or a journeyman getting tattooed more regularly than the cast of *Miami Ink*.

Collin Balester Bats: R Throws: R Height: 6' 5" Weight: 190 Born: June 6, 1986 Age: 22

YEAR	TEAM	LVL	AGE	W	L	SV	G	GS	IP	H	BB	SO	HR	GB%	BABIP	STUFF	WHIP	ERA	PERA	EqERA	EqH9	EqBB9	EqSO9	EqHR9	VORP	SN/WX
2005	SAV	A	19	8	6	0	24	23	125	105	42	95	11	43.1%	.257	-24	1.18	3.67	6.91	7.64	10.2	5.7	3.5	1.9	-24.0	—
2006	POT	A+	20	4	5	0	23	22	117²	126	53	87	12	43.9%	.325	-34	1.53	5.22	8.55	8.28	11.8	5.7	4.1	2.1	-31.1	—
2006	HAR	AA	20	1	0	0	3	3	19²	15	6	10	0	45.8%	.273	4	1.09	1.88	3.73	3.06	7.6	3.6	2.5	0.0	5.0	—
2007	HAR	AA	21	2	7	0	17	17	98²	103	25	77	9	45.7%	.314	-2	1.30	3.74	5.68	5.28	10.4	2.9	4.7	1.3	3.3	—
2007	COH	AAA	21	2	3	0	10	10	51²	49	23	40	3	35.0%	.309	3	1.39	4.18	4.95	5.66	9.3	4.4	4.9	0.7	-0.3	—
2008	WAS	MLB	22	6	10	0	23	23	125¹	141	56	79	21	41.8%	.297	0	1.57	5.45	5.90	5.81	9.9	3.6	5.1	1.4	-0.8	0.90

Breakout: 26% Improve: 55% Collapse: 17% Attrition: 13%   Comparables: Sean Douglass, Greg Hansell, Brian Rose, Buddy Carlyle

Balester has generally been considered the Nats' top pitching prospect at the upper levels, but that probably says more about the Washington system than anything else. That's not a total knock against Balester, but in other organizations, he'd be no more than a decent prospect—a solid arm with three average pitches and some idea of what to do with them. That's the description of a fourth starter in the big leagues.

Jason Bergmann Bats: R Throws: R Height: 6' 4" Weight: 205 Born: September 25, 1981 Age: 26

YEAR	TEAM	LVL	AGE	W	L	SV	G	GS	IP	H	BB	SO	HR	GB%	BABIP	STUFF	WHIP	ERA	PERA	EqERA	EqH9	EqBB9	EqSO9	EqHR9	VORP	SN/WX
2005	HAR	AA	23	2	0	5	21	0	37	27	16	37	3	35.1%	.255	-4	1.16	1.22	4.63	2.67	7.5	5.3	5.6	1.1	11.0	—
2005	NWO	AAA	23	3	2	2	20	0	37	26	13	39	5	40.0%	.250	1	1.05	3.16	4.04	4.11	6.7	3.6	6.9	1.5	5.8	—
2005	WAS	MLB	23	2	0	0	15	1	19²	14	11	21	1	33.3%	.271	16	1.27	2.74	3.23	2.75	6.4	4.6	8.7	0.5	5.8	0.52
2006	NWO	AAA	24	8	2	4	26	4	60²	54	20	62	5	28.5%	.318	2	1.23	3.29	4.83	4.18	9.3	3.4	7.1	1.1	8.8	—
2006	WAS	MLB	24	0	2	0	29	6	64²	81	27	54	12	33.3%	.356	-14	1.67	6.68	7.08	6.78	11.1	3.2	6.8	1.5	-6.7	-0.22
2007	COH	AAA	25	2	1	0	5	5	24	20	6	22	0	33.3%	.313	18	1.08	1.50	3.57	2.45	8.6	2.9	6.5	0.0	7.7	—
2007	WAS	MLB	25	6	6	0	21	21	115¹	99	42	86	18	36.3%	.249	4	1.22	4.45	3.88	4.37	7.6	2.8	6.2	1.3	15.5	3.19
2008	WAS	MLB	26	5	7	1	38	14	100¹	101	39	76	15	38.1%	.284	1	1.40	4.71	4.98	5.03	8.9	3.2	6.1	1.3	7.9	1.40

Breakout: 9% Improve: 36% Collapse: 36% Attrition: 24%   Comparables: Rob Bell, Eric Gagné, Chris Knapp, John Patterson

Bergmann's move to the rotation worked in that he delivered 11 quality starts (one blown) in his 21 tries despite losing time to injuries to his pitching elbow and hamstring. Still, his struggles with lefties make you wonder if the Grim Reaper and Max von Sydow are standing over his shoulder, watching to see which pitch comes to a messy end. Then again, maybe we're in an age in which big platoon splits are survivable in the rotation. Bergmann struggled in the second half, but it wasn't because people were loading up on spot starts for bench lefties; those guys mostly don't exist any more, their roster spots having been taken by the extra men in the bullpen. As a fairly extreme fly-ball pitcher, Bergmann is going to have an especially hard time with the team's move to a park with shallower power alleys.

Micah Bowie Bats: L Throws: L Height: 6' 4" Weight: 220 Born: November 10, 1974 Age: 33

YEAR	TEAM	LVL	AGE	W	L	SV	G	GS	IP	H	BB	SO	HR	GB%	BABIP	STUFF	WHIP	ERA	PERA	EqERA	EqH9	EqBB9	EqSO9	EqHR9	VORP	SN/WX
2005	HAR	AA	30	1	1	1	10	0	16¹	16	3	19	1	66.7%	.349	-3	1.17	4.42	5.21	6.14	10.4	2.5	6.8	1.2	-0.9	—
2006	NWO	AAA	31	2	0	1	31	0	42¹	33	24	57	0	45.6%	.337	20	1.35	3.85	4.12	5.05	8.1	5.5	9.0	0.2	2.5	—
2006	WAS	MLB	31	0	1	0	15	0	19²	11	7	11	1	36.8%	.182	1	0.92	1.37	2.16	1.37	4.6	2.7	4.6	0.5	10.1	0.68
2007	WAS	MLB	32	4	3	0	30	8	57¹	55	27	42	7	44.1%	.296	-5	1.43	4.55	4.60	4.63	8.8	3.7	6.2	1.1	6.9	1.22
2008	COL	MLB	33	2	3	1	28	5	41²	48	21	27	5	45.8%	.313	-10	1.65	5.57	5.15	5.34	9.3	4.0	5.6	1.0	2.9	0.40

Breakout: 3% Improve: 22% Collapse: 66% Attrition: 49%   Comparables: Joe Gibbon, Bill Krueger, Scott Radinsky, Ray Moore

A bum hip and a sports hernia cut into what was an otherwise triumphant return engagement in the majors for Bowie, who proved to be a relatively rare sort of utility pitcher by transforming from LOOGY into rotation regular for six weeks. The Nats put him in the disposable pile, and he signed a minor league deal with the Rockies. Already something of a soft-tosser, moving to Coors Field isn't going to help him, as his line-drive rates were pretty scary last year; if you enjoyed the ride, now would be a good time to get off.

Matt Chico   Bats: L   Throws: L   Height: 6' 0"   Weight: 205   Born: June 10, 1983   Age: 25

YEAR	TEAM	LVL	AGE	W	L	SV	G	GS	IP	H	BB	SO	HR	GB%	BABIP	STUFF	WHIP	ERA	PERA	EqERA	EqH9	EqBB9	EqSO9	EqHR9	VORP	SN/WX
2005	LNC	A+	22	7	2	0	18	18	110	101	39	102	13	43.4%	.293	-10	1.27	3.76	5.27	4.78	8.4	4.7	4.8	1.5	9.3	—
2005	TEN	AA	22	1	7	0	10	10	52²	75	15	35	8	36.1%	.379	-40	1.71	5.98	11.13	10.43	14.0	3.4	3.5	2.4	-25.9	—
2006	LNC	A+	23	3	4	0	10	10	50²	48	11	49	5	43.5%	.293	-7	1.18	3.76	4.61	5.15	8.2	3.0	4.6	1.4	2.5	—
2006	TEN	AA	23	7	2	0	13	13	81¹	62	21	63	6	40.6%	.249	2	1.02	2.22	3.85	3.39	7.5	2.7	4.6	1.2	18.9	—
2006	HAR	AA	23	2	0	0	4	4	22²	28	8	13	3	46.7%	.347	-27	1.62	3.24	11.51	6.63	14.2	4.7	3.3	2.4	-2.2	—
2007	WAS	MLB	24	7	9	0	31	31	167	183	74	94	26	34.5%	.295	-12	1.54	4.63	5.58	5.18	9.7	3.4	4.8	1.3	11.1	2.96
2008	WAS	MLB	25	4	6	0	25	12	81²	88	35	50	13	40.7%	.286	-6	1.50	5.01	5.46	5.34	9.5	3.5	4.9	1.4	4.2	0.90

Breakout: 18%   Improve: 43%   Collapse: 39%   Attrition: 38%   Comparables: Allen Watson, Arthur Rhodes, Skip Lockwood, Buster Narum

Chico wound up leading the Nats staff in most of the counting stats as a rookie last year simply by surviving the season (save for a brief late-August demotion to have him clean up his mechanics). Acta handled Chico with admirable care, monitoring his pitch counts, pulling him early, and only twice letting him go through an opposing lineup more than three times. The August demotion delivered tangible results—he made three quality starts in his last six after his recall (compared to seven in his first 25), with 18 Ks and eight unintentional walks in 34 2/3 innings pitched. That's still not as many strikeouts as you'd expect from a lefty who throws in the low 90s, but Chico's heat isn't overpowering or endowed with any extra english. He's more talented than your typical crafty lefty in the making, but still lacks an out pitch, and his extreme fly-ball rates aren't usually survivable for a rotation regular who isn't fooling people at home plate. His upside is as a fourth starter, which is pretty much what he is now.

Jesus Colome   Bats: R   Throws: R   Height: 6' 2"   Weight: 200   Born: December 23, 1977   Age: 30

YEAR	TEAM	LVL	AGE	W	L	SV	G	GS	IP	H	BB	SO	HR	GB%	BABIP	STUFF	WHIP	ERA	PERA	EqERA	EqH9	EqBB9	EqSO9	EqHR9	VORP	SN/WX
2005	TBA	MLB	27	2	3	0	36	0	45¹	54	18	28	7	40.9%	.301	-16	1.59	4.57	5.20	5.10	9.4	3.4	5.1	1.1	-0.5	-0.31
2006	COH	AAA	28	1	1	0	25	0	33	35	15	25	3	47.3%	.308	-22	1.52	3.82	5.53	5.51	9.6	4.7	4.7	1.4	0.3	—
2007	WAS	MLB	29	5	1	1	61	0	66	64	27	43	6	37.7%	.291	-4	1.38	3.82	3.96	3.93	8.5	3.1	5.4	0.8	12.4	1.70
2008	WAS	MLB	30	2	2	2	30	0	35¹	37	15	24	5	42.3%	.293	-8	1.47	4.46	4.99	4.80	9.3	3.5	5.5	1.1	4.1	0.30

Breakout: 18%   Improve: 41%   Collapse: 42%   Attrition: 40%   Comparables: Bill Sampen, Manuel Aybar, Bob Stoddard, Bobby Thigpen

Colome was another of the Nats' nice little retreading experiments, with extra credit given to special assistant Jose Rijo, who helped Colome clean up his delivery on his off-speed pitches, producing a slider and change that the hurler had confidence in for the first time in his career. Those pitches didn't help him against lefties (.311/.369/.491), so he's still essentially a situational right-hander, but that has value in a pen as heavily worked as Washington's. Acta used Colome with the same regularity as Rauch and Rivera; his 61 games came in little more than four months, as Colome missed almost eight weeks with an abscess on his *nalgas*. We'll see how well he holds up in a repeat engagement.

Chad Cordero   Bats: R   Throws: R   Height: 6' 0"   Weight: 195   Born: March 18, 1982   Age: 26

YEAR	TEAM	LVL	AGE	W	L	SV	G	GS	IP	H	BB	SO	HR	GB%	BABIP	STUFF	WHIP	ERA	PERA	EqERA	EqH9	EqBB9	EqSO9	EqHR9	VORP	SN/WX
2005	WAS	MLB	23	2	4	47	74	0	74¹	55	17	61	9	37.7%	.221	7	0.97	1.82	2.86	3.05	6.3	1.8	6.5	1.1	20.7	4.55
2006	WAS	MLB	24	7	4	29	68	0	73¹	59	22	69	13	38.5%	.240	4	1.10	3.19	3.35	2.83	6.7	2.2	7.4	1.4	21.5	3.88
2007	WAS	MLB	25	3	3	37	76	0	75	75	29	62	8	38.7%	.306	4	1.39	3.36	4.36	3.65	9.0	3.0	7.1	1.0	17.3	3.59
2008	WAS	MLB	26	3	5	23	50	0	57²	53	19	48	7	40.5%	.274	5	1.25	3.67	3.94	3.96	8.1	2.7	6.6	1.1	12.1	1.60

Breakout: 11%   Improve: 26%   Collapse: 52%   Attrition: 24%   Comparables: Eduardo Rodriguez, Gene Nelson, Frank Smith, Willie Fraser

There are only so many variants to a high-wire act: with or without a net, poles, unicycles, bears in tutus, whatever. After a certain point, you lose that sense of suspense, as even the falls seem routine. That's Cordero's lot—he'll log saves as long as he's closing, and he'll blow his share, but his ability to do either remains unimpressive. Part of the problem is a creeping tendency to drop his arm slot, especially dangerous for a short righty who leaves too many fastballs over the plate trying to set up his out pitch, a biting slider. After deadline-deal chatter and an offseason in which several teams went closer shopping, it's notable that none of the Cordero rumors panned out. His narrow margin for glory becomes more slender still with the move to Nationals Park, a workplace unlikely to be as amenable to his too-frequent mistakes as RFK.

Ross Detwiler

Bats: R   Throws: L   Height: 6' 5"   Weight: 185   Born: March 6, 1986   Age: 22

YEAR	TEAM	LVL	AGE	W	L	SV	G	GS	IP	H	BB	SO	HR	GB%	BABIP	STUFF	WHIP	ERA	PERA	EqERA	EqH9	EqBB9	EqSO9	EqHR9	VORP	SN/WX
2007	NAT	Rk	21	0	0	0	4	4	12	11	3	15	1	46.9%	.323	-11	1.17	2.25	8.35	5.06	11.8	5.1	5.1	2.5	0.6	—
2007	POT	A+	21	2	2	0	5	4	21¹	27	9	13	1	50.7%	.356	-25	1.69	4.23	8.49	7.45	13.0	5.6	2.8	0.9	-4.0	—
2008	WAS	MLB	22	5	11	0	24	24	125²	154	76	68	22	46.8%	.311	-13	1.83	6.63	7.07	7.11	10.8	4.9	4.3	1.5	-17.8	-1.00

Breakout: 8%   Improve: 30%   Collapse: 34%   Attrition: 4%   Comparables: Cesar Ramos, Kelly Wunsch, Jason Young, Matt Burch

Detwiler made his first start of his final college season on a Thursday. That's important because there were no other big games going on, and with plenty of scouting directors in attendance, he fired seven two-hit innings while striking out 13, launching the hype train that eventually got him selected sixth overall last June. He was certainly the most complete left-hander in the draft, with a low- to mid-90s fastball, a power curve, a solid changeup, and the ability to throw strikes. While he already has one game of big league experience, he's unlikely to make an impact with the Nats until next year.

Glenn Gibson

Bats: L   Throws: L   Height: 6' 4"   Weight: 195   Born: September 21, 1987   Age: 20

YEAR	TEAM	LVL	AGE	W	L	SV	G	GS	IP	H	BB	SO	HR	GB%	BABIP	STUFF	WHIP	ERA	PERA	EqERA	EqH9	EqBB9	EqSO9	EqHR9	VORP	SN/WX
2007	VER	A-	19	4	3	0	12	12	58	47	15	58	3	43.0%	.293	4	1.07	3.10	6.08	6.08	10.2	4.3	4.8	1.6	-2.7	—
2008	TBA	MLB	20	5	11	0	24	24	122	156	65	68	23	42.6%	.319	-9	1.82	6.87	6.86	6.41	11.3	4.4	4.5	1.8	-18.2	-1.10

Breakout: 12%   Improve: 42%   Collapse: 32%   Attrition: 13%   Comparables: Chris Narveson, Joel Adamson, Jimmy Gobble, Matt Anderson

The son of former big leaguer Paul Gibson, Glenn has as much polish as any teenager around. He locates his pitches with the mastery of a veteran, changes speeds well, and knows how to use his wide-ranging arsenal to set up young hitters. He lacks that one plus offering that would cause him to be projected as more than a back—end starter, but he's as safe a bet as you can find for a teenager who hasn't pitched in a full-season league yet, and that was enough to fetch Elijah Dukes in a trade with Tampa Bay.

Enrique Gonzalez

Bats: R   Throws: R   Height: 5' 10"   Weight: 210   Born: July 14, 1982   Age: 25

YEAR	TEAM	LVL	AGE	W	L	SV	G	GS	IP	H	BB	SO	HR	GB%	BABIP	STUFF	WHIP	ERA	PERA	EqERA	EqH9	EqBB9	EqSO9	EqHR9	VORP	SN/WX
2005	TEN	AA	22	11	8	0	27	27	161¹	160	52	146	8	48.9%	.336	7	1.31	3.46	4.88	5.17	9.6	3.5	5.2	0.8	7.2	—
2006	TUC	AAA	23	4	3	0	10	10	60²	61	14	35	2	53.0%	.303	7	1.25	2.24	3.95	3.70	9.1	2.5	3.5	0.5	12.3	—
2006	ARI	MLB	23	3	7	0	22	18	106¹	114	34	66	14	46.1%	.299	2	1.39	5.67	4.29	5.18	8.9	2.4	5.0	1.0	1.8	0.68
2007	TUC	AAA	24	8	10	0	27	27	153²	186	61	118	11	48.0%	.356	2	1.61	5.15	5.12	5.93	10.1	3.8	5.0	0.8	-5.6	—
2008	WAS	MLB	25	4	7	0	36	12	97	107	41	62	12	47.2%	.303	-5	1.52	5.12	5.33	5.56	9.7	3.4	5.2	1.1	2.0	0.60

Breakout: 14%   Improve: 48%   Collapse: 23%   Attrition: 22%   Comparables: Armando Reynoso, Calvin Maduro, Rodrigo Lopez, Juan Dominguez

Gonzalez went into spring training with a shot at a job in the Arizona rotation, but was lit up badly enough to get sent down to Triple-A Tucson for the season. After a nondescript year as a Sidewinder, he was snagged off waivers in September when the Snakes wasted a roster spot by adding Bob Wickman. Finding a role for Gonzalez isn't easy, as he throws hard and doesn't allow much power, but lacks the reliable off-speed stuff and control to start in the majors. He's probably best suited to a middle relief, utility/swingman role in which he could soak innings thereby allowing Acta to reserve his better relievers for late-game machinations.

Joel Hanrahan

Bats: R   Throws: R   Height: 6' 3"   Weight: 215   Born: October 6, 1981   Age: 26

YEAR	TEAM	LVL	AGE	W	L	SV	G	GS	IP	H	BB	SO	HR	GB%	BABIP	STUFF	WHIP	ERA	PERA	EqERA	EqH9	EqBB9	EqSO9	EqHR9	VORP	SN/WX
2005	VRO	A+	23	1	0	0	5	5	21^1	25	11	25	5	34.4%	.357	-32	1.69	5.92	19.05	13.75	14.8	8.2	6.6	4.1	-16.0	—
2005	JAX	AA	23	9	8	0	23	21	111^2	118	55	102	17	44.1%	.323	-45	1.55	4.91	9.95	8.76	11.9	5.5	5.6	2.6	-34.7	—
2006	JAX	AA	24	7	2	0	12	12	66	49	38	67	4	46.7%	.288	10	1.32	2.59	5.96	4.42	9.5	6.2	6.6	1.1	7.5	—
2006	LVG	AAA	24	4	3	0	14	14	74^1	70	39	46	7	41.2%	.276	-10	1.47	4.49	4.63	5.72	8.1	5.0	3.8	1.1	-1.0	—
2007	COH	AAA	25	5	4	0	15	15	75^1	65	36	71	10	39.3%	.266	-11	1.34	3.71	5.58	5.30	8.6	4.7	6.2	1.7	2.4	—
2007	WAS	MLB	25	5	3	0	12	11	51	59	38	43	9	34.9%	.325	-3	1.90	6.00	7.24	6.27	10.3	5.7	7.0	1.6	-2.2	0.71
2008	WAS	MLB	26	2	3	0	15	7	43	42	24	36	6	39.4%	.290	0	1.54	5.10	5.41	5.46	8.7	4.6	6.7	1.2	2.1	0.40

Breakout: 28% Improve: 53% Collapse: 24% Attrition: 54%   Comparables: *Jesse Jefferson, Colby Lewis, Aaron Myette, Eric Hetzel*

Say this for a Hanrahan start—stuff happens; strikeouts, walks, homers, hits, runs . . . few areas of a scorecard remain untouched. He's a junkballer, having lost the plus stuff he had years ago with the Dodgers to injuries. He probably would have gotten the call earlier last year if not for a pulled groin that cost him a month. If he's going to stick, it may have to be in the pen.

Shawn Hill

Bats: R   Throws: R   Height: 6' 2"   Weight: 180   Born: April 28, 1981   Age: 27

YEAR	TEAM	LVL	AGE	W	L	SV	G	GS	IP	H	BB	SO	HR	GB%	BABIP	STUFF	WHIP	ERA	PERA	EqERA	EqH9	EqBB9	EqSO9	EqHR9	VORP	SN/WX
2006	HAR	AA	25	3	3	0	10	10	50	46	5	32	2	63.0%	.275	0	1.02	2.70	3.85	4.69	8.8	1.5	3.4	0.6	4.9	—
2006	WAS	MLB	25	1	3	0	6	6	36^2	43	12	16	2	50.8%	.323	1	1.50	4.66	4.66	4.71	10.4	2.5	3.7	0.5	4.3	0.94
2007	WAS	MLB	26	4	5	0	16	16	97^1	86	25	65	9	55.9%	.264	19	1.14	3.42	3.39	3.82	7.8	2.0	5.7	0.7	20.8	3.19
2008	WAS	MLB	27	6	7	0	28	18	115^2	121	32	69	12	52.9%	.292	4	1.32	4.03	4.29	4.43	9.2	2.2	4.8	0.9	17.7	2.50

Breakout: 9% Improve: 31% Collapse: 36% Attrition: 24%   Comparables: *Clay Parker, Steve Ontiveros, Bobby Locke, Dennis Lamp*

The Canadian ace (man, that was a *really* terrible brand of cheap beer in the 1980s, down there with Blatz) of the 2004 Olympics, Hill missed 2005 after TJ surgery on his elbow, came back well in 2006, then alternated good work with trips to the DL last season, struggling through problems with his right forearm and elbow and his left (non-throwing) shoulder. All were addressed surgically, and he should be ready to go in camp. Hill's sinker devours right-handers wholesale, but he can't get lefties to bite on his breaking stuff, though that didn't stop him from delivering 11 quality starts in his first 14. There's a lot to like, and though he should make a solid rotation regular if he can stay healthy, the Nats seem to harbor higher expectations.

John Lannan

Bats: L   Throws: L   Height: 6' 5"   Weight: 200   Born: September 27, 1984   Age: 23

YEAR	TEAM	LVL	AGE	W	L	SV	G	GS	IP	H	BB	SO	HR	GB%	BABIP	STUFF	WHIP	ERA	PERA	EqERA	EqH9	EqBB9	EqSO9	EqHR9	VORP	SN/WX
2005	VER	A-	20	3	5	0	14	11	63^1	74	31	41	5	48.6%	.325	-46	1.66	5.26	11.10	11.18	13.2	8.9	1.9	2.4	-32.4	—
2006	SAV	A	21	6	8	0	27	25	138^1	149	54	114	11	52.2%	.332	-34	1.47	4.76	8.35	8.65	12.0	6.1	3.7	1.8	-41.2	—
2007	POT	A+	22	6	0	0	8	8	50^2	31	15	35	3	61.9%	.207	-6	0.91	2.13	4.10	3.97	6.4	4.2	3.8	1.2	8.2	—
2007	HAR	AA	22	3	2	0	6	5	36	31	15	20	2	57.5%	.261	-5	1.28	3.25	4.60	4.32	8.6	4.6	3.2	0.8	4.7	—
2007	COH	AAA	22	3	1	0	7	6	38	30	12	19	1	47.5%	.240	2	1.11	1.66	3.34	2.68	7.3	3.2	2.9	0.5	12.0	—
2007	WAS	MLB	22	2	2	0	6	6	34^2	36	17	10	3	52.4%	.277	-11	1.53	4.15	4.77	4.50	9.3	4.0	2.6	0.8	5.8	0.95
2008	WAS	MLB	23	6	11	0	49	23	141	169	76	64	20	50.3%	.304	-20	1.74	6.15	6.42	6.68	10.6	4.4	3.7	1.3	-13.2	-0.60

Breakout: 8% Improve: 31% Collapse: 41% Attrition: 14%   Comparables: *Jim Crowell, Todd James, Jimmy Osting, John Courtright*

Another product of Dana Brown's canny drafting, Lannan came to the organization as an 11th-round pick in 2005. A storky lefty with velocity that's developed since he was picked, he still doesn't hit the low 90s with regularity, but he's got some useful off-speed stuff. His promotions might seem as aggressive as Michael O'Connor's were in 2006, but Lannan tore through one challenge after another, getting hitters to pound pitches into the dirt, and earning a call-up. His promotion was premature, and he should be allowed to regroup in the minors and gear up for his next shot.

Shairon Martis

Bats: R   Throws: R   Height: 6' 1"   Weight: 175   Born: March 30, 1987   Age: 21

YEAR	TEAM	LVL	AGE	W	L	SV	G	GS	IP	H	BB	SO	HR	GB%	BABIP	STUFF	WHIP	ERA	PERA	EqERA	EqH9	EqBB9	EqSO9	EqHR9	VORP	SN/WX
2006	AUG	A	19	6	4	0	15	15	76¹	76	21	66	3	35.5%	.322	-2	1.27	3.67	6.57	7.62	11.5	4.5	4.0	1.1	-15.1	—
2006	SAV	A	19	1	1	0	4	4	21²	23	4	14	2	33.8%	.323	-12	1.27	3.82	8.30	7.00	12.5	3.5	3.0	2.0	-2.8	—
2006	POT	A+	19	0	2	0	2	2	12²	9	3	7	0	36.1%	.250	7	0.98	2.95	3.80	4.91	7.4	3.3	3.3	0.0	0.8	—
2007	POT	A+	20	14	8	0	27	26	151	150	52	108	9	35.8%	.304	-13	1.34	4.23	6.08	7.23	10.3	4.8	3.7	1.2	-24.8	—
2008	WAS	MLB	21	5	10	0	31	21	123	145	64	69	25	37.0%	.295	-13	1.69	6.37	6.71	6.73	10.4	4.2	4.5	1.7	-12.5	-0.50

Breakout: 34% Improve: 67% Collapse: 18% Attrition: 17%   Comparables: Scott Mathieson, Victor Santos, Calvin Maduro, Ken Cloude

The hero of Holland's World Baseball Classic appearance after no-hitting Panama, this flying Dutchman (Curaçaoan, in point of fact) might share Bert Blyleven's fly-ball tendencies, but the comparison ends there. He's had persistent location problems and becomes overreliant on his low-90s fastball. Improving command of his off-speed stuff would make a big difference as far as his surviving the jump to Double-A, but his durability and velocity give him some upside.

Garrett Mock

Bats: R   Throws: R   Height: 6' 4"   Weight: 215   Born: April 25, 1983   Age: 25

YEAR	TEAM	LVL	AGE	W	L	SV	G	GS	IP	H	BB	SO	HR	GB%	BABIP	STUFF	WHIP	ERA	PERA	EqERA	EqH9	EqBB9	EqSO9	EqHR9	VORP	SN/WX
2005	LNC	A+	22	14	7	0	28	28	174¹	202	33	160	19	50.8%	.344	-10	1.35	4.18	6.11	5.80	11.0	3.0	4.7	1.4	-3.6	—
2006	TEN	AA	23	4	8	0	23	23	131¹	144	50	117	14	50.6%	.339	-24	1.48	4.94	7.49	7.56	11.4	4.0	5.4	1.8	-26.7	—
2006	HAR	AA	23	0	4	0	4	4	16	29	5	9	2	42.6%	.422	-65	2.13	10.69	15.90	17.61	17.6	3.5	2.9	1.8	-20.4	—
2007	HAR	AA	24	1	5	0	11	11	51¹	66	28	41	5	50.5%	.367	-23	1.83	5.79	8.34	8.76	12.5	5.5	4.6	1.4	-17.7	—
2007	NAT	Rk	24	0	2	0	3	2	7²	11	1	8	3	68.0%	.364	-102	1.56	4.68	27.63	19.06	23.8	4.8	4.8	12.7	-8.5	—
2008	WAS	MLB	25	4	8	0	28	16	100²	123	47	61	15	48.8%	.320	-9	1.68	6.04	6.42	6.50	10.7	3.8	4.9	1.3	-8.0	-0.20

Breakout: 32% Improve: 65% Collapse: 18% Attrition: 15%   Comparables: Trevor Hutchinson, Clay Hensley, Paul Thornton, David Abbott

A frustrating pitcher, Mock has lost ground two years in a row after what seemed like a breakout in the California League in 2005. At its root, the problem has been with his plant knee, as he hasn't bounced back well from surgery on the joint. The knee disabled him for the first three months last season. It has also cost him velocity (he used to touch the mid-90s), while also generating problems with his release point because his mechanics are now a bit crooked. There's some thought that he needs to apply himself toward resolving these problems, so while he's been added to the 40-man and had a few good moments in the AFL, he's also going to have to work to get any further.

John Patterson

Bats: R   Throws: R   Height: 6' 6"   Weight: 210   Born: January 30, 1978   Age: 30

YEAR	TEAM	LVL	AGE	W	L	SV	G	GS	IP	H	BB	SO	HR	GB%	BABIP	STUFF	WHIP	ERA	PERA	EqERA	EqH9	EqBB9	EqSO9	EqHR9	VORP	SN/WX
2005	WAS	MLB	27	9	7	0	31	31	198¹	172	65	185	19	31.9%	.287	27	1.19	3.13	3.65	3.42	7.9	2.7	7.7	0.9	50.9	6.66
2006	WAS	MLB	28	1	2	0	8	8	40²	36	14	32	4	31.9%	.302	29	1.11	4.42	3.24	4.32	7.6	1.7	8.2	0.9	5.7	1.08
2007	WAS	MLB	29	1	5	0	7	7	31¹	39	22	15	5	37.4%	.321	-19	1.91	7.48	7.50	7.67	11.1	5.4	4.0	1.4	-5.1	0.35
2008	WAS	MLB	30	4	5	0	21	11	72¹	75	29	55	11	36.5%	.291	1	1.44	4.79	5.16	5.10	9.1	3.3	6.2	1.3	6.0	0.90

Breakout: 12% Improve: 30% Collapse: 49% Attrition: 38%   Comparables: John Ericks, Gary Glover, Charlie Lea, Roger Mason

This will be Year Three since Patterson's 2005 breakout, and there's still no certainty about whether his elbow is really right. He was last year's Opening Day starter, but the weak joint gave out a month into the season, and he spent the next four trying to get back before finally going under the knife in September. When Patterson is healthy, his electric curveball/fastball mix is something special. He's supposed to be back, and he's supposed to be fine, but we've heard that before. Give it ten starts before you drink the Kool-Aid.

Jon Rauch

Bats: R   Throws: R   Height: 6' 11"   Weight: 250   Born: September 27, 1978   Age: 29

YEAR	TEAM	LVL	AGE	W	L	SV	G	GS	IP	H	BB	SO	HR	GB%	BABIP	STUFF	WHIP	ERA	PERA	EqERA	EqH9	EqBB9	EqSO9	EqHR9	VORP	SN/WX
2005	NWO	AAA	26	1	1	0	7	5	21¹	19	2	25	3	31.6%	.296	16	0.99	2.54	4.48	3.66	9.2	1.4	7.8	1.4	4.2	—
2005	WAS	MLB	26	2	4	0	15	1	30	24	11	23	3	25.8%	.250	4	1.17	3.60	3.37	3.60	7.2	3.0	6.3	0.9	6.1	0.44
2006	WAS	MLB	27	4	5	2	85	0	91¹	78	36	86	13	31.3%	.272	5	1.25	3.35	3.75	3.25	7.5	3.1	7.7	1.2	23.5	1.71
2007	WAS	MLB	28	8	4	4	88	0	87¹	75	21	71	7	35.9%	.274	13	1.10	3.61	3.04	3.80	7.6	1.8	6.8	0.7	19.3	2.91
2008	WAS	MLB	29	3	3	5	56	0	63²	61	20	53	8	37.7%	.283	4	1.28	3.75	4.12	4.02	8.5	2.6	6.7	1.1	12.1	1.10

Breakout: 10% Improve: 35% Collapse: 42% Attrition: 24%   Comparables: Bobby Howry, Bill Dawley, Todd Worrell, Edwin Nuñez

How much do we know about survivable relief workloads? Not a lot. The expectation that Rauch's 2006 workload would break him seemed to be coming true when he carried a 5.76 ERA a week into June. Then, over the next month he allowed just one lone run and altogether allowed only 2.7 runs per nine over the rest of the season. Over that stretch, his strikeout rate improved, he induced popups at one of the highest rates in the game, and he finished strong while topping his "dangerous" 85-game workload from 2006. Rauch has noted that he had more trouble staying healthy while starting—which involves structured rest patterns—and last year he was actually better on no days' rest than with any. Should Cordero ever get dealt, it might be a mistake to move Rauch into the closer role, as that might mean he'd have to wait around for leads. The problem with generalizations is that there are always exceptions; Livan Hernandez's arm didn't fall off, and thus far, in a different kind of usage pattern, neither has Rauch's. Those exceptions no more disprove what we know than individual supporting examples prove it; in both cases, we're left trolling for more data.

Tim Redding

Bats: R　　Throws: R　　Height: 6' 0"　　Weight: 195　　Born: February 12, 1978　　Age: 30

YEAR	TEAM	LVL	AGE	W	L	SV	G	GS	IP	H	BB	SO	HR	GB%	BABIP	STUFF	WHIP	ERA	PERA	EqERA	EqH9	EqBB9	EqSO9	EqHR9	VORP	SN/WX
2005	SDN	MLB	27	0	5	0	9	6	29²	40	13	17	7	46.8%	.337	-38	1.79	9.09	9.02	11.27	11.6	3.6	4.5	2.1	-18.0	-0.64
2005	COH	AAA	27	3	4	0	10	10	51¹	62	13	47	5	43.0%	.361	-1	1.46	5.09	6.38	6.04	11.7	3.0	6.0	1.1	-2.3	—
2006	CHR	AAA	28	12	10	0	29	28	187	168	56	148	21	46.4%	.272	-14	1.20	3.42	5.62	5.31	9.6	3.4	5.2	1.6	5.6	—
2007	COH	AAA	29	9	5	0	17	16	89²	110	24	63	9	46.0%	.348	-21	1.49	5.32	7.35	7.62	12.4	2.9	4.7	1.4	-18.6	—
2007	WAS	MLB	29	3	6	0	15	15	84	84	38	47	10	41.9%	.285	0	1.45	3.64	4.74	3.70	9.0	3.5	4.8	1.0	19.4	2.76
2008	WAS	MLB	30	4	6	0	28	13	88	98	34	55	13	44.1%	.298	-6	1.49	4.94	5.33	5.31	9.8	3.2	5.1	1.2	4.6	0.90

Breakout: 25%　Improve: 47%　Collapse: 29%　Attrition: 28%　　　Comparables: Wayne Garland, Jae Weong Seo, Chris Brock, Duane Pillette

Redding is a nice comeback story. Having worn out his welcome with three organizations in less than two years, he spent all of 2006 pitching for the greater glory of the Triple-A Charlotte Knights. The Nats' open casting call last year made for a can't-miss opportunity, and as the team reached almost 100 percent turnover in its rotation by midseason, Redding's number came up. He delivered eight quality starts in his first 15 after his July call-up, but got handled roughly on his second pass around the league. His relative durability has him solidly in the mix this spring as both Hill and Patterson work their way back from injury, but he allows far too many hard-hit liners to make anyone comfortable, which is a symptom of his failure to fool many hitters much of the time.

Saul Rivera

Bats: S　　Throws: R　　Height: 5' 11"　　Weight: 155　　Born: December 7, 1977　　Age: 30

YEAR	TEAM	LVL	AGE	W	L	SV	G	GS	IP	H	BB	SO	HR	GB%	BABIP	STUFF	WHIP	ERA	PERA	EqERA	EqH9	EqBB9	EqSO9	EqHR9	VORP	SN/WX
2005	HAR	AA	27	3	3	9	40	0	76²	72	20	70	3	66.1%	.309	-6	1.20	2.46	4.71	4.78	9.7	3.5	5.2	0.6	6.4	—
2006	NWO	AAA	28	1	1	1	12	2	28²	25	12	25	1	58.3%	.300	0	1.31	1.60	4.33	2.93	8.5	4.2	5.5	0.3	8.2	—
2006	WAS	MLB	28	3	0	1	54	0	60¹	59	33	41	4	47.0%	.288	-3	1.52	3.43	3.93	3.71	8.3	4.0	5.4	0.6	12.0	1.11
2007	WAS	MLB	29	4	6	3	85	0	93	88	42	64	1	52.8%	.311	14	1.40	3.68	3.53	3.76	8.6	3.6	5.9	0.1	21.0	2.56
2008	WAS	MLB	30	2	3	3	49	0	56²	58	27	39	5	51.8%	.300	-7	1.50	4.23	4.65	4.66	9.1	3.8	5.5	0.7	6.9	0.60

Breakout: 5%　Improve: 20%　Collapse: 51%　Attrition: 38%　　　Comparables: Mike Koplove, Mike Proly, Gene Harris, Dooley Womack

A fun little reliever, Rivera works carefully, loses nothing to working from the stretch, almost never makes a mistake inside, and never passes up an opportunity to pitch, making him a perfect middle-man in a world in which not every reliever has to be an overpowering, flame-throwing giant. Rivera fit especially well with Acta's habit of going to his bullpen early and often. Sadly, Stumpy's probably the guy in this pen most likely to see his value drop to waiver bait with the move to the new park; he was allowing just over two runs per nine in RFK against five-plus on the road with ghastly peripherals. He's surprised people so far, though, so let's watch and see.

Chris Schroder

Bats: R   Throws: R   Height: 6' 3"   Weight: 210   Born: August 20, 1978   Age: 29

YEAR	TEAM	LVL	AGE	W	L	SV	G	GS	IP	H	BB	SO	HR	GB%	BABIP	STUFF	WHIP	ERA	PERA	EqERA	EqH9	EqBB9	EqSO9	EqHR9	VORP	SN/WX
2005	HAR	AA	26	2	3	0	16	0	23	20	11	28	4	33.3%	.308	-14	1.35	4.70	7.63	7.08	9.7	6.2	7.1	2.2	-3.3	—
2005	NWO	AAA	26	2	0	4	19	0	23	21	15	29	6	34.4%	.283	-12	1.57	7.83	8.60	9.55	9.6	6.2	8.3	2.9	-9.5	—
2006	HAR	AA	27	2	0	1	9	0	14	18	6	13	2	42.6%	.356	-30	1.71	5.14	10.27	8.31	13.2	4.8	5.5	2.1	-3.9	—
2006	NWO	AAA	27	2	1	1	28	0	47¹	25	16	60	2	44.4%	.223	21	0.87	1.53	2.86	2.49	5.2	3.3	8.2	0.6	16.2	—
2006	WAS	MLB	27	0	2	0	21	0	28¹	23	15	39	7	29.4%	.281	9	1.34	6.36	5.16	5.90	7.4	4.0	10.6	1.9	-2.4	-0.36
2007	COH	AAA	28	2	2	1	26	0	33	23	18	45	0	40.3%	.333	28	1.24	1.64	3.97	2.97	7.7	5.6	9.5	0.3	8.9	—
2007	WAS	MLB	28	2	3	0	37	0	45¹	36	15	43	2	35.6%	.266	18	1.13	3.18	2.74	3.80	6.8	2.5	7.6	0.4	10.3	0.51
2008	WAS	MLB	29	2	2	3	46	0	49¹	45	23	48	6	38.4%	.285	6	1.36	4.12	4.36	4.43	8.0	3.7	7.8	1.1	7.3	0.60

Breakout: 27% Improve: 49% Collapse: 27% Attrition: 28%   Comparables: Rich Croushore, Steve Montgomery, Russ Springer, Al Reyes

Another beneficiary of Jose Rijo's wisdom, Schroder picked up some depth on his slider, and suddenly people couldn't lay off of it. By adding that pitch to his already decent velocity, Schroder went from mere organizational soldier to potential relief asset, a working example of how relievers can sometimes be conjured up out of almost any farm system. He'll have to earn his job in camp, but he's shown more than guys like Ryan Wagner have.

Ryan Wagner

Bats: R   Throws: R   Height: 6' 4"   Weight: 210   Born: July 15, 1982   Age: 25

YEAR	TEAM	LVL	AGE	W	L	SV	G	GS	IP	H	BB	SO	HR	GB%	BABIP	STUFF	WHIP	ERA	PERA	EqERA	EqH9	EqBB9	EqSO9	EqHR9	VORP	SN/WX
2005	CIN	MLB	22	3	2	0	42	0	45²	56	17	39	4	62.7%	.366	2	1.60	6.11	5.20	6.26	10.4	2.9	6.8	0.8	-4.7	-0.50
2006	LOU	AAA	23	1	3	1	35	0	38²	55	14	28	3	61.9%	.403	-37	1.81	6.36	9.35	9.75	14.2	4.0	4.8	1.2	-16.6	—
2006	WAS	MLB	23	3	3	0	26	0	30²	36	15	20	3	63.5%	.330	-13	1.66	4.69	5.64	5.93	10.4	3.9	5.3	0.9	-0.6	-0.64
2007	WAS	MLB	24	0	2	0	14	0	15²	20	8	9	2	53.6%	.340	-24	1.79	5.73	7.00	6.46	11.7	4.1	5.3	1.2	-1.2	-0.22
2008	WAS	MLB	25	1	1	1	20	0	24¹	26	11	18	2	54.1%	.318	-2	1.52	4.46	4.62	4.96	9.6	3.6	5.8	0.6	2.4	0.20

Breakout: 46% Improve: 70% Collapse: 12% Attrition: 35%   Comparables: Craig Anderson, Bob Shaw, Jamie Arnold, Duaner Sanchez

In 2003, Wagner struck out 148 batters in 79 1/3 innings for the University of Houston, was picked 14th overall in the amateur draft by Jim Bowden and the Reds, threw nine innings across two upper levels of the minors, and wrapped things up by striking out 25 men in his first 21 2/3 innings in the majors while allowing just 13 hits. He threw 16 2/3 strong frames in Triple-A the next year, but otherwise he hasn't been the same pitcher since. Last year, a torn labrum required surgery and cost him much of the season. The Nats are still carrying him on the 40-man and still expect him to be back, but the odds that surgery will put the snap back on his slider or get him throwing hard again seem decidedly poor.

LINEOUTS

Hitters

PLAYER	TEAM	LVL	AGE	PA	R	2B	3B	HR	RBI	BB	SO	SB-CS	EqBRR	AVG/OBP/SLG	MLVr	EqAVG/EqOBP/EqSLG	EqA	VORP
PH T. Batista	COH	AAA	33	120	14	7	1	6	22	8	16	1-0	0.4	.290/.350/.542	.257	.278/.333/.546	.293	10.5
	WAS	MLB	33	118	10	3	0	2	16	12	14	0-0	0.3	.257/.347/.347	-.073	.257/.353/.337	.253	1.0
CF R. Bernadina*	HAR	AA	23	415	58	15	2	6	36	38	80	40-13	0.3	.270/.340/.369	-.040	.236/.300/.332	.231	-12.1
	COH	AAA	23	53	6	3	0	0	1	9	11	0-1	-0.6	.167/.327/.238	-.246	.163/.321/.256	.205	-2.8
OF M. Daniel*	HAG	A	22	236	38	15	1	7	37	19	50	9-5	0.1	.290/.365/.473	.174	.233/.291/.367	.229	-4.9
	POT	A+	22	320	37	20	5	4	41	29	62	16-6	-1.4	.296/.361/.446	.171	.234/.289/.362	.230	-14.6
3B L. Davis*	HAG	A	23	385	47	29	4	16	56	25	86	7-6	-4.8	.290/.344/.534	.227	.235/.277/.412	.234	-0.3
	POT	A+	23	87	8	4	0	4	10	1	22	0-2	-0.2	.262/.267/.452	.006	.224/.230/.353	.193	-4.5
C D. Ivany	POT	A+	24	144	18	5	0	5	19	7	26	4-2	0.9	.275/.313/.427	.051	.230/.257/.341	.209	-6.0
	HAR	AA	24	83	8	4	0	0	7	7	21	1-1	0.1	.178/.244/.233	-.429	.162/.220/.203	.142	-10.3
INF D. Jimenez#	COH	AAA	29	204	28	13	2	7	25	31	19	2-2	-3.0	.368/.461/.591	.553	.341/.431/.572	.334	34.5
	WAS	MLB	29	128	14	7	0	2	10	21	22	2-1	-2.1	.245/.379/.373	.015	.262/.397/.408	.284	4.6
INF S. King	HAG	A	19	142	16	4	0	2	9	13	51	5-4	-0.7	.180/.261/.258	-.352	.153/.213/.221	.131	-17.2
	NAT	Rk	19	179	20	6	1	9	30	12	47	1-2	-1.2	.248/.315/.466	.093	.190/.230/.327	.188	-30.5
CF B. Watson*	COH	AAA	25	440	47	11	6	2	29	21	51	17-8	-2.8	.313/.347/.386	.059	.288/.322/.367	.243	2.8

Another deathless extra, **Tony Batista** adapted extremely well to a pinch-hitting role, delivering at a .280/.397/.380 clip when the only leather he had to wear was a batting glove. ⊘ **Rogearvin Bernadina** is a fifth outfielder who can play center well, but has that wee bit of pop that might create better job security. ⊘ A 2005 seventh-rounder out of UNC, **Mike Daniel** has added enough pop to his stroke to start earning consideration as a future big-league reserve. ⊘ **Leonard Davis** tried to move from third to second, but it didn't take. His selectivity at the plate leaves a lot to be desired. ⊘ With a strong arm, good receiving skills, and some pop in his bat, **Devin Ivany** might eventually make it up as a backup backstop. ⊘ After a year spent knocking around between the Nats' bench and Triple-A Columbus, where he had played a decade earlier as a Yankee farmhand, **D'Angelo Jimenez** will be in Cardinals camp as a dark-horse contender for work in their messy middle infield. ⊘ **Stephen King**'s tools tend toward power and strength instead of terror, but a loopy swing handicaps his offensive potential. It looks like he's going to be moved to second base despite a good arm. ⊘ A singles machine even Timbaland might envy, **Brandon Watson** cranked out a 43-game hitting streak for Columbus last year. He deserves a better shot, and should get one with the Phillies in spring training.

Pitchers

PLAYER	TEAM	LVL	AGE	W	L	SV	IP	H	BB	SO	HR	GB%	BABIP	STUFF	WHIP	ERA	PERA	EqERA	EqH9	EqBB9	EqSO9	EqHR9	VORP
W. Abreu	COH	AAA	30	3	0	5	52¹	24	20	82	2	41.4%	.227	29	0.84	1.20	2.85	2.15	5.2	3.8	9.8	0.5	19.3
	WAS	MLB	30	0	1	0	30¹	37	9	26	7	32.7%	.337	-12	1.52	5.94	7.60	6.67	11.2	2.4	7.3	2.1	-1.7
J. Albaladejo	HAR	AA	24	4	3	2	36²	30	15	35	3	54.8%	.278	-10	1.23	4.17	4.61	5.86	8.2	4.3	5.9	1.3	-1.0
	COH	AAA	24	3	0	0	24	14	7	21	2	57.8%	.194	1	0.88	1.13	3.29	1.93	5.8	3.1	5.8	1.2	9.5
	WAS	MLB	24	1	1	0	14¹	7	2	12	1	61.1%	.176	14	0.63	1.89	2.00	1.93	4.5	1.3	7.1	0.6	6.3
C. Booker	COH	AAA	30	2	5	30	58	37	39	83	4	33.1%	.289	23	1.31	2.95	4.32	3.79	6.9	6.6	9.9	1.0	11.0
H. Carrasco	LAA	MLB	37	2	1	0	38¹	44	23	33	8	43.1%	.298	-17	1.75	6.58	5.90	6.97	8.9	4.4	6.5	1.7	-9.2
	COH	AAA	37	1	2	0	18¹	23	15	10	4	37.5%	.322	-59	2.08	8.85	15.18	15.12	13.0	8.1	3.2	3.2	-17.7
A. Muñoz*	COH	AAA	25	3	1	0	52²	46	18	46	5	38.7%	.273	-11	1.21	2.56	4.63	3.75	8.6	3.4	5.7	1.3	10.3
J. Nuñez	HAG	A	21	4	6	0	106²	97	48	86	10	43.2%	.281	-25	1.36	4.05	6.40	6.64	9.2	6.3	3.6	1.7	-11.4
J. Simontacchi	WAS	MLB	33	6	7	0	70²	95	23	42	13	35.8%	.352	-19	1.67	6.36	8.24	7.60	12.3	2.5	5.2	1.6	-8.1
L. Speigner	WAS	MLB	26	2	3	0	40	58	23	19	4	46.8%	.367	-31	2.08	8.78	7.94	9.37	12.7	4.5	4.0	0.9	-14.4
	COH	AAA	26	3	4	0	49	63	20	33	1	55.1%	.367	-15	1.69	4.96	6.05	6.80	12.1	4.0	4.2	0.4	-6.4
B. Traber*	COH	AAA	27	2	3	0	40¹	40	7	29	2	52.7%	.309	-5	1.17	2.90	4.11	5.72	9.4	1.8	4.6	0.7	-0.5
	WAS	MLB	27	2	2	0	39²	50	13	27	4	48.6%	.359	-7	1.59	4.76	5.70	5.18	11.0	2.5	5.6	0.9	3.4
C. Willems	VER	A-	18	3	2	0	58²	55	26	31	2	57.0%	.285	-14	1.38	1.84	6.61	6.31	10.5	6.5	1.8	1.1	-4.0
Z. Zinicola	HAR	AA	22	0	4	6	57²	53	36	45	3	54.9%	.301	-10	1.54	5.46	5.70	6.41	9.4	6.6	4.9	0.8	-4.8

Winston Abreu's fastball has always taught the bitter lesson that cooking with gas can get you burned. He'll be serving his flambé in Japan this year for the Chiba Lotte Marines. ⊘ Another minor league free agent who broke out as a Nat, **Jonathan Albaladejo** relies on snappy breaking stuff to get by. He was dealt to the Yankees over the winter for

Tyler Clippard. ⊘ **Chris Booker** still throws exceptionally hard, but with so little movement and command that it's hard to imagine he'll ever stick. ⊘ Having once cashed in on a comeback with the Nats, **Hector Carrasco** gave it another shot after being released by the Angels last summer, but was so flat he didn't earn a call-up from Columbus. ⊘ Southpaw stick-to-itiveness defines the diminutive **Arnie Muñoz** in his pursuit of a big-league LOOGY role, that and a curveball he'll throw any time against anybody. ⊘ It wasn't a great first season in the Nats organization for former Dodgers prospect **Jhonny Nuñez**, but he flashes power stuff in the 90s with a promising slider. ⊘ Need can make consenting adults do strange things, like bringing in **Jason Simontacchi** and then wondering how that could possibly have been a good idea. ⊘ The other Rule 5 pick on last year's team, **Levale Speigner** stuck around just long enough to prove carrying him was an undue burden; the Nats worked out a deal to keep and then demote him. ⊘ His days as a prospect are long gone, but **Billy Traber** might have a shot to make the Yankees as their second lefty as a non-roster invitee this spring. ⊘ A Florida high school product picked in the first round in 2006, **Colton Willems** is your basic big kid with a good arm and above-average heat; he needs to work on his secondary stuff, but he has promise. ⊘ When drafted in 2006, **Zech Zinicola** was considered a potential sleeper to make the 2007 big-league roster, but he struggled with his control last year, spoiling those premature expectations. He rebounded somewhat with a decent but hardly overpowering Arizona Fall League campaign.

MANAGER: MANNY ACTA

YEAR	TEAM	W-L	Pythag +/−	Avg PC	100+ P	120+ P	QS	BQS	REL	REL w Zero R	IBB	Subs	PH	PH Avg	PH HR	SB2	CS2	SB3	CS3	SAC Att	SAC %	POS SAC	Squeeze	Swing	In Play
2007	WAS	73-89	4	88.2	28	0	59	6	587	372	43	102	291	.198	5	59	20	10	2	90	70.0%	26	0	121	92

As the essay states, Acta was an active manager, leading the majors in relievers used, as well as how often he used them. Acta's relievers worked consecutive days 183 times, 40 more than his nearest competitor, Bobby Cox. He also used more pinch-hitters than anyone except Tony La Russa, and led the majors in defensive substitutions. Unlike most managers who take over a team with little scoring prowess, however, Acta didn't over-invest in one-run strategies. The players who had some chance of stealing, like Logan, ran; everyone else stayed put. He holstered the hit-and-run for the most part and didn't call for an extraordinary number of bunts. Where he saw he could have a positive effect—on the pitching staff and the defense—he was active, otherwise, he stayed out of the way. If Acta could be this effective with the 2007 Nats, one wonders what he might be capable of when he actually has a genuinely good team to manage. In the meantime, there are few in the dugout as fun to follow.

The Tortoise, the Hare, and Juan Pierre

Translating Baserunning into Runs

Dan Fox

> *In this game, you have to think about making plays, you can't worry about making mistakes.
> At times, a guy will get thrown out, but in the bigger scheme, the bases we're going to take will far
> outweigh that occasional misread. And it depends on what you call a mistake. If the outfielder puts
> the ball right on the money, he's out by a quarter-step and it's a bang-bang play, that's not a mistake.
> That's baseball. If you're out by four or five steps, it's ugly, it's a misread, but in the big picture,
> that aggressiveness is going to help us more than the occasional blunder will hurt.*
> **—ANGELS MANAGER MIKE SCIOSCIA,** as quoted by the *Los Angeles Times* in 2007

What makes a good baserunner? If you ask thinking fans, you'll likely get some combination of attributes including pure speed, quick thinking, daring, and the ability to balance risk and reward. Throughout the history of baseball, fans and even teams have relied largely on observation and intuition to determine just who is and isn't a good baserunner. The powers that be never saw fit to attempt to quantify baserunning outside of the rather narrow categories of stolen bases (consensus on the definition of the statistic was reached in 1898) and caught stealing (not tracked until 1912).

To be fair, there was a brief moment in early 1880 when former English cricket star Harry Wright proposed that a new statistic, "Total Bases Run," (sometimes also referred to as "Bases Touched") be tabulated to give individual players credit for each base gained during a game (save for reaching base on a force out). Wright's idea was implemented, but the stat was dropped after the season, leaving Chicago's Abner Dalrymple, who accumulated 501 Total Bases Run, as the sole league leader and, by default, career leader.

Time moves on and the availability of play-by-play data in the modern era has made the quantification of baserunning not only possible, but meaningful, as evidenced by James Click's 2005 essay in these pages titled "Station to Station: The Expensive Art of Baserunning." In this essay, we'll go a step beyond—actually four steps beyond—that work and discuss five metrics that, when combined, as they are in the player statistics under the column EqBRR (Equivalent Baserunning Runs), give us a fairly complete picture of baserunning. We'll still use subjective measures, as indeed we should, but now we'll have a more objective measure we can use to complement and augment our judgment. In that sense, you can think of it as a reincarnation of Harry Wright's Total Bases Run, albeit in a more sophisticated form.

Laying a Foundation

The gory details of all five of these metrics have been discussed in detail in my "Schrödinger's Bat" column on Base ballProspectus.com over the past two years, so I'll only touch on the framework briefly before diving into descriptions and results.

The framework is built on the foundations of Run Expectancy, comparison to a baseline, and the importance of context. We'll take them one at a time.

Run Expectancy (RX). Readers familiar with our work no doubt understand the usefulness of this tool in a whole host of applications. For the rest, RX is simply an accounting of the number of runs an average team would be expected to score from a particular point in an inning going forward. When calculated for all 24 possible base/out combinations you end up with a matrix like the one shown in Table 1 for the major leagues in 2007.

Table 1. 2007 Run Expectancy Matrix

Base/Out	0	1	2
xxx	0.54	0.28	0.11
1xx	0.93	0.54	0.24
x2x	1.19	0.73	0.35
xx3	1.41	0.99	0.39
12x	1.51	0.91	0.47
1x3	1.79	1.22	0.51
x23	2.12	1.44	0.64
123	2.35	1.61	0.79

For the baserunning framework, the trick is in crediting runners with how their actions on the bases change the expected number of runs for their team in that inning. For example, imagine Jose Reyes is on first with no one else on and nobody out, and Luis Castillo singles to left field. Reyes may be content with stopping on second but may try to take the extra base and motor around to third. If he stops at the second the RX for his team is 1.51 runs according to Table 1 (runners on first and second, none out). If, however, he makes it to third, his team's RX will be 1.79 (runners on the corners, none out). By taking the extra base, Reyes would thus raise the expected number of runs his team would score in that inning by +0.28. As a result, if Reyes takes the chance and makes it, we'll credit him with those +0.28 runs. We won't, however, give him any credit for stopping at second, since it was Castillo who essentially forced Reyes into that position. If, on the other hand, Reyes is thrown out trying to advance to third, the RX at the end of the play is 0.54 runs (runner on first with one out). The difference between this and 1.51 is -0.97 runs, which will be debited from Reyes' season total.

Fundamentally, it is the crediting and debiting of all of these individual events that gets us to a total number of theoretical runs contributed by each runner. Keep in mind that these are not actual runs. We are not concerned with whether or not the runner actually ended up scoring. We are only interested in is how his actions put his team in a better position to score potential runs.

Although the example above involved advancing on a hit, the same methodology applies to advancing on ground outs, fly balls, stolen base attempts, pickoffs, wild pitches, passed balls, and even balks. We can assign value to each outcome by comparing the RX after the play with the RX that would have resulted from the minimum necessary movement on the part of the runner. For example, a runner needn't leave his base on a wild pitch or a fly out, but he must attempt to advance one base on a single, two bases on a double, and so forth. Runners are not penalized for being forced out on groundballs to the infield, but are credited if they avoid an out in such situations. It should be noted that we use RX values averaged over a three-year period for each league in order to increase the sample size of the data.

Comparison to a Baseline. The second key concept in the framework involves comparing the credits and debits discussed above to a baseline. In doing so, we hope to uncover what the runner's contribution is above and beyond what an average runner's would be. To illustrate, let's go back to our scenario above in which Jose Reyes had the option of attempting to go from first to third on a single to left with nobody out. As shown in Table 2, runners in that situation made it to third base 14.7 percent of the time, stayed at second 84.4 percent of the time, came all the way around to score 0.5 percent of the time, and ran into an out 0.5 percent of the time.

If Reyes indeed makes it to third we don't want to credit him for that portion of the gain in RX represented by the av-

Table 2. Advancing from First to Third on a Single

Hit To	Outs	2nd	3rd	Scores	Out
Center	0	68.5%	30.0%	0.4%	1.0%
Center	1	70.8%	27.8%	0.5%	0.9%
Center	2	66.3%	31.7%	1.1%	1.0%
Left	0	84.4%	14.7%	0.5%	0.5%
Left	1	84.5%	14.4%	0.4%	0.7%
Left	2	81.1%	17.9%	0.3%	0.6%
Right	0	64.7%	33.8%	1.0%	0.5%
Right	1	60.0%	38.6%	0.5%	0.9%
Right	2	52.9%	44.7%	1.4%	0.9%

erage runner. To factor that portion in we can combine our calculations above with the percentages in Table 2 to calculate an expected number of runs over all four outcomes for this situation (mathletes can find the formula we use at the end of this essay). When we do so we find that the average runner would be expected to contribute +0.04 runs in this situation. Let's assume Reyes, being the speedy runner he is, did in fact take third. We then subtract the expected runs from +0.28 to credit him with +0.24, or about a quarter of a run.

Once again this process is followed on all forms of advancement from advancing on hits to advancing on ground-outs, fly outs, wild pitches, passed balls, and balks. We do not, however, apply this methodology to stolen base attempts, as attempted steals, and for that matter pickoffs, are initiated purely (well, almost purely) by the runner. In these cases, it doesn't seem right to debit a runner for not attempting to steal. Sometimes a manager will force a runner to run by calling for a hit and run. In those cases, if the batter swings through the pitch and the runner is thrown out, the runner will be dinged for the caught stealing, but this apparent injustice tends to evens out as the runner will receive the credit if the batter puts the ball in play and the runner advances to third or comes all the way around to score.

Context Matters. One of the many problems with the original formulation of Total Bases Run was that it lacked context. In other words, it had nothing to say about the quality of the bases the runner gained, or in what circumstances they were gained. In our baserunning framework, we strive to add as much context as is reasonable. For example, we look not only at the beginning and ending base states, but also the number of outs and which fielder fielded the ball. Knowing these last two are particularly important since, as illustrated in Table 2, the decisions runners make are largely predicated on these factors. The added advantage of accounting for the fielder who fielded the ball is that it similarly accounts for the handedness of the batter. This way, a player who is followed in the lineup by a left-handed pull hitter doesn't receive unwarranted credit for advancing from first to third on all those balls hit to right field. For two of the metrics described below we also take the home park of the runner into account since advancement on hits and fly balls are affected by park dimensions (which was illustrated beautifully in the 2007 postseason as Fenway Park's tiny left field was juxtaposed against the expansive outfield in Denver).

Taking context into account allows us to properly value runner advancement. For example, consider a runner on second base with nobody out. Believe it or not, when the batter hits a groundball to short that runner will advance to third 48.1 percent of the time. In doing so, he will gain +0.26 runs for his team at the risk of costing them -0.19 runs if he is thrown out. When the same scenario occurs with one out, the runner will also advance just over 48 percent of the time, but this time gain his team a mere +0.04 runs. The reason for this is that moving a runner from second to third on a groundout when there are zero outs, where he can now score on a sacrifice fly, is far more valuable than doing so when there is already one out. Factoring in the difference between these scenarios allows us to properly credit runners who make the more appropriate risk/reward decision. Finally, one of the realities that make taking the context into account so important is that in most cases runners don't have as many opportunities to advance as you may think (opportunities are defined for each metric in the following section). In 2007 the leader in number of opportunities to advance on hits was Juan Pierre with 75, on groundouts Brian Roberts led with 67 opportunities, and on fly outs Curtis Granderson with led with 56. These are the leaders; most regular players will be in the 20 to 30 range for all three types of advancement. With such small sample sizes, it is essential to adjust for context to prevent a cluster of similar scenarios (say, runner on first, ball hit to right field) from leading us astray in our determination of who is and who is not a good baserunner.

Of course, while we're considering much of the context, we don't have it all. Particularly, we don't consider the score (an extra base gained in a 1-0 game is more valuable than an extra base gained in a 10-1 contest), nor do we adjust the RX matrix for the run environment either at the team level or at the level of the actual play where the pitcher, upcoming hitters, weather and a thousand other factors have influence. It's important to remember that this framework is based on a model and as with any model is only an approximation of reality.

The Metrics

Now that you know the methodology behind them, let's define each of the five metrics.

Equivalent Air Advancement Runs (EqAAR). This measures the contributions of runners advancing, or not advancing as the case may be, on outs in the air. While this primarily includes sacrifice flies, it also incorporates opportunities to advance from second to third or first to second on a fly out in the following scenarios:

- Runner on first with second and third unoccupied, less than two outs

- Runner on second but not third, less than two outs
- Runner on third, less than two outs

This metric is park adjusted using a three-year park factors specific to each of the three outfield positions at each park. For example, a runner advancing on a fly ball to left field at the smaller Fenway Park receives more credit than doing so at spacious Coors Field. The range for this EqAAR is roughly -3.0 to +2.5 runs in a given season for individual players. Carl Crawford led the majors in EqAAR in 2007 by contributing +1.8 runs.

Equivalent Ground Advancement Runs (EqGAR). This measures the contributions of runners advancing on groundballs that were turned into outs, including sacrifice bunts. As such, you can think of it as the runner contribution to many of the so-called "productive outs" you hear about in the mainstream media. It includes the following opportunities:

- Runner on first with second and third unoccupied, less than two outs
- Runner on second but not third, less than two outs
- Runner on third, less than two outs

This metric is not park adjusted and its range is on the order of -2.0 to +4.0 runs per season. The 2007 leader in this category was Dave Roberts at +2.8 runs.

Equivalent Stolen Base Runs (EqSBR). This measures the contributions of runners resulting from stolen base attempts and times picked off when the player in question was not the trailing runner on a double or triple steal. That exception, as well as the inclusion of pickoffs, explains why some of the stolen base opportunity totals in Table 3 don't match the sum of that player's stolen bases and times caught stealing. The typical range for EqSBR is -6.0 to +5.0 runs per season, although the numbers have been rising in recent years as the overall stolen base percentage in the major leagues continues to climb. The 2007 leader in this metric was Brian Roberts at +6.0 runs.

Equivalent Hit Advancement Runs (EqHAR). This measures the contributions of runners who have the opportunity to advance on hits in the following scenarios:

- Runner on first, no runner on second, and the batter singles
- Runner on first, no runner on second, and the batter doubles
- Runner on second, no runner on third, and the batter singles

This metric is park adjusted using the same three-year park factor specific to each of the three outfield positions that is used in EqAAR. The typical range for this metric is -

Table 3. The Best and Worst in EqBRR for 2007

Name	Team	Opp	EqGAR	Opp	EqSBR	Opp	EqAAR	Opp	EqHAR	Opp	EqOAR	EqBRR
Juan Pierre	LAN	38	0.3	83	4.2	35	1.5	75	5.1	645	0.6	11.6
Luis Castillo	MIN/NYN	46	1.0	22	0.6	45	1.1	61	3.1	348	3.8	9.5
Jose Reyes	NYN	62	0.6	107	2.2	39	0.0	46	3.6	647	2.5	8.8
Brian Roberts	BAL	67	0.6	59	6.0	32	-0.4	56	2.6	616	-0.4	8.4
Coco Crisp	BOS	36	1.1	36	2.1	30	1.6	47	1.6	472	1.4	7.9
Grady Sizemore	CLE	44	0.5	45	-0.2	43	1.7	54	4.0	621	1.2	7.2
Jimmy Rollins	PHI	38	0.1	49	4.0	52	0.5	51	3.4	615	-0.8	7.2
Dave Roberts	SFN	41	2.8	38	2.9	33	-0.3	40	1.8	433	-0.1	7.1
Johnny Damon	NYA	41	0.3	30	3.3	38	1.7	59	1.9	539	-0.4	7.0
Ichiro Suzuki	SEA	58	-0.5	46	2.6	54	0.6	73	2.3	738	1.7	6.8
Casey Kotchman	ANA	25	0.1	7	-2.6	31	0.7	40	-4.7	369	0.4	-6.1
Mike Lowell	BOS	22	-0.4	5	-0.4	36	-2.1	41	-2.5	430	-0.8	-6.2
Carlos Delgado	NYN	30	-0.4	1	-0.2	32	-2.7	37	-3.6	381	-0.4	-7.3
Jorge Posada	NYA	34	-1.3	3	-0.1	40	-0.6	56	-4.0	494	-1.6	-7.6
Ryan Garko	CLE	20	-1.0	1	-0.4	27	0.4	52	-7.3	389	-0.5	-8.8

5.0 to +5.0 runs in a given season. Of all the metrics discussed here, this is the most persistent from year to year, both because of the larger number of opportunities (which produce a larger statistical sample), and because it involves a higher degree of skill. The 2007 leader in EqHAR was Juan Pierre at +5.1 runs.

Equivalent Other Advancement Runs (EqOAR). This measures the contributions of runners who take advantage of passed balls, wild pitches, and balks. Research has shown that runners have more influence on these events than one might think. Better baserunners cause more balks, as most balks result from an attempt to deceive the runner. Better baserunners also cause more passed balls and wild pitches, in a certain sense, as passed balls and wild pitches are only scored as such if the runner attempts to advance. As with the other metrics, EqOAR takes into consideration the number of opportunities the runner had, thus runners who reach base more frequently are expected to advance more often and do not receive extra credit for doing so. In 2007, Luis Castillo led baseball with +3.8 EqOAR, but the typical range is -3.0 to +3.0 runs per season.

The Results

These five metrics are added together to produce the numbers you see in the EqBRR (Equivalent Baserunning Runs) column. To spare you from having to sift through all of the player records (fun as that might be), Table 3 lists the top ten and bottom five players at the major league level in EqBRR.

Juan Pierre takes the title at +11.6 runs, which is almost two runs more than the next runner. Chone Figgins, who led the majors at +9.2 in 2006, fell to eleventh in 2007 because of his poor showing in EqOAR, while Luis Castillo, who split the 2007 season between Minnesota and New York, places second at +9.5 primarily on the strength of his major league-best EqOAR. There are no real surprises on this list

as speedsters such as Jose Reyes (+8.8) and Jimmy Rollins (+7.2) and runners with good reputations including Grady Sizemore (+7.2) and Dave Roberts (+7.1) help round out the top ten.

On the bottom of the list we find the Indians' Ryan Garko (-8.8), who had a disastrous season on the bases and who finished over a run worse than any other player. Garko led the major leagues by being thrown out five times while trying to advance on hits and failed to advance beyond the minimum number of bases in 42 of his 52 opportunities. Jorge Posada (-7.6), Carlos Delgado (-7.3), and Mike Lowell (-6.2) are no strangers to the bottom five, and routinely cost their teams around five runs on the bases over the course of a full season.

In between, several players did well despite not coming immediately to mind as plus baserunners. Alex Rodriguez placed 18th at +5.2 runs, picking up half his total in EqHAR. Gary Sheffield was 21st at +4.9. Kevin Youkilis was 24th at +4.5. However, all three were closer to average in the preceding seasons, clustering in the -0.4 to +1.5 range. One younger player who is gaining a deserved reputation as a good baserunner is Royals right fielder Mark Teahen, who followed up a +4.2 mark in 2006 with a +3.1 result in 2007. On the other hand, Dodgers catcher Russell Martin, who has developed a similarly positive reputation on the bases and posted an ever-so-slightly positive mark in 2006 (+0.3), finished at -2.2 last year while posting negative values in four of the five metrics. Two other players who saw a dramatic downturn in their EqBRR last year were Derrek Lee and Felipe Lopez. Lee had been roughly average in 2005 and 2006 (+0.5 and 0.0, respectively), but fell to -5.2 in 2007, recording negative values in all five metrics. Lopez, meanwhile, finished at -3.2 last year after recording a combined +3.5 in 2006 with the Reds and Nats and +0.4 in 2005 with the Reds. For the most, however, as you peruse the EqBRR totals throughout the book, you'll find that your notions about

Table 4. The Best and Worst for 2005 through 2007

Name	Opp	EqGAR	Opp	EqSBR	Opp	EqAAR	Opp	EqHAR	Opp	EqOAR	EqBRR
Juan Pierre	158	3.9	243	7.8	110	2.9	178	8.6	1285	3.4	26.6
Chone Figgins	122	7.0	202	3.2	120	4.2	167	12.0	1049	0.1	26.5
Jose Reyes	168	5.0	270	4.7	114	2.6	147	7.3	1156	3.1	22.6
Jimmy Rollins	134	2.3	140	10.8	136	2.4	185	4.3	1272	0.2	20.2
Grady Sizemore	136	2.0	109	-0.2	123	1.7	180	10.4	1307	4.9	18.7
Ichiro Suzuki	165	1.5	139	11.1	149	2.6	208	1.4	1460	1.6	18.2
Johnny Damon	132	0.9	86	6.4	128	5.6	177	5.2	1218	-0.3	17.7
Orlando Cabrera	95	2.7	80	5.0	98	-0.5	180	7.7	1073	0.1	15.0
Dave Roberts	108	4.2	134	6.0	109	0.1	132	3.4	926	0.1	13.9
Carlos Beltran	61	0.9	67	4.2	94	3.0	131	5.6	961	0.1	13.8
Mark Loretta	61	-0.5	24	-1.4	89	-1.3	144	-9.7	1000	0.9	-12.2
Paul Konerko	71	-2.0	2	-0.5	95	-0.9	147	-7.6	914	-1.6	-12.6
Bengie Molina	55	-0.7	5	-1.2	49	-2.6	82	-8.2	609	-0.2	-12.9
Pat Burrell	45	-1.3	3	-0.8	63	-1.5	117	-8.3	746	-1.5	-13.3
Jorge Posada	72	-2.0	8	-0.7	90	-0.7	144	-9.4	917	-2.4	-15.2

who is and who isn't a good baserunner line up pretty well with the numbers on the page.

Beyond confirming that Jorge Posada is a bad baserunner and Juan Pierre is a good one, facts which were already in our possession, this EqBRR helps us estimate the impact that baserunners can have. As ten runs are roughly equal to one win, we can see that, over the course of a season, a good runner can be worth a win or more, while a poor runner may cost his team almost as much. Of course, even the nearly 20-run difference between Pierre and Posada on the bases isn't enough close the gap in their production at the plate, as Posada was worth 57.2 runs more than Pierre last year according to VORP, which already accounts for stolen bases. Subtract Pierre's 4.3-run advantage over Posada in EqSBR from their overall baserunning numbers and he only makes up 14.9 of those 57.2 runs, meaning Posada was still more than four wins runs better than Pierre on offense in 2007.

If we expand our view to multiple seasons, we find that the range of impact shrinks, just as variability is wont to do when a sample is enlarged. This is illustrated in Table 4, which lists the overall leaders and trailers at the major league level over the last three seasons combined.

While we've only applied these metrics to individuals thus far, they also have meaning at the team level. When we add it all up, the Philadelphia Phillies come out on top with a total EqBRR of +14.9 in 2007 with the Texas Rangers a close second at +12.7 and the Los Angeles Dodgers at +9.6. Meanwhile the Astros finished well behind the pack at -17.9 runs and in what was a bad year on the bases in the NL Central, the Cubs (-11.7), Pirates (-11.1), and Cardinals (-10.8) took the next three spots. Overall, value range from best to the worst teams reveals that baserunning can have an impact worth around 30 equivalent runs or three wins.

As you browse through this book, you will notice that we have calculated EqBRR for the minor leagues and Mexican League as well (although not the Japanese leagues). The only difference in the way these statistics are formulated is that EqAAR and EqHAR are not park adjusted as they are for the major leagues. Since players below the major league level change leagues frequently, we thought it would be informative to show the top and bottom baserunners across all level of the minors in Table 5.

Our champion, 24-year-old outfielder Cesar Quintero (+10.9), split the 2007 season almost evenly between low-A Lexington and high-A Salem in the Astros' organization, totaling +6.8 EqBRR at the former stop and +4.1 at the latter. In second place, we find one of the principals of the deal that sent Edgar Renteria to the Tigers in Gorkys Hernandez (+10.2), who claimed the top spot at his level (low-A). Hernandez was excellent at going from first to third and from second to home on hits (he easily topped his level in EqHAR) and stole bases at an 83 percent rate, good for +2.5 runs.

Mets second-base prospect Hector Pellot (-9.5) had a turnaround season offensively at the tender age of 20, but the same cannot be said of his work on the bases. He finished dead last by managing to be caught stealing 18 times and picked off another five times. Perhaps incredibly, he was actually picked off five other times, but was either safe on throwing errors or charged with a caught stealing. At 27 years old, former *Moneyball* pinup Jeremy Brown found himself at the bottom of the list of triple-A baserunners, costing Sacramento 8.8 runs, 7.6 of those while attempting, or not attempting, to advance on hits. Brown was thrown out four times in 30 opportunities and only advanced farther than the batter pushed him twice, resulting in an EqHAR total almost 2.5 runs worse than anyone else at his level. Attempting to take the extra base just six times over a full season and still getting thrown out two-thirds of the time requires a unique lack of baserunning skill.

Future Directions

The baserunning framework presented in this essay is a work in progress and has evolved since its inception in early 2005. While it now includes many aspects of baserunning, it

Table 5. The Best and Worst in EqBRR at the Minor League Level in 2007

Name	Affil	Opp	EqGAR	Opp	EqSBR	Opp	EqAAR	Opp	EqHAR	Opp	EqOAR	EqBRR
Cesar Quintero	HOU	41	2.3	40	5.2	20	0.2	33	2.0	235	1.2	10.9
Gorkys Hernandez	ATL	33	-0.1	75	2.5	33	1.0	57	4.7	334	2.1	10.2
Wayne Lydon	TOR	37	2.3	41	1.8	45	0.1	47	3.6	356	2.1	9.8
Eric Reed	FLA	21	0.4	37	5.7	15	1.2	18	1.8	184	0.0	9.0
Mitchell Hilligoss	DET	31	1.1	43	1.8	39	1.9	45	2.4	374	1.7	8.9
Freddy Guzman	TEX	31	1.2	77	3.0	43	2.4	46	2.6	375	-0.6	8.6
Starling De Los Santos	MIN	19	0.0	38	3.3	14	1.0	15	1.9	186	2.3	8.5
Matthew Angle	BAL	23	1.0	41	4.8	30	1.6	24	1.0	230	-0.2	8.3
Daniel Figueroa	BAL	39	2.0	50	-0.5	30	0.2	39	4.0	331	2.4	8.2
Brent Lillibridge	ATL	26	0.7	58	1.5	26	0.1	30	1.5	290	4.3	8.1
Miguel Rodriguez	ARI	18	-0.3	12	-6.7	9	-1.5	16	-1.0	147	0.8	-8.8
Jeremy Brown	OAK	10	0.2	0	0.0	17	-1.1	30	-7.6	177	-0.3	-8.8
Carlos Sosa	SFN	40	-0.1	24	-4.0	24	0.1	64	-3.1	363	-1.9	-8.9
Hector Gomez	COL	33	0.3	50	-7.7	35	-0.3	53	-1.1	432	-0.5	-9.3
Hector Pellot	NYN	33	1.0	60	-5.2	16	-1.8	39	-2.0	292	-1.5	-9.5

is not complete. Accounting for hit-and-runs in EqSBR and EqHAR, looking at the different probabilities inherent in sacrifice hits within EqGAR, and examining differences in probabilities based on hit types (line drives versus groundballs, for example) when calculating EqHAR are all refinements that we'll hope to make in the future.

There is also hope that we will eventually be able to incorporate these baserunning values into VORP and WARP. Keith Woolner's Win Expectancy Framework, also discussed in the 2005 Prospectus, helps makes this possible and so it is certainly reasonable to expect movement in that direction as well.

One-hundred and twenty-seven years ago, Harry Wright planted the seeds of a good idea. Although that seed didn't sprout, it turns out that he was right to view baserunning as a quantifiable aspect of player performance and to suggest that players be given credit for putting their teams in a better position to score runs, which ultimately helps them win games. By including EqBRR among our offensive statistics, we believe we have taken a large step toward accomplishing that goal.

The Math. Our teachers always told us to show our work, so here's the math we skipped over in our Reyes example above.

$$ExR = \sum_{i=1}^{n} pr$$

We want to calculate the expected number of runs (call it *ExR*) for a runner in Reyes' situation and we need to incorporate all four possible outcomes: stopping at second, advancing to third, scoring, and being thrown out. Since we know the probability (call it *p*) of each outcome occurring for an average runner (Table 2), and since we can derive a run value (*r*) for each of those outcomes from Table 1, we have everything we need to use the formula:

First we need to calculate each of our four run values

from Table 1. If the runner stops at second there's no credit or debit, so $r_1 = 0$. Easy. In the explanation above we already calculated the run value for advancing to third and so $r_2 = 0.28$. If the runner scores the new run value will be calculated as 1 (in order to credit the run) plus the new RX value of a runner on first and nobody out (0.93) minus the RX if Reyes had not tried to advance (1.51). So $r_3 = 1.93 - 1.51$ or 0.42 runs. Finally, we calculated the run value associated with getting thrown out above and so $r_4 = -0.97$.

As our last step we'll expand our formula above, plugging in the *p* values from the row in Table 2 signifying a ball hit to left with zero outs. When we do so we end up with:

$$ExR = (.844 \times 0) + (.147 \times 0.28) + (.005 \times 0.42) + (.005 \times -0.97)$$

The result is *ExR* = 0.0385 which we can round up to 0.04. This is the number of runs an average runner would be expected to gain in this scenario and which we'll decrement from Reyes' actual outcome.

Expanding the Cannon
Quantifying the Impact of Outfield Throwing Arms

Dan Fox

To date, the effort spent on assessing defensive performance has focused on converting batted balls into outs, essentially measuring a player's range and sure-handedness. . . . [but] there are other, less-studied aspects to baseball defense. We'd want to start measuring the impact of an outfielder's arm, both in terms of cutting down baserunners and whether an outfielder with a cannon-arm reputation intimidates runners.

—**KEITH WOOLNER,** "Baseball's Hilbert Problems: 23 Burning Questions," *Baseball Prospectus 2000*

In the very early days of baseball, gloves were nothing more than a couple pieces of leather sewn together to fit over a player's hand, and it wasn't uncommon for there to be twenty or more "catches missed" (the predecessor to the modern "error") in a single game. It's thus no surprise that, as historian John Thorn has noted, "fielding skill was still the most highly sought after attribute of a ballplayer," through the end of the 19th century.

Fielding has come a long way since the 1800s, but fielding statistics have been historically stagnant, with the six official fielding stats adopted by the National League in 1876 (games played, total chances, putouts, assists, errors, and fielding percentage) being the same six in use 100 years later. There were some early efforts to develop a statistic that measured a fielder's range. Al Wright attempted to do so in 1875, and none other than the godfather of baseball statistics, Henry Chadwick, strongly advocated for such a stat by arguing that, "the best player in a nine is he who makes the most good plays in a match, not the one who commits the fewest errors." More than a century would pass before Wright and Chadwick's efforts would be rewarded.

Over the past quarter century, sabermetricians have at long last developed a number of new metrics to quantify fielding skill. These include early additions such as Bill James's Range Factor and Pete Palmer's Fielding Runs as well as newer metrics such as our own Clay Davenport's fielding translations, David Pinto's Probabilistic Model of Range, Baseball Info Solutions' Revised Zone Rating, Mitchell Lichtman's Ultimate Zone Rating, and most recently Baseball Info Solutions' Plus/Minus system, which first appeared in 2005's *The Fielding Bible*. All of these metrics, save the Plus/Minus system, translate fielding performance into the central currency of the game, runs.

These systems do an excellent job of measuring a fielder's range, which encompasses all aspects of defensive performance for infielders (specifically second and third basemen and shortstops) for whom unassisted plays are rare. For outfielders, for whom the unassisted play is the norm, however, range-based statistics do not take into consideration the contribution of a fielder's throwing arm in preventing opposition runs. In an attempt to compensate for this deficiency, I have worked to develop a method of quantifying the throwing prowess, or lack thereof, of those who patrol the outfield.*

A Methodological Redux

Although assists for fielders were recorded as early as the 1870s, the strength and accuracy of an outfielder's arm isn't fully represented by the number of assists he records. Advance scouting and an outfielder's reputation generally give runners and coaches an idea of which outfielders they'll take risks against and which they won't before such a play develops. For example, from 2005 through 2007, runners attempted to take an extra base on hits to right field 60 percent and 59 percent of the time, respectively, when Xavier Nady and Emil Brown were patrolling that pasture, but just 37 percent and 42 percent of the time when cannon-armed Alex Rios and Vladimir Guerrero were the right fielders on duty. Clearly, Rios and Guerrero have a significant effect on their opponent's baserunning that cannot be measured in assists, as runners would rather stay put than risk getting thrown out by them. Indeed, while an assist is a more valuable play, outfielders succeed in holding the runners far more often.

In order to incorporate holding runners into our evaluation of outfielders' throwing prowess, we've developed a method that is, to a large degree, the inverse of our methodology for measuring the impact of baserunners as, much like pitching and hitting, outfield throws and baserunning are two sides of the same coin. In developing our baserun-

*This method builds off work I have previously published on BaseballProspectus.com. I would also like to acknowledge the work of John Walsh of the *Hardball Times*, whose methodology is similar to my own, though we have each worked independently.

ning statistic EqBRR (Equivalent Baserunning Runs), we credited or debited runners for the impact their actions on the bases had on their team's Run Expectancy (RX). Run Expectancy was determined using the number of outs and base situation both before and after the play in question, and the frequency with which runners would successfully take the extra base when the ball was hit to left, center, or right field (see the preceding essay in this book, "The Tortoise, the Hare, and Juan Pierre: Translating Baserunning into Runs" for details). In attempting to quantify the impact of outfield arms, we turn that methodology on its head and credit the fielder if he keeps the opposing team from increasing their RX by taking the extra base, whether he does so by throwing a runner out and thus earning an assist (which, by this method, is often worth more than a run because it not only removes a runner from the bases entirely, but also increases the number of outs in the inning), or by simply preventing runners from advancing (be it because they're reacting to his reputation or a scouting report, or because he has fielded a hit quickly and cleanly).

As with our baserunning statistic, which of the three outfield positions the fielder in question plays is an important factor. Except in the most extreme cases, runners are less apt to try to advance on a ball hit to left field than one hit to right, regardless of who the fielder is at either position. As mentioned above, runners attempted to advance on balls hit to right field between 37 and 60 percent of the time. On balls hit to left field, they attempted advance just 29 to 44 percent of the time (with Carl Crawford and Eric Byrnes representing the low and high ends, respectively). Right fielders thus have more opportunity to differentiate themselves from their peers, as you'll see in the tables that follow.

Much in the same way that there are five distinct metrics which are added together to make our composite baserunning statistic EqBRR, our throwing arm stat has four components. They are:

Hit Advancement. In most respects this is analogous to the metric EqHAR (Equivalent Hit Advancement Runs) discussed for baserunners. It measures the impact of outfielders on baserunners attempting to take an extra base on hits. It considers the same three scenarios discussed for EqHAR:

• Runner on first and the batter singles
• Runner on first and the batter doubles
• Runner on second and the batter singles

The difference here is that we also consider the impact on trailing runners by not restricting the scenario to requiring that the subsequent base be open. This is done in order to account for the fielder taking the chance on nabbing the trailing runner going from first to third or second to home. As a result, if the fielder elects to try and gun down a runner attempting to score from second on a single and by doing so allows the runner on first to advance to third, he'll be debited for both advancements. On the other hand if the runner

on first is stopped from advancing to third while the runner on second scores, he'll be credited for keeping the trailing runner on second but debited for allowing the lead runner to score. In cases like this where the scenarios overlap, two advancement opportunities are tracked for the fielder.

Much like our baserunning statistics, this metric, as well as those that follow, compares performance to a baseline that represents what the average fielder would accomplish in the identical situation. Thus, a fielder who is exactly average in his ability to throw out and hold runners will neither save nor cost his team any runs. Additionally, because it is more difficult to prevent runners from advancing in some outfields than others (consider our comparison of Fenway Park's tiny left field area and Coors Field's vast outfield pastures in the preceding essay), the number of runs credited or debited to a fielder's total are park adjusted by outfield position for all major leaguers.

It's worth noting that, although our primary goal here is to measure the impact of a player's throwing arm, some of an outfielder's ability to hold runners results from his ability to field hits quickly and cleanly. In that sense, we are measuring an aspect of the fielder's range that is omitted from most range statistics, which concern themselves only with batted balls that are turned into outs, thus further compensating for the deficiencies of those statistics in evaluating outfielders' total impact on the game.

Fly Ball Advancement. This is essentially the inverse of EqAAR (Equivalent Air Advancement Runs) for baserunners and measures the impact of outfielders on the running game after catching a fly ball out. It considers the same three basic scenarios outlined in the baserunning essay, although here they are expanded as follows:

• Runner on first, less than two outs
• Runner on second, less than two outs
• Runner on third, less than two outs

Rather than restrict our accounting to the lead runners in these situations, as we did for EqAAR, here we consider all runners on base when an outfielder catches a fly ball, line drive, or popup with less than two outs. As a result, this works the same as hit advancement in that multiple advancement opportunities are tracked for a single play when more than one runner is on base. Fielders are credited both for assists on trailing runners and for holding trailing runners even as the lead runner advances, but are simultaneously debited for the advancement of the lead runner.

For example, on April 28 Grady Sizemore caught a fly ball with runners on first and third and one out. Rather than attempt to throw out the runner tagging from third, he threw the ball to first doubling up Nick Markakis of the Orioles to complete the double play and end the inning. Since the runner scored, we will charge Sizemore -0.14 runs according to the baseline calculations for a play of this type (the number is fairly low because centerfielders very rarely throw out a runner advancing from third on a fly ball). However, since he also doubled off the runner at first he is credited with saving +0.24 runs. For the play as a whole, Sizemore ends up with a credit of +0.10 runs.

Similarly, in a first-and-third situation, the outfielder would be credited with holding the runner at third, but debited if the trailing runner advanced to second. Once again this metric is park adjusted.

Stretching Hits. Here we find ourselves in deeper waters. While measuring an outfielder's impact on runners advancing on hits and fly balls is fairly straightforward, our capacity to measure an outfielder's ability to prevent batters from stretching singles into doubles or doubles into a triples is hampered by the limitations of the play-by-play data, which only tells us when a batter is thrown out attempting to stretch, but never when he is successful (this is why our baserunning system doesn't attempt to credit batters for stretching hits). Thus, while we may suspect that runners attempt to stretch singles into doubles more frequently when Juan Pierre is in center field than when Andruw Jones is on patrol, we simply don't have solid numbers to back it up.

As a result, what we do here is credit outfielders for the assists they record when throwing out batters attempting to stretch per the play-by-play data, then compare that to a league-wide baseline that is broken down by the type of hit and the outfield position that fielded the hit. That is, if league-wide batters were thrown out attempting to stretch 2 percent of all singles hit to centerfield, a fielder who recorded an assist on less than 2 percent of the singles hit to him is debited runs for the extra bases he theoretically allowed. As mentioned, this technique has its problems since fielders who intimidate or get to the ball quicker may wind up holding a portion of the batters on whom they might otherwise have recorded an assist. It is, however, the best we

can do absent video inspection of each hit or the creation of improved play-by-play data.

Other Assists. Because we want to provide as complete an accounting of outfielder's throwing as possible, we need to cast our net a little wider than the three metrics above to pick up any miscellaneous plays they do not cover. In 2007, there were eight outfield assists that weren't covered by any of the preceding three metrics. Although that number is small, assists have large impact on our statistics, so we want to make sure we account for all of them. While playing right field for the Astros in 2007, Luke Scott had two such plays. On July 25, the Dodgers' Derek Lowe hit a broken bat liner that fell in front of Scott, who fielded it on the first bounce and fired to first for the force out (9-3). On May 4 in St. Louis, David Eckstein hit a groundball to third baseman Morgan Ensberg with Yadier Molina on first. Ensberg, attempted to force out Molina, but threw wildly toward second and the ball skipped into right field. Scott charged Ensberg's wild throw and gunned down Molina as he tried to advance to third. Such plays are too unusual for us to develop a baseline of typical occurrences, thus the only calculation involved is to credit the outfielder for the run value associated with the assist.

Once we've calculated these four aspects of outfield defense, the individual run values credited to a given fielder are added together to produce what we call *Equivalent Throwing Runs* or EqThR, which represents the theoretical number of runs saved by the fielder above and beyond those measured by rate statistics.

Airing It Out

Tables 1, 2, and 3 list the top ten and bottom five outfielders in terms of EqThR at each of the three outfield positions for 2007. For each fielder in the tables below, we provide their

Table 1. 2007 Right Fielders

| Name | AdjG | Hit | | | Stretch | | Fly | | | Other | EqThR | EqThR Per 550 |
		Opps	Adv	A	Opps	A	Opps	Adv	A	A		
Jeff Francoeur	161	161	68	12	330	3	118	24	3	1	13.1	11.7
Michael Cuddyer	136	148	58	11	313	7	91	26	1	0	9.9	9.8
Delmon Young	127	156	56	6	287	3	102	23	7	0	9.3	9.2
Alex Rios	140	150	52	6	305	3	98	18	1	0	9.2	9.1
Shane Victorino	103	114	37	6	234	0	96	23	4	0	7.6	9.3
Mark Teahen	129	152	74	5	353	4	119	36	7	0	6.7	5.8
Jayson Werth	50	56	16	4	104	2	33	12	1	0	5.6	15.8
Ryan Doumit	35	33	8	2	65	0	34	12	3	0	5.1	20.7
Nick Markakis	156	193	95	1	337	7	116	28	4	0	2.3	2.0
Rick Ankiel	22	19	4	0	50	2	22	2	0	0	2.1	12.8
Brad Hawpe	138	138	75	2	297	2	72	26	2	0	-4.9	-5.2
Jermaine Dye	129	163	94	2	320	4	112	39	3	0	-5.2	-4.8
Corey Hart	97	132	63	2	218	2	95	27	0	0	-6.4	-7.9
Ken Griffey Jr.	130	135	76	1	325	2	103	40	2	0	-7.8	-7.6
Brian Giles	118	120	63	1	260	0	71	21	1	0	-7.8	-9.6

Table 2. 2007 Center Fielders

Name	AdjG	Hit			Stretch		Fly			Other	EqThR	EqThR Per 550
		Opps	Adv	A	Opps	A	Opps	Adv	A	A		
Ichiro Suzuki	149	164	77	2	387	3	175	37	3	0	6.0	4.5
Jacque Jones	72	60	29	3	155	5	50	13	0	0	4.3	9.0
Curtis Granderson	143	178	94	4	399	2	183	45	4	0	4.3	3.1
Andruw Jones	150	172	66	2	352	0	125	26	1	0	4.0	3.4
Josh Hamilton	62	61	33	4	145	0	35	4	2	0	3.9	8.9
Alfredo Amezaga	72	81	36	7	172	0	84	31	1	0	3.9	6.3
Jim Edmonds	92	110	53	3	235	1	90	24	4	0	3.5	4.4
Jason Lane	29	24	11	1	69	0	35	8	1	0	3.3	14.1
Bill Hall	114	134	55	5	295	0	106	23	0	0	3.1	3.2
B. J. Upton	74	99	54	3	210	6	69	14	2	0	2.5	3.6
Nook Logan	84	89	57	0	197	2	79	29	0	0	-3.5	-5.3
Jerry Owens	79	89	45	0	187	0	71	26	1	0	-3.9	-6.2
David DeJesus	151	158	84	2	358	3	137	39	0	0	-4.5	-3.8
Grady Sizemore	157	164	85	0	394	1	147	32	2	0	-4.6	-3.6
Juan Pierre	158	173	102	3	380	1	119	34	0	0	-7.3	-6.0

Table 3. 2007 Left Fielders

Name	AdjG	Hit			Stretch		Fly			Other	EqThR	EqThR Per 550
		Opps	Adv	A	Opps	A	Opps	Adv	A	A		
Alfonso Soriano	119	149	46	8	305	6	80	7	5	0	12.7	13.0
Hideki Matsui	109	122	33	4	284	1	72	13	1	0	3.6	4.1
Jose Cruz Jr.	41	38	7	1	86	2	21	3	1	0	2.8	10.5
Esteban German	5	11	4	2	16	0	0	0	0	0	2.5	51.1
Garret Anderson	81	88	27	4	190	3	58	9	0	0	2.4	3.9
Craig Monroe	90	99	34	3	218	2	69	7	1	0	2.1	3.0
Matt Kata	7	7	1	1	15	0	6	1	1	0	2.0	38.0
Andy Gonzalez	13	41	5	1	57	0	6	2	0	0	1.8	9.5
Norris Hopper	13	23	3	0	39	1	16	2	0	0	1.7	12.3
Timo Perez	18	31	10	1	50	1	10	1	0	0	1.7	10.2
Willie Harris	69	83	30	1	175	2	35	9	1	0	-2.5	-4.7
Luis Gonzalez	111	115	48	4	271	0	68	14	0	0	-3.2	-3.8
Barry Bonds	94	77	28	1	207	1	53	10	0	0	-3.4	-5.6
Adam Dunn	133	151	52	1	359	2	84	16	1	0	-5.3	-4.9
Shannon Stewart	129	145	62	2	326	1	91	18	1	0	-8.1	-7.9

adjusted number of nine-inning games played at the position (**AdjG**) by dividing their total innings played at that position by nine, the number of opportunities (**Opps**), advancements (**Adv**), and assists (**A**) in each of the first three scenarios listed above, and the number of Other Assists they recorded, per the final category above. In addition to each fielder's cumulative EqThR, a rate statistic is also provided that prorates each fielder's runs saved over 550 opportunities.

It's no surprise to see Jeff Francoeur, who is widely regarded as having a strong and accurate arm, atop Table 1. Francoeur also did well in his rookie season of 2005 (see Table 7). On a rate basis, however, Jayson Werth, relocated catcher Ryan Doumit, and repurposed pitching prospect Rick Ankiel did better. Rookie Delmon Young and relocated third baseman Mark Teahen shared the major league lead in throwing out runners trying to advance on fly balls, doing so seven times each and thus propelling themselves into the top ten. At the bottom of the heap, we find Brian Giles, who slipped below Ken Griffey Jr. by a mere fraction of a run after throwing out just two runners all season and allowing over 50 percent of runners to take the extra base on hits. Giles also came in last in EqThR per 550 opportunities among all starting outfielders across all three positions, although first baseman Lance Berkman (-16.5) did worse in part-time outfield duty while playing 26 adjusted games in right field. Surprisingly, Brad Hawpe fared poorly after enjoying a banner 2006 season (see Table 4).

Table 4. 2006 Right Fielders

Name	AdjG	Hit			Stretch		Fly			Other	EqThR	EqThR Per 550
		Opps	Adv	A	Opps	A	Opps	Adv	A	A		
Brad Hawpe	133	169	61	10	359	3	102	21	3	0	12.8	11.1
Ryan Freel	40	42	15	4	87	2	46	7	1	0	6.2	19.4
Magglio Ordonez	141	137	52	6	288	2	100	29	1	0	5.9	6.2
Alex Rios	106	106	29	3	214	2	91	16	2	0	5.6	7.5
Ichiro Suzuki	118	151	66	5	270	1	93	22	3	0	5.2	5.5
Geoff Jenkins	123	109	56	1	270	3	96	32	2	0	-3.9	-4.5
Xavier Nady	96	94	58	3	201	3	78	26	0	0	-6.3	-9.2
Shawn Green	125	131	83	0	275	0	71	20	1	0	-9.2	-10.6

Table 5. 2006 Center Fielders

Name	AdjG	Hit			Stretch		Fly			Other	EqThR	EqThR Per 550
		Opps	Adv	A	Opps	A	Opps	Adv	A	A		
Jose Bautista	47	73	33	3	146	3	42	9	1	0	4.8	10.0
Willy Taveras	124	98	51	2	243	5	98	19	2	0	4.5	5.6
Ryan Freel	45	42	16	2	115	2	43	8	0	0	3.8	10.5
David DeJesus	54	55	31	4	135	1	41	13	3	0	3.6	8.6
Shane Victorino	62	74	34	3	154	1	59	21	2	0	3.1	5.9
Mike Cameron	139	120	75	3	323	1	112	30	2	0	-3.7	-3.7
Johnny Damon	121	126	71	1	282	1	93	25	1	0	-4.3	-4.8
Joey Gathright	113	145	84	1	325	0	139	48	4	0	-4.7	-4.2

Table 6. 2006 Left Fielders

Name	AdjG	Hit			Stretch		Fly			Other	EqThR	EqThR Per 550
		Opps	Adv	A	Opps	A	Opps	Adv	A	A		
Reed Johnson	71	65	11	5	143	2	32	1	0	0	6.5	15.0
David DeJesus	61	109	27	4	197	1	70	9	0	0	5.4	8.0
Manny Ramirez	115	136	39	4	324	4	52	8	0	0	5.4	5.8
Alfonso Soriano	153	182	64	3	347	9	128	28	9	1	4.5	3.7
Juan Rivera	53	47	12	5	119	1	40	6	1	0	4.4	11.7
Jason Bay	153	203	77	4	389	4	124	17	1	1	-5.1	-3.9
Garret Anderson	90	91	38	0	186	1	55	3	0	0	-5.5	-9.1
Scott Podsednik	121	108	36	0	273	4	88	19	0	0	-6.3	-7.3

Ichiro Suzuki's move to center field paid off for the Mariners, as having his arm out there saved the team six runs, taking the top spot in Table 2. However, Jacque Jones, Josh Hamilton, Alfredo Amezaga, and Jason Lane all performed better in limited time per the rate stat on the far right. On the flip side, Juan Pierre, who recorded just four assists and allowed runners to advance on hits 59 percent of the time, cost his team more than seven runs, easily outdistancing the competition. Similarly, although Grady Sizemore does a lot of things very well, throwing is not one of them.

Table 3 is striking. Alfonso Soriano and his 19 assists saved the Cubs 12.7 runs, nine more than the next best left fielder, Hideki Matsui. Soriano was particularly effective at catching runners trying to stretch hits, picking up 6 assists in those situations, far and away the most among left fielders. The high impact of assists is evident elsewhere on Table 3 as infielders Esteban German, Matt Kata, and Andy Gonzalez all make the list despite very limited playing time in left field. Other left fielders with positive values and considerably more playing time who didn't make Table 3 include Josh Willingham (+1.5) in 132 adjusted games and Matt Holiday (+1.3) in 154 adjusted games. Shannon Stewart has consistently performed poorly over the past three years.

Table 7. 2005 Right Fielders

| Name | AdjG | Hit | | | Stretch | | Fly | | | Other | EqThR | EqThR Per 550 |
		Opps	Adv	A	Opps	A	Opps	Adv	A	A		
Jeff Francoeur	66	86	40	6	169	4	39	10	3	0	8.2	15.2
Geoff Jenkins	139	138	72	2	263	1	102	18	7	0	4.2	4.5
Alex Rios	118	135	50	3	259	2	93	24	2	0	3.8	4.3
Jermaine Dye	138	140	62	4	296	3	87	26	3	0	3.3	3.4
Michael Tucker	49	52	19	0	118	2	34	6	3	0	2.8	7.3
Casey Blake	133	143	77	2	276	1	83	29	0	0	-4.7	-5.2
Ichiro Suzuki	154	195	104	3	354	2	141	33	5	0	-5.6	-4.5
Emil Brown	122	168	95	4	312	3	82	27	0	0	-7.2	-7.0

Table 8. 2005 Center Fielders

| Name | AdjG | Hit | | | Stretch | | Fly | | | Other | EqThR | EqThR Per 550 |
		Opps	Adv	A	Opps	A	Opps	Adv	A	A		
Andruw Jones	152	164	71	7	381	3	111	18	1	0	9.0	7.6
Jason Repko	41	40	15	5	95	0	38	7	1	0	7.9	25.0
Jim Edmonds	128	143	51	4	297	0	122	26	2	0	4.5	4.4
Kenny Lofton	82	59	25	4	188	2	57	15	1	0	4.0	7.3
Vernon Wells	151	164	90	5	374	2	131	28	4	0	4.0	3.3
Jeremy Reed	128	140	77	2	329	3	143	39	2	0	-4.8	-4.3
Johnny Damon	137	130	71	1	364	2	127	54	2	0	-4.8	-4.3
Brady Clark	142	145	81	1	311	0	134	28	4	0	-5.5	-5.1

Table 9. 2005 Left Fielders

| Name | AdjG | Hit | | | Stretch | | Fly | | | Other | EqThR | EqThR Per 550 |
		Opps	Adv	A	Opps	A	Opps	Adv	A	A		
Manny Ramirez	137	179	54	8	384	9	83	16	0	0	8.5	7.2
Miguel Cabrera	123	139	37	6	292	3	81	14	3	0	7.6	8.2
Cliff Floyd	141	185	53	8	333	7	74	10	0	0	6.3	5.8
Ryan Freel	18	27	6	4	60	2	12	2	0	0	5.2	28.7
Kelly Johnson	72	91	23	4	181	1	65	8	1	0	4.3	7.0
Rondell White	60	48	15	0	125	0	37	8	0	0	-4.2	-11.0
Matt Holliday	117	139	50	1	290	2	84	16	2	0	-5.6	-6.0
Jason Bay	132	138	53	0	310	1	98	19	2	1	-5.9	-5.9

Comparing all three tables, we see that Jeff Francoeur is the major league leader in EqThR at +13.1, followed closely by Alfonso Soriano (+12.7), Michael Cuddyer (+9.9), and Delmon Young (+9.3). Meanwhile, Shannon Stewart brings up the rear at -8.1 with Brian Giles (-7.8) in a virtual tie with Ken Griffey Jr. (-7.8), and Juan Pierre (-7.3) not far behind. In comparing the tables, it's worth noting that, while we can compare EqThR values across positions, for the most part we cannot do the same for the advancement values in each category, as a comparison of Tables 1 and 3 in particular reveals. The advancement percentages for left fielders will always be lower than for right fielders. Even so, the range for

center fielders will usually be lower than that for corner outfielders who record more assists.

Wrapping It Up

Unlike the baserunning numbers, which can be applied to all hitters, we do not include EqThR in the player statistics in the team chapters because the statistic is relevant to outfielders only. Instead, we've included the following tables, which list the best and worst outfielders in EqThR at each position for the 2005 and 2006 seasons (Tables 4 through 9), the best and worst at each position for the last three seasons combined according to EqThR per 550 opportunities (100 or

Table 10. 2005-2007 Right Fielders

| Name | AdjG | Hit | | | Stretch | | Fly | | | Other | EqThR | EqThR Per 550 |
		Opps	Adv	A	Opps	A	Opps	Adv	A	A		
Delmon Young	155	209	75	8	367	5	117	29	7	0	13.0	10.2
Shane Victorino	121	125	43	6	265	2	107	27	5	0	8.4	9.2
Jeff Francoeur	385	442	197	22	896	12	276	59	10	1	25.2	8.5
Michael Cuddyer	291	288	110	15	646	11	197	45	3	1	14.9	7.2
Alex Rios	364	391	131	12	778	7	282	58	5	0	18.6	7.0
Mark Teahen	129	152	74	5	353	4	119	36	7	0	6.7	5.8
Brad Hawpe	348	424	197	16	873	8	230	62	7	0	8.5	3.0
Wily Mo Peña	100	121	54	2	235	2	50	7	0	0	1.8	2.5
Nick Markakis	258	308	151	3	577	11	210	56	4	1	4.5	2.2
Nelson Cruz	104	127	59	5	236	2	80	21	2	0	1.4	1.7
Shawn Green	343	320	174	1	730	3	221	67	1	0	-16.0	-6.9
Ken Griffey Jr.	130	135	76	1	325	2	103	40	2	0	-7.8	-7.6
Xavier Nady	188	184	105	5	405	4	151	48	1	0	-10.4	-7.7
Moises Alou	119	120	66	2	262	0	88	29	3	0	-6.8	-7.9
Corey Hart	129	171	89	2	288	5	131	35	0	0	-9.1	-8.5

Table 11. 2005-2007 Center Fielders

| Name | AdjG | Hit | | | Stretch | | Fly | | | Other | EqThR | EqThR Per 550 |
		Opps	Adv	A	Opps	A	Opps	Adv	A	A		
Ryan Freel	106	132	60	6	297	2	106	26	0	0	5.6	5.7
Ichiro Suzuki	187	198	95	2	471	4	198	37	3	0	5.8	3.7
Willy Taveras	344	296	151	12	777	10	296	71	4	0	9.1	3.6
Alfredo Amezaga	131	153	71	8	343	1	135	42	1	0	3.9	3.4
Jim Edmonds	309	350	158	9	743	3	301	67	6	0	8.5	3.4
Bill Hall	118	141	59	5	310	1	109	23	0	0	3.3	3.3
Marlon Byrd	110	133	71	3	311	1	72	17	1	0	2.9	3.1
Andruw Jones	450	499	225	12	1074	3	386	87	3	0	11.0	3.1
Cory Sullivan	191	225	121	3	532	4	168	44	3	0	3.5	2.1
Chone Figgins	137	115	62	3	323	2	118	28	3	0	1.7	1.7
Bernie Williams	118	116	69	4	301	1	111	38	1	0	-3.2	-3.3
Nook Logan	206	203	117	1	491	2	214	65	2	0	-7.3	-4.4
Johnny Damon	300	298	164	2	754	4	266	94	3	0	-11.2	-4.7
Joey Gathright	176	214	120	1	471	0	192	67	7	0	-7.6	-4.8
Brady Clark	256	274	154	2	553	0	228	62	4	0	-10.1	-5.3

more adjusted games) (Tables 10 through 12), and finally 2007's top minor league throwers by EqThR across positions (Table 13).

While this system isn't perfect, it does begin to shed some light on how important outfielder's arms are in terms of run prevention. The outfielders who are best at holding and throwing out runners can be worth a little more than a win per season (at the corners particularly), while the worst may cost their teams between a half win and a win, a range equal to about 20 runs over a full season. While the gap between the best and worst outfielder in the range-based statistics is certainly greater than this (on the order of 45 to 70 runs from 2003 through 2006), the addition of EqThR to the quantification of outfield defense should help us assemble a more complete picture of how much an outfielder contributes to his team on defense.

Table 12. 2005-2007 Left Fielders

| Name | AdjG | Hit | | | Stretch | | Fly | | | Other | EqThR | EqThR Per 550 |
		Opps	Adv	A	Opps	A	Opps	Adv	A	A		
Miguel Cabrera	123	139	37	6	292	3	81	14	3	0	7.6	8.2
Alfonso Soriano	272	331	110	11	652	15	208	35	14	1	17.2	7.8
Reed Johnson	193	181	44	9	415	5	99	9	1	0	7.2	5.7
Manny Ramirez	363	432	138	16	990	17	195	33	0	0	14.2	4.8
Andre Ethier	134	157	45	5	326	4	77	4	1	0	4.9	4.8
Melky Cabrera	127	164	51	5	323	7	70	12	1	1	4.4	4.4
Cliff Floyd	242	291	88	9	558	9	121	16	0	0	6.8	3.8
Chris Duncan	120	169	52	5	314	2	75	12	0	0	3.3	3.3
Craig Monroe	249	269	94	9	590	8	159	19	6	0	5.6	3.0
Emil Brown	157	202	64	6	451	6	124	23	4	0	2.8	2.0
Ryan Langerhans	147	147	46	1	322	1	108	20	0	0	-4.7	-4.5
Dave Roberts	118	85	33	1	215	0	82	11	0	0	-3.7	-5.3
Shannon Stewart	284	303	108	7	677	3	200	41	4	0	-11.8	-5.5
Barry Bonds	201	174	67	5	437	3	119	24	0	0	-7.6	-5.7
Rondell White	105	90	32	0	221	0	62	13	0	0	-6.6	-9.7

Table 13. 2007 Minor Leaguers by League Across Positions

| Name | LgId | Pos | AdjG | Hit | | | Stretch | | Fly | | | Other | EqThR | EqThR Per 550 |
				Opps	Adv	A	Opps	A	Opps	Adv	A	A		
Ruben Rivera	MEX	Center	97	137	48	4	248	5	93	10	2	0	12.1	13.8
Clete Thomas	EAS	Center	114	124	56	8	272	3	96	20	4	1	9.8	10.9
Matthew Joyce	EAS	Right	107	133	57	9	224	4	80	13	6	0	8.8	10.9
Ruben Martinez	DSL	Center	57	122	41	9	202	1	40	6	2	0	8.7	13.0
Francisco Plasencia	SAL	Center	67	83	29	9	173	1	67	25	1	0	8.0	13.5
Truan Mehl	CLF	Center	59	60	25	4	136	1	60	10	3	0	7.8	16.5
Amaury Marti	MEX	Left	90	167	49	7	277	9	81	10	0	0	7.8	8.1
Wilkin Ruan	PCL	Left	21	26	7	6	56	5	17	2	0	1	7.7	43.0
John Raynor	SAL	Left	103	97	22	4	216	7	65	9	0	2	7.6	11.0
Terry Serrano	VSL	Center	50	62	24	8	111	2	34	4	0	0	7.5	20.0
Noe Mata	MEX	Right	94	169	100	4	294	4	78	18	1	0	-6.6	-6.7
Daniel Perales	MDW	Left	96	122	50	2	257	2	74	7	1	0	-7.0	-8.5
Richie Robnett	TXS	Center	62	76	42	1	166	1	55	21	0	0	-7.1	-13.1
Brad Corley	CRL	Right	103	112	65	1	211	2	87	18	1	0	-7.1	-9.5
Demond Smith	MEX	Center	102	157	83	2	313	1	116	32	1	0	-7.9	-7.4

Enlightening Strikes
Why Pitchers Need to Work the Count, Too

Clay Davenport

There's a baseball adage that says strike one is your most important pitch. Of course that's true.
— AL LEITER

Is it? At Baseball Prospectus we have always advocated hitters who work the count, believing that Ted Williams' approach of waiting for a good pitch to drive and taking a walk if that pitch never comes was the way to go. We have seen that approach adopted at the team level by the Yankees, who learned it from another Hall of Fame Red Sock, Wade Boggs, in the early '90s; the A's, who had it imposed upon them from above by general manager Billy Beane in the latter part of that decade; and more recently, the Red Sox themselves, each team enjoying considerable success as a result. If controlling the count is that important for a hitter, then it follows that it is equally important for a pitcher. Certainly former Orioles pitching coach Ray Miller thought so ("throw strikes" was one of his simple rules for pitching), and certainly Al Leiter thinks so, but what do the numbers say?

First, let's look at typical batting performances by count by measuring the results of plate appearances that end at a given count, as well as those that pass through that count at any point (intentional walks have been removed). This data appears in Table 1. Note that, in addition to the standard slash stats, we've listed equivalent runs per 1,000 plate appearances (EqR/1KPA) rather than our total-offense metric EqA (equivalent average). This is because EqA is based on runs per out, and not only are outs highly variable in the

above statitstics, but we'll be applying them to situations in which no out is made at all, in which case EqA would become infinite.

Table 1 reveals that hitters go into a deep hole when they take their second strike. Hitters actually hit above league average in every count except for 0-2, 1-2, and 2-2, but those counts carry as much weight as the other nine (from the perspective of the mean). The pitchers face a similar explosion on the three-ball counts. Look at the OBP and EqR/1KPA columns for the 3-0 and 3-1 counts. Even with intentional walks removed, hitters reach base more than half the time when the count reaches 3-0 or 3-1, and a whopping 95 percent of all 3-0 counts end with the hitter reaching base.

In order to find the value of throwing a strike or ball on any given count, we can combine the run values in Table 1 with the frequencies of the various outcomes of those counts and plate appearances. For example, the first pitch of an at-bat:

- was taken for a ball 41.3 percent of the time, changing the count to 1-0
- was a strike (be it called, fouled, or swung on and missed) 47.2 of the time, changing the count to 0-1
- hit the batter 0.2 percent of the time
- was put into play 11.3 percent of the time; 65.6 percent of those balls in play were converted to outs, 22.5 percent landed for singles, 7.2 percent for doubles, 0.7 percent for triples, and 4.0 percent became home runs

Per Table 1, the value of plate appearances that pass through 1-0 counts is 156 EqR per 1,000 PA, thus the average value of throwing a first-pitch ball is 156 EqA/1KPA (technically the hit batsmen also factor into the results of throwing a ball, but they aren't common enough to affect the total value). By properly weighting the run values of the 81 percent of first-pitch strikes that send the count to 0-1 (91 EqR/1KPA) and the 19 percent of them that are put into play (170 EqR/1KPA), we can pin down the run value of a first-pitch strike at 104 EqR/1KPA. The difference between a first-pitch ball and a first-pitch strike is thus 156 minus 104, or 52

Table 1. Hitter Performance by Count

Count	Ends At				Passes Through			
	AVG	OBA	SLG	EqR/1KPA	AVG	OBA	SLG	EqR/1KPA
0-0	.344	.349	.551	170	.268	.331	.423	126
1-0	.341	.342	.562	171	.282	.383	.459	156
2-0	.350	.349	.615	191	.294	.492	.496	207
3-0	.396	.951	.816	360	.295	.723	.516	289
0-1	.324	.332	.481	141	.238	.281	.362	91
1-1	.327	.331	.512	151	.250	.321	.394	113
2-1	.339	.339	.554	167	.268	.403	.434	153
3-1	.368	.694	.641	289	.295	.593	.500	233
0-2	.167	.177	.235	37	.180	.211	.265	50
1-2	.179	.187	.263	44	.192	.242	.294	64
2-2	.195	.200	.300	54	.207	.306	.327	92
3-2	.233	.469	.385	166	.233	.469	.385	166

runs per 1,000 PA. That is roughly the same as the difference between the 2007 performances of NL MVP Jimmy Rollins (.290 EqA, 150 EqR) and Nationals shortstop Felipe Lopez (.239 EqA, 99 EqR), or between first basemen Prince Fielder (.323, 180) and Doug Mientkiewicz (.267, 125).

Repeating this method for every count, we can determine the value of a strike in every count (Table 2). The first thing we see here is that the first-pitch strike is actually one of the least valuable pitches. The most valuable strike-one pitch comes in 3-0 counts, but the alternative there is ball four, which puts the runner on base 100 percent of the time, so that's a bit misleading. Strike one on a 2-0 count ranks fifth on the list. Other than by the simple logic that you can't throw strike two without first throwing strike one, it's very difficult to find support for Leiter's statement in this data.

Table 2. The Value of a Strike

Count	Value	% Strike
3-2	199	78
2-1	169	70
3-1	154	71
3-0	126	69
2-0	125	70
2-2	99	70
1-0	78	66
1-1	73	64
0-1	71	58
0-0	52	59
1-2	41	63
0-2	22	54

The column on the far right in Table 2 shows the frequency with which pitchers throw strikes in each of the given counts. What's most interesting here is that the frequency of thrown strikes increases roughly relative to the run value of a strike in the given count. So while some pitchers, like Leiter, might echo the adage that strike one is the most important pitch they can throw, their actions betray their true, and surprisingly accurate, understanding of the importance of throwing a strike in a given count. The frequency of strikes not only increases with the value of strikes, but they do so at a fairly consistent rate, roughly equivalent to one-tenth of the run value of a strike in the given count plus 55 percent. The biggest outliers are 0-1 and 0-2 counts, in which the frequency is lower, and 2-2 and 3-2 counts in which the frequency is higher. It would appear that pitchers are being too careful when ahead 0-1 and 0-2, wasting pitches outside of the zone in an attempt to entice hitters who are in desperate situations; on 2-2 and 3-2 counts, however, it seems it is the batters who are being too careful, often swinging and missing at those pitches out of the zone. What tips the balance might be pitchers' historic tendency to throw a waste pitch on 0-2, and the batters' recognition that a waste pitch is what they're likely to see, whereas in full and 2-2 counts, the batter reasons that the pitcher can't afford to throw another ball, and is thus overly aggressive when he does.

The information in Table 1 allows us to estimate how many runs a pitcher should have allowed based only on the counts he faced. By comparing the equivalent runs per 1,000 PA for each count to the number of times a plate appearance against the pitcher in question ended on that count, we are able to explain 29 percent of the pitcher's ability to prevent runs from scoring. For example, Table 3 shows how often NL Cy Young award winner Jake Peavy ended an at-bat on each count along with the EqR/1KPA for each count across the major leagues (Table 3). After doing the math (dividing the EqRs by 1,000 and multiplying by the number of times Peavy faced each one), we can conclude that Peavy should have given up 105 runs based on the counts he faced. In reality, he only gave up 67. I'll address this discrepancy in a moment.

Table 3: Jake Peavy's 2007 Season by Count

Count	0-0	0-1	0-2	1-0	1-1	1-2	2-0	2-1	2-2	3-0	3-1	3-2
Number	95	67	83	47	68	170	14	41	150	13	35	115
EqR/1KPA	170	141	37	171	151	44	191	167	54	360	289	166

Table 4 lists the best and worst pitchers of 2007 according to their expected runs based on count frequency. I've adjusted all pitchers' workloads to 1,000 PA so as to compare pitchers on an equal basis and provided lists of the best and worst EqR/1KPA for pitchers with 200 or more batters faced and, since the former list is dominated by relief pitchers, those with 400 or more batters faced, which limits the list to starters.

Table 4. Expected Runs Based on Count Frequency

Best

200 PA	EqR/1KPA	400 PA	EqR/1KPA
Rafael Betancourt	101	Cole Hamels	115
Jonathan Papelbon	105	Johan Santana	115
Takashi Saito	108	Jake Peavy	118
Heath Bell	110	Erik Bedard	118
Mariano Rivera	111	Javier Vazquez	119

Worst

200 PA	EqR/1KPA	400 PA	EqR/1KPA
Danys Baez	157	Mike Maroth	149
J. C. Romero	153	Joe Kennedy	148
Ruddy Lugo	152	Tom Glavine	147
Jose Mesa	152	Doug Davis	145
Clay Hensley	151	Livan Hernandez	145

We can extend our tests of how important strike one is by using the information above to build a model that simulates plate appearances pitch-by-pitch determining the outcome of each pitch (strike, ball, type of hit, out, HBP, etc.) based on the league-wide frequency of that outcome, then doing the same for the next pitch and so forth until the plate appearance reaches a conclusion. By simulating plate appearances until 810 of them result in outs, we've in effect simulated a full season of pitching in which our baseline pitcher threw 30 complete games (27 outs x 30 games = 810 outs). Using the 2007 frequencies of events, the resulting baseline pitcher looks like this:

IP	H	HR	BB	SO	ERA	Pit/9	H/9	HR/9	BB/9	SO/9	WHIP
270	297	33	107	212	4.50	155	9.9	1.1	3.6	7.1	1.50

As per Table 2, that baseline pitcher throws a first-pitch strike 59 percent of the time, which is actually 58.5 percent rounded. If we simply change the frequency with which he throws a first-pitch strike—and absolutely nothing else—his pitching line changes in the manner seen in Table 5.

Table 5. Effects of Changing the Rate of First-Pitch Strikes

%	IP	H	HR	BB	SO	ERA	Pit/9	H/9	HR/9	BB/9	SO/9	WHIP
50	270	300	34	119	208	4.73	160	10.0	1.1	4.0	6.9	1.55
58.5	270	297	33	107	212	4.50	155	9.9	1.1	3.6	7.1	1.50
64.4	270	294	32	98	215	4.34	152	9.8	1.1	3.3	7.2	1.45
70	270	293	32	89	218	4.20	149	9.8	1.1	3.0	7.3	1.41
80	270	290	31	74	221	3.96	144	9.7	1.0	2.5	7.4	1.35
90	270	287	30	60	226	3.73	139	9.6	1.0	2.0	7.5	1.29
100	270	283	29	46	231	3.50	134	9.4	1.0	1.5	7.7	1.23

That's pretty impressive. Simply throwing a first-pitch strike every time out turns our (admittedly very durable) league-average baseline pitcher into a Cy Young award candidate by dropping his ERA by a full run and improving his K:BB ratio from 1.97 to 5.13. It's enough to make you wonder why everybody doesn't just throw strikes every time. The reason, of course, is that it's simply not possible to throw a first-pitch strike *and* have absolutely nothing else change. Our assumption is flawed. One of those unchanged assumptions is that batters will put the a first pitch strike into play 20 percent of the time, because that's how frequently hitters did so in 2007. In the real world, if you throw more first-pitch strikes, teams and players will recognize that and change their approach to swing more often. If you only increase your first-pitch strikes by 10 percent or so (a rate represented by the 64.4 percent statistics in Table 5), opposing hitters may not notice, but you can bet they will by the time you get to throwing 80 percent or more first-pitch strikes.

Looking at the pitcher and batter performance in all counts, we find that for every percentage point increase in strike frequency, the likelihood of a batter putting the ball in play also goes up by about a point. That suggests that a pitcher who throws a first pitch strike 100 percent of the time will have a little more than 60 percent of those strikes put into play, a drastic increase from the original 20 percent, and a figure which changes his results rather drastically as seen in Table 6.

These high-strike percentage lines in Table 6 look like

Table 6. Effects of Changing the Rate of First-Pitch Strikes, Adjusted for Change in Rate of Balls in Play

%	IP	H	HR	BB	SO	ERA	Pit/9	H/9	HR/9	BB/9	SO/9	WHIP
50	270	291	32	121	220	4.56	164	9.7	1.1	4.0	7.3	1.53
58.5	270	297	33	107	212	4.50	155	9.9	1.1	3.6	7.1	1.50
64.4	270	301	33	96	204	4.46	148	10.0	1.1	3.2	6.8	1.47
70	270	308	34	85	195	4.48	140	10.3	1.1	2.8	6.5	1.46
80	270	319	35	65	174	4.47	125	10.6	1.2	2.2	5.8	1.42
90	270	336	37	45	148	4.60	107	11.2	1.2	1.5	4.9	1.41
100	270	354	39	23	115	4.74	88	11.8	1.3	0.8	3.8	1.40

those of the game's more extreme contact and control pitchers such as Josh Towers and Carlos Silva. There's also a fairly broad equilibrium as the ERAs stay within 14 points of 4.60 and the increase in hits and decrease in walks are largely offset as seen by the only gradual change in WHIP relative to Table 5. The principal benefit is the reduction in pitch counts. The average pitcher is going to reach the 100-pitch mark in six innings, but he can get in another whole inning before reaching that point by raising his first-strike percentage to 80 percent. Doing so would have a negligible effect on his ERA, but his hit and strikeout numbers would be dramatically worse, and in these days of arbitration it is unlikely that any pitcher would be willing to make that exchange.

Still, we are jumping to unwarranted conclusions, because there is yet another hidden assumption in the analysis. When hitters are expecting a strike, they not only put a pitch into play more often, they put it into play better. The likelihood of a single actually goes down as strike percentage goes up, but that small decrease is dwarfed by the increases in extra-base hits, especially home runs. Home run rates more than double depending on the count, from a low of 2.2 percent of fair-batted balls on 0-2 counts up to 5.7 percent on 2-0 and 3-1 counts. That rate actually increases all the way to 9.4 percent on 3-0 counts, but that is an extremely restricted data set as the 3-0 count is such an automatic take for anybody except the very best hitters that we have to treat it as a highly biased outlier.

As such, if we make an additional adjustment for the increases in hit types as they correspond to the increases in strikes, we get a newer, and even worse, set of results for the pitcher as seen in Table 7.

Table 7. Effects of Changing the Rate of First-Pitch Strikes, Adjusted for Change in Rate of Balls in Play and for Change in Rate of Hits by Type

%	IP	H	HR	BB	SO	ERA	Pit/9	H/9	HR/9	BB/9	SO/9	WHIP
50	270	290	31	121	220	4.49	164	9.7	1.0	4.0	7.3	1.52
58.5	270	297	33	107	212	4.50	155	9.9	1.1	3.6	7.1	1.50
64.4	270	308	36	96	205	4.65	148	10.3	1.2	3.2	6.8	1.50
70	270	320	40	85	197	4.88	141	10.7	1.3	2.8	6.6	1.50
80	270	357	54	67	179	5.77	125	11.9	1.8	2.2	6.0	1.57
90	270	411	75	47	157	7.21	114	13.7	2.5	1.6	5.2	1.67
100	270	495	109	26	130	9.55	98	16.5	3.6	0.9	4.3	1.93

The drastic increase in run production that occurs somewhere above the 70 percent first-strike frequency in Table 7 can be explained by the simple logic of pitch selection and expectation. The more a pitcher needs a strike, the more likely he is to throw a fastball. Additionally, for the vast majority of pitchers, the fastball is the pitch they can locate most reliably. It is also the pitch that most major league hitters handle best. Once a pitcher surpasses a certain frequency of throwing first-pitch fastball strikes, hitters begin to look for them, and when a major league hitter is sitting dead red and gets his pitch, he's more often than not going to cream it. This is one reason why the run values of 3-0, 3-1, and 2-0 counts are so high in Table 1. In those counts the hitter knows the pitcher has to throw a strike (and per Table 2 is very likely to do so), which most likely means he's getting a fastball. It wouldn't be outrageous to say that the entire point of working the count, from the hitter's point of view, is to force the pitcher to throw him a fastball in the strike zone. Indeed, two-thirds of the run values of the various counts as seen in Table 1 can be explained simply by how often a fastball is thrown on that count.

If Al Leiter is your pitching coach and he tells you to throw more first-pitch strikes and you comply by pumping first-pitch fastballs in the zone, you're going to get killed. Strange as it may sound, even a pitcher with good control needs to throw some balls once in a while, as the most important thing for the pitcher is to make sure the hitter does not know what's coming. When a pitcher is wild, the hitter knows to rest his bat on his shoulder and take his walk. When a pitcher pounds the zone with fastballs, the hitter knows to load up and crush one of them. Only when a pitcher mixes his pitches and location, both in and out of the zone, to create deception is he going to be truly effective.

Let's illustrate that assertion with a simplified game theory table. Suppose we give the pitcher a choice of throwing either a ball or a strike knowing that he will successfully execute whichever pitch he chooses. Suppose also that the hitter commits to swing or not swing based on the count and frequency of strikes in that count, as opposed to by reacting to the pitch thrown. Simplifying even further, we can define the four most likely outcomes in Table 8 (Note that the typical ratio between balls hit fair and foul is closer to 2:1, but since we're focusing on contact made only with strikes I've rounded up to 3:1.)

Table 8. Game Theory Outcomes

Pitcher throws	Batter chooses to	Result
Ball	Take	Count advances by a ball
Ball	Swing	Misses, count advances by a strike
Strike	Take	Count advances by a strike
Strike	Swing	Hit into play 75%, fouled off 25%

Combine those with the run values for either ending or going through various counts, and we get:

Table 9. Run Value Results

Count	BT	BS	ST	SS	Should throw strikes	Do throw strikes
2-0	289	153	153	182	80%	70%
3-1	365	166	166	195	85%	71%
3-0	365	233	233	263	80%	69%
1-0	207	113	113	144	75%	66%
3-2	365	0	0	171	70%	78%
2-1	233	92	92	148	70%	70%
1-1	153	64	64	129	60%	64%
2-2	166	0	0	116	55%	70%
0-0	156	91	91	150	50%	59%
0-1	113	50	50	118	50%	58%
1-2	92	0	0	116	45%	63%
0-2	64	0	0	106	40%	54%

Using the four outcomes in Table 8 and the run values in Table 1, we can create a rough estimate of how often pitchers should throw strikes in each of the twelve counts. Those frequencies, along with how often pitchers actually do throw strikes in those counts (as per Table 2) can be found in Table 9. They confirm that pitchers, as a group, are pitching fairly close to their optimum frequencies, and the gaps between how often our model says pitchers should throw strikes and how often they actually do can be ascribed to our simplifying assumptions rather than to any lack of insight on the part of pitchers. Given this data, it seems that trying to improve by throwing more strikes is a fool's errand; unless it is accompanied by some sort of improvement in real command most pitchers will end up losing ground as a result. They will, however, realize a short-term gain until the hitters adapt, which could explain why a new coaching strategy will often seem to work. Such successes are fleeting.

The Baseball Prospectus
Top 100 Prospects

Kevin Goldstein

Welcome to the second Baseball Prospectus Top 100 prospects list. One of the challenges of assembling this list is that ranking prospects involves much more than simply perusing minor league statistics. There are no magic numbers for prospects, and often the guy with the 700 OPS is a much better prospect than his teammate who is leading the league in everything. We're not measuring what these kids are doing now, we're trying to evaluate what they are going to do in the future. Projecting them requires a bit of feel. You need the scouting reports, you need to understand what a player does and doesn't do well, and you need a sense of player development patterns to identify certain combinations of strengths and weaknesses and how those tend to play out over time. The wonderful thing about prospect hunting is that even then, even when you combine the scouting and the history and the kinds of tabletop projections we can do here at BP, there is still a possibility that something unanticipated will happen. There is always a chance that a 13th-round pick from an obscure Midwest junior college will grow up to be an MVP the way Albert Pujols did, or that a guy who had a 4.67 ERA in the Midwest League will get snapped up in the Rule 5 draft and blossom into Johan Santana. Studying prospects is not an exact science, and no matter how much great research we do, it never can be. In the end, I think that's why I like it so much.

1. Jay Bruce, OF, Reds

Bruce has consistently exceeded expectations to the point that he's now the best prospect in the game. When his senior year began, he was just a very good, athletic high school outfielder in Texas who most thought would end up somewhere around a third-round pick. However, between a strong senior showing and some impressive private workouts, he ended up as the 12th overall pick in the draft. Going into the Midwest League in 2006, he was overshadowed by Justin Upton and Cameron Maybin, but far outplayed them both and walked away with league MVP honors. Despite huge expectations going into 2007, Bruce moved through the system faster than expected, and by year's end the Reds had traded Josh Hamilton to open a full-time spot for him in the big leagues. Bruce won't turn 21 until just after Opening Day, but he has nothing left to prove in the minors; he can do it all. Think about Larry Walker and how great he was when he was healthy. That's Jay Bruce.

2. Clay Buchholz, RHP, Red Sox

Bucholz had an excellent full-season debut in 2006, but it was how he finished the year, with three dominating starts in the Carolina League, that had everyone so excited about 2007. That excitement was justified as Buchholz had nearly twice as many strikeouts (171) as hits allowed (87) in 125 1/3 innings before making a splash on the national scene with his big league no-hitter. A pitcher with three plus offerings is a rare thing, but Buchholz is just that, and his curveball and changeup are both ranked as plus-plus by some. Not only does he have ace potential, but his time is now. His inning count will be monitored closely this year, but it will be no surprise if he's among the top pitchers in the American League anyway.

3. Evan Longoria, 3B, Rays

The Rays have seemingly shuffled half their team to open up a spot for Longoria, the third overall pick in 2006. The Delmon Young trade allowed them to lock B. J. Upton in the outfield by relocating Akinori Iwamura to second, thereby opening up the hot corner for Longoria. That's a lot of dominoes to push over for one player, but Longoria should justify the effort. He doesn't have anything approaching Scott Rolen's glove, but at the plate, he's highly similar to Rolen in his peak years and will likely offer even more raw power. He's a special player and one the Devil Rays never thought they'd have a chance to draft, but on draft day the Rockies made a last-minute decision to take Greg Reynolds with the second overall pick instead. You'll read about Reynolds on this list about 80 players down.

4. Joba Chamberlain, RHP, Yankees

You've probably heard of this guy. So why, after limiting big-league hitters to a .145 average and striking out 34 in 24 innings is he not the best pitching prospect in baseball? It's pretty simple, really—Chamberlain's stuff isn't as good as Buchholz's. Buchholz has the three plus pitches to Joba's two, and Buchholz has better command. Now that Chamberlain is returning to the rotation, that's going to matter, because he'll have to do more than spot his upper–90s heat and uncork his nasty slider for two innings. He'll need to pace himself and work in his solid changeup as well as his curve (though the latter ranks far behind his other offerings). He'll need to, and he will; Chamberlain's the second best pitching prospect on the planet, and he's going to be a great major league starter.

5. Clayton Kershaw, LHP, Dodgers

One scout who had been covering the Midwest League for more than a decade said that Kershaw was the best left-hander he'd ever seen in that circuit. After dominating Low-A, Kershaw finished the year by whiffing more than a man per inning at Double-A, and he doesn't turn 20 until March. He has the perfect power-pitching frame, he throws in the mid-90s, and his fastball is often overshadowed by his hammer curve. I ranked Kershaw 16th on last year's list and got a lot of flack for putting him that high and finishing my comment with, "in the next 12 to 24 months, people will be taking about Kershaw the way they do about [Phil] Hughes and [Homer] Bailey." Twelve months later, he's passed Bailey and many GMs would take him over Hughes as well.

6. David Price, LHP, Rays

It's not easy to rank a player in the top ten when he has yet to don a professional uniform, but given the abilities of the first overall pick in the 2007 draft, it's just as hard not to. Price is like a left-handed Buchholz in that he has three plus pitches and fantastic command. He might not throw quite as hard as Buchholz, but being a southpaw makes up for that. No team in baseball can match the Rays' hitter/pitcher duo of Longoria and Price. Both have true impact potential, and if you think the balance of power in the game is tipped too far toward the AL East, well, it's about to get worse.

7. Travis Snider, OF, Blue Jays

Snider's .313/.377/.525 line last year was impressive enough, but the context in which he achieved it makes it even more so. Just 19, he was playing in the most pitcher-friendly league in professional baseball and led that league in slugging, doubles, and extra-base hits. Hitting is Snider's main skill as a ballplayer. He's about as wide as he is tall (he's not fat, just thick), but his bat is so special—and could get even better if he turns his patient approach into an aggressively patient approach—that it excuses his other limitations. The only Toronto farmhand on this list, Snider could be lined up for a Jay Bruce-like breakout in this year.

8. Colby Rasmus, OF, Cardinals

Last year, the Cardinals' premier athlete blossomed into a ballplayer, leading the Texas League in home runs and slugging percentage. Rasmus has added a significant amount of muscle to what was a very skinny frame when St. Louis made him their first-round pick in 2005. By dealing Jim Edmonds in the offseason, the Cardinals made it clear that the Rasmus era will begin sooner than expected, and while he won't be able to duplicate Edmonds' defensive value, his power/speed combination brings back memories of some of the best players of the 1980s.

9. Homer Bailey, RHP, Reds

Bailey was fourth on this list last year and is the highest ranked player this year to have experienced a decline in his stock. Inside the game, his 2007 is viewed as more of a bump in the road than any cause for real concern. Bailey's command took a huge step backward last year, and dealing with a groin injury all season didn't help matters. Still, his raw stuff—mid-90s fastball and fantastic curve—still gives him tremendous upside. No prospect could use a do-over more than Bailey, who still should be the Reds' ace by the end of this season.

10. Cameron Maybin, OF, Marlins

Maybin did practically nothing in his first taste of the majors last year, but it's hard to think of any way he could have succeeded given that he was allowed a grand total of 53 plate appearances in six weeks, including a 20-day stretch in September during which he got a whopping four at-bats. He remains baseball's ultimate tools prospect, a center fielder with true 30/30 abilities and a patient approach at the plate. His high strikeout rate is an indication that he could use a little more seasoning in the minors, but the trade to Florida puts additional pressure on him to perform immediately given the Marlins' hole in center.

11. Rick Porcello, RHP, Tigers

Another pitcher who has never pitched a professional inning, and a teenager to boot, Porcello was the best high school right-hander of the decade, the best since Josh Beckett in 1999. Six-foot-five with a long, skinny frame, Porcello is loaded with projection, but his stuff is already top notch, including a mid-90s fastball that can get up to 98 mph, two plus breaking balls, a rapidly developing changeup, and the ability to throw strikes with any of his offerings. While he was only the 27th overall pick due to bonus demands, he was the second-best talent in the draft (which tells you just how broken the process is). The Tigers already have some amazing young arms at the big league level. Porcello ranks with any of them.

12. Matt Wieters, C, Orioles

The Orioles put aside their conservative drafting habits to take a Scott Boras client with the fifth overall pick in last year's draft and give him the largest upfront bonus in draft history, a cool $6 million. They chose a good player to give in on, as Wieters was the top college position player in the draft. Catching talent is hard enough to find, impact catching talent, doubly so. Wieters, a switch hitter with tons of power, a patient approach, and excellent defensive skills, is definitely an impact talent. He could quickly become the face of the franchise.

13. Franklin Morales, LHP, Rockies

During the 2007 postseason, Morales showed off the kind of stuff that rarely comes out of anyone's hand, especially from the left side, with a mid-90s fastball and a curveball that some grade as an even better pitch. Morales is still not a finished product—he needs to hone his command—but his is the best pure arm the Rockies have ever had in their system.

14. Andy LaRoche, 3B, Dodgers

Everyone loves Andy LaRoche except, perhaps, for the Dodgers. Due to back problems, his big-league showing was poor, but he is a truly special hitter with a rare combination of plus power and a very low strikeout rate; in 128 Triple-A games he has 28 home runs, 64 walks, and just 74 whiffs. Perhaps because LaRoche is no better than a solid defensive player, the Dodgers keep blocking him, putting him behind what's left of Nomar Garciaparra to begin 2008 and making him the subject of trade rumors. They're missing out on something here, but then this is the same club that gave the big money to Juan Pierre.

15. Wade Davis, RHP, Rays

Davis is a 6-foot-5 right-hander with filthy power who used his mid-90s fastball and one of the better curves in the minors to dominate at both High- and Double-A last year. Tampa Bay's pitching has long been a joke, but their deep system (there are more arms to come on this list) is producing so much talent that it's going to be a Darwinian struggle for rotation spots, with the still-talented losers forced into the bullpen.

16. Jacoby Ellsbury, OF, Red Sox

Ellsbury hit .353 during his regular season stint in the big-leagues, then topped that with a .360 mark in the postseason. On a team of players that look more like softball sluggers from a local auto repair shop, he stands out as a sleek athlete. He can hit for average, runs like the wind, and utilizes that speed to play fantastic defense, but what he doesn't do is a bit of a concern. He doesn't have much power, and while that's okay on its own, he also doesn't draw many walks, so he's miscast as a leadoff man unless he keeps his average in batting title-territory. Even during Ellsbury's college days, the gimme comparison was Johnny Damon, and it still works.

17. Jordan Schafer, OF, Braves

No prospect in baseball took a larger step forward in 2007 than Schafer. In 2006, Schafer was an outstanding center fielder and a wonderful athlete, but not a very good offensive player. Last year, Schafer transformed into a multi-faceted player who can hit for average, get on base, and potentially provide 25 homers and 25 steals annually. While Schafer has yet to play above A-ball, he'll be given serious consideration as Andruw Jones' replacement in spring training with the understanding that he'll likely need another year.

18. Desmond Jennings, OF, Rays

Your runner-up for largest step forward goes to Jennings. Appropriately, he and Schafer are similar prospects. Rays officials found it hard to temper their enthusiasm for one of the best athletes in the game going into the season, but Jennings exceeded even internal expectations by hitting .315/.401/.465 at Low-A before going down for the year with a minor knee injury. He actually has a higher ceiling than Schafer, but he's not nearly as polished a product, so there's more risk involved. Jennings probably won't be ready until 2010 at the earliest, so it's too early to start worrying about where he fits in the outfield, but a trio of Jennings, Carl Crawford, and B. J. Upton would be among the fastest outfields in the game's history.

19. Mike Moustakas, SS, Royals

The second overall pick in last June's draft, Moose Tacos began the year behind high school teammate Matt Dominguez (who went 12th overall) on most draft worksheets, but by June he had set California state records for home runs in a season (24) and career (52) to establish himself as the top high school position player on the board. In his spare time, he also touched 97 mph on the mound as his team's closer. The only problem here is that Moustakas is just not a shortstop. That said, when you project to hit 35 to 40 home runs a year, no one cares if you're doing so at second or third instead of short.

20. Jarrod Parker, RHP, Diamondbacks

It's a bit of a scouting cliché, but every year some kid in the middle of nowhere starts firing bullets, forcing scouts to fire up MapQuest in order to find him. Last year, the middle of nowhere was Ossian, Indiana, and the kid was Jarrod Parker. The Cubs were locked in on him with the third overall pick, but when the Royals had a late change of direction at number two and took Moustakas, it made Josh Vitters available to Chicago and they took him. Somehow Parker slipped six notches to Arizona. Not only was he touching 98 mph throughout the season, but he consistently sat at 93 to 96 mph while also flashing an impressive power breaking ball. If anyone has the ability to dominate in his first full season the way Kershaw did last year, it's Parker.

21. Joey Votto, 1B, Reds

Votto continued to rake at Triple-A in 2007, and was actually a bit better during a 24-game big-league debut, cementing himself as the Reds' first baseman for 2008. Votto's bat is his only real tool, but it's one hell of a tool. Votto projects as a .300 hitter who draws 80-plus walks a year. It's still not clear just how much power he'll end up with; he's never hit more than 22 round-trippers in a minor league season. Those who think he'll hit 25 dingers a year project him as a very good player, while those that see 35 a year peg him as a borderline MVP candidate in the mold of fellow Canadian Justin Morneau.

22. Daric Barton, 1B, Athletics

Barton has always been one of the most advanced hitters in the minors, drawing 313 walks while striking out just 266 times in his five minor league seasons, but questions remain about how much power he has. Barton's .347/.429/.639 line in 18 big-league games provides plenty of room for optimism, and some feel that in the minors he was like the smart kid who gets C's because he's just plain bored. He'll be the offensive centerpiece to Oakland's rebuilding process.

23. Chase Headley, 3B, Padres

Headley could always hit, draw walks, and play a consistent third base, but many were left wondering if those skills would make up for his lack of power enough to let him be an everyday player. He showed up for the 2007 season with about ten pounds of new muscle, pounded out 38 doubles and 20 home runs at Double-A, and now those concerns are gone. San Diego is still trying to figure out what to do with him and Kevin Kouzmanoff; both are getting looks in the outfield.

24. Andrew McCutchen, OF, Pirates

McCutchen almost made the Pirates out of spring training last year. The organization successfully resisted what would have been a disastrous decision, but still made a bad one by skipping him up two levels to Double-A, where he struggled to get his OPS above 700. Though he's raw, McCutchen's tools still provide for a very high ceiling, and he's already shown enough baseball skills to make people believe that he can reach it. Of course, some things never change, as the Pirates are talking about opening this year with him on in the big leagues. To paraphrase Ronald Reagan, the most terrifying words in the English language are, "I'm from the Pirates and I'm here to help."

25. Reid Brignac, SS, Devil Rays

After winning California League MVP honors in 2006, Brignac's 2007 season was disappointing. That happens when a player not only moves to a higher level, but leaves behind the high-octane environment of the Cal League. The good news is that Brignac improved defensively to the point that he's now a viable shortstop, one who projects to hit 25 to 30 home runs a year. Paired with Evan Longoria on the left side during each of the last two years, Brignac will join him in the majors in 2009.

26. Carlos Gonzalez, OF, Athletics

Gonzalez was the best player the A's received in the Dan Haren deal. An outfielder with above-average power, speed, and a cannon arm, Gonzalez is supremely talented but has a tendency to fly on autopilot, knowing that his athleticism is more than enough on its own to achieve a modicum of success. If Mark Kotsay isn't around to begin the year for any reason, Gonzalez might be given a shot at the center-field job as early as spring training.

27. Nick Adenhart, RHP, Angels

Adenhart's numbers at Double-A were good but hardly eye-popping. Still, he was a 20-year-old in an advanced league who finished fourth in the league in ERA. With a 92 to 94 mph

fastball, an outstanding changeup, and a solid curve, Adenhart projects as a number-two starter in the big leagues. His struggles in 2007 were often self-inflicted; for the first time in his life he got hit hard, and he lost some aggressiveness because of it. Some pitchers need time to adjust to that kind of adversity. Fortunately, that's a luxury Adenhart has.

28. Chris Marrero, OF/1B, Nationals

Going into 2006, Marrero was generally considered the best pure hitter among potential high school draftees, but a disappointing senior year dropped him to the middle of the first round. In 2007, he hit like the early reviews were right, reaching High-A and slugging 23 home runs in the process. Marrero isn't some pull-happy monster, but a gifted hitter who focuses solely on hard contract, and his plate discipline made great strides throughout his first full season. Marrero's other tools fall well short of greatness, and he will likely be moved to first base to begin the season.

29. Angel Villalona, 3B, Giants

The Giants don't have a particularly strong presence in Latin America, so when Villalona, universally considered to be the best hitter to come out of the Dominican Republic in years, signed with them in 2006, it came as a complete surprise. In his pro debut, he looked to be worth every penny of the $2.1 million bonus he received. Just 17 years old and already as big as an ox, he's going to play his way off of third base pretty quickly, but with this kind of bat, it's not going to matter one bit.

30. Neftali Feliz, RHP, Rangers

Part of the Mark Teixiera haul, Feliz has been handled very carefully by both the Braves and Rangers, but in his 71 1/3 stateside innings, the Domincan hurler has allowed just 51 hits while striking out 97. He has as much raw stuff as any teenager; his fastball already sits in the mid-90s, and he should touch 90 mph more often as he fills out. Mix in a rapidly improving slider with some improvements in his command, and all systems are go for a spectacular takeoff in his full-season debut this year.

31. Matt LaPorta, OF, Brewers

LaPorta had as good a season as anyone in college baseball last year, hitting .402/.582/.817 for Florida in the ultra-tough SEC. Many saw him as the best pure hitter in the draft, but as a non-athlete who was limited to first base, he wasn't seen as much of an elite pick. Enter the Brewers, who made him the eighth overall selection. This was initially confusing, as the team already has a young star at first base, but Milwaukee immediately announced that LaPorta would move to left field. Even if he's not much more than acceptable there, his bat will carry his glove. With 12 home runs in just 115 pro at-bats, it already does.

32. Chin-Lung Hu, SS, Dodgers

Hu has astonished scouts for years with his defensive

prowess. He's a natural shortstop with the perfect combination of fundamentals and flashiness abetted by some of the quickest hands around. In 2007, he finally showed some life at the plate after adopting an Ichiro-like step in the bucket and an aggressive, contact-oriented approach that resulted in gap power that paid off with 40 doubles and 14 home runs. Hu is blocked for one more year by Rafael Furcal, but the Dodgers won't lose a shred of value when Hu takes over the following season.

33. Jeff Clement, C, Mariners

Always very aggressive with their assignments, the Mariners placed Clement at Double-A to begin his first full season in 2006, then inexplicably pushed him to Triple-A after he underwent a pair of minor surgeries to correct some knee and elbow issues. Healthy last year, Clement began to show the promise of his college days, projecting as a catcher who makes up for merely adequate defense with 30 home runs a year. Kenji Johjima is in the way for now, but the Mariners are considering easing Clement into the big leagues by having the two split time between catching and designated hitter, where they would represent an upgrade over Jose Vidro.

34. Ian Kennedy, RHP, Yankees

If you look at the numbers from Kennedy's full-season debut last year, this 34th-place ranking looks like an insult. He had a 1.89 ERA in 26 games spread over three levels, allowed just 91 hits in 146 1/3 innings and struck out 163. Still, he's a very good prospect but not a great one because he gets it done by being the ultimate finesse pitcher, painting spots at will and mixing his pitches well. His stuff is no better than average, so there's little room for error, but he's ready to be an average big-league starting pitcher right now, and a little more than that in the long run.

35. Ross Detwiler, RHP, Nationals

As the top talent in the draft, David Price was obviously also the top left-hander. Detwiler was the obvious number two southpaw to everyone but the Pirates, who confounded analysts when they selected Daniel Moskos (not on this list) with the fourth overall pick, leaving Detwiler to Washington at number six. The Nats are still pinching themselves, shocked that the Pirates would gift them with a 6-foot–4 projectable southpaw who can touch 95 mph with his fastball, has a plus curve, and was one of the more consistent performers throughout the college season. Detwiler could be up for good as early as the end of this season.

36. Jason Heyward, OF, Braves

Heyward frustrated scouts all spring. He played for a rural high school in Georgia, and the opposition invariably pitched around him. Few teams other than the Braves, who had been on him for years, got multiple looks at his swing. The Braves love taking local products and were thrilled when Heyward was still available with the 14th overall pick. He's 6-foot–4 with a ripped physique and is a true five-tool talent. One scout called him a better version of Jeff Francouer with more raw strength and a much better approach. He's the type of player who, the second he takes the field, makes you say, "I want one of those."

37. Geovany Soto, C, Cubs

The Cubs always thought Soto had the potential to develop into a big-league catcher, but nobody expected this. Soto got into the best shape of his life and exploded in 2007, finishing among the top three hitters in the Pacific Coast leagues in each of the slash-stat categories, walking away with PCL MVP honors, and stealing the Cubs' starting catcher job from Jason Kendall before the season was over. Kendall isn't in the way anymore, and Soto will be one of the NL's better catchers this year.

38. Brandon Wood, 3B/SS, Angels

Wood has made little progress since his borderline-historic season in 2005, when he amassed 101 extra-base hits in 134 games. His raw power, which comes not from pure strength, but from bat speed, remains tremendous, but pitchers at the upper levels have been able to take advantage of his impatient approach, consistently getting him to chase pitches out of the strike zone. Wood can play either position on the left side of the infield, but the Angels aren't making an opening for him in 2008, and will send him back to Triple-A to monitor the pitches he doesn't swing at as much as the ones he does.

39. Matt Antonelli, 2B, Padres

The Padres were the subject of some derision in 2006 after they selected Antonelli with their first-round pick only to watch him go homerless in his 60-game pro debut and look miscast as a third baseman who hit like a leadoff man. Those critics (myself included) jumped the gun. Antonelli made a successful transition to second base last year, hit 21 home runs while reaching Double-A, and continued his outstanding base-reaching ways, as evidenced by his scoring 123 runs in 131 contests. The Padres signed second baseman Tad Iguchi to a one-year deal, but it's just a stop-gap measure to give Antonelli a little more time in the oven.

40. Jacob McGee, LHP, Devil Rays

McGee gets some of the more diverse reviews out there. If we were able to get our hands on each team's prospect list, we would likely see McGee rank anywhere from the top 20 to somewhere in the 60 to 70 range. You don't need more than two hands to count the number of left-handers who can throw as hard as McGee; that velocity has served him well, as in the past two seasons he's struck out 346 men in 274 innings. The issue is that both his secondary offerings and his control lag behind. In a system loaded with starting-pitching prospects, it's only logical to expect some of them to move to relief roles, and McGee is the best candidate to not only do that, but to close.

41. Johnny Cueto, RHP, Reds

When you're a 5-foot–10 righty, you need to keep proving the doubters wrong. Despite Cueto's dominating 2006 campaign in A-ball, there were still plenty of skeptics last year. Cueto blew them away, just as he continued to blow away hitters, only this time at the upper levels of the Reds system. Despite his size, he's a power arm with a low- to mid-90s fastball and an above-average slider and changeup. While his stuff has held up for 160 innings, his frame still has people wondering if it will do so for 200-plus. Cueto has little left to prove in the minors, so the Reds could find out just how many innings are in that tiny body as early as this year.

42. Manny Parra, LHP, Brewers

Parra has teased the Brewers for years with his lefty power arm, but an inability to stay healthy has greatly slowed his path through the system. Healthy and outstanding since 2005 shoulder surgery, he had a brief but successful big-league debut last year that came to an unceremonious end when he broke his thumb. Parra has two plus pitches, a 92 to 95 mph fastball, and a hard biting curve, and projects as an above-average starter in the big leagues, a role he'll be given every opportunity to earn in spring training.

43. Steven Pearce, 1B, Pirates

Pearce was seen as just another generic senior when the Pirates selected him in the eighth round of the 2005 draft, but after popping 26 home runs in 2006 and 31 last year in 487 minor league at-bats, he's become one of the top power prospects in the game. His excellent contact rate (he struck out just 70 times in the minors last year) should allow him to hit for average as well. The Pirates hope he can make the conversion from first base to an outfield corner in order to provide a much-needed power bat in their lineup this year.

44. Chris Tillman, RHP, Mariners

Tillman had a 5.26 ERA at High-A this year, but he was just 19 and pitching in one of the biggest offensive parks in the minors, so ignore the numbers; he remains an outstanding prospect. With a tall, loose, and highly projectable frame, Tillman parks his fastball in the 92 to 95 mph zone with more to come and freezes batters with a hard 12-to-6 curveball. As with most teenagers, there are some issues with command and developing a changeup, but his ceiling is like that of the Sistine Chapel.

45. Josh Vitters, 3B, Cubs

The third overall pick in last year's draft, Vitters was the best pure hitter available, with some comparing him to Vladimir Guerrero for his combination of bat speed, hand-eye coordination, and plus power, while showing no weakness in terms of pitch type or location. Like many young hitters with this kind of talent, it comes at a price. Vitters has little plate discipline because he's never needed it—he simply hits everything. Guerrero learned to be a more patient hitter, while others players with this skill set, such as Alfonso Sori-

ano and Howie Kendrick, did not or have yet to. We won't know which way Vitters will go for a few more years.

46. Fautino de los Santos, RHP, Athletics

De los Santos was one of two big prizes the A's received from the White Sox in return for Nick Swisher (you'll find the other ten notches below). While de los Santos is a little short for a pitcher, he has a big, thick frame that bodes well for future durability. He gets outstanding leg drive on a 91 to 95 mph fastball that touches 98 and features a bit of cutting action and has also flashed a very good curveball at times. That combination alone was enough to limit Sally League hitters to just over one hit every two innings. The Oakland system was desperate for power arms, and de los Santos is just that.

47. Austin Jackson, OF, Yankees

Jackson is another one of those toolsy outfielders who went from great athlete/crappy ballplayer to great athlete/great ballplayer in the blink of an eye. Unlike many of these transformations, we actually know what happened here, as Yankees coaches re-engineered his swing (see his player comment in the Yankees' chapter for details). With his considerable tools and a .345/.398/.566 line at High-A under his belt, Jackson will now face a much bigger test in Double-A this year. If he passes it, he could provide 20 homers and 40 steals annually.

48. Jose Tabata, OF, Yankees

In some ways, Jose Tabata's development has been a disappointment, as his power has simply never come. At the same time, there are mitigating factors all over the place, beginning with the fact that he was at High-A last year and didn't turn 19 until the end of the year, and that he was dealing with a wrist injury all year that ultimately required surgery. Tabata is clearly a gifted hitter—hitting .307 in the Florida State League as a teenager is a remarkable feat—but even taking into account the wrist problems, he's not especially big, nor is there much loft or leverage in his swing. Is he a .300 hitter in the future? Hell yes. Is he a middle-of-the-order power source? The jury is still out.

49. Eric Hurley, RHP, Rangers

Hurley entered the year as the Rangers' top prospect, but while he pitched well at Double- and Triple-A, scouts are concerned about his lack of development. He's had the same weaknesses for years now, primarily a below-average changeup and a dangerous tendency to work up in the zone, so it's hard to see him suddenly fixing his issues to move into the elite class. What he has now is enough to be a solid third starter, and he's close to getting his opportunity.

50. Brett Anderson, LHP, Athletics

Anderson is the son of a major college coach, but even daddy was willing to admit that the kid was ready for pro ball when Arizona drafted him out of high school in 2006.

There is no teenage pitcher with more polish, command, or feel for his craft than Anderson, and his stuff isn't exactly pedestrian, as his fastball sits in the low 90s and he backs it up with a solid curveball and a downright nasty changeup. In a perfect world, he ends up as the left-handed version of the pitcher he was traded for, Dan Haren.

51. Fernando Martinez, OF, Mets

Martinez is the Mets' version of Tabata. He's a gifted hitter, but playing at levels far too high for his age has hampered his performance at High-A in 2006 (at age 17), and Double-A last year (at age 18). In the latter case, he was also dealing with a hand injury, again like Tabata. As young as he is, even holding his own at those levels was a remarkable achievement. Martinez remains an outstanding offensive prospect who will likely hit in the middle of a batting order one day.

52. Adam Miller, RHP, Indians

Miller has filthy stuff, with a fastball that gets into the upper 90s and a fantastic slider, but he has also shown an inability to stay healthy, missing significant portions for two of the last three seasons with arm troubles. Because of that, the Indians will exercise caution with him, likely beginning his major league career in the bullpen once they deem him ready. After not pitching during most of last year's second half, Miller looked promising in his Arizona Fall League showing.

53. Justin Masterson, RHP, Red Sox

Masterson was toiling away at a tiny Indiana college before transferring to San Diego State for his junior year, and it's been nothing but good things since. He arguably has the best sinker in the minors, a heavy pitch that he can get up to 94 mph and is nearly impossible to get any lift on. Scouts would like him even more if he would raise his arm angle to take more advantage of his 6-foot–6 frame, but the obvious comparisons to successful big-league sinkerballers such as Chien-Ming Wang, Fausto Carmona, and Derek Lowe are already being thrown out there.

54. J. R. Towles, C, Astros

Houston's utter offensive black hole behind the plate is about to be plugged. Towles might not be as heady a ballplayer as Ausmus, and he's no more than average as a defender, but he sure can hit. The only Astros prospect on this list, and the only one who even merited consideration, Towles projects as a .280 to .300 hitter with 12 to 18 home runs a year, which puts him in rare company at his position.

55. Carlos Triunfel, SS, Mariners

Another player for whom age plays a factor, Triunfel hit .288 at High-A last year despite the fact that, if he was an American, he wouldn't have been eligible to be drafted out of high school until this June. That takes a special kind of talent, but there are some holes in his game as well. In 371 at-bats last year, he had just 22 extra-base hits, including zero home runs, and walked just 17 times. While he's a good athlete, he's not especially quick, and his thick lower half means he's not likely to be a shortstop for long.

56. Gio Gonzalez, LHP, Athletics

Last year's minor league strikeout leader was the other big arm (along with de los Santos) to arrive from the White Sox in the Nick Swisher deal. Despite his strikeout numbers, Gonzalez is not the kind of guy who blows hitters away. He's short and has average velocity (which is good for a lefty), but his curveball is an absolute monster. Despite his size, Gonzalez has proven to be quite durable, and while he'll begin the year in Triple-A, the rebuilding A's are going to consider future options this year, including Gonzalez.

57. Jed Lowrie, SS, Red Sox

After a slow start to his career, last season Lowrie began to hit like he had in college, finishing the year with 47 doubles, eight triples, and 13 home runs in 133 games. Like most Stanford products, he's also a heady player and a guy who gets the maximum out of his skills, but unfortunately, those skills don't include playing shortstop, as his quickness just isn't good enough for the position. He's nearly ready to be an offensive second baseman in the majors, but there's no room for one of those in Boston.

58. Elvis Andrus, SS, Rangers

Scouts have drooled over Andrus's tools for years now, but his offensive production has yet to meet expectations. Defensively, Andrus is an absolute gem with the range, hands, instincts, and arm to play at a Gold Glove level. The question is how much his bat will develop. Just a few improvements would make him an ideal number-two hitter, capable of hitting .300 with not much in the way of secondary skills other than 30-plus stolen bases annually, but right now he looks like a guy who should hit seventh or eighth.

59. Jordan Walden, RHP, Angels

Walden was yet another steal for scouting director Eddie Bane. Three years ago, Bane drafted Nick Adenhart, who had just had Tommy John surgery, when other teams assumed he was going to college. In 2006, he used the now-dead draft-and-follow process to take Walden, who was throwing upper–90s gas as a junior but never came close to that in his draft year. After a season at junior college, the velocity came back, the Angels gave him seven figures to sign, and another power arm materialized in the Angels' system.

60. Ryan Kalish, OF, Red Sox

When the Red Sox gave Kalish $600,000 in 2006 to lure the eighth-round pick away from college baseball, they saw him as an unrefined athlete who would require patience. Instead of struggling, Kalish was the top positional player in the New York-Penn League last year before his season ended early due to a wrist injury. All of his tools grade out at least as average, and his bat, power, and speed all have plus potential.

61. Matt Latos, RHP, Padres

Latos's story is similar to Walden's. He was one of the top high school arms in the 2006 draft, but teams were turned off by his attitude. The Padres took a flyer on him as a draft-and-follow, and he had a great showing at a Florida junior college while also maturing a great deal. A power righty with a mid-90s fastball, Latos is the complete package when it comes to body and arm strength, but he still has a ways to go in developing the things he'll need to become a complete package as a pitcher, like breaking stuff and control.

62. Engel Beltre, OF, Rangers

The Rangers loaded up on young, high-ceiling prospects with their midseason housecleaning, and Beltre is the best of the position players they acquired. Coming from Boston in the Eric Gagné deal, Beltre offers big-time raw power from the left side, outstanding speed, and a right fielder's arm. The Rangers team at Low-A Clinton is going to be loaded this year, and Beltre will be the offensive leader.

63. Brent Lillibridge, SS, Braves

Positional scarcity plays into these rankings to a certain degree. Lillibridge is probably not a future superstar, but he is likely to be an above-average big league shortstop, which makes him a better prospect than some first basemen or corner outfielders who may project as more productive. Lillibridge is a solid hitter with a good approach and gap power, who draws his fair share of walks, has the speed and instincts to steal 40 bags a year, and is an above-average defender. There was some talk of moving him back to center field (which he played quite well in college), but the Braves have belayed that move, believing that Lillibridge will be big-league ready as a middle infielder by mid-2008.

64. Gerardo Parra, OF, Diamondbacks

When Parra and Carlos Gonzalez were in the same organization, Parra was generally seen as a Gonzalez starter kit—an athletic, toolsy Venezuelan who profiled as a classic right fielder. Now that Parra has had his big league debut, the perception has changed. Parra and Gonzalez are similar physically, but Gonzalez's power is far superior while Parra is the better all-around hitter. Parra is more of a contact hitter who projects to hit for a high average, but if he can't stay in center field—and he's already shaky there—he's going to have to *really* hit.

65. Carlos Gomez, OF, Mets

Gomez has so many tools, but none of them are big-league ready. Plenty of prospects have benefited from a swift rise, but plenty have been damaged by one as well as they never got the proper time to work on their weaknesses (we're looking at you, Cubs management who ruined Corey Patterson). Gomez would have been best served by a full year in the minor leagues last year, and that's still what he needs. His projection remains very high, but he's reaching the point at which he needs to fulfill it.

66. Scott Elbert, LHP, Dodgers

Elbert entered the year as one of the top left-handed pitching prospects in the minors, but he lasted just three starts before requiring shoulder surgery. The Dodgers insist he had only a minor procedure to clean up his labrum, but shoulder surgery is still shoulder surgery. We won't know how much of Elbert's power arsenal is still there until he takes the mound again. There's already some bad news, as players recovering from the procedure tend to struggle with their command, something which was already Elbert's biggest (and perhaps only) weakness.

67. Alan Horne, RHP, Yankees

It's been a long road for Horne, who was a first-round pick out of high school by the Indians in 2001 but didn't begin his pro career until four years, three colleges, and one Tommy John surgery later. In 2007, Horne finally had a taste of stability, staying at Double-A all year while leading the Eastern League in ERA and strikeouts. He's nearly a complete product, with four solid offerings and an excellent feel for his craft, but with the Yankees' glut of young pitching, he might start his career as a reliever.

68. Carlos Carrasco, RHP, Phillies

Carrasco is Philadelphia's top prospect thanks to his excellent fastball/changeup combination, but he encountered trouble for the first time in his career at Double-A last year. That was mostly due to command troubles and his inability to develop a consistent breaking ball, a combination which led to more walks and fewer missed bats, which meant more hits. There's still plenty of time for Carrasco to recover, as he was pitching at that level as a 20-year-old.

69. Chris Perez, RHP, Cardinals

Arguably the best pure closing prospect in the game, Perez was the closer at Miami when the Cardinals made him a first-round pick in 2006, and he had no trouble adjusting to pro ball last year, splitting time between Double- and Triple-A while allowing just 23 hits in 54 2/3 innings. He has classic closer stuff with a mid-90s fastball and a hard slider with a sharp, two-plane break. Jason Isringhausen can thank Perez for the fact that the final year of his contract is also likely be his last with the Cardinals.

70. Brandon Jones, OF, Braves

Arguably a better football than baseball player in high school and frequently delayed by minor injuries early in his career, Jones is a late bloomer. Last year, he conquered Double- and Triple-A on the way to his big-league debut, making 2007 one long coming-out party. While neither his power nor his speed is at the top of the charts, they're both above average, giving him 20/20 possibilities to go with a high batting average. Jones will compete for a starting job in spring training, but his poor defensive skills limit him to a corner, so though he'll help the Braves keep up their Jones quota, he's not going to replace Andruw.

71. Bryan Anderson, C, Cardinals

Anderson spent last season at Double-A as a 20-year-old and continued to show highly advanced hitting skills. He doesn't offer much in the way of power or walks, but a big-league catcher who can hit .300 is a rare commodity. Anderson will ultimately force the Cardinals to make a difficult decision, as he's the polar opposite of incumbent Yadier Molina, an offense-first catcher with little to offer on defense.

72. Luke Hochevar, RHP, Royals

Hochevar was the first overall pick in 2006. While he reached the big leagues in his full-season debut last year, his overall performance left much to be desired. Hochevar works off a low- to mid-90s fastball and an excellent curve, but he proved to be quite hittable. The scouting cliché "doesn't trust his stuff" came up often. Roughly translated, it means Hochevar was pitching scared, falling behind in the count and grooving fastballs. That's a correctable defect, so he should find success down the road.

73. Michael Main, RHP, Rangers

Main was arguably the best high school outfielder in the 2007 draft, but his upside as a pitcher was too good for teams to ignore. Because of his athleticism—he might be the fastest runner of any pitcher in the pros right now—he defines the word "projectable," which says something since he already pitches in the low 90s and has been clocked as high as 98 mph. Like many teenage pitchers, Main still requires a great deal of refinement, but he's already well on the way there.

74. Chris Davis, 3B, Rangers

A 2006 fifth-rounder, Davis hit 15 home runs in his pro debut, but even the most optimistic projections didn't anticipate his 2007 season in which he reached Double-A, hitting 36 home runs in the process. Does he need to develop a more patient approach? Sure. Is the high strikeout rate a concern? Absolutely. Will he be able to stay at third base? Probably not. Is there another prospect on whose potential to hit 40 home runs in a big-league season you'd want to put down as large a wager? No.

75. Chorye Spoone, RHP, Orioles

Just so you don't sound ignorant in your fantasy draft, it's pronounced "Cory." Spoone has endeared himself to scouts with a pair of plus fastballs. His four-seam heater touches 95 mph and misses bats like it has eyes, while his two-seam sinker also makes him an extreme groundball pitcher. Spoone's is a wide body, but so far all that has meant is outstanding stamina. He'll be spooning up extra helpings of game time as a big-league innings-eater by 2009.

76. Jeremy Jeffress, RHP, Brewers

If scouting reports and game performance automatically assured a prospects destiny, then Jeffress would rank in the top 25 of this list. He has size, stuff—he hit 100 mph on the radar gun several times last year—and draws comparisons to a young Doc Gooden. Unfortunately, he can't stay away from marijuana, making those Gooden comps somewhat ironic. He was hit with a 50-game suspension for a positive test during the year, and then tested positive again during the team's instructional league. The Brewers are hoping that an offseason spent near the team complex in Arizona and away from some bad influences, followed by an assignment to the Florida State League, will help prevent his career from going up in smoke.

77. Taylor Teagarden, C, Rangers

A Three True Outcomes hitter who has 34 home runs, 107 walks, and 167 strikeouts in 148 pro games, Teagarden is a valuable hitter and an outstanding defensive player who would rank much higher on this list if there was any confidence in his ability to stay behind the dish instead of breaking like one. Last year, a slow recovery from 2006 Tommy John surgery limited him to part-time backstoppage, and the elbow continues to flare up from time to time. If he's physically able to catch, he'll be a tremendous asset. If not, he'll be a one-dimensional first baseman.

78. Wes Hodges, 3B, Indians

Hodges had a disappointing final year at Georgia Tech, his numbers slipping while he tried to play though some minor injuries, but in his full-season debut, he looked to be worth every bit of the $1 million bonus he received as a 2006 second-round pick. He does nothing great, but also nothing poorly, as he projects as a .280- to .300-hitting third baseman with 20-plus home runs and 80 walks a year to go along with solid defense.

79. Deolis Guerra, RHP, Mets

Like Carlos Gomez and Fernando Martinez, Guerra is another prospect whom the Mets would best serve by not pushing so hard. Pitching in the Florida State League as an 18-year-old last year, Guerra more than held his own, but he has yet to prove he can last an entire season, not to mention get hitters out consistently. Six-foot-five and powerfully built, he has gained velocity each year since signing; his fastball now sits in the low 90s and touches 95 mph, and his changeup is a thing of beauty. The Mets need to let him stay where he is, crank out 120 innings, and work on his curveball before pitting him against players on the brink of the majors.

80. Chris Nelson, SS, Rockies

Nelson looked like an elite prospect after following his eighth-overall selection in 2004 with a monster pro debut. Two years later, he had all but vanished from human memory following a pair of subpar seasons at Low-A. His game finally began to coalesce in the Cal League last year with a .318/.386/.614 line in the second half and noticeable defensive growth. His performance in Double-A this year will show if those improvements were real and not just a Cal

League mirage. If they were, Nelson will rank much higher next year.

81. Michael Burgess, OF, Nationals

In 2006, high school slugger Chris Marrero fell to the Nationals at the 15th overall pick because of a poor senior year. Last year, the same set of circumstances allowed the Nats to snap up Burgess. He paid immediate dividends, crushing 11 home runs in his first 198 pro at-bats. Patience and power are Burgess's calling cards. He's the rare player who will be the idol of both scouts and analysts, not to mention the untold millions of civilians who are sadly unaware that they are witnesses to the great ideological battle of our time.

82. Greg Reynolds, RHP, Rockies

Colorado's selection of Reynolds over Longoria with the second overall pick in 2006 looks just as foolish now as it did then. That said, Reynolds looked very good last year in eight Texas League starts, limiting Double-A hitters to a .180 average before shoulder problems put him on the shelf. While his low–90s fastball isn't a pure sinker, Reynolds' 6-foot–7 frame and overhand delivery make him a groundball pitcher because of the natural downward leverage he gets on the pitch. That makes him a good candidate for success in Coors Field. If he stays healthy, he'll get his first pro visit there at some point during the season.

83. Gorkys Hernandez, OF, Braves

Hernandez was the 2007 Midwest League MVP, but Travis Snider was clearly the more deserving candidate, which shows you that they screw up awards at the minor league level too. One of two major prospects received from Detroit in the Edgar Renteria deal, Hernandez is one of the most exciting players in baseball with top marks for his speed and defense. Right now, however, he has little in the way of patience or power, which means he's just a guy who hits line drives and runs like the wind. He needs to add another wrinkle to stop the Braves from making like Peggy Lee and asking the musical question, "Is that all there is? … If that's all there is, my friends … let's break out the booze."

84. Henry Sosa, RHP, Giants

Thanks to a 97 mph fastball and a plus curve, Sosa had more than twice as many strikeouts (61) as hits allowed (30) in 13 Sally League games last year. He then moved up to High-A and struck out more than 11 men per nine innings. He's surprisingly raw for a 22-year-old and still needs to throw more strikes and learn how to set hitters up instead of trying to blow every batter away. Some think he's better suited to be a closer.

85. Radhames Liz, RHP, Orioles

Orioles fans got to see the best of Liz during his big-league debut late last season, as he struck out nearly a batter per inning. They also saw the worst of Liz, as he also walked nearly a batter per inning. The strongest arm in the O's system, Liz

pumps out mid- to upper–90s heat and a solid curve, but his violent mechanics and below-average changeup leave many projecting him as a closer in the end. His stuff should play either way.

86. Jair Jurrjens, RHP, Braves

Jurrjens' big-league success as a 21-year-old got him involved in the Renteria trade. A highly polished strike-thrower with an effective three-pitch mix, Jurrjens has probably already maxed out his talent. Fortunately, what he has is more than enough to be a middle-of-the-rotation starter right now.

87. Aaron Poreda, LHP, White Sox

The White Sox replaced their scouting department after years of safe, boring picks. Following general manager Kenny Williams' mandate to add a power arm, the new guys selected Poreda, a big, strong left-hander who can touch 99 mph with his fastball. Of course, that's pretty much all he has going for him, which is why he lasted until the second half of the first round in last year's draft. His secondary stuff is still in the pupa stage, but wow, what an arm.

88. Chris Volstad, RHP, Marlins

Volstad is the strangest of creatures, a strike-throwing machine with a finesse style packed into a 6-foot-7 power pitcher's frame. His fastball is more notable for its sink than its velocity, and though he has a good curve, he lacks that one go-to offering. Content to avoid walks and let his defense help him out, Volstad holds his stuff deep into games and projects to be eating innings in the majors by 2009.

89. Hank Conger, C, Angels

Hyun-Choi "Hank" Conger had his full-season debut marred by back issues (he's missing *X-Men* #136 and the first *Ambush Bug* mini-series), but when healthy, he showed off the power bat than got him drafted in 2006's first round. Conger gets tremendous loft in his swing, but much of his future depends on his ability to stay behind the plate, which right now is just a 50/50 proposition because the lad may be too big to squat.

90. Max Scherzer, RHP, Diamondbacks

Because of the new draft rules, Scherzer will go down in history as the last of the year-long draft holdouts. Drafted in June 2006 and signed in May 2007, Scherzer struck out 30 batters over 17 innings while allowing just five hits in his first three pro starts at High-A, but Double-A proved to be much more difficult, as he learned the tough lesson that man cannot live by fastball alone. Most now see him as a closer thanks to his upper–90s gas. He was dominant in short outings in the Arizona Fall League, which might accelerate his move to the pen.

91. Casey Weathers, RHP, Rockies

Every draft has that one college closer who's supposed to

move quickly. Last June, that closer was Casey Weathers, who finished his junior year at Vanderbilt by striking out three batters for every hit he allowed. There's nothing pretty about Weathers. He's a nasty, big-bodied righty with a violent delivery and questionable control, but batters are often helpless against his upper-90s fastball and a power slider that has been clocked as high as 92 mph. It won't take long for him to provide the Rockies with the first shut-down closer in franchise history.

92. Dexter Fowler, OF, Rockies

After an eye-popping full-season debut, Fowler got off to a slow start at High-A Modesto last year, but was hitting .349 in 16 June games when his season was cut short by a broken hand. Right now, he's just an on-base machine with plus speed and great center-field skills, but scouts believe he is a true five-tool athlete, and figure that power will eventually come out of his 6-foot-5 frame.

93. Wladimir Balentien, OF, Mariners

After hitting just .230 in Double-A in 2006, Balentien shortened his swing last year, and it paid off. He can still be prone to a high strikeout rate, and can look foolish against good breaking stuff, but shortening his swing didn't cost him any power—when he gets a hold of one, it's a thing of beauty. The Mariners opened up an outfield spot for Adam Jones in 2008; they might be forced to open another one for Balentien shortly thereafter.

94. Neil Walker, 3B, Pirates

The Pirates' first-round pick in 2004 made a successful transition from catcher to third base in 2007, and he had a good year at the plate as well. The problem is what the positional change does to his projection. If Walker was a 21-year-old backstop coming off a Double-A season with a .288/.362/.462 batting line, he'd be a special prospect. As a third baseman, he's merely good. Luckily for Walker, he's in Pittsburgh, where good is more than enough to make him the third baseman of the future.

95. Michael Bowden, RHP, Red Sox

Bowden seemingly achieved the impossible during the first half of 2007 by excelling for High-A Lancaster, whose average home game featured 16.3 runs. While he was unable to bring that success to Double-A, he was also among the youngest pitchers in the league. With above-average stuff and excellent command, Bowden has the upside of a third starter, but while his quirky mechanics give him deception, they also work against him at times when he gets out of synch.

96. Joe Savery, LHP, Phillies

The Phillies think they got one of the steals of the 2007 draft in the savory Savery, who was projected to be a top-ten pick going into the season, but underperformed as he recovered slowly from a minor procedure on his shoulder. The ultra-athletic Savery possesses power stuff with a fastball and changeup that are both plus pitches. If he makes any progress on his curveball, he could become something more than a number-three starter.

97. Ben Revere, OF, Twins

The Twins raised some eyebrows when they took Revere with their first-round pick (28th overall) last June, but his pro debut did much to cull the herd of doubters. An absolute burner who knows how to utilize his speed both offensively and defensively (yes, Revere rides again—someone wake up Henry Wadsworth Longfellow), he racked up 10 triples and 21 stolen bases in his 50-game pro debut. He needs to refine his approach in order to profile as a future leadoff hitter, but even though he's three or four years away from the majors, he's already the heir apparent to Torii Hunter in center field.

98. Trevor Cahill, RHP, Athletics

Oakland has a good high school arm on their hands; now we've seen everything. Then again, Cahill is not a young, lightning-armed stud, but more like a polished college product. The difference is that he'll be just 20 years old in this, his third pro season, so he has a little projection in him. He has impressive command of a three-pitch mix. The A's rotation at High-A Stockton will definitely be one to watch as it will include Cahill and two other Top 100 prospects in new additions Brett Anderson and Fautino de los Santos.

99. Chris Carter, 1B, Athletics

Another prospect from the Dan Haren gift-pack, Carter gives Oakland a much-needed power prospect, but his bat is his only tool. He's a big, plodding first baseman, but his bat is as quick as his body is slow, he has a solid approach at the plate, and he's so massively strong that he doesn't need to perfectly center a ball to get it out of the park. He's yet another top A's prospect headed for High-A. Putting his power in the California League could result in some tremendous numbers.

100. Lars Anderson, 1B, Red Sox

Anderson gets a lot of hype (being a Boston prospect doesn't hurt), but his pro debut was a mixed bag. While he hit for average and drew a ton of walks, he tended to leave his power in batting practice. That's a concern for an apprentice first baseman, as first-base prospects who don't project to post consistent 900-plus OPS figures in the majors are considered suspect in the minds of front office types. Anderson has plenty of promise, but right now, nobody is calling him a sure thing.

PECOTA Leaderboards

Compiled by Marc Normandin

PECOTA Leaderboards are a new addition to the annual this year. Below you will find PECOTA leaders in nine offensive categories and ten pitching categories. Both groups start off with the top 20 projections in each of the typical 5x5 fantasy scoring categories (AVG, HR, RBI, R, SB for hitters, W, K, ERA, WHIP, SV for pitchers). The one exception is stolen bases for which we've provided two different lists. Because the list of stolen base leaders is cluttered with players who are unlikely to see much if any playing time in the major leagues this year, we've provided both a top-15 list of stolen base projections for established major league players and a separate top-10 list of stolen base projections for minor leaguers. Despite this split, it is important to remember that PECOTA projects *all* players to the major leagues, so even the stolen base totals in the top 10 minor leaguers list represent *major* league steals.

In the Hitters section, we also present the top 10 projections for on-base percentage, isolated power, and Equivalent Average. Finally we present the top 10 VORP projections for each of the eight defensive positions and designated hitter, preceded by the top 10 VORP list for all hitters, regardless of position. Some players appear on the position lists despite the fact that they are not actually expected to crack their team's starting lineups at the start of the year. PECOTA is unaware of such managerial decisions and thus sheds light on the value that is being wasted by leaving players such as Matt Antonelli, Joe Dillon, J.R. Towles, and Jeff Keppinger on the bench or in the minors.

Finally we provide three lists to help you identify some of PECOTA's risers and fallers. The first two show the 15 established major leaguers whose VORP totals are expected to experience the largest increase from 2007 to 2008 and the 15 whose totals are expected to experience the largest decrease. The third and final list in the hitters' section shows the top 10 projected VORPs for players who retain rookie eligibility entering the 2008 season. These three lists are repeated for the pitchers at the end of the Pitcher section, which also includes top-10 lists for WXRL, Equivalent K/9IP, Peripheral ERA, and Stuff Score, and a list of the top 20 projected VORP totals for all pitchers.

HITTERS

Batting Average

RANK	NAME	TEAM	BA
1.	Albert Pujols	SLN	.327
2.	Matt Holliday	COL	.318
3.	Chipper Jones	ATL	.315
4.	Vladimir Guerrero	LAA	.310
5.	Todd Helton	COL	.309
6.	Moises Alou	NYN	.307
T7.	Magglio Ordoñez	DET	.306
T7.	Hanley Ramirez	FLO	.306
T9.	Placido Polanco	DET	.305
T9.	Jeff Keppinger	CIN	.305
T9.	David Wright	NYN	.305
12.	Ichiro Suzuki	SEA	.304
T13.	Derrek Lee	CHN	.303
T13.	Willy Taveras	COL	.303
T15.	Aramis Ramirez	CHN	.301
T15.	Garrett Atkins	COL	.301
T17.	Ryan Spilborghs	COL	.300
T17.	Miguel Cabrera	DET	.300
T17.	Ryan Braun	MIL	.300
20.	Robinson Cano	NYA	.299

Home Runs

RANK	NAME	TEAM	HR
1.	Ryan Howard	PHI	44
2.	Ryan Braun	MIL	39
3.	Prince Fielder	MIL	38
T4.	Adam Dunn	CIN	36
T4.	Alex Rodriguez	NYA	36
T6.	David Ortiz	BOS	35
T6.	Alfonso Soriano	CHN	35
8.	Carlos Peña	TBA	33
T9.	Albert Pujols	SLN	32
T9.	Mark Teixeira	ATL	32
11.	David Wright	NYN	31
T12.	Rick Ankiel	SLN	30
T12.	Lance Berkman	HOU	30
T14.	Jay Bruce	CIN	29
T14.	Matt Holliday	COL	29
T14.	Andruw Jones	LAN	29
T14.	Jim Thome	CHA	29
T18.	Miguel Cabrera	DET	28
T18.	Adrian Gonzalez	SDN	28

T18.	Travis Hafner	CLE	28
T18.	Aramis Ramirez	CHN	28
T18.	Mark Reynolds	ARI	28

Runs Batted In

RANK	NAME	TEAM	RBI
1.	Ryan Howard	PHI	122
2.	David Ortiz	BOS	119
3.	Ryan Braun	MIL	117
4.	Alex Rodriguez	NYA	116
5.	Albert Pujols	SLN	115
6.	Prince Fielder	MIL	111
7.	Matt Holliday	COL	108
8.	David Wright	NYN	105
T9.	Miguel Cabrera	DET	104
T9.	Alfonso Soriano	CHN	104
T11.	Aramis Ramirez	CHN	103
T11.	Mark Teixeira	ATL	103
13.	Rick Ankiel	SLN	101
T14.	Garrett Atkins	COL	100
T14.	Carlos Lee	HOU	100
T16.	Lance Berkman	HOU	99
T16.	Jay Bruce	CIN	99
T16.	Adrian Gonzalez	SDN	99
T16.	Vladimir Guerrero	LAA	99
T16.	Justin Morneau	MIN	99
T16.	Carlos Peña	TBA	99

Runs

RANK	NAME	TEAM	RUNS
T1.	Albert Pujols	SLN	120
T1.	Alex Rodriguez	NYA	120
3.	David Wright	NYN	119
4.	Hanley Ramirez	FLO	113
5.	Ryan Braun	MIL	111
6.	Jose Reyes	NYN	110
7.	David Ortiz	BOS	109
8.	Prince Fielder	MIL	106
9.	Matt Holliday	COL	105
10.	Grady Sizemore	CLE	103
T11.	Jimmy Rollins	PHI	102
T11.	Mark Teixeira	ATL	102
T11.	Chase Utley	PHI	102
14.	Brian Roberts	BAL	101
15.	Ryan Howard	PHI	100
T16.	Lance Berkman	HOU	99
T16.	Chipper Jones	ATL	99
T18.	Miguel Cabrera	DET	96
T18.	Adam Dunn	CIN	96
20.	Derrek Lee	CHN	94

Stolen Bases, Major Leaguers

RANK	NAME	TEAM	SB
1.	Jose Reyes	NYN	60
2.	Hanley Ramirez	FLO	38
3.	Juan Pierre	LAN	37

T4.	Carl Crawford	TBA	35
T4.	Brian Roberts	BAL	35
6.	Chone Figgins	LAA	33
7.	Jacoby Ellsbury	BOS	32
8.	Alexi Casilla	MIN	31
9.	Reggie Abercrombie	HOU	30
10.	B. J. Upton	TBA	30
11.	Jimmy Rollins	PHI	29
12.	Corey Patterson	BAL	29
13.	Willy Taveras	COL	26
14.	Rafael Furcal	LAN	25
T15.	Felix Lopez	WAS	23
T15.	Alex Rodriguez	NYY	23

Stolen Bases, Minor Leaguers

RANK	NAME	TEAM	SB
1.	Eric Young Jr.	COL	62
2.	Emmanuel Burriss	SFN	60
T3.	Darren Ford	MIL	47
T3.	Pedro Powell	PIT	47
5.	Eugenio Velez	SFN	41
6.	Freddy Guzman	TEX	37
7.	Josh Anderson	ATL	35
T8.	Quintin Berry	PHI	34
T8.	Brent Lillibridge	ATL	34
10.	Bradley Coon	LAA	33

On-Base Percentage

RANK	NAME	TEAM	OBP
1.	Albert Pujols	SLN	.427
2.	Barry Bonds	SFN	.419
3.	Todd Helton	COL	.415
4.	Chipper Jones	ATL	.410
T5.	David Ortiz	BOS	.402
T5.	Nick Johnson	WAS	.402
T7.	Alex Rodriguez	NYA	.401
T7.	Kosuke Fukudome	CHN	.401
9.	David Wright	NYN	.395
10.	Mark Teixeira	ATL	.394

Isolated Power

RANK	NAME	TEAM	ISO
1.	Ryan Howard	PHI	.302
2.	Adam Dunn	CIN	.288
3.	Ryan Braun	MIL	.275
4.	Prince Fielder	MIL	.273
5.	Alfonso Soriano	CHN	.266
6.	Jim Thome	CHA	.264
7.	David Ortiz	BOS	.259
8.	Alex Rodriguez	NYA	.256
9.	Pat Burrell	PHI	.255
10.	Mark Teixeira	ATL	.252

Equivalent Average

RANK	NAME	TEAM	EQA
1.	Albert Pujols	SLN	.335

2.	Alex Rodriguez	NYA	.333
3.	David Ortiz	BOS	.323
4.	Chipper Jones	ATL	.321
5.	David Wright	NYN	.319
6.	Mark Teixeira	ATL	.312
7.	Miguel Cabrera	FLO	.310
8.	Jim Thome	CHA	.309
T9.	Carlos Peña	TBA	.308
T9.	Prince Fielder	MIL	.308

Value Over Replacement Player, All Hitters

RANK	NAME	TEAM	VORP
1.	Albert Pujols	SLN	73.1
2.	David Wright	NYN	69.3
3.	Alex Rodriguez	NYA	63.3
4.	Ryan Braun	MIL	60.6
5.	Hanley Ramirez	FLO	59.7
6.	Chipper Jones	ATL	57.1
7.	David Ortiz	BOS	51.3
8.	Chase Utley	PHI	51.1
9.	Prince Fielder	MIL	49.3
10.	Mark Teixeira	ATL	48.8

Value Over Replacement Player, Catcher

RANK	NAME	TEAM	VORP
1.	Jorge Posada	NYA	37.1
2.	Victor Martinez	CLE	31.7
3.	Joe Mauer	MIN	30.4
4.	Russell Martin	LAN	29.9
5.	Brian McCann	ATL	29.7
6.	Josh Bard	SDN	26.7
7.	Geovany Soto	CHN	23.5
8.	J.R. Towles	HOU	20.0
9.	Jarrod Saltalamacchia	TEX	15.1
10.	Bengie Molina	SFN	14.8

Value Over Replacement Player, First Base

RANK	NAME	TEAM	VORP
1.	Albert Pujols	SLN	73.1
2.	Prince Fielder	MIL	49.3
3.	Mark Teixeira	ATL	48.8
4.	Ryan Howard	PHI	42.7
5.	Lance Berkman	HOU	42.0
6.	Derrek Lee	CHN	37.7
7.	Adrian Gonzalez	SDN	36.9
8.	Nick Johnson	WAS	30.9
9.	Carlos Peña	TBA	30.6
10.	Todd Helton	COL	24.1

Value Over Replacement Player, Second Base

RANK	NAME	TEAM	VORP
1.	Chase Utley	PHI	51.1
2.	Kelly Johnson	ATL	36.0
3.	Brian Roberts	BAL	33.5
4.	Jeff Kent	LAN	32.1
5.	Dan Uggla	FLO	31.7

6.	Robinson Cano	NYA	31.1
7.	Rickie Weeks	MIL	27.2
8.	Dustin Pedroia	BOS	26.2
9.	Freddy Sanchez	PIT	25.0
10.	Matt Antonelli	SDN	23.8

Value Over Replacement Player, Third Base

RANK	NAME	TEAM	VORP
1.	David Wright	NYN	69.3
2.	Alex Rodriguez	NYY	63.3
3.	Ryan Braun	MIL	60.6
4.	Chipper Jones	ATL	57.1
5.	Miguel Cabrera	FLO	47.8
6.	Ryan Zimmerman	WAS	41.0
7.	Aramis Ramirez	CHN	40.7
8.	Kevin Kouzmanoff	SDN	32.7
9.	Joe Dillon	MIL	30.3
10.	Edwin Encarnacion	CIN	30.2

Value Over Replacement Player, Shortstop

RANK	NAME	TEAM	VORP
1.	Hanley Ramirez	FLO	59.7
2.	Jose Reyes	NYN	44.5
3.	Jimmy Rollins	PHI	42.8
5.	Derek Jeter	NYA	31.7
6.	Khalil Greene	SDN	28.5
7.	Troy Tulowitzki	COL	28.3
8.	Felipe Lopez	WAS	24.2
9.	Miguel Tejada	BAL	24.0
T10.	Rafael Furcal	LAN	23.8
T10.	Jhonny Peralta	CLE	23.8

Value Over Replacement Player, Left Field

RANK	NAME	TEAM	VORP
1.	Adam Dunn	CIN	35.8
2.	Matt Holliday	COL	35.2
3.	Carlos Lee	HOU	32.7
4.	Alfonso Soriano	CHN	31.0
5.	Pat Burrell	PHI	28.1
6.	Josh Willingham	FLO	28.0
7.	Jason Bay	PIT	26.1
8.	Barry Bonds	SFN	24.8
9.	Hideki Matsui	NYA	23.7
10.	Manny Ramirez	BOS	23.3

Value Over Replacement Player, Center Field

RANK	NAME	TEAM	VORP
1.	Carlos Beltran	NYN	44.0
2.	Grady Sizemore	CLE	38.0
3.	Hunter Pence	HOU	31.6
4.	Jay Bruce	CIN	29.9
5.	Chris Young	ARI	29.2
6.	B. J. Upton	TBA	28.5
7.	Andruw Jones	LAN	27.9
8.	Mike Cameron	MIL	27.9
9.	Curtis Granderson	DET	26.2

10.	Lastings Milledge	WAS	26.0

Value Over Replacement Player, Right Field

RANK	NAME	TEAM	VORP
1.	Corey Hart	MIL	35.5
2.	Vladimir Guerrero	LAA	33.2
3.	Magglio Ordoñez	DET	31.1
4.	Kosuke Fukudome	CHN	29.2
5.	Jeremy Hermida	FLO	28.7
6.	Matt Kemp	LAN	27.2
7.	Nick Swisher	OAK	22.9
8.	Austin Kearns	WAS	19.9
9.	Delmon Young	MIN	19.4
10.	Bobby Abreu	NYY	19.0

Value Over Replacement Player, Designated Hitter

RANK	NAME	TEAM	VORP
1.	David Ortiz	BOS	51.3
2.	Travis Hafner	CLE	34.6
3.	Jim Thome	CHA	29.5
4.	Gary Sheffield	DET	21.1
5.	Jack Cust	OAK	20.4
6.	Billy Butler	KCA	19.7
7.	Frank Thomas	TOR	19.1
8.	Jonny Gomes	TBA	18.1
9.	Jason Giambi	NYA	11.0
10.	Jose Vidro	SEA	9.8

VORP Increase from 2007

			'07	'08	
RANK	NAME	TEAM	VORP	VORP	CHANGE
1.	Felix Pie	CHN	-5.7	21.4	+27.1
2.	Andy LaRoche	LAN	-0.8	25.6	+26.4
3.	Justin Upton	ARI	-5.3	19.2	+24.5
4.	Felipe Lopez	WAS	0.2	24.2	+24.0
5.	Joe Dillon	MIL	6.7	30.3	+23.6
6.	Nick Punto	MIN	-27.1	-3.9	+23.2
7.	Andruw Jones	LAN	5.4	27.9	+22.5
8.	Jason Bay	PIT	3.9	26.1	+22.2
9.	Cameron Maybin	FLO	-3.8	18.1	+21.9
10.	Adam Jones	SEA	-0.2	21.4	+21.6
11.	Stephen Drew	ARI	2.8	22.3	+19.5
12.	Ray Durham	SFN	-10.5	8.9	+19.4
13.	Marcus Giles	COL	-8.7	10.5	+19.2
T14.	Josh Barfield	CLE	-13.6	5.0	+18.6
T14.	Ben Zobrist	TBA	-11.6	7.0	+18.6

VORP Decrease from 2007

			'07	'08	
RANK	NAME	TEAM	VORP	VORP	CHANGE
1.	Magglio Ordoñez	DET	87.8	31.1	-56.7
2.	Ichiro Suzuki	SEA	63.5	14.7	-48.8
3.	Curtis Granderson	DET	67.3	26.2	-41.1
4.	Matt Holliday	COL	75.0	35.2	-39.8
5.	Carlos Peña	TBA	68.5	30.6	-37.9
6.	Jorge Posada	NYA	73.4	37.1	-36.3

7.	David Ortiz	BOS	86.2	51.3	-34.9
8.	Alex Rodriguez	NYA	96.6	63.3	-33.3
9.	Barry Bonds	SFN	55.2	24.8	-30.4
10.	Hanley Ramirez	FLO	89.5	59.7	-29.8
11.	Mike Lowell	BOS	46.5	16.9	-29.6
T12.	Vladimir Guerrero	LAA	62.6	33.2	-29.4
T12.	Edgar Renteria	DET	47.5	18.1	-29.4
14.	Aaron Rowand	SFN	52.0	23.4	-28.6
15.	Todd Helton	COL	51.9	24.1	-27.8

Rookie VORP

RANK	NAME	TEAM	VORP
1.	Jay Bruce	CIN	29.9
2.	Kosuke Fukudome	CHN	29.2
3.	Evan Longoria	TBA	25.4
4.	Joey Votto	CIN	24.6
5.	Matt Antonelli	SDN	23.8
6.	Geovany Soto	CHN	23.5
7.	J.R. Towles	HOU	20.0
8.	Colby Rasmus	SLN	19.4
9.	Brent Lillibridge	ATL	18.4
10.	Daric Barton	OAK	18.2

PITCHERS

Wins

RANK	NAME	TEAM	W
T1.	Jake Peavy	SDN	15
T1.	C. C. Sabathia	CLE	15
T1.	Johan Santana	MIN	15
T4.	Josh Beckett	BOS	14
T4.	Roy Halladay	TOR	14
T4.	John Smoltz	ATL	14
T7.	Erik Bedard	BAL	13
T7.	Cole Hamels	PHI	13
T7.	Aaron Harang	CIN	13
T7.	Dan Haren	ARI	13
T7.	John Lackey	LAA	13
T7.	Daisuke Matsuzaka	BOS	13
T7.	Roy Oswalt	HOU	13
T7.	Javier Vazquez	CHA	13
T7.	Justin Verlander	DET	13
T7.	Brandon Webb	ARI	13
T17.	Jeremy Bonderman	DET	12
T17.	A. J. Burnett	TOR	12
T17.	Fausto Carmona	CLE	12
T17.	Tim Hudson	ATL	12
T17.	Scott Kazmir	TBA	12
T17.	Andy Pettitte	NYA	12
T17.	Carlos Zambrano	CHN	12

Strikeouts

RANK	NAME	TEAM	SO
1.	Johan Santana	MIN	230

2.	Jake Peavy	SDN	223
3.	Erik Bedard	BAL	196
4.	Scott Kazmir	TBA	194
5.	C. C. Sabathia	CLE	179
T6.	Yovani Gallardo	MIL	177
T6.	Javier Vazquez	CHA	177
T8.	Josh Beckett	BOS	176
T8.	Cole Hamels	PHI	176
T8.	Aaron Harang	CIN	176
11.	Dan Haren	ARI	175
12.	Carlos Zambrano	CHN	173
13.	Daisuke Matsuzaka	BOS	170
14.	John Smoltz	ATL	169
15.	John Lackey	LAA	166
16.	A. J. Burnett	TOR	163
17.	Joba Chamberlain	NYA	162
18.	Justin Verlander	DET	161
19.	Rich Hill	CHN	160
20.	Brandon Webb	ARI	155

Earned Run Average (min. 125 IP)

RANK	NAME	TEAM	ERA
1.	Jake Peavy	SDN	2.98
2.	John Smoltz	ATL	3.28
3.	Johan Santana	MIN	3.32
4.	Brandon Webb	ARI	3.38
5.	Joba Chamberlain	NYA	3.39
6.	Cole Hamels	PHI	3.45
7.	C. C. Sabathia	CLE	3.51
T8.	Scott Kazmir	TBA	3.58
T8.	Tim Lincecum	SFN	3.58
T8.	Erik Bedard	BAL	3.58
11.	Roy Oswalt	HOU	3.62
T12.	A. J. Burnett	TOR	3.64
T12.	Josh Beckett	BOS	3.64
14.	Chris Young	SDN	3.73
15.	Aaron Harang	CIN	3.74
16.	John Lackey	LAA	3.77
17.	Dan Haren	ARI	3.78
18.	Carlos Zambrano	CHN	3.81
19.	Roy Halladay	TOR	3.85
20.	Yovani Gallardo	MIL	3.88

Walks plus Hits per Inning Pitched (min. 125 IP)

RANK	NAME	TEAM	WHIP
1.	Jake Peavy	SDN	1.13
2.	Johan Santana	MIN	1.14
3.	John Smoltz	ATL	1.18
4.	Cole Hamels	PHI	1.19
T5.	Josh Beckett	BOS	1.22
T5.	C. C. Sabathia	CLE	1.22
7.	Chris Young	SDN	1.23
T8.	Dan Haren	ARI	1.24
T8.	Javier Vazquez	CHA	1.24
T8.	Joba Chamberlain	NYA	1.24
T8.	Brandon Webb	ARI	1.24

T8.	Aaron Harang	CIN	1.24
T8.	Ben Sheets	MIL	1.24
14.	Rich Hill	CHN	1.25
T15.	A. J. Burnett	TOR	1.26
T15.	Kevin Slowey	MIN	1.26
T17.	Tim Lincecum	SFN	1.27
T17.	Roy Oswalt	HOU	1.27
T17.	Roy Halladay	TOR	1.27
T17.	Erik Bedard	BAL	1.27

Saves

RANK	NAME	TEAM	SV
1.	Jose Valverde	HOU	42
T2.	Joe Nathan	MIN	41
T2.	J. J. Putz	SEA	41
T4.	Francisco Cordero	CIN	40
T4.	Billy Wagner	NYN	40
T6.	Jonathan Papelbon	BOS	39
T6.	Takashi Saito	LAN	39
8.	Francisco Rodriguez	LAA	38
T9.	Trevor Hoffman	SDN	37
T9.	Bobby Jenks	CHA	37
11.	Eric Gagné	MIL	34
12.	Joe Borowski	CLE	30
13.	Mariano Rivera	NYA	29
14.	Chad Cordero	WAS	23
15.	Todd Jones	DET	22
T16.	Jason Isringhausen	SLN	21
T16.	Al Reyes	TBA	21
18.	Jeremy Accardo	TOR	20
19.	Huston Street	OAK	19
20.	Kevin Gregg	FLO	18

Win Expectancy over Replacement, Lineup-adjusted

RANK	NAME	TEAM	WXRL
1.	Jonathan Papelbon	BOS	3.97
2.	Francisco Rodriguez	LAA	3.60
3.	J. J. Putz	SEA	3.44
4.	Joe Nathan	MIN	3.34
5.	Mariano Rivera	NYA	2.99
6.	Billy Wagner	NYN	2.91
7.	Francisco Cordero	CIN	2.62
8.	Jose Valverde	HOU	2.60
9.	Bobby Jenks	CHA	2.58
10.	Joakim Soria	KCA	2.24

Equivalent Strikeouts per Nine Innings

RANK	NAME	TEAM	EQSO9
1.	Francisco Rodriguez	LAA	10.6
2.	Chris Perez	SLN	10.3
3.	Edwar Ramirez	NYA	10.2
4.	Jonathan Papelbon	BOS	9.9
5.	Huston Street	OAK	9.7
6.	Grant Balfour	TBA	9.6
T7.	George Sherrill	SEA	9.3
T7.	Stephen Randolph	HOU	9.3

T9.	Juan Cruz	ARI	9.2
T9.	Chris Booker	WAS	9.2

Peripheral Earned Run Average (min. 125 IP)

RANK	NAME	TEAM	PERA
1.	Johan Santana	MIN	3.28
T2.	A. J. Burnett	TOR	3.33
T2.	Joba Chamberlain	NYA	3.33
4.	Brandon Webb	ARI	3.36
5.	C. C. Sabathia	CLE	3.38
6.	Jake Peavy	SDN	3.40
7.	Josh Beckett	BOS	3.41
8.	Erik Bedard	BAL	3.43
9.	John Smoltz	ATL	3.57
10.	Javier Vazquez	CHA	3.60

Stuff Score

RANK	NAME	TEAM	STUFF
1.	Jake Peavy	SDN	32
2.	Huston Street	OAK	31
3.	Erik Bedard	BAL	31
4.	Francisco Rodriguez	LAA	31
5.	Scott Kazmir	TBA	31
6.	Johan Santana	MIN	30
7.	Jonathan Papelbon	BOS	29
8.	Yovani Gallardo	MIL	28
9.	Cole Hamels	PHI	27
T10.	Joba Chamberlain	NYA	26
T10.	Francisco Liriano	MIN	26

Value Over Replacement Player

RANK	NAME	TEAM	VORP
1.	Johan Santana	MIN	54.5
2.	Jake Peavy	SDN	52.3
3.	Brandon Webb	ARI	51.7
4.	C. C. Sabathia	CLE	47.6
5.	Cole Hamels	PHI	45.7
6.	Josh Beckett	BOS	44.6
7.	John Smoltz	ATL	43.4
8.	Dan Haren	ARI	43.3
9.	Aaron Harang	CIN	42.6
10.	Erik Bedard	BAL	42.2
11.	Scott Kazmir	TBA	40.7
12.	Roy Halladay	TOR	40.1
13.	Javier Vazquez	CHA	38.7
14.	John Lackey	LAA	38.4
15.	A. J. Burnett	TOR	38.0
16.	Roy Oswalt	HOU	37.0
17.	Daisuke Matsuzaka	BOS	36.8
18.	Carlos Zambrano	CHN	35.8
19.	Justin Verlander	DET	34.7
20.	Joba Chamberlain	NYA	33.7

VORP Increase from 2007

RANK	NAME	TEAM	'07 VORP	'08 VORP	CHANGE
1.	Scott Olsen	FLO	-23.1	7.9	+31.0
2.	Francisco Liriano	MIN	DNP	29.2	+29.2
3.	Mike Maroth	SLN	-26.1	1.1	+27.2
4.	J. P. Howell	TBA	-11.5	14.5	+26.0
5.	Byung-Hun Kim	FLO	-14.3	10.2	+24.5
6.	Dallas Braden	OAK	-11.7	10.8	+22.5
7.	B. J. Ryan	TOR	-4.1	18.1	+22.2
8.	Horacio Ramirez	SEA	-22.8	-1.1	+21.7
9.	Ervin Santana	LAA	-4.2	17.2	+21.4
T10.	Chris Carpenter	SLN	-1.1	20.1	+21.2
T10.	Rick Vanden Hurk	FLO	-11.3	9.9	+21.2
12.	Jeremy Bonderman	DET	10.1	30.5	+20.4
13.	Anthony Reyes	SLN	-6.9	13.3	+20.2
14.	Pedro Martinez	NYN	7.1	27.3	+20.2
15.	Jason Jennings	HOU	-8.2	11.6	+19.8

VORP Decrease from 2007

RANK	NAME	TEAM	'07 VORP	'08 VORP	CHANGE
1.	Brad Penny	LAN	61.7	20.9	-40.8
2.	Fausto Carmona	CLE	64.0	27.9	-36.1
3.	Tim Hudson	ATL	59.7	26.8	-32.9
4.	Mark Buehrle	CHA	49.3	18.3	-31.0
5.	Jeremy Guthrie	BAL	38.2	7.5	-30.7
6.	Chien-Ming Wang	NYA	48.5	19.0	-29.5
7.	Brian Bannister	KCA	34.9	6.3	-28.6
8.	Carlos Silva	SEA	35.5	7.0	-28.5
9.	Joe Blanton	OAK	46.3	19.0	-27.3
10.	Gil Meche	KCA	47.1	21.4	-25.7
T11.	Matt Guerrier	MIN	36.8	12.0	-24.8
T11.	Tom Glavine	ATL	28.1	3.3	-24.8
13.	Jake Peavy	SDN	77.0	52.3	-24.7
14.	Tom Gorzelanny	PIT	42.6	18.1	-24.5
15.	Heath Bell	SDN	39.7	15.8	-23.9

Rookie VORP

RANK	NAME	TEAM	VORP
1.	Joba Chamberlain	NYA	33.7
2.	Hiroki Kuroda	LAN	23.3
3.	Clay Buchholz	BOS	22.8
4.	Greg Reynolds	COL	18.6
5.	Aaron Laffey	CLE	15.1
6.	Brett Cecil	TOR	14.2
T7.	Dylan Owen	NYN	13.6
T7.	Max Scherzer	ARI	13.6
9.	Edwar Ramirez	NYA	13.5
10.	Cole Rohrbough	ATL	13.2

Team Name Key and Park Factors

Clay Davenport

Team		League (2007)	Affiliation (2007)	2005	2006	2007	Team		League (2007)	Affiliation (2007)	2005	2006	2007
ABE	Aberdeen	NYP	Orioles	965	964	934	CHT	Chattanooga	SOU	Reds	1033	1026	1040
ABQ	Albuquerque	PCL	Marlins	1116	1117	1120	CHU	Chunichi	JCL	Japan	941	943	957
AGU	Aguascaliente	MEX	Mexican	1084	1088	1094	CIN	Cincinnati	NL	Reds	1019	1037	1049
AKR	Akron	EAS	Indians	1026	1017	1009	CLE	Cleveland	AL	Indians	967	988	1013
ALT	Altoona	EAS	Pirates	987	1004	1004	CLN	Clinton	MDW	Rangers	1014	1011	1001
ANA	LA Angels	AL	Angels	971	982	998	CLR	Clearwater	FSL	Phillies	1016	1014	1000
ANG	AZL Angels	AZL	Angels	—	1020	1031	CMP	Campeche	MEX	Mexican	928	931	936
ARI	Arizona	NL	Diamondbacks	1049	1047	1049	COH	Columbus OH	INT	Nationals	978	982	997
ARK	Arkansas	TXS	Angels	1031	1035	1025	COL	Colorado	NL	Rockies	1091	1077	1067
ASH	Asheville	SAL	Rockies	1117	1104	1095	CRD	GCL Cardinal	GCL	Cardinals	—	—	1080
ATH	AZL Athletics	AZL	A's	—	999	999	CSC	Charleston SC	SAL	Yankees	972	973	955
ATL	Atlanta	NL	Braves	994	984	972	CSP	Colo Springs	PCL	Rockies	1060	1078	1091
AUB	Auburn	NYP	Blue Jays	991	988	976	CUB	AZL Cubs	AZL	Cubs	—	970	955
AUG	Augusta	SAL	Giants	967	958	974	DAY	Daytona	FSL	Cubs	1037	1047	1048
BAK	Bakersfield	CLF	Rangers	955	967	989	DEL	Delmarva	SAL	Orioles	981	966	939
BAL	Baltimore	AL	Orioles	989	999	1010	DET	Detroit	AL	Tigers	981	992	1005
BAT	Batavia	NYP	Cardinals	980	993	1019	DGR	GCL Dodgers	GCL	Dodgers	—	986	979
BIL	Billings	PIO	Reds	970	982	987	DNV	Danville	APL	Braves	901	911	922
BIN	Binghamton	EAS	Mets	1018	1009	995	DUN	Dunedin	FSL	Blue Jays	1040	1037	1019
BIR	Birmingham	SOU	White Sox	975	961	962	DUR	Durham	INT	Devil Rays	1034	1039	1052
BLJ	GCL BlueJays	GCL	Blue Jays	—	—	1018	DYT	Dayton	MDW	Reds	1022	1012	998
BLT	Beloit	MDW	Twins	1018	1011	1009	ELZ	Elizabethton	APL	Twins	973	970	973
BLU	Bluefield	APL	Orioles	1025	1014	1004	ERI	Erie	EAS	Tigers	1032	1024	1040
BNC	Burlington NC	APL	Royals	979	980	984	EUG	Eugene	NWN	Padres	1008	1009	1000
BOI	Boise	NWN	Cubs	1053	1047	1055	EVE	Everett	NWN	Mariners	1037	1025	998
BOS	Boston	AL	Red Sox	1030	1030	1039	FKU	SoftBank	JPL	Japan	952	962	983
BOW	Bowie	EAS	Orioles	960	974	973	FLO	Florida	NL	Marlins	954	963	982
BRA	GCL Braves	GCL	Braves	—	986	980	FRD	Frederick	CRL	Orioles	1023	1027	1018
BRI	Bristol VA	APL	White Sox	979	983	977	FRE	Fresno	PCL	Giants	966	967	962
BRO	Brooklyn	NYP	Mets	991	973	971	FRI	Frisco	TXS	Rangers	1001	1011	1017
BRR	AZL Brewers	AZL	Brewers	—	1010	1014	FTM	Ft Myers	FSL	Twins	984	983	979
BRV	Brevard County	FSL	Brewers	971	967	954	FTW	Ft Wayne	MDW	Padres	965	973	989
BUF	Buffalo	INT	Indians	1025	1043	1047	GIA	AZL Giants	AZL	Giants	—	979	968
BUR	Burlington IA	MDW	Royals	942	934	935	GRB	Greensboro	SAL	Marlins	1032	1042	1050
CAR	Carolina	SOU	Marlins	1001	1014	1020	GRF	Great Falls	PIO	White Sox	969	991	1014
CAS	Casper	PIO	Rockies	1025	1029	1034	GRL	Great Lakes	MDW	Dodgers	—	—	986
CCH	Corpus Christi	TXS	Astros	974	977	987	GRN	Greenville	SAL	Red Sox	1021	1021	1024
CCN	Cancun	MEX	Mexican	869	—	—	GRV	Greeneville	APL	Astros	961	976	1014
CDR	Cedar Rapids	MDW	Angels	1027	1014	997	HAG	Hagerstown	SAL	Nationals	985	986	1004
CGA	Columbus GA	SAL	Devil Rays	978	975	967	HAR	Harrisburg	EAS	Nationals	1021	1025	1035
CHA	Chicago W Sox	AL	White Sox	1026	1031	1032	HDS	High Desert	CLF	Mariners	1106	1107	1101
CHB	Chiba	JPL	Japan	926	938	962	HEL	Helena	PIO	Brewers	971	979	987
CHH	Chihuahua	MEX	Mexican	—	—	1053	HIC	Hickory	SAL	Pirates	998	993	1006
CHN	Chicago Cubs	NL	Cubs	1027	1038	1046	HNS	Hanshin	JCL	Japan	975	970	952
CHR	Charlotte	INT	White Sox	1010	1019	1028	HOU	Houston	NL	Astros	997	993	984

Team		League (2007)	Affiliation (2007)	2005	2006	2007	Team		League (2007)	Affiliation (2007)	2005	2006	2007
HRO	Hiroshima	JCL	Japan	1071	1075	1067	NYN	NY Mets	NL	Mets	973	964	959
HUD	Hudson Valley	NYP	Devil Rays	965	959	966	OAK	Oakland	AL	A's	981	968	948
HUN	Huntsville	SOU	Brewers	1023	1012	1005	OAX	Oaxaca	MEX	Mexican	1031	1051	1081
IDA	Idaho Falls	PIO	Royals	1034	1004	979	OGD	Ogden	PIO	Dodgers	1059	1059	1054
IDN	GCL Indians	GCL	Indians	—	990	984	OKL	Oklahoma	PCL	Rangers	949	939	939
IND	Indianapolis	INT	Pirates	990	951	997	OMA	Omaha	PCL	Royals	968	969	976
IOW	Iowa	PCL	Cubs	988	984	997	ONE	Oneonta	NYP	Tigers	1051	1061	1060
JAM	Jamestown	NYP	Marlins	1100	1105	1106	ORI	GCL Orioles	GCL	Orioles	—	—	1000
JAX	Jacksonville	SOU	Dodgers	966	970	952	ORM	Orem	PIO	Angels	905	908	919
JCY	Johnson City	APL	Cardinals	1019	986	961	ORX	Orix	JPL	Japan	997	984	978
JUP	Jupiter	FSL	Marlins	920	902	903	OTT	Ottawa	INT	Phillies	1005	997	968
KAN	Kannapolis	SAL	White Sox	999	1010	1015	PAW	Pawtucket	INT	Red Sox	1013	1025	1034
KCA	Kansas City	AL	Royals	1012	1016	1026	PDR	AZL Padres	AZL	Padres	—	1000	1059
KIN	Kinston	CRL	Indians	982	980	976	PEO	Peoria	MDW	Cubs	995	983	972
KNC	Kane County	MDW	A's	1046	1055	1048	PHI	Philadelphia	NL	Phillies	1029	1024	1020
KNG	Kingsport	APL	Mets	1020	1044	1061	PHL	GCL Phillies	GCL	Phillies	—	1020	1031
LAK	Lakeland	FSL	Tigers	1020	1029	1027	PIR	GCL Pirates	GCL	Pirates	—	999	998
LAN	LA Dodgers	NL	Dodgers	979	999	1010	PIT	Pittsburgh	NL	Pirates	996	998	993
LEL	Lake Elsinore	CLF	Padres	973	968	957	PMB	Palm Beach	FSL	Cardinals	952	951	959
LEX	Lexington	SAL	Astros	1024	1016	1014	PME	Portland ME	EAS	Red Sox	1023	1021	1018
LKC	Lake County	SAL	Indians	1009	1022	1015	POR	Portland OR	PCL	Padres	959	966	960
LNC	Lancaster	CLF	Red Sox	1095	1105	1114	POT	Potomac	CRL	Nationals	991	972	963
LNS	Lansing	MDW	Blue Jays	989	1002	1021	PRI	Princeton	APL	Devil Rays	1039	1046	1039
LOU	Louisville	INT	Reds	1001	988	993	PUE	Puebla	MEX	Mexican	1045	1046	1049
LOW	Lowell	NYP	Red Sox	1005	981	980	PUL	Pulaski	APL	Blue Jays	1065	1075	—
LVG	Las Vegas	PCL	Dodgers	1081	1084	1081	PZA	Minatitlan	MEX	Mexican	—	905	1036
LWD	Lakewood	SAL	Phillies	923	921	917	QUD	Quad Cities	MDW	Cardinals	990	989	984
LYN	Lynchburg	CRL	Pirates	990	1006	1025	RAK	Rakuten	JPL	Japan	1011	1012	1006
MCD	Mexico City	MEX	Mexican	1087	1085	1088	RCU	R Cucamonga	CLF	Angels	981	983	980
MCL	Monclova	MEX	Mexican	985	990	983	RDS	GCL Reds	GCL	Reds	—	989	984
MCT	Angelopolis	MEX	Mexican	1098	1094	—	REA	Reading	EAS	Phillies	1011	1003	1012
MEM	Memphis	PCL	Cardinals	925	932	934	RIC	Richmond	INT	Braves	999	1000	993
MHV	Mahoning Val	NYP	Indians	1018	1032	1048	RNG	AZL Rangers	AZL	Rangers	—	1019	1028
MID	Midland	TXS	A's	1006	1013	1021	ROC	Rochester	INT	Twins	1024	1023	1022
MIL	Milwaukee	NL	Brewers	1007	1006	1006	ROM	Rome	SAL	Braves	941	958	971
MIN	Minnesota	AL	Twins	997	985	971	ROU	Round Rock	PCL	Astros	946	937	943
MIS	Mississippi	SOU	Braves	960	962	960	ROY	AZL Royals	AZL	Royals	—	1004	1007
MNT	Montgomery	SOU	Devil Rays	987	997	992	RSX	GCL Red Sox	GCL	Red Sox	—	1014	1020
MOB	Mobile	SOU	Diamondbacks	1004	1006	1004	SAC	Sacramento	PCL	A's	943	928	909
MOD	Modesto	CLF	Rockies	971	965	947	SAN	San Antonio	TXS	Padres	928	918	905
MRL	GCL Marlins	GCL	Marlins	—	948	923	SAR	Sarasota	FSL	Reds	1005	1019	1031
MRN	AZL Mariners	AZL	Mariners	—	954	932	SAV	Savannah	SAL	Mets	972	973	976
MSO	Missoula	PIO	Diamondbacks	1000	1010	1011	SBN	South Bend	MDW	Diamondbacks	970	991	1013
MTR	Monterrey	MEX	Mexican	962	954	933	SBR	Inland Empire	CLF	Dodgers	954	950	938
MTS	GCL Mets	GCL	Mets	—	997	996	SCO	State College	NYP	Pirates	—	972	970
MYR	Myrtle Beach	CRL	Braves	957	970	968	SDN	San Diego	NL	Padres	920	919	910
NAS	Nashville	PCL	Brewers	949	962	953	SEA	Seattle	AL	Mariners	955	954	959
NAT	GCL National	GCL	Nationals	—	1038	1058	SEI	Seibu	JPL	Japan	1002	1004	1014
NBR	New Britain	EAS	Twins	1001	1019	1026	SFD	Springfield	TXS	Cardinals	976	979	989
NHP	New Hampshire	EAS	Blue Jays	975	994	1008	SFN	San Francisco	NL	Giants	1002	999	995
NIP	Nippon Ham	JPL	Japan	992	976	966	SJO	San Jose	CLF	Giants	892	878	868
NOR	Norfolk	INT	Orioles	915	903	901	SLC	Salt Lake	PCL	Angels	1087	1088	1088
NRW	Connecticut	EAS	Giants	978	877	862	SLM	Salem VA	CRL	Astros	958	961	970
NWJ	New Jersey	NYP	Cardinals	979	—	—	SLN	St Louis	NL	Cardinals	993	979	973
NWO	New Orleans	PCL	Mets	920	938	955	SLO	Salem-Keizer	NWN	Giants	983	991	1002
NYA	NY Yankees	AL	Yankees	988	993	1007	SLP	San Luis Potosi	MEX	Mexican	1046	1039	—

Team		League (2007)	Affiliation (2007)	2005	2006	2007	Team		League (2007)	Affiliation (2007)	2005	2006	2007
SLT	Saltillo	MEX	Mexican	1037	1035	1033	TWI	GCL Twins	GCL	Twins	—	1002	1002
SLU	St Lucie	FSL	Mets	1003	1001	1007	VAN	Vancouver	NWN	A's	936	948	960
SPO	Spokane	NWN	Rangers	1052	1068	1074	VAQ	Vaqueros	MEX	Mexican	1099	1054	1020
STA	Staten Island	NYP	Yankees	895	892	905	VER	Vermont	NYP	Nationals	1024	1038	1052
STO	Stockton	CLF	A's	961	964	973	VIS	Visalia	CLF	Diamondbacks	1000	992	992
SWB	Scranton/W-B	INT	Yankees	995	992	989	VRC	Veracruz	MEX	Mexican	909	891	877
SWM	SW Michigan	MDW	Devil Rays	1024	1027	—	VRO	Vero Beach	FSL	Devil Rays	1041	1039	1046
SYR	Syracuse	INT	Blue Jays	1034	1047	1044	WAS	Washington	NL	Nationals	949	950	946
TAB	Tabasco	MEX	Mexican	859	871	883	WIC	Wichita	TXS	Royals	991	1003	1020
TAC	Tacoma	PCL	Mariners	912	916	911	WIL	Wilmington	CRL	Royals	988	992	1006
TAM	Tampa	FSL	Yankees	998	998	1013	WIS	Wisconsin	MDW	Mariners	992	993	1004
TBA	Tampa Bay	AL	Devil Rays	984	987	984	WMI	W Michigan	MDW	Tigers	985	990	998
TCV	Tri-City	NYP	Astros	1038	1058	1073	WNS	Winston-Salem	CRL	White Sox	1057	1053	1055
TEN	Tennessee	SOU	Cubs	1032	1040	1056	WPT	Williamsport	NYP	Phillies	968	962	936
TEX	Texas	AL	Rangers	1040	1022	1005	WTN	W Tennessee	SOU	Mariners	997	1003	1008
TGR	GCL Tigers	GCL	Tigers	—	990	985	WVA	West Virginia	SAL	Brewers	997	1014	1010
TIJ	Tijuana	MEX	Mexican	1018	991	973	YAK	Yakima	NWN	Diamondbacks	971	947	932
TOL	Toledo	INT	Tigers	946	941	945	YAN	GCL Yankees	GCL	Yankees	—	1015	1023
TOR	Toronto	AL	Blue Jays	1024	1013	999	YKL	Yakult	JCL	Japan	1041	1065	1071
TRI	Tri-City	NWN	Rockies	918	920	938	YKO	Yokohama	JCL	Japan	1073	1068	1062
TRN	Trenton	EAS	Yankees	966	956	965	YOM	Yomiuri	JCL	Japan	950	950	950
TUC	Tucson	PCL	Diamondbacks	1067	1038	1025	YUC	Yucatan	MEX	Mexican	885	882	885
TUL	Tulsa	TXS	Rockies	1005	1008	1014							

League and Level Key

	League	Level
AFL	Arizona Fall	Winter
AL	American	MLB
APL	Appalachian	Rookie
AZL	Arizona	Rookie
CLF	California	A+
CRL	Carolina	A+
EAS	Eastern	AA
FSL	Florida State	A+
GCL	Gulf Coast	Rookie
HWB	Hawaiian Winter	Winter
INT	International	AAA
JCL	Japanese Central	Japan
JPL	Japanese Pacific	Japan
MDW	Midwest	A
MEX	Mexican	Mexico
NL	National	MLB
NWN	North Western	A-
NYP	New York-Penn	A-
PCL	Pacific Coast	AAA
PIO	Pioneer	Rookie
SAL	South Atlantic (Sally)	A
SOU	Southern	AA
TXS	Texas	AA

Index

Contributors

William Burke was brought on board to direct research and development efforts for Baseball Prospectus in 2007. This comes on the heels of several years spent wrangling statistics out of our vast array of databases as an outside contributor. He previously worked as lead researcher for *It Ain't Over 'Til It's Over* and took the helm for the annual for the first time this year. He lives in suburban Chicago with his wife Amanda, son Joey, and their dog Natty.

Clay Davenport is a meteorologist for the National Oceanic and Atmospheric Administration (NOAA) for whom he develops products to track rainfall from satellites so as to get an earlier jump on flash-flood warnings (tip: don't try to drive across a flooded road). He is one of the founders of Baseball Prospectus and lives in Maryland with his wife, Susan.

Dan Fox authors the weekly "Schrodinger's Bat" column for BaseballProspectus.com in which he delves into a variety of sabermetric analyses ranging from baserunning, to changes in the level of play over time, to what new technology can reveal about the game. Dan also works part-time as stats stringer for Major League Baseball Advanced Media and continues his analysis and commentary on his blog at Dan Agonistes.blogspot.com. When not crunching the numbers, Dan works as a Software Architect at Compassion International in beautiful Colorado Springs. He lives with his very understanding wife Beth and two lovely daughters, Laura and Anna.

Steven Goldman is the creator of the long-running "Pinstriped Bible" column and companion "Pinstriped Blog" at YesNetwork.com and the "You Could Look It Up" column for BaseballProspectus.com, and is a baseball columnist for the *New York Sun*. Steven is also the author of the biography *Forging Genius: The Making of Casey Stengel*, the editor of Baseball Prospectus's *Mind Game* and *It Ain't Over 'Til It's Over: The Baseball Prospectus Pennant Race Book* and a contributor to *Baseball Between the Numbers*. He has contributed to the annual since 2005 and has been the co-editor of the last three editions. Steven lives in New Jersey with his wife Stefanie, daughter Sarah, and son Clemens.

Kevin Goldstein covers baseball below the majors for Baseball Prospectus and is one of the nation's leading analysts on scouting, player development, and the draft. His 2007 season was marked by the purchase of a 1893 home in DeKalb, Illinois, a building that makes up for degrading tools with tons of makeup. He lives there with his one true love, Margaret, who hates baseball, as well as her two childen, Xander and Cameron, a white pit bull named Otto, and a pair of cats, Henry and Pickles. Outside of BP, he has also written for ESPN.com, SportsIllustrated.com, *Baseball America*, and various annual publications, was part of MLB.com's Draft Preview video program, and spent two innings in the booth during the televised broadcast of the 2007 Midwest League All-Star game. He is also available for weddings and bar mitzvahs.

Derek Jacques resides in New York City, where he works with his wife, Paula, running an editorial services firm, Kepos Media. Derek writes the "Prospectus Toolbox" column and also covers events such as the Caribbean Series for BaseballProspectus.com. This is his second time contributing to the annual. He has also written about baseball for the 2007 and 2008 editions of *Bombers Broadside*, for *Colorado Rockies Magazine*, and on his blog, the Weblog That Derek Built (weblogthat derekbuilt.blogspot.com).

Jay Jaffe is the founder of the seven-year-old Futility Infielder website (www.futilityinfielder.com), one of the oldest baseball blogs. In addition to covering the annual Hall of Fame ballot for BaseballProspectus.com, he writes the weekly "Prospectus Hit List" and "Prospectus Hit and Run" columns during the season. In recent years, he's contributed work to *It Ain't Over 'Til It's Over*, *Mind Game*, Will Carroll's *The Juice*, *Bombers Broadside*, and *Fantasy Baseball Index*. A graphic designer living in New York City, he's married to Andra, the most supportive gal in the world, and once came in third in the Milwaukee Brewers' famous sausage race.

Rany Jazayerli has written for all 13 editions of the Baseball Prospectus annual, during which time he has gotten married, helped raise his two young daughters, finished medical school, completed a dermatology residency, and opened his own medical practice. Fortunately, his beloved Royals have provided a rock of stability to his life by being bad the entire time.

Christina Kahrl is one of the founding five members of Baseball Prospectus, and the Managing Editor of BaseballProspectus.com. Beyond her regular "Transaction Analysis" column there, she's written about baseball and football for *Playboy*, the *New York Sun*, Salon.com, Slate.com, SportsIllustrated.com, ESPN.com, and Playboy.com and contributed to *Mind Game*, *It Ain't Over 'Til It's Over*, and the *ESPN Pro Football Encyclopedia*. During her five years as Sports Acquisitions Editor at Brassey's/Potomac Books, she helped launch the careers of several of her contemporaries. A graduate of the University of Chicago with a graduate degree in History from Loyola University, she's happily returned to sweet home Chicago with a new dog of almost manic energy. There, she's resumed her studied indifference to the fate of the local teams while continuing to observe her unswerving loyalty to the A's.

Marc Normandin is a student at Merrimack College, majoring in communication. This is his second year at Baseball Prospectus, as well as his second contributing to the annual. He lives outside of Boston, where he roots for the Red Sox and the cross-country San Diego Padres.

John Perrotto has covered Major League Baseball and the Pittsburgh Pirates, in particular, for the *Beaver County Times*, a newspaper in Western Pennsylvania, and other publications for twenty years. He began writing for Baseball Prospectus last year. He graduated from Geneva College, birthplace of college basketball, and lives in Beaver Falls, Pennsylvania, birthplace of Joe Willie Namath, with his wife Brenda.

Joe Sheehan is an original member of Baseball Prospectus. He writes the "Prospectus Today" column for Baseball Prospectus.com, has contributed to nine of the annuals, and serves as Executive Editor of BP's Premium content. Joe also serves as Managing Editor of the new BasketballProspectus.com. In addition, he contributes to *Sports Illustrated* and SI.com, and makes regular appearances on ESPN and ESPNews, as well as XM Radio, MLB.com's Baseball Channel, and local radio stations nationwide. He lives in New York City.

Nate Silver is the Managing Partner of Baseball Prospectus and the creator of the PECOTA projection system. In addition to his duties for BP, Nate has written for *Sports Illustrated*, ESPN.com, and Slate.com. He lives in Chicago, and his hobbies include poker, politics, eating burritos, and making fun of Rex Grossman.

Acknowledgments

Dan Arey, Andrew Baharlias, Jim Baker, Allen Barra, Kevin Baker, Sal Baxamusa, John Beamer, Alex Belth, Blackie and the dingo, Kent Bonham, Josh Boyd, Rick and Therese Boyd, Rico Brogna, Maury Brown, John Burnson, Jim Callis, Steve Canter, Alex Carnevale, Jay Catalano, James Click, Jon Coniff, John Coppolella, Kimball Crosley, Kevin Cuddihy, Jessica Curtis, John Daniels, Bobbie Dittmeier, Alex Early, Scott Engler, Eddie Epstein, John Erhardt, Dan Evans, Sean Forman, David Forst, Ted Frank, Lee Froehlich, Jeff Gambino, Peter Gammons, Sam Geaney, Gary Gillette, Fred Harner, Jeff Hem, M.J. Hindman, Alan and Alexandra Houghton, Gary Huckabay, Toby Hyde, David Gassko, Assorted Goldmans (Stefanie, Sarah, Clemens, Reuven, Eliane, and Ilana), Jordan Goldstein, Mike Janes, Stan Kasten, David Kaplan, Paula Kepos, Matthew Kleine, Carl Kline, Chris Kline, Dejan Kovacevic, Eric Kubota, John LaLonde, Mark Lamster, Jon Lane, Matthew Leach, Keith Lieppman, Chris Liss, Becky Lorig, Freddie Lutz, Diane Macedo, Dave Malpass, Hunter Manchak, John Marzano, Bruce Mathieson, Jonathan Mayo, Vizzy Micucci, John Mirabelli, Bill Mitchell, Dr. Richard Mohring, Matt Melzak, Ben Murphy, Mike and Jane Murphy, Rick O'Connor, Patrick O'Donnell, Steve Palazzolo, Jason Paré, Brian Parker, Caleb Peiffer, David Pinto, Peter Quadrino, Scott Raab, Jeff Sackmann, Ron Scarborough, Keith Scherer, John Schuerholz, Cory Schwartz, Dan Scotto, Jim Scully, Mark Shapiro, Stu Shea, John Shestakofsky, Mike Siano, Eric Simon, Nick Stone, Steve Stone, David Stoner, Paul Swydan, Cecilia Tan, Tom Tango, Bruce Taylor, Brett Trainor, Shawn Touney, Richard Wade, Brody Van Wagenen, Franklin Wagner Norm Wamer, Alasdair Wilkins, Chuck Wilson, Keith Woolner, Josh Yates, Geoff Young, Brad Ziegler, and Herbie Zucker. Joe Sheehan would like to thank more people than will fit in this space. Representing all of them this year is Pat McPartland. Thanks, Aunt Pat, for everything.